POETRY OF THE VICTORIAN PERIOD

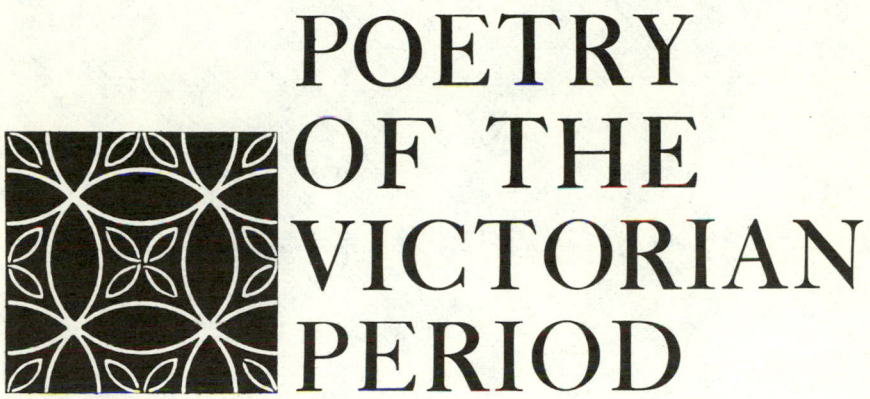

Third Edition

Selected and edited with critical and explanatory notes,
brief biographies, and bibliographies

JEROME HAMILTON BUCKLEY
Harvard University

GEORGE BENJAMIN WOODS

SCOTT, FORESMAN AND COMPANY

Library of Congress Catalog Card #65-11904.
Copyright © 1965 by Scott, Foresman and Company, Glenview, Illinois 60025.
Previous Copyright © 1955 by Scott, Foresman and Company.
All rights reserved.
Printed in the United States of America.
Regional offices of Scott, Foresman and Company are located in
Atlanta, Dallas, Glenview, Palo Alto, and Oakland, N.J.

PREFACE

Keats hoped that his first long poem, *Endymion*, might be appealing in its breadth and variety. "Do not Lovers of Poetry," he asked, "like to have a little Region to wander in where they may pick and choose, and in which the images are so numerous that many are forgotten and found anew in a second Reading...?" *Poetry of the Victorian Period* seeks to realize a similar intention. It offers the reader a wide area to explore and an ample opportunity to pick and choose. It represents as fully as possible the dozen or fifteen leading poets from Tennyson to Hardy—their early and late poems, their best work, their experiments, and even the failures that were crucial to their growth; and it includes also more than thirty significant minor poets whose verse, sometimes quite alien to modern tastes, sometimes astonishingly relevant, made a distinct contribution to the climate of opinion and feeling or to the literary tradition of the period. To leave the student freedom of judgment as well as choice, this anthology presents its varied materials with a minimum of editorial comment; it supplies many factual notes and glosses but prescribes no single critical approach or response. It assumes that the poetry should yield new meaning to every new reader.

Since 1930, when the late Dr. Benjamin Woods prepared the first edition of this anthology, the revaluation of Victorian culture has proceeded with a breadth of scholarship and a sympathetic concern that no one in the self-consciously "anti-Victorian" nineteen-twenties could well have imagined. And since 1955, when a second edition of *Poetry of the Victorian Period* appeared, the pace of the revival of interest has steadily increased, as a glance at the new bibliographies will suggest. The older fear of the epithet "Victorian" has been largely dissipated, and with it has gone much foolish indictment of those who willingly or not bore that label. Viewed for the first time as seriously and attentively as the poetry of any earlier age, Victorian poetry is now subjected to the same standards of judgment applied to all other carefully wrought verse. This anthology is intended to provide both text and context for continuing reappraisal: the accurate text of a particular poem selected for close analysis and the broader context for intelligent comparative estimate.

The present revision extends rather than alters Dr. Woods' original purposes. The representation of the major poets, who from the beginning commanded by far the greatest attention, has been, I believe, considerably strengthened. Important additions have been made to the selections from Browning, Arnold, and Meredith, and especially from Tennyson and Hopkins, the two poets who in

recent years have grown most in critical repute. *The Hesperides, Lucretius*, and *Demeter and Persephone* now take their places beside Tennyson's other and more familiar classical poems; *The Ancient Sage* stands as a late counterpart to *The Two Voices;* and *The Last Tournament* offers a powerful variation on the theme and story of Arnold's *Tristram and Iseult*. Hopkins' late sonnets extend our awareness of the strength and depth of his religious experience; his lyric *Spring and Fall* gives us a fresh view of his compassionate regard for man's mortality; and *The Leaden Echo and the Golden Echo* furnishes new evidence of his technical adroitness. *Bishop Blougram's Apology* affords a fine example of Browning's multiple irony. *The Woods of Westermain* illustrates at length Meredith's mature commitment to the life of nature. And the full text of *Empedocles on Etna* now invites our study of Arnold's most ambitious, though perhaps not most successful, poem. To make room for these additions and a number of others, I have had to sacrifice a few of the lesser writers. But I have hesitated to make extensive deletions, for it has been a constant object of this anthology to give a rounded impression of Victorian poetry as a whole. For this reason two rather interesting secondary figures have been added: Wilfrid Scawen Blunt, present in the first edition but omitted from the second, has been restored; and Richard Watson Dixon, member of the second Pre-Raphaelite circle and devoted friend of Hopkins, makes his first appearance.

From the beginning this anthology was designed to present, wherever possible, complete poems or at least complete units, in order that it be no random sampling, no thing of shreds and patches. The subsequent revisions have steadily advanced this aim. With both new and old selections, the present volume furnishes the full text of some twenty-five or thirty longer poems, many of them at first issued as whole books in themselves: the full sonnet cycles of Mrs. Browning, Dante Rossetti, and Meredith; complete dramas or "monodramas" like *Pippa Passes, Maud*, and *The Land of Heart's Desire;* all of *In Memoriam* and *The Rubáiyát, Laus Veneris* and *Goblin Market, Lancelot and Elaine* and *The Defence of Guenevere, Sohrab and Rustum* and *The Ballad of Reading Gaol, Tristram and Iseult* and *The Woods of Westermain, Lucretius* and *The Dream of Gerontius, The Holy Grail* and *The Wreck of the Deutschland* and *The City of Dreadful Night*. The mere listing of titles so various testifies to the enormous range of the verse that this volume seeks to represent. Yet, with all due regard for such larger units, we should not forget that the relatively short reflective lyric and the topical ballad, rather than the long narrative or the verse drama, established themselves as the most characteristic expressions of the Victorian poets; and the anthology fittingly reproduces hundreds of shorter pieces—love songs, sonnets, odes, monologues, hymns, elegies, parodies, limericks, triolets, descriptive vignettes, occasional poems, poems of image, poems of statement, satires, debates, propaganda verses. In short, it makes available virtually all the Victorian poetry that our generation chooses to remember and a great deal that it has perhaps too hastily ignored.

Since the major writers have been represented with unusual fullness, the reader

iv

may follow in detail their individual curves of development (for growth and diversity are surely tokens of their "majority"). But it is to be hoped that the reader will also find this anthology valuable for purposes of comparison and contrast and analysis of styles and genres, or for tracing parallel themes or traits common to the several "schools" of poets—the Pre-Raphaelites, the Aesthetes, the Decadents. If he is concerned with the social aspects of literature, he will note the attention accorded verse inspired by the public issues of Victoria's England—the demand for political reform and the fear of social change, the problem of the factory and the machine age, the promise of the new democracy, the idea of progress, the fear of decline, and the prophetic outcry against a merciless materialism. If, on the other hand, the reader's interest turns toward the spiritual crisis of the nineteenth century, this volume will offer him a many-sided reflection of the conflicts between science and religion, every shade of conviction, bewilderment, assent, and denial, and ample evidence of a sincere quest for faith, for a joy "whose grounds are real." For the Victorian period, when new philosophies were calling all in doubt, produced a poetry both of anxious questioning and of quiet certainty, ranging in tone from the darkness of Thomson's *City of Dreadful Night* and the gloom of Hardy's "God-forgotten" world to the hard intense light of Hopkins' faith or the quiet radiance of devotional lyrists as accomplished as Christina Rossetti and Alice Meynell.

Yet far from being the victims of their own earnestness, the Victorians were abundantly gifted with laughter; they were masters of nonsense no less than of sober debate, parodists *par excellence* undercutting their own solemnities with the comic spirit. And this anthology properly recalls to the student the light verses of Lear and Lewis Carroll and Calverley and Gilbert, Clough's pointed satire and Dobson's playful formalism, Swinburne's self-mimicry in *Nephelidia* and Hilton's hilarious burlesque of Swinburne's *Dolores*. Nor does it forget that the Victorian era was a great age of children's literature—of *Sing-Song* and *Goblin Market* and *A Child's Garden of Verses*, no less than of *Treasure Island* and the *Alice* books.

Represented rather fully is the Victorian concern with the arts and the function of the artist in society. A number of pieces—Tennyson's *Palace of Art*, for example, Arnold's *Resignation*, Morris's *Apology*, Browning's *How It Strikes a Contemporary*, the prefatory "Sonnet" to Rossetti's *House of Life*—develop explicitly or by implication the aesthetic credo of the poet. Many pay tribute to the old masters of literature or of painting; and as the long period advances, some of the later poems elegize such early Victorians as Dickens and Browning, who had already attained a more or less "classic" status in their own century. A few of the poems describe pictures. Many seem to invite illustration, and the age indeed was singularly rich in its graphic artists. Poetry in the Pre-Raphaelite mode approximates painting, while painting takes on a poetic dimension. Later, among the poets of the eighties and the nineties, graphic art and music serve as the stuff of direct inspiration; a good many of the selections from Wilde, Sharp, and Symons and several from Henley strive to reproduce in words the precise effect of visual and tonal harmonies. Though their standards of form may sometimes perplex us, the Victorians were from the outset much interested in the aesthetic process and by the end of their era were often self-consciously aware of their own aesthetic sensibilities.

If they seem to us at times completely immersed in the problems of a tumultuous present, the Victorian poets, nevertheless, like the Romantics, most typically looked to the past for their themes, their methods, their very language. Living in one of the world's great ages, they nonetheless felt that change was the most permanent element in their civilization and that every epoch was but a transition to the next. With Tennyson they were haunted by the passion of the past—the nostalgia of the individual for his lost youth but, more especially, the sense of the long traditions that had made their common culture, the best that men through the ages had thought and said. They borrowed much from established or newly revived sources: the Bible, Greek and Roman and Norse mythology, medieval legend, Renaissance biography. Their skill at translation called forth renditions that have all the freshness of original verse, poems as finely finished as FitzGerald's *Rubáiyát of Omar Khayyám*, or Rossetti's *Ballad of Dead Ladies* from Villon or his Pre-Raphaelite versions of Dante and the Italian sonneteers, or Dobson's *Ars Victrix* "imitated from Théophile Gautier," or Yeats's *When You Are Old* freely adapted from Ronsard. It may be that a good deal of Victorian poetry is too literary, that it suffers from its heavy indebtedness to an older literature and a spent archaic diction. Yet its strength is often retrospective; it succeeds repeatedly in revitalizing long-neglected genres, meters, prosodic conventions, and fixed verse patterns. And many of its finest effects are frankly achievements in the "grand style," in the high, deliberate, calculated, "poetic" language, freighted with connotation, that makes possible the superb artifice of Tennyson's songs from *The Princess* and the ornate rhetoric of Francis Thompson's *Hound of Heaven* and the overwhelming yet essentially "literary" eloquence of Swinburne's *Laus Veneris*.

Yet, for all their deep sense of history and tradition, the Victorian poets in various ways anticipated the shape of things to come. They were seldom bent on literal prophecy, though there may be something of that, too, as in the oft-quoted "vision" of *Locksley Hall* or even perhaps in Arnold's forecast of some distant world as yet powerless to be born. Their impact on later verse, at any rate, was for the most part quite involuntary. But they were in fact forerunners of modern poetry to a very considerable degree, in their use of imagery and symbols, in their desire for objectivity, in their concept of the lyric as springing from a situation dramatically conceived. Though a large part of his power lay in his conformity to an established convention, Tennyson did much to widen the thematic range of English verse, and as craftsman he displayed so rich a virtuosity, so tireless a will to experiment, that none of his disciples could keep pace with his development. Browning, who was metrically less inventive, evolved a mode of psychological analysis ultimately to be of influence on writers as remote from his point of view as Ezra Pound and T. S. Eliot. Moreover, he charged his verse with the energy of living speech, a quite "unliterary" colloquialism, which opened the way for the direct idiom and the spoken cadence of Kipling and Hardy and Housman. Arnold tentatively fashioned a kind of regular free verse which Henley later brought to the frontiers of modern *vers libre*. Above all, Hopkins, by turning back to the practice of the Welsh bards and the heavy beat of Anglo-Saxon rhythms, broke the old poetic line unit, found a new dissonantal music, and rediscovered something of the basic force and concretion of language. Though under no impression that the prime distinction of Victorian verse lies in having foreshadowed some of the poetic vogues of our time, this volume takes due cognizance of the links between the nineteenth century and the twentieth, for it assumes the general continuity of literature. It therefore pays far more than usual heed to the transitional late-Victorian poets, both to those whose innovation looks forward to modern poetry and to those whose reaction writes a quiet ending to their own particular literary tradition. The last one hundred and fifty-odd pages, from Henley to Hardy, in themselves constitute a fairly comprehensive anthology of the verse of the eighties and nineties. Prominent in this section is a representation of the early Yeats, to which are added three later poems indicative of Yeats's achievement as the greatest lyrist of our own century. Last of all, Hardy's *An Ancient to Ancients*, glancing with gentle nostalgia back from the nineteen-twenties to the world of Tennyson, stands as a fitting epilogue to the poetry of the Victorian period.

Readers of this volume in its earlier editions will be familiar with the arrangement of the text, notes, and appended aids to study. The poets appear in a roughly chronological sequence determined by the principal dates of writing and publishing. The poems of each have in turn been placed largely in the order of composition, if known, or else of first publication; and each piece has been marked at its close with the time of composition (in italics) and/or the publication date (in roman type). Wherever possible, direct glosses on the poems accompany the text as footnotes, so that reading need not be interrupted. The appendix is limited to ancillary materials: selected general and specific bibliographies, brief factual biographies, explanatory notes or comments on some of the poems, and suggestive appraisals often by late-Victorian essayists but also sometimes by more recent scholars and critics. A table of chronology lists the landmarks of Victorian literature and, in parallel columns, the most significant European and American publications of the same years. Finally, the acknowledgments record the indebtedness of the editors to the publishers and literary executors who have permitted the use of poems still in copyright. But no listing can begin to express the thanks due to countless friends, teachers, and students whose generous advice and trenchant criticisms over the years since 1930 have contributed much toward increasing the accuracy and usefulness of the whole anthology.

Jerome Hamilton Buckley

CONTENTS

Robert Browning

xii

xiii

xiv

xvi

JOHN HENRY NEWMAN (1801-1890)

THE SIGN OF THE CROSS

Whene'er across this sinful flesh of mine
  I draw the Holy Sign,
All good thoughts stir within me, and renew
  Their slumbering strength divine;
Till there springs up a courage high and true
  To suffer and to do.   6
.

And who shall say, but hateful spirits around,
  For their brief hour unbound,
Shudder to see, and wail their overthrow?
  While on far heathen ground   10
Some lonely Saint hails the fresh odor, though
  Its source he cannot know.   (*1832;* 1836)

ENGLAND

Tyre of the West, and glorying in the name
  More than in Faith's pure fame!
Oh, trust not crafty fort nor rock renowned
  Earned upon hostile ground;
Wielding Trade's master-keys, at thy proud
    will   5
To lock or loose its waters, England! trust
  not still.

Dread thine own power!   Since haughty
    Babel's prime,
  High towers have been man's crime.
Since her hoar age, when the huge moat lay
    bare,
  Strongholds have been man's snare.   10
Thy nest is in the crags; ah, refuge frail!
Mad counsel in its hour, or traitors, will
  prevail.

He who scanned Sodom for His righteous men
  Still spares thee for thy ten;
But, should vain tongues the Bride of Heaven
    defy,   15
  He will not pass thee by;
For, as earth's kings welcome their spotless
    guest,
So gives He them by turn, to suffer or be
  blest.   (*1832;* 1836)

England. 1. **Tyre,** a famous city of ancient Phoenicia on
the Mediterranean coast. It was noted for its worldliness and
commercial prosperity. A prophecy of its destruction is recorded in *Ezekiel,* 26-28; it was destroyed by Malik al Ashraf,
ruler of Egypt and Syria, in 1291. 3-4. **fort . . . ground,** a
reference to the Rock of Gibraltar, a British naval base and
fortification on the coast of Spain at the entrance to the
Mediterranean. It was taken from the Spanish in 1704. 7.
Babel, a reference to the confusion of tongues at the city and
tower of Babel, in the land of Shinar, as related in *Genesis,*
11:1-9. Because the descendants of Noah attempted to build
a tower that would reach to heaven, Jehovah, to prevent its
completion, "confounded their language" so that they could
not understand one another. 13-14. **Sodom . . . ten.** Sodom
was a city in Palestine destroyed because of its wickedness.
The Lord had promised Abraham that the city would be
saved if ten righteous men could be found in it (*Genesis,*
18:17-33; 19:1-25).

SENSITIVENESS

Time was, I shrank from what was right
  From fear of what was wrong;
I would not brave the sacred fight,
  Because the foe was strong.

But now I cast that finer sense   5
  And sorer shame aside;
Such dread of sin was indolence,
  Such aim at Heaven was pride.

So, when my Savior calls, I rise,
  And calmly do my best;   10
Leaving to Him, with silent eyes
  Of hope and fear, the rest.

I step, I mount where He has led;
  Men count my haltings o'er;—
I know them; yet, though self I dread,   15
  I love His precept more.   (*1833;* 1836)

THE PILLAR OF THE CLOUD

Lead, Kindly Light, amid the encircling
    gloom,
  Lead Thou me on!
The night is dark, and I am far from home—
  Lead Thou me on!
Keep Thou my feet; I do not ask to see   5
The distant scene—one step enough for me.

I was not ever thus, nor prayed that Thou
  Shouldst lead me on.
I loved to choose and see my path; but now
  Lead Thou me on!   10
I loved the garish day, and, spite of fears,
Pride ruled my will; remember not past years.

So long Thy power hath blessed me, sure it
    still
  Will lead me on,
O'er moor and fen, o'er crag and torrent, till
  The night is gone;   16
And with the morn those angel faces smile
Which I have loved long since, and lost awhile.
    (*1833;* 1836)

THE ELEMENTS

A TRAGIC CHORUS

Man is permitted much
  To scan and learn

The Pillar of the Cloud. This poem was written on shipboard
when Newman was returning from Italy. The title refers to
the incident of Moses leading the children of Israel out of
Egypt—"And the Lord went before them by day in a pillar
of a cloud, to lead them the way; and by night in a pillar of
fire, to give them light; . . ." (*Exodus,* 13:21).

In Nature's frame;
Till he well-nigh can tame
Brute mischiefs and can touch   5
Invisible things, and turn
All warring ills to purposes of good.
Thus, as a god below,
He can control,
And harmonize, what seems amiss to flow 10
As severed from the whole
And dimly understood.

But o'er the elements
One Hand alone,
One Hand has sway.   15
What influence day by day
In straiter belt prevents
The impious Ocean, thrown
Alternate o'er the ever-sounding shore?
Or who has eye to trace   20
How the Plague came?
Forerun the doublings of the Tempest's race?
Or the Air's weight and flame
On a set scale explore?

Thus God has willed   25
That man, when fully skilled,
Still gropes in twilight dim;
Encompassed all his hours
By fearfullest powers
Inflexible to him.   30
That so he may discern
His feebleness.
And e'en for earth's success
To Him in wisdom turn,
Who holds for us the keys of either home, 35
Earth and the world to come.

                        (*1833;* 1836)

THE DREAM OF GERONTIUS

I

Gerontius

Jesu, Maria—I am near to death,
And Thou art calling me; I know it now.
Not by the token of this faltering breath,
This chill at heart, this dampness on my
    brow,—
(Jesu, have mercy! Mary, pray for me!)   5
'Tis this new feeling, never felt before,
(Be with me, Lord, in my extremity!)
That I am going, that I am no more.
'Tis this strange innermost abandonment, 9
(Lover of souls! great God! I look to Thee,)

This emptying out of each constituent
And natural force, by which I come to be.
Pray for me, O my friends; a visitant
Is knocking his dire summons at my door,
The like of whom, to scare me and to daunt, 15
Has never, never come to me before;
'Tis death,—O loving friends, your prayers!
   —'tis he! . . .
As though my very being had given way,
As though I was no more a substance now,
And could fall back on naught to be my
    stay,   20
   (Help, loving Lord! Thou my sole Refuge,
    Thou,)
And turn no whither, but must needs decay
And drop from out the universal frame
Into that shapeless, scopeless, blank abyss,
That utter nothingness, of which I came: 25
This is it that has come to pass in me;
Oh, horror! this it is, my dearest, this;
So pray for me, my friends, who have not
    strength to pray.

Assistants

Kyrie eleïson, Christe eleïson, Kyrie eleïson.
Holy Mary, pray for him.   30
All holy Angels, pray for him.
Choirs of the righteous, pray for him.
Holy Abraham, pray for him.
St. John Baptist, St. Joseph, pray for him.
St. Peter, St. Paul, St. Andrew, St. John, 35
All Apostles, all Evangelists, pray for him.
All holy Disciples of the Lord, pray for him.
All holy Innocents, pray for him.
All holy Martyrs, all holy Confessors,
All holy Hermits, all holy Virgins,   40
All ye Saints of God, pray for him.

Gerontius

Rouse thee, my fainting soul, and play the
    man;
And through such waning span
Of life and thought as still has to be trod,
Prepare to meet thy God.   45
And while the storm of that bewilderment
Is for a season spent,
And, ere afresh the ruin on me fall,
Use well the interval.

Assistants

Be merciful, be gracious; spare him, Lord. 50
Be merciful, be gracious; Lord, deliver him.
From the sins that are past;
From Thy frown and Thine ire;

The Dream of Gerontius. This is a deeply religious poem that records the thoughts and emotions of Gerontius, an old man, as he lies dying. The lines enclosed in parentheses in the opening passage, uttered half-consciously by Gerontius, are responses to the Litany for the Dying.

23. **universal frame,** the world of space and time. 29. **Kyrie eleïson,** etc., Greek words meaning "Lord, have mercy; Christ, have mercy; Lord, have mercy." 46. **storm of that bewilderment,** his suffering at the thought of death.

From the perils of dying;
From any complying 55
With sin, or denying
His God, or relying
On self, at the last;
  From the nethermost fire;
From all that is evil; 60
From power of the devil;
Thy servant deliver,
For once and forever.

By Thy birth, and by Thy Cross,
Rescue him from endless loss; 65
By Thy death and burial,
Save him from a final fall;
By Thy rising from the tomb,
  By Thy mounting up above,
  By the Spirit's gracious love, 70
Save him in the day of doom.

Gerontius

Sanctus fortis, Sanctus Deus,
  De profundis oro te,
Miserere, Judex meus,
  Parce mihi, Domine. 75
Firmly I believe and truly
  God is three, and God is One;
And I next acknowledge duly
  Manhood taken by the Son.
And I trust and hope most fully 80
  In that Manhood crucified;
And each thought and deed unruly
  Do to death, as He has died.
Simply to His grace and wholly
  Light and life and strength belong, 85
And I love, supremely, solely,
  Him the holy, Him the strong.
Sanctus fortis, Sanctus Deus,
  De profundis oro te,
Miserere, Judex meus, 90
  Parce mihi, Domine.
And I hold in veneration,
  For the love of Him alone,
Holy Church, as His creation,
  And her teachings, as His own. 95
And I take with joy whatever
  Now besets me, pain or fear,
And with a strong will I sever
  All the ties which bind me here.
Adoration aye be given, 100
  With and through the angelic host,
To the God of earth and heaven,
  Father, Son, and Holy Ghost.
Sanctus fortis, Sanctus Deus,
  De profundis oro te, 105

Miserere, Judex meus,
  Mortis in discrimine.

I can no more; for now it comes again,
That sense of ruin, which is worse than pain,
That masterful negation and collapse 110
Of all that makes me man; as though I bent
Over the dizzy brink
Of some sheer infinite descent;
Or worse, as though
Down, down forever I was falling through 115
The solid framework of created things,
And needs must sink and sink
Into the vast abyss. And, crueler still,
A fierce and restless fright begins to fill
The mansion of my soul. And, worse and
  worse, 120
Some bodily form of ill
Floats on the wind, with many a loathsome
  curse
Tainting the hallowed air, and laughs, and
  flaps
Its hideous wings, 124
And makes me wild with horror and dismay.
O Jesu, help! pray for me, Mary, pray!
Some Angel, Jesu! such as came to Thee
In Thine own agony. . . .
Mary, pray for me. Joseph, pray for me.
  Mary, pray for me.

Assistants

Rescue him, O Lord, in this his evil hour, 130
As of old so many by Thy gracious power:—
  (Amen.)
Enoch and Elias from the common doom;
  (Amen.)
Noe from the waters in a saving home; (Amen.)
Abraham from the abounding guilt of Hea-
  thenesse; (Amen.)
Job from all his multiform and fell distress;
  (Amen.) 135
Isaac, when his father's knife was raised to
  slay; (Amen.)
Lot from burning Sodom on its judgment-
  day; (Amen.)
Moses from the land of bondage and despair;
  (Amen.)

72-75. **Sanctus . . . Domine,** Thou Holy, strong One, Holy God, from the depths I pray unto Thee; have mercy, my Judge, spare me, Lord. The words are taken in part from the service of Good Friday. 76-103. These lines are adapted from the Creed.

107. **Mortis in discrimine,** in the time of death. 127-128. **Angel . . . agony.** An angel came to comfort Christ in the garden of Gethsemane. See *Luke,* 22:41-46. 132. **Enoch and Elias,** Enoch and Elijah, two just men of the Old Testament, taken up bodily into heaven. See *Genesis,* 5:24 and *2 Kings,* 2:11. 133. **Noe.** Noah saved himself and his family by building an ark. See *Genesis,* 6:14 ff. 134. **Abraham.** He overcame hostile forces and became founder of the Hebrew race. See *Genesis,* 11 ff. 135. **Job.** He suffered many misfortunes. See *Book of Job.* 136. **Isaac.** Abraham, as a test of faithfulness, had been ordered by God to slay his son Isaac. About to obey, he was stopped by an angel. See *Genesis,* 22:1-12. 137. **Lot.** When the wicked city of Sodom was destroyed by fire, Lot escaped with his family through a warning by angels. See *Genesis,* 19:12-24. 138. **Moses.** Moses led the children of Israel out of bondage in Egypt. See *Exodus,* 12.

Daniel from the hungry lions in their lair;
    (Amen.)
And the Children Three amid the furnace-
    flame; (Amen.)   140
Chaste Susanna from the slander and the
    shame; (Amen.)
David from Golia and the wrath of Saul;
    (Amen.)
And the two Apostles from their prison-thrall;
    (Amen.)
Thecla from her torments; (Amen.)
                —so to show Thy power,   145
Rescue this Thy servant in his evil hour.

Gerontius

Novissima hora est; and I fain would sleep.
The pain has wearied me . . . Into Thy
    hands,
O Lord, into Thy hands. . . .   149

The Priest

Proficiscere, anima Christiana, de hoc mundo!
Go forth upon thy journey, Christian soul!
Go from this world! Go, in the Name of God
The Omnipotent Father, who created thee!
Go, in the Name of Jesus Christ, our Lord,
Son of the living God, who bled for thee! 155
Go, in the Name of the Holy Spirit, who
Hath been poured out on thee! Go, in the
    name
Of Angels and Archangels; in the name
Of Thrones and Dominations; in the name
Of Princedoms and of Powers; and in the
    name   160
Of Cherubim and Seraphim, go forth!
Go, in the name of Patriarchs and Prophets;
And of Apostles and Evangelists,
Of Martyrs and Confessors; in the name
Of holy Monks and Hermits; in the name 165
Of Holy Virgins; and all Saints of God,
Both men and women, go! Go on thy course;
And may thy place today be found in peace,
And may thy dwelling be the Holy Mount
Of Sion:—through the Same, through Christ,
    our Lord.   170

139. **Daniel.** Cast into a den of lions, the prophet Daniel
was left unharmed. See *Daniel*, 6. 140. **Children Three**,
the three Children of Israel who were cast into a fiery furnace
because they refused to worship a golden image. They were
saved by a miracle. See *Daniel*, 3. 141. **Susanna.** She was
falsely accused of adultery; her innocence was proved by Daniel. See "The History of Susanna" in the *Apocrypha*. 142.
David . . . Saul. David slew the giant Goliath and escaped
the jealous plots of Saul. See *I Samuel*, 17-31. 143. This refers
to the imprisonment and miraculous release of Paul and Silas.
See *Acts*, 16:19-27. 144. **Thecla**, St. Thecla, a Christian martyr of the second century who was miraculously saved from fire
and savage beasts of the arena. The story is told in *The Acts
of Paul and Thecla*, an apocryphal book. 147. **Novissima
hora est**, the final hour has come. The unexpressed part of
the prayer is "I commend my spirit." 150. **Proficiscere**, etc.,
Go forth, Christian soul, out of this world.

2

Soul of Gerontius

I went to sleep; and now I am refreshed,
A strange refreshment: for I feel in me
An inexpressive lightness, and a sense
Of freedom, as I were at length myself,
And ne'er had been before. How still it is! 175
I hear no more the busy beat of time,
No, nor my fluttering breath, nor struggling
    pulse;
Nor does one moment differ from the next.
I had a dream; yes:—someone softly said
"He's gone;" and then a sigh went round the
    room.   180
And then I surely heard a priestly voice
Cry "*Subvenite*"; and they knelt in prayer.
I seem to hear him still; but thin and low,
And fainter and more faint the accents come,
As at an ever-widening interval.   185
Ah! whence is this? What is this severance?
This silence pours a solitariness
Into the very essence of my soul;
And the deep rest, so soothing and so sweet,
Hath something too of sternness and of pain.
For it drives back my thoughts upon their
    spring   191
By a strange introversion, and perforce
I now begin to feed upon myself,
Because I have naught else to feed upon.—

Am I alive or dead? I am not dead,   195
But in the body still; for I possess
A sort of confidence which clings to me,
That each particular organ holds its place
As heretofore, combining with the rest 199
Into one symmetry, that wraps me round,
And makes me man; and surely I could move,
Did I but will it, every part of me.
And yet I cannot to my sense bring home
By very trial, that I have the power.
'Tis strange; I cannot stir a hand or foot, 205
I cannot make my fingers or my lips
By mutual pressure witness each to each,
Nor by the eyelid's instantaneous stroke
Assure myself I have a body still.
Nor do I know my very attitude,   210
Nor if I stand, or lie, or sit, or kneel.

So much I know, not knowing how I know,
That the vast universe, where I have dwelt,
Is quitting me, or I am quitting it.
Or I or it is rushing on the wings   215
Of light or lightning on an onward course,
And we e'en now are million miles apart.
Yet . . . is this peremptory severance

182. **Subvenite**, come to his assistance.

Wrought out in lengthening measurements of
    space,
Which grow and multiply by speed and time?
Or am I traversing infinity   221
By endless subdivision, hurrying back
From finite towards infinitesimal,
Thus dying out of the expansive world?

Another marvel: someone has me fast   225
Within his ample palm; 'tis not a grasp
Such as they use on earth, but all around
Over the surface of my subtle being,
As though I were a sphere, and capable
To be accosted thus, a uniform   230
And gentle pressure tells me I am not
Self-moving, but borne forward on my way.
And hark! I hear a singing; yet in sooth
I cannot of that music rightly say
Whether I hear, or touch, or taste the tones.
Oh, what a heart-subduing melody!   236

Angel

    My work is done,
      My task is o'er,
        And so I come,
        Taking it home,   240
    For the crown is won,
      Alleluia,
      Forevermore.

    My Father gave
      In charge to me   245
        This child of earth
        E'en from its birth,
    To serve and save,
      Alleluia,
    And saved is he.   250

    This child of clay
      To me was given,
        To rear and train
        By sorrow and pain
    In the narrow way,   255
      Alleluia,
    From earth to heaven.

Soul

It is a member of that family
Of wondrous beings, who, ere the worlds were
    made,
Millions of ages back, have stood around   260
The throne of God:—he never has known sin
But through those cycles all but infinite,
Has had a strong and pure celestial life,
And bore to gaze on the unveiled face of God,

And drank from the everlasting Fount of
    truth,   265
And served Him with a keen ecstatic love.
Hark! he begins again.

Angel

O Lord, how wonderful in depth and height,
    But most in man, how wonderful Thou
      art!   269
With what a love, what soft persuasive might
    Victorious o'er the stubborn fleshly heart,
    Thy tale complete of saints Thou dost pro-
      vide,
    To fill the thrones which angels lost through
      pride!

He lay a groveling babe upon the ground,
    Polluted in the blood of his first sire, 275
With his whole essence shattered and unsound,
    And coiled around his heart a demon dire,
    Which was not of his nature, but had skill
    To bind and form his opening mind to ill.

Then was I sent from heaven to set right 280
    The balance in his soul of truth and sin,
And I have waged a long relentless fight,
    Resolved that death-environed spirit to
      win,
    Which from its fallen state, when all was
      lost,
    Had been repurchased at so dread a cost. 285

Oh, what a shifting parti-colored scene
    Of hope and fear, of triumph and dismay,
Of recklessness and penitence, has been   288
    The history of that dreary, life-long fray!
    And oh, the grace to nerve him and to lead,
    How patient, prompt, and lavish at his need!

O man, strange composite of heaven and earth!
    Majesty dwarfed to baseness! fragrant
      flower
Running to poisonous seed! and seeming worth
    Cloking corruption! weakness mastering
      power!   295
    Who never art so near to crime and shame,
    As when thou hast achieved some deed of
      name;—

How should ethereal natures comprehend
    A thing made up of spirit and of clay,
Were we not tasked to nurse it and to tend, 300
    Linked one to one throughout its mortal day?
More than the Seraph in his height of place,
The Angel-guardian knows and loves the ran-
    somed race.

225. **someone**, the Guardian Angel who has been his constant invisible guide through his earthly life. 264. **bore**, dared, was able to.

273. **thrones . . . lost,** thrones vacated by Lucifer and his fallen angels. 274. **He,** Gerontius. 285. **so dread a cost,** by Christ on the Cross. 302. **Seraph,** celestial being.

Soul

Now know I surely that I am at length
Out of the body; had I part with earth,   305
I never could have drunk those accents in,
And not have worshiped as a god the voice
That was so musical; but now I am
So whole of heart, so calm, so self-possessed,
With such a full content, and with a sense   310
So apprehensive and discriminant,
As no temptation can intoxicate.
Nor have I even terror at the thought
That I am clasped by such a saintliness.   314

Angel

All praise to Him, at whose sublime decree
    The last are first, the first become the last;
By whom the suppliant prisoner is set free,
    By whom proud first-borns from their
       thrones are cast;
Who raises Mary to be Queen of heaven,   319
While Lucifer is left, condemned and unforgiven.

3

Soul

I will address him.   Mighty one, my Lord,
My Guardian Spirit, all hail!

Angel

           All hail, my child!
My child and brother, hail! what wouldest
    thou?

Soul

I would have nothing but to speak with thee 325
For speaking's sake.   I wish to hold with thee
Conscious communion; though I fain would
    know
A maze of things, were it but meet to ask,
And not a curiousness.

Angel

          You cannot now   330
Cherish a wish which ought not to be wished.

Soul

Then I will speak.   I ever had believed
That on the moment when the struggling soul
Quitted its mortal case, forthwith it fell
Under the awful Presence of its God,   335
There to be judged and sent to its own place.
What lets me now from going to my Lord?

<hr>

316. **last . . . last.** See *Mark*, 10:31—"But many that are
first shall be last; and the last first." 337. **lets**, hinders,
prevents.

Angel

Thou art not let; but with extremest speed
Art hurrying to the Just and Holy Judge:
For scarcely art thou disembodied yet.   340
Divide a moment, as men measure time,
Into its million-million-millionth part,
Yet even less than that the interval
Since thou didst leave the body; and the priest
Cried "*Subvenite*," and they fell to prayer; 345
Nay, scarcely yet have they begun to pray.

For spirits and men by different standards
       mete
The less and greater in the flow of time.
By sun and moon, primeval ordinances—
By stars which rise and set harmoniously— 350
By the recurring seasons, and the swing,
This way and that, of the suspended rod
Precise and punctual, men divide the hours,
Equal, continuous, for their common use.
Not so with us in the immaterial world;   355
But intervals in their succession
Are measured by the living thought alone,
And grow or wane with its intensity.
And time is not a common property;
But what is long is short, and swift is slow, 360
And near is distant, as received and grasped
By this mind and by that, and everyone
Is standard of his own chronology.
And memory lacks its natural resting-points
Of years, and centuries, and periods.   365
It is thy very energy of thought
Which keeps thee from thy God.

Soul

          Dear Angel, say,
Why have I now no fear at meeting Him?
Along my earthly life, the thought of death 370
And judgment was to me most terrible.
I had it aye before me, and I saw
The Judge severe e'en in the Crucifix.
Now that the hour is come, my fear is fled;
And at this balance of my destiny,   375
Now close upon me, I can forward look
With a serenest joy.

Angel

          It is because
Then thou didst fear, that now thou dost not
    fear.
Thou hast forestalled the agony, and so   380
For thee the bitterness of death is past.
Also, because already in thy soul
The judgment is begun.   That day of doom,
One and the same for the collected world,—
That solemn consummation for all flesh,   385
Is, in the case of each, anticipate
Upon his death; and, as the last great day

In the particular judgment is rehearsed,
So now, too, ere thou comest to the Throne,
A presage falls upon thee, as a ray   390
Straight from the Judge, expressive of thy lot.
That calm and joy uprising in thy soul
Is first-fruit to thee of thy recompense,
And heaven begun.

4

Soul

But hark! upon my sense
Comes a fierce hubbub, which would make
    me fear   396
Could I be frighted.

Angel

We are now arrived
Close on the judgment-court; that sullen howl
Is from the demons who assemble there.   400
It is the middle region, where of old
Satan appeared among the sons of God,
To cast his jibes and scoffs at holy Job.
So now his legions throng the vestibule,
Hungry and wild, to claim their property, 405
And gather souls for hell.   Hist to their cry.

Soul

How sour and how uncouth a dissonance!

Demons

Low-born clods
  Of brute earth,
    They aspire   410
To become gods,
  By a new birth,
And an extra grace,
  And a score of merits,
    As if aught   415
Could stand in place
    Of the high thought,
  And the glance of fire
Of the great spirits,
The powers blest,   420
  The lords by right,
    The primal owners,
      Of the proud dwelling
And realm of light,—
Dispossessed,   425
Aside thrust,
    Chucked down
By the sheer might
Of a despot's will,
    Of a tyrant's frown,   430
    Who after expelling
    Their hosts, gave,
Triumphant still,

And still unjust,
    Each forfeit crown   435
To psalm-droners,
And canting groaners,
  To every slave,
And pious cheat,
    And crawling knave,   440
Who licked the dust
Under his feet.

Angel

It is the restless panting of their being;
Like beasts of prey, who, caged within their
  bars,
In a deep hideous purring have their life,   445
And an incessant pacing to and fro.

Demons

The mind bold
  And independent,
    The purpose free,
So we are told,   450
Must not think
  To have the ascendant.
    What's a saint?
One whose breath
    Doth the air taint   455
Before his death;
    A bundle of bones,
  Which fools adore,
    Ha! ha!
When life is o'er;   460
Which rattle and stink,
  E'en in the flesh.
We cry his pardon!
    No flesh hath he;
    Ha! ha!   465
For it hath died,
  'Tis crucified
  Day by day,
Afresh, afresh,
    Ha! ha!   470
    That holy clay,
    Ha! ha!
This gains guerdon,
  So priestlings prate,
    Ha! ha!   475
Before the Judge,
    And pleads and atones
For spite and grudge,
    And bigot mood,
  And envy and hate,   480
  And greed of blood.

Soul

How impotent they are! and yet on earth
They have repute for wondrous power and
  skill;

And books describe, how that the very face
Of the Evil One, if seen, would have a force 485
Even to freeze the blood, and choke the life
Of him who saw it.

Angel

In thy trial-state
Thou hadst a traitor nestling close at home,
Connatural, who with the powers of hell 490
Was leagued, and of thy senses kept the keys,
And to that deadliest foe unlocked thy heart.
And therefore is it, in respect of man,
Those fallen ones show so majestical.
But, when some child of grace, Angel or Saint,
Pure and upright in his integrity   496
Of nature, meets the demons on their raid,
They scud away as cowards from the fight.
Nay, oft hath holy hermit in his cell,
Not yet disburdened of mortality,   500
Mocked at their threats and warlike overtures;
Or, dying, when they swarmed, like flies,
        around,
Defied them, and departed to his Judge.

Demons

Virtue and vice,
    A knave's pretense,   505
        'Tis all the same;
            Ha! ha!
                Dread of hell-fire,
        Of the venomous flame,
            A coward's plea.   510
Give him his price,
            Saint though he be,
Ha! ha!
    From shrewd good sense
        He'll slave for hire   515
    Ha! ha!
            And does but aspire
To the heaven above
    With sordid aim,
And not from love.   520
    Ha! ha!

Soul

I see not those false spirits; shall I see
My dearest Master, when I reach His Throne?
Or hear, at least, His awful judgment-word
With personal intonation, as I now   525
Hear thee, not see thee, Angel? Hitherto
All has been darkness since I left the earth;
Shall I remain thus sight-bereft all through
My penance-time? If so, how comes it then
That I have hearing still, and taste, and
        touch,   530

Yet not a glimmer of that princely sense
Which binds ideas in one, and makes them live?

Angel

Nor touch, nor taste, nor hearing hast thou
        now;
Thou livest in a world of signs and types,
The presentations of most holy truths,   535
Living and strong, which now encompass thee.
A disembodied soul, thou hast by right
No converse with aught else beside thyself;
But, lest so stern a solitude should load
And break thy being, in mercy are vouch-
        safed   540
Some lower measures of perception,
Which seem to thee, as though through chan-
        nels brought,
Through ear, or nerves, or palate, which are
        gone.
And thou art wrapped and swathed around in
        dreams,
Dreams that are true, yet enigmatical;   545
For the belongings of thy present state,
Save through such symbols, come not home
        to thee.
And thus thou tell'st of space, and time, and
        size,
Of fragrant, solid, bitter, musical,
Of fire, and of refreshment after fire; 550
As (let me use similitude of earth,
To aid thee in the knowledge thou dost ask)—
As ice which blisters may be said to burn.
Nor hast thou now extension, with its parts
Correlative,—long habit cozens thee,—   555
Nor power to move thyself, nor limbs to move.
Hast thou not heard of those, who after loss
Of hand or foot, still cried that they had pains
In hand or foot, as though they had it still?
So is it now with thee, who has not lost   560
Thy hand or foot, but all which made up man.
So will it be, until the joyous day
Of resurrection, when thou wilt regain
All thou hast lost, new-made and glorified.
How, even now, the consummated Saints 565
See God in heaven, I may not explicate;
Meanwhile, let it suffice thee to possess
Such means of converse as are granted thee,
Though, till that Beatific Vision, thou art
        blind;
For e'en thy purgatory, which comes like
        fire,   570
Is fire without its light.

Soul

His will be done!
I am not worthy e'er to see again
The face of day; far less His countenance,
Who is the very sun. Natheless in life, 575

---

489. **traitor**, the flesh. The three great enemies of the soul
are the world, the flesh, and the devil. See *1 John*, 2. Cf. C.
Rossetti's *The Three Enemies*, p. 563.

575. **Natheless**, nevertheless.

When I looked forward to my purgatory,
It ever was my solace to believe,
That, ere I plunged amid the avenging flame,
I had one sight of Him to strengthen me.

Angel

Nor rash nor vain is that presentiment;　580
Yes,—for one moment thou shalt see thy
　　Lord.
Thus will it be: what time thou art arraigned
Before the dread tribunal, and thy lot
Is cast forever, should it be to sit
On His right hand among His pure elect,　585
Then sight, or that which to the soul is sight,
As by a lightning-flash, will come to thee,
And thou shalt see, amid the dark profound,
Whom thy soul loveth, and would fain ap-
　　proach,
One moment; but thou knowest not, my
　　child,　590
What thou dost ask: that sight of the Most
　　Fair
Will gladden thee, but it will pierce thee too.

Soul

Thou speakest darkly, Angel; and an awe
Falls on me, and a fear lest I be rash.

Angel

There was a mortal, who is now above　595
In the mid glory: he, when near to die,
Was given communion with the Crucified,—
Such, that the Master's very wounds were
　　stamped
Upon his flesh; and, from the agony
Which thrilled through body and soul in that
　　embrace,　600
Learn that the flame of the Everlasting Love
Doth burn ere it transform. . . .

5

　　　. . . Hark to those sounds!
They come of tender beings angelical,
Least and most childlike of the sons of God.　605

First Choir of Angelicals

Praise to the Holiest in the height,
　　And in the depth be praise:
In all His words most wonderful;
　　Most sure in all His ways!

To us His elder race He gave　610
　　To battle and to win,

582. **arraigned**, summoned. 595. **mortal**, St. Francis of
Assisi (1182-1226), whose hands, feet, and right side were
marked with the five wounds of Christ's Passion.

Without the chastisement of pain,
　　Without the soil of sin.

The younger son He willed to be
　　A marvel in His birth:　615
Spirit and flesh his parents were;
　　His home was heaven and earth.

The Eternal blessed His child, and armed,
　　And sent him hence afar,
To serve as champion in the field　620
　　Of elemental war.

To be His Viceroy in the world
　　Of matter, and of sense;
Upon the frontier, towards the foe
　　A resolute defense.　625

Angel

We now have passed the gate, and are within
The House of Judgment; and whereas on earth
Temples and palaces are formed of parts
Costly and rare, but all material,
So in the world of spirits naught is found,　630
To mold withal, and form into a whole,
But what is immaterial; and thus
The smallest portions of this edifice,
Cornice, or frieze, or balustrade, or stair,
The very pavement is made up of life—　635
Of holy, blessed, and immortal beings,
Who hymn their Maker's praise continually.

Second Choir of Angelicals

Praise to the Holiest in the height,
　　And in the depth be praise:
In all His words most wonderful;　640
　　Most sure in all His ways!

Woe to thee, man! for he was found
　　A recreant in the fight;
And lost his heritage of heaven,
　　And fellowship with light.　645

Above him now the angry sky,
　　Around the tempest's din;
Who once had Angels for his friends,
　　Had but the brutes for kin.

O man! a savage kindred they;　650
　　To flee that monster brood
He scaled the seaside cave, and clomb
　　The giants of the wood.

With now a fear, and now a hope,
　　With aids which chance supplied,　655
From youth to eld, from sire to son,
　　He lived, and toiled, and died.

624. **foe**, Satan.

He dreed his penance age by age;
  And step by step began
Slowly to doff his savage garb,   660
  And be again a man.

And quickened by the Almighty's breath,
  And chastened by His rod,
And taught by angel-visitings,
  At length he sought his God;   665

And learned to call upon His Name,
  And in His faith create
A household and a father-land,
  A city and a state.

Glory to Him who from the mire,   670
  In patient length of days,
Elaborated into life
  A people to His praise!

Soul

The sound is like the rushing of the wind—
The summer wind—among the lofty pines; 675
Swelling and dying, echoing round about,
Now here, now distant, wild and beautiful;
While, scattered from the branches it has
    stirred
Descend ecstatic odors.

Third Choir of Angelicals

Praise to the Holiest in the height,   680
  And in the depth be praise:
In all His words most wonderful;
  Most sure in all His ways!

The Angels, as beseemingly
  To spirit-kind was given,   685
At once were tried and perfected,
  And took their seats in heaven.

For them no twilight or eclipse;
  No growth and no decay:
'Twas hopeless, all-ingulfing night,   690
  Or beatific day.

But to the younger race there rose
  A hope upon its fall;
And slowly, surely, gracefully,
  The morning dawned on all.   695

And ages, opening out, divide
  The precious, and the base,
And from the hard and sullen mass
  Mature the heirs of grace.

O man! albeit the quickening ray,   700
  Lit from his second birth,
Makes him at length what once he was,
  And heaven grows out of earth;

Yet still between that earth and heaven—
  His journey and his goal—   705
A double agony awaits
  His body and his soul.

A double debt he has to pay—
  The forfeit of his sins:
The chill of death is past, and now   710
  The penance-fire begins.

Glory to Him, who evermore
  By truth and justice reigns;
Who tears the soul from out its case,
  And burns away its stains!   715

Angel

They sing of thy approaching agony,
Which thou so eagerly didst question of:
It is the face of the Incarnate God
Shall smite thee with that keen and subtle
    pain;

And yet the memory which it leaves will be 720
A sovereign febrifuge to heal the wound;
And yet withal it will the wound provoke,
And aggravate and widen it the more.

Soul

Thou speakest mysteries; still methinks I know
To disengage the tangle of thy words: 725
Yet rather would I hear thy angel voice,
Than for myself be thy interpreter.

Angel

When then—if such thy lot—thou seest thy
    Judge,
The sight of Him will kindle in thy heart
All tender, gracious, reverential thoughts. 730
Thou wilt be sick with love, and yearn for Him,
And feel as though thou couldst but pity Him,
That one so sweet should e'er have placed
    Himself
At disadvantage such, as to be used
So vilely by a being so vile as thee.   735
There is a pleading in His pensive eyes
Will pierce thee to the quick, and trouble thee.
And thou wilt hate and loathe thyself; for,
    though
Now sinless, thou wilt feel that thou hast
    sinned,
As never thou didst feel; and wilt desire   740
To slink away, and hide thee from His sight:
And yet wilt have a longing aye to dwell
Within the beauty of His countenance   743
And these two pains, so counter and so keen,—
The longing for Him, when thou seest Him not;
The shame of self at thought of seeing Him,—
Will be thy veriest, sharpest purgatory.

Soul

My soul is in my hand: I have no fear,—
In His dear might prepared for weal or woe.
But hark! a grand, mysterious harmony: 750
It floods me like the deep and solemn sound
Of many waters.

Angel

          We have gained the stairs
Which rise towards the Presence-chamber;
          there
A band of mighty Angels keep the way   755
On either side, and hymn the Incarnate God.

Angels of the Sacred Stair

Father, whose goodness none can know, but
          they
     Who see Thee face to face,
By man hath come the infinite display
     Of thy victorious grace;   760
But fallen man—the creature of a day—
     Skills not that love to trace.
It needs, to tell the triumph Thou hast
     wrought,
An Angel's deathless fire, an Angel's reach of
     thought.

It needs that very Angel, who with awe,   765
     Amid the garden shade,
The great Creator in His sickness saw,
     Soothed by a creature's aid,
And agonized, as victim of the Law
     Which He Himself had made;   770
For who can praise Him in His depth and
     height,
But he who saw Him reel amid that solitary
     fight?

Soul

Hark! for the lintels of the presence-gate
Are vibrating and echoing back the strain.

Fourth Choir of Angelicals

Praise to the Holiest in the height,   775
     And in the depth be praise:
In all His words most wonderful;
     Most sure in all His ways!

The foe blasphemed the Holy Lord,
     As if He reckoned ill,   780
In that He placed His puppet man
     The frontier place to fill.

For, even in his best estate,
     With amplest gifts endued,
A sorry sentinel was he,   785
     A being of flesh and blood.

As though a thing, who for his help
     Must needs possess a wife,
Could cope with those proud rebel hosts
     Who had angelic life.   790

And when, by blandishment of Eve,
     That earth-born Adam fell,
He shrieked in triumph, and he cried,
     "A sorry sentinel;

"The Maker by His word is bound,   795
     Escape or cure is none;
He must abandon to his doom,
     And slay His darling son."

Angel

And now the threshold, as we traverse it,
Utters aloud its glad responsive chant.   800

Fifth Choir of Angelicals

Praise to the Holiest in the height,
     And in the depth be praise:
In all His words most wonderful;
     Most sure in all His ways!

O loving wisdom of our God!   805
     When all was sin and shame,
A second Adam to the fight
     And to the rescue came.

O wisest love! that flesh and blood
     Which did in Adam fail,   810
Should strive afresh against the foe,
     Should strive and should prevail;

And that a higher gift than grace
     Should flesh and blood refine,
God's Presence and His very Self,   815
     And Essence all-divine.

O generous love! that He who smote
     In man for man the foe,
The double agony in man
     For man should undergo;   820

And in the garden secretly,
     And on the cross on high,
Should teach His brethren and inspire
     To suffer and to die.

6

Angel

Thy judgment now is near, for we are come   825
Into the veiléd presence of our God.

791. **blandishment of Eve.** For this story see *Genesis*,
3:1-20.

Soul

I hear the voices that I left on earth.

Angel

It is the voice of friends around thy bed,
Who say the *"Subvenite"* with the priest.
Hither the echoes come; before the Throne 830
Stands the great Angel of the Agony,
The same who strengthened Him, what time
        He knelt
Lone in that garden shade, bedewed with
        blood.
That Angel best can plead with Him for all
Tormented souls, the dying and the dead. 835

Angel of the Agony

Jesu! by that shuddering dread which fell on
        Thee;
Jesu! by that cold dismay which sickened
        Thee;
Jesu! by that pang of heart which thrilled in
        Thee;
Jesu! by that mount of sins which crippled
        Thee;   839
Jesu! by that sense of guilt which stifled Thee;
Jesu! by that innocence which girdled Thee;
Jesu! by that sanctity which reigned in Thee;
Jesu! by that Godhead which was one with
        Thee;
Jesu! spare these souls which are so dear to
        Thee;
Souls, who in prison, calm and patient, wait
        for Thee;   845
Hasten, Lord, their hour, and bid them come
        to Thee,
To that glorious Home, where they shall ever
        gaze on Thee.

Soul

I go before my Judge. Ah! . . .

Angel

        . . . Praise to His Name!
The eager spirit has darted from my hold, 850
And, with the intemperate energy of love,
Flies to the dear feet of Emmanuel;
But, ere it reach them, the keen sanctity,
Which with its effluence, like a glory, clothes
And circles round the Crucified, has seized, 855
And scorched, and shriveled it; and now it lies
Passive and still before the awful Throne.
O happy, suffering soul! for it is safe,
Consumed, yet quickened, by the glance of
        God.

Soul

Take me away, and in the lowest deep   860
        There let me be,
And there in hope the lone night-watches keep,
        Told out for me.
There, motionless and happy in my pain,
        Lone, not forlorn,—   865
There will I sing my sad perpetual strain,
        Until the morn.
There will I sing, and soothe my stricken
        breast,
        Which ne'er can cease
To throb, and pine, and languish, till possest
        Of its Sole Peace.   871
There will I sing my absent Lord and Love:—
        Take me away,
That sooner I may rise, and go above,   874
And see Him in the truth of everlasting day.

7

Angel

Now let the golden prison ope its gates,
Making sweet music, as each fold revolves
Upon its ready hinge. And ye, great powers,
Angels of Purgatory, receive from me
My charge, a precious soul, until the day, 880
When, from all bond and forfeiture released,
I shall reclaim it for the courts of light.

Souls in Purgatory

1. Lord, Thou hast been our refuge: in every
        generation;
2. Before the hills were born, and the world
        was: from age to age Thou art God.
3. Bring us not, Lord, very low: for Thou hast
        said, Come back again, ye sons of
        Adam.   885
4. A thousand years before Thine eyes are but
        as yesterday: and as a watch of the
        night which is come and gone.
5. The grass springs up in the morning: at
        evening tide it shrivels up and dies.
6. So we fail in Thine anger: and in Thy wrath
        are we troubled.
7. Thou hast set our sins in Thy sight: and
        our round of days in the light of Thy
        countenance.
8. Come back, O Lord! how long: and be en-
        treated for Thy servants.   890
9. In Thy morning we shall be filled with Thy
        mercy: we shall rejoice and be in
        pleasure all our days.
10. We shall be glad according to the days of
        our humiliation: and the years in
        which we have seen evil.
11. Look, O Lord, upon Thy servants and on
        Thy work: and direct their children.

---

836 ff. These lines enumerate the mental tortures of Christ
on His journey from Gethsemane to Calvary. See *Luke*, 22-23.
852. **Emmanuel**, the Redeemer. See *Matthew*, 1:23.

883 ff. This passage is based upon the Ninetieth Psalm.

12. And let the beauty of the Lord our God be
    upon us: and the work of our hands,
    establish Thou it.
Glory be to the Father, and to the Son: and to
    the Holy Ghost.   895
As it was in the beginning, is now, and ever
    shall be: world without end. Amen.

Angel

Softly and gently, dearly-ransomed soul,
    In my most loving arms I now enfold thee,
And, o'er the penal waters, as they roll,
    I poise thee, and I lower thee, and hold
    thee.   900

And carefully I dip thee in the lake,
    And thou, without a sob or a resistance,
Dost through the flood thy rapid passage take,
    Sinking deep, deeper, into the dim dis-
    tance.

Angels, to whom the willing task is given, 905
    Shall tend, and nurse, and lull thee, as
    thou liest;
And masses on the earth, and prayers in
    heaven,
    Shall aid thee at the Throne of the Most
    Highest.

Farewell, but not forever! brother dear,
    Be brave and patient on thy bed of sor-
    row;   910
Swiftly shall pass thy night of trial here,
    And I will come and wake thee on the
    morrow.   (*1865;* 1865)

ALFRED, LORD TENNYSON
(1809-1892)

SONNET

She took the dappled partridge fleckt with
    blood,
    And in her hand the drooping pheasant bare,
    And by his feet she held the woolly hare,
And like a master-painting where she stood,
Lookt some new goddess of an English
    wood.   5
    Nor could I find an imperfection there,
    Nor blame the wanton act that showed so
    fair—
To me whatever freak she plays is good.

Hers is the fairest Life that breathes with
    breath,
    And *their* still plumes and azure eyelids
    closed   10
    Made quiet Death so beautiful to see
That Death lent grace to Life and Life to
    Death
    And in one image Life and Death reposed,
    To make my love an Immortality.
                              (*C. 1830;* 1931)

THE SLEEPING BEAUTY

I

Year after year unto her feet,
    She lying on her couch alone,
Across the purple coverlet,
    The maiden's jet-black hair has grown,
On either side her tranced form   5
    Forth streaming from a braid of pearl;
The slumbrous light is rich and warm,
    And moves not on the rounded curl.

2

The silk star-broider'd coverlid
    Unto her limbs itself doth mould   10
Languidly ever; and, amid
    Her full black ringlets downward roll'd,
Glows forth each softly-shadow'd arm
    With bracelets of the diamond bright;
Her constant beauty doth inform   15
    Stillness with love, and day with light.

3

She sleeps; her breathings are not heard
    In palace chambers far apart.
The fragrant tresses are not stirr'd
    That lie upon her charmed heart.   20
She sleeps; on either hand upswells
    The gold-fringed pillow lightly prest;
She sleeps, nor dreams, but ever dwells
    A perfect form in perfect rest. (*1830;* 1842)

THE KRAKEN

Below the thunders of the upper deep,
Far, far beneath in the abysmal sea,
His ancient, dreamless, uninvaded sleep

---

897 ff. These lines give beautiful expression to the doctrine
of purgatory.

The Kraken. The Kraken was a fabulous Scandinavian sea-
monster.

The Kraken sleepeth: faintest sunlights flee
About his shadowy sides; above him swell 5
Huge sponges of millennial growth and height;
And far away into the sickly light,
From many a wondrous grot and secret cell
Unnumbered and enormous polypi
Winnow with giant arms the slumbering
    green. 10
There hath he lain for ages, and will lie
Battening upon huge sea-worms in his sleep,
Until the latter fire shall heat the deep;
Then once by man and angels to be seen,
In roaring he shall rise and on the surface die.
                       (1830)

MARIANA

With blackest moss the flower-plots
    Were thickly crusted, one and all;
The rusted nails fell from the knots
    That held the pear to the gable-wall.
The broken sheds looked sad and strange: 5
    Unlifted was the clinking latch;
    Weeded and worn the ancient thatch
Upon the lonely moated grange.
        She only said, "My life is dreary,
            He cometh not," she said; 10
        She said, "I am aweary, aweary,
            I would that I were dead!"

Her tears fell with the dews at even;
    Her tears fell ere the dews were dried;
She could not look on the sweet heaven, 15
    Either at morn or eventide.
After the flitting of the bats,
    When thickest dark did trance the sky,
    She drew her casement-curtain by,
And glanced athwart the glooming flats. 20
        She only said, "The night is dreary,
            He cometh not," she said;
        She said, "I am aweary, aweary,
            I would that I were dead!"

Upon the middle of the night, 25
    Waking she heard the night-fowl crow;
The cock sung out an hour ere light;
    From the dark fen the oxen's low
Came to her; without hope of change,
    In sleep she seemed to walk forlorn, 30
    Till cold winds woke the gray-eyed morn
About the lonely moated grange.

She only said, "The day is dreary,
    He cometh not," she said;
She said, "I am aweary, aweary, 35
    I would that I were dead!"

About a stone-cast from the wall
    A sluice with blackened waters slept,
And o'er it many, round and small,
    The clustered marish-mosses crept. 40
Hard by a poplar shook alway,
    All silver-green with gnarlèd bark;
    For leagues no other tree did mark
The level waste, the rounding gray.
        She only said, "My life is dreary, 45
            He cometh not," she said;
        She said, "I am aweary, aweary,
            I would that I were dead!"

And ever when the moon was low,
    And the shrill winds were up and away, 50
In the white curtain, to and fro,
    She saw the gusty shadow sway.
But when the moon was very low,
    And wild winds bound within their cell,
    The shadow of the poplar fell 55
Upon her bed, across her brow.
        She only said, "The night is dreary,
            He cometh not," she said;
        She said, "I am aweary, aweary,
            I would that I were dead!" 60

All day within the dreamy house,
    The doors upon their hinges creaked;
The blue fly sung in the pane; the mouse
    Behind the moldering wainscot shrieked,
Or from the crevice peered about. 65
    Old faces glimmered through the doors,
    Old footsteps trod the upper floors,
Old voices called her from without.
        She only said, "My life is dreary,
            He cometh not," she said; 70
        She said, "I am aweary, aweary,
            I would that I were dead!"

The sparrow's chirrup on the roof,
    The slow clock ticking, and the sound
Which to the wooing wind aloof 75
    The poplar made, did all confound
Her sense; but most she loathed the hour
    When the thick-moted sunbeam lay
    Athwart the chambers, and the day
Was sloping toward his western bower. 80
        Then said she, "I am very dreary,
            He will not come," she said;
        She wept, "I am aweary, aweary,
            O God, that I were dead!" (1830)

Mariana. Mariana is a lady in Shakespeare's *Measure for Measure* deserted by her lover. She is described as waiting for him "at the moated grange" (III, i, 277). The scenery of the poem is that of Lincolnshire.
8. **moated grange,** a large country house surrounded by a moat, or ditch. Tennyson states that no particular house is meant. 18. **trance,** traverse.

40. **marish-mosses,** mosses that grow in a marsh.

RECOLLECTIONS OF THE ARABIAN NIGHTS

When the breeze of a joyful dawn blew free
In the silken sail of infancy,
The tide of time flowed back with me,
The forward-flowing tide of time;
And many a sheeny summer-morn, 5
Adown the Tigris I was borne,
By Bagdat's shrines of fretted gold,
High-walled gardens green and old;
True Mussulman was I and sworn,
  For it was in the golden prime 10
  Of good Haroun Alraschid.

Anight my shallop, rustling through
The low and blooméd foliage, drove
The fragrant, glistening deeps, and clove
The citron-shadows in the blue; 15
By garden porches on the brim,
The costly doors flung open wide,
Gold glittering through lamplight dim,
And broidered sofas on each side.
  In sooth it was a goodly time, 20
  For it was in the golden prime
  Of good Haroun Alraschid.

Often, where clear-stemmed platans guard
The outlet, did I turn away
The boat-head down a broad canal 25
From the main river sluiced, where all
The sloping of the moonlit sward
Was damask-work, and deep inlay
Of braided blooms unmown, which crept
Adown to where the water slept. 30
  A goodly place, a goodly time,
  For it was in the golden prime
  Of good Haroun Alraschid.

A motion from the river won
Ridged the smooth level, bearing on 35
My shallop through the star-strown calm,
Until another night in night
I entered, from the clearer light,
Embowered vaults of pillared palm,
Imprisoning sweets, which, as they clomb 40
Heavenward, were stayed beneath the dome
Of hollow boughs. A goodly time,
  For it was in the golden prime
  Of good Haroun Alraschid.

Still onward; and the clear canal 45
Is rounded to as clear a lake.

From the green rivage many a fall
Of diamond rillets musical,
Through little crystal arches low
Down from the central fountain's flow 50
Fallen silver-chiming, seemed to shake
The sparkling flints beneath the prow.
  A goodly place, a goodly time,
  For it was in the golden prime
  Of good Haroun Alraschid. 55

Above through many a bowery turn
A walk with vari-colored shells
Wandered engrained. On either side
All round about the fragrant marge
From fluted vase, and brazen urn 60
In order, eastern flowers large,
Some dropping low their crimson bells
Half-closed, and others studded wide
  With disks and tiars, fed the time
  With odor in the golden prime 65
  Of good Haroun Alraschid.

Far off, and where the lemon grove
In closest coverture upsprung,
The living airs of middle night
Died round the bulbul as he sung; 70
Not he, but something which possessed
The darkness of the world, delight,
Life, anguish, death, immortal love,
Ceasing not, mingled, unrepressed,
  Apart from place, withholding time, 75
  But flattering the golden prime
  Of good Haroun Alraschid.

Black the garden-bowers and grots
Slumbered; the solemn palms were ranged
Above, unwooed of summer wind; 80
A sudden splendor from behind
Flushed all the leaves with rich gold-green,
And, flowing rapidly between
Their interspaces, counterchanged
The level lake with diamond-plots 85
  Of dark and bright. A lovely time,
  For it was in the golden prime
  Of good Haroun Alraschid.

Dark-blue the deep sphere overhead,
Distinct with vivid stars inlaid, 90
Grew darker from that under-flame;
So, leaping lightly from the boat,
With silver anchor left afloat,
In marvel whence that glory came
Upon me, as in sleep I sank 95
In cool soft turf upon the bank,
  Entrancéd with that place and time,
  So worthy of the golden prime
  Of good Haroun Alraschid.

Recollections of the Arabian Nights. This poem is based upon descriptive portions of stories found in *The Arabian Nights' Entertainments.* The chief character in this famous collection is Harun al Rashid, the most renowned of the Bagdad caliphs. Under him, Bagdad, located on the Tigris River, in Mesopotamia, became famous for its poets and scholars and for its many beautiful mosques. He ruled 786-809.
23. **platans,** plane trees.

47. **rivage,** river bank. 58. **engrained.** The walk was inwrought or spotted with shells. 64. **tiars,** crowns. 70. **bulbul,** the Persian nightingale. 84. **counterchanged,** variegated; checkered.

Thence through the garden I was drawn —
A realm of pleasance, many a mound,   101
And many a shadow-checkered lawn
Full of the city's stilly sound,
And deep myrrh-thickets blowing round
The stately cedar, tamarisks,   105
Thick rosaries of scented thorn,
Tall orient shrubs, and obelisks
   Graven with emblems of the time,
   In honor of the golden prime
     Of good Haroun Alraschid.   110

With dazéd vision unawares
From the long alley's latticed shade
Emerged, I came upon the great
Pavilion of the Caliphat.
Right to the carven cedarn doors,   115
Flung inward over spangled floors,
Broad-baséd flights of marble stairs
Ran up with golden balustrade,
   After the fashion of the time,
   And humor of the golden prime   120
     Of good Haroun Alraschid.

The fourscore windows all alight
As with the quintessence of flame,
A million tapers flaring bright
From twisted silvers looked to shame   125
The hollow-vaulted dark, and streamed
Upon the moonéd domes aloof
In inmost Bagdat, till there seemed
Hundreds of crescents on the roof
   Of night new-risen, that marvelous time
   To celebrate the golden prime   131
     Of good Haroun Alraschid.

Then stole I up, and trancedly
Gazed on the Persian girl alone,
Serene with argent-lidded eyes   135
Amorous, and lashes like to rays
Of darkness, and a brow of pearl
Tressed with redolent ebony,
In many a dark delicious curl,
Flowing beneath her rose-hued zone—   140
   The sweetest lady of the time,
   Well worthy of the golden prime
     Of good Haroun Alraschid.

Six columns, three on either side,
Pure silver, underpropped a rich   145
Throne of the massive ore, from which
Down-drooped, in many a floating fold,
Engarlanded and diapered

With inwrought flowers, a cloth of gold.
Thereon, his deep eye laughter-stirred   150
With merriment of kingly pride,
   Sole star of all that place and time,
   I saw him — in his golden prime,
     THE GOOD HAROUN ALRASCHID.   (1830)

SONG

1

A spirit haunts the year's last hours
Dwelling amid these yellowing bowers.
   To himself he talks;
For at eventide, listening earnestly,
At his work you may hear him sob and sigh   5
   In the walks;
Earthward he boweth the heavy stalks
Of the moldering flowers.
   Heavily hangs the broad sunflower
     Over its grave i' the earth so chilly;   10
   Heavily hangs the hollyhock,
     Heavily hangs the tiger-lily.

2

The air is damp, and hushed, and close,
As a sick man's room when he taketh repose
   An hour before death;   15
My very heart faints and my whole soul
   grieves
At the moist rich smell of the rotting leaves,
   And the breath
Of the fading edges of box beneath,
   And the year's last rose.   20
   Heavily hangs the broad sunflower
     Over its grave i' the earth so chilly;
   Heavily hangs the hollyhock,
     Heavily hangs the tiger-lily.   (1830)

THE POET

The poet in a golden clime was born,
   With golden stars above;
Dowered with the hate of hate, the scorn of
   scorn,
   The love of love.

He saw through life and death, through good
   and ill,   5
   He saw through his own soul.
The marvel of the everlasting will,
   An open scroll,

101. pleasance, pleasure.   104. blowing, blooming.
105. tamarisk, a kind of shrub bearing masses of pink
flowers. 106. Thick . . . thorn. The thorn shrubs formed
circles. 107. orient, oriental. 127. moonéd, bearing the
crescent, or Turkish emblem. 135. argent, silvery. 140.
zone, hair-ribbon. 148. Engarlanded and diapered, ornamented with inwrought flowers and symmetrical figures.

Song. 19. box, a kind of evergreen shrub.
The Poet. See Critical Notes.
1-4. Tennyson said that when he wrote these lines he
meant that the poet is moved by a hatred for the quality of
hate, etc., but later he thought it a finer interpretation to
regard "hate of hate," etc., as meaning "the quintessence of
hate," etc. Hallam Tennyson says, "My father denounced
hate and scorn as if they were 'the sins of the Holy Ghost.'"

Before him lay; with echoing feet he threaded
    The secretest walks of fame: 10
The viewless arrows of his thoughts were
    headed
        And winged with flame.

Like Indian reeds blown from his silver
    tongue,
    And of so fierce a flight,
From Calpe unto Caucasus they sung,   15
    Filling with light

And vagrant melodies the winds which bore
    Them earthward till they lit;
Then, like the arrow-seeds of the field flower,
    The fruitful wit   20

Cleaving took root, and springing forth anew
    Where'er they fell, behold,
Like to the mother plant in semblance, grew
    A flower all gold,

And bravely furnished all abroad to fling   25
    The wingéd shafts of truth,
To throng with stately blooms the breathing
    spring
        Of Hope and Youth.

So many minds did gird their orbs with
    beams,
    Though one did fling the fire;   30
Heaven flowed upon the soul in many dreams
    Of high desire.

Thus truth was multiplied on truth, the world
    Like one great garden showed,
And through the wreaths of floating dark
    upcurled,   35
        Rare sunrise flowed.

And Freedom reared in that august sunrise
    Her beautiful bold brow,
When rites and forms before his burning eyes
    Melted like snow.   40

There was no blood upon her maiden robes
    Sunned by those orient skies;
But round about the circles of the globes
    Of her keen eyes

And in her raiment's hem was traced in
    flame   45
    WISDOM, a name to shake

All evil dreams of power—a sacred name.
    And when she spake,

Her words did gather thunder as they ran,
    And as the lightning to the thunder   50
Which follows it, riving the spirit of man,
    Making earth wonder,

So was their meaning to her words. No
    sword
    Of wrath her right arm whirled,
But one poor poet's scroll, and with *his*
    word   55
        She shook the world.   (1830)

THE LADY OF SHALOTT

PART I

On either side the river lie
Long fields of barley and of rye,
That clothe the wold and meet the sky;
And through the field the road runs by
    To many-towered Camelot;   5
And up and down the people go,
Gazing where the lilies blow
Round an island there below,
    The island of Shalott.

Willows whiten, aspens quiver,   10
Little breezes dusk and shiver
Through the wave that runs forever
By the island in the river
    Flowing down to Camelot.
Four gray walls, and four gray towers,   15
Overlook a space of flowers,
And the silent isle embowers
    The Lady of Shalott.

By the margin, willow-veiled,
Slide the heavy barges trailed   20
By slow horses; and unhailed
The shallop flitteth silken-sailed
    Skimming down to Camelot:
But who hath seen her wave her hand?
Or at the casement seen her stand?   25
Or is she known in all the land,
    The Lady of Shalott?

Only reapers, reaping early
In among the bearded barley,
Hear a song that echoes cheerly   30
From the river winding clearly,
    Down to towered Camelot;

---

13. **reeds,** darts or arrows blown from a pipe. 15. **From Calpe unto Caucasus,** from Gibraltar to the Caucasus Mountains, conventional western and eastern limits of Europe. 19. **field flower,** the dandelion, the seeds of which are attached to delicate shafts that the poet likens to arrows. 25. **bravely,** gloriously, admirably.

The Lady of Shalott. See Critical Notes.
5. **Camelot,** the city of King Arthur's court, in Cornwall. 7. **blow,** bloom. 10. **Willows whiten.** The wind turns up the white underside of the leaves.

And by the moon the reaper weary,
Piling sheaves in uplands airy,
Listening, whispers, " 'Tis the fairy   35
    Lady of Shalott."

PART 2

There she weaves by night and day
A magic web with colors gay.
She has heard a whisper say,
A curse is on her if she stay   40
    To look down to Camelot.
She knows not what the curse may be,
And so she weaveth steadily,
And little other care hath she,
    The Lady of Shalott.   45

And moving through a mirror clear
That hangs before her all the year,
Shadows of the world appear.
There she sees the highway near
    Winding down to Camelot;   50
There the river eddy whirls,
And there the surly village-churls,
And the red cloaks of market girls,
    Pass onward from Shalott.

Sometimes a troop of damsels glad,   55
An abbot on an ambling pad,
Sometimes a curly shepherd-lad,
Or long-haired page in crimson clad,
    Goes by to towered Camelot;
And sometimes through the mirror blue   60
The knights come riding two and two;
She hath no loyal knight and true,
    The Lady of Shalott.

But in her web she still delights
To weave the mirror's magic sights,   65
For often through the silent nights
A funeral, with plumes and lights
    And music, went to Camelot;
Or when the moon was overhead,
Came two young lovers lately wed;   70
"I am half sick of shadows," said
    The Lady of Shalott.

PART 3

A bow-shot from her bower eaves,
He rode between the barley-sheaves;
The sun came dazzling through the leaves,   75
And flamed upon the brazen greaves
    Of bold Sir Lancelot.
A red-cross knight forever kneeled
To a lady in his shield,

That sparkled on the yellow field,   80
    Beside remote Shalott.

The gemmy bridle glittered free,
Like to some branch of stars we see
Hung in the golden Galaxy.
The bridle bells rang merrily   85
    As he rode down to Camelot;
And from his blazoned baldric slung
A mighty silver bugle hung,
And as he rode his armor rung,
    Beside remote Shalott.   90

All in the blue unclouded weather
Thick-jewelled shone the saddle-leather,
The helmet and the helmet-feather
Burned like one burning flame together
    As he rode down to Camelot;   95
As often through the purple night,
Below the starry clusters bright,
Some bearded meteor, trailing light,
    Moves over still Shalott.

His broad clear brow in sunlight glowed;   100
On burnished hooves his war-horse trode;
From underneath his helmet flowed
His coal-black curls as on he rode,
    As he rode down to Camelot.
From the bank and from the river   105
He flashed into the crystal mirror,
"Tirra lirra," by the river
    Sang Sir Lancelot.

She left the web, she left the loom,
She made three paces through the room,   110
She saw the water-lily bloom,
She saw the helmet and the plume,
    She looked down to Camelot.
Out flew the web and floated wide;
The mirror cracked from side to side;   115
"The curse is come upon me," cried
    The Lady of Shalott.

PART 4

In the stormy east-wind straining,
The pale yellow woods were waning,
The broad stream in his banks complaining,
Heavily the low sky raining   121
    Over towered Camelot;
Down she came and found a boat
Beneath a willow left afloat,
And round about the prow she wrote   125
    The Lady of Shalott.

84. **Galaxy**, the Milky Way.

And down the river's dim expanse
Like some bold seër in a trance,
Seeing all his own mischance—
With a glassy countenance 130
    Did she look to Camelot.
And at the closing of the day
She loosed the chain, and down she lay;
The broad stream bore her far away,
    The Lady of Shalott. 135

Lying, robed in snowy white
That loosely flew to left and right—
The leaves upon her falling light—
Through the noises of the night
    She floated down to Camelot; 140
And as the boat-head wound along
The willowy hills and fields among,
They heard her singing her last song,
    The Lady of Shalott.

Heard a carol, mournful, holy, 145
Chanted loudly, chanted lowly,
Till her blood was frozen slowly,
And her eyes were darkened wholly,
    Turned to towered Camelot.
For ere she reached upon the tide 150
The first house by the water-side,
Singing in her song she died,
    The Lady of Shalott.

Under tower and balcony,
By garden-wall and gallery, 155
A gleaming shape she floated by,
Dead-pale between the houses high,
    Silent into Camelot.
Out upon the wharfs they came,
Knight and burgher, lord and dame, 160
And round the prow they read her name,
    The Lady of Shalott.

Who is this? and what is here?
And in the lighted palace near
Died the sound of royal cheer; 165
And they crossed themselves for fear,
    All the knights at Camelot.
But Lancelot mused a little space;
He said, "She has a lovely face;
God in his mercy lend her grace, 170
    The Lady of Shalott." (1832, 1842)

THE HESPERIDES

*"Hesperus and his daughters three,
That sing about the golden tree."*
                    Comus

The North-wind fall'n, in the new-starrèd
    night
Zidonian Hanno, voyaging beyond

The hoary promontory of Soloë
Past Thymiaterion, in calmèd bays,
Between the Southern and the Western
    Horn, 5
Heard neither warbling of the nightingale,
Nor melody of the Libyan lotusflute
Blown seaward from the shore; but from
    a slope
That ran bloombright into the Atlantic blue,
Beneath a highland leaning down a weight 10
Of cliffs, and zoned below with cedarshade,
Came voices, like the voices in a dream,
Continuous, till he reached the outer sea.

SONG

I

The golden apple, the golden apple, the
    hallowed fruit,
Guard it well, guard it warily, 15
Singing airily,
Standing about the charmèd root.
Round about all is mute,
As the snowfield on the mountain-peaks,
As the sandfield at the mountain-foot. 20
Crocodiles in briny creeks
Sleep and stir not: all is mute.
If ye sing not, if ye make false measure,
We shall lose eternal pleasure,
Worth eternal want of rest. 25
Laugh not loudly: watch the treasure
Of the wisdom of the West.
In a corner wisdom whispers. Five and three
(Let it not be preached abroad) make an
    awful mystery.
For the blossom unto threefold music bloweth;
Evermore it is born anew; 31
And the sap to threefold music floweth,
From the root
Drawn in the dark,
Up to the fruit, 35
Creeping under the fragrant bark,
Liquid gold, honeysweet, thro' and thro'.
Keen-eyed Sisters, singing airily,
Looking warily
Every way, 40
Guard the apple night and day,
Lest one from the East come and take it away.

The Hesperides. The Hesperides, daughters of the evening
star, Hesperus, were set along with their dragon, Ladon, to
guard a sacred tree of golden apples. The epilogue to Milton's
Comus describes their island garden in the western ocean.
2. **Zidonian Hanno,** Hanno of Carthage (5th century
B.C.), an explorer whose travels along the west coast of Africa
are mentioned in the following lines. 42. **one from the
East,** Hercules, whose eleventh labor was to steal the golden
apples.

2

Father Hesper, Father Hesper, watch, watch,
    ever and aye,
Looking under silver hair with a silver eye.
Father, twinkle not thy steadfast sight;   45
Kingdoms lapse, and climates change, and
    races die;
Honor comes with mystery;
Hoarded wisdom brings delight.
Number, tell them over and number
How many the mystic fruit-tree holds   50
Lest the red-combed dragon slumber
Rolled together in purple folds.
Look to him, father, lest he wink, and the
    golden apple be stol'n away,
For his ancient heart is drunk with over-
    watchings night and day,
Round about the hallowed fruit-tree curled—
Sing away, sing aloud evermore in the wind,
    without stop,   56
Lest his scalèd eyelid drop,
For he is older than the world.
If he waken, we waken,
Rapidly levelling eager eyes.   60
If he sleep, we sleep,
Dropping the eyelid over the eyes.
If the golden apple be taken,
The world will be overwise.
Five links, a golden chain, are we,   65
Hesper, the dragon, and sisters three,
Bound about the golden tree.

3

Father Hesper, Father Hesper, watch, watch,
    night and day,
Lest the old wound of the world be healèd,
The glory unsealèd,   70
The golden apple stol'n away,
And the ancient secret revealèd.
Look from west to east along:
Father, old Himala weakens, Caucasus is
    bold and strong.
Wandering waters unto wandering waters call;
Let them clash together, foam and fall.   76
Out of watchings, out of wiles,
Comes the bliss of secret smiles.
All things are not told to all.
Half-round the mantling night is drawn,   80
Purplefringéd with even and dawn.
Hesper hateth Phosphor, evening hateth
    morn.

4

Every flower and every fruit the redolent
    breath
Of this warm sea-wind ripeneth,
Arching the billow in his sleep;   85
But the land-wind wandereth,
Broken by the highland-steep,
Two streams upon the violet deep;
For the western sun and the western star,
And the low west-wind, breathing afar,   90
The end of day and beginning of night
Make the apple holy and bright;
Holy and bright, round and full, bright
    and blest,
Mellowed in a land of rest;
Watch it warily day and night;   95
All good things are in the west.
Till mid noon the cool east light
Is shut out by the round of the tall
    hillbrow.
But when the fullfaced sunset yellowly
Stays on the flowering arch of the bough,   100
The luscious fruitage clustereth mellowly,
Golden-kernelled, golden-cored,
Sunset-ripened, above on the tree.
The world is wasted with fire and sword,
But the apple of gold hangs over the sea   105
Five links, a golden chain are we,
Hesper, the dragon, and sisters three,
Daughters three,
Bound about
All round about   110
The gnarlèd bole of the charméd tree.
The golden apple, the golden apple, the
    hallowed fruit,
Guard it well, guard it warily,
Watch it warily,
Singing airily,   115
Standing about the charméd root.   (1832)

ŒNONE

There lies a vale in Ida, lovelier
Than all the valleys of Ionian hills.
The swimming vapor slopes athwart the
    glen,
Puts forth an arm, and creeps from pine to
    pine,

---

74. **Himala**, the Indian Himalayas. **Caucasus**, mountains between the Caspian and Black seas. The line means that the day is moving westward toward the garden of the Hesperides. 82. **Phosphor**, the morning star.

Œnone. Œnone was a nymph of Mt. Ida, in Troas, a country in Asia Minor. She was the wife of Paris, son of King Priam of Troy (Ilion). Paris has deserted Œnone for Helen of Troy. (See Critical Notes.)

And loiters, slowly drawn. On either hand 5
The lawns and meadow-ledges midway down
Hang rich in flowers, and far below them roars
The long brook falling through the cloven
ravine
In cataract after cataract to the sea.
Behind the valley topmost Gargarus 10
Stands up and takes the morning; but in front
The gorges, opening wide apart, reveal
Troas and Ilion's columned citadel,
The crown of Troas.

          Hither came at noon
Mournful Œnone, wandering forlorn 15
Of Paris, once her playmate on the hills.
Her cheek had lost the rose, and round her
neck
Floated her hair or seemed to float in rest.
She, leaning on a fragment twined with vine,
Sang to the stillness, till the mountain-shade
Sloped downward to her seat from the upper
cliff. 21

"O mother Ida, many-fountained Ida,
Dear mother Ida, harken ere I die.
For now the noonday quiet holds the hill;
The grasshopper is silent in the grass; 25
The lizard, with his shadow on the stone,
Rests like a shadow, and the winds are dead.
The purple flower droops, the golden bee
Is lily-cradled; I alone awake.
My eyes are full of tears, my heart of love, 30
My heart is breaking, and my eyes are dim,
And I am all aweary of my life.

"O mother Ida, many-fountained Ida,
Dear mother Ida, harken ere I die.
Hear me, O Earth, hear me, O Hills, O Caves
That house the cold crowned snake! O moun-
tain brooks, 36
I am the daughter of a river-god.
Hear me, for I will speak, and build up all
My sorrow with my song, as yonder walls
Rose slowly to a music slowly breathed, 40
A cloud that gathered shape; for it may be
That, while I speak of it, a little while
My heart may wander from its deeper woe.

"O mother Ida, many-fountained Ida,
Dear mother Ida, harken ere I die. 45
I waited underneath the dawning hills;
Aloft the mountain lawn was dewy-dark,
And dewy-dark aloft the mountain pine.

Beautiful Paris, evil-hearted Paris,
Leading a jet-black goat white-horned, white-
hoofed, 50
Came up from reedy Simois all alone.

"O mother Ida, harken ere I die.
Far-off the torrent called me from the cleft;
Far up the solitary morning smote
The streaks of virgin snow. With down-
dropped eyes 55
I sat alone; white-breasted like a star
Fronting the dawn he moved; a leopard skin
Drooped from his shoulder, but his sunny hair
Clustered about his temples like a god's;
And his cheek brightened as the foam-bow
brightens 60
When the wind blows the foam, and all my heart
Went forth to embrace him coming ere he
came.

"Dear mother Ida, harken ere I die.
He smiled, and opening out his milk-white
palm,
Disclosed a fruit of pure Hesperian gold, 65
That smelt ambrosially, and while I looked
And listened, the full-flowing river of speech
Came down upon my heart:
          'My own Œnone,
Beautiful-browed Œnone, my own soul,
Behold this fruit, whose gleaming rind in-
graven 70
"For the most fair," would seem to award it
thine,
As lovelier than whatever oread haunt
The knolls of Ida, loveliest in all grace
Of movement, and the charm of married
brows.'

"Dear mother Ida, harken ere I die. 75
He pressed the blossom of his lips to mine,
And added, 'This was cast upon the board,
When all the full-faced presence of the gods
Ranged in the halls of Peleus; whereupon
Rose feud, with question unto whom 'twere
due; 80
But light-foot Iris brought it yester-eve,
Delivering, that to me, by common voice
Elected umpire, Heré comes today,
Pallas and Aphrodite, claiming each
This meed of fairest. Thou, within the cave

6. **lawns,** open places in the woods. **meadow-ledges,** open flat spaces on the hillsides. 10. **Gargarus,** the highest part of Mt. Ida. 11. **takes,** charms, bewitches; receives (the rising sun). 22. **many-fountained.** Several rivers have their source on Mt. Ida. 36. **snake.** The snake was early recognized as a divinity; it symbolized the power of the under-world. 37. **river-god.** The river referred to is the Kebren, a small stream in Troas. 39-40. **walls . . . music.** According to Ovid, Troy was built to the music of Apollo's lyre.

51. **Simois,** a small stream in Troas. 65. **fruit . . . gold,** a golden apple from the garden of the Hesperides, daughters of Hesperus, or Night. 72. **oread,** a mountain nymph. 74. **married brows,** meeting eyebrows, regarded as a mark of beauty in the East. 79. **Peleus,** king of Thessaly, who had gathered the gods to witness his marriage to the sea nymph Thetis. 80. **feud.** Eris, the goddess of discord, angered at not being invited, threw among the guests a golden apple marked "for the most beautiful." It was claimed by Juno (Heré), wife of Jupiter and queen of heaven; by Minerva (Pallas), goddess of wisdom; and by Venus (Aphrodite), goddess of love. 81. **Iris,** goddess of the rainbow, the messenger of the gods.

Behind yon whispering tuft of oldest pine, 86
Mayst well behold them unbeheld, unheard
Hear all, and see thy Paris judge of gods.'

"Dear mother Ida, harken ere I die.
It was the deep midnoon; one silvery cloud 90
Had lost his way between the piny sides
Of this long glen.   Then to the bower they
     came,
Naked they came to that smooth-swarded
     bower,
And at their feet the crocus brake like fire,
Violet, amaracus, and asphodel,   95
Lotos and lilies; and a wind arose,
And overhead the wandering ivy and vine,
This way and that, in many a wild festoon
Ran riot, garlanding the gnarléd boughs
With bunch and berry and flower through and
     through.   100

"O mother Ida, harken ere I die.
On the tree-tops a crested peacock lit,
And o'er him flowed a golden cloud, and
     leaned
Upon him, slowly dropping fragrant dew.
Then first I heard the voice of her to whom
Coming through heaven, like a light that
     grows   106
Larger and clearer, with one mind the gods
Rise up for reverence.   She to Paris made
Proffer of royal power, ample rule
Unquestioned, overflowing revenue   110
Wherewith to embellish state, 'from many a
     vale
And river-sundered champaign clothed with
     corn,
Or labored mine undrainable of ore.
Honor,' she said, 'and homage, tax and toll,
From many an inland town and haven large,
Mast-thronged beneath her shadowing citadel
In glassy bays among her tallest towers.' 117

"O mother Ida, harken ere I die.
Still she spake on and still she spake of power,
'Which in all action is the end of all;   120
Power fitted to the season; wisdom-bred
And throned of wisdom — from all neighbor
     crowns
Alliance and allegiance, till thy hand
Fail from the scepter-staff.   Such boon from
     me,
From me, heaven's queen, Paris, to thee
     king-born,   125
A shepherd all thy life but yet king-born,

Should come most welcome, seeing men, in
     power
Only, are likest gods, who have attained
Rest in a happy place and quiet seats
Above the thunder, with undying bliss   130
In knowledge of their own supremacy.'

"Dear mother Ida, harken ere I die.
She ceased, and Paris held the costly fruit
Out at arm's-length, so much the thought of
     power
Flattered his spirit; but Pallas where she
     stood   135
Somewhat apart, her clear and baréd limbs
O'erthwarted with the brazen-headed spear
Upon her pearly shoulder leaning cold,
The while, above, her full and earnest eye
Over her snow-cold breast and angry cheek
Kept watch, waiting decision, made reply: 141

" 'Self-reverence, self-knowledge, self-con-
     trol,
These three alone lead life to sovereign power.
Yet not for power (power of herself
Would come uncalled for) but to live by law,
Acting the law we live by without fear;   146
And, because right is right, to follow right
Were wisdom in the scorn of consequence.'

"Dear mother Ida, harken ere I die.
Again she said: 'I woo thee not with gifts. 150
Sequel of guerdon could not alter me
To fairer.   Judge thou me by what I am,
So shalt thou find me fairest.
                         Yet, indeed,
If gazing on divinity disrobed
Thy mortal eyes are frail to judge of fair, 155
Unbiased by self-profit, oh, rest thee sure
That I shall love thee well and cleave to thee,
So that my vigor, wedded to thy blood,
Shall strike within thy pulses, like a god's,
To push thee forward through a life of shocks,
Dangers, and deeds, until endurance grow 161
Sinewed with action, and the full-grown will,
Circled through all experiences, pure law,
Commeasure perfect freedom.'
                         Here she ceased,
And Paris pondered, and I cried, 'O Paris,
Give it to Pallas!' but he heard me not,   166
Or hearing would not hear me, woe is me!

"O mother Ida, many-fountained Ida,
Dear mother Ida, harken ere I die.
Idalian Aphrodite beautiful,   170

102. peacock. The peacock was sacred to Juno. 112.
champaign, a stretch of flat open country. corn, grain,
wheat. 122. throned of wisdom, put in high place by
wisdom. 126. A shepherd . . . king-born. Because of a
prophecy at the birth of Paris that he would ruin his country
he was left to perish on Mt. Ida, but he was found by a
peasant and brought up as a shepherd.

136-137. limbs . . . spear. The spear was carried across
her body and over one shoulder. 151. Sequel of guerdon,
the giving of a reward for choosing me. 170. Idalian, so
called from one of her favorite seats, Idalium, a mountain
city in Cyprus.

Fresh as the foam, new-bathed in Paphian
   wells,
With rosy slender fingers backward drew
From her warm brows and bosom her deep
   hair
Ambrosial, golden round her lucid throat
And shoulder; from the violets her light foot
Shone rosy-white, and o'er her rounded form
Between the shadows of the vine-bunches 177
Floated the glowing sunlights, as she moved.

"Dear mother Ida, harken ere I die.
She with a subtle smile in her mild eyes,   180
The herald of her triumph, drawing nigh
Half-whispered in his ear, 'I promise thee
The fairest and most loving wife in Greece.'
She spoke and laughed; I shut my sight for
   fear;
But when I looked, Paris had raised his arm,
And I beheld great Heré's angry eyes,   186
As she withdrew into the golden cloud,
And I was left alone within the bower;
And from that time to this I am alone,
And I shall be alone until I die.   190

"Yet, mother Ida, harken ere I die.
Fairest — why fairest wife? am I not fair?
My love hath told me so a thousand times.
Methinks I must be fair, for yesterday,   194
When I passed by, a wild and wanton pard,
Eyed like the evening star, with playful tail
Crouched fawning in the weed. Most loving
   is she?
Ah me, my mountain shepherd, that my arms
Were wound about thee, and my hot lips
   pressed
Close, close to thine in that quick-falling
   dew
Of fruitful kisses, thick as autumn rains   201
Flash in the pools of whirling Simois!

"O mother, hear me yet before I die.
They came, they cut away my tallest pines,
My tall dark pines, that plumed the craggy
   ledge   205
High over the blue gorge, and all between
The snowy peak and snow-white cataract
Fostered the callow eaglet — from beneath
Whose thick mysterious boughs in the dark
   morn
The panther's roar came muffled, while I sat
Low in the valley. Never, never more   211
Shall lone Œnone see the morning mist
Sweep through them; never see them over-
   laid

With narrow moonlit slips of silver cloud,
Between the loud stream and the trembling
   stars.   215

"O mother, hear me yet before I die.
I wish that somewhere in the ruined folds,
Among the fragments tumbled from the glens,
Or the dry thickets, I could meet with her
The Abominable, that uninvited came   220
Into the fair Peleïan banquet-hall,
And cast the golden fruit upon the board,
And bred this change; that I might speak my
   mind,
And tell her to her face how much I hate
Her presence, hated both of gods and men.

"O mother, hear me yet before I die.   226
Hath he not sworn his love a thousand times,
In this green valley, under this green hill,
Even on this hand, and sitting on this stone?
Sealed it with kisses? watered it with tears?
O happy tears, and how unlike to these!   231
O happy heaven, how canst thou see my face?
O happy earth, how canst thou bear my
   weight?
O death, death, death, thou ever-floating
   cloud,
There are enough unhappy on this earth,   235
Pass by the happy souls, that love to live;
I pray thee, pass before my light of life,
And shadow all my soul, that I may die.
Thou weighest heavy on the heart within,
Weigh heavy on my eyelids; let me die.   240

"O mother, hear me yet before I die.
I will not die alone, for fiery thoughts
Do shape themselves within me, more and
   more,
Whereof I catch the issue, as I hear
Dead sounds at night come from the inmost
   hills,   245
Like footsteps upon wool. I dimly see
My far-off doubtful purpose, as a mother
Conjectures the features of her child
Ere it is born. Her child! — a shudder comes
Across me; never child be born of me,   250
Unblest, to vex me with his father's eyes!

"O mother, hear me yet before I die.
Hear me, O earth. I will not die alone,
Lest their shrill happy laughter come to me
Walking the cold and starless road of death
Uncomforted, leaving my ancient love   256
With the Greek woman. I will rise and go
Down into Troy, and ere the stars come forth

---

171. **Paphian.** The city of Paphos, in Cyprus, was the center of the worship of Venus. 183. **The fairest,** Helen of Troy. 195. **wanton pard,** sportive leopard. 204. **They,** the Trojan shipbuilders.

220. **The Abominable.** Eris. (See note on line 80.) 242. **I will not die alone.** Œnone was gifted with prophecy and the art of healing. She told Paris that he would be wounded and that she alone could cure him. When he came to her later, she avenged his act of desertion by refusing to aid him. 257. **the Greek woman,** Helen of Troy.

Talk with the wild Cassandra, for she says
A fire dances before her, and a sound   260
Rings ever in her ears of arméd men.
What this may be I know not, but I know
That, wheresoe'er I am by night and day,
All earth and air seem only burning fire."
(1832, 1842)

THE PALACE OF ART

I built my soul a lordly pleasure-house,
  Wherein at ease for aye to dwell.
I said, "O Soul, make merry and carouse,
  Dear soul, for all is well."

A huge crag-platform, smooth as burnished
    brass,   5
  I chose. The rangéd ramparts bright
From level meadow-bases of deep grass
  Suddenly scaled the light.

Thereon I built it firm. Of ledge or shelf
  The rock rose clear, or winding stair.   10
My soul would live alone unto herself
  In her high palace there.

And "while the world runs round and round,"
  I said,
  "Reign thou apart, a quiet king,
Still as, while Saturn whirls, his steadfast
    shade   15
  Sleeps on his luminous ring."

To which my soul made answer readily:
  "Trust me, in bliss I shall abide
In this great mansion, that is built for me,
  So royal-rich and wide."   20

   .   .   .   .   .

Four courts I made, East, West and South
    and North,
  In each a squaréd lawn, wherefrom
The golden gorge of dragons spouted forth
  A flood of fountain-foam.

And round the cool green courts there ran a
    row   25
  Of cloisters, branched like mighty woods,
Echoing all night to that sonorous flow
  Of spouted fountain-floods;

And round the roofs a gilded gallery
  That lent broad verge to distant lands,   30

Far as the wild swan wings, to where the sky
  Dipped down to sea and sands.

From those four jets four currents in one swell
  Across the mountain streamed below
In misty folds, that floating as they fell   35
  Lit up a torrent-bow.

And high on every peak a statue seemed
  To hang on tiptoe, tossing up
A cloud of incense of all odor steamed
  From out a golden cup.   40

So that she thought, "And who shall gaze
    upon
  My palace with unblinded eyes,
While this great bow will waver in the sun,
  And that sweet incense rise?"

For that sweet incense rose and never failed,
  And, while day sank or mounted higher,   46
The light aerial gallery, golden-railed,
  Burnt like a fringe of fire.

Likewise the deep-set windows, stained and
    traced,
  Would seem slow-flaming crimson fires   50
From shadowed grots of arches interlaced,
  And tipped with frost-like spires.

Full of long-sounding corridors it was,
  That over-vaulted grateful gloom,
Through which the livelong day my soul did
    pass,   55
  Well-pleased, from room to room.

Full of great rooms and small the palace stood,
  All various, each a perfect whole
From living Nature, fit for every mood
  And change of my still soul.   60

For some were hung with arras green and
    blue,
  Showing a gaudy summer-morn,
Where with puffed cheek the belted hunter
    blew
  His wreathéd bugle-horn.

One seemed all dark and red — a tract of
    sand,   65
  And someone pacing there alone,
Who paced forever in a glimmering land,
  Lit with a low large moon.

One showed an iron coast and angry waves.
  You seemed to hear them climb and fall   70
And roar rock-thwarted under bellowing
    caves,
  Beneath the windy wall.

And one, a full-fed river winding slow
   By herds upon an endless plain,
The ragged rims of thunder brooding low, 75
   With shadow-streaks of rain.

And one, the reapers at their sultry toil.
   In front they bound the sheaves. Behind
Were realms of upland, prodigal in oil,
   And hoary to the wind.   80

And one a foreground black with stones and
   slags;
Beyond, a line of heights; and higher
All barred with long white cloud the scornful
   crags;
   And highest, snow and fire.

And one, an English home — gray twilight
   poured   85
   On dewy pastures, dewy trees,
Softer than sleep — all things in order stored,
   A haunt of ancient Peace.

Nor these alone, but every landscape fair,
   As fit for every mood of mind,   90
Or gay, or grave, or sweet, or stern, was there,
   Not less than truth designed.

   .   .   .   .   .

Or the maid-mother by a crucifix,
   In tracts of pasture sunny-warm,
Beneath branch-work of costly sardonyx   95
   Sat smiling, babe in arm.

Or in a clear-walled city on the sea,
   Near gilded organ-pipes, her hair
Wound with white roses, slept Saint Cecily;
   An angel looked at her.   100

Or thronging all one porch of Paradise
   A group of Houris bowed to see
The dying Islamite, with hands and eyes
   That said, We wait for thee.

Or mythic Uther's deeply-wounded son   105
   In some fair space of sloping greens
Lay, dozing in the vale of Avalon,
   And watched by weeping queens.

Or hollowing one hand against his ear,
   To list a footfall, ere he saw   110

The wood-nymph, stayed the Ausonian king
   to hear
   Of wisdom and of law.

Or over hills with peaky tops engrailed,
   And many a tract of palm and rice,
The throne of Indian Cama slowly sailed   115
   A summer fanned with spice.

Or sweet Europa's mantle blew unclasped,
   From off her shoulder backward borne;
From one hand drooped a crocus; one hand
   grasped
   The mild bull's golden horn.   120

Or else flushed Ganymede, his rosy thigh
   Half-buried in the eagle's down,
Sole as a flying star shot through the sky
   Above the pillared town.

Nor these alone; but every legend fair   125
   Which the supreme Caucasian mind
Carved out of Nature for itself was there,
   Not less than life designed.

   .   .   .   .   .

Then in the towers I placed great bells that
   swung,
   Moved of themselves, with silver sound; 130
And with choice paintings of wise men I hung
   The royal dais round.

For there was Milton like a seraph strong,
   Beside him Shakespeare bland and mild;
And there the world-worn Dante grasped his
   song,   135
   And somewhat grimly smiled.

And there the Ionian father of the rest;
   A million wrinkles carved his skin;
A hundred winters snowed upon his breast,
   From cheek and throat and chin.   140

Above, the fair hall-ceiling stately-set
   Many an arch high up did lift,
And angels rising and descending met
   With interchange of gift.

Below was all mosaic choicely planned   145
   With cycles of the human tale

79. **prodigal in oil,** rich in olive oil. 80. **hoary to the
wind.** The wind turned up the whitish-gray undersides of
the olive leaves. 99. **Saint Cecily,** St. Cecilia, the patron
saint of music and inventor of the organ (3d cent.). 102.
Houris. According to the Moslem faith, the Houris are
beautiful maidens who will be the companions of true be-
lievers in paradise. The Moslems are known also as Islamites.
105. **Uther's . . . son,** King Arthur (see *Morte d'Arthur*, line
5, page 39). 107. **Avalon,** in Celtic mythology, the Land
of the Blessed, or Isle of Souls, an earthly paradise in the
western seas.

111. **Ausonian king.** Numa Pompilius, the legendary
second king of Rome, who is said to have been instructed by
the nymph Egeria. Ausonia is a poetic name for Italy. 113.
engrailed, indented in curved lines. 115. **Cama,** the god of
love in Hindu mythology. He is frequently represented as
riding on a parrot. 117. **Europa,** a princess of Phœnicia
whom Zeus, in the form of a white bull, carried off to Crete.
121. **Ganymede,** a beautiful Trojan boy whom Zeus, in the
form of an eagle, carried off to Olympus to be cupbearer to
the gods. 126. **supreme Caucasian mind,** i.e., the aggre-
gate of Western culture. Cf. *Locksley Hall*, 184, p. 49. 137.
the Ionian father, Homer.

Of this wide world, the times of every land
  So wrought they will not fail.

The people here, a beast of burden slow,
  Toiled onward, pricked with goads and
    stings;   150
Here played, a tiger, rolling to and fro
  The heads and crowns of kings;

Here rose, an athlete, strong to break or bind
  All force in bonds that might endure,
And here once more like some sick man
    declined,   155
  And trusted any cure.

But over these she trod; and those great bells
  Began to chime. She took her throne;
She sat betwixt the shining oriels,
  To sing her songs alone.   160

And through the topmost oriels' colored flame
  Two godlike faces gazed below:
Plato the wise, and large-browed Verulam,
  The first of those who know.

And all those names that in their motion were
  Full-welling fountain-heads of change, 166
Betwixt the slender shafts were blazoned fair
  In diverse raiment strange;

Through which the lights, rose, amber, em-
    erald, blue,
  Flushed in her temples and her eyes, 170
And from her lips, as morn from Memnon,
    drew
  Rivers of melodies.

No nightingale delighteth to prolong
  Her low preamble all alone,
More than my soul to hear her echoed song
  Throb through the ribbéd stone; 176

Singing and murmuring in her feastful mirth,
  Joying to feel herself alive,
Lord over Nature, lord of the visible earth,
  Lord of the senses five;   180

Communing with herself: "All these are mine,
  And let the world have peace or wars,
'Tis one to me." She — when young night
    divine
  Crowned dying day with stars,

Making sweet close of his delicious toils —
  Lit light in wreaths and anadems, 186
And pure quintessences of precious oils
  In hollowed moons of gems,

To mimic heaven; and clapped her hands and
    cried,
  "I marvel if my still delight   190
In this great house so royal-rich and wide
  Be flattered to the height.

"O all things fair to sate my various eyes!
  O shapes and hues that please me well!
O silent faces of the Great and Wise, 195
  My gods, with whom I dwell!

"O godlike isolation which art mine,
  I can but count thee perfect gain,
What time I watch the darkening droves of
    swine
  That range on yonder plain.   200

"In filthy sloughs they roll a prurient skin,
  They graze and wallow, breed and sleep;
And oft some brainless devil enters in,
  And drives them to the deep."

Then of the moral instinct would she prate
  And of the rising from the dead, 206
As hers by right of full-accomplished Fate;
  And at the last she said:

"I take possession of man's mind and deed.
  I care not what the sects may brawl. 210
I sit as God holding no form of creed,
  But contemplating all."

.   .   .   .   .

Full oft the riddle of the painful earth
  Flashed through her as she sat alone,
Yet not the less held she her solemn mirth,
  And intellectual throne.   216

And so she throve and prospered; so three
    years
  She prospered; on the fourth she fell,
Like Herod, when the shout was in his ears,
  Struck through with pangs of hell. 220

Lest she should fail and perish utterly,
  God, before whom ever lie bare
The abysmal deeps of personality,
  Plagued her with sore despair.

149-156. These lines refer to the people of France before
and during the French Revolution. The tiger (line 151) may
represent rebellion, the athlete (line 153) democracy, and the
sick man (line 155) anarchy. 163. **Plato**, a famous Greek
philosopher (427-347 B.C.). **Verulam**, Francis Bacon (1561-
1626), who was made Baron Verulam by James I in
1618. 171-172. **Memnon . . . melodies**, a large statue near
Thebes, in Upper Egypt, said to give forth music when hit
by the rays of the morning sun.

186. **anadems**, garlands. 188. **moons of gems**, gems
hollowed out for lamps. 203-204. **devil . . . deep**, a reference to the devils cast out of two men in *Matthew*, 8:32.
—"And he said unto them, 'Go.' And when they were come
out, they went into the herd of swine; and, behold, the whole
herd of swine ran violently down a steep place into the sea
and perished in the waters." 219. **Like Herod**, etc. After
Herod had spoken to the people from the throne, "the people
gave a shout, saying, 'It is the voice of a god, and not of a
man.' And immediately the angel of the Lord smote him,
because he gave not God the glory" (*Acts*, 12:21-23).

When she would think, where'er she turned
   her sight   225
The airy hand confusion wrought,
Wrote, "Mene, mene," and divided quite
   The kingdom of her thought.

Deep dread and loathing of her solitude
   Fell on her, from which mood was born 230
Scorn of herself; again, from out that mood
   Laughter at her self-scorn.

"What! is not this my place of strength," she
   said,
   "My spacious mansion built for me,
Whereof the strong foundation-stones were
   laid   235
   Since my first memory?"

But in dark corners of her palace stood
   Uncertain shapes; and unawares
On white-eyed phantasms weeping tears of
   blood,
   And horrible nightmares,   240

And hollow shades enclosing hearts of flame,
   And, with dim fretted foreheads all,
On corpses three-months-old at noon she
   came,
   That stood against the wall.

A spot of dull stagnation, without light   245
   Or power of movement, seemed my soul,
Mid onward-sloping motions infinite
   Making for one sure goal;

A still salt pool, locked in with bars of sand,
   Left on the shore, that hears all night   250
The plunging seas draw backward from the
   land
   Their moon-led waters white;

A star that with the choral starry dance
   Joined not, but stood, and standing saw
The hollow orb of moving Circumstance   255
   Rolled round by one fixed law.

Back on herself her serpent pride had curled.
   "No voice," she shrieked in that lone hall,
"No voice breaks through the stillness of this
   world;
   One deep, deep silence all!"   260

She, moldering with the dull earth's moldering sod,

227. **Mene,** the first word of the mysterious writing on
the wall of Belshazzar's palace, meaning "God hath numbered
thy kingdom and finished it." Daniel interpreted the writing.
(See *Daniel,* 5:17-31.) 242. **fretted,** wrinkled. 253-256.
star . . . law. The star represents the soul. It stood aloof
as the universe swept by, but it saw that life in all its seeming
confusion is yet subject to a controlling law.

Inwrapt tenfold in slothful shame,
Lay there exiled from eternal God,
   Lost to her place and name;

And death and life she hated equally,   265
   And nothing saw, for her despair,
But dreadful time, dreadful eternity,
   No comfort anywhere;

Remaining utterly confused with fears,
   And ever worse with growing time,   270
And ever unrelieved by dismal tears,
   And all alone in crime.

Shut up as in a crumbling tomb, girt round
   With blackness as a solid wall,
Far off she seemed to hear the dully sound
   Of human footsteps fall: 276

As in strange lands a traveler walking slow,
   In doubt and great perplexity,
A little before moonrise hears the low
   Moan of an unknown sea;   280

And knows not if it be thunder, or a sound
   Of rocks thrown down, or one deep cry
Of great wild beasts; then thinketh, "I have
   found
   A new land, but I die."

She howled aloud, "I am on fire within.   285
   There comes no murmur of reply.
What is it that will take away my sin,
   And save me lest I die?"

So when four years were wholly finished,
   She threw her royal robes away.   290
"Make me a cottage in the vale," she said,
   "Where I may mourn and pray.

"Yet pull not down my palace towers, that are
   So lightly, beautifully built;
Perchance I may return with others there 295
   When I have purged my guilt."
                (1832, 1842)

LADY CLARA VERE DE VERE

Lady Clara Vere de Vere,
   Of me you shall not win renown;
You thought to break a country heart
   For pastime, ere you went to town.
At me you smiled, but unbeguiled   5
   I saw the snare, and I retired;
The daughter of a hundred earls,
   You are not one to be desired.

Lady Clara Vere de Vere. See Critical Notes.

Lady Clara Vere de Vere,
  I know you proud to bear your name, 10
Your pride is yet no mate for mine,
  Too proud to care from whence I came.
Nor would I break for your sweet sake
  A heart that dotes on truer charms.
A simple maiden in her flower 15
  Is worth a hundred coats-of-arms.

Lady Clara Vere de Vere,
  Some meeker pupil you must find,
For, were you queen of all that is,
  I could not stoop to such a mind. 20
You sought to prove how I could love,
  And my disdain is my reply.
The lion on your old stone gates
  Is not more cold to you than I.

Lady Clara Vere de Vere, 25
  You put strange memories in my head.
Not thrice your branching limes have blown
  Since I beheld young Laurence dead.
Oh, your sweet eyes, your low replies!
  A great enchantress you may be; 30
But there was that across his throat
  Which you had hardly cared to see.

Lady Clara Vere de Vere,
  When thus he met his mother's view,
She had the passions of her kind, 35
  She spake some certain truths of you.
Indeed I heard one bitter word
  That scarce is fit for you to hear;
Her manners had not that repose
  Which stamps the caste of Vere de Vere. 40

Lady Clara Vere de Vere,
  There stands a specter in your hall;
The guilt of blood is at your door;
  You changed a wholesome heart to gall.
You held your course without remorse, 45
  To make him trust his modest worth,
And, last, you fixed a vacant stare,
  And slew him with your noble birth.

Trust me, Clara Vere de Vere,
  From yon blue heavens above us bent 50
The gardener Adam and his wife
  Smile at the claims of long descent.
Howe'er it be, it seems to me,
  'Tis only noble to be good.
Kind hearts are more than coronets, 55
  And simple faith than Norman blood.

I know you, Clara Vere de Vere,
  You pine among your halls and towers;
The languid light of your proud eyes
  Is wearied of the rolling hours. 60

In glowing health, with boundless wealth,
  But sickening of a vague disease,
You know so ill to deal with time,
  You needs must play such pranks as these.

Clara, Clara Vere de Vere, 65
  If time be heavy on your hands,
Are there no beggars at your gate,
  Nor any poor about your lands?
Oh, teach the orphan-boy to read,
  Or teach the orphan-girl to sew; 70
Pray Heaven for a human heart,
  And let the foolish yeoman go.

                       (*1833;* 1842)

THE LOTOS-EATERS

"Courage!" he said, and pointed toward the
    land,
"This mounting wave will roll us shoreward
    soon."
In the afternoon they came unto a land
In which it seemed always afternoon.
All round the coast the languid air did swoon,
Breathing like one that hath a weary dream. 6
Full-faced above the valley stood the moon;
And, like a downward smoke, the slender
    stream
Along the cliff to fall and pause and fall did
    seem.

A land of streams! some, like a downward
    smoke, 10
Slow-dropping veils of thinnest lawn, did go;
And some through wavering lights and
    shadows broke,
Rolling a slumbrous sheet of foam below.
They saw the gleaming river seaward flow
From the inner land; far off, three mountain-
    tops, 15
Three silent pinnacles of aged snow,
Stood sunset-flushed; and, dewed with show-
    ery drops,
Up-clomb the shadowy pine above the woven
    copse.

The charméd sunset lingered low adown
In the red West; through mountain clefts the
    dale 20
Was seen far inland, and the yellow down
Bordered with palm, and many a winding vale
And meadow, set with slender galingale;
A land where all things always seemed the
    same!
And round about the keel with faces pale, 25
Dark faces pale against that rosy flame,
The mild-eyed melancholy Lotos-eaters came.

The Lotos-Eaters. See Critical Notes.
23. **galingale,** a kind of grasslike herb.

Branches they bore of that enchanted stem,
Laden with flower and fruit, whereof they
    gave
To each, but whoso did receive of them 30
And taste, to him the gushing of the wave
Far far away did seem to mourn and rave
On alien shores; and if his fellow spake,
His voice was thin, as voices from the grave;
And deep-asleep he seemed, yet all awake, 35
And music in his ears his beating heart did
    make.

They sat them down upon the yellow sand
Between the sun and moon upon the shore;
And sweet it was to dream of Fatherland,
Of child, and wife, and slave; but evermore 40
Most weary seemed the sea, weary the oar,
Weary the wandering fields of barren foam.
Then someone said, "We will return no more";
And all at once they sang, "Our island home
Is far beyond the wave; we will no longer
    roam." 45

CHORIC SONG

1

There is sweet music here that softer falls
Than petals from blown roses on the grass,
Or night-dews on still waters between walls
Of shadowy granite, in a gleaming pass;
Music that gentlier on the spirit lies, 50
Than tired eyelids upon tired eyes;
Music that brings sweet sleep down from the
    blissful skies.
Here are cool mosses deep,
And through the moss the ivies creep,
And in the stream the long-leaved flowers
    weep, 55
And from the craggy ledge the poppy hangs
    in sleep.

2

Why are we weighed upon with heaviness,
And utterly consumed with sharp distress,
While all things else have rest from weariness?
All things have rest; why should we toil alone,
We only toil, who are the first of things, 61
And make perpetual moan,
Still from one sorrow to another thrown;
Nor ever fold our wings,
And cease from wanderings, 65
Nor steep our brows in slumber's holy balm;
Nor harken what the inner spirit sings,
"There is no joy but calm!"—
Why should we only toil, the roof and crown
    of things?

3

Lo! in the middle of the wood, 70
The folded leaf is wooed from out the bud
With winds upon the branch, and there
Grows green and broad, and takes no care,
Sun-steeped at noon, and in the moon
Nightly dew-fed; and turning yellow 75
Falls, and floats adown the air.
Lo! sweetened with the summer light,
The full-juiced apple, waxing over-mellow,
Drops in a silent autumn night.
All its allotted length of days 80
The flower ripens in its place,
Ripens and fades, and falls, and hath no toil,
Fast-rooted in the fruitful soil.

4

Hateful is the dark-blue sky,
Vaulted o'er the dark-blue sea. 85
Death is the end of life; ah, why
Should life all labor be?
Let us alone. Time driveth onward fast,
And in a little while our lips are dumb.
Let us alone. What is it that will last? 90
All things are taken from us, and become
Portions and parcels of the dreadful past.
Let us alone. What pleasure can we have
To war with evil? Is there any peace
In ever climbing up the climbing wave? 95
All things have rest, and ripen toward the
    grave
In silence — ripen, fall, and cease;
Give us long rest or death, dark death, or
    dreamful ease.

5

How sweet it were, hearing the downward
    stream
With half-shut eyes ever to seem 100
Falling asleep in a half-dream!
To dream and dream, like yonder amber light,
Which will not leave the myrrh-bush on the
    height;
To hear each other's whispered speech;
Eating the Lotos day by day, 105
To watch the crisping ripples on the beach,
And tender curving lines of creamy spray;
To lend our hearts and spirits wholly
To the influence of mild-minded melancholy;
To muse and brood and live again in memory,
With those old faces of our infancy 111
Heaped over with a mound of grass,
Two handfuls of white dust, shut in an urn
    of brass!

6

Dear is the memory of our wedded lives,
And dear the last embraces of our wives 115
And their warm tears; but all hath suffered
    change;

For surely now our household hearths are
    cold,
Our sons inherit us, our looks are strange,
And we should come like ghosts to trouble
    joy.
Or else the island princes over-bold   120
Have eat our substance, and the minstrel
    sings
Before them of the ten years' war in Troy,
And our great deeds, as half-forgotten things.
Is there confusion in the little isle?
Let what is broken so remain.   125
The gods are hard to reconcile;
'Tis hard to settle order once again.
There *is* confusion worse than death,
Trouble on trouble, pain on pain,
Long labor unto aged breath,   130
Sore task to hearts worn out by many wars
And eyes grown dim with gazing on the pilot-
    stars.

7

But, propped on beds of amaranth and moly,
How sweet — while warm airs lull us, blowing
    lowly —
With half-dropped eyelid still,   135
Beneath a heaven dark and holy,
To watch the long bright river drawing slowly
His waters from the purple hill —
To hear the dewy echoes calling
From cave to cave through the thick-twined
    vine —   140
To watch the emerald-colored water falling
Through many a woven acanthus-wreath
    divine!
Only to hear and see the far-off sparkling
    brine,
Only to hear were sweet, stretched out be-
    neath the pine.

8

The Lotos blooms below the barren peak, 145
The Lotos blows by every winding creek;
All day the wind breathes low with mellower
    tone;
Through every hollow cave and alley lone
Round and round the spicy downs the yellow
    Lotos-dust is blown.
We have had enough of action, and of motion
    we,   150
Rolled to starboard, rolled to larboard, when
    the surge was seething free,
Where the wallowing monster spouted his
    foam-fountains in the sea.

Let us swear an oath, and keep it with an
    equal mind,
In the hollow Lotos-land to live and lie re-
    clined
On the hills like gods together, careless of
    mankind.   155
For they lie beside their nectar, and the bolts
    are hurled
Far below them in the valleys, and the clouds
    are lightly curled
Round their golden houses, girdled with the
    gleaming world;
Where they smile in secret, looking over
    wasted lands,
Blight and famine, plague and earthquake,
    roaring deeps and fiery sands,   160
Clanging fights, and flaming towns, and sink-
    ing ships, and praying hands.
But they smile, they find a music centered in
    a doleful song
Steaming up, a lamentation and an ancient
    tale of wrong,
Like a tale of little meaning though the words
    are strong;
Chanted from an ill-used race of men that
    cleave the soil,   165
Sow the seed, and reap the harvest with
    enduring toil,
Storing yearly little dues of wheat, and wine
    and oil;
Till they perish and they suffer — some, 'tis
    whispered — down in hell
Suffer endless anguish, others in Elysian val-
    leys dwell,
Resting weary limbs at last on beds of as-
    phodel.   170
Surely, surely, slumber is more sweet than
    toil, the shore
Than labor in the deep mid-ocean, wind and
    wave and oar;
O rest ye, brother mariners, we will not wan-
    der more.   (1832, 1842)

THE TWO VOICES

A still small voice spake unto me,
"Thou art so full of misery,
Were it not better not to be?"

Then to the still small voice I said:
"Let me not cast in endless shade   5
What is so wonderfully made."

169-170. **Elysian . . . asphodel.** The Elysian Fields, the
paradise of the Greeks, were said by Homer to be covered
with asphodels (daffodils).
   The Two Voices. Originally "The Thoughts of a Suicide," this
poem was written soon after the death of Tennyson's friend,
Arthur Hallam. See Critical Note on *In Memoriam.*
   1. **still small voice.** See *1 Kings,* 19:12—"And after the
earthquake a fire; but the Lord was not in the fire: and after
the fire a still small voice."

120. **island princes,** princes from other islands near
Greece.   133. **amaranth,** an imaginary flower supposed
never to fade. **moly,** a fabulous herb of magic power. It
was given by Hermes (the messenger of the gods) to Ulysses
as a protection against Circe, the enchantress. 142. **acanthus-wreath.** The acanthus was a plant sacred to the gods.

To which the voice did urge reply:
"Today I saw the dragon-fly
Come from the wells where he did lie.

"An inner impulse rent the veil   10
Of his old husk; from head to tail
Came out clear plates of sapphire mail.

"He dried his wings; like gauze they grew;
Through crofts and pastures wet with dew
A living flash of light he flew."   15

I said: "When first the world began,
Young Nature through five cycles ran,
And in the sixth she molded man.

"She gave him mind, the lordliest
Proportion, and, above the rest,   20
Dominion in the head and breast."

Thereto the silent voice replied:
"Self-blinded are you by your pride;
Look up through night; the world is wide.

"This truth within thy mind rehearse,   25
That in a boundless universe
Is boundless better, boundless worse.

"Think you this mold of hopes and fears
Could find no statelier than his peers
In yonder hundred million spheres?"   30

It spake, moreover, in my mind:
"Though thou wert scattered to the wind,
Yet is there plenty of the kind."

Then did my response clearer fall:
"No compound of this earthly ball   35
Is like another, all in all."

To which he answered scoffingly:
"Good soul! suppose I grant it thee,
Who'll weep for thy deficiency?

"Or will one beam be less intense,   40
When thy peculiar difference
Is canceled in the world of sense?"

I would have said: "Thou canst not know,"
But my full heart, that worked below,
Rained through my sight its overflow.   45

Again the voice spake unto me:
"Thou art so steeped in misery,
Surely 'twere better not to be.

"Thine anguish will not let thee sleep,
Nor any train of reason keep;   50
Thou canst not think, but thou wilt weep."

I said: "The years with change advance;
If I make dark my countenance,
I shut my life from happier chance.

"Some turn this sickness yet might take,   55
Even yet."   But he: "What drug can make
A withered palsy cease to shake?"

I wept: "Though I should die, I know
That all about the thorn will blow
In tufts of rosy-tinted snow;   60

"And men, through novel spheres of thought
Still moving after truth long sought,
Will learn new things when I am not."

"Yet," said the secret voice, "sometime,
Sooner or later, will gray prime   65
Make thy grass hoar with early rime.

"Not less swift souls that yearn for light,
Rapt after heaven's starry flight,
Would sweep the tracts of day and night.

"Not less the bee would range her cells,   70
The furzy prickle fire the dells,
The foxglove cluster dappled bells."

I said that "all the years invent;
Each month is various to present
The world with some development.   75

"Were this not well, to bide mine hour,
Though watching from a ruined tower
How grows the day of human power?"

"The highest-mounted mind," he said,
"Still sees the sacred morning spread   80
The silent summit overhead.

"Will thirty seasons render plain
Those lonely lights that still remain,
Just breaking over land and main?

"Or make that morn, from his cold crown   85
And crystal silence creeping down,
Flood with full daylight glebe and town?

"Forerun thy peers, thy time, and let
Thy feet, millenniums hence, be set
In midst of knowledge, dreamed not yet.   90

"Thou has not gained a real height,
Nor art thou nearer to the light,
Because the scale is infinite.

16. world began. See *Genesis*, 1, the Creation.

57. withered palsy, a reference to the power of Christ to
cure a man afflicted with palsy (*Matthew*, 9:2-7) and to restore
a man's withered hand (*Matthew*, 12:9-13).   59. blow, blossom.   65. gray prime, dawn.   66. rime, frost.   89. glebe,
field.

" 'Twere better not to breathe or speak,
Than cry for strength, remaining weak,   95
And seem to find, but still to seek.

"Moreover, but to seem to find
Asks what thou lackest, thought resigned,
A healthy frame, a quiet mind."

I said: "When I am gone away,   100
'He dared not tarry,' men will say,
Doing dishonor to my clay."

"This is more vile," he made reply,
"To breathe and loathe, to live and sigh,
Than once from dread of pain to die.   105

"Sick art thou—a divided will
Still heaping on the fear of ill
The fear of men, a coward still.

"Do men love thee? Art thou so bound
To men, that how thy name may sound   110
Will vex thee lying underground?

"The memory of the withered leaf
In endless time is scarce more brief
Than of the garnered autumn-sheaf.

"Go, vexed spirit, sleep in trust;   115
The right ear that is filled with dust
Hears little of the false or just."

"Hard task, to pluck resolve," I cried,
"From emptiness and the waste wide
Of that abyss, or scornful pride!   120

"Nay—rather yet that I could raise
One hope that warmed me in the days
While still I yearned for human praise.

"When, wide in soul and bold of tongue,
Among the tents I paused and sung,   125
The distant battle flashed and rung.

"I sung the joyful Pæan clear,
And, sitting, burnished without fear
The brand, the buckler, and the spear—

"Waiting to strive a happy strife,   130
To war with falsehood to the knife,
And not to lose the good of life—

"Some hidden principle to move,
To put together, part and prove,
And mete the bounds of hate and love—   135

"As far as might be, to carve out
Free space for every human doubt,
That the whole mind might orb about—

"To search through all I felt or saw,
The springs of life, the depths of awe,   140
And reach the law within the law;

"At least, not rotting like a weed,
But, having sown some generous seed,
Fruitful of further thought and deed,

"To pass, when Life her light withdraws,   145
Not void of righteous self-applause,
Nor in a merely selfish cause—

"In some good cause, not in mine own,
To perish, wept for, honored, known,
And like a warrior overthrown;   150

"Whose eyes are dim with glorious tears,
When, soiled with noble dust, he hears
His country's war-song thrill his ears:

"Then dying of a mortal stroke,
What time the foeman's line is broke,   155
And all the war is rolled in smoke."

"Yea!" said the voice, "thy dream was good,
While thou abodest in the bud.
It was the stirring of the blood.

"If Nature put not forth her power   160
About the opening of the flower,
Who is it that could live an hour?

"Then comes the check, the change, the fall,
Pain rises up, old pleasures pall.
There is one remedy for all.   165

"Yet hadst thou, through enduring pain,
Linked month to month with such a chain
Of knitted purport, all were vain.

"Thou hadst not between death and birth
Dissolved the riddle of the earth.   170
So were thy labor little worth.

"That men with knowledge merely played,
I told thee—hardly nigher made,
Though scaling slow from grade to grade;

"Much less this dreamer, deaf and blind,   175
Named man, may hope some truth to find,
That bears relation to the mind.

"For every worm beneath the moon
Draws different threads, and late and soon
Spins, toiling out his own cocoon.   180

"Cry, faint not: either Truth is born
Beyond the polar gleam forlorn,
Or in the gateways of the morn.

"Cry, faint not, climb: the summits slope
Beyond the furthest flights of hope,   185
Wrapt in dense cloud from base to cope.

"Sometimes a little corner shines,
As over rainy mist inclines
A gleaming crag with belts of pines.

"I will go forward, sayest thou,   190
I shall not fail to find her now.
Look up, the fold is on her brow.

"If straight thy track, or if oblique,
Thou know'st not.   Shadows thou dost strike,
Embracing cloud, Ixion-like;   195

"And owning but a little more
Than beasts, abidest lame and poor,
Calling thyself a little lower

"Than angels.   Cease to wail and brawl!
Why inch by inch to darkness crawl?   200
There is one remedy for all."

"O dull, one-sided voice," said I,
"Wilt thou make everything a lie,
To flatter me that I may die?

"I know that age to age succeeds,   205
Blowing a noise of tongues and deeds,
A dust of systems and of creeds.

"I cannot hide that some have striven,
Achieving calm, to whom was given
The joy that mixes man with Heaven;   210

"Who, rowing hard against the stream,
Saw distant gates of Eden gleam,
And did not dream it was a dream;

"But heard, by secret transport led,
Even in the charnels of the dead,   215
The murmur of the fountain-head—

"Which did accomplish their desire,
Bore and forebore, and did not tire,
Like Stephen, an unquenched fire.

"He heeded not reviling tones,   220
Nor sold his heart to idle moans,
Though cursed and scorned, and bruised with
        stones;

"But looking upward, full of grace,
He prayed, and from a happy place
God's glory smote him on the face."   225

The sullen answer slid betwixt:
"Not that the grounds of hope were fixed,
The elements were kindlier mixed."

I said: "I toil beneath the curse,
But, knowing not the universe,   230
I fear to slide from bad to worse;

"And that, in seeking to undo
One riddle, and to find the true,
I knit a hundred others new;

"Or that this anguish fleeting hence,   235
Unmanacled from bonds of sense,
Be fixed and frozen to permanence:

"For I go, weak from suffering here;
Naked I go, and void of cheer:
What is it that I may not fear?"   240

"Consider well," the voice replied,
"His face, that two hours since hath died;
Wilt thou find passion, pain or pride?

"Will he obey when one commands?
Or answer should one press his hands?   245
He answers not, nor understands.

"His palms are folded on his breast;
There is no other thing expressed
But long disquiet merged in rest.

"His lips are very mild and meek;   250
Though one should smite him on the cheek,
And on the mouth, he will not speak.

"His little daughter, whose sweet face
He kissed, taking his last embrace,
Becomes dishonor to her race—   255

"His sons grow up that bear his name,
Some grow to honor, some to shame,—
But he is chill to praise or blame.

"He will not hear the north-wind rave,
Nor, moaning, household shelter crave   260
From winter rains that beat his grave.

"High up the vapors fold and swim;
About him broods the twilight dim;
The place he knew forgetteth him."

"If all be dark, vague voice," I said,   265
"These things are wrapt in doubt and dread,
Nor canst thou show the dead are dead.

"The sap dries up: the plant declines.
A deeper tale my heart divines.
Know I not Death? the outward signs?   270

195. **Ixion-like.** Ixion was bound to a wheel as punishment
for aspiring to the love of Hera, Zeus's wife. 198-199. **lower
. . . angels.** See *Psalms*, 8:5. 219. **Stephen.** See *Acts*, 7:54-60.

"I found him when my years were few;
A shadow on the graves I knew,
And darkness in the village yew.

"From grave to grave the shadow crept;
In her still place the morning wept: 275
Touched by his feet the daisy slept.

"The simple senses crowned his head:
'Omega! thou art Lord,' they said,
'We find no motion in the dead.'

"Why, if man rot in dreamless ease,   280
Should that plain fact, as taught by these,
Not make him sure that he shall cease?

"Who forged that other influence,
That heat of inward evidence,
By which he doubts against the sense?   285

"He owns the fatal gift of eyes,
That read his spirit blindly wise,
Not simple as a thing that dies.

"Here sits he shaping wings to fly;
His heart forebodes a mystery;   290
He names the name Eternity.

"That type of Perfect in his mind
In Nature can he nowhere find.
He sows himself on every wind.

"He seems to hear a Heavenly Friend,   295
And through thick veils to apprehend
A labor working to an end.

"The end and the beginning vex
His reason: many things perplex,
With motions, checks, and counterchecks. 300

"He knows a baseness in his blood
At such strange war with something good,
He may not do the thing he would.

"Heaven opens inward, chasms yawn,
Vast images in glimmering dawn,   305
Half shown, are broken and withdrawn.

"Ah! sure within him and without,
Could his dark wisdom find it out,
There must be answer to his doubt.

"But thou canst answer not again.   310
With thine own weapon art thou slain,
Or thou wilt answer but in vain.

"The doubt would rest, I dare not solve.
In the same circle we revolve.
Assurance only breeds resolve."   315

As when a billow, blown against,
Falls back, the voice with which I fenced
A little ceased, but recommenced:

"Where wert thou when thy father played
In his free field, and pastime made,   320
A merry boy in sun and shade?

"A merry boy they called him then.
He sat upon the knees of men
In days that never come again;

"Before the little ducts began   325
To feed thy bones with lime, and ran
Their course, till thou wert also man:

"Who took a wife, who reared his race,
Whose wrinkles gathered on his face,
Whose troubles number with his days;   330

"A life of nothings, nothing worth,
From that first nothing ere his birth
To that last nothing under earth!"

"These words," I said, "are like the rest;
No certain clearness, but at best   335
A vague suspicion of the breast:

"But if I grant, thou might'st defend
The thesis which thy words intend—
That to begin implies to end;

"Yet how should I for certain hold,   340
Because my memory is so cold,
That I first was in human mold?

"I cannot make this matter plain,
But I would shoot, howe'er in vain,
A random arrow from the brain.   345

"It may be that no life is found,
Which only to one engine bound
Falls off, but cycles always round.

"As old mythologies relate,
Some draft of Lethe might await   350
The slipping through from state to state;

"As here we find in trances, men
Forget the dream that happens then,
Until they fall in trance again;

---

278. **Omega**, the last letter of the Greek alphabet; hence, the last, the end.

350. **Lethe**, in classical mythology a river in Hades. A drink of its water produced forgetfulness of the past.

"So might we, if our state were such   355
As one before, remember much,
For those two likes might meet and touch.

"But, if I lapsed from nobler place,
Some legend of a fallen race
Alone might hint of my disgrace;   360

"Some vague emotion of delight
In gazing up an Alpine height,
Some yearning toward the lamps of night;

"Or if through lower lives I came—
Though all experience past became   365
Consolidate in mind and frame—

"I might forget my weaker lot;
For is not our first year forgot?
The haunts of memory echo not.

"And men, whose reason long was blind,   370
From cells of madness unconfined,
Oft lose whole years of darker mind.

"Much more, if first I floated free,
As naked essence, must I be
Incompetent of memory;   375

"For memory dealing but with time,
And he with matter, could she climb
Beyond her own material prime?

"Moreover, something is or seems,
That touches me with mystic gleams,   380
Like glimpses of forgotten dreams—

"Of something felt, like something here;
Of something done, I know not where;
Such as no language may declare."

The still voice laughed. "I talk," said he,
"Not with thy dreams. Suffice it thee   386
Thy pain is a reality."

"But thou," said I, "hast missed thy mark,
Who sought'st to wreck my mortal ark,
By making all the horizon dark.   390

"Why not set forth, if I should do
This rashness, that which might ensue
With this old soul in organs new?

"Whatever crazy sorrow saith,
No life that breathes with human breath 395
Has ever truly longed for death.

" 'Tis life, whereof our nerves are scant,
Oh life, not death, for which we pant;
More life, and fuller, that I want."

I ceased, and sat as one forlorn.   400
Then said the voice, in quiet scorn,
"Behold, it is the Sabbath morn."

And I arose, and I released
The casement, and the light increased
With freshness in the dawning east.   405

Like softened airs that blowing steal,
When meres begin to uncongeal,
The sweet church bells began to peal.

On to God's house the people pressed;
Passing the place where each must rest,   410
Each entered like a welcome guest.

One walked between his wife and child,
With measured footfall firm and mild,
And now and then he gravely smiled.

The prudent partner of his blood   415
Leaned on him, faithful, gentle, good,
Wearing the rose of womanhood.

And in their double love secure,
The little maiden walked demure,
Pacing with downward eyelids pure.   420

These three made unity so sweet,
My frozen heart began to beat,
Remembering its ancient heat.

I blessed them, and they wandered on;
I spoke, but answer came there none;   425
The dull and bitter voice was gone.

A second voice was at mine ear,
A little whisper silver-clear,
A murmur, "Be of better cheer."

As from some blissful neighborhood,   430
A notice faintly understood,
"I see the end, and know the good."

A little hint to solace woe,
A hint, a whisper breathing low,
"I may not speak of what I know."   435

Like an Æolian harp that wakes
No certain air, but overtakes
Far thought with music that it makes;

Such seemed the whisper at my side:
"What is it thou knowest, sweet voice?" I
        cried.   440
"A hidden hope," the voice replied;

436. **Æolian harp,** an instrument of several strings which
gave out musical sounds when currents of air passed over it.
It was named after Æolus, classical god of the winds.

So heavenly-toned, that in that hour
From out my sullen heart a power
Broke, like the rainbow from the shower,

To feel, although no tongue can prove,   445
That every cloud, that spreads above
And veileth love, itself is love.

And forth into the fields I went,
And Nature's living motion lent
The pulse of hope to discontent.   450

I wondered at the bounteous hours,
The slow result of winter showers;
You scarce could see the grass for flowers.

I wondered, while I paced along;
The woods were filled so full with song,   455
There seemed no room for sense of wrong;

So variously seemed all things wrought,
I marveled how the mind was brought
To anchor by one gloomy thought;

And wherefore rather I made choice   460
To commune with that barren voice,
Than him that said: "Rejoice! Rejoice!"
(*1833-1834;* 1842)

"MY LIFE IS FULL OF WEARY DAYS"

My life is full of weary days,
    But good things have not kept aloof,
Nor wandered into other ways;
    I have not lacked thy mild reproof,
Nor golden largess of thy praise.   5

And now shake hands across the brink
    Of that deep grave to which I go,
Shake hands once more; I cannot sink
    So far—far down, but I shall know
Thy voice, and answer from below.   10

When in the darkness over me
    The four-handed mole shall scrape,
Plant thou no dusky cypress-tree,
    Nor wreathe thy cap with doleful crape,
But pledge me in the flowing grape.   15

And when the sappy field and wood
    Grow green beneath the showery gray,
And rugged barks begin to bud,
    And through damp holts new-flushed with
        may,
    Ring sudden scritches of the jay,   20

Then let wise Nature work her will,
    And on my clay her darnel grow;
Come only, when the days are still,

And at my headstone whisper low,
And tell me if the woodbines blow.   25
(1833)

A FAREWELL

Flow down, cold rivulet, to the sea,
    Thy tribute wave deliver;
No more by thee my steps shall be,
    Forever and forever.

Flow, softly flow, by lawn and lea,   5
    A rivulet, then a river;
Nowhere by thee my steps shall be,
    Forever and forever.

But here will sigh thine alder-tree,
    And here thine aspen shiver;   10
And here by thee will hum the bee,
    Forever and forever.

A thousand suns will stream on thee,
    A thousand moons will quiver;
But not by thee my steps shall be,   15
    Forever and forever.   (1842)

ENGLAND AND AMERICA IN 1782

O thou that sendest out the man
    To rule by land and sea,
Strong mother of a Lion-line,
Be proud of those strong sons of thine
    Who wrenched their rights from thee!   5

What wonder if in noble heat
    Those men thine arms withstood,
Retaught the lesson thou hadst taught,
And in thy spirit with thee fought—
    Who sprang from English blood!   10

But thou rejoice with liberal joy,
    Lift up thy rocky face,
And shatter, when the storms are black,
In many a streaming torrent back,
    The seas that shock thy base!   15

Whatever harmonies of law
    The growing world assume,
Thy work is thine—the single note
From that deep chord which Hampden smote
    Will vibrate to the doom.   20
(1842)

England and America in 1782. Tennyson states that this
poem is supposed to be spoken by a liberal Englishman at the
time of the recognition of American independence.
    19. **Hampden,** John Hampden (1594-1643), a Parliamen-
tary leader who in 1635 refused to pay taxes to build warships on the principle that taxation without representation
is tyranny. This was the cry of the American revolutionists.
    20. **doom,** the Day of Judgment.

SAINT AGNES' EVE

Deep on the convent-roof the snows
  Are sparkling to the moon;
My breath to heaven like vapor goes;
  May my soul follow soon!
The shadows of the convent-towers   5
  Slant down the snowy sward,
Still creeping with the creeping hours
  That lead me to my Lord.
Make Thou my spirit pure and clear
  As are the frosty skies,   10
Or this first snowdrop of the year
  That in my bosom lies.

As these white robes are soiled and dark,
  To yonder shining ground;
As this pale taper's earthly spark,   15
  To yonder argent round;
So shows my soul before the Lamb,
  My spirit before Thee;
So in mine earthly house I am,
  To that I hope to be.   20
Break up the heavens, O Lord! and far,
  Through all yon starlight keen,
Draw me, thy bride, a glittering star,
  In raiment white and clean.

He lifts me to the golden doors;   25
  The flashes come and go;
All heaven bursts her starry floors,
  And strows her lights below,
And deepens on and up! the gates
  Roll back, and far within   30
For me the Heavenly Bridegroom waits,
  To make me pure of sin.
The Sabbaths of Eternity,
  One Sabbath deep and wide —
A light upon the shining sea —   35
  The Bridegroom with his bride!   (1837)

YOU ASK ME, WHY, THOUGH ILL AT EASE

You ask me, why, though ill at ease,
  Within this region I subsist,
  Whose spirits falter in the mist,
And languish for the purple seas.

It is the land that freemen till,   5
  That sober-suited Freedom chose,
  The land where, girt with friends or foes,
A man may speak the thing he will;

A land of settled government,
  A land of just and old renown,   10
  Where Freedom slowly broadens down
From precedent to precedent;

Where faction seldom gathers head,
  But, by degrees to fullness wrought,
  The strength of some diffusive thought   15
Hath time and space to work and spread.

Should banded unions persecute
  Opinion, and induce a time
  When single thought is civil crime,
And individual freedom mute,   20

Though power should make from land to land
  The name of Britain trebly great —
  Though every channel of the State
Should fill and choke with golden sand —

Yet waft me from the harbor-mouth,   25
  Wild wind! I seek a warmer sky,
  And I will see before I die
The palms and temples of the South.
        (c. 1833; 1842)

OF OLD SAT FREEDOM ON THE HEIGHTS

Of old sat Freedom on the heights,
  The thunders breaking at her feet;
Above her shook the starry lights;
  She heard the torrents meet.

There in her place she did rejoice,   5
  Self-gathered in her prophet-mind,
But fragments of her mighty voice
  Came rolling on the wind.

Then stepped she down through town and
    field
  To mingle with the human race,   10
And part by part to men revealed
  The fullness of her face —

Grave mother of majestic works,
  From her isle-altar gazing down,
Who, godlike, grasps the triple forks,   15
  And, king-like, wears the crown.

Her open eyes desire the truth.
  The wisdom of a thousand years
Is in them. May perpetual youth
  Keep dry their light from tears;   20

Saint Agnes' Eve. St. Agnes was a Roman virgin who suffered martyrdom about the year 300. According to ancient legend it was possible for a pure maiden on St. Agnes' Eve (January 21) to have a vision of her future husband. The poem is supposed to be spoken by a nun who embodies the spirit of St. Agnes. Here it is the Heavenly Bridegroom that the maiden longs to see. For a different treatment of the legend see Keats's *The Eve of St. Agnes.*
  16. **argent round,** the silver moon at the full.
You Ask Me, Why. See Critical Notes.

Of Old Sat Freedom. 14. **isle-altar,** England. 15. **Who . . . forks.** Rolfe quotes Tennyson for the 'atement that the figure represents Jove, the triple forks being his thunderbolts.

That her fair form may stand and shine,
  Make bright our days and light our dreams,
Turning to scorn with lips divine
  The falsehood of extremes! (*c. 1833;* 1842)

LOVE THOU THY LAND, WITH LOVE FAR-BROUGHT

Love thou thy land, with love far-brought
  From out the storied past, and used
  Within the present, but transfused
Through future time by power of thought;

True love turned round on fixéd poles,   5
  Love that endures not sordid ends,
  For English natures, freemen, friends,
Thy brothers and immortal souls.

But pamper not a hasty time,
  Nor feed with crude imaginings   10
  The herd, wild hearts and feeble wings
That every sophister can lime.

Deliver not the tasks of might
  To weakness, neither hide the ray
  From those, not blind, who wait for day,   15
Though sitting girt with doubtful light.

Make knowledge circle with the winds;
  But let her herald, Reverence, fly
  Before her to whatever sky
Bear seed of men and growth of minds.   20

Watch what main-currents draw the years;
  Cut Prejudice against the grain.
  But gentle words are always gain;
Regard the weakness of thy peers.

Nor toil for title, place, or touch   25
  Of pension, neither count on praise —
  It grows to guerdon after-days.
Nor deal in watch-words overmuch;

Not clinging to some ancient saw,
  Not mastered by some modern term,   30
  Not swift nor slow to change, but firm;
And in its season bring the law,

That from Discussion's lip may fall
  With Life that, working strongly, binds —
  Set in all lights by many minds,   35
To close the interests of all.

For Nature also, cold and warm,
  And moist and dry, devising long,
  Through many agents making strong,
Matures the individual form.   40

Meet is it changes should control
  Our being, lest we rust in ease.
  We all are changed by still degrees,
All but the basis of the soul.

So let the change which comes be free   45
  To ingroove itself with that which flies,
  And work, a joint of state, that plies
Its office, moved with sympathy.

A saying hard to shape in act;
  For all the past of Time reveals   50
  A bridal dawn of thunder-peals,
Wherever Thought hath wedded Fact.

Even now we hear with inward strife
  A motion toiling in the gloom —
  The Spirit of the years to come   55
Yearning to mix himself with Life.

A slow-developed strength awaits
  Completion in a painful school;
  Phantoms of other forms of rule,
New Majesties of mighty States —   60

The warders of the growing hour,
  But vague in vapor, hard to mark;
  And round them sea and air are dark
With great contrivances of Power.

Of many changes, aptly joined,   65
  Is bodied forth the second whole.
  Regard gradation, lest the soul
Of Discord race the rising wind;

A wind to puff your idol-fires,
  And heap their ashes on the head;   70
  To shame the boast so often made,
That we are wiser than our sires.

Oh, yet, if Nature's evil star
  Drive men in manhood, as in youth,
  To follow flying steps of Truth   75
Across the brazen bridge of war —

If New and Old, disastrous feud,
  Must ever shock, like arméd foes,
  And this be true, till Time shall close,
That Principles are rained in blood;   80

Not yet the wise of heart would cease
  To hold his hope through shame and guilt,
  But with his hand against the hilt,
Would pace the troubled land, like Peace;

Not less, though dogs of Faction bay,   85
  Would serve his kind in deed and word,

Love Thou Thy Land. **12. lime,** ensnare, trap. **37-40.**
For . . . form. According to medieval thinking, the nature
of a body was determined by the proportion of four qualities
—hot, cold, moist, and dry.

64. great contrivances, a reference to the building of
battleships and a prophecy of the airship. Cf. *Locksley Hall,*
lines 119-124, page 47.

Certain, if knowledge bring the sword,
That knowledge takes the sword away—

Would love the gleams of good that broke
    From either side, nor veil his eyes;   90
    And if some dreadful need should rise
Would strike, and firmly, and one stroke.

Tomorrow yet would reap today,
    As we bear blossom of the dead;
    Earn well the thrifty months, nor wed   95
Raw Haste, half-sister to Delay.
                                        (c. 1833; 1842)

THE EPIC

At Francis Allen's on the Christmas-eve—
The game of forfeits done—the girls all
        kissed
Beneath the sacred bush and passed away—
The parson Holmes, the poet Everard Hall,
The host, and I sat round the wassail-bowl, 5
Then half-way ebbed; and there we held a
        talk,
How all the old honor had from Christmas
        gone,
Or gone or dwindled down to some odd games
In some odd nooks like this; till I, tired out
With cutting eights that day upon the pond,
Where, three times slipping from the outer
        edge,   11
I bumped the ice into three several stars,
Fell in a doze; and half-awake I heard
The parson taking wide and wider sweeps,
Now harping on the church-commissioners,
Now hawking at geology and schism;   16
Until I woke, and found him settled down
Upon the general decay of faith
Right through the world: "at home was little
        left,
And none abroad; there was no anchor, none,
To hold by." Francis, laughing, clapped his
        hand
On Everard's shoulder, with "I hold by him."
"And I," quoth Everard, "by the wassail-
        bowl."
"Why yes," I said, "we knew your gift that
        way
At college; but another which you had—   25
I mean of verse (for so we held it then)—
What came of that?" "You know," said
        Frank, "he burnt
His epic, his King Arthur, some twelve
        books"—

And then to me, demanding why: "Oh, sir,
He thought that nothing new was said, or
        else   30
Something so said 'twas nothing—that a
        truth
Looks freshest in the fashion of the day;
God knows; he has a mint of reasons; ask.
It pleased *me* well enough." "Nay, nay,"
        said Hall,
"Why take the style of those heroic times?   35
For nature brings not back the mastodon,
Nor we those times; and why should any man
Remodel models? These twelve books of mine
Were faint Homeric echoes, nothing-worth,
Mere chaff and draff, much better burnt."
        "But I,"   40
Said Francis, "picked the eleventh from this
        hearth,
And have it; keep a thing, its use will come.
I hoard it as a sugar-plum for Holmes."
He laughed, and I, though sleepy, like a horse
That hears the corn-bin open, pricked my ears;
For I remembered Everard's college fame   46
When we were freshmen. Then at my request
He brought it; and the poet, little urged,
But with some prelude of disparagement,
Read, mouthing out his hollow oes and aes,
Deep-chested music, and to this result.   51
                                        (c. 1836; 1842)

MORTE D'ARTHUR

So all day long the noise of battle rolled
Among the mountains by the winter sea,
Until King Arthur's table, man by man,
Had fallen in Lyonnesse about their lord,
King Arthur; then, because his wound was
        deep,   5
The bold Sir Bedivere uplifted him,
Sir Bedivere, the last of all his knights,
And bore him to a chapel nigh the field,
A broken chancel with a broken cross,
That stood on a dark strait of barren land.   10
On one side lay the ocean, and on one
Lay a great water, and the moon was full.
    Then spake King Arthur to Sir Bedivere:
"The sequel of today unsolders all
The goodliest fellowship of famous knights
Whereof this world holds record. Such a
        sleep   16
They sleep—the men I loved. I think that
        we
Shall never more, at any future time,
Delight our souls with talk of knightly deeds,

The Epic. 3. **sacred bush,** mistletoe. 15. **church-com-missioners.** The Ecclesiastical Commission was a body formed in 1835-1836 especially for the purpose of administering the revenues of the Church of England. It had large powers. 16. **geology and schism,** a reference to the growing conflict between religion and science.

45. **corn-bin,** grain-bin.
Morte d'Arthur. See Critical Notes.
4. **Lyonnesse,** a district often mentioned in Arthurian romance. According to tradition it sank beneath the sea, its position being thereafter marked only by islands off the extreme point of Cornwall.

Walking about the gardens and the halls   20
Of Camelot, as in the days that were.
I perish by this people which I made—
Though Merlin sware that I should come
    again
To rule once more—but let what will be be,
I am so deeply smitten through the helm   25
That without help I cannot last till morn.
Thou therefore take my brand Excalibur,
Which was my pride; for thou rememberest
    how
In those old days, one summer noon, an arm
Rose up from out the bosom of the lake,   30
Clothed in white samite, mystic, wonderful,
Holding the sword—and how I rowed across
And took it, and have worn it, like a king;
And, wheresoever I am sung or told
In aftertime, this also shall be known.   35
But now delay not; take Excalibur,
And fling him far into the middle mere;
Watch what thou seest, and lightly bring me
    word."
    To him replied the bold Sir Bedivere:
"It is not meet, Sir King, to leave thee thus,
Aidless, alone, and smitten through the helm.
A little thing may harm a wounded man.   42
Yet I thy hest will all perform at full,
Watch what I see, and lightly bring thee
    word."
    So saying, from the ruined shrine he
        stepped   45
And in the moon athwart the place of tombs,
Where lay the mighty bones of ancient men,
Old knights, and over them the sea-wind sang
Shrill, chill, with flakes of foam. He, stepping
    down
By zigzag paths and juts of pointed rock,   50
Came on the shining levels of the lake.
    There drew he forth the brand Excalibur,
And o'er him, drawing it, the winter moon,
Brightening the skirts of a long cloud, ran
    forth
And sparkled keen with frost against the
    hilt;   55
For all the haft twinkled with diamond sparks,
Myriads of topaz-lights, and jacinth-work
Of subtlest jewelry. He gazed so long
That both his eyes were dazzled, as he stood,
This way and that dividing the swift mind,   60
In act to throw; but at the last it seemed
Better to leave Excalibur concealed
There in the many-knotted water-flags,
That whistled stiff and dry about the marge.
So strode he back slow to the wounded king.
    Then spake King Arthur to Sir Bedivere: 66
"Hast thou performed my mission which I
    gave?

What is it thou hast seen, or what hast
    heard?"
    And answer made the bold Sir Bedivere:
"I heard the ripple washing in the reeds,   70
And the wild water lapping on the crag."
    To whom replied King Arthur faint and
        pale,
"Thou hast betrayed thy nature and thy
    name,
Not rendering true answer, as beseemed
Thy fealty, nor like a noble knight;   75
For surer sign had followed, either hand,
Or voice, or else a motion of the mere.
This is a shameful thing for men to lie.
Yet now, I charge thee, quickly go again
As thou art lief and dear, and do the thing   80
I bade thee, watch, and lightly bring me
    word."
    Then went Sir Bedivere the second time
Across the ridge, and paced beside the mere,
Counting the dewy pebbles, fixed in thought;
But when he saw the wonder of the hilt,   85
How curiously and strangely chased, he smote
His palms together, and he cried aloud:
    "And if indeed I cast the brand away,
Surely a precious thing, one worthy note,
Should thus be lost forever from the earth,   90
Which might have pleased the eyes of many
    men.
What good should follow this, if this were
    done?
What harm, undone? deep harm to disobey,
Seeing obedience is the bond of rule.
Were it well to obey then, if a king demand
An act unprofitable, against himself?   96
The king is sick, and knows not what he does.
What record, or what relic of my lord
Should be to aftertime, but empty breath
And rumors of a doubt? But were this kept,
Stored in some treasure-house of mighty
    kings,   101
Someone might show it at a just of arms,
Saying, 'King Arthur's sword, Excalibur,
Wrought by the lonely maiden of the lake;
Nine years she wrought it, sitting in the
    deeps   105
Upon the hidden bases of the hills.'
So might some old man speak in the after-
    time
To all the people, winning reverence;
But now much honor and much fame were
    lost."
    So spake he, clouded with his own conceit,
And hid Excalibur the second time,   111
And so strode back slow to the wounded king.
    Then spoke King Arthur, breathing heavily,
"What is it thou hast seen, or what hast
    heard?"

21. Camelot, the city of King Arthur's court. 23. Merlin, the magician and prophet of Arthur's court. 31. samite, a kind of heavy silk stuff.

80. lief, beloved. 86. curiously, elaborately, elegantly.

And answer made the bold Sir Bedivere:
"I heard the water lapping on the crag,   116
And the long ripple washing in the reeds."
　　To whom replied King Arthur, much in
　　　wrath,
"Ah, miserable and unkind, untrue,
Unknightly, traitor-hearted! Woe is me!   120
Authority forgets a dying king,
Laid widowed of the power in his eye
That bowed the will. I see thee what thou
　　art,
For thou, the latest-left of all my knights,
In whom should meet the offices of all,   125
Thou wouldst betray me for the precious hilt;
Either from lust of gold, or like a girl
Valuing the giddy pleasure of the eyes.
Yet, for a man may fail in duty twice,
And the third time may prosper, get thee
　　hence;   130
But, if thou spare to fling Excalibur,
I will arise and slay thee with my hands."
　　Then quickly rose Sir Bedivere, and ran,
And, leaping down the ridges lightly, plunged
Among the bulrush-beds, and clutched the
　　sword,   135
And strongly wheeled and threw it. The
　　great brand
Made lightnings in the splendor of the moon,
And flashing round and round, and whirled
　　in an arch,
Shot like a streamer of the northern morn,
Seen where the moving isles of winter shock
By night, with noises of the northern sea.   141
So flashed and fell the brand Excalibur;
But ere he dipped the surface, rose an arm
Clothed in white samite, mystic, wonderful,
And caught him by the hilt, and brandished
　　him   145
Three times, and drew him under in the mere.
And lightly went the other to the king.
　　Then spoke King Arthur, drawing thicker
　　breath:
"Now see I by thine eyes that this is done.
Speak out; what is it thou hast heard, or
　　seen?"   150
　　And answer made the bold Sir Bedivere:
"Sir King, I closed mine eyelids, lest the gems
Should blind my purpose, for I never saw,
Nor shall see, here or elsewhere, till I die,
Not though I live three lives of mortal men,
So great a miracle as yonder hilt.   156
Then with both hands I flung him, wheeling
　　him;
But when I looked again, behold an arm,
Clothed in white samite, mystic, wonderful,
That caught him by the hilt, and brandished
　　him   160

Three times, and drew him under in the
　　mere."
　　And answer made King Arthur, breathing
　　hard:
"My end draws nigh; 'tis time that I were
　　gone.
Make broad thy shoulders to receive my
　　weight,
And bear me to the margin; yet I fear   165
My wound hath taken cold, and I shall die."
　　So saying, from the pavement he half rose,
Slowly, with pain, reclining on his arm,
And looking wistfully with wide blue eyes
As in a picture. Him Sir Bedivere   170
Remorsefully regarded through his tears,
And would have spoken, but he found not
　　words,
Then took with care, and kneeling on one
　　knee,
O'er both his shoulders drew the languid
　　hands,
And rising bore him through the place of
　　tombs.   175
But, as he walked, King Arthur panted hard,
Like one that feels a nightmare on his bed
When all the house is mute. So sighed the
　　king,
Muttering and murmuring at his ear, "Quick,
　　quick!
I fear it is too late, and I shall die."   180
But the other swiftly strode from ridge to
　　ridge,
Clothed with his breath, and looking, as he
　　walked,
Larger than human on the frozen hills.
He heard the deep behind him, and a cry
Before. His own thought drove him like a
　　goad.   185
Dry clashed his harness in the icy caves
And barren chasms, and all to left and right
The bare black cliff clanged round him, as he
　　based
His feet on juts of slippery crag that rang
Sharp-smitten with the dint of arméd heels—
And on a sudden, lo! the level lake,   191
And the long glories of the winter moon.
　　Then saw they how there hove a dusky
　　barge,
Dark as a funeral scarf from stem to stern,
Beneath them; and descending they were
　　ware   195
That all the decks were dense with stately
　　forms
Black-stoled, black-hooded, like a dream—
　　by these
Three queens with crowns of gold—and from
　　them rose
A cry that shivered to the tingling stars,

---

139. streamer . . . morn, the northern lights. 140. isles
of winter, icebergs.

186. Dry, a classical use of the word, meaning grating.

And, as it were one voice, an agony　　200
Of lamentation, like a wind that shrills
All night in a waste land, where no one comes,
Or hath come, since the making of the world.
　　Then murmured Arthur, "Place me in the
　　　　barge,"
And to the barge they came. There those
　　　three queens　　205
Put forth their hands, and took the king, and
　　wept.
But she that rose the tallest of them all
And fairest laid his head upon her lap,
And loosed the shattered casque, and chafed
　　his hands,
And called him by his name, complaining
　　loud,　　210
And dropping bitter tears against his brow
Striped with dark blood; for all his face was
　　white
And colorless, and like the withered moon
Smote by the fresh beam of the springing
　　east;
And all his greaves and cuisses dashed with
　　drops　　215
Of onset; and the light and lustrous curls—
That made his forehead like a rising sun
High from the dais-throne—were parched
　　with dust;
Or, clotted into points and hanging loose,
Mixed with the knightly growth that fringed
　　his lips.　　220
So like a shattered column lay the king;
Not like that Arthur who, with lance in rest,
From spur to plume a star of tournament,
Shot through the lists at Camelot, and charged
Before the eyes of ladies and of kings.　　225
　　Then loudly cried the bold Sir Bedivere:
"Ah! my Lord Arthur, whither shall I go?
Where shall I hide my forehead and my eyes?
For now I see the true old times are dead,
When every morning brought a noble chance,
And every chance brought out a noble knight.
Such times have been not since the light that
　　led　　232
The holy Elders with the gift of myrrh.
But now the whole ROUND TABLE is dis-
　　solved
Which was an image of the mighty world;
And I, the last, go forth companionless,　　236
And the days darken round me, and the years,
Among new men, strange faces, other minds."
　　And slowly answered Arthur from the
　　　barge:
"The old order changeth, yielding place to
　　new,　　240

And God fulfills himself in many ways,
Lest one good custom should corrupt the
　　world.
Comfort thyself; what comfort is in me?
I have lived my life, and that which I have
　　done
May He within himself make pure! but thou,
If thou shouldst never see my face again,　　246
Pray for my soul. More things are wrought
　　by prayer
Than this world dreams of. Wherefore, let
　　thy voice
Rise like a fountain for me night and day.
For what are men better than sheep or goats
That nourish a blind life within the brain,　　251
If, knowing God, they lift not hands of prayer
Both for themselves and those who call them
　　friend?
For so the whole round earth is every way
Bound by gold chains about the feet of God.
But now farewell. I am going a long way　　256
With these thou seest—if indeed I go—
For all my mind is clouded with a doubt—
To the island-valley of Avilion;
Where falls not hail, or rain, or any snow,　　260
Nor ever wind blows loudly, but it lies
Deep-meadowed, happy, fair with orchard
　　lawns
And bowery hollows crowned with summer
　　sea,
Where I will heal me of my grievous wound."
　　So said he, and the barge with oar and sail
Moved from the brink, like some full-breasted
　　swan　　266
That, fluting a wild carol ere her death,
Ruffles her pure cold plume, and takes the
　　flood
With swarthy webs. Long stood Sir Bedivere
Revolving many memories, till the hull　　270
Looked one black dot against the verge of
　　dawn,
And on the mere the wailing died away.

Here ended Hall, and our last light, that
　　long
Had winked and threatened darkness, flared
　　and fell;
At which the parson, sent to sleep with
　　sound,　　275
And waked with silence, grunted "Good!"
　　but we
Sat rapt; it was the tone with which he
　　read—

232. the light, the Star of Bethlehem. 240. The old . . .
new. This poem appeared in 1842, at the climax of the Oxford movement, the Chartist movement, and the Corn Law
agitation. The line may refer to many changes threatening
the old order of society.

254-255. The idea expressed here is a familiar one in literature, being found in Homer, Spenser, Milton, Dryden, and
others. See *Paradise Lost, II,* 1051. 259. Avilion, Avalon,
in Celtic mythology, the Land of the Blessed, or Isle of Souls,
an earthly paradise in the western seas. 266-267. According
to ancient tradition, the swan always sang immediately
before dying.

Perhaps some modern touches here and there
Redeemed it from the charge of nothingness—
Or else we loved the man, and prized his
   work; 280
I know not; but we sitting, as I said,
The cock crew loud, as at that time of year
The lusty bird takes every hour for dawn.
Then Francis, muttering, like a man ill-used,
"There now—that's nothing!" drew a little
   back, 285
And drove his heel into the smoldered log,
That sent a blast of sparkles up the flue.
And so to bed, where yet in sleep I seemed
To sail with Arthur under looming shores,
Point after point; till on to dawn, when
   dreams 290
Begin to feel the truth and stir of day,
To me, methought, who waited with the
   crowd,
There came a bark that, blowing forward,
   bore
King Arthur, like a modern gentleman
Of stateliest port; and all the people cried,
"Arthur is come again; he cannot die." 296
Then those that stood upon the hills behind
Repeated—"Come again, and thrice as fair";
And, further inland, voices echoed—"Come
With all good things, and war shall be no
   more." 300
At this a hundred bells began to peal,
That with the sound I woke, and heard indeed
The clear church-bells ring in the Christmas
   morn.

(c. 1835; 1842)

very hopeful of Senture

ULYSSES

It little profits that an idle king,
By this still hearth, among these barren crags,
Matched with an aged wife, I mete and dole
Unequal laws unto a savage race,
That hoard, and sleep, and feed, and know
   not me. 5
I cannot rest from travel; I will drink
Life to the lees. All times I have enjoyed
Greatly, have suffered greatly, both with
   those
That loved me, and alone; on shore, and
   when
Through scudding drifts the rainy Hyades 10

278. **modern touches.** See 1. 240 and note. In *The Idylls
of the King*, Tennyson was liberal with "modern touches."
See *To the Queen*, 35 ff., p. 160. 294. **a modern gentleman.**
Tennyson's *Dedication* (1862) to *The Idylls of the King* drew a
parallel between King Arthur and the modern gentleman
Prince Albert, the Consort of Queen Victoria.
   Ulysses. See Critical Notes.
   3. **an aged wife,** Penelope. The scene is in Ithaca, the
home of Ulysses. 10. **Hyades,** a group of seven stars in the
constellation Taurus. They were associated with the rainy
season.

Vexed the dim sea. I am become a name;
For always roaming with a hungry heart
Much have I seen and known—cities of men
And manners, climates, councils, govern-
   ments, 14
Myself not least, but honored of them all—
And drunk delight of battle with my peers,
Far on the ringing plains of windy Troy.
I am a part of all that I have met;
Yet all experience is an arch wherethrough
Gleams that untraveled world whose margin
   fades 20
Forever and forever when I move.
How dull it is to pause, to make an end,
To rust unburnished, not to shine in use!
As though to breathe were life! Life piled
   on life
Were all too little, and of one to me 25
Little remains; but every hour is saved
From that eternal silence, something more,
A bringer of new things; and vile it were
For some three suns to store and hoard my-
   self,
And this gray spirit yearning in desire 30
To follow knowledge like a sinking star,
Beyond the utmost bound of human thought.
   This is my son, mine own Telemachus,
To whom I leave the scepter and the isle—
Well-loved of me, discerning to fulfill 35
This labor, by slow prudence to make mild
A rugged people, and through soft degrees
Subdue them to the useful and the good.
Most blameless is he, centered in the sphere
Of common duties, decent not to fail 40
In offices of tenderness, and pay
Meet adoration to my household gods,
When I am gone. He works his work, I mine.
   There lies the port; the vessel puffs her sail;
There gloom the dark, broad seas. My
   mariners, 45
Souls that have toiled, and wrought, and
   thought with me—
That ever with a frolic welcome took
The thunder and the sunshine, and opposed
Free hearts, free foreheads—you and I are
   old;
Old age hath yet his honor and his toil. 50
Death closes all; but something ere the end,
Some work of noble note, may yet be done,
Not unbecoming men that strove with gods.
The lights begin to twinkle from the rocks;
The long day wanes; the slow moon climbs;
   the deep 55
Moans round with many voices. Come, my
   friends.
'Tis not too late to seek a newer world.
Push off, and sitting well in order smite

27. **eternal silence,** pagan conception of death. 49. **you,**
Ulysses's companions. Attitude expressed here is modern.

The sounding furrows; for my purpose holds
To sail beyond the sunset, and the baths   60
Of all the western stars, until I die.
It may be that the gulfs will wash us down;
It may be we shall touch the Happy Isles,
And see the great Achilles, whom we knew.
Though much is taken, much abides; and
    though   65
We are not now that strength which in old
    days
Moved earth and heaven, that which we are,
    we are —
One equal temper of heroic hearts,
Made weak by time and fate, but strong in
    will
To strive, to seek, to find, and not to yield. 70
                 (1842)

TITHONUS

The woods decay, the woods decay and fall,
The vapors weep their burthen to the ground;
Man comes and tills the field and lies beneath,
And after many a summer dies the swan.
Me only cruel immortality   5
Consumes; I wither slowly in thine arms,
Here at the quiet limit of the world,
A white-haired shadow roaming like a dream
The ever-silent spaces of the East,
Far-folded mists, and gleaming halls of morn.
    Alas! for this gray shadow, once a man —
So glorious in his beauty and thy choice,   12
Who madest him thy chosen, that he seemed
To his great heart none other than a god!
I asked thee, "Give me immortality."   15
Then didst thou grant mine asking with a
    smile,
Like wealthy men who care not how they
    give.
But thy strong Hours indignant worked their
    wills,
And beat me down and marred and wasted
    me,
And though they could not end me, left me
    maimed   20
To dwell in presence of immortal youth,

Immortal age beside immortal youth,
And all I was in ashes. Can thy love,
Thy beauty, make amends, though even now,
Close over us, the silver star, thy guide,   25
Shines in those tremulous eyes that fill with
    tears
To hear me? Let me go; take back thy gift.
Why should a man desire in any way
To vary from the kindly race of men,
Or pass beyond the goal of ordinance   30
Where all should pause, as is most meet for
    all?
A soft air fans the cloud apart; there comes
A glimpse of that dark world where I was
    born.
Once more the old mysterious glimmer steals
From thy pure brows, and from thy shoulders
    pure,   35
And bosom beating with a heart renewed.
Thy cheek begins to redden through the
    gloom,
Thy sweet eyes brighten slowly close to mine,
Ere yet they blind the stars, and the wild
    team
Which love thee, yearning for thy yoke, arise,
And shake the darkness from their loosened
    manes,   41
And beat the twilight into flakes of fire.
    Lo! ever thus thou growest beautiful
In silence; then, before thine answer given,
Departest, and thy tears are on my cheek. 45
    Why wilt thou ever scare me with thy tears,
And make me tremble lest a saying learnt,
In days far-off, on that dark earth, be true?
"The gods themselves cannot recall their
    gifts."
    Ay me! ay me! with what another heart 50
In days far-off, and with what other eyes
I used to watch — if I be he that watched —
The lucid outline forming round thee; saw
The dim curls kindle into sunny rings;
Changed with thy mystic change, and felt my
    blood   55
Glow with the glow that slowly crimsoned all
Thy presence and thy portals, while I lay,
Mouth, forehead, eyelids, growing dewy-warm
With kisses balmier than half-opening buds
Of April, and could hear the lips that kissed
Whispering I knew not what of wild and
    sweet,   61
Like that strange song I heard Apollo sing,
While Ilion like a mist rose into towers.
    Yet hold me not forever in thine East;
How can my nature longer mix with thine?
Coldly thy rosy shadows bathe me, cold   66

63. **the Happy Isles**, the Islands of the Blest, identified with the Elysian Fields as the abode of just men after death.
64. **Achilles**, the most famous of the Greek heroes in the Trojan War. At Troy he slew Hector and dragged his body three times around the walls. Achilles was finally killed by Paris, who wounded him with a poisoned arrow in the heel, his only vulnerable spot. The arms of Achilles were awarded to Ulysses. 65-70. These lines contain Tennyson's favorite doctrine of the unconquerable will.
Tithonus. Tithonus was the son of Laomedon, king of Troy, and the husband of Aurora, goddess of the dawn. Aurora asked the gods to grant Tithonus immortality, but she neglected to ask for him also eternal youth, and he became so withered and ugly that she turned him into a grasshopper. Cf. the fate of the Struldbrugs in Swift's *Gulliver's Travels*, III, 10.
18. **Hours**, the goddesses who cause all things to come into being, to ripen, and to decay at the appointed time.

25. **the silver star**, the morning star. 29. **kindly**, natural. 39. **team**, the steeds that drew Aurora's chariot up to Mt. Olympus to announce the coming of the day. 63. **Ilion**, Troy, the walls of which were said to have been built to the music of Apollo's lyre. Apollo (line 62) was the god of poetry and music.

Are all thy lights, and cold my wrinkled feet
Upon thy glimmering thresholds, when the
    steam
Floats up from those dim fields about the
    homes
Of happy men that have the power to die, 70
And grassy barrows of the happier dead.
Release me, and restore me to the ground.
Thou seest all things, thou wilt see my grave;
Thou wilt renew thy beauty morn by morn,
I earth in earth forget these empty courts, 75
And thee returning on thy silver wheels.

                      (c. 1842; 1860)

LOCKSLEY HALL

Comrades, leave me here a little, while as yet
    'tis early morn;
Leave me here, and when you want me, sound
    upon the bugle-horn.

'Tis the place, and all around it, as of old,
    the curlews call,
Dreary gleams about the moorland flying over
    Locksley Hall;

Locksley Hall, that in the distance overlooks
    the sandy tracts,   5
And the hollow ocean-ridges roaring into
    cataracts.

Many a night from yonder ivied casement,
    ere I went to rest,
Did I look on great Orion sloping slowly to
    the west.

Many a night I saw the Pleiads, rising through
    the mellow shade,
Glitter like a swarm of fireflies tangled in a
    silver braid.   10

Here about the beach I wandered, nourishing
    a youth sublime
With the fairy tales of science, and the long
    result of time;

When the centuries behind me like a fruitful
    land reposed;
When I clung to all the present for the promise
    that it closed;

When I dipped into the future far as human
    eye could see,   15
Saw the vision of the world and all the wonder
    that would be. —

Locksley Hall. See Critical Notes.
4. *gleams* may be taken as in apposition to *curlews* (line 3),
or the entire phrase may be an absolute construction. 8.
Orion, one of the most conspicuous constellations in the
heavens. 9. **the Pleiads,** a group of seven stars in the
constellation Taurus.

In the spring a fuller crimson comes upon
    the robin's breast;
In the spring the wanton lapwing gets him-
    self another crest;

In the spring a livelier iris changes on the
    burnished dove;
In the spring a young man's fancy lightly
    turns to thoughts of love.   20

Then her cheek was pale and thinner than
    should be for one so young,
And her eyes on all my motions with a mute
    observance hung.

And I said, "My cousin Amy, speak and
    speak the truth to me;
Trust me, cousin, all the current of my being
    sets to thee."

On her pallid cheek and forehead came a
    color and a light,   25
As I have seen the rosy red flushing in the
    northern night.

And she turned — her bosom shaken with a
    sudden storm of sighs —
All the spirit deeply dawning in the dark of
    hazel eyes —

Saying, "I have hid my feelings, fearing they
    should do me wrong";
Saying, "Dost thou love me, cousin?" weep-
    ing, "I have loved thee long."   30

Love took up the glass of Time, and turned
    it in his glowing hands;
Every moment, lightly shaken, ran itself in
    golden sands.

Love took up the harp of Life, and smote on
    all the chords with might;
Smote the chord of Self, that, trembling,
    passed in music out of sight.

Many a morning on the moorland did we hear
    the copses ring,   35
And her whisper thronged my pulses with the
    fullness of the spring.

Many an evening by the waters did we watch
    the stately ships,
And our spirits rushed together at the touch-
    ing of the lips.

O my cousin, shallow-hearted! O my Amy,
    mine no more!

19. **iris . . . dove.** The rainbow colors on the dove's neck
become brighter during the mating season.

O the dreary, dreary moorland! O the barren,
    barren shore!   40

Falser than all fancy fathoms, falser than all
    songs have sung,
Puppet to a father's threat, and servile to a
    shrewish tongue!

Is it well to wish thee happy? — having
    known me — to decline
On a range of lower feelings and a narrower
    heart than mine!

Yet it shall be; thou shalt lower to his level
    day by day,   45
What is fine within thee growing coarse to
    sympathize with clay.

As the husband is, the wife is; thou art mated
    with a clown,
And the grossness of his nature will have
    weight to drag thee down.

He will hold thee, when his passion shall have
    spent its novel force,
Something better than his dog, a little dearer
    than his horse.   50

What is this? his eyes are heavy; think not
    they are glazed with wine.
Go to him, it is thy duty; kiss him, take his
    hand in thine.

It may be my lord is weary, that his brain is
    overwrought;
Soothe him with thy finer fancies, touch him
    with thy lighter thought.

He will answer to the purpose, easy things to
    understand —   55
Better thou wert dead before me, though I
    slew thee with my hand!

Better thou and I were lying, hidden from
    the heart's disgrace,
Rolled in one another's arms, and silent in a
    last embrace.

Curséd be the social wants that sin against
    the strength of youth!
Curséd be the social lies that warp us from
    the living truth!   60

Curséd be the sickly forms that err from
    honest Nature's rule!
Curséd be the gold that gilds the straitened
    forehead of the fool!

42. **Puppet . . . tongue.** Her father and mother forced
her to marry another—a man of coarser nature.

Well — 'tis well that I should bluster! —
    Hadst thou less unworthy proved —
Would to God — for I had loved thee more
    than ever wife was loved.

Am I mad, that I should cherish that which
    bears but bitter fruit?   65
I will pluck it from my bosom, though my
    heart be at the root.

Never — though my mortal summers to such
    length of years should come
As the many-wintered crow that leads the
    clanging rookery home.

Where is comfort? in division of the records
    of the mind?
Can I part her from herself, and love her, as
    I knew her, kind?   70

I remember one that perished; sweetly did
    she speak and move;
Such a one do I remember, whom to look at
    was to love.

Can I think of her as dead, and love her for
    the love she bore?
No — she never loved me truly; love is love
    for evermore.

Comfort? comfort scorned of devils! this is
    truth the poet sings,   75
That a sorrow's crown of sorrow is remem-
    bering happier things.

Drug thy memories, lest thou learn it, lest
    thy heart be put to proof,
In the dead unhappy night, and when the
    rain is on the roof.

Like a dog, he hunts in dreams, and thou art
    staring at the wall,
Where the dying night-lamp flickers, and the
    shadows rise and fall.   80

Then a hand shall pass before thee, pointing
    to his drunken sleep,
To thy widowed marriage-pillows, to the tears
    that thou wilt weep.

Thou shalt hear the "Never, never," whis-
    pered by the phantom years,
And a song from out the distance in the ring-
    ing of thine ears;

68. **crow,** rook. 75. **comfort . . . devils,** as in *Paradise
Lost,* I and II. 76. **That . . . things.** Many poets express
this idea. Dante says in *Inferno,* 5, 121, "There is no greater
sorrow than to remember happy times when one is in misery."
79. **he,** Amy's husband, a fox-hunting squire.

And an eye shall vex thee looking ancient
    kindness on thy pain.   85
Turn thee, turn thee on thy pillow; get thee
    to thy rest again.

Nay, but Nature brings thee solace; for a
    tender voice will cry.
'Tis a purer life than thine, a lip to drain thy
    trouble dry.

Baby lips will laugh me down; my latest rival
    brings thee rest.
Baby fingers, waxen touches, press me from
    the mother's breast.   90

Oh, the child too clothes the father with a
    dearness not his due.
Half is thine and half is his; it will be worthy
    of the two.

Oh, I see thee old and formal, fitted to thy
    petty part,
With a little hoard of maxims preaching down
    a daughter's heart.

"They were dangerous guides, the feelings —
    she herself was not exempt —   95
Truly, she herself had suffered" — Perish in
    thy self-contempt!

Overlive it — lower yet — be happy! where-
    fore should I care?
I myself must mix with action, lest I wither
    by despair.

What is that which I should turn to, lighting
    upon days like these?
Every door is barred with gold, and opens
    but to golden keys.   100

Every gate is thronged with suitors, all the
    markets overflow.
I have but an angry fancy; what is that which
    I should do?

I had been content to perish, falling on the
    foeman's ground,
When the ranks are rolled in vapor, and the
    winds are laid with sound.

But the jingling of the guinea helps the hurt
    that Honor feels,   105
And the nations do but murmur, snarling at
    each other's heels.

Can I but relive in sadness? I will turn that
    earlier page.

Hide me from my deep emotion, O thou
    wondrous Mother-Age!

Make me feel the wild pulsation that I felt
    before the strife,
When I heard my days before me, and the
    tumult of my life;   110

Yearning for the large excitement that the
    coming years would yield,
Eager-hearted as a boy when first he leaves
    his father's field,

And at night along the dusky highway near
    and nearer drawn,
Sees in heaven the light of London flaring like
    a dreary dawn;

And his spirit leaps within him to be gone
    before him then,   115
Underneath the light he looks at, in among
    the throngs of men;

Men, my brothers, men the workers, ever
    reaping something new;
That which they have done but earnest of the
    things that they shall do.

For I dipped into the future, far as human eye
    could see,
Saw the Vision of the world, and all the
    wonder that would be;   120

Saw the heavens fill with commerce, argosies
    of magic sails,
Pilots of the purple twilight, dropping down
    with costly bales;

Heard the heavens fill with shouting, and
    there rained a ghastly dew
From the nations' airy navies grappling in
    the central blue;

Far along the world-wide whisper of the
    south-wind rushing warm,   125
With the standards of the peoples plunging
    through the thunder-storm;

Till the war-drum throbbed no longer, and
    the battle-flags were furled
In the Parliament of man, the Federation of
    the world.

There the common sense of most shall hold
    a fretful realm in awe,
And the kindly earth shall slumber, lapped in
    universal law.   130

---

104. **winds are laid.** There was an old idea that the discharge of cannon during a battle stilled the winds.

121-128. These lines are regarded as a prophetic glimpse of
modern aviation and of battles between airships. 128. Compare the idea of the present United Nations.

So I triumphed ere my passion sweeping
    through me left me dry,
Left me with the palsied heart, and left me
    with the jaundiced eye;

Eye, to which all order festers, all things here
    are out of joint.
Science moves, but slowly, slowly, creeping
    on from point to point;

Slowly comes a hungry people, as a lion,
    creeping nigher,   135
Glares at one that nods and winks behind a
    slowly-dying fire.

God as a purpose

Yet I doubt not through the ages one increas-
    ing purpose runs,
And the thoughts of men are widened with
    the process of the suns.

What is that to him that reaps not harvest
    of his youthful joys,
Though the deep heart of existence beat for-
    ever like a boy's?   140

Knowledge comes, but wisdom lingers, and I
    linger on the shore,
And the individual withers, and the world is
    more and more.

Knowledge comes, but wisdom lingers, and
    he bears a laden breast,
Full of sad experience, moving toward the
    stillness of his rest.

Hark, my merry comrades call me, sounding
    on the bugle-horn,   145
They to whom my foolish passion were a
    target for their scorn.

Shall it not be scorn to me to harp on such a
    moldered string?
I am shamed through all my nature to have
    loved so slight a thing.

Weakness to be wroth with weakness! woman's
    pleasure, woman's pain —
Nature made them blinder motions bounded
    in a shallower brain.   150

Woman is the lesser man, and all thy passions,
    matched with mine,
Are as moonlight unto sunlight, and as water
    unto wine —

Here at least, where nature sickens, nothing.
    Ah, for some retreat
Deep in yonder shining Orient, where my life
    began to beat,

Where in wild Mahratta-battle fell my father
    evil-starred —   155
I was left a trampled orphan, and a selfish
    uncle's ward.

Or to burst all links of habit — there to
    wander far away,
On from island unto island at the gateways
    of the day—

Larger constellations burning, mellow moons
    and happy skies,
Breadths of tropic shade and palms in clus-
    ter, knots of Paradise;   160

Never comes the trader, never floats an
    European flag,
Slides the bird o'er lustrous woodland, swings
    the trailer from the crag;

Droops the heavy-blossomed bower, hangs
    the heavy-fruited tree —
Summer isles of Eden lying in dark-purple
    spheres of sea.

There methinks would be enjoyment more
    than in this march of mind,   165
In the steamship, in the railway, in the
    thoughts that shake mankind.

escape

There the passions cramped no longer shall
    have scope and breathing space;
I will take some savage woman, she shall rear
    my dusky race.

Iron-jointed, supple-sinewed, they shall dive,
    and they shall run,
Catch the wild goat by the hair, and hurl
    their lances in the sun;   170

Whistle back the parrot's call, and leap the
    rainbows of the brooks,
Not with blinded eyesight poring over mis-
    erable books —

Fool, again the dream, the fancy! but I *know*
    my words are wild,
But I count the gray barbarian lower than
    the Christian child.

132. **jaundiced**, prejudiced. 135. **a hungry people**, a
reference to the "dangerous" advance of democracy felt in the
discontent which accompanied the Chartist movement. 138.
the process of the suns, the passing of the years. 141-142.
New facts of life crowd in upon us, but fundamental truths are
constant. Science and evolution show us that the mass of
humanity is more important than the individual. Cf. *In
Memoriam*, Section 114, p. 86. 150. **motions**, impulses.

155. The hero is represented as having been born in India,
the son of a British soldier who fell in battle against the
Mahrattas, a people living in central and western India.
162. **trailer**, a trailing vine.

I, to herd with narrow foreheads, vacant of
    our glorious gains,   175
Like a beast with lower pleasures, like a beast
    with lower pains!

Mated with a squalid savage — what to me
    were sun or clime?
I the heir of all the ages, in the foremost files
    of time —

I that rather held it better men should perish
    one by one,
Than that earth should stand at gaze like
    Joshua's moon in Ajalon!   180

Not in vain the distance beacons. Forward,
    forward let us range,
Let the great world spin forever down the
    ringing grooves of change.

Through the shadow of the globe we sweep
    into the younger day;
Better fifty years of Europe than a cycle of
    Cathay.

Mother-Age — for mine I knew not — help
    me as when life begun;   185
Rift the hills, and roll the waters, flash the
    lightnings, weigh the sun.

Oh, I see the crescent promise of my spirit
    hath not set.
Ancient founts of inspiration well through all
    my fancy yet.

Howsoever these things be, a long farewell to
    Locksley Hall!
Now for me the woods may wither, now for
    me the roof-tree fall.   190

Comes a vapor from the margin, blackening
    over heath and holt,
Cramming all the blast before it, in its breast
    a thunderbolt.

Let it fall on Locksley Hall, with rain or hail,
    or fire or snow;
For the mighty wind arises, roaring seaward,
    and I go.   (1842)

180. **Joshua's moon in Ajalon.** From *Joshua*, 10:12-13.
—"Then spake Joshua . . . in the sight of Israel, 'Sun, stand
thou still upon Gibeon; and thou, Moon, in the valley of
Ajalon.' And the sun stood still, and the moon stayed, until
the people had avenged themselves upon their enemies."
181. **beacons,** lights a signal for advance. 182. **grooves.**
When Tennyson first rode on a railroad train in 1830, he
thought that the wheels ran in a groove. He states that he
composed this line at that time (*Memoir*, I, 195). 184. **a
cycle of Cathay,** an indefinitely long period spent in China.
This passage reflects the common early-Victorian faith in
progress. 186. **Rift the hills,** etc. This line probably refers
to Francis Baily's experiments (1838-42) for determining the
mean density of the earth and the weight of the sun. 190. **for
me,** as far as I am concerned.

GODIVA

I waited for the train at Coventry;
I hung with grooms and porters on the bridge,
To watch the three tall spires; and there I shaped
The city's ancient legend into this:

Not only we, the latest seed of Time,   5
New men, that in the flying of a wheel
Cry down the past, not only we, that prate
Of rights and wrongs, have loved the people
    well,
And loathed to see them overtaxed; but she
Did more, and underwent, and overcame,   10
The woman of a thousand summers back,
Godiva, wife to that grim Earl, who ruled
In Coventry; for when he laid a tax
Upon his town, and all the mothers brought
Their children, clamoring, "If we pay, we
    starve!"   15
She sought her lord, and found him, where he
    strode
About the hall, among his dogs, alone,
His beard a foot before him, and his hair
A yard behind. She told him of their tears,
And prayed him, "If they pay this tax, they
    starve."   20
Whereat he stared, replying, half-amazed,
"You would not let your little finger ache
For such as *these?*" — "But I would die," said she.
He laughed, and swore by Peter and by Paul,
Then filliped at the diamond in her ear: 25
"Oh, ay, ay, ay, you talk!" — "Alas!" she
    said,
"But prove me what it is I would not do."
And from a heart as rough as Esau's hand,
He answered, "Ride you naked through the
    town,   29
And I repeal it"; and nodding, as in scorn,
He parted, with great strides among his dogs.
So left alone, the passions of her mind,
As winds from all the compass shift and blow,
Made war upon each other for an hour,
Till pity won. She sent a herald forth,   35
And bade him cry, with sound of trumpet, all
The hard condition, but that she would loose
The people; therefore, as they loved her well,
From then till noon no foot should pace the
    street,   39
No eye look down, she passing, but that all
Should keep within, door shut, and window
    barred.

Godiva. According to the legend here recorded, probably
partly true, Godiva was the wife of Leofric, who was Earl
of Mercia and Lord of Coventry about 1040; she rode naked
through the town as the price of remitting a burdensome tax
on her people.
3. **tall spires,** those of St. Michael's Church, Trinity
Church, and Christ Church. 28. **Esau,** the son of Isaac and
Rebekah. His hands and body were covered with hair. See
Genesis, 25:21-34.

Then fled she to her inmost bower, and
    there
Unclasped the wedded eagles of her belt,
The grim earl's gift; but ever at a breath
She lingered, looking like a summer moon 45
Half-dipped in cloud. Anon she shook her
    head,
And showered the rippled ringlets to her knee;
Unclad herself in haste; adown the stair
Stole on; and like a creeping sunbeam slid
From pillar unto pillar, until she reached 50
The gateway; there she found her palfrey
    trapped
In purple blazoned with armorial gold.
    Then she rode forth, clothed on with
    chastity.
The deep air listened round her as she rode,
And all the low wind hardly breathed for
    fear. 55
The little wide-mouthed heads upon the spout
Had cunning eyes to see; the barking cur
Made her cheek flame; her palfrey's footfall
    shot
Light horrors through her pulses; the blind
    walls
Were full of chinks and holes; and over-
    head
Fantastic gables, crowding, stared; but she 61
Not less through all bore up, till, last, she
    saw
The white-flowered elder-thicket from the
    field
Gleam through the Gothic archway in the
    wall.
    Then she rode back, clothed on with
    chastity. 65
And one low churl, compact of thankless
    earth,
The fatal byword of all years to come,
Boring a little auger-hole in fear,
Peeped — but his eyes, before they had their
    will,
Were shriveled into darkness in his head, 70
And dropped before him. So the Powers, who
    wait
On noble deeds, canceled a sense misused;
And she, that knew not, passed; and all at
    once,
With twelve great shocks of sound, the shame-
    less noon
Was clashed and hammered from a hundred
    towers, 75
One after one; but even then she gained
Her bower, whence reissuing, robed and
    crowned,
To meet her lord, she took the tax away
And built herself an everlasting name.
                    (1842)

66. **one low churl.** This was Peeping Tom, a tailor. The
name has been applied to others since his time.

SIR GALAHAD

My good blade carves the casques of men,
    My tough lance thrusteth sure,
My strength is as the strength of ten,
    Because my heart is pure.
The shattering trumpet shrilleth high, 5
    The hard brands shiver on the steel,
The splintered spear-shafts crack and fly,
    The horse and rider reel;
They reel, they roll in clanging lists,
    And when the tide of combat stands, 10
Perfume and flowers fall in showers,
    That lightly rain from ladies' hands.

How sweet are looks that ladies bend
    On whom their favors fall!
For them I battle till the end, 15
    To save from shame and thrall;
But all my heart is drawn above,
    My knees are bowed in crypt and shrine;
I never felt the kiss of love,
    Nor maiden's hand in mine. 20
More bounteous aspects on me beam,
    Me mightier transports move and thrill;
So keep I fair through faith and prayer
    A virgin heart in work and will.

When down the stormy crescent goes, 25
    A light before me swims,
Between dark stems the forest glows,
    I hear a noise of hymns.
Then by some secret shrine I ride;
    I hear a voice, but none are there; 30
The stalls are void, the doors are wide,
    The tapers burning fair.
Fair gleams the snowy altar-cloth,
    The silver vessels sparkle clean,
The shrill bell rings, the censer swings, 35
    And solemn chaunts resound between.

Sometimes on lonely mountain-meres
    I find a magic bark.
I leap on board; no helmsman steers;
    I float till all is dark. 40
A gentle sound, an awful light!
    Three angels bear the Holy Grail;
With folded feet, in stoles of white,
    On sleeping wings they sail.
Ah, blessed vision! blood of God! 45
    My spirit beats her mortal bars,
As down dark tides the glory slides,
    And starlike mingles with the stars.

When on my goodly charger borne
    Through dreaming towns I go, 50

Sir Galahad. In late versions of the Arthurian legends,
Sir Galahad was a famous knight of the Round Table who
achieved the quest of the Holy Grail. He was the son of
Lancelot. See Critical Notes.
    25. **the stormy crescent,** the new moon. 31. **stalls,**
seats in the choir and the chancel.

The cock crows ere the Christmas morn,
  The streets are dumb with snow.
The tempest crackles on the leads,
  And, ringing, springs from brand and mail;
But o'er the dark a glory spreads,   55
  And gilds the driving hail.
I leave the plain, I climb the height;
  No branchy thicket shelter yields;
But blessed forms in whistling storms
  Fly o'er waste fens and windy fields.   60

A maiden knight — to me is given
  Such hope, I know not fear;
I yearn to breathe the airs of heaven
  That often meet me here.
I muse on joy that will not cease,   65
  Pure spaces clothed in living beams,
Pure lilies of eternal peace,
  Whose odors haunt my dreams;
And, stricken by an angel's hand,
  This mortal armor that I wear,   70
This weight and size, this heart and eyes,
  Are touched, are turned to finest air.

The clouds are broken in the sky,
  And through the mountain-walls
A rolling organ-harmony   75
  Swells up and shakes and falls.
Then move the trees, the copses nod,
  Wings flutter, voices hover clear:
"O just and faithful knight of God!
  Ride on! the prize is near."   80
So pass I hostel, hall, and grange;
  By bridge and ford, by park and pale,
All-armed I ride, whate'er betide,
  Until I find the Holy Grail.   (1842)

THE BEGGAR MAID

Her arms across her breast she laid;
  She was more fair than words can say;
Barefooted came the beggar maid
  Before the king Cophetua.
In robe and crown the king stepped down,   5
  To meet and greet her on her way.
"It is no wonder," said the lords;
  "She is more beautiful than day."

As shines the moon in clouded skies,
  She in her poor attire was seen;   10
One praised her ankles, one her eyes,

One her dark hair and lovesome mien.
So sweet a face, such angel grace,
  In all that land had never been.
Cophetua sware a royal oath: 15
"This beggar maid shall be my queen!"
                          (1842)

THE VISION OF SIN

1

I had a vision when the night was late;
A youth came riding toward a palace-gate.
He rode a horse with wings, that would have
    flown,
But that his heavy rider kept him down.
And from the palace came a child of sin,   5
And took him by the curls, and led him in,
Where sat a company with heated eyes,
Expecting when a fountain should arise.
A sleepy light upon their brows and lips—
As when the sun, a crescent of eclipse,   10
Dreams over lake and lawn, and isles and
    capes —
Suffused them, sitting, lying, languid shapes,
By heaps of gourds, and skins of wine and
    piles of grapes.

2

Then methought I heard a mellow sound,
Gathering up from all the lower ground;   15
Narrowing in to where they sat assembled,
Low voluptuous music winding trembled,
Woven in circles. They that heard it sighed,
Panted hand-in-hand with faces pale,
Swung themselves, and in low tones replied;
Till the fountain spouted, showering wide   21
Sleet of diamond-drift and pearly hail.
Then the music touched the gates and died,
Rose again from where it seemed to fail,
Stormed in orbs of song, a growing gale;   25
Till thronging in and in, to where they waited,
As 'twere a hundred-throated nightingale,
The strong tempestuous treble throbbed and
    palpitated;
Ran into its giddiest whirl of sound,
Caught the sparkles, and in circles,   30
Purple gauzes, golden hazes, liquid mazes,
Flung the torrent rainbow round.
Then they started from their places,
Moved with violence, changed in hue,
Caught each other with wild grimaces,   35
Half-invisible to the view,
Wheeling with precipitate paces
To the melody, till they flew,
Hair and eyes and limbs and faces,
Twisted hard in fierce embraces,   40

---

51. The cock crows. According to an old superstition the cock crows all the night before Christmas to drive away evil spirits. **53. leads,** roofs covered with sheets of lead. **72.** See Critical Notes. **82. park,** a large piece of ground, consisting of woodland and pasture, attached to a country house. **pale,** an enclosed field.

The Beggar Maid. According to legend Cophetua, an African king, married a beggar maid, Penelophon. The story is told in Percy's *Reliques* in "King Cophetua and the Beggar Maid."

The Vision of Sin. See Critical Notes.
3. horse with wings, Pegasus, associated with the Muses, especially poetry. The youth seems therefore to be a poet kept earthbound by his sensuosity.

Like to Furies, like to Graces,
Dashed together in blinding dew;
Till, killed with some luxurious agony,
The nerve-dissolving melody
Fluttered headlong from the sky.   45

3

And then I looked up toward a mountain-
          tract,
That girt the region with high cliff and lawn.
I saw that every morning, far withdrawn
Beyond the darkness and the cataract,
God made Himself an awful rose of dawn, 50
Unheeded; and detaching, fold by fold,
From those still heights, and, slowly drawing
          near,
A vapor heavy, hueless, formless, cold,
Came floating on for many a month and year,
Unheeded; and I thought I would have
          spoken,   55
And warned that madman ere it grew too
          late,
But, as in dreams, I could not. Mine was
          broken,
When that cold vapor touched the palace
          gate,
And linked again. I saw within my head
A gray and gap-toothed man as lean as death,
Who slowly rode across a withered heath, 61
And lighted at a ruined inn, and said:

4

"Wrinkled ostler, grim and thin!
     Here is custom come your way;
Take my brute, and lead him in,   65
     Stuff his ribs with moldy hay.

"Bitter barmaid, waning fast!
     See that sheets are on my bed.
What! the flower of life is past;
     It is long before you wed.   70

"Slip-shod waiter, lank and sour,
     At the Dragon on the heath!
Let us have a quiet hour,
     Let us hob-and-nob with Death.

"I am old, but let me drink;   75
     Bring me spices, bring me wine;
I remember, when I think,
     That my youth was half divine.

"Wine is good for shriveled lips,
     When a blanket wraps the day,   80
When the rotten woodland drips,
     And the leaf is stamped in clay.

"Sit thee down, and have no shame,
     Cheek by jowl, and knee by knee;
What care I for any name?   85
     What for order or degree?

"Let me screw thee up a peg;
     Let me loose thy tongue with wine;
Callest thou that thing a leg?
     Which is thinnest? thine or mine?   90

"Thou shalt not be saved by works,
     Thou hast been a sinner too;
Ruined trunks on withered forks,
     Empty scarecrows, I and you!

"Fill the cup and fill the can,   95
     Have a rouse before the morn;
Every moment dies a man,
     Every moment one is born.

"We are men of ruined blood;
     Therefore comes it we are wise.   100
Fish are we that love the mud,
     Rising to no fancy-flies.

"Name and fame! to fly sublime
     Through the courts, the camps, the schools,
Is to be the ball of Time,   105
     Bandied by the hands of fools.

"Friendship! — to be two in one —
     Let the canting liar pack!
Well I know, when I am gone,
     How she mouths behind my back.   110

"Virtue! — to be good and just —
     Every heart, when sifted well,
Is a clot of warmer dust,
     Mixed with cunning sparks of hell.

"Oh, we two as well can look   115
     Whited thought and cleanly life
As the priest, above his book
     Leering at his neighbor's wife.

"Fill the cup and fill the can,
     Have a rouse before the morn;   120
Every moment dies a man,
     Every moment one is born.

"Drink, and let the parties rave;
     They are filled with idle spleen.
Rising, falling, like a wave,   125
     For they know not what they mean.

---

41. **Furies**, the three Greek goddesses of vengeance.
Graces, goddesses representing grace, gentleness, and beauty.
50. The poet's defection is measured against the unbroken
order of nature. 72. **Dragon**, the name of the inn.

96. **rouse**, a bumper of liquor. 99. **We . . . blood**. Cf.
Kipling's *Gentlemen-Rankers*, 13-14—
          "Gentlemen-rankers out on the spree,
          Damned from here to eternity."

"He that roars for liberty
  Faster binds a tyrant's power,
And the tyrant's cruel glee
  Forces on the freer hour. 130

"Fill the can and fill the cup;
  All the windy ways of men
Are but dust that rises up,
  And is lightly laid again.

"Greet her with applausive breath, 135
  Freedom, gayly doth she tread;
In her right a civic wreath,
  In her left a human head.

"No, I love not what is new;
  She is of an ancient house, 140
And I think we know the hue
  Of that cap upon her brows.

"Let her go! her thirst she slakes
  Where the bloody conduit runs,
Then her sweetest meal she makes 145
  On the first-born of her sons.

"Drink to lofty hopes that cool —
  Visions of a perfect State;
Drink we, last, the public fool,
  Frantic love and frantic hate. 150

"Chant me now some wicked stave,
  Till thy drooping courage rise,
And the glowworm of the grave
  Glimmer in thy rheumy eyes.

"Fear not thou to loose thy tongue, 155
  Set thy hoary fancies free;
What is loathsome to the young
  Savors well to thee and me.

"Change, reverting to the years,
  When thy nerves could understand 160
What there is in loving tears,
  And the warmth of hand in hand.

"Tell me tales of thy first love —
  April hopes, the fools of chance —
Till the graves begin to move, 165
  And the dead begin to dance.

"Fill the can and fill the cup;
  All the windy ways of men
Are but dust that rises up,
  And is lightly laid again. 170

"Trooping from their moldy dens
  The chap-fallen circle spreads —
Welcome, fellow-citizens,
  Hollow hearts and empty heads!

"You are bones, and what of that? 175
  Every face, however full,
Padded round with flesh and fat,
  Is but modeled on a skull.

"Death is king, and Vivat Rex!
  Tread a measure on the stones, 180
Madam — if I know your sex
  From the fashion of your bones.

"No, I cannot praise the fire
  In your eye — nor yet your lip;
All the more do I admire 185
  Joints of cunning workmanship.

"Lo! God's likeness — the ground-plan —
  Neither modeled, glazed, nor framed;
Buss me, thou rough sketch of man,
  Far too naked to be shamed! 190

"Drink to Fortune, drink to Chance,
  While we keep a little breath!
Drink to heavy Ignorance!
  Hob-and-nob with brother Death!

"Thou art mazed, the night is long, 195
  And the longer night is near —
What! I am not all as wrong
  As a bitter jest is dear.

"Youthful hopes, by scores, to all,
  When the locks are crisp and curled; 200
Unto me my maudlin gall
  And my mockeries of the world.

"Fill the cup and fill the can;
  Mingle madness, mingle scorn!
Dregs of life, and lees of man; 205
  Yet we will not die forlorn."

5

The voice grew faint; there came a further
    change;
Once more uprose the mystic mountain-range.
Below were men and horses pierced with
    worms,
And slowly quickening into lower forms; 210
By shards and scurf of salt, and scum of dross,
Old plash of rains, and refuse patched with
    moss.
Then someone spake: "Behold! it was a crime
Of sense avenged by sense that wore with
    time."

142. cap upon her brows. The Goddess of Liberty is represented as holding in her hand a cap, the symbol of freedom. The cap referred to here is the red cap of the French Revolutionists.

179. Vivat Rex, Long live the King! 189. Buss, kiss. 208. Once . . . -range. See lines 46ff.

Another said: "The crime of sense became 215
The crime of malice, and is equal blame."
And one: "He had not wholly quenched his
     power;
A little grain of conscience made him sour."
At last I heard a voice upon the slope
Cry to the summit, "Is there any hope?" 220
To which an answer pealed from that high
     land,
But in a tongue no man could understand;
And on the glimmering limit far withdrawn
God made Himself an awful rose of dawn.
                              (1842)

BREAK, BREAK, BREAK

Break, break, break,
     On thy cold gray stones, O Sea!
And I would that my tongue could utter
     The thoughts that arise in me.

O well for the fisherman's boy,   5
     That he shouts with his sister at play!
O well for the sailor lad,
     That he sings in his boat on the bay!

And the stately ships go on
     To their haven under the hill;   10
But O for the touch of a vanished hand,
     And the sound of a voice that is still!

Break, break, break,
     At the foot of thy crags, O Sea!
But the tender grace of a day that is dead 15
     Will never come back to me.   (1842)

THE POET'S SONG

The rain had fallen, the poet arose,
     He passed by the town and out of the
          street;
A light wind blew from the gates of the sun,
     And waves of shadow went over the wheat;
And he sat him down in a lonely place,   5
     And chanted a melody loud and sweet,
That made the wild-swan pause in her cloud,
     And the lark drop down at his feet.

The swallow stopped as he hunted the fly,
     The snake slipped under a spray,   10
The wild hawk stood with the down on his
          beak,
     And stared, with his foot on the prey;

Break, Break, Break. This is one of the poems inspired by
the death of Tennyson's intimate friend, Arthur Hallam. See
In Memoriam, page 57, and notes.
  11. a vanished hand, Hallam's.

And the nightingale thought, "I have sung
     many songs,
     But never a one so gay,
For he sings of what the world will be   15
     When the years have died away." (1842)

SONGS FROM *THE PRINCESS*

As through the Land at Eve We Went

As through the land at eve we went,
     And plucked the ripened ears,
We fell out, my wife and I,
O we fell out, I know not why,
     And kissed again with tears.   5
And blessings on the falling out
     That all the more endears,
When we fall out with those we love
     And kiss again with tears!
For when we came where lies the child   10
     We lost in other years,
There above the little grave,
O there above the little grave,
     We kissed again with tears.

Sweet and Low

Sweet and low, sweet and low,
     Wind of the western sea,
Low, low, breathe and blow,
     Wind of the western sea!
Over the rolling waters go,   5
Come from the dying moon, and blow,
     Blow him again to me;
While my little one, while my pretty one,
     sleeps.

Sleep and rest, sleep and rest,
     Father will come to thee soon;   10
Rest, rest, on mother's breast,
     Father will come to thee soon;
Father will come to his babe in the nest,
Silver sails all out of the west
     Under the silver moon;   15
Sleep, my little one, sleep, my pretty one,
     sleep.

The Splendor Falls on Castle Walls

The splendor falls on castle walls
     And snowy summits old in story;
The long light shakes across the lakes,

Songs from The Princess. See Critical Notes.
  As through the Land. This song stands between Part I
and Part II. It is in contrast with Ida's ideas about the
worth of children.
  Sweet and Low. This song stands between Part II and
Part III. It emphasizes the love for children.
  The Splendor Falls. This song stands between Part III and
Part IV. It emphasizes the immortality of the influence of
love. The song was suggested by the echoes from a bugle
heard by Tennyson on the Lakes of Killarney, in Ireland,
in 1848.

And the wild cataract leaps in glory.
Blow, bugle, blow, set the wild echoes fly-
    ing,
Blow, bugle; answer, echoes, dying, dying,
    dying.   6

O hark, O hear! how thin and clear,
    And thinner, clearer, farther going!
O sweet and far from cliff and scar
    The horns of Elfland faintly blowing! 10
Blow, let us hear the purple glens reply-
    ing,
Blow, bugle; answer, echoes, dying, dying,
    dying.

O love, they die in yon rich sky,
    They faint on hill or field or river;
Our echoes roll from soul to soul,   15
    And grow forever and forever.
Blow, bugle, blow, set the wild echoes fly-
    ing,
And answer, echoes, answer, dying, dying,
    dying.

Tears, Idle Tears

Tears, idle tears, I know not what they mean;
Tears from the depth of some divine despair
Rise in the heart, and gather to the eyes,
In looking on the happy autumn-fields,
And thinking of the days that are no more. 5

Fresh as the first beam glittering on a sail,
That brings our friends up from the under-
    world,
Sad as the last which reddens over one
That sinks with all we love below the verge;
So sad, so fresh, the days that are no more. 10

Ah, sad and strange as in dark summer
    dawns
The earliest pipe of half-awakened birds
To dying ears, when unto dying eyes
The casement slowly grows a glimmering
    square;
So sad, so strange, the days that are no more.

Dear as remembered kisses after death,   16
And sweet as those by hopeless fancy feigned
On lips that are for others; deep as love,
Deep as first love, and wild with all regret;
O Death in Life, the days that are no more! 20

10. **Elfland.** The echoes sound as if they came from fairyland, which in Ireland is always close to the world of mortals.
Tears, Idle Tears. This song, from Part IV, is sung by one
of the maidens in Ida's tent, in the presence of Ida and her
maidens and of the three men disguised as women. It expresses the maiden's longing for the past. See Critical Notes.

O Swallow, Swallow

O Swallow, Swallow, flying, flying south,
Fly to her, and fall upon her gilded eaves,
And tell her, tell her, what I tell to thee.

O tell her, Swallow, thou that knowest each,
That bright and fierce and fickle is the South,
And dark and true and tender is the North. 6

O Swallow, Swallow, if I could follow, and
    light
Upon her lattice, I would pipe and trill,
And cheep and twitter twenty million loves.

O were I thou that she might take me in, 10
And lay me on her bosom, and her heart
Would rock the snowy cradle till I died!

Why lingereth she to clothe her heart with
    love,
Delaying as the tender ash delays
To clothe herself, when all the woods are
    green?   15

O tell her, Swallow, that thy brood is flown;
Say to her, I do but wanton in the South,
But in the North long since my nest is made.

O tell her, brief is life but love is long,
And brief the sun of summer in the North, 20
And brief the moon of beauty in the South.

O Swallow, flying from the golden woods,
Fly to her, and pipe and woo her, and make
    her mine,
And tell her, tell her, that I follow thee.

Thy Voice Is Heard

Thy voice is heard through rolling drums
    That beat to battle where he stands;
Thy face across his fancy comes,
    And gives the battle to his hands.
A moment, while the trumpets blow,   5
    He sees his brood about thy knee;
The next, like fire he meets the foe,
    And strikes him dead for thine and thee.

O Swallow, Swallow. This song is sung by the disguised
prince in response to Ida's request for a song of promise
rather than one of retrospect like the one she had just heard,
Tears, Idle Tears. It is a song of a lover of the North as
he watches a swallow speed southward in the autumn.
His lady-love is in the South. In *The Princess* Ida is referred
to as the Princess "from the South."
4. **thou that knowest each.** The swallow knows both
the North and the South since it migrates from one to the
other according to the season of the year. 4-6. He fears a
rival in the South.
Thy Voice Is Heard. This song is sung by one of the maidens at the end of Part IV. It is a song of courage inspired
by domestic love, and strikes the keynote of the warlike
section that follows it.

Home They Brought Her Warrior Dead

Home they brought her warrior dead,
  She nor swooned nor uttered cry.
All her maidens, watching, said,
  "She must weep or she will die."

Then they praised him, soft and low,   5
  Called him worthy to be loved,
Truest friend and noblest foe;
  Yet she neither spoke nor moved.

Stole a maiden from her place,
  Lightly to the warrior stepped,   10
Took the face-cloth from the face;
  Yet she neither moved nor wept.

Rose a nurse of ninety years,
  Set his child upon her knee —
Like summer tempest came her tears —   15
  "Sweet my child, I live for thee."

Our Enemies Have Fallen

Our enemies have fallen, have fallen; the
    seed,
The little seed they laughed at in the dark,
Has risen and cleft the soil, and grown a bulk
Of spanless girth, that lays on every side
A thousand arms and rushes to the sun.   5

Our enemies have fallen, have fallen. They
    came;
The leaves were wet with women's tears; they
    heard
A noise of songs they would not understand;
They marked it with the red cross to the fall,
And would have strown it, and are fallen
    themselves.   10

Our enemies have fallen, have fallen; they
    came,
The woodmen with their axes; lo, the tree!
But we will make it faggots for the hearth,
And shape it plank and beam for roof and
    floor,
And boats and bridges for the use of men. 15

Our enemies have fallen, have fallen; they
    struck;
With their own blows they hurt themselves,
    nor knew

There dwelt an iron nature in the grain;
The glittering ax was broken in their arms,
Their arms were shattered to the shoulder
    blade.   20

Our enemies have fallen, but this shall grow
A night of summer from the heat, a breadth
Of autumn, dropping fruits of power; and
    rolled
With music in the growing breeze of Time,
The tops shall strike from star to star, the
    fangs   25
Shall move the stony bases of the world.

Ask Me No More

Ask me no more—the moon may draw the sea;
  The cloud may stoop from heaven and take
    the shape,
  With fold to fold, of mountain or of cape;
But O too fond, when have I answered thee?
    Ask me no more.   5

Ask me no more—what answer should I give?
  I love not hollow cheek or faded eye;
  Yet, O my friend, I will not have thee die!
Ask me no more, lest I should bid thee live;
    Ask me no more.   10

Ask me no more—thy fate and mine are sealed;
  I strove against the stream and all in vain;
  Let the great river take me to the main.
No more, dear love, for at a touch I yield;
    Ask me no more.   15

Now Sleeps the Crimson Petal

Now sleeps the crimson petal, now the
    white;
Nor waves the cypress in the palace walk;
Nor winks the gold fin in the porphyry font.
The firefly wakens; waken thou with me.

Now droops the milk-white peacock like a
    ghost,   5
And like a ghost she glimmers on to me.

Now lies the Earth all Danaë to the stars,
And all thy heart lies open unto me.

Home They Brought Her Warrior Dead. This song stands
between Part V and Part VI. It comes after the battle and
fittingly stresses the duty and the joy of motherhood.
Our Enemies Have Fallen. This song is sung by Ida in
Part VI, as she holds Psyche's babe in her arms. The battle
is over; the Prince's warriors have been defeated; many have
been wounded on both sides; and Ida has generously offered
"the tender ministries of female hands and hospitality."

Ask Me No More. This song stands between Part VI and
Part VII. It is an expression of the slow yielding of reluctant
love. The college has been turned into a hospital; Ida's
purpose has been abandoned, and many maidens have gone
home.
Now Sleeps the Crimson Petal. This song was read aloud
by the Princess as she watched at night by the wounded
Prince, in Part VII.
7. The earth is compared to Danaë, the princess whom
Zeus in the form of a golden shower visited in a tower of brass
in which her father had imprisoned her.

Now slides the silent meteor on, and leaves
A shining furrow, as thy thoughts in me.   10

Now folds the lily all her sweetness up,
And slips into the bosom of the lake.
So fold thyself, my dearest, thou, and slip
Into my bosom and be lost in me.

COME DOWN, O MAID

Come down, O maid, from yonder mountain
    height.
What pleasure lives in height (the shepherd
    sang),
In height and cold, the splendor of the hills?
But cease to move so near the heavens, and
    cease
To glide a sunbeam by the blasted pine,   5
To sit a star upon the sparkling spire;
And come, for Love is of the valley, come,
For Love is of the valley, come thou down
And find him; by the happy threshold, he,
Or hand in hand with Plenty in the maize,   10
Or red with spirted purple of the vats,
Or foxlike in the vine; nor cares to walk
With Death and Morning on the Silver Horns,
Nor wilt thou snare him in the white ra-
    vine,
Nor find him dropped upon the firths of
    ice;
That huddling slant in furrow-cloven falls   16
To roll the torrent out of dusky doors.
But follow; let the torrent dance thee down
To find him in the valley; let the wild
Lean-headed eagles yelp alone, and leave   20
The monstrous ledges there to slope, and spill
Their thousand wreaths of dangling water-
    smoke,
That like a broken purpose waste in air.
So waste not thou, but come; for all the vales
Await thee; azure pillars of the hearth   25
Arise to thee; the children call, and I,
Thy shepherd, pipe, and sweet is every
    sound,
Sweeter thy voice, but every sound is sweet;
Myriads of rivulets hurrying through the lawn,
The moan of doves in immemorial elms,   30
And murmuring of innumerable bees.
                    (1850)

Come Down, O Maid. This song also was read aloud by the Princess. It is a call for her to forsake a life of isolation and lonely thought and to ally herself with natural human needs and loves.
12. **foxlike in the vine.** Cf. *The Song of Solomon,* 2:15— "Take us the foxes, the little foxes, that spoil the vines; for our vines have tender grapes." 13. **the Silver Horns,** the peaks of the mountains. The Silberhorn is a spur of the Jungfrau, in the Alps. 15. **firths of ice,** glaciers. 16. **furrow-cloven,** split by crevasses. 17. **dusky doors,** the piled-up mass of refuse through which the stream emerges at the foot of the glacier. 25. **azure pillars of the hearth,** columns of blue smoke.

IN MEMORIAM

IN MEMORIAM A. H. H.
OBIIT 1833

PROLOGUE

Strong Son of God, immortal Love,
    Whom we, that have not seen thy face,
    By faith, and faith alone, embrace,
Believing where we cannot prove;

Thine are these orbs of light and shade;   5
    Thou madest Life in man and brute;
    Thou madest Death; and lo, thy foot
Is on the skull which thou hast made.

Thou wilt not leave us in the dust:
    Thou madest man, he knows not why,   10
    He thinks he was not made to die;
And thou hast made him; thou art just.

Thou seemest human and divine,
    The highest, holiest manhood, thou.
    Our wills are ours, we know not how;   15
Our wills are ours, to make them thine.

Our little systems have their day;
    They have their day and cease to be;
    They are but broken lights of thee,
And thou, O Lord, art more than they.   20

We have but faith; we cannot know,
    For knowledge is of things we see;
    And yet we trust it comes from thee,
A beam in darkness; let it grow.

Let knowledge grow from more to more,   25
    But more of reverence in us dwell;
    That mind and soul, according well,
May make one music as before,

But vaster. We are fools and slight;
    We mock thee when we do not fear.   30
    But help thy foolish ones to bear;
Help thy vain worlds to bear thy light.

Forgive what seemed my sin in me,
    What seemed my worth since I began;
    For merit lives from man to man,   35
And not from man, O Lord, to thee.

Forgive my grief for one removed,
    Thy creature, whom I found so fair.

In Memoriam. See Critical Notes.
Prologue. 5. **orbs of light and shade,** the planets, partly in the light of the sun and partly in shadow. 17. **systems,** i.e., systems of theology and philosophy. 28. **as before,** before mind and soul had become separated by the modern movement of science and skepticism. 32. **thy light,** the light of knowledge.

I trust he lives in thee, and there
I find him worthier to be loved.   40

Forgive these wild and wandering cries,
  Confusions of a wasted youth;
  Forgive them where they fail in truth,
And in thy wisdom make me wise.
                              (*1849; 1850*)

———————

1

I held it truth, with him who sings
  To one clear harp in divers tones,
  That men may rise on stepping-stones
Of their dead selves to higher things.

But who shall so forecast the years   5
  And find in loss a gain to match?
  Or reach a hand through time to catch
The far-off interest of tears?

Let Love clasp Grief lest both be drowned,
  Let darkness keep her raven gloss.   10
  Ah, sweeter to be drunk with loss,
To dance with Death, to beat the ground,

Than that the victor Hours should scorn
  The long result of love, and boast,
  "Behold the man that loved and lost,   15
But all he was is overworn."

2

Old yew, which graspest at the stones
  That name the underlying dead,
  Thy fibers net the dreamless head,
Thy roots are wrapped about the bones.

The seasons bring the flower again,   5
  And bring the firstling to the flock;
  And in the dusk of thee the clock
Beats out the little lives of men.

O not for thee the glow, the bloom,
  Who changest not in any gale,   10
  Nor branding summer suns avail
To touch thy thousand years of gloom;

And gazing on thee, sullen tree,
  Sick for thy stubborn hardihood,
  I seem to fail from out my blood   15
And grow incorporate into thee.

3

O Sorrow, cruel fellowship,
  O Priestess in the vaults of Death,

O sweet and bitter in a breath,
What whispers from thy lying lip?

"The stars," she whispers, "blindly run;   5
  A web is woven across the sky;
  From out waste places comes a cry,
And murmurs from the dying sun;

"And all the phantom, Nature, stands—
  With all the music in her tone,   10
  A hollow echo of my own—
A hollow form with empty hands."

And shall I take a thing so blind,
  Embrace her as my natural good;
  Or crush her, like a vice of blood,   15
Upon the threshold of the mind?

4

To Sleep I give my powers away;
  My will is bondsman to the dark;
  I sit within a helmless bark,
And with my heart I muse and say:

O heart, how fares it with thee now,   5
  That thou shouldst fail from thy desire,
  Who scarcely darest to inquire,
"What is it makes me beat so low?"

Something it is which thou hast lost,
  Some pleasure from thine early years.   10
  Break, thou deep vase of chilling tears,
That grief hath shaken into frost!

Such clouds of nameless trouble cross
  All night below the darkened eyes;
  With morning wakes the will, and cries,   15
"Thou shalt not be the fool of loss."

5

I sometimes hold it half a sin
  To put in words the grief I feel;
  For words, like Nature, half reveal
And half conceal the Soul within.

But, for the unquiet heart and brain,   5
  A use in measured language lies,
  The sad mechanic exercise,
Like dull narcotics, numbing pain.

In words, like weeds, I'll wrap me o'er,
  Like coarsest clothes against the cold;   10
  But that large grief which these enfold
Is given in outline and no more.

6

One writes that "other friends remain,"
  That "loss is common to the race"—

Prologue. 42. wasted, made desolate.
  Section 1. 1. him, Goethe, whom Tennyson ranked
highest among modern lyric poets because he was "consummate in so many different styles" (*Memoir*, II, 391).

Section 5. 9. weeds, garments.

And common is the commonplace,
And vacant chaff well meant for grain.

That loss is common would not make   5
My own less bitter, rather more.
Too common! Never morning wore
To evening but some heart did break.

O father, wheresoe'er thou be,
Who pledgest now thy gallant son,   10
A shot, ere half thy draft be done,
Hath stilled the life that beat from thee.

O mother, praying God will save
Thy sailor — while thy head is bowed,
His heavy-shotted hammock-shroud   15
Drops in his vast and wandering grave.

Ye know no more than I who wrought
At that last hour to please him well;
Who mused on all I had to tell,
And something written, something thought;

Expecting still his advent home;   21
And ever met him on his way
With wishes, thinking, "here today,"
Or "here tomorrow will he come."

O somewhere, meek, unconscious dove,   25
That sittest ranging golden hair;
And glad to find thyself so fair,
Poor child, that waitest for thy love!

For now her father's chimney glows
In expectation of a guest;   30
And thinking "this will please him best,"
She takes a riband or a rose;

For he will see them on tonight;
And with the thought her color burns;
And, having left the glass, she turns   35
Once more to set a ringlet right;

And, even when she turned, the curse
Had fallen, and her future lord
Was drowned in passing through the ford,
Or killed in falling from his horse.   40

O what to her shall be the end?
And what to me remains of good?
To her perpetual maidenhood,
And unto me no second friend.

7

Dark house, by which once more I stand
Here in the long unlovely street,

Section 6. 43. **To her,** i.e., to the girl of lines 25 ff., whose
fiancé is killed.
Section 7. 1. **Dark house,** Hallem's house at 67 Wimpole
Street in London.

Doors, where my heart was used to beat
So quickly, waiting for a hand,

A hand that can be clasped no more —   5
Behold me, for I cannot sleep,
And like a guilty thing I creep
At earliest morning to the door.

He is not here; but far away
The noise of life begins again,   10
And ghastly through the drizzling rain
On the bald street breaks the blank day.

8

A happy lover who has come
To look on her that loves him well,
Who 'lights and rings the gateway bell,
And learns her gone and far from home;

He saddens, all the magic light   5
Dies off at once from bower and hall,
And all the place is dark, and all
The chambers emptied of delight:

So find I every pleasant spot
In which we two were wont to meet —   10
The field, the chamber, and the street —
For all is dark where thou art not.

Yet as that other, wandering there
In those deserted walks, may find
A flower beat with rain and wind,   15
Which once she fostered up with care;

So seems it in my deep regret,
O my forsaken heart, with thee
And this poor flower of poesy
Which, little cared for, fades not yet.   20

But since it pleased a vanished eye,
I go to plant it on his tomb,
That if it can it there may bloom,
Or, dying, there at least may die.

9

Fair ship, that from the Italian shore
Sailest the placid ocean-plains
With my lost Arthur's loved remains,
Spread thy full wings, and waft him o'er.

So draw him home to those that mourn   5
In vain; a favorable speed
Ruffle thy mirrored mast, and lead
Through prosperous floods his holy urn.

All night no ruder air perplex
Thy sliding keel, till Phosphor, bright   10

Section 9. 1. **Fair ship,** etc. Hallam's body was brought
to England and buried at Clevedon, on the Severn River.
10. **Phosphor,** Lucifer, the morning star.

As our pure love, through early light
Shall glimmer on the dewy decks.

Sphere all your lights around, above;
  Sleep, gentle heavens, before the prow;
  Sleep, gentle winds, as he sleeps now,   15
My friend, the brother of my love;

My Arthur, whom I shall not see
  Till all my widowed race be run;
  Dear as the mother to the son,
More than my brothers are to me.   20

10

I hear the noise about thy keel;
  I hear the bell struck in the night;
  I see the cabin-window bright;
I see the sailor at the wheel.

Thou bring'st the sailor to his wife,   5
  And traveled men from foreign lands;
  And letters unto trembling hands;
And, thy dark freight, a vanished life.

So bring him; we have idle dreams;
  This look of quiet flatters thus   10
  Our home-bred fancies. O to us,
The fools of habit, sweeter seems

To rest beneath the clover sod,
  That takes the sunshine and the rains,
  Or where the kneeling hamlet drains   15
The chalice of the grapes of God,

Than if with thee the roaring wells
  Should gulf him fathom-deep in brine;
  And hands so often clasped in mine,
Should toss with tangle and with shells.   20

11

Calm is the morn without a sound,
  Calm as to suit a calmer grief,
  And only through the faded leaf
The chestnut pattering to the ground;

Calm and deep peace on this high wold,   5
  And on these dews that drench the furze,
  And all the silvery gossamers
That twinkle into green and gold;

Calm and still light on yon great plain
  That sweeps with all its autumn bowers,   10
  And crowded farms and lessening towers,
To mingle with the bounding main;

Calm and deep peace in this wide air,
  These leaves that redden to the fall —
  And in my heart, if calm at all,   15
If any calm, a calm despair;

Calm on the seas, and silver sleep,
  And waves that sway themselves in rest,
  And dead calm in that noble breast
Which heaves but with the heaving deep.   20

12

Lo, as a dove when up she springs
  To bear through heaven a tale of woe,
  Some dolorous message knit below
The wild pulsation of her wings;

Like her I go; I cannot stay;   5
  I leave this mortal ark behind,
  A weight of nerves without a mind,
And leave the cliffs, and haste away

O'er ocean-mirrors rounded large,
  And reach the glow of southern skies,   10
  And see the sails at distance rise,
And linger weeping on the marge,

And saying: "Comes he thus, my friend?
  Is this the end of all my care?"
  And circle moaning in the air: 15
"Is this the end? Is this the end?"

And forward dart again, and play
  About the prow, and back return
  To where the body sits, and learn
That I have been an hour away.   20

13

Tears of the widower, when he sees
  A late-lost form that sleep reveals,
  And moves his doubtful arms, and feels
Her place is empty, fall like these;

Which weep a loss forever new,   5
  A void where heart on heart reposed;
  And, where warm hands have pressed and
      closed,
Silence, till I be silent too;

Which weep the comrade of my choice,
  An awful thought, a life removed,   10
  The human-hearted man I loved,
A Spirit, not a breathing voice.

Come Time, and teach me, many years,
  I do not suffer in a dream;
  For now so strange do these things seem,   15
Mine eyes have leisure for their tears;

My fancies time to rise on wing,
  And glance about the approaching sails,

Section 10. 15-16. where . . . God, in the church, where
the people kneel at the altar for the communion service.
People were sometimes buried in English churches near or
under the altar. 20. tangle, a kind of seaweed.
  Section 11. 7. gossamers, cobwebs seen on grass and low
bushes. 11. lessening, diminishing by distance. 12.
bounding main, bordering sea.

  Section 13. 13. many years, in apposition with Time.

As though they brought but merchants'
bales,
And not the burthen that they bring.   20

14

If one should bring me this report,
  That thou hadst touched the land today,
  And I went down unto the quay,
And found thee lying in the port;

And standing, muffled round with woe,   5
  Should see thy passengers in rank
  Come stepping lightly down the plank,
And beckoning unto those they know;

And if along with these should come
  The man I held as half-divine;   10
  Should strike a sudden hand in mine,
And ask a thousand things of home;

And I should tell him all my pain,
  And how my life had drooped of late,
  And he should sorrow o'er my state   15
And marvel what possessed my brain;

And I perceived no touch of change,
  No hint of death in all his frame,
  But found him all in all the same,
I should not feel it to be strange.   20

15

Tonight the winds begin to rise
  And roar from yonder dropping day;
  The last red leaf is whirled away,
The rooks are blown about the skies;

The forest cracked, the waters curled,   5
  The cattle huddled on the lea;
  And wildly dashed on tower and tree
The sunbeam strikes along the world.

And but for fancies, which aver
  That all thy motions gently pass   10
  Athwart a plane of molten glass,
I scarce could brook the strain and stir

That makes the barren branches loud;
  And but for fear it is not so,
  The wild unrest that lives in woe   15
Would dote and pore on yonder cloud

That rises upward always higher,
  And onward drags a laboring breast,
  And topples round the dreary west,
A looming bastion fringed with fire.   20

Section 15. Compare this section with Section 11. 10.
thy motions, the motions of the ship.

16

What words are these have fallen from me?
  Can calm despair and wild unrest
  Be tenants of a single breast,
Or Sorrow such a changeling be?

Or doth she only seem to take   5
  The touch of change in calm or storm,
  But knows no more of transient form
In her deep self, than some dead lake

That holds the shadow of a lark
  Hung in the shadow of a heaven?   10
  Or has the shock, so harshly given,
Confused me like the unhappy bark

That strikes by night a craggy shelf,
  And staggers blindly ere she sink?
  And stunned me from my power to think
And all my knowledge of myself;   16

And made me that delirious man
  Whose fancy fuses old and new,
  And flashes into false and true,
And mingles all without a plan?   20

17

Thou comest, much wept for; such a breeze
  Compelled thy canvas, and my prayer
  Was as the whisper of an air
To breathe thee over lonely seas.

For I in spirit saw thee move   5
  Through circles of the bounding sky,
  Week after week; the days go by;
Come quick, thou bringest all I love.

Henceforth, wherever thou mayst roam,
  My blessing, like a line of light,   10
  Is on the waters day and night,
And like a beacon guards thee home.

So may whatever tempest mars
  Mid-ocean spare thee, sacred bark,
  And balmy drops in summer dark   15
Slide from the bosom of the stars;

So kind an office hath been done,
  Such precious relics brought by thee,
  The dust of him I shall not see
Till all my widowed race be run.   20

18

'Tis well; 'tis something; we may stand
  Where he in English earth is laid,

Section 16. 2. **calm despair and wild unrest,** as ex-
pressed in Sections 11 and 15 respectively.
Section 18. 2. **Where . . . laid,** in St. Andrew's Church,
Clevedon, in the west of England.

And from his ashes may be made
The violet of his native land.

'Tis little; but it looks in truth   5
　　As if the quiet bones were blest
　　Among familiar names to rest
And in the places of his youth.

Come then, pure hands, and bear the head
　　That sleeps or wears the mask of sleep,   10
　　And come, whatever loves to weep,
And hear the ritual of the dead.

Ah yet, even yet, if this might be,
　　I, falling on his faithful heart,
　　Would breathing through his lips impart   15
The life that almost dies in me;

That dies not, but endures with pain,
　　And slowly forms the firmer mind,
　　Treasuring the look it cannot find,
The words that are not heard again.   20

19

The Danube to the Severn gave
　　The darkened heart that beat no more;
　　They laid him by the pleasant shore,
And in the hearing of the wave.

There twice a day the Severn fills;   5
　　The salt sea-water passes by,
　　And hushes half the babbling Wye,
And makes a silence in the hills.

The Wye is hushed nor moved along,
　　And hushed my deepest grief of all,   10
　　When filled with tears that cannot fall,
I brim with sorrow drowning song.

The tide flows down, the wave again
　　Is vocal in its wooded walls;
　　My deeper anguish also falls,   15
And I can speak a little then.

20

The lesser griefs that may be said,
　　That breathe a thousand tender vows,
　　Are but as servants in a house
Where lies the master newly dead;   20

Who speak their feeling as it is,   5
　　And weep the fullness from the mind.
　　"It will be hard," they say, "to find
Another service such as this."

My lighter moods are like to these,
　　That out of words a comfort win;   10
　　But there are other griefs within,
And tears that at their fountain freeze;

For by the hearth the children sit
　　Cold in that atmosphere of death,
　　And scarce endure to draw the breath,   15
Or like to noiseless phantoms flit;

But open converse is there none,
　　So much the vital spirits sink
　　To see the vacant chair, and think,
"How good! how kind! and he is gone."   20

21

I sing to him that rests below,
　　And, since the grasses round me wave,
　　I take the grasses of the grave,
And make them pipes whereon to blow.

The traveler hears me now and then,   5
　　And sometimes harshly will he speak:
　　"This fellow would make weakness weak,
And melt the waxen hearts of men."

Another answers: "Let him be;
　　He loves to make parade of pain,   10
　　That with his piping he may gain
The praise that comes to constancy."

A third is wroth: "Is this an hour
　　For private sorrow's barren song,
　　When more and more the people throng   15
The chairs and thrones of civil power?

"A time to sicken and to swoon,
　　When Science reaches forth her arms
　　To feel from world to world, and charms
Her secret from the latest moon?"   20

Behold, ye speak an idle thing;
　　Ye never knew the sacred dust.
　　I do but sing because I must,
And pipe but as the linnets sing;

And one is glad; her note is gay,   25
　　For now her little ones have ranged;

Section 18. 9. **pure hands.** The bearers at the funeral were farmers on the Clevedon estate. 13-16. This stanza was suggested by the restoring of the Shunammite's son by Elisha, *2 Kings*, 4:32-37.—"And when Elisha was come into the house, behold, the child was dead and laid upon his bed. And he went up and lay upon the child, and put his mouth upon his mouth, and his eyes upon his eyes, and his hands upon his hands; and he stretched himself upon the child, and the flesh of the child waxed warm."
Section 19. 1. Vienna, where Hallam died, is on the Danube River. Clevedon overlooks the Severn where it flows into the Bristol Channel. The Wye (line 7) joins the Severn a short distance above Clevedon.

Section 21. 1-4. Tennyson, who had not visited Clevedon, at first assumed that Hallam was buried in the churchyard. Actually, he was buried in the church itself, as Section 67 indicates. 13-16. These lines may refer to the Chartist movement of 1836-48, which demanded radical reforms in social and industrial conditions. The platform was stated in a document called *The People's Charter.* 18-20. These lines may refer to the discovery of Neptune in 1846 and of the eighth satellite of Saturn in 1848. 24. Cf. Goethe's *Wilhelm Meisters Lehrjahre*, II, 11: "I sing but as the linnet sings."

And one is sad; her note is changed,
Because her brood is stolen away.

22

The path by which we twain did go,
　Which led by tracts that pleased us well,
　Through four sweet years arose and fell,
From flower to flower, from snow to snow;

And we with singing cheered the way,　　5
　And, crowned with all the season lent,
　From April on to April went,
And glad at heart from May to May.

But where the path we walked began
　To slant the fifth autumnal slope,　　10
　As we descended following Hope,
There sat the Shadow feared of man;

Who broke our fair companionship,
　And spread his mantle dark and cold,
　And wrapped thee formless in the fold,　　15
And dulled the murmur on thy lip,

And bore thee where I could not see
　Nor follow, though I walk in haste,
　And think that somewhere in the waste
The Shadow sits and waits for me.　　20

23

Now, sometimes in my sorrow shut,
　Or breaking into song by fits,
　Alone, alone, to where he sits,
The Shadow cloaked from head to foot,

Who keeps the keys of all the creeds,　　5
　I wander, often falling lame,
　And looking back to whence I came,
Or on to where the pathway leads;

And crying, How changed from where it ran
　Through lands where not a leaf was dumb,
　But all the lavish hills would hum　　11
The murmur of a happy Pan;

When each by turns was guide to each,
　And Fancy light from Fancy caught,
　And Thought leapt out to wed with
　　Thought　　15
Ere Thought could wed itself with Speech;

And all we met was fair and good,
　And all was good that Time could bring,
　And all the secret of the spring
Moved in the chambers of the blood;　　20

And many an old philosophy
　On Argive heights divinely sang,

And round us all the thicket rang
To many a flute of Arcady.

24

And was the day of my delight
　As pure and perfect as I say?
　The very source and fount of day
Is dashed with wandering isles of night.

If all was good and fair we met,　　5
　This earth had been the Paradise
　It never looked to human eyes
Since our first sun arose and set.

And is it that the haze of grief
　Makes former gladness loom so great?　　10
　The lowness of the present state,
That sets the past in this relief?

Or that the past will always win
　A glory from its being far,
　And orb into the perfect star　　15
We saw not when we moved therein?

25

I know that this was Life — the track
　Whereon with equal feet we fared;
　And then, as now, the day prepared
The daily burden for the back.

But this it was that made me move　　5
　As light as carrier-birds in air;
　I loved the weight I had to bear,
Because it needed help of Love;

Nor could I weary, heart or limb,
　When mighty Love would cleave in twain
　The lading of a single pain,　　11
And part it, giving half to him.

26

Still onward winds the dreary way;
　I with it, for I long to prove
　No lapse of moons can canker Love,
Whatever fickle tongues may say.

And if that eye which watches guilt　　5
　And goodness, and hath power to see
　Within the green the moldered tree,
And towers fallen as soon as built —

O if indeed that eye foresee
　Or see — in Him is no before —　　10
　In more of life true life no more
And Love the indifference to be,

Section 23. 2. **Or breaking**, etc., a reference to the casual
composition of the various sections of the poem at different
times and at different places. 12. **Pan**, the god of flocks
and shepherds and the symbol of nature. 22. **Argive, Greek.**

Section 23. 24. **Arcady**, the Greek center of pastoral
poetry.
Section 24. 4. **wandering isles of night**, a reference to
the spots on the sun.
Section 25. 11. **lading**, burden, weight.

Then might I find, ere yet the morn
  Breaks hither over Indian seas,
  That Shadow waiting with the keys,   15
To shroud me from my proper scorn.

27

I envy not in any moods
  The captive void of noble rage,
  The linnet born within the cage,
That never knew the summer woods;

I envy not the beast that takes   5
  His license in the field of time,
  Unfettered by the sense of crime,
To whom a conscience never wakes;

Nor, what may count itself as blest,
  The heart that never plighted troth   10
  But stagnates in the weeds of sloth;
Nor any want-begotten rest.

I hold it true, whate'er befall;
  I feel it, when I sorrow most —
  'Tis better to have loved and lost   15
Than never to have loved at all.

28

The time draws near the birth of Christ.
  The moon is hid; the night is still;
  The Christmas bells from hill to hill
Answer each other in the mist.

Four voices of four hamlets round,   5
  From far and near, on mead and moor,
  Swell out and fail, as if a door
Were shut between me and the sound;

Each voice four changes on the wind,
  That now dilate, and now decrease,   10
  Peace and goodwill, goodwill and peace,
Peace and goodwill, to all mankind.

This year I slept and woke with pain,
  I almost wished no more to wake,
  And that my hold on life would break   15
Before I heard those bells again.

But they my troubled spirit rule,
  For they controlled me when a boy;
  They bring me sorrow touched with joy,
The merry merry bells of Yule.   20

Section 26. 16. **my proper scorn**, scorn of myself.
Section 27. 15-16. **'Tis better . . . all.** Cf. Thomas
Campbell's *The Jilted Nymph*—
      "Better be courted and jilted
      Than never be courted at all."

Section 28. 5. **hamlets round**, hamlets near Somersby,
where Tennyson lived. 9. Each church has four bells. It
may be that the poet only imagined the sounds. 13. **This
year**, 1833. Hallam died in September of that year.

29

With such compelling cause to grieve
  As daily vexes household peace,
  And chains regret to his decease,
How dare we keep our Christmas Eve;

Which brings no more a welcome guest   5
  To enrich the threshold of the night
  With showered largess of delight
In dance and song and game and jest?

Yet go, and while the holly boughs
  Entwine the cold baptismal font,   10
  Make one wreath more for Use and Wont,
That guard the portals of the house;

Old sisters of a day gone by,
  Gray nurses, loving nothing new;
  Why should they miss their yearly due   15
Before their time? They too will die.

30

With trembling fingers did we weave
  The holly round the Christmas hearth;
  A rainy cloud possessed the earth,
And sadly fell our Christmas Eve.

At our old pastimes in the hall   5
  We gamboled, making vain pretense
  Of gladness, with an awful sense
Of one mute Shadow watching all.

We paused. The winds were in the beech;
  We heard them sweep the winter land;   10
  And in a circle hand-in-hand
Sat silent, looking each at each.

Then echo-like our voices rang;
  We sung, though every eye was dim,
  A merry song we sang with him   15
Last year; impetuously we sang.

We ceased; a gentler feeling crept
  Upon us: surely rest is meet.
  "They rest," we said, "their sleep is sweet,"
And silence followed, and we wept.   20

Our voices took a higher range;
  Once more we sang: "They do not die
  Nor lose their mortal sympathy,
Nor change to us, although they change;

"Rapt from the fickle and the frail   25
  With gathered power, yet the same,
  Pierces the keen seraphic flame
From orb to orb, from veil to veil."

Rise, happy morn, rise, holy morn,
  Draw forth the cheerful day from night; 30

Section 29. 13. **Old sisters**, Use and Wont of line 11.

O Father, touch the east, and light
The light that shone when Hope was born.

31

When Lazarus left his charnel-cave,
  And home to Mary's house returned,
  Was this demanded — if he yearned
To hear her weeping by his grave?

"Where wert thou, brother, those four days?"
  There lives no record of reply,   6
  Which telling what it is to die
Had surely added praise to praise.

From every house the neighbors met,
  The streets were filled with joyful sound,
  A solemn gladness even crowned   11
The purple brows of Olivet.

Behold a man raised up by Christ!
  The rest remaineth unrevealed;
  He told it not; or something sealed   15
The lips of that Evangelist.

32

Her eyes are homes of silent prayer,
  Nor other thought her mind admits
  But, he was dead, and there he sits,
And he that brought him back is there.

Then one deep love doth supersede   5
  All other, when her ardent gaze
  Roves from the living brother's face,
And rests upon the Life indeed.

All subtle thought, all curious fears,
  Borne down by gladness so complete,   10
  She bows, she bathes the Savior's feet
With costly spikenard and with tears.

Thrice blest whose lives are faithful prayers,
  Whose loves in higher love endure;
  What souls possess themselves so pure,   15
Or is there blessedness like theirs?

33

O thou that after toil and storm
  Mayst seem to have reached a purer air,
  Whose faith has center everywhere,
Nor cares to fix itself to form,

Leave thou thy sister when she prays,   5
  Her early Heaven, her happy views;

Nor thou with shadowed hint confuse
A life that leads melodious days.

Her faith through form is pure as thine,
  Her hands are quicker unto good;   10
  Oh, sacred be the flesh and blood
To which she links a truth divine!

See thou, that countest reason ripe
  In holding by the law within,
  Thou fail not in a world of sin,   15
And ev'n for want of such a type.

34

My own dim life should teach me this,
  That life shall live for evermore,
  Else earth is darkness at the core,
And dust and ashes all that is;

This round of green, this orb of flame,   5
  Fantastic beauty; such as lurks
  In some wild poet, when he works
Without a conscience or an aim.

What then were God to such as I?
  'Twere hardly worth my while to choose 10
  Of things all mortal, or to use
A little patience ere I die;

'Twere best at once to sink to peace,
  Like birds the charming serpent draws,
  To drop head-foremost in the jaws   15
Of vacant darkness and to cease.

35

Yet if some voice that man could trust
  Should murmur from the narrow house,
  "The cheeks drop in; the body bows;
Man dies, nor is there hope in dust" —

Might I not say, "Yet even here,   5
  But for one hour, O Love, I strive
  To keep so sweet a thing alive"?
But I should turn mine ears and hear

The moanings of the homeless sea,
  The sound of streams that swift or slow 10
  Draw down Æonian hills, and sow
The dust of continents to be;

And Love would answer with a sigh,
  "The sound of that forgetful shore
  Will change my sweetness more and more,
Half-dead to know that I shall die."   16

Section 31. 1-2. **Lazarus, Mary.** Lazarus, the brother of Mary and Martha, was raised by Christ from the dead. He had been buried in a cave. See *John*, 11:32-44. 12. **Olivet,** a hill hear Jerusalem. 16. **that Evangelist,** St. John, who alone records the miracle of the raising of Lazarus.
Section 32. 11-12. **She bows . . . tears,** a reference to Christ's visit in the home of Lazarus. See *John*, 12:1-3.— "Then took Mary a pound of ointment of spikenard, very costly, and anointed the feet of Jesus, and wiped his feet with her hair."
Section 33. This section is a plea for sympathy toward persons who cling to their simple traditional faith.

Section 34. 5. **This . . . flame,** the earth and the sun. 14. **charming serpent.** The boom-slang, a South-African snake, has power to attract birds to its mouth.
Section 35. 11. **Æonian hills,** hills that have existed for ages.

O me, what profits it to put
   An idle case? If Death were seen
   At first as Death, Love had not been,
Or been·in narrowest working shut,   20

Mere fellowship of sluggish moods,
   Or in his coarsest Satyr-shape
   Had bruised the herb and crushed the
     grape,
And basked and battened in the woods.

36

Though truths in manhood darkly join,
   Deep-seated in our mystic frame,
   We yield all blessing to the name
Of Him that made them current coin;

For Wisdom dealt with mortal powers,   5
   Where truth in closest words shall fail,
   When truth embodied in a tale
Shall enter in at lowly doors.

And so the Word had breath, and wrought
   With human hands the creed of creeds   10
   In loveliness of perfect deeds,
More strong than all poetic thought;

Which he may read that binds the sheaf,
   Or builds the house, or digs the grave,
   And those wild eyes that watch the wave
In roarings round the coral reef.   16

37

Urania speaks with darkened brow:
   "Thou pratest here where thou art least;
   This faith has many a purer priest,
And many an abler voice than thou.

"Go down beside thy native rill,   5
   On thy Parnassus set thy feet,
   And hear thy laurel whisper sweet
About the ledges of the hill."

And my Melpomene replies,
   A touch of shame upon her cheek: 10
   "I am not worthy even to speak
Of thy prevailing mysteries;

"For I am but an earthly Muse,
   And owning but a little art
   To lull with song an aching heart,   15
And render human love his dues;

Section 35. 22. **Satyr-shape,** half man and half beast, like the fabulous race of Satyrs.
   Section 36. 9. **the Word.** See *John,* 1-4.—"In the beginning was the Word, and the Word was with God, and the Word was God."
   Section 37. 1. **Urania,** the muse of loftiest poetry. 6. **Parnassus,** a mountain in Greece sacred to the muses. 7. **laurel.** Poets were crowned with laurel. 9. **Melpomene,** the muse of tragedy or elegy.

"But brooding on the dear one dead,
   And all he said of things divine —
   And dear to me as sacred wine
To dying lips is all he said —   20

"I murmured, as I came along,
   Of comfort clasped in truth revealed,
   And loitered in the master's field,
And darkened sanctities with song."

38

With weary steps I loiter on,
   Though always under altered skies
   The purple from the distance dies,
My prospect and horizon gone.

No joy the blowing season gives,   5
   The herald melodies of spring,
   But in the songs I love to sing
A doubtful gleam of solace lives.

If any care for what is here
   Survive in spirits rendered free,
   Then are these songs I sing of thee   10
Not all ungrateful to thine ear.

39

Old warder of these buried bones,
   And answering now my random stroke
   With fruitful cloud and living smoke,
Dark yew, that graspest at the stones

And dippest toward the dreamless head,   5
   To thee too comes the golden hour
   When flower is feeling after flower;
But Sorrow — fixed upon the dead,

And darkening the dark graves of men —
   What whispered from her lying lips?   10
   Thy gloom is kindled at the tips,
And passes into gloom again.

40

Could we forget the widowed hour
   And look on Spirits breathed away,
   As on a maiden in the day
When first she wears her orange-flower!

When crowned with blessing she doth rise   5
   To take her latest leave of home,
   And hopes and light regrets that come
Make April of her tender eyes;

And doubtful joys the father move,
   And tears are on the mother's face,   10
   As parting with a long embrace
She enters other realms of love;

Section 39. This section was added in 1869. Cf. Sections 2 and 3.
   3. **cloud . . . smoke,** clouds of yellow pollen.

Her office there to rear, to teach,
  Becoming as is meet and fit
  A link among the days, to knit   15
The generations each with each;

And, doubtless, unto thee is given
  A life that bears immortal fruit
  In those great offices that suit
The full-grown energies of heaven.   20

Ay me, the difference I discern!
  How often shall her old fireside
  Be cheered with tidings of the bride,
How often she herself return,

And tell them all they would have told,   25
  And bring her babe, and make her boast,
  Till even those that missed her most
Shall count new things as dear as old;

But thou and I have shaken hands,
  Till growing winters lay me low;   30
  My paths are in the fields I know,
And thine in undiscovered lands.

41

Thy spirit ere our fatal loss
  Did ever rise from high to higher,
  As mounts the heavenward altar-fire,
As flies the lighter through the gross.

But thou art turned to something strange, 5
  And I have lost the links that bound
  Thy changes; here upon the ground,
No more partaker of thy change.

Deep folly! yet that this could be —
  That I could wing my will with might   10
  To leap the grades of life and light,
And flash at once, my friend, to thee!

For though my nature rarely yields
  To that vague fear implied in death,
  Nor shudders at the gulfs beneath,   15
The howlings from forgotten fields;

Yet oft when sundown skirts the moor
  An inner trouble I behold,
  A spectral doubt which makes me cold,
That I shall be thy mate no more,   20

Though following with an upward mind
  The wonders that have come to thee,
  Through all the secular to-be,
But evermore a life behind.

Section 40. 17. thee, Hallam.
Section 41. 15-16. These lines probably refer to the
miseries of the Inferno, as described by Dante. 23. to-be,
the age-long future.

42

I vex my heart with fancies dim.
  He still outstripped me in the race;
  It was but unity of place
That made me dream I ranked with him.

And so may Place retain us still,   5
  And he the much-beloved again,
  A lord of large experience, train
To riper growth the mind and will;

And what delights can equal those
  That stir the spirit's inner deeps,   10
  When one that loves, but knows not, reaps
A truth from one that loves and knows?

43

If Sleep and Death be truly one,
  And every spirit's folded bloom
  Through all its intervital gloom
In some long trance should slumber on;

Unconscious of the sliding hour,   5
  Bare of the body, might it last,
  And silent traces of the past
Be all the color of the flower:

So then were nothing lost to man;
  So that still garden of the souls   10
  In many a figured leaf enrolls
The total world since life began;

And love will last as pure and whole
  As when he loved me here in Time,
  And at the spiritual prime   15
Rewaken with the dawning soul.

44

How fares it with the happy dead?
  For here the man is more and more;
  But he forgets the days before
God shut the doorways of his head.

The days have vanished, tone and tint,   5
  And yet perhaps the hoarding sense
  Gives out at times—he knows not whence—
A little flash, a mystic hint;

And in the long harmonious years —
  If Death so taste Lethean springs —   10
  May some dim touch of earthly things
Surprise thee ranging with thy peers.

Section 42. 2. still, always.
Section 43. 3. intervital gloom, the period between
death and the Resurrection. 15. the spiritual prime, the
resurrection morning.
Section 44. 2-4. here . . . head, the living man increases
in stored-up experience as he goes on; but the dead man
cannot remember the days of his life on earth. 10. Lethean.
Lethe was the mythical river of forgetfulness.

If such a dreamy touch should fall,
  O turn thee round, resolve the doubt;
  My guardian angel will speak out   15
In that high place, and tell thee all.

45

The baby new to earth and sky,
  What time his tender palm is prest
  Against the circle of the breast,
Has never thought that "this is I";

But as he grows he gathers much,   5
  And learns the use of "I" and "me,"
  And finds "I am not what I see,
And other than the things I touch."

So rounds he to a separate mind
  From whence clear memory may begin, 10
  As through the frame that binds him in
His isolation grows defined.

This use may lie in blood and breath,
  Which else were fruitless of their due,
  Had man to learn himself anew   15
Beyond the second birth of death.

46

We ranging down this lower track,
  The path we came by, thorn and flower,
  Is shadowed by the growing hour,
Lest life should fail in looking back.

So be it. There no shade can last   5
  In that deep dawn behind the tomb,
  But clear from marge to marge shall bloom
The eternal landscape of the past;

A lifelong tract of time revealed,
  The fruitful hours of still increase;
  Days ordered in a wealthy peace, 10
And those five years its richest field.

O Love, thy province were not large,
  A bounded field, nor stretching far;
  Look also, Love, a brooding star,   15
A rosy warmth from marge to marge.

47

That each, who seems a separate whole,
  Should move his rounds, and fusing all
  The skirts of self again, should fall
Remerging in the general Soul,

Is faith as vague as all unsweet.   5
  Eternal form shall still divide
  The eternal soul from all beside;
And I shall know him when we meet;

Section 47. In this section Tennyson rejects the doctrine that in the next life the individual will be merged into the general soul, and asserts the persistence of individuality.

And we shall sit at endless feast,
  Enjoying each the other's good.   10
  What vaster dream can hit the mood
Of Love on earth? He seeks at least

Upon the last and sharpest height,
  Before the spirits fade away,
  Some landing-place, to clasp and say,   15
"Farewell! We lose ourselves in light."

48

If these brief lays, of Sorrow born,
  Were taken to be such as closed
  Grave doubts and answers here proposed,
Then these were such as men might scorn.

Her care is not to part and prove;   5
  She takes, when harsher moods remit,
  What slender shade of doubt may flit,
And makes it vassal unto Love;

And hence, indeed, she sports with words,
  But better serves a wholesome law,   10
  And holds it sin and shame to draw
The deepest measure from the chords;

Nor dare she trust a larger lay,
  But rather loosens from the lip
  Short swallow-flights of song, that dip   15
Their wings in tears, and skim away.

49

From art, from nature, from the schools,
  Let random influences glance,
  Like light in many a shivered lance
That breaks about the dappled pools.

The lightest wave of thought shall lisp,   5
  The fancy's tenderest eddy wreathe,
  The slightest air of song shall breathe
To make the sullen surface crisp.

And look thy look, and go thy way,
  But blame not thou the winds that make
  The seeming-wanton ripple break,   11
The tender-penciled shadow play.

Beneath all fancied hopes and fears
  Ay me, the sorrow deepens down,
  Whose muffled motions blindly drown 15
The bases of my life in tears.

50

Be near me when my light is low,
  When the blood creeps, and the nerves prick
  And tingle; and the heart is sick,
And all the wheels of being slow.

Section 48. **13-16.** **Nor . . . away,** a reference to Tennyson's "spasmodic" method of writing the various sections.

Be near me when the sensuous frame   5
   Is racked with pangs that conquer trust;
   And Time, a maniac scattering dust,
And Life, a Fury slinging flame.

Be near me when my faith is dry,
   And men the flies of latter spring,   10
   That lay their eggs, and sting and sing
And weave their petty cells and die.

Be near me when I fade away,
   To point the term of human strife,
   And on the low dark verge of life   15
The twilight of eternal day.

51

Do we indeed desire the dead
   Should still be near us at our side?
   Is there no baseness we would hide?
No inner vileness that we dread?

Shall he for whose applause I strove,   5
   I had such reverence for his blame,
   See with clear eye some hidden shame
And I be lessened in his love?

I wrong the grave with fears untrue.
   Shall love be blamed for want of faith?   10
   There must be wisdom with great Death;
The dead shall look me through and through.

Be near us when we climb or fall;
   Ye watch, like God, the rolling hours
   With larger other eyes than ours,   15
To make allowance for us all.

52

I cannot love thee as I ought,
   For love reflects the thing beloved;
   My words are only words, and moved
Upon the topmost froth of thought.

"Yet blame not thou thy plaintive song,"   5
   The Spirit of true love replied;
   "Thou canst not move me from thy side,
Nor human frailty do me wrong.

"What keeps a spirit wholly true
   To that ideal which he bears?   10
   What record? not the sinless years
That breathed beneath the Syrian blue;

"So fret not, like an idle girl,
   That life is dashed with flecks of sin.
   Abide; thy wealth is gathered in,   15
When Time hath sundered shell from pearl."

53

How many a father have I seen,
   A sober man, among his boys,
   Whose youth was full of foolish noise,
Who wears his manhood hale and green;

And dare we to this fancy give,   5
   That had the wild oat not been sown,
   The soil, left barren, scarce had grown
The grain by which a man may live?

Or, if we held the doctrine sound
   For life outliving heats of youth,   10
   Yet who would preach it as a truth
To those that eddy round and round?

Hold thou the good, define it well;
   For fear divine Philosophy
   Should push beyond her mark, and be   15
Procuress to the Lords of Hell.

54

O yet we trust that somehow good
   Will be the final goal of ill,
   To pangs of nature, sins of will,
Defects of doubt, and taints of blood;

That nothing walks with aimless feet;   5
   That not one life shall be destroyed,
   Or cast as rubbish to the void,
When God hath made the pile complete;

That not a worm is cloven in vain;
   That not a moth with vain desire   10
   Is shriveled in a fruitless fire,
Or but subserves another's gain.

Behold, we know not anything;
   I can but trust that good shall fall
   At last — far off — at last, to all,   15
And every winter change to spring.

So runs my dream; but what am I?
   An infant crying in the night;
   An infant crying for the light,
And with no language but a cry.   20

55

The wish, that of the living whole
   No life may fail beyond the grave,
   Derives it not from what we have
The likest God within the soul?

Are God and Nature then at strife,   5
   That Nature lends such evil dreams?

Section 50. 8. **Fury slinging flame.** The Furies are represented as bearing torches.
Section 52. 11. **the sinless years**, the life of Christ.

Section 53. 5. **give,** yield, give in.
Section 55. 5. **at strife.** Tennyson attempts to reconcile the apparent conflict between science and faith then agitating the public.

So careful of the type she seems,
So careless of the single life,

That I, considering everywhere
  Her secret meaning in her deeds,   10
  And finding that of fifty seeds
She often brings but one to bear,

I falter where I firmly trod,
  And falling with my weight of cares
  Upon the great world's altar-stairs   15
That slope through darkness up to God,

I stretch lame hands of faith, and grope,
  And gather dust and chaff, and call
  To what I feel is Lord of all,
And faintly trust the larger hope.   20

56

"So careful of the type?" but no.
  From scarpéd cliff and quarried stone
She cries, "A thousand types are gone;
I care for nothing, all shall go.

"Thou makest thine appeal to me.   5
  I bring to life, I bring to death;
  The spirit does but mean the breath.
I know no more." And he, shall he,

Man, her last work, who seemed so fair,
  Such splendid purpose in his eyes,   10
  Who rolled the psalm to wintry skies,
Who built him fanes of fruitless prayer,

Who trusted God was love indeed
  And love Creation's final law —
  Though Nature, red in tooth and claw   15
With ravine, shrieked against his creed —

Who loved, who suffered countless ills,
  Who battled for the True, the Just,
  Be blown about the desert dust,
Or sealed within the iron hills?   20

No more? A monster then, a dream,
  A discord. Dragons of the prime,
  That tare each other in their slime,
Were mellow music matched with him.

O life as futile, then, as frail!   25
  O for thy voice to soothe and bless!
  What hope of answer, or redress?
Behind the veil, behind the veil.

57

Peace; come away: the song of woe
  Is after all an earthly song.
  Peace; come away: we do him wrong
To sing so wildly; let us go.

Come, let us go; your cheeks are pale;   5
  But half my life I leave behind.
  Methinks my friend is richly shrined;
But I shall pass, my work will fail.

Yet in these ears, till hearing dies,
  One set slow bell will seem to toll   10
  The passing of the sweetest soul
That ever looked with human eyes.

I hear it now, and o'er and o'er,
  Eternal greetings to the dead;
  And "Ave, Ave, Ave," said,   15
"Adieu, adieu," forevermore.

58

In those sad words I took farewell.
  Like echoes in sepulchral halls,
  As drop by drop the water falls
In vaults and catacombs, they fell;

And, falling, idly broke the peace   5
  Of hearts that beat from day to day,
  Half-conscious of their dying clay,
And those cold crypts where they shall cease.

The high Muse answered: "Wherefore grieve
  Thy brethren with a fruitless tear?   10
  Abide a little longer here,
And thou shalt take a nobler leave."

59

O Sorrow, wilt thou live with me
  No casual mistress, but a wife,
  My bosom-friend and half of life;
As I confess it needs must be;

O Sorrow, wilt thou rule my blood,   5
  Be sometimes lovely like a bride,
  And put thy harsher moods aside,
If thou wilt have me wise and good.

My centered passion cannot move,
  Nor will it lessen from today;   10
  But I'll have leave at times to play
As with the creature of my love;

And set thee forth, for thou art mine,
  With so much hope for years to come,

Section 55. 7-8. So careful . . . life. This doctrine of selection was explained later (1859) by Darwin in his *Origin of Species*. 20. the larger hope, i.e., that all humanity will eventually be purified and saved. (See *Memoir*, I, 321.)
Section 56. 2-3. cliff . . . gone. Geologic formations give evidence that form after form of life has vanished. 22. Dragons of the prime, monsters of prehistoric ages. 26. thy, Hallam's.

Section 57. This section may have been addressed to Tennyson's sister, who was betrothed to Hallam.
15. Ave, Ave, Ave, words of farewell to the dead, used by the Romans.
Section 58. 9. The high Muse, Urania, the muse of loftiest poetry.
Section 59. Compare this section with Section 3.

That, howsoe'er I know thee, some   15
Could hardly tell what name were thine.

60

He passed, a soul of nobler tone;
  My spirit loved and loves him yet,
  Like some poor girl whose heart is set
On one whose rank exceeds her own.

He mixing with his proper sphere,   5
  She finds the baseness of her lot,
  Half jealous of she knows not what,
And envying all that meet him there.

The little village looks forlorn;
  She sighs amid her narrow days,   10
  Moving about the household ways,
In that dark house where she was born.

The foolish neighbors come and go,
  And tease her till the day draws by;
  At night she weeps, "How vain am I!   15
How should he love a thing so low?"

61

If, in thy second state sublime,
  Thy ransomed reason change replies
  With all the circle of the wise,
The perfect flower of human time;

And if thou cast thine eyes below,   5
  How dimly charactered and slight,
  How dwarfed a growth of cold and night,
How blanched with darkness must I grow!

Yet turn thee to the doubtful shore,
  Where thy first form was made a man;   10
  I loved thee, Spirit, and love, nor can
The soul of Shakespeare love thee more.

62

Though if an eye that's downward cast
  Could make thee somewhat blench or fail,
  Then be my love an idle tale
And fading legend of the past;

And thou, as one that once declined,   5
  When he was little more than boy,
  On some unworthy heart with joy,
But lives to wed an equal mind,

And breathes a novel world, the while
  His other passion wholly dies,   10

Or in the light of deeper eyes
Is matter for a flying smile.

63

Yet pity for a horse o'er-driven,
  And love in which my hound has part,
  Can hang no weight upon my heart
In its assumptions up to heaven;

And I am so much more than these,   5
  As thou, perchance, art more than I,
  And yet I spare them sympathy,
And I would set their pains at ease.

So mayst thou watch me where I weep,
  As, unto vaster motions bound,   10
  The circuits of thine orbit round
A higher height, a deeper deep.

64

Dost thou look back on what hath been,
  As some divinely gifted man,
  Whose life in low estate began
And on a simple village green;

Who breaks his birth's invidious bar,   5
  And grasps the skirts of happy chance,
  And breasts the blows of circumstance,
And grapples with his evil star;

Who makes by force his merit known
  And lives to clutch the golden keys,   10
  To mold a mighty state's decrees,
And shape the whisper of the throne;

And moving up from high to higher,
  Becomes on Fortune's crowning slope
  The pillar of a people's hope,   15
The center of a world's desire;

Yet feels, as in a pensive dream,
  When all his active powers are still,
  A distant dearness in the hill,
A secret sweetness in the stream,   20

The limit of his narrower fate,
  While yet beside its vocal springs
  He played at counselors and kings,
With one that was his earliest mate;

Who plows with pain his native lea   25
  And reaps the labor of his hands,
  Or in the furrow musing stands:
"Does my old friend remember me?"

Section 60. 5. **proper,** own.
Section 61. 2. **change replies,** exchange replies. 8. **blanched with darkness,** like plants growing in the dark. 9. **the doubtful shore,** earthly existence. 12. **The soul . . . more.** Shakespeare's writings show that he deeply understood the nature and the power of love.
Section 62. 5-7. **declined . . . On,** stooped . . . to.

Section 63. 4. **assumptions,** aspirings.
Section 64. 10. **the golden keys,** the symbol of high office.

65

Sweet soul, do with me as thou wilt;
  I lull a fancy trouble-tost
  With "Love's too precious to be lost,
A little grain shall not be spilt."

And in that solace can I sing,   5
  Till out of painful phases wrought
  There flutters up a happy thought,
Self-balanced on a lightsome wing;

Since we deserved the name of friends,
  And thine effect so lives in me,   10
  A part of mine may live in thee
And move thee on to noble ends.

66

You thought my heart too far diseased;
  You wonder when my fancies play
  To find me gay among the gay,
Like one with any trifle pleased.

The shade by which my life was crost,   5
  Which makes a desert in the mind,
  Has made me kindly with my kind,
And like to him whose sight is lost;

Whose feet are guided through the land,
  Whose jest among his friends is free,   10
  Who takes the children on his knee,
And winds their curls about his hand.

He plays with threads, he beats his chair
  For pastime, dreaming of the sky;
  His inner day can never die,   15
His night of loss is always there.

67

When on my bed the moonlight falls,
  I know that in thy place of rest
  By that broad water of the west
There comes a glory on the walls;

Thy marble bright in dark appears,   5
  As slowly steals a silver flame
  Along the letters of thy name,
And o'er the number of thy years.

The mystic glory swims away,
  From off my bed the moonlight dies;   10
  And closing eaves of wearied eyes
I sleep till dusk is dipped in gray;

And then I know the mist is drawn,
  A lucid veil from coast to coast,

And in the dark church like a ghost   15
Thy tablet glimmers in the dawn.

68

When in the down I sink my head,
  Sleep, Death's twin-brother, times my
    breath;
  Sleep, Death's twin-brother, knows not
    Death,
Nor can I dream of thee as dead.

I walk as ere I walked forlorn,   5
  When all our path was fresh with dew,
  And all the bugle breezes blew
Reveillée to the breaking morn.

But what is this? I turn about;
  I find a trouble in thine eye,   10
  Which makes me sad I know not why,
Nor can my dream resolve the doubt;

But ere the lark hath left the lea
  I wake, and I discern the truth;
  It is the trouble of my youth   15
That foolish sleep transfers to thee.

69

I dreamed there would be spring no more,
  That Nature's ancient power was lost;
  The streets were black with smoke and
    frost,
They chattered trifles at the door;

I wandered from the noisy town,   5
  I found a wood with thorny boughs;
  I took the thorns to bind my brows,
I wore them like a civic crown;

I met with scoffs, I met with scorns
  From youth and babe and hoary hairs;   10
  They called me in the public squares
The fool that wears a crown of thorns.

They called me fool, they called me child.
  I found an angel of the night;
  The voice was low, the look was bright;   15
He looked upon my crown and smiled.

He reached the glory of a hand,
  That seemed to touch it into leaf;
  The voice was not the voice of grief,
The words were hard to understand.   20

70

I cannot see the features right,
  When on the gloom I strive to paint

Section 66. 1. diseased, made uneasy.
Section 67. 2. thy place of rest, in the church at Clevedon. 3. broad water of the west, the Severn, which is
nine miles wide at Clevedon.

Section 69. 14. an angel of the night. Explained by
Tennyson as "the divine Thing in the gloom."

The face I know; the hues are faint
And mix with hollow masks of night:

Cloud-towers by ghostly masons wrought,   5
  A gulf that ever shuts and gapes,
  A hand that points, and palléd shapes
In shadowy thoroughfares of thought;

And crowds that stream from yawning doors,
  And shoals of puckered faces drive;   10
  Dark bulks that tumble half alive,
And lazy lengths on boundless shores;

Till all at once beyond the will
  I hear a wizard music roll,
  And through a lattice on the soul   15
Looks thy fair face and makes it still.

71

Sleep, kinsman thou to death and trance
  And madness, thou hast forged at last
  A night-long present of the past
In which we went through summer France.

Hadst thou such credit with the soul?   5
  Then bring an opiate trebly strong,
  Drug down the blindfold sense of wrong,
That so my pleasure may be whole;

While now we talk as once we talked
  Of men and minds, the dust of change,   10
  The days that grow to something strange,
In walking as of old we walked

Beside the river's wooded reach,
  The fortress, and the mountain ridge,
  The cataract flashing from the bridge,   15
The breaker breaking on the beach.

72

Risest thou thus, dim dawn, again,
  And howlest, issuing out of night,
  With blasts that blow the poplar white,
And lash with storm the streaming pane?

Day, when my crowned estate begun   5
  To pine in that reverse of doom,
  Which sickened every living bloom,
And blurred the splendor of the sun;

Who usherest in the dolorous hour
  With thy quick tears that make the rose 10
  Pull sideways, and the daisy close
Her crimson fringes to the shower;

Section 70. **7. palléd,** wrapped in palls.
  Section 71. **4. In . . . France.** Tennyson and Hallam
visited France in the summer of 1830.
  Section 72. **1. dim dawn,** September 15, the anniversary
of Hallam's death. **3. that . . . white,** that turn up the
white underside of the poplar leaves. **5-9. Day . . . hour.** As
in the tradition of the pastoral elegy, Tennyson singles out the
precise time of death as a fateful day and hour of universal
doom. Cf. Shelley's reference to the time of Keats's death,
"sad Hour, selected from all years" (*Adonais,* l. 5).

Who mightest have heaved a windless flame
  Up the deep East, or, whispering, played
  A checker-work of beam and shade   15
Along the hills, yet looked the same,

As wan, as chill, as wild as now;
  Day, marked as with some hideous crime,
  When the dark hand struck down through
     time,
And canceled nature's best: but thou,   20

Lift as thou mayst thy burthened brows
  Through clouds that drench the morning
     star,
  And whirl the ungarnered sheaf afar,
And sow the sky with flying boughs,

And up thy vault with roaring sound   25
  Climb thy thick noon, disastrous day;
  Touch thy dull goal of joyless gray,
And hide thy shame beneath the ground.

73

So many worlds, so much to do,
  So little done, such things to be,
  How know I what had need of thee,
For thou wert strong as thou wert true?

The fame is quenched that I foresaw,   5
  The head hath missed an earthly wreath;
  I curse not Nature, no, nor Death,
For nothing is that errs from law.

We pass; the path that each man trod
  Is dim, or will be dim, with weeds.   10
  What fame is left for human deeds
In endless age? It rests with God.

O hollow wraith of dying fame,
  Fade wholly, while the soul exults,
  And self-infolds the large results   15
Of force that would have forged a name.

74

As sometimes in a dead man's face,
  To those that watch it more and more,
  A likeness, hardly seen before,
Comes out — to someone of his race;

So, dearest, now thy brows are cold,   5
  I see thee what thou art, and know
  Thy likeness to the wise below,
Thy kindred with the great of old.

But there is more than I can see,
  And what I see I leave unsaid,   10
  Nor speak it, knowing Death has made
His darkness beautiful with thee.

75

I leave thy praises unexpressed
  In verse that brings myself relief,
  And by the measure of my grief
I leave thy greatness to be guessed;

What practice howsoe'er expert   5
  In fitting aptest words to things,
  Or voice the richest-toned that sings,
Hath power to give thee as thou wert?

I care not in these fading days
  To raise a cry that lasts not long,   10
  And round thee with the breeze of song
To stir a little dust of praise.

Thy leaf has perished in the green,
  And, while we breathe beneath the sun,
  The world which credits what is done   15
Is cold to all that might have been.

So here shall silence guard thy fame;
  But somewhere, out of human view,
  Whate'er thy hands are set to do
Is wrought with tumult of acclaim.   20

76

Take wings of fancy, and ascend,
  And in a moment set thy face
  Where all the starry heavens of space
Are sharpened to a needle's end;

Take wings of foresight; lighten through   5
  The secular abyss to come,
  And lo, thy deepest lays are dumb
Before the moldering of a yew;

And if the matin songs, that woke
  The darkness of our planet, last,   10
  Thine own shall wither in the vast,
Ere half the lifetime of an oak.

Ere these have clothed their branchy bowers
  With fifty Mays, thy songs are vain;
  And what are they when these remain   15
The ruined shells of hollow towers?

77

What hope is here for modern rime
  To him who turns a musing eye
  On songs, and deeds, and lives, that lie
Foreshortened in the tract of time?

These mortal lullabies of pain   5
  May bind a book, may line a box,
  May serve to curl a maiden's locks;
Or when a thousand moons shall wane

A man upon a stall may find,
  And, passing, turn the page that tells   10
  A grief, then changed to something else,
Sung by a long-forgotten mind.

But what of that? My darkened ways
  Shall ring with music all the same;
  To breathe my loss is more than fame,   15
To utter love more sweet than praise.

78

Again at Christmas did we weave
  The holly round the Christmas hearth;
  The silent snow possessed the earth;
And calmly fell our Christmas Eve.

The yule-clog sparkled keen with frost,   5
  No wing of wind the region swept,
  But over all things brooding slept
The quiet sense of something lost.

As in the winters left behind,
  Again our ancient games had place,   10
  The mimic picture's breathing grace,
And dance and song and hoodman-blind.

Who showed a token of distress?
  No single tear, no mark of pain:
  O sorrow, then can sorrow wane?   15
O grief, can grief be changed to less?

O last regret, regret can die!
  No — mixed with all this mystic frame,
  Her deep relations are the same,
But with long use her tears are dry.   20

79

"More than my brothers are to me" —
  Let this not vex thee, noble heart!
  I know thee of what force thou art
To hold the costliest love in fee.

But thou and I are one in kind,   5
  As molded like in Nature's mint;
  And hill and wood and field did print
The same sweet forms in either mind.

For us the same cold streamlet curled
  Through all his eddying coves; the same   10
  All winds that roam the twilight came
In whispers of the beauteous world.

At one dear knee we proffered vows,
  One lesson from one book we learned,

Section 76. 8. **the moldering of a yew.** The yew lives several centuries. 9. **matin songs,** the songs of the great early poets.

Section 78. 1. **Christmas,** the second after Hallam's death. Cf. Sections 30 and 105. 5. **yule-clog,** the large log burned on Christmas Eve. 11. **mimic picture,** charades.
Section 79. 2. **thee,** addressed to Tennyson's brother Charles. See Section 9, line 20. 4. **in fee,** in absolute possession.

Ere childhood's flaxen ringlet turned   15
To black and brown on kindred brows.

And so my wealth resembles thine,
  But he was rich where I was poor,
  And he supplied my want the more
As his unlikeness fitted mine.   20

80

If any vague desire should rise,
  That holy Death ere Arthur died
  Had moved me kindly from his side,
And dropped the dust on tearless eyes;

Then fancy shapes, as fancy can,   5
  The grief my loss in him had wrought,
  A grief as deep as life or thought,
But stayed in peace with God and man.

I make a picture in the brain;
  I hear the sentence that he speaks;   10
  He bears the burthen of the weeks,
But turns his burthen into gain.

His credit thus shall set me free;
  And, influence-rich to soothe and save,
  Unused example from the grave   15
Reach out dead hands to comfort me.

81

Could I have said while he was here,
  "My love shall now no further range;
  There cannot come a mellower change,
For now is love mature in ear"?

Love, then, had hope of richer store;   5
  What end is here to my complaint?
  This haunting whisper makes me faint,
"More years had made me love thee more."

But Death returns an answer sweet:
  "My sudden frost was sudden gain,   10
  And gave all ripeness to the grain
It might have drawn from after-heat."

82

I wage not any feud with Death
  For changes wrought on form and face;
  No lower life that earth's embrace
May breed with him can fright my faith.

Eternal process moving on,   5
  From state to state the spirit walks;
  And these are but the shattered stalks,
Or ruined chrysalis of one.

Nor blame I Death, because he bare
  The use of virtue out of earth;   10

Section 82.   7. **these**, forms of "lower life," line 3.

I know transplanted human worth
Will bloom to profit, otherwhere.

For this alone on Death I wreak
  The wrath that garners in my heart:
  He put our lives so far apart   15
We cannot hear each other speak.

83

Dip down upon the northern shore,
  O sweet new-year delaying long;
  Thou doest expectant Nature wrong;
Delaying long, delay no more.

What stays thee from the clouded noons,   5
  Thy sweetness from its proper place?
  Can trouble live with April days,
Or sadness in the summer moons?

Bring orchis, bring the foxglove spire,
  The little speedwell's darling blue,   10
  Deep tulips dashed with fiery dew,
Laburnums, dropping-wells of fire.

O thou, new-year, delaying long,
  Delayest the sorrow in my blood,
  That longs to burst a frozen bud   15
And flood a fresher throat with song.

84

When I contemplate all alone
  The life that had been thine below,
  And fix my thoughts on all the glow
To which thy crescent would have grown,

I see thee sitting crowned with good,   5
  A central warmth diffusing bliss
  In glance and smile, and clasp and kiss,
On all the branches of thy blood;

Thy blood, my friend, and partly mine;
  For now the day was drawing on,   10
  When thou shouldst link thy life with one
Of mine own house, and boys of thine

Had babbled "Uncle" on my knee;
  But that remorseless iron hour
  Made cypress of her orange flower,   15
Despair of hope, and earth of thee.

I seem to meet their least desire,
  To clap their cheeks, to call them mine.
  I see their unborn faces shine
Beside the never-lighted fire.   20

Section 83.   1. **the northern shore**, England.   5. **the
clouded noons**, i.e., such as at that season overhung the
land.   12. **Laburnums . . . fire.** The laburnum blossoms
are of a bright yellow and hang in an inverted position.
  Section 84.   11. **with one.** Hallam was to have married
Tennyson's sister Emily.   15. **cypress, orange flower,** the
symbols respectively of death and marriage.

I see myself an honored guest,
  Thy partner in the flowery walk
  Of letters, genial table-talk,
Or deep dispute, and graceful jest;

While now thy prosperous labor fills   25
  The lips of men with honest praise,
  And sun by sun the happy days
Descend below the golden hills

With promise of a morn as fair;
  And all the train of bounteous hours ·   30
  Conduct, by paths of growing powers,
To reverence and the silver hair;

Till slowly worn her earthly robe,
  Her lavish mission richly wrought,
  Leaving great legacies of thought,   35
Thy spirit should fail from off the globe;

What time mine own might also flee,
  As linked with thine in love and fate,
  And, hovering o'er the dolorous strait
To the other shore, involved in thee,   40

Arrive at last the blessed goal,
  And He that died in Holy Land
  Would reach us out the shining hand,
And take us as a single soul.

What reed was that on which I leant?   45
  Ah, backward fancy, wherefore wake
  The old bitterness again, and break
The low beginnings of content?

85

This truth came borne with bier and pall,
  I felt it, when I sorrowed most:
  'Tis better to have loved and lost,
Than never to have loved at all —

O true in word, and tried in deed,   5
  Demanding, so to bring relief
  To this which is our common grief,
What kind of life is that I lead;

And whether trust in things above
  Be dimmed of sorrow, or sustained;   10
  And whether love for him have drained
My capabilities of love;

Your words have virtue such as draws
  A faithful answer from the breast,
  Through light reproaches, half expressed,   15
And loyal unto kindly laws.

My blood an even tenor kept,
  Till on mine ear this message falls,
  That in Vienna's fatal walls
God's finger touched him, and he slept.   20

The great Intelligences fair
  That range above our mortal state,
  In circle round the blessed gate,
Received and gave him welcome there;

And led him through the blissful climes,   25
  And showed him in the fountain fresh
  All knowledge that the sons of flesh
Shall gather in the cycled times.

But I remained, whose hopes were dim,
  Whose life, whose thoughts were little
    worth,   30
  To wander on a darkened earth,
Where all things round me breathed of him.

O friendship, equal-poised control,
  O heart, with kindliest motion warm,
  O sacred essence, other form,   35
O solemn ghost, O crownéd soul!

Yet none could better know than I,
  How much of act at human hands
  The sense of human will demands
By which we dare to live or die.   40

Whatever way my days decline,
  I felt and feel, though left alone,
  His being working in mine own,
The footsteps of his life in mine;

A life that all the Muses decked   45
  With gifts of grace, that might express
  All-comprehensive tenderness,
All-subtilizing intellect;

And so my passion hath not swerved
  To works of weakness, but I find   50
  An image comforting the mind,
And in my grief a strength reserved.

Likewise the imaginative woe,
  That loved to handle spiritual strife,
  Diffused the shock through all my life,   55
But in the present broke the blow.

My pulses therefore beat again
  For other friends that once I met;
  Nor can it suit me to forget
The mighty hopes that make us men.   60

I woo your love; I count it crime
  To mourn for any overmuch;

  Section 84. **33. earthly robe,** body. **37. What time,** at
which time.
  Section 85. 3-4. Cf. Section 27, lines 15-16. **5. O true,**
etc. Section 85 is addressed to Edmund Law Lushington,
Professor of Greek at the University of Glasgow. He
married Tennyson's youngest sister, Cecilia, on October 10,
1842. See the Epilogue to *In Memoriam*, page 90.

  21. Intelligences, angels. **28. the cycled times,** the
successive periods of human progress on earth. **48. All-subtilizing,** all-refining.

I, the divided half of such
A friendship as had mastered Time;

Which masters Time indeed, and is 65
Eternal, separate from fears.
The all-assuming months and years
Can take no part away from this;

But summer on the steaming floods,
And spring that swells the narrow brooks,
And autumn, with a noise of rooks, 71
That gather in the waning woods,

And every pulse of wind and wave
Recalls, in change of light or gloom,
My old affection of the tomb, 75
And my prime passion in the grave.

My old affection of the tomb,
A part of stillness, yearns to speak:
"Arise, and get thee forth and seek
A friendship for the years to come. 80

"I watch thee from the quiet shore;
Thy spirit up to mine can reach;
But in dear words of human speech
We two communicate no more."

And I, "Can clouds of nature stain 85
The starry clearness of the free?
How is it? Canst thou feel for me
Some painless sympathy with pain?"

And lightly does the whisper fall:
" 'Tis hard for thee to fathom this; 90
I triumph in conclusive bliss,
And that serene result of all."

So hold I commerce with the dead;
Or so methinks the dead would say;
Or so shall grief with symbols play 95
And pining life be fancy-fed.

Now looking to some settled end,
That these things pass, and I shall prove
A meeting somewhere, love with love,
I crave your pardon, O my friend; 100

If not so fresh, with love as true,
I, clasping brother-hands, aver
I could not, if I would, transfer
The whole I felt for him to you.

For which be they that hold apart 105
The promise of the golden hours?
First love, first friendship, equal powers,
That marry with the virgin heart.

Still mine, that cannot but deplore,
That beats within a lonely place, 110
That yet remembers his embrace,
But at his footstep leaps no more,

My heart, though widowed, may not rest
Quite in the love of what is gone,
But seeks to beat in time with one 115
That warms another living breast.

Ah, take the imperfect gift I bring,
Knowing the primrose yet is dear,
The primrose of the later year,
As not unlike to that of spring. 120

86

Sweet after showers, ambrosial air,
That rollest from the gorgeous gloom
Of evening over brake and bloom
And meadow, slowly breathing bare

The round of space, and rapt below 5
Through all the dewy tasseled wood,
And shadowing down the hornéd flood
In ripples, fan my brows and blow

The fever from my cheek, and sigh
The full new life that feeds thy breath 10
Throughout my frame, till Doubt and
 Death,
Ill brethren, let the fancy fly

From belt to belt of crimson seas
On leagues of odor streaming far,
To where in yonder orient star 15
A hundred spirits whisper "Peace."

' 87

I passed beside the reverend walls
In which of old I wore the gown;
I roved at random through the town,
And saw the tumult of the halls;

And heard once more in college fanes 5
The storm their high-built organs make,
And thunder-music, rolling, shake
The prophet blazoned on the panes;

And caught once more the distant shout,
The measured pulse of racing oars 10
Among the willows; paced the shores
And many a bridge, and all about

The same gray flats again, and felt
The same, but not the same; and last

67. **all-assuming**, all-devouring. 85. **nature**, human
nature. 86. **the free**, spirits freed from the body. 105.
hold apart, put aside.

Section 86. Tennyson frequently quoted this section to
illustrate his "sense of the joyous peace in Nature." Luce
regards it as the "very finest" section of the poem.
1. **ambrosial air**, the west wind. 4-5. **breathing** . . .
space, clearing the sky of clouds. 7. **hornéd**, winding, indented between points of land.
Section 87. 1. **walls**, those of **Trinity College**, Cambridge.

Up that long walk of limes I passed 15
To see the rooms in which he dwelt.

Another name was on the door.
  I lingered; all within was noise
  Of songs, and clapping hands, and boys
That crashed the glass and beat the floor; 20

Where once we held debate, a band
  Of youthful friends, on mind and art,
  And labor, and the changing mart,
And all the framework of the land;

When one would aim an arrow fair, 25
  But send it slackly from the string;
  And one would pierce an outer ring,
And one an inner, here and there;

And last the master-bowman, he,
  Would cleave the mark. A willing ear 30
  We lent him. Who but hung to hear
The rapt oration flowing free

From point to point, with power and grace
  And music in the bounds of law,
  To those conclusions when we saw 35
The God within him light his face,

And seem to lift the form, and glow
  In azure orbits heavenly-wise;
  And over those ethereal eyes
The bar of Michael Angelo? 40

88

Wild bird, whose warble, liquid sweet,
  Rings Eden through the budded quicks,
  O tell me where the senses mix,
O tell me where the passions meet,

Whence radiate. Fierce extremes employ 5
  Thy spirits in the darkening leaf,
  And in the midmost heart of grief
Thy passion clasps a secret joy;

And I — my harp would prelude woe —
  I cannot all command the strings; 10
  The glory of the sum of things
Will flash along the chords and go.

89

Witch-elms that counterchange the floor
  Of this flat lawn with dusk and bright;

And thou, with all thy breadth and height
Of foliage, towering sycamore;

How often, hither wandering down, 5
  My Arthur found your shadows fair,
  And shook to all the liberal air
The dust and din and steam of town!

He brought an eye for all he saw;
  He mixed in all our simple sports; 10
  They pleased him, fresh from brawling
      courts
And dusty purlieus of the law.

O joy to him in this retreat,
  Immantled in ambrosial dark,
  To drink the cooler air, and mark 15
The landscape winking through the heat!

O sound to rout the brood of cares,
  The sweep of scythe in morning dew,
  The gust that round the garden flew,
And tumbled half the mellowing pears! 20

O bliss, when all in circle drawn
  About him, heart and ear were fed
  To hear him, as he lay and read
The Tuscan poets on the lawn!

Or in the all-golden afternoon 25
  A guest, or happy sister, sung,
  Or here she brought the harp and flung
A ballad to the brightening moon.

Nor less it pleased in livelier moods,
  Beyond the bounding hill to stray, 30
  And break the livelong summer day
With banquet in the distant woods;

Whereat we glanced from theme to theme,
  Discussed the books to love or hate,
  Or touched the changes of the state, 35
Or threaded some Socratic dream;

But if I praised the busy town,
  He loved to rail against it still,
  For "ground in yonder social mill
We rub each other's angles down, 40

"And merge," he said, "in form and gloss
  The picturesque of man and man."
  We talked; the stream beneath us ran,
The wine-flask lying couched in moss,

Section 87. 21-22. a band Of youthful friends, known as "The Apostles," and also as "The Water Club" because there was no wine. 40. bar . . . Angelo. It is said that Michelangelo (1475-1564), the great Italian artist, had a distinct ridge above the eyes. Hallam once said to Tennyson: "Alfred, look over my eyes; surely I have the bar of Michael-Angelo" (*Memoir*, I, 38 note).
Section 88. 1. Wild bird, the nightingale. 2. quicks, the hawthorn hedges.
Section 89. 2. flat lawn, at Somersby. Cf. 8, 23, and 38.

12. purlieus of the law, the Inner Temple, where Hallam studied law. 24. The Tuscan poets. Hallam was an earnest student of Italian. He was especially fond of Dante and Petrarch, who wrote in the Tuscan language. 35-36. Or touched . . . dream. They discussed politics and the philosophy of Socrates and of his follower Plato. Hallam was especially fond of Plato.

Or cooled within the glooming wave;   45
  And last, returning from afar,
  Before the crimson-circled star
Had fallen into her father's grave,

And brushing ankle-deep in flowers,
  We heard behind the woodbine veil   50
  The milk that bubbled in the pail,
And buzzings of the honeyed hours.

90

He tasted love with half his mind,
  Nor ever drank the inviolate spring
  Where nighest heaven, who first could fling
This bitter seed among mankind:

That could the dead, whose dying eyes   5
  Were closed with wail, resume their life,
  They would but find in child and wife
An iron welcome when they rise.

'Twas well, indeed, when warm with wine,
  To pledge them with a kindly tear,   10
  To talk them o'er, to wish them here,
To count their memories half divine;

But if they came who passed away,
  Behold their brides in other hands;
  The hard heir strides about their lands,   15
And will not yield them for a day.

Yea, though their sons were none of these,
  Not less the yet-loved sire would make
  Confusion worse than death, and shake
The pillars of domestic peace.   20

Ah, dear, but come thou back to me!
  Whatever change the years have wrought,
  I find not yet one lonely thought
That cries against my wish for thee.

91

When rosy plumelets tuft the larch,
  And rarely pipes the mounted thrush,
  Or underneath the barren bush
Flits by the sea-blue bird of March;

Come, wear the form by which I know   5
  Thy spirit in time among thy peers;
  The hope of unaccomplished years
Be large and lucid round thy brow.

When summer's hourly-mellowing change
  May breathe, with many roses sweet,   10
  Upon the thousand waves of wheat
That ripple round the lowly grange,

Come; not in watches of the night,
  But where the sunbeam broodeth warm,
  Come, beauteous in thine after form,   15
And like a finer light in light.

92

If any vision should reveal
  Thy likeness, I might count it vain
  As but the canker of the brain;
Yea, though it spake and made appeal

To chances where our lots were cast   5
  Together in the days behind,
  I might but say, I hear a wind
Of memory murmuring the past.

Yea, though it spake and bared to view
  A fact within the coming year;   10
  And though the months, revolving near,
Should prove the phantom-warning true,

They might not seem thy prophecies,
  But spiritual presentiments,
  And such refraction of events   15
As often rises ere they rise.

93

I shall not see thee. Dare I say
  No spirit ever brake the band
  That stays him from the native land
Where first he walked when clasped in clay?

No visual shade of someone lost,   5
  But he, the Spirit himself, may come
  Where all the nerve of sense is numb,
Spirit to Spirit, Ghost to Ghost.

O therefore from thy sightless range
  With gods in unconjectured bliss,   10
  O from the distance of the abyss
Of tenfold-complicated change,

Descend, and touch, and enter; hear
  The wish too strong for words to name,
  That in this blindness of the frame   15
My Ghost may feel that thine is near.

94

How pure at heart and sound in head,
  With what divine affections bold
  Should be the man whose thought would hold
An hour's communion with the dead.

In vain shalt thou, or any, call   5
  The spirits from their golden day,

Except, like them, thou too canst say,
My spirit is at peace with all.

They haunt the silence of the breast,
  Imaginations calm and fair,   10
  The memory like a cloudless air,
The conscience as a sea at rest;

But when the heart is full of din,
  And doubt beside the portal waits,
  They can but listen at the gates,   15
And hear the household jar within.

95

By night we lingered on the lawn,
  For underfoot the herb was dry;
  And genial warmth; and o'er the sky
The silvery haze of summer drawn;

And calm that let the tapers burn   5
  Unwavering. Not a cricket chirred;
  The brook alone far-off was heard,
And on the board the fluttering urn.

And bats went round in fragrant skies,
  And wheeled or lit the filmy shapes   10
  That haunt the dusk, with ermine capes
And woolly breasts and beaded eyes;

While now we sang old songs that pealed
  From knoll to knoll, where, couched at ease,
  The white kine glimmered, and the trees 15
Laid their dark arms about the field.

But when those others, one by one,
  Withdrew themselves from me and night,
  And in the house light after light
Went out, and I was all alone,   20

A hunger seized my heart; I read
  Of that glad year which once had been,
  In those fallen leaves which kept their
      green,
The noble letters of the dead.

And strangely on the silence broke   25
  The silent-speaking words, and strange
  Was love's dumb cry defying change
To test his worth; and strangely spoke

The faith, the vigor, bold to dwell
  On doubts that drive the coward back,   30
  And keen through wordy snares to track
Suggestion to her inmost cell.

Section 95. This is the climax of the poem, the communion
with the dead prepared for in Sections 90-94.
  8. **the fluttering urn,** the boiling tea-urn. 10. **filmy
shapes,** night moths. 22. **that glad year,** the whole past
shared with Hallam.

So word by word, and line by line,
  The dead man touched me from the past,
  And all at once it seemed at last   35
The living soul was flashed on mine,

And mine in this was wound, and whirled
  About empyreal heights of thought,
  And came on that which is, and caught
The deep pulsations of the world,   40

Æonian music measuring out
  The steps of Time—the shocks of Chance—
  The blows of Death. At length my trance
Was canceled, stricken through with doubt.

Vague words! but ah, how hard to frame   45
  In matter-molded forms of speech,
  Or even for intellect to reach
Through memory that which I became;

Till now the doubtful dusk revealed
  The knolls once more where, couched at
      ease,   50
  The white kine glimmered, and the trees
Laid their dark arms about the field;

And sucked from out the distant gloom
  A breeze began to tremble o'er
  The large leaves of the sycamore,   55
And fluctuate all the still perfume,

And gathering freshlier overhead,
  Rocked the full-foliaged elms, and swung
  The heavy-folded rose, and flung
The lilies to and fro, and said,   60

"The dawn, the dawn," and died away;
  And East and West, without a breath,
  Mixed their dim lights, like life and death,
To broaden into boundless day.

96

You say, but with no touch of scorn,
  Sweet-hearted, you, whose light-blue eyes
  Are tender over drowning flies,
You tell me, doubt is Devil-born.

I know not. One indeed I knew   5
  In many a subtle question versed,
  Who touched a jarring lyre at first,
But ever strove to make it true;

Perplexed in faith, but pure in deeds,
  At last he beat his music out.   10

Section 95. 36-40. In a trance the poet is carried to
empyreal heights, where he could see the truth and purpose
of God in the universe. Tennyson states that he frequently
experienced "a kind of walking trance quite up from boyhood" (*Memoir,* I, 320). 41. *Æonian music,* music or harmony of the ages.
  Section 96. 1. **You,** some woman of simple faith. 5. **One,**
Hallam.

There lives more faith in honest doubt, 11
Believe me, than in half the creeds.

He fought his doubts and gathered strength,
    He would not make his judgment blind,
    He faced the specters of the mind   15
And laid them; thus he came at length

To find a stronger faith his own,
    And Power was with him in the night,
    Which makes the darkness and the light,
And dwells not in the light alone,   20

But in the darkness and the cloud,
    As over Sinaï's peaks of old,
    While Israel made their gods of gold,
Although the trumpet blew so loud.

97

My Love has talked with rocks and trees;
    He finds on misty mountain-ground
    His own vast shadow glory-crowned;
He sees himself in all he sees.

Two partners of a married life —   5
    I looked on these and thought of thee
    In vastness and in mystery,
And of my spirit as of a wife.

These two — they dwelt with eye on eye,
    Their hearts of old have beat in tune,   10
    Their meetings made December June,
Their every parting was to die.

Their love has never passed away;
    The days she never can forget
    Are earnest that he loves her yet,   15
Whate'er the faithless people say.

Her life is lone, he sits apart;
    He loves her yet, she will not weep,
    Though rapt in matters dark and deep
He seems to slight her simple heart.   20

He thrids the labyrinth of the mind,
    He reads the secret of the star,
    He seems so near and yet so far,
He looks so cold; she thinks him kind.

She keeps the gift of years before,   25
    A withered violet is her bliss;

She knows not what his greatness is,
For that, for all, she loves him more.

For him she plays, to him she sings
    Of early faith and plighted vows;   30
    She knows but matters of the house,
And he, he knows a thousand things.

Her faith is fixed and cannot move,
    She darkly feels him great and wise,
    She dwells on him with faithful eyes,   35
"I cannot understand; I love."

98

You leave us. You will see the Rhine,
    And those fair hills I sailed below,
    When I was there with him; and go
By summer belts of wheat and vine

To where he breathed his latest breath,   5
    That city. All her splendor seems
    No livelier than the wisp that gleams
On Lethe in the eyes of Death.

Let her great Danube rolling fair
    Enwind her isles, unmarked of me;   10
    I have not seen, I will not see
Vienna; rather dream that there,

A treble darkness, Evil haunts
    The birth, the bridal; friend from friend
    Is oftener parted, fathers bend   15
Above more graves, a thousand wants

Gnarr at the heels of men, and prey
    By each cold hearth, and sadness flings
    Her shadow on the blaze of kings.
And yet myself have heard him say   20

That not in any mother town
    With statelier progress to and fro
    The double tides of chariots flow
By park and suburb under brown

Of lustier leaves; nor more content,   25
    He told me, lives in any crowd,
    When all is gay with lamps, and loud
With sport and song, in booth and tent,

Imperial halls, or open plain;
    And wheels the circled dance, and breaks 30
    The rocket molten into flakes
Of crimson or in emerald rain.

99

Risest thou thus, dim dawn, again,
 So loud with voices of the birds,
 So thick with lowings of the herds,
Day, when I lost the flower of men;

Who tremblest through thy darkling red 5
 On yon swollen brook that bubbles fast
 By meadows breathing of the past,
And woodlands holy to the dead;

Who murmurest in the foliaged eaves
 A song that slights the coming care, 10
 And Autumn laying here and there
A fiery finger on the leaves;

Who wakenest with thy balmy breath
 To myriads on the genial earth,
 Memories of bridal, or of birth, 15
And unto myriads more, of death.

O wheresoever those may be,
 Betwixt the slumber of the poles,
 Today they count as kindred souls;
They know me not, but mourn with me. 20

100

I climb the hill. From end to end
 Of all the landscape underneath,
 I find no place that does not breathe
Some gracious memory of my friend;

No gray old grange, or lonely fold, 5
 Or low morass and whispering reed,
 Or simple stile from mead to mead,
Or sheepwalk up the windy wold;

Nor hoary knoll of ash and haw
 That hears the latest linnet trill, 10
 Nor quarry trenched along the hill
And haunted by the wrangling daw;

Nor runlet tinkling from the rock;
 Nor pastoral rivulet that swerves
 To left and right through meadowy curves,
That feed the mothers of the flock; 16

But each has pleased a kindred eye,
 And each reflects a kindlier day;
 And, leaving these, to pass away,
I think once more he seems to die. 20

101

Unwatched, the garden bough shall sway,
 The tender blossom flutter down,
Unloved, that beech will gather brown,
This maple burn itself away;

Unloved, the sunflower, shining fair, 5
 Ray round with flames her disk of seed,
 And many a rose-carnation feed
With summer spice the humming air;

Unloved, by many a sandy bar,
 The brook shall babble down the plain, 10
 At noon or when the Lesser Wain
Is twisting round the polar star;

Uncared for, gird the windy grove,
 And flood the haunts of hern and crake,
 Or into silver arrows break 15
The sailing moon in creek and cove;

Till from the garden and the wild
 A fresh association blow,
 And year by year the landscape grow
Familiar to the stranger's child; 20

As year by year the laborer tills
 His wonted glebe, or lops the glades,
 And year by year our memory fades
From all the circle of the hills.

102

We leave the well-beloved place
 Where first we gazed upon the sky;
 The roofs that heard our earliest cry
Will shelter one of stranger race.

We go, but ere we go from home, 5
 As down the garden-walks I move,
 Two spirits of a diverse love
Contend for loving masterdom.

One whispers, "Here thy boyhood sung
 Long since its matin song, and heard 10
 The low love-language of the bird
In native hazels tassel-hung."

The other answers, "Yea, but here
 Thy feet have strayed in after hours
 With thy lost friend among the bowers, 15
And this hath made them trebly dear."

These two have striven half the day,
 And each prefers his separate claim,
 Poor rivals in a losing game,
That will not yield each other way. 20

Section 99. 1. **dim dawn**, the second anniversary of Hallam's death. Compare Section 72.
Section 100. Sections 100, 101, and 102 were suggested by the removal of the Tennysons from Somersby in 1837 to High Beech, in Epping Forest, a few miles north of London.

Section 101. 4. **maple burn**, a reference to the red leaves of the maple in the fall. 11. **the Lesser Wain**, the constellation Ursa Minor, commonly called "The Little Dipper." It revolves around the Polar, or North, Star. 13. **gird**, shall girdle or encircle. *Brook* is the subject of *gird, flood*, and *break*. 22. **lops the glades**, trims out the thickets.
Section 102. 7. **Two spirits.** "First, the love of the native place; the second, this enhanced by the memory of A.H.H." (Tennyson's note). 10. **matin song**, a reference to Tennyson's earliest poems.

I turn to go; my feet are set
    To leave the pleasant fields and farms;
    They mix in one another's arms
To one pure image of regret.

103

On that last night before we went
    From out the doors where I was bred,
    I dreamed a vision of the dead,
Which left my after-morn content.

Methought I dwelt within a hall,   5
    And maidens with me; distant hills
    From hidden summits fed with rills
A river sliding by the wall.

The hall with harp and carol rang.
    They sang of what is wise and good   10
    And graceful.   In the center stood
A statue veiled, to which they sang;

And which, though veiled, was known to me,
    The shape of him I loved, and love
    Forever.   Then flew in a dove   15
And brought a summons from the sea;

And when they learnt that I must go,
    They wept and wailed, but led the way
    To where a little shallop lay
At anchor in the flood below;   20

And on by many a level mead,
    And shadowing bluff that made the banks,
    We glided winding under ranks
Of iris and the golden reed;

And still as vaster grew the shore   25
    And rolled the floods in grander space,
    The maidens gathered strength and grace
And presence, lordlier than before;

And I myself, who sat apart
    And watched them, waxed in every limb;
    I felt the thews of Anakim,   31
The pulses of a Titan's heart;

As one would sing the death of war,
    And one would chant the history
    Of that great race which is to be,   35
And one the shaping of a star;

Until the forward-creeping tides
    Began to foam, and we to draw
    From deep to deep, to where we saw
A great ship lift her shining sides.   40

The man we loved was there on deck,
    But thrice as large as man he bent
    To greet us.   Up the side I went,
And fell in silence on his neck;

Whereat those maidens with one mind   45
    Bewailed their lot; I did them wrong:
    "We served thee here," they said, "so long,
And wilt thou leave us now behind?"

So rapt I was, they could not win
    An answer from my lips; but he   50
    Replying, "Enter likewise ye
And go with us," they entered in.

And while the wind began to sweep
    A music out of sheet and shroud,
    We steered her toward a crimson cloud   55
That landlike slept along the deep.

104

The time draws near the birth of Christ;
    The moon is hid, the night is still;
    A single church below the hill
Is pealing, folded in the mist.

A single peal of bells below,   5
    That wakens at this hour of rest
    A single murmur in the breast,
That these are not the bells I know.

Like strangers' voices here they sound,
    In lands where not a memory strays,   10
    Nor landmark breathes of other days,
But all is new unhallowed ground.

105

Tonight ungathered let us leave
    This laurel, let this holly stand;
    We live within the stranger's land,
And strangely falls our Christmas Eve.

Our father's dust is left alone   5
    And silent under other snows;
    There in due time the woodbine blows,
The violet comes, but we are gone.

No more shall wayward grief abuse
    The genial hour with mask and mime;   10
    For change of place, like growth of time,
Has broke the bond of dying use.

Section 103. This section is an allegory. The maidens of line 6 are explained by Tennyson as "the Muses, poetry, arts—all that make life beautiful here, which we hope will pass with us beyond the grave." He also said that the maidens are "all the human powers and talents that do not pass with life but go along with it."   The hidden summits (line 7) are the divine source; the river (line 8) is life; the sea (line 16) is eternity.
31. **Anakim.** See *Numbers*, 13:33.—"And there we saw the giants, the sons of Anak, which come of the giants: and we were in our own sight as grasshoppers, and so we were in their sight." 32. **Titan's.** The Titans were fabulous giants of Greek mythology.

Section 104. 1. **The time,** etc., the Christmas of 1837. Compare Sections 28, 30, and 78. 3. **church,** Waltham Abbey Church, near the new home of the Tennysons. *Section 105.* 7. **blows,** blooms.

Let cares that petty shadows cast,
　By which our lives are chiefly proved,
　A little spare the night I loved,　　　15
And hold it solemn to the past.

But let no footstep beat the floor,
　Nor bowl of wassail mantle warm;
　For who would keep an ancient form
Through which the spirit breathes no more?

Be neither song, nor game, nor feast;　21
　Nor harp be touched, nor flute be blown;
　No dance, no motion, save alone
What lightens in the lucid East

Of rising worlds by yonder wood.　　25
　Long sleeps the summer in the seed;
　Run out your measured arcs, and lead
The closing cycle rich in good.

106

Ring out, wild bells, to the wild sky,
　The flying cloud, the frosty light;
　The year is dying in the night;
Ring out, wild bells, and let him die.

Ring out the old, ring in the new,　　5
　Ring, happy bells, across the snow;
　The year is going, let him go;
Ring out the false, ring in the true.

Ring out the grief that saps the mind,
　For those that here we see no more;　10
　Ring out the feud of rich and poor,
Ring in redress to all mankind.

Ring out a slowly dying cause,
　And ancient forms of party strife;
　Ring in the nobler modes of life,　　15
With sweeter manners, purer laws.

Ring out the want, the care, the sin,
　The faithless coldness of the times;
　Ring out, ring out my mournful rimes,
But ring the fuller minstrel in.　　　20

Ring out false pride in place and blood,
　The civic slander and the spite;
　Ring in the love of truth and right,
Ring in the common love of good.

Ring out old shapes of foul disease;　25
　Ring out the narrowing lust of gold;
　Ring out the thousand wars of old,
Ring in the thousand years of peace.

Ring in the valiant man and free,
　The larger heart, the kindlier hand;　30
　Ring out the darkness of the land,
Ring in the Christ that is to be.

107

It is the day when he was born,
　A bitter day that early sank
　Behind a purple-frosty bank
Of vapor, leaving night forlorn.

The time admits not flowers or leaves　5
　To deck the banquet.　Fiercely flies
　The blast of North and East, and ice
Makes daggers at the sharpened eaves,

And bristles all the brakes and thorns
　To yon hard crescent, as she hangs　10
　Above the wood which grides and clangs
Its leafless ribs and iron horns

Together, in the drifts that pass
　To darken on the rolling brine
　That breaks the coast.　But fetch the wine,
Arrange the board and brim the glass;　16

Bring in great logs and let them lie,
　To make a solid core of heat;
　Be cheerful-minded, talk and treat
Of all things even as he were by;　　20

We keep the day.　With festal cheer,
　With books and music, surely we
　Will drink to him, whate'er he be,
And sing the songs he loved to hear.

108

I will not shut me from my kind,
　And, lest I stiffen into stone,
　I will not eat my heart alone,
Nor feed with sighs a passing wind;

What profit lies in barren faith,　　5
　And vacant yearning, though with might
　To scale the heaven's highest height,
Or dive below the wells of death?

What find I in the highest place,
　But mine own phantom chanting hymns?
　And on the depths of death there swims　11
The reflex of a human face.

I'll rather take what fruit may be
　Of sorrow under human skies;

Section 105.　18. wassail . . . warm, wine become frothy.
25. rising worlds, the rising stars.　28. closing cycle, the
great final period when everything will be perfect.
　Section 106.　28. the thousand years of peace. Mentioned several times in Revelation, 20.

Section 106.　32. the Christ that is to be, a reference, as
Tennyson said, to a time "when Christianity without big-
otry will triumph, when the controversies of creeds shall
have vanished" (Memoir, I, 326).
　Section 107.　1. day, February 1.　12. iron horns, twigs
covered with ice.　13. drifts, variously defined as drifts of
snow, clouds, winds, drift-winds, and vapor.

'Tis held that sorrow makes us wise,   15
Whatever wisdom sleep with thee.

109

Heart-affluence in discursive talk
  From household fountains never dry;
  The critic clearness of an eye
That saw through all the Muses' walk;

Seraphic intellect and force   5
  To seize and throw the doubts of man;
  Impassioned logic, which outran
The hearer in its fiery course;

High nature amorous of the good,
  But touched with no ascetic gloom;   10
  And passion pure in snowy bloom
Through all the years of April blood;

A love of freedom rarely felt,
  Of freedom in her regal seat
  Of England; not the schoolboy heat,   15
The blind hysterics of the Celt;

And manhood fused with female grace
  In such a sort, the child would twine
  A trustful hand, unasked, in thine,
And find his comfort in thy face —   20

All these have been, and thee mine eyes
  Have looked on; if they looked in vain,
  My shame is greater who remain,
Nor let thy wisdom make me wise.

110

Thy converse drew us with delight,
  The men of rathe and riper years;
  The feeble soul, a haunt of fears,
Forgot his weakness in thy sight.

On thee the loyal-hearted hung,   5
  The proud was half disarmed of pride,
  Nor cared the serpent at thy side
To flicker with his double tongue.

The stern were mild when thou wert by,
  The flippant put himself to school   10
  And heard thee, and the brazen fool
Was softened, and he knew not why;

While I, thy nearest, sat apart,
  And felt thy triumph was as mine;
  And loved them more, that they were
    thine,   15
The graceful tact, the Christian art;

Nor mine the sweetness or the skill,
  But mine the love that will not tire,
  And, born of love, the vague desire
That spurs an imitative will.   20

111

The churl in spirit, up or down
  Along the scale of ranks, through all,
  To him who grasps a golden ball,
By blood a king, at heart a clown —

The churl in spirit, howe'er he veil   5
  'His want in forms for fashion's sake,
  Will let his coltish nature break
At seasons through the gilded pale;

For who can always act? but he,
  To whom a thousand memories call,   10
  Not being less but more than all
The gentleness he seemed to be,

Best seemed the thing he was, and joined
  Each office of the social hour
  To noble manners, as the flower   15
And native growth of noble mind;

Nor ever narrowness or spite,
  Or villain fancy fleeting by,
  Drew in the expression of an eye
Where God and Nature met in light;   20

And thus he bore without abuse
  The grand old name of gentleman,
  Defamed by every charlatan,
And soiled with all ignoble use.

112

High wisdom holds my wisdom less,
  That I, who gaze with temperate eyes
  On glorious insufficiencies,
Set light by narrower perfectness.

But thou, that fillest all the room   5
  Of all my love, art reason why
  I seem to cast a careless eye
On souls, the lesser lords of doom.

For what wert thou? some novel power
  Sprang up forever at a touch,   10
  And hope could never hope too much,
In watching thee from hour to hour,

Section 109. Tennyson here enumerates Hallam's qualities of heart and mind.
  16. The . . . Celt. Tennyson did not admire the revolutionary spirit in France; he was a conservative. Cf. Section 127, 7.
Section 110. 2. rathe, early. 7. serpent, deceiver.

Section 111. 3. golden ball. The crown and the scepter of a king are each decorated with a ball of gold. 18. villain, low-bred, ignoble, churlish. 19. Drew in, narrowed, contracted.
Section 112. 1-4. A wise friend takes the poet to task for being indifferent to great men who have defects and for making small account of lesser men who are perfect in their small way. Both groups fall far short of Hallam. 8. the lesser lords of doom, "those that have free will but less intellect" (Tennyson's note).

Large elements in order brought,
    And tracts of calm from tempest made,
    And world-wide fluctuations swayed   15
In vassal tides that followed thought.

113

'Tis held that sorrow makes us wise;
    Yet how much wisdom sleeps with thee
    Which not alone had guided me,
But served the seasons that may rise;

For can I doubt, who knew thee keen   5
    In intellect, with force and skill
    To strive, to fashion, to fulfill —
I doubt not what thou wouldst have been:

A life in civic action warm,
    A soul on highest mission sent,   10
    A potent voice of Parliament,
A pillar steadfast in the storm,

Should licensed boldness gather force,
    Becoming, when the time has birth,
    A lever to uplift the earth   15
And roll it in another course,

With thousand shocks that come and go,
    With agonies, with energies,
    With overthrowings, and with cries,
And undulations to and fro.   20

114

Who loves not Knowledge? Who shall rail
    Against her beauty? May she mix
    With men and prosper! Who shall fix
Her pillars? Let her work prevail.

But on her forehead sits a fire;   5
    She sets her forward countenance
    And leaps into the future chance,
Submitting all things to desire.

Half-grown as yet, a child, and vain —
    She cannot fight the fear of death.   10
    What is she, cut from love and faith,
But some wild Pallas from the brain

Of demons? fiery-hot to burst
    All barriers in her onward race
    For power. Let her know her place;   15
She is the second, not the first.

A higher hand must make her mild,
    If all be not in vain, and guide
    Her footsteps, moving side by side
With Wisdom, like the younger child;   20

Section 114. 12. **Pallas.** In Greek mythology Pallas
Athena (Minerva), the goddess of wisdom, sprang full-armed
from the brain of Zeus.

For she is earthly of the mind,
    But Wisdom heavenly of the soul.
    O friend, who camest to thy goal
So early, leaving me behind,

I would the great world grew like thee,   25
    Who grewest not alone in power
    And knowledge, but by year and hour
In reverence and in charity.

115

Now fades the last long streak of snow,
    Now burgeons every maze of quick
    About the flowering squares, and thick
By ashen roots the violets blow.

Now rings the woodland loud and long,   5
    The distance takes a lovelier hue,
    And drowned in yonder living blue
The lark becomes a sightless song.

Now dance the lights on lawn and lea,
    The flocks are whiter down the vale,   10
    And milkier every milky sail
On winding stream or distant sea;

Where now the seamew pipes, or dives
    In yonder greening gleam, and fly
    The happy birds, that change their sky   15
To build and brood, that live their lives

From land to land; and in my breast,
    Spring wakens too, and my regret
    Becomes an April violet,
And buds and blossoms like the rest.   20

116

Is it, then, regret for buried time
    That keenlier in sweet April wakes,
    And meets the year, and gives and takes
The colors of the crescent prime?

Not all: the songs, the stirring air,   5
    The life re-orient out of dust,
    Cry through the sense to hearten trust
In that which made the world so fair.

Not all regret: the face will shine
    Upon me, while I muse alone,   10
    And that dear voice, I once have known,
Still speak to me of me and mine.

Yet less of sorrow lives in me
    For days of happy commune dead,

Section 114. 21-22. **For she . . . soul.** Cf. *Locksley Hall*,
141, p. 48, and *The Ancient Sage*, 37 ff., p. 168.
Section 115. Compare this section with Sections 38, 83, and
91.
    2. **burgeons,** buds, sprouts. **maze of quick,** intricate
rows of hawthorn hedge. 3. **squares,** fields. 4. **ashen
roots,** roots of ash trees. 4. **blow,** bloom.
Section 116. 4. **crescent prime,** growing springtime.

Less yearning for the friendship fled   15
Than some strong bond which is to be.

117

O days and hours, your work is this,
    To hold me from my proper place,
    A little while from his embrace,
For fuller gain of after bliss;

That out of distance might ensue   5
    Desire of nearness doubly sweet,
    And unto meeting, when we meet,
Delight a hundredfold accrue,

For every grain of sand that runs,
    And every span of shade that steals,   10
    And every kiss of toothéd wheels,
And all the courses of the suns.

118

Contemplate all this work of Time,
    The giant laboring in his youth;
    Nor dream of human love and truth,
As dying Nature's earth and lime;

But trust that those we call the dead   5
    Are breathers of an ampler day
    For ever nobler ends.   They say
The solid earth whereon we tread

In tracts of fluent heat began,
    And grew to seeming-random forms,   10
    The seeming prey of cyclic storms,
Till at the last arose the man;

Who throve and branched from clime to clime,
    The herald of a higher race,
    And of himself in higher place,   15
If so he type this work of time

Within himself, from more to more;
    Or, crowned with attributes of woe
    Like glories, move his course, and show
That life is not as idle ore,   20

But iron dug from central gloom,
    And heated hot with burning fears,
    And dipped in baths of hissing tears,
And battered with the shocks of doom

To shape and use.   Arise and fly   25
    The reeling Faun, the sensual feast;

Move upward, working out the beast,
And let the ape and tiger die.

119

Doors, where my heart was used to beat
    So quickly, not as one that weeps
    I come once more; the city sleeps;
I smell the meadow in the street;

I hear a chirp of birds; I see   5
    Betwixt the black fronts long-withdrawn
    A light-blue lane of early dawn,
And think of early days and thee,

And bless thee, for thy lips are bland,
    And bright the friendship of thine eye;   10
    And in my thoughts with scarce a sigh
I take the pressure of thine hand.

120

I trust I have not wasted breath:
    I think we are not wholly brain,
    Magnetic mockeries; not in vain,
Like Paul with beasts, I fought with Death;

Not only cunning casts in clay.   5
    Let Science prove we are, and then
    What matters Science unto men,
At least to me?   I would not stay.

Let him, the wiser man who springs
    Hereafter, up from childhood shape   10
    His action like the greater ape,
But I was *born* to other things.

121

Sad Hesper o'er the buried sun
    And ready, thou, to die with him,
    Thou watchest all things ever dim
And dimmer, and a glory done.

The team is loosened from the wain,   5
    The boat is drawn upon the shore;
    Thou listenest to the closing door,
And life is darkened in the brain.

Bright Phosphor, fresher for the night,
    By thee the world's great work is heard   10

Section 118. 27-28. **Move . . . die.** Although Tennyson believed that man evolved from lower forms, he may here refer only to man's baser passions.
Section 119. 1. **Doors,** etc. Tennyson again visits the London house of Hallam.   See Section 7.   4. **the meadow,** loads of new hay.
Section 120. 3. **Magnetic mockeries,** i.e., automatic machines controlled by electric force.   4. **Like Paul,** etc. From *1 Corinthians*, 15:32.—"If after the manner of men I have fought with beasts at Ephesus, what advantageth it me if the dead rise not?"   6-8. Tennyson protests against materialism, not evolution. If science should establish the doctrine of materialism, he would not care to live.
Section 121. Gerard Manley Hopkins thought this section "terribly beautiful."
1. **Hesper** is the Greek name for Venus as the evening star, **Phosphor** (line 9), for Venus as the morning star.

Section 117. 9-12. This stanza mentions four ways of measuring time: by the hourglass (9); by the sundial (10); by the clock (11); and by the movements of the heavenly bodies (12).
Section 118. 3-4. **Nor dream . . . lime,** do not believe that a mere physical interpretation of love is possible.   9. **fluent heat,** a reference to the nebular hypothesis of the origin of the solar system as set forth by Laplace in the early 19th century.   26. **Faun,** a mythical creature, half man and half goat, here representing the grosser nature of man.

Beginning, and the wakeful bird;   11
Behind thee comes the greater light.

The market boat is on the stream,
    And voices hail it from the brink;
    Thou hear'st the village hammer clink,   15
And see'st the moving of the team.

Sweet Hesper-Phosphor, double name
    For what is one, the first, the last,
    Thou, like my present and my past,
Thy place is changed; thou art the same.   20

122

O wast thou with me, dearest, then,
    While I rose up against my doom,
    And yearned to burst the folded gloom,
To bare the eternal heavens again,

To feel once more, in placid awe,   5
    The strong imagination roll
    A sphere of stars about my soul,
In all her motion one with law?

If thou wert with me, and the grave
    Divide us not, be with me now,   10
    And enter in at breast and brow,
Till all my blood, a fuller wave,

Be quickened with a livelier breath,
    And like an inconsiderate boy,
    As in the former flash of joy,   15
I slip the thoughts of life and death;

And all the breeze of Fancy blows,
    And every dewdrop paints a bow,
    The wizard lightnings deeply glow,
And every thought breaks out a rose.   20

123

There rolls the deep where grew the tree.
O earth, what changes hast thou seen!
    There where the long street roars hath been
The stillness of the central sea.

The hills are shadows, and they flow   5
    From form to form, and nothing stands;
    They melt like mist, the solid lands,
Like clouds they shape themselves and go.

But in my spirit will I dwell,
    And dream my dream, and hold it true;   10
    For though my lips may breathe adieu,
I cannot think the thing farewell.

124

That which we dare invoke to bless;
    Our dearest faith; our ghastliest doubt;
    He, They, One, All; within, without;
The Power in darkness whom we guess —

I found Him not in world or sun,   5
    Or eagle's wing, or insect's eye,
    Nor through the questions men may try,
The petty cobwebs we have spun.

If e'er when faith had fallen asleep,
    I heard a voice, "believe no more,"   10
    And heard an ever-breaking shore
That tumbled in the Godless deep,

A warmth within the breast would melt
    The freezing reason's colder part,
    And like a man in wrath the heart   15
Stood up and answered, "I have felt."

No, like a child in doubt and fear:
    But that blind clamor made me wise;
    Then was I as a child that cries,
But, crying, knows his father near;   20

And what I am beheld again
    What is, and no man understands;
    And out of darkness came the hands
That reach through nature, molding men.

125

Whatever I have said or sung,
    Some bitter notes my harp would give,
    Yea, though there often seemed to live
A contradiction on the tongue

Yet Hope had never lost her youth;   5
    She did but look through dimmer eyes;
    Or Love but played with gracious lies,
Because he felt so fixed in truth.

And if the song were full of care,
    He breathed the spirit of the song;   10
    And if the words were sweet and strong
He set his royal signet there;

Abiding with me till I sail
    To seek thee on the mystic deeps,
    And this electric force, that keeps   15
A thousand pulses dancing, fail.

126

Love is and was my lord and king,
    And in his presence I attend
    To hear the tidings of my friend,
Which every hour his couriers bring.

Section 121. 11. the wakeful bird, the cock. 17-19.
Sweet . . . past. His past is like Hesper, his present like
Phosphor. (See note on line 1 of this Section.)
Section 122. 18. paints a bow, reveals the colors of the
rainbow.

Section 124. 9-12. This stanza refers to the materialistic
philosophy condemned in Section 120. 16. "I have felt."
Tennyson believed that the deepest revelation of God comes
not through science or through reason, but through the heart.

Love is and was my king and lord,   5
  And will be, though as yet I keep
  Within the court on earth, and sleep
Encompassed by his faithful guard,

And hear at times a sentinel
  Who moves about from place to place,   10
  And whispers to the worlds of space,
In the deep night, that all is well.

127

And all is well, though faith and form
  Be sundered in the night of fear;
  Well roars the storm to those that hear
A deeper voice across the storm,

Proclaiming social truth shall spread,   5
  And justice, even though thrice again
  The red fool-fury of the Seine
Should pile her barricades with dead.

But ill for him that wears a crown,
  And him, the lazar, in his rags!   10
  They tremble, the sustaining crags;
The spires of ice are toppled down,

And molten up, and roar in flood;
  The fortress crashes from on high,
  The brute earth lightens to the sky,   15
And the great Æon sinks in blood,

And compassed by the fires of hell;
  While thou, dear spirit, happy star,
  O'erlook'st the tumult from afar,
And smilest, knowing all is well.   20

128

The love that rose on stronger wings,
  Unpalsied when he met with Death,
  Is comrade of the lesser faith
That sees the course of human things.

No doubt vast eddies in the flood   5
  Of onward time shall yet be made,
  And thronèd races may degrade;
Yet, O ye mysteries of good,

Wild Hours that fly with Hope and Fear,
  If all your office had to do   10
  With old results that look like new —
If this were all your mission here,

To draw, to sheathe a useless sword,
  To fool the crowd with glorious lies,
  To cleave a creed in sects and cries,   15
To change the bearing of a word,

To shift an arbitrary power,
  To cramp the student at his desk,
  To make old bareness picturesque
And tuft with grass a feudal tower,   20

Why, then my scorn might well descend
  On you and yours. I see in part
  That all, as in some piece of art,
Is toil coöperant to an end.

129

Dear friend, far off, my lost desire,
  So far, so near in woe and weal,
  O loved the most, when most I feel
There is a lower and a higher;

Known and unknown, human, divine;   5
  Sweet human hand and lips and eye;
  Dear heavenly friend that canst not die,
Mine, mine, forever, ever mine;

Strange friend, past, present, and to be;
  Loved deeplier, darklier understood;   10
  Behold, I dream a dream of good,
And mingle all the world with thee.

130

Thy voice is on the rolling air;
  I hear thee where the waters run;
  Thou standest in the rising sun,
And in the setting thou art fair.

What art thou then? I cannot guess;   5
  But though I seem in star and flower
  To feel thee some diffusive power,
I do not therefore love thee less.

My love involves the love before;
  My love is vaster passion now;   10
  Though mixed with God and Nature thou,
I seem to love thee more and more.

Far off thou art, but ever nigh;
  I have thee still, and I rejoice;
  I prosper, circled with thy voice;   15
I shall not lose thee though I die.

131

O living will that shalt endure
  When all that seems shall suffer shock,
  Rise in the spiritual rock,
Flow through our deeds and make them pure,

That we may lift from out of dust   5
  A voice as unto him that hears,

Section 127. **6-8. thrice . . . dead,** that is, the French Revolution of 1789, even if repeated three times. **16. Æon,** the whole duration of the world or of the universe.
  Section 128. **7. degrade,** degenerate.

Section 131. **1. living will,** explained by Tennyson as "free-will, the higher and enduring part of man." **3. the spiritual rock.** See *1 Corinthians,* 10:4.—"And did all drink the same spiritual drink; for they drank of that spiritual Rock that followed them, and that Rock was Christ."

A cry above the conquered years
To one that with us works, and trust,

With faith that comes of self-control,
  The truths that never can be proved   10
  Until we close with all we loved,
And all we flow from, soul in soul.

EPILOGUE

O true and tried, so well and long,
  Demand not thou a marriage lay;
  In that it is thy marriage day
Is music more than any song.

Nor have I felt so much of bliss   5
  Since first he told me that he loved
  A daughter of our house, nor proved
Since that dark day a day like this;

Though I since then have numbered o'er
  Some thrice three years; they went and
     came,   10
  Remade the blood and changed the frame,
And yet is love not less, but more;

No longer caring to embalm
  In dying songs a dead regret,
  But like a statue solid-set,   15
And molded in colossal calm.

Regret is dead, but love is more
  Than in the summers that are flown,
  For I myself with these have grown
To something greater than before;   20

Which makes appear the songs I made
  As echoes out of weaker times,
  As half but idle brawling rimes,
The sport of random sun and shade.

But where is she, the bridal flower,   25
  That must be made a wife ere noon?
  She enters, glowing like the moon
Of Eden on its bridal bower.

On me she bends her blissful eyes
  And then on thee; they meet thy look   30
  And brighten like the star that shook
Betwixt the palms of Paradise.

Oh, when her life was yet in bud,
  He too foretold the perfect rose.

For thee she grew, for thee she grows   35
Forever, and as fair as good.

And thou art worthy, full of power;
  As gentle; liberal-minded, great,
  Consistent; wearing all that weight
Of learning lightly like a flower.   40

But now set out. The noon is near,
  And I must give away the bride;
  She fears not, or with thee beside
And me behind her, will not fear.

For I that danced her on my knee,   45
  That watched her on her nurse's arm,
  That shielded all her life from harm,
At last must part with her to thee;

Now waiting to be made a wife,
  Her feet, my darling, on the dead;   50
  Their pensive tablets round her head,
And the most living words of life

Breathed in her ear. The ring is on,
  The "Wilt thou?" answered, and again
  The "Wilt thou?" asked, till out of twain 55
Her sweet "I will" has made you one.

Now sign your names, which shall be read,
  Mute symbols of a joyful morn,
  By village eyes as yet unborn.
The names are signed, and overhead   60

Begins the clash and clang that tells
  The joy to every wandering breeze;
  The blind wall rocks, and on the trees
The dead leaf trembles to the bells.

O happy hour, and happier hours   65
  Await them. Many a merry face
  Salutes them — maidens of the place,
That pelt us in the porch with flowers.

O happy hour, behold the bride
  With him to whom her hand I gave.   70
  They leave the porch, they pass the grave
That has today its sunny side.

Today the grave is bright for me,
  For them the light of life increased,
  Who stay to share the morning feast,   75
Who rest tonight beside the sea.

Let all my genial spirits advance
  To meet and greet a whiter sun;

Section 131. **7. the conquered years,** the victor Hours
of Section 1, line 13, overcome by Love and Immortality.
  Epilogue. The Epilogue celebrates the marriage of Edmund
Law Lushington and Cecilia Tennyson, the poet's youngest
sister, October 10, 1842. ·
  2. Demand . . . lay. Since Tennyson could not write
the marriage ode for his sister Emily and Hallam, he has not
the heart to write an ode for others. **8. that dark day,** the
day of Hallam's death. **31-32. the star . . . Paradise.**
From Catullus, *Ode* 64, 206. The stars shook when Jupiter
nodded approval of the marriage of the sea nymph Thetis to
the river-god Peleus.

  39-40. that weight Of learning. Lushington was a
noted professor of Greek at Glasgow. **50. on the dead,**
on the slabs covering the graves beneath the chancel floor of
the church. **57. sign your names,** i.e., in the parish register,
as was the custom.

My drooping memory will not shun
The foaming grape of eastern France. 80

It circles round, and fancy plays,
 And hearts are warmed and faces bloom,
 As drinking health to bride and groom
We wish them store of happy days.

Nor count me all to blame if I 85
 Conjecture of a stiller guest,
 Perchance, perchance, among the rest,
And, though in silence, wishing joy.

But they must go, the time draws on,
 And those white-favored horses wait; 90
 They rise, but linger; it is late;
Farewell, we kiss, and they are gone.

A shade falls on us like the dark
 From little cloudlets on the grass,
 But sweeps away as out we pass 95
To range the woods, to roam the park,

Discussing how their courtship grew,
 And talk of others that are wed,
 And how she looked, and what he said,
And back we come at fall of dew. 100

Again the feast, the speech, the glee,
 The shade of passing thought, the wealth
 Of words and wit, the double health,
The crowning cup, the three-times-three,

And last the dance; — till I retire. 105
 Dumb is that tower which spake so loud,
 And high in heaven the streaming cloud,
And on the downs a rising fire.

And rise, O moon, from yonder down,
 Till over down and over dale 110
 All night the shining vapor sail
And pass the silent-lighted town,

The white-faced halls, the glancing rills,
 And catch at every mountain head,
 And o'er the friths that branch and spread
Their sleeping silver through the hills; 116

And touch with shade the bridal doors,
 With tender gloom the roof, the wall;
 And breaking let the splendor fall
To spangle all the happy shores 120

By which they rest, and ocean sounds,
 And, star and system rolling past,
 A soul shall draw from out the vast
And strike his being into bounds,

86. **a stiller guest,** the spirit of Hallam. 108. **a rising
fire,** the glow from the moon. 115. **friths,** narrow arms of
the sea. 121. **sounds,** used here as a verb.

And, moved through life of lower phase, 125
 Result in man, be born and think,
 And act and love, a closer link
Betwixt us and the crowning race

Of those that, eye to eye, shall look
 On knowledge; under whose command 130
 Is Earth and Earth's, and in their hand
Is Nature like an open book;

No longer half-akin to brute,
 For all we thought and loved and did,
 And hoped, and suffered, is but seed 135
Of what in them is flower and fruit;

Whereof the man that with me trod
 This planet was a noble type
 Appearing ere the times were ripe,
That friend of mine who lives in God, 140

That God, which ever lives and loves,
 One God, one law, one element,
 And one far-off divine event,
To which the whole creation moves.
(1850)

THE EAGLE

FRAGMENT

He clasps the crag with crooked hands;
Close to the sun in lonely lands,
Ringed with the azure world, he stands.

The wrinkled sea beneath him crawls;
He watches from his mountain walls, 5
And like a thunderbolt he falls.
(1851)

COME NOT, WHEN I AM DEAD

Come not, when I am dead,
 To drop thy foolish tears upon my grave,
To trample round my fallen head,
 And vex the unhappy dust thou wouldst
  not save.
There let the wind sweep and the plover cry;
 But thou, go by. 6

Child, if it were thine error or thy crime
 I care no longer, being all unblest:
Wed whom thou wilt, but I am sick of time,
 And I desire to rest. 10
Pass on, weak heart, and leave me where I
 lie;
 Go by, go by.
(1851)

ODE ON THE DEATH OF THE DUKE
OF WELLINGTON

1

Bury the Great Duke
  With an empire's lamentation;
Let us bury the Great Duke
  To the noise of the mourning of a mighty
      nation;
Mourning when their leaders fall,   5
Warriors carry the warrior's pall,
And sorrow darkens hamlet and hall.

2

Where shall we lay the man whom we deplore?
Here, in streaming London's central roar.
Let the sound of those he wrought for,   10
And the feet of those he fought for,
Echo round his bones for evermore.

3

Lead out the pageant; sad and slow,
As fits an universal woe,
Let the long, long procession go,   15
And let the sorrowing crowd about it grow,
And let the mournful martial music blow;
The last great Englishman is low.

4

Mourn, for to us he seems the last,
Remembering all his greatness in the past. 20
No more in soldier fashion will he greet
With lifted hand the gazer in the street.
O friends, our chief state-oracle is mute!
Mourn for the man of long-enduring blood,
The statesman-warrior, moderate, resolute, 25
Whole in himself, a common good.
Mourn for the man of amplest influence,
Yet clearest of ambitious crime,
Our greatest yet with least pretense,
Great in council and great in war,   30
Foremost captain of his time,
Rich in saving common-sense,
And, as the greatest only are,
In his simplicity sublime.
O good gray head which all men knew,   35
O voice from which their omens all men drew,
O iron nerve to true occasion true,
O fallen at length that tower of strength
Which stood four-square to all the winds that
    blew!
Such was he whom we deplore.   40

The long self-sacrifice of life is o'er.
The great World-victor's victor will be seen
  no more.

5

All is over and done.
Render thanks to the Giver,
England, for thy son.   45
Let the bell be tolled.
Render thanks to the Giver,
And render him to the mold.
Under the cross of gold
That shines over city and river,   50
There he shall rest forever
Among the wise and the bold.
Let the bell be tolled,
And a reverent people behold
The towering car, the sable steeds.   55
Bright let it be with its blazoned deeds,
Dark in its funeral fold.
Let the bell be tolled,
And a deeper knell in the heart be knolled;
And the sound of the sorrowing anthem rolled
Through the dome of the golden cross;   61
And the volleying cannon thunder his loss;
He knew their voices of old.
For many a time in many a clime
His captain's-ear has heard them boom   65
Bellowing victory, bellowing doom.
When he with those deep voices wrought,
Guarding realms and kings from shame,
With those deep voices our dead captain
    taught
The tyrant, and asserts his claim   70
In that dread sound to the great name
Which he has worn so pure of blame,
In praise and in dispraise the same,
A man of well-attempered frame,
O civic muse, to such a name,   75
To such a name for ages long,
To such a name,
Preserve a broad approach of fame,
And ever-echoing avenues of song!

6

"Who is he that cometh, like an honored
  guest,   80
With banner and with music, with soldier
  and with priest,
With a nation weeping, and breaking on my
  rest?" —
Mighty Seaman, this is he

Ode on the Death of the Duke of Wellington. Arthur Wellesley, Duke of Wellington (1769-1852), was at the time of his death the hero of the British nation. He had a distinguished record of military victories, the greatest being the defeat of Napoleon at Waterloo, in 1815. Tennyson had genuine enthusiasm for his subject. The poem is one of the first and most important of his "occasional" pieces as poet laureate.

9. Here . . . roar. Wellington was buried in St. Paul's Cathedral, located in the heart of London.

42. World-victor's victor, the conqueror of Napoleon, who had aimed at the conquest of Europe. **49. the cross of gold,** the cross on St. Paul's Cathedral. **56. blazoned deeds.** The funeral car was inscribed with the names of Wellington's victories. **66. Bellowing victory,** a reference to the many victories of Wellington—in Holland, India, Denmark, Portugal, Spain, France, and Belgium. **80-82.** These lines are spoken by Lord Nelson, the Mighty Seaman, who lay buried in St. Paul's. He was killed at Trafalgar in 1805.

Was great by land as thou by sea.
Thine island loves thee well, thou famous
   man,   85
The greatest sailor since our world began.
Now, to the roll of muffled drums,
To thee the greatest soldier comes;
For this is he
Was great by land as thou by sea.   90
His foes were thine; he kept us free;
Oh, give him welcome, this is he
Worthy of our gorgeous rites,
And worthy to be laid by thee;
For this is England's greatest son,   95
He that gained a hundred fights,
Nor ever lost an English gun;
This is he that far away
Against the myriads of Assaye
Clashed with his fiery few and won;   100
And underneath another sun,
Warring on a later day,
Round affrighted Lisbon drew
The treble works, the vast designs
Of his labored rampart-lines,   105
Where he greatly stood at bay,
Whence he issued forth anew,
And ever great and greater grew,
Beating from the wasted vines
Back to France her banded swarms,   110
Back to France with countless blows,
Till o'er the hills her eagles flew
Beyond the Pyrenean pines,
Followed up in valley and glen
With blare of bugle, clamor of men,   115
Roll of cannon and clash of arms,
And England pouring on her foes.
Such a war had such a close.
Again their ravening eagle rose
In anger, wheeled on Europe-shadowing wings,
And barking for the thrones of kings;   121
Till one that sought but Duty's iron crown
On that loud Sabbath shook the spoiler down;
A day of onsets of despair!
Dashed on every rocky square,   125
Their surging charges foamed themselves
   away;
Last, the Prussian trumpet blew;
Through the long-tormented air
Heaven flashed a sudden jubilant ray,
And down we swept and charged and over-
   threw.   130
So great a soldier taught us there

What long-enduring hearts could do
In that world-earthquake, Waterloo!
Mighty Seaman, tender and true,
And pure as he from taint of craven guile,   135
O savior of the silver-coasted isle,
O shaker of the Baltic and the Nile,
If aught of things that here befall
Touch a spirit among things divine,
If love of country move thee there at all,   140
Be glad, because his bones are laid by thine!
And through the centuries let a people's voice
In full acclaim,
A people's voice,
The proof and echo of all human fame,   145
A people's voice, when they rejoice
At civic revel and pomp and game,
Attest their great commander's claim
With honor, honor, honor, honor to him,
Eternal honor to his name.   150

7

A people's voice! we are a people yet.
Though all men else their nobler dreams for-
   get,
Confused by brainless mobs and lawless
   Powers,
Thank Him who isled us here, and roughly
   set
His Briton in blown seas and storming
   showers,   155
We have a voice with which to pay the debt
Of boundless love and reverence and regret
To those great men who fought, and kept it
   ours.
And keep it ours, O God, from brute control!
O Statesmen, guard us, guard the eye, the
   soul   160
Of Europe, keep our noble England whole,
And save the one true seed of freedom sown
Betwixt a people and their ancient throne,
That sober freedom out of which there springs
Our loyal passion for our temperate kings!   165
For, saving that, ye help to save mankind
Till public wrong be crumbled into dust,
And drill the raw world for the march of mind,
Till crowds at length be sane and crowns be
   just.
But wink no more in slothful overtrust.   170
Remember him who led your hosts;
He bade you guard the sacred coasts.
Your cannons molder on the seaward wall;
His voice is silent in your council-hall
Forever; and whatever tempests lour   175

---

99. **Assaye,** a small town in British India, where the
Duke (then General Wellesley) won his first great victory,
in 1803; he defeated an army of more than 40,000 with a force
of less than 5000. 103. **Round,** etc. In 1809-10 Wellington
constructed the lines of defense around Lisbon, Portugal,
against the French. In 1813 he drove the French across the
Pyrenees Mountains into France. 123. **Sabbath.** The
Battle of Waterloo was fought on Sunday, June 18, 1815.
129. **Heaven . . . ray.** The records state that the sun broke
through the clouds just as the British and the German forces
responded to the Duke's command to advance.

136. **the silver-coasted isle,** England. 137. **the Baltic
and the Nile,** victorious battles fought by Nelson against
Napoleon—the Baltic in 1801, the Nile in 1798. In the Battle
of the Baltic, Nelson crushed the naval power of Denmark,
one of Napoleon's northern allies, in four hours. 170. **wink,**
shut the eye, be blind. 172. **He . . . coasts.** In 1844-45
Wellington insisted upon the repair of coast defenses and upon
an increase of naval and military equipment.

Forever silent; even if they broke
In thunder, silent; yet remember all
He spoke among you, and the Man who
    spoke;
Who never sold the truth to serve the hour,
Nor paltered with Eternal God for power; 180
Who let the turbid streams of rumor flow
Through either babbling world of high and
    low;
Whose life was work, whose language rife
With rugged maxims hewn from life;
Who never spoke against a foe; 185
Whose eighty winters freeze with one rebuke
All great self-seekers trampling on the right.
Truth-teller was our England's Alfred named;
Truth-lover was our English Duke;
Whatever record leap to light 190
He never shall be shamed.

8

Lo! the leader in these glorious wars
Now to glorious burial slowly borne,
Followed by the brave of other lands,
He, on whom from both her open hands 195
Lavish Honor showered all her stars,
And affluent Fortune emptied all her horn.
Yea, let all good things await
Him who cares not to be great
But as he saves or serves the state. 200
Not once or twice in our rough island-story
The path of duty was the way to glory.
He that walks it, only thirsting
For the right, and learns to deaden
Love of self, before his journey closes, 205
He shall find the stubborn thistle bursting
Into glossy purples, which outredden
All voluptuous garden-roses.
Not once or twice in our fair island-story
The path of duty was the way to glory. 210
He, that ever following her commands,
On with toil of heart and knees and hands,
Through the long gorge to the far light has
    won
His path upward, and prevailed,
Shall find the toppling crags of Duty scaled
Are close upon the shining table-lands 216
To which our God Himself is moon and sun.
Such was he; his work is done.
But while the races of mankind endure
Let his great example stand 220
Colossal, seen of every land,
And keep the soldier firm, the statesman pure;
Till in all lands and through all human story

The path of duty be the way to glory.
And let the land whose hearths he saved from
    shame 225
For many and many an age proclaim
At civic revel and pomp and game,
And when the long-illumined cities flame,
Their ever-loyal iron leader's fame,
With honor, honor, honor, honor to him, 230
Eternal honor to his name.

9

Peace, his triumph will be sung
By some yet unmolded tongue
Far on in summers that we shall not see.
Peace, it is a day of pain 235
For one about whose patriarchal knee
Late the little children clung.
O peace, it is a day of pain
For one upon whose hand and heart and brain
Once the weight and fate of Europe hung. 240
Ours the pain, be his the gain!
More than is of man's degree
Must be with us, watching here
At this, our great solemnity.
Whom we see not we revere; 245
We revere, and we refrain
From talk of battles loud and vain,
And brawling memories all too free
For such a wise humility
As befits a solemn fane. 250
We revere, and while we hear
The tides of Music's golden sea
Setting toward eternity,
Uplifted high in heart and hope are we,
Until we doubt not that for one so true 255
There must be other nobler work to do
Than when he fought at Waterloo,
And Victor he must ever be.
For though the Giant Ages heave the hill
And break the shore, and evermore 260
Make and break, and work their will,
Though world on world in myriad myriads
    roll
Round us, each with different powers,
And other forms of life than ours,
What know we greater than the soul? 265
On God and Godlike men we build our trust.
Hush, the Dead March wails in the people's
    ears;
The dark crowd moves, and there are sobs
    and tears;
The black earth yawns; the mortal disappears;
Ashes to ashes, dust to dust; 270
He is gone who seemed so great.—
Gone, but nothing can bereave him
Of the force he made his own
Being here, and we believe him

<hr>

186. **eighty winters.** Wellington lived to be 83 years old.
188. **Truth-teller,** a name given to King Alfred the Great in
the old annals. 194. **Followed . . . lands.** Military
representatives of all the powers of Europe, except Austria,
were present at the funeral. 196. **Lavish Honor,** etc.
Besides being baron, viscount, earl, marquis, and duke,
Wellington was a knight of twenty-six orders and a marshal
of eight nations.

<hr>

252. **Music,** the music at the funeral service. 267. **the
Dead March,** from Handel's oratorio *Saul.*

Something far advanced in State,   275
And that he wears a truer crown
Than any wreath that man can weave him.
Speak no more of his renown,
Lay your earthly fancies down,
And in the vast cathedral leave him,   280
God accept him, Christ receive him!
                                    (*1852*; 1852)

THE CHARGE OF THE LIGHT
BRIGADE

Half a league, half a league,
Half a league onward,
All in the valley of Death
    Rode the six hundred.
"Forward the Light Brigade!   5
Charge for the guns!" he said.
Into the valley of Death
    Rode the six hundred.

"Forward, the Light Brigade!"
Was there a man dismayed?   10
Not though the soldier knew
    Someone had blundered.
Theirs not to make reply,
Theirs not to reason why,
Theirs but to do and die.   15
Into the valley of Death
    Rode the six hundred.

Cannon to right of them,
Cannon to left of them,
Cannon in front of them   20
    Volleyed and thundered;
Stormed at with shot and shell,
Boldly they rode and well,
Into the jaws of Death,
Into the mouth of hell   25
    Rode the six hundred.

Flashed all their sabers bare,
Flashed as they turned in air
Sabring the gunners there,
Charging an army, while   30
    All the world wondered.
Plunged in the battery-smoke
Right through the line they broke;
Cossack and Russian
Reeled from the saber-stroke   35
    Shattered and sundered.
Then they rode back, but not,
    Not the six hundred.

Cannon to right of them,
Cannon to left of them,   40
Cannon behind them
    Volleyed and thundered;
Stormed at with shot and shell,
While horse and hero fell,
They that had fought so well   45
Came through the jaws of Death,
Back from the mouth of hell,
All that was left of them,
    Left of six hundred.

When can their glory fade?   50
O the wild charge they made!
    All the world wondered.
Honor the charge they made!
Honor the Light Brigade,
    Noble six hundred!   55
                                (*1854*; 1854)

THE SONG OF THE BROOK

I come from haunts of coot and hern,
    I make a sudden sally,
And sparkle out among the fern,
    To bicker down a valley.

By thirty hills I hurry down,   5
    Or slip between the ridges,
By twenty thorps, a little town,
    And half a hundred bridges.

Till last by Philip's farm I flow
    To join the brimming river,   10
For men may come and men may go,
    But I go on forever.

I chatter over stony ways,
    In little sharps and trebles,
I bubble into eddying bays,   15
    I babble on the pebbles.

With many a curve my banks I fret
    By many a field and fallow,
And many a fairy foreland set
    With willow-weed and mallow.   20

I chatter, chatter, as I flow
    To join the brimming river,
For men may come and men may go,
    But I go on forever.

I wind about, and in and out,   25
    With here a blossom sailing,

The Charge of the Light Brigade. The charge here described
took place in 1854 at Balaklava, on the Black Sea, in the
Crimean War, fought against Russia by England, France,
Turkey, and Sardinia. For a spirited account of the charge, see
Cecil Woodham-Smith, *The Reason Why.*

The Song of the Brook. This lyric appears in a narrative
poem, an English idyl entitled *The Brook.* In the longer poem,
Lawrence Aylmer, returning home after an absence of twenty
years, wanders by the brook and recalls the past and the rime
of the brook written by his brother Edmund. No particular
brook is meant.
    9. Philip. Philip is a character in the idyl.

And here and there a lusty trout,
And here and there a grayling,

And here and there a foamy flake
Upon me, as I travel   30
With many a silvery water-break
Above the golden gravel,

And draw them all along and flow
To join the brimming river,
For men may come and men may go,   35
But I go on forever.

I steal by lawns and grassy plots,
I slide by hazel covers;
I move the sweet forget-me-nots
That grow for happy lovers.   40

I slip, I slide, I gloom, I glance,
Among my skimming swallows;
I make the netted sunbeam dance
Against my sandy shallows.

I murmur under moon and stars   45
In brambly wildernesses;
I linger by my shingly bars,
I loiter round my cresses;

And out again I curve and flow
To join the brimming river,   50
For men may come and men may go,
But I go on forever.

    (1855)

MAUD

PART ONE

I

1

I hate the dreadful hollow behind the little
    wood;
Its lips in the field above are dabbled with
    blood-red heath,
The red-ribbed ledges drip with a silent horror
    of blood,
And Echo there, whatever is asked her, an-
    swers "Death."

2

For there in the ghastly pit long since a body
    was found,   5

31. **water-break**, ripple.   **38. covers,** thickets.   47.
shingly bars, banks of loose, coarse gravel.
Maud. The speaker of this poem is a morbid, sentimental
young man in love with Maud, the rich playmate of his
youth. Each section is a stage in the hero's development.
After a tragic love affair, the hero goes insane, but he is
finally restored under the influence of the noble emotions
aroused by the Crimean War. (See Critical Notes.)

His who had given me life — O father! O
    God! was it well? —
Mangled, and flattened, and crushed, and
    dinted into the ground;
There yet lies the rock that fell with him
    when he fell.

3

Did he fling himself down? who knows? for a
    vast speculation had failed,
And ever he muttered and maddened, and
    ever wanned with despair,   10
And out he walked when the wind like a
    broken worldling wailed,
And the flying gold of the ruined woodlands
    drove through the air.

4

I remembered the time, for the roots of my
    hair were stirred
By a shuffled step, by a dead weight trailed,
    by a whispered fright,
And my pulses closed their gates with a shock
    on my heart as I heard   15
The shrill-edged shriek of a mother divide the
    shuddering night.

5

Villainy somewhere! whose? One says, we
    are villains all.
Not he; his honest fame should at least by
    me be maintained;
But that old man, now lord of the broad
    estate and the Hall,
Dropped off gorged from a scheme that had
    left us flaccid and drained.   20

6

Why do they prate of the blessings of peace?
    we have made them a curse,
Pickpockets, each hand lusting for all that is
    not its own;
And lust of gain, in the spirit of Cain, is it
    better or worse
Than the heart of the citizen hissing in war
    on his own hearthstone?

7

But these are the days of advance, the works
    of the men of mind,   25
When who but a fool would have faith in a
    tradesman's ware or his word?
Is it peace or war? Civil war, as I think, and
    that of a kind
The viler, as underhand, not openly bearing
    the sword.

8

Sooner or later I too may passively take the
   print
Of the golden age — why not? I have neither
   hope nor trust;   30
May make my heart as a millstone, set my
   face as a flint,
Cheat and be cheated, and die — who knows?
   we are ashes and dust.

9

Peace sitting under her olive, and slurring
   the days gone by,
When the poor are hoveled and hustled together, each sex, like swine,
When only the ledger lives, and when only
   not all men lie;   35
Peace in her vineyard — yes! — but a company forges the wine.

10

And the vitriol madness flushes up in the
   ruffian's head,
Till the filthy by-lane rings to the yell of the
   trampled wife,
And chalk and alum and plaster are sold to
   the poor for bread,
And the spirit of murder works in the very
   means of life,   40

11

And Sleep must lie down armed, for the villainous center-bits
Grind on the wakeful ear in the hush of the
   moonless nights,
While another is cheating the sick of a few
   last gasps, as he sits
To pestle a poisoned poison behind his crimson lights.

12

When a Mammonite mother kills her babe
   for a burial fee,   45
And Timour-Mammon grins on a pile of children's bones,
Is it peace or war? better, war! loud war by
   land and by sea,
War with a thousand battles, and shaking a
   hundred thrones!

13

For I trust if an enemy's fleet came yonder
   round by the hill,

41. **center-bit,** an instrument used for drilling holes; it
is a common tool of burglars. 45. **Mammonite,** one devoted
to the pursuit of wealth. Mammon is the god of wealth.
46. This line refers to the alleged brutalities of Timour, or
Tamerlane, the great Mongolian conqueror of the 14th
century. At the capture of Siwas he is said to have had a
thousand children crushed under the feet of his horsemen.

And the rushing battle-bolt sang from the
   three-decker out of the foam,   50
That the smooth-faced, snub-nosed rogue
   would leap from his counter and till,
And strike, if he could, were it but with his
   cheating yardwand, home. —

14

What! am I raging alone as my father raged
   in his mood?
Must *I* too creep to the hollow and dash
   myself down and die
Rather than hold by the law that I made,
   nevermore to brood   55
On a horror of shattered limbs and a wretched
   swindler's lie?

15

Would there be sorrow for *me?* there was *love*
   in the passionate shriek,
Love for the silent thing that had made false
   haste to the grave —
Wrapped in a cloak, as I saw him, and thought
   he would rise and speak
And rave at the lie and the liar, ah God, as
   he used to rave.   60

16

I am sick of the Hall and the hill, I am sick
   of the moor and the main.
Why should I stay? can a sweeter chance
   ever come to me here?
Oh, having the nerves of motion as well as
   the nerves of pain,
Were it not wise if I fled from the place and
   the pit and the fear?

17

Workmen up at the Hall! — they are coming
   back from abroad;   65
The dark old place will be gilt by the touch
   of a millionaire.
I have heard, I know not whence, of the
   singular beauty of Maud;
I played with the girl when a child; she promised then to be fair.

18

Maud, with her venturous climbings and
   tumbles and childish escapes,
Maud, the delight of the village, the ringing
   joy of the Hall,   70
Maud, with her sweet purse-mouth when my
   father dangled the grapes,
Maud, the beloved of my mother, the moon-
   faced darling of all —

19

What is she now? My dreams are bad. She
   may bring me a curse.

No, there is fatter game on the moor; she
    will let me alone.
Thanks; for the fiend best knows whether
    woman or man be the worse.   75
I will bury myself in myself, and the Devil
    may pipe to his own.

II

Long have I sighed for a calm; God grant I
    may find it at last!
It will never be broken by Maud; she has
    neither savor nor salt,
But a cold and clear-cut face, as I found when
    her carriage passed,
Perfectly beautiful; let it be granted her;
    where is the fault?   80
All that I saw — for her eyes were downcast,
    not to be seen —
Faultily faultless, icily regular, splendidly
    null,
Dead perfection, no more; nothing more, if it
    had not been
For a chance of travel, a paleness, an hour's
    defect of the rose,
Or an underlip, you may call it a little too
    ripe, too full,   85
Or the least little delicate aquiline curve in a
    sensitive nose,
From which I escaped heart-free, with the
    least little touch of spleen.

III

Cold and clear-cut face, why come you so
    cruelly meek,
Breaking a slumber in which all spleenful
    folly was drowned?
Pale with the golden beam of an eyelash dead
    on the cheek,   90
Passionless, pale, cold face, star-sweet on a
    gloom profound;
Womanlike, taking revenge too deep for a
    transient wrong
Done but in thought to your beauty, and
    ever as pale as before
Growing and fading and growing upon me
    without a sound,
Luminous, gemlike, ghostlike, deathlike, half
    the night long   95
Growing and fading and growing, till I could
    bear it no more,
But arose, and all by myself in my own dark
    garden ground,
Listening now to the tide in its broad-flung
    shipwrecking roar,
Now to the scream of a maddened beach
    dragged down by the wave,

Walked in a wintry wind by a ghastly glim-
    mer, and found   100
The shining daffodil dead, and Orion low in
    his grave.

IV

1

A million emeralds break from the ruby-
    budded lime
In the little grove where I sit — ah, where-
    fore cannot I be
Like things of the season gay, like the bounti-
    ful season bland,
When the far-off sail is blown by the breeze
    of a softer clime,   105
Half-lost in the liquid azure bloom of a cres-
    cent of sea,
The silent sapphire-spangled marriage ring of
    the land?

2

Below me, there, is the village, and looks how
    quiet and small!
And yet bubbles o'er like a city, with gossip,
    scandal, and spite;
And Jack on his ale-house bench has as many
    lies as a Czar;   110
And here on the landward side, by a red rock,
    glimmers the Hall;
And up in the high Hall-garden I see her pass
    like a light;
But sorrow seize me if ever that light be my
    leading star!

3

When have I bowed to her father, the wrinkled
    head of the race?
I met her today with her brother, but not to
    her brother I bowed;   115
I bowed to his lady-sister as she rode by on
    the moor,
But the fire of a foolish pride flashed over her
    beautiful face.
O child, you wrong your beauty, believe it,
    in being so proud;
Your father has wealth well-gotten, and I am
    nameless and poor.

4

I keep but a man and a maid, ever ready to
    slander and steal;   120
I know it, and smile a hard-set smile, like a
    stoic, or like
A wiser epicurean, and let the world have its
    way.
For nature is one with rapine, a harm no
    preacher can heal;

101. **Orion**, a large constellation in the shape of a man.

The Mayfly is torn by the swallow, the spar-
    row speared by the shrike,
And the whole little wood where I sit is a
    world of plunder and prey.   125

5

We are puppets, Man in his pride, and Beauty
    fair in her flower;
Do we move ourselves, or are moved by an
    unseen hand at a game
That pushes us off from the board, and others
    ever succeed?
Ah yet, we cannot be kind to each other here
    for an hour;
We whisper, and hint, and chuckle, and grin
    at a brother's shame;   130
However we brave it out, we men are a little
    breed.

6

A monstrous eft was of old the lord and
    master of earth,
For him did his high sun flame, and his river
    billowing ran,
And he felt himself in his force to be Nature's
    crowning race.
As nine months go to the shaping an infant
    ripe for his birth,   135
So many a million of ages have gone to the
    making of man;
He now is first, but is he the last? is he not
    too base?

7

The man of science himself is fonder of glory,
    and vain,
An eye well-practiced in nature, a spirit
    bounded and poor;
The passionate heart of the poet is whirled
    into folly and vice.   140
I would not marvel at either, but keep a
    temperate brain;
For not to desire or admire, if a man could
    learn it, were more
Than to walk all day like the sultan of old in
    a garden of spice.

8

For the drift of the Maker is dark, an Isis
    hid by the veil.
Who knows the ways of the world, how God
    will bring them about?   145
Our planet is one, the suns are many, the
    world is wide.
Shall I weep if a Poland fall? shall I shriek
    if a Hungary fail?

144. **Isis,** an Egyptian goddess of fruitfulness. 147.
Poland . . . fail, a reference to the final dismemberment of
Poland by Russia and Austria in 1846, and to the defeat of
the Hungarians in their revolt against Austrian rule in 1849.

Or an infant civilization be ruled with rod or
    with knout?
I have not made the world, and He that made
    it will guide.

9

Be mine a philosopher's life in the quiet
    woodland ways,   150
Where if I cannot be gay let a passionless
    peace be my lot,
Far-off from the clamor of liars belied in the
    hubbub of lies;
From the long-necked geese of the world that
    are ever hissing dispraise
Because their natures are little, and, whether
    he heed it or not,
Where each man walks with his head in a
    cloud of poisonous flies.   155

10

And most of all would I flee from the cruel
    madness of love,
The honey of poison-flowers and all the
    measureless ill.
Ah, Maud, you milk-white fawn, you are all
    unmeet for a wife.
Your mother is mute in her grave as her
    image in marble above;
Your father is ever in London, you wander
    about at your will;   160
You have but fed on the roses and lain in the
    lilies of life.

V

1

A voice by the cedar tree
In the meadow under the Hall!
She is singing an air that is known to me,
A passionate ballad gallant and gay,   165
A martial song like a trumpet's call!
Singing alone in the morning of life,
In the happy morning of life and of May,
Singing of men that in battle array,
Ready in heart and ready in hand,   170
March with banner and bugle and fife
To the death, for their native land.

2

Maud with her exquisite face,
And wild voice pealing up to the sunny sky,
And feet like sunny gems on an English green,
Maud in the light of her youth and her grace,
Singing of Death, and of Honor that cannot
    die,   177
Till I well could weep for a time so sordid
    and mean,
And myself so languid and base.

162. **A voice,** Maud's.

3

Silence, beautiful voice!   180
Be still, for you only trouble the mind
With a joy in which I cannot rejoice,
A glory I shall not find.
Still! I will hear you no more,
For your sweetness hardly leaves me a choice
But to move to the meadow and fall before 186
Her feet on the meadow grass, and adore,
Not her, who is neither courtly nor kind,
Not her, not her, but a voice.

VI

1

Morning arises stormy and pale,   190
No sun, but a wannish glare
In fold upon fold of hueless cloud;
And the budded peaks of the wood are bowed,
Caught, and cuffed by the gale;
I had fancied it would be fair.   195

2

Whom but Maud should I meet
Last night, when the sunset burned
On the blossomed gable-ends
At the head of the village street,
Whom but Maud should I meet?   200
And she touched my hand with a smile so
        sweet,
She made me divine amends
For a courtesy not returned.

3

And thus a delicate spark
Of glowing and growing light   205
Through the livelong hours of the dark
Kept itself warm in the heart of my dreams,
Ready to burst in a colored flame;
Till at last, when the morning came
In a cloud, it faded, and seems   210
But an ashen-gray delight.

4

What if with her sunny hair,
And smile as sunny as cold,
She meant to weave me a snare
Of some coquettish deceit,   215
Cleopatra-like as of old
To entangle me when we met,
To have her lion roll in a silken net
And fawn at a victor's feet?

5

Ah, what shall I be at fifty   220
Should Nature keep me alive,
If I find the world so bitter

When I am but twenty-five?
Yet, if she were not a cheat,
If Maud were all that she seemed,   225
And her smile were all that I dreamed,
Then the world were not so bitter
But a smile could make it sweet.

6

What if, though her eye seemed full
Of a kind intent to me,   230
What if that dandy-despot, he,
That jeweled mass of millinery,
That oiled and curled Assyrian bull
Smelling of musk and of insolence,
Her brother, from whom I keep aloof,   235
Who wants the finer politic sense
To mask, though but in his own behoof,
With a glassy smile his brutal scorn —
What if he had told her yestermorn
How prettily for his own sweet sake   240
A face of tenderness might be feigned,
And a moist mirage in desert eyes,
That so, when the rotten hustings shake
In another month to his brazen lies,
A wretched vote may be gained?   245

7

For a raven ever croaks, at my side,
Keep watch and ward, keep watch and ward,
Or thou wilt prove their tool.
Yea, too, myself from myself I guard,
For often a man's own angry pride   250
Is cap and bells for a fool.

8

Perhaps the smile and tender tone
Came out of her pitying womanhood,
For am I not, am I not, here alone
So many a summer since she died,   255
My mother, who was so gentle and good?
Living alone in an empty house,
Here half-hid in the gleaming wood,
Where I hear the dead at midday moan,
And the shrieking rush of the wainscot mouse,
And my own sad name in corners cried,   261
When the shiver of dancing leaves is thrown
About its echoing chambers wide,
Till a morbid hate and horror have grown
Of a world in which I have hardly mixed, 265
And a morbid eating lichen fixed
On a heart half-turned to stone.

9

O heart of stone, are you flesh, and caught
By that you swore to withstand?

203. courtesy, curtsy or bow.

233. **Assyrian bull.** Assyrian antiquities include sculptured bulls with wings and heavy-featured human heads. 243. **hustings,** a platform from which a candidate for Parliament addressed the electors. 251. **cap and bells,** a reference to the medieval fool's bauble, consisting of a representation of a fool's head with cap and bells.

For what was it else within me wrought 270
But, I fear, the new strong wine of love,
That made my tongue so stammer and trip
When I saw the treasured splendor, her hand,
Come sliding out of her sacred glove,
And the sunlight broke from her lip? 275

10

I have played with her when a child;
She remembers it now we meet.
Ah, well, well, well, I *may* be beguiled
By some coquettish deceit.
Yet, if she were not a cheat, 280
If Maud were all that she seemed,
And her smile had all that I dreamed,
Then the world were not so bitter
But a smile could make it sweet.

VII

1

Did I hear it half in a doze 285
  Long since, I know not where?
Did I dream it an hour ago,
  When asleep in this arm-chair?

2

Men were drinking together,
  Drinking and talking of me: 290
"Well, if it prove a girl, the boy
  Will have plenty; so let it be."

3

Is it an echo of something
  Read with a boy's delight,
Viziers nodding together 295
  In some Arabian night?

4

Strange, that I hear two men,
  Somewhere, talking of me:
"Well, if it prove a girl, my boy
  Will have plenty; so let it be." 300

VIII

She came to the village church,
And sat by a pillar alone;
An angel watching an urn
Wept over her, carved in stone;
And once, but once, she lifted her eyes, 305
And suddenly, sweetly, strangely blushed
To find they were met by my own;
And suddenly, sweetly, my heart beat stronger
And thicker, until I heard no longer
The snowy-banded, dilettante, 310
Delicate-handed priest intone;

295. **Viziers,** high officials of various Mohammedan countries.

And thought, is it pride? and mused and
  sighed,
"No surely, now it cannot be pride."

IX

I was walking a mile,
More than a mile from the shore, 315
The sun looked out with a smile
Betwixt the cloud and the moor;
And riding at set of day
Over the dark moor land,
Rapidly riding far away, 320
She waved to me with her hand.
There were two at her side,
Something flashed in the sun,
Down by the hill I saw them ride,
In a moment they were gone; 325
Like a sudden spark
Struck vainly in the night,
Then returns the dark
With no more hope of light.

X

1

Sick, am I sick of a jealous dread? 330
Was not one of the two at her side
This new-made lord, whose splendor plucks
The slavish hat from the villager's head?
Whose old grandfather has lately died,
Gone to a blacker pit, for whom 335
Grimy nakedness dragging his trucks
And laying his trams in a poisoned gloom
Wrought, till he crept from a gutted mine
Master of half a servile shire,
And left his coal all turned into gold 340
To a grandson, first of his noble line,
Rich in the grace all women desire,
Strong in the power that all men adore,
And simper and set their voices lower,
And soften as if to a girl, and hold 345
Awe-stricken breaths at a work divine,
Seeing his gewgaw castle shine,
New as his title, built last year,
There amid perky larches and pine,
And over the sullen-purple moor — 350
Look at it — pricking a cockney ear.

2

What, has he found my jewel out?
For one of the two that rode at her side
Bound for the Hall, I am sure was he;
Bound for the Hall, and I think for a bride.
Blithe would her brother's acceptance be. 356
Maud could be gracious too, no doubt,
To a lord, a captain, a padded shape,
A bought commission, a waxen face,
A rabbit mouth that is ever agape — 360

Bought? what is it he cannot buy?
And therefore splenetic, personal, base,
A wounded thing with a rancorous cry,
At war with myself and a wretched race,
Sick, sick to the heart of life, am I.   365

3

Last week came one to the county town,
To preach our poor little army down,
And play the game of the despot kings,
Though the state has done it and thrice as
      well.   369
This broad-brimmed hawker of holy things,
Whose ear is crammed with his cotton, and
      rings
Even in dreams to the chink of his pence,
This huckster put down war! can he tell
Whether war be a cause or a consequence?
Put down the passions that make earth hell!
Down with ambition, avarice, pride,   376
Jealousy, down! cut off from the mind
The bitter springs of anger and fear!
Down too, down at your own fireside,
With the evil tongue and the evil ear,   380
For each is at war with mankind!

4

I wish I could hear again
The chivalrous battle-song
That she warbled alone in her joy!
I might persuade myself then   385
She would not do herself this great wrong,
To take a wanton dissolute boy
For a man and leader of men.

5

Ah God, for a man with heart, head, hand,
Like some of the simple great ones gone   390
Forever and ever by,
One still strong man in a blatant land,
Whatever they call him — what care I? —
Aristocrat, democrat, autocrat — one
Who can rule and dare not lie!   395

6

And ah for a man to arise in me,
That the man I am may cease to be!

XI

1

Oh, let the solid ground
   Not fail beneath my feet
Before my life has found   400
   What some have found so sweet!

Then let come what come may,
What matter if I go mad,
I shall have had my day.

2

Let the sweet heavens endure,   405
   Not close and darken above me
Before I am quite, quite sure
   That there is one to love me!
Then let come what come may
To a life that has been so sad —   410
I shall have had my day.

XII

1

Birds in the high Hall-garden
   When twilight was falling,
Maud, Maud, Maud, Maud,
   They were crying and calling.   415

2

Where was Maud? in our wood;
   And I — who else? — was with her,
Gathering woodland lilies,
   Myriads blow together.

3

Birds in our wood sang   420
   Ringing through the valleys,
Maud is here, here, here
   In among the lilies.

4

I kissed her slender hand,
   She took the kiss sedately;   425
Maud is not seventeen,
   But she is tall and stately.

5

I to cry out on pride
   Who have won her favor!
Oh, Maud were sure of heaven   430
   If lowliness could save her!

6

I know the way she went
   Home with her maiden posy,
For her feet have touched the meadows
   And left the daisies rosy.   435

7

Birds in the high Hall-garden
   Were crying and calling to her,
Where is Maud, Maud, Maud?
   One is come to woo her.

---

370. **This broad-brimmed,** etc., someone who wore
the broad-brimmed hat of the Quakers; sometimes taken to
refer to John Bright (1811-1889), who was a Quaker and who
was prominent in the party opposing the war with Russia at
the time this poem was written.

419. **blow,** bloom. 434-435. **For . . . rosy.** The underside of the English daisy is rose-colored. Maud's dress
brushed the daisies and bent them over so that the underside
was visible.

8

Look, a horse at the door,	440

Look, a horse at the door, 440
    And little King Charley snarling!
Go back, my lord, across the moor,
    You are not her darling.

XIII

1

Scorned, to be scorned by one that I scorn,
Is that a matter to make me fret? 445
That a calamity hard to be borne?
Well, he may live to hate me yet.
Fool that I am to be vexed with his pride!
I passed him, I was crossing his lands;
He stood on the path a little aside; 450
His face, as I grant, in spite of spite,
Has a broad-blown comeliness, red and white,
And six feet two, as I think, he stands;
But his essences turned the live air sick,
And barbarous opulence jewel-thick 455
Sunned itself on his breast and his hands.

2

Who shall call me ungentle, unfair?
I longed so heartily then and there
To give him the grasp of fellowship;
But while I passed he was humming an air,
Stopped, and then with a riding-whip 461
Leisurely tapping a glossy boot,
And curving a contumelious lip,
Gorgonized me from head to foot
With a stony British stare. 465

3

Why sits he here in his father's chair?
That old man never comes to his place;
Shall I believe him ashamed to be seen?
For only once, in the village street,
Last year, I caught a glimpse of his face, 470
A gray old wolf and a lean.
Scarcely, now, would I call him a cheat;
For then, perhaps, as a child of deceit,
She might by a true descent be untrue;
And Maud is as true as Maud is sweet, 475
Though I fancy her sweetness only due
To the sweeter blood by the other side;
Her mother has been a thing complete,
However she came to be so allied.
And fair without, faithful within, 480
Maud to him is nothing akin.
Some peculiar mystic grace
Made her only the child of her mother,
And heaped the whole inherited sin
On that huge scapegoat of the race, 485
All, all upon the brother.

4

Peace, angry spirit, and let him be!
Has not his sister smiled on me?

XIV

1

Maud has a garden of roses
And lilies fair on a lawn; 490
There she walks in her state
And tends upon bed and bower,
And thither I climbed at dawn
And stood by her garden-gate.
A lion ramps at the top, 495
He is clasped by a passion-flower.

2

Maud's own little oak-room —
Which Maud, like a precious stone
Set in the heart of the carven gloom,
Lights with herself, when alone 500
She sits by her music and books
And her brother lingers late
With a roystering company — looks
Upon Maud's own garden-gate;
And I thought as I stood, if a hand, as white
As ocean-foam in the moon, were laid 506
On the hasp of the window, and my Delight
Had a sudden desire, like a glorious ghost, to
    glide,
Like a beam of the seventh heaven, down to
    my side,
There were but a step to be made. 510

3

The fancy flattered my mind,
And again seemed overbold;
Now I thought that she cared for me,
Now I thought she was kind
Only because she was cold. 515

4

I heard no sound where I stood
But the rivulet on from the lawn
Running down to my own dark wood,
Or the voice of the long sea-wave as it swelled
Now and then in the dim-gray dawn; 520
But I looked, and round, all round the house
    I beheld
The death-white curtain drawn,
Felt a horror over me creep,
Prickle my skin and catch my breath,

---

441. **Charley,** a spaniel. 464. **Gorgonized,** turned to stone (from *Gorgon,* a hideous monster of Greek mythology the sight of which turned the beholder to stone).

492. **bed and bower,** flower bed and arbor. 509. **the seventh heaven.** In ancient times the space around the earth was divided into a series of heavens of varying number. The seventh heaven represents the place or state of supreme bliss.

Knew that the death-white curtain meant
  but sleep,   525
Yet I shuddered and thought like a fool of
  the sleep of death.

XV

So dark a mind within me dwells,
  And I make myself such evil cheer,
That if *I* be dear to someone else,
  Then someone else may have much to fear;
But if *I* be dear to someone else,   531
  Then I should be to myself more dear.
Shall I not take care of all that I think,
Yea, even of wretched meat and drink,
If I be dear,   535
If I be dear to someone else?

XVI

I

This lump of earth has left his estate
The lighter by the loss of his weight;
And so that he find what he went to seek,
And fulsome pleasure clog him, and drown 540
His heart in the gross mud-honey of town,
He may stay for a year who has gone for a
  week.
But this is the day when I must speak,
And I see my oread coming down,
Oh, this is the day!   545
O beautiful creature, what am I
That I dare to look her way?
Think I may hold dominion sweet,
Lord of the pulse that is lord of her breast,
And dream of her beauty with tender dread,
From the delicate Arab arch of her feet   551
To the grace that, bright and light as the
  crest
Of a peacock, sits on her shining head,
And she knows it not — O if she knew it,
To know her beauty might half undo it!   555
I know it the one bright thing to save
My yet young life in the wilds of Time,
Perhaps from madness, perhaps from crime,
Perhaps from a selfish grave.

2

What, if she be fastened to this fool lord, 560
Dare I bid her abide by her word?
Should I love her so well if she
Had given her word to a thing so low?
Shall I love her as well if she
Can break her word were it even for me? 565
I trust that it is not so.

544. **oread,** a mountain nymph. 551. **Arab arch,** like
the arched neck of the Arabian horse.

3

Catch not my breath, O clamorous heart,
Let not my tongue be a thrall to my eye,
For I must tell her before we part,
I must tell her, or die.   570

XVII

Go not, happy day,
  From the shining fields,
Go not, happy day,
  Till the maiden yields.
Rosy is the West,   575
  Rosy is the South,
Roses are her cheeks,
  And a rose her mouth.
When the happy Yes
  Falters from her lips,   580
Pass and blush the news
  Over glowing ships;
Over blowing seas,
  Over seas at rest,
Pass the happy news,   585
  Blush it through the West;
Till the red man dance
  By his red cedar-tree,
And the red man's babe
  Leap, beyond the sea.   590
Blush from West to East,
  Blush from East to West,
Till the West is East,
  Blush it through the West.
Rosy is the West,   595
  Rosy is the South,
Roses are her cheeks,
  And a rose her mouth.

XVIII

I

I have led her home, my love, my only friend.
There is none like her, none.   600
And never yet so warmly ran my blood
And sweetly, on and on
Calming itself to the long-wished-for end,
Full to the banks, close on the promised good.

2

None like her, none.   605
Just now the dry-tongued laurels' pattering
  talk
Seemed her light foot along the garden walk,
And shook my heart to think she comes once
  more.

Section XVII. This section is commonly regarded as a
notable example of "the flowing richness of Tennyson's
rhythm." It is more operatic than rational, and Tennyson
read it aloud with great animation.

But even then I heard her close the door;
The gates of heaven are closed, and she is
    gone.   610

3

There is none like her, none,
Nor will be when our summers have deceased.
Oh, art thou sighing for Lebanon
In the long breeze that streams to thy de-
    licious East,
Sighing for Lebanon,   615
Dark cedar, though thy limbs have here in-
    creased,
Upon a pastoral slope as fair,
And looking to the South and fed
With honeyed rain and delicate air,
And haunted by the starry head   620
Of her whose gentle will has changed my fate,
And made my life a perfumed altar-flame;
And over whom thy darkness must have
    spread
With such delight as theirs of old, thy great
Forefathers of the thornless garden, there 625
Shadowing the snow-limbed Eve from whom
    she came?

4

Here will I lie, while these long branches
    sway,
And you fair stars that crown a happy day
Go in and out as if at merry play,
Who am no more so all forlorn   630
As when it seemed far better to be born
To labor and the mattock-hardened hand
Than nursed at ease and brought to under-
    stand
A sad astrology, the boundless plan
That makes you tyrants in your iron skies,
Innumerable, pitiless, passionless eyes,   636
Cold fires, yet with power to burn and brand
His nothingness into man.

5

But now shine on, and what care I,
Who in this stormy gulf have found a pearl 640
The countercharm of space and hollow sky,
And do accept my madness, and would die
To save from some slight shame one simple
    girl? —

6

Would die, for sullen-seeming Death may give
More life to Love than is or ever was   645
In our low world, where yet 'tis sweet to live.

Let no one ask me how it came to pass;
It seems that I am happy, that to me
A livelier emerald twinkles in the grass,
A purer sapphire melts into the sea.   650

7

Not die, but live a life of truest breath,
And teach true life to fight with mortal
    wrongs.
Oh, why should Love, like men in drinking-
    songs,
Spice his fair banquet with the dust of death?
Make answer, Maud my bliss,   655
Maud made my Maud by that long loving
    kiss,
Life of my life, wilt thou not answer this?
"The dusky strand of Death inwoven here
With dear Love's tie, makes Love himself
    more dear."

8

Is that enchanted moan only the swell   660
Of the long waves that roll in yonder bay?
And hark the clock within, the silver knell
Of twelve sweet hours that passed in bridal
    white,
And died, to live, long as my pulses play;
But now by this my love has closed her sight
And given false death her hand, and stolen
    away   666
To dreamful wastes where footless fancies
    dwell
Among the fragments of the golden day.
May nothing there her maiden grace affright!
Dear heart, I feel with thee the drowsy spell.
My bride to be, my evermore delight,   671
My own heart's heart, my ownest own, fare-
    well;
It is but for a little space I go.
And ye meanwhile far over moor and fell
Beat to the noiseless music of the night!   675
Has our whole earth gone nearer to the glow
Of your soft splendors that you look so bright?
I have climbed nearer out of lonely hell.
Beat, happy stars, timing with things below,
Beat with my heart more blest than heart
    can tell,   680
Blest, but for some dark undercurrent woe
That seems to draw — but it shall not be so;
Let all be well, be well.

XIX

I

Her brother is coming back tonight,
Breaking up my dream of delight.   685

---

616. **Dark cedar.** There was a famous cedar of Lebanon
in the grounds of Farringford, Tennyson's home on the Isle
of Wight. Lebanon is a mountain range in Syria.   625. **the
thornless garden.** The Garden of Eden was thornless until
the sin of Adam. Cf. *Genesis*, 3:18.—"Thorns also and
thistles shall it bring forth to thee."   634. **A sad astrology.**
The old astrology taught that the destinies of men were
controlled by the movement of the stars; modern science
teaches that the stars have no such power.

649. **livelier . . . grass.** Cf. *Locksley Hall*, 19-20, p. 45.
651. **Not . . . breath.** "This is the central idea, the holy
power of Love" (Tennyson's note).   666. **false death**, sleep.

2

My dream? do I dream of bliss?
I have walked awake with Truth.
Oh, when did a morning shine
So rich in atonement as this
For my dark-dawning youth,   690
Darkened watching a mother decline
And that dead man at her heart and mine;
For who was left to watch her but I?
Yet so did I let my freshness die.

3

I trust that I did not talk   695
To gentle Maud in our walk
For often in lonely wanderings
I have cursed him even to lifeless things —
But I trust that I did not talk,
Not touch on her father's sin.   700
I am sure I did but speak
Of my mother's faded cheek
When it slowly grew so thin
That I felt she was slowly dying
Vexed with lawyers and harassed with debt;
For how often I caught her with eyes all wet,
Shaking her head at her son and sighing   707
A world of trouble within!

4

And Maud too, Maud was moved
To speak of the mother she loved   710
As one scarce less forlorn,
Dying abroad and it seems apart
From him who had ceased to share her heart,
And ever mourning over the feud,
The household Fury sprinkled with blood 715
By which our houses are torn.
How strange was what she said,
When only Maud and the brother
Hung over her dying bed —
That Maud's dark father and mine   720
Had bound us one to the other,
Betrothed us over their wine,
On the day when Maud was born;
Sealed her mine from her first sweet breath!
Mine, mine by a right, from birth till death!
Mine, mine — our fathers have sworn!   726

5

But the true blood spilt had in it a heat
To dissolve the precious seal on a bond,
That, if left uncanceled, had been so sweet;
And none of us thought of a something
    beyond,   730
A desire that awoke in the heart of the child,
As it were a duty done to the tomb,
To be friends for her sake, to be reconciled;
And I was cursing them and my doom,
And letting a dangerous thought run wild 735

720-726. See Part One, Section VII, page 101.

While often abroad in the fragrant gloom
Of foreign churches — I see her there,
Bright English lily, breathing a prayer
To be friends, to be reconciled!

6

But then what a flint is he!   740
Abroad, at Florence, at Rome,
I find whenever she touched on me
This brother had laughed her down,
And at last, when each came home,
He had darkened into a frown,   745
Chid her, and forbid her to speak
To me, her friend of the years before;
And this was what had reddened her cheek
When I bowed to her on the moor.

7

Yet Maud, although not blind   750
To the faults of his heart and mind,
I see she cannot but love him,
And says he is rough but kind,
And wishes me to approve him,
And tells me, when she lay   755
Sick once, with a fear of worse,
That he left his wine and horses and play,
Sat with her, read to her, night and day,
And tended her like a nurse.

8

Kind? but the death-bed desire   760
Spurned by this heir of the liar —
Rough but kind? yet I know
He has plotted against me in this,
That he plots against me still.
Kind to Maud? that were not amiss.   765
Well, rough but kind; why, let it be so,
For shall not Maud have her will?

9

For, Maud, so tender and true,
As long as my life endures
I feel I shall owe you a debt   770
That I never can hope to pay;
And if ever I should forget
That I owe this debt to you
And for your sweet sake to yours,
Oh, then, what then shall I say? —   775
If ever I *should* forget,
May God make me more wretched
Than ever I have been yet!

10

So now I have sworn to bury
All this dead body of hate,   780
I feel so free and so clear
By the loss of that dead weight
That I should grow light-headed, I fear,
Fantastically merry,

But that her brother comes, like a blight 785
On my fresh hope, to the Hall tonight.

XX

1

Strange, that I felt so gay,
Strange, that *I* tried today
To beguile her melancholy;
The Sultan, as we name him —   790
She did not wish to blame him —
But he vexed her and perplexed her
With his worldly talk and folly.
Was it gentle to reprove her
For stealing out of view   795
From a little lazy lover
Who but claims her as his due?
Or for chilling his caresses
By the coldness of her manners,
Nay, the plainness of her dresses?   800
Now I know her but in two,
Nor can pronounce upon it
If one should ask me whether
The habit, hat, and feather,
Or the frock and gypsy bonnet   805
Be the neater and completer;
For nothing can be sweeter
Than maiden Maud in either.

2

But tomorrow, if we live,
Our ponderous squire will give   810
A grand political dinner
To half the squirelings near;
And Maud will wear her jewels,
And the bird of prey will hover,
And the titmouse hope to win her   815
With his chirrup at her ear.

3

A grand political dinner
To the men of many acres,
A gathering of the Tory,
A dinner and then a dance   820
For the maids and marriage-makers,
And every eye but mine will glance
At Maud in all her glory.

4

For I am not invited,
But, with the Sultan's pardon,   825
I am all as well delighted,
For I know her own rose-garden,
And mean to linger in it
Till the dancing will be over;
And then, O then, come out to me   830
For a minute, but for a minute,
Come out to your own true lover,
That your true lover may see

Your glory also, and render
All homage to his own darling,   835
Queen Maud in all her splendor.

XXI

Rivulet crossing my ground,
And bringing me down from the Hall
This garden-rose that I found,
Forgetful of Maud and me,   840
And lost in trouble and moving round
Here at the head of a tinkling fall,
And trying to pass to the sea;
O rivulet, born at the Hall,
My Maud has sent it by thee —   845
If I read her sweet will right —
On a blushing mission to me,
Saying in odor and color, "Ah, be
Among the roses tonight."

XXII

1

Come into the garden, Maud,   850
  For the black bat, night, has flown,
Come into the garden, Maud,
  I am here at the gate alone;
And the woodbine spices are wafted abroad,
  And the musk of the rose is blown.   855

2

For a breeze of morning moves,
  And the planet of Love is on high,
Beginning to faint in the light that she loves
  On a bed of daffodil sky,
To faint in the light of the sun she loves,   860
  To faint in his light, and to die.

3

All night have the roses heard
  The flute, violin, bassoon;
All night has the casement jessamine stirred
  To the dancers dancing in tune;   865
Till a silence fell with the waking bird,
  And a hush with the setting moon.

4

I said to the lily, "There is but one,
  With whom she has heart to be gay.
When will the dancers leave her alone?   870
  She is weary of dance and play."
Now half to the setting moon are gone,
  And half to the rising day;
Low on the sand and loud on the stone
  The last wheel echoes away.   875

Section XXII. The best known aria in *Maud.* Ruskin comments on its use of the "pathetic fallacy" in *Modern Painters*, III, 12.
857. **the planet of Love,** Venus.

5

I said to the rose, "The brief night goes
  In babble and revel and wine.
O young lord-lover, what sighs are those,
  For one that will never be thine?
But mine, but mine," so I sware to the rose,
  "Forever and ever, mine."   881

6

And the soul of the rose went into my blood,
  As the music clashed in the hall;
And long by the garden lake I stood,
  For I heard your rivulet fall   885
From the lake to the meadow and on to the
    wood,
  Our wood, that is dearer than all;

7

From the meadow your walks have left so
    sweet
  That whenever a March-wind sighs
He sets the jewel-print of your feet   890
  In violets blue as your eyes,
To the woody hollows in which we meet
  And the valleys of Paradise.

8

The slender acacia would not shake
  One long milk-bloom on the tree;   895
The white lake-blossom fell into the lake
  As the pimpernel dozed on the lea;
But the rose was awake all night for your sake,
  Knowing your promise to me;
The lilies and roses were all awake,   900
  They sighed for the dawn and thee.

9

Queen rose of the rosebud garden of girls,
  Come hither, the dances are done,
In gloss of satin and glimmer of pearls,
  Queen lily and rose in one;   905
Shine out, little head, sunning over with curls,
  To the flowers, and be their sun.

10

There has fallen a splendid tear
  From the passion-flower at the gate.
She is coming, my dove, my dear;   910
  She is coming, my life, my fate.
The red rose cries, "She is near, she is near";
  And the white rose weeps, "She is late";
The larkspur listens, "I hear, I hear";
  And the lily whispers, "I wait."   915

11

She is coming, my own, my sweet;
  Were it ever so airy a tread,
My heart would hear her and beat,
  Were it earth in an earthy bed;

My dust would hear her and beat,   920
  Had I lain for a century dead,
Would start and tremble under her feet,
  And blossom in purple and red.

PART TWO

I

1

"The fault was mine, the fault was mine" —
Why am I sitting here so stunned and still,
Plucking the harmless wild-flower on the
    hill? —
It is this guilty hand! —
And there rises ever a passionate cry   5
From underneath in the darkening land —
What is it that has been done?
O dawn of Eden bright over earth and sky,
The fires of hell brake out of thy rising sun,
The fires of hell and of hate;   10
For she, sweet soul, had hardly spoken a
    word,
When her brother ran in his rage to the gate,
He came with the babe-faced lord,
Heaped on her terms of disgrace;
And while she wept, and I strove to be cool,
He fiercely gave me the lie,   16
Till I with as fierce an anger spoke,
And he struck me, madman, over the face,
Struck me before the languid fool,
Who was gaping and grinning by;   20
Struck for himself an evil stroke,
Wrought for his house an irredeemable woe.
For front to front in an hour we stood,
And a million horrible bellowing echoes broke
From the red-ribbed hollow behind the wood,
And thundered up into heaven the Christless
    code   26
That must have life for a blow.
Ever and ever afresh they seemed to grow.
Was it he lay there with a fading eye?
"The fault was mine," he whispered, "fly!"
Then glided out of the joyous wood   31
The ghastly Wraith of one that I know,
And there rang on a sudden a passionate cry,
A cry for a brother's blood;
It will ring in my heart and my ears, till I
    die, till I die.   35

2

Is it gone? my pulses beat —
What was it? a lying trick of the brain?
Yet I thought I saw her stand,
A shadow there at my feet,
High over the shadowy land.   40

26. **the Christless code,** the unwritten law, which is invoked in settling "affairs of honor" in a duel. 32. **The ghastly Wraith of one,** the phantom of Maud.

It is gone; and the heavens fall in a gentle
    rain,
When they should burst and drown with
    deluging storms
The feeble vassals of wine and anger and lust,
The little hearts that know not how to for-
    give.
Arise, my God, and strike, for we hold Thee
    just,   45
Strike dead the whole weak race of venomous
    worms,
That sting each other here in the dust;
We are not worthy to live.

II

1

See what a lovely shell,
Small and pure as a pearl,   50
Lying close to my foot,
Frail, but a work divine,
Made so fairily well
With delicate spire and whorl,
How exquisitely minute,   55
A miracle of design!

2

What is it? a learned man
Could give it a clumsy name.
Let him name it who can;
The beauty would be the same.   60

3

The tiny cell is forlorn,
Void of the little living will
That made it stir on the shore.
Did he stand at the diamond door
Of his house in a rainbow frill?   65
Did he push, when he was uncurled,
A golden foot or a fairy horn
Through his dim water-world?

4

Slight, to be crushed with a tap
Of my finger-nail on the sand,   70
Small, but a work divine,
Frail, but of force to withstand,
Year upon year, the shock
Of cataract seas that snap
The three-decker's oaken spine   75
Athwart the ledges of rock,
Here on the Breton strand!

5

Breton, not Briton; here
Like a shipwrecked man on a coast

Of ancient fable and fear —   80
Plagued with a flitting to and fro,
A disease, a hard mechanic ghost
That never came from on high
Nor ever arose from below,
But only moves with the moving eye,   85
Flying along the land and the main —
Why should it look like Maud?
Am I to be overawed
By what I cannot but know
Is a juggle born of the brain?   90

6

Back from the Breton coast,
Sick of a nameless fear,
Back to the dark sea-line
Looking, thinking of all I have lost;
An old song vexes my ear,   95
But that of Lamech is mine.

7

For years, a measureless ill,
For years, forever, to part —
But she, she would love me still;
And as long, O God, as she   100
Have a grain of love for me,
So long, no doubt, no doubt,
Shall I nurse in my dark heart,
However weary, a spark of will
Not to be trampled out.   105

8

Strange, that the mind, when fraught
With a passion so intense
One would think that it well
Might drown all life in the eye —
That it should, by being so overwrought,   110
Suddenly strike on a sharper sense
For a shell, or a flower, little things
Which else would have been passed by!
And now I remember, I,
When he lay dying there,   115
I noticed one of his many rings —
For he had many, poor worm — and thought,
It is his mother's hair.

9

Who knows if he be dead?
Whether I need have fled?   120
Am I guilty of blood?
However this may be,
Comfort her, comfort her, all things good,
While I am over the sea!
Let me and my passionate love go by,   125
But speak to her all things holy and high,

---

49. **shell,** found on the coast of Brittany, after the duel
with Maud's brother. "The shell undestroyed amid the storm
perhaps symbolizes to him his own first and highest nature
preserved amid the storms of passion" (Tennyson's note).

96. **Lamech.** See *Genesis*, 4:23.—"And Lamech said unto
his wives, Adah and Zillah, 'Hear my voice; ye wives of
Lamech, hearken unto my speech; for I have slain a man
to my wounding, and a young man to my hurt.'"

Whatever happen to me!
Me and my harmful love go by;
But come to her waking, find her asleep,
Powers of the height, Powers of the deep, 130
And comfort her though I die!

III

Courage, poor heart of stone!
I will not ask thee why
Thou canst not understand
That thou art left forever alone; 135
Courage, poor stupid heart of stone! —
Or if I ask thee why,
Care not thou to reply:
She is but dead, and the time is at hand
When thou shalt more than die. 140

IV

1

O that 'twere possible
After long grief and pain
To find the arms of my true love
Round me once again!

2

When I was wont to meet her 145
In the silent woody places
By the home that gave me birth,
We stood tranced in long embraces
Mixed with kisses sweeter, sweeter
Than anything on earth. 150

3

A shadow flits before me,
Not thou, but like to thee.
Ah, Christ, that it were possible
For one short hour to see
The souls we loved, that they might tell us
What and where they be! 156

4

It leads me forth at evening,
It lightly winds and steals
In a cold white robe before me,
When all my spirit reels 160
At the shouts, the leagues of lights,
And the roaring of the wheels.

5

Half the night I waste in sighs,
Half in dreams I sorrow after
The delight of early skies; 165
In a wakeful doze I sorrow
For the hand, the lips, the eyes,
For the meeting of the morrow,

The delight of happy laughter,
The delight of low replies. 170

6

'Tis a morning pure and sweet,
And a dewy splendor falls
On the little flower that clings
To the turrets and the walls;
'Tis a morning pure and sweet, 175
And the light and shadow fleet.
She is walking in the meadow,
And the woodland echo rings;
In a moment we shall meet.
She is singing in the meadow, 180
And the rivulet at her feet
Ripples on in light and shadow
To the ballad that she sings.

7

Do I hear her sing as of old,
My bird with the shining head, 185
My own dove with the tender eye?
But there rings on a sudden a passionate cry,
There is someone dying or dead,
And a sullen thunder is rolled;
For a tumult shakes the city, 190
And I wake, my dream is fled.
In the shuddering dawn, behold,
Without knowledge, without pity,
By the curtains of my bed
That abiding phantom cold! 195

8

Get thee hence, nor come again,
Mix not memory with doubt,
Pass, thou deathlike type of pain,
Pass and cease to move about!
'Tis the blot upon the brain 200
That *will* show itself without.

9

Then I rise, the eave-drops fall,
And the yellow vapors choke
The great city sounding wide;
The day comes, a dull red ball 205
Wrapped in drifts of lurid smoke
On the misty river-tide.

10

Through the hubbub of the market
I steal, a wasted frame;
It crosses here, it crosses there, 210
Through all that crowd confused and loud,
The shadow still the same;
And on my heavy eyelids
My anguish hangs like shame.

11

Alas for her that met me, 215
That heard me softly call,

Section III. This lyric was added in 1856. It was one of
Tennyson's favorite "songs of the deeper kind."
Section IV. See Critical Notes.

Came glimmering through the laurels
At the quiet evenfall,
In the garden by the turrets
Of the old manorial hall!   220

12

Would the happy spirit descend
From the realms of light and song,
In the chamber or the street,
As she looks among the blest,
Should I fear to greet my friend   225
Or to say, "Forgive the wrong,"
Or to ask her, "Take me, sweet,
To the regions of thy rest"?

13

But the broad light glares and beats,
And the shadow flits and fleets   230
And will not let me be;
And I loathe the squares and streets,
And the faces that one meets,
Hearts with no love for me.
Always I long to creep   235
Into some still cavern deep,
There to weep, and weep, and weep
My whole soul out to thee.   (*1834; 1837*)

V

1

Dead, long dead,
Long dead!   240
And my heart is a handful of dust,
And the wheels go over my head,
And my bones are shaken with pain,
For into a shallow grave they are thrust,
Only a yard beneath the street,   245
And the hoofs of the horses beat, beat,
The hoofs of the horses beat,
Beat into my scalp and my brain,
With never an end to the stream of passing
     feet,
Driving, hurrying, marrying, burying,   250
Clamor and rumble, and ringing and clatter;
And here beneath it is all as bad,
For I thought the dead had peace, but it is
     not so.
To have no peace in the grave, is that not
     sad?
But up and down and to and fro,   255
Ever about me the dead men go;
And then to hear a dead man chatter
Is enough to drive one mad.

2

Wretchedest age, since Time began,
They cannot even bury a man;   260
And though we paid our tithes in the days
     that are gone,
Not a bell was rung, not a prayer was read.

It is that which makes us loud in the world
     of the dead;
There is none that does his work, not one.
A touch of their office might have sufficed,   265
But the churchmen fain would kill their
     church,
As the churches have killed their Christ.

3

See, there is one of us sobbing,
No limit to his distress;
And another, a lord of all things, praying   270
To his own great self, as I guess;
And another, a statesman there, betraying
His party-secret, fool, to the press;
And yonder a vile physician, blabbing
The case of his patient — all for what?   275
To tickle the maggot born in an empty head,
And wheedle a world that loves him not,
For it is but a world of the dead.

4

Nothing but idiot gabble!
For the prophecy given of old   280
And then not understood,
Has come to pass as foretold;
Not let any man think for the public good,
But babble, merely for babble.
For I never whispered a private affair   285
Within the hearing of cat or mouse,
No, not to myself in the closet alone,
But I heard it shouted at once from the top
     of the house;
Everything came to be known.
Who told *him* we were there?   290

5

Not that gray old wolf, for he came not back
From the wilderness, full of wolves, where he
     used to lie;
He has gathered the bones for his o'ergrown
     whelp to crack —
Crack them now for yourself, and howl, and
     die.

6

Prophet, curse me the blabbing lip,   295
And curse me the British vermin, the rat;
I know not whether he came in the Hanover
     ship,
But I know that he lies and listens mute

---

280. **the prophecy given of old**, a reference to *Luke*, 12:2-3.—"For there is nothing covered that shall not be revealed; neither hid that shall not be known. Therefore whatsoever ye have spoken in darkness shall be heard in the light; and that which ye have spoken in the ear in closets shall be proclaimed upon the housetops." 296. **the rat**, a reference to the Norwegian rat, which was carried to England in the 18th century. The Jacobites said that this rat had come to England with the House of Hanover in 1714, when George Ludwig, elector of Hanover, succeeded Anne on the English throne; hence it was called the "Hanoverian rat."

In an ancient mansion's crannies and holes.
Arsenic, arsenic, sure, would do it,   300
Except that now we poison our babes, poor
          souls!
It is all used up for that.

7

Tell him now: she is standing here at my
          head;
Not beautiful now, not even kind;
He may take her now; for she never speaks
          her mind,   305
But is ever the one thing silent here.
She is not *of* us, as I divine;
She comes from another stiller world of the
          dead,
Stiller, not fairer than mine.

8

But I know where a garden grows,   310
Fairer than aught in the world beside,
All made up of the lily and rose
That blow by night, when the season is good,
To the sound of dancing music and flutes.
It is only flowers, they had no fruits,   315
And I almost fear they are not roses, but
          blood;
For the keeper was one, so full of pride,
He linked a dead man there to a spectral
          bride;
For he, if he had not been a Sultan of brutes,
Would he have that hole in his side?   320

9

But what will the old man say?
He laid a cruel snare in a pit
To catch a friend of mine one stormy day;
Yet now I could even weep to think of it;
For what will the old man say   325
When he comes to the second corpse in the
          pit?

10

Friend, to be struck by the public foe,
Then to strike him and lay him low,
That were a public merit, far,
Whatever the Quaker holds, from sin;   330
But the red life spilt for a private blow —
I swear to you, lawful and lawless war
Are scarcely even akin.

11

O me, why have they not buried me deep
          enough?
Is it kind to have made me a grave so rough,

Me, that was never a quiet sleeper?   336
Maybe still I am but half-dead;
Then I cannot be wholly dumb.
I will cry to the steps above my head
And somebody, surely, some kind heart will
          come   340
To bury me, bury me
Deeper, ever so little deeper.

PART THREE

1

My life has crept so long on a broken wing
Through cells of madness, haunts of horror
          and fear,
That I come to be grateful at last for a little
          thing.
My mood is changed, for it fell at a time of
          year
When the face of night is fair on the dewy
          downs,   5
And the shining daffodil dies, and the Char-
          ioteer
And starry Gemini hang like glorious crowns
Over Orion's grave low down in the west,
That like a silent lightning under the stars
She seemed to divide in a dream from a band
          of the blest,   10
And spoke of a hope for the world in the
          coming wars —
"And in that hope, dear soul, let trouble
          have rest,
Knowing I tarry for thee," and pointed to
          Mars
As he glowed like a ruddy shield on the
          Lion's breast.

2

And it was but a dream, yet it yielded a dear
          delight   15
To have looked, though but in a dream, upon
          eyes so fair,
That had been in a weary world my one
          thing bright;
And it was but a dream, yet it lightened my
          despair
When I thought that a war would arise in
          defense of the right,
That an iron tyranny now should bend or
          cease,   20
The glory of manhood stand on his ancient
          height,

---

326. **the second corpse.** "The second corpse is Maud's
brother, the lover's father being the first corpse, whom the
lover thinks that Maud's father has murdered" (Tennyson's
note).   330. **Whatever the Quaker holds.** The Quakers,
or Friends, regard personal combats and public wars as contrary to the spirit of Christ. Cf. Part I, line 370n.

Part Three. Tennyson states that this part was written at
the outset of the Crimean War, fought against Russia by England, France, Turkey, and Sardinia, in 1854-56.
6. **the Charioteer,** the constellation Auriga, situated
midway between the Polar Star and Orion.   7. **Gemini,** the
Twins, two stars in the southern hemisphere, named Castor
and Pollux.   8. **Orion,** a large constellation in the shape of
a man.   14. **the Lion,** Leo, a northern constellation containing the bright star Regulus.

Nor Britain's one sole God be the millionaire.
No more shall commerce be all in all, and
    Peace
Pipe on her pastoral hillock a languid note,
And watch her harvest ripen, her herd in-
    crease,   25
Nor the cannon-bullet rust on a slothful shore,
And the cobweb woven across the cannon's
    throat
Shall shake its threaded tears in the wind no
    more.

3

And as months ran on and rumor of battle
    grew,
"It is time, it is time, O passionate heart,"
    said I —   30
For I cleaved to a cause that I felt to be pure
    and true —
"It is time, O passionate heart and morbid
    eye,
That old hysterical mock-disease should die."
And I stood on a giant deck and mixed my
    breath
With a loyal people shouting a battle-cry, 35
Till I saw the dreary phantom arise and fly
Far into the North, and battle, and seas of
    death.

4

Let it go or stay, so I wake to the higher aims
Of a land that has lost for a little her lust of
    gold,
And love of a peace that was full of wrongs
    and shames,   40
Horrible, hateful, monstrous, not to be told;
And hail once more to the banner of battle
    unrolled!
Though many a light shall darken, and many
    shall weep
For those that are crushed in the clash of
    jarring claims,
Yet God's just wrath shall be wreaked on a
    giant liar,   45
And many a darkness into the light shall leap,
And shine in the sudden making of splendid
    names,
And noble thought be freer under the sun,
And the heart of a people beat with one
    desire;
For the peace, that I deemed no peace, is
    over and done,   50
And now by the side of the Black and the
    Baltic deep,
And deathful-grinning mouths of the fortress,
    flames
The blood-red blossom of war with a heart
    of fire.

5

Let it flame or fade, and the war roll down
    like a wind,
We have proved we have hearts in a cause,
    we are noble still,   55
And myself have awaked, as it seems, to the
    better mind.
It is better to fight for the good than to rail
    at the ill;
I have felt with my native land, I am one
    with my kind,
I embrace the purpose of God, and the doom
    assigned.   (*1834-56; 1837-56*)

IN THE VALLEY OF CAUTERETZ

All along the valley, stream that flashest
    white,
Deepening thy voice with the deepening of
    the night,
All along the valley, where thy waters flow,
I walked with one I loved two and thirty
    years ago.
All along the valley, while I walked today, 5
The two and thirty years were a mist that
    rolls away;
For all along the valley, down thy rocky bed,
Thy living voice to me was as the voice of
    the dead,
And all along the valley, by rock and cave
    and tree,
The voice of the dead was a living voice to
    me.   10
                        (*1861; 1864*)

A WELCOME TO ALEXANDRA

MARCH 7, 1863

Sea-kings' daughter from over the sea,
    Alexandra!
Saxon and Norman and Dane are we,
But all of us Danes in our welcome of thee,
    Alexandra!   5
Welcome her, thunders of fort and of fleet!
Welcome her, thundering cheer of the street!
Welcome her, all things youthful and sweet,
Scatter the blossom under her feet!
Break, happy land, into earlier flowers!   10
Make music, O bird, in the new-budded
    bowers!
Blazon your mottoes of blessing and prayer!

---

36. **the dreary phantom**, probably the false phantom of
Maud, the "ghastly Wraith" of Part Two, 32, page 108.

In the Valley of Cauteretz. Cauteretz is a beautiful valley
in the Pyrenees Mountains, visited by Tennyson and Arthur
Hallam in 1830, and again by Tennyson in 1861. See *In
Memoriam*, Section 71, page 73.
    A Welcome to Alexandra. Alexandra was the daughter of
Christian IX, of Denmark. She married the Prince of Wales,
afterwards Edward VII, at Windsor on March 10, 1863. The
poem was written as a welcome to her upon her arrival in
England a few days before the wedding.

Welcome her, welcome her, all that is ours!
Warble, O bugle, and trumpet, blare!
Flags, flutter out upon turrets and towers! 15
Flames, on the windy headland flare!
Utter your jubilee, steeple and spire!
Clash, ye bells, in the merry March air!
Flash, ye cities, in rivers of fire!
Rush to the roof, sudden rocket, and higher
Melt into stars for the land's desire!   21
Roll and rejoice, jubilant voice,
Roll as a ground-swell dashed on the strand,
Roar as the sea when he welcomes the land,
And welcome her, welcome the land's desire,
The sea-kings' daughter as happy as fair, 26
Blissful bride of a blissful heir,
Bride of the heir of the kings of the sea —
O joy to the people and joy to the throne,
Come to us, love us and make us your own;
For Saxon or Dane or Norman we,   31
Teuton or Celt, or whatever we be,
We are each all Dane in our welcome of thee,
                    Alexandra!
                        (*1863;* 1863)

MILTON
(ALCAICS)

O mighty-mouthed inventor of harmonies,
O skilled to sing of Time or Eternity,
    God-gifted organ-voice of England,
        Milton, a name to resound for ages;
Whose Titan angels, Gabriel, Abdiel,   5
Starred from Jehovah's gorgeous armories,
    Tower, as the deep-domed empyrean
        Rings to the roar of an angel onset!
Me rather all that bowery loneliness,
The brooks of Eden mazily murmuring,   10
    And bloom profuse and cedar arches
        Charm, as a wanderer out in ocean,
Where some refulgent sunset of India
Streams o'er a rich ambrosial ocean isle,
    And crimson-hued the stately palm-woods
        Whisper in odorous heights of even.   16
                        (*1863;* 1864)

THE FLOWER

Once in a golden hour
    I cast to earth a seed.
Up there came a flower,
    The people said, a weed.

To and fro they went   5
    Through my garden-bower,
And muttering discontent
    Cursed me and my flower.

Then it grew so tall
    It wore a crown of light,   10
But thieves from o'er the wall
    Stole the seed by night;

Sowed it far and wide
    By every town and tower,
Till all the people cried,   15
    "Splendid is the flower."

Read my little fable:
    He that runs may read.
Most can raise the flowers now
    For all have got the seed.   20

And some are pretty enough,
    And some are poor indeed;
And now again the people
    Call it but a weed.   (1864)

A DEDICATION

Dear, near and true — no truer Time himself
Can prove you, though he make you evermore
Dearer and nearer, as the rapid of life
Shoots to the fall — take this and pray that he
Who wrote it, honoring your sweet faith in
                    him,   5
May trust himself; and after praise and scorn,
As one who feels the immeasurable world,
Attain the wise indifference of the wise;
And after autumn past — if left to pass
His autumn into seeming-leafless days —   10
Draw toward the long frost and longest night,
Wearing his wisdom lightly, like the fruit
Which in our winter woodland looks a flower.
                        (1864)

THE VOYAGE

We left behind the painted buoy
    That tosses at the harbor-mouth;
And madly danced our hearts with joy,
    As fast we fleeted to the south.
How fresh was every sight and sound   5
    On open main or winding shore!
We knew the merry world was round,
    And we might sail for evermore.

Milton. See Critical Notes.
5. Gabriel, Abdiel. In *Paradise Lost* Gabriel and Abdiel
withstood Satan in his revolt against God. (See Book 5.)
They are called Titans after the race of majestic giants of
Greek mythology.
The Flower. Although Tennyson states (*Memoir*, II, 10)
that this poem is "an universal apologue and parable," it
fittingly suggests that his own poetry, little cared for at first,
gained in popular approval after it found many imitators.

A Dedication. This poem is supposed to be addressed to
the poet's wife.
The Voyage. This poem is an allegory of earnest and noble
living. It represents a quest for a lofty ideal—never to be
attained, but never to be abandoned. Cf. *Ulysses,* 30-32, p.
43; *Locksley Hall,* 181, p. 49; and *Merlin and the Gleam,* p. 173.

Warm broke the breeze against the brow,
  Dry sang the tackle, sang the sail;   10
The Lady's-head upon the prow
  Caught the shrill salt, and sheered the gale.
The broad seas swelled to meet the keel,
  And swept behind; so quick the run,
We felt the good ship shake and reel,   15
  We seemed to sail into the sun!

How oft we saw the sun retire,
  And burn the threshold of the night,
Fall from his Ocean-lane of fire,
  And sleep beneath his pillared light!   20
How oft the purple-skirted robe
  Of twilight slowly downward drawn,
As through the slumber of the globe
  Again we dashed into the dawn!

New stars all night above the brim   25
  Of waters lightened into view;
They climbed as quickly, for the rim
  Changed every moment as we flew.
Far ran the naked moon across
  The houseless ocean's heaving field,   30
Or flying shone, the silver boss
  Of her own halo's dusky shield.

The peaky islet shifted shapes,
  High towns on hills were dimly seen;
We passed long lines of Northern capes   35
  And dewy Northern meadows green.
We came to warmer waves, and deep
  Across the boundless East we drove,
Where those long swells of breaker sweep
  The nutmeg rocks and isles of clove.   40

By peaks that flamed, or, all in shade,
  Gloomed the low coast and quivering brine
With ashy rains, that spreading made
  Fantastic plume or sable pine;
By sands and steaming flats, and floods   45
  Of mighty mouth, we scudded fast,
And hills and scarlet-mingled woods
  Glowed for a moment as we passed.

O hundred shores of happy climes,
  How swiftly streamed ye by the bark!   50
At times the whole sea burned, at times
  With wakes of fire we tore the dark;
At times a carven craft would shoot
  From havens hid in fairy bowers,
With naked limbs and flowers and fruit,   55
  But we nor paused for fruit nor flowers.

For one fair Vision ever fled
  Down the waste waters day and night,
And still we followed where she led,
  In hope to gain upon her flight.   60
Her face was evermore unseen,
  And fixed upon the far sea-line;

But each man murmured, "O my Queen,
  I follow till I make thee mine."

And now we lost her, now she gleamed   65
  Like Fancy made of golden air,
Now nearer to the prow she seemed
  Like Virtue firm, like Knowledge fair,
Now high on waves that idly burst
  Like Heavenly Hope she crowned the sea,
And now, the bloodless point reversed,   71
  She bore the blade of Liberty.

And only one among us — him
  We pleased not — he was seldom pleased;
He saw not far, his eyes were dim,   75
  But ours he swore were all diseased.
"A ship of fools," he shrieked in spite,
  "A ship of fools," he sneered and wept.
And overboard one stormy night
  He cast his body, and on we swept.   80

And never sail of ours was furled,
  Nor anchor dropped at eve or morn;
We loved the glories of the world,
  But laws of nature were our scorn.
For blasts would rise and rave and cease,   85
  But whence were those that drove the sail
Across the whirlwind's heart of peace,
  And to and through the counter gale?

Again to colder climes we came,
  For still we followed where she led;   90
Now mate is blind and captain lame,
  And half the crew are sick or dead,
But, blind or lame or sick or sound,
  We follow that which flies before;
We know the merry world is round,   95
  And we may sail for evermore.   (1864)

NORTHERN FARMER

OLD STYLE

Wheer 'asta beän saw long and meä liggin'
  'ere aloän?
Noorse? thoort nowt o' a noorse; whoy,
  Doctor's abeän an' agoän;
Says that I moänt 'a naw moor aäle, but I
  beänt a fool;

Northern Farmer (*Old Style*). Tennyson states that this poem is "founded on the dying words of a farm-bailiff as reported to me by a great-uncle of mine when verging upon 80—'God A'mighty little knows what He's about a-taking me. An' Squire will be so mad an' all.' I conjectured the man from that one saying" (*Memoir*, II, 9). The character belongs to Lincolnshire, a northern county of England. A farm-bailiff is an agent of the lord of the manor for collecting rents, managing the farm, etc. R. C. Trench wrote the Bishop of Oxford about the poem. He said: "Every clergyman ought to study it. It is a wonderful revelation of heathenism still in the land."
1. 'asta beän, hast thou been. liggin' 'ere aloän, lying here alone. 2. Noorse? . . . noorse, Nurse? thou art of no use as a nurse. abeän an' agoän, been and gone. 3. moänt 'a, may not have.

Git ma my aäle, fur I beänt a-gawin' to breäk
    my rule.

Doctors, they knaws nowt, fur a says what's
    nawways true;   5
Naw soort o' koind o' use to saäy the things
    that a do.
I've 'ed my point o' aäle ivry noight sin' I
    beän 'ere.
An' I've 'ed my quart ivry market-noight for
    foorty year.

Parson's a beän loikewoise, an' a sittin' ere
    o' my bed.
"The Amoighty's a taäkin o' you to 'issén,
    my friend," a said,   10
An' a towd ma my sins, an' 's toithe were
    due, an' I gied it in hond;
I done moy duty boy 'um, as I 'a done boy
    the lond.

Larned a ma' beä. I reckons I 'annot sa
    mooch to larn.
But a cast oop, thot a did, 'bout Bessy
    Marris's barne.
Thaw a knaws I hallus voäted wi' Squoire an'
    choorch an' staäte,   15
An' i' the woost o' toimes I wur niver agin
    the raäte.

An' I hallus coomed to 's choorch afoor moy
    Sally wur deäd,
An' 'eärd 'um a bummin' awaäy loike a
    buzzard-clock ower my 'eäd,
An' I niver knawed whot a meäned but I
    thowt a 'ad summut to saäy,
An' I thowt a said whot a owt to 'a said, an'
    I coomed awaäy.   20

Bessy Marris's barne! tha knaws she laäid it
    to meä.
Mowt a beän, mayhap, for she wur a bad un,
    sheä.
'Siver, I kep 'um, I kep 'um, my lass, tha
    mun understond;
I done moy duty boy 'um, as I 'a done boy
    the lond.

But Parson a cooms an' a goäs, an' a says it
    eäsy an' freeä: 25
"The Amoighty's a taäkin o' you to 'issén,
    my friend," says 'eä.
I weänt saäy men be loiars, thaw summun
    said it in 'aäste;

But 'e reäds wonn sarmin a weeäk, an' I 'a
    stubbed Thurnaby waäste.

D' ya moind the waäste, my lass? naw, naw,
    tha was not born then;
Theer wur a boggle in it, I often 'eärd 'um
    mysén;   30
Moäst loike a butter-bump, fur I 'eärd 'um
    about an' about,
But I stubbed 'um oop wi' the lot, an' raäved
    an' rembled 'um out.

Keäper's it wur; fo' they fun 'um theer
    a-laäid of 'is faäce
Down i' the woild 'enemies afoor I coomed
    to the plaäce.
Noäks or Thimbleby — toäner 'ed shot 'um
    as deäd as a naäil.   35
Noäks wur 'anged for it oop at 'soize — but
    git ma my aäle.

Dubbut looök at the waäste; theer warn't
    not feeäd for a cow;
Nowt at all but bracken an' fuzz, an' looök
    at it now —
Warn't worth nowt a haäcre, an' now theer
    's lots o' feeäd,
Fourscoor yows upon it, an' some on it down
    i' seeäd.   40

Nobbut a bit on it's left, an' I meäned to 'a
    stubbed it at fall,
Done it ta-year I meäned, an' runned plow
    thruff it an' all,
If Godamoighty an' parson 'ud nobbut let
    ma aloän —
Meä, wi' haäte hoonderd haäcre o' Squoire's,
    an' lond o' my oän.

Do Godamoighty knaw what a's doing, a-
    taäkin' o' meä?   45
I beänt wonn as saws 'ere a beän an' yonder
    a peä;
An' Squoire 'ull be sa mad an' all — a' dear,
    a' dear!
And I 'a managed for Squoire coom Michael-
    mas thutty year.

A mowt 'a taäen owd Joänes, as 'ant not a
    'aäpoth o' sense,

---

28. 'e, he (the parson). 'a stubbed, have cleared for cultivation. 30. boggle, bogie, ghost. 31. butter-bump, bittern (a bird with a loud, hollow note). 32. raäved an' rembled 'um out, plowed them up and threw them out. 33. Keäper's it wur, it was the ghost of the gamekeeper. a-laäid of 'is faäce, lying on his face. 34. i' the woild 'enemies, among the wild anemones. 35. toäner, one or the other (Noäks or Thimbleby). 36. at 'soize, at the assizes (court hearing).
37. Dubbut, do but. 38. bracken an' fuzz, fern and furze. 40. yows, ewes. i' seeäd, seeded to clover. 41. Nobbut, only. 42. ta-year, this year. 46. wonn as saws, such a one as sows. 48. Michaelmas, a church festival celebrated on September 29. 49. as . . . sense, who hasn't a half-penny worth of sense.

---

5. a, he. 7. point, pint. 10. you. *Ou* is pronounced as in *hour.* 'issén, himself. 11. towd, told. an' 's toithe, and his tithe. 12. boy, by. 13. Larned a ma' beä, learned he may be. 14. a cast oop, he brought up against me. barne, child. 16. the raäte, the poor tax. 18. buzzard-clock, cockchafer (a kind of buzzing insect). 23. 'Siver, I kep 'um, however, I supported him. 27. summun, someone (David; see *Psalms,* 116:11.—"I said in my haste, 'All men are liars.'").

Or a mowt 'a taäen young Robins — a niver
    mended a fence;   50
But Godamoighty a moost taäke meä an'
    taäke ma now,
Wi' aäf the cows to cauve an' Thurnaby
    hoälms to plow!

Looök 'ow quoloty smoiles when they seeäs
    ma a passin' boy,
Says to thessén, naw doubt, "What a man a
    beä sewer-loy!"
Fur they knaws what I beän to Squoire sin'
    fust a coomed to the 'All;   55
I done moy duty by Squoire an' I done moy
    duty boy hall.

Squoire's i' Lunnon, an' summun I reckons
    'ull 'a to wroite,
For whoä's to howd the lond ater meä thot
    muddles ma quoit;
Sartin-sewer I beä thot a weänt niver give it
    to Joänes,
Naw, nor a moänt to Robins — a niver rem-
    bles the stoäns.   60

But summun 'ull come ater meä mayhap wi'
    'is kittle o' steäm
Huzzin' an' maäzin' the blessed feälds wi'
    the divil's oän teäm.
Sin' I mun doy I mun doy, thaw loife they
    says is sweet,
But sin' I mun doy I mun doy, for I couldn
    abeär to see it.

What atta stannin' theer fur, an' doesn bring
    ma the aäle?   65
Doctor's a 'toättler, lass, an a's hallus i' the
    owd taäle;
I weänt breäk rules fur Doctor, a knaws naw
    moor nor a floy;
Git ma my aäle, I tell tha, an' if I mun doy
    I mun doy.   (1864)

NORTHERN FARMER

NEW STYLE

Dosn't thou 'ear my 'erse's legs, as they
    canters awaäy?

---

52. **cauve**, calve. 53. **quoloty**, quality; the gentry. 54.
thessén, themselves. **sewer-loy**, surely. 58. **howd**, hold.
61. **kittle o' steäm**, boiler of steam. (The steam thresher was
introduced into Lincolnshire in 1848.) 62. **Huzzin' an'
maäzin'**, worrying and frightening. 64. **it**, i.e., the presence
of the threshing machine. 65. **atta**, art thou. 66. **'toättler**,
teetotaler. **a's . . . taäle**, he is always telling the same story.
67. **floy**, fly.
  Northern Farmer (*New Style*). In this poem the independent farmer of large holdings has succeeded the farm agent
of the earlier poem. The poem grew out of a favorite saying
of a rich neighbor of Tennyson—"When I canters my 'erse
along the ramper [highway], I 'ears proputty, proputty,
proputty" (*Memoirs*, II, 9). The farmer and his son Sam
are on horseback. The speech to Sam is frequently broken
into by remarks to the horse.
  1. **'erse's**, horse's.

Proputty, proputty, proputty — that's what
    I 'ears 'em saäy.
Proputty, proputty, proputty — Sam, thou's
    an ass for thy pains;
Theer's moor sense i' one o' 'is legs nor in
    all thy braïns.

Woä — theer's a craw to pluck wi' tha, Sam;
    yon's parson's 'ouse —   5
Dosn't thou knaw that a man mun be eäther
    a man or a mouse?
Time to think on it then; for thou'll be
    twenty to weeäk.
Proputty, proputty — woä then, woä — let
    ma 'ear mysén speäk.

Me an' thy muther, Sammy, 'as beän a-
    talkin' o' thee;
Thou's beän talkin' to muther, an' she beän
    a-tellin' it me.   10
Thou'll not marry for munny — thou's sweet
    upo' parson's lass —
Noä — thou'll marry for luvv — an' we boäth
    on us thinks tha an ass.

Seeäed her todaäy goä by — Saäint's-daäy —
    they was ringing the bells.
She's a beauty, thou thinks — an' soä is
    scoors o' gells,
Them as 'as munny an' all — wot's a beauty?
    — the flower as blaws.   15
But proputty, proputty sticks, an' proputty,
    proputty graws.

Do'ant be stunt; taäke time. I knaws what
    maäkes tha sa mad.
Warn't I craäzed fur the lasses mysén when
    I wur a lad?
But I knawed a Quaäker feller as often 'as
    towd ma this:
"Doänt thou marry for munny, but goä
    wheer munny is!"   20

An' I went wheer munny war; an' thy muther
    coom to 'and,
Wi' lots o' munny laäïd by, an' a nicetish
    bit o' land.
Maäybe she warn't a beauty — I niver giv it
    a thowt —
But warn't she as good to cuddle an' kiss as
    a lass as 'ant nowt?

Parson's lass 'ant nowt, an' she weänt 'a
    nowt when 'e's deäd,   25
Mun be a guvness, lad, or summut, and addle
    her breäd.

---

2. **Proputty**, property. 5. **craw to pluck**, crow to pick;
something disagreeable to take up. 7. **to weeäk**, this week.
14. **scoors o' gells**, scores of girls. 17. **stunt**, stubborn.
24. **as 'ant nowt**, that has nothing. 25. **weänt 'a**, will not
have. 26. **addle her breäd**, earn her own living.

Why? fur 'e's nobbut a curate, an' weänt
    niver git hissén clear,
An' 'e maäde the bed as 'e ligs on afoor 'e
    coomed to the shere.

An' thin 'e coomed to the parish wi' lots o'
    Varsity debt,
Stook to his taaïl they did, an' 'e 'ant got
    shut on 'em yet.   30
An' 'e ligs on 'is back i' the grip, wi' noän
    to lend 'im a shove,
Woorse nor a far-weltered yowe; fur, Sammy,
    'e married fur luvv.

Luvv? what's luvv? thou can luvv thy lass
    an' 'er munny too,
Maäkin' 'em goä togither, as they've good
    right to do.
Couldn I luvv thy muther by cause o' 'er
    munny laaïd by?   35
Naäy—fur I luvved 'er a vast sight moor
    fur it; reäson why.

Ay, an' thy muther says thou wants to marry
    the lass,
Cooms of a gentleman burn; an' we boäth on
    us thinks tha an ass.
Woä then, proputty, wiltha?—an ass as near
    as mays nowt—
Woä then, wiltha? dangtha!—the bees is as
    fell as owt.   40

Breäk me a bit o' the esh for his 'eäd, lad,
    out o' the fence!
Gentleman burn! what's gentleman burn? is
    it shillins an' pence?
Proputty, proputty's ivrything 'ere, an',
    Sammy, I'm blest
If it isn't the saäme oop yonder, fur them as
    'as it's the best.

Tis'n them as 'as munny as breäks into 'ouses
    an' steäls,   45
Them as 'as coäts to their backs an' taäkes
    their regular meäls.
Noä, but it's them as niver knaws wheer a
    meäl's to be 'ad.
Taäke my word for it, Sammy, the poor in a
    loomp is bad.

Them or thir feythers, tha sees, mun 'a beän
    a laäzy lot,
Fur work mun 'a gone to the gittin' whiniver
    munny was got.   50
Feyther 'ad ammost nowt; leästways 'is
    munny was 'id.
But 'e tued an' moiled issén deäd, an' 'e died
    a good un, 'e did.

Locöök thou theer wheer Wrigglesby beck
    cooms out by the 'ill!
Feyther run oop to the farm, an' I runs oop
    to the mill;
An' I'll run oop to the brig, an' that thou'll
    live to see;   55
And if thou marries a good un I'll leäve the
    land to thee.

Thim's my noätions, Sammy, wheerby I
    meäns to stick;
But if thou marries a bad un, I'll leäve the
    land to Dick.—
Coom oop, proputty, proputty—that's what
    I 'ears 'im saäy—
Proputty, proputty, proputty—canter an'
    canter awaäy.   60
                       (1869)

LUCRETIUS

Lucilia, wedded to Lucretius, found
Her master cold; for when the morning flush
Of passion and the first embrace had died
Between them, tho' he loved her none the
    less,
Yet often when the woman heard his foot   5
Return from pacings in the field, and ran
To greet him with a kiss, the master took
Small notice, or austerely, for — his mind
Half buried in some weightier argument,
Or fancy-borne perhaps upon the rise   10
And long roll of the hexameter — he past
To turn and ponder those three hundred
    scrolls
Left by the Teacher, whom he held divine.

    51. **ammost**, almost. 52. **tued ... issén,** tugged and
toiled himself. 53. **beck**, brook. 54. **Feyther run oop,**
father extended his property to. 55. **brig,** bridge.
    Lucretius. Tennyson's commentary on the Roman phi-
losopher's great poem *De Rerum Natura (On the Nature of
Things)* (c. 55 B.C.) indicates both the strength and the
limitation of Lucretian materialism. Lucretius finds reason
unable to cope with the irrational lust engendered by a
love potion given him by his wife Lucilia. He is plagued
by evil dreams of chaos in the atom universe, which he has
conceived as orderly, and of bestiality in human conduct,
a token of the decadence of the Roman Republic.
    13. **the Teacher,** Epicurus (342-270 B.C.), Greek philos-
opher who taught that the highest intellectual and aesthetic
pleasure was the chief good.

    27. **nobbut**, only. **clear,** out of debt. 28. **ligs,** lies.
shere, shire, county. 30. **shut on 'em,** rid of them. 31.
grip, draining-ditch or trench. 32. **far-weltered yowe,**
ewe lying on its back. (When a sheep gets on its back, it cannot get up without help.) 38. **burn,** born. 39. **mays
nowt,** makes nothing. 40. **the bees ... owt,** the flies are
as fierce as anything. 41. **esh,** ash.

She brooked it not, but wrathful, petulant,
Dreaming some rival, sought and found a
   witch   15
Who brewed the philtre which had power,
   they said,
To lead an errant passion home again.
And this, at times, she mingled with his
   drink,
And this destroyed him; for the wicked broth
Confused the chemic labor of the blood,   20
And tickling the brute brain within the man's
Made havoc among those tender cells,
   and checked
His power to shape. He loathed himself,
   and once
After a tempest woke upon a morn
That mocked him with returning calm,
   and cried: 25

"Storm in the night! for thrice I heard
   the rain
Rushing; and once the flash of a thunder-
   bolt —
Methought I never saw so fierce a fork —
Struck out the streaming mountain-side,
   and showed
A riotous confluence of watercourses   30
Blanching and billowing in a hollow of it,
Where all but yester-eve was dusty-dry.

"Storm, and what dreams, ye holy Gods,
   what dreams!
For thrice I wakened after dreams.
   Perchance
We do but recollect the dreams that come   35
Just ere the waking. Terrible: for it seemed
A void was made in Nature; all her bonds
Cracked; and I saw the flaring atom-streams
And torrents of her myriad universe,
Ruining along the illimitable inane,   40
Fly on to clash together again, and make
Another and another frame of things
For ever. That was mine, my dream,
   I knew it —
Of and belonging to me, as the dog   44
With inward yelp and restless forefoot plies
His function of the woodland; but the next!
I thought that all the blood by Sylla shed
Came driving rainlike down again on earth,
And where it dashed the reddening meadow,
   sprang
No dragon warriors from Cadmean teeth,   50
For these I thought my dream would show
   to me,

But girls, Hetairai, curious in their art,
Hired animalisms, vile as those that made
The mulberry-faced Dictator's orgies worse
Than aught they fable of the quiet Gods.   55
And hands they mixt, and yelled and
   round me drove
In narrowing circles till I yelled again
Half-suffocated, and sprang up, and saw —
Was it the first beam of my latest day?

"Then, then, from utter gloom stood out
   the breasts,   60
The breasts of Helen, and hoveringly a sword
Now over and now under, now direct,
Pointed itself to pierce, but sank down
   shamed
At all that beauty; and as I stared, a fire,
The fire that left a roofless Ilion,   65
Shot out of them, and scorched me that
   I woke.

"Is this thy vengeance, holy Venus, thine,
Because I would not one of thine own doves,
Not even a rose, were offered to thee? thine,
Forgetful how my rich procœmion makes   70
Thy glory fly along the Italian field,
In lays that will outlast thy deity?

"Deity? nay, thy worshippers. My tongue
Trips, or I speak profanely. Which of these
Angers thee most, or angers thee at all?   75
Not if thou be'st of those who, far aloof
From envy, hate and pity, and spite and
   scorn,
Live the great life which all our greatest fain
Would follow, centered in eternal calm.

"Nay, if thou canst, O Goddess, like
   ourselves   80
Touch, and be touched, then would I cry to
   thee
To kiss thy Mavors, roll thy tender arms
Round him, and keep him from the lust
   of blood
That makes a steaming slaughter-house
   of Rome.

"Ay, but I meant not thee; I meant
   not her   85
Whom all the pines of Ida shook to see

---

47. **Sylla**, Sulla, the "mulberry-faced" Roman dictator
(82-79 B.C.) who reveled drunkenly with courtesans,
"Hetairai" (line 52). 50. **Cadmean**. Cadmus of Thebes
sowed the teeth of a dragon he had slain, and from the soil
sprang up armed warriors.

61. **Helen**, Helen of Troy, responsible for the war that
destroyed Ilion (Troy), line 65. 70. **procœmion**, the introduction to *De Rerum Natura*, celebrating Venus as the Cyprian
(Kypris, line 95), the "all-generating" power of nature, Aphrodite of Cyprus. 82. **Mavors**, Mars.

Slide from that quiet heaven of hers, and
    tempt
The Trojan, while his neatherds were abroad;
Nor her that o'er her wounded hunter wept
Her deity false in human-amorous tears; 90
Nor whom her beardless apple-arbiter
Decided fairest. Rather, O ye Gods,
Poet-like, as the great Sicilian called
Calliope to grace his golden verse —
Ay, and this Kypris also — did I take 95
That popular name of thine to shadow forth
The all-generating powers and genial heat
Of Nature, when she strikes thro' the
    thick blood
Of cattle, and light is large, and lambs are
    glad
Nosing the mother's udder, and the bird 100
Makes his heart voice amid the blaze of
    flowers;
Which things appear the work of mighty
    Gods.

"The Gods! and if I go *my* work is left
Unfinished — *if* I go. The Gods, who haunt
The lucid interspace of world and world, 105
Where never creeps a cloud, or moves a wind,
Nor ever falls the least white star of snow,
Nor ever lowest roll of thunder moans,
Nor sound of human sorrow mounts to mar
Their sacred everlasting calm! and such, 110
Not all so fine, nor so divine a calm,
Not such, nor all unlike it, man may gain
Letting his own life go. The Gods, the Gods!
If all be atoms, how then should the Gods
Being atomic not be dissoluble, 115
Not follow the great law? My master held
That Gods there are, for all men so believe.
I prest my footsteps into his, and meant
Surely to lead my Memmius in a train
Of flowery clauses onward to the proof 120
That Gods there are, and deathless. Meant?
    I meant?
I have forgotten what I meant; my mind
Stumbles, and all my faculties are lamed.

"Look where another of our Gods, the Sun,
Apollo, Delius, or of older use 125
All-seeing Hyperion — what you will —
Has mounted yonder; since he never sware,
Except his wrath were wreaked on
    wretched man,

That he would only shine among the dead
Hereafter — tales! for never yet on earth 130
Could dead flesh creep, or bits of roasting ox
Moan round the spit — nor knows he what
    he sees;
King of the East altho' he seem, and girt
With song and flame and fragrance,
    slowly lifts
His golden feet on those empurpled stairs 135
That climb into the windy halls of heaven
And here he glances on an eye new-born,
And gets for greeting but a wail of pain;
And here he stays upon a freezing orb
That fain would gaze upon him to the
    last; 140
And here upon a yellow eyelid fallen
And closed by those who mourn a friend
    in vain,
Not thankful that his troubles are no more.
And me, altho' his fire is on my face
Blinding, he sees not, nor at all can tell 145
Whether I mean this day to end myself.
Or lend an ear to Plato where he says,
That men like soldiers may not quit the post
Allotted by the Gods. But he that holds
The Gods are careless, wherefore need he
    care 150
Greatly for them, nor rather plunge at once,
Being troubled, wholly out of sight, and sink
Past earthquake — ay, and gout and stone,
    that break
Body toward death, and palsy, death-in-life,
And wretched age — and worst disease
    of all, 155
These prodigies of myriad nakednesses,
And twisted shapes of lust, unspeakable,
Abominable, strangers at my hearth
Not welcome, harpies miring every dish,
The phantom husks of something foully
    done, 160
And fleeting thro' the boundless universe,
And blasting the long quiet of my breast
With animal heat and dire insanity?

"How should the mind, except it loved
    them, clasp
These idols to herself? or do they fly 165
Now thinner, and now thicker, like the flakes
In a fall of snow, and so press in, perforce
Of multitude, as crowds that in an hour
Of civic tumult jam the doors, and bear
The keepers down, and throng, their rags
    and they 170
The basest, far into that council-hall
Where sit the best and stateliest of the land?

"Can I not fling this horror off me again,

---

88. **Trojan**, Anchises, father of Aeneas, seduced by Venus. 89. **hunter**, Adonis, wounded by a wild boar. 91. **apple-arbiter**, Paris, who gave the golden apple to Aphrodite. See *Œnone*, p. 20. 93. **great Sicilian**, Empedocles (see Arnold's *Empedocles on Etna*, p. 435), who invoked the muse of epic poetry, Calliope. 116. **master**, Epicurus. 119. **Memmius**, Caius Memmius Gamellus, to whom Lucretius dedicated his poem.

147-149. Plato so argues in his *Phaedo*.

Seeing with how great ease Nature can smile,
Balmier and nobler from her bath of
   storm,   175
At random ravage? and how easily
The mountain there has cast his cloudy
   slough,
Now towering o'er him in serenest air,
A mountain o'er a mountain, — ay, and
   within
All hollow as the hopes and fears of men? 180

"But who was he that in the garden snared
Picus and Faunus, rustic Gods? a tale
To laugh at — more to laugh at in myself —
For look! What is it? there? yon arbutus
Totters; a noiseless riot underneath   185
Strikes through the wood, sets all the tops
   quivering —
The mountain quickens into Nymph and
   Faun,
And here an Oread — how the sun delights
To glance and shift about her slippery sides,
And rosy knees and supple roundedness,   190
And budded bosom-peaks — who this way
   runs
Before the rest! — a satyr, a satyr, see,
Follows; but him I proved impossible;
Twy-natured is no nature. Yet he draws
Nearer and nearer, and I scan him now   195
Beastlier than any phantom of his kind
That ever butted his rough brother-brute
For lust or lusty blood or provender.
I hate, abhor, spit, sicken at him; and she
Loathes him as well; such a precipitate
   heel,   200
Fledged as it were with Mercury's ankle-wing,
Whirls her to me — but will she fling herself
Shameless upon me? Catch her, goatfoot! nay,
Hide, hide them, million-myrtled wilderness,
And cavern-shadowing laurels, hide! do I
   wish —   205
What? — that the bush were leafless? or to
   whelm
All of them in one massacre? O ye Gods,
I know you careless, yet, behold, to you
From childly wont and ancient use I call —
I thought I lived securely as yourselves — 210
No lewdness, narrowing envy, monkey-
   spite,
No madness of ambition, avarice, none;
No larger feast than under plane or pine
With neighbors laid along the grass, to take
Only such cups as left us friendly-warm,   215
Affirming each his own philosophy —

Nothing to mar the sober majesties
Of settled, sweet, Epicurean life.
But now it seems some unseen monster lays
His vast and filthy hands upon my will,   220
Wrenching it backward into his, and spoils
My bliss in being; and it was not great,
For save when shutting reasons up in rhythm,
Or Heliconian honey in living words,
To make a truth less harsh, I often grew   225
Tired of so much within our little life,
Or of so little in our little life —
Poor little life that toddles half an hour
Crowned with a flower or two, and there
   an end —
And since the nobler pleasure seems to
   fade,   230
Why should I, beastlike as I find myself,
Not manlike end myself? — our privilege —
What beast has heart to do it? And what man,
What Roman would be dragged in triumph
   thus?
Not I; not he, who bears one name with
   her   235
Whose death-blow struck the dateless doom
   of kings,
When, brooking not the Tarquin in her veins,
She made her blood in sight of Collatine
And all his peers, flushing the guiltless air,
Spout from the maiden fountain in her
   heart.   240
And from it sprang the Commonwealth,
   which breaks
As I am breaking now!

           "And therefore now
Let her, that is the womb and tomb of all,
Great Nature, take, and forcing far apart
Those blind beginnings that have made me
   man,   245
Dash them anew together at her will
Thro' all her cycles — into man once more,
Or beast or bird or fish, or opulent flower.
But till this cosmic order everywhere
Shattered into one earthquake in one day 250
Cracks all to pieces, — and that hour perhaps
Is not so far when momentary man
Shall seem no more a something to himself,
But he, his hopes and hates, his homes
   and fanes,
And even his bones long laid within the
   grave,   255
The very sides of the grave itself shall pass,
Vanishing, atom and void, atom and void,

---

182. Ovid tells of the legendary King Numa's capture of
these rustic deities to learn Jove's secrets. 194. **Twy-
natured**, double natured: the satyr was half goat and half
man; cf. "goat-foot," line 203. 208. **careless**, unconcerned
with mankind.

224. **Heliconian honey**, i.e., poetry (sweetness from the
home of the muses). 235. **her**, Lucretia, who, raped by the
son of King Tarquin, committed suicide and so set an example that led to the overthrow of the Tarquins and the establishment of the republic, which Lucretius sees now declining.

Into the unseen for ever, — till that hour,
My golden work in which I told a truth
That stays the rolling Ixionian wheel,   260
And numbs the Fury's ringlet-snake, and
          plucks
The mortal soul from out immortal hell,
Shall stand. Ay, surely; then it fails at last
And perishes as I must; for O Thou,
Passionless bride, divine Tranquillity,   265
Yearned after by the wisest of the wise,
Who fail to find thee, being as thou art
Without one pleasure and without one pain,
Howbeit I know thou surely must be mine
Or soon or late, yet out of season, thus   270
I woo thee roughly, for thou carest not
How roughly men may woo thee so they
          win —
Thus — thus — the soul flies out and dies
          in the air." .

With that he drove the knife into his side.
She heard him raging, heard him fall, ran
          in,   275
Beat breast, tore hair, cried out upon herself
As having failed in duty to him, shrieked
That she but meant to win him back, fell
          on him,
Clasped, kissed him, wailed. He answered,
          "Care not thou!
Thy duty? What is duty? Fare thee well!" 280
          (*1865;* 1868)

WAGES

Glory of warrior, glory of orator, glory of
          song,
     Paid with a voice flying by to be lost on
          an endless sea —
Glory of Virtue, to fight, to struggle, to right
          the wrong —
     Nay, but she aimed not at glory, no lover
          of glory she;
Give her the glory of going on, and still to be.

The wages of sin is death; if the wages of
          Virtue be dust,   6
     Would she have heart to endure for the
          life of the worm and the fly?
She desires no isles of the blest, no quiet seats
          of the just,
     To rest in a golden grove, or to bask in a
          summer sky;   9
Give her the wages of going on, and not to
          die.   (*1867;* 1868)

THE HIGHER PANTHEISM

The sun, the moon, the stars, the sea, the
          hills and the plains —
Are not these, O Soul, the Vision of Him
          who reigns?

Is not the Vision He, though He be not that
          which He seems?
Dreams are true while they last, and do we
          not live in dreams?

Earth, these solid stars, this weight of body
          and limb,   5
Are they not sign and symbol of thy division
          from Him?

Dark is the world to thee; thyself art the
          reason why,
For is He not all but thou, that hast power
          to feel "I am I"?

Glory about thee, without thee; and thou
          fulfillest thy doom,
Making Him broken gleams and a stifled
          splendor and gloom.   10

Speak to Him, thou, for He hears, and Spirit
          with Spirit can meet —
Closer is He than breathing, and nearer than
          hands and feet.

God is law, say the wise; O Soul, and let us
          rejoice,
For if He thunder by law the thunder is yet
          His voice.

Law is God, say some; no God at all, says
          the fool,   15
For all we have power to see is a straight
          staff bent in a pool;

And the ear of man cannot hear, and the eye
          of man cannot see;
But if we could see and hear, this Vision —
          were it not He?   (1869)

258-261. Lucretius' poem has denied the afterlife and the
torments of hell, such as the wheel to which Ixion in Greek
myth was forever bound for attempting to seduce Hera.
     Wages. **6. The . . . death.** Quoted from *Romans,* 6:23.

The Higher Pantheism. See Critical Notes and Swinburne's parody on the poem, *The Higher Pantheism in a
Nutshell,* 726.
     15. no God . . . fool. See *Psalms* 14:1.—"The fool hath
said in his heart. 'There is no God.' " The poem is full of
Bibilical allusions.

IN THE GARDEN AT SWAINSTON

Nightingales warbled without,
  Within was weeping for thee;
Shadows of three dead men
  Walked in the walks with me,
Shadows of three dead men, and thou wast
  one of the three.   5

Nightingales sang in his woods,
  The Master was far away;
Nightingales warbled and sang
  Of a passion that lasts but a day;
Still in the house in his coffin the Prince
  of courtesy lay.   10

Two dead men have I known
  In courtesy like to thee;
Two dead men have I loved
  With a love that ever will be;
Three dead men have I loved, and thou art
  last of the three.   15
             (*1870; 1874*)

FLOWER IN THE CRANNIED WALL

Flower in the crannied wall,
I pluck you out of the crannies,
I hold you here, root and all, in my hand,
Little flower — but *if* I could understand
What you are, root and all, and all in all,   5
I should know what God and man is.
             (1869)

From *THE IDYLLS OF THE KING*

LANCELOT AND ELAINE

Elaine the fair, Elaine the lovable,
Elaine, the lily maid of Astolat,
High in her chamber up a tower to the east
Guarded the sacred shield of Lancelot,
Which first she placed where morning's
  earliest ray   5
Might strike it, and awake her with the gleam;
Then, fearing rust or soilure, fashioned for it

A case of silk, and braided thereupon
All the devices blazoned on the shield
In their own tinct, and added, of her wit,   10
A border fantasy of branch and flower,
And yellow-throated nestling in the nest.
Nor rested thus content, but day by day,
Leaving her household and good father,
  climbed
That eastern tower, and, entering, barred her
  door,   15
Stripped off the case, and read the naked
  shield,
Now guessed a hidden meaning in his arms,
Now made a pretty history to herself
Of every dint a sword had beaten in it,
And every scratch a lance had made upon it,
Conjecturing when and where: this cut is
  fresh,   21
That ten years back; this dealt him at
  Caerlyle,
That at Caerleon — this at Camelot —
And, ah, God's mercy, what a stroke was
  there!
And here a thrust that might have killed,
  but God   25
Broke the strong lance, and rolled his enemy
  down,
And saved him. So she lived in fantasy.

How came the lily maid by that good
  shield
Of Lancelot, she that knew not even his
  name?
He left it with her, when he rode to tilt   30
For the great diamond in the diamond jousts,
Which Arthur had ordained, and by that
  name
Had named them, since a diamond was the
  prize.

For Arthur, long before they crowned him
  king,
Roving the trackless realms of Lyonnesse,   35
Had found a glen, gray boulder and black tarn.
A horror lived about the tarn, and clave
Like its own mists to all the mountain side;
For here two brothers, one a king, had met
And fought together, but their names were
  lost;   40
And each had slain his brother at a blow;
And down they fell and made the glen ab-
  horred.
And there they lay till all their bones were
  bleached,

In the Garden at Swainston. Swainston was the home of Tennyson's friend, Sir John Simeon. It was in the Isle of Wight, just off the south coast of England. Sir John died at Fribourg, Switzerland, in 1870. The other men referred to are Arthur Hallam and Henry Lushington (1812-55). Lushington was an admirer of Tennyson's youthful genius. *The Princess* was dedicated to him.
  The Idylls of the King. See Critical Notes.

8. **braided,** embroidered. 22. **Caerlyle,** Carlisle, in Cumberland. 23. **Caerleon,** an ancient town in Monmouthshire, where King Arthur frequently held court. **Camelot,** the place where Arthur had his palace and his court, and the place of the Round Table. 35. **Lyonnesse.** See note on *Morte d'Arthur,* line 4, p. 39.

And lichened into color with the crags.
And he that once was king had on a crown 45
Of diamonds, one in front and four aside.
And Arthur came, and laboring up the pass,
All in a misty moonshine, unawares
Had trodden that crowned skeleton, and the
  skull
Brake from the nape, and from the skull the
  crown   50
Rolled into light, and turning on its rims
Fled like a glittering rivulet to the tarn.
And down the shingly scaur he plunged, and
  caught,
And set it on his head, and in his heart
Heard murmurs, "Lo, thou likewise shalt be
  king."   55

  Thereafter, when a king, he had the gems
Plucked from the crown, and showed them
  to his knights,
Saying, "These jewels, whereupon I chanced
Divinely, are the kingdom's, not the King's —
For public use. Henceforward let there be, 60
Once every year, a just for one of these;
For so by nine years' proof we needs must
  learn
Which is our mightiest, and ourselves shall
  grow
In use of arms and manhood, till we drive
The heathen, who, some say, shall rule the
  land   65
Hereafter, which God hinder!" Thus he
  spoke.
And eight years past, eight justs had been,
  and still
Had Lancelot won the diamond of the year,
With purpose to present them to the Queen
When all were won; but, meaning all at once
To snare her royal fancy with a boon   71
Worth half her realm, had never spoken word.

  Now for the central diamond and the last
And largest, Arthur, holding then his court
Hard on the river nigh the place which now
Is this world's hugest, let proclaim a just 76
At Camelot, and when the time drew nigh
Spake — for she had been sick — to Guine-
  vere:
"Are you so sick, my Queen, you cannot move
To these fair justs?" "Yea, lord," she said,
  "ye know it."   80
"Then will ye miss," he answered, "the great
  deeds
Of Lancelot, and his prowess in the lists,
A sight ye love to look on." And the Queen
Lifted her eyes, and they dwelt languidly

On Lancelot, where he stood beside the King.
He, thinking that he read her meaning there,
"Stay with me, I am sick; my love is more 87
Than many diamonds," yielded; and a heart
Love-loyal to the least wish of the Queen —
However much he yearned to make complete
The tale of diamonds for his destined boon —
Urged him to speak against the truth, and
  say,   92
"Sir King, mine ancient wound is hardly
  whole,
And lets me from the saddle"; and the King
Glanced first at him, then her, and went his
  way.   95
No sooner gone than suddenly she began:

"To blame, my lord Sir Lancelot, much to
  blame!
Why go ye not to these fair justs? The
  knights
Are half of them our enemies, and the crowd
Will murmur, 'Lo, the shameless ones, who
  take   100
Their pastime now the trustful King is
  gone!'"
Then Lancelot, vexed at having lied in vain:
"Are ye so wise? Ye were not once so wise,
My Queen, that summer when ye loved me
  first.
Then of the crowd ye took no more account
Than of the myriad cricket of the mead, 106
When its own voice clings to each blade of
  grass,
And every voice is nothing. As to knights,
Them surely can I silence with all ease.
But now my loyal worship is allowed   110
Of all men; many a bard, without offense,
Has linked our names together in his lay,
Lancelot, the flower of bravery, Guinevere,
The pearl of beauty; and our knights at feast
Have pledged us in this union, while the King
Would listen smiling. How then? Is there
  more?   116
Has Arthur spoken aught? or would yourself,
Now weary of my service and devoir,
Henceforth be truer to your faultless lord?"

  She broke into a little scornful laugh: 120
"Arthur, my lord, Arthur, the faultless King,
That passionate perfection, my good lord —
But who can gaze upon the sun in heaven?
He never spake word of reproach to me,
He never had a glimpse of mine untruth, 125
He cares not for me. Only here today
There gleamed a vague suspicion in his
  eyes;
Some meddling rogue has tampered with him
  — else

---

44. lichened, became covered with lichen. 53. shingly
scaur, a steep cliff covered with stones. 59. Divinely, by
supernatural guidance. 65. The heathen, the Anglo-
Saxon invaders of Britain. 75. the place, London.

Rapt in this fancy of his Table Round,
And swearing men to vows impossible,   130
To make them like himself; but, friend, to me
He is all fault who hath no fault at all.
For who loves me must have a touch of earth;
The low sun makes the color. I am yours,
Not Arthur's, as ye know, save by the
    bond.
And therefore hear my words: go to the
    justs;   136
The tiny-trumpeting gnat can break our
    dream
When sweetest; and the vermin voices here
May buzz so loud — we scorn them, but they
    sting."

Then answered Lancelot, the chief of
    knights: 140
"And with what face, after my pretext made,
Shall I appear, O Queen, at Camelot, I
Before a king who honors his own word
As if it were his God's?"

                    "Yea," said the Queen,
"A moral child without the craft to rule,   145
Else had he not lost me; but listen to me,
If I must find you wit. We hear it said
That men go down before your spear at a
    touch,
But knowing you are Lancelot; your great
    name,
This conquers. Hide it therefore; go un-
    known.   150
Win! by this kiss you will; and our true King
Will then allow your pretext, O my knight,
As all for glory; for to speak him true,
Ye know right well, how meek soe'er he seem,
No keener hunter after glory breathes.   155
He loves it in his knights more than himself;
They prove to him his work. Win and return."

Then got Sir Lancelot suddenly to horse,
Wroth at himself. Not willing to be known,
He left the barren-beaten thoroughfare,   160
Chose the green path that showed the rarer
    foot,
And there among the solitary downs,
Full often lost in fancy, lost his way;
Till as he traced a faintly-shadowed track,
That all in loops and links among the dales
Ran to the Castle of Astolat, he saw   166
Fired from the west, far on a hill, the towers.
Thither he made, and blew the gateway horn.
Then came an old, dumb, myriad-wrinkled
    man,
Who let him into lodging and disarmed.   170
And Lancelot marveled at the wordless man;
And issuing found the Lord of Astolat

132. Cf. *Maud*, Part One, 82-84, page 98.

With two strong sons, Sir Torre and Sir
    Lavaine,
Moving to meet him in the castle court;
And close behind them stepped the lily maid
Elaine, his daughter; mother of the house 176
There was not. Some light jest among them
    rose
With laughter dying down as the great knight
Approached them; then the Lord of Astolat:
"Whence comest thou, my guest, and by what
    name   180
Livest between the lips? for by thy state
And presence I might guess thee chief of
    those,
After the King, who eat in Arthur's halls.
Him have I seen; the rest, his Table Round,
Known as they are, to me they are unknown."

Then answered Lancelot, the chief of
    knights: 186
"Known am I, and of Arthur's hall, and
    known,
What I by mere mischance have brought, my
    shield.
But since I go to just as one unknown
At Camelot for the diamond, ask me not;   190
Hereafter ye shall know me—and the shield—
I pray you lend me one, if such you have,
Blank, or at least with some device not mine."

Then said the Lord of Astolat: "Here is
    Torre's.   194
Hurt in his first tilt was my son, Sir Torre,
And so, God wot, his shield is blank enough.
His ye can have." Then added plain Sir
    Torre,
"Yea, since I cannot use it, ye may have it."
Here laughed the father, saying, "Fie, Sir
    Churl,
Is that an answer for a noble knight?   200
Allow him! but Lavaine, my younger here,
He is so full of lustihood, he will ride,
Just for it, and win, and bring it in an hour,
And set it in this damsel's golden hair,
To make her thrice as willful as before."   205

"Nay, father, nay, good father, shame me
    not
Before this noble knight," said young Lavaine,
"For nothing. Surely I but played on Torre—
He seemed so sullen, vexed he could not go —
A jest, no more! For, knight, the maiden
    dreamt   210
That someone put this diamond in her hand,
And that it was too slippery to be held,
And slipped and fell into some pool or stream,
The castle-well, belike; and then I said   214
That *if* I went and *if* I fought and won it —
But all was jest and joke among ourselves —
Then must she keep it safelier. All was jest.

But, father, give me leave, an if he will,
To ride to Camelot with this noble knight.
Win shall I not, but do my best to win; 220
Young as I am, yet would I do my best."

"So ye will grace me," answered Lancelot,
Smiling a moment, "with your fellowship
O'er these waste downs whereon I lost myself,
Then were I glad of you as guide and friend;
And you shall win this diamond — as I hear,
It is a fair large diamond — if ye may, 227
And yield it to this maiden, if ye will."
"A fair large diamond," added plain Sir Torre;
"Such be for queens, and not for simple
    maids." 230
Then she, who held her eyes upon the ground,
Elaine, and heard her name so tossed about,
Flushed slightly at the slight disparagement
Before the stranger knight, who, looking at
    her,
Full courtly, yet not falsely, thus returned:
"If what is fair be but for what is fair, 236
And only queens are to be counted so,
Rash were my judgment then, who deem this
    maid
Might wear as fair a jewel as is on earth,
Not violating the bond of like to like." 240

He spoke and ceased; the lily maid Elaine,
Won by the mellow voice before she looked,
Lifted her eyes and read his lineaments.
The great and guilty love he bare the Queen,
In battle with the love he bare his lord, 245
Had marred his face, and marked it ere his
    time.
Another sinning on such heights with one,
The flower of all the west and all the world,
Had been the sleeker for it; but in him
His mood was often like a fiend, and rose 250
And drove him into wastes and solitudes
For agony, who was yet a living soul.
Marred as he was, he seemed the goodliest
    man
That ever among ladies ate in hall,
And noblest, when she lifted up her eyes. 255
However marred, of more than twice her
    years,
Seamed with an ancient sword-cut on the
    cheek,
And bruised and bronzed, she lifted up her
    eyes
And loved him, with that love which was her
    doom.

Then the great knight, the darling of the
    court, 260
Loved of the loveliest, into that rude hall
Stepped with all grace, and not with half
    disdain

Hid under grace, as in a smaller time,
But kindly man moving among his kind;
Whom they with meats and vintage of their
    best 265
And talk and minstrel melody entertained.
And much they asked of court and Table
    Round,
And ever well and readily answered he;
But Lancelot, when they glanced at Guine-
    vere,
Suddenly speaking of the wordless man, 270
Heard from the baron that, ten years before,
The heathen caught and reft him of his
    tongue.
"He learned and warned me of their fierce
    design
Against my house, and him they caught and
    maimed;
But I, my sons, and little daughter fled 275
From bonds or death, and dwelt among the
    woods
By the great river in a boatman's hut.
Dull days were those, till our good Arthur
    broke
The Pagan yet once more on Badon hill."

"O there, great lord, doubtless," Lavaine
    said, rapt 280
By all the sweet and sudden passion of youth
Toward greatness in its elder, "you have
    fought.
O tell us — for we live apart — you know
Of Arthur's glorious wars." And Lancelot
    spoke 284
And answered him at full, as having been
With Arthur in the fight which all day long
Rang by the white mouth of the violent Glem;
And in the four loud battles by the shore
Of Duglas; that on Bassa; then the war
That thundered in and out the gloomy skirts
Of Celidon the forest; and again 291
By Castle Gurnion, where the glorious King
Had on his cuirass worn our Lady's Head,
Carved of one emerald centered in a sun
Of silver rays, that lightened as he breathed;
And at Caerleon had he helped his lord, 296
When the strong neighings of the wild White
    Horse
Set every gilded parapet shuddering;
And up in Agned-Cathregonion too,
And down the waste sand-shores of Trath
    Treroit, 300
Where many a heathen fell; "and on the
    mount

269. glanced at, spoke of. 279. The Pagan, the Saxons.
The battle was fought in 520 at Mount Badon, supposed to be
Badbury Hill, in Dorsetshire. The other battles mentioned
in lines 287-300 are regarded as mythical. Tennyson follows
the account given by Nennius in his *History of the Britons*
(8th century). 293. our Lady's Head, image of the Virgin
Mary. 297. the wild White Horse, the emblem of the Saxons.

Of Badon I myself beheld the King
Charge at the head of all his Table Round,
And all his legions crying Christ and him, 304
And break them; and I saw him, after, stand
High on a heap of slain, from spur to plume
Red as the rising sun with heathen blood,
And seeing me, with a great voice he cried,
'They are broken, they are broken!' for the
    King, 309
However mild he seems at home, nor cares
For triumph in our mimic wars, the justs —
For if his own knight casts him down, he
    laughs,
Saying his knights are better men than he —
Yet in this heathen war the fire of God
Fills him. I never saw his like; there lives 315
No greater leader."

        While he uttered this,
Low to her own heart said the lily maid,
"Save your great self, fair lord"; and when
    he fell
From talk of war to traits of pleasantry —
Being mirthful he, but in a stately kind — 320
She still took note that when the living smile
Died from his lips, across him came a cloud
Of melancholy severe, from which again,
Whenever in her hovering to and fro
The lily maid had striven to make him cheer,
There brake a sudden-beaming tenderness 326
Of manners and of nature; and she thought
That all was nature, all, perchance, for her.
And all night long his face before her lived,
As when a painter, poring on a face, 330
Divinely through all hindrance finds the
    man
Behind it, and so paints him that his face,
The shape and color of a mind and life,
Lives for his children, ever at its best
And fullest; so the face before her lived, 335
Dark-splendid, speaking in the silence, full
Of noble things, and held her from her sleep,
Till rathe she rose, half-cheated in the thought
She needs must bid farewell to sweet Lavaine.
First as in fear, step after step, she stole 340
Down the long tower-stairs, hesitating.
Anon, she heard Sir Lancelot cry in the court,
"This shield, my friend, where is it?" and
    Lavaine
Passed inward, as she came from out the
    tower.
There to his proud horse Lancelot turned,
    and smoothed 345
The glossy shoulder, humming to himself.
Half-envious of the flattering hand, she drew
Nearer and stood. He looked, and, more
    amazed
Than if seven men had set upon him, saw

338. rathe, early.

The maiden standing in the dewy light. 350
He had not dreamed she was so beautiful.
Then came on him a sort of sacred fear,
For silent, though he greeted her, she stood
Rapt on his face as if it were a god's.
Suddenly flashed on her a wild desire 355
That he should wear her favor at the tilt.
She braved a riotous heart in asking for it.
"Fair lord, whose name I know not — noble
    it is,
I well believe, the noblest — will you wear
My favor at this tourney?" "Nay," said he,
"Fair lady, since I never yet have worn 361
Favor of any lady in the lists.
Such is my wont, as those who know me
    know."
"Yea, so," she answered; "then in wearing
    mine 364
Needs must be lesser likelihood, noble lord,
That those who know should know you."
        And he turned
Her counsel up and down within his mind,
And found it true, and answered: "True, my
    child.
Well, I will wear it; fetch it out to me.
What is it?" and she told him, "A red sleeve
Broidered with pearls," and brought it. Then
    he bound 371
Her token on his helmet, with a smile,
Saying, "I never yet have done so much
For any maiden living," and the blood
Sprang to her face and filled her with delight;
But left her all the paler when Lavaine 376
Returning brought the yet-unblazoned shield,
His brother's, which he gave to Lancelot,
Who parted with his own to fair Elaine:
"Do me this grace, my child, to have my
    shield 380
In keeping till I come." "A grace to me,"
She answered, "twice today. I am your
    squire!"
Whereat Lavaine said, laughing: "Lily maid,
For fear our people call you lily maid
In earnest, let me bring your color back; 385
Once, twice, and thrice. Now get you hence
    to bed";
So kissed her, and Sir Lancelot his own hand,
And thus they moved away. She stayed a
    minute,
Then made a sudden step to the gate, and
    there —
Her bright hair blown about the serious face
Yet rosy-kindled with her brother's kiss — 391
Paused by the gateway, standing near the
    shield
In silence, while she watched their arms far-off
Sparkle, until they dipped below the downs.
Then to her tower she climbed, and took the
    shield, 395
There kept it, and so lived in fantasy.

Meanwhile the new companions passed
    away
Far o'er the long backs of the bushless downs,
To where Sir Lancelot knew there lived a
    knight   399
Not far from Camelot, now for forty years
A hermit, who had prayed, labored and
    prayed,
And ever laboring had scooped himself
In the white rock a chapel and a hall
On massive columns, like a shore-cliff cave,
And cells and chambers. All were fair and
    dry;   405
The green light from the meadows under-
    neath
Struck up and lived along the milky roofs;
And in the meadows tremulous aspen-trees
And poplars made a noise of falling showers.
And thither wending there that night they
    bode.   410

But when the next day broke from under-
    ground,
And shot red fire and shadows through the
    cave,
They rose, heard Mass, broke fast, and rode
    away.
Then Lancelot saying, "Hear, but hold my
    name   414
Hidden, you ride with Lancelot of the Lake,"
Abashed Lavaine, whose instant reverence,
Dearer to true young hearts than their own
    praise,
But left him leave to stammer, "Is it indeed?"
And after muttering, "The great Lancelot,"
At last he got his breath and answered:
    "One,   420
One have I seen — that other, our liege lord,
The dread Pendragon, Britain's King of kings,
Of whom the people talk mysteriously,
He will be there — then were I stricken blind
That minute, I might say that I had seen."

So spake Lavaine, and when they reached
    the lists   426
By Camelot in the meadow, let his eyes
Run through the peopled gallery which half
    round
Lay like a rainbow fallen upon the grass,
Until they found the clear-faced King, who
    sat   430
Robed in red samite, easily to be known,
Since to his crown the golden dragon clung,
And down his robe the dragon writhed in
    gold,
And from the carven-work behind him crept

Two dragons gilded, sloping down to make 435
Arms for his chair, while all the rest of them
Through knots and loops and folds innumer-
    able
Fled ever through the woodwork, till they
    found
The new design wherein they lost themselves,
Yet with all ease, so tender was the work; 440
And, in the costly canopy o'er him set,
Blazed the last diamond of the nameless
    king.

Then Lancelot answered young Lavaine
    and said:
"Me you call great; mine is the firmer seat,
The truer lance; but there is many a youth
Now crescent, who will come to all I am 446
And overcome it; and in me there dwells
No greatness, save it be some far-off touch
Of greatness to know well I am not great.
There is the man." And Lavaine gaped upon
    him   450
As on a thing miraculous, and anon
The trumpets blew: and then did either side,
They that assailed, and they that held the
    lists,
Set lance in rest, strike spur, suddenly move,
Meet in the midst, and there so furiously 455
Shock that a man far-off might well perceive,
If any man that day were left afield,
The hard earth shake, and a low thunder of
    arms.
And Lancelot bode a little, till he saw
Which were the weaker; then he hurled into it
Against the stronger. Little need to speak 461
Of Lancelot in his glory! King, duke, earl,
Count, baron — whom he smote, he over-
    threw.

But in the field were Lancelot's kith and
    kin,
Ranged with the Table Round that held the
    lists,   465
Strong men, and wrathful that a stranger
    knight
Should do and almost overdo the deeds
Of Lancelot; and one said to the other, "Lo!
What is he? I do not mean the force alone —
The grace and versatility of the man! 470
Is it not Lancelot?" "When has Lancelot
    worn
Favor of any lady in the lists?
Not such his wont, as we that know him
    know."
"How then? who then?" A fury seized them
    all,
A fiery family passion for the name 475
Of Lancelot, and a glory one with theirs.

422. **Pendragon**, a title given to the chief leader. 423.
talk mysteriously, a reference to the mystery of Arthur's
birth, told about in *The Coming of Arthur*. 431. **samite**, a
kind of heavy silk stuff.

446. **crescent**, in the period of promise.

They couched their spears and pricked their
    steeds, and thus,
Their plumes driven backward by the wind
    they made
In moving, all together down upon him
Bare, as a wild wave in the wide North Sea,
Green-glimmering toward the summit, bears,
    with all   481
Its stormy crests that smoke against the skies,
Down on a bark, and overbears the bark
And him that helms it; so they overbore
Sir Lancelot and his charger, and a spear   485
Down-glancing lamed the charger, and a spear
Pricked sharply his own cuirass, and the head
Pierced through his side, and there snapped
    and remained.

Then Sir Lavaine did well and worship-
    fully.
He bore a knight of old repute to the earth,
And brought his horse to Lancelot where he
    lay.   491
He up the side, sweating with agony, got,
But thought to do while he might yet endure,
And being lustily holpen by the rest,
His party — though it seemed half-miracle
To those he fought with — drave his kith and
    kin,   496
And all the Table Round that held the lists,
Back to the barrier; then the trumpets blew
Proclaiming his the prize who wore the sleeve
Of scarlet and the pearls; and all the knights
His party, cried, "Advance and take thy
    prize   501
The diamond"; but he answered: "Diamond
    me
No diamonds! for God's love, a little air!
Prize me no prizes, for my prize is death!
Hence will I, and I charge you, follow me
    not."   505

He spoke, and vanished suddenly from the
    field
With young Lavaine into the poplar grove.
There from his charger down he slid, and sat,
Gasping to Sir Lavaine, "Draw the lance-
    head."
"Ah, my sweet lord Sir Lancelot," said La-
    vaine,   510
"I dread me, if I draw it, you will die."
But he, "I die already with it; draw —
Draw" — and Lavaine drew, and Sir Lance-
    lot gave
A marvelous great shriek and ghastly groan,
And half his blood burst forth, and down he
    sank   515
For the pure pain, and wholly swooned away.
Then came the hermit out and bare him in,
There stanched his wound; and there, in daily
    doubt

Whether to live or die, for many a week
Hid from the wild world's rumor by the
    grove   520
Of poplars with their noise of falling showers,
And ever-tremulous aspen-trees, he lay.

But on that day when Lancelot fled the
    lists,
His party, knights of utmost North and
    West,
Lords of waste marshes, kings of desolate
    isles,   525
Came round their great Pendragon, saying
    to him,
"Lo, Sire, our knight, through whom we won
    the day,
Hath gone sore wounded, and hath left his
    prize
Untaken, crying that his prize is death."
"Heaven hinder," said the King, "that such
    an one,   530
So great a knight as we have seen today —
He seemed to me another Lancelot —
Yea, twenty times I thought him Lancelot —
He must not pass uncared for. Wherefore
    rise,
O Gawain, and ride forth and find the knight.
Wounded and wearied, needs must he be
    near.   536
I charge you that you get at once to horse.
And, knights and kings, there breathes not
    one of you
Will deem this prize of ours is rashly given;
His prowess was too wondrous. We will do
    him   540
No customary honor; since the knight
Came not to us, of us to claim the prize,
Ourselves will send it after. Rise and take
This diamond, and deliver it, and return, 544
And bring us where he is, and how he fares,
And cease not from your quest until ye find."

So saying, from the carven flower above,
To which it made a restless heart, he took
And gave the diamond. Then from where
    he sat
At Arthur's right, with smiling face arose, 550
With smiling face and frowning heart, a prince
In the mid might and flourish of his May,
Gawain, surnamed the Courteous, fair and
    strong,
And after Lancelot, Tristram, and Geraint,
And Gareth, a good knight, but therewithal
Sir Modred's brother, and the child of Lot, 556
Nor often loyal to his word, and now
Wroth that the King's command to sally
    forth

535. **Gawain**, son of King Lot of Orkney; he was the
nephew of King Arthur, the brother of Gareth, and the half-
brother of Modred. Modred was the traitor of the Round
Table.

In quest of whom he knew not, made him
    leave
The banquet and concourse of knights and
    kings.   560

So all in wrath he got to horse and went;
While Arthur to the banquet, dark in mood,
Passed, thinking, "Is it Lancelot who hath
    come
Despite the wound he spake of, all for gain
Of glory, and hath added wound to wound,
And ridden away to die?" So feared the
    King,   566
And, after two days' tarriance there, returned.
Then when he saw the Queen, embracing
    asked,
"Love, are you yet so sick?" "Nay, lord,"
    she said.
"And where is Lancelot?" Then the Queen
    amazed,   570
"Was he not with you? Won he not your
    prize?"
"Nay, but one like him." "Why, that like
    was he."
And when the King demanded how she knew,
Said: "Lord, no sooner had ye parted from us
Than Lancelot told me of a common talk 575
That men went down before his spear at a
    touch,
But knowing he was Lancelot; his great name
Conquered; and therefore would he hide his
    name   578
From all men, even the King, and to this end
Had made the pretext of a hindering wound,
That he might just unknown of all, and learn
If his old prowess were in aught decayed;
And added, 'Our true Arthur, when he learns,
Will well allow my pretext, as for gain
Of purer glory.'"

          Then replied the King: 585
"Far lovelier in our Lancelot had it been,
In lieu of idly dallying with the truth,
To have trusted me as he hath trusted thee.
Surely his King and most familiar friend
Might well have kept his secret. True, indeed,
Albeit I know my knights fantastical,   591
So fine a fear in our large Lancelot
Must needs have moved my laughter; now
    remains
But little cause for laughter. His own kin—
Ill news, my Queen, for all who love him,
    this!—   595
His kith and kin, not knowing, set upon him;
So that he went sore wounded from the field.
Yet good news too; for goodly hopes are mine
That Lancelot is no more a lonely heart.

592. **So fine a fear,** etc. There is a touch of sarcasm in
Arthur's words.

He wore, against his wont, upon his helm 600
A sleeve of scarlet, broidered with great
    pearls,
Some gentle maiden's gift."

             "Yea, lord," she said,
"Thy hopes are mine," and saying that, she
    choked,
And sharply turned about to hide her face,
Passed to her chamber, and there flung her-
    self   605
Down on the great King's couch, and writhed
    upon it,
And clenched her fingers till they bit the
    palm,
And shrieked out "Traitor!" to the unhear-
    ing wall,
Then flashed into wild tears, and rose again,
And moved about her palace, proud and pale.

Gawain the while through all the region
    round   611
Rode with his diamond, wearied of the quest,
Touched at all points except the poplar grove,
And came at last, though late, to Astolat;
Whom glittering in enameled arms the maid
Glanced at, and cried, "What news from
    Camelot, lord?   616
What of the knight with the red sleeve?"
    "He won."
"I knew it," she said. "But parted from the
    justs
Hurt in the side"; whereat she caught her
    breath.
Through her own side she felt the sharp lance
    go.   620
Thereon she smote her hand; wellnigh she
    swooned.
And, while he gazed wonderingly at her, came
The Lord of Astolat out, to whom the prince
Reported who he was, and on what quest
Sent, that he bore the prize and could not
    find   625
The victor, but had ridden a random round
To seek him, and had wearied of the search.
To whom the Lord of Astolat: "Bide with us,
And ride no more at random, noble prince!
Here was the knight, and here he left a
    shield;   630
This will he send or come for. Furthermore
Our son is with him; we shall hear anon;
Needs must we hear." To this the courteous
    prince
Accorded with his wonted courtesy,
Courtesy with a touch of traitor in it,   635
And stayed; and cast his eyes on fair Elaine.
Where could be found face daintier? Then
    her shape
From forehead down to foot, perfect; again
From foot to forehead exquisitely turned.

"Well — if I bide, lo! this wild flower for
    me!"   640
And oft they met among the garden yews,
And there he set himself to play upon her
With sallying wit, free flashes from a height
Above her, graces of the court, and songs,
Sighs, and low smiles, and golden eloquence
And amorous adulation, till the maid   646
Rebelled against it, saying to him: "Prince,
O loyal nephew of our noble King,
Why ask you not to see the shield he left,
Whence you might learn his name? Why
    slight your King,   650
And lose the quest he sent you on, and prove
No surer than our falcon yesterday,
Who lost the hern we slipped her at, and
    went
To all the winds?" "Nay, by mine head,"
    said he,
"I lose it, as we lose the lark in heaven,   655
O damsel, in the light of your blue eyes;
But an ye will it, let me see the shield."
And when the shield was brought, and Ga-
    wain saw
Sir Lancelot's azure lions, crowned with gold,
Ramp in the field, he smote his thigh, and
    mocked: 660
"Right was the King! our Lancelot! that true
    man!"
"And right was I," she answered merrily, "I,
Who dreamed my knight the greatest knight
    of all."
"And if *I* dreamed," said Gawain, "that you
    love
This greatest knight, your pardon! lo, ye
    know it!   665
Speak therefore; shall I waste myself in vain?"
Full simple was her answer: "What know
    I?
My brethren have been all my fellowship;
And I, when often they have talked of love,
Wished it had been my mother, for they
    talked,   670
Meseemed, of what they knew not; so my-
    self —
I know not if I know what true love is,
But if I know, then, if I love not him,
I know there is none other I can love."
"Yea, by God's death," said he, "ye love him
    well,   675
But would not, knew ye what all others know,
And whom he loves." "So be it," cried
    Elaine,
And lifted her fair face and moved away;
But he pursued her, calling, "Stay a little!
One golden minute's grace! He wore your
    sleeve;   680
Would he break faith with one I may not
    name?
Must our true man change like a leaf at last?

Nay — like enow. Why then, far be it from
    me
To cross our mighty Lancelot in his loves!
And, damsel, for I deem you know full well
Where your great knight is hidden, let me
    leave   686
My quest with you; the diamond also — here!
For if you love, it will be sweet to give it;
And if he love, it will be sweet to have it
From your own hand; and whether he love
    or not,   690
A diamond is a diamond. Fare you well
A thousand times! — a thousand times fare-
    well!
Yet, if he love, and his love hold, we two
May meet at court hereafter! There, I think,
So ye will learn the courtesies of the court,
We two shall know each other."   696

                    Then he gave,
And slightly kissed the hand to which he
    gave,
The diamond, and all wearied of the quest
Leaped on his horse, and caroling as he went
A true-love ballad, lightly rode away.   700

    Thence to the court he passed; there told
    the King
What the King knew, "Sir Lancelot is the
    knight."
And added, "Sire, my liege, so much I learned,
But failed to find him, though I rode all round
The region; but I lighted on the maid   705
Whose sleeve he wore. She loves him; and
    to her,
Deeming our courtesy is the truest law,
I gave the diamond. She will render it;
For by mine head she knows his hiding-
    place."

    The seldom-frowning King frowned, and
    replied,   710
"Too courteous truly! Ye shall go no more
On quest of mine, seeing that ye forget
Obedience is the courtesy due to kings."

    He spake and parted. Wroth, but all in
    awe,
For twenty strokes of the blood, without a
    word,   715
Lingered that other, staring after him;
Then shook his hair, strode off, and buzzed
    abroad
About the maid of Astolat, and her love.
All ears were pricked at once, all tongues
    were loosed:
"The maid of Astolat loves Sir Lancelot;   720
Sir Lancelot loves the maid of Astolat."
Some read the King's face, some the Queen's,
    and all

Had marvel what the maid might be, but most
Predoomed her as unworthy. One old dame
Came suddenly on the Queen with the sharp news.   725
She, that had heard the noise of it before,
But sorrowing Lancelot should have stooped so low,
Marred her friend's aim with pale tranquillity.
So ran the tale like fire about the court,
Fire in dry stubble a nine-days' wonder flared;   730
Till even the knights at banquet twice or thrice
Forgot to drink to Lancelot and the Queen,
And pledging Lancelot and the lily maid
Smiled at each other, while the Queen, who sat
With lips severely placid, felt the knot   735
Climb in her throat, and with her feet unseen
Crushed the wild passion out against the floor
Beneath the banquet, where the meats became
As wormwood, and she hated all who pledged.

But far away the maid in Astolat,   740
Her guiltless rival, she that ever kept
The one-day-seen Sir Lancelot in her heart,
Crept to her father, while he mused alone,
Sat on his knee, stroked his gray face, and said,   744
"Father, you call me willful, and the fault
Is yours who let me have my will; and now,
Sweet father, will you let me lose my wits?"
"Nay," said he, "surely." "Wherefore, let me hence,"
She answered, "and find out our dear Lavaine."
"Ye will not lose your wits for dear Lavaine.
Bide," answered he; "we needs must hear anon   751
Of him, and of that other." "Aye," she said,
"And of that other, for I needs must hence
And find that other, wheresoe'er he be,
And with mine own hand give his diamond to him,   755
Lest I be found as faithless in the quest
As yon proud prince who left the quest to me.
Sweet father, I behold him in my dreams
Gaunt as it were the skeleton of himself,
Death-pale, for the lack of gentle maiden's aid.   760
The gentler-born the maiden, the more bound,
My father, to be sweet and serviceable
To noble knights in sickness, as ye know,
When these have worn their tokens. Let me hence,
I pray you." Then her father nodding said:
"Aye, aye, the diamond. Wit ye well, my child,   766

Right fain were I to learn this knight were whole,
Being our greatest. Yea, and you must give it —
And sure I think this fruit is hung too high
For any mouth to gape for save a queen's —
Nay, I mean nothing; so then, get you gone,
Being so very willful you must go."   772

Lightly, her suit allowed, she slipped away,
And while she made her ready for her ride,
Her father's latest word hummed in her ear,
"Being so very willful you must go,"   776
And changed itself and echoed in her heart,
"Being so very willful you must die."
But she was happy enough and shook it off,
As we shake off the bee that buzzes at us; 780
And in her heart she answered it and said,
"What matter, so I help him back to life?"
Then far away with good Sir Torre for guide
Rode o'er the long backs of the bushless downs
To Camelot, and before the city-gates   785
Came on her brother with a happy face
Making a roan horse caper and curvet
For pleasure all about a field of flowers;
Whom when she saw, "Lavaine," she cried, "Lavaine,
How fares my lord Sir Lancelot?" He amazed,   790
"Torre and Elaine! why here? Sir Lancelot!
How know ye my lord's name is Lancelot?"
But when the maid had told him all her tale,
Then turned Sir Torre, and being in his moods
Left them, and under the strange-statued gate,   795
Where Arthur's wars were rendered mystically,
Passed up the still rich city to his kin,
His own far blood, which dwelt at Camelot;
And her, Lavaine across the poplar grove
Led to the caves. There first she saw the casque   800
Of Lancelot on the wall; her scarlet sleeve,
Though carved and cut, and half the pearls away,
Streamed from it still; and in her heart she laughed,
Because he had not loosed it from his helm,
But meant once more perchance to tourney in it.   805
And when they gained the cell wherein he slept,
His battle-writhen arms and mighty hands
Lay naked on the wolf-skin, and a dream
Of dragging down his enemy made them move.
Then she that saw him lying unsleek, unshorn,   810

798. **His own far blood,** his distant relatives.

Gaunt as it were the skeleton of himself,
Uttered a little tender, dolorous cry.
The sound not wonted in a place so still
Woke the sick knight, and while he rolled
    his eyes
Yet blank from sleep, she started to him,
    saying,   815
"Your prize, the diamond sent you by the
    King."
His eyes glistened; she fancied, "Is it for
    me?"
And when the maid had told him all the tale
Of king and prince, the diamond sent, the
    quest
Assigned to her not worthy of it, she knelt
Full lowly by the corners of his bed,   821
And laid the diamond in his open hand.
Her face was near, and as we kiss the child
That does the task assigned, he kissed her
    face.
At once she slipped like water to the floor. 825
"Alas," he said, "your ride hath wearied you.
Rest must you have." "No rest for me," she
    said;
"Nay, for near you, fair lord, I am at rest."
What might she mean by that? His large
    black eyes,
Yet larger through his leanness, dwelt upon
    her,   830
Till all her heart's sad secret blazed itself
In the heart's colors on her simple face;
And Lancelot looked and was perplexed in
    mind,
And being weak in body said no more,
But did not love the color; woman's love,   835
Save one, he not regarded, and so turned
Sighing, and feigned a sleep until he slept.

Then rose Elaine and glided through the
    fields,
And passed beneath the weirdly-sculptured
    gates
Far up the dim rich city to her kin;   840
There bode the night, but woke with dawn,
    and passed
Down through the dim rich city to the fields,
Thence to the cave. So day by day she passed
In either twilight ghost-like to and fro
Gliding, and every day she tended him,   845
And likewise many a night; and Lancelot
Would, though he called his wound a little
    hurt
Whereof he should be quickly whole, at times
Brain-feverous in his heat and agony, seem
Uncourteous, even he. But the meek maid
Sweetly forbore him ever, being to him   851
Meeker than any child to a rough nurse,
Milder than any mother to a sick child,
And never woman yet, since man's first fall,
Did kindlier unto man, but her deep love   855

Upbore her; till the hermit, skilled in all
The simples and the science of that time,
Told him that her fine care had saved his
    life.
And the sick man forgot her simple blush,
Would call her friend and sister, sweet Elaine,
Would listen for her coming and regret   861
Her parting step, and held her tenderly,
And loved her with all love except the love
Of man and woman when they love their best,
Closest and sweetest, and had died the death
In any knightly fashion for her sake.   866
And peradventure had he seen her first
She might have made this and that other
    world
Another world for the sick man; but now
The shackles of an old love straitened him, 870
His honor rooted in dishonor stood,
And faith unfaithful kept him falsely true.

Yet the great knight in his mid-sickness made
Full many a holy vow and pure resolve.   874
These, as but born of sickness, could not live;
For when the blood ran lustier in him again,
Full often the bright image of one face,
Making a treacherous quiet in his heart,
Dispersed his resolution like a cloud.   879
Then if the maiden, while that ghostly grace
Beamed on his fancy, spoke, he answered not,
Or short and coldly, and she knew right well
What the rough sickness meant, but what this
    meant
She knew not, and the sorrow dimmed her
    sight,
And drave her ere her time across the fields
Far into the rich city, where alone   886
She murmured, "Vain, in vain! it cannot be.
He will not love me. How then? Must I
    die?"
Then as a little helpless, innocent bird,   889
That has but one plain passage of few notes,
Will sing the simple passage o'er and o'er
For all an April morning, till the ear
Wearies to hear it, so the simple maid
Went half the night repeating, "Must I die?"
And now to right she turned, and now to left,
And found no ease in turning or in rest;   896
And "Him or death," she muttered, "death
    or him,"
Again and like a burthen, "Him or death."

But when Sir Lancelot's deadly hurt was
    whole,
To Astolat returning rode the three.   900
There morn by morn, arraying her sweet self
In that wherein she deemed she looked her
    best,
She came before Sir Lancelot, for she thought,

880. that ghostly grace, the vision of Guinevere. 883.
the rough sickness, delirium.

"If I be loved, these are my festal robes,
If not, the victim's flowers before he fall." 905
And Lancelot ever pressed upon the maid
That she should ask some goodly gift of him
For her own self or hers — "and do not shun
To speak the wish most near to your true
     heart;   909
Such service have ye done me that I make
My will of yours, and prince and lord am I
In mine own land, and what I will I can."
Then like a ghost she lifted up her face,
But like a ghost without the power to speak.
And Lancelot saw that she withheld her wish,
And bode among them yet a little space   916
Till he should learn it; and one morn it
     chanced
He found her in among the garden yews,
And said, "Delay no longer, speak your wish,
Seeing I go today." Then out she brake: 920
"Going? and we shall never see you more.
And I must die for want of one bold word."
"Speak; that I live to hear," he said, "is
     yours."
Then suddenly and passionately she spoke:
"I have gone mad. I love you; let me die."
"Ah, sister," answered Lancelot, "what is
     this?"   926
And innocently extending her white arms,
"Your love," she said, "your love — to be
     your wife."
And Lancelot answered, "Had I chosen to
     wed,
I had been wedded earlier, sweet Elaine; 930
But now there never will be wife of mine."
"No, no," she cried, "I care not to be wife,
But to be with you still, to see your face,
To serve you, and to follow you through the
     world."
And Lancelot answered: "Nay, the world, the
     world,   935
All ear and eye, with such a stupid heart
To interpret ear and eye, and such a tongue
To blare its own interpretation — nay,
Full ill then should I quit your brother's
     love,
And your good father's kindness." And she
     said,   940
"Not to be with you, not to see your face —
Alas for me then, my good days are done!"
"Nay, noble maid," he answered, "ten times
     nay!
This is not love, but love's first flash in youth,
Most common; yea, I know it of mine own
     self,   945
And you yourself will smile at your own self
Hereafter, when you yield your flower of life
To one more fitly yours, not thrice your age.
And then will I, for true you are and sweet

905. the victim's . . . fall, a reference to the ancient
custom of decorating animals for sacrifice.

Beyond mine old belief in womanhood,   950
More specially should your good knight be
     poor,
Endow you with broad land and territory
Even to the half my realm beyond the seas,
So that would make you happy; furthermore,
Even to the death, as though ye were my
     blood,   955
In all your quarrels will I be your knight.
This will I do, dear damsel, for your sake,
And more than this I cannot."

                         While he spoke
She neither blushed nor shook, but deathly-
     pale
Stood grasping what was nearest, then re-
     plied,   960
"Of all this will I nothing"; and so fell,
And thus they bore her swooning to her
     tower.

Then spake, to whom through those black
     walls of yew
Their talk had pierced, her father: "Aye, a
     flash,   964
I fear me, that will strike my blossom dead.
Too courteous are ye, fair Lord Lancelot.
I pray you, use some rough discourtesy
To blunt or break her passion."

                              Lancelot said,
"That were against me; what I can I will";
And there that day remained, and toward
     even   970
Sent for his shield. Full meekly rose the
     maid,
Stripped off the case, and gave the naked
     shield;
Then, when she heard his horse upon the
     stones,
Unclasping flung the casement back, and
     looked
Down on his helm, from which her sleeve
     had gone.   975
And Lancelot knew the little clinking sound;
And she by tact of love was well aware
That Lancelot knew that she was looking at
     him.
And yet he glanced not up, nor waved his
     hand,
Nor bade farewell, but sadly rode away. 980
This was the one discourtesy that he used.

So in her tower alone the maiden sat.
His very shield was gone; only the case,
Her own poor work, her empty labor, left
But still she heard him, still his picture
     formed   985
And grew between her and the pictured wall.

Then came her father, saying in low tones,
"Have comfort," whom she greeted quietly.
Then came her brethren saying, "Peace to thee,
Sweet sister," whom she answered with all calm.   990
But when they left her to herself again,
Death, like a friend's voice from a distant field
Approaching through the darkness, called; the owls
Wailing had power upon her, and she mixed 995
Her fancies with the sallow-rifted glooms
Of evening and the moanings of the wind.

And in those days she made a little song,
And called her song "The Song of Love and Death,"
And sang it; sweetly could she make and sing.

"Sweet is true love though given in vain, in vain;   1000
And sweet is death who puts an end to pain.
I know not which is sweeter, no, not I.

"Love, art thou sweet? Then bitter death must be.
Love, thou art bitter; sweet is death to me.
O Love, if death be sweeter, let me die. 1005

"Sweet love, that seems not made to fade away;
Sweet death, that seems to make us loveless clay;
I know not which is sweeter, no, not I.

"I fain would follow love, if that could be;
I needs must follow death, who calls for me;
Call and I follow, I follow! Let me die." 1011

High with the last line scaled her voice, and this,
All in a fiery dawning wild with wind
That shook her tower, the brothers heard, and thought
With shuddering, "Hark the Phantom of the house   1015
That ever shrieks before a death," and called
The father, and all three in hurry and fear
Ran to her, and lo! the blood-red light of dawn
Flared on her face, she shrilling, "Let me die!"

As when we dwell upon a word we know,
Repeating, till the word we know so well 1021
Becomes a wonder, and we know not why,

<hr/>

1015-1016. Phantom . . . death. In Celtic folklore a supernatural being, the banshee, was supposed to warn a family of approaching death by wailing or by singing in a mournful voice.

So dwelt the father on her face, and thought,
"Is this Elaine?" till back the maiden fell,
Then gave a languid hand to each, and lay,1025
Speaking a still good-morrow with her eyes.
At last she said: "Sweet brothers, yesternight
I seemed a curious little maid again,
As happy as when we dwelt among the woods,
And when ye used to take me with the flood
Up the great river in the boatman's boat. 1031
Only ye would not pass beyond the cape
That has the poplar on it; there ye fixed
Your limit, oft returning with the tide.
And yet I cried because ye would not pass
Beyond it, and far up the shining flood 1036
Until we found the palace of the King.
And yet ye would not; but this night I dreamed
That I was all alone upon the flood,
And then I said, 'Now shall I have my will';
And there I woke, but still the wish remained.   1041
So let me hence that I may pass at last
Beyond the poplar and far up the flood,
Until I find the palace of the King.
There will I enter in among them all,   1045
And no man there will dare to mock at me;
But there the fine Gawain will wonder at me,
And there the great Sir Lancelot muse at me;
Gawain, who bade a thousand farewells to me,
Lancelot, who coldly went, nor bade me one.
And there the King will know me and my love,   1051
And there the Queen herself will pity me,
And all the gentle court will welcome me,
And after my long voyage I shall rest!"

"Peace," said her father, "O my child, ye seem   1055
Light-headed, for what force is yours to go
So far, being sick? And wherefore would ye look
On this proud fellow again, who scorns us all?"

Then the rough Torre began to heave and move,
And bluster into stormy sobs and say: 1060
"I never loved him; an I meet with him,
I care not howsoever great he be,
Then will I strike at him and strike him down.
Give me good fortune, I will strike him dead,
For this discomfort he hath done the house."

To whom the gentle sister made reply: 1066
"Fret not yourself, dear brother, nor be wroth,
Seeing it is no more Sir Lancelot's fault
Not to love me than it is mine to love
Him of all men who seems to me the highest."

"Highest?" the father answered, echoing
    "highest?" —   1071
He meant to break the passion in her —
    "nay,
Daughter, I know not what you call the
    highest;
But this I know, for all the people know it,
He loves the Queen, and in an open shame,
And she returns his love in open shame;   1076
If this be high, what is it to be low?"

Then spake the lily maid of Astolat:
"Sweet father, all too faint and sick am I
For anger. These are slanders; never yet   1080
Was noble man but made ignoble talk.
He makes no friend who never made a foe,
But now it is my glory to have loved
One peerless, without stain; so let me pass,
My father, howsoe'er I seem to you,   1085
Not all unhappy, having loved God's best
And greatest, though my love had no return.
Yet, seeing you desire your child to live,
Thanks, but you work against your own
    desire,
For if I could believe the things you say   1090
I should but die the sooner; wherefore cease,
Sweet father, and bid call the ghostly man
Hither, and let me shrive me clean and die."

So when the ghostly man had come and
    gone,
She, with a face bright as for sin forgiven,   1095
Besought Lavaine to write as she devised
A letter, word for word; and when he asked,
"Is it for Lancelot, is it for my dear lord?
Then will I bear it gladly," she replied,
"For Lancelot and the Queen and all the
    world,   1100
But I myself must bear it." Then he wrote
The letter she devised, which being writ
And folded, "O sweet father, tender and true,
Deny me not," she said — "ye never yet
Denied my fancies — this, however strange,
My latest. Lay the letter in my hand   1106
A little ere I die, and close the hand
Upon it; I shall guard it even in death.
And when the heat has gone from out my
    heart,
Then take the little bed on which I died   1110
For Lancelot's love, and deck it like the
    Queen's
For richness, and me also like the Queen
In all I have of rich, and lay me on it.
And let there be prepared a chariot-bier
To take me to the river, and a barge   1115
Be ready on the river, clothed in black.
I go in state to court, to meet the Queen.
There surely I shall speak for mine own self,

1092. **the ghostly man**, the spiritual man, priest.

And none of you can speak for me so well.
And therefore let our dumb old man alone 1120
Go with me; he can steer and row, and he
Will guide me to that palace, to the doors."

She ceased. Her father promised; where-
    upon
She grew so cheerful that they deemed her
    death
Was rather in the fantasy than the blood.   1125
But ten slow mornings passed, and on the
    eleventh
Her father laid the letter in her hand,
And closed the hand upon it, and she died.
So that day there was dole in Astolat.

But when the next sun brake from under-
    ground,   1130
Then, those two brethren slowly with bent
    brows
Accompanying, the sad chariot-bier
Passed like a shadow through the field, that
    shone
Full-summer, to that stream whereon the
    barge,   1134
Palled all its length in blackest samite, lay.
There sat the lifelong creature of the house,
Loyal, the dumb old servitor, on deck,
Winking his eyes, and twisted all his face.
So those two brethren from the chariot took
And on the black decks laid her in her bed,
Set in her hand a lily, o'er her hung   1141
The silken case with braided blazonings,
And kissed her quiet brows, and saying to her,
"Sister, farewell forever," and again,
"Farewell, sweet sister," parted all in tears.
Then rose the dumb old servitor, and the
    dead,   1146
Oared by the dumb, went upward with the
    flood —
In her right hand the lily, in her left
The letter — all her bright hair streaming
    down —
And all the coverlid was cloth of gold   1150
Drawn to her waist, and she herself in white
All but her face, and that clear-featured face
Was lovely, for she did not seem as dead,
But fast asleep, and lay as though she smiled.

That day Sir Lancelot at the palace craved
Audience of Guinevere, to give at last   1156
The price of half a realm, his costly gift,
Hard-won and hardly won with bruise and
    blow,
With deaths of others, and almost his own,
The nine-years-fought-for diamonds; for he
    saw   1160
One of her house, and sent him to the Queen
Bearing his wish, whereto the Queen agreed
With such and so unmoved a majesty

She might have seemed her statue, but that
          he,
Low-drooping till he wellnigh kissed her feet
For loyal awe, saw with a sidelong eye   1166
The shadow of some piece of pointed lace,
In the Queen's shadow, vibrate on the walls,
And parted, laughing in his courtly heart.

          All in an oriel on the summer side,   1170
Vine-clad, of Arthur's palace toward the
          stream,
They met, and Lancelot kneeling uttered:
          "Queen,
Lady, my liege, in whom I have my joy,
Take, what I had not won except for you,
These jewels, and make me happy, making
          them   1175
An armlet for the roundest arm on earth,
Or necklace for a neck to which the swan's
Is tawnier than her cygnet's. These are words;
Your beauty is your beauty, and I sin
In speaking, yet O grant my worship of it 1180
Words, as we grant grief tears. Such sin in
          words,
Perchance, we both can pardon; but, my
          Queen,
I hear of rumors flying through your court.
Our bond, as not the bond of man and wife,
Should have in it an absoluter trust   1185
To make up that defect; let rumors be.
When did not rumors fly? These, as I trust
That you trust me in your own nobleness,
I may not well believe that you believe."

          While thus he spoke, half turned away, the
          Queen   1190
Brake from the vast oriel-embowering vine
Leaf after leaf, and tore, and cast them off,
Till all the place whereon she stood was green;
Then, when he ceased, in one cold, passive
          hand
Received at once and laid aside the gems 1195
There on a table near her, and replied:

          "It may be I am quicker of belief
Than you believe me, Lancelot of the Lake.
Our bond is not the bond of man and wife.
This good is in it, whatsoe'er of ill,   1200
It can be broken easier. I for you
This many a year have done despite and
          wrong
To one whom ever in my heart of hearts
I did acknowledge nobler. What are these?
Diamonds for me! They had been thrice their
          worth   1205
Being your gift, had you not lost your own.
To loyal hearts the value of all gifts

Must vary as the giver's. Not for me!
For her! for your new fancy. Only this   1209
Grant me, I pray you: have your joys apart.
I doubt not that, however changed, you keep
So much of what is graceful; and myself
Would shun to break those bounds of courtesy
In which as Arthur's Queen I move and rule,
So cannot speak my mind. An end to this!
A strange one! yet I take it with Amen.   1216
So pray you, add my diamonds to her pearls;
Deck her with these; tell her she shines me
          down;
An armlet for an arm to which the Queen's
Is haggard, or a necklace for a neck   1220
O as much fairer — as a faith once fair
Was richer than these diamonds — hers not
          mine —
Nay, by the mother of our Lord himself,
Or hers or mine, mine now to work my will —
She shall not have them."

                    Saying which she seized,   1225
And, through the casement standing wide for
          heat,
Flung them, and down they flashed, and
          smote the stream.
Then from the smitten surface flashed, as it
          were,
Diamonds to meet them, and they passed
          away.
Then while Sir Lancelot leaned, in half dis-
          dain   1230
At love, life, all things, on the window ledge,
Close underneath his eyes, and right across
Where these had fallen, slowly passed the
          barge
Whereon the lily maid of Astolat
Lay smiling, like a star in blackest night. 1235

          But the wild Queen, who saw not, burst
          away
To weep and wail in secret; and the barge,
On to the palace-doorway sliding, paused.
There two stood armed, and kept the door;
          to whom,
All up the marble stair, tier over tier,   1240
Were added mouths that gaped, and eyes
          that asked,
"What is it?" But that oarsman's haggard
          face,
As hard and still as is the face that men
Shape to their fancy's eye from broken rocks
On some cliff-side, appalled them, and they
          said,   1245
"He is enchanted, cannot speak — and she,
Look how she sleeps — the Fairy Queen, so
          fair!
Yea, but how pale! What are they? Flesh
          and blood?
Or come to take the King to Fairyland?

1170. oriel, a large bay window.   1178. tawnier . . .
cygnet's. The down of the cygnet, or young swan, is of a
brownish hue.

For some do hold our Arthur cannot die, 1250
But that he passes into Fairyland."

While thus they babbled of the King, the
    King
Came girt with knights. Then turned the
    tongueless man
From the half-face to the full eye, and rose
And pointed to the damsel and the doors.1255
So Arthur bade the meek Sir Percivale
And pure Sir Galahad to uplift the maid;
And reverently they bore her into hall.
Then came the fine Gawain and wondered at
    her,   1259
And Lancelot later came and mused at her,
And last the Queen herself, and pitied her;
But Arthur spied the letter in her hand,
Stooped, took, brake seal, and read it; this
    was all:

    "Most noble lord, Sir Lancelot of the
    Lake,
I, sometime called the maid of Astolat, 1265
Come, for you left me taking no farewell,
Hither, to take my last farewell of you.
I loved you, and my love had no return,
And therefore my true love has been my
    death.
And therefore to our Lady Guinevere, 1270
And to all other ladies, I make moan:
Pray for my soul, and yield me burial.
Pray for my soul thou too, Sir Lancelot,
As thou art a knight peerless."

                Thus he read;
And ever in the reading lords and dames 1275
Wept, looking often from his face who read
To hers which lay so silent, and at times,
So touched were they, half-thinking that her
    lips
Who had devised the letter moved again.

Then freely spoke Sir Lancelot to them
    all: 1280
"My lord liege Arthur, and all ye that hear,
Know that for this most gentle maiden's death
Right heavy am I; for good she was and true,
But loved me with a love beyond all love
In women, whomsoever I have known.   1285
Yet to be loved makes not to love again;
Not at my years, however it hold in youth.
I swear by truth and knighthood that I gave
No cause, not willingly, for such a love.
To this I call my friends in testimony,   1290
Her brethren, and her father, who himself
Besought me to be plain and blunt, and use,
To break her passion, some discourtesy

Against my nature; what I could, I did.
I left her and I bade her no farewell;   1295
Though, had I dreamt the damsel would have
    died,
I might have put my wits to some rough use,
And helped her from herself."

              Then said the Queen —
Sea was her wrath, yet working after storm:
"Ye might at least have done her so much
    grace,   1300
Fair lord, as would have helped her from her
    death."
He raised his head; their eyes met, and hers
    fell,
He adding: "Queen, she would not be content
Save that I wedded her, which could not be.
Then might she follow me through the world,
    she asked;   1305
It could not be. I told her that her love
Was but the flash of youth, would darken
    down,
To rise hereafter in a stiller flame
Toward one more worthy of her — then
    would I,   1309
More specially were he she wedded poor,
Estate them with large land and territory
In mine own realm beyond the narrow seas,
To keep them in all joyance. More than this
I could not; this she would not, and she
    died."

He pausing, Arthur answered: "O my
    knight,   1315
It will be to thy worship, as my knight,
And mine, as head of all our Table Round,
To see that she be buried worshipfully."

So toward that shrine which then in all
    the realm
Was richest, Arthur leading, slowly went   1320
The marshaled Order of their Table Round,
And Lancelot sad beyond his wont, to see
The maiden buried, not as one unknown,
Nor meanly, but with gorgeous obsequies,
And Mass, and rolling music, like a queen.
And when the knights had laid her comely
    head   1326
Low in the dust of half-forgotten kings,
Then Arthur spake among them: "Let her
    tomb
Be costly, and her image thereupon,
And let the shield of Lancelot at her feet 1330
Be carven, and her lily in her hand.
And let the story of her dolorous voyage
For all true hearts be blazoned on her tomb
In letters gold and azure!" which was wrought

1256-1257. **Sir Percivale, Sir Galahad.** These were the
purest knights of the Round Table.

1316. **worship,** honor. 1319-1320 **that shrine . . . rich-**
est, the burial place of kings.

Thereafter. But when now the lords and
    dames   1335
And people, from the high door streaming,
    brake
Disorderly, as homeward each, the Queen,
Who marked Sir Lancelot where he moved
    apart,
Drew near, and sighed in passing, "Lancelot,
Forgive me; mine was jealousy in love."   1340
He answered with his eyes upon the ground,
"That is love's curse; pass on, my Queen,
    forgiven."
But Arthur, who beheld his cloudy brows,
Approached him, and with full affection said:

"Lancelot, my Lancelot, thou in whom I
    have   1345
Most joy and most affiance, for I know
What thou hast been in battle by my side,
And many a time have watched thee at the
    tilt
Strike down the lusty and long practiced
    knight
And let the younger and unskilled go by   1350
To win his honor and to make his name,
And loved thy courtesies and thee, a man
Made to be loved; but now I would to God,
Seeing the homeless trouble in thine eyes,
Thou couldst have loved this maiden, shaped,
    it seems,   1355
By God for thee alone, and from her face,
If one may judge the living by the dead,
Delicately pure and marvelously fair,
Who might have brought thee, now a lonely
    man
Wifeless and heirless, noble issue, sons   1360
Born to the glory of thy name and fame,
My knight, the great Sir Lancelot of the
    Lake."

Then answered Lancelot: "Fair she was,
    my King,
Pure, as you ever wish your knights to be.
To doubt her fairness were to want an eye,
To doubt her pureness were to want a
    heart —   1366
Yea, to be loved, if what is worthy love
Could bind him, but free love will not be
    bound."

"Free love, so bound, were freest," said
    the King.   1369
"Let love be free; free love is for the best.
And, after heaven, on our dull side of death,
What should be best, if not so pure a love
Clothed in so pure a loveliness? Yet thee
She failed to bind, though being, as I think,
Unbound as yet, and gentle, as I know."   1375

And Lancelot answered nothing, but he
    went,

And at the inrunning of a little brook
Sat by the river in a cove, and watched
The high reed wave, and lifted up his eyes
And saw the barge that brought her moving
    down,   1380
Far-off, a blot upon the stream, and said
Low in himself: "Ah, simple heart and sweet,
Ye loved me, damsel, surely with a love
Far tenderer than my Queen's. Pray for thy
    soul?
Aye, that will I. Farewell too — now at
    last —   1385
Farewell, fair lily. 'Jealousy in love'?
Not rather dead love's harsh heir, jealous
    pride?
Queen, if I grant the jealousy as of love,
May not your crescent fear for name and
    fame
Speak, as it waxes, of a love that wanes? 1390
Why did the King dwell on my name to me?
Mine own name shames me, seeming a re-
    proach,
Lancelot, whom the Lady of the Lake
Caught from his mother's arms — the won-
    drous one   1394
Who passes through the vision of the night —
She chanted snatches of mysterious hymns
Heard on the winding waters; eve and morn
She kissed me, saying, 'Thou art fair, my
    child,
As a king's son,' and often in her arms
She bare me, pacing on the dusky mere.   1400
Would she had drowned me in it, where'er
    it be!
For what am I? What profits me my name
Of greatest knight? I fought for it, and
    have it.
Pleasure to have it, none; to lose it, pain;
Now grown a part of me; but what use in
    it?   1405
To make men worse by making my sin known?
Or sin seem less, the sinner seeming great?
Alas for Arthur's greatest knight, a man
Not after Arthur's heart! I needs must break
These bonds that so defame me. Not with-
    out   1410
She wills it — would I, if she willed it? Nay,
Who knows? But if I would not, then may
    God,
I pray him, send a sudden angel down
To seize me by the hair and bear me far,
And fling me deep in that forgotten mere, 1415
Among the tumbled fragments of the hills."

So groaned Sir Lancelot in remorseful pain,
Not knowing he should die a holy man. (1859)

1389. **crescent**, growing. 1417-1418. A full account of
Lancelot's repentance and death is given in Malory, 20 and
21. See Critical Notes; also *The Holy Grail*, 763-883, pp. 149-
150.

THE HOLY GRAIL

From noiseful arms, and acts of prowess done
In tournament or tilt, Sir Percivale
Whom Arthur and his knighthood called the
  Pure,
Had passed into the silent life of prayer,
Praise, fast, and alms; and leaving for the
  cowl   5
The helmet in an abbey far away
From Camelot, there, and not long after,
  died.

And one, a fellow-monk among the rest,
Ambrosius, loved him much beyond the rest,
And honored him, and wrought into his heart
A way by love that wakened love within,   11
To answer that which came; and as they sat
Beneath a world-old yew-tree, darkening half
The cloisters, on a gustful April morn
That puffed the swaying branches into smoke
Above them, ere the summer when he died, 16
The monk Ambrosius questioned Percivale:

"O brother, I have seen this yew-tree
  smoke,
Spring after spring, for half a hundred years;
For never have I known the world without, 20
Nor ever strayed beyond the pale. But thee,
When first thou camest — such a courtesy
Spake through the limbs and in the voice —
  I knew
For one of those who eat in Arthur's hall;
For good ye are and bad, and like to coins, 25
Some true, some light, but every one of you
Stamped with the image of the King; and
  now
Tell me, what drove thee from the Table
  Round,
My brother? Was it earthly passion crossed?"

"Nay," said the knight; "for no such pas-
  sion mine.   30
But the sweet vision of the Holy Grail
Drove me from all vainglories, rivalries,
And earthly heats that spring and sparkle out
Among us in the justs, while women watch
Who wins, who falls, and waste the spiritual
  strength   35
Within us, better offered up to heaven."

To whom the monk: "The Holy Grail! —
  I trust
We are green in Heaven's eyes; but here too
  much
We molder — as to things without, I mean —
Yet one of your own knights, a guest of ours,

Told us of this in our refectory,   41
But spake with such a sadness and so low
We heard not half of what he said. What
  is it?
The phantom of a cup that comes and goes?"

"Nay, monk! what phantom?" answered
  Percivale.   45
"The cup, the cup itself, from which our Lord
Drank at the last sad supper with his own.
This, from the blessed land of Aromat —
After the day of darkness, when the dead
Went wandering o'er Moriah — the good
  saint   50
Arimathæan Joseph, journeying brought
To Glastonbury, where the winter thorn
Blossoms at Christmas, mindful of our Lord.
And there awhile it bode; and if a man
Could touch or see it, he was healed at once,
By faith, of all his ills. But then the times 56
Grew to such evil that the holy cup
Was caught away to heaven, and disap-
  peared."

To whom the monk: "From our old books
  I know
That Joseph came of old to Glastonbury,   60
And there the heathen Prince, Arviragus,
Gave him an isle of marsh whereon to build;
And there he built with wattles from the
  marsh
A little lonely church in days of yore,
For so they say, these books of ours, but
  seem   65
Mute of this miracle, far as I have read.
But who first saw the holy thing today?"

"A woman," answered Percivale, "a nun,
And one no further off in blood from me
Than sister; and if ever holy maid   70
With knees of adoration wore the stone,
A holy maid; though never maiden glowed,
But that was in her earlier maidenhood,
With such a fervent flame of human love,
Which, being rudely blunted, glanced and
  shot   75
Only to holy things; to prayer and praise
She gave herself, to fast and alms. And yet,
Nun as she was, the scandal of the Court,
Sin against Arthur and the Table Round,
And the strange sound of an adulterous race,

48. Aromat, from Arimathea, a town in Palestine. 49.
the day of darkness, a reference to the darkness following
the Crucifixion. 50. Moriah, a mountain near Jerusalem, the site of Solomon's temple. See Matthew, 27:45-53.
—"And behold, the veil of the temple was rent in twain from
the top to the bottom, and the earth did quake, and the
rocks rent; and the graves were opened; and many bodies
of the saints which slept arose and came out of the graves
after his resurrection and went into the holy city" (vv. 51-
53). 61. Arviragus, supposed to have reigned as king of
Britain from 44 to 72 A.D.

The Holy Grail. See Critical Notes.
15. That puffed . . . smoke, a reference to the abundant
pollen of the yew. 21. the pale, the limits of the monastery
grounds.

Across the iron grating of her cell   81
Beat, and she prayed and fasted all the
      more.

"And he to whom she told her sins, or what
Her all but utter whiteness held for sin,
A man wellnigh a hundred winters old,   85
Spake often with her of the Holy Grail,
A legend handed down through five or six,
And each of these a hundred winters old,
From our Lord's time. And when King
      Arthur made
His Table Round, and all men's hearts became
Clean for a season, surely he had thought   91
That now the Holy Grail would come again;
But sin broke out. Ah, Christ, that it would
      come,
And heal the world of all their wickedness!
'O Father!' asked the maiden, 'might it come
To me by prayer and fasting?' 'Nay,' said he,
'I know not, for thy heart is pure as snow.'
And so she prayed and fasted, till the sun
Shone, and the wind blew, through her, and
      I thought
She might have risen and floated when I saw
      her.   100

"For on a day she sent to speak with me.
And when she came to speak, behold her eyes
Beyond my knowing of them, beautiful,
Beyond all knowing of them, wonderful,
Beautiful in the light of holiness!   105
And 'O my brother Percivale,' she said,
'Sweet brother, I have seen the Holy Grail;
For, waked at dead of night, I heard a sound
As of a silver horn from o'er the hills
Blown, and I thought, "It is not Arthur's use
To hunt by moonlight." And the slender
      sound   111
As from a distance beyond distance grew
Coming upon me — O never harp nor horn,
Nor aught we blow with breath, or touch
      with hand,
Was like that music as it came; and then   115
Streamed through my cell a cold and silver
      beam,
And down the long beam stole the Holy Grail,
Rose-red with beatings in it, as if alive,
Till all the white walls of my cell were dyed
With rosy colors leaping on the wall;   120
And then the music faded, and the Grail
Passed, and the beam decayed, and from the
      walls
The rosy quiverings died into the night.
So now the Holy Thing is here again   124
Among us, brother; fast thou too and pray,
And tell thy brother knights to fast and pray,
That so perchance the vision may be seen
By thee and those, and all the world be
      healed.'

"Then leaving the pale nun, I spake of this
To all men; and myself fasted and prayed 130
Always, and many among us many a week
Fasted and prayed even to the uttermost,
Expectant of the wonder that would be.

"And one there was among us, ever moved
Among us in white armor, Galahad.   135
'God make thee good as thou art beautiful!'
Said Arthur, when he dubbed him knight,
      and none
In so young youth was ever made a knight
Till Galahad; and this Galahad, when he
      heard
My sister's vision, filled me with amaze;   140
His eyes became so like her own, they seemed
Hers, and himself her brother more than I.

"Sister or brother none had he; but some
Called him a son of Lancelot, and some said
Begotten by enchantment — chatterers they,
Like birds of passage piping up and down, 146
That gape for flies — we know not whence
      they come;
For when was Lancelot wanderingly lewd?

"But she, the wan sweet maiden, shore
      away
Clean from her forehead all that wealth of
      hair   150
Which made a silken mat-work for her feet;
And out of this she plaited broad and long
A strong sword-belt, and wove with silver
      thread
And crimson in the belt a strange device,
A crimson grail within a silver beam;   155
And saw the bright boy-knight, and bound
      it on him,
Saying, 'My knight, my love, my knight of
      heaven,
O thou, my love, whose love is one with mine,
I, maiden, round thee, maiden, bind my belt.
Go forth, for thou shalt see what I have seen,
And break through all, till one will crown thee
      king   161
Far in the spiritual city'; and as she spake
She sent the deathless passion in her eyes
Through him, and made him hers, and laid
      her mind
On him, and he believed in her belief.   165

"Then came a year of miracle. O brother,
In our great hall there stood a vacant chair,
Fashioned by Merlin ere he passed away,
And carven with strange figures; and in and
      out
The figures, like a serpent, ran a scroll   170

135. **Galahad.** See *Sir Galahad*, page 50. 168. **Merlin**, the magician of Arthur's court. He made the Round Table at Camelot and built the castle to accommodate it.

Of letters in a tongue no man could read.
And Merlin called it 'the Siege Perilous,'
Perilous for good and ill; for there, he said,
No man could sit but he should lose himself.
And once by misadvertence Merlin sat   175
In his own chair, and so was lost; but he,
Galahad, when he heard of Merlin's doom,
Cried, 'If I lose myself, I save myself!'

"Then on a summer night it came to pass,
While the great banquet lay along the hall, 180
That Galahad would sit down in Merlin's
    chair.

"And all at once, as there we sat, we heard
A cracking and a riving of the roofs,
And rending, and a blast, and overhead
Thunder, and in the thunder was a cry.   185
And in the blast there smote along the hall
A beam of light seven times more clear than
    day;
And down the long beam stole the Holy Grail
All over covered with a luminous cloud,
And none might see who bare it, and it passed.
But every knight beheld his fellow's face 191
As in a glory, and all the knights arose,
And, staring each at other like dumb men,
Stood, till I found a voice and sware a vow.

"I sware a vow before them all, that I,   195
Because I had not seen the Grail, would ride
A twelvemonth and a day in quest of it,
Until I found and saw it, as the nun
My sister saw it; and Galahad sware the vow,
And good Sir Bors, our Lancelot's cousin,
    sware,   200
And Lancelot sware, and many among the
    knights,
And Gawain sware, and louder than the rest."

Then spake the monk Ambrosius, asking
    him,
"What said the King? Did Arthur take the
    vow?"

"Nay, for my lord," said Percivale, "the
    King,   205
Was not in hall; for early that same day,
Scaped through a cavern from a bandit bold,
An outraged maiden sprang into the hall
Crying on help; for all her shining hair

Was smeared with earth, and either milky
    arm   210
Red-rent with hooks of bramble, and all she
    wore
Torn as a sail that leaves the rope is torn
In tempest. So the King arose and went
To smoke the scandalous hive of those wild
    bees
That made such honey in his realm. Howbe-
    it
Some little of this marvel he too saw,   216
Returning o'er the plain that then began
To darken under Camelot; whence the King
Looked up, calling aloud, 'Lo, there! the roofs
Of our great hall are rolled in thundersmoke!
Pray heaven, they be not smitten by the
    bolt!'   221
For dear to Arthur was that hall of ours,
As having there so oft with all his knights
Feasted, and as the stateliest under heaven.

"O brother, had you known our mighty
    hall,
Which Merlin built for Arthur long ago!   226
For all the sacred mount of Camelot,
And all the dim rich city, roof by roof,
Tower after tower, spire beyond spire,
By grove, and garden-lawn, and rushing
    brook,   230
Climbs to the mighty hall that Merlin built.
And four great zones of sculpture, set betwixt
With many a mystic symbol, gird the hall;
And in the lowest beasts are slaying men,
And in the second men are slaying beasts, 235
And on the third are warriors, perfect men,
And on the fourth are men with growing
    wings,
And over all one statue in the mold
Of Arthur, made by Merlin, with a crown,
And peaked wings pointed to the Northern
    Star.   .   240
And eastward fronts the statue, and the crown
And both the wings are made of gold, and
    flame
At sunrise till the people in far fields
Wasted so often by the heathen hordes,
Behold it, crying, 'We have still a king.' 245

"And, brother, had you known our hall
    within,
Broader and higher than any in all the lands!
Where twelve great windows blazon Arthur's
    wars,
And all the light that falls upon the board
Streams through the twelve great battles of
    our King.   250

172. the Siege Perilous, the perilous seat, Merlin's magic
chair. It may represent some supreme test of spiritual worth.
Tennyson explained it as "spiritual imagination." Other explanations include "the temptation of sense," and "the chair
of knowledge." 175-176. Merlin . . . lost. In the medieval
romances Merlin is left under a spell by Vivien in a thorn
tree; in Tennyson's *Merlin and Vivien* he is overcome by
Vivien and confined in a hollow tower from which there is no
escape. 178. If I . . . myself. From *Matthew*, 10:39.—
"He that findeth his life shall lose it; and he that loseth his
life for my sake shall find it."

232. zones of sculpture. These zones represent four
stages in human progress, from the beastly to the spiritual.
250. twelve great battles. Cf. *Lancelot and Elaine*, 285 ff.,
p. 126.

Nay, one there is, and at the eastern end,
Wealthy with wandering lines of mount and
    mere,
Where Arthur finds the brand Excalibur.
And also one to the west, and counter to it,
And blank; and who shall blazon it? when
    and how? —   255
O there, perchance, when all our wars are
    done,
The brand Excalibur will be cast away!

"So to this hall full quickly rode the King,
In horror lest the work by Merlin wrought,
Dreamlike, should on the sudden vanish,
    wrapped   260
In unremorseful folds of rolling fire.
And in he rode, and up I glanced, and saw
The golden dragon sparkling over all;
And many of those who burned the hold,
    their arms
Hacked, and their foreheads grimed with
    smoke and seared,   265
Followed, and in among bright faces, ours,
Full of the vision, pressed; and then the
    King
Spake to me, being nearest, 'Percivale' —
Because the hall was all in tumult — some
Vowing, and some protesting — 'what is
    this?'   270

"O brother, when I told him what had
    chanced,
My sister's vision and the rest, his face
Darkened, as I have seen it more than once,
When some brave deed seemed to be done in
    vain,
Darken; and 'Woe is me, my knights,' he
    cried,   275
'Had I been here, ye had not sworn the vow.'
Bold was mine answer, 'Had thyself been
    here,
My King, thou wouldst have sworn.' 'Yea,
    yea,' said he,
'Art thou so bold and hast not seen the
    Grail?'

" 'Nay, lord, I heard the sound, I saw the
    light,   280
But since I did not see the holy thing,
I sware a vow to follow it till I saw.'

"Then when he asked us, knight by knight,
    if any
Had seen it, all their answers were as one:
'Nay, lord, and therefore have we sworn our
    vows.'   285

" 'Lo, now,' said Arthur, 'have ye seen a
    cloud?
What go ye into the wilderness to see?'

"Then Galahad on the sudden, and in a
    voice
Shrilling along the hall to Arthur, called,
'But I, Sir Arthur, saw the Holy Grail,   290
I saw the Holy Grail and heard a cry —
"O Galahad, and O Galahad, follow me!" '

" 'Ah, Galahad, Galahad,' said the King,
    'for such
As thou art is the vision, not for these.
Thy holy nun and thou have seen a sign —
Holier is none, my Percivale, than she —   296
A sign to maim this Order which I made.
But ye that follow but the leader's bell' —
Brother, the King was hard upon his knights—
'Taliessin is our fullest throat of song,   300
And one hath sung and all the dumb will
    sing.
Lancelot is Lancelot, and hath overborne
Five knights at once, and every younger
    knight,
Unproven, holds himself as Lancelot,
Till overborne by one, he learns — and ye, 305
What are ye? Galahads? — no, nor Per-
    civales' —
For thus it pleased the King to range me close
After Sir Galahad — 'nay,' said he, 'but men
With strength and will to right the wronged,
    of power
To lay the sudden heads of violence flat,   310
Knights that in twelve great battles splashed
    and dyed
The strong White Horse in his own heathen
    blood —
But one hath seen, and all the blind will see.
Go, since your vows are sacred, being made.
Yet — for ye know the cries of all my realm
Pass through this hall — how often, O my
    knights,   316
Your places being vacant at my side,
This chance of noble deeds will come and go
Unchallenged, while ye follow wandering fires
Lost in the quagmire! Many of you, yea
    most,   320
Return no more. Ye think I show myself
Too dark a prophet. Come now, let us meet
The morrow morn once more in one full field
Of gracious pastime, that once more the King,
Before ye leave him for this quest, may count

251-253. **Nay ... Excalibur.** Cf. *Morte d'Arthur*, 27 ff.,
page 40. 275-276. **Woe ... vow.** Arthur disapproves of
the quest since the knights have not the spiritual character
to succeed. He sees in it only the breaking-up of the Round
Table.

287. **What . . . see.** From *Matthew*, 11:7.—"And as they
departed, Jesus began to say unto the multitudes concerning
John, 'What went ye out into the wilderness to see? A reed
shaken in the wind?'" 298. **follow . . . bell,** like a flock of
stupid sheep. 300. **Taliessin,** a famous Welsh bard, said
to have lived in the sixth century. 312. **White Horse,** the
emblem of the Saxons, regarded as heathen. 319. **wandering
fires,** like the will-o'-the-wisp, made by the phosphorus in
plants and water.

The yet-unbroken strength of all his knights,
Rejoicing in that Order which he made.'

"So when the sun broke next from under-
ground,
All the great Table of our Arthur closed
And clashed in such a tourney and so full, 330
So many lances broken — never yet
Had Camelot seen the like since Arthur came;
And I myself and Galahad, for a strength
Was in us from the vision, overthrew
So many knights that all the people cried, 335
And almost burst the barriers in their heat,
Shouting, 'Sir Galahad and Sir Percivale!'

"But when the next day brake from under-
ground —
O brother, had you known our Camelot,
Built by old kings, age after age, so old 340
The King himself had fears that it would fall,
So strange, and rich, and dim; for where the
roofs
Tottered toward each other in the sky,
Met foreheads all along the street of those
Who watched us pass; and lower, and where
the long 345
Rich galleries, lady-laden, weighed the necks
Of dragons clinging to the crazy walls,
Thicker than drops from thunder, showers of
flowers
Fell as we passed; and men and boys astride
On wyvern, lion, dragon, griffin, swan, 350
At all the corners, named us each by name,
Calling 'God speed!' but in the ways below
The knights and ladies wept, and rich and
poor
Wept, and the King himself could hardly
speak
For grief, and all in middle street the Queen,
Who rode by Lancelot, wailed and shrieked
aloud, 356
'This madness has come on us for our sins.'
So to the Gate of the Three Queens we came,
Where Arthur's wars are rendered mystically,
And thence departed every one his way. 360

"And I was lifted up in heart, and thought
Of all my late-shown prowess in the lists,
How my strong lance had beaten down the
knights,
So many and famous names; and never yet
Had heaven appeared so blue, nor earth so
green, 365
For all my blood danced in me, and I knew
That I should light upon the Holy Grail.

"Thereafter, the dark warning of our King,
That most of us would follow wandering fires,
Came like a driving gloom across my mind.
Then every evil word I had spoken once, 371
And every evil thought I had thought of old,
And every evil deed I ever did,
Awoke and cried, 'This quest is not for thee.'
And lifting up mine eyes, I found myself 375
Alone, and in a land of sand and thorns,
And I was thirsty even unto death;
And I, too, cried, 'This quest is not for thee.'

"And on I rode, and when I thought my
thirst
Would slay me, saw deep lawns, and then a
brook, 380
With one sharp rapid, where the crisping
white
Played ever back upon the sloping wave
And took both ear and eye; and o'er the brook
Were apple-trees, and apples by the brook
Fallen, and on the lawns. 'I will rest here,'
I said; 'I am not worthy of the quest'; 386
But even while I drank the brook, and ate
The goodly apples, all these things at once
Fell into dust, and I was left alone
And thirsting in a land of sand and thorns. 390

"And then behold a woman at a door
Spinning; and fair the house whereby she sat,
And kind the woman's eyes and innocent,
And all her bearing gracious; and she rose,
Opening her arms to meet me, as who should
say, 395
'Rest here'; but when I touched her, lo! she,
too,
Fell into dust and nothing, and the house
Became no better than a broken shed,
And in it a dead babe; and also this
Fell into dust, and I was left alone. 400

"And on I rode, and greater was my thirst.
Then flashed a yellow gleam across the world,
And where it smote the plowshare in the field
The plowman left his plowing and fell down
Before it; where it glittered on her pail 405
The milkmaid left her milking and fell down
Before it, and I knew not why, but thought
'The sun is rising,' though the sun had risen.
Then was I ware of one that on me moved
In golden armor with a crown of gold 410
About a casque all jewels, and his horse
In golden armor jeweled everywhere;
And on the splendor came, flashing me blind,
And seemed to me the lord of all the world,
Being so huge. But when I thought he meant

---

350. **wyvern . . . swan.** These are all heraldic devices.
The wyvern was a two-legged dragon with wings and with
barbed tail tied in a knot. The griffin was half lion and half
eagle.

387-390. **But . . . thorns.** Percivale finds that the things
he has held most dear are only illusions: pleasures of the
senses (379-390); love of wife and family (391-400); wealth
and splendor (401-420); fame and glory (421-439).

To crush me, moving on me, lo! he, too,   416
Opened his arms to embrace me as he came,
And up I went and touched him, and he, too,
Fell into dust, and I was left alone
And wearying in a land of sand and thorns.

"And I rode on and found a mighty hill,
And on the top a city walled; the spires
Pricked with incredible pinnacles into heaven.
And by the gateway stirred a crowd; and
    these   424
Cried to me climbing, 'Welcome, Percivale!
Thou mightiest and thou purest among men!'
And glad was I and clomb, but found at top
No man, nor any voice. And thence I passed
Far through a ruinous city, and I saw
That man had once dwelt there; but there I
    found   430
Only one man of an exceeding age.
'Where is that goodly company,' said I,
'That so cried out upon me?' And he had
Scarce any voice to answer, and yet gasped,
'Whence and what art thou?' and even as he
    spoke   435
Fell into dust and disappeared, and I
Was left alone once more and cried in grief,
'Lo, if I find the Holy Grail itself
And touch it, it will crumble into dust!'

"And thence I dropped into a lowly vale,
Low as the hill was high, and where the vale
Was lowest found a chapel, and thereby
A holy hermit in a hermitage,
To whom I told my phantoms, and he said:

" 'O son, thou hast not true humility,   445
The highest virtue, mother of them all;
For when the Lord of all things made Himself
Naked of glory for His mortal change,
"Take thou my robe," she said, "for all is
    thine,"
And all her form shone forth with sudden
    light   450
So that the angels were amazed, and she
Followed Him down, and like a flying star
Led on the gray-haired wisdom of the East.
But her thou hast not known; for what is this
Thou thoughtest of thy prowess and thy sins?
Thou hast not lost thyself to save thyself   456
As Galahad.' When the hermit made an end,
In silver armor suddenly Galahad shone
Before us, and against the chapel door
Laid lance and entered, and we knelt in
    prayer.   460
And there the hermit slaked my burning
    thirst,
And at the sacring of the Mass I saw

449. she, humility. 453. the gray-haired . . . East, the
three Wise Men who visited the infant Christ on the night
of his birth (*Matthew*, 2). 462. the sacring of the Mass,
the consecration of the bread and wine.

The holy elements alone; but he,
'Saw ye no more? I, Galahad, saw the Grail,
The Holy Grail, descend upon the shrine.   465
I saw the fiery face as of a child
That smote itself into the bread and went;
And hither am I come; and never yet
Hath what thy sister taught me first to see,
This holy thing, failed from my side, nor come
Covered, but moving with me night and day,
Fainter by day, but always in the night
Blood-red, and sliding down the blackened
    marsh
Blood-red, and on the naked mountain top
Blood-red, and in the sleeping mere below 475
Blood-red. And in the strength of this I rode,
Shattering all evil customs everywhere,
And passed through Pagan realms, and made
    them mine,
And clashed with Pagan hordes, and bore
    them down,
And broke through all, and in the strength of
    this   480
Come victor. But my time is hard at hand,
And hence I go, and one will crown me king
Far in the spiritual city; and come thou, too,
For thou shalt see the vision when I go.'

"While thus he spake, his eye, dwelling on
    mine,   485
Drew me, with power upon me, till I grew
One with him, to believe as he believed.
Then, when the day began to wane, we went.

"There rose a hill that none but man could
    climb,   489
Scarred with a hundred wintry watercourses—
Storm at the top, and when we gained it,
    storm
Round us and death; for every moment
    glanced
His silver arms and gloomed, so quick and
    thick
The lightnings here and there to left and right
Struck, till the dry old trunks about us, dead,
Yea, rotten with a hundred years of death, 496
Sprang into fire. And at the base we found
On either hand, as far as eye could see,
A great black swamp and of an evil smell,
Part black, part whitened with the bones of
    men,   500
Not to be crossed, save that some ancient
    king
Had built a way, where, linked with many a
    bridge,
A thousand piers ran into the great Sea.
And Galahad fled along them bridge by
    bridge,
And every bridge as quickly as he crossed 505

489. See Critical Notes.

Sprang into fire and vanished, though I
    yearned
To follow; and thrice above him all the
    heavens
Opened and blazed with thunder such as
    seemed
Shoutings of all the sons of God. And first
At once I saw him far on the great Sea,   510
In silver-shining armor starry-clear;
And o'er his head the Holy Vessel hung
Clothed in white samite or a luminous cloud.
And with exceeding swiftness ran the boat,
If boat it were — I saw not whence it came.
And when the heavens opened and blazed
    again   516
Roaring, I saw him like a silver star —
And had he set the sail, or had the boat
Become a living creature clad with wings?
And o'er his head the Holy Vessel hung   520
Redder than any rose, a joy to me,
For now I knew the veil had been with-
    drawn.
Then in a moment when they blazed again
Opening, I saw the least of little stars
Down on the waste, and straight beyond the
    star   525
I saw the spiritual city and all her spires
And gateways in a glory like one pearl —
No larger, though the goal of all the saints —
Strike from the sea; and from the star there
    shot
A rose-red sparkle to the city, and there   530
Dwelt, and I knew it was the Holy Grail,
Which never eyes on earth again shall see.
Then fell the floods of heaven drowning the
    deep,
And how my feet recrossed the deathful ridge
No memory in me lives; but that I touched 535
The chapel-doors at dawn I know, and thence
Taking my war-horse from the holy man,
Glad that no phantom vexed me more, re-
    turned
To whence I came, the gate of Arthur's wars."

"O brother," asked Ambrosius — "for in
    sooth   540
These ancient books — and they would win
    thee — teem,
Only I find not there this Holy Grail,
With miracles and marvels like to these,
Not all unlike; which oftentime I read,
Who read but on my breviary with ease,   545
Till my head swims, and then go forth and
    pass
Down to the little thorpe that lies so close,
And almost plastered like a martin's nest

To these old walls — and mingle with our
    folk;
And knowing every honest face of theirs   550
As well as ever shepherd knew his sheep,
And every homely secret in their hearts,
Delight myself with gossip and old wives,
And ills and aches, and teethings, lyings-in,
And mirthful sayings, children of the place,
That have no meaning half a league away;
Or lulling random squabbles when they rise,
Chafferings and chatterings at the market-
    cross,   558
Rejoice, small man, in this small world of
    mine,
Yea, even in their hens and in their eggs —
O brother, saving this Sir Galahad,   561
Came ye on none but phantoms in your quest,
No man, no woman?"

        Then Sir Percivale:
"All men, to one so bound by such a vow,
And women were as phantoms. O my brother,
Why wilt thou shame me to confess to thee 566
How far I faltered from my quest and vow?
For after I had lain so many nights,
A bed-mate of the snail and eft and snake,
In grass and burdock, I was changed to
    wan   570
And meager, and the vision had not come;
And then I chanced upon a goodly town
With one great dwelling in the middle of it.
Thither I made, and there was I disarmed
By maidens each as fair as any flower;   575
But when they led me into hall, behold,
The princess of that castle was the one,
Brother, and that one only, who had ever
Made my heart leap; for when I moved of old
A slender page about her father's hall,   580
And she a slender maiden, all my heart
Went after her with longing, yet we twain
Had never kissed a kiss or vowed a vow.
And now I came upon her once again,
And one had wedded her, and he was dead,
And all his land and wealth and state were
    hers.   586
And while I tarried, every day she set
A banquet richer than the day before
By me, for all her longing and her will
Was toward me as of old; till one fair morn,
I walking to and fro beside a stream   591
That flashed across her orchard underneath
Her castle-walls, she stole upon my walk,
And calling me the greatest of all knights,
Embraced me, and so kissed me the first
    time,   595
And gave herself and all her wealth to me.
Then I remembered Arthur's warning word,
That most of us would follow wandering fires,

---

526. **the spiritual city**, the New Jerusalem, of *Revelation*,
21.—"And I John saw the holy city, new Jerusalem, coming
down from God out of heaven, prepared as a bride adorned for
her husband" (v. 2).

558. **the market-cross.** During the Middle Ages nearly
every town had a cross standing in the market-place.

And the quest faded in my heart. Anon,
The heads of all her people drew to me, 600
With supplication both of knees and tongue:
'We have heard of thee; thou art our greatest
    knight;
Our Lady says it, and we well believe.
Wed thou our Lady, and rule over us,
And thou shalt be as Arthur in our land.' 605
O me, my brother! but one night my vow
Burned me within, so that I rose and fled,
But wailed and wept, and hated mine own
    self,
And even the holy quest, and all but her;
Then, after I was joined with Galahad, 610
Cared not for her nor anything upon earth."

Then said the monk: "Poor men, when
    yule is cold,
Must be content to sit by little fires.
And this am I, so that ye care for me
Ever so little; yea, and blest be heaven 615
That brought thee here to this poor house of
    ours
Where all the brethren are so hard, to warm
My cold heart with a friend; but O the pity
To find thine own first love once more — to
    hold,
Hold her a wealthy bride within thine arms,
Or all but hold, and then — cast her aside, 621
Forgoing all her sweetness, like a weed!
For we that want the warmth of double life,
We that are plagued with dreams of some-
    thing sweet
Beyond all sweetness in a life so rich — 625
Ah, blessed Lord, I speak too earthly-wise,
Seeing I never strayed beyond the cell,
But live like an old badger in his earth,
With earth about him everywhere, despite
All fast and penance. Saw ye none beside, 630
None of your knights?"

        "Yea, so," said Percivale.
"One night my pathway swerving east, I saw
The pelican on the casque of our Sir Bors
All in the middle of the rising moon,
And toward him spurred, and hailed him, and
    he me, 635
And each made joy of either. Then he asked,
'Where is he? Hast thou seen him — Lance-
    lot? — Once,'
Said good Sir Bors, 'he dashed across me —
    mad,
And maddening what he rode; and when I
    cried,
"Ridest thou then so hotly on a quest 640
So holy?" Lancelot shouted, "Stay me not!

I have been the sluggard, and I ride apace,
For now there is a lion in the way!"
So vanished.'

        "Then Sir Bors had ridden on
Softly, and sorrowing for our Lancelot, 645
Because his former madness, once the talk
And scandal of our table, had returned;
For Lancelot's kith and kin so worship him
That ill to him is ill to them, to Bors
Beyond the rest. He well had been content
Not to have seen, so Lancelot might have
    seen, 651
The Holy Cup of healing; and, indeed,
Being so clouded with his grief and love,
Small heart was his after the holy quest.
If God would send the vision, well; if not, 655
The quest and he were in the hands of
    Heaven.

"And then, with small adventure met, Sir
    Bors
Rode to the lonest tract of all the realm,
And found a people there among their crags,
Our race and blood, a remnant that were left
Paynim amid their circles, and the stones 661
They pitch up straight to heaven; and their
    wise men
Were strong in that old magic which can trace
The wandering of the stars, and scoffed at
    him
And this high quest as at a simple thing, 665
Told him he followed — almost Arthur's
    words —
A mocking fire: 'What other fire than he
Whereby the blood beats, and the blossom
    blows,
And the sea rolls, and all the world is
    warmed?'
And when his answer chafed them, the rough
    crowd, 670
Hearing he had a difference with their priests,
Seized him, and bound and plunged him into
    a cell
Of great piled stones; and lying bounden
    there
In darkness through innumerable hours
He heard the hollow-ringing heavens sweep
Over him till by miracle — what else? — 676
Heavy as it was, a great stone slipped and
    fell,

---

643. For . . . way. He means his love for Guinevere;
from *Proverbs*, 22:13.—"The slothful man saith, 'There is a
lion without; I shall be slain in the streets.'" 646. madness.
Malory (11 and 12) tells of the madness of Lancelot, caused
by the anger of Guinevere when she thought he was in love
with the daughter of King Pelles. After two years he was
restored by the Grail. 661. Paynim . . . circles. These
pagans were still followers of the Druids, an ancient religious
order of the Celts. The circles were their places of worship,
like the ruins at Stonehenge. 667. he, the sun, worshiped
by these pagans. 668. blows, blooms. 675. the hollow-
ringing heavens. It was an old belief that the movement of
the heavenly bodies produced "the music of the spheres."

---

600. The heads of all her people, all her leading people.
612. when yule is cold, after the great fires of the Christmas yule log are passed.

Such as no wind could move; and through the
    gap
Glimmered the streaming scud. Then came
    a night
Still as the day was loud, and through the
    gap   680
The seven clear stars of Arthur's Table
    Round —
For, brother, so one night, because they roll
Through such a round in heaven, we named
    the stars,
Rejoicing in ourselves and in our King —
And these, like bright eyes of familiar friends,
In on him shone: 'And then to me, to me,' 686
Said good Sir Bors, 'beyond all hopes of
    mine,
Who scarce had prayed or asked it for my-
    self —
Across the seven clear stars — O grace to
    me! —
In color like the fingers of a hand   690
Before a burning taper, the sweet Grail
Glided and passed, and close upon it pealed
A sharp quick thunder.' Afterwards, a maid,
Who kept our holy faith among her kin
In secret, entering, loosed and let him go." 695

To whom the monk: "And I remember
    now
That pelican on the casque. Sir Bors it was
Who spake so low and sadly at our board,
And mighty reverent at our grace was he;
A square-set man and honest, and his eyes,
An outdoor sign of all the warmth within,
Smiled with his lips — a smile beneath a
    cloud,   702
But heaven had meant it for a sunny one.
Aye, aye, Sir Bors, who else? But when ye
    reached
The city, found ye all your knights returned,
Or was there sooth in Arthur's prophecy, 706
Tell me, and what said each, and what the
    King?"

Then answered Percivale: "And that can I,
Brother, and truly; since the living words
Of so great men as Lancelot and our King 710
Pass not from door to door and out again,
But sit within the house. O when we reached
The city, our horses stumbling as they trode
On heaps of ruin, hornless unicorns,
Cracked basilisks, and splintered cockatrices,
And shattered talbots, which had left the
    stones   716
Raw that they fell from, brought us to the
    hall.

"And there sat Arthur on the dais-throne,
And those that had gone out upon the quest,
Wasted and worn, and but a tithe of them,
And those that had not, stood before the
    King,   721
Who, when he saw me, rose and bade me
    hail,
Saying, 'A welfare in thine eyes reproves
Our fear of some disastrous chance for thee
On hill or plain, at sea or flooding ford. 725
So fierce a gale made havoc here of late
Among the strange devices of our kings,
Yea, shook this newer, stronger hall of ours,
And from the statue Merlin molded for us
Half-wrenched a golden wing; but now —
    the quest,   730
This vision — hast thou seen the Holy Cup
That Joseph brought of old to Glastonbury?'

"So when I told him all thyself hast heard,
Ambrosius, and my fresh but fixed resolve
To pass away into the quiet life,   735
He answered not, but, sharply turning, asked
Of Gawain, 'Gawain, was this quest for thee?'

" 'Nay, lord,' said Gawain, 'not for such
    as I.
Therefore I communed with a saintly man,
Who made me sure the quest was not for
    me;
For I was much a-wearied of the quest, 741
But found a silk pavilion in a field,
And merry maidens in it; and then this gale
Tore my pavilion from the tenting-pin,
And blew my merry maidens all about 745
With all discomfort; yea, and but for this,
My twelvemonth and a day were pleasant
    to me.'

"He ceased; and Arthur turned to whom
    at first
He saw not, for Sir Bors, on entering, pushed
Athwart the throng to Lancelot, caught his
    hand,   750
Held it, and there, half-hidden by him, stood,
Until the King espied him, saying to him,
'Hail, Bors! If ever loyal man and true
Could see it, thou hast seen the Grail'; and
    Bors:
'Ask me not, for I may not speak of it; 755
I saw it'; and the tears were in his eyes.

"Then there remained but Lancelot, for the
    rest
Spake but of sundry perils in the storm.

---

679. **the streaming scud,** vapory clouds. 681. **The seven
clear stars,** the seven stars of the constellation of the Great
Bear, which was called the Table Round because it revolves
around the Polar Star. 713-717. **The city . . . hall.** The
city had gone to decay since the knights' departure. The
wind had torn the carved decorations from the buildings.
The unicorn was a fabulous beast like a horse, but with a
single horn in the middle of the forehead; the basilisk was a
fabulous monster supposed to kill by its look; the cockatrice
was a winged snake; the talbot was a sort of hunting dog.

Perhaps, like him of Cana in Holy Writ,
Our Arthur kept his best until the last;   760
'Thou, too, my Lancelot,' asked the King,
     'my friend,
Our mightiest, hath this quest availed for
     thee?'

   " 'Our mightiest!' answered Lancelot, with
     a groan;
'O King!' — and when he paused methought
     I spied
A dying fire of madness in his eyes —   765
'O King, my friend, if friend of thine I be,
Happier are those that welter in their sin,
Swine in the mud, that cannot see for slime,
Slime of the ditch; but in me lived a sin
So strange, of such a kind, that all of pure,   770
Noble, and knightly in me twined and clung
Round that one sin, until the wholesome
     flower
And poisonous grew together, each as each,
Not to be plucked asunder; and when thy
     knights
Sware, I sware with them only in the hope   775
That could I touch or see the Holy Grail
They might be plucked asunder. Then I
     spake
To one most holy saint, who wept and said
That, save they could be plucked asunder, all
My quest were but in vain; to whom I vowed
That I would work according as he willed.   781
And forth I went, and while I yearned and
     strove
To tear the twain asunder in my heart,
My madness came upon me as of old,
And whipped me into waste fields far away.
There was I beaten down by little men,   786
Mean knights, to whom the moving of my
     sword
And shadow of my spear had been enow
To scare them from me once; and then I
     came
All in my folly to the naked shore,   790
Wide flats, where nothing but coarse grasses
     grew;
But such a blast, my King, began to blow,
So loud a blast along the shore and sea,
Ye could not hear the waters for the blast,
Though heaped in mounds and ridges all the
     sea   795
Drove like a cataract, and all the sand
Swept like a river, and the clouded heav-
     ens
Were shaken with the motion and the sound.

And blackening in the sea-foam swayed a
     boat,
Half-swallowed in it, anchored with a chain;
And in my madness to myself I said,   801
"I will embark and I will lose myself,
And in the great sea wash away my sin."
I burst the chain; I sprang into the boat.
Seven days I drove along the dreary deep,   805
And with me drove the moon and all the
     stars;
And the wind fell, and on the seventh night
I heard the shingle grinding in the surge,
And felt the boat shock earth, and looking up,
Behold, the enchanted towers of Carbonek,
A castle like a rock upon a rock,   811
With chasm-like portals open to the sea,
And steps that met the breaker! There was
     none
Stood near it but a lion on each side
That kept the entry, and the moon was full.
Then from the boat I leapt, and up the stairs,
There drew my sword. With sudden-flaring
     manes   817
Those two great beasts rose upright like a
     man,
Each gripped a shoulder, and I stood between,
And, when I would have smitten them, heard
     a voice,
"Doubt not, go forward; if thou doubt, the
     beasts   821
Will tear thee piecemeal." Then with vio-
     lence
The sword was dashed from out my hand,
     and fell.
And up into the sounding hall I passed;
But nothing in the sounding hall I saw —   825
No bench nor table, painting on the wall
Or shield of knight, only the rounded moon
Through the tall oriel on the rolling sea.
But always in the quiet house I heard,
Clear as a lark, high o'er me as a lark,   830
A sweet voice singing in the topmost tower
To the eastward. Up I climbed a thousand
     steps
With pain; as in a dream I seemed to climb
Forever. At the last I reached a door;
A light was in the crannies, and I heard,   835
"Glory and joy and honor to our Lord
And to the Holy Vessel of the Grail!"
Then in my madness I essayed the door;
It gave, and through a stormy glare, a heat
As from a seven-times-heated furnace, I,
Blasted and burnt, and blinded as I was,   841
With such a fierceness that I swooned away —

759–760. **like . . . last,** a reference to the wine served
at the marriage in Cana of Galilee, *John*, 2:1-10. The ruler
of the feast tasted the wine, not knowing that Jesus had
made it out of water, and said to the bridegroom, "Every
man at the beginning doth set forth good wine; and when
men have well drunk, then that which is worse; but thou hast
kept the good wine until now" (v. 10).

808. **shingle,** small rounded stones on the seashore. 810.
Carbonek, a castle mentioned several times by Malory, said
to be the place where the Holy Grail was kept. 828. **oriel,**
a large bay window. 840. **a seven-times-heated furnace,**
like the one in which Shadrach, Meshach, and Abednego
were cast because they refused to worship the golden image
set up by Nebuchadnezzar (*Daniel*, 3:1-30).

O yet methought I saw the Holy Grail,
All palled in crimson samite, and around
Great angels, awful shapes, and wings and
          eyes!   845
And but for all my madness and my sin,
And then my swooning, I had sworn I saw
That which I saw; but what I saw was veiled
And covered, and this quest was not for me.'

     "So speaking, and here ceasing, Lancelot
          left   850
The hall long silent, till Sir Gawain — nay,
Brother, I need not tell thee foolish words —
A reckless and irreverent knight was he,
Now boldened by the silence of his King —
Well, I will tell thee: 'O King, my liege,' he
          said,   855
'Hath Gawain failed in any quest of thine?
When have I stinted stroke in foughten field?
But as for thine, my good friend Percivale,
Thy holy nun and thou have driven men mad,
Yea, made our mightiest madder than our
          least.   860
But by mine eyes and by mine ears I swear,
I will be deafer than the blue-eyed cat,
And thrice as blind as any noonday owl,
To holy virgins in their ecstasies,
Henceforward.'

     " 'Deafer,' said the blameless King,
'Gawain, and blinder unto holy things,   866
Hope not to make thyself by idle vows,
Being too blind to have desire to see.
But if indeed there came a sign from heaven,
Blessed are Bors, Lancelot, and Percivale, 870
For these have seen according to their sight.
For every fiery prophet in old times,
And all the sacred madness of the bard,
When God made music through them, could
          but speak
His music by the framework and the chord;
And as ye saw it ye have spoken truth.   876

     " 'Nay — but thou errest, Lancelot; never
          yet
Could all of true and noble in knight and
          man
Twine round one sin, whatever it might be,
With such a closeness but apart there grew, 880
Save that he were the swine thou spakest of,
Some root of knighthood and pure nobleness;
Whereto see thou, that it may bear its flower.

     " 'And spake I not too truly, O my knights?
Was I too dark a prophet when I said   885
To those who went upon the Holy Quest,

That most of them would follow wandering
          fires,
Lost in the quagmire? — lost to me and gone,
And left me gazing at a barren board,   889
And a lean Order — scarce returned a tithe —
And out of those to whom the vision came
My greatest hardly will believe he saw.
Another hath beheld it afar off,
And, leaving human wrongs to right them-
          selves,
Cares but to pass into the silent life.   895
And one hath had the vision face to face,
And now his chair desires him here in vain,
However they may crown him otherwhere.

     " 'And some among you held that if the
          King
Had seen the sight he would have sworn the
          vow.   900
Not easily, seeing that the King must guard
That which he rules, and is but as the hind
To whom a space of land is given to plow,
Who may not wander from the allotted field
Before his work be done, but, being done, 905
Let visions of the night or of the day
Come as they will; and many a time they
          come,
Until this earth he walks on seems not earth,
This light that strikes his eyeball is not light,
This air that smites his forehead is not
          air   910
But vision — yea, his very hand and foot —
In moments when he feels he cannot die,
And knows himself no vision to himself,
Nor the high God a vision, nor that One
Who rose again. Ye have seen what ye have
          seen.'   915

     "So spake the King; I knew not all he
          meant."   (1869)

THE LAST TOURNAMENT

Dagonet, the fool, whom Gawain in his mood
Had made mock-knight of Arthur's Table
          Round,
At Camelot, high above the yellowing woods,
Danced like a withered leaf before the hall.
And toward him from the hall, with harp
          in hand,   5
And from the crown thereof a carcanet
Of ruby swaying to and fro, the prize
Of Tristram in the jousts of yesterday,
Came Tristram, saying, "Why skip ye so,
          Sir Fool?"

     For Arthur and Sir Lancelot riding once 10
Far down beneath a winding wall of rock

---

862. **deafer . . . cat.** Male white cats with blue eyes are
frequently deaf.

The Last Tournament. See Critical Notes.
6. **carcanet,** jeweled collar or necklace.

Heard a child wail. A stump of oak half-dead,
From roots like some black coil of carven
    snakes,
Clutched at the crag, and started thro' mid
    air
Bearing an eagle's nest; and thro' the tree 15
Rushed ever a rainy wind, and thro' the wind
Pierced ever a child's cry; and crag and tree
Scaling, Sir Lancelot from the perilous nest,
This ruby necklace thrice around her neck,
And all unscarred from beak or talon,
    brought 20
A maiden babe, which Arthur pitying took,
Then gave it to his Queen to rear. The Queen,
But coldly acquiescing, in her white arms
Received, and after loved it tenderly,
And named it Nestling; so forgot herself 25
A moment, and her cares; till that young life
Being smitten in mid heaven with mortal cold
Past from her, and in time the carcanet
Vext her with plaintive memories of the child.
So she, delivering it to Arthur, said, 30
"Take thou the jewels of this dead innocence,
And make them, an thou wilt, a tourney-
    prize."

To whom the King: "Peace to thine
    eagle-borne
Dead nestling, and this honor after death,
Following thy will! but, O my Queen, I
    muse 35
Why ye not wear on arm, or neck, or zone
Those diamonds that I rescued from the tarn,
And Lancelot won, methought, for thee to
    wear."

"Would rather you had let them fall,"
    she cried,
"Plunge and be lost — ill-fated as they were,
A bitterness to me! — ye look amazed, 41
Not knowing they were lost as soon as
    given —
Slid from my hands when I was leaning out
Above the river — that unhappy child
Past in her barge; but rosier luck will go 45
With these rich jewels, seeing that they came
Not from the skeleton of a brother-slayer,
But the sweet body of a maiden babe.
Perchance — who knows? — the purest of
    thy knights
May win them for the purest of my maids."

She ended, and the cry of a great jousts 51
With trumpet-blowings ran on all the ways
From Camelot in among the faded fields
To furthest towers; and everywhere the
    knights
Armed for a day of glory before the King. 55

But on the hither side of that loud morn
Into the hall staggered, his visage ribbed
From ear to ear with dogwhip-weals, his nose
Bridge-broken, one eye out, and one hand off,
And one with shatter'd fingers dangling
    lame, 60
A churl, to whom indignantly the King:

"My churl, for whom Christ died, what
    evil beast
Hath drawn his claws athwart thy face? or
    fiend?
Man was it who marred heaven's image in
    thee thus?"

Then, sputtering thro' the hedge of splin-
    tered teeth, 65
Yet strangers to the tongue, and with blunt
    stump
Pitch-blackened sawing the air, said the
    maimed churl:

"He took them and he drave them to his
    tower —
Some hold he was a table-knight of thine —
A hundred goodly ones — the Red Knight,
    he — 70
Lord, I was tending swine, and the Red
    Knight
Brake in upon me and drave them to his
    tower;
And when I called upon thy name as one
That doest right by gentle and by churl,
Maimed me and mauled, and would outright
    have slain, 75
Save that he sware me to a message, saying:
'Tell thou the King and all his lairs that I
Have founded my Round Table in the North,
And whatsoever his own knights have sworn
My knights have sworn the counter to it —
    and say 80
My tower is full of harlots, like his court,
But mine are worthier, seeing they profess
To be none other than themselves — and say
My knights are all adulterers like his own,
But mine are truer, seeing they profess 85
To be none other; and say his hour is come,
The heathen are upon him, his long lance
Broken, and his Excalibur a straw.' "

Then Arthur turned to Kay the seneschal:
"Take thou my churl, and tend him curi-
    ously 90
Like a king's heir, till all his hurts be whole.
The heathen — but that ever-climbing wave,
Hurled back again so often in empty foam,
Hath lain for years at rest — and renegades,
Thieves, bandits, leavings of confusion,
    whom 95
The wholesome realm is purged of other-
    where,

---

37. **diamonds**, see *Lancelot and Elaine*, 11. 1204-1229.

Friends, thro' your manhood and your
    fealty, — now
Make their last head like Satan in the North.
My younger knights, new-made, in whom
    your flower
Waits to be solid fruit of golden deeds,   100
Move with me toward their quelling, which
    achieved,
The loneliest ways are safe from shore to
    shore.
But thou, Sir Lancelot, sitting in my place
Enchaired to-morrow, arbitrate the field;
For wherefore shouldst thou care to mingle
    with it,   105
Only to yield my Queen her own again?
Speak, Lancelot, thou art silent; is it well?''

    Thereto Sir Lancelot answered: "It is well;
Yet better if the King abide, and leave
The leading of his younger knights to me.   110
Else, for the King has willed it, it is well.''

Then Arthur rose and Lancelot followed
    him,
And while they stood without the doors,
    the King
Turned to him saying: "Is it then so well?
Or mine the blame that oft I seem as he   115
Of whom was written, 'A sound is in his
    ears'?
The foot that loiters, bidden go, — the
    glance
That only seems half-loyal to command, —
A manner somewhat fallen from reverence —
Or have I dreamed the bearing of our
    knights   120
Tells of a manhood ever less and lower?
Or whence the fear lest this my realm, up-
    reared,
By noble deeds at one with noble vows,
From flat confusion and brute violences,
Reel back into the beast, and be no more?''   125

He spoke, and taking all his younger
    knights,
Down the slope city rode, and sharply
    turned
North by the gate. In her high bower the
    Queen,
Working a tapestry, lifted up her head,
Watched her lord pass, and knew not that
    she sighed.   130
Then ran across her memory the strange
    rhyme
Of bygone Merlin, "Where is he who knows?
From the great deep to the great deep he
    goes.''

But when the morning of a tournament,
By these in earnest, those in mockery
    called   135
The Tournament of the Dead Innocence,
Brake with a wet wind blowing, Lancelot,
Round whose sick head all night, like birds
    of prey,
The words of Arthur flying shrieked, arose,
And down a streetway hung with folds of
    pure   140
White samite, and by fountains running wine,
Where children sat in white with cups of gold,
Moved to the lists, and there, with slow
    sad steps
Ascending, filled his double-dragoned chair.

He glanced and saw the stately galleries, 145
Dame, damsel, each thro' worship of their
    Queen
White-robed in honor of the stainless child,
And some with scattered jewels, like a bank
Of maiden snow mingled with sparks of fire.
He looked but once, and vailed his eyes
    again.   150

The sudden trumpet sounded as in a dream
To ears but half-awaked, then one low roll
Of Autumn thunder, and the jousts began;
And ever the wind blew, and yellowing leaf,
And gloom and gleam, and shower and
    shorn plume   155
Went down it. Sighing weariedly, as one
Who sits and gazes on a faded fire,
When all the goodlier guests are past away,
Sat their great umpire looking o'er the lists.
He saw the laws that ruled the tourna-
    ment   160
Broken, but spake not; once, a knight cast
    down
Before his throne of arbitration cursed
The dead babe and the follies of the King;
And once the laces of a helmet crack'd,
And showed him, like a vermin in its hole, 165
Modred, a narrow face. Anon he heard
The voice that billowed round the barriers
    roar
An ocean-sounding welcome to one knight,
But newly-entered, taller than the rest,
And armored all in forest green, whereon 170
There tript a hundred tiny silver deer,
And wearing but a holly-spray for crest,
With ever-scattering berries, and on shield
A spear, a harp, a bugle — Tristram — late
From over-seas in Brittany returned,   175
And marriage with a princess of that realm,
Isolt the White — Sir Tristram of the
    Woods —

116. See *Job*, 15:20-21.—"The wicked man travaileth with
pain all his days . . . a dreadful sound is in his ears: in prosperity the destroyer shall come upon him.''

150. **vailed**, lowered.

Whom Lancelot knew, had held sometime
    with pain
His own against him, and now yearned to
    shake
The burthen off his heart in one full shock 180
With Tristram even to death. His strong
    hands gript
And dinted the gilt dragons right and left,
Until he groaned for wrath — so many of
    those
That ware their ladies' colors on the casque
Drew from before Sir Tristram to the
    bounds,   185
And there with gibes and flickering mockeries
Stood, while he muttered, "Craven crests!
    O shame!
What faith have these in whom they sware
    to love?
The glory of our Round Table is no more."

So Tristram won, and Lancelot gave, the
    gems,   190
Not speaking other word than, "Hast thou
    won?
Art thou the purest, brother? See, the hand
Wherewith thou takest this is red!" to whom
Tristram, half plagued by Lancelot's lan-
    guorous mood,
Made answer: "Ay, but wherefore toss me
    this   195
Like a dry bone cast to some hungry hound?
Let be thy fair Queen's fantasy. Strength
    of heart
And might of limb, but mainly use and skill,
Are winners in this pastime of our King.
My hand — belike the lance hath dript
    upon it —   200
No blood of mine, I trow; but O chief knight,
Right arm of Arthur in the battle-field,
Great brother, thou nor I have made the
    world;
Be happy in thy fair Queen as I in mine."

And Tristram round the gallery made
    his horse   205
Caracole; then bowed his homage, bluntly
    saying,
"Fair damsels, each to him who worships each
Sole Queen of Beauty and of love, behold
This day my Queen of Beauty is not here."
And most of these were mute, some angered,
    one   210
Murmuring, "All courtesy is dead," and one,
"The glory of our Round Table is no more."

Then fell thick rain, plume droopt and
    mantle clung,
And pettish cries awoke, and the wan day

206. **Caracole**, make half-turns to left and right.

Went glooming down in wet and weariness; 215
But under her black brows a swarthy one
Laughed shrilly, crying: "Praise the patient
    saints,
Our one white day of Innocence hath past,
Tho' somewhat draggled at the skirt. So be it.
The snowdrop only, flowering thro' the
    year,   220
Would make the world as blank as winter-tide.
Come — let us gladden their sad eyes, our
    Queen's
And Lancelot's, at this night's solemnity
With all the kindlier colors of the field."

So dame and damsel glittered at the
    feast   225
Variously gay; for he that tells the tale
Likened them, saying, as when an hour of
    cold
Falls on the mountain in midsummer snows,
And all the purple slopes of mountain flowers
Pass under white, till the warm hour re-
    turns   230
With veer of wind and all are flowers again,
So dame and damsel cast the simple white,
And glowing in all colors, the live grass,
Rose-campion, bluebell, kingcup, poppy,
    glanced
About the revels, and with mirth so loud 235
Beyond all use, that, half-amazed, the Queen,
And wroth at Tristram and the lawless jousts,
Brake up their sports, then slowly to her
    bower
Parted, and in her bosom pain was lord.

And little Dagonet on the morrow morn, 240
High over all the yellowing autumn-tide,
Danced like a withered leaf before the hall.
Then Tristram saying, "Why skip ye so,
    Sir Fool?"
Wheeled round on either heel, Dagonet
    replied,
"Belike for lack of wiser company;   245
Or being fool, and seeing too much wit
Makes the world rotten, why, belike I skip
To know myself the wisest knight of all."
"Ay, fool," said Tristram, "but 'tis eating
    dry
To dance without a catch, a roundelay   250
To dance to." Then he twangled on his harp,
And while he twangled little Dagonet stood
Quiet as any water-sodden log
Stayed in the wandering warble of a brook,
But when the twangling ended, skipt
    again;   255
And being asked, "Why skipt ye not, Sir
    Fool?"
Made answer, "I had liefer twenty years
Skip to the broken music of my brains

Than any broken music thou canst make."
Then Tristram, waiting for the quip to
   come,   260
"Good now, what music have I broken, fool?"
And little Dagonet, skipping, "Arthur, the
   King's;
For when thou playest that air with Queen
   Isolt,
Thou makest broken music with thy bride,
Her daintier namesake down in Brit-
   tany —   265
And so thou breakest Arthur's music, too."
"Save for that broken music in thy brains,
Sir Fool," said Tristram, "I would break
   thy head.
Fool, I came late, the heathen wars were o'er,
The life had flown, we sware but by the
   shell —   270
I am but a fool to reason with a fool —
Come, thou art crabbed and sour; but lean
   me down,
Sir Dagonet, one of thy long asses' ears,
And harken if my music be not true.

    " 'Free love — free field — we love but
      while we may.   275
  The woods are hushed, their music is no
    more;
  The leaf is dead, the yearning past away.
  New leaf, new life — the days of frost
    are o'er;
  New life, new love, to suit the newer day;
  New loves are sweet as those that went
    before.   280
  Free love — free field — we love but while
    we may.'

"Ye might have moved slow-measure to
   my tune,
Not stood stock-still. I made it in the woods,
And heard it ring as true as tested gold."

But Dagonet with one foot poised in his
   hand: 285
"Friend, did ye mark that fountain yesterday,
Made to run wine? — but this had run itself
All out like a long life to a sour end —
And them that round it sat with golden cups
To hand the wine to whosoever came —   290
The twelve small damosels white as
   Innocence,
In honor of poor Innocence the babe,
Who left the gems which Innocence the Queen
Lent to the King, and Innocence the King
Gave for a prize — and one of those white
   slips   295

Handed her cup and piped, the pretty one,
'Drink, drink, Sir Fool,' and thereupon I
   drank,
Spat — pish — the cup was gold, the
   draught was mud."

  And Tristram: "Was it muddier than thy
   gibes?
Is all the laughter gone dead out of thee? — 300
Not marking how the knighthood mock thee,
   fool —
'Fear God: honor the King — his one true
   knight —
Sole follower of the vows' — for here be they
Who knew thee swine enow before I came,
Smuttier than blasted grain. But when the
   King   305
Had made thee fool, thy vanity so shot up
It frighted all free fool from out thy heart;
Which left thee less than fool, and less
   than swine,
A naked aught — yet swine I hold thee still,
For I have flung thee pearls and find thee
   swine."   310

  And little Dagonet mincing with his feet:
"Knight, an ye fling those rubies round
   my neck
In lieu of hers, I'll hold thou hast some touch
Of music, since I care not for thy pearls.
Swine? I have wallowed, I have washed —
   the world   315
Is flesh and shadow — I have had my day.
The dirty nurse, Experience, in her kind
Hath fouled me — an I wallowed, then I
   washed —
I have had my day and my philosophies —
And thank the Lord I am King Arthur's
   fool.   320
Swine, say ye? swine, goats, asses, rams, and
   geese
Trooped round a Paynim harper once, who
   thrummed
On such a wire as musically as thou
Some such fine song — but never a king's
   fool."

  And Tristram, "Then were swine, goats,
   asses, geese   325
The wiser fools, seeing thy Paynim bard
Had such a mastery of his mystery
That he could harp his wife up out of hell."

  Then Dagonet, turning on the ball of his
   foot,
"And whither harp'st thou thine? down! and
   thyself   330

---

265. **daintier namesake,** Isolt of the White Hands, whom
Tristram married and left in Brittany.

322. **Paynim harper,** Orpheus in Greek myth (paynim =
pagan), who was to call back his wife Eurydice from the dead
by his playing (cf. line 328).

Down! and two more; a helpful harper thou,
That harpest downward! Dost thou know the
    star
We call the Harp of Arthur up in heaven?"

And Tristram, "Ay, Sir Fool, for when our
    King
Was victor wellnigh day by day, the
    knights,   335
Glorying in each new glory, set his name
High on all hills and in the signs of heaven."

And Dagonet answered: "Ay, and when
    the land
Was freed, and the Queen false, ye set yourself
To babble about him, all to show your
    wit —   340
And whether he were king by courtesy,
Or king by right — and so went harping
    down
The black king's highway, got so far and grew
So witty that ye played at ducks and drakes
With Arthur's vows on the great lake of
    fire.   345
Tuwhoo! do ye see it? do ye see the star?"

"Nay, fool," said Tristram, "not in open
    day."
And Dagonet: "Nay, nor will; I see it and
    hear.
It makes a silent music up in heaven,
And I and Arthur and the angels hear,   350
And then we skip." "Lo, fool," he said, "ye
    talk
Fool's treason; is the King thy brother fool?"
Then little Dagonet clapt his hands and
    shrilled:
"Ay, ay, my brother fool, the king of fools!
Conceits himself as God that he can make   355
Figs out of thistles, silk from bristles, milk
From burning spurge, honey from hornet-
    combs,
And men from beasts — Long life the king
    of fools!"

And down the city Dagonet danced away;
But thro' the slowly-mellowing avenues   360
And solitary passes of the wood
Rode Tristram toward Lyonnesse and the
    west.
Before him fled the face of Queen Isolt
With ruby-circled neck, but evermore
Past, as a rustle or twitter in the wood   365
Made dull his inner, keen his outer eye
For all that walked, or crept, or perched, or
    flew.
Anon the face, as, when a gust hath blown,
Unruffling waters re-collect the shape

Of one that in them sees himself, returned; 370
But at the slot or fewmets of a deer,
Or even a fallen feather, vanished again.

So on for all that day from lawn to lawn
Thro' many a league-long bower he rode. At
    length
A lodge of intertwisted beechen-boughs,   375
Furze-crammed and bracken-rooft, the which
    himself
Built for a summer day with Queen Isolt
Against a shower, dark in the golden grove
Appearing, sent his fancy back to where
She lived a moon in that low lodge with
    him;   380
Till Mark her lord had past, the Cornish King,
With six or seven, when Tristram was away,
And snatched her thence, yet, dreading worse
    than shame
Her warrior Tristram, spake not any word,
But bode his hour, devising wretchedness.   385

And now that desert lodge to Tristram lookt
So sweet that, halting, in he past and sank
Down on a drift of foliage random-blown;
But could not rest for musing how to smooth
And sleek his marriage over to the queen.   390
Perchance in lone Tintagil far from all
The tonguesters of the court she had not
    heard.
But then what folly had sent him over-seas
After she left him lonely here? a name?
Was it the name of one in Brittany,   395
Isolt, the daughter of the king? "Isolt
Of the White Hands" they called her: the
    sweet name
Allured him first, and then the maid herself,
Who served him well with those white hands
    of hers,
And loved him well, until himself had
    thought   400
He loved her also, wedded easily,
But left her all as easily, and returned.
The black-blue Irish hair and Irish eyes
Had drawn him home — what marvel? then
    he laid
His brows upon the drifted leaf and
    dreamed.   405

He seemed to pace the strand of Brittany
Between Isolt of Britain and his bride,
And showed them both the ruby-chain, and
    both
Began to struggle for it, till his Queen
Graspt it so hard that all her hand was
    red.   410
Then cried the Breton, "Look, her hand is
    red!

371. **slot,** footprints. **fewmets,** droppings. 391. **Tinta-gil,** castle in Cornwall.

These be no rubies, this is frozen blood,
And melts within her hand — her hand is hot
With ill desires, but this I gave thee, look,
Is all as cool and white as any flower."   415
Followed a rush of eagle's wings, and then
A whimpering of the spirit of the child,
Because the twain had spoiled her carcanet.

He dreamed; but Arthur with a hundred
    spears
Rode far, till o'er the illimitable reed,   420
And many a glancing plash and sallowy isle,
The wide-winged sunset of the misty marsh
Glared on a huge machicolated tower
That stood with open doors, whereout was
    rolled
A roar of riot, as from men secure   425
Amid their marshes, ruffians at their ease
Among their harlot-brides, an evil song.
"Lo there," said one of Arthur's youth, for
    there,
High on a grim dead tree before the tower,
A goodly brother of the Table Round   430
Swung by the neck; and on the boughs a
    shield
Showing a shower of blood in a field noir,
And therebeside a horn, inflamed the knights
At that dishonor done the gilded spur,
Till each would clash the shield and blow
    the horn.   435
But Arthur waved them back. Alone he rode.
Then at the dry harsh roar of the great horn,
That sent the face of all the marsh aloft
An ever upward-rushing storm and cloud
Of shriek and plume, the Red Knight heard,
    and all,   440
Even to tipmost lance and topmost helm,
In blood-red armor sallying, howled to the
    King:

"The teeth of Hell flay bare and gnash
    thee flat! —
Lo! art thou not that eunuch-hearted king
Who fain had clipt free manhood from the
    world —   445
The woman-worshipper? Yea, God's curse,
    and I!
Slain was the brother of my paramour
By a knight of thine, and I that heard her
    whine
And snivel, being eunuch-hearted too,
Sware by the scorpion-worm that twists in
    hell   450
And stings itself to everlasting death,
To hang whatever knight of thine I fought
And tumbled. Art thou King? — Look to
    thy life!"

432. **a field noir**, black background.

He ended. Arthur knew the voice; the face
Wellnigh was helmet-hidden, and the name 455
Went wandering somewhere darkling in his
    mind.
And Arthur deigned not use of word or sword,
But let the drunkard, as he stretched from
    horse
To strike him, overbalancing his bulk,
Down from the causeway heavily to the
    swamp   460
Fall, as the crest of some slow-arching wave,
Heard in dead night along that table-shore,
Drops flat, and after the great waters break
Whitening for half a league, and thin
    themselves,
Far over sands marbled with moon and
    cloud,   465
From less and less to nothing; thus he fell
Head-heavy. Then the knights, who watched
    him, roared
And shouted and leapt down upon the fallen,
There trampled out his face from being
    known,
And sank his head in mire, and slimed
    themselves;   470
Nor heard the King for their own cries, but
    sprang
Thro' open doors, and swording right and left
Men, women, on their sodden faces hurled
The tables over and the wines, and slew
Till all the rafters rang with woman-yells, 475
And all the pavement streamed with
    massacre.
Then, echoing yell with yell, they fired the
    tower,
Which half that autumn night, like the live
    North,
Red-pulsing up thro' Alioth and Alcor,
Made all above it, and a hundred meres   480
About it, as the water Moab saw
Come round by the east, and out beyond
    them flushed
The long low dune and lazy-plunging sea.

So all the ways were safe from shore to
    shore,
But in the heart of Arthur pain was lord. 485

Then, out of Tristram waking, the red
    dream
Fled with a shout, and that low lodge
    returned,
Mid-forest, and the wind among the boughs.
He whistled his good war-horse left to graze
Among the forest greens, vaulted upon
    him,   490

478. **live North**, the northern lights.   479. **Alioth, Alcor**,
stars in the Great Bear.   481. **water Moab saw**, the blood-
red water seen by the Moabites; see *II Kings*, 3:22.

And rode beneath an ever-showering leaf,
Till one lone woman, weeping near a cross,
Stayed him. "Why weep ye?" "Lord," she
   said, "my man
Hath left me or is dead;" whereon he
   thought —
"What, if she hate me now? I would not
   this.   495
What, if she love me still? I would not that.
I know not what I would" — but said to her,
"Yet weep not thou, lest, if thy mate return,
He find thy favor changed and love thee
   not" —
Then   pressing   day   by   day   thro'
   Lyonnesse   500
Last in a roky hollow, belling, heard
The hounds of Mark, and felt the goodly
   hounds
Yelp at his heart, but, turning, past and
   gained
Tintagil, half in sea and high on land,
A crown of towers.   505

              Down in a casement sat,
A low sea-sunset glorying round her hair
And glossy-throated grace, Isolt the Queen.
And when she heard the feet of Tristram
   grind
The spiring stone that scaled about her
   tower,
Flushed, started, met him at the doors, and
   there   510
Belted his body with her white embrace,
Crying aloud: "Not Mark — not Mark,
   my soul!
The footstep fluttered me at first — not he!
Catlike thro' his own castle steals my Mark,
But warrior-wise thou stridest thro' his
   halls   515
Who hates thee, as I him — even to the
   death.
My soul, I felt my hatred for my Mark
Quicken within me, and knew that thou
   wert nigh."
To whom Sir Tristram smiling, "I am here;
Let be thy Mark, seeing he is not thine."   520

   And   drawing   somewhat   backward   she
   replied:
"Can he be wronged who is not even his own,
But save for dread of thee had beaten me,
Scratched,   bitten,   blinded,   marred   me
   somehow — Mark?
What rights are his that dare not strike for
   them?   525
Not lift a hand — not, tho' he found me thus!
But harken! have ye met him? hence he went
To-day for three days' hunting — as he said —

And so returns belike within an hour.
Mark's way, my soul! — but eat not thou
   with Mark,   530
Because he hates thee even more than fears,
Nor drink; and when thou passest any wood
Close vizor, lest an arrow from the bush
Should leave me all alone with Mark and hell.
My God, the measure of my hate for
   Mark   535
Is as the measure of my love for thee!"

   So, plucked one way by hate and one by
   love,
Drained of her force, again she sat, and spake
To Tristram, as he knelt before her, saying:
"O hunter, and O blower of the horn,   540
Harper, and thou hast been a rover too,
For, ere I mated with my shambling king,
Ye twain had fallen out about the bride
Of one — his name is out of me — the prize,
If   prize she were — what   marvel? — she
   could see —   545
Thine, friend; and ever since my craven seeks
To wreck thee villainously — but, O Sir
   Knight,
What dame or damsel have ye kneeled to
   last?"

   And   Tristram, "Last   to   my   Queen
   Paramount,
Here now to my queen paramount of love 550
And loveliness — ay, lovelier than when first
Her light feet fell on our rough Lyonnesse,
Sailing from Ireland."

               Softly laughed Isolt:
"Flatter me not, for hath not our great
   Queen
My dole of beauty trebled?" and he
   said: 555
"Her beauty is her beauty, and thine thine,
And thine is more to me — soft, gracious,
   kind —
Save when thy Mark is kindled on thy lips
Most gracious; but she, haughty, even to
   him,
Lancelot; for I have seen him wan enow   560
To make one doubt if ever the great Queen
Have yielded him her love."

                     To whom Isolt:
"Ah, then, false hunter and false harper,
   thou
Who brakest thro' the scruple of my bond,
Calling me thy white hind, and saying to
   me   565
That   Guinevere   had   sinned   against   the
   highest,

---

501. **roky**, foggy.   546. **craven**, coward (i.e., Mark).

And I — misyoked with such a want of
 man —
That I could hardly sin against the lowest."

He answered: "O my soul, be comforted!
If this be sweet, to sin in leading-strings, 570
If here be comfort, and if ours be sin,
Crowned warrant had we for the crowning
 sin
That made us happy; but how ye greet me
 — fear
And fault and doubt — no word of that
 fond tale —
Thy deep heart-yearnings, thy sweet
 memories 575
Of Tristram in that year he was away."

And, saddening on the sudden, spake Isolt:
"I had forgotten all in my strong joy
To see thee — yearnings? — ay! for, hour
 by hour,
Here in the never-ended afternoon, 580
O, sweeter than all memories of thee,
Deeper than any yearnings after thee
Seemed those far-rolling, westward-smiling
 seas,
Watched from this tower. Isolt of Britain
 dashed
Before Isolt of Brittany on the strand, 585
Would that have chilled her bride-kiss?
 Wedded her?
Fought in her father's battles? wounded
 there?
The King was all fulfilled with gratefulness,
And she, my namesake of the hands, that
 healed
Thy hurt and heart with unguent and
 caress — 590
Well — can I wish her any huger wrong
Than having known thee? her too hast thou
 left
To pine and waste in those sweet memories.
O, were I not my Mark's, by whom all men
Are noble, I should hate thee more than
 love." 595

And Tristram, fondling her light hands,
 replied:
"Grace, Queen, for being loved; she loved
 me well.
Did I love her? the name at least I loved.
Isolt? — I fought his battles, for Isolt!
The night was dark; the true star set.
 Isolt! 600
The name was ruler of the dark — Isolt?
Care not for her! patient, and prayerful,
 meek,
Pale-blooded, she will yield herself to God."

And Isolt answered: "Yea, and why not I?

Mine is the larger need, who am not
 meek, 605
Pale-blooded, prayerful. Let me tell thee now.
Here one black, mute midsummer night I
 sat,
Lonely, but musing on thee, wondering where,
Murmuring a light song I had heard thee sing,
And once or twice I spake thy name
 aloud. 610
Then flashed a levin-brand; and near me
 stood,
In fuming sulphur blue and green, a fiend —
Mark's way to steal behind one in the dark —
For there was Mark: 'He has wedded her,'
 he said,
Not said, but hissed it; then this crown of
 towers 615
So shook to such a roar of all the sky,
That here in utter dark I swooned away,
And woke again in utter dark, and cried,
'I will flee hence and give myself to God' —
And thou wert lying in thy new leman's
 arms." 620

Then Tristram, ever dallying with her
 hand,
"May God be with thee, sweet, when old
 and gray,
And past desire!" a saying that angered her.
" 'May God be with thee, sweet, when thou
 art old,
And sweet no more to me!' I need Him
 now. 625
For when had Lancelot uttered aught so gross
Even to the swineherd's malkin in the mast?
The greater man the greater courtesy.
Far other was the Tristram, Arthur's knight!
But thou, thro' ever harrying thy wild
 beasts — 630
Save that to touch a harp, tilt with a lance
Becomes thee well — art grown wild beast
 thyself.
How darest thou, if lover, push me even
In fancy from thy side, and set me far
In the gray distance, half a life away. 635
Her to be loved no more? Unsay it, unswear!
Flatter me rather, seeing me so weak,
Broken with Mark and hate and solitude,
Thy marriage and mine own, that I should
 suck
Lies like sweet wines. Lie to me: I believe. 640
Will ye not lie? not swear, as there ye kneel,
And solemnly as when ye sware to him,
The man of men, our King — My God, the
 power
Was once in vows when men believed the
 King!

611. **levin-brand,** flash of lightning. 627. **malkin,** slattern. **mast,** hog-food.

They lied not then who sware, and thro'
    their vows   645
The King prevailing made his realm — I
    say,
Swear to me thou wilt love me even when
    old,
Gray-haired, and past desire, and in despair."

    Then Tristram, pacing moodily up and
    down:
"Vows! did you keep the vow you made to
    Mark   650
More than I mine? Lied, say ye? Nay, but
    learnt,
The vow that binds too strictly snaps itself —
My knighthood taught me this — ay, being
    snapt —
We run more counter to the soul thereof
Than had we never sworn. I swear no
    more.   655
I swore to the great King, and am forsworn.
For once — even to the height — I honored
    him.
'Man, is he man at all?' methought, when
    first
I rode from our rough Lyonnesse, and beheld
That victor of the Pagan throned in hall — 560
His hair, a sun that rayed from off a brow
Like hill-snow high in heaven, the steel-blue
    eyes,
The golden beard that clothed his lips with
    light —
Moreover, that weird legend of his birth,
With Merlin's mystic babble about his end
Amazed me; then, his foot was on a stool 666
Shaped as a dragon; he seemed to me no
    man,
But Michael trampling Satan; so I sware,
Being amazed. But this went by — The vows!
O, ay — the wholesome madness of an
    hour —   670
They served their use, their time; for
    every knight
Believed himself a greater than himself,
And every follower eyed him as a God;
Till he, being lifted up beyond himself,
Did mightier deeds than elsewise he had
    done,   675
And so the realm was made. But then
    their vows —
First mainly thro' that sullying of our
    Queen —
Began to gall the knighthood, asking whence
Had Arthur right to bind them to himself?
Dropt down from heaven? washed up from
    out the deep?   680
They failed to trace him thro' the flesh and
    blood
Of our old kings. Whence then? a doubtful
    lord

To bind them by inviolable vows,
Which flesh and blood perforce would violate;
For feel this arm of mine — the tide
    within   685
Red with free chase and heather-scented air,
Pulsing full man. Can Arthur make me pure
As any maiden child? lock up my tongue
From uttering freely what I freely hear?
Bind me to one? The wide world laughs
    at it.   690
And worldling of the world am I, and know
The ptarmigan that whitens ere his hour
Woos his own end; we are not angels here
Nor shall be. Vows — I am woodman of the
    woods,
And hear the garnet-headed yaffingale 695
Mock them — my soul, we love but while
    we may;
And therefore is my love so large for thee,
Seeing it is not bounded save by love."

    Here ending, he moved toward her, and
    she said:
"Good; an I turned away my love for
    thee   700
To some one thrice as courteous as thyself —
For courtesy wins woman all as well
As valor may, but he that closes both
Is perfect, he is Lancelot — taller indeed,
Rosier and comelier, thou — but say I
    loved   705
This knightliest of all knights, and cast
    thee back
Thine own small saw, 'We love but while
    we may,'
Well then, what answer?"

                     He that while she
    spake,
Mindful of what he brought to adorn her
    with,
The jewels, had let one finger lightly touch 710
The warm white apple of her throat, replied,
"Press this a little closer, sweet, until —
Come, I am hungered and half-angered —
    meat,
Wine, wine — and I will love thee to the
    death,
And out beyond into the dream to come." 715

    So then, when both were brought to full
    accord,
She rose, and set before him all he willed;
And after these had comforted the blood
With meats and wines, and satiated their
    hearts —
Now talking of their woodland paradise, 720

---

692. **ptarmigan**, grouse. 695. **yaffingale**, woodpecker.

The deer, the dews, the fern, the founts,
　the lawns;
Now mocking at the much ungainliness,
And craven shifts, and long crane legs of
　Mark —
Then Tristram laughing caught the harp
　and sang:

　　"Ay, ay, O, ay — the winds that bend
　　the brier!　　　　　　　　　　725
　A star in heaven, a star within the mere!
　Ay, ay, O, ay — a star was my desire,
　And one was far apart and one was near.
　Ay, ay, O, ay — the winds that bow the
　　grass!
　And one was water and one star was
　　fire,　　　　　　　　　　　　730
　And one will ever shine and one will pass.
　Ay, ay, O, ay — the winds that move
　　the mere!"

　Then in the light's last glimmer Tristram
　　showed
And swung the ruby carcanet. She cried,
"The collar of some Order, which our King　735
Hath thee, to yield thee grace beyond thy
　peers."

　"Not so, my Queen," he said, "but the
　　red fruit
Grown on a magic oak-tree in mid-heaven,
And won by Tristram as a tourney-prize,　740
And hither brought by Tristram for his last
Love-offering and peace-offering unto thee."

　He spoke, he turned, then, flinging round
　　her neck,
Claspt it, and cried, "Thine Order, O my
　　Queen!"
But, while he bowed to kiss the jewelled
　　throat,　　　　　　　　　　　745
Out of the dark, just as the lips had touched,
Behind him rose a shadow and a shriek —
"Mark's way," said Mark, and clove him
　thro' the brain.

　That night came Arthur home, and while
　　he climbed,
All in a death-dumb autumn-dripping
　gloom,　　　　　　　　　　　　750
The stairway to the hall, and looked and saw
The great Queen's bower was dark, — about
　his feet
A voice clung sobbing till he questioned it,
"What art thou?" and the voice about his
　feet
Sent up an answer, sobbing, "I am thy fool, 755
And I shall never make thee smile again."
　　　　　　　　　　　　　(1871)

TO THE QUEEN

O loyal to the royal in thyself,
And loyal to thy land, as this to thee —
Bear witness, that rememberable day,
When, pale as yet and fever-worn, the Prince
Who scarce had plucked his flickering life
　again　　　　　　　　　　　　5
From halfway down the shadow of the grave
Passed with thee through thy people and
　their love,
And London rolled one tide of joy through all
Her trebled millions, and loud leagues of man
And welcome! Witness, too, the silent cry,
The prayer of many a race and creed, and
　clime —　　　　　　　　　　　11
Thunderless lightnings striking under sea
From sunset and sunrise of all thy realm,
And that true North, whereof we lately heard
A strain to shame us, "Keep you to your-
　selves;　　　　　　　　　　　15
So loyal is too costly! friends — your love
Is but a burthen; loose the bond, and go."
Is this the tone of empire? here the faith
That made us rulers? this, indeed, her voice
And meaning whom the roar of Hougoumont
Left mightiest of all peoples under heaven? 21
What shock has fooled her since, that she
　·　should speak
So feebly? wealthier — wealthier — hour by
　hour!
The voice of Britain, or a sinking land,
Some third-rate isle half-lost among her seas?
There rang her voice, when the full city
　pealed　　　　　　　　　　　26
Thee and thy Prince! The loyal to their
　crown
Are loyal to their own far sons, who love
Our ocean-empire with her boundless homes
Forever-broadening England, and her throne
In our vast Orient, and one isle, one isle,　31
That knows not her own greatness; if she
　knows
And reads it we are fallen. — But thou, my
　Queen,
Not for itself, but through thy living love
For one to whom I made it o'er his grave　35
Sacred, accept this old imperfect tale,

To the Queen. The Queen is Victoria.
　3. **that rememberable day,** a reference to the public
thanksgiving in February 1872 upon the recovery of the
Prince of Wales from typhoid fever.　12. **Thunderless
lightnings,** cablegrams of congratulation.　14-17. **true
North . . . go.** When Manitoba was added to Canada in
1869, many persons in England complained of the cost of
maintaining the possessions in America and suggested that the
Canadians might well be left to care for themselves.　20.
Hougoumont, the Battle of Waterloo. During the battle
the Chateau of Hougoumont was occupied by British forces.
35. **one,** Prince Albert, husband of Victoria, to whose memory Tennyson dedicated *The Idylls of the King.* Tennyson
places Prince Albert above King Arthur the "gray king" of
line 39.

New-old, and shadowing Sense at war with
    Soul;
Ideal manhood closed in real man,
Rather than that gray king whose name, a
    ghost,
Streams like a cloud, man-shaped, from
    mountain peak,   40
And cleaves to cairn and cromlech still; or
    him
Of Geoffrey's book, or him of Malleor's, one
Touched by the adulterous finger of a time
That hovered between war and wantonness,
And crownings and dethronements. Take
    withal   45
Thy poet's blessing, and his trust that Heaven
Will blow the tempest in the distance back
From thine and ours; for some are scared,
    who mark,
Or wisely or unwisely, signs of storm,
Waverings of every vane with every wind,   50
And wordy trucklings to the transient hour,
And fierce or careless looseners of the faith,
And Softness breeding scorn of simple life,
Or Cowardice, the child of lust for gold,
Or Labor, with a groan and not a voice,   55
Or Art with poisonous honey stolen from
    France,
And that which knows, but careful for itself,
And that which knows not, ruling that which
    knows
To its own harm. The goal of this great
    world
Lies beyond sight; yet — if our slowly-grown
And crowned Republic's crowning common-
    sense,   61
That saved her many times, not fail — their
    fears
Are morning shadows huger than the shapes
That cast them, not those gloomier which
    forego
The darkness of that battle in the West   65
Where all of high and holy dies away.
    (1872)

THE VOICE AND THE PEAK

The voice and the Peak
    Far over summit and lawn,

The lone glow and long roar
    Green-rushing from the rosy thrones of
    dawn!

All night have I heard the voice   5
    Rave over the rocky bar,
But thou wert silent in heaven,
    Above thee glided the star.

Hast thou no voice, O Peak,
    That standest high above all?   10
"I am the voice of the Peak,
    I roar and rave, for I fall.

"A thousand voices go
    To North, South, East, and West;
They leave the heights and are troubled,   15
    And moan and sink to their rest.

"The fields are fair beside them,
    The chestnut towers in his bloom;
But they — they feel the desire of the deep —
    Fall, and follow their doom.   20

"The deep has power on the height,
    And the height has power on the deep;
They are raised forever and ever,
    And sink again into sleep."

Not raised forever and ever,   25
    But when their cycle is o'er,
The valley, the voice, the peak, the star
    Pass, and are found no more.

The Peak is high and flushed
    At his highest with sunrise fire;   30
The Peak is high, and the stars are high,
    And the thought of a man is higher.

A deep below the deep,
    And a height beyond the height!
Our hearing is not hearing,   35
    And our seeing is not sight.

The voice and the Peak
    Far into heaven withdrawn,
The lone glow and long roar   39
    Green-rushing from the rosy thrones of
    dawn!   (1874)

MONTENEGRO

They rose to where their sovran eagle sails,
They kept their faith, their freedom, on the
    height,

37. This line expresses the central meaning of *The Idylls of the King.* 41. **cairn and cromlech,** a reference to the followers of the Druids and their places of worship. See *The Holy Grail,* 661 ff., p. 146. A cromlech is a stone circle. 42. **Geoffrey,** Geoffrey of Monmouth (12th century), whose *Historia Regum Britanniæ* contains the earliest extended account of the achievements of King Arthur. **Malleor,** Sir Thomas Malory, whose *Morte Darthur* (1485) is the chief source of the *Idylls.* 56. **Art . . . France,** a reference to what Tennyson thought the lewdness of contemporary French fiction.
The Voice and the Peak. The thought of this poem is that the material is transient and that the spiritual is the only real and abiding principle of the universe. The utterance of peak and valley, of sea and star, is that everything of the senses perishes, but beyond the world of sense is a world that endures. See *In Memoriam,* 124, page 88.
2. **lawn,** an open place in a forest.

Montenegro. The word means *black mountains.* Montenegro was then the smallest independent state in Europe and the only portion of the Balkan peninsula never really subdued by the Turk. After centuries of warfare, the inhabitants won a decisive victory over Turkey in 1876. In 1918 the country became a part of Yugoslavia.

Chaste, frugal, savage, armed by day and
   night
Against the Turk; whose inroad nowhere
   scales
Their headlong passes, but his footsteps fails,
And red with blood the Crescent reels from
   fight   6
Before their daultless hundreds, in prone
   flight
By thousands down the crags and through
   the vales.
O smallest among peoples! rough rock-throne
Of Freedom! warriors beating back the swarm
Of Turkish Islam for five hundred years,   11
Great Tsernogora! Never since thine own
Black ridges drew the cloud and brake the
   storm
Has breathed a race of mightier mountaineers.
                        (1877)

THE REVENGE

A BALLAD OF THE FLEET

1

At Florés in the Azorés Sir Richard Grenville
   lay,
And a pinnace, like a fluttered bird, came
   flying from far away:
"Spanish ships of war at sea! We have sighted
   fifty-three!"
Then sware Lord Thomas Howard: " 'Fore
   God I am no coward;
But I cannot meet them here, for my ships
   are out of gear,   5
And the half my men are sick. I must fly,
   but follow quick.
We are six ships of the line; can we fight with
   fifty-three?"

2

Then spake Sir Richard Grenville: "I know
   you are no coward;
You fly them for a moment to fight with
   them again.
But I've ninety men and more that are lying
   sick ashore.   10
I should count myself the coward if I left
   them, my Lord Howard,
To these Inquisition dogs and the devildoms
   of Spain."

3

So Lord Howard passed away with five ships
   of war that day,
Till he melted like a cloud in the silent sum-
   mer heaven;
But Sir Richard bore in hand all his sick men
   from the land   15
Very carefully and slow,
Men of Bideford in Devon,
And we laid them on the ballast down below;
For we brought them all aboard,
And they blessed him in their pain, that they
   were not left to Spain,   20
To the thumb-screw and the stake, for the
   glory of the Lord.

4

He had only a hundred seamen to work the
   ship and to fight,
And he sailed away from Florés till the Span-
   iard came in sight,
With his huge sea-castles heaving upon the
   weather bow.
"Shall we fight or shall we fly?   25
Good Sir Richard, tell us now,
For to fight is but to die!
There'll be little of us left by the time this
   sun be set."
And Sir Richard said again, "We be all good
   English men.
Let us bang these dogs of Seville, the children
   of the devil,   30
For I never turned my back upon Don or
   devil yet."

5

Sir Richard spoke and he laughed, and we
   roared a hurrah, and so
The little *Revenge* ran on sheer into the heart
   of the foe,
With her hundred fighters on deck, and her
   ninety sick below;
For half of their fleet to the right and half
   to the left were seen,   35
And the little *Revenge* ran on through the long
   sea-lane between.

6

Thousands of their soldiers looked down from
   their decks and laughed,

---

6. **the Crescent,** the emblem of Turkey. 12. **Tserno-**
gora. the native name for Montenegro.
The Revenge. See Critical Notes.
7. **ships of the line.** A ship of line was one large enough
to have a place in the line of battle. It carried the heaviest
armament. 12. **Inquisition.** The Inquisition was a tribunal of the Roman Catholic Church for the discovery and
punishment of heretics and unbelievers. In Spain its proceedings were conducted with notorious cruelty, especially in the
16th century. It was abolished in 1834.

17. **Bideford,** an important seaport on the north coast of
Devonshire; the birthplace of Sir Richard Grenville. 21.
thumb-screw . . . the stake. Torturing by the use of an instrument for compressing the thumb, and burning at the stake
were methods employed by the Inquisition. 30. **Seville,** a
province in Spain. 31. **Don,** a title in Spain, formerly given
only to men of high rank.

Thousands of their seamen made mock at the
    mad little craft
Running on and on, till delayed
By their mountain-like *San Philip* that, of
    fifteen hundred tons,   40
And up-shadowing high above us with her
    yawning tiers of guns,
Took the breath from our sails, and we stayed.

7

And while now the great *San Philip* hung
    above us like a cloud
Whence the thunderbolt will fall
Long and loud,   45
Four galleons drew away
From the Spanish fleet that day,
And two upon the larboard and two upon
    the starboard lay,
And the battle-thunder broke from them all.

8

But anon the great *San Philip*, she bethought
    herself and went,   50
Having that within her womb that had left
    her ill content;
And the rest they came aboard us, and they
    fought us hand to hand,
For a dozen times they came with their pikes
    and musqueteers,
And a dozen times we shook 'em off as a dog
    that shakes his ears
When he leaps from the water to the land.   55

9

And the sun went down, and the stars came
    out far over the summer sea,
But never a moment ceased the fight of the
    one and the fifty-three.
Ship after ship, the whole night long, their
    high-built galleons came,
Ship after ship, the whole night long, with
    her battle-thunder and flame;
Ship after ship, the whole night long, drew
    back with her dead and her shame.   60
For some were sunk and many were shattered,
    and so could fight us no more —
God of battles, was ever a battle like this in
    the world before?

10

For he said, "Fight on! fight on!"
Though his vessel was all but a wreck;
And it chanced that, when half of the short
    summer night was gone,   65
With a grisly wound to be dressed he had
    left the deck,
But a bullet struck him that was dressing it
    suddenly dead,

40. **San Philip**, the flagship of the Spanish fleet.

And himself he was wounded again in the
    side and the head,
And he said, "Fight on! fight on!"

11

And the night went down, and the sun smiled
    out far over the summer sea,   70
And the Spanish fleet with broken sides lay
    round us all in a ring;
But they dared not touch us again, for they
    feared that we still could sting,
So they watched what the end would be.
And we had not fought them in vain,
But in perilous plight were we,   75
Seeing forty of our poor hundred were slain,
And half of the rest of us maimed for life
In the crash of the cannonades and the des-
    perate strife;
And the sick men down in the hold were
    most of them stark and cold,
And the pikes were all broken or bent, and
    the powder was all of it spent;   80
And the masts and the rigging were lying
    over the side;
But Sir Richard cried in his English pride,
"We have fought such a fight for a day and
    a night
As may never be fought again!
We have won great glory, my men!   85
And a day less or more
At sea or ashore,
We die — does it matter when?
Sink me the ship, Master Gunner — sink her,
    split her in twain!
Fall into the hands of God, not into the hands
    of Spain!"   90

12

And the gunner said, "Aye, aye," but the sea-
    men made reply,
"We have children, we have wives,
And the Lord hath spared our lives.
We will make the Spaniard promise, if we
    yield, to let us go;
We shall live to fight again and to strike an-
    other blow."   95
And the lion there lay dying, and they yielded
    to the foe.

13

And the stately Spanish men to their flagship
    bore him then,
Where they laid him by the mast, old Sir
    Richard caught at last,
And they praised him to his face with their
    courtly foreign grace;   99
But he rose upon their decks, and he cried,
"I have fought for Queen and Faith like a
    valiant man and true;

I have only done my duty as a man is bound
    to do.
With a joyful spirit I, Sir Richard Grenville,
    die!"
And he fell upon their decks, and he died.

14

And they stared at the dead that had been
    so valiant and true,   105
And had holden the power and glory of Spain
    so cheap
That he dared her with one little ship and
    his English few;
Was he devil or man? He was devil for aught
    they knew,
But they sank his body with honor down into
    the deep,
And they manned the *Revenge* with a swar-
    thier alien crew,   110
And away she sailed with her loss and longed
    for her own;
When a wind from the lands they had ruined
    awoke from sleep,
And the water began to heave and the weather
    to moan,
And or ever that evening ended a great gale
    blew,
And a wave like the wave that is raised by
    an earthquake grew,   115
Till it smote on their hulls and their sails and
    their masts and their flags,
And the whole sea plunged and fell on the
    shot-shattered navy of Spain,
And the little *Revenge* herself went down by
    the island crags
To be lost evermore in the main.   (1878)

RIZPAH

17—

Wailing, wailing, wailing, the wind over land
    and sea —
And Willy's voice in the wind, "O mother,
    come out to me!"
Why should he call me tonight, when he
    knows that I cannot go?
For the downs are as bright as day, and the
    full moon stares at the snow.

We should be seen, my dear; they would spy
    us out of the town.   5
The loud black nights for us, and the storm
    rushing over the down,
When I cannot see my own hand, but am
    led by the creak of the chain,
And grovel and grope for my son till I find
    myself drenched with the rain.

Rizpah. See Critical Notes.

Anything fallen again? nay — what was there
    left to fall?
I have taken them home, I have numbered
    the bones, I have hidden them all. 10
What am I saying? and what are *you?* Do
    you come as a spy?
Falls? what falls? who knows? As the tree
    falls so must it lie.

Who let her in? how long has she been? you
    — what have you heard?
Why did you sit so quiet? you never have
    spoken a word.
O — to pray with me — yes — a lady — none
    of their spies —   15
But the night has crept into my heart, and
    begun to darken my eyes.

Ah — you, that have lived so soft, what
    should *you* know of the night,
The blast and the burning shame and the
    bitter frost and the fright?
I have done it, while you were asleep — you
    were only made for the day.
I have gathered my baby together — and now
    you may go your way.   20

Nay — for it's kind of you, madam, to sit by
    an old dying wife.
But say nothing hard of my boy, I have only
    an hour of life.
I kissed my boy in the prison, before he went
    out to die.
"They dared me to do it," he said, and he
    never has told me a lie.
I whipped him for robbing an orchard once
    when he was but a child —   25
"The farmer dared me to do it," he said; he
    was always so wild —
And idle — and couldn't be idle — my Willy
    — he never could rest.
The King should have made him a soldier;
    he would have been one of his best.

But he lived with a lot of wild mates, and
    they never would let him be good;
They swore that he dare not rob the mail,
    and he swore that he would;   30
And he took no life, but he took one purse,
    and when all was done
He flung it among his fellows — "I'll none of
    it," said my son.

I came into court to the judge and the
    lawyers. I told them my tale,
God's own truth — but they killed him, they
    killed him for robbing the mail.
They hanged him in chains for a show — we
    had always borne a good name — 35
To be hanged for a thief — and then put
    away — isn't that enough shame?

Dust to dust — low down — let us hide! but
    they set him so high
That all the ships of the world could stare at
    him, passing by.
God 'ill pardon the hell-black raven and hor-
    rible fowls of the air,
But not the black heart of the lawyer who
    killed him and hanged him there.   40

And the jailer forced me away. I had bid
    him my last good-by;
They had fastened the door of his cell. "O
    mother!" I heard him cry.
I couldn't get back, though I tried; he had
    something further to say,
And now I never shall know it. The jailer
    forced me away.

Then since I couldn't but hear that cry of
    my boy that was dead,   45
They seized me and shut me up; they fas-
    tened me down on my bed.
"Mother, O mother!" — he called in the dark
    to me year after year —
They beat me for that, they beat me — you
    know that I couldn't but hear;
And then at the last they found I had grown
    so stupid and still
They let me abroad again — but the crea-
    tures had worked their will.   50

Flesh of my flesh was gone, but bone of my
    bone was left —
I stole them all from the lawyers — and you,
    will you call it a theft? —
My baby, the bones that had sucked me, the
    bones that had laughed and had cried—
Theirs? O, no! they are mine — not theirs —
    they had moved in my side.

Do you think I was scared by the bones? I
    kissed 'em, I buried 'em all —   55
I can't dig deep, I am old — in the night by
    the churchyard wall.
My Willy 'ill rise up whole when the trumpet
    of judgment 'ill sound,
But I charge you never to say that I laid
    him in holy ground.

They would scratch him up — they would
    hang him again on the cursed tree.
Sin? O yes, we are sinners, I know — let all
    that be,   60
And read me a Bible verse of the Lord's good-
    will toward men —

"Full of compassion and mercy, the Lord" —
    let me hear it again;
"Full of compassion and mercy — long-suf-
    fering." Yes, O yes!
For the lawyer is born but to murder — the
    Savior lives but to bless.
He'll never put on the black cap except for
    the worst of the worst,   65
And the first may be last — I have heard it in
    church — and the last may be first.
Suffering — O long-suffering — yes, as the
    Lord must know,
Year after year in the mist and the wind and
    the shower and the snow.

Heard, have you? what? they have told you
    he never repented his sin.
How do they know it? are *they* his mother? are
    you of his kin?   70
Heard! have you ever heard, when the storm
    of the downs began,
The wind that 'ill wail like a child and the
    sea that 'ill moan like a man?
Election, Election, and Reprobation — it's
    all very well.
But I go tonight to my boy, and I shall not
    find him in hell.
For I cared so much for my boy that the
    Lord has looked into my care.   75
And He means me I'm sure to be happy with
    Willy, I know not where.

And if *he* be lost — but to save *my* soul, that
    is all your desire —
Do you think that I care for *my* soul if my
    boy be gone to the fire?
I have been with God in the dark — go, go,
    you may leave me alone —
You never have borne a child — you are just
    as hard as a stone.   80

Madam, I beg your pardon! I think that
    you mean to be kind,
But I cannot hear what you say for my
    Willy's voice in the wind —
The snow and the sky so bright — he used
    but to call in the dark,
And he calls to me now from the church and
    not from the gibbet — for hark!
Nay — you can hear it yourself — it is com-
    ing — shaking the walls —   85
Willy — the moon's in a cloud —— Good-
    night. I am going. He calls.   (1880)

62. **Full . . . the Lord.** From *Psalms*, 86:15.—"But thou, O Lord, art a God full of compassion, and gracious, long-suffering, and plenteous in mercy and truth." 65. **the black cap**, worn by an English judge when he passes sentence of death upon a prisoner. 66. **the last may be first.** From *Matthew*, 19:30—"But many that are first shall be last; and the last shall be first." 73. **Election . . . Reprobation**, a reference to the belief that some persons are elected to be saved and others lost, regardless of personal character.

51. **Flesh . . . bone.** From *Genesis*, 2:23.—"And Adam said, 'This is now bone of my bones, and flesh of my flesh; she shall be called Woman, because she was taken out of Man.'" 58. **holy ground.** Executed persons were denied Christian burial.

"FRATER AVE ATQUE VALE"

Row us out from Desenzano, to your Sir-
    mione row!
So they rowed, and there we landed — "O
    venusta Sirmio!"
There to me through all the groves of olive in
    the summer glow,
There beneath the Roman ruin where the
    purple flowers grow,
Came that "Ave atque Vale" of the Poet's
    hopeless woe,   5
Tenderest of Roman poets nineteen hundred
    years ago,
"Frater Ave atque Vale" — as we wandered
    to and fro
Gazing at the Lydian laughter of the Garda
    Lake below
Sweet Catullus's all-but-island, olive-silvery
    Sirmio!   (*1880; 1883*)

TO VIRGIL

WRITTEN AT THE REQUEST OF THE MANTUANS
FOR THE NINETEENTH CENTENARY
OF VIRGIL'S DEATH

Roman Virgil, thou that singest Ilion's lofty
    temples robed in fire,
Ilion falling, Rome arising, wars, and filial
    faith, and Dido's pyre;

Landscape-lover, lord of language more than
    he that sang the "Works and Days,"
All the chosen coin of fancy flashing out from
    many a golden phrase;

Thou that singest wheat and woodland, tilth
    and vineyard, hive and horse and herd;
All the charm of all the Muses often flowering
    in a lonely word;   6

Poet of the happy Tityrus piping underneath
    his beechen bowers;
Poet of the poet-satyr whom the laughing
    shepherd bound with flowers;

Chanter of the Pollio, glorying in the blissful
    years again to be,
Summers of the snakeless meadow, unlabori-
    ous earth and oarless sea;   10

Thou that seest Universal Nature moved by
    Universal Mind;
Thou majestic in thy sadness at the doubtful
    doom of human kind;

Light among the vanished ages; star that
    gildest yet this phantom shore;
Golden branch amid the shadows, kings and
    realms that pass to rise no more;

Now thy Forum roars no longer, fallen every
    purple Cæsar's dome —   15
Though thine ocean-roll of rhythm sound for-
    ever of Imperial Rome —

Now the Rome of slaves hath perished, and
    the Rome of freemen holds her place,
I, from out the Northern Island sundered once
    from all the human race,

I salute thee, Mantovano, I that loved thee
    since my day began,
Wielder of the stateliest measure ever molded
    by the lips of man.   20
                                        (1882)

FREEDOM

O thou so fair in summers gone,
    While yet thy fresh and virgin soul
Informed the pillared Parthenon,
    The glittering Capitol;

So fair in southern sunshine bathed,   5
    But scarce of such majestic mien
As here with forehead vapor-swathed
    In meadows ever green;

For thou — when Athens reigned and Rome,
    Thy glorious eyes were dimmed with pain
To mark in many a freeman's home   11
    The slave, the scourge, the chain;

Frater Ave Atque Vale. The title, *Brother, Hail and Farewell,*
is quoted from a lament of the Roman poet Catullus (1st cent.)
for his brother. Tennyson visited Italy in 1880.
  1. Desenzano, a town on Lake Garda in northern Italy,
just west of Sirmione, a narrow peninsula, where Catullus
lived.   **2. O venusta Sirmio,** O beautiful Sirmio; quoted
from Catullus.   **8. Lydian.** The Etruscans, who settled
near Lake Garda, were supposed to be of Lydian origin.
  To Virgil. Virgil was born in Mantua, Italy. He died in
19 B.C. The poem is full of allusions to his works.
  1-2. This stanza refers to the chief incidents in Virgil's
Æneid—the burning of Troy (Ilion) and the death of Dido in
Carthage when Æneas left her.   **3. Works and Days,** the
title of a poem by Hesiod, a Greek poet of the 8th century B.C.
5-6. This stanza mentions themes of Virgil's *Georgics.*   **7.
Tityrus,** a shepherd in Virgil's first *Eclogue.*   **8. poet-satyr
. . . flowers,** an incident in the sixth *Eclogue.*

  9. Pollio, C. Asinius Pollio, a patron of Virgil, mentioned in
the fourth *Eclogue.*   **11-14.** These lines contain echoes of the
sixth book of the *Æneid.*   **15. Forum,** the famous market
place of ancient Rome, used for popular assemblies.   **purple,**
the color and symbol of authority. The Cæsars ruled during
the first century B.C.
  Freedom. This poem expresses Tennyson's favorite political
creed—that changes and reforms should be made gradually.
Cf. *Of Old Sat Freedom on the Heights,* page 37, and *The Poet,*
page 16.
  3. Parthenon, a celebrated temple built in Athens, Greece,
during the 5th century B.C.   **4. Capitol,** the temple of Jupiter
at Rome.   **12. The slave . . . chain.** Slavery held sway in
Greece and Rome for more than a thousand years.

O follower of the Vision, still
  In motion to the distant gleam
Howe'er blind force and brainless will   15
  May jar thy golden dream

Of Knowledge fusing class with class,
  Of civic Hate no more to be,
Of love to leaven all the mass,
  Till every soul be free;   20

Who yet, like Nature, wouldst not mar
  By changes all too fierce and fast
This order of her Human Star,
  This heritage of the past;

O scorner of the party cry   25
  That wanders from the public good,
Thou — when the nations rear on high
  Their idol smeared with blood,

And when they roll their idol down —
  Of saner worship sanely proud;   30
Thou loather of the lawless crown
  As of the lawless crowd;

How long thine ever-growing mind
  Hath stilled the blast and strown the wave,
Though some of late would raise a wind   35
  To sing thee to thy grave,

Men loud against all forms of power —
  Unfurnished brows, tempestuous tongues,
Expecting all things in an hour —
  Brass mouths and iron lungs!   40
        (1884)

VASTNESS

Many a hearth upon our dark globe sighs
  after many a vanished face,
Many a planet by many a sun may roll with
  the dust of a vanished race.

Raving politics, never at rest — as this poor
  earth's pale history runs —
What is it all but a trouble of ants in the
  gleam of a million million of suns?

Lies upon this side, lies upon that side, truth-
  less violence mourned by the wise,   5
Thousands of voices drowning his own in a
  popular torrent of lies upon lies;

Stately purposes, valor in battle, glorious
  annals of army and fleet,
Death for the right cause, death for the wrong
  cause, trumpets of victory, groans of
  defeat;

Vastness. See Critical Notes.

Innocence seethed in her mother's milk, and
  Charity setting the martyr aflame;
Thraldom who walks with the banner of Freedom, and recks not to ruin a realm in
  her name.   10

Faith at her zenith, or all but lost in the gloom
  of doubts that darken the schools;
Craft with a bunch of all-heal in her hand, followed up by her vassal legion of fools;

Trade flying over a thousand seas with her
  spice and her vintage, her silk and her
  corn;
Desolate offing, sailorless harbors, famishing
  populace, wharves forlorn;

Star of the morning, Hope in the sunrise;
  Gloom of the evening, Life at a close; 15
Pleasure who flaunts on her wide downway
  with her flying robe and her poisoned
  rose;

Pain, that has crawled from the corpse of
  Pleasure, a worm which writhes all
  day, and at night
Stirs up again in the heart of the sleeper, and
  stings him back to the curse of the
  light;

Wealth with his wines and his wedded harlots; honest Poverty, bare to the bone;
Opulent Avarice, lean as Poverty; Flattery
  gilding the rift in a throne;   20

Fame blowing out from her golden trumpet a
  jubilant challenge to Time and to Fate;
Slander, her shadow, sowing the nettle on all
  the laureled graves of the great;

Love for the maiden, crowned with marriage,
  no regrets for aught that has been,
Household happiness, gracious children, debt-
  less competence, golden mean;

National hatreds of whole generations, and
  pigmy spites of the village spire;   25
Vows that will last to the last death-ruckle,
  and vows that are snapped in a moment of fire;

He that has lived for the lust of the minute,
  and died in the doing it, flesh without
  mind;
He that has nailed all flesh to the Cross, till
  Self died out in the love of his kind;

12. **all-heal.** Many plants are so called from their supposed medicinal power. 13. **Corn,** grain, wheat. 26.
death-ruckle, a rattling sound sometimes produced in the
throat of a dying person. 28. **He . . . Cross.** From *Galatians,* 5:24.—"And they that are Christ's have crucified the
flesh with the affections and lusts."

Spring and Summer and Autumn and Winter,
  and all these old revolutions of earth;
All new-old revolutions of Empire — change
  of the tide — what is all of it worth?   30

What the philosophies, all the sciences, poesy,
  varying voices of prayer,
All that is noblest, all that is basest, all that
  is filthy with all that is fair?

What is it all, if we all of us end but in being
  our own corpse-coffins at last?
Swallowed in Vastness, lost in Silence, drowned
  in the deeps of a meaningless Past?

What but a murmur of gnats in the gloom,
  or a moment's anger of bees in their
  hive? —   35

·   ·   ·   ·   ·   ·   ·   ·

Peace, let it be! for I loved him, and love
  him forever; the dead are not dead but
  alive.   (1885)

THE ANCIENT SAGE

A thousand summers ere the time of Christ,
From out his ancient city came a Seer
Whom one that loved and honored him,
  and yet
Was no disciple, richly garbed, but worn
From wasteful living, followed — in his
  hand   5
A scroll of verse — till that old man before
A cavern whence an affluent fountain poured
From darkness into daylight, turned and
  spoke:

"This wealth of waters might but seem
  to draw
From yon dark cave, but, son, the source
  is higher,   10
Yon summit half-a-league in air — and higher
The cloud that hides it — higher still the
  heavens
Whereby the cloud was moulded, and
  whereout
The cloud descended. Force is from the
  heights.
I am wearied of our city, son, and go   15
To spend my one last year among the hills.
What hast thou there? Some death-song for
  the Ghouls
To make their banquet relish? let me read.

36. Originally this line was represented as spoken by another person in answer to the question in line 35. If the line is
spoken by the poet, *him* may refer to Arthur Hallam.
  The Ancient Sage. The sage is the Chinese philosopher,
Lao-tse (c. 604-531 B.C.), some of whose ideas are faithfully
reproduced; but he is also the aged Tennyson, describing
his lifelong experience of trances and quasi-mystical intuitions. In effect the poem is a late counterpart to *The Two
Voices*, p. 30; here the young poet's scroll serves as the voice
of negation.

" 'How far thro' all the bloom and brake
  That nightingale is heard!   20
What power but the bird's could make
  This music in the bird?
How summer-bright are yonder skies,
  And earth as fair in hue!
And yet what sign of aught that lies   25
  Behind the green and blue?
But man to-day is fancy's fool
  As man hath ever been.
The nameless Power, or Powers, that
  rule
Were never heard or seen.'   30

If thou wouldst hear the Nameless, and
  wilt dive
Into the temple-cave of thine own self,
There, brooding by the central altar, thou
Mayst haply learn the Nameless hath a voice,
By which thou wilt abide, if thou be wise,   35
As if thou knewest, tho' thou canst not know;
For Knowledge is the swallow on the lake
That sees and stirs the surface-shadow there
But never yet hath dipt into the abysm,
The abysm of all abysms, beneath,
  within   40
The blue of sky and sea, the green of earth,
And in the million-millionth of a grain
Which cleft and cleft again for evermore,
And ever vanishing, never vanishes,
To me, my son, more mystic than myself,   45
Or even than the Nameless is to me.
"And when thou sendest thy free soul
  thro' heaven,
Nor understandest bound nor boundlessness,
Thou seest the Nameless of the hundred
  names.
"And if the Nameless should withdraw
  from all   50
Thy frailty counts most real, all thy world
Might vanish like thy shadow in the dark.

" 'And since — from when this earth
  began —
  The Nameless never came
Among us, never spake with man,   55
  And never named the Name' —

Thou canst not prove the Nameless, O
  my son,
Nor canst thou prove the world thou
  movest in,
Thou canst not prove that thou art body
  alone,
Nor canst thou prove that thou are spirit
  alone,   60
Nor canst thou prove that thou art both
  in one.

Thou canst not prove thou art immortal, no,
Nor yet that thou art mortal — nay, my son,
Thou canst not prove that I, who speak
    with thee,
Am not thyself in converse with thyself,   65
For nothing worthy proving can be proven,
Nor yet disproven. Wherefore thou be wise,
Cleave ever to the sunnier side of doubt,
And cling to Faith beyond the forms of Faith!
She reels not in the storm of warring
    words,   70
She brightens at the clash of 'Yes' and 'No,'
She sees the best that glimmers thro' the
    worst,
She feels the sun is hid but for a night,
She spies the summer thro' the winter bud,
She tastes the fruit before the blossom
    falls,   75
She hears the lark within the songless egg,
She finds the fountain where they wailed
    'Mirage!'

  " 'What Power? aught akin to Mind,
    The mind in me and you?
    Or power as of the Gods gone blind   80
    Who see not what they do?'

But some in yonder city hold, my son,
That none but gods could build this house
    of ours,
So beautiful, vast, various, so beyond
All work of man, yet, like all work of man, 85
A beauty with defect — till That which
    knows,
And is not known, but felt thro' what we feel
Within ourselves is highest, shall descend
On this half-deed, and shape it at the last
According to the Highest in the Highest.   90

  " 'What Power but the Years that make
    And break the vase of clay,
    And stir the sleeping earth, and wake
    The bloom that fades away?
    What rulers but the Days and Hours 95
    That cancel weal with woe,
    And wind the front of youth with
    flowers,
    And cap our age with snow?'

The days and hours are ever glancing by,
And seem to flicker past thro' sun and
    shade,   100
Or short, or long, as Pleasure leads, or Pain,
But with the Nameless is nor day nor hour;
Tho' we, thin minds, who creep from
    thought to thought,
Break into 'Thens' and 'Whens' the Eternal
    Now —
This double seeming of the single
    world! —   105

My words are like the babblings in a dream
Of nightmare, when the babblings break
    the dream.
But thou be wise in this dream-world of ours,
Nor take thy dial for thy deity,
But make the passing shadow serve thy
    will.   110

  " 'The years that made the stripling wise
    Undo their work again,
    And leave him, blind of heart and eyes,
    The last and least of men;
    Who clings to earth, and once would
    dare   115
    Hell-heat or Arctic cold,
    And now one breath of cooler air
    Would loose him from his hold.
    His winter chills him to the root,
    He withers marrow and mind;   120
    The kernel of the shrivelled fruit
    Is jutting thro' the rind;
    The tiger spasms tear his chest,
    The palsy wags his head;
    The wife, the sons, who love him best 125
    Would fain that he were dead;
    The griefs by which he once was wrung
    Were never worth the while' —

Who knows? or whether this earth-narrow life
Be yet but yolk, and forming in the shell? 130

  " 'The shaft of scorn that once had stung
    But wakes a dotard smile.'

The placid gleam of sunset after storm!

  " 'The statesman's brain that swayed the
    past
    Is feebler than his knees;   135
    The passive sailor wrecks at last
    In ever-silent seas;
    The warrior hath forgot his arms,
    The learned all his lore;
    The changing market frets or charms 140
    The merchant's hope no more:
    The prophet's beacon burned in vain,
    And now is lost in cloud;
    The plowman passes, bent with pain,
    To mix with what he plowed;   145
    The poet whom his age would quote
    As heir of endless fame —
    He knows not even the book he wrote,
    Not even his own name.
    For man has overlived his day,   150
    And, darkening in the light,
    Scarce feels the senses break away
    To mix with ancient Night.'

The shell must break before the bird can fly.

" 'The years that when my youth began 155
    Had set the lily and rose
By all my ways where'er they ran,
    Have ended mortal foes;
My rose of love for ever gone,
    My lily of truth and trust —   160
They made her lily and rose in one,
    And changed her into dust.
O rose-tree planted in my grief,
    And growing on her tomb,
Her dust is greening in your leaf,   165
    Her blood is in your bloom.
O slender lily waving there,
    And laughing back the light,
In vain you tell me "Earth is fair"
    When all is dark as night.'   170

My son, the world is dark with griefs and
    graves,
So dark that men cry out against the heavens.
Who knows but that the darkness is in man?
The doors of Night may be the gates of
    Light;
For wert thou born or blind or deaf, and
    then   175
Suddenly healed, how wouldst thou glory in
    all
The splendors and the voices of the world!
And we, the poor earth's dying race, and yet
No phantoms, watching from a phantom
    shore
Await the last and largest sense to make   180
The phantom walls of this illusion fade,
And show us that the world is wholly fair.

" 'But vain the tears for darkened years
    As laughter over wine,
And vain the laughter as the tears,   185
    O brother, mine or thine,
For all that laugh, and all that weep
    And all that breathe are one
Slight ripple on the boundless deep
    That moves, and all is gone.'   190

But that one ripple on the boundless deep
Feels that the deep is boundless, and itself
For ever changing form, but evermore
One with the boundless motion of the deep.

" 'Yet wine and laughter, friends! and set
    The lamps alight, and call   196
    For golden music, and forget
    The darkness of the pall.'

If utter darkness closed the day, my son —
But earth's dark forehead flings athwart the
    heavens   200
Her shadow crowned with stars — and yonder
    — out
To northward — some that never set, but pass

From sight and night to lose themselves in
    day.
I hate the black negation of the bier,
And wish the dead, as happier than our-
    selves   205
And higher, having climbed one step beyond
Our village miseries, might be borne in white
To burial or to burning, hymned from hence
With songs in praise of death, and crowned
    with flowers!

" 'O worms and maggots of to-day   210
    Without their hope of wings!'

But louder than thy rhyme the silent Word
Of that world-prophet in the heart of man.

" 'Tho' some have gleams, or so they say,
    Of more than mortal things.'   215

To-day? but what of yesterday? for oft
On me, when boy, there came what then I
    called,
Who knew no books and no philosophies,
In my boy-phrase, 'The Passion of the Past.'
The first gray streak of earliest summer-
    dawn,   220
The last long stripe of waning crimson gloom,
As if the late and early were but one —
A height, a broken grange, a grove, a flower
Had murmurs, 'Lost and gone, and lost and
    gone!'
A breath, a whisper — some divine farewell —
Desolate sweetness — far and far away —   226
What had he loved, what had he lost, the
    boy?
I know not, and I speak of what has been.
    "And more, my son! for more than once
    when I
Sat all alone, revolving in myself   230
The word that is the symbol of myself,
The mortal limit of the Self was loosed,
And past into the Nameless, as a cloud
Melts into heaven. I touched my limbs, the
    limbs
Were strange, not mine — and yet no shade
    of doubt,   235
But utter clearness, and thro' loss of self
The gain of such large life as matched with
    ours
Were sun to spark — unshadowable in words,
Themselves but shadows of a shadow-world.

" 'And idle gleams will come and go,   240
    But still the clouds remain;'

The clouds themselves are children of the Sun.

219. "The Passion of the Past," see *Tears, Idle Tears,*
p. 55, and critical note to that poem.

" 'And Night and Shadow rule below
   When only Day should reign.'

And Day and Night are children of the Sun,
And idle gleams to thee are light to me.   246
Some say, the Light was father of the Night,
And some, the Night was father of the Light,
No night, no day! — I touch thy world
   again —
No ill, no good! such counter-terms, my
   son,   250
Are border-races, holding each its own
By endless war. But night enough is there
In yon dark city. Get thee back; and since
The key to that weird casket, which for thee
But holds a skull, is neither thine nor mine, 255
But in the hand of what is more than man,
Or in man's hand when man is more than man,
Let be thy wail, and help thy fellow-men,
And make thy gold thy vassal, not thy king,
And fling free alms into the beggar's bowl, 260
And send the day into the darkened heart;
Nor list for guerdon in the voice of men,
A dying echo from a falling wall;
Nor care — for Hunger hath the evil eye —
To vex the noon with fiery gems, or fold   265
Thy presence in the silk of sumptuous looms;
Nor roll thy viands on a luscious tongue,
Nor drown thyself with flies in honeyed wine;
Nor thou be rageful, like a handled bee,
And lose thy life by usage of thy sting;   270
Nor harm an adder thro' the lust for harm,
Nor make a snail's horn shrink for wantonness.
And more — think well! Do-well will follow
   thought,
And in the fatal sequence of this world
An evil thought may soil thy children's blood;
But curb the beast would cast thee in the
   mire,   276
And leave the hot swamp of voluptuousness,
A cloud between the Nameless and thyself,
And lay thine uphill shoulder to the wheel,
And climb the Mount of Blessing, whence, if
   thou   280
Look higher, then — perchance — thou mayest
   — beyond
A hundred ever-rising mountain lines,
And past the range of Night and Shadow —
   see
The high-heaven dawn of more than mortal
   day
Strike on the Mount of Vision!   285
                              So, farewell."
                                     (1885)

DEMETER AND PERSEPHONE

(IN ENNA)

Faint as a climate-changing bird that flies
All night across the darkness, and at dawn

Falls on the threshold of her native land,
And can no more, thou camest, O my child,
Led upward by the God of ghosts and dreams,
Who laid thee at Eleusis, dazed and dumb   6
With passing thro' at once from state to state,
Until I brought thee hither, that the day,
When here thy hands let fall the gathered
   flower,
Might break thro' clouded memories once
   again   10
On thy lost self. A sudden nightingale
Saw thee, and flashed into a frolic of song
And welcome; and a gleam as of the moon,
When first she peers along the tremulous
   deep,
Fled wavering o'er thy face, and chased away
That shadow of a likeness to the king   16
Of shadows, thy dark mate. Persephone!
Queen of the dead no more — my child! Thine
   eyes
Again were human-godlike, and the Sun
Burst from a swimming fleece of winter gray,
And robed thee in his day from head to feet —
"Mother!" and I was folded in thine arms.   22

Child, those imperial, disimpassioned eyes
Awed even me at first, thy mother — eyes
That oft had seen the serpent-wanded power
Draw downward into Hades with his drift   26
Of flickering spectres, lighted from below
By the red race of fiery Phlegethon;
But when before have Gods or men beheld
The Life that had descended re-arise,   30
And lighted from above him by the Sun?
So mighty was the mother's childless cry,
A cry that rang thro' Hades, Earth, and
   Heaven!

So in this pleasant vale we stand again,
The field of Enna, now once more ablaze   35
With flowers that brighten as thy footstep
   falls,
All flowers — but for one black blur of earth
Left by that closing chasm, thro' which the car
Of dark Aïdoneus rising rapt thee hence.
And here, my child, tho' folded in thine arms,
I feel the deathless heart of motherhood   41
Within me shudder, lest the naked glebe
Should yawn once more into the gulf, and
   thence
The shrilly whinnyings of the team of Hell,

Demeter and Persephone. In the Greek vegetation myth
Persephone, gathering flowers in the field of Enna, was
snatched away by Aïdoneus, king of the underworld. In
deep grief her mother, Demeter, goddess of the earth, neglected the harvest till Zeus restored Persephone to her for
three of the four seasons.
5. **God of ghosts,** Hermes. 6. **Eleusis,** a town near
Athens, noted for its shrine to Demeter. 25. **serpent-
wanded.** Hermes carried a staff twined with serpents as
he directed the dead to the underworld. 28. **Phlegethon,**
the fiery river of Hades.

Ascending, pierce the glad and songful air, 45
And all at once their arched necks, midnight-
    maned,
Jet upward thro' the midday blossom. No!
For, see, thy foot has touched it; all the space
Of blank earth-baldness clothes itself afresh,
And breaks into the crocus-purple hour   50
That saw thee vanish.

            Child, when thou wert gone,
I envied human wives, and nested birds,
Yea, the cubbed lioness; went in search of
    thee
Thro' many a palace, many a cot, and gave
Thy breast to ailing infants in the night,   55
And set the mother waking in a maze
To find her sick one whole; and forth again
Among the wail of midnight winds, and cried,
"Where is my loved one? Wherefore do ye
    wail?"
And out from all the night an answer shrilled,
"We know not, and we know not why we
    wail."   61
I climbed on all the cliffs of all the seas,
And asked the waves that moan about the
    world,
"Where? do ye make your moaning for my
    child?"
And round from all the world the voices
    came,   65
"We know not, and we know not why we
    moan."
"Where?" and I stared from every eagle-
    peak,
I thridded the black heart of all the woods,
I peered thro' tomb and cave, and in the
    storms
Of autumn swept across the city, and heard 70
The murmur of their temples chanting me,
Me, me, the desolate mother! "Where?" —
    and turned,
And fled by many a waste, forlorn of man,
And grieved for man thro' all my grief for
    thee, —
The jungle rooted in his shattered hearth, 75
The serpent coiled about his broken shaft,
The scorpion crawling over naked skulls; —
I saw the tiger in the ruined fane
Spring from his fallen God, but trace of thee
I saw not; and far on, and, following out   80
A league of labyrinthine darkness, came
On three gray heads beneath a gleaming rift.
"Where?" and I heard one voice from all the
    three,
"We know not, for we spin the lives of men,
And not of Gods, and know not why we spin!
There is a Fate beyond us." Nothing knew. 86

82. **three gray heads**, the three Fates.

Last as the likeness of a dying man,
Without his knowledge, from him flits to warn
A far-off friendship that he comes no more,
So he, the God of dreams, who heard my cry, 90
Drew from thyself the likeness of thyself
Without thy knowledge, and thy shadow past
Before me, crying, "The Bright one in the
    highest
Is brother of the Dark one in the lowest,
And Bright and Dark have sworn that I, the
    child   95
Of thee, the great Earth-Mother, thee, the
    Power
That lifts her buried life from gloom to bloom,
Should be for ever and for evermore
The Bride of Darkness."

                    So the Shadow wailed.
Then I, Earth-Goddess, cursed the Gods of
    heaven.   100
I would not mingle with their feasts; to me
Their nectar smacked of hemlock on the lips,
Their rich ambrosia tasted aconite.
That man, that only lives and loves an hour,
Seemed nobler than their hard eternities.   105
My quick tears killed the flower, my ravings
    hushed
The bird, and lost in utter grief I failed
To send my life thro' olive-yard and vine
And golden-grain, my gift to helpless man.
Rain-rotten died the wheat, the barley-spears
Were hollow-husked, the leaf fell, and the
    Sun,   111
Pale at my grief, drew down before his time
Sickening, and Ætna kept her winter snow.

  Then He, the brother of this Darkness, He
Who still is highest, glancing from his height 115
On earth a fruitless fallow, when he missed
The wonted steam of sacrifice, the praise
And prayer of men, decreed that thou shouldst
    dwell
For nine white moons of each whole year with
    me,
Three dark ones in the shadow with thy
    king.   120

  Once more the reaper in the gleam of dawn
Will see me by the landmark far away,
Blessing his field, or seated in the dusk
Of even, by the lonely threshing-floor,
Rejoicing in the harvest and the grange.   125

  Yet I, Earth-Goddess, am but ill-content
With them who still are highest. Those gray
    heads,
What meant they by their "Fate beyond the
    Fates"?

But younger kindlier Gods to bear us down,
As we bore down the Gods before us? Gods, 130
To quench, not hurl the thunderbolt, to stay,
Not spread the plague, the famine; Gods
  indeed,
To send the noon into the night and break
The sunless halls of Hades into Heaven?
Till thy dark lord accept and love the Sun, 135
And all the Shadow die into the Light,
When thou shalt dwell the whole bright year
  with me,
And souls of men, who grew beyond their race,
And made themselves as Gods against the
  fear
Of Death and Hell; and thou that hast from
  men, 140
As Queen of Death, that worship which is
  Fear,
Henceforth, as having risen from out the dead,
Shalt ever send thy life along with mine
From buried grain thro' springing blade, and
  bless
Their garnered autumn also, reap with me, 145
Earth-mother, in the harvest hymns of Earth
The worship which is Love, and see no more
The Stone, the Wheel, the dimly-glimmering
  lawns
Of that Elysium, all the hateful fires
Of torment, and the shadowy warrior glide 150
Along the silent field of Asphodel.

(1889)

MERLIN AND THE GLEAM

I

O young Mariner,
You from the haven
Under the sea-cliff,
You that are watching
The gray Magician   5
With eyes of wonder,
I am Merlin,
And *I* am dying,
I am Merlin
Who follow the Gleam.   10

2

Mighty the Wizard
Who found me at sunrise
Sleeping, and woke me
And learned me Magic!
Great the Master,   15
And sweet the Magic,
When over the valley,
In early summers,
Over the mountain,
On human faces,   20
And all around me,
Moving to melody,
Floated the Gleam.

3

Once at the croak of a Raven who crossed it,
A barbarous people,   25
Blind to the magic
And deaf to the melody,
Snarled at and cursed me.
A demon vexed me,
The light retreated,   30
The landskip darkened,
The melody deadened,
The Master whispered,
"Follow the Gleam."

4

Then to the melody,   35
Over a wilderness
Gliding, and glancing at
Elf of the woodland,
Gnome of the cavern,
Griffin and Giant,   40
And dancing of Fairies
In desolate hollows,
And wraiths of the mountain,
And rolling of dragons
By warble of water,   45
Or cataract music
Of falling torrents,
Flitted the Gleam.

Stanza 2. This stanza refers to Tennyson's early poetry, as in the 1827 volume.
Stanza 3. This stanza refers to the hostility of reviewers of the 1830 volume of poems and to the period of Tennyson's silence from 1833 to 1842. The "Raven" of line 24 may refer to Christopher North (John Wilson), whose criticism appeared in *Blackwood's Magazine*, May, 1832. The following poem by Tennyson appeared in the volume of 1832:

TO CHRISTOPHER NORTH

You did late review my lays,
    Crusty Christopher;
You did mingle blame and praise,
    Rusty Christopher.
When I learnt from whom it came
I forgave you all the blame,
    Musty Christopher;
I could *not* forgive the praise,
    Fusty Christopher.

Stanza 4. This stanza refers to the period of imaginative poems, as found in the 1842 volume.

129. **younger kindlier Gods**: in the strength of her mother-love Demeter imagines a vital new religion—in effect, Christianity—which will defeat the forces of death. 148. **the Stone, the Wheel** symbolize the torments of Hades. The stone of Sisyphus rolled back as often as he pushed it to the top of a hill. Ixion was bound to an eternally revolving wheel. 149. **Elysium**, a region of the nether world. 151. **Asphodel**, a barren plain in Hades.
Merlin and the Gleam. Merlin was the magician of Arthur's court. The poem is an allegory of Tennyson's poetical career. Merlin is Tennyson; the Gleam is "the higher poetic imagination."

5

Down from the mountain
And over the level,   50
And streaming and shining on
Silent river,
Silvery willow,
Pasture and plowland,
Innocent maidens,   55
Garrulous children,
Homestead and harvest,
Reaper and gleaner,
And rough-ruddy faces
Of lowly labor,   60
Slided the Gleam —

6

Then, with a melody
Stronger and statelier,
Led me at length
To the city and palace   65
Of Arthur the King;
Touched at the golden
Cross of the churches,
Flashed on the tournament,
Flickered and bickered   70
From helmet to helmet,
And last on the forehead
Of Arthur the blameless
Rested the Gleam.

7

Clouds and darkness   75
Closed upon Camelot;
Arthur had vanished
I knew not whither,
The king who loved me,
And cannot die;   80
For out of the darkness
Silent and slowly
The Gleam, that had waned to a wintry
    glimmer
On icy fallow
And faded forest,   85
Drew to the valley
Named of the shadow,
And slowly brightening
Out of the glimmer,
And slowly moving again to a melody   90
Yearningly tender,
Fell on the shadow,
No longer a shadow,
But clothed with the Gleam.

8

And broader and brighter   95
The Gleam flying onward,
Wed to the melody,
Sang through the world;
And slower and fainter,
Old and weary,   100
But eager to follow,
I saw, whenever
In passing it glanced upon
Hamlet or city,
That under the Crosses   105
The dead man's garden,
The mortal hillock,
Would break into blossom;
And so to the land's
Last limit I came —   110
And can no longer,
But die rejoicing,
For through the Magic
Of Him the Mighty,
Who taught me in childhood,   115
There on the border
Of boundless Ocean,
And all but in Heaven
Hovers the Gleam.

9

Not of the sunlight,   120
Not of the moonlight,
Not of the starlight!
O young Mariner,
Down to the haven,
Call your companions,   125
Launch your vessel
And crowd your canvas,
And, ere it vanishes
Over the margin,
After it, follow it,   130
Follow the Gleam.   (1889)

BY AN EVOLUTIONIST

The Lord let the house of a brute to the soul
    of a man,
    And the man said, "Am I your debtor?"
And the Lord — "Not yet; but make it as
    clean as you can,
    And then I will let you a better."

I

If my body come from brutes, my soul uncer-
    tain or a fable,   5
Why not bask amid the senses while the
    sun of morning shines,

Stanza 5. This stanza refers to the period of pastorals and English idyls, as found in the 1842 volume.
Stanza 6. This stanza refers to *The Idylls of the King.*
Stanza 7. This stanza refers to the experiences related in *In Memoriam.*
87. the shadow. Cf. *Psalms,* 23:4—"Though I walk through the valley of the shadow of death, I will fear no evil."

Stanza 8. This stanza refers to later poetic activity and particularly to an increased social concern. Cf. the image of the "boundless Ocean" with that of *Crossing the Bar,* p. 176.

I, the finer brute rejoicing in my hounds, and
    in my stable,
Youth and health, and birth and wealth,
    and choice of women and of wines?

2

What hast thou done for me, grim Old Age,
    save breaking my bones on the rack?
Would I had passed in the morning that
    looks so bright from afar!   10

Old Age

Done for thee? starved the wild beast that
    was linked with thee eighty years back.
Less weight now for the ladder-of-heaven
    that hangs on a star.

1

If my body come from brutes, though some-
    what finer than their own,
I am heir, and this my kingdom. Shall the
    royal voice be mute?
No, but if the rebel subject seek to drag me
    from the throne,   15
    Hold the scepter, Human Soul, and rule
    thy province of the brute.

2

I have climbed to the snows of Age, and I
    gaze at a field in the Past,
    Where I sank with the body at times in
    the sloughs of a low desire,
But I hear no yelp of the beast, and the Man
    is quiet at last,
    As he stands on the heights of his life with
    a glimpse of a height that is higher. 20
                        (1889)

FAR — FAR — AWAY

(FOR MUSIC)

What sight so lured him through the fields
    he knew
As where earth's green stole into heaven's
    own hue,
    Far — far — away?

What sound was dearest in his native dells?
The mellow lin-lan-lone of evening bells   5
    Far — far — away.

What vague world-whisper, mystic pain or
    joy,
Through those three words would haunt him
    when a boy,
    Far — far — away?

A whisper from his dawn of life? a breath   10
From some fair dawn beyond the doors of
    death
    Far — far — away?

Far, far, how far? from o'er the gates of birth,
The faint horizons, all the bounds of earth,
    Far — far — away?   15

What charm in words, a charm no words
    could give?
O dying words, can Music make you live
    Far — far — away?   (1889)

THE THROSTLE

"Summer is coming, summer is coming.
    I know it, I know it, I know it.
Light again, leaf again, life again, love again!"
    Yes, my wild little Poet.

Sing the new year in under the blue.   5
    Last year you sang it as gladly.
"New, new, new, new!" Is it then *so* new
    That you should carol so madly?

"Love again, song again, nest again, young
    again,"
    Never a prophet so crazy!   10
And hardly a daisy as yet, little friend,
    See, there is hardly a daisy.

"Here again, here, here, here, happy year!"
    O warble unchidden, unbidden!
Summer is coming, is coming, my dear,   15
    And all the winters are hidden.   (1889)

THE OAK

Live thy Life,
    Young and old,
Like yon oak,
    Bright in spring,
Living gold;   5

Summer-rich
    Then; and then
Autumn-changed,
    Soberer-hued
Gold again.   10

All his leaves
    Fallen at length,
Look, he stands,
    Trunk and bough,
Naked strength.   (1889)

Far—Far—Away. Compare this poem with *Tears, Idle Tears*, page 55.

The Throstle. In this poem Tennyson sets words to the music of the song thrush. Cf. *O Swallow, Swallow*, p. 55, and Swinburne's *Itylus*, p. 685.

JUNE BRACKEN AND HEATHER

TO ——

There on the top of the down,
The wild heather round me and over me
    June's high blue,
When I looked at the bracken so bright and
    the heather so brown,
I thought to myself I would offer this book
    to you,
This, and my love together,   5
To you that are seventy-seven,
With a faith as clear as the heights of the
    June-blue heaven,
And a fancy as summer-new
As the green of the bracken amid the gloom
    of the heather.   (1892)

From AKBAR'S DREAM
HYMN

Once again thou flamest heavenward, once
    again we see thee rise.
Every morning is thy birthday gladdening
    human hearts and eyes.
    Every morning here we greet it, bowing
    lowly down before thee,
Thee the Godlike, thee the changeless in thine
    ever-changing skies.

Shadow-maker, shadow-slayer, arrowing light
    from clime to clime,   5
Hear thy myriad laureates hail thee monarch
    in their woodland rime.
    Warble bird, and open flower, and, men,
    below the dome of azure
Kneel adoring Him the Timeless in the flame
    that measures Time!   (1892)

CROSSING THE BAR

Sunset and evening star,
    And one clear call for me!
And may there be no moaning of the bar,
    When I put out to sea,

But such a tide as moving seems asleep,   5
    Too full for sound and foam,
When that which drew from out the bound-
    less deep
    Turns again home.

Twilight and evening bell,
    And after that the dark!   10
And may there be no sadness of farewell,
    When I embark;

For though from out our bourne of Time and
    Place
    The flood may bear me far,
I hope to see my Pilot face to face   15
    When I have crossed the bar.
                                              (1889)

ROBERT BROWNING (1812-1889)

From PARACELSUS

HEAP CASSIA, SANDAL-BUDS, AND STRIPES

Heap cassia, sandal-buds, and stripes
Of labdanum, and aloe-balls,
Smeared with dull nard an Indian wipes
    From out her hair; such balsam falls
    Down sea-side mountain pedestals,   5
From tree-tops where tired winds are fain,
Spent with the vast and howling main,
To treasure half their island-gain.

And strew faint sweetness from some old
    Egyptian's fine worm-eaten shroud   10
Which breaks to dust when once unrolled;
    Or shredded perfume, like a cloud
From closet long to quiet vowed,
With mothed and dropping arras hung,
Moldering her lute and books among,   15
As when a queen, long dead, was young.

OVER THE SEA OUR GALLEYS WENT

Over the sea our galleys went,
With cleaving prows in order brave
To a speeding wind and a bounding wave —
    A gallant armament;
Each bark built out of a forest-tree   5
    Left leafy and rough as first it grew,
And nailed all over the gaping sides,
Within and without, with black bull-hides,
Seethed in fat and suppled in flame,
To bear the playful billows' game;   10
So, each good ship was rude to see,
Rude and bare to the outward view,
    But each upbore a stately tent

June Bracken and Heather. This poem is the dedication to Tennyson's last volume of poetry, *The Death of Œnone and Other Poems.* It is addressed to his wife. Cf. *A Dedication,* page 114.
Akbar's Dream. See Critical Notes.
Crossing the Bar. A few days before he died, Tennyson gave instructions that this lyric should be put at the end of all editions of his poems

Paracelsus. See Critical Notes.
Heap Cassia. The items mentioned in this poem are noted for their fragrance. They have long been associated in poetry. 4. **balsam,** fragrance, balm. 5. **mountain pedestals,** cliffs.
12. **shredded,** a transferred epithet; it applies to *arras,* line 14.
Over The Sea. See Critical Notes.

Where cedar pales in scented row
Kept out the flakes of the dancing brine,   15
And an awning drooped the mast below,
In fold on fold of the purple fine,
That neither noontide nor starshine
Nor moonlight cold which maketh mad,
    Might pierce the regal tenement.   20
When the sun dawned, oh, gay and glad
We set the sail and plied the oar;
But when the night-wind blew like breath,
For joy of one day's voyage more,
We sang together on the wide sea,   25
Like men at peace on a peaceful shore;
Each sail was loosed to the wind so free,
Each helm made sure by the twilight star,
And in a sleep as calm as death,
We, the voyagers from afar,   30
    Lay stretched along, each weary crew
In a circle round its wondrous tent
Whence gleamed soft light and curled rich
        scent,
    And with light and perfume, music, too.
So the stars wheeled round, and the darkness
        past,   35
And at morn we started beside the mast,
And still each ship was sailing fast.

Now, one morn, land appeared — a speck
Dim trembling betwixt sea and sky —
"Avoid it," cried our pilot, "check   40
    The shout, restrain the eager eye!"
But the heaving sea was black behind
For many a night and many a day,
And land, though but a rock, drew nigh;
So, we broke the cedar pales away,   45
Let the purple awning flap in the wind,
    And a statue bright was on every deck!
We shouted, every man of us,
And steered right into the harbor thus,
With pomp and pæan glorious.   50

A hundred shapes of lucid stone!
    All day we built its shrine for each,
A shrine of rock for every one,
Nor paused till in the westering sun
    We sat together on the beach   55
To sing because our task was done.
When lo! what shouts and merry songs!
What laughter all the distance stirs!
A loaded raft with happy throngs
Of gentle islanders!   60
"Our isles are just at hand," they cried,
    "Like cloudlets faint in even sleeping.
Our temple-gates are opened wide,
    Our olive-groves thick shade are keeping
For these majestic forms" — they cried.   65
Oh, then we awoke with sudden start

From our deep dream, and knew, too late,
How bare the rock, how desolate,
Which had received our precious freight;
    Yet we called out — "Depart!   70
Our gifts, once given, must here abide.
    Our work is done; we have no heart
To mar our work" — we cried.

THUS THE MAYNE GLIDETH

    Thus the Mayne glideth
Where my Love abideth.
Sleep's no softer; it proceeds
On through lawns, on through meads,
On and on, whate'er befall,   5
Meandering and musical,
Though the niggard pasturage
Bears not on its shaven ledge
Aught but weeds and waving grasses
To view the river as it passes,   10
Save here and there a scanty patch
Of primroses too faint to catch
A weary bee. And scarce it pushes
Its gentle way through strangling rushes
Where the glossy kingfisher   15
Flutters when noon-heats are near,
Glad the shelving banks to shun,
Red and steaming in the sun,
Where the shrew-mouse with pale throat
Burrows, and the speckled stoat;   20
Where the quick sandpipers flit
In and out the marl and grit
That seems to breed them, brown as they.
Naught disturbs its quiet way,
Save some lazy stork that springs,   25
Trailing it with legs and wings,
Whom the shy fox from the hill
Rouses, creep he ne'er so still.   (1835)

PORPHYRIA'S LOVER

The rain set early in tonight;
    The sullen wind was soon awake —
It tore the elm-tops down for spite,
    And did its worst to vex the lake.
I listened with heart fit to break.   5
When glided in Porphyria; straight
    She shut the cold out and the storm,
And kneeled and made the cheerless grate
    Blaze up, and all the cottage warm;
Which done, she rose, and from her form   10
Withdrew the dripping cloak and shawl,
    And laid her soiled gloves by, untied

---

19. **moonlight . . . mad.** The moon was long thought
to cause madness.

Thus the Mayne Glideth. The Mayne River is a tributary
of the Rhine. See Critical Notes.
    4. **lawns,** open spaces in the woods. 20. **speckled
stoat,** ermine. 22. **marl and grit,** earth and sand.
    Porphyria's Lover. This poem, together with the one fol-
lowing, first appeared under the title *Madhouse Cells.* It is
the earliest of Browning's dramatic monologues.

Her hat and let the damp hair fall,
  And, last, she sat down by my side
And called me. When no voice replied,   15
She put my arm about her waist,
  And made her smooth white shoulder bare
And all her yellow hair displaced,
  And, stooping, made my cheek lie there,
And spread, o'er all, her yellow hair,   20
Murmuring how she loved me — she
  Too weak, for all her heart's endeavor,
To set its struggling passion free
  From pride, and vainer ties dissever,
And give herself to me forever.   25
But passion sometimes would prevail,
  Nor could tonight's gay feast restrain
A sudden thought of one so pale
  For love of her, and all in vain:
So, she was come through wind and rain.   30
Be sure I looked up at her eyes
  Happy and proud; at last I knew
Porphyria worshiped me; surprise
  Made my heart swell, and still it grew
While I debated what to do.   35
That moment she was mine, mine, fair,
  Perfectly pure and good; I found
A thing to do, and all her hair
  In one long yellow string I wound
Three times her little throat around,   40
And strangled her. No pain felt she;
  I am quite sure she felt no pain.
As a shut bud that holds a bee,
  I warily oped her lids; again
Laughed the blue eyes without a stain.   45
And I untightened next the tress
  About her neck; her cheek once more
Blushed bright beneath my burning kiss.
  I propped her head up as before,
Only, this time my shoulder bore   50
Her head, which droops upon it still —
  The smiling rosy little head,
So glad it has its utmost will,
  That all it scorned at once is fled,
And I, its love, am gained instead!   55
Porphyria's love — she guessed not how
  Her darling one wish would be heard.
And thus we sit together now,
  And all night long we have not stirred,
And yet God has not said a word!   (1836)

JOHANNES AGRICOLA IN MEDITATION

There's heaven above, and night by night
  I look right through its gorgeous roof;
No suns and moons though e'er so bright

Johannes Agricola in Meditation. Johannes Agricola, a German reformer of the 16th century, was the reputed founder of the Antinomians, a sect of Christians who held that the moral law is of no value or force on the ground that faith only is necessary to salvation.

Avail to stop me; splendor-proof
I keep the broods of stars aloof.   5
For I intend to get to God,
  For 'tis to God I speed so fast,
For in God's breast, my own abode,
  Those shoals of dazzling glory, passed,
I lay my spirit down at last.   10
I lie where I have always lain,
  God smiles as he has always smiled;
Ere suns and moons could wax and wane,
  Ere stars were thundergirt, or piled
The heavens, God thought on me his child;
Ordained a life for me, arrayed   16
  Its circumstances every one
To the minutest; aye, God said
  This head this hand should rest upon
Thus, ere he fashioned star or sun.   20
And having thus created me,
  Thus rooted me, he bade me grow,
Guiltless forever, like a tree
  That buds and blooms, nor seeks to know
The law by which it prospers so.   25
But sure that thought and word and deed
  All go to swell his love for me,
Me, made because that love had need
  Of something irreversibly
Pledged solely its content to be.   30
Yes, yes, a tree which must ascend,
  No poison-gourd foredoomed to stoop!
I have God's warrant, could I blend
  All hideous sins, as in a cup,
To drink the mingled venoms up;   35
Secure my nature will convert
  The draft to blossoming gladness fast;
While sweet dews turn to the gourd's hurt,
  And bloat, and while they bloat it, blast,
As from the first its lot was cast.   40
For as I lie, smiled on, full-fed
  By unexhausted power to bless,
I gaze below on hell's fierce bed,
  And those its waves of flame oppress,
Swarming in ghastly wretchedness;   45
Whose life on earth aspired to be
  One altar-smoke, so pure! — to win
If not one like God's love for me,
  At least to keep his anger in;
And all their striving turned to sin.   50
Priest, doctor, hermit, monk grown white
  With prayer, the broken-hearted nun,
The martyr, the wan acolyte,
  The incense-swinging child — undone
Before God fashioned star or sun!   55
God, whom I praise; how could I praise,
  If such as I might understand,
Make out and reckon on his ways,
  And bargain for his love, and stand,
Paying a price, at his right hand?   (1836)

53. **acolyte,** one who carries the wine, the water, and the lights at the Mass.

PIPPA PASSES

A DRAMA

PERSONS

PIPPA	JULES
OTTIMA	PHENE
SEBALD	Austrian Police
Foreign Students	BLUPHOCKS
GOTTLIEB	LUIGI and his mother
SCHRAMM	Poor Girls

MONSIGNOR and his attendants

INTRODUCTION

NEW YEAR'S DAY AT ASOLO IN THE TREVISAN

SCENE: *A large mean airy chamber. A girl*, PIPPA, *from the silk-mills, springing out of bed.*

Day!
Faster and more fast,
O'er night's brim, day boils at last;
Boils, pure gold, o'er the cloud-cup's brim
Where spurting and suppressed it lay,   5
For not a froth-flake touched the rim
Of yonder gap in the solid gray
Of the eastern cloud, an hour away;
But forth one wavelet, then another, curled,
Till the whole sunrise, not to be suppressed,
Rose, reddened, and its seething breast   11
Flickered in bounds, grew gold, then over-
flowed the world.

O Day, if I squander a wavelet of thee,
A mite of my twelve-hours' treasure,
The least of thy gazes or glances   15
(Be they grants thou art bound to or gifts
above measure)
One of thy choices or one of thy chances
(Be they tasks God imposed thee or freaks at
thy pleasure)
— My Day, if I squander such labor or leisure,
Then shame fall on Asolo, mischief on me!   20

Thy long blue solemn hours serenely flowing,
Whence earth, we feel, gets steady help and
good —
Thy fitful sunshine-minutes, coming, going,
As if earth turned from work in gamesome
mood —   24
All shall be mine! But thou must treat me not
As prosperous ones are treated, those who live
At hand here, and enjoy the higher lot,
In readiness to take what thou wilt give,
And free to let alone what thou refusest;
For, Day, my holiday, if thou ill-usest   30
Me, who am only Pippa — old-year's sorrow,
Cast off last night, will come again tomorrow;

Whereas, if thou prove gentle, I shall borrow
Sufficient strength of thee for new-year's
sorrow.
All other men and women that this earth   35
Belongs to, who all days alike possess,
Make general plenty cure particular dearth,
Get more joy one way, if another, less;
Thou art my single day, God lends to leaven
What were all earth else, with a feel of
heaven —   40
Sole light that helps me through the year, thy
sun's!
Try now! Take Asolo's Four Happiest Ones —
And let thy morning rain on that superb
Great haughty Ottima; can rain disturb
Her Sebald's homage? All the while thy rain
Beats fiercest on her shrub-house window-
pane,   46
He will but press the closer, breathe more
warm
Against her cheek; how should she mind the
storm?
And, morning past, if mid-day shed a gloom
O'er Jules and Phene — what care bride and
groom   50
Save for their dear selves? 'Tis their mar-
riage-day;
And while they leave church and go home
their way,
Hand clasping hand, within each breast
would be
Sunbeams and pleasant weather spite of thee.
Then, for another trial, obscure thy eve   55
With mist—will Luigi and his mother grieve—
The lady and her child, unmatched, forsooth,
She in her age, as Luigi in his youth,
For true content? The cheerful town, warm,
close
And safe, the sooner that thou art morose,   60
Receives them. And yet once again, outbreak
In storm at night on Monsignor, they make
Such stir about — whom they expect from
Rome
To visit Asolo, his brothers' home,
And say here masses proper to release   65
A soul from pain — what storm dares hurt
his peace?
Calm would he pray, with his own thoughts
to ward
Thy thunder off, nor want the angels' guard.
But Pippa — just one such mischance would
spoil
Her day that lightens the next twelvemonth's
toil   70
At wearisome silk-winding, coil on coil!
And here I let time slip for naught!
Aha, you foolhardy sunbeam, caught

Pippa Passes. See Critical Notes. The scene of the introduction is Asolo, a small town in the province of Treviso, about 30 miles from Venice, Italy.

62. **Monsignor**, an ecclesiastical title bestowed by the Pope upon high church officials.

With a single splash from my ewer!
You that would mock the best pursuer,   75
Was my basin over-deep?
One splash of water ruins you asleep,
And up, up, fleet your brilliant bits
Wheeling and counterwheeling,
Reeling, broken beyond healing —   80
Now grow together on the ceiling!
That will task your wits.
Whoever it was quenched fire first, hoped to
    see
Morsel after morsel flee
As merrily, as giddily . . .   85
Meantime, what lights my sunbeam on,
Where settles by degrees the radiant cripple?
Oh, is it surely blown, my martagon?
New-blown and ruddy as St. Agnes' nipple,
Plump as the flesh-bunch on some Turk bird's
    poll!   90
Be sure if corals, branching 'neath the ripple
Of ocean, bud there — fairies watch unroll
Such turban-flowers; I say, such lamps dis-
    perse
Thick red flame through that dusk green uni-
    verse!
I am queen of thee, floweret!   95
And each fleshy blossom
Preserve I not — safer
Than leaves that embower it,
Or shells that embosom —
From weevil and chafer?   100
Laugh through my pane then; solicit the bee;
Gibe him, be sure; and, in midst of thy glee,
Love thy queen, worship me!

—Worship whom else? For am I not, this day,
Whate'er I please? What shall I please today?
My morn, noon, eve, and night — how spend
    my day?   106
Tomorrow I must be Pippa who winds silk,
The whole year round, to earn just bread and
    milk;
But, this one day, I have leave to go,
And play out my fancy's fullest games;   110
I may fancy all day — and it shall be so —
That I taste of the pleasures, am called by the
    names
Of the Happiest Four in our Asolo!

See! Up the hillside yonder, through the
    morning,
Someone shall love me, as the world calls love;
I am no less than Ottima, take warning!   116
The gardens, and the great stone house above,
And other house for shrubs, all glass in front,

Are mine; where Sebald steals, as he is wont,
To court me, while old Luca yet reposes;   120
And therefore, till the shrub-house door un-
    closes,
I — what now? — give abundant cause for
    prate
About me — Ottima, I mean — of late,
Too bold, too confident she'll still face down
The spitefullest of talkers in our town.   125
How we talk in the little town below!
    But love, love, love — there's better love,
      I know!
This foolish love was only day's first offer;
I choose my next love to defy the scoffer;
For do not our Bride and Bridegroom sally   130
Out of Possagno church at noon?
Their house looks over Orcana valley;
Why should not I be the bride as soon
As Ottima? For I saw, beside,
Arrive last night that little bride —   135
Saw, if you call it seeing her, one flash
Of the pale snow-pure cheek and black bright
    tresses,
Blacker than all except the black eyelash;
I wonder she contrives those lids no dresses!
— So strict was she, the veil   140
Should cover close her pale
Pure cheeks — a bride to look at and scarce
    touch,
Scarce touch, remember, Jules! For are not
    such
Used to be tended, flower-like, every feature,
As if one's breath would fray the lily of a
    creature?   145
A soft and easy life these ladies lead;
Whiteness in us were wonderful indeed.
Oh, save that brow its virgin dimness,
Keep that foot its lady primness,
Let those ankles never swerve   150
From their exquisite reserve,
Yet have to trip along the streets like me,
All but naked to the knee!
How will she ever grant her Jules a bliss
So startling as her real first infant kiss?   155
Oh, no — not envy, this!

— Not envy, sure! — for if you gave me
Leave to take or to refuse,
In earnest, do you think I'd choose
That sort of new love to enslave me?   160
Mine should have lapped me round from the
    beginning;
As little fear of losing it as winning:
Lovers grow cold, men learn to hate their
    wives,
And only parents' love can last our lives.
At eve the Son and Mother, gentle pair,   165

---

88. martagon, a kind of lily, called the "Turk's cap."
89. St. Agnes, a virgin martyr of the fourth century. Pippa
had no doubt seen a painting of her in the church. 90. Turk
bird's, turkey's. The common turkey is supposed to have
come from Turkey. 93. turban, turban-shaped, like the
lily. 100. weevil and chafer, insects of the beetle family.

120. Luca, Ottima's despised husband. 131. Possagno,
a village four miles from Asolo.

Commune inside our turret; what prevents
My being Luigi? While that mossy lair
Of lizards through the winter-time is stirred
With each to each imparting sweet intents
For this new-year, as brooding bird to bird
(For I observe of late, the evening walk   171
Of Luigi and his mother, always ends
Inside our ruined turret, where they talk,
Calmer than lovers, yet more kind than
    friends),
Let me be cared about, kept out of harm,   175
And schemed for, safe in love as with a charm;
Let me be Luigi! If I only knew
What was my mother's face — my father, too!
  Nay, if you come to that, best love of all
Is God's; then why not have God's love befall
Myself as, in the palace by the Dome,   181
Monsignor? — who tonight will bless the home
Of his dead brother; and God bless in turn
That heart which beats, those eyes which
    mildly burn
With love for all men! I, tonight at least, 185
Would be that holy and beloved priest.

Now wait! — even I already seem to share
In God's love; what does New-year's hymn
    declare?
What other meaning do these verses bear?

  All service ranks the same with God: 190
  If now, as formerly he trod
  Paradise, his presence fills
  Our earth, each only as God wills
  Can work — God's puppets, best and worst,
  Are we; there is no last nor first.   195

  Say not "a small event!" Why "small"?
  Costs it more pain that this, ye call
  A "great event," should come to pass,
  Than that? Untwine me from the mass
  Of deeds which make up life, one deed   200
  Power shall fall short in or exceed!

And more of it, and more of it! — oh, yes —
I will pass each, and see their happiness,
And envy none — being just as great, no
    doubt,
Useful to men, and dear to God, as they! 205
A pretty thing to care about
So mightily, this single holiday!
But let the sun shine! Wherefore repine?
—With thee to lead me, O Day of mine,
Down the grass path gray with dew,   210
Under the pine-wood, blind with boughs,
Where the swallow never flew
Nor yet cicala dared carouse —
No, dared carouse!   [*She enters the street.*

  169. **each to each,** Luigi and his mother. 181. **the
Dome,** the Duomo, or cathedral. Near it was the Bishop's
palace.

I. MORNING

SCENE: *Up the Hillside, inside the Shrub-house.*
  LUCA'S *Wife,* OTTIMA, *and her Paramour, the*
    German SEBALD.

Sebald [*sings*].

  Let the watching lids wink!
  Day's ablaze with eyes, think!
  Deep into the night, drink!

  Ottima. Night? Such may be your Rhine-
    land nights, perhaps;
But this blood-red beam through the shutter's
    chink   5
—We call such light, the morning; let us
    see!
Mind how you grope your way, though! How
    these tall
Naked geraniums straggle! Push the lattice
Behind that frame! — Nay, do I bid you? —
    Sebald,
It shakes the dust down on me! Why, of
    course   10
The slide-bolt catches. Well, are you content,
Or must I find you something else to spoil?
Kiss and be friends, my Sebald! Is't full
    morning?
Oh, don't speak then!
  Seb.   Aye, thus it used to be!
Ever your house was, I remember, shut   15
Till mid-day; I observed that, as I strolled
On mornings through the vale here; country
    girls
Were noisy, washing garments in the brook,
Hinds drove the slow white oxen up the hills;
But no, your house was mute, would ope no
    eye!   20
And wisely; you were plotting one thing there,
Nature, another outside. I looked up —
Rough white wood shutters, rusty iron bars,
Silent as death, blind in a flood of light.
Oh, I remember! — and the peasants laughed
And said, "The old man sleeps with the young
    wife."   26
This house was his, this chair, this window —
    his.
  Otti. Ah, the clear morning! I can see
    Saint Mark's;
That black streak is the belfry. Stop; Vicenza
Should lie — there's Padua, plain enough,
    that blue!   30
Look o'er my shoulder, follow my finger!
  Seb.   Morning?
It seems to me a night with a sun added.
Where's dew, where's freshness? That bruised
    plant, I bruised
In getting through the lattice yestereve,

  28. **St. Mark's,** the cathedral in Venice. The cities of
Vicenza and Padua (lines 29, 30) are also plainly visible.

Droops as it did. See, here's my elbow's mark
I' the dust o' the sill.
    Otti.   Oh, shut the lattice, pray! 36
    Seb. Let me lean out. I cannot scent blood
here,
Foul as the morn may be.
                There, shut the world out!
How do you feel now, Ottima? There, curse
The world and all outside! Let us throw off
This mask; how do you bear yourself? Let's
out   41
With all of it!
    Otti.   Best never speak of it.
    Seb. Best speak again and yet again of it,
Till words cease to be more than words. "His
blood,"
For instance — let those two words mean "his
blood"   45
And nothing more. Notice, I'll say them now,
"His blood."
    Otti.   Assuredly if I repented
The deed —
    Seb.   Repent? Who should repent, or
why?
What puts that in your head? Did I once say
That I repented?
    Otti.   No; I said the deed —   50
    Seb. "The deed" and "the event" — just
now it was
"Our passion's fruit" — the devil take such
cant!
Say, once and always, Luca was a wittol,
I am his cutthroat, you are —
    Otti.   Here's the wine;
I brought it when we left the house above, 55
And glasses too — wine of both sorts. Black?
White then?
    Seb. But am not I his cutthroat? What
are you?
    Otti. There trudges on his business from
the Duomo
Benet the Capuchin, with his brown hood 59
And bare feet; always in one place at church,
Close under the stone wall by the south entry.
I used to take him for a brown cold piece
Of the wall's self, as out of it he rose
To let me pass — at first, I say, I used;   64
Now, so has that dumb figure fastened on
me,
I rather should account the plastered wall
A piece of him, so chilly does it strike.
This, Sebald?
    Seb.   No, the white wine — the white
wine!
Well, Ottima, I promised no new year
Should rise on us the ancient shameful way; 70
Nor does it rise. Pour on! To your black
eyes!

Do you remember last damned New Year's
day?
    Otti. You brought those foreign prints. We
looked at them
Over the wine and fruit. I had to scheme 74
To get him from the fire. Nothing but saying
His own set wants the proof-mark, roused
him up
To hunt them out.
    Seb.   'Faith, he is not alive
To fondle you before my face.
    Otti.   Do you
Fondle me then! Who means to take your life
For that, my Sebald?
    Seb.   Hark you, Ottima!   80
One thing to guard against. We'll not make
much
One of the other — that is, not make more
Parade of warmth, childish officious coil,
Than yesterday — as if, sweet, I supposed
Proof upon proof were needed now, now first,
To show I love you — yes, still love you —
love you   86
In spite of Luca and what's come to him —
Sure sign we had him ever in our thoughts,
White sneering old reproachful face and all!
We'll even quarrel, love, at times, as if   90
We still could lose each other, were not tied
By this; conceive you?
    Otti.   Love!
    Seb.   Not tied so sure!
Because though I was wrought upon, have
struck
His insolence back into him — am I
So surely yours? — therefore forever yours?
    Otti. Love, to be wise (one counsel pays
another),   96
Should we have — months ago, when first we
loved,
For instance that May morning we two stole
Under the green ascent of sycamores —
If we had come upon a thing like that   100
Suddenly —
    Seb.   "A thing" — there again — "a
thing!"
    Otti. Then, Venus' body, had we come
upon
My husband Luca Gaddi's murdered corpse
Within there, at his couch-foot, covered
close —   104
Would you have pored upon it? Why persist
In poring now upon it? For 'tis here
As much as there in the deserted house;
You cannot rid your eyes of it. For me,
Now he is dead I hate him worse; I hate —
Dare you stay here? I would go back and
hold   110

---

59. Capuchin . . . brown hood. The Capuchins, a
branch of the Franciscan order, wear a brown habit.

76. the proof-mark, the mark that indicates that a
print is one of the first impressions from the plate. **83. coil,**
fuss, ado. **102. Venus'.** Venus was the goddess of love.

His two dead hands, and say, "I hate you
  worse,
Luca, than" —
  Seb.   Off, off — take your hands off
  mine,
'Tis the hot evening — off! oh, morning is it?
  Otti. There's one thing must be done; you
  know what thing.
Come in and help to carry. We may sleep 115
Anywhere in the whole wide house tonight.
  Seb. What would come, think you, if we
  let him lie
Just as he is? Let him lie there until
The angels take him! He is turned by this
Off from his face beside, as you will see. 120
  Otti. This dusty pane might serve for look-
  ing-glass.
Three, four — four gray hairs! Is it so you
  said
A plait of hair should wave across my neck?
No — this way.
  Seb.   Ottima, I would give your neck,
Each splendid shoulder, both those breasts of
  yours,   125
That this were undone! Killing! Kill the
  world,
So Luca lives again! — aye, lives to sputter
His fulsome dotage on you — yes, and feign
Surprise that I return at eve to sup,
When all the morning I was loitering here —
Bid me dispatch my business and begone. 131
I would —
  Otti. See!
  Seb.   No, I'll finish. Do you think
I fear to speak the bare truth once for all?
All we have talked of, is, at bottom, fine
To suffer; there's a recompense in guilt;   135
One must be venturous and fortunate —
What is one young for, else?' In age we'll sigh
O'er the wild reckless wicked days flown
  over;
Still, we have lived; the vice was in its place.
But to have eaten Luca's bread, have worn
His clothes, have felt his money swell my
  purse —   141
Do lovers in romances sin that way?
Why, I was starving when I used to call
And teach you music, starving while you
  plucked me
These flowers to smell!
  Otti.   My poor lost friend!
  Seb.   He gave me 145
Life, nothing less; what if he did reproach
My perfidy, and threaten, and do more —
Had he no right? What was to wonder at?
He sat by us at table quietly;
Why must you lean across till our cheeks
  touched?   150

119-120. **turned . . . face.** It was believed that the face of
a murdered man looks toward heaven for vengeance.

Could he do less than make pretense to strike?
'Tis not the crime's sake — I'd commit ten
  crimes
Greater, to have this crime wiped out, un-
  done!
And you — O how feel you? Feel you for me?
  Otti. Well then, I love you better now than
  ever,   155
And best (look at me while I speak to you) —
Best for the crime; nor do I grieve, in truth,
This mask, this simulated ignorance,
This affectation of simplicity,   159
Falls off our crime; this naked crime of ours
May not now be looked over — look it down!
Great? Let it be great; but the joys it brought,
Pay they or no its price? Come: they or it!
Speak not! The past, would you give up the
  past
Such as it is, pleasure and crime together? 165
Give up that noon I owned my love for you?
The garden's silence: even the single bee
Persisting in his toil, suddenly stopped,
And where he hid you only could surmise
By some campanula chalice set a-swing.   170
Who stammered — "Yes, I love you?"
  Seb.   And I drew
Back; put far back your face with both my
  hands
Lest you should grow too full of me — your
  face
So seemed athirst for my whole soul and body!
  Otti. And when I ventured to receive you
  here,   175
Made you steal hither in the mornings —
  Seb.   When
I used to look up 'neath the shrub-house here,
Till the red fire on its glazed windows spread
To a yellow haze?
  Otti.   Ah — my sign was, the sun
Inflamed the sear side of yon chestnut-tree 180
Nipped by the first frost.
  Seb.   You would always laugh
At my wet boots; I had to stride through
  grass
Over my ankles.
  Otti.   Then our crowning night!
  Seb. The July night?
  Otti.   The day of it too, Sebald!
When heaven's pillars seemed o'erbowed with
  heat,   185
Its black-blue canopy suffered descend
Close on us both, to weigh down each to each
And smother up all life except our life.
So lay we till the storm came.
  Seb.   How it came!
  Otti. Buried in woods we lay, you recollect;
Swift ran the searching tempest overhead; 191
And ever and anon some bright white shaft
Burned through the pine-tree roof, here burned
  and there,

As if God's messenger through the close wood
   screen
Plunged and replunged his weapon at a ven-
   ture,   195
Feeling for guilty thee and me; then broke
The thunder like a whole sea overhead —
    Seb.   Yes!
    Otti. — While I stretched myself upon you,
    hands
To hands, my mouth to your hot mouth, and
   shook
All my locks loose, and covered you with
   them —   200
You, Sebald, the same you!
    Seb.   Slower, Ottima!
    Otti. And as we lay —
    Seb.   Less vehemently! Love me!
Forgive me! Take not words, mere words, to
   heart!
Your breath is worse than wine. Breathe slow,
   speak slow!
Do not lean on me!
    Otti.   Sebald, as we lay,   205
Rising and falling only with our pants,
Who said, "Let death come now! 'Tis right
   to die!
Right to be punished! Naught completes such
   bliss
But woe!" Who said that?
    Seb.   How did we ever rise?
Was 't that we slept? Why did it end?
    Otti.   I felt you   210
Taper into a point the ruffled ends
Of my loose locks 'twixt both your humid lips.
My hair is fallen now; knot it again!
    Seb. I kiss you now, dear Ottima, now and
   now!
This way? Will you forgive me — be once
   more   215
My great queen?
    Otti.   Bind it thrice about my brow;
Crown me your queen, your spirit's arbitress,
Magnificent in sin. Say that!
    Seb.   I crown you
My great white queen, my spirit's arbitress,
   Magnificent —   220

    [*From without is heard the voice of* PIPPA *singing —*
       The year's at the spring
       And day's at the morn;
       Morning's at seven;
       The hillside's dew-pearled;
       The lark's on the wing;   225
       The snail's on the thorn:
       God's in his heaven —
       All's right with the world!

               [PIPPA *passes.*

    Seb. God's in his heaven! Do you hear
   that? Who spoke?
You, you spoke!

    Otti.   Oh — that little ragged girl! 230
She must have rested on the step; we give
   them
But this one holiday the whole year round.
Did you ever see our silk-mills — their inside?
There are ten silk-mills now belong to you.
She stoops to pick my double heartsease —
   Sh!   235
She does not hear; call you out louder!
    Seb.   Leave me!
Go, get your clothes on — dress those
   shoulders!
    Otti.   Sebald?
    Seb. Wipe off that paint! I hate you.
    Otti.   Miserable!
    Seb. My God, and she is emptied of it now!
Outright now! — how miraculously gone 240
All of the grace — had she not strange grace
   once?
Why, the blank cheek hangs listless as it
   likes,
No purpose holds the features up together,
Only the cloven brow and puckered chin
Stay in their places; and the very hair, 245
That seemed to have a sort of life in it,
Drops, a dead web!
    Otti.   Speak to me — not of me!
    Seb. — That round great full-orbed face,
   where not an angle
Broke the delicious indolence — all broken!
    Otti. To me — not of me! Ungrateful, per-
   jured cheat!   250
A coward too; but ingrate's worse than all!
Beggar — my slave — a fawning, cringing lie!
Leave me! Betray me! I can see your drift!
A lie that walks and eats and drinks!
    Seb.   My God!
Those morbid olive faultless shoulder-blades—
I should have known there was no blood be-
   neath!   256
    Otti. You hate me then? You hate me
   then?
    Seb.   To think
She would succeed in her absurd attempt,
And fascinate by sinning, show herself
Superior — guilt from its excess superior 260
To innocence! That little peasant's voice
Has righted all again. Though I be lost,
I know which is the better, never fear,
Of vice or virtue, purity or lust,
Nature or trick! I see what I have done, 265
Entirely now! Oh, I am proud to feel
Such torments — let the world take credit
   thence —
I, having done my deed, pay too its price!
I hate, hate — curse you! God's in his heaven!
    Otti.   — Me! 269
Me! no, no, Sebald, not yourself — kill me!

247. **Speak to me—not of me!** This is generally regarded as one of the great dramatic lines in the drama.

Mine is the whole crime. Do but kill me —
   then
Yourself — then — presently — first hear me
   speak!
I always meant to kill myself — wait, you!
Lean on my breast — not as a breast; don't
   love me   274
The more because you lean on me, my own
Heart's Sebald! There, there, both deaths
   presently!
   Seb. My brain is drowned now — quite
   drowned; all I feel
Is . . . is, at swift-recurring intervals,
A hurry-down within me, as of waters
Loosened to smother up some ghastly pit; 280
There they go — whirls from a black fiery sea!
   Otti. Not me — to him, O God, be merciful!

SCENE: *Talk by the way, while* PIPPA *is passing
from the hillside to Orcana. Foreign Students of
painting and sculpture, from Venice, assembled
opposite the house of* JULES, *a young French
statuary, at Possagno.*

   1st Student. Attention! My own post is
beneath this window, but the pomegranate
clump yonder will hide three or four of you
with a little squeezing, and Schramm and his
pipe must lie flat in the balcony. Four, five —
who's a defaulter? We want everybody, for
Jules must not be suffered to hurt his bride
when the jest's found out.
   2d Stud. All here! Only our poet's away
— never having much meant to be present,
moonstrike him! The airs of that fellow, that
Giovacchino! He was in violent love with
himself, and had a fair prospect of thriving in
his suit, so unmolested was it—when suddenly
a woman falls in love with him, too; and out
of pure jealousy he takes himself off to Trieste,
immortal poem and all: whereto is this prophetical epitaph appended already, as Bluphocks assures me — *"Here a mammoth-poem
lies, Fouled to death by butterflies."* His own
fault, the simpleton! Instead of cramp couplets, each like a knife in your entrails, he
should write, says Bluphocks, both classically
and intelligibly.—*Æsculapius, an Epic. Catalogue of the drugs: Hebe's plaister — One strip
Cools your lip. Phœbus' emulsion — One bottle
Clears your throttle. Mercury's bolus — One box
Cures —*
   3d Stud. Subside, my fine fellow! If the
marriage was over by ten o'clock, Jules will
certainly be here in a minute with his bride.

   2d Stud. Good! — only, so should the poet's
muse have been universally acceptable, says
Bluphocks, *et canibus nostris* — and Delia not
better known to our literary dogs than the 35
boy Giovacchino!
   1st Stud. To the point, now. Where's Gottlieb, the new-comer? Oh — listen, Gottlieb,
to what has called down this piece of friendly
vengeance on Jules, of which we now assemble 40
to witness the winding-up. We are all agreed,
all in a tale, observe, when Jules shall burst out
on us in a fury by and by: I am spokesman —
the verses that are to undeceive Jules bear my
name of Lutwyche — but each professes him- 45
self alike insulted by this strutting stone-
squarer, who came alone from Paris to Munich,
and thence with a crowd of us to Venice and
Possagno here, but proceeds in a day or two
alone again — oh, alone indubitably! — to 50
Rome and Florence. He, forsooth, take up his
portion with these dissolute, brutalized, heartless bunglers! — so he was heard to call us all.
Now, is Schramm brutalized, I should like to
know? Am I heartless?   55
   Gottlieb. Why, somewhat heartless; for, suppose Jules a coxcomb as much as you choose,
still, for this mere coxcombry, you will have
brushed off — what do folks style it? — the
bloom of his life. Is it too late to alter? 60
These love-letters now, you call his — I can't
laugh at them.
   4th Stud. Because you never read the sham
letters of our inditing which drew forth these.
   Gott. His discovery of the truth will be 65
frightful.
   4th Stud. That's the joke. But you should
have joined us at the beginning; there's no
doubt he loves the girl — loves a model he
might hire by the hour!   70
   Gott. See here! "He has been accustomed,"
he writes, "to have Canova's women about
him, in stone, and the world's women beside
him, in flesh; these being as much below, as
those above, his soul's aspiration; but now he 75
is to have the reality." There you laugh
again! I say, you wipe off the very dew of his
youth.
   1st Stud. Schramm! (Take the pipe out of
his mouth, somebody!) Will Jules lose the 80
bloom of his youth?
   Schramm. Nothing worth keeping is ever
lost in this world: look at a blossom — it drops

34. et canibus nostris . . . Delia. From Virgil's *Eclogues*,
3, 67: "So that now not Delia herself is more familiar to
our dogs." In the Eclogue, which is a poetry contest, Delia
is the mistress of one of the singers. She runs no risk in
calling upon him at night, because she knows the watchdogs
and they know her. 42. all in a tale, bound to tell the
same story. 72. Canova's women. Antonio Canova
(1757-1822) was an Italian sculptor. He designed the church
at Possagno, his birthplace; in it are several of his statues of
women.

Stage Directions: statuary, one who makes statues.
16. Trieste, a city in Austria. 24. Æsculapius, the god of
medicine. Giovacchino is ridiculed for regarding love as a
disease to be cured by drugs, pills, etc., instead of as a passion to be enjoyed. 25. Hebe, the goddess of youth and
cupbearer to the gods. 26. Phœbus, Apollo, the sun god.
27. Mercury, the messenger of the gods. bolus, pill.

presently, having done its service and lasted its
85 time; but fruits succeed, and where would be
the blossom's place could it continue? As well
affirm that your eye is no longer in your body,
because its earliest favorite, whatever it may
have first loved to look on, is dead and done
90 with — as that any affection is lost to the soul
when its first object, whatever happened first
to satisfy it, is superseded in due course. Keep
but ever looking, whether with the body's eye
or the mind's, and you will soon find something
95 to look on! Has a man done wondering at
women? — there follow men, dead and alive,
to wonder at. Has he done wondering at men?
— there's God to wonder at; and the faculty
of wonder may be, at the same time, old and
100 tired enough with respect to its first object,
and yet young and fresh sufficiently, so far as
concerns its novel one. Thus —

1st Stud. Put Schramm's pipe into his
mouth again! There, you see! Well, this
105 Jules — a wretched fribble — oh, I watched
his disportings at Possagno, the other day!
Canova's gallery—you know: there he marches
first resolvedly past great works by the dozen
without vouchsafing an eye; all at once he
110 stops full at the *Psiche-fanciulla*—cannot pass
that old acquaintance without a nod of encouragement — "In your new place, beauty?
Then behave yourself as well here as at
Munich — I see you!" Next he posts himself
115 deliberately before the unfinished *Pietà* for
half an hour without moving, till up he starts
of a sudden, and thrusts his very nose into —
I say, into — the group; by which gesture you
are informed that precisely the sole point he
120 had not fully mastered in Canova's practice
was a certain method of using the drill in the
articulation of the knee-joint — and that, likewise, has he mastered at length! Good-by,
therefore, to poor Canova — whose gallery no
125 longer needs detain his successor Jules, the
predestinated novel thinker in marble!

5th Stud. Tell him about the women; go
on to the women!

1st Stud. Why, on that matter he could
130 never be supercilious enough. How should we
be other (he said) than the poor devils you
see, with those debasing habits we cherish?
He was not to wallow in that mire, at least;
he would wait, and love only at the proper
135 time, and meanwhile put up with the *Psiche-
fanciulla.* Now, I happened to hear of a young
Greek — real Greek girl at Malamocco; a true

Islander, do you see, with Alciphron's "hair
like sea-moss" — Schramm knows! — white
and quiet as an apparition, and fourteen years 140
old at farthest — a daughter of Natalia, so
she swears — that hag Natalia, who helps us
to models at three *lire* an hour. We selected
this girl for the heroine of our jest. So first,
Jules received a scented letter — somebody 145
had seen his Tydeus at the Academy, and my
picture was nothing to it; a profound admirer
bade him persevere — would make herself
known to him ere long. (Paolina, my little
friend of the *Fenice*, transcribes divinely.) 150
And in due time, the mysterious correspondent gave certain hints of her peculiar charms
— the pale cheeks, the black hair — whatever, in short, had struck us in our Malamocco model; we retained her name, too — 155
Phene, which is, by interpretation, sea-eagle.
Now, think of Jules finding himself distinguished from the herd of us by such a creature!
In his very first answer he proposed marrying
his monitress; and fancy us over these letters, 160
two, three times a day, to receive and dispatch! I concocted the main of it: relations
were in the way — secrecy must be observed
— in fine, would he wed her on trust, and only
speak to her when they were indissolubly 165
united? St — st — Here they come!

6th Stud. Both of them! Heaven's love,
speak softly, speak within yourselves!

5th Stud. Look at the bridegroom! Half
his hair in storm and half in calm — patted 170
down over the left temple — like a frothy cup
one blows on to cool it; and the same old
blouse that he murders the marble in.

2d Stud. Not a rich vest like yours, Hannibal Scratchy! — rich, that your face may the 175
better set it off.

6th Stud. And the bride! Yes, sure enough,
our Phene! Should you have known her in
her clothes? How magnificently pale!

Gott. She does not also take it for earnest, 180
I hope?

1st Stud. Oh, Natalia's concern, that is!
We settle with Natalia.

6th Stud. She does not speak — has evidently let out no word. The only thing is, will 185
she equally remember the rest of her lesson,
and repeat correctly all those verses which are
to break the secret to Jules?

Gott. How he gazes on her! Pity — pity!

---

105. **fribble**, a frivolous person. 110. **Psiche-fanciulla**,
one of the most faultless of Canova's works, representing
Psyche as a maiden with a butterfly. *Fanciulla* is Italian for
young girl. Psyche was the beautiful maiden loved by Cupid.
The statue is in the gallery at Possagno. 115. **Pietà**, a
statue of the Virgin with the dead Christ in her arms. It is
in the church at Possagno. 137. **Malamocco**, a small town
on an island of the same name near Venice.

138. **Alciphron**, the most distinguished of the Greek
epistolary writers of the second century A.D. 143. **lire**,
plural of *lira*, an Italian coin worth about twenty cents.
146. **Tydeus**, an Homeric hero, one of the leaders in the
expedition against Thebes. Jules is supposed to have made
a statue of him for the Academy of Fine Arts in Venice.
150. **Fenice**, Phenix, the principal theater in Venice. Paolina
(l. 149) was an actress at the theater. 174. **Hannibal Scratchy**,
a burlesque spelling of the name of the noted Italian painter,
Annibale Caracci, attached in jest to one of the group.

190 1st Stud. They go in; now, silence! You
three — not nearer the window, mind, than
that pomegranate — just where the little girl,
who a few minutes ago passed us singing, is
seated!

II. NOON

SCENE: *Over Orcana. The house of* JULES, *who
crosses its threshold with* PHENE: *she is silent,
on which* JULES *begins —*

Do not die, Phene! I am yours now, you
Are mine now; let fate reach me how she likes,
If you'll not die; so, never die! Sit here —
My workroom's single seat. I over-lean
This length of hair and lustrous front; they
     turn   5
Like an entire flower upward: eyes, lips, last
Your chin — no, last your throat turns: 'tis
     their scent
Pulls down my face upon you. Nay, look ever
This one way till I change, grow you — I
     could
Change into you, beloved!
                              You by me,   10
And I by you; this is your hand in mine,
And side by side we sit; all's true. Thank
     God!
I have spoken; speak you!
                        O my life to come!
My Tydeus must be carved that's there in
     clay;
Yet how be carved, with you about the room?
Where must I place you? When I think that
     once   16
This room-full of rough block-work seemed
     my heaven
Without you! Shall I ever work again,
Get fairly into my old ways again,
Bid each conception stand while, trait by
     trait,   20
My hand transfers its lineaments to stone?
Will my mere fancies live near you, their
     truth —
The live truth, passing and repassing me,
Sitting beside me?
                    Now speak!
                        Only first,
See, all your letters! Was 't not well con-
     trived?   25
Their hiding-place is Psyche's robe; she keeps
Your letters next her skin. Which drops out
     foremost?
Ah — this that swam down like a first moon-
     beam
Into my world!
                Again those eyes complete
Their melancholy survey, sweet and slow,   30
Of all my room holds; to return and rest
On me, with pity, yet some wonder too;
As if God bade some spirit plague a world,

And this were the one moment of surprise
And sorrow while she took her station, paus-
     ing   35
O'er what she sees, finds good, and must de-
     stroy!
What gaze you at? Those? Books, I told
     you of;
Let your first word to me rejoice them, too:
This minion, a Coluthus, writ in red,
Bister and azure by Bessarion's scribe —   40
Read this line — no, shame — Homer's be the
     Greek
First breathed me from the lips of my Greek
     girl!
This Odyssey in coarse black vivid type
With faded yellow blossoms 'twixt page and
     page,
To mark great places with due gratitude;   45
*"He said, and on Antinous directed
A bitter shaft"* — a flower blots out the rest!
Again upon your search? My statues, then!
— Ah, do not mind that — better that will
     look
When cast in bronze — an Almaign Kaiser,
     that,   50
Swart-green and gold, with truncheon based
     on hip.
This, rather, turn to! What, unrecognized?
I thought you would have seen that here you
     sit
As I imagined you — Hippolyta,
Naked upon her bright Numidian horse.   55
Recall you this then? "Carve in bold relief"—
So you commanded — "carve, against I come,
A Greek, in Athens, as our fashion was,
Feasting, bay-filleted and thunder-free,
Who rises 'neath the lifted myrtle-branch. 60
'Praise those who slew Hipparchus!' cry the
     guests,
'While o'er thy head the singer's myrtle waves
As erst above our champion: stand up, all!' "
See, I have labored to express your thought.
Quite round, a cluster of mere hands and arms
(Thrust in all senses, all ways, from all sides,
Only consenting at the branch's end   67
They strain toward) serves for frame to a sole
     face,

39. **minion**, favorite. **Coluthus**, a Greek epic poet of
the 6th century. His *The Rape of Helen* was discovered by
Cardinal Bessarion (1395-1472), a noted Greek scholar.
40. **Bister**, brown. **46-47. He said . . . shaft**, from the
Odyssey, 22, 10. Upon returning home from his wanderings,
Ulysses found his wife Penelope besieged with suitors. When
he attacked them, Antinous was the first to fall. The flower
that blotted out the rest of the story symbolizes Phene's
love that robbed Lutwyche's plot of its bitterness. **50.
Almaign Kaiser**, German emperor. **54. Hippolyta**, queen
of the Amazons, a race of women warriors. **55. Numidian.**
Numidia was a country in northern Africa, now Algeria.
59. bay-filleted and thunder-free. A crown of bay or
laurel was supposed to be a protection against thunder and
lightning because the tree was sacred to Apollo, the sun god.
61. Hipparchus, a tyrant of Athens slain in 514 B.C. by
Harmodius and Aristogeiton, who carried their swords concealed in myrtle branches. **67. consenting**, coming together.

The Praiser's, in the center: who with eyes
Sightless, so bend they back to light inside 70
His brain where visionary forms throng up,
Sings, minding not that palpitating arch
Of hands and arms, nor the quick drip of wine
From the drenched leaves o'erhead, nor crowns
    cast off,
Violet and parsley crowns to trample on — 75
Sings, pausing as the patron-ghosts approve,
Devoutly their unconquerable hymn.
But you must say a "well" to that — say
    "well!"
Because you gaze — am I fantastic, sweet?
Gaze like my very life's-stuff, marble — mar-
    bly   80
Even to the silence! Why, before I found
The real flesh Phene, I inured myself
To see, throughout all nature, varied stuff
For better nature's birth by means of art;
With me, each substance tended to one form
Of beauty — to the human archetype.   86
On every side occurred suggestive germs
Of that — the tree, the flower — or take the
    fruit —
Some rosy shape, continuing the peach,
Curved beewise o'er its bough; as rosy limbs,
Depending, nestled in the leaves; and just 91
From a cleft rose-peach the whole Dryad
    sprang.
But of the stuffs one can be master of,
How I divined their capabilities!
From the soft-rinded smoothening facile chalk
That yields your outline to the air's embrace,
Half-softened by a halo's pearly gloom;   97
Down to the crisp imperious steel, so sure
To cut its one confided thought clean out
Of all the world. But marble! — 'neath my
    tools   100
More pliable than jelly — as it were
Some clear primordial creature dug from
    depths
In the earth's heart, where itself breeds itself,
And whence all baser substance may be
    worked;
Refine it off to air, you may — condense it 105
Down to the diamond — is not metal there,
When o'er the sudden speck my chisel trips?
— Not flesh, as flake off flake I scale, ap-
    proach,
Lay bare those bluish veins of blood asleep?
Lurks flame in no strange windings where,
    surprised   110
By the swift implement sent home at once,
Flushes and glowings radiate and hover
About its track?
            Phene? what — why is this?
That whitening cheek, those still dilating eyes!

<hr>

75. **parsley**, frequently used by the ancients in crowns
worn at feasts because of its strong fragrance. 92. **Dryad**,
a wood nymph.

Ah, you will die — I knew that you would
    die!   115

PHENE *begins, on his having long remained silent*

Now the end's coming; to be sure, it must
Have ended sometime! Tush, why need I
    speak
Their foolish speech? I cannot bring to mind
One half of it, beside; and do not care
For old Natalia now, nor any of them.   120
Oh, you — what are you? — if I do not try
To say the words Natalia made me learn,
To please your friends — it is to keep myself
Where your voice lifted me, by letting that
Proceed; but can it? Even you, perhaps, 125
Cannot take up, now you have once let fall,
The music's life, and me along with that —
No, or you would! We'll stay, then, as we are —
Above the world.
         You creature with the eyes!
If I could look forever up to them,   130
As now you let me — I believe all sin,
All memory of wrong done, suffering borne,
Would drop down, low and lower, to the earth
Whence all that's low comes, and there touch
    and stay —
Never to overtake the rest of me,   135
All that, unspotted, reaches up to you,
Drawn by those eyes! What rises is myself,
Not me the shame and suffering; but they
    sink,
Are left, I rise above them. Keep me so,
Above the world!
         But you sink, for your eyes 140
Are altering — altered! Stay — "I love you,
    love" —
I could prevent it if I understood:
More of your words to me; was 't in the tone
Or the words, your power?
         Or stay — I will repeat
Their speech, if that contents you! Only
    change   145
No more, and I shall find it presently
Far back here, in the brain yourself filled up.
Natalia threatened me that harm should
    follow
Unless I spoke their lesson to the end,
But harm to me, I thought she meant, not
    you.   150
Your friends — Natalia said they were your
    friends
And meant you well — because, I doubted it,
Observing (what was very strange to see)
On every face, so different in all else,
The same smile girls like me are used to bear,
But never men, men cannot stoop so low; 156
Yet your friends, speaking of you, used that
    smile,
That hateful smirk of boundless self-conceit
Which seems to take possession of the world

And make of God a tame confederate, 160
Purveyor to their appetites — you know!
But still Natalia said they were your friends,
And they assented though they smiled the
     more,
And all came round me — that thin English-
     man 164
With light lank hair seemed leader of the rest;
He held a paper — "What we want," said he,
Ending some explanation to his friends —
"Is something slow, involved and mystical,
To hold Jules long in doubt, yet take his taste
And lure him on until, at innermost 170
Where he seeks sweetness' soul, he may find
     — this!
— As in the apple's core, the noisome fly;
For insects on the rind are seen at once,
And brushed aside as soon, but this is found
Only when on the lips or loathing tongue." 175
And so he read what I have got by heart:
I'll speak it — "Do not die, love! I am
     yours" —
No — is not that, or like that, part of words
Yourself began by speaking? Strange to lose
What cost such pains to learn! Is this more
     right? 180

I am a painter who cannot paint;
In my life, a devil rather than saint;
In my brain, as poor a creature too:
No end to all I cannot do!
Yet do one thing at least I can — 185
Love a man or hate a man
Supremely; thus my lore began.
Through the Valley of Love I went,
In the lovingest spot to abide,
And just on the verge where I pitched my tent,
I found Hate dwelling beside. 191
(Let the Bridegroom ask what the painter
     meant,
Of his Bride, of the peerless Bride!)
And further, I traversed Hate's grove,
In the hatefullest nook to dwell; 195
But lo, where I flung myself prone, couched
     Love
Where the shadow threefold fell.
(The meaning—those black bride's-eyes above,
Not a painter's lip should tell!)

"And here," said he, "Jules probably will
     ask, 200
'You have black eyes, Love — you are, sure
     enough,
My peerless bride — then do you tell indeed
What needs some explanation! What means
     this?' "
— And I am to go on, without a word —

So, I grew wise in Love and Hate, 205
From simple that I was of late.
Once, when I loved, I would enlace
Breast, eyelids, hands, feet, form, and face
Of her I loved, in one embrace —
As if by mere love I could love immensely! 210
Once, when I hated, I would plunge
My sword, and wipe with the first lunge
My foe's whole life out like a sponge —
As if by mere hate I could hate intensely!
But now I am wiser, know better the fashion
How passion seeks aid from its opposite pas-
     sion; 216
And if I see cause to love more, hate more
Than ever man loved, ever hated before —
And seek in the Valley of Love
The nest, or the nook in Hate's Grove 220
Where my soul may surely reach
The essence, naught less, of each,
The Hate of all Hates, the Love
Of all Loves, in the Valley or Grove —
I find them the very warders 225
Each of the other's borders.
When I love most, Love is disguised
In Hate; and when Hate is surprised
In Love, then I hate most: ask 229
How Love smiles through Hate's iron casque,
Hate grins through Love's rose-braided mask—
And how, having hated thee,
I sought long and painfully
To reach thy heart, nor prick
The skin but pierce to the quick — 235
Ask this, my Jules, and be answered straight
By thy bride — how the painter Lutwyche can
hate!

JULES *interposes*

Lutwyche! Who else? But all of them, no
     doubt,
Hated me: they at Venice — presently 239
Their turn, however! You I shall not meet;
If I dreamed, saying this would wake me.
                                        Keep
What's here, the gold—we cannot meet again,
Consider! and the money was but meant
For two years' travel, which is over now,
All chance or hope or care or need of it. 245
This — and what comes from selling these,
     my casts
And books and medals, except — let them go
Together, so the produce keeps you safe
Out of Natalia's clutches! If by chance
(For all's chance here) I should survive the
     gang 250
At Venice, root out all fifteen of them,
We might meet somewhere, since the world is
     wide.

181-237. Although these lines are intentionally involved in
manner, they reveal the hateful plot to Jules, and he learns
what Phene has been.

241. **If I dreamed, etc.** If I have been in love with a
phantom-Phene, saying as I do, "It's over," will bring me
back to the harsh truth.

From without is heard the voice of PIPPA, *singing* —

> *Give her but a least excuse to love me!*
> *When — where —*
> *How — can this arm establish her above me,*
> *If fortune fixed her as my lady there,*   256
> *There already, to eternally reprove me?*
> *("Hist!" — said Kate the Queen;*
> *But "Oh!" cried the maiden, binding her*
>   *tresses,*
> *" 'Tis only a page that carols unseen,*   260
> *Crumbling your hounds their messes!")*
>
> *Is she wronged? —To the rescue of her honor,*
> *My heart!*
> *Is she poor? — What costs it to be styled a*
>   *donor?*
> *Merely an earth to cleave, a sea to part.*   265
> *But that fortune should have thrust all this*
>   *upon her!*
> *("Nay, list!" — bade Kate the Queen;*
> *And still cried the maiden, binding her tresses,*
> *" 'Tis only a page that carols unseen,*
> *Fitting your hawks their jesses!")*   270

[PIPPA *passes*

JULES *resumes*

What name was that the little girl sang forth?
Kate? The Cornaro, doubtless, who renounced
The crown of Cyprus to be lady here
At Asolo, where still her memory stays,
And peasants sing how once a certain page 275
Pined for the grace of her so far above
His power of doing good to, "Kate the Queen—
She never could be wronged, be poor," he
      sighed,
"Need him to help her!"
                            Yes, a bitter thing
To see our lady above all need of us;   280
Yet so we look ere we will love; not I,
But the world looks so. If whoever loves
Must be, in some sort, god or worshiper,
The blessing or the blest one, queen or page,
Why should we always choose the page's
      part?   285
Here is a woman with utter need of me —
I find myself queen here, it seems!
                            How strange!
Look at the woman here with the new soul,
Like my own Psyche — fresh upon her lips
Alit, the visionary butterfly,   290
Waiting my word to enter and make bright,
Or flutter off and leave all blank as first.
This body had no soul before, but slept

Or stirred, was beauteous or ungainly, free
From taint or foul with stain, as outward
      things   295
Fastened their image on its passiveness;
Now, it will wake, feel, live — or die again!
Shall to produce form out of unshaped stuff
Be Art — and further, to evoke a soul
From form be nothing? This new soul is
      mine!   300

Now, to kill Lutwyche, what would that do?
      — save
A wretched dauber, men will hoot to death
Without me, from their hooting. Oh, to hear
God's voice plain as I heard it first, before
They broke in with their laughter! I heard
      them   305
Henceforth, not God.
                     To Ancona — Greece — some isle!
I wanted silence only; there is clay
Everywhere. One may do whate'er one likes
In Art; the only thing is, to make sure
That one does like it — which takes pains to
      know.   310
      Scatter all this, my Phene—this mad dream!
Who, what is Lutwyche, what Natalia's
      friends,
What the whole world except our love — my
      own,
Own Phene? But I told you, did I not,
Ere night we travel for your land — some isle
With the sea's silence on it? Stand aside— 316
I do but break these paltry models up
To begin Art afresh. Meet Lutwyche, I —
And save him from my statue meeting him?
Some unsuspected isle in the far seas!   320
Like a god going through his world, there
      stands
One mountain for a moment in the dusk,
Whole brotherhoods of cedars on its brow;
And you are ever by me while I gaze
— Are in my arms as now — as now — as
      now!   325
Some unsuspected isle in the far seas!
Some unsuspected isle in far-off seas!

SCENE: *Talk by the way, while* PIPPA *is passing from
Orcana to the Turret. Two or three of the Austrian
Police loitering with* BLUPHOCKS, *an English
vagabond, just in view of the Turret.*

Bluphocks. So, that is your Pippa, the little girl who passed us singing? Well, your
Bishop's Intendant's money shall be honestly

---

258. **Kate the Queen.** Caterina Cornaro, the last queen
of the island of Cyprus, off the coast of Turkey, was induced
to yield her kingdom to the Republic of Venice in 1489. She
was received in Venice with great honor and was assigned a
palace and a court at Asolo (line 274). 270. **jesses.** A jess
is a strap of leather or silk fastened round the leg of a hawk
and usually fitted with a ring to which the leash of the hunter
is attached. 290. **butterfly,** symbol of the soul and of immortality.

306. **Ancona,** a city on the east coast of Italy. 318-319.
Meet . . . him? Jules means, "I will not kill Lutwyche in a
duel, because I want him to have the pain of seeing a fine
complete work of mine in marble."
3. **Intendant's money.** The Bishop's Superintendent
(Maffeo, or Ugo) has bribed Bluphocks to seduce Pippa, the
rightful heir to the estate that the Bishop has just inherited
from his brother. Maffeo, who is in charge of the estate, will
expect a large reward for his services.

earned: — now, don't make me that sour face
5 because I bring the Bishop's name into the
business; we know he can have nothing to do
with such horrors; we know that he is a saint
and all that a bishop should be, who is a great
man beside. *Oh, were but every worm a maggot,*
10 *Every fly a grig, Every bough a Christmas faggot,*
Every tune a jig! In fact, I have abjured all
religions; but the last I inclined to was the
Armenian: for I have traveled, do you see,
and at Koenigsberg, Prussia Improper (so
15 styled because there's a sort of bleak hungry
sun there), you might remark, over a vener-
able house-porch, a certain Chaldee inscription; and brief as it is, a mere glance at it
used absolutely to change the mood of every
20 bearded passenger. In they turned, one and
all; the young and lightsome, with no irreverent pause, the aged and decrepit, with a sen-
sible alacrity: 'twas the Grand Rabbi's abode,
in short. Struck with curiosity, I lost no time
25 in learning Syriac — (these are vowels, you
dogs — follow my stick's end in the mud —
Celarent, Darii, Ferio!) and one morning presented myself, spelling-book in hand, a, b, c,
— I picked it out letter by letter, and what
30 was the purport of this miraculous posy?
Some cherished legend of the past, you'll say
— *"How Moses hocus-pocussed Egypt's land*
with fly and locust" — or *"How to Jonah*
sounded harshish, Get thee up and go to Tar-
35 *shish"* — or *"How the angel meeting Balaam,*
Straight his ass returned a salaam." In no
wise! *"Shackabrack — Boach — somebody or*
other — Isaach, Re-cei-ver, Pur-cha-ser, and
Ex-chan-ger of — Stolen Goods!" So, talk to
40 me of the religion of a bishop! I have renounced all bishops save Bishop Beveridge!
— mean to live so — and die — *As some*
Greek dog-sage, dead and merry, Hellward
bound in Charon's wherry, With food for both
45 *worlds, under and upper, Lupine-seed and*
Hecate's supper, And never an obolus . . .
(though thanks to you, or this Intendant

10. **grig,** cricket. 13. **Armenian.** Bluphocks has always adopted the form of religion best suited to his immediate
purpose. 14. **Koenigsberg,** a fortified city of East Prussia,
beyond the border of "Prussia Proper," the name applied to
the arm of land between Poland and the Baltic Sea. 17.
Chaldee inscription. The Chaldeans spoke a Semitic
dialect. They were the leading people in ancient Babylonia.
25. **Syriac,** the common language of Western Asia from the
third to the eighth century. It has five vowels. 27. **Celarent, Darii, Ferio,** coined words used in formal logic to
designate certain types of reasoning. 34. **harshish,** harsh.
Tarshish, an ancient city; mentioned in the Old Testament
(see *Jonah,* 1:1-2). 35. **Balaam.** See *Numbers,* 22. 41.
Bishop Beveridge. Bluphocks is making a pun on the name
of a Calvinist theologian who lived in the 17th century.
44. **Charon's wherry.** Charon was a god of hell. It was
his task to carry the shades of the dead across the river Styx
(the Stygian Ferry of line 50). The price of the passage was
an obolus (line 46), a small silver coin worth about fifteen
cents, found in the mouth of the body. 45. **Lupine,** a kind
of plant. *Lupine* means *wolfish.* 46. **Hecate's supper.**
Hecate was a goddess of hell who was propitiated by frequent
gifts of food, usually placed at cross-roads.

through you, or this Bishop through his
Intendant — I possess a burning pocket-full
of *zwanzigers*) . . . *To pay the Stygian Ferry!* 50
1st Policeman. There is the girl, then; go
and deserve them the moment you have
pointed out to us Signor Luigi and his mother.
[*To the rest.*] I have been noticing a house
yonder, this long while — not a shutter un- 55
closed since morning!
2d Pol. Old Luca Gaddi's, that owns the
silk-mills here. He dozes by the hour, wakes
up, sighs deeply, says he should like to be
Prince Metternich, and then dozes again after 60
having bidden young Sebald, the foreigner, set
his wife to playing draughts. Never molest
such a household; they mean well.
Blup. Only, cannot you tell me something
of this little Pippa, I must have to do with? 65
One could make something of that name.
Pippa — that is, short for Felippa — riming
to *Panurge consults Hertrippa—Believest thou,*
King Agrippa? Something might be done
with that name. 70
2d Pol. Put into rime that your head and
a ripe muskmelon would not be dear at half a
zwanziger! Leave this fooling, and look out;
the afternoon's over or nearly so.
3d Pol. Where in this passport of Signor 75
Luigi does our Principal instruct you to watch
him so narrowly? There? What's there beside a simple signature? (That English fool's
busy watching.)
2d Pol. Flourish all round — "Put all pos- 80
sible obstacles in his way;" oblong dot at the
end — "Detain him till further advices reach
you"; scratch at bottom — "Send him back
on pretense of some informality in the above";
ink-spirt on right-hand side (which is the case 85
here) — "Arrest him at once." Why and
wherefore, I don't concern myself, but my
instructions amount to this: if Signor Luigi
leaves home tonight for Vienna — well and
good, the passport deposed with us for our 90
visa is really for his own use, they have mis-
informed the Office, and he means well; but
let him stay over tonight — there has been
the pretense we suspect, the accounts of his
corresponding and holding intelligence with 95

50. **zwanzigers.** A zwanziger is an Austrian coin worth
about fifteen cents. 60. **Metternich,** a famous Austrian
statesman (1773-1859) noted for his policy of conservatism
and repression. He was an enemy of Italy. Cf. *The Italian in
England,* page 209. 68. **Panurge . . . Hertrippa.** Panurge
is a character in *Gargantua and Pantagruel,* a romance by the
French writer Rabelais (1490-1553). Panurge consults the
magician Hertrippa in regard to marriage. 68-69. **Believest
. . . Agrippa.** From *Acts,* 26:27. Paul tells the story of
his conversion to Christianity to Festus and Agrippa, and
asks, "King Agrippa, believest thou the prophets? I know
thou believest." 71-73. **Put into rime . . . zwanziger.**
The policeman ridicules Bluphocks by telling him to make a
rime out of the fact that his head and a ripe muskmelon
together are worth only seven and a half cents, the value of
a muskmelon alone.

the Carbonari are correct, we arrest him at
once, tomorrow comes Venice, and presently
Spielberg. Bluphocks makes the signal, sure
enough! That is he, entering the turret with
100 his mother, no doubt.

III. EVENING

SCENE: *Inside the Turret on the Hill above Asolo.*
LUIGI *and his* MOTHER *entering.*

Mother. If there blew wind, you'd hear a
    long sigh, easing
The utmost heaviness of music's heart.
    Luigi. Here in the archway?
    Mother.   Oh no, no — in farther,
Where the echo is made, on the ridge.
    Luigi.   Here surely, then.
How plain the tap of my heel as I leaped up!
Hark — "Lucius Junius!" The very ghost of
    a voice   6
Whose body is caught and kept by . . . what
    are those?
Mere withered wallflowers, waving overhead?
They seem an elvish group with thin bleached
    hair
That lean out of their topmost fortress — look
And listen, mountain men, to what we say, 11
Hand under chin of each grave earthy face.
Up and show faces all of you! — "All of you!"
That's the king dwarf with the scarlet comb;
    old Franz,
Come down and meet your fate? Hark —
    "Meet your fate!"   15
    Mother. Let him not meet it, my Luigi —
    do not
Go to his City! Putting crime aside,
Half of these ills of Italy are feigned;
Your Pellicos and writers for effect,
Write for effect.
    Luigi.   Hush! Say A writes, and B. 20
    Mother. These A's and B's write for effect,
    I say.
Then, evil is in its nature loud, while good
Is silent; you hear each petty injury,
None of his virtues; he is old beside,
Quiet and kind, and densely stupid. Why 25
Do A and B kill not him themselves?
    Luigi.   They teach
Others to kill him — me — and, if I fail,
Others to succeed; now, if A tried and failed,
I could not teach that; mine's the lesser task.
Mother, they visit night by night . . .

96. **Carbonari**, a secret society of Italian patriots organized in 1820 to help free Italy from the control of Austria.
98. **Spielberg**, an Austrian prison.
Evening. 6. **Lucius Junius**, Lucius Junius Brutus, who
led the revolt against the Tarquins in Rome and established
the Roman Republic in 509 B.C. Luigi is contemplating a similar deed. 14. **Franz**, Francis I, emperor of Austria (1804-
1835). 19. **Pellicos.** Silvio Pellico (1788-1854) was an Italian
patriot and a member of the Carbonari. He was imprisoned
for eleven years, part of the time in Spielberg Castle.

    Mother.   — You, Luigi? 30
Ah, will you let me tell you what you are?
    Luigi. Why not? Oh, the one thing you
    fear to hint,
You may assure yourself I say and say
Ever to myself! At times — nay, even as now
We sit — I think my mind is touched, suspect
All is not sound; but is not knowing that, 36
What constitutes one sane or otherwise?
I know I am thus — so, all is right again.
I laugh at myself as through the town I walk,
And see men merry as if no Italy   40
Were suffering; then I ponder — "I am rich,
Young, healthy; why should this fact trouble
    me,
More than it troubles these?" But it does
    trouble.
No, trouble's a bad word; for as I walk
There's springing and melody and giddiness,
And old quaint turns and passages of my
    youth,   46
Dreams long forgotten, little in themselves,
Return to me — whatever may amuse me.
And earth seems in a truce with me, and
    heaven
Accords with me, all things suspend their
    strife,   50
The very cicala laughs "There goes he, and
    there!
Feast him, the time is short; he is on his
    way
For the world's sake; feast him this once, our
    friend!"
And in return for all this, I can trip
Cheerfully up the scaffold-steps. I go   55
This evening, mother!
    Mother.   But mistrust yourself —
Mistrust the judgment you pronounce on him!
    Luigi. Oh, there I feel — am sure that I
    am right!
    Mother. Mistrust your judgment then, of
    the mere means
To this wild enterprise; say, you are right —
How should one in your state e'er bring to
    pass   61
What would require a cool head, a cool heart,
And a calm hand? You never will escape.
    Luigi. Escape? To even wish that would
    spoil all.
The dying is best part of it. Too much   65
Have I enjoyed these fifteen years of mine,
To leave myself excuse for longer life;
Was not life pressed down, running o'er with
    joy,
That I might finish with it ere my fellows
Who, sparelier feasted, make a longer stay? 70
I was put at the board-head, helped to all
At first; I rise up happy and content.
God must be glad one loves his world so
    much.
I can give news of earth to all the dead

Who ask me: — last year's sunsets, and great
    stars   75
Which had a right to come first and see ebb
The crimson wave that drifts the sun away —
Those crescent moons with notched and burn-
    ing rims
That strengthened into sharp fire, and there
    stood,
Impatient of the azure — and that day   80
In March, a double rainbow stopped the
    storm —
May's warm slow yellow moonlit summer
    nights —
Gone are they, but I have them in my soul!
    Mother. (He will not go!)
    Luigi.   You smile at me? 'Tis true —
Voluptuousness, grotesqueness, ghastliness, 85
Environ my devotedness as quaintly
As round about some antique altar wreathe
The rose festoons, goats' horns, and oxen's
    skulls.
    Mother. See now; you reach the city, you
    must cross
His threshold — how?
    Luigi.   Oh, that's if we conspired!   90
Then would come pains in plenty, as you
    guess —
But guess not how the qualities most fit
For such an office, qualities I have,
Would little stead me, otherwise employed,
Yet prove of rarest merit only here.   95
Everyone knows for what his excellence
Will serve, but no one ever will consider
For what his worst defect might serve; and
    yet
Have you not seen me range our coppice
    yonder
In search of a distorted ash? — I find   100
The wry spoilt branch a natural perfect bow.
Fancy the thrice-sage, thrice-precautioned
    man
Arriving at the palace on my errand!
No, no! I have a handsome dress packed up—
White satin here, to set off my black hair; 105
In I shall march — for you may watch your
    life out
Behind thick walls, make friends there to be-
    tray you;
More than one man spoils everything. March
    straight —
Only, no clumsy knife to fumble for,
Take the great gate, and walk (not saunter)
    on   110
Through guards and guards — I have re-
    hearsed it all
Inside the turret here a hundred times.
Don't ask the way of whom you meet, observe!
But where they cluster thickliest is the door
Of doors; they'll let you pass — they'll never
    blab   115
Each to the other, he knows not the favorite,

Whence he is bound and what's his business
    now.
Walk in — straight up to him; you have no
    knife.
Be prompt, how should he scream? Then, out
    with you!
Italy, Italy, my Italy!   120
You're free, you're free! Oh, mother, I could
    dream
They got about me — Andrea from his exile,
Pier from his dungeon, Gualtier from his
    grave!
    Mother. Well, you shall go. Yet seems this
    patriotism
The easiest virtue for a selfish man   125
To acquire; he loves himself — and next, the
    world —
If he must love beyond — but naught be-
    tween:
As a short-sighted man sees naught midway
His body and the sun above. But you
Are my adored Luigi, ever obedient   130
To my least wish, and running o'er with love;
I could not call you cruel or unkind.
Once more, your ground for killing him! —
    then go!
    Luigi. Now do you try me, or make sport
    of me?
How first the Austrians got these provinces...
(If that is all, I'll satisfy you soon)   136
— Never by conquest but by cunning, for
That treaty whereby . . .
    Mother.   Well?
    Luigi.   (Sure, he's arrived,
The tell-tale cuckoo; spring's his confidant,
And he lets out her April purposes!)   140
Or . . . better go at once to modern time.
He has . . . they have . . . in fact, I under-
    stand
But can't restate the matter; that's my boast:
Others could reason it out to you, and prove
Things they have made me feel.
    Mother.   Why go tonight?   145
Morn's for adventure. Jupiter is now
A morning-star. I cannot hear you, Luigi!
    Luigi. "I am the bright and morning-
    star," saith God —
And, "to such an one I give the morning-
    star."
The gift of the morning-star! Have I God's
    gift   150
Of the morning-star?

122-123. **Andrea, Pier, Gualtier,** imaginary former con-
spirators against the tyranny of Austria. 135. **How . . .
provinces.** Austria gained part of Northern Italy by conquest in 1813, and the rest by the terms of the treaty made at
the Congress of Vienna in 1815. 146-147. **Jupiter . . . morning-star.** When a planet rises after midnight, it is called a
morning-star. It is now evening, and the mother urges Luigi
to wait until morning—until Jupiter rises. 148. **I am,** etc.
From *Revelation,* 22:16.—"I Jesus . . . am the bright and
morning star." 149. **to . . . star.** From *Revelation,* 2:26-28.
—"And he that overcometh, and keepeth my works to the
end, to him will I give . . . the morning star."

Mother. Chiara will love to see
That Jupiter an evening-star next June.
   Luigi. True, mother. Well for those who
      live through June!
Great noontides, thunder-storms, all glaring
      pomps
That triumph at the heels of June the god 155
Leading his revel through our leafy world.
Yes, Chiara will be here.
   Mother. In June: remember,
Yourself appointed that month for her com-
      ing.
   Luigi. Was that low noise the echo?
   Mother. The night-wind.
She must be grown — with her blue eyes up-
      turned   160
As if life were one long and sweet surprise:
In June she comes.
   Luigi. We were to see together
The Titian at Treviso. There, again!

[*From without is heard the voice of* PIPPA, *singing* —

A king lived long ago,
In the morning of the world,   165
When earth was nigher heaven than now;
And the king's locks curled,
Disparting o'er a forehead full
As the milk-white space 'twixt horn and horn
Of some sacrificial bull —   170
Only calm as a babe new-born:
For he was got to a sleepy mood,
So safe from all decrepitude,
Age with its bane, so sure gone by,
(The gods so loved him while he dreamed) 175
That, having lived thus long, there seemed
No need the king should ever die.

   Luigi. No need that sort of king should
      ever die!

Among the rocks his city was;
Before his palace, in the sun,   180
He sat to see his people pass,
And judge them every one
From its threshold of smooth stone.
They haled him many a valley-thief
Caught in the sheep-pens, robber-chief   185
Swarthy and shameless, beggar-cheat,
Spy-prowler, or rough pirate found
On the sea-sand left aground;
And sometimes clung about his feet,
With bleeding lip and burning cheek,   190
A woman, bitterest wrong to speak

151. **Chiara,** Luigi's betrothed. The mother hopes to
keep Luigi from going by reminding him of her. 163. **The
Titian,** an altar-piece by Titian, a noted Venetian painter
(1477–1576), in the Cathedral of San Pietro, at Treviso, an
Italian town seventeen miles from Venice. 164. **A king,**
etc. This song was first published in 1835; it was changed
considerably when adapted to this drama.

Of one with sullen thickset brows:
And sometimes from the prison-house
The angry priests a pale wretch brought,
Who through some chink had pushed and
     pressed   195
On knees and elbows, belly and breast,
Worm-like into the temple — caught
He was by the very god,
Who ever in the darkness strode
Backward and forward, keeping watch   200
O'er his brazen bowls, such rogues to catch!
These, all and every one,
The king judged, sitting in the sun.

   Luigi. That king should still judge sitting in
      the sun!

His councilors, on left and right,   205
Looked anxious up — but no surprise
Disturbed the king's old smiling eyes
Where the very blue had turned to white.
'Tis said, a Python scared one day
The breathless city, till he came,   210
With forky tongue and eyes on flame,
Where the old king sat to judge alway;
But when he saw the sweepy hair
Girt with a crown of berries rare
Which the god will hardly give to wear   215
To the maiden who singeth, dancing bare
In the altar-smoke by the pine-torch lights,
At his wondrous forest rites —
Seeing this, he did not dare
Approach that threshold in the sun,   220
Assault the old king smiling there.
Such grace had kings when the world begun!
               [PIPPA *passes*

   Luigi. And such grace have they, now that
      the world ends!
The Python at the city, on the throne,
And brave men, God would crown for slaying
      him,   225
Lurk in by-corners lest they fall his prey.
Are crowns yet to be won in this late time,
Which weakness makes me hesitate to reach?
'Tis God's voice calls; how could I stay?
      Farewell!

SCENE: *Talk by the way, while* PIPPA *is passing
from the Turret to the Bishop's Brother's House,
close to the Duomo S. Maria. Poor* GIRLS *sitting
on the steps.*

   1st Girl. There goes a swallow to Venice —
      the stout seafarer!
Seeing those birds fly makes one wish for
      wings.
Let us all wish; you wish first!
   2d Girl. I? This sunset
To finish.
   3d Girl. That old — somebody I know,
Grayer and older than my grandfather,   5

To give me the same treat he gave last week —
Feeding me on his knee with fig-peckers,
Lampreys and red Breganze-wine, and mum-
    bling
The while some folly about how well I fare,
Let sit and eat my supper quietly;.   10
Since had he not himself been late this morn-
    ing
Detained at — never mind where — had he
    not —
"Eh, baggage, had I not!" —
    2d Girl.   How she can lie!
    3d Girl. Look there — by the nails!
    2d Girl.   What makes your fingers red?
    3d Girl. Dipping them into wine to write
        bad words with   15
On the bright table; how he laughed!
    1st Girl.   My turn.
Spring's come and summer's coming. I would
    wear
A long loose gown, down to the feet and hands,
With plaits here, close about the throat, all
    day;
And all night lie, the cool long nights, in bed;
And have new milk to drink, apples to eat,   21
Deuzans and junetings, leather-coats — ah, I
    should say,
This is away in the fields — miles!
    3d Girl.   Say at once
You'd be at home; she'd always be at home!
Now comes the story of the farm among   25
The cherry orchards, and how April snowed
White blossoms on her as she ran. Why, fool,
They've rubbed the chalk-mark out, how tall
    you were,
Twisted your starling's neck, broken his cage,
Made a dung-hill of your garden!
    1st Girl.   They destroy 30
My garden since I left them? well — perhaps
I would have done so; so I hope they have!
A fig-tree curled out of our cottage wall;
They called it mine—I have forgotten why—
It must have been there long ere I was born;
Cric — cric — I think I hear the wasps o'er-
    head   36
Pricking the papers strung to flutter there
And keep off birds in fruit-time — coarse long
    papers,
And the wasps eat them, prick them through
    and through.
    3d Girl. How her mouth twitches! Where
        was I? — before   40
She broke in with her wishes and long gowns
And wasps — would I be such a fool! — Oh,
    here!
This is my way: I answer everyone

Who asks me why I make so much of him —
(If you say, "you love him" — straight "he'll
    not be gulled!")   45
"He that seduced me when I was a girl
Thus high — had eyes like yours, or hair like
    yours,
Brown, red, white," — as the case may be;
    that pleases!
See how that beetle burnishes in the path! 49
There sparkles he along the dust; and, there—
Your journey to that maize-tuft spoiled at
    least!
    1st Girl. When I was young, they said if
        you killed one
Of those sunshiny beetles that his friend
Up there would shine no more that day nor
    next.
    2d Girl. When you were young? Nor are
        you young, that's true.   55
How your plump arms, that were, have
    dropped away!
Why, I can span them.   Cecco beats you
    still?
No matter, so you keep your curious hair.
I wish they'd find a way to dye our hair
Your color — any lighter tint, indeed,   60
Than black; the men say they are sick of
    black,
Black eyes, black hair!
    4th Girl.   Sick of yours, like enough.
Do you pretend you ever tasted lampreys
And ortolans? Giovita, of the palace,
Engaged (but there's no trusting him) to slice
    me   65
Polenta with a knife that had cut up
An ortolan.
    2d Girl.   Why, there! Is not that Pippa
We are to talk to, under the window —
    quick! —
Where the lights are?
    1st Girl.   That she? No, or she would sing,
For the Intendant said—
    3d Girl.   Oh, you sing first!   70
Then, if she listens and comes close — I'll
    tell you —
Sing that song the young English noble made,
Who took you for the purest of the pure,
And meant to leave the world for you — what
    fun!
    2d Girl. [Sings.]

    You'll love me yet! — and I can tarry   75
      Your love's protracted growing:
    June reared that bunch of flowers you carry,
      From seeds of April's sowing.

    I plant a heartfull now: some seed
      At least is sure to strike,   80

---

7. **fig-peckers**, birds that feed on figs.   8. **Lampreys**,
eel-like fish, considered a delicacy.   **Breganze-wine**, wine
made at Breganza, a village in northern Italy.   22. **Deuzans,
junetings, leather-coats**, varieties of apples.

64. **ortolan**, a small singing bird, regarded as a table
delicacy.   66. **Polenta**, corn-meal porridge.

And yield — *what you'll not pluck indeed,*
Not love, but, may be, like.

You'll look at least on love's remains,
   A grave's one violet:
Your look? — that pays a thousand pains.
What's death? You'll love me yet!   86

3d Girl. [*To* PIPPA *who approaches.*] Oh,
you may come closer — we shall not eat you!
Why, you seem the very person that the great
rich handsome Englishman has fallen so violently in love with. I'll tell you all about it.

IV. NIGHT

SCENE: *Inside the Palace by the Duomo.* MONSIG-
    NOR, *dismissing his* Attendants.

Monsignor. Thanks, friends, many thanks!
I chiefly desire life now, that I may recompense every one of you. Most I know something of already. What, a repast prepared?
5 *Benedicto benedicatur* . . . ugh, ugh! Where
was I? Oh, as you were remarking, Ugo, the
weather is mild, very unlike winter-weather;
but I am a Sicilian, you know, and shiver in
your Julys here. To be sure, when 'twas full
10 summer at Messina, as we priests used to
cross in procession the great square on
Assumption Day, you might see our thickest
yellow tapers twist suddenly in two, each like
a falling star, or sink down on themselves in
15 a gore of wax. But go, my friends, but go!
[*To the* Intendant.] Not you, Ugo! [*The
others leave the apartment.*] I have long wanted
to converse with you, Ugo.
Intendant. Uguccio —
20 *Mon.* . . . . 'guccio Stefani, man! of Ascoli,
Fermo, and Fossombruno;—what I do need
instructing about, are these accounts of your
administration of my poor brother's affairs.
Ugh! I shall never get through a third part
25 of your accounts; take some of these dainties
before we attempt it, however. Are you bashful to that degree? For me, a crust and water
suffice.
Inten. Do you choose this especial night to
30 question me?
Mon. This night, Ugo. You have managed
my late brother's affairs since the death of our
elder brother: fourteen years and a month, all
but three days. On the Third of December, I
35 find him —

Inten. If you have so intimate an acquaintance with your brother's affairs, you will be
tender of turning so far back; they will hardly
bear looking into, so far back.
Mon. Aye, aye, ugh, ugh — nothing but 40
disappointments here below! I remark a considerable payment made to yourself on this
Third of December. Talk of disappointments!
There was a young fellow here, Jules, a foreign sculptor — I did my utmost to advance, 45
that the Church might be a gainer by us both:
he was going on hopefully enough, and of a
sudden he notifies to me some marvelous
change that has happened in his notions of
Art. Here's his letter — "He never had a 50
clearly conceived Ideal within his brain till
today. Yet since his hand could manage a
chisel, he has practiced expressing other men's
Ideals; and, in the very perfection he has
attained to, he foresees an ultimate failure: 55
his unconscious hand will pursue its prescribed
course of old years, and will reproduce with a
fatal expertness the ancient types, let the
novel one appear never so palpably to his
spirit. There is but one method of escape: 60
confiding the virgin type to as chaste a hand,
he will turn painter instead of sculptor, and
paint, not carve, its characteristics" — strike
out, I dare say, a school like Correggio. How
think you, Ugo?   65
Inten. Is Correggio a painter?
Mon. Foolish Jules! and yet, after all, why
foolish? He may — probably will — fail egre-
giously; but if there should arise a new painter,
will it not be in some such way, by a poet 70
now, or a musician (spirits who have conceived and perfected an Ideal through some
other channel), transferring it to this, and
escaping our conventional roads by pure
ignorance of them; eh, Ugo? If you have no 75
appetite, talk at least, Ugo!
Inten. Sir, I can submit no longer to this
course of yours. First, you select the group
of which I formed one — next you thin it
gradually — always retaining me with your 80
smile — and so do you proceed till you have
fairly got me alone with you between four
stone walls. And now then? Let this farce,
this chatter end now; what is it you want
with me?   85
Mon. Ugo!
Inten. From the instant you arrived, I felt
your smile on me as you questioned me about
this and the other article in those papers —
why your brother should have given me this 90
villa, that *podere* — and your nod at the end
meant — what?

---

90. **Englishman,** Bluphocks.
   Night. 5. **Benedicto benedicatur,** a form of blessing
for the food—"Let it be consecrated with a good saying."
8. **a Sicilian.** The Bishop has come from Messina, in
Sicily, to take charge of his brother's estate. 12. **Assumption Day,** a church festival celebrated on August 15 to
commemorate the Ascension of the Virgin Mary. 20-21.
Ascoli, Fermo, Fossombruno, towns of central Italy.

54-55. **perfection . . . failure,** a favorite doctrine with
Browning. Cf. *Andrea del Sarto,* 97, p. 289. 64. **Correggio,**
a famous Italian painter (1494-1534). 91. **podere,** a small
farm or manor.

Mon. Possibly that I wished for no loud talk here. If once you set me coughing,
95 Ugo! —

Inten. I have your brother's hand and seal to all I possess; now ask me what for! what service I did him — ask me!

Mon. I would better not; I should rip up
100 old disgraces, let out my poor brother's weaknesses. By the way, Maffeo of Forli (which, I forgot to observe, is your true name), was the interdict ever taken off you for robbing that church at Cesena?

105 *Inten.* No, nor needs be; for when I murdered your brother's friend, Pasquale, for him —

Mon. Ah, he employed you in that business, did he? Well, I must let you keep, as
110 you say, this villa and that *podere*, for fear the world should find out my relations were of so indifferent a stamp? Maffeo, my family is the oldest in Messina, and century after century have my progenitors gone on polluting them-
115 selves with every wickedness under heaven. My own father — rest his soul! — I have, I know, a chapel to support that it may rest; my dear two dead brothers were — what you know tolerably well; I, the youngest, might
120 have rivaled them in vice, if not in wealth, but from my boyhood I came out from among them, and so am not partaker of their plagues. My glory springs from another source; or if from this, by contrast only—for I, the bishop,
125 am the brother of your employers, Ugo. I hope to repair some of their wrong, however; so far as my brother's ill-gotten treasure reverts to me, I can stop the consequences of his crime; and not one *soldo* shall escape me.
130 Maffeo, the sword we quiet men spurn away, you shrewd knaves pick up and commit murders with; what opportunities the virtuous forego, the villainous seize. Because, to pleasure myself apart from other considerations,
135 my food would be millet-cake, my dress sackcloth, and my couch straw — am I therefore to let you, the off-scouring of the earth, seduce the poor and ignorant by appropriating a pomp these will be sure to think lessens the
140 abominations so unaccountably and exclusively associated with it? Must I let villas and *poderi* go to you, a murderer and thief, that you may beget by means of them other murderers and thieves? No — if my cough
145 would but allow me to speak!

Inten. What am I to expect? You are going to punish me?

Mon. Must punish you, Maffeo. I cannot afford to cast away a chance. I have whole

centuries of sin to redeem, and only a month 150 or two of life to do it in. How should I dare to say —

Inten. "Forgive us our trespasses"?

Mon. My friend, it is because I avow myself a very worm, sinful beyond measure, 155 that I reject a line of conduct you would applaud perhaps. Shall I proceed, as it were, a-pardoning? — I? — who have no symptom of reason to assume that aught less than my strenuousest efforts will keep myself out of 160 mortal sin, much less keep others out. No; I do trespass, but will not double that by allowing you to trespass.

Inten. And suppose the villas are not your brother's to give, nor yours to take? Oh, you 165 are hasty enough just now!

Mon. 1, 2 — No. 3! — aye, can you read the substance of a letter, No. 3, I have received from Rome? It is precisely on the ground there mentioned, of the suspicion I 170 have that a certain child of my late elder brother, who would have succeeded to his estates, was murdered in infancy by you, Maffeo, at the instigation of my late younger brother — that the Pontiff enjoins on me not 175 merely the bringing that Maffeo to condign punishment, but the taking all pains, a guardian of the infant's heritage for the Church, to recover it parcel by parcel, howsoever, whensoever, and wheresoever. While you are 180 now gnawing those fingers, the police are engaged in sealing up your papers, Maffeo, and the mere raising my voice brings my people from the next room to dispose of yourself. But I want you to confess quietly, and 185 save me raising my voice. Why, man, do I not know the old story? The heir between the succeeding heir, and this heir's ruffianly instrument, and their complot's effect, and the life of fear and bribes and ominous smiling 190 silence? Did you throttle or stab my brother's infant? Come now!

Inten. So old a story, and tell it no better? When did such an instrument ever produce such an effect? Either the child smiles in his 195 face; or, most likely, he is not fool enough to put himself in the employer's power so thoroughly; the child is always ready to produce — as you say — howsoever, wheresoever, and whensoever. 200

Mon. Liar!

Inten. Strike me? Ah, so might a father chastise! I shall sleep soundly tonight at least, though the gallows await me tomorrow; for what a life did I lead! Carlo of Cesena 205 reminds me of his connivance, every time I pay his annuity; which happens commonly thrice a year. If I remonstrate, he will confess all to the good bishop — you!

101. **Forli**, a city of central Italy. 104. **Cesena**, a city near Forli. 129. **soldo**, an Italian coin worth about one cent.

210   *Mon.* I see through the trick, caitiff! I
would you spoke truth for once. All shall be
sifted, however — seven times sifted.

  Inten. And how my absurd riches encum-
bered me! I dared not lay claim to above half
215 my possessions. Let me but once unbosom
myself, glorify Heaven, and die!

  Sir, you are no brutal dastardly idiot like
your brother I frightened to death; let us
understand one another. Sir, I will make
220 away with her for you — the girl — here close
at hand; not the stupid obvious kind of killing; do not speak — know nothing of her nor
of me! I see her every day — saw her this
morning. Of course there is to be no killing;
225 but at Rome the courtesans perish off every
three years, and I can entice her thither—have
indeed begun operations already. There's a
certain lusty, blue-eyed, florid-complexioned
English knave, I and the Police employ occa-
230 sionally. You assent, I perceive — no, that's
not it — assent I do not say — but you will let
me convert my present havings and holdings
into cash, and give me time to cross the Alps?
'Tis but a little black-eyed pretty singing Fe-
235 lippa, gay silk-winding girl. I have kept her
out of harm's way up to this present; for I
always intended to make your life a plague to
you with her. 'Tis as well settled once and
forever. Some women I have procured will
240 pass Bluphocks, my handsome scoundrel, off
for somebody; and once Pippa entangled! —
you conceive? Through her singing? Is it a
bargain?

  [*From without is heard the voice of* PIPPA, *singing* —

  Overhead the tree-tops meet,   244
  Flowers and grass spring 'neath one's feet;
  There was naught above me, naught below,
  My childhood had not learned to know;
  For, what are the voices of birds
  —Aye, and of beasts — but words, our words,
  Only so much more sweet?   250
  The knowledge of that with my life begun.
  But I had so near made out the sun,
  And counted your stars, the seven and one,
  Like the fingers of my hand.
  Nay, I could all but understand   255
  Wherefore through heaven the white moon
        ranges;
  And just when out of her soft fifty changes
  No unfamiliar face might overlook me —
  Suddenly God took me.

                            [PIPPA *passes*

260   *Mon.* [*Springing up.*] My people — one
and all — all — within there! Gag this villain — tie him hand and foot! He dares — I
know not half he dares — but remove him —
quick! *Miserere mei, Domine!* Quick, I say! 264

SCENE: PIPPA's *Chamber again. She enters it.*

  The bee with his comb,
  The mouse at her dray,
  The grub in his tomb,
  While winter away;
  But the firefly and hedge-shrew and lob-
        worm, I pray,   5
  How fare they?
  Ha, ha, thanks for your counsel, my Zanze!
  "Feast upon lampreys, quaff Breganze" —
  The summer of life so easy to spend,
  And care for tomorrow so soon put away!   10
  But winter hastens at summer's end,
  And firefly, hedge-shrew, lob-worm, pray,
  How fare they?
  No bidding me then to — what did Zanze
        say?
  "Pare your nails pearlwise, get your small feet
        shoes   15
  More like" — (what said she?) — "and less
        like canoes!"
  How pert that girl was! — would I be those
        pert
  Impudent staring women! It had done me,
  However, surely no such mighty hurt
  To learn his name who passed that jest upon
        me;   20
  No foreigner, that I can recollect,
  Came, as she says, a month since, to inspect
  Our silk-mills — none with blue eyes and
        thick rings
  Of raw-silk-colored hair, at all events.
  Well, if old Luca keep his good intents,   25
  We shall do better, see what next year brings!
  I may buy shoes, my Zanze, not appear
  More destitute than you perhaps next year!
  Bluph . . . something! I had caught the un-
        couth name   29
  But for Monsignor's people's sudden clatter
  Above us — bound to spoil such idle chatter
  As ours; it were indeed a serious matter
  If silly talk like ours should put to shame
  The pious man, the man devoid of blame,
  The — ah but — ah but, all the same,   35
  No mere mortal has a right
  To carry that exalted air;
  Best people are not angels quite:
  While — not the worst of people's doings
        scare   39
  ' The devil; so there's that proud look to spare!

---

229. **English knave,** Bluphocks. 253. **stars, seven and
one,** the Pleiades (consisting of seven stars) and one other.

264. **Miserere mei, Domine,** Have mercy on me, O Lord.
Scene: Pippa's Chamber. 2. **dray,** nest (usually of a
squirrel). 5. **hedge-shrew,** field mouse. **lob-worm,** lug-
worm, a kind of giant earthworm. 7. **Zanze,** the third girl
that waited for Pippa, pp. 194-195. 40. **that proud look to
spare.** The "exalted air" of the Monsignor can well be spared.

Which is mere counsel to myself, mind!
    for
I have just been the holy Monsignor;
And I was you too, Luigi's gentle mother,
And you too, Luigi! — how that Luigi started
Out of the turret — doubtlessly departed   45
On some good errand or another,
For he passed just now in a traveler's trim,
And the sullen company that prowled
About his path, I noticed, scowled
As if they had lost a prey in him.   50
And I was Jules the sculptor's bride,
And I was Ottima beside,
And now what am I? — tired of fooling.
Day for folly, night for schooling!
New-year's day is over and spent,   55
Ill or well, I must be content.

  Even my lily's asleep, I vow;
Wake up — here's a friend I've plucked you!
Call this flower a heart's-ease now!
Something rare, let me instruct you,   60
Is this, with petals triply swollen,
Three times spotted, thrice the pollen;
While the leaves and parts that witness
Old proportions and their fitness,
Here remain unchanged, unmoved now;   65
Call this pampered thing improved now!
Suppose there's a king of the flowers
And a girl-show held in his bowers —
"Look ye, buds, this growth of ours,"
Says he, "Zanze from the Brenta,   70
I have made her gorge polenta
Till both cheeks are near as bouncing
As her—name there's no pronouncing!
See this heightened color too,
For she swilled Breganze wine   75
Till her nose turned deep carmine;
'Twas but white when wild she grew.
And only by this Zanze's eyes
Of which we could not change the size,
The magnitude of all achieved   80
Otherwise, may be perceived."

Oh, what a drear dark close to my poor day!
How could that red sun drop in that black
    cloud?
Ah, Pippa, morning's rule is moved away,
Dispensed with, never more to be allowed!   85
Day's turn is over, now arrives the night's.
O lark, be day's apostle
To mavis, merle, and throstle,
Bid them their betters jostle
From day and its delights!   90
But at night, brother owlet, over the woods,
Toll the world to thy chantry;
Sing to the bats' sleek sisterhoods

Full complines with gallantry:
Then, owls and bats,   95
Cowls and twats,
Monks and nuns, in a cloister's moods,
Adjourn to the oak-stump pantry!
    [After she has begun to undress herself
Now, one thing I should like to really know:
How near I ever might approach all these   100
I only fancied being, this long day —
Approach, I mean, so as to touch them, so
As to — in some way — move them — if you
    please,
Do good or evil to them some slight way.
For instance, if I wind   105
Silk tomorrow, my silk may bind
    [Sitting on the bedside
And border Ottima's cloak's hem.
Ah me, and my important part with them,
This morning's hymn half promised when I
    rose!
True in some sense or other, I suppose.   110
    [As she lies down
God bless me! I can pray no more tonight.
No doubt, some way or other, hymns say
    right.

All service ranks the same with God —
With God, whose puppets, best and worst,
Are we; there is no last nor first.   115
    [She sleeps
(1841)

CAVALIER TUNES

1. Marching Along

Kentish Sir Byng stood for his King,
Bidding the crop-headed Parliament swing;
And, pressing a troop unable to stoop
And see the rogues flourish and honest folk
    droop,
Marched them along, fifty-score strong,   5
Great-hearted gentlemen, singing this song:

God for King Charles! Pym and such carles
To the Devil that prompts 'em their treason-
    ous parles!
Cavaliers, up! Lips from the cup,
Hands from the pasty, nor bite take nor sup
Till you're —   11

---

47. **in . . . trim,** dressed for travel. 70. **the Brenta,** a river of northern Italy. 88. **mavis, merle, and throstle,** songthrush, blackbird, and thrush.

94. **compline,** an ecclesiastical term—the last of the canonical hours. 96. **twat,** part of a nun's garb, corresponding to the cowl of a monk.
Cavalier Tunes. The three songs under this title express the loyalty of the Cavaliers to King Charles I of England (1625-49) and their contempt for his Puritan enemies.
Marching Along. 2. **the crop-headed Parliament,** the Parliament of 1640, controlled by the Puritans, who wore their hair short in protest against the vain fashion of the Cavaliers, who wore their hair long and in curls. The Puritans were called "Roundheads." 7. **Pym,** John Pym (1584-1643), a leader of Parliament against the king.

Chorus —

> *Marching along, fifty-score strong,*
> *Great-hearted gentlemen, singing this*
> *song.*

Hampden to hell, and his obsequies' knell
Serve Hazelrig, Fiennes, and young Harry as
    well!   15
England, good cheer! Rupert is near!
Kentish and loyalists, keep we not here,

Chorus —

> *Marching along, fifty-score strong,*
> *Great-hearted gentlemen, singing this*
> *song?*

Then, God for King Charles! Pym and his
    snarls   20
To the Devil that pricks on such pestilent
    carles!
Hold by the right, you double your might;
So, onward to Nottingham, fresh for the fight,

Chorus —

> *March we along, fifty-score strong,*
> *Great-hearted gentlemen, singing this*
> *song.*

2. GIVE A ROUSE

King Charles, and who'll do him right now?
King Charles, and who's ripe for fight now?
Give a rouse; here's, in hell's despite now,
King Charles!

Who gave me the goods that went since?   5
Who raised me the house that sank once?
Who helped me to gold I spent since?
Who found me in wine you drank once?

Chorus —

> *King Charles, and who'll do him right*
> *now?*
> *King Charles, and who's ripe for fight*
> *now?*
> *Give a rouse; here's, in hell's despite now,*
> *King Charles.*

To whom used my boy George quaff else,
By the old fool's side that begot him?

---

14. **Hampden,** John Hampden (1594-1643), associated with
Pym in Parliament in opposition to the king. 15. **Hazelrig,**
Fiennes, young Harry. The Puritans were aided by Sir
Arthur Hazelrig, Nathaniel Fiennes, and Sir Henry Vane, son
of the elder Sir Henry Vane, one of Charles's secretaries.
Young Harry was Governor of Massachusetts Bay, 1636-37.
He was executed for treason after the accession of Charles II.
16. **Rupert,** Rupert, Prince of Bavaria (1619-82), a nephew
of Charles I. 23. **Nottingham.** The first stand of the
Royalists was made at Nottingham, a city in central England
in August, 1642.
Give a Rouse. Title: **rouse,** a shout that accompanies
drinking.

For whom did he cheer and laugh else,   15
While Noll's damned troopers shot him?

Chorus —

> *King Charles, and who'll do him right*
> *now?*
> *King Charles, and who's ripe for fight*
> *now?*
> *Give a rouse; here's, in hell's despite now,*
> *King Charles.*   20

3. BOOT AND SADDLE

Boot, saddle, to horse, and away!
Rescue my castle before the hot day
Brightens to blue from its silvery gray.

Chorus —

> *Boot, saddle, to horse, and away!*

Ride past the suburbs, asleep as you'd say;   5
Many's the friend there, will listen and pray
"God's luck to gallants that strike up the
    lay —

Chorus—

> *Boot, saddle, to horse, and away!"*

Forty miles off, like a roebuck at bay,
Flouts Castle Brancepeth the Roundheads'
    array;   10
Who laughs, "Good fellows ere this, by my
    fay,

Chorus —

> *Boot, saddle, to horse, and away!"*

Who? My wife Gertrude; that, honest and
    gay,
Laughs when you talk of surrendering, "Nay!
I've better counselors; what counsel they?   15

Chorus —

> *Boot, saddle, to horse, and away!"*
>   (1842)

THROUGH THE METIDJA TO ABD-EL-KADR

As I ride, as I ride,
With a full heart for my guide,
So its tide rocks my side,
As I ride, as I ride,

---

16. **Noll,** a contemptuous nickname for Cromwell, leader
of the Puritans.
Boot and Saddle. This song is supposed to be sung by a
Royalist nobleman who is riding to rescue Castle Brancepeth,
near Durham, from an attack of the Roundheads, or Puritans.
His wife Gertrude held the castle.
Through the Metidja. The speaker of the poem is an Arab
who is riding through the great Metidja Plain in Algeria to
join his chieftain Abd-el-Kadr (1807-83), who at the head of

That, as I were double-eyed,   5
He, in whom our Tribes confide,
Is descried, ways untried,
As I ride, as I ride.

As I ride, as I ride
To our Chief and his Allied,   10
Who dares chide my heart's pride
As I ride, as I ride?
Or are witnesses denied —
Through the desert waste and wide
Do I glide unespied   15
As I ride, as I ride?

As I ride, as I ride,
When an inner voice has cried,
The sands slide, nor abide
(As I ride, as I ride)   20
O'er each visioned homicide
That came vaunting (has he lied?)
To reside — where he died,
As I ride, as I ride.

As I ride, as I ride,   25
Ne'er has spur my swift horse plied,
Yet his hide, streaked and pied,
As I ride, as I ride,
Shows where sweat has sprung and dried
— Zebra-footed, ostrich-thighed —   30
How has vied stride with stride
As I ride, as I ride!

As I ride, as I ride,
Could I loose what Fate has tied,
Ere I pried, she should hide   35
(As I ride, as I ride)
All that's meant me — satisfied
When the Prophet and the Bride
Stop veins I'd have subside
As I ride, as I ride!   40
                                           (1842)

RUDEL TO THE LADY OF TRIPOLI

I

I know a Mount, the gracious Sun perceives
First, when he visits, last, too, when he leaves
The world; and, vainly favored, it repays
The day-long glory of his steadfast gaze
By no change of its large calm front of snow. 5
And underneath the Mount, a Flower I know,

He cannot have perceived, that changes ever
At his approach; and, in the lost endeavor
To live his life, has parted, one by one,
With all a flower's true graces, for the grace 10
Of being but a foolish mimic sun,
With ray-like florets round a disk-like face.
Men nobly call by many a name the Mount
As over many a land of theirs its large
Calm front of snow like a triumphal targe 15
Is reared, and still with old names, fresh
       names vie,
Each to its proper praise and own account:
Men call the Flower the Sunflower, spor-
       tively.

2

Oh, Angel of the East, one, one gold look
Across the waters to this twilight nook — 20
The far sad waters, Angel, to this nook!

3

Dear Pilgrim, art thou for the East indeed?
Go! — saying ever as thou dost proceed,
That I, French Rudel, choose for my device
A sunflower outspread like a sacrifice 25
Before its idol. See! These inexpert
And hurried fingers could not fail to hurt
The woven picture; 'tis a woman's skill
Indeed; but nothing baffled me, so, ill
Or well, the work is finished. Say, men feed 30
On songs I sing, and therefore bask the bees
On my flower's breast as on a platform broad;
But, as the flower's concern is not for these
But solely for the sun, so men applaud
In vain this Rudel, he not looking here 35
But to the East — the East! Go, say this,
       Pilgrim dear!   (1842)

CRISTINA

She should never have looked at me
    If she meant I should not love her!
There are plenty — men, you call such,
    I suppose — she may discover
All her soul to, if she pleases,   5
    And yet leave much as she found them;
But I'm not so, and she knew it
    When she fixed me, glancing round them.

What? To fix me thus meant nothing?
    But I can't tell (there's my weakness)   10
What her look said! — no vile cant, sure,
    About "need to strew the bleakness

---

allied tribes is resisting a French invasion. As he gallops
along, his spiritual fervor reveals Mohammed (line 6) in a
new light. The rider rejoices in his visions of the dead bodies
of the slain Frenchmen, buried in the desert and seemingly
uncovered by the shifting sands. His own future is concealed, but he will be content to accept death when Mohammed pleases. Or the last stanza may mean that Fate
will be satisfied when Mohammed allows the rider to slay his
enemies.
Rudel to the Lady of Tripoli. See Critical Notes.

17. **proper,** own. 28. **'tis a woman's skill,** the weaving
requires the skill of a woman.
Cristina. Maria Christina (1806-78) was the daughter of
Francis I, king of Sicily. In 1829 she married Ferdinand VII,
king of Spain, and upon his death in 1833 she became queen
dowager. Before her marriage she had the reputation of
being a coquette and a political intriguer.

Of some lone shore with its pearl-seed,
   That the sea feels" — no "strange yearning
That such souls have, most to lavish   15
   Where there's chance of least returning."

Oh, we're sunk enough here, God knows!
   But not quite so sunk that moments,
Sure though seldom, are denied us,
   When the spirit's true endowments   20
Stand out plainly from its false ones,
   And apprise it if pursuing
Or the right way or the wrong way,
   To its triumph or undoing.

There are flashes struck from midnights,   25
   There are fire-flames noondays kindle,
Whereby piled-up honors perish,
   Whereby swollen ambitions dwindle,
While just this or that poor impulse,
   Which for once had play unstifled,   30
Seems the sole work of a lifetime,
   That away the rest have trifled.

Doubt you if, in some such moment,
   As she fixed me, she felt clearly,
Ages past the soul existed,   35
   Here an age 'tis resting merely,
And hence fleets again for ages,
   While the true end, sole and single,
It stops here for is, this love-way,
   With some other soul to mingle?   40

Else it loses what it lived for,
   And eternally must lose it;
Better ends may be in prospect,   .
   Deeper blisses (if you choose it),
But this life's end and this love-bliss   45
Have been lost here. Doubt you whether
This she felt as, looking at me,
   Mine and her souls rushed together?

Oh, observe! Of course, next moment,
   The world's honors, in derision,   50
Trampled out the light forever;
   Never fear but there's provision
Of the devil's to quench knowledge
   Lest we walk the earth in rapture!
— Making those who catch God's secret   55
Just so much more prize their capture!

Such am I; the secret's mine now!
   She has lost me, I have gained her;
Her soul's mine: and thus, grown perfect,
   I shall pass my life's remainder.   60
Life will just hold out the proving
   Both our powers, alone and blended;
And then, come the next life quickly!
   This world's use will have been ended.
                       (1842)

INCIDENT OF THE FRENCH CAMP

You know, we French stormed Ratisbon;
   A mile or so away,
On a little mound, Napoleon
   Stood on our storming-day;
With neck out-thrust, you fancy how,   5
   Legs wide, arms locked behind,
As if to balance the prone brow
   Oppressive with its mind.

Just as perhaps he mused, "My plans
   That soar, to earth may fall,   10
Let once my army-leader Lannes
   Waver at yonder wall" —
Out 'twixt the battery-smokes there flew
   A rider, bound on bound
Full-galloping; nor bridle drew   15
   Until he reached the mound.

Then off there flung in smiling joy,
   And held himself erect
By just his horse's mane, a boy;
   You hardly could suspect —   20
(So tight he kept his lips compressed,
   Scarce any blood came through)
You looked twice ere you saw his breast
   Was all but shot in two.

"Well," cried he, "Emperor, by God's grace
   We've got you Ratisbon!   26
The Marshal's in the market-place,
   And you'll be there anon
To see your flag-bird flap his vans
   Where I, to heart's desire,   30
Perched him!" The chief's eye flashed; his plans
   Soared up again like fire.

The chief's eye flashed; but presently
   Softened itself, as sheathes
A film the mother-eagle's eye   35
   When her bruised eaglet breathes;
"You're wounded!" "Nay," the soldier's pride
   Touched to the quick, he said:
"I'm killed, Sire!" And his chief beside,
   Smiling the boy fell dead.   (1842)

SOLILOQUY OF THE SPANISH CLOISTER

Gr-r-r — there go, my heart's abhorrence!
   Water your damned flower-pots, do!
If hate killed men, Brother Lawrence,
   God's blood, would not mine kill you!

Incident of the French Camp. The incident is said to be
true, but the actual hero was a man. Ratisbon, a city in
Bavaria, was taken by Napoleon in 1809.
   11. **Lannes**, Jean Lannes (1769-1809), a distinguished
marshal of Napoleon. 29. **flag-bird**, eagle.

What? your myrtle-bush wants trimming? 5
  Oh, that rose has prior claims —
Needs its leaden vase filled brimming?
  Hell dry you up with its flames!

At the meal we sit together:
  Salve tibi! I must hear 10
Wise talk of the kind of weather,
  Sort of season, time of year:
Not a plenteous cork-crop; scarcely
  Dare we hope oak-galls, I doubt;
What's the Latin name for "parsley"? 15
  What's the Greek name for Swine's Snout?

Whew! We'll have our platter burnished,
  Laid with care on our own shelf!
With a fire-new spoon we're furnished,
  And a goblet for ourself, 20
Rinsed like something sacrificial
  Ere 'tis fit to touch our chaps —
Marked with L for our initial!
  (He-he! There his lily snaps!)

Saint, forsooth! While brown Dolores 25
  Squats outside the Convent bank
With Sanchicha, telling stories,
  Steeping tresses in the tank,
Blue-black, lustrous, thick like horsehairs
  — Can't I see his dead eye glow, 30
Bright as 'twere a Barbary corsair's?
  (That is, if he'd let it show!)

When he finishes refection,
  Knife and fork he never lays
Cross-wise, to my recollection, 35
  As do I, in Jesu's praise.
I the Trinity illustrate,
  Drinking watered orange-pulp —
In three sips the Arian frustrate;
  While he drains his at one gulp. 40

Oh, those melons! If he's able
  We're to have a feast! so nice!
One goes to the Abbot's table,
  All of us get each a slice.
How go on your flowers? None double? 45
  Not one fruit-sort can you spy?
Strange! — And I, too, at such trouble
  Keep them close-nipped on the sly!

There's a great text in Galatians,
  Once you trip on it, entails 50

Twenty-nine distinct damnations,
  One sure, if another fails:
If I trip him just a-dying,
  Sure of heaven as sure can be,
Spin him round and send him flying 55
  Off to hell, a Manichee?

Or, my scrofulous French novel
  On gray paper with blunt type!
Simply glance at it, you grovel
  Hand and foot in Belial's gripe; 60
If I double down its pages
  At the woeful sixteenth print,
When he gathers his greengages,
  Ope a sieve and slip it in 't?

Or, there's Satan! — one might venture 65
  Pledge one's soul to him, yet leave
Such a flaw in the indenture
  As he'd miss till, past retrieve,
Blasted lay that rose-acacia
  We're so proud of! *Hy, Zy, Hine* . . . 70
'St, there's Vespers! *Plena gratiâ,*
  Ave, Virgo! Gr-r-r — you swine!

(1842)

MY LAST DUCHESS
FERRARA

That's my last Duchess painted on the wall,
Looking as if she were alive. I call
That piece a wonder, now; Frà Pandolf's
    hands
Worked busily a day, and there she stands.
Will 't please you sit and look at her? I said 5
"Frà Pandolf" by design, for never read
Strangers like you that pictured counte-
    nance,
The depth and passion of its earnest glance,
But to myself they turned (since none puts by
The curtain I have drawn for you, but I) 10
And seemed as they would ask me, if they
    durst,
How such a glance came there; so, not the first
Are you to turn and ask thus. Sir, 'twas not
Her husband's presence only, called that spot
Of joy into the Duchess' cheek; perhaps 15
Frà Pandolf chanced to say, "Her mantle
    laps

10. **Salve tibi**, hail to thee. 14. **oak-galls**, swellings on oak leaves, a very rich source of tannic acid widely used by the monks in making black ink. 31. **Barbary corsair**. Barbary includes the countries on the north coast of Africa. A corsair was originally a Turkish or Saracen pirate. 39. **Arian**, a follower of Arius, a fourth-century priest who held that Christ is not the Eternal Son of God, and who denied the Trinity. 49. **text in Galatians**, probably a reference to *Galatians*, 5:19-21, which enumerates seventeen "works of the flesh" and states that "they which do such things shall not inherit the kingdom of God." See also *Galatians*, 3:10 for another possible reference.

56. **Manichee**, a believer in the doctrines of Manichaeus, a Persian of the third century, who held that man's body is the product of evil and his soul the product of good. 60. **Belial's**, the devil's. 70. **Hy, Zy, Hine**, perhaps part of a magic formula. 71-72. **Plena . . . Virgo**, Hail, Virgin, full of grace (a form of prayer used when the vesper bell sounds). *My Last Duchess*. The speaker in this poem is a duke of Ferrara, a famous Italian city in northern Italy, near Venice. He is negotiating with an envoy for the hand of the Count's daughter. This is one of Browning's most famous dramatic monologues. 3. **Frà Pandolf**, Brother Pandolf, an imaginary painter represented as a monk.

Over my lady's wrist too much," or "Paint
Must never hope to reproduce the faint
Half-flush that dies along her throat." Such
    stuff
Was courtesy, she thought, and cause enough
For calling up that spot of joy. She had   21
A heart — how shall I say? — too soon made
    glad,
Too easily impressed; she liked whate'er
She looked on, and her looks went every-
    where.
Sir, 'twas all one! My favor at her breast, 25
The dropping of the daylight in the West,
The bough of cherries some officious fool
Broke in the orchard for her, the white mule
She rode with round the terrace — all and
    each
Would draw from her alike the approving
    speech,   30
Or blush, at least. She thanked men,— good!
    but thanked
Somehow — I know not how — as if she
    ranked
My gift of a nine-hundred-years-old name
With anybody's gift. Who'd stoop to blame
This sort of trifling? Even had you skill   35
In speech — which I have not — to make your
    will
Quite clear to such an one, and say, "Just
    this
Or that in you disgusts me; here you miss,
Or there exceed the mark" — and if she let
Herself be lessoned so, nor plainly set   40
Her wits to yours, forsooth, and made excuse—
E'en then would be some stooping; and I
    choose
Never to stoop. Oh, sir, she smiled, no doubt,
Whene'er I passed her; but who passed with-
    out
Much the same smile? This grew; I gave
    commands;   45
Then all smiles stopped together. There she
    stands
As if alive. Will 't please you rise? We'll meet
The company below, then. I repeat,
The Count your master's known munificence
Is ample warrant that no just pretense   50
Of mine for dowry will be disallowed;
Though his fair daughter's self, as I avowed
At starting, is my object. Nay, we'll go
Together down, sir. Notice Neptune, though,
Taming a sea-horse, thought a rarity,   55
Which Claus of Innsbruck cast in bronze for
    me!   (1842)

45-46. commands . . . together. In response to an inquiry from Professor Corson (*Introduction to Browning*),
Browning said that he meant that "the commands were that
she should be put to death, or he might have had her shut up
in a convent." 54. Neptune, the god of the sea. 56. Claus
of Innsbruck, an imaginary sculptor. Innsbruck, the
capital of Tyrol in Austria, is noted for its bronze work on
the tomb of the Emperor Maximilian (1459-1519).

IN A GONDOLA

He sings:

I send my heart up to thee, all my heart
  In this my singing.
For the stars help me, and the sea bears part;
  The very night is clinging
Closer to Venice' streets to leave one space   5
  Above me, whence thy face
May light my joyous heart to thee its dwelling
  place.

She speaks:

Say after me, and try to say
My very words, as if each word
Came from you of your own accord,   10
In your own voice, in your own way:
"This woman's heart and soul and brain
Are mine as much as this gold chain
She bids me wear; which" (say again)
"I choose to make by cherishing   15
A precious thing, or choose to fling
Over the boat-side, ring by ring."
And yet once more say — no word more!
Since words are only words. Give o'er!

Unless you call me, all the same,   20
Familiarly by my pet name,
Which if the Three should hear you call,
And me reply to, would proclaim
At once our secret to them all.
Ask of me, too, command me, blame —   25
Do, break down the partition-wall
'Twixt us, the daylight world beholds
Curtained in dusk and splendid folds!
What's left but — all of me to take?
I am the Three's; prevent them, slake   30
Your thirst! 'Tis said, the Arab sage,
In practicing with gems, can loose
Their subtle spirit in his cruce
And leave but ashes; so, sweet mage,
Leave them my ashes when thy use   35
Sucks out my soul, thy heritage!

He sings:

Past we glide, and past, and past!
  What's that poor Agnese doing
Where they make the shutters fast?
  Gray Zanobi's just a-wooing   40
To his couch the purchased bride;
  Past we glide!

Past we glide, and past, and past!
  Why's the Pucci Palace flaring
Like a beacon to the blast?   45
  Guests by hundreds, not one caring

In a Gondola. See Critical Notes.
22. the three, Paul, Gian, and Himself (see note on ll.
106-107). 33. cruce, crucible. 34. mage, magician.

If the dear host's neck were wried;
  Past we glide!

She sings:

The moth's kiss, first!
Kiss me as if you made believe   50
You were not sure, this eve,
How my face, your flower, had pursed
Its petals up; so, here and there
You brush it, till I grow aware
Who wants me, and wide ope I burst.   55

The bee's kiss, now!
Kiss me as if you entered gay
My heart at some noonday,
A bud that dares not disallow
The claim, so all is rendered up,   60
And passively its shattered cup
Over your head to sleep I bow.

He sings:

What are we two?
I am a Jew,
And carry thee, farther than friends can
    pursue,   65
To a feast of our tribe;
Where they need thee to bribe
The devil that blasts them unless he imbibe
Thy — Scatter the vision forever! And now,
As of old, I am I, thou art thou!   70

Say again, what we are?
The sprite of a star,
I lure thee above where the destinies bar
My plumes their full play
Till a ruddier ray   75
Than my pale one announce there is withering
    away
Some — Scatter the vision forever! And now,
As of old, I am I, thou art thou!

He muses:

Oh, which were best, to roam or rest?
The land's lap or the water's breast?   80
To sleep on yellow millet-sheaves,
Or swim in lucid shallows just
Eluding water-lily leaves,
An inch from Death's black fingers, thrust
To lock you, whom release he must;   85
Which life were best on summer eves?

He speaks, musing:

Lie back; could thought of mine improve you?
From this shoulder let there spring
A wing; from this, another wing;
Wings, not legs and feet, shall move you!   90
Snow-white must they spring, to blend
With your flesh, but I intend
They shall deepen to the end,

Broader, into burning gold,
Till both wings crescent-wise enfold   95
Your perfect self, from 'neath your feet
To o'er your head, where, lo, they meet
As if a million sword-blades hurled
Defiance from you to the world!

Rescue me thou, the only real!   100
And scare away this mad ideal
That came, nor motions to depart!
Thanks! Now, stay ever as thou art!

Still he muses:

What if the Three should catch at last
Thy serenader? While there's cast   105
Paul's cloak about my head, and fast
Gian pinions me, Himself has past
His stylet through my back; I reel;
And — is it thou I feel?

They trail me, these three godless knaves, 110
Past every church that saints and saves,
Nor stop till, where the cold sea raves
By Lido's wet accursèd graves,
They scoop mine, roll me to its brink,
And — on thy breast I sink!   115

She replies, musing:

Dip your arm o'er the boat-side, elbow-deep,
As I do — thus; were death so unlike sleep,
Caught this way? Death's to fear from flame
    or steel,
Or poison doubtless; but from water — feel!

Go find the bottom! Would you stay me?
    There!   120
Now pluck a great blade of that ribbon-grass
To plait in where the foolish jewel was,
I flung away; since you have praised my hair,
'Tis proper to be choice in what I wear.

He speaks:

Row home? must we row home? Too surely
Know I where its front's demurely   126
Over the Giudecca piled;
Window just with window mating,
Door on door exactly waiting,
All's the set face of a child;   130
But behind it, where's a trace
Of the staidness and reserve,
And formal lines without a curve,
In the same child's playing-face?
No two windows look one way   135
O'er the small sea-water thread
Below them. Ah, the autumn day
I, passing, saw you overhead!

106-107. **Paul's . . . past.** Paul and Gian are friends or
relatives of Himself, the lady's husband. 113. **Lido's . . .
graves,** the ancient graves of Jews at Lido, near Venice.
127. **the Giudecca,** one of the canals of Venice.

First, out a cloud of curtain blew,
Then a sweet cry, and last came you —   140
To catch your lory that must needs
Escape just then, of all times then,
To peck a tall plant's fleecy seeds,
And make me happiest of men.
I scarce could breathe to see you reach   145
So far back o'er the balcony
To catch him ere he climbed too high
Above you in the Smyrna peach,
That quick the round smooth cord of gold,
This coiled hair on your head, unrolled,   150
Fell down you like a gorgeous snake
The Roman girls were wont, of old,
When Rome there was, for coolness' sake
To let lie curling o'er their bosoms.
Dear lory, may his beak retain   155
Ever its delicate rose stain
As if the wounded lotus-blossoms
Had marked their thief to know again!

Stay longer yet, for others' sake
Than mine! What should your chamber do?
— With all its rarities that ache   161
In silence while day lasts, but wake
At night-time and their life renew,
Suspended just to pleasure you
Who brought against their will together   165
These objects, and, while day lasts, weave
Around them such a magic tether
That dumb they look; your harp, believe,
With all the sensitive tight strings
Which dare not speak, now to itself   170
Breathes slumberously, as if some elf
Went in and out the chords, his wings
Make murmur wheresoe'er they graze,
As an angel may, between the maze
Of midnight palace-pillars, on   175
And on, to sow God's plagues, have gone
Through guilty glorious Babylon.
And while such murmurs flow, the nymph
Bends o'er the harp-top from her shell
As the dry limpet for the lymph   180
Come with a tune he knows so well.
And how your statues' hearts must swell!
And how your pictures must descend
To see each other, friend with friend!
Oh, could you take them by surprise,   185
You'd find Schidone's eager Duke
Doing the quaintest courtesies
To that prim saint by Haste-thee-Luke!
And, deeper into her rock den,

Bold Castelfranco's Magdalen   190
You'd find retreated from the ken
Of that robed counsel-keeping Ser —
As if the Tizian thinks of her,
And is not, rather, gravely bent
On seeing for himself what toys   195
Are these, his progeny invent,
What litter now the board employs
Whereon he signed a document
That got him murdered! Each enjoys
Its night so well, you cannot break   200
The sport up, so, indeed must make
More stay with me, for others' sake.

She speaks:

Tomorrow, if a harp-string, say,
Is used to tie the jasmine back
That overfloods my room with sweets,   205
Contrive your Zorzi somehow meets
My Zanze! If the ribbon's black,
The Three are watching; keep away!

Your gondola — let Zorzi wreathe
A mesh of water-weeds about   210
Its prow, as if he unaware
Had struck some quay or bridge-foot stair!
That I may throw a paper out
As you and he go underneath.

There's Zanze's vigilant taper; safe are we. 215
Only one minute more tonight with me?
Resume your past self of a month ago!
Be you the bashful gallant; I will be
The lady with the colder breast than snow.
Now bow you, as becomes, nor touch my hand
More than I touch yours when I step to
    land,
And say, "All thanks, Siora!" —
                    Heart to heart 222
And lips to lips! Yet once more, ere we part,
Clasp me and make me thine, as mine thou
    art!

He is surprised, and stabbed.

It was ordained to be so, sweet! — and best
Comes now, beneath thine eyes, upon thy
    breast.   226
Still kiss me! Care not for the cowards! Care
Only to put aside thy beauteous hair
My blood will hurt! The Three, I do not scorn
To death, because they never lived; but I 230
Have lived indeed, and so — (yet one more
    kiss) — can die!   (1842)

---

141. **lory**, a kind of parrot. 148. **the Smyrna peach**, a peach tree native of Smyrna, a province of Turkey. 151-154. **snake . . . bosoms.** Various classical authors—Lucian, Pliny, Cicero, Seneca, and others—speak of snakes being kept as pets in both Greece and Rome. Cf. Martial, 7, 87.—"If Glaucilla twines a cold serpent round her neck." 177. **Babylon**, the capital of the ancient empire of Babylon, noted for its wealth and wickedness. 180-181. **the dry limpet . . . well**, the dry limpet on the rock or shore extends himself from his shell as he hears the familiar sound of water. 186. **Schidone's eager Duke**, a painting by Bartolommeo

Schidone (1560-1616), an Italian artist. 188. **Haste-thee-Luke**, Luca Giordana (1632-1705), a painter of Naples. The nickname came from the fact that he was constantly being urged by his father to hurry. 190. **Castelfranco**, Giorgio Barbarelli (1478-1511), a painter born at Castelfranco, in northern Italy. 192. **Ser**, an Italian title of courtesy, like *sir* or *gentleman*. 193. **Tizian**, Tiziano Vecellio (1477-1576), a famous Venetian painter surnamed "Il Divino." 206-207. **Zorzi, Zanze.** Zorzi was his servant, Zanze hers. 222. **Siora**, Venetian for the Italian *Signora*, Lady.

THE PIED PIPER OF HAMELIN

A CHILD'S STORY

I

Hamelin Town's in Brunswick,
By famous Hanover city;
  The river Weser, deep and wide,
  Washes its wall on the southern side;
A pleasanter spot you never spied;   5
But, when begins my ditty,
  Almost five hundred years ago,
  To see the townsfolk suffer so
    From vermin, was a pity.

2

Rats!   10
They fought the dogs and killed the cats,
  And bit the babies in the cradles,
And ate the cheeses out of the vats,
  And licked the soup from the cooks' own
    ladles,
Split open the kegs of salted sprats,   15
Made nests inside men's Sunday hats,
And even spoiled the women's chats
  By drowning their speaking
  With shrieking and squeaking
In fifty different sharps and flats.   20

3

At last the people in a body
  To the Town Hall came flocking.
" 'Tis clear," cried they, "our Mayor's a
  noddy;
And as for our Corporation — shocking
To think we buy gowns lined with ermine 25
For dolts that can't or won't determine
What's best to rid us of our vermin!
You hope, because you're old and obese,
To find in the furry civic robe ease?
Rouse up, sirs! Give your brains a racking 30
To find the remedy we're lacking,
Or, sure as fate, we'll send you packing!"
At this the Mayor and Corporation
Quaked with a mighty consternation.

4

An hour they sat in council;   35
  At length the Mayor broke silence:
"For a guilder I'd my ermine gown sell,
  I wish I were a mile hence!
It's easy to bid one rack one's brain —
I'm sure my poor head aches again,   40

The Pied Piper of Hamelin. This poem is based upon an
old legend found in many forms, all dealing with the attempt
to cheat a magician out of his promised reward. (See Brew-
er's *Reader's Handbook* under "Pied Piper.") Browning
wrote the poem to amuse Willy (line 300), the son of the
famous actor William Macready (1793-1873). The boy was
ill and desired a subject for which he could make illustrations.
  1. **Brunswick,** a state in north-central Germany. 24.
Corporation, the governing body of the city. 37. **guilder,**
a coin worth about forty cents.

I've scratched it so, and all in vain.
Oh, for a trap, a trap, a trap!"
Just as he said this, what should hap
At the chamber-door but a gentle tap?
"Bless us," cried the Mayor, "what's that?"
(With the Corporation as he sat,   46
Looking little though wondrous fat;
Nor brighter was his eye, nor moister
Than a too-long-opened oyster,
Save when at noon his paunch grew mutinous
For a plate of turtle green and glutinous), 51
"Only a scraping of shoes on the mat?
Anything like the sound of a rat
Makes my heart go pit-a-pat!"

5

"Come in!" — the Mayor cried, looking big-
  ger;   55
And in did come the strangest figure!
His queer long coat from heel to head
Was half of yellow and half of red,
And he himself was tall and thin,
With sharp blue eyes, each like a pin,   60
And light loose hair, yet swarthy skin,
No tuft on cheek nor beard on chin,
But lips where smiles went out and in;
There was no guessing his kith and kin;
And nobody could enough admire   65
The tall man and his quaint attire.
Quoth one, "It's as my great-grandsire,
Starting up at the Trump of Doom's tone,
Had walked this way from his painted tomb-
  stone!"

6

He advanced to the council-table;   70
And, "Please your honors," said he, "I'm able,
By means of a secret charm, to draw
All creatures living beneath the sun,
That creep or swim or fly or run,
After me so as you never saw!   75
And I chiefly use my charm
On creatures that do people harm,
The mole and toad and newt and viper;
And people call me the Pied Piper."
(And here they noticed round his neck   80
A scarf of red and yellow stripe,
To match with his coat of the self-same check;
And at the scarf's end hung a pipe;
And his fingers, they noticed, were ever stray-
  ing
As if impatient to be playing   85
Upon this pipe, as low it dangled
Over his vesture so old-fangled.)
"Yet," said he, "poor piper as I am,
In Tartary I freed the Cham,
Last June, from his huge swarm of gnats; 90

  89. **Cham,** the title of the ruler of the Tartar Empire in
Central Asia.

I eased in Asia the Nizam
Of a monstrous brood of vampire-bats;
And as for what your brain bewilders,
If I can rid your town of rats
Will you give me a thousand guilders?"   95
"One? fifty thousand!" — was the exclama-
tion
Of the astonished Mayor and Corporation.

7

Into the street the Piper stepped,
  Smiling first a little smile,
As if he knew what magic slept   100
  In his quiet pipe the while;
Then, like a musical adept,
To blow the pipe his lips he wrinkled,
And green and blue his sharp eyes twinkled,
Like a candle-flame where salt is sprinkled; 105
And ere three shrill notes the pipe uttered,
You heard as if an army muttered;
And the muttering grew to a grumbling;
And the grumbling grew to a mighty rum-
  bling;   109
And out of the houses the rats came tum-
  bling.
Great rats, small rats, lean rats, brawny rats,
Brown rats, black rats, gray rats, tawny rats,
Grave old plodders, gay young friskers,
  Fathers, mothers, uncles, cousins,
Cocking tails and pricking whiskers,   115
  Families by tens and dozens,
Brothers, sisters, husbands, wives —
Followed the Piper for their lives.
From street to street he piped advancing,
And step for step they followed dancing,   120
Until they came to the river Weser,
Wherein all plunged and perished!
— Save one who, stout as Julius Cæsar,
Swam across and lived to carry
(As he, the manuscript he cherished)   125
To Rat-land home his commentary—
Which was, "At the first shrill notes of the
  pipe,
I heard a sound as of scraping tripe,
And putting apples, wondrous ripe,
Into a cider-press's gripe,   130
And a moving away of pickle-tub-boards,
And a leaving ajar of conserve-cupboards,
And a drawing the corks of train-oil-flasks,
And a breaking the hoops of butter-casks;
And it seemed as if a voice   135
(Sweeter far than by harp or by psaltery
Is breathed) called out, 'O rats, rejoice!
The world is grown to one vast drysaltery!

So munch on, crunch on, take your nunch-
  eon,
Breakfast, supper, dinner, luncheon!'   140
And just as a bulky sugar-puncheon,
All ready staved, like a great sun shone
Glorious scarce an inch before me,
Just as methought it said, 'Come, bore me!'
— I found the Weser rolling o'er me."   145

8

You should have heard the Hamelin people
Ringing the bells till they rocked the steeple.
"Go," cried the Mayor, "and get long poles,
Poke out the nests and block up the holes!
Consult with carpenters and builders,   150
And leave in our town not even a trace
Of the rats!" — when suddenly, up the face
Of the Piper perked in the market-place,
With a "First, if you please, my thousand
  guilders!"

9

A thousand guilders! The Mayor looked blue;
So did the Corporation too.   156
For council dinners made rare havoc
With Claret, Moselle, Vin-de-Grave, Hock;
And half the money would replenish
Their cellar's biggest butt with Rhenish.   160
To pay this sum to a wandering fellow
With a gypsy coat of red and yellow!
"Beside," quoth the Mayor with a knowing
  wink,
"Our business was done at the river's brink;
We saw with our eyes the vermin sink,   165
And what's dead can't come to life, I think.
So, friend, we're not the folks to shrink
From the duty of giving you something for
  drink,
And a matter of money to put in your poke;
But as for the guilders, what we spoke   170
Of them, as you very well know, was in joke.
Beside, our losses have made us thrifty.
A thousand guilders! Come, take fifty!"

10

The Piper's face fell, and he cried,
"No trifling! I can't wait, beside!   175
I've promised to visit by dinner time
Bagdat, and accept the prime
Of the Head-Cook's pottage, all he's rich in,
For having left, in the Caliph's kitchen,
Of a nest of scorpions no survivor;   180
With him I proved no bargain-driver,
With you, don't think I'll bate a stiver!
And folks who put me in a passion
May find me pipe after another fashion."

---

91. **Nizam**, the title of the ruler of Hyderabad, the chief state of India. 123-126. **Cæsar . . . commentary.** At the siege of Alexandria, Egypt, in 48 B.C., Cæsar's ship was captured, and Cæsar had to swim for his life. It is said that he carried with him the manuscript of his *Commentaries on the Gallic War*, a record of his campaign in Gaul. 133. **train-oil-flasks**, bottles containing whale oil.

139. **nuncheon**, light lunch. 158. **Claret . . . Hock.** These are all names of wines. 177. **Bagdat**, Bagdad, a city in Mesopotamia, in Asia. 182. **stiver**, a Dutch coin worth about two cents.

11

"How?" cried the Mayor, "d'ye think I brook
Being worse treated than a Cook?   186
Insulted by a lazy ribald
With idle pipe and vesture piebald?
You threaten us, fellow? Do your worst,
Blow your pipe there till you burst!"   190

12

Once more he stepped into the street,
    And to his lips again
Laid his long pipe of smooth straight cane;
    And ere he blew three notes (such sweet
Soft notes as yet musician's cunning   195
    Never gave the enraptured air)
There was a rustling that seemed like a bus-
    tling
Of merry crowds justling at pitching and hus-
    tling;
Small feet were pattering, wooden shoes clat-
    tering,
Little hands clapping and little tongues chat-
    tering,   200
And, like fowls in a farm-yard when barley is
    scattering,
Out came the children running.
All the little boys and girls,
With rosy cheeks and flaxen curls,
And sparkling eyes and teeth like pearls,   205
Tripping and skipping, ran merrily after
The wonderful music with shouting and laugh-
    ter.

13

The Mayor was dumb, and the Council stood
As if they were changed into blocks of wood,
Unable to move a step, or cry   210
To the children merrily skipping by,
— Could only follow with the eye
That joyous crowd at the Piper's back.
But how the Mayor was on the rack,
And the wretched Council's bosoms beat, 215
As the Piper turned from the High Street
To where the Weser rolled its waters
Right in the way of their sons and daughters!
However, he turned from South to West,
And to Koppelberg Hill his steps addressed,
And after him the children pressed;   221
Great was the joy in every breast.
"He never can cross that mighty top!
He's forced to let the piping drop,
And we shall see our children stop!"   225
When, lo, as they reached the mountain-side,
A wondrous portal opened wide,
As if a cavern was suddenly hollowed;
And the Piper advanced and the children fol-
    lowed,
And when all were in to the very last,   230
The door in the mountain-side shut fast.
Did I say all? No! One was lame,

And could not dance the whole of the way;
And in after years, if you would blame
His sadness, he was used to say —   235
"It's dull in our town since my playmates left!
I can't forget that I'm bereft
Of all the pleasant sights they see,
Which the Piper also promised me.
For he led us, he said, to a joyous land,   240
Joining the town and just at hand,
Where waters gushed and fruit-trees grew
And flowers put forth a fairer hue,
And everything was strange and new;
The sparrows were brighter than peacocks
    here,   245
And their dogs outran our fallow deer,
And honey-bees had lost their stings,
And horses were born with eagles' wings;
And just as I became assured
My lame foot would be speedily cured,   250
The music stopped and I stood still,
And found myself outside the hill,
Left alone against my will,
To go now limping as before,
And never hear of that country more!"   255

14

Alas, alas for Hamelin!
    There came into many a burgher's pate
    A text which says that heaven's gate
    Opes to the rich at as easy rate
As the needle's eye takes a camel in!   260
The Mayor sent East, West, North and South,
To offer the Piper, by word of mouth,
    Wherever it was men's lot to find him,
Silver and gold to his heart's content,
If he'd only return the way he went,   265
    And bring the children behind him.
But when they saw 'twas a lost endeavor,
And Piper and dancers were gone forever,
They made a decree that lawyers never
    Should think their records dated duly   270
If, after the day of the month and year,
These words did not as well appear,
"And so long after what happened here
    On the Twenty-second of July,
Thirteen hundred and seventy-six":   275
And the better in memory to fix
The place of the children's last retreat,
They called it, the Pied Piper's Street —
Where anyone playing on pipe or tabor
Was sure for the future to lose his labor.   280
Nor suffered they hostelry or tavern
    To shock with mirth a street so solemn;
But opposite the place of the cavern
    They wrote the story on a column,
And on the great church-window painted 285
The same, to make the world acquainted

258-260. A text . . . camel in. From *Matthew*, 19:24.—
"It is easier for a camel to go through the eye of a needle
than for a rich man to enter into the kingdom of God."

How their children were stolen away,
And there it stands to this very day.
And I must not omit to say
That in Transylvania there's a tribe   290
Of alien people who ascribe
.The outlandish ways and dress
On which their neighbors lay such stress,
To their fathers and mothers having risen
Out of some subterraneous prison   295
Into which they were trepanned
Long time ago in a mighty band
Out of Hamelin town in Brunswick land,
But how or why, they don't understand.

15

So, Willy, let me and you be wipers   300
Of scores out with all men — especially pipers!
And, whether they pipe us free frόm rats or
     frόm mice,
If we've promised them aught, let us keep our
     promise!   (1842)

COUNT GISMOND

AIX IN PROVENCE

Christ God who savest man, save most
   Of men Count Gismond, who saved me!
Count Gauthier, when he chose his post,
   Chose time and place and company
To suit it; when he struck at length   5
My honor, 'twas with all his strength.

And doubtlessly ere he could draw
   All points to one, he must have schemed!
That miserable morning saw
   Few half so happy as I seemed,   10
While being dressed in queen's array
To give our tourney prize away.

I thought they loved me, did me grace
   To please themselves; 'twas all their deed;
God makes, or fair or foul, our face;   15
   If showing mine so caused to bleed
My cousins' hearts, they should have dropped
A word, and straight the play had stopped.

They, too, so beauteous! Each a queen
   By virtue of her brow and breast;   20
Not needing to be crowned, I mean,
   As I do. E'en when I was dressed,
Had either of them spoke, instead
Of glancing sideways with still head!

But no; they let me laugh, and sing   25
   My birthday song quite through, adjust

The last rose in my garland, fling
   A last look on the mirror, trust
My arms to each an arm of theirs,
And so descend the castle-stairs —   30

And come out on the morning-troop
   Of merry friends who kissed my cheek,
And called me queen, and made me stoop
   Under the canopy — a streak
That pierced it, of the outside sun,   35
Powdered with gold its gloom's soft dun —

And they could let me take my state
   And foolish throne amid applause
Of all come there to celebrate
   My queen's-day — oh, I think the cause   40
Of much was, they forgot no crowd
Makes up for parents in their shroud!

Howe'er that be, all eyes were bent
   Upon me, when my cousins cast
Theirs down; 'twas time I should present   45
   The victor's crown, but . . . there, 'twill last
No long time . . . the old mist again
Blinds me as then it did. How vain!

See! Gismond's at the gate, in talk
   With his two boys; I can proceed.   50
Well, at that moment, who should stalk
   Forth boldly — to my face, indeed —
But Gauthier, and he thundered, "Stay!"
And all stayed. "Bring no crowns, I say!

"Bring torches! Wind the penance-sheet   55
   About her! Let her shun the chaste,
Or lay herself before their feet!
   Shall she whose body I embraced
A night long, queen it in the day?
For honor's sake no crowns, I say!"   60

I? What I answered? As I live,
   I never fancied such a thing
As answer possible to give.
   What says the body when they spring
Some monstrous torture-engine's whole   65
Strength on it? No more says the soul.

Till out strode Gismond; then I knew
   That I was saved. I never met
His face before, but, at first view,
   I felt quite sure that God had set   70
Himself to Satan; who would spend
A minute's mistrust on the end?

He strode to Gauthier, in his throat
   Gave him the lie, then struck his mouth
With one back-handed blow that wrote   75

290. **Transylvania,** a region in northwest Rumania, formerly a part of Hungary.
   Count Gismond. The poem is spoken by a lady of the
court of Aix, in Provence, an old province in southeastern
France.

73-74. **in his throat . . . lie.** To lie in the throat is to
lie abominably. It is therefore more serious to accuse one
of lying in the throat than to accuse one of merely lying.

In blood men's verdict there. North, South,
East, West, I looked. The lie was dead,
And damned, and truth stood up instead.

This glads me most, that I enjoyed
  The heart of the joy, with my content 80
In watching Gismond unalloyed
  By any doubt of the event;
God took that on him — I was bid
Watch Gismond for my part. I did.

Did I not watch him while he let   85
  His armorer just brace his greaves,
Rivet his hauberk, on the fret
  The while! His foot . . . my memory leaves
No least stamp out, nor how anon
He pulled his ringing gauntlets on.   90

And e'en before the trumpet's sound
  Was finished, prone lay the false knight,
Prone as his lie, upon the ground;
  Gismond flew at him, used no sleight
O' the sword, but open-breasted drove,   95
Cleaving till out the truth he clove.

Which done, he dragged him to my feet
  And said, "Here die, but end thy breath
In full confession, lest thou fleet
  From my first, to God's second death! 100
Say, hast thou lied?" And, "I have lied
To God and her," he said, and died.

Then Gismond, kneeling to me, asked —
  What safe my heart holds, though no word
Could I repeat now, if I tasked   105
  My powers forever, to a third
Dear even as you are. Pass the rest
Until I sank upon his breast.

Over my head his arm he flung
  Against the world; and scarce I felt   110
His sword (that dripped by me and swung)
  A little shifted in its belt;
For he began to say the while
How South our home lay many a mile.

So 'mid the shouting multitude   115
  We two walked forth to never more
Return. My cousins have pursued
  Their life, untroubled as before
I vexed them. Gauthier's dwelling-place
God lighten! May his soul find grace!   120

Our elder boy has got the clear
  Great brow; though when his brother's black
Full eye shows scorn, it . . . Gismond here?
  And have you brought my tercel back?
I just was telling Adela   125
How many birds it struck since May. (1842)

124. **tercel**, a male falcon, used in hunting.

THE LABORATORY
ANCIEN RÉGIME

Now that I, tying thy glass mask tightly,
May gaze through these faint smokes curling
    whitely,
As thou pliest thy trade in this devil's-
    smithy —
Which is the poison to poison her, prithee?

He is with her, and they know that I know 5
Where they are, what they do; they believe
    my tears flow
While they laugh, laugh at me, at me fled to
    the drear
Empty church, to pray God in, for them! — I
    am here.

Grind away, moisten and mash up thy paste,
Pound at thy powder — I am not in haste! 10
Better sit thus, and observe thy strange things,
Than go where men wait me and dance at the
    King's.

That in the mortar — you call it a gum?
Ah, the brave tree whence such gold oozings
    come!
And yonder soft phial, the exquisite blue, 15
Sure to taste sweetly — is that poison too?

Had I but all of them, thee and thy treasures,
What a wild crowd of invisible pleasures!
To carry pure death in an earring, a casket,
A signet, a fan-mount, a filigree basket! 20

Soon, at the King's, a mere lozenge to give,
And Pauline should have just thirty minutes
    to live!
But to light a pastile, and Elise, with her head
And her breast and her arms and her hands,
    should drop dead!

Quick — is it finished? The color's too grim!
Why not soft like the phial's, enticing and
    dim? 26
Let it brighten her drink, let her turn it and
    stir,
And try it and taste, ere she fix and prefer!

What a drop! She's not little, no minion like
    me!
That's why she ensnared him; this never will
    free 30

The Laboratory. See Critical Notes. The subtitle suggests
the setting: the "old order," i.e., pre-Revolutionary France,
actually the time of Louis XIV. Browning's original seems to
have been Madame de Brinvilliers, an accomplished poisoner.
29. **minion**, a dainty or delicate person.

The soul from those masculine eyes — say
    "no!"
To that pulse's magnificent come-and-go.

For only last night, as they whispered, I
    brought
My own eyes to bear on her so, that I thought
Could I keep them one half minute fixed, she
    would fall   35
Shriveled; she fell not; yet this does it all!

Not that I bid you spare her the pain;
Let death be felt and the proof remain;
Brand, burn up, bite into its grace —
He is sure to remember her dying face!   40

Is it done? Take my mask off! Nay, be not
    morose;
It kills her, and this prevents seeing it close:
The delicate droplet, my whole fortune's fee!
If it hurts her, beside, can it ever hurt me?

Now, take all my jewels, gorge gold to your
    fill,   45
You may kiss me, old man, on my mouth if
    you will!
But brush this dust off me, lest horror it brings
Ere I know it — next moment I dance at the
    King's!   (1844)

THE BOY AND THE ANGEL

Morning, evening, noon, and night,
"Praise God!" said Theocrite.

Then to his poor trade he turned,
Whereby the daily meal was earned.

Hard he labored, long and well;   5
O'er his work the boy's curls fell.

But ever, at each period,
He stopped and sang, "Praise God!"

Then back again his curls he threw,
And cheerful turned to work anew.   10

Said Blaise, the listening monk, "Well done;
I doubt not thou art heard, my son,

"As well as if thy voice today
Were praising God, the Pope's great way.

"This Easter Day, the Pope at Rome   15
Praises God from Peter's dome."

Said Theocrite, "Would God that I
Might praise him that great way, and die!"

Night passed, day shone,
And Theocrite was gone.   20

With God a day endures alway,
A thousand years are but a day.

God said in heaven, "Nor day nor night
Now brings the voice of my delight."

Then Gabriel, like a rainbow's birth,   25
Spread his wings and sank to earth;

Entered, in flesh, the empty cell,
Lived there, and played the craftsman well;

And morning, evening, noon, and night,
Praised God in place of Theocrite.   30

And from a boy, to youth he grew;
The man put off the stripling's hue;

The man matured and fell away
Into the season of decay;

And ever o'er the trade he bent,   35
And ever lived on earth content.

(He did God's will; to him, all one
If on the earth or in the sun.)

God said, "A praise is in mine ear;
There is no doubt in it, no fear;   40

"So sing old worlds, and so
New worlds that from my footstool go.

"Clearer loves sound other ways;
I miss my little human praise."

Then forth sprang Gabriel's wings, off fell   45
The flesh disguise, remained the cell.

'Twas Easter Day; he flew to Rome,
And paused above Saint Peter's dome.

In the tiring-room close by
The great outer gallery,   50

With his holy vestments dight,
Stood the new Pope, Theocrite;

And all his past career
Came back upon him clear,

Since when, a boy, he plied his trade,   55
Till on his life the sickness weighed;

The Boy and the Angel. This legend presents one of Browning's deepest convictions, expressed in lines 37-38 and 78—
namely, that in service to God, the humblest is equal with the
highest. Cf. *Pippa Passes*, 190-195, p. 181. For a variation
of the theme, see Longfellow's *King Robert of Sicily.*

25. **Gabriel,** an angel whose duty was to bear comfort and
sympathy to man.

And in his cell, when death drew near,
An angel in a dream brought cheer;

And rising from the sickness drear,
He grew a priest, and now stood here. 60

To the East with praise he turned,
And on his sight the angel burned.

"I bore thee from thy craftsman's cell,
And set thee here; I did not well.

"Vainly I left my angel-sphere, 65
Vain was thy dream of many a year.

"Thy voice's praise seemed weak; it dropped—
Creation's chorus stopped!

"Go back and praise again
The early way, while I remain. 70

"With that weak voice of our disdain,
Take up creation's pausing strain.

"Back to the cell and poor employ;
Resume the craftsman and the boy!"

Theocrite grew old at home; 75
A new Pope dwelt in Peter's dome.

One vanished as the other died;
They sought God side by side. (1844)

"HOW THEY BROUGHT THE GOOD NEWS FROM GHENT TO AIX"

[16—]

I sprang to the stirrup, and Joris, and he;
I galloped, Dirck galloped, we galloped all
three;
"Good speed!" cried the watch, as the gate-
bolts undrew;
"Speed!" echoed the wall to us galloping
through;
Behind shut the postern, the lights sank to
rest, 5
And into the midnight we galloped abreast.

Not a word to each other; we kept the great
pace
Neck by neck, stride by stride, never changing
our place;
I turned in my saddle and made its girths
tight,

Then shortened each stirrup, and set the pique
right, 10
Rebuckled the cheek-strap, chained slacker
the bit,
Nor galloped less steadily Roland a whit.

'Twas moonset at starting; but while we drew
near
Lokeren, the cocks crew and twilight dawned
clear;
At Boom, a great yellow star came out to see;
At Düffeld, 'twas morning as plain as could
be; 16
And from Mecheln church-steeple we heard
the half-chime,
So Joris broke silence with, "Yet there is
time!"

At Aershot, up leaped of a sudden the sun,
And against him the cattle stood black every
one, 20
To stare through the mist at us galloping past,
And I saw my stout galloper Roland at last,
With resolute shoulders, each butting away
The haze, as some bluff river headland its
spray;

And his low head and crest, just one sharp ear
bent back 25
For my voice, and the other pricked out on
his track;
And one eye's black intelligence — ever that
glance
O'er its white edge at me, his own master,
askance!
And the thick heavy spume-flakes which aye
and anon
His fierce lips shook upwards in galloping on.

By Hasselt, Dirck groaned; and cried Joris,
"Stay spur!
Your Roos galloped bravely, the fault's not
in her, 31
We'll remember at Aix" — for one heard the
quick wheeze
Of her chest, saw the stretched neck and stag-
gering knees,
And sunk tail, and horrible heave of the flank,
As down on her haunches she shuddered and
sank. 36

So we were left galloping, Joris and I,
Past Looz and past Tongres, no cloud in the
sky;

How They Brought the Good News from Ghent to Aix. Ghent
is an important city in Belgium, about 100 miles from Aix,
or Aix-la-Chapelle, in West Prussia, Germany. The other
places mentioned in the poem lie between Ghent and Aix.
The date 16— suggests that the incident might have happened in the conflict between the Netherlands and Spain or
during the Thirty Years War. See Critical Notes.
5. postern, the rear gate of a castle or of a fortified city.

10. pique, the pommel of the saddle. 14. Lokeren,
12 miles from Ghent. 15. Boom, 16 miles from Lokeren.
16. Düffeld, 12 miles from Boom. 17. Mecheln, near
Düffeld. 19. Aershot, 15 miles from Düffeld. 31. Hasselt, 80 miles from Ghent. 38. Looz, Tongres. These
towns, and Dalhem (line 41), are off the direct route.

The broad sun above laughed a pitiless laugh,
'Neath our feet broke the brittle bright stub-
    ble like chaff;   40
Till over by Dalhem a dome-spire sprang
    white,
And "Gallop," gasped Joris, "for Aix is in
    sight!"

"How they'll greet us!" — and all in a mo-
    ment his roan
Rolled neck and croup over, lay dead as a
    stone;
And there was my Roland to bear the whole
    weight   45
Of the news which alone could save Aix from
    her fate,
With his nostrils like pits full of blood to the
    brim,
And with circles of red for his eye-sockets' rim.

Then I cast loose my buffcoat, each holster
    let fall,
Shook off both my jack-boots, let go belt and
    all,   50
Stood up in the stirrup, leaned, patted his ear,
Called my Roland his pet-name, my horse
    without peer;
Clapped my hands, laughed and sang, any
    noise, bad or good,
Till at length into Aix Roland galloped and
    stood.

And all I remember is—friends flocking round
As I sat with his head 'twixt my knees on the
    ground;   56
And no voice but was praising this Roland of
    mine,
As I poured down his throat our last measure
    of wine,
Which (the burgesses voted by common con-
    sent)
Was no more than his due who brought good
    news from Ghent.   60
                  (1845)

THE LOST LEADER

Just for a handful of silver he left us,
    Just for a riband to stick in his coat —
Found the one gift of which fortune bereft us,
    Lost all the others she lets us devote;
They, with the gold to give, doled him out
    silver,   5
    So much was theirs who so little allowed;
How all our copper had gone for his service!
    Rags — were they purple, his heart had
    been proud!

We that had loved him so, followed him,
    honored him,
    Lived in his mild and magnificent eye,   10
Learned his great language, caught his clear
    accents,
    Made him our pattern to live and to die!
Shakespeare was of us, Milton was for us,
    Burns, Shelley, were with us — they watch
    from their graves!
He alone breaks from the van and the free-
    men —   15
    He alone sinks to the rear and the slaves!

We shall march prospering — not through his
    presence;
    Songs may inspirit us — not from his lyre;
Deeds will be done — while he boasts his
    quiescence,
    Still bidding crouch whom the rest bade
    aspire;   20
Blot out his name, then, record one lost soul
    more,
    One task more declined, one more footpath
    untrod,
One more devils'-triumph and sorrow for
    angels,
    One wrong more to man, one more insult to
    God!
Life's night begins; let him never come back
    to us!   25
    There would be doubt, hesitation, and pain,
Forced praise on our part — the glimmer of
    twilight,
    Never glad confident morning again!
Best fight on well, for we taught him — strike
    gallantly,   29
    Menace our heart ere we master his own;
Then let him receive the new knowledge and
    wait us,
    Pardoned in heaven, the first by the throne!
                  (1845)

THE LOST MISTRESS

All's over, then; does truth sound bitter
    As one at first believes?
Hark, 'tis the sparrows' good-night twitter
    About your cottage eaves!

And the leaf-buds on the vine are woolly;   5
    I noticed that, today;
One day more bursts them open fully—
    You know the red turns gray.

Tomorrow we meet the same then, dearest?
    May I take your hand in mine?   10

The Lost Leader. See Critical Notes.

20. **whom,** the people generally, especially the lower
classes. 29. **Best fight on well,** addressed to the lost leader.

Mere friends are we — well, friends the merest
Keep much that I resign:

For each glance of the eye so bright and black
Though I keep with heart's endeavor —
Your voice, when you wish the snowdrops
    back,   15
Though it stay in my soul forever! —

Yet I will but say what mere friends say,
Or only a thought stronger;
I will hold your hand but as long as all may,
Or so very little longer!   20
                                      (1845)

EARTH'S IMMORTALITIES

FAME

See, as the prettiest graves will do in time,
Our poet's wants the freshness of its prime;
Spite of the sexton's browsing horse, the sods
Have struggled through its binding osier rods;
Headstone and half-sunk footstone lean awry,
Wanting the brick-work promised by-and-by;
How the minute gray lichens, plate o'er plate,
Have softened down the crisp-cut name and
    date!

LOVE

So, the year's done with!
    (*Love me forever!*)
All March begun with,
    April's endeavor;
May-wreaths that bound me   5
    June needs must sever;
Now snows fall round me,
    Quenching June's fever —
    (*Love me forever!*)   (1845)

MEETING AT NIGHT

The gray sea and the long black land;
And the yellow half-moon large and low;
And the startled little waves that leap
In fiery ringlets from their sleep,
As I gain the cove with pushing prow,   5
And quench its speed i' the slushy sand.

Then a mile of warm sea-scented beach;
Three fields to cross till a farm appears;
A tap at the pane, the quick sharp scratch
And blue spurt of a lighted match,   10
And a voice less loud, through its joys and
    fears,
Than the two hearts beating each to each!
                                      (1845)

PARTING AT MORNING

Round the cape of a sudden came the sea,
And the sun looked over the mountain's rim:
And straight was a path of gold for him,
And the need of a world of men for me.
                                      (1845)

SONG

Nay but you, who do not love her,
    Is she not pure gold, my mistress?
Holds earth aught — speak truth — above
    her?
    Aught like this tress, see, and this tress,
And this last fairest tress of all,   5
So fair, see, ere I let it fall?

Because you spend your lives in praising;
    To praise, you search the wide world over;
Then why not witness, calmly gazing,
    If earth holds aught — speak truth — above
        her?   10
Above this tress, and this, I touch
But cannot praise, I love so much!
                                      (1845)

HOME-THOUGHTS, FROM ABROAD

Oh, to be in England
Now that April's there,
And whoever wakes in England
Sees, some morning, unaware,
That the lowest boughs and the brushwood
    sheaf   5
Round the elm-tree bole are in tiny leaf,
While the chaffinch sings on the orchard bough
In England — now!

And after April, when May follows,
And the whitethroat builds, and all the swal-
    lows!   10
Hark, where my blossomed pear-tree in the
    hedge
Leans to the field and scatters on the clover
Blossoms and dewdrops — at the bent spray's
    edge —
That's the wise thrush; he sings each song
    twice over,
Lest you should think he never could recap-
    ture   15
The first fine careless rapture!
And though the fields look rough with hoary
    dew,

Parting at Morning. This is a sequel to the poem preceding. Here the speaker, the same man, emphasizes the fact
that with the morning the need of activity among men comes
to him. *Him* in line 3 refers to the sun.

All will be gay when noontide wakes anew
The buttercups, the little children's dower —
Far brighter than this gaudy melon-flower! 20
                                        (1845)

HOME-THOUGHTS, FROM THE SEA

Nobly, nobly Cape Saint Vincent to the
    Northwest died away;
Sunset ran, one glorious blood-red, reeking
    into Cadiz Bay;
Bluish 'mid the burning water, full in face
    Trafalgar lay;
In the dimmest Northeast distance dawned
    Gibraltar grand and gray;
"Here and here did England help me; how
    can I help England?" — say,   5
Whoso turns as I, this evening, turn to God
    to praise and pray,
While Jove's planet rises yonder, silent over
    Africa.
                                        (1845)

THE CONFESSIONAL
SPAIN

It is a lie — their Priests, their Pope,
Their Saints, their . . . all they fear or hope
Are lies, and lies — there! through my door
And ceiling, there! and walls and floor,
There, lies, they lie — shall still be hurled 5
Till spite of them I reach the world!

You think Priests just and holy men!
Before they put me in this den
I was a human creature too,
With flesh and blood like one of you,   10
A girl that laughed in beauty's pride
Like lilies in your world outside.

I had a lover — shame avaunt!
This poor wrenched body, grim and gaunt,
Was kissed all over till it burned,   15
By lips the truest, love e'er turned
His heart's own tint; one night they kissed
My soul out in a burning mist.

Home-Thoughts, from the Sea. Browning wrote this poem
one evening in April while on shipboard off the northwest
coast of Africa on his first voyage to Italy.
    1. **Cape Saint Vincent**, the southwestern point of Portu-
gal, near which in 1797 England won a naval victory over
Spain. 2. **Cadiz Bay**, on the southern coast of Spain, east
of Cape St. Vincent, where in 1596 an English fleet destroyed
the second Spanish Armada. 3. **Trafalgar**, a cape east of
Cadiz Bay, off which Lord Nelson won his greatest victory
over the French and Spanish fleets in 1805. 4. **Gibraltar**,
the famous British stronghold at the entrance to the Mediterranean. It was acquired from Spain by the Peace of Utrecht
in 1713. 7. **Jove's planet**, Jupiter.
    The Confessional. This poem relates an incident as of
the period of the persecutions by the Spanish Inquisition of
the sixteenth century and later.

So, next day when the accustomed train
Of things grew round my sense again,   20
"That is a sin," I said; and slow
With downcast eyes to church I go,
And pass to the confession-chair,
And tell the old mild father there.

But when I falter Beltran's name,   25
"Ha!" quoth the father, "much I blame
The sin; yet wherefore idly grieve?
Despair not — strenuously retrieve!
Nay, I will turn this love of thine
To lawful love, almost divine;   30

"For he is young, and led astray,
This Beltran, and he schemes, men say,
To change the laws of church and state;
So, thine shall be an angel's fate,
Who, ere the thunder breaks, should roll 35
Its cloud away and save his soul.

"For, when he lies upon thy breast,
Thou mayest demand and be possessed
Of all his plans, and next day steal
To me, and all those plans reveal,   40
That I and every priest, to purge
His soul, may fast and use the scourge."

That father's beard was long and white,
With love and truth his brow seemed bright;
I went back, all on fire with joy,   45
And, that same evening, bade the boy
Tell me, as lovers should, heart-free,
Something to prove his love of me.

He told me what he would not tell
For hope of heaven or fear of hell;   50
And I lay listening in such pride!
And, soon as he had left my side,
Tripped to the church by morning-light
To save his soul in his despite.

I told the father all his schemes,   55
Who were his comrades, what their dreams;
"And now make haste," I said, "to pray
The one spot from his soul away;
Tonight he comes, but not the same
Will look!" At night he never came.   60

Nor next night; on the after-morn,
I went forth with a strength new-born.
The church was empty; something drew
My steps into the street; I knew
It led me to the market-place—   65
Where, lo, on high, the father's face!

That horrible black scaffold dressed,
That stapled block — God sink the rest!
That head strapped back, that blinding vest,
Those knotted hands and naked breast,   70

Till near one busy hangman pressed,
And on the neck these arms caressed . . .

No part in aught they hope or fear!
No heaven with them, no hell! — and here,
No earth, not so much space as pens   75
My body in their worst of dens
But shall bear God and man my cry,
Lies — lies, again — and still, they lie!

                                        (1845)

THE GLOVE

(PETER RONSARD *loquitur*)

"Heigho," yawned one day King Francis,
"Distance all value enhances!
When a man's busy, why, leisure
Strikes him as wonderful pleasure;
'Faith, and at leisure once is he?   5
Straightway he wants to be busy.
Here we've got peace; and aghast I'm
Caught thinking war the true pastime.
Is there a reason in meter?
Give us your speech, master Peter!"   10
I who, if mortal dare say so,
Ne'er am at loss with my Naso,
"Sire," I replied, "joys prove cloudlets;
Men are the merest Ixions" —
Here the King whistled aloud, "Let's   15
— Heigho — go look at our lions!"
Such are the sorrowful chances
If you talk fine to King Francis.

And so, to the courtyard proceeding
Our company, Francis was leading,   20
Increased by new followers tenfold
Before he arrived at the penfold;
Lords, ladies, like clouds which bedizen
At sunset the western horizon.
And Sir De Lorge pressed 'mid the foremost
With the dame he professed to adore most. 26
Oh, what a face! One by fits eyed
Her, and the horrible pitside;
For the penfold surrounded a hollow
Which led where the eye scarce dared follow,
And shelved to the chamber secluded   31
Where Bluebeard, the great lion, brooded.
The King hailed his keeper, an Arab
As glossy and black as a scarab,

And bade him make sport and at once stir 35
Up and out of his den the old monster.
They opened a hole in the wire-work
Across it, and dropped there a firework,
And fled; one's heart's beating redoubled;
A pause, while the pit's mouth was troubled,
The blackness and silence so utter,   41
By the firework's slow sparkling and sputter;
Then earth in a sudden contortion
Gave out to our gaze her abortion.
Such a brute! Were I friend Clement Marot
(Whose experience of nature's but narrow, 46
And whose faculties move in no small mist
When he versifies David the Psalmist)
I should study that brute to describe you
Illum Juda Leonem de Tribu.   50

One's whole blood grew curdling and creepy
To see the black mane, vast and heapy,
The tail in the air stiff and straining,
The wide eyes, nor waxing nor waning,
As over the barrier which bounded   55
His platform, and us who surrounded
The barrier, they reached and they rested
On space that might stand him in best stead;
For who knew, he thought, what the amaze-
          ment,
The eruption of clatter and blaze meant, 60
And if, in this minute of wonder,
No outlet, 'mid lightning and thunder,
Lay broad, and, his shackles all shivered,
The lion at last was delivered?
Aye, that was the open sky o'er head!   65
And you saw by the flash on his forehead,
By the hope in those eyes wide and steady,
He was leagues in the desert already,
Driving the flocks up the mountain,
Or catlike couched hard by the fountain   70
To waylay the date-gathering negress;
So guarded he entrance or egress.
"How he stands!" quoth the King; "we may
          well swear
(No novice, we've won our spurs elsewhere
And so can afford the confession)   75
We exercise wholesome discretion
In keeping aloof from his threshold;
Once hold you, those jaws want no fresh
          hold—
Their first would too pleasantly purloin
The visitor's brisket or surloin;   80
But who's he would prove so foolhardy?
Not the best man of Marignan, pardie!"

The sentence no sooner was uttered,
Than over the rails a glove fluttered,

The Glove. The incident here related is supposed to be
told by Pierre de Ronsard, a famous French poet of the 16th
century. The story has also been told by a French writer,
St. Croix (1746-1809) in *Essais Historiques sur Paris;* by
the German poet Schiller (1759-1805) in *Der Handschuh;*
and by Leigh Hunt (1784-1859) in *The Glove and the Lions.*
1. **King Francis,** Francis I (1494-1547), king of France.
12. **Naso,** Ovid (Publius Ovidius Naso), a famous Roman
poet (43 B.C.-18 A.D.). 14. **Ixions.** Ixion was a king in
Greek mythology who loved Hera, queen of the gods and wife
of Zeus. She sent him a cloud in her shape, by which he
became father of the race of centaurs. For his presumption
he was bound in Hades to an endlessly revolving wheel.
34. **scarab,** a large black dung beetle.

45. **Clement Marot,** a famous French court poet (1496-
1544) who versified forty-nine of the Psalms, ascribed to
David. 50. **Illum . . . Tribu,** that lion of the tribe of
Judah. 82. **Marignan,** Melegnano, an Italian town ten
miles southeast of Milan. **pardie,** surely (originally an oath,
meaning *by God*).

Fell close to the lion, and rested;   85
The dame 'twas, who flung it and jested
With life so, De Lorge had been wooing
For months past; he sat there pursuing
His suit, weighing out with nonchalance
Fine speeches like gold from a balance.   90

Sound the trumpet, no true knight's a tarrier!
De Lorge made one leap at the barrier,
Walked straight to the glove — while the lion
Ne'er moved, kept his far-reaching eye on
The palm-tree-edged desert-spring's sapphire,
And the musky oiled skin of the Kaffir —   96
Picked it up, and as calmly retreated,
Leaped back where the lady was seated,
And full in the face of its owner
Flung the glove.

"Your heart's queen, you dethrone her?   100
So should I!" — cried the King — " 'twas
          mere vanity,
Not love, set that task to humanity!"
Lords and ladies alike turned with loathing
From such a proved wolf in sheep's clothing.

Not so, I; for I caught an expression   105
In her brow's undisturbed self-possession
Amid the Court's scoffing and merriment —
As if from no pleasing experiment
She rose, yet of pain not much heedful
So long as the process was needful —   110
As if she had tried in a crucible,
To what "speeches like gold" were reducible,
And, finding the finest prove copper,
Felt the smoke in her face was but proper;
To know what she had *not* to trust to,   115
Was worth all the ashes and dust too.
She went out 'mid hooting and laughter;
Clement Marot stayed; I followed after,
And asked, as a grace, what it all meant?
If she wished not the rash deed's recallment?
"For I" — so I spoke — "am a poet;   121
Human nature — behooves that I know it!"

She told me, "Too long had I heard
Of the deed proved alone by the word;
For my love — what De Lorge would not dare!
With my scorn — what De Lorge could com-
          pare!   126
And the endless descriptions of death
He would brave when my lip formed a breath,
I must reckon as braved, or, of course,
Doubt his word — and moreover, perforce,   130
For such gifts as no lady could spurn,
Must offer my love in return.
When I looked on your lion, it brought
All the dangers at once to my thought,

Encountered by all sorts of men,   135
Before he was lodged in his den —
From the poor slave whose club or bare hands
Dug the trap, set the snare on the sands,
With no King and no Court to applaud,
By no shame, should he shrink, overawed,   140
Yet to capture the creature made shift,
That his rude boys might laugh at the gift
—To the page who last leaped o'er the fence
Of the pit, on no greater pretense
Than to get back the bonnet he dropped,   145
Lest his pay for a week should be stopped.
So, wiser I judged it to make
One trial what 'death for my sake'
Really meant, while the power was yet mine,
Than to wait until time should define   150
Such a phrase not so simply as I,
Who took it to mean just 'to die.'
The blow a glove gives is but weak;
Does the mark yet discolor my cheek?
But when the heart suffers a blow,   155
Will the pain pass so soon, do you know?"

I looked, as away she was sweeping,
And saw a youth eagerly keeping
As close as he dared to the doorway.
No doubt that a noble should more weigh   160
His life than befits a plebeian;
And yet, had our brute been Nemean —
I judge by a certain calm fervor
The youth stepped with, forward to serve her
—He'd have scarce thought you did him the
          worst turn   165
If you whispered, "Friend, what you'd get,
          first earn!"
And when, shortly after, she carried
Her shame from the Court, and they married,
To that marriage some happiness, maugre
The voice of the Court, I dared augur.   170

For De Lorge, he made women with men vie,
Those in wonder and praise, these in envy;
And in short stood so plain a head taller
That he wooed and won — how do you call
          her?
The beauty, that rose in the sequel   175
To the King's love, who loved her a week well.
And 'twas noticed he never would honor
De Lorge (who looked daggers upon her)
With the easy commission of stretching
His legs in the service, and fetching   180
His wife, from her chamber, those straying
Sad gloves she was always mislaying,
While the King took the closet to chat in —
But of course this adventure came pat in.
And never the King told the story,   185
How bringing a glove brought such glory,

96. **Kaffir,** a member of a South African tribe noted as lion hunters.

162. **our brute been Nemean,** referring to a monstrous lion in the valley of Nemea, in ancient Greece, slain by Hercules.

But the wife smiled — "His nerves are grown
    firmer;
Mine he brings now and utters no murmur."

Venienti occurrite morbo!
With which moral I drop my theorbo.   190
                      (1845)

TIME'S REVENGES

I've a Friend, over the sea;
I like him, but he loves me.
It all grew out of the books I write;
They find such favor in his sight
That he slaughters you with savage looks   5
Because you don't admire my books.
He does himself though — and if some vein
Were to snap tonight in this heavy brain,
Tomorrow month, if I lived to try,
Round should I just turn quietly,   10
Or out of the bedclothes stretch my hand
Till I found him, come from his foreign land
To be my nurse in this poor place,
And make my broth and wash my face
And light my fire and, all the while,   15
Bear with his old good-humored smile
That I told him "Better have kept away
Than come and kill me, night and day,
With, worse than fever throbs and shoots,
The creaking of his clumsy boots."   20
I am as sure that this he would do,
As that Saint Paul's is striking two.
And I think I rather . . . woe is me!

— Yes, rather should see him than not see,
If lifting a hand could seat him there   25
Before me in the empty chair
Tonight, when my head aches indeed,
And I can neither think nor read,
Nor make these purple fingers hold
The pen; this garret's freezing cold!   30

And I've a Lady — there he wakes,
The laughing fiend and prince of snakes
Within me, at her name, to pray
Fate send some creature in the way
Of my love for her, to be down-torn,   35
Upthrust and outward-borne,
So I might prove myself that sea
Of passion which I needs must be!
Call my thoughts false and my fancies quaint
And my style infirm and its figures faint,   40
All the critics say, and more blame yet,
And not one angry word you get.
But, please you, wonder I would put
My cheek beneath that lady's foot

Rather than trample under mine   45
The laurels of the Florentine,
And you shall see how the devil spends
A fire God gave for other ends!
I tell you, I stride up and down
This garret, crowned with love's best crown,
And feasted with love's perfect feast,   51
To think I kill for her, at least,
Body and soul and peace and fame,
Alike youth's end and manhood's aim —
So is my spirit, as flesh with sin,   55
Filled full, eaten out and in
With the face of her, the eyes of her,
The lips, the little chin, the stir
Of shadow round her mouth; and she
(I'll tell you) calmly would decree   60
That I should roast at a slow fire,
If that would compass her desire
And make her one whom they invite
To the famous ball tomorrow night.

There may be heaven; there must be hell; 65
Meantime, there is our earth here — well!
                      (1845)

THE ITALIAN IN ENGLAND

That second time they hunted me
From hill to plain, from shore to sea,
And Austria, hounding far and wide
Her blood-hounds through the country-side,
Breathed hot and instant on my trace —   5
I made six days a hiding-place
Of that dry green old aqueduct
Where I and Charles, when boys, have plucked
The fire-flies from the roof above,
Bright creeping through the moss they love —
How long it seems since Charles was lost! 11
Six days the soldiers crossed and crossed
The country in my very sight;
And when that peril ceased at night,
The sky broke out in red dismay   15
With signal fires; well, there I lay
Close covered o'er in my recess,
Up to the neck in ferns and cress,
Thinking on Metternich our friend,
And Charles's miserable end,   20

The Italian in England. The speaker is represented as an Italian patriot of the early 19th century active in one of the uprisings against the rule of Austria. He is a refugee in England. Mazzini (1805-1872), the famous revolutionary leader of Italy, who spent seven years of his exile in England, may well have gone through such experiences as are here related. The poem shows Browning's enthusiasm for Italian liberty. Cf. the story of Luigi and the Austrian police in *Pippa Passes*, III, pp. 192-194.
    8. **Charles**, Carlo Alberto (1798-1849), king of Sardinia, who had made terms with Austria. In 1831 he dealt severely with Mazzini's "Young Italy" and other patriotic secret societies. In 1848 he took the lead in a revolt against Austrian rule, but was defeated and forced to abdicate. 19. **Metternich**, a noted Austrian statesman (1773-1859), one of the most powerful enemies of Italian liberty.

189. **Venienti**, etc., encounter the approaching disease; or, meet trouble as it comes. 190. **theorbo**, a light stringed instrument.
    Time's Revenges. 22. **Saint Paul's**, a cathedral in London.

And much beside, two days; the third,
Hunger o'ercame me when I heard
The peasants from the village go
To work among the maize; you know,
With us in Lombardy, they bring   25
Provisions packed on mules, a string
With little bells that cheer their task,
And casks, and boughs on every cask
To keep the sun's heat from the wine;
These I let pass in jingling line,   30
And, close on them, dear noisy crew,
The peasants from the village, too;
For at the very rear would troop
Their wives and sisters in a group
To help, I knew. When these had passed, 35
I threw my glove to strike the last,
Taking the chance; she did not start,
Much less cry out, but stooped apart,
One instant rapidly glanced round,
And saw me beckon from the ground;   40
A wild bush grows and hides my crypt;
She picked my glove up while she stripped
A branch off, then rejoined the rest
With that; my glove lay in her breast.
Then I drew breath; they disappeared;   45
It was for Italy I feared.

  An hour, and she returned alone
Exactly where my glove was thrown.
Meanwhile came many thoughts; on me
Rested the hopes of Italy;   50
I had devised a certain tale
Which, when 'twas told her, could not fail
Persuade a peasant of its truth;
I meant to call a freak of youth
This hiding, and give hopes of pay,   55
And no temptation to betray.
But when I saw that woman's face,
Its calm simplicity of grace,
Our Italy's own attitude
In which she walked thus far, and stood,   60
Planting each naked foot so firm,
To crush the snake and spare the worm —
At first sight of her eyes, I said,
"I am that man upon whose head
They fix the price, because I hate   65
The Austrians over us; the State
Will give you gold — oh, gold so much! —
If you betray me to their clutch,
And be your death, for aught I know,
If once they find you saved their foe.   70
Now, you must bring me food and drink,
And also paper, pen, and ink,
And carry safe what I shall write
To Padua, which you'll reach at night
Before the duomo shuts; go in,   75
And wait till Tenebræ begin;

74. **Padua,** an important Italian city, about twenty miles
west of Venice. 75. **the duomo,** the most famous church in
Padua. 76. **Tenebræ,** Darkness, a religious service in the
Roman Catholic Church commemorating the Crucifixion.

Walk to the third confessional,
Between the pillar and the wall,
And kneeling whisper, *Whence comes peace?*
Say it a second time, then cease;   80
And if the voice inside returns,
From Christ and Freedom; what concerns
The cause of Peace? — for answer, slip
My letter where you placed your lip;
Then come back happy we have done   85
Our mother service — I, the son,
As you the daughter of our land!"

  Three mornings more, she took her stand
In the same place, with the same eyes;
I was no surer of sunrise   90
Than of her coming. We conferred
Of her own prospects, and I heard
She had a lover — stout and tall,
She said — then let her eyelids fall,
"He could do much" — as if some doubt   95
Entered her heart — then, passing out,
"She could not speak for others, who
Had other thoughts; herself she knew";
And so she brought me drink and food.
After four days, the scouts pursued   100
Another path; at last arrived
The help my Paduan friends contrived
To furnish me; she brought the news.
For the first time I could not choose
But kiss her hand, and lay my own   105
Upon her head — "This faith was shown
To Italy, our mother; she
Uses my hand and blesses thee."
She followed down to the seashore;
I left and never saw her more.   110

  How very long since I have thought
Concerning — much less wished for — aught
Beside the good of Italy,
For which I live and mean to die!
I never was in love; and since   115
Charles proved false, what shall now convince
My inmost heart I have a friend?
However, if I pleased to spend
Real wishes on myself — say, three —
I know at least what one should be.   120
I would grasp Metternich until
I felt his red wet throat distill
In blood through these two hands. And next—
Nor much for that am I perplexed —
Charles, perjured traitor, for his part,   125
Should die slow of a broken heart
Under his new employers. Last —
Ah, there, what should I wish? For fast
Do I grow old and out of strength.
If I resolved to seek at length   130
My father's house again, how scared
They all would look, and unprepared!
My brothers live in Austria's pay —
Disowned me long ago, men say;
And all my early mates who used   135

To praise me so — perhaps induced
More than one early step of mine —
Are turning wise; while some opine
"Freedom grows license," some suspect
"Haste breeds delay," and recollect   140
They always said, such premature
Beginnings never could endure!
So, with a sullen "All's for best,"
The land seems settling to its rest.
I think, then, I should wish to stand   145
This evening in that dear, lost land,
Over the sea the thousand miles,
And know if yet that woman smiles
With the calm smile; some little farm
She lives in there, no doubt. What harm 150
If I sat on the door-side bench,
And, while her spindle made a trench
Fantastically in the dust,
Inquired of all her fortunes — just
Her children's ages and their names,   155
And what may be the husband's aims
For each of them. I'd talk this out,
And sit there, for an hour about,
Then kiss her hand once more, and lay
Mine on her head, and go my way.   160

So much for idle wishing — how
It steals the time! To business now.

(1845)

PICTOR IGNOTUS

FLORENCE, 15—

I could have painted pictures like that youth's
Ye praise so. How my soul springs up!
No bar
Stayed me — ah, thought which saddens while
it soothes!
— Never did fate forbid me, star by star,
To outburst on your night with all my gift 5
Of fires from God; nor would my flesh have
shrunk
From seconding my soul, with eyes uplift
And wide to heaven, or, straight like thun-
der, sunk
To the center, of an instant; or around
Turned calmly and inquisitive, to scan 10
The license and the limit, space and bound,
Allowed to truth made visible in man.
And, like that youth ye praise so, all I saw,
Over the canvas could my hand have flung,
Each face obedient to its passion's law, 15
Each passion clear proclaimed without a
tongue;
Whether Hope rose at once in all the blood,
A-tiptoe for the blessing of embrace,
Or Rapture drooped the eyes, as when her
brood

Pictor Ignotus. The title means *The Unknown Painter.*
He is placed in Florence, Italy, in the 16th century.

Pull down the nesting dove's heart to its
place;   20
Or Confidence lit swift the forehead up,
And locked the mouth fast, like a castle
braved —
O human faces, hath it spilt, my cup?
What did ye give me that I have not saved?
Nor will I say I have not dreamed (how
well!)   25
Of going — I, in each new picture — forth,
As, making new hearts beat and bosoms swell,
To Pope or Kaiser, East, West, South, or
North,
Bound for the calmly satisfied great State,
Or glad aspiring little burgh, it went,   30
Flowers cast upon the car which bore the
freight,
Through old streets named afresh from the
event,
Till it reached home, where learned age should
greet
My face, and youth, the star not yet dis-
tinct
Above his hair, lie learning at my feet! — 35
Oh, thus to live, I and my picture, linked
With love about, and praise, till life should
end,
And then not go to heaven, but linger here,
Here on my earth, earth's every man my
friend —
The thought grew frightful, 'twas so wildly
dear!   40
But a voice changed it. Glimpses of such
sights
Have scared me, like the revels through a
door
Of some strange house of idols at its rites!
This world seemed not the world it was
before;
Mixed with my loving trusting ones, there
trooped   45
. . . Who summoned those cold faces that
begun
To press on me and judge me? Though I
stooped
Shrinking, as from the soldiery a nun,
They drew me forth, and spite of me . . .
enough!
These buy and sell our pictures, take and
give,   50
Count them for garniture and household-stuff,
And where they live needs must our pic-
tures live
And see their faces, listen to their prate,
Partakers of their daily pettiness,
Discussed of — "This I love, or this I hate, 55
This likes me more, and this affects me
less!"
Wherefore I chose my portion. If at whiles

41. **a voice,** the voice of his own peculiar genius.

My heart sinks, as monotonous I paint
These endless cloisters and eternal aisles
  With the same series, Virgin, Babe, and
    Saint,   60
With the same cold calm beautiful regard —
  At least no merchant traffics in my heart;
The sanctuary's gloom at least shall ward
  Vain tongues from where my pictures stand
    apart;
Only prayer breaks the silence of the shrine 65
  While, blackening in the daily candle-
    smoke,
They molder on the damp wall's travertine,
  'Mid echoes the light footstep never woke.
So, die my pictures! surely, gently die!
  O youth, men praise so — holds their praise
    its worth?   70
Blown harshly, keeps the trump its golden
  cry?
  Tastes sweet the water with such specks of
    earth?   (1845)

THE BISHOP ORDERS HIS TOMB AT SAINT PRAXED'S CHURCH

ROME, 15—

Vanity, saith the preacher, vanity!
Draw round my bed; is Anselm keeping back?
Nephews — sons mine . . . ah, God, I know
  not! Well —
She, men would have to be your mother once,
Old Gandolf envied me, so fair she was!   5
What's done is done, and she is dead beside,
Dead long ago, and I am Bishop since,
And as she died so must we die ourselves,
And thence ye may perceive the world's a
  dream.
Life, how and what is it? As here I lie   10
In this state-chamber, dying by degrees,
Hours and long hours in the dead night, I
  ask
"Do I live, am I dead?" Peace, peace seems
  all.
Saint Praxed's ever was the church for peace;
And so, about this tomb of mine. I fought 15
With tooth and nail to save my niche, ye
  know —
Old Gandolf cozened me, despite my care;
Shrewd was that snatch from out the corner
  South

He graced his carrion with, God curse the
  same!
Yet still my niche is not so cramped but
  thence   20
One sees the pulpit o' the epistle-side,
And somewhat of the choir, those silent seats,
And up into the aery dome where live
The angels, and a sunbeam's sure to lurk;
And I shall fill my slab of basalt there,   25
And 'neath my tabernacle take my rest,
With those nine columns round me, two and
  two,
The odd one at my feet where Anselm stands:
Peach-blossom marble all, the rare, the ripe
As fresh-poured red wine of a mighty pulse. 30
— Old Gandolf with his paltry onion-stone,
Put me where I may look at him! True peach,
Rosy and flawless; how I earned the prize!
Draw close; that conflagration of my church—
What then? So much was saved if aught
  were missed!   35
My sons, ye would not be my death? Go dig
The white-grape vineyard where the oil-press
  stood,
Drop water gently till the surface sink,
And if ye find . . . Ah, God, I know not, I! . . .
Bedded in store of rotten fig-leaves soft,   40
And corded up in a tight olive-frail,
Some lump, ah, God, of *lapis lazuli*,
Big as a Jew's head cut off at the nape,
Blue as a vein o'er the Madonna's breast . . .
Sons, all have I bequeathed you, villas, all, 45
That brave Frascati villa with its bath,
So, let the blue lump poise between my
  knees,
Like God the Father's globe on both his hands
Ye worship in the Jesu Church so gay,
For Gandolf shall not choose but see and
  burst!   50
Swift as a weaver's shuttle fleet our years;
Man goeth to the grave, and where is he?
Did I say basalt for my slab, sons? Black —
'Twas ever antique-black I meant! How else
Shall ye contrast my frieze to come beneath?
The bas-relief in bronze ye promised me,   56
Those Pans and Nymphs ye wot of, and per-
  chance

21. the epistle-side, the right-hand side as one faces the altar. The left is the gospel-side. **25. basalt,** a hard rock of dark color. **26. tabernacle,** a protecting canopy. **29. Peach-blossom marble,** exceptionally fine marble of a pinkish hue. **30. pulse,** a fruit mash. **31. onion-stone,** an inferior greenish marble that easily splits into thin layers like those of the onion. It is called *cipollino,* from *cipolla* (onion). **41. olive-frail,** a basket used for holding olives. **42. lapis lazuli,** a valuable blue stone, stolen by the Bishop from his own church. **46. Frascati,** a wealthy resort near Rome. **49. Jesu Church,** Il Gesu, the church of the Jesuits in Rome; it contains an image of God holding a globe made of lapis lazuli. **51. Swift . . . years.** From *Job,* 7:6.—"My days are swifter than a weaver's shuttle, and are spent without hope." **54. antique-black,** Nero-antico, a beautiful black marble. **57. Pans.** Pan was the god of flocks and pastures. The bas-relief was to contain a curious mixture of pagan and Christian symbols.

67. travertine, a kind of white limestone used for building.
  The Bishop Orders His Tomb at Saint Praxed's Church. This old church in Rome was named after a virgin, St. Praxed, or Praxedes, a Christian saint of the first century who used her riches in aiding the poor and the persecuted Christians. Both the Bishop and the tomb are imaginary. See Critical Notes.
1. Vanity, etc. From *Ecclesiastes,* 1:2.—"Vanity of vanities, saith the Preacher, vanity of vanities; all is vanity."
5. Old Gandolf, the Bishop's predecessor and rival.

Some tripod, thyrsus, with a vase or so,
The Savior at his sermon on the mount,
Saint Praxed in a glory, and one Pan 60
Ready to twitch the Nymph's last garment off,
And Moses with the tables . . . but I know
Ye mark me not! What do they whisper thee,
Child of my bowels, Anselm? Ah, ye hope
To revel down my villas while I gasp 65
Bricked o'er with beggar's moldy travertine
Which Gandolf from his tomb-top chuckles at!
Nay, boys, ye love me — all of jasper, then!
'Tis jasper ye stand pledged to, lest I grieve
My bath must needs be left behind, alas! 70
One block, pure green as a pistachio-nut,
There's plenty jasper somewhere in the
            world —
And have I not Saint Praxed's ear to pray
Horses for ye, and brown Greek manuscripts,
And mistresses with great smooth marbly
            limbs? 75
— That's if ye carve my epitaph aright,
Choice Latin, picked phrase, Tully's every
            word,
No gaudy ware like Gandolf's second line —
Tully, my masters? Ulpian serves his need!
And then how I shall lie through centuries, 80
And hear the blessed mutter of the Mass,
And see God made and eaten all day long,
And feel the steady candle-flame, and taste
Good strong thick stupefying incense-smoke!
For as I lie here, hours of the dead night, 85
Dying in state and by such slow degrees,
I fold my arms as if they clasped a crook,
And stretch my feet forth straight as stone
            can point,
And let the bedclothes, for a mortcloth, drop
Into great laps and folds of sculptor's-work; 90
And as yon tapers dwindle, and strange
            thoughts
Grow, with a certain humming in my ears,
About the life before I lived this life,
And this life too, popes, cardinals, and priests,
Saint Praxed at his sermon on the mount, 95
Your tall pale mother with her talking eyes,
And new-found agate urns as fresh as day,
And marble's language, Latin pure, discreet—
Aha, ELUCESCEBAT quoth our friend?

No Tully, said I, Ulpian at the best! 100
Evil and brief hath been my pilgrimage.
All *lapis*, all, sons! Else I give the Pope
My villas! Will ye ever eat my heart?
Ever your eyes were as a lizard's quick,
They glitter like your mother's for my soul, 105
Or ye would heighten my impoverished frieze,
Piece out its starved design, and fill my vase
With grapes, and add a visor and a term,
And to the tripod ye would tie a lynx
That in his struggle throws the thyrsus down,
To comfort me on my entablature 111
Whereon I am to lie till I must ask,
"Do I live, am I dead?" There, leave me,
            there!
For ye have stabbed me with ingratitude
To death — ye wish it — God, ye wish it!
            Stone — 115
Gritstone, a-crumble! Clammy squares which
            sweat
As if the corpse they keep were oozing
            through —
And no more *lapis* to delight the world!
Well, go! I bless ye. Fewer tapers there,
But in a row; and, going, turn your backs —
Aye, like departing altar-ministrants, 121
And leave me in my church, the church for
            peace,
That I may watch at leisure if he leers —
Old Gandolf — at me, from his onion-stone,
As still he envied me, so fair she was! (1845)

SAUL

I

Said Abner, "At last thou art come! Ere I
            tell, ere thou speak,
Kiss my cheek, wish me well!" Then I wished
            it, and did kiss his cheek.
And he: "Since the King, O my friend, for thy
            countenance sent,
Neither drunken nor eaten have we; nor until
            from his tent
Thou return with the joyful assurance the
            King liveth yet, 5
Shall our lip with the honey be bright, with
            the water be wet.
For out of the black mid-tent's silence, a space
            of three days,
Not a sound hath escaped to thy servants, of
            prayer nor of praise,

To betoken that Saul and the Spirit have
    ended their strife,
And that, faint in his triumph, the monarch
    sinks back upon life.   .10

2

"Yet now my heart leaps, O beloved! God's
    child with his dew
On thy gracious gold hair, and those lilies still
    living and blue
Just broken to twine round thy harp-strings,
    as if no wild heat
Were now raging to torture the desert!"

3

                        Then I, as was meet,
Knelt down to the God of my fathers, and
    rose on my feet,   15
And ran o'er the sand burnt to powder. The
    tent was unlooped;
I pulled up the spear that obstructed, and
    under I stooped;
Hands and knees on the slippery grass-patch,
    all withered and gone,
That extends to the second enclosure, I groped
    my way on
Till I felt where the foldskirts fly open. Then
    once more I prayed,   20
And opened the foldskirts and entered, and
    was not afraid
But spoke, "Here is David, thy servant!"
    And no voice replied.
At the first I saw naught but the blackness;
    but soon I descried
A something more black than the blackness —
    the vast, the upright
Main prop which sustains the pavilion; and
    slow into sight   25
Grew a figure against it, gigantic and blackest
    of all.
Then a sunbeam, that burst through the tent-
    roof, showed Saul.

4

He stood as erect as that tent-prop, both arms
    stretched out wide
On the great cross-support in the center, that
    goes to each side;
He relaxed not a muscle, but hung there as,
    caught in his pangs   30
And waiting his change, the king-serpent all
    heavily hangs,
Far away from his kind, in the pine, till deliv-
    erance come
With the spring-time — so agonized Saul,
    drear and stark, blind and dumb.

5

Then I tuned my harp — took off the lilies
    we twine round its chords
Lest they snap 'neath the stress of the noon-
    tide — those sunbeams like swords! 35
And I first played the tune all our sheep know,
    as, one after one,
So docile they come to the pen-door till folding
    be done.
They are white and untorn by the bushes, for
    lo, they have fed
Where the long grasses stifle the water within
    the stream's bed;
And now one after one seeks its lodging, as
    star follows star   40
Into eve and the blue far above us — so blue
    and so far!

6

— Then the tune for which quails on the corn-
    land will each leave his mate
To fly after the player; then, what makes the
    crickets elate
Till for boldness they fight one another; and
    then, what has weight
To set the quick jerboa a-musing outside his
    sand house —   45
There are none such as he for a wonder, half
    bird and half mouse!
God made all the creatures and gave them
    our love and our fear,
To give sign, we and they are his children, one
    family here.

7

Then I played the help-tune of our reapers,
    their wine-song, when hand
Grasps at hand, eye lights eye in good friend-
    ship, and great hearts expand   50
And grow one in the sense of this world's life.
    — And then, the last song
When the dead man is praised on his journey
    — "Bear, bear him along,
With his few faults shut up like dead flowerets!
    Are balm seeds not here
To console us? The land has none left such as
    he on the bier.
Oh, would we might keep thee, my brother!"
    — And then, the glad chaunt   55
Of the marriage — first go the young maidens;
    next, she whom we vaunt
As the beauty, the pride of our dwelling. —
    And then, the great march
Wherein man runs to man to assist him and
    buttress an arch
Naught can break; who shall harm them, our
    friends? Then, the chorus intoned

---

31. **king-serpent**, probably the boa-constrictor, waiting
the change that will come with the sloughing of his skin in
the spring.

42. **corn-land**, grain-land. 45. **jerboa**, the jumping hare,
a small jumping animal of the rat family.

As the Levites go up to the altar in glory
    enthroned.   60
But I stopped here; for here in the darkness
    Saul groaned.

8

And I paused, held my breath in such silence,
    and listened apart;
And the tent shook, for mighty Saul shud-
    dered; and sparkles 'gan dart
From the jewels that woke in his turban, at
    once with a start,
All its lordly male-sapphires, and rubies coura-
    geous at heart.   65
So the head; but the body still moved not,
    still hung there erect.
And I bent once again to my playing, pursued
    it unchecked,
As I sang:

9

"Oh, our manhood's prime vigor! No spirit
    feels waste,
Not a muscle is stopped in its playing nor
    sinew unbraced.
Oh, the wild joys of living! the leaping from
    rock up to rock,   70
The strong rending of boughs from the fir-
    tree, the cool silver shock
Of the plunge in a pool's living water, the hunt
    of the bear,
And the sultriness showing the lion is couched
    in his lair.
And the meal, the rich dates yellowed over
    with gold dust divine,
And the locust-flesh steeped in the pitcher,
    the full draft of wine,   75
And the sleep in the dried river-channel where
    bulrushes tell
That the water was wont to go warbling so
    softly and well.
How good is man's life, the mere living! how
    fit to employ
All the heart and the soul and the senses for-
    ever in joy!
Hast thou loved the white locks of thy father,
    whose sword thou didst guard   80
When he trusted thee forth with the armies,
    for glorious reward?
Didst thou see the thin hands of thy mother
    held up as men sung
The low song of the nearly-departed, and hear
    her faint tongue
Joining in while it could to the witness, 'Let
    one more attest,

I have lived, seen God's hand through a life-
    time, and all was for best'?   85
Then they sung through their tears in strong
    triumph, not much, but the rest.
And thy brothers, the help and the contest,
    the working whence grew
Such result as, from seething grape-bundles,
    the spirit strained true;
And the friends of thy boyhood—that boy-
    hood of wonder and hope,
Present promise and wealth of the future be-
    yond the eye's scope —   90
Till lo, thou art grown to a monarch; a people
    is thine;
And all gifts, which the world offers singly,
    on one head combine!
On one head, all the beauty and strength, love
    and rage (like the throe
That, a-work in the rock, helps its labor and
    lets the gold go),
High ambition and deeds which surpass it,
    fame crowning them — all   95
Brought to blaze on the head of one creature
    — King Saul!"

10

And lo, with that leap of my spirit — heart,
    hand, harp, and voice,
Each lifting Saul's name out of sorrow, each
    bidding rejoice
Saul's fame in the light it was made for — as
    when, dare I say,
The Lord's army, in rapture of service, strains
    through its array,   100
And upsoareth the cherubim-chariot—"Saul!"
    cried I, and stopped,
And waited the thing that should follow. Then
    Saul, who hung propped
By the tent's cross-support in the center, was
    struck by his name.
Have ye seen when Spring's arrowy summons
    goes right to the aim,
And some mountain — the last to withstand
    her, that held (he alone,   105
While the vale laughed in freedom and flowers)
    on a broad bust of stone
A year's snow bound about for a breastplate
    — leaves grasp of the sheet?
Fold on fold all at once it crowds thunderously
    down to his feet,
And there fronts you, stark, black, but alive
    yet, your mountain of old,
With his rents, the successive bequeathings of
    ages untold —   110
Yea, each harm got in fighting your battles,
    each furrow and scar
Of his head thrust 'twixt you and the tempest
    — all hail, there they are!
— Now again to be softened with verdure,
    again hold the nest

---

60. **Levites . . . enthroned.** The sons of Levi were
priests. An account of the service required of them appears
in *1 Chronicles*, 23:24-32. 65. **male-sapphire.** It reveals
a star of bright rays. The ruby shows a bright red light at
the center.

Of the dove, tempt the goat and its young to
    the green on his crest
For their food in the ardors of summer. One
    long shudder thrilled   115
All the tent till the very air tingled, then sank
    and was stilled
At the King's self left standing before me, re-
    leased and aware.
What was gone, what remained? All to tra-
    verse 'twixt hope and despair,
Death was past, life not come; so he waited.
    Awhile his right hand
Held the brow, helped the eyes left too vacant
    forthwith to remand   120
To their place what new objects should enter;
    'twas Saul as before.
I looked up and dared gaze at those eyes, nor
    was hurt any more
Than by slow pallid sunsets in autumn, ye
    watch from the shore,
At their sad level gaze o'er the ocean — a sun's
    slow decline
Over hills which, resolved in stern silence, o'er-
    lap and entwine   125
Base with base to knit strength more intensely;
    so, arm folded arm
O'er the chest whose slow heavings subsided.

11

            What spell or what charm
(For awhile there was trouble within me),
    what next should I urge
To sustain him where song had restored him?
    — Song filled to the verge
His cup with the wine of this life, pressing all
    that it yields   130
Of mere fruitage, the strength and the beauty;
    beyond, on what fields,
Glean a vintage more potent and perfect to
    brighten the eye
And bring blood to the lip, and commend them
    the cup they put by?
He saith, "It is good"; still he drinks not; he
    lets me praise life,
Gives assent, yet would die for his own part.

12

            Then fancies grew rife
Which had come long ago on the pasture,
    when round me the sheep   136
Fed in silence — above, the one eagle wheeled
    slow as in sleep;
And I lay in my hollow and mused on the
    world that might lie
'Neath his ken, though I saw but the strip
    'twixt the hill and the sky;
And I laughed — "Since my days are ordained
    to be passed with my flocks,   140

135. Pippa had fancies similar to those expressed in this
section. See *Pippa Passes*, 104-113, p. 180.

Let me people at least, with my fancies, the
    plains and the rocks,
Dream the life I am never to mix with, and
    image the show
Of mankind as they live in those fashions I
    hardly shall know!
Schemes of life, its best rules and right uses,
    the courage that gains,
And the prudence that keeps what men strive
    for." And now these old trains   145
Of vague thought came again; I grew surer;
    so, once more the string
Of my harp made response to my spirit, as
    thus —

13

          "Yea, my King,"
I began — "thou dost well in rejecting mere
    comforts that spring
From the mere mortal life held in common by
    man and by brute;
In our flesh grows the branch of this life, in
    our soul it bears fruit.
Thou hast marked the slow rise of the tree —
    how its stem trembled first   151
Till it passed the kid's lip, the stag's antler;
    then safely outburst
The fan-branches all round; and thou mindest
    when these too, in turn,
Broke a-bloom and the palm-tree seemed per-
    fect; yet more was to learn,
E'en the good that comes in with the palm-
    fruit. Our dates shall we slight,   155
When their juice brings a cure for all sorrow?
    or care for the plight
Of the palm's self whose slow growth produced
    them? Not so! stem and branch
Shall decay, nor be known in their place, while
    the palm-wine shall stanch
Every wound of man's spirit in winter. I pour
    thee such wine.
Leave the flesh to the fate it was fit for! the
    spirit be thine!   160
By the spirit, when age shall o'ercome thee,
    thou still shalt enjoy
More indeed, than at first when inconscious,
    the life of a boy.
Crush that life, and behold its wine running!
    Each deed thou hast done
Dies, revives, goes to work in the world; until
    e'en as the sun
Looking down on the earth, though clouds
    spoil him, though tempests efface, 165
Can find nothing his own deed produced not,
    must everywhere trace
The results of his past summer-prime — so,
    each ray of thy will,
Every flash of thy passion and prowess, long
    over, shall thrill
Thy whole people, the countless, with ardor,
    till they too give forth

A like cheer to their sons, who in turn, fill
    the South and the North   170
With the radiance thy deed was the germ of.
    Carouse in the past!
But the license of age has its limit; thou diest
    at last:
As the lion when age dims his eyeball, the rose
    at her height,
So with man — so his power and his beauty
    forever take flight.
No! Again a long draft of my soul-wine!
    Look forth o'er the years!   175
Thou hast done now with eyes for the actual;
    begin with the seer's!
Is Saul dead? In the depth of the vale make
    his tomb — bid arise
A gray mountain of marble heaped four-
    square, till, built to the skies,
Let it mark where the great First King slum-
    bers; whose fame would ye know?
Up above see the rock's naked face, where
    the record shall go   180
In great characters cut by the scribe — Such
    was Saul, so he did;
With the sages directing the work, by the
    populace chid —
For not half, they'll affirm, is comprised there!
    Which fault to amend,
In the grove with his kind grows the cedar,
    whereon they shall spend
(See, in tablets 'tis level before them) their
    praise, and record   185
With the gold of the graver, Saul's story —
    the statesman's great word
Side by side with the poet's sweet comment.
    The river's a-wave
With smooth paper-reeds grazing each other
    when prophet-winds rave;
So the pen gives unborn generations their due
    and their part
In thy being! Then, first of the mighty,
    thank God that thou art!"   190

14

And behold while I sang . . . but O Thou who
    didst grant me that day,
And before it not seldom hast granted thy
    help to essay,
Carry on and complete an adventure — my
    shield and my sword
In that act where my soul was thy servant,
    thy word was my word —
Still be with me, who then at the summit of
    human endeavor   195
And scaling the highest, man's thought could,
    gazed hopeless as ever
On the new stretch of heaven above me — till,
    mighty to save,

Just one lift of thy hand cleared that distance
    — God's throne from man's grave!
Let me tell out my tale to its ending — my
    voice to my heart
Which can scarce dare believe in what marvels
    last night I took part,   200
As this morning I gather the fragments, alone
    with my sheep,
And still fear lest the terrible glory evanish
    like sleep!
For I wake in the gray dewy covert, while
    Hebron upheaves
The dawn struggling with night on his shoul-
    der, and Kidron retrieves
Slow the damage of yesterday's sunshine.

15
           I say then — my song
While I sang thus, assuring the monarch, and
    ever more strong   206
Made a proffer of good to console him — he
    slowly resumed
His old motions and habitudes kingly. The
    right hand replumed
His black locks to their wonted composure,
    adjusted the swathes
Of his turban, and see — the huge sweat that
    his countenance bathes,   210
He wipes off with the robe; and he girds now
    his loins as of yore,
And feels slow for the armlets of price, with
    the clasp set before.
He is Saul ye remember in glory — ere error
    had bent
The broad brow from the daily communion;
    and still, though much spent
Be the life and the bearing that front you, the
    same God did choose   215
To receive what a man may waste, desecrate,
    never quite lose.
So sank he along by the tent-prop till, stayed
    by the pile
Of his armor and war-cloak and garments, he
    leaned there awhile,
And sat out my singing — one arm round the
    tent-prop, to raise
His bent head, and the other hung slack —
    till I touched on the praise   220
I foresaw from all men in all time, to the man
    patient there;
And thus ended, the harp falling forward.
    Then first I was 'ware
That he sat, as I say, with my head just above
    his vast knees,
Which were thrust out on each side around
    me, like oak roots which please

---

188. **paper-reeds,** papyrus plants, used as paper for writing
by the ancient Egyptians, Greeks, and Romans.

203. **Hebron,** one of the oldest cities of Palestine, situated
on a hill. 204. **Kidron,** a small brook near Jerusalem.
213-214. ere error . . . **communion,** a reference to God's
rejection of Saul because he disobeyed the command to
destroy all the Amalekites and all their possessions. See
the account in *1 Samuel*, 15.

To encircle a lamb when it slumbers. I looked
   up to know   225
If the best I could do had brought solace; he
   spoke not, but slow
Lifted up the hand slack at his side, till he
   laid it with care
Soft and grave, but in mild settled will, on my
   brow; through my hair
The large fingers were pushed, and he bent
   back my head, with kind power —
All my face back, intent to peruse it, as men
   do a flower.   230
Thus held he me there with his great eyes that
   scrutinized mine —
And, oh, all my heart how it loved him! but
   where was the sign?
I yearned — "Could I help thee, my father,
   inventing a bliss,
I would add, to that life of the past, both the
   future and this;
I would give thee new life altogether, as good,
   ages hence,   235
As this moment — had love but the warrant,
   love's heart to dispense!"

16

Then the truth came upon me. No harp more
   — no song more! Outbroke:

17

"I have gone the whole round of creation; I
   saw and I spoke;
I, a work of God's hand for that purpose, re-
   ceived in my brain
And pronounced on the rest of his handwork
   — returned him again   240
His creation's approval or censure; I spoke as
   I saw;
I report, as a man may of God's work — all's
   love, yet all's law.
Now I lay down the judgeship he lent me.
   Each faculty tasked
To perceive him, has gained an abyss, where
   a dewdrop was asked.
Have I knowledge? confounded it shrivels at
   Wisdom laid bare.   245
Have I forethought? how purblind, how blank,
   to the Infinite Care!
Do I task any faculty highest, to image suc-
   cess?
I but open my eyes — and perfection, no more
   and no less,
In the kind I imagined, full-fronts me, and
   God is seen God
In the star, in the stone, in the flesh, in the
   soul and the clod.   250

237. **Outbroke.** David first played on his harp (lines
36-60); then he sang (lines 68-190); and finally he spoke
(lines 238-312).

And thus looking within and around me, I
   ever renew
(With that stoop of the soul which in bending
   upraises it too)
The submission of man's nothing-perfect to
   God's all-complete,
As by each new obeisance in spirit, I climb to
   his feet.
Yet with all this abounding experience, this
   deity known,   255
I shall dare to discover some province, some
   gift of my own.
There's a faculty pleasant to exercise, hard to
   hoodwink,
I am fain to keep still in abeyance (I laugh as
   I think),
Lest, insisting to claim and parade in it, wot
   ye, I worst
E'en the Giver in one gift. — Behold, I could
   love if I durst!   260
But I sink the pretension as fearing a man
   may o'ertake
God's own speed in the one way of love; I
   abstain for love's sake.
—What, my soul? see thus far and no far-
   ther? when doors great and small,
Nine-and-ninety flew ope at our touch, should
   the hundredth appall?
In the least things have faith, yet distrust in
   the greatest of all?   265
Do I find love so full in my nature, God's
   ultimate gift,
That I doubt his own love can compete with
   it? Here, the parts shift?
Here, the creature surpass the Creator — the
   end, what Began?
Would I fain in my impotent yearning do all
   for this man,
And dare doubt he alone shall not help him,
   who yet alone can?   270
Would it ever have entered my mind, the bare
   will, much less power,
To bestow on this Saul what I sang of, the
   marvelous dower
Of the life he was gifted and filled with? to
   make such a soul,
Such a body, and then such an earth for in-
   sphering the whole?
And doth it not enter my mind (as my warm
   tears attest)   275
These good things being given, to go on, and
   give one more, the best?
Aye, to save and redeem and restore him,
   maintain at the height
This perfection — succeed with life's dayspring, death's minute of night?
Interpose at the difficult minute, snatch Saul
   the mistake,
Saul the failure, the ruin he seems now — and
   bid him awake   280

From the dream, the probation, the prelude,
    to find himself set
Clear and safe in new light and new life — a
    new harmony yet
To be run, and continued, and ended — who
    knows? — or endure!
The man taught enough by life's dream, of
    the rest to make sure;
By the pain-throb, triumphantly winning in-
    tensified bliss,   285
And the next world's reward and repose, by
    the struggles in this.

18

"I believe it! 'Tis thou, God, that givest,
    'tis I who receive;
In the first is the last, in thy will is my power
    to believe.
All's one gift; thou canst grant it moreover,
    as prompt to my prayer
As I breathe out this breath, as I open these
    arms to the air.   290
From thy will stream the worlds, life and na-
    ture, thy dread Sabaoth;
I will? — the mere atoms despise me! Why
    am I not loath
To look that, even that, in the face too? Why
    is it I dare
Think but lightly of such impuissance? What
    stops my despair?
This — 'tis not what man Does which exalts
    him, but what man Would do!   295
See the King — I would help him but cannot
    — the wishes fall through.
Could I wrestle to raise him from sorrow,
    grow poor to enrich,
To fill up his life, starve my own out, I would
    — knowing which,
I know that my service is perfect. Oh, speak
    through me now!
Would I suffer for him that I love? So wouldst
    thou — so wilt thou!   300
So shall crown thee the topmost, ineffablest,
    uttermost crown —
And thy love fill infinitude wholly, nor leave
    up nor down
One spot for the creature to stand in! It is by
    no breath,
Turn of eye, wave of hand, that salvation
    joins issue with death!
As thy Love is discovered almighty, almighty
    be proved   305
Thy power, that exists with and for it, of being
    Beloved!
He who did most shall bear most; the strong-
    est shall stand the most weak.
'Tis the weakness in strength that I cry for!
    my flesh, that I seek

In the Godhead! I seek and I find it. O Saul,
    it shall be
A Face like my face that receives thee; a Man
    like to me,   310
Thou shalt love and be loved by, forever; a
    Hand like this hand
Shall throw open the gates of new life to thee!
    See the Christ stand!"

19

I know not too well how I found my way
    home in the night.
There were witnesses, cohorts about me, to
    left and to right,
Angels, powers, the unuttered, unseen, the
    alive, the aware;   315
I repressed, I got through them as hardly, as
    strugglingly there,
As a runner beset by the populace famished
    for news —
Life or death. The whole earth was awakened,
    hell loosed with her crews;
And the stars of night beat with emotion, and
    tingled and shot
Out in fire the strong pain of pent knowledge;
    but I fainted not,   320
For the Hand still impelled me at once and
    supported, suppressed
All the tumult, and quenched it with quiet,
    and holy behest,
Till the rapture was shut in itself, and the
    earth sank to rest.
Anon at the dawn, all that trouble had with-
    ered from earth —
Not so much, but I saw it die out in the day's
    tender birth;   325
In the gathered intensity brought to the gray
    of the hills;
In the shuddering forests' held breath; in the
    sudden wind-thrills;
In the startled wild beasts that bore off, each
    with eye sidling still
Though averted with wonder and dread; in the
    birds stiff and chill
That rose heavily, as I approached them,
    made stupid with awe;   330
E'en the serpent that slid away silent — he
    felt the new law.
The same stared in the white humid faces up-
    turned by the flowers;
The same worked in the heart of the cedar
    and moved the vine-bowers;
And the little brooks, witnessing, murmured,
    persistent and low,
With their obstinate, all but hushed voices —
    "E'en so, it is so!"

                 (1845, 1855)

---

291. Sabaoth. The word literally means *armies* or *hosts.*
It indicates the omnipotence of God.

331. the new law, i.e., that God is infinite in love as well
as in power.

A WOMAN'S LAST WORD

Let's contend no more, Love,
  Strive nor weep;
All be as before, Love,
  —Only sleep!

What so wild as words are?   5
  I and thou
In debate, as birds are,
  Hawk on bough!

See the creature stalking
  While we speak!   10
Hush and hide the talking,
  Cheek on cheek!

What so false as truth is,
  False to thee?
Where the serpent's tooth is   15
  Shun the tree —

Where the apple reddens
  Never pry —
Lest we lose our Edens,
  Eve and I.   20

Be a god and hold me
  With a charm!
Be a man and fold me
  With thine arm!

Teach me, only teach, Love!   25
  As I ought
I will speak thy speech, Love,
  Think thy thought —

Meet, if thou require it,
  Both demands,   30
Laying flesh and spirit
  In thy hands.

That shall be tomorrow,
  Not tonight;
I must bury sorrow   35
  Out of sight —

Must a little weep, Love
  (Foolish me!),
And so fall asleep, Love,
  Loved by thee.   40
                    (1855)

EVELYN HOPE

Beautiful Evelyn Hope is dead!
  Sit and watch by her side an hour.
That is her book-shelf, this her bed;
  She plucked that piece of geranium-flower,
Beginning to die too, in the glass;   5

Little has yet been changed, I think:
The shutters are shut, no light may pass,
  Save two long rays through the hinge's
    chink.

Sixteen years old when she died!
  Perhaps she had scarcely heard my name;   10
It was not her time to love; beside,
  Her life had many a hope and aim,
Duties enough and little cares,
  And now was quiet, now astir,
Till God's hand beckoned unawares—   15
  And the sweet white brow is all of her.

Is it too late then, Evelyn Hope?
  What, your soul was pure and true,
The good stars met in your horoscope,
  Made you of spirit, fire, and dew—   20
And, just because I was thrice as old
  And our paths in the world diverged so wide,
Each was naught to each, must I be told?
  We were fellow mortals, naught beside?

No, indeed! for God above   25
  Is great to grant, as mighty to make,
And creates the love to reward the love;
  I claim you still, for my own love's sake!
Delayed it may be for more lives yet,
  Through worlds I shall traverse, not a few;
Much is to learn, much to forget   31
  Ere the time be come for taking you.

But the time will come — at last it will,
  When, Evelyn Hope, what meant (I shall
    say)
In the lower earth, in the years long still,   35
  That body and soul so pure and gay?
Why your hair was amber, I shall divine,
  And your mouth of your own geranium's
    red—
And what you would do with me, in fine,
  In the new life come in the old one's
    stead.   40

I have lived (I shall say) so much since then,
  Given up myself so many times,
Gained me the gains of various men,
  Ransacked the ages, spoiled the climes;
Yet one thing, one, in my soul's full scope,   45
  Either I missed or itself missed me:
And I want and find you, Evelyn Hope!
  What is the issue? let us see!

I loved you, Evelyn, all the while!
  My heart seemed full as it could hold;   50
There was place and to spare for the frank
    young smile,
  And the red young mouth, and the hair's
    young gold.
So, hush — I will give you this leaf to keep;

See, I shut it inside the sweet cold hand!
There, that is our secret; go to sleep!   55
   You will wake, and remember, and under-
     stand.   (1855)

LOVE AMONG THE RUINS

Where the quiet-colored end of evening smiles
   Miles and miles
On the solitary pastures where our sheep
   Half-asleep
Tinkle homeward through the twilight, stray
   or stop   5
     As they crop —
Was the site once of a city great and gay
   (So they say),
Of our country's very capital, its prince
   Ages since   10
Held his court in, gathered councils, wielding
   far
     Peace or war.

Now — the country does not even boast a
   tree,
     As you see,
To distinguish slopes of verdure, certain rills
   From the hills   16
Intersect and give a name to (else they run
   Into one),
Where the domed and daring palace shot its
   spires
     Up like fires   20
O'er the hundred-gated circuit of a wall
   Bounding all,
Made of marble, men might march on nor be
   pressed,
     Twelve abreast.

And such plenty and perfection, see, of grass
   Never was!   26
Such a carpet as, this summer-time, o'er-
   spreads
     And embeds
Every vestige of the city, guessed alone,
   Stock or stone —   30
Where a multitude of men breathed joy and
   woe
     Long ago;
Lust of glory pricked their hearts up, dread
   of shame
     Struck them tame;
And that glory and that shame alike, the gold
   Bought and sold.   36

Now — the single little turret that remains
   On the plains,
By the caper overrooted, by the gourd

Love among the Ruins. **39. caper,** a low prickly shrub of
the Mediterranean region.

Overscored,   40
While the patching houseleek's head of blossom winks
     Through the chinks —
Marks the basement whence a tower in ancient time
     Sprang sublime,
And a burning ring, all round, the chariots
   traced   45
     As they raced,
And the monarch and his minions and his
   dames
     Viewed the games.

And I know, while thus the quiet-colored eve
   Smiles to leave   50
To their folding, all our many-tinkling fleece
   In such peace,
And the slopes and rills in undistinguished
   gray
     Melt away —
That a girl with eager eyes and yellow hair
   Waits me there   56
In the turret whence the charioteers caught
   soul
     For the goal,
When the king looked, where she looks now,
   breathless, dumb
     Till I come.   60

But he looked upon the city, every side,
   Far and wide,
All the mountains topped with temples, all
   the glades'
     Colonnades,
All the causeys, bridges, aqueducts — and
   then,   65
     All the men!
When I do come, she will speak not, she will
   stand,
     Either hand
On my shoulder, give her eyes the first em-
   brace
     Of my face,   70
Ere we rush, ere we extinguish sight and
   speech
     Each on each.

In one year they sent a million fighters forth
   South and North,
And they built their gods a brazen pillar high
   As the sky,   76
Yet reserved a thousand chariots in full
   force —
     Gold, of course.
O heart! O blood that freezes, blood that
   burns!

41. houseleek, a common European plant with leaves
clustered in a kind of rosette. **65. causeys,** causeways—
that is, raised roads across low ground.

Earth's returns   80
For whole centuries of folly, noise and sin!
    Shut them in,
With their triumphs and their glories and the
    rest!
        Love is best.

                                        (1855)

UP AT A VILLA — DOWN IN THE CITY

(AS DISTINGUISHED BY AN ITALIAN PERSON OF
QUALITY)

Had I but plenty of money, money enough
    and to spare,
The house for me, no doubt, were a house in
    the city-square;
Ah, such a life, such a life, as one leads at the
    window there!

Something to see, by Bacchus, something to
    hear, at least!
There, the whole day long, one's life is a per-
    fect feast;   5
While up at a villa one lives, I maintain it,
    no more than a beast.

Well now, look at our villa! stuck like the
    horn of a bull
Just on a mountain-edge as bare as the crea-
    ture's skull,
Save a mere shag of a bush with hardly a leaf
    to pull!
— I scratch my own, sometimes, to see if the
    hair's turned wool.   10

But the city, oh, the city — the square with
    the houses! Why?
They are stone-faced, white as a curd, there's
    something to take the eye!
Houses in four straight lines, not a single front
    awry;
You watch who crosses and gossips, who
    saunters, who hurries by;
Green blinds, as a matter of course, to draw
    when the sun gets high;   15
And the shops with fanciful signs which are
    painted properly.

What of a villa? Though winter be over in
    March by rights,
'Tis May perhaps ere the snow shall have
    withered well off the heights;
You've the brown plowed land before, where
    the oxen steam and wheeze,
And the hills over-smoked behind by the faint
    gray olive-trees.   20

Up at a Villa—Down in the City. **4. Bacchus,** the god of
wine.

Is it better in May, I ask you? You've sum-
    mer all at once;
In a day he leaps complete with a few strong
    April suns.
'Mid the sharp short emerald wheat, scarce
    risen three fingers well,
The wild tulip, at end of its tube, blows out
    its great red bell
Like a thin clear bubble of blood, for the
    children to pick and sell.   25

Is it ever hot in the square? There's a foun-
    tain to spout and splash!
In the shade it sings and springs; in the shine
    such foambows flash
On the horses with curling fish-tails, that
    prance and paddle and pash
Round the lady atop in her conch — fifty
    gazers do not abash,
Though all that she wears is some weeds
    round her waist in a sort of sash.   30

All the year long at the villa, nothing to see
    though you linger,
Except yon cypress that points like death's
    lean lifted forefinger.
Some think fireflies pretty, when they mix i'
    the corn and mingle,
Or thrid the stinking hemp till the stalks of
    it seem a-tingle.
Late August or early September, the stun-
    ning cicala is shrill,   35
And the bees keep their tiresome whine round
    the resinous firs on the hill.
Enough of the seasons — I spare you the
    months of the fever and chill.

Ere you open your eyes in the city, the
    blessed church-bells begin;
No sooner the bells leave off than the dili-
    gence rattles in;
You get the pick of the news, and it costs you
    never a pin.   40
By and by there's the traveling doctor gives
    pills, lets blood, draws teeth;
Or the Pulcinello-trumpet breaks up the mar-
    ket beneath.
At the post-office such a scene-picture — the
    new play, piping hot!
And a notice how, only this morning, three
    liberal thieves were shot.

29. **conch,** shell. 32. **cypress.** The cypress, an emblem
of mourning, is a common tree in graveyards. 33. **corn,**
wheat and other small grains; not maize. 34. **thrid,** thread,
fly through. 42. **Pulcinello-trumpet,** the signal of strolling
players, announcing the coming of Pulcinello, the clown or
buffoon of the puppet show. 43. **scene-picture,** a picture
advertising some new play. 44. **liberal thieves,** members of
the liberal, or revolutionary, party, working for Italian freedom from Austrian control.

Above it, behold the Archbishop's most fa-
    therly of rebukes,   45
And beneath, with his crown and his lion,
    some little new law of the Duke's!
Or a sonnet with flowery marge, to the Rev-
    erend Don So-and-so,
Who is Dante, Boccaccio, Petrarca, Saint Je-
    rome, and Cicero,
"And moreover" (the sonnet goes riming),
    "the skirts of Saint Paul has reached,
Having preached us those six Lent-lectures
    more unctuous than ever he preached."
Noon strikes — here sweeps the procession!
    our Lady borne smiling and smart   51
With a pink gauze gown all spangles, and
    seven swords stuck in her heart!
Bang-whang-whang goes the drum, *tootle-te-*
    tootle the fife;
No keeping one's haunches still; it's the great-
    est pleasure in life.

But bless you, it's dear — it's dear! fowls,
    wine, at double the rate.   55
They have clapped a new tax upon salt, and
    what oil pays passing the gate
It's a horror to think of. And so, the villa for
    me, not the city!
Beggars can scarcely be choosers: but still —
    ah, the pity, the pity!
Look, two and two go the priests, then the
    monks with cowls and sandals,
And the penitents dressed in white shirts,
    a-holding the yellow candles;   60
Once, he carries a flag up straight, and another
    a cross with handles,
And the Duke's guard brings up the rear, for
    the better prevention of scandals;
Bang-whang-whang goes the drum, *tootle-te-*
    tootle the fife.
Oh, a day in the city-square, there is no such
    pleasure in life!

                (1855)

A TOCCATA OF GALUPPI'S

O Galuppi, Baldassare, this is very sad to
    find!
I can hardly misconceive you; it would prove
    me deaf and blind;
But although I take your meaning, 'tis with
    such a heavy mind!

Here you come with your old music, and
    here's all the good it brings.
What, they lived once thus at Venice where
    the merchants were the kings,   5
Where St. Mark's is, where the Doges used
    to wed the sea with rings?

Aye, because the sea's the street there; and
    'tis arched by—what you call —
Shylock's bridge with houses on it, where
    they kept the carnival.
I was never out of England — it's as if I saw
    it all.

Did young people take their pleasure when
    the sea was warm in May?   10
Balls and masks begun at midnight, burning
    ever to mid-day,
When they made up fresh adventures for the
    morrow, do you say?

Was a lady such a lady, cheeks so round and
    lips so red —
On her neck the small face buoyant, like a
    bell-flower on its bed,
O'er the breast's superb abundance where a
    man might base his head?   15

Well, and it was graceful of them — they'd
    break talk off and afford —
She, to bite her mask's black velvet — he, to
    finger on his sword,
While you sat and played Toccatas, stately
    at the clavichord?

47-50. sonnet . . . preached. The sonnet ranks the Reverend So-and-So with Dante (1265-1321), Boccaccio (1313-75), and Petrarch (1304-74), the three greatest Italian writers; with St. Jerome (340?-420), the most learned of the early Fathers of the Latin Church; with Cicero (106-43 B.C.), the famous Roman orator and statesman; and with St. Paul, the great Christian preacher of the first century A.D. **51. procession . . . borne,** a religious procession bearing an image of the Virgin Mary. **52. seven swords.** These symbolize the seven traditional sorrows of the Virgin Mary. These are: (1) her grief at the prophecy of Simeon that a sword should pierce her soul because of her Son (*Luke*, 2:34-35); (2) her affliction during the flight into Egypt (*Matthew*, 2:13-15); (3) her distress at the loss of her Son before finding Him in the Temple (*Luke*, 2:41-51); (4) her sorrow when she met her Son bearing His cross (*John*, 19:17); (5) her suffering at the sight of His agony (*John*, 19:25-30); (6) the wound to her heart when His side was pierced (*John*, 19:34); and (7) her agony at His burial (*Matthew*, 27:58-61). **56. a new tax upon salt.** A tax was levied upon all country produce brought into the city.

A Toccata of Galuppi's. A toccata (Italian *toccare*, to touch) is a musical composition characterized by lightness of tone and freedom of movement. Baldassare Galuppi (1706-1785) was a noted popular Italian musician and composer. During his last years he was organist at St. Mark's Cathedral in Venice. In the poem the toccata reveals to a serious Victorian the gay, empty life of Venice of the 18th century. Browning himself was fond of playing Galuppi. *A Toccata* is regarded as one of the finest of his music poems. Cf. *Abt Vogler*, p. 300. **6. St. Mark's,** the great cathedral in Venice. **Doges.** The Doge was the chief magistrate of the city. **to wed . . . rings.** The ceremony of "wedding the Adriatic" was instituted by Pope Alexander III in 1174. He gave the doge a ring in token of the victory of the Venetians over Frederick Barbarossa, emperor of Germany, and desired the doge to throw a similar ring into the sea annually in commemoration of the event. The ceremony denoted that the Adriatic Sea was subject to Venice as a wife was subject to her husband. **8. Shylock's bridge,** the Rialto, a bridge over the Grand Canal. **18. clavichord,** an old fashioned instrument with keys and strings, the predecessor of the modern piano.

What? Those lesser thirds so plaintive, sixths
    diminished, sigh on sigh,
Told them something? Those suspensions,
    those solutions — "Must we die?"   20
Those commiserating sevenths — "Life might
    last! we can but try!"

"Were you happy?"—"Yes."—"And are you
    still as happy?"—"Yes. And you?"
—"Then, more kisses!"—"Did *I* stop them,
    when a million seemed so few?"
Hark, the dominant's persistence till it must
    be answered to!

So, an octave struck the answer. Oh, they
    praised you, I dare say!   25
"Brave Galuppi! that was music! good alike
    at grave and gay!
I can always leave off talking when I hear a
    master play!"

Then they left you for their pleasure; till in
    due time, one by one,
Some with lives that came to nothing, some
    with deeds as well undone,
Death stepped tacitly and took them where
    they never see the sun.   30

But when I sit down to reason, think to take
    my stand nor swerve,
While I triumph o'er a secret wrung from
    nature's close reserve,
In you come with your cold music till I creep
    through every nerve.

Yes, you, like a ghostly cricket, creaking
    where a house was burned:
"Dust and ashes, dead and done with, Venice
    spent what Venice earned.   35
The soul, doubtless, is immortal — where a
    soul can be discerned.

"Yours for instance: you know physics, some-
    thing of geology,
Mathematics are your pastime; souls shall rise
    in their degree;
Butterflies may dread extinction — you'll not
    die, it cannot be!

"As for Venice and her people, merely born
    to bloom and drop,   40
Here on earth they bore their fruitage, mirth
    and folly were the crop;
What of soul was left, I wonder, when the
    kissing had to stop?

19-24. In these lines Browning uses a number of technical
musical terms the general meaning of which is made clear by
accompanying phrases. 35-43. The quotation in these lines
is what the music says to the speaker in the monologue concerning the men and women for whom life meant merely a
butterfly pleasure.

"Dust and ashes!" So you creak it, and I
    want the heart to scold.
Dear dead women, with such hair, too —
    what's become of all the gold
Used to hang and brush their bosoms? I feel
    chilly and grown old.   45

                (1855)

OLD PICTURES IN FLORENCE

The morn when first it thunders in March,
    The eel in the pond gives a leap, they say.
As I leaned and looked over the aloed arch
    Of the villa-gate this warm March day,
No flash snapped, no dumb thunder rolled   5
    In the valley beneath where, white and wide
And washed by the morning water-gold,
    Florence lay out on the mountain-side.

River and bridge and street and square
    Lay mine, as much at my beck and call,   10
Through the live translucent bath of air,
    As the sights in a magic crystal ball.
And of all I saw and of all I praised,
    The most to praise and the best to see,
Was the startling bell-tower Giotto raised;   15
    But why did it more than startle me?

Giotto, how, with that soul of yours,
    Could you play me false who loved you so?
Some slights if a certain heart endures
    Yet it feels, I would have your fellows
      know!   20
I' faith, I perceive not why I should care
    To break a silence that suits them best,
But the thing grows somewhat hard to bear
    When I find a Giotto join the rest.

On the arch where olives overhead   25
    Print the blue sky with twig and leaf
(That sharp-curled leaf which they never
      shed),
'Twixt the aloes, I used to lean in chief,
And mark through the winter afternoons,
    By a gift God grants me now and then,   30

Old Pictures in Florence. In this poem Browning emphasizes the idea that art is continuous, that each period of art
derives from the periods preceding. With this thought in
mind, the poet pays homage to the great souls of the past and
laments the fact that the world has forgotten them while
in the presence of later masters. He stresses also the idea that
the spiritual quality of art is far more important than perfection of artistic technique, that the soul surpasses the body as
a theme of art. Cf. *Andrea del Sarto,* 97-98, 112-117, 194-197,
pp. 289, 290.
    12. **a magic crystal ball,** a crystal sphere used in fortune-
telling. 15. **Giotto,** Giotto di Bondone (1276-1337), the
greatest of the early Florentine artists. The bell-tower, or
campanile, is that of the Cathedral of Florence. Giotto did
not live to complete the tower; it was to have had a spire 100
feet high. See lines 136, 276. 17-18. **Giotto . . . so.** For
an explanation of this humorous rebuke, see lines 233-40.
30. **a gift,** the gift of spiritual vision, the power to re-create
the past.

In the mild decline of those suns like moons,
  Who walked in Florence, besides her men.

They might chirp and chaffer, come and go
  For pleasure or profit, her men alive —
My business was hardly with them, I trow, 35
  But with empty cells of the human hive;
—With the chapter-room, the cloister-porch,
  The church's apsis, aisle or nave,
Its crypt, one fingers along with a torch,
  Its face set full for the sun to shave.   40

Wherever a fresco peels and drops,
  Wherever an outline weakens and wanes
Till the latest life in the painting stops,
  Stands One whom each fainter pulse-tick
    pains;
One, wishful each scrap should clutch the
    brick,   45
  Each tinge not wholly escape the plaster,
A lion who dies of an ass's kick,
  The wronged great soul of an ancient
    Master.

For, oh, this world and the wrong it does!
  They are safe in heaven with their backs
    to it,   50
The Michaels and Rafaels, you hum and buzz
  Round the works of, you of the little wit!
Do their eyes contract to the earth's old
    scope,
  Now that they see God face to face,
And have all attained to be poets, I hope? 55
  'Tis their holiday now, in any case.

Much they reck of your praise and you!
  But the wronged great souls — can they
    be quit
Of a world where their work is all to do,
  Where you style them, you of the little wit,
Old Master This and Early the Other,   61
  Not dreaming that Old and New are fel-
    lows;
A younger succeeds to an elder brother,
  Da Vincis derive in good time from Dellos.

And here where your praise might yield re-
    turns,   65
  And a handsome word or two give help,
Here, after your kind, the mastiff girns
  And the puppy pack of poodles yelp.
What, not a word for Stefano there,
  Of brow once prominent and starry,   70

Called Nature's Ape, and the world's despair
  For his peerless painting? (See Vasari.)

There stands the Master. Study, my friends,
  What a man's work comes to! So he plans
    it,
Performs it, perfects it, makes amends   75
  For the toiling and moiling, and then, *sic
    transit!*
Happier the thrifty blind-folk labor,
  With upturned eye while the hand is busy,
Not sidling a glance at the coin of their
    neighbor!
  'Tis looking downward that makes one
    dizzy.   80

"If you knew their work you would deal your
    dole."
  May I take upon me to instruct you?
When Greek Art ran and reached the goal,
  Thus much had the world to boast *in
    fructu—*
The Truth of Man, as by God first spoken,
  Which the actual generations garble,   86
Was re-uttered, and Soul (which Limbs be-
    token)
  And Limbs (Soul informs) made new in
    marble.

So you saw yourself as you wished you were,
  As you might have been, as you cannot be;
Earth here, rebuked by Olympus there;   91
  And grew content in your poor degree
With your little power, by those statues' god-
    head,
  And your little scope, by their eyes' full
    sway,
And your little grace, by their grace em-
    bodied,   95
  And your little date, by their forms that
    stay,

You would fain be kinglier, say, than I am?
  Even so, you will not sit like Theseus.
You would prove a model? The Son of Priam
  Has yet the advantage in arms' and knees'
    use.   100
You're wroth — can you slay your snake like
  Apollo?

72. **Vasari,** Giorgio Vasari (1511-74), author of *Lives of the Most Excellent Italian Architects, Painters, and Sculptors,* a work much used by Browning. 76. **sic transit,** a short form of *Sic transit gloria mundi*—so departs the glory of the world. 81. **If . . . dole,** the remark of a conventional critic. 84. **in fructu,** as fruit. Greek art achieved perfection of the human form in marble. 98. **Theseus,** the subject of a kingly statue in the frieze of the Parthenon, now in the British Museum. Theseus was a legendary hero, son of Ægeus, king of Athens. 99. **The Son of Priam,** Paris, the subject of a portion of the sculptures of Ægina. He is kneeling and drawing the bow, a model of grace and beauty. Priam was the last king of Troy. 101. **Apollo,** a statue of the god of manly youth and beauty, of wisdom, etc. At Delphi he slew an enormous python.

44. **One,** the spirit of one of the unappreciated early artists, lamenting the decay and the neglect of his frescoes. 50. **They,** the great artists like Michelangelo (1475-1564) and Raphael (1483-1520). 64. **Da Vinci,** Leonardo da Vinci (1452-1519), the famous medieval painter, musician, and engineer. **Dello.** Dello di Niccolo Delli was a painter and sculptor of the early 15th century. 67. **girns,** snarls. (When the influential critic speaks, all the little critics imitate him.) 69. **Stefano,** a pupil of Giotto, called "Nature's Ape" because of his marked realistic tendencies.

You're grieved — still Niobe's the grander!
You live — there's the Racers' frieze to fol-
　　low;
You die — there's the dying Alexander.

So, testing your weakness by their strength,
　　Your meager charms by their rounded
　　　beauty,　　　　　　　　　　　　106
Measured by Art in your breadth and length,
　　You learned — to submit is a mortal's duty.
—When I say "you" 'tis the common soul,
　　The collective, I mean: the race of Man 110
That receives life in parts to live in a whole,
　　And grow here according to God's clear
　　　plan.

Growth came when, looking your last on them
　　all,
　　You turned your eyes inwardly one fine day
And cried with a start — What if we so small
　　Be greater and grander the while than
　　　they?　　　　　　　　　　　　116
Are they perfect of lineament, perfect of stat-
　　ure?
In both, of such lower types are we
Precisely because of our wider nature;
　　For time, theirs — ours, for eternity.　　120

Today's brief passion limits their range;
　　It seethes with the morrow for us and more.
They are perfect — how else? they shall never
　　change.
　　We are faulty — why not? we have time in
　　　store.
The Artificer's hand is not arrested　　125
　　With us; we are rough-hewn, nowise pol-
　　　ished;
They stand for our copy, and, once invested
　　With all they can teach, we shall see them
　　　abolished.

'Tis a life-long toil till our lump be leaven —
　　The better! What's come to perfection
　　　perishes.　　　　　　　　　　130
Things learned on earth, we shall practice in
　　heaven;
　　Works done least rapidly, Art most cher-
　　　ishes.
Thyself shalt afford the example, Giotto!
　　Thy one work, not to decrease or diminish,
Done at a stroke, was just (was it not?)
　　"O!"　　　　　　　　　　　　135
　　Thy great Campanile is still to finish.

Is it true that we are now, and shall be here-
　　after,
　　But what and where depend on life's min-
　　　ute?
Hails heavenly cheer or infernal laughter
　　Our first step out of the gulf or in it?　140
Shall Man, such step within his endeavor,
　　Man's face, have no more play and action
Than joy which is crystallized forever,
　　Or grief, an eternal petrifaction?

On which I conclude, that the early painters,
　　To cries of "Greek Art and what more wish
　　　you?" —　　　　　　　　　146
Replied, "To become now self-acquainters,
　　And paint man, man, whatever the issue!
Make new hopes shine through the flesh they
　　fray,
　　New fears aggrandize the rags and tatters;
To bring the invisible full into play!　　151
　　Let the visible go to the dogs — what mat-
　　　ters?"

Give these, I exhort you, their guerdon and
　　glory
　　For daring so much, before they well did it.
The first of the new, in our race's story,　155
　　Beats the last of the old; 'tis no idle quiddit.
The worthies began a revolution,
　　Which if on earth you intend to acknowl-
　　　edge,
Why, honor them now! (ends my allocution)
　　Nor confer your degree when the folk leave
　　　college.　　　　　　　　　160

There's a fancy some lean to and others
　　hate —
　　That, when this life is ended, begins
New work for the soul in another state,
　　Where it strives and gets weary, loses and
　　　wins;
Where the strong and the weak, this world's
　　congeries,　　　　　　　　　165
　　Repeat in large what they practiced in
　　　small,
Through life after life in unlimited series;
　　Only the scale's to be changed, that's all.

Yet I hardly know. When a soul has seen
　　By the means of Evil that Good is best, 170
And, through earth and its noise, what is
　　heaven's serene —
　　When our faith in the same has stood the
　　　test —
Why, the child grown man, you burn the rod,

The uses of labor are surely done;
There remaineth a rest for the people of God;
And I have had troubles enough, for one. 176

But at any rate I have loved the season
　Of Art's spring-birth so dim and dewy;
My sculptor is Nicolo the Pisan,
　My painter — who but Cimabue? 180
Nor ever was man of them all indeed,
　From these to Ghiberti and Ghirlandajo,
Could say that he missed my critic-meed.
　So, now to my special grievance — heigh-
　ho!

Their ghosts still stand, as I said before, 185
　Watching each fresco flaked and rasped,
Blocked up, knocked out, or whitewashed
　o'er —
　No getting again what the church has
　grasped!
The works on the wall must take their chance;
　"Works never conceded to England's thick
　clime!" 190
(I hope they prefer their inheritance
　Of a bucketful of Italian quick-lime.)

When they go at length, with such a shaking
　Of heads o'er the old delusion, sadly
Each master his way through the black streets
　taking, 195
　Where many a lost work breathes though
　badly —
Why don't they bethink them of who has
　merited?
Why not reveal, while their pictures dree
Such doom, how a captive might be out-
　ferreted?
Why is it they never remember me? 200

Not that I expect the great Bigordi,
　Nor Sandro to hear me, chivalric, bellicose;
Nor the wronged Lippino; and not a word I
　Say of a scrap of Frà Angelico's;
But are you too fine, Taddeo Gaddi, 205

To grant me a taste of your intonaco,
　Some Jerome that seeks the heaven with a
　sad eye?
Not a churlish saint, Lorenzo Monaco?

Could not the ghost with the close red cap,
　My Pollajolo, the twice a craftsman, 210
Save me a sample, give me the hap
　Of a muscular Christ that shows the drafts-
　man?
No Virgin by him the somewhat petty,
　Of finical touch and tempera crumbly —
Could not Alesso Baldovinetti 215
　Contribute so much, I ask him humbly?

Margheritone of Arezzo,
　With the grave-clothes garb and swaddling
　barret
(Why purse up mouth and beak in a pet so,
　You bald old saturnine poll-clawed parrot?),
Not a poor glimmering Crucifixion, 221
　Where in the foreground kneels the donor?
If such remain, as is my conviction,
　The hoarding it does you but little honor.

They pass; for them the panels may thrill, 225
　The tempera grow alive and tinglish;
Their pictures are left to the mercies still
　Of dealers and stealers, Jews and the Eng-
　lish,
Who, seeing mere money's worth in their
　prize,
　Will sell it to somebody calm as Zeno 230
At naked High Art, and in ecstasies
　Before some clay-cold vile Carlino!

No matter for these! But Giotto, you,
　Have you allowed, as the town-tongues
　babble it —
Oh, never! it shall not be counted true — 235
　That a certain precious little tablet
Which Buonarroti eyed like a lover —
　Was buried so long in oblivion's womb
And, left for another than I to discover,
　Turns up at last! and to whom? — to
　whom? 240

179. **Nicolo the Pisan**, a famous architect and sculptor of the 13th century. 180. **Cimabue**, Giovanni Cimabue (1240-1302), noted for his beautiful Madonnas, was the inspiration of Giotto. 182. **Ghiberti**, Lorenzo Ghiberti (1381-1455), the great Florentine sculptor whose bronze doors of the Baptistery of Florence were said by Michelangelo to be worthy to be the gates of Paradise. **Ghirlandajo**, Domenico Ghirlandajo ("garland-maker"), a famous fresco painter of the 15th century. 185. **as I said before.** See lines 41-48. 192. **quick-lime.** They have been given a coat of whitewash. 198. **dree,** suffer, endure. 201. **Bigordi,** Ghirlandajo (see note on line 182). Bigordi was his family name. 202. **Sandro,** Sandro Botticelli (1457-1515), one of the most famous of Florentine painters. 203. **Lippino,** Filippino Lippi (1460-1505), son of Frà Lippo Lippi, a noted Florentine painter. He was wronged in the fact that others were credited with his work. 204. **Frà Angelico,** the professional name of Giovanni da Fiesole (1387-1455). He was a Dominican friar, the greatest of the distinctly Christian painters. 205. **Taddeo Gaddi,** both an architect and a painter (1300-1366). He was the godson and the pupil of Giotto and worked on the campanile after Giotto's death.

206. **intonaco,** the plaster-ground for fresco work. 207. **Jerome,** Saint Jerome (340?-420), the most learned of the early Fathers of the Latin Church. He translated the Bible into the Latin Vulgate. 208. **Lorenzo Monaco,** a monk and a conservative artist of the 14th century. 210. **Pollajolo,** Antonio Pollajolo (1430-98), a Florentine painter, sculptor, and goldsmith. 211. **the hap,** the good luck of finding. 214. **tempera,** paint made by mixing pigment and some substance like white of egg. 215. **Alesso Baldovinetti,** a Florentine painter and worker in mosaic (1422-99). 217. **Margheritone of Arezzo,** a painter, sculptor, and architect (1236-1313). His chief subject was the Crucifixion. 218. **barret,** a little flat cap. 230. **Zeno,** a Greek philosopher of the 3d century B.C. He founded the school of Stoics, noted for their calmness. 232. **some . . . Carlino,** that is, some inane picture by Carlo Dolci, an uninspired artist of the 17th century. 236. **a certain . . . tablet,** a beautiful *Last Supper* by Giotto, lost from the church of San Spirito and found while Browning was in Florence. The poet chides Giotto for allowing someone else to find the treasure. 237. **Buonarroti,** Michelangelo.

I, that have haunted the dim San Spirito
  (Or was it rather the Ognissanti?),
Patient on altar-step planting a weary toe!
  Nay, I shall have it yet! *Detur amanti!*
My Koh-i-noor — or (if that's a platitude) 245
  Jewel of Giamschid, the Persian Sofi's eye;
So, in anticipative gratitude,
  What if I take up my hope and prophesy?

When the hour grows ripe, and a certain
    dotard   249
  Is pitched, no parcel that needs invoicing,
To the worse side of the Mont St. Gothard,
  We shall begin by way of rejoicing;
None of that shooting the sky (blank cart-
    ridge),
  Nor a civic guard, all plumes and lacquer,
Hunting Radetzky's soul like a partridge 255
  Over Morello with squib and cracker.

This time we'll shoot better game and bag
    'em hot —
  No mere display at the stone of Dante,
But a kind of sober Witanagemot
  (Ex: "Casa Guidi," *quod videas ante*)   260
Shall ponder, once Freedom restored to Flor-
    ence,
  How Art may return that departed with
    her.
Go, hated house, go each trace of the Lor-
    aine's,
  And bring us the days of Orgagna hither!

How we shall prologuize, how we shall per-
    orate,   265
  Utter fit things upon art and history,
Feel truth at blood-heat and falsehood at
    zero rate,
  Make of the want of the age no mystery;
Contrast the fructuous and sterile eras,
  Show — monarchy ever its uncouth cub
    licks   270
Out of the bear's shape into Chimæra's,
  While Pure Art's birth is still the republic's.

Then one shall propose in a speech (curt
    Tuscan,
  Expurgate and sober, with scarcely an
    "*issimo*")
To end now our half-told tale of Cambuscan,
  And turn the bell-tower's *alt* to *altissimo;* 276
And fine as the beak of a young beccaccia
  The Campanile, the Duomo's fit ally,
Shall soar up in gold full fifty braccia,
  Completing Florence, as Florence Italy. 280

Shall I be alive that morning the scaffold
  Is broken away, and the long-pent fire,
Like the golden hope of the world, unbaffled
  Springs from its sleep, and up goes the
    spire
While "God and the People" plain for its
    motto,   285
  Thence the new tricolor flaps at the sky?
At least to foresee that glory of Giotto
  And Florence together, the first am I!
            (1855)

"DE GUSTIBUS — "

Your ghost will walk, you lover of trees,
  (If our loves remain)
    In an English lane,
By a cornfield-side a-flutter with poppies.
Hark, those two in the hazel coppice —   5
  A boy and a girl, if the good fates please,
    Making love, say —
    The happier they!
Draw yourself up from the light of the moon,
And let them pass, as they will too soon,   10
    With the beanflowers' boon,
    And the blackbird's tune,
    And May, and June!

What I love best in all the world
Is a castle, precipice-encurled,   15
  In a gash of the wind-grieved Apennine.
Or look for me, old fellow of mine,
  (If I get my head from out the mouth
  O' the grave, and loose my spirit's bands,
  And come again to the land of lands)   20
In a sea-side house to the farther South,
  Where the baked cicala dies of drouth,
  And one sharp tree — 'tis a cypress — stands, ·
By the many hundred years red-rusted,
Rough iron-spiked, ripe fruit-o'ercrusted,   25

241. **San Spirito,** a church of the 14th century in Florence. The name means *Holy Spirit.* 242. **the Ognissanti,** All Saints Church in Florence. 244. **Detur amanti,** Let it be given to the one who loves it. 245. **Koh-i-noor,** a famous Indian diamond given to Queen Victoria in 1850. 246. **Jewel of Giamschid,** the fabulous ruby of Sultan Giamschid, owned by the Sofi—the shah of Persia. 251. **Mont St. Gothard,** a mountain range of the Alps. The "worse side" of the range is the side toward Switzerland—that is, out of Italy. 255. **Radetzky,** Joseph Wenzel Radetzky (1766-1858), an Austrian count and governor of the Austrian possessions in Upper Italy. 256. **Morello,** a mountain near Florence. 258. **the stone of Dante,** the stone where Dante often sat in Florence. It was often the place of patriotic gatherings. 259. **Witanagemot,** the name of the famous Anglo-Saxon assembly, the forerunner of Parliament. 260. **Casa Guidi,** a reference to Mrs. Browning's *Casa Guidi Windows,* a long poem which was inspired by love of Italy. (See page 373.) **quod videas ante,** which you may have seen before. 263. **hated house,** the House of Lorraine, which through Duke Francis of Lorraine came into control of Tuscany in 1737. 264. **Orgagna,** a Florentine painter of the 14th century, when Italy was free. He was one of the most noted successors of Giotto.

273. **Tuscan,** the literary language of Italy. 274. **issimo,** a Latin superlative ending. 275. **half-told tale of Cambuscan,** a reference to *The Squire's Tale,* left unfinished by Chaucer. Browning has in mind the unfinished Campanile of Giotto. 276. **alt to altissimo,** high to highest. 277. **beccaccia,** woodcock. 278. **the Duomo's,** the Cathedral's. 279. **braccia,** cubits. (Giotto's plan included a spire 100 feet high. It has never been built.)

"**De Gustibus—".** The full form of the Latin proverb is *De gustibus non est disputandum*—There is no disputing about tastes. 2. **If our loves remain,** if we live after death. 4. **cornfield,** grainfield, wheatfield.

My sentinel to guard the sands
To the water's edge.   For, what expands
Before the house, but the great opaque
Blue breadth of sea without a break?
While, in the house, forever crumbles   30
Some fragment of the frescoed walls,
From blisters where a scorpion sprawls.
A girl barefooted brings, and tumbles
Down on the pavement, green-flesh melons,
And says there's news today — the king   35
Was shot at, touched in the liver-wing,
Goes with his Bourbon arm in a sling—
She hopes they have not caught the felons.
Italy, my Italy!
Queen Mary's saying serves for me —   40
    (When fortune's malice
      Lost her, Calais) —
Open my heart and you will see
Graved inside of it, "Italy."
Such lovers old are I and she;   45
So it always was, so shall ever be!   (1855)

MY STAR

All that I know
  Of a certain star
Is, it can throw
  (Like the angled spar)
Now a dart of red,   5
  Now a dart of blue;
Till my friends have said
  They would fain see, too,
My star that dartles the red and the blue!
Then it stops like a bird; like a flower, hangs
    furled.   10
  They must solace themselves with the
    Saturn above it.
What matter to me if their star is a world?
  Mine has opened its soul to me; therefore
    I love it.   (1855)

ANY WIFE TO ANY HUSBAND

My love, this is the bitterest, that thou —
Who art all truth, and who dost love me now
  As thine eyes say, as thy voice breaks to
    say —

36. **the liver-wing,** the right wing—that is, the right arm.
37. **Bourbon.** Ferdinand II, king of the Two Sicilies, was a
member of the House of Bourbon. Browning rejoices that the
people of Italy are taking action against the Bourbons. See
The Italian in England, p. 219.   40. **Queen Mary's saying.**
The French seaport of Calais was taken from England by the
French in 1558, the last year of the reign of Queen Mary.
She grieved for the loss so much that she declared that the
word *Calais* would be found written on her heart.
    My Star.   This lyric is supposed to refer to Mrs. Browning.
The idea expressed is expanded in *One Word More*, lines 187-
197, p. 298.   Cf. the lines from Book I of *The Ring and the
Book*, p. 320, and *Prospice*, p. 317.
    4. **Like . . . spar,** like a prism, which reflects different
colors from different angles.

Shouldst love so truly, and couldst love me
    still
A whole long life through, had but love its
    will,   5
  Would death that leads me from thee brook
    delay.

I have but to be by thee, and thy hand
Will never let mine go, nor heart withstand
  The beating of my heart to reach its place.
When shall I look for thee and feel thee gone?
When cry for the old comfort and find none? 11
  Never, I know! Thy soul is in thy face.

Oh, I should fade — 'tis willed so! Might I
    save,
Gladly I would, whatever beauty gave
  Joy to thy sense, for that was precious too.
It is not to be granted. But the soul   16
Whence the love comes, all ravage leaves that
    whole;
  Vainly the flesh fades; soul makes all things
    new.

It would not be because my eye grew dim
Thou couldst not find the love there, thanks
    to Him   20
  Who never is dishonored in the spark
He gave us from his fire of fires, and bade
Remember whence it sprang, nor be afraid
  While that burns on, though all the rest
    grow dark.

So, how thou wouldst be perfect, white and
    clean   25
Outside as inside, soul and soul's demesne
  Alike, this body given to show it by!
Oh, three-parts through the worst of life's
    abyss,
What plaudits from the next world after this,
  Couldst thou repeat a stroke and gain the
    sky!   30

And is it not the bitterer to think
That disengage our hands and thou wilt sink
  Although thy love was love in very deed?
I know that nature! Pass a festive day,
Thou dost not throw its relic-flower away   35
  Nor bid its music's loitering echo speed.

Thou let'st the stranger's glove lie where it
    fell;
If old things remain old things all is well,
  For thou art grateful as becomes man best;
And hadst thou only heard me play one tune,
Or viewed me from a window, not so soon   41
  With thee would such things fade as with
    the rest.

I seem to see! We meet and part; 'tis brief;
The book I opened keeps a folded leaf,

The very chair I sat on, breaks the rank;
That is a portrait of me on the wall —   46
Three lines, my face comes at so slight a call;
And for all this, one little hour to thank!

But now, because the hour through years was
    fixed,
Because our inmost beings met and mixed, 50
    Because thou once hast loved me — wilt
        thou dare
Say to thy soul and Who may list beside,
"Therefore she is immortally my bride;
    Chance cannot change my love, nor time
        impair.

"So, what if in the dusk of life that's left, 55
I, a tired traveler of my sun bereft,
    Look from my path when, mimicking the
        same,
The fire-fly glimpses past me, come and gone?
—Where was it till the sunset? Where anon
It will be at the sunrise! What's to blame?"

Is it so helpful to thee? Canst thou take   61
The mimic up, nor, for the true thing's sake,
    Put gently by such efforts at a beam?
Is the remainder of the way so long,
Thou need'st the little solace, thou the strong?
    Watch out thy watch, let weak ones doze
        and dream!   66

Ah, but the fresher faces! "Is it true,"
Thou'lt ask, "some eyes are beautiful and
    new?
    Some hair — how can one choose but grasp
        such wealth?
And if a man would press his lips to lips   70
Fresh as the wilding hedge-rose-cup there
    slips
    The dewdrop out of, must it be by stealth?

"It cannot change the love still kept for Her,
More than if such a picture I prefer
    Passing a day with, to a room's bare side; 75
The painted form takes nothing she possessed,
Yet, while the Titian's Venus lies at rest,
    A man looks. Once more, what is there to
        chide?"

So must I see, from where I sit and watch,
My own self sell myself, my hand attach   80
Its warrant to the very thefts from me —
Thy singleness of soul that made me proud,
Thy purity of heart I loved aloud,
    Thy man's-truth I was bold to bid God see!

Love so, then, if thou wilt! Give all thou
    canst   85

---

77. **Titian's Venus,** a painting of Venus, goddess of love,
by Titian (1477-1576), one of the most illustrious artists of
Italy.

Away to the new faces — disentranced,
    (Say it and think it) obdurate no more;
Re-issue looks and words from the old mint,
Pass them afresh, no matter whose the print
Image and superscription once they bore! 90

Re-coin thyself and give it them to spend —
It all comes to the same thing at the end,
    Since mine thou wast, mine art and mine
        shalt be,
Faithful or faithless, sealing up the sum
Or lavish of my treasure, thou must come 95
    Back to the heart's place here I keep for
        thee!

Only, why should it be with stain at all?
Why must I, 'twixt the leaves of coronal,
    Put any kiss of pardon on thy brow?
Why need the other women know so much, 100
And talk together, "Such the look and such
    The smile he used to love with, then as
        now!"

Might I die last and show thee! Should I find
Such hardship in the few years left behind,
    If free to take and light my lamp, and go
Into thy tomb, and shut the door and sit, 106
Seeing thy face on those four sides of it
    The better that they are so blank, I know!

Why, time was what I wanted, to turn o'er
Within my mind each look, get more and
    more   110
    By heart each word, too much to learn at
        first:
And join thee all the fitter for the pause
'Neath the low doorway's lintel. That were
    cause
    For lingering, though thou calledst, if I
        durst!

And yet thou art the nobler of us two;   115
What dare I dream of, that thou canst not do,
    Outstripping my ten small steps with one
        stride?
I'll say then, here's a trial and a task —
Is it to bear? — if easy, I'll not ask:
    Though love fail, I can trust on in thy
        pride.   120

Pride? — when those eyes forestall the life
    behind
The death I have to go through! — when I
    find,
    Now that I want thy help most, all of thee!
What did I fear? Thy love shall hold me fast
Until the little minute's sleep is past   125
    And I wake saved. — And yet it will not
        be!   (1855)

TWO IN THE CAMPAGNA

I wonder do you feel today
  As I have felt since, hand in hand,
We sat down on the grass, to stray
  In spirit better through the land,
This morn of Rome and May?   5

For me, I touched a thought, I know,
  Has tantalized me many times
(Like turns of thread the spiders throw
  Mocking across our path) for rhymes
To catch at and let go.   10

Help me to hold it! First it left
  The yellowing fennel, run to seed
There, branching from the brickwork's cleft,
  Some old tomb's ruin; yonder weed
Took up the floating weft,   15

Where one small orange cup amassed
  Five beetles — blind and green they grope
Among the honey-meal; and last,
  Everywhere on the grassy slope
I traced it. Hold it fast!   20

The champaign with its endless fleece
  Of feathery grasses everywhere!
Silence and passion, joy and peace,
  An everlasting wash of air —
Rome's ghost since her decease.   25

Such life here, through such lengths of hours,
  Such miracles performed in play,
Such primal naked forms of flowers,
  Such letting nature have her way
While heaven looks from its towers!   30

How say you? Let us, O my dove,
  Let us be unashamed of soul,
As earth lies bare to heaven above!
  How is it under our control
To love or not to love?   35

I would that you were all to me,
  You that are just so much, no more.
Nor yours nor mine, nor slave nor free!
  Where does the fault lie? What the core
O' the wound, since wound must be?   40

I would I could adopt your will,
  See with your eyes, and set my heart

Beating by yours, and drink my fill
  At your soul's springs — your part my part
In life, for good and ill.   45

No. I yearn upward, touch you close,
  Then stand away. I kiss your cheek,
Catch your soul's warmth — I pluck the rose
  And love it more than tongue can speak —
Then the good minute goes.   50

Already how am I so far
  Out of that minute? Must I go
Still like the thistle-ball, no bar,
  Onward, whenever light winds blow,
Fixed by no friendly star?   55

Just when I seemed about to learn!
  Where is the thread now? Off again!
The old trick! Only I discern —
  Infinite passion, and the pain
Of finite hearts that yearn.   (1855)

MISCONCEPTIONS

This is a spray the Bird clung to,
  Making it blossom with pleasure,
Ere the high tree-top she sprung to,
  Fit for her nest and her treasure.
  Oh, what a hope beyond measure   5
Was the poor spray's, which the flying feet
    hung to —
So to be singled out, built in, and sung to!

This is a heart the Queen leant on,
  Thrilled in a minute erratic,
Ere the true bosom she bent on,   10
  Meet for love's regal dalmatic.
  Oh, what a fancy ecstatic
Was the poor heart's, ere the wanderer went
    on —
Love to be saved for it, proffered to, spent on!
          (1855)

ONE WAY OF LOVE

All June I bound the rose in sheaves.
Now, rose by rose, I strip the leaves
And strew them where Pauline may pass.
She will not turn aside? Alas!
Let them lie. Suppose they die?   5
The chance was they might take her eye.

How many a month I strove to suit
These stubborn fingers to the lute!
Today I venture all I know.
She will not hear my music? So!   10

Two in the Campagna. The Campagna di Roma is the large
open space that lies around the city of Rome. It is called
"Rome's ghost" (line 25), because it is dotted with ruins of
ancient cities. It provides an admirable setting for the poem,
which expresses the idea that no matter how close love brings
two persons, they are still, forever, immutably alone. Cf.
Arnold's *Switzerland* (*Isolation*), p. 456.
15. **weft,** the cross threads in weaving. 21. **champaign,**
the open space of the Campagna.

Misconceptions. 11. **dalmatic,** a robe worn by kings and
high church officials.

Break the string; fold music's wing:
Suppose Pauline had bade me sing!

My whole life long I learned to love.
This hour my utmost art I prove
And speak my passion — heaven or hell?   15
She will not give me heaven? 'Tis well!
Lose who may — I still can say,
Those who win heaven, blest are they!
                                                    (1855)

ANOTHER WAY OF LOVE

June was not over
    Though past the full,
And the best of her roses
    Had yet to blow,
When a man I know   5
(But shall not discover,
    Since ears are dull,
And time discloses)
Turned him and said with a man's true air,
Half sighing a smile in a yawn, as 'twere —   10
"If I tire of your June, will she greatly care?"

Well, dear, in-doors with you!
    True! serene deadness
Tries a man's temper.
    What's in the blossom   15
June wears on her bosom?
    Can it clear scores with you?
    Sweetness and redness,
Eadem semper!
Go, let me care for it greatly or slightly!   20
If June mend her bower now, your hand left
    unsightly
By plucking the roses — my June will do
    rightly.

And after, for pastime,
    If June be refulgent
With flowers in completeness,   25
    All petals, no prickles,
    Delicious as trickles
Of wine poured at mass-time —
    And choose One indulgent
To redness and sweetness;   30
Or if, with experience of man and of spider,
June use my June-lightning, the strong insect-
    ridder,
And stop the fresh film-work — why, June
    will consider.
                                                    (1855)

Another Way of Love. This poem is spoken by a woman to
an indifferent and impatient lover who tires of the monotony
of roses always sweet and red. She bids him depart, and adds
that to a more appreciative lover she may respond, or on the
basis of present experience she may scorn the would-be lover.
June symbolizes the speaker.
6. **discover,** disclose. 19. **Eadem semper,** always the
same. 32. **June-lightning,** scorn.

RESPECTABILITY

Dear, had the world in its caprice
    Deigned to proclaim, "I know you both,
    Have recognized your plighted troth,
Am sponsor for you; live in peace!" —
How many precious months and years   5
    Of youth had passed, that speed so fast,
    Before we found it out at last,
The world, and what it fears!

How much of priceless life were spent
    With men that every virtue decks,   10
    And women models of their sex,
Society's true ornament —
Ere we dared wander, nights like this,
    Through wind and rain, and watch the
        Seine,
    And feel the Boulevard break again   15
To warmth and light and bliss!

I know! the world proscribes not love;
    Allows my finger to caress
    Your lips' contour and downiness,
Provided it supply a glove.   20
The world's good word! — the Institute!
    Guizot receives Montalembert!
    Eh? Down the court three lampions flare;
Put forward your best foot!   (1855)

LOVE IN A LIFE

Room after room,
I hunt the house through
We inhabit together.
Heart, fear nothing, for, heart, thou shalt
    find her —
Next time, herself! — not the trouble behind
    her   5
Left in the curtain, the couch's perfume!
As she brushed it, the cornice-wreath blos-
    somed anew;
Yon looking-glass gleamed at the wave of her
    feather.

Respectability. In this poem a lover speaks ironically
of respectability that is purchased by paying homage to
convention. The scene is laid in Paris.
17-20. **the world . . . glove.** The world will allow the
caress if we buy gloves from it—if we pay the price by being
conventional. 21. **the Institute,** the Institute of France, a
national society established in 1795 to promote science, literature, and art. 22. **Guizot,** François Guizot (1787-1874),
a French statesman and historian and a member of the Constitutional Royalist party. **Montalembert.** Charles Montalembert (1810-70), a French publicist and historian and a
member of the Liberal party. Guizot disliked Montalembert
but welcomed him into the Institute as a matter of convention. 23. **lampions,** lamps, which indicate a place where
respectables are gathered; hence you must be conventional
as you approach, or be condemned.
Love in a Life. This poem and the poem following are sup-
plementary in thought. In the first the lover finds his love
always eluding him, like ideals, but he is confident that at
any moment he may catch her. In the second poem the
lover realizes that he cannot achieve his love, or ideal, but he
resolves to devote his life to the quest.

Yet the day wears,
And door succeeds door;   10
I try the fresh fortune —
Range the wide house from the wing to the
    center.
Still the same chance! she goes out as I enter.
Spend my whole day in the quest — who
    cares?
But 'tis twilight, you see — with such suites
    to explore,   15
Such closets to search, such alcoves to impor-
    tune!   (1855)

LIFE IN A LOVE

Escape me?
Never —
Beloved!
While I am I, and you are you,
    So long as the world contains us both,   5
    Me the loving and you the loath,
While the one eludes, must the other pursue.
My life is a fault at last, I fear;
    It seems too much like a fate, indeed!
    Though I do my best I shall scarce succeed.
But what if I fail of my purpose here?   11
It is but to keep the nerves at strain,
    To dry one's eyes and laugh at a fall,
And, baffled, get up and begin again —
    So the chase takes up one's life, that's all. 15
While, look but once from your farthest
    bound
    At me so deep in the dust and dark,
No sooner the old hope goes to ground
    Than a new one, straight to the selfsame
        mark,
    I shape me —   20
Ever
    Removed!   (1855)

IN THREE DAYS

So, I shall see her in three days
And just one night, but nights are short,
Then two long hours, and that is morn.
See how I come, unchanged, unworn!
Feel, where my life broke off from thine,   5
How fresh the splinters keep and fine —
Only a touch and we combine!

Too long, this time of year, the days!
But nights, at least the nights are short.
As night shows where her one moon is,   10
A hand's-breadth of pure light and bliss,
So life's night gives my lady birth
And my eyes hold her! What is worth
The rest of heaven, the rest of earth?

O loaded curls, release your store   15
Of warmth and scent, as once before
The tingling hair did, lights and darks
Outbreaking into fairy sparks,
When under curl and curl I pried
After the warmth and scent inside,   20
Through lights and darks how manifold —
The dark inspired, the light controlled!
As early Art embrowns the gold.

What great fear, should one say, "Three days
That change the world might change as well
Your fortune; and if joy delays,   26
Be happy that no worse befell!"
What small fear, if another says,
"Three days and one short night beside
May throw no shadow on your ways;   30
But years must teem with change untried,
With chance not easily defied,
With an end somewhere undescried."
No fear! — or if a fear be born
This minute, it dies out in scorn.   35
Fear? I shall see her in three days
And one night, now the nights are short,
Then just two hours, and that is morn.
                                             (1855)

THE GUARDIAN-ANGEL

A PICTURE AT FANO

Dear and great Angel, wouldst thou only
    leave
    That child, when thou hast done with him,
        for me!
Let me sit all the day here, that when eve
    Shall find performed thy special ministry,
And time come for departure, thou, suspend-
    ing   5
Thy flight, may'st see another child for
    tending,
    Another still, to quiet and retrieve.

Then I shall feel thee step one step, no more,
    From where thou standest now, to where I
        gaze,
—And suddenly my head is covered o'er   10
    With those wings, white above the child
        who prays
Now on that tomb — and I shall feel thee
    guarding
Me, out of all the world; for me, discard-
    ing
    Yon heaven thy home, that waits and opes
        its door.

The Guardian-Angel. The title is taken from that of a
painting by Giovanni Francesco Barbieri (1590-1666), nicknamed Guercino (line 36), "the squint-eyed." The picture
is in the Church of San Agostino at Fano, an Italian city on
the Adriatic Sea.

I would not look up thither past thy head 15
  Because the door opes, like that child, I
    know,
For I should have thy gracious face instead,
  Thou bird of God! And wilt thou bend me
    low
Like him, and lay, like his, my hands together,
And lift them up to pray, and gently tether
  Me, as thy lamb there, with thy garment's
    spread?   21

If this was ever granted, I would rest
  My head beneath thine, while thy healing
    hands
Close-covered both my eyes beside thy breast,
  Pressing the brain, which too much thought
    expands,   25
Back to its proper size again, and smoothing
Distortion down till every nerve had sooth-
  ing,
And all lay quiet, happy, and suppressed.

How soon all worldly wrong would be re-
  paired!
  I think how I should view the earth and
    skies   30
And sea, when once again my brow was bared
  After thy healing, with such different eyes.
O world, as God has made it! All is beauty;
And knowing this is love, and love is duty.
  What further may be sought for or de-
    clared?   35

Guercino drew this angel I saw teach
  (Alfred, dear friend!) — that little child to
    pray,
Holding the little hands up, each to each
  Pressed gently — with his own head turned
    away
Over the earth where so much lay before him
Of work to do, though heaven was opening
  o'er him,   41
And he was left at Fano by the beach.

We were at Fano, and three times we went
  To sit and see him in his chapel there,
And drink his beauty to our soul's content —45
  My angel with me too; and since I care
For dear Guercino's fame (to which in power
And glory comes this picture for a dower,
  Fraught with a pathos so magnificent) —

And since he did not work thus earnestly 50
  At all times, and has else endured some
    wrong —

I took one thought his picture struck from
  me,
  And spread it out, translating it to song.
My love is here. Where are you, dear old
  friend?
How rolls the Wairoa at your world's far
  end?   55
  This is Ancona, yonder is the sea.
                    (*1848;* 1855)

MEMORABILIA

Ah, did you once see Shelley plain,
  And did he stop and speak to you,
And did you speak to him again?
  How strange it seems and new!

But you were living before that,   5
  And also you are living after;
And the memory I started at —
  My starting moves your laughter!

I crossed a moor, with a name of its own
  And a certain use in the world no doubt, 10
Yet a hand's-breadth of it shines alone
  'Mid the blank miles round about;

For there I picked up on the heather,
  And there I put inside my breast
A molted feather, an eagle-feather!   15
  Well, I forget the rest.
                    (1855)

POPULARITY

Stand still, true poet that you are!
  I know you; let me try and draw you.
Some night you'll fail us; when afar
  You rise, remember one man saw you,
Knew you, and named a star!   5

My star, God's glowworm! Why extend
  That loving hand of his which leads you,
Yet locks you safe from end to end
  Of this dark world, unless he needs you,
Just saves your light to spend?   10

His clenched hand shall unclose at last,
  I know, and let out all the beauty;
My poet holds the future fast,
  Accepts the coming ages' duty,
Their present for this past.   15

That day, the earth's feast-master's brow
  Shall clear, to God the chalice raising;

37. **Alfred.** The poem is addressed to Alfred Domett, one of Browning's warm friends, who was then in New Zealand. 43. **We ... went.** When the poem was written, Browning and Mrs. Browning (the "angel" of line 46) were staying at Ancona (line 56), about 30 miles south of Fano.

55. **the Wairoa,** a river in New Zealand.
Memorabilia. The title means *Things Worth Remembering.* Browning first became acquainted with Shelley's poetry about 1825 and instantly fell under its spell.

"Others give best at first, but thou
  Forever set'st our table praising,
Keep'st the good wine till now!"   20

Meantime, I'll draw you as you stand,
  With few or none to watch and wonder;
I'll say — a fisher, on the sand
  By Tyre the old, with ocean-plunder,
A netful, brought to land.   25

Who has not heard how Tyrian shells
  Enclosed the blue, that dye of dyes
Whereof one drop worked miracles,
  And colored like Astarte's eyes
Raw silk the merchant sells?   30

And each bystander of them all
  Could criticize, and quote tradition
How depths of blue sublimed some pall —
  To get which, pricked a king's ambition;
Worth scepter, crown, and ball.   35

Yet there's the dye, in that rough mesh,
  The sea has only just o'er-whispered!
Live whelks, each lip's beard dripping fresh,
  As if they still the water's lisp heard
Through foam the rock-weeds thresh.   40

Enough to furnish Solomon
  Such hangings for his cedar-house,
That, when gold-robed he took the throne
  In that abyss of blue, the Spouse
Might swear his presence shone   45

Most like the center-spike of gold
  Which burns deep in the bluebell's womb
What time, with ardors manifold,
  The bee goes singing to her groom,
Drunken and overbold.   50

Mere conchs! not fit for warp or woof!
  Till cunning come to pound and squeeze
And clarify — refine to proof
  The liquor filtered by degrees,
While the world stands aloof.   55

And there's the extract, flasked and fine,
  And priced and salable at last!
And Hobbs, Nobbs, Stokes, and Nokes com-
  bine

To paint the future from the past,
  Put blue into their line.   60

Hobbs hints blue — straight he turtle eats;
  Nobbs prints blue — claret crowns his cup;
Nokes outdares Stokes in azure feats —
  Both gorge. Who fished the murex up?
What porridge had John Keats?   65
                                                  (1855)

THE PATRIOT

AN OLD STORY

It was roses, roses, all the way,
  With myrtle mixed in my path like mad;
The house-roofs seemed to heave and sway,
  The church-spires flamed, such flags they
    had,
A year ago on this very day.   5

The air broke into a mist with bells,
  The old walls rocked with the crowd and
    cries.
Had I said, "Good folk, mere noise repels —
  But give me your sun from yonder skies!"
They had answered, "And afterward, what
    else?"   10

Alack, it was I who leaped at the sun
  To give it my loving friends to keep!
Naught man could do, have I left undone;
  And you see my harvest, what I reap
This very day, now a year is run.   15

There's nobody on the house-tops now —
  Just a palsied few at the windows set;
For the best of the sight is, all allow,
  At the Shambles' Gate — or, better yet,
By the very scaffold's foot, I trow.   20

I go in the rain, and, more than needs,
  A rope cuts both my wrists behind;
And I think, by the feel, my forehead bleeds,
  For they fling, whoever has a mind,
Stones at me for my year's misdeeds.   25

Thus I entered, and thus I go!
  In triumphs, people have dropped down
    dead.
"Paid by the world, what dost thou owe
  Me?" — God might question; now instead,
'Tis God shall repay; I am safer so.   (1855)

18-20. **Others . . . now.** See note on lines 759-760, p. 149.
24. **Tyre**, a famous city of ancient Phœnicia, on the Mediterranean coast. The Phœnicians discovered the dye mentioned in the lines following. 29. **Astarte**, a Phœnician
goddess of love and beauty. 33. **pall**, a rich cloth used as
a covering. 38. **whelks**, shellfish. 41-44. **Solomon**, etc.
For the description of Solomon's temple and palace, see *1
Kings*, 6-7. 44. **the Spouse**, Solomon's wife, Pharaoh's
daughter. 48. **What time**, at the time when. 51. **conchs**,
shells. 58. **Hobbs . . . Nokes**, the common run of humanity; like Tom, Dick, and Harry.

64. **murex**, the shellfish from which the famous dye was
made. 65. **What . . . Keats?** Browning imagines Keats as
the literary fisherman who discovers the rich dye of words
and images but gets nothing for it; other poets follow im-
itatively and get much.
  The Patriot. This poem contains no direct historical
reference. It is called "an old story" because it presents
universal truth—the fickleness of popular approval.
  19. **Shambles' Gate.** The shambles is a place for
slaughtering animals.

A LIGHT WOMAN

So far as our story approaches the end,
    Which do you pity the most of us three? —
My friend, or the mistress of my friend
    With her wanton eyes, or me?

My friend was already too good to lose,   5
    And seemed in the way of improvement
        yet,
When she crossed his path with her hunting-
        noose,
    And over him drew her net.

When I saw him tangled in her toils,
    A shame, said I, if she adds just him   10
To her nine-and-ninety other spoils,
    The hundredth for a whim!

And before my friend be wholly hers,
    How easy to prove to him, I said,
An eagle's the game her pride prefers,   15
    Though she snaps at a wren instead!

So I gave her eyes my own eyes to take,
    My hand sought hers as in earnest need,
And round she turned for my noble sake,
    And gave me herself indeed.   20

The eagle am I, with my fame in the world,
    The wren is he, with his maiden face.
—You look away and your lip is curled?
    Patience, a moment's space!

For see, my friend goes shaking and white;
    He eyes me as the basilisk;   26
I have turned, it appears, his day to night,
    Eclipsing his sun's disk.

And I did it, he thinks, as a very thief:
    "Though I love her — that, he compre-
        hends —   30
One should master one's passions (love, in
        chief),
    And be loyal to one's friends!"

And she — she lies in my hand as tame
    As a pear late basking over a wall;
Just a touch to try and off it came;   35
    'Tis mine — can I let it fall?

With no mind to eat it, that's the worst!
    Were it thrown in the road, would the case
        assist?
'Twas quenching a dozen blue-flies' thirst
    When I gave its stalk a twist.   40

26. **basilisk,** a fabulous monster said to be able to kill with a look.

And I — what I seem to my friend, you see;
    What I soon shall seem to his love, you
        guess;
What I seem to myself, do you ask of me?
    No hero, I confess.

'Tis an awkward thing to play with souls,   45
    And matter enough to save one's own;
Yet think of my friend, and the burning coals
    He played with for bits of stone!

One likes to show the truth for the truth;
    That the woman was light is very true;   50
But suppose she says—Never mind that
        youth!
    What wrong have I done to you?

Well, anyhow, here the story stays,
    So far at least as I understand;
And, Robert Browning, you writer of plays,   55
    Here's a subject made to your hand!
                (1855)

THE LAST RIDE TOGETHER

I said—Then, dearest, since 'tis so,
Since now at length my fate I know,
Since nothing all my love avails,
Since all my life seemed meant for, fails,
    Since this was written and needs must be— 5
My whole heart rises up to bless
Your name in pride and thankfulness!
Take back the hope you gave—I claim
Only a memory of the same,
    —And this beside, if you will not blame,   10
    Your leave for one more last ride with me.

My mistress bent that brow of hers;
Those deep dark eyes where pride demurs
When pity would be softening through,
Fixed me a breathing-while or two   15
    With life or death in the balance: right!
The blood replenished me again;
My last thought was at least not vain:
I and my mistress, side by side
Shall be together, breathe and ride,   20
So, one day more am I deified.
    Who knows but the world may end tonight?

Hush! If you saw some western cloud
All billowy-bosomed, over-bowed
By many benedictions—sun's   25
And moon's and evening-star's at once—
    And so, you, looking and loving best,
Conscious grew, your passion drew
Cloud, sunset, moonrise, star-shine too,
Down on you, near and yet more near,   30
Till flesh must fade for heaven was here!—

Thus leant she and lingered—joy and fear!
  Thus lay she a moment on my breast.

Then we began to ride. My soul
Smoothed itself out, a long-cramped scroll 35
Freshening and fluttering in the wind.
Past hopes already lay behind.
  What need to strive with a life awry?
Had I said that, had I done this,
So might I gain, so might I miss.   40
Might she have loved me? Just as well
She might have hated; who can tell!
Where had I been now if the worst befell?
  And here we are riding, she and I.

Fail I alone, in words and deeds?   45
Why, all men strive, and who succeeds?
We rode; it seemed my spirit flew,
Saw other regions, cities new,
  As the world rushed by on either side.
I thought—All labor, yet no less   50
Bear up beneath their unsuccess.
Look at the end of work, contrast
The petty done, the undone vast,
This present of theirs with the hopeful past!
  I hoped she would love me; here we ride. 55

What hand and brain went ever paired?
What heart alike conceived and dared?
What act proved all its thought had been?
What will but felt the fleshly screen?
  We ride and I see her bosom heave.   60
There's many a crown for who can reach.
Ten lines, a statesman's life in each!
The flag stuck on a heap of bones,
A soldier's doing! what atones!
They scratch his name on the Abbey-stones. 65
  My riding is better, by their leave.

What does it all mean, poet? Well,
Your brains beat into rhythm, you tell
What we felt only; you expressed
You hold things beautiful the best,   70
  And place them in rime so, side by side.
'Tis something, nay 'tis much; but then,
Have you yourself what's best for men?
Are you—poor, sick, old ere your time—
Nearer one whit your own sublime   75
Than we who never have turned a rime?
  Sing, riding's a joy! For me, I ride.

And you, great sculptor—so, you gave
A score of years to Art, her slave,
And that's your Venus, whence we turn   80
To yonder girl that fords the burn!
  You acquiesce, and shall I repine?
What, man of music, you grown gray
With notes and nothing else to say,

  81. **burn,** brook.

Is this your sole praise from a friend, 85
"Greatly his opera's strains intend,
But in music we know how fashions end!"
  I gave my youth; but we ride, in fine.

Who knows what's fit for us? Had fate
Proposed bliss here should sublimate   90
My being—had I signed the bond—
Still one must lead some life beyond,
  Have a bliss to die with, dim-descried.
This foot once planted on the goal,
This glory-garland round my soul,   95
Could I descry such? Try and test!
I sink back shuddering from the quest.
Earth being so good, would heaven seem best?
  Now, heaven and she are beyond this ride.

And yet—she has not spoke so long!   100
What if heaven be that, fair and strong
At life's best, with our eyes upturned
Whither life's flower is first discerned,
  We, fixed so, ever should so abide?
What if we still ride on, we two,   105
With life forever old yet new,
Changed not in kind but in degree,
The instant made eternity—
  And heaven just prove that I and she
    Ride, ride together, forever ride?   110

              (1855)

A GRAMMARIAN'S FUNERAL

SHORTLY AFTER THE REVIVAL OF LEARNING
IN EUROPE

Let us begin and carry up this corpse,
  Singing together.
Leave we the common crofts, the vulgar
    thorpes,
  Each in its tether
Sleeping safe on the bosom of the plain,   5
  Cared-for till cock-crow;
Look out if yonder be not day again
  Rimming the rock-row!
That's the appropriate country; there, man's
    thought,
  Rarer, intenser,
Self-gathered for an outbreak, as it ought,
  Chafes in the censer.
Leave we the unlettered plain its herd and
    crop;

  86. **Greatly . . . intend,** have high aims. 90. **sublimate,**
lift to its highest pitch.
  A Grammarian's Funeral. The speaker of the poem is a
disciple of a dead scholar of the early Renaissance, noted for
his passion for knowledge. He leads other disciples as they
bear the body of their master to the top of a lofty mountain
for burial at sunrise. See Critical Notes.
  3. **crofts,** enclosed farm lands. **thorpes,** small villages.
7-8. **day . . . rock-row.** The sun's rays are just hitting the
rocky tops of the mountains. 12. **in the censer,** in the
crater of a smoking volcano.

Seek we sepulture
On a tall mountain, citied to the top,   15
  Crowded with culture!
All the peaks soar, but one the rest excels;
  Clouds overcome it;
No! yonder sparkle is the citadel's
  Circling its summit.   20
Thither our path lies; wind we up the heights;
  Wait ye the warning?
Our low life was the level's and the night's;
  He's for the morning.
Step to a tune, square chests, erect each head,
  'Ware the beholders!   26
This is our master, famous, calm and dead,
  Borne on our shoulders.

Sleep, crop and herd! sleep, darkling thorpe
    and croft,
  Safe from the weather!   30
He whom we convoy to his grave aloft,
  Singing together,
He was a man born with thy face and throat,
  Lyric Apollo!
Long he lived nameless; how should Spring
    take note   35
  Winter would follow?
Till lo, the little touch, and youth was gone!
  Cramped and diminished,
Moaned he, "New measures, other feet anon!
  My dance is finished"?   40
No, that's the world's way (keep the moun-
    tain-side,
  Make for the city!);
He knew the signal, and stepped on with pride
  Over men's pity;
Left play for work, and grappled with the
    world
  Bent on escaping;
"What's in the scroll," quoth he, "thou
    keepest furled?
  Show me their shaping,
Theirs who most studied man, the bard and
    sage—
  Give!"—So, he gowned him,   50
Straight got by heart that book to its last
    page;
  Learned, we found him.
Yea, but we found him bald too, eyes like lead,
  Accents uncertain;
"Time to taste life," another would have said,
  "Up with the curtain!"   56
This man said rather, "Actual life comes next?
  Patience a moment!
Grant I have mastered learning's crabbed
    text,

Still there's the comment.   60
Let me know all! Prate not of most or least,
  Painful or easy!
Even to the crumbs I'd fain eat up the feast,
  Aye, nor feel queasy."
Oh, such a life as he resolved to live,   65
  When he had learned it,
When he had gathered all books had to give!
  Sooner, he spurned it.
Image the whole, then execute the parts—
  Fancy the fabric   70
Quite, ere you build, ere steel strike fire from
    quartz,
  Ere mortar dab brick!

(Here's the town-gate reached; there's the
    market-place
  Gaping before us.)
Yea, this in him was the peculiar grace   75
  (Hearten our chorus!)
That before living he'd learn how to live—
  No end to learning;
Earn the means first—God surely will contrive
  Use for our earning.   80
Others mistrust and say, "But time escapes;
  Live now or never!"
He said, "What's time? Leave Now for dogs
    and apes!
  Man has Forever."
Back to his book then; deeper drooped his
    head;
  Calculus racked him;
Leaden before, his eyes grew dross of lead;
  Tussis attacked him.
"Now, master, take a little rest!"—not he!
  (Caution redoubled,   90
Step two abreast, the way winds narrowly!)
  Not a whit troubled,
Back to his studies, fresher than at first,
  Fierce as a dragon
He (soul-hydroptic with a sacred thirst)   95
  Sucked at the flagon.
Oh, if we draw a circle premature,
  Heedless of far gain,
Greedy for quick returns of profit, sure
  Bad is our bargain!   100
Was it not great? did not he throw on God
  (He loves the burthen)—
God's task to make the heavenly period
  Perfect the earthen?
Did not he magnify the mind, show clear 105
  Just what it all meant?
He would not discount life, as fools do here,
  Paid by instalment.
He ventured neck or nothing—heaven's suc-
    cess
  Found, or earth's failure: 110

25-26. These lines are directions to the bearers, as are the
passages in parentheses in lines 41, 73, 76, 90. 34. **Apollo,**
the Greek god of manly beauty and of music. 47. **scroll,**
manuscript. This was before the time of books. 50. **he
gowned him,** he put on the scholastic gown. 55-72. With
these lines compare *Cleon,* 214-220 and 278-283, pp. 293, 294.

86. **Calculus,** the disease called the stone. 88. **Tussis,**
a bronchial cough. 95. **soul-hydroptic,** soul-thirsty.

"Wilt thou trust death or not?" He answered
        "Yes!
    Hence with life's pale lure!"
That low man seeks a little thing to do,
    Sees it and does it;
This high man, with a great thing to pursue,
    Dies ere he knows it.   116
That low man goes on adding one to one,
    His hundred's soon hit;
This high man, aiming at a million,
    Misses an unit.   120
That, has the world here — should he need
        the next,
    Let the world mind him!
This, throws himself on God, and unperplexed
    Seeking shall find him.
So, with the throttling hands of death at
        strife,   125
    Ground he at grammar;
Still, through the rattle, parts of speech were
        rife;
    While he could stammer
He settled *Hoti's* business — let it be! —
    Properly based *Oun* —   130
Gave us the doctrine of the enclitic *De*,
    Dead from the waist down.
Well, here's the platform, here's the proper
        place;
    Hail to your purlieus,
All ye highfliers of the feathered race,   135
    Swallows and curlews!
Here's the top-peak; the multitude below
    Live, for they can, there;
This man decided not to Live but Know —
    Bury this man there?   140
Here — here's his place, where meteors shoot,
        clouds form,
    Lightnings are loosened,
Stars come and go! Let joy break with the
        storm,
    Peace let the dew send!
Lofty designs must close in like effects;   145
    Loftily lying,
Leave him — still loftier than the world sus-
        pects,
    Living and dying.   (1855)

THE STATUE AND THE BUST

There's a palace in Florence, the world knows
        well,
And a statue watches it from the square,
And this story of both do our townsmen tell.

Ages ago, a lady there,
At the farthest window facing the East,   5
Asked, "Who rides by with the royal air?"

The bridesmaids' prattle around her ceased;
She leaned forth, one on either hand;
They saw how the blush of the bride in-
        creased —

They felt by its beats her heart expand —   10
As one at each ear and both in a breath
Whispered, "The Great-Duke Ferdinand."

That selfsame instant, underneath,
The Duke rode past in his idle way,
Empty and fine like a swordless sheath.   15

Gay he rode, with a friend as gay,
Till he threw his head back — "Who is she?"
—"A bride the Riccardi brings home today."

Hair in heaps lay heavily
Over a pale brow spirit-pure —   20
Carved like the heart of the coal-black tree,

Crisped like a war-steed's encolure —
And vainly sought to dissemble her eyes
Of the blackest black our eyes endure,

And lo, a blade for a knight's emprise   25
Filled the fine empty sheath of a man —
The Duke grew straightway brave and wise.

He looked at her, as a lover can;
She looked at him, as one who awakes;
The past was a sleep, and her life began.   30

Now, love so ordered for both their sakes,
A feast was held that selfsame night
In the pile which the mighty shadow makes.

(For Via Larga is three-parts light,
But the palace overshadows one,   35
Because of a crime, which may God requite!

To Florence and God the wrong was done,
Through the first republic's murder there
By Cosimo and his cursed son.)

The Duke (with the statue's face in the
        square)   40
Turned in the midst of his multitude
At the bright approach of the bridal pair.

113-124. These lines express a favorite doctrine with
Browning. Cf. *Andrea del Sarto*, p. 288. 127. **the rattle**,
the death rattle in his throat. 129-131. *Hoti*, *oun*, and *de*
are Greek particles meaning respectively *that, therefore*, and
toward. They involve critical points of syntax. 134. **purlieus**, haunts.
   The Statue and the Bust. See Critical Notes.

22. **encolure**, mane. 25. **emprise**, enterprise. 33. **the
pile**, a large building—the Duke's palace. 36. **a crime**, the
crime committed by Cosimo de' Medici (1389-1464) and his
grandson Lorenzo (1449-1492) in destroying the liberties of
Florence. Both were absolute lords and rulers of Florence,
virtually tyrants.

Face to face the lovers stood
A single minute and no more,
While the bridegroom bent as a man sub-
　　dued —　　　　　　　　　　　　　45

Bowed till his bonnet brushed the floor —
For the Duke on the lady a kiss conferred,
As the courtly custom was of yore.

In a minute can lovers exchange a word?
If a word did pass, which I do not think,　50
Only one out of a thousand heard.

That was the bridegroom. At day's brink
He and his bride were alone at last
In a bed chamber by a taper's blink.

Calmly he said that her lot was cast,　　55
That the door she had passed was shut on
　　her
Till the final catafalk repassed.

The world meanwhile, its noise and stir,
Through a certain window facing the East
She could watch like a convent's chronicler. 60

Since passing the door might lead to a feast,
And a feast might lead to so much beside,
He, of many evils, chose the least.

"Freely I choose, too," said the bride —
"Your window and its world suffice,"　　65
Replied the tongue, while the heart replied —

"If I spend the night with that devil twice,
May his window serve as my loop of hell
Whence a damned soul looks on paradise!

"I fly to the Duke who loves me well,　　70
Sit by his side and laugh at sorrow
Ere I count another ave-bell.

" 'Tis only the coat of a page to borrow,
And tie my hair in a horse-boy's trim.
And I save my soul — but not tomorrow" —

(She checked herself and her eye grew dim) 76
"My father tarries to bless my state;
I must keep it one day more for him.

"Is one day more so long to wait?
Moreover the Duke rides past, I know;　　80
We shall see each other, sure as fate."

She turned on her side and slept. Just so!
So we resolve on a thing and sleep;
So did the lady, ages ago.

That night the Duke said, "Dear or cheap 85
As the cost of this cup of bliss may prove
To body or soul, I will drain it deep."

And on the morrow, bold with love,
He beckoned the bridegroom (close on call,
As his duty bade, by the Duke's alcove)　90

And smiled " 'Twas a very funeral,
Your lady will think, this feast of ours —
A shame to efface, whate'er befall!

"What if we break from the Arno bowers,
And try if Petraja, cool and green,　　　95
Cure last night's fault with this morning's
　　flowers?"

The bridegroom, not a thought to be seen
On his steady brow and quiet mouth,
Said, "Too much favor for me so mean!

"But, alas! my lady leaves the South;　　100
Each wind that comes from the Apennine
Is a menace to her tender youth;

"Nor a way exists, the wise opine,
If she quits her palace twice this year,
To avert the flower of life's decline."　105

Quoth the Duke, "A sage and a kindly fear.
Moreover Petraja is cold this spring;
Be our feast tonight as usual here!"

And then to himself — "Which night shall
　　bring
Thy bride to her lover's embraces, fool — 110
Or I am the fool, and thou art the king!

"Yet my passion must wait a night, nor cool —
For tonight the Envoy arrives from France
Whose heart I unlock with thyself, my tool.

"I need thee still and might miss perchance.
Today is not wholly lost, beside,　　　116
With its hope of my lady's countenance:

"For I ride — what should I do but ride?
And passing her palace, if I list,
May glance at its window — well betide!" 120

So said, so done; nor the lady missed
One ray that broke from the ardent brow,
Nor a curl of the lips where the spirit kissed.

Be sure that each renewed the vow,
No morrow's sun should arise and set　　125
And leave them then as it left them now.

---

57. **catafalk,** a kind of open hearse or funeral car. 72.
ave-bell, the bell sounded in the evening or at early dawn
when the people repeat the devotional *Ave Maria* (*Hail,
Mary*) of the Roman Catholic Church.

94. **the Arno,** the river that flows through Florence.
95. **Petraja,** the Duke's country seat, a villa near Florence.
101. **the Apennine,** a mountain range near Florence.

But next day passed, and next day yet,
With still fresh cause to wait one day more
Ere each leaped over the parapet.

And still, as love's brief morning wore,   130
With a gentle start, half smile, half sigh,
They found love not as it seemed before.

They thought it would work infallibly,
But not in despite of heaven and earth;
The rose would blow when the storm passed
     by.   135

Meantime they could profit in winter's dearth
By store of fruits that supplant the rose;
The world and its ways have a certain
     worth—

And to press a point while these oppose
Were simple policy; better wait: 140
We lose no friends and we gain no foes.

Meantime, worse fates than a lover's fate,
Who daily may ride and pass and look
Where his lady watches behind the grate!

And she — she watched the square like a book
Holding one picture and only one,   146
Which daily to find she undertook;

When the picture was reached the book was
     done,
And she turned from the picture at night to
     scheme
Of tearing it out for herself next sun.   150

So weeks grew months, years; gleam by gleam
The glory dropped from their youth and love,
And both perceived they had dreamed a
     dream,

Which hovered, as dreams do, still above;
But who can take a dream for a truth?   155
Oh, hide our eyes from the next remove!

One day as the lady saw her youth
Depart, and the silver thread that streaked
Her hair, and, worn by the serpent's tooth,

The brow so puckered, the chin so peaked —
And wondered who the woman was,   161
Hollow-eyed and haggard-cheeked,

Fronting her silent in the glass —
"Summon here," she suddenly said,
"Before the rest of my old self pass,   165

"Him, the Carver, a hand to aid,
Who fashions the clay no love will change,
And fixes a beauty never to fade.

"Let Robbia's craft so apt and strange
Arrest the remains of young and fair,   170
And rivet them while the seasons range.

"Make me a face on the window there,
Waiting as ever, mute the while,
My love to pass below in the square!

"And let me think that it may beguile   175
Dreary days which the dead must spend
Down in their darkness under the aisle,

"To say, 'What matters it at the end?
I did no more while my heart was warm
Than does that image, my pale-faced friend.'

"Where is the use of the lip's red charm,   181
The heaven of hair, the pride of the brow,
And the blood that blues the inside arm —

"Unless we turn, as the soul knows how,
The earthly gift to an end divine?   185
A lady of clay is as good, I trow."

But long ere Robbia's cornice, fine,
With flowers and fruits which leaves enlace,
Was set where now is the empty shrine —

(And, leaning out of a bright blue space,   190
As a ghost might lean from a chink of sky,
The passionate pale lady's face —

Eying ever, with earnest eye
And quick-turned neck at its breathless
     stretch,
Someone who ever is passing by —)   195

The Duke had sighed like the simplest wretch
In Florence, "Youth — my dream escapes!
Will its record stay?" And he bade them fetch

Some subtle molder of brazen shapes —
"Can the soul, the will, die out of a man   200
Ere his body find the grave that gapes?

"John of Douay shall effect my plan,
Set me on horseback here aloft,
Alive, as the crafty sculptor can,

"In the very square I have crossed so oft, 205
That men may admire, when future suns
Shall touch the eyes to a purpose soft,

129. **the parapet,** the barrier between them. **159. the
serpent's tooth,** probably ingratitude and dilatoriness on
the part of her lover, the Duke.

169. **Robbia's craft.** Della Robbia is the name of a
distinguished family of Florentine artists, the last one of
whom died in 1566. "Robbia's craft" refers to relief work
in marble, bronze, and terra-cotta. **202. John of Douay,**
usually called Giovanni da Bologna (1524-1608), a noted
sculptor of Italy.

"While the mouth and the brow stay brave
      in bronze —
Admire and say, 'When he was alive
How he would take his pleasure once!'   210

"And it shall go hard but I contrive
To listen the while, and laugh in my tomb
At idleness which aspires to strive."

So! While these wait the trump of doom,
How do their spirits pass, I wonder,   215
Nights and days in the narrow room?

Still, I suppose, they sit and ponder
What a gift life was, ages ago,
Six steps out of the chapel yonder.

Only they see not God, I know,   220
Nor all that chivalry of his,
The soldier-saints who, row on row,

Burn upward each to his point of bliss —
Since, the end of life being manifest,
He had burned his way through the world to
      this.   225

I hear you reproach, "But delay was best,
For their end was a crime." — Oh, a crime
      will do
As well, I reply, to serve for a test,

As a virtue golden through and through,
Sufficient to vindicate itself   230
And prove its worth at a moment's view!

Must a game be played for the sake of pelf?
Where a button goes, 'twere an epigram
To offer the stamp of the very Guelph.

The true has no value beyond the sham;   235
As well the counter as coin, I submit,
When your table's a hat, and your prize, a
      dram.

Stake your counter as boldly every whit,
Venture as warily, use the same skill,
Do your best, whether winning or losing it,

If you choose to play! — is my principle.   241
Let a man contend to the uttermost
For his life's set prize, be it what it will!

The counter our lovers staked was lost
As surely as if it were lawful coin;   245
And the sin I impute to each frustrate ghost

Is — the unlit lamp and the ungirt loin,
Though the end in sight was a vice, I say.
You of the virtue (we issue join)
How strive you? *De te, fabula!*   250
                                    (1855)

"CHILDE ROLAND TO THE DARK TOWER CAME"

My first thought was, he lied in every word,
      That hoary cripple, with malicious eye
      Askance to watch the working of his lie
On mine, and mouth scarce able to afford
Suppression of the glee, that pursed and
      scored   5
      Its edge, at one more victim gained there-
      by.

What else should he be set for, with his staff?
      What, save to waylay with his lies, ensnare
      All travelers who might find him posted
      there,
And ask the road? I guessed what skull-like
      laugh   10
Would break, what crutch 'gin write my epi-
      taph
      For pastime in the dusty thoroughfare,

If at his counsel I should turn aside
      Into that ominous tract which, all agree,
      Hides the Dark Tower. Yet acquiescingly
I did turn as he pointed — neither pride   16
Nor hope rekindling at the end descried,
      So much as gladness that some end might
      be.

For, what with my whole world-wide wander-
      ing,
      What with my search drawn out through
      years, my hope   20
      Dwindled into a ghost not fit to cope
With that obstreperous joy success would
      bring —
I hardly tried now to rebuke the spring
      My heart made, finding failure in its scope.

As when a sick man very near to death   25
      Seems dead indeed, and feels begin and end
      The tears, and takes the farewell of each
      friend,
And hears one bid the other go, draw breath
Freelier outside ("since all is o'er," he saith,
      "And the blow fallen no grieving can
      amend"),   30

234. **To offer . . . Guelph**, to offer real money bearing
the impress of the crown. The Guelphs were the ruling faction in Italy from the 12th to the 15th centuries.

250. **De te, fabula**, the fable is told concerning yourself.
See Critical Notes.
   Childe Roland to the Dark Tower Came. The title *Childe* was
given to a young knight who had not yet distinguished himself. See Critical Notes.
   14. **all agree.** So the cripple says.

While some discuss if near the other graves
  Be room enough for this, and when a day
  Suits best for carrying the corpse away,
With care about the banners, scarves and
    staves;
And still the man hears all, and only craves 35
  He may not shame such tender love and
    stay.

Thus, I had so long suffered in this quest,
  Heard failure prophesied so oft, been writ
  So many times among "The Band" — to
    wit,
The knights who to the Dark Tower's search
    addressed   40
Their steps — that just to fail as they, seemed
    best,
  And all the doubt was now — should I be
    fit?

So, quiet as despair, I turned from him,
  That hateful cripple, out of his highway
  Into the path he pointed. All the day   45
Had been a dreary one at best, and dim
  Was settling to its close, yet shot one grim
  Red leer to see the plain catch its estray.

For mark! no sooner was I fairly found
  Pledged to the plain, after a pace or two, 50
  Than, pausing to throw backward a last
    view
O'er the safe road, 'twas gone; gray plain all
    round—
Nothing but plain to the horizon's bound.
  I might go on; naught else remained to do.

So, on I went. I think I never saw   55
  Such starved ignoble nature; nothing
    throve;
  For flowers — as well expect a cedar grove!
But cockle, spurge, according to their law
Might propagate their kind, with none to awe,
  You'd think; a burr had been a treasure
    trove.   60

No! penury, inertness, and grimace,
  In some strange sort, were the land's por-
    tion. "See
  Or shut your eyes," said Nature peevishly,
"It nothing skills — I cannot help my case;
'Tis the Last Judgment's fire must cure this
    place,   65
  Calcine its clods, and set my prisoners free."

If there pushed any ragged thistle-stalk
  Above its mates, the head was chopped; the
    bents

48. **estray,** the one who has strayed—namely, Childe
Roland. 64. **skills,** matters. 66. **Calcine,** reduce to powder by heat. 68. **bents,** coarse grasses.

Were jealous else. What made those holes
  and rents
In the dock's harsh swarth leaves, bruised as
  to balk   70
All hope of greenness? 'Tis a brute must walk
Pashing their life out, with a brute's intents.

As for the grass, it grew as scant as hair
  In leprosy; thin dry blades pricked the mud,
  Which underneath looked kneaded up with
    blood.   .   75
One stiff blind horse, his every bone a-stare,
Stood stupefied, however he came there—
  Thrust out past service from the devil's
    stud!

Alive? he might be dead for aught I know,
  With that red gaunt and colloped neck
    a-strain,   80
  And shut eyes underneath the rusty mane;
Seldom went such grotesqueness with such
    woe;
I never saw a brute I hated so;
  He must be wicked to deserve such pain.

I shut my eyes and turned them on my heart.
  As a man calls for wine before he fights, 86
  I asked one draft of earlier, happier sights,
Ere fitly I could hope to play my part.
Think first, fight afterwards — the soldier's
    art;
  One taste of the old time sets all to rights. 90

Not it! I fancied Cuthbert's reddening face
  Beneath its garniture of curly gold,
  Dear fellow, till I almost felt him fold
An arm in mine to fix me to the place,
That way he used. Alas, one night's dis-
    grace!   95
  Out went my heart's new fire and left it
    cold.

Giles then, the soul of honor — there he stands
  Frank as ten years ago when knighted first.
  What honest man should dare (he said) he
    durst.
Good — but the scene shifts — faugh! what
    hangman hands   100
Pin to his breast a parchment? His own bands
Read it. Poor traitor, spit upon and curst!

Better this present than a past like that;
  Back therefore to my darkening path again!
  No sound, no sight as far as eye could
    strain.   105
Will the night send a howlet or a bat?
I asked — when something on the dismal flat
  Came to arrest my thoughts and change
    their train.

80. **colloped,** marked with ridges.

A sudden little river crossed my path
  As unexpected as a serpent comes.   110
No sluggish tide congenial to the glooms;
This, as it frothed by, might have been a bath
For the fiend's glowing hoof — to see the
    wrath
  Of its black eddy bespate with flakes and
    spumes.

So petty yet so spiteful! All along,   115
  Low scrubby alders kneeled down over it;
Drenched willows flung them headlong in a
    fit
Of mute despair, a suicidal throng;
The river which had done them all the wrong,
  Whate'er that was, rolled by, deterred no
    whit.   120

Which, while I forded — good saints, how I
    feared
  To set my foot upon a dead man's cheek,
Each step, or feel the spear I thrust to seek
For hollows, tangled in his hair or beard!
— It may have been a water-rat I speared, 125
  But, ugh! it sounded like a baby's shriek.

Glad was I when I reached the other bank.
  Now for a better country. Vain presage!
Who were the strugglers, what war did they
    wage,
Whose savage trample thus could pad the
    dank   130
Soil to a plash? Toads in a poisoned tank,
  Or wild cats in a red-hot iron cage —

The fight must so have seemed in that fell
    cirque.
  What penned them there, with all the plain
    to choose?
No footprint leading to that horrid mews,
None out of it. Mad brewage set to work 136
Their brains, no doubt, like galley-slaves the
    Turk
  Pits for his pastime, Christians against
    Jews.

And more than that — a furlong on — why,
    there!
  What bad use was that engine for, that
    wheel,   140
  Or brake, not wheel — that harrow fit to
    reel
Men's bodies out like silk? with all the air
Of Tophet's tool, on earth left unaware,
  Or brought to sharpen its rusty teeth of
    steel.

Then came a bit of stubbed ground, once a
    wood,   145
Next a marsh, it would seem, and now mere
    earth
Desperate and done with — so a fool finds
    mirth,
Makes a thing and then mars it, till his mood
Changes and off he goes! — within a rood,
  Bog, clay and rubble, sand and stark black
    dearth.   150

Now blotches rankling, colored gay and grim,
  Now patches where some leanness of the
    soil's
Broke into moss or substances like boils;
Then came some palsied oak, a cleft in him
Like a distorted mouth that splits its rim 155
  Gaping at death, and dies while it recoils.

And just as far as ever from the end!
  Naught in the distance but the evening,
    naught
To point my footstep further! At the
    thought,
A great black bird, Apollyon's bosom-friend,
Sailed past, nor beat his wide wing dragon-
    penned   161
  That brushed my cap — perchance the
    guide I sought.

For, looking up, aware I somehow grew,
  'Spite of the dusk, the plain had given place
All round to mountains — with such name
    to grace   165
Mere ugly heights and heaps now stolen in
    view.
How thus they had surprised me — solve it,
    you!
  How to get from them was no clearer case.

Yet half I seemed to recognize some trick
  Of mischief happened to me, God knows
    when —   170
In a bad dream perhaps. Here ended, then,
Progress this way. When, in the very nick
Of giving up, one time more, came a click
  As when a trap shuts — you're inside the
    den!

Burningly it came on me all at once,   175
  This was the place! those two hills on the
    right,
Crouched like two bulls locked horn in horn
    in fight;

---

114. **bespate**, spattered. 130. **pad**, tread down. 131.
plash, puddle. 135. **mews**, enclosure, pen. 143. **Tophet**,
an Old Testament name for hell.

150. **rubble**, broken stone. 160. **Apollyon's**, the devil's;
from *Revelation*, 9:11.—"And they had a king over them,
which is the angel of the bottomless pit, whose name . . . is
Apollyon." 161. **dragon-penned**, furnished with feathers
like those in a dragon's wing. 174. **As when**, etc. Cf. *Love
in a Life*, p. 242.

While to the left, a tall scalped mountain . . .
    Dunce,
Dotard, a-dozing at the very nonce,
    After a life spent training for the sight! 180

What in the midst lay but the Tower itself?
    The round squat turret, blind as the fool's
        heart,
    Built of brown stone, without a counterpart
In the whole world. The tempest's mocking
    elf
Points to the shipman thus the unseen shelf 185
He strikes on, only when the timbers start.

Not see? because of night perhaps? — why,
    day
    Came back again for that! before it left,
    The dying sunset kindled through a cleft;
The hills, like giants at a hunting, lay, 190
Chin upon hand, to see the game at bay —
    "Now stab and end the creature — to the
        heft!"

Not hear? when noise was everywhere! it
    tolled
    Increasing like a bell. Names in my ears,
    Of all the lost adventurers my peers — 195
How such a one was strong, and such was
    bold,
And such was fortunate, yet each of old
    Lost, lost! one moment knelled the woe of
        years.

There they stood, ranged along the hillsides,
    met
    To view the last of me, a living frame 200
    For one more picture! in a sheet of flame
I saw them and I knew them all. And yet
Dauntless the slug-horn to my lips I set,
    And blew. "*Childe Roland to the Dark
        Tower came.*"   (*1852; 1855*)

IN A BALCONY

Persons { NORBERT
{ CONSTANCE
{ THE QUEEN

CONSTANCE *and* NORBERT

Norbert. Now!
Constance.   Not now!
Nor. Give me them again, those hands;
Put them upon my forehead — how it throbs!
Press them before my eyes; the fire comes
    through!

179. **nonce**, moment. 203. **slug-horn**, trumpet. The
word is really *slogan*. It had formerly been misused by
Chatterton to mean *trumpet*.
In a Balcony. See Critical Notes.

You cruellest, you dearest in the world,
Let me! The Queen must grant whate'er I
    ask —   5
How can I gain you and not ask the Queen?
There she stays waiting for me, here stand
    you;
Some time or other this was to be asked;
Now is the one time — what I ask, I gain.
Let me ask now, Love!
    Con.   Do, and ruin us! 10
    Nor. Let it be now, Love! All my soul
        breaks forth.
How I do love you! Give my love its way!
A man can have but one life and one death,
One heaven, one hell. Let me fulfill my fate—
Grant me my heaven now! Let me know you
    mine,   15
Prove you mine, write my name upon your
    brow,
Hold you and have you, and then die away,
If God please, with completion in my soul!
    Con. I am not yours then? How content
        this man!
I am not his — who change into himself, 20
Have passed into his heart and beat its beats,
Who give my hands to him, my eyes, my hair,
Give all that was of me away to him —
So well, that now, my spirit turned his own,
Takes part with him against the woman here,
Bids him not stumble at so mere a straw 26
As caring that the world be cognizant
How he loves her and how she worships him.
You have this woman, not as yet that world.
Go on, I bid, nor stop to care for me 30
By saving what I cease to care about,
The courtly name and pride of circumstance—
The name you'll pick up and be cumbered
    with
Just for the poor parade's sake, nothing more;
Just that the world may slip from under
    you —   35
Just that the world may cry, "So much for
    him —
The man predestined to the heap of crowns;
There goes his chance of winning one, at
    least!"
    Nor. The world!
    Con.   You love it! Love me quite as well,
And see if I shall pray for this in vain! 40
Why must you ponder what it knows or
    thinks?
    Nor. You pray for — what, in vain?
    Con.   Oh, my heart's heart,
How I do love you, Norbert! That is right.
But listen, or I take my hands away! 44
You say, "Let it be now"; you would go
    now

20. **who.** The antecedent of *who* is *I*. 25. **the woman
here**, that is, myself. 40. **for this**, for the concealment of
our love.

And tell the Queen, perhaps six steps from us,
You love me — so you do, thank God!
  Nor.   Thank God!
  Con. Yes, Norbert — but you fain would
    tell your love,
And, what succeeds the telling, ask of her
My hand. Now take this rose and look at it,
Listening to me. You are the minister,   51
The Queen's first favorite, nor without a
    cause.
Tonight completes your wonderful year's-
    work
(This palace-feast is held to celebrate),
Made memorable by her life's success,   55
The junction of two crowns, on her sole head,
Her house had only dreamed of anciently;
That this mere dream is grown a stable truth,
Tonight's feast makes authentic. Whose the
    praise?
Whose genius, patience, energy, achieved   60
What turned the many heads and broke the
    hearts?
You are the fate, your minute's in the heaven.
Next comes the Queen's turn. "Name your
    own reward!"
With leave to clench the past, chain the to-
    come,
Put out an arm and touch and take the sun
And fix it ever full-faced on your earth,   66
Possess yourself supremely of her life —
You choose the single thing she will not grant;
Nay, very declaration of which choice
Will turn the scale and neutralize your work;
At best she will forgive you, if she can.   71
You think I'll let you choose — her cousin's
    hand?
  Nor. Wait. First, do you retain your old
    belief
The Queen is generous — nay, is just?
  Con.   There, there!
So men make women love them, while they
    know   75
No more of women's hearts than . . . look
    you here,
You that are just and generous beside.
Make it your own case! For example now,
I'll say — I let you kiss me, hold my hands —
Why? do you know why? I'll instruct you,
    then —   80
The kiss, because you have a name at court;
This hand and this, that you may shut in
    each
A jewel, if you please to pick up such.
That's horrible? Apply it to the Queen —
Suppose I am the Queen to whom you speak.
"I was a nameless man; you needed me;   86
Why did I proffer you my aid? — There stood
A certain pretty cousin at your side.

Why did I make such common cause with
    you?
Access to her had not been easy else.   90
You give my labor here abundant praise?
'Faith, labor, which she overlooked, grew
    play.
How shall your gratitude discharge itself?
Give me her hand!"
  Nor.   And still I urge the same.
Is the Queen just? just — generous or no!   95
  Con. Yes, just. You love a rose (no harm
    in that),
But was it for the rose's sake or mine
You put it in your bosom? Mine, you said —
Then, mine you still must say or else be false.
You told the Queen you served her for her-
    self;   100
If so, to serve her was to serve yourself,
She thinks, for all your unbelieving face!
I know her. In the hall, six steps from us,
One sees the twenty pictures; there's a life
Better than life, and yet no life at all.   105
Conceive her born in such a magic dome,
Pictures all round her! Why, she sees the
    world,
Can recognize its given things and facts,
The fight of giants or the feast of gods,
Sages in senate, beauties at the bath,   110
Chases and battles, the whole earth's display,
Landscape and sea-piece, down to flowers and
    fruit —
And who shall question that she knows them
    all,
In better semblance than the things outside?
Yet bring into the silent gallery   115
Some live thing to contrast in breath and
    blood,
Some lion, with the painted lion there —
You think she'll understand composedly?
— Say, "That's his fellow in the hunting-
    piece
Yonder, I've turned to praise a hundred
    times?"   120
Not so. Her knowledge of our actual earth,
Its hopes and fears, concerns and sympathies,
Must be too far, too mediate, too unreal.
The real exists for us outside, not her;
How should it, with that life in these four
    walls,   125
That father and that mother, first to last
No father and no mother — friends, a heap,
Lovers, no lack — a husband in due time,
And every one of them alike a lie!
Things painted by a Rubens out of naught 130
Into what kindness, friendship, love should be;
All better, all more grandiose than the life,
Only no life; mere cloth and surface-paint,

---

49. **succeeds,** follows. 62. **your . . . heaven,** this is your
supreme moment—the stars are favorable to you.

92. **overlooked,** supervised. 123. **mediate,** indirect.
130. **Rubens,** Peter Paul Rubens (1577-1640), a noted
Flemish painter.

You feel, while you admire. How should she
 feel?
Yet now that she has stood thus fifty years 135
The sole spectator in that gallery,
You think to bring this warm real struggling
 love
In to her of a sudden, and suppose
She'll keep her state untroubled? Here's the
 truth —
She'll apprehend truth's value at a glance, 140
Prefer it to the pictured loyalty?
You only have to say, "So men are made,
For this they act; the thing has many names,
But this the right one; and now, Queen, be
 just!"
Your life slips back; you lose her at the word:
You do not even for amends gain me. 146
He will not understand! oh, Norbert, Norbert,
Do you not understand?
   Nor.   The Queen's the Queen,
I am myself — no picture, but alive
In every nerve and every muscle, here 150
At the palace-window o'er the people's street,
As she in the gallery where the pictures glow;
The good of life is precious to us both.
She cannot love; what do I want with rule?
When first I saw your face a year ago 155
I knew my life's good, my soul heard one
 voice —
"The woman yonder, there's no use of life
But just to obtain her! heap earth's woes in
 one
And bear them — make a pile of all earth's
 joys
And spurn them, as they help or help not
 this; 160
Only, obtain her!" How was it to be?
I found you were the cousin of the Queen;
I must then serve the Queen to get to you.
No other way. Suppose there had been one,
And I, by saying prayers to some white star
With promise of my body and my soul, 166
Might gain you — should I pray the star or
 no?
Instead, there was the Queen to serve! I
 served,
Helped, did what other servants failed to do.
Neither she sought nor I declared my end. 170
Her good is hers, my recompense be mine —
I therefore name you as that recompense.
She dreamed that such a thing could never be?
Let her wake now. She thinks there was
 more cause
In love of power, high fame, pure loyalty? 175
Perhaps she fancies men wear out their lives
Chasing such shades. Then, I've a fancy too;
I worked because I want you with my soul;
I therefore ask your hand. Let it be now!
   Con. Had I not loved you from the very
 first, 180

Were I not yours, could we not steal out thus
So wickedly, so wildly, and so well,
You might become impatient. What's con-
 ceived
Of us without here, by the folk within?
Where are you now? immersed in cares of
 state — 185
Where am I now? intent on festal robes —
We two, embracing under death's spread
 hand!
What was this thought for, what that scruple
 of yours
Which broke the council up? — to bring about
One minute's meeting in the corridor! 190
And then the sudden sleights, strange se-
 crecies,
Complots inscrutable, deep telegraphs,
Long-planned chance-meetings, hazards of a
 look,
"Does she know? does she not know? saved
 or lost?"
A year of this compression's ecstasy 195
All goes for nothing! you would give this up
For the old way, the open way, the world's,
His way who beats, and his who sells his wife!
What tempts you? — their notorious happi-
 ness
Makes you ashamed of ours? The best you'll
 gain 200
Will be — the Queen grants all that you re-
 quire,
Concedes the cousin, rids herself of you
And me at once, and gives us ample leave
To live like our five hundred happy friends.
The world will show us with officious hand 205
Our chamber-entry, and stand sentinel
Where we so oft have stolen across its traps!
Get the world's warrant, ring the falcons' feet,
And make it duty to be bold and swift,
Which long ago was nature. Have it so! 210
We never hawked by rights till flung from
 fist?
Oh, the man's thought! no woman's such a
 fool.
   Nor. Yes, the man's thought and my
 thought, which is more —
One made to love you, let the world take note!
Have I done worthy work? Be love's the
 praise, 215
Though hampered by restrictions, barred
 against
By set forms, blinded by forced secrecies!
Set free my love, and see what love can do
Shown in my life — what work will spring
 from that!
The world is used to have its business done 220

205-207. With these lines cf. lines 232-233 and 625-627.
208. **ring the falcons' feet.** Rings in which to fasten the
leashes were put on the feet of the falcons preparatory to
hunting.

On other grounds, find great effects produced
For power's sake, fame's sake, motives in
    men's mouth.
So, good; but let my low ground shame their
    high!
Truth is the strong thing. Let man's life be
    true!
And love's the truth of mine. Time prove
    the rest!   225
I choose to wear you stamped all over me,
Your name upon my forehead and my breast,
You, from the sword's blade to the ribbon's
    edge,
That men may see, all over, you in me —
That pale loves may die out of their pretense
In face of mine, shames thrown on love fall
    off.   231
Permit this, Constance! Love has been so
    long
Subdued in me, eating me through and
    through,
That now 'tis all of me and must have way.
Think of my work, that chaos of intrigues, 235
Those hopes and fears, surprises and delays,
That long endeavor, earnest, patient, slow,
Trembling at last to its assured result;
Then think of this revulsion! I resume
Life after death (it is no less than life,   240
After such long unlovely laboring days),
And liberate to beauty life's great need
O' the beautiful, which, while it prompted
    work,
Suppressed itself erewhile. This eve's the
    time,
This eve intense with yon first trembling star
We seem to pant and reach; scarce aught be-
    tween   246
The earth that rises and the heaven that bends;
All nature self-abandoned, every tree
Flung as it will, pursuing its own thoughts
And fixed so, every flower and every weed, 250
No pride, no shame, no victory, no defeat;
All under God, each measured by itself.
These statues round us stand abrupt, distinct,
The strong in strength, the weak in weakness
    fixed,
The Muse forever wedded to her lyre,   255
Nymph to her fawn, and Silence to her rose;
See God's approval on his universe!
Let us do so — aspire to live as these
In harmony with truth, ourselves being true!
Take the first way, and let the second come!
My first is to possess myself of you;   261
The music sets the march-step — forward,
    then!
And there's the Queen, I go to claim you of,
The world to witness, wonder, and applaud.
Our flower of life breaks open. No delay! 265
    Con. And so shall we be ruined, both of us.
Norbert, I know her to the skin and bone;

You do not know her, were not born to it,
To feel what she can see or cannot see.
Love, she is generous — aye, despite your
    smile,   270
Generous as you are; for, in that thin frame,
Pain-twisted, punctured through and through
    with cares,
There lived a lavish soul until it starved,
Debarred of healthy food. Look to the soul —
Pity that, stoop to that, ere you begin   275
(The true man's-way) on justice and your
    rights,
Exactions and acquittance of the past!
Begin so — see what justice she will deal!
We women hate a debt as men a gift.
Suppose her some poor keeper of a school 280
Whose business is to sit through summer
    months
And dole out children leave to go and play,
Herself superior to such lightness — she
In the arm-chair's state and pedagogic
    pomp —
To the life, the laughter, sun and youth out-
    side —   285
We wonder such a face looks black on us?
I do not bid you wake her tenderness
(That were vain truly — none is left to wake),
But let her think her justice is engaged
To take the shape of tenderness, and mark 290
If she'll not coldly pay its warmest debt!
Does she love me, I ask you? not a whit;
Yet, thinking that her justice was engaged
To help a kinswoman, she took me up —
Did more on that bare ground than other
    loves   295
Would do on greater argument. For me,
I have no equivalent of such cold kind
To pay her with, but love alone to give
If I give anything. I give her love;
I feel I ought to help her, and I will.   300
So, for her sake, as yours, I tell you twice
That women hate a debt as men a gift.
If I were you, I could obtain this grace —
Could lay the whole I did to love's account,
Nor yet be very false as courtiers go —   305
Declaring my success was recompense;
It would be so, in fact — what were it else?
And then, once loose her generosity —
Oh, how I see it! then, were I but you
To turn it, let it seem to move itself,   310
And make it offer what I really take,
Accepting just, in the poor cousin's hand,
Her value as the next thing to the Queen's —
Since none love queens directly, none dare
    that,   314
And a thing's shadow or a name's mere echo
Suffices those who miss the name and thing!
You pick up just a ribbon she has worn,
To keep in proof how near her breath you
    came.

Say, I'm so near I seem a piece of her — 319
Ask for me that way — oh, you understand —
You'd find the same gift yielded with a grace,
Which, if you make the least show to ex-
    tort . . .
—You'll see! and when you have ruined both
    of us,
Dissertate on the Queen's ingratitude!
    Nor.   Then, if I turn it that way, you con-
        sent?   325
'Tis not my way; I have more hope in truth.
Still, if you won't have truth — why, this in-
    deed,
Were scarcely false, as I'd express the sense.
Will you remain here?
    Con.   O best heart of mine,
How I have loved you! then, you take my
    way?   330
Are mine as you have been her minister,
Work out my thought, give it effect for me,
Paint plain my poor conceit and make it
    serve?
I owe that withered woman everything —
Life, fortune, you, remember! Take my
    part —   335
Help me to pay her! Stand upon your rights?
You, with my rose, my hands, my heart on
    you?
Your rights are mine — you have no rights
    but mine.
    Nor.   Remain here. How you know me!
    Con.   Ah, but still —
[*He breaks from her; she remains. Dance-music
    from within.*

(*Enter the* QUEEN)

    Queen.   Constance? She is here, as he said.
        Speak quick!   340
Is it so? Is it true or false? One word!
    Con.   True.
    Queen.   Mercifullest Mother, thanks to
        thee!
    Con.   Madam?
    Queen.   I love you, Constance, from my
        soul.
Now say once more, with any words you will,
'Tis true, all true, as true as that I speak. 345
    Con.   Why should you doubt it?
    Queen.   Ah, why doubt? why doubt?
Dear, make me see it! Do you see it so?
None see themselves; another sees them best.
You say "why doubt it?" — you see him and
    me.
It is because the Mother has such grace   350
That if we had but faith — wherein we fail —
Whate'er we yearn for would be granted us;
Yet still we let our whims prescribe despair,
Our fancies thwart and cramp our will and
    power,
And while accepting life, abjure its use. 355

Constance, I had abjured the hope of love
And being loved, as truly as yon palm
The hope of seeing Egypt from that plot.
    Con.   Heaven!
    Queen.   But it was so, Constance, it was so!
Men say — or do men say it? fancies say — 360
"Stop here, your life is set, you are grown
    old.
Too late — no love for you, too late for love —
Leave love to girls. Be queen; let Constance
    love!"
One takes the hint — half meets it like a
    child,
Ashamed at any feelings that oppose.   365
"O love, true, never think of love again!
I am a queen; I rule, not love, forsooth."
So it goes on; so a face grows like this,
Hair like this hair, poor arms as lean as these,
Till — nay, it does not end so, I thank God!
    Con.   I cannot understand —
    Queen.   The happier you! 371
Constance, I know not how it is with men;
For women (I am a woman now like you)
There is no good of life but love — but love!
What else looks good, is some shade flung
    from love;   375
Love gilds it, gives it worth. Be warned by
    me,
Never you cheat yourself one instant! Love,
Give love, ask only love, and leave the rest!
O Constance, how I love you!
    Con.   I love you.
    Queen.   I do believe that all is come through
        you.   380
I took you to my heart to keep it warm
When the last chance of love seemed dead in
    me;
I thought your fresh youth warmed my with-
    ered heart.
Oh, I am very old now, am I not?
Not so! it is true and it shall be true!   385
    Con.   Tell it me; let me judge if true or
        false.
    Queen.   Ah, but I fear you! You will look
        at me
And say, "She's old, she's grown unlovely
    quite
Who ne'er was beauteous; men want beauty
    still."   389
Well, so I feared — the curse! so I felt sure!
    Con.   Be calm. And now you feel not sure,
        you say?
    Queen.   Constance, he came — the coming
        was not strange —
Do not I stand and see men come and go?
I turned a half-look from my pedestal
Where I grow marble — "one young man the
    more!   395

362. **Too late . . . for love.** Cf. Christina Rossetti's *Too
Late for Love* (from *The Prince's Progress*), p. 573.

He will love someone; that is naught to me;
What would he with my marble stateliness?"
Yet this seemed somewhat worse than here-
    tofore;
The man more gracious, youthful, like a god,
And I still older, with less flesh to change —
We two those dear extremes that long to
    touch.   401
It seemed still harder when he first began
To labor at those state-affairs, absorbed
The old way for the old end — interest.   404
Oh, to live with a thousand beating hearts
Around you, swift eyes, serviceable hands,
Professing they've no care but for your cause,
Thought but to help you, love but for your-
    self —
And you the marble statue all the time   409
They praise and point at as preferred to life,
Yet leave for the first breathing woman's
    smile,
First dancer's, gypsy's, or street baladine's!
Why, how I have ground my teeth to hear
    men's speech
Stifled for fear it should alarm my ear,   414
Their gait subdued lest step should startle me,
Their eyes declined, such queendom to re-
    spect,
Their hands alert, such treasure to preserve,
While not a man of them broke rank and
    spoke,
Wrote me a vulgar letter all of love,   419
Or caught my hand and pressed it like a hand!
There have been moments, if the sentinel
Lowering his halbert to salute the queen,
Had flung it brutally and clasped my knees,
I would have stooped and kissed him with
    my soul.
   Con.   Who could have comprehended?
   Queen.   Aye, who — who?   425
Why, no one, Constance, but this one who did.
Not they, not you, not I. Even now perhaps
It comes too late — would you but tell the
    truth.
   Con.   I wait to tell it.
   Queen.   Well, you see, he came,
Outfaced the others, did a work this year   430
Exceeds in value all was ever done,
You know — it is not I who say it — all
Say it. And so (a second pang and worse)
I grew aware not only of what he did,
But why so wondrously. Oh, never work 435
Like his was done for work's ignoble sake —
Souls need a finer aim to light and lure!
I felt, I saw, he loved — loved somebody.
And Constance, my dear Constance, do you
    know,
I did believe this while 'twas you he loved.
   Con.   Me, madam?

<hr>

412. **baladine,** a singer of ballads, a street dancer.

• *Queen.*   It did seem to me, your face 441
Met him where'er he looked; and whom but
    you
Was such a man to love? It seemed to me,
You saw he loved you, and approved his love,
And both of you were in intelligence.   445
You could not loiter in that garden, step
Into this balcony, but I straight was stung
And forced to understand. It seemed so true,
So right, so beautiful, so like you both,
That all this work should have been done by
    him   450
Not for the vulgar hope of recompense,
But that at last — suppose, some night like
    this —
Borne on to claim his due reward of me,
He might say, "Give her hand and pay me
    so."   454
And I (O Constance, you shall love me now!)
I thought, surmounting all the bitterness,
"And he shall have it. I will make her blest,
My flower of youth, my woman's self that
    was,
My happiest woman's self that might have
    been!
These two shall have their joy and leave me
    here."   460
Yes — yes!
   Con.   Thanks!
   Queen.   And the word was on my lips
When he burst in upon me. I looked to hear
A mere calm statement of his just desire
For payment of his labor. When — O heaven,
How can I tell you? Lightning on my eyes 465
And thunder in my ears proved that first
    word
Which told 'twas love of me, of me, did all —
He loved me — from the first step to the last,
Loved me!
   Con.   You hardly saw, scarce heard him
    speak
Of love; what if you should mistake?
   Queen.   No, no —   470
No mistake! Ha, there shall be no mistake!
He had not dared to hint the love he felt —
You were my reflex — (how I understood!)
He said you were the ribbon I had worn,   474
He kissed my hand, he looked into my eyes,
And love, love came at end of every phrase.
Love is begun; this much is come to pass;
The rest is easy. Constance, I am yours!
I will learn, I will place my life on you;   479
Teach me but how to keep what I have won!
Am I so old? This hair was early gray;
But joy ere now has brought hair brown again,
And joy will bring the cheek's red back, I feel.
I could sing once too; that was in my youth.
Still, when men paint me, they declare me
    . . . yes,   485
Beautiful — for the last French painter did!

I know they flatter somewhat; you are
    frank —
I trust you. How I loved you from the first!
Some queens would hardly seek a cousin out
And set her by their side to take the eye; 490
I must have felt that good would come from
    you.
I am not generous — like him — like you!
But he is not your lover after all;
It was not you he looked at. Saw you him?
You have not been mistaking words or looks?
He said you were the reflex of myself.   496
And yet he is not such a paragon
To you, to younger women who may choose
Among a thousand Norberts. Speak the
    truth!   499
You know you never named his name to me;
You know, I cannot give him up — ah God,
Not up now, even to you!
Con.   Then calm yourself.
Queen. See, I am old — look here, you
    happy girl!
I will not play the fool, deceive — ah, whom?
'Tis all gone; put your cheek beside my cheek
And what a contrast does the moon behold! 506
But then I set my life upon one chance,
The last chance and the best — am *I* not left,
My soul, myself? All women love great men
If young or old; it is in all the tales;   510
Young beauties love old poets who can love —
Why should not he, the poems in my soul,
The passionate faith, the pride of sacrifice,
Life-long, death-long? I throw them at his
    feet.   514
Who cares to see the fountain's very shape,
Whether it be a Triton's or a Nymph's
That pours the foam, makes rainbows all
    around?
You could not praise indeed the empty conch;
But I'll pour floods of love and hide myself.
How I will love him! Cannot men love
    love?   520
Who was a queen and loved a poet once,
Humpbacked, a dwarf? Ah, women can do
    that!
Well, but men too; at least, they tell you so.
They love so many women in their youth,
And even in age they all love whom they
    please;   525
And yet the best of them confide to friends
That 'tis not beauty makes the lasting love —
They spend a day with such and tire the next.
They like soul — well then, they like phan-
    tasy,
Novelty even. Let us confess the truth,   530

516. **Triton**, a sea-god, part man, part horse, and part
fish. He blew a twisted seashell to calm or raise the waves.
521. **a queen . . . once.** This may refer to Françoise d'Au-
bigne, Marquise de Maintenon (1635–1719), who first married
the deformed Scarron, a French poet and dramatist, and after
his death became the consort of King Louis XIV.

Horrible though it be, that prejudice,
Prescription . . . curses! they will love a queen.
They will, they do; and will not, does not —
    he?
Con. How can he? You are wedded; 'tis
    a name,
We know, but still a bond. Your rank re-
    mains,   535
His rank remains. How can he, nobly souled
As you believe and I incline to think,
Aspire to be your favorite, shame and all?
Queen. Hear her! There, there now —
    could she love like me?
What did I say of smooth-cheeked youth and
    grace?   540
See all it does or could do! so youth loves!
Oh, tell him, Constance, you could never do
What I will — you, it was not born in!
Will drive these difficulties far and fast   544
As yonder mists curdling before the moon.
I'll use my light too, gloriously retrieve
My youth from its enforced calamity,
Dissolve that hateful marriage, and be his,
His own in the eyes alike of God and man.
Con. You will do — dare do . . . pause on
    what you say!   550
Queen. Hear her! I thank you, sweet, for
    that surprise.
You have the fair face; for the soul, see mine!
I have the strong soul; let me teach you,
    here.
I think I have borne enough and long enough,
And patiently enough, the world remarks, 555
To have my own way now, unblamed by all.
It does so happen (I rejoice for it)
This most unhoped-for issue cuts the knot.
There's not a better way of settling claims 559
Than this; God sends the accident express.
And were it for my subjects' good, no more,
'Twere best thus ordered. I am thankful now,
Mute, passive, acquiescent. I receive,
And bless God simply, or should almost fear
To walk so smoothly to my ends at last.   565
Why, how I baffle obstacles, spurn fate!
How strong I am! Could Norbert see me
    now!
Con. Let me consider. It is all too strange.
Queen. You, Constance, learn of me; do
    you, like me!   569
You are young, beautiful; my own, best girl,
You will have many lovers, and love one —
Light hair, not hair like Norbert's, to suit
    yours,
Taller than he is, since yourself are tall.
Love him, like me! Give all away to him; 574
Think never of yourself; throw by your pride,
Hope, fear — your own good as you saw it
    once,
And love him simply for his very self.
Remember, I (and what am I to you?)

Would give up all for one, leave throne, lose
    life,   579
Do all but just unlove him! He loves me.
  Con. He shall.
  Queen. You, step inside my inmost heart!
Give me your own heart; let us have one
    heart!
I'll come to you for counsel; "this he says,
This he does; what should this amount to,
    pray?
Beseech you, change it into current coin! 585
Is that worth kisses? Shall I please him
    there?"
And then we'll speak in turn of you — what
    else?
Your love, according to your beauty's worth,
For you shall have some noble love, all gold;
Whom choose you? We will get him at your
    choice.   590
— Constance, I leave you. Just a minute
    since,
I felt as I must die or be alone,
Breathing my soul into an ear like yours;
Now, I would face the world with my new
    life,
Wear my new crown. I'll walk around the
    rooms,   595
And then come back and tell you how it feels.
How soon a smile of God can change the
    world!
How we are made for happiness — how work
Grows play, adversity a winning fight!
True, I have lost so many years; what then?
Many remain; God has been very good. 601
You, stay here! 'Tis as different from dreams,
From the mind's cold calm estimate of bliss,
As these stone statues from the flesh and
    blood.
The comfort thou hast caused mankind, God's
    moon!   605
She goes out, leaving CONSTANCE. *Dance-music*
    from within.

(NORBERT *enters.*)

  Nor. Well? we have but one minute and
    one word!
  Con. I am yours, Norbert!
  Nor.   Yes, mine.
  Con.   Not till now!
You were mine. Now I give myself to you.
  Nor. Constance?
  Con.   Your own! I know the thriftier
    way
Of giving — haply, 'tis the wiser way.   610
Meaning to give a treasure, I might dole
Coin after coin out (each, as that were all,
With a new largess still at each despair)
And force you keep in sight the deed, pre-
    serve   614
Exhaustless till the end my part and yours,

My giving and your taking; both our joys
Dying together. Is it the wiser way?
I choose the simpler; I give all at once.
Know what you have to trust to, trade upon!
Use it, abuse it — anything but think   620
Hereafter, "Had I known she loved me so,
And what my means, I might have thriven
    with it."
This is your means. I give you all myself.
  Nor. I take you and thank God.
  Con.   Look on through years!
We cannot kiss, a second day like this; 625
Else were this earth no earth.
  Nor.   With this day's heat
We shall go on through years of cold.
  Con.   So, best!
— I try to see those years — I think I see.
You walk quick, and new warmth comes; you
    look back   629
And lay all to the first glow — not sit down
Forever brooding on a day like this
While seeing embers whiten and love die.
Yes, love lives best in its effect; and mine,
Full in its own life, yearns to live in yours.
  Nor. Just so. I take and know you all at
    once.   635
Your soul is disengaged so easily,
Your face is there, I know you; give me time,
Let me be proud and think you shall know me.
My soul is slower; in a life I roll   639
The minute out whereto you condense yours —
The whole slow circle round you I must move,
To be just you. I look to a long life
To decompose this minute, prove its worth.
'Tis the sparks' long succession one by one
Shall you, in the end, what fire was
    crammed   645
In that mere stone you struck; how could you
    know,
If it lay ever unproved in your sight,
As now my heart lies? Your own warmth
    would hide
Its coldness, were it cold.
  Con.   But how prove, how?
  Nor. Prove in my life, you ask?
  Con.   Quick, Norbert — how? 650
  Nor. That's easy told. I count life just a
    stuff
To try the soul's strength on, educe the man.
Who keeps one end in view makes all things
    serve
As with the body — he who hurls a lance
Or heaps up stone on stone, shows strength
    alike;   655
So must I seize and task all means to prove
And show this soul of mine, you crown as
    yours,
And justify us both.

652. **educe**, draw forth.

Con.　　　　Could you write books,
Paint pictures! One sits down in poverty 659
And writes or paints, with pity for the rich.
　Nor.　And loves one's painting and one's
　　　writing, then,
And not one's mistress! All is best, believe,
And we best as no other than we are.
We live, and they experiment on life —　664
Those poets, painters, all who stand aloof
To overlook the farther. Let us be
The thing they look at! I might take your
　　face
And write of it and paint it — to what end?
For whom? What pale dictatress in the air 669
Feeds, smiling sadly, her fine ghost-like form
With earth's real blood and breath, the beau-
　　teous life
She makes despised forever? You are mine,
Made for me, not for others in the world,
Nor yet for that which I should call my art,
The cold calm power to see how fair you
　　look.　　　　　　　　　　　675
I come to you; I leave you not, to write
Or paint. You are, I am; let Rubens there
Paint us!
　Con.　So, best!
　Nor.　　　　I understand your soul;
You live, and rightly sympathize with life,
With action, power, success. This way is
　　straight;　　　　　　　　680
And time were short beside, to let me change
The craft my childhood learnt; my craft
　　shall serve.
Men set me here to subjugate, enclose,
Manure their barren lives, and force thence
　　fruit　　　　　　　　　684
First for themselves, and afterward for me
In the due tithe; the task of some one soul,
Through ways of work appointed by the
　　world.
I am not bid create — men see no star
Transfiguring my brow to warrant that —
But find and bind and bring to bear their
　　wills.　　　　　　　　690
So I began; tonight sees how I end.
What if it see, too, power's first outbreak here
Amid the warmth, surprise, and sympathy,
And instincts of the heart that teach the
　　head?　　　　　　　　694
What if the people have discerned at length
The dawn of the next nature, novel brain
Whose will they venture in the place of theirs,
Whose work, they trust, shall find them as
　　novel ways
To untried heights which yet he only sees? 699
I felt it when you kissed me. See this Queen,
This people — in our phrase this mass of
　　men —
See how the mass lies passive to my hand
Now that my hand is plastic, with you by

To make the muscles iron! Oh, an end　704
Shall crown this issue as this crowns the first!
My will be on the people! then, the strain,
The grappling of the potter with his clay,
The long uncertain struggle — the success
And consummation of the spirit-work,　709
Some vase shape to the curl of the god's lip,
While rounded fair for human sense to see
The Graces in a dance men recognize
With turbulent applause and laughs of heart!
So triumph ever shall renew itself;
Ever shall end in efforts higher yet,　715
Ever begin . . .
　Con.　　　　I ever helping?
　Nor.　　　　　　　Thus!

(As he embraces her, the QUEEN *enters.)*

Con.　Hist, madam! So have I performed
　　my part.
You see your gratitude's true decency,
Norbert? A little slow in seeing it!
Begin, to end the sooner! What's a kiss? 720
　Nor.　Constance?
　Con.　　　　Why, must I teach it you again?
You want a witness to your dullness, sir?
What was I saying these ten minutes long?
Then I repeat—when some young handsome
　　man
Like you has acted out a part like yours, 725
Is pleased to fall in love with one beyond,
So very far beyond him, as he says —
So hopelessly in love that but to speak
Would prove him mad — he thinks judicious-
　　ly,
And makes some insignificant good soul,　730
Like me, his friend, adviser, confidant,
And very stalking-horse to cover him
In following after what he dares not face —
When his end's gained (sir, do you under-
　　stand?) —
When she, he dares not face, has loved him
　　first —　　　　　　　735
May I not say so, madam? — tops his hope,
And overpasses so his wildest dream,
With glad consent of all, and most of her
The confidant who brought the same about —
Why, in the moment when such joy explodes,
I do hold that the merest gentleman　741
Will not start rudely from the stalking-horse,
Dismiss it with a "There, enough of you!"
Forget it, show his back unmannerly;
But like a liberal heart will rather turn　745
And say, "A tingling time of hope was ours;
Betwixt the fears and falterings, we two lived
A chanceful time in waiting for the prize;
The confidant, the Constance, served not ill.
And though I shall forget her in good time, 750
Her use being answered now, as reason bids,
Nay as herself bids from her heart of hearts —
Still, she has rights, the first thanks go to her,

The first good praise goes to the prosperous
    tool,
And the first — which is the last — rewarding
    kiss."   755

    Nor. Constance, it is a dream — ah, see,
    you smile!

    Con. So, now his part being properly per-
    formed,
Madam, I turn to you and finish mine
As duly; I do justice in my turn.
Yes, madam, he has loved you — long and
    well;   760
He could not hope to tell you so — 'twas I
Who served to prove your soul accessible;
I led his thoughts on, drew them to their place
When they had wandered else into despair,
And kept love constant toward its natural
    aim.   765
Enough, my part is played; you stoop half-
    way
And meet us royally and spare our fears;
'Tis like yourself. He thanks you, so do I.
Take him — with my full heart! my work is
    praised   769
By what comes of it. Be you happy, both!
Yourself — the only one on earth who can —
Do all for him, much more than a mere heart
Which though warm is not useful in its
    warmth
As the silk vesture of a queen! fold that
Around him gently, tenderly. For him — 775
For him — he knows his own part!
    Nor.   Have you done?
I take the jest at last. Should I speak now?
Was yours the wager, Constance, foolish child,
Or did you but accept it? Well — at least
You lose by it.
    Con.   Nay, madam, 'tis your turn!   780
Restrain him still from speech a little more,
And make him happier as more confident!
Pity him, madam; he is timid yet!
Mark, Norbert! Do not shrink now! Here
    I yield   784
My whole right in you to the Queen, observe!
With her go put in practice the great schemes
You teem with, follow the career else closed —
Be all you cannot be except by her!
Behold her! — Madam, say for pity's sake   789
Anything — frankly say you love him! Else
He'll not believe it; there's more earnest in
His fear than you conceive — I know the man!
    Nor. I know the woman somewhat, and
    confess
I thought she had jested better; she begins
To overcharge her part. I gravely wait   795
Your pleasure, madam; where is my reward?
    Queen. Norbert, this wild girl — whom I
    recognize
Scarce more than you do, in her fancy-fit,
Eccentric speech, and variable mirth,   799

Not very wise perhaps and somewhat bold,
Yet suitable, the whole night's work being
    strange —
May still be right; I may do well to speak
And make authentic what appears a dream
To even myself. For, what she says is true;
Yes, Norbert — what you spoke just now of
    love,   805
Devotion, stirred no novel sense in me,
But justified a warmth felt long before.
Yes, from the first — I loved you, I shall say.
Strange! but I do grow stronger, now 'tis
    said.
Your courage helps mine; you did well to
    speak   810
Tonight, the night that crowns your twelve-
    months' toil;
But still I had not waited to discern
Your heart so long, believe me! From the
    first
The source of so much zeal was almost plain,
In absence even of your own words just now
Which hazarded the truth. 'Tis very strange,
But takes a happy ending — in your love 817
Which mine meets; be it so! as you choose
    me,
So I choose you.
    Nor.   And worthily you choose.
I will not be unworthy your esteem,   820
No, madam. I do love you; I will meet
Your nature, now I know it. This was well.
I see — you dare and you are justified;
But none had ventured such experiment,
Less versed than you in nobleness of heart,
Less confident of finding such in me.   826
I joy that thus you test me ere you grant
The dearest, richest, beauteousest, and best
Of women to my arms; 'tis like yourself.
So — back again into my part's set words —
Devotion to the uttermost is yours,   831
But no, you cannot, madam, even you,
Create in me the love our Constance does.
Or — something truer to the tragic phrase —
Not yon magnolia-bell superb with scent 835
Invites a certain insect — that's myself —
But the small eye-flower nearer to the ground.
I take this lady.
    Con.   Stay — not hers, the trap —
Stay, Norbert — that mistake were worst of
    all!
He is too cunning, madam! It was I,   840
I, Norbert, who . . .
    Nor.   You, was it, Constance? Then,
But for the grace of this divinest hour
Which gives me you, I might not pardon here!
I am the Queen's; she only knows my brain;
She may experiment upon my heart   845
And I instruct her too by the result.
But you, Sweet, you who know me, who so
    long

Have told my heartbeats over, held my life
In those white hands of yours — it is not
    well!
  Con. Tush! I have said it, did I not say
    it all? 850
The life, for her — the heartbeats, for her sake!
  Nor. Enough! My cheek grows red, I
    think. Your test?
There's not the meanest woman in the world,
Not she I least could love in all the world,
Whom, did she love me, had love proved
    itself, 855
I dare insult as you insult me now.
Constance, I could say, if it must be said,
"Take back the soul you offer, I keep mine!"
But — "Take the soul still quivering on your
    hand,
The soul so offered, which I cannot use, 860
And, please you, give it to some playful friend,
For — what's the trifle he requites me with?"
I, tempt a woman, to amuse a man,
That two may mock her heart if it succumb?
No; fearing God and standing 'neath his
    heaven, 865
I would not dare insult a woman so,
Were she the meanest woman in the world,
And he, I cared to please, ten emperors!
  Con. Norbert!
  Nor. I love once as I live but once. 869
What case is this to think or talk about?
I love you. Would it mend the case at all
If such a step as this killed love in me?
Your part were done; account to God for it!
But mine — could murdered love get up again,
And kneel to whom you please to designate,
And make you mirth? It is too horrible. 876
You did not know this, Constance? Now you
    know
That body and soul have each one life, but
    one;
And here's my love, here, living, at your feet.
  Con. See the Queen! Norbert — this one
    more last word — 880
If thus you have taken jest for earnest — thus
Loved me in earnest . . .
  Nor. Ah, no jest holds here!
Where is the laughter in which jests break up,
And what this horror that grows palpable? 884
Madam — why grasp you thus the balcony?
Have I done ill? Have I not spoken truth?
How could I other? Was it not your test,
To try me, what my love for Constance
    meant?
Madam, your royal soul itself approves,
The first, that I should choose thus! so one
    takes 890
A beggar — asks him, what would buy his
    child?
And then approves the expected laugh of
    scorn

Returned as something noble from the rags.
Speak, Constance, I'm the beggar! Ha, what's
    this? 894
You two glare each at each like panthers now.
Constance, the world fades; only you stand
    there!
You did not, in tonight's wild whirl of things,
Sell me — your soul of souls, for any price?
No — no — 'tis easy to believe in you!
Was it your love's mad trial to o'ertop 900
Mine by this vain self-sacrifice? Well, still —
Though I might curse, I love you. I am love
And cannot change; love's self is at your feet!
    [*The* QUEEN *goes out.*
  Con. Feel my heart; let it die against your
    own!
  Nor. Against my own. Explain not; let
    this be! 905
This is life's height.
  Con. Yours, yours, yours!
  Nor. You and I —
Why care by what meanders we are here
I' the center of the labyrinth? Men have died
Trying to find this place, which we have
    found.
  Con. Found, found! 909
  Nor. Sweet, never fear what she can do!
We are past harm now.
  Con. On the breast of God.
I thought of men — as if you were a man.
Tempting him with a crown!
  Nor. This must end here;
It is too perfect.
  Con. There's the music stopped. 914
What measured heavy tread? It is one blaze
About me and within me.
  Nor. Oh, some death
Will run its sudden finger round this spark
And sever us from the rest!
  Con. And so do well.
Now the doors open —
  Nor. 'Tis the guard comes.
  Con. Kiss!
    (*1853;* 1855)

"TRANSCENDENTALISM: A POEM IN TWELVE BOOKS"

Stop playing, poet! May a brother speak?
'Tis you speak, that's your error. Song's our
    art:
Whereas you please to speak these naked
    thoughts
Instead of draping them in sights and sounds.

"Transcendentalism: A Poem in Twelve Books." This is addressed to an imaginary poet who is supposed to be writing
a poem on transcendentalism, a system of speculative philosophy. Berdoe thinks that Browning intended the poem as an
answer to the critics who had accused him of philosophizing
instead of writing poetry.

— True thoughts, good thoughts, thoughts
    fit to treasure up!   5
But why such long prolusion and display,
Such turning and adjustment of the harp,
And taking it upon your breast, at length,
Only to speak dry words across its strings?
Stark-naked thought is in request enough; 10
Speak prose and hollo it till Europe hears!
The six-foot Swiss tube, braced about with
    bark,
Which helps the hunter's voice from Alp to
    Alp —
Exchange our harp for that — who hinders
    you?

    But here's your fault; grown men want
       thought, you think;   15
Thought's what they mean by verse, and seek
    in verse;
Boys seek for images and melody,
Men must have reason — so, you aim at
    men.
Quite otherwise! Objects throng our youth,
    'tis true;
We see and hear and do not wonder much: 20
If you could tell us what they mean, indeed!
As German Boehme never cared for plants
Until it happed, a-walking in the fields,
He noticed all at once that plants could speak,
Nay, turned with loosened tongue to talk
    with him.   25
That day the daisy had an eye indeed —
Colloquized with the cowslip on such themes!
We find them extant yet in Jacob's prose.
But by the time youth slips a stage or two
While reading prose in that tough book he
    wrote   30
(Collating and emendating the same
And settling on the sense most to our mind),
We shut the clasps and find life's summer
    past.
Then, who helps more, pray, to repair our
    loss —
Another Boehme with a tougher book   35
And subtler meanings of what roses say —
Or some stout Mage like him of Halberstadt,
John, who made things Boehme wrote
    thoughts about?
He with a "look you!" vents a brace of rimes,
And in there breaks the sudden rose herself,
Over us, under, round us every side,   41
Nay, in and out the tables and the chairs
And musty volumes, Boehme's book and all —

Buries us with a glory, young once more,
Pouring heaven into this shut house of life. 45

So come, the harp back to your heart again!
You are a poem, though your poem's naught.
The best of all you showed before, believe,
Was your own boy-face o'er the finer chords
Bent, following the cherub at the top   50
That points to God with his paired half-moon
    wings.

                          (1855)

HOW IT STRIKES A CONTEMPORARY

I only knew one poet in my life;
And this, or something like it, was his way.

    You saw go up and down Valladolid,
A man of mark, to know next time you saw.
His very serviceable suit of black   5
Was courtly once and conscientious still,
And many might have worn it, though none
    did;
The cloak, that somewhat shone and showed
    the threads,
Had purpose, and the ruff, significance.
He walked and tapped the pavement with his
    cane,   10
Scenting the world, looking it full in face,
An old dog, bald and blindish, at his heels.
They turned up, now, the alley by the church,
That leads nowhither; now, they breathed
    themselves
On the main promenade just at the wrong
    time.   15
You'd come upon his scrutinizing hat,
Making a peaked shade blacker than itself
Against the single window spared some house
Intact yet with its moldered Moorish work —
Or else surprise the ferrel of his stick   20
Trying the mortar's temper 'tween the chinks
Of some new shop a-building, French and fine.
He stood and watched the cobbler at his trade,
The man who slices lemons into drink,
The coffee-roaster's brazier, and the boys 25
That volunteer to help him turn its winch.
He glanced o'er books on stalls with half an
    eye,
And fly-leaf ballads on the vender's string,
And broad-edge bold-print posters by the wall.
He took such cognizance of men and things,
If any beat a horse, you felt he saw;   31

---

12. **The six-foot Swiss tube,** a kind of wooden trumpet
used by Alpine hunters. 22. **Boehme,** Jacob Boehme
(1575–1624), a German mystical writer who professed to
know all mysteries through actual observation of them. He
declared that he was able to see into the being of God and
into the heart of things. 37. **him of Halberstadt,** John of
Halberstadt, a German magician and astrologer who is said
to have made flowers bloom in winter by magic. Cf. Chaucer's *Franklin's Tale* for a story of a similar feat.

How It Strikes a Contemporary. This poem, spoken by a
Spanish gentleman from the city of Valladolid, in northern
Spain, suggests that the function of the poet is "scenting the
world, looking it full in face" (line 11).
    7. **many might . . . none did,** that is, it was out of
style. 11–32. **Scenting . . . note.** These lines are said to
reflect Browning's own habits. 28. **fly-leaf ballads,** flying
ballads, or broadsides—i.e., ballads printed on one side of
large sheets of paper.

If any cursed a woman, he took note;
Yet stared at nobody — you stared at him,
And found, less to your pleasure than sur-
   prise,
He seemed to know you and expect as much.
So, next time that a neighbor's tongue was
   loosed,   36
It marked the shameful and notorious fact,
We had among us, not so much a spy,
As a recording chief-inquisitor,
The town's true master if the town but knew!
We merely kept a governor for form,   41
While this man walked about and took
   account
Of all thought, said, and acted, then went
   home,
And wrote it fully to our Lord the King,
Who has an itch to know things, he knows
   why,   45
And reads them in his bedroom of a night.
Oh, you might smile! there wanted not a
   touch,
A tang of . . . well, it was not wholly ease
As back into your mind the man's look came.
Stricken in years a little — such a brow   50
His eyes had to live under! — clear as flint
On either side the formidable nose
Curved, cut, and colored like an eagle's claw.
Had he to do with A's surprising fate?
When altogether old B disappeared   55
And young C got his mistress — was't our
   friend,
His letter to the King, that did it all?
What paid the bloodless man for so much
   pains?
Our Lord the King has favorites manifold,
And shifts his ministry some once a month; 60
Our city gets new governors at whiles —
But never word or sign, that I could hear,
Notified to this man about the streets
The King's approval of those letters conned
The last thing duly at the dead of night.   65
Did the man love his office? Frowned our
   Lord,
Exhorting, when none heard — "Beseech me .
   not!
Too far above my people — beneath me!
I set the watch — how should the people
   know?   69
Forget them, keep me all the more in
   mind!"
Was some such understanding 'twixt the two?

I found no truth in one report at least —
That if you tracked him to his home, down
   lanes
Beyond the Jewry, and as clean to pace,
You found he ate his supper in a room   75

Blazing with lights, four Titians on the wall,
And twenty naked girls to change his plate!
Poor man, he lived another kind of life
In that new stuccoed third house by the
   bridge,
Fresh-painted, rather smart than otherwise!
The whole street might o'erlook him as he
   sat,   81
Leg crossing leg, one foot on the dog's back,
Playing a decent cribbage with his maid
(Jacynth, you're sure her name was) o'er the
   cheese
And fruit, three red halves of starved winter-
   pears,   85
Or treat of radishes in April. Nine,
Ten, struck the church clock; straight to bed
   went he.

My father, like the man of sense he was,
Would point him out to me a dozen times;
" 'St — 'St," he'd whisper, "the Corregidor!"
I had been used to think that personage   91
Was one with lacquered breeches, lustrous
   belt,
And feathers like a forest in his hat,
Who blew a trumpet and proclaimed the
   news,
Announced the bull-fights, gave each church
   its turn,   95
And memorized the miracle in vogue!
He had a great observance from us boys;
We were in error; that was not the man.

I'd like now, yet had haply been afraid,
To have just looked, when this man came to
   die,   100
And seen who lined the clean gay garret-sides
And stood about the neat low truckle-bed,
With the heavenly manner of relieving guard.
Here had been, mark, the general-in-chief,
Through a whole campaign of the world's life
   and death,   105
Doing the King's work all the dim day long,
In his old coat and up to knees in mud,
Smoked like a herring, dining on a crust —
And, now the day was won, relieved at once!
No further show or need for that old coat, 110
You are sure, for one thing! Bless us, all the
   while
How sprucely we are dressed out, you and I!
A second, and the angels alter that.
Well, I could never write a verse — could you?
Let's to the Prado and make the most of
   time.   115

(1855)

74. the Jewry, the Jewish section.

76. Titians, paintings by Titian (1477-1575), a noted
Italian painter. 90. the Corregidor, the title of the chief
magistrate of the city. 115. the Prado, the name of the
fashionable promenade of Madrid, copied by other Spanish
cities.

BISHOP BLOUGRAM'S APOLOGY

No more wine? then we'll push back chairs
    and talk.
A final glass for me, though: cool, i' faith!
We ought to have our Abbey back, you see.
It's different, preaching in basilicas,
And doing duty in some masterpiece   5
Like this of brother Pugin's, bless his heart!
I doubt if they're half baked, those chalk
    rosettes,
Ciphers and stucco-twiddlings everywhere;
It's just like breathing in a lime-kiln: eh?
These hot long ceremonies of our church   10
Cost us a little — oh, they pay the price,
You take me — amply pay it! Now, we'll talk.

So, you despise me, Mr. Gigadibs.
No deprecation, — nay, I beg you, sir!
Beside 'tis our engagement: don't you know,
I promised, if you'd watch a dinner out,   16
We'd see truth dawn together? — truth that
    peeps
Over the glasses' edge when dinner's done,
And body gets its sop and holds its noise
And leaves soul free a little. Now's the time: 20
Truth's break of day! You do despise me
    then.
And if I say, "despise me," — never fear!
I know you do not in a certain sense —
Not in my arm-chair, for example: here,
I well imagine you respect my place   25
(*Status, entourage,* worldly circumstance)
Quite to its value — very much indeed:
— Are up to the protesting eyes of you
In pride at being seated here for once —
You'll turn it to such capital account!   30
When somebody, through years and years to
    come,
Hints of the bishop, — names me — that's
    enough:
"Blougram? I knew him" — (into it you slide)
"Dined with him once, a Corpus Christi Day,
All alone, we two; he's a clever man: 35
And after dinner, — why, the wine you
    know, —
Oh, there was wine, and good! — what with
    the wine . . .
Faith, we began upon all sorts of talk!
He's no bad fellow, Blougram; he had seen
Something of mine he relished, some review: 40
He's quite above their humbug in his heart,
Half-said as much, indeed — the thing's his
    trade.
I warrant, Blougram's skeptical at times:

How otherwise? I liked him, I confess!"
Che che, my dear sir, as we say at Rome,   45
Don't you protest now! It's fair give and
    take;
You have had your turn and spoken your
    home-truths:
The hand's mine now, and here you follow
    suit.

Thus much conceded, still the first fact
    stays —
You do despise me; your ideal of life   50
Is not the bishop's: you would not be I.
You would like better to be Goethe, now,
Or Buonaparte, or, bless me, lower still,
Count D'Orsay, — so you did what you pre-
    ferred,
Spoke as you thought, and, as you cannot
    help,   55
Believed or disbelieved, no matter what,
So long as on that point, whate'er it was,
You loosed your mind, were whole and sole
    yourself.
— That, my ideal never can include,
Upon that element of truth and worth   60
Never be based! for say they make me Pope —
(They can't — suppose it for our argument!)
Why, there I'm at my tether's end, I've
    reached
My height, and not a height which pleases
    you:
An unbelieving Pope won't do, you say.   65
It's like those eerie stories nurses tell,
Of how some actor on a stage played Death,
With pasteboard crown, sham orb and tin-
    selled dart,
And called himself the monarch of the world;
Then, going in the tire-room afterward,   70
Because the play was done, to shift himself,
Got touched upon the sleeve familiarly,
The moment he had shut the closet door,
By Death himself. Thus God might touch a
    Pope
At unawares, ask what his baubles mean,   75
And whose part he presumed to play just now.
Best be yourself, imperial, plain and true!

So, drawing comfortable breath again,
You weigh and find, whatever more or less
I boast of my ideal realized   80
Is nothing in the balance when opposed
To your ideal, your grand simple life,
Of which you will not realize one jot.
I am much, you are nothing; you would be all,
I would be merely much: you beat me there.   85

No, friend, you do not beat me: hearken
    why!

Bishop Blougram's Apology. See Critical Notes.
  3. **our Abbey,** Westminster Abbey, Roman Catholic until
the Reformation. 6. **Pugin,** A. N. W. Pugin (1812-1852),
Catholic architect of Neo-Gothic churches. 34. **Corpus
Christi,** feast day, the Thursday after Trinity Sunday, kept
in honor of the Eucharist.

45. **Che, che,** what, what (Italian). 54. **Count D'Orsay**
(1798-1852), a well known early-Victorian dandy.

The common problem, yours, mine, every
    one's,
Is — not to fancy what were fair in life
Provided it could be, — but, finding first
What may be, then find how to make it fair 90
Up to our means: a very different thing!
No abstract intellectual plan of life
Quite irrespective of life's plainest laws,
But one, a man, who is man and nothing more,
May lead within a world which (by your
    leave) 95
Is Rome or London, not Fool's-paradise.
Embellish Rome, idealize away,
Make paradise of London if you can,
You're welcome, nay, you're wise.

                  A simile!
We mortals cross the ocean of this world 100
Each in his average cabin of a life;
The best's not big, the worst yields elbow-
    room.
Now for our six months' voyage — how pre-
    pare?
You come on shipboard with a landsman's
    list
Of things he calls convenient: so they are! 105
An India screen is pretty furniture,
A piano-forte is a fine resource,
All Balzac's novels occupy one shelf,
The new edition fifty volumes long;
And little Greek books, with the funny type
They get up well at Leipsic, fill the next: 111
Go on! slabbed marble, what a bath it makes!
And Parma's pride, the Jerome, let us add!
'Twere pleasant could Corregio's fleeting glow
Hang full in face of one where'er one roams,
Since he more than the others brings with
    him 116
Italy's self, — the marvellous Modenese! —
Yet was not on your list before, perhaps.
— Alas, friend, here's the agent . . . is't the
    name?
The captain, or whoever's master here — 120
You see him screw his face up; what's his cry
Ere you set foot on shipboard? "Six feet
    square!"
If you won't understand what six feet mean,
Compute and purchase stores accordingly —
And if, in pique because he overhauls 125
Your Jerome, piano, bath, you come on board
Bare — why, you cut a figure at the first
While sympathetic landsmen see you off;
Not afterward, when long ere half seas over,
You peep up from your utterly naked boards
Into some snug and well-appointed berth, 131

Like mine for instance (try the cooler jug —
Put back the other, but don't jog the ice!)
And mortified you mutter "Well and good;
He sits enjoying his sea-furniture; 135
'Tis stout and proper, and there's store of it:
Though I've the better notion, all agree,
Of fitting rooms up. Hang the carpenter,
Neat ship-shape fixings and contrivances —
I would have brought my Jerome, frame and
    all!" 140
And meantime you bring nothing: never
    mind —
You've proved your artist-nature: what you
    don't
You might bring, so despise me, as I say.

    Now come, let's backward to the starting-
    place.
See my way: we're two college friends, sup-
    pose. 145
Prepare together for our voyage, then;
Each note and check the other in his work,—
Here's mine, a bishop's outfit; criticise!
What's wrong? why won't you be a bishop
    too?

    Why first, you don't believe, you don't and
    can't, 150
(Not statedly, that is, and fixedly
And absolutely and exclusively)
In any revelation called divine.
No dogmas nail your faith; and what remains
But say so, like the honest man you are? 155
First, therefore, overhaul theology!
Nay, I too, not a fool, you please to think,
Must find believing every whit as hard:
And if I do not frankly say as much,
The ugly consequence is clear enough. 160

    Now wait, my friend: well, I do not be-
    lieve —
If you'll accept no faith that is not fixed,
Absolute and exclusive, as you say.
You're wrong — I mean to prove it in due
    time.
Meanwhile, I know where difficulties lie 165
I could not, cannot solve, nor ever shall,
So give up hope accordingly to solve —
(To you, and over the wine). Our dogmas
    then
With both of us, though in unlike degree,
Missing full credence — overboard with them!
I mean to meet you on your own premise: 171
Good, there go mine in company with yours!

    And now what are we? unbelievers both,
Calm and complete, determinately fixed
To-day, to-morrow and forever, pray? 175
You'll guarantee me that? Not so, I think!
In no wise! all we've gained is, that belief,

---

108. **Balzac** (1799-1850), the great French "realist," author
of *The Human Comedy* in many volumes. 113-114. **Parma's**
. . . **Correggio**, the painting of Saint Jerome in the Ducal
Academy at Parma by Correggio (1494-1534), who studied at
Modena (cf. line 117).

As unbelief before, shakes us by fits,
Confounds us like its predecessor. Where's
The gain? how can we guard our unbelief, 180
Make it bear fruit to us? — the problem here.
Just when we are safest, there's a sunset-
    touch,
A fancy from a flower-bell, some one's death,
A chorus-ending from Euripides, —
And that's enough for fifty hopes and fears
As old and new at once as nature's self, 186
To rap and knock and enter in our soul,
Take hands and dance there, a fantastic ring,
Round the ancient idol, on his base again, —
The grand Perhaps! We look on helplessly. 190
There the old misgivings, crooked questions
    are —
This good God, — what he could do, if he
    would,
Would, if he could — then must have done
    long since:
If so, when, where and how? some way must
    be, —
Once feel about, and soon or late you hit 195
Some sense, in which it might be, after all.
Why not, "The Way, the Truth, the Life?"

                        — That way
Over the mountain, which who stands upon
Is apt to doubt if it be meant for a road;
While, if he views it from the waste itself, 200
Up goes the line there, plain from base to
    brow,
Not vague, mistakable! what's a break or two
Seen from the unbroken desert either side?
And then (to bring in fresh philosophy)
What if the breaks themselves should prove
    at last   205
The most consummate of contrivances
To train a man's eye, teach him what is faith?
And so we stumble at truth's very test!
All we have gained then by our unbelief
Is a life of doubt diversified by faith, 210
For one of faith diversified by doubt:
We called the chess-board white, — we call it
    black.

    "Well," you rejoin, "the end's no worse, at
        least;
We've reason for both colors on the board:
Why not confess then, where I drop the faith
And you the doubt, that I'm as right as you?"

    Because, friend, in the next place, this being
        so,   217
And both things even, — faith and unbelief
Left to a man's choice, — we'll proceed a step,
Returning to our image, which I like.   220

197. **"The Way . . . the Life,"** see *John,* 14:6. "Jesus
saith . . . . I am the way, the truth, and the life: no man cometh unto the Father, but by me."

A man's choice, yes — but a cabin-pas-
    senger's —
The man made for the special life o' the
    world —
Do you forget him? I remember though!
Consult our ship's conditions and you find
One and but one choice suitable to all; 225
The choice, that you unluckily prefer,
Turning things topsy-turvy — they or it
Going to the ground. Belief or unbelief
Bears upon life, determines its whole course,
Begins at its beginning. See the world   230
Such as it is, — you made it not, nor I;
I mean to take it as it is, — and you,
Not so you'll take it, — though you get naught
    else.
I know the special kind of life I like,
What suits the most my idiosyncrasy,   235
Brings out the best of me and bears me fruit
In power, peace, pleasantness and length of
    days.
I find that positive belief does this
For me, and unbelief, no whit of this.
— For you, it does, however? — that, we'll
    try!   240
'Tis clear, I cannot lead my life, at least,
Induce the world to let me peaceably,
Without declaring at the outset, "Friends,
I absolutely and peremptorily
Believe!" — I say, faith is my waking life: 245
One sleeps, indeed, and dreams at intervals,
We know, but waking's the main point with
    us,
And my provision's for life's waking part.
Accordingly, I use heart, head and hand
All day, I build, scheme, study, and make
    friends;   250
And when night overtakes me, down I lie,
Sleep, dream a little, and get done with it,
The sooner the better, to begin afresh.
What's midnight doubt before the dayspring's
    faith?
You, the philosopher, that disbelieve,   255
That recognize the night, give dreams their
    weight —
To be consistent you should keep your bed,
Abstain from healthy acts that prove you
    man,
For fear you drowse perhaps at unawares!
And certainly at night you'll sleep and dream,
Live through the day and bustle as you
    please.   261
And so you live to sleep as I to wake,
To unbelieve as I to still believe?
Well, and the common sense o' the world calls
    you
Bed-ridden, — and its good things come to
    me.   265
Its estimation, which is half the fight,
That's the first-cabin comfort I secure:

The next . . . but you perceive with half an
  eye!
Come, come, it's best believing, if we may;
You can't but own that!

            Next, concede again, 270
If once we choose belief, on all accounts
We can't be too decisive in our faith,
Conclusive and exclusive in its terms,
To suit the world which gives us the good
  things.
In every man's career are certain points 275
Whereon he dares not be indifferent;
The world detects him clearly, if he dare,
As baffled at the game, and losing life.
He may care little or he may care much
For riches, honor, pleasure, work, repose, 280
Since various theories of life and life's
Success are extant which might easily
Comport with either estimate of these;
And whoso chooses wealth or poverty,
Labor or quiet, is not judged a fool 285
Because his fellow would choose otherwise:
We let him choose upon his own account
So long as he's consistent with his choice,
But certain points, left wholly to himself,
When once a man has arbitrated on, 290
We say he must succeed there or go hang.
Thus, he should wed the woman he loves
  most
Or needs most, whatsoe'er the love or need —
For he can't wed twice. Then, he must avouch,
Or follow, at the least, sufficiently, 295
The form of faith his conscience holds the
  best,
Whate'er the process of conviction was:
For nothing can compensate his mistake
On such a point, the man himself being judge:
He cannot wed twice, nor twice lose his soul.

Well now, there's one great form of Chris-
  tian faith 301
I happened to be born in — which to teach
Was given me as I grew up, on all hands,
As best and readiest means of living by;
The same on examination being proved 305
The most pronounced moreover, fixed, precise
And absolute form of faith in the whole
  world —
Accordingly, most potent of all forms
For working on the world. Observe my friend!
Such as you know me, I am free to say, 310
In these hard latter days which hamper one,
Myself — by no immoderate exercise
Of intellect and learning, but the tact
To let external forces work for me,
— Bid the street's stones be bread and they
  are bread; 315

Bid Peter's creed, or rather, Hildebrand's,
Exalt me o'er my fellows in the world
And make my life an ease and joy and pride;
It does so, — which for me's a great point
  gained, —
Who have a soul and body that exact 320
A comfortable care in many ways.
There's power in me and will to dominate
Which I must exercise, they hurt me else:
In many ways I need mankind's respect,
Obedience, and the love that's born of fear: 325
While at the same time, there's a taste I
  have,
A toy of soul, a titillating thing,
Refuses to digest these dainties crude.
The naked life is gross till clothed upon:
I must take what men offer, with a grace 330
As though I would not, could I help it, take!
An uniform I wear though over-rich —
Something imposed on me, no choice of mine;
No fancy-dress worn for pure fancy's sake
And despicable therefore! now folk kneel 335
And kiss my hand — of course the Church's
  hand.
Thus I am made, thus life is best for me,
And thus that it should be I have procured;
And thus it could not be another way,
I venture to imagine.

            You'll reply, 340
So far my choice, no doubt, is a success;
But were I made of better elements,
With nobler instincts, purer tastes, like you,
I hardly would account the thing success
Though it did all for me I say.

            But, friend, 345
We speak of what is; not of what might be,
And how 'twere better if 'twere otherwise.
I am the man you see here plain enough:
Grant I'm a beast, why, beasts must lead
  beasts' lives!
Suppose I own at once to tail and claws; 350
The tailless man exceeds me: but being tailed
I'll lash out lion fashion, and leave apes
To dock their stump and dress their haunches
  up.
My business is not to remake myself,
But make the absolute best of what God
  made. 355
Or — our first simile — though you prove me
  doomed
To a viler berth still, to the steerage-hole,
The sheep-pen or the pig-stye, I should strive
To make what use of each were possible;
And as this cabin gets upholstery, 360
That hutch should rustle with sufficient straw.

316. **Peter . . . Hildebrand.** The Church traces its beginnings to Saint Peter, but Hildebrand, Pope Gregory VII
(1073-1085), asserted its temporal power.

But, friend, I don't acknowledge quite so
    fast
I fail of all your manhood's lofty tastes
Enumerated so complacently,
On the mere ground that you forsooth can
    find   365
In this particular life I choose to lead
No fit provision for them. Can you not?
Say you, my fault is I address myself
To grosser estimators than should judge?
And that's no way of holding up the soul, 370
Which, nobler, needs men's praise perhaps,
    yet knows
One wise man's verdict outweighs all the
    fools' —
Would like the two, but, forced to choose,
    takes that.
I pine among my million imbeciles
(You think) aware some dozen men of sense
Eye me and know me, whether I believe   376
In the last winking Virgin, as I vow,
And am a fool, or disbelieve in her
And am a knave,— approve in neither case,
Withhold their voices though I look their
    way: 380
Like Verdi when, at his worst opera's end
(The thing they gave at Florence, — what's
    its name?)
While the mad houseful's plaudits near out-
    bang
His orchestra of salt-box, tongs and bones,
He looks through all the roaring and the
    wreaths   385
Where sits Rossini patient in his stall.

Nay, friend, I meet you with an answer
    here —
That even your prime men who appraise their
    kind
Are men still, catch a wheel within a wheel,
See more in a truth than the truth's simple
    self,   390
Confuse themselves. You see lads walk the
    street
Sixty the minute; what's to note in that?
You see one lad o'erstride a chimney-stack;
Him you must watch — he's sure to fall, yet
    stands!
Our interest's on the dangerous edge of things.
The honest thief, the tender murderer,   396
The superstitious atheist, demirep
That loves and saves her soul in new French
    books —

We watch while these in equilibrium keep
The giddy line midway: one step aside,   400
They're classed and done with. I, then, keep
    the line
Before your sages, — just the men to shrink
From the gross weights, coarse scales and
    labels broad
You offer their refinement. Fool or knave?
Why needs a bishop be a fool or knave   405
When there's a thousand diamond weights
    between?
So, I enlist them. Your picked twelve, you'll
    find,
Profess themselves indignant, scandalized
At thus being held unable to explain
How a superior man who disbelieves   410
May not believe as well: that's Schelling's
    way!
It's through my coming in the tail of time,
Nicking the minute with a happy tact.
Had I been born three hundred years ago
They'd say, "What's strange? Blougram of
    course believes;"   415
And, seventy years since, "disbelieves of
    course."
But now, "He may believe; and yet, and yet
How can he?" All eyes turn with interest.
Whereas, step off the line on either side —
You, for example, clever to a fault,   420
The rough and ready man who write apace,
Read somewhat seldomer, think perhaps even
    less —
You disbelieve! Who wonders and who cares?
Lord So-and-so — his coat bedropped with
    wax,
All Peter's chains about his waist, his back 425
Brave with the needlework of Noodledom —
Believes! Again, who wonders and who cares?
But I, the man of sense and learning too,
The able to think yet act, the this, the that,
I, to believe at this late time of day!   430
Enough; you see, I need not fear contempt.

— Except it's yours! Admire me as these
    may,
You don't. But whom at least do you admire?
Present your own perfection, your ideal,
Your pattern man for a minute — oh, make
    haste,   435
Is it Napoleon you would have us grow?
Concede the means; allow his head and hand,
(A large concession, clever as you are)
Good! In our common primal element
Of unbelief (we can't believe, you know—   440
We're still at that admission, recollect!)
Where do you find — apart from, towering
    o'er

---

377. **winking Virgin**, a statue of the Virgin reported miraculously to have moved its eyes.   381-386. **Verdi . . . Rossini**. Despite public applause, the true value of a minor opera
by Giuseppe Verdi (1813-1901) is to be judged by the knowing
silence of Gioacchino Rossini (1792-1868), an older and less
flamboyant composer.   397. **demirep**, woman of dubious
reputation. The courtesan with the heart of gold was a
familiar character in French fiction of the period.

407. **picked twelve**, a jury.   411. **Schelling**, Friedrich
von Schelling (1775-1854), German idealist who believed intuitive knowledge more reliable than practical reason.

The secondary temporary aims
Which satisfy the gross taste you despise —
Where do you find his star? — his crazy
  trust   445
God knows through what or in what? it's
  alive
And shines and leads him, and that's all we
  want.
Have we aught in our sober night shall point
Such ends as his were, and direct the means
Of working out our purpose straight as his, 450
Nor bring a moment's trouble on success
With after-care to justify the same?
— Be a Napoleon, and yet disbelieve —
Why, the man's mad, friend, take his light
  away!
What's the vague good o' the world, for which
  you dare   455
With comfort to yourself blow millions up?
We neither of us see it! we do see
The blown-up millions — spatter of their
  brains
And writhing of their bowels and so forth,
In that bewildering entanglement   460
Of horrible eventualities
Past calculation to the end of time!
Can I mistake for some clear word of God
(Which were my ample warrant for it all)
His puff of hazy instinct, idle talk,   465
"The State, that's I," quack-nonsense about
  crowns,
And (when one beats the man to his last hold)
A vague idea of setting things to rights,
Policing people efficaciously,
More to their profit, most of all to his own; 470
The whole to end that dismallest of ends
By an Austrian marriage, cant to us the
  Church,
And resurrection of the old *régime?*
Would I, who hope to live a dozen years,
Fight Austerlitz for reasons such and such?
No: for, concede me but the merest chance
Doubt may be wrong — there's judgment,
  life to come!   477
With just that chance, I dare not. Doubt
  proves right?
This present life is all? — you offer me
Its dozen noisy years, without a chance   480
That wedding an archduchess, wearing lace,
And getting called by divers new-coined
  names,
Will drive off ugly thoughts and let me dine,
Sleep, read and chat in quiet as I like!
Therefore I will not.

Take another case; 485
Fit up the cabin yet another way.
What say you to the poets? shall we write
Hamlet, Othello — make the world our own,
Without a risk to run of either sort?
I can't! — to put the strongest reason first. 490
"But try," you urge, "the trying shall suffice;
The aim, if reached or not, makes great the
  life:
Try to be Shakespeare, leave the rest to fate!"
Spare my self-knowledge — there's no fooling
  me!
If I prefer remaining my poor self,   495
I say so not in self-dispraise but praise.
If I'm a Shakespeare, let the well alone;
Why should I try to be what now I am?
If I'm no Shakespeare, as too probable, —
His power and consciousness and self-
  delight   500
And all we want in common, shall I find —
Trying forever? while on points of taste
Wherewith, to speak it humbly, he and I
Are dowered alike — I'll ask you, I or he,
Which in our two lives realizes most?   505
Much, he imagined — somewhat, I possess.
He had the imagination; stick to that!
Let him say, "In the face of my soul's works
Your world is worthless and I touch it not
Lest I should wrong them" — I'll withdraw
  my plea.   510
But does he say so? look upon his life!
Himself, who only can, gives judgment there.
He leaves his towers and gorgeous palaces
To build the trimmest house in Stratford
  town;
Saves money, spends it, owns the worth of
  things,   515
Giulio Romano's pictures, Dowland's lute;
Enjoys a show, respects the puppets, too,
And none more, had he seen its entry once,
Than "Pandulph, of fair Milan cardinal."
Why then should I who play that person-
  age,   520
The very Pandulph Shakespeare's fancy made,
Be told that had the poet chanced to start
From where I stand now (some degree like
  mine
Being just the goal he ran his race to reach)
He would have run the whole race back,
  forsooth,   525
And left being Pandulph, to begin write plays?
Ah, the earth's best can be but the earth's
  best!
Did Shakespeare live, he could but sit at
  home

---

472. **Austrian marriage.** By marrying Mary Louise,
Hapsburg princess of Austria, Napoleon made the reactionary
gesture that completed the betrayal of his early revolutionary
position. Several years earlier he had crushed the Austrian
forces at Austerlitz (cf. line 475).

516. **Giulio Romano**, Italian painter (1492-1546) whose
work was known to Shakespeare. **Dowland.** John Dowland
(1563-1626), Elizabethan lutanist and composer. 519. **Pandulph**, medieval Italian Churchman, mentioned in Shakespeare's *King John*, III, i, 138.

And get himself in dreams the Vatican,
Greek busts, Venetian paintings, Roman
        walls,   530
And English books, none equal to his own,
Which I read, bound in gold (he never did).
— Terni's fall, Naples' bay and Gothard's
        top —
Eh, friend? I could not fancy one of these;
But, as I pour this claret, there they are: 535
I've gained them — crossed St. Gothard last
        July
With ten mules to the carriage and a bed
Slung inside; is my hap the worse for that?
We want the same things, Shakespeare and
        myself,
And what I want, I have: he, gifted more, 540
Could fancy he too had them when he liked,
But not so thoroughly that, if fate allowed,
He would not have them also in my sense.
We play one game; I send the ball aloft
No less adroitly that of fifty strokes   545
Scarce five go o'er the wall so wide and high
Which sends them back to me: I wish and
        get.
He struck balls higher and with better skill,
But at a poor fence level with his head,
And hit — his Stratford house, a coat of
        arms,   550
Successful dealings in his grain and wool, —
While I receive heaven's incense in my nose
And style myself the cousin of Queen Bess.
Ask him, if this life's all, who wins the game?

Believe — and our whole argument breaks
        up.   555
Enthusiasm's the best thing, I repeat;
Only, we can't command it; fire and life
Are all, dead matter's nothing, we agree:
And be it a mad dream or God's very breath,
The fact's the same, — belief's fire, once in
        us,   560
Makes of all else mere stuff to show itself:
We penetrate our life with such a glow
As fire lends wood and iron — this turns
        steel,
That burns to ash — all's one, fire proves its
        power
For good or ill, since men call flare success. 565
But paint a fire, it will not therefore burn.
Light one in me, I'll find it food enough!
Why, to be Luther — that's a life to lead,
Incomparably better than my own.
He comes, reclaims God's earth for God, he
        says,   570
Sets up God's rule again by simple means,
Re-opens a shut book, and all is done.
He flared out in the flaring of mankind;

Such Luther's luck was: how shall such be
        mine?
If he succeeded, nothing's left to do: 575
And if he did not altogether — well,
Strauss is the next advance. All Strauss
        should be
I might be also. But to what result?
He looks upon no future: Luther did.
What can I gain on the denying side?   580
Ice makes no conflagration. State the facts,
Read the text right, emancipate the world —
The emancipated world enjoys itself
With scarce a thank-you: Blougram told it
        first
It could not owe a farthing — not to him 585
More than Saint Paul! 'twould press its pay,
        you think?
Then add there's still that plaguy hundredth
        chance
Strauss may be wrong. And so a risk is run —
For what gain? not for Luther's, who secured
A real heaven in his heart throughout his
        life,   590
Supposing death a little altered things.

"Ay, but since really you lack faith," you
        cry,
"You run the same risk really on all sides,
In cool indifference as bold unbelief.
As well be Strauss as swing 'twixt Paul and
        him.   595
It's not worth having, such imperfect faith,
No more available to do faith's work
Than unbelief like mine. Whole faith, or
        none!"

Softly, my friend! I must dispute that point.
Once own the use of faith, I'll find you faith.
We're back on Christian ground. You call
        for faith: 601
I show you doubt, to prove that faith exists.
The more of doubt, the stronger faith, I say,
If faith o'ercomes doubt. How I know it
        does?
By life and man's free will, God gave for
        that!   605
To mould life as we choose it, shows our
        choice:
That's our one act, the previous work's his
        own.
You criticise the soul? it reared this tree —
This broad life and whatever fruit it bears!
What matter though I doubt at every pore, 610
Head-doubts, heart-doubts, doubts at my
        fingers' ends,
Doubts in the trivial work of every day,
Doubts at the very bases of my soul

533. **Terni's fall,** waterfall north of Rome. **Gothard,**
St. Gothard, pass between Italy and Switzerland.

577. **Strauss,** David Friedrich Strauss (1808-1874), author
of a rationalistic *Life of Jesus,* influenced by the Higher Criticism (historical Biblical research).

In the grand moments when she probes her-
self —
If finally I have a life to show, 615
The thing I did, brought out in evidence
Against the thing done to me underground
By hell and all its brood, for aught I know?
I say, whence sprang this? shows it faith or
doubt?
All's doubt in me; where's break of faith in
this? 620
It is the idea, the feeling and the love,
God means mankind should strive for and
show forth
Whatever be the process to that end, —
And not historic knowledge, logic sound,
And metaphysical acumen, sure! 625
"What think ye of Christ," friend? when all's
done and said,
Like you this Christianity or not?
It may be false, but will you wish it true?
Has it your vote to be so if it can?
Trust you an instinct silenced long ago 630
That will break silence and enjoin you love
What mortified philosophy is hoarse,
And all in vain, with bidding you despise?
If you desire faith — then you've faith
enough:
What else seeks God — nay, what else seek
ourselves? 635
You form a notion of me, we'll suppose,
On hearsay; it's a favorable one:
"But still" (you add), "there was no such
good man,
Because of contradiction in the facts.
One proves, for instance, he was born in
Rome, 640
This Blougram; yet throughout the tales of
him
I see he figures as an Englishman."
Well, the two things are reconcilable.
But would I rather you discover that,
Subjoining — "Still, what matter though
they be? 645
Blougram concerns me naught, born here or
there."

Pure faith indeed — you know not what
you ask!
Naked belief in God the Omnipotent,
Omniscient, Omnipresent, sears too much
The sense of conscious creatures to be borne.
It were the seeing him, no flesh shall dare. 651
Some think, Creation's meant to show him
forth:
I say it's meant to hide him all it can,
And that's what all the blessed evil's for.
Its use in Time is to environ us, 655
Our breath, our drop of dew, with shield
enough
Against that sight till we can bear its stress.

Under a vertical sun, the exposed brain
And lidless eye and disemprisoned heart
Less certainly would wither up at once 660
Than mind, confronted with the truth of him.
But time and earth case-harden us to live;
The feeblest sense is trusted most; the child
Feels God a moment, ichors o'er the place,
Plays on and grows to be a man like us. 665
With me, faith means perpetual unbelief
Kept quiet like the snake 'neath Michael's
foot
Who stands calm just because he feels it
writhe.
Or, if that's too ambitious, — here's my
box —
I need the excitation of a pinch 670
Threatening the torpor of the inside-nose
Nigh on the imminent sneeze that never
comes.
"Leave it in peace" advise the simple folk:
Make it aware of peace by itching-fits,
Say I — let doubt occasion still more faith! 675

You'll say, once all believed, man, woman,
child,
In that dear middle-age these noodles praise.
How you'd exult if I could put you back
Six hundred years, blot out cosmogony,
Geology, ethnology, what not, 680
(Greek endings, each the little passing-bell
That signifies some faith's about to die),
And set you square with Genesis again, —
When such a traveller told you his last news,
He saw the ark a-top of Ararat 685
But did not climb there since 'twas getting
dusk
And robber-bands infest the mountain's foot!
How should you feel, I ask, in such an age,
How act? As other people felt and did;
With soul more blank than this decanter's
knob, 690
Believe — and yet lie, kill, rob, fornicate
Full in belief's face, like the beast you'd be!

No, when the fight begins within himself,
A man's worth something. God stoops o'er
his head,
Satan looks up between his feet — both tug —
He's left, himself, i' the middle: the soul
wakes 696
And grows. Prolong that battle through his
life!
Never leave growing till the life to come!
Here, we've got callous to the Virgin's winks
That used to puzzle people wholesomely: 700
Men have outgrown the shame of being fools.
What are the laws of nature, not to bend

---

664. **ichors,** discharges, as does a wound before healing.
667. **snake . . . foot.** The Archangel Michael is often depicted as crushing the serpentine Satan. 685. **Ararat,** mountain in Turkey; see *Genesis,* 8:4.

If the Church bid them? — brother Newman
   asks.
Up with the Immaculate Conception, then —
On to the rack with faith! — is my advice. 705
Will not that hurry us upon our knees,
Knocking our breasts, "It can't be — yet it
   shall!
Who am I, the worm, to argue with my Pope?
Low things confound the high things!" and
   so forth.
That's better than acquitting God with
   grace   710
As some folk do. He's tried — no case is
   proved,
Philosophy is lenient — he may go!

You'll say, the old system's not so obsolete
But men believe still: ay, but who and where?
King Bomba's lazzaroni foster yet   715
The sacred flame, so Antonelli writes;
But even of these, what ragamuffin-saint
Believes God watches him continually,
As he believes in fire that it will burn,
Or rain that it will drench him? Break fire's
   law,   720
Sin against rain, although the penalty
Be just a singe or soaking? "No," he smiles;
"Those laws are laws that can enforce them-
   selves."

The sum of all is — yes, my doubt is great,
My faith's still greater, then my faith's
   enough.   725
I have read much, thought much, experi-
   enced much,
Yet would die rather than avow my fear
The Naples' liquefaction may be false,
When set to happen by the palace-clock
According to the clouds or dinner-time.   730
I hear you recommend, I might at least
Eliminate, decrassify my faith
Since I adopt it; keeping what I must
And leaving what I can — such points as this.
I won't — that is, I can't throw one away. 735
Supposing there's no truth in what I hold
About the need of trial to man's faith,
Still, when you bid me purify the same,
To such a process I discern no end.
Clearing off one excrescence to see two,   740
There's ever a next in size, now grown as big,
That meets the knife: I cut and cut again!
First cut the Liquefaction, what comes last
But Fichte's clever cut at God himself?

Experimentalize on sacred things!   745
I trust nor hand nor eye nor heart nor brain
To stop betimes: they all get drunk alike.
The first step, I am master not to take.

You'd find the cutting-process to your taste
As much as leaving growths of lies unpruned,
Nor see more danger in it, — you retort. 751
Your taste's worth mine; but my taste proves
   more wise
When we consider that the steadfast hold
On the extreme end of the chain of faith
Gives all the advantage, makes the difference
With the rough purblind mass we seek to
   rule: 756
We are their lords, or they are free of us,
Just as we tighten or relax our hold.
So, other matters equal, we'll revert
To the first problem — which, if solved my
   way   760
And thrown into the balance, turns the
   scale —
How we may lead a comfortable life,
How suit our luggage to the cabin's size.

Of course you are remarking all this time
How narrowly and grossly I view life,   765
Respect the creature-comforts, care to rule
The masses, and regard complacently
"The cabin," in our old phrase. Well, I do.
I act for, talk for, live for this world now,
As this world prizes action, life and talk: 770
No prejudice to what next world may prove,
Whose new laws and requirements, my best
   pledge
To observe then, is that I observe these now,
Shall do hereafter what I do meanwhile.
Let us concede (gratuitously though)   775
Next life relieves the soul of body, yields
Pure spiritual enjoyment: well, my friend,
Why lose this life i' the meantime, since its
   use
May be to make the next life more intense?

Do you know, I have often had a dream 780
(Work it up in your next month's article)
Of man's poor spirit in its progress, still
Losing true life forever and a day
Through ever trying to be and ever being —
In the evolution of successive spheres —   785
Before its actual sphere and place of life,
Halfway into the next, which having reached,
It shoots with corresponding foolery
Halfway into the next still, on and off!
As when a traveller, bound from North to
   South,   790
Scouts fur in Russia: what's its use in France?
In France spurns flannel: where's its need in
   Spain?

703. Newman, J. H. Newman, who defended miracles in his *Present Position of Catholics in England* (1851), including the liquefaction of the blood of St. Januarius, patron saint of Naples, on the saint's feast day (Sept. 19) each year; cf. line 728. **704. Immaculate Conception.** This dogma (that the Virgin Mary was free, from the time of her conception, of all taint of original sin) was promulgated by Pope Pius IX in 1854. **715. King Bomba's lazzaroni**, the beggarly subjects of Ferdinand II (1810-1859) of the Two Sicilies. **716. Antonelli**, cardinal, secretary to Pius IX.

744. Fichte, German idealist (1762-1814) who defined God as man's idea of the moral order of the universe.

In Spain drops cloth, too cumbrous for Al-
  giers!
Linen goes next, and last the skin itself,
A superfluity at Timbuctoo.   795
When, through his journey, was the fool at
  ease?
I'm at ease now, friend; worldly in this world,
I take and like its way of life; I think
My brothers, who administer the means,
Live better for my comfort — that's good
  too;   800
And God, if he pronounce upon such life,
Approves my service, which is better still.
If he keep silence, — why, for you or me
Or that brute beast pulled-up in to-day's
  "Times,"
What odds is 't, save to ourselves, what life
  we lead?   805

You meet me at this issue: you declare, —
All special-pleading done with — truth is
  truth,
And justifies itself by undreamed ways.
You don't fear but it's better, if we doubt,
To say so, act up to our truth perceived   810
However feebly. Do then, — act away!
'Tis there I'm on the watch for you. How one
  acts
Is, both of us agree, our chief concern:
And how you'll act is what I fain would see
If, like the candid person you appear,   815
You dare to make the most of your life's
  scheme
As I of mine, live up to its full law
Since there's no higher law that counter-
  checks.
Put natural religion to the test
You've just demolished the revealed with —
  quick,   820
Down to the root of all that checks your
  will,
All prohibition to lie, kill and thieve,
Or even to be an atheistic priest!
Suppose a pricking to incontinence —
Philosophers deduce you chastity   825
Or shame, from just the fact that at the first
Whoso embraced a woman in the field,
Threw club down and forewent his brains
  beside,
So, stood a ready victim in the reach
Of any brother savage, club in hand;   830
Hence saw the use of going out of sight
In wood or cave to prosecute his loves:
I read this in a French book t' other day.
Does law so analyzed coerce you much?
Oh, men spin clouds of fuzz where matters
  end,   835
But you who reach where the first thread
  begins,
You'll soon cut that! — which means you can,
  but won't,

Through certain instincts, blind, unreasoned-
  out,
You dare not set aside, you can't tell why,
But there they are, and so you let them
  rule.   840
Then, friend, you seem as much a slave as I,
A liar, conscious coward and hypocrite,
Without the good the slave expects to get,
In case he has a master after all!
You own your instincts? why, what else do
  I,   845
Who want, am made for, and must have a
  God
Ere I can be aught, do aught? — no mere
  name
Want, but the true thing with what proves its
  truth,
To wit, a relation from that thing to me,
Touching from head to foot — which touch I
  feel,   850
And with it take the rest, this life of ours!
I live my life here; yours you dare not live.

— Not as I state it, who (you please
  subjoin)
Disfigure such a life and call it names.
While, to your mind, remains another way   855
For simple men: knowledge and power have
  rights,
But ignorance and weakness have rights too.
There needs no crucial effort to find truth
If here or there or anywhere about:
We ought to turn each side, try hard and
  see,   860
And if we can't, be glad we've earned at least
The right, by one laborious proof the more,
To graze in peace earth's pleasant pasturage.
Men are not angels, neither are they brutes:
Something we may see, all we cannot see.   865
What need of lying? I say, I see all,
And swear to each detail the most minute
In what I think a Pan's face — you, mere
  cloud:
I swear I hear him speak and see him wink,
For fear, if once I drop the emphasis,   870
Mankind may doubt there's any cloud at all.
You take the simple life — ready to see,
Willing to see (for no cloud's worth a face) —
And leaving quiet what no strength can move,
And which, who bids you move? who has the
  right?   875
I bid you; but you are God's sheep, not mine:
"*Pastor est tui Dominus.*" You find
In this the pleasant pasture of our life
Much you may eat without the least offence,
Much you don't eat because your maw ob-
  jects,   880
Much you would eat but that your fellow-flock

877. **"Pastor . . . Dominus,"** "The Lord is thy shepherd," an ironic misquotation of Psalm 23.

Open great eyes at you and even butt,
And thereupon you like your mates so well
You cannot please yourself, offending them;
Though when they seem exorbitantly sheep,
You weigh your pleasure with their butts
    and bleats   886
And strike the balance. Sometimes certain
    fears
Restrain you, real checks since you find them
    so;
Sometimes you please yourself and nothing
    checks:
And thus you graze through life with not one
    lie,   890
And like it best.
                But do you, in truth's name?
If so, you beat — which means you are not
    I —
Who needs must make earth mine and feed
    my fill
Not simply unbutted at, unbickered with,
But motioned to the velvet of the sward   895
By those obsequious wethers' very selves.
Look at me, sir; my age is double yours:
At yours, I knew beforehand, so enjoyed,
What now I should be — as, permit the word,
I pretty well imagine your whole range   900
And stretch of tether twenty years to come.
We both have minds and bodies much alike:
In truth's name, don't you want my bishopric,
My daily bread, my influence and my state?
You're young. I'm old; you must be old one
    day;   905
Will you find then, as I do hour by hour,
Women their lovers kneel to, who cut curls
From your fat lap-dog's ear to grace a
    brooch —
Dukes, who petition just to kiss your ring —
With much beside you know or may con-
    ceive?   910
Suppose we die to-night: well, here am I,
Such were my gains, life bore this fruit to me,
While writing all the same my articles
On music, poetry, the fictile vase
Found at Albano, chess, Anacreon's Greek. 915
But you — the highest honor in your life,
The thing you'll crown yourself with, all your
    days,
Is — dining here and drinking this last glass
I pour you out in sign of amity
Before we part forever. Of your power   920
And social influence, worldly worth in short,
Judge what's my estimation by the fact,
I do not condescend to enjoin, beseech,
Hint secrecy on one of all these words!
You're shrewd and know that should you
    publish one   925

The world would brand the lie — my ene-
    mies first,
Who'd sneer — "the bishop's an arch-hypo-
    crite
And knave perhaps, but not so frank a fool."
Whereas I should not dare for both my ears
Breathe one such syllable, smile one such
    smile,   930
Before the chaplain who reflects myself —
My shade's so much more potent than your
    flesh.
What's your reward, self-abnegating friend?
Stood you confessed of those exceptional
And privileged great natures that dwarf
    mine —   935
A zealot with a mad ideal in reach,
A poet just about to print his ode,
A statesman with a scheme to stop this war,
An artist whose religion is his art —
I should have nothing to object: such men 940
Carry the fire, all things grow warm to them,
Their drugget's worth my purple, they beat
    me.
But you, — you're just as little those as I —
You, Gigadibs, who, thirty years of age,
Write statedly for Blackwood's Magazine, 945
Believe you see two points in Hamlet's soul
Unseized by the Germans yet — which view
    you'll print —
Meantime the best you have to show being
    still
That lively lightsome article we took
Almost for the true Dickens — what's its
    name?   950
"The Slum and Cellar, or Whitechapel life
Limned after dark!" it made me laugh, I
    know,
And pleased a month, and brought you in
    ten pounds.
— Success I recognize and compliment,
And therefore give you, if you choose, three
    words   955
(The card and pencil-scratch is quite enough)
Which whether here, in Dublin or New York,
Will get you, prompt as at my eyebrow's wink,
Such terms as never you aspired to get
In all our own reviews and some not ours. 960
Go write your lively sketches! be the first
"Blougram, or The Eccentric Confidence" —
Or better simply say, "The Outward-bound."
Why, men as soon would throw it in my teeth
As copy and quote the infamy chalked broad
About me on the church-door opposite.   966
You will not wait for that experience though,
I fancy, howsoever you decide,
To discontinue — not detesting, not
Defaming, but at least — despising me!   970

913-915. The *Dublin Review*, founded by Wiseman (the prototype of Blougram), carried articles on similar subjects. **Albano**, a town in Italy. **Anacreon**, Greek lyric poet of the sixth century B.C.

942. **drugget**, rough woolen cloth. 945. **Blackwood's,** *Blackwood's Edinburgh Magazine*, a literary monthly founded in 1817.

Over his wine so smiled and talked his hour
Sylvester Blougram, styled *in partibus*
Episcopus, nec non — (the deuce knows what
It's changed to by our novel hierarchy)
With Gigadibs the literary man,   975
Who played with spoons, explored his plate's
    design,
And ranged the olive-stones about its edge,
While the great bishop rolled him out a mind
Long crumpled, till creased consciousness lay
    smooth.

    For Blougram, he believed, say, half he
        spoke.   980
The other portion, as he shaped it thus
For argumentatory purposes,
He felt his foe was foolish to dispute.
Some arbitrary accidental thoughts
That crossed his mind, amusing because new,
He chose to represent as fixtures there,   986
Invariable convictions (such they seemed
Beside his interlocutor's loose cards
Flung daily down, and not the same way
    twice)
While certain hell-deep instincts, man's weak
    tongue   990
Is never bold to utter in their truth
Because styled hell-deep ('tis an old mistake
To place hell at the bottom of the earth)
He ignored these, — not having in readiness
Their nomenclature and philosophy: 995
He said true things, but called them by wrong
    names.
"On the whole," he thought, "I justify myself
On every point where cavillers like this
Oppugn my life: he tries one kind of fence,
I close, he's worsted, that's enough for him.
He's on the ground: if ground should break
    away   1001
I take my stand on, there's a firmer yet
Beneath it, both of us may sink and reach.
His ground was over mine and broke the first:
So, let him sit with me this many a year!" 1005

    He did not sit five minutes. Just a week
Sufficed his sudden healthy vehemence.
Something had struck him in the "Outward-
    bound"
Another way than Blougram's purpose was:
And having bought, not cabin-furniture 1010
But settler's-implements (enough for three)
And started for Australia — there, I hope,
By this time he has tested his first plough,
And studied his last chapter of St. John.
                                        (1855)

972-974. The Roman Catholic hierarchy was re-established
in England in 1850, and Wiseman was named Cardinal and
Archbishop of Westminster. He had earlier been Bishop *in*
partibus infidelium (i.e., in the territory of the unfaithful).
Presumably Blougram's title was also changed. 1014. This
last line may mean that Gigadibs has given up his Germanic
study of the Gospels or that he has begun to take a serious
view of religious faith.

WOMEN AND ROSES

I dream of a red-rose tree.
And which of its roses three
Is the dearest rose to me?

Round and round, like a dance of snow
In a dazzling drift, as its guardians, go   5
Floating the women faded for ages,
Sculptured in stone, on the poet's pages.
Then follow the women fresh and gay,
Living and loving and loved today.
Last, in the rear, flee the multitude of 10
    maidens,
Beauties unborn. And all, to one cadence,
They circle their rose on my rose tree.

    Dear rose, thy term is reached,
    Thy leaf hangs loose and bleached:
    Bees pass it unimpeached.   15

Stay then, stoop, since I cannot climb,
You, great shapes of the antique time!
How shall I fix you, fire you, freeze you,
Break my heart at your feet to please you?
Oh, to possess and be possessed!   20
Hearts that beat 'neath each pallid breast!
But once of love, the poesy, the passion,
Drink once and die! — In vain, the same
    fashion,
They circle their rose on my rose-tree.

    Dear rose, thy joy's undimmed;   25
    Thy cup is ruby-rimmed,
    Thy cup's heart nectar-brimmed.

Deep as drops from a statue's plinth
The bee sucked in by the hyacinth,
So will I bury me while burning,   30
Quench like him at a plunge my yearning.
Eyes in your eyes, lips on your lips!
Fold me fast where the cincture slips,
Prison all my soul in eternities of pleasure,
Girdle me for once! But no — the old measure,
They circle their rose on my rose tree.   36

    Dear rose, without a thorn,
    Thy bud's the babe unborn:
    First streak of a new morn.

Wings, lend wings for the cold, the clear!
What's far conquers what is near.   41
Roses will bloom nor want beholders,
Sprung from the dust where our own flesh
    moulders.
What shall arrive with the cycle's change?
A novel grace and a beauty strange.   45
I will make an Eve, be the artist that began
    her,
Shaped her to his mind! — Alas! in like
    manner,
They circle their rose on my rose tree. (1855)

AN EPISTLE

CONTAINING THE STRANGE MEDICAL EXPERI-
ENCE OF KARSHISH, THE ARAB PHYSICIAN

Karshish, the picker-up of learning's crumbs,
The not-incurious in God's handiwork—
This man's-flesh He hath admirably made,
Blown like a bubble, kneaded like a paste,
To coop up and keep down on earth a space 5
That puff of vapor from His mouth, man's
    soul—
To Abib, all-sagacious in our art,
Breeder in me of what poor skill I boast,
Like me inquisitive how pricks and cracks
Befall the flesh through too much stress and
    strain, 10
Whereby the wily vapor fain would slip
Back and rejoin its source before the term—
And aptest in contrivance (under God)
To baffle it by deftly stopping such—
The vagrant Scholar to his Sage at home 15
Sends greeting (health and knowledge, fame
    with peace)
Three samples of true snake-stone—rarer
    still,
One of the other sort, the melon-shaped
(But fitter, pounded fine, for charms than
    drugs);
And writeth now the twenty-second time. 20

My journeyings were brought to Jericho;
Thus I resume. Who studious in our art
Shall count a little labor unrepaid?
I have shed sweat enough, left flesh and bone
On many a flinty furlong of this land. 25
Also, the country-side is all on fire
With rumors of a marching hitherward;
Some say Vespasian cometh, some, his son.
A black lynx snarled and pricked a tufted ear;
Lust of my blood inflamed his yellow balls; 30
I cried and threw my staff and he was gone.
Twice have the robbers stripped and beaten
    me,
And once a town declared me for a spy;
But at the end, I reach Jerusalem, 34
Since this poor covert where I pass the night,
This Bethany, lies scarce the distance thence
A man with plague-sores at the third degree
Runs till he drops down dead. Thou laughest
    here!
'Sooth, it elates me, thus reposed and safe,
To void the stuffing of my travel-scrip 40

And share with thee whatever Jewry yields.
A viscid choler is observable
In tertians, I was nearly bold to say;
And falling-sickness hath a happier cure
Than our school wots of; there's a spider
    here 45
Weaves no web, watches on the ledge of
    tombs,
Sprinkled with mottles on an ash-gray back;
Take five and drop them . . . but who knows
    his mind,
The Syrian runagate I trust this to?
His service payeth me a sublimate 50
Blown up his nose to help the ailing eye.
Best wait; I reach Jerusalem at morn,
There set in order my experiences,
Gather what most deserves, and give thee
    all—
Or I might add, Judæa's gum-tragacanth 55
Scales off in purer flakes, shines clearer-
    grained,
Cracks 'twixt the pestle and the porphyry—
In fine, exceeds our produce. Scalp-disease
Confounds me, crossing so with leprosy—
Thou hadst admired one sort I gained at
    Zoar— 60
But zeal outruns discretion. Here I end.

Yet stay; my Syrian blinketh gratefully,
Protesteth his devotion is my price—
Suppose I write what harms not, though he
    steal?
I half resolve to tell thee, yet I blush, 65
What set me off a-writing first of all.
An itch I had, a sting to write, a tang!
For, be it this town's barrenness—or else—
The Man had something in the look of him—
His case has struck me far more than 'tis
    worth. 70
So, pardon if—lest presently I lose
In the great press of novelty at hand
The care and pains this somehow stole from
    me—
I bid thee take the thing while fresh in mind,
Almost in sight—for, wilt thou have the
    truth? 75
The very man is gone from me but now,
Whose ailment is the subject of discourse.
Thus then, and let thy better wit help all!

'Tis but a case of mania—subinduced
By epilepsy, at the turning-point 80

An Epistle. This poem is based upon the account of
Christ's raising of Lazarus from the dead told in *John*, 11:
1–44. Cf. Tennyson's *In Memoriam*, 31–32, page 65. The
epistle is written from Bethany in Judea by a wandering
scholar-physician to the sage Abib, his master in the science
of medicine. Both Karshish and Abib are imaginary.
17. **snake-stone**, a stone used as a charm to cure snake
bites. 21. **Jericho**, an important city of ancient Palestine.
Karshish's last letter covered his travels as far as Jericho.
28. **Vespasian** (9–79 A.D.). He led a campaign against the
Jews in 67. His son Titus destroyed Jerusalem in 70.

43. **tertians**, persons afflicted with intermittent fever.
44. **falling-sickness**, epilepsy. This disease was ascribed
by Karshish to Lazarus, who exemplified the "happier cure."
45. **a spider**, probably the Zebra spider. The use of spiders
in medicine is an old practice. 48. **his mind**, the mind of
the messenger who is to carry the letter. 50. **a sublimate**,
some kind of medicine. 55. **gum-tragacanth**, a kind of
gum used in medicine. 57. **the porphyry**, a kind of stone
used for pulverizing drugs. 60. **Zoar**, a city southeast of
the Dead Sea. It is mentioned in *Genesis*, 13:10 and in
Deuteronomy, 34:3. 69. **The Man**, Lazarus.

Of trance prolonged unduly some three days;
When, by the exhibition of some drug
Or spell, exorcization, stroke of art
Unknown to me and which 'twere well to
    know,
The evil thing out-breaking all at once   85
Left the man whole and sound of body in-
    deed —
But, flinging (so to speak) life's gates too wide,
Making a clear house of it too suddenly,
The first conceit that entered might inscribe
Whatever it was minded on the wall   90
So plainly at that vantage, as it were,
(First come, first served) that nothing subse-
    quent
Attaineth to erase those fancy-scrawls
The just-returned and new-established soul
Hath gotten now so thoroughly by heart   95
That henceforth she will read or these or none.
And first — the man's own firm conviction
    rests
That he was dead (in fact they buried him)
— That he was dead and then restored to life
By a Nazarene physician of his tribe: 100
— 'Sayeth, the same bade "Rise," and he did
    rise.
"Such cases are diurnal," thou wilt cry.
Not so this figment! — not, that such a fume,
Instead of giving way to time and health,
Should eat itself into the life of life,   105
As saffron tingeth flesh, blood, bones and all!
For see, how he takes up the after-life.
The man — it is one Lazarus, a Jew,
Sanguine, proportioned, fifty years of age,
The body's habit wholly laudable,   110
As much, indeed, beyond the common health
As he were made and put aside to show.
Think, could we penetrate by any drug
And bathe the wearied soul and worried flesh,
And bring it clear and fair, by three days'
    sleep!   115
Whence has the man the balm that brightens
    all?
This grown man eyes the world now like a
    child.
Some elders of his tribe, I should premise,
Led in their friend, obedient as a sheep,
To bear my inquisition. While they spoke,
Now sharply, now with sorrow — told the
    case —   121
He listened not except I spoke to him,
But folded his two hands and let them talk,
Watching the flies that buzzed: and yet no
    fool.
And that's a sample how his years must go.
Look, if a beggar, in fixed middle-life,   126

Should find a treasure — can he use the same
With straitened habits and with tastes starved
    small,
And take at once to his impoverished brain
The sudden element that changes things,   130
That sets the undreamed-of rapture at his
    hand
And puts the cheap old joy in the scorned
    dust?
Is he not such an one as moves to mirth —
Warily parsimonious, when no need,
Wasteful as drunkenness at undue times?   135
All prudent counsel as to what befits
The golden mean, is lost on such an one;
The man's fantastic will is the man's law.
So here — we call the treasure knowledge, say,
Increased beyond the fleshly faculty —   140
Heaven opened to a soul while yet on earth,
Earth forced on a soul's use while seeing
    heaven;
The man is witless of the size, the sum,
The value in proportion of all things,
Or whether it be little or be much.   145
Discourse to him of prodigious armaments
Assembled to besiege his city now,
And of the passing of a mule with gourds —
'Tis one! Then take it on the other side,
Speak of some trifling fact — he will gaze rapt
With stupor at its very littleness   151
(Far as I see), as if in that indeed
He caught prodigious import, whole results;
And so will turn to us the bystanders
In ever the same stupor (note this point)   155
That we too see not with his opened eyes.
Wonder and doubt come wrongly into play,
Preposterously, at cross purposes.
Should his child sicken unto death — why,
    look
For scarce abatement of his cheerfulness,   160
Or pretermission of the daily craft!
While a word, gesture, glance from that same
    child
At play or in the school or laid asleep
Will startle him to an agony of fear,
Exasperation, just as like. Demand   165
The reason why — "'Tis but a word," ob-
    ject —
"A gesture" — he regards thee as our lord
Who lived there in the pyramid alone,
Looked at us (dost thou mind?) when, being
    young,
We both would unadvisedly recite   170
Some charm's beginning, from that book of
    his,
Able to bid the sun throb wide and burst
All into stars, as suns grown old are wont.
Thou and the child have each a veil alike

---

82. **exhibition,** the act of administering a remedy. 83.
exorcization, the act of expelling an evil spirit by the use
of a holy name. 102. **diurnal,** daily. 103. **such a fume,**
such a vaporish fancy. 113. **could we,** if only we could.

161. **pretermission,** omission, interruption. 167. **our
lord,** some sage under whom they had studied. Cf. line 254,
p. 282.

Thrown o'er your heads, from under which ye
    both   175
Stretch your blind hands and trifle with a
    match
Over a mine of Greek fire, did ye know!
He holds on firmly to some thread of life
(It is the life to lead perforcedly)
Which runs across some vast distracting orb
Of glory on either side that meager thread, 181
Which, conscious of, he must not enter yet —
The spiritual life around the earthly life.
The law of that is known to him as this,
His heart and brain move there, his feet stay
    here.   185
So is the man perplexed with impulses
Sudden to start off crosswise, not straight on,
Proclaiming what is right and wrong across,
And not along, this black thread through the
    blaze —
"It should be" balked by "here it cannot be."
And oft the man's soul springs into his face 191
As if he saw again and heard again
His sage that bade him "Rise" and he did
    rise.
Something, a word, a tick o' the blood within
Admonishes; then back he sinks at once   195
To ashes, who was very fire before,
In sedulous recurrence to his trade
Whereby he earneth him the daily bread;
And studiously the humbler for that pride,
Professedly the faultier that he knows   200
God's secret, while he holds the thread of life.
Indeed the especial marking of the man
Is prone submission to the heavenly will —
Seeing it, what it is, and why it is.
'Sayeth, he will wait patient to the last   205
For that same death which must restore his
    being
To equilibrium, body loosening soul
Divorced even now by premature full growth;
He will live, nay, it pleaseth him to live
So long as God please, and just how God
    please.   210
He even seeketh not to please God more
(Which meaneth, otherwise) than as God
    please.
Hence, I perceive not he affects to preach
The doctrine of his sect whate'er it be,
Make proselytes as madmen thirst to do;   215
How can he give his neighbor the real ground,
His own conviction? Ardent as he is —
Call his great truth a lie, why, still the old
"Be it as God please" reassureth him.
I probed the sore as thy disciple should.   220
"How, beast," said I, "this stolid carelessness
Sufficeth thee, when Rome is on her march

To stamp out like a little spark thy town,
Thy tribe, thy crazy tale, and thee at once?"
He merely looked with his large eyes on me.
The man is apathetic, you deduce?   226
Contrariwise, he loves both old and young,
Able and weak, affects the very brutes
And birds — how say I? flowers of the field —
As a wise workman recognizes tools   230
In a master's workshop, loving what they
    make.
Thus is the man as harmless as a lamb;
Only impatient, let him do his best,
At ignorance and carelessness and sin —
An indignation which is promptly curbed: 235
As when in certain travel I have feigned
To be an ignoramus in our art
According to some preconceived design,
And happed to hear the land's practitioners,
Steeped in conceit sublimed by ignorance, 240
Prattle fantastically on disease,
Its cause and cure — and I must hold my
    peace!

    Thou wilt object — Why have I not ere this
Sought out the sage himself, the Nazarene
Who wrought this cure, inquiring at the
    source,   245
Conferring with the frankness that befits?
Alas! it grieveth me, the learned leech
Perished in a tumult many years ago,
Accused — our learning's fate — of wizardry,
Rebellion, to the setting up a rule   250
And creed prodigious as described to me.
His death, which happened when the earth-
    quake fell
(Prefiguring, as soon appeared, the loss
To occult learning in our lord the sage
Who lived there in the pyramid alone),   255
Was wrought by the mad people — that's
    their wont!
On vain recourse, as I conjecture it,
To his tried virtue, for miraculous help —
How could he stop the earthquake? That's
    their way!
The other imputations must be lies;   260
But take one, though I loathe to give it thee,
In mere respect for any good man's fame.
(And after all, our patient Lazarus
Is stark mad; should we count on what he
    says?
Perhaps not; though in writing to a leech 265
'Tis well to keep back nothing of a case.)
This man so cured regards the curer, then,
As — God forgive me! who but God himself,
Creator and sustainer of the world,

---

177. **Greek fire,** some highly inflammable substance, supposed to contain sulphur, niter, and naphtha. Since it was
first used in 673 A.D. in the siege of Constantinople by the
Saracens, the reference here is an anachronism.

252. **the earthquake.** The record of the earthquake at
the time of the Crucifixion is found in *Matthew,* 27:51.—"And
behold, the vail of the temple was rent in twain from the
top to the bottom; and the earth did quake, and the rocks
rent."

That came and dwelt in flesh on it awhile! 270
— 'Sayeth that such an one was born and
lived,
Taught, healed the sick, broke bread at his
own house,
Then died, with Lazarus by, for aught I know,
And yet was . . . what I said nor choose re-
peat,
And must have so avouched himself, in fact,
In hearing of this very Lazarus, 276
Who saith — but why all this of what he
saith?
Why write of trivial matters, things of price
Calling at every moment for remark?
I noticed on the margin of a pool 280
Blue-flowering borage, the Aleppo sort,
Aboundeth, very nitrous. It is strange!

Thy pardon for this long and tedious case,
Which, now that I review it, needs must seem
Unduly dwelt on, prolixly set forth! 285
Nor I myself discern in what is writ
Good cause for the peculiar interest
And awe indeed this man has touched me
with.
Perhaps the journey's end, the weariness
Had wrought upon me first. I met him thus:
I crossed a ridge of short sharp broken hills 291
Like an old lion's cheek teeth. Out there
came
A moon made like a face with certain spots
Multiform, manifold, and menacing;
Then a wind rose behind me. So we met 295
In this old sleepy town at unaware,
The man and I. I send thee what is writ.
Regard it as a chance, a matter risked
To this ambiguous Syrian — he may lose,
Or steal, or give it thee with equal good. 300
Jerusalem's repose shall make amends
For time this letter wastes, thy time and
mine;
Till when, once more thy pardon and fare-
well!

The very God! think, Abib; dost thou
think? 304
So, the All-Great, were the All-Loving too —
So, through the thunder comes a human voice
Saying, "O heart I made, a heart beats here!
Face, my hands fashioned, see it in myself!
Thou hast no power nor mayst conceive of
mine,
But love I gave thee, with myself to love, 310
And thou must love me who have died for
thee!"
The madman saith He said so; it is strange.
(1855)

281. **borage**, a plant supposed to have properties of exhil-aration. Aleppo is a town in Syria. 304-312. **The . . . strange.** Compare the closing lines of *Saul*, p. 229; of *Caponsacchi*, pp. 344-345; and of *Cleon*, p. 295.

FRA LIPPO LIPPI

I am poor brother Lippo, by your leave!
You need not clap your torches to my face.
Zooks, what's to blame? you think you see a
monk!
What, 'tis past midnight, and you go the
rounds,
And here you catch me at an alley's end   5
Where sportive ladies leave their doors ajar?
The Carmine's my cloister; hunt it up,
Do — harry out, if you must show your zeal,
Whatever rat, there, haps on his wrong hole,
And nip each softling of a wee white mouse,
Weke, weke, that's crept to keep him com-
pany! 11
Aha, you know your betters! Then, you'll
take
Your hand away that's fiddling on my throat,
And please to know me likewise. Who am I?
Why, one, sir, who is lodging with a friend 15
Three streets off — he's a certain . . . how d'
ye call?
Master — a . . . Cosimo of the Medici,
I' the house that caps the corner. Boh! you
were best!
Remember and tell me, the day you're hanged,
How you affected such a gullet's-gripe! 20
But you, sir, it concerns you that your knaves
Pick up a manner nor discredit you;
Zooks, are we pilchards, that they sweep the
streets
And count fair prize what comes into their
net?
He's Judas to a tittle, that man is! 25
Just such a face! Why, sir, you make amends.
Lord, I'm not angry! Bid your hangdogs go
Drink out this quarter-florin to the health
Of the munificent House that harbors me
(And many more beside, lads! more beside!)
And all's come square again. I'd like his
face — 31
His, elbowing on his comrade in the door
With the pike and lantern — for the slave
that holds
John Baptist's head a-dangle by the hair
With one hand ("Look you, now," as who
should say) 35

Fra Lippo Lippi. Fra Lippo Lippi (1406-69) was a famous Florentine painter of the 15th century. The account upon which Browning based his interpretation of Lippo's life and art was found in Vasari's *Lives of the Painters.* The poem is addressed to Florentine guards who have caught Lippo in a nocturnal frolic. See Critical Notes.
3. **Zooks,** an oath shortened from *Gadzooks.* 7. **The Carmine's.** Lippo entered the monastery of the Carmelite friars of the Carmine in Florence in 1420. 17. **Cosimo of the Medici.** Cosimo de' Medici (1389-1464) was a rich Florentine banker, statesman, and patron of art and literature. The Medici palace, now known as the Palazzo Riccardi, is on the corner of Via Cavour and Via Gori. See *The Statue and the Bust,* p. 249. 23. **pilchards,** a kind of cheap common fish. 33-34. **the slave . . . hair,** an imaginary picture. In Lippo's real picture of the beheading of John the Baptist, the head is carried on a great platter by Salome, the daughter of Herodias. The account is found in *Matthew,* 14:1-11.

And his weapon in the other, yet unwiped!
It's not your chance to have a bit of chalk,
A wood-coal or the like? or you should see!
Yes, I'm the painter, since you style me so.
What, brother Lippo's doings, up and down,
You know them and they take you? like
    enough!   41
I saw the proper twinkle in your eye —
'Tell you, I liked your looks at very first.
Let's sit and set things straight now, hip to
    haunch.
Here's spring come, and the nights one makes
    up bands   45
To roam the town and sing out carnival,
And I've been three weeks shut within my
    mew,
A-painting for the great man, saints and saints
And saints again. I could not paint all night —
Ouf! I leaned out of window for fresh air. 50
There came a hurry of feet and little feet,
A sweep of lute-strings, laughs, and whiffs of
    song —
Flower o' the broom,
Take away love, and our earth is a tomb!
Flower o' the quince,   55
I let Lisa go, and what good in life since?
Flower o' the thyme — and so on. Round they
    went.
Scarce had they turned the corner when a
    titter
Like the skipping of rabbits by moonlight —
    three slim shapes,
And a face that looked up . . . zooks, sir,
    flesh and blood,   60
That's all I'm made of! Into shreds it went,
Curtain and counterpane and coverlet,
All the bed-furniture — a dozen knots,
There was a ladder! Down I let myself,
Hands and feet, scrambling somehow, and so
    dropped,   65
And after them. I came up with the fun
Hard by Saint Laurence, hail fellow, well
    met —
Flower o' the rose,
If I've been merry, what matter who knows?
And so as I was stealing back again   70
To get to bed and have a bit of sleep
Ere I rise up tomorrow and go work
On Jerome knocking at his poor old breast
With his great round stone to subdue the
    flesh,

46. **carnival,** a period of gayety preceding Lent. 47.
mew, coop, pen. (Lippo had been engaged to paint pictures
in the palace and had been locked in a room until the work
should be done.) 52. **song.** The song that follows is
a stornello, a kind of short folk song of the Italians usually
improvised on the name of a flower or some other familiar
object. 67. **Saint Laurence,** the Church of San Lorenzo.
73. **Jerome . . . breast.** Saint Jerome (340?–420) was the
most learned of the early Fathers of the Latin Church. He
lived in the desert for several years as a penance for his
youthful sins. Early Christian art depicted him on his knees
before a crucifix, beating his breast with a stone.

You snap me of the sudden. Ah, I see!   75
Though your eye twinkles still, you shake
    your head —
Mine's shaved — a monk, you say — the
    sting's in that!
If Master Cosimo announced himself,
Mum's the word naturally; but a monk!
Come, what am I a beast for? tell us, now! 80
I was a baby when my mother died
And father died and left me in the street.
I starved there, God knows how, a year or
    two
On fig-skins, melon-parings, rinds and shucks,
Refuse and rubbish. One fine frosty day,   85
My stomach being empty as your hat,
The wind doubled me up and down I went.
Old Aunt Lapaccia trussed me with one hand
(Its fellow was a stinger as I knew),
And so along the wall, over the bridge,   90
By the straight cut to the convent. Six words
    there,
While I stood munching my first bread that
    month:
"So, boy, you're minded," quoth the good fat
    father,
Wiping his own mouth — 'twas refection-
    time —
"To quit this very miserable world?   95
Will you renounce" . . . "the mouthful of
    bread?" thought I;
By no means! Brief, they made a monk of
    me;
I did renounce the world, its pride and greed,
Palace, farm, villa, shop, and banking-house,
Trash, such as these poor devils of Medici
Have given their hearts to — all at eight years
    old.   101
Well, sir, I found in time, you may be sure,
'Twas not for nothing — the good bellyful,
The warm serge and the rope that goes all
    round,
And day-long blessed idleness beside!   105
"Let's see what the urchin's fit for" — that
    came next.
Not overmuch their way, I must confess.
Such a to-do! They tried me with their books;
Lord, they'd have taught me Latin in pure
    waste!
Flower o' the clove,   110
All the Latin I construe is "amo," I love!
But, mind you, when a boy starves in the
    streets
Eight years together, as my fortune was,
Watching folk's faces to know who will fling
The bit of half-stripped grape-bunch he
    desires,   115
And who will curse or kick him for his pains —

88. **Aunt Lapaccia.** Mona Lapaccia, his father's sister.
trussed, held firmly.

Which gentleman processional and fine,
Holding a candle to the Sacrament,
Will wink and let him lift a plate and catch
The droppings of the wax to sell again, 120
Or holla for the Eight and have him whipped —
How say I? — nay, which dog bites, which
    lets drop
His bone from the heap of offal in the street —
Why, soul and sense of him grow sharp alike;
He learns the look of things, and none the less
For admonition from the hunger-pinch. 126
I had a store of such remarks, be sure,
Which, after I found leisure, turned to use.
I drew men's faces on my copy-books,
Scrawled them within the antiphonary's
    marge, 130
Joined legs and arms to the long music-notes,
Found eyes and nose and chin for A's and B's,
And made a string of pictures of the world
Betwixt the ins and outs of verb and noun,
On the wall, the bench, the door. The monks
    looked black. 135
"Nay," quoth the Prior, "turn him out, d' ye
    say?
In no wise. Lose a crow and catch a lark.
What if at last we get our man of parts,
We Carmelites, like those Camaldolese
And Preaching Friars, to do our church up
    fine 140
And put the front on it that ought to be!"
And hereupon he bade me daub away.
Thank you! my head being crammed, the
    walls a blank,
Never was such prompt disemburdening.
First, every sort of monk, the black and white,
I drew them, fat and lean; then, folk at
    church, 146
From good old gossips waiting to confess
Their cribs of barrel-droppings, candle-ends —
To the breathless fellow at the altar-foot,
Fresh from his murder, safe and sitting there
With the little children round him in a row 151
Of admiration, half for his beard and half
For that white anger of his victim's son
Shaking a fist at him with one fierce arm,
Signing himself with the other because of
    Christ 155

(Whose sad face on the cross sees only this
After the passion of a thousand years),
Till some poor girl, her apron o'er her head
(Which the intense eyes looked through),
    came at eve
On tiptoe, said a word, dropped in a loaf, 160
Her pair of earrings and a bunch of flowers
(The brute took growling), prayed, and so
    was gone.
I painted all, then cried, " 'Tis ask and have;
Choose, for more's ready!'" — laid the ladder
    flat, 164
And showed my covered bit of cloister-wall.
The monks closed in a circle and praised loud
Till checked, taught what to see and not to
    see,
Being simple bodies — "That's the very man!
Look at the boy who stoops to pat the dog!
That woman's like the Prior's niece who comes
To care about his asthma; it's the life!" 171
But there my triumph's straw-fire flared and
    funked;
Their betters took their turn to see and say;
The Prior and the learned pulled a face
And stopped all that in no time. "How?
    what's here? 175
Quite from the mark of painting, bless us all!
Faces, arms, legs, and bodies like the true
As much as pea and pea! It's devil's-game!
Your business is not to catch men with show,
With homage to the perishable clay, 180
But lift them over it, ignore it all,
Make them forget there's such a thing as flesh.
Your business is to paint the souls of men —
Man's soul, and it's a fire, smoke . . . no,
    it's not . . .
It's vapor done up like a new-born babe 185
(In that shape when you die it leaves your
    mouth) —
It's . . . well, what matters talking, it's the
    soul!
Give us no more of body than shows soul!
Here's Giotto, with his Saint a-praising God,
That sets us praising — why not stop with
    him? 190
Why put all thoughts of praise out of our head
With wonder at lines, colors, and what not?
Paint the soul, never mind the legs and arms!
Rub all out, try at it a second time.
Oh, that white smallish female with the
    breasts, 195
She's just my niece . . . Herodias, I would
    say —
Who went and danced and got men's heads
    cut off!

117. **gentleman processional**, etc., gentlemen wearing fine ecclesiastical robes and walking in the religious procession. 121. **the Eight**, the magistrates who governed Florence. 130. **the antiphonary's marge**, the margins of the books used by the choir. 131. **the long music-notes**. The medieval music notes were square or oblong, with long stems. 139-140. **Carmelites, Camaldolese, Preaching Friars.** The Carmelites were monks of the Order of Mount Carmel in Syria; the Camaldolese belonged to the convent of Camaldoli, near Florence; the Preaching Friars are the Dominicans, named after St. Dominic. They were called Brothers Preachers by Pope Innocent III in 1215. These orders owned various monasteries and churches and wanted to possess the greatest religious paintings. 148. **Their cribs**, etc., small thefts of wine, wax, etc. 150. **safe**, because he is in a sacred place, which by the law of the medieval church protected him from arrest. 154-155. **Shaking . . . Christ**. Revenge and religion are at war in him.

157. **passion**, suffering. 189. **Giotto**, Giotto di Bondone (1276-1337), a famous Florentine painter, architect, and sculptor. See note on line 15, p. 234. His work is marked by an intense spirituality, whereas Lippi's and Guidi's paintings (line 276) were considerably more physical or "realistic" in appeal. 196. **Herodias**. See note on lines 33-34, p. 283.

Have it all out!" Now, is this sense, I ask?
A fine way to paint soul, by painting body
So ill the eye can't stop there, must go further
And can't fare worse! Thus, yellow does for
    white   201
When what you put for yellow's simply black,
And any sort of meaning looks intense
When all beside itself means and looks naught.
Why can't a painter lift each foot in turn, 205
Left foot and right foot, go a double step,
Make his flesh liker and his soul more like,
Both in their order? Take the prettiest face,
The Prior's niece . . . patron-saint — is it so
    pretty
You can't discover if it means hope, fear, 210
Sorrow or joy? won't beauty go with these?
Suppose I've made her eyes all right and blue,
Can't I take breath and try to add life's flash,
And then add soul and heighten them three-
    fold?
Or say there's beauty with no soul at all 215
(I never saw it — put the case the same);
If you get simple beauty and naught else,
You get about the best thing God invents—
That's somewhat; and you'll find the soul you
    have missed,
Within yourself, when you return him thanks.
"Rub all out!" Well, well, there's my life, in
    short,   221
And so the thing has gone on ever since.
I'm grown a man no doubt, I've broken
    bounds;
You should not take a fellow eight years old
And make him swear to never kiss the girls. 225
I'm my own master, paint now as I please —
Having a friend, you see, in the Corner-house!
Lord, it's fast holding by the rings in front —
Those great rings serve more purposes than
    just
To plant a flag in, or tie up a horse!   230
And yet the old schooling sticks, the old grave
    eyes
Are peeping o'er my shoulder as I work,
The heads shake still — "It's art's decline,
    my son!
You're not of the true painters, great and old;
Brother Angelico's the man, you'll find; 235
Brother Lorenzo stands his single peer —
Fag on at flesh, you'll never make the third!"
Flower o' the pine,
You keep your mistr . . . manners, and I'll
*   stick to mine!*
I'm not the third, then; bless us, they must
    know!   240

Don't you think they're the likeliest to know,
They with their Latin? So, I swallow my
    rage,
Clench my teeth, suck my lips in tight, and
    paint
To please them — sometimes do and some-
    times don't;
For, doing most, there's pretty sure to come
A turn, some warm eve finds me at my
    saints —   246
A laugh, a cry, the business of the world
(*Flower o' the peach,*
Death for us all, and his own life for each!) —
And my whole soul revolves, the cup runs
    over,   250
The world and life's too big to pass for a
    dream,
And I do these wild things in sheer despite,
And play the fooleries you catch me at,
In pure rage! The old mill-horse, out at grass
After hard years, throws up his stiff heels so,
Although the miller does not preach to him 256
The only good of grass is to make chaff.
What would men have? Do they like grass
    or no —
May they or mayn't they? All I want's the
    thing
Settled forever one way. As it is,   260
You tell too many lies and hurt yourself;
You don't like what you only like too much,
You do like what, if given you at your word,
You find abundantly detestable.
For me, I think I speak as I was taught; 265
I always see the garden and God there
A-making man's wife; and, my lesson learned—
The value and significance of flesh —
I can't unlearn ten minutes afterwards.

You understand me; I'm a beast, I know.
But see, now — why, I see as certainly 271
As that the morning-star's about to shine,
What will hap some day. We've a youngster
    here
Comes to our convent, studies what I do,
Slouches and stares and lets no atom drop. 275
His name is Guidi — he'll not mind the
    monks —
They call him Hulking Tom, he lets them
    talk;
He picks my practice up — he'll paint apace,
I hope so — though I never live so long,
I know what's sure to follow. You be judge!
You speak no Latin more than I, belike; 281
However, you're my man, you've seen the
    world —
The beauty and the wonder and the power,

228. **the rings in front,** big iron rings on the front of the palace. Lippi used them in climbing in and out of his window. 235. **Brother Angelico,** Fra Angelico, Giovanni da Fiesole (1387-1455), the greatest of the medieval school of religious artists who "painted souls." 236. **Brother Lorenzo,** Lorenzo Monaco, a painter of the Order of the Camaldolese, who also "painted souls."

276. **Guidi,** Tommaso Guidi, or Masaccio (1401-28), nicknamed Hulking Tom. He is said to have been the first Italian artist to paint a nude figure. He was Lippo's master, not his disciple.

The shapes of things, their colors, lights and
    shades,
Changes, surprises — and God made it all! 285
— For what? Do you feel thankful, aye or
    no,
For this fair town's face, yonder river's line,
The mountain round it and the sky above,
Much more the figures of man, woman, child,
These are the frame to? What's it all about?
To be passed over, despised? or dwelt upon,
Wondered at? Oh, this last of course! — you
    say.   292
But why not do as well as say — paint these
Just as they are, careless what comes of it?
God's works — paint any one, and count it
    crime   295
To let a truth slip. Don't object, "His works
Are here already; nature is complete:
Suppose you reproduce her — which you
    can't —
There's no advantage! you must beat her,
    then."
For, don't you mark? we're made so that we
    love   300
First when we see them painted, things we
    have passed
Perhaps a hundred times nor cared to see;
And so they are better, painted — better to
    us,
Which is the same thing. Art was given for
    that;
God uses us to help each other so,   305
Lending our minds out. Have you noticed,
    now,
Your cullion's hanging face? A bit of chalk,
And trust me but you should, though! How
    much more,
If I drew higher things with the same truth!
That were to take the Prior's pulpit-place, 310
Interpret God to all of you! Oh, oh,
It makes me mad to see what men shall do
And we in our graves! This world's no blot
    for us,
Nor blank; it means intensely, and means
    good —
To find its meaning is my meat and drink. 315
"Aye, but you don't so instigate to prayer!"
Strikes in the Prior; "when your meaning's
    plain
It does not say to folk — remember matins,
Or, mind you fast next Friday!" Why, for
    this
What need of art at all? A skull and bones,
Two bits of stick nailed crosswise, or, what's
    best,   321
A bell to chime the hour with, does as well.
I painted a Saint Laurence six months since

307. cullion, a low fellow. 323. a Saint Laurence, a
picture of St. Laurence, who was martyred in 258 by being
burned to death on a gridiron.

At Prato, splashed the fresco in fine style;
"How looks my painting, now the scaffold's
    down?"   325
I ask a brother. "Hugely," he returns —
"Already not one phiz of your three slaves
Who turn the Deacon off his toasted side,
But's scratched and prodded to our heart's
    content,
The pious people have so eased their own 330
With coming to say prayers there in a rage;
We get on fast to see the bricks beneath.
Expect another job this time next year,
For pity and religion grow i' the crowd —
Your painting serves its purpose!" Hang the
    fools!   335

— That is — you'll not mistake an idle word
Spoke in a huff by a poor monk, God wot,
Tasting the air this spicy night, which turns
The unaccustomed head like Chianti wine!
Oh, the church knows! don't misreport me,
    now!   340
It's natural a poor monk out of bounds
Should have his apt word to excuse himself;
And hearken how I plot to make amends.
I have bethought me: I shall paint a piece
. . . There's for you! Give me six months,
    then go, see   345
Something in Sant' Ambrogio's! Bless the
    nuns!
They want a cast o' my office. I shall paint
God in the midst, Madonna and her babe,
Ringed by a bowery, flowery angel-brood,
Lilies and vestments and white faces, sweet
As puff on puff of grated orris-root   351
When ladies crowd to Church at midsummer.
And then i' the front, of course a saint or
    two —
Saint John, because he saves the Florentines,
Saint Ambrose, who puts down in black and
    white   355
The convent's friends and gives them a long
    day,
And Job, I must have him there past mistake,
The man of Uz (and Us without the z,
Painters who need his patience). Well, all
    these
Secured at their devotion, up shall come   360
Out of a corner when you least expect,
As one by a dark stair into a great light,
Music and talking, who but Lippo! I! —

324. At Prato. Some of Lippo's most important work is
in the Cathedral at Prato, a town near Florence. 339. Chianti wine, wine from Chianti, a region south of Florence.
346. Sant' Ambrogio's, Saint Ambrose' Church in Florence. Saint Ambrose was a famous church leader during the
fourth century. He became Bishop of Milan in 374. 347-
389. I shall paint, etc. The picture described is The Corona-
tion of the Virgin, now in the Academy of Fine Arts, Florence.
The model for the Virgin was Lucrezia Buti, Lippo's mistress.
361-363. Out of a corner . . . I. Browning mistook a head
in the lower right-hand corner for Lippo's self-portrait.

Mazed, motionless, and moonstruck — I'm
   the man!
Back I shrink — what is this I see and hear?
I, caught up with my monk's-things by mis-
   take,   366
My old serge gown and rope that goes all
   round,
I, in this presence, this pure company!
Where's a hole, where's a corner for escape?
Then steps a sweet angelic slip of a thing 370
Forward, puts out a soft palm: "Not so fast!"
— Addresses the celestial presence, "Nay,
He made you and devised you, after all,
Though he's none of you! Could Saint John
   there draw —
His camel-hair make up a painting-brush? 375
We come to brother Lippo for all that,
Iste perfecit opus!" So, all smile —
I shuffle sideways with my blushing face
Under the cover of a hundred wings
Thrown like a spread of kirtles when you're
   gay   380
And play hot cockles, all the doors being shut,
Till, wholly unexpected, in there pops
The hothead husband! Thus I scuttle off
To some safe bench behind, not letting go
The palm of her, the little lily thing   385
That spoke the good word for me in the
   nick,
Like the Prior's niece . . . Saint Lucy, I
   would say.
And so all's saved for me, and for the church
A pretty picture gained. Go, six months
   hence!
Your hand, sir, and good-by; no lights, no
   lights!   390
The street's hushed, and I know my own way
   back,
Don't fear me! There's the gray beginning.
   Zooks!   (1855)

ANDREA DEL SARTO

CALLED "THE FAULTLESS PAINTER"

But do not let us quarrel any more,
No, my Lucrezia; bear with me for once.
Sit down and all shall happen as you wish.
You turn your face, but does it bring your
   heart?

374-375. **Saint John . . . camel-hair.** Cf. *Mark,* 1:6.—
"And John was clothed with camel's hair." 377. **Iste**
perfecit opus, this one did the work. The inscription is on
a scroll in the picture. 381. **hot cockles,** an old English game
in which a blindfolded player tries to guess who strikes him.
Andrea del Sarto. Andrea d'Angelo di Francesca (1486-
1531) was called "del Sarto" because he was the son of a
tailor (sarto). The perfection of his frescoes in the Church
of the Annuziata in Florence won him the title of "The
Faultless Painter." In 1512 he married Lucrezia del Fede,
whose influence led Andrea to neglect his art work. The
poem is based upon the account of Andrea found in Vasari's
Lives of the Painters. See Critical Notes.

I'll work then for your friend's friend, never
   fear,   5
Treat his own subject after his own way,
Fix his own time, accept too his own price,
And shut the money into this small hand
When next it takes mine. Will it? tenderly?
Oh, I'll content him — but tomorrow, Love!
I often am much wearier than you think, 11
This evening more than usual, and it seems
As if — forgive now — should you let me sit
Here by the window with your hand in mine
And look a half-hour forth on Fiesole, 15
Both of one mind, as married people use,
Quietly, quietly the evening through,
I might get up tomorrow to my work
Cheerful and fresh as ever. Let us try.
Tomorrow, how you shall be glad for this! 20
Your soft hand is a woman of itself,
And mine the man's bared breast she curls
   inside.
Don't count the time lost, neither; you must
   serve
For each of the five pictures we require —
It saves a model. So! keep looking so — 25
My serpentining beauty, rounds on rounds!
— How could you ever prick those perfect
   ears,
Even to put the pearl there! oh, so sweet —
My face, my moon, my everybody's moon,
Which everybody looks on and calls his, 30
And, I suppose, is looked on by in turn,
While she looks — no one's: very dear, no less.
You smile? why, there's my picture ready
   made,
There's what we painters call our harmony!
A common grayness silvers everything — 35
All in a twilight, you and I alike —
You, at the point of your first pride in me
(That's gone, you know), but I, at every
   point;
My youth, my hope, my art, being all toned
   down
To yonder sober pleasant Fiesole. 40
There's the bell clinking from the chapel-top;
That length of convent-wall across the way
Holds the trees safer, huddled more inside;
The last monk leaves the garden; days de-
   crease,
And autumn grows, autumn in everything. 45
Eh? the whole seems to fall into a shape
As if I saw alike my work and self
And all that I was born to be and do,
A twilight-piece. Love, we are in God's hand.
How strange now looks the life he makes us
   lead;   50
So free we seem, so fettered fast we are!
I feel he laid the fetter; let it lie!

15. **Fiesole,** a suburb of Florence. 23-25. **you must**
serve . . . a model. Lucrezia is discernible in almost all
of the women of Andrea's pictures.

This chamber, for example — turn your
  head —
All that's behind us! You don't understand,
Nor care to understand, about my art,   55
But you can hear at least when people speak;
And that cartoon, the second from the door —
It is the thing, Love! so such thing should
  be —
Behold Madonna! — I am bold to say.
I can do with my pencil what I know,   60
What I see, what at bottom of my heart
I wish for, if I ever wish so deep —
Do easily, too — when I say perfectly,
I do not boast, perhaps; yourself are judge,
Who listened to the Legate's talk last week, 65
And just as much they used to say in France.
At any rate, 'tis easy, all of it!
No sketches first, no studies — that's long
  past;
I do what many dream of all their lives —
Dream? strive to do, and agonize to do,   70
And fail in doing. I could count twenty such
On twice your fingers, and not leave this town,
Who strive — you don't know how the others
  strive
To paint a little thing like that you smeared
Carelessly passing with your robes afloat — 75
Yet do much less, so much less, Someone
  says
(I know his name, no matter) — so much less!
Well, less is more, Lucrezia; I am judged.
There burns a truer light of God in them,
In their vexed, beating, stuffed, and stopped-
  up brain,   80
Heart, or whate'er else, than goes on to
  prompt
This low-pulsed forthright craftsman's hand
  of mine.
Their works drop groundward, but them-
  selves, I know,
Reach many a time a heaven that's shut to
  me,
Enter and take their place there sure enough,
Though they come back and cannot tell the
  world.   86
My works are nearer heaven, but I sit here.
The sudden blood of these men! at a word —
Praise them, it boils; or blame them, it boils
  too.
I, painting from myself and to myself,   90
Know what I do, am unmoved by men's blame
Or their praise either. Somebody remarks
Morello's outline there is wrongly traced,
His hue mistaken; what of that? or else,
Rightly traced and well ordered; what of that?
Speak as they please, what does the mountain
  care?   96

Ah, but a man's reach should exceed his grasp,
Or what's a heaven for? All is silver-gray
Placid and perfect with my art: the worse!
I know both what I want and what might
  gain,   100
And yet how profitless to know, to sigh,
"Had I been two, another and myself,
Our head would have o'erlooked the world!"
  No doubt.
Yonder's a work now, of that famous youth,
The Urbinate, who died five years ago.   105
('Tis copied; George Vasari sent it me.)
Well, I can fancy how he did it all,
Pouring his soul, with kings and popes to see,
Reaching, that heaven might so replenish him,
Above and through his art — for it gives way:
That arm is wrongly put — and there again —
A fault to pardon in the drawing's lines,   112
Its body, so to speak: its soul is right,
He means right — that, a child may under-
  stand.
Still, what an arm! and I could alter it;
But all the play, the insight, and the stretch —
Out of me, out of me! And wherefore out?   117
Had you enjoined them on me, given me soul,
We might have risen to Rafael, I and you!
Nay, Love, you did give all I asked, I think —
More than I merit, yes, by many times.
But had you — oh, with the same perfect
  brow,
And perfect eyes, and more than perfect
  mouth,
And the low voice my soul hears, as a bird
The fowler's pipe, and follows to the snare —
Had you, with these the same, but brought a
  mind!   126
Some women do so. Had the mouth there
  urged,
"God and the glory! never care for gain.
The present by the future, what is that?
Live for fame, side by side with Agnolo!   130
Rafael is waiting; up to God, all three!"
I might have done it for you. So it seems;
Perhaps not. All is as God overrules.
Beside, incentives come from the soul's self;
The rest avail not. Why do I need you?   135
What wife had Rafael, or has Agnolo?
In this world, who can do a thing, will not;
And who would do it, cannot, I perceive;
Yet the will's somewhat — somewhat, too,
  the power —
And thus we half-men struggle. At the end,

65. the Legate's talk. The Legate was the representative of the Pope. 93. Morello's outline. Morello is a
high peak of the Apennines, north of Florence.

97-98. Ah . . . heaven for. Cf. *A Death in the Desert*,
424-431, p. 309; *Cleon*, 114, p. 292; *Rabbi Ben Ezra*, 40-41,
p. 302; and *Saul*, 295, p. 229. 105. The Urbinate, Raphael
Sanzio (1483-1520), one of the greatest of Italian painters.
He was born in the city of Urbino. 106. George Vasari
(1512-1574), a pupil of Andrea del Sarto and author of *The
Lives of the Most Eminent Painters, Sculptors, and Architects*.
130. Agnolo, Michelangelo (1475-1564), famous as a painter,
sculptor, architect, and poet.

God, I conclude, compensates, punishes.   141
'Tis safer for me, if the award be strict,
That I am something underrated here,
Poor this long while, despised, to speak the
    truth.
I dared not, do you know, leave home all day,
For fear of chancing on the Paris lords.   146
The best is when they pass and look aside;
But they speak sometimes; I must bear it all.
Well may they speak! That Francis, that first
    time,
And that long festal year at Fontainebleau!
I surely then could sometimes leave the
    ground,   151
Put on the glory, Rafael's daily wear,
In that humane great monarch's golden
    look —
One finger in his beard or twisted curl
Over his mouth's good mark that made the
    smile;   155
One arm about my shoulder, round my neck;
The jingle of his gold chain in my ear —
I painting proudly with his breath on me,
All his Court round him, seeing with his eyes,
Such frank French eyes, and such a fire of
    souls   160
Profuse, my hand kept plying by those hearts;
And, best of all, this, this, this face beyond,
This in the background, waiting on my work,
To crown the issue with a last reward!
A good time, was it not, my kingly days?   165
And had you not grown restless . . . but I
    know —
'Tis done and past; 'twas right, my instinct
    said;
Too live the life grew, golden and not gray,
And I'm the weak-eyed bat no sun should
    tempt
Out of the grange whose four walls make his
    world.   170
How could it end in any other way?
You called me, and I came home to your
    heart.
The triumph was — to reach and stay there;
    since
I reached it ere the triumph, what is lost?
Let my hands frame your face in your hair's
    gold,   175
You beautiful Lucrezia that are mine!
"Rafael did this, Andrea painted that;
The Roman's is the better when you pray,
But still the other's Virgin was his wife" —
Men will excuse me. I am glad to judge   180
Both pictures in your presence; clearer grows

My better fortune, I resolve to think.
For, do you know, Lucrezia, as God lives,
Said one day Agnolo, his very self,
To Rafael . . . I have known it all these
    years . . .   185
(When the young man was flaming out his
    thoughts
Upon a palace-wall for Rome to see,
Too lifted up in heart because of it),
"Friend, there's a certain sorry little scrub
Goes up and down our Florence, none cares
    how,   190
Who, were he set to plan and execute
As you are, pricked on by your popes and
    kings,
Would bring the sweat into that brow of
    yours!"
To Rafael's! — And indeed the arm is wrong.
I hardly dare . . . yet, only you to see,   195
Give the chalk here — quick, thus the line
    should go!
Ay, but the soul! he's Rafael! rub it out!
Still, all I care for, if he spoke the truth
(What he? why, who but Michel Agnolo?
Do you forget already words like those?),   200
If really there was such a chance, so lost —
Is, whether you're — not grateful — but
    more pleased.
Well, let me think so. And you smile in-
    deed!
This hour has been an hour! Another smile?
If you would sit thus by me every night,   205
I should work better, do you comprehend?
I mean that I should earn more, give you
    more.
See, it is settled dusk now; there's a star;
Morello's gone, the watch-lights show the
    wall,
The cue-owls speak the name we call them
    by.   210
Come from the window, love — come in, at
    last,
Inside the melancholy little house
We built to be so gay with. God is just.
King Francis may forgive me; oft at nights
When I look up from painting, eyes tired
    out,   215
The walls become illumined, brick from brick
Distinct, instead of mortar, fierce bright gold,
That gold of his I did cement them with!
Let us but love each other. Must you go?
That Cousin here again? he waits outside?
Must see you — you, and not with me?
    Those loans?   221
More gaming debts to pay? you smiled for
    that?

149. **That Francis**, Francis I, king of France (1494-1547).
He had invited Andrea to come to Fontainebleau, the seat of
the richest of the royal palaces. While engaged upon important work there, Andrea was suddenly called home by
Lucrezia. He was given money with which to secure works
of art for the French king, but he purchased a house with it
for Lucrezia. 178. **The Roman's**, Raphael's.

186-188. **When . . . it**, probably a reference to Raphael's
decorations made in certain rooms of the Vatican under
Julius II (1443-1513). 210. **cue-owls**, small European owls.
220. **Cousin**, a euphemism for *lover*. Cf. lines 29-32.

Well, let smiles buy me! have you more to
　　spend?
While hand and eye and something of a heart
Are left me, work's my ware, and what's it
　　worth?   225
I'll pay my fancy.   Only let me sit
The gray remainder of the evening out,
Idle, you call it, and muse perfectly
How I could paint, were I but back in France,
One picture, just one more — the Virgin's
　　face,   230
Not yours this time! I want you at my
　　side
To hear them — that is, Michel Agnolo —
Judge all I do and tell you of its worth.
Will you?   Tomorrow, satisfy your friend.
I take the subjects for his corridor,   235
Finish the portrait out of hand — there, there,
And throw him in another thing or two
If he demurs; the whole should prove enough
To pay for this same Cousin's freak.   Be-
　　side —
What's better and what's all I care about —
Get you the thirteen scudi for the ruff!   241
Love, does that please you? Ah, but what
　　does he,
The Cousin! what does he to please you more?

I am grown peaceful as old age tonight.
I regret little, I would change still less.   245
Since there my past life lies, why alter it?
The very wrong to Francis! — it is true
I took his coin, was tempted and complied,
And built this house and sinned, and all is
　　said.
My father and my mother died of want.   250
Well, had I riches of my own? you see
How one gets rich!   Let each one bear his
　　lot.
They were born poor, lived poor, and poor
　　they died;
And I have labored somewhat in my time
And not been paid profusely.   Some good
　　son   255
Paint my two hundred pictures — let him
　　try!
No doubt, there's something strikes a bal-
　　ance.   Yes,
You loved me quite enough, it seems tonight.
This must suffice me here.   What would one
　　have?
In heaven, perhaps, new chances, one more
　　chance —   260
Four great walls in the New Jerusalem,
Meted on each side by the angel's reed,
For Leonard, Rafael, Agnolo, and me

To cover — the three first without a wife, 264
While I have mine! So — still they overcome
Because there's still Lucrezia — as I choose.

　　Again the Cousin's whistle! Go, my Love.
　　　　　　　　　　　　　　　　　　　　(1855)

CLEON

"As certain also of your own poets have said"—

Cleon the poet (from the sprinkled isles,
Lily on lily, that o'erlace the sea,
And laugh their pride when the light wave
　　lisps "Greece") —
To Protus in his Tyranny: much health!

　　They give thy letter to me, even now;   5
I read and seem as if I heard thee speak.
The master of thy galley still unlades
Gift after gift; they block my court at last
And pile themselves along its portico
Royal with sunset, like a thought of thee;   10
And one white she-slave from the group dis-
　　persed
Of black and white slaves (like the checker-
　　work
Pavement, at once my nation's work and gift,
Now covered with this settle-down of doves),
One lyric woman, in her crocus vest   15
Woven of sea-wools, with her two white hands
Commends to me the strainer and the cup
Thy lip hath bettered ere it blesses mine.

　　Well-counseled, king, in thy munificence!
For so shall men remark, in such an act   20
Of love for him whose song gives life its joy,
Thy recognition of the use of life;
Nor call thy spirit barely adequate
To help on life in straight ways, broad enough
For vulgar souls, by ruling and the rest.   25
Thou, in the daily building of thy tower —
Whether in fierce and sudden spasms of toil,
Or through dim lulls of unapparent growth,
Or when the general work 'mid good acclaim
Climbed with the eye to cheer the architect —
Didst ne'er engage in work for mere work's
　　sake —   31
Hadst ever in thy heart the luring hope
Of some eventual rest a-top of it,
Whence, all the tumult of the building hushed,
Thou first of men mightst look out to the
　　East;   35

241. scudi, plural of *scudo*, an Italian coin worth about
one dollar. 261. the New Jerusalem. For a description
of the New Jerusalem and its walls, see *Revelation*, 21:10-21.
263. Leonard, Leonardo da Vinci (1452-1519), one of the
greatest of Italian painters.

Cleon. In this poem Cleon is imagined as a Greek poet
replying to a letter written by Protus, an imaginary king,
who has been his friend and patron. The quotation is
from *Acts*, 17:28. The thought expressed in the poem is
characteristic of that of the Greek philosophers of the first
century.
1. the sprinkled isles, probably the Sporades, lying east
of Greece. 4. Tyranny, used in the ancient Greek sense,
referring to any ruler who had absolute power.

The vulgar saw thy tower, thou sawest the
   sun.
For this, I promise on thy festival
To pour libation, looking o'er the sea,
Making this slave narrate thy fortunes, speak
Thy great words, and describe thy royal
   face —   40
Wishing thee wholly where Zeus lives the
   most,
Within the eventual element of calm.

   Thy letter's first requirement meets me
   here.
It is as thou hast heard: in one short life
I, Cleon, have effected all those things   45
Thou wonderingly dost enumerate.
That epos on thy hundred plates of gold
Is mine — and also mine the little chant,
So sure to rise from every fishing-bark
When, lights at prow, the seamen haul their
   net.   50
The image of the sun-god on the phare,
Men turn from the sun's self to see, is mine;
The Pœcile, o'er-storied its whole length,
As thou didst hear, with painting, is mine too.
I know the true proportions of a man   55
And woman also, not observed before;
And I have written three books on the soul,
Proving absurd all written hitherto,
And putting us to ignorance again.
For music — why, I have combined the
   moods,   60
Inventing one.   In brief, all arts are mine;
Thus much the people know and recognize,
Throughout our seventeen islands.   Marvel
   not.
We of these latter days, with greater mind
Than our forerunners, since more composite,
Look not so great, beside their simple way,   66
To a judge who only sees one way at once,
One mind-point and no other at a time —
Compares the small part of a man of us
With some whole man of the heroic age,   70
Great in his way — not ours, nor meant for
   ours.
And ours is greater, had we skill to know;
For, what we call this life of men on earth,
This sequence of the soul's achievements here
Being, as I find much reason to conceive,   75
Intended to be viewed eventually
As a great whole, not analyzed to parts,
But each part having reference to all —
How shall a certain part, pronounced com-
   plete,

Endure effacement by another part?   80
Was the thing done? — then, what's to do
   again?
See, in the checkered pavement opposite,
Suppose the artist made a perfect rhomb,
And next a lozenge, then a trapezoid —
He did not overlay them, superimpose   85
The new upon the old and blot it out,
But laid them on a level in his work,
Making at last a picture; there it lies.
So, first the perfect separate forms were made,
The portions of mankind; and after, so,   90
Occurred the combination of the same.
For where had been a progress, otherwise?
Mankind, made up of all the single men —
In such a synthesis the labor ends.
Now mark me! those divine men of old time
Have reached, thou sayest well, each at one
   point   96
The outside verge that rounds our faculty;
And where they reached, who can do more
   than reach?
It takes but little water just to touch
At some one point the inside of a sphere,   100
And, as we turn the sphere, touch all the rest
In due succession; but the finer air,
Which not so palpably nor obviously
(Though no less universally) can touch
The whole circumference of that emptied
   sphere,   105
Fills it more fully than the water did;
Holds thrice the weight of water in itself
Resolved into a subtler element.
And yet the vulgar call the sphere first full
Up to the visible height — and after, void;   110
Not knowing air's more hidden properties.
And thus our soul, misknown, cries out to
   Zeus
To vindicate his purpose in our life:
Why stay we on the earth unless to grow?
Long since, I imaged, wrote the fiction out,   115
That he or other god descended here
And, once for all, showed simultaneously
What, in its nature, never can be shown,
Piecemeal or in succession — showed, I say,
The worth both absolute and relative   120
Of all his children from the birth of time,
His instruments for all appointed work.
I now go on to image — might we hear
The judgment which should give the due to
   each,   124
Show where the labor lay and where the ease,
And prove Zeus' self, the latent everywhere!
This is a dream — but no dream, let us hope,
That years and days, the summers and the
   springs,
Follow each other with unwaning powers.   129
The grapes which dye thy wine are richer far,

---

41. **Zeus,** the chief of the Grecian gods. 47. **That epos
. . . gold,** epic poem, engraved on golden plates. 51. **sun-
god . . . phare,** the statue of Apollo on the lighthouse. The
word *phare* is derived from the island of Pharos, the site of
a great lighthouse. 53. **The Pœcile,** the Portico at Athens,
covered with painted scenes of war. 60. **moods.** In
Greek music the moods were the scales.

114. **Why stay . . . to grow?** Cf. *Andrea del Sarto,* 97-98,
p. 289, and *A Death in the Desert,* 424-431, p. 309.

Through culture, than the wild wealth of the
    rock;
The suave plum than the savage-tasted drupe;
The pastured honey-bee drops choicer sweet;
The flowers turn double, and the leaves turn
    flowers;
That young and tender crescent-moon, thy
    slave,   135
Sleeping above her robe as buoyed by clouds,
Refines upon the women of my youth.
What, and the soul alone deteriorates?
I have not chanted verse like Homer, no —
Nor swept string like Terpander, no — nor
    carved   140
And painted men like Phidias and his friend;
I am not great as they are, point by point.
But I have entered into sympathy
With these four, running these into one soul,
Who, separate, ignored each other's art.   145
Say, is it nothing that I know them all?
The wild flower was the larger; I have dashed
Rose-blood upon its petals, pricked its cup's
Honey with wine, and driven its seed to fruit,
And show a better flower if not so large: 150
I stand myself. Refer this to the gods
Whose gift alone it is! which, shall I dare
(All pride apart) upon the absurd pretext
That such a gift by chance lay in my hand,
Discourse of lightly or depreciate?   155
It might have fallen to another's hand; what
    then?
I pass too surely; let at least truth stay!

    And next, of what thou followest on to ask.
This being with me as I declare, O king,
My works, in all these varicolored kinds,   160
So done by me, accepted so by men —
Thou askest, if (my soul thus in men's hearts)
I must not be accounted to attain
The very crown and proper end of life?
Inquiring thence how, now life closeth up,   165
I face death with success in my right hand:
Whether I fear death less than dost thyself
The fortunate of men? "For" (writest thou)
"Thou leavest much behind, while I leave
    naught.
Thy life stays in the poems men shall sing,   170
The pictures men shall study; while my life,
Complete and whole now in its power and joy,
Dies altogether with my brain and arm,
Is lost indeed; since, what survives myself?
The brazen statue to o'erlook my grave,   175
Set on the promontory which I named.
And that — some supple courtier of my heir

Shall use its robed and sceptered arm, per-
    haps,
To fix the rope to, which best drags it down.
I go then; triumph thou, who dost not go!"

    Nay, thou art worthy of hearing my whole
        mind.   181
Is this apparent, when thou turn'st to muse
Upon the scheme of earth and man in chief,
That admiration grows as knowledge grows?
That imperfection means perfection hid,   185
Reserved in part, to grace the after-time?
If, in the morning of philosophy,
Ere aught had been recorded, nay perceived,
Thou, with the light now in thee, couldst have
    looked
On all earth's tenantry, from worm to bird,   190
Ere man, her last, appeared upon the stage —
Thou wouldst have seen them perfect, and
    deduced
The perfectness of others yet unseen.
Conceding which — had Zeus then questioned
    thee,
"Shall I go on a step, improve on this,   195
· Do more for visible creatures than is done?"
Thou wouldst have answered, "Aye, by mak-
    ing each
Grow conscious in himself — by that alone.
All's perfect else; the shell sucks fast the rock,
The fish strikes through the sea, the snake
    both swims   200
And slides, forth range the beasts, the birds
    take flight,
Till life's mechanics can no further go —
And all this joy in natural life is put
Like fire from off thy finger into each,
So exquisitely perfect is the same.   205
But 'tis pure fire, and they mere matter are;
It has them, not they it; and so I choose
For man, thy last premeditated work
(If I might add a glory to the scheme),
That a third thing should stand apart from
    both,   210
A quality arise within his soul,
Which, intro-active, made to supervise
And feel the force it has, may view itself,
And so be happy." Man might live at first
The animal life; but is there nothing more?
In due time, let him critically learn   216
How he lives; and, the more he gets to know
Of his own life's adaptabilities,
The more joy-giving will his life become.
Thus man, who hath this quality, is best.   220

    But thou, king, hadst more reasonably said:
"Let progress end at once — man make no
    step

132. drupe, any fruit containing a stone, like a plum or
a peach. Cleon contrasts the cultivated plum and the wild
plum. 140. Terpander, a famous Greek musician of the
seventh century B.C. He was known as "the father of Greek
music." 141. Phidias, a great Athenian sculptor of the
fifth century B.C. His friend was Pericles, the ruler of Athens
(444-429 B.C).

181-186. Nay . . . after-time. Compare *Abt Vogler*, 65-
96, p. 301. 214-220. Man . . . best. Compare *A Grammarian's Funeral*, 56-72, p. 248.

Beyond the natural man, the better beast,
Using his senses, not the sense of sense."
In man there's failure, only since he left 225
The lower and inconscious forms of life.
We called it an advance, the rendering plain
Man's spirit might grow conscious of man's
life,
And, by new lore so added to the old,
Take each step higher over the brute's head.
This grew the only life, the pleasure-house, 231
Watch-tower, and treasure-fortress of the
soul,
Which whole surrounding flats of natural life
Seemed only fit to yield subsistence to;
A tower that crowns a country. But alas, 235
The soul now climbs it just to perish there!
For thence we have discovered ('tis no
dream —
We know this, which we had not else per-
ceived)
That there's a world of capability
For joy, spread round about us, meant for
us,
Inviting us; and still the soul craves all, 241
And still the flesh replies, "Take no jot more
Than ere thou clombst the tower to look
abroad!
Nay, so much less as that fatigue has brought
Deduction to it." We struggle, fain to
enlarge 245
Our bounded physical recipiency,
Increase our power, supply fresh oil to life,
Repair the waste of age and sickness; no,
It skills not! — life's inadequate to joy,
As the soul sees joy, tempting life to take. 250
They praise a fountain in my garden here
Wherein a Naiad sends the water-bow
Thin from her tube; she smiles to see it rise.
What if I told her, it is just a thread
From that great river which the hills shut
up,
And mock her with my leave to take the
same? 256
The artificer has given her one small tube
Past power to widen or exchange — what
boots
To know she might spout oceans if she could?
She cannot lift beyond her first thin thread;
And so a man can use but a man's joy 261
While he sees God's. Is it for Zeus to boast,
"See, man, how happy I live, and despair —
That I may be still happier — for thy use!"
If this were so, we could not thank our lord,
As hearts beat on to doing; 'tis not so — 266
Malice it is not. Is it carelessness?
Still, no. If care — where is the sign? I ask,
And get no answer, and agree in sum,
O king, with thy profound discouragement,

Who seest the wider but to sigh the more. 271
Most progress is most failure; thou sayest
well.

The last point now: — thou dost except a
case —
Holding joy not impossible to one
With artist-gifts — to such a man as I 275
Who leave behind me living works indeed;
For, such a poem, such a painting lives.
What? dost thou verily trip upon a word,
Confound the accurate view of what joy is
(Caught somewhat clearer by my eyes than
thine) 280
With feeling joy? confound the knowing how
And showing how to live (my faculty)
With actually living? — Otherwise
Where is the artist's vantage o'er the king?
Because in my great epos I display 285
How divers men young, strong, fair, wise, can
act —
Is this as though I acted? If I paint,
Carve the young Phœbus, am I therefore
young?
Methinks I'm older that I bowed myself
The many years of pain that taught me
art!
Indeed, to know is something, and to prove 291
How all this beauty might be enjoyed, is more;
But, knowing naught, to enjoy is something
too.
Yon rower, with the molded muscles there,
Lowering the sail, is nearer it than I. 295
I can write love-odes; thy fair slave's an ode.
I get to sing of love, when grown too gray
For being beloved; she turns to that young
man,
The muscles all a-ripple on his back.
I know the joy of kingship; well, thou art
king! 300

"But," sayest thou — and I marvel, I
repeat,
To find thee trip on such a mere word —
"what
Thou writest, paintest, stays; that does not
die:
Sappho survives, because we sing her songs,
And Æschylus, because we read his plays!" 305
Why, if they live still, let them come and
take
Thy slave in my despite, drink from thy
cup,
Speak in my place. Thou diest while I
survive?
Say rather that my fate is deadlier still,

288. **Phœbus,** Apollo. See line 51. 296. **I . . . ode.** Cf.
Transcendentalism, p. 265. 304. **Sappho,** a famous Greek
poetess of 600 B.C. 305. **Æschylus** (525-456 B.C.), one of
the three greatest writers of Greek tragedy.

In this, that every day my sense of joy   310
Grows more acute, my soul (intensified
By power and insight) more enlarged, more
   keen;
While every day my hairs fall more and more,
My hand shakes, and the heavy years in-
   crease —
The horror quickening still from year to year,
The consummation coming past escape,   316
When I shall know most, and yet least en-
   joy —
When all my works wherein I prove my
   worth,
Being present still to mock me in men's
   mouths,
Alive still, in the praise of such as thou,   320
I, I the feeling, thinking, acting man,
The man who loved his life so over-much,
Sleep in my urn. It is so horrible,
I dare at times imagine to my need
Some future state revealed to us by Zeus,   325
Unlimited in capability
For joy, as this is in desire for joy —
To seek which, the joy-hunger forces us:
That, stung by straitness of our life, made
   strait   329
On purpose to make prized the life at large —
Freed by the throbbing impulse we call death,
We burst there as the worm into the fly,
Who, while a worm still, wants his wings.
   But no!
Zeus has not yet revealed it; and alas,
He must have done so, were it possible!   335

Live long and happy, and in that thought
   die —
Glad for what was! Farewell. And for the
   rest,
I cannot tell thy messenger aright
Where to deliver what he bears of thine
To one called Paulus; we have heard his fame
Indeed, if Christus be not one with him —   341
I know not, nor am troubled much to know.
Thou canst not think a mere barbarian Jew,
As Paulus proves to be, one circumcised,
Hath access to a secret shut from us?   345
Thou wrongest our philosophy, O king,
In stooping to inquire of such an one,
As if his answer could impose at all!
He writeth, doth he? well, and he may write.
Oh, the Jew findeth scholars! certain slaves
Who touched on this same isle, preached him
   and Christ;   351
And (as I gathered from a bystander)
Their doctrine could be held by no sane man.
   (1855)

336-353. **Live long . . . sane man.** Cf. the closing lines
of *An Epistle*, p. 283. 340-341. **Paulus . . . him.** Paul died
about 67 A.D. Cleon is not sure whether Paul and Christ are
different persons.

ONE WORD MORE

TO E. B. B.

I

There they are, my fifty men and women
Naming me the fifty poems finished!
Take them, Love, the book and me together;
Where the heart lies, let the brain lie also.

2

Rafael made a century of sonnets,   5
Made and wrote them in a certain volume
Dinted with the silver-pointed pencil
Else he only used to draw Madonnas;
These, the world might view — but one, the
   volume.
Who that one, you ask? Your heart instructs
   you.   10
Did she live and love it all her lifetime?
Did she drop, his lady of the sonnets,
Die, and let it drop beside her pillow
Where it lay in place of Rafael's glory,
Rafael's cheek so duteous and so loving —   15
Cheek, the world was wont to hail a painter's,
Rafael's cheek, her love had turned a poet's?

3

You and I would rather read that volume
(Taken to his beating bosom by it),
Lean and list the bosom-beats of Rafael,   20
Would we not? than wonder at Madonnas —
Her, San Sisto names, and Her, Foligno,
Her, that visits Florence in a vision,
Her, that's left with lilies in the Louvre —
Seen by us and all the world in circle.   25

4

You and I will never read that volume.
Guido Reni, like his own eye's apple
Guarded long the treasure-book and loved it.
Guido Reni dying, all Bologna

One Word More. This poem was originally appended to the
volume of Browning's poems called *Men and Women.* It is a
deeply personal poem addressed to Mrs. Browning. Other
poems written by Browning in praise of his wife are *My Star,*
p. 239, the selection from Book I of *The Ring and the Book,* p.
320, Proem to *The Two Poets of Croisic,* and *By the Fireside.*

2. **Naming me,** furnishing me with the name of the
volume. 5. **Rafael,** Raphael Sanzio (1483-1520), one of
the greatest of Italian painters. Only four of his sonnets
exist, and there is no authentic record of the others having
been written. The "lady of the sonnets" of line 12 is said
to have been named Margharita; her likeness appears in
several of Raphael's paintings. 21-24. **Madonnas . . .
Louvre.** Of the fifty or more Madonnas painted by Raphael,
the four mentioned here are the most important: the *Sistine
Madonna,* at Dresden; the *Madonna of Foligno,* at Rome;
the *Madonna del Granduca,* at Florence; and probably the
Madonna of the Garden (La Belle Jardinière), at the Louvre,
in Paris. The one at Rome was painted as a votive offering
for Sigismond Corti of Foligno; in the one at Florence the
Madonna is represented as appearing to a votary in a vision.
27. **Guido Reni** (1575-1642), a painter of Bologna, a city in
northern Italy The "treasure-book" he owned contained
one hundred of Raphael's original designs, but no sonnets.

Cried, and the world cried too, "Ours, the
    treasure!"   30
Suddenly, as rare things will, it vanished.

5

Dante once prepared to paint an angel—
Whom to please? You whisper "Beatrice."
While he mused and traced it and retraced it
(Peradventure with a pen corroded   35
Still by drops of that hot ink he dipped for,
When, his left-hand i' the hair o' the wicked,
Back he held the brow and pricked its stigma,
Bit into the live man's flesh for parchment,
Loosed him, laughed to see the writing rankle,
Let the wretch go festering through Flor-
    ence) —   41
Dante, who loved well because he hated,
Hated wickedness that hinders loving,
Dante standing, studying his angel —
In there broke the folk of his Inferno.   45
Says he — "Certain people of importance"
(Such he gave his daily dreadful line to)
"Entered and would seize, forsooth, the poet."
Says the poet — "Then I stopped my paint-
    ing."

6

You and I would rather see that angel,   50
Painted by the tenderness of Dante —
Would we not? — than read a fresh Inferno.

7

You and I will never see that picture.
While he mused on love and Beatrice,
While he softened o'er his outlined angel,   55
In they broke, those "people of importance";
We and Bice bear the loss forever.

8

What of Rafael's sonnets, Dante's picture?
This: no artist lives and loves, that longs not
Once, and only once, and for one only   60
(Ah, the prize!), to find his love a language
Fit and fair and simple and sufficient —
Using nature that's an art to others,
Not, this one time, art that's turned his
    nature.
Aye, of all the artists living, loving,   65
None but would forego his proper dowry —
Does he paint? he fain would write a poem —
Does he write? he fain would paint a picture,

Put to proof art alien to the artist's,
Once, and only once, and for one only,   70
So to be the man and leave the artist,
Gain the man's joy, miss the artist's sorrow.

9

Wherefore? Heaven's gift takes earth's abate-
    ment!
He who smites the rock and spreads the water,
Bidding drink and live a crowd beneath him,
Even he, the minute makes immortal,   76
Proves, perchance, but mortal in the minute,
Desecrates, belike, the deed in doing.
While he smites, how can he but remember,
So he smote before, in such a peril,   80
When they stood and mocked — "Shall smit-
    ing help us?"
When they drank and sneered — "A stroke is
    easy!"
When they wiped their mouths and went their
    journey,
Throwing him for thanks — "But drought
    was pleasant."
Thus old memories mar the actual triumph;
Thus the doing savors of disrelish;   86
Thus achievement lacks a gracious somewhat;
O'er-importuned brows becloud the mandate,
Carelessness or consciousness — the gesture.
For he bears an ancient wrong about him,   90
Sees and knows again those phalanxed faces,
Hears, yet one time more, the 'customed pre-
    lude —
"How shouldst thou, of all men, smite, and
    save us?"
Guesses what is like to prove the sequel —
"Egypt's flesh-pots — nay, the drought was
    better."   95

10

Oh, the crowd must have emphatic warrant!
Theirs, the Sinai-forehead's cloven brilliance,
Right-arm's rod-sweep, tongue's imperial fiat.
Never dares the man put off the prophet.

11

Did he love one face from out the thousands
(Were she Jethro's daughter, white and wifely,
Were she but the Ethiopian bondslave),   102
He would envy yon dumb patient camel,
Keeping a reserve of scanty water
Meant to save his own life in the desert;   105

32-33. **Dante . . . Beatrice.** Dante, Italy's greatest
poet (1265-1321), loved Beatrice Portinari, whom he immortalized in his *Vita Nuova* and his *Divina Commedia*. At
the close of the *Vita Nuova* Dante states that on the first
anniversary of the death of Beatrice he wished to paint an
angel as a memorial to her. He says too that he was interrupted by "certain people of importance" (line 46). 35-41.
Peradventure . . . Florence. The *Divina Commedia* consists of the *Inferno*, the *Purgatorio*, and the *Paradiso*. Dante
freely consigned his enemies, living or dead, to appropriate
places in Inferno or Purgatory. Lines 35-41 refer to incidents in sections 32-33 of the *Inferno*. The man referred
to in lines 37-38 was dead, but the man of lines 39-41 was
alive. 57. **Bice,** Beatrice.

74. **He who,** etc. The experience of Moses is cited as an
example of the "artist's sorrow." The story of the smiting
of the rock by Moses is found in *Exodus*, 16-19, and in *Numbers*, 20. 95. **Egypt's . . . better.** The Israelites murmured
against Moses in the wilderness because they had no food and
said, "Would to God we had died by the hand of the Lord in
the land of Egypt, when we sat by the flesh pots, and when
we did eat bread to the full" (*Exodus*, 16:3). 97. **Sinai-
forehead's . . . brilliance,** a reference to the appearance
of God in the thunder and lightning on Mount Sinai, as told
in *Exodus*, 19. 101. **Jethro's daughter,** Zipporah, the
wife of Moses (see *Exodus*, 2 and 18). 102. **the Ethiopian
bondslave,** the Ethiopian woman whom Moses married
(see *Numbers*, 12:1).

Ready in the desert to deliver
(Kneeling down to let his breast be opened)
Hoard and life together for his mistress.

12

I shall never, in the years remaining,   109
Paint you pictures, no, nor carve you statues,
Make you music that should all-express me;
So it seems — I stand on my attainment.
This of verse alone, one life allows me;
Verse and nothing else have I to give you.
Other heights in other lives, God willing;   115
All the gifts from all the heights, your own,
    Love!

13

Yet a semblance of resource avails us —
Shade so finely touched, love's sense must
    seize it.
Take these lines, look lovingly and nearly, 119
Lines I write the first time and the last time.
He who works in fresco, steals a hair-brush,
Curbs the liberal hand, subservient proudly,
Cramps his spirit, crowds its all in little,
Makes a strange art of an art familiar,
Fills his lady's missal-marge with flowerets.
He who blows through bronze may breathe
    through silver,   126
Fitly serenade a slumbrous princess.
He who writes may write for once as I do.

14

Love, you saw me gather men and women,
Live or dead or fashioned by my fancy,   130
Enter each and all, and use their service,
Speak from every mouth — the speech, a
    poem.
Hardly shall I tell my joys and sorrows,
Hopes and fears, belief and disbelieving;
I am mine and yours — the rest be all men's,
Karshish, Cleon, Norbert, and the fifty.   136
Let me speak this once in my true person,
Not as Lippo, Roland, or Andrea,
Though the fruit of speech be just this sen-
    tence:
Pray you, look on these my men and women,
Take and keep my fifty poems finished;   141
Where my heart lies, let my brain lie also!
Poor the speech; be how I speak, for all things.

15

Not but that you know me! Lo, the moon's
    self!
Here in London, yonder late in Florence,   145
Still we find her face, the thrice-transfigured.

Curving on a sky imbrued with color,
Drifted over Fiesole by twilight,
Came she, our new crescent of a hair's-
    breadth,
Full she flared it, lamping Samminiato,   150
Rounder 'twixt the cypresses and rounder,
Perfect till the nightingales applauded.
Now, a piece of her old self, impoverished,
Hard to greet, she traverses the house-roofs,
Hurries with unhandsome thrift of silver,   155
Goes dispiritedly, glad to finish.

16

What, there's nothing in the moon note-
    worthy?
Nay; for if that moon could love a mortal,
Use, to charm him (so to fit a fancy),
All her magic ('tis the old sweet mythos),   160
She would turn a new side to her mortal,
Side unseen of herdsman, huntsman, steers-
    man —
Blank to Zoroaster on his terrace,
Blind to Galileo on his turret,
Dumb to Homer, dumb to Keats — him,
    even!   165
Think, the wonder of the moonstruck mor-
    tal —
When she turns round, comes again in heaven,
Opens out anew for worse or better!
Proves she like some portent of an iceberg
Swimming full upon the ship it founders,   170
Hungry with huge teeth of splintered crys-
    tals?
Proves she as the paved work of a sapphire
Seen by Moses when he climbed the moun-
    tain?
Moses, Aaron, Nadab, and Abihu
Climbed and saw the very God, the Highest,
Stand upon the paved work of a sapphire.   176
Like the bodied heaven in his clearness
Shone the stone, the sapphire of that paved
    work,
When they ate and drank and saw God also!

17

What were seen? None knows, none ever
    shall know.   180
Only this is sure — the sight were other,

148. **Fiesole,** a suburb of Florence. 150. **Samminiato,** San Miniato, a church on the height above Florence, opposite Fiesole. 160. **mythos,** legend, myth. Lines 158-162 refer to myths concerning Endymion, the youth loved by Diana (the moon). 163. **Zoroaster,** the founder of the Persian religion, about 500 B.C. He studied the heavenly bodies while meditating upon religious themes. 164. **Galileo,** the great Italian physicist and astronomer (1564-1642). 165. **Homer,** a reference to Homer's "Hymn to Diana" in Book 21 of the *Iliad.* **Keats,** a reference to Keats's *Endymion.* Even Keats, whom Browning thus exalts above all others who had been entranced by the moon, had not caught all her magic. 176-179. **paved work . . . God also.** Cf. *Exodus,* 24:9-10.—"Then went up Moses, and Aaron, Nadab, and Abihu, and seventy of the elders of Israel; and they saw the God of Israel; and there was under his feet as it were a paved work of a sapphire stone, and as it were the body of heaven in his clearness."

120. **Lines . . . time.** This is the only poem of Browning's written in rimeless five-foot trochaics. 125. **missal-marge,** border of the prayer-book. 136-138. **Karshish . . . Andrea.** Lines 136-138 mention the characters found in six of the poems included in *Men and Women.* 144-146. **Lo . . . thrice-transfigured.** They had recently watched the new moon in Florence; now in London they see her in her last quarter.

Not the moon's same side, born late in Flor-
    ence,
Dying now impoverished here in London.
God be thanked, the meanest of his creatures
Boasts two soul-sides, one to face the world
    with,   185
One to show a woman when he loves her!

18

This I say of me, but think of you, Love!
This to you — yourself my moon of poets!
Ah, but that's the world's side, there's the
    wonder,
Thus they see you, praise you, think they
    know you!   190
There, in turn I stand with them and praise
    you —
Out of my own self, I dare to phrase it.
But the best is when I glide from out them,
Cross a step or two of dubious twilight,
Come out on the other side, the novel   195
Silent silver lights and darks undreamed of,
Where I hush and bless myself with silence.

19

Oh, their Rafael of the dear Madonnas,
Oh, their Dante of the dread Inferno,   199
Wrote one song — and in my brain I sing it,
Drew one angel — borne, see, on my bosom!
                     R. B.
                (*1855; 1855*)

BEN KARSHOOK'S WISDOM

I

"Would a man 'scape the rod?"
    Rabbi Ben Karshook saith,
"See that he turn to God
    The day before his death."

"Aye, could a man inquire   5
    When it shall come!" I say.
The Rabbi's eye shoots fire —
    "Then let him turn today!"

2

Quoth a young Sadducee:
    "Reader of many rolls,   10
Is it so certain we
    Have, as they tell us, souls?"

"Son, there is no reply!"
    The Rabbi bit his beard:

"Certain, a soul have *I* —   15
    We may have none," he sneered.

Thus Karshook, the Hiram's-Hammer,
    The Right-hand Temple-column,
Taught babes in grace their grammar,
    And struck the simple, solemn.   20
                (*1854; 1856*)

TOO LATE

Here was I with my arm and heart
    And brain, all yours for a word, a want
Put into a look — just a look, your part —
    While mine, to repay it . . . vainest vaunt.
Were the woman, that's dead, alive to hear, 5
    Had her lover, that's lost, love's proof to
        show!
But I cannot show it; you cannot speak
    From the churchyard neither, miles re-
        moved,
Though I feel by a pulse within my cheek,
    Which stabs and stops, that the woman I
        loved   10
Needs help in her grave and finds none near,
    Wants warmth from the heart which sends
        it — so!

Did I speak once angrily, all the drear days
    You lived, you woman I loved so well,
Who married the other? Blame or praise,   15
    Where was the use then? Time would tell,
And the end declare what man for you,
    What woman for me, was the choice of God.
But, Edith dead! no doubting more!
    I used to sit and look at my life   20
As it rippled and ran till, right before,
    A great stone stopped it; oh, the strife
Of waves at the stone some devil threw
    In my life's midcurrent, thwarting God!

But either I thought, "They may churn and
    chide   25
    Awhile, my waves which came for their joy
And found this horrible stone full-tide;
    Yet I see just a thread escape, deploy
Through the evening-country, silent and safe,
    And it suffers no more till it finds the sea."
Or else I would think, "Perhaps some night 31
    When new things happen, a meteor-ball
May slip through the sky in a line of light,
    And earth breathe hard, and landmarks
        fall,

Ben Karshook's Wisdom.   *Karshook* is Hebrew for *thistle.*
The character is imaginary.
9. **Sadducee.** The Sadducees were a sect of the Jews
composed largely of the priestly aristocracy (2d century B.C.
to 1st century A.D.). They denied the Resurrection, personal
immortality, etc.

17-18. **Hiram's-Hammer . . . Temple-column,** a reference to Hiram, a Phœnician king, described as a skillful
worker in brass on Solomon's Temple. He set up two brass
pillars—the one on the right was named Jachin, signifying
stability; the one on the left, Boaz, signifying strength (see
1 Kings, 7:13-22).

And my waves no longer champ nor chafe, 35
  Since a stone will have rolled from its place;
    let be!"

But, dead! All's done with; wait who may,
  Watch and wear and wonder who will.
Oh, my whole life that ends today!
  Oh, my soul's sentence, sounding still, 40
"The woman is dead that was none of his;
  And the man that was none of hers may
    go!"
There's only the past left; worry that!
  Wreak, like a bull, on the empty coat,
  Rage, its late wearer is laughing at! 45
  Tear the collar to rags, having missed his
    throat;
Strike stupidly on — "This, this, and this,
  Where I would that a bosom received the
    blow!"

I ought to have done more; once my speech,
  And once your answer, and there, the end,
And Edith was henceforth out of reach! 51
  Why, men do more to deserve a friend,
Be rid of a foe, get rich, grow wise,
  Nor, folding their arms, stare fate in the
    face.
Why, better even have burst like a thief 55
  And borne you away to a rock for us two,
In a moment's horror, bright, bloody, and
    brief,
  Then changed to myself again — "I slew
Myself in that moment; a ruffian lies
  Somewhere; your slave, see, born in his
    place!" 60

What did the other do? You be judge!
  Look at us, Edith! Here are we both!
Give him his six whole years; I grudge
  None of the life with you, nay, loathe
Myself that I grudged his start in advance 65
  Of me who could overtake and pass.
But, as if he loved you! No, not he,
  Nor any one else in the world, 'tis plain;
Who ever heard that another, free 69
  As I, young, prosperous, sound, and sane,
Poured life out, proffered it — "Half a glance
  Of those eyes of yours and I drop the glass!"

Handsome, were you? 'Tis more than they
    held,
  More than they said; I was 'ware and
    watched;
I was the scapegrace, this rat belled 75
  The cat, this fool got his whiskers scratched.
The others? No head that was turned, no
    heart
  Broken, my lady, assure yourself!
Each soon made his mind up; so and so
  Married a dancer, such and such 80

Stole his friend's wife, stagnated slow,
  Or maundered, unable to do as much,
And muttered of peace where he had no part;
  While, hid in the closet, laid on the shelf —

On the whole, you were let alone, I think! 85
  So you looked to the other, who acquiesced;
My rival, the proud man — prize your pink
  Of poets! A poet he was! I've guessed;
He rimed you his rubbish nobody read,
  Loved you and doved you — did not I
    laugh! 90
There was a prize! But we both were tried.
  Oh, heart of mine, marked broad with her
    mark,
Tekel, found wanting, set aside,
  Scorned! See. I bleed these tears in the
    dark
Till comfort come and the last be bled; 95
  He? He is tagging your epitaph.

If it would only come over again!
  — Time to be patient with me, and probe
This heart till you punctured the proper vein,
  Just to learn what blood is; twitch the
    robe 100
From that blank lay-figure your fancy draped,
  Prick the leathern heart till the — verses
    spirt!
And late it was easy; late, you walked
  Where a friend might meet you; Edith's
    name
Arose to one's lip if one laughed or talked; 105
  If I heard good news, you heard the same;
When I woke, I knew that your breath es-
    caped;
  I could bide my time, keep alive, alert.

And alive I shall keep and long, you will see!
  I knew a man, was kicked like a dog 110
From gutter to cesspool; what cared he
  So long as he picked from the filth his prog?
He saw youth, beauty, and genius die,
  And jollily lived to his hundredth year.
But I will live otherwise; none of such life!
  At once I begin as I mean to end. 116
Go on with the world, get gold in its strife,
  Give your spouse the slip and betray your
    friend!
There are two who decline, a woman and I,
  And enjoy our death in the darkness here.

I liked that way you had with your curls 121
  Wound to a ball in a net behind;
Your cheek was chaste as a Quaker-girl's;

93. **Tekel**, one of the words of the mysterious writing on the wall of Belshazzar's palace, interpreted by Daniel (*Daniel*, 5:1-31). It means "Thou art weighed in the balances and art found wanting" (v. 27). 96. **tagging**, supplying with rimes. 112. **prog**, food.

And your mouth — there was never, to my
    mind,
Such a funny mouth, for it would not shut; 125
And the dented chin too — what a chin!
There were certain ways when you spoke,
    some words
That you know you never could pronounce.
You were thin, however; like a bird's
    Your hand seemed — some would say, the
    pounce   130
Of a scaly-footed hawk — all but!
The world was right when it called you thin.

But I turn my back on the world; I take
    Your hand, and kneel, and lay to my lips.
Bid me live, Edith! Let me slake   135
    Thirst at your presence! Fear no slips;
'Tis your slave shall pay, while his soul en-
    dures,
Full due, love's whole debt, *summum jus*.
My queen shall have high observance, planned
    Courtship made perfect, no least line   140
Crossed without warrant. There you stand,
    Warm too, and white too; would this wine
Had washed all over that body of yours,
Ere I drank it, and you down with it, thus!
                      (1864)

ABT VOGLER

(AFTER HE HAS BEEN EXTEMPORIZING
UPON THE MUSICAL INSTRUMENT
OF HIS INVENTION)

Would that the structure brave, the manifold
    music I build,
    Bidding my organ obey, calling its keys to
    their work,
Claiming each slave of the sound, at a touch,
    as when Solomon willed
Armies of angels that soar, legions of de-
    mons that lurk,
Man, brute, reptile, fly — alien of end and of
    aim,   5
    Adverse, each from the other heaven-high,
    hell-deep removed —
Should rush into sight at once as he named
    the ineffable Name,
    And pile him a palace straight, to pleasure
    the princess he loved!

Would it might tarry like his, the beautiful
    building of mine,

This which my keys in a crowd pressed and
    importuned to raise!   10
Ah, one and all, how they helped, would dis-
    part now and now combine,
    Zealous to hasten the work, heighten their
    master his praise!
And one would bury his brow with a blind
    plunge down to hell,
    Burrow awhile and build, broad on the
    roots of things,
Then up again swim into sight, having based
    me my palace well,   15
    Founded it, fearless of flame, flat on the
    nether springs.

And another would mount and march, like the
    excellent minion he was,
    Aye, another and yet another, one crowd
    but with many a crest,
Raising my rampired walls of gold as trans-
    parent as glass,
    Eager to do and die, yield each his place to
    the rest;   20
For higher still and higher (as a runner tips
    with fire,
    When a great illumination surprises a festal
    night —
Outlined round and round Rome's dome from
    space to spire)
    Up, the pinnacled glory reached, and the
    pride of my soul was in sight.

In sight? Not half! for it seemed, it was
    certain, to match man's birth,   25
    Nature in turn conceived, obeying an im-
    pulse as I;
And the emulous heaven yearned down, made
    effort to reach the earth,
    As the earth had done her best, in my pas-
    sion, to scale the sky;
Novel splendors burst forth, grew familiar
    and dwelt with mine;
    Not a point nor peak but found and fixed
    its wandering star —   30
Meteor-moons, balls of blaze; and they did
    not pale nor pine,
    For earth had attained to heaven — there
    was no more near nor far.

Nay, more; for there wanted not who walked
    in the glare and glow,
    Presences plain in the place; or, fresh from
    the Protoplast,

---

138. summum jus, exact law, highest right.
    Abt Vogler. Georg Joseph Vogler (1749-1814), also known
as Abbé (or Abt) Vogler, was a noted German musician. He
invented a kind of small organ called the orchestrion. He was
a skilled organist and composer.
    3. as when Solomon willed. According to legend,
Solomon had power over supernatural beings through a seal
bearing the name of God, the "ineffable Name" of line 7.

16. nether springs, deepest sources. 17. minion,
servant. 19. rampired, having ramparts. 21-23. For
higher . . . spire. The structure rises in his imagination
like the fire that ascends streamers and illuminates St. Peter's
from the open space between the colonnades to the cross on
top of the dome. The cathedral is often illuminated for
special festivals. 34. fresh . . . Protoplast, fresh from
the mass of protoplasm—i.e., just created.

Furnished for ages to come, when a kindlier
    wind should blow,   35
    Lured now to begin and live, in a house to
        their liking at last;
Or else the wonderful Dead who have passed
    through the body and gone,
    But were back once more to breathe in an
        old world worth their new.
What never had been, was now; what was, as
    it shall be anon;
    And what is — shall I say, matched both? for
        I was made perfect, too.   40

All through my keys that gave their sounds
    to a wish of my soul,
    All through my soul that praised as its wish
        flowed visibly forth,
All through music and me! For think, had I
    painted the whole,
    Why, there it had stood, to see, nor the
        process so wonder-worth;
Had I written the same, made verse — still,
    effect proceeds from cause,   45
    Ye know why the forms are fair, ye hear
        how the tale is told;
It is all triumphant art, but art in obedience
    to laws,
    Painter and poet are proud in the artist-
        list enrolled: —

But here is the finger of God, a flash of the
    will that can,
    Existent behind all laws, that made them
        and, lo, they are!   50
And I know not if, save in this, such gift be
    allowed to man,
    That out of three sounds he frame, not a
        fourth sound, but a star.
Consider it well: each tone of our scale in
    itself is naught;
    It is everywhere in the world — loud, soft,
    and all is said —
Give it to me to use! I mix it with two in
    my thought —   55
    And there! Ye have heard and seen; con-
    sider, and bow the head!

Well, it is gone at last, the palace of music I
    reared;
    Gone! and the good tears start, the praises
        that come too slow;
For one is assured at first, one scarce can say
    that he feared,
    That he even gave it a thought, the gone
    thing was to go.   60

Never to be again! But many more of the
    kind
    As good, nay, better perchance; is this your
        comfort to me?
To me, who must be saved because I cling
    with my mind
    To the same, same self, same love, same
        God; aye, what was, shall be.

Therefore to whom turn I but to thee, the
    ineffable Name?   65
    Builder and maker, thou, of houses not
    made with hands!
What, have fear of change from thee who art
    ever the same?
    Doubt that thy power can fill the heart that
        thy power expands?
There shall never be one lost good! What
    was, shall live as before;
    The evil is null, is naught, is silence imply-
        ing sound;   70
What was good shall be good, with, for evil,
    so much good more;
    On the earth the broken arcs; in the heaven
    a perfect round.

All we have willed or hoped or dreamed of
    good shall exist;
    Not its semblance, but itself; no beauty, nor
    good, nor power
Whose voice has gone forth, but each survives
    for the melodist   75
    When eternity affirms the conception of an
    hour.
The high that proved too high, the heroic for
    earth too hard,
    The passion that left the ground to lose
    itself in the sky,
Are music sent up to God by the lover and
    the bard.
    Enough that he heard it once; we shall hear
    it by and by.   80

And what is our failure here but a triumph's
    evidence
    For the fullness of the days? Have we
    withered or agonized?
Why else was the pause prolonged but that
    singing might issue thence?
    Why rushed the discords in, but that har-
    mony should be prized?
Sorrow is hard to bear, and doubt is slow to
    clear,   85
    Each sufferer says his say, his scheme of the
    weal and woe.

43-44. **had I painted . . . wonder-worth,** if I had
painted the structure, there it would be to look at; but the
greater permanence of paint would have left less to the imagination than the dissolving notes.

66. **Builder and maker.** Abraham "looked for a city
which hath foundations, whose builder and maker is God"
(*Hebrews*, 11:10). **houses . . . hands.** "For we know
that if our earthly house . . . were dissolved, we have a building of God, an house not made with hands, eternal in the
heavens" (*2 Corinthians*, 5:1).

But God has a few of us whom he whispers
    in the ear;
The rest may reason and welcome; 'tis we
    musicians know.

Well, it is earth with me; silence resumes her
    reign.
    I will be patient and proud, and soberly
      acquiesce.   90
Give me the keys. I feel for the common
    chord again,
Sliding by semitones till I sink to the minor
    — yes,
And I blunt it into a ninth, and I stand on
    alien ground,
Surveying awhile the heights I rolled from
    into the deep;
Which, hark, I have dared and done, for my
    resting-place is found,   95
The C Major of this life; so, now I will try
    to sleep.   (1864)

RABBI BEN EZRA

Grow old along with me!
The best is yet to be,
The last of life, for which the first was made.
Our times are in his hand
Who saith, "A whole I planned;   5
Youth shows but half. Trust God; see all,
    nor be afraid!"

Not that, amassing flowers,
Youth sighed, "Which rose make ours,
Which lily leave and then as best recall?"
Not that, admiring stars,   10
It yearned, "Nor Jove, nor Mars;
Mine be some figured flame which blends,
    transcends them all!"

Not for such hopes and fears
Annulling youth's brief years,
Do I remonstrate — folly wide the mark!   15
Rather I prize the doubt
Low kinds exist without,
Finished and finite clods, untroubled by a
    spark.

Poor vaunt of life indeed,
Were man but formed to feed   20
On joy, to solely seek and find and feast.
Such feasting ended, then
As sure an end to men;
Irks care the crop-full bird? Frets doubt the
    maw-crammed beast?

Rejoice we are allied   25
To that which doth provide
And not partake, effect and not receive!
A spark disturbs our clod;
Nearer we hold of God
Who gives, than of his tribes that take, I must
    believe.   30

Then, welcome each rebuff
That turns earth's smoothness rough,
Each sting that bids nor sit nor stand but go!
Be our joys three-parts pain!
Strive, and hold cheap the strain;   35
Learn, nor account the pang; dare, never
    grudge the throe!

For thence — a paradox
Which comforts while it mocks —
Shall life succeed in that it seems to fail:
What I aspired to be,   40
And was not, comforts me;
A brute I might have been, but would not
    sink i' the scale.

What is he but a brute
Whose flesh has soul to suit,
Whose spirit works lest arms and legs want
    play?   45
To man, propose this test —
Thy body at its best,
How far can that project thy soul on its lone
    way?

Yet gifts should prove their use:
I own the Past profuse   50
Of power each side, perfection every turn;
Eyes, ears took in their dole,
Brain treasured up the whole;
Should not the heart beat once, "How good to
    live and learn"?

Not once beat, "Praise be thine!   55
I see the whole design,
I, who saw power, see now Love perfect too;
Perfect I call thy plan.
Thanks that I was a man!
Maker, remake, complete — I trust what
    thou shalt do!"   60

91-96. common chord, etc. As the musician had mounted to supreme heights of thought through the medium of his art, so he now descends to level ground. He strikes different chords—plaintive and poignant minors, then reassuring harmonies that lead at last to C major, the natural scale without variations of sharps and flats, hence symbolic of the common level of everyday life.

Rabbi Ben Ezra. Rabbi Ben Ezra was a distinguished Jewish philosopher, physician, astronomer, and poet of the 12th century. Although the ideas in the poem are drawn largely from his writings, the poem is one of the best expressions of Browning's own philosophy of life.

1. Grow . . . me. Cf. *Saul,* 161-164, p. 226. The poem may be compared with FitzGerald's *Rubáiyát,* p. 425, and Arnold's *Growing Old,* p. 500. **7. Not that.** *Not that* of lines 7 and 10 and *Not for* of line 13 go with *Do I remonstrate* of line 15.

24. Irks . . . bird, does care irk the crop-full bird? **40-41. What . . . me.** Cf. *Saul,* 295-296, p. 229. **57. I . . . too.** Cf. *Saul,* 242, 305-306, pp. 228, 229.

For pleasant is this flesh;
Our soul, in its rose-mesh
Pulled ever to the earth, still yearns for rest.
Would we some prize might hold
To match those manifold   65
Possessions of the brute — gain most, as we
    did best!

Let us not always say,
"Spite of this flesh today
I strove, made head, gained ground upon the
    whole!"
As the bird wings and sings,   70
Let us cry, "All good things
Are ours, nor soul helps flesh more, now, than
    flesh helps soul!"

Therefore I summon age
To grant youth's heritage,
Life's struggle having so far reached its term.
Thence shall I pass, approved   76
A man, for aye removed
From the developed brute — a god, though
    in the germ.

And I shall thereupon
Take rest, ere I be gone   80
Once more on my adventure brave and new;
Fearless and unperplexed,
When I wage battle next,
What weapons to select, what armor to indue.

Youth ended, I shall try   85
My gain or loss thereby;
Leave the fire ashes, what survives is gold.
And I shall weigh the same,
Give life its praise or blame.
Young, all lay in dispute; I shall know, being
    old.   90

For note, when evening shuts,
A certain moment cuts
The deed off, calls the glory from the gray;
A whisper from the west
Shoots — "Add this to the rest,   95
Take it and try its worth. Here dies another
    day."

So, still within this life,
Though lifted o'er its strife,
Let me discern, compare, pronounce at last,
"This rage was right i' the main,   100
That acquiescence vain;
The Future I may face, now I have proved
    the Past."

For more is not reserved
To man, with soul just nerved
To act tomorrow what he learns today;   105
Here, work enough to watch
The Master work, and catch
Hints of the proper craft, tricks of the tool's
    true play.

As it was better, youth
Should strive, through acts uncouth,   110
Toward making, than repose on aught found
    made;
So, better, age, exempt
From strife, should know, than tempt
Further. Thou waitedst age; wait death nor
    be afraid!

Enough now, if the Right   115
And Good and Infinite
Be named here, as thou callest thy hand
    thine own,
With knowledge absolute,
Subject to no dispute
From fools that crowded youth, nor let thee
    feel alone.   120

Be there, for once and all,
Severed great minds from small,
Announced to each his station in the Past!
Was I, the world arraigned,
Were they, my soul disdained,   125
Right? Let age speak the truth and give us
    peace at last!

Now, who shall arbitrate?
Ten men love what I hate,
Shun what I follow, slight what I receive;
Ten, who in ears and eyes   130
Match me. We all surmise,
They this thing, and I that; whom shall my
    soul believe?

Not on the vulgar mass
Called "work," must sentence pass —
Things done, that took the eye and had the
    price;   135
O'er which, from level stand,
The low world laid its hand,
Found straightway to its mind, could value in
    a trice:

But all, the world's coarse thumb
And finger failed to plumb,   140
So passed in making up the main account;
All instincts immature,

61-72. **For pleasant**, etc. Cf. *Fra Lippo Lippi*, 205-214, p. 286. 81. **adventure . . . new**, the life after death. 84. **to indue**, to put on. 87. **Leave . . . ashes**, if the fire leaves ashes.

109-111. **As . . . made.** Cf. *Old Pictures in Florence*, p. 234, in which Browning applies the idea of these lines to the development of art. 124. **Was I.** Supply *whom* after *I* and also after *they*, line 125.

All purposes unsure,
That weighed not as his work, yet swelled
    the man's amount:

Thoughts hardly to be packed   145
Into a narrow act,
Fancies that broke through language and
    escaped;
All I could never be,
All, men ignored in me,
This, I was worth to God, whose wheel the
    pitcher shaped.   150

Aye, note that Potter's wheel,
That metaphor! and feel
Why time spins fast, why passive lies our
    clay —
Thou, to whom fools propound,
When the wine makes its round,   155
"Since life fleets, all is change; the Past gone,
    seize today!"

Fool! All that is, at all,
Lasts ever, past recall;
Earth changes, but thy soul and God stand
    sure.
What entered into thee,   160
That was, is, and shall be.
Time's wheel runs back or stops; Potter and
    clay endure.

He fixed thee 'mid this dance
Of plastic circumstance,
This Present, thou, forsooth, would fain ar-
    rest —   165
Machinery just meant
To give thy soul its bent,
Try thee and turn thee forth, sufficiently im-
    pressed.

What though the earlier grooves,
Which ran the laughing loves   170
Around thy base, no longer pause and press?
What though, about thy rim,
Skull-things in order grim
Grow out, in graver mood, obey the sterner
    stress?

Look not thou down but up!   175
To uses of a cup,
The festal board, lamp's flash, and trumpet's
    peal,
The new wine's foaming flow,
The Master's lips aglow!
Thou, heaven's consummate cup, what needst
    thou with earth's wheel?   180

But I need, now as then,
Thee, God, who moldest men;
And since, not even while the whirl was worst,
Did I — to the wheel of life
With shapes and colors rife,   185
Bound dizzily — mistake my end, to slake
    Thy thirst,

So, take and use Thy work;
Amend what flaws may lurk,
What strain o' the stuff, what warpings past
    the aim!
My times be in Thy hand!   190
Perfect the cup as planned!
Let age approve of youth, and death complete
    the same!   (1864)

A DEATH IN THE DESERT

[Supposed of Pamphylax the Antiochene:
It is a parchment, of my rolls the fifth,
Hath three skins glued together, is all Greek,
And goeth from *Epsilon* down to *Mu;*
Lies second in the surnamed Chosen Chest, 5
Stained and conserved with juice of terebinth,
Covered with cloth of hair, and lettered *Xi,*
From Xanthus, my wife's uncle now at peace;
Mu and *Epsilon* stand for my own name.
I may not write it, but I make a cross   10
To show I wait His coming, with the rest,
And leave off here; beginneth Pamphylax.]

I said, "If one should wet his lips with wine,
And slip the broadest plantain-leaf we find,
Or else the lappet of a linen robe,   15
Into the water-vessel, lay it right,
And cool his forehead just above the eyes,
The while a brother, kneeling either side,
Should chafe each hand and try to make it
    warm —
He is not so far gone but he might speak." 20

This did not happen in the outer cave,
Nor in the secret chamber of the rock —
Where, sixty days since the decree was out,
We had him, bedded on a camel-skin,
And waited for his dying all the while —   25
But in the midmost grotto, since noon's light

---

151. **that Potter's wheel.** Cf. *Isaiah*, 64:8.—"But now,
O Lord, thou art our father; we are the clay, and thou our
potter: and we all are the work of thy hand." Cf. also Fitz-
Gerald's *Rubáiyát,* 325-360, pp. 430-431. 157-162. **Fool,**
etc. Compare *Abt Vogler,* 69-80, p. 301.

A Death in the Desert. This poem presents the account of
an imaginary scene in which the aged Apostle St. John lies
dying in a cave in the desert. He is attended and guarded
by five devoted companions. The opening lines, 1-12, purport
to have been written by the owner of the parchment in which
the famous incident is recorded. The supposed author of the
narrative was Pamphylax, of the city of Antioch, in Syria.
He and Xanthus were present at the death of the Apostle.
  2. **rolls,** manuscripts rolled up. 4. *Epsilon* and *Mu* and
Xi (line 7) are letters of the Greek alphabet. *Epsilon* and
Mu mark divisions of the parchment; *Xi* is its letter or
number. 6. **terebinth,** the turpentine tree. 23. **the decree,**
i.e., one of many for persecuting the Christians, probably
the one issued by Domitian (51-96 A.D.), the emperor of
Rome. (81-96).

Reached there a little, and we would not lose
The last of what might happen on his face.
I at the head, and Xanthus at the feet,
With Valens and the Boy, had lifted him,   30
And brought him from the chamber in the
depths,
And laid him in the light where we might see;
For certain smiles began about his mouth,
And his lids moved, presageful of the end.

Beyond, and halfway up the mouth o' the
cave,   35
The Bactrian convert, having his desire,
Kept watch, and made pretense to graze a
goat
That gave us milk, on rags of various herb,
Plantain and quitch, the rocks' shade keeps
alive—
So that if any thief or soldier passed   40
(Because the persecution was aware),
Yielding the goat up promptly with his life,
Such man might pass on, joyful at a prize,
Nor care to pry into the cool o' the cave.
Outside was all noon and the burning blue. 45

"Here is wine," answered Xanthus — dropped
a drop;
I stooped and placed the lap of cloth aright,
Then chafed his right hand, and the Boy his
left;
But Valens had bethought him, and produced
And broke a ball of nard, and made perfume.
Only, he did — not so much wake, as — turn
And smile a little, as a sleeper does   52
If any dear one call him, touch his face —
And smiles and loves, but will not be dis-
turbed.

Then Xanthus said a prayer, but still he slept.
It is the Xanthus that escaped to Rome,   56
Was burned, and could not write the chron-
icle.

Then the Boy sprang up from his knees, and
ran,
Stung by the splendor of a sudden thought,
And fetched the seventh plate of graven lead
Out of the secret chamber, found a place,   61
Pressing with finger on the deeper dints,
And spoke, as 'twere his mouth proclaiming
first,
"I am the Resurrection and the Life."

Whereat he opened his eyes wide at once,   65
And sat up of himself, and looked at us;

And thenceforth nobody pronounced a word.
Only, outside, the Bactrian cried his cry
Like the lone desert-bird that wears the ruff,
As signal we were safe, from time to time. 70

First he said, "If a friend declared to me,
This my son Valens, this my other son,
Were James and Peter — nay, declared as
well
This lad was very John — I could believe!
— Could, for a moment, doubtlessly believe;
So is myself withdrawn into my depths,   76
The soul retreated from the perished brain
Whence it was wont to feel and use the world
Through these dull members, done with long
ago.
Yet I myself remain; I feel myself—   80
And there is nothing lost. Let be, awhile!"

[This is the doctrine he was wont to teach,
How divers persons witness in each man,
Three souls which make up one soul: first, to
wit,
A soul of each and all the bodily parts,   85
Seated therein, which works, and is what
Does,
And has the use of earth, and ends the man
Downward; but, tending upward for advice,
Grows into, and again is grown into
By the next soul, which, seated in the brain,
Useth the first with its collected use,   91
And feeleth, thinketh, willeth — is what
Knows;
Which, duly tending upward in its turn,
Grows into, and again is grown into
By the last soul, that uses both the first,   95
Subsisting whether they assist or no,
And, constituting man's self, is what Is —
And leans upon the former, makes it play,
As that played off the first: and, tending up,
Holds, is upheld by, God, and ends the man
Upward in that dread point of intercourse, 101
Nor needs a place, for it returns to Him.
What Does, what Knows, what Is; three
souls, one man.
I give the glossa as Theotypas.]

And then, "A stick, once fire from end to
end;   105
Now, ashes save the tip that holds a spark!
Yet, blow the spark, it runs back, spreads
itself
A little where the fire was. Thus I urge
The soul that served me, till it task once more

30. Valens, one of the companions. 36. The Bactrian
convert, one of St. John's converts from Bactria, a district of
Afghanistan. 39. quitch, a kind of hardy grass. 41.
aware, active, on the lookout. 50. nard, a kind of fragrant
ointment. 60. seventh plate, one of the plates on which
the Gospel of John was engraved. 61. a place, verse 25 of
Chapter 11, of John.

69. the lone desert-bird, the sand grouse. 76. my
depths, the depths of his absolute being, as explained in
lines 93-102. 82-104. This...Theotypas. Lines 82-104
are inserted by Pamphylax on the authority of Theotypas
(line 104), an imaginary commentator. 83. witness, show,
appear. 104. give the glossa as Theotypas, supply a
commentary or marginal note as Theotypas did.

What ashes of my brain have kept their
    shape,   110
And these make effort on the last o' the flesh,
Trying to taste again the truth of things"
(He smiled) — "their very superficial truth;
As that ye are my sons, that it is long
Since James and Peter had release by death,
And I am only he, your brother John,   116
Who saw and heard, and could remember all.
Remember all! It is not much to say.
What if the truth broke on me from above
As once and ofttimes? Such might hap again;
Doubtlessly He might stand in presence here,
With head wool-white, eyes flame, and feet
    like brass,   122
The sword and the seven stars, as I have
    seen —
I who now shudder only and surmise,
'How did your brother bear that sight and
    live?'   125

"If I live yet, it is for good, more love
Through me to men; be naught but ashes here
That keep awhile my semblance, who was
    John —
Still, when they scatter, there is left on earth
No one alive who knew (consider this!),   130
Saw with his eyes and handled with his hands
That which was from the first, the Word of
    Life.
How will it be when none more saith 'I saw'?

"Such ever was love's way: to rise, it stoops.
Since I, whom Christ's mouth taught, was
    bidden teach,   135
I went, for many years, about the world,
Saying 'It was so; so I heard and saw,'
Speaking as the case asked; and men believed.
Afterward came the message to myself
In Patmos isle; I was not bidden teach,   140
But simply listen, take a book and write,
Nor set down other than the given word,
With nothing left to my arbitrament
To choose or change. I wrote, and men be-
    lieved.
Then — for my time grew brief, no message
    more,   145
No call to write again — I found a way,
And, reasoning from my knowledge, merely
    taught

Men should, for love's sake, in love's strength
    believe;
Or I would pen a letter to a friend
And urge the same as friend, nor less nor
    more.   150
Friends said I reasoned rightly, and believed.
But at the last, why, I seemed left alive
Like a sea-jelly weak on Patmos strand,
To tell dry sea-beach gazers how I fared
When there was mid-sea, and the mighty
    things;   155
Left to repeat, 'I saw, I heard, I knew,'
And go all over the old ground again,
With Antichrist already in the world,
And many Antichrists, who answered prompt,
'Am I not Jasper as thyself art John?   160
Nay, young, whereas through age thou may-
    est forget;
Wherefore, explain, or how shall we be-
    lieve?'
I never thought to call down fire on such,
Or, as in wonderful and early days,
Pick up the scorpion, tread the serpent
    dumb;
But patient stated much of the Lord's life 166
Forgotten or misdelivered, and let it work,
Since much that at the first, in deed and word,
Lay simply and sufficiently exposed,
Had grown (or else my soul was grown to
    match,   170
Fed through such years, familiar with such
    light,
Guarded and guided still to see and speak)
Of new significance and fresh result;
What first were guessed as points, I now knew
    stars,
And named them in the Gospel I have writ.
For men said, 'It is getting long ago;   176
Where is the promise of his coming?' —
    asked
These young ones in their strength, as loath to
    wait,
Of me who, when their sires were born, was
    old.
I, for I loved them, answered, joyfully,   180
Since I was there, and helpful in my age;
And, in the main, I think such men believed.
Finally, thus endeavoring, I fell sick;
Ye brought me here, and I supposed the end,
And went to sleep with one thought that, at
    least,   185
Though the whole earth should lie in wicked-
    ness,
We had the truth, might leave the rest to
    God.

122-123. **With head . . . seven stars.** Based on *Revelation*, 1:12-17.—"I saw seven golden candlesticks; And in the midst . . . one like unto the Son of man . . . His head and his hairs were white like wool, as white as snow; and his eyes were as a flame of fire; And his feet like unto fine brass . . . And he had in his right hand seven stars; and out of his mouth went a sharp two-edged sword; and his countenance was as the sun shineth in his strength. And when I saw him, I fell at his feet as dead." 125. **your brother,** that is, himself. 130. **No one,** etc. St. John was the last of the men who had seen Christ. 140. **Patmos isle.** He was banished by Domitian, emperor of Rome (81-96), to the Isle of Patmos, in the Ægean Sea, in the year 95. 141. **take . . . write,** a reference to the command to write his vision, as told in Chapter 1 of *Revelation*.

148. **Men . . . believe.** The Gospel of John, in its mildness of tone and spirit, stresses the Godlikeness of Christ through his manifestation of divine love. 156. **I saw . . . knew.** These expressions appear frequently in *Revelation*. 158. **Antichrist,** a personification of sin and evil in the world. See *John*, 2:18, 22.

Yet now I wake in such decrepitude
As I have slidden down and fallen afar,
Past even the presence of my former self, 190
Grasping the while for stay at facts which
    snap,
Till I am found away from my own world,
Feeling for foothold through a blank pro-
    found,
Along with unborn people in strange lands,
Who say — I hear said or conceive they say —
'Was John at all, and did he say he saw?' 196
Assure us, ere we ask what he might see!'

"And how shall I assure them? Can they
    share —
They, who have flesh, a veil of youth and
    strength
About each spirit, that needs must bide its
    time, 200
Living and learning still as years assist
Which wear the thickness thin, and let man
    see —
With me who hardly am withheld at all,
But shudderingly, scarce a shred between,
Lie bare to the universal prick of light? 205
Is it for nothing we grow old and weak,
We whom God loves? When pain ends, gain
    ends too.
To me, that story — aye, that Life and Death
Of which I wrote 'it was' — to me, it is;
— Is, here and now; I apprehend naught
    else.
Is not God now i' the world his power first
    made? 211
Is not his love at issue still with sin,
Visibly when a wrong is done on earth?
Love, wrong, and pain, what see I else around?
Yea, and the Resurrection and Uprise 215
To the right hand of the throne — what is it
    beside,
When such truth, breaking bounds, o'erfloods
    my soul,
And, as I saw the sin and death, even so
See I the need yet transiency of both,
The good and glory consummated thence? 220
I saw the power; I see the Love, once weak,
Resume the Power; and in this word 'I see,'
Lo, there is recognized the Spirit of both,
That moving o'er the spirit of man, unblinds
His eye and bids him look. These are, I see;
But ye, the children, his beloved ones too, 226
Ye need — as I should use an optic glass

I wondered at erewhile, somewhere i' the
    world,
It had been given a crafty smith to make;
A tube, he turned on objects brought too
    close, 230
Lying confusedly insubordinate
For the unassisted eye to master once:
Look through his tube, at distance now they
    lay,
Become succinct, distinct, so small, so clear!
Just thus, ye needs must apprehend what
    truth 235
I see, reduced to plain historic fact,
Diminished into clearness, proved a point
And far away; ye would withdraw your sense
From out eternity, strain it upon time,
Then stand before that fact, that Life and
    Death, 240
Stay there at gaze, till it dispart, dispread,
As though a star should open out, all sides,
Grow the world on you, as it is my world.

"For life, with all it yields of joy and woe,
And hope and fear — believe the aged
    friend — 245
Is just our chance o' the prize of learning love,
How love might be, hath been indeed, and is;
And that we hold thenceforth to the uttermost
Such prize despite the envy of the world,
And, having gained truth, keep truth; that is
    all. 250
But see the double way wherein we are led,
How the soul learns diversely from the flesh!
With flesh, that hath so little time to stay,
And yields mere basement for the soul's em-
    prise,
Expect prompt teaching. Helpful was the
    light, 255
And warmth was cherishing, and food was
    choice
To every man's flesh, thousand years ago,
As now to yours and mine; the body sprang
At once to the height, and stayed: but the
    soul — no!
Since sages who, this noontide, meditate 260
In Rome or Athens, may descry some point
Of the eternal power, hid yestereve;
And, as thereby the power's whole mass ex-
    tends,
So much extends the ether floating o'er
The love that tops the might, the Christ in
    God. 265
Then, as new lessons shall be learned in these
Till earth's work stop and useless time run out,
So duly, daily, needs provision be
For keeping the soul's prowess possible,
Building new barriers as the old decay, 270
Saving us from evasion of life's proof,
Putting the question ever, 'Does God love,
And will ye hold that truth against the world?'

188-197. **Yet now ... might see.** In these lines Browning prepares for the prophetic utterances of John against later
attacks on Christian belief. Dying persons were long regarded as gifted with prophecy. Cf. Arnold's *Sohrab and
Rustum*, 656, p. 483, and the dying prophecy of Gaunt in
Shakespeare's *Richard II*, II, 1, 5-16. 208. **that story,** as
recorded in the *Gospel of John*. 221-222. **I see ... Power.**
Cf. *Saul*, 305-306, p. 229. 227. **optic glass,** some kind of
optical toy or magnifying glass set in a tube.

Ye know there needs no second proof with
    good   274
Gained for our flesh from any earthly source;
We might go freezing, ages; give us fire —
Thereafter we judge fire at its full worth,
And guard it safe through every chance, ye
    know!
That fable of Prometheus and his theft,
How mortals gained Jove's fiery flower, grows
    old   280
(I have been used to hear the pagans own)
And out of mind; but fire, howe'er its birth,
Here is it, precious to the sophist now
Who laughs the myth of Æschylus to scorn,
As precious to those satyrs of his play,   285
Who touched it in gay wonder at the thing.
While were it so with the soul — this gift of
    truth,
Once grasped, were this our soul's gain safe,
    and sure
To prosper as the body's gain is wont —
Why, man's probation would conclude, his
    earth   290
Crumble; for he both reasons and decides,
Weighs first, then chooses: will he give up fire
For gold or purple, once he knows its worth?
Could he give Christ up were his worth as
    plain?
Therefore, I say, to test man, the proofs shift,
Nor may he grasp that fact like other fact,   296
And straightway in his life acknowledge it,
As, say, the indubitable bliss of fire.
Sigh ye, 'It had been easier once than now'?
To give you answer I am left alive;   300
Look at me who was present from the first!
Ye know what things I saw; then came a test,
My first, befitting me who so had seen:
'Forsake the Christ thou sawest transfigured,
    him
Who trod the sea and brought the dead to
    life?   305
What should wring this from thee!' — ye
    laugh and ask.
What wrung it? Even a torchlight and a
    noise,
The sudden Roman faces, violent hands,
And fear of what the Jews might do! Just
    that.

And it is written, 'I forsook and fled.'   310
There was my trial, and it ended thus.
Aye, but my soul had gained its truth, could
    grow;
Another year or two — what little child,
What tender woman, that had seen no least
Of all my sights, but barely heard them told,
Who did not clasp the cross with a light
    laugh,   316
Or wrap the burning robe round, thanking
    God?
Well, was truth safe forever, then? Not so.
Already had begun the silent work
Whereby truth, deadened of its absolute blaze,
Might need love's eye to pierce the o'er-
    stretched doubt.   321
Teachers were busy, whispering 'All is true
As the aged ones report; but youth can reach
Where age gropes dimly, weak with stir and
    strain,
And the full doctrine slumbers till today.' 325
Thus, what the Roman's lowered spear was
    found,
A bar to me who touched and handled truth,
Now proved the glozing of some new shrewd
    tongue,
This Ebion, this Cerinthus, or their mates,
Till imminent was the outcry 'Save our
    Christ!'   330
Whereon I stated much of the Lord's life
Forgotten or misdelivered, and let it work.
Such work done, as it will be, what comes next?
What do I hear say, or conceive men say,
'Was John at all, and did he say he saw? 335
Assure us, ere we ask what he might see!'

"Is this indeed a burden for late days,
And may I help to bear it with you all,
Using my weakness which becomes your
    strength?
For if a babe were born inside this grot,   340
Grew to a boy here, heard us praise the sun,
Yet had but yon sole glimmer in light's
    place —
One, loving him and wishful he should learn,
Would much rejoice himself was blinded first
Month by month here, so made to under-
    stand   345
How eyes, born darkling, apprehend amiss.
I think I could explain to such a child
There was more glow outside than gleams he
    caught,

279. **Prometheus . . . theft.** Grieved at the neglect of mankind by the gods, Prometheus stole fire from heaven and carried it in a hollow reed to man. In anger Zeus (Jove) bound Prometheus to a mountain where a vulture daily fed upon his liver. 283-285. **sophist . . . play.** The sophists were teachers of rhetoric, philosophy, and conduct, in ancient Greece. They flourished in the 5th century B.C. They ridiculed traditional mythology, such as the myth of Prometheus, which was used by Æschylus (525-456 B.C.), the great Greek tragic dramatist, in his *Prometheus Bound.* This was a dramatic trilogy, only one part of which is preserved; in the lost parts the satyrs may have touched the fire as Browning imagines. The satyrs were demigods, half man and half goat, given to riotous merriment. 305. **Who . . . life,** incidents recorded in *John,* 6:15-21, and 11:1-44.

310. **I forsook and fled.** The account of Christ's desertion by his disciples when he was betrayed and taken by the mob is found in *Matthew,* 26:47-56; *Mark,* 14:43-50; and *John,* 18:1-12. 326. **found,** i.e., found to be. 328. **proved,** i.e., proved to be. 329. **Ebion, Cerinthus.** Ebion and Cerinthus were early heretics who believed Jesus to have been a mere man, though possessed of divine power. The *Gospel of St. John* is said to have been written against them. St. Luke and St. Paul were also said to have written against them.

Aye, nor need urge 'I saw it, so believe!'
It is a heavy burden you shall bear   350
In latter days, new lands, or old grown
      strange,
Left without me, which must be very soon.
What is the doubt, my brothers? Quick with it!
I see you stand conversing, each new face,
Either in fields, of yellow summer eves,   355
On islets yet unnamed amid the sea;
Or pace for shelter 'neath a portico
Out of the crowd in some enormous town
Where now the larks sing in a solitude;
Or muse upon blank heaps of stone and sand
Idly conjectured to be Ephesus;   361
And no one asks his fellow any more
'Where is the promise of his coming?' but
'Was he revealed in any of his lives,
As Power, as Love, as Influencing Soul?'   365

"Quick, for time presses, tell the whole mind
      out,
And let us ask and answer and be saved!
My book speaks on, because it cannot pass;
One listens quietly, nor scoffs but pleads,
'Here is a tale of things done ages since;   370
What truth was ever told the second day?
Wonders, that would prove doctrine, go for
      naught.
Remains the doctrine, love; well, we must
      love,
And what we love most, power and love in
      one,
Let us acknowledge on the record here,   375
Accepting these in Christ. Must Christ then
      be?
Has he been? Did not we ourselves make
      him?
Our mind receives but what it holds, no more.
First of the love, then; we acknowledge
      Christ —
A proof we comprehend his love, a proof   380
We had such love already in ourselves,
Knew first what else we should not recognize.
'Tis mere projection from man's inmost mind,
And, what he loves, thus falls reflected back,
Becomes accounted somewhat out of him;   385
He throws it up in air, it drops down earth's,
With shape, name, story added, man's old
      way.
How prove you Christ came otherwise at
      least?
Next try the power: he made and rules the
      world;
Certes there is a world once made, now ruled,
Unless things have been ever as we see.   391

Our sires declared a charioteer's yoked steeds
Brought the sun up the east and down the
      west,
Which only of itself now rises, sets,
As if a hand impelled it and a will —   395
Thus they long thought, they who had will
      and hands;
But the new question's whisper is distinct,
Wherefore must all force needs be like our-
      selves?
We have the hands, the will; what made and
      drives
The sun is force, is law, is named, not known,
While will and love we do know; marks of
      these,   401
Eye-witnesses attest, so books declare —
As that, to punish or reward our race,
The sun at undue times arose or set
Or else stood still: what do not men affirm?
But earth requires as urgently reward   406
Or punishment today as years ago,
And none expects the sun will interpose;
Therefore it was mere passion and mistake,
Or erring zeal for right, which changed the
      truth.   410
Go back, far, farther, to the birth of things;
Ever the will, the intelligence, the love,
Man's! — which he gives, supposing he but
      finds,
As late he gave head, body, hands, and feet,
To help these in what forms he called his gods.
First, Jove's brow, Juno's eyes were swept
      away,   416
But Jove's wrath, Juno's pride continued long;
As last, will, power, and love discarded these,
So law in turn discards power, love, and will.
What proveth God is otherwise at least?   420
All else, projection from the mind of man!'

"Nay, do not give me wine, for I am strong,
But place my gospel where I put my hands.

"I say that man was made to grow, not stop;
That help, he needed once, and needs no
      more,   425
Having grown but an inch by, is withdrawn:
For he hath new needs, and new helps to
      these.
This imports solely, man should mount on
      each
New height in view; the help whereby he
      mounts,

353. my brothers, Christians of the distant future.
361. Ephesus, an ancient Greek city on the coast of Asia
Minor. 368. speaks on, i.e., to future ages. 371. What
. . . day. He seems to mean that tradition cannot be
trusted. 385. somewhat out of him, something beyond
himself.

392-393. a charioteer's . . . west. In Greek mythology
Phœbus Apollo, the sun god, drove westerly all day in his
flaming chariot of the sun. 405. stood still. At Joshua's
command the sun stood still until the Gibeonites had avenged
themselves upon their enemies (see Joshua, 10:12-14). 416.
Jove's . . . Juno's. Juno was queen of the gods and wife of
Jove. 418. these, Jove's wrath and Juno's pride. 424-431.
I say . . . the Truth. These lines contain a favorite doctrine
of Browning. Cf. Andrea del Sarto, 97-98, p. 289; Cleon, 114,
p. 292; and Rabbi Ben Ezra, 40-41, p. 302.

The ladder-rung his foot has left, may fall, 430
Since all things suffer change save God the
    Truth.
Man apprehends him newly at each stage
Whereat earth's ladder drops, its service
    done;
And nothing shall prove twice what once was
    proved.
You stick a garden-plot with ordered twigs 435
To show inside lie germs of herbs unborn,
And check the careless step would spoil their
    birth;
But when herbs wave, the guardian twigs may
    go,
Since should ye doubt of virtues, question
    kinds,
It is no longer for old twigs ye look,   440
Which proved once underneath lay store of
    seed,
But to the herb's self, by what light ye boast,
For what fruit's signs are. This book's fruit
    is plain,
Nor miracles need prove it any more.
Doth the fruit show? Then miracles bade
    'ware   445
At first of root and stem, saved both till now
From trampling ox, rough boar, and wanton
    goat.
What? Was man made a wheelwork to wind
    up,
And be discharged, and straight wound up
    anew?
No! — grown, his growth lasts; taught, he
    ne'er forgets;   450
May learn a thousand things, not twice the
    same.

"This might be pagan teaching; now hear
    mine.

"I say, that as the babe, you feed awhile,
Becomes a boy and fit to feed himself,
So, minds at first must be spoon-fed with
    truth;   455
When they can eat, babe's nurture is with-
    drawn.
I fed the babe whether it would or no;
I bid the boy or feed himself or starve.
I cried once, 'That ye may believe in Christ,
Behold this blind man shall receive his sight!'
I cry now, 'Urgest thou, *for I am shrewd* 461
And smile at stories how John's word could
    cure —
Repeat that miracle and take my faith?'
I say, that miracle was duly wrought
When, save for it, no faith was possible.   465

460. **Behold . . . sight.** The healing of the blind man is
recorded in *John,* 9:1-25. In 20:30-31 John states that the
miracles "are written that ye might believe that Jesus is the
Christ, the Son of God."

Whether a change were wrought i' the shows
    o' the world,
Whether the change came from our minds
    which see
Of shows o' the world so much as and no more
Than God wills for his purpose — what do I
See now, suppose you, there where you see
    rock   470
Round us? — I know not; such was the effect,
So faith grew, making void more miracles
Because too much; they would compel, not
    help.
I say, the acknowledgment of God in Christ
Accepted by thy reason, solves for thee   475
All questions in the earth and out of it,
And has so far advanced thee to be wise.
Wouldst thou unprove this to re-prove the
    proved?
In life's mere minute, with power to use that
    proof,
Leave knowledge and revert to how it sprung?
Thou hast it; use it and forthwith, or die! 481

"For I say, this is death and the sole death,
When a man's loss comes to him from his
    gain,
Darkness from light, from knowledge ignor-
    ance,
And lack of love from love made manifest; 485
A lamp's death when, replete with oil, it
    chokes;
A stomach's when, surcharged with food, it
    starves.
With ignorance was surety of a cure.
When man, appalled at nature, questioned
    first,
'What if there lurk a might behind this might?'
He needed satisfaction God could give,   491
And did give, as ye have the written word;
But when he finds might still redouble might,
Yet asks, 'Since all is might, what use of will?'
— Will, the one source of might — he being
    man   495
With a man's will and a man's might, to teach
In little how the two combine in large —
That man has turned round on himself and
    stands,
Which in the course of nature is, to die.

"And when man questioned, 'What if there
    be love   500
Behind the will and might, as real as they?' —
He needed satisfaction God could give,
And did give, as ye have the written word;
But when, beholding that love everywhere,
He reasons, 'Since such love is everywhere,
And since ourselves can love and would be
    loved,   506

498. **stands,** i.e., stands still.

We ourselves make the love, and Christ was
    not' —
How shall ye help this man who knows him-
    self
That he must love and would be loved again,
Yet, owning his own love that proveth Christ,
Rejecteth Christ through very need of him?
The lamp o'erswims with oil, the stomach
    flags   512
Loaded with nurture, and that man's soul
    dies.

"If he rejoin, 'But this was all the while
A trick; the fault was, first of all, in thee,   515
Thy story of the places, names, and dates,
Where, when, and how the ultimate truth had
    rise —
Thy prior truth, at last discovered none,
Whence now the second suffers detriment.
What good of giving knowledge if, because 520
O' the manner of the gift, its profit fail?
And why refuse what modicum of help
Had stopped the after-doubt, impossible
I' the face of truth — truth absolute, uniform?
Why must I hit of this and miss of that,   525
Distinguish just as I be weak or strong,
And not ask of thee and have answer prompt,
Was this once, was it not once? — then and
    now
And evermore, plain truth from man to man.
Is John's procedure just the heathen bard's?
Put question of his famous play again,   531
How, for the ephemerals' sake, Jove's fire was
    filched,
And carried in a cane and brought to earth;
The fact is in the fable, cry the wise,
Mortals obtained the boon, so much is fact,   535
Though fire be spirit and produced on earth.
As with the Titan's, so now with thy tale;
Why breed in us perplexity, mistake,
Nor tell the whole truth in the proper words?'

"I answer, Have ye yet to argue out   540
The very primal thesis, plainest law—
Man is not God, but hath God's end to serve,
A master to obey, a course to take,
Somewhat to cast off, somewhat to become?
Grant this, then man must pass from old to
    new,   545
From vain to real, from mistake to fact,
From what once seemed good, to what now
    proves best.
How could man have progression otherwise?
Before the point was mooted 'What is God?'
No savage man inquired 'What am myself?'

Much less replied, 'First, last, and best of
    things.'   551
Man takes that title now if he believes
Might can exist with neither will nor love,
In God's case — what he names now Nature's
    Law —
While in himself he recognizes love   555
No less than might and will: and rightly
    takes.
Since if man prove the sole existent thing
Where these combine, whatever their degree,
However weak the might or will or love,
So they be found there, put in evidence —   560
He is as surely higher in the scale
Than any might with neither love nor will,
As life, apparent in the poorest midge
(When the faint dust-speck flits, ye guess its
    wing),
Is marvelous beyond dead Atlas' self —   565
Given to the nobler midge for resting-place!
Thus, man proves best and highest — God,
    in fine,
And thus the victory leads but to defeat,
The gain to loss, best rise to the worst fall,
His life becomes impossible, which is death.

"But if, appealing thence, he cower, avouch
He is mere man, and in humility   572
Neither may know God nor mistake himself;
I point to the immediate consequence
And say, by such confession straight he falls
Into man's place, a thing nor God nor beast,
Made to know that he can know and not
    more;
Lower than God, who knows all and can all,
Higher than beasts, which know and can so
    far
As each beast's limit, perfect to an end,   580
Nor conscious that they know, nor craving
    more;
While man knows partly but conceives beside,
Creeps ever on from fancies to the fact,
And in this striving, this converting air
Into a solid he may grasp and use,   585
Finds progress, man's distinctive mark alone,
Not God's, and not the beasts' — God is,
    they are,
Man partly is and wholly hopes to be.
Such progress could no more attend his soul,
Were all it struggles after found at first   590
And guesses changed to knowledge absolute,
Than motion wait his body, were all else
Than it the solid earth on every side,
Where now through space he moves from rest
    to rest.
Man, therefore, thus conditioned, must expect

523. Had stopped, would have stopped. **530. the
heathen bard's,** Æschylus's. **531. famous play,** *Prometheus Bound.* **532. ephemerals', mortals'. 537. the Titan's.**
Prometheus belonged to the giant race of Titans. **540. I
answer.** Lines 540-633 express Browning's own philosophy.

552. that title, the title of "First, last, and best of things."
565. Atlas' self. Atlas was a giant Titan who warred
against Zeus and who was forced to carry the heavens on his
head and hands.

He could not, what he knows now, know at
    first;   596
What he considers that he knows today,
Come but tomorrow, he will find misknown;
Getting increase of knowledge, since he learns
Because he lives, which is to be a man,   600
Set to instruct himself by his past self:
First, like the brute, obliged by facts to learn,
Next, as man may, obliged by his own mind,
Bent, habit, nature, knowledge turned to
    law.
God's gift was that man should conceive of
    truth   605
And yearn to gain it, catching at mistake,
As midway help till he reach fact indeed.
The statuary, ere he mold a shape,
Boasts a like gift — the shape's idea — and
    next
The aspiration to produce the same;   610
So, taking clay, he calls his shape thereout,
Cries ever, 'Now I have the thing I see';
Yet all the while goes changing what was
    wrought,
From falsehood like the truth, to truth itself.
How were it had he cried, 'I see no face,   615
No breast, no feet i' the ineffectual clay'?
Rather commend him that he clapped his
    hands,
And laughed, 'It is my shape and lives again!'
Enjoyed the falsehood, touched it on to truth,
Until yourselves applaud the flesh indeed   620
In what is still flesh-imitating clay.
Right in you, right in him, such way be
    man's!
God only makes the live shape at a jet.
Will ye renounce this pact of creatureship?
The pattern on the Mount subsists no more,
Seemed awhile, then returned to nothing-
    ness;
But copies, Moses strove to make thereby, 627
Serve still and are replaced as time requires.
By these, make newest vessels, reach the type!
If ye demur, this judgment on your head,   630
Never to reach the ultimate, angels' law,
Indulging every instinct of the soul
There where law, life, joy, impulse are one
    thing!

"Such is the burden of the latest time.
I have survived to hear it with my ears,   635
Answer it with my lips; does this suffice?
For if there be a further woe than such,
Wherein my brothers struggling need a hand,
So long as any pulse is left in mine,
May I be absent even longer yet,   640
Plucking the blind ones back from the abyss,
Though I should tarry a new hundred years!"

623. at a jet, in a moment. 625. pattern on the Mount,
a reference to the commandments given to Moses by God
on Mount Sinai (see *Exodus*, 19-20).

But he was dead; 'twas about noon, the day
Somewhat declining. We five buried him
That eve, and then, dividing, went five ways,
And I, disguised, returned to Ephesus.   646

By this, the cave's mouth must be filled with
    sand.
Valens is lost, I know not of his trace;
The Bactrian was but a wild childish man,
And could not write nor speak, but only loved.
So, lest the memory of this go quite,   651
Seeing that I tomorrow fight the beasts,
I tell the same to Phœbas, whom believe!
For many look again to find that face,
Beloved John's to whom I ministered,   655
Somewhere in life about the world; they err—
Either mistaking what was darkly spoke
At ending of his book, as he relates,
Or misconceiving somewhat of this speech
Scattered from mouth to mouth, as I suppose.
Believe ye will not see him any more   661
About the world with his divine regard!
For all was as I say, and now the man
Lies as he lay once, breast to breast with God.

[Cerinthus read and mused; one added this:

"If Christ, as thou affirmest, be of men   666
Mere man, the first and best but nothing
    more —
Account him, for reward of what he was,
Now and forever, wretchedest of all.
For see; himself conceived of life as love, 670
Conceived of love as what must enter in,
Fill up, make one with his each soul he loved:
Thus much for man's joy, all men's joy for
    him.
Well, he is gone, thou sayest, to fit reward.
But by this time are many souls set free, 675
And very many still retained alive;
Nay, should his coming be delayed awhile,
Say, ten years longer (twelve years, some com-
    pute),
See if, for every finger of thy hands,
There be not found, that day the world shall
    end,   680
Hundreds of souls, each holding by Christ's
    word
That he will grow incorporate with all,

652. fight the beasts. This was the method of his
martyrdom. 653. Phœbas, the person to whom Pamphylax told the incident related in the poem. 658. as he
relates, a reference to *John*, 21:20-25. When Christ appeared
to the disciples after the Resurrection, Peter asked him what
John should do. Jesus replied: "If I will that he tarry till
I come, what is that to thee? Follow thou me." Verse
23 states that "then went this saying abroad among the
brethren, that that disciple should not die. Yet Jesus said
not unto him, He should not die; but, 'If I will that he tarry
till I come, what is that to thee?'" 662. regard, look.
666-687. If Christ, etc. These lines are addressed to
Cerinthus (see note on line 329). Pamphylax states that
Cerinthus could not be saved unless he accepted Christ as God.

With me as Pamphylax, with him as John,
Groom for each bride! Can a mere man do
    this?
Yet Christ saith, this he lived and died to do.
Call Christ, then, the illimitable God,   686
Or lost!"

But 'twas Cerinthus that is lost.]
                                    (1864)

CALIBAN UPON SETEBOS;

OR, NATURAL THEOLOGY IN THE ISLAND

"Thou thoughtest that I was altogether such an
    one as thyself."

['Will sprawl, now that the heat of day is best,
Flat on his belly in the pit's much mire,
With elbows wide, fists clenched to prop his
    chin.
And, while he kicks both feet in the cool slush,
And feels about his spine small eft-things
    course,   5
Run in and out each arm, and make him
    laugh;
And while above his head a pompion-plant,
Coating the cave-top as a brow its eye,
Creeps down to touch and tickle hair and
    beard,
And now a flower drops with a bee inside,   10
And now a fruit to snap at, catch and crunch—
He looks out o'er yon sea, which sunbeams
    cross
And recross till they weave a spider-web
(Meshes of fire, some great fish breaks at
    times),
And talks to his own self, howe'er he please,
Touching that other, whom his dam called
    God.   16
Because to talk about Him, vexes — ha,
Could He but know! and time to vex is now,
When talk is safer than in winter-time.
Moreover Prosper and Miranda sleep   20
In confidence he drudges at their task;

683. **With me . . . John.** Christ and Pamphylax are
to be one; so Christ and John.
  Caliban upon Setebos. Caliban is a kind of semi-intellec-
tual monster, one of the servants of Prospero and his daughter
Miranda on the island in Shakespeare's *The Tempest.* He
was the son of the witch Sycorax, who worshiped a god
called Setebos, the god of the Patagonians. Caliban sees
this god as a capricious and willful being like himself. The
poem is therefore a satire on Calvinism and the anthropo-
morphic idea of God. The quotation at the head of the
poem is taken from *Psalms,* 50:21. It is spoken by God
to the wicked.
  1-23. **'Will . . . speech.** In the first twenty-three lines
Caliban describes his physical background and the reason
for his theological speculations. In most of the poem he
speaks of himself in the third person. 5. **eft-things,**
lizard-like animals. 7. **pompion-plant,** a vine of the
pumpkin family. 17. **Him.** Pronouns referring to Setebos
are capitalized. 18. **time . . . now,** in summer, when Setebos
is likely to be away from the island. In winter he would
usually be at home, on or near the island.

And it is good to cheat the pair, and gibe,
Letting the rank tongue blossom into speech.]

Setebos, Setebos, and Setebos!   24
'Thinketh He dwelleth i' the cold o' the moon.

'Thinketh He made it, with the sun to match,
But not the stars; the stars came otherwise;
Only made clouds, winds, meteors, such as
    that;
Also this isle, what lives and grows thereon,
And snaky sea which rounds and ends the
    same.   30

'Thinketh, it came of being ill at ease;
He hated that He cannot change His cold,
Nor cure its ache. 'Hath spied an icy fish
That longed to 'scape the rock-stream where
    she lived,
And thaw herself within the lukewarm brine
O' the lazy sea her stream thrusts far amid, 36
A crystal spike 'twixt two warm walls of wave;
Only, she ever sickened, found repulse
At the other kind of water, not her life
(Green-dense and dim-delicious, bred o' the
    sun),   40
Flounced back from bliss she was not born to
    breathe,
And in her old bounds buried her despair,
Hating and loving warmth alike: so He.

'Thinketh, He made thereat the sun, this isle,
Trees and the fowls here, beast and creeping
    thing;   45
Yon otter, sleek-wet, black, lithe as a leech;
Yon auk, one fire-eye in a ball of foam,
That floats and feeds; a certain badger brown
He hath watched hunt with that slant white-
    wedge eye
By moonlight; and the pie with the long
    tongue   50
That pricks deep into oakwarts for a worm,
And says a plain word when she finds her
    prize,
But will not eat the ants; the ants themselves
That build a wall of seeds and settled stalks
About their hole — He made all these and
    more,   55
Made all we see, and us, in spite; how else?
He could not, Himself, make a second self
To be His mate—as well have made Himself;
He would not make what He mislikes or
    slights,
An eyesore to Him, or not worth His pains;
But did, in envy, listlessness, or sport,   61
Make what Himself would fain, in a manner,
    be —
Weaker in most points, stronger in a few,

33. **'Hath,** he (Caliban) hath. 50. **pie,** magpie.

Worthy, and yet mere playthings all the while,
Things He admires and mocks too — that
   is it.   65
Because, so brave, so better though they be,
It nothing skills if He begin to plague.
Look now, I melt a gourd-fruit into mash,
Add honeycomb and pods, I have perceived,
Which bite like finches when they bill and
   kiss —   70
Then, when froth rises bladdery, drink up all,
Quick, quick, till maggots scamper through
   my brain;
Last, throw me on my back i' the seeded
   thyme,
And wanton, wishing I were born a bird.
Put case, unable to be what I wish,   75
I yet could make a live bird out of clay;
Would not I take clay, pinch my Caliban
Able to fly? — for, there, see, he hath wings,
And great comb like the hoopoe's to admire,
And there, a sting to do his foes offense;   80
There, and I will that he begin to live,
Fly to yon rock-top, nip me off the horns
Of grigs high up that make the merry din,
Saucy through their veined wings, and mind
   me not.
In which feat, if his leg snapped, brittle clay,
And he lay stupid-like — why, I should laugh;
And if he, spying me, should fall to weep,   87
Beseech me to be good, repair his wrong,
Bid his poor leg smart less or grow again —
Well, as the chance were, this might take or
   else   90
Not take my fancy; I might hear his cry,
And give the manikin three sound legs for one,
Or pluck the other off, leave him like an egg,
And lessoned he was mine and merely clay.
Were this no pleasure, lying in the thyme,   95
Drinking the mash, with brain become alive,
Making and marring clay at will? So He.

'Thinketh, such shows nor right nor wrong in
   Him,
Nor kind, nor cruel; He is strong and Lord.
'Am strong myself compared to yonder crabs
That march now from the mountain to the
   sea;   101
'Let twenty pass, and stone the twenty-first,
Loving not, hating not, just choosing so.
'Say, the first straggler that boasts purple
   spots
Shall join the file, one pincer twisted off;   105
'Say, this bruised fellow shall receive a worm,

And two worms he whose nippers end in red;
As it likes me each time, I do. So He.

Well then, 'supposeth He is good i' the main,
Placable if His mind and ways were guessed,
But rougher than His handiwork, be sure!   111
Oh, He hath made things worthier than Him-
   self,
And envieth that, so helped, such things do
   more
Than He who made them! What consoles but
   this?
That they, unless through Him, do naught at
   all,   115
And must submit; what other use in things?
'Hath cut a pipe of pithless elder-joint
That, blown through, gives exact the scream
   o' the jay
When from her wing you twitch the feathers
   blue;
Sound this, and little birds that hate the jay
Flock within stone's throw, glad their foe is
   hurt.   121
Put case such pipe could prattle and boast
   forsooth,
"I catch the birds, I am the crafty thing,
I make the cry my maker cannot make
With his great round mouth; he must blow
   through mine!"   125
Would not I smash it with my foot? So He.

But wherefore rough, why cold and ill at ease?
Aha, that is a question! Ask, for that,
What knows — the something over Setebos
That made Him, or He, may be, found and
   fought,   130
Worsted, drove off, and did to nothing, per-
   chance.
There may be something quiet o'er His head,
Out of His reach, that feels nor joy nor grief,
Since both derive from weakness in some way.
I joy because the quails come; would not
   joy   135
Could I bring quails here when I have a mind;
This Quiet, all it hath a mind to, doth.
'Esteemeth stars the outposts of its couch,
But never spends much thought nor care that
   way.
It may look up, work up — the worse for
   those   140
It works on! 'Careth but for Setebos
The many-handed as a cuttle-fish,
Who, making Himself feared through what
   He does,
Looks up, first, and perceives he cannot soar
To what is quiet and hath happy life;   145
Next looks down here, and out of very spite
Makes this a bauble-world to ape yon real,
These good things to match those as hips do
   grapes.

71. **bladdery**, in bubbles like bladders. 75. **Put case**, etc.
If Caliban were the Creator, he would do things out of spite
or envy, or as an exercise of absolute will; so does Setebos.
79. **hoopoe**, a kind of bird with a beautiful crest. 83.
grigs, crickets. 103. **Loving . . . so.** This line and
lines 98-108 correspond with the Calvinistic doctrine of
election and reprobation, whereby some persons are predestined to eternal life and others to eternal death.

'Tis solace making baubles, aye, and sport.
Himself peeped late, eyed Prosper at his books
Careless and lofty, lord now of the isle;   151
Vexed, 'stitched a book of broad leaves, arrow-
    shaped,
Wrote thereon, he knows what, prodigious
    words;
Has peeled a wand and called it by a name;
Weareth at whiles for an enchanter's robe 155
The eyed skin of a supple oncelot;
And hath an ounce sleeker than youngling
    mole,
A four-legged serpent he makes cower and
    couch,
Now snarl, now hold its breath and mind his
    eye,
And saith she is Miranda and my wife.   160
'Keeps for his Ariel a tall pouch-bill crane
He bids go wade for fish and straight disgorge;
Also a sea-beast, lumpish, which he snared,
Blinded the eyes of, and brought somewhat
    tame,
And split its toe-webs, and now pens the
    drudge   165
In a hole o' the rock and calls him Caliban —
A bitter heart that bides its time and bites.
'Plays thus at being Prosper in a way,
Taketh his mirth with make-believes. So He.

His dam held that the Quiet made all things
Which Setebos vexed only; 'holds not so.   171
Who made them weak, meant weakness He
    might vex.
Had He meant other, while His hand was in,
Why not make horny eyes no thorn could
    prick,
Or plate my scalp with bone against the snow,
Or overscale my flesh 'neath joint and joint,
Like an orc's armor? Aye — so spoil His
    sport!   177
He is the One now; only He doth all.

'Saith, He may like, perchance, what profits
    Him.
Aye, himself loves what does him good; but
    why?   180
'Gets good no otherwise. This blinded beast
Loves whoso places flesh-meat on his nose,
But, had he eyes, would want no help, but
    hate
Or love, just as it liked him; He hath eyes.
Also it pleaseth Setebos to work,   185
Use all His hands, and exercise much craft,
By no means for the love of what is worked.
'Tasteth, himself, no finer good i' the world
When all goes right, in this safe summer-time,
And he wants little, hungers, aches not
    much,   190
Than trying what to do with wit and strength.
'Falls to make something; 'piled yon pile of
    turfs,
And squared and stuck there squares of soft
    white chalk,
And, with a fish-tooth, scratched a moon on
    each,
And set up endwise certain spikes of tree,   195
And crowned the whole with a sloth's skull
    a-top,
Found dead i' the woods, too hard for one to
    kill.
No use at all i' the work, for work's sole sake;
'Shall some day knock it down again. So He.

'Saith He is terrible; watch His feats in proof!
One hurricane will spoil six good months'
    hope.   201
He hath a spite against me, that I know,
Just as He favors Prosper, who knows why?
So it is, all the same, as well I find.
'Wove wattles half the winter, fenced them
    firm   205
With stone and stake to stop she-tortoises
Crawling to lay their eggs here; well, one
    wave,
Feeling the foot of Him upon its neck,
Gaped as a snake does, lolled out its large
    tongue,
And licked the whole labor flat — so much
    for spite.   210

'Saw a ball flame down late (yonder it lies)
Where, half an hour before, I slept i' the
    shade.
Often they scatter sparkles; there is force!
'Dug up a newt He may have envied once
And turned to stone, shut up inside a stone.
Please Him and hinder this? — What Prosper
    does?   216
Aha, if He would tell me how! Not He!
There is the sport; discover how or die!
All need not die, for of the things o' the isle
Some flee afar, some dive, some run up trees.
Those at His mercy — why, they please Him
    most   221
When . . . when . . . well, never try the same
    way twice!
Repeat what act has pleased, He may grow
    wroth.
You must not know His ways, and play Him
    off,
Sure of the issue. 'Doth the like himself: 225
'Spareth a squirrel that it nothing fears
But steals the nut from underneath my
    thumb,

---

156. **oncelot**, the ounce, or snow leopard.   161. **Ariel**, an airy spirit in the service of Prospero.   177. **orc**, a sea monster.

196. **sloth**, a slow-moving animal resembling the anteater.   205. **wattles**, twigs.

And when I threat, bites stoutly in defense;
'Spareth an urchin that contrariwise,
Curls up into a ball, pretending death   230
For fright at my approach — the two ways
     please.
But what would move my choler more than
     this,
That either creature counted on its life
Tomorrow and next day and all days to come,
Saying, forsooth, in the inmost of its heart, 235
"Because he did so yesterday with me,
And otherwise with such another brute,
So must he do henceforth and always." —
     Aye?
Would teach the reasoning couple what
     "must" means!
'Doth as he likes, or wherefore Lord? So He.

'Conceiveth all things will continue thus, 241
And we shall have to live in fear of Him
So long as He lives, keeps His strength; no
     change,
If He have done His best, make no new world
To please Him more, so leave off watching
     this —   245
If He surprise not even the Quiet's self
Some strange day — or, suppose, grow into it
As grubs grow butterflies; else, here we are,
And there is He, and nowhere help at all.

'Believeth with the life, the pain shall stop.
His dam held different, that after death   251
He both plagued enemies and feasted friends:
Idly! He doth His worst in this our life,
Giving just respite lest we die through pain,
Saving last pain for worst — with which, an
     end.   255
Meanwhile, the best way to escape His ire
Is, not to seem too happy. 'Sees, himself,
Yonder two flies, with purple films and pink,
Bask on the pompion-bell above; kills both.
'Sees two black painful beetles roll their ball
On head and tail as if to save their lives; 261
Moves them the stick away they strive to
     clear.

Even so, 'would have Him misconceive, sup-
     pose
This Caliban strives hard and ails no less,
And always, above all else, envies Him;   265
Wherefore he mainly dances on dark nights,
Moans in the sun, gets under holes to laugh,
And never speaks his mind save housed as
     now:
Outside, 'groans, curses. If He caught me
     here,
O'erheard this speech, and asked "What
     chucklest at?"   270
'Would, to appease Him, cut a finger off,
Or of my three kid yearlings burn the best,

Or let the toothsome apples rot on tree,
Or push my tame beast for the orc to taste —
While myself lit a fire, and made a song   275
And sung it, *"What I hate, be consecrate*
To celebrate Thee and Thy state, no mate
For Thee; what see for envy in poor me?"
Hoping the while, since evils sometimes mend,
Warts rub away, and sores are cured with
     slime,   280
That some strange day, will either the Quiet
     catch
And conquer Setebos, or likelier He
Decrepit may doze, doze, as good as die.

[What, what? A curtain o'er the world at
     once!
Crickets stop hissing; not a bird — or, yes, 285
There scuds His raven that has told Him all!
It was fool's play, this prattling! Ha! The
     wind
Shoulders the pillared dust, death's house o'
     the move,
And fast invading fires begin! White blaze —
A tree's head snaps — and there, there, there,
     there, there,   290
His thunder follows! Fool to gibe at Him!
Lo! 'Lieth flat and loveth Setebos!
'Maketh his teeth meet through his upper lip,
Will let those quails fly, will not eat this
     month
One little mess of whelks, so he may
     'scape!]   (1864)

CONFESSIONS

What is he buzzing in my ears?
     "Now that I come to die,
Do I view the world as a vale of tears?"
     Ah, reverend sir, not I!

What I viewed there once, what I view again
     Where the physic bottles stand   6
On the table's edge — is a suburb lane,
     With a wall to my bedside hand.

That lane sloped, much as the bottles do,
     From a house you could descry   10
O'er the garden-wall; is the curtain blue
     Or green to a healthy eye?

To mine, it serves for the old June weather
     Blue above lane and wall;
And that farthest bottle labeled "Ether"   15
     Is the house o'ertopping all.

At a terrace, somewhere near the stopper,
     There watched for me, one June,
A girl; I know, sir, it's improper,
     My poor mind's out of tune.   20

Only, there was a way . . . you crept
  Close by the side, to dodge
Eyes in the house, two eyes except;
  They styled their house "The Lodge."

What right had a lounger up their lane? 25
  But, by creeping very close,
With the good wall's help — their eyes might strain
  And stretch themselves to Oes,

Yet never catch her and me together,
  As she left the attic, there, 30
By the rim of the bottle labeled "Ether,"
  And stole from stair to stair,

And stood by the rose-wreathed gate. Alas,
  We loved, sir — used to meet;
How sad and bad and mad it was — 35
  But then, how it was sweet!   (1864)

PROSPICE

Fear death? — to feel the fog in my throat,
  The mist in my face,
When the snows begin, and the blasts denote
  I am nearing the place,
The power of the night, the press of the storm,
  The post of the foe; 6
Where he stands, the Arch Fear in a visible form,
  Yet the strong man must go.
For the journey is done and the summit attained,
  And the barriers fall, 10
Though a battle's to fight ere the guerdon be gained,
  The reward of it all.
I was ever a fighter, so — one fight more,
  The best and the last!
I would hate that death bandaged my eyes, and forbore, 15
  And bade me creep past.
No! let me taste the whole of it, fare like my peers,
  The heroes of old,
Bear the brunt, in a minute pay glad life's arrears
  Of pain, darkness, and cold. 20
For sudden the worst turns the best to the brave,
  The black minute's at end,
And the elements' rage, the fiend-voices that rave,
  Shall dwindle, shall blend,

Shall change, shall become first a peace out of pain, 25
  Then a light, then thy breast,
O thou soul of my soul! I shall clasp thee again,
  And with God be the rest!

               (1861; 1864)

YOUTH AND ART

It once might have been, once only:
  We lodged in a street together,
You, a sparrow on the housetop lonely,
  I, a lone she-bird of his feather.

Your trade was with sticks and clay, 5
  You thumbed, thrust, patted, and polished,
Then laughed "They will see some day
  Smith made, and Gibson demolished."

My business was song, song, song;
  I chirped, cheeped, trilled, and twittered,10
"Kate Brown's on the boards ere long,
  And Grisi's existence embittered!"

I earned no more by a warble
  Than you by a sketch in plaster;
You wanted a piece of marble, 15
  I needed a music-master.

We studied hard in our styles,
  Chipped each at a crust like Hindus,
For air, looked out on the tiles,
  For fun, watched each other's windows. 20

You lounged, like a boy of the South,
  Cap and blouse — nay, a bit of beard too;
Or you got it, rubbing your mouth
  With fingers the clay adhered to.

And I — soon managed to find 25
  Weak points in the flower-fence facing,
Was forced to put up a blind
  And be safe in my corset-lacing.

No harm! It was not my fault
  If you never turned your eye's tail up 30
As I shook upon E in alt.,
  Or ran the chromatic scale up;

For spring bade the sparrows pair,
  And the boys and girls gave guesses,
And stalls in our street looked rare 35
  With bulrush and watercresses.

---

28. **Oes**, plural of *O*.
Prospice. The title means *Look Forward.* The poem was written shortly after the death of Mrs. Browning. See Critical Notes. Cf. *My Star*, p. 239, and Tennyson's *Crossing the Bar*, p. 176.

Youth and Art. Cf. *The Statue and the Bust*, p. 249.
8. **Gibson**, John Gibson (1790-1866), a noted English sculptor. 12. **Grisi.** Giulia Grisi (1811-1869) was a famous Italian singer. 18. **Chipped . . . Hindus.** Hindus are vegetarians. 31. **E in alt.**, high E.

Why did not you pinch a flower
  In a pellet of clay and fling it?
Why did not I put a power
  Of thanks in a look, or sing it?   40

I did look, sharp as a lynx
  (And yet the memory rankles),
When models arrived, some minx
  Tripped upstairs, she and her ankles.

But I think I gave you as good!   45
  "That foreign fellow — who can know
How she pays, in a playful mood,
  For his tuning her that piano?"

Could you say so, and never say,
  "Suppose we join hands and fortunes, 50
And I fetch her from over the way,
  Her, piano, and long tunes and short tunes"?

No, no; you would not be rash,
  Nor I rasher and something over.
You've to settle yet Gibson's hash,   55
  And Grisi yet lives in clover.

But you meet the Prince at the Board,
  I'm queen myself at *bals-paré*,
I've married a rich old lord,
  And you're dubbed knight and an R. A. 60

Each life unfulfilled, you see;
  It hangs still, patchy and scrappy.
We have not sighed deep, laughed free,
  Starved, feasted, despaired — been happy.

And nobody calls you a dunce,   65
  And people suppose me clever;
This could but have happened once,
  And we missed it, lost it forever.
                    (1864)

A FACE

If one could have that little head of hers
Painted upon a background of pale gold,
Such as the Tuscan's early art prefers!
No shade encroaching on the matchless mold
Of those two lips, which should be opening
  soft   5
In the pure profile — not as when she laughs,
For that spoils all, but rather as if aloft
Yon hyacinth, she loves so, leaned its staff's
Burden of honey-colored buds to kiss
And capture 'twixt the lips apart for this. 10
Then her lithe neck, three fingers might sur-
  round,

57. **meet . . . Board**, dine with the Prince at Board of
Trade dinners. 58. **bals-paré**, fancy-dress balls. 60. **R. A.**,
member of the Royal Academy, a British society for the
promotion of painting, sculpture, and architecture.

How it should waver on the pale gold ground
Up to the fruit-shaped, perfect chin it lifts!
I know, Correggio loves to mass, in rifts
Of heaven, his angel faces, orb on orb   15
Breaking its outline, burning shades absorb;
But these are only massed there, I should
  think,
Waiting to see some wonder momently
Grow out, stand full, fade slow against the sky
(That's the pale ground you'd see this sweet
  face by),   20
All heaven, meanwhile, condensed into one
  eye
Which fears to lose the wonder, should it
  wink.   (1864)

A LIKENESS

Some people hang portraits up
In a room where they dine or sup;
And the wife clinks tea-things under,
And her cousin, he stirs his cup,
Asks, "Who was the lady, I wonder?"   5
" 'Tis a daub John bought at a sale,"
Quoth the wife — looks black as thunder.
"What a shade beneath her nose!
Snuff-taking, I suppose" —
Adds the cousin, while John's corns ail.   10

Or else, there's no wife in the case,
But the portrait's queen of the place,
Alone 'mid the other spoils
Of youth — masks, gloves, and foils,
And pipe-sticks, rose, cherry-tree, jasmine, 15
And the long whip, the tandem-lasher,
And the cast from a fist ("not, alas! mine,
But my master's, the Tipton Slasher"),
And the cards where pistol-balls mark ace,
And a satin shoe used for cigar-case,   20
And the chamois-horns ("shot in the Chab-
  lais"),
And prints — Rarey drumming on Cruiser,
And Sayers, our champion, the bruiser,
And the little edition of Rabelais:
Where a friend, with both hands in his
  pockets,   25
May saunter up close to examine it,
And remark a good deal of Jane Lamb in it,
"But the eyes are half out of their sockets;
That hair's not so bad, where the gloss is,
But they've made the girl's nose a proboscis;
Jane Lamb, that we danced with at Vichy! 31
What, is not she Jane? Then, who is she?"

14. **Correggio**, a famous Italian painter (1494-1534).
A Likeness. 18. **the Tipton Slasher**, an English boxer.
21. **Chablais**, a district in southeastern France. 22. **Rarey**,
J. S. Rarey (c. 1825-66), a famous American horse tamer
who subdued vicious animals by firm but gentle treatment.
Cruiser, the name of one of Rarey's horses. 23. **Sayers**,
Tom Sayers (1826-65), an English prize fighter. 24. **Rabelais**,
a celebrated French satirist and humorist of the early 16th
century. 31. **Vichy**, a town in central France.

All that I own is a print,
An etching, a mezzotint;
'Tis a study, a fancy, a fiction,   35
Yet a fact (take my conviction)
Because it has more than a hint
Of a certain face I never
Saw elsewhere touch or trace of
In women I've seen the face of: 40
Just an etching, and, so far, clever.

I keep my prints, an imbroglio,
Fifty in one portfolio.
When somebody tries my claret,
We turn round chairs to the fire,   45
Chirp over days in a garret,
Chuckle o'er increase of salary,
Taste the good fruits of our leisure,
Talk about pencil and lyre,
And the National Portrait Gallery;   50
Then I exhibit my treasure.
After we've turned over twenty,
And the debt of wonder my crony owes
Is paid to my Marc Antonios,
He stops me — "*Festina lentè!*   55
What's that sweet thing there, the etching?"
How my waistcoat-strings want stretching,
How my cheeks grow red as tomatoes,
How my heart leaps! But hearts, after leaps,
     ache.

"By the bye, you must take, for a keepsake,
That other, you praised, of Volpato's."   61
The fool! would he try a flight further and
     say —
He never saw, never before today,
What was able to take his breath away,
A face to lose youth for, to occupy age   65
With the dream of, meet death with — why,
     I'll not engage
But that, half in a rapture and half in a rage,
I should toss him the thing's self — " 'Tis
     only a duplicate,
A thing of no value! Take it, I supplicate!"
                                                   (1864)

APPARENT FAILURE

"We shall soon lose a celebrated building."
                      ——*Paris Newspaper*

No, for I'll save it! Seven years since,
     I passed through Paris, stopped a day
To see the baptism of your Prince;
     Saw, made my bow, and went my way.

Walking the heat and headache off,   5
     I took the Seine-side, you surmise,
Thought of the Congress, Gortschakoff,
     Cavour's appeal and Buol's replies,
So sauntered till — what met my eyes?

Only the Doric little Morgue!   10
     The dead-house where you show your
          drowned.
Petrarch's Vaucluse makes proud the Sorgue;
     Your Morgue has made the Seine renowned.
One pays one's debt in such a case;
     I plucked up heart and entered — stalked,
Keeping a tolerable face   16
     Compared with some whose cheeks were
          chalked.
Let them! No Briton's to be balked!

First came the silent gazers; next,
     A screen of glass, we're thankful for;   20
Last, the sight's self, the sermon's text,
     The three men who did most abhor
Their life in Paris yesterday,
     So killed themselves; and now, enthroned
Each on his copper couch, they lay   25
     Fronting me, waiting to be owned.
I thought, and think, their sin's atoned.

Poor men, God made, and all for that!
     The reverence struck me; o'er each head
Religiously was hung its hat,   30
     Each coat dripped by the owner's bed,
Sacred from touch; each had his berth,
     His bounds, his proper place of rest,
Who last night tenanted on earth
     Some arch, where twelve such slept
          abreast —
Unless the plain asphalt seemed best.   36

How did it happen, my poor boy?
     You wanted to be Buonaparte
And have the Tuileries for toy,
     And could not, so it broke your heart?   40
You, old one by his side, I judge,
     Were, red as blood, a socialist,
A leveler! Does the Empire grudge
     You've gained what no Republic missed?
Be quiet, and unclench your fist!   45

And this — why, he was red in vain,
     Or black — poor fellow that is blue!
What fancy was it turned your brain?

---

42. **imbroglio**, a confused mass. 54. **Marc Antonios**,
pictures by Marcantonio Raimondi (c. 1480-1540), a noted
Italian engraver. 55. **Festina lentè**, make haste slowly.
61. **Volpato**, Giovanni Volpato (c. 1735-1803), an eminent
Italian engraver.
Apparent Failure. Browning wrote this poem in an effort
to save from destruction the famous Paris Morgue on the
bank of the Seine River. He had visited the Morgue in
1856, when he was first in Paris to see the baptism of Prince
Louis Napoleon, son of Emperor Napoleon III, born March
16, 1856.

7. **the Congress.** The Congress of Paris, composed of
representatives of several European powers, met in Paris in
1856 to discuss the unity of Italy. Prince Alexander Gortcha-
koff (1798-1883) represented Russia; Count Camillo di
Cavour (1810-61), Sardinia; Count von Buol-Schauenstein
(1797-1865), Austria. Cavour was the great unifier of Italy.
12. **Vaucluse.** The Fountain of Vaucluse is the source of
the Sorgue River in southeastern France. The famous
Italian poet Petrarch (1304-74) once lived in Vaucluse, near
Avignon. 39. **Tuileries**, the royal palace in Paris. 46-47.
red . . . black, a reference to the gambling game of *rouge-
et-noir*—red and black—named from colors on the table.

Oh, women were the prize for you!
Money gets women, cards and dice   50
    Get money, and ill-luck gets just
The copper couch and one clear nice
    Cool squirt of water o'er your bust,
The right thing to extinguish lust!

It's wiser being good than bad;   55
    It's safer being meek than fierce;
It's fitter being sane than mad.
    My own hope is, a sun will pierce
The thickest cloud earth ever stretched;
    That, after Last, returns the First,   60
Though a wide compass round be fetched;
    That what began best, can't end worst,
Nor what God blessed once, prove accurst.
                            (1864)

From THE RING AND THE BOOK

From BOOK I

THE RING AND THE BOOK

O lyric Love, half angel and half bird,
And all a wonder and a wild desire —
Boldest of hearts that ever braved the sun,
Took sanctuary within the holier blue,
And sang a kindred soul out to his face —   5
Yet human at the red-ripe of the heart —
When the first summons from the darkling
    earth
Reached thee amid thy chambers, blanched
    their blue,
And bared them of the glory — to drop down,
To toil for man, to suffer or to die —   10
This is the same voice: can thy soul know
    change?
Hail then, and hearken from the realms of
    help!
Never may I commence my song, my due
To God who best taught song by gift of thee,
Except with bent head and beseeching
    hand —   15
That still, despite the distance and the dark,
What was, again may be; some interchange
Of grace, some splendor once thy very
    thought,
Some benediction anciently thy smile:
— Never conclude, but raising hand and head
Thither where eyes, that cannot reach, yet
    yearn   21
For all hope, all sustainment, all reward,
Their utmost up and on — so blessing back

In those thy realms of help, that heaven thy
    home,
Some whiteness which, I judge, thy face makes
    proud,   25
Some wanness where, I think, thy foot may
    fall!

BOOK VI

GIUSEPPE CAPONSACCHI

Answer you, Sirs? Do I understand aright?
Have patience! In this sudden smoke from
    hell —
So things disguise themselves — I cannot see
My own hand held thus broad before my face
And know it again. Answer you? Then that
    means   5
Tell over twice what I, the first time, told
Six months ago, 'twas here, I do believe,
Fronting you same three in this very room,
I stood and told you; yet now no one laughs,
Who then . . . nay, dear my lords, but laugh
    you did,   10
As good as laugh, what in a judge we style
Laughter — no levity, nothing indecorous,
    lords!
Only — I think I apprehend the mood:
There was the blameless shrug, permissible
    smirk,
The pen's pretense at play with the pursed
    mouth,   15
The titter stifled in the hollow palm
Which rubbed the eyebrow and caressed the
    nose,
When I first told my tale; they meant, you
    know,
"The sly one, all this we are bound believe!
Well, he can say no other than what he says.
We have been young, too — come, there's
    greater guilt!   21
Let him but decently disembroil himself,
Scramble from out the scrape nor move the
    mud —
We solid ones may risk a finger-stretch!"
And now you sit as grave, stare as aghast   25
As if I were a phantom; now 'tis — "Friend,
Collect yourself!" — no laughing matter
    more —
"Counsel the Court in this extremity,
Tell us again!" — tell that, for telling which,
I got the jocular piece of punishment,   30
Was sent to lounge a little in the place
Whence now of a sudden here you summon me

The Ring and the Book. See Critical Notes.
Book I. 1-25. **O lyric Love,** etc. These are the closing lines of Book I. They are intended as an invocation to Mrs. Browning, who died in 1861. 23. **so blessing back,** etc. My eyes yearn for reward from you in heaven — a glimpse of some whiteness glorified by your presence, of some wanness reflected wherever you walk, which will be evidence of your blessing to me. *Blessing* is a participle modifying *whiteness* and *wanness;* both nouns are parallel in construction with *hope* and *reward* (line 22).

Book VI. Giuseppe Caponsacchi. Caponsacchi, summoned before the Court, tells the story of his efforts to help Pompilia. He had told the same story some months before when on trial with Pompilia. While he is speaking, Pompilia is in the hospital, dying from wounds inflicted by Guido.
30. **jocular . . . punishment.** The Court had previously decided against Pompilia and Caponsacchi and had banished Caponsacchi for three years to Civita Vecchia, a seaport near Rome. Pompilia had been sent to a convent.

To take the intelligence from just — your lips!
You, Judge Tommati, who then tittered
  most —
That she I helped eight months since to escape
Her husband, was retaken by the same, 36
Three days ago, if I have seized your sense
(I being disallowed to interfere,
Meddle or make in a matter none of mine, 39
For you and law were guardians quite enough
O' the innocent, without a pert priest's help)—
And that he has butchered her according-
  ly,
As she foretold and as myself believed —
And, so foretelling and believing so, 44
We were punished, both of us, the merry way:
Therefore, tell once again the tale! For what?
Pompilia is only dying while I speak!
Why does the mirth hang fire and miss the
  smile?
My masters, there's an old book, you should
  con
For strange adventures, applicable yet, 50
'Tis stuffed with. Do you know that there
  was once
This thing: a multitude of worthy folk
Took recreation, watched a certain group
Of soldiery intent upon a game —
How first they wrangled, but soon fell to
  play, 55
Threw dice — the best diversion in the world.
A word in your ear — they are now casting
  lots,
Aye, with that gesture quaint and cry un-
  couth,
For the coat of One murdered an hour ago!
I am a priest — talk of what I have learned.
Pompilia is bleeding out her life belike, 61
Gasping away the latest breath of all,
This minute, while I talk — not while you
  laugh.

Yet, being sobered now, what is it you ask
By way of explanation? There's the fact! 65
It seems to fill the universe with sight
And sound — from the four corners of this
  earth
Tells itself over, to my sense at least.
But you may want it lower set i' the scale —
Too vast, too close it clangs in the ear, per-
  haps; 70
You'd stand back just to comprehend it more.
Well then, let me, the hollow rock, condense
The voice o' the sea and wind, interpret you
The mystery of this murder. God above!
It is too paltry, such a transference 75
O' the storm's roar to the cranny of the stone!

This deed, you saw begin — why does its end
Surprise you? Why should the event enforce
The lesson, we ourselves learned, she and I,
From the first o' the fact, and taught you, all
  in vain? 80
This Guido from whose throat you took my
  grasp,
Was this man to be favored, now, or feared,
Let do his will, or have his will restrained,
In the relation with Pompilia? — say!
Did any other man need interpose — 85
Oh, though first comer, though as strange at
  the work
As fribble must be, coxcomb, fool that's near
To knave as, say, a priest who fears the
  world —
Was he bound brave the peril, save the
  doomed, 89
Or go on, sing his snatch and pluck his flower,
Keep the straight path and let the victim die?
I held so; you decided otherwise,
Saw no such peril, therefore no such need
To stop song, loosen flower, and leave path.
  Law,
Law was aware and watching, would suffice,
Wanted no priest's intrusion, palpably 96
Pretense, too manifest a subterfuge!
Whereupon I, priest, coxcomb, fribble, and
  fool,
Ensconced me in my corner, thus rebuked,
A kind of culprit, over-zealous hound 100
Kicked for his pains to kennel; I gave place
To you, and let the law reign paramount.
I left Pompilia to your watch and ward,
And now you point me — there and thus she
  lies!

Men, for the last time, what do you want
  with me? 105
Is it — you acknowledge, as it were, a use,
A profit in employing me? — at length
I may conceivably help the august law?
I am free to break the blow, next hawk that
  swoops
On next dove, nor miss much of good repute?
Or what if this your summons, after all, 111
Be but the form of mere release, no more,
Which turns the key and lets the captive go?
I have paid enough in person at Civita,
Am free — what more need I concern me
  with? 115
Thank you! I am rehabilitated then,
A very reputable priest. But she —
The glory of life, the beauty of the world,
The splendor of heaven . . . well, Sirs, does
  no one move?
Do I speak ambiguously? The glory, I say,
And the beauty, I say, and splendor, still
  say I, 121

57-59. **casting lots . . . One.** Cf. *Matthew*, 27:35.—"And
they crucified him, and parted his garments, casting lots:
that it might be fulfilled which was spoken by the prophet,
'They parted my garments among them, and upon my
vesture did they cast lots.' "

87. **fribble,** a frivolous person.

Who, priest and trained to live my whole life
    long
On beauty and splendor, solely at their source,
God — have thus recognized my food in her,
You tell me, that's fast dying while we talk,
Pompilia! How does lenity to me   126
Remit one death-bed pang to her? Come,
    smile!
The proper wink at the hot-headed youth
Who lets his soul show, through transparent
    words,
The mundane love that's sin and scandal too!
You are all struck acquiescent now, it seems;
It seems the oldest, gravest signor here,   132
Even the redoubtable Tommati, sits
Chopfallen — understands how law might
    take
Service like mine, of brain and heart and hand,
In good part. Better late than never, law! 136
You understand of a sudden, gospel too
Has a claim here, may possibly pronounce
Consistent with my priesthood, worthy Christ,
That I endeavored to save Pompilia?

                   Then,   140
You were wrong, you see. That's well to see,
    though late.
That's all we may expect of man, this side
The grave; his good is — knowing he is bad.
Thus will it be with us when the books ope
And we stand at the bar on judgment-day. 145
Well, then, I have a mind to speak, see cause
To relume the quenched flax by this dreadful
    light,
Burn my soul out in showing you the truth.
I heard, last time I stood here to be judged,
What is priest's-duty — labor to pluck tares
And weed the corn of Molinism; let me   151
Make you hear, this time, how, in such a case,
Man, be he in the priesthood or at plow,
Mindful of Christ or marching step by step
With . . . what's his style, the other potentate
Who bids have courage and keep honor safe,
Nor let minuter admonition tease? —   157
How he is bound, better or worse, to act.
Earth will not end through this misjudgment,
    no!
For you and the others like you sure to come,
Fresh work is sure to follow — wickedness 161
That wants withstanding. Many a man of
    blood,
Many a man of guile will clamor yet,
Bid you redress his grievance — as he clutched
The prey, forsooth a stranger stepped be-
    tween,

151. **Molinism**, the doctrine taught by Miguel de Molinos
(1640-97), a Spanish priest who lived in Rome. He considered
abstinence, penance, etc., of little value except at the beginning of a course of self-discipline. His teaching was
condemned by the Pope in 1687. 155. **potentate**, a satirical
reference to Satan.

And there's the good gripe in pure waste!
    My part   166
Is done; i' the doing it, I pass away
Out of the world. I want no more with earth.
Let me, in heaven's name, use the very snuff
O' the taper in one last spark shall show truth
For a moment, show Pompilia who was true!
Not for her sake, but yours; if she is dead, 172
Oh, Sirs, she can be loved by none of you
Most or least priestly! Saints, to do us good,
Must be in heaven, I seem to understand; 175
We never find them saints before, at least.
Be her first prayer then presently for you —
She has done the good to me . . .
                What is all this?
There, I was born, have lived, shall die, a fool!
This is a foolish outset — might with cause 180
Give color to the very lie o' the man,
The murderer — make as if I loved his wife
In the way he called love. He is the fool
    there!
Why, had there been in me the touch of taint,
I had picked up so much of knaves'-policy 185
As hide it, keep one hand pressed on the place
Suspected of a spot would damn us both.
Or no, not her! — not even if any of you
Dares think that I, i' the face of death, her
    death
That's in my eyes and ears and brain and
    heart,   190
Lie — if he does, let him! I mean to say,
So he stop there, stay thought from smirching
    her
The snow-white soul that angels fear to take
Untenderly. But, all the same, I know
I too am taintless, and I bare my breast.   195
You can't think, men as you are, all of you,
But that, to hear thus suddenly such an end
Of such a wonderful white soul, that comes
Of a man and murderer calling the white
    black,
Must shake me, trouble and disadvantage.
    Sirs,   200
Only seventeen!

              Why, good and wise you are!
You might at the beginning stop my mouth;
So, none would be to speak for her, that knew.
I talk impertinently, and you bear,
All the same. This it is to have to do   205
With honest hearts; they easily may err,
But in the main they wish well to the truth.
You are Christians; somehow, no one ever
    plucked
A rag, even, from the body of the Lord,
To wear and mock with, but, despite him-
    self,
He looked the greater and was the better.
    Yes,   211
I shall go on now. Does she need or not

I keep calm? Calm I'll keep as monk that croons
Transcribing battle, earthquake, famine, plague,
From parchment to his cloister's chronicle. 215
Not one word more from the point now!

                                    I begin.
Yes, I am one of your body and a priest.
Also I am younger son o' the House
Oldest now, greatest once, in my birth-town
Arezzo, I recognize no equal there— 220
(I want all arguments, all sorts of arms
That seem to serve — use this for a reason, wait!),
Not therefore thrust into the Church, because
O' the piece of bread one gets there. We were first
Of Fiesole, that rings still with the fame 225
Of Capo-in-Sacco, our progenitor.
When Florence ruined Fiesole, our folk
Migrated to the victor-city, and there
Flourished — our palace and our tower attest,
In the Old Mercato — this was years ago, 230
Four hundred, full — no, it wants fourteen just.
Our arms are those of Fiesole itself,
The shield quartered with white and red; a branch
Are the Salviati of us, nothing more.
That were good help to the Church? But better still — 235
Not simply for the advantage of my birth
I' the way of the world, was I proposed for priest;
But because there's an illustration, late
I' the day, that's loved and looked to as a saint
Still in Arezzo, he was bishop of, 240
Sixty years since; he spent to the last doit
His bishop's-revenue among the poor,
And used to tend the needy and the sick,
Barefoot, because of his humility.
He it was — when the Granduke Ferdinand
Swore he would raze our city, plow the place
And sow it with salt, because we Aretines 247
Had tied a rope about the neck, to hale

The statue of his father from its base
For hate's sake — he availed by prayers and tears 250
To pacify the Duke and save the town.
This was my father's father's brother. You see,
For his sake, how it was I had a right
To the selfsame office, bishop in the egg,
So, grew i' the garb and prattled in the school,
Was made expect, from infancy almost, 256
The proper mood o' the priest; till time ran by
And brought the day when I must read the vows,
Declare the world renounced, and undertake
To become priest and leave probation — leap
Over the ledge into the other life, 261
Having gone trippingly hitherto up to the height
O'er the wan water. Just a vow to read!

I stopped short, awe-struck. "How shall holiest flesh
Engage to keep such vow inviolate, 265
How much less mine? I know myself too weak,
Unworthy! Choose a worthier, stronger man!"
And the very Bishop smiled and stopped my mouth
In its mid-protestation. "Incapable?
Qualmish of conscience? Thou ingenuous boy! 270
Clear up the clouds and cast thy scruples far!
I satisfy thee there's an easier sense
Wherein to take such vow than suits the first
Rough rigid reading. Mark what makes all smooth,
Nay, has been even a solace to myself! 275
The Jews who needs must, in their synagogue,
Utter sometimes the holy name of God,
A thing their superstition boggles at,
Pronounce aloud the ineffable sacrosanct —
How does their shrewdness help them? In this wise: 280
Another set of sounds they substitute,
Jumble so consonants and vowels — how
Should I know? — that there grows from out the old
Quite a new word that means the very same —
And o'er the hard place slide they with a smile. 285
Giuseppe Maria Caponsacchi mine,
Nobody wants you in these latter days
To prop the Church by breaking your backbone —
As the necessary way was once, we know,

---

217. one of . . . priest. Caponsacchi's church was that of S. Maria della Pieve, in Arezzo, a city about 100 miles north of Rome. 222. use . . . wait, I use this reference to my family for a reason that will appear later. 225. Fiesole, a suburb of Florence. 226. Capo-in-Sacco. The name means *Head in the Sack.* 227. Florence ruined Fiesole. This happened in 1125, although Caponsacchi's exact figures (line 231) would place the event in 1312, which is 386 years before the time of his speech—1698. Dante refers to the moving of the Caponsacchi family from Fiesole to Florence in *Paradiso,* 15:139-148, written about 1312. It is mentioned by one of Dante's ancestors who died about 1148. A lady of the Caponsacchi family was the mother of Dante's Beatrice. 230. Old Mercato, the old market-place in Florence. 234. Salviati, a well-known Italian family. 241. doit, a small Dutch coin, worth about one-fourth of a cent. 245. the Granduke Ferdinand, Ferdinand II, Grand Duke of Tuscany, 1621-70, grandson of Ferdinand I. 247. Aretines the men of Arezzo.

249. statue of his father, the statue of Ferdinand I (1549-1609), erected in front of the cathedral in 1595. Cf. *The Statue and the Bust,* p. 249. 279. ineffable sacrosanct, the unspeakable holy name. The Jews, out of reverence, do not pronounce the name of Jehovah; they substitute the name *Adonai,* meaning *Lord.*

When Diocletian flourished and his like. 290
That building of the buttress-work was done
By martyrs and confessors; let it bide,
Add not a brick, but, where you see a chink,
Stick in a sprig of ivy or root a rose
Shall make amends and beautify the pile! 295
We profit as you were the painfullest
O' the martyrs, and you prove yourself a
      match
For the cruellest confessor ever was,
If you march boldly up and take your stand
Where their blood soaks, their bones yet strew
      the soil,   300
And cry 'Take notice, I the young and free
And well-to-do i' the world, thus leave the
      world,
Cast in my lot thus with no gay young world
But the grand old Church; she tempts me of
      the two!'
Renounce the world? Nay, keep and give
      it us!   305
Let us have you, and boast of what you bring.
We want the pick o' the earth to practice
      with,
Not its offscouring, halt and deaf and blind
In soul and body. There's a rubble-stone
Unfit for the front o' the building, stuff to
      stow   310
In a gap behind and keep us weather-tight;
There's porphyry for the prominent place.
      Good lack!
Saint Paul has had enough and to spare, I
      trow,
Of ragged runaway Onesimus;
He wants the right-hand with the signet-ring
Of King Agrippa, now, to shake and use. 316
I have a heavy scholar cloistered up,
Close under lock and key, kept at his task
Of letting Fénelon know the fool he is,
In a book I promise Christendom next spring.
Why, if he covets so much meat, the clown, 321
As a lark's wing next Friday, or, any day,
Diversion beyond catching his own fleas,
He shall be properly swinged, I promise him.
But you, who are so quite another paste 325
Of a man — do you obey me? Cultivate
Assiduous that superior gift you have
Of making madrigals (who told me? Ah!);
Get done a Marinesque Adoniad straight
With a pulse o' the blood a-pricking, here and
      there,   330
That I may tell the lady, 'And he's ours!'"

So I became a priest. Those terms changed
      all —
I was good enough for that, nor cheated so;
I could live thus and still hold head erect.
Now you see why I may have been before 335
A fribble and coxcomb, yet, as priest, break
      word
Nowise, to make you disbelieve me now.
I need that you should know my truth. Well,
      then,
According to prescription did I live —
Conformed myself, both read the breviary 340
And wrote the rimes, was punctual to my
      place
I' the Pieve, and as diligent at my post
Where beauty and fashion rule. I throve
      apace,
Sub-deacon, Canon, the authority
For delicate play at tarocs, and arbiter 345
O' the magnitude of fan-mounts; all the while
Wanting no whit the advantage of a hint
Benignant to the promising pupil — thus:
"Enough attention to the Countess now,
The young one; 'tis her mother rules the
      roast,   350
We know where, and puts in a word; go pay
Devoir tomorrow morning after Mass!
Break that rash promise to preach, Passion-
      week!
Has it escaped you the Archbishop grunts
And snuffles when one grieves to tell his
      Grace ·   355
No soul dares treat the subject of the day
Since his own masterly handling it (ha, ha!)
Five years ago — when somebody could help
And touch up an odd phrase in time of need
(He, he!) — and somebody helps you, my son!
Therefore, don't prove so indispensable 361
At the Pieve, sit more loose i' the seat, nor
      grow
A fixture by attendance morn and eve!
Arezzo's just a haven midway Rome —
Rome's the eventual harbor — make for port,
Crowd sail, crack cordage! And your cargo
      be   366
A polished presence, a genteel manner, wit
At will, and tact at every pore of you!
I sent our lump of learning, Brother Clout,
And Father Slouch, our piece of piety, 370
To see Rome and try suit the Cardinal.
Thither they clump-clumped, beads and book
      in hand,
And ever since 'tis meat for man and maid
How both flopped down, prayed blessing on
      bent pate   374
Bald many an inch beyond the tonsure's need,
Never once dreaming, the two moony dolts,

290. **Diocletian**, emperor of Rome (284-305). He per-
secuted the Christians. 314. **Onesimus**, mentioned in
Paul's *Epistle to Philemon*, 1:10-18. 316. **King Agrippa**.
Paul, while held a prisoner by Festus, was brought before
King Agrippa. The account appears in *Acts*, 25-26. 319.
Fénelon, a French preacher, Archbishop of Cambrai (1651-
1751), who adopted the doctrines of Molinos (see note on
line 151). 329. **Marinesque Adoniad,** a poem in the
manner of a popular poem called *L'Adone*, written by Giovanni
Marino, an Italian poet (1569-1625).

342. **the Pieve**, his church. 345. **tarocs**, a kind of card
game. 353. **Passion-week**, the week before Easter, in
which Christ's sufferings are commemorated.

There's nothing moves his Eminence so much
As — far from all this awe at sanctitude —
Heads that wag, eyes that twinkle, modified
    mirth
At the closet-lectures on the Latin tongue 380
A lady learns so much by, we know where.
Why, body o' Bacchus, you should crave his
    rule
For pauses in the elegiac couplet, chasms
Permissible only to Catullus! There!
Now go to duty; brisk, break Priscian's head
By reading the day's office — there's no help.
You've Ovid in your poke to plaster that; 387
Amen's at the end of all. Then sup with me!''

Well, after three or four years of this life,
In prosecution of my calling, I   390
Found myself at the theater one night
With a brother Canon, in a mood and mind
Proper enough for the place, amused or no;
When I saw enter, stand, and seat herself
A lady, young, tall, beautiful, strange and sad.
It was as when, in our cathedral once,   396
As I got yawningly through matin-song,
I saw *facchini* bear a burden up,
Base it on the high-altar, break away
A board or two, and leave the thing inside 400
Lofty and lone; and lo, when next I looked,
There was the Rafael! I was still one stare,
When — "Nay, I'll make her give you back
    your gaze" —
Said Canon Conti; and at the word he tossed
A paper-twist of comfits to her lap,   405
And dodged and in a trice was at my back
Nodding from over my shoulder. Then she
    turned,
Looked our way, smiled the beautiful sad
    strange smile.
"Is not she fair? 'Tis my new cousin," said he.
"The fellow lurking there i' the black o' the
    box   410
Is Guido, the old scapegrace; she's his wife,
Married three years since. How his Count-
    ship sulks!
He has brought little back from Rome beside,
After the bragging, bullying. A fair face,
And — they do say — a pocketful of gold 415
When he can worry both her parents dead.
I don't go much there, for the chamber's cold
And the coffee pale. I got a turn at first
Paying my duty; I observed they crouched —
The two old frightened family specters —
    close   420

In a corner, each on each like mouse on mouse
I' the cat's cage. Ever since, I stay at home.
Hallo, there's Guido, the black, mean, and
    small,
Bends his brows on us — please to bend your
    own
On the shapely nether limbs of Light-skirts
    there   425
By way of a diversion! I was a fool
To fling the sweetmeats. Prudence, for God's
    love!
Tomorrow I'll make my peace, e'en tell some
    fib,
Try if I can't find means to take you there.''

That night and next day did the gaze endure,
Burnt to my brain, as sunbeam through shut
    eyes,   431
And not once changed the beautiful sad
    strange smile.
At vespers Conti leaned beside my seat
I' the choir — part said, part sung — "*In
    ex-cel-sis —*
All's to no purpose; I have louted low,   435
But he saw you staring — *quia sub* — don't
    incline
To know you nearer; him we would not hold
For Hercules — the man would lick your shoe
If you and certain efficacious friends
Managed him warily — but there's the wife.
Spare her, because he beats her; as it is, 441
She's breaking her heart quite fast enough —
    jam tu —
So, be you rational and make amends
With little Light-skirts yonder — *in secula
Secu-lo-o-o-rum.* Ah, you rogue! Everyone
    knows   445
What great dame she makes jealous; one
    against one,
Play, and win both!''
            Sirs, ere the week was out,
I saw and said to myself, "Light-skirts hides
    teeth
Would make a dog sick — the great dame
    shows spite
Should drive a cat mad; 'tis but poor work
    this —   450
Counting one's fingers till the sonnet's
    crowned.
I doubt much if Marino really be
A better bard than Dante after all.
'Tis more amusing to go pace at eve
I' the Duomo — watch the day's last gleam
    outside   455
Turn, as into a skirt of God's own robe,

382. **Bacchus,** the god of wine.   384. **Catullus,** a Latin
poet (87-47 B.C.), noted for the polish of his verse.   385.
break Priscian's head, violate the rules of grammar. Priscian was a famous Latin grammarian of the fifth century.
387. **Ovid,** a favorite Latin poet (43 B.C.-18 A.D.), noted for
his love poems and stories of pagan gods. 398. **facchini,**
porters. 402. **Rafael,** Santi Raphael (1483-1520), one of
the greatest of Italian painters. 420. **two . . . specters.**
Pompilia's foster-parents lived for a time in Guido's home.

434. **In ex-cel-sis,** etc., in the highest . . . forever and
ever. These Latin phrases are found in numerous places in
the ritual of the Roman Catholic Church. 438. **Hercules,**
a famous hero in Greek and Roman mythology. 452-453.
I doubt . . . after all. See line 329. 455. **the Duomo,** the
cathedral.

Those lancet-windows' jeweled miracle —
Than go eat the Archbishop's ortolans,
Digest his jokes. Luckily Lent is near;
Who cares to look will find me in my stall 460
At the Pieve, constant to this faith at least —
Never to write a canzonet any more."

So, next week, 'twas my patron spoke abrupt,
In altered guise, "Young man, can it be true
That after all your promise of sound fruit, 465
You have kept away from Countess young or
    old
And gone play truant in church all day long?
Are you turning Molinist?" I answered quick:
"Sir, what if I turned Christian? It might be.
The fact is, I am troubled in my mind, 470
Beset and pressed hard by some novel
    thoughts.
This your Arezzo is a limited world;
There's a strange Pope — 'tis said, a priest
    who thinks.
Rome is the port, you say; to Rome I go. 474
I will live alone — one does so in a crowd —
And look into my heart a little." "Lent
Ended" — I told friends — "I shall go to
    Rome."

One evening I was sitting in a muse
Over the opened "Summa," darkened round
By the mid-March twilight, thinking how my
    life 480
Had shaken under me — broke short indeed
And showed the gap 'twixt what is, what
    should be —
And into what abysm the soul may slip,
Leave aspiration here, achievement there,
Lacking omnipotence to connect extremes —
Thinking moreover . . . oh, thinking, if you
    like, 486
How utterly dissociated was I,
A priest and celibate, from the sad strange
    wife
Of Guido — just as an instance to the point,
Naught more — how I had a whole store of
    strengths 490
Eating into my heart, which craved employ,
And she, perhaps, need of a finger's help —
And yet there was no way in the wide world
To stretch out mine and so relieve myself —
How when the page o' the "Summa" preached
    its best, 495
Her smile kept glowing out of it, as to mock
The silence we could break by no one word —
There came a tap without the chamber-door,

And a whisper, when I bade who tapped speak
    out,
And, in obedience to my summons, last 500
In glided a masked muffled mystery,
Laid lightly a letter on the opened book,
Then stood with folded arms and foot demure,
Pointing as if to mark the minutes' flight.

I took the letter, read to the effect 505
That she, I lately flung the comfits to,
Had a warm heart to give me in exchange,
And gave it — loved me and confessed it thus,
And bade me render thanks by word of mouth,
Going that night to such a side o' the house 510
Where the small terrace overhangs a street
Blind and deserted, not the street in front:
Her husband being away, the surly patch,
At his villa of Vittiano.

            "And you?" — I asked;
"What may you be?" "Count Guido's kind of
    maid — 515
Most of us have two functions in his house.
We all hate him, the lady suffers much,
'Tis just we show compassion, furnish help,
Specially since her choice is fixed so well,
What answer may I bring to cheer the sweet
Pompilia?"

            Then I took a pen and wrote: 521
"No more of this! That you are fair, I know;
But other thoughts now occupy my mind.
I should not thus have played the insensible
Once on a time. What made you — may one
    ask — 525
Marry your hideous husband? 'Twas a fault,
And now you taste the fruit of it. Farewell."

"There!" smiled I as she snatched it and was
    gone —
"There, let the jealous miscreant — Guido's
    self,
Whose mean soul grins through this trans-
    parent trick — 530
Be balked so far, defrauded of his aim!
What fund of satisfaction to the knave,
Had I kicked this his messenger downstairs,
Trussed to the middle of her impudence,
And set his heart at ease so! No, indeed! 535
There's the reply which he shall turn and
    twist
At pleasure, snuff at till his brain grow drunk,
As the bear does when he finds a scented glove
That puzzles him — a hand and yet no hand,
Of other perfume than his own foul paw! 540
Last month, I had doubtless chosen to play
    the dupe,
Accepted the mock-invitation, kept

---

457. **lancet-window**, window shaped like a lance. 458.
ortolan, a kind of bird, regarded as a table delicacy. 462.
canzonet, a short song in one, two, or three parts. 473. **a
strange Pope**, Pope Innocent XII (1691-1700). 479. **Summa**, *Summa Theologiæ* (*Summary of Theology*), a work by
Thomas Aquinas (1227-74), a famous theologian and philosopher.

---

513. **patch**, dolt, clown. 514. **Vittiano**, a village **nine**
miles from Arezzo on the road to Perugia.

The sham appointment, cudgel beneath cloak,
Prepared myself to pull the appointer's self
Out of the window from his hiding-place 545
Behind the gown of this part-messenger
Part-mistress who would personate the wife.
Such had seemed once a jest permissible;
Now, I am not i' the mood."

     Back next morn brought
The messenger, a second letter in hand. 550
"You are cruel, Thyrsis, and Myrtilla moans
Neglected but adores you, makes request
For mercy: why is it you dare not come?
Such virtue is scarce natural to your age —
You must love someone else; I hear you do, 555
The Baron's daughter or the Advocate's wife,
Or both — all's one, would you make me the
 third —
I take the crumbs from table gratefully
Nor grudge who feasts there. 'Faith, I blush
 and blaze!
Yet if I break all bounds, there's reason sure.
Are you determinedly bent on Rome? 561
I am wretched here, a monster tortures me;
Carry me with you! Come and say you will!
Concert this very evening! Do not write!
I am ever at the window of my room 565
Over the terrace, at the *Ave.* Come!"

I questioned — lifting half the woman's mask
To let her smile loose. "So, you gave my line
To the merry lady?" "She kissed off the
 wax,
And put what paper was not kissed away 570
In her bosom to go burn; but merry, no!
She wept all night when evening brought no
 friend,
Alone, the unkind missive at her breast;
Thus Philomel, the thorn at her breast too,
Sings" . . . "Writes this second letter?"
 "Even so! 575
Then she may peep at vespers forth?" —
 "What risk
Do we run o' the husband?" — "Ah — no
 risk at all!
He is more stupid even than jealous. Ah —
That was the reason? Why, the man's away!
Beside, his bugbear is that friend of yours, 580
Fat little Canon Conti. He fears him;
How should he dream of you? I told you
 truth:
He goes to the villa at Vittiano — 'tis
The time when Spring-sap rises in the vine —
Spends the night there. And then his wife's
 a child; 585

551. **Thyrsis, Myrtilla.** These are common names of
lovers in pastoral poetry. 566. **at the Ave,** at the hour of
evening prayer, when the *Ave Maria* (*Hail Mary*) is sung.
574-575. **Thus Philomel . . . Sings.** The nightingale
(Philomel) was said to sing from pain. See note to Arnold's
Philomela, p. 486.

Does he think a child outwits him? A mere
 child —
Yet so full-grown, a dish for any duke.
Don't quarrel longer with such cates, but
 come!"

I wrote, "In vain do you solicit me.
I am a priest; and you are wedded wife, 590
Whatever kind of brute your husband prove.
I have scruples, in short. Yet should you
 really show
Sign at the window . . . but nay, best be
 good!
My thoughts are elsewhere." — "Take her
 that!"
      — "Again
Let the incarnate meanness, cheat and spy, 595
Mean to the marrow of him, make his heart
His food, anticipate hell's worm once more!
Let him watch shivering at the window — aye,
And let this hybrid, this his light-of-love
And lackey-of-lies — a sage economy — 600
Paid with embracings for the rank brass
 coin —
Let her report and make him chuckle o'er
The breakdown of my resolution now,
And lour at disappointment in good time!
— So tantalize and so enrage by turns, 605
Until the two fall each on the other like
Two famished spiders, as the coveted fly,
That toys long, leaves their net and them at
 last!"

And so the missives followed thick and fast
For a month, say — I still came at every
 turn 610
On the soft sly adder, endlong 'neath my
 tread.
I was met i' the street, made sign to in the
 church,
A slip was found i' the door-sill, scribbled
 word
'Twixt page and page o' the prayer-book in
 my place.
A crumpled thing dropped even before my
 feet, 615
Pushed through the blind, above the terrace-
 rail,
As I passed, by day, the very window once.
And ever from corners would be peering up
The messenger, with the selfsame demand,
"Obdurate still, no flesh but adamant? 620
Nothing to cure the wound, assuage the throe
O' the sweetest lamb that ever loved a bear?"
And ever my one answer in one tone —
"Go your ways, temptress! Let a priest read,
 pray,
Unplagued of vain talk, visions not for him!

588. **cates.** delicacies.

In the end, you'll have your will and ruin
  me!"   626

One day, a variation; thus I read:
"You have gained little by timidity.
My husband has found out my love at length,
Sees cousin Conti was the stalking-horse, 630
And you the game he covered, poor fat soul!
My husband is a formidable foe,
Will stick at nothing to destroy you. Stand
Prepared, or better, run till you reach Rome!
I bade you visit me, when the last place   635
My tyrant would have turned suspicious at,
Or cared to seek you in, was . . . why say,
  where?
But now all's changed; beside, the season's
  past
At the villa — wants the master's eye no
  more.
Anyhow, I beseech you, stay away   640
From the window! He might well be posted
  there."

I wrote — "You raise my courage, or call up
My curiosity, who am but man.
Tell him he owns the palace, not the street
Under — that's his and yours and mine alike.
If it should please me pad the path this eve,
Guido will have two troubles — first to get 647
Into a rage, and then get out again.
Be cautious, though: at the *Ave!*"
                 You of the court,
When I stood question here and reached this
  point   650
O' the narrative — search notes and see and
  say
If someone did not interpose with smile
And sneer, "And prithee why so confident
That the husband must, of all needs, not the
  wife,
Fabricate thus — what if the lady loved? 655
What if she wrote the letters?"

                        Learned Sir,
I told you there's a picture in our church.
Well, if a low-browed verger sidled up
Bringing me, like a blotch, on his prod's point,
A transfixed scorpion, let the reptile writhe,
And then said, "See a thing that Rafael
  made —   661
This venom issued from Madonna's mouth!"
I should reply, "Rather, the soul of you
Has issued from your body, like from like,
By way of the ordure-corner!"

                 But no less,   665
I tired of the same long black teasing lie
Obtruded thus at every turn; the pest

Was far too near the picture, anyhow:
One does Madonna service, making clowns
Remove their dung-heap from the sacristy. 670
"I will to the window, as he tempts," said I:
"Yes, whom the easy love has failed allure,
This new bait of adventure tempts — thinks
  he.
Though the imprisoned lady keeps afar,
There will they lie in ambush, heads alert, 675
Kith, kin, and Count mustered to bite my
  heel.
No mother nor brother viper of the brood
Shall scuttle off without the instructive
  bruise!"

So I went; crossed street and street: "The
  next street's turn,
I stand beneath the terrace, see, above,   680
The black of the ambush-window. Then, in
  place
Of hand's throw of soft prelude over lute,
And cough that clears way for the ditty
  last" —
I began to laugh already — "he will have
'Out of the hole you hide in, on to the front,
Count Guido Franceschini, show yourself! 686
Hear what a man thinks of a thing like you,
And after, take this foulness in your face!'"

The words lay living on my lip; I made
The one turn more — and there at the window
  stood,   690
Framed in its black square length, with lamp
  in hand,
Pompilia; the same great, grave, griefful air
As stands i' the dusk, on altar that I know,
Left alone with one moonbeam in her cell,
Our Lady of all the Sorrows. Ere I knelt — 695
Assured myself that she was flesh and blood —
She had looked one look and vanished.
                  I thought — "Just so;
It was herself, they have set her there to
  watch —
Stationed to see some wedding-band go by,
On fair pretense that she must bless the
  bride,   700
Or wait some funeral with friends wind past,
And crave peace for the corpse that claims
  its due.
She never dreams they used her for a snare,
And now withdraw the bait has served its
  turn.
Well done, the husband, who shall fare the
  worse!"   705
And on my lip again was — "Out with thee,

Guido!" When all at once she reappeared;
But, this time, on the terrace overhead,
So close above me, she could almost touch
My head if she bent down; and she did bend,
While I stood still as stone, all eye, all ear. 711

She began — "You have sent me letters, Sir:
I have read none — I can neither read nor
    write;
But she you gave them to, a woman here,
One of the people in whose power I am,   715
Partly explained their sense, I think, to me
Obliged to listen while she inculcates
That you, a priest, can dare love me, a wife,
Desire to live or die as I shall bid
(She makes me listen if I will or no),   720
Because you saw my face a single time.
It cannot be she says the thing you mean;
Such wickedness were deadly to us both.
But good true love would help me now so
    much —
I tell myself, you may mean good and true.
You offer me, I seem to understand,   726
Because I am in poverty and starve,
Much money, where one piece would save my
    life.
The silver cup upon the altar-cloth
Is neither yours to give nor mine to take; 730
But I might take one bit of bread therefrom,
Since I am starving, and return the rest,
Yet do no harm: this is my very case.
I am in that strait, I may not dare abstain
From so much of assistance as would bring 735
The guilt of theft on neither you nor me;
But no superfluous particle of aid.
I think, if you will let me state my case,
Even had you been so fancy-fevered here,
Not your sound self, you must grow healthy
    now —   740
Care only to bestow what I can take.
That it is only you in the wide world,
Knowing me nor in thought nor word nor
    deed,
Who, all unprompted save by your own heart,
Came proffering assistance now—were strange
But that my whole life is so strange; as
    strange   746
It is, my husband, whom I have not wronged,
Should hate and harm me. For his own soul's
    sake,
Hinder the harm! But there is something
    more,
And that the strangest: it has got to be   750
Somehow for my sake too, and yet not mine
— This is a riddle — for some kind of sake
Not any clearer to myself than you,
And yet as certain as that I draw breath —
I would fain live, not die — oh no, not die!
My case is, I was dwelling happily   756
At Rome with those dear Comparini, called

Father and mother to me; when at once
I found I had become Count Guido's wife,
Who then, not waiting for a moment, changed
Into a fury of fire, if once he was   761
Merely a man. His face threw fire at mine,
He laid a hand on me that burned all peace,
All joy, all hope, and last all fear away,
Dipping the bough of life, so pleasant once, 765
In fire which shriveled leaf and bud alike,
Burning not only present life but past,
Which you might think was safe beyond his
    reach.
He reached it, though, since that beloved pair,
My father once, my mother all those years, 770
That loved me so, now say I dreamed a dream
And bid me wake, henceforth no child of
    theirs,
Never in all the time their child at all.
Do you understand? I cannot; yet so it is.
Just so I say of you that proffer help: 775
I cannot understand what prompts your soul,
I simply needs must see that it is so,
Only one strange and wonderful thing more.
They came here with me, those two dear ones,
    kept
All the old love up, till my husband, till   780
His people here so tortured them, they fled.
And now, is it because I grow in flesh
And spirit one with him their torturer,
That they, renouncing him, must cast off me?
If I were graced by God to have a child,   785
Could I one day deny God graced me so?
Then, since my husband hates me, I shall
    break
No law that reigns in this fell house of hate,
By using — letting have effect so much
Of hate as hides me from that whole of hate
Would take my life which I want and must
    have —   791
Just as I take from your excess of love
Enough to save my life with, all I need.
The Archbishop said to murder me were sin;
My leaving Guido were a kind of death   795
With no sin — more death, he must answer
    for.
Hear now what death to him and life to you
I wish to pay and owe. Take me to Rome!
You go to Rome, the servant makes me hear.
Take me as you would take a dog, I think, 800
Masterless left for strangers to maltreat;
Take me home like that — leave me in the
    house
Where the father and the mother are; and
    soon
They'll come to know and call me by my
    name,
Their child once more, since child I am, for
    all   805
They now forget me, which is the worst o'
    the dream —

And the way to end dreams is to break them,
    stand,
Walk, go. Then help me to stand, walk, and
    go!
The Governor said the strong should help the
    weak;
You know how weak the strongest women are.
How could I find my way there by myself? 811
I cannot even call out, make them hear —
Just as in dreams; I have tried and proved
    the fact.
I have told this story and more to good great
    men,
The Archbishop and the Governor; they
    smiled.   815
'Stop your mouth, fair one!' — presently they
    frowned,
'Get you gone, disengage you from our feet!'
I went in my despair to an old priest,
Only a friar, no great man like these two,
But good, the Augustinian, people name 820
Romano — he confessed me two months since.
He fears God; why then needs he fear the
    world?
And when he questioned how it came about
That I was found in danger of a sin —
Despair of any help from providence —   825
'Since, though your husband outrage you,'
    said he,
'That is a case too common, the wives die
Or live, but do not sin so deep as this' —
Then I told — what I never will tell you —
How, worse than husband's hate, I had to
    bear   830
The love — soliciting to shame called love —
Of his brother — the young idle priest i' the
    house
With only the devil to meet there. 'This is
    grave —
Yes, we must interfere. I counsel — write
To those who used to be your parents once, 835
Of dangers here, bid them convey you hence!'
'But,' said I, 'when I neither read nor write?'
Then he took pity and promised 'I will write.'
If he did so — why, they are dumb or dead;
Either they give no credit to the tale,   840
Or else, wrapped wholly up in their own joy
Of such escape, they care not who cries, still
I' the clutches. Anyhow, no word arrives.
All such extravagance and dreadfulness   844
Seems incident to dreaming, cured one way —
Wake me! The letter I received this morn
Said — if the woman spoke your very sense —
'You would die for me.' I can believe it now;
For now the dream gets to involve yourself.
First of all, you seemed wicked and not good,
In writing me those letters; you came in 851
Like a thief upon me. I this morning said
In my extremity, entreat the thief!
Try if he have in him no honest touch!

A thief might save me from a murderer. 855
'Twas a thief said the last kind word to Christ.
Christ took the kindness and forgave the
    theft;
And so did I prepare what I now say.
But now, that you stand and I see your face,
Though you have never uttered word yet —
    well, I know,   860
Here too has been dream-work, delusion too,
And that at no time, you with the eyes here,
Ever intended to do wrong by me,
Nor wrote such letters therefore. It is false,
And you are true, have been true, will be
    true.   865
To Rome then — when is it you take me
    there?
Each minute lost is mortal. When? — I ask.'

I answered, "It shall be when it can be.
I will go hence and do your pleasure, find
The sure and speedy means of travel, then 870
Come back and take you to your friends in
    Rome.
There wants a carriage, money, and the rest —
A day's work by tomorrow at this time.
How shall I see you and assure escape?"

She replied, "Pass, tomorrow at this hour. 875
If I am at the open window, well;
If I am absent, drop a handkerchief
And walk by! I shall see from where I watch,
And know that all is done. Return next
    eve,
And next, and so till we can meet and speak!"
"Tomorrow at this hour I pass," said I.   881
She was withdrawn.

                    Here is another point
I bid you pause at. When I told thus far,
Someone said, subtly, "Here at least was found
Your confidence in error — you perceived 885
The spirit of the letters, in a sort,
Had been the lady's, if the body should be
Supplied by Guido: say, he forged them all!
Here was the unforged fact — she sent for
    you,
Spontaneously elected you to help,   890
— What men call, loved you; Guido read her
    mind,
Gave it expression to assure the world
The case was just as he foresaw. He wrote;
She spoke."
            Sirs, that first simile serves still —
That falsehood of a scorpion hatched, I say,

---

856. **the last kind word to Christ.** See the account of
the Crucifixion in *Luke*, 23:32-34. One of the thieves "said
unto Jesus, 'Lord, remember me when thou comest into thy
kingdom.' And Jesus said unto him, 'Verily I say unto thee,
Today shalt thou be with me in paradise.'" 894. **that first
simile.** See lines 656-665, p. 328.

Nowhere i' the world but in Madonna's
    mouth.   896
Go on! Suppose, that falsehood foiled, next
    eve
Pictured Madonna raised her painted hand,
Fixed the face Rafael bent above the Babe,
On my face as I flung me at her feet;   900
Such miracle vouchsafed and manifest,
Would that prove the first lying tale was true?
Pompilia spoke, and I at once received,
Accepted my own fact, my miracle
Self-authorized and self-explained — she chose
To summon me and signify her choice.   906
Afterward — oh! I gave a passing glance
To a certain ugly cloud-shape, goblin-shred
Of hell-smoke hurrying past the splendid
    moon
Out now to tolerate no darkness more,   910
And saw right through the thing that tried to
    pass
For truth and solid, not an empty lie:
"So, he not only forged the words for her
But words for me, made letters he called
    mine;
What I sent, he retained, gave these in place,
All by the mistress-messenger! As I   916
Recognized her, at potency of truth,
So she, by the crystalline soul, knew me,
Never mistook the signs. Enough of this —
Let the wraith go to nothingness again,   920
Here is the orb, have only thought for her!"

"Thought?" nay, Sirs, what shall follow was
    not thought;
I have thought sometimes, and thought long
    and hard.
I have stood before, gone round a serious
    thing,
Tasked my whole mind to touch and clasp it
    close,   925
As I stretch forth my arm to touch this bar.
God and man, and what duty I owe both —
I dare to say I have confronted these
In thought; but no such faculty helped here.
I put forth no thought — powerless, all that
    night   930
I paced the city; it was the first spring.
By the invasion I lay passive to,
In rushed new things, the old were rapt away;
Alike abolished — the imprisonment
Of the outside air, the inside weight o' the
    world   935
That pulled me down. Death meant, to spurn
    the ground,
Soar to the sky — die well and you do that.
The very immolation made the bliss;
Death was the heart of life, and all the harm
My folly had crouched to avoid, now proved
    a veil   940
Hiding all gain my wisdom strove to grasp —

As if the intense center of the flame
Should turn a heaven to that devoted fly
Which hitherto, sophist alike and sage,
Saint Thomas with his sober gray goose-quill,
And sinner Plato by Cephisian reed,   946
Would fain, pretending just the insect's good,
Whisk off, drive back, consign to shade again.
Into another state, under new rule
I knew myself was passing swift and sure;   950
Whereof the initiatory pang approached,
Felicitous annoy, as bitter-sweet
As when the virgin-band, the victors chaste,
Feel at the end the earthly garments drop,
And rise with something of a rosy shame   955
Into immortal nakedness: so I
Lay, and let come the proper throe would
    thrill
Into the ecstasy and outthrob pain.

I' the gray of dawn it was I found myself
Facing the pillared front o' the Pieve — mine,
My church; it seemed to say for the first
    time,
"But am not I the Bride, the mystic love   962
O' the Lamb, who took thy plighted troth,
    my priest,
To fold thy warm heart on my heart of stone
And freeze thee nor unfasten any more?   965
This is a fleshly woman — let the free
Bestow their life-blood; thou art pulseless
    now!"
See! Day by day I had risen and left this
    church
At the signal waved me by some foolish fan,
With half a curse and half a pitying smile 970
For the monk I stumbled over in my haste,
Prostrate and corpse-like at the altar-foot
Intent on his *corona;* then the church
Was ready with her quip, if word conduced,
To quicken my pace nor stop for prating —
    "There!
Be thankful you are no such ninny, go   976
Rather to teach a black-eyed novice cards
Than gabble Latin and protrude that nose
Smooth to a sheep's through no brains and
    much faith!"
That sort of incentive! Now the church
    changed tone —   980
Now, when I found out first that life and
    death
Are means to an end, that passion uses both,
Indisputably mistress of the man
Whose form of worship is self-sacrifice;
Now, from the stone lungs sighed the scrannel
    voice,   985

945. **Saint Thomas,** Saint Thomas Aquinas (see note on
line 479, p. 326). 946. **sinner Plato by Cephisian reed.**
Plato (427-347 B.C.) was a famous Greek philosopher. He
was called sinner because he was a pagan. The Cephisus
was a river near Athens. 963. **the Lamb,** Christ. 973.
corona, rosary. 985. **scrannel,** harsh, unmelodious.

"Leave that live passion, come be dead with
   me!"   986
As if, i' the fabled garden, I had gone
On great adventure, plucked in ignorance
Hedge-fruit, and feasted to satiety,
Laughing at such high fame for hips and haws,
And scorned the achievement; then come all
   at once   991
O' the prize o' the place, the thing of perfect
   gold,
The apple's self — and, scarce my eye on that,
Was 'ware as well o' the seven-fold dragon's
   watch.

Sirs, I obeyed. Obedience was too strange —
This new thing that had been struck into me
By the look o' the lady — to dare disobey 997
The first authoritative word. 'Twas God's.
I had been lifted to the level of her,
Could take such sounds into my sense. I said,
"We two are cognizant o' the Master now;
She it is bids me bow the head. How true, 1002
I am a priest! I see the function here;
I thought the other way self-sacrifice:
This is the true, seals up the perfect sum.
I pay it, sit down, silently obey."   1006

So, I went home. Dawn broke, noon broad-
   ened, I —
I sat stone-still, let time run over me.
The sun slanted into my room, had reached
The west. I opened book — Aquinas blazed
With one black name only on the white page.
I looked up, saw the sunset; vespers rang. 1012
"She counts the minutes till I keep my word
And come say all is ready. I am a priest.
Duty to God is duty to her; I think   1015
God, who created her, will save her too
Some new way, by one miracle the more,
Without me. Then, prayer may avail per-
   haps."
I went to my own place i' the Pieve, read
The office; I was back at home again   1020
Sitting i' the dark. "Could she but know —
   but know
That, were there good in this distinct from
   God's,
Really good as it reached her, though pro-
   cured
By a sin of mine — I should sin; God forgives.
She knows it is no fear withholds me — fear?
Of what? Suspense here is the terrible thing.
If she should, as she counts the minutes, come
On the fantastic notion that I fear   1028
The world now, fear the Archbishop, fear
   perhaps
Count Guido, he who, having forged the lies,

May wait the work, attend the effect — I
   fear   1031
The sword of Guido! Let God see to that —
Hating lies, let not her believe a lie!"

Again the morning found me. "I will work,
Tie down my foolish thoughts. Thank God
   so far!   1035
I have saved her from a scandal, stopped the
   tongues
Had broken else into a cackle and hiss
Around the noble name. Duty is still
Wisdom; I have been wise." So the day wore.

At evening — "But, achieving victory,   1040
I must not blink the priest's peculiar part,
Nor shrink to counsel, comfort. Priest and
   friend —
How do we discontinue to be friends?
I will go minister, advise her seek
Help at the source — above all, not despair.
There may be other happier help at hand. 1046
I hope it — wherefore then neglect to say?"

There she stood — leaned there, for the second
   time,
Over the terrace, looked at me, then spoke:
"Why is it you have suffered me to stay 1050
Breaking my heart two days more than was
   need?
Why delay help, your own heart yearns to
   give?
You are again here, in the selfsame mind,
I see here, steadfast in the face of you —
You grudge to do no one thing that I ask.
Why then is nothing done? You know my
   need.   1056
Still, through God's pity on me, there is
   time
And one day more; shall I be saved or no?"
I answered — "Lady, waste no thought, no
   word
Even to forgive me! Care for what I care —
Only! Now follow me as I were fate!   1061
Leave this house in the dark tomorrow night,
Just before daybreak; there's new moon this
   eve —
It sets, and then begins the solid black.
Descend, proceed to the Torrione, step   1065
Over the low dilapidated wall,
Take San Clemente; there's no other gate
Unguarded at the hour. Some paces thence
An inn stands; cross to it; I shall be there."

She answered, "If I can but find the way. 1070
But I shall find it. Go now!"

---

987. **fabled garden**, the Garden of the Hesperides, where
the golden apple was guarded by a dragon (line 994).

1065-1067. **Torrione . . . San Clemente.** The Torrione
was a part of the wall adjacent to the San Clemente gate at
the extreme north end of Arezzo.

I did go,
Took rapidly the route myself prescribed,
Stopped at Torrione, climbed the ruined place,
Proved that the gate was practicable, reached
The inn, no eye, despite the dark, could miss,
Knocked there and entered, made the host
    secure: 1076
"With Caponsacchi it is ask and have;
I know my betters. Are you bound for Rome?
I get swift horse and trusty man," said he.

Then I retraced my steps, was found once
    more
In my own house for the last time; there lay
The broad pale opened "Summa." "Shut his
    book,   1082
There's other showing! 'Twas a Thomas too
Obtained — more favored than his namesake
    here —
A gift, tied faith fast, foiled the tug of doubt—
Our Lady's girdle; down he saw it drop   1086
As she ascended into heaven, they say.
He kept that safe and bade all doubt adieu.
I too have seen a lady and hold a grace."

I know not how the night passed. Morning
    broke;   1090
Presently came my servant. "Sir, this eve —
Do you forget?" I started. "How forget?
What is it you know?" "With due submis-
    sion, Sir,
This being last Monday in the month but one,
And a vigil, since tomorrow is Saint George,
And feast-day, and moreover day for copes,
And Canon Conti now away a month,   1097
And Canon Crispi sour because, forsooth,
You let him sulk in stall and bear the brunt
Of the octave . . . Well, Sir, 'tis important!"
        "True!
Hearken, I have to start for Rome this night.
No word, lest Crispi overboil and burst! 1102
Provide me with a laic dress! Throw dust
I' the Canon's eye, stop his tongue's scandal
    so!
See there's a sword in case of accident."
I knew the knave; the knave knew me.

    And thus 1106
Through each familiar hindrance of the day
Did I make steadily for its hour and end —
Felt time's old barrier-growth of right and fit
Give way through all its twines, and let me
    go.   1110

Use and wont recognized the excepted man,
Let speed the special service — and I sped
Till, at the dead between midnight and morn,
There was I at the goal, before the gate,
With a tune in the ears, low leading up to
    loud,   1115
A light in the eyes, faint that would soon be
    flare,
Ever some spiritual witness new and new
In faster frequence, crowding solitude
To watch the way o' the warfare — till, at
    last,
When the ecstatic minute must bring birth,
Began a whiteness in the distance, waxed 1121
Whiter and whiter, near grew and more near,
Till it was she; there did Pompilia come.
The white I saw shine through her was her
    soul's,
Certainly, for the body was one black,   1125
Black from head down to foot. She did not
    speak,
Glided into the carriage — so a cloud
Gathers the moon up. "By San Spirito,
To Rome, as if the road burned underneath!
Reach Rome, then hold my head in pledge, I
    pay   1130
The run and the risk to heart's content!"
    Just that
I said — then, in another tick of time,
Sprang, was beside her, she and I alone.

So it began, our flight through dusk to clear,
Through day and night and day again to night
Once more, and to last dreadful dawn of all.
Sirs, how should I lie quiet in my grave 1137
Unless you suffer me wring, drop by drop,
My brain dry, make a riddance of the drench
Of minutes with a memory in each,   1140
Recorded motion, breath or look of hers,
Which poured forth would present you one
    pure glass,
Mirror you plain — as God's sea, glassed in
    gold,
His saints — the perfect soul Pompilia? Men,
You must know that a man gets drunk with
    truth   1145
Stagnant inside him! Oh, they've killed her,
    Sirs!
Can I be calm?
        Calmly! Each incident
Proves, I maintain, that action of the flight
For the true thing it was. The first faint
    scratch
O' the stone will test its nature, teach its
    worth   1150
To idiots who name Parian — coprolite.

1086-1087. **Our Lady's girdle . . . heaven.** As the
Virgin Mary ascended into heaven, tradition reports that
her girdle, which had been loosened, fell into the hands of
St. Thomas, the doubting apostle. 1095. **Saint George,**
the patron saint of England. His day is April 23. 1096.
cope, an ecclesiastical vestment. 1099. **stall,** a seat in the
choir of a church, for officiating clergy. 1100. **octave,** the
week after a church festival; in this instance, April 14 to 21
inclusive. 1103. **laic,** secular.

1128. **San Spirito,** a gate at the south end of Arezzo.
1143. **God's sea, glassed.** Cf. *Revelation,* 4:6.—"And
before the throne there was a sea of glass like unto crystal."
1151. **Parian,** pure marble from Paros, a Greek island in the
Ægean Sea. **coprolite,** a piece of petrified dung.

After all, I shall give no glare — at best
Only display you certain scattered lights
Lamping the rush and roll of the abyss;
Nothing but here and there a fire-point pricks
Wavelet from wavelet. Well!
               For the first hour 1156
We both were silent in the night, I know;
Sometimes I did not see nor understand.
Blackness engulfed me—partial stupor, say—
Then I would break way, breathe through
    the surprise,   1160
And be aware again, and see who sat
In the dark vest with the white face and
    hands.
I said to myself — "I have caught it, I con-
    ceive
The mind o' the mystery; 'tis the way they
    wake
And wait, two martyrs somewhere in a tomb,
Each by each as their blessing was to die; 1166
Some signal they are promised and expect —
When to arise before the trumpet scares:
So, through the whole course of the world
    they wait
The last day, but so fearless and so safe! 1170
No otherwise, in safety and not fear,
I lie, because she lies too by my side."
You know this is not love, Sirs — it is faith,
The feeling that there's God, he reigns and
    rules   1174
Out of this low world — that is all; no harm!
At times she drew a soft sigh—music seemed
Always to hover just above her lips,
Not settle — break a silence music too.

In the determined morning, I first found
Her head erect, her face turned full to me, 1180
Her soul intent on mine through two wide
    eyes.
I answered them. "You are saved hitherto.
We have passed Perugia — gone round by the
    wood,
Not through, I seem to think — and opposite
I know Assisi; this is holy ground."   1185
Then she resumed. "How long since we both
    left
Arezzo?" — "Years — and certain hours be-
    side."
It was at . . . ah, but I forget the names!
'Tis a mere post-house and a hovel or two;
I left the carriage and got bread and wine
And brought it her. — "Does it detain to
    eat?"   1191
" — They stay perforce, change horses —
    therefore eat!
We lose no minute; we arrive, be sure!"

1183. **Perugia,** a city about forty miles from Arezzo, on
the road to Rome. 1185. **holy ground,** holy because St.
Francis was born there in 1182. He was the founder of the
Order of Franciscan monks and of the monastery of St.
Francis.

This was — I know not where — there's a
    great hill
Close over, and the stream has lost its bridge;
One fords it. She began — "I have heard say
Of some sick body that my mother knew, 1197
'Twas no good sign when in a limb diseased
All the pain suddenly departs — as if
The guardian angel discontinued pain   1200
Because the hope of cure was gone at last;
The limb will not again exert itself,
It needs be pained no longer: so with me —
My soul whence all the pain is past at once;
All pain must be to work some good in the
    end.   1205
True, this I feel now, this may be that good,
Pain was because of — otherwise, I fear!"

She said — a long while later in the day,
When I had let the silence be — abrupt —
"Have you a mother?" "She died, I was
    born."   1210
"A sister then?" "No sister." "Who was
    it —
What woman were you used to serve this way,
Be kind to, till I called you and you came?"
I did not like that word. Soon afterward —
"Tell me, are men unhappy, in some kind 1215
Of mere unhappiness at being men,
As women suffer, being womanish?
Have you, now, some unhappiness, I mean,
Born of what may be man's strength over-
    much,
To match the undue susceptibility,   1220
The sense at every pore when hate is close?
It hurts us if a baby hides its face
Or child strikes at us punily, calls names
Or makes a mouth — much more if stranger
    men
Laugh or frown — just as that were much to
    bear!   1225
Yet rocks split — and the blow-ball does no
    more,
Quivers to feathery nothing at a touch;
And strength may have its drawback, weak-
    ness 'scapes."

Once she asked, "What is it that made you
    smile,
At the great gate with the eagles and the
    snakes,   1230
Where the company entered, 'tis a long time
    since?"
" — Forgive — I think you would not under-
    stand.
Ah, but you ask me — therefore, it was this:
That was a certain bishop's villa-gate
(I knew it by the eagles), and at once   1235
Remember this same bishop was just he

1226. **blow-ball,** the flower of the dandelion.

People of old were wont to bid me please
If I would catch preferment; so, I smiled
Because an impulse came to me, a whim —
What if I prayed the prelate leave to speak,
Began upon him in his presence-hall   1241
— 'What, still at work so gray and obsolete?
Still rocheted and mitered more or less?
Don't you feel all that out of fashion now?
I find out when the day of things is done!' "

At eve we heard the *angelus;* she turned — 1246
"I told you I can neither read nor write.
My life stopped with the play-time; I will
      learn,
If I begin to live again; but you —
Who are a priest — wherefore do you not read
The service at this hour? Read Gabriel's
      song,   1251
The lesson, and then read the little prayer
To Raphael, proper for us travelers!"
I did not like that, neither, but I read.

When we stopped at Foligno it was dark. 1255
The people of the post came out with lights.
The driver said, "This time tomorrow, may
Saints only help, relays continue good,
Nor robbers hinder, we arrive at Rome."
I urged — "Why tax your strength a second
      night?   1260
Trust me, alight here and take brief repose!
We are out of harm's reach, past pursuit; go
      sleep
If but an hour! I keep watch, guard the
      while
Here in the doorway." But her whole face
      changed —
The misery grew again about her mouth; 1265
The eyes burned up from faintness, like the
      fawn's
Tired to death in the thicket, when she feels
The probing spear o' the huntsman. "Oh, no
      stay!"
She cried, in the fawn's cry, "On to Rome,
      on, on —
Unless 'tis you who fear — which cannot be!"

We did go on all night; but at its close 1271
She was troubled, restless, moaned low, talked
      at whiles
To herself, her brow on quiver with the
      dream.

1243. **rocheted and mitered.** The rochet is a close-fitting linen vestment resembling the surplice. The miter is
the official headdress of a bishop. 1246. **the angelus,** a
prayer spoken at the sound of the bell at morning, noon, and
night. It consists of Gabriel's salutation (line 1251) to
Mary—*Ave Maria* (*Hail Mary*), etc. 1251. **Gabriel's
song,** a hymn in the Roman Catholic breviary for the feast
of St. Gabriel, the Archangel. 1252-1253. **prayer To
Raphael,** a prayer in the Roman Catholic breviary for the
feast of St. Raphael, an angel mentioned in the apocryphal
book of Tobit. He is represented as a traveler. 1255.
Foligno, a small town about twenty miles from Perugia,
and ten from Assisi.

Once, wide awake, she menaced, at arms'
      length
Waved away something — "Never again with
      you!   1275
My soul is mine, my body is my soul's;
You and I are divided evermore
In soul and body. Get you gone!" Then I —
"Why, in my whole life I have never prayed!
Oh, if the God, that only can, would help!
Am I his priest with power to cast out fiends?
Let God arise and all his enemies   1282
Be scattered!" By morn, there was peace,
      no sigh
Out of the deep sleep.

                          When she woke at last,
I answered the first look — "Scarce twelve
      hours more,   1285
Then, Rome! There probably was no pur-
      suit,
There cannot now be peril; bear up brave!
Just some twelve hours to press through to
      the prize;
Then, no more of the terrible journey!"
"Then,   1289
No more o' the journey; if it might but last!
Always, my life long, thus to journey still!
It is the interruption that I dread —
With no dread, ever to be here and thus!
Never to see a face nor hear a voice!
Yours is no voice; you speak when you are
      dumb;   1295
Nor face — I see it in the dark. I want
No face nor voice that change and grow
      unkind."
That I liked; that was the best thing she said.

In the broad day, I dared entreat, "Descend!"
I told a woman, at the garden-gate   1300
By the post-house, white and pleasant in the
      sun,
"It is my sister — talk with her apart!
She is married and unhappy, you perceive;
I take her home because her head is hurt;
Comfort her as you women understand!"   1305
So, there I left them by the garden-wall,
Paced the road, then bade put the horses to,
Came back, and there she sat. Close to her
      knee,
A black-eyed child still held the bowl of milk,
Wondered to see how little she could drink,
And in her arms the woman's infant lay. 1311
She smiled at me, "How much good this has
      done!
This is a whole night's rest and how much
      more!
I can proceed now, though I wish to stay.
How do you call that tree with the thick top
That holds in all its leafy green and gold 1316
The sun now like an immense egg of fire?"

(It was a million-leaved mimosa.) "Take
The babe away from me and let me go!"
And in the carriage, "Still a day, my friend!
And perhaps half a night, the woman fears.
I pray it finish, since it cannot last.   1322
There may be more misfortune at the close,
And where will you be? God suffice me
          then!"
And presently — for there was a roadside-
          shrine —   1325
"When I was taken first to my own church,
Lorenzo in Lucina, being a girl,
And bid confess my faults, I interposed,
'But teach me what fault to confess and
          know!'
So, the priest said — 'You should bethink
          yourself;   1330
Each human being needs must have done
          wrong!'
Now, be you candid and no priest but friend—
Were I surprised and killed here on the spot,
A runaway from husband and his home,
Do you account it were in sin I died?   1335
My husband used to seem to harm me, not —
Not on pretense he punished sin of mine,
Nor for sin's sake and lust of cruelty,
But as I heard him bid a farming-man
At the villa take a lamb once to the wood 1340
And there ill-treat it, meaning that the wolf
Should hear its cries, and so come, quick be
          caught,
Enticed to the trap. He practiced thus with
          me
That so, whatever were his gain thereby, 1344
Others than I might become prey and spoil.
Had it been only between our two selves —
His pleasure and my pain — why, pleasure
          him
By dying, nor such need to make a coil!
But this was worth an effort, that my pain
Should not become a snare, prove pain three-
          fold   1350
To other people — strangers — or unborn —
How should I know? I sought release from
          that —
I think, or else from — dare I say, some cause
Such as is put into a tree, which turns
Away from the north wind with what nest it
          holds —   1355
The woman said that trees so turn. Now,
          friend,
Tell me — because I cannot trust myself!
You are a man — what have I done amiss?"
You must conceive my answer — I forget —
Taken up wholly with the thought, per-
          haps,
This time she might have said — might, did
          not say —   1361

"You are a priest." She said "my friend."
                              Day wore,
We passed the places, somehow the calm went,
Again the restless eyes began to rove
In new fear of the foe mine could not see. 1365
She wandered in her mind — addressed me
          once
"Gaetano!" — that is not my name; whose
          name?
I grew alarmed, my head seemed turning too.
I quickened pace with promise now, now
          threat;
Bade drive and drive, nor any stopping more.
"Too deep i' the thick of the struggle, struggle
          through!   1371
Then drench her in repose though death's self
          pour
The plenitude of quiet — help us, God,
Whom the winds carry!"

                    Suddenly I saw
The old tower, and the little white-walled
          clump   1375
Of buildings and the cypress-tree or two —
"Already Castelnuovo — Rome!" I cried,
"As good as Rome — Rome is the next stage,
          think!
This is where travelers' hearts are wont to
          beat.
Say you are saved, sweet lady!" Up she
          woke.   1380
The sky was fierce with color from the sun
Setting. She screamed out, "No, I must not
          die!
Take me no farther, I should die; stay here!
I have more life to save than mine!"
                              She swooned.
We seemed safe; what was it foreboded so?
Out of the coach into the inn I bore   1386
The motionless and breathless pure and pale
Pompilia — bore her through a pitying group
And laid her on a couch, still calm and cured
By deep sleep of all woes at once. The host
Was urgent, "Let her stay an hour or two! 1391
Leave her to us, all will be right by morn!"
Oh, my foreboding! But I could not choose.
I paced the passage, kept watch all night long,
I listened — not one movement, not one sigh.
"Fear not; she sleeps so sound!" they said.
          But I   1396
Feared, all the same, kept fearing more and
          more,
Found myself throb with fear from head to
          foot,
Filled with a sense of such impending woe
That, at first pause of night, pretense of gray,

1327. **Lorenzo in Lucina**, the Church of San Lorenzo-
in-Lucina, in Rome. 1348. **coil**, fuss, confusion.

1367. **Gaetano.** This was the name of Pompilia's son;
he was named after St. Gaetan (1480-1547), founder of the
Order of Theatins. (See *Pompilia*, 99ff., p. 346.) 1377.
Castelnuovo, a village about fifteen miles from Rome.

I made my mind up it was morn. — "Reach
    Rome,   1401
Lest hell reach her! A dozen miles to make,
Another long breath, and we emerge!" I stood
I' the courtyard, roused the sleepy grooms.
"Have out
Carriage and horse, give haste, take gold!"
    said I.   1405
While they made ready in the doubtful
    morn —
'Twas the last minute — needs must I ascend
And break her sleep; I turned to go.
                And there
Faced me Count Guido, there posed the mean
    man
As master — took the field, encamped his
    rights,   1410
Challenged the world; there leered new tri-
    umph, there
Scowled the old malice in the visage bad
And black o' the scamp. Soon triumph sup-
    pled the tongue
A little, malice glued to his dry throat,
And he part howled, part hissed . . . oh, how
    he kept   1415
Well out o' the way, at arm's length and to
    spare! —
"My salutation to your priestship! What?
Matutinal, busy with book so soon
Of an April day that's damp as tears that
    now
Deluge Arezzo at its darling's flight? —   1420
'Tis unfair, wrongs feminity at large,
To let a single dame monopolize
A heart the whole sex claims, should share
    alike.
Therefore I overtake you, Canon! Come! 1424
The lady — could you leave her side so soon?
You have not yet experienced at her hands
My treatment; you lay down undrugged, I
    see!
Hence this alertness — hence no death-in-life
Like what held arms fast when she stole from
    mine.
To be sure, you took the solace and repose 1430
That first night at Foligno! — news abound
O' the road by this time — men regaled me
    much,
As past them I came halting after you,
Vulcan pursuing Mars, as poets sing —
Still at the last here pant I, but arrive,   1435
Vulcan — and not without my Cyclops too,
The Commissary and the unpoisoned arm
O' the Civil Force, should Mars turn mutineer.
Enough of fooling; capture the culprits, friend!

Here is the lover in the smart disguise   1440
With the sword — he is a priest, so mine lies
    still.
There upstairs hides my wife the runaway,
His leman; the two plotted, poisoned first,
Plundered me after, and eloped thus far
Where now you find them. Do your duty
    quick!   1445
Arrest and hold him! That's done; now catch
    her!"
During this speech of that man — well, I
    stood
Away, as he managed; still, I stood as near
The throat of him — with these two hands,
    my own —
As now I stand near yours, Sir — one quick
    spring,   1450
One great good satisfying gripe, and lo!
There had he lain abolished with his lie,
Creation purged o' the miscreate, man re-
    deemed,
A spittle wiped off from the face of God!
I, in some measure, seek a poor excuse   1455
For what I left undone, in just this fact
That my first feeling at the speech I quote
Was — not of what a blasphemy was dared,
Not what a bag of venomed purulence   1459
Was split and noisome — but how splendidly
Mirthful, how ludicrous a lie was launched!
Would Molière's self wish more than hear
    such man
Call, claim such woman for his own, his wife,
Even though, in due amazement at the boast,
He had stammered, she moreover was divine?
She to be his — were hardly less absurd   1466
Than that he took her name into his mouth,
Licked, and then let it go again, the beast,
Signed with his slaver. Oh, she poisoned him,
Plundered him, and the rest! Well, what I
    wished   1470
Was, that he would but go on, say once more
So to the world, and get his meed of men,
The fist's reply to the filth. And while I
    mused,
The minute, oh, the misery, was gone!
On either idle hand of me there stood   1475
Really an officer, nor laughed i' the least;
Nay, rendered justice to his reason, laid
Logic to heart, as 'twere submitted them
"Twice two makes four."
             "And now, catch her!" he cried.
That sobered me. "Let myself lead the way —
Ere you arrest me, who am somebody,   1481
Being, as you hear, a priest and privileged —
To the lady's chamber! I presume you —
    men

1418. **Matutinal,** early. 1434. **Vulcan . . . Mars.**
Vulcan was the blacksmith of the gods and the consort of
Venus, goddess of love. He objected to the love of Venus
for Mars, god of war. The story is told in the *Odyssey.*
1436. **Cyclops,** a race of giants said to have assisted in the
workshop of Vulcan under Mt. Etna.

1459. **purulence,** pus, matter. 1462. **Molière,** the great
French dramatist of the 17th century. Lines 1462-64 refer
to his play *Don Juan,* in which the libertine husband claims
Donna Elvire, the nun, as his wife.

Expert, instructed how to find out truth,
Familiar with the guise of guilt. Detect 1485
Guilt on her face when it meets mine, then
    judge
Between us and the mad dog howling there!"
Up we all went together; in they broke
O' the chamber late my chapel. There she
    lay,
Composed as when I laid her, that last eve,
O' the couch, still breathless, motionless,
    sleep's self,   1491
Wax-white, seraphic, saturate with the sun
O' the morning that now flooded from the
    front
And filled the window with a light like blood.
"Behold the poisoner, the adulteress —   1495
And feigning sleep too! Seize, bind!" Guido
    hissed.

She started up, stood erect, face to face
With the husband; back he fell, was but-
    tressed there
By the window all aflame with morning-red,
He the black figure, the opprobrious blur   1500
Against all peace and joy and light and life.
"Away from between me and hell!" she cried;
"Hell for me, no embracing any more!
I am God's, I love God, God — whose knees
    I clasp,
Whose utterly most just award I take,   1505
But bear no more love-making devils; hence!"
I may have made an effort to reach her side
From where I stood i' the doorway — any-
    how
I found the arms, I wanted, pinioned fast,
Was powerless in the clutch to left and right
O' the rabble pouring in, rascality   1511
Enlisted, rampant on the side of hearth,
Home and the husband — pay in prospect
    too!
They heaped themselves upon me. "Ha! —
    and him   1514
Also you outrage? Him, too, my sole friend,
Guardian, and savior? That I balk you of,
Since — see how God can help at last and
    worst!"
She sprang at the sword that hung beside him,
    seized,
Drew, brandished it (the sunrise burned for
    joy
O' the blade), "Die," cried she, "devil, in
    God's name!"   1520
Ah, but they all closed round her, twelve to
    one —
The unmanly men, no woman-mother made,
Spawned somehow! Dead-white and dis-
    armed she lay.
No matter for the sword, her word sufficed
To spike the coward through and through; he
    shook,   1525

Could only spit between the teeth — "You
    see?
You hear? Bear witness, then! Write down
    . . . but no —
Carry these criminals to the prison-house,
For first thing! I begin my search meanwhile
After the stolen effects, gold, jewels, plate, 1530
Money and clothes, they robbed me of and
    fled,
With no few amorous pieces, verse and prose,
I have much reason to expect to find."

When I saw that — no more than the first
    mad speech,
Made out the speaker mad and a laughing-
    stock,   1535
So neither did this next device explode
One listener's indignation — that a scribe
Did sit down; set himself to write indeed,
While sundry knaves began to peer and pry
In corner and hole — that Guido, wiping
    brow   1540
And getting him a countenance, was fast
Losing his fear, beginning to strut free
O' the stage of his exploit, snuff here, sniff
    there —
Then I took truth in, guessed sufficiently
The service for the moment. "What I say,
Slight at your peril! We are aliens here, 1546
My adversary and I, called noble both;
I am the nobler, and a name men know.
I could refer our cause to our own court
In our own country, but prefer appeal   1550
To the nearer jurisdiction. Being a priest,
Though in a secular garb — for reasons good
I shall adduce in due time to my peers —
I demand that the Church I serve, decide
Between us, right the slandered lady there. 1555
A Tuscan noble, I might claim the Duke;
A priest, I rather choose the Church — bid
    Rome
Cover the wronged with her inviolate shield."

There was no refusing this; they bore me off,
They bore her off, to separate cells o' the same
Ignoble prison, and, separate, thence to
    Rome.   1561
Pompilia's face, then and thus, looked on me
The last time in this life — not one sight since,
Never another sight to be! And yet
I thought I had saved her. I appealed to
    Rome;   1565
It seems I simply sent her to her death.
You tell me she is dying now, or dead;
I cannot bring myself to quite believe
This is a place you torture people in.
What if this your intelligence were just   1570
A subtlety, an honest wile to work
On a man at unawares? 'Twere worthy you.
No, Sirs, I cannot have the lady dead!

That erect form, flashing brow, fulgurant eye,
That voice immortal (oh, that voice of hers!),
That vision in the blood-red daybreak — that
Leap to life of the pale electric sword   1577
Angels go armed with — that was not the last
O' the lady! Come, I see through it, you
    find —
Know the maneuver! Also herself said   1580
I had saved her; do you dare say she spoke
    false?
Let me see for myself if it be so!
Though she were dying, a priest might be of
    use,
The more when he's a friend too — she called
    me
Far beyond "friend." Come, let me see her —
    indeed
It is my duty, being a priest; I hope   1586
I stand confessed, established, proved a priest?
My punishment had motive that, a priest
I, in a laic garb, a mundane mode,
Did what were harmlessly done otherwise.
I never touched her with my finger-tip   1591
Except to carry her to the couch, that eve,
Against my heart, beneath my head, bowed
    low,
As we priests carry the paten; that is why
— To get leave and go see her of your grace —
I have told you this whole story over again. 1596
Do I deserve grace? For I might lock lips,
Laugh at your jurisdiction; what have you
To do with me in the matter? I suppose
You hardly think I donned a bravo's dress
To have a hand in the new crime; on the old,
Judgment's delivered, penalty imposed,   1602
I was chained fast at Civita hand and foot —
She had only you to trust to, you and Rome,
Rome and the Church, and no pert meddling
    priest   1605
Two days ago, when Guido, with the right,
Hacked her to pieces. One might well be
    wroth;
I have been patient, done my best to help.
I come from Civita and punishment
As friend of the court — and for pure friend-
    ship's sake   1610
Have told my tale to the end — nay, not the
    end —
For, wait — I'll end — not leave you that
    excuse!

When we were parted — shall I go on there?
I was presently brought to Rome — yes, here
    I stood
Opposite yonder very crucifix —   1615
And there sat you and you, Sirs, quite the
    same.

I heard charge, and bore question, and told
    tale
Noted down in the book there — turn and see
If, by one jot or tittle, I vary now!
I' the color the tale takes, there's change per-
    haps;   1620
'Tis natural, since the sky is different,
Eclipse in the air now; still, the outline stays.
I showed you how it came to be my part
To save the lady. Then your clerk produced
Papers, a pack of stupid and impure   1625
Banalities called letters about love —
Love, indeed — I could teach who styled
    them so,
Better, I think, though priest and loveless
    both!
" — How was it that a wife, young, innocent,
And stranger to your person, wrote this
    page?" —   1630
" — She wrote it when the Holy Father wrote
The bestiality that posts through Rome,
Put in his mouth by Pasquin." "Nor per-
    haps
Did you return these answers, verse and prose,
Signed, sealed and sent the lady? There's
    your hand!"   1635
" — This precious piece of verse, I really
    judge,
Is meant to copy my own character,
A clumsy mimic; and this other prose,
Not so much even; both rank forgery.
Verse, quotha? Bembo's verse! When Saint
    John wrote   1640
The tract 'De Tribus,' I wrote this to match."
" —- How came it, then, the documents were
    found
At the inn on your departure?" — "I opine,
Because there were no documents to find
In my presence — you must hide before you
    find.   1645
Who forged them hardly practiced in my
    view;
Who found them waited till I turned my
    back."
" — And what of the clandestine visits paid,
Nocturnal passage in and out the house
With its lord absent? 'Tis alleged you
    climbed" . . .   1650
" — Flew on a broomstick to the man i' the
    moon!
Who witnessed or will testify this trash?"

1574. fulgurant, bright, flashing. 1594. paten, the plate
on which the sacred bread of the communion service is
carried.

1633. Pasquin, the Roman Pasquino, an imaginary person
to whom anonymous lampoons were ascribed. The name
was popularly given to a statue discovered in 1501 near the
shop of a man named Pasquino. Satires and lampoons
were frequently fastened to the statue, which had been set
up in Rome. 1637. character, handwriting. 1640. Bembo,
Cardinal Pietro Bembo (1470-1547), of Venice. He was a'
great scholar and an elegant writer of both prose and verse.
The reference is ironical. 1641. De Tribus, the title of a
blasphemous and legendary pamphlet entitled De Tribus
Impostoribus (The Three Impostors). It referred to Moses,
Christ, and Mahomet.

"— The trusty servant, Margherita's self,
Even she who brought you letters, you con-
    fess,
And, you confess, took letters in reply;   1655
Forget not we have knowledge of the facts!"
"— Sirs, who have knowledge of the facts,
    defray
The expenditure of wit I waste in vain,
Trying to find out just one fact of all!
She who brought letters from who could not
    write,   1660
And took back letters to who could not
    read —
Who was that messenger, of your charity?"
"— Well, so far favors you the circumstance
That this same messenger . . . how shall we
    say? . . .
Sub imputatione meretricis   1665
Laborat — which makes accusation null;
We waive this woman's. — Naught makes
    void the next.
Borsi, called Venerino, he who drove,
O' the first night when you fled away, at
    length
Deposes to your kissings in the coach,   1670
— Frequent, frenetic" . . . "When deposed
    he so?"
"After some weeks of sharp imprison-
    ment" . . .
"Granted by friend the Governor, I engage"—
"— For his participation in your flight!
At length his obduracy melting made   1675
The avowal mentioned" . . . "Was dismissed
    forthwith
To liberty, poor knave, for recompense.
Sirs, give what credit to the lie you can!
For me, no word in my defense I speak,
And God shall argue for the lady!"
                  So   1680
Did I stand question, and make answer, still
With the same result of smiling disbelief,
Polite impossibility of faith
In such affected virtue in a priest;
But a showing fair play, an indulgence, even,
To one no worse than others after all —   1686
Who had not brought disgrace to the order,
    played
Discreetly, ruffled gown nor ripped the cloth
In a bungling game at romps; I have told
    you, Sirs —
If I pretended simply to be pure,   1690
Honest, and Christian in the case — absurd!
As well go boast myself above the needs
O' the human nature, careless how meat
    smells,
Wine tastes — a saint above the smack! But
    once   1694

Abate my crest, own flaws i' the flesh, agree
To go with the herd, be hog no more nor less,
Why, hogs in common herd have common
    rights;
I must not be unduly borne upon,   1698
Who just romanced a little, sowed wild oats,
But 'scaped without a scandal, flagrant fault.
My name helped to a mirthful circumstance:
"Joseph" would do well to amend his plea;
Undoubtedly — some toying with the wife,
But as for ruffian violence and rape,   1704
Potiphar pressed too much on the other side!
The intrigue, the elopement, the disguise —
    well charged!
The letters and verse looked hardly like the
    truth.
Your apprehension was — of guilt enough
To be compatible with innocence,   1709
So, punished best a little and not too much.
Had I struck Guido Franceschini's face,
You had counseled me withdraw for my own
    sake,
Balk him of bravo-hiring. Friends came
    round,
Congratulated, "Nobody mistakes!
The pettiness o' the forfeiture defines   1715
The peccadillo: Guido gets his share;
His wife is free of husband and hook-nose,
The moldy viands and the mother-in-law.
To Civita with you and amuse the time,
Travesty us '*De Raptu Helenæ!*'   1720
A funny figure must the husband cut
When the wife makes him skip — too ticklish,
    eh?
Do it in Latin, not the Vulgar, then!
Scazons — we'll copy and send his Eminence.
Mind — one iambus in the final foot!   1725
He'll rectify it, be your friend for life!"
Oh, Sirs, depend on me for much new light
Thrown on the justice and religion here
By this proceeding, much fresh food for
    thought!

And I was just set down to study these   1730
In relegation, two short days ago,
Admiring how you read the rules, when, clap,
A thunder comes into my solitude —
I am caught up in a whirlwind and cast here,
Told of a sudden, in this room where so late
You dealt out law adroitly, that those
    scales,   1736

1665-1666. **Sub . . . Laborat**, labors under the imputation
of unchastity.   1671. **frenetic**, uncontrolled, passionate.
1694. above the smack, superior to the sense of taste.

1702-1705. **Joseph . . . Potiphar.** The story of Joseph
and Potiphar's wife is told in *Genesis*, 39. As the result of her
false report, Joseph was imprisoned. **1716. peccadillo**,
fault. **1720. De Raptu Helenæ,** *Of the Carrying off of
Helen* (of Troy); the title of a Greek poem by Coluthus (c.
500 A.D.). It is a bad imitation of Homer. **1723. Vulgar,**
common Italian. **1724. Scazon,** a line of verse consisting
of six feet; five are iambic and one (the last) is trochaic.
Caponsacchi is told to write an imperfect line, with an iambus
for the trochee so that the Cardinal may detect it, thus
proving his acumen.

I meekly bowed to, took my allotment from,
Guido has snatched at, broken in your hands,
Metes to himself the murder of his wife,.
Full measure, pressed down, running over
  now!   1740
Can I assist to an explanation? — Yes,
I rise in your esteem, sagacious Sirs,
Stand up a renderer of reasons, not
The officious priest would personate Saint
  George
For a mock Princess in undragoned days. 1745
What, the blood startles you? What, after all
The priest who needs must carry sword on
  thigh
May find imperative use for it? Then, there
  was
A Princess, was a dragon belching flame,
And should have been a Saint George also?
  Then,   1750
There might be worse schemes than to break
  the bonds
At Arezzo, lead her by the little hand,
Till she reached Rome, and let her try to live?
But you were law and gospel — would one
  please   1754
Stand back, allow your faculty elbow-room?
You blind guides who must needs lead eyes
  that see!
Fools, alike ignorant of man and God!
What was there here should have perplexed
  your wit
For a wink of the owl-eyes of you? How miss,
  then,
What's now forced on you by this flare of
  fact —   1760
As if Saint Peter failed to recognize
Nero as no apostle, John or James,
Till some one burned a martyr, made a torch
O' the blood and fat to show his features by!
Could you fail read this cartulary aright 1765
On head and front of Franceschini there —
Large-lettered like hell's masterpiece of
  print
That he, from the beginning pricked at heart
By some lust, letch of hate against his wife,
Plotted to plague her into overt sin   1770
And shame, would slay Pompilia body and
  soul,
And save his mean self — miserably caught
I' the quagmire of his own tricks, cheats, and
  lies?
— That himself wrote those papers — from
  himself

To himself — which, i' the name of me and
  her,   1775
His mistress-messenger gave her and me,
Touching us with such pustules of the soul
That she and I might take the taint, be shown
To the world and shuddered over, speckled
  so?
— That the agent put her sense into my
  words,   1780
Made substitution of the thing she hoped,
For the thing she had and held, its opposite,
While the husband in the background bit his
  lips
At each fresh failure of his precious plot?
— That when at the last we did rush each on
  each,   1785
By no chance but because God willed it so —
The spark of truth was struck from out our
  souls —
Made all of me, descried in the first glance,
Seem fair and honest and permissible love
O' the good and true — as the first glance told
  me   1790
There was no duty patent in the world
Like daring try be good and true myself,
Leaving the shows of things to the Lord of
  Show
And Prince o' the Power of the Air. Our very
  flight,
Even to its most ambiguous circumstance, 1795
Irrefragably proved how futile, false . . .
Why, men — men and not boys — boys and
  not babes —
Babes and not beasts — beasts and not stocks
  and stones! —
Had the liar's lie been true one pin-point
  speck,
Were I the accepted suitor, free o' the place,
Disposer of the time, to come at a call   1801
And go at a wink as who should say me nay —
What need of flight, what were the gain there-
  from
But just damnation, failure or success?
Damnation pure and simple to her the wife
And me the priest — who bartered private
  bliss   1806
For public reprobation, the safe shade
For the sunshine which men see to pelt me by;
What other advantage — we who led the days
And nights alone i' the house — was flight to
  find?   1810
In our whole journey did we stop an hour,
Diverge a foot from straight road till we
  reached
Or would have reached — but for that fate of
  ours —
The father and mother, in the eye of Rome,

1740. Full· measure . . . running over. From *Luke*,
6:38.—"Give and it shall be given unto you; good measure,
pressed down and shaken together, and running over, shall
men give into your bosom." 1744-1745. Saint George . . .
Princess. Saint George, the patron saint of England,
according to tradition killed a dragon in Lybia and rescued
the princess Sabra. 1762. Nero, a profligate and tyrannical
Roman emperor (54-68 A.D.) He persecuted the Christians.
1765. cartulary, a register. 1769. letch, passion.

1794. Prince . . . Air, a designation of Satan in *Ephesians*,
2:2.

The eye of yourselves we made aware of us
At the first fall of misfortune? And indeed
You did so far give sanction to our flight,   1817
Confirm its purpose, as lend helping hand,
Deliver up Pompilia not to him
She fled, but those the flight was ventured for.
Why then could you, who stopped short, not
    go on   1821
One poor step more, and justify the means,
Having allowed the end? — not see and say,
"Here's the exceptional conduct that should
    claim
To be exceptionally judged on rules   1825
Which, understood, make no exception here"
— Why play instead into the devil's hands
By dealing so ambiguously as gave
Guido the power to intervene like me,   1829
Prove one exception more? I saved his wife
Against law; against law he slays her now —
Deal with him!

           I have done with being judged.
I stand here guiltless in thought, word, and
    deed,
To the point that I apprise you — in con-
    tempt
For all misapprehending ignorance   1835
O' the human heart, much more the mind of
    Christ —
That I assuredly did bow, was blessed
By the revelation of Pompilia. There!
Such is the final fact I fling you, Sirs,
To mouth and mumble and misinterpret;
    there!   1840
"The priest's in love," have it the vulgar
    way!
Unpriest me, rend the rags o' the vestment,
    do —
Degrade deep, disenfranchise all you dare —
Remove me from the midst, no longer priest
And fit companion for the like of you —   1845
Your gay Abati with the well-turned leg
And rose i' the hat-rim, Canons, cross at neck
And silk mask in the pocket of the gown,
Brisk bishops with the world's musk still un-
    brushed
From the rochet; I'll no more of these good
    things.   1850
There's a crack somewhere, something that's
    unsound
I' the rattle!

         For Pompilia — be advised,
Build churches, go pray! You will find me
    there,
I know, if you come — and you will come, I
    know.

Why, there's a Judge weeping! Did not I
    say   1855
You were good and true at bottom? You see
    the truth —
I am glad I helped you; she helped me just so.

But for Count Guido — you must counsel
    there!
I bow my head, bend to the very dust,
Break myself up in shame of faultiness.   1860
I had him one whole moment, as I said --
As I remember, as will never out
O' the thoughts of me — I had him in arm's
    reach
There — as you stand, Sir, now you cease to
    sit —
I could have killed him ere he killed his wife,
And did not; he went off alive and well   1866
And then effected this last feat — through me!
Me — not through you — dismiss that fear!
    'Twas you
Hindered me staying here to save her — not
From leaving you and going back to him   1870
And doing service in Arezzo. Come,
Instruct me in procedure! I conceive —
In all due self-abasement might I speak —
How you will deal with Guido. Oh, not
    death!
Death, if it let her life be; otherwise   1875
Not death — your lights will teach you clear-
    er! I
Certainly have an instinct of my own
I' the matter; bear with me and weigh its
    worth!
Let us go away — leave Guido all alone
Back on the world again that knows him now!
I think he will be found (indulge so far!)   1881
Not to die so much as slide out of life,
Pushed by the general horror and common
    hate
Low, lower — left o' the very ledge of things,
I seem to see him catch convulsively   1885
One by one at all honest forms of life,
At reason, order, decency, and use —
To cramp him and get foothold by at least;
And still they disengage them from his clutch.
"What, you are he, then, had Pompilia once
And so forwent her? Take not up with
    us!"   1891
And thus I see him slowly and surely edged
Off all the table-land whence life upsprings
Aspiring to be immortality,
As the snake, hatched on hill-top by mis-
    chance,   1895
Despite his wriggling, slips, slides, slidders
    down
Hillside, lies low and prostrate on the smooth
Level of the outer place, lapsed in the vale.

1846. **Abati,** a name applied to all persons wearing ecclesiastical garb. 1850. **rochet.** See note on line 1243, p. 335.

1891. **forwent her,** gave her up.

So I lose Guido in the loneliness,
Silence, and dusk, till at the dole end,   1900
At the horizontal line, creation's verge,
From what just is to absolute nothingness —
Whom is it, straining onward still, he meets?
What other man deep further in the fate,
Who, turning at the prize of a footfall   1905
To flatter him and promise fellowship,
Discovers in the act a frightful face —
Judas, made monstrous by much solitude!
The two are at one now! Let them love their
    love
That bites and claws like hate, or hate their
    hate   1910
That mops and mows and makes as it were
    love!
There, let them each tear each in devil's-
    fun,
Or fondle this the other while malice aches —
Both teach, both learn detestability!
Kiss him the kiss, Iscariot! Pay that back,
That smatch o' the slaver blistering on your
    lip,   1916
By the better trick, the insult he spared
    Christ —
Lure him the lure o' the letters, Aretine!
Lick him o'er slimy-smooth with jelly-filth
O' the verse-and-prose pollution in love's
    guise!   1920
The cockatrice is with the basilisk!
There let them grapple, denizens o' the dark,
Foes or friends, but indissolubly bound,
In their one spot out of the ken of God
Or care of man, forever and evermore!   1925

Why, Sirs, what's this? Why, this is sorry
    and strange!
Futility, divagation; this from me
Bound to be rational, justify an act
Of sober man! — whereas, being moved so
    much,
I give you cause to doubt the lady's mind:
A pretty sarcasm for the world! I fear   1931
You do her wit injustice — all through me!
Like my fate all through — ineffective help!
A poor rash advocate I prove myself.
You might be angry with good cause; but sure
At the advocate — only at the undue zeal 1936
That spoils the force of his own plea, I think?
My part was just to tell you how things stand,
State facts and not be flustered at their fume.
But then 'tis a priest speaks; as for love —
    no!   1940
If you let buzz a vulgar fly like that
About your brains, as if I loved, forsooth,

Indeed, Sirs, you do wrong! We had no
    thought
Of such infatuation, she and I.
There are many points that prove it; do be
    just!   1945
I told you — at one little roadside-place
I spent a good half-hour, paced to and fro
The garden; just to leave her free awhile,
I plucked a handful of spring herb and bloom.
I might have sat beside her on the bench
Where the children were. I wish the thing
    had been,   1951
Indeed; the event could not be worse, you
    know —
One more half-hour of her saved! She's dead
    now, Sirs!
While I was running on at such a rate,
Friends should have plucked me by the sleeve;
    I went
Too much o' the trivial outside of her face 1956
And the purity that shone there — plain to
    me,
Not to you — what more natural? Nor am I
Infatuated — oh, I saw, be sure!
Her brow had not the right line — leaned too
    much,   1960
Painters would say — they like the straight-
    up Greek;
This seemed bent somewhat with an invisible
    crown
Of martyr and saint, not such as art approves.
And how the dark orbs dwelt deep under-
    neath,
Looked out of such a sad sweet heaven on me!
The lips, compressed a little, came forward
    too,   1966
Careful for a whole world of sin and pain.
That was the face, her husband makes his
    plea,
He sought just to disfigure — no offense
Beyond that! Sirs, let us be rational!   1970
He needs must vindicate his honor — aye,
Yet shirks, the coward, in a clown's disguise,
Away from the scene, endeavors to escape.
Now, had he done so, slain and left no trace
O' the slayer — what were vindicated, pray?
You had found his wife disfigured or a corpse,
For what and by whom? It is too palpable!
Then, here's another point involving law:
I use this argument to show you meant
No calumny against us by that title   1980
O' the sentence — liars try to twist it so;
What penalty it bore, I had to pay
Till further proof should follow of innocence—
Probationis ob defectum — proof?
How could you get proof without trying us?
You went through the preliminary form,   1986

1917. **the better trick**, i.e., spitting upon him, a common
form of insult. 1918. **Aretine**, man of Arezzo (addressed
to Guido). 1921. **cockatrice, basilisk.** These were both
fabulous monsters supposed to kill with a look. 1927.
divagation, digression.

1984. **Probationis ob defectum**, for want of sufficient
proof.

Stopped there, contrived this sentence to
    amuse
The adversary. If the title ran
For more than fault imputed and not proved,
That was a simple penman's error, else   1990
A slip i' the phrase — as when we say of you
"Charged with injustice" — which may either
    be
Or not be — 'tis a name that sticks mean-
    while.
Another relevant matter (fool that I am!) 1994
Not what I wish true, yet a point friends urge;
It is not true — yet, since friends think it
    helps):
She only tried me when some others failed —
Began with Conti, whom I told you of,
And Guillichini, Guido's kinsfolk both,   1999
And when abandoned by them, not before,
Turned to me. That's conclusive why she
    turned.
Much good they got by the happy cowardice!
Conti is dead, poisoned a month ago;
Does that much strike you as a sin? Not
    much,
After the present murder — one mark more
On the Moor's skin — what is black by
    blacker still?   2006
Conti had come here and told truth. And so
With Guillichini; he's condemned of course
To the galleys, as a friend in this affair,
Tried and condemned for no one thing i' the
    world,   2010
A fortnight since by who but the Governor?
The just judge, who refused Pompilia help
At first blush, being her husband's friend, you
    know.
There are two tales to suit the separate courts,
Arezzo and Rome: he tells you here, we fled
Alone, unhelped — lays stress on the main
    fault,   2016
The spiritual sin, Rome looks to; but else-
    where
He likes best we should break in, steal, bear
    off,
Be fit to brand and pillory and flog —
That's the charge goes to the heart of the
    Governor.   2020
If these unpriest me, you and I may yet
Converse, Vincenzo Marzi-Medici!
Oh, Sirs, there are worse men than you, I say!
More easily duped, I mean; this stupid lie,
Its liar never dared propound in Rome,   2025
He gets Arezzo to receive — nay more,

Gets Florence and the Duke to authorize!
This is their Rota's sentence, their Granduke
Signs and seals! Rome for me hencefor-
    ward — Rome,
Where better men are — most of all, that
    man   2030
The Augustinian of the Hospital,
Who writes the letter — he confessed, he says,
Many a dying person, never one
So sweet and true and pure and beautiful.
A good man! Will you make him Pope one
    day?   2035
Not that he is not good too, this we have —
But old — else he would have his word to
    speak,
His truth to teach the world. I thirst for
    truth,
But shall not drink it till I reach the source.

Sirs, I am quiet again. You see, we are   2040
So very pitiable, she and I,
Who had conceivably been otherwise.
Forget distemperature and idle heat!
Apart from truth's sake, what's to move so
    much?
Pompilia will be presently with God;   2045
I am, on earth, as good as out of it,
A relegated priest; when exile ends,
I mean to do my duty and live long.
She and I are mere strangers now; but priests
Should study passion — how else cure man-
    kind,   2050
Who come for help in passionate extremes?
I do but play with an imagined life
Of who, unfettered by a vow, unblessed
By the higher call — since you will have it
    so —
Leads it companioned by the woman there.
To live, and see her learn, and learn by
    her,   2056
Out of the low obscure and petty world —
Or only see one purpose and one will
Evolve themselves i' the world, change wrong
    to right;
To have to do with nothing but the true, 2060
The good, the eternal — and these, not alone
In the main current of the general life,
But small experiences of every day,
Concerns of the particular hearth and home;
To learn not only by a comet's rush   2065
But a rose's birth — not by the grandeur,
    God —
But the comfort, Christ. All this, how far
    away!

1988. **The adversary,** Guido. One of Browning's sources
states that the judges sent Caponsacchi to prison to give
"the Franceschini brothers satisfaction in their pressing
solicitations rather than because of the claims of justice."
2006. **the Moor's skin,** a reference to Othello the Moor, in
Shakespeare's *Othello,* who killed his wife Desdemona on a
charge of infidelity that later was shown to be false. 2022.
Vincenzo Marzi-Medici, the governor of Arezzo, before
whom the first trial was held.

2028. **Rota's sentence.** The Rota is an ecclesiastical
court that hears appeals. 2031. **The Augustinian . . .
Hospital,** Frà Celestino Angelo di Sant Anna, the Augustinian
monk who received the confession of Pompilia. The letter
is his deposition, given in a pamphlet describing the case.
This came into Browning's possession in London just before
he began writing the poem.

Mere delectation, meet for a minute's
 dream! —
Just as a drudging student trims his lamp,
Opens his Plutarch, puts him in the place 2070
Of Roman, Grecian; draws the patched gown
 close,
Dreams, "Thus should I fight, save or rule
 the world!"
Then smilingly, contentedly, awakes
To the old solitary nothingness.
So I, from such communion, pass content . . .

O great, just, good God! Miserable me! 2076

BOOK VII

POMPILIA

I am just seventeen years and five months old,
And, if I lived one day more, three full weeks;
'Tis writ so in the church's register,
Lorenzo in Lucina, all my names
At length, so many names for one poor child —
Francesca Camilla Vittoria Angela 6
Pompilia Comparini — laughable!
Also 'tis writ that I was married there
Four years ago; and they will add, I hope,
When they insert my death, a word or two —
Omitting all about the mode of death — 11
This, in its place, this which one cares to
 know —
That I had been a mother of a son
Exactly two weeks. It will be through grace
O' the Curate, not through any claim I have;
Because the boy was born at, so baptized 16
Close to, the Villa, in the proper church —
A pretty church, I say no word against,
Yet stranger-like — while this Lorenzo seems
My own particular place, I always say. 20
I used to wonder, when I stood scarce high
As the bed here, what the marble lion meant,
With half his body rushing from the wall,
Eating the figure of a prostrate man
(To the right, it is, of entry by the door) — 25
An ominous sign to one baptized like me,
Married, and to be buried there, I hope.
And they should add, to have my life com-
 plete,
He is a boy and Gaetan by name —
Gaetano, for a reason — if the friar 30

2070. **Plutarch.** Plutarch was a Greek biographer and
moralist of the first century. His chief work contains the
lives of Greek and Roman heroes.
 Pompilia. In this Book Pompilia tells the story of her
life as she lies dying in the hospital, where she was taken
after being attacked by Guido and left for dead. The date
is January 6, 1698.
 4. **Lorenzo in Lucina,** the Church of San Lorenzo-in-
Lucina, in Rome. 22-24. **marble lion . . . man.** A lion
preying upon a man symbolized the severity of the church
toward impenitents or disbelievers. 30. **for a reason.** See
lines 99-102.

Don Celestine will ask this grace for me
Of Curate Ottoboni. He it was
Baptized me; he remembers my whole life
As I do his gray hair.

     All these few things
I know are true — will you remember
 them? 35
Because time flies. The surgeon cared for me,
To count my wounds — twenty-two dagger-
 wounds,
Five deadly, but I do not suffer much —
Or too much pain — and am to die tonight.

Oh, how good God is that my babe was born —
Better than born, baptized and hid away 41
Before this happened, safe from being hurt!
That had been sin God could not well forgive;
He was too young to smile and save himself.
When they took, two days after he was born,
My babe away from me to be baptized 46
And hidden awhile, for fear his foe should
 find —
The country-woman, used to nursing babes,
Said, "Why take on so? where is the great
 loss?
These next three weeks he will but sleep and
 feed, 50
Only begin to smile at the month's end;
He would not know you, if you kept him here,
Sooner than that; so, spend three merry weeks
Snug in the Villa, getting strong and stout,
And then I bring him back to be your own, 55
And both of you may steal to — we know
 where!"
The month — there wants of it two weeks
 this day!
Still, I half fancied when I heard the knock
At the Villa in the dusk, it might prove she —
Come to say, "Since he smiles before the
 time, 60
Why should I cheat you out of one good hour?
Back I have brought him; speak to him and
 judge!"
Now I shall never see him; what is worse,
When he grows up and gets to be my age,
He will seem hardly more than a great
 boy; 65
And if he asks, "What was my mother like?"
People may answer, "Like girls of seven-
 teen" —
And how can he but think of this and that,
Lucias, Marias, Sofias, who titter or blush
When he regards them as such boys may do?
Therefore I wish someone will please to say 71
I looked already old though I was young;
Do I not — say, if you are by to speak —

31. **Don Celestine,** the monk who heard Pompilia's
confession.

Look nearer twenty? No more like, at least,
Girls who look arch or redden when boys
   laugh,   75
Than the poor Virgin that I used to know
At our street-corner in a lonely niche —
The babe, that sat upon her knees, broke
   off —
Thin white glazed clay, you pitied her the
   more.
She, not the gay ones, always got my rose. 80

How happy those are who know how to write!
Such could write what their son should read
   in time,
Had they a whole day to live out like me.
Also my name is not a common name,
"Pompilia," and may help to keep apart   85
A little the thing I am from what girls are.
But then how far away, how hard to find
Will anything about me have become,
Even if the boy bethink himself and ask!
No father that he ever knew at all,   90
Nor ever had—no, never had, I say!
That is the truth — nor any mother left,
Out of the little two weeks that she lived,
Fit for such memory as might assist;
As good too as no family, no name,   95
Not even poor old Pietro's name, nor hers,
Poor kind unwise Violante, since it seems
They must not be my parents any more.
That is why something put it in my head
To call the boy "Gaetano"—no old name   100
For sorrow's sake; I looked up to the sky
And took a new saint to begin anew.
One who has only been made saint — how
   long?
Twenty-five years; so, carefuller, perhaps,
To guard a namesake than those old saints
   grow,   105
Tired out by this time — see my own five
   saints!

On second thoughts, I hope he will regard
The history of me as what some one dreamed,
And get to disbelieve it at the last;
Since to myself it dwindles fast to that,   110
Sheer dreaming and impossibility —
Just in four days too! All the seventeen years,
Not once did a suspicion visit me
How very different a lot is mine
From any other woman's in the world.   115
The reason must be, 'twas by step and step
It got to grow so terrible and strange.
These strange woes stole on tiptoe, as it were,
Into my neighborhood and privacy,   119
Sat down where I sat, laid them where I lay;
And I was found familiarized with fear,

When friends broke in, held up a torch and
   cried,
"Why, you Pompilia in the cavern thus,
How comes that arm of yours about a wolf?
And the soft length — lies in and out your
   feet   125
And laps you round the knee — a snake it is!"
And so on.

      Well, and they are right enough,
By the torch they hold up now; for first,
   observe,
I never had a father — no, nor yet
A mother; my own boy can say at least,   130
"I had a mother whom I kept two weeks!"
Not I, who little used to doubt . . . I doubt
Good Pietro, kind Violante, gave me birth?
They loved me always as I love my babe 134
(Nearly so, that is — quite so could not be),
Did for me all I meant to do for him,
Till one surprising day, three years ago,
They both declared, at Rome, before some
   judge
In some court where the people flocked to
   hear,
That really I had never been their child, 140
Was a mere castaway, the careless crime
Of an unknown man, the crime and care too
   much
Of a woman known too well — little to these,
Therefore, of whom I was the flesh and blood;
What then to Pietro and Violante, both
No more my relatives than you or you?   145
Nothing to them! You know what they de-
   clared.

So with my husband — just such a surprise,
Such a mistake, in that relationship!   149
Everyone says that husbands love their wives,
Guard them and guide them, give them
   happiness;
'Tis duty, law, pleasure, religion. Well,
You see how much of this comes true in mine!
People indeed would fain have somehow
   proved
He was no husband; but he did not hear, 155
Or would not wait, and so has killed us all.
Then there is . . . only let me name one more!
There is the friend — men will not ask about,
But tell untruths of, and give nicknames to,
And think my lover, most surprise of all! 160
Do only hear, it is the priest they mean,
Giuseppe Caponsacchi: a priest — love,
And love me! Well, yet people think he did.
I am married, he has taken priestly vows, 164
They know that, and yet go on, say, the same,
"Yes, how he loves you!" "That was love"
   — they say,

<hr />

102. **a new saint,** St. Gaetan (1480-1547), who was canonized by Pope Clement X in 1671.   106. **my own five saints.**
She had five names (see lines 6-7).

155. **He . . . husband.**   Pompilia brought suit for divorce,
but it was never given a hearing.

When anything is answered that they ask;
Or else "No wonder you love him" — they
　　say.
Then they shake heads, pity much, scarcely
　　blame —
As if we neither of us lacked excuse,　170
And anyhow are punished to the full,
And downright love atones for everything!
Nay, I heard read out in the public court
Before the judge, in presence of my friends,
Letters 'twas said the priest had sent to me,
And other letters sent him by myself,　176
We being lovers!

　　　　　Listen what this is like!
When I was a mere child, my mother . . .
　　that's
Violante, you must let me call her so,　179
Nor waste time, trying to unlearn the word . . .
She brought a neighbor's child of my own
　　age
To play with me of rainy afternoons;
And, since there hung a tapestry on the wall,
We two agreed to find each other out
Among the figures. "Tisbe, that is you,　185
With half-moon on your hair-knot, spear in
　　hand,
Flying, but no wings, only the great scarf
Blown to a bluish rainbow at your back;
Call off your hound and leave the stag
　　alone!"
" — And there are you, Pompilia, such green
　　leaves　190
Flourishing out of your five finger-ends,
And all the rest of you so brown and rough;
Why is it you are turned a sort of tree?"
You know the figures never were ourselves,
Though we nicknamed them so. Thus, all
　　my life —　195
As well what was, as what, like this, was
　　not —
Looks old, fantastic, and impossible;
I touch a fairy thing that fades and fades.
— Even to my babe! I thought, when he
　　was born,
Something began for once that would not end,
Nor change into a laugh at me, but stay　201
Forevermore, eternally quite mine.
Well, so he is — but yet they bore him off,
The third day, lest my husband should lay
　　traps
And catch him, and by means of him catch
　　me.　205
Since they have saved him so, it was well
　　done;
Yet thence comes such confusion of what was

With what will be — that late seems long ago,
And, what years should bring round, already
　　come,
Till even he withdraws into a dream　210
As the rest do. I fancy him grown great,
Strong, stern, a tall young man who tutors
　　me,
Frowns with the others, "Poor imprudent
　　child!
Why did you venture out of the safe street?
Why go so far from help to that lone house?
Why open at the whisper and the knock?"　216

Six days ago when it was New Year's day,
We bent above the fire and talked of him,
What he should do when he was grown and
　　great.
Violante, Pietro, each had given the arm　220
I leant on, to walk by, from couch to chair
And fireside — laughed, as I lay safe at last,
"Pompilia's march from bed to board is made,
Pompilia back again and with a babe,
Shall one day lend his arm and help her
　　walk!"　225
Then we all wished each other more New
　　Years.
Pietro began to scheme — "Our cause is
　　gained;
The law is stronger than a wicked man —
Let him henceforth go his way, leave us ours!
We will avoid the city, tempt no more　230
The greedy ones by feasting and parade —
Live at the other villa, we know where,
Still farther off, and we can watch the babe
Grow fast in the good air; and wood is cheap
And wine sincere outside the city gate.　235
I still have two or three old friends will grope
Their way along the mere half-mile of road,
With staff and lantern on a moonless night
When one needs talk; they'll find me, never
　　fear,
And I'll find them a flask of the old sort
　　yet!"　240
Violante said, "You chatter like a crow;
Pompilia tires o' the tattle, and shall to bed.
Do not too much the first day — somewhat
　　more
Tomorrow, and, the next, begin the cape　244
And hood and coat! I have spun wool
　　enough."
Oh, what a happy friendly eve was that!

And, next day, about noon, out Pietro went —
He was so happy and would talk so much,　248
Until Violante pushed and laughed him forth
Sight-seeing in the cold — "So much to see
I' the churches! Swathe your throat three
　　times!" she cried,

---

189. **Call . . . alone.** This refers to a figure of Diana, goddess of the chase. 193. **you . . . tree,** a figure of Daphne, a beautiful nymph pursued by Apollo and changed into a laurel tree.

235. **sincere,** pure, unadulterated.

"And, above all, beware the slippery ways,
And bring us all the news by supper-time!"
He came back late, laid by cloak, staff, and
hat,
Powdered so thick with snow it made us
laugh; 255
Rolled a great log upon the ash o' the hearth,
And bade Violante treat us to a flask,
Because he had obeyed her faithfully,
Gone sight-see through the seven, and found
no church
To his mind like San Giovanni — "There's
the fold, 260
And all the sheep together, big as cats!
And such a shepherd, half the size of life,
Starts up and hears the angel" — when, at
the door,
A tap. We started up; you know the rest.

Pietro at least had done no harm, I know; 265
Nor even Violante, so much harm as makes
Such revenge lawful. Certainly she erred —
Did wrong, how shall I dare say otherwise? —
In telling that first falsehood, buying me
From my poor faulty mother at a price, 270
To pass off upon Pietro as his child.
If one babe take my babe, give him a name,
Say he was not Gaetano and my own,
But that some other woman made his mouth
And hands and feet — how very false were
that! 275
No good could come of that; and all harm
did.
Yet if a stranger were to represent,
"Needs must you either give your babe to me
And let me call him mine forevermore,
Or let your husband get him" — ah, my God,
That were a trial I refuse to face! 281
Well, just so here; it proved wrong but
seemed right
To poor Violante — for there lay, she said,
My poor real dying mother in her rags, 284
Who put me from her with the life and all,
Poverty, pain, shame, and disease at once,
To die the easier by what price I fetched —
Also (I hope) because I should be spared
Sorrow and sin — why may not that have
helped?
My father — he was no one, anyone — 290
The worse, the likelier — call him — he who
came,
Was wicked for his pleasure, went his way,
And left no trace to track by; there remained
Nothing but me, the unnecessary life,
To catch up or let fall — and yet a thing 295
She could make happy, be made happy with,
This poor Violante — who would frown there-
at?

Well, God, you see! God plants us where we
grow.
It is not that, because a bud is born
At a wild brier's end, full i' the wild beast's
way, 300
We ought to pluck and put it out of reach
On the oak-tree top — say, "There the bud
belongs!"
She thought, moreover, real lies were lies told
For harm's sake; whereas this had good at
heart, 304
Good for my mother, good for me, and good
For Pietro who was meant to love a babe,
And needed one to make his life of use,
Receive his house and land when he should
die.
Wrong, wrong, and always wrong! how plainly
wrong! 309
For see, this fault kept pricking, as faults do,
All the same at her heart. This falsehood
hatched,
She could not let it go nor keep it fast.
She told me so — the first time I was found
Locked in her arms once more after the pain,
When the nuns let me leave them and go
home, 315
And both of us cried all the cares away —
This it was set her on to make amends,
This brought about the marriage — simply
this!
Do let me speak for her you blame so much!
When Paul, my husband's brother, found me
out, 320
Heard there was wealth for who should marry
me,
So, came and made a speech to ask my hand
For Guido — she, instead of piercing straight
Through the pretense to the ignoble truth,
Fancied she saw God's very finger point, 325
Designate just the time for planting me
(The wild-brier slip she plucked to love and
wear)
In soil where I could strike real root, and
grow,
And get to be the thing I called myself; 329
For, wife and husband are one flesh, God says,
And I, whose parents seemed such and were
none,
Should in a husband have a husband now,
Find nothing, this time, but was what it
seemed —
All truth and no confusion any more.
I know she meant all good to me, all pain 335
To herself — since how could it be aught but
pain
To give me up, so, from her very breast,
The wilding flower-tree-branch that, all those
years,

---

259. the seven, the seven hills of Rome.

330. God says, in *Genesis*, 2:24, and in *Mark*, 10:8.

She had got used to feel for and find fixed?
She meant well; has it been so ill i' the main?
That is but fair to ask; one cannot judge   341
Of what has been the ill or well of life,
The day that one is dying — sorrows change
Into not altogether sorrow-like.
I do see strangeness but scarce misery,   345
Now it is over, and no danger more.
My child is safe; there seems not so much
    pain.
It comes, most like, that I am just absolved,
Purged of the past, the foul in me, washed
    fair —
One cannot both have and not have, you
    know —   350
Being right now, I am happy and color things.
Yes, everybody that leaves life sees all
Softened and bettered; so with other sights.
To me at least was never evening yet
But seemed far beautifuller than its day,   355
For past is past.

                There was a fancy came,
When somewhere, in the journey with my
    friend,
We stepped into a hovel to get food;
And there began a yelp here, a bark there —
Misunderstanding creatures that were wroth
And vexed themselves and us till we re-
    tired.
The hovel is life; no matter what dogs bit
Or cat scratched in the hovel I break from,
All outside is lone field, moon and such
    peace —
Flowing in, filling up as with a sea   365
Whereon comes Someone, walks fast on the
    white,
Jesus Christ's self, Don Celestine declares,
To meet me and calm all things back again.

Beside, up to my marriage, thirteen years 369
Were, each day, happy as the day was long;
This may have made the change too terrible.
I know that when Violante told me first
The cavalier — she meant to bring next
    morn,
Whom I must also let take, kiss my hand —
Would be at San Lorenzo the same eve   375
And marry me — which over, we should go
Home both of us without him as before,
And, till she bade speak, I must hold my
    tongue,
Such being the correct way with girl-brides,
From whom one word would make a father
    blush —   380
I know, I say, that when she told me this —
Well, I no more saw sense in what she said
Than a lamb does in people clipping wool;
Only lay down and let myself be clipped.
And when next day the cavalier who came 385

(Tisbe had told me that the slim young man
With wings at head, and wings at feet, and
    sword
Threatening a monster, in our tapestry,
Would eat a girl else — was a cavalier) — 389
When he proved Guido Franceschini — old
And nothing like so tall as I myself,
Hook-nosed and yellow in a bush of beard,
Much like a thing I saw on a boy's wrist,
He called an owl and used for catching
    birds —
And when he took my hand and made a
    smile —   395
Why, the uncomfortableness of it all
Seemed hardly more important in the case
Than — when one gives you, say, a coin to
    spend —
Its newness or its oldness; if the piece   399
Weigh properly and buy you what you wish,
No matter whether you get grime or glare!
Men take the coin, return you grapes and figs.
Here, marriage was the coin, a dirty piece
Would purchase me the praise of those I
    loved;
About what else should I concern myself?   405

So, hardly knowing what a husband meant,
I supposed this or any man would serve,
No whit the worse for being so uncouth;
For I was ill once and a doctor came
With a great ugly hat, no plume thereto, 410
Black jerkin and black buckles and black
    sword,
And white sharp beard over the ruff in front,
And, oh, so lean, so sour-faced and austere! —
Who felt my pulse, made me put out my
    tongue,
Then oped a phial, dripped a drop or two 415
Of a black bitter something — I was cured!
What mattered the fierce beard or the grim
    face?
It was the physic beautified the man,
Master Malpichi — never met his match 419
In Rome, they said — so ugly all the same!

However, I was hurried through a storm,
Next dark eve of December's deadest day —
How it rained! — through our street and the
    Lion's-mouth
And the bit of Corso — cloaked round, cov-
    ered close,   424
I was like something strange or contraband —
Into blank San Lorenzo, up the aisle,

386-388. **young man . . . monster,** a reference to Perseus, the hero in Greek mythology who rescued Andromeda,
the daughter of the king of Ethiopia, from a sea-monster.
419. **Master Malpichi,** probably Marcello Malpighi (1628-
94), a famous physician of Bologna. He became physician
to Pope Innocent XII in Rome in 1691. 423. **the Lion's-
mouth,** the name of a street in Rome, Via della Bocca di
Leone. 424. **Corso,** the principal thoroughfare of Rome.

My mother keeping hold of me so tight,
I fancied we were come to see a corpse
Before the altar which she pulled me toward.
There we found waiting an unpleasant priest,
Who proved the brother, not our parish
    friend,   431
But one with mischief-making mouth and eye,
Paul, whom I know since to my cost. And
    then
I heard the heavy church-door lock out help
Behind us; for the customary warmth,   435
Two tapers shivered on the altar. "Quick —
Lose no time!" cried the priest. And straight-
    way down
From . . . what's behind the altar where he
    hid —
Hawk-nose and yellowness and bush and all,
Stepped Guido, caught my hand, and there
    was I   440
O' the chancel, and the priest had opened
    book,
Read here and there, made me say that and
    this,
And after, told me I was now a wife,
Honored indeed, since Christ thus weds the
    Church,
And therefore turned he water into wine, 445
To show I should obey my spouse like Christ.
Then the two slipped aside and talked apart,
And I, silent and scared, got down again
And joined my mother, who was weeping now.
Nobody seemed to mind us any more,   450
And both of us on tiptoe found our way
To the door which was unlocked by this, and
    wide.
When we were in the street, the rain had
    stopped;
All things looked better. At our own house-
    door,
Violante whispered, "No one syllable   455
To Pietro! Girl-brides never breathe a word!"
" — Well treated to a wetting, draggle-tails!"
Laughed Pietro as he opened — "Very near
You made me brave the gutter's roaring sea
To carry off from roost old dove and young,
Trussed up in church, the cote, by me, the
    kite!   461
What do these priests mean, praying folk to
    death
On stormy afternoons, with Christmas close
To wash our sins off nor require the rain?"
Violante gave my hand a timely squeeze; 465
Madonna saved me from immodest speech.
I kissed him and was quiet, being a bride.

When I saw nothing more, the next three
    weeks,

Of Guido — "Nor the Church sees Christ,"
    thought I.
"Nothing is changed, however; wine is wine
And water only water in our house.   471
Nor did I see that ugly doctor since
That cure of the illness; just as I was cured,
I am married — neither scarecrow will re-
    turn."

Three weeks, I chuckled — "How would
    Giulia stare,   475
And Tecla smile and Tisbe laugh outright,
Were it not impudent for brides to talk!" —
Until one morning, as I sat and sang
At the broidery-frame alone i' the chamber —
    loud
Voices, two, three together, sobbings too, 480
And my name, "Guido," "Paolo," flung like
    stones
From each to the other! In I ran to see.
There stood the very Guido and the priest
With sly face — formal but nowise afraid —
While Pietro seemed all red and angry, scarce
Able to stutter out his wrath in words; 486
And this it was that made my mother sob,
As he reproached her — "You have murdered
    us,
Me and yourself and this our child beside!"
Then Guido interposed, "Murdered or not,
Be it enough your child is now my wife! 491
I claim and come to take her." Paul put in,
"Consider — kinsman, dare I term you so?
What is the good of your sagacity
Except to counsel in a strait like this?   495
I guarantee the parties man and wife
Whether you like or loathe it, bless or ban.
May spilt milk be put back within the
    bowl —
The done thing, undone? You, it is, we look
For counsel to, you fitliest will advise!   500
Since milk, though spilt and spoilt, does
    marble good,
Better we down on knees and scrub the floor,
Than sigh, 'the waste would make a syllabub!'
Help us so turn disaster to account,
So predispose the groom, he needs shall grace
The bride with favor from the very first,   506
Not begin marriage an embittered man!"
He smiled — the game so wholly in his hands!
While fast and faster sobbed Violante —
    "Aye,
All of us murdered, past averting now!   510
O my sin, O my secret!" and such like.

Then I began to half surmise the truth;
Something had happened, low, mean, under-
    hand,
False, and my mother was to blame, and I

---

445. **turned . . . wine.** This took place at the marriage
feast in Cana in Galilee; told in *John*, 2:1-10.

503. **syllabub**, a dish made by mixing wine with milk.

To pity, whom all spoke of, none addressed.
I was the chattel that had caused a crime.
I stood mute — those who tangled must untie
The embroilment. Pietro cried, "Withdraw,
    my child!
She is not helpful to the sacrifice   519
At this stage — do you want the victim by
While you discuss the value of her blood?
For her sake, I consent to hear you talk;
Go, child, and pray God help the innocent!"

I did go and was praying God, when came 524
Violante, with eyes swollen and red enough,
But movement on her mouth for make-believe
Matters were somehow getting right again.
She bade me sit down by her side and
    hear.
"You are too young and cannot understand,
Nor did your father understand at first. 530
I wished to benefit all three of us,
And when he failed to take my meaning —
    why,
I tried to have my way at unaware —
Obtained him the advantage he refused.
As if I put before him wholesome food   535
Instead of broken victual — he finds change
I' the viands, never cares to reason why,
But falls to blaming me, would fling the
    plate
From window, scandalize the neighborhood,
Even while he smacks his lips — men's way,
    my child!   540
But either you have prayed him unperverse
Or I have talked him back into his wits;
And Paolo was a help in time of need —
Guido, not much — my child, the way of
    men!
A priest is more a woman than a man,   545
And Paul did wonders to persuade. In short,
Yes, he was wrong, your father sees and says;
My scheme was worth attempting, and bears
    fruit —
Gives you a husband and a noble name,
A palace and no end of pleasant things. 550
What do you care about a handsome youth?
They are so volatile, and tease their wives!
This is the kind of man to keep the house.
We lose no daughter — gain a son, that's all;
For 'tis arranged we never separate,   555
Nor miss, in our gray time of life, the tints
Of you that color eve to match with morn.
In good or ill, we share and share alike,
And cast our lots into a common lap,
And all three die together as we lived!   560
Only, at Arezzo — that's a Tuscan town,
Not so large as this noisy Rome, no doubt,
But older far and finer much, say folk —
In a great palace where you will be queen,
Know the Archbishop and the Governor, 565
And we see homage done you ere we die.

Therefore, be good and pardon!" — "Pardon
    what?
You know things, I am very ignorant;
All is right if you only will not cry!"

And so an end! Because a blank begins 570
From when, at the word, she kissed me hard
    and hot,
And took me back to where my father leaned
Opposite Guido — who stood eying him,
As eyes the butcher the cast panting ox
That feels his fate is come, nor struggles
    more —   575
While Paul looked archly on, pricked brow
    at whiles
With the pen-point as to punish triumph
    there —
And said, "Count Guido, take your lawful
    wife
Until death part you!"

                        All since is one blank,
Over and ended; a terrific dream.   580
It is the good of dreams — so soon they go!
Wake in a horror of heart-beats, you may —
Cry, "The dread thing will never from my
    thoughts!"
Still, a few daylight doses of plain life,
Cock-crow and sparrow-chirp, or bleat and
    bell   585
Of goats that trot by, tinkling, to be milked;
And when you rub your eyes awake and wide,
Where is the harm o' the horror? Gone! So
    here.
I know I wake — but from what? Blank, I
    say!   590
This is the note of evil; for good lasts.
Even when Don Celestine bade, "Search and
    find!
For your soul's sake, remember what is past,
The better to forgive it" — all in vain!
What was fast getting indistinct before,
Vanished outright. By special grace perhaps,
Between that first calm and this last, four
    years   596
Vanish — one quarter of my life, you know.
I am held up, amid the nothingness,
By one or two truths only — thence I hang,
And there I live — the rest is death or dream,
All but those points of my support. I think
Of what I saw at Rome once in the Square
O' the Spaniards, opposite the Spanish House:
There was a foreigner had trained a goat,
A shuddering white woman of a beast,   605
To climb up, stand straight on a pile of sticks
Put close, which gave the creature room
    enough;

When she was settled there, he, one by one,
Took away all the sticks, left just the four
Whereon the little hoofs did really rest; 610
There she kept firm; all underneath was air.
So, what I hold by, are my prayer to God,
My hope, that came in answer to the pray-
    er,
Some hand would interpose and save me —
    hand
Which proved to be my friend's hand; and —
    blest bliss —   615
That fancy which began so faint at first,
That thrill of dawn's suffusion through my
    dark,
Which I perceive was promise of my child,
The light his unborn face sent long before —
God's way of breaking the good news to flesh.
That is all left now of those four bad years.
Don Celestine urged, "But remember more!
Other men's faults may help me find your
    own.
I need the cruelty exposed, explained,
Or how can I advise you to forgive?"   625
He thought I could not properly forgive
Unless I ceased forgetting — which is true;
For, bringing back reluctantly to mind
My husband's treatment of me — by a light
That's later than my lifetime, I review   630
And comprehend much and imagine more,
And have but little to forgive at last.
For now — be fair and say — is it not true
He was ill-used and cheated of his hope   634
To get enriched by marriage? Marriage gave
Me and no money, broke the compact so.
He had a right to ask me on those terms,
As Pietro and Violante to declare
They would not give me; so the bargain stood.
They broke it, and he felt himself aggrieved,
Became unkind with me to punish them. 641
They said 'twas he began deception first,
Nor, in one point whereto he pledged himself,
Kept promise; what of that, suppose it were?
Echoes die off, scarcely reverberate   645
Forever — why should ill keep echoing ill,
And never let our ears have done with noise?
Then my poor parents took the violent way
To thwart him — he must needs retaliate —
    wrong,
Wrong, and all wrong — better say, all blind!
As I myself was, that is sure, who else   651
Had understood the mystery; for his wife
Was bound in some sort to help somehow
    there.
It seems as if I might have interposed,
Blunted the edge of their resentment so, 655

Since he vexed me because they first vexed
    him;
"I will entreat them to desist, submit,
Give him the money and be poor in peace —
Certainly not go tell the world; perhaps   659
He will grow quiet with his gains."

                                    Yes, say
Something to this effect and you do well!
But then you have to see first; I was blind.
That is the fruit of all such wormy ways,
The indirect, the unapproved of God —   664
You cannot find their author's end and aim,
Not even to substitute your good for bad,
Your straight for the irregular; you stand
Stupefied, profitless, as cow or sheep
That miss a man's mind; anger him just twice
By trial at repairing the first fault.   670
Thus, when he blamed me, "You are a co-
    quette,
A lure-owl posturing to attract birds;
You look love-lures at theater and church,
In walk, at window!" — that, I knew, was
    false.
But why he charged me falsely, whither
    sought   675
To drive me by such charge — how could I
    know?
So, unaware, I only made things worse.
I tried to soothe him by abjuring walk,
Window, church, theater, for good and all, 679
As if he had been in earnest; that, you know,
Was nothing like the object of his charge.
Yes, when I got my maid to supplicate
The priest, whose name she read when she
    would read
Those feigned false letters I was forced to hear
Though I could read no word of — he should
    cease   685
Writing — nay, if he minded prayer of mine,
Cease from so much as even pass the street
Whereon our house looked — in my ignorance
I was just thwarting Guido's true intent; 689
Which was, to bring about a wicked change
Of sport to earnest, tempt a thoughtless man
To write indeed, and pass the house, and
    more,
Till both of us were taken in a crime.
He ought not to have wished me thus act lies,
Simulate folly; but — wrong or right, the
    wish —   695
I failed to apprehend its drift. How plain
It follows — if I fell into such fault,
He also may have overreached the mark,
Made mistake, by perversity of brain,
I' the whole sad strange plot, the grotesque
    intrigue   700
To make me and my friend unself ourselves,

630. That's . . . lifetime, that has come to me on my
deathbed. 642. began deception, i.e., by pretending that
his income was larger than it really was. 643. one point . . .
pledged himself, namely, to maintain Pietro and Violante
at Arezzo.

693. were, should be.

Be other man and woman than we were!
Think it out, you who have the time! for
   me —
I cannot say less; more I will not say.
Leave it to God to cover and undo!   705
Only, my dullness should not prove too much!
— Not prove that in a certain other point
Wherein my husband blamed me — and you
   blame,
If I interpret smiles and shakes of head —
I was dull too. Oh, if I dared but speak! 710
Must I speak? I am blamed that I forwent
A way to make my husband's favor come.
That is true; I was firm, withstood, re-
   fused . . .
— Women as you are, how can I find the
   words?

I felt there was just one thing Guido claimed
I had no right to give nor he to take,   716
We being in estrangement, soul from soul;
Till, when I sought help, the Archbishop
   smiled,
Inquiring into privacies of life —
Said I was blamable (he stands for God) —
Nowise entitled to exemption there.
Then I obeyed — as surely had obeyed
Were the injunction "Since your husband
   bids,
Swallow the burning coal he proffers you!"
But I did wrong, and he gave wrong advice,
Though he were thrice Archbishop — that, I
   know! —   726
Now I have got to die and see things clear.
Remember I was barely twelve years old —
A child at marriage. I was let alone
For weeks, I told you, lived my child-life still
Even at Arezzo, when I woke and found 731
First . . . but I need not think of that again —
Over and ended! Try and take the sense
Of what I signify, if it must be so.
After the first, my husband, for hate's sake,
Said one eve, when the simpler cruelty 736
Seemed somewhat dull at edge and fit to bear,
"We have been man and wife six months
   almost;
How long is this your comedy to last?
Go this night to my chamber, not your own!"
At which word, I did rush — most true the
   charge —   741
And gain the Archbishop's house — he stands
   for God —
And fall upon my knees and clasp his feet,
Praying him hinder what my estranged soul
Refused to bear, though patient of the rest.
"Place me within a convent," I implored —
"Let me henceforward lead the virgin life
You praise in Her you bid me imitate!"
What did he answer? "Folly of ignorance!
Know, daughter, circumstances make or mar

Virginity — 'tis virtue or 'tis vice.   751
That which was glory in the Mother of God
Had been, for instance, damnable in Eve,
Created to be mother of mankind.
Had Eve, in answer to her Maker's speech —
'Be fruitful, multiply, replenish earth' — 756
Pouted, 'But I choose rather to remain
Single' — why, she had spared herself forth-
   with
Further probation by the apple and snake,
Been pushed straight out of Paradise! For
   see —   760
If motherhood be qualified impure,
I catch you making God command Eve sin!
— A blasphemy so like these Molinists',
I must suspect you dip into their books."
Then he pursued, " 'Twas in your covenant!"

No! There my husband never used deceit.
He never did by speech nor act imply,
"Because of our souls' yearning that we meet
And mix in soul through flesh, which yours
   and mine
Wear and impress, and make their visible
   selves,   770
— All which means, for the love of you and
   me,
Let us become one flesh, being one soul!"
He only stipulated for the wealth;
Honest so far. But when he spoke as plain —
Dreadfully honest also — "Since our souls 775
Stand each from each, a whole world's width
   between,
Give me the fleshly vesture I can reach
And rend and leave just fit for hell to burn!"—
Why, in God's name, for Guido's soul's own
   sake
Imperiled by polluting mine — I say,   780
I did resist; would I had overcome!

My heart died out at the Archbishop's smile;
— It seemed so stale and worn a way o' the
   world,
As though 'twere nature frowning — "Here is
   spring,
The sun shines as he shone at Adam's fall, 785
The earth requires that warmth reach every-
   where;
What, must your patch of snow be saved for-
   sooth
Because you rather fancy snow than flowers?"
Something in this style he began with me.
Last he said, savagely for a good man,   790
"This explains why you call your husband
   harsh,
Harsh to you, harsh to whom you love. God's
   Bread!
The poor Count has to manage a mere child

756. **Be fruitful**, etc. Quoted from *Genesis*, 1:28. 763.
Molinists'. See *Caponsacchi*, 151, and note, p. 322.

Whose parents leave untaught the simplest
       things
Their duty was and privilege to teach — 795
Goodwives' instruction, gossips' lore; they
       laugh
And leave the Count the task — or leave it
       me!"
Then I resolved to tell a frightful thing.
"I am not ignorant — know what I say, 799
Declaring this is sought for hate, not love.
Sir, you may hear things like almighty God.
I tell you that my housemate, yes — the
       priest
My husband's brother, Canon Girolamo —
Has taught me what depraved and misnamed
       love   804
Means, and what outward signs denote the
       sin,
For he solicits me and says he loves,
The idle young priest with naught else to do.
My husband sees this, knows this, and lets be.
Is it your counsel I bear this beside?"
" — More scandal, and against a priest this
       time!   810
What, 'tis the Canon now?" — less snap-
       pishly —
"Rise up, my child, for such a child you are,
The rod were too advanced a punishment!
Let's try the honeyed cake. A parable!
'Without a parable spake he not to them.' 815
There was a ripe round long black toothsome
       fruit,
Even a flower-fig, the prime boast of May;
And, to the tree, said . . . either the spirit o'
       the fig,
Or, if we bring in men, the gardener,
Archbishop of the orchard — had I time 820
To try o' the two which fits in best; indeed
It might be the Creator's self, but then
The tree should bear an apple, I suppose —
Well, anyhow, one with authority said,
'Ripe fig, burst skin, regale the fig-pecker —
The bird whereof thou art a perquisite!' 826
'Nay,' with a flounce, replied the restif fig,
'I much prefer to keep my pulp myself;
He may go breakfastless and dinnerless,
Supperless of one crimson seed, for me!' 830
So, back she flopped into her bunch of leaves.
He flew off, left her — did the natural lord —
And lo, three hundred thousand bees and
       wasps   833
Found her out, feasted on her to the shuck.
Such gain the fig's that gave its bird no bite!
The moral — fools elude their proper lot,
Tempt other fools, get ruined all alike.
Therefore go home, embrace your husband
       quick!

Which if his Canon brother chance to see,
He will the sooner back to book again." 840

So, home I did go; so, the worst befell;
So, I had proof the Archbishop was just man,
And hardly that, and certainly no more.
For, miserable consequence to me,   844
My husband's hatred waxed nor waned at
       all,
His brother's boldness grew effrontery soon,
And my last stay and comfort in myself
Was forced from me; henceforth I looked to
       God
Only, nor cared my desecrated soul
Should have fair walls, gay windows for the
       world.   850
God's glimmer, that came through the ruin-
       top,
Was witness why all lights were quenched
       inside;
Henceforth I asked God counsel, not man-
       kind.

So, when I made the effort, freed myself,
They said — "No care to save appearance
       here!   855
How cynic — when, how wanton, were
       enough!"
— Adding, it all came of my mother's life —
My own real mother, whom I never knew,
Who did wrong (if she needs must have done
       wrong)   859
Through being all her life, not my four years,
At mercy of the hateful; every beast
O' the field was wont to break that fountain-
       fence,
Trample the silver into mud so murk
Heaven could not find itself reflected there.
Now they cry, "Out on her, who, plashy pool,
Bequeathed turbidity and bitterness   866
To the daughter-stream where Guido dipped
       and drank!"

Well, since she had to bear this brand — let
       me!
The rather do I understand her now —
From my experience of what hate calls love —
Much love might be in what their love called
       hate.
If she sold . . . what they call, sold . . . me,
       her child —
I shall believe she hoped in her poor heart
That I at least might try be good and pure,
Begin to live untempted, not go doomed 875
And done with ere once found in fault, as she.
O and, my mother, it all came to this?
Why should I trust those that speak ill of you,
When I mistrust who speaks even well of
       them?
Why, since all bound to do me good, did
       harm,   880

May not you, seeming as you harmed me
    most,
Have meant to do most good — and feed your
    child
From bramble-bush, whom not one orchard-
    tree
But drew bough back from, nor let one fruit
    fall?
This it was for you sacrificed your babe?
Gained just this, giving your heart's hope
    away
As I might give mine, loving it as you,
If . . . but that never could be asked of
    me!

There, enough! I have my support again, 889
Again the knowledge that my babe was, is,
Will be mine only. Him, by death, I give
Outright to God, without a further care —
But not to any parent in the world —
So to be safe; why is it we repine?
What guardianship were safer could we
    choose?   895
All human plans and projects come to naught;
My life, and what I know of other lives,
Prove that — no plan nor project! God shall
    care!

And now you are not tired? How patient
    then   899
All of you — oh yes, patient this long while
Listening, and understanding, I am sure!
Four days ago, when I was sound and well
And like to live, no one would understand.
People were kind, but smiled, "And what of
    him,
Your friend, whose tonsure the rich dark-
    brown hides?   905
There, there! — your lover, do we dream he
    was?
A priest too — never were such naughtiness!
Still, he thinks many a long think, never fear,
After the shy pale lady — lay so light
For a moment in his arms, the lucky one!" 910
And so on; wherefore should I blame you
    much?
So we are made, such difference in minds,
Such difference too in eyes that see the minds!
That man, you misinterpret and misprise —
The glory of his nature, I had thought,   915
Shot itself out in white light, blazed the truth
Through every atom of his act with me.
Yet where I point you, through the crystal
    shrine,
Purity in quintessence, one dew-drop,
You all descry a spider in the midst.   920
One says, "The head of it is plain to see,"
And one, "They are the feet by which I
    judge,"
All say, "Those films were spun by nothing
    else."

Then, I must lay my babe away with God,
Nor think of him again for gratitude.   925
Yes, my last breath shall wholly spend itself
In one attempt more to disperse the stain,
The mist from other breath fond mouths have
    made,
About a lustrous and pellucid soul;   929
So that, when I am gone but sorrow stays,
And people need assurance in their doubt
If God yet have a servant, man a friend,
The weak a savior, and the vile a foe —
Let him be present, by the name invoked,
Giuseppe-Maria Caponsacchi!

                                    There, 935
Strength comes already with the utterance!
I will remember once more for his sake
The sorrow; for he lives and is belied.
Could he be here, how he would speak for me!

I had been miserable three drear years   940
In that dread palace and lay passive now,
When I first learned there could be such a
    man.
Thus it fell: I was at a public play,
In the last days of Carnival last March,
Brought there I knew not why, but now
    know well.   945
My husband put me where I sat, in front;
Then crouched down, breathed cold through
    me from behind,
Stationed i' the shadow — none in front could
    see —
I, it was, faced the stranger-throng beneath,
The crowd with upturned faces, eyes one
    stare,   950
Voices one buzz. I looked but to the stage,
Whereon two lovers sang and interchanged,
"True life is only love, love only bliss:
I love thee — thee I love!" then they em-
    braced.   954
I looked thence to the ceiling and the walls —
Over the crowd, those voices and those eyes —
My thoughts went through the roof and out,
    to Rome
On wings of music, waft of measured words —
Set me down there, a happy child again,
Sure that tomorrow would be festa-day,   960
Hearing my parents praise past festas more,
And seeing they were old if I was young,
Yet wondering why they still would end dis-
    course
With "We must soon go, you abide your time,
And — might we haply see the proper friend
Throw his arm over you and make you safe!"

Sudden I saw him; into my lap there fell
A foolish twist of comfits, broke my dream
And brought me from the air and laid me low,
As ruined as the soaring bee that's reached 970
(So Pietro told me at the Villa once)

By the dust-handful. There the comfits lay;
I looked to see who flung them, and I faced
This Caponsacchi, looking up in turn.
Ere I could reason out why, I felt sure, 975
Whoever flung them, his was not the hand —
Up rose the round face and good-natured grin
Of one who, in effect, had played the prank,
From covert close beside the earnest face —
Fat waggish Conti, friend of all the world. 980
He was my husband's cousin, privileged
To throw the thing; the other, silent, grave,
Solemn almost, saw me, as I saw him.

There is a psalm Don Celestine recites,
"Had I a dove's wings, how I fain would
    flee!" 985
The psalm runs not "I hope, I pray for
    wings" —
Not "If wings fall from heaven, I fix them
    fast" —
Simply "How good it were to fly and rest,
Have hope now, and one day expect content!
How well to do what I shall never do!" 990
So I said, "Had there been a man like that,
To lift me with his strength out of all strife
Into the calm, how I could fly and rest!
I have a keeper in the garden here 994
Whose sole employment is to strike me low
If ever I, for solace, seek the sun.
Life means with me successful feigning death,
Lying stone-like, eluding notice so,
Forgoing here the turf and there the sky.
Suppose that man had been instead of this!"

Presently Conti laughed into my ear — 1001
Had tripped up to the raised place where I
    sat —
"Cousin, I flung them brutishly and hard!
Because you must be hurt, to look austere
As Caponsacchi yonder, my tall friend 1005
A-gazing now. Ah, Guido, you so close?
Keep on your knees, do! Beg her to forgive!
My cornet battered like a cannon-ball.
Good-by, I'm gone!" — nor waited the
    reply. 1009
That night at supper, out my husband broke,
"Why was that throwing, that buffoonery?
Do you think I am your dupe? What man
    would dare
Throw comfits in a stranger lady's lap?
'Twas knowledge of you bred such insolence
In Caponsacchi; he dared shoot the bolt, 1015
Using that Conti for his stalking-horse.
How could you see him this once and no more,
When he is always haunting hereabout

At the street-corner or the palace-side,
Publishing my shame and your impudence?
You are a wanton — I a dupe, you think?
O Christ, what hinders that I kill her quick?"
Whereat he drew his sword and feigned a
    thrust.

All this, now — being not so strange to me,
Used to such misconception day by day 1025
And broken-in to bear — I bore, this time,
More quietly than woman should perhaps;
Repeated the mere truth and held my tongue.

Then he said, "Since you play the ignorant,
I shall instruct you. This amour — com-
    menced 1030
Or finished or midway in act, all's one —
'Tis the town-talk; so my revenge shall be.
Does he presume because he is a priest? 1033
I warn him that the sword I wear shall pink
His lily-scented cassock through and through,
Next time I catch him underneath your
    eaves!" 1036
But he had threatened with the sword so oft
And, after all, not kept his promise. All
I said was, "Let God save the innocent!
Moreover, death is far from a bad fate. 1040
I shall go pray for you and me, not him;
And then I look to sleep, come death or,
    worse,
Life." So, I slept.

           There may have elapsed a week,
When Margherita — called my waiting-
    maid,
Whom it is said my husband found too fair —
Who stood and heard the charge and the
    reply, 1046
Who never once would let the matter rest
From that night forward, but rang changes
    still
On this the thrust and that the shame, and
    how
Good cause for jealousy cures jealous fools,
And what a paragon was this same priest
She talked about until I stopped my ears —
She said, "A week is gone; you comb your
    hair,
Then go mope in a corner, cheek on palm,
Till night comes round again — so, waste a
    week 1055
As if your husband menaced you in sport.
Have not I some acquaintance with his tricks?
Oh no, he did not stab the serving-man
Who made and sang the rimes about me once!
For why? They sent him to the wars next
    day. 1060
Nor poisoned he the foreigner, my friend,

---

981. **cousin.** The word is loosely used. His brother had
married Guido's sister. 985. **Had I . . . flee.** Cf. *Psalms,*
55:6.—"Oh, that I had wings like a dove! for then would I
fly away and be at rest." 1008. **cornet,** a piece of paper
twisted into the shape of a cone.

1034. **pink,** pierce.

Who wagered on the whiteness of my breast —
The swarth skins of our city in dispute;
For, though he paid me proper compli-
 ment,   1064
The Count well knew he was besotted with
Somebody else, a skin as black as ink
(As all the town knew save my foreigner) —
He found and wedded presently — 'Why need
Better revenge?' — the Count asked. But
 what's here?   1069
A priest that does not fight, and cannot wed,
Yet must be dealt with! If the Count took
 fire
For the poor pastime of a minute — me —
What were the conflagration for yourself,
Countess and lady-wife and all the rest? 1074
The priest will perish; you will grieve too late.
So shall the city-ladies' handsomest,
Frankest, and liberalest gentleman
Die for you, to appease a scurvy dog
Hanging's too good for. Is there no escape?
Were it not simple Christian charity 1080
To warn the priest be on his guard — save
 him
Assured death, save yourself from causing it?
I meet him in the street. Give me a glove,
A ring to show for token! Mum's the
 word!"   1084
I answered, "If you were, as styled, my maid,
I would command you; as you are, you say,
My husband's intimate — assist his wife,
Who can do nothing but entreat 'Be still!'
Even if you speak truth and a crime is
 planned,
Leave help to God as I am forced to do! 1090
There is no other help, or we should craze,
Seeing such evil with no human cure.
Reflect that God, who makes the storm de-
 sist,
Can make an angry violent heart subside.
Why should we venture teach him govern-
 ance?   1095
Never address me on this subject more!"

Next night she said, "But I went, all the
 same —
Aye, saw your Caponsacchi in his house,
And come back stuffed with news I must out-
 pour.
I told him, 'Sir, my mistress is a stone; 1100
Why should you harm her for no good you
 get?
For you do harm her — prowl about our
 place,
With the Count never distant half the street,
Lurking at every corner, would you look! 1104
'Tis certain she has witched you with a spell.
Are there not other beauties at your beck?
We all know, Donna This and Monna That
Die for a glance of yours, yet here you gaze!

Go make them grateful, leave the stone its
 cold!'
And he — oh, he turned first white and then
 red,   1110
And then — 'To her behest I bow myself,
Whom I love with my body and my soul;
Only a word i' the bowing! See, I write
One little word, no harm to see or hear!
Then, fear no further!' This is what he
 wrote.   1115
I know you cannot read — therefore, let me!
'My idol!' " . . .

      But I took it from her hand
And tore it into shreds. "Why, join the rest
Who harm me? Have I ever done you
 wrong?
People have told me 'tis you wrong myself;
Let it suffice I either feel no wrong 1121
Or else forgive it — yet you turn my foe!
The others hunt me, and you throw a noose!"

She muttered, "Have your willful way!" I
 slept.   1124

Whereupon . . . no, I leave my husband out!
It is not to do him more hurt, I speak.
Let it suffice, when misery was most,
One day, I swooned and got a respite so.
She stooped as I was slowly coming to.
This Margherita, ever on my trace, 1130
And whispered — "Caponsacchi!"

        If I drowned,
But woke afloat i' the wave with upturned
 eyes,
And found their first sight was a star! I
 turned —
For the first time, I let her have her will,
Heard passively — "The imposthume at such
 head,   1135
One touch, one lancet-puncture would re-
 lieve —
And still no glance the good physician's way
Who rids you of the torment in a trice!
Still he writes letters you refuse to hear. 1139
He may prevent your husband, kill himself,
So desperate and all fordone is he!
Just hear the pretty verse he made today!
A sonnet from Mirtillo. 'Peerless fair. . . .'
All poetry is difficult to read —
The sense of it is, anyhow, he seeks 1145
Leave to contrive you an escape from hell,
And for that purpose asks an interview.
I can write, I can grant it in your name,
Or, what is better, lead you to his house.
Your husband dashes you against the stones—

1135. **imposthume**, abscess. 1140. **prevent**, anticipate.
1143. **Mirtillo.** One of the letters introduced at the trial
was signed "Mirtillo." See *Caponsacchi*, 551, and note, p. 327.

This man would place each fragment in a
  shrine;   1151
You hate him, love your husband!"

        I returned,
"It is not true I love my husband — no,
Nor hate this man. I listen while you speak —
Assured that what you say is false, the same;
Much as when once, to me a little child, 1156
A rough gaunt man in rags, with eyes on fire,
A crowd of boys and idlers at his heels,
Rushed as I crossed the Square, and held my
  head
In his two hands, 'Here's she will let me
  speak!   1160
You little girl, whose eyes do good to mine,
I am the Pope, am Sextus, now the Sixth;
And that Twelfth Innocent, proclaimed today,
Is Lucifer disguised in human flesh!
The angels, met in conclave, crowned me!' —
  thus   1165
He gibbered and I listened; but I knew
All was delusion, ere folk interposed,
'Unfasten him, the maniac!' Thus I know
All your report of Caponsacchi false,
Folly or dreaming. I have seen so much 1170
By that adventure at the spectacle,
The face I fronted that one first, last time;
He would belie it by such words and thoughts.
Therefore while you profess to show him me,
I ever see his own face. Get you gone!" 1175

" — That will I, nor once open mouth again —
No, by Saint Joseph and the Holy Ghost!
On your head be the damage, so adieu!"

And so more days, more deeds I must forget,
Till . . . what a strange thing now is to de-
  clare!   1180
Since I say anything, say all if true!
And how my life seems lengthened as to serve!
It may be idle or inopportune,
But, true? — why, what was all I said but
  truth,   1184
Even when I found that such as are untrue
Could only take the truth in through a lie?
Now — I am speaking truth to the Truth's
  self;
God will lend credit to my words this time.

It had got half through April. I arose 1189
One vivid daybreak — who had gone to bed
In the old way my wont those last three
  years,
Careless until, the cup drained, I should die.
The last sound in my ear, the over-night,
Had been a something let drop on the sly

In prattle by Margherita, "Soon enough 1195
Gayeties end, now Easter's past; a week,
And the Archbishop gets him back to Rome —
Everyone leaves the town for Rome, this
  spring —
Even Caponsacchi, out of heart and hope, 1199
Resigns himself and follows with the flock."
I heard this drop and drop like rain outside
Fast-falling through the darkness while she
  spoke;
So had I heard with like indifference,
"And Michael's pair of wings will arrive first
At Rome, to introduce the company, 1205
And bear him from our picture where he fights
Satan — expect to have that dragon loose
And never a defender!" — my sole thought
Being still, as night came, "Done, another
  day!   1209
How good to sleep and so get nearer death!"—
When, what, first thing at daybreak, pierced
  the sleep
With a summons to me? Up I sprang alive,
Light in me, light without me, everywhere
Change! A broad yellow sunbeam was let
  fall
From heaven to earth — a sudden drawbridge
  lay,   1215
Along which marched a myriad merry motes,
Mocking the flies that crossed them and re-
  crossed
In rival dance, companions new-born too.
On the house-eaves, a dripping shag of weed
Shook diamonds on each dull gray lattice-
  square,   1220
As first one, then another bird leapt by,
And light was off, and, lo, was back again,
Always with one voice — where are two such
  joys? —
The blessed building-sparrow! I stepped
  forth,
Stood on the terrace — o'er the roofs, such
  sky!   1225
My heart sang, "I too am to go away,
I too have something I must care about,
Carry away with me to Rome, to Rome!
The bird brings hither sticks and hairs and
  wool,
And nowhere else i' the world; what fly breaks
  rank,   1230
Falls out of the procession that befits,
From window here to window there, with all
The world to choose — so well he knows his
  course?
I have my purpose and my motive too,
My march to Rome, like any bird or fly! 1235
Had I been dead! How right to be alive!
Last night I almost prayed for leave to die,

1163. **that Twelfth Innocent, proclaimed today.**
Innocent XII (1615-1700) was proclaimed pope on July 12,
1691. There has never been a Pope Sextus (the Sixth).

1204-1208. **And Michael's . . . defender.** Lines 1204-
1208 refer to a fresco in the Church of San Francesco at
Arezzo.

Wished Guido all his pleasure with the sword
Or the poison — poison, sword, was but a
    trick,   1239
Harmless, may God forgive him the poor jest!
My life is charmed, will last till I reach Rome!
Yesterday, but for the sin — ah, nameless
    be
The deed I could have dared against myself!
Now — see if I will touch an unripe fruit, 1244
And risk the health I want to have and use!
Not to live, now, would be the wickedness —
For life means to make haste and go to Rome
And leave Arezzo, leave all woes at once!"

Now, understand here, by no means mistake!
Long ago had I tried to leave that house 1250
When it seemed such procedure would stop
    sin;
And still failed more the more I tried — at
    first
The Archbishop, as I told you; next, our lord
The Governor — indeed I found my way;
I went to the great palace where he rules, 1255
Though I knew well 'twas he who — when I
    gave
A jewel or two, themselves had given me,
Back to my parents — since they wanted
    bread,
They who had never let me want a nosegay
    — he
Spoke of the jail for felons, if they kept 1260
What was first theirs, then mine, so doubly
    theirs,
Though all the while my husband's most of
    all!
I knew well who had spoke the word wrought
    this;
Yet, being in extremity, I fled
To the Governor, as I say — scarce opened
    lip   1265
When — the cold cruel snicker close behind —
Guido was on my trace, already there,
Exchanging nod and wink for shrug and smile,
And I — pushed back to him and, for my
    pains,
Paid with . . . but why remember what is
    past?   1270
I sought out a poor friar the people call
The Roman, and confessed my sin which came
Of their sin — that fact could not be re-
    pressed —
The frightfulness of my despair in God;
And feeling, through the grate, his horror
    shake,   1275
Implored him, "Write for me who cannot
    write,
Apprise my parents, make them rescue me!
You bid me be courageous and trust God.

Do you in turn dare somewhat, trust and
    write,
'Dear friends, who used to be my parents
    once,   1280
And now declare you have no part in me,
This is some riddle I want wit to solve,
Since you must love me with no difference.
Even suppose you altered — there's your hate,
To ask for; hate of you two dearest ones 1285
I shall find liker love than love found here,
If husbands love their wives. Take me away
And hate me as you do the gnats and fleas,
Even the scorpions! How I shall rejoice!'
Write that and save me!" And he promised
    — wrote   1290
Or did not write; things never changed at all.
He was not like the Augustinian here!
Last, in a desperation, I appealed
To friends, whoever wished me better days,
To Guillichini, that's of kin — "What, I —
Travel to Rome with you? A flying gout 1296
Bids me deny my heart and mind my leg!"
Then I tried Conti, used to brave — laugh
    back
The louring thunder when his cousin scowled
At me protected by his presence: "You —
Who well know what you cannot save me
    from —   1301
Carry me off! What frightens you, a priest?"
He shook his head, looked grave — "Above
    my strength!
Guido has claws that scratch, shows feline
    teeth;
A formidabler foe than I dare fret —   1305
Give me a dog to deal with, twice the size!
Of course I am a priest and Canon too,
But . . . by the bye . . . though both, not
    quite so bold
As he, my fellow-Canon, brother-priest,
The personage in such ill odor here   1310
Because of the reports — pure birth o' the
    brain!
Our Caponsacchi, he's your true Saint George
To slay the monster, set the Princess free,
And have the whole High-Altar to himself.
I always think so when I see that piece 1315
I' the Pieve (that's his church and mine, you
    know),
Though you drop eyes at mention of his
    name!"

That name had got to take a half-grotesque,
Half-ominous, wholly enigmatic sense,
Like any by-word, broken bit of song   1320

1263. **who had spoke.** It was Guido.

1292. **He was . . . here.** See *Caponsacchi*, 2031, and note,
p. 344. 1295. **That's of kin.** He was related to Guido.
1312-1313. **Saint George . . . free.** See note on lines 1744-
1745, p. 341. 1315. **that piece**, a picture of St. George killing the dragon, by Giorgio Vasari (an Italian painter of the
16th century). It is at the high altar of the church of S.
Maria della Pieve, in Arezzo.

Born with a meaning, changed by mouth and
   mouth
That mix it in a sneer or smile, as chance
Bids, till it now means naught but ugliness
And perhaps shame.

             — All this intends to say,
That, over-night, the notion of escape   1325
Had seemed distemper, dreaming; and the
   name —
Not the man, but the name of him, thus made
Into a mockery and disgrace — why, she
Who uttered it persistently, had laughed,
"I name his name, and there you start and
   wince   1330
As criminal from the red tongs' touch!" —
   yet now,
Now, as I stood letting morn bathe me bright,
Choosing which butterfly should bear my
   news —
The white, the brown one, or that tinier
   blue —
The Margherita, I detested so,   1335
In she came — "The fine day, the good
   spring time!
What, up and out at window? That is best.
No thought of Caponsacchi? — who stood
   there
All night on one leg, like the sentry crane,
Under the pelting of your water-spout — 1340
Looked last look at your lattice ere he leave
Our city, bury his dead hope at Rome.
Aye, go to looking-glass and make you fine,
While he may die ere touch one least loose
   hair   1344
You drag at with the comb in such a rage!"

I turned — "Tell Caponsacchi he may come!"

"Tell him to come? Ah, but, for charity,
A truce to fooling! Come? What — come
   this eve?
Peter and Paul! But I see through the trick!
Yes, come, and take a flower-pot on his head,
Flung from your terrace! No joke, sincere
   truth?"   1351

How plainly I perceived hell flash and fade
O' the face of her — the doubt that first paled
   joy,
Then, final reassurance I indeed
Was caught now, never to be free again! 1355
What did I care? — who felt myself of force
To play with silk, and spurn the horsehair-
   springe.

"But — do you know that I have bade him
   come,   1358

1357. horsehair-springe, a trap made of horsehair.

And in your own name? I presumed so much,
Knowing the thing you needed in your heart.
But somehow — what had I to show in proof?
He would not come: half-promised, that was
   all,
And wrote the letters you refused to read.
What is the message that shall move him
   now?"

"After the Ave Maria, at first dark,   1365
I will be standing on the terrace, say!"

"I would I had a good long lock of hair
Should prove I was not lying! Never mind!"

Off she went — "May he not refuse, that's
   all —   1369
Fearing a trick!"

           I answered, "He will come."
And, all day, I sent prayer like incense up
To God the strong, God the beneficent,
God ever mindful in all strife and strait,
Who, for our own good, makes the need ex-
   treme,   1374
Till at the last he puts forth might and saves.
An old rime came into my head and rang
Of how a virgin, for the faith of God,
Hid herself, from the Paynims that pursued,
In a cave's heart; until a thunderstone, 1379
Wrapped in a flame, revealed the couch and
   prey;
And they laughed — "Thanks to lightning,
   ours at last!"
And she cried, "Wrath of God, assert his
   love!
Servant of God, thou fire, befriend his child!"
And lo, the fire she grasped at, fixed its
   flash,   1384
Lay in her hand a calm, cold, dreadful sword
She brandished till pursuers strewed the
   ground,
So did the souls within them die away,
As o'er the prostrate bodies, sworded, safe,
She walked forth to the solitudes and Christ:
So should I grasp the lightning and be saved!

And still, as the day wore, the trouble grew
Whereby I guessed there would be born a
   star,
Until at an intense throe of the dusk,   1393
I started up, was pushed, I dare to say,
Out on the terrace, leaned and looked at last
Where the deliverer waited me — the same
Silent and solemn face, I first descried
At the spectacle, confronted mine once more.

1365. Ave Maria, the evening prayer, which begins with
these words, meaning Hail Mary. 1378. Paynims, pagans.
1379. thunderstone, a stone supposed to be the material part of lightning.

So was that minute twice vouchsafed me,
so
The manhood, wasted then, was still at watch
To save me yet a second time: no change 1401
Here, though all else changed in the changing
world!

I spoke on the instant, as my duty bade,
In some such sense as this, whatever the
phrase,

"Friend, foolish words were borne from you
to me; 1405
Your soul behind them is the pure strong
wind,
Not dust and feathers which its breath may
bear.
These to the witless seem the wind itself,
Since proving thus the first of it they feel. 1409
If by mischance you blew offense my way,
The straws are dropped, the wind desists no
whit,
And how such strays were caught up in the
street
And took a motion from you, why inquire?
I speak to the strong soul, no weak disguise.
If it be truth — why should I doubt it
truth? — 1415
You serve God specially, as priests are bound,
And care about me, stranger as I am,
So far as wish my good, that—miracle
I take to intimate he wills you serve
By saving me—what else can he direct? 1420
Here is the service. Since a long while now,
I am in course of being put to death;
While death concerned nothing but me, I
bowed
The head and bade, in heart, my husband
strike.
Now I imperil something more, it seems, 1425
Something that's trulier me than this myself,
Something I trust in God and you to save.
You go to Rome, they tell me: take me there;
Put me back with my people!"

He replied —
The first word I heard ever from his lips, 1430
All himself in it — an eternity
Of speech, to match the immeasurable depth
O' the soul that then broke silence — "I am
yours."

So did the star rise, soon to lead my step,1434
Lead on, nor pause before it should stand still
Above the House o' the Babe — my babe to
be,
That knew me first and thus made me know
him,
That had his right of life and claim on mine,
And would not let me die till he was born, 1439

But pricked me at the heart to save us both,
Saying, "Have you the will? Leave God the
way!"
And the way was Caponsacchi — "mine,"
thank God!
He was mine, he is mine, he will be mine. 1443

No pause i' the leading and the light! I know,
Next night there was a cloud came, and not
he,
But I prayed through the darkness till it
broke
And let him shine. The second night, he
came.

"The plan is rash; the project desperate.
In such a flight needs must I risk your life,
Give food for falsehood, folly or mistake, 1450
Ground for your husband's rancor and re-
venge" —
So he began again, with the same face.
I felt that, the same loyalty — one star
Turning now red that was so white before —
One service apprehended newly; just 1455
A word of mine and there the white was back!

"No, friend, for you will take me! 'Tis your-
self
Risk all, not I — who let you, for I trust
In the compensating great God; enough!
I know you; when is it that you will come?"

"Tomorrow at the day's dawn." Then I
heard 1461
What I should do: how to prepare for flight
And where to fly.

That night my husband bade
" — You, whom I loathe, beware you break
my sleep
This whole night! Couch beside me like the
corpse 1465
I would you were!" The rest you know, I
think —
How I found Caponsacchi and escaped.

And this man, men call sinner? Jesus Christ!
Of whom men said, with mouths Thyself
mad'st once, 1469
"He hath a devil" — say he was Thy saint,
My Caponsacchi! Shield and show — un-
shroud
In Thine own time the glory of the soul
If aught obscure — if ink-spot, from vile pens
Scribbling a charge against him (I was glad
Then, for the first time, that I could not
write) — 1475
Flirted his way, have flecked the blaze!

1470. **He hath a devil,** Jesus is so referred to in *John*
7:20 and 8:48 by people who disliked his teachings.

For me,
'Tis otherwise; let men take, sift my
        thoughts —
Thoughts I throw like the flax for sun to
        bleach!   1478
I did pray, do pray, in the prayer shall die,
"Oh, to have Caponsacchi for my guide!"
Ever the face upturned to mine, the hand
Holding my hand across the world — a sense
That reads, as only such can read, the mark
God sets on woman, signifying so   1484
She should — shall peradventure — be divine;
Yet 'ware, the while, how weakness mars the
        print
And makes confusion, leaves the thing men
        see —
Not this man sees — who from his soul, re-
        writes
The obliterated charter — love and strength
Mending what's marred. "So kneels a vo-
        tarist,   1490
Weeds some poor waste traditionary plot
Where shrine once was, where temple yet
        may be,
Purging the place but worshiping the while,
By faith and not by sight, sight clearest so —
Such way the saints work" — says Don Ce-
        lestine.   1495
But I, not privileged to see a saint
Of old when such walked earth with crown
        and palm,
If I call "saint" what saints call something
        else —
The saints must bear with me, impute the
        fault   1499
To a soul i' the bud, so starved by ignorance,
Stinted of warmth, it will not blow this year
Nor recognize the orb which spring-flowers
        know.
But if meanwhile some insect with a heart
Worth floods of lazy music, spendthrift joy —
Some firefly renounced spring for my dwarfed
        cup,   1505
Crept close to me, brought luster for the dark,
Comfort against the cold — what though
        excess
Of comfort should miscall the creature — sun?
What did the sun to hinder while harsh hands,
Petal by petal, crude and colorless,   1510
Tore me? This one heart gave me all the
        spring!

Is all told? There's the journey; and where's
        time
To tell you how that heart burst out in shine?
Yet certain points do press on me too hard.
Each place must have a name, though I for-
        get.   1515

How strange it was — there where the plain
        begins
And the small river mitigates its flow —
When eve was fading fast, and my soul sank,
And he divined what surge of bitterness,
In overtaking me, would float me back   1520
Whence I was carried by the striding day —
So — "This gray place was famous once,"
        said he —
And he began that legend of the place
As if in answer to the unspoken fear,   1524
And told me all about a brave man dead,
Which lifted me and let my soul go on!
How did he know too — at that town's ap-
        proach
By the rock-side — that in coming near the
        signs
Of life, the house-roofs and the church and
        tower,   1529
I saw the old boundary and wall o' the world
Rise plain as ever round me, hard and cold,
As if the broken circlet joined again,
Tightened itself about me with no break —
As if the town would turn Arezzo's self — 1534
The husband there — the friends my enemies,
All ranged against me, not an avenue
To try, but would be blocked and drive me
        back
On him — this other . . . oh, the heart in
        that!
Did not he find, bring, put into my arms 1539
A new-born babe? — and I saw faces beam:
Of the young mother proud to teach me joy,
And gossips round expecting my surprise
At the sudden hole through earth that lets in
        heaven.
I could believe himself by his strong will 1544
Had woven around me what I thought the
        world
We went along in, every circumstance,
Towns, flowers and faces, all things helped so
        well!
For, through the journey, was it natural
Such comfort should arise from first to last?
As I look back, all is one milky way;   1550
Still bettered more, the more remembered,
        so
Do new stars bud while I but search for old,
And fill all gaps i' the glory, and grow him —
Him I now see make the shine everywhere.
Even at the last when the bewildered flesh,
The cloud of weariness about my soul   1556
Clogging too heavily, sucked down all sense —
Still its last voice was, "He will watch and
        care;
Let the strength go, I am content — he
        stays!"   1559
I doubt not he did stay and care for all —
From that sick minute when the head swam
        round,

1514. **too hard**, i.e., for me to keep silent.

And the eyes looked their last and died on
    him,
As in his arms he caught me, and, you say,
Carried me in, that tragical red eve,
And laid me where I next returned to life 1565
In the other red of morning, two red plates
That crushed together, crushed the time be-
    tween,
And are since then a solid fire to me — 1568
When in, my dreadful husband and the world
Broke — and I saw him, master, by hell's
    right,
And saw my angel helplessly held back
By guards that helped the malice — the lamb
    prone,
The serpent towering and triumphant — then
Came all the strength back in a sudden
    swell,   1574
I did for once see right, do right, give tongue
The adequate protest; for a worm must turn
If it would have its wrong observed by God.
I did spring up, attempt to thrust aside
That ice-block 'twixt the sun and me, lay low
The neutralizer of all good and truth.   1580
If I sinned so — never obey voice more
O' the Just and Terrible, who bids us —
    "Bear!"
Not — "Stand by, bear to see my angels
    bear!"
I am clear it was on impulse to serve God, 1584
Not save myself — no — nor my child un-
    born!
Had I else waited patiently till now? —
Who saw my old kind parents, silly-sooth
And too much trustful, for their worst of
    faults,
Cheated, browbeaten, stripped and starved,
    cast out   1589
Into the kennel. I remonstrated,
Then sank to silence, for — their woes at end,
Themselves gone — only I was left to plague.
If only I was threatened and belied,
What matter? I could bear it and did bear;
It was a comfort, still one lot for all — 1595
They were not persecuted for my sake
And I, estranged, the single happy one.
But when at last, all by myself I stood
Obeying the clear voice which bade me rise,
Not for my own sake but my babe unborn,
And take the angel's hand was sent to help —
And found the old adversary athwart the
    path —   1602
Not my hand simply struck from the angel's,
    but
The very angel's self made foul i' the face
By the fiend who struck there — that I would
    not bear,   1605
That only I resisted! So, my first

1587. **silly-sooth,** unsuspecting.

And last resistance was invincible.
Prayers move God; threats, and nothing else,
    move men!
I must have prayed a man as he were God
When I implored the Governor to right   1610
My parents' wrongs; the answer was a smile.
The Archbishop — did I clasp his feet enough,
Hide my face hotly on them, while I told
More than I dared make my own mother
    know?
The profit was — compassion and a jest. 1615
This time, the foolish prayers were done with,
    right
Used might, and solemnized the sport at once.
All was against the combat; vantage, mine?
The runaway avowed, the accomplice-wife,
In company with the plan-contriving priest?
Yet, shame thus rank and patent, I struck,
    bare,   1621
At foe from head to foot in magic mail,
And off it withered, cobweb-armory
Against the lightning! 'Twas truth singed
    the lies
And saved me, not the vain sword nor weak
    speech!   1625

You see, I will not have the service fail!
I say, the angel saved me; I am safe!
Others may want and wish, I wish nor want
One point o' the circle plainer, where I stand
Traced round about with white to front the
    world.   1630
What of the calumny I came across,
What o' the way to the end? — the end
    crowns all.
The judges judged aright i' the main, gave me
The uttermost of my heart's desire, a truce
From torture and Arezzo, balm for hurt, 1635
With the quiet nuns — God recompense the
    good! —
Who said and sang away the ugly past.
And, when my final fortune was revealed,
What safety, while, amid my parents' arms,
My babe was given me! Yes, he saved my
    babe;   1640
It would not have peeped forth, the bird-like
    thing,
Through that Arezzo noise and trouble; back
Had it returned nor ever let me see!
But the sweet peace cured all, and let me live
And give my bird the life among the leaves
God meant him! Weeks and months of quie-
    tude,   1646
I could lie in such peace and learn so much —
Begin the task, I see how needful now,
Of understanding somewhat of my past —
Know life a little, I should leave so soon. 1650
Therefore, because this man restored my soul,
All has been right; I have gained my gain,
    enjoyed

As well as suffered — nay, got foretaste too
Of better life beginning where this ends —
All through the breathing-while allowed me
    thus,   1655
Which let good premonitions reach my soul
Unthwarted, and benignant influence flow
And interpenetrate and change my heart,
Uncrossed by what was wicked — nay, un-
    kind.   1659
For, as the weakness of my time drew nigh,
Nobody did me one disservice more,
Spoke coldly or looked strangely, broke the
    love
I lay in the arms of, till my boy was born,
Born all in love, with naught to spoil the bliss
A whole long fortnight. In a life like mine 1665
A fortnight filled with bliss is long and much.
All women are not mothers of a boy,
Though they live twice the length of my
    whole life,
And, as they fancy, happily all the same. 1669
There I lay, then, all my great fortnight long,
As if it would continue, broaden out
Happily more and more, and lead to heaven.
Christmas before me — was not that a chance?
I never realized God's birth before —
How he grew likest God in being born.   1675
This time I felt like Mary, had my babe
Lying a little on my breast like hers.
So all went on till, just four days ago —
The night and the tap.

                    Oh, it shall be success
To the whole of our poor family! My friends
. . . Nay, father and mother — give me back
    my word!   1681
They have been rudely stripped of life, dis-
    graced
Like children who must needs go clothed too
    fine,
Carry the garb of Carnival in Lent.
If they too much affected frippery,   1685
They have been punished and submit them-
    selves,
Say no word. All is over; they see God,
Who will not be extreme to mark their fault
Or he had granted respite. They are safe. 1689

For that most woeful man my husband once,
Who, needing respite, still draws vital breath,
I — pardon him? So far as lies in me,
I give him for his good the life he takes,
Praying the world will therefore acquiesce.
Let him make God amends — none, none to
    me   1695
Who thank him rather that, whereas strange
    fate
Mockingly styled him husband and me wife,
Himself this way at least pronounced divorce,
Blotted the marriage-bond; this blood of mine
Flies forth exultingly at any door,   1700

Washes the parchment white, and thanks the
    blow.
We shall not meet in this world nor the next,
But where will God be absent? In his face
Is light, but in his shadow healing too;   1704
Let Guido touch the shadow and be healed!
And as my presence was importunate —
My earthly good, temptation and a snare —
Nothing about me but drew somehow down
His hate upon me — somewhat so excused
Therefore, since hate was thus the truth of
    him —   1710
May my evanishment forevermore
Help further to relieve the heart that cast
Such object of its natural loathing forth!
So he was made; he nowise made himself.
I could not love him, but his mother did.   1715
His soul has never lain beside my soul;
But for the unresisting body — thanks!
He burned that garment spotted by the flesh.
Whatever he touched is rightly ruined; plague
It caught, and disinfection it had craved 1720
Still but for Guido. I am saved through him
So as by fire; to him — thanks and fare-
    well!

Even for my babe, my boy, there's safety
    thence —
From the sudden death of me, I mean; we
    poor   1724
Weak souls, how we endeavor to be strong!
I was already using up my life —
This portion, now, should do him such a good,
This other go to keep off such an ill!
The great life; see, a breath and it is gone!
So is detached, so left all by itself   1730
The little life, the fact which means so much.
Shall not God stoop the kindlier to his work,
His marvel of creation, foot would crush,
Now that the hand he trusted to receive 1734
And hold it, lets the treasure fall perforce?
The better; he shall have in orphanage
His own way all the clearlier. If my babe
Outlived the hour — and he has lived two
    weeks —
It is through God who knows I am not by.
Who is it makes the soft gold hair turn black,
And sets the tongue, might lie so long at rest,
Trying to talk? Let us leave God alone! 1742
Why should I doubt he will explain in time
What I feel now, but fail to find the words?
My babe nor was, nor is, nor yet shall be
Count Guido Franceschini's child at all —
Only his mother's, born of love, not hate!
So shall I have my rights in after-time.
It seems absurd, impossible today;   1749
So seems so much else, not explained but
    known!

Ah! Friends, I thank and bless you every
    one!

No more now; I withdraw from earth and
    man
To my own soul, compose myself for God.

Well, and there is more! Yes, my end of
    breath
Shall bear away my soul in being true! 1755
He is still here, not outside with the world,
Here, here, I have him in his rightful place!
'Tis now, when I am most upon the move,
I feel for what I verily find — again
The face, again the eyes, again, through all,
The heart and its immeasurable love   1761
Of my one friend, my only, all my own,
Who put his breast between the spears and
    me.
Ever with Caponsacchi! Otherwise
Here alone would be failure, loss to me —
How much more loss to him, with life debarred
From giving life, love locked from love's dis-
    play,
The day-star stopped its task that makes
    night morn!
O lover of my life, O soldier-saint,   1769
No work begun shall ever pause for death!
Love will be helpful to me more and more
I' the coming course, the new path I must
    tread —
My weak hand in thy strong hand, strong for
    that!
Tell him that if I seem without him now, 1774
That's the world's insight! Oh, he under-
    stands!
He is at Civita — do I once doubt
The world again is holding us apart?
He had been here, displayed in my behalf
The broad brow that reverberates the truth,
And flashed the word God gave him, back to
    man!   1780
I know where the free soul is flown! My
    fate
Will have been hard for even him to bear;
Let it confirm him in the trust of God,
Showing how holily he dared the deed!
And, for the rest — say, from the deed, no
    touch   1785
Of harm came, but all good, all happiness,
Not one faint fleck of failure! Why explain?
What I see, oh, he sees and how much more!
Tell him — I know not wherefore the true
    word   1789
Should fade and fall unuttered at the last —
It was the name of him I sprang to meet
When came the knock, the summons, and the
    end.
"My great heart, my strong hand are back
    again!"
I would have sprung to these, beckoning
    across

1776. He is at Civita. Caponsacchi had been banished to
Civita Vecchia, a seaport near Rome.

Murder and hell gigantic and distinct   1795
O' the threshold, posted to exclude me heaven;
He is ordained to call and I to come!
Do not the dead wear flowers when dressed
    for God?
Say — I am all in flowers from head to foot!
Say — not one flower of all he said and did,
Might seem to flit unnoticed, fade unknown,
But dropped a seed, has grown a balsam-tree
Whereof the blossoming perfumes the place
At this supreme of moments! He is a priest;
He cannot marry therefore, which is right;
I think he would not marry if he could. 1806
Marriage on earth seems such a counterfeit,
Mere imitation of the inimitable;
In heaven we have the real and true and sure.
'Tis there they neither marry nor are given
In marriage but are as the angels; right, 1811
Oh, how right that is, how like Jesus Christ
To say that! Marriage-making for the earth,
With gold so much — birth, power, repute so
    much,
Or beauty, youth so much, in lack of these!
Be as the angels rather, who, apart,   1816
Know themselves into one, are found at length
Married, but marry never, no, nor give
In marriage; they are man and wife at once
When the true time is: here we have to wait
—Not so long neither! Could we by a wish 1821
Have what we will and get the future now,
Would we wish aught done undone in the
    past?
So, let him wait God's instant men call years;
Meantime hold hard by truth and his great
    soul,   1825
Do out the duty! Through such souls alone
God stooping shows sufficient of his light
For us i' the dark to rise by. And I rise.
                              (1868-1869)

HERVÉ RIEL

I

On the sea and at the Hogue, sixteen hundred
        ninety-two,
    Did the English fight the French — woe to
    France!

1810-1811. 'Tis there, etc. From *Matthew*, 22:30.—"For
in the resurrection they neither marry, nor are given in
marriage, but are as the angels of God in heaven."
  Hervé Riel. This poem is based upon an incident of the
war between France and England in 1692, over the succession
of William of Orange to the English throne. The French
took the side of James II, who had been deposed, and were
fighting for his restoration. The united fleets of England
and Holland, under Admiral Russell, crushed the French
fleet, under Admiral Tourville (line 43), but several of the
French ships under Damfreville (line 8) were saved from
capture as related in the poem.
  Browning found the story among the town records of Saint
Malo when, in 1867, he visited Le Croisic, the home of Hervé
Riel, in Brittany.
  1. the Hogue, the name of a fort and of a cape on the
northeast coast of France.

And, the thirty-first of May, helter-skelter
   through the blue,
Like a crowd of frightened porpoises a shoal
   of sharks pursue,
Came crowding ship on ship to Saint Malo
   on the Rance,   5
With the English fleet in view.

2

'Twas the squadron that escaped, with the
   victor in full chase;
First and foremost of the drove, in his great
   ship, Damfreville;
   Close on him fled, great and small,
   Twenty-two good ships in all;   10
And they signaled to the place,
"Help the winners of a race!
   Get us guidance, give us harbor, take us
   quick — or, quicker still,
   Here's the English can and will!"

3

Then the pilots of the place put out brisk and
   leapt on board;   15
   "Why, what hope or chance have ships like
   these to pass?" laughed they.
"Rocks to starboard, rocks to port, all the
   passage scarred and scored,
Shall the *Formidable* here, with her twelve and
   eighty guns,
   Think to make the river-mouth by the
   single narrow way,
Trust to enter where 'tis ticklish for a craft
   of twenty tons,   20
   And with flow at full beside?
   Now, 'tis slackest ebb of tide.
Reach the mooring? Rather say,
While rock stands or water runs,
   Not a ship will leave the bay!"   25

4

Then was called a council straight.
Brief and bitter the debate:
"Here's the English at our heels; would you
   have them take in tow
All that's left us of the fleet, linked together
   stern and bow,
For a prize to Plymouth Sound?   30
Better run the ships aground!"
   (Ended Damfreville his speech).
"Not a minute more to wait!
   Let the Captains all and each
   Shove ashore, then blow up, burn the ves-
   sels on the beach!   35
France must undergo her fate.

5

"Give the word!" But no such word
Was ever spoke or heard;
   For up stood, for out stepped, for in struck
   amid all these
— A Captain? A Lieutenant? A Mate — first,
   second, third?   40
   No such man of mark, and meet
   With his betters to compete!
   But a simple Breton sailor pressed by
   Tourville for the fleet,
A poor coasting-pilot he, Hervé Riel the Croi-
   sickese.   44

6

And "What mockery or malice have we
   here?" cries Hervé Riel;
   "Are you mad, you Malouins? Are you
   cowards, fools, or rogues?
Talk to me of rocks and shoals, me who took
   the soundings, tell
On my fingers every bank, every shallow,
   every swell
'Twixt the offing here and Grève, where the
   river disembogues?
Are you bought by English gold? Is it love
   the lying's for?   50
   Morn and eve, night and day,
   Have I piloted your bay,
Entered free and anchored fast at the foot of
   Solidor.
   Burn the fleet and ruin France? That were
   worse than fifty Hogues!
   Sirs, they know I speak the truth! Sirs,
   believe me there's a way!   55
Only let me lead the line,
   Have the biggest ship to steer,
   Get this *Formidable* clear,
Make the others follow mine,
And I lead them, most and least, by a pas-
   sage I know well,   60
   Right to Solidor past Grève,
   And there lay them safe and sound;
   And if one ship misbehave
   Keel so much as grate the ground —
Why, I've nothing but my life — here's my
   head!" cries Hervé Riel.   65

7

Not a minute more to wait.
"Steer us in, then, small and great!
   Take the helm, lead the line, save the
   squadron!" cried its chief.
Captains, give the sailor place!
He is Admiral, in brief.   70

---

5. **Saint Malo,** a fortified seaport on an island at the mouth of the Rance River, west of the cape. 18. **the Formidable,** the name of the leading French ship. 30. **Plymouth Sound.** Plymouth is a great British naval station on the southern coast of England.

44. **Croisickese,** a native of Croisic, in Brittany. 46. **Malouins,** people of Saint Malo. 49. **Grève,** the sands between St. Malo and Mont St. Michel, a rocky island off the coast of Normandy. **disembogues,** empties. 53. **Solidor,** a fortified town at the mouth of the Rance; also the name of a fort in the town.

Still the north-wind, by God's grace!
  See the noble fellow's face
As the big ship, with a bound,
Clears the entry like a hound,
Keeps the passage as its inch of way were the
    wide sea's profound!   75
  See, safe through shoal and rock,
  How they follow in a flock,
Not a ship that misbehaves, not a keel that
    grates the ground,
  Not a spar that comes to grief!
The peril, see, is past,   80
All are harbored to the last,
And just as Hervé Riel hollas "Anchor!" —
    sure as fate,
Up the English come — too late!

8

So, the storm subsides to calm;
  They see the green trees wave   85
  On the heights o'erlooking Grève.
Hearts that bled are stanched with balm.
"Just our rapture to enhance,
  Let the English rake the bay,
Gnash their teeth and glare askance   90
  As they cannonade away!
'Neath rampired Solidor pleasant riding on
    the Rance!"
How hope succeeds despair on each Captain's
    countenance!
Out burst all with one accord,
  "This is Paradise for Hell!   95
  Let France, let France's King
  Thank the man that did the thing!"
What a shout, and all one word,
  "Hervé Riel!"
As he stepped in front once more,   100
  Not a symptom of surprise
  In the frank blue Breton eyes,
Just the same man as before.

9

Then said Damfreville, "My friend,
I must speak out at the end,   105
  Though I find the speaking hard.
Praise is deeper than the lips;
You have saved the King his ships,
  You must name your own reward.
'Faith, our sun was near eclipse!   110
Demand whate'er you will,
France remains your debtor still.
Ask to heart's content and have! or my
    name's not Damfreville."

10

Then a beam of fun outbroke
On the bearded mouth that spoke,   115
As the honest heart laughed through

92. rampired, protected with ramparts.

Those frank eyes of Breton blue:
"Since I needs must say my say,
  Since on board the duty's done,
  And from Malo Roads to Croisic Point,
    what is it but a run? —   120
Since 'tis ask and have, I may —
  Since the others go ashore —
Come! A good whole holiday!
  Leave to go and see my wife, whom I call
    the Belle Aurore!"
That he asked and that he got — nothing
    more.   125

11

Name and deed alike are lost:
Not a pillar nor a post
  In his Croisic keeps alive the feat as it
    befell;
Not a head in white and black
On a single fishing-smack,   130
In memory of the man but for whom had
    gone to wrack
  All that France saved from the fight whence
    England bore the bell.
Go to Paris; rank on rank
  Search the heroes flung pell-mell
On the Louvre, face and flank!   135
  You shall look long enough ere you come
    to Hervé Riel.
So, for better and for worse,
Hervé Riel, accept my verse!
In my verse, Hervé Riel, do thou once more
Save the squadron, honor France, love thy
    wife, the Belle Aurore!   140

          (*1867; 1871*)

HOUSE

Shall I sonnet-sing you about myself?
  Do I live in a house you would like to see?
Is it scant of gear, has it store of pelf?
  "Unlock my heart with a sonnet-key"?

Invite the world, as my betters have done? 5
  "Take notice: this building remains on
    view,
Its suites of reception every one,
  Its private apartment and bedroom too;

"For a ticket, apply to the Publisher."
  No; thanking the public, I must decline. 10
A peep through my window, if folk prefer;
  But, please you, no foot over threshold of
    mine!

124. Leave . . . Belle Aurore. The hero asked for a permanent release, but Browning departs from the historic fact to heighten the dramatic value of the story. 129. head, figurehead. 135. the Louvre, the great palace and art gallery of Paris.

I have mixed with a crowd and heard free talk
   In a foreign land where an earthquake
     chanced
And a house stood gaping, naught to balk 15
   Man's eye wherever he gazed or glanced.

The whole of the frontage shaven sheer,
   The inside gaped; exposed to day,
Right and wrong and common and queer,
   Bare, as the palm of your hand, it lay. 20

The owner? Oh, he had been crushed, no
   doubt!
   "Odd tables and chairs for a man of wealth!
What a parcel of musty old books about!
   He smoked — no wonder he lost his health!

"I doubt if he bathed before he dressed. 25
   A brasier? — the pagan, he burned per-
     fumes!
You see it is proved, what the neighbors
   guessed:
   His wife and himself had separate rooms."

Friends, the goodman of the house at least
   Kept house to himself till an earthquake
     came; 30
'Tis the fall of its frontage permits you feast
   On the inside arrangement you praise or
     blame.

Outside should suffice for evidence;
   And whoso desires to penetrate
Deeper, must dive by the spirit-sense — 35
   No optics like yours, at any rate!

"Hoity-toity! A street to explore,
   Your house the exception! '*With this same
     key*
Shakespeare unlocked his heart,' once more!"
   Did Shakespeare? If so, the less Shake-
   speare he!   (1876)

SHOP

So, friend, your shop was all your house!
   Its front, astonishing the street,
Invited view from man and mouse
   To what diversity of treat
   Behind its glass — the single sheet! 5

What gimcracks, genuine Japanese —
   Gape-jaw and goggle-eye, the frog;
Dragons, owls, monkeys, beetles, geese;

Some crush-nosed human-hearted dog —
   Queer names, too, such a catalogue! 10

I thought "And he who owns the wealth
   Which blocks the window's vastitude —
Ah, could I peep at him by stealth
   Behind his ware, pass shop, intrude
   On house itself, what scenes were viewed!15

"If wide and showy thus the shop,
   What must the habitation prove?
The true house with no name a-top —
   The mansion, distant one remove,
   Once get him off his traffic-groove! 20

"Pictures he likes, or books perhaps;
   And as for buying most and best,
Commend me to these city chaps!
   Or else he's social, takes his rest
   On Sundays, with a Lord for guest. 25

"Some suburb-palace, parked about
   And gated grandly, built last year —
The four-mile walk to keep off gout;
   Or big seat sold by bankrupt peer —
   But then he takes the rail, that's clear. 30

"Or, stop! I wager, taste selects
   Some out-o'-the-way, some all-unknown
Retreat; the neighborhood suspects
   Little that he who rambles lone
   Makes Rothschild tremble on his throne!"

Nowise! Nor Mayfair residence 36
   Fit to receive and entertain —
Nor Hampstead villa's kind defense
   From noise and crowd, from dust and
     drain —
   Nor country-box was soul's domain! 40

Nowise! At back of all that spread
   Of merchandise, woe's me, I find
A hole i' the wall where, heels by head,
   The owner couched, his ware behind —
   In cupboard suited to his mind. 45

For why? He saw no use of life
   But, while he drove a roaring trade,
To chuckle, "Customers are rife!"
   To chafe, "So much hard cash outlaid,
   Yet zero in my profits made! 50

"This novelty costs pains, but — takes?
   Cumbers my counter! Stock no more!
This article, no such great shakes,
   Fizzes like wildfire? Underscore
   The cheap thing — thousands to the fore!"

38-39. **With this . . . heart.** Quoted from Wordsworth's
Scorn Not the Sonnet, 2-3. Many poets have sung about them-
selves in sonnets—Dante, Petrarch, Sidney, Spenser, Milton,
Keats, Mrs. Browning, D. G. Rossetti.
   Shop. 5. **single sheet,** single pane of glass.

30. **takes the rail,** gets an advantage (a term from horse-
racing). 35. **Rothschild,** the name of a famous Jewish family of bankers, noted for enormous wealth and influence. 36,
38. **Mayfair, Hampstead,** fashionable sections of London.

'Twas lodging best to live most nigh   56
  (Cramp, coffinlike as crib might be)
Receipt of Custom; ear and eye
  Wanted no outworld: "Hear and see
The bustle in the shop!" quoth he.   60

My fancy of a merchant-prince
  Was different. Through his wares we groped
Our darkling way to — not to mince
  The matter — no black den where moped
The master if we interloped!   65

Shop was shop only; household-stuff?
  What did he want with comforts there?
"Walls, ceiling, floor, stay blank and rough,
  So goods on sale show rich and rare!
'*Sell and scud home*' be shop's affair!"   70

What might he deal in? Gems, suppose!
  Since somehow business must be done
At cost of trouble — see, he throws
  You choice of jewels, every one,
Good, better, best, star, moon, and sun!   75

Which lies within your power of purse?
  This ruby that would tip aright
Solomon's scepter? Oh, your nurse
  Wants simply coral, the delight
Of teething baby — stuff to bite!   80

Howe'er your choice fell, straight you took
  Your purchase, prompt your money rang
On counter — scarce the man forsook
  His study of the *Times*, just swang
Till-ward his hand that stopped the clang —

Then off made buyer with a prize,   86
  Then seller to his *Times* returned;
And so did day wear, wear, till eyes
  Brightened apace, for rest was earned.
He locked door long ere candle burned.   90

And whither went he? Ask himself,
  Not me! To change of scene, I think.
Once sold the ware and pursed the pelf,
  Chaffer was scarce his meat and drink,
Nor all his music — money-chink.   95

Because a man has shop to mind
  In time and place, since flesh must live,
Needs spirit lack all life behind,
  All stray thoughts, fancies fugitive,
All loves except what trade can give?   100

I want to know a butcher paints,
  A baker rimes for his pursuit,
Candlestick-maker much acquaints

84. **the Times**, the leading paper of London.

His soul with song, or, haply mute,
  Blows out his brains upon the flute!   105

But — shop each day and all day long!
  Friend, your good angel slept, your star
Suffered eclipse, fate did you wrong!
  From where these sorts of treasures are,
There should our hearts be — Christ, how
  far!   110
                 (1876)

PISGAH-SIGHTS

1

Over the ball of it,
  Peering and prying,
How I see all of it,
  Life there, outlying!
Roughness and smoothness,   5
  Shine and defilement,
Grace and uncouthness:
  One reconcilement.

Orbed as appointed,
  Sister with brother   10
Joins, ne'er disjointed
  One from the other.
All's lend-and-borrow;
  Good, see, wants evil,
Joy demands sorrow,   15
  Angel weds devil!

"Which things must — *why* be?"
  Vain our endeavor!
So shall things aye be
  As they were ever.   20
"Such things should *so* be!"
  Sage our desistence!
Rough-smooth let globe be,
  Mixed — man's existence!

Man — wise and foolish,   25
  Lover and scorner,
Docile and mulish —
  Keep each his corner!
Honey yet gall of it!
  There's the life lying,   30
And I see all of it,
  Only, I'm dying!

2

Could I but live again
  Twice my life over,
Would I once strive again?   35
  Would not I cover

109-110. **where ... hearts be.** Cf. *Matthew*, 6:21.—"For where your treasure is, there will your heart be also."
Pisgah-Sights. Pisgah is the name of a mountain in Palestine from which Moses saw the Promised Land (*Deuteronomy*, 34:1-4).

Quietly all of it —
  Greed and ambition —
So, from the pall of it,
  Pass to fruition?   40

"Soft!" I'd say, "Soul mine!
  Three-score and ten years,
Let the blind mole mine
  Digging out deniers!
Let the dazed hawk soar,   45
  Claim the sun's rights too!
Turf 'tis thy walk's o'er,
  Foliage thy flight's to."

Only a learner,
  Quick one or slow one,   50
Just a discerner,
  I would teach no one.
I am earth's native. —
  No rearranging it!
I be creative,   55
  Chopping and changing it?

March, men, my fellows!
  Those who, above me
(Distance so mellows),
  Fancy you love me;   60
Those who, below me
  (Distance makes great so),
Free to forego me,
  Fancy you hate so!

Praising, reviling,   65
  Worst head and best head,
Past me defiling,
  Never arrested,
Wanters, abounders,
  March, in gay mixture,   70
Men, my surrounders!
  I am the fixture.

So shall I fear thee,
  Mightiness yonder!
Mock-sun — more near thee,   75
  What is to wonder?
So shall I love thee,
  Down in the dark — lest
Glowworm I prove thee,
  Star that now sparklest!   80
                                    (1876)

NATURAL MAGIC

All I can say is — I saw it!
The room was as bare as your hand.
I locked in the swarth little lady — I swear,
From the head to the foot of her — well,
  quite as bare!

44. **denier,** a small copper French coin of little value.

"No Nautch shall cheat me," said I, "taking
  my stand   5
At this bolt which I draw!" And this bolt —
  I withdraw it,
And there laughs the lady, not bare, but em-
  bowered
With — who knows what verdure, o'erfruited,
  o'erflowered?
Impossible! Only — I saw it!

All I can sing is — I feel it!   10
This life was as blank as that room;
I let you pass in here. Precaution, indeed?
Walls, ceiling, and floor — not a chance for a
  weed!
Wide opens the entrance; where's cold now,
  where's gloom?
No May to sow seed here, no June to reveal
  it,   15
Behold you enshrined in these blooms of your
  bringing,
These fruits of your bearing — nay, birds of
  your winging!
A fairy-tale! Only — I feel it!   (1876)

MAGICAL NATURE

Flower — I never fancied; jewel — I profess
  you!
  Bright I see and soft I feel the outside of a
    flower.
Save but glow inside and — jewel, I should
  guess you,
  Dim to sight and rough to touch; the glory
    is the dower.

You, forsooth, a flower? Nay, my love, a
  jewel —   5
  Jewel at no mercy of a moment in your
    prime!
Time may fray the flower-face; kind be time
  or cruel,
  Jewel, from each facet, flash your laugh at
    time!   (1876)

APPEARANCES

And so you found that poor room dull,
  Dark, hardly to your taste, my dear?
Its features seemed unbeautiful;
  But this I know — 'twas there, not here,
You plighted troth to me, the word   5
Which — ask that poor room how it heard.

And this rich room obtains your praise
  Unqualified — so bright, so fair,

Natural Magic. 5. **Nautch,** an Indian dancing girl, to
whom are ascribed the powers of a magician, as in producing
a flowering tree out of nothing.

So all whereat perfection stays?
  Aye, but remember — here, not there,   10
The other word was spoken! — Ask
This rich room how you dropped the mask!
                             (1876)

PROLOGUE to LA SAISIAZ

Good, to forgive;
  Best, to forget!
  Living, we fret;
Dying, we live.
Fretless and free,   5
  Soul, clap thy pinion!
  Earth have dominion,
Body, o'er thee!

Wander at will,
  Day after day —   10
  Wander away,
Wandering still —
Soul that canst soar!
  Body may slumber;
  Body shall cumber   15
Soul-flight no more.

Waft of soul's wing!
  What lies above?
  Sunshine and Love,
Skyblue and Spring!   20
Body hides — where?
  Ferns of all feather,
  Mosses and heather,
Yours be the care!   (1878)

PHEIDIPPIDES

Χαίρετε, νικῶμεν

First I salute this soil of the blessed, river and
  rock!
Gods of my birthplace, dæmons and heroes,
  honor to all!
Then I name thee, claim thee for our patron,
  co-equal in praise —
Aye, with Zeus the Defender, with Her of
  the ægis and spear!

Also, ye of the bow and the buskin, praised be
  your peer,   5
Now, henceforth and forever — O latest to
  whom I upraise
Hand and heart and voice! For Athens, leave
  pasture and flock!
Present to help, potent to save, Pan — patron
  I call!

Archons of Athens, topped by the tettix, see,
  I return!
See, 'tis myself here standing alive, no specter
  that speaks!   10
Crowned with the myrtle, did you command
  me, Athens and you,
"Run, Pheidippides, run and race, reach
  Sparta for aid!
Persia has come, we are here, where is She?"
  Your command I obeyed,
Ran and raced; like stubble, some field which
  a fire runs through,
Was the space between city and city. Two
  days, two nights did I burn   15
Over the hills, under the dales, down pits and
  up peaks.

Into their midst I broke; breath served but
  for "Persia has come!
Persia bids Athens proffer slaves'-tribute,
  water and earth;
Razed to the ground is Eretria — but Athens,
  shall Athens sink,
Drop into dust and die — the flower of Hellas
  utterly die,   20
Die, with the wide world spitting at Sparta,
  the stupid, the stander-by?
Answer me quick, what help, what hand do
  you stretch o'er destruction's brink?
How — when? No care for my limbs! —
  there's lightning in all and some —
Fresh and fit your message to bear, once lips
  give it birth!"

O my Athens — Sparta love thee? Did Sparta
  respond?   25
Every face of her leered in a furrow of envy,
  mistrust,
Malice — each eye of her gave me its glitter
  of gratified hate!
Gravely they turned to take counsel, to cast
  for excuses. I stood

Prologue to La Saisiaz. La Saisiaz, meaning *The Sun*, was the name of the villa near Geneva, Switzerland, where Browning stayed during the autumn of 1877 with his sister and a friend, Miss Ann Egerton-Smith. The sudden death of Miss Egerton-Smith called forth this poem, in which Browning discusses questions of death, God, the soul, and immortality.

Pheidippides. Pheidippides, the hero of this poem, was a Greek athlete who had been commissioned by Athens in 493 B.C. to run 140 miles to Sparta to ask for aid against the attacking Persians. The runner has returned and is reporting to the rulers of Athens. The story is from Book 6 of Herodotus, the famous Greek historian of the fourth century B.C.
  The Greek legend means *Rejoice, we conquer.* These were the words spoken by Pheidippides (line 111) when he carried to Athens the report of the victory at Marathon in 490 B.C.
  2. **dæmons**, guardian spirits of Greek families. 4. **Zeus**, chief of the Greek gods. **Her . . . spear**, Athena (Minerva), goddess of wisdom and warfare. The ægis was a shield.

5. **ye . . . buskin**, Artemis (Diana), goddess of the moon and of the chase. The buskin was a shoe laced about the ankle. 8. **Pan**, the god of all nature. He was thought by the Greeks to be half man and half goat, hence the goat-god (line 77). 9. **Archons**, rulers. They wore the golden grasshopper (tettix) to signify their right to their territory as descendants of earth-born possessors. The grasshopper was supposed to have sprung from the earth. 11. **myrtle**, often used in crowning heroes. 18. **water and earth.** To carry earth and water to an invading enemy was a symbol of submission. 20. **Hellas**, Greece.

Quivering — the limbs of me fretting as fire
    frets, an inch from dry wood:
"Persia has come, Athens asks aid, and still
    they debate? 30
Thunder, thou Zeus! Athené, are Spartans a
    quarry beyond
Swing of thy spear? Phoibos and Artemis,
    clang them 'Ye must!' "

No bolt launched from Olumpos! Lo, their
    answer at last!
"Has Persia come — does Athens ask aid —
    may Sparta befriend?
Nowise precipitate judgment — too weighty
    the issue at stake! 35
Count we no time lost time which lags through
    respect to the gods!
Ponder that precept of old, 'No warfare, what-
    ever the odds
In your favor, so long as the moon, half-
    orbed, is unable to take
Full-circle her state in the sky!' Already she
    rounds to it fast;
Athens must wait, patient as we — who judg-
    ment suspend." 40

Athens — except for that sparkle — thy name,
    I had moldered to ash!
That sent a blaze through my blood; off, off
    and away was I back —
Not one word to waste, one look to lose on
    the false and the vile!
Yet "O gods of my land!" I cried, as each
    hillock and plain,
Wood and stream, I knew, I named, rushing
    past them again, 45
"Have ye kept faith, proved mindful of honors
    we paid you erewhile?
Vain was the filleted victim, the fulsome liba-
    tion! Too rash
Love in its choice, paid you so largely service
    so slack!

"Oak and olive and bay — I bid you cease to
    enwreathe
Brows made bold by your leaf! Fade at the
    Persian's foot, 50
You that, our patrons were pledged, should
    never adorn a slave!
Rather I hail thee, Parnes — trust to thy wild
    waste tract!
Treeless, herbless, lifeless mountain! What
    matter if slacked
My speed may hardly be, for homage to crag
    and to cave

No deity deigns to drape with verdure? At
    least I can breathe, 55
Fear in thee no fraud from the blind, no lie
    from the mute!"

Such my cry as, rapid, I ran over Parnes'
    ridge;
Gully and gap I clambered and cleared till,
    sudden, a bar
Jutted, a stoppage of stone against me, block-
    ing the way.
Right! for I minded the hollow to traverse,
    the fissure across; 60
"Where I could enter, there I depart by!
    Night in the fosse?
Athens to aid? Though the dive were through
    Erebos, thus I obey —
Out of the day dive, into the day as bravely
    arise! No bridge
Better!" — when — ha! what was it I came
    on, of wonders that are?

There, in the cool of a cleft, sat he — majes-
    tical Pan! 65
Ivy drooped wanton, kissed his head, moss
    cushioned his hoof;
All the great god was good in the eyes grave-
    kindly — the curl
Carved on the bearded cheek, amused at a
    mortal's awe,
As, under the human trunk, the goat-thighs
    grand I saw.
"Halt, Pheidippides!" — halt I did, my brain
    of a whirl. 70
"Hither to me! Why pale in my presence?"
    he gracious began;
"How is it — Athens, only in Hellas, holds me
    aloof?

"Athens, she only, rears me no fane, makes
    me no feast!
Wherefore? Than I what godship to Athens
    more helpful of old?
Aye, and still, and forever her friend! Test
    Pan, trust me! 75
Go, bid Athens take heart, laugh Persia to
    scorn, have faith
In the temples and tombs! Go, say to Athens,
    'The Goat-God saith:
When Persia — so much as strews not the soil
    — is cast in the sea,
Then praise Pan who fought in the ranks with
    your most and least,
Goat-thigh to greaved-thigh, made one cause
    with the free and the bold!' 80

"Say Pan saith: 'Let this, foreshowing the
    place, be the pledge!' "

32. **Phoibos**, Phœbus Apollo, god of the sun. 33.
Olumpos, Olympus, a mountain in Greece; the abode of the
gods. 47. **filleted victim.** Animals for sacrifice were be-
decked with ribbons. 49. **Oak and olive and bay.** These
were sacred trees, the leaves and branches of which were
often used in wreaths bestowed as prizes for victory or excellence. 52. **Parnes,** a mountain north of Athens.

61. **fosse**, ditch. 62. **Erebos**, the dark space between
earth and Hades.

(Gay, the liberal hand held out this herbage I
    bear
— Fennel — I grasped it a-tremble with dew
    — whatever it bode.)
"While, as for thee" . . . But enough! He
    was gone. If I ran hitherto —
Be sure that, the rest of my journey, I ran no
    longer, but flew.   85
Parnes to Athens — earth no more, the air
    was my road;
Here am I back. Praise Pan, we stand no
    more on the razor's edge!
Pan for Athens, Pan for me! I too have a
    guerdon rare!

Then spoke Miltiades. "And thee, best run-
    ner of Greece,
Whose limbs did duty indeed — what gift is
    promised thyself?   90
Tell it us straightway — Athens the mother
    demands of her son!"
Rosily blushed the youth; he paused; but,
    lifting at length
His eyes from the ground, it seemed as he
    gathered the rest of his strength
Into the utterance — "Pan spoke thus: 'For
    what thou hast done
Count on a worthy reward! Henceforth be
    allowed thee release   95
From the racer's toil, no vulgar reward in
    praise or in pelf!'

"I am bold to believe, Pan means reward the
    most to my mind!
Fight I shall, with our foremost, wherever this
    fennel may grow —
Pound — Pan helping us — Persia to dust,
    and, under the deep,
Whelm her away forever; and then — no
    Athens to save —   100
Marry a certain maid, I know keeps faith to
    the brave —
Hie to my house and home; and, when my
    children shall creep
Close to my knees — recount how the god
    was awful yet kind,
Promised their sire reward to the full — re-
    warding him — so!"

Unforeseeing one! Yes, he fought on the
    Marathon day;   105
So, when Persia was dust, all cried, "To Akrop-
    olis!

Run, Pheidippides, one race more! the meed
    is thy due!
'Athens is saved, thank Pan,' go shout!" He
    flung down his shield,
Ran like fire once more; and the space 'twixt
    the Fennel-field
And Athens was stubble again, a field which
    a fire runs through,   110
Till in he broke: "Rejoice, we conquer!"
    Like wine through clay,
Joy in his blood bursting his heart, he died —
    the bliss!

So, to this day, when friend meets friend, the
    word of salute
Is still "Rejoice!" — his word which brought
    rejoicing indeed.
So is Pheidippides happy forever — the noble
    strong man   115
Who could race like a god, bear the face of a
    god, whom a god loved so well;
He saw the land saved he had helped to save,
    and was suffered to tell
Such tidings, yet never decline, but, gloriously
    as he began,
So to end gloriously — once to shout, there-
    after be mute:
"Athens is saved!" — Pheidippides dies in the
    shout for his meed.   120
                  (1879)

EPILOGUE TO *DRAMATIC IDYLS*

"Touch him ne'er so lightly, into song he
    broke;
Soil so quick-receptive — not one feather-
    seed,
Not one flower-dust fell but straight its fall
    awoke
Vitalizing virtue; song would song succeed
Sudden as spontaneous — prove a poet-soul!"
             Indeed?   5
Rock's the song-soil rather, surface hard and
    bare;
Sun and dew their mildness, storm and frost
    their rage
Vainly both expend — few flowers awaken
    there;
Quiet in its cleft broods — what the after-
    age   9
Knows and names a pine, a nation's heritage.

Thus I wrote in London, musing on my betters,
Poets dead and gone; and lo, the critics cried,

83. **Fennel**, a prophecy that Pan would aid the Athenians at Marathon, which means *fennel*. 89. **Miltiades**, the Greek general who won the victory over the Persians at Marathon in 490 B.C. 106. **Akropolis**, the citadel of Athens.

Epilogue to Dramatic Idyls. The first ten lines of this poem were published as an epilogue to the second series of *Dramatic Idyls* in 1880; the remaining lines were added in an album of a young American girl in Venice later in the same year.

"Out on such a boast!" as if I dreamed that
    fetters
Binding Dante bind up — me! as if true pride
Were not also humble!
                    So I smiled and sighed   15
As I oped your book in Venice this bright
    morning,
Sweet new friend of mine! and felt the clay
    or sand,
Whatsoe'er my soil be, break — for praise or
    scorning —
Out in grateful fancies — weeds; but weeds
    expand   19
Almost into flowers, held by such a kindly
    hand.   (1880)

WANTING IS —WHAT?

Wanting is — what?
Summer redundant,
Blueness abundant,
—Where is the blot?
Beamy the world, yet a blank all the same, 5
— Framework which waits for a picture to
    frame.
What of the leafage, what of the flower?
Roses embowering with naught they em-
    bower!
Come then, complete incompletion, O comer,
Pant through the blueness, perfect the sum-
    mer!   10
Breathe but one breath
Rose-beauty above,
And all that was death
Grows life, grows love,
Grows love!   (1883)

ADAM, LILITH, AND EVE

One day, it thundered and lightened.
Two women, fairly frightened,
Sank to their knees, transformed, transfixed,
At the feet of the man who sat betwixt;
And "Mercy!" cried each — "if I tell the
    truth   5
Of a passage in my youth!"

Said This: "Do you mind the morning
I met your love with scorning?
As the worst of the venom left my lips,
I thought, 'If, despite this lie, he strips   10
The mask from my soul with a kiss — I crawl
His slave — soul, body, and all!' "

Said That: "We stood to be married;
The priest, or someone, tarried;
'If Paradise-door prove locked?' smiled you.
I thought, as I nodded, smiling too,   16
'Did one, that's away, arrive — nor late
Nor soon should unlock Hell's gate!' "

It ceased to lighten and thunder.
Up started both in wonder,   20
Looked round and saw that the sky was clear,
Then laughed, "Confess you believed us,
    Dear!"
"I saw through the joke!" the man replied.
They re-seated themselves beside.   (1883)

NEVER THE TIME AND THE PLACE

Never the time and the place
    And the loved one all together!
This path — how soft to pace!
    This May — what magic weather!
Where is the loved one's face?   5
In a dream that loved one's face meets mine,
    But the house is narrow, the place is bleak
Where, outside, rain and wind combine
    With a furtive ear, if I strive to speak,
    With a hostile eye at my flushing cheek,   10
With a malice that marks each word, each
    sign!
O enemy sly and serpentine,
    Uncoil thee from the waking man!
        Do I hold the Past
        Thus firm and fast   15
    Yet doubt if the Future hold I can?
This path so soft to pace shall lead
Through the magic of May to herself in-
    deed!
Or narrow if needs the house must be,
Outside are the storms and strangers; we —
Oh, close, safe, warm sleep I and she —   21
    I and she!   (1883)

WHY I AM A LIBERAL

"Why?" Because all I haply can and do,
All that I am now, all I hope to be —
Whence comes it save from fortune setting
    free
Body and soul the purpose to pursue,
God traced for both? If fetters not a few,   5
Of prejudice, convention, fall from me,
These shall I bid men — each in his degree
Also God-guided — bear, and gayly, too?

But little do or can the best of us;
That little is achieved through Liberty.   10
Who, then, dares hold, emancipated thus,

Wanting Is—What? This poem stands as an introduction to a group of poems published in 1883 under the title of *Jocoseria.* The two following poems are from the same volume. Each poem in the collection shows the lack of something necessary to make human action or experience more nearly perfect. In this poem the spirit of love is invoked.
Adam, Lilith, and Eve. Lilith was the traditional first wife of Adam; she is reputed to have been the mother of demons.
Why I Am a Liberal. Compare *The Lost Leader*, p. 214.

His fellow shall continue bound? Not I,
Who live, love, labor freely, nor discuss
A brother's right to freedom. That is "Why."
(1885)

PROLOGUE TO *ASOLANDO*

"The Poet's age is sad; for why?
  In youth, the natural world could show
No common object but his eye
  At once involved with alien glow —
His own soul's iris-bow.   5

"And now a flower is just a flower;
  Man, bird, beast are but beast, bird, man —
Simply themselves, uncinct by dower
  Of dyes which, when life's day began,
Round each in glory ran."   10

Friend, did you need an optic glass,
  Which were your choice? A lens to drape
In ruby, emerald, chrysopras,
  Each object — or reveal its shape
Clear outlined, past escape,   15

The naked very thing? — so clear
  That, when you had the chance to gaze,
You found its inmost self appear
  Through outer seeming — truth ablaze,
Not falsehood's fancy-haze?   20

How many a year, my Asolo,
  Since — one step just from sea to land —
I found you, loved yet feared you so —
  For natural objects seemed to stand
Palpably fire-clothed! No —   25

No mastery of mine o'er these!
  Terror with beauty, like the Bush
Burning but unconsumed. Bend knees,
  Drop eyes to earthward! Language? Tush!
Silence 'tis awe decrees.   30

And now? The lambent flame is — where?
  Lost from the naked world; earth, sky,
Hill, vale, tree, flower — Italia's rare
  O'er-running beauty crowds the eye —
But flame? The Bush is bare.   35

Hill, vale, tree, flower — they stand distinct,
  Nature to know and name. What then?

Prologue to Asolando. The remaining poems of Browning
in this volume were published in 1889 in a book entitled
Asolando: Fancies and Facts. Browning had been living in
Asolo, not far from Venice. He derives the title from *asolare,*
meaning *to disport in the open air, to amuse oneself at random.* The book appeared on the day of Browning's death.
  5. **iris-bow,** rainbow (so called from Iris, goddess of the
rainbow). 13. **chrysopras,** a kind of apple-green onyx.
27–28. **the Bush . . . unconsumed,** a reference to an experience of Moses related in *Exodus,* 3:2.—"And the angel of
the Lord appeared unto him in a flame of fire out of the midst
of a bush; and he looked, and, behold, the bush burned with
fire, and the bush was not consumed."

A Voice spoke thence which straight unlinked
  Fancy from fact; see, all's in ken;
Has once my eyelid winked?   40

No, for the purged ear apprehends
  Earth's import, not the eye late dazed.
The Voice said, "Call my works thy friends!
  At Nature dost thou shrink amazed?
God is it who transcends."   45
                (*1889;* 1889)

DUBIETY

I will be happy if but for once;
  Only help me, Autumn weather,
Me and my cares to screen, ensconce
  In luxury's sofa-lap of leather!

Sleep? Nay, comfort — with just a cloud   5
  Suffusing day too clear and bright;
Eve's essence, the single drop allowed
  To sully, like milk, Noon's water-white.

Let gauziness shade, not shroud — adjust,
  Dim, and not deaden — somehow sheathe 10
Aught sharp in the rough world's busy thrust,
  If it reach me through dreaming's vapor-
    wreath.

Be life so, all things ever the same!
  For, what has disarmed the world? Out-
    side,
Quiet and peace; inside, nor blame   15
  Nor want, nor wish whate'er betide.

What is it like that has happened before?
  A dream? No dream, more real by much.
A vision? But fanciful days of yore
  Brought many; mere musing seems not
    such.   20

Perhaps but a memory, after all!
  — Of what came once when a woman leant
To feel for my brow where her kiss might fall.
  Truth ever, truth only the excellent!
                (1889)

NOW

Out of your whole life give but a moment!
All of your life that has gone before,
All to come after it — so you ignore,
So you make perfect the present — condense,
In a rapture of rage, for perfection's endow-
    ment,   5
Thought and feeling and soul and sense —
Merged in a moment which gives me at last
You around me for once, you beneath me,
    above me —

Me — sure that despite of time future, time
    past —
This tick of our lifetime's one moment you
    love me!   10
How long such suspension may linger? Ah,
    Sweet —
The moment eternal — just that and no
    more —
When ecstasy's utmost we clutch at the core
While cheeks burn, arms open, eyes shut, and
    lips meet!   (1889)

HUMILITY

What girl but, having gathered flowers,
Stripped the beds and spoilt the bowers,
From the lapful light she carries
Drops a careless bud? — nor tarries
To regain the waif and stray: 5
"Store enough for home" — she'll say.

So say I too; give your lover
Heaps of loving — under, over,
Whelm him — make the one the wealthy!
Am I all so poor who — stealthy   10
Work it was! — picked up what fell:
Not the worst bud — who can tell?
                (1889)

POETICS

"So say the foolish!" Say the foolish so,
    Love?
  "Flower she is, my rose" — or else, "My
    very swan is she" —
Or perhaps, "Yon maid-moon, blessing earth
    below, Love,
  That art thou!" — to them, belike; no such
    vain words from me.

"Hush, rose, blush! no balm like breath," I
    chide it;   5
  "Bend thy neck its best, swan — hers the
    whiter curve!"
Be the moon the moon; my Love I place be-
    side it.
  What is she? Her human self — no lower
    word will serve.   (1889)

SUMMUM BONUM

All the breath and the bloom of the year in
    the bag of one bee;
  All the wonder and wealth of the mine in
    the heart of one gem;

Summum Bonum. The title means *The Highest Good.*

In the core of one pearl all the shade and the
    shine of the sea;
  Breath and bloom, shade and shine — won-
    der, wealth, and — how far above
    them —
        Truth, that's brighter than gem, 5
        Trust, that's purer than pearl —
Brightest truth, purest trust in the universe
    — all were for me
        In the kiss of one girl.
                (1889)

A PEARL, A GIRL

A simple ring with a single stone,
  To the vulgar eye no stone of price;
Whisper the right word, that alone —
  Forth starts a sprite, like fire from ice,
And lo, you are lord (says an Eastern scroll) 5
Of heaven and earth, lord whole and sole
  Through the power in a pearl.

A woman ('tis I this time that say)
  With little the world counts worthy praise;
Utter the true word — out and away   10
  Escapes her soul: I am wrapped in blaze,
Creation's lord, of heaven and earth
Lord whole and sole — by a minute's birth —
  Through the love in a girl!
                (1889)

SPECULATIVE

Others may need new life in Heaven —
  Man, Nature, Art — made new, assume!
Man with new mind old sense to leaven,
  Nature — new light to clear old gloom,
Art that breaks bounds, gets soaring-room. 5

I shall pray: "Fugitive as precious —
  Minutes which passed — return, remain!
Let earth's old life once more enmesh us,
  You with old pleasure, me — old pain,
So we but meet nor part again!"   10

                (1889)

BAD DREAMS

Last night I saw you in my sleep;
  And how your charm of face was changed!
I asked, "Some love, some faith you keep?"
  You answered, "Faith gone, love estranged."

Whereat I woke — a twofold bliss: 5
  Waking was one, but next there came
This other — "Though I felt, for this,
  My heart break, I loved on the same."
                (1889)

MUCKLE-MOUTH MEG

Frowned the Laird on the Lord: "So, red-
  handed I catch thee?
Death-doomed by our Law of the Border!
We've a gallows outside and a chiel to dis-
  patch thee.
Who trespasses — hangs; all's in order."

He met frown with smile, did the young English gallant.   5
Then the Laird's dame: "Nay, Husband, I
  beg!
He's comely; be merciful! Grace for the callant —
If he marries our Muckle-mouth Meg!"

"No mile-wide-mouthed monster of yours do
  I marry;
Grant rather the gallows!" laughed he.   10
"Foul fare kith and kin of you — why do you
  tarry?"
"To tame your fierce temper!" quoth she.

"Shove him quick in the Hole, shut him fast
  for a week.
Cold, darkness, and hunger work wonders;
Who lion-like roars now, mouse-fashion will
  squeak,   15
And 'it rains' soon succeed to 'it thunders.' "

A week did he bide in the cold and the dark
— Not hunger; for duly at morning
In flitted a lass, and a voice like a lark
Chirped, "Muckle-mouth Meg still ye're
  scorning?   20

"Go hang, but here's parritch to hearten ye
  first!"
"Did Meg's muckle-mouth boast within
  some
Such music as yours, mine should match it or
  burst;
No frog-jaws! So tell folk, my Winsome!"

Soon week came to end, and, from Hole's
  door set wide,   25
Out he marched, and there waited the
  lassie.
"Yon gallows, or Muckle-mouth Meg for a
  bride!
Consider! Sky's blue and turf's grassy;

"Life's sweet; shall I say ye wed Muckle-
  mouth Meg?"
"Not I," quoth the stout heart; "too
  eerie   30

Muckle-Mouth Meg. The title means *Big-mouthed Margaret.* See Critical Notes.
  3. **chiel,** young fellow. 7. **callant,** fine fellow. 21.
parritch, porridge.

The mouth that can swallow a bubblyjock's
  egg;
Shall I let it munch mine? Never, Dearie!"

"Not Muckle-mouth Meg? Wow, the obstin-
  ate man!
Perhaps he would rather wed me!"
"Aye, would he — with just for a dowry your
  can!"   35
"I'm Muckle-mouth Meg," chirruped she.

"Then so — so — so — so — " as he kissed
  her apace —
"Will I widen thee out till thou turnest
From Margaret Minnikin-mou', by God's
  grace,
To Muckle-mouth Meg in good earnest!" 40
                                         (1889)

DEVELOPMENT

My father was a scholar and knew Greek.
When I was five years old, I asked him once,
"What do you read about?"
                        "The siege of Troy."
"What is a siege, and what is Troy?"
                                    Whereat
He piled up chairs and tables for a town,   5
Set me a-top for Priam, called our cat —
Helen, enticed away from home (he said)
By wicked Paris, who couched somewhere
  close
Under the footstool, being cowardly,
But whom — since she was worth the pains,
  poor puss —   10
Towzer and Tray — our dogs, the Atreidai —
  sought
By taking Troy to get possession of
— Always when great Achilles ceased to sulk
(My pony in the stable) — forth would prance
And put to flight Hector — our page-boy's
  self.   15
This taught me who was who and what was
  what,
So far I rightly understood the case
At five years old; a huge delight it proved

And still proves — thanks to that instructor
    sage,   19
My father, who knew better than turn straight
Learning's full flare on weak-eyed ignorance,
Or, worse yet, leave weak eyes to grow sand-
    blind,
Content with darkness and vacuity.

It happened, two or three years afterward,
That — I and playmates playing at Troy's
    Siege —   25
My father came upon our make-believe.
"How would you like to read yourself the tale
Properly told, of which I gave you first
Merely such notion as a boy could bear?
Pope, now, would give you the precise account
Of what, some day, by dint of scholarship,   31
You'll hear — who knows? — from Homer's
    very mouth.
Learn Greek by all means, read the 'Blind
    Old Man,
Sweetest of Singers' — *tuphlos* which means
    'blind,'
Hedistos which means 'sweetest.' Time
    enough!   35
Try, anyhow, to master him some day;
Until when, take what serves for substitute,
Read Pope, by all means!"
                So I ran through Pope,
Enjoyed the tale — what history so true?
Also attacked my Primer, duly drudged,   40
Grew fitter thus for what was promised next—
The very thing itself, the actual words,
When I could turn — say, Buttmann to ac-
    count.

Time passed, I ripened somewhat; one fine
    day,
"Quite ready for the Iliad, nothing less?   45
There's Heine, where the big books block the
    shelf;
Don't skip a word, thumb well the Lexicon!"

I thumbed well and skipped nowise till I
    learned
Who was who, what was what, from Homer's
    tongue,   49
And there an end of learning. Had you asked
The all-accomplished scholar, twelve years
    old,
"Who was it wrote the Iliad?" — what a
    laugh!
"Why, Homer, all the world knows. Of his
    life

Doubtless some facts exist; it's everywhere. 54
We have not settled, though, his place of birth;
He begged, for certain, and was blind beside;
Seven cities claimed him — Scio, with best
    right,
Thinks Byron. What he wrote? Those
    Hymns we have.
Then there's the 'Battle of the Frogs and
    Mice,'
That's all — unless they dig 'Margites' up 60
(I'd like that), nothing more remains to
    know."

Thus did youth spend a comfortable time;
Until — "What's this the Germans say in fact
That Wolf found out first? It's unpleasant
    work
Their chop and change, unsettling one's be-
    lief;   65
All the same, where we live, we learn, that's
    sure."
So, I bent brow o'er *Prolegomena*.
And after Wolf, a dozen of his like
Proved there was never any Troy at all,
Neither Besiegers nor Besieged—nay, worse—
No actual Homer, no authentic text,   71
No warrant for the fiction I, as fact,
Had treasured in my heart and soul so long —
Aye, mark you! and as fact held still, still
    hold,
Spite of new knowledge, in my heart of
    hearts   75
And soul of souls, fact's essence freed and
    fixed
From accidental fancy's guardian sheath.
Assuredly thenceforward—thank my stars!—
However it got there, deprive who could —
Wring from the shrine my precious tenantry,
Helen, Ulysses, Hector and his Spouse,   81
Achilles and his Friend? — though Wolf —
    ah, Wolf!
Why must he needs come doubting, spoil a
    dream?

But then, "No dream's worth waking" —
    Browning says;
And here's the reason why I tell thus much.
I, now mature man, you anticipate,   86
May blame my father justifiably

57. **Seven cities.** The seven cities were Chios (Scio),
Colophon, Smyrna, Rhodes, Athens, Argos, and Salamis.
These are all located in the region of Greece and Asia Minor.
58. **Hymns.** These were hymns to the gods, called *Homeric
Hymns* but actually composed by various authors after the
death of Homer. 59. **Battle . . . Mice.** This is a mock
epic poem attributed to Homer. 60. **Margites,** a humorous
poem no longer ascribed to Homer. 64. **Wolf,** Friedrich
August Wolf (1759-1842), a German scholar who advanced
the theory in his *Prolegomena in Homerum* (1795), that the
Iliad and the *Odyssey* were not the work of one man but the
compilation of various writers' songs handed down through
a long period of oral tradition. 81. **Ulysses,** one of the
Greek heroes in the Trojan War. **his Spouse.** The wife of
Hector was Andromache.

22. **sand-blind,** weak-sighted. 30. **Pope.** Alexander
Pope (1688-1744) published an English translation of the
Iliad in 1720 and of the *Odyssey* in 1725. 40. **Primer,** the
first book in Greek. 43. **Buttmann,** Philipp Karl Buttmann
(1764-1829), a German scholar, famous for his studies in
Greek grammar. 46. **Heine,** Christian Gottlob Heyne
(1729-1812), a German philologist who edited the *Iliad*.

For letting me dream out my nonage thus,
And only by such slow and sure degrees
Permitting me to sift the grain from chaff, 90
Get truth and falsehood known and named as
    such.
Why did he ever let me dream at all,
Not bid me taste the story in its strength?
Suppose my childhood was scarce qualified
To rightly understand mythology;   95
Silence at least was in his power to keep.
I might have—somehow—correspondingly—
Well, who knows by what method, gained my
    gains,
Been taught, by forthrights not meanderings,
My aim should be to loathe, like Peleus' son,
A lie as Hell's Gate, love my wedded wife, 101
Like Hector, and so on with all the rest.
Could not I have excogitated this
Without believing such man really were?
That is — he might have put into my
    hand   105
The "Ethics"? In translation, if you please,
Exact, no pretty lying that improves,
To suit the modern taste: no more, no less —
The "Ethics." 'Tis a treatise I find hard
To read aright now that my hair is gray, 110
And I can manage the original.
At five years old — how ill had fared its
    leaves!
Now, growing double o'er the Stagirite,
At least I soil no page with bread and milk,
Nor crumple, dogs-ear and deface — boys'
    way.   115
                                (1889)

EPILOGUE TO *ASOLANDO*

At the midnight in the silence of the sleep-
    time,
    When you set your fancies free,
Will they pass to where — by death, fools
    think, imprisoned —
Low he lies who once so loved you, whom you
    loved so,
        — Pity me?   5

Oh, to love so, be so loved, yet so mistaken!
    What had I on earth to do
With the slothful, with the mawkish, the un-
    manly?

Like the aimless, helpless, hopeless, did I
    drivel —
        Being — who?   10

One who never turned his back but marched
    breast forward,
    Never doubted clouds would break,
Never dreamed, though right were worsted,
    wrong would triumph,
Held we fall to rise, are baffled to fight better,
    Sleep to wake.   15

No! At noonday, in the bustle of man's work-
    time,
    Greet the unseen with a cheer!
Bid him forward, breast and back as either
    should be,
"Strive and thrive!" cry, "Speed — fight on,
    fare ever
        There as here!"   (1889)

ELIZABETH BARRETT BROWNING
(1806-1861)

CONSOLATION

All are not taken; there are left behind
Living Belovéds, tender looks to bring
And make the daylight still a happy thing,
And tender voices, to make soft the wind.
But if it were not so — if I could find   5
No love in all the world for comforting,
Nor any path but hollowly did ring
Where "dust to dust" the love from life dis-
    joined,
And if, before those sepulchers unmoving
I stood alone (as some forsaken lamb   10
Goes bleating up the moors in weary dearth),
Crying, "Where are ye, O my loved and
    loving?" —
I know a Voice would sound, "Daughter, I
    AM.
Can I suffice for HEAVEN and not for earth?"
                                (1838)

COWPER'S GRAVE

It is a place where poets crowned may feel
    the heart's decaying;
It is a place where happy saints may weep
    amid their praying.

100. **Peleus' son**, Achilles, who considered the action of Agamemnon regarding Briseis as a breach of faith. (See note on line 3.) 101-102. **wedded . . . Hector.** See Hector's famous farewell to his wife, Andromache, in Book 6 of the *Iliad*, 486 ff. 103. **excogitated**, thought out. 106. **The "Ethics,"** the *Nicomachean Ethics*, the great work of Aristotle (384-322 B.C.), the famous Greek philosopher. 113. **the Stagirite**, Aristotle, so called because he was born at Stagira, an ancient city of Chalcidice, a peninsula of northeastern Greece.
Epilogue to Asolando. This is Browning's last poem. It should be compared with Tennyson's *Crossing the Bar*, p. 176.

Cowper's Grave. William Cowper (1731-1800) is buried in Dereham Church, Norfolk, England. Throughout his life he suffered from attacks of melancholy which at times led to actual insanity. He often saw himself as one forsaken by God. His poetry includes a number of hymns and passages that show a sympathetic interest in nature, in man, and in animals and birds. He was especially fond of hares (see line 25), and kept some as pets.

Yet let the grief and humbleness, as low as
  silence, languish;
Earth surely now may give her calm to whom
  she gave her anguish.

O poets, from a maniac's tongue was poured
  the deathless singing!   5
O Christians, at your cross of hope, a hopeless hand was clinging!
O men, this man in brotherhood your weary
  paths beguiling,
Groaned inly while he taught you peace, and
  died while ye were smiling!

And now, what time ye all may read through
  dimming tears his story,
How discord on the music fell and darkness
  on the glory,   10
And how when, one by one, sweet sounds and
  wandering lights departed,
He wore no less a loving face because so
  broken-hearted,

He shall be strong to sanctify the poet's high
  vocation,
And bow the meekest Christian down in
  meeker adoration;
Nor ever shall he be, in praise, by wise or
  good forsaken,   15
Named softly as the household name of one
  whom God hath taken.

With quiet sadness and no gloom I learn to
  think upon him,
With meekness that is gratefulness to God
  whose heaven hath won him,
Who suffered once the madness-cloud to his
  own love to blind him,
But gently led the blind along where breath
  and bird could find him;   20

And wrought within his shattered brain such
  quick poetic senses
As hills have language for, and stars, harmonious influences.
The pulse of dew upon the grass kept his
  within its number,
And silent shadows from the trees refreshed
  him like a slumber.

Wild timid hares were drawn from woods to
  share his home-caresses,   25
Uplooking to his human eyes with sylvan
  tendernesses;
The very world, by God's constraint, from
  falsehood's ways removing,
Its women and its men became, beside him,
  true and loving.

And though, in blindness, he remained unconscious of that guiding,
And things provided came without the sweet
  sense of providing,   30
He testified this solemn truth, while frenzy
  desolated —
Nor man nor nature satisfies whom only God
  created.

Like a sick child that knoweth not his mother
  while she blesses
And drops upon his burning brow the coolness of her kisses —
That turns his fevered eyes around — "My
  mother! where's my mother?" —   35
As if such tender words and deeds could come
  from any other! —

The fever gone, with leaps of heart he sees
  her bending o'er him,
Her face all pale from watchful love, the
  unweary love she bore him!
Thus woke the poet from the dream his life's
  long fever gave him,
Beneath those deep pathetic Eyes which
  closed in death to save him.   40

Thus? Oh, not *thus!* No type of earth can
  image that awaking,
Wherein he scarcely heard the chant of
  seraphs, round him breaking,
Or felt the new immortal throb of soul from
  body parted,
But felt those eyes alone, and knew — "*My*
  Savior! *not* deserted!"

Deserted! Who hath dreamt that when the
  cross in darkness rested,   45
Upon the Victim's hidden face no love was
  manifested?
What frantic hands outstretched have e'er
  the atoning drops averted?
What tears have washed them from the soul,
  that *one* should be deserted?

Deserted! God could separate from his own
  essence rather;
And Adam's sins *have* swept between the
  righteous Son and Father.   50
Yea, once, Immanuel's orphaned cry his universe hath shaken —
It went up single, echoless, "My God, I am
  forsaken!"

It went up from the Holy's lips amid his lost
  creation,

33-38. **Like . . . him.** See Cowper's *On the Receipt of My
Mother's Picture out of Norfolk.* 51. **Immanuel,** an appellation of Christ (*Matthew*, 1:23). 52. "**My God, I am forsaken!**" Cf. Christ's words from the Cross: "My God, my
God, why hast thou forsaken me?" (*Matthew*, 27:46.)

That, of the lost, no son should use those
    words of desolation!
That Earth's worst frenzies, marring hope,
    should mar not hope's fruition,   55
And I, on Cowper's grave, should see his
    rapture in a vision.   (1838)

THE CRY OF THE HUMAN

"There is no God," the foolish saith,
    But none "There is no sorrow";
And nature oft the cry of faith
    In bitter need will borrow.
Eyes, which the preacher could not school, 5
    By wayside graves are raiséd,
And lips say, "God be pitiful,"
    Who ne'er said, "God be praiséd."
                Be pitiful, O God!

The tempest stretches from the steep   10
    The shadow of its coming,
The beasts grow tame and near us creep,
    As help were in the human;
Yet, while the cloud-wheels roll and grind,
    We spirits tremble under —   15
The hills have echoes, but we find
    No answer for the thunder.
                Be pitiful, O God!

The battle hurtles on the plains,
    Earth feels new scythes upon her; 20
We reap our brothers for the wains,
    And call the harvest — honor:
Draw face to face, front line to line,
    One image all inherit —
Then kill, curse on, by that same sign, 25
    Clay — clay, and spirit — spirit.
                Be pitiful, O God!

The plague runs festering through the town,
    And never a bell is tolling,
And corpses, jostled 'neath the moon, 30
    Nod to the dead-cart's rolling;
The young child calleth for the cup,
    The strong man brings it weeping,
The mother from her babe looks up,
    And shrieks away its sleeping. 35
                Be pitiful, O God!

The plague of gold strikes far and near,
    And deep and strong it enters;
This purple chimar which we wear
    Makes madder than the centaur's. 40

Our thoughts grow blank, our words grow
    strange,
We cheer the pale gold-diggers,
Each soul is worth so much on 'Change,
    And marked, like sheep, with figures.
                Be pitiful, O God!

The curse of gold upon the land   46
    The lack of bread enforces;
The rail-cars snort from strand to strand,
    Like more of Death's White Horses.
The rich preach "rights" and "future days,"
    And hear no angel scoffing; 51
The poor die mute, with starving gaze
    On corn-ships in the offing.
                Be pitiful, O God!

We meet together at the feast, 55
    To private mirth betake us;
We stare down in the winecup, lest
    Some vacant chair should shake us.
We name delight, and pledge it round —
    "It shall be ours tomorrow!" 60
God's seraphs, do your voices sound
    As sad, in naming sorrow?
                Be pitiful, O God!

We sit together, with the skies,
    The steadfast skies, above us, 65
We look into each other's eyes,
    "And how long will you love us?"
The eyes grow dim with prophecy,
    The voices, low and breathless —
"Till death us part!" — O words, to be 70
    Our best, for love the deathless!
                Be pitiful, O God!

We tremble by the harmless bed
    Of one loved and departed;
Our tears drop on the lips that said 75
    Last night, "Be stronger-hearted!"
O God — to clasp those fingers close,
    And yet to feel so lonely!
To see a light upon such brows,
    Which is the daylight only! 80
                Be pitiful, O God!

The happy children come to us
    And look up in our faces;

The Cry of the Human. 1. **"There is no God."** From *Psalms,* 14:1.—"The fool hath said in his heart, There is no God." 21. **wains,** wagons. 39. **chimar,** robe. 40. **centaur's.** Because Nessus the centaur made love to Hercules's wife, Dejanira, Hercules shot him with a poisoned arrow. In obedience to the dying advice of Nessus, Dejanira steeped her husband's shirt in the blood of the centaur as a love charm; but it poisoned Hercules, who, after venting his anger upon the messenger who brought the garment, gave himself up to die.

43. **'Change,** Exchange, the financial center of London. 48. **rail-cars.** Railway trains were first introduced into England in 1823, and for more than twenty years they were regarded as very dangerous. 49. **Death's White Horses.** In Scandinavian mythology the white horse is regarded as an omen of death. The fourth beast of the Apocalypse (*Revelation,* 6:8) was "a pale horse; and his name that sat on him was Death . . ." 50. **"rights" and "future days,"** slogans of the members of the new capitalistic group, who protested against innovations and reforms, held out for the private exercise of property rights, and regarded the accumulation of wealth for the future as a guarantee of public welfare. 53. **corn-ships,** wheat-ships. Much suffering was occasioned among the lower classes because of the Corn Laws, which prohibited or greatly restricted the importation of grain. The laws were repealed in 1846.

They ask us, "Was it thus, and thus,
  When we were in their places?"   85
We cannot speak — we see anew
  The hills we used to live in,
And feel our mother's smile press through
  The kisses she is giving.
               Be pitiful, O God!

We pray together at the kirk   91
  For mercy, mercy solely;
Hands weary with the evil work,
  We lift them to the Holy.
The corpse is calm below our knee,   95
  Its spirit, bright before Thee;
Between them, worse than either, we —
  Without the rest or glory.
               Be pitiful, O God!

We leave the communing of men,   100
  The murmur of the passions,
And live alone, to live again
  With endless generations;
Are we so brave? The sea and sky
  In silence lift their mirrors,   105
And, glassed therein, our spirits high
  Recoil from their own terrors.
               Be pitiful, O God!

We sit on hills our childhood wist,
  Woods, hamlets, streams, beholding   110
The sun strikes through the farthest mist
  The city's spire to golden;
The city's golden spire it was,
  When hope and health were strongest,
But now it is the churchyard grass   115
  We look upon the longest.
               Be pitiful, O God!

And soon all vision waxeth dull;
  Men whisper, "He is dying";
We cry no more, "Be pitiful!"   120
  We have no strength for crying —
No strength, no need. Then, soul of mine,
  Look up and triumph rather!
Lo, in the depth of God's Divine,
  The Son adjures the Father,   125
              BE PITIFUL, O GOD!
                     (1842)

THE CRY OF THE CHILDREN

Do ye hear the children weeping, O my
  brothers,
  Ere the sorrow comes with years?

109. **wist**, knew.
The Cry of the Children. This poem was suggested by an official report on the employment of children in mines and factories. The poem is a product of the humanitarian movement of the period. In reply to a complaint against the rhythm of the poem, Mrs. Browning said, "The first stanza came into my head in a hurricane, and I was obliged to make the other stanzas like it."

They are leaning their young heads against
  their mothers,
  And *that* cannot stop their tears.
The young lambs are bleating in the meadows,
  The young birds are chirping in the nest,   6
The young fawns are playing with the
  shadows,
  The young flowers are blowing toward the
    west —
But the young, young children, O my brothers,
  They are weeping bitterly!   10
They are weeping in the playtime of the
  others,
  In the country of the free.

Do you question the young children in the
  sorrow
  Why their tears are falling so?
The old man may weep for his tomorrow   15
  Which is lost in Long Ago;
The old tree is leafless in the forest,
  The old year is ending in the frost,
The old wound, if stricken, is the sorest,
  The old hope is hardest to be lost.   20
But the young, young children, O my brothers,
  Do you ask them why they stand
Weeping sore before the bosoms of their
  mothers,
  In our happy Fatherland?

They look up with their pale and sunken
  faces,   25
  And their looks are sad to see,
For the man's hoary anguish draws and
  presses
  Down the cheeks of infancy;
"Your old earth," they say, "is very dreary;
  Our young feet," they say, "are very weak;
Few paces have we taken, yet are weary —   31
  Our grave-rest is very far to seek.
Ask the aged why they weep, and not the
  children,
  For the outside earth is cold,
And we young ones stand without, in our
  bewildering,   35
  And the graves are for the old.

"True," say the children, "it may happen
  That we die before our time.
Little Alice died last year; her grave is shapen
  Like a snowball, in the rime.   40
We looked into the pit prepared to take her;
  Was no room for any work in the close
    clay!
From the sleep wherein she lieth none will
  wake her,
  Crying, 'Get up, little Alice! it is day.'   44
If you listen by that grave, in sun and shower,
  With your ear down, little Alice never cries;

40. **rime**, hoarfrost.

Could we see her face, be sure we should not
    know her,
    For the smile has time for growing in her
      eyes;
And merry go her moments, lulled and stilled
    in
    The shroud by the kirk-chime.   50
It is good when it happens," say the children,
    "That we die before our time."

Alas, alas, the children! they are seeking
    Death in life, as best to have;
They are binding up their hearts away from
    breaking,   55
    With a cerement from the grave.
Go out, children, from the mine and from the
    city,
    Sing out, children, as the little thrushes do;
Pluck your handfuls of the meadow-cowslips
    pretty.
    Laugh aloud, to feel your fingers let them
      through!   60
But they answer, "Are your cowslips of the
    meadows
    Like our weeds anear the mine?
Leave us quiet in the dark of the coal-
    shadows,
    From your pleasures fair and fine!

"For, oh," say the children, "we are weary,
    And we cannot run or leap;   66
If we cared for any meadows, it were mere-
    ly
    To drop down in them and sleep.
Our knees tremble sorely in the stooping,
    We fall upon our faces, trying to go;   70
And, underneath our heavy eyelids drooping
    The reddest flower would look as pale as
      snow.
For, all day, we drag our burden tiring
    Through the coal-dark, underground;
Or, all day, we drive the wheels of iron   75
    In the factories, round and round.

"For all day the wheels are droning, turning;
    Their wind comes in our faces,
Till our hearts turn, our heads with pulses
    burning,
    And the walls turn in their places.   80
Turns the sky in the high window, blank and
    reeling,
    Turns the long light that drops adown the
      wall,
Turn the black flies that crawl along the
    ceiling;
    All are turning, all the day — and we with
    all.
And all day the iron wheels are droning,   85
    And sometimes we could pray,

56. cerement, grave-cloth.

'O ye wheels' (breaking out in a mad moaning),
    'Stop! be silent for today!' "

Aye, be silent! Let them hear each other
    breathing
    For a moment, mouth to mouth!   90
Let them touch each other's hands, in a fresh
    wreathing
    Of their tender human youth!
Let them feel that this cold metallic motion
    Is not all the life God fashions or reveals;
Let them prove their living souls against the
    notion   95
    That they live in you, or under you, O
      wheels!
Still, all day, the iron wheels go onward,
    Grinding life down from its mark;
And the children's souls, which God is calling
    sunward,
    Spin on blindly in the dark.   100

Now tell the poor young children, O my
    brothers,
    To look up to Him and pray;
So the blessèd One who blesseth all the others,
    Will bless them another day.
They answer, "Who is God that He should
    hear us,   105
    While the rushing of the iron wheels is
      stirred?
When we sob aloud, the human creatures
    near us
    Pass by, hearing not, or answer not a word.
And we hear not (for the wheels in their
    resounding)
    Strangers speaking at the door;   110
Is it likely God, with angels singing round
    Him,
    Hears our weeping any more?

"Two words, indeed, of praying we remember,
    And at midnight's hour of harm,
'Our Father,' looking upward in the chamber,
    We say softly for a charm.   116
We know no other words except 'Our Father,'
    And we think that, in some pause of angels'
      song,
God may pluck them with the silence sweet
    to gather,
    And hold both within his right hand, which
    is strong.   120
'Our Father!' If He heard us, He would
    surely
    (For they call Him good and mild)
Answer, smiling down the steep world very
    purely,
    'Come and rest with me, my child.'

"But, no!" say the children, weeping faster,
    "He is speechless as a stone;   126

And they tell us, of His image is the master
    Who commands us to work on.
Go to!" say the children — "up in Heaven,
    Dark, wheel-like, turning clouds are all we
        find.   130
Do not mock us; grief has made us un-
    believing:
    We look up for God, but tears have made
        us blind."
Do you hear the children weeping and dis-
    proving,
    O my brothers, what ye preach?
For God's possible is taught by his world's
    loving,   135
    And the children doubt of each.

And well may the children weep before you!
    They are weary ere they run;
They have never seen the sunshine, nor the
        glory
    Which is brighter than the sun.   140
They know the grief of man, without its
        wisdom;
    They sink in man's despair, without its
        calm —
Are slaves, without the liberty in Christdom,
    Are martyrs, by the pang without the palm,
Are worn as if with age, yet unretrievingly 145
    The harvest of its memories cannot
        reap —
Are orphans of the earthly love and heavenly.
    Let them weep! let them weep!

They look up with their pale and sunken
        faces,
    And their look is dread to see,   150
For they mind you of their angels in high
        places,
    With eyes turned on Deity.
"How long," they say, "how long, O cruel
        nation,
    Will you stand, to move the world, on a
        child's heart —
Stifle down with a mailéd heel its palpitation,
    And tread onward to your throne amid the
        mart?   156
Our blood splashes upward, O gold-heaper,
    And your purple shows your path!
But the child's sob in the silence curses
        deeper
    Than the strong man in his wrath."   160
                                       (1843)

GRIEF

I tell you, hopeless grief is passionless;
That only men incredulous of despair,
Half-taught in anguish, through the midnight
        air

144. **palm**, palm branch, the symbol of victory, the prize.

Beat upward to God's throne in loud access
Of shrieking and reproach. Full desertness,
In souls as countries, lieth silent-bare   6
Under the blanching, vertical eye-glare
Of the absolute Heavens. Deep-hearted man,
        express
Grief for thy Dead in silence like to death —
Most like a monumental statue set   10
In everlasting watch and moveless woe
Till itself crumble to the dust beneath.
Touch it; the marble eyelids are not wet.
If it could weep, it could arise and go. (1844)

CHEERFULNESS TAUGHT BY REASON

I think we are too ready with complaint
In this fair world of God's. Had we no hope
Indeed beyond the zenith and the slope
Of yon gray blank of sky, we might grow
        faint
To muse upon eternity's constraint   5
Round our aspirant souls; but since the scope
Must widen early, is it well to droop,
For a few days consumed in loss and taint?
O pusillanimous Heart, be comforted
And, like a cheerful traveler, take the road, 10
Singing beside the hedge. What if the bread
Be bitter in thine inn, and thou unshod
To meet the flints? At least it may be said
"Because the way is *short*, I thank thee,
        God."   (1844)

THE DEAD PAN

Gods of Hellas, gods of Hellas,
Can ye listen in your silence?
Can your mystic voices tell us
Where ye hide? In floating islands,
With a wind that evermore   5
Keeps you out of sight of shore?
        Pan, Pan is dead.

In what revels are ye sunken
In old Æthiopia?
Have the Pygmies made you drunken,   10
Bathing in mandragora
Your divine pale lips that shiver
Like the lotus in the river?
        Pan, Pan is dead.

The Dead Pan. Pan was the Greek god of pastures, flocks,
and forests. He was part man and part goat. He was fond of
music and invented the shepherd's flute. (See *A Musical
Instrument*, p. 398.) Mrs. Browning states that this poem
was "excited by Schiller's *Götter Griechenlands* and partly
founded on a well-known tradition mentioned in a treatise
of Plutarch (*De Oraculorum Defectu*), according to which, at
the hour of the Savior's agony, a cry of 'Great Pan is dead!'
swept across the waves in the hearing of certain mariners—
and the oracles ceased."
1. **Hellas**, ancient Greece. 9. **Æthiopia**, a country in
northern Africa. 10. **Pygmies**, according to Greek legend,
a race of dwarfs that lived on the banks of the Upper Nile.
11. **mandragora**, a narcotic herb, the subject of many super-
stitions. 13. **lotus**, the Egyptian water lily.

Responsibility to sway people to the right path.

to poetic

Do ye sit there still in slumber,   15
In gigantic Alpine rows?
The black poppies out of number
Nodding, dripping from your brows
To the red lees of your wine,
And so kept alive and fine?   20
          Pan, Pan is dead.

Or lie crushed your stagnant corses
Where the silver spheres roll on,
Stung to life by centric forces
Thrown like rays out from the sun? —   25
While the smoke of your old altars
Is the shroud that round you welters?
          Great Pan is dead.

"Gods of Hellas, gods of Hellas,"
Said the old Hellenic tongue —   30
Said the hero-oaths, as well as
Poets' songs the sweetest sung —
Have ye grown deaf in a day?
Can ye speak not yea or nay,
          Since Pan is dead?   35

Do ye leave your rivers flowing
All alone, O Naiades,
While your drenchéd locks dry slow in
This cold feeble sun and breeze?
Not a word the Naiads say,   40
Though the rivers run for aye;
          For Pan is dead.

From the gloaming of the oak-wood,
O ye Dryads, could ye flee?
At the rushing thunderstroke, would   45
No sob tremble through the tree?
Not a word the Dryads say,
Though the forests wave for aye;
          For Pan is dead.

Have ye left the mountain places,   50
Oreads wild, for other tryst?
Shall we see no sudden faces
Strike a glory through the mist?
Not a sound the silence thrills
Of the everlasting hills;   55
          Pan, Pan is dead.

O twelve gods of Plato's vision,
Crowned to starry wanderings,
With your chariots in procession

And your silver clash of wings!   60
Very pale ye seem to rise,
Ghosts of Grecian deities,
          Now Pan is dead!

Jove, that right hand is unloaded
Whence the thunder did prevail,   65
While in idiocy of godhead
Thou art scaring the stars pale!
And thine eagle, blind and old,
Roughs his feathers in the cold.
          Pan, Pan is dead.   70

Where, O Juno, is the glory
Of thy regal look and tread?
Will they lay, for evermore, thee
On thy dim, strait, golden bed?
Will thy queendom all lie hid   75
Meekly under either lid?
          Pan, Pan is dead.

Ha, Apollo! floats his golden
Hair all mist-like where he stands,
While the Muses hang enfolding   80
Knee and foot with faint wild hands?
'Neath the clanging of thy bow,
Niobe looked lost as thou!
          Pan, Pan is dead.

Shall the casque with its brown iron   85
Pallas' broad blue eyes eclipse,
And no hero take inspiring
From the god-Greek of her lips?
'Neath her olive dost thou sit,
Mars the mighty, cursing it?   90
          Pan, Pan is dead.

Bacchus, Bacchus! on the panther
He swoons, bound with his own vines;
And his Mænads slowly saunter,
Head aside, among the pines,   95
While they murmur dreamingly,
"Evohe! — ah — evohe! —
          Ah, Pan is dead!"

Neptune lies beside the trident,
Dull and senseless as a stone;   100
And old Pluto deaf and silent
Is cast out into the sun;

22. **corses,** bodies. 23. **silver spheres.** According to the Ptolemaic system of astrology, nine spheres, containing the sun, the moon, and the stars, revolved around the earth, which was stationary. As they revolved, the spheres produced music. 24. **centric,** central. 37. **Naiades,** water nymphs. 44. **Dryads,** wood nymphs. 51. **Oreads,** mountain nymphs. 57. **Plato's vision,** etc., a reference to Plato's *Phædrus*, Sec. 247 (Jowett's translation): "Zeus, the mighty lord, holding the reins of a winged chariot, leads the way in heaven, ordering all and caring for all; and there follows him the heavenly array of gods and demi-gods, divided into eleven bands; for only Hestia is left at home in the house of heaven; but the rest of the twelve greater deities march in their appointed order."

Jove. Zeus, the chief god of the Greeks. The eagle was his attendant bird. 71. **Juno,** queen of the gods. 78. **Apollo,** the god of youth and beauty, of poetry and music. His attributes were the bow and the lyre. 80. **Muses,** the nine daughters of Jove, goddesses of poetry, art, music, etc. 83. **Niobe.** See note on line 102, p. 236. 86. **Pallas,** Athene, or Minerva, goddess of wisdom and war. The olive tree was sacred to her. 90. **Mars,** god of war. 92. **Bacchus,** god of wine. His forehead was crowned with vine leaves or ivy. He frequently rode upon a panther or a tiger and was attended by the Maenads (l. 94), women who, as they danced and sang, waved a staff entwined with ivy and surmounted by a pine cone. 97. **Evohe,** the cry of the devotees of Bacchus; usually a shout of joy. 99. **Neptune,** god of the sea. He carried a trident, a three-pronged spear. 101. **Pluto,** god of the lower world.

Ceres smileth stern thereat,
"We *all* now are desolate —
        Now Pan is dead." 105

Aphrodite! dead and driven
As thy native foam thou art;
With the cestus long done heaving
On the white calm of thine heart!
Ai Adonis! at that shriek   110
Not a tear runs down her cheek —
        Pan, Pan is dead.

And the Loves, we used to know from
One another, huddled lie,
Frore as taken in a snow-storm,   115
Close beside her tenderly;
As if each had weakly tried
Once to kiss her as he died.
        Pan, Pan is dead.

What, and Hermes? Time enthralleth   120
All thy cunning, Hermes, thus,
And the ivy blindly crawleth
Round thy brave caduceus?
Hast thou no new message for us,
Full of thunder and Jove-glories?   125
        Nay, Pan is dead.

Crownéd Cybele's great turret
Rocks and crumbles on her head;
Roar the lions of her chariot
Toward the wilderness, unfed;   130
Scornful children are not mute —
"Mother, mother, walk afoot,
        Since Pan is dead!"

In the fiery-hearted center
Of the solemn universe,   135
Ancient Vesta — who could enter
To consume thee with this curse?
Drop thy gray chin on thy knee,
O thou palsied Mystery!
        For Pan is dead.   140

Gods, we vainly do adjure you —
Ye return nor voice nor sign!
Not a votary could secure you
Even a grave for your Divine;

Not a grave, to show thereby   145
Here these gray old gods do lie.
        Pan, Pan is dead.

Even that Greece who took your wages
Calls the obolus outworn;
And the hoarse, deep-throated ages   150
Laugh your godships unto scorn;
And the poets do disclaim you,
Or grow colder if they name you —
        And Pan is dead.

Gods bereavéd, gods belated,   155
With your purples rent asunder!
Gods discrowned and desecrated,
Disinherited of thunder!
Now, the goats may climb and crop
The soft grass on Ida's top —   160
        Now Pan is dead.

Calm, of old, the bark went onward,
When a cry more loud than wind
Rose up, deepened, and swept sunward
From the piléd Dark behind;   165
And the sun shrank and grew pale,
Breathed against by the great wail —
        "Pan, Pan is dead."

And the rowers from the benches
Fell, each shuddering on his face,   170
While departing Influences
Struck a cold back through the place;
And the shadow of the ship
Reeled along the passive deep —
        "Pan, Pan is dead." 175

And that dismal cry rose slowly
And sank slowly through the air,
Full of spirit's melancholy
And eternity's despair!
And they heard the words it said —   180
PAN IS DEAD — GREAT PAN IS DEAD —
        PAN, PAN IS DEAD.

'Twas the hour when One in Sion
Hung for love's sake on a cross;
When his brow was chill with dying   185
And his soul was faint with loss;
When his priestly blood dropped downward —
And his kingly eyes looked throneward —
        Then, Pan was dead.

By the love, He stood alone in,   190
His sole Godhead rose complete,
And the false gods fell down moaning

103. **Ceres,** goddess of the harvest. 106. **Aphrodite,**
Venus, goddess of love and beauty. She was worshiped also
as goddess of the sea; according to one tradition she was
born of the foam of the sea. Her girdle, or cestus (l. 108), had
the power of exciting the wearer to love. 110. **Ai Adonis,**
a cry of woe—*alas, Adonis.* Adonis was the beautiful youth
loved by Venus. 115. **frore,** frozen. 120. **Hermes,** Mercury, the messenger of the gods. He carried a wand, the
caduceus (l. 123), entwined with ivy. 127. **Cybele,** Rhea,
the mother of the gods. She wore a turreted crown and rode
in a chariot drawn by lions. 136. **Vesta,** the goddess of the
hearth. She was the eldest sister of Jupiter and mysteriously
elected to remain single. In the center of her temple at
Rome a fire was kept burning by her six virgin priestesses.

149. **obolus,** a small Greek coin. 160. **Ida's top,** Mt.
Ida, in Crete, the birthplace of Zeus. 162-181. **Calm . . .
dead.** These lines refer to Plutarch's story (see introductory
note). 165. **piléd Dark,** the piled up, or heavy, darkness at
the time of the Crucifixion.

Each from off his golden seat;
All the false gods with a cry
Rendered up their deity —   195
      Pan, Pan was dead.

Wailing wide across the islands,
They rent, vest-like, their Divine;
And a darkness and a silence
Quenched the light of every shrine;   200
And Dodona's oak swang lonely
Henceforth, to the tempest only;
      Pan, Pan was dead.

Pythia staggered, feeling o'er her
Her lost god's forsaking look;   205
Straight her eyeballs filmed with horror,
And her crispy fillets shook,
And her lips gasped, through their foam,
For a word that did not come.
      Pan, Pan was dead.210

O ye vain false gods of Hellas,
Ye are silent evermore!
And I dash down this old chalice
Whence libations ran of yore.
See, the wine crawls in the dust   215
Wormlike — as your glories must,
      Since Pan is dead.

Get to dust, as common mortals,
By a common doom and track!
Let no Schiller from the portals   220
Of that Hades call you back,
Or instruct us to weep all
At your antique funeral.
      Pan, Pan is dead.

By your beauty, which confesses   225
Some chief Beauty conquering you —
By our grand heroic guesses
Through your falsehood at the True —
We will weep *not!* earth shall roll
Heir to each god's aureole —   230
      And Pan is dead.

Earth outgrows the mythic fancies
Sung beside her in her youth,
And those debonair romances
Sound but dull beside the truth.   235
Phœbus' chariot-course is run!
Look up, poets, to the sun!
      Pan, Pan is dead.

201. **Dodona,** the seat of the oracle of Zeus in Epirus. The responses were given by the rustling of the leaves of the sacred oak tree. 204. **Pythia,** the priestess of the oracle of Apollo at Delphi. 207. **crispy fillets,** curly hair. 220. **Schiller.** In his poem *The Gods of Greece* Schiller suggests that with the death of the gods poetry and art and beauty perished. Mrs. Browning says, "It is in all veneration to the memory of the deathless Schiller that I oppose a doctrine still more dishonoring to poetry than to Christianity." 230. **aureole,** a kind of luminous halo. 236. **Phœbus' chariot-course.** Phœbus Apollo, the god of the sun, drove westerly all day in a flaming chariot.

Christ hath sent us down the angels;
And the whole earth and the skies   240
Are illumed by altar-candles
Lit for blesséd mysteries;
And a Priest's hand through creation
Waveth calm and consecration.
      And Pan is dead.   245

Truth is fair; should we forgo it?
Can we sigh right for a wrong?
God Himself is the best Poet,
And the Real is his song.
Sing his truth out fair and full,   250
And secure his beautiful!
      Let Pan be dead!

Truth is large; our aspiration
Scarce embraces half we be.
Shame, to stand in his creation   255
And doubt truth's sufficiency! —
To think God's song unexcelling
The poor tales of our own telling —
      When Pan is dead!

What is true and just and honest,   260
What is lovely, what is pure,
All of praise that hath admonisht,
All of virtue — shall endure;
These are themes for poets' uses,
Stirring nobler than the Muses,   265
      Ere Pan was dead.

O brave poets, keep back nothing,
Nor mix falsehood with the whole!
Look up Godward; speak the truth in
Worthy song from earnest soul;   270
Hold, in high poetic duty,
Truest Truth the fairest Beauty!
      Pan, Pan is dead.
          (1844)

God the best poet

SONNETS FROM THE PORTUGUESE

I

I thought once how Theocritus had sung
Of the sweet years, the dear and wished-for
    years,
Who each one in a gracious hand appears
To bear a gift for mortals, old or young;
And, as I mused it in his antique tongue,   5

260-263. **What is true ... virtue.** Based on *Philippians,* 4:8.—"Whatsoever things are true, whatsoever things are honest, whatsoever things are just, whatsoever things are pure, whatsoever things are lovely, whatsoever things are of good report: if there be any virtue, and if there be any praise, think on these things." 272. **Truth ... Beauty.** Cf. Keats's *Ode on a Grecian Urn,* 49: "Beauty is truth, truth beauty." *Sonnets from the Portuguese.* See Critical Notes. *Sonnet 1.* 1. **Theocritus,** a famous Greek pastoral poet of the third century B.C. See *Idylls,* 15, 1044 ff.

I saw, in gradual vision through my tears,
The sweet, sad years, the melancholy years,
Those of my own life, who by turns had flung
A shadow across me. Straightway I was
   'ware,
So weeping, how a mystic Shape did move 10
Behind me, and drew me backward by the
   hair;
And a voice said in mastery, while I strove —
"Guess now who holds thee?" — "Death,"
   I said. But, there,
The silver answer rang — "Not Death, but
   Love."

2

But only three in all God's universe
Have heard this word thou hast said —
   Himself, beside
Thee speaking, and me listening! and replied
One of us . . . *that* was God . . . and laid the
   curse
So darkly on my eyelids, as to amerce   5
My sight from seeing thee — that if I had
   died,
The deathweights, placed there, would have
   signified
Less absolute exclusion. "Nay" is worse
From God than from all others, O my friend!
Men could not part us with their worldly
   jars,   10
Nor the seas change us, nor the tempests
   bend;
Our hands would touch for all the mountain-
   bars:
And, heaven being rolled between us at the
   end,
We should but vow the faster for the stars.

3

Unlike are we, unlike, O princely Heart!
Unlike our uses and our destinies.
Our ministering two angels look surprise
On one another, as they strike athwart
Their wings in passing. Thou, bethink thee,
   art   5
A guest for queens to social pageantries,
With gages from a hundred brighter eyes
Than tears even can make mine, to play thy
   part
Of chief musician. What hast *thou* to do
With looking from the lattice-lights at me, 10
A poor, tired, wandering singer, singing
   through
The dark, and leaning up a cypress tree?

The chrism is on thine head — on mine, the
   dew —
And Death must dig the level where these
   agree.

4

Thou hast thy calling to some palace-floor,
Most gracious singer of high poems! where
The dancers will break footing, from the care
Of watching up thy pregnant lips for more.
And dost thou lift this house's latch too poor
For hand of thine? and canst thou think and
   bear   6
To let thy music drop here unaware
In folds of golden fullness at my door?
Look up and see the casement broken in,
The bats and owlets builders in the roof!   10
My cricket chirps against thy mandolin.
Hush, call no echo up in further proof
Of desolation! there's a voice within
That weeps . . . as thou must sing . . . alone,
   aloof.

5

I lift my heavy heart up solemnly,
As once Electra her sepulchral urn,
And, looking in thine eyes, I overturn
The ashes at thy feet. Behold and see
What a great heap of grief lay hid in me,   5
And how the red wild sparkles dimly burn
Through the ashen grayness. If thy foot in
   scorn
Could tread them out to darkness utterly,
It might be well perhaps. But if instead
Thou wait beside me for the wind to blow 10
The gray dust up . . . those laurels on thine
   head,
O my Belovéd, will not shield thee so,
That none of all the fires shall scorch and
   shred
The hair beneath. Stand farther off then! go.

6

Go from me. Yet I feel that I shall stand
Henceforward in thy shadow. Nevermore
Alone upon the threshold of my door
Of individual life, I shall command
The uses of my soul, nor lift my hand   5
Serenely in the sunshine as before,
Without the sense of that which I forbore —
Thy touch upon the palm. The widest land
Doom takes to part us, leaves thy heart in
   mine

Sonnet 1. 13. **Death.** Miss Barrett had been an invalid for years.
Sonnet 2. 5. **amerce,** deprive of, as by way of punishment. 7. **deathweights,** small weights placed upon the eyelids of a dead person to hold them shut.
Sonnet 3. 7. **gages,** pledges. 12. **cypress tree,** a symbol of death. (See note on *Sonnet 1*, line 13).

Sonnet 3. 13. **chrism,** consecrated oil, used in various anointing ceremonies.
Sonnet 5. 2. **Electra,** daughter of Agamemnon, king of Mycenæ. With her brother Orestes, she avenged the murder of her father. As a part of the plan Orestes feigned death, and Electra was given possession of an urn supposed to contain his ashes. When she saw him alive, she expressed a sudden revulsion of feeling. 11. **laurels,** crowns of laurel, signifying poetic fame.

With pulses that beat double. What I do 10
And what I dream include thee, as the wine
Must taste of its own grapes. And when I sue
God for myself, He hears that name of thine,
And sees within my eyes the tears of two.

7

The face of all the world is changed, I think,
Since first I heard the footsteps of thy soul
Move still, oh, still, beside me, as they stole
Betwixt me and the dreadful outer brink
Of obvious death, where I, who thought to
    sink, 5
Was caught up into love, and taught the
    whole
Of life in a new rhythm. The cup of dole
God gave for baptism, I am fain to drink,
And praise its sweetness, Sweet, with thee
    anear.
The names of country, heaven, are changed
    away 10
For where thou art or shalt be, there or here;
And this . . . this lute and song . . . loved
    yesterday
(The singing angels know), are only dear
Because thy name moves right in what they
    say.

8

What can I give thee back, O liberal
And princely giver, who hast brought the
    gold
And purple of thine heart, unstained, untold,
And laid them on the outside of the wall
For such as I to take or leave withal, 5
In unexpected largesse? Am I cold,
Ungrateful, that for these most manifold
High gifts, I render nothing back at all?
Not so; not cold — but very poor instead.
Ask God, who knows. For frequent tears
    have run 10
The colors from my life, and left so dead
And pale a stuff, it were not fitly done
To give the same as pillow to thy head.
Go farther! let it serve to trample on.

9

Can it be right to give what I can give?
To let thee sit beneath the fall of tears
As salt as mine, and hear the sighing years
Re-sighing on my lips renunciative
Through those infrequent smiles which fail to
    live 5
For all thy adjurations? O my fears,
That this can scarce be right! We are not
    peers,
So to be lovers; and I own, and grieve,
That givers of such gifts as mine are, must
Be counted with the ungenerous. Out, alas!
I will not soil thy purple with my dust, 11

Nor breathe my poison on thy Venice-glass,
Nor give thee any love — which were unjust.
Belovéd, I only love thee! let it pass.

10

Yet, love, mere love, is beautiful indeed
And worthy of acceptation. Fire is bright,
Let temple burn, or flax; an equal light
Leaps in the flame from cedar-plank or weed:
And love is fire. And when I say at need, 5
I love thee . . . mark! . . . *I love thee* — in
    thy sight
I stand transfigured, glorified aright,
With conscience of the new rays that proceed
Out of my face toward thine. There's nothing
    low
In love, when love the lowest; meanest
    creatures 10
Who love God, God accepts while loving so.
And what I *feel*, across the inferior features
Of what I *am*, doth flash itself, and show
How that great work of Love enhances
    Nature's.

11

And therefore if to love can be desert,
I am not all unworthy. Cheeks as pale
As these you see, and trembling knees that
    fail
To bear the burden of a heavy heart —
This weary minstrel-life that once was girt 5
To climb Aornus, and can scarce avail
To pipe now 'gainst the valley nightingale
A melancholy music — why advert
To these things? O Belovéd, it is plain
I am not of thy worth nor for thy place! 10
And yet, because I love thee, I obtain
From that same love this vindicating grace,
To live on still in love, and yet in vain —
To bless thee, yet renounce thee to thy face.

12

Indeed this very love which is my boast,
And which, when rising up from breast to
    brow,
Doth crown me with a ruby large enow
To draw men's eyes and prove the inner
    cost —
This love even, all my worth, to the utter-
    most, 5
I should not love withal, unless that thou
Hadst set me an example, shown me how,
When first thine earnest eyes with mine were
    crossed,
And love called love. And thus, I cannot
    speak
Of love even, as a good thing of my own: 10

Sonnet 9. 12. **Venice-glass.** There was a tradition that
poison would break this especially thin and delicate ware.
Sonnet 11. 6. **Aornus,** a mountain in India.

Thy soul hath snatched up mine all faint and
    weak,
And placed it by thee on a golden throne —
And that I love (O soul, we must be meek!)
Is by thee only, whom I love alone.

13

And wilt thou have me fashion into speech
The love I bear thee, finding words enough,
And hold the torch out, while the winds are
    rough,
Between our faces, to cast lignt on each? —
I drop it at thy feet. I cannot teach   5
My hand to hold my spirit so far off
From myself — me — that I should bring
    thee proof
In words, of love hid in me out of reach.
Nay, let the silence of my womanhood
Commend my woman-love to thy belief — 10
Seeing that I stand unwon, however wooed,
And rend the garment of my life, in brief,
By a most dauntless, voiceless fortitude,
Lest one touch of this heart convey its grief.

14

If thou must love me, let it be for naught
Except for love's sake only. Do not say
"I love her for her smile — her look — her
    way
Of speaking gently — for a trick of thought
That falls in well with mine, and certes
    brought   5
A sense of pleasant ease on such a day" —
For these things in themselves, Belovéd, may
Be changed, or change for thee — and love,
    so wrought,
May be unwrought so. Neither love me for
Thine own dear pity's wiping my cheeks
    dry —   .   10
A creature might forget to weep, who bore
Thy comfort long, and lose thy love thereby!
But love me for love's sake, that evermore
Thou mayst love on, through love's eternity.

15

Accuse me not, beseech thee, that I wear
Too calm and sad a face in front of thine;
For we two look two ways, and cannot shine
With the same sunlight on our brow and hair.
On me thou lookest with no doubting care, 5
As on a bee shut in a crystalline;
Since sorrow hath shut me safe in love's
    divine,
And to spread wing and fly in the outer air
Were most impossible failure, if I strove
To fail so. But I look on thee — on thee —
Beholding, besides love, the end of love, 11
Hearing oblivion beyond memory;
As one who sits and gazes from above,
Over the rivers to the bitter sea.

16

And yet, because thou overcomest so,
Because thou art more noble and like a king,
Thou canst prevail against my fears and fling
Thy purple round me, till my heart shall
    grow
Too close against thine heart henceforth to
    know   5
How it shook when alone. Why, conquer-
    ing
May prove as lordly and complete a thing
In lifting upward, as in crushing low!
And as a vanquished soldier yields his sword
To one who lifts him from the bloody earth,
Even so, Belovéd, I at last record,   11
Here ends my strife. If *thou* invite me forth,
I rise above abasement at the word.
Make thy love larger to enlarge my worth.

17

My poet, thou canst touch on all the notes
God set between his After and Before,
And strike up and strike off the general roar
Of the rushing worlds a melody that floats
In the serene air purely. Antidotes   5
Of medicated music, answering for
Mankind's forlornest uses, thou canst pour
From thence into their ears. God's will
    devotes
Thine to such ends, and mine to wait on
    thine.
How, Dearest, wilt thou have me for most
    use?   10
A hope, to sing by gladly? or a fine
Sad memory, with thy songs to interfuse?
A shade, in which to sing — of palm or pine?
A grave, on which to rest from singing?
    Choose.

18

I never gave a lock of hair away
To a man, Dearest, except this to thee,
Which now upon my fingers thoughtfully,
I ring out to the full brown length and say
"Take it." My day of youth went yester-
    day;
My hair no longer bounds to my foot's glee, 6
Nor plant I it from rose or myrtle-tree,
As girls do, any more. It only may
Now shade on two pale cheeks the mark of
    tears,
Taught drooping from the head that hangs
    aside   10
Through sorrow's trick. I thought the fun-
    eral-shears
Would take this first, but Love is justified —
Take it thou, finding pure, from all those
    years,
The kiss my mother left here when she died.

19

The soul's Rialto hath its merchandise;
I barter curl for curl upon that mart,
And from my poet's forehead to my heart
Receive this lock which outweighs argosies —
As purply black, as erst to Pindar's eyes   5
The dim purpureal tresses gloomed athwart
The nine white Muse-brows. For this coun-
    terpart, . . .
The bay-crown's shade, Belovéd, I surmise,
Still lingers on thy curl, it is so black!
Thus, with a fillet of smooth-kissing breath,
I tie the shadows safe from gliding back,   11
And lay the gift where nothing hindereth;
Here on my heart, as on thy brow, to lack
No natural heat till mine grows cold in death.

20

Belovéd, my Belovéd, when I think
That thou wast in the world a year ago,
What time I sat alone here in the snow
And saw no footprint, heard the silence sink
No moment at thy voice, but, link by link,   5
Went counting all my chains as if that so
They never could fall off at any blow
Struck by thy possible hand — why, thus I
    drink
Of life's great cup of wonder! Wonderful,
Never to feel thee thrill the day or night   10
With personal act or speech — nor ever cull
Some prescience of thee with the blossoms
    white
Thou sawest growing! Atheists are as dull,
Who cannot guess God's presence out of sight.

21

Say over again, and yet once over again,
That thou dost love me. Though the word
    repeated
Should seem "a cuckoo-song," as thou dost
    treat it,
Remember, never to the hill or plain,
Valley and wood, without her cuckoo-strain
Comes the fresh Spring in all her green com-
    pleted.   6
Belovéd, I, amid the darkness greeted
By a doubtful spirit-voice, in that doubt's
    pain
Cry, "Speak once more — thou lovest!" Who
    can fear
Too many stars, though each in heaven shall
    roll,   10
Too many flowers, though each shall crown
    the year?

Sonnet 19. 1. **Rialto**, a bridge over the Grand Canal in
Venice. It is lined with shops. 5. **Pindar**, a famous Greek
lyric poet (518-446?, B.C.) 7. **nine . . . Muse-brows**, the
brows of the nine Muses. They were daughters of Jove and
goddesses of poetry, art, music, etc. 8. **bay-crown**, a
wreath of laurel bestowed upon a poet. 10. **fillet**, a white
and red band worn in ancient times upon the forehead as a
sign of religious consecration and of inviolability.

"Flush"

Say thou dost love me, love me, love me —
    toll
The silver iterance! — only minding, Dear,
To love me also in silence with thy soul.

22

When our two souls stand up erect and strong,
Face to face, silent, drawing nigh and nigher,
Until the lengthening wings break into fire
At either curvéd point — what bitter wrong
Can the earth do to us, that we should not
    long   5
Be here contented? Think. In mounting
    higher,
The angels would press on us and aspire
To drop some golden orb of perfect song
Into our deep, dear silence. Let us stay
Rather on earth, Belovéd — where the unfit
Contrarious moods of men recoil away   11
And isolate pure spirits, and permit
A place to stand and love in for a day,
With darkness and the death-hour round-
    ing it.

23

Is it indeed so? If I lay here dead,
Wouldst thou miss any life in losing mine?
And would the sun for thee more coldly shine
Because of grave-damps falling round my
    head?
I marveled, my Belovéd, when I read   5
Thy thought so in the letter. I am thine —
But . . . *so* much to thee? Can I pour thy
    wine
While my hands tremble? Then my soul,
    instead
Of dreams of death, resumes life's lower
    range.
Then, love me, Love! look on me — breathe
    on me!   10
As brighter ladies do not count it strange,
For love, to give up acres and degree,
I yield the grave for thy sake, and exchange
My near sweet view of Heaven, for earth
    with thee!

24

Let the world's sharpness, like a clasping
    knife,
Shut in upon itself and do no harm
In this close hand of Love, now soft and
    warm,
And let us hear no sound of human strife
After the click of the shutting. Life to life —
I lean upon thee, Dear, without alarm,   6
And feel as safe as guarded by a charm
Against the stab of worldlings, who if rife
Are weak to injure. Very whitely still
The lilies of our lives may reassure   10
Their blossoms from their roots, accessible

Alone to heavenly dews that drop not fewer,
Growing straight, out of man's reach, on the
    hill.
God only, who made us rich, can make us
    poor.

25

A heavy heart, Belovéd, have I borne
From year to year until I saw thy face,
And sorrow after sorrow took the place
Of all those natural joys as lightly worn
As the stringed pearls, each lifted in its turn
By a beating heart at dance-time. Hopes
    apace   6
Were changed to long despairs, till God's own
    grace
Could scarcely lift above the world forlorn
My heavy heart. Then *thou* didst bid me
    bring
And let it drop adown thy calmly great   10
Deep being! Fast it sinketh, as a thing
Which its own nature doth precipitate,
While thine doth close above it, mediating
Betwixt the stars and the unaccomplished
    fate.

26

I lived with visions for my company
Instead of men and women, years ago,
And found them gentle mates, nor thought
    to know
A sweeter music than they played to me.
But soon their trailing purple was not free   5
Of this world's dust, their lutes did silent
    grow,
And I myself grew faint and blind below
Their vanishing eyes. Then THOU didst come
    — to be,
Belovéd, what they seemed. Their shining
    fronts,
Their songs, their splendors (better, yet the
    same,   10
As river-water hallowed into fonts),
Met in thee, and from out thee overcame
My soul with satisfaction of all wants:
Because God's gifts put man's best dreams
    to shame.

27

My own Belovéd, who hast lifted me
From this drear flat of earth where I was
    thrown,
And, in betwixt the languid ringlets, blown
A life-breath, till the forehead hopefully
Shines out again, as all the angels see,   5
Before thy saving kiss! My own, my own,
Who camest to me when the world was gone,
And I who looked for only God, found
    thee!
I find thee; I am safe, and strong, and glad.

As one who stands in dewless asphodel   10
Looks backward on the tedious time he had
In the upper life — so I, with bosom-swell,
Make witness, here, between the good and
    bad,
That Love, as strong as Death, retrieves as
    well.

28

My letters! all dead paper, mute and white!
And yet they seem alive and quivering
Against my tremulous hands which loose the
    string
And let them drop down on my knee tonight.
This said — he wished to have me in his
    sight   5
Once, as a friend; this fixed a day in spring
To come and touch my hand . . . a simple
    thing,
Yet I wept for it! — this, . . . the paper's
    light . . .
Said, *Dear, I love thee;* and I sank and quailed
As if God's future thundered on my past.   10
This said, *I am thine* — and so its ink has
    paled
With lying at my heart that beat too fast.
And this . . . O Love, thy words have ill
    availed
If, what this said, I dared repeat at last!

29

I think of thee! — my thoughts do twine and
    bud
About thee, as wild vines, about a tree,
Put out broad leaves, and soon there's naught
    to see
Except the straggling green which hides the
    wood.
Yet, O my palm-tree, be it understood   5
I will not have my thoughts instead of thee
Who art dearer, better! Rather, instantly
Renew thy presence; as a strong tree should,
Rustle thy boughs and set thy trunk all bare,
And let these bands of greenery which in-
    sphere thee   10
Drop heavily down — burst, shattered, every-
    where!
Because, in this deep joy to see and hear thee
And breathe within thy shadow a new air,
I do not think of thee — I am too near thee.

30

I see thine image through my tears tonight,
And yet today I saw thee smiling. How
Refer the cause? — Belovéd, is it thou
Or I, who makes me sad? The acolyte
Amid the chanted joy and thankful rite   5

Sonnet 27. 10. **asphodel**, a lily-like flower supposed by
the Greeks to grow in Hades.
Sonnet 30. 4. **acolyte**. See note on line 53, p. 178.

May so fall flat, with pale insensate brow,
On the altar-stair. I hear thy voice and vow,
Perplexed, uncertain, since thou art out of
   sight,
As he, in his swooning ears, the choir's Amen.
Belovéd, dost thou love? or did I see all   10
The glory as I dreamed, and fainted when
Too vehement light dilated my ideal,
For my soul's eyes? Will that light come
   again,
As now these tears come — falling hot and
   real?

31

Thou comest! all is said without a word.
I sit beneath thy looks, as children do
In the noon-sun, with souls that tremble
   through
Their happy eyelids from an unaverred
Yet prodigal inward joy. Behold, I erred   5
In that last doubt! and yet I cannot rue
The sin most, but the occasion — that we two
Should for a moment stand unministered
By a mutual presence. Ah, keep near and
   close,
Thou dovelike help! and, when my fears
   would rise,   10
With thy broad heart serenely interpose;
Brood down with thy divine sufficiencies
These thoughts which tremble when bereft
   of those,
Like callow birds left desert to the skies.

32

The first time that the sun rose on thine oath
To love me, I looked forward to the moon
To slacken all those bonds which seemed too
   soon
And quickly tied to make a lasting troth.
Quick-loving hearts, I thought, may quickly
   loathe;   5
And, looking on myself, I seemed not one
For such man's love! — more like an out-of-
   tune
Worn viol, a good singer would be wroth
To spoil his song with, and which, snatched
   in haste,
Is laid down at the first ill-sounding note.   10
I did not wrong myself so, but I placed
A wrong on *thee*. For perfect strains may float
'Neath master-hands, from instruments de-
   faced —
And great souls, at one stroke, may do and
   doat.

33

Yes, call me by my pet-name! let me hear
The name I used to run at, when a child,

Sonnet 33. 1. pet-name. "Ba," pronounced as if spelled
Bay.

From innocent play, and leave the cowslips
   piled,
To glance up in some face that proved me
   dear
With the look of its eyes. I miss the clear   5
Fond voices which, being drawn and recon-
   ciled
Into the music of Heaven's undefiled,
Call me no longer. Silence on the bier,
While I call God — call God! — So let thy
   mouth
Be heir to those who are now exanimate.   10
Gather the north flowers to complete the
   south,
And catch the early love up in the late.
Yes, call me by that name — and I, in truth,
With the same heart, will answer and not
   wait.

34

With the same heart, I said, I'll answer thee
As those, when thou shalt call me by my
   name —
Lo, the vain promise! is the same, the same,
Perplexed and ruffled by life's strategy?
When called before, I told how hastily   5
I dropped my flowers or brake off from a
   game,
To run and answer with the smile that came
At play last moment, and went on with me
Through my obedience. When I answer now,
I drop a grave thought, break from soli-
   tude;
Yet still my heart goes to thee — ponder
   how —   11
Not as to a single good, but all my good!
Lay thy hand on it, best one, and allow
That no child's foot could run fast as this
   blood.

35

If I leave all for thee, wilt thou exchange
And be all to me? Shall I never miss
Home-talk and blessing and the common kiss
That comes to each in turn, nor count it
   strange,
When I look up, to drop on a new range   5
Of walls and floors, another home than this?
Nay, wilt thou fill that place by me which is
Filled by dead eyes too tender to know
   change?
That's hardest. If to conquer love, has tried,
To conquer grief, tries more, as all things
   prove;   10
For grief indeed is love and grief beside.
Alas, I have grieved so I am hard to love.

Sonnet 33. 10. exanimate, lifeless.
Sonnet 35. 1. leave all. Because of the attitude of the
father of Miss Barrett, her marriage involved the severance
of all home ties.

Yet love me — wilt thou? Open thine heart
    wide,
And fold within the wet wings of thy dove.

36

When we met first and loved, I did not build
Upon the event with marble. Could it mean
To last, a love set pendulous between
Sorrow and sorrow? Nay, I rather thrilled,
Distrusting every light that seemed to gild 5
The onward path, and feared to overlean
A finger even. And, though I have grown
    serene
And strong since then, I think that God has
    willed
A still renewable fear . . . O love, O troth . . .
Lest these enclaspéd hands should never
    hold, 10
This mutual kiss drop down between us both
As an unowned thing, once the lips being cold.
And Love, be false! if *he*, to keep one oath,
Must lose one joy, by his life's star foretold.

37

Pardon, oh, pardon, that my soul should
    make,
Of all that strong divineness which I know
For thine and thee, an image only so
Formed of the sand, and fit to shift and
    break.
It is that distant years which did not take 5
Thy sovranty, recoiling with a blow,
Have forced my swimming brain to undergo
Their doubt and dread, and blindly to forsake
Thy purity of likeness and distort
Thy worthiest love to a worthless counterfeit:
As if a shipwrecked Pagan, safe in port, 11
His guardian sea-god to commemorate,
Should set a sculptured porpoise, gills a-snort
And vibrant tail, within the temple-gate.

38

First time he kissed me, he but only kissed
The fingers of this hand wherewith I write;
And ever since, it grew more clean and white,
Slow to world-greetings, quick with its "Oh,
    list,"
When the angels speak. A ring of amethyst
I could not wear here, plainer to my sight, 6
Than that first kiss. The second passed in
    height
The first, and sought the forehead, and half
    missed,
Half falling on the hair. O beyond meed!
That was the chrism of love, which love's own
    crown, 10
With sanctifying sweetness, did precede.
The third upon my lips was folded down
In perfect, purple state; since when, indeed,
I have been proud and said, "My love, my
    own."

39

Because thou hast the power and own'st the
    grace
To look through and behind this mask of me
(Against which years have beat thus blanch-
    ingly
With their rains), and behold my soul's true
    face,
The dim and weary witness of life's race — 5
Because thou hast the faith and love to see,
Through that same soul's distracting lethargy,
The patient angel waiting for a place
In the new Heavens — because nor sin nor
    woe,
Nor God's infliction, nor death's neighbor-
    hood, 10
Nor all which others viewing, turn to go,
Nor all which makes me tired of all, self-
    viewed —
Nothing repels thee . . . Dearest, teach me so
To pour out gratitude, as thou dost, good!

40

Oh, yes! they love through all this world of
    ours!
I will not gainsay love, called love forsooth.
I have heard love talked in my early youth,
And since, not so long back but that the
    flowers
Then gathered, smell still. Mussulmans and
    Giaours 5
Throw kerchiefs at a smile, and have no ruth
For any weeping. Polypheme's white tooth
Slips on the nut if, after frequent showers,
The shell is over-smooth — and not so much
Will turn the thing called love, aside to hate
Or else to oblivion. But thou art not such 11
A lover, my Belovéd! Thou canst wait
Through sorrow and sickness, to bring souls
    to touch,
And think it soon when others cry, "Too
    late."

41

I thank all who have loved me in their hearts,
With thanks and love from mine. Deep
    thanks to all
Who paused a little near the prison-wall
To hear my music in its louder parts
Ere they went onward, each one to the mart's
Or temple's occupation, beyond call. 6
But thou, who, in my voice's sink and fall
When the sob took it, thy divinest Art's
Own instrument didst drop down at thy foot

Sonnet 39. 10. **God's infliction**, her illness, which delayed her acceptance of Browning's proposal of marriage.
  Sonnet 40. 5. **Mussulmans**, Mohammedans. **Giaours**,
the name applied by Mohammedans to disbelievers in their
religion, especially Christians. 7. **Polypheme**, Polyphemus,
the one-eyed monster who imprisoned Odysseus and his
companions and devoured two of them daily until Odysseus
got the monster drunk, put out his eye, and escaped.

To hearken what I said between my tears ...
Instruct me how to thank thee! Oh, to
   shoot   11
My soul's full meaning into future years,
That *they* should lend it utterance, and sa-
   lute
Love that endures, from Life that disappears!

42

"My future will not copy fair my past" —
I wrote that once; and thinking at my side
My ministering life-angel justified
The word by his appealing look upcast
To the white throne of God, I turned at last,
And there, instead, saw thee, not unallied   6
To angels in thy soul! Then I, long tried
By natural ills, received the comfort fast,
While budding, at thy sight, my pilgrim's
   staff
Gave out green leaves with morning dews
   impearled.   10
I seek no copy now of life's first half;
Leave here the pages with long musing curled,
And write me new my future's epigraph,
New angel mine, unhoped for in the world!

43

How do I love thee? Let me count the ways.
I love thee to the depth and breadth and
   height
My soul can reach, when feeling out of sight
For the ends of Being and ideal Grace.
I love thee to the level of everyday's   5
Most quiet need, by sun and candle-light.
I love thee freely, as men strive for Right;
I love thee purely, as they turn from Praise.
I love thee with the passion put to use
In my old griefs, and with my childhood's
   faith.   10
I love thee with a love I seemed to lose
With my lost saints — I love thee with the
   breath,
Smiles, tears, of all my life! — and, if God
   choose,
I shall but love thee better after death.

44

Belovéd, thou hast brought me many flowers
Plucked in the garden, all the summer through
And winter, and it seemed as if they grew
In this close room, nor missed the sun and
   showers.
So, in the like name of that love of ours,   5
Take back these thoughts which here un-
   folded too,

And which on warm and cold days I withdrew
From my heart's ground. Indeed, those beds
   and bowers
Be overgrown with bitter weeds and rue,
And wait thy weeding; yet here's eglantine, 10
Here's ivy! — take them, as I used to do
Thy flowers, and keep them where they shall
   not pine.
Instruct thine eyes to keep their colors true,
And tell thy soul their roots are left in mine.
                (1845-1846; 1850)

LIFE AND LOVE

Fast this Life of mine was dying,
   Blind already and calm as death,
Snowflakes on her bosom lying
   Scarcely heaving with her breath.

Love came by, and having known her   5
   In a dream of fabled lands,
Gently stooped, and laid upon her
   Mystic chrism of holy hands;

Drew his smile across her folded
   Eyelids, as the swallow dips;   10
Breathed as finely as the cold did
   Through the locking of her lips.

So, when Life looked upward, being
   Warmed and breathed on from above,
What sight could she have for seeing,   15
   Evermore ... but only LOVE?   *(1850)*

From *CASA GUIDI WINDOWS*

From PART II

A cry is up in England, which doth ring
   The hollow world through, that for ends of
      trade
And virtue and God's better worshiping, 375
   We henceforth should exalt the name of
      Peace
And leave those rusty wars that eat the soul —
   Besides their clippings at our golden fleece.
I, too, have loved peace, and from bole to
      bole
Of immemorial undeciduous trees   380
Would write, as lovers use upon a scroll,
   The holy name of Peace and set it high
Where none could pluck it down. On trees,
      I say —

Sonnet 42. 9. **pilgrim's staff**, like the rod of Aaron, which "budded and brought forth buds, and bloomed blossoms" (*Numbers*, 17:8). See *Ave Atque Vale*, 166, and note, p. 704.
Sonnet 43. 14. **I shall ... death.** See Browning's *Prospice*, p. 317.

Casa Guidi Windows. The house in which the Brownings lived in Florence was called Casa Guidi. *Casa Guidi Windows* is a long poem in which Mrs. Browning voices the cause of Italian liberty. It contains descriptions of Florence, of noted personages of Italian history, etc. See Browning's *The Italian in England*, p. 219. See also the Critical Notes.

Not upon gibbets! — With the greenery
Of dewy branches and the flowery May, 385
Sweet mediation betwixt earth and sky
Providing, for the shepherd's holiday.
Not upon gibbets! though the vulture leaves
The bones to quiet, which he first picked bare.
Not upon dungeons! though the wretch
who grieves 390
And groans within less stirs the outer air
Than any little field-mouse stirs the
sheaves.
Not upon chain-bolts! though the slave's
despair
Has dulled his helpless miserable brain
And left him blank beneath the freeman's
whip 395
To sing and laugh out idiocies of pain.
Nor yet on starving homes! where many a lip
Has sobbed itself asleep through curses
vain.
I love no peace which is not fellowship
And which includes not mercy. I would
have 400
Rather the raking of the guns across
The world, and shrieks against Heaven's
architrave;
Rather the struggle in the slippery fosse
Of dying men and horses, and the wave
Blood-bubbling. . . . Enough said! — by
Christ's own cross, 405
And by this faint heart of my womanhood,
Such things are better than a Peace that sits
Beside a hearth in self-commended mood,
And takes no thought how wind and rain by
fits
Are howling out of doors against the good
Of the poor wanderer. What! your peace
admits 411
Of outside anguish while it keeps at home?
I loathe to take its name upon my tongue.
'Tis nowise peace; 'tis treason, stiff with
doom —
'Tis gagged despair and inarticulate wrong —
Annihilated Poland, stifled Rome, 416
Dazed Naples, Hungary fainting 'neath the
thong,
And Austria wearing a smooth olive-leaf
On her brute forehead, while her hoofs out-
press
The life from these Italian souls, in brief.
O Lord of Peace, who art Lord of Right-
eousness, 421

Constrain the anguished worlds from sin
and grief,
Pierce them with conscience, purge them with
redress,
And give us peace which is no counterfeit!

* * *

(*1851; 1851*)

A CURSE FOR A NATION

PROLOGUE

I heard an angel speak last night,
    And he said, "Write!
Write a Nation's curse for me,
And send it over the Western Sea."

I faltered, taking up the word: 5
    "Not so, my lord!
If curses must be, choose another
To send thy curse against my brother.

"For I am bound by gratitude,
    By love and blood, 10
To brothers of mine across the sea,
Who stretch out kindly hands to me."

"Therefore," the voice said, "shalt thou write
    My curse tonight.
From the summits of love a curse is driven,
As lightning is from the tops of heaven." 16

"Not so," I answered. "Evermore
    My heart is sore
For my own land's sins; for little feet
Of children bleeding along the street; 20

"For parked-up honors that gainsay
    The right of way;
For almsgiving through a door that is
Not open enough for two friends to kiss;

"For love of freedom which abates 25
    Beyond the Straits;
For patriot virtue starved to vice on
Self-praise, self-interest, and suspicion;

"For an oligarchic parliament,
    And bribes well-meant. 30

416. **Poland.** Poland, once a powerful and important nation, had been dismembered in 1772, 1793, and 1795 and annexed by Russia, Prussia, and Austria. An uprising in 1830-32 was put down with great cruelty. When this poem was written, Hungary and Italy were both under the despotic control of Austria. Mrs. Browning was in Florence in 1847-49 when attempts were made by both Hungary and Italy to throw off the hated rule of Austria.

A Curse for a Nation. This poem is directed at the United States in its practice of slavery. When it appeared it was wrongly interpreted as an attack upon England. It was written in Italy.
2. **Write.** a command like that given by the angel to St. John.—". . . And he said unto me, Write: for these words are true and faithful." (*Revelation*, 21:5) 21. **parked-up honors,** probably the great estates in England closed to the people. 26. **the Straits,** the Straits of Dover, which separate England from the Continent. The reference is to Hungary, Italy, and Poland. See note on *Casa Guidi Windows*, 416, preceding column.

What curse to another land assign,
When heavy-souled for the sins of mine?"

"Therefore," the voice said, "shalt thou write
    My curse tonight,
Because thou hast strength to see and hate 35
A foul thing done *within* thy gate."

"Not so," I answered once again.
    "To curse, choose men.
For I, a woman, have only known
How the heart melts and the tears run
    down."   40

"Therefore," the voice said, "shalt thou write
    My curse tonight.
Some women weep and curse, I say
(And no one marvels), night and day.

"And thou shalt take their part tonight, 45
    Weep and write.
A curse from the depths of womanhood
Is very salt, and bitter, and good."

So thus I wrote, and mourned indeed,
    What all may read. 50
And thus, as was enjoined on me,
I send it over the Western Sea.

THE CURSE

I

Because ye have broken your own chain
    With the strain
Of brave men climbing a Nation's height,
Yet thence bear down with brand and thong
On souls of others — for this wrong 5
    This is the curse. Write.

Because yourselves are standing straight
    In the state
Of Freedom's foremost acolyte,
Yet keep calm footing all the time 10
On writhing bond slaves — for this crime
    This is the curse. Write.

Because ye prosper in God's name,
    With a claim
To honor in the old world's sight, 15
Yet do the fiend's work perfectly
In strangling martyrs — for this lie
    This is the curse. Write.

2

Ye shall watch while kings conspire
Round the people's smoldering fire, 20

And, warm for your part,
Shall never dare — O shame! —
To utter the thought into flame
    Which burns at your heart.
    This is the curse. Write. 25

Ye shall watch while nations strive
With the bloodhounds, die or survive,
    Drop faint from their jaws,
Or throttle them backward to death;
And only under your breath 30
    Shall favor the cause.
    This is the curse. Write.

Ye shall watch while strong men draw
The nets of feudal law
    To strangle the weak; 35
And, counting the sin for a sin,
Your soul shall be sadder within
    Than the word ye shall speak.
    This is the curse. Write.

When good men are praying erect 40
That Christ may avenge his elect
    And deliver the earth,
The prayer in your ears, said low,
Shall sound like the tramp of a foe
    That's driving you forth. 45
    This is the curse. Write.

When wise men give you their praise,
They shall pause in the heat of the phrase,
    As if carried too far.
When ye boast your own charters kept
    true,
Ye shall blush; for the thing which ye do 51
    Derides what ye are.
    This is the curse. Write.

When fools cast taunts at your gate,
Your scorn ye shall somewhat abate 55
    As ye look o'er the wall;
For your conscience, tradition, and name
Explode with a deadlier blame
    Than the worst of them all.
    This is the curse. Write. 60

Go, wherever ill deeds shall be done,
Go, plant your flag in the sun
    Beside the ill-doers!
And recoil from clenching the curse
Of God's witnessing Universe 65
    With a curse of yours.
    THIS is the curse. Write.

          (1860)

The Curse. **1. chain**, the chain that tied the American colonies to England. **9. acolyte**, an assistant at the altar in the Mass.

26. nations, especially Italy and Hungary, then under control of Austria.

THE FORCED RECRUIT

In the ranks of the Austrian you found him,
    He died with his face to you all;
Yet bury him here where around him
    You honor your bravest that fall.

Venetian, fair-featured and slender,   5
    He lies shot to death in his youth,
With a smile on his lips over-tender
    For any mere soldier's dead mouth.

No stranger, and yet not a traitor,
    Though alien the cloth on his breast,   10
Underneath it how seldom a greater
    Young heart has a shot sent to rest!

By your enemy tortured and goaded
    To march with them, stand in their file,
His musket (see) never was loaded,   15
    He facing your guns with that smile!

As orphans yearn on to their mothers,
    He yearned to your patriot bands —
"Let me die for our Italy, brothers,
    If not in your ranks, by your hands!   20

"Aim straightly, fire steadily! spare me
    A ball in the body which may
Deliver my heart here, and tear me
    This badge of the Austrian away!"

So thought he, so died he this morning.   25
    What then? — many others have died.
Aye, but easy for men to die scorning
    The death-stroke, who fought side by side—

One tricolor floating above them;
    Struck down 'mid triumphant acclaims   30
Of an Italy rescued to love them
    And blazon the brass with their names.

But he — without witness or honor,
    Mixed, shamed in his country's regard,
With the tyrants who march in upon her —
    Died faithful and passive; 'twas hard.   36

'Twas sublime. In a cruel restriction
    Cut off from the guerdon of sons,
With most filial obedience, conviction,
    His soul kissed the lips of her guns.   40

That moves you? Nay, grudge not to show
    it,
    While digging a grave for him here;

The others who died, says your poet,
    Have glory — let *him* have a tear.
                   (*1859;* 1860)

A MUSICAL INSTRUMENT

What was he doing, the great god Pan,
    Down in the reeds by the river?
Spreading ruin and scattering ban,
Splashing and paddling with hoofs of a goat,
And breaking the golden lilies afloat   5
    With the dragon-fly on the river.

He tore out a reed, the great god Pan,
    From the deep cool bed of the river;
The limpid water turbidly ran,
And the broken lilies a-dying lay,   10
And the dragon-fly had fled away,
    Ere he brought it out of the river.

High on the shore sat the great god Pan
    While turbidly flowed the river;
And hacked and hewed as a great god can, 15
With his hard bleak steel at the patient reed,
Till there was not a sign of the leaf indeed
    To prove it fresh from the river.

He cut it short, did the great god Pan
    (How tall it stood in the river!),   20
Then drew the pith, like the heart of a man,
Steadily from the outside ring,
And notched the poor dry empty thing
    In holes, as he sat by the river.

"This is the way," laughed the great god Pan
    (Laughed while he sat by the river),   26
"The only way, since gods began
To make sweet music, they could succeed."
Then, dropping his mouth to a hole in the
    reed,
    He blew in power by the river.   30

Sweet, sweet, sweet, O Pan!
    Piercing sweet by the river!
Blinding sweet, O great god Pan!
The sun on the hill forgot to die,
And the lilies revived, and the dragon-fly   35
    Came back to dream on the river.

Yet half a beast is the great god Pan,
    To laugh as he sits by the river,
Making a poet out of a man;
The true gods sigh for the cost and pain — 40
For the reed which grows nevermore again
    As a reed with the reeds in the river.
                   (1860)

The Forced Recruit. This poem is based upon an actual
incident of an Italian soldier's being forced to serve in the
Austrian army.

A Musical Instrument. See introductory note on *The Dead
Pan*, p. 384.

EMILY BRONTË (1818-1848)

REMEMBRANCE

Cold·in the earth — and the deep snow piled
    above thee,
Far, far removed, cold in the dreary grave!
Have I forgot, my only Love, to love thee,
Severed at last by Time's all-severing wave?

Now, when alone, do my thoughts no longer
    hover   5
Over the mountains, on that northern shore,
Resting their wings where heath and fern-
    leaves cover
Thy noble heart for ever, ever more?

Cold in the earth — and fifteen wild Decem-
    bers,
From those brown hills, have melted into
    spring;   10
Faithful, indeed, is the spirit that remem-
    bers
After such years of change and suffering!

Sweet Love of youth, forgive, if I forget thee,
While the world's tide is bearing me along;
Other desires and other hopes beset me,   15
Hopes which obscure, but cannot do thee
    wrong!

No later light has lightened up my heaven,
No second morn has ever shone for me;
All my life's bliss from thy dear life was
    given,
All my life's bliss is in the grave with thee. 20

But, when the days of golden dreams had
    perished,
And ev'n Despair was powerless to destroy;
Then did I learn how existence could be
    cherished,
Strengthened, and fed without the aid of joy.

Then did I check the tears of useless pas-
    sion —   25
Weaned my young soul from yearning after
    thine;
Sternly denied its burning wish to hasten
Down to that tomb already more than mine.

And, even yet, I dare not let it languish, 29
Dare not indulge in memory's rapturous pain;
Once drinking deep of that divinest anguish,
How could I seek the empty world again?
                    (*1845;* 1846)

Remembrance. The persons referred to in Miss Brontë's poems are imaginary, many of them characters in a Brontë cycle of fiction.

SONG

The linnet in the rocky dells,
    The moor-lark in the air,
The bee among the heather bells
    That hide my lady fair:

The wild deer browse above her breast;   5
    The wild birds raise their brood;
And they, her smiles of love caressed,
    Have left her solitude.

I ween that, when the grave's dark wall
    Did first her form retain,   10
They thought their hearts could ne'er recall
    The light of joy again.

They thought the tide of grief would flow
    Unchecked through future years;
But where is all their anguish now,   15
    And where are all their tears?

Well, let them fight for honor's breath,
    Or pleasure's shade pursue —
The dweller in the land of death
    Is changed and careless too.   20

And, if their eyes should watch and weep
    Till sorrow's source were dry,
She would not, in her tranquil sleep,
    Return a single sigh.

Blow, west-wind, by the lonely mound,   25
    And murmur, summer streams!
There is no need of other sound
    To soothe my lady's dreams.   (*1844;* 1846)

THE OLD STOIC

Riches I hold in light esteem,
    And Love I laugh to scorn;
And lust of fame was but a dream
    That vanished with the morn;

And if I pray, the only prayer   5
    That moves my lips for me
Is, "Leave the heart that now I bear,
    And give me liberty!"

Yes, as my swift days near their goal,
    'Tis all that I implore: 10
In life and death a chainless soul,
    With courage to endure.   (*1841;* 1846)

WARNING AND REPLY

In the earth — the earth — thou shalt be laid,
    A gray stone standing over thee;
Black mold beneath thee spread,
    And black mold to cover thee.

The Old Stoic. The Stoics were a school of Greek philosophers (2d century B.C.) who held that virtue was the highest good and that all feelings should be rigidly subdued.

"Well — there is rest there,　　　　　　5
　　So fast come thy prophecy;
The time when my sunny hair
　　Shall with grass roots entwinéd be."

But cold — cold is that resting-place,
　　Shut out from joy and liberty,　　　10
And all who loved thy living face
　　Will shrink from it shudderingly.

"Not so. Here the world is chill,
　　And sworn friends fall from me;
But there — they will own me still,　　15
　　And prize my memory."

Farewell, then, all that love,
　　All that deep sympathy.
Sleep on; Heaven laughs above,
　　Earth never misses thee.　　　　　20

Turf-sod and tombstone drear
　　Part human company;
One heart breaks only — here,
　　But that heart was worthy thee!
　　　　　　　　　　　　　(1843; 1850)

OFTEN REBUKED, YET ALWAYS BACK RETURNING

Often rebuked, yet always back returning
　　To those first feelings that were born with
　　　　me,
And leaving busy chase of wealth and learning
　　For idle dreams of things which cannot be:

Today, I will seek not the shadowy region;　5
　　Its unsustaining vastness waxes drear;
And visions rising, legion after legion,
　　Bring the unreal world too strangely near.

I'll walk, but not in old heroic traces,
　　And not in paths of high morality,　　　10
And not among the half-distinguished faces,
　　The clouded forms of long-past history.

I'll walk where my own nature would be
　　leading —
　　It vexes me to choose another guide —
Where the gray flocks in ferny glens are
　　feeding,　　　　　　　　　　　　　15
Where the wild wind blows on the mountain-
　　side.

What have those lonely mountains worth re-
　　vealing?
　　More glory and more grief than I can tell:

Often Rebuked. 17. **those lonely mountains,** the moors
in Yorkshire, where Miss Brontë lived.

The earth that wakes one human heart to
　　feeling
　　Can center both the worlds of Heaven and
　　　Hell.　　　　　　　　　　　　(1850)

LOVE AND FRIENDSHIP

Love is like the wild rose-brier;
　　Friendship like the holly-tree.
The holly is dark when the rose-brier blooms,
　　But which will bloom most constantly?

The wild rose-brier is sweet in spring,　　5
　　Its summer blossoms scent the air;
Yet wait till winter comes again,
　　And who will call the wild-brier fair?

Then, scorn the silly rose-wreath now,
　　And deck thee with the holly's sheen,　10
That, when December blights thy brow,
　　He still may leave thy garland green.
　　　　　　　　　　　　　　　(1850)

NO COWARD SOUL IS MINE

No coward soul is mine,
No trembler in the world's storm-troubled
　　　sphere;
　　I see Heaven's glories shine,
And faith shines equal, arming me from fear.

O God within my breast,　　　　　　5
Almighty, ever-present Deity!
　　Life — that in me has rest,
As I — undying Life — have power in Thee!

Vain are the thousand creeds
That move men's hearts — unutterably vain;
　　Worthless as withered weeds,　　　11
Or idlest froth amid the boundless main,

To waken doubt in one
Holding so fast by Thine infinity;
　　So surely anchored on　　　　　　15
The steadfast rock of immortality.

With wide-embracing love
Thy spirit animates eternal years,
　　Pervades and broods above,
Changes, sustains, dissolves, creates, and rears.

Though earth and man were gone,　　21
And suns and universes ceased to be,
　　And Thou were left alone,
Every existence would exist in Thee.

There is not room for Death,　　　　25
Nor atom that his might could render void;
　　Thou — Thou art Being and Breath,
And what Thou art may never be destroyed.
　　　　　　　　　　　　　(1846; 1850)

AUBREY THOMAS DE VERE
(1814-1902)

EPITAPH

He roamed half-round the world of woe,
    Where toil and labor never cease;
Then dropped one little span below
    In search of peace.

And now to him mild beams and showers, 5
    All that he needs to grace his tomb,
From loneliest regions at all hours,
    Unsought-for, come.   (1842)

THE SUN-GOD

I saw the Master of the Sun. He stood
High in his luminous car, himself more
    bright —
An Archer of immeasurable might.
On his left shoulder hung his quivered load;
Spurned by his steeds the eastern mountains
    glowed;   5
Forward his eagle eye and bow of Light
He bent, and while both hands that arch
    embowed,
Shaft after shaft pursued the flying night.
No wings profaned that godlike form; around
His neck high-held an ever-moving crowd   10
Of locks hung glistening, while such perfect
    sound
Fell from his bowstring that th' ethereal dome
Thrilled as a dew-drop; and each passing cloud
Expanded, whitening like the ocean foam.
    (1843)

From *MAY CAROLS*
MATER CHRISTI

He willed to lack; He willed to bear;
    He willed by suffering to be schooled;
He willed the chains of flesh to wear:
    Yet from her arms the worlds He ruled.

As tapers 'mid the noontide glow   5
    With merged yet separate radiance burn,
With human taste and touch, even so,
    The things He knew He willed to learn.

He sat beside the lowly door;
    His homeless eyes appeared to trace   10
In evening skies remembered lore,
    And shadows of His Father's face.

One only knew Him. She alone
    Who nightly to His cradle crept,

And lying like the moonbeams prone,   15
    Worshiped her Maker as He slept.   (1857)

TURRIS EBURNEA

This scheme of worlds, which vast we call,
    Is only vast compared with man;
Compared with God, the One yet All,
    Its greatness dwindles to a span.

A Lily with its isles of buds   5
    Asleep on some unmeasured sea —
O God, the starry multitudes,
    What are they more than this to Thee?

Yet girt by Nature's petty pale
    Each tenant holds the place assigned   10
To each in Being's awful scale —
    The last of creatures leaves behind

The abyss of nothingness; the first
    Into the abyss of Godhead peers,
Waiting that vision which shall burst   15
    In glory on the eternal years.

Tower of our Hope! through thee we climb
    Finite creation's topmost stair;
Through thee from Sion's height sublime
    Toward God we gaze through purer air.   20

Infinite distance still divides
    Created from Creative Power;
But all which intercepts and hides
    Lies dwarfed by that surpassing Tower!
    (1857)

FEST. PURITATIS

Cloud-piercing mountains! Chance and Change
    More high than you their thrones advance.
Self-vanquished Nature's rockiest range
    Gives way before them like the trance

Of one that wakes. From morn to eve   5
    Through fissured clefts her mists make way;
At Night's cold touch they freeze, and cleave
    Her crags; and, with a Titan's sway,

Flake off and peel the rotting rocks,
    And heap the glacier tide below   10
With isles of sand and floating blocks,
    As leaves on streams when tempests blow.

Lo, thus the great decree all-just,
    O Earth, thy mountains hear; and learn

The Sun God. The sun-god is Phœbus Apollo.
May Carols. This is a series of poems on the Christian mystery of the Incarnation and on devotion to Mary as the Mother of Christ. De Vere was urged to write such a collection by Pope Pius IX (1846-78).
Mater Christi. The title means *Mother of Christ.*

Turris Eburnea. The title means *The Ivory Tower.* This is an imaginary structure conceived of as an ideal of beauty and symmetry. Cf. *Song of Solomon,* 7:4.—"Thy neck is as a tower of ivory."
19. **Sion's height,** the heavenly Jerusalem.
Fest. Puritatis. The title means *Festival of the Purification.* This is a feast in commemoration of the ceremonial purification of the Virgin Mary, celebrated on February 2. See *Leviticus,* 12, and *Luke,* 2:22.

From fire and frost its import — "Dust 15
Thou art; and shalt to dust return."

He only *is* Who ever was—
The All-measuring Mind, the Will Supreme,
Rocks, mountains, worlds, like bubbles pass;
God is; the things not God but seem. 20
(1857)

SONG

Seek not the tree of silkiest bark
And balmiest bud
To carve her name, while yet 'tis dark,
Upon the wood!
The world is full of noble tasks, 5
And wreaths hard won;
Each work demands strong hearts, strong
hands,
Till day is done.

Sing not that violet-veinéd skin,
That cheek's pale roses; 10
The lily of that form wherein
Her soul reposes!
Forth to the fight, true man! true knight!
The clash of arms
Shall more prevail than whispered tale 15
To win her charms.

The warrior for the True, the Right,
Fights in Love's name;
The love that lures thee from the fight
Lures thee to shame: 20
That love which lifts the heart, yet leaves
The spirit free —
That love, or none, is fit for one
Man-shaped like thee.

WILLIAM BARNES (1801-1886)

EASTER ZUNDAY

Last Easter Jim put on his blue
Frock cwoat, the vu'st time — vier new;
Wi' yollow buttons all o' brass,
That glittered in the zun lik' glass;
An' poked 'ithin the button-hole 5
A tutty he'd a-begged or stole.
A span-new wes'cot, too, he wore,
Wi' yollow stripes all down avore;
An' tied his breeches' lags below
The knee, wi' ribbon in a bow; 10
An' drowed his kitty-boots azide,
An' put his laggéns on, an' tied
(1885)

His shoes wi' strings two vingers wide,
Because 'twer Easter Zunday.

An' after mornén church wer out 15
He come back hwome, an' strolled about
All down the vields, an' drough the leäne,
Wi' sister Kit an' cousin Jeäne,
A-turnén proudly to their view
His yollow breast an' back o' blue. 20
The lambs did play, the grounds wer green,
The trees did bud, the zun did sheen;
The lark did zing below the sky,
An' roads wer all a-blown so dry,
As if the zummer wer begun; 25
An' he had sich a bit o' fun!
He meäde the maïdens squeäl an' run,
Because 'twer Easter Zunday. (1844)

EASTER MONDAY

An' zoo o' Monday we got drough
Our work betimes, an axed a vew
Young vo'k vrom Stowe an' Coom, an' zome
Vrom uncle's down at Grange, to come.
An' they so spry, wi' merry smiles, 5
Did beät the path an leäp the stiles,
Wi' two or dree young chaps bezide,
To meet an' keep up Easter tide;
Vor we'd a-zaid avore, we'd git
Zome friends to come, an' have a bit 10
O' fun wi' me, an' Jeäne, an' Kit,
Because 'twer Easter Monday.

An' there we played away at quaïts,
An' weighed ourzelves wi' sceäles an' waïghts;
An' jumped to zee who jumped the spryest,
An' sprung the vurdest an' the highest; 16
An' rung the bells vor vull an hour,
An' pläyed at vives ageän the tower.
An' then we went an' had a taït,
An' cousin Sammy, wi' his waïght, 20
Broke off the bar, he wer so fat!
An' toppled off, an' vell down flat
Upon his head, an' squot his hat,
Because 'twer Easter Monday. (1844)

THE GIRT WOAK TREE THAT'S IN THE DELL

The girt woak tree that's in the dell!
There's noo tree I do love so well;
Vor times an' times when I wer young,
I there've a-climbed, an' there've a-zwung,
An' picked the eäcorns green, a-shed 5
In wrestlén storms vrom his broad head.
An' down below's the cloty brook
Where I did vish with line an' hook,

An' beät, in plaÿsome dips and zwims,
The foamy stream, wi' white-skinned lim's. 10
An' there my mother nimbly shot
Her knittén-needles, as she zot
At evenén down below the wide
Woak's head, wi' father at her zide.
An' I've a-plaÿed wi' many a bwoy, 15
That's now a man an' gone awoy;
  Zoo I do like noo tree so well
  'S the girt woak tree that's in the dell.

An' there, in leäter years, I roved
Wi' thik poor maïd I fondly loved — 20
The maïd too feäir to die so soon —
When evenén twilight, or the moon,
Cast light enough 'ithin the pleäce
To show the smiles upon her feäce,
Wi' eyes so clear's the glassy pool, 25
An' lips an' cheäks so soft as wool.
There han' in han', wi' bosoms warm,
Wi' love that burned but thought noo harm,
Below the wide-boughed tree we past
The happy hours that went too vast; 30
An' though she'll never be my wife,
She's still my leäden star o' life.
She's gone, an' she've a-left to me
Her mem'ry in the girt woak tree;
  Zoo I do love noo tree so well 35
  'S the girt woak tree that's in the dell.

An' oh! mid never ax nor hook
Be brought to spweil his steätely look;
Nor ever roun' his ribby zides
Mid cattle rub ther heäiry hides; 40
Nor pigs rout up his turf, but keep
His lwonesome sheäde vor harmless sheep;
An' let en grow, an' let en spread,
An' let en live when I be dead.
But oh! if men should come an' vell 45
The girt woak tree that's in the dell,
An' build his planks 'ithin the zide
O' some girt ship to plow the tide,
Then, life or death! I'd goo to sea,
A saïlén wi' the girt woak tree; 50
An' I upon his planks would stand,
An' die a-fightén vor the land —
The land so dear — the land so free —
The land that bore the girt woak tree;
  Vor I do love noo tree so well 55
  'S the girt woak tree that's in the dell.
                (1844)

JEANE'S WEDDEN DAY IN MORNEN

At last Jeäne come down stairs, a-drest
Wi' weddén knots upon her breast,
A-blushén, while a tear did lie
Upon her burnén cheäk half dry;
An' then her Robert, drawén nigh 5

20. thik, that. 32. leäden, leading. 37. mid, might.
38. spweil, spoil. 43. en, him. 45. vell, fell, cut down.

Wi' tothers, took her han' wi' pride,
To meäke her at the church his bride,
  Her weddén day in mornén.

Wi' litty voot an' beäten heart
She stepped up in the new light cart, 10
An' took her bridemaïd up to ride
Along wi' Robert at her zide;
An' uncle's meäre looked roun' wi' pride
To zee that, if the cart wer vull,
'Twer Jenny that he had to pull, 15
  Her weddén day in mornén.

An' aunt an' uncle stood stock-still,
An' watched em trottén down the hill;
An' when they turned off out o' groun'
Down into leäne, two tears run down 20
Aunt's feäce; an' uncle, turnén roun',
Sighed woonce, an' stumped off wi' his stick,
Because did touch en to the quick
  To peärt wi' Jeäne thik mornén.

"Now Jeäne's agone," Tom muttered, "we 25
Shall mwope lik' owls 'ithin a tree;
Vor she did zet us all agog
Vor fun, avore the burnén log."
An' as he zot an' talked, the dog
Put up his nose athirt his thighs, 30
But coulden meäke en turn his eyes,
  Jeäne's weddén day in mornén.

An' then the naïghbors round us, all
By woones an' twos begun to call,
To meet the young vo'k, when the meäre 35
Mid bring em back a married peäir;
An' all o'm zaid, to Robert's sheäre,
There had a-vell the feärest feäce,
An' kindest heart in all the pleäce,
  Jeäne's weddén day in mornén.   (1844)

THE WOODLANDS

O spread agen your leaves an' flow'rs,
  Luonesome woodlands! zunny woodlands!
Here underneath the dewy show'rs
  O' warm-aired spring-time, zunny wood-
    lands!
As when, in drong or oben groun', 5
Wi' happy buoyish heart I voun'
The twitt'ren birds a-builden roun'
  Your high-boughed hedges, zunny wood-
    lands!

Ya gie'd me life, ya gie'd me jay,
  Luonesome woodlands! zunny woodlands!
Ya gie'd me health, as in my play 11

9. litty voot, lightsome foot. 14. vull, full. 23. en,
him. 24. peärt, part. thik, that. 30. athirt, athwart.
36. Mid, might. 38. a-vell, fallen.
The Woodlands. 5. drong or oben groun', lane or open
field. 6. voun', found. 9. gie'd, gave.

I rambled droo ye, zunny woodlands!
Ya gie'd me freedom var to rove
In airy mead or sheädy grove;
Ya gie'd me smilen Fanny's love,   15
    The best ov all o't, zunny woodlands!

My vust shill skylark whivered high,
    Luonesome woodlands! zunny woodlands!
To zing below your deep-blue sky
    An' white spring-clouds, O zunny wood-
        lands!   20
An' boughs o' trees that oonce stood here,
Wer glossy green the happy year
That gie'd me oon I loved so dear,
    An' now ha' lost, O zunny woodlands!

O let me rove agen unspied,   25
    Luonesome woodlands! zunny woodlands!
Along your green-boughed hedges' zide,
    As then I rambled, zunny woodlands!
An' where the missén trees oonce stood,
Or tongues oonce rung among the wood,   30
My memory shall miäke em good,
    Though you've a-lost em, zunny wood-
        lands!

            (1844)

BLACKMWORE MAIDENS

The primrwose in the sheäde do blow,
    The cowslip in the zun,
The thyme upon the down do grow,
    The clote where streams do run;
An' where do pretty maïdens grow   5
    An' blow, but where the tow'r
Do rise among the bricken tuns,
    In Blackmwore by the Stour.

If you could zee their comely gaït,
    An' prettÿ feäces' smiles,   10
A-trippén on so light o' waïght,
    An' steppén off the stiles;
A-gwaïn to church, as bells do swing
    An' ring 'ithin the tow'r,
You'd own the pretty maïdens' pleäce   15
    Is Blackmwore by the Stour.

If you vrom Wimborne took your road,
    To Stower or Paladore,
An' all the farmers' housen showed
    Their daeters at the door,   20
You'd cry to bachelors at hwome —

"Here, come; 'ithin an hour
You'll vind ten maïdens to your mind,
    In Blackmwore by the Stour."

An' if you looked 'ithin their door,   25
    To zee 'em in their pleäce,
A-doén housework up avore
    Their smilén mother's feäce,
You'd cry — "Why, if a man would wive
    An' thrive, 'ithout a dow'r,   30
Then let en look en out a wife
    In Blackmwore by the Stour."

As I upon my road did pass
    A school-house back in Maÿ,
There out upon the beäten grass   35
    Wer maïdens at their plaÿ;
An' as the pretty souls did twile
    An' smile, I cried, "The flow'r
O' beauty, then, is still in bud
    In Blackmwore by the Stour."

            (1859)

THE SURPRISE

As there I left the road in May,
And took my way along a ground,
I found a glade with girls at play,
By leafy boughs close-hemmed around,
And there, with stores of harmless joys,   5
They plied their tongues, in merry noise;
Though little did they seem to fear
So queer a stranger might be near;
Teeh-hee! Look here! Hah! ha! Look there!
And oh! so playsome, oh! so fair.   10

And one would dance as one would spring,
Or bob or bow with leering smiles,
And one would swing, or sit and sing,
Or sew a stitch or two at whiles,
And one skipped on with downcast face,   15
All heedless, to my very place,
And there, in fright, with one foot out,
Made one dead step and turned about.
Heeh, hee, oh! oh! ooh! oo! — Look there!
And oh! so playsome, oh! so fair.   20

Away they scampered all, full speed,
By boughs that swung along their track,
As rabbits out of wood at feed,
At sight of men all scamper back.
And one pulled on behind her heel,   25
A thread of cotton, off her reel,
And oh! to follow that white clue,
I felt I fain could scamper too.
Teeh, hee, run here. Eeh! ee! Look there!
And oh! so playsome, oh! so fair.   (1869)

---

12. **droo,** through. 17. **vust shill,** first shrill. **whivered,**
hovered. 29. **missén,** missing.

Blackmwore Maidens. Blackmoor is a hamlet in East
Somerset; it is on the Stour River, which flows through
Somerset and Dorset.

4. **clote,** water lily. 7. **bricken tuns,** chimneys made
of bricks. 17. **Wimborne,** a town in Dorset, on the Stour
River. 18. **Stower, Paladore.** East Stower and West
Stower are villages about twenty miles northwest of Wim-
borne; Paladore is an old name for Shaftesbury, in North
Dorset.

37. **twile,** move about.

THE MOTHER'S DREAM

I'd a dream tonight
As I fell asleep —
Oh! the touching sight
Makes me still to weep —
Of my little lad, 5
Gone to leave me sad,
Aye, the child I had,
But was not to keep.

As in heaven high,
I my child did seek, 10
There, in train, came by
Children fair and meek,
Each in lily white,
With a lamp alight;
Each was clear to sight, 15
But they did not speak.

Then, a little sad,
Came my child in turn,
But the lamp he had,
Oh! it did not burn; 20
He, to clear my doubt,
Said, half turned about,
"Your tears put it out;
Mother, never mourn."   (1869)

THE BROKEN JUG

JENNY AND TOM

(*Tom idly swings about Jenny's jug, and breaks
it against a stone.*)

J. As if you could not leave the jug alone!
Now you have smacked my jug;
Now you have whacked my jug;
Now you have cracked my jug,
Against the stone. 5

T. The jug was cracked before, unknown to
you;
So don't belie the stone.
It scarce went nigh the stone;
It just went by the stone,
And broke in two. 10

J. Oh! cracked before! no! that was sound
enough,
From back to lip was sound,
To stand or tip was sound,
To hold or dip, was sound.
Don't talk such stuff. 15

T. How high then must I take its price to
reach?
I'd buy some more as good;
I'd buy a score as good;
I'd buy a store as good;
For twopence each. 20

J. Indeed; when stonen jugs are sold so
dear!
No, there's a tap for lies;
And there's a slap for lies;
And there's a rap for lies,
About your ear. 25

T. Oh! there are pretty hands! a little dear!
(1869)

CHARLES KINGSLEY (1819-1875)

AIRLY BEACON

Airly Beacon, Airly Beacon;
Oh, the pleasant sight to see
Shires and towns from Airly Beacon,
While my love climbed up to me!

Airly Beacon, Airly Beacon; 5
Oh, the happy hours we lay
Deep in fern on Airly Beacon,
Courting through the summer's day!

Airly Beacon, Airly Beacon;
Oh, the weary haunt for me, 10
All alone on Airly Beacon,
With his baby on my knee!   (1847)

From *THE SAINT'S TRAGEDY*

WHEN I WAS A GREENHORN AND YOUNG

When I was a greenhorn and young,
And wanted to be and to do,
I puzzled my brains about choosing my
line,
Till I found out the way that things go.

The same piece of clay makes a tile, 5
A pitcher, a taw, or a brick.
Dan Horace knew life; you may cut out a
saint,
Or a bench, from the selfsame stick.

The urchin who squalls in a gaol,
By circumstance turns out a rogue; 10
While the castle-born brat is a senator born,
Or a saint, if religion's in vogue

We fall on our legs in this world,
Blind kittens, tossed in neck and heels;

Airly Beacon. This poem may refer to a hill in the parish
of Airlie, Forfarshire, Scotland, formerly used as a signal
station.
The Saint's Tragedy. This is a drama of the life of St.
Elizabeth of Hungary. The song given here is sung by the
Fool to offset a song sung by one of the Saint's ladies who
had learned it from a nun, formerly a shepherdess.
6. **taw**, a marble used as a shooter. 7. **Horace**, a famous
Latin poet (65-8 B.C.), whose *Satires* give a complete and vivid
picture of the life of his period. The title *Dan* is from Latin
Dominus, meaning *master*.

'Tis Dame Circumstance licks Nature's cubs
　　into shape — 15
She's the mill-head, if we are the wheels.

Then why puzzle and fret, plot and dream?
He that's wise will just follow his nose;
Contentedly fish, while he swims with the
　　stream;
'Tis no business of his where it goes.　20
　　　　　　　　　　　　　　　　(1848; 1848)

From ALTON LOCKE

THE SANDS OF DEE

"O Mary, go and call the cattle home,
　　And call the cattle home,
　　And call the cattle home
　　Across the sands of Dee!"
The western wind was wild and dank with
　　foam,　5
　　And all alone went she.

The western tide crept up along the sand,
　　And o'er and o'er the sand,
　　And round and round the sand,
　　As far as eye could see.　10
The rolling mist came down and hid the
　　land —
　　And never home came she.

"Oh! is it weed, or fish, or floating hair —
　　A tress of golden hair,
　　A drownéd maiden's hair　15
　　Above the nets at sea?
Was never salmon yet that shone so fair
　　Among the stakes on Dee."

They rowed her in across the rolling foam,
　　The cruel crawling foam,　20
　　The cruel hungry foam,
　　To her grave beside the sea;
But still the boatmen hear her call the cattle
　　home
　　Across the sands of Dee.　(1849; 1850)

THE THREE FISHERS

Three fishers went sailing away to the West,
　　Away to the West as the sun went down;
Each thought on the woman who loved him
　　the best;

And the children stood watching them out
　　of the town;
For men must work, and women must weep,
And there's little to earn, and many to keep,
　　Though the harbor bar be moaning.

Three wives sat up in the lighthouse tower,
And they trimmed the lamps as the sun went
　　down;
They looked at the squall, and they looked at
　　the shower,　10
　　And the night-rack came rolling up ragged
　　and brown.
But men must work, and women must weep,
Though storms be sudden, and waters deep,
　　And the harbor bar be moaning.

Three corpses lay out on the shining sands 15
　　In the morning gleam as the tide went
　　down,
And the women are weeping and wringing
　　their hands
　　For those who will never come home to the
　　town;
For men must work, and women must weep,
And the sooner it's over, the sooner to
　　sleep;　20
　　And good-by to the bar and its moaning.
　　　　　　　　　　　　　　　　(1851)

DOLCINO TO MARGARET

The world goes up and the world goes down,
　　And the sunshine follows the rain;
And yesterday's sneer and yesterday's frown
　　Can never come over again,
　　　　Sweet wife;　5
　　No never come over again.

For woman is warm though man be cold,
　　And the night will hallow the day;
Till the heart which at even was weary and old
　　Can rise in the morning gay,　10
　　　　Sweet wife;
　　To its work in the morning gay.　(1851)

THE OUBIT

It was an hairy oubit, sae proud he crept
　　alang;
A feckless hairy oubit, and merrily he sang —
"My Minnie bade me bide at hame until I
　　won my wings;
I shew her soon my soul's aboon the warks o'
　　creeping things."

Alton Locke. This is a novel presenting a study of industrial conditions in England. Because of its picture of
Alton Locke and his radical Chartist friends, it won for
Kingsley the title of "The Chartist Clergyman." See Meredith's *The Old Chartist.*
The Sands of Dee. The Dee is a river in England and
North Wales. This song, from Chapter 26, was composed
by Alton Locke (the purported author of the novel) after
he had heard a song about a drowned girl.
20-21. **cruel . . . foam.** See Ruskin's comment on these
lines in Critical Notes.

Dolcino to Margaret. Dolcino is a man's name. Compare
the poem with Browning's *Parting at Morning*, p. 215.
The Oubit. The oubit is a woobut, a hairy caterpillar.
2. **feckless,** worthless.

This feckless hairy oubit cam' hirpling by the
   linn,   5
A swirl o' wind cam' doun the glen, and blew
   that oubit in;
O when he took the water, the saumon fry
   they rose,
And tigged him a' to pieces sma', by head and
   tail and toes.

Tak' warning then, young poets a', by this
   poor oubit's shame;
Though Pegasus may nicher loud, keep Pegasus at hame.   10
O haud your hands frae inkhorns, though a'
   the Muses woo;
For critics lie, like saumon fry, to mak' their
   meals o' you.
                        (1851)

A FAREWELL

TO C. E. G.

My fairest child, I have no song to give you;
   No lark could pipe in skies so dull and gray;
Yet, if you will, one quiet hint I'll leave you,
   For every day.

I'll tell you how to sing a clearer carol   5
   Than lark who hails the dawn or breezy
     down;
To earn yourself a purer poet's laurel
   Than Shakespeare's crown.

Be good, sweet maid, and let who can be
   clever;
   Do lovely things, not dream them, all day
     long;   10
And so make Life, and Death, and that For
   Ever,
   One grand sweet song.
                        (1856)

THE LAST BUCCANEER

Oh, England is a pleasant place for them
   that's rich and high;
But England is a cruel place for such poor
   folks as I;
And such a port for mariners I ne'er shall see
   again,
As the pleasant Isle of Avès, beside the
   Spanish main.

There were forty craft in Avès that were
   both swift and stout,   5
All furnished well with small arms and cannons round about;
And a thousand men in Avès made laws so
   fair and free
To choose their valiant captains and obey
   them loyally.

Thence we sailed against the Spaniard with
   his hoards of plate and gold,
Which he wrung by cruel tortures from Indian
   folk of old;   10
Likewise the merchant captains, with hearts
   as hard as stone,
Who flog men and keel-haul them, and starve
   them to the bone.

Oh, the palms grew high in Avès and fruits
   that shone like gold,
And the colibris and parrots they were gorgeous to behold;
And the negro maids to Avès from bondage
   fast did flee,   15
To welcome gallant sailors a-sweeping in from
   sea.

Oh, sweet it was in Avès to hear the landward
   breeze,
A-swing with good tobacco in a net between
   the trees,
With a negro lass to fan you while you listened
   to the roar
Of the breakers on the reef outside, that
   never touched the shore.   20

But Scripture saith, an ending to all fine
   things must be;
So the King's ships sailed on Avès and quite
   put down were we.
All day we fought like bulldogs, but they
   burst the booms at night;
And I fled in a piragua, sore wounded, from
   the fight.

Nine days I floated starving, and a negro lass
   beside,   25
Till for all I tried to cheer her, the poor
   young thing she died;
But as I lay a-gasping, a Bristol sail came by,
And brought me home to England here, to
   beg until I die.

And now I'm old and going — I'm sure I
   can't tell where;
One comfort is, this world's so hard, I can't
   be worse off there.   30

---

5. **hirpling by the linn**, crawling by the pool. 8. **tigged**,
pulled, tore. 10. **Pegasus**, a fabled winged horse whose
hoof caused the fountain of the Muses to spring forth from
Mt. Helicon, in Greece. He is associated with poetic inspiration. **nicher**, neigh.

The Last Buccaneer. Compare this poem with Macaulay's
The Last Buccaneer.

4. **Isle of Avès**, the Bird Islands, in the Venezuelan group
of the West Indies. **Spanish main**, the southern portion
of the Caribbean Sea. The phrase was applied also to the
mainland of Spanish America from Panama to the Amazon
River.

12. **keel-haul**, haul by ropes under the keel of a ship.
This was a method of torture used by pirates. It was also
a method of punishment once used in the Dutch and English
navies. 14. **colibris**, humming-birds. 21. **ending . . . be.**
Cf. *1 Peter*, 4:7.—"But the end of all things is at hand."
24. **piragua**, a two-masted, flat-bottomed boat.

If I might but be a sea-dove, I'd fly across
    the main,
To the pleasant Isle of Avès, to look at it
    once again.   (1856)

From THE WATER-BABIES

THE TIDE RIVER

Clear and cool, clear and cool,
By laughing shallow, and dreaming pool;
    Cool and clear, cool and clear,
By shining shingle, and foaming weir;
Under the crag where the ouzel sings,   5
And the ivied wall where the church-bell
    rings,
    Undefiled, for the undefiled;
Play by me, bathe in me, mother and child.

Dank and foul, dank and foul,
By the smoky town in its murky cowl;   10
    Foul and dank, foul and dank,
By wharf and sewer and slimy bank;
Darker and darker the further I go,
Baser and baser the richer I grow;
    Who dare sport with the sin-defiled?   15
    Shrink from me, turn from me, mother and
    child.

Strong and free, strong and free,
The floodgates are open, away to the sea;
    Free and strong, free and strong,
Cleansing my streams as I hurry along   20
To the golden sands and the leaping bar,
And the taintless tide that awaits me afar,
As I lose myself in the infinite main,
Like a soul that has sinned and is pardoned
    again.
    Undefiled, for the undefiled;   25
    Play by me, bathe in me, mother and child.
        (1862; 1862)

YOUNG AND OLD

When all the world is young, lad,
    And all the trees are green;
And every goose a swan, lad,
    And every lass a queen;
Then hey for boot and horse, lad,   5
    And round the world away;
Young blood must have its course, lad,
    And every dog his day.

When all the world is old, lad,
    And all the trees are brown;   10
And all the sport is stale, lad,
    And all the wheels run down;

4. shingle, weir, gravel, dam. 5. ouzel, the water ouzel.

Creep home, and take your place there,
    The spent and maimed among.
God grant you find one face there   15
    You loved when all was young.
        (1862; 1862)

LORRAINE, LORRAINE, LORRÈE

"Are you ready for your Steeple-chase, Lor-
    raine, Lorraine, Lorrèe?
    Barum, Barum, Barum, Barum,
    Barum, Barum, Baree.
You're booked to ride your capping race
    today at Coulterlee,
You're booked to ride Vindictive, for all the
    world to see,
To keep him straight, and keep him first, and
    win the run for me.   5
    Barum, Barum," etc.

She clasped her new-born baby, poor Lor-
    raine, Lorraine, Lorrèe.
"I cannot ride Vindictive, as any man might
    see,
And I will not ride Vindictive, with this baby
    on my knee;
He's killed a boy, he's killed a man, and why
    must he kill me?"   10

"Unless you ride Vindictive, Lorraine, Lor-
    raine, Lorrèe,
Unless you ride Vindictive today at Coul-
    terlee,
And land him safe across the brook, and win
    the blank for me,
It's you may keep your baby, for you'll get
    no keep from me."

"That husbands could be cruel," said Lor-
    raine, Lorraine, Lorrèe,   15
"That husbands could be cruel, I have known
    for seasons three;
But oh! to ride Vindictive while a baby cries
    for me,
And be killed across a fence at last for all the
    world to see!"

She mastered young Vindictive — oh! the
    gallant lass was she!
And kept him straight and won the race as
    near as near could be;   20
But he killed her at the brook against a pol-
    lard willow tree;
Oh! he killed her at the brook, the brute, for
    all the world to see,
And no one but the baby cried for poor
    Lorraine, Lorrèe.   (1874; 1874)

Lorraine, Lorraine, Lorrèe. 3. capping, chief, best. 21.
pollard, a tree cut back to the trunk.

ARTHUR HUGH CLOUGH
(1819-1861)

IN A LECTURE-ROOM

Away, haunt thou not me,
Thou vain Philosophy!
Little hast thou bestead,
Save to perplex the head,
And leave the spirit dead.   5
Unto thy broken cisterns wherefore go,
While from the secret treasure-depths below,
Fed by the skyey shower,
And clouds that sink and rest on hilltops high,
Wisdom at once, and Power,   10
Are welling, bubbling forth, unseen, incessantly?
Why labor at the dull mechanic oar,
When the fresh breeze is blowing,
And the strong current flowing,
Right onward to the Eternal Shore?   15
     (*1840;* 1849)

Tὸ καλόν

I have seen higher, holier things than these,
   And therefore must to these refuse my
     heart,
Yet am I panting for a little ease;
   I'll take, and so depart.

Ah, hold! the heart is prone to fall away,   5
   Her high and cherished visions to forget,
And if thou takest, how wilt thou repay
   So vast, so dread a debt?

How will the heart, which now thou trustest,
     then
   Corrupt, yet in corruption mindful yet,   10
Turn with sharp stings upon itself! Again,
   Bethink thee of the debt!

— Hast thou seen higher, holier things than
     these,
   And therefore must to these thy heart
     refuse?
With the true best, alack, how ill agrees   15
   That best that thou would'st choose!

The Summum Pulchrum rests in heaven
     above;
   Do thou, as best thou may'st, thy duty do.

Amid the things allowed thee, live and love;
   Some day thou shalt it view.   (*1841;* 1849)

QUA CURSUM VENTUS

As ships, becalmed at eve, that lay
   With canvas drooping, side by side,
Two towers of sail at dawn of day
   And scarce long leagues apart descried;

When fell the night, upsprung the breeze,   5
   And all the darkling hours they plied,
Nor dreamt but each the self-same seas
   By each was cleaving, side by side:

E'en so, but why the tale reveal
   Of those, whom year by year unchanged, 10
Brief absence joined anew to feel,
   Astounded, soul from soul estranged?

At dead of night their sails were filled,
   And onward each rejoicing steered —
Ah, neither blame, for neither willed,   15
   Or wist, what first with dawn appeared!

To veer, how vain! On, onward strain,
   Brave barks! In light, in darkness too,
Through winds and tides one compass
     guides—
   To that, and your own selves, be true.   20

But O blithe breeze; and O great seas,
   Though ne'er, that earliest parting past,
On your wide plain they join again,
   Together lead them home at last.

One port, methought, alike they sought,   25
   One purpose hold where'er they fare—
O bounding breeze, O rushing seas!
   At last, at last, unite them there!
     (*1845;* 1849)

"WEN GOTT BETRÜGT, IST WOHL BETROGEN"

Is it true, ye gods, who treat us
As the gambling fool is treated;
O ye, who ever cheat us,
And let us feel we're cheated!
Is it true that poetical power,   5
The gift of heaven, the dower
Of Apollo and the Nine,

In a Lecture-Room. The first three lines of this poem are
an echo of the opening lines of Milton's *Il Penseroso*—

   "Hence, vain deluding Joys,
   The brood of Folly without father bred!
   How little you bestéd,
   Or fill the fixéd mind with all your toys."

Tὸ κaλόν. The title means *Moral Virtue.*
17. Summum Pulchrum, the highest beauty.

Qua Cursum Ventus. The title means *As the Wind Blows,
So the Vessel Takes Its Course.* The words are taken from
Virgil's *Æneid,* 3, 269. The poem suggests the break between
Clough and W. G. Ward (1812-1882), a religious thinker who
became a Roman Catholic in 1845.
   "Wen Gott Betrügt, Ist Wohl Betrogen." The title means *He
Whom God Deludes Is Well Deluded.* This is an old German
proverb found in a collection published by Johannes Agricola
(1529-1548). See *Dipsychus,* 94-97, p. 417, and note, p. 178.
   7. Apollo and the Nine. Apollo was the god of poetry
and music. For the Nine Muses, see note on *In the Depths,*
2, p. 413.

The inborn sense, "the vision and the faculty
   divine,"
All we glorify and bless
In our rapturous exaltation,   10
All invention, and creation,
Exuberance of fancy, and sublime imagina-
   tion,
All a poet's fame is built on,
The fame of Shakespeare, Milton,
Of Wordsworth, Byron, Shelley,   15
Is in reason's grave precision,
Nothing more, nothing less,
Than a peculiar conformation,
Constitution, and condition
Of the brain and of the belly?   20
Is it true, ye gods who cheat us?
And that's the way ye treat us?

Oh, say it, all who think it,
Look straight, and never blink it!
If it is so, let it be so,   25
And we will all agree so;
But the plot has counterplot,
It may be, and yet be not.   (*1842;* 1849)

THE NEW SINAI

Lo, here is God, and there is God!
   Believe it not, O Man;
In such vain sort to this and that
   The ancient heathen ran:
Though Old Religion shake her head,   5
   And say in bitter grief,
The day behold, at first foretold,
   Of atheist unbelief:
Take better part, with manly heart,
   Thine adult spirit can;   10
Receive it not, believe it not,
   Believe it not, O Man!

As men at dead of night awaked
   With cries, "The king is here,"
Rush forth and greet whome'er they meet,   15
   Whoe'er shall first appear;
And still repeat, to all the street,
   " 'Tis he — the king is here";
The long procession moveth on,
   Each nobler form they see,   20
With changeful suit they still salute
   And cry, " 'Tis he, 'tis he!"

So, even so, when men were young,
   And earth and heaven were new,
And His immediate presence He   25

From human hearts withdrew,
The soul perplexed and daily vexed
   With sensuous False and True,
Amazed, bereaved, no less believed,
   And fain would see Him too.   30
"He is!" the prophet-tongues proclaimed;
   In joy and hasty fear,
"He is!" aloud replied the crowd,
   "Is here, and here, and here."

"He is! They are!" in distance seen   35
   On yon Olympus high,
In those Avernian woods abide
   And walk this azure sky;
"They are! They are!" — to every show
   Its eyes the baby turned,   40
And blazes sacrificial, tall,
   On thousand altars burned;
"They are! They are!" — On Sinai's top
   Far seen the lightnings shone,
The thunder broke, a trumpet spoke,   45
   And God said, "I am One."

God spake it out, "I, God, am One";
   The unheeding ages ran.
And baby-thoughts again, again,
   Have dogged the growing man;   50
And as of old from Sinai's top
   God said that God is One,
By Science strict so speaks He now
   To tell us, There is None!
Earth goes by chemic forces; Heaven's   55
   A Mécanique Céleste!
And heart and mind of human kind
   A watch-work as the rest!

Is this a Voice, as was the Voice,
   Whose speaking told abroad,   60
When thunder pealed, and mountain reeled,
   The ancient truth of God?
Ah, not the Voice; 'tis but the cloud,
   The outer-darkness dense,
Where image none, nor e'er was seen   65
   Similitude of sense.
'Tis but the cloudy darkness dense
   That wrapped the Mount around;
While in amaze the people stays,
   To hear the Coming Sound.   70

Is there no prophet-soul the while
   To dare, sublimely meek,
Within the shroud of blackest cloud
   The Deity to seek?

8. **the vision . . . divine.** From Wordsworth's *Excursion,*
1, 79.
   The New Sinai. Sinai was the mountain upon which God
appeared to Moses and gave him the Ten Commandments.
See *Exodus,* 19, 20, and 34. Clough's poem bears upon the
conflict that raged in his day between science and religion.

36. **Olympus,** Mt. Olympus, in Greece, the fabled home
of the Greek gods. 37. **Avernian woods,** on the shore of
Lake Avernus, nine miles west of Naples, Italy. The lake
is supposed to fill the crater of an extinct volcano regarded
as the entrance to the infernal regions. 43-46. **On Sinai's
top,** etc. From *Exodus,* 19:16.—"There were thunders, and
lightnings, and a thick cloud upon the mount, and the voice
of the trumpet exceeding loud; so that all the people . . .
trembled." 56. **Mécanique Céleste,** a celestial mechanism.

'Midst atheistic systems dark, 75
  And darker hearts' despair,
That soul has heard perchance His word,
  And on the dusky air
His skirts, as passed He by, to see
  Hath strained on their behalf, 80
Who on the plain, with dance amain,
  Adore the Golden Calf.

'Tis but the cloudy darkness dense;
  Though blank the tale it tells,
No God, no Truth! yet He, in sooth, 85
  Is there — within it dwells;
Within the skeptic darkness deep
  He dwells that none may see,
Till idol forms and idle thoughts
  Have passed and ceased to be. 90
No God, no Truth! ah, though, in sooth
  So stand the doctrine's half;
On Egypt's track return not back,
  Nor own the Golden Calf.

Take better part, with manlier heart, 95
  Thine adult spirit can;
No God, no Truth, receive it ne'er —
  Believe it ne'er — O Man!
But turn not then to seek again
  What first the ill began; 100
No God, it saith; ah, wait in faith
  God's self-completing plan;
Receive it not, but leave it not,
  And wait it out, O Man!

"The Man that went the cloud within 105
  Is gone and vanished quite;
He cometh not," the people cries,
  "Nor bringeth God to sight.
Lo, these thy gods, that safety give,
  Adore and keep the feast!" 110
Deluding and deluded, cries
  The Prophet's brother-Priest;
And Israel all bows down to fall
  Before the gilded beast.

Devout, indeed! that priestly creed, 115
  O Man, reject as sin;
The clouded hill attend thou still,
  And him that went within.
He yet shall bring some worthy thing
  For waiting souls to see; 120
Some sacred word that he hath heard
  Their light and life shall be;
Some lofty part, than which the heart
  Adopt no nobler can,
Thou shalt receive, thou shalt believe 125
And thou shalt do, O Man! (1845; 1862)

82. **Golden Calf**, an image made by Aaron and worshiped by the Israelites (*Exodus*, 32:1-4). 105. **Man.** Moses. 112. **brother-Priest**, Aaron.

THE QUESTIONING SPIRIT

The human spirits saw I on a day,
Sitting and looking each a different way;
And hardly tasking, subtly questioning,
Another spirit went around the ring
To each and each. And as he ceased his say,
Each after each, I heard them singly sing, 6
Some querulously high, some softly, sadly low,
We know not — what avails to know?
We know not — wherefore need we know?
This answer gave they still unto his suing, 10
We know not, let us do as we are doing.

Dost thou not know that these things only seem?—
I know not, let me dream my dream.
Are dust and ashes fit to make a treasure?—
I know not, let me take my pleasure. 15
What shall avail the knowledge thou hast sought? —
I know not, let me think my thought.
What is the end of strife? —
I know not, let me live my life.
How many days or e'er thou mean'st to move? — 20
I know not, let me love my love.
Were not things old once new? —
I know not, let me do as others do.
And when the rest were over past,
I know not, I will do my duty, said the last.

Thy duty do? rejoined the voice, 26
Ah, do it, do it, and rejoice;
But shalt thou then, when all is done,
Enjoy a love, embrace a beauty
Like these, that may be seen and won 30
In life, whose course will then be run;
Or wilt thou be where there is none?
I know not, I will do my duty.

And taking up the word around, above, below,
Some querulously high, some softly, sadly low,
We know not, sang they all, nor ever need we know. 36
We know not, sang they, what avails to know?
Whereat the questioning spirit, some short space,
Though unabashed, stood quiet in his place.
But as the echoing chorus died away 40
And to their dreams the rest returned apace,
By the one spirit I saw him kneeling low,
And in a silvery whisper heard him say:
Truly, thou know'st not, and thou need'st not know;
Hope only, hope thou, and believe alway; 45
I also know not, and I need not know,
Only with questionings pass I to and fro,
Perplexing these that sleep, and in their folly
Imbreeding doubt and skeptic melancholy;

Till that, their dreams deserting, they with
   me   50
Come all to this true ignorance and thee.
               (*1844; 1862*)

BETHESDA

A SEQUEL

I saw again the spirits on a day,
Where on the earth in mournful case they
   lay;
Five porches were there, and a pool, and
   round,
Huddling in blankets, strewn upon the ground,
Tied-up and bandaged, weary, sore, and
   spent,   5
The maimed and halt, diseased and impotent.

For a great angel came, 'twas said, and stirred
The pool at certain seasons, and the word
Was, with this people of the sick, that they
Who in the waters here their limbs should
   lay   10
Before the motion on the surface ceased
Should of their torment straightway be re-
   leased.
So with shrunk bodies and with heads down-
   dropped,
Stretched on the steps, and at the pillars
   propped,
Watching by day and listening through the
   night,   15
They filled the place, a miserable sight.

And I beheld that on the stony floor
He too, that spoke of duty once before,
No otherwise than others here today,
Foredone and sick and sadly muttering lay. 20
"I know not, I will do — what is it I would
   say;
What was that word which once sufficed alone
   for all,
Which now I seek in vain, and never can
   recall?"
And then, as weary of in vain renewing
His question, thus his mournful thought pur-
   suing,   25
"I know not, I must do as other men are
   doing."

But what the waters of that pool might be,
Of Lethe were they, or Philosophy;
And whether he, long waiting, did attain
Deliverance from the burden of his pain   30
There with the rest; or whether, yet before,

Some more diviner stranger passed the door
With his small company into that sad place,
And breathing hope into the sick man's face,
Bade him take up his bed, and rise and go, 35
What the end were, and whether it were so,
Further than this I saw not, neither know.
               (*1849; 1862*)

PESCHIERA

What voice did on my spirit fall,
Peschiera, when thy bridge I crost?
" 'Tis better to have fought and lost,
Than never to have fought at all."

The tricolor — a trampled rag —   5
Lies, dirt and dust; the lines I track
By sentry boxes yellow-black,
Lead up to no Italian flag.

I see the Croat soldier stand
Upon the grass of your redoubts;   10
The eagle with his black wings flouts
The breadth and beauty of your land.

Yet not in vain, although in vain,
O men of Brescia, on the day
Of loss past hope, I heard you say   15
Your welcome to the noble pain.

You say, "Since so it is — good-by,
Sweet life, high hope; but whatsoe'er
May be, or must, no tongue shall dare
To tell, 'The Lombard feared to die!' "   20

You said (there shall be answer fit),
"And if our children must obey,
They must; but thinking on this day
'Twill less debase them to submit."

You said (oh, not in vain you said),   25
"Haste, brothers, haste, while yet we may;
The hours ebb fast of this one day
When blood may yet be nobly shed."

Ah! not for idle hatred, not
For honor, fame, nor self-applause,   30
But for the glory of the cause,
You did what will not be forgot.

35. **take up . . . go**, the command of Jesus to the sick
man by the pool (*John*, 5:5-9).
   Peschiera. Peschiera is a fortified town in the province
of Verona, Italy. The poem refers to a defeat of the Italians
in their struggle for freedom from Austria.
   3-4. **'Tis better**, etc. Cf. Tennyson's *In Memoriam*, 27,
lines 15-16, p. 64. 5. **The tricolor**, the flag of Italy—red,
white, and green. 9. **Croat**, a native of Croatia, a part of
Yugoslavia. Croatia was formerly a province of Hungary.
11. **eagle**, on the standard of the Croats. 14. **Brescia**, an
ancient city in Italy, at the foot of the Alps. 20. **Lombard**,
a native of Lombardy, in northern Italy.

Bethesda. Bethesda is the name of a pool near Jerusalem,
said to have curative powers. (See *John*, 5:1-9.) This poem
is a sequel to *The Questioning Spirit*.
   28. **Lethe**, the river of forgetfulness, in Hades.

And though the stranger stand, 'tis true,
By force and fortune's right he stands;
By fortune, which is in God's hands,   35
And strength, which yet shall spring in you.

This voice did on my spirit fall,
Peschiera, when thy bridge I crost,
"'Tis better to have fought and lost,
Than never to have fought at all."   40
         (*1850; 1854*)

ALTERAM PARTEM

Or shall I say, Vain word, false thought,
Since Prudence hath her martyrs too,
And Wisdom dictates not to do,
Till doing shall be not for naught?

Not ours to give or lose is life;   5
Will Nature, when her brave ones fall,
Remake her work? or songs recall
Death's victim slain in useless strife?

That rivers flow into the sea
Is loss and waste, the foolish say,   10
Nor know that back they find their way,
Unseen, to where they wont to be.

Showers fall upon the hills, springs flow,
The river runneth still at hand,
Brave men are born into the land,   15
And whence the foolish do not know.

No! no vain voice did on me fall,
Peschiera, when thy bridge I crost,
"'Tis better to have fought and lost,
Than never to have fought at all."   20
         (*1850; 1862*)

IN THE DEPTHS

It is not sweet content, be sure,
  That moves the nobler Muse to song,
Yet when could truth come whole and pure
  From hearts that inly writhe with wrong?

'Tis not the calm and peaceful breast   5
  That sees or reads the problem true;
They only know, on whom 't has prest
  Too hard to hope to solve it too.

Our ills are worse than at their ease
  These blameless happy souls suspect;   10
They only study the disease,
  Alas, who live not to detect. (*1851; 1869*)

EASTER DAY

NAPLES, 1849

Through the great sinful streets of Naples as
    I passed,
  With fiercer heat than flamed above my
    head
My heart was hot within me; till at last
  My brain was lightened when my tongue
    had said —
    Christ is not risen!   5
    Christ is not risen, no —
      He lies and molders low;
    Christ is not risen!

What though the stone were rolled away, and
    though
  The grave found empty there? —   10
  If not there, then elsewhere;
If not where Joseph laid Him first, why then
  Where other men
Translaid Him after, in some humbler clay.
  Long ere today   15
Corruption that sad perfect work hath done,
Which here she scarcely, lightly had begun;
  The foul engendered worm
Feeds on the flesh of the life-giving form
Of our most Holy and Anointed One.   20
    He is not risen, no —
    He lies and molders low;
    Christ is not risen!

What if the women, ere the dawn was gray,
Saw one or more great angels, as they say 25
(Angels, or Him himself)? Yet neither there,
    nor then,
Nor afterwards, nor elsewhere, nor at all,
Hath He appeared to Peter or the Ten;
Nor save in thunderous terror, to blind Saul;
Save in an after Gospel and late Creed,   30
    He is not risen, indeed —
    Christ is not risen!

Alteram Partem. The title means *On the Other Side.*
18. **Peschiera.** See note on previous poem.
In the Depths. 2. **nobler Muse**, Melpomene, the muse of
tragedy. The other muses, daughters of Jove, were Calliope,
epic poetry; Clio, history; Euterpe, lyric poetry; Terpsichore,
choral dance and song; Erato, love poetry; Polyhymnia,
sacred poetry; Urania, astronomy; and Thalia, comedy.

Easter Day. Clough was in Naples on Easter Day, 1849.
12. **where . . . laid Him first**, in Joseph's tomb (*Matthew*,
27:57-60). 24-25. **women . . . angels.** See *Matthew*, 28;
Mark, 16:5; *Luke*, 24:4; *John*, 20:22. 28. **Peter . . . Ten.**
After the Resurrection, as reported in *John* 21, Christ appeared to Peter and the other disciples on the shore of the
Sea of Galilee. (See *Luke*, 24:34-43; *John*, 20:19-25.) 29.
Saul. While Saul was on the road to Damascus, "suddenly
there shined round about him a light from heaven: And
he fell to the earth, and heard a voice saying unto him,
'Saul, Saul, why persecutest thou me?'" (*Acts*, 9:3-4).
30. **late Creed.** The Resurrection of Christ was affirmed
in the creed adopted by a church council held at Nicæa,
an ancient city of Asia Minor, in 325 A.D. It is also a part of
the so-called Apostles' Creed, of unknown origin, dating
possibly from the second century.

Or, what if e'en, as runs a tale, the Ten
Saw, heard, and touched, again and yet again?
What if at Emmaüs' inn, and by Caper-
    naum's Lake, 35
    Came One, the bread that brake —
Came One that spake as never mortal spake,
And with them ate, and drank, and stood,
    and walked about?
    Ah? "some" did well to "doubt"!
Ah! the true Christ, while these things came
    to pass, 40
Nor heard, nor spake, nor walked, nor lived
    alas!
    He was not risen, no —
    He lay and moldered low,
    Christ was not risen!

As circulates in some great city crowd 45
A rumor, changeful, vague, importunate, and
    loud,
From no determined center or of fact
    Or authorship exact,
    Which no man can deny
    Nor verify; 50
So spread the wondrous fame;
    He all the same
    Lay senseless, moldering, low:
    He was not risen, no —
    Christ was not risen! 55

Ashes to ashes, dust to dust;
As of the unjust, also of the just —
    Yea, of that Just One, too!
This is the one sad Gospel that is true —
    Christ is not risen! 60

Is He not risen, and shall we not rise?
    Oh, we unwise!
What did we dream, what wake we to dis-
    cover?
Ye hills, fall on us, and ye mountains, cover!
    In darkness and great gloom 65
Come ere we thought it is *our* day of doom;
From the cursed world, which is one tomb,
    Christ is not risen!

Eat, drink, and play, and think that this is
    bliss:
There is no heaven but this; 70
    There is no hell,
Save earth, which serves the purpose doubly
    well,

Seeing it visits still
With equalest apportionment of ill
Both good and bad alike, and brings to one
    same dust 75
    The unjust and the just
    With Christ, who is not risen.

Eat, drink, and die, for we are souls bereaved;
Of all the creatures under heaven's wide cope
    We are most hopeless, who had once most
    hope, 80
And most beliefless, that had most believed.
    Ashes to ashes, dust to dust;
    As of the unjust, also of the just —
    Yea, of that Just One too!
    It is the one sad Gospel that is true — 85
    Christ is not risen!

Weep not beside the tomb,
    Ye women, unto whom
He was great solace while ye tendered him;
    Ye who with napkin o'er the head 90
And folds of linen round each wounded limb
    Laid out the Sacred Dead;
And thou that bar'st Him in thy wondering
    womb;
Yea, Daughters of Jerusalem, depart,
Bind up as best ye may your own sad bleeding
    heart. 95

Go to your homes, your living children tend,
    Your earthly spouses love;
    Set your affections *not* on things above,
Which moth and rust corrupt, which quick-
    liest come to end;
Or pray, if pray ye must, and pray, if pray
    ye can, 100
For death; since dead is He whom ye deemed
    more than man,
    Who is not risen: no —
    But lies and molders low —
    Who is not risen!

Ye men of Galilee! 105
Why stand ye looking up to heaven, where
    Him ye ne'er may see,
Neither ascending hence, nor returning hither
    again?
    Ye ignorant and idle fishermen!
Hence to your huts, and boats, and inland
    native shore,
    And catch not men, but fish; 110
    Whate'er things ye might wish,
Him neither here nor there ye e'er shall meet
    with more.

33-34. **Ten saw,** etc., as in the account recorded in *Luke,* 24:36-48. 35. **Emmaüs,** a village near Jerusalem. After the Resurrection Christ appeared to two of his disciples on the road to Emmaüs, walked with them to the village, and tarried with them during part of the night (*Luke,* 24:13-31; *John,* 21:1-24). **Capernaum's Lake,** the Sea of Galilee, bordering the city of Capernaum. 39. **"some"** . . . **"doubt."** "And when they saw him, they worshiped him; but some doubted" (*Matthew,* 28:17). 56. **Ashes . . . dust,** words of the burial service.

98-99. **Set . . . corrupt.** From *Matthew,* 6:20.—"Lay up for yourselves treasures in heaven, where neither moth nor rust doth corrupt." 110. **catch not men.** Jesus found Simon and Andrew casting a net into the sea, "for they were fishers. And Jesus said unto them, 'Come ye after me, and I will make you to become fishers of men'" (*Mark,* 1:16-17).

Ye poor deluded youths, go home,
Mend the old nets ye left to roam,
Tie the split oar, patch the torn sail; 115
It was indeed an "idle tale" —
    He was not risen!
And, oh, good men of ages yet to be,
Who shall believe *because* ye did not see —
    Oh, be ye warned, be wise!   120
Nor more with pleading eyes,
And sobs of strong desire,
Unto the empty vacant void aspire,
Seeking another and impossible birth
That is not of your own, and only mother
    earth.   125
But if there is no other life for you,
Sit down and be content, since this must
    even do;
    He is not risen!
One look, and then depart,
Ye humble and ye holy men of heart;   130
And ye! ye ministers and stewards of a Word
Which ye would preach, because another
    heard —
Ye worshipers of that ye do not know,
Take these things hence and go —
    He is not risen!   135

    Here, on our Easter Day
We rise, we come, and lo! we find Him not,
Gardener nor other, on the sacred spot.
Where they have laid Him there is none to
    say;
No sound, nor in, nor out — no word   140
Of where to seek the dead or meet the living
    Lord.
There is no glistering of an angel's wings,
There is no voice of heavenly clear behest.
Let us go hence, and think upon these things
    In silence, which is best.   145
    Is He not risen? No—
    But lies and molders low?
    Christ is not risen?   (*1849;* 1865)

EASTER DAY

II

So in the sinful streets, abstracted and alone,
I with my secret self held communing of
    mine own.
    So in the southern city spake the tongue
Of one that somewhat overwildly sung,
But in a later hour I sat and heard   5
Another voice that spake — another graver
    word.
Weep not, it bade, whatever hath been said,
Though He be dead, He is not dead.
    In the true creed
    He is yet risen indeed;   10
    Christ is yet risen.

Weep not beside His Tomb,
Ye women unto whom
He was great comfort and yet greater grief;
Nor ye, ye faithful few that wont with Him
    to roam,   15
Seek sadly what for Him ye left, go hopeless
    to your home;
Nor ye despair, ye sharers yet to be of their
    belief;
    Though He be dead, He is not dead,
    Nor gone, though fled,
    Not lost, though vanished;   20
    Though He return not, though
    He lies and molders low;
    In the true creed
    He is yet risen indeed;
    Christ is yet risen.   25

Sit if ye will, sit down upon the ground,
Yet not to weep and wail, but calmly look
    around.
    Whate'er befell,
    Earth is not hell;
Now, too, as when it first began,   30
Life is yet life, and man is man.
For all that breathe beneath the heaven's
    high cope,
Joy with grief mixes, with despondence hope.
Hope conquers cowardice, joy grief;
Or at least, faith unbelief.   35
    Though dead, not dead;
    Not gone, though fled;
    Not lost, though vanished.
    In the great gospel and true creed,
    He is yet risen indeed;   40
    Christ is yet risen.

                              (*1849;* 1869)

From DIPSYCHUS

From PART I, SCENE V

"There is no God," the wicked saith,
    "And truly it's a blessing,
For what He might have done with us
    It's better only guessing."

"There is no God," a youngster thinks,   5
    "Or really, if there may be,
He surely did not mean a man
    Always to be a baby."

' There is no God, or if there is,"
    The tradesman thinks, " 'twere funny   10

Dipsychus. This poem consists of a series of conversations
between Dipsychus and a Mephistophelian Spirit. They go
together about Venice, apparently to see the sights, and
whenever they come to a well-known place they stop and
converse. See Critical Notes.
    1. "**There is no God.**" See note on line 1, *The Cry of
the Human,* p. 381. This poem is spoken by the Spirit to
Dipsychus, who had been troubled all night by a dream in
which a bell kept tolling out the words "There is no God!"

If He should take it ill in me
To make a little money."

"Whether there be," the rich man says,
"It matters very little,
For I and mine, thank somebody,   15
Are not in want of victual."

Some others, also, to themselves,
Who scarce so much as doubt it,
Think there is none, when they are well
And do not think about it.   20

But country folks who live beneath
The shadow of the steeple;
The parson and the parson's wife,
And mostly married people;

Youths green and happy in first love,   25
So thankful for illusion;
And men caught out in what the world
Calls guilt, in first confusion;

And almost everyone when age,
Disease, or sorrows strike him,   30
Inclines to think there is a God,
Or something very like Him.   (*1850; 1865*)

From PART II

SCENE II. — *In a Gondola*

Sp. Per ora. To the Grand Canal.
Afterwards e'en as fancy shall.

Di. Afloat; we move. Delicious! Ah,
What else is like the gondola?
This level floor of liquid glass   5
Begins beneath us swift to pass.
It goes as though it went alone
By some impulsion of its own.
(How light it moves, how softly! Ah,
Were all things like the gondola!)   10

How light it moves, how softly! Ah,
Could life, as does our gondola,
Unvexed with quarrels, aims, and cares,
And moral duties and affairs,
Unswaying, noiseless, swift and strong,   15
Forever thus — thus glide along!
(How light we move, how softly! Ah,
Were life but as the gondola!)

With no more motion than should bear
A freshness to the languid air;   20
With no more effort than exprest
The need and naturalness of rest,

Part II, Scene II: In a Gondola. **1. Per ora,** now, for the
time being.

Which we beneath a grateful shade
Should take on peaceful pillows laid!
(How light we move, how softly! Ah,   25
Were life but as the gondola!)

In one unbroken passage borne
To closing night from opening morn,
Uplift at whiles slow eyes to mark
Some palace front, some passing bark;   30
Through windows catch the varying shore,
And hear the soft turns of the oar!
(How light we move, how softly! Ah,
Were life but as the gondola!)

So live, nor need to call to mind   35
Our slaving brother here behind!

Sp. Pooh! Nature meant him for no better
Than our most humble menial debtor:
Who thanks us for his day's employment
As we our purse for our enjoyment.   40

Di. To make one's fellow-man an instrument —

Sp. Is just the thing that makes him most
  content.

Di. Our gayeties, our luxuries,
    Our pleasures and our glee,
  Mere insolence and wantonness,   45
    Alas! they feel to me.

Life—it is beautiful truly, my brothers, I
    grant it you duly;
But for perfection attaining is one method
    only, abstaining;
Let us abstain, for we should so, if only we
    thought that we could so.

Sp. Bravo, bravissimo! this time though   50
You rather were run short for rime though;
Not that on that account your verse
Could be much better or much worse.

  This world is very odd, we see;
    We do not comprehend it;   55
  But in one fact we all agree —
    God won't, and we can't, mend it.

  Being common-sense, it can't be sin
    To take it as I find it;
  The pleasure to take pleasure in;   60
    The pain, try not to mind it.

Di. O let me love my love unto myself
    alone,
And know my knowledge to the world un-
    known;
No witness to the vision call,

Beholding, unbeheld of all; 65
And worship thee, with thee withdrawn, apart,
Whoe'er, whate'er thou art,
Within the closest veil of mine own inmost heart.

Better it were, thou sayest, to consent,
Feast while we may, and live ere life be spent;
Close up clear eyes, and call the unstable sure, 71
The unlovely lovely, and the filthy pure;
In self-belyings, self-deceivings roll,
And lose in Action, Passion, Talk, the soul.

Nay, better far to mark off thus much air, 75
And call it heaven; place bliss and glory there;
Fix perfect homes in the unsubstantial sky,
And say, what is not, will be by-and-by;
What here exists not must exist elsewhere.
But play no tricks upon thy soul, O man; 80
Let fact be fact, and life the thing it can.

Sp. To these remarks so sage and clerkly,
Worthy of Malebranche or Berkeley,
I trust it won't be deemed a sin
If I too answer "with a grin." 85

These juicy meats, this flashing wine,
May be an unreal mere appearance;
Only — for my inside, in fine,
They have a singular coherence.

Oh, yes, my pensive youth, abstain; 90
And any empty sick sensation,
Remember, anything like pain
Is only your imagination.

Trust me, I've read your German sage
To far more purpose e'er than you did; 95
You find it in his wisest page,
Whom God deludes is well deluded.

Di. Where are the great, whom thou would'st wish to praise thee?
Where are the pure, whom thou would'st choose to love thee?
Where are the brave, to stand supreme above thee, 100
Whose high commands would cheer, whose chiding raise thee?
Seek, seeker, in thyself; submit to find
In the stones, bread, and life in the blank mind.

82. **clerkly**, wise, learned. 83. **Malebranche**, a famous French philosopher (1638-1715). Berkeley, George Berkeley (1685-1753), a noted English philosopher, political economist, and bishop. The next stanza is a refutation of Berkeley's idealism. 97. **Whom . . . deluded**. Cf. "*Wen Gott Betrügt*," p. 409.

(Written in London, standing in the Park,
One evening in July, just before dark.) 105

Sp. As I sat at the café, I said to myself,
They may talk as they please about what they call pelf,
They may sneer as they like about eating and drinking,
But help it I cannot, I cannot help thinking,
How pleasant it is to have money, heigh-ho!
How pleasant it is to have money. 111

I sit at my table *en grand seigneur*,
And when I have done, throw a crust to the poor;
Not only the pleasure, one's self, of good living, 114
But also the pleasure of now and then giving.
So pleasant it is to have money, heigh ho!
So pleasant it is to have money.

It was but last winter I came up to town,
But already I'm getting a little renown; 119
I make new acquaintance where'er I appear;
I am not too shy, and have nothing to fear.
So pleasant it is to have money, heigh ho!
So pleasant it is to have money.

I drive through the streets, and I care not a d——n;
The people they stare, and they ask who I am; 125
And if I should chance to run over a cad,
I can pay for the damage if ever so bad.
So pleasant it is to have money, heigh ho!
So pleasant it is to have money.

We stroll to our box and look down on the pit, 130
And if it weren't low should be tempted to spit;
We loll and we talk until people look up,
And when it's half over we go out to sup.
So pleasant it is to have money, heigh ho!
So pleasant it is to have money. 135

The best of the tables and the best of the fare —
And as for the others, the devil may care;
It isn't our fault if they dare not afford
To sup like a prince and be drunk as a lord.
So pleasant it is to have money, heigh ho!
So pleasant it is to have money. 141

We sit at our tables and tipple champagne;
Ere one bottle goes, comes another again;
The waiters they skip and they scuttle about,
And the landlord attends us so civilly out. 145

112. **en grand seigneur**, as a noble lord.

So pleasant it is to have money, heigh ho!
So pleasant it is to have money.

It was but last winter I came up to town,
But already I'm getting a little renown;
I get to good houses without much ado,   150
Am beginning to see the nobility too.
  So pleasant it is to have money, heigh ho!
  So pleasant it is to have money.

O dear! what a pity they ever should lose it!
For they are the gentry that know how to
    use it;   155
So grand and so graceful, such manners, such
    dinners,
But yet, after all, it is we are the winners.
  So pleasant it is to have money, heigh ho!
  So pleasant it is to have money.

Thus I sat at my table *en grand seigneur*, 160
And when I had done threw a crust to the
    poor;
Not only the pleasure, one's self, of good
    eating,
But also the pleasure of now and then
    treating.
  So pleasant it is to have money, heigh ho!
  So pleasant it is to have money.   165

They may talk as they please about what
    they call pelf,
And how one ought never to think of one's
    self,
And how pleasures of thought surpass eating
    and drinking —
My pleasure of thought is the pleasure of
    thinking
  How pleasant it is to have money, heigh ho!
  How pleasant it is to have money.   171

(Written in Venice, but for all parts true,
'Twas not a crust I gave him, but a sou.)

A gondola here, and a gondola there,
'Tis the pleasantest fashion of taking the air.
To right and to left; stop, turn, and go
    yonder,   176
And let us repeat, o'er the tide as we wander,
  How pleasant it is to have money, heigh ho!
  How pleasant it is to have money.

      Come, leave your Gothic, worn-out story,
      San Giorgio and the Redentore;   181
      I from no building, gay or solemn,

Can spare the shapely Grecian column.
'Tis not, these centuries four, for naught
Our European world of thought   185
Hath made familiar to its home
The classic mind of Greece and Rome;
In all new work that would look forth
To more than antiquarian worth,
Palladio's pediments and bases,   190
Or something such, will find their places:
Maturer optics don't delight
In childish dim religious light,
In evanescent vague effects
That shirk, not face, one's intellects;   195
They love not fancies just betrayed,
And artful tricks of light and shade,
But pure form nakedly displayed,
And all things absolutely made.
The Doge's palace though, from hence,
In spite of doctrinaire pretense,   201
The tide now level with the quay,
Is certainly a thing to see.
We'll turn to the Rialto soon;
One's told to see it by the moon.   205

A gondola here, and a gondola there,
'Tis the pleasantest fashion of taking the air.
To right and to left; stop, turn, and go
    yonder,
And let us reflect, o'er the flood as we wander,
  How pleasant it is to have money, heigh ho!
  How pleasant it is to have money.   211

Di. How light we go, how soft we skim,
And all in moonlight seem to swim!
The south side rises o'er our bark,
A wall impenetrably dark;   215
The north is seen profusely bright;
The water, is it shade or light?
Say, gentle moon, which conquers now
The flood, those massy hulls, or thou?
(How light we go, how softly! Ah,   220
Were life but as the gondola!)

How light we go, how soft we skim,
And all in moonlight seem to swim!
In moonlight is it now, or shade?
In planes of sure division made,   225
By angles sharp of palace walls
The clear light and the shadow falls;
O sight of glory, sight of wonder!
Seen, a pictorial portent, under,
O great Rialto, the vast round   230
Of thy thrice-solid arch profound!

---

173. **sou,** a French coin worth about one cent. 180-181. **leave . . . Redentore.** The Spirit dislikes Gothic architecture and evidently some features of the two famous Renaissance churches in Venice—San Giorgio Maggiore and Redentore. These were both built by Andrea Palladio (line 190), an Italian architect of the 16th century for whom the classical Italian style is named.

184. **centuries four,** the period since the dawn of the Renaissance. 193. **dim . . . light.** From Milton's *Il Penseroso*, 160. 200. **Doge's palace,** the building in which the rulers of Venice formerly held their court. It is located on the Piazza of St. Mark. A magnificent example of Italian architecture, it is considered one of the most picturesque buildings in the world. 204. **Rialto,** a bridge over the Grand Canal in Venice.

(How light we go, how softly! Ah,
Life should be as the gondola!)

How light we go, how softly —

Sp.   Nay;
'Fore heaven, enough of that today.   235
I'm deadly weary of your tune,
And half-ennuyé with the moon;
The shadows lie, the glories fall,
And are but moonshine, after all.
It goes against my conscience really   240
To let myself feel so ideally.
Come, for the Piazzetta steer;
'Tis nine o'clock or very near.
These airy blisses, skyey joys
Of vague romantic girls and boys,   245
Which melt the heart and the brain soften,
When not affected, as too often
They are, remind me, I protest,
Of nothing better at the best
Than Timon's feast to his ancient lovers,   250
Warm water under silver covers;
"Lap, dogs!" I think I hear him say;
And lap who will, so I'm away.

Di. How light we go, how soft we skim,
And all in moonlight seem to swim!   255
Against bright clouds projected dark,
The white dome now, reclined I mark,
And, by o'er-brilliant lamps displayed,
The Doge's columns and arcade;
Over still waters mildly come   260
The distant laughter and the hum.
(How light we go, how softly! Ah,
Life should be as the gondola!)

How light we go, how soft we skim,
And all in open moonlight swim!   265
Ah, gondolier, slow, slow, more slow!
We go; but wherefore thus should go?
Ah, let not muscle all too strong
Beguile, betray thee to our wrong!
On to the landing, onward. Nay,   270
Sweet dream, a little longer stay!
On to the landing; here. And, ah!
Life is not as the gondola.

Sp. Tre ore. So. The Parthenone
Is it? you haunt for your limone.   275

237. **half-ennuyé**, half-wearied. 242. **Piazzetta**, the
small piazza leading from the Piazza of St. Mark's to the
waterfront. It is flanked by the Doge's palace and the library
of St. Mark's. 250 ff. **Timon's feast**, etc., a reference to the
banquet scene in Shakespeare's *Timon of Athens*, III, 6.
Timon was a famous misanthrope who lived during the fifth
century B.C. For a time he was rich and generous and was
surrounded by numerous parasites. When his wealth failed,
his friends deserted him, and he invited the parasites (lovers)
to a pretended banquet. With the dishes containing only
warm water before them, Timon shouted, "Uncover, dogs,
and lap"; then he threw the water and dishes at the guests
and drove them out. 274. **Tre ore**, three hours later.
Parthenone, the name of a café. 275. **limone**, lemonade.

Let me induce you to join me,
In gramolate persiche.   (*1850; 1865*)

SCENE VII. — *At Torcello. Dipsychus alone*

Di. I had a vision; was it in my sleep?
And if it were, what then? But sleep or wake,
I saw a great light open o'er my head;
And sleep or wake, uplifted to that light,
Out of that light proceeding heard a voice 5
Uttering high words, which, whether sleep or
    wake,
In me were fixed, and in me must abide.

When the enemy is near thee,
        Call on us!
In our hands we will upbear thee,   10
He shall neither scathe nor scare thee,
He shall fly thee, and shall fear thee.
        Call on us!
Call when all good friends have left thee,
Of all good sights and sounds bereft thee; 15
Call when hope and heart are sinking,
And the brain is sick with thinking,
        Help, O help!
Call, and following close behind thee
There shall haste, and there shall find thee,
        Help, sure help.   21

When the panic comes upon thee,
When necessity seems on thee,
Hope and choice have all forgone thee,
Fate and force are closing o'er thee,   25
And but one way stands before thee —
        Call on us!
Oh, and if thou dost not call,
Be but faithful, that is all.
Go right on, and close behind thee   30
There shall follow still and find thee,
        Help, sure help.   (*1849; 1865*)

SAY NOT THE STRUGGLE NAUGHT
AVAILETH

Say not the struggle naught availeth,
    The labor and the wounds are vain,
The enemy faints not, nor faileth,
    And as things have been they remain.

If hopes were dupes, fears may be liars;   5
    It may be, in yon smoke concealed,
Your comrades chase e'en now the fliers,
    And, but for you, possess the field.

277. **gramolate persiche**, a kind of ice pudding.
Scene VII. **Torcello**, on the island of Burano, below
Venice. In the sections omitted Dipsychus longs for action
and bids farewell to the "sweet simplicities of life"; but he
is admonished by the spirit to submit to the "stern necessity
of things" as they are.

For while the tired waves, vainly breaking,
  Seem here no painful inch to gain,   10
Far back, through creeks and inlets making,
  Comes silent, flooding in, the main.

And not by eastern windows only,
  When daylight comes, comes in the light,
In front, the sun climbs slow, how slowly,   15
  But westward, look, the land is bright.
                                   (*1850;* 1865)

IN STRATIS VIARUM

Blessed are those who have not seen,
  And who have yet believed
The witness, here that has not been,
  From heaven they have received.

Blessed are those who have not known 5
The things that stand before them,
And for a vision of their own
  Can piously ignore them.

So let me think whate'er befall,
  That in the city duly   10
Some men there are who love at all,
  Some women who love truly;

And that upon two millions odd
  Transgressors in sad plenty,
Mercy will of a gracious God   15
  Be shown — because of twenty. (1862)

"WHAT WENT YE OUT FOR TO SEE?"

Across the sea, along the shore,
In numbers more and ever more,
From lonely hut and busy town,
The valley through, the mountain down,
What was it ye went out to see,   5
Ye silly folk of Galilee?
The reed that in the wind doth shake?
The weed that washes in the lake?
The reeds that waver, the weeds that float? —
A young man preaching in a boat.   10

What was it ye went out to hear
By sea and land, from far and near?
A teacher? Rather seek the feet
Of those who sit in Moses' seat.
Go humbly seek, and bow to them,   15

Far off in great Jerusalem.
From them that in her courts ye saw,
Her perfect doctors of the law,
What is it ye came here to note? —
A young man preaching in a boat.   20

A prophet! Boys and women weak!
Declare or cease to rave;
Whence is it he hath learned to speak?
  Say, who his doctrine gave?
A prophet? Prophet wherefore he   25
Of all in Israel tribes? —
He teacheth with authority,
  And not as do the Scribes.   (1851; 1862)

IN THE GREAT METROPOLIS

Each for himself is still the rule;
We learn it when we go to school —
  The devil take the hindmost, O!

And when the schoolboys grow to men,
In life they learn it o'er again —   5
  The devil take the hindmost, O!

For in the church, and at the bar,
On 'Change, at court, where'er they are,
  The devil takes the hindmost, O!

Husband for husband, wife for wife, 10
Are careful that in married life
  The devil takes the hindmost, O!

From youth to age, whate'er the game,
The unvarying practice is the same—
  The devil takes the hindmost, O!   15

And after death, we do not know,
But scarce can doubt, where'er we go,
  The devil takes the hindmost, O!

Ti rol de rol, ti rol de ro,
  The devil takes the hindmost, O!   20
                       (*1852;* 1863)

QUI LABORAT, ORAT

O only Source of all our light and life,
  Whom as our truth, our strength, we see
    and feel,
But whom the hours of mortal moral strife
  Alone aright reveal!

In Stratis Viarum. The title means *In Narrow Streets.*
1. **Blessed . . . seen.** From *John,* 20:29.—"Jesus said
unto him, 'Thomas, because thou hast seen me, thou hast
believed: blessed are they that have not seen, and yet have
believed.'" 16. **twenty.** The Lord promised Abraham
that the wicked city of Sodom would be saved if twenty
righteous persons could be found in it (*Genesis,* 18:17-33).
  "What Went Ye Out for to See?" The title is taken from
Matthew, 11:7.—"What went ye out in the wilderness to see?
A reed shaken with the wind?"

27-28. **He teacheth,** etc. The people were astonished at
Christ's teaching in the synagogue, for "he taught them as
one that had authority, and not as the scribes" (*Mark,* 1:22).
  In the Great Metropolis. 8. **On 'Change,** on the Exchange,
the financial center of London.
  Qui Laborat, Orat. The title means *He who Labors, Prays.*

Mine inmost soul, before Thee inly brought,
  Thy presence owns ineffable, divine;   6
Chastised each rebel self-encentered thought,
  My will adoreth Thine.

With eye down-dropped, if then this earthly
    mind
  Speechless remain, or speechless e'en de-
    part;   10
Nor seek to see — for what of earthly kind
  Can see Thee as Thou art? —

If well-assured 'tis but profanely bold
  In thought's abstractest forms to seem to
    see,
It dare not dare the dread communion hold 15
  In ways unworthy Thee,

O not unowned, thou shalt unnamed forgive,
  In worldly walks the prayerless heart pre-
    pare;
And if in work its life it seem to live,
  Shalt make that work be prayer.   20

Nor times shall lack, when while the work it
    plies,
  Unsummoned powers the blinding film
    shall part,
And scarce by happy tears made dim, the
    eyes
  In recognition start.

But, as thou willest, give or e'en forbear   25
  The beatific supersensual sight,
So, with Thy blessing blessed, that humbler
    prayer
  Approach Thee morn and night.   (1849)

Ὕμνος ἄυμνος

O Thou whose image in the shrine
Of human spirits dwells divine;
Which from that precinct once conveyed,
To be to outer day displayed,
Doth vanish, part, and leave behind   5
Mere blank and void of empty mind,
Which willful fancy seeks in vain
With casual shapes to fill again!

O Thou that in our bosom's shrine
Dost dwell, unknown because divine!   10
I thought to speak, I thought to say,
"The light is here," "behold the way,"
"The voice was thus," and "thus the word,"
And "thus I saw," and "that I heard" —
But from the lips that half essayed   15
The imperfect utterance fell unmade.

Ὕμνος ἄυμνος. The title means *The Unsung Hymn.*

O Thou, in that mysterious shrine
Enthroned, as I must say, divine!
I will not frame one thought of what
Thou mayest either be or not.   20
I will not prate of "thus" and "so,"
And be profane with "yes" and "no";
Enough that in our soul and heart
Thou, whatsoe'er Thou may'st be, art.

Unseen, secure in that high shrine   25
Acknowledged present and divine,
I will not ask some upper air,
Some future day to place Thee there;
Nor say, nor yet deny, such men
And women saw Thee thus and then;   30
Thy name was such, and there or here
To him or her Thou didst appear.

Do only Thou in that dim shrine,
Unknown or known, remain, divine;
There, or if not, at least in eyes   35
That scan the fact that round them lies,
The hand to sway, the judgment guide,
In sight and sense Thyself divide;
Be Thou but there—in soul and heart,
I will not ask to feel Thou art.   40
                (*1851; 1862*)

AH! YET CONSIDER IT AGAIN!

"Old things need not be therefore true."
O brother men, nor yet the new;
Ah! still awhile the old thought retain,
And yet consider it again!

The souls of now two thousand years   5
Have laid up here their toils and fears,
And all the earnings of their pain —
Ah, yet consider it again!

We! what do we see? each a space
Of some few yards before his face;   10
Does that the whole wide plan explain?
Ah, yet consider it again!

Alas! the great world goes its way,
And takes its truth from each new day;
They do not quit, nor can retain,   15
Far less consider it again.   (*1851; 1862*)

NOLI ÆMULARI

In controversial foul impureness
  The peace that is thy light to thee
Quench not; in faith and inner sureness
  Possess thy soul and let it be.

Noli Æmulari. The title means *Do not Try to Emulate.*

No violence — perverse — persistent —   5
  What cannot be can bring to be;
No zeal what is make more existent,
  And strife but blinds the eyes that see.

What though in blood their souls embruing,
  The great, the good and wise they curse, 10
Still sinning, what they know not doing;
  Stand still, forbear, nor make it worse.

By curses, by denunciation,
  The coming fate they cannot stay;
Nor thou, by fiery indignation,   15
  Though just, accelerate the day.
              (*1849;* 1869)

From *SONGS IN ABSENCE*

Ye Flags of Piccadilly

Ye flags of Piccadilly,
  Where I posted up and down,
And wished myself so often
  Well away from you and town —

Are the people walking quietly   5
  And steady on their feet,
Cabs and omnibuses plying
  Just as usual in the street?

Do the houses look as upright
  As of old they used to be,   10
And does nothing seem affected
  By the pitching of the sea?

Through the Green Park iron railings
  Do the quick pedestrians pass?
Are the little children playing   15
  Round the plane-tree in the grass?

This squally wild north-wester
  With which our vessel fights,
Does it merely serve with you to
  Carry up some paper kites?   20

Ye flags of Piccadilly,
  Which I hated so, I vow
I could wish with all my heart
  You were underneath me now!

O Ship, Ship, Ship

O ship, ship, ship,
  That comest over the sea,
Whatever it be thou bringest,   15
  Come quickly with it to me.   (*1853;* 1869)

Are they tidings of comfort and joy,   5
  That shall make me seem to see

The sweet lips softly moving
  And whispering love to me?

Or are they of trouble and grief,
  Estrangement, sorrow, and doubt,   10
To turn into torture my hopes,
  And drive me from Paradise out?

O ship, ship, ship,
  That comest over the sea,
Whatever it be thou bringest,   15
  Come quickly with it to me.
              (*1852;* 1862)

HOPE EVERMORE AND BELIEVE!

Hope evermore and believe, O man, for e'en
  as thy thought
So are the things that thou see'st; e'en as
  thy hope and belief.
Cowardly art thou and timid? they rise to
  provoke thee against them;
Hast thou courage? enough, see them exult-
  ing to yield.
Yea, the rough rock, the dull earth, the wild
  sea's furying waters   5
(Violent say'st thou and hard, mighty thou
  think'st to destroy),
All with ineffable longing are waiting their
  Invader,

All with one varying voice, call to him.
  Come and subdue;
Still for their Conqueror call, and, but for the
  joy of being conquered
(Rapture they will not forego), dare to
  resist and rebel;   10
Still, when resisting and raging, in soft under-
  voice say unto him,
Fear not, retire not, O man; hope ever-
  more and believe.

Go from the east to the west, as the sun and
  the stars direct thee,
Go with the girdle of man, go and encom-
  pass the earth.
Not for the gain of the gold; for the getting,
  the hoarding, the having,   15
But for the joy of the deed; but for the
  Duty to do.
Go with the spiritual life, the higher volition
  and action,
With the great girdle of God, go and encom-
  pass the earth.

Go; say not in thy heart, And what then were
  it accomplished,
Were the wild impulse allayed, what were
  the use or the good!   20

Songs in Absence. This title covers a group of lyrics written by Clough on a journey to the United States in 1852.
Most of the lyrics are addressed to the lady who became his
wife.
  1. **flags of Piccadilly**, flagstones of Piccadilly, a famous
street in London.

Go, when the instinct is stilled, and when the
    deed is accomplished,
What thou hast done and shalt do, shall be
    declared to thee then.
Go with the sun and the stars, and yet ever-
    more in thy spirit
    Say to thyself: It is good; yet is there
    better than it.
This that I see is not all, and this that I do
    is but little;   25
    Nevertheless it is good, though there is
    better than it.

          (1862)

THE LATEST DECALOGUE

Thou shalt have one God only; who
Would be at the expense of two?
No graven images may be
Worshiped, except the currency.
Swear not at all; for, for thy curse   5
Thine enemy is none the worse.
At church on Sunday to attend
Will serve to keep the world thy friend.
Honor thy parents; that is, all
From whom advancement may befall.   10
Thou shalt not kill; but need'st not strive
Officiously to keep alive.
Do not adultery commit;
Advantage rarely comes of it.
Thou shalt not steal; an empty feat,   15
When it's so lucrative to cheat.
Bear not false witness; let the lie
Have time on its own wings to fly.
Thou shalt not covet, but tradition
Approves all forms of competition.   20

          (1862)

"WITH WHOM IS NO VARIABLENESS, NEITHER SHADOW OF TURNING"

It fortifies my soul to know
That, though I perish, Truth is so;
That, howsoe'er I stray and range,
Whate'er I do, Thou dost not change.
I steadier step when I recall   5
That, if I slip, Thou dost not fall.

        (1850; 1862)

THROUGH A GLASS DARKLY

What we, when face to face we see
The Father of our souls, shall be,   ▸

John tells us, doth not yet appear;
Ah! did he tell what we are here!

A mind for thoughts to pass into,   5
A heart for loves to travel through,
Five senses to detect things near —
Is this the whole that we are here?

Rules baffle instincts — instincts rules,
Wise men are bad — and good are fools,   10
Facts evil — wishes vain appear;
We cannot go, why are we here?

Oh, may we for assurance' sake,
Some arbitrary judgment take,
And willfully pronounce it clear,   15
For this or that 'tis we are here?

Or is it right, and will it do,
To pace the sad confusion through,
And say: it doth not yet appear,
What we shall be, what we are here?   20

Ah, yet, when all is thought and said,
The heart still overrules the head;
Still what we hope we must believe,
And what is given us receive;

Must still believe, for still we hope   25
That in a world of larger scope,
What here is faithfully begun
Will be completed, not undone.

My child, we still must think, when we
That ampler life together see,   30
Some true result will yet appear
Of what we are, together, here.

          (1862)

ITE DOMUM SATURÆ, VENIT HESPERUS

The skies have sunk, and hid the upper snow
(Home, Rose, and home, Provence and La
    Palie),
The rainy clouds are filing fast below,
And wet will be the path, and wet shall we.
Home, Rose, and home, Provence and La
    Palie.   5

Hope Evermore and Believe! 24. **good . . . better than it.**
Cf. Browning's *Saul,* 295, p. 229.
    Through a Glass Darkly. The title is taken from *1 Corin-thians,* 13:12.—"For now we see through a glass darkly; but then face to face."

    3. John tells us, in *1 John,* 3:2.—"Beloved, now are we the sons of God, and it doth not yet appear what we shall be: but we know that, when he shall appear, we shall be like him; for we shall see him as he is."
    Ite Domum Saturæ, Venit Hesperus. The title means *Go Home Satisfied; Hesperus [the evening star] Comes.* It is taken from a line in the tenth *Eclogue* of Virgil, in which a goatherd is addressing his herd: "Go home full-fed; Hesperus comes." Clough makes the speaker a peasant girl who is driving home her cows, named Rose, Provence, and La Palie.

Ah dear, and where is he, a year agone,
Who stepped beside and cheered us on and
on?
My sweetheart wanders far away from me,
In foreign land or on a foreign sea.
Home, Rose, and home, Provence and La
Palie.   10

The lightning zigzags shoot across the sky
(Home, Rose, and home, Provence and La
Palie),
And through the vale the rains go sweeping
by;
Ah me, and when in shelter shall we be?
Home, Rose, and home, Provence and La
Palie.   15

Cold, dreary cold, the stormy winds feel they
O'er foreign lands and foreign seas that stray
(Home, Rose, and home, Provence and La
Palie).
And doth he e'er, I wonder, bring to mind
The pleasant huts and herds he left behind?
And doth he sometimes in his slumbering
see   21
The feeding kine, and doth he think of me,
My sweetheart wandering wheresoe'er it be?
Home, Rose, and home, Provence and La
Palie.
The thunder bellows far from snow to snow
(Home, Rose, and home, Provence and La
Palie),   26
And loud and louder roars the flood below.
Heigho! but soon in shelter shall we be;
Home, Rose, and home, Provence and La
Palie.

Or shall he find before his term be sped,   30
Some comelier maid that he shall wish to
wed?
(Home, Rose, and home, Provence and La
Palie),
For weary is work, and weary day by day
To have your comfort miles on miles away.
Home, Rose, and home, Provence and La
Palie.   35

Or may it be that I shall find my mate,
And he returning see himself too late?
For work we must, and what we see, we see,
And God, He knows, and what must be,
must be,
When sweethearts wander far away from me.
Home, Rose, and home, Provence and La
Palie.   41

The sky behind is brightening up anew
(Home, Rose, and home, Provence and La
Palie),

The rain is ending, and our journey too;
Heigho! aha! for here at home are we—   45
In, Rose, and in, Provence and La Palie.
(1849; 1862)

PERCHE PENSA? PENSANDO S'INVECCHIA

To spend uncounted years of pain,
Again, again, and yet again,
In working out in heart and brain
The problem of our being here;
To gather facts from far and near,   5
Upon the mind to hold them clear,
And, knowing more may yet appear,
Unto one's latest breath to fear,
The premature result to draw —
Is this the object, end and law,   10
And purpose of our being here?
(1851; 1853)

LIFE IS STRUGGLE

To wear out heart, and nerves, and brain,
And give oneself a world of pain;
Be eager, angry, fierce, and hot,
Imperious, supple — God knows what,
For what's all one to have or not;   5
O false, unwise, absurd, and vain!
For 'tis not joy, it is not gain,
It is not in itself a bliss,
Only it is precisely this
That keeps us all alive.   10

To say we truly feel the pain,
And quite are sinking with the strain; —
Entirely, simply, undeceived,
Believe, and say we ne'er believed
The object, e'en were it achieved,   15
A thing we e'er had cared to keep;
With heart and soul to hold it cheap,
And then to go and try it again;
O false, unwise, absurd, and vain!
Oh, 'tis not joy, and 'tis not bliss,   20
Only it is precisely this
That keeps us still alive.   *(1851; 1869)*

IN A LONDON SQUARE

Put forth thy leaf, thou lofty plane —
East wind and frost are safely gone;
With zephyr mild and balmy rain
The summer comes serenely on;
Earth, air, and sun and skies combine   5
To promise all that's kind and fair.

Perche Pensa? Pensando S'Invecchia. The title means
Why Think? By Thinking You Grow Old.

But thou, O human heart of mine,
 Be still, contain thyself, and bear.

December days were brief and chill,
 The winds of March were wild and drear,
And, nearing and receding still, 11
 Spring never would, we thought, be here.
The leaves that burst, the suns that shine,
 Had, not the less, their certain date—
And thou, O human heart of mine, 15
 Be still, refrain thyself, and wait. (1862)

ALL IS WELL

Whate'er you dream, with doubt possessed,
Keep, keep it snug within your breast,
And lay you down and take your rest;
Forget in sleep the doubt and pain,
And when you wake, to work again. 5
The wind it blows, the vessel goes,
And where and whither, no one knows.

'Twill all be well—no need of care;
Though how it will, and when, and where,
We cannot see, and can't declare. 10
In spite of dreams, in spite of thought,
'Tis not in vain, and not for naught,
The wind it blows, the ship it goes,
Though where and whither, no one knows.
(1851; 1869)

EDWARD FITZGERALD (1809–1883)

not trying to resolve

THE RUBÁIYÁT OF OMAR KHAYYÁM

naturalism + transcendentalism

1

Wake! For the Sun, who scattered into flight
The Stars before him from the Field of Night,
 Drives Night along with them from Heav'n
 and strikes
The Sultán's Turret with a Shaft of Light.

2

Before the phantom of False morning died, 5
Methought a Voice within the Tavern cried,
 "When all the Temple is prepared within,
Why nods the drowsy Worshiper outside?"

3

And, as the Cock crew, those who stood before
The Tavern shouted — "Open, then, the
 Door! 10

You know how little while we have to
 stay,
And, once departed, may return no more."

4

Now the New Year reviving old Desires,
The thoughtful Soul to Solitude retires,
 Where the WHITE HAND OF MOSES on the
 Bough 15
Puts out, and Jesus from the Ground suspires.

5

Iram indeed is gone with all his Rose,
And Jamshyd's Sev'n-ringed Cup where no
 one knows;
 But still a Ruby kindles in the Vine,
And many a Garden by the Water blows. 20

6

And David's lips are locked; but in divine
High-piping Pehleví, with "Wine! Wine!
 Wine!
 Red Wine!" — the Nightingale cries to
 the Rose
That sallow cheek of hers to incarnadine.

7

Come, fill the Cup, and in the fire of Spring 25
Your Winter-garment of Repentance fling;
 The Bird of Time has but a little way
To flutter — and the Bird is on the Wing.

8

Whether at Naishápúr or Babylon,
Whether the Cup with sweet or bitter run, 30
 The Wine of Life keeps oozing drop by
 drop,
The Leaves of Life keep falling one by one.

9

Each Morn a thousand Roses brings, you
 say;
Yes, but where leaves the Rose of Yesterday?
 And this first Summer month that brings
 the Rose 35
Shall take Jamshyd and Kaikobád away.

The Rubáiyát of Omar Khayyám. Omar Khayyám (Omar the Tent-Maker) was a Persian poet and astronomer of the 11th century. *Rubáiyát* is the plural form of *rubái*, meaning *quatrain.* See Critical Notes.
5. **False morning,** a transient light on the horizon about an hour before the true dawn—a common phenomenon in the East. (FitzGerald's note.)

13. **New Year.** The Persian new year begins with the vernal equinox. 15. **White Hand . . . Bough.** At the command of the Lord, Moses put his hand into his bosom and "when he took it out, behold, his hand was leprous as snow" (*Exodus*, 4:6). The metaphor is applied to the blooming of the flowers. 16. **Jesus . . . suspires.** The Persians believed that the healing power of Jesus resided in his breath. 17. **Iram,** an ancient Persian garden, now obliterated. 18. **Jamshyd,** a legendary king of Persia. His seven-ringed cup was symbolical of the seven heavens, the seven planets, the seven seas, etc. 21-22. **David . . . Pehleví.** David's tongue is forgotten, but the nightingale still cries in Pehleví, the ancient literary language of Persia. 29. **Naishápúr,** a village in Persia; Omar's native place. 36. **Kaikobád,** the founder of the most celebrated of the dynasties of ancient Persia.

10

Well, let it take them! What have we to do
With Kaikobád the Great, or Kaikhosrú?
⟩ Let Zál and Rustum bluster as they will,
Or Hátim call to Supper — heed not you. 40

11

With me along the strip of Herbage strown
That just divides the desert from the sown,
  Where name of Slave and Sultán is forgot —
And Peace to Mahmúd on his golden Throne!

12

A Book of Verses underneath the Bough, 45
A Jug of Wine, a Loaf of Bread — and Thou
  Beside me singing in the Wilderness —
Oh, Wilderness were Paradise enow!

13

Some for the Glories of This World; and some
Sigh for the Prophet's Paradise to come; 50
  Ah, take the Cash, and let the Credit go,
Nor heed the rumble of a distant Drum!

14

Look to the blowing Rose about us — "Lo,
Laughing," she says, "into the world I blow,
  At once the silken tassel of my Purse 55
Tear, and its Treasure on the Garden throw."

15

And those who husbanded the Golden Grain,
And those who flung it to the winds like Rain,
  Alike to no such aureate Earth are turned
As, buried once, Men want dug up again. 60

16

The Worldly Hope men set their Hearts upon
Turns Ashes — or it prospers; and anon,
  Like Snow upon the Desert's dusty Face,
Lighting a little hour or two — is gone.

17

Think, in this battered Caravanserai 65
Whose Portals are alternate Night and Day,
  How Sultán after Sultán with his Pomp
Abode his destined Hour, and went his way.

18

They say the Lion and the Lizard keep
The Courts where Jamshyd gloried and drank
    deep; 70
  And Bahrám, that great Hunter — the
    Wild Ass
Stamps o'er his Head, but cannot break his
    Sleep.

19

I sometimes think that never blows so red
The Rose as where some buried Cæsar bled;
  That every Hyacinth the Garden wears 75
Dropped in her Lap from some once lovely
    Head.

20

And this reviving Herb whose tender Green
Fledges the River-Lip on which we lean —
  Ah, lean upon it lightly! for who knows
From what once lovely Lip it springs unseen!

21

Ah, my Belovéd, fill the Cup that clears 81
TODAY of past Regrets and future Fears:
  Tomorrow! — Why, Tomorrow I may be
Myself with Yesterday's Sev'n thousand
    Years.

22

For some we loved, the loveliest and the
    best 85
That from his Vintage rolling Time hath prest,
  Have drunk their Cup a Round or two be-
    fore,
And one by one crept silently to rest.

23

And we, that now make merry in the Room
They left, and Summer dresses in new bloom,
  Ourselves must we beneath the Couch of
    Earth 91
Descend — ourselves to make a Couch — for
    whom?

24

Ah, make the most of what we yet may spend,
Before we too into the Dust descend;
  Dust into Dust, and under Dust, to lie, 95
Sans Wine, sans Song, sans Singer, and —
    sans End!

38. **Kaikhosrú,** a famous Persian hero, identified with
Cyrus the Great (6th century B.C.), the founder of the Persian
Empire. 39. **Zál and Rustum,** famous Persian heroes; Zál
was the father of Rustum. (See Arnold's *Sohrab and Rustum*
and introductory note, p. 475.) 40. **Hátim,** a type of
Oriental Generosity. (FitzGerald's note.) 44. **Mahmúd,**
the Sultan. Mahmúd the Great (c. 970-1030) was the famous
Mohammedan conqueror of India. He was sultan of Ghazni,
the city of his birth in Afghanistan. 50. **the Prophet,**
Mohammed. 57. **Golden grain,** wealth. 65. **Caravanserai,**
a kind of Oriental inn, where caravans rest at night.

70. **Courts.** Jamshyd's capital was Persepolis. 71. **Bahrám,** a Persian ruler who lost his life in a swamp while
hunting a wild ass. 75. **Hyacinth,** a flower named after
Hyacinthus, a youth accidentally killed by his friend, Apollo,
god of the sun. The flower sprang up where the blood of
Hyacinthus flowed upon the ground. 84. **Sev'n thousand
Years,** a thousand years to each planet, or, the time by
Moslem computation from the creation of Adam to Dooms-
day. 96. **Sans,** without.

25

Alike for those who for TODAY prepare,
And those that after some TOMORROW stare,
  A Muezzín from the Tower of Darkness
    cries,
"Fools, your Reward is neither Here nor
    There."   100

26

Why, all the Saints and Sages who discussed
Of the Two Worlds so wisely — they are
    thrust
  Like foolish Prophets forth; their Words to
    Scorn
Are scattered, and their Mouths are stopped
    with Dust.

27

Myself when young did eagerly frequent   105
Doctor and Saint, and heard great argument
  About it and about; but evermore
Came out by the same door where in I went.

28

With them the seed of Wisdom did I sow,
And with mine own hand wrought to make it
    grow;   110
  And this was all the Harvest that I
    reaped —
"I came like Water, and like Wind I go."

29

Into this Universe, and *Why* not knowing
Nor *Whence*, like Water willy-nilly flowing;
  And out of it, as Wind along the Waste,   115
I know not *Whither*, willy-nilly blowing.

30

What, without asking, hither hurried *Whence?*
And, without asking, *Whither* hurried hence!
  Oh, many a Cup of this forbidden Wine
Must drown the memory of that insolence!

31

Up from the Earth's Center through the
    Seventh Gate   121
I rose, and on the Throne of Saturn sate,
  And many a Knot unraveled by the Road;
But not the Master-knot of Human Fate.

32

There was the Door to which I found no Key;
There was the Veil through which I might
    not see;   126

Some little talk awhile of ME and THEE
There was — and then no more of THEE and
    ME.

33

Earth could not answer; nor the Seas that
    mourn
In flowing Purple, of their Lord forlorn;   130
  Nor rolling Heaven, with all his Signs
    revealed
And hidden by the sleeve of Night and Morn.

34

Then of the THEE IN ME who works behind
The Veil, I lifted up my hands to find   134
  A lamp amid the Darkness; and I heard,
As from Without — "THE ME WITHIN THEE
    BLIND!"

35

Then to the Lip of this poor earthen Urn
I leaned, the Secret of my Life to learn;
  And Lip to Lip it murmured — "While you
    live,
Drink! — for, once dead, you never shall
    return."   140

36

I think the Vessel, that with fugitive
Articulation answered, once did live,
  And drink; and Ah! the passive Lip I
    kissed,
How many Kisses might it take — and give!

37

For I remember stopping by the way   145
To watch a Potter thumping his wet Clay;
  And with its all-obliterated Tongue
It murmured — "Gently, Brother, gently,
    pray!"

38

And has not such a Story from of Old
Down Man's successive generations rolled   150
  Of such a clod of saturated Earth
Cast by the Maker into Human mold?

39

And not a drop that from our Cups we
    throw
For Earth to drink of, but may steal below
  To quench the fire of Anguish in some
    Eye
There hidden — far beneath, and long ago.   156

99. Muezzín, the officer who summons the faithful to
prayer in Mohammedan countries. 119. forbidden Wine.
Orthodox Mohammedanism regards the use of wine as one
of twelve capital sins. 122. Saturn, the lord of the seventh
heaven, one of the concentric spheres into which, according to
the ancients, the space around the earth was divided.

131. Signs, the signs of the zodiac. 153-154. drop . . .
Earth. It was an old custom to throw a little wine on the
ground before drinking; it refreshed some wine-drinker who
had gone before.

40

As then the Tulip, for her morning sup
Of Heav'nly Vintage, from the soil looks up,
   Do you devoutly do the like, till Heav'n
To Earth invert you — like an empty Cup. 160

41

Perplexed no more with Human or Divine,
Tomorrow's tangle to the winds resign,
   And lose your fingers in the tresses of
The Cypress-slender Minister of Wine.

42

And if the Wine you drink, the Lip you press,
End in what All begins and ends in — Yes; 166
   Think that you are TODAY what YESTER-
     DAY
You were — TOMORROW you shall not be less.

43

So when that Angel of the darker Drink
At last shall find you by the river-brink, 170
   And offering his Cup, invite your Soul
Forth to your Lips to quaff — you shall not
     shrink.

44

Why, if the Soul can fling the Dust aside,
And naked on the Air of Heaven ride,
   Were 't not a Shame — were 't not a
     Shame for him 175
In this clay carcass crippled to abide?

45

'Tis but a Tent where takes his one day's rest
A Sultán to the realm of Death addrest;
   The Sultán rises, and the dark Ferrásh
Strikes, and prepares it for another Guest. 180

46

And fear not lest Existence closing your
Account, and mine, should know the like no
     more;
   The Eternal Sákí from that Bowl has poured
Millions of Bubbles like us, and will pour.

47

When You and I behind the Veil are past, 185
Oh, but the long, long while the World shall
     last,
   Which of our Coming and Departure heeds
As the Sea's self should heed a pebble-cast.

164. Cypress-slender . . . Wine, the maiden who passes
the wine; she is as slender as a cypress. Stanza 42 stresses
the joy of wine mingled with the joy of love. 179. Ferrásh,
a servant, a camp-follower. 183. Sákí, wine-bearer.

48

A Moment's Halt — a momentary taste 189
Of BEING from the Well amid the Waste —
And Lo!—the phantom Caravan has reached
The NOTHING it set out from — Oh, make
     haste!

49

Would you that spangle of Existence spend
About THE SECRET — quick about it, Friend!
   A Hair perhaps divides the False and
     True — 195
And upon what, prithee, does life depend?

50

A Hair perhaps divides the False and True —
Yes; and a single Alif were the clue —
   Could you but find it — to the Treasure-
     house,
And peradventure to THE MASTER too; 200

51

Whose secret Presence, through Creation's
     veins
Running Quicksilver-like, eludes your pains;
   Taking all shapes from Máh to Máhi; and
They change and perish all — but He remains;

52

A moment guessed — then back behind the
     Fold 205
Immersed of Darkness round the Drama
     rolled
   Which, for the Pastime of Eternity,
He doth Himself contrive, enact, behold.

53

But if in vain, down on the stubborn floor
Of Earth, and up to Heav'n's unopening Door,
   You gaze TODAY, while You are You —
     how then 211
TOMORROW, when You shall be You no more?

54

Waste not your Hour, nor in the vain pursuit
Of This and That endeavor and dispute;
   Better be jocund with the fruitful Grape
Than sadden after none, or bitter, Fruit. 216

55

You know, my Friends, with what a brave
     Carouse
I made a Second Marriage in my house;
   Divorced old barren Reason from my Bed,
And took the Daughter of the Vine to Spouse.

198. Alif, the first letter of the Arabic alphabet. 203.
from Máh to Máhi, from fish to moon.

(handwritten notes in margin: "like live now", "light heartedness — refreshing humor")

56

For "Is" and "Is-not" though with Rule and
Line,   221
And "Up-and-down" by Logic, I define,
Of all that one should care to fathom, I
Was never deep in anything but — Wine.

57

Ah, but my Computations, People say,   225
Reduced the Year to better reckoning? —
    Nay,
'Twas only striking from the Calendar
Unborn Tomorrow, and dead Yesterday.

58

And lately, by the Tavern Door agape,
Came shining through the Dusk an Angel
    Shape   230
Bearing a Vessel on his Shoulder; and
He bid me taste of it; and 'twas — the Grape!

59

The Grape that can with Logic absolute
The Two-and-Seventy jarring Sects confute;
    The sovereign Alchemist that in a trice   235
Life's leaden metal into Gold transmute;

60

The mighty Mahmúd, Allah-breathing Lord,
That all the misbelieving and black Horde
Of fears and Sorrows that infest the Soul
Scatters before him with his whirlwind Sword.

61

Why, be this Juice the growth of God, who
    dare   241
Blaspheme the twisted tendril as a Snare?
    A Blessing, we should use it, should we not?
And if a Curse — why, then, Who set it there?

62

I must abjure the Balm of Life, I must,   245
Scared by some After-reckoning ta'en on trust
Or lured with Hope of some Diviner Drink,
To fill the Cup — when crumbled into Dust!

63

Oh threats of Hell and Hopes of Paradise!
One thing at least is certain — *This* Life
    flies;   250
One thing is certain and the rest is Lies —
The Flower that once has blown forever dies.

64

Strange, is it not? that of the myriads who
Before us passed the door of Darkness
    through,
    Not one returns to tell us of the Road,   255
Which to discover we must travel too.

65

The Revelations of Devout and Learned
Who rose before us, and as Prophets burned,
    Are all but Stories, which, awoke from Sleep,
They told their comrades, and to Sleep
    returned.   260

66

I sent my Soul through the Invisible,
Some letter of that After-life to spell;
    And by and by my Soul returned to me,
And answered, "I Myself am Heav'n and
    Hell" —

67

Heav'n but the Vision of fulfilled Desire,   265
And Hell the Shadow from a Soul on fire
    Cast on the Darkness into which Ourselves,
So late emerged from, shall so soon expire.

68

We are no other than a moving row   269
Of Magic Shadow-shapes that come and go
    Round with the Sun-illumined Lantern held
In Midnight by the Master of the Show;

69

But helpless Pieces of the Game He plays
Upon this Checker-board of Nights and Days;
    Hither and thither moves, and checks, and
        slays,   275
And one by one back in the Closet lays.

70

The Ball no question makes of Ayes and Noes,
But Here or There as strikes the Player goes;
    And He that tossed you down into the
        Field,
He knows about it all — HE knows — HE
    knows!   280

71

The Moving Finger writes, and, having writ,
Moves on; nor all your Piety nor Wit
    Shall lure it back to cancel half a Line,
Nor all your Tears wash out a Word of it.

72

And that inverted Bowl they call the Sky,   285
Whereunder crawling cooped we live and die,

---

225. **Computations.** Omar was a learned astronomer
and was one of eight men employed to reform the calendar.
234. **Two-and-Seventy**, the seventy-two sects of Islam, said
to be in schism while one sect only clings to the true faith.
237. **Mahmúd.** See note on line 44. **Allah-breathing.**
Mahmúd worshiped Allah, the deity among the Mohammedans, and forced others to do so. 252. **blown**, bloomed.

277. **The Ball,** etc., a reference to the game of polo, of
ancient Persian origin.

Lift not your hands to *It* for help — for It
As impotently moves as you or I.

73

With Earth's first Clay They did the Last Man
    knead,   289
And there of the Last Harvest sowed the Seed;
    And the first Morning of Creation wrote
What the Last Dawn of Reckoning shall read.

74

YESTERDAY *This* Day's Madness did prepare;
TOMORROW's Silence, Triumph, or Despair.
    Drink! for you know not whence you came,
        nor why;   295
Drink, for you know not why you go, nor
    where.

75

I tell you this — When, started from the Goal,
Over the flaming shoulders of the Foal
    Of Heav'n Parwín and Mushtarí they flung,
In my predestined Plot of Dust and Soul   300

76

The Vine had struck a fiber; which about
If clings my Being — let the Dervish flout;
    Of my Base metal may be filed a Key,
That shall unlock the Door he howls without.

77

And this I know: whether the one True
    Light   305
Kindle to love, or Wrath-consume me quite,
    One Flash of It within the Tavern caught
Better than in the Temple lost outright.

78

What! out of senseless Nothing to provoke
A conscious Something to resent the yoke   310
    Of unpermitted Pleasure, under pain
Of Everlasting Penalties, if broke!

79

What! from his helpless Creature be repaid
Pure Gold for what he lent him dross-
    allayed —
    Sue for a Debt he never did contract,   315
And cannot answer — Oh, the sorry trade!

80

O Thou, who didst with pitfall and with gin
Beset the Road I was to wander in,

Thou wilt not with Predestined Evil round
Enmesh, and then impute my Fall to Sin!   320

81

Oh Thou, who Man of Baser Earth didst make,
And ev'n with Paradise devise the Snake,
    For all the Sin wherewith the Face of Man
Is blackened — Man's forgiveness give — and
    take!

    ·   ·   ·   ·   ·

82

As under cover of departing Day   325
Slunk hunger-stricken Ramazán away,
    Once more within the Potter's house alone
I stood, surrounded by the Shapes of Clay —

83

Shapes of all Sorts and Sizes, great and small,
That stood along the floor and by the wall;   330
    And some loquacious Vessels were; and
    some
Listened perhaps, but never talked at all.

84

Said one among them — "Surely not in vain
My substance of the common Earth was ta'en
    And to this Figure molded, to be broke,   335
Or trampled back to shapeless Earth again."

85

Then said a Second — "Ne'er a peevish Boy
Would break the Bowl from which he drank
    in joy;
    And He that with his hand the Vessel made
Will surely not in after Wrath destroy."   340

86

After a momentary silence spake
Some Vessel of a more ungainly Make:
    "They sneer at me for leaning all awry;
What! did the Hand, then, of the Potter
    shake?"

87

Whereat someone of the loquacious Lot —   345
I think a Súfi pipkin — waxing hot —
    "All this of Pot and Potter — Tell me then,
Who is the Potter, pray, and who the Pot?"

88

"Why," said another, "Some there are who
    tell
Of one who threatens he will toss to Hell   350

298-299. **Foal Of Heav'n,** an equatorial constellation
known as Equuleus (the Little Horse). 299. **Parwín and
Mushtarí,** the Pleiades and Jupiter. 302. **Dervish,** a
Mohammedan devotee. 317. **gin,** trap.

326. **Ramazán,** the fasting month of the Mohammedans,
during which no food is eaten between sunrise and sunset.
346. **Súfi,** a member of a Persian sect of mystics whose
purpose was to gain insight into the Divine Being through
ecstasy and contemplation.

The luckless Pots he marred in making —
Pish!
He's a Good Fellow, and 'twill all be well."

89

"Well," murmured one, "Let whoso make or
buy,
My Clay with long Oblivion is gone dry;
But fill me with the old familiar Juice, 355
Methinks I might recover by and by."

90

So while the Vessels one by one were speaking
The little Moon looked in that all were
seeking;
And then they jogged each other, "Brother!
Brother!
Now for the Porter's shoulder-knot a-creak-
ing!"   360

.   .   .   .   .   .

91

Ah, with the Grape my fading Life provide,
And wash the Body whence the Life has died,
And lay me, shrouded in the living Leaf,
By some not unfrequented Garden-side—

92

That ev'n my buried Ashes such a snare   365
Of Vintage shall fling up into the Air
As not a True-believer passing by
But shall be overtaken unaware.

93

Indeed the Idols I have loved so long
Have done my credit in this World much
wrong,   370
Have drowned my Glory in a shallow Cup,
And sold my Reputation for a Song.

94

Indeed, indeed, Repentance oft before
I swore — but was I sober when I swore?
And then and then came Spring, and Rose-
in-hand   375
My thread-bare Penitence apieces tore.

95

And much as Wine has played the Infidel,
And robbed me of my Robe of Honor — Well,
I wonder often what the Vintners buy
One-half so precious as the stuff they sell.   380

96

Yet Ah, that Spring should vanish with the
Rose!
That Youth's sweet-scented manuscript
should close!
The Nightingale that in the branches sang,
Ah whence, and whither flown again, who
knows!

97

Would but the Desert of the Fountain yield 385
One glimpse — if dimly, yet indeed, revealed,
To which the fainting Traveler might
spring,
As springs the trampled herbage of the field!

98

Would but some wingéd Angel ere too late
Arrest the yet unfolded Roll of Fate,   390
And make the stern Recorder otherwise
Enregister, or quite obliterate!

99

Ah, Love! could you and I with Him conspire
To grasp this sorry Scheme of Things entire,
Would not we shatter it to bits — and then
Remold it nearer to the Heart's Desire!   396

.   .   .   .   .   .

100

Yon rising Moon that looks for us again —
How oft hereafter will she wax and wane;
How oft hereafter rising look for us
Through this same Garden — and for *one* in
vain!   400

101

And when like her, O Sákí, you shall pass
Among the Guests Star-scattered on the
Grass,
And in your joyous errand reach the spot
Where I made One — turn down an empty
Glass!   (1859, 1868, 1872, 1879)

MATTHEW ARNOLD (1822-1888)

QUIET WORK

One lesson, Nature, let me learn of thee,
One lesson which in every wind is blown,
One lesson of two duties kept at one
Though the loud world proclaim their en-
mity —
Of toil unsevered from tranquillity!   5
Of labor, that in lasting fruit outgrows
Far noisier schemes, accomplished in repose,
Too great for haste, too high for rivalry!

358. **Moon . . . seeking**, the new moon, which would mark the end of the fasting period. 360. **shoulder-knot a-creaking**, with the load of wine he was carrying. The shoulder-knot was a strap on which the jars were hung. 369. **Idols**, wine and wine-poetry.

401. **Sákí**, wine-bearer.

Yes, while on earth a thousand discords ring,
Man's fitful uproar mingling with his toil, 10
Still do thy sleepless ministers move on,
Their glorious tasks in silence perfecting;
Still working, blaming still our vain turmoil,
Laborers that shall not fail, when man is
    gone.   (1849)

MYCERINUS

"Not by the justice that my father spurned,
Not for the thousands whom my father slew,
Altars unfed and temples overturned,
Cold hearts and thankless tongues, where
    thanks are due;   4
Fell this dread voice from lips that cannot lie,
Stern sentence of the Powers of Destiny.

"I will unfold my sentence and my crime.
My crime — that, rapt in reverential awe,
I sate obedient, in the fiery prime
Of youth, self-governed, at the feet of Law; 10
Ennobling this dull pomp, the life of kings,
By contemplation of diviner things.

"My father loved injustice, and lived long;
Crowned with gray hairs he died, and full of
    sway.
I loved the good he scorned, and hated
    wrong —   15
The gods declare my recompense today.
I looked for life more lasting, rule more high;
And when six years are measured, lo, I die!

"Yet surely, O my people, did I deem   19
Man's justice from the all-just gods was given;
A light that from some upper fount did beam,
Some better archetype, whose seat was
    heaven;
A light that, shining from the blest abodes,
Did shadow somewhat of the life of gods.

"Mere phantoms of man's self-tormenting
    heart,   25
Which on the sweets that woo it dares not
    feed!
Vain dreams, which quench our pleasures,
    then depart,
When the duped soul, self-mastered, claims
    its meed;
When, on the strenuous just man, Heaven
    bestows,
Crown of his struggling life, an unjust close!

"Seems it so light a thing, then, austere
    Powers,   31
To spurn man's common lure, life's pleasant
    things?
Seems there no joy in dances crowned with
    flowers,
Love, free to range, and regal banquetings?
Bend ye on these, indeed, an unmoved eye, 35
Not gods but ghosts, in frozen apathy?

"Or is it that some Force, too wise, too
    strong,
Even for yourselves to conquer or beguile,
Sweeps earth, and heaven, and men, and gods
    along,
Like the broad volume of the insurgent Nile?
And the great powers we serve, themselves
    may be   41
Slaves of a tyrannous necessity?

"Or in mid-heaven, perhaps, your golden cars,
Where earthly voice climbs never, wing their
    flight,
And in wild hunt, through mazy tracts of
    stars,   45
Sweep in the sounding stillness of the night?
Or in deaf ease, on thrones of dazzling sheen,
Drinking deep drafts of joy, ye dwell serene?

"Oh, wherefore cheat our youth, if thus it be,
Of one short joy, one lust, one pleasant
    dream?   50
Stringing vain words of powers we cannot see,
Blind divinations of a will supreme;
Lost labor! when the circumambient gloom
But hides, if gods, gods careless of our doom?

"The rest I give to joy. Even while I speak,
My sand runs short; and — as yon star-shot
    ray,   56
Hemmed by two banks of cloud, peers pale
    and weak,
Now, as the barrier closes, dies away —
Even so do past and future intertwine,
Blotting this six years' space, which yet is
    mine.   60

"Six years — six little years — six drops of
    time!
Yet suns shall rise, and many moons shall
    wane,
And old men die, and young men pass their
    prime,
And languid pleasure fade and flower again,
And the dull gods behold, ere these are
    flown,   65
Revels more deep, joy keener than their own.

Mycerinus. Mycerinus, or Mankaura, was king of Egypt about 2800 B.C. His father, Cheops, was noted for his unjust rule and a long happy life. Mycerinus was warned by an oracle that he would live only six years, and in the poem he protests against the injustice of his fate. The story is told by the Greek historian Herodotus (4th century B.C.) in Book II, Chapter 129.

40. insurgent Nile. The Nile is called "insurgent" because it overflows its banks each spring.

"Into the silence of the groves and woods
I will go forth, though something would I
    say —
Something — yet what, I know not; for the
    gods   69
The doom they pass revoke not, nor delay;
And prayers, and gifts, and tears, are fruit-
    less all,
And the night waxes, and the shadows fall.

"Ye men of Egypt, ye have heard your king!
I go, and I return not. But the will
Of the great gods is plain; and ye must bring
Ill deeds, ill passions, zealous to fulfill   76
Their pleasure, to their feet; and reap their
    praise,
The praise of gods, rich boon! and length of
    days."

— So spake he, half in anger, half in scorn;
And one loud cry of grief and of amaze   80
Broke from his sorrowing people; so he spake,
And turning, left them there; and with brief
    pause,
Girt with a throng of revelers, bent his way
To the cool region of the groves he loved.
There by the river-banks he wandered on, 85
From palm-grove on to palm-grove, happy
    trees,
Their smooth tops shining sunward, and be-
    neath
Burying their unsunned stems in grass and
    flowers;
Where in one dream the feverish time of youth
Might fade in slumber, and the feet of joy 90
Might wander all day long and never tire.
Here came the king, holding high feast, at
    morn,
Rose-crowned; and ever, when the sun went
    down,
A hundred lamps beamed in the tranquil
    gloom,
From tree to tree all through the twinkling
    grove,   95
Revealing all the tumult of the feast —
Flushed guests, and golden goblets foamed
    with wine;
While the deep-burnished foliage overhead
Splintered the silver arrows of the moon.
    It may be that sometimes his wondering
        soul   100
From the loud joyful laughter of his lips
Might shrink half startled, like a guilty man
Who wrestles with his dream; as some pale
    shape
Gliding half hidden through the dusky stems,
Would thrust a hand before the lifted bowl,
Whispering, "A little space, and thou art
    mine!"   106
It may be on that joyless feast his eye

Dwelt with mere outward seeming; he, within,
Took measure of his soul, and knew its
    strength,
And by that silent knowledge, day by day, 110
Was calmed, ennobled, comforted, sustained.
It may be; but not less his brow was smooth,
And his clear laugh fled ringing through the
    gloom,
And his mirth quailed not at the mild reproof
Sighed out by winter's sad tranquillity;   115
Nor, palled with its own fullness, ebbed and
    died
In the rich languor of long summer-days;
Nor withered when the palm-tree plumes,
    that roofed
With their mild dark his grassy banquet-
    hall,
Bent to the cold winds of the showerless
    spring;   120
No, nor grew dark when autumn brought the
    clouds.

So six long years he reveled, night and day,
And when the mirth waxed loudest, with dull
    sound
Sometimes from the grove's center echoes
    came,
To tell his wondering people of their king; 125
In the still night, across the steaming flats,
Mixed with the murmur of the moving Nile.
                                        (1849)

TO A FRIEND

Who prop, thou ask'st, in these bad days, my
    mind? —
He much, the old man, who, clearest-souled
    of men,
Saw The Wide Prospect, and the Asian Fen,
And Tmolus' Hill, and Smyrna Bay, though
    blind.
Much he, whose friendship I not long since
    won,   5
That halting slave, who in Nicopolis
Taught Arrian, when Vespasian's brutal son
Cleared Rome of what most shamed him.
    But be his
My special thanks, whose even-balanced soul,

108-112. **he, within . . . smooth.** These lines sound the
Stoic note of Arnold's poetry.
    To a Friend. 2. **the old man,** Homer, who was said to be
blind. 3. **The Wide Prospect,** Europe (a literal translation
of the Greek word Εὐρώπη). **Asian Fens,** the marshy,
low-lying districts along the rivers in Asia Minor. 4. **Tmolus'
Hill,** a mountain in Lydia, Asia Minor. **Smyrna Bay.**
Smyrna is the chief seaport of Asia Minor. 6. **slave,**
Epictetus (c. 60- c. 120 A.D.), the Stoic philosopher, who was
lame and at one time a slave. He lived at Nicopolis, Greece,
after he was banished from Rome by the Emperor Domitian,
the brutal son of Vespasian. One of the pupils of Epictetus
was Arrian, a famous philosopher and historian. 8. **his,**
a reference to Sophocles (497-406 B.C.), the Athenian dramatist whose plays are noted for their serenity. He was born
at Colonus (line 14), a village near Athens.

From first youth tested up to extreme old
 age,   10
Business could not make dull, nor passion
 wild;
Who saw life steadily, and saw it whole;
The mellow glory of the Attic stage,
Singer of sweet Colonus, and its child.
         (1849)

THE SICK KING IN BOKHARA

HUSSEIN

O most just Vizier, send away
The cloth-merchants, and let them be,
Them and their dues, this day! The King
Is ill at ease, and calls for thee.

THE VIZIER

O merchants, tarry yet a day   5
Here in Bokhara! but at noon,
Tomorrow, come, and ye shall pay
Each fortieth web of cloth to me,
As the law is, and go your way.
O Hussein, lead me to the King! 10
Thou teller of sweet tales, thine own,
Ferdousi's, and the others', lead!
How is it with my lord?

HUSSEIN

     Alone,
Ever since prayer-time, he doth wait,
O Vizier! without lying down, 15
In the great window of the gate,
Looking into the Registàn,
Where through the sellers' booths the slaves
Are this way bringing the dead man. —
O Vizier, here is the King's door! 20

THE KING

O Vizier, I may bury him?

THE VIZIER

O King, thou know'st, I have been sick
These many days, and heard no thing
(For Allah shut my ears and mind),
Not even what thou dost, O King! 25
Wherefore, that I may counsel thee,
Let Hussein, if thou wilt, make haste
To speak in order what hath chanced.

THE KING

O Vizier, be it as thou say'st!

The Sick King in Bokhara. Bokhara was the ancient capital of a large area in central Asia. It was a famous money market, the chief trade center between China and Western Asia. The Vizier was a minister of state.
 12. **Ferdousi,** the epic poet of Persia (940-1020). His *Shah Namak (Book of Kings)* contains the legends of his country, including the story of Sohrab and Rustum. 17. **the Registàn,** the market-place. 24. **Allah,** the name of the Mohammedan God; the word means *worthy to be adored.*

HUSSEIN

Three days since, at the time of prayer 30
A certain Moollah, with his robe
All rent, and dust upon his hair,
Watched my lord's coming forth, and pushed
The golden mace-bearers aside,
And fell at the King's feet, and cried: 35

"Justice, O King, and on myself!
On this great sinner, who did break
The law, and by the law must die!
Vengeance, O King!"

     But the King spake:
"What fool is this, that hurts our ears 40
With folly? or what drunken slave?
My guards, what, prick him with your spears!
Prick me the fellow from the path!"
As the King said, so it was done,
And to the mosque my lord passed on. 45

But on the morrow, when the King
Went forth again, the holy book
Carried before him, as is right,
And through the square his way he took;
My man comes running, flecked with blood 50
From yesterday, and falling down,
Cries out most earnestly: "O King,
My lord, O King, do right, I pray!

"How canst thou, ere thou hear, discern
If I speak folly? but a king,   55
Whether a thing be great or small,
Like Allah, hears and judges all.

"Wherefore hear thou! Thou know'st, how
 fierce
In these last days the sun hath burned;
That the green water in the tanks 60
Is to a putrid puddle turned;
And the canal, which from the stream
Of Samarcand is brought this way,
Wastes, and runs thinner every day.

"Now I at nightfall had gone forth 65
Alone, and in a darksome place
Under some mulberry-trees I found
A little pool; and in short space,
With all the water that was there
I filled my pitcher, and stole home 70
Unseen; and having drink to spare,
I hid the can behind the door,
And went up on the roof to sleep.

"But in the night, which was with wind
And burning dust, again I creep 75
Down, having fever, for a drink.

 31. **Moollah,** a learned teacher of Mohammedan law and dogma. 62-63. **stream Of Samarcand,** the Zerafshan River, which supplied water to the city of Samarcand, east of Bokhara.

"Now meanwhile had my brethren found
The water-pitcher, where it stood
Behind the door upon the ground,
And called my mother; and they all,   80
As they were thirsty, and the night
Most sultry, drained the pitcher there;
That they sate with it, in my sight,
Their lips still wet, when I came down.

"Now mark! I, being fevered, sick   85
(Most unblest also), at that sight
Brake forth, and cursed them — dost thou
    hear? —
One was my mother — Now, do right!"

But my lord mused a space, and said:
"Send him away, Sirs, and make on!   90
It is some madman!" the King said.
As the King bade, so was it done.

The morrow, at the self-same hour,
In the King's path, behold, the man,
Not kneeling, sternly fixed! he stood   95
Right opposite, and thus began,
Frowning grim down: "Thou wicked King,
Most deaf where thou shouldst most give ear!
What, must I howl in the next world,
Because thou wilt not listen here?   100

"What, wilt thou pray, and get thee grace,
And all grace shall to me be grudged?
Nay but, I swear, from this thy path
I will not stir till I be judged!"
Then they who stood about the King   105
Drew close together and conferred;
Till that the King stood forth and said:
"Before the priests thou shalt be heard."

But when the Ulemas were met,
And the thing heard, they doubted not;   110
But sentenced him, as the law is,
To die by stoning on the spot.

Now the King charged us secretly:
"Stoned must he be, the law stands so.
Yet, if he seek to fly, give way;   115
Hinder him not, but let him go."

So saying, the King took a stone,
And cast it softly — but the man,
With a great joy upon his face,
Kneeled down, and cried not, neither ran. 120

So they, whose lot it was, cast stones,
That they flew thick and bruised him sore.
But he praised Allah with loud voice,
And remained kneeling as before.

My lord had covered up his face;   125
But when one told him, "He is dead,"

109. Ulemas, the wise men who interpreted the law.

Turning him quickly to go in,
"Bring thou to me his corpse," he said.

And truly, while I speak, O King,
I hear the bearers on the stair;   130
Wilt thou they straightway bring him in?
— Ho! enter ye who tarry there!

THE VIZIER

O King, in this I praise thee not!
Now must I call thy grief not wise.
Is he thy friend, or of thy blood,   135
To find such favor in thine eyes?

Nay, were he thine own mother's son,
Still, thou art king, and the law stands.
It were not meet the balance swerved,
The sword were broken in thy hands.   140

But being nothing, as he is,
Why for no cause make sad thy face? —
Lo, I am old! three kings, ere thee,
Have I seen reigning in this place.

But who, through all this length of time,   145
Could bear the burden of his years,
If he for strangers pained his heart
Not less than those who merit tears?

Fathers we *must* have, wife and child,
And grievous is the grief for these;   150
This pain alone, which *must* be borne,
Makes the head white, and bows the knees.

But other loads than this his own
One man is not well made to bear.
Besides, to each are his own friends,   155
To mourn with him, and show him care.

Look, this is but one single place,
Though it be great; all the earth round,
If a man bear to have it so,
Things which might vex him shall be found.

Upon the Russian frontier, where   161
The watchers of two armies stand
Near one another, many a man,
Seeking a prey unto his hand,

Hath snatched a little fair-haired slave;   165
They snatch also, toward Mervè,
The Shiah dogs, who pasture sheep,
And up from thence to Orgunjè.

And these all, laboring for a lord,
Eat not the fruit of their own hands;   170

166. Mervè, a city south of Bokhara. 167. Shiah dogs,
the Shiites, one of the two sects of Mohammedans who do
not consider the body of traditions regarding Mohammed
as a part of the law. 168. Orgunjè, a city on the Amu River
near the Aral Sea, in central Asia.

Which is the heaviest of all plagues,
To that man's mind, who understands.

The kaffirs also (whom God curse!)
Vex one another, night and day;
There are the lepers, and all sick;   175
There are the poor, who faint alway.

All these have sorrow, and keep still,
Whilst other men make cheer, and sing.
Wilt thou have pity on all these?
No, nor on this dead dog, O King!   180

THE KING

O Vizier, thou art old, I young!
Clear in these things I cannot see.
My head is burning, and a heat
Is in my skin which angers me.

But hear ye this, ye sons of men!   185
They that bear rule, and are obeyed,
Unto a rule more strong than theirs
Are in their turn obedient made.

In vain therefore, with wistful eyes
Gazing up hither, the poor man,   190
Who loiters by the high-heaped booths,
Below there, in the Registàn,

Says: "Happy he, who lodges there!
With silken raiment, store of rice,
And for this drought, all kinds of fruits,   195
Grape-syrup, squares of colored ice,

"With cherries served in drifts of snow."
In vain hath a king power to build
Houses, arcades, enameled mosques;
And to make orchard-closes, filled   200

With curious fruit-trees brought from far,
With cisterns for the winter-rain,
And, in the desert, spacious inns
In divers places — if that pain

Is not more lightened, which he feels,   205
If his will be not satisfied;
And that it be not, from all time
The law is planted, to abide.

Thou wast a sinner, thou poor man!
Thou wast athirst; and didst not see,   210
That, though we take what we desire,
We must not snatch it eagerly.

And I have meat and drink at will,
And rooms of treasures, not a few.
But I am sick, nor heed I these;   215
And what I would, I cannot do.

173. **kaffirs,** disbelievers in the Mohammedan religion.

Even the great honor which I have,
When I am dead, will soon grow still;
So have I neither joy nor fame.
But what I can do, that I will.   220

I have a fretted brick-work tomb
Upon a hill on the right hand,
Hard by a close of apricots,
Upon the road of Samarcand;

Thither, O Vizier, will I bear   225
This man my pity could not save,
And, plucking up the marble flags,
There lay his body in my grave.

Bring water, nard, and linen rolls!
Wash off all blood, set smooth each limb! 230
Then say: "He was not wholly vile,
Because a king shall bury him."   (1849)

SHAKESPEARE

Others abide our question. Thou art free.
We ask and ask — thou smilest and art still,
Out-topping knowledge. For the loftiest hill,
Who to the stars uncrowns his majesty,
Planting his steadfast footsteps in the sea, 5
Making the heaven of heavens his dwelling-
    place,
Spares but the cloudy border of his base
To the foiled searching of mortality;
And thou, who didst the stars and sunbeams
    know,
Self-schooled, self-scanned, self-honored, self-
    secure,   10
Didst tread on earth unguessed at. — Better
    so!
All pains the immortal spirit must endure,
All weakness which impairs, all griefs which
    bow,
Find their sole speech in that victorious brow.
    (1849)

IN HARMONY WITH NATURE

TO A PREACHER

"In harmony with Nature?" Restless fool,
Who with such heat dost preach what were
    to thee,
When true, the last impossibility —
To be like Nature strong, like Nature cool!
Know, man hath all which Nature hath, but
    more,   5

223. **close,** an enclosed place. 229. **nard,** a kind of ointment.
   Shakespeare. 1. **Others . . . free.** We may question the
work of other poets; Shakespeare eludes our inquiry.
   In Harmony with Nature. This poem is addressed to a
preacher who had urged his audience to live in harmony
with nature.

man must move forward ideal

And in that *more* lie all his hopes of good.
Nature is cruel, man is sick of blood;
Nature is stubborn, man would fain adore;
Nature is fickle, man hath need of rest;
Nature forgives no debt, and fears no grave;
Man would be mild, and with safe conscience
   blest.   11
Man must begin, know this, where Nature
   ends;
Nature and man can never be fast friends.
Fool, if thou canst not pass her, rest her slave!
                                           (1849)

TO A REPUBLICAN FRIEND, 1848

God knows it, I am with you. If to prize
Those virtues, prized and practiced by too
   few,
But prized, but loved, but eminent in you,
Man's fundamental life; if to despise
The barren optimistic sophistries   5
Of comfortable moles, whom what they do
Teaches the limit of the just and true
(And for such doing they require not eyes);
If sadness at the long heart-wasting show
Wherein earth's great ones are disquieted; 10
If thoughts, not idle, while before me flow
The armies of the homeless and unfed —
If these are yours, if this is what you are,
Then am I yours, and what you feel, I share.
                                           (1849)

CONTINUED

Yet, when I muse on what life is, I seem
Rather to patience prompted, than that proud
Prospect of hope which France proclaims so
   loud —
France, famed in all great arts, in none
   supreme;
Seeing this vale, this earth, whereon we
   dream,   5
Is on all sides o'ershadowd by the high
Uno'erleaped Mountains of Necessity,
Sparing us narrower margin than we deem.
Nor will that day dawn at a human nod,
When, bursting through the network super-
   posed   10
By selfish occupation — plot and plan,
Lust, avarice, envy — liberated man,
All difference with his fellow-mortal closed,
Shall be left standing face to face with God.
                                           (1849)

T[...]

Joy comes and g[...]
   Like the [...]
Change doth unkn[...]
       men.
   Love lends life [...]
   A few sad smiles [...] [...]en,   5
   Both are laid in one cold place,
   In the grave.

Dreams dawn and fly; friends smile and die,
   Like spring flowers.
Our vaunted life is one long funeral.   10
   Men dig graves, with bitter tears,
   For their dead hopes; and all,
   Mazed with doubts, and sick with fears,
   Count the hours.

We count the hours; these dreams of ours,   15
   False and hollow,
Shall we go hence and find they are not dead?
   Joys we dimly apprehend,
   Faces that smiled and fled,
Hopes born here, and born to end,   20
   Shall we follow?   (1849)

THE FORSAKEN MERMAN

Come, dear children, let us away;
Down and away below!
Now my brothers call from the bay,
Now the great winds shoreward blow,
Now the salt tides seaward flow;   5
Now the wild white horses play,
Champ and chafe and toss in the spray.
Children dear, let us away!
This way, this way!

Call her once before you go —   10
Call once yet!
In a voice that she will know:
"Margaret! Margaret!"
Children's voices should be dear
(Call once more) to a mother's ear;   15
Children's voices, wild with pain —
Surely she will come again!
Call her once and come away;
This way, this way!
"Mother dear, we cannot stay!   20
The wild white horses foam and fret."
Margaret! Margaret!

Come, dear children, come away down;
Call no more!

To a Republican Friend. The friend is probably Clough.
The year 1848 was marked by various revolutions on the
Continent, beginning with the overthrow of the monarchy
in France.
   Continued. With this sonnet cf. Tennyson's *You Ask Me,
Why* and *Love Thou Thy Land,* pages 37, 38.
   3. **France proclaims,** referring to the establishment of
the republic in 1848.

To Fausta. Fausta was Arnold's sister Jane.
   The Forsaken Merman. Folklore has many tales dealing
with relations between mortals and mermen or mermaids.
This story belongs to Danish legend.
   13. **Margaret,** a favorite name with Arnold. See *Switzerland,* p. 456.

...ast look at the white-walled town,   25
...d the little gray church on the windy shore,
Then come down!
She will not come though you call all day;
Come away, come away!

Children dear, was it yesterday   30
We heard the sweet bells over the bay?
In the caverns where we lay,
Through the surf and through the swell,
The far-off sound of a silver bell?
Sand-strewn caverns, cool and deep,   35
Where the winds are all asleep;
Where the spent lights quiver and gleam,
Where the salt weed sways in the stream,
Where the sea-beasts, ranged all round,
Feed in the ooze of their pasture-ground;   40
Where the sea-snakes coil and twine,
Dry their mail and bask in the brine;
Where great whales come sailing by,
Sail and sail, with unshut eye,
Round the world for ever and aye?   45
When did music come this way?
Children dear, was it yesterday?

Children dear, was it yesterday
(Call yet once) that she went away?
Once she sate with you and me,   50
On a red gold throne in the heart of the sea,
And the youngest sate on her knee.
She combed its bright hair, and she tended it
    well,
When down swung the sound of a far-off bell.
She sighed, she looked up through the clear
    green sea;   55
She said: "I must go, for my kinsfolk pray
In the little gray church on the shore today.
'Twill be Easter-time in the world — ah me!
And I lose my poor soul, Merman! here with
    thee."
I said: "Go up, dear heart, through the waves;
Say thy prayer, and come back to the kind
    sea-caves!"   61
She smiled, she went up through the surf in
    the bay.
Children dear, was it yesterday?

Children dear, were we long alone?   64
"The sea grows stormy, the little ones moan;
Long prayers," I said, "in the world they say;
Come!" I said; and we rose through the surf
    in the bay.
We went up the beach, by the sandy down
Where the sea-stocks bloom, to the white-
    walled town;
Through the narrow paved streets, where all
    was still,   70
To the little gray church on the windy hill.

69. **sea-stocks**, sea gillyflowers.

From the church came a murmur of folk at
    their prayers,
But we stood without in the cold blowing airs.
We climbed on the graves, on the stones worn
    with rains,
And we gazed up the aisle through the small
    leaded panes.   75
She sate by the pillar; we saw her clear:
"Margaret, hist! come quick, we are here!
Dear heart," I said, "we are long alone;
The sea grows stormy, the little ones moan."
But, ah, she gave me never a look,   80
For her eyes were sealed to the holy book!
Loud prays the priest; shut stands the door.
Come away, children, call no more!
Come away, come down, call no more!

Down, down, down!   85
Down to the depths of the sea!
She sits at her wheel in the humming town,
Singing most joyfully.
Hark what she sings: "O joy, O joy,
For the humming street, and the child with
    its toy!   90
For the priest, and the bell, and the holy
    well;
For the wheel where I spun,
And the blessed light of the sun!"
And so she sings her fill,
Singing most joyfully,   95
Till the spindle drops from her hand,
And the whizzing wheel stands still.
She steals to the window, and looks at the
    sand,
And over the sand at the sea;
And her eyes are set in a stare;   100
And anon there breaks a sigh,
And anon there drops a tear,
From a sorrow-clouded eye,
And a heart sorrow-laden,
A long, long sigh;   105
For the cold strange eyes of a little Mermaiden
And the gleam of her golden hair.

Come away, away children;
Come children, come down!
The hoarse wind blows coldly;   110
Lights shine in the town.
She will start from her slumber
When gusts shake the door;
She will hear the winds howling,
Will hear the waves roar.   115
We shall see, while above us
The waves roar and whirl,
A ceiling of amber,
A pavement of pearl.
Singing: "Here came a mortal,   120

82. **shut . . . door.** According to popular belief, heaven
and the benefits of Christianity are denied fairies and certain
other supernatural beings.

But faithless was she!
And alone dwell forever
The kings of the sea."

But, children, at midnight,
When soft the winds blow,   125
When clear falls the moonlight,
When spring-tides are low;
When sweet airs come seaward
From heaths starred with broom,
And high rocks throw mildly   130
On the blanched sands a gloom;
Up the still, glistening beaches,
Up the creeks we will hie,
Over banks of bright seaweed
The ebb-tide leaves dry.   135
We will gaze, from the sand-hills,
At the white, sleeping town;
At the church on the hillside —
And then come back down,
Singing: "There dwells a loved one,   140
But cruel is she!
She left lonely forever
The kings of the sea."   (1849)

IN UTRUMQUE PARATUS

If, in the silent mind of One all-pure,
     At first imagined lay
The sacred world; and by procession sure
From those still deeps, in form and color
     drest,
Seasons alternating, and night and day,   5
The long-mused thought to north, south, east,
     and west,
     Took then its all-seen way;

O waking on a world which thus-wise springs!
     Whether it needs thee count
Betwixt thy waking and the birth of things 10
Ages or hours — O waking on life's stream!
By lonely pureness to the all-pure fount
(Only by this thou canst) the colored dream
     Of life remount!

Thin, thin the pleasant human noises grow, 15
     And faint the city gleams;
Rare the lone pastoral huts — marvel not
     thou!
The solemn peaks but to the stars are known,
But to the stars, and the cold lunar beams;
Alone the sun arises, and alone   20
     Spring the great streams.

But, if the wild unfathered mass no birth
     In divine seats hath known;

In the blank, echoing solitude if Earth,
Rocking her obscure body to and fro,   25
Ceases not from all time to heave and groan,
Unfruitful oft, and at her happiest throe
     Forms, what she forms, alone;

O seeming sole to awake, thy sun-bathed head
     Piercing the solemn cloud   30
Round thy still dreaming brother-world out-
     spread!
O man, whom Earth, thy long-vexed mother,
     bare
Not without joy — so radiant, so endowed
(Such happy issue crowned her painful care)—
     Be not too proud!   35

Oh, when most self-exalted, most alone,
     Chief dreamer, own thy dream!
Thy brother-world stirs at thy feet unknown,
Who hath a monarch's hath no brother's part;
Yet doth thine inmost soul with yearning
     teem.   40
— Oh, what a spasm shakes the dreamer's
     heart!
     "I, too, but seem."   (1849)

RESIGNATION

TO FAUSTA

"To die be given us, or attain!
Fierce work it were, to do again."
So pilgrims, bound for Mecca, prayed
At burning noon; so warriors said,
Scarfed with the cross, who watched the
     miles   5
Of dust which wreathed their struggling files
Down Lydian mountains; so, when snows
Round Alpine summits, eddying, rose,
The Goth, bound Rome-wards; so the Hun,
Crouched on his saddle, while the sun   10
Went lurid down o'er flooded plains
Through which the groaning Danube strains
To the drear Euxine; — so pray all,
Whom labors, self-ordained, enthrall;
Because they to themselves propose   15
On this side the all-common close
A goal which, gained, may give repose.
So pray they; and to stand again
Where they stood once, to them were pain;
Pain to thread back and to renew   20
Past straits, and currents long steered through.

But milder natures, and more free —
Whom an unblamed serenity

In Utrumque Paratus. The title means Prepared for
Either—that is, for either explanation of the origin of the
world as given in the poem.

Resignation. See To Fausta, p. 437.
  3. Mecca, the holy city of the Mohammedans, in Arabia.
4. warriors, crusaders on their way across Lydia, in Asia
Minor, to Palestine. 9. Goth . . . Hun. The Goths under
Alaric, and the Huns under Attila, made attacks upon Rome
in the 4th century. 13. Euxine, the Black Sea.

Hath freed from passions, and the state
Of struggle these necessitate;   25
Whom schooling of the stubborn mind
Hath made, or birth hath found, resigned —
These mourn not, that their goings pay
Obedience to the passing day.
These claim not every laughing Hour   30
For handmaid to their striding power;
Each in her turn, with torch upreared,
To await their march; and when appeared,
Through the cold gloom, with measured race,
To usher for a destined space   35
(Her own sweet errands all forgone)
The too imperious traveler on.
These, Fausta, ask not this; nor thou,
Time's chafing prisoner, ask it now!

We left, just ten years since, you say,   40
That wayside inn we left today.
Our jovial host, as forth we fare,
Shouts greeting from his easy chair.
High on a bank our leader stands,
Reviews and ranks his motley bands,   45
Makes clear our goal to every eye —
The valley's western boundary.
A gate swings to! our tide hath flowed
Already from the silent road.
The valley-pastures, one by one,   50
Are threaded, quiet in the sun;
And now beyond the rude stone bridge
Slopes gracious up the western ridge.
Its woody border, and the last
Of its dark upland farms, is past —   55
Cool farms, with open-lying stores,
Under their burnished sycamores;
All past! and through the trees we glide,
Emerging on the green hillside.
There climbing hangs, a far-seen sign,   60
Our wavering, many-colored line;
There winds, upstreaming slowly still
Over the summit of the hill.
And now, in front, behold outspread
Those upper regions we must tread!   65
Mild hollows, and clear heathy swells,
The cheerful silence of the fells.
Some two hours' march with serious air,
Through the deep noontide heats we fare;
The red-grouse, springing at our sound,   70
Skims, now and then, the shining ground;
No life, save his and ours, intrudes
Upon these breathless solitudes.
O joy! again the farms appear.
Cool shade is there, and rustic cheer;   75

38. ask not this. Milder natures than those mentioned
in lines 1-21 do not ask that Time shall stand still while
they accomplish their ambitions. **41. wayside inn,** the
inn at Wythburn, Cumberland. The walk described in
lines 40-85 was probably taken in 1833, when the Arnolds
were living at Grasmere. Under the leadership of Arnold's
father (line 44) the group passed through Keswick (the
"noisy town" of line 77) on the way to the sea.

There springs the brook will guide us down,
Bright comrade, to the noisy town.
Lingering, we follow down; we gain
The town, the highway, and the plain.
And many a mile of dusty way,   80
Parched and road-worn, we made that day;
But, Fausta, I remember well,
That as the balmy darkness fell
We bathed our hands with speechless glee,
That night, in the wide-glimmering sea.   85

Once more we tread this self-same road,
Fausta, which ten years since we trod;
Alone we tread it, you and I,
Ghosts of that boisterous company.
Here, where the brook shines, near its head,
In its clear, shallow, turf-fringed bed;   91
Here, whence the eye first sees, far down,
Capped with faint smoke, the noisy town;
Here sit we, and again unroll,
Though slowly, the familiar whole.   95
The solemn wastes of heathy hill
Sleep in the July sunshine still;
The self-same shadows now, as then,
Play through this grassy upland glen;
The loose dark stones on the green way   100
Lie strewn, it seems, where then they lay; —
On this mild bank above the stream
(You crush them!), the blue gentians gleam.
Still this wild brook, the rushes cool,
The sailing foam, the shining pool!   105
These are not changed; and we, you say,
Are scarce more changed, in truth, than they.

The gypsies, whom we met below,
They, too, have long roamed to and fro;
They ramble, leaving, where they pass,   110
Their fragments on the cumbered grass.
And often to some kindly place
Chance guides the migratory race,
Where, though long wanderings intervene,
They recognize a former scene.   115
The dingy tents are pitched; the fires
Give to the wind their wavering spires;
In dark knots crouch round the wild flame
Their children, as when first they came;
They see their shackled beasts again   120
Move, browsing, up the gray-walled lane.
Signs are not wanting, which might raise
The ghost in them of former days —
Signs are not wanting, if they would;
Suggestions to disquietude.   125
For them, for all, time's busy touch,
While it mends little, troubles much.
Their joints grow stiffer — but the year
Runs his old round of dubious cheer;
Chilly they grow — yet winds in March,   130
Still, sharp as ever, freeze and parch;
They must live still — and yet, God knows,
Crowded and keen the country grows;

It seems as if, in their decay,
The law grew stronger every day. 135
So might they reason, so compare,
Fausta, times past with times that are.
But no! — they rubbed through yesterday
In their hereditary way,
And they will rub through, if they can, 140
Tomorrow on the self-same plan,
Till death arrive to supersede,
For them, vicissitude and need.

The poet, to whose mighty heart
Heaven doth a quicker pulse impart, 145
Subdues that energy to scan
Not his own course, but that of man.
Though he move mountains, though his day
Be passed on the proud heights of sway,
Though he hath loosed a thousand chains, 150
Though he hath borne immortal pains,
Action and suffering though he know —
He hath not lived, if he lives so.
He sees, in some great-historied land,
A ruler of the people stand, 155
Sees his strong thought in fiery flood
Roll through the heaving multitude,
Exults — yet for no moment's space
Envies the all-regarded place.
Beautiful eyes meet his — and he 160
Bears to admire uncravingly;
They pass — he, mingled with the crowd,
Is in their far-off triumphs proud.
From some high station he looks down,
At sunset, on a populous town; 165
Surveys each happy group, which fleets,
Toil ended, through the shining streets,
Each with some errand of its own —
And does not say, "I am alone."
He sees the gentle stir of birth 170
When morning purifies the earth;
He leans upon a gate and sees
The pastures, and the quiet trees.
Low, woody hill, with gracious bound,
Folds the still valley almost round; 175
The cuckoo, loud on some high lawn,
Is answered from the depth of dawn;
In the hedge straggling to the stream,
Pale, dew-drenched, half-shut roses gleam;
But, where the farther side slopes down, 180
He sees the drowsy new-waked clown
In his white quaint-embroidered frock
Make, whistling, tow'rd his mist-wreathed
    flock —
Slowly, behind his heavy tread,
The wet, flowered grass heaves up its head.
Leaned on his gate, he gazes — tears 186
Are in his eyes, and in his ears
The murmur of a thousand years.
Before him he sees life unroll,

A placid and continuous whole — 190
That general life, which does not cease,
Whose secret is not joy, but peace;
That life, whose dumb wish is not missed
If birth proceeds, if things subsist;
The life of plants, and stones, and rain, 195
The life he craves — if not in vain
Fate gave, what chance shall not control,
His sad lucidity of soul.

You listen — but that wandering smile,
Fausta, betrays you cold the while! 200
Your eyes pursue the bells of foam
Washed, eddying, from this bank, their home.
"Those gypsies," so your thoughts I scan,
"Are less, the poet more, than man.
They feel not, though they move and see; 205
Deeper the poet feels; but he
Breathes, when he will, immortal air,
Where Orpheus and where Homer are.
In the day's life, whose iron round
Hems us all in, he is not bound; 210
He leaves his kind, o'erleaps their pen,
And flees the common life of men.
He escapes thence, but we abide —
Not deep the poet sees, but wide."

The world in which we live and move 215
Outlasts aversion, outlasts love,
Outlasts each effort, interest, hope,
Remorse, grief, joy — and were the scope
Of these affections wider made,
Man still would see, and see dismayed, 220
Beyond his passion's widest range,
Far regions of eternal change.
Nay, and since death, which wipes out man,
Finds him with many an unsolved plan,
With much unknown, and much untried, 225
Wonder not dead, and thirst not dried,
Still gazing on the ever full
Eternal mundane spectacle —
This world in which we draw our breath,
In some sense, Fausta, outlasts death. 230

Blame thou not, therefore, him who dares
Judge vain beforehand human cares;
Whose natural insight can discern
What through experience others learn;
Who needs not love and power, to know 235
Love transient, power an unreal show;
Who treads at ease life's uncheered ways —
Him blame not, Fausta, rather praise!
Rather thyself for some aim pray
Nobler than this, to fill the day; 240
Rather that heart, which burns in thee,
Ask, not to amuse, but to set free;
Be passionate hopes not ill resigned
For quiet, and a fearless mind.

181. clown, a country fellow.

208. Orpheus, a famous musician of Greek mythology.

And though fate grudge to thee and me   245
The poet's rapt security,
Yet they, believe me, who await
No gifts from chance, have conquered fate.
They, winning room to see and hear,
And to men's business not too near,   250
Through clouds of individual strife
Draw homeward to the general life.
Like leaves by suns not yet uncurled;
To the wise, foolish; to the world,
Weak — yet not weak, I might reply,   255
Not foolish, Fausta, in His eye,
To whom each moment in its race,
Crowd as we will its neutral space,
Is but a quiet watershed
Whence, equally, the seas of life and death
     are fed.   260

Enough, we live! — and if a life,
With large results so little rife,
Though bearable, seem hardly worth
This pomp of worlds, this pain of birth;
Yet, Fausta, the mute turf we tread,   265
The solemn hills around us spread,
This stream which falls incessantly,
The strange-scrawled rocks, the lonely sky,
If I might lend their life a voice,
Seem to bear rather than rejoice.   270
And even could the intemperate prayer
Man iterates, while these forbear,
For movement, for an ampler sphere,
Pierce Fate's impenetrable ear;
Not milder is the general lot   275
Because our spirits have forgot,
In action's dizzying eddy whirled,
The something that infects the world.   (1849)

MEMORIAL VERSES

APRIL, 1850

Goethe in Weimar sleeps, and Greece,
Long since, saw Byron's struggle cease.
But one such death remained to come;
The last poetic voice is dumb —
We stand today by Wordsworth's tomb.   5

When Byron's eyes were shut in death,
We bowed our head and held our breath.
He taught us little; but our soul
Had *felt* him like the thunder's roll.
With shivering heart the strife we saw   10
Of passion with eternal law;
And yet with reverential awe

We watched the fount of fiery life
Which served for that Titanic strife.

When Goethe's death was told, we said: 15
Sunk, then, is Europe's sagest head.
Physician of the iron age,
Goethe has done his pilgrimage.
He took the suffering human race,
He read each wound, each weakness clear;   20
And struck his finger on the place,
And said: *Thou ailest here, and here!*
He looked on Europe's dying hour
Of fitful dream and feverish power;
His eye plunged down the weltering strife,   25
The turmoil of expiring life —
He said: *The end is everywhere,*
Art still has truth, take refuge there!
And he was happy, if to know
Causes of things, and far below   30
His feet to see the lurid flow
Of terror, and insane distress,
And headlong fate, be happiness.

And Wordsworth! — Ah, pale ghosts, rejoice!
For never has such soothing voice   35
Been to your shadowy world conveyed,
Since erst, at morn, some wandering shade
Heard the clear song of Orpheus come
Through Hades, and the mournful gloom.
Wordsworth has gone from us — and ye,   40
Ah, may ye feel his voice as we!
He too upon a wintry clime
Had fallen — on this iron time
Of doubts, disputes, distractions, fears.
He found us when the age had bound   45
Our souls in its benumbing round;
He spoke, and loosed our heart in tears.
He laid us, as we lay at birth,
On the cool flowery lap of earth;
Smiles broke from us and we had ease;   50
The hills were round us, and the breeze
Went o'er the sun-lit fields again;
Our foreheads felt the wind and rain.
Our youth returned; for there was shed
On spirits that had long been dead,   55
Spirits dried up and closely furled,
The freshness of the early world.

Ah! since dark days still bring to light
Man's prudence and man's fiery might,

---

246. **security,** freedom from care, due to his detachment from affairs of the world. 278. **something . . . world,** possibly, doubt and pessimism.
Memorial Verses. Goethe died in 1832 and was buried in Weimar, Germany. Byron died in 1824 while aiding the Greeks in their fight for independence. Wordsworth died in 1850. Arnold gave high place to all three poets; he was influenced especially by the poetry of Wordsworth.

14. **Titanic strife.** Byron was noted for his fiery, passionate nature, and the word *Titanic* is fittingly applied to him. The Titans were superhuman beings of great size who rebelled against the gods. 17. **iron age,** so called because of the terrible years of the French Revolution and the period following. To Goethe they seemed to portend the destruction of Europe. 29-33. **And he . . . happiness.** These lines are translated from Virgil's *Georgics,* 2, 490-492. 38. **Orpheus,** the famous musician of Greek mythology who descended to the lower world to rescue his wife Eurydice. He was allowed by Pluto, god of the underworld, to lead her to the upper world on condition that he should not look back. He broke the condition, however, and saw Eurydice vanish.

Time may restore us in his course 60
Goethe's sage mind and Byron's force;
But where will Europe's latter hour
Again find Wordsworth's healing power?
Others will teach us how to dare,
And against fear our breast to steel; 65
Others will strengthen us to bear —
But who, ah! who, will make us feel?
The cloud of mortal destiny,
Others will front it fearlessly —
But who, like him, will put it by? 70

Keep fresh the grass upon his grave,
O Rotha, with thy living wave!
Sing him thy best! for few or none
Hears thy voice right, now he is gone. (1850)

EMPEDOCLES ON ETNA

A DRAMATIC POEM

PERSONS

EMPEDOCLES
PAUSANIAS, *a Physician*
CALLICLES, *a young Harp-player*

*The scene of the Poem is on Mount Etna; at first
in the forest region, afterwards on the
summit of the mountain.*

ACT I, SCENE I.

Morning. A Pass in the forest region of Etna.

Callicles
(Alone, resting on a rock by the path).

The mules, I think, will not be here this hour;
They feel the cool wet turf under their feet
By the stream-side, after the dusty lanes
In which they have toiled all night from
  Catana,
And scarcely will they budge a yard. O Pan, 5
How gracious is the mountain at this hour!
A thousand times have I been here alone,
Or with the revellers from the mountain-
  towns,

But never on so fair a morn; — the sun
Is shining on the brilliant mountain-crests, 10
And on the highest pines; but farther down,
Here in the valley, is in shade; the sward
Is dark, and on the stream the mist still
  hangs;
One sees one's footprints crushed in the wet
  grass,
One's breath curls in the air; and on these
  pines 15
That climb from the stream's edge, the long
  grey tufts,
Which the goats love, are jewelled thick with
  dew.
Here will I stay till the slow litter comes.
I have my harp too — that is well. — Apollo!
What mortal could be sick or sorry here? 20
I know not in what mind Empedocles,
Whose mules I followed, may be coming up,
But if, as most men say, he is half mad
With exile, and with brooding on his wrongs,
Pausanias, his sage friend, who mounts with
  him, 25
Could scarce have lighted on a lovelier cure.
The mules must be below, far down. I hear
Their tinkling bells, mixed with the song of
  birds,
Rise faintly to me — now it stops! — Who's
  here?
Pausanias! and on foot? alone?

Pausanias. And thou, then? 30
I left thee supping with Peisianax,
With thy head full of wine, and thy hair
  crowned,
Touching thy harp as the whim came on thee,
And praised and spoiled by master and by
  guests
Almost as much as the new dancing-girl. 35
Why hast thou followed us?

Callicles. The night was hot,
And the feast past its prime; so we slipped
  out,
Some of us, to the portico to breathe; —
Peisianax, thou know'st, drinks late; — and
  then,
As I was lifting my soiled garland off, 40
I saw the mules and litter in the court,
And in the litter sate Empedocles;
Thou, too, wast with him. Straightway I sped
  home;
I saddled my white mule, and all night long
Through the cool lovely country followed
  you, 45
Passed you a little since as morning dawn'd,
And have this hour sate by the torrent here,

---

72. **Rotha**, a small stream near Grasmere, Westmoreland,
where Wordsworth is buried.
Empedocles on Etna. Empedocles was a poet and a philosopher who lived in Sicily in the fifth century B.C. He was
noted as a teacher of rhetoric and as a musician, and was
reputed to be able to perform miracles. In the drama
he is represented as an exile on Mount Etna, on the east
coast of Sicily.
Act I, Scene I. 4. **Catana**, a town at the foot of Mt. Etna.

31. **Peisianax**, a wealthy patron of Empedocles.

Till the slow mules should climb in sight
again.
And now?

Pausanias. And now, back to the town with
speed!
Crouch in the wood first, till the mules have
passed;   50
They do but halt, they will be here anon.
Thou must be viewless to Empedocles;
Save mine, he must not meet a human eye.
One of his moods is on him that thou know'st;
I think, thou wouldst not vex him.

Callicles. No—and yet   55
I would fain stay, and help thee tend him.
Once
He knew me well, and would oft notice me;
And still, I know not how, he draws me to
him,
And I could watch him with his proud sad
face,
His flowing locks and gold-encircled brow   60
And kingly gait, for ever; such a spell
In his severe looks, such a majesty
As drew of old the people after him,
In Agrigentum and Olympia,
When his star reigned, before his banishment,
Is potent still on me in his decline.   66
But oh! Pausanias, he is changed of late;
There is a settled trouble in his air
Admits no momentary brightening now,
And when he comes among his friends at
feasts,   70
'Tis as an orphan among prosperous boys.
Thou know'st of old he loved this harp of
mine,
When first he sojourned with Peisianax;
He is now always moody, and I fear him;
But I would serve him, soothe him, if I could,
Dared one but try.   76

Pausanias. Thou wast a kind child ever!
He loves thee, but he must not see thee now.
Thou hast indeed a rare touch on thy harp,
He loves that in thee, too;— there was a
time
(But that is passed), he would have paid thy
strain   80
With music to have drawn the stars from
heaven.
He hath his harp and laurel with him still,
But he has laid the use of music by,
And all which might relax his settled gloom.
Yet thou may'st try thy playing, if thou
wilt—   85

But thou must keep unseen; follow us on,
But at a distance! in these solitudes,
In this clear mountain-air, a voice will rise,
Though from afar, distinctly; it may soothe
him.
Play when we halt, and, when the evening
comes   90
And I must leave him (for his pleasure is
To be left musing these soft nights alone
In the high unfrequented mountain-spots),
Then watch him, for he ranges swift and far,
Sometimes to Etna's top, and to the cone; 95
But hide thee in the rocks a great way down,
And try thy noblest strains, my Callicles,
With the sweet night to help thy harmony!
Thou wilt earn my thanks sure, and perhaps
his.

Callicles. More than a day and night, Pau-
sanias,   100
Of this fair summer-weather, on these hills,
Would I bestow to help Empedocles.
That needs no thanks; one is far better here
Than in the broiling city in these heats.
But tell me, how hast thou persuaded him 105
In this his present fierce, man-hating mood,
To bring thee out with him alone on Etna?

Pausanias. Thou hast heard all men speak-
ing of Pantheia
The woman who at Agrigentum lay
Thirty long days in a cold trance of death, 110
And whom Empedocles called back to life.
Thou art too young to note it, but his power
Swells with the swelling evil of this time,
And holds men mute to see where it will rise.
He could stay swift diseases in old days,   115
Chain madmen by the music of his lyre,
Cleanse to sweet airs the breath of poisonous
streams,
And in the mountain-chinks inter the winds.
This he could do of old; but, now since all
Clouds and grows daily worse in Sicily,   120
Since broils tear us in twain, since this new
swarm
Of sophists has got empire in our schools
Where he was paramount, since he is ban-
ished
And lives a lonely man in triple gloom—
He grasps the very reins of life and death. 125
I asked him of Pantheia yesterday,
When we were gathered with Peisianax,
And he made answer, I should come at night
On Etna here, and be alone with him,
And he would tell me, as his old, tried friend,
Who still was faithful, what might profit me;
That is, the secret of this miracle.   132

---

64. **Agrigentum**, town in Sicily. **Olympia**, in Greece,
site of Olympian Games. Empedocles was driven from his
native Agrigentum by political enemies.

122. **sophists**, teachers of rhetoric, given to specious argument.

Callicles. Bah! Thou a doctor! Thou art
    superstitious.
Simple Pausanias, 'twas no miracle!
Pantheia, for I know her kinsmen well,   135
Was subject to these trances from a girl.
Empedocles would say so, did he deign;
But he still lets the people, whom he scorns,
Gape and cry *wizard* at him, if they list.

But thou, thou art no company for him!   140
Thou art as cross, as soured as himself!
Thou hast some wrong from thine own citi-
    zens,
And then thy friend is banished, and on that,
Straightway thou fallest to arraign the times,
As if the sky was impious not to fall.   145
The sophists are no enemies of his;
I hear, Gorgias, their chief, speaks nobly of
    him,
As of his gifted master, and once friend.
He is too scornful, too high-wrought, too
    bitter.
'Tis not the times, 'tis not the sophists vex
    him;   150
There is some root of suffering in himself,
Some secret and unfollowed vein of woe,
Which makes the time look black and sad to
    him.
Pester him not in this his sombre mood
With questionings about an idle tale,   155
But lead him through the lovely mountain-
    paths,
And keep his mind from preying on itself,
And talk to him of things at hand and com-
    mon,
Not miracles! thou art a learned man,
But credulous of fables as a girl.   160

Pausanias. And thou, a boy whose tongue
    outruns his knowledge,
And on whose lightness blame is thrown away.
Enough of this! I see the litter wind
Up by the torrent-side, under the pines.
I must rejoin Empedocles. Do thou   165
Crouch in the brushwood till the mules have
    passed;
Then play thy kind part well. Farewell till
    night!

SCENE II

*Noon. A Glen on the highest skirts of the woody
region of Etna.*

EMPEDOCLES—PAUSANIAS

Pausanias. The noon is hot. When we
    have crossed the stream,

We shall have left the woody tract and come
Upon the open shoulder of the hill.
See how the giant spires of yellow bloom
Of the sun-loving gentian, in the heat,   5
Are shining on those naked slopes like flame!
Let us rest here; and now, Empedocles,
Pantheia's history!
          [*A harp-note below is heard.*
    Empedocles. Hark! what sound was that
Rose from below? If it were possible,
And we were not so far from human haunt,
I should have said that some one touched a
    harp.   11
Hark! there again!
    Pausanias. 'Tis the boy Callicles,
The sweetest harp-player in Catana.
He is forever coming on these hills,
In summer, to all country-festivals,   15
With a gay reveling band; he breaks from
    them
Sometimes, and wanders far among the glens.
But heed him not, he will not mount to us;
I spoke with him this morning. Once more,
    therefore,
Instruct me of Pantheia's story, Master,   20
As I have prayed thee.
    Empedocles. That? and to what end?
    Pausanias. It is enough that all men speak
    of it.
But I will also say, that when the gods
Visit us as they do with sign and plague,
To know those spells of thine which stay their
    hand   25
Were to live free from terror.
    Empedocles.   Spells? Mistrust them!
Mind is the spell which governs earth and
    heaven.
Man has a mind with which to plan his safety;
Know that, and help thyself!
    Pausanias.   But thine own words?—
"The wit and counsel of man was never clear,
Troubles confound the little wit he has."   31
Mind is a light which the gods mock us with,
To lead those false who trust it.
          [*The harp sounds again.*
    Empedocles. Hist! once more!
Listen, Pausanias! — Aye, 'tis Callicles;
I know these notes among a thousand. Hark!

Callicles

(*Sings unseen, from below*)

The track winds down to the clear stream,   36
To cross the sparkling shallows; there
The cattle love to gather, on their way
To the high mountain-pastures, and to stay,
Till the rough cowherds drive them past,   40
Knee-deep in the cool ford; for 'tis the last
Of all the woody, high well-watered dells

On Etna; and the beam
Of noon is broken there by chestnut-boughs
Down its steep verdant sides; the air　45
Is freshened by the leaping stream, which
　　throws
Eternal showers of spray on the mossed roots
Of trees, and veins of turf, and long dark
　　shoots
Of ivy-plants, and fragrant hanging bells
Of hyacinths, and on late anemones,　50
That muffle its wet banks; but glade,
And stream, and sward, and chestnut-trees,
End here; Etna beyond, in the broad glare
Of the hot noon, without a shade,
Slope behind slope, up to the peak, lies
　　bare;　55
The peak, round which the white clouds play.

In such a glen, on such a day,
On Pelion, on the grassy ground,
Chiron, the aged Centaur lay,
The young Achilles standing by.　60
The Centaur taught him to explore
The mountains; where the glens are dry
And the tired Centaurs come to rest,
And where the soaking springs abound
And the straight ashes grow for spears,　65
And where the hill-goats come to feed,
And the sea-eagles build their nest.
He showed him Phthia far away,
And said, "O boy, I taught this lore
To Peleus in long distant years!"　70
He told him of the gods, the stars,
The tides — and then of mortal wars,
And of the life which heroes lead
Before they reach the Elysian place
And rest in the immortal mead;　75
And all the wisdom of his race.

The music below ceases, and EMPEDOCLES
speaks, accompanying himself in a solemn
　　manner on his harp.

The outspread world to span
A cord the gods first slung,
And then the soul of man
There, like a mirror, hung,
And bade the winds through space impel the
　　gusty toy.　80

Hither and thither spins
The wind-borne, mirroring soul,

---

58. **Pelion**, a mountain in Thessaly, the haunt of the
Centaurs—fabled monsters, half man and half horse. The
most famous of the Centaurs was Chiron, noted for his wisdom. He was the instructor of Achilles, the son of Peleus.
Achilles was the famous Greek hero in the Trojan War. He
was born at Phthia, in Thessaly. 74. **Elysian place**, the
abode of the blessed after death.

A thousand glimpses wins,
And never sees a whole;　85
Looks once, and drives elsewhere, and leaves
　　its last employ.

The gods laugh in their sleeve
To watch man doubt and fear,
Who knows not what to believe
Since he sees nothing clear,　90
And dares stamp nothing false where he finds
　　nothing sure.

Is this, Pausanias, so?
And can our souls not strive,
But with the winds must go,
And hurry where they drive?　95
Is fate indeed so strong, man's strength indeed
　　so poor?

I will not judge. That man,
Howbeit, I judge as lost,
Whose mind allows a plan,
Which would degrade it most;　100
And he treats doubt the best who tries to see
　　least ill.

Be not, then, fear's blind slave!
Thou art my friend; to thee,
All knowledge that I have,
All skill I wield, are free.　105
Ask not the latest news of the last miracle,

Ask not what days and nights
In trance Pantheia lay,
But ask how thou such sights
May'st see without dismay;　110
Ask what most helps when known, thou son
　　of Anchitus!

What? hate, and awe, and shame
Fill thee to see our time;
Thou feelest thy soul's frame
Shaken and out of chime?　115
What? life and chance go hard with thee too,
　　as with us;

Thy citizens, 'tis said,
Envy thee and oppress,
Thy goodness no men aid,
All strive to make it less;　120
Tyranny, pride, and lust fill Sicily's abodes;

Heaven is with earth at strife,
Signs make thy soul afraid,
The dead return to life,
Rivers are dried, winds stayed;　125

Scarce can one think in calm, so threatening
 are the gods;

And we feel, day and night,
The burden of ourselves —
Well, then, the wiser wight
In his own bosom delves,   130
And asks what ails him so, and gets what
 cure he can.

The sophist sneers: Fool, take
Thy pleasure, right or wrong!
The pious wail: Forsake
A world these sophists throng! —   135
Be neither saint nor sophist-led, but be a man!

These hundred doctors try
To preach thee to their school.
We have the truth! they cry;
And yet their oracle,   140
Trumpet it as they will, is but the same as
 thine.

Once read thy own breast right,
And thou hast done with fears;
Man gets no other light,
Search he a thousand years.   145
Sink in thyself! there ask what ails thee, at
 that shrine!

What makes thee struggle and rave?
Why are men ill at ease? —
'Tis that the lot they have
Fails their own will to please;   150
For man would make no murmuring, were his
 will obeyed.

And why is it, that still
Man with his lot thus fights? —
'Tis that he makes this *will*
The measure of his *rights*,   155
And believes Nature outraged if his will's
 gainsaid.

Couldst thou, Pausanias, learn
How deep a fault is this;
Couldst thou but once discern
Thou hast no *right* to bliss,   160
No title from the gods to welfare and repose;

Then thou wouldst look less mazed
Whene'er of bliss debarred,
Nor think the gods were crazed
When thy own lot went hard.   165

But we are all the same — the fools of our
 own woes!

For, from the first faint morn
Of life, the thirst for bliss
Deep in man's heart is born;
And, skeptic as he is,   170
He fails not to judge clear if this be quenched
 or no.

Nor is the thirst to blame.
Man errs not that he deems
His welfare his true aim;
He errs because he dreams   175
The world does but exist that welfare to
 bestow.

We mortals are no kings
For each of whom to sway
A new-made world up-springs,
Meant merely for his play;   180
No, we are strangers here; the world is from
 of old.

In vain our pent wills fret,
And would the world subdue.
Limits we did not set
Condition all we do;   185
Born into life we are, and life must be our
 mold.

Born into life! — man grows
Forth from his parents' stem,
And blends their bloods, as those
Of theirs are blent in them;   190
So each new man strikes root into a far fore-
 time.

Born into life! — we bring
A bias with us here,
And, when here, each new thing
Affects us we come near;   195
To tunes we did not call our being must keep
 chime.

Born into life! — in vain,
Opinions, those or these,
Unaltered to retain
The obstinate mind decrees;   200
Experience, like a sea, soaks all-effacing in.

Born into life! — who lists
May what is false hold dear,
And for himself make mists
Through which to see less clear;   205
The world is what it is, for all our dust and
 din.

129. **wight**, person.

Born into life! — 'tis we,
And not the world, are new;
Our cry for bliss, our plea,
Others have urged it too —   210
Our wants have all been felt, our errors made
  before.

No eye could be too sound
To observe a world so vast,
No patience too profound
To sort what's here amassed;   215
How man may here best live no care too great
  to explore.

But we — as some rude guest
Would change, where'er he roam,
The manners there professed
To those he brings from home —   220
We mark not the world's course, but would
  have it take ours.

The world's course proves the terms
On which man wins content;
Reason the proof confirms —
We spurn it, and invent   225
A false course for the world, and for our-
  selves, false powers.

Riches we wish to get,
Yet remain spendthrifts still;
We would have health, and yet
Still use our bodies ill;   230
Bafflers of our own prayers, from youth to
  life's last scenes.

We would have inward peace,
Yet will not look within;
We would have misery cease,
Yet will not cease from sin;   235
We want all pleasant ends, but will use no
  harsh means;

We do not what we ought,
What we ought not, we do,
And lean upon the thought
That chance will bring us through;   240
But our own acts for good, or ill, are mightier
  powers.

Yet, even when man forsakes
All sin — is just, is pure,
Abandons all which makes
His welfare insecure —   245
Other existences there are, that clash with
  ours.

Like us, the lightning-fires
Love to have scope and play;

The stream, like us, desires
An unimpeded way;   250
Like us, the Libyan wind delights to roam at
  large.

Streams will not curb their pride
The just man not to entomb,
Nor lightnings go aside
To give his virtues room;   255
Nor is that wind less rough which blows a
  good man's barge.

Nature, with equal mind,
Sees all her sons at play;
Sees man control the wind,
The wind sweep man away;   260
Allows the proudly-riding and the foundering
  bark.

And, lastly, though of ours
No weakness spoil our lot,
Though the non-human powers
Of Nature harm us not,   265
The ill deeds of other men make often our
  life dark.

What were the wise man's plan? —
Through this sharp, toil-set life,
To work as best he can,
And win what's won by strife. —   270
But we an easier way to cheat our pains have
  found.

Scratched by a fall, with moans
As children of weak age
Lend life to the dumb stones
Whereon to vent their rage,   275
And bend their little fists, and rate the sense-
  less ground;

So, loath to suffer mute,
We, peopling the void air,
Make gods to whom to impute
The ills we ought to bear;   280
With God and Fate to rail at, suffering easily.

Yet grant — as sense long missed
Things that are now perceived,
And much may still exist
Which is not yet believed —   285

251. **Libyan,** from Libya, a part of northern Africa.
252-256. **Streams ... barge.** Cf. *Matthew,* 5:44-46.—"But
I say unto you, Love your enemies ... that ye may be the
children of your Father which is in heaven: for he maketh his
sun to rise on the evil and on the good, and sendeth rain on
the just and on the unjust." 276. **rate,** berate, scold.

Grant that the world were full of gods we
    cannot see;

All things the world which fill
Of but one stuff are spun,
That we who rail are still,
With what we rail at, one;   290
One with the o'erlabored Power that through
    the breadth and length

Of earth, and air, and sea,
In men, and plants, and stones,
Hath toil perpetually,
And travails, pants, and moans;   295
Fain would do all things well, but sometimes
    fails in strength.

And patiently exact
This universal God
Alike to any act
Proceeds at any nod,   300
And quietly declaims the cursings of himself.

This is not what man hates,
Yet he can curse but this.
Harsh gods and hostile Fates
Are dreams! this only *is* —   305
Is everywhere; sustains the wise, the foolish
    elf.

Nor only, in the intent
To attach blame elsewhere,
Do we at will invent
Stern Powers who make their care   310
To embitter human life, malignant Deities;

But, next, we would reverse
The scheme ourselves have spun,
And what we made to curse
We now would lean upon,   315
And feign kind gods who perfect what man
    vainly tries.

Look, the world tempts our eye,
And we would know it all!
We map the starry sky,
We mine this earthen ball,   320
We measure the sea-tides, we number the
    sea-sands;

We scrutinize the dates
Of long-past human things,
The bounds of effaced states,
The lines of deceased kings;   325

306. **elf**, person.

We search out dead men's words, and works
    of dead men's hands;

We shut our eyes, and muse
How our own minds are made,
What springs of thought they use,
How rightened, how betrayed —   330
And spend our wit to name what most em-
    ploy unnamed.

But still, as we proceed
The mass swells more and more
Of volumes yet to read,
Of secrets yet to explore.   335
Our hair grows gray, our eyes are dimmed,
    our heat is tamed;

We rest our faculties,
And thus address the gods:
"True science if there is,
It stays in your abodes!   340
Man's measures cannot mete the immeasur-
    able All.

"You only can take in
The world's immense design.
Our desperate search was sin,
Which henceforth we resign,   345
Sure only that your mind sees all things
    which befall."

Fools! That in man's brief term
He cannot all things view,
Affords no ground to affirm
That there are gods who do;   350
Nor does being weary prove that he has
    where to rest.

Again. — Our youthful blood
Claims rapture as its right;
The world, a rolling flood
Of newness and delight,   355
Draws in the enamored gazer to its shining
    breast;

Pleasure, to our hot grasp,
Gives flowers, after flowers;
With passionate warmth we clasp
Hand after hand in ours;   360
Now do we soon perceive how fast our youth
    is spent.

At once our eyes grow clear!
We see, in blank dismay,
Year posting after year,
Sense after sense decay;   365

Our shivering heart is mined by secret discontent;

Yet still, in spite of truth,
In spite of hopes entombed,
That longing of our youth
Burns ever unconsumed,   370
Still hungrier for delight as delights grow
   more rare.

We pause; we hush our heart,
And thus address the gods:
"The world hath failed to impart
The joy our youth forebodes,   375
Failed to fill up the void which in our breasts
   we bear.

"Changeful till now, we still
Looked on to something new;
Let us, with changeless will,
Henceforth look on to you,   380
To find with you the joy we in vain here re-
   quire!"

Fools! That so often here
Happiness mocked our prayer,
I think, might make us fear
A like event elsewhere;   385
Make us, not fly to dreams, but moderate
   desire.

And yet, for those who know
Themselves, who wisely take
Their way through life, and bow
To what they cannot break,   390
Why should I say that life need yield but
   moderate bliss?

Shall we, with temper spoiled,
Health sapped by living ill,
And judgment all embroiled
By sadness and self-will,   395
Shall *we* judge what for man is not true bliss
   or is?

Is it so small a thing
To have enjoyed the sun,
To have lived light in the spring,
To have loved, to have thought, to have
   done;   400
To have advanced true friends, and beat
   down baffling foes —

That we must feign a bliss
Of doubtful future date,
And, while we dream on this,

Lose all our present state,   405
And relegate to worlds yet distant our repose?

Not much, I know, you prize
What pleasures may be had,
Who look on life with eyes
Estranged, like mine, and sad;   410
And yet the village-churl feels the truth more
   than you,

Who's loath to leave this life
Which to him little yields —
His hard-tasked sunburnt wife,
His often-labored fields,   415
The boors with whom he talked, the country-
   spots he knew.

But thou, because thou hear'st
Men scoff at heaven and fate,
Because the gods thou fear'st
Fail to make blest thy state,   420
Tremblest, and wilt not dare to trust the joys
   there are!

I say: Fear not! Life still
Leaves human effort scope.
But, since life teems with ill,
Nurse no extravagant hope;   425
Because thou must not dream, thou need'st
   not then despair!

A long pause. At the end of it the notes of a
harp below are again heard, and CALLICLES
sings:

Far, far from here,
The Adriatic breaks in a warm bay
Among the green Illyrian hills; and there
The sunshine in the happy glens is fair,   430
And by the sea, and in the brakes.
The grass is cool, the seaside air
Buoyant and fresh, the mountain flowers
More virginal and sweet than ours.
And there, they say, two bright and agéd
   snakes,   435
Who once were Cadmus and Harmonia,
Bask in the glens or on the warm sea-shore,
In breathless quiet, after all their ills;

429. **Illyrian hills,** mountains in ancient Illyria, a region
north of Greece. 436. **Cadmus and Harmonia.** Cadmus
was the legendary founder of Thebes, in Greece. He married
Harmonia, the daughter of Mars and Venus; but because
Cadmus had previously slain a crested snake sacred to Mars,
a fatal vengeance hung over the family. The children of
Cadmus perished by violence, and Cadmus and Harmonia left
Thebes for Illyria. Their misfortunes weighed so heavily upon
their minds that the gods granted their wish to be changed
into serpents.

Nor do they see their country, nor the place
Where the Sphinx lived among the frowning
    hills,   440
Nor the unhappy palace of their race,
Nor Thebes, nor the Ismenus, any more.

  There those two live, far in the Illyrian
    brakes!
They had stayed long enough to see,
In Thebes, the billow of calamity   445
Over their own dear children rolled,
Curse upon curse, pang upon pang,
For years, they sitting helpless in their home,
A gray old man and woman; yet of old
The gods had to their marriage come,   450
And at the banquet all the Muses sang.

Therefore they did not end their days
In sight of blood; but were rapt, far away,
To where the west-wind plays,
And murmurs of the Adriatic come   455
To those untrodden mountain-lawns; and
    there
Placed safely in changed forms, the pair
Wholly forget their first sad life, and home,
And all that Theban woe, and stray
Forever through the glens, placid and dumb.

  Empedocles. That was my harp-player
    again! — where is he?   461
Down by the stream?
  Pausanias. Yes, Master, in the wood.
  Empedocles. He ever loved the Theban
    story well!
But the day wears. Go now, Pausanias,
For I must be alone. Leave me one mule;   465
Take down with thee the rest to Catana.
And for young Callicles, thank him from me;
Tell him, I never failed to love his lyre —
But he must follow me no more tonight.
  Pausanias. Thou wilt return tomorrow to
    the city?   470
  Empedocles. Either tomorrow or some
    other day,
In the sure revolutions of the world,
Good friend, I shall revisit Catana.
I have seen many cities in my time,
Till mine eyes ache with the long spectacle,
And I shall doubtless see them all again;   476
Thou know'st me for a wanderer from of old.
Meanwhile, stay me not now. Farewell,
    Pausanias!
    [*He departs on his way up the mountain.*

440. **Sphinx**, the monster—half woman and half lion—
sent to Thebes by Juno, mother of Mars, to punish the family
of Cadmus. The monster propounded a riddle to all passers-
by and killed those who could not solve it. 442. **Ismenus**.
a small river near Thebes.

Pausanias (alone)

I dare not urge him further — he must go;
But he is strangely wrought! — I will speed
    back.   480
And bring Peisianax to him from the city;
His counsel could once soothe him. But,
    Apollo!
How his brow lightened as the music rose!
Callicles must wait here, and play to him;
I saw him through the chestnuts far below,   485
Just since, down at the stream. — Ho! Cal-
    licles!

    [*He descends, calling.*

ACT II

Evening. The Summit of Etna.

EMPEDOCLES

                 Alone! —
On this charred, blackened, melancholy waste,
Crowned by the awful peak, Etna's great
    mouth.
Round which the sullen vapour rolls —
    alone!
Pausanias is far hence, and that is well,   5
For I must henceforth speak no more with
    man.
He hath his lesson too, and that debt's paid;
And the good, learned, friendly, quiet man
May bravelier front his life, and in himself
Find henceforth energy and heart. But I —   10
The weary man, the banished citizen,
Whose banishment is not his greatest ill,
Whose weariness no energy can reach,
And for whose hurt courage is not the cure —
What should I do with life and living more? 15

  No, thou art come too late, Empedocles!
And the world hath the day, and must break
    thee,
Not thou the world. With men thou canst
    not live,
Their thoughts, their ways, their wishes, are
    not thine;
And being lonely thou art miserable,   20
For something has impaired thy spirit's
    strength,
And dried its self-sufficing fount of joy.
Thou canst not live with men nor with thy-
    self —
O sage! O sage! — Take then the one way
    left;
And turn thee to the elements, thy friends, 25

482. **Apollo**, god of music and poetry.

Thy well-tried friends, thy willing ministers,
And say: Ye helpers, hear Empedocles,
Who asks this final service at your hands!
Before the sophist-brood hath overlaid
The last spark of man's consciousness with
    words —   30
Ere quite the being of man, ere quite the
    world
Be disarrayed of their divinity —
Before the soul lose all her solemn joys,
And awe be dead, and hope impossible,
And the soul's deep eternal night come on —
Receive me, hide me, quench me, take me
    home!   36

*He advances to the edge of the crater. Smoke and
fire break forth with a loud noise, and* CALLICLES
is heard below singing:

The lyre's voice is lovely everywhere;
In the court of Gods, in the city of men,
And in the lonely rock-strewn mountain-glen,
In the still mountain air.   40

Only to Typho it sounds hatefully;
To Typho only, the rebel o'erthrown,
Through whose heart Etna drives her roots
    of stone
To imbed them in the sea.

Wherefore dost thou groan so loud?   45
Wherefore do thy nostrils flash,
Through the dark night, suddenly,
Typho, such red jets of flame? —
Is thy tortured heart still proud?
Is thy fire-scathed arm still rash?   50
Still alert thy stone-crushed frame?
Doth thy fierce soul still deplore
Thine ancient rout by the Cilician hills,
And that curst treachery on the Mount of
    Gore?
Do thy bloodshot eyes still weep   55
The fight which crowned thine ills,
Thy last mischance on this Sicilian deep?
Hast thou sworn, in thy sad lair,
Where erst the strong sea-currents sucked
    thee down,
Never to cease to writhe, and try to rest, 60
Letting the sea-stream wander through thy
    hair?
That thy groans, like thunder prest,
Begin to roll, and almost drown
The sweet notes whose lulling spell
Gods and the race of mortals love so well, 65

Act II. 41. **Typho,** giant who warred on Zeus and in defeat was buried under Mount Etna, from the crater of which
he spews forth fire. 54. **Mount of Gore,** Mount Haemus
(Blood), where Typho bled when finally overcome by Zeus.
119-120. The circlet and the robe are symbols of Empedocles'
public role as healer and worker of magic.

When through thy caves thou hearest music
    swell?

But an awful pleasure bland
Spreading o'er the Thunderer's face,
When the sound climbs near his seat,
The Olympian council sees;   70
As he lets his lax right hand,
Which the lightnings doth embrace,
Sink upon his mighty knees.
And the eagle, at the beck
Of the appeasing, gracious harmony,   75
Droops all his sheeny, brown, deep-feathered
    neck,
Nestling nearer to Jove's feet;
While o'er his sovran eye
The curtains of the blue films slowly meet
And the white Olympus-peaks   80
Rosily brighten, and the soothed Gods smile
At one another from their golden chairs,
And no one round the charmed circle speaks.
Only the loved Hebe bears
The cup about, whose draughts beguile   85
Pain and care, with a dark store
Of fresh-pulled violets wreathed and nodding
    o'er;
And her flushed feet glow on the marble floor.

Empedocles. He fables, yet speaks truth!
The brave, impetuous heart yields every-
    where   90
To the subtle, contriving head;
Great qualities are trodden down,
And littleness united
Is become invincible.

These rumblings are not Typho's groans, I
    know!   95
These angry smoke-bursts
Are not the passionate breath
Of the mountain-crushed, tortured, intract-
    able Titan king —
But over all the world
What suffering is there not seen   100
Of plainness oppressed by cunning,
As the well-counselled Zeus oppressed
That self-helping son of earth!
What anguish of greatness,
Railed and hunted from the world,   105
Because its simplicity rebukes
This envious, miserable age!

I am weary of it.
— Lie there, ye ensigns
Of my unloved preëminence   110
In an age like this!
Among a people of children,
Who thronged me in their cities,
Who worshipped me in their houses,
And asked, not wisdom,   115

But drugs to charm with,
But spells to mutter —
All the fool's-armoury of magic! — Lie there,
My golden circlet,
My purple robe! 120

Callicles (from below)

As the sky-brightening south-wind clears the
    day,
And makes the massed clouds roll,
The music of the lyre blows away
The clouds which wrap the soul.

Oh! that Fate had let me see 125
That triumph of the sweet persuasive lyre,
That famous, final victory,
When jealous Pan with Marsyas did con-
    spire;
When, from far Parnassus' side,
Young Apollo, all the pride 130
Of the Phrygian flutes to tame,
To the Phrygian highlands came;
Where the long green reed-beds sway
In the rippled waters grey
Of that solitary lake 135
Where Mæander's springs are born;
Whence the ridged pine-wooded roots
Of Messogis westward break,
Mounting westward, high and higher.
There was held the famous strife; 140
There the Phrygian brought his flutes,
And Apollo brought his lyre;
And, when now the westering sun
Touched the hills, the strife was done,
And the attentive Muses said: 145
'Marsyas, thou art vanquished!'
Then Apollo's minister
Hanged upon a branching fir
Marsyas, that unhappy Faun,
And began to whet his knife. 150
But the Mænads, who were there,
Left their friend, and with robes flowing
In the wind, and loose dark hair
O'er their polished bosoms blowing,
Each her ribboned tambourine 155
Flinging on the mountain-sod,
With a lovely frightened mien
Came about the youthful God.
But he turned his beauteous face
Haughtily another way, 160
From the grassy sun-warmed place
Where in proud repose he lay,
With one arm over his head,
Watching how the whetting sped.

But aloof, on the lake-strand, 165
Did the young Olympus stand,
Weeping at his master's end;
For the Faun had been his friend.
For he taught him how to sing,
And he taught him flute-playing. 170
Many a morning had they gone
To the glimmering mountain-lakes,
And had torn up by the roots
The tall crested water-reeds
With long plumes and soft brown seeds, 175
And had carved them into flutes,
Sitting on a tabled stone
Where the shoreward ripple breaks.
And he taught him how to please
The red-snooded Phrygian girls, 180
Whom the summer evening sees
Flashing in the dance's whirls
Underneath the starlit trees
In the mountain-villages.
Therefore now Olympus stands, 185
At his master's piteous cries
Pressing fast with both his hands
His white garment to his eyes,
Not to see Apollo's scorn; —
Ah, poor Faun, poor Faun! ah, poor Faun! 190

Empedocles. And lie thou there,
My laurel bough!
Scornful Apollo's ensign, lie thou there!
Though thou hast been my shade in the
    world's heat —
Though I have loved thee, lived in honour-
    ing thee — 195
Yet lie thou there,
My laurel bough!

I am weary of thee.
I am weary of the solitude
Where he who bears thee must abide — 200
Of the rocks of Parnassus,
Of the gorge of Delphi,
Of the moonlit peaks, and the caves.
Thou guardest them, Apollo!
Over the grave of the slain Pytho, 205
Though young, intolerably severe!
Thou keepest aloof the profane,
But the solitude oppresses thy votary!
The jars of men reach him not in thy valley —
But can life reach him? 210
Thou fencest him from the multitude —
Who will fence him from himself?
He hears nothing but the cry of the torrents,
And the beating of his own heart.
The air is thin, the veins swell, 215
The temples tighten and throb there —

---

128. **Marsyas**, a satyr who, encouraged by Pan, challenged Apollo to a flute-playing contest with the understanding that the winner might treat the loser as he would; when Apollo won, he had Marsyas flayed alive. 151. **Mænads**, female attendants of Dionysus.

166. **Olympus**, a poet of Mysia, taught by Marsyas. 193. **Apollo's ensign**, i.e., the symbol of poetry and the intellectual life. 205. **Pytho**, or python, a dragon slain by Apollo at Delphi.

Air! air!

Take thy bough, set me free from my soli-
    tude;
I have been enough alone!

Where shall thy votary fly then? back to
    men? —   220
But they will gladly welcome him once more,
And help him to unbend his too tense thought,
And rid him of the presence of himself,
And keep their friendly chatter at his ear,
And haunt him, till the absence from himself,
That other torment, grow unbearable;   226
And he will fly to solitude again,
And he will find its air too keen for him,
And so change back; and many thousand
    times
Be miserably bandied to and fro   230
Like a sea-wave, betwixt the world and thee,
Thou young, implacable God! and only death
Can cut his oscillations short, and so
Bring him to poise. There is no other way.

And yet what days were those, Parmenides!
When we were young, when we could number
    friends   236
In all the Italian cities like ourselves,
When with elated hearts we joined your train,
Ye Sun-born Virgins! on the road of truth.
Then we could still enjoy, then neither
    thought   240
Nor outward things were closed and dead to
    us;
But we received the shock of mighty thoughts
On simple minds with a pure natural joy;
And if the sacred load oppressed our brain,
We had the power to feel the pressure eased,
The brow unbound, the thoughts flow free
    again,   246
In the delightful commerce of the world.
We had not lost our balance then, nor grown
Thought's slaves, and dead to every natural
    joy.
The smallest thing could give us pleasure
    then —   250
The sports of the country-people,
A flute-note from the woods,
Sunset over the sea;
Seed-time and harvest,
The reapers in the corn,   255
The vinedresser in his vineyard,
The village-girl at her wheel.

Fulness of life and power of feeling, ye
Are for the happy, for the souls at ease,
Who dwell on a firm basis of content!   260

239. **Sun-born Virgins**, daughters of the Sun-god who
presided over Sicily.

But he, who has outlived his prosperous
    days —
But he, whose youth fell on a different world
From that on which his exiled age is thrown —
Whose mind was fed on other food, was
    trained
By other rules than are in vogue to-day — 265
Whose habit of thought is fixed, who will not
    change,
But, in a world he loves not, must subsist
In ceaseless opposition, be the guard
Of his own breast, fettered to what he guards,
That the world win no mastery over him — 270
Who has no friend, no fellow left, not one;
Who has no minute's breathing space allowed
To nurse his dwindling faculty of joy ——
Joy and the outward world must die to him,
As they are dead to me.   275

A long pause, during which EMPEDOCLES *remains motionless, plunged in thought. The night
deepens. He moves forward and gazes round
him, and proceeds:*

And you, ye stars,
Who slowly begin to marshal,
As of old, in the fields of heaven,
Your distant, melancholy lines!
Have you, too, survived yourselves?   280
Are you, too, what I fear to become?
You, too, once lived;
You, too, moved joyfully
Among august companions,
In an older world, peopled by Gods,   285
In a mightier order,
The radiant, rejoicing, intelligent Sons of
    Heaven.
But now, ye kindle
Your lonely, cold-shining lights,
Unwilling lingerers   290
In the heavenly wilderness,
For a younger, ignoble world;
And renew, by necessity,
Night after night your courses,
In echoing, unneared silence,   295
Above a race you know not —
Uncaring and undelighted,
Without friend and without home;
Weary like us, though not
Weary with our weariness.   300

No, no, ye stars! there is no death with you,
No languor, no decay! languor and death,
They are with me, not you! ye are alive —
Ye, and the pure dark ether where ye ride
Brilliant above me! And thou, fiery world, 305
That sapp'st the vitals of this terrible mount
Upon whose charred and quaking crust I
    stand —

Thou, too, brimmest with life! — the sea of
    cloud,
That heaves its white and billowy vapours up
To moat this isle of ashes from the world, 310
Lives; and that other fainter sea, far down,
O'er whose lit floor a road of moonbeams
    leads
To Etna's Liparëan sister-fires
And the long dusky line of Italy —
That mild and luminous floor of waters
    lives,   315
With held-in joy swelling its heart; I only,
Whose spring of hope is dried, whose spirit
    has failed,
I, who have not, like these, in solitude
Maintained courage and force, and in myself
Nursed an immortal vigour — I alone   320
Am dead to life and joy, therefore I read
In all things my own deadness.

A long silence. He continues:

Oh, that I could glow like this mountain!
Oh, that my heart bounded with the swell of
    the sea!
Oh, that my soul were full of light as the
    stars!   325
Oh, that it brooded over the world like the
    air!

But no, this heart will glow no more; thou art
A living man no more, Empedocles!
Nothing but a devouring flame of thought —
But a naked, eternally restless mind!   330

After a pause:

To the elements it came from
Everything will return —
Our bodies to earth,
Our blood to water,
Heat to fire,   335
Breath to air.
They were well born, they will be well en-
    tombed —
But mind? . . .

And we might gladly share the fruitful stir
Down in our mother earth's miraculous womb;
Well would it be   341
With what rolled of us in the stormy main;
We might have joy, blent with the all-bathing
    air,
Or with the nimble, radiant life of fire.

But mind, but thought —   345
If these have been the master part of us —
Where will *they* find their parent element?
What will receive *them*, who will call *them*
    home?
But we shall still be in them, and they in us,
And we shall be the strangers of the world, 350

And they will be our lords, as they are now;
And keep us prisoners of our consciousness,
And never let us clasp and feel the All
But through their forms, and modes, and sti-
    fling veils.
And we shall be unsatisfied as now;   355
And we shall feel the agony of thirst,
The ineffable longing for the life of life
Baffled for ever; and still thought and mind
Will hurry us with them on their homeless
    march,
Over the unallied unopening earth,   360
Over the unrecognising sea; while air
Will blow us fiercely back to sea and earth,
And fire repel us from its living waves.
And then we shall unwillingly return
Back to this meadow of calamity,   365
This uncongenial place, this human life;
And in our individual human state
Go through the sad probation all again,
To see if we will poise our life at last,
To see if we will now at last be true   370
To our own only true, deep-buried selves,
Being one with which we are one with the
    whole world;
Or whether we will once more fall away
Into some bondage of the flesh or mind,
Some slough of sense, or some fantastic maze
Forged by the imperious lonely thinking-
    power.   376
And each succeeding age in which we are
    born
Will have more peril for us than the last;
Will goad our senses with a sharper spur,
Will fret our minds to an intenser play,   380
Will make ourselves harder to be discerned.
And we shall struggle awhile, gasp and
    rebel —
And we shall fly for refuge to past times,
Their soul of unworn youth, their breath of
    greatness;
And the reality will pluck us back,   385
Knead us in its hot hand, and change our
    nature
And we shall feel our powers of effort flag,
And rally them for one last fight — and fail;
And we shall sink in the impossible strife,
And be astray for ever.

              Slave of sense   390
I have in no wise been; — but slave of
    thought? . . .
And who can say: I have been always free,
Lived ever in the light of my own soul? —
I cannot; I have lived in wrath and gloom,
Fierce, disputatious, ever at war with man, 395
Far from my own soul, far from warmth and
    light.
But I have not grown easy in these bonds —
But I have not denied what bonds these were.

Yea, I take myself to witness,
That I have loved no darkness,   400
Sophisticated no truth,
Nursed no delusion,
Allowed no fear!

And therefore, O ye elements! I know —
Ye know it too — it hath been granted me 405
Not to die wholly, not to be all enslaved.
I feel it in this hour. The numbing cloud
Mounts off my soul; I feel it, I breathe free.

Is it but for a moment?
— Ah, boil up, ye vapours!   410
Leap and roar, thou sea of fire!
My soul glows to meet you.
Ere it flag, ere the mists
Of despondency and gloom
Rush over it again,   415
Receive me, save me!
            [*He plunges into the crater.*

Callicles (from below)

Through the black, rushing smoke-bursts,
Thick breaks the red flame;
All Etna heaves fiercely
Her forest-clothed frame.   420

Not here, O Apollo!
Are haunts meet for thee.
But, where Helicon breaks down
In cliff to the sea,

Where the moon-silvered inlets   425
Send far their light voice
Up the still vale of Thisbe,
O speed, and rejoice!

On the sward at the cliff-top
Lie strewn the white flocks,   430
On the cliff-side the pigeons
Roost deep in the rocks.

In the moonlight the shepherds,
Soft lulled by the rills,
Lie wrapped in their blankets,   435
Asleep on the hills.

— What forms are these coming
So white through the gloom?
What garments out-glistening
The gold-flowered broom?   440

What sweet-breathing presence
Out-perfumes the thyme?
What voices enrapture
The night's balmy prime? —

'Tis Apollo comes leading   445
His choir, the Nine.
— The leader is fairest,
But all are divine.

They are lost in the hollows!
They stream up again!   450
What seeks on this mountain
The glorified train? —

They bathe on this mountain,
In the spring by their road;
Then on to Olympus,   455
Their endless abode.

— Whose praise do they mention?
Of what is it told? —
What will be forever;
What was from of old.   460

First hymn they the Father
Of all things; and then,
The rest of immortals,
The action of men.

The day in his hotness,   465
The strife with the palm;
The night in her silence,
The stars in their calm.   (1852)

From SWITZERLAND

4. ISOLATION.   TO MARGUERITE

We were apart; yet, day by day,
I bade my heart more constant be.
I bade it keep the world away,
And grow a home for only thee;
Nor feared but thy love likewise grew,   5
Like mine, each day, more tried, more true.

The fault was grave! I might have known,
What far too soon, alas! I learned —
The heart can bind itself alone,
And faith may oft be unreturned.   10
Self-swayed our feelings ebb and swell —
Thou lov'st no more; — Farewell! Farewell!

Farewell! — and thou, thou lonely heart,
Which never yet without remorse
Even for a moment didst depart   15
From thy remote and sphered course

446. **the Nine,** the nine Muses. See note on Clough's *In
the Depths,* p. 405.   454. **the spring,** a spring flowing from
Mount Helicon, sacred to the Muses.   455. **Olympus,** a
mountain in Greece, the abode of the gods.   466. **the palm,**
the reward of victory.
   Switzerland. This title is given to a group of six love poems.
The three omitted are entitled *Meeting, Parting,* and *A Farewell.* Marguerite seems to have been a French girl whom
Arnold met in Switzerland and who played an important part
in his emotional development.

423. **Helicon,** a mountain in Greece, sacred to Apollo.
427. **Thisbe,** a town situated in a valley in Bœotia, Greece.

To haunt the place where passions reign —
Back to thy solitude again!

Back! with the conscious thrill of shame
Which Luna felt, that summer-night,   20
Flash through her pure immortal frame,
When she forsook the starry height
To hang over Endymion's sleep
Upon the pine-grown Latmian steep.

Yet she, chaste queen, had never proved   25
How vain a thing is mortal love,
Wandering in heaven, far removed.
But thou hast long had place to prove
This truth — to prove, and make thine own:
"Thou hast been, shalt be, art, alone."   30

Or, if not quite alone, yet they
Which touch thee are unmating things —
Ocean and clouds and night and day;
Lorn autumns and triumphant springs;
And life, and others' joy and pain,   35
And love, if love, of happier men.

Of happier men — for they, at least,
Have *dreamed* two human hearts might blend
In one, and were through faith released
From isolation without end   40
Prolonged; nor knew, although not less
Alone than thou, their loneliness.
                                        (1855)

5. TO MARGUERITE — CONTINUED

Yes! in the sea of life enisled,
With echoing straits between us thrown,
Dotting the shoreless watery wild,
We mortal millions live *alone*.
The islands feel the enclasping flow,   5
And then their endless bounds they know.

But when the moon their hollows lights,
And they are swept by balms of spring,
And in their glens, on starry nights,
The nightingales divinely sing;   10
And lovely notes, from shore to shore,
Across the sounds and channels pour —

Oh! then a longing like despair
Is to their farthest caverns sent;
For surely once, they feel, we were   15
Parts of a single continent!
Now round us spreads the watery plain —
Oh, might our marges meet again!

Who ordered, that their longing's fire
Should be, as soon as kindled, cooled?   20

20. **Luna,** Diana, the goddess of the moon and the goddess
of chastity. She fell in love with Endymion, the shepherd boy
whom she found sleeping on Mt. Latmos, in Asia Minor.

Who renders vain their deep desire? —
A god, a god their severance ruled!
And bade betwixt their shores to be
The unplumbed, salt, estranging sea.   (1852)

6. ABSENCE

In this fair stranger's eyes of gray
Thine eyes, my love! I see.
I shiver; for the passing day
Had borne me far from thee.

This is the curse of life! that not   5
A nobler, calmer train
Of wiser thoughts and feelings blot
Our passions from our brain;

But each day brings its petty dust
Our soon-choked souls to fill,   10
And we forget because we must
And not because we will.

I struggle toward the light; and ye,
Once-longed-for storms of love!
If with the light ye cannot be,   15
I bear that ye remove.

I struggle toward the light — but oh,
While yet the night is chill,
Upon time's barren, stormy flow,
Stay with me, Marguerite, still!   20
                                        (1852)

DESPONDENCY

The thoughts that rain their steady glow
Like stars on life's cold sea,
Which others know, or say they know —
They never shone for me.

Thoughts light, like gleams, my spirit's sky,
But they will not remain.   6
They light me once, they hurry by;
And never come again.   (1852)

SELF-DECEPTION

Say, what blinds us, that we claim the glory
Of possessing powers not our share?
— Since man woke on earth, he knows his
        story,
But, before we woke on earth, we were.

Long, long since, undowered yet, our spirit 5
Roamed, ere birth, the treasuries of God;
Saw the gifts, the powers it might inherit,
Asked an outfit for its earthly road.

Then, as now, this tremulous, eager being
Strained and longed and grasped each gift it
    saw;   10
Then, as now, a Power beyond our seeing
Staved us back, and gave our choice the law.

Ah, whose hand that day through heaven
    guided
Man's new spirit, since it was not we?
Ah, who swayed our choice, and who decided
What our gifts, and what our wants should
    be?   16

For, alas! he left us each retaining
Shreds of gifts which he refused in full.
Still these waste us with their hopeless
    straining,
Still the attempt to use them proves them
    null.   20

And on earth we wander, groping, reeling;
Powers stir in us, stir and disappear.
Ah! and he, who placed our master-feeling,
Failed to place that master-feeling clear.

We but dream we have our wished-for powers,
Ends we seek we never shall attain.   26
Ah! *some* power exists there, which is ours?
Some end is there, we indeed may gain?
        (1852)

TRISTRAM AND ISEULT

I. TRISTRAM

Tristram

Is she not come? The messenger was sure.
Prop me upon the pillows once again —
Raise me, my page! this cannot long endure.
— Christ, what a night! how the sleet whips
    the pane!
What lights will those out to the northward
    be?   5

The Page

The lanterns of the fishing-boats at sea.

Tristram

Soft — who is that stands by the dying fire?

The Page

Iseult.

Tristram

Ah! not the Iseult I desire.

.   .   .   .   .

What knight is this so weak and pale,
Though the locks are yet brown on his noble
    head,   10
Propped on pillows in his bed,
Gazing seaward for the light
Of some ship that fights the gale
On this wild December night?
Over the sick man's feet is spread   15
A dark green forest-dress;
A gold harp leans against the bed,
Ruddy in the fire's light.
I know him by his harp of gold,
Famous in Arthur's court of old;   20
I know him by his forest-dress —
The peerless hunter, harper, knight,
Tristram of Lyoness.

What lady is this, whose silk attire
Gleams so rich in the light of the fire?   25
The ringlets on her shoulders lying
In their flitting luster vying
With the clasp of burnished gold
Which her heavy robe doth hold.
Her looks are mild, her fingers slight   30
As the driven snow are white;
But her cheeks are sunk and pale.
Is it that the bleak sea-gale
Beating from the Atlantic sea
On this coast of Brittany,   35
Nips too keenly the sweet flower?
Is it that a deep fatigue
Hath come on her, a chilly fear,
Passing all her youthful hour
Spinning with her maidens here,   40
Listlessly through the window-bars
Gazing seawards many a league,
From her lonely shore-built tower,
While the knights are at the wars?
Or, perhaps, has her young heart   45
Felt already some deeper smart,
Of those that in secret the heart-strings rive,
Leaving her sunk and pale, though fair?
Who is this snowdrop by the sea? —
I know her by her mildness rare,   50
Her snow-white hands, her golden hair;
I know her by her rich silk dress,
And her fragile loveliness —

---

12. **Staved us back,** held us back as with a staff.
Tristram and Iseult. Tristram was a famous hero of Celtic legend. His home was in Lyoness, a region which, according to tradition, sank beneath the sea, its position thereafter being marked by islands off the point of Cornwall. Tristram was sent to Ireland by his uncle, King Mark of Cornwall, to bring back Iseult, the King's bride, to the castle of Tintagel. On the return voyage Tristram and Iseult both drank of a potion that made them permanent lovers. Forced by his uncle to leave Cornwall, Tristram went to Brittany and married Iseult of the White Hands. Afterwards he became attached to Arthur's Court as one of the Knights of the Round Table. The story of Tristram is found in Malory's *Morte Darthur*, Books 10-12. Tennyson treated the theme in *The Last Tournament* (p. 153), Swinburne in *Tristram of Lyonesse* (p. 717), and Edwin Arlington Robinson in *Tristram*. In Arnold's poem Tristram is lying ill in Brittany waiting for an answer to the message he has sent to Iseult of Ireland asking her to come to him. The story is told partly in dialogue and partly in narrative.

The sweetest Christian soul alive,
Iseult of Brittany.   55

Iseult of Brittany? — but where
Is that other Iseult fair,
That proud, first Iseult, Cornwall's queen?
She, whom Tristram's ship of yore
From Ireland to Cornwall bore,   60
To Tyntagel, to the side
Of King Marc, to be his bride?
She who, as they voyaged, quaffed
With Tristram that spiced magic draft,
Which since then forever rolls   65
Through their blood, and binds their souls,
Working love, but working teen? —
There were two Iseults who did sway
Each her hour of Tristram's day;
But one possessed his waning time,   70
The other his resplendent prime.
Behold her here, the patient flower,
Who possessed his darker hour!
Iseult of the Snow-White Hand
Watches pale by Tristram's bed.   75
She is here who had his gloom,
Where art thou who hadst his bloom?
One such kiss as those of yore
Might thy dying knight restore!
Does the love-draft work no more?   80
Art thou cold, or false, or dead,
Iseult of Ireland?

            .   .   .   .   .

Loud howls the wind, sharp patters the rain,
And the knight sinks back on his pillows
      again.
He is weak with fever and pain,   85
And his spirit is not clear.
Hark! he mutters in his sleep,
As he wanders far from here,
Changes place and time of year,
And his closéd eye doth sweep   90
O'er some fair unwintry sea,
Not this fierce Atlantic deep,
While he mutters brokenly:

Tristram

The calm sea shines, loose hang the vessel's
      sails;   94
Before us are the sweet green fields of Wales,
And overhead the cloudless sky of May. —
"Ah, would I were in those green fields at play,
Not pent on shipboard this delicious day!
Tristram, I pray thee, of thy courtesy,
Reach me my golden phial stands by thee,   100
But pledge me in it first for courtesy. —"
Ha! dost thou start? are thy lips blanched
      like mine?

67. **teen**, grief.

Child, 'tis no true draft this 'tis poisoned
      wine!
Iseult! . . .
                    .   .   .   .   .

Ah, sweet angels, let him dream!   105
Keep his eyelids! let him seem
Not this fever-wasted wight
Thinned and paled before his time,
But the brilliant youthful knight
In the glory of his prime,   110
Sitting in the gilded barge,
At thy side, thou lovely charge,
Bending gaily o'er thy hand,
Iseult of Ireland!
And she too, that princess fair,   115
If her bloom be now less rare,
Let her have her youth again —
Let her be as she was then!
Let her have her proud dark eyes,
And her petulant quick replies —   120
Let her sweep her dazzling hand
With its gesture of command,
And shake back her raven hair
With the old imperious air!
As of old, so let her be,   125
That first Iseult, princess bright,
Chatting with her youthful knight
As she steers her o'er the sea,
Quitting at her father's will
The green isle where she was bred,   130
And her bower in Ireland,
For the surge-beat Cornish strand;
Where the prince whom she must wed
Dwells on loud Tyntagel's hill,
High above the sounding sea.   135
And that potion rare her mother
Gave her, that her future lord,
Gave her, that King Marc and she,
Might drink it on their marriage-day,
And forever love each other —   140
Let her, as she sits on board,
Ah, sweet saints, unwittingly!
See it shine, and take it up,
And to Tristram laughing say:
"Sir Tristram, of thy courtesy,   145
Pledge me in my golden cup!"
Let them drink it — let their hands
Tremble, and their cheeks be flame,
As they feel the fatal bands
Of a love they dare not name,   150
With a wild delicious pain,
Twine about their hearts again!
Let the early summer be
Once more round them, and the sea
Blue, and o'er its mirror kind   155
Let the breath of the May-wind,
Wandering through their drooping sails,
Die on the green fields of Wales!

Let a dream like this restore
What his eye must see no more!   160

Tristram

Chill blows the wind, the pleasaunce-walks
    are drear—
Madcap, what jest was this, to meet me here?
Were feet like those made for so wild a way?
The southern winter-parlor, by my fay,   164
Had been the likeliest trysting-place today!
"*Tristram!* — *nay, nay* — *thou must not take
    my hand!* —
Tristram! — *sweet love!* — *we are betrayed* —
    out-planned.
Fly — *save thyself* — *save me!* — *I dare not
    stay.*"—
One last kiss first! — " '*Tis vain* — *to horse
    — away!*"

.   .   .   .   .

Ah! sweet saints, his dream doth move   170
Faster surely than it should,
From the fever in his blood!
All the springtime of his love
Is already gone and past,
And instead thereof is seen   175
Its winter, which endureth still —
Tyntagel on its surge-beat hill,
The pleasaunce-walks, the weeping queen,
The flying leaves, the straining blast,
And that long, wild kiss — their last.   180
And this rough December-night,
And his burning fever-pain,
Mingle with his hurrying dream,
Till they rule it, till he seem
The pressed fugitive again,   185
The love-desperate banished knight
With a fire in his brain
Flying o'er the stormy main.
—Whither does he wander now?
Haply in his dreams the wind   190
Wafts him here, and lets him find
The lovely orphan child again
In her castle by the coast;
The youngest, fairest chatelaine
Whom this realm of France can boast,   195
Our snowdrop by the Atlantic sea,
Iseult of Brittany.
And — for through the haggard air,
The stained arms, the matted hair
Of that stranger-knight ill-starred,   200
There gleamed something, which recalled
The Tristram who in better days
Was Launcelot's guest at Joyous Gard —
Welcomed here, and here installed,

Tended of his fever here,   205
Haply he seems again to move
His young guardian's heart with love;
In his exiled loneliness,
In his stately, deep distress,
Without a word, without a tear.   210
— Ah! 'tis well he should retrace
His tranquil life in this lone place;
His gentle bearing at the side
Of his timid youthful bride;
His long rambles by the shore   215
On winter-evenings, when the roar
Of the near waves came, sadly grand,
Through the dark, up the drowned sand,
Or his endless reveries
In the woods, where the gleams play   220
On the grass under the trees,
Passing the long summer's day
Idle as a mossy stone
In the forest-depths alone,
The chase neglected, and his hound   225
Couched beside him on the ground.
— Ah! what trouble's on his brow?
Hither let him wander now;
Hither, to the quiet hours
Passed among these heaths of ours   230
By the gray Atlantic sea;
Hours, if not of ecstasy,
From violent anguish surely free!

Tristram

All red with blood the whirling river flows,
The wide plain rings, the dazed air throbs
    with blows.   235
Upon us are the chivalry of Rome —
Their spears are down, their steeds are bathed
    in foam.
"Up, Tristram, up," men cry, "thou moon-
    struck knight!
What foul fiend rides thee? On into the
    fight!"
— Above the din her voice is in my ears;   240
I see her form glide through the crossing
    spears. —
Iseult! . . .

.   .   .   .   .   .

Ah! he wanders forth again;
We cannot keep him; now, as then,
There's a secret in his breast   245
Which will never let him rest.
These musing fits in the green wood
They cloud the brain, they dull the blood!
— His sword is sharp, his horse is good;
Beyond the mountains will he see   250
The famous towns of Italy,

---

161. **pleasaunce-walks**, the walks in the pleasance, an enclosure with fountains, flower gardens, etc. 164. **fay**, faith. 194. **chatelaine**, lady of a castle. 203. **Launcelot**. See Tennyson's *Lancelot and Elaine*, p. 123, and Critical Notes. **Joyous Gard**, Launcelot's home, reputed to have been near Berwick, in northern England.

236. **chivalry of Rome.** Early tradition states that King Arthur and his knights conquered Scandinavia, Gaul, and Rome. 238. **moonstruck.** The moon was long thought to cause madness.

And label with the blessed sign
The heathen Saxons on the Rhine.
At Arthur's side he fights once more
With the Roman emperor.   255
There's many a gay knight where he goes
Will help him to forget his care;
The march, the leaguer, heaven's blithe air,
The neighing steeds, the ringing blows —
Sick pining comes not where these are.   260
Ah! what boots it that the jest
Lightens every other brow,
What, that every other breast
Dances as the trumpets blow,
If one's own heart beats not light   265
On the waves of the tossed fight,
If oneself cannot get free
From the clog of misery?
Thy lovely youthful wife grows pale
Watching by the salt sea-tide   270
With her children at her side
For the gleam of thy white sail.
Home, Tristram, to thy halls again!
To our lonely sea complain,
To our forests tell thy pain!   275

Tristram

All round the forest sweeps off, black in shade,
But it is moonlight in the open glade;
And in the bottom of the glade shine clear
The forest-chapel and the fountain near.
— I think I have a fever in my blood;   280
Come, let me leave the shadow of this wood,
Ride down, and bathe my hot brow in the
      flood.
— Mild shines the cold spring in the moon's
      clear light;
God! 'tis *her* face plays in the waters bright.
"Fair love," she says, "canst thou forget so
      soon,   285
At this soft hour, under this sweet moon?" —
Iseult! . . .

　　　．　　．　　．　　．　　．

Ah, poor soul! if this be so,
Only death can balm thy woe.
The solitudes of the green wood   290
Had no medicine for thy mood;
The rushing battle cleared thy blood
As little as did solitude.
— Ah! his eyelids slowly break
Their hot seals, and let him wake;   295
What new change shall we now see?
A happier? Worse it cannot be.

Tristram

Is my page here? Come, turn me to the fire!

258. leaguer, siege.

Upon the window-panes the moon shines
      bright;
The wind is down — but she'll not come
      tonight.   300
Ah no! she is asleep in Cornwall now,
Far hence; her dreams are fair — smooth is
      her brow.
Of me she recks not, nor my vain desire.
— I have had dreams, I have had dreams,
      my page,
Would take a score years from a strong man's
      age;   305
And with a blood like mine, will leave, I fear,
Scant leisure for a second messenger.
— My princess, art thou there? Sweet, do
      not wait!
To bed, and sleep! my fever is gone by;   309
Tonight my page shall keep me company.
Where do the children sleep? kiss them for
      me!
Poor child, thou art almost as pale as I;
This comes of nursing long and watching late.
To bed — good night!

　　　．　　．　　．　　．　　．

She left the gleam-lit fireplace,   315
She came to the bedside;
She took his hands in hers — her tears
Down on his wasted fingers rained.
She raised her eyes upon his face —
Not with a look of wounded pride,   320
A look as if the heart complained —
Her look was like a sad embrace;
The gaze of one who can divine
A grief, and sympathize.
Sweet flower! thy children's eyes   325
Are not more innocent than thine.
  But they sleep in sheltered rest,
Like helpless birds in the warm nest,
On the castle's southern side;
Where feebly comes the mournful roar   330
Of buffeting wind and surging tide
Through many a room and corridor.
— Full on their window the moon's ray
Makes their chamber as bright as day.
It shines upon the blank white walls,   335
And on the snowy pillow falls,
And on two angel-heads doth play
Turned to each other — the eyes closed,
The lashes on the cheeks reposed.
Round each sweet brow the cap close-set   340
Hardly lets peep the golden hair;
Through the soft-opened lips the air
Scarcely moves the coverlet.
One little wandering arm is thrown
At random on the counterpane,   345
And often the fingers close in haste
As if their baby-owner chased
The butterflies again.
This stir they have, and this alone;

But else they are so still!   350
— Ah, tired madcaps! you lie still;
But were you at the window now,
To look forth on the fairy sight
Of your illumined haunts by night,
To see the park-glades where you play   355
Far lovelier than they are by day,
To see the sparkle on the eaves,
And upon every giant-bough
Of those old oaks, whose wet red leaves
Are jeweled with bright drops of rain —   360
How would your voices run again!
And far beyond the sparkling trees
Of the castle-park one sees
The bare heaths spreading, clear as day,
Moor behind moor, far, far away,   365
Into the heart of Brittany.
And here and there, locked by the land,
Long inlets of smooth glittering sea,
And many a stretch of watery sand
All shining in the white moonbeams —   370
But you see fairer in your dreams!
What voices are these on the clear night-air?
What lights in the court — what steps on the
   stair?

II. ISEULT OF IRELAND

Tristram

Raise the light, my page! that I may see
   her. —
   Thou art come at last, then, haughty
     Queen!
Long I've waited, long I've fought my fever;
   Late thou comest, cruel thou hast been.

Iseult

Blame me not, poor sufferer! that I tarried; 5
   Bound I was, I could not break the band.
Chide not with the past, but feel the present!
   I am here— we meet — I hold thy hand.

Tristram

Thou art come, indeed — thou hast rejoined
   me;
   Thou hast dared it — but too late to save.
Fear not now that men should tax thine
   honor!   11
   I am dying; build (thou may'st) my grave!

Iseult

Tristram, ah, for love of Heaven, speak
   kindly!
   What, I hear these bitter words from thee?
Sick with grief I am, and faint with travel —
   Take my hand — dear Tristram, look on
     me!   16

Tristram

I forgot, thou comest from thy voyage —
   Yes, the spray is on thy cloak and hair.
But thy dark eyes are not dimmed, proud
   Iseult!
   And thy beauty never was more fair.   20

Iseult

Ah, harsh flatterer! let alone my beauty!
   I, like thee, have left my youth afar.
Take my hand, and touch these wasted
   fingers —
   See my cheek and lips, how white they are!

Tristram

Thou art paler — but thy sweet charm,
   Iseult!   25
   Would not fade with the dull years away.
Ah, how fair thou standest in the moonlight!
   I forgive thee, Iseult! — thou wilt stay?

Iseult

Fear me not, I will be always with thee;
   I will watch thee, tend thee, soothe thy
     pain;   30
Sing thee tales of true, long-parted lovers,
   Joined at evening of their days again.

Tristram

No, thou shalt not speak! I should be finding
   Something altered in thy courtly tone.
Sit — sit by me! I will think, we've lived so
   In the greenwood, all our lives, alone.   36

Iseult

Altered, Tristram? Not in courts, believe me;
   Love like mine is altered in the breast.
Courtly life is light and cannot reach it —
   Ah! it lives, because so deep-suppressed! 40

What, thou think'st men speak in courtly
   chambers
   Words by which the wretched are consoled?
What, thou think'st this aching brow was
   cooler,
   Circled, Tristram, by a band of gold?

Royal state with Marc, my deep-wronged
   husband —   45
   That was bliss to make my sorrows flee!
Silken courtiers whispering honeyed noth-
   ings —
   Those were friends to make me false to
     thee!

Ah, on which, if both our lots were balanced,
   Was indeed the heaviest burden thrown —

Thee, a pining exile in thy forest,   51
  Me, a smiling queen upon my throne?

Vain and strange debate, where both have
    suffered,
  Both have passed a youth consumed and
    sad,
Both have brought their anxious day to
    evening,   55
  And have now short space for being glad!

Joined we are henceforth; nor will thy people,
  Nor thy younger Iseult take it ill,
That a former rival shares her office,
  When she sees her humbled, pale, and still.

I, a faded watcher by thy pillow,   61
  I, a statue on thy chapel-floor,
Poured in prayer before the Virgin-Mother,
  Rouse no anger, make no rivals more.

She will cry: "Is this the foe I dreaded?   65
  This his idol? this that royal bride?
Ah, an hour of health would purge his eye-
    sight!
  Stay, pale queen! forever by my side."

Hush, no words! that smile, I see, forgives me.
  I am now thy nurse, I bid thee sleep.   70
Close thine eyes — this flooding moonlight
    blinds them! —
  Nay, all's well again! thou must not weep.

Tristram

I am happy! yet I feel there's something
  Swells my heart, and takes my breath
    away.
Through a mist I see thee; near — come
    nearer!   75
  Bend — bend down! — I yet have much to
    say.

Iseult

Heaven! his head sinks back upon the pillow—
  Tristram! Tristram! let thy heart not fail!
Call on God and on the holy angels!
  What, love, courage! — Christ! he is so
    pale.   80

Tristram

Hush, 'tis vain, I feel my end approaching!
  This is what my mother said should be,
When the fierce pains took her in the forest,
  The deep drafts of death, in bearing me.

"Son," she said, "thy name shall be of
    sorrow;   85

---

85. **name . . . of sorrow.** The name *Tristram* is from the
Latin word *tristis*, meaning *sorrow*.

Tristram art thou called for my death's
    sake."
So she said, and died in the drear forest.
  Grief since then his home with me doth
    make.

I am dying. — Start not, nor look wildly!
  Me, thy living friend, thou canst not save.
But, since living we were ununited,   91
  Go not far, O Iseult! from my grave.

Close mine eyes, then seek the princess Iseult;
  Speak her fair, she is of royal blood!
Say, I willed so, that thou stay beside me —
  She will grant it; she is kind and good.   96

Now to sail the seas of death I leave thee —
  One last kiss upon the living shore!

Iseult

Tristram! — Tristram! — stay — receive me
    with thee!
  Iseult leaves thee, Tristram! never more. 100

        .   .   .   .   .

You see them clear — the moon shines bright.
Slow, slow and softly, where she stood,
She sinks upon the ground; — her hood
Had fallen back; her arms outspread
Still hold her lover's hand; her head   105
Is bowed, half-buried, on the bed.
O'er the blanched sheet her raven hair
Lies in disordered streams; and there,
Strung like white stars, the pearls still are,
And the golden bracelets, heavy and rare, 110
Flash on her white arms still—
The very same which yesternight
Flashed in the silver sconces' light,
When the feast was gay and the laughter loud
In Tyntagel's palace proud.   115
But then they decked a restless ghost
With hot-flushed cheeks and brilliant eyes,
And quivering lips on which the tide
Of courtly speech abruptly died,
And a glance which over the crowded floor,
The dancers, and the festive host,   121
Flew ever to the door.
That the knights eyed her in surprise,
And the dames whispered scoffingly:
"Her moods, good lack, they pass like showers!
But yesternight and she would be   126
As pale and still as withered flowers,
And now tonight she laughs and speaks
And has a color in her cheeks;
Christ keep us from such fantasy!" —   130

Yes, now the longing is o'erpast,
Which, dogged by fear and fought by shame,

---

113. **sconce**, a bracket for holding a light.   130. **fantasy**,
queer behavior.

Shook her weak bosom day and night,
Consumed her beauty like a flame,
And dimmed it like the desert-blast.   135
And though the bedclothes hide her face,
Yet were it lifted to the light,
The sweet expression of her brow
Would charm the gazer, till his thought
Erased the ravages of time,   140
Filled up the hollow cheek, and brought
A freshness back as of her prime —
So healing is her quiet now.
So perfectly the lines express
A tranquil, settled loveliness,   145
Her younger rival's purest grace.

The air of the December-night
Steals coldly around the chamber bright,
Where those lifeless lovers be;
Swinging with it, in the light   150
Flaps the ghostlike tapestry.
And on the arras wrought you see
A stately huntsman, clad in green,
And round him a fresh forest-scene.
On that clear forest-knoll he stays,   155
With his pack round him, and delays.
He stares and stares, with troubled face,
At this huge, gleam-lit fireplace,
At that bright, iron-figured door,
And those blown rushes on the floor.   160
He gazes down into the room
With heated cheeks and flurried air,
And to himself he seems to say:
"What place is this, and who are they?
Who is that kneeling lady fair?.   165
And on his pillows that pale knight
Who seems of marble on a tomb?
How comes it here, this chamber bright,
Through whose mullioned windows clear
The castle-court all wet with rain,   170
The drawbridge and the moat appear,
And then the beach, and, marked with spray,
The sunken reefs, and far away
The unquiet bright Atlantic plain?
—What, has some glamour made me sleep,   175
And sent me with my dogs to sweep,
By night, with boisterous bugle-peal,
Through some old, seaside, knightly hall,
Not in the free greenwood at all?
That knight's asleep, and at her prayer   180
That lady by the bed doth kneel —
Then hush, thou boisterous bugle-peal!"
— The wild boar rustles in his lair;
The fierce hounds snuff the tainted air;
But lord and hounds keep rooted there.   185

Cheer, cheer thy dogs into the brake,
O hunter! and without a fear

Thy golden-tasseled bugle blow,
And through the glades thy pastime take —
For thou wilt rouse no sleepers here!   190
For these thou seest are unmoved;
Cold, cold as those who lived and loved
A thousand years ago.

III. ISEULT OF BRITTANY

A year had flown, and o'er the sea away,
In Cornwall, Tristram and Queen Iseult lay;
In King Marc's chapel, in Tyntagel old —
There in a ship they bore those lovers cold.

The young surviving Iseult, one bright day, 5
Had wandered forth. Her children were at
     play
In a green circular hollow in the heath
Which borders the sea-shore — a country
     path
Creeps over it from the tilled fields behind.
The hollow's grassy banks are soft-inclined,10
And to one standing on them, far and near
The lone unbroken view spreads bright and
     clear
Over the waste. This cirque of open ground
Is light and green; the heather, which all
     round
Creeps thickly, grows not here; but the pale
     grass   15
Is strewn with rocks, and many a shivered
     mass
Of veined white-gleaming quartz, and here
     and there
Dotted with holly-trees and juniper.
In the smooth center of the opening stood
Three hollies side by side, and made a
     screen,   20
Warm with the winter-sun, of burnished green
With scarlet berries gemmed, the fell-fare's
     food.
Under the glittering hollies Iseult stands,
Watching her children play; their little hands
Are busy gathering spars of quartz, and
     streams   25
Of stagshorn for their hats; anon, with
     screams
Of mad delight they drop their spoils, and
     bound
Among the holly-clumps and broken ground,
Racing full speed, and startling in their rush
The fell-fares and the speckled missel-
     thrush   30
Out of their glossy coverts; — but when now
Their cheeks were flushed, and over each hot
     brow,

---

169. **mullioned windows,** windows with panes of glass
divided by upright stone bars.

22. **fell-fare,** field-fare, a kind of thrush. 25. **spars of
quartz,** pieces of quartz crystal. 26. **stagshorn,** a kind
of moss. 30. **missel-thrush,** a large European thrush that
feeds on mistletoe berries.

Under the feathered hats of the sweet pair,
In blinding masses showered the golden hair—
Then Iseult called them to her, and the three
Clustered under the holly-screen, and she   36
Told them an old-world Breton history.

Warm in their mantles wrapped the three
    stood there,
Under the hollies, in the clear still air —
Mantles with those rich furs deep glistering 40
Which Venice ships do from swart Egypt
    bring.
Long they stayed still — then, pacing at their
    ease,
Moved up and down under the glossy trees.
But still, as they pursued their warm dry
    road,   44
From Iseult's lips the unbroken story flowed,
And still the children listened, their blue eyes
Fixed on their mother's face in wide surprise;
Nor did their looks stray once to the seaside,
Nor to the brown heaths round them, bright
    and wide,
Nor to the snow, which, though 'twas all
    away   50
From the open heath, still by the hedgerows
    lay,
Nor to the shining sea-fowl, that with screams
Bore up from where the bright Atlantic
    gleams,
Swooping to landward; nor to where, quite
    clear,
The fell-fares settled on the thickets near. 55
And they would still have listened, till dark
    night
Came keen and chill down on the heather
    bright;
But, when the red glow on the sea grew cold,
And the gray turrets of the castle old
Looked sternly through the frosty evening-
    air,   60
Then Iseult took by the hand those children
    fair,
And brought her tale to an end, and found
    the path,
And led them home over the darkening heath.

And is she happy? Does she see unmoved
The days in which she might have lived and
    loved   65
Slip without bringing bliss slowly away,
One after one, tomorrow like today?
Joy has not found her yet, nor ever will —
Is it this thought which makes her mien so
    still,
Her features so fatigued, her eyes, though
    sweet,   70
So sunk, so rarely lifted save to meet

Her children's? She moves slow; her voice
    alone
Hath yet an infantine and silver tone,
But even that comes languidly; in truth,
She seems one dying in a mask of youth.   75
And now she will go home, and softly lay
Her laughing children in their beds, and play
Awhile with them before they sleep; and then
She'll light her silver lamp, which fishermen
Dragging their nets through the rough waves,
    afar,   80
Along this iron coast, know like a star,
And take her broidery-frame, and there she'll
    sit
Hour after hour, her gold curls sweeping it;
Lifting her soft-bent head only to mind
Her children, or to listen to the wind.   85
And when the clock peals midnight, she will
    move
Her work away, and let her fingers rove
Across the shaggy brows of Tristram's hound,
Who lies, guarding her feet, along the ground;
Or else she will fall musing, her blue eyes   90
Fixed, her slight hands clasped on her lap;
    then rise,
And at her pric-dieu kneel, until she have told
Her rosary-beads of ebony tipped with gold,
Then to her soft sleep — and tomorrow 'll be
Today's exact repeated effigy.   95

Yes, it is lonely for her in her hall.
The children, and the gray-haired seneschal,
Her women, and Sir Tristram's agéd hound,
Are there the sole companions to be found.
But these she loves; and noisier life than this
She would find ill to bear, weak as she is. 101
She has her children, too, and night and day
Is with them; and the wide heaths where they
    play,
The hollies, and the cliff, and the seashore,
The sand, the sea-birds, and the distant sails,
These are to her dear as to them; the tales 106
With which this day the children she beguiled
She gleaned from Breton grandames, when a
    child,
In every hut along this seacoast wild.
She herself loves them still, and, when they
    are told,   110
Can forget all to hear them, as of old.

Dear saints, it is not sorrow, as I hear,
Not suffering, which shuts up eye and ear
To all that has delighted them before,
And lets us be what we were once no more.
No, we may suffer deeply, yet retain   116
Power to be moved and soothed, for all our
    pain,
By what of old pleased us, and will again.

---

37. **Breton history,** story of Brittany.

92. **pric-dieu,** prayer desk. 97. **seneschal,** steward.

No, 'tis the gradual furnace of the world,
In whose hot air our spirits are upcurled 120
Until they crumble, or else grow like steel —
Which kills in us the bloom, the youth, the
    spring —
Which leaves the fierce necessity to feel,
But takes away the power — this can avail,
By drying up our joy in everything, 125
To make our former pleasures all seem stale.
This, or some tyrannous single thought, some
    fit
Of passion, which subdues our souls to it,
Till for its sake alone we live and move —
Call it ambition, or remorse, or love — 130
This too can change us wholly, and make seem
All which we did before, shadow and dream.

And yet, I swear, it angers me to see
How this fool passion gulls men potently;
Being, in truth, but a diseased unrest, 135
And an unnatural overheat at best.
How they are full of languor and distress
Not having it; which when they do possess,
They straightway are burnt up with fume
    and care,
And spend their lives in posting here and
    there 140
Where this plague drives them; and have
    little ease,
Are furious with themselves, and hard to
    please,
Like that bold Cæsar, the famed Roman
    wight,
Who wept at reading of a Grecian knight
Who made a name at younger years than he;
Or that renowned mirror of chivalry, 146
Prince Alexander, Philip's peerless son,
Who carried the great war from Macedon
Into the Soudan's realm, and thundered on
To die at thirty-five in Babylon. 150

What tale did Iseult to the children say,
Under the hollies, that bright winter's day?

She told them of the fairy-haunted land
Away the other side of Brittany,
Beyond the heaths, edged by the lonely sea;
Of the deep forest-glades of Broce-liande, 156
Through whose green boughs the golden sun-
    shine creeps,

Where Merlin by the enchanted thorn-tree
    sleeps.
For here he came with the fay Vivian,
One April, when the warm days first
    began. 160
He was on foot, and that false fay, his friend,
On her white palfrey; here he met his end,
In these lone sylvan glades, that April-day.
This tale of Merlin and the lovely fay
Was the one Iseult chose, and she brought
    clear 165
Before the children's fancy him and her.

Blowing between the stems, the forest-air
Had loosened the brown locks of Vivian's
    hair,
Which played on her flushed cheek, and her
    blue eyes
Sparkled with mocking glee and exercise. 170
Her palfrey's flanks were mired and bathed
    in sweat,
For they had traveled far and not stopped
    yet.
A brier in that tangled wilderness
Had scored her white right hand, which she
    allows
To rest ungloved on her green riding-dress; 175
The other warded off the drooping boughs.
But still she chatted on, with her blue eyes
Fixed full on Merlin's face, her stately prize.
Her 'haviour had the morning's fresh clear
    grace,
The spirit of the woods was in her face. 180
She looked so witching fair, that learned wight
Forgot his craft, and his best wits took flight;
And he grew fond, and eager to obey
His mistress, use her empire as she may.

They came to where the brushwood ceased,
    and day 185
Peered 'twixt the stems; and the ground
    broke away,
In a sloped sward down to a brawling brook;
And up as high as where they stood to look
On the brook's farther side was clear, but then
The underwood and trees began again. 190
This open glen was studded thick with thorns
Then white with blossom; and you saw the
    horns,
Through last year's fern, of the shy fallow-
    deer
Who come at noon down to the water here.
You saw the bright-eyed squirrels dart along
Under the thorns on the greensward; and
    strong 196
The blackbird whistled from the dingles near,
And the weird chipping of the woodpecker
Rang lonelily and sharp; the sky was fair,

139. fume, passion. 143-150. Cæsar . . . Babylon. The
Roman historian Suetonius (c. 75-160 A.D.) relates that
Julius Cæsar wept when he heard of the conquests of Alexander the Great (356-323 B.C.), son of Philip, king of Macedon.
Alexander became king of Macedon when he was twenty
years old and conquered Persia when he was twenty-five.
149. Soudan's, Sultan's. 156. Broce-liande, a forest
supposed to have been in Brittany. At one end of it was the
tomb of Merlin, the magician of Arthur's Court, who was
induced by his mistress Vivien to tell her the secret of his
magic power. Having learned that secret, she used it to
overcome him. See Tennyson's *Merlin and Vivien*.

174. scored, scratched.   197. dingles, small valleys.

And a fresh breath of spring stirred every-
    where. 200
Merlin and Vivian stopped on the slope's
    brow,
To gaze on the light sea of leaf and bough
Which glistering plays all round them, lone
    and mild,
As if to itself the quiet forest smiled.
Upon the brow-top grew a thorn, and here 205
The grass was dry and mossed, and you saw
    clear
Across the hollow; white anemones
Starred the cool turf, and clumps of prim-
    roses
Ran out from the dark underwood behind.
No fairer resting-place a man could find. 210
"Here let us halt," said Merlin then; and she
Nodded, and tied her palfrey to a tree.

They sate them down together, and a sleep
Fell upon Merlin, more like death, so deep.
Her finger on her lips, then Vivian rose, 215
And from her brown-locked head the wimple
    throws,
And takes it in her hand, and waves it over
The blossomed thorn-tree and her sleeping
    lover.
Nine times she waved the fluttering wimple
    round,
And made a little plot of magic ground. 220
And in that daisied circle, as men say,
Is Merlin prisoner till the judgment-day;
But she herself whither she will can rove —
For she was passing weary of his love. (1852)

SELF-DEPENDENCE

Weary of myself, and sick of asking
What I am, and what I ought to be,
At this vessel's prow I stand, which bears me
Forwards, forwards, o'er the starlit sea.

And a look of passionate desire 5
O'er the sea and to the stars I send:
"Ye who from my childhood up have calmed
    me,
Calm me, ah, compose me to the end!

"Ah, once more," I cried, "ye stars, ye waters,
On my heart your mighty charm renew; 10
Still, still let me, as I gaze upon you,
Feel my soul becoming vast like you!"

From the intense, clear, star-sown vault of
    heaven,
Over the lit sea's unquiet way,
In the rustling night-air came the answer: 15
"Wouldst thou *be* as these are? *Live* as they.

216. **wimple,** a linen head covering.

"Unaffrighted by the silence round them,
Undistracted by the sights they see,
These demand not that the things without
    them
Yield them love, amusement, sympathy. 20

"And with joy the stars perform their shining,
And the sea its long moon-silvered roll;
For self-poised they live, nor pine with noting
All the fever of some differing soul.

"Bounded by themselves, and unregardful 25
In what state God's other works may be,
In their own tasks all their powers pouring,
These attain the mighty life you see."

O air-born voice! long since, severely clear,
A cry like thine in mine own heart I hear: 30
"Resolve to be thyself; and know that he
Who finds himself loses his misery!"
                       (1852)

A SUMMER NIGHT

In the deserted, moon-blanched street,
How lonely rings the echo of my feet!
Those windows, which I gaze at, frown,
Silent and white, unopening down,
Repellent as the world — but see, 5
A break between the housetops shows
The moon! and, lost behind her, fading dim
Into the dewy dark obscurity
Down at the far horizon's rim,
Doth a whole tract of heaven disclose! 10

And to my mind the thought
Is on a sudden brought
Of a past night, and a far different scene.
Headlands stood out into the moonlit deep
As clearly as at noon; 15
The spring-tide's brimming flow
Heaved dazzlingly between;
Houses, with long white sweep,
Girdled the glistening bay;
Behind, through the soft air, 20
The blue haze-cradled mountains spread
    away.
That night was far more fair —
But the same restless pacings to and fro,
And the same vainly throbbing heart was
    there,
And the same bright, calm moon. 25

And the calm moonlight seems to say:
Hast thou then still the old unquiet breast,
Which neither deadens into rest,
Nor ever feels the fiery glow
That whirls the spirit from itself away, 30
But fluctuates to and fro,

Never by passion quite possessed
And never quite benumbed by the world's
　　sway? —
And I, I know not if to pray
Still to be what I am, or yield and be　　35
Like all the other men I see.

For most men in a brazen prison live,
Where, in the sun's hot eye,
With heads bent o'er their toil, they languidly
Their lives to some unmeaning taskwork give,
Dreaming of naught beyond their prison-wall.
And as, year after year,
Fresh products of their barren labor fall
From their tired hands, and rest
Never yet comes more near,　　45
Gloom settles slowly down over their breast;
And while they try to stem
The waves of mournful thought by which
　　they are prest
Death in their prison reaches them,
Unfreed, having seen nothing, still unblest. 50

And the rest, a few,
Escape their prison and depart
On the wide ocean of life anew.
There the freed prisoner, where'er his heart
Listeth, will sail;　　55
Nor doth he know how there prevail,
Despotic on that sea,
Trade-winds which cross it from eternity.
Awhile he holds some false way, undebarred
By thwarting signs, and braves　　60
The freshening wind and blackening waves,
And then the tempest strikes him; and be-
　　tween
The lightning-bursts is seen
Only a driving wreck,
And the pale master on his spar-strewn deck
With anguished face and flying hair　　66
Grasping the rudder hard,
Still bent to make some port he knows not
　　where,
Still standing for some false, impossible shore.
And sterner comes the roar　　70
Of sea and wind, and through the deepening
　　gloom
Fainter and fainter wreck and helmsman
　　loom,
And he too disappears, and comes no more.

Is there no life, but these alone?
Madman or slave, must man be one?　　75

Plainness and clearness without shadow of
　　stain!
Clearness divine!

<hr>

75. **Madman or slave**, a reference to the types of life
just described—one (madman) in lines 51-73; the other
(slave) in lines 37-50.

Ye heavens, whose pure dark regions have no
　　sign
Of languor, though so calm, and, though so
　　great,
Are yet untroubled and unpassionate;　　80
Who, though so noble, share in the world's
　　toil,
And, though so tasked, keep free from dust
　　and soil!
I will not say that your mild deeps retain
A tinge, it may be, of their silent pain
Who have longed deeply once, and longed in
　　vain —　　85
But I will rather say that you remain
A world above man's head, to let him see
How boundless might his soul's horizons
　　be,
How vast, yet of what clear transparency!
How it were good to abide there, and breathe
　　free;　　90
How fair a lot to fill
Is left to each man still!

　　　　　　　　　　　　　　　(1852)

THE BURIED LIFE

Light flows our war of mocking words, and
　　yet,
Behold, with tears mine eyes are wet!
I feel a nameless sadness o'er me roll.
Yes, yes, we know that we can jest,
We know, we know that we can smile!　　5
But there's a something in this breast,
To which thy light words bring no rest,
And thy gay smiles no anodyne.
Give me thy hand, and hush awhile,
And turn those limpid eyes on mine,　　10
And let me read there, love! thy inmost soul.

Alas! is even love too weak
To unlock the heart, and let it speak?
Are even lovers powerless to reveal
To one another what indeed they feel?　　15
I knew the mass of men concealed
Their thoughts, for fear that if revealed
They would by other men be met
With blank indifference, or with blame re-
　　proved;
I knew they lived and moved　　20
Tricked in disguises, alien to the rest
Of men, and alien to themselves — and yet
The same heart beats in every human breast!

But we, my love! — doth a like spell be-
　　numb
Our hearts, our voices? — must we too be
　　dumb?　　25

<hr>

The Buried Life. The title refers to man's hidden self—
the source of his thought and his feeling.

Ah! well for us, if even we,
Even for a moment, can get free
Our heart, and have our lips unchained;
For that which seals them hath been deep-
    ordained!

Fate, which foresaw   30
How frivolous a baby man would be —
By what distractions he would be possessed,
How he would pour himself in every strife,
And well-nigh change his own identity —
That it might keep from his capricious play
His genuine self, and force him to obey   36
Even in his own despite his being's law,
Bade through the deep recesses of our breast
The unregarded river of our life
Pursue with indiscernible flow its way;   40
And that we should not see
The buried stream, and seem to be
Eddying at large in blind uncertainty,
Though driving on with it eternally.

But often, in the world's most crowded streets,
But often, in the din of strife,   46
There rises an unspeakable desire
After the knowledge of our buried life;
A thirst to spend our fire and restless force
In tracking out our true, original course;   50
A longing to inquire
Into the mystery of this heart which beats
So wild, so deep in us — to know
Whence our lives come and where they go.
And many a man in his own breast then
    delves,   55
But deep enough, alas! none ever mines.
And we have been on many thousand lines,
And we have shown, on each, spirit and
    power;
But hardly have we, for one little hour,
Been on our own line, have we been our-
    selves —   60
Hardly had skill to utter one of all
The nameless feelings that course through
    our breast,
But they course on for ever unexpressed.
And long we try in vain to speak and act
Our hidden self, and what we say and do   65
Is eloquent, is well — but 'tis not true!
And then we will no more be racked
With inward striving, and demand
Of all the thousand nothings of the hour
Their stupefying power;   70
Ah yes, and they benumb us at our call!
Yet still, from time to time, vague and for-
    lorn,
From the soul's subterranean depth upborne
As from an infinitely distant land,
Come airs, and floating echoes, and con-
    vey
A melancholy into all our day   76

Only — but this is rare —
When a belovéd hand is laid in ours,
When, jaded with the rush and glare
Of the interminable hours,   80
Our eyes can in another's eyes read clear,
When our world-deafened ear
Is by the tones of a loved voice caressed —
A bolt is shot back somewhere in our breast,
And a lost pulse of feeling stirs again;   85
The eye sinks inward, and the heart lies plain,
And what we mean, we say, and what we
    would, we know.
A man becomes aware of his life's flow,
And hears its winding murmur; and he sees
The meadows where it glides, the sun, the
    breeze.   90

And there arrives a lull in the hot race
Wherein he doth forever chase
That flying and elusive shadow, rest.
An air of coolness plays upon his face,
And an unwonted calm pervades his breast.
And then he thinks he knows   96
The hills where his life rose,
And the sea where it goes.   (1852)

STANZAS IN MEMORY OF THE AUTHOR OF "OBERMANN"

In front the awful Alpine track
Crawls up its rocky stair;
The autumn storm-winds drive the rack,
Close o'er it, in the air.

Behind are the abandoned baths   5
Mute in their meadows lone;
The leaves are on the valley-paths,
The mists are on the Rhone —

The white mists rolling like a sea!
I hear the torrents roar.   10
—Yes, Obermann, all speaks of thee;
I feel thee near once more!

I turn thy leaves! I feel their breath
Once more upon me roll;
That air of languor, cold, and death,   15
Which brooded o'er thy soul.

Fly hence, poor wretch, whoe'er thou art,
Condemned to cast about,

77-98. **Only . . . goes.** Cf. *Dover Beach,* lines 29-37, p. 499.
    Stanzas in Memory of the Author of "Obermann." Étienne
Pivert de Senancour (1770-1846) was the author of a French
philosophic romance called *Obermann.* It is in the form of letters, many of which are supposed to have been written in a
lonely Alpine valley in Switzerland where the hero of the romance lived. The book is devoted to descriptions of nature
and discussions of the human soul. The tone is melancholy.
    5. **abandoned baths,** the baths of Leuk, a village in the
canton of Valais.

All shipwreck in thy own weak heart,
For comfort from without! 20

A fever in these pages burns
Beneath the calm they feign;
A wounded human spirit turns,
Here, on its bed of pain.

Yes, though the virgin mountain-air 25
Fresh through these pages blows;
Though to these leaves the glaciers spare
The soul of their white snows;

Though here a mountain-murmur swells
Of many a dark-boughed pine; 30
Though, as you read, you hear the bells
Of the high-pasturing kine —

Yet, through the hum of torrent lone,
And brooding mountain-bee,
There sobs I know not what ground-tone 35
Of human agony.

Is it for this, because the sound
Is fraught too deep with pain,
That, Obermann! the world around
So little loves thy strain? 40

Some secrets may the poet tell,
For the world loves new ways;
To tell too deep ones is not well —
It knows not what he says.

Yet, of the spirits who have reigned 45
In this our troubled day,
I know but two who have attained,
Save thee, to see their way.

By England's lakes, in gray old age,
His quiet home one keeps; 50
And one, the strong much-toiling sage,
In German Weimar sleeps.

But Wordsworth's eyes avert their ken
From half of human fate;
And Goethe's course few sons of men 55
May think to emulate.

For he pursued a lonely road,
His eyes on Nature's plan;
Neither made man too much a God,
Nor God too much a man. 60

Strong was he, with a spirit free
From mists, and sane, and clear;
Clearer, how much! than ours — yet we
Have a worse course to steer.

For though his manhood bore the blast 65
Of a tremendous time,
Yet in a tranquil world was passed
His tenderer youthful prime.

But we, brought forth and reared in hours
Of change, alarm, surprise — 70
What shelter to grow ripe is ours?
What leisure to grow wise?

Like children bathing on the shore,
Buried a wave beneath,
The second wave succeeds, before 75
We have had time to breathe.

Too fast we live, too much are tried,
Too harrassed, to attain
Wordsworth's sweet calm, or Goethe's wide
And luminous view to gain. 80

And then we turn, thou sadder sage,
To thee! we feel thy spell!
— The hopeless tangle of our age,
Thou, too, hast scanned it well!

Immovable thou sittest, still 85
As death, composed to bear!
Thy head is clear, thy feeling chill,
And icy thy despair.

Yes, as the son of Thetis said,
I hear thee saying now: 90
Greater by far than thou are dead;
Strive not! die also thou!

Ah! two desires toss about
The poet's feverish blood.
One drives him to the world without, 95
And one to solitude.

The glow, he cries, *the thrill of life,*
Where, where do these abound? —
Not in the world, not in the strife
Of men, shall they be found. 100

He who hath watched, not shared, the strife,
Knows how the day hath gone.
He only lives with the world's life,
Who hath renounced his own.

To thee we come, then! Clouds are rolled 105
Where thou, O seer! art set;
Thy realm of thought is drear and cold —
The world is colder yet!

---

50. **one,** Wordsworth (1770-1850). Cf. *Memorial Verses*, p. 442. 51. **sage,** Goethe (1749-1832), who was buried at Weimar, Germany. Cf. *Memorial Verses*, p. 442.

89. **son of Thetis,** Achilles, the famous Greek hero of the Trojan War. He preferred a short career of military glory to a long life of obscurity. When Lycaon asked Achilles (his captor) for mercy, Achilles, angered by the death of his friend Patroclus, made a long speech in which he said in part, "My friend, do thou too die; Patroclus is also dead, who was better far than thou art, and behold what kind of man I am; I too must die" (the *Iliad*, 21, 34 ff.).

And thou hast pleasures, too, to share
With those who come to thee —— 110
Balms floating on thy mountain-air,
And healing sights to see.

How often, where the slopes are green
On Jaman, hast thou sate
By some high chalet-door, and seen 115
The summer-day grow late;

And darkness steal o'er the wet grass
With the pale crocus starred,
And reach that glimmering sheet of glass
Beneath the piny sward, 120

Lake Leman's waters, far below!
And watched the rosy light
Fade from the distant peaks of snow;
And on the air of night

Heard accents of the eternal tongue 125
Through the pine branches play —
Listened, and felt thyself grow young!
Listened and wept —— Away!

Away the dreams that but deceive
And thou, sad guide, adieu! 130
I go, fate drives me; but I leave
Half of my life with you.

We, in some unknown Power's employ,
Move on a rigorous line;
Can neither, when we will, enjoy, 135
Nor, when we will, resign.

I in the world must live; but thou,
Thou melancholy shade!
Wilt not, if thou canst see me now,
Condemn me, nor upbraid. 140

For thou art gone away from earth,
And place with those dost claim,
The Children of the Second Birth,
Whom the world could not tame;

And with that small, transfigured band, 145
Whom many a different way
Conducted to their common land,
Thou learn'st to think as they.

Christian and pagan, king and slave,
Soldier and anchorite, 150
Distinctions we esteem so grave,
Are nothing in their sight.

They do not ask, who pined unseen,
Who was on action hurled,

Whose one bond is, that all have been 155
Unspotted by the world.

There without anger thou wilt see
Him who obeys thy spell
No more, so he but rest, like thee,
Unsoiled! — and so, farewell. 160

Farewell! — Whether thou now liest near
That much-loved inland sea,
The ripples of whose blue waves cheer
Vevey and Meillerie:

And in that gracious region bland, 165
Where with clear-rustling wave
The scented pines of Switzerland
Stand dark round thy green grave,

Between the dusty vineyard-walls
Issuing on that green place 170
The early peasant still recalls
The pensive stranger's face,

And stoops to clear thy moss-grown date
Ere he plods on again —
Or whether, by maligner fate, 175
Among the swarms of men,

Where between granite terraces
The blue Seine rolls her wave,
The Capital of Pleasure sees
The hardly-heard-of grave — 180

Farewell! Under the sky we part,
In this stern Alpine dell.
O unstrung will! O broken heart!
A last, a last farewell! (1852)

LINES

WRITTEN IN KENSINGTON GARDENS

In this lone, open glade I lie,
Screened by deep boughs on either hand;
And at its end, to stay the eye,
Those black-crowned, red-boled pine-trees
stand!

Birds here make song, each bird has his, 5
Across the girdling city's hum.
How green under the boughs it is!
How thick the tremulous sheep-cries come!

Sometimes a child will cross the glade
To take his nurse his broken toy; 10

114. **Jaman,** one of the Alpine peaks. 121. **Lake Leman,** Lake Geneva, Switzerland. 150. **anchorite,** a religious recluse.

164. **Vevey and Meillerie,** towns on Lake Geneva, Switzerland. 179. **Capital of Pleasure,** Paris.
Lines Written in Kensington Gardens. Kensington is a borough in the western part of London. The Gardens are surrounded by busy streets. This poem is regarded as one of the most Wordsworthian of Arnold's poems.
4. **red-boled pine-trees,** pine-trees with reddish trunks.

Sometimes a thrush flits overhead
Deep in her unknown day's employ.

Here at my feet what wonders pass,
What endless, active life is here!
What blowing daisies, fragrant grass!   15
An air-stirred forest, fresh and clear.

Scarce fresher is the mountain-sod
Where the tired angler lies, stretched out,
And, eased of basket and of rod,
Counts his day's spoil, the spotted trout.   20

In the huge world, which roars hard by,
Be others happy if they can!
But in my helpless cradle I
Was breathed on by the rural Pan.

I, on men's impious uproar hurled,   25
Think often, as I hear them rave,
That peace has left the upper world
And now keeps only in the grave.

Yet here is peace forever new!
When I who watch them am away,   30
Still all things in this glade go through
The changes of their quiet day.

Then to their happy rest they pass!
The flowers upclose, the birds are fed,
The night comes down upon the grass,   35
The child sleeps warmly in his bed.

Calm soul of all things! make it mine
To feel, amid the city's jar,
That there abides a peace of thine,
Man did not make, and cannot mar.   40

The will to neither strive nor cry,
The power to feel with others give!
Calm, calm me more! nor let me die
Before I have begun to live.   (1852)

REVOLUTIONS

Before man parted for this earthly strand,
While yet upon the verge of heaven he stood,
God put a heap of letters in his hand,
And bade him make with them what word
he could.

And man has turned them many times; made
Greece,   5
Rome, England, France — yes, nor in vain
essayed

18. **angler.** Arnold was an enthusiastic fisherman. 24.
breathed . . . Pan. Pan was the god of shepherds and the
country. Arnold was born at Laleham, a country village in
Middlesex.

Way after way, changes that never cease!
The letters have combined, something was
made.

But ah! an inextinguishable sense
Haunts him that he has not made what he
should;   10
That he has still, though old, to recommence,
Since he has not yet found the word God
would.

And empire after empire, at their height
Of sway, have felt this boding sense come on;
Have felt their huge frames not constructed
right,   15
And drooped, and slowly died upon their
throne.

One day, thou say'st, there will at last appear
The word, the order, which God meant
should be.
— Ah! we shall know *that* well when it comes
near;
The band will quit man's heart, he will
breathe free.   20
(1852)

THE YOUTH OF NATURE

Raised are the dripping oars,
Silent, the boat! the lake,
Lovely and soft as a dream,
Swims in the sheen of the moon.
The mountains stand at its head   5
Clear in the pure June-night,
But the valleys are flooded with haze.
Rydal and Fairfield are there;
In the shadow Wordsworth lies dead.
So it is, so it will be for aye.   10
Nature is fresh as of old,
Is lovely; a mortal is dead.

The spots which recall him survive,
For he lent a new life to these hills.
The Pillar still broods o'er the fields   15
Which border Ennerdale Lake,
And Egremont sleeps by the sea.
The gleam of The Evening Star

The Youth of Nature. This poem is a tribute to Wordsworth; it was written shortly after his death in 1850. See
Memorial Verses, p. 442.
2. **the lake.** Rydal or Grasmere, in the Lake District,
England. 8. **Rydal and Fairfield.** Wordsworth lived at
Rydal Mount from 1813 till his death. Fairfield is a mountain
north of Rydal Mount. 15. **The Pillar,** a prominent rock
on a mountain in Cumberland. 17. **Egremont,** a town near
the sea; it is seven miles from Ennerdale Lake (line 16).
The places of lines 15-17 are mentioned in Wordsworth's
The Brothers. 18. **The Evening Star,** the name of Michael's
cottage above Grasmere, Westmoreland. It was so called
because it was visible from a long distance. (See Wordsworth's *Michael.*)

Twinkles on Grasmere no more,
But ruined and solemn and gray   20
The sheepfold of Michael survives;
And, far to the south, the heath
Still blows in the Quantock coombs,
By the favorite waters of Ruth.
These survive! — yet not without pain,   25
Pain and dejection tonight,
Can I feel that their poet is gone.

He grew old in an age he condemned.
He looked on the rushing decay
Of the times which had sheltered his youth,
Felt the dissolving throes   31
Of a social order he loved;
Outlived his brethren, his peers,
And, like the Theban seer,
Died in his enemies' day.   35

Cold bubbled the spring of Tilphusa,
Copais lay bright in the moon,
Helicon glassed in the lake
Its firs, and afar rose the peaks
Of Parnassus, snowily clear;   40
Thebes was behind him in flames,
And the clang of arms in his ear,
When his awe-struck captors led
The Theban seer to the spring.
Tiresias drank and died.   45
Nor did reviving Thebes
See such a prophet again.

Well may we mourn, when the head
Of a sacred poet lies low
In an age which can rear them no more!   50
The complaining millions of men
Darken in labor and pain;
But he was a priest to us all
Of the wonder and bloom of the world,
Which we saw with his eyes, and were glad.
He is dead, and the fruit-bearing day   56
Of his race is past on the earth;
And darkness returns to our eyes.

For, oh! is it you, is it you,
Moonlight, and shadow, and lake,   60
And mountains, that fill us with joy,
Or the poet who sings you so well?

Is it you, O beauty, O grace,
O charm, O romance, that we feel,
Or the voice which reveals what you are?   65
Are ye, like daylight and sun,
Shared and rejoiced in by all?
Or are ye immersed in the mass
Of matter, and hard to extract,
Or sunk at the core of the world   70
Too deep for the most to discern?
Like stars in the deep of the sky,
Which arise on the glass of the sage,
But are lost when their watcher is gone.

"They are here" — I heard, as men heard   75
In Mysian Ida the voice
Of the Mighty Mother, or Crete,
The murmur of Nature reply —
"Loveliness, magic, and grace,
They are here! they are set in the world,   80
They abide; and the finest of souls
Hath not been thrilled by them all,
Nor the dullest been dead to them quite.
The poet who sings them may die,
But they are immortal and live,   85
For they are the life of the world.
Will ye not learn it, and know,
When ye mourn that a poet is dead,
That the singer was less than his themes,
Life, and emotion, and I?   90

"More than the singer are these.
Weak is the tremor of pain
That thrills in his mournfullest chord
To that which once ran through his soul.
Cold the elation of joy   95
In his gladdest, airiest song,
To that which of old in his youth
Filled him and made him divine.
Hardly his voice at its best
Gives us a sense of the awe,   100
The vastness, the grandeur, the gloom
Of the unlit gulf of himself.

"Ye know not yourselves; and your bards —
The clearest, the best, who have read
Most in themselves — have beheld   105
Less than they left unrevealed.
Ye express not yourselves — can you make
With marble, with color, with word,
What charmed you in others re-live?
Can thy pencil, O artist! restore   110
The figure, the bloom of thy love,
As she was in her morning of spring?
Canst thou paint the ineffable smile
Of her eyes as they rested on thine?

23. **Quantock coombs,** valleys among the Quantock Hills in Somerset. Ruth (line 24), in Wordsworth's *Ruth,* visited these hills. 28. **He grew old . . . condemned.** In his youth Wordsworth sympathized with the French Revolution, but he later became disgusted with its excesses. The "dissolving throes" of line 31 refer to such movements as the Reform Bill of 1832 and the Repeal of the Corn Laws of 1846. By those dates Wordsworth had become a conservative. 33. **brethren . . . peers,** Coleridge and Southey, who were often associated with Wordsworth. They died in 1834 and 1843 respectively. 34. **Theban seer,** Tiresias, who is said to have met his death by drinking from a stream on Mount Tilphusa (line 36), in Bœotia. Copais (line 37) was a lake near Thebes. Mt. Helicon (line 38), sacred to the Muses, and Mt. Parnassus (line 40), sacred to Apollo, were also in Bœotia. 56-58. **He is dead . . . eyes.** Lines 56-58 express Arnold's usual pessimism about his own age.

77. **Mighty Mother,** Cybele, the great goddess of nature. As the "Mother of the Gods" she was worshiped on Mt. Ida in Mysia, Asia Minor. She was identified with Rhea, who was worshiped in Crete, a Greek island in the Mediterranean. 90. **I,** Nature. 91-102. Cf. Shelley's *Defence of Poetry.*

Can the image of life have the glow,   115
The motion of life itself?

"Yourselves and your fellows ye know not;
     and me,
The mateless, the one, will ye know?
Will ye scan me, and read me, and tell
Of the thoughts that ferment in my breast,
My longing, my sadness, my joy?   121
Will ye claim for your great ones the gift
To have rendered the gleam of my skies,
To have echoed the moan of my seas,
Uttered the voice of my hills?   125
When your great ones depart, will ye say:
*All things have suffered a loss,
Nature is hid in their grave?*

"Race after race, man after man,
Have thought that my secret was theirs,   130
Have dreamed that I lived but for them,
That they were my glory and joy.
— They are dust, they are changed, they are
     gone!
I remain."   (1852)

MORALITY

We cannot kindle when we will
The fire which in the heart resides;
The spirit bloweth and is still,
In mystery our soul abides.
     But tasks in hours of insight willed   5
     Can be through hours of gloom fulfilled.

With aching hands and bleeding feet
We dig and heap, lay stone on stone;
We bear the burden and the heat
Of the long day, and wish 'twere done.   10
     Not till the hours of light return,
     All we have built do we discern.

Then, when the clouds are off the soul,
When thou dost bask in Nature's eye,
Ask, how *she* viewed thy self-control,   15
Thy struggling, tasked morality —
     Nature, whose free, light, cheerful air,
     Oft made thee, in thy gloom, despair.

And she, whose censure thou dost dread,
Whose eye thou wast afraid to seek,   20
See, on her face a glow is spread,
A strong emotion on her cheek!
     "Ah, child!" she cries, "that strife divine,
     Whence was it, for it is not mine?

"There is no effort on *my* brow —   25
I do not strive, I do not weep;
I rush with the swift spheres and glow
In joy, and when I will, I sleep.

Yet that severe, that earnest air,
I saw, I felt it once — but where?   30

"I knew not yet the gauge of time,
Nor wore the manacles of space;
I felt it in some other clime,
I saw it in some other place.
'Twas when the heavenly house I trod,   35
And lay upon the breast of God."   (1852)

THE FUTURE

A wanderer is man from his birth.
He was born in a ship
On the breast of the river of Time;
Brimming with wonder and joy
He spreads out his arms to the light,   5
Rivets his gaze on the banks of the stream.

As what he sees is, so have his thoughts been.
Whether he wakes,
Where the snowy mountainous pass,
Echoing the screams of the eagles,   10
Hems in its gorges the bed
Of the new-born clear-flowing stream;
Whether he first sees light
Where the river in gleaming rings
Sluggishly winds through the plain;   15
Whether in sound of the swallowing sea —
As is the world on the banks,
So is the mind of the man.

Vainly does each, as he glides,
Fable and dream   20
Of the lands which the river of Time
Had left ere he woke on its breast,
Or shall reach when his eyes have been closed.
Only the tract where he sails
He wots of; only the thoughts,   25
Raised by the objects he passes, are his.

Who can see the green earth any more
As she was by the sources of Time?
Who imagines her fields as they lay
In the sunshine, unworn by the plow?   30
Who thinks as they thought,
The tribes who then roamed on her breast,
Her vigorous, primitive sons?

What girl
Now reads in her bosom as clear   35
As Rebekah read, when she sate
At eve by the palm-shaded well?
Who guards in her breast

The Future. This is one of the earliest of Arnold's poems
to strike an optimistic note.
    36-37. **Rebekah . . . well.** Rebekah was found at the
well by the servant who had been sent by Abraham to get a
wife for his son Isaac. (See *Genesis,* 24.)

As deep, as pellucid a spring
Of feeling, as tranquil, as sure? 40

What bard,
At the height of his vision, can deem
Of God, of the world, of the soul,
With a plainness as near,
As flashing as Moses felt 45
When he lay in the night by his flock
On the starlit Arabian waste?
Can rise and obey
The beck of the Spirit like him?

This tract which the river of Time 50
Now flows through with us, is the plain.
Gone is the calm of its earlier shore.
Bordered by cities and hoarse
With a thousand cries is its stream.
And we on its breast, our minds 55
Are confused as the cries which we hear,
Changing and shot as the sights which we see.

And we say that repose has fled
Forever the course of the river of Time.
That cities will crowd to its edge 60
In a blacker, incessanter line;
That the din will be more on its banks,
Denser the trade on its stream,
Flatter the plain where it flows,
Fiercer the sun overhead. 65
That never will those on its breast
See an ennobling sight,
Drink of the feeling of quiet again.

But what was before us we know not,
And we know not what shall succeed. 70

Haply, the river of Time —
As it grows, as the towns on its marge
Fling their wavering lights
On a wider, statelier stream —
May acquire, if not the calm 75
Of its early mountainous shore,
Yet a solemn peace of its own.

And the width of the waters, the hush
Of the gray expanse where he floats,
Freshening its current and spotted with foam
As it draws to the Ocean, may strike 81
Peace to the soul of the man on its breast —
As the pale waste widens around him,
As the banks fade dimmer away,
As the stars come out, and the night-wind 85
Brings up the stream
Murmurs and scents of the infinite sea.

(1852)

45. **Moses felt.** When Moses was watching sheep in "the backside of the desert" near Mt. Horeb (Sinai), in Arabia, God appeared to him in a burning bush and commanded him to lead the children of Israel out of Egypt. (See *Exodus*, 3.) 57. **shot**, variegated. Cf. *shot silk*.

SOHRAB AND RUSTUM

AN EPISODE

And the first gray of morning filled the east,
And the fog rose out of the Oxus stream.
But all the Tartar camp along the stream
Was hushed, and still the men were plunged
      in sleep.
Sohrab alone, he slept not; all night long 5
He had lain wakeful, tossing on his bed;
But when the gray dawn stole into his tent,
He rose, and clad himself, and girt his sword,
And took his horseman's cloak, and left his
      tent,
And went abroad into the cold wet fog, 10
Through the dim camp to Peran-Wisa's tent.
   Through the black Tartar tents he passed,
      which stood
Clustering like beehives on the low flat strand
Of Oxus, where the summer-floods o'erflow
When the sun melts the snows in high Pamere;
Through the black tents he passed, o'er that
      low strand,
And to a hillock came, a little back 16
From the stream's brink — the spot where
      first a boat,
Crossing the stream in summer, scrapes the
      land.
The men of former times had crowned the top
With a clay fort; but that was fallen, and now
The Tartars built there Peran-Wisa's tent,
A dome of laths, and o'er it felts were spread.
And Sohrab came there, and went in, and
      stood
Upon the thick-piled carpets in the tent, 25
And found the old man sleeping on his bed
Of rugs and felts, and near him lay his arms.
And Peran-Wisa heard him, though the step
Was dulled; for he slept light, an old man's
      sleep;
And he rose quickly on one arm, and said: 30
   "Who art thou? for it is not yet clear dawn.
Speak! is there news, or any night alarm?"
   But Sohrab came to the bedside, and said:
"Thou know'st me, Peran-Wisa! it is I.
The sun is not yet risen, and the foe 35
Sleep; but I sleep not; all night long I lie
Tossing and wakeful, and I come to thee.
For so did King Afrasiab bid me seek

Sohrab and Rustum. This narrative poem is based upon an episode in the great Persian epic *Shah Namah* (*Book of Kings*) written by the poet Firdausi about 1000 A.D. Rustum was the most illustrious of Persian heroes. His combat with Sohrab, his unknown son, which belongs to the realm of folklore, was supposed to have taken place about 600 B.C. Arnold found the story in Sir John Malcolm's *History of Persia.* See Critical Notes.
2. **Oxus,** the chief river of central Asia. 3. **Tartar.** The Tartars were wandering savage tribes in central Asia and southern Russia. Although a Persian by birth, Sohrab is serving under Afrasiab, the Tartar king. 11. **Peran-Wisa,** leader of the Tartar army. 15. **Pamere,** a lofty plateau in central Asia. 25. **thick-piled,** having a thick pile, or nap.

Thy counsel, and to heed thee as thy son,
In Samarcand, before the army marched;　40
And I will tell thee what my heart desires.
Thou know'st if, since from Ader-baijan first
I came among the Tartars and bore arms,
I have still served Afrasiab well, and shown,
At my boy's years, the courage of a man.　45
This too thou know'st, that while I still bear
　　　on
The conquering Tartar ensigns through the
　　　world,
And beat the Persians back on every field,
I seek one man, one man, and one alone —
Rustum, my father; who I hoped should greet,
Should one day greet, upon some well-fought
　　　field,　51
His not unworthy, not inglorious son.
So I long hoped, but him I never find.
Come then, hear now, and grant me what I
　　　ask.
Let the two armies rest today; but I　55
Will challenge forth the bravest Persian lords
To meet me, man to man; if I prevail,
Rustum will surely hear it; if I fall —
Old man, the dead need no one, claim no kin.
Dim is the rumor of a common fight,　60
Where host meets host, and many names are
　　　sunk;
But of a single combat fame speaks clear."
　　He spoke; and Peran-Wisa took the hand
Of the young man in his, and sighed, and said:
"O Sohrab, an unquiet heart is thine!　65
Canst thou not rest among the Tartar chiefs,
And share the battle's common chance with us
Who love thee, but must press forever first,
In single fight incurring single risk,
To find a father thou hast never seen?　70
That were far best, my son, to stay with us
Unmurmuring; in our tents, while it is war,
And when 'tis truce, then in Afrasiab's towns.
But, if this one desire indeed rules all,
To seek out Rustum — seek him not through
　　　fight!　75
Seek him in peace, and carry to his arms,
O Sohrab, carry an unwounded son!
But far hence seek him, for he is not here.
For now it is not as when I was young,
When Rustum was in front of every fray;　80
But now he keeps apart, and sits at home,
In Seistan, with Zal, his father old,
Whether that his own mighty strength at last
Feels the abhorred approaches of old age,
Or in some quarrel with the Persian King.　85
There go! — Thou wilt not? Yet my heart
　　　forebodes

Danger or death awaits thee on this field.
Fain would I know thee safe and well, though
　　　lost
To us; fain therefore send thee hence, in peace
To seek thy father, not seek single fights　90
In vain — but who can keep the lion's cub
From ravening, and who govern Rustum's
　　　son?
Go, I will grant thee what thy heart desires."
　　So said he, and dropped Sohrab's hand, and
　　　left
His bed, and the warm rugs whereon he lay;
And o'er his chilly limbs his woolen coat　96
He passed, and tied his sandals on his feet,
And threw a white cloak round him, and he
　　　took
In his right hand a ruler's staff, no sword;
And on his head he set his sheepskin cap,　100
Black, glossy, curled, the fleece of Kara-Kul;
And raised the curtain of his tent, and called
His herald to his side, and went abroad.
　　The sun by this had risen, and cleared the
　　　fog　104
From the broad Oxus and the glittering sands.
And from their tents the Tartar horsemen filed
Into the open plain; so Haman bade —
Haman, who next to Peran-Wisa ruled
The host, and still was in his lusty prime.
From their black tents, long files of horse,
　　　they streamed;　110
As when some gray November morn the files,
In marching order spread, of long-neck
　　　cranes
Stream over Casbin and the southern slopes
Of Elburz, from the Aralian estuaries,
Or some frore Caspian reed-bed, southward
　　　bound　115
For the warm Persian seaboard — so they
　　　streamed:
The Tartars of the Oxus, the King's guard,
First, with black sheepskin caps and with
　　　long spears —
Large men, large steeds, who from Bokhara
　　　come
And Khiva, and ferment the milk of mares;
Next, the more temperate Toorkmuns of the
　　　south,　121
The Tukas, and the lances of Salore,
And those from Attruck and the Caspian
　　　sands —
Light men and on light steeds, who only drink

101. **Kara-Kul**, a district in south-central Asia. 111 ff. **As when**, etc. This is an example of the so-called epic simile—that is, a simile, common in epic poetry, which plays upon minute details of comparison. 113. **Casbin**, a city in northern Persia. 114. **Elburz**, mountains on the northern border of Persia. 115. **frore**, frozen. 119. **Bokhara**, a large district in central Asia. 120. **Khiva**, a district in the valley of the lower Oxus. 121. **Toorkmuns**, a branch of the Turkish race, living in central Asia. 122. **Tukas**, from northwest Persia. **Salore**, a tribe living east of the Caspian Sea. 123. **Attruck**, a river in northern Persia.

40. **Samarcand**, a city in Turkestan; once the capital of Tartary. 42. **Ader-baijan**, a province in northwestern Persia. It was the home of Sohrab's mother Tahminah (line 590). 60. **common**, general. 82. **Seistan**, a district bordering Persia and Afghanistan. 85. **Persian King**, Kai Khosroo (line 223).

The acrid milk of camels, and their wells; 125
And then a swarm of wandering horse, who
   came
From far, and a more doubtful service owned,
The Tartars of Ferghana, from the banks
Of the Jaxartes — men with scanty beards
And close-set skull-caps; and those wilder
   hordes   130
Who roam o'er Kipchak and the northern
   waste,
Kalmucks and unkempt Kuzzaks, tribes who
   stray
Nearest the Pole, and wandering Kirghizzes,
Who come on shaggy ponies from Pamere.
These all filed out from camp into the plain.
And on the other side the Persians formed: 136
First, a light cloud of horse, Tartars they
   seemed,
The Ilyats of Khorassan; and behind,
The royal troops of Persia, horse and foot,
Marshaled battalions bright in burnished
   steel.   140
But Peran-Wisa with his herald came,
Threading the Tartar squadrons to the front,
And with his staff kept back the foremost
   ranks,
And when Ferood, who led the Persians, saw
That Peran-Wisa kept the Tartars back, 145
He took his spear, and to the front he came,
And checked his ranks, and fixed them where
   they stood.
And the old Tartar came upon the sand
Betwixt the silent hosts, and spake, and said:
"Ferood, and ye, Persians and Tartars
   hear!   150
Let there be truce between the hosts to-
   day.
But choose a champion from the Persian lords
To fight our champion Sohrab, man to man."
   As, in the country, on a morn in June,
When the dew glistens on the pearléd ears, 155
A shiver runs through the deep corn for joy —
So, when they heard what Peran-Wisa said,
A thrill through all the Tartar squadrons ran
Of pride and hope for Sohrab, whom they
   loved.
   But as a troop of peddlers, from Caboool, 160
Cross underneath the Indian Caucasus,
That vast sky-neighboring mountain of milk
   snow,

Crossing so high, that, as they mount, they
   pass
Long flocks of traveling birds dead on the
   snow,
Choked by the air, and scarce can they them-
   selves   165
Slake their parched throats with sugared
   mulberries —
In single file they move, and stop their breath,
For fear they should dislodge the o'erhanging
   snows —
So the pale Persians held their breath with
   fear.
   And to Ferood his brother chiefs came up
To counsel; Gudurz and Zoarrah came, 171
And Feraburz, who ruled the Persian host
Second, and was the uncle of the King;
These came and counseled, and then Gudurz
   said:
"Ferood, shame bids us take their challenge
   up,   175
Yet champion have we none to match this
   youth.
He has the wild stag's foot, the lion's heart.
But Rustum came last night; aloof he sits
And sullen, and has pitched his tents apart.
Him will I seek, and carry to his ear   180
The Tartar challenge, and this young man's
   name.
Haply he will forget his wrath, and fight.
Stand forth the while, and take their challenge
   up."
   So spake he; and Ferood stood forth and
   cried:
"Old man, be it agreed as thou hast said! 185
Let Sohrab arm, and we will find a man."
   He spake; and Peran-Wisa turned and
   strode
Back through the opening squadrons to his
   tent.
But through the anxious Persians Gudurz ran,
And crossed the camp which lay behind, and
   reached,   190
Out on the sands beyond it, Rustum's tents.
Of scarlet cloth they were, and glittering gay,
Just pitched; the high pavilion in the midst
Was Rustum's, and his men lay camped
   around.
And Gudurz entered Rustum's tent, and
   found   195
Rustum; his morning meal was done, but still
The table stood before him, charged with
   food —
A side of roasted sheep, and cakes of bread
And dark green melons; and there Rustum
   sate
Listless, and held a falcon on his wrist, 200
And played with it; but Gudurz came and
   stood
Before him; and he looked, and saw him stand,

128. Ferghana, a district in Turkestan, south of Samarcand. 129. Jaxartes, an early name of the Sir-Daria
River, which flows through Turkestan into the Aral Sea.
131. Kipchak, a district in central Asia. 132. Kalmucks,
wandering Mongolian tribes living in western Siberia.
Kuzzaks, Cossacks, a warlike people in southern Russia
and southwestern Asia. 133. Pole, the north pole. Kirghizzes, a nomadic people of northern Turkestan. 138. Ilyats
of Khorassan, tribes of Khorassan, a province in northeastern Persia. 156. corn, grain. 160 Caboool, Kabul, an
important commercial city in northern Afghanistan. 161.
Indian Caucasus, a mountain range between Turkestan
and Afghanistan.

And with a cry sprang up and dropped the
   bird,
And greeted Gudurz with both hands, and
   said:
  "Welcome! these eyes could see no better
    sight.   205
What news? but sit down first, and eat and
   drink."
  But Gudurz stood in the tent-door, and
   said:
"Not now! a time will come to eat and drink,
But not today; today has other needs.
The armies are drawn out, and stand at
   gaze;   210
For from the Tartars is a challenge brought
To pick a champion from the Persian lords
To fight their champion — and thou know'st
   his name —
Sohrab men call him, but his birth is hid. 214
O Rustum, like thy might is this young man's!
He has the wild stag's foot, the lion's heart;
And he is young, and Iran's chiefs are old,
Or else too weak; and all eyes turn to thee.
Come down and help us, Rustum, or we lose!"
  He spoke; but Rustum answered with a
   smile: 220
"Go to! if Iran's chiefs are old, then I
Am older; if the young are weak, the King
Errs strangely; for the King, for Kai Khosroo,
Himself is young, and honors younger men,
And lets the aged molder to their graves. 225
Rustum he loves no more, but loves the
   young —
The young may rise at Sohrab's vaunts, not I.
For what care I, though all speak Sohrab's
   fame?
For would that I myself had such a son,
And not that one slight helpless girl I have —
A son so famed, so brave, to send to war, 231
And I to tarry with the snow-haired Zal,
My father, whom the robber Afghans vex,
And clip his borders short, and drive his herds,
And he has none to guard his weak old age. 235
There would I go, and hang my armor up,
And with my great name fence that weak old
   man,
And spend the goodly treasures I have got,
And rest my age, and hear of Sohrab's fame,
And leave to death the hosts of thankless
   kings,   240
And with these slaughterous hands draw
   sword no more."
  He spoke, and smiled; and Gudurz made
   reply:
"What then, O Rustum, will men say to this,
When Sohrab dares our bravest forth, and
   seeks

Thee most of all, and thou, whom most he
   seeks,   245
Hidest thy face? Take heed lest men should
   say,
'Like some old miser, Rustum hoards his fame,
And shuns to peril it with younger men.'"
  And, greatly moved, then Rustum made
   reply:
"O Gudurz, wherefore dost thou say such
   words?   250
Thou knowest better words than this to say.
What is one more, one less, obscure or famed,
Valiant or craven, young or old, to me?
Are not they mortal, am not I myself?
But who for men of naught would do great
   deeds?   255
Come, thou shalt see how Rustum hoards his
   fame!
But I will fight unknown, and in plain arms;
Let not men say of Rustum, he was matched
In single fight with any mortal man."
  He spoke, and frowned; and Gudurz turned
   and ran   260
Back quickly through the camp in fear and
   joy —
Fear at his wrath, but joy that Rustum came.
But Rustum strode to his tent-door and called
His followers in, and bade them bring his
   arms,   264
And clad himself in steel; the arms he chose
Were plain, and on his shield was no de-
   vice,
Only his helm was rich, inlaid with gold,
And, from the fluted spine atop, a plume
Of horsehair waved, a scarlet horsehair plume.
So armed, he issued forth; and Ruksh, his
   horse,   270
Followed him like a faithful hound at heel —
Ruksh, whose renown was noised through all
   the earth,
The horse, whom Rustum on a foray once
Did in Bokhara by the river find
A colt beneath its dam, and drove him home,
And reared him; a bright bay, with lofty
   crest,   276
Dight with a saddle-cloth of broidered green
Crusted with gold, and on the ground were
   worked
All beasts of chase, all beasts which hunters
   know.
So followed, Rustum left his tents, and
   crossed   280
The camp, and to the Persian host appeared.
And all the Persians knew him, and with
   shouts
Hailed; but the Tartars knew not who he was.
And dear as the wet diver to the eyes
Of his pale wife who waits and weeps on shore,

---

217. **Iran,** Persia. 223. **Kai Khosroo,** thought to be
Cyrus the Great, the founder of the Persian Empire, sixth
century B.C.

257. **plain arms,** arms devoid of devices that would betray his identity. 277. **dight,** decorated, adorned.

By sandy Bahrein, in the Persian Gulf, 286
Plunging all day in the blue waves, at night,
Having made up his tale of precious pearls,
Rejoins her in their hut upon the sands —
So dear to the pale Persians Rustum came. 290
  And Rustum to the Persian front advanced;
And Sohrab armed in Haman's tent, and
  came.
And as afield the reapers cut a swath
Down through the middle of a rich man's
  corn, 294
And on each side are squares of standing corn,
And in the midst a stubble, short and bare —
So on each side were squares of men, with
  spears
Bristling, and in the midst, the open sand.
And Rustum came upon the sand, and cast
His eyes toward the Tartar tents, and saw 300
Sohrab come forth, and eyed him as he came.
  As some rich woman, on a winter's morn,
Eyes through her silken curtains the poor
  drudge
Who with numb blackened fingers makes her
  fire
At cock-crow, on a starlit winter's morn, 305
When the frost flowers the whitened window-
  panes,
And wonders how she lives, and what the
  thoughts
Of that poor drudge may be — so Rustum
  eyed
The unknown adventurous youth, who from
  afar
Came seeking Rustum, and defying forth 310
All the most valiant chiefs. Long he perused
His spirited air, and wondered who he was;
For very young he seemed, tenderly reared:
Like some young cypress, tall, and dark, and
  straight,
Which in a queen's secluded garden throws 315
Its slight dark shadow on the moonlit turf,
By midnight, to a bubbling fountain's sound—
So slender Sohrab seemed, so softly reared.
And a deep pity entered Rustum's soul
As he beheld him coming; and he stood, 320
And beckoned to him with his hand, and said:
  "O thou young man, the air of heaven is
  soft,
And warm, and pleasant; but the grave is
  cold!
Heaven's air is better than the cold dead
  grave.
Behold me! I am vast, and clad in iron, 325
And tried; and I have stood on many a field
Of blood, and I have fought with many a
  foe —
Never was that field lost, or that foe saved.
O Sohrab, wherefore wilt thou rush on death?

286. Bahrein, the Aval Islands, in the Persian Gulf, noted for their pearl fisheries. 288. tale, count.

Be governed! quit the Tartar host, and come
To Iran, and be as my son to me, 330
And fight beneath my banner till I die!
There are no youths in Iran brave as
  thou."
  So he spake, mildly; Sohrab heard his voice,
The mighty voice of Rustum, and he saw 335
His giant figure planted on the sand,
Sole, like some single tower, which a chief
Hath builded on the waste in former years
Against the robbers; and he saw that head,
Streaked with its first gray hairs; hope filled
  his soul, 340
And he ran forward and embraced his knees,
And clasped his hand within his own, and
  said:
  "Oh, by thy father's head! by thine own
  soul!
Art thou not Rustum? speak! art thou not
  he?"
  But Rustum eyed askance the kneeling
  youth, 345
And turned away, and spake to his own soul:
  "Ah me, I muse what this young fox may
  mean!
False, wily, boastful, are these Tartar boys.
For if I now confess this thing he asks,
And hide it not, but say: 'Rustum is here!' 350
He will not yield indeed, nor quit our foes,
But he will find some pretext not to fight,
And praise my fame, and proffer courteous
  gifts,
A belt or sword perhaps, and go his way.
And on a feast-tide, in Afrasiab's hall, 355
In Samarcand, he will arise and cry:
'I challenged once, when the two armies
  camped
Beside the Oxus, all the Persian lords
To cope with me in single fight; but they
Shrank, only Rustum dared; then he and I 360
Changed gifts, and went on equal terms away.'
So will he speak, perhaps, while men applaud;
Then were the chiefs of Iran shamed through
  me."
  And then he turned, and sternly spake
  aloud:
  "Rise! wherefore dost thou vainly question
  thus 365
Of Rustum? I am here, whom thou hast
  called
By challenge forth; make good thy vaunt, or
  yield!
Is it with Rustum only thou wouldst fight?
Rash boy, men look on Rustum's face and
  flee! 369
For well I know that did great Rustum stand
Before thy face this day, and were revealed,
There would be then no talk of fighting more.
But being what I am, I tell thee this —
Do thou record it in thine inmost soul:

Either thou shalt renounce thy vaunt and
　　yield,　　　　　　　　　　　　　　　375
Or else thy bones shall strew this sand, till
　　winds
Bleach them, or Oxus with his summer-floods,
Oxus in summer wash them all away."
　　He spoke; and Sohrab answered, on his feet:
"Art thou so fierce? Thou wilt not fright
　　me so!　　　　　　　　　　　　　　　380
I am no girl, to be made pale by words.
Yet this thou hast said well, did Rustum
　　stand
Here on this field, there were no fighting
　　then.
But Rustum is far hence, and we stand here.
Begin! thou art more vast, more dread than I,
And thou art proved, I know, and I am
　　young —　　　　　　　　　　　　　　386
But yet success sways with the breath of
　　Heaven.
And though thou thinkest that thou knowest
　　sure
Thy victory, yet thou canst not surely know.
For we are all, like swimmers in the sea,　390
Poised on the top of a huge wave of fate,
Which hangs uncertain to which side to fall.
And whether it will heave us up to land,
Or whether it will roll us out to sea,
Back out to sea, to the deep waves of death,
We know not, and no search will make us
　　know;　　　　　　　　　　　　　　　396
Only the event will teach us in its hour."
　　He spoke, and Rustum answered not, but
　　hurled
His spear; down from the shoulder, down it
　　came,
As on some partridge in the corn a hawk,　400
That long has towered in the airy clouds,
Drops like a plummet; Sohrab saw it come,
And sprang aside, quick as a flash; the spear
Hissed, and went quivering down into the
　　sand,
Which it sent flying wide; then Sohrab threw
In turn, and full struck Rustum's shield;
　　sharp rang,　　　　　　　　　　　　406
The iron plates rang sharp, but turned the
　　spear.
And Rustum seized his club, which none but
　　he
Could wield; an unlopped trunk it was, and
　　huge,
Still rough — like those which men in treeless
　　plains　　　　　　　　　　　　　　　410
To build them boats fish from the flooded
　　rivers,
Hyphasis or Hydaspes, when, high up
By their dark springs, the wind in winter-time
Hath made in Himalayan forests wrack,

And strewn the channels with torn boughs —
　　so huge　　　　　　　　　.　　　　415
The club which Rustum lifted now, and struck
One stroke; but again Sohrab sprang aside,
Lithe as the glancing snake, and the club came
Thundering to earth, and leapt from Rustum's
　　hand.
And Rustum followed his own blow, and fell
To his knees, and with his fingers clutched the
　　sand;　　　　　　　　　　　　　　　421
And now might Sohrab have unsheathed his
　　sword,
And pierced the mighty Rustum while he lay
Dizzy, and on his knees, and choked with
　　sand;
But he looked on, and smiled, nor bared his
　　sword,　　　　　　　　　　　　　　425
But courteously drew back, and spoke, and
　　said:
　　"Thou strik'st too hard! that club of thine
　　will float
Upon the summer-floods, and not my bones.
But rise, and be not wroth! not wroth am I;
No, when I see thee, wrath forsakes my soul.
Thou say'st thou art not Rustum; be it so! 431
Who art thou then, that canst so touch my
　　soul?
Boy as I am, I have seen battles too —
Have waded foremost in their bloody waves,
And heard their hollow roar of dying men; 435
But never was my heart thus touched before.
Are they from Heaven, these softenings of the
　　heart?
O thou old warrior, let us yield to Heaven!
Come, plant we here in earth our angry spears,
And make a truce, and sit upon this sand, 440
And pledge each other in red wine, like friends,
And thou shalt talk to me of Rustum's deeds.
There are enough foes in the Persian host,
Whom I may meet, and strike, and feel no
　　pang;
Champions enough Afrasiab has, whom thou
Mayst fight; fight *them*, when they confront
　　thy spear!　　　　　　　　　　　446
But oh, let there be peace 'twixt thee and
　　me!"
　　He ceased, but while he spake, Rustum had
　　risen,
And stood erect, trembling with rage; his club
He left to lie, but had regained his spear, 450
Whose fiery point now in his mailed right-
　　hand
Blazed bright and baleful, like that autumn
　　star,
The baleful sign of fevers; dust had soiled
His stately crest, and dimmed his glittering
　　arms.

---

412. **Hyphasis or Hydaspes**, rivers in northern India.

452. **autumn star**, Sirius, the Dog Star, associated among
certain ancient peoples with hot, dry weather and with
fevers.

His breast heaved, his lips foamed, and twice
 his voice   455
Was choked with rage; at last these words
 broke way:
"Girl! nimble with thy feet, not with thy
 hands!
Curled minion, dancer, coiner of sweet words!
Fight, let me hear thy hateful voice no more!
Thou art not in Afrasiab's gardens now 460
With Tartar girls, with whom thou art wont
 to dance;
But on the Oxus-sands, and in the dance
Of battle, and with me, who make no play
Of war; I fight it out, and hand to hand.
Speak not to me of truce, and pledge, and
 wine!   465
Remember all thy valor; try thy feints
And cunning! all the pity I had is gone,
Because thou hast shamed me before both
 the hosts
With thy light skipping tricks, and thy girl's
 wiles."
 He spoke; and Sohrab kindled at his taunts,
And he too drew his sword. At once they
 rushed   471
Together, as two eagles on one prey
Come rushing down together from the clouds,
One from the east, one from the west; their
 shields
Dashed with a clang together, and a din 475
Rose, such as that the sinewy woodcutters
Make often in the forest's heart at morn,
Of hewing axes, crashing trees — such blows
Rustum and Sohrab on each other hailed.
And you would say that sun and stars took
 part   480
In that unnatural conflict; for a cloud
Grew suddenly in heaven, and darked the sun
Over the fighters' heads; and a wind rose
Under their feet, and moaning swept the
 plain,
And in a sandy whirlwind wrapped the pair.
In gloom they twain were wrapped, and they
 alone;   486
For both the on-looking hosts on either hand
Stood in broad daylight, and the sky was
 pure,
And the sun sparkled on the Oxus stream.
But in the gloom they fought, with bloodshot
 eyes   490
And laboring breath: first Rustum struck the
 shield
Which Sohrab held stiff out; the steel-spiked
 spear
Rent the tough plates, but failed to reach the
 skin,
And Rustum plucked it back with angry
 groan.
Then Sohrab with his sword smote Rustum's
 helm,   495

Nor clove its steel quite through; but all the
 crest
He shore away, and that proud horsehair
 plume,
Never till now defiled, sank to the dust;
And Rustum bowed his head; but then the
 gloom
Grew blacker, thunder rumbled in the air, 500
And lightnings rent the cloud; and Ruksh,
 the horse,
Who stood at hand, uttered a dreadful cry —
No horse's cry was that, most like the roar
Of some pained desert-lion, who all day
Hath trailed the hunter's javelin in his side,
And comes at night to die upon the sand. 506
The two hosts heard that cry, and quaked for
 fear,
And Oxus curdled as it crossed his stream.
But Sohrab heard, and quailed not, but
 rushed on,
And struck again; and again Rustum bowed
His head; but this time all the blade, like
 glass,   511
Sprang in a thousand shivers on the helm,
And in the hand the hilt remained alone.
Then Rustum raised his head; his dreadful
 eyes
Glared, and he shook on high his menacing
 spear,   515
And shouted, "Rustum!" Sohrab heard that
 shout,
And shrank amazed; back he recoiled one
 step,
And scanned with blinking eyes the advanc-
 ing form;
And then he stood bewildered; and he dropped
His covering shield, and the spear pierced his
 side.   520
He reeled and, staggering back, sank to the
 ground;
And then the gloom dispersed, and the wind
 fell,
And the bright sun broke forth, and melted all
The cloud; and the two armies saw the pair—
Saw Rustum standing, safe upon his feet, 525
And Sohrab, wounded, on the bloody sand.
 Then, with a bitter smile, Rustum began:
"Sohrab, thou thoughtest in thy mind to kill
A Persian lord this day, and strip his corpse,
And bear thy trophies to Afrasiab's tent, 530
Or else that the great Rustum would come
 down
Himself to fight, and that thy wiles would
 move
His heart to take a gift, and let thee go.
And then that all the Tartar host would
 praise
Thy courage or thy craft, and spread thy
 fame,   535
To glad thy father in his weak old age.

Fool, thou art slain, and by an unknown man!
Dearer to the red jackals shalt thou be
Than to thy friends, and to thy father old."
  And, with a fearless mien, Sohrab replied:
"Unknown thou art; yet thy fierce vaunt is
      vain. 541
Thou dost not slay me, proud and boastful
      man!
No! Rustum slays me, and this filial heart.
For were I matched with ten such men as thee,
And I were that which till today I was, 545
They should be lying here, I standing there.
But that belovéd name unnerved my arm —
That name, and something, I confess, in thee,
Which troubles all my heart, and made my
      shield
Fall; and thy spear transfixed an unarmed
      foe. 550
And now thou boastest, and insult'st my fate.
But hear thou this, fierce man, tremble to
      hear:
The mighty Rustum shall avenge my death!
My father, whom I seek through all the world,
He shall avenge my death, and punish thee!"
  As when some hunter in the spring hath
      found 556
A breeding eagle sitting on her nest,
Upon the craggy isle of a hill-lake,
And pierced her with an arrow as she rose,
And followed her to find her where she fell 560
Far off — anon her mate comes winging back
From hunting, and a great way off descries
His huddling young left sole; at that, he
      checks
His pinion, and with short uneasy sweeps
Circles above his eyry, with loud screams 565
Chiding his mate back to her nest; but she
Lies dying, with the arrow in her side,
In some far stony gorge out of his ken,
A heap of fluttering feathers — never more
Shall the lake glass her, flying over it; 570
Never the black and dripping precipices
Echo her stormy scream as she sails by —
As that poor bird flies home, nor knows his
      loss,
So Rustum knew not his own loss, but stood
Over his dying son, and knew him not. 575
  But, with a cold incredulous voice, he said:
"What prate is this of fathers and revenge?
The mighty Rustum never had a son."
  And, with a failing voice, Sohrab replied:
"Ah yes, he had! and that lost son am I. 580
Surely the news will one day reach his ear,
Reach Rustum, where he sits, and tarries long,
Somewhere, I know not where, but far from
      here,
And pierce him like a stab, and make him
      leap
To arms, and cry for vengeance upon thee. 585
Fierce man, bethink thee! for an only son

What will that grief, what will that vengeance
      be?
Oh, could I live, till I that grief had seen!
Yet him I pity not so much, but her,
My mother, who in Ader-baijan dwells 590
With that old king, her father, who grows
      gray
With age, and rules over the valiant Koords.
Her most I pity, who no more will see
Sohrab returning from the Tartar camp,
With spoils and honor, when the war is done.
But a dark rumor will be bruited up, 596
From tribe to tribe, until it reach her ear;
And then will that defenseless woman learn
That Sohrab will rejoice her sight no more,
But that in battle with a nameless foe, 600
By the far-distant Oxus, he is slain."
  He spoke; and as he ceased, he wept aloud,
Thinking of her he left, and his own death.
He spoke; but Rustum listened, plunged in
      thought.
Nor did he yet believe it was his son 605
Who spoke, although he called back names
      he knew;
For he had had sure tidings that the babe,
Which was in Ader-baijan born to him,
Had been a puny girl, no boy at all —
So that sad mother sent him word, for fear 610
Rustum should seek the boy, to train in arms.
And so he deemed that either Sohrab took,
By a false boast, the style of Rustum's son,
Or that men gave it him, to swell his fame.
So deemed he; yet he listened, plunged in
      thought. 615
And his soul set to grief, as the vast tide
Of the bright rocking ocean sets to shore
At the full moon; tears gathered in his eyes;
For he remembered his own early youth,
And all its bounding rapture; as, at dawn, 620
The shepherd from his mountain-lodge de-
      scries
A far, bright city, smitten by the sun,
Through many rolling clouds — so Rustum
      saw
His youth; saw Sohrab's mother, in her bloom;
And that old king, her father, who loved well
His wandering guest, and gave him his fair
      child 626
With joy; and all the pleasant life they led,
They three, in that long-distant summer-
      time —
The castle, and the dewy woods, and hunt
And hound, and morn on those delightful
      hills 630
In Ader-baijan. And he saw that youth,
Of age and looks to be his own dear son,
Piteous and lovely, lying on the sand,
Like some rich hyacinth which by the scythe

592. **Koords,** Curds, a warlike people of northwestern
Persia. 596. **bruited up,** noised abroad. 613. **style,** name.

Of an unskillful gardener has been cut,   635
Mowing the garden grass-plots near its bed,
And lies, a fragrant tower of purple bloom,
On the mown, dying grass — so Sohrab lay,
Lovely in death, upon the common sand.
And Rustum gazed on him with grief, and
    said: 640
"O Sohrab, thou indeed art such a son
Whom Rustum, wert thou his, might well
    have loved.
Yet here thou errest, Sohrab, or else men
Have told thee false — thou art not Rustum's
    son.   644
For Rustum had no son; one child he had —
But one — a girl; who with her mother now
Plies some light female task, nor dreams of
    us —
Of us she dreams not, nor of wounds, nor
    war."
    But Sohrab answered him in wrath; for now
The anguish of the deep-fixed spear grew
    fierce,   650
And he desiréd to draw forth the steel,
And let the blood flow free, and so to die —
But first he would convince his stubborn foe;
And, rising sternly on one arm, he said:
    "Man, who art thou who dost deny my
    words?   655
Truth sits upon the lips of dying men,
And falsehood, while I lived, was far from
    mine.
I tell thee, pricked upon this arm I bear
That seal which Rustum to my mother gave,
That she might prick it on the babe she bore."
    He spoke; and all the blood left Rustum's
    cheeks,   661
And his knees tottered, and he smote his hand
Against his breast, his heavy mailed hand,
That the hard iron corslet clanked aloud;
And to his heart he pressed the other hand, 665
And in a hollow voice he spake, and said:
    "Sohrab, that were a proof which could
    not lie!
If thou show this, then art thou Rustum's
    son."
    Then, with weak, hasty fingers, Sohrab
    loosed   669
His belt, and near the shoulder bared his arm,
And showed a sign in faint vermilion points
Pricked. As a cunning workman, in Pekin,
Pricks with vermilion some clear porcelain
    vase,
An emperor's gift; at early morn he paints,
And all day long, and, when night comes, the
    lamp   675
Lights up his studious forehead and thin
    hands —
So delicately pricked the sign appeared

656. **Truth ... men**. Cf. Browning's *A Death in the
Desert*, lines 188-197, and note, p. 307.

On Sohrab's arm, the sign of Rustum's seal.
It was that griffin which of old reared Zal,
Rustum's great father, whom they left to
    die,   680
A helpless babe, among the mountain-rocks;
Him that kind creature found, and reared,
    and loved —
Then Rustum took it for his glorious sign.
And Sohrab bared that image on his arm,
And himself scanned it long with mournful
    eyes,   685
And then he touched it with his hand and
    said:
    "How say'st thou? Is that sign the proper
    sign
Of Rustum's son, or of some other man's?"
    He spoke; but Rustum gazed, and gazed,
    and stood
Speechless; and then he uttered one sharp
    cry: 690
"O boy — thy father!" — and his voice
    choked there.
And then a dark cloud passed before his eyes,
And his head swam, and he sank down to
    earth.
But Sohrab crawled to where he lay, and cast
His arms about his neck, and kissed his lips,
And with fond, faltering fingers stroked his
    cheeks,   696
Trying to call him back to life; and life
Came back to Rustum, and he oped his eyes,
And they stood wide with horror; and he
    seized
In both his hands the dust which lay around,
And threw it on his head, and smirched his
    hair —   701
His hair, and face, and beard, and glittering
    arms;
And strong, convulsive groanings shook his
    breast,
And his sobs choked him; and he clutched his
    sword,
To draw it and forever let life out.   705
But Sohrab saw his thought, and held his
    hands,
And with a soothing voice he spake, and said:
    "Father, forbear! for I but meet today
The doom which at my birth was written
    down
In Heaven, and thou art Heaven's uncon-
    scious hand.   710
Surely my heart cried out that it was thou,
When first I saw thee; and thy heart spoke
    too,
I know it! but fate trod those promptings
    down
Under its iron heel; fate, fate engaged
The strife, and hurled me on my father's
    spear.   715
But let us speak no more of this! I find

My father; let me feel that I have found!
Come, sit beside me on this sand, and take
My head betwixt thy hands, and kiss my
   cheeks,
And wash them with thy tears, and say,
   'My son!'   720
Quick! quick! for numbered are my sands of
   life,
And swift; for like the lightning to this field
I came, and like the wind I go away —
Sudden, and swift, and like a passing wind.
But it was writ in Heaven that this should
   be."   725
   So said he, and his voice released the heart
Of Rustum, and his tears broke forth; he cast
His arms round his son's neck, and wept
   aloud,
And kissed him. And awe fell on both the
   hosts,
When they saw Rustum's grief; and Ruksh,
   the horse,   730
With his head bowing to the ground and mane
Sweeping the dust, came near, and in mute
   woe
First to the one then to the other moved
His head, as if inquiring what their grief
Might mean; and from his dark, compassion-
   ate eyes,   735
The big warm tears rolled down, and caked
   the sand.
But Rustum chid him with stern voice, and
   said: —
   "Ruksh, now thou grievest; but, O Ruksh,
   thy feet
Should first have rotted on their nimble
   joints,   739
Or ere they brought thy master to this field!"
   But Sohrab looked upon the horse and said:
"Is this, then, Ruksh? How often, in past
   days,
My mother told me of thee, thou brave steed,
My terrible father's terrible horse! and said,
That I should one day find thy lord and thee.
Come, let me lay my hand upon thy mane! 746
O Ruksh, thou art more fortunate than I;
For thou hast gone where I shall never go,
And snuffed the breezes of my father's home.
And thou hast trod the sands of Seistan,   750
And seen the River of Helmund, and the Lake
Of Zirrah; and the aged Zal himself
Has often stroked thy neck, and given thee
   food,
Corn in a golden platter soaked with wine,
And said, 'O Ruksh! bear Rustum well!' —
   but I   755
Have never known my grandsire's furrowed
   face,
Nor seen his lofty house in Seistan,

Nor slaked my thirst at the clear Helmund
   stream;
But lodged among my father's foes, and seen
Afrasiab's cities only, Samarcand,   760
Bokhara, and lone Khiva in the waste,
And the black Toorkmun tents; and only
   drunk
The desert rivers, Moorghab and Tejend,
Kohik, and where the Kalmuks feed their
   sheep,
The northern Sir; and this great Oxus stream,
The yellow Oxus, by whose brink I die."   766
   Then, with a heavy groan, Rustum be-
   wailed:
"Oh, that its waves were flowing over me!
Oh, that I saw its grains of yellow silt
Roll tumbling in the current o'er my head!"
   But, with a grave, mild voice, Sohrab
   replied: 771
"Desire not that, my father! thou must live;
For some are born to do great deeds, and live,
As some are born to be obscured, and die.
Do thou the deeds I die too young to do, 775
And reap a second glory in thine age;
Thou art my father, and thy gain is mine.
But come! thou seest this great host of men
Which follow me; I pray thee, slay not these!
Let me entreat for them; what have they
   done?   780
They followed me, my hope, my fame, my
   star.
Let them all cross the Oxus back in peace.
But me thou must bear hence, not send with
   them,
But carry me with thee to Seistan,
And place me on a bed, and mourn for me,
Thou, and the snow-haired Zal, and all thy
   friends.   786
And thou must lay me in that lovely earth,
And heap a stately mound above my bones,
And plant a far-seen pillar over all,
That so the passing horseman on the waste 790
May see my tomb a great way off, and cry,
'Sohrab, the mighty Rustum's son, lies there,
Whom his great father did in ignorance kill!'
And I be not forgotten in my grave."
   And, with a mournful voice, Rustum re-
   plied: 795
"Fear not! as thou hast said, Sohrab, my son,
So shall it be; for I will burn my tents,
And quit the host, and bear thee hence with
   me,
And carry thee away to Seistan,   799
And place thee on a bed, and mourn for thee,
With the snow-headed Zal, and all my friends.
And I will lay thee in that lovely earth,
And heap a stately mound above thy bones,

751-752. **Helmund . . . Zirrah**, in the district of Seistan,
Afghanistan.

763-764. **Moorghab, Tejend, Kohik**, rivers in Afghanistan.   765. **Sir**, the Jaxartes River, in Turkestan. (See line
129 and note, p. 477.)

And plant a far-seen pillar over all,
And men shall not forget thee in thy grave. 805
And I will spare thy host; yea, let them go!
Let them all cross the Oxus back in peace!
What should I do with slaying any more?
For would that all that I have ever slain
Might be once more alive; my bitterest foes,
And they who were called champions in their
    time,   811
And through whose death I won that fame I
    have —
And I were nothing but a common man,
A poor, mean soldier, and without renown,
So thou mightest live too, my son, my son! 815
Or rather would that I, even I myself,
Might now be lying on this bloody sand,
Near death, and by an ignorant stroke of
  ‛ thine,
Not thou of mine! and I might die, not thou;
And I, not thou, be borne to Seistan;   820
And Zal might weep above my grave, not
    thine;
And say: 'O son, I weep thee not too sore,
For willingly, I know, thou met'st thine end!'
But now in blood and battles was my youth,
And full of blood and battles is my age, 825
And I shall never end this life of blood."
    Then, at the point of death, Sohrab replied:
"A life of blood indeed, thou dreadful man!
But thou shalt yet have peace; only not now,
Not yet! but thou shalt have it on that day,
When thou shalt sail in a high-masted ship, 831
Thou and the other peers of Kai Khosroo,
Returning home over the salt blue sea,
From laying thy dear master in his grave."
    And Rustum gazed in Sohrab's face, and
    said: 835
"Soon be that day, my son, and deep that sea!
Till then, if fate so wills, let me endure."
    He spoke; and Sohrab smiled on him, and
    took
The spear, and drew it from his side, and
    eased
His wound's imperious anguish; but the blood
Came welling from the open gash, and life 841
Flowed with the stream — all down his cold
    white side
The crimson torrent ran, dim now and soiled,
Like the soiled tissue of white violets   844
Left, freshly gathered, on their native bank,
By children whom their nurses call with haste
Indoors from the sun's eye; his head drooped
    low,
His limbs grew slack; motionless, white, he
    lay —
White, with eyes closed; only when heavy
    gasps,
Deep heavy gasps quivering through all his
    frame,   850
Convulsed him back to life, he opened them,

And fixed them feebly on his father's face;
Till now all strength was ebbed, and from his
    limbs
Unwillingly the spirit fled away,
Regretting the warm mansion which it left,
And youth, and bloom, and this delightful
    world.   856
    So, on the bloody sand, Sohrab lay dead;
And the great Rustum drew his horseman's
    cloak
Down o'er his face, and sate by his dead son.
As those black granite pillars, once high-
    reared   860
By Jemshid in Persepolis, to bear
His house, now 'mid their broken flights of
    steps
Lie prone, enormous, down the mountain
    side —
So in the sand lay Rustum by his son.
    And night came down over the solemn
    waste,   865
And the two gazing hosts, and that sole pair,
And darkened all; and a cold fog, with night,
Crept from the Oxus. Soon a hum arose,
As of a great assembly loosed, and fires
Began to twinkle through the fog; for now 870
Both armies moved to camp, and took their
    meal;
The Persians took it on the open sands
Southward, the Tartars by the river marge;
And Rustum and his son were left alone.
    But the majestic river floated on,   875
Out of the mist and hum of that low land,
Into the frosty starlight, and there moved,
Rejoicing, through the hushed Chorasmian
    waste,
Under the solitary moon — he flowed
Right for the polar star, past Orgunjè,   880
Brimming, and bright, and large; then sands
    begin
To hem his watery march, and dam his
    streams,
And split his currents; that for many a league
The shorn and parceled Oxus strains along
Through beds of sand and matted rushy
    isles —   885
Oxus, forgetting the bright speed he had
In his high mountain-cradle in Pamere,
A foiled circuitous wanderer — till at last
The longed-for dash of waves is heard, and
    wide
His luminous home of waters opens, bright
And tranquil, from whose floor the new-
    bathed stars   891
Emerge, and shine upon the Aral Sea.

                  (1853)

861. **Jemshid**, a mythical king of Persia; his capital was
Persepolis. **878. Chorasmian waste**, a region in Turkes-
tan; the modern Khiva. **880. Orgunjè**, a village on the
Oxus, near the Aral Sea. **890. home of waters**, the Aral
Sea.

PHILOMELA

Hark! ah, the nightingale —
The tawny-throated!
Hark, from that moonlit cedar what a burst!
What triumph! hark! — what pain!

O wanderer from a Grecian shore,   5
Still, after many years, in distant lands,
Still nourishing in thy bewildered brain
That wild, unquenched, deep-sunken, old-
          world pain —
Say, will it never heal?
And can this fragrant lawn   10
With its cool trees, and night,
And the sweet, tranquil Thames,
And moonshine, and the dew,
To thy racked heart and brain
Afford no balm?   15

Dost thou tonight behold,
Here, through the moonlight on this English
          grass,
The unfriendly palace in the Thracian wild?
Dost thou again peruse
With hot cheeks and seared eyes   20
The too clear web, and thy dumb sister's
          shame?
Dost thou once more assay
Thy flight, and feel come over thee,
Poor fugitive, the feathery change
Once more, and once more seem to make
          resound   25
With love and hate, triumph and agony,
Lone Daulis, and the high Cephissian vale?
Listen, Eugenia —
How thick the bursts come crowding through
          the leaves!
Again — thou hearest?   30
Eternal passion!
Eternal pain!   (1853)

REQUIESCAT

Strew on her roses, roses,
     And never a spray of yew!
In quiet she reposes;
     Ah, would that I did too!

Her mirth the world required;   5
     She bathed it in smiles of glee.
But her heart was tired, tired,
     And now they let her be.

Her life was turning, turning,
     In mazes of heat and sound.   10
But for peace her soul was yearning,
     And now peace laps her round.

Her cabined, ample spirit,
     It fluttered and failed for breath.
Tonight it doth inherit   15
     The vasty hall of death.   (1853)

From THE CHURCH OF BROU

3.   THE TOMB

So rest, forever rest, O princely pair!
In your high church, 'mid the still mountain-
          air,
Where horn, and hound, and vassals, never
          come.
Only the blessed saints are smiling dumb,
From the rich painted windows of the nave, 5
On aisle, and transept, and your marble
          grave;
Where thou, young prince! shalt never more
          arise
From the fringed mattress where thy duchess
          lies,
On autumn-mornings, when the bugle sounds,
And ride across the drawbridge with thy
          hounds   10
To hunt the boar in the crisp woods till eve;
And thou, O princess! shalt no more receive,
Thou and thy ladies, in the hall of state,
The jaded hunters with their bloody freight,
Coming benighted to the castle-gate.   15
     So sleep, forever sleep, O marble pair!
Or, if ye wake, let it be then, when fair
On the carved western front a flood of light
Streams from the setting sun, and colors
          bright
Prophets, transfigured saints, and martyrs
          brave,   20
In the vast western window of the nave;
And on the pavement round the tomb there
          glints
A checker-work of glowing sapphire-tints,

Philomela. Philomela and Procne were daughters of Pan-
dion, king of Athens. Procne was the wife of Tereus, king of
Thrace. Tereus dishonored Philomela and then cut out her
tongue that she might not betray him; but Philomela wove
the story in a piece of tapestry, which she gave to her sister.
Procne then killed her son Itys (Itylus), served him as food
to his father, and fled with Philomela. On being pursued by
Tereus, the sisters prayed for deliverance and were changed
into birds—Philomela into a nightingale and Procne into a
swallow. In the poem Arnold has reversed the positions of the
sisters. See Swinburne's *Itylus*, p. 685.
27. **Daulis,** the scene of the tragedy, in Phocis, Greece.
The Cephissus was the chief river of Phocis. 28. **Eugenia,**
an imaginary person.
Requiescat. The title means *May She Rest.*
2. **yew,** a common tree in graveyards.

13. **cabined,** shut up, as in a cabin.
The Church of Brou. The Church of Notre Dame de Brou
is about a mile from Bourg-en-Bresse, an important town
in east-central France. It contains the tombs of Philibert II,
Duke of Savoy, and his wife, Margaret of Austria. These
are the "princely pair" of line 1. Philibert died in 1504 after
drinking cold water when he was heated from hunting.
His wife built the church to his memory in 1511-36. Following a French writer, Arnold wrongly placed Brou among
the mountains. The section of the poem here printed was
originally published separately, under the title *A Tomb
among the Mountains.* It is greatly superior to the rest of the
poem.

And amethyst, and ruby — then unclose
Your eyelids on the stone where ye repose, 25
And from your broidered pillows lift your
heads,
And rise upon your cold white marble beds;
And, looking down on the warm rosy tints,
Which checker, at your feet, the illumined
flints,
Say: *What is this? we are in bliss — forgiven —*
Behold the pavement of the courts of heaven! 31
Or let it be on autumn nights, when rain
Doth rustlingly above your heads complain
On the smooth leaden roof, and on the walls
Shedding her pensive light at intervals 35
The moon through the clere-story windows
shines,
And the wind washes through the mountain-
pines.
Then, gazing up 'mid the dim pillars high,
The foliaged marble forest where ye lie,
Hush, ye will say, *it is eternity!* 40
This is the glimmering verge of heaven, and
these
The columns of the heavenly palaces!
And, in the sweeping of the wind, your ear
The passage of the angels' wings will hear,
And on the lichen-crusted leads above 45
The rustle of the eternal rain of love.

(1853)

THE SCHOLAR-GYPSY

Go, for they call you, shepherd, from the hill;
Go, shepherd, and untie the wattled cotes!
No longer leave thy wistful flock unfed,
Nor let thy bawling fellows rack their
throats,
Nor the cropped herbage shoot another
head. 5
But when the fields are still,
And the tired men and dogs all gone to
rest,
And only the white sheep are sometimes
seen
Cross and recross the strips of moon-
blanched green,
Come, shepherd, and again begin the
quest! 10

Here, where the reaper was at work of late —
In this high field's dark corner, where he
leaves
His coat, his basket, and his earthen
cruse,

And in the sun all morning binds the
sheaves,
Then here, at noon, comes back his stores
to use — 15
Here will I sit and wait,
While to my ear from uplands far away
The bleating of the folded flocks is borne,
With distant cries of reapers in the corn—
All the live murmur of a summer's day. 20

Screened is this nook o'er the high, half-
reaped field,
And here till sun-down, shepherd! will I be.
Through the thick corn the scarlet pop-
pies peep,
And round green roots and yellowing stalks
I see
Pale pink convolvulus in tendrils creep;
And air-swept lindens yield 26
Their scent, and rustle down their per-
fumed showers
Of bloom on the bent grass where I am
laid,
And bower me from the August sun with
shade;
And the eye travels down to Oxford's
towers. 30

And near me on the grass lies Glanvil's book—
Come, let me read the oft-read tale again!
The story of the Oxford scholar poor,
Of pregnant parts and quick inventive
brain,
Who, tired of knocking at preferment's
door, 35
One summer-morn forsook
His friends, and went to learn the gypsy-
lore,
And roamed the world with that wild
brotherhood,
And came, as most men deemed, to little
good,
But came to Oxford and his friends no
more. 40

But once, years after, in the country-lanes,
Two scholars, whom at college erst he knew,
Met him, and of his way of life inquired;
Whereat he answered that the gypsy-crew,
His mates, had arts to rule as they desired
The workings of men's brains, 46
And they can bind them to what thoughts
they will.
"And I," he said, "the secret of their art,
When fully learned, will to the world
impart;
But it needs heaven-sent moments for this
skill." 50

36. clere-story, the upper wall of a church containing
windows through which light is admitted into the nave.
45. leads, roofs made of lead.
The Scholar-Gypsy. See Critical Notes.
2. wattled cotes, sheepfolds built of wattles, or interwoven twigs. 10. the quest, the search for the Scholar-
Gypsy, who is supposed still to haunt the vicinity.

19. corn, grain, wheat. 25. convolvulus, a species of
morning-glory. 31. Glanvil's book. See Critical Note on
title. 34. pregnant parts, inventive faculties.

This said, he left them, and returned no
  more. —
But rumors hung about the country-side,
  That the lost scholar long was seen to
    stray,
  Seen by rare glimpses, pensive and tongue-
    tied,
  In hat of antique shape, and cloak of
    gray,   55
    The same the gypsies wore.
Shepherds had met him on the Hurst in
    spring;
  At some lone alehouse in the Berkshire
    moors,
  On the warm ingle-bench, the smock-
    frocked boors
  Had found him seated at their entering. 60

But, 'mid their drink and clatter, he would fly.
  And I myself seem half to know thy looks,
  And put the shepherds, wanderer! on thy
    trace;
  And boys who in lone wheatfields scare the
    rooks
  I ask if thou hast passed their quiet place;
    Or in my boat I lie   66
  Moored to the cool bank in the summer-
    heats,
  'Mid wide grass meadows which the sun-
    shine fills,
  And watch the warm, green-muffled
    Cumner hills,
  And wonder if thou haunt'st their shy
    retreats.   70

For most, I know, thou lov'st retired ground!
  Thee at the ferry Oxford riders blithe,
  Returning home on summer-nights, have
    met
  Crossing the stripling Thames at Bab-lock-
    hithe,
  Trailing in the cool stream thy fingers wet,
    As the punt's rope chops round;   76
  And leaning backward in a pensive dream,
  And fostering in thy lap a heap of flowers
  Plucked in shy fields and distant Wych-
    wood bowers,
  And thine eyes resting on the moonlit
    stream.   80

And then they land, and thou art seen no
    more! —

Maidens, who from the distant hamlets
    come
  To dance around the Fyfield elm in May,
  Oft through the darkening fields have seen
    thee roam,
  Or cross a stile into the public way.   85
    Oft thou hast given them store
  Of flowers—the frail-leafed, white anemo-
    ne,
  Dark bluebells drenched with dews of
    . summer eves,
  And purple orchises with spotted leaves—
  But none hath words she can report of thee.

And, above Godstow Bridge, when hay-time's
    here   91
  In June, and many a scythe in sunshine
    flames,
  Men who through those wide fields of
    breezy grass
  Where black-winged swallows haunt the
    glittering Thames,
  To bathe in the abandoned lasher pass,
    Have often passed thee near   96
  Sitting upon the river bank o'ergrown;
  Marked thine outlandish garb, thy figure
    spare,
  Thy dark vague eyes, and soft abstracted
    air —
  But, when they came from bathing, thou
    wast gone!   100

At some lone homestead in the Cumner hills,
  Where at her open door the housewife
    darns,
  Thou hast been seen, or hanging on a
    gate
  To watch the threshers in the mossy barns.
  Children, who early range these slopes
    and late   105
    For cresses from the rills,
  Have known thee eying, all an April-day,
  The springing pastures and the feeding
    kine;
  And marked thee, when the stars come
    out and shine,
  Through the long dewy grass move slow
    away.   110

In autumn, on the skirts of Bagley Wood —
  Where most the gypsies by the turf-edged
    way
    Pitch their smoked tents, and every bush
    you see

---

57. **Hurst**, Cumner Hurst, a prominent hill in the parish
of Cumner, southwest of Oxford. 58. **Berkshire**, a county
south of Oxford. 59. **ingle-bench**, bench in the chimney
corner. 74. **Bab-lock-hithe**, a ferry over the Thames
about two miles west of the village of Cumner. 76. **punt's...
round.** The Scholar-Gypsy is seen reposing in a boat
moored to the bank. The punt, or ferryboat, is pulled across
the stream by a rope, and the boat moves in a kind of curve.
The rope "chops" or suddenly shifts with the wind or current.
79. **Wychwood**, a forest about ten miles northwest of
Oxford.

83. **Fyfield . . . May**, a reference to the maypole dance
at Fyfield, a village six miles southwest of Oxford. The
large elm was a landmark for all the countryside. 91. **Godstow Bridge**, about two miles up the Thames from Oxford.
95. **lasher**, pool below a dam. 111. **Bagley Wood**, southwest of Oxford. It had been a favorite place of Arnold's
father.

With scarlet patches tagged and shreds of
    gray,
  Above the forest-ground called Thes-
    saly —   115
    The blackbird, picking food,
Sees thee, nor stops his meal, nor fears at
    all;
  So often has he known thee past him
    stray,
Rapt, twirling in thy hand a withered
    spray,
And waiting for the spark from heaven to
    fall.   120

And once, in winter, on the causeway chill
Where home through flooded fields foot-
    travelers go,
  Have I not passed thee on the wooden
    bridge,
Wrapped in thy cloak and battling with the
    snow,
  Thy face tow'rd Hinksey and its wintry
    ridge?   125
    And thou hast climbed the hill,
And gained the white brow of the Cumner
    range;
  Turned once to watch, while thick the
    snowflakes fall,
  The line of festal light in Christ-Church
    hall —
Then sought thy straw in some sequestered
    grange.   130

But what — I dream! Two hundred years
    are flown
Since first thy story ran through Oxford
    halls,
  And the grave Glanvil did the tale
    inscribe
That thou wert wandered from the studi-
    ous walls
  To learn strange arts, and join a gypsy
    tribe;   135
    And thou from earth art gone
Long since, and in some quiet churchyard
    laid —
  Some country-nook, where o'er thy un-
    known grave
Tall grasses and white flowering nettles
    wave,
Under a dark, red-fruited yew-tree's shade.

— No, no, thou hast not felt the lapse of
    hours!   141
For what wears out the life of mortal men?

'Tis that from change to change their
    being rolls;
'Tis that repeated shocks, again, again,
  Exhaust the energy of strongest souls 145
    And numb the elastic powers,
Till having used our nerves with bliss and
    teen,
  And tired upon a thousand schemes our
    wit,
  To the just-pausing Genius we remit
Our worn-out life, and are — what we have
    been.   150

Thou hast not lived, why should'st thou per-
    ish, so?
  Thou hadst *one* aim, *one* business, *one*
    desire;
  Else wert thou long since numbered with
    the dead!
Else hadst thou spent, like other men, thy
    fire!
  The generations of thy peers are fled, 155
    And we ourselves shall go;
But thou possessest an immortal lot,
  And we imagine thee exempt from age
  And living as thou liv'st on Glanvil's
    page,
Because thou hadst — what we, alas! have
    not.   160

For early didst thou leave the world, with
    powers
Fresh, undiverted to the world without,
  Firm to their mark, not spent on other
    things;
  Free from the sick fatigue, the languid
    doubt,
  Which much to have tried, in much been
    baffled, brings.   165
    O life unlike to ours!
Who fluctuate idly without term or scope,
  Of whom each strives, nor knows for
    what he strives,
  And each half lives a hundred different
    lives;
Who wait like thee, but not, like thee, in
    hope.   170

Thou waitest for the spark from heaven!
    and we,
Light half-believers of our casual creeds,
  Who never deeply felt, nor clearly willed,
  Whose insight never has borne fruit in
    deeds,
  Whose vague resolves never have been
    fulfilled;   175

114. scarlet patches . . . gray. The bright-colored, tattered garments of the gypsies were hung on the bushes.
115. Thessaly, a piece of forest ground near Bagley Wood.
125. Hinksey, a village south of Oxford. 129. Christ-
Church hall, the dining-hall in Christ Church College,
Oxford.

147. teen, sorrow. 149. just-pausing Genius. According to the ancients the Genius of a man was his spirit
or guardian angel. The phrase may mean that the Genius
pauses just for a moment before departing, or that the even-
handed spirit of the world impartially ends individual lives.

For whom each year we see
Breeds new beginnings, disappointments
    new;
Who hesitate and falter life away,
And lose tomorrow the ground won
    today —
Ah! do not we, wanderer! await it too? 180

Yes, we await it!—but it still delays,
And then we suffer! and amongst us one,
Who most has suffered, takes dejectedly
His seat upon the intellectual throne;
And all his store of sad experience he 185
    Lays bare of wretched days;
Tells us his misery's birth and growth and
    signs,
And how the dying spark of hope was
    fed,
And how the breast was soothed, and
    how the head,
And all his hourly varied anodynes.   190

This for our wisest! and we others pine,
And wish the long unhappy dream would
    end,
And waive all claim to bliss, and try to
    bear;
With close-lipped patience for our only
    friend,
Sad patience, too near neighbor to
    despair —   195
    But none has hope like thine!
Thou through the fields and through the
    woods dost stray,
Roaming the country-side, a truant boy,
Nursing thy project in unclouded joy,
And every doubt long blown by time away.

O born in days when wits were fresh and
    clear,   201
And life ran gayly as the sparkling Thames;
Before this strange disease of modern life,
With its sick hurry, its divided aims,
    Its heads o'ertaxed, its palsied hearts, was
    rife—   205
    Fly hence, our contact fear!
Still fly, plunge deeper in the bowering
    wood!
Averse, as Dido did with gesture stern
From her false friend's approach in Hades
    turn,
Wave us away, and keep thy solitude!   210

Still nursing the unconquerable hope,
Still clutching the inviolable shade,
    With a free, onward impulse brushing
    through,
By night, the silvered branches of the
    glade —
    Far on the forest-skirts, where none
    pursue,   215
    On some mild pastoral slope
Emerge, and resting on the moonlit pales
Freshen thy flowers as in former years
With dew, or listen with enchanted ears,
From the dark dingles, to the nightingales!

But fly our paths, our feverish contact fly! 221
For strong the infection of our mental strife,
    Which, though it gives no bliss, yet spoils
    for rest;
And we should win thee from thy own fair
    life,
Like us distracted, and like us unblest.
    Soon, soon thy cheer would die,   226
Thy hopes grow timorous, and unfixed thy
    powers,
And thy clear aims be cross and shifting
    made;
And then thy glad perennial youth would
    fade,
Fade, and grow old at last, and die like
    ours.   230

Then fly our greetings, fly our speech and
    smiles!
— As some grave Tyrian trader, from the
    sea,
Descried at sunrise an emerging prow
Lifting the cool-haired creepers stealthily,
    The fringes of a southward-facing brow
    Among the Ægæan isles;   236
And saw the merry Grecian coaster come,
Freighted with amber grapes, and Chian
    wine,
Green, bursting figs, and tunnies steeped
    in brine —
And knew the intruders on his ancient home,

The young light-hearted masters of the
    waves —   241
And snatched his rudder, and shook out
    more sail;
    And day and night held on indignantly
O'er the blue Midland waters with the gale,

182 ff. one . . . suffered, etc., probably Tennyson, who
had recently been chosen poet laureate. See *In Memoriam*,
Section 5, lines 5-8, p. 58.   190. anodynes, drugs to soothe
pain.   208-209. Dido . . . turn. Dido, queen of Carthage,
killed herself because she was deserted by Æneas. On his
journey through Hades, Æneas met the shade of Dido, but
she turned scornfully away from him. The incident is related
in Virgil's *Æneid*, 6, 450-471.

220. dingles, wooded dells.   232. Tyrian trader. The
Phœnicians of the city of Tyre were the chief traders in
the Mediterranean from 900 to 700 B.C. They were gradually displaced by the Greeks.   234. cool-haired creepers,
foliage overhanging the entrance to some cavern or inlet.
236. Ægæan isles, islands in the Ægæan Sea, between Greece
and Asia Minor.   238. Chian wine, wine from Chios, an
island in the Ægæan Sea.   239. tunnies, a kind of large
fish.   244. Midland waters, Mediterranean Sea.

Betwixt the Syrtes and soft Sicily,   245
  To where the Atlantic raves
Outside the western straits; and unbent
    sails
  There, where down cloudy cliffs, through
    sheets of foam,
Shy traffickers, the dark Iberians come;
  And on the beach undid his corded
    bales.   250
                                   (1853)

STANZAS FROM THE GRANDE CHARTREUSE

Through Alpine meadows soft-suffused
With rain, where thick the crocus blows,
Past the dark forges long disused,
The mule-track from Saint Laurent goes.
The bridge is crossed, and slow we ride,   5
Through forest, up the mountain-side.

The autumnal evening darkens round,
The wind is up, and drives the rain;
While, hark! far down, with strangled sound
Doth the Dead Guier's stream complain,   10
Where that wet smoke, among the woods,
Over his boiling caldron broods.

Swift rush the spectral vapors white
Past limestone scars with ragged pines,
Showing — then blotting from our sight! —
Halt — through the cloud-drift something
    shines!   16
High in the valley, wet and drear,
The huts of Courrerie appear.

Strike leftward! cries our guide; and higher
Mounts up the stony forest-way.   20
At last the encircling trees retire;
Look! through the showery twilight gray
What pointed roofs are these advance? —
A palace of the kings of France?

Approach, for what we seek is here!   25
Alight, and sparely sup, and wait
For rest in this outbuilding near;
Then cross the sward and reach that gate.

Knock; pass the wicket! Thou art come
To the Carthusians' world-famed home.   30

The silent courts, where night and day
Into their stone-carved basins cold
The splashing icy fountains play —
The humid corridors behold!
Where, ghostlike in the deepening night,   35
Cowled forms brush by in gleaming white.

The chapel, where no organ's peal
Invests the stern and naked prayer —
With penitential cries they kneel
And wrestle; rising then, with bare   40
And white uplifted faces stand,
Passing the Host from hand to hand;

Each takes, and then his visage wan
Is buried in his cowl once more.
The cells! — the suffering Son of Man   45
Upon the wall — the knee-worn floor —
And where they sleep, that wooden bed,
Which shall their coffin be, when dead!

The library, where tract and tome
Not to feed priestly pride are there,   50
To hymn the conquering march of Rome,
Nor yet to amuse, as ours are!
They paint of souls the inner strife,
Their drops of blood, their death in life.

The garden, overgrown — yet mild,   55
See, fragrant herbs are flowering there!
Strong children of the Alpine wild
Whose culture is the brethren's care;
Of human tasks their only one,
And cheerful works beneath the sun.   60

Those halls, too, destined to contain
Each its own pilgrim-host of old,
From England, Germany, or Spain —
All are before me! I behold
The House, the Brotherhood austere!   65
— And what am I, that I am here?

Repudiates the dream

For rigorous teachers seized my youth,
And purged its faith, and trimmed its fire,
Showed me the high, white star of Truth,
There bade me gaze, and there aspire.   70
Even now their whispers pierce the gloom:
What dost thou in this living tomb?

Forgive me, masters of the mind!
At whose behest I long ago
So much unlearnt, so much resigned —   75
I come not here to be your foe!

245. **Syrtes,** the Gulf of Sidra, on the northern coast of Africa. 247. **western straits,** Strait of Gibraltar. 249. **Iberians,** early inhabitants of Spain and Portugal.
    Stanzas from the Grande Chartreuse. The Grande Chartreuse, located in the French Alps about fourteen miles from Grenoble, was formerly a monastery of the Order of Carthusians. It was founded by St. Bruno, about 1084, but the present building dates from 1678. The monks were compelled to leave France in 1903. Arnold had visited the Grande Chartreuse in 1852. Cf. Dowson, p. 844.
    4. **Saint Laurent,** about five miles from the monastery. 10. **Dead Guier's stream,** the Guiers Mort River, which rises near the monastery. 14. **scars,** cliffs. 18. **Courrerie,** a village in the mountains.

42. **Host,** the consecrated bread used in the Mass. 67. **rigorous teachers,** like Arnold's own father, Dr. Thomas Arnold, of Rugby.

I seek these anchorites, not in ruth,
To curse and to deny your truth;

Not as their friend, or child, I speak!
But as, on some far northern strand,   80
Thinking of his own gods, a Greek
In pity and mournful awe might stand
Before some fallen Runic stone —
For both were faiths, and both are gone.

Wandering between two worlds, one dead, 85
The other powerless to be born,
With nowhere yet to rest my head,
Like these, on earth I wait forlorn.
Their faith, my tears, the world deride —
I come to shed them at their side.   90

Oh, hide me in your gloom profound,
Ye solemn seats of holy pain!
Take me, cowled forms, and fence me round,
Till I possess my soul again;
Till free my thoughts before me roll,   95
Not chafed by hourly false control!

For the world cries your faith is now
But a dead time's exploded dream;
My melancholy, sciolists vow,
Is a passed mode, an outworn theme —   100
As if the world had ever had
A faith, or sciolists been sad!

Ah, if it *be* passed, take away,
At least, the restlessness, the pain;
Be man henceforth no more a prey   105
To these out-dated stings again!
The nobleness of grief is gone —
Ah, leave us not the fret alone!

But — if you cannot give us ease —
Last of the race of them who grieve   110
Here leave us to die out with these
Last of the people who believe!
Silent, while years engrave the brow;
Silent — the best are silent now.

Achilles ponders in his tent,   115
The kings of modern thought are dumb;
Silent they are, though not content,
And wait to see the future come.

They have the grief men had of yore,
But they contend and cry no more.   120
Our fathers watered with their tears
This sea of time whereon we sail,
Their voices were in all men's ears
Who passed within their puissant hail.
Still the same ocean round us raves,   125
But we stand mute, and watch the waves.

For what availed it, all the noise
And outcry of the former men? —
Say, have their sons achieved more joys?
Say, is life lighter now than then?   130
The sufferers died, they left their pain —
The pangs which tortured them remain.

What helps it now that Byron bore,
With haughty scorn which mocked the smart,
Through Europe to the Ætolian shore,   135
The pageant of his bleeding heart?
That thousands counted every groan,
And Europe made his woe her own?

What boots it, Shelley! that the breeze
Carried thy lovely wail away,   140
Musical through Italian trees
Which fringe thy soft blue Spezzian bay?
Inheritors of thy distress
Have restless hearts one throb the less?

Or are we easier, to have read,   145
O Obermann! the sad, stern page,
Which tells us how thou hidd'st thy head
From the fierce tempest of thine age
In the lone brakes of Fontainebleau,
Or chalets near the Alpine snow?   150

Ye slumber in your silent grave! —
The world, which for an idle day
Grace to your mood of sadness gave,
Long since hath flung her weeds away.
The eternal trifler breaks your spell;   155
But we — we learned your lore too well!

Years hence, perhaps, may dawn an age,
More fortunate, alas! than we,
Which without hardness will be sage,
And gay without frivolity.   160
Sons of the world, oh, speed those years;
But, while we wait, allow our tears!

77. **anchorites**, religious hermits. **ruth**, repentance.
83. **Runic stone**, a stone bearing runes, a form of lettering
used by the early people of northern Europe. 85. **two
worlds**, the old age of faith with its worn-out conventions
and the new age that will establish faith on some new and
acceptable basis of unity and harmony. 99. **sciolists**, persons of superficial knowledge; from Latin *scio* (*know*).
115. **Achilles . . . tent.** During the siege of Troy, Achilles,
one of the Greek heroes, retired to his tent and refused to
take part in the war because he had been deprived of his
captive maiden. It has been suggested that Arnold here
refers to Newman's two years of quiet study, 1843-45, before he was received into the Roman Catholic Church.

133. **Byron.** Byron died at Missolonghi, on the shores of
Ætolia, Greece, in 1824. When exiled from England, Byron
traveled through France and Italy to Greece, and displayed
his hurts in all that he wrote during these years. Byron and
his writings exercised a strange hold upon Europe. 139.
Shelley. After his union with Mary Godwin, Shelley spent
most of his life abroad. He was drowned in the Gulf of
Spezzia, south of Genoa, Italy, in 1822. 146. **Obermann.**
See note on *Stanzas in Memory of the Author of "Obermann,"*
p. 469. 149. **Fontainebleau**, a city south of Paris.

Allow them! We admire with awe
The exulting thunder of your race;
You give the universe your law,   165
You triumph over time and space!
Your pride of life, your tireless powers,
We laud them, but they are not ours.

We are like children reared in shade
Beneath some old-world abbey wall,   170
Forgotten in a forest-glade,
And secret from the eyes of all.
Deep, deep the greenwood round them waves,
Their abbey, and its close of graves!

But, where the road runs near the stream, 175
Oft through the trees they catch a glance
Of passing troops in the sun's beam —
Pennon, and plume, and flashing lance!
Forth to the world those soldiers fare,
To life, to cities, and to war!   180

And through the wood, another way,
Faint bugle-notes from far are borne,
Where hunters gather, staghounds bay,
Round some fair forest-lodge at morn.
Gay dames are there, in sylvan green;   185
Laughter and cries — those notes between!

The banners flashing through the trees
Make their blood dance and chain their eyes;
That bugle-music on the breeze
Arrests them with a charmed surprise.   190
Banner by turns and bugle woo:
Ye shy recluses, follow too!

O children, what do ye reply? —
"Action and pleasure, will ye roam
Through these secluded dells to cry   195
And call us? — but too late ye come!
Too late for us your call ye blow,
Whose bent was taken long ago.

"Long since we pace this shadowed nave;
We watch those yellow tapers shine,   200
Emblems of hope over the grave,
In the high altar's depth divine;
The organ carries to our ear
Its accents of another sphere.

"Fenced early in this cloistral round   205
Of reverie, of shade, of prayer,
How should we grow in other ground?
How can we flower in foreign air?
— Pass, banners, pass, and bugles, cease;
And leave our desert to its peace!"   210
                                        (1855)

174. **close,** enclosure. 210. **desert,** our life devoid of
action, in the cloister.

THYRSIS

A MONODY, *to commemorate the author's
friend,* ARTHUR HUGH CLOUGH,
who died at Florence, 1861

How changed is here each spot man makes
      or fills!
In the two Hinkseys nothing keeps the
      same;
   The village street its haunted mansion
      lacks,
And from the sign is gone Sibylla's name,
   And from the roofs the twisted chimney-
      stacks —   5
   Are ye too changed, ye hills?
See, 'tis no foot of unfamiliar men
   Tonight from Oxford up your pathway
      strays!
   Here came I often, often, in old days —
Thyrsis and I; we still had Thyrsis then. 10

Runs it not here, the track by Childsworth
      Farm,
   Past the high wood, to where the elm-tree
      crowns
      The hill behind whose ridge the sunset
      flames?
The signal-elm, that looks on Ilsley Downs,
   The Vale, the three lone weirs, the youth-
      ful Thames? —   15
   This winter's-eve is warm,
Humid the air! leafless, yet soft as spring,
   The tender purple spray on copse and
      briers!
   And that sweet city with her dreaming
      spires,
She needs not June for beauty's heighten-
      ing,   20

Lovely all times she lies, lovely tonight! —
   Only, methinks, some loss of habit's power
      Befalls me wandering through this up-
      land dim;
   Once passed I blindfold here, at any hour;
   Now seldom come I, since I came with
      him.   25

Thyrsis. See Critical Notes. In the poem Arnold speaks of
himself as Corydon (line 80) and of Clough as Thyrsis. These
are conventional names in pastoral poetry; they are found in
Virgil's Seventh *Eclogue,* Milton's *L'Allegro,* and elsewhere.
Arnold's poem is full of reminiscences of the days spent with
Clough in Oxford and its environs.
   2. **two Hinkseys,** villages southwest of Oxford, across the
river. 4. **Sibylla's name.** Sibylla Kerr was keeper of a pub
in South Hinksey. 5. **twisted,** set at an angle. 11. **Childsworth Farm,** modern Chilswell Farm, three miles from
Oxford. 14. **signal-elm.** This famous tree has frequently
been identified with an oak tree standing at the top of the
knoll on the Oxford side of the ridge. A large elm a short distance below the summit of the ridge better fits the description.
Ilsley Downs. Ilsley is a parish in West Berkshire. 15.
weirs, dams. **youthful Thames.** The Thames River is
about fifty yards wide at Oxford. 19. **sweet city,** Oxford.

That single elm-tree bright
Against the west — I miss it! is it gone?
We prized it dearly; while it stood, we
    said,
Our friend, the gypsy-scholar, was not
    dead;
While the tree lived, he in these fields
    lived on.   30

Too rare, too rare, grow now my visits here,
But once I knew each field, each flower,
    each stick;
And with the country-folk acquaintance
    made
By barn in threshing-time, by new-built
    rick.
Here, too, our shepherd-pipes we first
    assayed.   35
    Ah me! this many a year
My pipe is lost, my shepherd's holiday!
Needs must I lose them, needs with
    heavy heart
Into the world and wave of men de-
    part;
But Thyrsis of his own will went away. 40

It irked him to be here; he could not rest.
He loved each simple joy the country yields,
He loved his mates; but yet he could
    not keep,
For that a shadow lowered on the fields,
Here with the shepherds and the silly
    sheep.   45
    Some life of men unblest
He knew, which made him droop, and filled
    his head.
He went; his piping took a troubled
    sound
Of storms that rage outside our happy
    ground;
He could not wait their passing, he is dead.

So, some tempestuous morn in early June, 51
When the year's primal burst of bloom is
    o'er,
Before the roses and the longest day —
When garden-walks and all the grassy floor
With blossoms red and white of fallen
    May   55
And chestnut-flowers are strewn —
So have I heard the cuckoo's parting cry,
From the wet field, through the vexed
    garden-trees,

Come with the volleying rain and tossing
    breeze: 59
The bloom is gone, and with the bloom go I!

Too quick despairer, wherefore wilt thou go?
Soon will the high midsummer pomps come
    on,
Soon will the musk carnations break and
    swell,
Soon shall we have gold-dusted snapdragon,
Sweet-William with his homely cottage-
    smell,   65
And stocks in fragrant blow;
Roses that down the alleys shine afar,
And open, jasmine-muffled lattices,
And groups under the dreaming garden-
    trees,
And the full moon, and the white evening-
    star.   70

He hearkens not! light comer, he is flown!
What matters it? next year he will return,
And we shall have him in the sweet
    spring-days,
With whitening hedges, and uncrumpling
    fern,
And bluebells trembling by the forest-
    ways,   75
And scent of hay new-mown.
But Thyrsis never more we swains shall
    see;
See him come back, and cut a smoother
    reed,
And blow a strain the world at last shall
    heed —
For Time, not Corydon, hath conquered
    thee!   80

Alack, for Corydon no rival now! —
But when Sicilian shepherds lost a mate,
Some good survivor with his flute would
    go,
Piping a ditty sad for Bion's fate;
And cross the unpermitted ferry's flow,
And relax Pluto's brow,   86
And make leap up with joy the beauteous
    head
Of Proserpine, among whose crownéd
    hair
Are flowers first opened on Sicilian air,
And flute his friend, like Orpheus, from the
    dead.   90

29. **gypsy-scholar.** See *The Scholar-Gypsy*, p. 487, and
Critical Notes. 35. **shepherd-pipes,** poetry. 36-37.
many a year . . . lost. Arnold had not published any poetry
for nine years. 40. **Thyrsis . . . away.** Clough resigned his
fellowship in Oriel College, Oxford, in 1848, partly on religious
grounds. 45. **silly,** simple. 49. **storms that rage.** Much
of the poetry of Clough reflects his spiritual struggles.

62. **pomps,** shows, displays. 66. **stocks,** gillyflowers.
82. **Sicilian shepherds,** pastoral poets of Sicily; a reference
to the lament for Bion, a Sicilian pastoral poet, written by his
friend Moschus, 2d century B.C. 85. **unpermitted . . .
flow,** the river Styx, over which only the dead were permitted
to pass. 86. **Pluto,** god of the underworld. He is said to
have carried off Proserpine to be his wife. He found her in
the vale of Enna (line 95), in Sicily, where she was gathering
lilies and violets. 90. **Orpheus.** See note on *Memorial
Verses,* line 38, p. 442.

O easy access to the hearer's grace
  When Dorian shepherds sang to Proser-
    pine!
For she herself had trod Sicilian fields,
She knew the Dorian water's gush divine,
  She knew each lily white which Enna
    yields,   95
    Each rose with blushing face;
She loved the Dorian pipe, the Dorian
    strain.
But, ah, of our poor Thames she never
    heard!
Her foot the Cumner cowslips never
    stirred;
And we should tease her with our plaint
    in vain!   100

Well! wind-dispersed and vain the words will
    be, .
Yet, Thyrsis, let me give my grief its hour
  In the old haunt, and find our tree-
    topped hill!
Who, if not I, for questing here hath power?
  I know the wood which hides the daffodil,
    I know the Fyfield tree,   106
I know what white, what purple fritillaries
  The grassy harvest of the river-fields,
    Above by Ensham, down by Sandford,
    yields,
And what sedged brooks are Thames's
    tributaries;   110

I know these slopes; who knows them if
    not I? —
But many a dingle on the loved hillside,
  With thorns once studded, old, white-
    blossomed trees,
  Where thick the cowslips grew, and far
    descried
  High towered the spikes of purple
    orchises,   115
    Hath since our day put by
The coronals of that forgotten time;
  Down each green bank hath gone the
    plowboy's team,
And only in the hidden brookside gleam
Primroses, orphans of the flowery prime.120

Where is the girl, who by the boatman's door,
  Above the locks, above the boating throng,
    Unmoored our skiff when through the
    Wytham flats,
  Red loosestrife and blond meadow-sweet
    among

And darting swallows and light water-
    gnats,   125
    We tracked the shy Thames shore?
Where are the mowers, who, as the tiny
    swell
Of our boat passing heaved the river-
    grass,
  Stood with suspended scythe to see us
    pass? —
They all are gone, and thou art gone as
    well!   130

Yes, thou art gone! and round me too the
    night
  In ever-nearing circle weaves her shade.
    I see her veil draw soft across the day,
  I feel her slowly chilling breath invade
    The cheek grown thin, the brown hair
    sprent with gray;   135
    I feel her finger light
Laid pausefully upon life's headlong train—
  The foot less prompt to meet the morn-
    ing dew,
  The heart less bounding at emotion new,
And hope, once crushed, less quick to
    spring again.   140

And long the way appears, which seemed so
    short
  To the less practiced eye of sanguine youth;
    And high the mountain-tops, in cloudy
    air,
  The mountain-tops where is the throne of
    Truth,
    Tops in life's morning-sun so bright and
    bare!   145
    Unbreachable the fort
Of the long-battered world uplifts its wall;
  And strange and vain the earthly tur-
    moil grows,
  And near and real the charm of thy
    repose,
And night as welcome as a friend would
    fall.   150

But hush! the upland hath a sudden loss
  Of quiet! — Look, adown the dusk hillside,
    A troop of Oxford hunters going home,
  As in old days, jovial and talking, ride!
    From hunting with the Berkshire hounds
    they come.   155
    Quick! let me fly, and cross
Into yon farther field! — 'Tis done; and
    see,
  Backed by the sunset, which doth glorify
    The orange and pale violet evening-sky,
Bare on its lonely ridge, the Tree! the Tree!

92. **Dorian**, Sicilian. 99. **Cumner**, hills near Oxford.
106. **Fyfield tree**, a giant elm near the village of Fyfield,
six miles southwest of Oxford. 107. **fritillaries**, lily-like
flowers. 109. **Ensham**, Eynsham, a village northwest of
Oxford. Sandford is south of Oxford. 112. **dingle**, wooded
dell. 123. **Wytham flats**, about two miles northwest of
Oxford, between the village of Wytham and the Thames.

135. **sprent**, sprinkled. 137. **pausefully**, so as to make
it pause. 155. **Berkshire**, a county south of Oxford.
160. **the Tree**. See lines 12-14.

I take the omen! Eve lets down her veil, 161
  The white fog creeps from bush to bush
      about,
  The west unflushes, the high stars grow
      bright,
And in the scattered farms the lights come
      out.
  I cannot reach the signal-tree tonight,165
    Yet, happy omen, hail!
Hear it from thy broad lucent Arno-vale
  (For there thine earth-forgetting eyelids
      keep
  The morningless and unawakening sleep
Under the flowery oleanders pale),   170

Hear it, O Thyrsis, still our tree is there! —
  Ah, vain! These English fields, this upland
      dim,
  These brambles pale with mist engar-
      landed,
That lone, sky-pointing tree, are not for
      him;
  To a boon southern country he is fled, 175
    And now in happier air,
  Wandering with the great Mother's train
      divine
  (And purer or more subtle soul than thee,
  I trow, the mighty Mother doth not see)
Within a folding of the Apennine,   180

Thou hearest the immortal chants of old! —
  Putting his sickle to the perilous grain
  In the hot cornfield of the Phrygian king,
For thee the Lityerses-song again
  Young Daphnis with his silver voice doth
      sing;   185
    Sings his Sicilian fold,
  His sheep, his hapless love, his blinded
      eyes —
  And how a call celestial round him rang,
  And heavenward from the fountain-
      brink he sprang,
And all the marvel of the golden skies. 190

There thou art gone, and me thou leavest here
  Sole in these fields! yet will I not despair.
  Despair I will not, while I yet descry
  'Neath the mild canopy of English air
    That lonely tree against the western sky.

Still, still these slopes, 'tis clear,   196
  Our gypsy-scholar haunts, outliving thee!
  Fields where soft sheep from cages pull
      the hay,
  Woods with anemones in flower till May,
Know him a wanderer still; then why not
    me?   200

A fugitive and gracious light he seeks,
  Shy to illumine; and I seek it too.
  This does not come with houses or with
      gold,
  With place, with honor, and a flattering
      crew;
  'Tis not in the world's market bought
      and sold —   205
  But the smooth-slipping weeks
Drop by, and leave its seeker still untired;
  Out of the heed of mortals he is gone,
  He wends unfollowed, he must house
      alone;
Yet on he fares, by his own heart inspired.

Thou too, O Thyrsis, on like quest wast
    bound;   211
  Thou wanderedst with me for a little hour!
  Men gave thee nothing; but this happy
      quest,
  If men esteemed thee feeble, gave thee
      power,
  If men procured thee trouble, gave thee
      rest.   215
    And this rude Cumner ground,
  Its fir-topped Hurst, its farms, its quiet
      fields,
  Here cam'st thou in thy jocund youthful
      time,
  Here was thine height of strength, thy
      golden prime!   219
And still the haunt beloved a virtue yields.

What though the music of thy rustic flute
  Kept not for long its happy, country tone;
  Lost it too soon, and learned a stormy
      note
  Of men contention-tossed, of men who
      groan,
    Which tasked thy pipe too sore, and
      tired thy throat —   225
    It failed, and thou wast mute!
Yet hadst thou alway visions of our light,
  And long with men of care thou couldst
      not stay,
  And soon thy foot resumed its wandering
      way,
Left human haunt, and on alone till
  night.   230

---

167. **Arno.** Clough died in Italy and was buried in Florence by the Arno River. 175. **boon,** rich, benign. 177.
great Mother. See note on *The Youth of Nature*, line 77, p.
473. 183. **Phrygian king,** Lityerses, who made strangers
contest with him in reaping grain. If he defeated them, he put
them to death. The Sicilian shepherd Daphnis (line 185), son
of Hermes (messenger of the gods), engaged in such a contest
in order to release his mistress, who was in the power of the
king. Hercules reaped the grain for Daphnis and killed Lityerses. The Lityerses-song connected with the tradition used
to be sung by Greek grain reapers. Another tradition represented Daphnis as having been blinded by a nymph whose
love he slighted. His father raised Daphnis to heaven and
caused a fountain to spring up in the place from which he
ascended.

202. **Shy to illumine,** reluctant to shine forth. 217.
Hurst, a prominent hill in the parish of Cumner.

Too rare, too rare, grow now my visits here!
  'Mid city-noise, not, as with thee of yore,
    Thyrsis! in reach of sheep-bells is my
    home.
— Then through the great town's harsh,
    heart-wearying roar,
  Let in thy voice a whisper often come,
    To chase fatigue and fear: 236
Why faintest thou? I wandered till I died.
Roam on! The light we sought is shining
    still.
Dost thou ask proof? Our tree yet crowns
    the hill,
Our scholar travels yet the loved hillside. 240
                         (1866)

SAINT BRANDAN

Saint Brandan sails the northern main;
The brotherhoods of saints are glad.
He greets them once, he sails again;
So late! — such storms! — The Saint is mad!

He heard, across the howling seas,   5
Chime convent-bells on wintry nights;
He saw, on spray-swept Hebrides,
Twinkle the monastery-lights.

But north, still north, Saint Brandan steered —
And now no bells, no convents more!   10
The hurtling Polar lights are neared,
The sea without a human shore.

At last — (it was the Christmas night;
Stars shone after a day of storm) —
He sees float past an iceberg white,   15
And on it — Christ! — a living form.

That furtive mien, that scowling eye,
Of hair that red and tufted fell ——
It is — oh, where shall Brandan fly? —
The traitor Judas, out of hell!   20

Palsied with terror, Brandan sate;
The moon was bright, the iceberg near.
He hears a voice sigh humbly, "Wait!
By high permission I am here.

"One moment wait, thou holy man!   25
On earth my crime, my death, they knew;
My name is under all men's ban —
Ah, tell them of my respite too!

"Tell them, one blessed Christmas-night
(It was the first after I came,   30

Breathing self-murder, frenzy, spite,
To rue my guilt in endless flame) —

"I felt, as I in torment lay
'Mid the souls plagued by heavenly power,
An angel touch mine arm, and say,   35
Go hence and cool thyself an hour!

" 'Ah, whence this mercy, Lord?' I said.
The Leper recollect, said he,
Who asked the passers-by for aid,
In Joppa, and thy charity.   40

"Then I remembered how I went,
In Joppa, through the public street,
One morn when the sirocco spent
Its storms of dust with burning heat;

"And in the street a leper sate,   45
Shivering with fever, naked, old;
Sand raked his sores from heel to pate,
The hot wind fevered him five-fold.

"He gazed upon me as I passed,
And murmured: *Help me, or I die!*   50
To the poor wretch my cloak I cast,
Saw him look eased, and hurried by.

"Oh, Brandan, think what grace divine,
What blessing must full goodness shower,
When fragment of it small, like mine,   55
Hath such inestimable power!

"Well-fed, well-clothed, well-friended, I
Did that chance act of good, that one!
Then went my way to kill and lie —
Forgot my good as soon as done.   60

"That germ of kindness, in the womb
Of mercy caught, did not expire;
Outlives my guilt, outlives my doom,
And friends me in the pit of fire.

"Once every year, when carols wake,   65
On earth, the Christmas-night's repose,
Arising from the sinners' lake,
I journey to these healing snows.

"I stanch with ice my burning breast,
With silence balm my whirling brain.   70
O Brandan! to this hour of rest
That Joppan leper's ease was pain." ——

Tears started to Saint Brandan's eyes;
He bowed his head, he breathed a prayer —
Then looked, and lo, the frosty skies!   75
The iceberg, and no Judas there!   (1867)

Saint Brandan. Saint Brandan was an Irish saint (c. 484-578) who, according to medieval tradition, went on a voyage across the Atlantic to the "Promised Land of the Saints." The legend is found in many languages.
7. **Hebrides,** islands off the west coast of Scotland. 11. **hurtling,** darting. 18. **fell,** matted hair. Judas is traditionally represented as having red hair.

40. **Joppa,** a port of Palestine on the Mediterranean, thirty-five miles northwest of Jerusalem. 43. **sirocco,** a hot south wind.

WORLDLY PLACE

Even in a palace, life may be led well!
So spake the imperial sage, purest of men,
Marcus Aurelius. But the stifling den
Of common life, where, crowded up pell-mell,
Our freedom for a little bread we sell,   5
And drudge under some foolish master's ken
Who rates us if we peer outside our pen —
Matched with a palace, is not this a hell?
Even in a palace! On his truth sincere,
Who spoke these words, no shadow ever
          came;   10
And when my ill-schooled spirit is aflame
Some nobler, ampler stage of life to win,
I'll stop, and say, "There were no succor here!
The aids to noble life are all within." (1867)

EAST LONDON

'Twas August, and the fierce sun overhead
Smote on the squalid streets of Bethnal Green,
And the pale weaver, through his windows
          seen
In Spitalfields, looked thrice dispirited.
I met a preacher there I knew, and said: 5
"Ill and o'erworked, how fare you in this
          scene?" —
"Bravely!" said he; "for I of late have been
Much cheered with thoughts of Christ, *the
          living bread.*"
O human soul! as long as thou canst so
Set up a mark of everlasting light,   10
Above the howling senses' ebb and flow,
To cheer thee, and to right thee if thou
          roam —
Not with lost toil thou laborest through the
          night!
Thou mak'st the heaven thou hop'st indeed
          thy home.   (1867)

WEST LONDON

Crouched on the pavement, close by Belgrave
          Square,
A tramp I saw, ill, moody, and tongue-tied.
A babe was in her arms, and at her side
A girl; their clothes were rags, their feet were
          bare.
Some laboring men, whose work lay some-
          where there,   5

Passed opposite; she touched her girl, who
          hied
Across, and begged, and came back satisfied.
The rich she had let pass with frozen stare.
Thought I: "Above her state this spirit
          towers;
She will not ask of aliens, but of friends,   10
Of sharers in a common human fate.
She turns from that cold succor, which attends
The unknown little from the unknowing great,
And points us to a better time than ours."
                                             (1867)

THE BETTER PART

Long fed on boundless hopes, O race of man,
How angrily thou spurn'st all simpler fare!
"Christ," someone says, "was human as we
          are;
No judge eyes us from heaven, our sin to
          scan;
We live no more, when we have done our
          span." —   5
"Well, then, for Christ," thou answerest,
          "who can care?
From sin, which heaven records not, why
          forbear?
Live we like brutes our life without a plan!"
So answerest thou; but why not rather say:
"Hath man no second life? — *Pitch this one
          high!*   10
Sits there no judge in heaven, our sin to see?
More strictly, then, the inward judge obey!
Was Christ a man like us? *Ah! let us try
If we then, too, can be such men as he!*" (1867)

IMMORTALITY

Foiled by our fellow-men, depressed, outworn,
We leave the brutal world to take its way,
And, *Patience! in another life*, we say,
*The world shall be thrust down, and we up-
          borne.*
And will not, then, the immortal armies scorn
The world's poor, routed leavings? or will
          they,   6
Who failed under the heat of this life's day,
Support the fervors of the heavenly morn?
No, no! the energy of life may be
Kept on after the grave, but not begun;   10
And he who flagged not in the earthly strife,
From strength to strength advancing — only
          he,
His soul well-knit, and all his battles won,
Mounts, and that hardly, to eternal life.
                                             (1867)

Worldly Place. **3. Marcus Aurelius,** a famous Roman
emperor (161-180 A.D.) and philosopher; author of *Meditations,* a book highly valued by Arnold. Cf. *Meditations,* 5,
15.—"Wheresoever thou mayest live, there it is in thy power
to live well and happy. But thou mayest live at the Court,
there then also mayest thou live well and happy."
    East London. **2. Bethnal Green,** one of the poor dis-
tricts of London. **4. Spitalfields.** This is the famous
district of silk-weavers; it has been the scene of numerous
riots.
    West London. **1. Belgrave Square,** the place of residence
of members of the nobility and of distinguished foreigners.

The Better Part. Originally called *Anti-Desperation.*
1. boundless hopes, as of immortality, future reward,
etc.

THE GOOD SHEPHERD WITH THE KID

He saves the sheep, the goats he doth not save.
So rang Tertullian's sentence, on the side
Of that unpitying Phrygian sect which cried,
"Him can no fount of fresh forgiveness lave,
Who sins, once washed by the baptismal
    wave." —   5
So spake the fierce Tertullian. But she sighed,
The infant Church! of love she felt the tide
Stream on her from her Lord's yet recent
    grave.
And then she smiled; and in the Catacombs,
With eye suffused but heart inspired true, 10
On those walls subterranean, where she hid
Her head 'mid ignominy, death, and tombs,
She her Good Shepherd's hasty image drew —
And on his shoulders, not a lamb, a kid.
                    (1867)

AUSTERITY OF POETRY

That son of Italy who tried to blow,
Ere Dante came, the trump of sacred song,
In his light youth amid a festal throng
Sate with his bride to see a public show.
Fair was the bride, and on her front did glow 5
Youth like a star; and what to youth belong —
Gay raiment, sparkling gauds, elation strong.
A prop gave way! crash fell a platform! lo,
'Mid struggling sufferers, hurt to death, she
    lay!
Shuddering, they drew her garments off —
    and found   10
A robe of sackcloth next the smooth, white
    skin.
Such, poets, is your bride, the Muse! young,
    gay,
Radiant, adorned outside; a hidden ground
Of thought and of austerity within.   (1867)

DOVER BEACH

The sea is calm tonight,
The tide is full, the moon lies fair
Upon the straits; — on the French coast the
    light
Gleams and is gone; the cliffs of England
    stand,   4
Glimmering and vast, out in the tranquil bay.
Come to the window, sweet is the night-air!

Only, from the long line of spray
Where the sea meets the moon-blanched land,
Listen! you hear the grating roar
Of pebbles which the waves draw back, and
    fling,   10
At their return, up the high strand,
Begin, and cease, and then again begin,
With tremulous cadence slow, and bring
The eternal note of sadness in.

Sophocles long ago   15
Heard it on the Ægæan, and it brought
Into his mind the turbid ebb and flow
Of human misery; we
Find also in the sound a thought,
Hearing it by this distant northern sea.   20

The Sea of Faith
Was once, too, at the full, and round earth's
    shore
Lay like the folds of a bright girdle furled.
But now I only hear
Its melancholy, long, withdrawing roar,   25
Retreating, to the breath
Of the night-wind, down the vast edges drear
And naked shingles of the world.

Ah, love, let us be true
To one another! for the world, which seems
To lie before us like a land of dreams,   31
So various, so beautiful, so new,
Hath really neither joy, nor love, nor light,
Nor certitude, nor peace, nor help for pain;
And we are here as on a darkling plain   35
Swept with confused alarms of struggle and
    flight,
Where ignorant armies clash by night. (1867)

PALLADIUM

Set where the upper streams of Simois flow
Was the Palladium, high 'mid rock and wood;
And Hector was in Ilium, far below,
And fought, and saw it not — but there it
    stood!

It stood, and sun and moonshine rained their
    light   5
On the pure columns of its glen-built hall.

Dover Beach. 15. **Sophocles**, the famous Greek tragic dramatist of the 4th century B.C. The reference is to a passage in *Antigone*, 583 ff. 28. **shingles**, beaches covered with shingle, i.e., coarse gravel or round stones. 29-37. **Ah, love . . . night**. Cf. *The Buried Life*, lines 79-98, p. 469.
Palladium. The Palladium was a statue of Pallas Athena, goddess of wisdom, which was supposed to have fallen from heaven when the city of Troy (Ilium, line 3) was being built, and upon which the safety of the city depended. The statue was stolen by the Greeks, and the city then fell.
1. **Simois**, one of the two rivers of Troy; the other was Xanthus (line 14). 3. **Hector**, son of King Priam of Troy and the city's greatest hero.

The Good Shepherd with the Kid. 2. **Tertullian**, one of the greatest of the early Church fathers (c. 155-220). 3. **Phrygian sect**, the Montanists, a religious sect founded by Montanus, a Phrygian enthusiast of the 2d century. They held very strict views of life and advocated complete segregation of Christians from the world. 9. **Catacombs**, underground tombs used as a place of burial and also of refuge by the early Christians in Rome.
Austerity of Poetry. 1. **son of Italy**, Giacopone di Todi, a poet of the 13th century. Upon the death of his bride, as related in the poem, he became a Franciscan monk.

Backward and forward rolled the waves of
   fight
Round Troy — but while this stood, Troy
   could not fall.

So, in its lovely moonlight, lives the soul.
Mountains surround it, and sweet virgin air;
Cold plashing, past it, crystal waters roll;   11
We visit it by moments, ah, too rare!

We shall renew the battle in the plain
Tomorrow; — red with blood will Xanthus be;
Hector and Ajax will be there again,   15
Helen will come upon the wall to see.

Then we shall rust in shade, or shine in strife,
And fluctuate 'twixt blind hopes and blind
   despairs,
And fancy that we put forth all our life,   19
And never know how with the soul it fares.

Still doth the soul, from its lone fastness high,
Upon our life a ruling effluence send.
And when it fails, fight as we will, we die;
And while it lasts, we cannot wholly end.
                            (1867)

YOUTH AND CALM

'Tis death! and peace, indeed, is here,
And ease from shame, and rest from fear.
There's nothing can dismarble now
The smoothness of that limpid brow.
But is a calm like this, in truth,   5
The crowning end of life and youth,
And when this boon rewards the dead,
Are all debts paid, has all been said?
And is the heart of youth so light,
Its step so firm, its eyes so bright,   10
Because on its hot brow there blows
A wind of promise and repose
From the far grave, to which it goes;
Because it hath the hope to come,
One day, to harbor in the tomb?   15
Ah no, the bliss youth dreams is one
For daylight, for the cheerful sun,
For feeling nerves and living breath —
Youth dreams a bliss on this side death.
It dreams a rest, if not more deep,   20
More grateful than this marble sleep;
It hears a voice within it tell:
Calm's not life's crown, though calm is well.
'Tis all perhaps which man acquires,
But 'tis not what our youth desires.   25
                            (1867)

GROWING OLD

What is it to grow old?
Is it to lose the glory of the form,
The luster of the eye?
Is it for beauty to forego her wreath?
—Yes, but not this alone.   5

Is it to feel our strength —
Not our bloom only, but our strength —
   decay?
Is it to feel each limb
Grow stiffer, every function less exact,
Each nerve more loosely strung?   10

Yes, this, and more; but not,
Ah, 'tis not what in youth we dreamed
   'twould be!
'Tis not to have our life
Mellowed and softened as with sunset-glow,
A golden day's decline.   15

'Tis not to see the world
As from a height, with rapt prophetic eyes,
And heart profoundly stirred;
And weep, and feel the fullness of the past,
The years that are no more.   20

It is to spend long days
And not once feel that we were ever young;
It is to add, immured
In the hot prison of the present, month
To month with weary pain.   25

It is to suffer this,
And feel but half, and feebly, what we feel.
Deep in our hidden heart
Festers the dull remembrance of a change,
But no emotion — none.   30

It is — last stage of all —
When we are frozen up within, and quite
The phantom of ourselves,
To hear the world applaud the hollow ghost
Which blamed the living man.   35
                            (1867)

THE PROGRESS OF POESY

A VARIATION

Youth rambles on life's arid mount,
And strikes the rock, and finds the vein,
And brings the water from the fount,
The fount which shall not flow again.

---

15. **Ajax,** a famous Greek hero. 16. **Helen,** wife of
Menelaus, king of Sparta. She was carried off by Paris,
brother of Hector, and thus became the cause of the Trojan
War.

Growing Old. Cf. Browning's *Rabbi Ben Ezra*, p. 302.
The Progress of Poesy. 2. **strikes the rock,** a reference
to Moses, who secured water for the Israelites by smiting a
rock on Mt. Horeb. (See *Exodus*, 17:1-6.)

The man mature with labor chops   5
For the bright stream a channel grand,
And sees not that the sacred drops
Ran off and vanished out of hand.

And then the old man totters nigh,
And feebly rakes among the stones.   10
The mount is mute, the channel dry;
And down he lays his weary bones.   (1867)

PERSISTENCY OF POETRY

Though the Muse be gone away,
Though she move not earth today,
Souls, erewhile who caught her word,
Ah! still harp on what they heard.   (1867)

A CAUTION TO POETS

What poets feel not, when they make,
  A pleasure in creating,
The world, in *its* turn, will not take
  Pleasure in contemplating.   (1867)

THE LAST WORD

Creep into thy narrow bed,
Creep, and let no more be said!
Vain thy onset! all stands fast.
Thou thyself must break at last.

Let the long contention cease!   5
Geese are swans, and swans are geese.
Let them have it how they will!
Thou art tired; best be still.

They out-talked thee, hissed thee, tore thee?
Better men fared thus before thee;   10
Fired their ringing shot and passed,
Hotly charged — and sank at last.

Charge once more, then, and be dumb!
Let the victors, when they come,
When the forts of folly fall,   15
Find thy body by the wall!   (1867)

PIS-ALLER

"Man is blind because of sin;
Revelation makes him sure.
Without that, who looks within,
Looks in vain, for all's obscure."

The Last Word. **16. body ... wall,** where it fell in attacking the forts of folly.
Pis-Aller. The title means *A Last Resource.*

Nay, look closer into man!   5
Tell me, can you find indeed
Nothing sure, no moral plan
Clear prescribed, without your creed?

"No, I nothing can perceive!
Without that, all's dark for men.   10
That, or nothing, I believe." —
For God's sake, believe it then!   (1867)

A WISH

I ask not that my bed of death
From bands of greedy heirs be free;
For these besiege the latest breath
Of fortune's favored sons, not me.

I ask not each kind soul to keep   5
Tearless, when of my death he hears.
Let those who will, if any, weep!
There are worse plagues on earth than tears.

I ask but that my death may find
The freedom to my life denied;   10
Ask but the folly of mankind
Then, then at last, to quit my side.

Spare me the whispering, crowded room,
The friends who come, and gape, and go;
The ceremonious air of gloom —   15
All which makes death a hideous show!

Nor bring, to see me cease to live,
Some doctor full of phrase and fame,
To shake his sapient head, and give
The ill he cannot cure a name.   20

Nor fetch, to take the accustomed toll
Of the poor sinner bound for death,
His brother-doctor of the soul,
To canvass with official breath

The future and its viewless things —   25
That undiscovered mystery
Which one who feels death's winnowing wings
Must needs read clearer, sure, than he!

Bring none of these; but let me be,
While all around in silence lies,   30
Moved to the window near, and see
Once more, before my dying eyes,

Bathed in the sacred dews of morn
The wide aerial landscape spread —
The world which was ere I was born,   35
The world which lasts when I am dead;

Which never was the friend of *one*,
Nor promised love it could not give,
But lit for all its generous sun,
And lived itself, and made us live.   40

There let me gaze, till I become
In soul, with what I gaze on, wed!
To feel the universe my home;
To have before my mind — instead

Of the sick room, the mortal strife,   45
The turmoil for a little breath —
The pure eternal course of life,
Not human combatings with death!

Thus feeling, gazing, might I grow
Composed, refreshed, ennobled, clear;   50
Then willing let my spirit go
To work or wait elsewhere or here!   (1867)

BACCHANALIA;

OR, THE NEW AGE

I

The evening comes, the fields are still.
The tinkle of the thirsty rill,
Unheard all day, ascends again;
Deserted is the half-mown plain,
Silent the swaths! the ringing wain,   5
The mower's cry, the dog's alarms,
All housed within the sleeping farms!
The business of the day is done,
The last-left haymaker is gone.
And from the thyme upon the height,   10
And from the elder-blossom white
And pale dog-roses in the hedge,
And from the mint-plant in the sedge,
In puffs of balm the night-air blows
The perfume which the day forgoes.   15
And on the pure horizon far,
See, pulsing with the first-born star,
The liquid sky above the hill!
The evening comes, the fields are still.
Loitering and leaping,   20
With saunter, with bounds —
Flickering and circling
In files and in rounds —
Gayly their pine-staff green
Tossing in air,   25
Loose o'er their shoulders white
Showering their hair —
See! the wild Mænads
Break from the wood,
Youth and Iacchus   30
Maddening their blood.
See! through the quiet land
Rioting they pass —
Fling the fresh heaps about,
Trample the grass,   35

Tear from the rifled hedge
Garlands, their prize;
Fill with their sports the field,
Fill with their cries.

Shepherd, what ails thee, then?   40
Shepherd, why mute?
Forth with thy joyous song!
Forth with thy flute!
Tempts not the revel blithe?
Lure not their cries?   45
Glow not their shoulders smooth?
Melt not their eyes?
Is not, on cheeks like those,
Lovely the flush?
—*Ah, so the quiet was!*   50
So was the hush!

2

The epoch ends, the world is still.
The age has talked and worked its fill —
The famous orators have shone,
The famous poets sung and gone,   55
The famous men of war have fought,
The famous speculators thought,
The famous players, sculptors, wrought.
The famous painters filled their wall,
The famous critics judged it all.   60
The combatants are parted now —
Uphung the spear, unbent the bow,
The puissant crowned, the weak laid low.
And in the after-silence sweet,
Now strifes are hushed, our ears doth meet,
Ascending pure, the bell-like fame   66
Of this or that down-trodden name,
Delicate spirits, pushed away
In the hot press of the noon-day.
And o'er the plain, where the dead age   70
Did its now silent warfare wage —
O'er that wide plain, now wrapped in gloom,
Where many a splendor finds its tomb,
Many spent fames and fallen mights —
The one or two immortal lights   75
Rise slowly up into the sky
To shine there everlastingly,
Like stars over the bounding hill.
The epoch ends, the world is still.

Thundering and bursting   80
In torrents, in waves —
Caroling and shouting
Over tombs, amid graves —
See! on the cumbered plain
Clearing a stage,   85
Scattering the past about,
Comes the new age.
Bards make new poems,
Thinkers new schools,

Bacchanalia. The title indicates a festival or revelry of Bacchus, god of wine.
5. **ringing wain**, wagon with bells. 28. **Mænads**, priestesses of Bacchus.   The name is derived from a Greek word meaning *to be frenzied.* 30. **Iacchus**, another name for Bacchus.

78. **bounding hill**, hill that bounds or marks the horizon.

Statesmen new systems, 90
Critics new rules.
All things begin again;
Life is their prize;
Earth with their deeds they fill,
Fill with their cries. 95

Poet, what ails thee, then?
Say, why so mute?
Forth with thy praising voice!
Forth with thy flute!
Loiterer! why sittest thou 100
Sunk in thy dream?
Tempts not the bright new age?
Shines not its stream?
Look, ah, what genius,
Art, science, wit! 105
Soldiers like Cæsar,
Statesmen like Pitt!
Sculptors like Phidias,
Raphaels in shoals,
Poets like Shakespeare — 110
Beautiful souls!
See, on their glowing cheeks
Heavenly the flush!
—*Ah, so the silence was!*
So was the hush! 115

The world but feels the present's spell,
The poet feels the past as well;
Whatever men have done, might do,
Whatever thought, might think it too. (1867)

RUGBY CHAPEL
NOVEMBER, 1857

Coldly, sadly descends
The autumn evening. The field
Strewn with its dank yellow drifts
Of withered leaves, and the elms,
Fade into dimness apace, 5
Silent — hardly a shout
From a few boys late at their play!
The lights come out in the street,
In the schoolroom windows; — but cold,
Solemn, unlighted, austere, 10
Through the gathering darkness, arise
The chapel-walls, in whose bound
Thou, my father! art laid.

There thou dost lie, in the gloom
Of the autumn evening. But ah! 15
That word, *gloom*, to my mind
Brings thee back, in the light

107. **Pitt**, William Pitt (1708-78), a famous British
statesman. 108. **Phidias**, the greatest of Athenian sculptors (4th century B.C.) 109. **Raphael** (1483-1520), one of
the greatest of the Italian painters.
  Rugby Chapel. This poem was written in memory of the
poet's father, Dr. Thomas Arnold, the famous headmaster of
Rugby School. He died suddenly in June, 1842, and was
buried in the College Chapel.

Of thy radiant vigor, again;
In the gloom of November we passed
Days not dark at thy side; 20
Seasons impaired not the ray
Of thy buoyant cheerfulness clear.
Such thou wast! and I stand
In the autumn evening, and think
Of by-gone autumns with thee. 25

Fifteen years have gone round
Since thou arosest to tread,
In the summer-morning, the road
Of death, at a call unforeseen,
Sudden. For fifteen years, 30
We who till then in thy shade
Rested as under the boughs
Of a mighty oak, have endured
Sunshine and rain as we might,
Bare, unshaded, alone, 35
Lacking the shelter of thee.

O strong soul, by what shore
Tarriest thou now? For that force,
Surely, has not been left vain!
Somewhere, surely, afar, 40
In the sounding labor-house vast
Of being, is practiced that strength,
Zealous, beneficent, firm!

Yes, in some far-shining sphere,
Conscious or not of the past, 45
Still thou performest the word
Of the Spirit in whom thou dost live —
Prompt, unwearied, as here!
Still thou upraisest with zeal
The humble good from the ground, 50
Sternly repressest the bad!
Still, like a trumpet, dost rouse
Those who with half-open eyes
Tread the border-land dim
'Twixt vice and virtue; reviv'st, 55
Succorest! — this was thy work,
This was thy life upon earth.

What is the course of the life
Of mortal men on the earth? —
Most men eddy about 60
Here and there — eat and drink,
Chatter and love and hate,
Gather and squander, are raised
Aloft, are hurled in the dust,
Striving blindly, achieving 65
Nothing; and then they die —
Perish; — and no one asks
Who or what they have been,
More than he asks what waves,
In the moonlit solitudes mild 70
Of the midmost Ocean, have swelled,
Foamed for a moment, and gone.

And there are some, whom a thirst
Ardent, unquenchable, fires,
Not with the crowd to be spent,   75
Not without aim to go round
In an eddy of purposeless dust,
Effort unmeaning and vain.
Ah, yes! some of us strive
Not without action to die   80
Fruitless, but something to snatch
From dull oblivion, nor all
Glut the devouring grave!
We, we have chosen our path —
Path to a clear-purposed goal,   85
Path of advance! — but it leads
A long, steep journey, through sunk
Gorges, o'er mountains in snow.
Cheerful, with friends, we set forth —
Then, on the height, comes the storm.   90
Thunder crashes from rock
To rock, the cataracts reply,
Lightnings dazzle our eyes.
Roaring torrents have breached
The track, the stream-bed descends   95
In the place where the wayfarer once
Planted his footstep — the spray
Boils o'er its borders! aloft
The unseen snow-beds dislodge
Their hanging ruin; alas,   100
Havoc is made in our train!
Friends, who set forth at our side,
Falter, are lost in the storm.
We, we only are left!
With frowning foreheads, with lips   105
Sternly compressed, we strain on,
On — and at nightfall at last
Come to the end of our way,
To the lonely inn 'mid the rocks;
Where the gaunt and taciturn host   110
Stands on the threshold, the wind
Shaking his thin white hairs —
Holds his lantern to scan
Our storm-beat figures, and asks:
Whom in our party we bring?   115
Whom we have left in the snow?

Sadly we answer: We bring
Only ourselves! we lost
Sight of the rest in the storm.
Hardly ourselves we fought through,   120
Stripped, without friends, as we are.
Friends, companions, and train,
The avalanche swept from our side.

But thou would'st not *alone*
Be saved, my father! *alone*   125
Conquer and come to thy goal,
Leaving the rest in the wild.
We were weary, and we

Fearful, and we in our march
Fain to drop down and to die.   130
Still thou turnedst, and still
Beckonedst the trembler, and still
Gavest the weary thy hand.

If, in the paths of the world,
Stones might have wounded thy feet,   135
Toil or dejection have tried
Thy spirit, of that we saw
Nothing — to us thou wast still
Cheerful, and helpful, and firm!
Therefore to thee it was given   140
Many to save with thyself;
And, at the end of thy day,
O faithful shepherd! to come,
Bringing thy sheep in thy hand.
And through thee I believe   145
In the noble and great who are gone;
Pure souls honored and blessed
By former ages, who else —
Such, so soulless, so poor,
Is the race of men whom I see —   150
Seemed but a dream of the heart,
Seemed but a cry of desire.
Yes! I believe that there lived
Others like thee in the past,
Not like the men of the crowd   155
Who all round me today
Bluster or cringe, and make life
Hideous, and arid, and vile;
But souls tempered with fire,
Fervent, heroic, and good,   160
Helpers and friends of mankind.

Servants of God! — or sons
Shall I not call you? because
Not as servants ye knew .
Your Father's innermost mind,   165
His, who unwillingly sees
One of his little ones lost —
Yours is the praise, if mankind
Hath not as yet in its march
Fainted, and fallen, and died!   170

See! In the rocks of the world
Marches the host of mankind,
A feeble, wavering line.
Where are they tending? — A God
Marshaled them, gave them their goal.   175
Ah, but the way is so long!
Years they have been in the wild!
Sore thirst plagues them, the rocks,
Rising all round, overawe;
Factions divide them, their host   180
Threatens to break, to dissolve.

79-84. Cf. Horace, *Odes*, III, 30: "I shall not all die; and of me many a portion shall unharmed flee from Libitina." 110. **host,** probably Time, or Death.

148. **who else,** etc., who, but for what I have known of thee, would have seemed a dream. 162. **Servants ... sons.** Cf. *John*, 1:12.—"But as many as received him, to them gave he power to become the sons of God."

— Ah, keep, keep them combined!
Else, of the myriads who fill
That army, not one shall arrive;
Sole they shall stray; in the rocks   185
Stagger forever in vain,
Die one by one in the waste.

Then, in such hour of need
Of your fainting, dispirited race,
Ye, like angels, appear,   190
Radiant with ardor divine!
Beacons of hope, ye appear!
Languor is not in your heart,
Weakness is not in your word,
Weariness not on your brow.   195
Ye alight in our van! at your voice,
Panic, despair, flee away.
Ye move through the ranks, recall
The stragglers, refresh the outworn,
Praise, re-inspire the brave!   200
Order, courage, return.
Eyes rekindling, and prayers,
Follow your steps as ye go.
Ye fill up the gaps in our files,
Strengthen the wavering line,   205
Stablish, continue our march,
On, to the bound of the waste,
On, to the City of God.   (1867)

CHARLES TENNYSON TURNER
(1808-1879)

THE STEAM THRESHING-MACHINE

WITH THE STRAW-CARRIER

Flush with the pond the lurid furnace burned
At eve, while smoke and vapor filled the yard;
The gloomy winter sky was dimly starred,
The fly-wheel with a mellow murmur turned;
While, ever rising on its mystic stair   5
In the dim light, from secret chambers borne,
The straw of harvest, severed from the corn,
Climbed, and fell over, in the murky air.
I thought of mind and matter, will and law,
And then of him, who set his stately seal   10
Of Roman words on all the forms he saw
Of old-world husbandry; *I* could but feel
With what a rich precision *he* would draw
The endless ladder, and the booming wheel!

190. **Ye,** the servants of God of line 162.
The Steam Threshing-Machine. 7. **corn,** wheat. 10-12. **him
. . . husbandry,** Virgil (70-19 B.C.), whose *Georgics,* devoted to
rural life, contains descriptions of farm implements. Cf. the
picture of the plow in *Georgics,* 1, 166 ff.

Did any seer of ancient time forebode
This mighty engine, which we daily see
Accepting our full harvests, like a god,
With clouds about his shoulders — it might be
Some poet-husbandman, some lord of verse, 5
Old Hesiod, or the wizard Mantuan,
Who catalogued in rich hexameters
The rake, the roller, and the mystic van;
Or else some priest of Ceres, it might seem,
Who witnessed, as he trod the silent fane, 10
The notes and auguries of coming change,
Of other ministrants in shrine and grange —
The sweating statue, and her sacred wain
Low-booming with the prophecy of steam!
                                            (1868)

DANTE GABRIEL ROSSETTI
(1828-1882)

THE BLESSED DAMOZEL

The blessed damozel leaned out
    From the gold bar of heaven;
Her eyes were deeper than the depth
    Of waters stilled at even;
She had three lilies in her hand,   5
    And the stars in her hair were seven.

Her robe, ungirt from clasp to hem,
    No wrought flowers did adorn,
But a white rose of Mary's gift,
    For service meetly worn;   10
Her hair that lay along her back
    Was yellow like ripe corn.

Herseemed she scarce had been a day
    One of God's choristers;
The wonder was not yet quite gone   15
    From that still look of hers;
Albeit, to them she left, her day
    Had counted as ten years.

Continued. 6. **Hesiod** (8th century B.C.), the father of
Greek didactic poetry. He drew many faithful pictures of
the life of his period. **Mantuan,** Virgil, who was born in the
city of Mantua. 8. **van,** a fan or other winnowing device.
The implements mentioned in this line were all sacred to
Ceres, Italian goddess of agriculture. 13. **sweating statue.**
Drops of water that sometimes appeared on the statues of
the gods were interpreted as foretelling disaster. **wain,**
wagon, chariot; it was drawn by serpents.
The Blessed Damozel. The theme of this poem was suggested by Poe's *The Raven,* published in 1845. "I saw,"
Rossetti said, "that Poe had done the utmost it was possible
to do with the grief of the lover on earth, and I determined to
reverse the conditions, and give utterance to the yearning of
the loved one in heaven." See Critical Notes.
    10. **For . . . worn,** fittingly worn in the service of the Virgin
Mary. 13. **Herseemed,** it seemed to her.

(To *one* it is ten years of years.
   . . . Yet now, and in this place,   20
Surely she leaned o'er me—her hair
   Fell all about my face. . . .
Nothing: the autumn fall of leaves.
   The whole year sets apace.)

It was the rampart of God's house   25
   That she was standing on;
By God built over the sheer depth
   The which is Space begun;
So high, that looking downward thence
   She scarce could see the sun.   30

It lies in heaven, across the flood
   Of ether, as a bridge.
Beneath the tides of day and night
   With flame and darkness ridge
The void, as low as where this earth   35
   Spins like a fretful midge.

Around her, lovers, newly met
   'Mid deathless love's acclaims,
Spoke evermore among themselves
   Their heart-remembered names;   40
And the souls mounting up to God
   Went by her like thin flames.

And still she bowed herself and stooped
   Out of the circling charm;
Until her bosom must have made   45
   The bar she leaned on warm,
And the lilies lay as if asleep
   Along her bended arm.

From the fixed place of heaven she saw
   Time like a pulse shake fierce   50
Through all the worlds. Her gaze still strove
   Within the gulf to pierce
Its path; and now she spoke as when
   The stars sang in their spheres.

The sun was gone now; the curled moon   55
   Was like a little feather
Fluttering far down the gulf; and now
   She spoke through the still weather.
Her voice was like the voice the stars
   Had when they sang together.   60

(Ah, sweet! Even now, in that bird's song,
   Strove not her accents there,
Fain to be harkened? When those bells
   Possessed the mid-day air,
Strove not her steps to reach my side   65
   Down all the echoing stair?)

"I wish that he were come to me,
   For he will come," she said.
"Have I not prayed in heaven?—on earth,
   Lord, Lord, has he not prayed?   70
Are not two prayers a perfect strength?
   And shall I feel afraid?

"When round his head the aureole clings,
   And he is clothed in white,
I'll take his hand and go with him   75
   To the deep wells of light;
As unto a stream we will step down,
   And bathe there in God's sight.

"We two will stand beside that shrine,
   Occult, withheld, untrod,   80
Whose lamps are stirred continually
   With prayers sent up to God;
And see our old prayers, granted, melt
   Each like a little cloud.

"We two will lie i' the shadow of   85
   That living mystic tree
Within whose secret growth the Dove
   Is sometimes felt to be,
While every leaf that His plumes touch
   Saith His Name audibly.   90

"And I myself will teach to him,
   I myself, lying so,
The songs I sing here; which his voice
   Shall pause in, hushed and slow,
And find some knowledge at each pause,   95
   Or some new thing to know."

(Alas! We two, we two, thou say'st!
   Yea, one wast thou with me
That once of old. But shall God lift
   To endless unity   100
The soul whose likeness with thy soul
   Was but its love for thee?)

"We two," she said, "will seek the groves
   Where the lady Mary is,
With her five handmaidens, whose names   105
   Are five sweet symphonies,
Cecily, Gertrude, Magdalen,
   Margaret, and Rosalys.

"Circlewise sit they, with bound locks
   And foreheads garlanded;   110

86. **living . . . tree**, the tree of life (see *Revelation*, 22:2).
87. **Dove**, a symbol of the Holy Spirit, the third member of the Trinity. 107–108. **Cicily . . . Rosalys.** These are names of famous Christian saints. St. Cecilia (3d century) is the patron saint of the blind and of musicians. (See Chaucer's *Second Nun's Tale* and odes in her honor by Dryden and Pope.) St. Gertrude (7th century) is the patron saint of travelers. St. Mary Magdalene is the patron saint of penitents (see *Mary Magdalene*, p. 524). St. Margaret is the chosen type of female innocence and meekness. St. Rosalie (12th century) is the patron saint of the city of Palermo, Sicily.

36. **midge,** a kind of small gnat or fly. 54. **stars . . . spheres.** These words are taken from *Job*, 38:4–7.— "Where wast thou . . . When the morning stars sang together, and all the sons of God shouted for joy?" The ancients believed that the stars made music as they revolved in their spheres.

Into the fine cloth white like flame
  Weaving the golden thread,
To fashion the birth-robes for them
  Who are just born, being dead.

"He shall fear, haply, and be dumb; 115
  Then will I lay my cheek
To his, and tell about our love,
  Not once abashed or weak;
And the dear Mother will approve
  My pride, and let me speak. 120

"Herself shall bring us, hand in hand,
  To Him round whom all souls
Kneel, the clear-ranged unnumbered heads
  Bowed with their aureoles;
And angels meeting us shall sing 125
  To their citherns and citoles.

"There will I ask of Christ the Lord
  Thus much for him and me—
Only to live as once on earth
  With Love, only to be, 130
As then awhile, forever now,
  Together, I and he."

She gazed and listened and then said,
  Less sad of speech than mild—
"All this is when he comes." She ceased. 135
  The light thrilled toward her, filled
With angels in strong, level flight.
  Her eyes prayed, and she smiled.

(I saw her smile.) But soon their path
  Was vague in distant spheres; 140
And then she cast her arms along
  The golden barriers,
And laid her face between her hands,
  And wept. (I heard her tears.)

Ideal world is actually here (1847; 1850, 1856, 1870)

MY SISTER'S SLEEP

She fell asleep on Christmas Eve;
  At length the long-ungranted shade
Of weary eyelids overweighed
The pain naught else might yet relieve.

Our mother, who had leaned all day 5
  Over the bed from chime to chime,
  Then raised herself for the first time,
And as she sat her down, did pray.

Her little work-table was spread
  With work to finish. For the glare, 10

126. **citherns and citoles**, medieval stringed musical instruments.
My Sister's Sleep. This is an imaginative poem without basis of fact in Rossetti's life.

Made by her candle, she had care
To work some distance from the bed.

Without, there was a cold moon up,
  Of winter radiance sheer and thin;
  The hollow halo it was in 15
Was like an icy crystal cup.

Through the small room, with subtle sound
  Of flame, by vents the fireshine drove
  And reddened. In its dim alcove
The mirror shed a clearness round. 20

I had been sitting up some nights,
  And my tired mind felt weak and blank;
  Like a sharp strengthening wine it drank
The stillness and the broken lights.

Twelve struck. That sound, by dwindling
    years 25
  Heard in each hour, crept off; and then
  The ruffled silence spread again,
Like water that a pebble stirs.

Our mother rose from where she sat;
  Her needles, as she laid them down, 30
  Met lightly, and her silken gown
Settled—no other noise than that.

"Glory unto the Newly Born!"
  So, as said angels, she did say;
  Because we were in Christmas Day, 35
Though it would still be long till morn.

Just then in the room over us
  There was a pushing back of chairs,
  As some who had sat unawares
So late, now heard the hour, and rose. 40

With anxious, softly-stepping haste
  Our mother went where Margaret lay,
  Fearing the sounds o'erhead—should they
Have broken her long watched-for rest!

She stooped an instant, calm, and turned, 45
  But suddenly turned back again;
  And all her features seemed in pain
With woe, and her eyes gazed and yearned.

For my part, I but hid my face,
  And held my breath, and spoke no word. 50
  There was none spoken; but I heard
The silence for a little space.

Our mother bowed herself and wept;
  And both my arms fell, and I said,
  "God knows I knew that she was dead." 55
And there, all white, my sister slept.

25. **dwindling years**, old persons.

Then kneeling, upon Christmas morn
  A little after twelve o'clock
We said, ere the first quarter struck,
"Christ's blessing on the newly born!"   60
                 (*1847;* 1850)

THE PORTRAIT

This is her picture as she was;
  It seems a thing to wonder on,
As though mine image in the glass
  Should tarry when myself am gone.
I gaze until she seems to stir,   5
Until mine eyes almost aver
  That now, even now, the sweet lips part
  To breathe the words of the sweet heart—
And yet the earth is over her.

Alas! even such the thin-drawn ray   10
  That makes the prison-depths more rude—
The drip of water night and day
  Giving a tongue to solitude.
Yet only this, of love's whole prize,
Remains; save what in mournful guise   15
  Takes counsel with my soul alone—
  Save what is secret and unknown,
Below the earth, above the skies.

In painting her I shrined her face
  'Mid mystic trees, where light falls in   20
Hardly at all; a covert place
  Where you might think to find a din
Of doubtful talk, and a live flame
Wandering, and many a shape whose name
  Not itself knoweth, and old dew,   25
  And your own footsteps meeting you,
And all things going as they came.

A deep dim wood; and there she stands
  As in that wood that day—for so
Was the still movement of her hands   30
  And such the pure line's gracious flow.
And passing fair the type must seem,
Unknown the presence and the dream.
  'Tis she—though of herself, alas!
  Less than her shadow on the grass   35
Or than her image in the stream.

That day we met there, I and she
  One with the other all alone;
And we were blithe; yet memory
  Saddens those hours, as when the moon   40
Looks upon daylight. And with her
I stooped to drink the spring-water,
  Athirst where other waters sprang;
  And where the echo is, she sang—
My soul another echo there.   45

The Portrait. The subject of the portrait is imaginary.

But when that hour my soul won strength
  For words whose silence wastes and kills,
Dull raindrops smote us, and at length
  Thundered the heat within the hills.
That eve I spoke those words again   50
Beside the pelted window-pane;
  And there she harkened what I said,
  With under-glances that surveyed
The empty pastures blind with rain.

Next day the memories of these things,   55
  Like leaves through which a bird has flown,
Still vibrated with Love's warm wings;
  Till I must make them all my own
And paint this picture. So, 'twixt ease
Of talk and sweet, long silences,   60
  She stood among the plants in bloom
  At windows of a summer room,
To feign the shadow of the trees.

And as I wrought, while all above
  And all around was fragrant air,   65
In the sick burthen of my love
  It seemed each sun-thrilled blossom there
Beat like a heart among the leaves.
O heart that never beats nor heaves,
  In that one darkness lying still,   70
  What now to thee my love's great will,
Or the fine web the sunshine weaves?

For now doth daylight disavow
  Those days—naught left to see or hear.
Only in solemn whispers now   75
  At night-time these things reach mine ear,
When the leaf-shadows at a breath
Shrink in the road, and all the heath,
  Forest and water, far and wide,
  In limpid starlight glorified,   80
Lie like the mystery of death.

Last night at last I could have slept,
  And yet delayed my sleep till dawn,
Still wandering. Then it was I wept;
  For unawares I came upon   85
Those glades where once she walked with me;
And as I stood there suddenly,
  All wan with traversing the night,
  Upon the desolate verge of light
Yearned loud the iron-bosomed sea.   90

Even so, where Heaven holds breath and
    hears
  The beating heart of Love's own breast—
Where round the secret of all spheres
  All angels lay their wings to rest—
How shall my soul stand rapt and awed,   95
When, by the new birth borne abroad
  Throughout the music of the suns,
  It enters in her soul at once
And knows the silence there for God!

Here with her face doth memory sit   100
  Meanwhile, and wait the day's decline,
Till other eyes shall look from it,
  Eyes of the spirit's Palestine,
Even than the old gaze tenderer;
While hopes and aims long lost with her   105
  Stand round her image side by side,
  Like tombs of pilgrims that have died
About the Holy Sepulcher.   (*1847; 1870*)

AT THE SUNRISE IN 1848

God said, Let there be light! and there was
    light.
Then heard we sounds as though the Earth
    did sing
And the Earth's angel cried upon the wing;
We saw priests fall together and turn white;
And covered in the dust from the sun's sight,
A king was spied, and yet another king.   6
We said: "The round world keeps its bal-
    ancing;
On this globe, they and we are opposite—
If it is day with us, with them 'tis night.
Still, Man, in thy just pride, remember this:
Thou hadst not made that thy sons' sons
    shall ask   11
What the word *king* may mean in their day's
    task,
But for the light that led; and if light is,
It is because God said, Let there be light."
    (*1848; 1886*)

ON REFUSAL OF AID BETWEEN NATIONS

Not that the earth is changing, O my God!
Nor that the seasons totter in their walk—
Not that the virulent ill of act and talk
Seethes ever as a winepress ever trod—
Not therefore are we certain that the rod   5
Weighs in thine hand to smite thy world;
    though now
Beneath thine hand so many nations bow,
So many kings—not therefore, O my God!—
But because Man is parceled out in men
Today; because, for any wrongful blow,   10
No man not stricken asks, "I would be told
Why thou dost thus"; but his heart whispers
    then,
"He is he, I am I." By this we know
That the earth falls asunder, being old.
    (*1848; 1870*)

MARY'S GIRLHOOD
(*For a Picture*)

I

This is that blessed Mary, pre-elect
God's Virgin. Gone is a great while, and she
Dwelt young in Nazareth of Galilee.
Unto God's will she brought devout respect,
Profound simplicity of intellect,   5
And supreme patience. From her mother's
    knee
Faithful and hopeful; wise in charity;
Strong in grave peace; in pity circumspect.
So held she through her girlhood; as it were
An angel-watered lily, that near God   10
Grows and is quiet. Till, one dawn at home
She woke in her white bed, and had no fear
At all—yet wept till sunshine, and felt awed,
Because the fullness of the time was come.

2

These are the symbols. On that cloth of red
I' the center is the Tripoint; perfect each,
Except the second of its points, to teach
That Christ is not yet born. The books—
    whose head
Is golden Charity, as Paul hath said—   5
Those virtues are wherein the soul is rich;
Therefore on them the lily standeth, which
Is Innocence, being interpreted.
The seven-thorned briar and the palm seven-
    leaved
Are her great sorrow and her great reward.   10
Until the end be full, the Holy One
Abides without. She soon shall have achieved
Her perfect purity; yea, God the Lord
Shall soon vouchsafe His Son to be her Son.
    (*1848; 1849*)

FOR A VENETIAN PASTORAL
BY GIORGIONE
(*In the Louvre*)

Water, for anguish of the solstice—nay,
But dip the vessel, slowly—nay, but lean
And hark how at its verge the wave sighs in,

At the Sunrise in 1848. The poem refers to the European revolutions of 1848. Cf. Mrs. Browning's *Casa Guidi Windows*, p. 395.
  1. **God ... light.** Quoted from *Genesis*, 1:3.
On Refusal of Aid between Nations. This poem refers to the indifference of other nations to the struggles of Italy and Hungary against the tyranny of Austria in the mid 1800's.

Mary's Girlhood. These two sonnets were written for Rossetti's first exhibited picture, painted in 1848.
  Sonnet 2. 1. **symbols.** The symbols mentioned are in the picture. 2. **the Tripoint,** a triangle symbolizing God the Father, God the Son, and God the Holy Ghost. 5. **Paul hath said,** in *I Corinthians*, 13:13.—"And now abideth faith, hope, charity, these three; but the greatest of these is charity." 10. **sorrow ... reward.** For the seven sorrows of Mary, see note on Browning's *Up at a Villa—Down in the City*, 52, p. 233. The seven joys are as follows: the annunciation of the angel Gabriel (*Luke*, 1:26-38); the visitation (*Luke*, 1:39-56); the Nativity (*Luke*, 2:6-7); the adoration of the Magi (*Matthew*, 2:1-12); the presentation in the Temple (*Luke*, 2:22-33); the finding of the lost child (*Luke*, 2:41-51); and the assumption (*Luke*, 24:50-53).
For a Venetian Pastoral. This sonnet was written for a picture in which two cavaliers and a nude woman are seated

Reluctant. Hush! Beyond all depth away
The heat lies silent at the brink of day;   5
Now the hand trails upon the viol-string
That sobs, and the brown faces cease to sing,
Sad with the whole of pleasure. Whither stray
Her eyes now, from whose mouth the slim
    pipes creep
And leave it pouting, while the shadowed
    grass   10
Is cool against her naked side? Let be—
Say nothing now unto her lest she weep—
Nor name this ever. Be it as it was—
Life touching lips with Immortality.   (1850)

THE CARD-DEALER

Could you not drink her gaze like wine?
    Yet though its splendor swoon
Into the silence languidly
    As a tune into a tune,
Those eyes unravel the coiled night   5
    And know the stars at noon.

The gold that's heaped beside her hand,
    In truth rich prize it were;
And rich the dreams that wreathe her brows
    With magic stillness there;   10
And he were rich who should unwind
    That woven golden hair.

Around her, where she sits, the dance
    Now breathes its eager heat;
And not more lightly or more true   15
    Fall there the dancers' feet
Than fall her cards on the bright board
    As 'twere an heart that beat.

Her fingers let them softly through,
    Smooth polished silent things;   20
And each one as it falls reflects
    In swift light-shadowings,
Blood-red and purple, green and blue,
    The great eyes of her rings.

Whom plays she with? With thee, who lov'st
    Those gems upon her hand;   26
With me, who search her secret brows;
    With all men, blessed or banned.
We play together, she and we,
    Within a vain strange land: 30

A land without any order—
    Day even as night (one saith)—
Where who lieth down ariseth not

Nor the sleeper awakeneth;
A land of darkness as darkness itself   35
    And of the shadow of death.

What be her cards, you ask? Even these:
    The heart, that doth but crave
More, having fed; the diamond,
    Skilled to make base seem brave;   40
The club, for smiting in the dark;
    The spade, to dig a grave.

And do you ask what game she plays?
    With me 'tis lost or won;
With thee it is playing still; with him   45
    It is not well begun;
But 'tis a game she plays with all
    Beneath the sway o' the sun.

Thou seest the card that falls, she knows
    The card that followeth;   50
Her game in thy tongue is called Life,
    As ebbs thy daily breath.
When she shall speak, thou'lt learn her tongue
    And know she calls it Death.   (*1849;* 1870)

ON THE "VITA NUOVA" OF DANTE

As he that loves oft looks on the dear form
And guesses how it grew to womanhood,
And gladly would have watched the beauties
    bud
And the mild fire of precious life wax warm—
So I, long bound within the threefold charm 5
Of Dante's love sublimed to heavenly mood,
Had marveled, touching his Beatitude,
How grew such presence from man's shameful
    swarm.
At length within this book I found portrayed
Newborn that Paradisal Love of his,   10
And simple like a child; with whose clear aid
I understood. To such a child as this,
Christ, charging well his chosen ones, forbade
Offense: "For lo! of such my kingdom is."
    (1870)

WORLD'S WORTH

'Tis of the Father Hilary.
    He strove, but could not pray; so took
    The steep-coiled stair, where his feet shook
A sad blind echo. Ever up

on the grass, with musical instruments, while another woman
dips a vase into a well for water. The picture was painted by
Giorgione da Castelfranco (1478?-1511), a Venetian artist. .
    1. **anguish of the solstice,** parching by summer heat.
  The Card-dealer. 31-36. The lines echo *Job,* 10:22.—"A
land of darkness, as darkness itself: and of the shadow of death,
without any order, and where the light is as darkness."

On the "Vita Nuova" of Dante. The *Vita Nuova* (*New Life*)
is an early lyrical sequence with prose commentary presenting the story of Dante's love life.
  5. **threefold charm,** a reference to the three parts of *The
Divine Comedy—Inferno, Purgatory,* and *Paradise.* 6. **sublimed,** raised to a sublime plane. 7. **Beatitude,** Dante's
blessed state, which came as a result of *The Divine Comedy.*
14. **of such . . . is.** From *Mark,* 10:14.—". . . Suffer the little
children to come unto me, and forbid them not: for of such
is the kingdom of God."
  World's Worth. 1. **Father Hilary,** an early saint and
bishop of the fourth century.

He toiled. 'Twas a sick sway of air 5
That autumn noon within the stair,
As dizzy as a turning cup.
  His brain benumbed him, void and thin;
  He shut his eyes and felt it spin;
  The obscure deafness hemmed him in. 10
He said, "O world, what world for me?"

He leaned unto the balcony
  Where the chime keeps the night and day;
  It hurt his brain, he could not pray.
He had his face upon the stone; 15
  Deep 'twixt the narrow shafts, his eye
  Passed all the roofs to the stark sky,
Swept with no wing, with wind alone.
  Close to his feet the sky did shake
  With wind in pools that the rains make; 20
  The ripple set his eyes to ache.
He said, "O world, what world for me?"

He stood within the mystery
  Girding God's blessed Eucharist;
  The organ and the chant had ceased. 25
The last words paused against his ear
  Said from the altar; drawn round him
  The gathering rest was dumb and dim.
And now the sacring-bell rang clear
  And ceased; and all was awe—the breath
Of God in man that warranteth 31
  The inmost utmost things of faith.
He said, "O God, my world in Thee!" (1850)

THE SEA-LIMITS

Consider the sea's listless chime:
  Time's self it is, made audible—
  The murmur of the earth's own shell.
Secret continuance sublime
  Is the sea's end; our sight may pass 5
  No furlong further. Since time was,
This sound hath told the lapse of time.

No quiet, which is death's—it hath
  The mournfulness of ancient life,
  Enduring always at dull strife. 10
As the world's heart of rest and wrath,
  Its painful pulse is in the sands.
  Last utterly, the whole sky stands,
Gray and not known, along its path.

Listen alone beside the sea, 15
  Listen alone among the woods;
  Those voices of twin solitudes
Shall have one sound alike to thee.
  Hark where the murmurs of thronged men
  Surge and sink back and surge again— 20
Still the one voice of wave and tree.

Gather a shell from the strown beach
  And listen at its lips; they sigh
  The same desire and mystery,
The echo of the whole sea's speech. 25
  And all mankind is thus at heart
  Not anything but what thou art;
And Earth, Sea, Man, are all in each.
                  (*1849;* 1850)

—THE BURDEN OF NINEVEH

In our Museum galleries
Today I lingered o'er the prize
Dead Greece vouchsafes to living eyes—
Her Art forever in fresh wise
  From hour to hour rejoicing me. 5
Sighing I turned at last to win
Once more the London dirt and din;
And as I made the swing-door spin
And issued, they were hoisting in
  A wingéd beast from Nineveh. 10

A human face the creature wore,
And hoofs behind and hoofs before,
And flanks with dark runes fretted o'er.
'Twas bull, 'twas mitered Minotaur,
  A dead disboweled mystery; 15
The mummy of a buried faith
Stark from the charnel without scathe,
Its wings stood for the light to bathe—
Such fossil cerements as might swathe
  The very corpse of Nineveh. 20

The print of its first rush-wrapping,
Wound ere it dried, still ribbed the thing.
What song did the brown maidens sing,
From purple mouths alternating,
  When that was woven languidly? 25
What vows, what rites, what prayers preferred,
What songs has the strange image heard?
In what blind vigil stood interred
For ages, till an English word
  Broke silence first at Nineveh? 30

Oh, when upon each sculptured court,
Where even the wind might not resort—

---

24. **Eucharist,** the sacrament of the Lord's Supper. 29. **sacring-bell,** a bell rung at certain times during the Mass, or the Communion Service.

The Burden of Nineveh. The title is identical with the opening words of *Nahum.* Nineveh was the famous capital of the ancient Assyrian Empire. The city was destroyed by the Medes and the Chaldeans in 600 B.C. and during the centuries that followed was completely buried under drifting sands. In 1845-51 excavations on the site, under the direction of Sir Austen Layard (1817-94) of England, revealed ancient palaces, libraries, and sculptures, including colossal winged man-headed statues of bulls and lions. Rossetti got the suggestion for the poem while watching some of the sculptures being unpacked at the British Museum in London.
13. **runes,** ancient characters used in writing. They are called "dark" because their meaning is concealed. 14. **Minotaur,** a mythological monster slain by Theseus, a great hero of Athens. The beast was half man and half bull.

O'er which Time passed, of like import
With the wild Arab boys at sport —
 A living face looked in to see.— 35
Oh, seemed it not — the spell once broke —
As though the carven warriors woke,
As though the shaft the string forsook,
The cymbals clashed, the chariots shook,
 And there was life in Nineveh? 40

On London stones our sun anew
The beast's recovered shadow threw.
(No shade that plague of darkness knew,
No light, no shade, while older grew
 By ages the old earth and sea.) 45
Lo thou! could all thy priests have shown
Such proof to make thy godhead known?
From their dead Past thou liv'st alone;
And still thy shadow is thine own,
 Even as of yore in Nineveh. 50

That day whereof we keep record,
When near thy city-gates the Lord
Sheltered his Jonah with a gourd,
This sun (I said), here present, poured
 Even thus this shadow that I see. 55
This shadow has been shed the same
From sun and moon — from lamps which
  came
For prayer — from fifteen days of flame,
The last, while smoldered to a name
 Sardanapalus' Nineveh. 60

Within thy shadow, haply, once
Sennacherib has knelt, whose sons
Smote him between the altar-stones;
Or pale Semiramis her zones
 Of gold, her incense brought to thee, 65
In love for grace, in war for aid . . .
Aye, and who else? . . . till 'neath thy shade
Within his trenches newly made
Last year the Christian knelt and prayed —
 Not to thy strength — in Nineveh. 70

Now, thou poor god, within this hall
Where the blank windows blind the wall
From pedestal to pedestal,
The kind of light shall on thee fall
 Which London takes the day to be; 75

While school-foundations in the act
Of holiday, three files compact,
Shall learn to view thee as a fact
Connected with that zealous tract:
 "Rome — Babylon and Nineveh." 80

Deemed they of this, those worshipers,
When, in some mythic chain of verse
Which man shall not again rehearse,
The faces of thy ministers
 Yearned pale with bitter ecstasy? 85
Greece, Egypt, Rome — did any god
Before whose feet men knelt unshod
Deem that in this unblest abode
Another scarce more unknown god
 Should house with him, from Nineveh? 90

Ah! in what quarries lay the stone
From which this pygmy pile has grown,
Unto man's need how long unknown,
Since thy vast temples, court, and cone,
 Rose far in desert history? 95
Ah! what is here that does not lie
All strange to thine awakened eye?
Ah! what is here can testify
(Save that dumb presence of the sky)
 Unto thy day and Nineveh? 100

Why, of those mummies in the room
Above, there might indeed have come
One out of Egypt to thy home,
An alien. Nay, but were not some
 Of these thine own "antiquity"? 105
And now — they and their gods and thou
All relics here together — now
Whose profit? whether bull or cow,
Isis or Ibis, who or how,
 Whether of Thebes or Nineveh? 110

The consecrated metals found,
And ivory tablets, underground,
Winged teraphim and creatures crowned
When air and daylight filled the mound,
 Fell into dust immediately. 115
And even as these, the images
Of awe and worship — even as these —
So, smitten with the sun's increase,
Her glory moldered and did cease
 From immemorial Nineveh. 120

The day her builders made their halt,
Those cities of the lake of salt

53. Jonah . . . gourd. Angry because the repentant city of Nineveh was not to be destroyed by the Lord, Jonah "went out of the city and sat on the east side . . . And the Lord God prepared a gourd and made it to come up over Jonah that it might be a shadow over his head to deliver him from his grief" (*Jonah*, 4:5-6). **60. Sardanapalus,** the Greek name of the last great Assyrian king, Assurbanipal (8th century B.C.). According to tradition he burned his wives, his treasures, and himself to avoid capture by the enemy. **62. Sennacherib,** king of Assyria (705-681 B.C.); a great warrior and builder of Nineveh. His palace was discovered by the excavators of 1846-51. **64. Semiramis,** a famous queen of Assyria; according to legend, the half-divine wife and successor of Ninus, the founder of Nineveh, c. 2000 B.C. **69. Last year . . . prayed.** During the excavations the workmen conducted their worship in the shadow of the great bulls.

76. school-foundations, endowed schools. **109. Isis,** the chief Egyptian goddess, sometimes represented with the head of a cow. **Ibis,** the sacred ibis, a wading bird venerated by the Egyptians. **110. Thebes,** the ancient capital of Upper Egypt, on the Nile. **113. teraphim,** household idols. **122. cities . . . salt,** the ancient cities of Sodom and Gomorrah, situated in the plain of the Jordan River, which flowed into the Dead Sea (Salt Sea) southwest of Jerusalem. The cities were destroyed because of their wickedness. (See *Genesis*, 13:10-13; 19:1-29.)

Stood firmly 'stablished without fault,
Made proud with pillars of basalt,
   With sardonyx and porphyry.   125
The day that Jonah bore abroad
To Nineveh the voice of God,
A brackish lake lay in his road,
Where erst Pride fixed her sure abode,
   As then in royal Nineveh.   130

The day when he, Pride's lord and Man's,
Showed all the kingdoms at a glance
To Him before whose countenance
The years recede, the years advance,
   And said, Fall down and worship me — 135
'Mid all the pomp beneath that look,
Then stirred there, haply, some rebuke,
Where to the wind the salt pools shook,
And in those tracts, of life forsook,
   That knew thee not, O Nineveh!   140

Delicate harlot! On thy throne
Thou with a world beneath thee prone
In state for ages sat'st alone;
And needs were years and lusters flown
   Ere strength of man could vanquish thee, 145
Whom even thy victor foes must bring,
Still royal, among maids that sing
As with doves' voices, taboring
Upon their breasts, unto the King —
   A kingly conquest, Nineveh!   150

. . . Here woke my thought. The wind's
   slow sway
Had waxed; and like the human play
Of scorn that smiling spreads away,
The sunshine shivered off the day;
   The callous wind, it seemed to me,   155
Swept up the shadow from the ground;
And pale as whom the Fates astound,
The god forlorn stood winged and crowned;
Within I knew the cry lay bound
   Of the dumb soul of Nineveh.   160

And as I turned, my sense half shut
Still saw the crowds of curb and rut
Go past as marshaled to the strut
Of ranks in gypsum quaintly cut.
   It seemed in one same pageantry   165
They followed forms which had been erst;
To pass, till on my sight should burst
That future of the best or worst
When some may question which was first,
   Of London or of Nineveh.   170

For as that Bull-god once did stand
And watched the burial-clouds of sand,

Till these at last without a hand
Rose o'er his eyes, another land,
   And blinded him with destiny —   175
So may he stand again; till now,
In ships of unknown sail and prow,
Some tribe of the Australian plow
Bear him afar — a relic now
   Of London, not of Nineveh!   180

Or it may chance indeed that when
Man's age is hoary among men —
His centuries threescore and ten —
His furthest childhood shall seem then
   More clear than later times may be; 185
Who, finding in this desert place
This form, shall hold us for some race
That walked not in Christ's lowly ways,
But bowed its pride and vowed its praise
   Unto the god of Nineveh.   190

The smile rose first — anon drew nigh
The thought: . . . Those heavy wings spread
   high
So sure of flight, which do not fly;
That set gaze never on the sky;
   Those scriptured flanks it cannot see; 195
Its crown, a brow-contracting load;
Its planted feet which trust the sod: . . .
(So grew the image as I trod)
O Nineveh, was this thy God —
   Thine also, mighty Nineveh?   200
                         (1870)

THE STAFF AND SCRIP

"Who owns these lands?" the Pilgrim said.
  "Stranger, Queen Blanchelys."
"And who has thus harried them?" he said.
  "It was Duke Luke did this;
    God's ban be his!"   5

The Pilgrim said: "Where is your house?
  I'll rest there, with your will."
"You've but to climb these blackened boughs
  And you'll see it over the hill,
    For it burns still."   10

"Which road, to seek your Queen?" said he.
  "Nay, nay, but with some wound
You'll fly back hither, it may be,
  And by your blood i' the ground
    My place be found."   15

"Friend, stay in peace. God keep your head,
  And mine, where I will go;

---

127. **voice of God.** Jonah was commanded to go to Nineveh and "cry against it" because of its wickedness. As he entered the city he said, "Yet forty days, and Nineveh shall be overthrown" (*Jonah*, 3:4). 148. **taboring,** striking lightly, as upon a tabor (a small drum). 162. **crowds of curb and rut,** crowds of common people—those of the curbstone and gutter.

The Staff and Scrip. This poem is based upon a story in the *Gesta Romanorum* (*Deeds of the Romans*), a famous collection of short tales in Latin, popular during the late Middle Ages. All pilgrims carried staff and scrip (a small bag). 5. **ban,** curse.

For He is here and there," he said.
    He passed the hillside, slow,
        And stood below.   20

The Queen sat idle by her loom;
    She heard the arras stir,
And looked up sadly; through the room
    The sweetness sickened her
        Of musk and myrrh.   25

Her women, standing two and two,
    In silence combed the fleece.
The Pilgrim said, "Peace be with you,
    Lady," and bent his knees.
        She answered, "Peace."   30

Her eyes were like the wave within;
    Like water-reeds the poise
Of her soft body, dainty thin;
    And like the water's noise
        Her plaintive voice.   35

For him, the stream had never welled
    In desert tracts malign
So sweet; nor had he ever felt
    So faint in the sunshine
        Of Palestine.   40

Right so, he knew that he saw weep
    Each night through every dream
The Queen's own face, confused in sleep
    With visages supreme
        Not known to him.   45

"Lady," he said, "your lands lie burnt
    And waste. To meet your foe
All fear; this I have seen and learnt.
    Say that it shall be so,
        And I will go."   50

She gazed at him. "Your cause is just,
    For I have heard the same."
He said: "God's strength shall be my trust.
    Fall it to good or grame,
        'Tis in His name."   55

"Sir, you are thanked. My cause is dead.
    Why should you toil to break
A grave, and fall therein?" she said.
    He did not pause but spake:
        "For my vow's sake."   60

"Can such vows be, sir — to God's ear,
    Not to God's will?" "My vow
Remains; God heard me there as here,"
    He said with reverent brow,
        "Both then and now."   65

They gazed together, he and she,
    The minute while he spoke;

54. **grame**, harm, sorrow.

And when he ceased, she suddenly
    Looked round upon her folk
        As though she woke.   70

"Fight, sir," she said; "my prayers in pain
    Shall be your fellowship."
He whispered one among her train —
    "Tomorrow bid her keep
        This staff and scrip."   75

She sent him a sharp sword, whose belt
    About his body there
As sweet as her own arms he felt.
    He kissed its blade, all bare,
        Instead of her.   80

She sent him a green banner wrought
    With one white lily stem,
To bind his lance with when he fought.
    He writ upon the same
        And kissed her name.   85

She sent him a white shield, whereon
    She bade that he should trace
His will. He blent fair hues that shone,
    And in a golden space
        He kissed her face.   90

Right so, the sunset skies unsealed,
    Like lands he never knew,
Beyond tomorrow's battlefield
    Lay open out of view
        To ride into.   95

Next day till dark the women prayed;
    Nor any might know there
How the fight went — the Queen has bade
    That there do come to her
        No messenger.   100

Weak now to them the voice o' the priest
    As any trance affords;
And when each anthem failed and ceased,
    It seemed that the last chords
        Still sang the words.   105

Lo, Father, is thine ear inclined,
    And hath thine angel passed?
For these thy watchers now are blind
    With vigil, and at last
        Dizzy with fast.   110

"Oh, what is the light that shines so red?
    'Tis long since the sun set";
Quoth the youngest to the eldest maid:
    " 'Twas dim but now, and yet
        The light is great."   115

Quoth the other: " 'Tis our sight is dazed
    That we see flame i' the air."

But the Queen held her brows and gazed,
  And said, "It is the glare
    Of torches there."   120

"Oh, what are the sounds that rise and spread?
  All day it was so still";
Quoth the youngest to the eldest maid:
  "Unto the furthest hill
    The air they fill."   125

Quoth the other: " 'Tis our sense is blurred
  With all the chants gone by."
But the Queen held her breath and heard,
  And said, "It is the cry
    Of victory."   130

The first of all the rout was sound,
  The next were dust and flame,
And then the horses shook the ground;
  And in the thick of them
    A still band came.   135

"Oh, what do ye bring out of the fight,
  Thus hid beneath these boughs?"
"Even him, thy conquering guest tonight,
  Who yet shall not carouse,
    Queen, in thy house."   140

"Uncover ye his face," she said.
  "O changed in little space!"
She cried, "O pale that was so red!
  O God, O God of grace!
    Cover his face."   145

His sword was broken in his hand
  Where he had kissed the blade.
"O soft steel that could not withstand!
  O my hard heart unstayed,
    That prayed and prayed!"   150

His bloodied banner crossed his mouth
  Where he had kissed her name.
"O east, and west, and north, and south,
  Fair flew my web, for shame,
    To guide Death's aim!"   155

The tints were shredded from his shield
  Where he had kissed her face.
"Oh, of all gifts that I could yield,
  Death only keeps its place,
    My gift and grace!"   160

Then stepped a damsel to her side,
  And spoke, and needs must weep:
"For his sake, lady, if he died,
  He prayed of thee to keep
    This staff and scrip."   165

That night they hung above her bed,
  Till morning wet with tears.

Year after year above her head
  Her bed his token wears,
    Five years, ten years.   170

That night the passion of her grief
  Shook them as there they hung.
Each year the wind that shed the leaf
  Shook them and in its tongue
    A message flung.   175

And once she woke with a clear mind
  That letters writ to calm
Her soul lay in the scrip; to find
  Only a torpid balm
    And dust of palm.   180

They shook far off with palace sport
  When just and dance were rife;
And the hunt shook them from the court;
  For hers, in peace or strife,
    Was a queen's life.   185

A queen's death now; as now they shake
  To gusts in chapel dim —
Hung where she sleeps, not seen to wake
  (Carved lovely white and slim),
    With them by him.   190

Stand up today, still armed, with her,
  Good knight, before His brow
Who then as now was here and there,
  Who had in mind thy vow
    Then even as now.   195

The lists are set in heaven today,
  The bright pavilions shine;
Fair hangs thy shield, and none gainsay;
  The trumpets sound in sign
    That she is thine.   200

Not tithed with days' and years' decease
  He pays thy wage He owed,
But with imperishable peace
  Here in His own abode,
    Thy jealous God.   (*1849-1853; 1870*)

SISTER HELEN

"Why did you melt your waxen man,
     Sister Helen?
Today is the third since you began."
"The time was long, yet the time ran,
     Little brother."   5
    (*O Mother, Mary Mother,*
Three days today, between Hell and Heaven!)

201 ff. **Not tithed,** etc. His reward is not to be limited
in time but is to be everlasting.
Sister Helen. This poem is founded upon the old superstition that burning a waxen image of a person will bring
suffering and death upon him. The false lover whom Helen
is punishing is Keith of Ewern (line 87).

"But if you have done your work aright,
                Sister Helen,
You'll let me play, for you said I might."   10
"Be very still in your play tonight,
                Little brother."
        (*O Mother, Mary Mother,*
Third night, tonight, between Hell and Heaven!)

"You said it must melt ere vesper-bell,   15
                Sister Helen;
If now it be molten, all is well."
"Even so — nay, peace! you cannot tell,
                Little brother."
        (*O Mother, Mary Mother,*   20
Oh, what is this, between Hell and Heaven?)

"Oh, the waxen knave was plump today,
                Sister Helen;
How like dead folk he has dropped away!"
"Nay now, of the dead what can you say,   25
                Little brother?"
        (*O Mother, Mary Mother,*
What of the dead, between Hell and Heaven?)

"See, see, the sunken pile of wood,
                Sister Helen,   30
Shines through the thinned wax red as blood!"
"Nay now, when looked you yet on blood,
                Little brother?"
        (*O Mother, Mary Mother,*
How pale she is, between Hell and Heaven!)   35

"Now close your eyes, for they're sick and
                sore,
                Sister Helen,
And I'll play without the gallery door."
"Aye, let me rest — I'll lie on the floor,
                Little brother."   40
        (*O Mother, Mary Mother,*
What rest tonight, between Hell and Heaven?)

"Here high up in the balcony,
                Sister Helen,
The moon flies face to face with me."   45
"Aye, look and say whatever you see,
                Little brother."
        (*O Mother, Mary Mother,*
What sight tonight, between Hell and Heaven?)

"Outside it's merry in the wind's wake,   50
                Sister Helen;
In the shaken trees the chill stars shake."
"Hush, heard you a horse-tread as you spake,
                Little brother?"
        (*O Mother, Mary Mother,*   55
What sound tonight, between Hell and Heaven?)

"I hear a horse-tread, and I see,
                Sister Helen,
Three horsemen that ride terribly."

"Little brother, whence come the three,   60
                Little brother?"
        (*O Mother, Mary Mother,*
*Whence should they come, between Hell and
                Heaven?*)

"They come by the hill-verge from Boyne Bar,
                Sister Helen,   65
And one draws nigh, but two are afar."
"Look, look, do you know them who they are,
                Little brother?"
        (*O Mother, Mary Mother,*
Who should they be, between Hell and Heaven?)

"Oh, it's Keith of Eastholm rides so fast,   71
                Sister Helen,
For I know the white mane on the blast."
"The hour has come, has come at last,
                Little brother!"   75
        (*O Mother, Mary Mother,*
Her hour at last, between Hell and Heaven!)

"He has made a sign and called Halloo!
                Sister Helen,
And he says that he would speak with you."
"Oh, tell him I fear the frozen dew,   81
                Little brother."
        (*O Mother, Mary Mother,*
Why laughs she thus, between Hell and Heaven?)

"The wind is loud, but I hear him cry,   85
                Sister Helen,
That Keith of Ewern's like to die."
"And he and thou, and thou and I,
                Little brother."
        (*O Mother, Mary Mother,*   90
And they and we, between Hell and Heaven!)

"Three days ago, on his marriage-morn,
                Sister Helen,
He sickened, and lies since then forlorn."
"For bridegroom's side is the bride a thorn,   95
                Little brother?"
        (*O Mother, Mary Mother,*
Cold bridal cheer, between Hell and Heaven!)

"Three days and nights now he has lain abed,
                Sister Helen,   100
And he prays in torment to be dead."
"The thing may chance, if he have prayed,
                Little brother!"
        (*O Mother, Mary Mother,*
If he have prayed, between Hell and Heaven!)

"But he has not ceased to cry today,   106
                Sister Helen,
That you should take your curse away."

---

64. **Boyne Bar**, a famous bar at the mouth of the **Boyne**
River, Leinster, Ireland.

"*My* prayer was heard — he need but pray,
    Little brother!"   110
    (*O Mother, Mary Mother,*
Shall God not hear, between Hell and Heaven?)

"But he says, till you take back your ban,
    Sister Helen,
His soul would pass, yet never can."   115
"Nay then, shall I slay a living man,
    Little brother?"
    (*O Mother, Mary Mother,*
A living soul, between Hell and Heaven!)

"But he calls forever on your name,   120
    Sister Helen,
And says that he melts before a flame."
"My heart for his pleasure fared the same,
    Little brother."   124
    (*O Mother, Mary Mother,*
Fire at the heart, between Hell and Heaven!)

"Here's Keith of Westholm riding fast,
    Sister Helen,
For I know the white plume on the blast."
"The hour, the sweet hour I forecast,   130
    Little brother!"
    (*O Mother, Mary Mother,*
Is the hour sweet, between Hell and Heaven?)

"He stops to speak, and he stills his horse,
    Sister Helen;   135
But his words are drowned in the wind's
    course."
"Nay hear, nay hear, you must hear perforce,
    Little brother!"
    (*O Mother, Mary Mother,*
What word now heard, between Hell and
    Heaven!)

"Oh, he says that Keith of Ewern's cry,   141
    Sister Helen,
Is ever to see you ere he die."
"In all that his soul sees, there am I,
    Little brother!"   145
    (*O Mother, Mary Mother,*
The soul's one sight, between Hell and Heaven!)

"He sends a ring and a broken coin,
    Sister Helen,
And bids you mind the banks of Boyne."   150
"What else he broke will he ever join,
    Little brother?"
    (*O Mother, Mary Mother,*
No, never joined, between Hell and Heaven!)

"He yields you these and craves full fain,   155
    Sister Helen,
You pardon him in his mortal pain."

148. broken coin. The two had broken a coin, and each
had kept half as a pledge.

"What else he took will he give again,
    Little brother?"
    (*O Mother, Mary Mother,* 160
Not twice to give, between Hell and Heaven!)

"He calls your name in an agony,
    Sister Helen,
That even dead Love must weep to see."
"Hate, born of Love, is blind as he,   165
    Little brother!"
    (*O Mother, Mary Mother,* 160
Love turned to hate, between Hell and Heaven!)

"Oh, it's Keith of Keith now that rides fast,
    170
For I know the white hair on the blast."
"The short, short hour will soon be past,
    Little brother!"
    (*O Mother, Mary Mother,*
Will soon be past, between Hell and Heaven!)

"He looks at me and he tries to speak,   176
    Sister Helen,
But oh! his voice is sad and weak!"
"What here should the mighty Baron seek,
    Little brother?"   180
    (*O Mother, Mary Mother,*
Is this the end, between Hell and Heaven?)

"Oh, his son still cries, if you forgive,
    Sister Helen,
The body dies, but the soul shall live."   185
"Fire shall forgive me as I forgive,
    Little brother!"
    (*O Mother, Mary Mother,*
As she forgives, between Hell and Heaven!)

"Oh, he prays you, as his heart would rive,
    Sister Helen,   191
To save his dear son's soul alive."
"Fire cannot slay it; it shall thrive,
    Little brother!"
    (*O Mother, Mary Mother,* 195
Alas, alas, between Hell and Heaven!)

"He cries to you, kneeling in the road,
    Sister Helen,
To go with him for the love of God!"
"The way is long to his son's abode,   200
    Little brother."
    (*O Mother, Mary Mother,*
The way is long, between Hell and Heaven!)

"A lady's here, by a dark steed brought,
    Sister Helen,   205
So darkly clad, I saw her not."
"See her now or never see aught,
    Little brother!"
    (*O Mother, Mary Mother,*)
What more to see, between Hell and Heaven!

"Her hood falls back, and the moon shines
    fair,   211
        Sister Helen,
On the Lady of Ewern's golden hair."
"Blest hour of my power and her despair,
        Little brother!"   215
      (*O Mother, Mary Mother,*
Hour blest and banned, between Hell and
Heaven!)

"Pale, pale her cheeks, that in pride did glow,
        Sister Helen,
'Neath the bridal-wreath three days ago."
"One morn for pride and three days for woe,
        Little brother!"   221
      (*O Mother, Mary Mother,*
Three days, three nights, between Hell and
Heaven!)

"Her clasped hands stretch from her bending
    head,   225
        Sister Helen;
With the loud wind's wail her sobs are wed."
"What wedding-strains hath her bridal-bed,
        Little brother?"
      (*O Mother, Mary Mother,* 230
What strain but death's, between Hell and
Heaven!)

"She may not speak, she sinks in a swoon,
        Sister Helen—
She lifts her lips and gasps on the moon."
"Oh! might I but hear her soul's blithe tune,
        Little brother!"   236
      (*O Mother, Mary Mother,*
Her woe's dumb cry, between Hell and Heaven!)

"They've caught her to Westholm's saddle-
    bow,
        Sister Helen,   240
And her moonlit hair gleams white in its
    flow."
"Let it turn whiter than winter snow,
        Little brother!"
      (*O Mother, Mary Mother,*
Woe-withered gold, between Hell and Heaven!)

"O Sister Helen, you heard the bell,
        Sister Helen!
More loud than the vesper-chime it fell."
"No vesper-chime, but a dying knell,
        Little brother!"   250
      (*O Mother, Mary Mother,*
His dying knell, between Hell and Heaven!)

"Alas! but I fear the heavy sound,
        Sister Helen;
Is it in the sky or in the ground?"   255

"Say, have they turned their horses round,
        Little brother?"
      (*O Mother, Mary Mother,*
What would she more, between Hell and
Heaven?)

"They have raised the old man from his knee,
        Sister Helen,   261
And they ride in silence hastily."
"More fast the naked soul doth flee,
        Little brother!"
      (*O Mother, Mary Mother,*
The naked soul, between Hell and Heaven!)

"Flank to flank are the three steeds gone,
        Sister Helen,
But the lady's dark steed goes alone."
"And lonely her bridegroom's soul hath flown,
        Little brother."   271
      (*O Mother, Mary Mother,*
The lonely ghost, between Hell and Heaven!)

"Oh, the wind is sad in the iron chill,
        Sister Helen,   275
And weary sad they look by the hill."
"But he and I are sadder still,
        Little brother!"
      (*O Mother, Mary Mother,*
Most sad of all, between Hell and Heaven!) 280

"See, see, the wax has dropped from its place,
        Sister Helen,
And the flames are winning up apace!"
"Yet here they burn but for a space,
        Little brother!"   285
      (*O Mother, Mary Mother,*
Here for a space, between Hell and Heaven!)

"Ah! what white thing at the door has crossed,
        Sister Helen?
Ah! what is this that sighs in the frost?" 290
"A soul that's lost as mine is lost,
        Little brother!"
      (*O Mother, Mary Mother,*
Lost, lost, all lost, between Hell and Heaven!)
        (*1851-1852; 1853, 1870*)

PENUMBRA

I did not look upon her eyes
(Though scarcely seen, with no surprise,
'Mid many eyes a single look),
Because they should not gaze rebuke,
At night, from stars in sky and brook.   5

Penumbra. A penumbra is a partial shadow.

I did not take her by the hand
(Though little was to understand
From touch of hand all friends might take),
Because it should not prove a flake
Burnt in my palm to boil and ache.　　　10

I did not listen to her voice
(Though none had noted, where at choice
All might rejoice in listening),
Because no such a thing should cling
In the wood's moan at evening.　　　15

I did not cross her shadow once
(Though from the hollow west the sun's
Last shadow runs along so far),
Because in June it should not bar
My ways, at noon when fevers are.　　　20

They told me she was sad that day
(Though wherefore tell what love's soothsay,
Sooner than they, did register?),
And my heart leapt and wept to her,
And yet I did not speak nor stir.　　　25

So shall the tongues of the sea's foam
(Though many voices therewith come
From drowned hope's home to cry to me),
Bewail one hour the more, when sea
And wind are one with memory.　　　(1870)

FIRST LOVE REMEMBERED

Peace in her chamber, wheresoe'er
　　It be, a holy place;
　　The thought still brings my soul such grace
As morning meadows wear.

Whether it still be small and light,　　　5
　　A maid's who dreams alone,
　　As from her orchard-gate the moon
Its ceiling showed at night;

Or whether, in a shadow dense
　　As nuptial hymns invoke,　　　10
　　Innocent maidenhood awoke
To married innocence —

There still the thanks unheard await
　　The unconscious gift bequeathed;
　　For there my soul this hour has breathed　15
An air inviolate.
　　　　　　　　(1870)

SUDDEN LIGHT

I have been here before,
　　But when or how I cannot tell.
I know the grass beyond the door,
　　The sweet keen smell,
The sighing sound, the lights around the
　　shore.　　　5

You have been mine before —
　　How long ago I may not know;
But just when at that swallow's soar
　　Your neck turned so,
Some veil did fall — I knew it all of yore.　10

Has this been thus before?
　　And shall not thus time's eddying flight
Still with our lives our loves restore
　　In death's despite,
And day and night yield one delight once
　　more?　　　15
　　　　　　　　(1870)

THE WOODSPURGE

The wind flapped loose, the wind was still,
Shaken out dead from tree and hill;
I had walked on at the wind's will —
I sat now, for the wind was still.

Between my knees my forehead was —　　5
My lips, drawn in, said not Alas!
My hair was over in the grass,
My naked ears heard the day pass.

My eyes, wide open, had the run
Of some ten weeds to fix upon;　　　10
Among those few, out of the sun,
The woodspurge flowered, three cups in one.

From perfect grief there need not be
Wisdom or even memory;
One thing then learned remains to me —　15
The woodspurge has a cup of three.　　(1870)

THE HONEYSUCKLE

I plucked a honeysuckle where
　　The hedge on high is quick with thorn,
　　And climbing for the prize, was torn,
And fouled my feet in quag-water;
　　And by the thorns and by the wind　　5
　　The blossom that I took was thinned,
And yet I found it sweet and fair.

Thence to a richer growth I came,
　　Where, nursed in mellow intercourse,
　　The honeysuckles sprang by scores,　10
Not harried like my single stem,
　　All virgin lamps of scent and dew.
　　So from my hand that first I threw,
Yet plucked not any more of them.
　　　　　　　　(1870)

The Woodspurge. Woodspurge is a species of weed that
exudes a milky fluid. Rossetti wrote the poem after he
noticed a drawing of the plant in a botanical book.

THE SONG OF THE BOWER

Say, is it day, is it dusk in thy bower,
  Thou whom I long for, who longest for me?
Oh! be it light, be it night, 'tis Love's hour,
  Love's that is fettered as Love's that is free,
Free Love has leaped to that innermost
    chamber,   5
  Oh! the last time, and the hundred before;
Fettered Love, motionless, can but remember,
  Yet something that sighs from him passes
    the door.

Nay, but my heart when it flies to thy bower,
  What does it find there that knows it again?
There it must droop like a shower-beaten
    flower,   11
  Red at the rent core and dark with the rain.
Ah! yet what shelter is still shed above it —
  What waters still image its leaves torn
    apart?
Thy soul is the shade that clings round it to
    love it,   15
  And tears are its mirror deep down in thy
    heart.

What were my prize, could I enter thy bower,
  This day, tomorrow, at eve or at morn?
Large lovely arms and a neck like a tower,
  Bosom then heaving that now lies forlorn.
Kindled with love-breath (the sun's kiss is
    colder!)   21
  Thy sweetness all near me, so distant today;
My hand round thy neck and thy hand on
    my shoulder,
  My mouth to thy mouth as the world
    melts away.   24

What is it keeps me afar from thy bower —
  My spirit, my body, so fain to be there?
Waters engulfing or fires that devour? —
  Earth heaped against me or death in the
    air?
Nay, but in day-dreams, for terror, for pity,
  The trees wave their heads with an omen
    to tell;   30
Nay, but in night-dreams, throughout the
    dark city,
  The hours, clashed together, lose count in
    the bell.

Shall I not one day remember thy bower,
  One day when all days are one day to
    me?
Thinking, "I stirred not, and yet had the
    power" —   35
  Yearning, "Ah, God, if again it might be!"
Peace, peace! such a small lamp illumes, on
    this highway,
So dimly so few steps in front of my feet —

Yet shows me that her way is parted from
    my way. . . .
Out of sight, beyond light, at what goal
    may we meet?   40
                  (1870)

AN OLD SONG ENDED

"How should I your true love know
  From another one?"
"By his cockle-hat and staff
  And his sandal-shoon."

"And what signs have told you now   5
  That he hastens home?"
"Lo! the spring is nearly gone,
  He is nearly come."

"For a token is there naught,
  Say, that he should bring?"   10
"He will bear a ring I gave
  And another ring."

"How may I, when he shall ask,
  Tell him who lies there?"
"Nay, but leave my face unveiled   15
  And unbound my hair."

"Can you say to me some word
  I shall say to him?"
"Say I'm looking in his eyes
  Though my eyes are dim."   20

ASPECTA MEDUSA
(For a Drawing)

Andromeda, by Perseus saved and wed,
Hankered each day to see the Gorgon's head;
Till o'er a fount he held it, bade her lean,
And mirrored in the wave was safely seen
That death she lived by.   5

        Let not thine eyes know
Any forbidden thing itself, although
It once should save as well as kill; but be
Its shadow upon life enough for thee.
             (*1865*; 1870)

An Old Song Ended. The first stanza is quoted from
Ophelia's song in *Hamlet*, IV, 5, 23-26.
  Aspecta Medusa. These lines were written for a design
from which Rossetti intended to paint a picture of Perseus
allowing Andromeda to look at the severed head of Medusa
as it was reflected from a tank of water. The picture,
however, was never painted. Medusa was one of the Gorgons,
fabulous monsters with snaky hair and of terrible aspect
that turned the beholder to stone. Perseus, the son of Zeus,
king of the gods, cut off Medusa's head by looking at its
reflection in his shield. Andromeda was the daughter of
Cassiopeia, king of Ethiopia. In order to expiate a curse
upon her father's land, she was chained to a cliff to be devoured by a monster. Perseus slew the monster and married
Andromeda.

EDEN BOWER

It was Lilith the wife of Adam;
(*Eden bower's in flower.*)
Not a drop of her blood was human,
But she was made like a soft sweet woman.

Lilith stood on the skirts of Eden;   5
(*And O the bower and the hour!*)
She was the first that thence was driven;
With her was hell and with Eve was heaven.

In the ear of the Snake said Lilith:
(*Eden bower's in flower.*)   10
"To thee I come when the rest is over;
A snake was I when thou wast my lover.

"I was the fairest snake in Eden;
(*And O the bower and the hour!*)
By the earth's will, new form and feature   15
Made me a wife for the earth's new creature.

"Take me thou as I come from Adam.
(*Eden bower's in flower.*)
Once again shall my love subdue thee;
The past is past and I am come to thee.   20

"O but Adam was thrall to Lilith!
(*And O the bower and the hour!*)
All the threads of my hair are golden,
And there in a net his heart was holden.

"O and Lilith was queen of Adam!   25
(*Eden bower's in flower.*)
All the day and the night together
My breath could shake his soul like a feather.

"What great joys had Adam and Lilith! —
(*And O the bower and the hour!*)   30
Sweet close rings of the serpent's twining,
As heart in heart lay sighing and pining.

"What bright babes had Lilith and Adam! —
(*Eden bower's in flower.*)
Shapes that coiled in the woods and waters,   35
Glittering sons and radiant daughters.

"O thou God, the Lord God of Eden!
(*And O the bower and the hour!*)
Say, was this fair body for no man,
That of Adam's flesh thou mak'st him a
    woman?   40

"O thou Snake, the King-snake of Eden!
(*Eden bower's in flower.*)
God's strong will our necks are under,
But thou and I may cleave it in sunder.

Eden Bower. This poem is based upon an ancient legend
that regarded Lilith as the first wife of Adam. Cf. Browning's
Adam, Lilith, and Eve, p. 374.

"Help, sweet Snake, sweet lover of Lilith! 45
(*And O the bower and the hour!*)
And let God learn how I loved and hated
Man in the image of God created.

"Help me once against Eve and Adam!
(*Eden bower's in flower.*)   50
Help me once for this one endeavor,
And then my love shall be thine forever!

"Strong is God, the fell foe of Lilith —
(*And O the bower and the hour!*)   54
Naught in heaven or earth may affright him;
But join thou with me and we will smite him

"Strong is God, the great God of Eden;
(*Eden bower's in flower.*)
Over all He made He hath power;
But lend me thou thy shape for an hour!   60

"Lend thy shape for the love of Lilith!
(*And O the bower and the hour!*)
Look, my mouth and my cheek are ruddy,
And thou art cold, and fire is my body.

"Lend thy shape for the hate of Adam!   65
(*Eden bower's in flower.*)
That he may wail my joy that forsook him,
And curse the day when the bride-sleep took
    him.

"Lend thy shape for the shame of Eden!
(*And O the bower and the hour!*)   70
Is not the foe-God weak as the foeman
When love grows hate in the heart of a
    woman?

"Would'st thou know the heart's hope of
    Lilith?
(*Eden bower's in flower.*)
Then bring thou close thine head till it glisten
Along my breast, and lip me and listen.   76

"Am I sweet, O sweet Snake of Eden?
(*And O the bower and the hour!*)
Then ope thine ear to my warm mouth's
    cooing
And learn what deed remains for our doing. 80

"Thou didst hear when God said to Adam:
(*Eden bower's in flower.*)
'Of all this wealth I have made thee warden;
Thou'rt free to eat of the trees of the garden;

"'Only of one tree eat not in Eden;   85
(*And O the bower and the hour!*)
All save one I give to thy freewill —
The Tree of the Knowledge of Good and
    Evil.'

"O my love, come nearer to Lilith!
(*Eden bower's in flower.*)   90

In thy sweet folds bind me and bend me,
And let me feel the shape thou shalt lend me!

"In thy shape I'll go back to Eden;
    (*And O the bower and the hour!*)
In these coils that Tree will I grapple,   95
And stretch this crowned head forth by the
    apple.

"Lo, Eve bends to the breath of Lilith!
    (*Eden bower's in flower.*)
O how then shall my heart desire
All her blood as food to its fire!   100

"Lo, Eve bends to the words of Lilith! —
    (*And O the bower and the hour!*)
'Nay, this Tree's fruit — why should ye
    hate it,
Or Death be born the day that ye ate it?

" 'Nay, but on that great day in Eden,   105
    (*Eden bower's in flower.*)
By the help that in this wise Tree is,'
God knows well ye shall be as He is.'

"Then Eve shall eat and give unto Adam;
    (*And O the bower and the hour!*)   110
And then they both shall know they are
    naked,
And their hearts ache as my heart hath achéd.

"Aye, let them hide in the trees of Eden,
    (*Eden bower's in flower.*)
As in the cool of the day in the garden   115
God shall walk without pity or pardon.

"Hear, thou Eve, the man's heart in Adam!
    (*And O the bower and the hour!*)
Of his brave words hark to the bravest:
'This the woman gave that thou gavest.'   120

"Hear Eve speak, yea, list to her, Lilith!
    (*Eden bower's in flower.*)
Feast thine heart with words that shall sate
    it —
'This the serpent gave and I ate it.'

"O proud Eve, cling close to thine Adam,   125
    (*And O the bower and the hour!*)
Driven forth as the beasts of his naming
By the sword that forever is flaming.

"Know, thy path is known unto Lilith!
    (*Eden bower's in flower.*)   130
While the blithe birds sang at thy wedding,
There her tears grew thorns for thy threading.

"O my love, thou Love-snake of Eden!
    (*And O the bower and the hour!*)
O today and the day to come after!   135
Loose me, love — give breath to my laughter!

"O bright Snake, the Death-worm of Adam!
    (*Eden bower's in flower.*)
Wreathe thy neck with my hair's bright
    tether,
And wear my gold and thy gold together!   140

"On that day on the skirts of Eden,
    (*And O the bower and the hour!*)
In thy shape shall I glide back to thee,
And in my shape for an instant view thee.

"But when thou'rt thou and Lilith is Lilith,
    (*Eden bower's in flower.*)   146
In what bliss past hearing or seeing
Shall each one drink of the other's being!

"With cries of 'Eve!' and 'Eden!' and 'Adam!'
    (*And O the bower and the hour!*)   150
How shall we mingle our love's caresses,
I in thy coils, and thou in my tresses!

"With those names, ye echoes of Eden,
    (*Eden bower's in flower.*)
Fire shall cry from my heart that burneth —
'Dust he is and to dust returneth!'   156

"Yet today, thou master of Lilith —
    (*And O the bower and the hour!*)
Wrap me round in the form I'll borrow
And let me tell thee of sweet tomorrow.   160

"In the planted garden eastward in Eden,
    (*Eden bower's in flower.*)
Where the river goes forth to water the gar-
    den,
The springs shall dry and the soil shall harden.

"Yea, where the bride-sleep fell upon Adam,
    (*And O the bower and the hour!*)   166
None shall hear when the storm-wind whistles
Through roses choked among thorns and
    thistles.

"Yea, beside the east-gate of Eden,
    (*Eden bower's in flower.*)   170
Where God joined them and none might sever
The sword turns this way and that forever.

"What of Adam cast out of Eden?
    (*And O the bower and the hour!*)
Lo! with care like a shadow shaken,   175
He tills the hard earth whence he was taken.

"What of Eve too, cast out of Eden?
    (*Eden bower's in flower.*)
Nay, but she, the bride of God's giving,
Must yet be mother of all men living.   180

156. **Dust . . . returneth.** Cf. *Ecclesiastes*, 3:20.—"All
go unto one place; all are of the dust, and all turn to dust
again."

"Lo, God's grace, by the grace of Lilith!
   (*And O the bower and the hour!*)
To Eve's womb, from our sweet tomorrow,
God shall greatly multiply sorrow.

"Fold me fast, O God-snake of Eden!   185
   (*Eden bower's in flower.*)
What more prize than love to impel thee?
Grip and lip my limbs as I tell thee!

"Lo! two babes for Eve and for Adam!
   (*And O the bower and the hour!*)   190
Lo! sweet Snake, the travail and treasure —
Two men-children born for their pleasure!

"The first is Cain and the second Abel;
   (*Eden bower's in flower.*)
The soul of one shall be made thy brother,
And thy tongue shall lap the blood of the
   other."   196
   (*And O the bower and the hour!*)
               (1870)

THE BALLAD OF DEAD LADIES

(FROM FRANÇOIS VILLON)

Tell me now in what hidden way is
   Lady Flora the lovely Roman?
Where's Hipparchia, and where is Thais,
   Neither of them the fairer woman?
Where is Echo, beheld of no man,   5
Only heard on river and mere —
   She whose beauty was more than hu-
      man? . . .
But where are the snows of yester-year?

Where's Héloise, the learned nun,
   For whose sake Abeillard, I ween,   10
Lost manhood and put priesthood on?

(From Love he won such dule and teen!)
   And where, I pray you, is the Queen
Who willed that Buridan should steer
   Sewed in a sack's mouth down the Seine? . . .
But where are the snows of yester-year?   16

White Queen Blanche, like a queen of lilies,
   With a voice like any mermaiden —
Bertha Broadfoot, Beatrice, Alice,
   And Ermengarde the lady of Maine —   20
   And that good Joan whom Englishmen
At Rouen doomed and burned her there —
   Mother of God, where are they then? . . .
But where are the snows of yester-year?

Nay, never ask this week, fair lord,   25
   Where they are gone, nor yet this year,
Except with this for an overword —
   But where are the snows of yester-year?
               (*1869;* 1869)

JOHN OF TOURS

(*Old French*)

John of Tours is back with peace,
But he comes home ill at ease.

"Good-morrow, mother." "Good-morrow,
   son;
Your wife has borne you a little one."

"Go now, mother, go before,   5
Make me a bed upon the floor;

"Very low your foot must fall,
That my wife hear not at all."

As it neared the midnight toll,
John of Tours gave up his soul.   10

"Tell me now, my mother my dear,
What's the crying that I hear?"

The Ballad of Dead Ladies. This is a translation of *Ballade des Dames du Temps Jadis*, by François Villon, the greatest of the French medieval poets. (See Swinburne's *A Ballad of François Villon*, p. 725.) The next two poems are also translations from the Old French.
  2. Lady Flora, perhaps the Roman goddess of flowers and spring; late tradition made her a wealthy and beautiful woman. Other identifications include several famous courtesans of Rome named Flora. **3. Hipparchia**, the wife of Crates, the famous Cynic philosopher of Thebes, Greece. She lived during the 3d century B.C. **Thais**, perhaps the celebrated Athenian courtesan who accompanied Alexander the Great on his expedition into Asia, 331 B.C.; see Dryden's *Alexander's Feast*. Another Thais was the famous Egyptian courtesan who became a saint. **5. Echo**, a beautiful nymph who for love of Narcissus pined away until nothing was left of her but her voice. **9. Héloise**, the beautiful niece of Canon Fulbert, of Paris. She fell in love with her teacher, Pierre Abélard (1079-1142), a scholastic philosopher and theologian. After they eloped and were married, she returned to her uncle's house and denied the marriage in order that her love might not be a hindrance to Abélard's advancement in the church. Fulbert was so enraged at this move that he caused Abélard to be emasculated in order to make him canonically incapable of ecclesiastical preferment. Abélard then became a monk in the abbey of St. Denis, in Paris, and induced Héloise to become a nun. **10. ween**, think.

12. dule and teen, grief and pain. **13. the Queen**, Marguerite de Bourgogne, wife of Louis le Hutin (14th century). She is the heroine of the legend of the Tour de Nesle, according to which she had her numerous lovers killed and thrown into the Seine. Jean Buridan, rector of the University of Paris, escaped this fate. **17. Queen Blanche**, probably Blanche of Castille, mother of Louis IX, king of France (1226-70). **19. Bertha Broadfoot**, the mother of Charlemagne, king of the Franks and emperor of the West (742-814). She is a prominent character in medieval romances dealing with Charlemagne and his court. **Beatrice, Alice**. These were names of various well-known women of the Middle Ages, and it is impossible to tell the exact persons meant. Beatrice might be the young beloved of Dante or, more probably, Béatrix de Provence, wife of Charles, son of Louis VIII, king of France (1223-1226). Alice may be Ælis, one of the characters in the romance *Aliscans*, or Alix de Champagne, wife of Louis le Jeune (12th century). **20. Ermengarde**, the daughter of d'Helie, Count of Maine, an old province in northwestern France. She died in 1126. **21. Joan**, Joan of Arc (1412-31), who saved France from conquest, but who later was imprisoned at Rouen, France, by the English, convicted of witchcraft and heresy, and burned at the stake. She was canonized in 1920.

"Daughter, it's the children wake
Crying with their teeth that ache."

"Tell me though, my mother my dear,　15
What's the knocking that I hear?"

"Daughter, it's the carpenter
Mending planks upon the stair."

"Tell me too, my mother my dear,
What's the singing that I hear?"　20

"Daughter, it's the priests in rows
Going round about our house."

"Tell me then, my mother my dear,
What's the dress that I should wear?"

"Daughter, any reds or blues,　25
But the black is most in use."

"Nay, but say, my mother my dear,
Why do you fall weeping here?"

"Oh! the truth must be said —
It's that John of Tours is dead."　30

"Mother, let the sexton know
That the grave must be for two;

"Aye, and still have room to spare,
For you must shut the baby there."　(1870)

MY FATHER'S CLOSE
(Old French)

Inside my father's close
　　(Fly away, O my heart, away!)
Sweet apple-blossom blows
　　So sweet.

Three kings' daughters fair,　5
　　(Fly away, O my heart, away!)
They lie below it there
　　So sweet.

"Ah!" says the eldest one,
　　(Fly away, O my heart, away!)　10
"I think the day's begun
　　So sweet."

"Ah!" says the second one,
　　(Fly away, O my heart, away!)
"Far off I hear the drum　15
　　So sweet."

"Ah!" says the youngest one,
　　(Fly away, O my heart, away!)
"It's my true love, my own,
　　So sweet.　20

My Father's Close.　A close is an enclosed place.

"Oh! if he fight and win,"
　　(Fly away, O my heart, away!)
"I keep my love for him,
　　So sweet;
Oh! let him lose or win,　25
　　He hath it still complete."　(1870)

MARY MAGDALENE
AT THE DOOR OF SIMON THE PHARISEE
(For a Drawing)

"Why wilt thou cast the roses from thine hair?
Nay, be thou all a rose — wreath, lips, and
　　cheek.
Nay, not this house — that banquet-house we
　　seek;
See how they kiss and enter; come thou there.
This delicate day of love we two will share　5
Till at our ear love's whispering night shall
　　speak.
What, sweet one — hold'st thou still the
　　foolish freak?
Nay, when I kiss thy feet they'll leave the
　　stair."

"Oh, loose me! See'st thou not my Bride-
　　groom's face
That draws me to Him? For His feet my
　　kiss,　10
My hair, my tears He craves today — and oh!
What words can tell what other day and place
Shall see me clasp those blood-stained feet of
　　His?
He needs me, calls me, loves me; let me go!"
　　　　(1869?; 1870)

TROY TOWN

Heavenborn Helen, Sparta's queen,
　　　　(O Troy Town!)
Had two breasts of heavenly sheen,
The sun and moon of the heart's desire;
All Love's lordship lay between.　5
　　　　(O Troy's down,
　　　　Tall Troy's on fire!)

Mary Magdalene. When Jesus was being entertained at
the home of Simon the Pharisee, "a woman in the city, which
was a sinner . . . brought an alabaster box of ointment, And
stood at his feet before him weeping, and began to wash his
feet with tears, and did wipe them with the hairs of her head,
and kissed his feet, and anointed them with the ointment"
(Luke, 7:37-38). For Rossetti's prose description of the picture see Critical Notes. In the drawing Mary has left a procession of revelers and is ascending the steps of the house
where she sees Christ. Her lover has followed her and is
trying to turn her back.
　Troy Town. The theme of this poem is Helen's dedication
of a goblet molded in the shape of her breast to Venus, goddess
of love. The legend is found in Pliny (23-79 A.D.), a famous
Roman historian and naturalist. For Helen's place in the
story of Troy, see introductory note to Browning's Development, p. 377.

Helen knelt at Venus' shrine,
   (O Troy Town!)
Saying, "A little gift is mine,   10
A little gift for a heart's desire.
Hear me speak and make me a sign!
   (O Troy's down,
   Tall Troy's on fire!)

"Look, I bring thee a carven cup; 15
   (O Troy Town!)
See it here as I hold it up —
Shaped it is to the heart's desire,
Fit to fill when the gods would sup.
   (O Troy's down, 20
   Tall Troy's on fire!)

"It was molded like my breast;
   (O Troy Town!)
He that sees it may not rest,
Rest at all for his heart's desire. 25
O give ear to my heart's behest!
   (O Troy's down,
   Tall Troy's on fire!)

"See my breast, how like it is;
   (O Troy Town!) 30
See it bare for the air to kiss!
Is the cup to thy heart's desire?
O for the breast, O make it his!
   (O Troy's down,
   Tall Troy's on fire!) 35

"Yea, for my bosom here I sue;
   (O Troy Town!)
Thou must give it where 'tis due,
Give it there to the heart's desire.
Whom do I give my bosom to? 40
   (O Troy's down,
   Tall Troy's on fire!)

"Each twin breast is an apple sweet!
   (O Troy Town!)
Once an apple stirred the beat 45
Of thy heart with the heart's desire;
Say, who brought it then to thy feet?
   (O Troy's down,
   Tall Troy's on fire!)

"They that claimed it then were three; 50
   (O Troy Town!)
For thy sake two hearts did he
Make forlorn of the heart's desire.
Do for him as he did for thee!
   (O Troy's down, 55
   Tall Troy's on fire!)

"Mine are apples grown to the south,
   (O Troy Town!)
Grown to taste in the days of drouth,

Taste and waste to the heart's desire; 60
Mine are apples meet for his mouth!"
   (O Troy's down,
   Tall Troy's on fire!)

Venus looked on Helen's gift,
   (O Troy Town!) 65
Looked and smiled with subtle drift,
Saw the work of her heart's desire —
"There thou kneel'st for Love to lift!"
   (O Troy's down,
   Tall Troy's on fire!) 70

Venus looked in Helen's face,
   (O Troy Town!)
Knew far off an hour and place,
And fire lit from the heart's desire;
Laughed and said, "Thy gift hath grace!" 75
   (O Troy's down,
   Tall Troy's on fire!)

Cupid looked on Helen's breast,
   (O Troy Town!)
Saw the heart within its nest, 80
Saw the flame of the heart's desire —
Marked his arrow's burning crest.
   (O Troy's down,
   Tall Troy's on fire!)

Cupid took another dart, 85
   (O Troy Town!)
Fledged it for another heart,
Winged the shaft with the heart's desire,
Drew the string and said, "Depart!"
   (O Troy's down, 90
   Tall Troy's on fire!)

Paris turned upon his bed,
   (O Troy Town!)
Turned upon his bed and said,
Dead at heart with the heart's desire — 95
"O to clasp her golden head!"
   (O Troy's down,
   Tall Troy's on fire!)
   (1870)

LOVE-LILY

Between the hands, between the brows,
 Between the lips of Love-lily,
A spirit is born whose birth endows
 My blood with fire to burn through me;
Who breathes upon my gazing eyes, 5
 Who laughs and murmurs in mine ear,
At whose least touch my color flies,
 And whom my life grows faint to hear.

Within the voice, within the heart,
 Within the mind of Love-Lily, 10

---

45. **apple.** The golden apple marked "for the most beautiful" was awarded by Paris, son of King Priam, of Troy, to Venus. See Tennyson's *Œnone*, page 21, and note on line 80.

78. **Cupid,** the god of love.

A spirit is born who lifts apart
  His tremulous wings and looks at me;
Who on my mouth his finger lays,
  And shows, while whispering lutes confer,
That Eden of Love's watered ways   15
  Whose winds and spirits worship her.

Brows, hands, and lips, heart, mind, and
    voice,
  Kisses and words of Love-Lily —
Oh! bid me with your joy rejoice
  Till riotous longing rest in me!   20
Ah! let not hope be still distraught,
  But find in her its gracious goal,
Whose speech Truth knows not from her
    thought,
  Nor Love her body from her soul.
                          (*1869; 1870*)

THE HOUSE OF LIFE

THE SONNET

A sonnet is a moment's monument—
Memorial from the Soul's eternity
To one dead deathless hour. Look that it be,
Whether for lustral rite or dire portent,
Of its own arduous fulness reverent.   5
Carve it in ivory or in ebony,
As Day or Night may rule; and let Time see
Its flowering crest impearled and orient.
A sonnet is a coin; its face reveals
The Soul—its converse, to what Power 'tis
    due:—   10
Whether for tribute to the august appeals
Of Life, or dower in Love's high retinue,
It serve; or 'mid the dark wharf's cavernous
    breath,
In Charon's palm it pay the toll to Death.
                          (*1880; 1881*)

PART I.   YOUTH AND CHANGE

I. LOVE ENTHRONED

I marked all kindred Powers the heart finds
    fair:—
Truth, with awed lips; and Hope, with eyes
    upcast;
And Fame, whose loud wings fan the ashen
    Past

The House of Life. These sonnets were written during a
period of thirty-three years—1848-81. Although they do not
form an organic whole, they fulfill the mission indicated in
the introductory sonnet. The title came from Rossetti's
interest in astrology, as if the heavens were regarded as
divided into "houses," the most important of which was the
"house of human life." The sonnets are largely autobiographical. They were inspired by Elizabeth Siddal and various
other women and sometimes simply by the idea of Woman.
The Sonnet. See Critical Notes.
  4. **lustral rite,** ceremony of purification. 14. **Charon**
...Death. Charon was the boatman who ferried the souls
of the dead over the Styx, one of the rivers of Hades. His
pay was a coin found in the mouth of the passenger.

To signal-fires, Oblivion's flight to scare;
And Youth, with still some single golden hair
Unto his shoulder clinging, since the last   6
  Embrace wherein two sweet arms held him
    fast;
And Life, still wreathing flowers for Death to
    wear.
Love's throne was not with these; but far
    above
All passionate wind of welcome and farewell
He sat in breathless bowers they dream not
    of;   11
Though Truth foreknow Love's heart, and
    Hope foretell,
And Flame be for Love's sake desirable,
And Youth be dear, and Life be sweet to
    Love.   (*1881*)

2. BRIDAL BIRTH

As when desire, long darkling, dawns, and
    first
The mother looks upon the newborn child,
Even so my Lady stood at gaze and smiled
When her soul knew at length the Love it
    nursed.
Born with her life, creature of poignant thirst
And exquisite hunger, at her heart Love lay   6
Quickening in darkness, till a voice that day
Cried on him, and the bonds of birth were
    burst.
Now, shadowed by his wings, our faces yearn
Together, as his fullgrown feet now range   10
The grove, and his warm hands our couch
    prepare;
Till to his song our bodiless souls in turn
Be born his children, when Death's nuptial
    change
Leaves us for light the halo of his hair.   (*1870*)

3. LOVE'S TESTAMENT

O thou who at Love's hour ecstatically
Unto my heart dost evermore present,
Clothed with his fire, thy heart his testament;
Whom I have neared and felt thy breath to be
The inmost incense of his sanctuary;   5
Who without speech hast owned him, and,
    intent
Upon his will, thy life with mine hast blent,
And murmured, "I am thine, thou'rt one
    with me!"
O what from thee the grace, to me the prize,·
And what to Love the glory,—when the
    whole   10
Of the deep stair thou tread'st to the dim
    shoal
And weary water of the place of sighs,
And there dost work deliverance, as thine eyes
Draw up my prisoned spirit to thy soul!
                          (*1870*)

4. LOVESIGHT

When do I see thee most, beloved one?
When in the light the spirits of mine eyes
Before thy face, their altar, solemnize
The worship of that Love through thee made
    known?
Or when in the dusk hours (we two alone)   5
Close-kissed and eloquent of still replies
Thy twilight-hidden glimmering visage lies,
And my soul only sees thy soul its own?
O love, my love! if I no more should see
Thyself, nor on the earth the shadow of thee,
Nor image of thine eyes in any spring,—   11
How then should sound upon Life's darkening
    slope
The ground-whirl of the perished leaves of
    Hope,
The wind of Death's imperishable wing?
                    (1870)

5. HEART'S HOPE

By what word's power, the key of paths
    untrod,
Shall I the difficult deeps of Love explore,
Till parted waves of Song yield up the shore
Even as that sea which Israel crossed dryshod?
For lo! in some poor rhythmic period,   5
Lady, I fain would tell how evermore
Thy soul I know not from thy body, nor
Thee from myself, neither our love from God.
Yea, in God's name, and Love's, and thine,
    would I
Draw from one loving heart such evidence   10
As to all hearts all things shall signify;
Tender as dawn's first hill-fire, and intense
As instantaneous penetrating sense,
In Spring's birth-hour, of other Springs gone
    by.   (1881)

6. THE KISS

What smouldering senses in death's sick delay
Or seizure of malign vicissitude
Can rob this body of honor, or denude
This soul of wedding-raiment worn today?
For lo! even now my lady's lips did play   5
With these my lips such consonant interlude
As laureled Orpheus longed for when he wooed

Sonnet 5. *Heart's Hope.* 4. **sea ... dryshod.** The
Israelites escaped from the Egyptians by passing through the
Red Sea, which became dry ground by the power of the Lord
(*Exodus*, 14).
Sonnet 6. *The Kiss.* 7. **Orpheus**, in Greek mythology a
Thracian poet and musician, whose lyre could charm beasts
and make trees and rocks move. When his wife, Eurydice,
died, he descended to Hades and so pleased the god Pluto by
his music that he was permitted to lead Eurydice back to
earth on condition that he should not look behind him until
he reached the upper world. His love for his wife was so great
that he violated the condition, and as a result she vanished
among the shades. In great grief Orpheus then withdrew to
the wild mountains, where shortly he was slain.

The half-drawn hungering face with that last
    lay.
I was a child beneath her touch,—a man
When breast to breast we clung, even I and
    she,—   10
A spirit when her spirit looked through me,—
A god when all our life-breath met to fan
Our life-blood, till love's emulous ardors ran,
Fire within fire, desire in deity.
                    (1870)

7. SUPREME SURRENDER

To all the spirits of Love that wander by
Along his love-sown harvest-field of sleep
My lady lies apparent; and the deep
Calls to the deep; and no man sees but I.
The bliss so long afar, at length so nigh,   5
Rests there attained. Methinks proud Love
    must weep
When Fate's control doth from his harvest
    reap
The sacred hour for which the years did sigh.
First touched, the hand now warm around
    my neck
Taught memory long to mock desire: and
    lo!   10
Across my breast the abandoned hair doth
    flow,
Where one shorn tress long stirred the long-
    ing ache:
And next the heart that trembled for its
    sake
Lies the queen-heart in sovereign overthrow.
                    (1870)

8. LOVE'S LOVERS

Some ladies love the jewels in Love's zone,
And gold-tipped darts he hath for painless
    play
In idle scornful hours he flings away;
And some that listen to his lute's soft tone
Do love to vaunt the silver praise their own;   5
Some prize his blindfold sight; and there be
    they
Who kissed his wings which brought him
    yesterday
And thank his wings today that he is flown.
My lady only loves the heart of Love:
Therefore Love's heart, my lady, hath for
    thee   10
His bower of unimagined flower and tree:
There kneels he now, and all-anhungered of
Thine eyes gray-lit in shadowing hair a-
    bove,
Seals with thy mouth his immortality.
                    (1870)

Sonnet 8. *Love's Lovers.* 1. **zone**, girdle.

9. PASSION AND WORSHIP

One flame-winged brought a white-winged
    harp-player
Even where my lady and I lay all alone;
Saying: "Behold, this minstrel is unknown;
Bid him depart, for I am minstrel here:
Only my strains are to Love's dear ones dear."
Then said I: "Through thine hautboy's rap-
    turous tone   6
Unto my lady still this harp makes moan,
And still she deems the cadence deep and
    clear."
Then said my lady: "Thou art Passion of
    Love,
And this Love's Worship: both he plights to
    me.   10
Thy mastering music walks the sunlit sea:
But where wan water trembles in the grove
And the wan moon is all the light thereof,
This harp still makes my name its voluntary."
    (1870)

10. THE PORTRAIT

O Lord of all compassionate control,
O Love! let this my lady's picture glow
Under my hand to praise her name, and show
Even of her inner self the perfect whole: 4
That he who seeks her beauty's furthest goal,
Beyond the light that the sweet glances throw
And refluent wave of the sweet smile, may
    know
The very sky and sea-line of her soul.
Lo! it is done. Above the enthroning throat
The mouth's mold testifies of voice and kiss, 10
The shadowed eyes remember and foresee.
Her face is made her shrine. Let all men note
That in all years (O Love, thy gift is this!)
They that would look on her must come to
    me.
    (1870)

11. THE LOVE-LETTER

Warmed by her hand and shadowed by her
    hair
As close she leaned and poured her heart
    through thee,
Whereof the articulate throbs accompany
The smooth black stream that makes thy
    whiteness fair,—
Sweet fluttering sheet, even of her breath
    aware,—   5
Oh, let thy silent song diclose to me
That soul wherewith her lips and eyes agree
Like married music in Love's answering air.

Fain had I watched her when, at some fond
    thought,
Her bosom to the writing closelier pressed,   10
And her breast's secrets peered into her breast;
When, through eyes raised an instant, her
    soul sought
My soul, and from the sudden confluence
    caught
The words that made her love the loveliest.
    (1870)

12. THE LOVERS' WALK

Sweet twining hedgeflowers wind-stirred in no
    wise
On this June day; and hand that clings in
    hand:—
Still glades; and meeting faces scarcely
    fanned:—
An osier-odored stream that draws the skies
Deep to its heart; and mirrored eyes in
    eyes:—   5
Fresh hourly wonder o'er the Summer land
Of light and cloud; and two souls softly
    spanned
With one o'erarching heaven of smiles and
    sighs:—
Even such their path, whose bodies lean unto
Each other's visible sweetness amorously,— 10
Whose passionate hearts lean by Love's high
    decree
Together on his heart forever true,
As the cloud-foaming firmamental blue
Rests on the blue line of a foamless sea.
    (1871; 1881)

13. YOUTH'S ANTIPHONY

"I love you, sweet: how can you ever learn
How much I love you?" "You I love even so,
And so I learn it." "Sweet, you cannot know
How fair you are." "If fair enough to earn
Your love, so much is all my love's concern."
"My love grows hourly, sweet." "Mine too
    doth grow,   6
Yet love seemed full so many hours ago!"
Thus lovers speak, till kisses claim their turn.
Ah! happy they to whom such words as these
In youth have served for speech the whole
    day long,   10
Hour after hour, remote from the world's
    throng,
Work, contest, fame, all life's confederate
    pleas,—
What while Love breathed in sighs and
    silences
Through two blent souls one rapturous under-
    song.
    (1881)

Sonnet 9. Passion and Worship. 6. **hautboy,** oboe, a
wind instrument.

14. YOUTH'S SPRING-TRIBUTE

On this sweet bank your head thrice sweet
    and dear
I lay, and spread your hair on either side,
And see the newborn woodflowers bashful-
    eyed
Look through the golden tresses here and
    there.
On these debatable borders of the year   5
Spring's foot half falters; scarce she yet may
    know
The leafless blackthorn-blossom from the
    snow;
And through her bowers the wind's way still
    is clear.
But April's sun strikes down the glades today;
So shut your eyes upturned, and feel my kiss 10
Creep, as the Spring now thrills through every
    spray,
Up your warm throat to your warm lips: for
    this
Is even the hour of Love's sworn suitservice,
With whom cold hearts are counted castaway.
                    (1870; 1881)

15. THE BIRTH-BOND

Have you not noted, in some family
Where two were born of a first marriage-bed,
How still they own their gracious bond,
    though fed
And nursed on the forgotten breast and
    knee?—
How to their father's children they shall
    be   5
In act and thought of one goodwill; but each
Shall for the other have, in silence speech,
And in a word complete community?
Even so, when first I saw you, seemed it,
    love,
That among souls allied to mine was yet   10
One nearer kindred than life hinted of.
O born with me somewhere that men forget,
And though in years of sight and sound
    unmet,
Known for my soul's birth-partner well
    enough!   *(1854; 1870)*

16. A DAY OF LOVE

Those envied places which do know her well,
And are so scornful of this lonely place,
Even now for once are emptied of her grace:
Nowhere but here she is: and while Love's spell
From his predominant presence doth compel 5
All alien hours, an outworn populace,
The hours of Love fill full the echoing space

With sweet confederate music favorable.
Now many memories make solicitous
The delicate love-lines of her mouth, till, lit 10
With quivering fire, the words take wing from
    it;
As here between our kisses we sit thus
Speaking of things remembered, and so sit
Speechless while things forgotten call to us.
                        (1870)

17. BEAUTY'S PAGEANT

What dawn-pulse at the heart of heaven, or
    last
Incarnate flower of culminating day,—
What marshaled marvels on the skirts of May,
Or song full-quired, sweet June's encomiast;
What glory of change by nature's hand
    amassed   5
Can vie with all those moods of varying grace
Which o'er one loveliest woman's form and
    face
Within this hour, within this room, have
    passed?
Love's very vesture and elect disguise   9
Was each fine movement,—wonder new-begot
Of lily or swan or swan-stemmed galiot;
Joy to his sight who now the sadlier sighs,
Parted again; and sorrow yet for eyes
Unborn, that read these words and saw her
    not.   *(c. 1871; 1881)*

18. GENIUS IN BEAUTY

Beauty like hers is genius. Not the call
Of Homer's or of Dante's heart sublime,—
Not Michael's hand furrowing the zones of
    time,—
Is more with compassed mysteries musical;
Nay, not in Spring's or Summer's sweet
    footfall   5
More gathered gifts exuberant Life bequeaths
Than doth this sovereign face, whose love-
    spell breathes
Even from its shadowed contour on the wall.
As many men are poets in their youth,
But for one sweet-strung soul the wires pro-
    long   10
Even through all change the indomitable
    song;
So in likewise the envenomed years, whose
    tooth
Rends shallower grace with ruin void of ruth,
Upon this beauty's power shall wreak no
    wrong.   *(1881)*

Sonnet 17. Beauty's Pageant. 11. **swan-stemmed galiot,**
kind of small ship with the stem built in the likeness of a swan.
Sonnet 18. Genius in Beauty. 3. **Michael,** Michelangelo
(1475-1564), famous Italian painter, sculptor, architect,
and poet. The reference is to his figures of Night, Day,
Evening, etc.

Sonnet 15. The Birth-Bond. 5. **father's children,** i.e.,
children by a second marriage.

19. SILENT NOON

Your hands lie open in the long fresh grass,—
The finger-points look through like rosy
    blooms:
Your eyes smile peace. The pasture gleams
    and glooms
'Neath billowing skies that scatter and amass.
All round our nest, far as the eye can pass, 5
Are golden kingcup-fields with silver edge
Where the cow-parsley skirts the hawthorn-
    hedge.
'Tis visible silence, still as the hour-glass.
Deep in the sun-searched growths the dragon-
    fly
Hangs like a blue thread loosened from the
    sky:—   10
So this winged hour is dropped to us from
    above.
Oh! clasp we to our hearts, for deathless
    dower,
This close-companioned inarticulate hour
When twofold silence was the song of love.
    (1881)

20. GRACIOUS MOONLIGHT

Even as the moon grows queenlier in mid-space
When the sky darkens, and her cloud-rapt car
Thrills with intenser radiance from afar,—
So lambent, lady, beams thy sovereign grace
When the drear soul desires thee. Of that
    face   5
What shall be said,—which, like a governing
    star,
Gathers and garners from all things that are
Their silent penetrative loveliness?
O'er water-daisies and wild waifs of Spring,
There where the iris rears its gold-crowned
    sheaf   10
With flowering rush and sceptered arrow-leaf,
So have I marked Queen Dian, in bright ring
Of cloud above and wave below, take wing
And chase night's gloom, as thou the spirit's
    grief.
    (c. 1871; 1881)

21. LOVE-SWEETNESS

Sweet dimness of her loosened hair's down-
    fall
About thy face; her sweet hands round thy
    head
In gracious fostering union garlanded;
Her tremulous smiles; her glances' sweet
    recall
Of love; her murmuring sighs memorial;   5
Her mouth's culled sweetness by thy kisses
    shed

Sonnet 20. Gracious Moonlight. 12. **Queen Dian**, the moon.

On cheeks and neck and eyelids, and so led
Back to her mouth which answers there for
    all:—
What sweeter than these things, except the
    thing
In lacking which all these would lose their
    sweet:—   10
The confident heart's still fervor: the swift
    beat
And soft subsidence of the spirit's wing,
Then when it feels in cloud-girt wayfaring,
The breath of kindred plumes against its
    feet?
    (1870)

22. HEART'S HAVEN

Sometimes she is a child within mine arms,
Cowering beneath dark wings that love must
    chase,—
With still tears showering and averted face,
Inexplicably filled with faint alarms:
And oft from mine own spirit's hurtling
    harms   5
I crave the refuge of her deep embrace,—
Against all ills the fortified strong place
And sweet reserve of sovereign counter-
    charms.
And Love, our light at night and shade at
    noon,
Lulls us to rest with songs, and turns away 10
All shafts of shelterless tumultuous day.
Like the moon's growth, his face gleams
    through his tune;
And as soft waters warble to the moon,
Our answering spirits chime one roundelay.
    (*1871;* 1881)

23. LOVE'S BAUBLES

I stood where Love in brimming armfuls bore
Slight wanton flowers and foolish toys of
    fruit:
And round him ladies thronged in warm pur-
    suit,
Fingered and lipped and proffered the strange
    store.
And from one hand the petal and the core   5
Savored of sleep; and cluster and curled shoot
Seemed from another hand like shame's sa-
    lute,—
Gifts that I felt my cheek was blushing for.
At last Love bade my Lady give the same:
And as I looked, the dew was light thereon; 10
And as I took them, at her touch they shone
With inmost heaven-hue of the heart of flame.
And then Love said: "Lo! when the hand is
    hers,
Follies of love are love's true ministers."
    (1870)

24. PRIDE OF YOUTH

Even as a child, of sorrow that we give
The dead, but little in his heart can find,
Since without need of thought to his clear
    mind
Their turn it is to die and his to live:—
Even so the winged New Love smiles to
    receive   5
Along his eddying plumes the auroral wind,
Nor, forward glorying, casts one look be-
    hind
Where night-rack shrouds the Old Love
    fugitive.
There is a change in every hour's recall,
And the last cowslip in the fields we see   10
On the same day with the first corn-poppy.
Alas for hourly change! Alas for all
The loves that from his hand proud Youth
    lets fall,
Even as the beads of a told rosary!
                         (1881)

25. WINGED HOURS

Each hour until we meet is as a bird
That wings from far his gradual way along
The rustling covert of my soul,—his song
Still loudlier trilled through leaves more
    deeply stirred.
But at the hour of meeting, a clear word   5
Is every note he sings, in Love's own tongue;
Yet, Love, thou know'st the sweet strain
    suffers wrong,
Full oft through our contending joys unheard.
What of that hour at last, when for her sake
No wing may fly to me nor song may flow;
When, wandering round my life unleaved, I
    know   11
The bloodied feathers scattered in the brake,
And think how she, far from me, with like eyes
Sees through the untuneful bough the wing-
    less skies?   (1869)

26. MID-RAPTURE

Thou lovely and beloved, thou my love;
Whose kiss seems still the first; whose sum-
    moning eyes,
Even now, as for our love-world's new sunrise,
Shed very dawn; whose voice, attuned above
All modulation of the deep-bowered dove,   5
Is like a hand laid softly on the soul;
Whose hand is like a sweet voice to control
Those worn tired brows it hath the keeping
    of:—
What word can answer to thy word,—what
    gaze   9
To thine, which now absorbs within its sphere
My worshiping face, till I am mirrored there

Light-circled in a heaven of deep-drawn rays?
What clasp, what kiss mine inmost heart can
    prove,
O lovely and beloved, O my love?
                    (c. 1871; 1881)

27. HEART'S COMPASS

Sometimes thou seem'st not as thyself alone,
But as the meaning of all things that are;
A breathless wonder, shadowing forth afar
Some heavenly solstice hushed and halcyon;
Whose unstirred lips are music's visible tone; 5
Whose eyes the sun-gate of the soul unbar,
Being of its furthest fires oracular;—
The evident heart of all life sown and mown.
Even such Love is; and is not thy name Love?
Yea, by thy hand the Love-god rends apart
All gathering clouds of Night's ambiguous
    art;   11
Flings them far down, and sets thine eyes
    above;
And simply, as some gage of flower or glove,
Stakes with a smile the world against thy
    heart.   (1881)

28. SOUL-LIGHT

What other woman could be loved like you,
Or how of you should love possess his fill?
After the fulness of all rapture, still,—
As at the end of some deep avenue
A tender glamor of day,—there comes to
    view   5
Far in your eyes a yet more hungering thrill,—
Such fire as Love's soul-winnowing hands
    distil
Even from his inmost ark of light and dew.
And as the traveler triumphs with the sun,
Glorying in heat's mid-height, yet startide
    brings   10
Wonder new-born, and still fresh transport
    springs
From limpid lambent hours of day begun;—
Even so, through eyes and voice, your soul
    doth move
My soul with changeful light of infinite love.
                    (c. 1871; 1881)

29. THE MOONSTAR

Lady, I thank thee for thy loveliness,
Because my lady is more lovely still.
Glorying I gaze, and yield with glad goodwill
To thee thy tribute; by whose sweet-spun dress
Of delicate life Love labors to assess   5
My lady's absolute queendom; saying, "Lo!
How high this beauty is, which yet doth show

Sonnet 27. Heart's Compass. **4. halcyon,** calm.

But as that beauty's sovereign votaress."
Lady, I saw thee with her, side by side;
And as, when night's fair fires their queen
    surround,   10
An emulous star too near the moon will ride,—
Even so thy rays within her luminous bound
Were traced no more; and by the light so
    drowned,
Lady, not thou but she was glorified.
                   (*c. 1871;* 1881)

30. LAST FIRE

Love, through your spirit and mine what
    summer eve
Now glows with glory of all things possessed,
Since this day's sun of rapture filled the west
And the light sweetened as the fire took leave?
Awhile now softlier let your bosom heave,   5
As in Love's harbor, even that loving breast,
All care takes refuge while we sink to rest,
And mutual dreams the bygone bliss retrieve.
Many the days that Winter keeps in store,
Sunless throughout, or whose brief sun-
    glimpses   10
Scarce shed the heaped snow through the
    naked trees.
This day at least was Summer's paramour,
Sun-colored to the imperishable core
With sweet well-being of love and full heart's
    ease.
                   (*c. 1871;* 1881)

31. HER GIFTS

High grace, the dower of queens; and there-
    withal
Some wood-born wonder's sweet simplicity;
A glance like water brimming with the sky
Or hyacinth-light where forest-shadows fall;
Such thrilling pallor of cheek as doth enthrall
The heart; a mouth whose passionate forms
    imply   6
All music and all silence held thereby;
Deep golden locks, her sovereign coronal;
A round reared neck, meet column of Love's
    shrine
To cling to when the heart takes sanctuary;
Hands which forever at Love's bidding be,   11
And soft-stirred feet still answering to his
    sign—
These are her gifts, as tongue may tell them
    o'er.
Breathe low her name, my soul; for that
    means more.   (*c. 1871;* 1881)

32. EQUAL TROTH

Not by one measure mayst thou mete our love;
For how should I be loved as I love thee?—

I, graceless, joyless, lacking absolutely
All gifts that with thy queenship best be-
    hove;—
Thou, throned in every heart's elect alcove,   5
And crowned with garlands culled from every
    tree,
Which for no head but thine, by Love's decree,
All beauties and all mysteries interwove.
But here thine eyes and lips yield soft re-
    buke:—
"Then only" (say'st thou) "could I love thee
    less,   10
When thou couldst doubt my love's equality."
Peace, sweet! If not to sum but worth we
    look,—
Thy heart's transcendence, not my heart's
    excess,—
Then more a thousandfold thou lov'st than I.
                   (*c. 1871;* 1881)

33. VENUS VICTRIX

Could Juno's self more sovereign presence
    wear
Than thou, 'mid other ladies throned in
    grace?—
Or Pallas, when thou bend'st with soul-stilled
    face   3
O'er poet's page gold-shadowed in thy hair?
Dost thou than Venus seem less heavenly fair
When o'er the sea of love's tumultuous trance
Hovers thy smile, and mingles with thy glance
That sweet voice like the last wave murmuring
    there?
Before such triune loveliness divine
Awestruck I ask, which goddess here most
    claims   10
The prize that, howsoe'er adjudged, is thine?
Then Love breathes low the sweetest of thy
    names;
And Venus Victrix to my heart doth bring
Herself, the Helen of thy guerdoning.
                 (*c. 1871;* 1881)

34. THE DARK GLASS

Not I myself know all my love for thee:
How should I reach so far, who cannot weigh
Tomorrow's dower by gage of yesterday?
Shall birth and death, and all dark names that
    be

Sonnet 33. Venus Victrix. The title means *Venus the Conqueror.* Venus was the goddess of love. Juno (l. 1) was the wife of Jupiter and queen of the gods; Pallas Athena (l. 3) was a civic goddess, identified with Minerva. These three goddesses were competitors for a golden apple marked "for the fairest." Paris, son of King Priam of Troy, was selected to make the decision. Each woman promised Paris a reward if she were chosen: Juno promised power; Pallas promised glory; Venus promised the fairest of women for his wife. Aided by Venus, Paris persuaded Helen, the beautiful wife of Menelaus, King of Sparta, to elope with him, and he carried her off to Troy. This action started the great Trojan War.

As doors and windows bared to some loud sea,
Lash deaf mine ears and blind my face with
    spray;   6
And shall my sense pierce love,—the last
    relay
And ultimate outpost of eternity?
Lo! what am I to Love, the lord of all?
One murmuring shell he gathers from the
    sand,—   10
One little heart-flame sheltered in his hand.
Yet through thine eyes he grants me clearest
    call
And veriest touch of powers primordial
That any hour-girt life may understand.

                (*1871;* 1881)

35. THE LAMP'S SHRINE

Sometimes I fain would find in thee some
    fault,
That I might love thee still in spite of it:
Yet how should our Lord Love curtail one whit
Thy perfect praise whom most he would exalt?
Alas! he can but make my heart's low vault   5
Even in men's sight unworthier, being lit
By thee, who thereby show'st more exquisite
Like fiery chrysoprase in deep basalt.
Yet will I nowise shrink; but at Love's shrine
Myself within the beams his brow doth dart 10
Will set the flashing jewel of thy heart
In that dull chamber where it deigns to shine:
For lo! in honor of thine excellencies
My heart takes pride to show how poor it is.

              (*c. 1871;* 1881)

36. LIFE-IN-LOVE

Not in thy body is thy life at all,
But in this lady's lips and hands and eyes;
Through these she yields thee life that vivifies
What else were sorrow's servant and death's
    thrall.
Look on thyself without her, and recall   5
The waste remembrance and forlorn surmise
That lived but in a dead-drawn breath of sighs
O'er vanished hours and hours eventual.
Even so much life hath the poor tress of hair
Which, stored apart, is all love hath to show 10
For heart-beats and for fire-heats long ago;
Even so much life endures unknown, even
    where,
'Mid change the changeless night environeth,
Lies all that golden hair undimmed in death.

                 (1870)

37. THE LOVE-MOON

"When that dead face, bowered in the fur-
    thest years,
Which once was all the life years held for thee,
Can now scarce bid the tides of memory
Cast on thy soul a little spray of tears,—
How canst thou gaze into these eyes of hers 5
Whom now thy heart delights in, and not see
Within each orb Love's philtered euphrasy
Make them of buried troth remembrancers?"
"Nay, pitiful Love, nay, loving Pity! Well
Thou knowest that in these twain I have con-
    fessed   10
Two very voices of thy summoning bell.
Nay, Master, shall not Death make manifest
In these the culminant changes which approve
The love-moon that must light my soul to
    Love?"

                 (1870)

38. THE MORROW'S MESSAGE

"Thou Ghost," I said, "and is thy name
    Today?—
Yesterday's son, with such an abject brow!—
And can Tomorrow be more pale than thou?"
While yet I spoke, the silence answered: "Yea,
Henceforth our issue is all grieved and gray, 5
And each beforehand makes such poor avow
As of old leaves beneath the budding bough
Or night-drift that the sundawn shreds away."
Then cried I: "Mother of many malisons,
O Earth, receive me to thy dusty bed!"   10
But therewithal the tremulous silence said:
"Lo! Love yet bids thy lady greet thee
    once:—
Yea, twice,—whereby thy life is still the
    sun's;
And thrice,—whereby the shadow of death is
    dead."

                 (1870)

39. SLEEPLESS DREAMS

Girt in dark growths, yet glimmering with one
    star,
O night desirous as the nights of youth!
Why should my heart within thy spell, for-
    sooth,
Now beat, as the bride's finger-pulses are
Quickened within the girdling golden bar? 5
What wings are these that fan my pillow
    smooth?
And why does Sleep, waved back by Joy and
    Ruth,

Sonnet 34. The Dark Glass. 9. The earthly love of line 1
has now become an index of the Divine. This is the finest
statement of Rossetti's "mystical" philosophy.
   Sonnet 35. The Lamp's Shrine. 8. **chrysoprase,** a kind of
light green quartz, sometimes valued as a gem.
   Sonnet 36. Life-in-Love. 2. **this lady,** the first direct
reference to the second or new beloved.

Sonnet 37. The Love-Moon. 7. **euphrasy,** eyebright, a
small plant formerly used as a remedy for diseases of the
eye.
   Sonnet 38. The Morrow's Message. 9. **malisons,** curses.
   Sonnet 39. Sleepless Dreams. 7. **Ruth,** sorrow.

Tread softly round and gaze at me from far?
Nay, night deep-leaved!   And would Love
    feign in thee
Some shadowy palpitating grove that bears 10
Rest for man's eyes and music for his ears?
O lonely night! art thou not known to me,
A thicket hung with masks of mockery
And watered with the wasteful warmth of
    tears?
                   (c. 1869; 1870)

40. SEVERED SELVES

Two separate divided silences,
Which, brought together, would find loving
    voice;
Two glances, which together would rejoice
In love, now lost like stars beyond dark trees;
Two hands apart whose touch alone gives
    ease;   5
Two bosoms which, heart-shrined with mu-
    tual flame,
Would, meeting in one clasp, be made the
    same;
Two souls, the shores wave-mocked of sunder-
    ing seas:—
Such are we now.   Ah! may our hope fore-
    cast
Indeed one hour again, when on this stream
Of darkened love once more the light shall
    gleam?—   11
An hour how slow to come, how quickly
    past,—
Which blooms and fades, and only leaves at
    last,
Faint as shed flowers, the attenuated dream.
                   (1881)

41. THROUGH DEATH TO LOVE

Like labor-laden moonclouds faint to flee
From winds that sweep the winter-bitten
    wold,—
Like multiform circumfluence manifold
Of night's flood-tide,—like terrors that agree
Of hoarse-tongued fire and inarticulate sea,— 5
Even such, within some glass dimmed by our
    breath,
Our hearts discern wild images of Death,
Shadows and shoals that edge eternity.
Howbeit athwart Death's imminent shade
    doth soar
One Power, than flow of stream or flight of
    dove   10
Sweeter to glide around, to brood above.
Tell me, my heart,—what angel-greeted door
Or threshold of wing-winnowed threshing-floor
Hath guest fire-fledged as thine, whose lord is
    Love?
               (1871; 1881)

42. HOPE OVERTAKEN

I deemed thy garments, O my Hope, were
    gray,
So far I viewed thee.   Now the space between
Is passed at length; and garmented in green
Even as in days of yore thou stand'st today.
Ah God! and but for lingering dull dismay, 5
On all that road our footsteps erst had been
Even thus commingled, and our shadows seen
Blent on the hedgerows and the water-way.
O Hope of mine whose eyes are living love,
No eyes but hers,—O Love and Hope the
    same!—   10
Lean close to me, for now the sinking sun
That warmed our feet scarce gilds our hair
    above.
O hers thy voice and very hers thy name!
Alas, cling round me, for the day is done!
              (c. 1871; 1881)

43. LOVE AND HOPE

Bless love and hope.   Full many a withered
    year
Whirled past us, eddying to its chill dooms-
    day;
And clasped together where the blown leaves
    lay,
We long have knelt and wept full many a tear.
Yet lo! one hour at last, the Spring's compeer,
Flutes softly to us from some green byway: 6
Those years, those tears are dead, but only
    they:—
Bless love and hope, true soul; for we are here.
Cling heart to heart; nor of this hour demand
Whether in very truth, when we are dead, 10
Our hearts shall wake to know Love's golden
    head
Sole sunshine of the imperishable land;
Or but discern, through night's unfeatured
    scope,
Scorn-fired at length the illusive eyes of Hope.
              (c. 1871; 1881)

44. CLOUD AND WIND

Love, should I fear death most for you or me?
Yet if you die, can I not follow you,
Forcing the straits of change?   Alas! but who
Shall wrest a bond from night's inveteracy,
Ere yet my hazardous soul put forth, to be 5
Her warrant against all her haste might rue?—
Ah! in your eyes so reached what dumb adieu,
What unsunned gyres of waste eternity?
And if I die the first, shall death be then
A lampless watchtower whence I see you
    weep?—   10

Sonnet 44. Cloud and Wind. **8.** gyres, spirals.

Or (woe is me!) a bed wherein my sleep
Ne'er notes (as death's dear cup at last you
    drain)
The hour when you too learn that all is vain
And that Hope sows what Love shall never
    reap?

             (c. 1871; 1881)

45. SECRET PARTING

Because our talk was of the cloud-control
And moon-track of the journeying face of
    Fate,
Her tremulous kisses faltered at love's gate
And her eyes dreamed against a distant goal:
But soon, remembering her how brief the
    whole   5
Of joy, which its own hours annihilate,
Her set gaze gathered, thirstier than of late,
And as she kissed, her mouth became her soul.
Thence in what ways we wandered, and how
    strove
To build with fire-tried vows the piteous
    home   10
Which memory haunts and whither sleep may
    roam,—
They only know for whom the roof of Love
Is the still-seated secret of the grove,
Nor spire may rise nor bell be heard there-
    from.

          (c. 1868-1869; 1881)

46. PARTED LOVE

What shall be said of this embattled day
And arméd occupation of this night
By all thy foes beleaguered,—now when sight
Nor sound denotes the loved one far away?
Of these thy vanquished hours what shalt
    thou say,—   5
As every sense to which she dealt delight
Now labors lonely o'er the stark noon-height
To reach the sunset's desolate disarray?
Stand still, fond fettered wretch! while
    Memory's art
Parades the Past before thy face, and lures 10
Thy spirit to her passionate portraitures:
Till the tempestuous tide-gates flung apart
Flood with wild will the hollows of thy heart,
And thy heart rends thee, and thy body en-
    dures.

              (1870)

47. BROKEN MUSIC

The mother will not turn, who thinks she
    hears
Her nursling's speech first grow articulate;
But breathless with averted eyes elate
She sits, with open lips and open ears,

That it may call her twice. 'Mid doubts and
    fears   5
Thus oft my soul has hearkened; till the song,
A central moan for days, at length found
    tongue,
And the sweet music welled and the sweet
    tears.
But now, whatever while the soul is fain
To list that wonted murmur, as it were   10
The speech-bound sea-shell's low importunate
    strain,—
No breath of song, thy voice alone is there,
O bitterly beloved! and all her gain
Is but the pang of unpermitted prayer.

          (c. 1869; 1870)

48. DEATH-IN-LOVE

There came an image in Life's retinue
That had Love's wings and bore his gon-
    falon:
Fair was the web, and nobly wrought
    thereon,
O soul-sequestered face, thy form and hue!
Bewildering sounds, such as spring wakens
    to,   5
Shook in its folds; and through my heart
    its power
Sped trackless as the immemorable hour
When birth's dark portal groaned and all
    was new.
But a veiled woman followed, and she caught
The banner round its staff, to furl and cling,—
Then plucked a feather from the bearer's
    wing,   11
And held it to his lips that stirred it not,
And said to me, "Behold, there is no breath:
I and this Love are one, and I am Death."

              (1870)

49. WILLOWWOOD — I

I sat with Love upon a woodside well,
Leaning across the water, I and he;
Nor ever did he speak nor looked at me,
But touched his lute wherein was audible
The certain secret thing he had to tell.   5
Only our mirrored eyes met silently
In the low wave; and that sound came to be
The passionate voice I knew; and my tears
    fell.
And at their fall, his eyes beneath grew hers;
And with his foot and with his wing-feathers
He swept the spring that watered my heart's
    drouth.   11
Then the dark ripples spread to waving hair,

Sonnet 48. Death-in-Love. 2. **gonfalon**, banner.
Sonnets 49-52. Willowwood. The title given to this series
of four sonnets is poetical for *The Woodland of Weeping.*
The willow is a symbol of mourning.

And as I stooped, her own lips rising there
Bubbled with brimming kisses at my mouth.

(1868; 1869)

50. WILLOWWOOD — 2

And now Love sang: but his was such a song,
So meshed with half-remembrance hard to
    free,
As souls disused in death's sterility
May sing when the new birthday tarries long.
And I was made aware of a dumb throng   5
That stood aloof, one form by every tree,
All mournful forms, for each was I or she,
The shades of those our days that had no
    tongue.
They looked on us, and knew us and were
    known;
While fast together, alive from the abyss,   10
Clung the soul-wrung implacable close kiss;
And pity of self through all made broken
    moan
Which said, "For once, for once, for once
    alone!"
And still Love sang, and what he sang was
    this:

(1868; 1869)

51. WILLOWWOOD — 3

"O ye, all ye that walk in Willowwood,
That walk with hollow faces burning white:
What fathom-depth of soul-struck widow-
    hood,
What long, what longer hours, one lifelong
    night,
Ere ye again, who so in vain have wooed   5
Your last hope lost, who so in vain invite
Your lips to that their unforgotten food,
Ere ye, ere ye again shall see the light!
Alas! the bitter banks in Willowwood,
With tear-spurge wan, with blood-wort burn-
    ing red: 10
Alas! if ever such a pillow could
Steep deep the soul in sleep till she were
    dead,—
Better all life forget her than this thing,
That Willowwood should hold her wander-
    ing!"   *(1868; 1869)*

52. WILLOWWOOD — 4

So sang he: and as meeting rose and rose
Together cling through the wind's wellaway
Nor change at once, yet near the end of day
The leaves drop loosened where the heart-
    stain glows,—
So when the song died did the kiss unclose;   5
And her face fell back drowned, and was as
    gray

As its gray eyes; and if it ever may
Meet mine again I know not if Love knows.
Only I know that I leaned low and drank
A long draft from the water where she sank,   10
Her breath and all her tears and all her soul:
And as I leaned, I know I felt Love's face
Pressed on my neck with moan of pity and
    grace,
Till both our heads were in his aureole.

(1868; 1869)

53. WITHOUT HER

What of her glass without her? The blank.
    gray
There where the pool is blind of the moon's
    face.
Her dress without her? The tossed empty
    space
Of cloud-rack whence the moon has passed
    away.
Her paths without her? Day's appointed
    sway   5
Usurped by desolate night. Her pillowed place
Without her? Tears, ah me! for love's good
    grace,
And cold forgetfulness of night or day.
What of the heart without her? Nay, poor
    heart,
Of thee what word remains ere speech be
    still?   10
A wayfarer by barren ways and chill,
Steep ways and weary, without her thou art,
Where the long cloud, the long wood's coun-
    terpart,
Sheds doubled darkness up the laboring hill.

(1881)

54. LOVE'S FATALITY

Sweet Love,—but oh! most dread Desire of
    Love
Life-thwarted. Linked in gyves I saw them
    stand,
Love shackled with Vain-longing, hand to
    hand:
And one was eyed as the blue vault above:
But hope tempestuous like a fire-cloud hove   5
I' the other's gaze, even as in his whose wand
Vainly all night with spell-wrought power has
    spanned
The unyielding caves of some deep treasure-
    trove.
Also his lips, two writhen flakes of flame,
Made moan: "Alas O Love, thus leashed with
    me!   10
Wing-footed thou, wing-shouldered, once born
    free:
And I, thy cowering self, in chains grown
    tame,—

Bound to thy body and soul, named with thy
    name,—
Life's iron heart, even Love's Fatality."
                (*1871;* 1881)

55. STILLBORN LOVE

The hour which might have been yet might
    not be,
Which man's and woman's heart conceived
    and bore
Yet whereof life was barren,—on what shore
Bides it the breaking of Time's weary sea?
Bondchild of all consummate joys set free,   5
It somewhere sighs and serves, and mute
    before
The house of Love, hears through the echoing
    door
His hours elect in choral consonancy.
But lo! what wedded souls now hand in hand
Together tread at last the immortal strand 10
With eyes where burning memory lights love
    home?
Lo! how the little outcast hour has turned
And leaped to them and in their faces
    yearned:—
"I am your child: O parents, ye have come!"
                (*1869;* 1870)

56. TRUE WOMAN—1. HERSELF

To be a sweetness more desired than Spring;
A bodily beauty more acceptable
Than the wild rose-tree's arch that crowns
    the fell;
To be an essence more environing   4
Than wine's drained juice; a music ravishing
More than the passionate pulse of Philomel:
To be all this 'neath one soft bosom's swell
That is the flower of life:—how strange a
    thing!
How strange a thing to be what Man can
    know
But as a sacred secret! Heaven's own screen
Hides her soul's purest depth and loveliest
    glow;   11
Closely withheld, as all things most unseen,—
The wave-bowered pearl,—the heart-shaped
    seal of green
That flecks the snowdrop underneath the
    snow.
             (*c. 1881;* 1881)

57. TRUE WOMAN—2. HER LOVE

She loves him; for her infinite soul is Love,
And he her lodestar. Passion in her is

A glass facing his fire, where the bright bliss
Is mirrored, and the heat returned. Yet move
That glass, a stranger's amorous flame to
    prove,   5
And it shall turn, by instant contraries,
Ice to the moon; while her pure fire to his
For whom it burns, clings close i' the heart's
    alcove.
Lo! they are one. With wifely breast to
    breast
And circling arms, she welcomes all com-
    mand   10
Of love,—her soul to answering ardors
    fanned;
Yet as morn springs or twilight sinks to rest,
Ah! who shall say she deems not loveliest
The hour of sisterly sweet hand-in-hand?
               (1881)

58. TRUE WOMAN—3. HER HEAVEN

If to grow old in Heaven is to grow young,
(As the Seer saw and said,) then blest were he
With youth forevermore, whose heaven should
    be
True Woman, she whom these weak notes
    have sung.
Here and hereafter,—choir-strains of her
    tongue,—   5
Sky-spaces of her eyes,—sweet signs that flee
About her soul's immediate sanctuary,—
Were Paradise all uttermost worlds among.
The sunrise blooms and withers on the hill
Like any hillflower; and the noblest troth   10
Dies here to dust. Yet shall Heaven's prom-
    ise clothe
Even yet those lovers who have cherished
    still
This test for love:—in every kiss sealed fast
To feel the first kiss and forbode the last.
               (1881)

59. LOVE'S LAST GIFT

Love to his singer held a glistening leaf,
And said: "The rose-tree and the apple-tree
Have fruits to vaunt or flowers to lure the
    bee;
And golden shafts are in the feathered sheaf
Of the great harvest-marshal, the year's chief,
Victorious Summer; aye, and 'neath warm sea
Strange secret grasses lurk inviolably   7
Between the filtering channels of sunk reef.
All are my blooms; and all sweet blooms of love
To thee I gave while Spring and Summer
    sang;   10

Sonnet 56. *True Woman, 1.* 3. **fell**, moor. 7. **Philomel**,
the nightingale. (See Arnold's *Philomela*, p. 486.)

Sonnet 57. *True Woman, 2.* 7. **Ice to the moon**, as cold
as ice under moonlight.
Sonnet 58. *True Woman, 3.* 2. **Seer**, Emanuel Sweden-
borg (1688-1772), a Swedish theologian and mystic.

But Autumn stops to listen, with some pang
From those worse things the wind is moaning
    of.
Only this laurel dreads no winter days:
Take my last gift; thy heart hath sung my
    praise."

              (*c. 1871;* 1881)

PART II. CHANGE AND FATE

60. TRANSFIGURED LIFE

As growth of form or momentary glance
In a child's features will recall to mind
The father's with the mother's face com-
    bined,—
Sweet interchange that memories still en-
    hance:
And yet as childhood's years and youth's
    advance,   5
The gradual moldings leave one stamp be-
    hind,
Till in the blended likeness now we find
A separate man's or woman's countenance—
So in the Song, the singer's Joy and Pain,
Its very parents, evermore expand   10
To bid the passion's fullgrown birth remain,
By Art's transfiguring essence subtly spanned;
And from that song-cloud shaped as a man's
    hand
There comes the sound as of abundant rain.

              (1881)

61. THE SONG-THROE

By thine own tears thy song must tears beget,
O Singer! Magic mirror thou hast none
Except thy manifest heart; and save thine own
Anguish or ardor, else no amulet.
Cisterned in Pride, verse is the feathery jet 5
Of soulless air-flung fountains; nay, more dry
Than the Dead Sea for throats that thirst and
    sigh,
That song o'er which no singer's lids grew wet.
The Song-god—He the Sun-god—is no slave
Of thine: thy Hunter he, who for thy soul 10
Fledges his shaft: to no august control
Of thy skilled hand his quivered store he gave:
But if thy lips' loud cry leap to his smart,
The inspired recoil shall pierce thy brother's
    heart.

            (*1880;* 1881)

    Sonnet 60. Transfigured Life. **14. sound . . . rain.** Rain is
considered as the symbol of fertility and purification. For
the phrase, see *I Kings,* 18:41.
    Sonnet 61. The Song-Throe. **7. Dead Sea,** a salt lake south-
east of Jerusalem. **9. Song-god,** Apollo, god of poetry and
music, identified with the sun god Helios. His constant
attributes were the bow and the lyre. **11. Fledges,** furnishes
with feathers ready for shooting. **12. quivered store,** stock
of arrows.

62. THE SOUL'S SPHERE

Some prisoned moon in steep cloud-fast-
    nesses,—
Throned queen and thralled; some dying sun
    whose pyre
Blazed with momentous memorable fire;—
Who hath not yearned and fed his heart with
    these?   4
Who, sleepless, hath not anguished to appease
Tragical shadow's realm of sound and sight
Conjectured in the lamentable night? . . .
Lo! the soul's sphere of infinite images!
What sense shall count them? Whether it
    forecast   9
The rose-winged hours that flutter in the van
Of Love's unquestioning unrevealéd span,—
Visions of golden futures: or that last
Wild pageant of the accumulated past
That clangs and flashes for a drowning man.

            (*c. 1871;* 1881)

63. INCLUSIVENESS

The changing guests, each in a different mood,
Sit at the roadside table and arise:
And every life among them in likewise
Is a soul's board set daily with new food.
What man has bent o'er his son's sleep, to
    brood   5
How that face shall watch his when cold it
    lies?—
Or thought, as his own mother kissed his eyes,
Of what her kiss was when his father wooed?
May not this ancient room thou sitt'st in
    dwell
In separate living souls for joy or pain?   10
Nay, all its corners may be painted plain
Where Heaven shows pictures of some life
    spent well;
And may be stamped, a memory all in vain,
Upon the sight of lidless eyes in Hell.

            (1869)

64. ARDOR AND MEMORY

The cuckoo-throb, the heartbeat of the Spring;
The rosebud's blush that leaves it as it grows
Into the full-eyed fair unblushing rose;
The summer clouds that visit every wing
With fires of sunrise and of sunsetting;   5
The furtive flickering streams to light reborn
'Mid airs new-fledged and valorous lusts of
    morn,
While all the daughters of the daybreak
    sing:—
These ardor loves, and memory: and when
    flown
All joys, and through dark forest-boughs in
    flight   10

The wind swoops onward brandishing the
    light,
Even yet the rose-tree's verdure left alone
Will flush all ruddy though the rose be gone;
With ditties and with dirges infinite.
                (*1879;* 1881)

65. KNOWN IN VAIN

As two whose love, first foolish, widening
    scope,
Knows suddenly, with music high and soft,
The Holy of holies; who because they
    scoffed
Are now amazed with shame, nor dare to
    cope
With the whole truth aloud, lest heaven
    should ope;   5
Yet, at their meetings, laugh not as they
    laughed
In speech; nor speak, at length; but sitting
    oft
Together, within hopeless sight of hope
For hours are silent:—so it happeneth
When Work and Will awake too late, to
    gaze   10
After their life sailed by, and hold their
    breath.
Ah! who shall dare to search through what
    sad maze
Thenceforth their incommunicable ways
Follow the desultory feet of Death?
                      (1869)

66. THE HEART OF THE NIGHT

From child to youth; from youth to arduous
    man;
From lethargy to fever of the heart;
From faithful life to dream-dowered days
    apart;
From trust to doubt; from doubt to brink of
    ban;—
Thus much of change in one swift cycle ran   5
Till now. Alas, the soul!—how soon must
    she
Accept her primal immortality,—
The flesh resume its dust whence it began?
O Lord of work and peace! O Lord of life!
O Lord, the awful Lord of will! though late,
Even yet renew this soul with duteous
    breath: 11
That when the peace is garnered in from
    strife,
The work retrieved, the will regenerate,
This soul may see thy face, O Lord of death!
                    (1881)

Sonnet 66. The Heart of the Night. **4. ban,** condemnation.

67. THE LANDMARK

Was *that* the landmark? What,—the foolish
    well
Whose wave, low down, I did not stoop to
    drink,
But sat and flung the pebbles from its brink
In sport to send its imaged skies pell-mell,
(And mine own image, had I noted well!)— 5
Was that my point of turning?—I had thought
The stations of my course should rise un-
    sought,
As altar-stone or ensigned citadel.
But lo! the path is missed, I must go back,
And thirst to drink when next I reach the
    spring   10
Which once I stained, which since may have
    grown black.
Yet though no light be left nor bird now sing
As here I turn, I'll thank God, hastening,
That the same goal is still on the same track.
                (*1854;* 1870)

68. A DARK DAY

The gloom that breathes upon me with these
    airs
Is like the drops which strike the traveler's
    brow
Who knows not, darkling, if they bring him
    now
Fresh storm, or be old rain the covert bears.
Ah! bodes this hour some harvest of new
    tares,   5
Or hath but memory of the day whose plow
Sowed hunger once,—the night at length when
    thou,
O prayer found vain, didst fall from out my
    prayers?
How prickly were the growths which yet how
    smooth,
Along the hedgerows of this journey shed, 10
Lie by Time's grace till night and sleep may
    soothe!
Even as the thistledown from pathsides dead
Gleaned by a girl in autumns of her youth,
Which one new year makes soft her marriage-
    bed.   (*1855;* 1870)

69. AUTUMN IDLENESS

This sunlight shames November where he
    grieves
In dead red leaves, and will not let him shun
The day, though bough with bough be over-
    run.
But with a blessing every glade receives
High salutation; while from hillock-eaves 5
The deer gaze calling, dappled white and dun,
As if, being foresters of old, the sun

Had marked them with the shade of forest-
    leaves.
Here dawn today unveiled her magic glass;
Here noon now gives the thirst and takes the
    dew;   10
Till eve bring rest when other good things
    pass.
And here the lost hours the lost hours renew
While I still lead my shadow o'er the grass,
Nor know, for longing, that which I should
    do.
                              (*1850;* 1881)

70. THE HILL SUMMIT

This feast-day of the sun, his altar there
In the broad west has blazed for vesper-song;
And I have loitered in the vale too long
And gaze now a belated worshiper.
Yet may I not forget that I was 'ware,   5
So journeying, of his face at intervals
Transfigured where the fringed horizon falls,—
A fiery bush with coruscating hair.
And now that I have climbed and won this
    height,
I must tread downward through the sloping
    shade   10
And travel the bewildered tracks till night.
Yet for this hour I still may here be stayed
And see the gold air and the silver fade
And the last bird fly into the last light.
                            (*1853;* 1870)

71. THE CHOICE — 1

Eat thou and drink; tomorrow thou shalt
    die.
Surely the earth, that's wise being very old,
Needs not our help. Then loose me, love,
    and hold
Thy sultry hair up from my face; that I
May pour for thee this golden wine, brim-
    high,   5
Till round the glass thy fingers glow like gold.
We'll drown all hours: thy song, while hours
    are tolled,
Shall leap, as fountains veil the changing sky.
Now kiss, and think that there are really
    those,
My own high-bosomed beauty, who increase
Vain gold, vain lore, and yet might choose
    our way!   11

Sonnets 71-73. The Choice. Of the three sonnets under this title, William Rossetti, the poet's brother, says: "This trio is important as indicating Rossetti's youthful conception of life as a moral discipline and problem. He propounds three theories: 1, Eat thou and drink, tomorrow thou shalt die; 2, Watch thou and pray; 3, Think thou and act. It is manifest, however, that Rossetti intends us to set aside the 'Eat thou and drink' theory of life, and not to accept without much reservation the 'Watch thou and pray' theory. 'Think thou and act' is what he abides by."

Through many years they toil; then on a day
They die not,—for their life was death,—
    but cease;
And round their narrow lips the mold falls
    close.   (*1848;* 1870)

72. THE CHOICE — 2

Watch thou and fear; tomorrow thou shalt
    die.
Or art thou sure thou shalt have time for
    death?
Is not the day which God's word promiseth
To come man knows not when? In yonder
    sky,
Now while we speak, the sun speeds forth;
    can I   5
Or thou assure him of his goal? God's breath
Even at this moment haply quickeneth
The air to a flame; till spirits, always nigh
Though screened and hid, shall walk the day-
    light here.
And dost thou prate of all that man shall do?
Canst thou, who hast but plagues, presume
    to be   11
Glad in his gladness that comes after thee?
Will *his* strength slay *thy* worm in Hell?
    Go to:
Cover thy countenance, and watch, and fear.
                          (*1848;* 1870)

73. THE CHOICE — 3

Think thou and act; tomorrow thou shalt die.
Outstretched in the sun's warmth upon the
    shore,
Thou say'st: "Man's measured path is all
    gone o'er:
Up all his years, steeply, with strain and sigh,
Man clomb until he touched the truth; and I,
Even I, am he whom it was destined for."   6
How should this be? Art thou then so much
    more
Than they who sowed, that thou shouldst
    reap thereby?
Nay, come up hither. From this wave-washed
    mound
Unto the furthest flood-brim look with me;
Then reach on with thy thought till it be
    drowned.   11
Miles and miles distant though the last line
    be,
And though thy soul sail leagues and leagues
    beyond,—
Still, leagues beyond those leagues, there is
    more sea.   (*1848;* 1870)

Sonnet 71. The Choice, 1. 13. **They die not,** etc. Cf. Browning's *In a Gondola,* 229 ff., p. 206. Rossetti states that he wrote the sonnet before he had read Browning's poem, but that he was annoyed by the resemblance.

74. OLD AND NEW ART— I. ST. LUKE THE PAINTER

Give honor unto Luke Evangelist;
For he it was (the aged legends say)
Who first taught Art to fold her hands and
pray.
Scarcely at once she dared to rend the mist
Of devious symbols: but soon having wist 5
How sky-breadth and field-silence and this day
Are symbols also in some deeper way,
She looked through these to God and was
God's priest.
And if, past noon, her toil began to irk, 9
And she sought talismans, and turned in vain
To soulless self-reflections of man's skill,—
Yet now, in this the twilight, she might still
Kneel in the latter grass to pray again,
Ere the night cometh and she may not work.
(*1849;* 1881)

75. OLD AND NEW ART—2. NOT AS THESE

"I am not as these are," the poet saith
In youth's pride, and the painter, among men
At bay, where never pencil comes nor pen,
And shut about with his own frozen breath.
To others, for whom only rhyme wins faith 5
As poets,—only paint as painters,—then
He turns in the cold silence; and again
Shrinking, "I am not as these are," he saith.
And say that this is so, what follows it?
For were thine eyes set backwards in thine
head, 10
Such words were well; but they see on, and
far.
Unto the lights of the great Past, new-lit
Fair for the Future's track, look thou in-
stead,—
Say thou instead, "I am not as *these* are."
(*1849;* 1881)

76. OLD AND NEW ART—3. THE HUSBANDMAN

Though God, as one that is an householder,
Called these to labor in His vineyard first,
Before the husk of darkness was well burst
Bidding them grope their way out and bestir,
(Who, questioned of their wages, answered,
"Sir, 5

Unto each man a penny":) though the worst
Burthen of heat was theirs and the dry thirst:
Though God hath since found none such as
these were
To do their work like them:—Because of this
Stand not ye idle in the market-place. 10
Which of ye knoweth *he* is not that last
Who may be first by faith and will?—yea, his
The hand which after the appointed days
And hours shall give a Future to their Past?
(*1849;* 1881)

77. SOUL'S BEAUTY

(*Sibylla Palmifera*)

Under the arch of Life, where love and death,
Terror and mystery, guard her shrine, I saw
Beauty enthroned; and though her gaze struck
awe,
I drew it in as simply as my breath.
Hers are the eyes which, over and beneath, 5
The sky and sea bend on thee,—which can
draw,
By sea or sky or woman, to one law,
The allotted bondman of her palm and
wreath.
This is that Lady Beauty, in whose praise
Thy voice and hand shake still,—long known
to thee 10
By flying hair and fluttering hem,—the beat
Following her daily of thy heart and feet,
How passionately and irretrievably,
In what fond flight, how many ways and
days!
(*1866;* 1870)

78. BODY'S BEAUTY

(*Lilith*)

Of Adam's first wife, Lilith, it is told
(The witch he loved before the gift of Eve,)
That, ere the snake's, her sweet tongue could
deceive,
And her enchanted hair was the first gold.
And still she sits, young while the earth is
old, 5
And, subtly of herself contemplative,
Draws men to watch the bright web she can
weave,

Sonnet 74. *Old and New Art, 1.* St. Luke was a patron saint
of painters and physicians. Tradition says that he painted a
portrait of the Virgin Mary and that he was the founder of a
true religious art.

Sonnet 76. *Old and New Art, 3.* This sonnet applies to art
the parable of the householder who early in the morning hired
laborers for a penny a day and at later hours at the same price
hired men standing idle in the market place. At the end of the
day, when all received the same pay, those hired first objected,
but the householder said: ". . . didst not thou agree with me
for a penny? . . . So the last shall be first, and the first last:
. . ." (*Matthew*, 20:1-16). Rossetti is saying in effect, "Though
we of the present came last, we may equal or surpass the great
early Italian painters" (*these* of ll. 2 and 8).

Sonnet 77. *Soul's Beauty.* This sonnet, originally called
Sibylla Palmifera, was written for a painting of that name
representing the palm-bearing Sibyl, or prophetess. In the
picture she bears a branch of palm and is seated on a throne
beneath a stone canopy overlooking a temple court.

Sonnet 78. *Body's Beauty.* This sonnet was originally called
Lilith, after the traditional first wife of Adam. (See Brown-
ing's *Adam, Lilith, and Eve*, p. 374, and Rossetti's *Eden
Bower*, p. 521.) The sonnet was written for a painting entitled
Lady Lilith. In both the painting and the sonnet, Lilith
represents fleshly beauty and amorous passion.

Till heart and body and life are in its hold.
The rose and poppy are her flowers; for where
Is he not found, O Lilith, whom shed scent   10
And soft-shed kisses and soft sleep shall snare?
Lo! as that youth's eyes burned at thine, so
    went
Thy spell through him, and left his straight
    neck bent
And round his heart one strangling golden
    hair.

                          (*1864; 1870*)

79. THE MONOCHORD

Is it this sky's vast vault or ocean's sound
That is Life's self and draws my life from me,
And by instinct ineffable decree
Holds my breath quailing on the bitter
    bound?
Nay, is it Life or Death, thus thunder-
    crowned,   5
That 'mid the tide of all emergency
Now notes my separate wave, and to what
    sea
Its difficult eddies labor in the ground?
Oh! what is this that knows the road I came,
The flame turned cloud, the cloud returned to
    flame,   10
The lifted shifted steeps and all the way?—
That draws round me at last this wind-warm
    space,
And in regenerate rapture turns my face
Upon the devious coverts of dismay?

                          (*1870*)

80. FROM DAWN TO NOON

As the child knows not if his mother's face
Be fair; nor of his elders yet can deem
What each most is; but as of hill or stream
At dawn, all glimmering life surrounds his
    place:
Who yet, toward noon of his half-weary race, 5
Pausing awhile beneath the high sun-beam
And gazing steadily back,—as through a
    dream,
In things long past new features now can
    trace:—
Even so the thought that is at length full-
    grown
Turns back to note the sun-smit paths, all
    gray   10
And marvelous once, where first it walked
    alone;
And haply doubts, amid the unblenching day,
Which most or least impelled its onward
    way,—
Those unknown things or these things over-
    known.

                      (*c. 1871; 1881*)

81. MEMORIAL THRESHOLDS

What place so strange,—though unrevealéd
    snow
With unimaginable fires arise
At the earth's end,—what passion of surprise
Like frost-bound fire-girt scenes of long ago?
Lo! this is none but I this hour; and lo!   5
This is the very place which to mine eyes
Those mortal hours in vain immortalize,
'Mid hurrying crowds, with what alone I
    know.
City, of thine a single simple door,
By some new Power reduplicate, must be   10
Even yet my life-porch in eternity,
Even with one presence filled, as once of yore:
Or mocking winds whirl round a chaff-strown
    floor
Thee and thy years and these my words and
    me.

                          (*1874; 1881*)

82. HOARDED JOY

I said: "Nay, pluck not,—let the first fruit
    be:
Even as thou sayest, it is sweet and red,
But let it ripen still. The tree's bent head
Sees in the stream its own fecundity
And bides the day of fullness. Shall not we   5
At the sun's hour that day possess the shade,
And claim our fruit before its ripeness fade,
And eat it from the branch and praise the
    tree?"
I say: "Alas! our fruit hath wooed the sun
Too long,—'tis fallen and floats adown the
    stream.   10
Lo, the last clusters! Pluck them every one,
And let us sup with summer; ere the gleam
Of autumn set the year's pent sorrow free,
And the woods wail like echoes from the sea."

                          (*1870*)

83. BARREN SPRING

Once more the changed year's turning wheel
    returns:
And as a girl sails balanced in the wind,
And now before and now again behind
Stoops as it swoops, with cheek that laughs
    and burns,—
So Spring comes merry toward me here, but
    earns   5
No answering smile from me, whose life is
    twined
With the dead boughs that winter still must
    bind,

Sonnet 81. *Memorial Thresholds.* 1-4. W. M. Rossetti
traced the imagery of these lines to the ending of Edgar Allan
Poe's story, *The Narrative of Arthur Gordon Pym.*

And whom today the Spring no more con-
cerns.
Behold, this crocus is a withering flame;
This snowdrop, snow; this apple-blossom's
part   10
To breed the fruit that breeds the serpent's
art.
Nay, for these Spring-flowers, turn thy face
from them,
Nor stay till on the year's last lily-stem
The white cup shrivels round the golden
heart.

(1870)

84. FAREWELL TO THE GLEN

Sweet stream-fed glen, why say "farewell" to
thee
Who far'st so well and find'st forever smooth
The brow of Time where man may read no
ruth?
Nay, do thou rather say "farewell" to me,
Who now fare forth in bitterer fantasy   5
Than erst was mine where other shade might
soothe
By other streams, what while in fragrant
youth
The bliss of being sad made melancholy.
And yet, farewell! For better shalt thou fare
When children bathe sweet faces in thy flow 10
And happy lovers blend sweet shadows there
In hours to come, than when an hour ago
Thine echoes had but one man's sighs to bear
And thy trees whispered what he feared to
know.

(1869; 1881)

85. VAIN VIRTUES

What is the sorriest thing that enters Hell?
None of the sins,—but this and that fair deed
Which a soul's sin at length could supersede.
These yet are virgins, whom death's timely
knell
Might once have sainted; whom the fiends
compel   5
Together now, in snake-bound shuddering
sheaves
Of anguish, while the pit's pollution leaves
Their refuse maidenhood abominable.
Night sucks them down, the tribute of the pit,
Whose names, half entered in the book of
Life,   10
Were God's desire at noon. And as their hair
And eyes sink last, the Torturer deigns no
whit
To gaze, but, yearning, waits his destined wife,
The Sin still blithe on earth that sent them
there.

(1870)

86. LOST DAYS

The lost days of my life until today,
What were they, could I see them on the
street
Lie as they fell? Would they be ears of wheat
Sown once for food but trodden into clay?
Or golden coins squandered and still to pay? 5
Or drops of blood dabbling the guilty feet?
Or such spilt water as in dreams must cheat
The undying throats of Hell, athirst alway?
I do not see them here; but after death
God knows I know the faces I shall see,   10
Each one a murdered self, with low last
breath.
"I am thyself,—what hast thou done to
me?"
"And I—and I—thyself," (lo! each one
saith,)
"And thou thyself to all eternity!"

(1858; 1869)

87. DEATH'S SONGSTERS

When first that horse, within whose populous
womb
The birth was death, o'ershadowed Troy with
fate,
Her elders, dubious of its Grecian freight,
Brought Helen there to sing the songs of
home;
She whispered, "Friends, I am alone; come,
come!"   5
Then, crouched within, Ulysses waxed afraid,
And on his comrades' quivering mouths he
laid
His hands, and held them till the voice was
dumb.
The same was he who, lashed to his own mast,
There where the sea-flowers screen the char-
nel-caves,   10
Beside the sirens' singing island passed,
Till sweetness failed along the inveterate
waves . . .
Say, soul,—are songs of Death no heaven to
thee,
Nor shames her lip the cheek of Victory?

(1870)

Sonnet 87. *Death's Songsters.* **1. horse.** See *Sonnet 33*
and note. In attacking the city of Troy, the Greeks, following
the advice of crafty Ulysses, King of Ithaca, built a large
wooden horse, filled it with armed men, and left it to be
captured by the Trojans, who took it within the gates of
the city. At night the men were let out by a fellow Greek,
the gates were opened to the attackers, the city was set on
fire, the Trojans were subdued, and Helen was returned home.
9. he . . . mast. After the fall of Troy, Ulysses started on
his return voyage to Ithaca. The journey took his ship past
the coast of the Sirens, nymphs whose sweet singing so
charmed all who heard it that they cast themselves into the
sea. To avoid this fate Ulysses filled the ears of his seamen
with wax and had himself bound to the mast of his ship.
The story is told in Homer's *Odyssey.* See Tennyson's *The
Lotos-Eaters,* page 28.

88. HERO'S LAMP

That lamp thou fill'st in Eros' name tonight,
O Hero, shall the Sestian augurs take
Tomorrow, and for drowned Leander's sake
To Anteros its fireless lip shall plight.
Aye, waft the unspoken vow: yet dawn's first
    light   5
On ebbing storm and life twice ebbed must
    break;
While 'neath no sunrise, by the Avernian
    Lake,
Lo where Love walks, Death's pallid neo-
    phyte.
That lamp within Anteros' shadowy shrine
Shall stand unlit (for so the gods decree)   10
Till some one man the happy issue see
Of a life's love, and bid its flame to shine:
Which still may rest unfired; for, theirs or
    thine,
O brother, what brought love to them or
    thee?

                         (c. 1875; 1881)

89. THE TREES OF THE GARDEN

Ye who have passed Death's haggard hills;
    and ye
Whom trees that knew your sires shall cease
    to know
And still stand silent:—is it all a show,—
A wisp that laughs upon the wall?—decree
Of some inexorable supremacy   5
Which ever, as man strains his blind surmise
From depth to ominous depth, looks past his
    eyes,
Sphinx-faced with unabashéd augury?
Nay, rather question the Earth's self. In-
    voke
The storm-felled forest-trees moss-grown to-
    day   10
Whose roots are hillocks where the children
    play;
Or ask the silver sapling 'neath what yoke
Those stars, his spray-crown's clustering
    gems, shall wage
Their journey still when his boughs shrink
    with age.

                         (c. 1875; 1881)

90. "RETRO ME, SATHANA!"

Get thee behind me. Even as, heavy-curled,
Stooping against the wind, a charioteer
Is snatched from out his chariot by the
    hair,
So shall Time be; and as the void car, hurled
Abroad by reinless steeds, even so the world:
Yea, even as chariot-dust upon the air,   6
It shall be sought and not found anywhere.
Get thee behind me, Satan. Oft unfurled,
Thy perilous wings can beat and break like
    lath
Much mightiness of men to win thee praise. 10
Leave these weak feet to tread in narrow
    ways.
Thou still, upon the broad vine-sheltered
    path,
Mayst wait the turning of the phials of wrath
For certain years, for certain months and
    days.

                         (1847; 1870)

91. LOST ON BOTH SIDES

As when two men have loved a woman well,
Each hating each, through Love's and Death's
    deceit;
Since not for either this stark marriage-sheet
And the long pauses of this wedding-bell;
Yet o'er her grave the night and day dispel 5
At last their feud forlorn, with cold and heat;
Nor other than dear friends to death may fleet
The two lives left that most of her can tell:—
So separate hopes, which in a soul had wooed
The one same Peace, strove with each other
    long,   10
And Peace before their faces perished since:
So through that soul, in restless brotherhood,
They roam together now, and wind among
Its by-streets, knocking at the dusty inns.

                         (1854; 1870)

92. THE SUN'S SHAME—I

Beholding youth and hope in mockery caught
From life; and mocking pulses that remain
When the soul's death of bodily death is fain;
Honor unknown, and honor known unsought;
And penury's sedulous self-torturing thought 5
On gold, whose master therewith buys his
    bane;
And longed-for woman longing all in vain
For lonely man with love's desire distraught;

Sonnet 88. Hero's Lamp. Hero (l. 2) was a priestess of Aphrodite, goddess of love, at Sestos, on the Hellespont (the Dardanelles). Leander (l. 3), her lover, who lived at Abydos, on the other side of the strait, nightly swam across to visit her, guided by a torch which she held. One night he was drowned, and Hero, in grief, cast herself into the sea. After the death of the lovers the signal torch was dedicated to Anteros (l. 4), a god who was opposed to Eros (l. 1), god of love, with the edict that no man should light it unless his love had proved fortunate. **7. Avernian Lake,** Avernus, the infernal regions.
Sonnet 89. The Trees of the Garden. **8. Sphinx-faced,** a face like that of the sphinx, which conceals its character and purposes.

Sonnet 90. "Retro Me, Sathana!" The title means *Get behind Me, Satan.* These are the words spoken by Christ to Satan at the time of the temptation, as told in *Luke,* 4:8.
Sonnet 91. Lost on Both Sides. W. M. Rossetti suggested that the sestet reflects his brother's "separate hopes," his twin ambitions in painting and in poetry, neither realized to his own full satisfaction.

And wealth, and strength, and power, and
    pleasantness,
Given unto bodies of whose souls men say, 10
None poor and weak, slavish and foul, as
    they:—
Beholding these things, I behold no less
The blushing morn and blushing eve confess
The shame that loads the intolerable day.

                (1870)

93. THE SUN'S SHAME—2

As some true chief of men, bowed down with
    stress
Of life's disastrous eld, on blossoming youth
May gaze, and murmur with self-pity and
    ruth,—
"Might I thy fruitless treasure but possess,
Such blessing of mine all coming years should
    bless";—   5
Then sends one sigh forth to the unknown
    goal,
And bitterly feels breathe against his soul
The hour swift-winged of nearer nothingness:—
Even so the World's gray Soul to the green
    World
Perchance one hour must cry: "Woe's me, for
    whom   10
Inveteracy of ill portends the doom,—
Whose heart's old fire in shadow of shame is
    furled:
While thou even as of yore art journeying,
All soulless now, yet merry with the Spring!"

                (1870)

94. MICHELANGELO'S KISS

Great Michelangelo, with age grown bleak
And uttermost labors, having once o'ersaid
All grievous memories on his long life shed,
This worst regret to one true heart could
    speak:—
That when, with sorrowing love and rev-
    erence meek,   5
He stooped o'er sweet Colonna's dying bed,
His Muse and dominant Lady, spirit-wed,—
Her hand he kissed, but not her brow or
    cheek.
O Buonarroti,—good at Art's fire-wheels
To urge her chariot!—even thus the Soul, 10

Sonnet 94. Michelangelo's Kiss. Michelangelo Buonarroti (1475-1564) was a famous Italian painter, sculptor,
architect, and poet.
   4. **one true heart**, Ascanio Condivi, who published a
biography of his master Michelangelo, in 1553. He is
authority for the statement contained in lines 5-8 of the
sonnet. 6. **Colonna**, Vittoria Colonna (1490-1547), an
Italian poet, beloved friend of Michelangelo. She is referred
to as one of the most beautiful characters of the Italian
Renaissance. 9. **good . . . fire-wheels.** Rossetti uses this
as a play on the name Buonarroti; but he follows a mistaken
etymology. The name would have to be *Buoni ruoti* to mean
good wheels.

Touching at length some sorely-chastened
    goal,
Earns oftenest but a little: her appeals
Were deep and mute,—lowly her claim.
    Let be:
What holds for her Death's garner? And
    for thee?

                (1881)

95. THE VASE OF LIFE

Around the vase of Life at your slow pace
He has not crept, but turned it with his hands,
And all its sides already understands.
There, girt, one breathes alert for some great
    race;
Whose road runs far by sands and fruitful
    space;   5
Who laughs, yet through the jolly throng has
    passed;
Who weeps, nor stays for weeping; who at last,
A youth, stands somewhere crowned, with
    silent face.
And he has filled this vase with wine for blood,
With blood for tears, with spice for burning
    vow,   10
With watered flowers for buried love most fit;
And would have cast it shattered to the flood,
Yet in Fate's name has kept it whole; which
    now
Stands empty till his ashes fall in it.

                (1870)

96. LIFE THE BELOVED

As thy friend's face, with shadow of soul
    o'erspread,
Somewhile unto thy sight perchance hath been
Ghastly and strange, yet never so is seen
In thought, but to all fortunate favor wed;
As thy love's death-bound features never
    dead   5
To memory's glass return, but contravene
Frail fugitive days, and always keep, I ween,
Than all new life a livelier lovelihead:—
So Life herself, thy spirit's friend and love,
Even still as Spring's authentic harbinger 10
Glows with fresh hours for hope to glorify;
Though pale she lay when in the winter grove
Her funeral flowers were snow-flakes shed on
    her
And the red wings of frost-fire rent the sky.

           (*c. 1871;* 1881)

97. A SUPERSCRIPTION

Look in my face; my name is Might-have-
    been;
I am also called No-more, Too-late, Fare-
    well;

Unto thine ear I hold the dead-sea shell
Cast up thy Life's foam-fretted feet between;
Unto thine eyes the glass where that is seen
Which had Life's form and Love's, but by
    my spell   6
Is now a shaken shadow intolerable,
Of ultimate things unuttered the frail screen.
Mark me, how still I am! But should there
    dart
One moment through thy soul the soft sur-
    prise   10
Of that winged Peace which lulls the breath
    of sighs,—
Then shalt thou see me smile, and turn apart
Thy visage to mine ambush at thy heart
Sleepless with cold commemorative eyes.
                (*1869;* 1869)

98. HE AND I

Whence came his feet into my field, and why?
How is it that he sees it all so drear?
How do I see his seeing, and how hear
The name his bitter silence knows it by?
This was the little fold of separate sky   5
Whose pasturing clouds in the soul's atmos-
    phere
Drew living light from one continual year:
How should he find it lifeless? He, or I?
Lo! this new Self now wanders round my field,
With plaints for every flower, and for each
    tree   10
A moan, the sighing wind's auxiliary:
And o'er sweet waters of my life, that yield
Unto his lips no draft but tears unsealed,
Even in my place he weeps. Even I, not he.
                (1870)

99. NEWBORN DEATH—1

Today Death seems to me an infant child
Which her worn mother Life upon my knee
Has set to grow my friend and play with
    me;
If haply so my heart might be beguiled
To find no terrors in a face so mild,—   5
If haply so my weary heart might be
Unto the newborn milky eyes of thee,
O Death, before resentment reconciled.
How long, O Death? And shall thy feet
    depart
Still a young child's with mine, or wilt thou
    stand   10
Fullgrown the helpful daughter of my heart,
What time with thee indeed I reach the
    strand
Of the pale wave which knows thee what
    thou art,
And drink it in the hollow of thy hand?
                (1869)

100. NEWBORN DEATH—2

And thou, O Life, the lady of all bliss,
With whom, when our first heart beat full
    and fast,
I wandered till the haunts of men were
    passed,
And in fair places found all bowers amiss
Till only woods and waves might hear our
    kiss,   5
While to the winds all thought of Death
    we cast:—
Ah, Life! and must I have from thee at last
No smile to greet me and no babe but this?
Lo! Love, the child once ours; and Song,
    whose hair
Blew like a flame and blossomed like a
    wreath;   10
And Art, whose eyes were worlds by God
    found fair:
These o'er the book of Nature mixed their
    breath
With neck-twined arms, as oft we watched
    them there;
And did these die that thou mightst bear me
    Death?   (*1868;* 1870)

101. THE ONE HOPE

When vain desire at last and vain regret
Go hand in hand to death, and all is vain,
What shall assuage the unforgotten pain
And teach the unforgetful to forget?
Shall Peace be still a sunk stream long
    unmet,—   5
Or may the soul at once in a green plain
Stoop through the spray of some sweet life-
    fountain
And cull the dew-drenched flowering amulet?
Ah! when the wan soul in that golden air
Between the scriptured petals softly blown 10
Peers breathless for the gift of grace unknown,
Ah! let none other alien spell soe'er
But only the one Hope's one name be there,—
Not less nor more, but even that word alone.
            (*1869;* 1870)

THREE SHADOWS

I looked and saw your eyes
    In the shadow of your hair,
As a traveler sees the stream
    In the shadow of the wood;
And I said, "My faint heart sighs,   5
    Ah me! to linger there,
To drink deep and to dream
    In that sweet solitude."

I looked and saw your heart
    In the shadow of your eyes,   10

As a seeker sees the gold
  In the shadow of the stream;
And I said, "Ah me! what art
  Should win the immortal prize,
Whose want must make life cold   15
  And heaven a hollow dream?"

I looked and saw your love
  In the shadow of your heart,
As a diver sees the pearl
  In the shadow of the sea;   20
And I murmured, not above
  My breath, but all apart —
"Ah! you can love, true girl,
  And is your love for me?"

(*1876; 1881*)

THE WHITE SHIP

HENRY I OF ENGLAND. — 25TH NOV., 1120

By none but me can the tale be told,
The butcher of Rouen, poor Berold.
(*Lands are swayed by a King on a throne.*)
'Twas a royal train put forth to sea,
Yet the tale can be told by none but me.   5
(*The sea hath no King but God alone.*)

King Henry held it as life's whole gain
That after his death his son should reign.

'Twas so in my youth I heard men say,
And my old age calls it back today.   10

King Henry of England's realm was he,
And Henry Duke of Normandy.

The times had changed when on either coast
"Clerkly Harry" was all his boast.

Of ruthless strokes full many an one   15
He had struck to crown himself and his son;
And his elder brother's eyes were gone.

And when to the chase his court would crowd,
The poor flung plowshares on his road,
And shrieked: "Our cry is from King to
  God!"   20

But all the chiefs of the English land
Had knelt and kissed the Prince's hand.

The White Ship. This poem relates an actual incident.
Henry I ruled in England from 1100 to 1135. He conquered
Normandy in 1106.
2. **Rouen,** an important city in France, the ancient
capital of Normandy. 14. **Clerkly,** learned, scholarly.
Henry was called "Beauclerk" because of his scholarly
tastes. 17. **elder . . . gone.** Henry seized the throne
when his elder brother Robert, the rightful heir, was on a
crusade to the Holy Land. When Henry conquered Normandy in 1106, he captured his brother and imprisoned him
for the rest of his life.

And next with his son he sailed to France
To claim the Norman allegiance;

And every baron in Normandy   25
Had taken the oath of fealty.

'Twas sworn and sealed, and the day had
  come
When the King and the Prince might journey
  home;

For Christmas cheer is to home hearts dear,
And Christmas now was drawing near.   30

Stout Fitz-Stephen came to the King —
A pilot famous in seafaring;

And he held to the King, in all men's sight,
A mark of gold for his tribute's right.

"Liege Lord! my father guided the ship   35
From whose boat your father's foot did slip
When he caught the English soil in his grip,

"And cried: 'By this clasp I claim command
O'er every rood of English land!'

"He was borne to the realm you rule o'er now
In that ship with the archer carved at her
  prow;   41

"And thither I'll bear, an' it be my due,
Your father's son and his grandson too.

"The famed White Ship is mine in the bay;
From Harfleur's harbor she sails today,   45

"With masts fair-pennoned as Norman spears
And with fifty well-tried mariners."

Quoth the King: "My ships are chosen each
  one,
But I'll not say nay to Stephen's son.

"My son and daughter and fellowship   50
Shall cross the water in the White Ship."

The King set sail with the eve's south wind,
And soon he left that coast behind.

The Prince and all his, a princely show,
Remained in the good White Ship to go.   55

With noble knights and with ladies fair,
With courtiers and sailors gathered there,
Three hundred living souls we were;

And I Berold was the meanest hind
In all that train to the Prince assigned.   60

45. **Harfleur,** a town in northern France.

The Prince was a lawless shameless youth;
From his father's loins he sprang without
   ruth.

Eighteen years till then he had seen,
And the devil's dues in him were eighteen.

And now he cried: "Bring wine from below;
Let the sailors revel ere yet they row.   66

"Our speed shall o'ertake my father's flight
Though we sail from the harbor at midnight."

The rowers made good cheer without check;
The lords and ladies obeyed his beck;   70
The night was light, and they danced on the
   deck.

But at midnight's stroke they cleared the
   bay,
And the White Ship furrowed the waterway.

The sails were set, and the oars kept tune
To the double flight of the ship and the moon.

Swifter and swifter the White Ship sped   76
Till she flew as the spirit flies from the dead;

As white as a lily glimmered she
Like a ship's fair ghost upon the sea.

And the Prince cried, "Friends, 'tis the hour
   to sing!   80
Is a songbird's course so swift on the wing?"

And under the winter stars' still throng,
From brown throats, white throats, merry and
   strong,
The knights and the ladies raised a song.

A song — nay, a shriek that rent the sky,   85
That leaped o'er the deep! — the grievous cry
Of three hundred living that now must die.

An instant shriek that sprang to the shock
As the ship's keel felt the sunken rock.

'Tis said that afar — a shrill strange sigh —   90
The King's ships heard it and knew not why.

Pale Fitz-Stephen stood by the helm
'Mid all those folk that the waves must
   whelm.

A great King's heir for the waves to whelm,
And the helpless pilot pale at the helm!   95

The ship was eager and sucked athirst,
By the stealthy stab of the sharp reef pierced;

And like the moil round a sinking cup,
The waters against her crowded up.

A moment the pilot's senses spin —   100
The next he snatched the Prince 'mid the din,
Cut the boat loose, and the youth leaped in.

A few friends leaped with him, standing near.
"Row! the sea's smooth and the night is
   clear!"   104

"What! none to be saved but these and I?"
"Row, row as you'd live! All here must die!"

Out of the churn of the choking ship,
Which the gulf grapples and the waves strip,
They struck with the strained oars' flash and
   dip.   109

'Twas then o'er the splitting bulwarks' brim
The Prince's sister screamed to him.

He gazed aloft, still rowing apace,
And through the whirled surf he knew her
   face.

To the toppling decks clave one and all
As a fly cleaves to a chamber-wall.   115

I Berold was clinging anear;
I prayed for myself and quaked with fear,
But I saw his eyes as he looked at her.

He knew her face and he heard her cry,   119
And he said, "Put back! she must not die!"

And back with the current's force they reel
Like a leaf that's drawn to a water-wheel.

'Neath the ship's travail they scarce might
   float,
But he rose and stood in the rocking boat.

Low the poor ship leaned on the tide;   125
O'er the naked keel as she best might slide,
The sister toiled to the brother's side.

He reached an oar to her from below,
And stiffened his arms to clutch her so.   129

But now from the ship some spied the boat,
And "Saved!" was the cry from many a
   throat.

And down to the boat they leaped and fell;
It turned as a bucket turns in a well,
And nothing was there but the surge and
   swell.   134

The Prince that was and the King to come,
There in an instant gone to his doom,

Despite of all England's bended knee
And maugre the Norman fealty!

He was a Prince of lust and pride;
He showed no grace till the hour he died. 140

When he should be King, he oft would vow,
He'd yoke the peasant to his own plow.
O'er him the ships score their furrows now.

God only knows where his soul did wake,
But I saw him die for his sister's sake. 145

By none but me can the tale be told,
The butcher of Rouen, poor Berold.
  (*Lands are swayed by a King on a throne.*)
'Twas a royal train put forth to sea,
Yet the tale can be told by none but me. 150
  (*The sea hath no King but God alone.*)

And now the end came o'er the water's womb
Like the last great Day that's yet to come.

With prayers in vain and curses in vain, 154
The White Ship sundered on the mid-main;

And what were men and what was a ship
Were toys and splinters in the sea's grip.

I Berold was down in the sea;
And passing strange though the thing may be,
Of dreams then known I remember me. 160

Blithe is the shout on Harfleur's strand
When morning lights the sails to land;

And blithe is Honfleur's echoing gloam
When mothers call the children home;

And high do the bells of Rouen beat 165
When the Body of Christ goes down the street.

These things and the like were heard and
    shown
In a moment's trance 'neath the sea alone;

And when I rose, 'twas the sea did seem,
And not these things, to be all a dream. 170

The ship was gone and the crowd was gone,
And the deep shuddered and the moon shone;

And in a strait grasp my arms did span
The mainyard rent from the mast where it
    ran;
And on it with me was another man. 175

163. **Honfleur,** a town in northwestern France.

Where lands were none 'neath the dim sea-
    sky,
We told our names, that man and I.

"O I am Godefroy de l'Aigle hight,
And son I am to a belted knight."

"And I am Berold the butcher's son 180
Who slays the beasts in Rouen town."

Then cried we upon God's name, as we
Did drift on the bitter winter sea.

But lo! a third man rose o'er the wave,
And we said, "Thank God! us three may He
    save!" 185

He clutched to the yard with panting stare,
And we looked and knew Fitz-Stephen there.

He clung, and "What of the Prince?" quoth
    he.
"Lost, lost!" we cried. He cried, "Woe on
    me!" 189
And loosed his hold and sank through the sea.

And soul with soul again in that space
We two were together face to face;

And each knew each, as the moments sped,
Less for one living than for one dead;

And every still star overhead 195
Seemed an eye that knew we were but dead.

And the hours passed; till the noble's son
Sighed, "God be thy help! my strength's fore-
    done!

"O farewell, friend, for I can no more!"
"Christ take thee!" I moaned; and his life
    was o'er. 200

Three hundred souls were all lost but one,
And I drifted over the sea alone.

At last the morning rose on the sea
Like an angel's wing that beat toward me.

Sore numbed I was in my sheepskin coat; 205
Half dead I hung, and might nothing note,
Till I woke sun-warmed in a fisher-boat.

The sun was high o'er the eastern brim
As I praised God and gave thanks to Him.

That day I told my tale to a priest, 210
Who charged me, till the shrift were released,
That I should keep it in mine own breast.

And with the priest I thence did fare
To King Henry's court at Winchester.   214

We spoke with the King's high chamberlain,
And he wept and mourned again and again,
As if his own son had been slain;

And round us ever there crowded fast
Great men with faces all aghast.   219

And who so bold that might tell the thing
Which now they knew to their lord the King?
Much woe I learnt in their communing.

The King had watched with a heart sore
    stirred
For two whole days, and this was the third;

And still to all his court would he say,   225
"What keeps my son so long away?"

And they said: "The ports lie far and wide
That skirt the swell of the English tide;

"And England's cliffs are not more white
Than her women are, and scarce so light   230
Her skies as their eyes are blue and bright;

"And in some port that he reached from
    France
The Prince has lingered for his pleasaunce."

But once the King asked: "What distant cry
Was that we heard 'twixt the sea and sky?"

And one said: "With suchlike shouts, pardie!
Do the fishers fling their nets at sea."   237

And one: "Who knows not the shrieking quest
When the sea-mew misses its young from the
    nest?"

'Twas thus till now they had soothed his
    dread,   240
Albeit they knew not what they said;

But who should speak today of the thing
That all knew there except the King?

Then pondering much they found a way,   244
And met round the King's high seat that day;

And the King sat with a heart sore stirred,
And seldom he spoke and seldom heard.

'Twas then through the hall the King was
    'ware
Of a little boy with golden hair,

As bright as the golden poppy is   250
That the beach breeds for the surf to kiss;

Yet pale his cheek as the thorn in spring,
And his garb black like the raven's wing.

Nothing heard but his foot through the hall,
For now the lords were silent all.   255

And the King wondered, and said, "Alack!
Who send me a fair boy dressed in black?

"Why, sweet heart, do you pace through the
    hall
As though my court were a funeral?"

Then lowly knelt the child at the dais,   260
And looked up weeping in the King's face.

"O wherefore, O King, ye may say,
For white is the hue of death today.

"Your son and all his fellowship
Lie low in the sea with the White Ship."   265

King Henry fell as a man struck dead;
And speechless still he stared from his bed
When to him next day my rede I read.

There's many an hour must needs beguile   269
A King's high heart that he should smile —

Full many a lordly hour, full fain
Of his realm's rule and pride of his reign —

But this King never smiled again.

By none but me can the tale be told,
The butcher of Rouen, poor Berold.   275
    (*Lands are swayed by a King on a throne.*)
'Twas a royal train put forth to sea,
Yet the tale can be told by none but me.
    (*The sea hath no King but God alone.*)
                     (1880)

ASTARTE SYRIACA
(*For a Picture*)

Mystery: lo! betwixt the sun and moon
    Astarte of the Syrians; Venus Queen
    Ere Aphrodite was. In silver sheen
Her twofold girdle clasps the infinite boon
Of bliss whereof the heaven and earth com-
    mune;   5
    And from her neck's inclining flower-stem
    lean

---

214. **Winchester**, a city in Wessex, England, sixty miles
southwest of London. It was the residence of the early
English kings. 233. **pleasaunce**, pleasure. 236. **pardie**, a
French oath—*par Dieu*, meaning *by God.*

268. **rede**, story, counsel.
Astarte Syriaca. Astarte is Ishtar, an Assyrian goddess
known as queen of the gods. She was identified with the
planet Venus. Aphrodite was the Greek goddess of love and
beauty. Many of her attributes were derived from the
Assyrian goddess.

Love-freighted lips and absolute eyes that
  wean
The pulse of hearts to the spheres' dominant
  tune.

Torch-bearing, her sweet ministers compel
  All thrones of light beyond the sky and sea
  The witnesses of Beauty's face to be;   11
That face, of Love's all-penetrative spell
Amulet, talisman, and oracle —
  Betwixt the sun and moon a mystery.

INSOMNIA

Thin are the night-skirts left behind
  By daybreak hours that onward creep,
  And thin, alas! the shred of sleep
That wavers with the spirit's wind;
But in half-dreams that shift and roll   5
  And still remember and forget,
  My soul this hour has drawn your soul
A little nearer yet.

Our lives, most dear, are never near,
  Our thoughts are never far apart,   10
  Though all that draws us heart to heart
Seems fainter now and now more clear.
Tonight Love claims his full control,
  And with desire and with regret
  My soul this hour has drawn your soul   15
A little nearer yet.

Is there a home where heavy earth
  Melts to bright air that breathes no pain,
  Where water leaves no thirst again
And springing fire is Love's new birth?   20
If faith long bound to one true goal
  May there at length its hope beget,
  My soul that hour shall draw your soul
Forever nearer yet.   (1881)

ALAS, SO LONG!

Ah! dear one, we were young so long,
  It seemed that youth would never go,
For skies and trees were ever in song
  And water in singing flow
In the days we never again shall know.   5
    Alas, so long!
  Ah! then was it all spring weather?
  Nay, but we were young and together.

Ah! dear one, I've been old so long,
  It seems that age is loath to part,   10
Though days and years have never a song,
  And oh! have they still the art
That warmed the pulses of heart to heart?
    Alas, so long!

Ah! then was it all spring weather?   15
  Nay, but we were young and together.

Ah! dear one, you've been dead so long —
  How long until we meet again,
Where hours may never lose their song
  Nor flowers forget the rain   20
In glad noonlight that never shall wane?
    Alas, so long!
  Ah! shall it be then spring weather,
  And ah! shall we be young together?

FIVE ENGLISH POETS

I. THOMAS CHATTERTON

With Shakespeare's manhood at a boy's wild
  heart —
Through Hamlet's doubt to Shakespeare near
  allied,
And kin to Milton through his Satan's pride —
At Death's sole door he stooped, and craved
  a dart;
And to the dear new bower of England's
  art —   5
Even to that shrine Time else had deified,
The unuttered heart that soared against his
  side —
Drove the fell point, and smote life's seals
  apart.
Thy nested home-loves, noble Chatterton;
The angel-trodden stair thy soul could trace
Up Redcliffe's spire; and in the world's armed
  space   11
Thy gallant sword-play — these to many an
  one
Are sweet forever, as thy grave unknown
And love-dream of thine unrecorded face.
      (1881)

2. WILLIAM BLAKE

This is the place. Even here the dauntless
  soul,
The unflinching hand, wrought on; till in that
  nook,

Five English Poets. Rossetti was an enthusiastic admirer
of the five poets enshrined in these sonnets.
1. Thomas Chatterton. Chatterton was born in 1752; he
died, by suicide, in 1770. He was unable to find employment
in London, and he was too proud to become the object of
charity.
2. Hamlet's doubt. Hamlet doubted the propriety and
the expediency of suicide. See his speech beginning "To be or
not to be," *Hamlet,* III, 1, 56 ff. **9. nested home-loves,**
a reference to the deep love of Chatterton for Bristol, the city
of his birth. **11. Redcliffe's spire.** Chatterton spent much of
his time in the attic of the church St. Mary Redcliffe, in
Bristol. In his visions he saw angels going up and down the
spire. **12. gallant sword-play,** a reference to Chatterton's
dreams of chivalrous encounter as expressed in *The Bristowe
Tragedie* and other poems.
2. William Blake. Blake (1757-1827) was a mystic poet
and artist. Rossetti addressed the poem to Frederick Shields,
who had made a sketch of Blake's workroom and death-room
at 3 Fountain Court, Strand, near the Thames River, London.
Cf. Thomson's *William Blake,* p. 584.

8. spheres' . . . **tune.** The ancients believed that the
stars made music as they revolved in their spheres.

As on that very bed, his life partook
New birth, and passed. Yon river's dusky
    shoal,
Whereto the close-built coiling lanes unroll, 5
Faced his work-window, whence his eyes
    would stare,
Thought-wandering, unto naught that met
    them there,
But to the unfettered irreversible goal.
This cupboard, Holy of Holies, held the cloud
Of his soul writ and limned; this other one, 10
His true wife's charge, full oft to their abode
Yielded for daily bread the martyr's stone,
Ere yet their food might be that Bread alone,
The words now home-speech of the mouth of
    God.   (*1880;* 1881)

3. SAMUEL TAYLOR COLERIDGE

His Soul fared forth (as from the deep home
    grove
The father-songster plies the hour-long quest)
To feed his soul-brood hungering in the nest;
But his warm Heart, the mother-bird, above
Their callow fledgling progeny still hove   5
With tented roof of wings and fostering breast
Till the Soul fed the soul-brood. Richly blest
From Heaven their growth, whose food was
    Human Love.
Yet ah! Like desert pools that show the stars
Once in long leagues — even such the scarce-
    snatched hours   10
Which deepening pain left to his lordliest
    powers —
Heaven lost through spider-trammeled prison-
    bars.
Six years, from sixty saved! Yet kindling
    skies
Own them, a beacon to our centuries.
                                    (*1880;* 1881)

4. JOHN KEATS

The weltering London ways where children
    weep
And girls whom none call maidens laugh —
    strange road
Miring his outward steps, who inly trode

The bright Castalian brink and Latmos'
    steep —
Even such his life's cross-paths; till deathly
    deep   5
He toiled through sands of Lethe; and long
    pain,
Weary with labor spurned and love found
    vain,
In dead Rome's sheltering shadow wrapped
    his sleep.
O pang-dowered Poet, whose reverberant lips
And heart-strung lyre awoke the Moon's
    eclipse —   10
Thou whom the daisies glory in growing
    o'er —
Their fragrance clings around thy name, not
    writ
But rumored in water, while the fame of it
Along Time's flood goes echoing evermore.
                                    (*1880;* 1881)

5. PERCY BYSSHE SHELLEY

(INSCRIPTION FOR THE COUCH, STILL PRESERVED,
ON WHICH HE PASSED THE LAST NIGHT OF HIS
LIFE.)

'Twixt those twin worlds — the world of
    Sleep, which gave
No dream to warm, the tidal world of Death,
Which the earth's sea, as the earth, replen-
    isheth —
Shelley, Song's orient sun, to breast the wave,
Rose from this couch that morn. Ah! did he
    brave   5
Only the sea? — or did man's deed of hell
Engulf his bark 'mid mists impenetrable? . . .
No eye discerned, nor any power might save.
When that mist cleared, O Shelley! what
    dread veil
Was rent for thee, to whom far-darkling Truth
Reigned sovereign guide through thy brief
    ageless youth?   11
Was the Truth *thy* Truth, Shelley? — Hush!
    All-Hail,
Past doubt, thou gav'st it; and in Truth's
    bright sphere
Art first of praisers, being most praiséd here.
                                    (*1870;* 1881)

10. writ and limned, written and painted or sketched.
11. wife. Mrs. Blake was regarded as an almost perfect
wife. **12. martyr's stone.** In the sermon on the mount,
Christ asked his listeners, "What man is there of you, whom
if his son ask bread, will he give him a stone?" (*Matthew,*
7:9). Rossetti suggests that Blake was neglected and abused
by his contemporaries.
3. Samuel Taylor Coleridge. **11. deepening pain.** In
order to relieve physical pain, Coleridge took opium. His
later life was marked by fits of despondency induced by the
habitual use of this drug. **12. lost . . . prison-bars.**
Coleridge sacrificed his poetic gift when he began to spin cobwebs of philosophy. Nearly all his great poems were
written during the six years from 1797 to 1803.
4. John Keats. Rossetti uses classical names in this poem
to suggest the classical element in Keats's poems.

4. Castalian brink. Castalia was a fountain on Mt.
Parnassus, in Greece, sacred to Apollo, god of poetry and
music, and the Muses; hence the source of inspiration. Latmos was a mountain in Asia Minor, the scene of the story
of the love of Selene (the moon goddess) and Endymion (the
shepherd boy) as told in Keats's *Endymion.* **6. Lethe,** the
river of forgetfulness. **8. Rome's . . . shadow.** Keats
died in Rome. His life was marked with sadness because of
a hopeless love affair and ill health. **11. daisies . . . o'er,**
suggested by the famous remark of Keats when he was
near death—"I feel the flowers growing over me." **12-13.
writ . . . in water,** a reference to "Here lies one whose name
was writ in water," the epitaph that Keats wrote for himself in the melancholy days when he despaired of winning
that fame for which he ardently longed.
5. Percy Bysshe Shelley. **4. orient,** brilliant, lustrous.
6. Only the sea. Shelley lost his life by drowning.

FOR "THE WINE OF CIRCE"

(BY EDWARD BURNE-JONES)

Dusk-haired and gold-robed o'er the golden
    wine
She stoops, wherein, distilled of death and
    shame,
Sink the black drops; while, lit with fragrant
    flame,
Round her spread board the golden sun-
    flowers shine.
Doth Helios here with Hecaté combine   5
(O Circe, thou their votaress!) to proclaim
For these thy guests all rapture in Love's
    name,
Till pitiless Night give Day the countersign?
Lords of their hour, they come. And by her
    knee
Those cowering beasts, their equals hereto-
    fore,   10
Wait; who with them in new equality
Tonight shall echo back the unchanging roar
Which sounds forever from the tide-strown
    shore
Where the disheveled seaweed hates the sea.

"FOUND"

(For a Picture)

"There is a budding morrow in midnight" —
So sang our Keats, our English nightingale.
And here, as lamps across the bridge turn
    pale
In London's smokeless resurrection-light,
Dark breaks to dawn. But o'er the deadly
    blight   5
Of love deflowered and sorrow of none avail
Which makes this man gasp and this woman
    quail,
Can day from darkness ever again take flight?
Ah! gave not these two hearts their mutual
    pledge,
Under one mantle sheltered 'neath the hedge
In gloaming courtship? And O God! today   11
He only knows he holds her — but what part
Can life now take? She cries in her locked
    heart,
"Leave me — I do not know you — go away!"
                      (1881; 1881)

THE KING'S TRAGEDY

JAMES I OF SCOTS. — 20TH FEBRUARY, 1437

I Catherine am a Douglas born,
    A name to all Scots dear;
And Kate Barlass they've called me now
    Through many a waning year.

This old arm's withered now. 'Twas once 5
    Most deft 'mong maidens all
To rein the steed, to wing the shaft,
    To smite the palm-play ball.

In hall adown the close-linked dance
    It has shone most white and fair;   10
It has been the rest for a true lord's head,
And many a sweet babe's nursing-bed,
    And the bar to a King's chambère.

Aye, lasses, draw round Kate Barlass,
    And hark with bated breath   15
How good King James, King Robert's son,
    Was foully done to death.

Through all the days of his gallant youth
    The princely James was pent,
By his friends at first and then by his foes,
    In long imprisonment.   21

For the elder Prince, the kingdom's heir,
    By treason's murderous brood
Was slain; and the father quaked for the
    child
    With the royal mortal blood.   25

I' the Bass Rock fort, by his father's care,
    Was his childhood's life assured;
And Henry the subtle Bolingbroke,
Proud England's King, 'neath the southron
    yoke
    His youth for long years immured.   30

The King's Tragedy. The events recorded in this ballad are historical, as are also the persons mentioned. Because of his violent suppression of the nobles, James was murdered on Feb. 20, 1437, by Sir Robert Graham (who had previously been banished) and his band at the instigation of Walter Stewart, earl of Atholl, whose hope of the throne had been destroyed by the birth of James's son.

"Tradition says that Catherine Douglas, in honor of her heroic act when she barred the door with her arm against the murderers of James the First of Scots, received popularly the name of 'Barlass.' The name remains to her descendants, the Barlas family, in Scotland, who bear for their crest a broken arm. . . . A few stanzas from King James's lovely poem, known as *The King's Quair* [*Quair* means *Book*], are quoted in the course of this ballad. The writer must express regret for the necessity which has compelled him to shorten the ten-syllabled lines to eight syllables, in order that they might harmonize with the ballad meter." (Rossetti's note.)

8. **palm-play ball,** ball struck by the hand in a game. 16. **King Robert,** Robert III (1390-1424). 19. **James was pent.** On the death of his elder brother David, James was sent to France for safety, but the vessel was stopped by the English and James was taken into custody and kept as a prisoner in various places in England for nearly twenty years, until 1424. 26. **Bass Rock fort,** a small island at the entrance to the Firth of Forth, on the east coast of Scotland, where James embarked for France. 28. **Henry,** Henry IV, king of England (1399-1413). 29. **southron,** archaic for *southern.* See note on line 19. 30. **His,** James's.

For "The Wine of Circe." This poem was written for a picture by Sir Edward Burne-Jones (1833-98), an English painter noted for highly decorative design. He was a pupil of Rossetti. Circe was a sorceress who could turn men into beasts.

5. **Helios,** god of the sun, representing day. **Hecaté,** goddess of the night.

"Found." The picture for which this sonnet was written represents a lost girl found in the city streets by her former lover, a countryman bound to market with a white calf in his cart.

1. **"There . . . midnight,"** quoted from Keats's *To Homer,* line 11.

Yet in all things meet for a kingly man
  Himself did he approve;
And the nightingale through his prison-wall
  Taught him both lore and love.

For once, when the bird's song drew him
    close   35
  To the opened window-pane,
In her bowers beneath a lady stood,
A light of life to his sorrowful mood,
  Like a lily amid the rain.

And for her sake, to the sweet bird's note, 40
  He framed a sweeter song,
More sweet than ever a poet's heart
  Gave yet to the English tongue.

She was a lady of royal blood;
  And when, past sorrow and teen,   45
He stood where still through his crownless
    years
  His Scottish realm had been,
At Scone were the happy lovers crowned,
  A heart-wed King and Queen.

But the bird may fall from the bough of
    youth,   50
  And song be turned to moan,
And Love's storm-cloud be the shadow of
    Hate,
When the tempest-waves of a troubled State
  Are beating against a throne.

Yet well they loved; and the god of Love, 55
  Whom well the King had sung,
Might find on the earth no truer hearts
  His lowliest swains among.

From the days when first she rode abroad
  With Scottish maids in her train,   60
I Catherine Douglas won the trust
  Of my mistress sweet Queen Jane.

And oft she sighed, "To be born a King!"
  And oft along the way
When she saw the homely lovers pass   65
  She has said, "Alack the day!"

Years waned — the loving and toiling
    years —
  Till England's wrong renewed

Drove James, by outrage cast on his crown,
  To the open field of feud.   70

'Twas when the King and his host were met
  At the leaguer of Roxbro' hold,
The Queen o' the sudden sought his camp
  With a tale of dread to be told.

And she showed him a secret letter writ 75
  That spoke of treasonous strife,
And how a band of his noblest lords
  Were sworn to take his life.

"And it may be here or it may be there,
  In the camp or the court," she said;   80
"But for my sake come to your people's arms
  And guard your royal head."

Quoth he, "'Tis the fifteenth day of the siege,
  And the castle's nigh to yield."
"Oh, face your foes on your throne," she cried,
  "And show the power you wield;   86
And under your Scottish people's love
  You shall sit as under your shield."

At the fair Queen's side I stood that day
  When he bade them raise the siege,   90
And back to his Court he sped to know
  How the lords would meet their Liege.

But when he summoned his Parliament,
  The louring brows hung round,
Like clouds that circle the mountain-head
  Ere the first low thunders sound.   96

For he had tamed the nobles' lust
  And curbed their power and pride,
And reached out an arm to right the poor
  Through Scotland far and wide;   100
And many a lordly wrongdoer
  By the headsman's ax had died.

'Twas then upspoke Sir Robert Græme,
  The bold o'ermastering man,
"O King, in the name of your Three Estates
  I set you under their ban!   106

"For, as your lords made oath to you
  Of service and fealty,
Even in likewise you pledged your oath
  Their faithful sire to be;   110

"Yet all we here that are nobly sprung
  Have mourned dear kith and kin
Since first for the Scottish Barons' curse
  Did your bloody rule begin."

With that he laid his hands on his King — 115
"Is this not so, my lords?"
But of all who had sworn to league with him
Not one spake back to his words.

Quoth the King: "Thou speak'st but for one
Estate,
Nor doth it avow thy gage. 120
Let my liege lords hale this traitor hence!"
The Græme fired dark with rage,
"Who works for lesser men than himself,
He earns but a witless wage!"

But soon from the dungeon where he lay 125
He won by privy plots,
And forth he fled with a price on his head
To the country of the Wild Scots.

And word there came from Sir Robert Græme
To the King at Edinbro': 130
"No Liege of mine thou art; but I see
From this day forth alone in thee
God's creature, my mortal foe.

"Through thee are my wife and children lost,
My heritage and lands; 135
And when my God shall show me a way,
Thyself my mortal foe will I slay
With these my proper hands."

Against the coming of Christmastide
That year the King bade call 140
I' the Black Friars' Charterhouse of Perth
A solemn festival.

And we of his household rode with him
In a close-ranked company;
But not till the sun had sunk from his throne
Did we reach the Scottish Sea. 146

That eve was clenched for a boding storm,
'Neath a toilsome moon half seen;
The cloud stooped low and the surf rose high;
And where there was a line of the sky, 150
Wild wings loomed dark between.

And on a rock of the black beach-side
By the veiled moon dimly lit,
There was something seemed to heave with
life
As the King drew nigh to it. 155

And was it only the tossing furze
Or brake of the waste sea-wold?

Or was it an eagle bent to the blast?
When near we came, we knew it at last
For a woman tattered and old. 160

But it seemed as though by a fire within
Her writhen limbs were wrung;
And as soon as the King was close to her,
She stood up gaunt and strong.

'Twas then the moon sailed clear of the rack
On high in her hollow dome; 166
And still as aloft with hoary crest
Each clamorous wave rang home,
Like fire in snow the moonlight blazed
Amid the champing foam. 170

And the woman held his eyes with her eyes:
"O King, thou art come at last;
But thy wraith has haunted the Scottish Sea
To my sight for four years past.

"Four years it is since first I met, 175
'Twixt the Duchray and the Dhu,
A shape whose feet clung close in a shroud,
And that shape for thine I knew.

"A year again, and on Inchkeith Isle
I saw thee pass in the breeze, 180
With the cerecloth risen above thy feet
And wound about thy knees.

"And yet a year, in the Links of Forth,
As a wanderer without rest,
Thou cam'st with both thine arms i' the
shroud 185
That clung high up thy breast.

"And in this hour I find thee here,
And well mine eyes may note
That the winding-sheet hath passed thy
breast
And risen around thy throat. 190

"And when I meet thee again, O King,
That of death hast such sore drouth —
Except thou turn again on this shore —
The winding-sheet shall have moved once
more
And covered thine eyes and mouth. 195

"O King, whom poor men bless for their King,
Of thy fate be not so fain;
But these my words for God's message take,
And turn thy steed, O King, for her sake
Who rides beside thy rein!" 200

119. **one Estate,** the nobility. 120. **avow thy gage,** support thy challenge. 128. **country . . . Scots,** the Highlands, in northern Scotland. 138. **proper,** own. 141. **Perth,** a city in Perthshire, the seat of government at the time. The Charterhouse was the monastery of the Black Friars, an order of Dominican Friars, so called from their black mantles. 157. **sea-wold,** open land along the sea.

162. **writhen, twisted.** 165. **rack,** floating mass of clouds. 176. **Duchray . . . Dhu.** Duchray is a small stream west of Loch Lomond. Dhu is a lake in Aberdeenshire. Perthshire lies between Duchray and Dhu. 179. **Inchkeith Isle,** a small island in the Firth of Forth. 181. **cerecloth,** waxed cloth, used in burial. 183. **Links of Forth,** the windings of the River Forth, together with the adjacent land, near Stirling, Scotland. 192. **drouth,** thirst.

While the woman spoke, the King's horse
    reared
    As if it would breast the sea,
And the Queen turned pale as she heard on
    the gale
    The voice die dolorously.

When the woman ceased, the steed was still,
    But the King gazed on her yet,   206
And in silence save for the wail of the sea
    His eyes and her eyes met.

At last he said, "God's ways are His own;
    Man is but shadow and dust.   210
Last night I prayed by His altar-stone;
Tonight I wend to the Feast of His Son;
    And in Him I set my trust.

"I have held my people in sacred charge,
    And have not feared the sting   215
Of proud men's hate — to His will resigned
Who has but one same death for a hind
    And one same death for a King.

"And if God in His wisdom have brought
    close
    The day when I must die,   220
That day by water or fire or air
My feet shall fall in the destined snare
    Wherever my road may lie.

"What man can say but the Fiend hath set
    Thy sorcery on my path,   225
My heart with the fear of death to fill,
And turn me against God's very will
    To sink in His burning wrath?"

The woman stood as the train rode past,
    And moved nor limb nor eye;   230
And when we were shipped, we saw her there
    Still standing against the sky.

As the ship made way, the moon once more
    Sank slow in her rising pall;
And I thought of the shrouded wraith of the
    King,   235
    And I said, "The Heavens know all."

And now, ye lasses, must ye hear
    How my name is Kate Barlass —
But a little thing, when all the tale
    Is told of the weary mass   240
Of crime and woe which in Scotland's realm
    God's will let come to pass.

'Twas in the Charterhouse of Perth
    That the King and all his Court
Were met, the Christmas Feast being done,
    For solace and disport.   246

217. **hind**, peasant.

'Twas a wind-wild eve in February,
    And against the casement-pane
The branches smote like summoning hands
    And muttered the driving rain.   250

And when the wind swooped over the lift
    And made the whole heaven frown,
It seemed a grip was laid on the walls
    To tug the housetop down.

And the Queen was there, more stately fair 255
    Than a lily in garden set;
And the King was loath to stir from her side,
For as on the day when she was his bride,
    Even so he loved her yet.

And the Earl of Athole, the King's false
    friend,   260
    Sat with him at the board;
And Robert Stuart the chamberlain
    Who had sold his sovereign Lord.

Yet the traitor Christopher Chaumber there
    Would fain have told him all,   265
And vainly four times that night he strove
    To reach the King through the hall.

But the wine is bright at the goblet's brim
    Though the poison lurk beneath;
And the apples still are red on the tree   270
    Within whose shade may the adder be
    That shall turn thy life to death.

There was a knight of the King's fast friends
    Whom he called the King of Love;
And to such bright cheer and courtesy   275
    That name might best behove.

And the King and Queen both loved him well
    For his gentle knightliness;
And with him the King, as that eve wore on,
    Was playing at the chess.   280

And the King said (for he thought to jest
    And soothe the Queen thereby),
"In a book 'tis writ that this same year
    A King shall in Scotland die.

"And I have pondered the matter o'er,   285
    And this have I found, Sir Hugh —
There are but two kings on Scottish ground,
    And those kings are I and you.

"And I have a wife and a newborn heir,
    And you are yourself alone;   290
So stand you stark at my side with me
    To guard our double throne.

"For here sit I and my wife and child,
    As well your heart shall approve,

251. **lift**, sky, air.

In full surrender and soothfastness,   295
  Beneath your Kingdom of Love."

And the Knight laughed, and the Queen too
    smiled;
  But I knew her heavy thought,
And I strove to find in the good King's jest
  What cheer might thence be wrought.   300

And I said, "My Liege, for the Queen's dear
    love
  Now sing the song that of old
You made, when a captive Prince you lay,
And the nightingale sang sweet on the spray,
  In Windsor's castle-hold."   305

Then he smiled the smile I knew so well
  When he thought to please the Queen;
The smile which under all bitter frowns
  Of hate that rose between,
Forever dwelt at the poet's heart   310
  Like the bird of love unseen.

And he kissed her hand and took his harp,
  And the music sweetly rang;
And when the song burst forth, it seemed
  'Twas the nightingale that sang.   315

"Worship, ye lovers, on this May;
  Of bliss your kalends are begun.
Sing with us, Away, Winter, away!
  Come, Summer, the sweet season and sun!
Awake for shame — your heaven is won —
  And amorously your heads lift all;   321
Thank Love, that you to his grace doth call!"

But when he bent to the Queen, and sang
  The speech whose praise was hers,
It seemed his voice was the voice of the spring
  And the voice of the bygone years.   326

"The fairest and the freshest flower
  That ever I saw before that hour,
The which o' the sudden made to start
  The blood of my body to my heart.   330

   .   .   .   .   .

Ah sweet, are ye a worldly creature
Or heavenly thing in form of nature?"

And the song was long, and richly stored
  With wonder and beauteous things;
And the harp was tuned to every change   335
  Of minstrel ministerings;
But when he spoke of the Queen at the last,
  Its strings were his own heart-strings.

"Unworthy but only of her grace,
  Upon Love's rock that's easy and sure,   340
In guerdon of all my love's space
  She took me her humble creäture.
Thus fell my blissful aventure
In youth of love that from day to day
Flowereth aye new, and further I say.   345

"To reckon all the circumstance
  As happed when lessen gan my sore,
Of my rancor and woeful chance,
  It were too long — I have done therefor.
And of this flower I say no more   350
But unto my help her heart hath tended
And even from death her man defended."

"Aye, even from death," to myself I said;
  For I thought of the day when she
Had borne him the news, at Roxbro' siege,
  Of the fell confederacy.   366

But Death even then took aim as he sang
  With an arrow deadly bright;
And the grinning skull lurked grimly aloof,
And the wings were spread far over the roof
  More dark than the winter night.   361

Yet truly along the amorous song
  Of Love's high pomp and state,
There were words of Fortune's trackless doom
  And the dreadful face of Fate.   365

And oft have I heard again in dreams
  The voice of dire appeal
In which the King then sang of the pit
  That is under Fortune's wheel.

"And under the wheel beheld I there   370
  An ugly Pit as deep as hell,
That to behold I quaked for fear.
  And this I heard, that who therein fell
  Came no more up, tidings to tell;
Whereat, astound of the fearful sight,   375
  I wist not what to do for fright."

And oft has my thought called up again
  These words of the changeful song:
"Wist thou thy pain and thy travàil
To come, well might'st thou weep and wail!"
  And our wail, O God! is long.   381

But the song's end was all of his love;
  And well his heart was graced
With her smiling lips and her tear-bright eyes
  As his arm went round her waist. 385

And on the swell of her long fair throat
  Close clung the necklet-chain
As he bent her pearl-tired head aside,

And in the warmth of his love and pride
  He kissed her lips full fain.   390

And her true face was a rosy red,
  The very red of the rose
That, couched on the happy garden-bed,
  In the summer sunlight glows.

And all the wondrous things of love   395
  That sang so sweet through the song
Were in the look that met in their eyes,
  And the look was deep and long.

'Twas then a knock came at the outer gate,
  And the usher sought the King.   400
"The woman you met by the Scottish Sea,
  My Liege, would tell you a thing;
And she says that her present need for speech
  Will bear no gainsaying."

And the King said: "The hour is late;   405
  Tomorrow will serve, I ween."
Then he charged the usher strictly, and said:
  "No word of this to the Queen."

But the usher came again to the King.
  "Shall I call her back?" quoth he;   410
"For as she went on her way, she cried,
  'Woe! Woe! then the thing must be!'"

And the King paused, but he did not speak.
  Then he called for the Voidee-cup;
And as we heard the twelfth hour strike,   415
There by true lips and false lips alike
  Was the draft of trust drained up.

So with reverence meet to King and Queen,
  To bed went all from the board;
And the last to leave of the courtly train   420
Was Robert Stuart the chamberlain
  Who had sold his sovereign lord.

And all the locks of the chamber door
  Had the traitor riven and brast;
And that Fate might win sure way from afar
He had drawn out every bolt and bar   426
  That made the entrance fast.

And now at midnight he stole his way
  To the moat of the outer wall,
And laid strong hurdles closely across   430
  Where the traitors' tread should fall.

But we that were the Queen's bower-maids
  Alone were left behind;
And with heed we drew the curtains close
  Against the winter wind.   435

And now that all was still through the hall,
  More clearly we heard the rain
That clamored ever against the glass
  And the boughs that beat on the pane.

But the fire was bright in the ingle-nook,   440
  And through empty space around
The shadows cast on the arrased wall
'Mid the pictured kings stood sudden and tall
  Like specters sprung from the ground.

And the bed was dight in a deep alcove;   445
  And as he stood by the fire
The King was still in talk with the Queen
  While he doffed his goodly attire.

And the song had brought the image back
  Of many a bygone year;   450
And many a loving word they said
With hand in hand and head laid to head;
  And none of us went anear.

But Love was weeping outside the house,
  A child in the piteous rain;   455
And as he watched the arrow of Death,
He wailed for his own shafts close in the
    sheath
  That never should fly again.

And now beneath the window arose
  A wild voice suddenly;   460
And the King reared straight, but the Queen
    fell back
  As for bitter dule to dree;
And all of us knew the woman's voice
  Who spoke by the Scottish Sea.

"O King," she cried, "in an evil hour   465
  They drove me from thy gate;
And yet my voice must rise to thine ears;
  But alas! it comes too late!

"Last night at mid-watch, by Aberdour,
  When the moon was dead in the skies,   470
O King, in a death-light of thine own
  I saw thy shape arise.

"And in full season, as erst I said,
  The doom had gained its growth;
And the shroud had risen above thy neck 475
  And covered thine eyes and mouth.

"And no moon woke, but the pale dawn broke,
  And still thy soul stood there;
And I thought its silence cried to my soul
  As the first rays crowned its hair.   480

---

414. Voidee-cup, a spiced wine served late in the evening before bedtime. **424. riven and brast,** torn and broken. **430. hurdles,** narrow boards.

445. dight, prepared. **462. dule to dree,** sorrow to suffer. **469. Aberdour,** a town on the north shore of the Firth of Forth, across from Edinburgh.

"Since then have I journeyed fast and fain
  In very despite of Fate,
Lest Hope might still be found in God's will;
  But they drove me from thy gate.

"For every man on God's ground, O King, 485
  His death grows up from his birth
In a shadow-plant perpetually;
And thine towers high, a black yew-tree,
  O'er the Charterhouse of Perth!"

That room was built far out from the house;
  And none but we in the room 491
Might hear the voice that rose beneath,
  Nor the tread of the coming doom.

For now there came a torchlight-glare,
  And a clang of arms there came; 495
And not a soul in that space but thought
  Of the foe Sir Robert Græme.

Yea, from the country of the Wild Scots,
  O'er mountain, valley, and glen,
He had brought with him in murderous
    league 500
  Three hundred arméd men.

The King knew all in an instant's flash,
  And like a King did he stand;
But there was no armor in all the room,
  Nor weapon lay to his hand. 505

And all we women flew to the door
  And thought to have made it fast;
But the bolts were gone and the bars were
    gone
  And the locks were riven and brast.

And he caught the pale pale Queen in his
    arms 510
  As the iron footsteps fell —
Then loosed her, standing alone, and said,
  "Our bliss was our farewell!"

And 'twixt his lips he murmured a prayer,
  And he crossed his brow and breast; 515
And proudly in royal hardihood
Even so with folded arms he stood —
  The prize of the bloody quest.

Then on me leaped the Queen like a deer —
  "O Catherine, help!" she cried. 520
And low at his feet we clasped his knees
  Together side by side.
"Oh! even a king, for his people's sake,
  From treasonous death must hide!"

"For *her* sake most!" I cried, and I marked
  The pang that my words could wring. 526
And the iron tongs from the chimney-nook

I snatched and held to the King —
"Wrench up the plank! and the vault beneath
  Shall yield safe harboring." 530

With brows low-bent, from my eager hand
  The heavy heft did he take;
And the plank at his feet he wrenched and
    tore;
And as he frowned through the open floor,
  Again I said, "For her sake!" 535

Then he cried to the Queen, "God's will be
    done!"
  For her hands were clasped in prayer.
And down he sprang to the inner crypt;
And straight we closed the plank he had
    ripped
  And toiled to smoothe it fair. 540

(Alas! in that vault a gap once was
  Wherethrough the King might have fled;
But three days since close-walled had it been
By his will; for the ball would roll therein
  When without at the palm he played.) 545

Then the Queen cried, "Catherine, keep the
    door,
  And I to this will suffice!"
At her word I rose all dazed to my feet,
  And my heart was fire and ice.

And louder ever the voices grew, 550
  And the tramp of men in mail;
Until to my brain it seemed to be
As though I tossed on a ship at sea
  In the teeth of a crashing gale.

Then back I flew to the rest; and hard 555
  We strove with sinews knit
To force the table against the door;
  But we might not compass it.

Then my wild gaze sped far down the hall
  To the place of the hearthstone-sill; 560
And the Queen bent ever above the floor,
  For the plank was rising still.

And now the rush was heard on the stair,
  And "God, what help?" was our cry.
And was I frenzied or was I bold? 565
I looked at each empty stanchion-hold,
  And no bar but my arm had I!

Like iron felt my arm, as through
  The staple I made it pass —
Alack! it was flesh and bone — no more! 570
'Twas Catherine Douglas sprang to the door,
  But I fell back Kate Barlass.

532. **heft,** handle. 545. **at the palm.** See note on line
8, p. 553. 566. **stanchion-hold,** a large staple or socket
for securing the bar that fastened the door.

With that they all thronged into the hall,
　　Half dim to my failing ken;
And the space that was but a void before 575
　　Was a crowd of wrathful men.

Behind the door I had fall'n and lay,
　　Yet my sense was wildly aware,
And for all the pain of my shattered arm
　　I never fainted there.　　　　　　580

Even as I fell, my eyes were cast
　　Where the King leaped down to the pit;
And lo! the plank was smooth in its place,
　　And the Queen stood far from it.

And under the litters and through the bed
　　And within the presses all　　　　586
The traitors sought for the King, and pierced
　　The arras around the wall.

And through the chamber they ramped and
　　stormed
　　Like lions loose in the lair,　　　　590
And scarce could trust to their very eyes —
　　For behold! no King was there.

Then one of them seized the Queen, and cried,
　　"Now tell us, where is thy lord?"
And he held the sharp point over her heart.
She drooped not her eyes nor did she start, 596
　　But she answered never a word.

Then the sword half pierced the true true
　　breast;
　　But it was the Græme's own son
Cried, "This is a woman — we seek a man!"
　　And away from her girdle-zone　　　601
He struck the point of the murderous steel;
　　And that foul deed was not done.

And forth flowed all the throng like a sea,
　　And 'twas empty space once more;　　605
And my eyes sought out the wounded Queen
　　As I lay behind the door.

And I said, "Dear Lady, leave me here,
　　For I cannot help you now;
But fly while you may, and none shall reck
　　Of my place here lying low."　　　611

And she said, "My Catherine, God help thee!"
　　Then she looked to the distant floor,
And clasping her hands, "O God help *him*,"
　　She sobbed, "for we can no more!"　615

But God He knows what help may mean,
　　If it mean to live or to die;
And what sore sorrow and mighty moan
On earth it may cost ere yet a throne
　　Be filled in His house on high.　　620

And now the ladies fled with the Queen;
　　And through the open door
The night-wind wailed round the empty room
　　And the rushes shook on the floor.

And the bed drooped low in the dark recess
　　Whence the arras was rent away;　　626
And the firelight still shone over the space
　　Where our hidden secret lay.

And the rain had ceased, and the moonbeams
　　lit
　　The window high in the wall —　　630
Bright beams that on the plank that I knew
　　Through the painted pane did fall
And gleamed with the splendor of Scotland's
　　crown
　　And shield armorial.

But then a great wind swept up the skies, 635
　　And the climbing moon fell back;
And the royal blazon fled from the floor,
　　And naught remained on its track;
And high in the darkened window-pane
　　The shield and the crown were black.　640

And what I say next I partly saw
　　And partly I heard in sooth,
And partly since from the murderers' lips
　　The torture wrung the truth.

For now again came the arméd tread,　　645
　　And fast through the hall it fell;
But the throng was less — and ere I saw,
　　By the voice without I could tell
That Robert Stuart had come with them
　　Who knew that chamber well.　　　650

And over the space the Græme strode dark
　　With his mantle round him flung;
And in his eye was a flaming light
　　But not a word on his tongue.

And Stuart held a torch to the floor,　　655
　　And he found the thing he sought;
And they slashed the plank away with their
　　swords;
　　And O God! I fainted not!

And the traitor held his torch in the gap,
　　All smoking and smoldering;　　　660
And through the vapor and fire, beneath
　　In the dark crypt's narrow ring,
With a shout that pealed to the room's high
　　roof
　　They saw their naked King.

Half naked he stood, but stood as one　665
　　Who yet could do and dare;

664. **naked**, unarmed.

With the crown, the King was stript away —
The Knight was reft of his battle-array —
  But still the Man was there.

From the rout then stepped a villain forth —
Sir John Hall was his name;   671
With a knife unsheathed he leapt to the vault
  Beneath the torchlight-flame.

Of his person and stature was the King
A man right manly strong,   675
And mightily by the shoulder-blades
  His foe to his feet he flung.

Then the traitor's brother, Sir Thomas Hall,
Sprang down to work his worst;
And the King caught the second man by the
  neck   680
  And flung him above the first.

And he smote and trampled them under him;
And a long month thence they bare
All black their throats with the grip of his
  hands
  When the hangman's hand came there. 685

And sore he strove to have had their knives,
But the sharp blades gashed his hands.
Oh, James! so armed, thou hadst battled
  there
  Till help had come of thy bands;
And oh! once more thou hadst held our
  throne   690
  And ruled thy Scottish lands!

But while the King o'er his foes still raged
With a heart that naught could tame,
Another man sprang down to the crypt;
And with his sword in his hand hard-gripped
  There stood Sir Robert Græme.   696

(Now shame on the recreant traitor's heart
Who durst not face his King
Till the body unarmed was wearied out
  With twofold combating!   700

Ah! well might the people sing and say,
As oft ye have heard aright —
"O Robert Græme, O Robert Græme,
Who slew our King, God give thee shame!"
  For he slew him not as a knight.)   705

And the naked King turned round at bay,
But his strength had passed the goal,
And he could but gasp, "Mine hour is come;
But oh! to succor thine own soul's doom,
  Let a priest now shrive my soul!"   710

And the traitor looked on the King's spent
  strength
And said, "Have I kept my word? —

Yea, King, the mortal pledge that I gave?
No black friar's shrift thy soul shall save,
  But the shrift of this red sword!"   715

With that he smote his King through the
  breast;
And all they three in the pen
Fell on him and stabbed and stabbed him
  there
  Like merciless murderous men.

Yet seemed it now that Sir Robert Græme,
Ere the King's last breath was o'er,   721
Turned sick at heart with the deadly sight
  And would have done no more.

But a cry came from the troop above:
"If him thou do not slay,   725
The price of his life that thou dost spare
  Thy forfeit life shall pay!"

O God! what more did I hear or see,
Or how should I tell the rest?
But there at length our King lay slain   730
  With sixteen wounds in his breast.

O God! and now did a bell boom forth,
And the murderers turned and fled; —
Too late, too late, O God, did it sound! —
And I heard the true men mustering round,
  And the cries and the coming tread.   736

But ere they came, to the black death-gap
Somewise did I creep and steal;
And lo! or ever I swooned away,
Through the dusk I saw where the white face
  lay   740
  In the Pit of Fortune's Wheel.

And now, ye Scottish maids who have heard
Dread things of the days grown old —
Even at the last, of true Queen Jane
May somewhat yet be told,   745
And how she dealt for her dear lord's sake
  Dire vengeance manifold.

'Twas in the Charterhouse of Perth,
In the fair-lit Death-chapelle,
That the slain King's corpse on bier was laid
  With chaunt and requiem-knell.   751

And all with royal wealth of balm
Was the body purified;
And none could trace on the brow and lips
  The death that he had died.   755

In his robes of state he lay asleep
  With orb and scepter in hand;

751. **requiem-knell**, the bell sounded at requiem-mass for the dead. 757. **orb**, a small globe and cross mounted on the scepter, a part of the royal regalia.

And by the crown he wore on his throne
  Was his kingly forehead spanned.

And, girls, 'twas a sweet sad thing to see   760
  How the curling golden hair,
As in the day of the poet's youth,
  From the King's crown clustered there.

And if all had come to pass in the brain
  That throbbed beneath those curls,   765
Then Scots had said in the days to come
That this their soil was a different home
  And a different Scotland, girls!

And the Queen sat by him night and day,
  And oft she knelt in prayer,   770
All wan and pale in the widow's veil
  That shrouded her shining hair.

And I had got good help of my hurt,
  And only to me some sign
She made; and save the priests that were
    there   775
  No face would she see but mine.

And the month of March wore on apace;
  And now fresh couriers fared
Still from the country of the Wild Scots
  With news of the traitors snared.   780

And still as I told her day by day,
  Her pallor changed to sight,
And the frost grew to a furnace-flame
  That burnt her visage white.

And evermore as I brought her word,   785
  She bent to her dead King James,
And in the cold ear with fire-drawn breath
  She spoke the traitors' names.

But when the name of Sir Robert Græme
  Was the one she had to give,   790
I ran to hold her up from the floor;
For the froth was on her lips, and sore
  I feared that she could not live.

And the month of March wore nigh to its end,
  And still was the death-pall spread;   795
For she would not bury her slaughtered lord
  Till his slayers all were dead.

And now of their dooms dread tidings came,
  And of torments fierce and dire;
And naught she spake — she had ceased to
    speak —   800
  But her eyes were a soul on fire.

But when I told her the bitter end
  Of the stern and just award,
She leaned o'er the bier, and thrice three
    times
  She kissed the lips of her lord.   805

And then she said, "My King, they are dead!"
  And she knelt on the chapel-floor,
And whispered low with a strange proud
    smile —
  "James, James, they suffered more!"

Last she stood up to her queenly height,   810
  But she shook like an autumn leaf,
As though the fire wherein she burned
Then left her body, and all were turned
  To winter of life-long grief.

And "O James!" she said — "My James!"
    she said —   815
  "Alas for the woeful thing,
That a poet true and a friend of man,
In desperate days of bale and ban,
  Should needs be born a King!"

                         (*1881;* 1881)

CHRISTINA ROSSETTI (1830-1894)

SONG

When I am dead, my dearest,
  Sing no sad songs for me;
Plant thou no roses at my head,
  Nor shady cypress tree.
Be the green grass above me   5
  With showers and dewdrops wet;
And if thou wilt, remember,
  And if thou wilt, forget.

I shall not see the shadows,
  I shall not feel the rain;   10
I shall not hear the nightingale
  Sing on as if in pain.
And dreaming through the twilight
  That doth not rise nor set,
Haply I may remember,   15
  And haply may forget.   (*1848;* 1862)

DREAM LAND

Where sunless rivers weep
Their waves into the deep,
She sleeps a charmèd sleep;
  Awake her not.
Led by a single star,   5
She came from very far
To seek where shadows are
  Her pleasant lot.

She left the rosy morn,
She left the fields of corn,   10

818. **bale and ban**, evil and enmity.
Song. 4. **cypress tree.** The cypress is a symbol of mourn-
ing; it is a common tree in graveyards.
Dream Land. 10. **corn**, wheat.

For twilight cold and lorn
    And water springs.
Through sleep, as through a veil,
She sees the sky look pale,
And hears the nightingale   15
    That sadly sings.

Rest, rest, a perfect rest
Shed over brow and breast;
Her face is toward the west,
    The purple land.   20
She cannot see the grain
Ripening on hill and plain,
She cannot feel the rain
    Upon her hand.

Rest, rest, for evermore   25
Upon a mossy shore;
Rest, rest at the heart's core
    Till time shall cease:
Sleep that no pain shall wake;
Night that no morn shall break,   30
Till joy shall overtake
    Her perfect peace.   (*1849; 1850*)

AFTER DEATH

The curtains were half drawn; the floor was
    swept
And strewn with rushes; rosemary and may
Lay thick upon the bed on which I lay,
Where, through the lattice, ivy-shadows crept.
He leaned above me, thinking that I slept   5
And could not hear him; but I heard him
    say,
"Poor child, poor child"; and as he turned
    away
Came a deep silence, and I knew he wept.
He did not touch the shroud, or raise the fold
That hid my face, or take my hand in his,   10
Or ruffle the smooth pillows for my head.
He did not love me living; but once dead
He pitied me; and very sweet it is
To know he still is warm though I am cold.
                              (*1849; 1862*)

REMEMBER

Remember me when I am gone away,
Gone far away into the silent land;
When you can no more hold me by the hand,
Nor I half turn to go yet turning stay.
Remember me when no more day by day   5
You tell me of our future that you planned.
Only remember me; you understand
It will be late to counsel then or pray.
Yet if you should forget me for a while
And afterwards remember, do not grieve;   10

After Death. 2. **rosemary**, a fragrant shrub, the emblem
of fidelity. **may**, hawthorn.

For if the darkness and corruption leave
A vestige of the thoughts that once I had,
Better by far you should forget and smile
Than that you should remember and be sad.
                              (*1849; 1862*)

THE THREE ENEMIES

THE FLESH

"Sweet, thou art pale."
                    "More pale to see,
Christ hung upon the cruel tree
And bore His Father's wrath for me."

"Sweet, thou art sad."
                    "Beneath a rod
More heavy, Christ for my sake trod   5
The winepress of the wrath of God."

"Sweet, thou art weary."
                    "Not so Christ,
Whose mighty love of me sufficed
For Strength, Salvation, Eucharist."

"Sweet, thou art footsore."
                          "If I bleed,   10
His feet have bled; yea, in my need
His Heart once bled for mine indeed."

THE WORLD

"Sweet, thou art young."
                    "So He was young
Who for my sake in silence hung
Upon the Cross with Passion wrung."   15

"Look, thou art fair."
                    "He was more fair
Than men, Who deigned for me to wear
A visage marred beyond compare."

"And thou hast riches."
                    "Daily bread;
All else is His — Who, living, dead,   20
For me lacked where to lay His Head."

"And life is sweet."
                    "It was not so
To Him, Whose Cup did overflow
With mine unutterable woe."

THE DEVIL

"Thou drinkest deep."
                    "When Christ would sup   25
He drained the dregs from out my cup;
So how should I be lifted up?"

The Three Enemies. 6. **winepress ... God.** See *Isaiah,*
63:2-3. 9. **Eucharist,** the sacrament of the Lord's Supper,
the communion.

"Thou shalt win Glory."
               "In the skies,
Lord Jesus, cover up mine eyes
Lest they should look on vanities."   30

"Thou shalt have Knowledge."
               "Helpless dust!
In thee, O Lord, I put my trust;
Answer Thou for me, Wise and Just."

"And Might." —
         "Get thee behind me. Lord,
Who hast redeemed and not abhorred   35
My soul, oh, keep it by Thy Word."
                       (1851; 1862)

PARADISE

Once in a dream I saw the flowers
   That bud and bloom in Paradise;
More fair they are than waking eyes
Have seen in all this world of ours.
And faint the perfume-bearing rose,   5
   And faint the lily on its stem,
And faint the perfect violet,
   Compared with them.

I heard the songs of Paradise:
   Each bird sat singing in his place;   10
   A tender song so full of grace
It soared like incense to the skies.
Each bird sat singing to his mate
   Soft cooing notes among the trees;
The nightingale herself were cold   15
   To such as these.

I saw the fourfold River flow,
   And deep it was, with golden sand;
   It flowed between a mossy land
With murmured music grave and low.   20
It hath refreshment for all thirst,
   For fainting spirits strength and rest;
Earth holds not such a draft as this
   From east to west.

The Tree of Life stood budding there,   25
   Abundant with its twelvefold fruits;
   Eternal sap sustains its roots,
Its shadowing branches fill the air.
Its leaves are healing for the world,
   Its fruit the hungry world can feed,   30

Sweeter than honey to the taste
   And balm indeed.

I saw the Gate called Beautiful,
   And looked, but scarce could look within;
   I saw the golden streets begin,   35
And outskirts of the glassy pool.
O harps, O crowns of plenteous stars,
   O green palm branches many-leaved —
Eye hath not seen, nor ear hath heard,
   Nor heart conceived.   40

I hope to see these things again,
   But not as once in dreams by night;
   To see them with my very sight,
And touch and handle and attain —
To have all heaven beneath my feet   45
   For narrow way that once they trod;
To have my part with all the saints,
   And with my God.   *(1854; 1865)*

A BETTER RESURRECTION

I have no wit, no words, no tears;
   My heart within me like a stone
Is numbed too much for hopes or fears.
   Look right, look left, I dwell alone;
I lift mine eyes, but dimmed with grief   5
   No everlasting hills I see.
My life is in the falling leaf;
   O Jesus, quicken me.

My life is like a faded leaf,
   My harvest dwindled to a husk;   10
Truly my life is void and brief
   And tedious in the barren dusk;
My life is like a frozen thing,
   No bud nor greenness can I see;
Yet rise it shall — the sap of Spring;   15
   O Jesus, rise in me.

My life is like a broken bowl,
   A broken bowl that cannot hold
One drop of water for my soul
   Or cordial in the searching cold;   20
Cast in the fire the perished thing;
   Melt and remold it, till it be
A royal cup for Him, my King;
   O Jesus, drink of me.   *(1857; 1862)*

A BIRTHDAY

My heart is like a singing bird
   Whose nest is in a watered shoot;
My heart is like an apple-tree

---

34. Get . . . me. See note on *"Retro Me, Sathana!"* p. 544.
  Paradise. This poem is based upon John's vision of the New Jerusalem in *Revelation*, 21-22. **17. fourfold River,** the river of the water of life (*Revelation*, 22:1). Cf. *Genesis*, 2:10.—"And a river went out of Eden to water the garden; and from thence it was parted, and became into four heads." **25 ff. Tree of life,** etc. From *Revelation*, 22:2.—"On either side of the river was there the tree of life, which bare twelve manner of fruits. . . . and the leaves of the tree were for the healing of the nations."

35. golden streets. "The street of the city was pure gold, as it were transparent glass" (*Revelation*, 21:21). **36. glassy pool.** See note on line 6 of *The Convent Threshold*, p. 566. **39-40. Eye . . . conceived.** From *1 Corinthians*, 2:9.—"Eye hath not seen, nor ear heard, neither have entered into the heart of man, the things which God hath prepared for them that love him."

Whose boughs are bent with thickset fruit;
My heart is like a rainbow shell   5
   That paddles in a halcyon sea;
My heart is gladder than all these
   Because my love is come to me.

Raise me a dais of silk and down;
   Hang it with vair and purple dyes;   10
Carve it in doves and pomegranates,
   And peacocks with a hundred eyes;
Work it in gold and silver grapes,
   In leaves and silver fleurs-de-lys;
Because the birthday of my life   15
   Is come, my love is come to me.

                     (*1857; 1861*)

AN APPLE GATHERING

I plucked pink blossoms from mine apple-tree
   And wore them all that evening in my hair;
Then in due season when I went to see,
   I found no apples there.

With dangling basket all along the grass   5
   As I had come I went the self-same track;
My neighbors mocked me while they saw me pass
   So empty-handed back.

Lilian and Lilias smiled in trudging by,
   Their heaped-up basket teased me like a jeer;   10
Sweet-voiced they sang beneath the sunset sky —
   Their mother's home was near.

Plump Gertrude passed me with her basket full,
   A stronger hand than hers helped it along;
A voice talked with her through the shadows cool   15
   More sweet to me than song.

Ah Willie, Willie, was my love less worth
   Than apples with their green leaves piled above?
I counted rosiest apples on the earth
   Of far less worth than love.   20

So once it was with me you stooped to talk,
   Laughing and listening in this very lane;
To think that by this way we used to walk
   We shall not walk again!

I let my neighbors pass me, ones and twos   25
   And groups; the latest said the night grew chill,
And hastened. But I loitered; while the dews
   Fell fast I loitered still.   (*1857; 1862*)

---

6. **halcyon,** calm. 10. **vair,** a fine fur, made from the skin of a gray squirrel, used for lining robes.

ADVENT

This Advent moon shines cold and clear,
   These Advent nights are long;
Our lamps have burned year after year,
   And still their flame is strong.
"Watchman, what of the night?" we cry,   5
   Heart-sick with hope deferred;
"No speaking signs are in the sky,"
   Is still the watchman's word.

The Porter watches at the gate,
   The servants watch within;   10
The watch is long betimes and late,
   The prize is slow to win.
"Watchman, what of the night?" But still
   His answer sounds the same:
"No daybreak tops the utmost hill,   15
   Nor pale our lamps of flame."

One to another hear them speak
   The patient virgins wise:
"Surely He is not far to seek" —
   "All night we watch and rise."   20
"The days are evil looking back,
   The coming days are dim;
Yet count we not His promise slack,
   But watch and wait for Him."

One with another, soul with soul,   25
   They kindle fire from fire:
"Friends watch us who have touched the goal."
   "They urge us, come up higher."
"With them shall rest our waysore feet,
   With them is built our home,   30
With Christ." — "They sweet, but He most sweet,
   Sweeter than honeycomb."

There no more parting, no more pain,
   The distant ones brought near,
The lost so long are found again,   35
   Long lost but longer dear;
Eye hath not seen, ear hath not heard,
   Nor heart conceived that rest,
With them our good things long deferred,
   With Jesus Christ our Best.   40

We weep because the night is long,
   We laugh for day shall rise,
We sing a slow contented song
   And knock at Paradise.
Weeping we hold Him fast Who wept   45
   For us, we hold Him fast;

Advent. Advent is the period including the four Sundays preceding Christmas.
  5. **Watchman . . . night.** Quoted from *Isaiah,* 21:11.
6. **Heart-sick . . . deferred.** From *Proverbs,* 13:12.—"Hope deferred maketh the heart sick." 18 ff. **virgins,** etc. See the parable of the ten virgins, *Matthew,* 25:1-13. 32. **sweeter than honeycomb.** Quoted from *Psalms,* 19:10. 37-38. **Eye . . . rest.** See note on lines 39-40 of *Paradise,* p. 564.

And will not let Him go except
　　He bless us first or last.

Weeping we hold Him fast tonight;
　　We will not let Him go　　　　　　　　　50
Till daybreak smite our wearied sight
　　And summer smite the snow.
Then figs shall bud, and dove with dove
　　Shall coo the livelong day;
Then He shall say, "Arise, My love,　　　55
　　My fair one, come away."　　(*1858; 1862*)

AT HOME

When I was dead, my spirit turned
　　To seek the much-frequented house.
I passed the door, and saw my friends
　　Feasting beneath green orange-boughs;
From hand to hand they pushed the wine,　5
　　They sucked the pulp of plum and peach;
They sang, they jested, and they laughed,
　　For each was loved of each.

I listened to their honest chat.
　　Said one: "Tomorrow we shall be　　　10
Plod plod along the featureless sands,
　　And coasting miles and miles of sea."
Said one: "Before the turn of tide
　　We will achieve the eyrie-seat."
Said one: "Tomorrow shall be like　　　15
　　Today, but much more sweet."

"Tomorrow," said they, strong with hope,
　　And dwelt upon the pleasant way.
"Tomorrow," cried they one and all,
　　While no one spoke of yesterday.　　　20
Their life stood full at blessed noon;
　　I, only I, had passed away.
"Tomorrow and today," they cried;
　　I was of yesterday.

I shivered comfortless, but cast　　　　25
　　No chill across the tablecloth;
I, all-forgotten, shivered, sad
　　To stay and yet to part how loath;
I passed from the familiar room,
　　I who from love had passed away,　　　30
Like the remembrance of a guest
　　That tarrieth but a day.　　(*1858;* 1862)

UPHILL

Does the road wind uphill all the way?
　　Yes, to the very end.
Will the day's journey take the whole long
　　day?
　　From morn to night, my friend.

But is there for the night a resting-place?　5
　　A roof for when the slow dark hours begin.

May not the darkness hide it from my face?
　　You cannot miss that inn.

Shall I meet other wayfarers at night?
　　Those who have gone before.　　　　　10
Then must I knock, or call when just in sight?
　　They will not keep you standing at that
　　door.

Shall I find comfort, travel-sore and weak?
　　Of labor you shall find the sum.
Will there be beds for me and all who seek?
　　Yea, beds for all who come.　　　　　16
　　　　　　　　　　　　　　(*1858;* 1861)

THE CONVENT THRESHOLD

There's blood between us, love, my love,
There's father's blood, there's brother's blood
And blood's a bar I cannot pass.
I choose the stairs that mount above,
Stair after golden sky-ward stair,　　　　5
To city and to sea of glass.
My lily feet are soiled with mud,
With scarlet mud which tells a tale
Of hope that was, of guilt that was,
Of love that shall not yet avail;　　　　10
Alas, my heart, if I could bare
My heart, this selfsame stain is there.
I seek the sea of glass and fire
To wash the spot, to burn the snare;
Lo, stairs are meant to lift us higher —　15
Mount with me, mount the kindled stair.

Your eyes look earthward, mine look up.
I see the far-off city grand,
Beyond the hills a watered land,
Beyond the gulf a gleaming strand　　　20
Of mansions where the righteous sup;
Who sleep at ease among their trees,
Or wake to sing a cadenced hymn
With Cherubim and Seraphim.
They bore the Cross, they drained the cup, 25
Racked, roasted, crushed, wrenched limb from
　　limb,
They the offscouring of the world.
The heaven of starry heavens unfurled,
The sun before their face is dim.

You looking earthward, what see you?　　30
Milk-white, wine-flushed among the vines,
Up and down leaping, to and fro,
Most glad, most full, made strong with wines,
Blooming as peaches pearled with dew,

11-12. **knock . . . door.** From *Revelation*, 3:20.—"Behold,
I stand at the door and knock."
　　The Convent Threshold. **6. sea of glass.** In one of his
visions John saw "a sea of glass mingled with fire" (*Revelation*, 15:2; 4:6). **24. Cherubim and Seraphim,** two
orders of angels.　The first place in the hierarchy was given
to the Seraphim, angels of love; the next place was given to
the Cherubim, angels of light.

Their golden windy hair afloat, 35
Love-music warbling in their throat,
Young men and women come and go.

You linger, yet the time is short.
Flee for your life, gird up your strength
To flee; the shadows stretched at length 40
Show that day wanes, that night draws nigh;
Flee to the mountain, tarry not.
Is this a time for smile and sigh,
For songs among the secret trees
Where sudden blue birds nest and sport? 45
The time is short and yet you stay.
Today, while it is called today,
Kneel, wrestle, knock, do violence, pray;
Today is short, tomorrow nigh —
Why will you die? why will you die? 50

You sinned with me a pleasant sin;
Repent with me, for I repent.
Woe's me the lore I must unlearn!
Woe's me that easy way we went,
So rugged when I would return! 55
How long until my sleep begin,
How long shall stretch these nights and days?
Surely, clean angels cry, she prays;
She laves her soul with tedious tears;
How long must stretch these years and years?

I turn from you my cheeks and eyes, 61
My hair which you shall see no more —
Alas for joy that went before,
For joy that dies, for love that dies!
Only my lips still turn to you, 65
My livid lips that cry "Repent!"
O weary life, O weary Lent,
O weary time whose stars are few!
How should I rest in paradise,
Or sit on steps of heaven alone? 70
If saints and angels spoke of love,
Should I not answer from my throne,
"Have pity upon me, ye my friends,
For I have heard the sound thereof"?
Should I not turn with yearning eyes, 75
Turn earthwards with a pitiful pang?
Oh, save me from a pang in heaven!
By all the gifts we took and gave,
Repent, repent, and be forgiven.
This life is long, but yet it ends; 80
Repent and purge your soul and save —
No gladder song the morning stars
Upon their birthday morning sang
Than angels sing when one repents.

I tell you what I dreamed last night. 85
A spirit with transfigured face

Fire-footed clomb an infinite space.
I heard his hundred pinions clang,
Heaven-bells rejoicing rang and rang,
Heaven-air was thrilled with subtle scents, 90
Worlds spun upon their rushing cars.
He mounted, shrieking, "Give me light!"
Still light was poured on him, more light;
Angels, archangels he outstripped,
Exulting in exceeding might, 95
And trod the skirts of cherubim.
Still "Give me light," he shrieked; and dipped
His thirsty face, and drank a sea,
Athirst with thirst it could not slake.
I saw him, drunk with knowledge, take 100
From aching brows the aureole crown —
His locks writhe like a cloven snake —
He left his throne to grovel down
And lick the dust of seraphs' feet;
For what is knowledge duly weighed? 105
Knowledge is strong, but love is sweet;
Yea, all the progress he had made
Was but to learn that all is small
Save love, for love is all in all.

I tell you what I dreamed last night. 110
It was not dark, it was not light,
Cold dews had drenched my plenteous hair
Through clay; you came to seek me there,
And "Do you dream of me?" you said.
My heart was dust that used to leap 115
To you; I answered half asleep:
"My pillow is damp, my sheets are red,
There's a leaden tester to my bed;
Find you a warmer playfellow,
A warmer pillow for your head, 120
A kinder love to love than mine."
You wrung your hands, while I, like lead,
Crushed downwards through the sodden earth;
You smote your hands but not in mirth,
And reeled but were not drunk with wine. 125

For all night long I dreamed of you;
I woke and prayed against my will,
Then slept to dream of you again.
At length I rose and knelt and prayed.
I cannot write the words I said — 130
My words were slow, my tears were few;
But through the dark my silence spoke
Like thunder. When this morning broke,
My face was pinched, my hair was gray,
And frozen blood was on the sill 135
Where stifling in my struggle I lay.

If now you saw me you would say:
"Where is the face I used to love?"
And I would answer: "Gone before;
It tarries veiled in paradise. 140
When once the morning star shall rise,
When earth with shadow flees away

82–83. morning stars . . . sang. From *Job*, 38:7.—
"When the morning stars sang together, and all the sons of
God shouted for joy." 84. angels . . . repents. From
Luke, 15:7.—"I say unto you, that likewise joy shall be in
heaven over one sinner that repenteth."

118. tester, a canopy over a bed.

And we stand safe within the door,
Then you shall lift the veil thereof.
Look up, rise up, for far above   145
Our palms are grown, our place is set;
There we shall meet as once we met,
And love with old familiar love."
                              (*1858;* 1862)

GOBLIN MARKET

Morning and evening
Maids heard the goblins cry,
"Come buy our orchard fruits,
Come buy, come buy:
Apples and quinces,   5
Lemons and oranges,
Plump unpecked cherries,
Melons and raspberries,
Bloom-down-cheeked peaches,
Swart-headed mulberries,   10
Wild free-born cranberries,
Crab-apples, dewberries,
Pineapples, blackberries,
Apricots, strawberries —
All ripe together   15
In summer weather —
Morns that pass by,
Fair eves that fly;
Come buy, come buy:
Our grapes fresh from the vine,   20
Pomegranates full and fine,
Dates and sharp bullaces,
Rare pears and greengages,
Damsons and bilberries,
Taste them and try;   25
Currants and gooseberries,
Bright-fire-like barberries,
Figs to fill your mouth,
Citrons from the South,
Sweet to tongue and sound to eye;   30
Come buy, come buy."

Evening by evening
Among the brook-side rushes,
Laura bowed her head to hear,
Lizzie veiled her blushes;   35
Crouching close together
In the cooling weather,
With clasping arms and cautioning lips,
With tingling cheeks and finger tips.
"Lie close," Laura said,   40
Pricking up her golden head.
"We must not look at goblin men,
We must not buy their fruits;
Who knows upon what soil they fed
Their hungry thirsty roots?"   45
"Come buy," call the goblins

Hobbling down the glen.
"Oh," cried Lizzie, "Laura, Laura,
You should not peep at goblin men."
Lizzie covered up her eyes,   50
Covered close lest they should look;
Laura reared her glossy head,
And whispered like the restless brook:
"Look, Lizzie, look, Lizzie,
Down the glen tramp little men.   55
One hauls a basket,
One bears a plate,
One lugs a golden dish
Of many pounds' weight.
How fair the vine must grow   60
Whose grapes are so luscious!
How warm the wind must blow
Through those fruit bushes!"
"No," said Lizzie, "No, no, no;
Their offers should not charm us,   65
Their evil gifts would harm us."
She thrust a dimpled finger
In each ear, shut eyes and ran.
Curious Laura chose to linger,
Wondering at each merchant man.   70
One had a cat's face,
One whisked a tail,
One tramped at a rat's pace,
One crawled like a snail,
One like a wombat prowled obtuse and furry,
One like a ratel tumbled hurry-skurry.   76
She heard a voice like voice of doves
Cooing all together;
They sounded kind and full of loves
In the pleasant weather.   80

Laura stretched her gleaming neck
Like a rush-imbedded swan,
Like a lily from the beck,
Like a moonlit poplar branch,
Like a vessel at the launch   85
When its last restraint is gone.

Backward up the mossy glen
Turned and trooped the goblin men,
With their shrill repeated cry,
"Come buy, come buy."   90
When they reached where Laura was
They stood stock still upon the moss,
Leering at each other,
Brother with queer brother;
Signaling each other,   95
Brother with sly brother.
One set his basket down,
One reared his plate;
One began to weave a crown
Of tendrils, leaves, and rough nuts brown 100

Goblin Market. See Critical Notes.
22. **bullaces,** small European plums.

75. **wombat,** an animal of Australia that looks like a small bear. It carries its young in a pouch, like the kangaroo. 76. **ratel,** a South African animal, like the badger in size, form, and habits. 83. **beck,** a small brook.

(Men sell not such in any town);
One heaved the golden weight
Of dish and fruit to offer her;
"Come buy, come buy" was still their cry.
Laura stared but did not stir, 105
Longed but had no money.
The whisk-tailed merchant bade her taste
In tones as smooth as honey,
The cat-faced purred,
The rat-paced spoke a word 110
Of welcome, and the snail-paced even was
    heard;
One parrot-voiced and jolly
Cried, "Pretty Goblin" still for "Pretty
    Polly";
One whistled like a bird.

But sweet-tooth Laura spoke in haste: 115
"Good folk, I have no coin;
To take were to purloin.
I have no copper in my purse,
I have no silver either,
And all my gold is on the furze 120
That shakes in windy weather
Above the rusty heather."
"You have much gold upon your head,"
They answered all together;
"Buy from us with a golden curl." 125
She clipped a precious golden lock,
She dropped a tear more rare than pearl,
Then sucked their fruit globes fair or red.
Sweeter than honey from the rock,
Stronger than man-rejoicing wine, 130
Clearer than water flowed that juice;
She never tasted such before,
How should it cloy with length of use?
She sucked and sucked and sucked the more
Fruits which that unknown orchard bore; 135
She sucked until her lips were sore;
Then flung the emptied rinds away,
But gathered up one kernel stone,
And knew not was it night or day
As she turned home alone. 140

Lizzie met her at the gate,
Full of wise upbraidings:
"Dear, you should not stay so late,
Twilight is not good for maidens;
Should not loiter in the glen 145
In the haunts of goblin men.
Do you not remember Jeanie,
How she met them in the moonlight,
Took their gifts both choice and many,
Ate their fruits and wore their flowers 150
Plucked from bowers
Where summer ripens at all hours?
But ever in the moonlight
She pined and pined away;
Sought them by night and day, 155

Found them no more, but dwindled and grew
    gray;
Then fell with the first snow,
While to this day no grass will grow
Where she lies low;
I planted daisies there a year ago 160
That never blow.
You should not loiter so."
"Nay, hush," said Laura;
"Nay, hush, my sister.
I ate and ate my fill, 165
Yet my mouth waters still;
Tomorrow night I will
Buy more"; and kissed her.
"Have done with sorrow;
I'll bring you plums tomorrow 170
Fresh on their mother twigs,
Cherries worth getting;
You cannot think what figs
My teeth have met in,
What melons icy-cold 175
Piled on a dish of gold
Too huge for me to hold,
What peaches with a velvet nap,
Pellucid grapes without one seed.
Odorous indeed must be the mead 180
Whereon they grow, and pure the wave they
    drink
With lilies at the brink,
And sugar-sweet their sap."

Golden head by golden head,
Like two pigeons in one nest 185
Folded in each other's wings,
They lay down in their curtained bed;
Like two blossoms on one stem,
Like two flakes of new-fall'n snow,
Like two wands of ivory 190
Tipped with gold for awful kings.
Moon and stars gazed in at them,
Wind sang to them lullaby,
Lumbering owls forebore to fly,
Not a bat flapped to and fro 195
Round their nest;
Cheek to cheek and breast to breast
Locked together in one nest.

Early in the morning
When the first cock crowed his warning, 200
Neat like bees, as sweet and busy,
Laura rose with Lizzie;
Fetched in honey, milked the cows,
Aired and set to rights the house,
Kneaded cakes of whitest wheat, 205
Cakes for dainty mouths to eat,
Next churned butter, whipped up cream,
Fed their poultry, sat and sewed;
Talked as modest maidens should —
Lizzie with an open heart, 210

Laura in an absent dream,
One content, one sick in part;
One warbling for the mere bright day's
        delight,
One longing for the night.

At length slow evening came.   215
They went with pitchers to the reedy brook;
Lizzie most placid in her look,
Laura most like a leaping fiame.
They drew the gurgling water from its deep.
Lizzie plucked purple and rich golden flags,
Then turning homeward said: "The sunset
        flushes   221
Those furthest loftiest crags;
Come, Laura, not another maiden lags.
No willful squirrel wags;
The beasts and birds are fast asleep."   225

But Laura loitered still among the rushes,
And said the bank was steep,
And said the hour was early still,
The dew not fall'n, the wind not chill;
Listening ever, but not catching   230
The customary cry,
"Come buy, come buy,"
With its iterated jingle
Of sugar-baited words;
Not for all her watching   235
Once discerning even one goblin
Racing, whisking, tumbling, hobbling —
Let alone the herds
That used to tramp along the glen,
In groups or single,   240
Of brisk fruit-merchant men.

Till Lizzie urged, "O Laura, come;
I hear the fruit-call, but I dare not look.
You should not loiter longer at this brook;
Come with me home.   245
The stars rise, the moon bends her arc,
Each glowworm winks her spark.
Let us get home before the night grows dark,
For clouds may gather
Though this is summer weather,   250
Put out the lights and drench us through;
Then if we lost our way what should we do?"

Laura turned cold as stone
To find her sister heard that cry alone,
That goblin cry,   255
"Come buy our fruits, come buy."
Must she then buy no more such dainty fruit?
Must she no more such succous pasture find,
Gone deaf and blind?
Her tree of life drooped from the root;   260
She said not one word in her heart's sore ache;

258. **succous**, juicy.

But peering through the dimness, naught
        discerning,
Trudged home, her pitcher dripping all the
        way;
So crept to bed, and lay
Silent till Lizzie slept;   265
Then sat up in a passionate yearning,
And gnashed her teeth for balked desire, and
        wept
As if her heart would break.

Day after day, night after night,
Laura kept watch in vain   270
In sullen silence of exceeding pain.
She never caught again the goblin cry,
"Come buy, come buy";
She never spied the goblin men
Hawking their fruits along the glen.   275
But when the noon waxed bright
Her hair grew thin and gray;
She dwindled, as the fair full moon doth turn
To swift decay and burn
Her fire away.   280

One day, remembering her kernel-stone,
She set it by a wall that faced the south;
Dewed it with tears, hoped for a root,
Watched for a waxing shoot,
But there came none.   285
It never saw the sun,
It never felt the trickling moisture run;
While with sunk eyes and faded mouth
She dreamed of melons, as a traveler sees
False waves in desert drouth   290
With shade of leaf-crowned trees,
And burns the thirstier in the sandful breeze.

She no more swept the house,
Tended the fowls or cows,
Fetched honey, kneaded cakes of wheat,   295
Brought water from the brook;
But sat down listless in the chimney-nook
And would not eat.

Tender Lizzie could not bear
To watch her sister's cankerous care,   300
Yet not to share.
She night and morning
Caught the goblins' cry:
"Come buy our orchard fruits,
Come buy, come buy."   305
Beside the brook, along the glen,
She heard the tramp of goblin men,
The voice and stir
Poor Laura could not hear;
Longed to buy fruit to comfort her,   310
But feared to pay too dear.
She thought of Jeanie in her grave,
Who should have been a bride;

But who for joys brides hope to have
Fell sick and died 315
In her gay prime,
In earliest winter time,
With the first glazing rime,
With the first snow-fall of crisp winter time.

Till Laura dwindling 320
Seemed knocking at Death's door.
Then Lizzie weighed no more
Better and worse;
But put a silver penny in her purse,
Kissed Laura, crossed the heath with clumps
    of furze 325
At twilight, halted by the brook,
And for the first time in her life
Began to listen and look.

Laughed every goblin
When they spied her peeping; 330
Came toward her hobbling,
Flying, running, leaping,
Puffing and blowing,
Chuckling, clapping, crowing,
Clucking and gobbling, 335
Mopping and mowing,
Full of airs and graces,
Pulling wry faces,
Demure grimaces,
Cat-like and rat-like, 340
Ratel- and wombat-like,
Snail-paced in a hurry,
Parrot-voiced and whistler,
Helter-skelter, hurry-skurry,
Chattering like magpies, 345
Fluttering like pigeons,
Gliding like fishes —
Hugged her and kissed her,
Squeezed and caressed her,
Stretched up their dishes, 350
Panniers, and plates:
"Look at our apples
Russet and dun,
Bob at our cherries,
Bite at our peaches, 355
Citrons and dates,
Grapes for the asking,
Pears red with basking
Out in the sun,
Plums on their twigs; 360
Pluck them and suck them —
Pomegranates, figs."

"Good folk," said Lizzie,
Mindful of Jeanie,
"Give me much and many"; 365
Held out her apron,
Tossed them her penny.
"Nay, take a seat with us,
Honor and eat with us,"

They answered, grinning; 370
"Our feast is but beginning.
Night yet is early,
Warm and dew-pearly,
Wakeful and starry.
Such fruits as these 375
No man can carry;
Half their bloom would fly,
Half their dew would dry,
Half their flavor would pass by.
Sit down and feast with us, 380
Be welcome guest with us,
Cheer you and rest with us." —
"Thank you," said Lizzie, "but one waits
At home alone for me;
So without further parleying, 385
If you will not sell me any
Of your fruits though much and many,
Give me back my silver penny
I tossed you for a fee." —
They began to scratch their pates, 390
No longer wagging, purring,
But visibly demurring,
Grunting and snarling.
One called her proud,
Cross-grained, uncivil; 395
Their tones waxed loud,
Their looks were evil.
Lashing their tails,
They trod and hustled her,
Elbowed and jostled her, 400
Clawed with their nails,
Barking, mewing, hissing, mocking,
Tore her gown and soiled her stocking,
Twitched her hair out by the roots,
Stamped upon her tender feet, 405
Held her hands and squeezed their fruits
Against her mouth to make her eat.

White and golden Lizzie stood,
Like a lily in a flood —
Like a rock of blue-veined stone 410
Lashed by tides obstreperously —
Like a beacon left alone
In a hoary, roaring sea,
Sending up a golden fire —
Like a fruit-crowned orange-tree 415
White with blossoms honey-sweet
Sore beset by wasp and bee —
Like a royal virgin town
Topped with gilded dome and spire
Close beleaguered by a fleet 420
Mad to tug her standard down.

One may lead a horse to water;
Twenty cannot make him drink.
Though the goblins cuffed and caught her,
Coaxed and fought her, 425
Bullied and besought her,
Scratched her, pinched her black as ink,

Kicked and knocked her,
Mauled and mocked her,
Lizzie uttered not a word;   430
Would not open lip from lip
Lest they should cram a mouthful in;
But laughed in heart to feel the drip
Of juice that siruped all her face,
And lodged in dimples of her chin,   435
And streaked her neck which quaked like
          curd.
At last the evil people,
Worn out by her resistance,
Flung back her penny, kicked their fruit
Along whichever road they took,   440
Not leaving root or stone or shoot;
Some writhed into the ground,
Some dived into the brook
With ring and ripple,
Some scudded on the gale without a sound,
Some vanished in the distance.   446

In a smart, ache, tingle,
Lizzie went her way;
Knew not was it night or day;
Sprang up the bank, tore through the furze,
Threaded copse and dingle,   451
And heard her penny jingle
Bouncing in her purse —
Its bounce was music to her ear.
She ran and ran   455
As if she feared some goblin man
Dogged her with gibe or curse
Or something worse;
But not one goblin skurried after,
Nor was she pricked by fear;   460
The kind heart made her windy-paced
That urged her home quite out of breath with
          haste
And inward laughter.

She cried, "Laura," up the garden,
"Did you miss me?   465
Come and kiss me.
Never mind my bruises,
Hug me, kiss me, suck my juices
Squeezed from goblin fruits for you,
Goblin pulp and goblin dew.   470
Eat me, drink me, love me;
Laura, make much of me;
For your sake I have braved the glen
And had to do with goblin merchant men."

Laura started from her chair,   475
Flung her arms up in the air,
Clutched her hair:
"Lizzie, Lizzie, have you tasted
For my sake the fruit forbidden?
Must your light like mine be hidden,   480
Your young life like mine be wasted,
Undone in mine undoing,

And ruined in my ruin,
Thirsty, cankered, goblin-ridden?" —
She clung about her sister,   485
Kissed and kissed and kissed her;
Tears once again
Refreshed her shrunken eyes,
Dropping like rain
After long sultry drouth;   490
Shaking with aguish fear, and pain,
She kissed and kissed her with a hungry
          mouth.

Her lips began to scorch,
That juice was wormwood to her tongue,
She loathed the feast.   495
Writhing as one possessed, she leaped and
          sung,
Rent all her robe, and wrung
Her hands in lamentable haste,
And beat her breast.
Her locks streamed like the torch   500
Borne by a racer at full speed,
Or like the mane of horses in their flight,
Or like an eagle when she stems the light
Straight toward the sun,
Or like a caged thing freed,   505
Or like a flying flag when armies run.

Swift fire spread through her veins, knocked
          at her heart,
Met the fire smoldering there
And overbore its lesser flame;
She gorged on bitterness without a name —
Ah, fool, to choose such part   511
Of soul-consuming care!
Sense failed in the mortal strife;
Like the watch-tower of a town
Which an earthquake shatters down,   515
Like a lightning-stricken mast,
Like a wind-uprooted tree
Spun about,
Like a foam-topped waterspout
Cast down headlong in the sea,   520
She fell at last;
Pleasure past and anguish past,
Is it death or is it life?

Life out of death.
That night long Lizzie watched by her,   525
Counted her pulse's flagging stir,
Felt for her breath,
Held water to her lips, and cooled her face
With tears and fanning leaves.
But when the first birds chirped about their
          eaves,   530
And early reapers plodded to the place
Of golden sheaves,
And dew-wet grass
Bowed in the morning winds so brisk to pass,
And new buds with new day   535

Opened of cup-like lilies on the stream,
Laura awoke as from a dream,
Laughed in the innocent old way,
Hugged Lizzie but not twice or thrice;
Her gleaming locks showed not one thread
    of gray,   540
Her breath was sweet as May,
And light danced in her eyes.

Days, weeks, months, years
Afterwards, when both were wives
With children of their own;   545
Their mother-hearts beset with fears,
Their lives bound up in tender lives;
Laura would call the little ones
And tell them of her early prime,
Those pleasant days long gone   550
Of not-returning time;
Would talk about the haunted glen,
The wicked quaint fruit-merchant men,
Their fruits like honey to the throat
But poison in the blood   555
(Men sell not such in any town);
Would tell them how her sister stood
In deadly peril to do her good,
And win the fiery antidote;
Then joining hands to little hands   560
Would bid them cling together —
"For there is no friend like a sister
In calm or stormy weather;
To cheer one on the tedious way,
To fetch one if one goes astray,   565
To lift one if one totters down,
To strengthen whilst one stands."
                    (1859; 1862)

AMOR MUNDI

"Oh, where are you going with your love-
    locks flowing,
  On the west wind blowing along this valley
    track?"
"The downhill path is easy, come with me an
    it please ye,
  We shall escape the uphill by never turning
    back."

So they two went together in glowing August
    weather,   5
  The honey-breathing heather lay to their
    left and right;
And dear she was to doat on, her swift feet
    seemed to float on
  The air like soft twin pigeons too sportive
    to alight.

"Oh, what is that in heaven where gray
    cloud-flakes are seven,

Where blackest clouds hang riven just at
    the rainy skirt?"   10
"Oh, that's a meteor sent us, a message
    dumb, portentous,
  An undeciphered solemn signal of help or
    hurt."

"Oh, what is that glides quickly where velvet
    flowers grow thickly,
  Their scent comes rich and sickly?" "A
    scaled and hooded worm."
"Oh, what's that in the hollow, so pale I
    quake to follow?"   15
  "Oh, that's a thin dead body which waits
    the eternal term."

"Turn again, O my sweetest — turn again,
    false and fleetest;
  This beaten way thou beatest, I fear, is
    hell's own track."
"Nay, too steep for hill mounting; nay, too
    late for cost counting;
  This downhill path is easy, but there's no
    turning back."   *(1865; 1865)*

EVE

"While I sit at the door,
Sick to gaze within,
Mine eye weepeth sore
For sorrow and sin:
As a tree my sin stands   5
To darken all lands;
Death is the fruit it bore.

"How have Eden bowers grown
Without Adam to bend them!
How have Eden flowers blown,   10
Squandering their sweet breath,
Without me to tend them!
The Tree of Life was ours,
Tree twelvefold-fruited,
Most lofty tree that flowers,   15
Most deeply rooted:
I chose the Tree of Death.

"Hadst thou but said me nay,
Adam, my brother,
I might have pined away;   20
I, but none other:
God might have let thee stay
Safe in our garden,
By putting me away
Beyond all pardon.   25

"I, Eve, sad mother
Of all who must live,
I, not another,

Amor Mundi. The title means *Love of the World.*
3. **an**, if.

16. **the ... term**, the day of judgment.

Plucked bitterest fruit to give
My friend, husband, lover.   30
O wanton eyes run over;
Who but I should grieve? —
Cain hath slain his brother:
Of all who must die mother,
Miserable Eve!"   35

Thus she sat weeping,
Thus Eve our mother,
Where one lay sleeping
Slain by his brother.
Greatest and least,   40
Each piteous beast
To hear her voice
Forgot his joys
And set aside his feast.

The mouse paused in his walk   45
And dropped his wheaten stalk;
Grave cattle wagged their heads
In rumination;
The eagle gave a cry
From his cloud station: 50
Larks on thyme beds
Forbore to mount or sing;
Bees drooped upon the wing;
The raven perched on high
Forgot his ration;   55
The conies in their rock,
A feeble nation,
Quaked sympathetical;
The mocking-bird left off to mock;
Huge camels knelt as if   60
In deprecation;
The kind hart's tears were falling;
Chattered the wistful stork;
Dove-voices with a dying fall
Cooed desolation,   65
Answering grief by grief.

Only the serpent in the dust,
Wriggling and crawling,
Grinned an evil grin and thrust
His tongue out with its fork.   70
                                   (1866)

"TODAY FOR ME"

She sitteth still who used to dance,
She weepeth sore and more and more —
Let us sit with thee weeping sore,
    O fair France.

She trembleth as the days advance   5
Who used to be so light of heart —

We in thy trembling bear a part,
    Sister France.

Her eyes shine tearful as they glance;
"Who shall give back my slaughtered sons? 10
"Bind up," she saith, "my wounded ones." —
    Alas, France!

She struggles in a deathly trance,
As in a dream her pulses stir,
She hears the nations calling her,   15
    "France, France, France!"

Thou people of the lifted lance,
Forbear her tears, forbear her blood;
Roll back, roll back, thy whelming flood,
    Back from France.   20

Eye not her loveliness askance,
Forge not for her a galling chain;
Leave her at peace to bloom again,
    Vine-clad France.

A time there is for change and chance,   25
A time for passing of the cup;
And One abides can yet bind up
    Broken France.

A time there is for change and chance;
Who next shall drink the trembling cup,   30
Wring out its dregs and suck them up
    After France?   (1871)

From *SING-SONG*

"If I were a queen,
    What would I do?
I'd make you king,
    And I'd wait on you."

"If I were a king,   5
    What would I do?
I'd make you queen,
    For I'd marry you."

——

Mother shake the cherry-tree,
    Susan catch a cherry;
Oh, how funny that will be —
    Let's be merry!

——

One for brother, one for sister,   5
    Two for mother more,
Six for father, hot and tired,
    Knocking at the door.

——

The wind has such a rainy sound
    Moaning through the town,
The sea has such a windy sound —
    Will the ships go down?

"Today For Me." Dante Gabriel Rossetti regarded this poem as the greatest of all his sister's poems. It was written during the agonized suspense of the German-French campaign of 1870-71.

17. **people . . . lance**, people of Germany.
Sing-Song. This is a happy title given by Miss Rossetti to a collection of lyrics, some of which are suggestive of Mother Goose. Cf. Stevenson's poems beginning on p. 801.

The apples in the orchard   5
   Tumble from their tree. —
Oh, will the ships go down, go down,
   In the windy sea?

———

Fly away, fly away over the sea,
   Sun-loving swallow, for summer is done;
Come again, come again, come back to me,
   Bringing the summer and bringing the sun.

———

Who has seen the wind?
   Neither I nor you;
But when the leaves hang trembling
   The wind is passing through.

Who has seen the wind?   5
   Neither you nor I;
But when the trees bow down their heads
   The wind is passing by.

———

Boats sail on the rivers,
   And ships sail on the seas;
But clouds that sail across the sky
   Are prettier far than these.

There are bridges on the rivers,   5
   As pretty as you please;
But the bow that bridges heaven,
   And overtops the trees,
And builds a road from earth to sky,
   Is prettier far than these.   10
                (1872)

From MONNA INNOMINATA

II

Vien dietro a me e lascia dir le genti.
                  — DANTE.
   Contando i casi della vita nostra.
                 — PETRARCA.

Many in aftertimes will say of you
"He loved her" — while of me what will they
   say?
Not that I loved you more than just in play,

Monna Innominata. The title means *My Nameless Lady.* The poem consists of fourteen sonnets, supposed, from Miss Rossetti's introductory note, to be spoken by one of the numerous unnamed ladies exalted by poets before Dante and Petrarch. "One can imagine," she says, "many a lady as sharing her lover's poetic aptitude, while the barrier between them might be one held sacred by both, yet not such as to render mutual love incompatible with mutual honor." W. M. Rossetti states that the real speaker in the sonnets is "Christina herself giving expression to her love for Charles Cayley," a scholarly recluse whom she declined to marry because of his liberal religious views.

The quotation from Dante may be translated, "Come after me and let the people talk" (*Purgatory*, 5, 13). The quotation from Petrarch is translated, "Relating the casualties of our life" (*Sonnet*, 244, 12).

For fashion's sake as idle women do.
Even let them prate; who know not what we
   knew   5
Of love and parting in exceeding pain,
Of parting hopeless here to meet again,
Hopeless on earth, and heaven is out of view.
But by my heart of love laid bare to you,
My love that you can make not void nor
   vain,   10
Love that foregoes you but to claim anew
Beyond this passage of the gate of death,
I charge you at the Judgment make it plain
My love of you was life and not a breath.
                (*Before 1882*)

DE PROFUNDIS

Oh, why is heaven built so far,
   Oh, why is earth set so remote?
I cannot reach the nearest star
   That hangs afloat.

I would not care to reach the moon,   5
   One round monotonous of change;
Yet even she repeats her tune
   Beyond my range.

I never watch the scattered fire
   Of stars, or sun's far-trailing train,   10
But all my heart is one desire,
   And all in vain.

For I am bound with fleshly bands,
   Joy, beauty, lie beyond my scope;
I strain my heart, I stretch my hands, 15
   And catch at hope.   (*Before 1882*)

THE HILLS ARE TIPPED WITH SUNSHINE

The hills are tipped with sunshine, while I
   walk
   In shadows dim and cold;
The unawakened rose sleeps on her stalk
   In a bud's fold,
   Until the sun flood all the world with gold.

The hills are crowned with glory, and the
   glow   6
   Flows widening down apace;
Unto the sunny hilltops I, set low,
   Lift a tired face —
   Ah, happy rose, content to wait for grace!

How tired a face, how tired a brain, how
   tired   11
   A heart I lift, who long

De Profundis. The title means *From the Depths.*

For something never felt but still desired;
  Sunshine and song,
Song where the choirs of sunny heaven
    stand choired.   15
               (*Before 1893*)

SLEEPING AT LAST

Sleeping at last, the trouble and tumult over,
  Sleeping at last, the struggle and horror
    past,
Cold and white, out of sight of friend and of
    lover,
      Sleeping at last.

No more a tired heart downcast or over-
    cast,   5
No more pangs that wring or shifting fears
    that hover,
Sleeping at last in a dreamless sleep locked
    fast.

Fast asleep. Singing birds in their leafy cover
Cannot wake her, nor shake her the gusty
    blast.
Under the purple thyme and the purple clover
    Sleeping at last.   11
          (*1893; 1896*)

COVENTRY PATMORE (1823-1896)

From *THE ANGEL IN THE HOUSE*

THE IMPOSSIBILITY

Lo, Love's obeyed by all. 'Tis right
  That all should know what they obey,
Lest erring conscience damp delight,
  And folly laugh our joys away.
Thou Primal Love, who grantest wings   5
  And voices to the woodland birds,
Grant me the power of saying things
  Too simple and too sweet for words! (1854)

LOVE'S REALITY

I walk, I trust, with open eyes;
  I've traveled half my worldly course;
And in the way behind me lies
  Much vanity and some remorse;

I've lived to feel how pride may part   5
  Spirits, though matched like hand and
    glove;
I've blushed for love's abode, the heart;
  But have not disbelieved in love;
Nor unto love, sole mortal thing
  Of worth immortal, done the wrong   10
To count it, with the rest that sing,
  Unworthy of a serious song;
And love is my reward, for now,
  When most of dead'ning time complain,
The myrtle blooms upon my brow,   15
  Its odor quickens all my brain.   (1854)

LOVE AT LARGE

Whene'er I come where ladies are,
  How sad soever I was before,
Though like a ship frost-bound and far
  Withheld in ice from the ocean's roar,
Third-wintered in that dreadful dock,   5
  With stiffened cordage, sails decayed,
And crew that care for calm and shock
  Alike, too dull to be dismayed,
Yet, if I come where ladies are,
  How sad soever I was before,   10
Then is my sadness banished far,
  And I am like that ship no more;
Or like that ship if the ice-field splits,
  Burst by the sudden polar spring,
And all thank God with their warming wits,
  And kiss each other and dance and sing, 16
And hoist fresh sails, that make the breeze
  Blow them along the liquid sea,
Out of the North, where life did freeze,
  Into the haven where they would be.   20
               (1854)

THE LOVER

He meets, by heavenly chance express,
  The destined maid; some hidden hand
Unveils to him that loveliness
  Which others cannot understand.
His merits in her presence grow,   5
  To match the promise in her eyes,
And round her happy footsteps blow
  The authentic airs of paradise.
For joy of her he cannot sleep;
  Her beauty haunts him all the night;   10
It melts his heart, it makes him weep
  For wonder, worship, and delight.
Oh, paradox of love, he longs,
  Most humble when he most aspires,
To suffer scorn and cruel wrongs   15
  From her he honors and desires.
Her graces make him rich, and ask
  No guerdon; this imperial style
Affronts him; he disdains to bask,
  The pensioner of her priceless smile.   20

Sleeping at Last. W. M. Rossetti regarded this poem as the last one written by his sister. He found it after her death.
  The Angel in the House. In the Prologue to this poem, Patmore introduces Vaughan, a poet who seeks fame largely to please his wife. He therefore decides to write a poem with his wife Honoria and love as the theme; *The Angel in the House* is the result. The poem is made up of a number of brief episodes, each prefaced by several short preludes. The selections given here are all preludes except "The Wedding Sermon," which is a section of *The Wedding*, one of the narratives. Honoria, the "Angel of the House," is the daughter of the Dean of Salisbury Cathedral.

Love's Reality. 15. **myrtle . . . brow.** In ancient times poets were often crowned with myrtle.

He prays for some hard thing to do,
  Some work of fame and labor immense,
To stretch the languid bulk and thew
  Of love's fresh-born magnipotence.
No smallest boon were bought too dear, 25
  Though bartered for his love-sick life;
Yet trusts he, with undoubted cheer,
  To vanquish heaven, and call her wife.
He notes how queens of sweetness still
  Neglect their crowns, and stoop to mate; 30
How, self-consigned with lavish will,
  They ask but love proportionate;
How swift pursuit by small degrees,
  Love's tactic, works like miracle;
How valor, clothed in courtesies, 35
  Brings down the haughtiest citadel;
And therefore, though he merits not
  To kiss the braid upon her skirt,
His hope, discouraged ne'er a jot, 39
  Out-soars all possible desert. (1854)

The Wedding Sermon

"Now, while she's changing," said the Dean,
  "Her bridal for her traveling dress,
I'll preach allegiance to your queen!
  Preaching's the thing which I profess;
And one more minute's mine! You know 5
  I've paid my girl a father's debt,
And this last charge is all I owe.
  She's yours; but I love more than yet
You can; such fondness only wakes
  When time has raised the heart above 10
The prejudice of youth, which makes
  Beauty conditional to love.
Prepare to meet the weak alarms
  Of novel nearness; recollect
The eye which magnifies her charms 15
  Is microscopic for defect.
Fear comes at first; but soon, rejoiced,
  You'll find your strong and tender loves,
Like holy rocks by Druids poised,
  The least force shakes, but none removes.
Her strength is your esteem; beware 21
  Of finding fault; her will's unnerved
By blame; from you 'twould be despair;
  But praise that is not quite deserved
Will all her noble nature move 25
  To make your utmost wishes true.
Yet think, while mending thus your Love,
  Of matching her ideal too!
The death of nuptial joy is sloth;
  To keep your mistress in your wife, 30
Keep to the very height your oath,
  And honor her with arduous life.
Lastly, no personal reverence doff.

Life's all externals unto those
  Who pluck the blushing petals off, 35
  To find the secret of the rose. —
How long she's tarrying! Green's Hotel
  I'm sure you'll like. The charge is fair,
The wines good. I remember well
  I stayed once, with her mother, there. 40
A tender conscience of her vow
  That mother had! She's so like her!"
But Mrs. Fife, much flurried, now
  Whispered, "Miss Honor's ready, sir."
                         (1854)

The Married Lover

Why, having won her, do I woo?
  Because her spirit's vestal grace
Provokes me always to pursue,
  But, spirit-like, eludes embrace;
Because her womanhood is such 5
  That, as on court-days subjects kiss
The Queen's hand, yet so near a touch
  Affirms no mean familiarness,
Nay, rather marks more fair the height
  Which can with safety so neglect 10
To dread, as lower ladies might,
  That grace could meet with disrespect;
Thus she with happy favor feeds
  Allegiance from a love so high
That thence no false conceit proceeds 15
  Of difference bridged, or state put by;
Because, although in act and word
  As lowly as a wife can be,
Her manners, when they call me lord,
  Remind me 'tis by courtesy; 20
Not with her least consent of will,
  Which would my proud affection hurt,
But by the noble style that still
  Imputes an unattained desert;
Because her gay and lofty brows, 25
  When all is won which hope can ask,
Reflect a light of hopeless snows
  That bright in virgin ether bask;
Because, though free of the outer court
  I am, this Temple keeps its shrine 30
Sacred to heaven; because, in short,
  She's not and never can be mine. (1854)

PROPHETS WHO CANNOT SING

Ponder, ye Just, the scoffs that frequent go
From forth the foe:
  "The holders of the Truth in Verity

<hr>

24. **magnipotence,** great power.
The Wedding Sermon. 19. **Druids,** members of a religious
order among the ancient Celts. Their places of worship
were circles of rocks like those at Stonehenge, near Salisbury,
England.

The Married Lover. 2. **vestal,** chaste. 29-31. **though
free . . . heaven.** He thinks of his lover as a temple, like
that at Jerusalem with its outer court and a sacred inaccessible inner shrine. The shrine is that part of the wife's personality which the husband cannot approach. Cf. Browning's
Two in the Campagna, p. 241.
Prophets Who Cannot Sing. This ode and the three that
follow are taken from the volume of Odes published in 1868.
They were later incorporated in *The Unknown Eros* (1877).

Are people of a harsh and stammering tongue!
The hedge-flower hath its song; 5
Meadow and wandering cloud
Find Seers who see,
And, with convincing music clear and loud,
Startle the adder-deafness of the crowd
By tones, O Love, from thee. 10
Views of the unveiled heavens alone forth
    bring
Prophets who cannot sing,
Praise that in chiming numbers will not run;
At least, from David until Dante, none,
And none since him. 15
Fish, and not swim?
They think they somehow should, and so they
    try;
But (haply 'tis they screw the pitch too high)
'Tis still their fates
To warble tunes that nails might draw from
    slates. 20
Poor Seraphim!
They mean to spoil our sleep, and do, but all
    their gains
Are curses for their pains!"

    Now who but knows
That truth to learn from foes 25
Is wisdom ripe?
Therefore no longer let us stretch our throats
Till hoarse as frogs
With straining after notes
Which but to touch would burst an organ-
    pipe. 30
Far better be dumb dogs.
                    (1868)

"FAINT YET PURSUING"

    Heroic Good, target for which the young
Dream in their dreams that every bow is
    strung,
And, missing, sigh
Unfruitful, or as disbelievers die,
Thee having missed, I will not so revolt, 5
But lowlier shoot my bolt,
And lowlier still, if still I may not reach,
And my proud stomach teach
That less than highest is good, and may be
    high.
An even walk in life's uneven way, 10
Though to have dreamt of flight and not to
    fly
Be strange and sad,
Is not a boon that's given to all who pray.
If this I had
I'd envy none! 15
Nay, trod I straight for one

Year, month, or week,
Should Heaven withdraw, and Satan me
    amerce
Of power and joy, still would I seek
Another victory with a like reverse; 20
Because the god of victory does not die,
As dies the failure's curse,
And what we have to gain
Is, not one battle, but a weary life's campaign.
Yet meaner lot being sent 25
Should more than me content;
Yea, if I lie
Among vile shards, though born for silver
    wings,
In the strong flight and feathers gold
Of whatsoever heavenward mounts and
    sings 30
I must by admiration so comply
That there I should my own delight behold.
Yea, though I sin each day times seven,
And dare not lift the fearfullest eyes to
    Heaven,
Thanks must I give 35
Because that seven times are not eight or
    nine,
And that my darkness is all mine,
And that I live
Within this oak-shade one more minute even,
Hearing the winds their Maker magnify. 40
                    (1868)

THE TWO DESERTS

    Not greatly moved with awe am I
To learn that we may spy
Five thousand firmaments beyond our own.
The best that's known
Of the heavenly bodies does them credit
    small. 5
Viewed close, the Moon's fair ball
Is of ill objects worst,
A corpse in Night's highway, naked, fire-
    scarred, accurst;
And now they tell
That the Sun is plainly seen to boil and
    burst 10
Too horribly for hell.
So, judging from these two,
As we must do,
The Universe, outside our living Earth,
Was all conceived in the Creator's mirth, 15
Forecasting at the time Man's spirit deep,
To make dirt cheap.
Put by the Telescope!
Better without it man may see,
Stretched awful in the hushed midnight, 20
The ghost of his eternity.

---

14. **David,** the author of many of the Psalms. **Dante,**
Dante Alighieri (1265-1321). 21. **Seraphim,** the highest
order of angels—angels of love.

18. **amerce of,** punish by taking away.

Give me the nobler glass that swells to the
    eye
The things which near us lie,
Till Science rapturously hails,
In the minutest water-drop,   25
A torment of innumerable tails.
These at the least do live.
But rather give
A mind not much to pry
Beyond our royal-fair estate   30
Betwixt these deserts blank of small and
    great.
Wonder and beauty our own courtiers are,
Pressing to catch our gaze,
And out of obvious ways
Ne'er wandering far.   35
            (1868)

DELICIÆ SAPIENTIÆ DE AMORE

Love, light for me
Thy ruddiest blazing torch,
That I, albeit a beggar by the Porch
Of the glad Palace of Virginity,
May gaze within, and sing the pomp I see; 5
For, crowned with roses all,
'Tis there, O Love, they keep thy festival!
But first warn off the beatific spot
Those wretched who have not
Even afar beheld the shining wall,   10
And those who, once beholding, have forgot,
And those, most vile, who dress
The charnel specter drear
Of utterly dishallowed nothingness
In that refulgent fame,   15
And cry Lo, here!
And name
The Lady whose smiles inflame
The sphere.
Bring, Love, anear,   20
And bid be not afraid
Young Lover true, and love-foreboding Maid,
And wedded Spouse, if virginal of thought;
For I will sing of naught
Less sweet to hear   25
Than seems
A music in their half-remembered dreams.

The magnet calls the steel:
Answers the iron to the magnet's breath;
What do they feel   30
But death!
The clouds of summer kiss in flame and rain,
And are not found again;
But the heavens themselves eternal are with
    fire
Of unapproached desire,   35

By the aching heart of Love, which cannot
    rest,
In blissfullest pathos so indeed possessed.
Oh, spousals high;
Oh, doctrine blest,
Unutterable in even the happiest sigh;   40
This know ye all
Who can recall
With what a welling of indignant tears
Love's simpleness first hears
The meaning of his mortal covenant,   45
And from what pride comes down
To wear the crown
Of which 'twas very heaven to feel the want.
How envies he the ways
Of yonder hopeless star,   50
And so would laugh and yearn
With trembling lids eterne,
Ineffably content from infinitely far
Only to gaze
On his bright Mistress's responding rays,   55
That never know eclipse;
And, once in his long year,
With præternuptial ecstasy and fear,
By the delicious law of that ellipse
Wherein all citizens of ether move,   60
With hastening pace to come
Nearer, though never near,
His Love
And always inaccessible sweet Home;
There on his path doubly to burn.   65
Kissed by her doubled light
That whispers of its source,
The ardent secret ever clothed with Night,
Then go forth in new force
Toward a new return,   70
Rejoicing as a Bridegroom on his course!
This know ye all;
Therefore gaze bold,
That so in you be joyful hope increased,
Thorough the Palace portals, and behold   75
The dainty and unsating Marriage-Feast.
Oh, hear
Them singing clear
"Cor meum et caro mea" round the "I Am,"
The Husband of the Heavens, and the
    Lamb   80
Whom they forever follow there that kept,
Or losing, never slept
Till they reconquered had in mortal fight
The standard white.
Oh, hear   85
From the harps they bore from Earth, five-
    strung, what music springs,
While the glad Spirits chide
The wondering strings!
And how the shining sacrificial Choirs,
Offering for aye their dearest hearts' desires, 90

Deliciæ Sapientiæ de Amore. The title means *Delights
of Knowledge about Love.*

79. "Cor . . . mea," my heart and my flesh.

Which to their hearts come back beatified,
Hymn, the bright aisles along,
The nuptial song,
Song ever new to us and them, that saith,
"Hail Virgin in Virginity a Spouse!"   95
Heard first below
Within the little house
At Nazareth;
Heard yet in many a cell where brides of
          Christ
Lie hid, emparadised,   100
And where, although
By the hour 'tis night,
There's light,
The Day still lingering in the lap of snow.
Gaze and be not afraid,   105
Ye wedded few that honor, in sweet thought
And glittering will,
So freshly from the garden gather still
The lily sacrificed;
For ye, though self-suspected here for
          naught,   110
Are highly styled
With the thousands twelve times twelve of
          undefiled.
Gaze and be not afraid,
Young Lover true and love-foreboding Maid.
The full noon of deific vision bright   115
Abashes nor abates
No spark minute of Nature's keen delight.
'Tis there your Hymen waits!
There where in courts afar, all unconfused,
          they crowd,
As fumes the starlight soft   120
In gulfs of cloud,
And each to the other, well-content,
Sighs oft,
" 'Twas this we meant!"
Gaze without blame   125
Ye in whom living Love yet blushes for dead
          shame.
There of pure Virgins none
Is fairer seen,
Save One,
Than Mary Magdalene,   130
Gaze without doubt or fear,
Ye to whom generous Love, by any name, is
          dear.
Love makes the life to be
A fount perpetual of virginity;
For, lo, the Elect   135
Of generous Love, how named soe'er, affect
Nothing but God,
Or mediate or direct,
Nothing but God,
The Husband of the Heavens: 140

96. **Heard first**, by Mary from the angel Gabriel at Nazareth in Galilee (*Luke*, 1:26-38).   118. **Hymen,** god of marriage.   130. **Mary Magdalene.** See *Mary Magdalene and note, p. 524.

And who Him love, in potence great or
          small,
Are, one and all,
Heirs of the Palace glad,
And inly clad
With the bridal robes of ardor virginal.   145
                                       (1868)

From *THE UNKNOWN EROS*

A FAREWELL

With all my will, but much against my heart,
     We two now part.
My Very Dear,
     Our solace is, the sad road lies so clear.
It needs no art,   5
With faint, averted feet
     And many a tear,
In our opposéd paths to persevere.
     Go thou to East, I West.
We will not say   10
There's any hope, it is so far away.
But, O my Best!
When the one darling of our widowhead,
     The nursling Grief,
Is dead,   15
And no dews blur our eyes
To see the peach-bloom come in evening skies,
     Perchance we may,
Where now this night is day,
And even through faith of still averted feet, 20
Making full circle of our banishment,
     Amazéd meet;
The bitter journey to the bourne so sweet
Seasoning the termless feast of our content
With tears of recognition never dry.   25
                                       (1877)

THE TOYS

My little son, who looked from thoughtful
          eyes,
And moved and spoke in quiet grown-up wise,
Having my law the seventh time disobeyed,
I struck him, and dismissed
With hard words and unkissed,   5
His mother, who was patient, being dead.
Then, fearing lest his grief should hinder
          sleep,
I visited his bed,
But found him slumbering deep,
With darkened eyelids, and their lashes yet
From his late sobbing wet.   11
And I, with moan,

The Unknown Eros. Eros was the Greek god of love. The poem is really a collection of odes, forty-six in number, on various subjects. Some of the odes were reprinted from an earlier volume.
The Toys. See Critical Notes.

Kissing away his tears, left others of my own;
For, on a table drawn beside his head,
He had put, within his reach,   15
A box of counters and a red-veined stone,
A piece of glass abraded by the beach
And six or seven shells,
A bottle with bluebells
And two French copper coins, ranged there
    with careful art,   20
To comfort his sad heart.
So when that night I prayed
To God, I wept, and said:
"Ah, when at last we lie with trancéd breath,
Not vexing Thee in death,   25
And Thou rememberest of what toys
We made our joys,
How weakly understood,
Thy great commanded good,
Then, fatherly not less   30
Than I whom Thou hast molded from the
    clay,
Thou'lt leave Thy wrath, and say,
'I will be sorry for their childishness.' "
                  (1877)

MAGNA EST VERITAS

Here, in this little bay,
Full of tumultuous life and great repose,
Where, twice a day,
The purposeless, glad ocean comes and goes,
Under high cliffs, and far from the huge town,
I sit me down.   6
For want of me the world's course will not
    fail —
When all its work is done, the lie shall rot;
The truth is great, and shall prevail
When none cares whether it prevail or not. 10
                  (1877)

DEPARTURE

It was not like your great and gracious ways!
Do you, that have naught other to lament,
Never, my love, repent
Of how, that July afternoon,
You went,   5
With sudden, unintelligible phrase,
And frightened eye,
Upon your journey of so many days,
Without a single kiss or a good-by?
I knew, indeed, that you were parting soon;
And so we sate, within the low sun's rays, 11
You whispering to me, for your voice was
    weak,
Your harrowing praise.

Well, it was well, my wife,
To hear you such things speak,   15
And see your love
Make of your eyes a growing gloom of life,
As a warm south-wind sombers a March
    grove.
And it was like your great and gracious ways
To turn your talk on daily things, my dear,
Lifting the luminous, pathetic lash   21
To let the laughter flash,
Whilst I drew near,
Because you spoke so low that I could scarcely
    hear.
But all at once to leave me at the last,   25
More at the wonder than the loss aghast,
With huddled, unintelligible phrase,
And frightened eye,
And go your journey of all days
With not one kiss or a good-by,   30
And the only loveless look the look with
    which you passed,
'Twas all unlike your great and gracious ways.
                  (1877)

THE AZALEA

There, where the sun shines first
Against our room,
She trained the gold azalea, whose perfume
She, spring-like, from her breathing grace
    dispersed.
Last night the delicate crests of saffron bloom,
For this their dainty likeness watched and
    nurst,   6
Were just at point to burst.
At dawn I dreamed, O God, that she was
    dead,
And groaned aloud upon my wretched bed,
And waked, ah, God, and did not waken her,
But lay, with eyes still closed,   11
Perfectly blessed in the delicious sphere
By which I knew so well that she was near,
My heart to speechless thankfulness com-
    posed.
Till 'gan to stir   15
A dizzy somewhat in my troubled head —
It *was* the azalea's breath, and she *was* dead!
The warm night had the lingering buds dis-
    closed;
And I had fall'n asleep with to my breast
A chance-found letter pressed   20
In which she said,
"So, till tomorrow eve, my own, adieu!
Parting's well-paid with soon again to meet,
Soon in your arms to feel so small and sweet,
Sweet to myself that am so sweet to you!"   25
                  (1877)

17. **abraded . . . beach,** worn down by the waves and the
sand.
  Magna Est Veritas. The title means *Great Is Truth.* It
is taken from the Apocryphal Book of *1 Esdras,* 4:41.—
"Great is truth and strong above all things."

The Azalea. The azalea is a beautiful shrub with masses
of pink, red, or yellow blossoms.

REGINA CŒLI

Say, did his sisters wonder what could Joseph
          see
In a mild, silent little maid like thee?
And was it awful, in that narrow house,
With God for Babe and Spouse?
Nay, like thy simple, female sort, each one 5
Apt to find Him in Husband and in Son,
Nothing to thee came strange in this.
Thy wonder was but wondrous bliss:
Wondrous, for, though
True Virgin lives not but does know   10
(Howbeit none ever yet confessed),
That God lies really in her breast,
Of thine He made His special nest!
And so
All mothers worship little feet,   15
And kiss the very ground they've trod;
But, ah, thy little Baby sweet
Who was indeed thy God!   (1878)

JAMES THOMSON (1834-1882)

ONCE IN A SAINTLY PASSION

Once in a saintly passion
    I cried with desperate grief,
"O Lord, my heart is black with guile,
    Of sinners I am chief."
Then stooped my guardian angel   5
    And whispered from behind,
"Vanity, my little man,
    You're nothing of the kind."

FOR I MUST SING OF ALL
I FEEL AND KNOW

For I must sing of all I feel and know,
    Waiting with Memnon passive near the
        palms,
Until the heavenly light doth dawn and grow
    And thrill my silence into mystic psalms;
From unknown realms the wind streams sad
        or gay,   5
The trees give voice responsive to its sway.

For I must sing: of mountains, deserts, seas,
    Of rivers ever flowing, ever flowing;
Of beasts and birds, of grass and flowers and
        trees
    Forever fading and forever growing;   10

Of calm and storm, of night and eve and noon,
Of boundless space, and sun and stars and
        moon;

And of the secret sympathies that bind
    All beings to their wondrous dwelling-place;
And of the perfect Unity enshrined   15
    In omnipresence throughout time and space,
Alike informing with its full control
The dust, the stars, the worm, the human
        soul;

And most supremely of my human kin —
    Their thoughts and deeds, their valors and
        their fears,   20
Their griefs and joys, their virtue and their
        sin,
    Their feasts and wars, their cradles and
        their biers,
Their temples, prisons, homes and ships and
        marts,
The subtlest windings of their brains and
        hearts.

So rich and sweet is Life.   And what is
        Death? —   25
    The tranquil slumbers dear and strange and
        boon
That feed at whiles our waking being's breath;
    The solemn midnight of this glorious noon,
With countless distant stars, and each a sun,
Revealed harmonious with our daily one.   30
                        (1857; 1859)

TWO SONNETS

I

"Why are your songs all wild and bitter sad
As funeral dirges with the orphans' cries?
Each night since first the world was made
        hath had
A sequent day to laugh it down the skies.
Chant us a glee to make our hearts rejoice, 5
Or seal in silence this unmanly moan."
My friend, I have no power to rule my
        voice —
A spirit lifts me where I lie alone,
And thrills me into song by its own laws;
That which I feel, but seldom know, indeed
Tempering the melody it could not cause.   11
The bleeding heart cannot forever bleed
Inwardly solely; on the wan lips, too,
Dark blood will bubble ghastly into view.

2

Striving to sing glad songs, I but attain
Wild discords sadder than Grief's saddest
        tune;

Regina Cœli. The title means *Queen of Heaven.*
For I Must Sing of All I Feel and Know. 2. **Memnon,** a
colossal statue near Thebes, Egypt, which was supposed to
give forth a musical sound at daybreak.

17. **informing,** animating, giving form to.

As if an owl with his harsh screech should
    strain
To over-gratulate a thrush of June.
The nightingale upon its thorny spray   5
Finds inspiration in the sullen dark;
The kindling dawn, the world-wide joyous day
Are inspiration to the soaring lark;
The seas are silent in the sunny calm,
Their anthem surges in the tempest boom;   10
The skies outroll no solemn thunder psalm
Till they have clothed themselves with clouds
    of gloom.
My mirth can laugh and talk, but cannot sing;
My grief finds harmonies in everything.
                   (1860)

"AS WE RUSH, AS WE RUSH
IN THE TRAIN"

As we rush, as we rush in the train,
    The trees and the houses go wheeling back,
But the starry heavens above the plain
    Come flying on our track.

All the beautiful stars of the sky,   5
    The silver doves of the forest of Night,
Over the dull earth swarm and fly,
    Companions of our flight.

We will rush ever on without fear;
    Let the goal be far, the flight be fleet!   10
For we carry the Heavens with us, Dear,
    While the Earth slips from our feet!
                  (*1863;* 1865)

THE FIRE THAT FILLED MY HEART
OF OLD

The fire that filled my heart of old
    Gave luster while it burned;
Now only ashes gray and cold
    Are in its silence urned.
Ah! better was the furious flame,   5
    The splendor with the smart;
I never cared for the singer's fame,
    But, oh! for the singer's heart
      Once more —
    The burning fulgent heart!   10

No love, no hate, no hope, no fear,
    No anguish and no mirth;
Thus life extends from year to year,
    A flat of sullen dearth.
Ah! life's blood creepeth cold and tame,   15
    Life's thought plays no new part;

4. **over-gratulate**, surpass in expressing a feeling of joy.
5. **nightingale . . . spray.** The nightingale was supposed
to sing more sweetly when a thorn was at its breast.

I never cared for the singer's fame,
    But, oh! for the singer's heart
      Once more —
    The bleeding passionate heart!   20
                  (1864)

From ART

"What precious thing are you making fast
    In all these silken lines?
And where and to whom will it go at last?
    Such subtle knots and twines!"

"I am tying up all my love in this,   5
    With all its hopes and fears,
With all its anguish and all its bliss,
    And its hours as heavy as years.

"I am going to send it afar, afar,
    To I know not where above;   10
To that sphere beyond the highest star
    Where dwells the soul of my Love.

"But in vain, in vain, would I make it fast
    With countless subtle twines;
Forever its fire breaks out at last,   15
    And shrivels all the lines."   (1865)

From SUNDAY UP THE RIVER

1

I looked out into the morning,
    I looked out into the west:
The soft blue eye of the quiet sky
    Still drooped in dreamy rest;

The trees were still like clouds there,   5
    The clouds like mountains dim;
The broad mist lay, a silver bay
    Whose tide was at the brim.

I looked out into the morning,
    I looked out into the east: 10
The flood of light upon the night
    Had silently increased;

The sky was pale with fervor,
    The distant trees were gray,
The hill-lines drawn like waves of dawn   15
    Dissolving in the day.

I looked out into the morning,
    Looked east, looked west, with glee;
O richest day of happy May,
    My love will spend with me!   20

2

"Oh, what are you waiting for here, young
    man?
    What are you looking for over the bridge?"

A little straw hat with the streaming blue
    ribbons
Is soon to come dancing over the bridge.

Her heart beats the measure that keeps her
    feet dancing,   5
    Dancing along like a wave o' the sea;
Her heart pours the sunshine with which her
    eyes glancing
    Light up strange faces in looking for me.

The strange faces brighten in meeting her
    glances;
    The strangers all bless her, pure, lovely,
    and free.   10
She fancies she walks, but her walk skips and
    dances,
    Her heart makes such music in coming to
    me.

Oh, thousands and thousands of happy
    young maidens
Are tripping this morning their sweethearts
    to see;
But none whose heart beats to a sweeter
    love-cadence   15
    Than hers who will brighten the sunshine
    for me.

"Oh, what are you waiting for here, young
    man?
    What are you looking for over the bridge?"
A little straw hat with the streaming blue
    ribbons;   19
— And here it comes dancing over the bridge!

15

Give a man a horse he can ride,
    Give a man a boat he can sail;
And his rank and wealth, his strength and
    health,
    On sea nor shore shall fail.

Give a man a pipe he can smoke,   5
    Give a man a book he can read;
And his home is bright with a calm delight,
    Though the room be poor indeed.

Give a man a girl he can love,
    As I, O my Love, love thee;   10
And his heart is great with the pulse of Fate,
    At home, on land, on sea.

17

Let my voice ring out and over the earth,
    Through all the grief and strife,
With a golden joy in a silver mirth:
    Thank God for Life!

Let my voice swell out through the great
    abyss   5

To the azure dome above,
With a chord of faith in the harp of bliss:
    Thank God for Love!

Let my voice thrill out beneath and above,
    The whole world through: 10
O my Love and Life, O my Life and Love,
    Thank God for you!

18

The wine of Love is music,
    And the feast of Love is song;
And when Love sits down to the banquet,
    Love sits long;

Sits long and ariseth drunken,   5
    But not with the feast and the wine;
He reeleth with his own heart,
    That great rich Vine.   (*1865;* 1869)

WILLIAM BLAKE

He came to the desert of London town
    Gray miles long;
He wandered up and he wandered down,
    Singing a quiet song.

He came to the desert of London town,   5
    Mirk miles broad;
He wandered up and he wandered down,
    Ever alone with God.

There were thousands and thousands of
    human kind
    In this desert of brick and stone;   10
But some were deaf and some were blind,
    And he was there alone.

At length the good hour came; he died
    As he had lived, alone.
He was not missed from the desert wide;   15
    Perhaps he was found at the Throne.
                  (1866)

L' ANCIEN REGIME

OR, THE GOOD OLD RULE

Who has a thing to bring
For a gift to our lord the king,
Our king all kings above?
A young girl brought him love;
And he dowered her with shame,   5
With a sort of infamous fame,
And then with lonely years
Of penance and bitter tears —
Love is scarcely the thing
To bring as a gift for our king.   10

William Blake. Cf. Rossetti's *William Blake*, p. 551.

Who has a thing to bring
For a gift to our lord the king?
A statesman brought him planned
Justice for all the land;
And he in recompense got   15
Fierce struggle with brigue and plot,
Then a fall from lofty place
Into exile and disgrace —
Justice is never the thing
To bring as a gift for our king.   20

Who has a thing to bring
For a gift to our lord the king?
A writer brought him truth;
And first he imprisoned the youth,
And then he bestowed a free pyre   25
That the works might have plenty of fire,
And also to cure the pain
Of the headache called thought in the brain —
Truth is a very bad thing
To bring as a gift for our king.   30

Who has a thing to bring
For a gift to our lord the king?
The people brought their sure
Loyalty fervid and pure;
And he gave them bountiful spoil   35
Of taxes and hunger and toil,
Ignorance, brutish plight,
And wholesale slaughter in fight —
Loyalty's quite the worst thing
To bring as a gift for our king.   40

Who has a thing to bring
For a gift to our lord the king?
A courtier brought to his feet
Servility graceful and sweet,
With an ever ready smile   45
And an ever supple guile;
And he got in reward the place
Of the statesman in disgrace —
Servility's always a thing
To bring as a gift for our king.   50

Who has a thing to bring
For a gift to our lord the king?
A soldier brought him war,
La gloire, la victoire,
Ravage and carnage and groans,   55
For the pious *Te Deum* tones;
And he got in return for himself
Rank and honors and pelf —
War is a very fine thing
To bring as a gift for our king.   60

Who has a thing to bring
For a gift to our lord the king?

A harlot brought him her flesh,
Her lusts, and the manifold mesh
Of her wiles intervolved with caprice;   65
And he gave her his realm to fleece,
To corrupt, to ruin, and gave
Himself for her toy and her slave —
Harlotry's just the thing
To bring as a gift for our king.   70

Who has a thing to bring
For a gift to our lord the king,
Our king who fears to die?
A priest brought him a lie,
The blackness of hell uprolled   75
In heaven's shining gold;
And he got as guerdon for that
A see and a cardinal's hat —
A lie is an excellent thing
To bring as a gift for our king.   80

Has any one yet a thing
For a gift to our lord the king?
The country gave him a tomb,
A magnificent sleeping-room;
And for this it obtained some rest,   85
Clear riddance of many a pest,
And a hope which it much enjoyed
That the throne would continue void —
A tomb is the very best thing
For a gift to our lord the king.   *(1867)*

THE CITY OF DREADFUL NIGHT

PROEM

Lo, thus, as prostrate, "In the dust I write
   My heart's deep languor and my soul's sad
      tears."
Yet why evoke the specters of black night
   To blot the sunshine of exultant years?
Why disinter dead faith from moldering
   hidden?   5
Why break the seals of mute despair un-
   bidden,
   And wail life's discords into careless ears?

Because a cold rage seizes one at whiles
   To show the bitter old and wrinkled truth
Stripped naked of all vesture that beguiles, 10
   False dreams, false hopes, false masks and
      modes of youth;
Because it gives some sense of power and
   passion

16. **brigue,** intrigue. 54. **La gloire, la victoire,** the glory, the victory. 56. **Te Deum,** the name of an ancient and famous Christian hymn beginning *"Te Deum laudamus"* ("We praise thee, O God").

The City of Dreadful Night. Many of the images and ideas of this poem pressed themselves upon Thomson as he wandered about the streets of London during periods of insomnia. What he presents, however, is a city of modern society, conceived as the result of a vast single process without objective aim. It thus becomes an imaginary City of Despair. The poem shows the influence of Dante's *Inferno.* Cf. also, in imagery and idea, *The Waste Land* of T. S. Eliot.

In helpless impotence to try to fashion
　Our woe in living words howe'er uncouth.

Surely I write not for the hopeful young,　15
　Or those who deem their happiness of
　　worth,
Or such as pasture and grow fat among
　The shows of life and feel nor doubt nor
　　dearth,
Or pious spirits with a God above them
To sanctify and glorify and love them,　20
　Or sages who foresee a heaven on earth.

For none of these I write, and none of these
　Could read the writing if they deigned to
　　try;
So may they flourish, in their due degrees,
　On our sweet earth and in their unplaced
　　sky.　25
If any cares for the weak words here written,
It must be someone desolate, Fate-smitten,
　Whose faith and hope are dead, and who
　　would die.

Yes, here and there some weary wanderer
　In that same city of tremendous night,　30
Will understand the speech, and feel a stir
　Of fellowship in all-disastrous fight;
"I suffer mute and lonely, yet another
Uplifts his voice to let me know a brother
　Travels the same wild paths though out of
　　sight."　35

O sad Fraternity, do I unfold
　Your dolorous mysteries shrouded from of
　　yore?
Nay, be assured — no secret can be told
　To any who divined it not before;
None uninitiate by many a presage　40
Will comprehend the language of the message,
　Although proclaimed aloud for evermore.

I

The City is of Night; perchance of Death,
　But certainly of Night; for never there
Can come the lucid morning's fragrant breath
　After the dewy dawning's cold gray air;　46
The moon and stars may shine with scorn or
　pity;
The sun has never visited that city,
　For it dissolveth in the daylight fair;

Dissolveth like a dream of night away,　50
　Though present in distempered gloom of
　　thought
And deadly weariness of heart all day.
　But when a dream night after night is
　　brought
Throughout a week, and such weeks few or
　many
Recur each year for several years, can any　55
　Discern that dream from real life in aught?

For life is but a dream whose shapes return,
　Some frequently, some seldom, some by
　　night
And some by day, some night and day; we
　learn,
　The while all change and many vanish
　　quite,　60
In their recurrence with recurrent changes
A certain seeming order; where this ranges ·
　We count things real; such is memory's
　　might.

A river girds the city west and south,　64
　The main north channel of a broad lagoon,
Regurging with the salt tides from the mouth;
　Waste marshes shine and glister to the
　　moon
For leagues, then moorland black, then stony
　ridges;
Great piers and causeways, many noble
　bridges,
　Connect the town and islet suburbs strewn.

Upon an easy slope it lies at large,　71
　And scarcely overlaps the long curved crest
Which swells out two leagues from the river
　marge.
　A trackless wilderness rolls north and west,
Savannahs, savage woods, enormous moun-
　tains,　75
Bleak uplands, black ravines with torrent
　fountains;
　And eastward rolls the shipless sea's unrest.

The city is not ruinous, although
　Great ruins of an unremembered past,
With others of a few short years ago,　80
　More sad, are found within its precincts
　　vast.
The street-lamps always burn; but scarce a
　casement
In house or palace front from roof to base-
　ment
　Doth glow or gleam athwart the mirk air
　　cast.

The street-lamps burn amidst the baleful
　glooms,　85
　Amidst the soundless solitudes immense
Of rangéd mansions dark and still as tombs.
　The silence which benumbs or strains the
　　sense
Fulfills with awe the soul's despair unweeping;
Myriads of habitants are ever sleeping,　90
　Or dead, or fled from nameless pestilence!

Yet, as in some necropolis you find
　Perchance one mourner to a thousand dead,
So there: worn faces that look deaf and blind

66. **Regurging**, surging back.　75. **Savannahs**, open,
level regions.　92. **necropolis**, a city of the dead.

Like tragic masks of stone. With weary
   tread,   95
Each wrapped in his own doom, they wander,
   wander,
Or sit foredone and desolately ponder
   Through sleepless hours with heavy drooping head.

Mature men chiefly, few in age or youth,
   A woman rarely, now and then a child —
A child! If here the heart turns sick with
   ruth   101
   To see a little one from birth defiled,
Or lame or blind, as preordained to languish
Through youthless life, think how it bleeds
   with anguish   104
   To meet one erring in that homeless wild.

They often murmur to themselves, they speak
   To one another seldom, for their woe
Broods maddening inwardly and scorns to
   wreak
   Itself abroad; and if at whiles it grow
To frenzy which must rave, none heeds the
   clamor,   110
Unless there waits some victim of like glamour,
   To rave in turn, who lends attentive show.

The City is of Night, but not of Sleep;
   There sweet sleep is not for the weary brain;
The pitiless hours like years and ages creep,
   A night seems termless hell. This dreadful
   strain   116
Of thought and consciousness, which never
   ceases,
Or which some moments' stupor but increases,
   This, worse than woe, makes wretches there
   insane.   119

They leave all hope behind who enter there;
   One certitude while sane they cannot leave,
One anodyne for torture and despair —
   The certitude of Death, which no reprieve
Can put off long; and which, divinely tender,
But waits the outstretched hand to promptly
   render   125
   That draft whose slumber nothing can
   bereave.

2

Because he seemed to walk with an intent
   I followed him; who, shadowlike and frail,
Unswervingly though slowly onward went, 129
   Regardless, wrapped in thought as in a veil.
Thus step for step with lonely sounding feet
We traveled many a long dim silent street.

105. erring, wandering. 120. They . . . there. Cf.
the description over the portal to hell in Dante's *Inferno*—
"Leave all hope, ye that enter."

At length he paused — a black mass in the
   gloom,
   A tower that merged into the heavy sky;
Around, the huddled stones of grave and
   tomb —   135
Some old God's-acre now corruption's sty:
He murmured to himself with dull despair,
   "Here Faith died, poisoned by this charnel
   air."

Then, turning to the right, went on once more,
   And traveled weary roads without sus-
   pense;   140
And reached at last a low wall's open door,
   Whose villa gleamed beyond the foliage
   dense.
He gazed, and muttered with a hard despair,
   "Here Love died, stabbed by its own wor-
   shiped pair."

Then, turning to the right, resumed his
   march,   145
   And traveled streets and lanes with won-
   drous strength,
Until on stooping through a narrow arch
   We stood before a squalid house at length.
He gazed, and whispered with a cold despair,
   "Here Hope died, starved out in its utmost
   lair."   150

When he had spoken thus, before he stirred,
   I spoke, perplexed by something in the
   signs
Of desolation I had seen and heard
   In this drear pilgrimage to ruined shrines:
"When Faith and Love and Hope are dead
   indeed,   155
Can Life still live? By what doth it pro-
   ceed?"

As whom his one intense thought overpowers,
   He answered coldly, "Take a watch, erase
The signs and figures of the circling hours,
   Detach the hands, remove the dial-face; 160
The works proceed until run down, although
Bereft of purpose, void of use, still go."

Then, turning to the right, paced on again,
   And traversed squares and traveled streets
   whose glooms
Seemed more and more familiar to my ken;
   And reached that sullen temple of the
   tombs;   166
And paused to murmur with the old despair,
   "Here Faith died, poisoned by this charnel
   air."

I ceased to follow, for the knot of doubt
   Was severed sharply with a cruel knife; 170

136. God's-acre, cemetery.

He circled thus forever tracing out
  The series of the fraction left of Life;
Perpetual recurrence in the scope
Of but three terms, dead Faith, dead Love,
    dead Hope.   174

3

Although lamps burn along the silent streets,
  Even when moonlight silvers empty squares,
The dark holds countless lanes and close
    retreats;
  But when the night its sphereless mantle
    wears,
The open spaces yawn with gloom abysmal,
The somber mansions loom immense and
    dismal,   180
The lanes are black as subterranean lairs.

And soon the eye a strange new vision learns:
  The night remains for it as dark and dense,
Yet clearly in this darkness it discerns   184
  As in the daylight with its natural sense;
Perceives a shade in shadow not obscurely,
Pursues a stir of black in blackness surely,
  Sees specters also in the gloom intense.

The ear, too, with the silence vast and deep
  Becomes familiar though unreconciled;   190
Hears breathings as of hidden life asleep,
  And muffled throbs as of pent passions
    wild,
Far murmurs, speech of pity or derision;
But all more dubious than the things of vision,
  So that it knows not when it is beguiled. 195

No time abates the first despair and awe,
  But wonder ceases soon; the weirdest thing
Is felt least strange beneath the lawless law
  Where Death-in-Life is the eternal king;
Crushed impotent beneath this reign of terror,
Dazed with such mysteries of woe and error,
  The soul is too outworn for wondering.   202

4

He stood alone within the spacious square,
  Declaiming from the central grassy mound,
With head uncovered and with streaming
    hair,   205
  As if large multitudes were gathered round—
A stalwart shape, the gestures full of might,
The glances burning with unnatural light:

"As I came through the desert thus it was,
As I came through the desert: All was black,
In heaven no single star, on earth no track;
A brooding hush without a stir or note,   212
The air so thick it clotted in my throat;
And thus for hours; then some enormous
    things

Swooped past with savage cries and clanking
    wings.   215
  But I strode on austere;
  No hope could have no fear.

"As I came through the desert thus it was,
As I came through the desert: Eyes of fire   219
Glared at me throbbing with a starved desire;
The hoarse and heavy and carnivorous breath
Was hot upon me from deep jaws of death;
Sharp claws, swift talons, fleshless fingers cold
Plucked at me from the bushes, tried to hold.
  But I strode on austere;   225
  No hope could have no fear.

"As I came through the desert thus it was,
As I came through the desert: Lo you, there,
That hillock burning with a brazen glare;
Those myriad dusky flames with points a-glow
Which writhed and hissed and darted to and
    fro;   231
A Sabbath of the Serpents, heaped pell-mell
For Devil's roll-call and some fête of hell.
  Yet I strode on austere;
  No hope could have no fear.   235

"As I came through the desert thus it was,
As I came through the desert: Meteors ran
And crossed their javelins on the black sky-
    span;
The zenith opened to a gulf of flame,
The dreadful thunderbolts jarred earth's fixed
    frame;   240
The ground all heaved in waves of fire that
    surged
And weltered round me sole there unsub-
    merged.
  Yet I strode on austere;
  No hope could have no fear.

"As I came through the desert thus it was, 245
As I came through the desert: Air once more,
And I was close upon a wild seashore;
Enormous cliffs arose on either hand,
The deep tide thundered up a league-broad
    strand;
White foambelts seethed there, wan spray
    swept and flew;   250
The sky broke, moon and stars and clouds
    and blue.
  And I strode on austere;
  No hope could have no fear.

"As I came through the desert thus it was,
As I came through the desert: On the left 255
The sun arose and crowned a broad crag-
    cleft;

---

232. **Sabbath of the Serpents,** a midnight meeting supposed to be held annually by demons, witches, etc., under
the leadership of Satan, for the purpose of celebrating their
orgies.

There stopped and burned out black, except
   a rim,
A bleeding, eyeless socket, red and dim;
Whereon the moon fell suddenly southwest,
And stood above the right-hand cliffs at rest.
    Still I strode on austere;   261
    No hope could have no fear.

"As I came through the desert thus it was,
As I came through the desert: From the right
A shape came slowly with a ruddy light;   265
A woman with a red lamp in her hand,
Bareheaded and barefooted on that strand;
O desolation moving with such grace!
O anguish with such beauty in thy face!
    I fell as on my bier,   270
    Hope travailed with such fear.

"As I came through the desert thus it was,
As I came through the desert: I was twain,
Two selves distinct that cannot join again;
One stood apart and knew but could not stir,
And watched the other stark in swoon and
   her;   276
And she came on, and never turned aside,
Between such sun and moon and roaring tide.
    And as she came more near
    My soul grew mad with fear.   280

"As I came through the desert thus it was,
As I came through the desert: Hell is mild
And piteous matched with that accurséd wild;
A large black sign was on her breast that
   bowed,
A broad black band ran down her snow-white
   shroud;   285
That lamp she held was her own burning
   heart,
Whose blood-drops trickled step by step apart.
    The mystery was clear;
    Mad rage had swallowed fear.

"As I came through the desert thus it was, 290
As I came through the desert: By the sea
She knelt and bent above that senseless me;
Those lamp-drops fell upon my white brow
   there,
She tried to cleanse them with her tears and
   hair;
She murmured words of pity, love, and woe,
She heeded not the level rushing flow.   296
    And mad with rage and fear,
    I stood stonebound so near.

"As I came through the desert thus it was, 299
As I came through the desert: When the tide
Swept up to her there kneeling by my side,
She clasped that corpse-like me, and they
   were borne
Away, and this vile me was left forlorn;

I know the whole sea cannot quench that
   heart,
Or cleanse that brow, or wash those two
   apart.   305
    They love; their doom is drear,
    Yet they nor hope nor fear;
    But I, what do I here?"

5

How he arrives there none can clearly know;
   Athwart the mountains and immense wild
    tracts,   310
Or flung a waif upon that vast sea-flow,
   Or down the river's boiling cataracts.
To reach it is as dying fever-stricken;
To leave it, slow faint birth intense pangs
   quicken;
   And memory swoons in both the tragic
    acts.   315

But being there one feels a citizen;
   Escape seems hopeless to the heart forlorn—
Can Death-in-Life be brought to life again?
   And yet release does come; there comes a
    morn
When he awakes from slumbering so sweetly
That all the world is changed for him com-
   pletely,   321
   And he is verily as if new-born.

He scarcely can believe the blissful change,
   He weeps perchance who wept not while
    accurst;
Never again will he approach the range   325
   Infected by that evil spell now burst.
Poor wretch! who once hath paced that dolent
   city
Shall pace it often, doomed beyond all pity,
   With horror ever deepening from the first.

Though he possess sweet babes and loving
   wife,   330
   A home of peace by loyal friendships
    cheered,
And love them more than death or happy
   life,
   They shall avail not; he must dree his
    weird;
Renounce all blessings for that imprecation,
Steal forth and haunt that builded desolation,
   Of woe and terrors and thick darkness
    reared.   336

6

I sat forlornly by the river-side,
   And watched the bridge-lamps glow like
    golden stars
Above the blackness of the swelling tide,

327. **dolent,** sorrowful. 333. **dree his weird,** endure
his fate.

Down which they struck rough gold in
   ruddier bars;   340
And heard the heave and splashing of the
   flow
Against the wall a dozen feet below.

Large elm-trees stood along that river-walk;
   And under one, a few steps from my seat,
I heard strange voices join in stranger talk,
   Although I had not heard approaching
   feet;   346
These bodiless voices in my waking dream
Flowed dark words blending with the somber
   stream:

"And you have after all come back; come
   back.
I was about to follow on your track.   350
And you have failed; our spark of hope is
   black."

"That I have failed is proved by my return;
The spark is quenched, nor ever more will
   burn.
But listen; and the story you shall learn.

"I reached the portal common spirits fear, 355
And read the words above it, dark yet clear,
'Leave hope behind, all ye who enter here';

"And would have passed in, gratified to gain
That positive eternity of pain,
Instead of this insufferable inane.   360

"A demon warder clutched me, 'Not so fast;
First leave your hopes behind!' — 'But years
   have passed
Since I left all behind me, to the last.

" 'You cannot count for hope, with all your
   wit,
This bleak despair that drives me to the Pit;
How could I seek to enter void of it?'   366

"He snarled, 'What thing is this which apes
   a soul,
And would find entrance to our gulf of dole
Without the payment of the settled toll?'

"Outside the gate he showed an open chest.
'Here pay their entrance fees the souls un-
   blest;   371
Cast in some hope, you enter with the rest.

" 'This is Pandora's box, whose lid shall shut,

And Hell-gate too, when hopes have filled it;
   but
They are so thin that it will never glut.' 375

"I stood a few steps backwards, desolate;
And watched the spirits pass me to their fate,
And fling off hope, and enter at the gate.

"When one casts off a load he springs upright,
Squares back his shoulders, breathes with all
   his might,   380
And briskly paces forward strong and light;

"But these, as if they took some burden,
   bowed;
The whole frame sank; however strong and
   proud
Before, they crept in quite infirm and cowed.

"And as they passed me, earnestly from each
A morsel of his hope I did beseech,   386
To pay my entrance; but all mocked my
   speech.

"Not one would cede a tittle of his store,
Though knowing that in instants three or
   four
He must resign the whole for evermore.   390

"So I returned. Our destiny is fell;
For in this Limbo we must ever dwell,
Shut out alike from heaven and earth and
   hell."

The other sighed back, "Yea; but if we grope
With care through all this Limbo's dreary
   scope,   395
We yet may pick up some minute lost hope;

"And, sharing it between us, entrance win,
In spite of fiends so jealous for gross sin.
Let us without delay our search begin."

7

Some say that phantoms haunt those shad-
   owy streets,   400
   And mingle freely there with sparse man-
   kind;
And tell of ancient woes and black de-
   feats,
   And murmur mysteries in the grave en-
   shrined.
But others think them visions of illusion,
Or even men gone far in self-confusion,   405
   No man there being wholly sane in mind.

---

373. **Pandora's box.** Pandora, a beautiful woman created
to punish mankind because Prometheus had stolen fire from
heaven, opened a box containing all human ills, which
escaped over the earth. A later tradition had the blessings
of the gods escape from the box, with the exception of hope,
which was saved for the human race.

391. **fell,** cruel. 392. **Limbo,** a region supposed to lie
on the border of hell as the abode of the just who died before
Christ's coming.

And yet a man who raves, however mad,
  Who bares his heart and tells of his own
    fall,
Reserves some inmost secret good or bad;
  The phantoms have no reticence at all— 410
The nudity of flesh will blush though tame-
  less,
The extreme nudity of bone grins shameless,
  The unsexed skeleton mocks shroud and
    pall.

I have seen phantoms there that were as men
  And men that were as phantoms flit and
    roam;   415
Marked shapes that were not living to my
  ken,
  Caught breathings acrid as with Dead Sea
    foam.
The City rests for man so weird and awful,
That his intrusion there might seem unlawful,
  And phantoms there may have their proper
    home.   420

8

While I still lingered on that river-walk,
  And watched the tide as black as our black
    doom,
I heard another couple join in talk,
  And saw them to the left hand in the gloom
Seated against an elm bole on the ground, 425
Their eyes intent upon the stream profound.

"I never knew another man on earth
  But had some joy and solace in his life,
  Some chance of triumph in the dreadful
    strife;
My doom has been unmitigated dearth."   430

"We gaze upon the river, and we note
The various vessels large and small that float,
  Ignoring every wrecked and sunken boat."

"And yet I asked no splendid dower, no spoil
  Of sway or fame or rank or even wealth; 435
  But homely love with common food and
    health,
And nightly sleep to balance daily toil."

"This all-too humble soul would arrogate
Unto itself some signalizing hate
From the supreme indifference of Fate!"   440

"Who is most wretched in this dolorous place?
  I think myself; yet I would rather be
  My miserable self than He, than He
Who formed such creatures to His own dis-
  grace.

"The vilest thing must be less vile than Thou
  From whom it had its being, God and
    Lord!   446

Creator of all woe and sin! abhorred,
Malignant and implacable! I vow

"That not for all Thy power furled and
  unfurled,
  For all the temples to Thy glory built, 450
  Would I assume the ignominious guilt
Of having made such men in such a world."

"As if a Being, God or Fiend, could reign,
At once so wicked, foolish, and insane,
As to produce men when He might refrain! 455

"The world rolls round forever like a mill;
It grinds out death and life and good and ill;
It has no purpose, heart or mind or will.

"While air of Space and Time's full river flow
The mill must blindly whirl unresting so; 460
It may be wearing out, but who can know?

"Man might know one thing were his sight
  less dim;
That it whirls not to suit his petty whim,
That it is quite indifferent to him.

"Nay, does it treat him harshly as he saith?
It grinds him some slow years of bitter
  breath,   466
Then grinds him back into eternal death."

9

It is full strange to him who hears and feels,
  When wandering there in some deserted
    street,   469
The booming and the jar of ponderous wheels,
  The trampling clash of heavy ironshod feet:
Who in this Venice of the Black Sea rideth?
Who in this city of the stars abideth
  To buy or sell as those in daylight sweet?

The rolling thunder seems to fill the sky 475
  As it comes on; the horses snort and strain,
The harness jingles, as it passes by;
  The hugeness of an overburthened wain —
A man sits nodding on the shaft or trudges,
Three parts asleep beside his fellow-drudges;
  And so it rolls into the night again.   481

What merchandise? whence, whither, and for
  whom?
  Perchance it is a Fate-appointed hearse,
Bearing away to some mysterious tomb
  Or Limbo of the scornful universe   485
The joy, the peace, the life-hope, the abor-
  tions
Of all things good which should have been
  our portions,
  But have been strangled by that City's
    curse.

472. Venice . . . Sea, the City of Dreadful Night. 478.
wain, wagon.

10

The mansion stood apart in its own ground;
  In front thereof a fragrant garden-lawn, 490
High trees about it, and the whole walled
    round.
    The massive iron gates were both with-
      drawn;
And every window of its front shed light,
  Portentous in that City of the Night.

But though thus lighted, it was deadly still
  As all the countless bulks of solid gloom; 496
Perchance a congregation to fulfill
  Solemnities of silence in this doom,
Mysterious rites of dolor and despair
Permitting not a breath of chant or prayer?

Broad steps ascended to a terrace broad   501
  Whereon lay still light from the open door;
The hall was noble, and its aspect awed,
  Hung round with heavy black from dome
    to floor;
And ample stairways rose to left and right 505
Whose balustrades were also draped with
    night.

I paced from room to room, from hall to hall,
  Nor any life throughout the maze dis-
    cerned;
But each was hung with its funereal pall,
  And held a shrine, around which tapers
    burned,   510
With picture or with statue or with bust,
All copied from the same fair form of dust —

A woman very young and very fair;
  Beloved by bounteous life and joy and
    youth,
And loving these sweet lovers, so that care 515
  And age and death seemed not for her in
    sooth.
Alike as stars, all beautiful and bright,
These shapes lit up that mausoléan night.

At length I heard a murmur as of lips,
  And reached an open oratory hung   520
With heaviest blackness of the whole eclipse;
  Beneath the dome a fuming censer swung;
And one lay there upon a low white bed,
With tapers burning at the foot and head —

The Lady of the images. Supine,   525
  Deathstill, lifesweet, with folded palms she
    lay;
And kneeling there, as at a sacred shrine,
  A young man wan and worn who seemed to
    pray;
A crucifix of dim and ghostly white
Surmounted the large altar left in night — 530

520. **oratory**, a room or chapel set apart for private
devotions.

"The chambers of the mansion of my heart,
In every one whereof thine image dwells,
Are black with grief eternal for thy sake.

"The inmost oratory of my soul,
Wherein thou ever dwellest quick or dead, 535
Is black with grief eternal for thy sake.

"I kneel beside thee and I clasp the cross
With eyes forever fixed upon that face,
So beautiful and dreadful in its calm.

"I kneel here patient as thou liest there;   540
As patient as a statue carved in stone,
Of adoration and eternal grief.

"Whilst thou dost not awake I cannot move;
And something tells me thou wilt never wake
And I alive feel turning into stone.   545

"Most beautiful were Death to end my grief,
Most hateful to destroy the sight of thee,
Dear vision better than all death or life.

"But I renounce all choice of life or death,
For either shall be ever at thy side,   550
And thus in bliss or woe be ever well."

He murmured thus and thus in monotone,
  Intent upon that uncorrupted face,
Entranced except his moving lips alone.
  I glided with hushed footsteps from the
    place.   555
This was the festival that filled with light
That palace in the City of the Night.

11

What men are they who haunt these fatal
    glooms,
  And fill their living mouths with dust of
    death,
And make their habitations in the tombs, 560
  And breathe eternal sighs with mortal
    breath,
And pierce life's pleasant veil of various error
To reach that void of darkness and old terror
  Wherein expire the lamps of hope and
    faith?

They have much wisdom, yet they are not
    wise;   565
  They have much goodness, yet they do
    not well
(The fools we know have their own paradise,
  The wicked also have their proper hell);
They have much strength, but still their
    doom is stronger;
Much patience, but their time endureth
    longer;   570
  Much valor, but life mocks it with some
    spell.

They are most rational and yet insane —
An outward madness, not to be controlled;
A perfect reason in the central brain,
　Which has no power, but sitteth wan and
　　cold, 575
And sees the madness, and foresees as plainly
The ruin in its path, and trieth vainly
　To cheat itself refusing to behold.

And some are great in rank and wealth and
　　power,
　And some renowned for genius and for
　　worth; 580
And some are poor and mean, who brood and
　　cower
　And shrink from notice, and accept all
　　dearth
Of body, heart and soul, and leave to others
All boons of life; yet these and those are
　　brothers, 584
　The saddest and the weariest men on earth.

12

Our isolated units could be brought
　To act together for some common end?
For one by one, each silent with his thought,
　I marked a long loose line approach and
　　wend
Athwart the great cathedral's cloistered
　　square, 590
And slowly vanish from the moonlit air.

Then I would follow in among the last;
　And in the porch a shrouded figure stood,
Who challenged each one pausing ere he
　　passed,
　With deep eyes burning through a blank
　　white hood: 595
"Whence come you in the world of life and
　　light
To this our City of Tremendous Night?"

"From pleading in a senate of rich lords
For some scant justice to our countless hordes
Who toil half-starved with scarce a human
　　right — 600
I wake from daydreams to this real night."

"From wandering through many a solemn
　　scene
Of opium visions, with a heart serene
And intellect miraculously bright —
I wake from daydreams to this real night."

"From making hundreds laugh and roar with
　　glee 606
By my transcendent feats of mimicry,
And humor wanton as an elfish sprite —
I wake from daydreams to this real night."

"From prayer and fasting in a lonely cell, 610
Which brought an ecstasy ineffable
Of love and adoration and delight —
I wake from daydreams to this real night."

"From ruling on a splendid kingly throne 614
A nation which beneath my rule has grown
Year after year in wealth and arts and
　　might —
I wake from daydreams to this real night."

"From preaching to an audience fired with
　　faith
The Lamb who died to save our souls from
　　death,
Whose blood hath washed our scarlet sins
　　wool-white — 620
I wake from daydreams to this real night."

"From drinking fiery poison in a den
Crowded with tawdry girls and squalid men,
Who hoarsely laugh and curse and brawl and
　　fight — 624
I wake from daydreams to this real night."

"From picturing with all beauty and all grace
First Eden and the parents of our race,
A luminous rapture unto all men's sight —
I wake from daydreams to this real night."

"From writing a great work with patient plan
To justify the ways of God to man, 631
And show how ill must fade and perish
　　quite —
I wake from daydreams to this real night."

"From desperate fighting with a little band
Against the powerful tyrants of our land, 635
To free our brethren in their own despite —
I wake from daydreams to this real night."

Thus, challenged by that warder sad and
　　stern,
　Each one responded with his countersign,
Then entered the cathedral; and in turn 640
　I entered also, having given mine,
But lingered near until I heard no more,
And marked the closing of the massive door.

13

'Of all things human which are strange and
　　wild
　This is perchance the wildest and most
　　strange, 645

620. **blood . . . wool-white.** From *Isaiah*, 1:18.—
"Though your sins be . . . red like crimson, they shall be as
wool." 631. **justify . . . man.** Milton thus states his
purpose in writing *Paradise Lost*—
　　"That to the height of this great argument
　　I may assert eternal Providence,
　　And justify the ways of God to man." (I, 24-26)

And showeth man most utterly beguiled,
  To those who haunt that sunless City's
    range —
That he bemoans himself for aye, repeating
How time is deadly swift, how life is fleeting,
  How naught is constant on the earth but
    change.   650

The hours are heavy on him and the days;
The burden of the months he scarce can bear;
And often in his secret soul he prays
  To sleep through barren periods unaware,
Arousing at some longed-for date of pleasure;
Which having passed and yielded him small
    treasure,   656
  He would outsleep another term of care.

Yet in his marvelous fancy he must make
  Quick wings for Time, and see it fly from
    us—
This Time which crawleth like a monstrous
    snake,   660
Wounded and slow and very venomous;
Which creeps blindwormlike round the earth
  and ocean,
Distilling poison at each painful motion,
And seems condemned to circle ever thus.

And since he cannot spend and use aright 665
  The little time here given him in trust,
But wasteth it in weary undelight
  Of foolish toil and trouble, strife and lust,
He naturally claimeth to inherit
The everlasting Future, that his merit   670
  May have full scope—as surely is most just.

O length of the intolerable hours,
  O nights that are as æons of slow pain,
O Time, too ample for our vital powers,
  O Life, whose woeful vanities remain   675
Immutable for all of all our legions
Through all the centuries and in all the
    regions,
  Not of your speed and variance *we* com-
    plain.

We do not ask a longer term of strife,
  Weakness and weariness and nameless
    woes;   680
We do not claim renewed and endless life
  When this which is our torment here shall
    close,
An everlasting conscious inanition!
We yearn for speedy death in full fruition,
  Dateless oblivion and divine repose.   685

14

Large glooms were gathered in the mighty
    fane,
  With tinted moongleams slanting here and
    there;

And all was hush — no swelling organ-strain,
  No chant, no voice or murmuring of prayer;
No priests came forth, no tinkling censers
    fumed,   690
And the high altar space was unillumed.

Around the pillars and against the walls
  Leaned men and shadows; others seemed
    to brood,
Bent or recumbent, in secluded stalls.
  Perchance they were not a great multitude
Save in that city of so lonely streets   696
Where one may count up every face he meets.

All patiently awaited the event
  Without a stir or sound, as if no less
Self-occupied, doomstricken, while attent. 700
  And then we heard a voice of solemn stress
From the dark pulpit, and our gaze there met
Two eyes which burned as never eyes burned
    yet —

Two steadfast and intolerable eyes
  Burning beneath a broad and rugged brow;
The head behind it of enormous size.   706
  And as black fir-groves in a large wind bow,
Our rooted congregation, gloom-arrayed,
By that great sad voice deep and full were
    swayed:

"O melancholy Brothers, dark, dark, dark! 710
O battling in black floods without an ark!
  O spectral wanderers of unholy Night!
My soul hath bled for you these sunless years,
With bitter blood-drops running down like
    tears;
  Oh, dark, dark, dark, withdrawn from joy
    and light!   715

"My heart is sick with anguish for your bale;
Your woe hath been my anguish; yea, I quail
  And perish in your perishing unblest.
And I have searched the heights and depths,
    the scope
Of all our universe, with desperate hope 720
  To find some solace for your wild unrest.

"And now at last authentic word I bring,
Witnessed by every dead and living thing;
  Good tidings of great joy for you, for all;
There is no God; no Fiend with names divine
Made us and tortures us; if we must pine, 726
  It is to satiate no Being's gall.

"It was the dark delusion of a dream,
That living Person conscious and supreme,
  Whom we must curse for cursing us with
    life;   730
Whom we must curse because the life He
    gave

Could not be buried in the quiet grave,
  Could not be killed by poison or by knife.

"This little life is all we must endure,
The grave's most holy peace is ever sure, 735
  We fall asleep and never wake again;
Nothing is of us but the moldering flesh,
Whose elements dissolve and merge afresh
  In earth, air, water, plants, and other men.

"We finish thus; and all our wretched race
Shall finish with its cycle, and give place 741
  To other beings, with their own time-doom;
Infinite æons ere our kind began;
Infinite æons after the last man
  Has joined the mammoth in earth's tomb
  and womb.   745

"We bow down to the universal laws,
Which never had for man a special clause
  Of cruelty or kindness, love or hate;
If toads and vultures are obscene to sight,
If tigers burn with beauty and with might, 750
  Is it by favor or by wrath of fate?

"All substance lives and struggles evermore
Through countless shapes continually at war,
  By countless interactions interknit;
If one is born a certain day on earth,   755
All times and forces tended to that birth,
  Not all the world could change or hinder it.

"I find no hint throughout the Universe
Of good or ill, of blessing or of curse;
  I find alone Necessity Supreme;   760
With infinite Mystery, abysmal, dark,
Unlighted ever by the faintest spark
  For us the flitting shadows of a dream.

"O Brothers of sad lives! they are so brief;
A few short years must bring us all relief —
  Can we not bear these years of laboring
  breath?   766
But if you would not this poor life fulfill,
Lo, you are free to end it when you will,
  Without the fear of waking after death."

The organ-like vibrations of his voice   770
  Thrilled through the vaulted aisles and died
  away;
The yearning of the tones which bade rejoice
  Was sad and tender as a requiem lay;
Our shadowy congregation rested still
As brooding on that "End it when you will."

15

Wherever men are gathered, all the air   776
  Is charged with human feeling, human
  thought;

Each shout and cry and laugh, each curse
  and prayer,
  Are into its vibrations surely wrought;
Unspoken passion, wordless meditation,   780
Are breathed into it with our respiration;
  It is with our life fraught and overfraught.

So that no man there breathes earth's simple
  breath,
  As if alone on mountains or wide seas;
But nourishes warm life or hastens death 785
  With joys and sorrows, health and foul
  disease,
Wisdom and folly, good and evil labors,
Incessant of his multitudinous neighbors;
  He in his turn affecting all of these.

That City's atmosphere is dark and dense, 790
  Although not many exiles wander there,
With many a potent evil influence,
  Each adding poison to the poisoned air;
Infections of unutterable sadness,
Infections of incalculable madness,   795
  Infections of incurable despair.

16

Our shadowy congregation rested still,
  As musing on that message we had heard
And brooding on that "End it when you
  will";
  Perchance awaiting yet some other word;
When keen as lightning through a muffled
  sky   801
Sprang forth a shrill and lamentable cry —

"The man speaks sooth, alas! the man speaks
  sooth;
  We have no personal life beyond the grave;
There is no God; Fate knows nor wrath nor
  ruth.   805
  Can I find here the comfort which I crave?

"In all eternity I had one chance,
  One few years' term of gracious human life:
The splendors of the intellect's advance;
  The sweetness of the home with babes and
  wife;   810

"The social pleasures with their genial wit;
  The fascination of the worlds of art;
The glories of the worlds of nature, lit
  By large imagination's glowing heart;

"The rapture of mere being, full of health; 815
  The careless childhood and the ardent
  youth,
The strenuous manhood winning various
  wealth,
  The reverend age serene with life's long
  truth —

"All the sublime prerogatives of Man;
  The storied memories of the times of old,
The patient tracking of the world's great
    plan   821
  Through sequences and changes myriad-
    fold.

"This chance was never offered me before;
  For me the infinite Past is blank and dumb.
This chance recurreth never, nevermore; 825
  Blank, blank for me the infinite To-come.

"And this sole chance was frustrate from my
    birth,
A mockery, a delusion; and my breath
Of noble human life upon this earth
  So racks me that I sigh for senseless death.

"My wine of life is poison mixed with gall, 831
  My noonday passes in a nightmare dream,
I worse than lose the years which are my all;
  What can console me for the loss supreme?

"Speak not of comfort where no comfort is,
  Speak not at all; can words make foul
    things fair?   836
Our life's a cheat, our death a black abyss;
  Hush and be mute, envisaging despair."

This vehement voice came from the northern
    aisle,
  Rapid and shrill to its abrupt harsh close;
And none gave answer for a certain while, 841
  For words must shrink from these most
    wordless woes;
At last the pulpit speaker simply said,
With humid eyes and thoughtful drooping
    head:

"My brother, my poor brothers, it is thus:
This life itself holds nothing good for us, 846
  But it ends soon and nevermore can be;
And we knew nothing of it ere our birth,
And shall know nothing when consigned to
    earth.
  I ponder these thoughts, and they comfort
    me."   850

17

How the moon triumphs through the endless
    nights!
  How the stars throb and glitter as they
    wheel
Their thick processions of supernal lights
  Around the blue vault obdurate as steel!
And men regard with passionate awe and
    yearning   855
The mighty marching and the golden burning,
  And think the heavens respond to what
    they feel.

Boats gliding like dark shadows of a dream,
  Are glorified from vision as they pass
The quivering moonbridge on the deep black
    stream;   860
  Cold windows kindle their dead glooms of
    glass
To restless crystals; cornice, dome, and
    column
Emerge from chaos in the splendor solemn;
  Like faëry lakes gleam lawns of dewy grass.

With such a living light these dead eyes shine,
  These eyes of sightless heaven, that as we
    gaze   866
We read a pity, tremulous, divine,
  Or cold majestic scorn in their pure rays.
Fond man! they are not haughty, are not
    tender;
There is no heart or mind in all their splendor,
  They thread mere puppets all their mar-
    velous maze.   871

If we could near them with the flight unflown,
  We should but find them worlds as sad as
    this,
Or suns all self-consuming like our own
  Enringed by planet worlds as much amiss.
They wax and wane through fusion and con-
    fusion;   876
The spheres eternal are a grand illusion,
  The empyréan is a void abyss.

18

I wandered in a suburb of the north,
  And reached a spot whence three close lanes
    led down,   880
Beneath thick trees and hedgerows winding
    forth
  Like deep brook channels, deep and dark
    and lown.
The air above was wan with misty light;
  The dull gray south showed one vague blur
    of white.

I took the left-hand lane and slowly trod 885
  Its earthen footpath, brushing as I went
The humid leafage; and my feet were shod
  With heavy languor, and my frame down-
    bent,
With infinite sleepless weariness outworn,
So many nights I thus had paced forlorn. 890

After a hundred steps I grew aware
  Of something crawling in the lane below;
It seemed a wounded creature prostrate there
  That sobbed with pangs in making progress
    slow,
The hind limbs stretched to push, the fore
    limbs then   895
To drag; for it would die in its own den.

But coming level with it I discerned
  That it had been a man; for at my tread
It stopped in its sore travail and half turned,
  Leaning upon its right, and raised its head,
And with the left hand twitched back as in
  ire   901
Long gray unreverend locks befouled with
  mire —

A haggard filthy face with bloodshot eyes,
  An infamy for manhood to behold.
He gasped all trembling, "What, you want
  my prize?   905
  You leave, to rob me, wine and lust and
  gold
And all that men go mad upon, since you
Have traced my sacred secret of the clue?

"You think that I am weak and must submit;
  Yet I but scratch you with this poisoned
  blade,   910
And you are dead as if I clove with it
  That false fierce greedy heart. Betrayed!
  betrayed!
I fling this phial if you seek to pass,
And you are forthwith shriveled up like
  grass."

And then with sudden change, "Take thought!
  take thought!   915
  Have pity on me! it is mine alone.
If you could find, it would avail you naught;
  Seek elsewhere on the pathway of your
  own.
For who of mortal or immortal race
The lifetrack of another can retrace?   920

"Did you but know my agony and toil!
  Two lanes diverge up yonder from this
  lane;
My thin blood marks the long length of their
  soil;
  Such clue I left, who sought my clue in
  vain.
My hands and knees are worn both flesh and
  bone;   925
I cannot move but with continual moan.

"But I am in the very way at last
  To find the long-lost broken golden thread
Which reunites my present with my past,
  If you but go your own way." And I said,
"I will retire as soon as you have told   931
Whereunto leadeth this lost thread of gold."

"And so you know it not!" he hissed with
  scorn;
  "I feared you, imbecile! It leads me back
From this accursèd night without a morn,   935
  And through the deserts which have else
  no track,

And through vast wastes of horror-haunted
  time,
  To Eden innocence in Eden's clime;

"And I become a nursling soft and pure,
  An infant cradled on its mother's knee, 940
Without a past, love-cherished and secure;
  Which if it saw this loathsome present Me,
Would plunge its face into the pillowing
  breast,
And scream abhorrence hard to lull to rest."

He turned to grope; and I, retiring, brushed
  Thin shreds of gossamer from off my face,
And mused, His life would grow, the germ
  uncrushed;   947
He should to antenatal night retrace,
And hide his elements in that large womb
Beyond the reach of man-evolving Doom. 950

And even thus, what weary way were planned,
  To seek oblivion through the far-off gate
Of birth, when that of death is close at hand!
  For this is law, if law there be in Fate:
What never has been, yet may have its when;
The thing which has been, never is again. 956

19

The mighty river flowing dark and deep,
  With ebb and flood from the remote sea-
  tides
Vague-sounding through the City's sleepless
  sleep,
  Is named the River of the Suicides;   960
For night by night some lorn wretch over-
  weary,
And shuddering from the future yet more
  dreary,
  Within its cold secure oblivion hides.

One plunges from a bridge's parapet,   964
  As by some blind and sudden frenzy hurled;
Another wades in slow with purpose set
  Until the waters are above him furled;
Another in a boat with dreamlike motion
Glides drifting down into the desert ocean,
  To starve or sink from out the desert
  world.   970

They perish from their suffering surely thus,
  For none beholding them attempts to save,
The while each thinks how soon, solicitous,
  He may seek refuge in the selfsame wave;
Some hour when tired of ever-vain endurance
Impatience will forerun the sweet assurance
  Of perfect peace eventual in the grave. 977

When this poor tragic-farce has palled us long,
  Why actors and spectators do we stay? —
To fill our so-short *rôles* out right or wrong;

To see what shifts are yet in the dull play
For our illusion; to refrain from grieving   982
Dear foolish friends by our untimely leaving—
    But those asleep at home, how blest are
        they!

Yet it is but for one night after all;   985
    What matters one brief night of dreary
        pain?
When after it the weary eyelids fall
    Upon the weary eyes and wasted brain;
And all sad scenes and thoughts and feelings
        vanish
    In that sweet sleep no power can ever banish,
    That one best sleep which never wakes
        again.   991

20

I sat me weary on a pillar's base,
    And leaned against the shaft; for broad
        moonlight
O'erflowed the peacefulness of cloistered
        space,
    A shore of shadow slanting from the right.
The great cathedral's western front stood
        there,   996
A wave-worn rock in that calm sea of air.

Before it, opposite my place of rest,
    Two figures faced each other, large, au-
        stere;   999
A couchant sphinx in shadow to the breast,
    An angel standing in the moonlight clear;
So mighty by magnificence of form,
They were not dwarfed beneath that mass
        enorm.

Upon the cross-hilt of a naked sword
    The angel's hands, as prompt to smite,
        were held;   1005
His vigilant, intense regard was poured
    Upon the creature placidly unquelled,
Whose front was set at level gaze which took
No heed of aught, a solemn trance-like look.

And as I pondered these opposéd shapes 1010
    My eyelids sank in stupor, that dull swoon
Which drugs and with a leaden mantle drapes
    The outworn to worse weariness. But soon
A sharp and clashing noise the stillness broke,
And from the evil lethargy I woke.   1015

The angel's wings had fallen, stone on stone,
    And lay there shattered; hence the sudden
        sound.
A warrior leaning on his sword alone
    Now watched the sphinx with that regard
        profound;
The sphinx unchanged looked forthright, as
        aware   1020
Of nothing in the vast abyss of air.

Again I sank in that repose unsweet,
    Again a clashing noise my slumber rent;
The warrior's sword lay broken at his feet;
    An unarmed man with raised hands im-
        potent   1025
Now stood before the sphinx, which ever kept
Such mien as if with open eyes it slept.

My eyelids sank in spite of wonder grown;
    A louder crash upstartled me in dread —
The man had fallen forward, stone on stone,
    And lay there shattered, with his trunkless
        head   1031
Between the monster's large quiescent paws,
Beneath its grand front changeless as life's
        laws.

The moon had circled westward full and
        bright,
    And made the temple-front a mystic dream,
And bathed the whole enclosure with its light,
    The sworded angel's wrecks, the sphinx
        supreme.   1037
I pondered long that cold majestic face
Whose vision seemed of infinite void space.

21

Anear the center of that northern crest   1040
    Stands out a level upland bleak and bare,
From which the city east and south and
        west
    Sinks gently in long waves; and throned
        there
An Image sits, stupendous, superhuman,
The bronze colossus of a wingéd Woman, 1045
    Upon a graded granite base foursquare.

Low-seated she leans forward massively,
    With cheek on clenched left hand, the fore-
        arm's might
Erect, its elbow on her rounded knee;
    Across a clasped book in her lap the right
Upholds a pair of compasses; she gazes   1051
    With full set eyes, but wandering in thick
        mazes
    Of somber thought beholds no outward
        sight.

Words cannot picture her; but all men know
    That solemn sketch the pure sad artist
        wrought   1055
Three centuries and threescore years ago,
    With phantasies of his peculiar thought:
The instruments of carpentry and science
Scattered about her feet, in strange alliance
    With the keen wolf-hound sleeping undis-
        traught;   1060

1055. **sad artist.** Albrecht Dürer (1471-1528), a famous
German painter and engraver. His *Melancholia* is one of
his most noted engravings.

Scales, hour-glass, bell, and magic-square
   above;
The grave and solid infant perched beside,
With open winglets that might bear a dove,
Intent upon its tablets, heavy-eyed;
Her folded wings as of a mighty eagle,   1065
But all too impotent to lift the regal
   Robustness of her earth-born strength and
   pride;

And with those wings, and that light wreath
   which seems
To mock her grand head and the knotted
   frown
Of forehead charged with baleful thoughts
   and dreams,   1070
   The household bunch of keys, the house-
   wife's gown
Voluminous, indented, and yet rigid
As if a shell of burnished metal frigid,
   The feet thick-shod to tread all weakness
   down;   1074

The comet hanging o'er the waste dark seas,
   The massy rainbow curved in front of it,
Beyond the village with the masts and trees;
   The snaky imp, dog-headed, from the Pit,
Bearing upon its batlike leathern pinions   1079
Her name unfolded in the sun's dominions,
The "Melencolia" that transcends all
   wit.

Thus has the artist copied her, and thus
   Surrounded to expound her form sublime,
Her fate heroic and calamitous;   1084
   Fronting the dreadful mysteries of Time,
Unvanquished in defeat and desolation,
Undaunted in the hopeless conflagration
Of the day setting on her baffled prime.

Baffled and beaten back she works on still,
   Weary and sick of soul she works the more,
Sustained by her indomitable will;   1091
   The hands shall fashion and the brain shall
   pore,
And all her sorrow shall be turned to labor,
Till Death, the friend-foe, piercing with his
   saber
That mighty heart of hearts, ends bitter
   war.   1095

But as if blacker night could dawn on night,
   With tenfold gloom on moonless night
   unstarred,
A sense more tragic than defeat and blight,

More desperate than strife with hope de-
   barred,
More fatal than the adamantine Never   1100
Encompassing her passionate endeavor,
   Dawns glooming in her tenebrous regard —

The sense that every struggle brings defeat
   Because Fate holds no prize to crown suc-
   cess;
That all the oracles are dumb or cheat   1105
   Because they have no secret to express;
That none can pierce the vast black veil
   uncertain
Because there is no light beyond the curtain;
   That all is vanity and nothingness.   1109

Titanic from her high throne in the north,
   That City's somber Patroness and Queen,
In bronze sublimity she gazes forth.
   Over her Capital of teen and threne,
Over the river with its isles and bridges,
The marsh and moorland, to the stern rock-
   ridges,   1115
   Confronting them with a coëval mien.

The moving moon and stars from east to
   west
   Circle before her in the sea of air;
Shadows and gleams glide round her solemn
   rest.
   Her subjects often gaze up to her there:
The strong to drink new strength of iron
   endurance,   1121
The weak new terrors; all, renewed assurance
And confirmation of the old despair.

   (*1870-1874; 1874*)

GEORGE MEREDITH (1828-1909)

MODERN LOVE

I

By this he knew she wept with waking eyes:
That, at his hand's light quiver by her head,
The strange low sobs that shook their com-
   mon bed
Were called into her with a sharp surprise,
And strangled mute, like little gaping snakes,
Dreadfully venomous to him. She lay   6
Stone-still, and the long darkness flowed away
With muffled pulses.   Then, as midnight
   makes

1061. **bell, and magic-square.** The bell, a symbol of
faith, summons people to prayer. The magic-square, a symbol of equality, is a square diagram consisting of a number of
small squares each containing a number. The numbers are
so arranged that the sum of those in each of the various rows
is the same.

1102. **tenebrous regard,** dusky look. 1113. **teen and
threne,** sorrow and lamentation.
Modern Love. This sequence of 16-line poems records the
thoughts and feelings of a married couple who realize that
their love for each other is dying. The husband sometimes
speaks in his own person as "I." He then refers to his wife as
"Madam" and to the other woman as "the Lady."

Her giant heart of Memory and Tears
Drink the pale drug of silence, and so beat   10
Sleep's heavy measure, they from head to feet
Were moveless, looking through their dead
        black years
By vain regret scrawled over the blank wall.
Like sculptured effigies they might be seen
Upon their marriage-tomb, the sword be-
        tween;   15
Each wishing for the sword that severs all.

2

It ended, and the morrow brought the task.
Her eyes were guilty gates, that let him in
By shutting all too zealous for their sin:
Each sucked a secret, and each wore a mask.
But, oh, the bitter taste her beauty had!   5
He sickened as at breath of poison-flowers:
A languid humor stole among the hours,
And if their smiles encountered, he went mad,
And raged deep inward, till the light was
        brown
Before his vision, and the world, forgot,   10
Looked wicked as some old dull murder-spot.
A star with lurid beams, she seemed to crown
The pit of infamy: and then again
He fainted on his vengefulness, and strove
To ape the magnanimity of love,   15
And smote himself, a shuddering heap of pain.

3

This was the woman; what now of the man?
But pass him. If he comes beneath a heel,
He shall be crushed until he cannot feel,
Or, being callous, haply till he can.
But he is nothing:—nothing? Only mark   5
The rich light striking out from her on him!
Ha! what a sense it is when her eyes swim
Across the man she singles, leaving dark
All else! Lord God, who mad'st the thing so
        fair,
See that I am drawn to her even now!   10
It cannot be such harm on her cool brow
To put a kiss? Yet if I meet him there!
But she is mine! Ah, no! I know too well
I claim a star whose light is overcast:
I claim a phantom-woman in the Past.   15
The hour has struck, though I heard not the
        bell!

4

All other joys of life he strove to warm,
And magnify, and catch them to his lip:

But they had suffered shipwreck with the ship,
And gazed upon him sallow from the storm.
Or if Delusion came, 'twas but to show   5
The coming minute mock the one that went.
Cold as a mountain in its star-pitched tent,
Stood high Philosophy, less friend than foe:
Whom self-caged Passion, from its prison-
        bars,
Is always watching with a wondering hate.   10
Not till the fire is dying in the grate,
Look we for any kinship with the stars.
Oh, wisdom never comes when it is gold,
And the great price we pay for it full worth:
We have it only when we are half earth.   15
Little avails that coinage to the old!

5

A message from her set his brain aflame.
A world of household matters filled her mind,
Wherein he saw hypocrisy designed:
She treated him as something that is tame,
And but at other provocation bites.   5
Familiar was her shoulder in the glass,
Through that dark rain: yet it may come to
        pass
That a changed eye finds such familiar sights
More keenly tempting than new loveliness.
The "What has been" a moment seemed his
        own: 10
The splendors, mysteries, dearer because
        known,
Nor less divine: Love's inmost sacredness
Called to him, "Come!"—In his restraining
        start,
Eyes nurtured to be looked at scarce could
        see
A wave of the great waves of Destiny   15
Convulsed at a checked impulse of the heart.

6

It chanced his lips did meet her forehead cool.
She had no blush, but slanted down her eye.
Shamed nature, then, confesses love can die:
And most she punishes the tender fool
Who will believe what honors her the most!   5
Dead! is it dead? She has a pulse, and flow
Of tears, the price of blood-drops, as I know,
For whom the midnight sobs around Love's
        ghost,
Since then I heard her, and so will sob on.
The love is here; it has but changed its aim. 10
O bitter barren woman! what's the name?
The name, the name, the new name thou hast
        won?
Behold me striking the world's coward stroke!
That will I not do, though the sting is dire.
—Beneath the surface this, while by the fire
They sat, she laughing at a quiet joke.   16

Poem 1.   15. **the sword between.** In medieval romances,
chastity between lovers was insured by the naked sword. See
Of the Passing Away of Brynhild, 141-143, p. 654.
Poem 3.   1. **the man**, the other man, whom the wife regards with favor. Meredith was married in 1849; his wife
deserted him in 1858 and eloped with an artist. She died
in 1861.

7

She issues radiant from her dressing-room,
Like one prepared to scale an upper sphere:
—By stirring up a lower, much I fear!
How deftly that oiled barber lays his bloom!
That long-shanked dapper Cupid with frisked
    curls   5
Can make known women torturingly fair;
The gold-eyed serpent dwelling in rich hair
Awakes beneath his magic whisks and twirls.
His art can take the eyes from out my head,
Until I see with eyes of other men;   10
While deeper knowledge crouches in its den,
And sends a spark up:—is it true we are wed?
Yea! filthiness of body is most vile,
But faithlessness of heart I do hold worse.
The former, it were not so great a curse   15
To read on the steel-mirror of her smile.

8

Yet it was plain she struggled, and that salt
Of righteous feeling made her pitiful.
Poor twisting worm, so queenly beautiful!
Where came the cleft between us? whose the
    fault?
My tears are on thee, that have rarely
    dropped   5
As balm for any bitter wound of mine:
My breast will open for thee at a sign!
But, no: we are two reed-pipes, coarsely
    stopped:
The God once filled them with his mellow
    breath;   9
And they were music till he flung them down,
Used! used! Hear now the discord-loving
    clown
Puff his gross spirit in them, worse than death!
I do not know myself without thee more:
In this unholy battle I grow base:
If the same soul be under the same face,   15
Speak, and a taste of that old time restore!

9

He felt the wild beast in him betweenwhiles
So masterfully rude, that he would grieve
To see the helpless delicate thing receive
His guardianship through certain dark defiles.
Had he not teeth to rend, and hunger too? 5
But still! he spared her. Once: "Have you no
    fear?"
He said: 'twas dusk; she in his grasp; none
    near.
She laughed: "No, surely; am I not with
    you?"
And uttering that soft starry "you," she
    leaned

*Poem 8. 9. **The God**, Apollo, god of music and poetry.*

Her gentle body near him, looking up;   10
And from her eyes, as from a poison-cup,
He drank until the flittering eyelids screened.
Devilish malignant witch! and oh, young
    beam
Of heaven's circle-glory! Here thy shape
To squeeze like an intoxicating grape—   15
I might, and yet thou goest safe, supreme.

10

But where began the change; and what's my
    crime?
The wretch condemned, who has not been
    arraigned,
Chafes at his sentence. Shall I, unsustained,
Drag on Love's nerveless body through all
    time?   4
I must have slept, since now I wake. Prepare,
You lovers, to know Love a thing of moods:
Not, like hard life, of laws. In Love's deep
    woods,
I dreamt of loyal Life:—the offense is there!
Love's jealous woods about the sun are curled;
At least, the sun far brighter there did beam.—
My crime is, that the puppet of a dream,   11
I plotted to be worthy of the world.
Oh, had I with my darling helped to mince
The facts of life, you still had seen me go
With hindward feather and with forward toe,
Her much-adored delightful Fairy Prince!   16

11

Out in the yellow meadows, where the bee
Hums by us with the honey of the Spring,
And showers of sweet notes from the larks on
    wing
Are dropping like a noon-dew, wander we.
Or is it now? or was it then? for now,   5
As then, the larks from running rings pour
    showers:
The golden foot of May is on the flowers,
And friendly shadows dance upon her brow.
What's this, when Nature swears there is no
    change
To challenge eyesight? Now, as then, the
    grace   10
Of heaven seems holding earth in its embrace.
Nor eyes, nor heart, has she to feel it strange?
Look, woman, in the West. There wilt thou
    see
An amber cradle near the sun's decline:
Within it, featured even in death divine,   15
Is lying a dead infant, slain by thee.

12

Not solely that the Future she destroys,
And the fair life which in the distance lies

For all men, beckoning out from dim rich
    skies:
Nor that the passing hour's supporting joys
Have lost the keen-edged flavor, which begat 5
Distinction in old times, and still should breed
Sweet Memory, and Hope,—earth's modest
    seed,
And heaven's high-prompting: not that the
    world is flat
Since that soft-luring creature I embraced
Among the children of Illusion went: 10
Methinks with all this loss I were content,
If the mad Past, on which my foot is based,
Were firm, or might be blotted: but the whole
Of life is mixed: the mocking Past will stay:
And if I drink oblivion of a day,   15
So shorten I the stature of my soul.

13

"I play for Seasons; not Eternities!"
Says Nature, laughing on her way. "So must
All those whose stake is nothing more than
    dust!"
And lo, she wins, and of her harmonies
She is full sure! Upon her dying rose   5
She drops a look of fondness, and goes by,
Scarce any retrospection in her eye;
For she the laws of growth most deeply knows,
Whose hands bear, here, a seed-bag—there,
    an urn.
Pledged she herself to aught, 'twould mark
    her end!   10
This lesson of our only visible friend
Can we not teach our foolish hearts to learn?
Yes! yes!—but, oh, our human rose is fair
Surpassingly! Lose calmly Love's great bliss,
When the renewed forever of a kiss   15
Whirls life within the shower of loosened hair!

14

What soul would bargain for a cure that brings
Contempt the nobler agony to kill?
Rather let me bear on the bitter ill,
And strike this rusty bosom with new stings!
It seems there is another veering fit,   5
Since on a gold-haired lady's eyeballs pure
I looked with little prospect of a cure,
The while her mouth's red bow loosed shafts
    of wit.
Just heaven! can it be true that jealousy
Has decked the woman thus? and does her
    head   10
Swim somewhat for possessions forfeited?
Madam, you teach me many things that be.
I open an old book, and there I find

Poem 14.   6. **gold-haired lady**, the other woman, with
whom the husband sought distraction (see *Poems 27, 28, 31*).

That "Women still may love whom they
    deceive."
Such love I prize not, madam: by your leave,
The game you play at is not to my mind.   16

15

I think she sleeps: it must be sleep, when low
Hangs that abandoned arm toward the floor;
The face turned with it. Now make fast the
    door.
Sleep on: it is your husband, not your foe.
The Poet's black stage-lion of wronged love 5
Frights not our modern dames:—well if he
    did!
Now will I pour new light upon that lid,
Full-sloping like the breasts beneath. "Sweet
    dove,   8
Your sleep is pure. Nay, pardon: I disturb.
I do not? good!" Her waking infant-stare
Grows woman to the burden my hands bear:
Her own handwriting to me when no curb
Was left on Passion's tongue. She trembles
    through;
A woman's tremble—the whole instrument:—
I show another letter lately sent.   15
The words are very like: the name is new.

16

In our old shipwrecked days there was an
    hour,
When in the firelight steadily aglow,
Joined slackly, we beheld the red chasm grow
Among the clicking coals. Our library-bower
That eve was left to us: and hushed we sat 5
As lovers to whom Time is whispering.
From sudden-opened doors we heard them
    sing:
The nodding elders mixed good wine with
    chat.
Well knew we that Life's greatest treasure
    lay
With us, and of it was our talk. "Ah, yes! 10
Love dies!" I said: I never thought it less.
She yearned to me that sentence to unsay.
Then when the fire domed blackening, I found
Her cheek was salt against my kiss, and swift
Up the sharp scale of sobs her breast did
    lift:—   15
Now am I haunted by that taste! that sound!

17

At dinner, she is hostess, I am host.
Went the feast ever cheerfuller? She keeps
The Topic over intellectual deeps
In buoyancy afloat. They see no ghost.
With sparkling surface-eyes we ply the ball: 5
It is in truth a most contagious game:

Hiding the Skeleton, shall be its name.
Such play as this the devils might appal!
But here's the greater wonder: in that we,
Enamored of an acting naught can tire,   10
Each other, like true hypocrites, admire;
Warm-lighted looks, Love's ephemeridæ,
Shoot gayly o'er the dishes and the wine.
We waken envy of our happy lot.
Fast, sweet, and golden, shows the marriage-
          knot.   15
Dear guests, you now have seen Love's
          corpse-light shine.

18

Here Jack and Tom are paired with Moll and
          Meg.
Curved open to the river-reach is seen
A country merry-making on the green.
Fair space for signal shakings of the leg.
That little screwy fiddler from his booth,   5
Whence flows one nut-brown stream, com-
          mands the joints
Of all who caper here at various points.
I have known rustic revels in my youth:
The May-fly pleasures of a mind at ease.
An early goddess was a country lass: 10
A charmed Amphion-oak she tripped the
          grass.
What life was that I lived?   The life of these?
Heaven keep them happy!   Nature they seem
          near.
They must, I think, be wiser than I am;
They have the secret of the bull and lamb. 15
'Tis true that when we trace its source, 'tis
          beer.

19

No state is enviable.   To the luck alone
Of some few favored men I would put claim.
I bleed, but her who wounds I will not blame.
Have I not felt her heart as 'twere my own
Beat through me? could I hurt her? heaven
          and hell!   5
But I could hurt her cruelly! Can I let
My Love's old time-piece to another set,
Swear it can't stop, and must forever swell?
Sure, that's one way Love drifts into the mart
Where goat-legged buyers throng.   I see not
          plain:—   10
My meaning is, it must not be again.

Great God! the maddest gambler throws his
          heart.
If any state be enviable on earth,
'Tis yon born idiot's, who, as days go by,
Still rubs his hands before him, like a fly,   15
In a queer sort of meditative mirth.

20

I am not of those miserable males
Who sniff at vice and, daring not to snap,
Do therefore hope for heaven. I take the hap
Of all my deeds.   The wind that fills my sails
Propels; but I am helmsman. Am I wrecked,
I know the devil has sufficient weight   6
To bear: I lay it not on him, or fate.
Besides, he's damned. That man I do suspect
A coward, who would burden the poor deuce
With what ensues from his own slipperiness. 10
I have just found a wanton-scented tress
In an old desk, dusty for lack of use.
Of days and nights it is demonstrative,
That, like some aged star, gleam luridly.
If for those times I must ask charity,   15
Have I not any charity to give?

21

We three are on the cedar-shadowed lawn;
My friend being third.   He who at love once
          laughed
Is in the weak rib by a fatal shaft
Struck through, and tells his passion's bashful
          dawn
And radiant culmination, glorious crown,   5
When "this" she said: went "thus": most
          wondrous she.
Our eyes grow white, encountering: that we
          are three,
Forgetful; then together we look down.
But he demands our blessing; is convinced
That words of wedded lovers must bring
          good.   10
We question; if we dare! or if we should!
And pat him, with light laugh. We have
          not winced.
Next, she has fallen. Fainting points the sign
To happy things in wedlock. When she
          wakes,
She looks the star that through the cedar
          shakes: 15
Her lost moist hand clings mortally to mine.

22

What may the woman labor to confess?
There is about her mouth a nervous twitch.
'Tis something to be told, or hidden:—which?
I get a glimpse of hell in this mild guess.
She has desires of touch, as if to feel   5

Poem 17. 7. **Hiding the Skeleton.** They not only do not
love each other, but each has another attraction—the wife, a
man mentioned in *Poem 3*, line 1; the husband, a lady with
golden hair mentioned in *Poem 14*, line 6. 12. **ephemeridæ,**
delicate insects that live for only a few hours or days. 16.
corpse-light, a luminous appearance resembling the flame of
a candle, sometimes seen in graveyards and damp places; it is
thought to portend death.
      Poem 18. 11. **Amphion,** a legendary singer of Greece whose
music made trees dance.

That all the household things are things she
    knew.
She stops before the glass. What sight in view?
A face that seems the latest to reveal!
For she turns from it hastily, and tossed
Irresolute steals shadow-like to where   10
I stand; and wavering pale before me there,
Her tears fall still as oak-leaves after frost.
She will not speak. I will not ask. We are
League-sundered by the silent gulf between.
You burly lovers on the village green,   15
Yours is a lower, and a happier star!

23

'Tis Christmas weather, and a country house
Receives us: rooms are full: we can but get
An attic-crib. Such lovers will not fret
At that, it is half-said. The great carouse
Knocks hard upon the midnight's hollow
    door,   5
But when I knock at hers, I see the pit.
Why did I come here in that dullard fit?
I enter, and lie couched upon the floor.
Passing, I caught the coverlet's quick beat:—
Come, Shame, burn to my soul! and Pride,
    and Pain—   10
Foul demons that have tortured me, enchain!
Out in the freezing darkness the lambs bleat.
The small bird stiffens in the low starlight.
I know not how, but shuddering as I slept,
I dreamed a banished angel to me crept: 15
My feet were nourished on her breasts all
    night.

24

The misery is greater, as I live!
To know her flesh so pure, so keen her sense,
That she does penance now for no offense,
Save against Love. The less can I forgive!
The less can I forgive, though I adore   5
That cruel lovely pallor which surrounds
Her footsteps; and the low vibrating sounds
That come on me, as from a magic shore.
Low are they, but most subtle to find out   9
The shrinking soul. Madam, 'tis understood
When women play upon their womanhood,
It means, a Season gone. And yet I doubt
But I am duped. That nun-like look waylays
My fancy. Oh! I do but wait a sign!
Pluck out the eyes of pride! thy mouth to
    mine!   15
Never! though I die thirsting. Go thy ways!

25

You like not that French novel? Tell me why.
You think it quite unnatural. Let us see.
The actors are, it seems, the usual three:

Husband, and wife, and lover. She—but fie!
In England we'll not hear of it. Edmond, 5
The lover, her devout chagrin doth share;
Blancmange and absinthe are his penitent
    fare,
Till his pale aspect makes her over-fond:
So, to preclude fresh sin, he tries *rosbif*.
Meantime the husband is no more abused: 10
Auguste forgives her ere the tear is used.
Then hangeth all on one tremendous IF:—
If she will choose between them. She does
    choose;
And takes her husband, like a proper wife.
Unnatural? My dear, these things are life: 15
And life, some think, is worthy of the Muse.

26

Love ere he bleeds, an eagle in high skies,
Has earth beneath his wings: from reddened
    eve
He views the rosy dawn. In vain they weave
The fatal web below while far he flies.
But when the arrow strikes him, there's a
    change.   5
He moves but in the track of his spent pain,
Whose red drops are the links of a harsh chain,
Binding him to the ground, with narrow range.
A subtle serpent then has Love become.
I had the eagle in my bosom erst: 10
Henceforward with the serpent I am cursed.
I can interpret where the mouth is dumb.
Speak, and I see the side-lie of a truth.
Perchance my heart may pardon you this
    deed:
But be no coward:—you that made Love
    bleed,   15
You must bear all the venom of his tooth!

27

Distraction is the panacea, Sir!
I hear my oracle of Medicine say.
Doctor! that same specific yesterday
I tried, and the result will not deter
A second trial. Is the devil's line   5
Of golden hair, or raven black, composed?
And does a cheek, like any sea-shell rosed,
Or clear as widowed sky, seem most divine?
No matter, so I taste forgetfulness.
And if the devil snare me, body and mind, 10
Here gratefully I score:—he seeméd kind,
When not a soul would comfort my distress!
O sweet new world, in which I rise new made!
O Lady, once I gave love: now I take!
Lady, I must be flattered. Shouldst thou
    wake   15
The passion of a demon, be not afraid.

Poem 25. 9. **rosbif**, roast beef, as pronounced by the
Frenchman. 10. **abused**, deceived.

28

I must be flattered.   The imperious
Desire speaks out. Lady, I am content
To play with you the game of Sentiment,
And with you enter on paths perilous;
But if across your beauty I throw light,   5
To make it threefold, it must be all mine.
First secret; then avowed.   For I must shine
Envied,—I, lessened in my proper sight!
Be watchful of your beauty, Lady dear!
How much hangs on that lamp you cannot
   tell.   10
Most earnestly I pray you, tend it well:
And men shall see me as a burning sphere;
And men shall mark you eyeing me, and groan
To be the God of such a grand sunflower!
I feel the promptings of Satanic power,   15
While you do homage unto me alone.

29

Am I failing? For no longer can I cast
A glory round about this head of gold.
Glory she wears, but springing from the mold;
Not like the consecration of the Past!
Is my soul beggared? Something more than
   earth   5
I cry for still; I cannot be at peace
In having Love upon a mortal lease.
I cannot take the woman at her worth!
Where is the ancient wealth wherewith I
   clothed
Our human nakedness, and could endow   10
With spiritual splendor a white brow
That else had grinned at me the fact I
   loathed?
A kiss is but a kiss now! and no wave
Of a great flood that whirls me to the sea.
But, as you will! we'll sit contentedly,   15
And eat our pot of honey on the grave.

30

What are we first?   First, animals; and next
Intelligences at a leap; on whom
Pale lies the distant shadow of the tomb,
And all that draweth on the tomb for text.
Into which state comes Love, the crowning
   sun: 5
Beneath whose light the shadow loses form.
We are the lords of life, and life is warm.
Intelligence and instinct now are one.
But Nature says: "My children most they
   seem
When they least know me: therefore I decree 10
That they shall suffer."   Swift doth young
   Love flee,
And we stand wakened, shivering from our
   dream.
Then if we study Nature we are wise.

Thus do the few who live but with the day:
The scientific animals are they.—   15
Lady, this is my sonnet to your eyes.

31

This golden head has wit in it.   I live
Again, and a far higher life, near her.
Some women like a young philosopher;
Perchance because he is diminutive.
For woman's manly god must not exceed   5
Proportions of the natural nursing size.
Great poets and great sages draw no prize
With women: but the little lap-dog breed,
Who can be hugged, or on a mantel-piece
Perched up for adoration, these obtain   10
Her homage.   And of this we men are vain?
Of this!   'Tis ordered for the world's increase!
Small flattery!   Yet she has that rare gift
To beauty, Common Sense.   I am approved.
It is not half so nice as being loved,   15
And yet I do prefer it.   What's my drift?

32

Full faith I have she holds that rarest gift
To beauty, Common Sense.   To see her lie
With her fair visage an inverted sky
Bloom-covered, while the underlids uplift,
Would almost wreck the faith; but when her
   mouth   5
(Can it kiss sweetly? sweetly!) would address
The inner me that thirsts for her no less,
And has so long been languishing in drouth,
I feel that I am matched; that I am man!
One restless corner of my heart or head,   10
That holds a dying something never dead,
Still frets, though Nature giveth all she can.
It means, that woman is not, I opine,
Her sex's antidote.   Who seeks the asp
For serpents' bites?   'Twould calm me could
   I clasp   15
Shrieking Bacchantes with their souls of wine!

33

"In Paris, at the Louvre, there have I seen
The sumptuously-feathered angel pierce
Prone Lucifer, descending.   Looked he fierce,
Showing the fight a fair one?   Too serene!
The young Pharsalians did not disarray   5
Less willingly their locks of floating silk:
That suckling mouth of his upon the milk
Of heaven might still be feasting through the
   fray.
Oh, Raphael! when men the Fiend do fight,

Poem 33. 1. **Louvre**, the well-known art gallery in Paris. The reference is to "St. Michael" by Raphael (1483–1520). This painting shows the serene young archangel slaying Lucifer, the devil. 5. **Pharsalians**, the young Roman dandies who fought in the Battle of Pharsalus, 48 B.C.

They conquer not upon such easy terms. 10
Half serpent in the struggle grow these
    worms.
And does he grow half human, all is right."
This to my Lady in a distant spot,
Upon the theme: *While mind is mastering clay,*
Gross clay invades it. If the spy you play, 15
My wife, read this! Strange love-talk, is it
    not?

34

Madam would speak with me. So, now it
    comes:
The Deluge or else Fire! She's well; she
    thanks
My husbandship. Our chain on silence
    clanks.
Time leers between, above his twiddling
    thumbs.
Am I quite well? Most excellent in health! 5
The journals, too, I diligently peruse.
Vesuvius is expected to give news:
Niagara is no noisier. By stealth
Our eyes dart scrutinizing snakes. She's glad
I'm happy, says her quivering under-lip. 10
"And are not you?" "How can I be?"
    "Take ship!
For happiness is somewhere to be had."
"Nowhere for me!" Her voice is barely
    heard.
I am not melted, and make no pretense.
With commonplace I freeze her, tongue and
    sense. 15
Niagara or Vesuvius is deferred.

35

It is no vulgar nature I have wived.
Secretive, sensitive, she takes a wound
Deep to her soul, as if the sense had swooned,
And not a thought of vengeance had survived.
No confidences has she: but relief 5
Must come to one whose suffering is acute.
O have a care of natures that are mute!
They punish you in acts: their steps are brief.
What is she doing? What does she demand
From Providence or me? She is not one 10
Long to endure this torpidly, and shun
The drugs that crowd about a woman's hand.
At Forfeits during snow we played, and I
Must kiss her. "Well performed!" I said:
    then she:
" 'Tis hardly worth the money, you agree?" 15
Save her? What for? To act this wedded lie!

36

My lady unto Madam makes her bow.
The charm of women is, that even while

You're probed by them for tears, you yet
    may smile,
Nay, laugh outright, as I have done just now.
The interview was gracious: they anoint 5
(To me aside) each other with fine praise:
Discriminating compliments they raise,
That hit with wondrous aim on the weak
    point:
My Lady's nose of Nature might complain.
It is not fashioned aptly to express 10
Her character of large-browed steadfastness.
But Madam says: Thereof she may be vain!
Now, Madam's faulty feature is a glazed
And inaccessible eye, that has soft fires,
Wide gates, at love-time, only. This admires
My Lady. At the two I stand amazed. 16

37

Along the garden terrace, under which
A purple valley (lighted at its edge
By smoky torch-flame on the long cloud-ledge
Whereunder dropped the chariot) glimmers
    rich,
A quiet company we pace, and wait 5
The dinner-bell in prae-digestive calm.
So sweet up violet banks the Southern balm
Breathes round, we care not if the bell be late:
Though here and there gray seniors question
    Time
In irritable coughings. With slow foot 10
The low rosed moon, the face of Music mute,
Begins among her silent bars to climb.
As in and out, in silvery dusk, we thread,
I hear the laugh of Madam, and discern
My Lady's heel before me at each turn. 15
Our tragedy, is it alive or dead?

38

Give to imagination some pure light
In human form to fix it, or you shame
The devils with that hideous human game:—
Imagination urging appetite!
Thus fallen have earth's greatest Gogmagogs,
Who dazzle us, whom we cannot revere: 6
Imagination is the charioteer
That, in default of better, drives the hogs.
So, therefore, my dear Lady, let me love!
My soul is arrowy to the light in you. 10
You know me that I never can renew
The bond that woman broke: what would you
    have?
'Tis Love, or Vileness! not a choice between,
Save petrifaction! What does Pity here?
She killed a thing, and now it's dead, 'tis
    dear. 15
Oh, when you counsel me, think what you
    mean!

Poem 38. 5. **Gogmagogs,** giants.

39

She yields: my Lady in her noblest mood
Has yielded: she, my golden-crownéd rose!
The bride of every sense! more sweet than
those
Who breathe the violet breath of maidenhood.
O visage of still music in the sky! 5
Soft moon! I feel thy song, my fairest friend!
True harmony within can apprehend
Dumb harmony without. And hark! 'tis
nigh!
Belief has struck the note of sound: a gleam
Of living silver shows me where she shook 10
Her long white fingers down the shadowy
brook,
That sings her song, half waking, half in
dream.
What two come here to mar this heavenly
tune?
A man is one: the woman bears my name,
And honor. Their hands touch! Am I still
tame? 15
God, what a dancing specter seems the moon!

40

I bade my Lady think what she might mean.
Know I my meaning, I? Can I love one,
And yet be jealous of another? None
Commits such folly. Terrible Love, I ween,
Has might, even dead, half sighing to up-
heave 5
The lightless seas of selfishness amain:
Seas that in a man's heart have no rain
To fall and still them. Peace can I achieve,
By turning to this fountain-source of woe,
This woman, who's to Love as fire to wood? 10
She breathed the violet breath of maidenhood
Against my kisses once! but I say, No!
The thing is mocked at! Helplessly afloat,
I know not what I do, whereto I strive.
The dread that my old love may be alive 15
Has seized my nursling new love by the throat.

41

How many a thing which we cast to the
ground,
When others pick it up becomes a gem!
We grasp at all the wealth it is to them;
And by reflected light its worth is found.
Yet for us still 'tis nothing! and that zeal 5
Of false appreciation quickly fades.
This truth is little known to human shades,
How rare from their own instinct 'tis to feel!
They waste the soul with spurious desire,
That is not the ripe flame upon the bough. 10
We two have taken up a lifeless vow
To rob a living passion: dust for fire!

Madam is grave, and eyes the clock that tells
Approaching midnight. We have struck
despair
Into two hearts. Oh, look we like a pair 15
Who for fresh nuptials joyfully yield all else?

42

I am to follow her. There is much grace
In women when thus bent on martyrdom.
They think that dignity of soul may come,
Perchance, with dignity of body. Base!
But I was taken by that air of cold 5
And statuesque sedateness, when she said
"I'm going"; lit a taper, bowed her head,
And went, as with the stride of Pallas bold.
Fleshly indifference horrible! The hands
Of Time now signal: O, she's safe from me! 10
Within those secret walls what do I see?
Where first she set the taper down she stands:
Not Pallas: Hebe shamed! Thoughts black
as death
Like a stirred pool in sunshine break. Her
wrists
I catch: she faltering, as she half resists, 15
"You love . . . ? love . . . ? love . . . ?"
all on an indrawn breath.

43

Mark where the pressing wind shoots javelin-
like
Its skeleton shadow on the broad-backed
wave!
Here is a fitting spot to dig Love's grave;
Here where the ponderous breakers plunge
and strike,
And dart their hissing tongues high up the
sand: 5
In hearing of the ocean, and in sight
Of those ribbed wind-streaks running into
white.
If I the death of Love had deeply planned,
I never could have made it half so sure,
As by the unblest kisses which upbraid 10
The full-waked sense; or failing that, degrade!
'Tis morning: but no morning can restore
What we have forfeited. I see no sin:
The wrong is mixed. In tragic life, God wot,
No villain need be! Passions spin the plot: 15
We are betrayed by what is false within.

44

They say, that Pity in Love's service dwells,
A porter at the rosy temple's gate.
I missed him going: but it is my fate

Poem 42. 8. **Pallas**, Pallas Athena, the Greek goddess of
wisdom. 13. **Hebe**, the goddess of youth and spring, and cupbearer to the gods.
Poem 43. 14. **wot**, knows.

To come upon him now beside his wells;
Whereby I know that I Love's temple leave, 5
And that the purple doors have closed be-
    hind.
Poor soul! if, in those early days unkind,
Thy power to sting had been but power to
    grieve,
We now might with an equal spirit meet,
And not be matched like innocence and vice.
She for the Temple's worship has paid price, 11
And takes the coin of Pity as a cheat.
She sees through simulation to the bone:
What's best in her impels her to the worst:
Never, she cries, shall Pity soothe Love's
    thirst,   15
Or foul hypocrisy for truth atone!

45

It is the season of the sweet wild rose,
My Lady's emblem in the heart of me!
So golden-crownéd shines she gloriously,
And with that softest dream of blood she
    glows:
Mild as an evening heaven round Hesper
    bright!   5
I pluck the flower, and smell it, and revive
The time when in her eyes I stood alive.
I seem to look upon it out of Night.
Here's Madam, stepping hastily.   Her whims
Bid her demand the flower, which I let drop. 10
As I proceed, I feel her sharply stop,
And crush it under heel with trembling limbs.
She joins me in a cat-like way, and talks
Of company, and even condescends
To utter laughing scandal of old friends. 15
These are the summer days, and these our
    walks.

46

At last we parley: we so strangely dumb
In such a close communion!   It befell
About the sounding of the Matin-bell,
And lo! her place was vacant, and the hum
Of loneliness was round me.   Then I rose, 5
And my disordered brain did guide my foot
To that old wood where our first love-salute
Was interchanged: the source of many throes!
There did I see her, not alone.   I moved
Toward her, and made proffer of my arm. 10
She took it simply, with no rude alarm;
And that disturbing shadow passed reproved.
I felt the pained speech coming, and declared
My firm belief in her, ere she could speak.
A ghastly morning came into her cheek, 15
While with a widening soul on me she stared.

47

We saw the swallows gathering in the sky,
And in the osier-isle we heard them noise.
We had not to look back on summer joys,
Or forward to a summer of bright dye;
But in the largeness of the evening earth 5
Our spirits grew as we went side by side.
The hour became her husband and my bride.
Love, that had robbed us so, thus blessed our
    dearth!
The pilgrims of the year waxed very loud
In multitudinous chatterings, as the flood 10
Full brown came from the West, and like pale
    blood
Expanded to the upper crimson cloud.
Love, that had robbed us of immortal things,
This little moment mercifully gave,
Where I have seen across the twilight wave 15
The swan sail with her young beneath her
    wings.

48

Their sense is with their senses all mixed in,
Destroyed by subtleties these women are!
More brain, O Lord, more brain! or we shall
    mar
Utterly this fair garden we might win.
Behold!   I looked for peace, and thought it
    near.   5
Our inmost hearts had opened, each to each.
We drank the pure daylight of honest speech.
Alas! that was the fatal draft, I fear.
For when of my lost Lady came the word,
This woman, O this agony of flesh! 10
Jealous devotion bade her break the mesh,
That I might seek that other like a bird.
I do adore the nobleness! despise
The act!   She has gone forth, I know not
    where.
Will the hard world my sentience of her share?
I feel the truth; so let the world surmise. 16

49

He found her by the ocean's moaning verge.
Nor any wicked change in her discerned;
And she believed his old love had returned,
Which was her exultation, and her scourge.
She took his hand, and walked with him, and
    seemed   5
The wife he sought, though shadow-like and
    dry.
She had one terror, lest her heart should sigh,
And tell her loudly she no longer dreamed.

Poem 45. 5. **Hesper**, the evening star.
Poem 46. 3. **Matin-bell**, the bell calling people to morning
prayer.

Poem 47. 2. **osier-isle**, willow-isle. 9. **pilgrims of the
year**, migrating birds.
Poem 48. 9. **lost Lady**, the other woman. 10. **This woman**,
his wife.
Poem 49. 1. **He found her**. The husband found his wife.

She dared not say, "This is my breast: look
    in."
But there's a strength to help the desperate
    weak.   10
That night he learned how silence best can
    speak
The awful things when Pity pleads for Sin.
About the middle of the night her call
Was heard, and he came wondering to the bed.
"Now kiss me, dear! it may be, now!" she
    said.   15
Lethe had passed those lips, and he knew all.

50

Thus piteously Love closed what he begat:
The union of this ever-diverse pair!
These two were rapid falcons in a snare,
Condemned to do the flitting of the bat.
Lovers beneath the singing sky of May,   5
They wandered once; clear as the dew on
    flowers:
But they fed not on the advancing hours:
Their hearts held cravings for the buried day.
Then each applied to each that fatal knife,
Deep questioning, which probes to endless
    dole.   10
Ah, what a dusty answer gets the soul
When hot for certainties in this our life!—
In tragic hints here see what evermore
Moves dark as yonder midnight ocean's force,
Thundering like ramping hosts of warrior
    horse,   15
To throw that faint thin line upon the shore!
                                        (1862)

DIRGE IN WOODS

A wind sways the pines,
        And below
Not a breath of wild air—
Still as the mosses that glow
On the flooring and over the lines   5
Of the roots here and there.
The pine-tree drops its dead;
They are quiet, as under the sea.
Overhead, overhead
Rushes life in a race,   10
As the clouds the clouds chase;
        And we go,
And we drop like the fruits of the tree,
        Even we,
        Even so.   (1870)

A BALLAD OF PAST MERIDIAN

Last night returning from my twilight walk
I met the gray mist Death, whose eyeless
    brow

Was bent on me, and from his hand of chalk
He reached me flowers as from a withered
    bough.
O Death, what bitter nosegays givest thou!   5

Death said, "I gather," and pursued his way
Another stood by me, a shape in stone,
Sword-hacked and iron-stained, with breasts
    of clay,
And metal veins that sometimes fiery shone. 9
O Life, how naked and how hard when known!

Life said, "As thou hast carved me, such am
    I."
Then Memory, like the nightjar on the pine,
And sightless Hope, a woodlark in night sky,
Joined notes of Death and Life till night's
    decline.   14
Of Death, of Life, those inwound notes are
    mine.   (1876)

LOVE IN THE VALLEY

Under yonder beech-tree single on the green-
    sward,
    Couched with her arms behind her golden
        head,
Knees and tresses folded to slip and ripple
    idly,
    Lies my young love sleeping in the shade.
Had I the heart to slide an arm beneath her,
    Press her parting lips as her waist I gather
        slow,   6
Waking in amazement she could not but em-
        brace me;
    Then would she hold me and never let me
        go?

.   .   .   .   .

Shy as the squirrel and wayward as the
        swallow,
    Swift as the swallow along the river's light
Circleting the surface to meet his mirrored
        winglets,   11
    Fleeter she seems in her stay than in her
        flight.
Shy as the squirrel that leaps among the
        pine-tops,
    Wayward as the swallow overhead at set
        of sun,
She whom I love is hard to catch and con-
        quer,   15
    Hard, but O the glory of the winning were
        she won!

When her mother tends her before the laugh-
        ing mirror,
    Tying up her laces, looping up her hair,
Often she thinks, were this wild thing wedded,

12. **nightjar**, the European goatsucker, a night bird similar
to the whippoorwill.

More love should I have, and much less
　　care.　20
When her mother tends her before the lighted
　　mirror,
　Loosening her laces, combing down her
　　curls,
.Often she thinks, were this wild thing wedded,
　　I should miss but one for many boys and
　　girls.

.　　　.　　　.　　　.

Heartless she is as the shadow in the meadows
　　Flying to the hills on a blue and breezy
　　noon.　26
No, she is athirst and drinking up her wonder;
　　Earth to her is young as the slip of the
　　new moon.
Deals she an unkindness, 'tis but her rapid
　　measure,
　Even as in a dance; and her smile can heal
　　no less;　30
Like the swinging May-cloud that pelts the
　　flowers with hailstones
　Off a sunny border, she was made to bruise
　　and bless.

Lovely are the curves of the white owl
　　sweeping
　Wavy in the dusk lit by one large star.
Lone on the fir-branch, his rattle-note un-
　　varied,　35
　Brooding o'er the gloom, spins the brown
　　evejar.
Darker grows the valley, more and more for-
　　getting;
　So were it with me if forgetting could be
　　willed.
Tell the grassy hollow that holds the bubbling
　　well-spring,
　Tell it to forget the source that keeps it
　　filled.　40

.　　　.　　　.　　　.

Stepping down the hill with her fair com-
　　panions,
　Arm in arm, all against the raying West,
Boldly she sings, to the merry tune she
　　marches,
　Brave is her shape, and sweeter unpos-
　　sessed.
Sweeter, for she is what my heart first
　　awaking　45
　Whispered the world was; morning light
　　is she.
Love that so desires would fain keep her
　　changeless;
　Fain would fling the net, and fain have her
　　free.

36. everjar, nightjar (see note on line 12, p. 609).

Happy, happy time, when the white star
　　hovers
　Low over dim fields fresh with bloomy dew,
Near the face of dawn, that draws athwart
　　the darkness,　51
　Threading it with color, like yewberries the
　　yew.
Thicker crowd the shades as the grave East
　　deepens
　Glowing, and with crimson a long cloud
　　swells.
Maiden still the morn is; and strange she is,
　　and secret;　55
　Strange her eyes; her cheeks are cold as
　　cold sea-shells.

.　　　.　　　.　　　.

Sunrays, leaning on our southern hills and
　　lighting
　Wild cloud-mountains that drag the hills
　　along,
Oft ends the day of your shifting brilliant
　　laughter
　Chill as a dull face frowning on a song.　60
Aye, but shows the Southwest a ripple-
　　feathered bosom
　Blown to silver while the clouds are shaken
　　and ascend,
Scaling the mid-heavens as they stream—there
　　comes a sunset
　Rich, deep like love in beauty without end.

When at dawn she sighs, and like an infant
　　to the window　65
　Turns grave eyes craving light, released
　　from dreams,
Beautiful she looks, like a white water-lily
　　Bursting out of bud in havens of the
　　streams.
When from bed she rises clothed from neck
　　to ankle
　In her long nightgown sweet as boughs of
　　May,　70
Beautiful she looks, like a tall garden lily
　　Pure from the night, and splendid for the
　　day.

.　　　.　　　.　　　.

Mother of the dews, dark eye-lashed twilight,
　　Low-lidded twilight, o'er the valley's brim,
Rounding on thy breast sings the dew-
　　delighted skylark,　75
　Clear as though the dewdrops had their
　　voice in him.
Hidden where the rose-flush drinks the ray-
　　less planet,
　Fountain-full he pours the spraying foun-
　　tain-showers.

77. rayless planet, the morning star bereft of its rays
by the dawn.

Let me hear her laughter, I would have her
ever
   Cool as dew in twilight, the lark above the
flowers. 80

All the girls are out with their baskets for
the primrose;
   Up lanes, woods through, they troop in
joyful bands.
My sweet leads; she knows not why, but now
she loiters,
   Eyes the bent anemones, and hangs her
hands.
Such a look will tell that the violets are
peeping, 85
   Coming the rose; and unaware a cry
Springs in her bosom for odors and for
color,
   Covert and the nightingale — she knows
not why.

.   .   .   .   .

Kerchiefed head and chin she darts between
her tulips,
   Streaming like a willow gray in arrowy
rain. 90
Some bend beaten cheek to gravel, and their
angel
   She will be; she lifts them, and on she
speeds again.
Black the driving raincloud breasts the iron
gateway;
   She is forth to cheer a neighbor lacking
mirth.
So when sky and grass met rolling dumb for
thunder 95
   Saw I once a white dove, sole light of earth.

Prim little scholars are the flowers of her
garden,
   Trained to stand in rows, and asking if
they please.
I might love them well but for loving more
the wild ones —
   O my wild ones! they tell me more than
these. 100
You, my wild one, you tell of honeyed field-
rose,
   Violet, blushing eglantine in life; and even
as they,
They by the wayside are earnest of your
goodness,
   You are of life's, on the banks that line
the way.

.   .   .   .   .

Peering at her chamber the white crowns the
red rose, 105
   Jasmine winds the porch with stars two
and three.

Parted is the window; she sleeps; the starry
jasmine
   Breathes a falling breath that carries
thoughts of me.
Sweeter unpossessed, have I said of her my
sweetest?
   Not while she sleeps — while she sleeps the
jasmine breathes, 110
Luring her to love; she sleeps; the starry
jasmine
   Bears me to her pillow under white rose-
wreaths.

Yeilow with birdfoot-trefoil are the grass-
glades;
   Yellow with cinquefoil of the dew-gray
leaf;
Yellow with stonecrop; the moss-mounds are
yellow; 115
   Blue-necked the wheat sways, yellowing to
the sheaf.
Green-yellow bursts from the copse the laughing yaffle;
   Sharp as a sickle is the edge of shade and
shine.
Earth in her heart laughs looking at the
heavens,
   Thinking of the harvest: I look and think
of mine. 120

.   .   .   .   .

This I may know: her dressing and undress-
ing
   Such a change of light shows as when the
skies in sport
Shift from cloud to moonlight; or edging over
thunder
   Slips a ray of sun; or sweeping into port
White sails furl; or on the ocean borders 125
   White sails lean along the waves leaping
green.
Visions of her shower before me, but from
eyesight
   Guarded she would be like the sun were
she seen.

Front door and back of the mossed old farm-
house
   Open with the morn; and in a breezy link
Freshly sparkles garden to stripe-shadowed
orchard, 131
   Green across a rill where on sand the min-
nows wink.
Busy in the grass the early sun of summer
   Swarms, and the blackbird's mellow flut-
ing notes

113. **birdfoot-trefoil,** a three-lobed flower or leaf resembling the foot of a bird. 114. **cinquefoil,** a plant having
leaves with five leaflets. 117. **yaffle,** the green woodpecker.
130. **link,** a part of a winding stream and its adjacent land.

Call my darling up with round and roguish
    challenge —   135
  Quaintest, richest carol of all the singing
    throats!

.   .   .   .   .

Cool was the woodside; cool as her white
    dairy
  Keeping sweet the cream-pan; and there
    the boys from school,
Cricketing below, rushed brown and red with
    sunshine;
  O the dark translucence of the deep-eyed
    cool!   140
Spying from the farm, herself she fetched a
    pitcher
  Full of milk, and tilted for each in turn
    the beak.
Then a little fellow, mouth up and on tiptoe,
  Said, "I will kiss you"; she laughed and
    leaned her cheek.

Doves of the fir-wood walling high our red
    roof   145
  Through the long noon coo, crooning
    through the coo.
Loose droop the leaves, and down the sleepy
    roadway
  Sometimes pipes a chaffinch; loose droops
    the blue.
Cows flap a slow tail knee-deep in the river,
  Breathless, given up to sun and gnat and
    fly.   150
Nowhere is she seen; and if I see her nowhere,
  Lightning may come, straight rains and
    tiger sky.

.   .   .   .   .

O the golden sheaf, the rustling treasure-
    armful!
  O the nutbrown tresses nodding interlaced!
O the treasure-tresses one another over   155
  Nodding! O the girdle slack about the
    waist!
Slain are the poppies that shot their random
    scarlet
  Quick amid the wheatears; wound about
    the waist,
Gathered, see these brides of Earth one blush
    of ripeness!
  O the nutbrown tresses nodding interlaced!

Large and smoky red the sun's cold disk
    drops,   161
  Clipped by naked hills, on violet shaded
    snow;
Eastward large and still lights up a bower of
    moonrise,
  Whence at her leisure steps the moon
    aglow.

Nightlong on black print-branches our beech-
    tree   165
  Gazes in this whiteness; nightlong could I.
Here may life on death or death on life be
    painted.
  Let me clasp her soul to know she cannot
    die!

.   .   .   .   .

Gossips count her faults; they scour a narrow
    chamber
  Where there is no window, read not heaven
    or her.   170
"When she was a tiny," one aged woman
    quavers,
  Plucks at my heart and leads me by the
    ear.
Faults she had once as she learned to run
    and tumbled;
  Faults of feature some see, beauty not
    complete.
Yet, good gossips, beauty that makes holy
  Earth and air, may have faults from head
    to feet.   176

Hither she comes; she comes to me; she
    lingers,
  Deepens her brown eyebrows, while in new
    surprise
High rise the lashes in wonder of a stranger;
  Yet am I the light and living of her eyes.
Something friends have told her fills her heart
    to brimming,   181
  Nets her in her blushes, and wounds her,
    and tames. —
Sure of her haven, O like a dove alighting,
  Arms up, she dropped; our souls were in
    our names.

.   .   .   .   .

Soon will she lie like a white-frost sunrise.
  Yellow oats and brown wheat, barley pale
    as rye,   186
Long since your sheaves have yielded to the
    thresher,
  Felt the girdle loosened, seen the tresses
    fly.
Soon will she lie like a blood-red sunset.
  Swift with the tomorrow, green-winged
    Spring!   190
Sing from the Southwest, bring her back the
    truants,
  Nightingale and swallow, song and dipping
    wing.

Soft new beech-leaves, up to beamy April
  Spreading bough on bough a primrose
    mountain, you

165. **print-branches**, shadows of the branches of the
beech-tree.

Lucid in the moon, raise lilies to the sky-
    fields, 195
  Youngest green transfused in silver shining
    through —
Fairer than the lily, than the wild white
    cherry;
  Fair as in image my seraph love appears
Borne to me by dreams when dawn is at my
    eyelids;
  Fair as in the flesh she swims to me on
    tears. 200

.   .   .   .   .

Could I find a place to be alone with heaven,
  I would speak my heart out; heaven is my
    need.
Every woodland tree is flushing like the dog-
    wood,
  Flashing like the whitebeam, swaying like
    the reed —
Flushing like the dogwood crimson in Octo-
    ber; 205
  Streaming like the flag-reed Southwest blown;
Flashing as in gusts the sudden-lighted white-
    beam.
  All seem to know what is for heaven alone.
                        (1851; 1878)

THE LARK ASCENDING

He rises and begins to round;
He drops the silver chain of sound,
Of many links without a break,
In chirrup, whistle, slur, and shake —
All intervolved and spreading wide, 5
Like water-dimples down a tide
Where ripple ripple overcurls
And eddy into eddy whirls;
A press of hurried notes that run
So fleet they scarce are more than one, 10
Yet changingly the trills repeat
And linger ringing while they fleet —
Sweet to the quick o' the ear, and dear
To her beyond the handmaid ear,
Who sits beside our inner springs, 15
Too often dry for this he brings,
Which seems the very jet of earth
At sight of sun, her music's mirth,
As up he wings the spiral stair,
A song of light, and pierces air 20
With fountain ardor, fountain play,
To reach the shining tops of day,
And drink in everything discerned,
An ecstasy to music turned —
Impelled by what his happy bill 25
Disperses; drinking, showering still,

Unthinking save that he may give
His voice the outlet, there to live
Renewed in endless notes of glee,
So thirsty of his voice is he, 30
For all to hear and all to know
That he is joy, awake, aglow —
The tumult of the heart to hear
Through pureness filtered crystal-clear—
And know the pleasure sprinkled bright 35
By simple singing of delight,
Shrill, irreflective, unrestrained,
Rapt, ringing, on the jet sustained
Without a break, without a fall,
Sweet-silvery, sheer lyrical, 40
Perennial, quavering up the chord
Like myriad dews of sunny sward
That trembling into fullness shine,
And sparkle dropping argentine;
Such wooing as the ear receives 45
From zephyr caught in choric leaves
Of aspens when their chattering net
Is flushed to white with shivers wet;
And such the water-spirit's chime
On mountain heights in mornings prime, 50
Too freshly sweet to seem excess,
Too animate to need a stress;
But wider over many heads
The starry voice ascending spreads,
Awakening, as it waxes thin, 55
The best in us to him akin;
And every face to watch him raised
Puts on the light of children praised —
So rich our human pleasure ripes
When sweetness on sincereness pipes, 60
Though naught be promised from the seas—
But only a soft-ruffling breeze
Sweep glittering on a still content,
Serenity in ravishment.

For singing till his heaven fills, 65
'Tis love of earth that he instills,
And ever winging up and up,
Our valley is his golden cup,
And he the wine which overflows
To lift us with him as he goes — 70
But not from earth is he divorced,
He joyfully to fly enforced.
The woods and brooks, the sheep and kine,
He is, the hills, the human line,
The meadows green, the fallows brown, 75
The dreams of labor in the town;
He sings the sap, the quickened veins;
The wedding song of sun and rains
He is, the dance of children, thanks
Of sowers, shout of primrose-banks, 80
And eye of violets while they breathe;
All these the circling song will wreathe,
And you shall hear the herb and tree,

---

204. **whitebeam**, a small tree with leaves white on the
underside.
The Lark Ascending. 14. **her**, the spirit of earth or
nature within us.

44. **argentine**, silver-like substance.

The better heart of men shall see,
Shall feel celestially — as long   85
As you crave nothing save the song.

Was never voice of ours could say
Our inmost in the sweetest way,
Like yonder voice aloft, and link
All hearers in the song they drink.   90
Our wisdom speaks from failing blood,
Our passion is too full in flood;
We want the key of his wild note
Of truthful in a tuneful throat,
The song seraphically free   95
Of taint of personality —
So pure that it salutes the suns,
The voice of one for millions,
In whom the millions rejoice
For giving their one spirit voice.   100

Yet men have we, whom we revere,
Now names — and men still housing here —
Whose lives, by many a battle-dint
Defaced, and grinding wheels on flint,
Yield substance, though they sing not, sweet
For song our highest heaven to greet;   106
Whom heavenly singing gives us new,
Enspheres them brilliant in our blue,
From firmest base to farthest leap,
Because their love of Earth is deep,   110
And they are warriors in accord
With life to serve, and pass reward —
So touching purest and so heard
In the brain's reflex of yon bird.
Wherefore their soul in me — or mine,   115
Through self-forgetfulness divine,
In them — that song aloft maintains,
To fill the sky and thrill the plains
With showerings drawn from human stores,
As he to silence nearer soars,   120
Extends the world at wings and dome,
More spacious making more our home,
Till lost on his aërial rings
In light — and then the fancy sings.
                              (*1881;* 1881)

LUCIFER IN STARLIGHT

On a starred night Prince Lucifer uprose.
Tired of his dark dominion, swung the fiend
Above the rolling ball, in cloud part screened,
Where sinners hugged their specter of repose.
Poor prey to his hot fit of pride were those. 5
And now upon his western wing he leaned,
Now his huge bulk o'er Afric's sands careened,
Now the black planet shadowed Arctic snows.

Soaring through wider zones that pricked his
      scars
With memory of the old revolt from Awe, 10
He reached a middle height, and at the stars,
Which are the brain of heaven, he looked, .
      and sank.
Around the ancient track marched, rank on
      rank,
The army of unalterable law.
                              (1883)

SENSE AND SPIRIT

The senses loving Earth or well or ill,
Raven yet more the riddle of our lot.
The mind is in their trammels, and lights not
By trimming fear-bred tales; nor does the will
To find in nature things which less may chill
An ardor that desires, unknowing what.
Till we conceive her living we go distraught,
At best but circle-windsails of a mill.
Seeing she lives, and of her joy of life
Creatively has given us blood and breath   10
For endless war and never wound unhealed,
The gloomy Wherefore of our battlefield
Solves in the Spirit, wrought of her through
      strife
To read her own and trust her down to death.
                              (1883)

THE WOODS OF WESTERMAIN

I

Enter these enchanted woods,
      You who dare.
Nothing harms beneath the leaves
More than waves a swimmer cleaves.
Toss your heart up with the lark,   5
Foot at peace with mouse and worm,
      Fair you fare.
Only at a dread of dark
Quaver, and they quit their form:
Thousand eyeballs under hoods   10
      Have you by the hair.
Enter these enchanted woods,
      You who dare.

---

96. **taint of personality**, egotism. 112. **pass**, do without. 114. **brain's reflex**, mind's reflection or interpretation. 122. **More . . . home**, extending our habitat.
Lucifer in Starlight. 2. **his dark dominion**, hell.

9. **scars**, those received in his battle with the angels and
in his fall through the regions of air with the rebel hosts.
Sense and Spirit. 4. **nor does the will.** The will does not
give us our true relation with Nature any more than do the
senses.
The Woods of Westermain. The woods, near Meredith's
home in Surrey, here represent the whole world of nature,
which man must "enter," i.e., learn to accept with love and
courage. The poem is Meredith's most important commentary on Darwinian evolution and the elements of blood,
brain, and spirit (line 353) that mark the human being.

II

Here the snake across your path
Stretches in his golden bath: 15
Mossy-footed squirrels leap
Soft as winnowing plumes of Sleep:
Yaffles on a chuckle skim
Low to laugh from branches dim:
Up the pine, where sits the star,   20
Rattles deep the moth-winged jar
Each has business of his own;
But should you distrust a tone,
   Then beware.
Shudder all the haunted roods,   25
All the eyeballs under hoods
   Shroud you in their glare.
Enter these enchanted woods,
   You who dare.

III

Open hither, open hence,   30
Scarce a bramble weaves a fence,
Where the strawberry runs red,
With white star-flower overhead;
Cumbered by dry twig and cone,
Shredded husks of seedlings flown,   35
Mine of mole and spotted flint:
Of dire wizardry no hint,
Save mayhap the print that shows
Hasty outward-tripping toes,
Heels to terror, on the mould.   40
These, the woods of Westermain,
Are as others to behold,
Rich of wreathing sun and rain;
Foliage lustreful around
Shadowed leagues of slumbering sound.   45
Wavy tree-tops, yellow whins,
Shelter eager minikins,
Myriads, free to peck and pipe:
Would you better? would you worse?
You with them may gather ripe   50
Pleasures flowing not from purse.
Quick and far as Colour flies
Taking the delighted eyes,
You of any well that springs
May unfold the heaven of things;   55
Have it homely and within,
And thereof its likeness win,
Will you so in soul's desire:
This do sages grant t' the lyre.
This is being bird and more,   60
More than glad musician this;
Granaries you will have a store
Past the world of woe and bliss;
Sharing still its bliss and woe;
Harnessed to its hungers, no.   65

On the throne Success usurps
You shall seat the joy you feel
Where a race of water chirps,
Twisting hues of flourished steel:
Or where light is caught in hoop   70
Up a clearing's leafy rise,
Where the crossing deerherds troop
Classic splendours, knightly dyes.
Or, where old-eyed oxen chew
Speculation with the cud,   75
Read their pool of vision through,
Back to hours when mind was mud;
Nigh the knot, which did untwine
Timelessly to drowsy suns;
Seeing Earth a slimy spine,   80
Heaven a space for winging tons.
Farther, deeper, may you read,
Have you sight for things afield,
Where peeps she, the Nurse of seed,
Cloaked, but in the peep revealed;   85
Showing a kind face and sweet:
Look you with the soul you see 't.
Glory narrowing to grace,
Grace to glory magnified,
Following that will you embrace   90
Close in arms or aëry wide.
Banished is the white Foam-born
Not from here, nor under ban
Phoebus lyrist, Phoebe's horn,
Pipings of the reedy Pan.   95
Loved of Earth of old they were,
Loving did interpret her;
And the sterner worship bars
None whom Song has made her stars.
You have seen the huntress moon   100
Radiantly facing dawn,
Dusky meads between them strewn
Glimmering like downy awn:
Argent Westward glows the hunt,
East the blush about to climb;   105
One another fair they front,
Transient, yet outshine the time;
Even as dewlight off the rose
In the mind a jewel sows.
Thus opposing grandeurs live   110
Here if Beauty be their dower:
Doth she of her spirit give,
Fleetingness will spare her flower.
This is in the tune we play,
Which no spring of strength would quell;   115
In subduing does not slay;
Guides the channel, guards the well:
Tempered holds the young blood-heat,
Yet through measured grave accord
Hears the heart of wildness beat   120
Like a centaur's hoof on sward.

18. **yaffles**, woodpeckers. 21. **jar**, nightjar, a bird.
46. **whins**, gorse plants. 47. **minikins**, tiny animals and
birds.

84. **Nurse of seed**, Mother Earth. 92. **Foam-born**,
Venus, Love goddess. 94. **Phoebus**, Apollo, god of the
sun and of poetry. **Phoebe**, moon goddess. 95. **Pan**, god of
nature. 103. **awn**, tip of grain, beard.

Drink the sense the notes infuse,
You a larger self will find:
Sweetest fellowship ensues
With the creatures of your kind.   125
Ay, and Love, if Love it be
Flaming over *I* and *ME*,
Love meet they who do not shove
Cravings in the van of Love.
Courtly dames are here to woo,   130
Knowing love if it be true.
Reverence the blossom-shoot
Fervently, they are the fruit.
Mark them stepping, hear them talk,
Goddess is no myth inane,   135
You will say of those who walk
In the woods of Westermain.
Waters that from throat and thigh
Dart the sun his arrows back;
Leaves that on a woodland sigh   140
Chat of secret things no lack;
Shadowy branch-leaves, waters clear,
Bare or veiled they move sincere;
Not by slavish terrors tripped;
Being anew in nature dipped,   145
Growths of what they step on, these;
With the roots the grace of trees.
Casket-breasts they give, nor hide,
For a tyrant's flattered pride,
Mind, which nourished not by light,   150
Lurks the shuffling trickster sprite:
Whereof are strange tales to tell;
Some in blood writ, tombed in hell.
Here the ancient battle ends,
Joining two astonished friends,   155
Who the kiss can give and take
With more warmth than in that world
Where the tiger claws the snake,
Snake her tiger clasps infurled,
And the issue of their fight   160
Peoples lands in snarling plight.
Here her splendid beast she leads
Silken-leashed and decked with weeds
Wild as he, but breathing faint
Sweetness of unfelt constraint.   165
Love, the great volcano, flings
Fires of lower Earth to sky;
Love, the sole permitted sings
Sovereignly of *ME* and *I*.
Bowers he has of sacred shade,   170
Spaces of superb parade,
Voiceful. . . . But bring you a note
Wrangling, howsoe'er remote,
Discords out of discord spin
Round and round derisive din: 175
Sudden will a pallor pant
Chill at screeches miscreant;
Owls or spectres, thick they flee;
Nightmare upon horror broods;
Hooded laughter, monkish glee,   180
    Gaps the vital air.

Enter these enchanted woods
    You who dare.

IV

You must love the light so well
That no darkness will seem fell.   185
Love it so you could accost
Fellowly a livid ghost.
Whish! the phantom wisps away,
Owns him smoke to cocks of day.
In your breast the light must burn   190
Fed of you, like corn in quern
Ever plumping while the wheel
Speeds the mill and drains the meal.
Light to light sees little strange,
Only features heavenly new;   195
Then you touch the nerve of Change,
Then of Earth you have the clue;
Then her two-sexed meanings melt
Through you, wed the thought and felt.
Sameness locks no scurfy pond   200
Here for Custom, crazy-fond:
Change is on the wing to bud
Rose in brain from rose in blood.
Wisdom throbbing shall you see
Central in complexity;   205
From her pasture 'mid the beasts
Rise to her ethereal feasts,
Not, though lightnings track your wit
Starward, scorning them you quit:
For be sure the bravest wing   210
Preens it in our common spring,
Thence along the vault to soar,
You with others, gathering more,
Glad of more, till you reject
Your proud title of elect,   215
Perilous even here while few
Roam the arched greenwood with you.
    Heed that snare.
Muffled by his cavern-cowl
Squats the scaly Dragon-fowl,   220
Who was lord ere light you drank,
And lest blood of knightly rank
Stream, let not your fair princess
Stray: he holds the leagues in stress,
    Watches keenly there.   225
Oft has he been riven; slain
Is no force in Westermain.
Wait, and we shall forge him curbs,
Put his fangs to uses, tame,
Teach him, quick as cunning herbs,   230
How to cure him sick and lame.
Much restricted, much enringed,
Much he frets, the hooked and winged,
    Never known to spare.
'Tis enough: the name of Sage   235
Hits no thing in nature, nought;
Man the least, save when grave Age

191. **quern**, small hand mill. 220. **Dragon-fowl**, i.e.,
egoism.

From yon Dragon guards his thought.
Eye him when you hearken dumb
To what words from Wisdom come.   240
When she says how few are by
Listening to her, eye his eye.
  Self, his name declare.
Him shall Change, transforming late,
Wonderously renovate.   245
Hug himself the creature may:
What he hugs is loathed decay.
Crying, slip thy scales, and slough!
Change will strip his armour off;
Make of him who was all maw,   250
Inly only thrilling-shrewd,
Such a servant as none saw
Through his days of dragonhood:
Days when growling o'er his bone,
Sharpened he for mine and thine;   255
Sensitive within alone;
Scaly as in clefts of pine.
Change. the strongest son of Life,
Has the Spirit here to wife.
Lo, their young of vivid breed   260
Bear the lights that onward speed,
Threading thickets, mounting glades,
Up the verdurous colonnades,
Round the fluttered curves, and down,
Out of sight of Earth's blue crown,   265
Whither, in her central space,
Spouts the Fount and Lure o' the chase.
Fount unresting, Lure divine!
There meet all: too late look most.
Fire in water hued as wine   270
Springs amid a shadowy host;
Circled: one close-headed mob,
Breathless, scanning divers heaps
Where a Heart begins to throb,
Where it ceases, slow, with leaps: 275
And 'tis very strange, 'tis said,
How you spy in each of them
Semblance of that Dragon red,
As the oak in bracken-stem.
And, 'tis said, how each and each: 280
Which commences, which subsides:
First my Dragon! doth beseech
Her who food for all provides.
And she answers with no sign;
Utters neither yea nor nay;   285
Fires the water hued as wine;
Kneads another spark in clay.
Terror is about her hid;
Silence of the thunders locked;
Lightnings lining the shut lid;   290
Fixity on quaking rocked.
Lo, you look at Flow and Drought
Interflashed and interwrought:
Ended is begun, begun
Ended, quick as torrents run.   295

267. **Fount and Lure**, love.

Young Impulsion spouts to sink;
Luridness and lustre link;
'Tis your come and go of breath;
Mirrored pants the Life, the Death;
Each of either reaped and sown: 300
Rosiest rosy wanes to crone.
See you so? your senses drift;
'Tis a shuttle weaving swift.
Look with spirit past the sense,
Spirit shines in permanence.   305
That is She, the view of whom
Is the dust within the tomb,
Is the inner blush above,
Look to loathe, or look to love;
Think her Lump, or know her Flame;   310
Dread her scourge, or read her aim;
Shoot your hungers from their nerve;
Or, in her example, serve.
Some have found her sitting grave;
Laughing, some; or, browed with sweat,   315
Hurling dust of fool and knave
In a hissing smithy's jet.
More it were not well to speak;
Burn to see, you need but seek.
Once beheld she gives the key   320
Airing every doorway, she;
Little can you stop or steer
Ere of her you are the seër,
On the surface she will witch,
Rendering Beauty yours, but gaze   325
Under, and the soul is rich
Past computing, past amaze.
Then is courage that endures
Even her awful tremble yours.
Then, the reflex of that Fount   330
Spied below, will Reason mount
Lordly and a quenchless force,
Lighting Pain to its mad source,
Scaring Fear till Fear escapes,
Shot through all its phantom shapes.   335
Then your spirit will perceive
Fleshly seed of fleshly sins;
Where the passions interweave,
How the serpent tangle spins
Of the sense of Earth misprised,   340
Brainlessly unrecognized;
She being Spirit in her clods,
Footway to the God of Gods.
Then for you are pleasures pure,
Sureties as the stars are sure: 345
Not the wanton beckoning flags
Which, of flattery and delight,
Wax to the grim Habit-Hags
Riding souls of men to night:
Pleasures that through blood run sane,   350
Quickening spirit from the brain.
Each of each in sequent birth,
Blood and brain and spirit, three
(Say the deepest gnomes of Earth),
Join for true felicity.   355

Are they parted, then expect
Some one sailing will be wrecked:
Separate hunting are they sped,
Scan the morsel coveted.
Earth that Triad is: she hides   360
Joy from him who that divides;
Showers it when the three are one
Glassing her in union.
Earth your haven, Earth your helm,
You command a double realm;   365
Labouring here to pay your debt,
Till your little sun shall set;
Leaving her the future task:
Loving her too well to ask.
Eglantine that climbs the yew,   370
She her darkest wreathes for those
Knowing her the Ever-new,
And themselves the kin o' the rose.
Life, the chisel, axe and sword,
Wield who have her depths explored: 375
Life, the dream, shall be their robe,
Large as air about the globe;
Life, the question, hear its cry
Echoed with concordant Why;
Life, the small self-dragon ramped,   380
Thrill for service to be stamped.
Ay, and over every height
Life for them shall wave a wand:
That, the last, where sits affright,
Homely shows the stream beyond.   385
Love the light and be its lynx,
You will track her and attain;
Read her as no cruel Sphinx
In the woods of Westermain.
Daily fresh the woods are ranged;   390
Glooms which otherwhere appal,
Sounded: here, their worths exchanged,
Urban joins with pastoral:
Little lost, save what may drop
Husk-like, and the mind preserves.   395
Natural overgrowths they lop,
Yet from nature neither swerves,
Trained or savage: for this cause:
Of our Earth they ply the laws,
Have in Earth their feeding root,   400
Mind of man and bent of brute.
Hear that song; both wild and ruled.
Hear it: is it wail or mirth?
Ordered, bubbled, quite unschooled?
None, and all: it springs of Earth.   405
O but hear it! 'tis the mind;
Mind that with deep Earth unites,
Round the solid trunk to wind
Rings of clasping parasites.
Music have you there to feed   410
Simplest and most soaring need.
Free to wind, and in desire
Winding, they to her attached
Feel the trunk a spring of fire,
And ascend to heights unmatched,   415

Whence the tidal world is viewed
As a sea of windy wheat,
Momently black, barren, rude;
Golden-brown, for harvest meet;
Dragon-reaped from folly-sown;   420
Bride-like to the sickle-blade:
Quick it varies, while the moan,
Moan of a sad creature strayed,
Chiefly is its voice. So flesh
Conjures tempest-flails to thresh   425
Good from worthless. Some clear lamps
Light it; more of dead marsh-damps.
Monster is it still, and blind,
Fit but to be led by Pain.
Glance we at the paths behind,   430
Fruitful sight has Westermain.
There we laboured, and in turn
Forward our blown lamps discern,
As you see on the dark deep
Far the loftier billows leap,   435
     Foam for beacon bear.
Hither, hither, if you will,
Drink instruction, or instil,
Run the woods like vernal sap,
Crying, hail to luminousness!   440
     But have care.
In yourself may lurk the trap:
On conditions they caress.
Here you meet the light invoked:
Here is never secret cloaked.   445
Doubt you with the monster's fry
All his orbit may exclude;
Are you of the stiff, the dry,
Cursing the not understood;
Grasp you with the monster's claws;   450
Govern with his truncheon-saws;
Hate, the shadow of a grain;
You are lost in Westermain:
Earthward swoops a vulture sun,
Nighted upon carrion: 455
Straightway venom winecups shout
Toasts to One whose eyes are out:
Flowers along the reeling floor
Drip henbane and hellebore:
Beauty, of her tresses shorn,   460
Shrieks as nature's maniac:
Hideousness on hoof and horn
Tumbles, yapping in her track:
Haggard Wisdom, stately once,
Leers fantastical and trips: 465
Allegory drums the sconce,
Impiousness nibblenips.
Imp that dances, imp that flits,
Imp o' the demon-growing girl,
Maddest! whirl with imp o' the pits   470
Round you, and with them you whirl

446. **monster,** the dragon of self as in I. 220.   451. **truncheon-saws,** oppressive precepts.   457. **One,** Death.   459. **henbane and hellebore,** poisonous herbs.   466. **drums the sconce,** taps on the skull.

Fast where pours the fountain-rout
Out of Him whose eyes are out:
Multitudes on multitudes,
Drenched in wallowing devilry: 475
And you ask where you may be,
  In what reek of a lair
Given to bones and ogre-broods:
  And they yell you Where.
Enter these enchanted woods,   480
  You who dare.   (1883)

WILLIAM MORRIS
(1834-1896)

THE DEFENCE OF GUENEVERE

But, knowing now that they would have her
  speak,
She threw her wet hair backward from her
  brow,
Her hand close to her mouth touching her
  cheek,

As though she had had there a shameful
  blow,
And feeling it shameful to feel aught but
  shame   5
All through her heart, yet felt her cheek
  burned so,

She must a little touch it; like one lame
She walked away from Gauwaine, with her
  head
Still lifted up; and on her cheek of flame

The tears dried quick; she stopped at last
  and said: 10
"O knights and lords, it seems but little skill
To talk of well-known things past now and
  dead.

"God wot I ought to say, I have done ill,
And pray you all forgiveness heartily!
Because you must be right, such great lords;
  still   15

"Listen — suppose your time were come to die,
And you were quite alone and very weak;
Yea, laid a-dying, while very mightily

"The wind was ruffling up the narrow streak
Of river through your broad lands running
  well;   20

Suppose a hush should come, then someone
  speak:

" 'One of these cloths is heaven, and one is
  hell;
Now choose one cloth forever — which they
  be,
I will not tell you; you must somehow tell

" 'Of your own strength and mightiness; here,
  see!'   25
Yea, yea, my lord, and you to ope your eyes,
At foot of your familiar bed to see

"A great God's angel standing, with such dyes,
Not known on earth, on his great wings, and
  hands,
Held out two ways, light from the inner skies

"Showing him well, and making his com-
  mands   31
Seem to be God's commands, moreover, too,
Holding within his hands the cloths on wands;

"And one of these strange choosing cloths
  was blue,
Wavy and long, and one cut short and red;
No man could tell the better of the two.   36

"After a shivering half-hour you said:
'God help! heaven's color, the blue'; and he
  said, 'hell.'
Perhaps you would then roll upon your bed,

"And cry to all good men that loved you well,
'Ah, Christ! if only I had known, known,
  known';   41
Launcelot went away, then I could tell,

"Like wisest man how all things would be,
  moan,
And roll and hurt myself, and long to die,
And yet fear much to die for what was sown.

"Nevertheless, you, O Sir Gauwaine, lie;   46
Whatever may have happened through these
  years,
God knows I speak truth, saying that you
  lie."

Her voice was low at first, being full of tears,
But as it cleared, it grew full loud and shrill,
Growing a windy shriek in all men's ears,   51

The Defence of Guenevere. See Critical Notes.
11. **skill**, reason, wisdom. 13. **wot**, knows.

46. **you . . . lie.** Gawaine is here presented as an accuser.
See Critical Note on title.

A ringing in their startled brains, until
She said that Gauwaine lied, then her voice
    sunk,
And her great eyes began again to fill,

Though still she stood right up, and never
    shrunk,   55
But spoke on bravely, glorious lady fair!
Whatever tears her full lips may have drunk,

She stood, and seemed to think, and wrung
    her hair,
Spoke out at last with no more trace of
    shame,
With passionate twisting of her body there: 60

"It chanced upon a day that Launcelot came
To dwell at Arthur's court — at Christmas-
    time
This happened; when the heralds sung his
    name,

"Son of King Ban of Benwick, seemed to
    chime
Along with all the bells that rang that day, 65
O'er the white roofs, with little change of
    rime.

"Christmas and whitened winter passed away,
And over me the April sunshine came,
Made very awful with black hail-clouds;
    yea,

"And in the summer I grew white with flame,
And bowed my head down; autumn, and the
    sick   71
Sure knowledge things would never be the
    same,

"However often spring might be most thick
Of blossoms and buds, smote on me, and I
    grew
Careless of most things, let the clock tick,
    tick,   75

"To my unhappy pulse, that beat right
    through
My eager body; while I laughed out loud,
And let my lips curl up at false or true,

"Seemed cold and shallow without any cloud.
Behold, my judges, then the cloths were
    brought;   80
While I was dizzied thus, old thoughts would
    crowd,

"Belonging to the time ere I was bought
By Arthur's great name and his little love;
Must I give up forever then, I thought,

80. **the cloths.** See lines 21 ff.

"That which I deemed would ever round me
    move   85
Glorifying all things; for a little word,
Scarce ever meant at all, must I now prove

"Stone-cold forever? Pray you, does the Lord
Will that all folks should be quite happy and
    good?
I love God now a little, if this cord   90

"Were broken, once for all what striving could
Make me love anything in earth or heaven?
So day by day it grew, as if one should

"Slip slowly down some path worn smooth
    and even,
Down to a cool sea on a summer day;   95
Yet still in slipping there was some small
    leaven

"Of stretched hands catching small stones by
    the way,
Until one surely reached the sea at last,
And felt strange new joy as the worn head
    lay

"Back, with the hair like sea-weed; yea, all
    past   100
Sweat of the forehead, dryness of the lips,
Washed utterly out by the dear waves o'er-
    cast,

"In the lone sea, far off from any ships!
Do I not know now of a day in spring?
No minute of that wild day ever slips   105

"From out my memory; I hear thrushes sing,
And wheresoever I may be, straightway
Thoughts of it all come up with most fresh
    sting.

"I was half mad with beauty on that day,
And went, without my ladies, all alone,   110
In a quiet garden walled round every way;

"I was right joyful of that wall of stone,
That shut the flowers and trees up with the
    sky,
And trebled all the beauty; to the bone —

"Yea, right through to my heart, grown very
    shy   115
With wary thoughts — it pierced, and made
    me glad,
Exceedingly glad, and I knew verily,

"A little thing just then had made me mad;
I dared not think, as I was wont to do,
Sometimes, upon my beauty; if I had   120

"Held out my long hand up against the blue,

And, looking on the tenderly darkened fingers,
Thought that by rights one ought to see quite
   through,

"There, see you, where the soft still light yet
   lingers,   124
Round by the edges; what should I have done,
If this had joined with yellow spotted singers,

"And startling green drawn upward by the
   sun?
But shouting, loosed out, see now! all my
   hair,
And trancedly stood watching the west wind
   run

"With faintest half-heard breathing sound —
   why there   130
I lose my head e'en now in doing this.
But shortly listen: In that garden fair

"Came Launcelot walking; this is true, the
   kiss
Wherewith we kissed in meeting that spring
   day,
I scarce dare talk of the remembered bliss,135

"When both our mouths went wandering in
   one way,
And aching sorely, met among the leaves;
Our hands, being left behind, strained far
   away.

"Never within a yard of my bright sleeves
Had Launcelot come before — and now so
   nigh!   140
After that day why is it Guenevere grieves?

"Nevertheless, you, O Sir Gauwaine, lie,
Whatever happened on through all those
   years —
God knows I speak truth, saying that you
   lie.   144

"Being such a lady, could I weep these tears
If this were true? A great queen such as I,
Having sinned this way, straight her con-
   science sears;

"And afterwards she liveth hatefully,
Slaying and poisoning — certes never weeps;
Gauwaine, be friends now, speak me lov-
   ingly.   150

"Do I not see how God's dear pity creeps
All through your frame, and trembles in your
   mouth?
Remember in what grave your mother sleeps,

"Buried in some place far down in the south,
Men are forgetting as I speak to you;   155
By her head, severed in that awful drouth

"Of pity that drew Agravaine's fell blow,
I pray your pity! let me not scream out
Forever after, when the shrill winds blow

"Through half your castle-locks! let me not
   shout   160
Forever after in the winter night
When you ride out alone! in battle-rout

"Let not my rusting tears make your sword
   light!
Ah! God of mercy, how he turns away!
So, ever must I dress me to the fight,   165

"So — let God's justice work! Gauwaine, I
   say,
See me hew down your proofs; yea, all men
   know,
Even as you said, how Mellyagraunce one
   day,

"One bitter day in *la Fausse Garde*, for so
All good knights held it after, saw —   170
Yea, sirs, by cursed unknightly outrage,
   though

"You, Gauwaine, held his word without a
   flaw,
This Mellyagraunce saw blood upon my
   bed —
Whose blood then pray you? is there any law

"To make a queen say why some spots of
   red   175
Lie on her coverlet? or will you say,
'Your hands are white, lady, as when you wed,

" 'Where did you bleed?' and must I stammer
   out — 'Nay,
I blush indeed, fair lord, only to rend
My sleeve up to my shoulder, where there
   lay   180

" ' A knife-point last night': so must I defend
The honor of the Lady Guenevere?
Not so, fair lords, even if the world should
   end

"This very day, and you were judges here
Instead of God. Did you see Mellyagraunce

---

126. **yellow spotted singers,** thrushes (line 106). 153.
your mother. According to Malory she was Morgawse,
Arthur's sister. She was slain by her son Sir Gaheris (not
Agravaine) when he found her faithless to her husband, King
Lot, in Orkney. (*Le Morte Darthur,* 10, 24.)

168. **Mellyagraunce.** See Critical Note on title. 169.
la Fausse Garde, the false prison. 171. **unknightly outrage.** Meliagrance had entered the chamber of Guenevere
before she was up.

When Launcelot stood by him? — what white
    fear   186

"Curdled his blood, and how his teeth did
    dance,
His side sink in? as my knight cried and said:
'Slayer of unarmed men, here is a chance!

" 'Setter of traps, I pray you guard your
    head;   190
By God, I am so glad to fight with you,
Stripper of ladies, that my hand feels lead

" 'For driving weight; hurrah now! draw and
    do,
For all my wounds are moving in my breast,
And I am getting mad with waiting so.' 195

"He struck his hands together o'er the beast,
Who fell down flat, and groveled at his feet,
And groaned at being slain so young. 'At
    least,'

"My knight said, 'Rise you, sir, who are so
    fleet
At catching ladies; half-armed will I fight, 200
My left side all uncovered!' Then, I weet,

"Up sprang Sir Mellyagraunce with great
    delight
Upon his knave's face; not until just then
Did I quite hate him, as I saw my knight

"Along the lists look to my stake and pen 205
With such a joyous smile, it made me sigh
From agony beneath my waist-chain, when

"The fight began, and to me they drew nigh;
Ever Sir Launcelot kept him on the right,
And traversed warily, and ever high   210

"And fast leapt caitiff's sword, until my
    knight
Sudden threw up his sword to his left hand,
Caught it, and swung it; that was all the
    fight,

"Except a spout of blood on the hot land;
For it was hottest summer; and I know   215
I wondered how the fire, while I should stand,

"And burn, against the heat, would quiver so,
Yards above my head; thus these matters
    went;
Which things were only warnings of the woe

"That fell on me. Yet Mellyagraunce was
    shent,   220
For Mellyagraunce had fought against the
    Lord;
Therefore, my lords, take heed lest you be
    blent

"With all his wickedness—say no rash word
Against me, being so beautiful; my eyes,
Wept all away to gray, may bring some sword

"To drown you in your blood; see my breast
    rise,   226
Like waves of purple sea, as here I stand;
And how my arms are moved in wonderful
    wise;

"Yea, also at my full heart's strong command,
See through my long throat how the words
    go up   230
In ripples to my mouth; how in my hand

"The shadow lies like wine within a cup
Of marvelously colored gold; yea, now
This little wind is rising, look you up,

"And wonder how the light is falling so   235
Within my moving tresses. Will you dare
When you have looked a little on my brow,

"To say this thing is vile? or will you care
For any plausible lies of cunning woof,
When you can see my face with no lie there

"Forever? Am I not a gracious proof?— 241
'But in your chamber Launcelot was found'—
Is there a good knight then would stand aloof,

"When a queen says with gentle queenly
    sound,
'O true as steel, come now and talk with
    me;   245
I love to see your step upon the ground

" 'Unwavering; also well I love to see
That gracious smile light up your face, and
    hear
Your wonderful words, that all mean verily

" 'The thing they seem to mean. Good
    friend, so dear   250
To me in everything, come here tonight,
Or else the hours will pass most dull and
    drear.

" 'If you come not, I fear this time I
    might

---

190. **Setter of traps.** See Critical Note on title.   201.
weet, observed, knew.   216-217. **while I should stand
And burn.** Upon the testimony of Meliagrance she was
sentenced to be burned. The appearance and victory of
Launcelot saved her.

220. **shent**, destroyed. 222. **blent**, blinded. 242. **But
. . . found.** See Critical Notes.

Get thinking overmuch of times gone by,
When I was young, and green hope was in
    sight;   255

" 'For no man cares now to know why I
    sigh;
And no man comes to sing me pleasant songs,
Nor any brings me the sweet flowers that lie

" 'So thick in the gardens; therefore one so
    longs
To see you, Launcelot, that we may be   260
Like children once again, free from all wrongs

" 'Just for one night.' Did he not come to
    me?
What thing could keep true Launcelot away
If I said, 'Come'? There was one less than
    three

"In my quiet room that night, and we were
    gay;   265
Till sudden I rose up, weak, pale, and sick,
Because a bawling broke our dream up; yea,

"I looked at Launcelot's face and could not
    speak,
For he looked helpless, too, for a little while;
Then I remember how I tried to shriek,   270

"And could not, but fell down; from tile to
    tile
The stones they threw up rattled o'er my
    head
And made me dizzier; till within a while

"My maids were all about me, and my head
On Launcelot's breast was being soothed
    away   275
From its white chattering, until Launcelot
    said . . .

"By God! I will not tell you more today—
Judge any way you will; what matters it?
You know quite well the story of that fray,

"How Launcelot stilled their bawling, the
    mad fit   280
That caught up Gauwaine, all, all, verily,
But just that which would save me; these
    things flit.

"Nevertheless, you, O Sir Gauwaine, lie;
Whatever may have happened these long
    years,
God knows I speak truth, saying that you
    lie!   285

"All I have said is truth, by Christ's dear
    tears."
She would not speak another word, but stood
Turned sideways, listening, like a man who
    hears

His brother's trumpet sounding through the
    wood
Of his foes' lances. She leaned eagerly,   290
And gave a slight spring sometimes, as she
    could

At last hear something really; joyfully
Her cheek grew crimson, as the headlong
    speed
Of the roan charger drew all men to see,   294
The knight who came was Launcelot at good
    need.   (1858)

RAPUNZEL

The Prince (*being in the wood near the tower
in the evening*)

I could not even think
  What made me weep that day
When out of the council-hall
  The courtiers passed away—

The Witch

Rapunzel, Rapunzel,   5
Let down your hair!

Rapunzel

Is it not true that every day
She climbeth up the same strange way,
Her scarlet cloak spread broad and gay,
  Over my golden hair?   10

The Prince

And left me there alone,
  To think on what they said:
"Thou art a king's own son,
  'Tis fit that thou should'st wed."

The Witch

Rapunzel, Rapunzel,   15
Let down your hair!

Rapunzel

When I undo the knotted mass,
Fathoms below the shadows pass
Over my hair along the grass.
  O my golden hair!   20

---

280. **mad fit.** Gawaine was not present. See Critical
Note on title. 282. **that . . . me,** her innocence.

291. **as,** as if. 295. **knight . . . need.** Launcelot and his
kinsmen rescued the Queen from the fire.
Rapunzel. This poem is based upon the story of Rapunzel
as told in *Grimms' Fairy Tales.* See Critical Notes.

The Prince

I put my armor on,
   Thinking on what they said:
"Thou art a king's own son,
   'Tis fit that thou should'st wed."

The Witch

   Rapunzel, Rapunzel,   25
   Let down your hair!

Rapunzel

See on the marble parapet
I lean my brow, strive to forget
That fathoms below my hair grows wet
   With the dew, my golden hair.   30

The Prince

I rode throughout the town,
   Men did not bow the head,
Though I was the king's own son;
   "He rides to dream," they said.

The Witch

   Rapunzel, Rapunzel,   35
   Wind up your hair!

Rapunzel

See, on the marble parapet
The faint red stains with tears are wet;
The long years pass, no help comes yet
   To free my golden hair.   40

The Prince

For leagues and leagues I rode,
   Till hot my armor grew,
Till underneath the leaves
   I felt the evening dew.

The Witch

   Rapunzel, Rapunzel,   45
   Weep through your hair!

Rapunzel

And yet—but I am growing old,
For want of love my heart is cold;
Years pass, the while I loose and fold
   The fathoms of my hair.   50

The Prince (in the morning)

I have heard tales of men, who in the night
   Saw paths of stars let down to earth from
      heaven,
Who followed them until they reached the
      light
   Wherein they dwell, whose sins are all for-
      given;

But who went backward when they saw the
      gate   55
   Of diamond, nor dared to enter in;
All their life long they were content to wait,
   Purging them patiently of every sin.

I must have had a dream of some such thing,
   And now am just awaking from that
      dream;   60
For even in gray dawn those strange words
      ring
   Through heart and brain, and still I see
      that gleam.

For in my dream at sunset-time I lay
   Beneath these beeches, mail and helmet off,
Right full of joy that I had come away   65
   From court; for I was patient of the scoff

That met me always there from day to day,
   From any knave or coward of them all;
I was content to live that wretched way;
   For truly till I left the council-hall,   70

And rode forth armed beneath the burning
      sun,
   My gleams of happiness were faint and
      few,
But then I saw my real life had begun,
   And that I should be strong, quite well I
      knew.

For I was riding out to look for love,   75
   Therefore the birds within the thickets
      sung;
Even in hot noontide, as I passed, above
   The elms o'erswayed with longing toward
      me hung.

Now some few fathoms from the place
      where I
   Lay in the beech-wood, was a tower fair, 80
The marble corners faint against the sky;
   And dreamily I wondered what lived there,

Because it seemed a dwelling for a queen,
   No belfry for the swinging of great bells;
No bolt or stone had ever crushed the green
   Shafts, amber and rose walls, no soot that
      tells   86

Of the Norse torches burning up the roofs,
   On the flower-carven marble could I see;
But rather on all sides I saw the proofs
   Of a great loneliness that sickened me, 90

55-56. **gate Of diamond.** In *Revelation*, 21, John sees
the New Jerusalem with twelve gates of pearl, and the walls
with twelve foundations "garnished with all manner of
precious stones." 87. **Norse torches**, a reference to the
burning of houses in the early raids of the Norsemen.

Making me feel a doubt that was not fear,
   Whether my whole life long had been a
      dream,
And I should wake up soon in some place,
    where
   The piled-up arms of the fighting angels
      gleam;

Not born as yet, but going to be born,   95
   No naked baby as I was at first,
But an arméd knight, whom fire, hate, and
    scorn
   Could turn from nothing; my heart almost
      burst

Beneath the beeches, as I lay a-dreaming,
   I tried so hard to read this riddle through,
To catch some golden cord that I saw gleam-
    ing   101
.   Like gossamer against the autumn blue.

But while I pondered these things, from the
    wood
   There came a black-haired woman, tall and
      bold,
Who strode straight up to where the tower
    stood,   105
And cried out shrilly words, whereon be-
    hold—

The Witch (*from the tower*)

   Rapunzel, Rapunzel,
   Let down your hair!

The Prince

Ah, Christ! it was no dream then, but there
    stood   109
(She comes again) a maiden passing fair,
Against the roof, with face turned to the wood,
   Bearing within her arms waves of her yel-
    low hair.

I read my riddle when I saw her stand,
   Poor love! her face quite pale against her
    hair,
Praying to all the leagues of empty land   115
   To save her from the woe she suffered there.

To think! they trod upon her golden hair
   In the witches' sabbaths; it was a delight
For these foul things, while she, with thin
    feet bare,
   Stood on the roof upon the winter night, 120

To plait her dear hair into many plaits,
   And then, while God's eye looked upon the
    thing,

---

118. **witches' sabbaths,** nocturnal gatherings of witches
and demons to concoct mischief. They participated in
various orgies under the leadership of Satan.

In the very likenesses of Devil's bats,
   Upon the ends of her long hair to swing.

And now she stood above the parapet,   125
   And, spreading out her arms, let her hair
    flow,
Beneath that veil her smooth white forehead
    set
   Upon the marble; more I do not know,

Because before my eyes a film of gold   129
   Floated, as now it floats. O unknown love,
Would that I could thy yellow stair behold,
   If still thou standest with lead roof above!

The Witch (*as she passes*)

   Is there any who will dare
   To climb up the yellow stair,
   Glorious Rapunzel's golden hair?   135

The Prince

If it would please God make you sing again,
   I think that I might very sweetly die,
My soul somehow reach heaven in joyous
    pain,
   My heavy body on the beech-nuts lie.

Now I remember; what a most strange year,
   Most strange and awful, in the beechen
    wood   141
I have passed now; I still have a faint fear
   It is a kind of dream not understood.

I have seen no one in this wood except
   The witch and her; have heard no human
    tones,   145
But when the witches' revelry has crept
   Between the very jointing of my bones.

Ah! I know now; I could not go away,
   But needs must stop to hear her sing that
    song
She always sings at dawning of the day. 150
   I am not happy here, for I am strong.

And every morning do I whet my sword,
   Yet Rapunzel still weeps within the tower,
And still God ties me down to the green
    sward,
   Because I cannot see the gold stair floating
    lower.   155

Rapunzel (*sings from the tower*)

My mother taught me prayers
To say when I had need;
I have so many cares,
That I can take no heed
Of many words in them;   160
But I remember this:
Christ, bring me to thy bliss.

Mary, maid withouten wem,
Keep me! I am lone, I wis,
Yet besides I have made this   165
By myself: *Give me a kiss,*
Dear God, dwelling up in heaven!
Also: *Send me a true knight,*
Lord Christ, with a steel sword, bright,
Broad and trenchant; yea, and seven   170
Spans from hilt to point, O Lord!
And let the handle of his sword
Be gold on silver, Lord in heaven!
Such a sword as I see gleam
Sometimes, when they let me dream.   175

 Yea, besides, I have made this:
Lord, give Mary a dear kiss,
And let gold Michael, who looked down,
When I was there, on Rouen town
From the spire, bring me that kiss   180
On a lily!   Lord, do this!

 These prayers on the dreadful nights
When the witches plait my hair,
And the fearfullest of sights
On the earth and in the air,   185
Will not let me close my eyes,
I murmur often, mixed with sighs,
That my weak heart will not hold
At some things that I behold.
Nay, not sighs, but quiet groans,   190
That swell out the little bones
Of my bosom; till a trance
God sends in middle of that dance,
And I behold the countenance
Of Michael, and can feel no more   195
The bitter east wind biting sore
My naked feet; can see no more
The crayfish on the leaden floor,
That mock with feeler and grim claw.

 Yea, often in that happy trance,   200
Beside the blessed countenance
Of golden Michael, on the spire
Glowing all crimson in the fire
Of sunset, I behold a face,
Which sometime, if God give me grace,   205
May kiss me in this very place.

   (Evening in the tower)
    Rapunzel

It grows half way between the dark and
  light;
 Love, we have been six hours here alone;
I fear that she will come before the night,
 And if she finds us thus we are undone. 210

    The Prince

Nay, draw a little nearer, that your breath
 May touch my lips, let my cheek feel your
  arm;
Now tell me, did you ever see a death,
 Or ever see a man take mortal harm!

    Rapunzel

Once came two knights and fought with
 swords below,   215
 And while they fought I scarce could look
  at all,
My head swam so, after a moaning low
 Drew my eyes down; I saw against the wall

One knight lean dead, bleeding from head
 and breast,
 Yet seemed it like a line of poppies red 220
In the golden twilight, as he took his rest,
 In the dusky time he scarcely seemed dead.

But the other, on his face six paces off,
 Lay moaning, and the old familiar name
He muttered through the grass, seemed like
 a scoff   225
 Of some lost soul remembering his past
  fame.

His helm all dinted lay beside him there,
 The visor-bars were twisted toward the
  face,
The crest, which was a lady very fair,
 Wrought wonderfully, was shifted from its
  place.   230

The showered mail-rings on the speed-walk
  lay;
 Perhaps my eyes were dazzled with the
  light
That blazed in the west, yet surely on that
  day
 Some crimson thing had changed the grass
  from bright

Pure green I love so. But the knight who
 died   235
 Lay there for days after the other went;
Until one day I heard a voice that cried,
 "Fair knight, I see Sir Robert we were sent

"To carry dead or living to the king."
 So the knights came and bore him straight
  away   240
On their lance truncheons, such a battered
  thing,
 His mother had not known him on that
  day,

---

163. **withouten wem,** without blemish. 164. **wis,** know.
178. **gold Michael,** a statue of the archangel Michael (*Reve-lation,* 12:7) on the spire of the cathedral in Rouen, a city in
northern France.

241. **lance truncheons,** shafts of spears.

But for his helm-crest, a gold lady fair
Wrought wonderfully.

The Prince

Ah, they were brothers then,
And often rode together, doubtless where 245
  The swords were thickest, and were loyal
    men,

Until they fell in these same evil dreams.

Rapunzel

Yea, love; but shall we not depart from
  hence?
The white moon groweth golden fast, and
  gleams
  Between the aspen stems; I fear—and yet
    a sense   250

Of fluttering victory comes over me,
  That will not let me fear aright; my heart—
Feel how it beats, love, strives to get to
  thee—
  I breathe so fast that my lips need must
    part;

Your breath swims round my mouth, but
  let us go.   255

The Prince

I, Sebald, also, pluck from off the staff
The crimson banner, let it lie below,
  Above it in the wind let grasses laugh.

Now let us go, love, down the winding stair,
  With fingers intertwined; aye, feel my
    sword!   260
I wrought it long ago, with golden hair
  Flowing about the hilts, because a word,

Sung by a minstrel old, had set me dreaming
  Of a sweet bowed-down face with yellow
    hair;
Betwixt green leaves I used to see it gleam-
  ing,   265
  A half smile on the lips, though lines of
    care

Had sunk the cheeks, and made the great
  eyes hollow;
  What other work in all the world had I,
But through all turns of fate that face to
  follow?
  But wars and business kept me there to
    die.   270

O child, I should have slain my brother, too,
  My brother, Love, lain moaning in the
    grass,

Had I not ridden out to look for you,
  When I had watched the gilded courtiers
    pass

From the golden hall. But it is strange your
  name   275
Is not the same the minstrel sung of yore;
You called it Rapunzel, 'tis not the name.
  See, love, the stems shine through the open
    door.

(Morning in the woods)
Rapunzel

O Love! me and my unknown name you have
  well won;
  The witch's name was Rapunzel; eh! not
    so sweet?   280
No!—but is this real grass, love, that I tread
  upon?
  What call they these blue flowers that lean
    across my feet?

The Prince

Dip down your dear face in the dewy grass,
  O love!
  And ever let the sweet slim harebells,
    tenderly hung,
Kiss both your parted lips; and I will hang
  above,   285
  And try to sing that song the dreamy
    harper sung.

He sings

'Twixt the sunlight and the shade
Float up memories of my maid,
  God, remember Guendolen!

Gold or gems she did not wear,   290
But her yellow rippled hair,
  Like a veil, hid Guendolen!

'Twixt the sunlight and the shade,
My rough hands so strangely made,
  Folded Golden Guendolen;   **295**

Hands used to grip the sword-hilt hard,
Framed her face, while on the sward;
  Tears fell down from Guendolen.

Guendolen now speaks no word,
Hands fold around about the sword,   300
  Now no more of Guendolen.

Only 'twixt the light and shade
Floating memories of my maid
  Make me pray for Guendolen.

287. **'Twixt the sunlight**, etc. This song was first published in 1856 under the title of *Hands*.

Guendolen

I kiss thee, new-found name; but I will never
　　go;　　　　　　　　　　　　　　　　305
　　Your hands need never grip the hammered
　　　　sword again
But all my golden hair shall ever round you
　　flow,
　　Between the light and shade from Golden
　　　　Guendolen.

(Afterwards, in the Palace)
King Sebald

I took my armor off,
　　Put on king's robes of gold;　　　　310
Over her kirtle green
　　The gold fell fold on fold.

The Witch (out of hell)

　　Guendolen! Guendolen!
　　One lock of hair!

Guendolen

I am so glad, for every day　　　　　315
He kisses me much the same way
　　As in the tower; under the sway
　　Of all my golden hair.

King Sebald

We rode throughout the town,
　　A gold crown on my head,　　　　　320
Through all the gold-hung streets,
　　"Praise God!" the people said.

The Witch

　　Guendolen! Guendolen!
　　Lend me your hair!

Guendolen

Verily, I seem like one　　　　　　　325
Who, when day is almost done,
　　Through a thick wood meets the sun
　　That blazes in her hair.

King Sebald

Yea, at the palace gates,
　　"Praise God!" the great knights said,　330
"For Sebald the high king,
　　And the lady's golden head."

The Witch

　　Woe is me! Guendolen
　　Sweeps back her hair.

Guendolen

Nothing wretched now, no screams;　　335
I was unhappy once in dreams,
　　And even now a harsh voice seems
　　To hang about my hair.

The Witch

WOE! THAT ANY MAN COULD DARE
To CLIMB UP THE YELLOW STAIR,　　340
GLORIOUS GUENDOLEN'S GOLDEN HAIR.

(1858)

CONCERNING GEFFRAY TESTE NOIRE

And if you meet the Canon of Chimay,
　　As going to Ortaise you well may do,
Greet him from John of Castel Neuf, and say
　　All that I tell you, for all this is true.

This Geffray Teste Noire was a Gascon
　　thief,　　　　　　　　　　　　　　5
　　Who, under shadow of the English name,
Pilled all such towns and countries as were
　　lief
　　To King Charles and St. Dennis; thought
　　　　it blame

If anything escaped him; so my lord,
　　The Duke of Berry, sent Sir John Bonne
　　　　Lance,　　　　　　　　　　　　10
And other knights, good players with the
　　sword,
　　To check this thief, and give the land a
　　　　chance.

Therefore we set out bastides round the
　　tower
　　That Geffray held, the strong thief! like a
　　　　king,　　　　　　　　　　　　14
High perched upon the rock of Ventadour,
　　Hopelessly strong by Christ! It was mid
　　　　spring

When first I joined the little army there
　　With ten good spears. Auvergne is hot;
　　　　each day
We sweated, armed before the barrier;
　　Good feats of arms were done there often
　　　　—eh?　　　　　　　　　　　　20

Concerning Geffray Teste Noire. Geffray with the Black
Head was a freebooter from the province of Gascony, in
southern France, during the period of 1375-88. His stronghold
was Ventadour (line 15), a castle in the province of Auvergne.
The poem is addressed to a man named Alleyne (line 27) by
John of Newcastle (line 3), who, with Sir John of the Good
Lance (line 10), Aldovrand (line 90), and other warriors, took
part in the attack upon Geffray's band. Geffray appears
in the *Chronicles* of Jean Froissart (1337-1410?), the famous
French historian and poet, Volume 1, Chapter 345; Volume 2,
Chapters 147-148.
　1. **Canon of Chimay,** Froissart. Chimay is a town in
Belgium near the French border. 2. **Ortaise,** the name of
the house of the Earl of Foiz and Béarn, a favorite gathering
place of knights, in the province of Béarn, in southern France.
7. **Pilled,** pillaged, plundered. **lief,** dear. 8. **King Charles,**
Charles V of France (1337-80). **St. Dennis,** the first bishop
of Paris and the patron saint of France (3d century). 10.
Duke of Berry, Jean de France (1340-1416), Count of
Poictiers. He was the son of John II, king of France (1350-
64), and the King's lieutenant in southern France. 13. **bastides,** temporary huts or towers erected for besieging purposes.

Your brother was slain there? I mind me
    now,
  A right good man-at-arms, God pardon
    him!
I think 'twas Geffray smote him on the
    brow
  With some spiked ax, and while he tottered,
    dim

About the eyes, the spear of Alleyne Roux 25
  Slipped through his camaille and his
    throat; well, well!
Alleyne is paid now; your name Alleyne too?
  Mary! how strange—but this tale I would
    tell—

For spite of all our bastides, damned Black-
    head
  Would ride abroad whene'er he chose to
    ride— 30
We could not stop him; many a burgher
    bled
  Dear gold all around his girdle; far and
    wide

The villaynes dwelt in utter misery
  'Twixt us and thief Sir Geffray; hauled this
    way
By Sir Bonne Lance at one time, he gone
    by, 35
  Down comes this Teste Noire on another
    day.

And therefore they dig up the stone, grind
    corn,
  Hew wood, draw water—yea, they lived, in
    short,
As I said just now, utterly forlorn,
  Till this our knave and Blackhead was out-
    fought. 40

So Bonne Lance fretted, thinking of some
    trap
  Day after day, till on a time he said:
"John of Newcastle, if we have good hap,
  We catch our thief in two days." "How?"
    I said.

"Why, sir, today he rideth out again, 45
  Hoping to take well certain sumpter mules
From Carcassonne, going with little train,
  Because, forsooth, he thinketh us mere
    fools;

"But if we set an ambush in some wood,
  He is but dead; so, sir, take thirty spears 50

To Verville forest, if it seem you good."
  Then felt I like the horse in Job, who hears

The dancing trumpet sound, and we went
    forth;
  And my red lion on the spear-head flapped,
As faster than the cool wind we rode north, 55
  Toward the wood of Verville; thus it
    happed.

We rode a soft space on that day while spies
  Got news about Sir Geffray; the red wine
Under the roadside bush was clear; the flies,
  The dragon-flies I mind me most, did
    shine 60

In brighter arms than ever I put on;
  So—"Geffray," said our spies, "would pass
    that way
Next day at sundown"; then he must be won;
  And so we entered Verville wood next day,

In the afternoon; through it the highway
    runs, 65
'Twixt copses of green hazel, very thick,
And underneath, with glimmering of suns,
  The primroses are happy; the dews lick

The soft green moss. "Put cloths about your
    arms
  Lest they should glitter; surely they will
    go 70
In a long thin line, watchful for alarms,
  With all their carriages of booty, so—

"Lay down my pennon in the grass—Lord
    God!
  What have we lying here? will they be cold,
I wonder, being so bare, above the sod, 75
  Instead of under? This was a knight, too,
    fold

"Lying on fold of ancient rusted mail;
  No plate at all, gold rowels to the spurs,
And see the quiet gleam of turquoise pale
  Along the ceinture; but the long time
    blurs 80

"Even the tinder of his coat to naught,
  Except these scraps of leather; see how
    white
The skull is, loose within the coif! He fought
  A good fight, maybe, ere he was slain quite.

---

25. **Alleyne Roux**, a nephew of Geffray. 26. **camaille**, a
piece of armor protecting the neck and shoulders. 33. **villaynes**, peasants. 46. **sumpter mules**, pack mules. 47.
Carcassonne, a manufacturing city in southern France.

52. **horse in Job.** *Job*, 39:19-25.—"He paweth in the
valley, and rejoiceth in his strength; he goeth on to meet the
armed men. He mocketh at fear, and is not affrighted;
neither turneth he back from the sword" (verses 21-22). 73.
pennon, banner. 80. **ceinture**, girdle, belt. 81. **tinder of
his coat**, the inflammable fabric of his coat. 83. **coif**, a
defensive skullcap made of iron.

"No armor on the legs, too; strange in faith—
A little skeleton for a knight though—ah! 86
This one is bigger; truly without scathe
His enemies escaped not—ribs driven out
far—

"That must have reached the heart, I doubt
—how now,
What say you, Aldovrand—a woman?
why?" 90
"Under the coif a gold wreath on the brow,
Yea, see the hair not gone to powder, lie,

"Golden, no doubt, once—yea, and very
small—
This for a knight; but for a dame, my lord,
These loose-hung bones seem shapely still,
and tall— 95
Didst ever see a woman's bones, my lord?"

Often, God help me! I remember when
I was a simple boy, fifteen years old,
The Jacquerie froze up the blood of men
With their fell deeds, not fit now to be
told. 100

God help again! we entered Beauvais town,
Slaying them fast, whereto I helped, mere
boy
As I was then; we gentles cut them down,
These burners and defilers, with great joy.

Reason for that, too, in the great church
there 105
These fiends had lit a fire, that soon went
out,
The church at Beauvais being so great and
fair—
My father, who was by me, gave a shout

Between a beast's howl and a woman's
scream,
Then, panting, chuckled to me: "John,
look! look! 110
Count the dames' skeletons!" From some
bad dream
Like a man just awaked, my father shook;

And I, being faint with smelling the burnt
bones,
And very hot with fighting down the street,
And sick of such a life, fell down; with
groans 115
My head went weakly nodding to my
feet.—

—An arrow had gone through her tender
throat,

And her right wrist was broken; then I saw
The reason why she had on that warcoat—
Their story came out clear without a
flaw; 120

For when he knew that they were being waylaid,
He threw it over her, yea, hood and all;
Whereby he was much hacked, while they
were stayed
By those their murderers; many an one
did fall

Beneath his arm, no doubt, so that he cleared
Their circle, bore his death-wound out of
it; 126
But as they rode, some archer least afeared
Drew a strong bow, and thereby she was
hit.

Still as he rode he knew not she was dead—
Thought her but fainted from her broken
wrist, 130
He bound with his great leathern belt—she
bled?
Who knows! he bled too; neither was there
missed

The beating of her heart, his heart beat well
For both of them, till here, within this
wood,
He died scarce sorry; easy this to tell; 135
After these years the flowers forget their
blood.—

How could it be? Never before that day,
However much a soldier I might be,
Could I look on a skeleton and say 139
I care not for it, shudder not—now see,

Over those bones I sat and pored for hours,
And thought, and dreamed, and still I
scarce could see
The small white bones that lay upon the
flowers,
But evermore I saw the lady; she

With her dear gentle walking leading in, 145
By a chain of silver twined about her
wrists,
Her loving knight, mounted and armed to win
Great honor for her, fighting in the lists.

O most pale face, that brings such joy and
sorrow
Into men's hearts—yea, too, so piercing
sharp 150
That joy is, that it marcheth nigh to sorrow
Forever—like an overwinded harp.

Your face must hurt me always; pray you
now,

99. The Jacquerie, a revolt of the French peasants
against the nobles in 1358. 101. Beauvais, an important
city in northern France. 117. An arrow, etc. This line
connects with line 96.

Doth it not hurt you too? seemeth some
   pain
To hold you always, pain to hold your
   brow   155
So smooth, unwrinkled ever; yea, again,

Your long eyes where the lids seem like to
   drop,
Would you not, lady, were they shut fast
   feel
Far merrier?   There so high they will not
   stop,
They are most sly to glide forth and to
   steal   160

Into my heart; *I kiss their soft lids there,*
And in green garden scarce can stop my lips
From wandering on your face, but that your
   hair
Falls down and tangles me, back my face
   slips.

Or say your mouth—I saw you drink red
   wine   165
Once at a feast; how slowly it sank in,
As though you feared that some wild fate
   might twine
Within that cup, and slay you for a sin.

And when you talk your lips do arch and
   move   169
In such wise that a language new I know
Besides their sound; they quiver, too, with
   love
When you are standing silent; know this,
   too,

I saw you kissing once, like a curved sword
   That bites with all its edge, did your lips
   lie,
Curled gently, slowly, long time could afford
   For caught-up breathings; like a dying
   sigh   176

They gathered up their lines and went away,
   And still kept twitching with a sort of
   smile,
As likely to be weeping presently —
   Your hands, too — how I watched them
   all the while!   180

"Cry out St. Peter now," quoth Aldovrand;
   I cried, "St. Peter," broke out from the
   wood
With all my spears; we met them hand to
   hand,
   And shortly slew them; natheless, by the
   rood, .

We caught not Blackhead then, or any day;
   Months after that he died at last in bed, 186

From a wound picked up at a barrier-fray;
   That same year's end a steel bolt in the
   head,

And much bad living killed Teste Noire at
   last;   189
John Froissart knoweth he is dead by now,
No doubt, but knoweth not this tale just past;
   Perchance then you can tell him what I
   show.

In my new castle, down beside the Eure,
   There is a little chapel of squared stone,
Painted inside and out; in green nook pure 195
   There did I lay them, every wearied bone;

And over it they lay, with stone-white hands
   Clasped fast together, hair made bright
   with gold
This Jaques Picard, known through many
   lands,
   Wrought cunningly; he's dead now — I am
   old.   200
                   (1858)

THE GILLYFLOWER OF GOLD

A golden gillyflower today
I wore upon my helm alway,
And won the prize of this tourney.
   Hah! hah! la belle jaune giroflée.

However well Sir Giles might sit,   5
His sun was weak to wither it;
Lord Miles's blood was dew on it.
   Hah! hah! la belle jaune giroflée.

Although my spear in splinters flew,
From John's steel-coat, my eye was true; 10
I wheeled about, and cried for you,
   Hah! hah! la belle jaune giroflée.

Yea, do not doubt my heart was good,
Though my sword flew like rotten wood,
To shout, although I scarcely stood,   15
   Hah! hah! la belle jaune giroflée.

My hand was steady too, to take
My ax from round my neck, and break
John's steel-coat up for my love's sake.
   Hah! hah! la belle jaune giroflée —   20

When I stood in my tent again,
Arming afresh, I felt a pain
Take hold of me, I was so fain —
   Hah! hah! la belle jaune giroflée —

193. **the Eure,** a river in northern France; it empties into
the Seine. 199. **Jaques Picard,** an imaginary sculptor.
   The Gillyflower of Gold. 4. **la belle jaune giroflée,** the
beautiful yellow gillyflower.

To hear *Honneur aux fils des preux!*   25
Right in my ears again, and shew
The gillyflower blossomed new.
  Hah! hah! la belle jaune giroflée.

The Sieur Guillaume against me came,
His tabard bore three points of flame   30
From a red heart; with little blame —
  Hah! hah! la belle jaune giroflée —

Our tough spears crackled up like straw;
He was the first to turn and draw
His sword, that had nor speck nor flaw;   35
  Hah! hah! la belle jaune giroflée.

But I felt weaker than a maid,
And my brain, dizzied and afraid,
Within my helm a fierce tune played,
  Hah! hah! la belle jaune giroflée,   40

Until I thought of your dear head,
Bowed to the gillyflower bed,
The yellow flowers stained with red;
  Hah! hah! la belle jaune giroflée.

Crash! how the swords met — *giroflée!*   45
The fierce tune in my helm would play,
La belle! la belle! jaune giroflée!
  Hah! hah! la belle jaune giroflée.

Once more the great swords met again;
"*La belle! la belle!*" but who fell then?   50
Le Sieur Guillaume, who struck down ten;
  Hah! hah! la belle jaune giroflée.

And as with mazed and unarmed face
Toward my own crown and the Queen's place,
They led me at a gentle pace —   55
  Hah! hah! la belle jaune giroflée —

I almost saw your quiet head
Bowed o'er the gillyflower bed,
The yellow flowers stained with red.
  Hah! hah! la belle jaune giroflée.   60
                    (1858)

SHAMEFUL DEATH

There were four of us about that bed:
  The mass-priest knelt at the side,
I and his mother stood at the head,
  Over his feet lay the bride;
We were quite sure that he was dead,   5
  Though his eyes were open wide.

He did not die in the night,
  He did not die in the day,
But in the morning twilight
  His spirit passed away,   10
When neither sun nor moon was bright,
  And the trees were merely gray.

He was not slain with the sword,
  Knight's ax, or the knightly spear,
Yet spoke he never a word   15
  After he came in here;
I cut away the cord
  From the neck of my brother dear.

He did not strike one blow,
  For the recreants came behind,   20
In a place where the hornbeams grow,
  A path right hard to find,
For the hornbeam boughs swing so
  That the twilight makes it blind.

They lighted a great torch then,   25
  When his arms were pinioned fast,
Sir John the knight of the Fen,
  Sir Guy of the Dolorous Blast,
With knights threescore and ten,
  Hung brave Lord Hugh at last.   30

I am threescore and ten,
  And my hair is all turned gray,
But I met Sir John of the Fen,
  Long ago on a summer day,
And am glad to think of the moment when 35
  I took his life away.

I am threescore and ten,
  And my strength is mostly passed,
But long ago I and my men,
  When the sky was overcast,   40
And the smoke rolled over the reeds of the fen,
  Slew Guy of the Dolorous Blast.

And now, knights all of you,
  I pray you pray for Sir Hugh,
A good knight and a true,   45
  And for Alice, his wife, pray too.   (1858)

THE EVE OF CRÉCY

Gold on her head, and gold on her feet,
And gold where the hems of her kirtle meet,
And a golden girdle round my sweet;
  Ah! qu'elle est belle La Marguerite.

21. **hornbeams,** trees with smooth gray bark and leaves resembling those of the beech.
  The Eve of Crécy. Crécy is a village in northern France, the scene of a famous battle won by the English over the French in 1346. The poem is spoken by a French knight (Sir Lambert of the Wood, line 18), as he muses before the battle on what the chance of victory may bring him.
  4. **qu'elle est belle La Marguerite,** how beautiful is Margaret.

25. **Honneur . . . preux,** honor to the sons of valiant knights. 30. **tabard,** a kind of cloak or mantle worn by knights. 31. **blame,** damage.
  Shameful Death. 2. **mass-priest,** a priest whose special duty was to say mass for the dead.

Margaret's maids are fair to see,   5
Freshly dressed and pleasantly;
Margaret's hair falls down to her knee;
    Ah! qu'elle est belle La Marguerite.

If I were rich I would kiss her feet;
I would kiss the place where the gold hems
    meet,   10
And the golden kirtle round my sweet —
    Ah! qu'elle est belle La Marguerite.

Ah me! I have never touched her hand;
When the arrière-ban goes through the land,
Six basnets under my pennon stand;   15
    Ah! qu'elle est belle La Marguerite.

And many an one grins under his hood:
Sir Lambert du Bois, with all his men good,
Has neither food nor firewood;
    Ah! qu'elle est belle La Marguerite.   20

If I were rich I would kiss her feet,
And the golden girdle of my sweet,
And thereabouts where the gold hems meet;
    Ah! qu'elle est belle La Marguerite.

Yet even now it is good to think,   25
While my poor varlets grumble and drink
In my desolate hall, where the fires sink —
    Ah! qu'elle est belle La Marguerite —

Of Margaret sitting glorious there,
In glory of gold and glory of hair,   30
And glory of glorious face most fair;
    Ah! qu'elle est belle La Marguerite.

Likewise tonight I make good cheer,
Because this battle draweth near;
For what have I to lose or fear?   35
    Ah! qu'elle est belle La Marguerite.

For, look you, my horse is good to prance
A right fair measure in this war-dance
Before the eyes of Philip of France;
    Ah! qu'elle est belle La Marguerite.   40

And sometime it may hap, perdie,
While my new towers stand up three and
    three,
And my hall gets painted fair to see —
    Ah! qu'elle est belle La Marguerite —

That folks may say: Times change, by the
    rood,   45
For Lambert, banneret of the wood,

Has heaps of food and firewood;
    Ah! qu'elle est belle La Marguerite.

And wonderful eyes, too, under the hood
Of a damsel of right noble blood.   50
St. Ives, for Lambert of the Wood!
    Ah! qu'elle est belle La Marguerite. (1858)

THE SAILING OF THE SWORD

Across the empty garden-beds,
    When the Sword went out to sea,
I scarcely saw my sisters' heads
    Bowed each beside a tree.
I could not see the castle-leads,   5
    When the Sword went out to sea.

Alicia wore a scarlet gown,
    When the Sword went out to sea,
But Ursula's was russet brown;
    For the mist we could not see   10
The scarlet roofs of the good town,
    When the Sword went out to sea.

Green holly in Alicia's hand,
    When the Sword went out to sea;
With sear oak-leaves did Ursula stand;   15
    O! yet alas for me!
I did but bear a peeled white wand,
    When the Sword went out to sea.

Oh, russet brown and scarlet bright,
    When the Sword went out to sea,   20
My sisters wore; I wore but white.
    Red, brown, and white are three;
Three damozels; each had a knight,
    When the Sword went out to sea.

Sir Robert shouted loud, and said,   25
    When the Sword went out to sea,
"Alicia, while I see thy head,
    What shall I bring for thee?"
"Oh, my sweet lord, a ruby red —"
    The Sword went out to sea.   30

Sir Miles said, while the sails hung down,
    When the Sword went out to sea,
"Oh, Ursula! while I see the town,
    What shall I bring for thee?"
"Dear knight, bring back a falcon brown" —
    The Sword went out to sea.   36

But my Roland, no word he said
    When the Sword went out to sea,
But only turned away his head —

---

14. **arrière-ban**, a proclamation calling men to arms; also,
a body of vassals called to arms. 15. **basnets**, light steel
helmets. **pennon**, banner. 39. **Philip of France**, Philip
VI, king of France (1328-50). 41. **perdie**, a French oath,
par Dieu, meaning *by God*. 46. **banneret**, a knight who could
lead vassals into the field under his own banner.

51. **St. Ives**, the patron saint of lawyers (died 1303). The
name is used here as a battle-cry.
The Sailing of the Sword. 5. **castle-leads**, leaden roofs of
the castle.

A quick shriek came from me: 40
"Come back, dear lord, to your white maid"—
  The Sword went out to sea.

The hot sun bit the garden-beds,
  When the Sword came back from sea;
Beneath an apple-tree our heads   45
  Stretched out toward the sea;
Gray gleamed the thirsty castle-leads,
  When the Sword came back from sea.

Lord Robert brought a ruby red,
  When the Sword came back from sea;   50
He kissed Alicia on the head —
  "I am come back to thee;
'Tis time, sweet love, that we were wed,
  Now the Sword is back from sea!"

Sir Miles he bore a falcon brown,   55
  When the Sword came back from sea;
His arms went round tall Ursula's gown —
  "What joy, O love, but thee?
Let us be wed in the good town,
  Now the Sword is back from sea!"   60

My heart grew sick, no more afraid,
  When the Sword came back from sea;
Upon the deck a tall white maid
  Sat on Lord Roland's knee;
His chin was pressed upon her head,   65
  When the Sword came back from sea! (1858)

THE WIND

Ah! no, no, it is nothing, surely nothing at all,
Only the wild-going wind round by the gar-
  den-wall,
For the dawn just now is breaking, the wind
  beginning to fall.
  Wind, wind! thou art sad, art thou kind?
  Wind, wind, unhappy! thou art blind,   5
  Yet still thou wanderest the lily-seed to find.

So I will sit, and think and think of the days
  gone by,
Never moving my chair for fear the dogs
  should cry,
Making no noise at all while the flambeau
  burns awry.
For my chair is heavy and carved, and with
  sweeping green behind   10
It is hung, and the dragons thereon grin out
  in the gusts of the wind;
On its folds an orange lies, with a deep gash
  cut in the rind.

The Wind. This poem is spoken by a Norse knight who is
haunted by visions of the past. Apparently crazed by unrequited love, he had killed his sweetheart. The carvings
on the chair and the decorations on the hangings are meant to
be indefinitely symbolical.
  9. **flambeau**, a flaming torch.

Wind, wind! thou art sad, art thou kind?
Wind, wind, unhappy! thou art blind,
Yet still thou wanderest the lily-seed to find.

If I move my chair it will scream, and the
  orange will roll out far,   16
And the faint yellow juice ooze out like blood
  from a wizard's jar;
And the dogs will howl for those who went
  last month to the war.
  Wind, wind! thou art sad, art thou kind?
  Wind, wind, unhappy! thou art blind,   20
  Yet still thou wanderest the lily-seed to find.

So I will sit and think of love that is over
  and past,
O! so long ago — yes, I will be quiet at last;
Whether I like it or not, a grim half-slumber
  is cast
Over my worn old brains, that touches the
  roots of my heart,   25
And above my half-shut eyes the blue roof
  'gins to part,
And show the blue spring sky, till I am ready
  to start
From out of the green-hung chair; but some-
  thing keeps me still,
And I fall in a dream that I walked with her
  on the side of a hill,
Dotted — for was it not spring? — with tufts
  of the daffodil.   30
  Wind, wind! thou art sad, art thou kind?
  Wind, wind, unhappy! thou art blind,
  Yet still thou wanderest the lily-seed to find.

And Margaret, as she walked, held a painted
  book in her hand;
Her finger kept the place; I caught her; we
  both did stand   35
Face to face, on the top of the highest hill in
  the land.
  Wind, wind! thou art sad, art thou kind?
  Wind, wind, unhappy! thou art blind,
  Yet still thou wanderest the lily-seed to find.

I held to her long bare arms, but she shuddered away from me,   40
While the flush went out of her face as her
  head fell back on a tree,
And a spasm caught her mouth, fearful for
  me to see;

And still I held to her arms till her shoulder
  touched my mail;
Weeping, she tottered forward, so glad that I
  should prevail,
And her hair went over my robe, like a gold
  flag over a sail.   45
  Wind, wind! thou art sad, art thou kind?
  Wind, wind, unhappy! thou art blind,
  Yet still thou wanderest the lily-seed to find.

I kissed her hard by the ear, and she kissed
    me on the brow,
And then lay down on the grass, where the
    mark on the moss is now,   50
And spread her arms out wide while I went
    down below.
Wind, wind! thou art sad, art thou kind?
Wind, wind, unhappy! thou art blind,
Yet still thou wanderest the lily-seed to find.

And then I walked for a space to and fro on
    the side of the hill,   55
Till I gathered and held in my arms great
    sheaves of the daffodil,
And when I came again my Margaret lay
    there still.

I piled them high and high above her heaving
    breast —
How they were caught and held in her loose
    ungirded vest!
But one beneath her arm died, happy so to
    be prest!   60
Wind, wind! thou art sad, art thou kind?
Wind, wind, unhappy! thou art blind,
Yet still thou wanderest the lily-seed to find.

Again I turned my back and went away for
    an hour;
She said no word when I came again, so,
    flower by flower,   65
I counted the daffodils over, and cast them
    languidly lower.
Wind, wind! thou art sad, art thou kind?
Wind, wind, unhappy! thou art blind,
Yet still thou wanderest the lily-seed to find.

My dry hands shook and shook as the green
    gown showed again,   70
Cleared from the yellow flowers, and I grew
    hollow with pain,
And on to us both there fell from the sun-
    shower drops of rain.
Wind, wind! thou art sad, art thou kind?
Wind, wind, unhappy! thou art blind,
Yet still thou wanderest the lily-seed to find.

Alas! alas! there was blood on the very quiet
    breast,   76
Blood lay in the many folds of the loose
    ungirded vest,
Blood lay upon her arm where the flower had
    been prest.

I shrieked and leapt from my chair, and the
    orange rolled out far,
The faint yellow juice oozed out like blood
    from a wizard's jar;   80

79. **I shrieked,** etc. The memory of the experience is so
vivid that he shrieks.

And then in marched the ghosts of those that
    had gone to the war.
I knew them by the arms that I was used to
    paint
Upon their long thin shields; but the colors
    were all grown faint,
And faint upon their banner was Olaf, king
    and saint.
Wind, wind! thou art sad, art thou kind?   85
Wind, wind, unhappy! thou art blind,
Yet still thou wanderest the lily-seed to find.
(1858)

THE BLUE CLOSET

The Damozels

Lady Alice, Lady Louise,
Between the wash of the tumbling seas
We are ready to sing, if so ye please;
So lay your long hands on the keys;
        Sing, "*Laudate pueri.*"   5

And ever the great bell overhead
Boomed in the wind a knell for the dead,
Though no one tolled it, a knell for the dead.

Lady Louise

Sister, let the measure swell
Not too loud; for you sing not well   10
If you drown the faint boom of the bell;
        He is weary, so am I.

And ever the chevron overhead
Flapped on the banner of the dead;
(Was he asleep, or was he dead?)   15

Lady Alice

Alice the Queen, and Louise the Queen,
Two damozels wearing purple and green
Four lone ladies dwelling here
From day to day and year to year;
And there is none to let us go;   20
To break the locks of the doors below,
Or shovel away the heaped-up snow;
And when we die no man will know
That we are dead; but they give us leave,
Once every year on Christmas-eve,   25
To sing in the Closet Blue one song;
And we should be so long, so long,
If we dared, in singing; for dream on dream,

84. **Olaf,** Olaf II (995-1030), king and patron saint of
Norway.
   The Blue Closet. This poem was written for a picture by
Rossetti. It presents the story of Lady Louise, whose lover
Arthur (line 66) had gone away wearing her token. He never
returned except in the Lady's dreams when she and Lady
Alice, with their two Damozels, were gathered in the Blue
Closet once a year, on Christmas Eve. See Critical Notes.
   5. **Laudate pueri,** Let the children praise. These are the
opening words of a version of the famous church hymn *Te
Deum* used in Ireland; it is found in the Bangor Antiphonary,
dated 680-691. 13. **chevron,** a device of honor on a banner.
Arthur's banner had been left in the Blue Closet.

They float on in a happy stream;
Float from the gold strings, float from the
   keys,   30
Float from the opened lips of Louise;
But, alas! the sea-salt oozes through
The chinks of the tiles of the Closet Blue;

And ever the great bell overhead
Booms in the wind a knell for the dead,   35
The wind plays on it a knell for the dead.

[*They sing all together*]

How long ago was it, how long ago,
He came to this tower with hands full of
   snow?
"Kneel down, O love Louise, kneel down,"
   he said,
And sprinkled the dusty snow over my head.

He watched the snow melting, it ran through
   my hair,   41
Ran over my shoulders, white shoulders and
   bare.

"I cannot weep for thee, poor love Louise,
For my tears are all hidden deep under the
   seas;

"In a gold and blue casket she keeps all my
   tears,   45
But my eyes are no longer blue, as in old
   years;

"Yea, they grow gray with time, grow small
   and dry;
I am so feeble now, would I might die."

And in truth the great bell overhead
Left off his pealing for the dead,   50
Perchance, because the wind was dead.

Will he come back again, or is he dead?
Oh! is he sleeping, my scarf round his head?

Or did they strangle him as he lay there,
With the long scarlet scarf I used to wear? 55

Only I pray thee, Lord, let him come here!
Both his soul and his body to me are most
   dear.

Dear Lord, that loves me, I wait to receive
Either body or spirit this wild Christmas-eve.

Through the floor shot up a lily red,   60
With a patch of earth from the land of the dead,
For he was strong in the land of the dead.

What matter that his cheeks were pale,
   His kind kissed lips all gray?

"O love Louise, have you waited long?"   65
"O my lord Arthur, yea."

What if his hair that brushed her cheek
   Was stiff with frozen rime?
His eyes were grown quite blue again,
   As in the happy time.   70

"O love Louise, this is the key
   Of the happy golden land!
O sisters, cross the bridge with me,
   My eyes are full of sand.
What matter that I cannot see,   75
   If ye take me by the hand?"

And ever the great bell overhead,
And the tumbling seas mourned for the dead;
For their song ceased, and they were dead.
         (1858)

THE TUNE OF SEVEN TOWERS

No one goes there now;
   For what is left to fetch away
From the desolate battlements all arow,
   And the lead roof heavy and gray?
"Therefore," said fair Yoland of the flowers, 5
"This is the tune of Seven Towers."

No one walks there now,
   Except in the white moonlight
The white ghosts walk in a row;
   If one could see it, an awful sight —   10
"Listen!" said fair Yoland of the flowers,
"This is the tune of Seven Towers."

But none can see them now,
   Though they sit by the side of the moat,
Feet half in the water, there in a row,   15
   Long hair in the wind afloat.
"Therefore," said fair Yoland of the flowers,
"This is the tune of Seven Towers."

If any will go to it now,
   He must go to it all alone,   20
Its gates will not open to any row
   Of glittering spears — will *you* go alone?
"Listen!" said fair Yoland of the flowers,
"This is the tune of Seven Towers."

By my love go there now,   25
   To fetch me my coif away,
My coif and my kirtle, with pearls arow,
   Oliver, go today!
"Therefore," said fair Yoland of the flowers,
"This is the tune of Seven Towers."   30

The Tune of Seven Towers. 26. **coif,** a tight-fitting cap.
27. **kirtle,** a short skirt.

I am unhappy now,
  I cannot tell you why;
If you go, the priests and I in a row
  Will pray that you may not die.
"Listen!" said fair Yoland of the flowers,   35
"This is the tune of Seven Towers."

If you will go for me now,
  I will kiss your mouth at last;
    [*She sayeth inwardly.*]
(*The graves stand gray in a row*),   40
  Oliver, hold me fast!
"Therefore," said fair Yoland of the flowers,
"This is the tune of Seven Towers."   (1858)

THE HAYSTACK IN THE FLOODS

Had she come all the way for this,
To part at last without a kiss?
Yea, had she borne the dirt and rain
That her own eyes might see him slain
Beside the haystack in the floods?   5

Along the dripping, leafless woods,
The stirrup touching either shoe,
She rode astride as troopers do;
With kirtle kilted to her knee,
To which the mud splashed wretchedly;   10
And the wet dripped from every tree
Upon her head and heavy hair,
And on her eyelids broad and fair;
The tears and rain ran down her face.

By fits and starts they rode apace,   15
And very often was his place
Far off from her; he had to ride
Ahead, to see what might betide
When the roads crossed; and sometimes, when
There rose a murmuring from his men,   20
Had to turn back with promises.
Ah me! she had but little ease;
And often for pure doubt and dread
She sobbed, made giddy in the head
By the swift riding; while, for cold,   25
Her slender fingers scarce could hold
The wet reins; yea, and scarcely, too,
She felt the foot within her shoe
Against the stirrup; all for this,
To part at last without a kiss   30
Beside the haystack in the floods.

For when they neared that old soaked hay,
They saw across the only way
That Judas, Godmar, and the three

Red running lions dismally   35
Grinned from his pennon, under which
In one straight line along the ditch,
They counted thirty heads.
           So then
While Robert turned round to his men,
She saw at once the wretched end,   40
And, stooping down, tried hard to rend
Her coif the wrong way from her head,
And hid her eyes; while Robert said,
"Nay, love, 'tis scarcely two to one;
At Poictiers where we made them run   45
So fast — why, sweet my love, good cheer,
The Gascon frontier is so near,
Naught after us."
        But "O!" she said,
"My God! my God! I have to tread
The long way back without you; then   50
The court at Paris; those six men;
The gratings of the Chatelet;
The swift Seine on some rainy day
Like this, and people standing by,
And laughing, while my weak hands try   55
To recollect how strong men swim.
All this, or else a life with him,
For which I should be damned at last;
Would God that this next hour were past!"

He answered not, but cried his cry,   60
"St. George for Marny!" cheerily;
And laid his hand upon her rein.
Alas! no man of all his train
Gave back that cheery cry again;
And, while for rage his thumb beat fast   65
Upon his sword-hilt, someone cast
About his neck a kerchief long,
And bound him.

      Then they went along
To Godmar; who said: "Now, Jehane,
Your lover's life is on the wane   70
So fast, that, if this very hour
You yield not as my paramour,
He will not see the rain leave off;
Nay, keep your tongue from gibe and scoff,
Sir Robert, or I slay you now."   75

She laid her hand upon her brow,
Then gazed upon the palm, as though

The Haystack in the Floods. In this poem Sir Robert de Marny, an English knight who had fought at Poictiers (1356), is riding through France with Jehane, his mistress, and a small company. They are confronted by Godmar, a traitorous French knight, who was waiting to slay Robert and carry off Jehane.
9. **kirtle kilted**, skirt tucked up.

36. **pennon**, banner. 42. **coif . . head.** The coif was a close-fitting cap tied under the chin. Jehane tried to pull her coif down over her eyes so that she might not see her lover slain. 45. **Poictiers.** At the Battle of Poictiers the French outnumbered the English five to one, but the English won. 47. **Gascon frontier.** Robert would be safe in the province of Gascony, since during the reign of Edward III of England (1327–77) Gascony was English territory. 51. **those six men,** the judges who would try her as a witch and imprison her in the Grand Châtelet, the most terrible of the Paris prisons. She would be flung into the Seine to test her guilt— if she swam she would be declared guilty; if she drowned she was innocent. 61. **St. George for Marny.** St. George was the patron saint of the English. **Marny is Robert.**

She thought her forehead bled, and "No!"
She said, and turned her head away,
As there was nothing else to say, 80
And everything was settled; red
Grew Godmar's face from chin to head —
"Jehane, on yonder hill there stands
My castle, guarding well my lands;
What hinders me from taking you, 85
And doing that I list to do
To your fair willful body, while
Your knight lies dead?"

        A wicked smile
Wrinkled her face, her lips grew thin,
A long way out she thrust her chin: 90
"You know that I should strangle you
While you were sleeping; or bite through
Your throat, by God's help; ah!" she said,
"Lord Jesus, pity your poor maid!
For in such wise they hem me in, 95
I cannot choose but sin and sin,
Whatever happens; yet I think
They could not make me eat or drink,
And so should I just reach my rest."

"Nay, if you do not my behest, 100
O Jehane! though I love you well,"
Said Godmar, "would I fail to tell
All that I know?" "Foul lies," she said.
"Eh? lies, my Jehane? by God's head,
At Paris folks would deem them true! 105
Do you know, Jehane, they cry for you:
'Jehane the brown! Jehane the brown!
Give us Jehane to burn or drown!
Eh! — gag me Robert! — sweet my friend,
This were indeed a piteous end 110
For those long fingers, and long feet,
And long neck, and smooth shoulders sweet;
An end that few men would forget
That saw it. So, an hour yet —
Consider, Jehane, which to take 115
Of life or death!"

        So, scarce awake,
Dismounting, did she leave that place,
And totter some yards; with her face
Turned upward to the sky she lay,
Her head on a wet heap of hay, 120
And fell asleep; and while she slept,
And did not dream, the minutes crept
Round to the twelve again; but she,
Being waked at last, sighed quietly,
And strangely childlike came, and said: 125
"I will not." Straightway Godmar's head,
As though it hung on strong wires, turned
Most sharply round, and his face burned.

For Robert, both his eyes were dry —
He could not weep—but gloomily 130
He seemed to watch the rain; yea, too,

His lips were firm; he tried once more
To touch her lips; she reached out, sore
And vain desire so tortured them,
The poor gray lips, and now the hem 135
Of his sleeve brushed them.

        With a start
Up Godmar rose, thrust them apart;
From Robert's throat he loosed the bands
Of silk and mail; with empty hands
Held out, she stood and gazed, and saw, 140
The long bright blade without a flaw
Glide out from Godmar's sheath, his hand
In Robert's hair; she saw him bend
Back Robert's head; she saw him send
The thin steel down; the blow told well — 145
Right backward the knight Robert fell,
And moaned as dogs do, being half dead,
Unwitting, as I deem; so then
Godmar turned grinning to his men,
Who ran, some five or six, and beat 150
His head to pieces at their feet.

Then Godmar turned again and said:
"So, Jehane, the first fitte is read!
Take note, my lady, that your way
Lies backward to the Chatelet!" 155
She shook her head and gazed awhile
At her cold hands with a rueful smile,
As though this thing had made her mad.

This was the parting that they had
Beside the haystack in the floods. 160
        (1858)

TWO RED ROSES ACROSS THE MOON

There was a lady lived in a hall,
Large of her eyes and slim and tall;
And ever she sung from noon to noon,
Two red roses across the moon.

There was a knight came riding by 5
In early spring, when the roads were dry;
And he heard that lady sing at the noon,
Two red roses across the moon.

Yet none the more he stopped at all,
But he rode a-gallop past the hall; 10
And left that lady singing at noon,
Two red roses across the moon.

Because, forsooth, the battle was set,
And the scarlet and blue had got to be met,
He rode on the spur till the next warm
      noon; 15
Two red roses across the moon.

153. **fitte**, a division of a poem, song, or story.

But the battle was scattered from hill to hill,
From the windmill to the watermill;
And he said to himself, as it neared the noon,
Two red roses across the moon. 20

You scarce could see for the scarlet and blue,
A golden helm or a golden shoe;
So he cried, as the fight grew thick at the
    noon,
Two red roses across the moon!

Verily then the gold bore through 25
The huddled spears of the scarlet and blue;
And they cried, as they cut them down at the
    noon,
Two red roses across the moon!

I trow he stopped when he rode again
By the hall, though draggled sore with the
    rain; 30
And his lips were pinched to kiss at the noon
Two red roses across the moon.

Under the may she stooped to the crown;
All was gold, there was nothing of brown,
And the horns blew up in the hall at noon, 35
Two red roses across the moon. (1858)

SIR GILES'S WAR-SONG

Ho! is there any will ride with me,
  Sir Giles, le bon des barrières?

The clink of arms is good to hear,
The flap of pennons fair to see;
  Ho! is there any will ride with me, 5
    Sir Giles, le bon des barrières?

The leopards and lilies are fair to see;
St. George Guienne! right good to hear;
  Ho! is there any will ride with me;
    Sir Giles, le bon des barrières? 10

I stood by the barrier,
My coat being blazoned fair to see;
  Ho! is there any will ride with me,
    Sir Giles, le bon des barrières?

Clisson put out his head to see, 15
And lifted his basnet up to hear;
  I pulled him through the bars to ME,
    Sir Giles, le bon des barrières.
           (1858)

33. may, hawthorn.
Sir Giles's War-Song. 2. le bon des barrières, the good
one of the lists. 7. leopards and lilies, Sir Giles's device.
8. St. George Guienne. St. George was the patron saint
of England. Guienne, a province in southern France, was
English territory during the reign of Edward III (1327-77).
12. blazoned, adorned. 16. basnet, a light steel helmet.

NEAR AVALON

A ship with shields before the sun,
Six maidens round the mast,
A red-gold crown on every one,
A green gown on the last.

The fluttering green banners there 5
Are wrought with ladies' heads most fair,
And a portraiture of Guenevere
The middle of each sail doth bear.

A ship which sails before the wind,
And round the helm six knights, 10
Their heaumes are on, whereby, half blind,
They pass by many sights.

The tattered scarlet banners there,
Right soon will leave the spear-heads bare,
Those six knights sorrowfully bear, 15
In all their heaumes some yellow hair. (1858)

PRAISE OF MY LADY

My lady seems of ivory
Forehead, straight nose, and cheeks that be
Hollowed a little mournfully.
    Beata mea Domina!

Her forehead, overshadowed much 5
By bows of hair, has a wave such
As God was good to make for me.
    Beata mea Domina!

Not greatly long my lady's hair,
Nor yet with yellow color fair, 10
But thick and crispéd wonderfully;
    Beata mea Domina!

Heavy to make the pale face sad,
And dark, but dead as though it had
Been forged by God most wonderfully 15
    — *Beata mea Domina!* —

Of some strange metal, thread by thread,
To stand out from my lady's head,
Not moving much to tangle me.
    Beata mea Domina! 20

Beneath her brows the lids fall slow,
The lashes a clear shadow throw

Near Avalon. In medieval romance, Avalon was an ocean
island, the earthly paradise, where, according to legend,
Arthur is waiting to return. The poem symbolizes the hopeless love of knights for gay maidens.
  11. heaumes, helmets. 16. yellow hair, a love token.
Most ladies of romance had golden hair.
  Praise of My Lady. The details in this poem fit almost
exactly Rossetti's portrait of Jane Burden, whom Morris
married in 1859. Morris and Rossetti had met her at Oxford
in 1856.
  4. Beata mea Domina, my blessed lady. 11. crispéd,
curled.

Where I would wish my lips to be.
Beata mea Domina!

Her great eyes, standing far apart,   25
Draw up some memory from her heart,
And gaze out very mournfully
— *Beata mea Domina!* —

So beautiful and kind they are,
But most times looking out afar,   30
Waiting for something, not for me.
Beata mea Domina!

I wonder if the lashes long
Are those that do her bright eyes wrong,
For always half tears seem to be   35
— *Beata mea Domina!* —

Lurking below the underlid,
Darkening the place where they lie hid —
If they should rise and flow for me!
Beata mea Domina!   40

Her full lips being made to kiss,
Curled up and pensive each one is;
This makes me faint to stand and see.
Beata mea Domina!

Her lips are not contented now,   45
Because the hours pass so slow
Toward a sweet time (pray for me),
— *Beata mea Domina!* —

Nay, hold thy peace! for who can tell;
But this at least I know full well,   50
Her lips are parted longingly,
— *Beata mea Domina!* —

So passionate and swift to move,
To pluck at any flying love,
That I grow faint to stand and see.   55
Beata mea Domina!

Yea! there beneath them is her chin,
So fine and round, it were a sin
To feel no weaker when I see
— *Beata mea Domina!* —   60

God's dealings; for with so much care
And troublous, faint lines wrought in there,
He finishes her face for me.
Beata mea Domina!

Of her long neck what shall I say?   65
What things about her body's sway,
Like a knight's pennon or slim tree
— *Beata mea Domina!* —

Set gently waving in the wind;
Or her long hands that I may find   70
On some day sweet to move o'er me?
Beata mea Domina!

God pity me though, if I missed
The telling, how along her wrist
The veins creep, dying languidly   75
— *Beata mea Domina!* —

Inside her tender palm and thin,
Now give me pardon, dear, wherein
My voice is weak and vexes thee.
Beata mea Domina!   80

All men that see her any time,
I charge you straightly in this rime,
What, and wherever you may be,
— *Beata mea Domina!* —

To kneel before her; as for me,   85
I choke and grow quite faint to see
My lady moving graciously.
Beata mea Domina! .(*1857; 1858*)

IN PRISON

Wearily, drearily,
Half the day long,
Flap the great banners
High over the stone;
Strangely and eerily   5
Sounds the wind's song,
Bending the banner-poles.

While, all alone,
Watching the loophole's spark,
Lie I, with life all dark,   10
Feet tethered, hands fettered
Fast to the stone,
The grim wall, square lettered
With prisoned men's groan.

Still strain the banner-poles   15
Through the wind's song
Westward the banner rolls
Over my wrong.

(*1858*)

From *THE LIFE AND DEATH OF JASON*

O BITTER SEA

O bitter sea, tumultuous sea,
Full many an ill is wrought by thee! —
Unto the wasters of the land
Thou holdest out thy wrinkled hand;
And when they leave the conquered town,   5
Whose black smoke makes thy surges brown,
Driven betwixt thee and the sun,

The Life and Death of Jason. See Critical Notes.
O Bitter Sea. This lyric, in Book 4, is sung by Orpheus, the
famous musician, as the ship *Argo* moves out into the sea on
its journey from the shore of Thessaly, Greece.

As the long day of blood is done,
From many a league of glittering waves
Thou smilest on them and their slaves.   10
    The thin bright-eyed Phœnician
Thou drawest to thy waters wan;
With ruddy eve and golden morn
Thou temptest him, until, forlorn,
Unburied, under alien skies   15
Cast up ashore his body lies.
    Yea, whoso sees thee from his door,
Must ever long for more and more;
Nor will the beechen bowl suffice,
Or homespun robe of little price,   20
Or hood well-woven of the fleece
Undyed, or unspiced wine of Greece;
So sore his heart is set upon
Purple, and gold, and cinnamon;
For as thou cravest, so he craves,   25
Until he rolls beneath thy waves.
Nor in some landlocked, unknown bay,
Can satiate thee for one day.

    Now, therefore, O thou bitter sea,
With no long words we pray to thee,   30
But ask thee, hast thou felt before
Such strokes of the long ashen oar?
And hast thou yet seen such a prow
Thy rich and niggard waters plow?
    Nor yet, O sea, shalt thou be cursed,   35
If at thy hands we gain the worst,
And, wrapped in water, roll about
Blind-eyed, unheeding song or shout,
Within thine eddies far from shore,
Warmed by no sunlight any more.   40
    Therefore, indeed, we joy in thee,
And praise thy greatness, and will we
Take at thy hands both good and ill,
Yea, what thou wilt, and praise thee still,
Enduring not to sit at home,   45
And wait until the last days come,
When we no more may care to hold
White bosoms under crowns of gold,
And our dulled hearts no longer are
Stirred by the clangorous noise of war,   50
And hope within our souls is dead,
And no joy is rememberéd.
    So, if thou hast a mind to slay,
Fair prize thou hast of us today;
And if thou hast a mind to save,   55
Great praise and honor shalt thou have;
But whatso thou wilt do with us,
Our end shall not be piteous,
Because our memories shall live
When folk forget the way to drive   60
The black keel through the heaped-up sea,
And half dried up thy waters be.
                      (1867)

11. **Phœnician**, a native of Phœnicia, along the coast of
Asia Minor. The Phœnicians were noted for their commerce.

A GARDEN BY THE SEA

I know a little garden close
Set thick with lily and red rose,
Where I would wander if I might
From dewy dawn to dewy night,
And have one with me wandering.   5

And though within it no birds sing,
And though no pillared house is there,
And though the apple boughs are bare
Of fruit and blossom, would to God,
Her feet upon the green grass trod,   10
And I beheld them as before.

There comes a murmur from the shore,
And in the close two fair streams are,
Drawn from the purple hills afar,
Drawn down unto the restless sea: 15
Dark hills whose heath-bloom feeds no bee,
Dark shore no ship has ever seen,
Still beaten by the billows green,
Whose murmur comes unceasingly
Unto the place for which I cry.   20

For which I cry both day and night,
For which I let slip all delight,
That maketh me both deaf and blind,
Careless to win, unskilled to find,
And quick to lose what all men seek.   25

Yet tottering as I am, and weak,
Still have I left a little breath
To seek within the jaws of death
An entrance to that happy place,
To seek the unforgotten face   30
Once seen, once kissed, once reft from me
Anigh the murmuring of the sea.   (1867)

O DEATH, THAT MAKETH LIFE SO SWEET

O death, that maketh life so sweet,
O fear, with mirth before thy feet,
What have ye yet in store for us,
The conquerors, the glorious?
    Men say: "For fear that thou shouldst die
Tomorrow, let today pass by   6
Flower-crowned and singing"; yet have we
Passed our today upon the sea,
Or in a poisonous unknown land,
With fear and death on either hand,   10
And listless when the day was done

A Garden by The Sea. This lyric, in Book 4, is the "sweet
song sung not yet to any man" by the water-nymph as she
lulls to sleep the Theban youth Hylas. He had wandered
away from his companions who had landed on the shore of
Mysia, Asia Minor, in search of fresh water. Hylas was left
behind by his companions.
  1. **close**, enclosure.
  O Death, That Maketh Life So Sweet. This song, in Book 12,
is sung by Orpheus to inspire his comrades on their homeward
voyage after a hard winter passed on the shore of a northern
river; they are tossing upon the Atlantic near the Pillars of
Hercules (Strait of Gibraltar).

Have scarcely hoped to see the sun
Dawn on the morrow of the earth,
Nor in our hearts have thought of mirth.
And while the world lasts, scarce again   15
Shall any sons of men bear pain
Like we have borne, yet be alive.
   So surely not in vain we strive
Like other men for our reward;
Sweet peace and deep, the checkered sward
Beneath the ancient mulberry trees,   21
The smooth-paved gilded palaces,
Where the shy thin-clad damsels sweet
Make music with their gold-ringed feet,
The fountain court amidst of it,   25
Where the short-haired slave-maidens sit,
While on the veinéd pavement lie
The honeyed things and spicery
Their arms have borne from out the town.
   The dancers on the thymy down   30
In summer twilight, when the earth
Is still of all things but their mirth,
And echoes borne upon the wind
Of others in like way entwined.
   The merchant-town's fair market-place, 35
Where over many a changing face
The pigeons of the temple flit,
And still the outland merchants sit
Like kings above their merchandise,
Lying to foolish men and wise.   40
   Ah! if they heard that we were come
Into the bay, and bringing home
That which all men have talked about,
Some men with rage, and some with doubt,
Some with desire, and some with praise; 45
Then would the people throng the ways,
Nor heed the outland merchandise,
Nor any talk, from fools or wise,
But tales of our accomplished quest.
   What soul within the house shall rest 50
When we come home? The wily king
Shall leave his throne to see the thing;
No man shall keep the landward gate;
The hurried traveler shall wait
Until our bulwarks graze the quay;   55
Unslain the milk-white bull shall be
Beside the quivering altar-flame;
Scarce shall the maiden clasp for shame
Over her breast the raiment thin,
The morn that *Argo* cometh in.   60
   Then cometh happy life again
That payeth well our toil and pain
In that sweet hour, when all our woe
But as a pensive tale we know,
Nor yet remember deadly fear;   65
For surely now if death be near,
Unthought-of is it, and unseen
When sweet is, that hath bitter been.
                      (1867)

43. **That . . . about,** the Golden Fleece. 60. **Argo,** the
name of their ship, from which they were called Argonauts.

From *THE EARTHLY PARADISE*

AN APOLOGY

Of Heaven or Hell I have no power to sing;
I cannot ease the burden of your fears,
Or make quick-coming death a little thing,
Or bring again the pleasure of past years;
Nor for my words shall ye forget your tears, 6
Or hope again for aught that I can say —
The idle singer of an empty day.

But rather, when aweary of your mirth,
From full hearts still unsatisfied ye sigh,
And, feeling kindly unto all the earth,   10
Grudge every minute as it passes by,
Made the more mindful that the sweet days
    die —
Remember me a little then, I pray,
The idle singer of an empty day.

The heavy trouble, the bewildering care   15
That weighs us down who live and earn our
    bread,
These idle verses have no power to bear;
So let me sing of names rememberéd,
Because they, living not, can ne'er be dead,
Or long time take their memory quite away
From us poor singers of an empty day.   21

Dreamer of dreams, born out of my due time,
Why should I strive to set the crooked
    straight?
Let it suffice me that my murmuring rime,
Beats with light wing against the ivory gate,
Telling a tale not too importunate   26
To those who in the sleepy region stay,
Lulled by the singer of an empty day.

Folk say, a wizard to a northern king
At Christmas-tide such wondrous things did
    show,   30
That through one window men beheld the
    spring,
And through another saw the summer glow,
And through a third the fruited vines a-row,
While still, unheard, but in its wonted way,
Piped the drear wind of that December day.

So with this Earthly Paradise it is,   36
If ye will read aright, and pardon me,
Who strive to build a shadowy isle of bliss
Midmost the beating of the steely sea,
Where tossed about all hearts of men must
    be;

The Earthly Paradise. See Critical Notes.
An Apology. **1. Of Heaven or Hell.** Morris disclaims
equality with earlier poets who used these themes—Virgil,
Dante, Milton.　**25. the ivory gate.**　The house of Mor-
pheus, god of sleep, had two gates through which dreams
issued.　True dreams passed through a gate of horn; false
dreams, through a gate of ivory.

Whose ravening monsters mighty men shall
   slay — 41
Not the poor singer of an empty day.

(1868-1870)

JUNE

O June, O June, that we desired so,
Wilt thou not make us happy on this day?
Across the river thy soft breezes blow,
Sweet with the scent of beanfields far away;
Above our heads rustle the aspens gray; 5
Calm is the sky with harmless clouds beset —
No thought of storm the morning vexes yet.

See, we have left our hopes and fears behind
To give our very hearts up unto thee;
What better place than this, then, could we
   find 10
By this sweet stream that knows not of the
   sea,
That guesses not the city's misery —
This little stream whose hamlets scarce have
   names,
This far-off, lonely mother of the Thames?

Here then, O June, thy kindness will we take;
And if indeed but pensive men we seem, 16
What should we do? Thou wouldst not have
   us wake
From out the arms of this rare happy dream
And wish to leave the murmur of the stream,
The rustling boughs, the twitter of the birds,
And all thy thousand peaceful happy words. 21

(1868)

THE LADY OF THE LAND

Argument: A certain man, having landed on an
island in the Greek Sea, found there a beautiful
damsel, whom he fain would have delivered
from a strange and dreadful doom, but failing
herein, he died soon afterwards.

It happened once, some men of Italy
Midst the Greek Islands went a sea-roving,
And much good fortune had they on the sea:
Of many a man they had the ransoming, 4
And many a chain they gat, and goodly thing;
And midst their voyage to an isle they came,
Whereof my story keepeth not the name.

Now though but little was there left to
   gain,
Because the richer folk had gone away,
Yet since, by this, of water they were fain, 10
They came to anchor in a land-locked bay,

The Lady of the Land. This is the eighth story of the cycle.
Cf. Browning's *Muckle-Mouth Meg*, page 355. The source of
the poem is found in Book 4 of John Maundeville's *Voiage
and Travaile.* See Critical Notes.

Whence in a while some went ashore to play,
Going but lightly armed in twos or threes,
For midst that folk they feared no enemies.

And of these fellows that thus went
   ashore, 15
One was there who left all his friends behind;
Who going inland ever more and more,
And being left quite alone, at last did find
A lonely valley sheltered from the wind,
Wherein, amidst an ancient cypress wood, 20
A long-deserted ruined castle stood.

The wood, once ordered in fair grove and
   glade,
With gardens overlooked by terraces,
And marble-pavéd pools for pleasure made,
Was tangled now, and choked with fallen
   trees; 25
And he who went there, with but little ease
Must stumble by the stream's side, once
   made meet
For tender women's dainty wandering feet.

The raven's croak, the low wind choked
   and drear,
The baffled stream, the gray wolf's doleful
   cry, 30
Were all the sounds that mariner could hear,
As through the wood he wandered painfully;
But as unto the house he drew anigh,
The pillars of a ruined shrine he saw,
The once fair temple of a fallen law. 35

No image was there left behind to tell
Before whose face the knees of men had
   bowed;
An altar of black stone, of old wrought well,
Alone beneath a ruined roof now showed
The goal whereto the folk were wont to
   crowd, 40
Seeking for things forgotten long ago,
Praying for heads long ages laid a-low.

Close to the temple was the castle-gate,
Doorless and crumbling; there our fellow
   turned,
Trembling indeed at what might chance to
   wait 45
The prey entrapped, yet with a heart that
   burned
To know the most of what might there be
   learned,
And hoping somewhat too, amid his fear,
To light on such things as all men hold dear.

Noble the house was, nor seemed built for
   war, 50
But rather like the work of other days,

35. law, belief, religion.

When men, in better peace than now they
    are,
Had leisure on the world around to gaze,
And noted well the past times' changing ways;
And fair with sculptured stories it was
    wrought,   55
By lapse of time unto dim ruin brought.

Now as he looked about on all these things,
And strove to read the moldering histories,
Above the door an image with wise wings,
Whose unclad limbs a serpent seemed to
    seize,   60
He dimly saw, although the western breeze,
And years of biting frost and washing rain,
Had made the carver's labor wellnigh vain.

But this, though perished sore, and worn
    away,
He noted well, because it seemed to be,   65
After the fashion of another day,
Some great man's badge of war, or armory,
And round it a carved wreath he seemed to
    see;
But taking note of these things, at the last
The mariner beneath the gateway passed.   70

And there a lovely cloistered court he
    found,
A fountain in the midst, o'erthrown and dry,
And in the cloister briers twining round
The slender shafts; the wondrous imagery
Outworn by more than many years gone
    by,
Because the country people, in their fear   76
Of wizardry, had wrought destruction here;

And piteously these fair things had been
    maimed —
There stood great Jove, lacking his head of
    might;
Here was the archer, swift Apollo, lamed;   80
The shapely limbs of Venus hid from sight
By weeds and shards; Diana's ankles light
Bound with the cable of some coasting ship;
And rusty nails through Helen's maddening
    lip.

Therefrom unto the chambers did he pass,
And found them fair still, midst of their
    decay,   86
Though in them now no sign of man there
    was,
And everything but stone had passed away
That made them lovely in that vanished day;

79. **Jove,** ruler of the gods. 80. **Apollo,** god of manly
youth and beauty, of poetry and music. His attributes were
the bow and the lyre. 81. **Venus,** goddess of love. 82.
Diana, goddess of the moon and of the chase. 84. **Helen,**
Helen of Troy.

Nay, the mere walls themselves would soon
    be gone   90
And naught be left but heaps of moldering
    stone.

But he, when all the place he had gone o'er,
And with much trouble clomb the broken
    stair,
And from the topmost turret seen the shore
And his good ship drawn up at anchor there,
Came down again, and found a crypt most
    fair,   96
Built wonderfully beneath the greatest hall;
And there he saw a door within the wall,

Well-hinged, close-shut; nor was there in
    that place
Another on its hinges — therefore he   100
Stood there and pondered for a little space,
And thought, "Perchance some marvel I shall
    see,
For surely here some dweller there must be,
Because this door seems whole, and new, and
    sound,
While naught but ruin I can see around."   105

So with that word, moved by a strong
    desire,
He tried the hasp, that yielded to his hand,
And in a strange place, lit as by a fire
Unseen but near, he presently did stand;
And by an odorous breeze his face was fanned,
As though in some Arabian plain he stood,   111
Anigh the border of a spice-tree wood.

He moved not for a while, but looking
    round,
He wondered much to see the place so fair,
Because, unlike the castle above ground,   115
No pillager or wrecker had been there;
It seemed that time had passed on other-
    where,
Nor laid a finger on this hidden place,
Rich with the wealth of some forgotten race.

With hangings, fresh as when they left the
    loom,   120
The walls were hung a space above the head;
Slim ivory chairs were set about the room;
And in one corner was a dainty bed,
That seemed for some fair queen appareléd;
And marble was the worst stone of the floor,
That with rich Indian webs was covered o'er.

The wanderer trembled when he saw all
    this,
Because he deemed by magic it was wrought;
Yet in his heart a longing for some bliss,
Whereof the hard and changing world knows
    naught,   130

Arose and urged him on, and dimmed the
    thought
That there perchance some devil lurked to
    slay
The heedless wanderer from the light of day.

Over against him was another door
Set in the wall; so, casting fear aside,   135
With hurried steps he crossed the varied floor,
And there again the silver latch he tried,
And with no pain the door he opened wide,
And entering the new chamber cautiously
The glory of great heaps of gold could see. 140

Upon the floor uncounted medals lay,
Like things of little value; here and there
Stood golden caldrons, that might well out-
    weigh
The biggest midst an emperor's copper-ware,
And golden cups were set on tables fair,   145
Themselves of gold; and in all hollow things
Were stored great gems, worthy the crowns
    of kings.

The walls and roof with gold were overlaid,
And precious raiment from the wall hung
    down;
The fall of kings that treasure might have
    stayed,   150
Or gained some longing conqueror great
    renown,
Or built again some god-destroyed old town;
What wonder, if this plunderer of the sea
Stood gazing at it long and dizzily?

But at the last his troubled eyes and dazed
He lifted from the glory of that gold,   156
And then the image, that, wellnigh erased,
Over the castle-gate he did behold,
Above a door well wrought in colored gold
Again he saw — a naked girl with wings   160
Enfolded in a serpent's scaly rings.

And even as his eyes were fixed on it
A woman's voice came from the other side,
And through his heart strange hopes began
    to flit
That in some wondrous land he might abide
Not dying, master of a deathless bride;   166
So o'er the gold he scarcely now could see
He went, and passed this last door eagerly.

Then in a room he stood wherein there
    was
A marble bath, whose brimming water yet 170
Was scarcely still; a vessel of green glass
Half full of odorous ointment was there set
Upon the topmost step that still was wet,
And jeweled shoes and women's dainty gear,
Lay cast upon the varied pavement near. 175

In one quick glance these things his eyes
    did see,
But speedily they turned round to behold
Another sight, for throned on ivory
There sat a girl, whose dripping tresses
    rolled
On to the floor in waves of gleaming gold, 180
Cast back from such a form as, erewhile
    shown
To one poor shepherd, lighted up Troy town.

Naked she was; the kisses of her feet
Upon the floor a dying path had made
From the full bath unto her ivory seat;   185
In her right hand, upon her bosom laid,
She held a golden comb; a mirror weighed
Her left hand down; aback her fair head lay,
Dreaming, awake, of some long vanished day.

Her eyes were shut, but she seemed not to
    sleep;   190
Her lips were murmuring things unheard and
    low,
Or sometimes twitched as though she needs
    must weep
Though from her eyes the tears refused to
    flow;
And oft with heavenly red her cheek did
    glow,
As if remembrance of some half-sweet shame
Across the web of many memories came.   196

There stood the man, scarce daring to draw
    breath
For fear the lovely sight should fade away;
Forgetting heaven, forgetting life and death,
Trembling for fear lest something he should
    say   200
Unwitting, lest some sob should yet betray
His presence there, for to his eager eyes
Already did the tears begin to rise.

But as he gazed, she moved, and with a
    sigh
Bent forward, dropping down her golden
    head;   205
"Alas, alas! another day gone by,
Another day and no soul come," she said;
"Another year, and still I am not dead!"
And with that word once more her head she
    raised,
And on the trembling man with great eyes
    gazed.   210

Then he imploring hands to her did reach,
And toward her very slowly 'gan to move
And with wet eyes her pity did beseech,
And seeing her about to speak, he strove

182. **shepherd . . . town**, a reference to Paris and Helen
of Troy. See *Œnone* and notes, page 20.

From trembling lips to utter words of love; 215
And with a look she stayed his doubtful feet,
And made sweet music as their eyes did meet.

For now she spoke in gentle voice and clear,
Using the Greek tongue that he knew full well:
"What man art thou, that thus hast wan-
　　dered here,   220
And found this lonely chamber where I dwell?
Beware, beware! for I have many a spell;
If greed of power and gold have led thee on,
Not lightly shall this untold wealth be won.

"But if thou com'st here, knowing of my
　　tale,   225
In hope to bear away my body fair,
Stout must thine heart be, nor shall that avail
If thou a wicked heart in thee dost bear;
So once again I bid thee to beware,
Because no base man things like this may see,
And live thereafter long and happily."   231

"Lady," he said, "in Florence is my home,
And in my city noble is my name;
Neither on peddling voyage am I come,
But, like my fathers, bent to gather fame; 235
And though thy face has set my heart a-flame,
Yet of thy story nothing do I know,
But here have wandered heedlessly enow.

"But since the sight of thee mine eyes did
　　bless,
What can I be but thine? what wouldst thou
　　have?   240
From those thy words, I deem from some
　　distress
By deeds of mine thy dear life I might save;
Oh, then, delay not! if one ever gave
His life to any, mine I give to thee;
Come, tell me what the price of love must
　　be? —   245

"Swift death, to be with thee a day and
　　night
And with the earliest dawning to be slain?
Or better, a long year of great delight,
And many years of misery and pain?
Or worse, and this poor hour for all my gain?
A sorry merchant am I on this day;   251
E'en as thou willest, so must I obey."

She said, "What brave words! Naught
　　divine am I,
But an unhappy and unheard-of maid,
Compelled by evil fate and destiny   255
To live, who long ago should have been laid
Under the earth within the cypress shade.

238. enow, enough. 257. cypress shade. The cypress, a
tree common in cemeteries, is an emblem of mourning.

Hearken awhile, and quickly shalt thou know
What deed I pray thee to accomplish now.

"God grant indeed thy words are not for
　　naught!   260
Then shalt thou save me, since for many a
　　day
To such a dreadful life I have been brought.
Nor will I spare with all my heart to pay
What man soever takes my grief away;
Ah! I will love thee, if thou lovest me   265
But well enough my savior now to be.

"My father lived a many years agone,
Lord of this land, master of all cunning,
Who ruddy gold could draw from out gray
　　stone,
And gather wealth from many an uncouth
　　thing;   270
He made the wilderness rejoice and sing,
And such a leech he was that none could say
Without his word what soul should pass away.

"Unto Diana such a gift he gave,
Goddess above, below, and on the earth,   275
That I should be her virgin and her slave
From the first hour of my most wretched
　　birth;
Therefore my life had known but little mirth
When I had come unto my twentieth year
And the last time of hallowing drew anear. 280

"So in her temple had I lived and died
And all would long ago have passed away,
But ere that time came, did strange things
　　betide,
Whereby I am alive unto this day;
Alas, the bitter words that I must say!   285
Ah! can I bring my wretched tongue to tell
How I was brought unto this fearful hell?

"A queen I was; what gods I knew I loved,
And nothing evil was there in my thought,
And yet by love my wretched heart was
　　moved   290
Until to utter ruin I was brought!
Alas! thou sayest our gods were vain and
　　naught;
Wait, wait, till thou hast heard this tale of
　　mine —
Then shalt thou think them devilish or divine.

"Hearken! in spite of father and of vow,
I loved a man; but for that sin I think   296
Men had forgiven me — yea, yea, even thou;
But from the gods the full cup must I drink,
And into misery unheard of sink,
Tormented, when their own names are forgot,
And men must doubt e'er if they lived or
　　not.   301

"Glorious my lover was unto my sight,
Most beautiful — of love we grew so fain
That we at last agreed that on a night
We should be happy, but that he were slain 305
Or shut in hold; and neither joy nor pain
Should else forbid that hoped-for time to be;
So came the night that made a wretch of me.

"Ah! well do I remember all that night,
When through the window shone the orb
    of June,   310
And by the bed flickered the taper's light,
Whereby I trembled, gazing at the moon;
Ah me! the meeting that we had, when soon
Into his strong, well-trusted arms I fell,
And many a sorrow we began to tell.   315

"Ah me! what parting on that night we
    had!
I think the story of my great despair
A little while might merry folk make sad;
For, as he swept away my yellow hair
To make my shoulder and my bosom bare,
I raised mine eyes, and shuddering could
    behold   321
A shadow cast upon the bed of gold;

"Then suddenly was quenched my hot
    desire,
And he untwined his arms; the moon, so pale
A while ago, seemed changed to blood and
    fire,   325
And yet my limbs beneath me did not fail,
And neither had I strength to cry or wail,
But stood there helpless, bare, and shivering,
With staring eyes still fixed upon the thing.

"Because the shade that on the bed of gold
The changed and dreadful moon was throw-
    ing down   331
Was of Diana, whom I did behold,
With knotted hair, and shining girt-up gown,
And on the high white brow, a deadly frown
Bent upon us, who stood scarce drawing
    breath,   335
Striving to meet the horrible sure death,

"No word at all the dreadful goddess said,
But soon across my feet my lover lay,
And well indeed I knew that he was dead;
And would that I had died on that same day!
For in a while the image turned away,   341
And without words my doom I understood,
And felt a horror change my human blood.

"And there I fell, and on the floor I lay
By the dead man, till daylight came on me, 345
And not a word thenceforward could I say
For three years; till of grief and misery,
The lingering pest, the cruel enemy,

My father and his folk were dead and gone,
And in this castle I was left alone.   350

"And then the doom foreseen upon me fell,
For Queen Diana did my body change
Into a fork-tongued dragon flesh and fell,
And through the island nightly do I range,
Or in the green sea mate with monsters
    strange,   355
When in the middle of the moonlit night
The sleepy mariner I do affright.

"But all day long upon this gold I lie,
Within this place, where never mason's hand
Smote trowel on the marble noisily;   360
Drowsy I lie, no folk at my command,
Who once was called the Lady of the Land;
Who might have bought a kingdom with a
    kiss,
Yea, half the world with such a sight as this."

And therewithal, with rosy fingers light, 365
Backward her heavy-hanging hair she threw,
To give her naked beauty more to sight;
But when, forgetting all the things he knew,
Maddened with love unto the prize he drew,
She cried, "Nay, wait! for wherefore wilt thou
    die;   370
Why should we not be happy, thou and I?

"Wilt thou not save me? Once in every
    year
This rightful form of mine that thou dost see
By favor of the goddess have I here
From sunrise unto sunset given me,   375
That some brave man may end my misery.
And thou — art thou not brave? can thy
    heart fail,
Whose eyes e'en now are weeping at my tale?

"Then listen! when this day is overpast,
A fearful monster shall I be again,   380
And thou mayst be my savior at the last —
Unless, once more, thy words are naught and
    vain.
If thou of love and sovereignty art fain,
Come thou next morn, and when thou seest
    here
A hideous dragon, have thereof no fear. 385

"But take the loathsome head up in thine
    hands,
And kiss it, and be master presently
Of twice the wealth that is in all the lands,
From Cathay to the head of Italy;
And master also, if it pleaseth thee,   390
Of all thou praisest as so fresh and bright,
Of what thou callest crown of all delight.

353. **flesh and fell,** body and skin. 389. **Cathay,** a
poetic name for China; used vaguely during the Middle Ages
for regions in the Far East.

"Ah! with what joy then shall I see again
The sunlight on the green grass and the trees,
And hear the clatter of the summer rain,   395
And see the joyous folk beyond the seas;
Ah, me! to hold my child upon my knees,
After the weeping of unkindly tears,
And all the wrongs of these four hundred
    years.

"Go now, go quick! leave this gray heap of
    stone;   400
And from thy glad heart think upon thy
    way,
How I shall love thee — yea, love thee alone,
That bringest me from dark death unto
    day;
For this shall be thy wages and thy pay;   404
Unheard-of wealth, unheard-of love is near,
If thou hast heart a little dread to bear."

Therewith she turned to go; but he cried
    out,
"Ah! wilt thou leave me then without one
    kiss,
To slay the very seeds of fear and doubt,
That glad tomorrow may bring certain bliss?
Hast thou forgotten how love lives by this, 411
The memory of some hopeful close embrace,
Low whispered words within some lonely
    place?"

But she, when his bright glittering eyes she
    saw,
And burning cheeks, cried out, "Alas, alas! 415
Must I be quite undone, and wilt thou draw
A worse fate on me than the first one was?
Oh, haste thee from this fatal place to pass!
Yet, ere thou goest, take this, lest thou
    shouldst deem
Thou hast been fooled by some strange mid-
    day dream."   420

So saying, blushing like a new-kissed maid,
From off her neck a little gem she drew,
That, 'twixt those snowy rose-tinged hillocks
    laid,
The secrets of her glorious beauty knew;   424
And ere he well perceived what she would do,
She touched his hand, the gem within it lay,
And, turning, from his sight she fled away.

Then at the doorway where her rosy heel
Had glanced and vanished, he awhile did
    stare,   429
And still upon his hand he seemed to feel
The varying kisses of her fingers fair;
Then turned he toward the dreary crypt and
    bare,
And dizzily throughout the castle passed,
Till by the ruined fane he stood at last.

Then weighing still the gem within his
    hand,   434
He stumbled backward though the cypress
    wood,
Thinking the while of some strange lovely
    land,
Where all his life should be most fair and
    good
Till on the valley's wall of hills he stood, 439
And slowly thence passed down unto the
    bay
Red with the death of that bewildering
    day.

The next day came, and he, who all the
    night
Had ceaselessly been turning in his bed,
Arose and clad himself in armor bright,
And many a danger he rememberéd —   445
Storming of towns, lone sieges full of dread,
That with renown his heart had borne him
    through —
And this thing seemed a little thing to do.

So on he went, and on the way he thought
Of all the glorious things of yesterday,   450
Naught of the price whereat they must be
    bought,
But ever to himself did softly say,
"No roaming now, my wars are passed away;
No long dull days devoid of happiness,
When such a love my yearning heart shall
    bless."   455

Thus to the castle did he come at last,
But when unto the gateway he drew near,
And underneath its ruined archway passed
Into the court, a strange noise did he hear,
And through his heart there shot a pang of
    fear;   460
Trembling, he gat his sword into his hand,
And midmost of the cloisters took his stand.

But for a while that unknown noise in-
    creased,
A rattling, that with strident roars did blend,
And whining moans; but suddenly it ceased—
A fearful thing stood at the cloister's end, 466
And eyed him for a while, then 'gan to wend
Adown the cloisters, and began again
That rattling, and the moan like fiends in
    pain.

And as it came on toward him, with its
    teeth   470
The body of a slain goat did it tear,
The blood whereof in its hot jaws did seethe,
And on its tongue he saw the smoking hair;
Then his heart sank, and standing trembling
    there,

Throughout his mind wild thoughts and fear-
    ful ran,   475
"Some fiend she was," he said, "the bane of
    man."

Yet he abode her still, although his blood
Curdled within him. The thing dropped the
    goat,
And creeping on, came close to where he
    stood,
And raised its head to him, and wrinkled
    throat;   480
Then he cried out and wildly at her smote,
Shutting his eyes, and turned and from the
    place
Ran swiftly, with a white and ghastly face.

But little things rough stones and tree-
    trunks seemed,
And if he fell, he rose and ran on still.   485
No more he felt his hurts than if he dreamed;
He made no stay for valley or steep hill;
Heedless, he dashed through many a foaming
    rill,
Until he came unto the ship at last,
And with no word into the deep hold passed.

Meanwhile the dragon, seeing him clean
    gone,   491
Followed him not, but crying horribly,
Caught up within her jaws a block of stone
And ground it into powder, then turned she,
With cries that folk could hear far out at
    sea,
And reached the treasure set apart of old, 496
To brood above the hidden heaps of gold.

Yet was she seen again on many a day
By some half-waking mariner, or heard, .
Playing amid the ripples of the bay,   500
Or on the hills making all things afeard,
Or in the wood, that did that castle gird,
But never any man again durst go
To seek her woman's form, and end her woe.

As for the man, who knows what things he
    bore?   505
What mournful faces peopled the sad night,
What wailings vexed him with reproaches
    sore,
What images of that nigh-gained delight!
What dreamed caresses from soft hands and
    white,
Turning to horrors ere they reached the best!
What struggles vain, what shame, what huge
    unrest!   511

No man he knew; three days he lay and
    raved,
And cried for death, until a lethargy

Fell on him, and his fellows thought him
    saved;
But on the third night he awoke to die; 515
And at Byzantium doth his body lie
Between two blossoming pomegranate trees,
Within the churchyard of the Genoese.(1868)

Song from OGIER THE DANE

Hæc

In the white-flowered hawthorn brake,
Love, be merry for my sake;
Twine the blossoms in my hair,
Kiss me where I am most fair --
Kiss me, love! for who knoweth   5
What thing cometh after death?

Ille

Nay, the garlanded gold hair
Hides thee where thou art most fair;
Hides the rose-tinged hills of snow —
Ah, sweet love, I have thee now!   10
Kiss me, love! for who knoweth
What thing cometh after death?

Hæc

Shall we weep for a dead day,
Or set Sorrow in our way?
Hidden by my golden hair,   15
Wilt thou weep that sweet days wear?
Kiss me, love! for who knoweth
What thing cometh after death?

Ille

Weep, O love, the days that flit,
    Now, while I can feel thy breath; 20
Then may I remember it
    Sad and old, and near my death.
Kiss me, love! for who knoweth
What thing cometh after death?   (1868)

Song from THE HILL OF VENUS

Before our lady came on earth
Little there was of joy or mirth;
About the borders of the sea
The sea-folk wandered heavily;
About the wintry river side   5
The weary fishers would abide.

516. **Byzantium,** an ancient Greek city on the site of
Constantinople. It contained a cemetery for natives of
Genoa who had moved there.
   Song from Ogier the Dane. Ogier was a Danish prince, a
hero of medieval French romances. The song given here was
heard by Ogier as it was sung by two young voices early in the
morning; it seemed to him to be the farewell of the Queen of
France, whom he loved. *Haec* and *Ille* are *She* and *He.*
   Song from The Hill of Venus. See note on *Laus Veneris,*
line 25, p. 675. The song given here was heard by a knight
as he awoke from a swoon. It was sung by a group of young
men and maidens deeply in love.

Alone within the weaving-room
The girls would sit before the loom,
And sing no song, and play no play;
Alone from dawn to hot mid-day,   10
From mid-day unto evening,
The men afield would work, nor sing,
'Mid weary thoughts of man and God,
Before thy feet the wet ways trod.

Unkissed, the merchant bore his care;   15
Unkissed, the knights went out to war;
Unkissed, the mariner came home;
Unkissed, the minstrel men did roam.

Or in the stream the maids would stare,
Nor know why they were made so fair;   20
Their yellow locks, their bosoms white,
Their limbs well wrought for all delight,
Seemed foolish things that waited death,
As hopeless as the flowers beneath
The weariness of unkissed feet.   25
No life was bitter then, or sweet.

Therefore, O Venus, well may we
Praise the green ridges of the sea
O'er which, upon a happy day,
Thou cam'st to take our shame away.   30
Well may we praise the curdling foam
Amidst the which thy feet did bloom,
Flowers of the gods; the yellow sand
They kissed atwixt the sea and land;
The bee-beset, ripe-seeded grass,   35
Through which thy fine limbs first did pass;
The purple-dusted butterfly,
First blown against thy quivering thigh;
The first red rose that touched thy side,
And over-blown and fainting died;   40
The flickering of the orange shade,
Where first in sleep thy limbs were laid;
The happy day's sweet life and death,
Whose air first caught thy balmy breath —
Yea, all these things well praised may be,   45
But with what words shall we praise thee —
O Venus, O thou love alive,
Born to give peace to souls that strive?
                                    (1870)

L'ENVOI

Here are we for the last time face to face,
Thou and I, Book, before I bid thee speed
Upon thy perilous journey to that place
For which I have done on thee pilgrim's weed,
Striving to get thee all things for thy need —
I love thee, whatso time or men may say   6
Of the poor singer of an empty day.

Good reason why I love thee, e'en if thou
Be mocked or clean forgot as time wears on;

For ever as thy fashioning did grow,   10
Kind word and praise because of thee I won
From those without whom were my world all
        gone,
My hope fallen dead, my singing cast away,
And I set soothly in an empty day.

I love thee; yet this last time must it be   15
That thou must hold thy peace and I must
        speak,
Lest if thou babble I begin to see
Thy gear too thin, thy limbs and heart too
        weak,
To find the land thou goest forth to seek —
Though what harm if thou die upon the way,
Thou idle singer of an empty day?   21

But though this land desired thou never
        reach,
Yet folk who know it mayst thou meet, or
        death;
Therefore a word unto thee would I teach
To answer these, who, noting thy weak
        breath,   25
Thy wandering eyes, thy heart of little faith,
May make thy fond desire a sport and play
Mocking the singer of an empty day.

That land's name, say'st thou? and the road
        thereto?
Nay, Book, thou mockest, saying thou
        know'st it not;   30
Surely no book of verse I ever knew
But ever was the heart within him hot
To gain the Land of Matters Unforgot —
There, now we both laugh — as the whole
        world may,
At us poor singers of an empty day.   35

Nay, let it pass, and harken! Hast thou heard
That therein I believe I have a friend,
Of whom for love I may not be afeared?
It is to him indeed I bid thee wend;
Yea, he perchance may meet thee ere thou
        end,   40
Dying so far off from the hedge of bay,
Thou idle singer of an empty day!

Well, think of him, I bid thee, on the road,
And if it hap that midst of thy defeat,
Fainting beneath thy follies' heavy load,   45
My Master, GEOFFREY CHAUCER, thou do
        meet,
Then shalt thou win a space of rest full sweet;
Then be thou bold, and speak the words I say,
The idle singer of an empty day!

L'Envoi. 4. done . . . weed, put on thee the garments of a
pilgrim preparatory to a journey—i.e., got you printed.

41. bay, laurel. In ancient times poets were crowned with
wreaths of laurel or myrtle. 46. Geoffrey Chaucer. The
framework of Chaucer's Canterbury Tales is similar to that of
The Earthly Paradise.

"O Master, O thou great of heart and tongue,
Thou well mayst ask me why I wander here,
In raiment rent of stories oft besung!   52
But of thy gentleness draw thou anear,
And then the heart of one who held thee dear
Mayst thou behold! So near as that I lay 55
Unto the singer of an empty day.

"For this he ever said, who sent me forth
To seek a place amid thy company:
That howsoever little was my worth,
Yet was he worth e'en just so much as I; 60
He said that rime hath little skill to lie;
Nor feigned to cast his worser part away:
In idle singing for an empty day.

"I have beheld him tremble oft enough
At things he could not choose but trust to me,
Although he knew the world was wise and
        rough;   66
And never did he fail to let me see
His love — his folly and faithlessness, maybe;
And still in turn I gave him voice to pray
Such prayers as cling about an empty day. 70

"Thou, keen-eyed, reading me, mayst read
        him through,
For surely little is there left behind;
No power great deeds unnameable to do;
No knowledge for which words he may not
        find,
No love of things as vague as autumn wind —
Earth of the earth lies hidden by my clay, 76
The idle singer of an empty day!

"Children we twain are, saith he, late made
        wise
In love, but in all else most childish still,
And seeking still the pleasure of our eyes, 80
And what our ears with sweetest sounds may
        fill;
Not fearing Love, lest these things he should
        kill;
Howe'er his pain by pleasure doth he lay,
Making a strange tale of an empty day.

"Death have we hated, knowing not what it
        meant;   85
Life had we loved, through green leaf and
        through sere,
Though still the less we knew of its intent;
The Earth and Heaven through countless
        year on year,
Slow changing, were to us but curtains fair,
Hung round about a little room, where play 90
Weeping and laughter of man's empty day.

"O Master, if thine heart could love us yet,
Spite of things left undone, and wrongly done,
Some place in loving hearts then should we
        get,

For thou, sweet-souled, didst never stand
        alone,   95
But knew'st the joy and woe of many an
        one —
By lovers dead, who live through thee, we
        pray,
Help thou us singers of an empty day!"

Fearest thou, Book, what answer thou mayst
        gain
Lest he should scorn thee, and thereof thou
        die?   100
Nay, it shall not be. — Thou mayst toil in
        vain,
And never draw the House of Fame anigh;
Yet he and his shall know whereof we cry,
Shall call it not ill done to strive to lay
The ghosts that crowd about life's empty day.

Then let the others go! and if indeed   106
In some old garden thou and I have wrought,
And made fresh flowers spring up from
        hoarded seed,
And fragrance of old days and deeds have
        brought
Back to folk weary, all was not for naught.
— No little part it was for me to play — 111
The idle singer of an empty day.   (1870)

From THE STORY OF SIGURD THE VOLSUNG

OF THE PASSING AWAY OF BRYNHILD

Once more on the morrow-morning fair shin-
        eth the glorious sun,
And the Niblung children labor on a deed
        that shall be done.
For out in the people's meadows they raise a
        bale on high,
The oak and the ash together, and thereon
        shall the Mighty lie;
Nor gold nor steel shall be lacking, nor savor
        of sweet spice,   5
Nor cloths in the Southlands woven, nor webs
        of untold price.
The work grows, toil is as nothing; long blasts
        of the mighty horn
From the topmost tower out-wailing o'er the
        woeful world are borne.

But Brynhild lay in her chamber, and her
        women went and came,
And they feared and trembled before her, and
        none spake Sigurd's name;   10

102. **House of Fame**, a punning reference to Chaucer's
Hous of Fame.
The Story of Sigurd the Volsung. See Critical Notes.
Of the Passing Away of Brynhild. 3. **bale**, funeral pyre
for Sigurd, the Mighty.

But whiles they deemed her weeping, and
    whiles they deemed indeed
That she spake, if they might but hearken,
    but no words their ears might heed;
Till at last she spake out clearly:
        "I know not what ye would;
For ye come and go in my chamber, and ye
    seem of wavering mood
To thrust me on, or to stay me; to help my
    heart in woe,   15
Or to bid my days of sorrow midst nameless
    folly go."

None answered the word of Brynhild, none
    knew of her intent;
But she spake: "Bid hither Gunnar, lest the
    sun sink o'er the bent,
And leave the words unspoken I yet have will
    to speak."

Then her maidens go from before her, and
    that lord of war they seek,   20
And he stands by the bed of Brynhild and
    strives to entreat and beseech,
But her eyes gaze awfully on him, and his
    lips may learn no speech.
And she saith:
        "I slept in the morning, or I dreamed
    in the waking-hour,
And my dream was of thee, O Gunnar, and
    the bed in thy kingly bower,
And the house that I blessed in my sorrow,
    and cursed in my sorrow and shame, 25
The gates of an ancient people, the towers of
    a mighty name.
King, cold was the hall I have dwelt in, and
    no brand burned on the hearth;
Dead-cold was thy bed, O Gunnar, and thy
    land was parched with dearth;

"But I saw a great king riding, and a master
    of the harp,
And he rode amidst of the foemen, and the
    swords were bitter-sharp,   30
But his hand in the hand-gyves smote not,
    and his feet in the fetters were fast,
While many a word of mocking at his speech-
    less face was cast.
Then I heard a voice in the world: 'O woe
    for the broken troth,
And the heavy Need of the Niblungs, and the
    Sorrow of Odin the Goth!'
Then I saw the halls of the strangers, and the
    hills, and the dark-blue sea,   35
Nor knew of their names and their nations,
    for earth was afar from me,
But brother rose up against brother, and
    blood swam over the board,

18. **bent**, heath, moor.

And women smote and spared not, and the
    fire was master and lord.
Then, then was the moonless mid-mirk, and
    I woke to the day and the deed,
The deed that earth shall name not, the day
    of its bitterest need.   40
Many words have I said in my life-days, and
    little more shall I say.
Ye have heard the dream of a woman — deal
    with it as ye may;
For meseems the world-ways sunder, and the
    dusk and the dark is mine,
Till I come to the hall of Freyia, where the
    deeds of the mighty shall shine."

So hearkened Gunnar the Niblung, that her
    words he understood,   45
And he knew she was set on the death-stroke,
    and he deemed it nothing good.
But he said: "I have hearkened, and heeded
    thy death and mine in thy words;
I have done the deed and abide it, and my
    face shall laugh on the swords.
But thee, woman, I bid thee abide here till
    thy grief of soul abate;
Meseems naught lowly nor shameful shall be
    the Niblung fate;   50
And here shalt thou rule and be mighty, and
    be queen of the measureless Gold,
And abase the kings and upraise them; and
    anew shall thy fame be told,
And as fair shall thy glory blossom as the
    fresh fields under the spring."

Then he casteth his arms about her, and hot
    is the heart of the King
For the glory of Queen Brynhild and the hope
    of her days of gain,   55
And he clean forgetteth Sigurd and the foster-
    brother slain;
But she shrank aback from before him, and
    cried: "Woe worth the while
For the thoughts ye drive back on me, and
    the memory of your guile!
The Kings of Earth were gathered, the wise
    of men were met;
On the death of a woman's pleasure their
    glorious hearts were set,   60
And I was alone amidst them — ah, hold thy
    peace hereof!
Lest the thought of the bitterest hours this
    little hour should move."

He rose abashed from before her, and yet he
    lingered there;

39. **mid-mirk**, mid-gloom, deepest gloom. **the deed**, her
suicide. 44. **Freyia**, the goddess who presides over the regions
of the dead. 48. **the deed**, his part in deceiving Brynhild.
(See Critical Note on title.) 56. **foster-brother slain**,
Guttorm.

Then she said: "O King of the Niblungs,
  what noise do I hearken and hear?
Why ring the axes and hammers, while feet
  of men go past,   65
And shields from the wall are shaken, and
  swords on the pavement cast,
And the door of the treasure is open, and the
  horn cries loud and long,
And the feet of the Niblung children to the
  people's meadows throng?"

His face was troubled before her, and again
  she spake and said:
"Meseemeth this is the hour when men array
  the dead;   70
Wilt thou tell me tidings, Gunnar, that the
  children of thy folk
Pile up the bale for Guttorm, and the hand
  that smote the stroke?"

He said: "It is not so, Brynhild; for that
  Giuki's son was burned
When the moon of the middle heaven last
  night toward dawning turned."

They looked on each other and spake not; but
  Gunnar gat him gone,   75
And came to his brother Hogni, the wise-
  heart Giuki's son,
And spake: "Thou art wise, O Hogni; go in
  to Brynhild the queen,
And stay her swift departing; or the last of
  her days hath she seen."

"It is naught, thy word," said Hogni, "wilt
  thou bring dead men aback,
Or the souls of kings departed midst the
  battle and the wrack?   80
Yet this shall be easier to thee than the turning Brynhild's heart;
She came to dwell among us, but in us she
  had no part;
Let her go her ways from the Niblungs with
  her hand in Sigurd's hand.
Will the grass grow up henceforward where
  her feet have trodden the land?"

"O evil day," said Gunnar, "when my queen
  must perish and die!"   85

"Such oft betide," saith Hogni, "as the lives
  of men flit by;
But the evil day is a day, and on each day
  groweth a deed,
And a thing that never dieth; and the fateful
  tale shall speed.
Lo now, let us harden our hearts and set our
  brows as the brass,
Lest men say it, 'They loathed the evil, and
  they brought the evil to pass.'"   90

So they spake, and their hearts were heavy,
  and they longed for the morrow morn,
And the morrow of tomorrow, and the new
  day yet to be born.

But Brynhild cried to her maidens: "Now
  open ark and chest,
And draw forth queenly raiment of the loveliest and the best,
Red rings that the Dwarf-lords fashioned, fair
  cloths that queens have sewed   95
To array the bride for the mighty, and the
  traveler for the road."

They wept as they wrought her bidding and
  did on her goodliest gear,
But she laughed amid the dainty linen, and
  the gold-rings fashioned fair;
She arose from the bed of the Niblungs, and
  her face no more was wan;
As a star in the dawn-tide heavens, mid the
  dusky house she shone.   100
And they that stood about her, their hearts
  were raised aloft
Amid their fear and wonder; then she spake
  them kind and soft:

"Now give me my sword, O maidens, wherewith I sheared the wind
When the Kings of Earth were gathered to
  know the Chooser's mind."

All sheathed the maidens brought it, and
  feared the hidden blade,   105
But the naked blue-white edges across her
  knees she laid,
And spake: "The heaped-up riches, the gear
  my fathers left,
All dear-bought woven wonders, all rings
  from battle reft,
All goods of men desired, now strew them on
  the floor,
And so share among you, maidens, the gifts
  of Brynhild's store."   110

They brought them mid their weeping, but
  none put forth a hand
To take that wealth desired, the spoils of
  many a land.
There stand and weep before her, and
  some are moved to speech,
And they cast their arms about her and strive
  with her, and beseech
That she look on her loved-ones' sorrow and
  the glory of the day.   115

97. **did on . . . gear**, put on her best raiment. 103-104.
sword . . . mind. Brynhild was one of the Old Norse
Valkyries (the Choosers of the Slain), twelve nymphs who,
mounted on swift horses and holding drawn swords, rushed
into the thick of the battle and chose those destined to
death. 107. **gear**, property.

It was naught; she scarce might see them,
and she put their hands away,
And she said: "Peace, ye that love me! and
take the gifts and the gold
In remembrance of my fathers and the faithful deeds of old."

Then she spake: "Where now is Gunnar, that
I may speak with him?
For new things are mine eyes beholding and
the Niblung house grows dim,   120
And new sounds gather about me, that may
hinder me to speak
When the breath is near to flitting, and the
voice is waxen weak."

Then upright by the bed of the Niblungs for
a moment doth she stand,
And the blade flasheth bright in the chamber,
but no more they hinder her hand
Than if a god were smiting to rend the world
in two;   125
Then dulled are the glittering edges, and the
bitter point cleaves through
The breast of the all-wise Brynhild, and her
feet from the pavement fail,
And the sigh of her heart is hearkened mid
the hush of the maidens' wail.
Chill, deep is the fear upon them, but they
bring her aback to the bed,
And her hand is yet on the hilts, and sidelong
droopeth her head.   130

Then there cometh a cry from withoutward,
and Gunnar's hurrying feet
Are swift on the kingly threshold, and Bryn-
hild's blood they meet.
Low down o'er the bed he hangeth and heark-
eneth for her word,
And her heavy lids are opened to look on the
Niblung lord,
And she saith:
          "I pray thee a prayer, the last word
in the world I speak,   135
That ye bear me forth to Sigurd, and the
hand my hand would seek;
The bale for the dead is builded, it is wrought
full wide on the plain,
It is raised for Earth's best Helper, and there-
on is room for twain.
Ye have hung the shields about it, and the
Southland hangings spread;
There lay me adown by Sigurd and my head
beside his head;   140
But ere ye leave us sleeping, draw his Wrath
from out the sheath,
And lay that Light of the Branstock, and the
blade that frighted death

Betwixt my side and Sigurd's, as it lay that
while agone,
When once in one bed together we twain were
laid alone.
How then when the flames flare upward may
I be left behind?   145
How then may the road he wendeth be hard
for my feet to find?
How then in the gates of Valhall may the
door of the gleaming ring
Clash to on the heel of Sigurd, as I follow on
my king?"

Then she raised herself on her elbow, but
again her eyelids sank,
And the wound by the sword-edge whispered,
as her heart from the iron shrank,   150
And she moaned: "O lives of man-folk, for
unrest all overlong
By the Father were ye fashioned; and what
hope amendeth wrong?
Now at last, O my belovéd, all is gone; none
else is near.
Through the ages of all ages, never sundered,
shall we wear."

Scarce more than a sigh was the word, as
back on the bed she fell,   155
Nor was there need in the chamber of the
passing of Brynhild to tell;
And no more their lamentation might the
maidens hold aback,
But the sound of their bitter mourning was
as if red-handed wrack
Ran wild in the Burg of the Niblungs, and
the fire were master of all.

Then the voice of Gunnar the war-king cried
out o'er the weeping hall: 160
"Wail on, O women forsaken, for the might-
iest woman born!
Now the hearth is cold and joyless, and the
waste bed lieth forlorn.
Wail on, but amid your weeping lay hand to
the glorious dead,
That not alone for an hour may lie Queen
Brynhild's head;
For here have been heavy tidings, and the
Mightiest under shield   165
Is laid on the bale high-builded in the Nib-
lungs' hallowed field.
Fare forth! for he abideth, and we do All-
father wrong,
If the shining Valhall's pavement await their
feet o'erlong."

Then they took the body of Brynhild in the
raiment that she wore,

---

141. **Wrath**, the name of Sigurd's sword. 142. **Light of the Branstock**, the bright sword that Sigmund, son of Vol-sung, drew from Branstock, the great oak tree about which the Hall of the Volsungs had been built. 143. **lay . . . agone.** See Critical Note on title. 147. **Valhall**, Valhalla—in Norse mythology the hall of Odin, father of the gods. With him dwelt all warriors slain in battle. 165. **under shield**, that ever bore shield. 167. **All-father**, Odin, the Father of All.

And out through the gate of the Niblungs
the holy corpse they bore, 170
And thence forth to the mead of the people
and the high-built shielded bale;
Then afresh in the open meadows breaks
forth the women's wail
When they see the bed of Sigurd and the
glittering of his gear;
And fresh is the wail of the people as Brynhild draweth anear,
And the tidings go before her that for twain
the bale is built, 175
That for twain is the oak-wood shielded and
the pleasant odors spilt.

There is peace on the bale of Sigurd, and the
gods look down from on high,
And they see the lids of the Volsung close
shut against the sky,
As he lies with his shield beside him in the
Hauberk all of gold,
That has not its like in the heavens, nor has
earth of its fellow told; 180
And forth from the Helm of Aweing are the
sunbeams flashing wide,
And the sheathéd Wrath of Sigurd lies still
by his mighty side.
Then cometh an elder of days, a man of the
ancient times,
Who is long past sorrow and joy, and the
steep of the bale he climbs;
And he kneeleth down by Sigurd, and bareth
the Wrath to the sun 185
That the beams are gathered about it, and
from hilt to blood-point run,
And wide o'er the plain of the Niblungs doth
the Light of the Branstock glare,
Till the wondering mountain-shepherds on
that star of noontide stare,
And fear for many an evil; but the ancient
man stands still
With the war-flame on his shoulder, nor thinks
of good or of ill, 190
Till the feet of Brynhild's bearers on the topmost bale are laid,
And her bed is dight by Sigurd's; then he
sinks the pale white blade
And lays it 'twixt the sleepers, and leaves
them there alone —
He, the last that shall ever behold them —
and his days are wellnigh done.

There is silence over the plain; in the noon
shine the torches pale, 195
As the best of the Niblung Earl-folk bear fire
to the builded bale;

Then a wind in the west ariseth, and the
white flames leap on high,
And with one voice crieth the people a great
and mighty cry,
And men cast up hands to the Heavens, and
pray without a word,
As they that have seen God's visage, and the
voice of the Father have heard. 200

They are gone — the lovely, the mighty, the
hope of the ancient Earth;
It shall labor and bear the burden as before
that day of their birth;
It shall groan in its blind abiding for the day
that Sigurd hath sped,
And the hour that Brynhild hath hastened,
and the dawn that waketh the dead.
It shall yearn, and be ofttimes holpen, and
forget their deeds no more, 205
Till the new sun beams on Baldur, and the
happy sealess shore.

(1876)

GUNNAR IN THE PIT OF ADDERS

Then was Gunnar silent a little, and the shout
in the hall had died,
And he spoke as a man awakening, and turned
on Atli's pride.
"Thou all-rich King of the Eastlands, e'en
such a man might I be
That I might utter a word, and the heart
should be glad in thee,
And I should live and be sorry; for I, I only
am left 5
To tell of the ransom of Odin, and the wealth
from the toiler reft.
Lo, once it lay in the water, hid, deep adown
it lay,
Till the gods were grieved and lacking, and
men saw it and the day;
Let it lie in the water once more, let the gods
be rich and in peace!
But I at least in the world from the words
and the babble shall cease." 10

So he spake and Atli beheld him, and before
his eyes he shrank;
Still deep of the cup of desire the mighty
Atli drank,
And to overcome seemed little if the Gold he
might not have,
And his hard heart craved for a while to hold
the King for a slave,
A bondman blind and guarded in his glorious
house and great. 15
But he thought of the overbold, and of kings
who have dallied with fate,

176. **oak-wood shielded,** the funeral pyre, built of oak
(and ash, line 4), covered with shields. 181. **Helm of Aweing,** helmet of Sigurd, that frightened foes. 192. **dight,**
prepared. 196. **Earl-folk,** Norse chieftains, ranking just
below the king. Lower-ranking people were known as carles.

206. **Baldur,** son of Odin, and the Norse god of light and
peace.
Gunnar in the Pit of Adders. See Critical Note on title.

And died bemocked and smitten; and he
deemed it worser than well
While the last of the sons of Giuki hangeth
back from his journey to Hell;
So he turneth away from the stranger, and
beholdeth Gudrun his wife,
Not glad nor sorry by seeming, no stirrer nor
stayer of strife.   20
Then he looked at his living earl-folk, and
thought of his groves of war,
And his realm and the kindred nations, and
his measureless guarded store.
And he thought: Shall Atli perish, shall his
name be cast to the dead,
Though the feeble folk go wailing? Then he
cried aloud and said:

"Why tarry ye, Sons of the Morning? The
wain for the bondman is dight;   25
And the folk that are waiting his body have
néed of no sunshine to smite.
Go forth 'neath the stars and night-wind; go
forth by the cloud and the moon,
And come back with the word in the dawning,
that my house may be merry at noon!"

Then the sword-folk rise round Gunnar, round
the fettered and bound they throng,
As men in the bitter battle round the God-
kin over-strong;   30
They bore him away to the doorway, and
the winds were awake in the night,
And the wood of the thorns of battle in the
moon shone sharp and bright;
But Gunnar looked to the heavens, and
blessed the promise of rain,
And the windy drift of the clouds, and the
dew on the builded wain;
And the sword-folk tarried a little, and the
sons of the wise were there,   35
And beheld his face o'er the war-helms, and
the wavy night of his hair.
Then they feared for the weal of Atli, and
the Niblung's harp they brought,
And they dealt with the thralls of the sword,
and commanded and besought,
Till men loosened the gyves of Gunnar, and
laid the harp by his side.
Then the yoke-beasts lowed in the forecourt,
and the wheels of the wagon cried,   40
And the war-thorns clashed in the night, and
the men went dark on their way,
And the city was silent before them; on the
roofs the white moon lay.

Now they left the gate and the highway, and
came to a lonely place,
Where the sun all day had been shining on
the desert's empty face;
Then the moon ran forth from a cloud, the
gray light shone and showed   45
The pit of King Atli's adders in the land
without a road,
Digged deep adown in the desert with shining
walls and smooth
For the Serpent's habitation, and folk that
know not ruth.
Therein they thrust King Gunnar, and he
bare of his kingly weed,
But they gave his harp to the Niblung, and
his hands of the gyves they freed;   50
They stood around in their war-gear to note
what next should befall
For the comfort of King Atli, and the glee of
the Eastland hall.

Still hot was that close with the sun, and
thronged with the coiling folk,
And about the feet of Gunnar their hissing
mouths awoke;
But he heeded them not nor beheld them,
and his hands in the harp-strings ran,   55
As he sat him down in the midmost on a sun-
scorched rock and wan;
And he sighed as one who resteth on a flowery
bank by the way
When the wind is in the blossoms at the eventide of day.
But his harp was murmuring low, and he
mused: Am I come to the death,
And I, who was Gunnar the Niblung? Nay,
nay, how I draw my breath,   60
And love my life as the living! and so I ever
shall do,
Though wrack be loosed in the heavens and
the world be fashioned anew.

But the worms were beholding their prey,
and they drew around and nigher,
Smooth coil, and flickering tongue, and eyes
as the gold in the fire;
And he looked and beheld them and spake,
nor stilled his harp meanwhile: 65
"What will ye, O thralls of Atli, O images of
guile?"

Then he rose at once to his feet, and smote
the harp with his hand,
And it rang as if with a cry in the dream of
a lonely land;
Then he fondled its wail as it faded, and
orderly over the strings

Went the marvelous sound of its sweetness,
   like the march of Odin's kings   70
New-risen for play in the morning when o'er
   meadows of God-home they wend,
And hero playeth with hero, that their hands
   may be deft in the end.
But the crests of the worms were uplifted,
   though coil on coil was stayed,
And they moved but as dark-green rushes by
   the summer river swayed.
Then uprose the Song of Gunnar, and sang
   o'er his crafty hands,   75
And told of the World of Aforetime, un-
   shapen, void of lands;
Yet it wrought, for its memory bideth, and
   it died and abode its doom;
It shaped, and the Upper-Heavens, and the
   hope came forth from its womb.

Great then grew the voice of Gunnar, and
   his speech was sweet on the wild,
And the moon on his harp was shining, and
   the hands of the Niblung child: 80

"So perished the Gap of the Gaping, and the
   cold sea swayed and sang.
And the wind came down on the waters, and
   the beaten rock-walls rang;
Then the Sun from the south came shining,
   and the Starry Host stood round,
And the wandering Moon of the heavens his
   habitation found;
And they knew not why they were gathered,
   nor the deeds of their shaping they knew.
But lo, Mid-Earth the Noble 'neath their
   might and their glory grew,   86
And the grass spread over its face, and the
   Night and the Day were born,
And it cried on the Death in the even, and
   it cried on the Life in the morn;
Yet it waxed and waxed, and knew not, and
   it lived and had not learned;
And where were the Framers that framed,
   and the Soul and the Might that had
   yearned?   90

"On the Thrones are the Powers that fashioned, and they name the Night and the
   Day,
And the tide of the Moon's increasing, and
   the tide of his waning away;
And they name the years for the story; and
   the Lands they change and change,

The great and the mean and the little, that
   this unto that may be strange.
They met, and they fashioned dwellings, and
   the House of Glory they built;   95
They met, and they fashioned the Dwarf-
   kind, and the Gold and the Gifts and the
   Guilt.

"There were twain, and they went upon earth,
   and were speechless unmighty and wan;
They were hopeless, deathless, lifeless, and
   the Mighty named them Man.
Then they gave them speech and power, and
   they gave them color and breath;
And deeds and the hope they gave them, and
   they gave them Life and Death —   100
Yea, hope, as the hope of the Framers; yea,
   might, as the Fashioners had,
Till they wrought, and rejoiced in their bodies,
   and saw their sons and were glad;
And they changed their lives and departed,
   and came back as the leaves of the trees
Come back and increase in the summer —
   and I, I, I am of these;
And I know of Them that have fashioned,
   and the deeds that have blossomed and
   grow;   105
But naught of the gods' repentance, or the
   gods' undoing I know."

Then falleth the speech of Gunnar, and his
   lips the word forget,
But his crafty hands are busy, and the harp
   is murmuring yet.

And the crests of the worms have fallen, and
   their flickering tongues are still,
The Roller and the Coiler, and Grayback,
   lord of ill,   110
Grave-groper and Death-swaddler, the Slum-
   berer of the Heath,
Gold-wallower, Venom-smiter, lie still, forgetting death,
And loose are coils of Long-back; yea, all as
   soft are laid
As the kine in midmost summer about the
   elmy glade —
All save the Gray and Ancient, that holds his
   crest aloft,   115
Light-wavering as the flame-tongue when the
   evening wind is soft;
For he comes of the kin of the Serpent once
   wrought all wrong to nurse,
The bond of earthly evil, and Midworld's
   ancient curse.

70. march of Odin's kings. Odin was the father of the
gods of Norse mythology. When he and his heroes in Valhalla
were not feasting, they amused themselves with fighting.
Every day they rode out into the field and fought until they
cut each other to pieces; but they soon recovered from their
wounds and returned to feast in Valhalla. **81. Gap of the
Gaping,** Ginungagap, the bottomless deep of the Norse story
of creation, which is the theme of Gunnar's song, lines 81-106,
123-144. The abode of man was Midgard, or Mid-Earth
(line 86).

106. gods' undoing, the period of Ragnarok, the Twilight of the Gods, when the world was destroyed. **118.
Midworld's . . . curse,** the Midgard Serpent, the child of
Loki, who is described in Norse mythology as the calumniator
of the gods and the contriver of all evil.

But Gunnar looked and considered, and wise
and wary he grew,
And the dark of night was waning and chill
in the dawning it grew;   120
But his hands were strong and mighty and
the fainting harp he woke,
And cried in the deadly desert, and the song
from his soul out-broke:

"O Hearken, Kindreds and Nations, and all
Kings of the plenteous earth,
Heed, ye that shall come hereafter, and are
far and far from the birth!
I have dwelt in the world aforetime, and I
called it the garden of God;   125
I have stayed my heart with its sweetness,
and fair on its freshness I trod;
I have seen its tempest and wondered, I have
cowered adown from its rain,
And desired the brightening sunshine, and
seen it and been fain;
I have waked, time was, in its dawning; its
noon and its even I wore;
I have slept unafraid of its darkness, and the
days have been many and more.   130
I have dwelt with the deeds of the mighty; I
have woven the web of the sword;
I have borne up the guilt nor repented; I
have sorrowed nor spoken the word;
And I fought and was glad in the morning,
and I sing in the night and the end;
So let him stand forth, the Accuser, and do
on the death-shoon to wend;
For not here on the earth shall I hearken, nor
on earth for the dooming shall stay,   135
Nor stretch out mine hand for the pleading;
for I see the spring of the day
Round the doors of the golden Valhall, and I
see the mighty arise,
And I hearken the voice of Odin, and his
mouth on Gunnar cries,
And he nameth the Son of Giuki, and cries on
deeds long done,
And the fathers of my fathers, and the sons
of yore agone.   140

"O Odin, I see, and I hearken; but, lo thou,
the bonds on my feet,
And the walls of the wilderness round me, ere
the light of thy land I meet!
I crave and I weary, Allfather, and long and
dark is the road;
And the feet of the mighty are weakened, and
the back is bent with the load."

Then fainted the song of Gunnar, and the
harp from his hand fell down,   145
And he cried: "Ah, what hath betided? for
cold the world hath grown,

134. do . . . wend, put on the death shoes that I may go.
135. dooming, judging.

And cold is the heart within me, and my hand
is heavy and strange;
What voice is the voice I hearken in the chill
and the dusk and the change?
Where art thou, God of the war-fain? for this
is the death indeed;
And I unsworded, unshielded, in the Day of
the Niblungs' Need!"   150

He fell to the earth as he spake, and life left
Gunnar the King,
For his heart was chilled forever by the sleep-
less serpent's sting,
The gray Worm, Great and Ancient — and
day in the East began,
And the moon was low in the heavens, and
the light clouds over him ran.

(1876)

THE DAY IS COMING

Come hither, lads, and harken, for a tale
there is to tell,
Of the wonderful days a-coming, when all
shall be better than well.

And the tale shall be told of a country, a land
in the midst of the sea,
And folk shall call it England in the days that
are going to be.

There more than one in a thousand in the
days that are yet to come,   5
Shall have some hope of the morrow, some
joy of the ancient home.

For then — laugh not, but listen to this
strange tale of mine —
All folk that are in England shall be better
lodged than swine.

Then a man shall work and bethink him, and
rejoice in the deeds of his hand,
Nor yet come home in the even too faint and
weary to stand.   10

Men in that time a-coming shall work and
have no fear
For tomorrow's lack of earning and the hun-
ger-wolf anear.

I tell you this for a wonder, that no man
then shall be glad
Of his fellow's fall and mishap to snatch at
the work he had,

The Day Is Coming. In 1883 Morris declared himself a
Socialist and for the next seven years devoted much of his
time and energy to the Socialist cause. This poem, together
with others that follow, expresses his interest in the welfare
of the lower classes. It was published with *The Voice of Toil,
No Master, Down among the Dead Men,* and other poems in a
pamphlet entitled *Chants for Socialists.*

For that which the worker winneth shall then
    be his indeed,   15
Nor shall half be reaped for nothing by him
    that sowed no seed.

O strange new wonderful justice! But for
    whom shall we gather the gain?
For ourselves and for each of our fellows, and
    no hand shall labor in vain.

Then all Mine and all Thine shall be Ours,
    and no more shall any man crave
For riches that serve for nothing but to fetter
    a friend for a slave.   20

And what wealth then shall be left us when
    none shall gather gold
To buy his friend in the market, and pinch
    and pine the sold?

Nay, what save the lovely city, and the little
    house on the hill,
And the wastes and the woodland beauty,
    and the happy fields we till;

And the homes of ancient stories, the tombs
    of the mighty dead;   25
And the wise men seeking out marvels, and
    the poet's teeming head;

And the painter's hand of wonder; and the
    marvelous fiddle-bow,
And the banded choirs of music — all those
    that do and know.

For all these shall be ours and all men's; nor
    shall any lack a share
Of the toil and the gain of living in the days
    when the world grows fair.   30

Ah! such are the days that shall be! But what
    are the deeds of today,
In the days of the years we dwell in, that
    wear our lives away?

Why, then, and for what are we waiting?
    There are three words to speak —
WE WILL IT — and what is the foeman but
    the dream-strong wakened and weak?

O why and for what are we waiting? while our
    brothers droop and die,   35
And on every wind of the heavens a wasted
    life goes by.

How long shall they reproach us where crowd
    on crowd they dwell,
Poor ghosts of the wicked city, the gold-
    crushed, hungry hell?

Through squalid life they labored, in sordid
    grief they died,

Those sons of a mighty mother, those props
    of England's pride.   40

They are gone; there is none can undo it, nor
    save our souls from the curse;
But many a million cometh, and shall they be
    better or worse?

It is we must answer and hasten, and open
    wide the door
For the rich man's hurrying terror, and the
    slow-foot hope of the poor.

Yea, the voiceless wrath of the wretched, and
    their unlearned discontent,   45
We must give it voice and wisdom till the
    waiting-tide be spent.

Come, then, since all things call us, the living
    and the dead,
And o'er the weltering tangle a glimmering
    light is shed.

Come, then, let us cast off fooling, and put
    by ease and rest,
For the Cause alone is worthy till the good
    days bring the best.   50

Come, join in the only battle wherein no man
    can fail,
Where whoso fadeth and dieth, yet his deed
    shall still prevail.

Ah! come, cast off all fooling, for this, at
    least, we know:
That the Dawn and the Day is coming, and
    forth the Banners go.
        (1884)

THE VOICE OF TOIL

I heard men saying, Leave hope and praying,
All days shall be as all have been;
Today and tomorrow bring fear and sorrow,
The never ending toil between.

When Earth was younger mid toil and hunger,
In hope we strove, and our hands were strong;
Then great men led us, with words they fed us,
And bade us right the earthly wrong.

Go read in story their deeds and glory,
Their names amidst the nameless dead;   10
Turn then from lying to us slow-dying
In that good world to which they led;

Where fast and faster our iron master,
The thing we made, forever drives,
Bids us grind treasure and fashion pleasure 15
For other hopes and other lives.

Where home is a hovel and dull we grovel,
Forgetting that the world is fair;
Where no babe we cherish, lest its very soul
    perish;
Where mirth is crime, and love a snare.   20

Who now shall lead us, what god shall heed us
As we lie in the hell our hands have won?
For us are no rulers but fools and befoolers;
The great are fallen, the wise men gone.

I heard men saying, Leave tears and praying,
The sharp knife heedeth not the sheep;   26
Are we not stronger than the rich and the
    wronger,
When day breaks over dreams and sleep?

Come, shoulder to shoulder, ere the world
    grows older!
Help lies in naught but thee and me;   30
Hope is before us, the long years that bore us
Bore leaders more than men may be.

Let dead hearts tarry and trade and marry,
And trembling nurse their dreams of mirth,
While we the living our lives are giving   35
To bring the bright new world to birth.

Come, shoulder to shoulder, ere earth grows
    older!
The cause spreads over land and sea;
Now the world shaketh, and fear awaketh,
And joy at last for thee and me.   40
                (1884)

NO MASTER

Saith man to man, We've heard and known
    That we no master need
To live upon this earth our own,
    In fair and manly deed.
The grief of slaves long passed away   5
    For us hath forged the chain,
Till now each worker's patient day
    Builds up the House of Pain.

And we, shall we too, crouch and quail,
    Ashamed, afraid of strife,   10
And lest our lives untimely fail
    Embrace the Death in Life?
Nay, cry aloud, and have no fear,
    We few against the world;
Awake, arise! the hope we bear   15
    Against the curse is hurled.

It grows and grows — are we the same,
    The feeble band, the few?
Or what are these with eyes aflame,
    And hands to deal and do?   20
This is the host that bears the word,

"NO MASTER HIGH OR LOW" —
A lightning flame, a shearing sword,
A storm to overthrow.   (1884)

DOWN AMONG THE DEAD MEN

Come, comrades, come, your glasses clink;
Up with your hands a health to drink,
The health of all that workers be,
In every land, on every sea.
    And he that will this health deny,   5
    Down among the dead men, down among
        the dead men,
    Down, down, down, down,
    Down among the dead men let him lie!

Well done! Now drink another toast,
And pledge the gath'ring of the host,   10
The people armed in brain and hand,
To claim their rights in every land.
    And he that will, etc.

There's liquor left; come, let's be kind,
And drink the rich a better mind,   15
That when we knock upon the door,
They may be off and say no more.
    And he that will, etc.

Now, comrades, let the glass blush red,
Drink we the unforgotten dead   20
That did their deeds and went away,
Before the bright sun brought the day.
    And he that will, etc.

The Day? Ah, friends, late grows the night;
Drink to the glimmering spark of light,   25
The herald of the joy to be,
The battle-torch of thee and me!
    And he that will, etc.

Take yet another cup in hand
And drink in hope our little band;   30
Drink strife in hope while lasteth breath,
And brotherhood in life and death;
    And he that will, etc.
                (1885)

From *A DREAM OF JOHN BALL*
The Sheriff

The Sheriff is made a mighty lord,
    Of goodly gold he hath enow,
And many a sergeant girt with sword;
    But forth will we and bend the bow.
        We shall bend the bow on the lily lea   5
        Betwixt the thorn and the oaken tree.

A Dream of John Ball. See Critical Notes.

With stone and lime is the burg wall built,
   And pit and prison are stark and strong,
And many a true man there is spilt,
   And many a right man doomed by wrong.
     So forth shall we and bend the bow   11
     And the king's writ never the road shall
      know.

Now yeomen walk ye warily,
   And heed ye the houses where ye go,
For as fair and as fine as they may be,   15
   Lest behind your heels the door clap to.
     Fare forth with the bow to the lily lea
     Betwixt the thorn and the oaken tree.

Now bills and bows! and out a-gate!
   And turn about on the lily lea!   20
And though their company be great
   The gray-goose wing shall set us free.
     Now bent is the bow in the green abode
     And the king's writ knoweth not the road.

So over the mead and over the hithe,   25
   And away to the wild-wood wend we forth;
There dwell we yeomen bold and blithe
   Where the Sheriff's word is naught of worth.
     Bent is the bow on the lily lea
     Betwixt the thorn and the oaken tree. 30
                   (1886)

THE DAY OF DAYS

Each eve earth falleth down the dark,
As though its hope were o'er;
Yet lurks the sun when day is done
Behind tomorrow's door.

Gray grows the dawn while men-folk sleep; 5
Unseen spreads on the light,
Till the thrush sings to the colored things,
And earth forgets the night.

No otherwise wends on our Hope —
E'en as a tale that's told   10
Are fair lives lost, and all the cost
Of wise and true and bold.

We've toiled and failed; we spake the word;
None harkened; dumb we lie;
Our Hope is dead, the seed we spread   15
Fell o'er the earth to die.

What's this? For joy our hearts stand still,
And life is loved and dear,
The lost and found the Cause hath crowned,
The Day of Days is here.   20
                (1890)

THE BURGHERS' BATTLE

Thick rise the spear-shafts o'er the land
That erst the harvest bore;
The sword is heavy in the hand,
And we return no more.

The light wind waves the Ruddy Fox,   5
Our banner of the war,
And ripples in the Running Ox,
And we return no more.

Across our stubble acres now
The teams go four and four;   10
But out-worn elders guide the plow,
And we return no more.

And now the women, heavy-eyed,
Turn through the open door
From gazing down the highway wide,   15
Where we return no more.

The shadows of the fruited close
Dapple the feast-hall floor;
There lie our dogs and dream and doze,
And we return no more.   20

Down from the minster tower today
Fall the soft chimes of yore
Amidst the chattering jackdaws' play;
And we return no more.

But underneath the streets are still;   25
Noon, and the market's o'er!
Back go the goodwives o'er the hill;
For we return no more.

What merchant to our gates shall come?
What wise man bring us lore?   30
What abbot ride away to Rome,
Now we return no more?

What mayor shall rule the hall we built?
Whose scarlet sweep the floor?
What judge shall doom the robber's guilt, 35
Now we return no more?

New houses in the streets shall rise
Where builded we before,
Of other stone wrought otherwise;
For we return no more.   40

And crops shall cover field and hill
Unlike what once they bore,
And all be done without our will,
Now we return no more.

---

19. **bills,** battle weapons consisting of a long staff with a hook-shaped blade on the end. 22. **gray-goose wing,** arrow. 25. **hithe,** dale.

17. **fruited close,** orchard. 27. **goodwives.** A goodwife was a mistress of a house. The term was formerly used as an appellation of civility, like our *Mrs.* 35. **doom,** judge.

Look up! the arrows streak the sky,　45
The horns of battle roar;
The long spears lower and draw nigh,
And we return no more.

Remember how beside the wain,
We spoke the word of war,　50
And sowed this harvest of the plain,
And we return no more.

Lay spears about the Ruddy Fox!
The days of old are o'er;
Heave sword about the Running Ox!　55
For we return no more.　(1891)

TO THE MUSE OF THE NORTH

O muse that swayest the sad Northern Song,
Thy right hand full of smiting and of wrong,
Thy left hand holding pity, and thy breast
Heaving with hope of that so certain rest;
Thou, with the gray eyes kind and unafraid,
The soft lips trembling not, though they have said　6
The doom of the World and those that dwell therein,
The lips that smile not though thy children win
The fated Love that draws the fated Death —
O, borne adown the fresh stream of thy breath,
Let some word reach my ears and touch my heart,　11
That, if it may be, I may have a part
In that great sorrow of thy children dead
That vexed the brow, and bowed adown the head,
Whitened the hair, made life a wondrous dream,　15
And death the murmur of a restful stream,
But left no stain upon those souls of thine
Whose greatness through the tangled world doth shine.
O Mother, and Love and Sister all in one,
Come thou; for sure I am enough alone　20
That thou thine arms about my heart shouldst throw,
And wrap me in the grief of long ago. (1891)

ICELAND FIRST SEEN

Lo, from our loitering ship a new land at last to be seen;
Toothed rocks down the side of the firth on the east guard a weary wide lea,

To the Muse of the North. This poem emphasizes the important place that Fate held among the early Teutonic people. The Scandinavian Norns were the dispensers of fate in Norse mythology. The poem also stresses Morris's interest in Scandinavian material.
Iceland First Seen. Morris visited Iceland in 1871 and again in 1873.

And black slope the hillsides above, striped adown with their desolate green;
And a peak rises up on the west from the meeting of cloud and of sea,
Foursquare from base unto point like the building of gods that have been,　5
The last of that waste of the mountains all cloud-wreathed and snow-flecked and gray,
And bright with the dawn that began just now at the ending of day.

Ah! what came we forth for to see that our hearts are so hot with desire?
Is it enough for our rest the sight of this desolate strand,
And the mountain-waste voiceless as death but for winds that may sleep not nor tire?
Why do we long to wend forth through the length and breadth of a land,　11
Dreadful with grinding of ice, and record of scarce hidden fire,
But that there 'mid the gray grassy dales sore scarred by the ruining streams
Lives the tale of the Northland of old and the undying glory of dreams?

O land, as some cave by the sea where the treasures of old have been laid,　15
The sword it may be of a king whose name was the turning of fight;
Or the staff of some wise of the world that many things made and unmade,
Or the ring of a woman maybe whose woe is grown wealth and delight.
No wheat and no wine grows above it, no orchard for blossom and shade;
The few ships that sail by its blackness but deem it the mouth of a grave;　20
Yet sure when the world shall awaken, this too shall be mighty to save.

Or rather, O land, if a marvel it seemeth that men ever sought
Thy wastes for a field and a garden fulfilled of all wonder and doubt,
And feasted amidst of the winter when the fight of the year had been fought,
Whose plunder all gathered together was little to babble about —　25
Cry aloud from thy wastes, O thou land, "Not for this nor for that was I wrought
Amid waning of realms and of riches and death of things worshiped and sure;
I abide here the spouse of a god, and I made and I make and endure."

O Queen of the grief without knowledge, of the courage that may not avail,
Of the longing that may not attain, or the love that shall never forget　30

More joy than the gladness of laughter thy
    voice hath amidst of its wail;
More hope than of pleasure fulfilled amidst
    of thy blindness is set;
More glorious than gaining of all, thine unfal-
    tering hand that shall fail;
For what is the mark on thy brow but the
    brand that thy Brynhild doth bear?
Lone once, and loved and undone by a love
    that no ages outwear.   35

Ah! when thy Balder comes back, and bears
    from the heart of the Sun,
Peace and the healing of pain, and the wis-
    dom that waiteth no more;
And the lilies are laid on thy brow 'mid the
    crown of the deeds thou hast done;
And the roses spring up by thy feet that the
    rocks of the wilderness wore —
Ah! when thy Balder comes back and we
    gather the gains he hath won,   40
Shall we not linger a little to talk of thy
    sweetness of old,
Yea, turn back awhile to thy travail whence
    the gods stood aloof to behold?   (1891)

A DEATH SONG

What cometh here from west to east a-wend-
    ing?
And who are these, the marchers stern and
    slow?
We bear the message that the rich are sending
Aback to those who bade them wake and
    know.
Not one, not one, nor thousands must they slay,
But one and all if they would dusk the day.   6

We asked them for a life of toilsome earn-
    ing —
They bade us bide their leisure for our bread;
We craved to speak to tell our woeful learn-
    ing —
We come back speechless, bearing back our
    dead.   10
Not one, not one, nor thousands must they slay,
But one and all if they would dusk the day.

They will not learn; they have no ears to
    hearken;
They turn their faces from the eyes of fate;
Their gay-lit halls shut out the skies that
    darken.   15
But, lo! this dead man knocking at the gate.

Not one, not one, nor thousands must they slay,
But one and all if they would dusk the day.

Here lies the sign that we shall break our
    prison;
Amidst the storm he won a prisoner's rest; 20
But in the cloudy dawn the sun arisen
Brings us our day of work to win the best.
Not one, not one, nor thousands must they slay,
But one and all if they would dusk the day.
                   (1891)

AGNES AND THE HILL-MAN
TRANSLATED FROM THE DANISH

Agnes went through the meadows a-weeping,
Fowl are a-singing.
There stood the hill-man, heed thereof keep-
    ing.
Agnes, fair Agnes!
"Come to the hill, fair Agnes, with me;   5
The reddest of gold will I give unto thee!"

Twice went Agnes the hill round about,
Then wended within, left the fair world with-
    out.

In the hillside bode Agnes, three years thrice
    told o'er,
For the green earth sithence fell she longing
    full sore.   10

There she sat, and lullaby sang in her singing,
And she heard how the bells of England were
    ringing.

Agnes before her true-love did stand:
"May I wend to the church of the English
    Land?"

"To England's Church well mayst thou be
    gone,   15
So that no hand thou lay the red gold upon.

"So that when thou art come the churchyard
    anear
Thou cast not abroad thy golden hair.

"So that when thou standest the church
    within
To thy mother on bench thou never win.   20

"So that when thou hearest the high God's
    name,
No knee unto earth thou bow to the same."

---

34. Brynhild. See *The Story of Sigurd the Volsung*, p. 651,
and note on lines 103-104, p. 653. **36. Balder**, son of Odin,
and the Norse god of light and peace.
A Death Song. This poem was written to be sold as a penny
pamphlet to aid the children of Morris's friend Alfred Linnell,
who died from injuries received when the police attacked
marchers in a great Socialist parade in London, November 13,
1887. Morris was one of the marchers.

Agnes and the Hill-Man. The hill-man is a kind of dwarf
or troll living in the side of a hill. He belongs to the realm of
folklore. Compare the poem with Arnold's *The Forsaken
Merman*, p. 437.
10. sithence, afterwards. **20. win,** go.

Hand she laid on all gold that was there,
And cast abroad her golden hair.

And when the church she stood within　25
To her mother on bench straight did she win.

And when she heard the high God's name,
Knee unto earth she bowed to the same.

When all the Mass was sung to its end
Home with her mother dear did she wend. 30

"Come, Agnes, into the hillside to me,
For thy seven small sons greet sorely for
　　thee!"

"Let them greet, let them greet, as they will
　　have to do;
For never again will I hearken thereto!"

Weird laid he on her, sore sickness he wrought,
Fowl are a-singing.　　　　　　　　　　36
That selfsame hour to death was she brought.
Agnes, fair Agnes!　　　　　　(1891)

FOR THE BED AT KELMSCOTT

The wind's on the wold
And the night is a-cold,
And Thames runs chill
Twixt mead and hill;
But kind and dear　　　　　5
Is the old house here,
And my heart is warm
Midst winter's harm.

Rest, then, and rest,
And think of the best　　　　10
'Twixt summer and spring,
When all birds sing
In the town of the tree,
And ye lie in me
And scarce dare move,　　　15
Lest the earth and its love
Should fade away
Ere the full of the day.

I am old and have seen
Many things that have been —　　20
Both grief and peace
And wane and increase.
No tale I tell
Of ill or well,

But this I say:　　　　　　　　　25
Night treadeth on day,
And for worst or best
Right good is rest.　　　(*1893;* 1893)

ALGERNON CHARLES SWINBURNE
(1837-1909)

A SONG IN TIME OF ORDER
1852

Push hard across the sand,
　For the salt wind gathers breath;
Shoulder and wrist and hand,
　Push hard as the push of death.

The wind is as iron that rings,　　　　5
　The foam-heads loosen and flee;
It swells and welters and swings,
　The pulse of the tide of the sea.

And up on the yellow cliff
　The long corn flickers and shakes;　　10
Push, for the wind holds stiff,
　And the gunwale dips and rakes.

Good hap to the fresh fierce weather,
　The quiver and beat of the sea!
While three men hold together,　　　15
　The kingdoms are less by three.

Out to the sea with her there,
　Out with her over the sand;
Let the kings keep the earth for their share!
　We have done with the sharers of land.　20

They have tied the world in a tether,
　They have bought over God with a fee;
While three men hold together,
　The kingdoms are less by three.

We have done with the kisses that sting,　25
　The thief's mouth red from the feast,
The blood on the hands of the king
　And the lie at the lips of the priest.

Will they tie the winds in a tether,
　Put a bit in the jaws of the sea?　　30
While three men hold together,
　The kingdoms are less by three.

Let our flag run out straight in the wind!
　The old red shall be floated again　　34

---

30. wend, go. 32. greet, weep. 35. Weird, fate; a spell.
For the Bed at Kelmscott. This poem was written for the
embroidered hangings that belonged to a carved oak bedstead at Kelmscott Manor, Morris's home in Lechlade, about
thirty miles above Oxford. The poem first appeared in the
Catalogue of the Arts and Crafts Exhibition, 1893. The old
bedstead is the speaker.

A Song in Time of Order. See Critical Notes.
10. corn, grain, wheat. 34. The old red, the flag of the
Revolution.

When the ranks that are thin shall be thinned,
  When the names that were twenty are ten;

When the devil's riddle is mastered
  And the galley-bench creaks with a pope,
We shall see Buonaparte the bastard
  Kick heels with his throat in a rope.   40

While the shepherd sets wolves on his sheep
  And the emperor halters his kine,
While Shame is a watchman asleep
  And Faith is a keeper of swine,

Let the wind shake our flag like a feather, 45
  Like the plumes of the foam of the sea!
While three men hold together,
  The kingdoms are less by three.

All the world has its burdens to bear,
  From Cayenne to the Austrian whips; 50
Forth, with the rain in our hair
  And the salt sweet foam in our lips;

In the teeth of the hard glad weather,
  In the blown wet face of the sea;
While three men hold together,   55
  The kingdoms are less by three.   (1862)

FAUSTINE

Ave Faustina Imperatrix morituri te salutant

Lean back, and get some minutes' peace;
  Let your head lean
Back to the shoulder with its fleece
  Of locks, Faustine.

The shapely silver shoulder stoops,   5
  Weighted over clean
With state of splendid hair that droops
  Each side, Faustine.

Let me go over your good gifts
  That crown you queen,   10
A queen whose kingdom ebbs and shifts
  Each week, Faustine:

Bright heavy brows well gathered up—
  White gloss and sheen;

Carved lips that make my lips a cup   15
  To drink, Faustine,

Wine and rank poison, milk and blood,
  Being mixed therein
Since first the devil threw dice with God
  For you, Faustine.   20

Your naked new-born soul, their stake,
  Stood blind between;
God said, "Let him that wins her take
  And keep Faustine."

But this time Satan throve, no doubt;   25
  Long since, I ween,
God's part in you was battered out—
  Long since, Faustine.

The die rang sideways as it fell,
  Rang cracked and thin,   30
Like a man's laughter heard in hell
  Far down, Faustine.

A shadow of laughter like a sigh,
  Dead sorrow's kin;
So rang, thrown down, the devil's die   35
  That won Faustine.

A suckling of his breed you were,
  One hard to wean;
But God, who lost you, left you fair,
  We see, Faustine.   40

You have the face that suits a woman
  For her soul's screen—
The sort of beauty that's called human
  In hell, Faustine.

You could do all things but be good   45
  Or chaste of mien;
And that you would not if you could,
  We know, Faustine.

Even He who cast seven devils out
  Of Magdalene   50
Could hardly do as much, I doubt,
  For you, Faustine.

Did Satan make you to spite God?
  Or did God mean
To scourge with scorpions for a rod   55
  Our sins, Faustine?

I know what queen at first you were,
  As though I had seen

38. a pope, Pius IX (1846-78), who was driven from Rome during the Italian Revolution of 1848 and who returned in 1850 by the aid of foreign arms. Swinburne wanted him sentenced to die in the galleys. **39. Buonaparte the bastard,** Napoleon III, emperor of the French (1852-70), who is called a bastard because as president of the Republic (1848-52) he overthrew the old constitution and made a new one that gave him unlimited power. He was thus an illegitimate emperor. **50. Cayenne,** the capital of French Guiana, used as a place of banishment for political prisoners. **Austrian whips,** a reference to the Austrian oppression of Italy during the period.
Faustine. See Critical Notes.
Ave Faustina, etc. Hail, Faustina, Empress, those about to die salute thee. This is adapted from the traditional words of the Roman gladiators about to engage in mortal combat: "Hail Cæsar, Emperor! those about to die salute thee!"

50. Magdalene. See Rossetti's *Mary Magdalene,* p. 524.
57. what queen . . . were, a reference to Faustina (104?-141 A.D.), the wife of the Roman emperor Antoninus. She was notorious for her licentiousness. Her daughter, also named Faustina, was the wife of Marcus Aurelius, Roman emperor (161-180). She is said to have been more profligate than her mother.

Red gold and black imperious hair
  Twice crown Faustine.   60

As if your fed sarcophagus
  Spared flesh and skin,
You come back face to face with us,
  The same Faustine.

She loved the games men played with death, 65
  Where death must win;
As though the slain man's blood and breath
  Revived Faustine.

Nets caught the pike, pikes tore the net;
  Lithe limbs and lean   70
From drained-out pores dripped thick red
    sweat
  To soothe Faustine.

She drank the steaming drift and dust
  Blown off the scene;
Blood could not ease the bitter lust   75
  That galled Faustine.

All round the foul fat furrows reeked,
  Where blood sank in;
The circus splashed and seethed and shrieked
  All round Faustine.   80

But these are gone now; years entomb
  The dust and din;
Yea, even the bath's fierce reek and fume
  That slew Faustine.

Was life worth living then? and now   85
  Is life worth sin?
Where are the imperial years? and how
  Are you Faustine?

Your soul forgot her joys, forgot
  Her times of teen;   90
Yea, this life likewise will you not
  Forget, Faustine?

For in the time we know not of
  Did fate begin
Weaving the web of days that wove   95
  Your doom, Faustine.

The threads were wet with wine, and all
  Were smooth to spin;
They wove you like a Bacchanal,
  The first Faustine.   100

And Bacchus cast your mates and you
  Wild grapes to glean;
Your flower-like lips were dashed with dew
  From his, Faustine.

90. **teen,** sorrow, grief.   99. **Bacchanal,** a devotee of Bacchus, god of wine.

Your drenched loose hands were stretched to
    hold   105
  The vine's wet green,
Long ere they coined in Roman gold
  Your face, Faustine.

Then after change of soaring feather
  And winnowing fin,   110
You woke in weeks of feverish weather,
  A new Faustine.

A star upon your birthday burned,
  Whose fierce serene
Red pulseless planet never yearned   115
  In heaven, Faustine.

Stray breaths of Sapphic song that blew
  Through Mitylene
Shook the fierce quivering blood in you
  By night, Faustine.   120

The shameless nameless love that makes
  Hell's iron gin
Shut on you like a trap that breaks
  The soul, Faustine.

And when your veins were void and dead, 125
  What ghosts unclean
Swarmed round the straitened barren bed
  That hid Faustine?

What sterile growths of sexless root
  Or epicene?   130
What flower of kisses without fruit
  Of love, Faustine?

What adders came to shed their coats?
  What coiled obscene
Small serpents with soft stretching throats 135
  Caressed Faustine?

But the time came of famished hours,
  Maimed loves and mean,
This ghastly thin-faced time of ours,
  To spoil Faustine.   140

You seem a thing that hinges hold,
  A love-machine
With clockwork joints of supple gold—
  No more, Faustine.

Not godless, for you serve one god, 145
  The Lampsacene,

117. **Sapphic song,** poetry of Sappho, a noted Greek poetess (c. 600 B.C.), famous for the erotic quality of her verse. She was born in the city of Mitylene, on the island of Lesbos, off the coast of Asia Minor. 122. **gin,** engine of torture. 130. **epicene,** common to both sexes. 146. **Lampsacene,** Priapus, the Greek god of fertility and gardens. In later times he was regarded as the chief deity of lasciviousness and obscenity. His worship began in the city of Lampsacus, in Asia Minor.

Who metes the gardens with his rod;
Your lord, Faustine.

If one should love you with real love
(Such things have been, 150
Things your fair face knows nothing of,
It seems, Faustine);

That clear hair heavily bound back,
The lights wherein
Shift from dead blue to burnt-up black; 155
Your throat, Faustine,

Strong, heavy, throwing out the face
And hard bright chin
And shameful scornful lips that grace
Their shame, Faustine, 160

Curled lips, long since half kissed away,
Still sweet and keen;
You'd give him—poison shall we say?
Or what, Faustine? (1862)

From *ATALANTA IN CALYDON*

INVOCATION

Maiden, and mistress of the months and stars
Now folded in the flowerless fields of heaven,
Goddess whom all gods love with threefold
heart,
Being treble in thy divided deity,
A light for dead men and dark hours, a foot 5
Swift on the hills as morning, and a hand
To all things fierce and fleet that roar and
range
Mortal, with gentler shafts than snow or
sleep—
Hear now and help and lift no violent hand,
But favorable and fair as thine eye's beam 10
Hidden and shown in heaven; for I all night
Amid the king's hounds and the hunting men
Have wrought and worshiped toward thee;
nor shall man
See goodlier hounds or deadlier edge of spears;
But for the end, that lies unreached as yet 15
Between the hands and on the knees of gods.
O fair-faced sun, killing the stars and dews
And dreams and desolation of the night!
Rise up, shine, stretch thine hand out, with
thy bow
Touch the most dimmest height of trembling
heaven, 20
And burn and break the dark about thy ways,
Shot through and through with arrows; let
thine hair

Lighten as flame above that flameless shell
Which was the moon, and thine eyes fill the
world
And thy lips kindle with swift beams; let
earth 25
Laugh, and the long sea fiery from thy feet
Through all the roar and ripple of streaming
springs
And foam in reddening flakes and flying
flowers
Shaken from hands and blown from lips of
nymphs
Whose hair or breast divides the wandering
wave 30
With salt close tresses cleaving lock to lock,
All gold, or shuddering and unfurrowed snow;
And all the winds about thee with their wings,
And fountain-heads of all the watered world;
Each horn of Acheloüs, and the green 35
Euenus, wedded with the straitening sea.
For in fair time thou comest; come also thou,
Twin-born with him, and virgin, Artemis,
And give our spears their spoil, the wild boar's
hide,
Sent in thine anger against us for sin done 40
And bloodless altars without wine or fire.
Him now consume thou; for thy sacrifice
With sanguine-shining steam divides the
dawn,
And one, the maiden rose of all thy maids,
Arcadian Atalanta, snowy-souled, 45
Fair as the snow and footed as the wind,
From Ladon and well-wooded Mænalus
Over the firm hills and the fleeting sea
Hast thou drawn hither, and many an arméd
king,
Heroes, the crown of men, like gods in fight. 50
Moreover out of all the Ætolian land,
From the full-flowered Lelantian pasturage
To what of fruitful field the son of Zeus
Won from the roaring river and laboring sea
When the wild god shrank in his horn and
fled 55
And foamed and lessened through his wrath-
ful fords,
Leaving clear lands that steamed with sudden
sun,

---

28. **foam**, a verb parallel with *laugh* understood. The construction is: Let earth laugh, the long sea laugh and foam, the winds laugh (line 33), etc. 32. **shuddering**, refers to *breast* (line 30). 35. **Acheloüs**, a river in western Greece. 36. **Euenus**, a river in western Greece; it flows into the Ionian Sea where it narrows at the entrance to the Gulf of Corinth. 38. **Twin-born**. Apollo and Artemis were twin children of Zeus and Leto. 45. **Atalanta**, a maiden of Arcadia, Greece, famous for her beauty and her fleetness of foot. 47. **Ladon**, a river in Arcadia. **Mænalus**, a mountain in Arcadia. 51. **Ætolian land**, Ætolia, in western Greece, the province in which Calydon was located. 52. **Lelantian pasturage**, a region at the mouth of the River Euenus. 53. **son of Zeus**, etc., Hercules, who defeated the river god Acheloüs in a combat over Dejanira of Calydon, whom they both loved. Acheloüs, who assumed the form of a bull, lost one of his horns in the fight.

Atalanta in Calydon. See Critical Notes.
1. **Maiden . . . stars**, Artemis, goddess of maidenhood and of the moon. She was often mentioned as having a three-fold form—Luna in the sky, Diana on earth, and Hecate in Hades. 8. **Mortal**, deadly; the word refers to *hand* (line 6). 17. **fair-faced sun**, Apollo, god of the sun. One of his attributes was the bow.

These virgins with the lightening of the day
Bring thee fresh wreaths and their own
    sweeter hair,
Luxurious locks and flower-like mixed with
    flowers,   60
Clean offering, and chaste hymns; but me the
    time
Divides from these things; whom do thou not
    less
Help and give honor, and to mine hounds
    good speed,
And edge to spears, and luck to each man's
    hand.   (1865)

WHEN THE HOUNDS OF SPRING

When the hounds of spring are on winter's
    traces,
    The mother of months in meadow or plain
Fills the shadows and windy places
    With lisp of leaves and ripple of rain;
And the brown bright nightingale amorous 5
Is half assuaged for Itylus,
For the Thracian ships and the foreign faces,
    The tongueless vigil, and all the pain.

Come with bows bent and with emptying of
    quivers,
    Maiden most perfect, lady of light,   10
With a noise of winds and many rivers,
    With a clamor of waters, and with might;
Bind on thy sandals, O thou most fleet,
Over the splendor and speed of thy feet;
For the faint east quickens, the wan west
    shivers,   15
    Round the feet of the day and the feet of
    the night.

Where shall we find her, how shall we sing to
    her,
    Fold our hands round her knees, and cling?
Oh, that man's heart were as fire and could
    spring to her,
    Fire, or the strength of the streams that
    spring!   20
For the stars and the winds are unto her
As raiment, as songs of the harp-player;
For the risen stars and the fallen cling to her,
    And the southwest-wind and the west-wind
    sing.

For winter's rains and ruins are over,   25
    And all the season of snows and sins;
The days dividing lover and lover,

The light that loses, the night that wins;
And time remembered is grief forgotten,
And frosts are slain and flowers begotten,   30
And in green underwood and cover
    Blossom by blossom the spring begins.

The full streams feed on flower of rushes,
    Ripe grasses trammel a traveling foot,
The faint fresh flame of the young year flushes
    From leaf to flower and flower to fruit;   36
And fruit and leaf are as gold and fire,
And the oat is heard above the lyre,
And the hoofèd heel of a satyr crushes
    The chestnut-husk at the chestnut-root.   40

And Pan by noon and Bacchus by night,
    Fleeter of foot than the fleet-foot kid,
Follows with dancing and fills with delight
    The Mænad and the Bassarid;
And soft as lips that laugh and hide   45
The laughing leaves of the trees divide,
And screen from seeing and leave in sight
    The god pursuing, the maiden hid.

The ivy falls with the Bacchanal's hair
    Over her eyebrows hiding her eyes;   50
The wild vine slipping down leaves bare
    Her bright breast shortening into sighs;
The wild vine slips with the weight of its
    leaves,
But the berried ivy catches and cleaves   54
    To the limbs that glitter, the feet that scare
The wolf that follows, the fawn that flies.
                                    (1865)

BEFORE THE BEGINNING OF YEARS

Before the beginning of years
    There came to the making of man
Time, with a gift of tears;
    Grief, with a glass that ran;
Pleasure, with pain for leaven;   5
    Summer, with flowers that fell;
Remembrance fallen from heaven,
    And madness risen from hell;
Strength without hands to smite;
    Love that endures for a breath;   10
Night, the shadow of light,
    And life, the shadow of death.

28. **light . . . wins,** a reference to the short days and long nights of winter.   38. **oat,** the shepherd's pipe of oaten straw.   39. **satyr,** a sylvan demigod, half man and half goat.   41. **Pan,** god of flocks and pastures. **Bacchus,** god of wine.   44. **Mænad,** a female worshiper of Bacchus. The name is derived from a Greek word meaning *to be frenzied.* **Bassarid,** a Thracian worshiper of Bacchus. The celebrations of the Bassarids included licentious excesses and a sacrifice of some animal on the altar of the god. The participants ate the flesh raw. 47-48. **screen . . . hid.** As the god and the maiden slip through the forest, they are alternately concealed and revealed by the wind-swayed foliage.

Before the Beginning of Years. This song is sung by the Chorus after Althæa had departed to prepare her son Meleager for the hunt, "lest love or some man's anger work him harm."

58. **These virgins,** maidens of Ætolia who form the chorus of the drama.

When the Hounds of Spring. This is the opening chorus of the drama, sung by a group of Ætolian maidens; it follows the Invocation.

2. **mother of months,** Artemis, goddess of the moon.
6. **Itylus.** See note on Arnold's *Philomela,* p. 486.

And the high gods took in hand
  Fire, and the falling of tears,
And a measure of sliding sand   15
  From under the feet of the years;
And froth and drift of the sea;
  And dust of the laboring earth;
And bodies of things to be
  In the houses of death and of birth;   20
And wrought with weeping and laughter,
  And fashioned with loathing and love,
With life before and after
  And death beneath and above,
For a day and a night and a morrow,   25
  That his strength might endure for a span
With travail and heavy sorrow,
  The holy spirit of man.

From the winds of the north and the south
  They gathered as unto strife;   30
  They breathed upon his mouth,
  They filled his body with life;
Eyesight and speech they wrought
  For the veils of the soul therein,
A time for labor and thought,   35
  A time to serve and to sin;
They gave him light in his ways,
  And love, and a space for delight,
And beauty and length of days,
  And night, and sleep in the night.   40
His speech is a burning fire;
  With his lips he travaileth;
In his heart is a blind desire,
  In his eyes foreknowledge of death;
He weaves, and is clothed with derision;   45
  Sows, and he shall not reap;
His life is a watch or a vision
  Between a sleep and a sleep.   (1865)

We Have Seen Thee, O Love

We have seen thee, O Love; thou art fair;
  thou art goodly, O Love;
Thy wings make light in the air as the wings
  of a dove.
Thy feet are as winds that divide the stream
  of the sea;
Earth is thy covering to hide thee, the garment of thee.
Thou art swift and subtle and blind as a flame
  of fire;   5
Before thee the laughter, behind thee the tears
  of desire;
And twain go forth beside thee, a man with a
  maid;
Her eyes are the eyes of a bride whom delight
  makes afraid;

As the breath in the buds that stir is her
  bridal breath;
But Fate is the name of her; and his name is
  Death.   (1865)

Not As with Sundering of the Earth

Not as with sundering of the earth,
  Nor as the cleaving of the sea,
Nor fierce foreshadowings of a birth,
  Nor flying dreams of death to be,
Nor loosening of the large world's girth   5
And quickening of the body of night,
  And sound of thunder in men's ears,
And fire of lightning in men's sight,
  Fate, mother of desires and fears,
  Bore unto men the law of tears;   10
But sudden, an unfathered flame,
  And broken out of night, she shone,
She, without body, without name,
  In days forgotten and foregone;
And heaven rang round her as she came,   15
Like smitten cymbals, and lay bare;
  Clouds and great stars, thunders and snows,
The blue sad fields and folds of air,
  The life that breathes, the life that grows,
  All wind, all fire, that burns or blows,   20
Even all these knew her — for she is great;
  The daughter of doom, the mother of death,
The sister of sorrow; a lifelong weight
  That no man's finger lighteneth,
Nor any god can lighten fate;   25
  A landmark seen across the way
Where one race treads as the other trod;
  An evil scepter, an evil stay,
  Wrought for a staff, wrought for a rod,
  The bitter jealousy of God.   30

For death is deep as the sea,
  And fate as the waves thereof.
Shall the waves take pity on thee
  Or the south-wind offer thee love?
Wilt thou take the night for thy day   35
Or the darkness for light on thy way,
  Till thou say in thine heart, Enough?

Behold, thou art over-fair, thou art over-wise;
The sweetness of spring in thine hair, and the
  light in thine eyes.
The light of the spring in thine eyes, and the
  sound in thine ears;   40
Yet thine heart shall wax heavy with sighs
  and thine eyelids with tears.
Wilt thou cover thine hair with gold, and with
  silver thy feet?

We Have Seen Thee, O Love. These are the opening lines of a chorus on the coming of Love in the form of Aphrodite. The first two lines are from *The Song of Solomon*, 4:1.— "Behold, thou art fair, my love; behold, thou art fair; thou hast doves' eyes within thy locks."

Not As with Sundering of the Earth. This song is sung by the Chorus after Althæa has determined to sacrifice her son for killing her brothers.
9. **Fate.** According to the Greeks, fate was the necessity behind and above gods as well as men.

Hast thou taken the purple to fold thee, and
    made thy mouth sweet?
Behold, when thy face is made bare, he that
    loved thee shall hate;
Thy face shall be no more fair at the fall of
    thy fate.   45
For thy life shall fall as a leaf and be shed as
    the rain;
And the veil of thine head shall be grief; and
    the crown shall be pain.   (1865)

THE DEATH OF MELEAGER

Meleager

Let your hands meet
    Round the weight of my head;
Lift ye my feet
    As the feet of the dead;
For the flesh of my body is molten, the limbs
    of it molten as lead.   5

Chorus

O thy luminous face,
    Thine imperious eyes!
O the grief, O the grace,
    As of day when it dies!
Who is this bending over thee, lord, with tears
    and suppression of sighs?   10

Meleager

Is a bride so fair?
    Is a maid so meek?
With unchapleted hair,
    With unfilleted cheek,
Atalanta, the pure among women, whose
    name is as blessing to speak.   15

Atalanta

I would that with feet
    Unsandaled, unshod,
Overbold, overfleet,
    I had swum not nor trod
From Arcadia to Calydon, northward, a blast
    of the envy of God.   20

Meleager

Unto each man his fate;
    Unto each as he saith
In whose fingers the weight
    Of the world is as breath;
Yet I would that in clamor of battle mine
    hands had laid hold upon death.   25

Chorus

Not with cleaving of shields
    And their clash in thine ear,

The Death of Meleager. This incident occurs after Althæa
throws the brand into the fire. See Critical Note on title.
11-15. **bride . . . Atalanta.** A bride with her chaplet
or garland worn on her head, and a maiden with her fillet or
band of ribbon around her forehead, are not so fair or so
meek as Atalanta, who wears neither decoration.

When the lord of fought fields
    Breaketh spearshaft from spear,
Thou art broken, our lord, thou art broken,
    with travail and labor and fear.   30

Meleager

Would God he had found me
    Beneath fresh boughs!
Would God he had bound me
    Unawares in mine house,
With light in mine eyes, and songs in my lips,
    and a crown on my brows!   35

Chorus

Whence art thou sent from us?
    Whither thy goal?
How art thou rent from us,
    Thou that wert whole,
As with severing of eyelids and eyes, as with
    sundering of body and soul!   40

Meleager

My heart is within me
    As an ash in the fire;
Whosoever hath seen me,
    Without lute, without lyre,
Shall sing of me grievous things, even things
    that were ill to desire.   45

Chorus

Who shall raise thee
    From the house of the dead?
Or what man praise thee
    That thy praise may be said?
Alas thy beauty! alas thy body! alas thine
    head!   50

Meleager

But thou, O mother,
    The dreamer of dreams,
Wilt thou bring forth another
    To feel the sun's beams
When I move among shadows a shadow, and
    wail by impassable streams?   55

Œneus

What thing wilt thou leave me
    Now this thing is done?
A man wilt thou give me,
    A son for my son,
For the light of mine eyes, the desire of my
    life, the desirable one?   60

Chorus

Thou wert glad above others,
    Yea, fair beyond word;
Thou wert glad among mothers;
    For each man that heard
Of thee, praise there was added unto thee, as
    wings to the feet of a bird.   65

Œneus

Who shall give back
Thy face of old years
With travail made black,
Grown gray among fears,
Mother of sorrow, mother of cursing, mother
of tears?   70

Meleager

Though thou art as fire
Fed with fuel in vain,
My delight, my desire,
Is more chaste than the rain,
More pure than the dewfall, more holy than
stars are that live without stain.   75

Atalanta

I would that as water
My life's blood had thawn,
Or as winter's wan daughter
Leaves lowland and lawn
Spring-stricken, or ever mine eyes had beheld
thee made dark in thy dawn.   80

Chorus

When thou dravest the men
Of the chosen of Thrace,
None turned him again
Nor endured he thy face
Clothed round with the blush of the battle,
with light from a terrible place.   85

Œneus

Thou shouldst die as he dies
For whom none sheddeth tears;
Filling thine eyes
And fulfilling thine ears
With the brilliance of battle, the bloom and
the beauty, the splendor of spears.   90

Chorus

In the ears of the world
It is sung, it is told,
And the light thereof hurled
And the noise thereof rolled
From the Acroceraunian snow to the ford of
the fleece of gold.   95

Meleager

Would God ye could carry me
Forth of all these;
Heap sand and bury me
By the Chersonese

Where the thundering Bosphorus answers the
thunder of Pontic seas.   100

Œneus

Dost thou mock at our praise
And the singing begun
And the men of strange days
Praising my son
In the folds of the hills of home, high places
of Calydon?   105

Meleager

For the dead man no home is;
Ah, better to be
What the flower of the foam is
In fields of the sea,
That the sea-waves might be as my raiment,
the gulf-stream a garment for me.   110

Chorus

Who shall seek thee and bring
And restore thee thy day,
When the dove dipped her wing
And the oars won their way
Where the narrowing Symplegades whitened
the straits of Propontis with spray?   115

Meleager

Will ye crown me my tomb
Or exalt me my name,
Now my spirits consume,
Now my flesh is a flame?
Let the sea slake it once, and men speak of
me sleeping to praise me or shame.   120

Chorus

Turn back now, turn thee,
As who turns him to wake;
Though the life in thee burn thee,
Couldst thou bathe it and slake
Where the sea-ridge of Helle hangs heavier,
and east upon west waters break?   125

Meleager

Would the winds blow me back
Or the waves hurl me home?
Ah, to touch in the track
Where the pine learned to roam
Cold girdles and crowns of the sea-gods, cool
blossoms of water and foam!   130

Chorus

The gods may release
That they made fast;
Thy soul shall have ease

---

77. **thawn,** become thin. 95. **From . . . gold,** from one
end of the Greek world to the other. The Acroceraunian
Mountains are on the west coast of Epirus, in northwestern
Greece. The ford of the fleece of gold is the Hellespont.
See Critical Note on *The Life and Death of Jason.* 99-100.
Chersonese . . . seas. Meleager desired to be buried as far
away as possible from the scene of his death. The Chersonese
was a peninsula north of the Hellespont; it is modern Gallip-
oli. The Bosphorus (line 100) is a strait connecting the
Black Sea (Pontic Sea, line 100) with the Sea of Marmora.

115. **Symplegades,** two rocks at the entrance of the Black
Sea. They clashed together at intervals, but remained apart
when the Argonauts passed through on their quest for the
Golden Fleece. **Propontis,** the Sea of Marmora. 125.
Helle, the Hellespont.

In thy limbs at the last;
But what shall they give thee for life, sweet
life that is overpast?   135

Meleager

Not the life of men's veins,
    Not of flesh that conceives;
But the grace that remains,
    The fair beauty that cleaves
To the life of the rains in the grasses, the life
of the dews on the leaves.   140

Chorus

Thou wert helmsman and chief;
    Wilt thou turn in an hour,
Thy limbs to the leaf,
    Thy face to the flower,
Thy blood to the water, thy soul to the gods
who divide and devour?   145

Meleager

The years are hungry,
    They wail all their days;
The gods wax angry
    And weary of praise;
And who shall bridle their lips? and who shall
straighten their ways?   150

Chorus

The gods guard over us
    With sword and with rod;
Weaving shadow to cover us,
    Heaping the sod,
That law may fulfill herself wholly, to darken
man's face before God.   155
    (1865)

From CHASTELARD

BETWEEN THE SUNSET AND THE SEA

Between the sunset and the sea
My love laid hands and lips on me;
Of sweet came sour, of day came night,
Of long desire came brief delight,
Ah, love, and what thing came of thee   5
Between the sea-downs and the sea?

Between the sea-mark and the sea
Joy grew to grief, grief grew to me;
Love turned to tears, and tears to fire,
And dead delight to new desire;   10

Love's talk, love's touch there seemed to be
Between the sea-sand and the sea.

Between the sundown and the sea
Love watched one hour of love with me;
Then down the all-golden waterways   15
His feet flew after yesterdays;
I saw them come and saw them flee
Between the sea-foam and the sea.

Between the sea-strand and the sea
Love fell on sleep, sleep fell on me;   20
The first star saw twain turn to one
Between the moonrise and the sun;
The next, that saw not love, saw me
Between the sea-banks and the sea.
    (1865)

A BALLAD OF LIFE

I found in dreams a place of wind and flowers,
    Full of sweet trees and color of glad grass,
        In midst whereof there was
A lady clothed like summer with sweet hours.
Her beauty, fervent as a fiery moon,   5
    Made my blood burn and swoon
        Like a flame rained upon.
Sorrow had filled her shaken eyelids' blue,
And her mouth's sad red heavy rose all
        through
    Seemed sad with glad things gone.   10

She held a little cithern by the strings,
    Shaped heartwise, strung with subtle-col-
        ored hair
    Of some dead lute player
That in dead years had done delicious things.
The seven strings were named accordingly: 15
    The first string charity,
        The second tenderness;
The rest were pleasure, sorrow, sleep, and sin,
And loving-kindness, that is pity's kin
        And is most pitiless.   20

There were three men with her, each gar-
        mented
    With gold and shod with gold upon the
        feet;
    And with plucked ears of wheat
The first man's hair was wound upon his head.
His face was red, and his mouth curled and
        sad;   25
    All his gold garment had
        Pale stains of dust and rust.
A riven hood was pulled across his eyes;

155. law . . . God. At Mt. Sinai (*Exodus*, 19), the people
were forbidden to look upon the presence of God concealed
in darkness on the Mount.
Chastelard. Chastelard is the first of a series of three tragedies on Mary, Queen of Scots. Mary Beaton, one of the
Queen's ladies, in love with Chastelard, sang the lyric given
here. Pierre de Boscosel de Chastelard was a French poet
at the court of Queen Mary, with whom he was violently in
love. He had followed her to Scotland from France in 1561.
His intrigue with Mary cost him his life in 1563.

A Ballad of Life. This poem and *A Ballad of Death* (page
663), with their ornateness of style and wealth of sensuous
beauty, illustrate the influence of the Pre-Raphaelite movement upon the early work of Swinburne. See Critical Note
on the Pre-Raphaelites (under Rossetti).
11. cithern, a kind of stringed instrument.

The token of him being upon this wise
 Made for a sign of Lust.   30

The next was Shame, with hollow heavy face
 Colored like green wood when flame
   kindles it.
 He hath such feeble feet
They may not well endure in any place.
His face was full of gray old miseries,   35
 And all his blood's increase
  Was even increase of pain.
The last was Fear, that is akin to Death;
He is Shame's friend, and always as Shame
  saith
 Fear answers him again.   40

My soul said in me: This is marvelous,
 Seeing the air's face is not so delicate
  Nor the sun's grace so great,
If sin and she be kin or amorous.
And seeing where maidens served her on their
  knees,   45
 I bade one crave of these
  To know the cause thereof.
Then Fear said: I am Pity that was dead.
And Shame said: I am Sorrow comforted.
  And Lust said: I am Love.   50

Thereat her hands began a lute-playing
 And her sweet mouth a song in a strange
   tongue;
 And all the while she sung
There was no sound but long tears following
Long tears upon men's faces, waxen white   55
 With extreme sad delight.
  But those three following men
Became as men raised up among the dead;
Great glad mouths open and fair cheeks made
  red
 With child's blood come again.   60

Then I said: Now assuredly I see
 My lady is perfect, and transfigureth
  All sin and sorrow and death,
Making them fair as her own eyelids be,
Or lips wherein my whole soul's life abides; 65
 Or as her sweet white sides
  And bosom carved to kiss.
Now therefore, if her pity further me,
Doubtless for her sake all my days shall be
 As righteous as she is.   70

Forth, ballad, and take roses in both arms,
 Even till the top rose touch thee in the
   throat
Where the least thornprick harms;
 And girdled in thy golden singing-coat,
Come thou before my lady and say this: 75

71. **Forth**, go forth.

Borgia, thy gold hair's color burns in me,
 Thy mouth makes beat my blood in
  feverish rimes;
Therefore so many as these roses be,
 Kiss me so many times.
Then it may be, seeing how sweet she is, 80
 That she will stoop herself none otherwise
  Than a blown vine-branch doth,
And kiss thee with soft laughter on thine eyes,
 Ballad, and on thy mouth.   (1866)

A BALLAD OF DEATH

Kneel down, fair Love, and fill thyself with
  tears,
Girdle thyself with sighing for a girth
Upon the sides of mirth,
Cover thy lips and eyelids, let thine ears
Be filled with rumor of people sorrowing;   5
Make thee soft raiment out of woven sighs
Upon the flesh to cleave,
Set pains therein and many a grievous thing,
And many sorrows after each his wise
For armlet and for gorget and for sleeve.   10

O Love's lute heard about the lands of death,
Left hanged upon the trees that were therein;
O Love and Time and Sin,
Three singing mouths that mourn now under-
  breath,
Three lovers, each one evil spoken of;   15
O smitten lips wherethrough this voice of mine
Came softer with her praise;
Abide a little for our lady's love.
The kisses of her mouth were more than wine,
And more than peace the passage of her days.

O Love, thou knowest if she were good to see.
O Time, thou shalt not find in any land,
Till, cast out of thine hand,
The sunlight and the moonlight fail from thee,
Another woman fashioned like as this.   25
O Sin, thou knowest that all thy shame in her
Was made a goodly thing;
Yea, she caught Shame and shamed him with
  her kiss,
With her fair kiss, and lips much lovelier
Than lips of amorous roses in late spring.   30

By night there stood over against my bed
Queen Venus with a hood striped gold and
  black,

76. **Borgia**, Lucrezia di Borgia (1480-1519), daughter of
Pope Alexander VI and wife of Alfonso, Duke of Ferrara.
Although she was represented as a veritable monster of
wickedness, as Duchess of Ferrara she was noted for her
charm and beauty.
 A Ballad of Death. 10. **gorget**, a neck covering or ornament. 19. **kisses . . . wine.** From *The Song of Solomon,*
1:2.—"Let him kiss me with the kisses of his mouth; for thy
love is better than wine." 32. **Queen Venus**, goddess of
love. According to one tradition she was born of the sea-
foam (line 36).

Both sides drawn fully back
From brows wherein the sad blood failed of
      red,
And temples drained of purple and full of
      death.   35
Her curled hair had the wave of sea-water
And the sea's gold in it.
Her eyes were as a dove's that sickeneth.
Strewn dust of gold she had shed over her,
And pearl and purple and amber on her feet.

Upon her raiment of dyed sendaline   41
Were painted all the secret ways of love
And covered things thereof,
That hold delight as grape-flowers hold their
      wine;   44
Red mouths of maidens and red feet of doves,
And brides that kept within the bride-cham-
      ber
Their garment of soft shame,
And weeping faces of the wearied loves
That swoon in sleep and awake wearier,   49
With heat of lips and hair shed out like flame.

The tears that through her eyelids fell on
      me
Made mine own bitter where they ran be-
      tween
As blood had fallen therein,
She saying: Arise, lift up thine eyes and see
If any glad thing be or any good   55
Now the best thing is taken forth of us;
Even she to whom all praise
Was as one flower in a great multitude,
One glorious flower of many and glorious,
One day found gracious among many days;

Even she whose handmaiden was Love — to
      whom   61
At kissing times across her stateliest bed
Kings bowed themselves and shed
Pale wine, and honey with the honeycomb,
And spikenard bruised for a burnt-offering;
Even she between whose lips the kiss became
As fire and frankincense;
Whose hair was as gold raiment on a king,
Whose eyes were as the morning purged with
      flame,   69
Whose eyelids as sweet savor issuing thence.

Then I beheld, and lo, on the other side
My lady's likeness crowned and robed and
      dead.
Sweet still, but now not red,
Was the shut mouth whereby men lived and
      died.

And sweet, but emptied of the blood's blue
      shade,   75
The great curled eyelids that withheld her
      eyes.
And sweet, but like spoilt gold,
The weight of color in her tresses weighed.
And sweet, but as a vesture with new dyes,
The body that was clothed with love of old. 80

Ah! that my tears filled all her woven hair
And all the hollow bosom of her gown —
Ah! that my tears ran down
Even to the place where many kisses were,
Even where her parted breast-flowers have
      place,   85
Even where they are cloven apart — who
      knows not this?
Ah! the flowers cleave apart
And their sweet fills the tender interspace;
Ah! the leaves grown thereof were things to
      kiss   89
Ere their fine gold was tarnished at the heart.

Ah! in the days when God did good to me,
Each part about her was a righteous thing;
Her mouth an almsgiving,
The glory of her garments charity,
The beauty of her bosom a good deed,   95
In the good days when God kept sight of us;
Love lay upon her eyes,
And on that hair whereof the world takes
      heed;
And all her body was more virtuous
Than souls of women fashioned otherwise. 100

Now, ballad, gather poppies in thine hands
And sheaves of briar and many rusted sheaves
Rain-rotten in rank lands,
Waste marigold and late unhappy leaves
And grass that fades ere any of it be mown,
And when thy bosom is filled full thereof 106
Seek out Death's face ere the light altereth,
And say: "My master that was thrall to Love
Is become thrall to Death."
Bow down before him, ballad, sigh and groan,
But make no sojourn in thy outgoing;   111
For haply it may be
That when thy feet return at evening
Death shall come in with thee.   (1866)

LAUS VENERIS

Asleep or waking is it? for her neck,
Kissed over close, wears yet a purple speck
      Wherein the pained blood falters and goes
      out;
Soft, and stung softly — fairer for a fleck.

---

41. **sendaline**, a light silk fabric used in the Middle Ages.
65. **spikenard**, a plant from which a costly fragrant ointment was made.   67. **frankincense**, a fragrant ointment
valued by the ancients for fumigation, embalming, etc.

Laus Veneris. The title means *Praise of Venus.* Cf. *Hymn
to Proserpine*, p. 686; see also Critical Notes.

But though my lips shut sucking on the place,
There is no vein at work upon her face; 6
Her eyelids are so peaceable, no doubt
Deep sleep has warmed her blood through all
its ways.

Lo, this is she that was the world's delight; 9
The old gray years were parcels of her might;
The strewings of the ways wherein she trod
Were the twain seasons of the day and night.

Lo, she was thus when her clear limbs enticed
All lips that now grow sad with kissing Christ,
Stained with blood fallen from the feet of
God, 15
The feet and hands whereat our souls were
priced.

Alas, Lord, surely thou art great and fair.
But, lo, her wonderfully woven hair!
And thou didst heal us with thy piteous
kiss;
But see now, Lord, her mouth is lovelier. 20

She is right fair; what hath she done to thee?
Nay, fair Lord Christ, lift up thine eyes and
see;
Had now thy mother such a lip — like this?
Thou knowest how sweet a thing it is to me.

Inside the Horsel here the air is hot; 25
Right little peace one hath for it, God wot;
The scented dusty daylight burns the air,
And my heart chokes me till I hear it not.

Behold, my Venus, my soul's body, lies
With my love laid upon her garment-wise, 30
Feeling my love in all her limbs and hair
And shed between her eyelids through her
eyes.

She holds my heart in her sweet open hands
Hanging asleep; hard by her head there
stands,
Crowned with gilt thorns and clothed with
flesh like fire, 35
Love, wan as foam blown up the salt burnt
sands —

Hot as the brackish waifs of yellow spume
That shift and steam — loose clots of arid
fume
From the sea's panting mouth of dry desire;
There stands he, like one laboring at a loom.

The warp holds fast across; and every thread
That makes the woof up has dry specks of red;

Always the shuttle cleaves clean through,
and he
Weaves with the hair of many a ruined head.

Love is not glad nor sorry, as I deem; 45
Laboring he dreams, and labors in the dream,
Till when the spool is finished, lo, I see
His web, reeled off, curls and goes out like
steam.

Night falls like fire; the heavy lights run low,
And as they drop, my blood and body so 50
Shake as the flame shakes, full of days and
hours
That sleep not neither weep they as they go.

Ah, yet would God, this flesh of mine might be
Where air might wash and long leaves cover
me,
Where tides of grass break into foam of
flowers, 55
Or where the wind's feet shine along the sea.

Ah, yet would God that stems and roots were
bred
Out of my weary body and my head,
That sleep were sealed upon me with a seal
And I were as the least of all his dead. 60

Would God my blood were dew to feed the
grass,
Mine ears made deaf and mine eyes blind as
glass,
My body broken as a turning wheel,
And my mouth stricken ere it saith Alas!

Ah, God, that love were as a flower or flame,
That life were as the naming of a name, 66
That death were not more pitiful than
desire,
That these things were not one thing and the
same!

Behold now, surely somewhere there is death;
For each man hath some space of years, he
saith, 70
A little space of time ere time expire,
A little day, a little way of breath.

And, lo, between the sundawn and the sun,
His day's work and his night's work are
undone; 74
And, lo, between the nightfall and the night,
He is not, and none knoweth of such an one.

Ah, God, that I were as all souls that be,
As any herb or leaf of any tree,
As men that toil through hours of laboring
light, 80
As bones of men under the deep sharp sea.

25. **Horsel**, Hörselberg, the Mountain of Venus, in central
Germany. In medieval tradition Venus was an enchantress
who held her court with pagan splendor and revelry in a
cavern in this mountain. This tradition is the theme of the
legend of Tannhäuser. See Morris's *The Hill of Venus*, p. 649.
26. **wot**, knows.

Outside it must be winter among men;
For at the gold bars of the gates again
   I heard all night and all the hours of it
The wind's wet wings and fingers drip with
     rain.

Knights gather, riding sharp for cold; I know
The ways and woods are strangled with the
     snow;   86
   And with short song the maidens spin and
     sit
Until Christ's birthnight, lily-like, arow.

The scent and shadow shed about me make
The very soul in all my senses ache;   90
   The hot hard night is fed upon my breath,
And sleep beholds me from afar awake.

Alas, but surely where the hills grow deep,
Or where the wild ways of the sea are steep,
   Or in strange places somewhere there is
     death,   95
And on death's face the scattered hair of
     sleep.

There lover-like with lips and limbs that meet
They lie, they pluck sweet fruit of life and eat;
   But me the hot and hungry days devour,
And in my mouth no fruit of theirs is sweet. 100

No fruit of theirs, but fruit of my desire,
For her love's sake whose lips through mine
     respire;
   Her eyelids on her eyes like flower on flower,
Mine eyelids on mine eyes like fire on fire.

So lie we, not as sleep that lies by death, 105
With heavy kisses and with happy breath;   ·
   Not as man lies by woman, when the bride
Laughs low for love's sake and the words he
     saith.

For she lies, laughing low with love; she lies
And turns his kisses on her lips to sighs, 110
   To sighing sound of lips unsatisfied,
And the sweet tears are tender with her eyes.

Ah, not as they, but as the souls that were
Slain in the old time, having found her fair;
   Who, sleeping with her lips upon their eyes,
Heard sudden serpents hiss across her hair. 116

Their blood runs round the roots of time like
     rain;
She casts them forth and gathers them again;
   With nerve and bone she weaves and mul-
     tiplies
Exceeding pleasure out of extreme pain.   120

102. respire, breathe.

Her little chambers drip with flower-like red,
Her girdles, and the chaplets of her head,
   Her armlets and her anklets; with her feet
She tramples all that wine-press of the dead.

Her gateways smoke with fume of flowers and
     fires,   125
With loves burnt out and unassuaged desires;
   Between her lips the steam of them is sweet,
The languor in her ears of many lyres.

Her beds are full of perfume and sad sound,
Her doors are made with music, and barred
     round   130
   With sighing and with laughter and with
     tears,
With tears whereby strong souls of men are
     bound.

There is the knight Adonis that was slain;
With flesh and blood she chains him for a
     chain;
   The body and the spirit in her ears   135
Cry, for her lips divide him vein by vein.

Yea, all she slayeth; yea, every man save me;
Me, love, thy lover that must cleave to thee
   Till the ending of the days and ways of
     earth,
The shaking of the sources of the sea.   140

Me, most forsaken of all souls that fell;
Me, satiated with things insatiable;
   Me, for whose sake the extreme hell makes
     mirth,
Yea, laughter kindles at the heart of hell.

Alas thy beauty! for thy mouth's sweet sake
My soul is bitter to me, my limbs quake 146
   As water, as the flesh of men that weep,
As their heart's vein whose heart goes nigh
     to break.

Ah, God, that sleep with flower-sweet finger-
     tips
Would crush the fruit of death upon my lips;
   Ah, God, that death would tread the grapes
     of sleep   151
And wring their juice upon me as it drips.

There is no change of cheer for many days,
But change of chimes high up in the air, that
     sways
   Rung by the running fingers of the wind; 155
And singing sorrows heard on hidden ways.

122. chaplets, wreaths.   133. Adonis, the beautiful
youth loved by Venus, goddess of love. He was slain while
hunting. Because of the great sorrow of Venus, the gods of
the lower world allowed Adonis to spend half of each year
with her in the upper world.

Day smiteth day in twain, night sundereth
    night,
And on mine eyes the dark sits as the light;
    Yea, Lord, thou knowest I know not, hav-
      ing sinned,
If heaven be clean or unclean in thy sight. 160

Yea, as if earth were sprinkled over me,
Such chafed harsh earth as chokes a sandy
    sea,
    Each pore doth yearn, and the dried blood
      thereof
Gasps by sick fits; my heart swims heavily;

There is a feverish famine in my veins; 165
Below her bosom, where a crushed grape stains
    The white and blue, there my lips caught
      and clove
An hour since, and what mark of me remains?

I dare not always touch her, lest the kiss
Leave my lips charred. Yea, Lord, a little
    bliss, 170
    Brief bitter bliss, one hath for a great sin;
Nathless thou knowest how sweet a thing it is.

Sin, is it sin whereby men's souls are thrust
Into the pit? yet had I a good trust
    To save my soul before it slipped therein,
    Trod under by the fire-shod feet of lust. 176

For if mine eyes fail and my soul takes breath,
I look between the iron sides of death
    Into sad hell, where all sweet love hath
      end —
All but the pain that never finisheth. 180

There are the naked faces of great kings,
The singing folk with all their lute-playings;
    There when one cometh he shall have to
      friend
The grave that covets and the worm that
    clings.

There sit the knights that were so great of
    hand, 185
The ladies that were queens of fair green land,
    Grown gray and black now, brought unto
      the dust,
Soiled, without raiment, clad about with sand.

There is one end for all of them; they sit
Naked and sad, they drink the dregs of it, 190
    Trodden as grapes in the wine-press of lust,
    Trampled and trodden by the fiery feet.

I see the marvelous mouth whereby there fell
Cities and people whom the gods loved well,
    Yet for her sake on them the fire gat hold,
And for their sakes on her the fire of hell. 196

And softer than the Egyptian lote-leaf is,
The queen whose face was worth the world
    to kiss,
    Wearing at breast a suckling snake of gold;
And large pale lips of strong Semiramis, 200

Curled like a tiger's that curl back to feed;
Red only where the last kiss made them bleed;
    Her hair most thick with many a carven
      gem,
Deep in the mane, great-chested, like a steed.

Yea, with red sin the faces of them shine; 205
But in all these there was no sin like mine;
    No, not in all the strange great sins of them
That made the wine-press froth and foam with
    wine.

For I was of Christ's choosing, I God's knight,
No blinkard heathen stumbling for scant light;
    I can well see, for all the dusty days 211
Gone past, the clean great time of goodly fight.

I smell the breathing battle sharp with blows,
With shriek of shafts and snapping short of
    bows;
    The fair pure sword smites out in subtle
      ways, 215
Sounds and long lights are shed between the
    rows

Of beautiful mailed men; the edged light slips,
Most like a snake that takes short breath and
    dips
    Sharp from the beautifully bending head,
With all its gracious body lithe as lips 220

That curl in touching you; right in this wise
My sword doth, seeming fire in mine own eyes,
    Leaving all colors in them brown and red
And flecked with death; then the keen breaths
    like sighs,

The caught-up choked dry laughters following
    them, 225
When all the fighting face is grown a flame
    For pleasure, and the pulse that stuns the
      ears,
And the heart's gladness of the goodly game.

---

172. **Nathless,** nevertheless. 181 ff. **There ... kings,**
etc. See Critical Notes. 186. **queens ... land,** such as
Helen of Troy, wife of King Menelaus of Sparta, and Cleopatra, queen of Egypt. 191-192. **Trodden ... feet.** See
Isaiah, 63:2-3.

197. **lote-leaf,** the leaf of the lotus. See *The Lotos-Eaters,*
page 28, and Critical Note. 198. **The queen,** Cleopatra.
Dryden's drama on Antony and Cleopatra was entitled *All
for Love; or the World Well Lost.* 200. **Semiramis,** in legendary history the queen of Assyria. She is said to have built
the city of Babylon and its famous hanging gardens. 210.
blinkard, blinking, stupid.

Let me think yet a little; I do know
These things were sweet, but sweet such years
    ago,   230
    Their savor is all turned now into tears;
Yea, ten years since, where the blue ripples
    blow,

The blue curled eddies of the blowing Rhine,
I felt the sharp wind shaking grass and vine
    Touch my blood, too, and sting me with
    delight   235
Through all this waste and weary body of
    mine

That never feels clear air; right gladly then
I rode alone, a great way off my men,
    And heard the chiming bridle smite and
    smite,
And gave each rime thereof some rime again,

Till my song shifted to that iron one;   241
Seeing there rode up between me and the sun
    Some certain of my foe's men, for his three
White wolves across their painted coats did
    run.

The first red-bearded, with square cheeks —
    alack,   245
I made my knave's blood turn his beard to
    black;
    The slaying of him was a joy to see.
Perchance, too, when at night he came not
    back,

Some woman fell a-weeping, whom this thief
Would beat when he had drunken; yet small
    grief   250
    Hath any for the ridding of such knaves;
Yea, if one wept, I doubt her teen was brief.

This bitter love is sorrow in all lands,
Draining of eyelids, wringing of drenched
    hands,
    Sighing of hearts and filling up of graves; 255
A sign across the head of the world he stands,

As one that hath a plague-mark on his brows;
Dust and spilt blood do track him to his house
    Down under earth; sweet smells of lip and
    cheek,
Like a sweet snake's breath made more poi-
    sonous   260

With chewing of some perfumed deadly grass,
Are shed all round his passage if he pass,
    And their quenched savor leaves the whole
    soul weak,
Sick with keen guessing whence the perfume
    was.

252. **teen**, grief, sorrow.

As one who hidden in deep sedge and reeds
Smells the rare scent made where a panther
    feeds,   266
    And tracking ever slotwise the warm smell
Is snapped upon by the sweet mouth and
    bleeds,

His head far down the hot sweet throat of
    her —   269
So one tracks love, whose breath is deadlier,
    And, lo, one springe and you are fast in hell,
Fast as the gin's grip of a wayfarer.

I think now, as the heavy hours decease
One after one, and bitter thoughts increase
    One upon one, of all sweet finished things:
The breaking of the battle; the long peace 276

Wherein we sat clothed softly, each man's hair
Crowned with green leaves beneath white
    hoods of vair;
    The sounds of sharp spears at great tour-
    neyings,   279
And noise of singing in the late sweet air.

I sang of love too, knowing naught thereof;
"Sweeter," I said, "the little laugh of love
    Than tears out of the eyes of Magdalen,
Or any fallen feather of the Dove.

"The broken little laugh that spoils a kiss, 285
The ache of purple pulses, and the bliss
    Of blinded eyelids that expand again —
Love draws them open with those lips of his;

"Lips that cling hard till the kissed face has
    grown
Of one same fire and color with their own; 290
    Then ere one sleep, appeased with sacrifice,
Where his lips wounded, there his lips atone."

I sang these things long since and knew them
    not:
"Lo, here is love, or there is love, God wot,
    This man and that finds favor in his eyes,"
I said, "but I, what guerdon have I got?   296

"The dust of praise that is blown everywhere
In all men's faces with the common air;
    The bay-leaf that wants chafing to be sweet
Before they wind it in a singer's hair."   300

267. **slotwise**, in the way one follows a slot—that is, a track or trace of an animal. 271-2. **springe, gin,** snares or traps for catching game. 278. **vair,** the skin of a species of squirrel, much used in the Middle Ages as fur for costly dresses and robes. 283. **Magdalen.** See Rossetti's *Mary Magdalene* and note, p. 524. 284. **the Dove.** Cf. *Matthew,* 3:16-17.—"And Jesus, when he was baptized, went up straightway out of the water; and, lo, the heavens were opened unto him, and he saw the Spirit of God descending like a dove, and lighting upon him: And lo a voice from heaven, saying, 'This is my beloved Son, in whom I am well pleased.'" 299. **bay-leaf,** laurel, often used in wreaths for crowning poets and heroes in ancient times.

So that one dawn I rode forth sorrowing;
I had no hope but of some evil thing,
  And so rode slowly past the windy wheat
And past the vineyard and the water-spring,

Up to the Horsel. A great elder-tree   305
Held back its heaps of flowers to let me see
  The ripe tall grass, and one that walked
    therein,
Naked, with hair shed over to the knee.

She walked between the blossom and the grass;
I knew the beauty of her, what she was,   310
  The beauty of her body and her sin,
And in my flesh the sin of hers, alas!

Alas! for sorrow is all the end of this.
O sad kissed mouth, how sorrowful it is!
  O breast whereat some suckling sorrow
    clings,   315
Red with the bitter blossom of a kiss!

Ah, with blind lips I felt for you, and found
About my neck your hands and hair enwound,
  The hands that stifle and the hair that
    stings,   319
I felt them fasten sharply without sound.

Yea, for my sin I had great store of bliss;
Rise up, make answer for me, let thy kiss
  Seal my lips hard from speaking of my sin,
Lest one go mad to hear how sweet it is.

Yet I waxed faint with fume of barren bowers,
And murmuring of the heavy-headed hours;
  And let the dove's beak fret and peck within
My lips in vain, and Love shed fruitless
    flowers.

So that God looked upon me when your hands
Were hot about me; yea, God brake my bands
  To save my soul alive, and I came forth   331
Like a man blind and naked in strange lands

That hears men laugh and weep, and knows
  not whence
Nor wherefore, but is broken in his sense;
  Howbeit I met folk riding from the north
Toward Rome, to purge them of their souls'
    offense.   336

And rode with them, and spake to none; the
  day
Stunned me like lights upon some wizard way,
  And ate like fire mine eyes and mine eye-
    sight;   339
So rode I, hearing all these chant and pray,

And marveled; till before us rose and fell
White curséd hills, like outer skirts of hell

Seen where men's eyes look through the
  day to night,
Like a jagged shell's lips, harsh, untunable,

Blown in between by devils' wrangling
  breath;   345
Nathless we won well past that hell and death,
  Down to the sweet land where all airs are
    good,
Even unto Rome where God's grace tarrieth.

Then came each man and worshiped at his
  knees
Who in the Lord God's likeness bears the keys
  To bind or loose, and called on Christ's shed
    blood,   351
And so the sweet-souled father gave him ease.

But when I came I fell down at his feet,
Saying, "Father, though the Lord's blood be
  right sweet,   354
  The spot it takes not off the panther's skin,
Nor shall an Ethiop's stain be bleached
    with it.

"Lo, I have sinned and have spat out at God,
Wherefore his hand is heavier and his rod
  More sharp because of mine exceeding sin,
And all his raiment redder than bright blood

"Before mine eyes; yea, for my sake I wot   361
The heat of hell is waxen seven times hot
  Through my great sin." Then spake he
    some sweet word,
Giving me cheer; which thing availed me not;

Yea, scarce I wist if such indeed were said;   365
For when I ceased — lo, as one newly dead
  Who hears a great cry out of hell, I heard
The crying of his voice across my head.

"Until this dry shred staff, that hath no whit
Of leaf nor bark, bear blossom and smell
  sweet,   370
  Seek thou not any mercy in God's sight,
For so long shalt thou be cast out from it."

Yea, what if dried-up stems wax red and
  green,
Shall that thing be which is not nor has been?
  Yea, what if sapless bark wax green and
    white,   375
Shall any good fruit grow upon my sin?

Nay, though sweet fruit were plucked of a
  dry tree,

352. **sweet-souled father,** Pope Urban IV (1261-64), according to the legend. 355-356. **spot . . . with it.** From *Jeremiah*, 13:23.—"Can the Ethiopian change his skin, or the leopard his spots?"

And though men drew sweet waters of the
  sea,
  There should not grow sweet leaves on this
    dead stem,   379
This waste wan body and shaken soul of me.

Yea, though God search it warily enough,
There is not one sound thing in all thereof;
  Though he search all my veins through,
    searching them
He shall find nothing whole therein but love.

For I came home right heavy, with small
  cheer,   385
And, lo, my love, mine own soul's heart, more
  dear
  Than mine own soul, more beautiful than
    God,
Who hath my being between the hands of
  her —

Fair still, but fair for no man saving me,
As when she came out of the naked sea   390
  Making the foam as fire whereon she trod,
And as the inner flower of fire was she.

Yea, she laid hold upon me, and her mouth
Clove unto mine as soul to body doth,
  And, laughing, made her lips luxurious; 395
Her hair had smells of all the sunburnt south,

Strange spice and flower, strange savor of
  crushed fruit,
And perfume the swart kings tread underfoot
  For pleasure when their minds wax amor-
    ous,
Charred frankincense and grated sandal-root.

And I forgot fear and all weary things,   401
All ended prayers and perished thanksgivings,
  Feeling her face with all her eager hair
Cleave to me, clinging as a fire that clings

To the body and to the raiment, burning
  them;   405
As after death I know that such-like flame
  Shall cleave to me forever; yea, what care,
Albeit I burn then, having felt the same?

Ah, love, there is no better life than this; 409
To have known love, how bitter a thing it is,
  And afterward be cast out of God's sight;
Yea, these that know not, shall they have such
  bliss

High up in barren heaven before his face
As we twain in the heavy-hearted place,

Remembering love and all the dead delight,   415
And all that time was sweet with for a space?

For till the thunder in the trumpet be,
Soul may divide from body, but not we
  One from another; I hold thee with my
    hand,
I let mine eyes have all their will of thee, 420

I seal myself upon thee with my might,
Abiding alway out of all men's sight
  Until God loosen over sea and land
The thunder of the trumpets of the night.
                (1866)

THE TRIUMPH OF TIME

Before our lives divide forever,
  While time is with us and hands are free
(Time, swift to fasten and swift to sever
  Hand from hand, as we stand by the sea),
I will say no word that a man might say   5
Whose whole life's love goes down in a day;
For this could never have been, and never —
  Though the gods and the years relent —
    shall be.

Is it worth a tear, is it worth an hour,
  To think of things that are well outworn?
Of fruitless husk and fugitive flower,   11
  The dream foregone and the deed forborne?
Though joy be done with and grief be vain,
Time shall not sever us wholly in twain;
Earth is not spoilt for a single shower;   15
  But the rain has ruined the ungrown corn.

It will grow not again, this fruit of my heart,
  Smitten with sunbeams, ruined with rain.
The singing seasons divide and depart,
  Winter and summer depart in twain.   20
It will grow not again, it is ruined at root,
The bloodlike blossom, the dull red fruit;
Though the heart yet sickens, the lips yet
  smart,
With sullen savor of poisonous pain.

I have given no man of my fruit to eat;   25
  I trod the grapes, I have drunken the wine.
Had you eaten and drunken and found it
  sweet,
This wild new growth of the corn and vine,
This wine and bread without lees or leaven,
We had grown as gods, as the gods in heaven,

---

417. **thunder in the trumpet**, the sound of the trumpet
on the Day of Judgment.
  The Triumph of Time. This poem was written soon after
Swinburne's rejection by a young girl whom he ardently
loved.
  16. **corn**, grain, wheat.

390. **when she . . . sea.** According to tradition Aphrodite (Venus) sprang from the foam of the sea.

Souls fair to look upon, goodly to greet,   31
  One splendid spirit, your soul and mine.

In the change of years, in the coil of things,
  In the clamor and rumor of life to be,
We, drinking love at the furthest springs,   35
  Covered with love as a covering tree,
We had grown as gods, as the gods above,
Filled from the heart to the lips with love,
Held fast in his hands, clothed warm with his
    wings,
  O love, my love, had you loved but me!   40

We had stood as the sure stars stand, and
    moved
  As the moon moves, loving the world; and
    seen
Grief collapse as a thing disproved,
  Death consume as a thing unclean;
Twain halves of a perfect heart, made fast   45
Soul to soul while the years fell past —
Had you loved me once, as you have not
    loved;
  Had the chance been with us that has not
    been.

I have put my days and dreams out of mind,
  Days that are over, dreams that are done.
Though we seek life through, we shall surely
    find   51
  There is none of them clear to us now, not
    one.
But clear are these things; the grass and the
    sand,
Where, sure as the eyes reach, ever at hand,
With lips wide open and face burnt blind,   55
  The strong sea-daisies feast on the sun.

The low downs lean to the sea; the stream,
  One loose thin pulseless tremulous vein,
Rapid and vivid and dumb as a dream,
  Works downward, sick of the sun and the
    rain;   60
No wind is rough with the rank rare flowers;
The sweet sea, mother of loves and hours,
Shudders and shines as the gray winds gleam,
  Turning her smile to a fugitive pain.

Mother of loves that are swift to fade,   65
  Mother of mutable winds and hours;
A barren mother, a mother-maid,
  Cold and clean as her faint salt flowers —
I would we twain were even as she,
Lost in the night and the light of the sea,   70
Where faint sounds falter and wan beams
    wade,
  Break, and are broken, and shed into
    showers.

65. **Mother of loves,** the sea.

The loves and hours of the life of a man,
  They are swift and sad, being born of the
    sea:
Hours that rejoice and regret for a span,   75
  Born with a man's breath, mortal as he;
Loves that are lost ere they come to birth,
Weeds of the wave, without fruit upon earth.
I lose what I long for, save what I can,
  My love, my love, and no love for me!   80

It is not much that a man can save
  On the sands of life, in the straits of time,
Who swims in sight of the great third wave
  That never a swimmer shall cross or climb.
Some waif washed up with the strays and
    spars   85
That ebb-tide shows to the shore and the
    stars;
Weed from the water, grass from a grave,
  A broken blossom, a ruined rime.

There will no man do for your sake, I think,
  What I would have done for the least word
    said.   90
I had wrung life dry for your lips to drink,
  Broken it up for your daily bread;
Body for body and blood for blood,
As the flow of the full sea risen to flood
That yearns and trembles before it sink,   95
  I had given, and lain down for you, glad
    and dead.

Yea, hope at highest and all her fruit,
  And time at fullest and all his dower,
I had given you surely, and life to boot,
  Were we once made one for a single
    hour.   100
But now, you are twain, you are cloven apart,
Flesh of his flesh, but heart of my heart;
And deep in one is the bitter root,
And sweet for one is the lifelong flower.

To have died if you cared I should die for
    you, clung   105
  To my life if you bade me, played my part
As it pleased you — these were the thoughts
    that stung,
  The dreams that smote with a keener dart
Than shafts of love or arrows of death;
These were but as fire is, dust, or breath,   110
Or poisonous foam on the tender tongue
  Of the little snakes that eat my heart.

I wish we were dead together today,
  Lost sight of, hidden away out of sight,
Clasped and clothed in the cloven clay,   115
  Out of the world's way, out of the light,
Out of the ages of worldly weather,

83. **the great third wave,** a reference to the belief that
each third wave is bigger than the two preceding.

Forgotten of all men altogether,
As the world's first dead, taken wholly away,
    Made one with death, filled full of the
        night.   120

How we should slumber, how we should sleep,
    Far in the dark with the dreams and the
        dews!
And dreaming, grow to each other, and weep,
    Laugh low, live softly, murmur and muse;
Yea, and it may be, struck through by the
        dream,   125
Feel the dust quicken and quiver, and seem
Alive as of old to the lips, and leap
    Spirit to spirit as lovers use.

Sick dreams and sad of a dull delight;
    For what shall it profit when men are dead
To have dreamed, to have loved with the
        whole soul's might,   131
    To have looked for day when the day was
        fled?
Let come what will, there is one thing worth:
To have had fair love in the life upon earth;
To have held love safe till the day grew night,
    While skies had color and lips were red. 136

Would I lose you now? would I take you then,
    If I lose you now that my heart has need?
And come what may after death to men,
    What thing worth this will the dead years
        breed?   140
Lose life, lose all; but at least I know,
O sweet life's love, having loved you so,
Had I reached you on earth, I should lose not
        again,
    In death nor life, nor in dream or deed.

Yea, I know this well: were you once sealed
        mine,   145
    Mine in the blood's beat, mine in the breath,
Mixed into me as honey in wine,
    Not time, that sayeth and gainsayeth,
Nor all strong things had severed us then;
Not wrath of gods, nor wisdom of men,   150
    Nor all things earthly, nor all divine,
    Nor joy nor sorrow, nor life nor death.

I had grown pure as the dawn and the dew;
    You had grown strong as the sun or the sea.
But none shall triumph a whole life through;
    For death is one, and the fates are three. 156
At the door of life, by the gate of breath,
There are worse things waiting for men than
        death;
Death could not sever my soul and you,
    As these have severed your soul from me.

156. **fates are three**, Clotho, who spins the thread of life;
Lachesis, who determines its length, and Atropos, who cuts
it off.

You have chosen and clung to the chance they
        sent you,   161
    Life sweet as perfume and pure as prayer.
But will it not one day in heaven repent you?
    Will they solace you wholly, the days that
        were?
Will you lift up your eyes between sadness
        and bliss,   165
Meet mine, and see where the great love is,
And tremble and turn and be changed? Con-
        tent you;
    The gate is strait; I shall not be there.

But you, had you chosen, had you stretched
        hand,
    Had you seen good such a thing were done,
I too might have stood with the souls that
        stand   171
    In the sun's sight, clothed with the light of
        the sun;
But who now on earth need care how I live?
Have the high gods anything left to give,
Save dust and laurels and gold and sand? 175
    Which gifts are goodly; but I will none.

O all fair lovers about the world,
    There is none of you, none, that shall com-
        fort me.
My thoughts are as dead things, wrecked and
        whirled
    Round and round in a gulf of the sea;   180
And still, through the sound and the straining
        stream,
Through the coil and chafe, they gleam in a
        dream,
The bright fine lips so cruelly curled,
    And strange swift eyes where the soul sits
        free.

Free, without pity, withheld from woe,   185
    Ignorant; fair as the eyes are fair.
Would I have you change now, change at a
        blow,
    Startled and stricken, awake and aware?
Yea, if I could, would I have you see
My very love of you filling me,   190
And know my soul to the quick, as I know
    The likeness and look of your throat and
        hair?

I shall not change you. Nay, though I might,
    Would I change my sweet one love with a
        word?
I had rather your hair should change in a
        night,   195
    Clear now as the plume of a black bright
        bird;
Your face fail suddenly, cease, turn gray,
    Die as a leaf that dies in a day.
I will keep my soul in a place out of sight,
    Far off, where the pulse of it is not heard.

Far off it walks, in a bleak blown space,   201
  Full of the sound of the sorrow of years.
I have woven a veil for the weeping face,
  Whose lips have drunken the wine of tears;
I have found a way for the failing feet,   205
A place for slumber and sorrow to meet;
There is no rumor about the place,
  Nor light, nor any that sees or hears.

I have hidden my soul out of sight and said,
  "Let none take pity upon thee, none   210
Comfort thy crying, for, lo, thou art dead;
  Lie still now, safe out of sight of the sun.
Have I not built thee a grave, and wrought
Thy grave-clothes on thee of grievous thought,
With soft spun verses and tears unshed,   215
  And sweet light visions of things undone?

"I have given thee garments and balm and
    myrrh,
  And gold, and beautiful burial things.
But thou, be at peace now, make no stir;
  Is not thy grave as a royal king's?   220
Fret not thyself though the end were sore;
Sleep, be patient, vex me no more.
Sleep; what hast thou to do with her?
  The eyes that weep, with the mouth that
    sings?"

Where the dead red leaves of the years lie
    rotten,   225
  The cold old crimes and the deeds thrown
    by,
The misconceived and the misbegotten,
  I would find a sin to do ere I die,
Sure to dissolve and destroy me all through,
That would set you higher in heaven, serve
    you   230
And leave you happy, when clean forgotten,
  As a dead man out of mind, am I.

Your lithe hands draw me, your face burns
    through me,
  I am swift to follow you, keen to see;
But love lacks might to redeem or undo me;
  As I have been, I know I shall surely be; 236
"What should such fellows as I do?" Nay,
  My part were worse if I chose to play;
For the worst is this, after all — if they knew
    me,
  Not a soul upon earth would pity me.   240

And I play not for pity of these; but you,
  If you saw with your soul what man am I,
You would praise me at least that my soul all
    through
  Clove to you, loathing the lives that lie;
The souls and lips that are bought and sold,
The smiles of silver and kisses of gold,   246

217. myrrh, a kind of rich perfume.

The lapdog loves that whine as they chew,
  The little lovers that curse and cry.

There are fairer women, I hear; that may be;
  But I, that I love you and find you fair, 250
Who are more than fair in my eyes if they be,
  Do the high gods know or the great gods
    care?
Though the swords in my heart for one were
    seven,
Should the iron hollow of doubtful heaven,
That knows not itself whether night-time or
    day be,   255
  Reverberate words and a foolish prayer?

I will go back to the great sweet mother,
  Mother and lover of men, the sea.
I will go down to her, I and none other,
  Close with her, kiss her, and mix her with
    me;   260
Cling to her, strive with her, hold her fast.
O fair white mother, in days long past
Born without sister, born without brother,
  Set free my soul as thy soul is free.

O fair green-girdled mother of mine,   265
  Sea, that art clothed with the sun and the
    rain,
Thy sweet hard kisses are strong like wine,
  Thy large embraces are keen like pain.
Save me and hide me with all thy waves,
Find me one grave of thy thousand graves, 270
Those pure cold populous graves of thine
  Wrought without hand in a world without
    stain.

I shall sleep, and move with the moving ships,
  Change as the winds change, veer in the
    tide;
My lips will feast on the foam of thy lips, 275
  I shall rise with thy rising, with thee sub-
    side;
Sleep, and not know if she be, if she were,
Filled full with life to the eyes and hair,
As a rose is fulfilled to the roseleaf tips
  With splendid summer and perfume and
    pride.   280

This woven raiment of nights and days,
  Were it once cast off and unwound from me,
Naked and glad would I walk in thy ways,
  Alive and aware of thy ways and thee;
Clear of the whole world, hidden at home, 285
Clothed with the green and crowned with the
    foam,
A pulse of the life of thy straits and bays,
  A vein in the heart of the streams of the
    sea.

253. swords . . . seven, a reference to the seven sorrows
of Mary. (See note on Browning's *Up at a Villa—Down in
the City*, 52, p. 233.)

Fair mother, fed with the lives of men,   289
  Thou art subtle and cruel of heart, men say.
Thou hast taken, and shalt not render again;
  Thou art full of thy dead, and cold as they.
But death is the worst that comes of thee;
Thou art fed with our dead, O mother, O sea,
But when hast thou fed on our hearts? or
     when,   295
  Having given us love, hast thou taken
     away?

O tender-hearted, O perfect lover,
  Thy lips are bitter, and sweet thine heart.
The hopes that hurt and the dreams that
     hover,
  Shall they not vanish away and apart? 300
But thou, thou art sure, thou art older than
     earth;
Thou art strong for death and fruitful of
     birth;
Thy depths conceal and thy gulfs discover;
  From the first thou wert; in the end thou
     art.   304

And grief shall endure not forever, I know.
  As things that are not shall these things be;
We shall live through seasons of sun and of
     snow,
  And none be grievous as this to me.
We shall hear, as one in a trance that hears,
The sound of time, the rime of the years; 310
Wrecked hope and passionate pain will grow
  As tender things of a springtide sea,

Sea-fruit that swings in the waves that hiss,
  Drowned gold and purple and royal rings.
And all time past, was it all for this?   315
  Times unforgotten, and treasures of things?
Swift years of liking, and sweet long laughter,
That wist not well of the years thereafter
Till love woke, smitten at heart by a kiss,
  With lips that trembled and trailing wings?

There lived a singer in France of old   321
  By the tideless dolorous midland sea.
In a land of sand and ruin and gold
  There shone one woman, and none but she.
And finding life for her love's sake fail,   325
Being fain to see her, he bade set sail,
Touched land, and saw her as life grew cold,
  And praised God, seeing; and so died he —

Died, praising God for his gift and grace;
  For she bowed down to him weeping, and
     said
                            330
"Live"; and her tears were shed on his face
Or ever the life in his face was shed.

The sharp tears fell through her hair, and
     stung
Once, and her close lips touched him and
     clung   334
Once, and grew one with his lips for a space;
  And so drew back, and the man was dead.

O brother, the gods were good to you.
  Sleep, and be glad while the world endures.
Be well content as the years wear through;
  Give thanks for life, and the loves and lures;
Give thanks for life, O brother, and death, 341
For the sweet last sound of her feet, her
     breath,
For gifts she gave you, gracious and few,
  Tears and kisses, that lady of yours.

Rest and be glad of the gods; but I,   345
  How shall I praise them, or how take rest?
There is not room under all the sky
  For me that know not of worst or best,
Dream or desire of the days before,
Sweet things or bitterness, any more.   350
Love will not come to me now though I
     die,
  As love came close to you, breast to breast.

I shall never be friends again with roses;
  I shall loathe sweet tunes, where a note
     grown strong   354
Relents and recoils, and climbs and closes,
  As a wave of the sea turned back by song.
There are sounds where the soul's delight
     takes fire,
Face to face with its own desire;
A delight that rebels, a desire that reposes;
  I shall hate sweet music my whole life long.

The pulse of war and passion of wonder, 361
  The heavens that murmur, the sounds that
     shine,
The stars that sing and the loves that thunder,
  The music burning at heart like wine,
An armed archangel whose hands raise up 365
All senses mixed in the spirit's cup
Till flesh and spirit are molten in sunder —
  These things are over, and no more mine.

These were a part of the playing I heard
  Once, ere my love and my heart were at
     strife;   370
Love that sings and hath wings as a bird,
  Balm of the wound and heft of the knife.
Fairer than earth is the sea, and sleep
Than overwatching of eyes that weep,
Now time has done with his one sweet word,
  The wine and leaven of lovely life.   376

---

321. **singer . . . old**, a reference to the story of the love of
Geoffrey Rudel, a Provençal poet of the 12th century, for the
Countess of Tripoli (see Browning's *Rudel to the Lady of
Tripoli*, p. 195, and Critical Note).

363. **stars that sing**, a reference to the ancient belief
that the stars made music as they revolved in their spheres.

I shall go my ways, tread out my measure,
  Fill the days of my daily breath
With fugitive things not good to treasure,
  Do as the world doth, say as it saith;   380
But if we had loved each other — O sweet,
  Had you felt, lying under the palms of your
      feet,
The heart of my heart, beating harder with
      pleasure
  To feel you tread it to dust and death —

Ah, had I not taken my life up and given 385
  All that life gives and the years let go,
The wine and honey, the balm and leaven,
  The dreams reared high and the hopes
      brought low?
Come life, come death, not a word be said;
  Should I lose you living, and vex you
      dead?   390
I never shall tell you on earth; and in heaven,
  If I cry to you then, will you hear or know?
             (1866)

A LEAVE-TAKING

Let us go hence, my songs; she will not hear.
Let us go hence together without fear;
Keep silence now, for singing-time is over,
And over all old things and all things dear.
She loves not you nor me as all we love her.
Yea, though we sang as angels in her ear,   6
  She would not hear.

Let us rise up and part; she will not know.
Let us go seaward as the great winds go,
Full of blown sand and foam; what help is
    here?   10
There is no help, for all these things are so,
And all the world is bitter as a tear.
And how these things are, though ye strove
    to show,
  She would not know.   14

Let us go home and hence; she will not weep.
We gave love many dreams and days to keep,
Flowers without scent, and fruits that would
    not grow,
Saying, "If thou wilt, thrust in thy sickle and
    reap."
All is reaped now; no grass is left to mow; 19
And we that sowed, though all we fell on sleep,
  She would not weep.

Let us go hence and rest; she will not love.
She shall not hear us if we sing hereof,
Nor see love's ways, how sore they are and
    steep.
Come hence, let be, lie still; it is enough.   25
Love is a barren sea, bitter and deep;
And though she saw all heaven in flower
    above,
  She would not love.

Let us give up, go down; she will not care.
Though all the stars made gold of all the air,
And the sea moving saw before it move   31
One moon-flower making all the foam-flowers
    fair;
Though all those waves went over us, and
    drove
Deep down the stifling lips and drowning hair,
  She would not care.   35

Let us go hence, go hence; she will not see.
Sing all once more together; surely she,
She too, remembering days and words that
    were,
Will turn a little toward us, sighing; but we,
We are hence, we are gone, as though we had
    not been there.   40
Nay, and though all men seeing had pity on
    me,
  She would not see.   (1866)

ITYLUS

Swallow, my sister, O sister swallow,
  How can thine heart be full of the spring?
    A thousand summers are over and dead.
What hast thou found in the spring to follow?
  What hast thou found in thine heart to
    sing?   5
    What wilt thou do when the summer is
    shed?

O swallow, sister, O fair swift swallow,
  Why wilt thou fly after spring to the south,
    The soft south whither thine heart is set?
Shall not the grief of the old time follow?   10
  Shall not the song thereof cleave to thy
    mouth?
    Hast thou forgotten ere I forget?

Sister, my sister, O fleet sweet swallow,
  Thy way is long to the sun and the south;
    But I, fulfilled of my heart's desire,   15
Shedding my song upon height, upon hollow,
  From tawny body and sweet small mouth
    Feed the heart of the night with fire.

I the nightingale all spring through,
  O swallow, sister, O changing swallow,   20
    All spring through till the spring be done,
Clothed with the light of the night on the dew,
  Sing, while the hours and the wild birds
    follow,
    Take flight and follow and find the sun.

Sister, my sister, O soft light swallow,   25
  Though all things feast in the spring's guest-
    chamber,

Itylus. See Arnold's *Philomela* and note, p. 486.

How hast thou heart to be glad thereof
yet?
For where thou fliest I shall not follow,
Till life forget and death remember,
Till thou remember and I forget.   30

Swallow, my sister, O singing swallow,
I know not how thou hast heart to sing.
Hast thou the heart? is it all past over?
Thy lord the summer is good to follow,
And fair the feet of thy lover the spring; 35
But what wilt thou say to the spring, thy
lover?

O swallow, sister, O fleeting swallow,
My heart in me is a molten ember,
And over my head the waves have met.
But thou wouldst tarry or I would follow, 40
Could I forget or thou remember,
Couldst thou remember and I forget.

O sweet stray sister, O shifting swallow,
The heart's division divideth us.
Thy heart is light as a leaf of a tree;   45
But mine goes forth among sea-gulfs hollow
To the place of the slaying of Itylus,
The feast of Daulis, the Thracian sea.

O swallow, sister, O rapid swallow,
I pray thee sing not a little space.   50
Are not the roofs and the lintels wet?
The woven web that was plain to follow,
The small slain body, the flowerlike face,
Can I remember if thou forget?

O sister, sister, thy first-begotten!   55
The hands that cling and the feet that
follow,
The voice of the child's blood crying yet
Who hath remembered me? who hath forgotten?
Thou hast forgotten, O summer swallow,
But the world shall end when I forget. 60
(1866)

HYMN TO PROSERPINE

(AFTER THE PROCLAMATION IN ROME OF THE
CHRISTIAN FAITH)

Vicisti, Galilœe

I have lived long enough, having seen one
thing, that love hath an end;
Goddess and maiden and queen, be near me
now and befriend.

Thou art more than the day or the morrow,
the seasons that laugh or that weep;
For these give joy and sorrow; but thou,
Proserpina, sleep.
Sweet is the treading of wine, and sweet the
feet of the dove;   5
But a goodlier gift is thine than foam of the
grapes or love.
Yea, is not even Apollo, with hair and harp-
string of gold,
A bitter god to follow, a beautiful god to
behold?
I am sick of singing; the bays burn deep and
chafe. I am fain
To rest a little from praise and grievous
pleasure and pain.   10
For the gods we know not of, who give us our
daily breath,
We know they are cruel as love or life, and
lovely as death.

O gods dethroned and deceased, cast forth,
wiped out in a day!
From your wrath is the world released, redeemed from your chains, men say.
New gods are crowned in the city; their flowers
have broken your rods;   15
They are merciful, clothed with pity, the
young compassionate gods.
But for me their new device is barren, the
days are bare;
Things long past over suffice, and men forgotten that were.
Time and the gods are at strife; ye dwell in
the midst thereof,
Draining a little life from the barren breasts
of love.   20
I say to you, cease, take rest; yea, I say to you
all, be at peace,
Till the bitter milk of her breast and the
barren bosom shall cease.

Wilt thou yet take all, Galilean? But these
thou shalt not take—
The laurel, the palms, and the pæan, the
breasts of the nymphs in the brake,
Breasts more soft than a dove's, that tremble
with tenderer breath;   25

48. **feast of Daulis**, the feast in the city of Daulis, in
Phocis, Greece, at which Tereus, king of Thrace, ate the
flesh of his son Itylus.
Hymn to Proserpine. Proserpine was the goddess and
queen of the lower world. As a maiden (line 2) she was
carried off from Sicily by Pluto, god of the lower world, and
became his wife. The Proclamation of Christian faith may
be identified with the Edict of Milan promulgated by the
Roman emperors Constantine and Licinius in 313. It

recognized Christianity and restored to Christians their
civil and religious rights.
Vicisti, Galilæe, Thou hast conquered, Galilean (line 35).
These words were attributed by early Christian writers to
the Roman emperor, Julian (331-63), who had renounced
Christianity but who is said to have died with this confession
on his lips.
The poem, represented as spoken by a noble pagan who
regrets the overthrow of the Greek deities, presents an essential part of Swinburne's philosophy of life. Swinburne
characterized this poem and the *Hymn of Man* (page 699) as
"the deathsong of spiritual decadence and the birthsong of
spiritual renascence."
5. **Sweet . . . dove.** The dove was sacred to Venus. 7.
Apollo, the god of the sun, of poetry, and of youth and manly
beauty. His attributes were the bow and the lyre. 9. **bays,**
the poet's crown of laurel. 16. **compassionate gods.** Cf.
Tennyson's *Demeter and Persephone*, line 129, p. 173.

And all the wings of the Loves, and all the joy
   before death;
All the feet of the hours that sound as a single
   lyre,
Dropped and deep in the flowers, with strings
   that flicker like fire.
More than these wilt thou give, things fairer
   than all these things?
Nay, for a little we live, and life hath mutable
   wings.   30
A little while and we die; shall life not thrive as
   it may?
For no man under the sky lives twice, outliving his day.
And grief is a grievous thing, and a man hath
   enough of his tears;
Why should he labor, and bring fresh grief to
   blacken his years?

Thou hast conquered, O pale Galilean; the
   world has grown gray from thy breath;   35
We have drunken of things Lethean, and fed
   on the fullness of death.
Laurel is green for a season, and love is sweet
   for a day;
But love grows bitter with treason, and laurel
   outlives not May.
Sleep, shall we sleep after all? for the world is
   not sweet in the end;
For the old faiths loosen and fall, the new
   years ruin and rend.   40
Fate is a sea without shore, and the soul is a
   rock that abides;
But her ears are vexed with the roar and her
   face with the foam of the tides.
O lips that the live blood faints in, the leavings
   of racks and rods!
O ghastly glories of saints, dead limbs of
   gibbeted gods!
Though all men abase them before you in
   spirit, and all knees bend,   45
I kneel not, neither adore you, but standing,
   look to the end.

All delicate days and pleasant, all spirits and
   sorrows are cast
Far out with the foam of the present that
   sweeps to the surf of the past;
Where beyond the extreme sea-wall, and
   between the remote sea-gates,
Waste water washes, and tall ships founder,
   and deep death waits;   50
Where, mighty with deepening sides, clad
   about with the seas as with wings,
And impelled of invisible tides, and fulfilled
   of unspeakable things,

White-eyed and poisonous-finned, shark-
   toothed and serpentine-curled,
Rolls, under the whitening wind of the future,
   the wave of the world.
The depths stand naked in sunder behind it,
   the storms flee away;   55
In the hollow before it the thunder is taken
   and snared as a prey;
In its sides is the north-wind bound; and its
   salt is of all men's tears,
With light of ruin, and sound of changes, and
   pulse of years;
With travail of day after day, and with
   trouble of hour upon hour.
And bitter as blood is the spray; and the
   crests are as fangs that devour;   60
And its vapor and storm of its steam as the
   sighing of spirits to be;
And its noise as the noise in a dream; and its
   depths as the roots of the sea;
And the height of its heads as the height of the
   utmost stars of the air;
And the ends of the earth at the might thereof
   tremble, and time is made bare.
Will ye bridle the deep sea with reins, will ye
   chasten the high sea with rods?   65
Will ye take her to chain her with chains, who
   is older than all ye gods?
All ye as a wind shall go by, as a fire shall ye
   pass and be past;
Ye are gods, and behold, ye shall die, and the
   waves be upon you at last.
In the darkness of time, in the deeps of the
   years, in the changes of things,
Ye shall sleep as a slain man sleeps, and the
   world shall forget you for kings.   70
Though the feet of thine high priests tread
   where thy lords and our forefathers trod,
Though these that were gods are dead, and
   thou being dead art a god,
Though before thee the throned Cytherean be
   fallen, and hidden her head,
Yet thy kingdom shall pass, Galilean, thy
   dead shall go down to thee dead.

Of the maiden thy mother men sing as a goddess with grace clad around;   75
Thou art throned where another was king;
   where another was queen she is crowned.
Yea, once we had sight of another; but now
   she is queen, say these.
Not as thine, not as thine was our mother, a
   blossom of flowering seas,
Clothed round with the world's desire as with
   raiment, and fair as the foam,
And fleeter than kindled fire, and a goddess,
   and mother of Rome.   80

---

36. Lethean, causing forgetfulness. Lethe was the river of forgetfulness in Hades. **43. racks and rods,** a reference to the early persecution of the Christians and to their self-inflicted torture as a means of penance. **44. ghastly . . . gods,** a reference to the worship of saints' relics and the crucified Christ.

73. Cytherean, Aphrodite, who, according to tradition, rose from the foam of the sea and landed at Cythera, an island southeast of Greece. See lines 85-87. **80. mother of Rome,** Aphrodite, mother of Aeneas, founder of Rome.

For thine came pale and a maiden, and sister
   to sorrow; but ours,
Her deep hair heavily laden with odor and
   color of flowers,
White rose of the rose-white water, a silver
   splendor, a flame,
Bent down unto us that besought her, and
   earth grew sweet with her name.
For thine came weeping, a slave among slaves,
   and rejected; but she   85
Came flushed from the full-flushed wave, and
   imperial, her foot on the sea.
And the wonderful waters knew her, the winds
   and the viewless ways,
And the roses grew rosier, and bluer the sea-
   blue stream of the bays.

Ye are fallen, our lords, by what token? we
   wist that ye should not fall.
Ye were all so fair that are broken; and one
   more fair than ye all.   90
But I turn to her still, having seen she shall
   surely abide in the end;
Goddess and maiden and queen, be near me
   now and befriend.
O daughter of earth, of my mother, her crown
   and blossom of birth,
I am also, I also, thy brother; I go as I came
   unto earth.
In the night where thine eyes are as moons are
   in heaven, the night where thou art,   95
Where the silence is more than all tunes, where
   sleep overflows from the heart,
Where the poppies are sweet as the rose in our
   world, and the red rose is white,
And the wind falls faint as it blows with the
   fume of the flowers of the night,
And the murmur of spirits that sleep in the
   shadow of gods from afar
Grows dim in thine ears and deep as the deep
   dim soul of a star,   100
In the sweet low light of thy face, under
   heavens untrod by the sun,
Let my soul with their souls find place, and
   forget what is done and undone.
Thou art more than the gods who number the
   days of our temporal breath;
For these give labor and slumber; but thou,
   Proserpina, death.
Therefore now at thy feet I abide for a season
   in silence. I know   105
I shall die as my fathers died, and sleep as
   they sleep; even so.
For the glass of the years is brittle wherein we
   gaze for a span.
A little soul for a little bears up this corpse
   which is man.

91. her, Proserpine. 97. poppies, flowers of oblivion,
sacred to Proserpine. 108. A little soul, etc. Swinburne
refers in a note to a line from Epictetus, a Greek Stoic philosopher of the 1st century A. D.—"Thou art a little soul bearing up a corpse."

So long I endure, no longer; and laugh not
   again, neither weep.
For there is no god found stronger than death;
   and death is a sleep.   110
                  (1866)

ILICET

There is an end of joy and sorrow;
Peace all day long, all night, all morrow,
   But never a time to laugh or weep.
The end is come of pleasant places,
The end of tender words and faces,   5
   The end of all, the poppied sleep.

No place for sound within their hearing,
No room to hope, no time for fearing,
   No lips to laugh, no lids for tears.
The old years have run out all their measure;10
No chance of pain, no chance of pleasure,
   No fragment of the broken years.

Outside of all the worlds and ages,
There where the fool is as the sage is,
   There where the slayer is clean of blood,   15
No end, no passage, no beginning,
There where the sinner leaves off sinning,
   There where the good man is not good.

There is not one thing with another,
But Evil saith to Good: My brother,   20
   My brother, I am one with thee.
They shall not strive nor cry forever;
No man shall choose between them; never
   Shall this thing end and that thing be.

Wind wherein seas and stars are shaken   25
Shall shake them, and they shall not waken;
   None that has lain down shall arise;
The stones are sealed across their places;
One shadow is shed on all their faces,
   One blindness cast on all their eyes.   30

Sleep, is it sleep perchance that covers
Each face, as each face were his lover's?
   Farewell; as men that sleep fare well.
The grave's mouth laughs unto derision
Desire and dread and dream and vision,   35
   Delight of heaven and sorrow of hell.

No soul shall tell nor lip shall number
The names and tribes of you that slumber;
   No memory, no memorial.
"Thou knowest"—who shall say thou knowest?
There is none highest and none lowest;   41
   An end, an end, an end of all.

Good night, good sleep, good rest from sorrow
To these that shall not have good morrow;

Ilicet. The title means *It Is Not Permitted*—that is, one
is not permitted to know what follows death.
6. the poppied sleep. The poppy was the flower of
oblivion; it was sacred to Proserpine, queen of Hades.

The gods be gentle to all these.   45
Nay, if death be not, how shall they be?
Nay, is there help in heaven? it may be
  All things and lords of things shall cease.

The stooped urn, filling, dips and flashes;
The bronzéd brims are deep in ashes;   50
  The pale old lips of death are fed.
Shall this dust gather flesh hereafter?
Shall one shed tears or fall to laughter,
  At sight of all these poor old dead?

Nay, as thou wilt; these know not of it;   55
Thine eyes' strong weeping shall not profit,
  Thy laughter shall not give thee ease;
Cry aloud, spare not, cease not crying,
Sigh, till thou cleave thy sides with sighing,
  Thou shalt not raise up one of these.   60

Burnt spices flash, and burnt wine hisses,
The breathing flame's mouth curls and kisses
  The small dried rows of frankincense;
All round the sad red blossoms smolder,
Flowers colored like the fire, but colder,   65
  In sign of sweet things taken hence;

Yea, for their sake and in death's favor
Things of sweet shape and of sweet savor
  We yield them, spice and flower and wine;
Yea, costlier things than wine or spices,   70
Whereof none knoweth how great the price
    is,
  And fruit that comes not of the vine.

From boy's pierced throat and girl's pierced
    bosom
Drips, reddening round the blood-red blos-
    som,
  The slow delicious bright soft blood,   75
Bathing the spices and the pyre,
Bathing the flowers and fallen fire,
  Bathing the blossom by the bud.

Roses whose lips the flame has deadened
Drink till the lapping leaves are reddened   80
  And warm wet inner petals weep;
The flower whereof sick sleep gets leisure,
Barren of balm and purple pleasure,
  Fumes with no native steam of sleep.

Why will ye weep? what do ye weeping?   85
For waking folk and people sleeping,
  And sands that fill and sands that fall,
The days rose-red, the poppied hours,
Blood, wine, and spice and fire and flowers,
  There is one end of one and all.   90

Shall such an one lend love or borrow?
Shall these be sorry for thy sorrow?

79. Roses. The rose was sacred to Venus.

Shall these give thanks for words or breath?
Their hate is as their loving-kindness;
The frontlet of their brows is blindness,   95
  The armlet of their arms is death.

Lo, for no noise or light of thunder
Shall these grave-clothes be rent in sunder;
  He that hath taken, shall he give?
He hath rent them; shall he bind together? 100
He hath bound them; shall he break the
    tether?
  He hath slain them; shall he bid them live?

A little sorrow, a little pleasure,
Fate metes us from the dusty measure
  That holds the date of all of us;   105
We are born with travail and strong crying,
And from the birth-day to the dying
  The likeness of our life is thus.

One girds himself to serve another,
Whose father was the dust, whose mother 110
  The little dead red worm therein;
They find no fruit of things they cherish;
The goodness of a man shall perish,
  It shall be one thing with his sin.

In deep wet ways by gray old gardens   115
Fed with sharp spring the sweet fruit hard-
    ens;
  They know not what fruits wane or grow;
Red summer burns to the utmost ember;
They know not, neither can remember,
  The old years and flowers they used to
    know.   120

Ah, for their sakes, so trapped and taken,
For theirs, forgotten and forsaken,
  Watch, sleep not, gird thyself with prayer.
Nay, where the heart of wrath is broken,
Where long love ends as a thing spoken, 125
  How shall thy crying enter there?

Though the iron sides of the old world falter,
The likeness of them shall not alter
  For all the rumor of periods,
The stars and seasons that come after,   130
The tears of latter men, the laughter
  Of the old unalterable gods.

Far up above the years and nations,
The high gods, clothed and crowned with
    patience,
  Endure through days of deathlike date; 135
They bear the witness of things hidden;
Before their eyes all life stands chidden,
  As they before the eyes of Fate.

Not for their love shall Fate retire,
Nor they relent for our desire,   140
  Nor the graves open for their call.
The end is more than joy and anguish,

Than lives that laugh and lives that languish,
The poppied sleep, the end of all.
                                    (1866)

A MATCH

If love were what the rose is,
    And I were like the leaf,
Our lives would grow together
In sad or singing weather,
Blown fields or flowerful closes,   5
    Green pleasure or gray grief;
If love were what the rose is,
    And I were like the leaf.

If I were what the words are,
    And love were like the tune,   10
With double sound and single
Delight our lips would mingle,
With kisses glad as birds are
    That get sweet rain at noon;
If I were what the words are,   15
    And love were like the tune.

If you were life, my darling,
    And I your love were death,
We'd shine and snow together
Ere March made sweet the weather   20
With daffodil and starling
    And hours of fruitful breath;
If you were life, my darling,
    And I your love were death.

If you were thrall to sorrow,   25
    And I were page to joy,
We'd play for lives and seasons
With loving looks and treasons
And tears of night and morrow
    And laughs of maid and boy;   30
If you were thrall to sorrow,
    And I were page to joy.

If you were April's lady,
    And I were lord in May,
We'd throw with leaves for hours   35
And draw for days with flowers,
Till day like night were shady
    And night were bright like day:
If you were April's lady,
    And I were lord in May.   40

If you were queen of pleasure,
    And I were king of pain,
We'd hunt down love together,
Pluck out his flying-feather,
And teach his feet a measure,   45
    And find his mouth a rein;
If you were queen of pleasure,
    And I were king of pain.   (1866)

A Match. 5. **closes**, enclosures.

A BALLAD OF BURDENS

The burden of fair women. Vain delight,
    And love self-slain in some sweet shameful
        way,
And sorrowful old age that comes by night
    As a thief comes that has no heart by
        day,
    And change that finds fair cheeks and leaves
        them gray,   5
And weariness that keeps awake for hire,
    And grief that says what pleasure used to
        say;
This is the end of every man's desire.

The burden of bought kisses. This is sore,
    A burden without fruit in childbearing; 10
Between the nightfall and the dawn three-
        score,
    Threescore between the dawn and evening.
    The shuddering in thy lips, the shudder-
        ing
In thy sad eyelids tremulous like fire,
    Makes love seem shameful and a wretched
        thing.   15
This is the end of every man's desire.

The burden of sweet speeches. Nay, kneel
        down,
    Cover thy head, and weep; for verily
These market-men that buy thy white and
        brown
    In the last days shall take no thought for
        thee.   20
    In the last days like earth thy face shall be,
Yea, like sea-marsh made thick with brine and
        mire,
    Sad with sick leavings of the sterile sea.
This is the end of every man's desire.

The burden of long living. Thou shalt fear 25
    Waking, and sleeping mourn upon thy bed;
And say at night, "Would God the day were
        here,"
    And say at dawn, "Would God the day were
        dead."
    With weary days thou shalt be clothed and
        fed,
And wear remorse of heart for thine attire, 30
    Pain for thy girdle and sorrow upon thine
        head;
This is the end of every man's desire.

The burden of bright colors. Thou shalt see
    Gold tarnished, and the gray above the
        green;
And as the thing thou seest thy face shall be, 35
    And no more as the thing beforetime seen.

A Ballad of Burdens. This poem is arranged in a modified
form of the French *ballade.* See note on *A Ballad of Dreamland,* p. 723.

And the same ... "It hath
been,"
And living, watch the old lips and loves expire,
  And talking, tears shall take thy breath
    between;
This is the end of every man's desire.   40

The burden of sad sayings. In that day
  Thou shalt tell all thy days and hours, and
    tell
Thy times and ways and words of love, and
    say
  How one was dear and one desirable,
  And sweet was life to hear and sweet to
    smell,   45
But now with lights reverse the old hours re-
    tire
And the last hour is shod with fire from hell;
This is the end of every man's desire.

The burden of four seasons. Rain in spring,
  White rain and wind among the tender
    trees;   50
A summer of green sorrows gathering,
  Rank autumn in a mist of miseries,
With sad face set toward the year, that sees
The charred ash drop out of the dropping pyre,
  And winter wan with many maladies;   55
This is the end of every man's desire.

The burden of dead faces. Out of sight
  And out of love, beyond the reach of hands,
Changed in the changing of the dark and light,
  They walk and weep about the barren lands
Where no seed is nor any garner stands,   61
Where in short breaths the doubtful days
    respire,
  And time's turned glass lets through the
    sighing sands;
This is the end of every man's desire.   64

The burden of much gladness. Life and lust
  Forsake thee, and the face of thy delight;
And underfoot the heavy hour strews dust,
  And overhead strange weathers burn and
    bite;
  And where the red was, lo, the bloodless
    white,
And where truth was, the likeness of a liar, 70
  And where day was, the likeness of the
    night;
This is the end of every man's desire.

L'ENVOY

Princes, and ye whom pleasure quickeneth,
  Heed well this rime before your pleasure
    tire;
For life is sweet, but after life is death.   75
  This is the end of every man's desire.
                                     (1866)

RONDEL

Kissing her hair I sat against her feet,
  Wove and unwove it, wound and found it
    sweet;
Made fast therewith her hands, drew down
    her eyes,
Deep as deep flowers and dreamy like dim
    skies;
With her own tresses bound and found her
    fair,   5
      Kissing her hair.

Sleep were no sweeter than her face to me,
Sleep of cold sea-bloom under the cold sea;
What pain could get between my face and
    hers?
What new sweet thing would love not relish
    worse?   10
Unless, perhaps, white death had kissed me
    there,
      Kissing her hair?   (1866)

IN MEMORY OF WALTER SAVAGE
LANDOR

Back to the flower-town, side by side,
  The bright months bring,
New-born, the bridegroom and the bride,
  Freedom and spring.

The sweet land laughs from sea to sea,   5
  Filled full of sun;
All things come back to her, being free;
  All things but one.

In many a tender wheaten plot
  Flowers that were dead   10
Live, and old suns revive; but not
  That holier head.

By this white wandering waste of sea,
  Far north, I hear
One face shall never turn to me   15
  As once this year;

Shall never smile and turn and rest
  On mine as there,
Nor one most sacred hand be prest
  Upon my hair.   20

I came as one whose thoughts half linger,
  Half run before;

Rondel. The rondel is a French lyric form consisting of
ten to fourteen lines usually running on two rimes. It contains a refrain taken from the beginning of the first line.
In Memory of Walter Savage Landor. See Critical Notes.
1. **flower-town**, Florence, where Landor died in September, 1864. 4. **Freedom.** Both Landor and Swinburne were
greatly interested in Italy's struggle for freedom from the
rule of Austria. In 1865, about the time this poem was
written, Florence was chosen as the capital of United Italy.
21. **I came**, etc. Swinburne had visited Landor at Florence
in the spring of 1864.

The youngest to the oldest singer
   That England bore.

I found him whom I shall not find   25
   Till all grief end,
In holiest age our mightiest mind,
   Father and friend.

But thou, if anything endure,
   If hope there be,   30
O spirit that man's life left pure,
   Man's death set free,

Not with disdain of days that were
   Look earthward now;
Let dreams revive the reverend hair,   35
   The imperial brow;

Come back in sleep, for in the life
   Where thou art not
We find none like thee. Time and strife
   And the world's lot   40

Move thee no more; but love at least
   And reverent heart
May move thee, royal and released,
   Soul, as thou art.

And thou, his Florence, to thy trust   45
   Receive and keep,
Keep safe his dedicated dust,
   His sacred sleep.

So shall thy lovers, come from far,
   Mix with thy name   50
As morning-star with evening-star
   His faultless fame.   (1866)

DOLORES

NOTRE-DAME DES SEPT DOULEURS

Cold eyelids that hide like a jewel
   Hard eyes that grow soft for an hour;
The heavy white limbs, and the cruel
   Red mouth like a venomous flower;
When these are gone by with their glories, 5
   What shall rest of thee then, what remain,
O mystic and somber Dolores,
   Our Lady of Pain?

Seven sorrows the priests give their Virgin;
   But thy sins, which are seventy times seven,
Seven ages would fail thee to purge in,   11
   And then they would haunt thee in heaven:
Fierce midnights and famishing morrows,
   And the loves that complete and control
All the joys of the flesh, all the sorrows   15
   That wear out the soul.

Dolores. See Critical Notes.
Subtitle. **Notre-Dame,** etc., Our Lady of the Seven Sorrows. (See note on Browning's *Up at a Villa—Down in the City,* 52, p. 233.)

O garment not golden but gilded,
   O garden where all men may dwell,
O tower not of ivory, but builded
   By hands that reach heaven from hell;   20
O mystical rose of the mire,
   O house not of gold but of gain,
O house of unquenchable fire,
   Our Lady of Pain!

O lips full of lust and of laughter,   25
   Curled snakes that are fed from my breast,
Bite hard, lest remembrance come after
   And press with new lips where you pressed.
For my heart too springs up at the pressure,
   Mine eyelids too moisten and burn;   30
Ah, feed me and fill me with pleasure,
   Ere pain come in turn.

In yesterday's reach and tomorrow's,
   Out of sight though they lie of today,
There have been and there yet shall be
    sorrows   35
   That smite not and bite not in play.
The life and the love thou despisest,
   These hurt us indeed, and in vain,
O wise among women, and wisest,
   Our Lady of Pain.   40

Who gave thee thy wisdom? what stories
   That stung thee, what visions that smote?
Wert thou pure and a maiden, Dolores,
   When desire took thee first by the throat?
What bud was the shell of a blossom   45
   That all men may smell to and pluck?
What milk fed thee first at what bosom?
   What sins gave thee suck?

We shift and bedeck and bedrape us,
   Thou art noble and nude and antique;   50
Libitina thy mother, Priapus
   Thy father, a Tuscan and Greek.
We play with light loves in the portal,
   And wince and relent and refrain;
Loves die, and we know thee immortal,   55
   Our Lady of Pain.

Fruits fail and love dies and time ranges;
   Thou art fed with perpetual breath,
And alive after infinite changes,
   And fresh from the kisses of death;   60
Of languors rekindled and rallied,
   Of barren delights and unclean,
Things monstrous and fruitless, a pallid
   And poisonous queen.

19. **tower ... ivory.** Cf. *Song of Solomon,* 7:4.—"Thy neck is as a tower of ivory." 49-52. **We shift ... Greek.** These lines are quoted in Kipling's story of "In the Rukh," *The Jungle Book.* See Critical Notes. 51. **Libitina,** an ancient Italian goddess of gardens and voluptuous pleasures. She is the Tuscan of line 52. **Priapus.** See note on *Faustine,* 146, p. 666.

Could you hurt me, sweet lips, though I hurt
    you?   65
Men touch them, and change in a trice
The lilies and languors of virtue
    For the raptures and roses of vice;
Those lie where thy foot on the floor is,
    These crown and caress thee and chain,   70
O splendid and sterile Dolores,
    Our Lady of Pain.

There are sins it may be to discover,
    There are deeds it may be to delight.   74
What new work wilt thou find for thy lover,
    What new passions for daytime or night?
What spells that they know not a word of
    Whose lives are as leaves overblown?
What tortures undreamt of, unheard of,
    Unwritten, unknown?   80

Ah, beautiful passionate body
    That never has ached with a heart!
On thy mouth though the kisses are bloody,
    Though they sting till it shudder and smart,
More kind than the love we adore is,   85
    They hurt not the heart or the brain,
O bitter and tender Dolores,
    Our Lady of Pain.

As our kisses relax and redouble,
    From the lips and the foam and the fangs
Shall no new sin be born for men's trouble, 91
    No dream of impossible pangs?
With the sweet of the sins of old ages
    Wilt thou satiate thy soul as of yore?
Too sweet is the rind, say the sages,   95
    Too bitter the core.

Hast thou told all thy secrets the last time,
    And bared all thy beauties to one?
Ah, where shall we go then for pastime,
    If the worst that can be has been done? 100
But sweet as the rind was the core is;
    We are fain of thee still, we are fain,
O sanguine and subtle Dolores,
    Our Lady of Pain.

By the hunger of change and emotion,   105
    By the thirst of unbearable things,
By despair, the twin-born of devotion,
    By the pleasure that winces and stings,
The delight that consumes the desire,
    The desire that outruns the delight,   110
By the cruelty deaf as a fire
    And blind as the night,

By the ravenous teeth that have smitten
    Through the kisses that blossom and bud,

By the lips intertwisted and bitten   115
    Till the foam has a savor of blood,
By the pulse as it rises and falters,
    By the hands as they slacken and strain,
I adjure thee, respond from thine altars,
    Our Lady of Pain.   120

Wilt thou smile as a woman disdaining
    The light fire in the veins of a boy?
But he comes to thee sad, without feigning,
    Who has wearied of sorrow and joy;
Less careful of labor and glory   125
    Than the elders whose hair has uncurled;
And young, but with fancies as hoary
    And gray as the world.

I have passed from the outermost portal
    To the shrine where a sin is a prayer; 130
What care though the service be mortal?
    O our Lady of Torture, what care?
All thine the last wine that I pour is,
    The last in the chalice we drain,
O fierce and luxurious Dolores,   135
    Our Lady of Pain.

All thine the new wine of desire,
    The fruit of four lips as they clung
Till the hair and the eyelids took fire,
    The foam of a serpentine tongue,   140
The froth of the serpents of pleasure,
    More salt than the foam of the sea,
Now felt as a flame, now at leisure
    As wine shed for me.

Ah, thy people, thy children, thy chosen,   145
    Marked cross from the womb and perverse!
They have found out the secret to cozen
    The gods that constrain us and curse;
They alone, they are wise, and none other;
    Give me place, even me, in their train, 150
O my sister, my spouse, and my mother,
    Our Lady of Pain.

For the crown of our life as it closes
    Is darkness, the fruit thereof dust;
No thorns go as deep as a rose's,   155
    And love is more cruel than lust.
Time turns the old days to derision,
    Our loves into corpses or wives;
And marriage and death and division
    Make barren our lives.   160

And pale from the past we draw nigh thee,
    And satiate with comfortless hours;
And we know thee, how all men belie thee,
    And we gather the fruit of thy flowers;
The passion that slays and recovers,   165
    The pangs and the kisses that rain
On the lips and the limbs of thy lovers,
    Our Lady of Pain.

67-68. **The lilies . . . vice.** See Critical Notes for Chesterton's comment on these lines.

The desire of thy furious embraces
  Is more than the wisdom of years,   170
On the blossom though blood lie in traces,
  Though the foliage be sodden with tears.
For the lords in whose keeping the door is
  That opens on all who draw breath
Gave the cypress to love, my Dolores,   175
  The myrtle to death.

And they laughed, changing hands in the
    measure,
  And they mixed and made peace after strife;
Pain melted in tears, and was pleasure;
  Death tingled with blood, and was life.   180
Like lovers they melted and tingled,
  In the dusk of thine innermost fane;
In the darkness they murmured and mingled,
  Our Lady of Pain.

In a twilight where virtues are vices,   185
  In thy chapels, unknown of the sun,
To a tune that enthralls and entices,
  They were wed, and the twain were as one.
For the tune from thine altar hath sounded
  Since God bade the world's work begin,   190
And the fume of thine incense abounded,
  To sweeten the sin.

Love listens, and paler than ashes,
  Through his curls as the crown on them
    slips,
Lifts languid wet eyelids and lashes,   195
  And laughs with insatiable lips.
Thou shalt hush him with heavy caresses,
  With music that scares the profane;
Thou shalt darken his eyes with thy tresses,
  Our Lady of Pain.   200

Thou shalt blind his bright eyes though he
    wrestle,
  Thou shalt chain his light limbs though he
    strive;
In his lips all thy serpents shall nestle,
  In his hands all thy cruelties thrive.
In the daytime thy voice shall go through
    him,   205
  In his dreams he shall feel thee and ache;
Thou shalt kindle by night and subdue him
  Asleep and awake.

Thou shalt touch and make redder his roses
  With juice not of fruit nor of bud;   210
When the sense in the spirit reposes,
  Thou shalt quicken the soul through the
    blood.
Thine, thine the one grace we implore is,
  Who would live and not languish or feign,

O sleepless and deadly Dolores,   215
  Our Lady of Pain.

Dost thou dream, in a respite of slumber,
  In a lull of the fires of thy life,
Of the days without name, without number,
  When thy will stung the world into strife;
When, a goddess, the pulse of thy passion   221
  Smote kings as they reveled in Rome;
And they hailed thee re-risen, O Thalassian,
  Foam-white, from the foam?

When thy lips had such lovers to flatter;   225
  When the city lay red from thy rods,
And thine hands were as arrows to scatter
  The children of change and their gods;
When the blood of thy foemen made fervent
  A sand never moist from the main,   230
As one smote them, their lord and thy servant,
  Our Lady of Pain.

On sands by the storm never shaken,
  Nor wet from the washing of tides;
Nor by foam of the waves overtaken,   235
  Nor winds that the thunder bestrides;
But red from the print of thy paces,
  Made smooth for the world and its lords,
Ringed round with a flame of fair faces,
  And splendid with swords.   240

There the gladiator, pale for thy pleasure,
  Drew bitter and perilous breath;
There torments laid hold on the treasure
  Of limbs too delicious for death;   244
When thy gardens were lit with live torches;
  When the world was a steed for thy rein;
When the nations lay prone in thy porches,
  Our Lady of Pain.

When, with flame all around him aspirant,
  Stood flushed, as a harp-player stands,   250
The implacable beautiful tyrant,
  Rose-crowned, having death in his hands;
And a sound as the sound of loud water
  Smote far through the flight of the fires,
And mixed with the lightning of slaughter   255
  A thunder of lyres.

Dost thou dream of what was and no more is,
  The old kingdoms of earth and the kings?
Dost thou hunger for these things, Dolores,
  For these, in a world of new things?   260

---

223. **Thalassian**, Venus (Aphrodite). The word means *born of the sea*. According to tradition Aphrodite was born of the foam of the sea. 228. **children of change**, those who introduced the new religion of Christianity. 229. **blood of thy foemen**, a reference to the persecution of the Christians by the Roman Cæsars, pagan followers of Venus. 230. **A sand**, the arena of the Coliseum. 231. **one**, Nero, Roman emperor (54-68). 245. **gardens . . . torches.** Nero used burning Christians as torches in his garden. 251. **beautiful tyrant**, Nero, who is said to have played upon the harp while Rome burned.

175. **cypress.** The cypress was an emblem of mourning; the myrtle was sacred to Venus. Swinburne reverses the traditions.

But thy bosom no fasts could emaciate,
  No hunger compel to complain
Those lips that no bloodshed could satiate,
  Our Lady of Pain.

As of old when the world's heart was lighter,
  Through thy garments the grace of thee
    glows,   266
The white wealth of thy body made whiter
  By the blushes of amorous blows,
And seamed with sharp lips and fierce fingers,
  And branded by kisses that bruise;   270
When all shall be gone that now lingers,
  Ah, what shall we lose?

Thou wert fair in the fearless old fashion,
  And thy limbs are as melodies yet,
And move to the music of passion   275
  With lithe and lascivious regret.
What ailed us, O gods, to desert you
  For creeds that refuse and restrain?
Come down and redeem us from virtue,
  Our Lady of Pain.   280

All shrines that were Vestal are flameless,
  But the flame has not fallen from this;
Though obscure be the god, and though name-
    less
  The eyes and the hair that we kiss;
Low fires that love sits by and forges   285
  Fresh heads for his arrows and thine;
Hair loosened and soiled in mid orgies
  With kisses and wine.

Thy skin changes country and color,
  And shrivels or swells to a snake's.   290
Let it brighten and bloat and grow duller,
  We know it, the flames and the flakes,
Red brands on it smitten and bitten,
  Round skies where a star is a stain,
And the leaves with their litanies written,   295
  Our Lady of Pain.

On thy bosom though many a kiss be,
  There are none such as knew it of old.
Was it Alciphron once or Arisbe,
  Male ringlets or feminine gold,   300
That thy lips met with under the statue,
  Whence a look shot out sharp after thieves
From the eyes of the garden god at you
  Across the fig-leaves?

Then still, through dry seasons and moister,
  One god had a wreath to his shrine;   306

Then love was the pearl of his oyster,
  And Venus rose red out of wine.
We have all done amiss, choosing rather
  Such loves as the wise gods disdain;   310
Intercede for us thou with thy father,
  Our Lady of Pain.

In spring he had crowns of his garden,
  Red corn in the heat of the year,
Then hoary green olives that harden   315
  When the grape-blossom freezes with fear;
And milk-budded myrtles with Venus
  And vine-leaves with Bacchus he trod;
And ye said, "We have seen, he hath seen us,
  A visible god."   320

What broke off the garlands that girt you?
  What sundered you spirit and clay?
Weak sins yet alive are as virtue
  To the strength of the sins of that day.
For dried is the blood of thy lover,   325
  Ipsithilla, contracted the vein;
Cry aloud, "Will he rise and recover,
  Our Lady of Pain?"

Cry aloud; for the old world is broken.
  Cry out; for the Phrygian is priest,   330
And rears not the bountiful token
  And spreads not the fatherly feast.
From the midmost of Ida, from shady
  Recesses that murmur at morn,
They have brought and baptized her, Our
    Lady,   335
  A goddess new-born.

And the chaplets of old are above us,
  And the oyster-bed teems out of reach;
Old poets outsing and outlove us,
  And Catullus makes mouths at our speech.
Who shall kiss, in thy father's own city,   341
  With such lips as he sang with, again?
Intercede for us all of thy pity,
  Our Lady of Pain.

Out of Dindymus heavily laden   345
  Her lions draw bound and unfed
A mother, a mortal, a maiden,
  A queen over death and the dead.
She is cold, and her habit is lowly,
  Her temple of branches and sods;   350
Most fruitful and virginal, holy,
  A mother of gods.

---

281. **shrines . . . flameless.** It was the duty of the Vestal virgins to keep burning the sacred fire of Vesta, goddess of the hearth. 299. **Alciphron,** a Greek rhetorician of the 2d century A.D. He was the author of letters supposed to have been written by celebrated courtesans. **Arisbe,** according to Greek tradition, the wife of King Priam, of Troy. 303. **the garden god,** Priapus. See note on *Faustine,* 146, p. 666.

311. **thy father,** Priapus. 314. **corn,** grain, wheat. 318. **Bacchus,** god of wine. 326. **Ipsithilla.** Hypsithilla is one of the lovers mentioned by Catullus in *Carmina,* 32. 330. **the Phrygian,** Cybele, who was worshiped in Phrygia, Asia Minor, as the mother of the gods. Swinburne explains that her devotees were more restrained than those of Venus. Mt. Ida (line 333), in Asia Minor, was a seat of the worship of Cybele. 340. **Catullus,** a famous Roman lyric poet (84-54 B.C.) His love lyrics are noted for their grace and finish. 345. **Dindymus,** a mountain in Phrygia, sacred to Cybele. From her shrine she traveled over the surrounding country in a chariot drawn by lions.

She hath wasted with fire thine high places,
  She hath hidden and marred and made sad
The fair limbs of the Loves, the fair faces 355
  Of gods that were goodly and glad.
She slays, and her hands are not bloody;
  She moves as a moon in the wane,
White-robed, and thy raiment is ruddy,
  Our Lady of Pain. 360

They shall pass and their places be taken,
  The gods and the priests that are pure.
They shall pass, and shalt thou not be shaken?
  They shall perish, and shalt thou endure?
Death laughs, breathing close and relent-
  less
  In the nostrils and eyelids of lust, 366
With a pinch in his fingers of scentless
  And delicate dust.

But the worm shall revive thee with kisses;
  Thou shalt change and transmute as a god,
As the rod to a serpent that hisses, 371
  As the serpent again to a rod.
Thy life shall not cease though thou doff
  it;
  Thou shalt live until evil be slain,
And good shall die first, said thy prophet, 375
  Our Lady of Pain.

Did he lie? did he laugh? does he know it,
  Now he lies out of reach, out of breath,
Thy prophet, thy preacher, thy poet,
  Sin's child by incestuous Death? 380
Did he find out in fire at his waking,
  Or discern as his eyelids lost light,
When the bands of the body were break-
  ing
  And all came in sight?

Who has known all the evil before us, 385
  Or the tyrannous secrets of time?
Though we match not the dead men that
  bore us
  At a song, at a kiss, at a crime —
Though the heathen outface and outlive us,
  And our lives and our longings are twain —
Ah, forgive us our virtues, forgive us, 391
  Our Lady of Pain.

Who are we that embalm and embrace thee
  With spices and savors of song?

What is time, that his children should face
  thee? 395
  What am I, that my lips do thee wrong?
I could hurt thee — but pain would delight
  thee;
  Or caress thee — but love would repel;
And the lovers whose lips would excite thee
  Are serpents in hell. 400

Who now shall content thee as they did,
  Thy lovers, when temples were built
And the hair of the sacrifice braided
  And the blood of the sacrifice spilt,
In Lampsacus fervent with faces, 405
  In Aphaca red from thy reign,
Who embraced thee with awful embraces,
  Our Lady of Pain?

Where are they, Cotytto or Venus,
  Astarte or Ashtaroth, where? 410
Do their hands as we touch come between us?
  Is the breath of them hot in thy hair?
From their lips have thy lips taken fever,
  With the blood of their bodies grown red?
Hast thou left upon earth a believer 415
  If these men are dead?

They were purple of raiment and golden,
  Filled full of thee, fiery with wine,
Thy lovers, in haunts unbeholden,
  In marvelous chambers of thine. 420
They are fled, and their footprints escape us,
  Who appraise thee, adore, and abstain,
O daughter of Death and Priapus,
  Our Lady of Pain.

What ails us to fear overmeasure, 425
  To praise thee with timorous breath,
O mistress and mother of pleasure,
  The one thing as certain as death?
We shall change as the things that we cherish,
  Shall fade as they faded before, 430
As foam upon water shall perish,
  As sand upon shore.

We shall know what the darkness discovers,
  If the grave-pit be shallow or deep;
And our fathers of old, and our lovers, 435
  We shall know if they sleep not or sleep.
We shall see whether hell be not heaven,
  Find out whether tares be not grain,
And the joys of thee seventy times seven,
  Our Lady of Pain. 440

(1866)

---

371. **rod to a serpent.** Cf. *Exodus*, 7:8-10.—"And the
Lord spake unto Moses and unto Aaron, saying, 'When
Pharaoh shall speak unto you, saying, Show a miracle for
you, then thou shalt say unto Aaron, Take thy rod and cast
it before Pharaoh, and it shall become a serpent.'" 375.
good . . . first. Cf. "He whom the gods love dies young"
(Plautus, *Bacchides*, 4, 7, 18). Cf. also Wordsworth's *Excursion*, 1, 500-502.—"The good die first, And they whose hearts
are dry as summer dust Burn to the socket." 380. **Sin's . . .
Death.** Milton makes Death the son of Sin and Satan, and
he makes Death and his mother the parents of the barking
hounds of Hell (*Paradise Lost*, 2, 747 ff.).

405. **Lampsacus.** See note on *Faustine*, 146, p. 666.
406. **Aphaca**, a city in Asia Minor associated with the worship of Priapus and Venus. 409. **Cotytto**, a Thracian goddess whose festivals were marked with great revelry. 410.
Astarte or Ashtaroth, the goddess of love and fertility,
called Ishtar by the Assyrians. **tares be not grain**,
a reference to the parable of the tares sown among the wheat
(*Matthew*, 13:25-40).

THE GARDEN OF PROSERPINE

Here, where the world is quiet;
  Here, where all trouble seems
Dead winds' and spent waves' riot
  In doubtful dreams of dreams;
I watch the green field growing   5
For reaping folk and sowing,
For harvest-time and mowing,
  A sleepy world of streams.

I am tired of tears and laughter,
  And men that laugh and weep,   10
Of what may come hereafter
  For men that sow to reap;
I am weary of days and hours,
Blown buds of barren flowers,
Desires and dreams and powers   15
  And everything but sleep.

Here life has death for neighbor,
  And far from eye or ear
Wan waves and wet winds labor,
  Weak ships and spirits steer;   20
They drive adrift, and whither
They wot not who make thither;
But no such winds blow hither,
  And no such things grow here.

No growth of moor or coppice,   25
  No heather-flower or vine,
But bloomless buds of poppies,
  Green grapes of Proserpine,
Pale beds of blowing rushes
Where no leaf blooms or blushes   30
Save this whereout she crushes
  For dead men deadly wine.

Pale, without name or number,
  In fruitless fields of corn,
They bow themselves and slumber   35
  All night till light is born;
And like a soul belated,
In hell and heaven unmated,
By cloud and mist abated
  Comes out of darkness morn.   40

Though one were strong as seven,
  He too with death shall dwell,
Nor wake with wings in heaven,

Nor weep for pains in hell;
Though one were fair as roses,   45
His beauty clouds and closes;
And well though love reposes,
  In the end it is not well.

Pale, beyond porch and portal,
  Crowned with calm leaves, she stands 50
Who gathers all things mortal
  With cold immortal hands;
Her languid lips are sweeter
Than love's who fears to greet her
To men that mix and meet her   55
  From many times and lands.

She waits for each and other,
  She waits for all men born;
Forgets the earth her mother,
  The life of fruits and corn;   60
And spring and seed and swallow
Take wing for her and follow
Where summer song rings hollow
  And flowers are put to scorn.

There go the loves that wither,   65
  The old loves with wearier wings;
And all dead years draw thither,
  And all disastrous things;
Dead dreams of days forsaken,
Blind buds that snows have shaken,   70
Wild leaves that winds have taken,
  Red strays of ruined springs.

We are not sure of sorrow,
  And joy was never sure;
Today will die tomorrow;   75
  Time stoops to no man's lure;
And love, grown faint and fretful,
With lips but half regretful
Sighs, and with eyes forgetful
  Weeps that no loves endure.   80

From too much love of living,
  From hope and fear set free,
We thank with brief thanksgiving
  Whatever gods may be
That no life lives forever;   85
That dead men rise up never;
That even the weariest river
  Winds somewhere safe to sea.

Then star nor sun shall waken,
  Nor any change of light;   90
Nor sound of waters shaken,
  Nor any sound or sight;
Nor wintry leaves nor vernal,
Nor days nor things diurnal;
Only the sleep eternal   95
  In an eternal night.   (1866)

The Garden of Proserpine. Proserpine was the daughter of Demeter, the mother earth (see line 59). While gathering flowers in Sicily she was carried off by Pluto, god of Hades, to his realm of darkness and death. Certain groves at the entrance to Hades were sacred to her. By action of the gods, she was allowed to return to the upper world for half of each year. The myth symbolizes the changes in the seasons. The poem is spoken by a Roman pagan. Cf. C. Rossetti's *Dream Land*, p. 562, and Tennyson's *Demeter and Persephone*, p. 171.
14. Blown . . . flowers, blossoming flowers that will produce no fruit. They are used as a symbol of unfulfilled desires and dreams. **22. wot**, know. **27. poppies**, the flowers of oblivion, sacred to Proserpine, who was often represented with a crown of them on her head (line 50). **34. corn**, grain, wheat.

83-84. thank . . . may be. Cf. Henley's *Invictus*, p. 794.
94. diurnal, belonging to the daylight.

SAPPHICS

All the night sleep came not upon my eyelids,
Shed not dew, nor shook nor unclosed a
    feather,
Yet with lips shut close and with eyes of iron
    Stood and beheld me.

Then to me so lying awake a vision   5
Came without sleep over the seas and touched
    me,
Softly touched mine eyelids and lips; and I,
    too,
    Full of the vision

Saw the white implacable Aphrodite,
Saw the hair unbound and the feet unsandaled
Shine as fire of sunset on western waters; 11
    Saw the reluctant

Feet, the straining plumes of the doves that
    drew her,
Looking always, looking with necks reverted,
Back to Lesbos, back to the hills whereunder
    Shone Mitylene;   16

Heard the flying feet of the Loves behind her
Make a sudden thunder upon the waters,
As the thunder flung from the strong unclosing
    Wings of a great wind.   20

So the goddess fled from her place, with awful
Sound of feet and thunder of wings around
    her;
While behind a clamor of singing women
    Severed the twilight.

Ah, the singing, ah, the delight, the passion!
All the Loves wept, listening; sick with an-
    guish,   26
Stood the crowned nine Muses about Apollo;
    Fear was upon them,

While the tenth sang wonderful things they
    knew not.
Ah, the tenth, the Lesbian! the nine were
    silent,   30
None endured the sound of her song for
    weeping;
    Laurel by laurel,

Sapphics. The title is a term used to designate a verse
form employed by Sappho (c. 600 B.C.), a Greek poetess of
the city of Mitylene, on the island of Lesbos, off the coast of
Asia Minor. Each stanza consists of three lines of five feet
each and a fourth line of two feet. The prevailing measure
is trochaic with a dactyl in the third foot of the long lines
and in the first foot of the short lines.
9. **Aphrodite,** goddess of love. She was often represented
as drawn by doves. 27. **nine Muses.** See note on Clough's
In the Depths, 2, p. 413. Apollo was the god of music and
poetry. He presided over the Muses. 29. **the tenth.**
Sappho was called the "tenth muse." 32. **laurel.** The
laurel, used in crowning poets, was sacred to the gods.

Faded all their crowns; but about her fore-
    head,
Round her woven tresses and ashen temples
White as dead snow, paler than grass in
    summer,   35
    Ravaged with kisses,

Shone a light of fire as a crown forever.
Yea, almost the implacable Aphrodite
Paused, and almost wept; such a song was
    that song.
    Yea, by her name, too,   40

Called her, saying, "Turn to me, O my
    Sappho";
Yet she turned her face from the Loves, she
    saw not
Tears for laughter darken immortal eyelids,
    Heard not about her

Fearful fitful wings of the doves departing, 45
Saw not how the bosom of Aphrodite
Shook with weeping, saw not her shaken
    raiment,
    Saw not her hands wrung;

Saw the Lesbians kissing across their smitten
Lutes with lips more sweet than the sound of
    lute-strings,   50
Mouth to mouth and hand upon hand, her
    chosen,
    Fairer than all men;

Only saw the beautiful lips and fingers,
Full of songs and kisses and little whispers,
Full of music; only beheld among them   55
    Soar, as a bird soars

Newly fledged, her visible song, a marvel,
Made of perfect sound and exceeding passion,
Sweetly shapen, terrible, full of thunders,
    Clothed with the wind's wings.   60

Then rejoiced she, laughing with love, and
    scattered
Roses, awful roses of holy blossom;
Then the Loves thronged sadly with hidden
    faces
    Round Aphrodite,

Then the Muses, stricken at heart, were
    silent;   65
Yea, the gods waxed pale; such a song was
    that song.
All reluctant, all with a fresh repulsion,
    Fled from before her.

All withdrew long since, and the land was
    barren,
Full of fruitless women and music only.   70

Now perchance, when winds are assuaged at
    sunset,
  Lulled at the dewfall,

By the gray seaside, unassuaged, unheard of,
Unbeloved, unseen in the ebb of twilight,
Ghosts of outcast women return lamenting,
  Purged not in Lethe,   76

Clothed about with flame and with tears, and
    singing
Songs that move the heart of the shaken
    heaven,
Songs that break the heart of the earth with
    pity,
  Hearing, to hear them.   80
        (1866)

DEDICATION TO *POEMS AND BALLADS*

The sea gives her shells to the shingle,
  The earth gives her streams to the sea;
They are many, but my gift is single,
  My verses, the first fruits of me.
Let the wind take the green and the gray
    leaf,
  Cast forth without fruit upon air;   6
Take rose-leaf and vine-leaf and bay-leaf
  Blown loose from the hair.

The night shakes them round me in legions,
  Dawn drives them before her like dreams;
Time sheds them like snows on strange
    regions,   11
  Swept shoreward on infinite streams;
Leaves pallid and somber and ruddy,
  Dead fruits of the fugitive years;
Some stained as with wine and made bloody,
  And some as with tears.   16

Some scattered in seven years' traces,
  As they fell from the boy that was then;
Long left among idle green places,
  Or gathered but now among men;   20
On seas full of wonder and peril,
  Blown white round the capes of the north;
Or in islands where myrtles are sterile
  And loves bring not forth.

O daughters of dreams and of stories   25
  That life is not wearied of yet,
Faustine, Fragoletta, Dolores,
  Félise and Yolande and Juliette,
Shall I find you not still, shall I miss you,
  When sleep, that is true or that seems,   30
Comes back to me hopeless to kiss you,
  O daughters of dreams?

They are past as a slumber that passes,
  As the dew of a dawn of old time;
More frail than the shadows on glasses,   35
  More fleet than a wave or a rime.
As the waves after ebb drawing seaward,
  When their hollows are full of the night,
So the birds that flew singing to me-ward
  Recede out of sight.   40

The songs of dead seasons, that wander
  On wings of articulate words;
Lost leaves that the shore-wind may squan-
    der,
  Light flocks of untameable birds;
Some sang to me dreaming in class time   45
  And truant in hand as in tongue;
For the youngest were born of boy's pas-
    time,
  The eldest are young.

Is there shelter while life in them lingers,
  Is there hearing for songs that recede,   50
Tunes touched from a harp with man's
    fingers
  Or blown with boy's mouth in a reed?
Is there place in the land of your labor,
  Is there room in your world of delight,
Where change has not sorrow for neighbor 55
  And day has not night?

In their wings though the sea-wind yet
    quivers,
  Will you spare not a space for them there
Made green with the running of rivers
  And gracious with temperate air;   60
In the fields and the turreted cities,
  That cover from sunshine and rain
Fair passions and bountiful pities
  And loves without stain?

In a land of clear colors and stories,   65
  In a region of shadowless hours,
Where earth has a garment of glories
  And a murmur of musical flowers;
In woods where the spring half uncovers
  The flush of her amorous face,   70
By the waters that listen for lovers,
  For these is there place?

---

76. **Purged not in Lethe**, unable to secure oblivion by
drinking of the water of Lethe, the river of forgetfulness in
Hades.
  Dedication to Poems and Ballads. This dedication to the
first series of Swinburne's *Poems and Ballads* was addressed
to Sir Edward Burne-Jones (1833-98), an English painter
noted for highly decorative design. He was a member of the
Pre-Raphaelite group of artists, a pupil of Rossetti, and a
friend of Swinburne.
  1. **shingle**, coarse rounded stones on the seashore. 7.
bay-leaf, laurel-leaf, sacred to the gods. 17. **seven years'
traces.** Evidently the poems in the volume were written
between 1859 and 1866. 23. **myrtles.** Poets were crowned
with wreaths of myrtle, sacred to the gods.

27-28. **Faustine . . . Juliette**, names of women appearing
in the poems of the 1866 volume. 45. **in class time**, while
he was at Eton, 1849-53. He was at Oxford 1856-59.

For the song-birds of sorrow, that muffle
　Their music as clouds do their fire;
For the storm-birds of passion, that ruffle　75
　Wild wings in a wind of desire;
In the stream of the storm as it settles
　Blown seaward, borne far from the sun,
Shaken loose on the darkness like petals
　Dropped one after one?　　　　　　80

Though the world of your hands be more
　　gracious
　And lovelier in lordship of things
Clothed round by sweet art with the spacious
　Warm heaven of her imminent wings,
Let them enter, unfledged and nigh fainting,
　For the love of old loves and lost times; 86
And receive in your palace of painting
　This revel of rimes.

Though the seasons of man full of losses
　Make empty the years full of youth,　90
If but one thing be constant in crosses,
　Change lays not her hand upon truth;
Hopes die, and their tombs are for token
　That the grief as the joy of them ends
Ere time that breaks all men has broken　95
　The faith between friends.

Though the many lights dwindle to one light,
　There is help if the heaven has one;
Though the skies be discrowned of the sun-
　　light
　And the earth dispossessed of the sun,　100
They have moonlight and sleep for repay-
　　ment,
　When, refreshed as a bride and set free,
With stars and sea-winds in her raiment,
　Night sinks on the sea.　　　　(1866)

AVE ATQUE VALE

IN MEMORY OF CHARLES BAUDELAIRE

Shall I strew on thee rose or rue or laurel,
　Brother, on this that was the veil of thee?
　Or quiet sea-flower molded by the sea,
Or simplest growth of meadow-sweet or sorrel,
　Such as the summer-sleepy Dryads weave,
　Waked up by snow-soft sudden rains at
　　eve?　　　　　　　　　　　　6
Or wilt thou rather, as on earth before,
　Half-faded fiery blossoms, pale with heat
　And full of bitter summer, but more sweet

To thee than gleanings of a northern shore 10
　Trod by no tropic feet?

For always thee the fervid languid glories
　Allured of heavier suns in mightier skies;
　Thine ears knew all the wandering watery
　　sighs
Where the sea sobs round Lesbian promon-
　　tories,　　　　　　　　　　　　15
　The barren kiss of piteous wave to wave
　That knows not where is that Leucadian
　　grave
Which hides too deep the supreme head of
　　song.
　Ah, salt and sterile as her kisses were,
　The wild sea winds her and the green gulfs
　　bear　　　　　　　　　　　　　20
Hither and thither, and vex and work her
　　wrong,
　Blind gods that cannot spare.

Thou sawest, in thine old singing season,
　　brother,
　Secrets and sorrows unbeheld of us;　24
　Fierce loves, and lovely leaf-buds poison-
　　ous,
Bare to thy subtler eye, but for none other
　Blowing by night in some unbreathed-in
　　clime;
　The hidden harvest of luxurious time,
Sin without shape, and pleasure without
　　speech;
　And where strange dreams in a tumultuous
　　sleep　　　　　　　　　　　　30
　Make the shut eyes of stricken spirits weep;
And with each face thou sawest the shadow
　　on each,
　Seeing as men sow men reap.

O sleepless heart and somber soul unsleeping,
　That were athirst for sleep and no more
　　life　　　　　　　　　　　　35
　And no more love, for peace and no more
　　strife!
Now the dim gods of death have in their
　　keeping
　Spirit and body and all the springs of song,
　Is it well now where love can do no wrong,
Where stingless pleasure has no foam or fang
　Behind the unopening closure of her lips? 41
　Is it not well where soul from body slips
And flesh from bone divides without a pang
　As dew from flower-bell drips?

---

81. **the world . . . hands,** the paintings of Burne-Jones.
Ave Atque Vale. See note on Tennyson's *Frater Ave Atque
Vale,* p. 165. Baudelaire (1821-67) was a French poet. See
Critical Notes.
　1. **rose . . . laurel.** The rose is a symbol of love, rue of
remembrance; the laurel is sacred to poetry. 2. **veil,** the
body of Baudelaire. 5. **Dryads,** wood nymphs. 8-11. **fiery
blossoms,** etc., a reference to the morbid and passionate
verse of Baudelaire, and to his visit to Mauritius in 1841-42.

15. **Where the sea sobs,** etc., a reference to the tradition
that because of disdained love the Greek poetess Sappho
(c. 600 B.C.), born on the island of Lesbos off the coast of
Asia Minor, cast herself into the sea from the rocky heights
of Leucas, one of the Ionian Islands, west of Greece. Baudelaire refers to Sappho's death in his *Lesbos.* 33. **as men . . .
reap.** Cf. "Whatsoever a man soweth, that shall he also
reap" (*Galatians,* 6:7).

It is enough; the end and the beginning   45
  Are one thing to thee, who art past the end.
O hand unclasped of unbeholden friend,
For thee no fruits to pluck, no palms for
    winning,
No triumph and no labor and no lust,
  Only dead yew-leaves and a little dust.   50
O quiet eyes wherein the light saith naught,
  Whereto the day is dumb, nor any night
  With obscure finger silences your sight,
Nor in your speech the sudden soul speaks
    thought,
  Sleep, and have sleep for light.   55

Now all strange hours and all strange loves
    are over,
  Dreams and desires and somber songs and
    sweet,
  Hast thou found place at the great knees
    and feet
Of some pale Titan-woman like a lover,
  Such as thy vision here solicited,   60
  Under the shadow of her fair vast head,
The deep division of prodigious breasts,
  The solemn slope of mighty limbs asleep,
  The weight of awful tresses that still keep
The savor and shade of old-world pine-
    forests   65
  Where the wet hill-winds weep?

Hast thou found any likeness for thy vision?
  O gardener of strange flowers, what bud,
    what bloom,
  Hast thou found sown, what gathered in
    the gloom?
What of despair, of rapture, of derision,   70
  What of life is there, what of ill or good?
  Are the fruits gray like dust or bright like
    blood?
Does the dim ground grow any seed of ours,
  The faint fields quicken any terrene root,
  In low lands where the sun and moon are
    mute   75
And all the stars keep silence? Are there
    flowers
  At all, or any fruit?

Alas, but though my flying song flies after,
  O sweet strange elder singer, thy more fleet
  Singing, and footprints of thy fleeter feet, 80
Some dim derision of mysterious laughter
  From the blind tongueless warders of the
    dead,
  Some gainless glimpse of Proserpine's veiled
    head,
Some little sound of unregarded tears

Wept by effaced unprofitable eyes,   85
  And from pale mouths some cadence of
    dead sighs —
These only, these the hearkening spirit hears,
  Sees only such things rise.

Thou art far too far for wings of words to
    follow,
  Far too far off for thought or any prayer.
What ails us with thee, who art wind and
    air?   91
What ails us gazing where all seen is hollow?
  Yet with some fancy, yet with some desire,
  Dreams pursue death as winds a flying fire,
Our dreams pursue our dead and do not find.
  Still, and more swift than they, the thin
    flame flies,   96
  The low light fails us in elusive skies,
Still the foiled earnest ear is deaf, and blind
  Are still the eluded eyes.

Not thee, O never thee, in all time's changes,
  Not thee, but this the sound of thy sad
    soul,   101
  The shadow of thy swift spirit, this shut
    scroll
I lay my hand on, and not death estranges
  My spirit from communion of thy song —
  These memories and these melodies that
    throng   105
Veiled porches of a Muse funereal —
  These I salute, these touch, these clasp and
    fold
  As though a hand were in my hand to hold,
Or through mine ears a mourning musical
  Of many mourners rolled.   110

I among these, I also, in such station
  As when the pyre was charred, and piled
    the sods,
  And offering to the dead made, and their
    gods,
The old mourners had, standing to make
    libation,
  I stand, and to the gods and to the dead 115
  Do reverence without prayer or praise and
    shed
Offering to these unknown, the gods of gloom,
  And what of honey and spice my seedlands
    bear,
  And what I may of fruits in this chilled air,
And lay, Orestes-like, across the tomb   120
  A curl of severed hair.

59. **Titan-woman,** a reference to Baudelaire's poem *La
Géante* (*The Giantess*). The Titans were giants of Greek
mythology who rebelled against the gods. 74. **terrene,**
earthly. 83. **Proserpine's . . . head.** See note on *The
Garden of Proserpine,* p. 697.

106. **Muse funereal.** See note on Clough's *In the Depths,*
2, p. 413. 120-121. **Orestes-like,** etc. Orestes was the son
of Agamemnon, king of Mycenæ, Greece, who led the expedition against Troy. The incident of Orestes's offering a tress
of his hair as a sacrifice to the dead is found in the opening
scene of the *Choephori,* a drama by Æschylus (525-456 B.C.),
the great Greek tragic dramatist. The King (line 123) is
Agamemnon. Electra (line 129) is the sister of Orestes. They
meet at the bier of their father slain by his wife (Clytemnestra)
and her paramour, Ægisthus.

But by no hand nor any treason stricken,
  Not like the low-lying head of Him, the
      King,
  The flame that made of Troy a ruinous
      thing,
Thou liest, and on this dust no tears could
    quicken   125
  There fall no tears like theirs that all men
      hear
  Fall tear by sweet imperishable tear
Down the opening leaves of holy poet's pages.
  Thee not Orestes, not Electra mourns;
  But bending us-ward with memorial urns
The most high Muses that fulfill all ages 131
  Weep, and our god's heart yearns.

For, sparing of his sacred strength, not often
  Among us darkling here the lord of light
Makes manifest his music and his might 135
  In hearts that open and in lips that soften
  With the soft flame and heat of songs that
      shine.
Thy lips indeed he touched with bitter
    wine,
  And nourished them indeed with bitter bread;
  Yet surely from his hand thy soul's food
      came,   140
  The fire that scarred thy spirit at his flame
Was lighted, and thine hungering heart he fed
  Who feeds our hearts with fame.

Therefore he too now at thy soul's sunsetting,
  God of all suns and songs, he too bends
      down   145
  To mix his laurel with thy cypress crown,
And save thy dust from blame and from
    forgetting.
  Therefore he too, seeing all thou wert and
      art,
  Compassionate, with sad and sacred heart,
Mourns thee of many his children the last
    dead,   150
  And hallows with strange tears and alien
      sighs
  Thine unmelodious mouth and sunless eyes,
And over thine irrevocable head
  Sheds light from the under skies.

And one weeps with him in the ways Lethean,
  And stains with tears her changing bosom
      chill —   156
  That obscure Venus of the hollow hill,

That thing transformed which was the
    Cytherean,
  With lips that lost their Grecian laugh
      divine
  Long since, and face no more called Ery-
      cine;   160
A ghost, a bitter and luxurious god.
  Thee also with fair flesh and singing spell
  Did she, a sad and second prey, compel
Into the footless places once more trod,
  And shadows hot from hell.   165

And now no sacred staff shall break in blos-
    som,
  No choral salutation lure to light
  A spirit sick with perfume and sweet night
And love's tired eyes and hands and barren
    bosom.
  There is no help for these things; none to
      mend   170
  And none to mar; not all our songs, O
      friend,
Will make death clear or make life durable.
  Howbeit with rose and ivy and wild vine
  And with wild notes about this dust of thine
At least I fill the place where white dreams
    dwell   175
  And wreathe an unseen shrine.

Sleep; and if life was bitter to thee, pardon,
  If sweet, give thanks; thou hast no more
      to live;
  And to give thanks is good, and to forgive.
Out of the mystic and the mournful garden
  Where all day through thine hands in bar-
      ren braid   181
  Wove the sick flowers of secrecy and shade,
Green buds of sorrow and sin, and remnants
    gray,
  Sweet-smelling, pale with poison, sanguine-
      hearted,
  Passions that sprang from sleep and
      thoughts that started,   185
Shall death not bring us all as thee one day
  Among the days departed?

For thee, O now a silent soul, my brother,
  Take at my hands this garland, and fare-
      well.
  Thin is the leaf, and chill the wintry smell,

---

158. **the Cytherean.** Aphrodite (Venus), who according
to tradition arose from the foam of the sea near the island of
Cythera, southeast of Greece. 160. **Erycine,** a title of Venus
derived from Mt. Eryx, in Sicily, where she was worshiped
as the goddess of heavenly love. 166. **staff . . . blossom.**
After the knight Tannhäuser had spent a year with Venus
in her cavern, he made a visit of penance to Rome and asked
for absolution, but Pope Urban IV (1261-64) said that he
would grant no mercy until his staff should burst into bloom.
Shortly thereafter the staff began to bud, but the knight had
returned to Venus. See *Laus Veneris,* 346-372, p. 679. Cf.
the story of the blossoming of Aaron's rod (*Numbers,* 17).
See Morris's *The Hill of Venus,* p. 649.

134. **lord of light,** Apollo, god of the sun and of poetry
and music. 146. **cypress.** The cypress is a symbol of
mourning and is a common tree in graveyards. See note on
line 1. 155. **ways Lethean,** the paths of forgetfulness.
Lethe was the river of forgetfulness in Hades. 157. **Venus
. . . hill.** In the medieval legend of Tannhäuser, Venus
appears transformed into an enchantress who lures victims
into the caverns of Hörselberg (the Mountain of Venus), a
mountain between the cities of Eisenach and Gotha, in
Germany.

And chill the solemn earth, a fatal mother, 191
  With sadder than the Niobean womb,
  And in the hollow of her breasts a tomb.
Content thee, howsoe'er, whose days are done;
  There lies not any troublous thing before,
  Nor sight nor sound to war against thee
    more, 196
For whom all winds are quiet as the sun,
  All waters as the shore. (1868)

PRELUDE TO *SONGS BEFORE SUNRISE*

Between the green bud and the red
Youth sat and sang by Time, and shed
  From eyes and tresses flowers and tears,
  From heart and spirit hopes and fears,
Upon the hollow stream whose bed 5
  Is channeled by the foamless years;
And with the white the gold-haired head
  Mixed running locks, and in Time's ears
Youth's dreams hung singing, and Time's truth
Was half not harsh in the ears of Youth. 10

Between the bud and the blown flower
Youth talked with joy and grief an hour,
  With footless joy and wingless grief
  And twin-born faith and disbelief
Who share the seasons to devour; 15
  And long ere these made up their sheaf
Felt the winds round him shake and shower
  The rose-red and the blood-red leaf,
Delight whose germ grew never grain,
And passion dyed in its own pain. 20

Then he stood up, and trod to dust
Fear and desire, mistrust and trust,
  And dreams of bitter sleep and sweet,
  And bound for sandals on his feet
Knowledge and patience of what must 25
  And what things may be, in the heat
And cold of years that rot and rust
  And alter; and his spirit's meat
Was freedom, and his staff was wrought
Of strength, and his cloak woven of thought.

For what has he whose will sees clear 31
To do with doubt and faith and fear,
  Swift hopes and slow despondencies?

His heart is equal with the sea's
And with the sea-wind's, and his ear 35
  Is level to the speech of these,
And his soul communes and takes cheer
  With the actual earth's equalities,
Air, light, and night, hills, winds, and streams,
And seeks not strength from strengthless
  dreams. 40

His soul is even with the sun
Whose spirit and whose eye are one,
  Who seeks not stars by day, nor light
  And heavy heat of day by night.
Him can no god cast down, whom none 45
  Can lift in hope beyond the height
Of fate and nature and things done
  By the calm rule of might and right
That bids men be and bear and do,
And die beneath blind skies or blue. 50

To him the lights of even and morn
Speak no vain things of love or scorn,
  Fancies and passions miscreate
  By man in things dispassionate.
Nor holds he fellowship forlorn 55
  With souls that pray and hope and hate,
And doubt they had better not been born,
  And fain would lure or scare off fate
And charm their doomsman from their doom
And make fear dig its own false tomb. 60

He builds not half of doubts and half
Of dreams his own soul's cenotaph,
  Whence hopes and fears with helpless eyes,
Wrapped loose in cast-off cerecloths, rise 64
And dance and wring their hands and laugh,
  And weep thin tears and sigh light sighs,
And without living lips would quaff
  The living spring in man that lies,
And drain his soul of faith and strength
It might have lived on a life's length. 70

He hath given himself and hath not sold
To God for heaven or man for gold,
  Or grief for comfort that it gives,
  Or joy for grief's restoratives.
He hath given himself to time, whose fold 75
  Shuts in the mortal flock that lives
On its plain pasture's heat and cold
  And the equal year's alternatives.
Earth, heaven, and time, death, life, and he,
Endure while they shall be to be. 80

"Yet between death and life are hours
To flush with love and hide in flowers;
  What profit save in these?" men cry.
"Ah, see, between soft earth and sky,
What only good things here are ours!" 85

192. **sadder ... womb.** See note on Robert Browning's
Old Pictures in Florence, 102. p. 236.
  Prelude to Songs before Sunrise. In this Prelude Swinburne
explains that his former interest in love, as expressed in his
first volume of verse, has given place to a new devotion to the
spirit of Freedom—freedom from the tyranny of government,
of religion, of passion and prejudice, etc. Some of the poems
in the volume entitled *Songs before Sunrise* were inspired
chiefly by Italy's long struggle for freedom from the rule of
Austria. Poems on pages 705-717 of this volume were included in *Songs before Sunrise.*
  1. **Between the green bud**, etc. Lines 1-2 refer to the
composition of the poems in the first series of *Poems and
Ballads*, published in 1866.

62. **cenotaph,** tomb or monument. 64. **cerecloths,**
waxed grave clothes.

They say, "what better wouldst thou try,
What sweeter sing of? or what powers
    Serve, that will give thee ere thou die
More joy to sing and be less sad,
More heart to play and grow more glad?" 90

Play then and sing; we too have played,
We likewise, in that subtle shade.
    We too have twisted through our hair
Such tendrils as the wild Loves wear,
And heard what mirth the Mænads made, 95
    Till the wind blew our garlands bare
And left their roses disarrayed,
    And smote the summer with strange air,
And disengirdled and discrowned
The limbs and locks that vine-wreaths bound.

We too have tracked by star-proof trees 101
The tempest of the Thyiades
    Scare the loud night on hills that hid
    The blood-feasts of the Bassarid,
Heard their song's iron cadences 105
    Fright the wolf hungering from the kid,
    Outroar the lion-throated seas,
    Outchide the north-wind if it chid,
And hush the torrent-tongued ravines
With thunders of their tambourines. 110

But the fierce flute whose notes acclaim
Dim goddesses of fiery fame,
    Cymbal and clamorous kettledrum,
    Timbrels and tabrets, all are dumb
That turned the high chill air to flame; 115
    The singing tongues of fire are numb
That called on Cotys by her name
    Edonian, till they felt her come
And maddened, and her mystic face
Lightened along the streams of Thrace. 120

For Pleasure slumberless and pale,
And Passion with rejected veil,
    Pass, and the tempest-footed throng
    Of hours that follow them with song
Till their feet flag and voices fail, 125
    And lips that were so loud so long
Learn silence, or a wearier wail;
    So keen is change, and time so strong,
To weave the robes of life and rend
And weave again till life have end. 130

But weak is change, but strengthless time,
To take the light from heaven, or climb

The hills of heaven with wasting feet.
Songs they can stop that earth found meet,
But the stars keep their ageless rime; 135
    Flowers they can slay that spring thought
        sweet,
But the stars keep their spring sublime;
    Passions and pleasures can defeat,
Actions and agonies control,
And life and death, but not the soul. 140

Because man's soul is man's God still,
What wind soever waft his will
    Across the waves of day and night
    To port or shipwreck, left or right,
By shores and shoals of good and ill; 145
    And still its flame at mainmast height
Through the rent air that foam-flakes fill
    Sustains the indomitable light
Whence only man hath strength to steer
Or helm to handle without fear. 150

Save his own soul's light overhead,
None leads him, and none ever led,
    Across birth's hidden harbor-bar,
    Past youth where shoreward shallows are,
Through age that drives on toward the red
    Vast void of sunset hailed from far, 156
To the equal waters of the dead;
    Save his own soul he hath no star,
And sinks, except his own soul guide,
Helmless in middle turn of tide. 160

No blast of air or fire of sun
Puts out the light whereby we run
    With girdled loins our lamplit race.
    And each from each takes heart of grace
And spirit till his turn be done, 165
    And light of face from each man's face
In whom the light of trust is one;
    Since only souls that keep their place
By their own light, and watch things roll,
And stand, have light for any soul. 170

A little time we gain from time
To set our seasons in some chime,
    For harsh or sweet or loud or low,
    With seasons played out long ago
And souls that in their time and prime 175
    Took part with summer or with snow,
Lived abject lives out or sublime,
    And had their chance of seed to sow
For service or disservice done
To those days dead and this their son. 180

A little time that we may fill
Or with such good works or such ill
    As loose the bonds or make them strong
    Wherein all manhood suffers wrong.

95. **Mænads.** See note on line 44, p. 668. 101 ff.
tracked . . . tempest . . . Scare, seen the tempests of the
Thyiades scare, etc. The Thyiades were women of Attica,
Greece, who worshiped Bacchus with great debauchery.
104. **Bassarid**, a worshiper of Bacchus in Lydia and Thrace,
Greece. The celebration included licentious excesses and a
sacrifice of some animal on the altar of the god. The participants ate the flesh raw. 114. **Timbrels and tabrets**, kinds
of small drums, like tambourines. 117. **Cotys**, the same as
Cotytto, a goddess whose festivals were marked with licentiousness. Her worship was associated with Mt. Edon, in
Thrace, Greece.

163ff. **lamplit race**, etc., a reference to the ancient
lampadedromy, a kind of relay race in which a torch or
lighted lamp was passed by each runner to the next. The
race was run in honor of some god or goddess.

By rose-hung river and light-foot rill 185
  There are who rest not; who think long
Till they discern as from a hill
  At the sun's hour of morning song,
Known of souls only, and those souls free,
The sacred spaces of the sea. 190
  (1871)

SUPER FLUMINA BABYLONIS

By the waters of Babylon we sat down and
    wept,
  Remembering thee,
That for ages of agony hast endured, and
    slept,
  And wouldst not see.

By the waters of Babylon we stood up and
    sang, 5
  Considering thee,
That a blast of deliverance in the darkness
    rang,
  To set thee free.

And with trumpets and thunderings and with
    morning song
  Came up the light; 10
And thy spirit uplifted thee to forget thy
    wrong
  As day doth night.

And thy sons were dejected not any more, as
    then
  When thou wast shamed;
When thy lovers went heavily without heart,
    as men 15
  Whose life was maimed.

In the desolate distances, with a great desire,
  For thy love's sake,
With our hearts going back to thee, they were
    filled with fire,
  Were nigh to break. 20

It was said to us: "Verily ye are great of
    heart,
  But ye shall bend;
Ye are bondmen and bondwomen, to be
    scourged and smart,
  To toil and tend."

And with harrows men harrowed us, and sub-
    dued with spears, 25
  And crushed with shame;

And the summer and winter was, and the
    length of years,
  And no change came.

By the rivers of Italy, by the sacred streams,
  By town, by tower, 30
There was feasting with reveling, there was
    sleep with dreams,
  Until thine hour.

And they slept and they rioted on their rose-
    hung beds,
  With mouths on flame,
And with love-locks vine-chapleted, and with
    rose-crowned heads 35
  And robes of shame.

And they knew not their forefathers, nor the
    hills and streams
  And words of power,
Nor the gods that were good to them, but
    with songs and dreams
  Filled up their hour. 40

By the rivers of Italy, by the dry streams'
    beds,
  When thy time came,
There was casting of crowns from them, from
    their young men's heads,
  The crowns of shame.

By the horn of Eridanus, by the Tiber mouth,
  As thy day rose, 46
They arose up and girded them to the north
    and south,
  By seas, by snows.

As a water in January the frost confines,
  Thy kings bound thee; 50
As a water in April is, in the new-blown vines,
  Thy sons made free.

And thy lovers that looked for thee, and that
    mourned from far,
  For thy sake dead,
We rejoiced in the light of thee, in the signal
    star 55
  Above thine head.

In thy grief had we followed thee, in thy pas-
    sion loved,
  Loved in thy loss;
In thy shame we stood fast to thee, with thy
    pangs were moved,
  Clung to thy cross. 60

By the hillside of Calvary we beheld thy
    blood,
  Thy blood-red tears,

Super Flumina Babylonis. The title is translated in the first line, which is quoted from *Psalms,* 137:1.—"By the rivers of Babylon, there we sat down, yea, we wept, when we remembered Zion." The Psalm refers to the afflictions of the Jews in captivity in Babylon, the great empire of western Asia. Swinburne has Italy in mind. (See note of Prelude to *Songs before Sunrise,* p. 703.)

45. the horn of Eridanus, the delta of the River Po. Eridanus is its Greek name.

As a mother's in bitterness, an unebbing flood,
   Years upon years.

And the north was Gethsemane, without leaf
   or bloom,   65
   A garden sealed;
And the south was Aceldama, for a sanguine
   fume
   Hid all the field.

By the stone of the sepulcher we returned to
   weep,
   From far, from prison;   70
And the guards by it keeping it we beheld
   asleep,
   But thou wast risen.

And an angel's similitude by the unsealed
   grave,
   And by the stone;
And the voice was angelical, to whose words
   God gave   75
   Strength like his own.

"Lo, the graveclothes of Italy that are folded
   up
   In the grave's gloom!
And the guards as men wrought upon with a
   charméd cup,
   By the open tomb.   80

"And her body most beautiful, and her shin-
   ing head,
   These are not here;
For your mother, for Italy, is not surely dead;
   Have ye no fear.

"As of old time she spake to you, and you
   hardly heard,   85
   Hardly took heed,
So now also she saith to you, yet another
   word,
   Who is risen indeed.

"By my saying she saith to you, in your ears
   she saith,
   Who hear these things,   90
Put no trust in men's royalties, nor in great
   men's breath,
   Nor words of kings.

"For the life of them vanishes and is no more
   seen,
   Nor no more known;
Nor shall any remember him if a crown hath
   been,   95
   Or where a throne.

"Unto each man his handiwork, unto each
   his crown,
   The just Fate gives;
Whoso takes the world's life on him and his
   own lays down,
   He, dying so, lives.   100

"Whoso bears the whole heaviness of the
   wronged world's weight
   And puts it by,
It is well with him suffering, though he face
   man's fate;
   How should he die?

"Seeing death has no part in him any more,
   no power   105
   Upon his head;
He has bought his eternity with a little hour,
   And is not dead.

"For an hour, if ye look for him, he is no
   more found,
   For one hour's space;   110
Then ye lift up your eyes to him and be-
   hold him crowned,
   A deathless face.

"On the mountains of memory, by the world's
   well-springs,
   In all men's eyes,
Where the light of the life of him is on all
   past things,   115
   Death only dies.

"Not the light that was quenched for us, nor
   the deeds that were,
   Nor the ancient days,
Nor the sorrows not sorrowful, nor the face
   most fair
   Of perfect praise."   120

So the angel of Italy's resurrection said,
   So yet he saith;
So the son of her suffering, that from breasts
   nigh dead
   Drew life, not death.

That the pavement of Golgotha should be
   white as snow,   125
   Not red, but white;
That the waters of Babylon should no longer
   flow,
   And men see light.

                              (1871)

65. **Gethsemane,** the garden outside Jerusalem; the scene of the agony and the arrest of Jesus. 67. **Aceldama,** mentioned in *Acts,* 1:18, as the scene of the suicide of Judas; later called the "Field of Blood." 73. **angel's similitude,** the angel of Italy's resurrection (see line 121).

99ff. **Whoso takes the world's life,** etc. Cf. *Matthew,* 16:25.—"Whosoever will save his life shall lose it; and who-soever will lose his life for my sake shall find it." 125. **Golgotha,** the place of the Crucifixion.

HERTHA

I am that which began;
  Out of me the years roll;
  Out of me God and man;
    I am equal and whole;
God changes, and man, and the form of them
  bodily; I am the soul.   5

Before ever land was,
  Before ever the sea,
  Or soft hair of the grass,
    Or fair limbs of the tree,
Or the flesh-colored fruit of my branches, I
  was, and thy soul was in me.   10

First life on my sources
  First drifted and swam;
  Out of me are the forces
    That save it or damn;
Out of me man and woman, and wild-beast
  and bird; before God was, I am.   15

Beside or above me
  Naught is there to go;
  Love or unlove me,
    Unknow me or know,
I am that which unloves me and loves; I am
  stricken, and I am the blow.   20

I the mark that is missed
  And the arrows that miss,
  I the mouth that is kissed
    And the breath in the kiss,
The search, and the sought, and the seeker,
  the soul and the body that is.   25

I am that thing which blesses
  My spirit elate;
  That which caresses
    With hands uncreate
My limbs unbegotten that measure the length
  of the measure of fate.   30

But what thing dost thou now,
  Looking Godward, to cry,
  "I am I, thou art thou,
    I am low, thou art high"?

I am thou, whom thou seekest to find him;
  find thou but thyself, thou art I.   35

I the grain and the furrow,
  The plow-cloven clod
  And the plowshare drawn thorough,
    The germ and the sod,
The deed and the doer, the seed and the
  sower, the dust which is God.   40

Hast thou known how I fashioned thee,
  Child, underground?
  Fire that impassioned thee,
    Iron that bound,
Dim changes of water, what thing of all these
  hast thou known of or found?   45

Canst thou say in thine heart
  Thou has seen with thine eyes
  With what cunning of art
    Thou wast wrought in what wise,
By what force of what stuff thou wast shapen,
  and shown on my breast to the skies? 50

Who hath given, who hath sold it thee,
  Knowledge of me?
  Hath the wilderness told it thee?
    Hast thou learnt of the sea?
Hast thou communed in spirit with night?
  Have the winds taken counsel with thee?

Have I set such a star   56
  To show light on thy brow
  That thou sawest from afar
    What I show to thee now?
Have ye spoken as brethren together, the sun
  and the mountains and thou?   60

What is here, dost thou know it?
  What was, hast thou known?
  Prophet nor poet
    Nor tripod nor throne
Nor spirit nor flesh can make answer, but
  only thy mother alone.   65

Mother, not maker,
  Born, and not made;
  Though her children forsake her,
    Allured or afraid,
Praying prayers to the God of their fashion,
  she stirs not for all that have prayed. 70

A creed is a rod,
  And a crown is of night;

Hertha. Hertha was the ancient Germanic goddess of the earth, of fertility, and of growth. In Swinburne's conception, she is much vaster, being regarded as the evolution of the world-soul. Swinburne said of the poem: "Of all I have done I rate *Hertha* highest as a single piece, finding in it the most of lyric force and music combined with the most of condensed and clarified thought" (letter to Stedman, Feb. 21, 1875).
15. before God was, I am. Cf. *Exodus,* 3:14.—"And God said unto Moses, 'I AM THAT I AM'"; and *John,* 8:58.— "Jesus said unto them, 'Verily, verily, I say unto you, Before Abraham was, I am.'" **20-40. I am the,** etc. The thought of these lines is suggestive of Emerson's *Brahma,* especially lines 10-12.—
    "When me they fly, I am the wings;
    I am the doubter and the doubt,
    And I the hymn the Brahmin sings."

41ff. Hast thou known, etc. With these questions compare the words spoken to Job by the Lord out of the whirlwind (*Job,* 38-39). **64. Nor tripod nor throne,** neither priest nor king. The tripod was the altar, supported on three legs, on which the priestesses of Apollo at Delphi sat when they delivered their oracles. **67. Born, and not made.** These lines are a protest against the idea of a single act of creation. Swinburne conceives nature as a continuous process of evolution.

But this thing is God,
   To be man with thy might,
To grow straight in the strength of thy spirit,
   and live out thy life as the light.   75

I am in thee to save thee,
   As my soul in thee saith;
Give thou as I gave thee,
   Thy life-blood and breath,
Green leaves of thy labor, white flowers of
   thy thought, and red fruit of thy death.

Be the ways of thy giving   81
   As mine were to thee;
The free life of thy living,
   Be the gift of it free;
Not as servant to lord, nor as master to slave,
   shalt thou give thee to me.   85

O children of banishment,
   Souls overcast,
Were the lights ye see vanish meant
   Alway to last,
Ye would know not the sun overshining the
   shadows and stars overpast.   90

I that saw where ye trod
   The dim paths of the night
Set the shadow called God
   In your skies to give light;
But the morning of manhood is risen, and the
   shadowless soul is in sight.   95

The tree many-rooted
   That swells to the sky
With frondage red-fruited,
   The life-tree am I;
In the buds of your lives is the sap of my
   leaves; ye shall live and not die.   100

But the gods of your fashion
   That take and that give,
In their pity and passion
   That scourge and forgive,
They are worms that are bred in the bark that
   falls off; they shall die and not live.   105

My own blood is what stanches
   The wounds in my bark;
Stars caught in my branches
   Make day of the dark,
And are worshiped as suns till the sunrise shall
   tread out their fires as a spark.   110

Where dead ages hide under
   The live roots of the tree,
In my darkness the thunder
   Makes utterance of me;

88. **lights,** religious creeds and dogmas. 96. **The tree
many-rooted,** the mighty ash tree Yggdrasill, supposed, in
Norse mythology, to support the entire universe.

In the clash of my boughs with each other ye
   hear the waves sound of the sea.   115

That noise is of Time,
   As his feathers are spread
And his feet set to climb
   Through the boughs overhead,
And my foliage rings round him and rustles,
   and branches are bent with his tread.   120

The storm-winds of ages
   Blow through me and cease,
The war-wind that rages,
   The spring-wind of peace,
Ere the breath of them roughen my tresses,
   ere one of my blossoms increase.   125

All sounds of all changes,
   All shadows and lights
On the world's mountain-ranges
   And stream-riven heights,
Whose tongue is the wind's tongue and lan-
   guage of storm-clouds on earth-shaking
   nights;   130

All forms of all faces,
   All works of all hands
In unsearchable places
   Of time-stricken lands,
All death and all life, and all reigns and all
   ruins, drop through me as sands.   135

Though sore be my burden
   And more than ye know,
And my growth have no guerdon
   But only to grow,
Yet I fail not of growing for lightnings above
   me or deathworms below.   140

These too have their part in me,
   As I too in these;
Such fire is at heart in me,
   Such sap is this tree's,
Which hath in it all sounds and all secrets of
   infinite lands and of seas.   145

In the spring-colored hours
   When my mind was as May's,
There brake forth of me flowers
   By centuries of days,
Strong blossoms with perfume of manhood,
   shot out from my spirit as rays.   150

And the sound of them springing
   And smell of their shoots
Were as warmth and sweet singing
   And strength to my roots;
And the lives of my children made perfect
   with freedom of soul were my fruits.   155

I bid you but be;
   I have need not of prayer;

I have need of you free
  As your mouths of mine air;
That my heart may be greater within me,
  beholding the fruits of me fair.   160

More fair than strange fruit is
  Of faiths ye espouse;
In me only the root is
  That blooms in your boughs;
Behold now your God that ye made you, to
  feed him with faith of your vows.   165

In the darkening and whitening
  Abysses adored,
With dayspring and lightning
  For lamp and for sword,
God thunders in heaven, and his angels are
  red with the wrath of the Lord.   170

O my sons, O too dutiful
  Toward gods not of me,
Was not I enough beautiful?
  Was it hard to be free?
For behold, I am with you, am in you and
  of you; look forth now and see.   175

Lo, winged with world's wonders,
  With miracles shod,
With the fires of his thunders
  For raiment and rod,
God trembles in heaven, and his angels are
  white with the terror of God.   180

For his twilight is come on him,
  His anguish is here;
And his spirits gaze dumb on him,
  Grown gray from his fear;
And his hour taketh hold on him stricken, the
  last of his infinite year.   185

Thought made him and breaks him,
  Truth slays and forgives;
But to you, as time takes him,
  This new thing it gives,
Even love, the beloved Republic, that feeds
  upon freedom and lives.   190

For truth only is living,
  Truth only is whole,
And the love of his giving
  Man's polestar and pole;
Man, pulse of my center, and fruit of my
  body, and seed of my soul;   195

One birth of my bosom;
  One beam of mine eye;
One topmost blossom

That scales the sky;
Man, equal and one with me, man that is
  made of me, man that is I.   200
                                      (1871)

HYMN OF MAN

(DURING THE SESSION IN ROME OF THE
ŒCUMENICAL COUNCIL)

In the gray beginning of years, in the twilight
    of things that began,
The word of the earth in the ears of the world,
    was it God? was it man?
The word of the earth to the spheres her
    sisters, the note of her song,
The sound of her speech in the ears of the
    starry and sisterly throng,
Was it praise or passion or prayer, was it love
    or devotion or dread,   5
When the veils of the shining air first wrapped
    her jubilant head?
When her eyes new-born of the night saw yet
    no star out of reach;
When her maiden mouth was alight with the
    flame of musical speech;
When her virgin feet were set on the terrible
    heavenly way,
And her virginal lids were wet with the dew
    of the birth of the day —   10
Eyes that had looked not on time, and ears
    that had heard not of death;
Lips that had learned not the rime of change
    and passionate breath,
The rhythmic anguish of growth, and the
    motion of mutable things,
Of love that longs and is loath, and plume-
    plucked hope without wings,
Passions and pains without number, and life
    that runs and is lame,   15
From slumber again to slumber, the same race
    set for the same,
Where the runners outwear each other, but
    running with lampless hands
No man takes light from his brother till blind
    at the goal he stands —
Ah, did they know, did they dream of it,
    counting the cost and the worth?
The ways of her days, did they seem then
    good to the new-souled earth?   20
Did her heart rejoice, and the might of her
    spirit exult in her then,
Child yet no child of the night, and mother-
    less mother of men?

---

181. **his twilight.** The idea of the twilight of the gods is
derived from Norse mythology. This is the period, known as
Ragnarok, which involves the destruction of the universe.
After this period a new heaven and a new earth will arise
out of the sea.

Hymn of Man. The twenty-first Œcumenical (general)
Council of the church met in Rome from December, 1869, to
July, 1870. It voted for the dogma of the infallibility of the
Pope on July 18, 1870. Swinburne characterized the *Hymn
to Proserpine* (p. 686) and the *Hymn of Man* as "the death-
song of spiritual decadence and the birthsong of spiritual
renascence."

21 ff. **Did her heart rejoice,** etc. The idea expressed in
these lines is frequently found in literature. See Critical
Notes.

Was it Love brake forth flower-fashion, a bird
    with gold on his wings,
Lovely, her firstborn passion, and impulse of
    firstborn things?
Was Love that nestling indeed that under the
    plumes of the night   25
Was hatched and hidden as seed in the fur-
    row, and brought forth bright?
Was it Love lay shut in the shell world-
    shaped, having over him there
Black world-wide wings that impel the might
    of the night through air?
And bursting his shell as a bird, night shook
    through her sail-stretched vans,
And her heart as a water was stirred, and its
    heat was the firstborn man's.   30
For the waste of the dead void air took form
    of a world at birth,
And the waters and firmaments were, and
    light, and the life-giving earth.
The beautiful bird unbegotten that night
    brought forth without pain
In the fathomless years forgotten whereover
    the dead gods reign,
Was it love, life, godhead, or fate? We say
    the spirit is one   35
That moved on the dark to create out of
    darkness the stars and the sun.
Before the growth was the grower, and the
    seed ere the plant was sown;
But what was seed of the sower? and the grain
    of him, whence was it grown?
Foot after foot ye go back and travail and
    make yourselves mad;
Blind feet that feel for the track where high-
    way is none to be had.   40
Therefore the God that ye make you is griev-
    ous, and gives not aid,
Because it is but for your sake that the God
    of your making is made.
Thou and I and he are not gods made men
    for a span,
But God, if a God there be, is the substance
    of men which is man.
Our lives are as pulses of pores of his mani-
    fold body and breath;   45
As waves of his sea on the shores where birth
    is the beacon of death.
We men, the multiform features of man, what-
    soever we be,
Re-create him of whom we are creatures, and
    all we only are he.
For each man of all men is God, but God is
    the fruit of the whole;
Indivisible spirit and blood, indiscernible body
    from soul.   50
Not men's but man's is the glory of godhead,
    the kingdom of time,

35-36. **spirit . . . sun.** Cf. the story of creation in
Genesis, 1.

The mountainous ages made hoary with snows
    for the spirit to climb.
A God with the world inwound whose clay to
    his footsole clings;
A manifold God fast-bound as with iron of
    adverse things.
A soul that labors and lives, an emotion, a
    strenuous breath,   55
From the flame that its own mouth gives
    reillumed, and refreshed with death.
In the sea whereof centuries are waves the
    live God plunges and swims;
His bed is in all men's graves, but the worm
    hath not hold on his limbs.
Night puts out not his eyes, nor time sheds
    change on his head;
With such fire as the stars of the skies are the
    roots of his heart are fed.   60
Men are the thoughts passing through it, the
    veins that fulfill it with blood,
With spirit of sense to renew it as springs ful-
    filling a flood.
Men are the heartbeats of man, the plumes
    that feather his wings,
Storm-worn, since being began, with the wind
    and thunder of things.
Things are cruel and blind; their strength
    detains and deforms;   65
And the wearying wings of the mind still beat
    up the stream of their storms.
Still, as one swimming upstream, they strike
    out blind in the blast,
In thunders of vision and dream, and light-
    nings of future and past.
We are baffled and caught in the current and
    bruised upon edges of shoals;
As weeds or as reeds in the torrent of things
    are the wind-shaken souls.   70
Spirit by spirit goes under, a foam-bell's
    bubble of breath,
That blows and opens in sunder and blurs not
    the mirror of death.
For a worm or a thorn in his path is a man's
    soul quenched as a flame;
For his lust of an hour or his wrath shall the
    worm and the man be the same.
O God sore stricken of things! they have
    wrought him a raiment of pain;   75
Can a God shut eyelids and wings at a touch
    on the nerves of the brain?
O shamed and sorrowful God, whose force
    goes out at a blow!
What world shall shake at his nod? at his
    coming what wilderness glow?
What help in the work of his hands? what
    light in the track of his feet?
His days are snowflakes or sands, with cold
    to consume him and heat.   80
He is servant with Change for lord, and for
    wages he hath to his hire

Folly and force, and a sword that devours,
and a ravening fire.
From the bed of his birth to his grave he is
driven as a wind at their will;
Lest Change bow down as his slave, and the
storm and the sword be still;
Lest earth spread open her wings to the sunward, and sing with the spheres; 85
Lest man be master of things, to prevail on
their forces and fears.
By the spirit are things overcome; they are
stark, and the spirit hath breath;
It hath speech, and their forces are dumb; it
is living, and things are of death.
But they know not the spirit for master, they
feel not force from above,
While man makes love to disaster, and woos
desolation with love. 90
Yea, himself too hath made himself chains,
and his own hands plucked out his eyes;
For his own soul only constrains him, his own
mouth only denies.
The herds of kings and their hosts and the
flocks of the high priests bow
To a master whose face is a ghost's; O thou
that wast God, is it thou?
Thou madest man in the garden; thou tempt-
edst man, and he fell; 95
Thou gavest him poison and pardon for blood
and burnt-offering to sell.
Thou hast sealed thine elect to salvation, fast
locked with faith for the key;
Make now for thyself expiation, and be thine
atonement for thee.
Ah, thou that darkenest heaven — ah, thou
that bringest a sword —
By the crimes of thine hands unforgiven they
beseech thee to hear them, O Lord. 100
By the balefires of ages that burn for thine
incense, by creed and by rood,
By the famine and passion that yearn and
that hunger to find of thee food,
By the children that asked at thy throne of
the priests that were fat with thine hire
For bread, and thou gavest a stone; for light,
and thou madest them fire;
By the kiss of thy peace like a snake's kiss,
that leaves the soul rotten at root; 105
By the savors of gibbets and stakes thou hast
planted to bear to thee fruit;
By torture and terror and treason, that make
to thee weapons and wings;
By thy power upon men for a season, made
out of the malice of things;

O thou that hast built thee a shrine of the
madness of man and his shame,
And hast hung in the midst for a sign of his
worship the lamp of thy name; 110
That hast shown him for heaven in a vision
a void world's shadow and shell,
And hast fed thy delight and derision with
fire of belief as of hell;
That hast fleshed on the souls that believe
thee the fang of the death-worm fear,
With anguish of dreams to deceive them whose
faith cries out in thine ear;
By the face of the spirit confounded before
thee humbled in dust, 115
By the dread wherewith life was astounded
and shamed out of sense of its trust,
By the scourges of doubt and repentance that
fell on the soul at thy nod,
Thou art judged, O judge, and the sentence is
gone forth against thee, O God.
Thy slave that slept is awake; thy slave but
slept for a span;
Yea, man thy slave shall unmake thee, who
made thee lord over man. 120
For his face is set to the east, his feet on the
past and its dead;
The sun rearisen is his priest, and the heat
thereof hallows his head.
His eyes take part in the morning; his spirit
outsounding the sea
Asks no more witness or warning from temple
or tripod or tree.
He hath set the centuries at union; the night
is afraid at his name; 125
Equal with life, in communion with death, he
hath found them the same.
Past the wall unsurmounted that bars out our
vision with iron and fire
He hath sent forth his soul for the stars to
comply with and suns to conspire.
His thought takes flight for the center wherethrough it hath part in the whole;
The abysses forbid it not enter — the stars
make room for the soul. 130
Space is the soul's to inherit; the night is hers
as the day;
Lo, saith man, this is my spirit; how shall not
the worlds make way?
Space is thought's, and the wonders thereof,
and the secret of space;
Is thought not more than the thunders and
lightnings? shall thought give place?
Is the body not more than the vesture, the life
not more than the meat? 135
The will than the word or the gesture, the
heart than the hands or the feet?

85. **sing with the spheres.** The ancients believed that
the stars made music as they revolved in their spheres. 99.
thou . . . sword. Cf. *Matthew*, 10:34.—"Think not that
I am come to send peace on earth; I came not to send peace,
but a sword." 101. **balefires,** funeral pyres. **rood,** cross.
104. **bread . . . stone.** From Christ's Sermon on the Mount,
Matthew, 7:9.—"What man is there of you, whom if his son
ask bread, will he give him a stone?"

124. **tripod.** See note on *Hertha*, 64, p. 707. **tree,** the
cross. 135. **body . . . meat.** From Christ's Sermon on the
Mount, *Matthew*, 6:25.—"Is not the life more than meat, and
body than raiment?"

Is the tongue not more than the speech is? the
   head not more than the crown?
And if higher than is heaven be the reach of
   the soul, shall not heaven bow down?
Time, father of life, and more great than the
   life it begat and began,
Earth's keeper and heaven's and their fate,
   lives, thinks, and hath substance in
   man.   140
Time's motion that throbs in his blood is the
   thought that gives heart to the skies,
And the springs of the fire that is food to the
   sunbeams are light to his eyes.
The minutes that beat with his heart are the
   words to which worlds keep chime,
And the thought in his pulses is part of the
   blood and the spirit of time.
He saith to the ages, Give; and his soul forgoes not her share;   145
Who are ye that forbid him to live, and would
   feed him with heavenlier air?
Will ye feed him with poisonous dust, and restore him with hemlock for drink,
Till he yield you his soul up in trust, and have
   heart not to know or to think?
He hath stirred him, and found out the flaw
   in his fetters, and cast them behind;
His soul to his soul is a law, and his mind is
   a light to his mind.   150
The seal of his knowledge is sure, the truth
   and his spirit are wed;
Men perish, but man shall endure; lives die,
   but the life is not dead.
He hath sight of the secrets of season, the
   roots of the years and the fruits;
His soul is at one with the reason of things
   that is sap to the roots.
He can hear in their changes a sound as the
   conscience of consonant spheres;   155
He can see through the years flowing round
   him the law lying under the years.
Who are ye that would bind him with curses
   and blind him with vapor of prayer?
Your might is as night that disperses when
   light is alive in the air.
The bow of your godhead is broken, the arm
   of your conquest is stayed;
Though ye call down God to bear token, for
   fear of you none is afraid.   160
Will ye turn back times, and the courses of
   stars, and the season of souls?
Shall God's breath dry up the sources that
   feed time full as it rolls?
Nay, cry on him then till he show you a sign,
   till he lift up a rod;
Hath he made not the nations to know him
   of old if indeed he be God?
Is no heat of him left in the ashes of thousands
   burnt up for his sake?   165

Can prayer not rekindle the flashes that shone
   in his face from the stake?
Cry aloud; for your God is a God and a
   Savior; cry, make yourselves lean;
Is he drunk or asleep, that the rod of his
   wrath is unfelt and unseen?
Is the fire of his old loving-kindness gone out,
   that his pyres are acold?
Hath he gazed on himself unto blindness, who
   made men blind to behold?   170
Cry out, for his kingdom is shaken; cry out,
   for the people blaspheme;
Cry aloud till his godhead awaken; what doth
   he to sleep and to dream?
Cry, cut yourselves, gash you with knives and
   with scourges, heap on to you dust;
Is his life but as other gods' lives? is not this
   the Lord God of your trust?
Is not this the great God of your sires, that
   with souls and with bodies was fed, 175
And the world was on flame with his fires?
   O fools, he was God, and is dead.
He will hear not again the strong crying of
   earth in his ears as before,
And the fume of his multitudes dying shall
   flatter his nostrils no more.
By the spirit he ruled as his slave is he slain
   who was mighty to slay,
And the stone that is sealed on his grave he
   shall rise not and roll not away.   180
Yea, weep to him, lift up your hands; be your
   eyes as a fountain of tears;
Where he stood there is nothing that stands;
   if he call, there is no man that hears.
He hath doffed his king's raiment of lies now
   the wane of his kingdom is come;
Ears hath he, and hears not; and eyes, and he
   sees not; and mouth, and is dumb.
His red king's raiment is ripped from him
   naked, his staff broken down;   185
And the signs of his empire are stripped from
   him shuddering; and where is his crown?
And in vain by the wellsprings refrozen ye
   cry for the warmth of his sun —
O God, the Lord God of thy chosen, thy will
   in thy kingdom be done.
Kingdom and will hath he none in him left
   him, nor warmth in his breath;
Till his corpse be cast out of the sun will ye
   know not the truth of his death?   190
Surely, ye say, he is strong, though the times
   be against him and men;

---

147. **hemlock,** a drug prepared from the leaves of the
poisonous hemlock herb.   155. **consonant,** harmonious.

167ff. **Cry aloud,** etc. Taken from *1 Kings*, 18:19-40,
where Elijah rebukes and destroys the prophets of Baal.—
"And it came to pass at noon that Elijah mocked them, and
said, 'Cry aloud: for he is a god; either he is talking, or he is
pursuing, or he is in a journey, or peradventure he sleepeth,
and must be awaked.' And they cried aloud, and cut themselves after their manner with knives and lancets, till the
blood gushed out upon them" (verses 27-28). 184. **Ears . . .
dumb.** Cf. *Psalms,* 115:4-6.—"Their idols are silver and gold,
the work of men's hands. They have mouths, but they
speak not; eyes have they, but they see not; they have ears,
but they hear not."

Yet a little, ye say, and how long, till he come
    to show judgment again?
Shall God then die as the beasts die? who is it
    hath broken his rod?
O God, Lord God of thy priests, rise up now
    and show thyself God.
They cry out, thine elect, thine aspirants to
    heavenward, whose faith is as flame;
O thou the Lord God of our tyrants, they call
    thee, their God, by thy name. 196
By thy name that in hell-fire was written, and
    burned at the point of thy sword,
Thou art smitten, thou God, thou art smitten,
    thy death is upon thee, O Lord.
And the love-song of earth as thou diest re-
    sounds through the wind of her wings—
Glory to Man in the highest! for Man is the
    master of things. 200
                  (1871)

THE PILGRIMS

Who is your lady of love, O ye that pass
Singing? and is it for sorrow of that which was
    That ye sing sadly, or dream of what shall
    be?
      For gladly at once and sadly it seems
      ye sing.
— Our lady of love by you is unbeholden; 5
For hands she hath none, nor eyes, nor lips,
    nor golden
    Treasure of hair, nor face nor form; but we
      That love, we know her more fair than
      anything.

— Is she a queen, having great gifts to give?
— Yea, these: that whoso hath seen her shall
    not live 10
Except he serve her sorrowing, with strange
    pain,
    Travail and bloodshedding and bit-
    terer tears;
And when she bids die he shall surely die.
And he shall leave all things under the sky
    And go forth naked under sun and rain 15
    And work and wait and watch out all
    his years.

— Hath she on earth no place of habitation?
— Age to age calling, nation answering nation,
    Cries out, Where is she? and there is none
    to say; 19
      For if she be not in the spirit of men,
For if in the inward soul she hath no place,
In vain they cry unto her, seeking her face,

In vain their mouths make much of her;
    for they
    Cry with vain tongues, till the heart lives
    again.

— O ye that follow, and have ye no repent-
    ance? 25
For on your brows is written a mortal sen-
    tence,
    An hieroglyph of sorrow, a fiery sign,
    That in your lives ye shall not pause or
    rest,
Nor have the sure sweet common love, nor
    keep
Friends and safe days, nor joy of life nor
    sleep. 30
— These have we not, who have one thing,
    the divine
    Face and clear eyes of faith and fruitful
    breast.

— And ye shall die before your thrones be
    won.
— Yea, and the changed world and the
    liberal sun
    Shall move and shine without us, and we
    lie 35
    Dead; but if she too move on earth and
    live,
But if the old world with all the old irons rent
Laugh and give thanks, shall we be not con-
    tent?
    Nay, we shall rather live, we shall not die,
    Life being so little and death so good to
    give. 40

— And these men shall forget you. — Yea,
    but we
Shall be a part of the earth and the ancient
    sea,
    And heaven-high air august, and awful fire,
    And all things good; and no man's heart
    shall beat
But somewhat in it of our blood once shed 45
Shall quiver and quicken, as now in us the
    dead
    Blood of men slain and the old same life's
    desire
    Plants in their fiery footprints our fresh
    feet.

— But ye that might be clothed with all
    things pleasant,
Ye are foolish that put off the fair soft
    present, 50
That clothe yourselves with the cold future
    air;
    When mother and father and tender sis-
    ter and brother

---

200. **Glory . . . highest.** Cf. *Luke,* 2:14.—"Glory to God
in the highest, and on earth peace, good will toward men."
  The Pilgrims. This poem pays tribute to the great spirits
of the earth who in spite of hardship and death have dedicated
themselves to the cause of humanity, the lady of love of line 1.
It is in the form of a dialogue between those spirits and their
fellowmen who live only for themselves.

41-42. **we . . . earth,** etc. Cf. Prelude to *Songs before
Sunrise,* 31-40, p. 703.

And the old live love that was shall be as ye,
Dust, and no fruit of loving life shall be.
— She shall be yet who is more than all
        these were,   55
    Than sister or wife or father unto us or
        mother.

— Is this worth life, is this, to win for wages?
Lo, the dead mouths of the awful gray-grown
        ages,
    The venerable, in the past that is their
        prison,
    In the outer darkness, in the unopening
        grave,   60
Laugh, knowing how many as ye now say
        have said,
How many, and all are fallen, are fallen and
        dead;
Shall ye dead rise, and these dead have not
        risen?
    — Not we but she, who is tender and swift
        to save.

— Are ye not weary and faint not by the
        way,   65
Seeing night by night devoured of day by day,
    Seeing hour by hour consumed in sleepless
        fire?
    Sleepless; and ye too, when shall ye too
        sleep?
— We are weary in heart and head, in hands
        and feet,
And surely more than all things sleep were
        sweet,   70
    Than all things save the inexorable desire
    Which whoso knoweth shall neither faint
        nor weep.

— Is this so sweet that one were fain to follow?
Is this so sure where all men's hopes are
        hollow,
    Even this your dream, that by much trib-
        ulation   75
    Ye shall make whole flawed hearts, and
        bowed necks straight?
— Nay, though our life were blind, our death
        were fruitless,
Not therefore were the whole world's high
        hope rootless;
    But man to man, nation would turn to
        nation,
    And the old life live, and the old great
        word be great.   80

— Pass on then and pass by us and let us be,
For what light think ye after life to see?
And if the world fare better will ye know?

And if man triumph who shall seek you and
        say?
— Enough of light is this for one life's span, 85
That all men born are mortal, but not man;
    And we men bring death lives by night to
        sow,
    That man may reap and eat and live by
        day.   (1871)

TO WALT WHITMAN IN AMERICA

Send but a song oversea for us,
    Heart of their hearts who are free,
Heart of their singer, to be for us
    More than our singing can be;
Ours, in the tempest at error,   5
With no light but the twilight of terror;
    Send us a song oversea!

Sweet-smelling of pine-leaves and grasses,
    And blown as a tree through and through
With the winds of the keen mountain-passes,
    And tender as sun-smitten dew;   11
Sharp-tongued as the winter that shakes
The wastes of your limitless lakes,
    Wide-eyed as the sea-line's blue.

O strong-winged soul with prophetic   15
    Lips hot with the bloodbeats of song,
With tremor of heartstrings magnetic,
    With thoughts as thunders in throng,
With consonant ardors of chords
That pierce men's souls as with swords   20
    And hale them hearing along,

Make us, too, music, to be with us
    As a word from a world's heart warm;
To sail the dark as a sea with us,
    Full-sailed, outsinging the storm,   25
A song to put fire in our ears
Whose burning shall burn up tears,
    Whose sign bid battle reform;

A note in the ranks of a clarion,
    A word in the wind of cheer,   30
To consume as with lightning the carrion
    That makes time foul for us here;
In the air that our dead things infest
A blast of the breath of the west,
    Till east way as west way is clear.   35

Out of the sun beyond sunset,
    From the evening whence morning shall be,
With the rollers in measureless onset,
    With the van of the storming sea,

---

56. **Than sister,** etc. Cf. *Luke,* 14:26.—"If any man
come to me, and hate not his father, and mother, and wife,
and children, and brethren, and sister, yea, and his own life
also, he cannot be my disciple."

87. **bring . . . sow.** Cf. *I Corinthians,* 15:36-38.—". . . that
which thou sowest is not quickened, except it die. And that
which thou sowest, thou sowest not that body that shall be,
but bare grain, . . . But God giveth it a body as it hath
pleased him, and to every seed his own body."
To Walt Whitman in America. See Critical Notes.
19. **consonant,** harmonious.

With the world-wide wind, with the breath 40
That breaks ships driven upon death,
  With the passion of all things free,

With the sea-steeds footless and frantic,
  White myriads for death to bestride
In the charge of the ruining Atlantic   45
  Where deaths by regiments ride,
With clouds and clamors of waters,
With a long note shriller than slaughter's
  On the furrowless fields world-wide,

With terror, with ardor and wonder,   50
  With the soul of the season that wakes
When the weight of a whole year's thunder
  In the tidestream of autumn breaks,
Let the flight of the wide-winged word
Come over, come in and be heard,   55
  Take form and fire for our sakes.

For a continent bloodless with travail
  Here toils and brawls as it can,
And the web of it who shall unravel
  Of all that peer on the plan;   60
Would fain grow men, but they grow not,
And fain be free, but they know not
  One name for freedom and man?

One name, not twain for division;
  One thing, not twain, from the birth;   65
Spirit and substance and vision,
  Worth more than worship is worth;
Unbeheld, unadored, undivined,
The cause, the center, the mind,
  The secret and sense of the earth.   70

Here as a weakling in irons,
  Here as a weanling in bands,
As a prey that the stake-net environs,
  Our life that we looked for stands;
And the man-child naked and dear,   75
Democracy, turns on us here
  Eyes trembling, with tremulous hands.

It sees not what season shall bring to it
  Sweet fruit of its bitter desire;
Few voices it hears yet sing to it,   80
  Few pulses of hearts reaspire;
Foresees not time, nor forehears
The noises of imminent years,
  Earthquake, and thunder, and fire;

When crowned and weaponed and curbless 85
  It shall walk, without helm or shield,
The bare burnt furrows and herbless
  Of war's last flame-stricken field —
Till godlike, equal with time,
It stand in the sun sublime,   90
  In the godhead of man revealed.

73. **stake-net**, a fishing net usually set in shallow water,
held in a vertical position by means of stakes.

Round your people and over them
  Light like raiment is drawn,
Close as a garment to cover them,
  Wrought not of mail nor of lawn;   95
Here, with hope hardly to wear,
Naked nations and bare
  Swim, sink, strike out for the dawn.

Chains are here, and a prison,
  Kings, and subjects, and shame;   100
If the God upon you be arisen,
  How should our songs be the same?
How, in confusion of change,
How shall we sing, in a strange
  Land, songs praising his name?   105

God is buried and dead to us,
  Even the spirit of earth,
Freedom; so have they said to us,
  Some with mocking and mirth,
Some with heartbreak and tears;   110
And a God without eyes, without ears,
  Who shall sing of him, dead in the birth?

The earth god Freedom, the lonely
  Face lightening, the footprint unshod,
Not as one man crucified only,   115
  Nor scourged with but one life's rod;
The soul that is substance of nations,
Reincarnate with fresh generations;
  The great god Man, which is God.

But in weariest of years and obscurest   120
  Doth it live not at heart of all things,
The one God and one spirit, a purest
  Life, fed from unstanchable springs?
Within love, within hatred it is,
And its seed in the stripe as the kiss,   125
  And in slaves is the germ, and in kings.

Freedom we call it, for holier
  Name of the soul's there is none;
Surelier it labors, if slowlier,
  Than the meters of star or of sun;   130
Slowlier than life into breath,
Surelier than time into death,
  It moves till its labor be done —

Till the motion be done and the measure
  Circling through season and clime,   135
Slumber and sorrow and pleasure,
  Vision of virtue and crime;
Till consummate with conquering eyes,
A soul disembodied, it rise
  From the body transfigured of time;   140

Till it rise and remain and take station
  With the stars of the worlds that rejoice;

104-105. **How ... name.** See Psalm 137:4. 115. **Not as
one man**, etc. Swinburne means that others besides Christ
have suffered martyrdom in the name of Freedom. 125. **the
stripe**, the mark of the lash.

Till the voice of its heart's exultation
  Be as theirs an invariable voice;
By no discord of evil estranged,   145
By no pause, by no breach in it changed,
  By no clash in the chord of its choice.

It is one with the world's generations,
  With the spirit, the star and the sod;   149
With the kingless and king-stricken nations,
  With the cross, the chain, and the rod;
The most high, the most secret, most lonely,
  The earth-soul Freedom, that only
Lives, and that only is God.

                       (1871)

COR CORDIUM

O heart of hearts, the chalice of love's fire,
Hid round with flowers and all the bounty
    of bloom,
O wonderful and perfect heart, for whom
The lyrist liberty made life a lyre;
O heavenly heart, at whose most dear desire
Dead love, living and singing, cleft his
    tomb,   6
And with him risen and regent in death's
    room
All day thy choral pulses rang full choir;
O heart whose beating blood was running
    song,
O sole thing sweeter than thine own songs
    were,   10
Help us for thy free love's sake to be free,
True for thy truth's sake, for thy strength's
    sake strong,
Till very liberty make clean and fair
The nursing earth as the sepulchral sea.

                       (1871)

THE SONG OF THE STANDARD

Maiden most beautiful, mother most bountiful, lady of lands,
Queen and republican, crowned of the centuries whose years are thy sands,
See for thy sake what we bring to thee, Italy,
  here in our hands.

This is the banner thy gonfalon, fair in the
  front of thy fight,

Red from the hearts that were pierced for
  thee, white as thy mountains are white,
Green as the spring of thy soul everlasting,
  whose life-blood is light.   6

Take to thy bosom thy banner, a fair bird fit
  for the nest,
Feathered for flight into sunrise or sunset, for
  eastward or west,
Fledged for the flight everlasting, but held
  yet warm to thy breast.

Gather it close to thee, song-bird or storm-
  bearer, eagle or dove,   10
Lift it to sunward, a beacon beneath to the
  beacon above,
Green as our hope in it, white as our faith in
  it, red as our love.

Thunder and splendor of lightning are hid in
  the folds of it furled;
Who shall unroll it but thou, as thy bolt to
  be handled and hurled,
Out of whose lips is the honey, whose bosom
  the milk of the world?   15

Out of thine hands hast thou fed us with
  pasture of color and song;
Glory and beauty by birthright to thee as
  thy garments belong;
Out of thine hands thou shalt give us as
  surely deliverance from wrong.

Out of thine eyes thou hast shed on us love
  as a lamp in our night,
Wisdom a lodestar to ships, and remembrance
  a flame-colored light;   20
Out of thine eyes thou shalt show us as surely
  the sundawn of right.

Turn to us, speak to us, Italy, mother, but
  once and a word,
None shall not follow thee, none shall not
  serve thee, not one that has heard;
Twice hast thou spoken a message, and time
  is athirst for the third.

Kingdom and empire of peoples thou hadst,
  and thy lordship made one   25
North sea and south sea and east men and
  west men that look on the sun;
Spirit was in thee and counsel, when soul in
  the nations was none.

Banner and beacon thou wast to the centuries of storm-wind and foam,

---

Cor Cordium. The title means *Heart of Hearts.* These are the words inscribed upon Shelley's tomb in Rome; they were suggested by Leigh Hunt, Shelley's friend.

The Song of the Standard. This poem is addressed to Italy with her flag of three colors—red, white, and green. Although the country had won its freedom and was set up as a limited monarchy under Victor Emmanuel, the first king of Italy (1861-78), Swinburne still cherished the idea of an Italian republic.

4. **gonfalon,** an ensign or standard hung from a crosspiece or frame instead of from a staff.

24. **Twice . . . message.** The first time (lines 25-27) was when Rome exercised sovereignty over the nations of the ancient world. The second (lines 28-30) was when Rome, through the Renaissance, saved Europe from the chaos of the Dark Ages.

Ages that clashed in the dark with each other,
   and years without home;
Empress and prophetess wast thou, and what
   wilt thou now be, O Rome? 30

Ah, by the faith and the hope and the love
   that have need of thee now,
Shines not thy face with the forethought of
   freedom, and burns not thy brow?
Who is against her but all men? and who is
   beside her but thou?

Art thou not better than all men? and where
   shall she turn but to thee?
Lo, not a breath, not a beam, not a beacon
   from midland to sea; 35
Freedom cries out for a sign among nations,
   and none will be free.

England in doubt of her, France in despair of
   her, all without heart —
Stand on her side in the vanward of ages, and
   strike on her part!
Strike but one stroke for the love of her love
   of thee, sweet that thou art!

Take in thy right hand thy banner, a strong
   staff fit for thine hand; 40
Forth at the light of it lifted shall foul things
   flock from the land;
Faster than stars from the sun shall they fly,
   being lighter than sand.

Green thing to green in the summer makes
   answer, and rose-tree to rose;
Lily by lily the year becomes perfect; and
   none of us knows
What thing is fairest of all things on earth as
   it brightens and blows. 45

This thing is fairest in all time of all things,
   in all time is best —
Freedom, that made thee, our mother, and
   suckled her sons at thy breast;
Take to thy bosom the nations, and there
   shall the world come to rest. (1871)

"NON DOLET"

It does not hurt. She looked along the knife
  Smiling, and watched the thick drops mix
    and run
  Down the sheer blade; not that which had
    been done

"Non Dolet." The title means *It Does Not Hurt.* When
Pætus Cæcina, who was ordered by Claudius I, emperor of
Rome (41-54 A.D.), to kill himself, hesitated to strike the blow,
his wife Arria seized the dagger, plunged it into her own
breast, and handed the bloody weapon to her husband, saying: "Pæte, non dolet." The incident is mentioned by Pliny,
Letter 316, 6.

Could hurt the sweet sense of the Roman
  wife, 4
But that which was to do yet ere the strife
  Could end for each forever, and the sun;
Nor was the palm yet, nor was peace yet
   won,
While pain had power upon her husband's life.

It does not hurt, Italia. Thou art more
  Than bride to bridegroom; how shalt thou
   not take 10
  The gift love's blood has reddened for thy
   sake?
Was not thy lifeblood given for us before?
And if love's heartblood can avail thy need,
And thou not die, how should it hurt
  indeed? (1871)

THE OBLATION

Ask nothing more of me, sweet;
  All I can give you I give.
    Heart of my heart, were it more,
More would be laid at your feet —
    Love that should help you to live, 5
    Song that should spur you to soar.

All things were nothing to give,
  Once to have sense of you more,
    Touch you and taste of you, sweet,
Think you and breathe you and live, 10
    Swept of your wings as they soar,
    Trodden by chance of your feet.

I that have love and no more
  Give you but love of you, sweet.
    He that hath more, let him give; 15
He that hath wings, let him soar;
    Mine is the heart at your feet
    Here, that must love you to live.
      (1871)

From *TRISTRAM OF LYONESSE*

PRELUDE: TRISTRAM AND ISEULT

Love, that is first and last of all things made,
The light that has the living world for shade,
The spirit that for temporal veil has on
The souls of all men woven in unison,
One fiery raiment with all lives inwrought 5
And lights of sunny and starry deed and
  thought,
And alway through new act and passion new
Shines the divine same body and beauty
  through,
The body spiritual of fire and light
That is to worldly noon as noon to night; 10

The Oblation. This poem is addressed to Liberty.
Tristram of Lyonesse. See Critical Notes.

Love, that is flesh upon the spirit of man
And spirit within the flesh whence breath
   began;
Love, that keeps all the choir of lives in
   chime;
Love, that is blood within the veins of time;
That wrought the whole world without stroke
   of hand,   15
Shaping the breadth of sea, the length of land,
And with the pulse and motion of his breath
Through the great heart of the earth strikes
   life and death,
The sweet twain chords that make the sweet
   tune live
Through day and night of things alternative,
Through silence and through sound of stress
   and strife,   21
And ebb and flow of dying death and life;
Love, that sounds loud or light in all men's
   ears,
Whence all men's eyes take fire from sparks
   of tears,
That binds on all men's feet or chains or
   wings;   25
Love, that is root and fruit of terrene things;
Love, that the whole world's waters shall not
   drown,
The whole world's fiery forces not burn down;
Love, that what time his own hands guard
   his head
The whole world's wrath and strength shall
   not strike dead;   30
Love, that if once his own hands make his
   grave
The whole world's pity and sorrow shall not
   save;
Love, that for very life shall not be sold,
Nor bought nor bound with iron nor with
   gold;
So strong that heaven, could love bid heaven
   farewell,   35
Would turn to fruitless and unflowering hell;
So sweet that hell, to hell could love be given,
Would turn to splendid and sonorous heaven;
Love that is fire within thee and light above,
And lives by grace of nothing but of love;   40
Through many and lovely thoughts and much
   desire
Led these twain to the life of tears and fire;
Through many and lovely days and much
   delight
Led these twain to the lifeless life of night.
   Yea, but what then? albeit all this were
   thus,   45
And soul smote soul and left it ruinous,
And love led love as eyeless men lead
   men,

Through chance by chance to deathward —
   ah, what then?
Hath love not likewise led them further
   yet,
Out through the years where memories rise
   and set,   50
Some large as suns, some moon-like warm
   and pale,
Some starry-sighted, some through clouds
   that sail
Seen as red flame through spectral float of
   fume,
Each with the blush of its own special bloom
On the fair face of its own colored light,   55
Distinguishable in all the host of night,
Divisible from all the radiant rest
And separable in splendor? Hath the best
Light of love's all, of all that burn and move,
A better heaven than heaven is? Hath not
   love   60
Made for all these their sweet particular air
To shine in, their own beams and names to
   bear,
Their ways to wander and their wards to keep,
Till story and song and glory and all things
   sleep?
Hath he not plucked from death of lovers
   dead   65
Their musical soft memories, and kept red
The rose of their remembrance in men's eyes,
The sunsets of their stories in his skies,
The blush of their dead blood in lips that
   speak
Of their dead lives, and in the listener's cheek
That trembles with the kindling pity lit   71
In gracious hearts for some sweet fever-fit,
A fiery pity enkindled of pure thought
By tales that make their honey out of naught,
The faithless faith that lives without belief   75
Its light life through, the griefless ghost of
   grief?
Yea, as warm night refashions the sear blood
In storm-struck petal or in sun-struck bud,
With tender hours and tempering dew to cure
The hunger and thirst of day's distemperature
And ravin of the dry discoloring hours,   81
Hath he not bid relume their flameless flowers
With summer fire and heat of lamping song,
And bid the short-lived things, long dead, live
   long,   84
And thought remake their wan funereal fames,
And the sweet shining signs of women's names
That mark the months out and the weeks
   anew
He moves in changeless change of seasons
   through
To fill the days up of his dateless year

---

26. **terrene,** earthly.   42. **these twain,** Tristram and Iseult.

81. **ravin,** ravenous hunger. 83. **lamping,** lighting, illuminating. 89. **dateless year,** eternity.

Flame from Queen Helen to Queen Guene-
    vere? 90
For first of all the sphery signs whereby
Love severs light from darkness, and most
    high,
In the white front of January there glows
The rose-red sign of Helen like a rose;
And gold-eyed as the shore-flower shelterless
Whereon the sharp-breathed sea blows bitter-
    ness, 96
A storm-star that the seafarers of love
Strain their wind-wearied eyes for glimpses of,
Shoots keen through February's gray frost
    and damp
The lamplike star of Hero for a lamp; 100
The star that Marlowe sang into our skies
With mouth of gold, and morning in his eyes;
And in clear March across the rough blue sea
The signal sapphire of Alcyone
Makes bright the blown brows of the wind-
    foot year; 105
And shining like a sunbeam-smitten tear
Full ere it fall, the fair next sign in sight
Burns opal-wise with April-colored light
When air is quick with song and rain and
    flame,
My birth-month star that in love's heaven
    hath name 110
Iseult, a light of blossom and beam and
    shower,
My singing sign that makes the song-tree
    flower;
Next like a pale and burning pearl beyond
The rose-white sphere of flower-named Rosa-
    mond
Signs the sweet head of Maytime; and for
    June 115
Flares like an angered and storm-reddening
    moon
Her signal sphere, whose Carthaginian pyre
Shadowed her traitor's flying sail with fire;
Next, glittering as the wine-bright jacinth-
    stone,

A star south-risen that first to music shone,
The keen girl-star of golden Juliet bears 121
Light northward to the month whose fore-
    head wears
Her name for flower upon it, and his trees
Mix their deep English song with Veronese;
And like an awful sovereign chrysolite 125
Burning, the supreme fire that blinds the
    night,
The hot gold head of Venus kissed by Mars,
A sun-flower among small spheréd flowers of
    stars,
The light of Cleopatra fills and burns
The hollow of heaven whence ardent August
    yearns; 130
And fixed and shining as the sister-shed
Sweet tears for Phæthon disorbed and dead,
The pale bright autumn's amber-colored
    sphere,
That through September sees the saddening
    year
As love sees change through sorrow, hath to
    name 135
Francesca's; and the star that watches flame
The embers of the harvest overgone
Is Thisbe's, slain of love in Babylon,
Set in the golden girdle of sweet signs
A blood-bright ruby; last save one light shines
An eastern wonder of sphery chrysopras, 141
The star that made men mad, Angelica's;
And latest named and lordliest, with a sound
Of swords and harps in heaven that ring it
    round,
Last love-light and last love-song of the year's
Gleams like a glorious emerald Guenevere's.
These are the signs wherethrough the year
    sees move,
Full of the sun, the sun-god which is love,
A fiery body blood-red from the heart
Outward, with fire-white wings made wide
    apart, 150
That close not and unclose not, but upright

---

90. **Flame.** The construction is: Hath he not bid . . . the sweet signs of women's names . . . flame from, etc. Supply *that* before line 88; it refers to *months* and *weeks*. **Queen Helen**, beautiful Helen of Troy, of Greek mythology. **Queen Guenevere.** See *Idylls of the King*, p. 123, and Critical Notes. 91. **sphery signs**, the signs of the zodiac. Swinburne assigns a heroine to each sign. 100. **Hero**, a priestess of Aphrodite (Venus) in the city of Sestos, on the Hellespont; she was loved by Leander, who swam the Hellespont nightly to see her. Marlowe treated the theme in his *Hero and Leander*. 104. **Alcyone**, Halcyone, the daughter of Æolus, god of the winds. When Halcyone learned that her husband Ceyx was drowned, she threw herself into the sea and was changed into a kingfisher. 105. **wind-foot**, swiftly passing. 110. **My . . . star.** Swinburne was born in April. 111. **Iseult.** This Iseult was the wife of King Mark, of Cornwall. See Arnold's *Tristram and Iseult* and note, p. 458. 114. **Rosamond.** Rosamond Clifford, the mistress of Henry II (1154-89), said to have been slain or forced to drink poison by Henry's jealous queen, Eleanor, at Woodstock in 1177. 117. **Her signal sphere.** After Dido, queen of Carthage, was deserted by Æneas, she ascended a funeral pyre and was burned. The story is told in Virgil's *Æneid*, Book 4.

121. **Juliet**, of Shakespeare's *Romeo and Juliet*. The scene of the drama is laid in Verona, Italy (line 124). 125. **chryso-lite**, a yellowish or greenish crystal. 127. **Venus**, goddess of love. **Mars**, god of war. Venus and Mars stand for Cleopatra and Antony. 129. **Cleopatra.** See note on *Laus Veneris*, 186, p. 677. 132. **Phæthon**, son of Phœbus Apollo, god of the sun. To prove his divine origin, Phæthon was permitted for one day to drive the chariot of the sun, but he lost control of the horses and fell into the river Eridanus. His sisters, the Heliades, lamenting his fate, were turned into poplar trees, and their tears, which continued to flow, became amber as they dropped into the stream. 136. **Francesca**, Francesca da Rimini (13th century). She fell in love with her husband's brother Paolo and both lovers were killed by the husband. 138. **Thisbe**, the beautiful girl loved by Pyramus, of Babylon. Arriving first at the appointed meeting place, Thisbe, frightened by a lion, fled and dropped her veil, which the lion besmeared with blood. Pyramus, thinking that Thisbe was devoured, slew himself, and Thisbe returning to the scene stabbed herself also. 141. **chrysopras**, an apple-green variety of quartz. 142. **Angelica**, the fickle lover of Orlando, one of the great heroes of medieval romance. Because she did not return his love, Orlando went mad.

Steered without wind by their own light and
    might
Sweep through the flameless fire of air that
    rings
From heaven to heaven with thunder of
    wheels and wings
And antiphones of motion-molded rime   155
Through spaces out of space and timeless
    time.
    So shine above dead chance and conquered
      change
The spheréd signs, and leave without their
    range
Doubt and desire, and hope with fear for wife,
Pale pains, and pleasures long worn out of
    life.   160
Yea, even the shadows of them spiritless,
Through the dim door of sleep that seem to
    press,
Forms without form, a piteous people and
    blind,
Men and no men, whose lamentable kind
The shadow of death and shadow of life
    compel   165
Through semblances of heaven and false-
    faced hell,
Through dreams of light and dreams of dark-
    ness tost
On waves innavigable, are these so lost?
Shapes that wax pale and shift in swift
    strange wise,
Void faces with unspeculative eyes,   170
Dim things that gaze and glare, dead mouths
    that move,
Featureless heads discrowned of hate and
    love,
Mockeries and masks of motion and mute
    breath,
Leavings of life, the superflux of death —
If these things and no more than these things
    be   175
Left when man ends or changes, who can see?
Or who can say with what more subtle sense
Their subtler natures taste in air less dense
A life less thick and palpable than ours,
Warmed with faint fires and sweetened with
    dead flowers   180
And measured by low music? how time fares
In that wan time-forgotten world of theirs,
Their pale poor world too deep for sun or star
To live in, where the eyes of Helen are,
And hers who made as God's own eyes to
    shine   185
The eyes that met them of the Florentine,
Wherein the godhead thence transfigured lit
All time for all men with the shadow of it?

Ah, and these, too, felt on them as God's
    grace
The pity and glory of this man's breathing
    face;   190
For these, too, these my lovers, these my
    twain,
Saw Dante, saw God visible by pain,
With lips that thundered and with feet that
    trod
Before men's eyes incognizable God;
Saw love and wrath and light and night and
    fire   195
Live with one life and at one mouth respire,
And in one golden sound their whole soul
    heard
Sounding, one sweet immitigable word.
    They have the night, who had like us the
      day;
We, whom day binds, shall have the night as
    they.   200
We, from the fetters of the light unbound,
Healed of our wound of living, shall sleep
    sound.
All gifts but one the jealous God may keep
From our soul's longing, one he cannot —
    sleep.
This, though he grudge all other grace to
    prayer,   205
This grace his closed hand cannot choose but
    spare.
This, though his ear be sealed to all that live,
Be it lightly given or loathly, God must give.
We, as the men whose name on earth is none,
We too shall surely pass out of the sun;   210
Out of the sound and eyeless light of things,
Wide as the stretch of life's time-wandering
    wings,
Wide as the naked world and shadowless,
And long-lived as the world's own weariness.
Us too, when all the fires of time are cold, 215
The heights shall hide us and the depths shall
    hold.
Us too, when all the tears of time are dry,
The night shall lighten from her tearless eye.
Blind is the day and eyeless all its light,
But the large unbewildered eye of night   220
Hath sense and speculation; and the sheer
Limitless length of lifeless life and clear,
The timeless space wherein the brief worlds
    move
Clothed with light life and fruitful with light
    love,
With hopes that threaten, and with fears that
    cease,   225
Past fear and hope, hath in it only peace.

---

155. **antiphones,** anthems or psalms sung alternately by
parts of a choir. 185. **And hers,** a reference to Beatrice,
loved by Dante, the Florentine. She influenced the course of
his later life.

191-2. **these . . . Saw Dante.** Tristram and Isolde are
represented in the fifth canto of Dante's *Inferno* as sharing
the fate of a multitude of guilty lovers. Dante sees them
as they are tossed about in the dark air by the blasts of hell.
196. **respire,** breathe.

Yet of these lives inlaid with hopes and
  fears,
Spun fine as fire and jeweled thick with
  tears,
These lives made out of loves that long since
  were,
Lives wrought as ours of earth and burning
  air,   230
Fugitive flame, and water of secret springs,
And clothed with joys and sorrows as with
  wings,
Some yet are good, if aught be good, to save
Some while from washing wreck and wrecking
  wave.
Was such not theirs, the twain I take, and
  give   235
Out of my life to make their dead life live
Some days of mine, and blow my living breath
Between dead lips forgotten even of death?
So many and many of old have given my
  twain
Love and live song and honey-hearted pain,
Whose root is sweetness and whose fruit is
  sweet,   241
So many and with such joy have tracked
  their feet,
What should I do to follow? Yet I too,
I have the heart to follow, many or few
Be the feet gone before me; for the way,   245
Rose-red with remnant roses of the day
Westward, and eastward white with stars
  that break,
Between the green and foam is fair to take
For any sail the sea-wind steers for me
From morning into morning, sea to sea.   250
                 (*1869*; *1871*)

A VISION OF SPRING IN WINTER

O tender time that love thinks long to see,
  Sweet foot of spring that with her footfall
    sows
  Late snowlike flowery leavings of the
    snows,
Be not too long irresolute to be;
O mother-month, where have they hidden
  thee?   5
  Out of the pale time of the flowerless rose
I reach my heart out toward the springtime
  lands,
  I stretch my spirit forth to the fair hours,
    The purplest of the prime;
I lean my soul down over them, with hands 10

Made wide to take the ghostly growths of
  flowers;
  I send my love back to the lovely time.

Where has the greenwood hid thy gracious
  head?
  Veiled with what visions while the gray
    world grieves,
  Or muffled with what shadows of green
    leaves,   15
What warm intangible green shadows spread
To sweeten the sweet twilight for thy bed?
  What sleep enchants thee? what delight
    deceives?
Where the deep dreamlike dew before the
  dawn
  Feels not the fingers of the sunlight yet   20
  Its silver web unweave,
Thy footless ghost on some unfooted lawn
  Whose air the unrisen sunbeams fear to
    fret
    Lives a ghost's life of daylong dawn and
    eve.

Sunrise it sees not, neither set of star,   25
  Large nightfall, nor imperial plenilune,
  Nor strong sweet shape of the full-breasted
    noon;
But where the silver-sandaled shadows are,
Too soft for arrows of the sun to mar,
  Moves with the mild gait of an ungrown
    moon: 30
Hard overhead the half-lit crescent swims,
  The tender-colored night draws hardly
    breath,
    The light is listening;
They watch the dawn of slender-shapen
  limbs,
  Virginal, born again of doubtful death, 35
  Chill foster-father of the weanling spring.

As sweet desire of day before the day,
  As dreams of love before the true love born,
  From the outer edge of winter overworn
The ghost arisen of May before the May   40
Takes through dim air her unawakened way,
  The gracious ghost of morning risen ere
    morn.
With little unblown breasts and child-eyed
  looks
  Following, the very maid, the girl-child
    spring,
    Lifts windward her bright brows,   45
Dips her light feet in warm and moving
  brooks,
And kindles with her own mouth's coloring
    The fearful firstlings of the plumeless
    boughs.

239. So many. The love of Tristram and Iseult was a
favorite theme of medieval romance. It was treated by
Malory, by Tennyson, and by Arnold; also by Wagner in
his opera *Tristan and Isolde* (1865).
A Vision of Spring in Winter. Swinburne had a very
great love for spring. **5. mother-month,** April, the month
of Swinburne's birth.

26. plenilune, the time of full moon.

I seek thee sleeping, and awhile I see,
Fair face that art not, how thy maiden
breath   50
Shall put at last the deadly days to death
And fill the fields and fire the woods with thee
And seaward hollows where my feet would
be
When heaven shall hear the word that
April saith
To change the cold heart of the weary time, 55
To stir and soften all the time to tears,
Tears joyfuller than mirth;
As even to May's clear height the young days
climb
With feet not swifter than those fair first
years
Whose flowers revive not with thy flow-
ers on earth.   60

I would not bid thee, though I might, give
back
One good thing youth has given and borne
away;
I crave not any comfort of the day
That is not, nor on time's retrodden track
Would turn to meet the white-robed hours or
black   65
That long since left me on their mortal way;
Nor light nor love that has been, nor the
breath
That comes with morning from the sun to
be
And sets light hope on fire;
No fruit, no flower thought once too fair for
death,   70
No flower nor hour once fallen from life's
green tree,
No leaf once plucked or once fulfilled
desire.

The morning song beneath the stars that fled
With twilight through the moonless moun-
tain air,
While youth with burning lips and wreath-
less hair   75
Sang toward the sun that was to crown his
head,
Rising; the hopes that triumphed and fell
dead,
The sweet swift eyes and songs of hours
that were;
These may'st thou not give back forever;
these,
As at the sea's heart all her wrecks lie
waste,   80
Lie deeper than the sea;
But flowers thou may'st, and winds, and
hours of ease,
And all its April to the world thou may'st
Give back, and half my April back to me.
                                          (1875)

A FORSAKEN GARDEN

In a coign of the cliff between lowland and
highland,
At the sea-down's edge between windward
and lee,
Walled round with rocks as an inland island,
The ghost of a garden fronts the sea.
A girdle of brushwood and thorn encloses   5
The steep square slope of the blossomless
bed
Where the weeds that grew green from the
graves of its roses
Now lie dead.

The fields fall southward, abrupt and broken,
To the low last edge of the long lone
land.   10
If a step should sound or a word be spoken,
Would a ghost not rise at the strange
guest's hand?
So long have the gray bare walks lain guest-
less,
Through branches and briars if a man make
way,
He shall find no life, but the sea-wind's, rest-
less   15
Night and day.

The dense hard passage is blind and stifled
That crawls by a track none turn to climb
To the strait waste place that the years have
rifled
Of all but the thorns that are touched not
of time.   20
The thorns he spares when the rose is taken;
The rocks are left when he wastes the plain.
The wind that wanders, the weeds wind-
shaken,
These remain.

Not a flower to be pressed of the foot that
falls not;   25
As the heart of a dead man the seed-plots
are dry;
From the thicket of thorns whence the night-
ingale calls not,
Could she call, there were never a rose to
reply.
Over the meadows that blossom and wither
Wings but the note of a sea-bird's song;   30
Only the sun and the rain come hither
All year long.

The sun burns sear and the rain dishevels
One gaunt bleak blossom of scentless
breath.

A Forsaken Garden. The scene of this poem is East Dene,
on the Isle of Wight, where Swinburne spent much of his
youth.
1. **coign**, corner, projection.

Only the wind here hovers and revels   35
In a round where life seems barren as death.
Here there was laughing of old, there was
  weeping,
Haply, of lovers none ever will know,
Whose eyes went seaward a hundred sleeping
  Years ago.   40

Heart handfast in heart as they stood, "Look
  thither,"
  Did he whisper? "look forth from the
  flowers to the sea;
For the foam-flowers endure when the rose-
  blossoms wither,
  And men that love lightly may die — but
  we?"
And the same wind sang and the same waves
  whitened,   45
  And or ever the garden's last petals were
  shed,
In the lips that had whispered, the eyes that
  had lightened,
  Love was dead.

Or they loved their life through, and then
  went whither?
  And were one to the end — but what end
  who knows?   50
Love deep as the sea as a rose must wither,
  As the rose-red seaweed that mocks the
  rose.
Shall the dead take thought for the dead to
  love them?
  What love was ever as deep as a grave?
They are loveless now as the grass above them
  Or the wave.   56

All are at one now, roses and lovers,
  Not known of the cliffs and the fields and
  the sea.
Not a breath of the time that has been hovers
  In the air now soft with a summer to be. 60
Not a breath shall there sweeten the seasons
  hereafter
  Of the flowers or the lovers that laugh now
  or weep,
When as they that are free now of weeping
  and laughter
  We shall sleep.

Here death may deal not again forever;   65
  Here change may come not till all change
  end.
From the graves they have made they shall
  rise up never,
  Who have left naught living to ravage and
  rend.
Earth, stones, and thorns of the wild ground
  growing,
  While the sun and the rain live, these shall
  be;   70

Till a last wind's breath upon all these blowing
  Roll the sea.

Till the slow sea rise and the sheer cliff
  crumble,
  Till terrace and meadow the deep gulfs
  drink,
Till the strength of the waves of the high
  tides humble   75
  The fields that lessen, the rocks that shrink,
Here now in his triumph where all things
  falter,
  Stretched out on the spoils that his own
  hand spread,
As a god self-slain on his own strange altar,
  Death lies dead.   80
  (1876)

A BALLAD OF DREAMLAND

I hid my heart in a nest of roses,
  Out of the sun's way, hidden apart;
In a softer bed than the soft white snow's
  is,
  Under the roses I hid my heart.
  Why would it sleep not? why should it
  start,   5
When never a leaf of the rose-tree stirred?
  What made sleep flutter his wings and part?
Only the song of a secret bird.

Lie still, I said, for the wind's wing closes,
  And mild leaves muffle the keen sun's
  dart;   10
Lie still, for the wind on the warm sea dozes,
  And the wind is unquieter yet than thou
  art.
  Does a thought in thee still as a thorn's
  wound smart?
Does the fang still fret thee of hope deferred?
  What bids the lids of thy sleep dispart?   15
Only the song of a secret bird.

The green land's name that a charm encloses,
  It never was writ in the traveler's chart,
And sweet on its trees as the fruit that grows
  is,
  It never was sold in the merchant's mart.
  The swallows of dreams through its dim
  fields dart,   21
And sleep's are the tunes in its tree-tops
  heard;
  No hound's note wakens the wildwood
  hart,
Only the song of a secret bird.

A Ballad of Dreamland. This lyric is generally regarded as
one of the best examples in English of the French *ballade*—a
poem composed of three stanzas of eight or ten lines each and
a concluding *envoi.* Each of the stanzas ends with the same
refrain, and only three or four rimes are used in the entire
poem.

In the world of dreams I have chosen my
    part,   25
  To sleep for a season and hear no word
Of true love's truth or of light love's art,
  Only the song of a secret bird.
                             (1876)

A LYKE-WAKE SONG

Fair of face, full of pride,
Sit ye down by a dead man's side.

Ye sang songs a' the day;
Sit down at night in the red worm's way.

Proud ye were a' day long;   5
Ye'll be but lean at evensong.

Ye had gowd kells on your hair;
Nae man kens what ye were.

Ye set scorn by the silken stuff;
Now the grave is clean enough.   10

Ye set scorn by the rubis ring;
Now the worm is a saft sweet thing.

Fine gold and blithe fair face,
Ye are come to a grimly place.

Gold hair and glad grey een,   15
Nae man kens if ye have been.   (1877)

A JACOBITE'S FAREWELL

1716

There's nae mair lands to tyne, my dear,
  And nae mair lives to gie;
Though a man think sair to live nae mair,
  There's but one day to die.

For a' things come and a' days gane,   5
  What needs ye rend your hair?
But kiss me till the morn's morrow,
  Then I'll kiss ye nae mair.

O lands are lost and life's losing,
  And what were they to gie?   10

Fu' mony a man gives all he can,
  But nae man else gives ye.

Our king wons ower the sea's water,
  And I in prison sair;
But I'll win out the morn's morrow,   15
  And ye'll see me nae mair.
                             (1877)

THE TYNESIDE WIDOW

There's mony a man loves land and life,
  Loves life and land and fee;
And mony a man loves fair women,
  But never a man loves me, my love,
  But never a man loves me.   5

O weel and weel for a' lovers,
  I wot weel may they be;
And weel and weel for a' fair maidens,
  But aye mair woe for me, my love,
  But aye mair woe for me.   10

O weel be wi' you, ye sma' flowers,
  Ye flowers and every tree;
And weel be wi' you, a' birdies,
  But teen and tears wi' me, my love,
  But teen and tears wi' me.   15

O weel be yours, my three brethren,
  And ever weel be ye,
Wi' deeds for doing and loves for wooing;
  But never a love for me, my love,
  But never a love for me.   20

And weel be yours, my seven sisters,
  And good love-days to see,
And long life-days and true lovers;
  But never a day for me, my love,
  But never a day for me.   25

Good times wi' you, ye bauld riders,
  By the hieland and the lee;
And by the leeland and by the hieland
  It's weary times wi' me, my love,
  It's weary times wi' me.   30

Good days wi' you, ye good sailors,
  Sail in and out the sea;
And by the beaches and by the reaches
  It's heavy days wi' me, my love,
  It's heavy days wi' me.   35

I had his kiss upon my mouth,
  His bairn upon my knee;
I would my soul and body were twain,

A Lyke-Wake Song. A lyke-wake is a watch over a dead
body.
7. **gowd kells**, gold hairnets.
A Jacobite's Farewell. The Jacobites were partisans of
James II of England. See Aytoun's *The Old Scottish Cavalier*,
page 388. The date 1716, linked with this poem, marked
the end of the unsuccessful attempt to secure the English
throne for James Stuart (1688-1766), known as the Old Pretender. He was the son of James II. Swinburne belonged to
a family noted for its Jacobite sympathies, and he was proud
of the sacrifices made by his ancestors for the cause of the
Stuarts.
1. **to tyne**, to lose.

13. **wons**, dwells. The Pretender lived for a while in
France.
The Tyneside Widow. The Tyne is a river in Northumber-
land; it was the scene of frequent border strife.
2. **fee**, money. 14. **teen**, sorrow, grief. 27. **hieland
and the lee**, highland and the lowland. 33. **reaches**,
extended portions of land or water.

And the bairn and the kiss wi' me, my love,
And the bairn and the kiss wi' me.   40

The bairn down in the mools, my dear,
  O saft and saft lies she;
I would the mools were ower my head,
  And the young bairn fast wi' me, my love,
  And the young bairn fast wi' me.   45

The father under the faem, my dear,
  O sound and sound sleeps he;
I would the faem were ower my face,
  And the father lay by me, my love,
  And the father lay by me.   50

I would the faem were ower my face,
  Or the mools on my ee-bree;
And waking-time with a' lovers,
  But sleeping-time wi' me, my love,
  But sleeping-time wi' me.   55

I would the mools were meat in my mouth,
  The saut faem in my ee;
And the land-worm and the water-worm
  To feed fu' sweet on me, my love,
  To feed fu' sweet on me.   60

My life is sealed with a seal of love,
  And locked with love for a key;
And I lie wrang and I wake lang,
  But ye tak' nae thought for me, my love,
  But ye tak' nae thought for me.   65

We were weel fain of love, my dear,
  O fain and fain were we;
It was weel with a' the weary world,
  But O, sae weel wi' me, my love,
  But O, sae weel wi' me.   70

We were nane ower mony to sleep, my dear,
  I wot we were but three;
And never a bed in the weary world
  For my bairn and my dear and me, my love,
  For my bairn and my dear and me.   75
         (1877)

A BALLAD OF FRANÇOIS VILLON

PRINCE OF ALL BALLAD-MAKERS

Bird of the bitter bright gray golden morn
Scarce risen upon the dusk of dolorous
    years,

First of us all and sweetest singer born
  Whose far shrill note the world of new men
    hears
Cleave the cold shuddering shade as twi-
    light clears;   5
When song new-born put off the old world's
    attire
And felt its tune on her changed lips ex-
    pire,
  Writ foremost on the roll of them that
    came
Fresh girt for service of the latter lyre,
  Villon, our sad bad glad mad brother's
    name!   10

Alas the joy, the sorrow, and the scorn,
  That clothed thy life with hopes and sins
    and fears,
And gave thee stones for bread and tares for
    corn
  And plume-plucked gaol-birds for thy
    starveling peers
Till death clipped close their flight with
    shameful shears;   15
Till shifts came short and loves were hard
    to hire,
When lilt of song nor twitch of twangling wire
  Could buy thee bread or kisses; when light
    fame
Spurned like a ball and haled through brake
    and briar,
  Villon, our sad bad glad mad brother's
    name!   20

Poor splendid wings so frayed and soiled and
    torn!
  Poor kind wild eyes so dashed with light
    quick tears!
Poor perfect voice, most blithe when most
    forlorn,
  That rings athwart the sea whence no man
    steers
Like joy-bells crossed with death-bells in
    our ears!   25
What far delight has cooled the fierce de-
    sire
That like some ravenous bird was strong to
    tire
  On that frail flesh and soul consumed with
    flame,
But left more sweet than roses to respire,
  Villon, our sad bad glad mad brother's
    name?   30

---

41. **mools**, molds, earth. 46. **faem**, foam of the sea.
52. **ee-bree**, eyebrow. 63. **I lie wrang**, I lie tortured on
my bed.
  A Ballad of François Villon. François Villon (1431-63?)
was a French poet and vagabond, famous for his *ballades*.
On the *ballade* form see note on *A Ballad of Dreamland*, p. 723.
See also Rossetti's *The Ballad of Dead Ladies* and note, p. 523.
  1. **golden morn**, the Renaissance, which succeeded the
"dusk" of the Middle Ages.

6. **song new-born.** Villon is regarded as the first and one
of the greatest of the French lyric poets of the modern school.
His verse, characterized by polish, raciness, and intense sub-
jectivity, had great influence. 13. **stones for bread.** See
note on *Hymn of Man*, 104, p. 711. **corn**, wheat. See note
on *Dolores*, 438, p. 696. 14. **gaol-birds . . . peers.** For a
number of years Villon was the leader of a band of vagabonds
and thieves that infested the streets of Paris. He was arrested
and imprisoned several times for robbery. 16. **shifts came
short**, his expedients for a livelihood were exhausted. 29.
respire, breathe.

ENVOI

Prince of sweet songs made out of tears and
    fire,
A harlot was thy nurse, a god thy sire;
    Shame soiled thy song, and song assoiled
      thy shame.
But from thy feet now death has washed the
    mire,   34
Love reads out first at head of all our quire,
    Villon, our sad bad glad mad brother's
      name.   (1877)

CHILD'S SONG

What is gold worth, say,
Worth for work or play,
Worth to keep or pay,
Hide or throw away,
    Hope about or fear?   5
What is love worth, pray?
    Worth a tear?

Golden on the mold
Lie the dead leaves rolled
Of the wet woods old,   10
Yellow leaves and cold,
    Woods without a dove;
Gold is worth but gold;
    Love's worth love.   (1878)

TRIADS

1

The word of the sun to the sky,
The word of the wind to the sea,
The word of the moon to the night,
    What may it be?

The sense of the flower to the fly,   5
The sense of the bird to the tree,
The sense of the cloud to the light,
    Who can tell me?

The song of the fields to the kye,
The song of the lime to the bee,   10
The song of the depth to the height,
    Who knows all three?

2

The message of April to May,
    That May sends on into June
And June gives out to July   15
    For birthday boon;

The delight of the dawn in the day,
    The delight of the day in the noon,
The delight of a song in a sigh
    That breaks the tune;   20

The secret of passing away,
    The cast of the change of the moon,
None knows it with ear or with eye,
    But all will soon.

3

The live wave's love for the shore,   25
    The shore's for the wave as it dies,
The love of the thunder-fire
    That sears the skies —

We shall know not though life wax hoar,
    Till all life, spent into sighs,   30
Burn out as consumed with desire
    Of death's strange eyes;

Till the secret be secret no more
    In the light of one hour as it flies,
Be the hour as of suns that expire   35
    Or suns that rise.   (1878)

THALASSIUS

Upon the flowery forefront of the year,
One wandering by the gray-green April sea
Found on a reach of shingle and shallower
    sand
Inlaid with starrier glimmering jewelry
Left for the sun's love and the light wind's
    cheer   5
Along the foam-flowered strand,
Breeze-brightened, something nearer sea than
    land
Though the last shoreward blossom-fringe
    was near,
A babe asleep with flower-soft face that
    gleamed
To sun and seaward as it laughed and
    dreamed,   10
Too sure of either love for either's fear,
Albeit so birdlike slight and light, it seemed
Nor man nor mortal child of man, but fair
As even its twin-born tenderer spray-flowers
    were,
That the wind scatters like an Oread's hair. 15

For when July strewed fire on earth and sea
The last time ere that year,

Thalassius. The title means *From the Sea* and refers to the
origin of the child, the central figure in the poem. *Thalassius*
is intimately autobiographical. It portrays the early influences that shaped the life of Swinburne and traces the
progress of his spiritual development. Cf. the Prelude to
Songs before Sunrise, p. 703. See Critical Notes.
3. **shingle,** stony seashore. 15. **Oread's hair.** The
Oreads were mountain nymphs.

---

32. **harlot . . . sire.** Many poets have sprung from
humble origins, but few have shown so startling a combination of artistic fineness and baseness of life.
Triads. A triad is a group of three things closely related.
9. **kye,** cows.

Out of the flame of morn Cymothoë
Beheld one brighter than the sunbright sphere
Move toward her from its fieriest heart,
   whence trod   20
The live sun's very god,
Across the foam-bright waterways that are
As heavenlier heavens with star for answering
   star,
And on her eyes and hair and maiden mouth
Felt a kiss falling fierier than the South, 25
And heard above afar
A noise of songs and wind-enamored wings
And lutes and lyres of milder and mightier
   strings,
And round the resonant radiance of his car
Where depth is one with height,   30
Light heard as music, music seen as light,
And with that second moondawn of the
   spring's
That fosters the first rose,
A sun-child whiter than the sunlit snows
Was born out of the world of sunless things 35
That round the round earth flows and ebbs
   and flows.

But he that found the sea-flower by the sea
And took to foster like a graft of earth
Was born of man's most highest and heaven-
   liest birth,
Free-born as winds and stars and waves are
   free;   40
A warrior gray with glories more than years,
Though more of years than change the quick
   to dead
Had rained their light and darkness on his
   head;
A singer that in time's and memory's ears
Should leave such words to sing as all his
   peers   45
Might praise with hallowing heat of raptur-
   ous tears
Till all the days of human flight were fled.
And at his knees his fosterling was fed
Not with man's wine and bread
Nor mortal mother-milk of hopes and fears, 50
But food of deep memorial days long sped;
For bread with wisdom and with song for
   wine
Clear as the full calm's emerald hyaline.
And from his grave glad lips the boy would
   gather
Fine honey of song-notes goldener than gold,
More sweet than bees make of the breathing
   heather,   56
That he, as glad and bold,

Might drink as they, and keep his spirit from
   cold.
And the boy loved his laurel-laden hair
As his own father's risen on the eastern air, 60
And that less white brow-binding bayleaf
   bloom
More than all flowers his father's eyes re-
   lume;
And those high songs he heard,
More than all notes of any landward bird,
More than all sounds less free   65
Than the wind's quiring to the choral sea.

High things the high song taught him—
   how the breath
Too frail for life may be more strong than
   death;
And this poor flash of sense in life, that
   gleams
As a ghost's glory in dreams,   70
More stable than the world's own heart's
   root seems,
By that strong faith of lordliest love which
   gives
To death's own sightless-seeming eyes a light
Clearer, to death's bare bones a verier might,
Than shines or strikes from any man that
   lives.   75
How he that loves life overmuch shall die
The dog's death, utterly:
And he that much less loves it than he hates
All wrongdoing that is done
Anywhere always underneath the sun   80
Shall live a mightier life than time's or fate's.
One fairer thing he shewed him, and in might
More strong than day and night
Whose strengths build up time's towering
   period:
Yea, one thing stronger and more high than
   God,   85
Which if man had not, then should God not
   be:
And that was Liberty.
And gladly should man die to gain, he said,
Freedom; and gladlier, having lost, lie dead.
For man's earth was not, nor the sweet sea-
   waves   90
His, nor his own land, nor its very graves,
Except they bred not, bore not, hid not
   slaves:
But all of all that is,
Were one man free in body and soul, were
   his.

18. **Cymothoë,** a sea nymph. 21. **sun's very god,**
Phœbus Apollo. 37. **he that found,** etc. This has been
identified as Landor. See *In Memory of Walter Savage Landor,*
p. 691. 53. **hyaline,** a poetic term for the sea or for clear
atmosphere.

59. **laurel-laden,** crowned with the poet's laurel-wreath
of honor. 61. **bayleaf,** myrtle, used in crowning poets. 76.
he that . . . die. Cf. *Matthew,* 16:25.—"Whosoever will
save his life shall lose it; and whosoever will lose his life for
my sake shall find it." 88-89. **gladly . . . lie dead,** a free
translation of the Latin inscription written by Landor for
the Spanish patriots who died resisting the invasion of
Napoleon in the campaign of 1811-12.

And the song softened, even as heaven by
    night   95
Softens, from sunnier down to starrier light,
And with its moonbright breath
Blessed life for death's sake, and for life's
    sake death,
Till as the moon's own beam and breath con-
    fuse,
In one clear hueless haze of glimmering
    hues,   100
The sea's line and the land's line and the sky's,
And light for love of darkness almost dies,
As darkness only lives for light's dear love,
Whose hands the web of night is woven of;
So in that heaven of wondrous words were
    life   105
And death brought out of strife;
Yea, by that strong spell of serene increase
Brought out of strife to peace.

And the song lightened, as the wind at
    morn
Flashes, and even with lightning of the
    wind   110
Night's thick-spun web is thinned
And all its weft unwoven and overworn
Shrinks, as might love from scorn,
And as when wind and light on water and
    land
Leap as twin gods from heavenward hand in
    hand,   115
And with the sound and splendor of their
    leap
Strike darkness dead, and daunt the spirit of
    sleep,
And burn it up with fire;
So with the light that lightened from the
    lyre
Was all the bright heat in the child's heart
    stirred   120
And blown with blasts of music into flame
Till even his sense became
Fire, as the sense that fires the singing bird
Whose song calls night by name.
And in the soul within the sense began   125
The manlike passion of a godlike man,
And in the sense within the soul again
Thoughts that make men of gods and gods of
    men.

For love the high song taught him—love
    that turns
God's heart toward man as man's to God-
    ward; love   130
That life and death and life are fashioned of,
From the first breath that burns
Half-kindled on the flowerlike yeanling's lip,
So light and faint that life seems like to slip,
To that yet weaklier drawn   135
When sunset dies of night's devouring dawn.
But the man dying not wholly as all men dies

If aught be left of his in live men's eyes
Out of the dawnless dark of death to rise;
If aught of deed or word   140
Be seen for all time or of all time heard.
Love, that though body and soul were over-
    thrown
Should live for love's sake of itself alone,
Though spirit and flesh were one thing
    doomed and dead,
Not wholly annihilated.   145
Seeing even the hoariest ash-flake that the
    pyre
Drops, and forgets the thing was once afire
And gave its heart to feed the pile's full flame
Till its own heart its own heat overcame,
Outlives its own life, though by scarce a
    span,   150
As such men dying outlive themselves in man,
Outlive themselves forever; if the heat
Outburn the heart that kindled it, the sweet
Outlast the flower whose soul it was, and flit
Forth of the body of it   155
Into some new shape of a strange perfume
More potent than its light live spirit of bloom,
How shall not something of that soul relive,
That only soul that had such gifts to give
As lighten something even of all men's
    doom,   160
Even from the laboring womb,
Even to the seal set on the unopening tomb?
And these the loving light of song and love
Shall wrap and lap round and impend above,
Imperishable; and all springs born illume 165
Their sleep with brighter thoughts than wake
    the dove
To music, when the hillside winds resume
The marriage-song of heather-flower and
    broom
And all the joy thereof.

And hate the song too taught him—hate
    of all   170
That brings or holds in thrall
Of spirit or flesh, free-born ere God began,
The holy body and sacred soul of man.
And wheresoever a curse was or a chain,
A throne for torment or a crown for bane 175
Rose, molded out of poor men's molten pain,
There, said he, should man's heaviest hate be
    set
Inexorably, to faint not or forget
Till the last warmth bled forth of the last vein
In flesh that none should call a king's again,
Seeing wolves and dogs and birds that
    plague-strike air   181
Leave the last bone of all the carrion bare.

And hope the high song taught him—hope
    whose eyes
Can sound the seas unsoundable, the skies
Inaccessible of eyesight; that can see   185

What earth beholds not, hear what wind and
 sea
Hear not, and speak what all these crying in
 one
Can speak not to the sun.
For in her sovereign eyelight all things are
Clear as the closest seen and kindlier star 190
That marries morn and even and winter and
 spring
With one love's golden ring.
For she can see the days of man, the birth
Of good and death of evil things on earth
Inevitable and infinite, and sure 195
As present pain is, or herself is pure.
Yea, she can hear and see, beyond all things
That lighten from before Time's thunderous
 wings
Through the awful circle of wheel-winged
 periods,
The tempest of the twilight of all gods; 200
And higher than all the circling course they
 ran
The sundawn of the spirit that was man.

And fear the song too taught him—fear to
 be
Worthless the dear love of the wind and sea
That bred him fearless, like a sea-mew
 reared 205
In rocks of man's foot feared,
Where naught of wingless life may sing or
 shine.
Fear to wax worthless of that heaven he had
When all the life in all his limbs was glad,
And all the drops in all his veins were wine, 210
And all the pulses music; when his heart,
Singing, bade heaven and wind and sea bear
 part
In one live song's reiterance, and they bore;
Fear to go crownless of the flower he wore
When the winds loved him and the waters
 knew, 215
The blithest life that clove their blithe life
 through
With living limbs exultant, or held strife
More amorous than all dalliance aye anew
With the bright breath and strength of their
 large life,
With all strong wrath of all sheer winds that
 blew, 220
All glories of all storms of the air that fell
Prone, ineluctable,
With roar from heaven of revel, and with hue
As of a heaven turned hell.
For when the red blast of their breath had
 made 225
All heaven aflush with light more dire than
 shade,

He felt it in his blood and eyes and hair
Burn as if all the fires of the earth and air
Had laid strong hold upon his flesh, and stung
The soul behind it as with serpent's tongue,
Forked like the loveliest lightnings; nor could
 bear 231
But hardly, half distraught with strong
 delight,
The joy that like a garment wrapped him
 round
And lapped him over and under
With raiment of great light 235
And rapture of great sound
At every loud leap earthward of the thunder
From heaven's most furthest bound;
So seemed all heaven in hearing and in sight,
Alive and mad with glory and angry joy, 240
That something of its marvelous mirth and
 might
Moved even to madness, fledged as even for
 flight,
The blood and spirit of one but mortal boy.

So, clothed with love and fear that love
 makes great,
And armed with hope and hate, 245
He set first foot upon the spring-flowered
 ways
That all feet pass and praise.
And one dim dawn between the winter and
 spring,
In the sharp harsh wind harrying heaven and
 earth
To put back April that had borne his birth 250
From sunward on her sunniest shower-struck
 wing,
With tears and laughter for the dew-dropped
 thing,
Slight as indeed a dew-drop, by the sea
One met him lovelier than all men may be,
God-featured, with god's eyes; and in their
 might 255
Somewhat that drew men's own to mar their
 sight,
Even of all eyes drawn toward him; and his
 mouth
Was as the very rose of all men's youth,
One rose of all the rose-beds in the world.
But round his brows the curls were snakes
 that curled, 260
And like his tongue a serpent's; and his voice
Speaks death, and bids rejoice.
Yet then he spake no word, seeming as dumb,
A dumb thing mild and hurtless; nor at first
From his bowed eyes seemed any light to
 come, 265
Nor his meek lips for blood or tears to thirst;
But as one blind and mute in mild sweet wise
Pleading for pity of piteous lips and eyes,
He strayed with faint bare lily-lovely feet
Helpless, and flowerlike sweet; 270

205. **like a sea-mew.** Swinburne frequently compares
himself to a sea gull. 222. **ineluctable,** inescapable.

Nor might man see, not having word hereof,
That this of all gods was the great god Love.

And seeing him lovely and like a little child
That wellnigh wept for wonder that it smiled
And was so feeble and fearful, with soft
    speech   275
The youth bespake him softly; but there fell
From the sweet lips no sweet word audible
That ear or thought might reach—
No sound to make the dim cold silence glad,
No breath to thaw the hard harsh air with
    heat;   280
Only the saddest smile of all things sweet,
Only the sweetest smile of all things sad.

And so they went together one green way
Till April dying made free the world for May;
And on his guide suddenly Love's face
    turned,   285
And in his blind eyes burned
Hard light and heat of laughter; and like flame
That opens in a mountain's ravening mouth
To blear and sear the sunlight from the south,
His mute mouth opened, and his first word
    came: 290
"Knowest thou me now by name?"
And all his stature waxed immeasurable,
As of one shadowing heaven and lightening
    hell;
And statelier stood he than a tower that
    stands
And darkens with its darkness far-off sands
Whereon the sky leans red;   296
And with a voice that stilled the winds he
    said:
"I am he that was thy lord before thy birth,
I am he that is thy lord till thou turn earth;
I make the night more dark, and all the mor-
    row   300
Dark as the night whose darkness was my
    breath.
O fool, my name is sorrow;
Thou fool, my name is death."

And he that heard spake not, and looked
    right on
Again, and Love was gone.   305

Through many a night toward many a
    wearier day
His spirit bore his body down its way.
Through many a day toward many a wearier
    night
His soul sustained his sorrows in her sight.
And earth was bitter, and heaven, and even
    the sea   310

Sorrowful even as he.
And the wind helped not, and the sun was
    dumb;
And with too long stress of grief to be
His heart grew sear and numb.

And one bright even ere summer in autumn
    sank   315
At stardawn standing on a gray sea-bank,
He felt the wind fitfully shift and heave
As toward a stormier eve;
And all the wan wide sea shuddered; and
    earth
Shook underfoot as toward some timeless
    birth,   320
Intolerable and inevitable; and all
Heaven, darkling, trembled like a stricken
    thrall.
And far out of the quivering east, and far
From past the moonrise and its guiding star,
Began a noise of tempest and a light   325
That was not of the lightning; and a sound
Rang with it round and round
That was not of the thunder; and a flight
As of blown clouds by night,
That was not of them; and with songs and
    cries   330
That sang and shrieked their soul out at the
    skies
A shapeless earthly storm of shapes began
From all ways round to move in on the
    man,
Clamorous against him silent; and their feet
Were as the wind's are fleet,   335
And their shrill songs were as wild birds' are
    sweet.

And as when all the world of earth was
    wronged
And all the host of all men driven afoam
By the red hand of Rome,
Round some fierce amphitheater over-
    thronged   340
With fair clear faces full of bloodier lust
Than swells and stings the tiger when his
    mood
Is fieriest after blood
And drunk with trampling of the murderous
    must
That soaks and stains the tortuous close-
    coiled wood   345
Made monstrous with its myriad-mustering
    brood,
Face by fair face panted and gleamed and
    pressed,
And breast by passionate breast

281-82 **Only the saddest . . . sad.** With these lines compare Shelley's *To a Skylark,* 90.—"Our sweetest songs are those that tell of saddest thought."

339. **red hand of Rome,** etc., a reference to the Roman revels under Nero. Cf. *Dolores,* 225-256, p. 694. 344. **must,** decayed vegetation of the forest. 346. **myriad-mustering brood,** life on the floor of the jungle.

Heaved hot with ravenous rapture, as they
    quaffed
The red ripe full fume of the deep live
    draft,   350
The sharp quick reek of keen fresh bloodshed,
    blown
Through the dense deep drift up to the em-
    peror's throne
From the under steaming sands
With clamor of all-applausive throats and
    hands,
Mingling in mirthful time   355
With shrill blithe mockeries of the lithe-limbed
    mime:
So from somewhence far forth of the un-
    beholden,
Dreadfully driven from over and after and
    under,
Fierce, blown through fifes of brazen blast
    and golden,
With sound of chiming waves that drown the
    thunder   360
Or thunder that strikes dumb the sea's own
    chimes,
Began the bellowing of the bull-voiced mimes,
Terrible; firs bowed down as briars or palms
Even at the breathless blast as of a breeze
Fulfilled with clamor and clangor and storms
    of psalms;   365
Red hands rent up the roots of old-world
    trees,
Thick flames of torches tossed as tumbling
    seas
Made mad the moonless and infuriate air
That, ravening, reveled in the riotous hair
And raiment of the furred Bassarides.   370

So came all those in on him; and his heart,
As out of sleep suddenly struck astart,
Danced, and his flesh took fire of theirs, and
    grief
Was as a last year's leaf
Blown dead far down the wind's way; and he
    set   375
His pale mouth to the brightest mouth it
    met
That laughed for love against his lips, and bade
Follow; and in following all his blood grew
    glad
And as again a sea-bird's; for the wind
Took him to bathe him deep round breast
    and brow   380

Not as it takes a dead leaf drained and
    thinned,
But as the brightest bay-flower blown on
    bough,
Set springing toward it singing; and they rode
By many a vine-leaved, many a rose-hung
    road,
Exalt with exultation; many a night   385
Set all its stars upon them as for spies
On many a moon-bewildering mountain-
    height
Where he rode only by the fierier light
Of his dread lady's hot sweet hungering eyes.
For the moon wandered witless of her
    way,   390
Spell-stricken by strong magic in such wise
As wizards use to set the stars astray.
And in his ears the music that makes mad
Beat always; and what way the music bade,
That alway rode he; nor was any sleep   395
His, nor from height nor deep.
But heaven was as red iron, slumberless,
And had no heart to bless;
And earth lay sear and darkling as distraught,
And help in her was naught.   400

Then many a midnight, many a morn and
    even,
His mother, passing forth of her fair heaven,
With goodlier gifts than all save gods can give
From earth or from the heaven where sea-
    things live,
With shine of sea-flowers through the bay-
    leaf braid   405
Woven for a crown her foam-white hands had
    made
To crown him with land's laurel and sea-
    dew,
Sought the sea-bird that was her boy; but he
Sat panther-throned beside Erigone,
Riding the red ways of the revel through   410
Midmost of pale-mouthed passion's crownless
    crew.
Till on some winter'd dawn of some dim year
He let the vine-bit on the panther's lip
Slide, and the green rein slip,
And set his eyes to seaward, nor gave ear   415
If sound from landward hailed him, dire or
    dear;
And passing forth of all those fair fierce
    ranks
Back to the gray sea-banks,
Against a sea-rock lying, aslant the steep,
Fell after many sleepless dreams on sleep. 420

356. **mime,** an actor in the ancient mime, a kind of drama
in which scenes from life were imitated and generally represented in a ridiculous manner. 370. **furred Bassarides,**
devotees of Bacchus, god of wine. They were noted for their
wild orgies, which included sacrifices of animals, eaten raw
by the participants. They wore garments made of fur. 373.
flesh . . . theirs. This symbolizes the mood in which Swinburne wrote the poems in the first series of *Poems and Ballads.*
Poems on pages 672-699 of this volume were included in
Poems and Ballads.

409. **panther-throned beside Erigone.** Erigone was
the daughter of Icarius, who was taught by Dionysus (god
of wine) the culture of the grape. He gave wine to some
shepherds who, thinking it poison, killed him. Overcome
with grief, Erigone took her own life. She was later placed
by Zeus among the stars as the constellation Virgo (Virgin)
The panther was sacred to Dionysus.

And in his sleep the dun green light was
   shed
Heavily round his head
That through the veil of sea falls fathom-deep,
Blurred like a lamp's that when the night
   drops dead
Dies; and his eyes gat grace of sleep to see 425
The deep divine dark dayshine of the sea,
Dense water-walls and clear dusk water-
   ways,
Broad-based, or branching as a sea-flower
   sprays
That side or this dividing; and anew
The glory of all her glories that he knew.   430
And in sharp rapture of recovering tears
He woke on fire with yearnings of old years,
Pure as one purged of pain that passion bore,
Ill child of bitter mother; for his own
Looked laughing toward him from her midsea
   throne,   435
Up toward him there ashore.

   Thence in his heart the great same joy
   began,
Of child that made him man;
And turned again from all hearts else on
   quest,
He communed with his own heart, and had
   rest.   440
And like sea-winds upon loud waters ran
His days and dreams together, till the joy
Burned in him of the boy.
Till the earth's great comfort and the sweet
   sea's breath
Breathed and blew life in where was heartless
   death,   445
Death spirit-stricken of soul-sick days, where
   strife
Of thought and flesh made mock of death and
   life.
And grace returned upon him of his birth
Where heaven was mixed with heavenlike sea
   and earth;
And song shot forth strong wings that took
   the sun   450
From inward, fledged with might of sorrow
   and mirth
And father's fire made mortal in his son.
Nor was not spirit of strength in blast and
   breeze
To exalt again the sun's child and the sea's;
For as wild mares in Thessaly grow great   455
With child of ravishing winds, that violate
Their leaping length of limb with manes like
   fire
And eyes outburning heaven's

With fires more violent than the lightning
   levin's
And breath drained out and desperate of
   desire,   460
Even so the spirit in him, when winds grew
   strong,
Grew great with child of song.
Nor less than when his veins first leapt for
   joy
To draw delight in such as burns a boy,
Now too the soul of all his senses felt   465
The passionate pride of deep sea-pulses dealt
Through nerve and jubilant vein
As from the love and largess of old time,
And with his heart again
The tidal throb of all the tides keep rime   470
And charm him from his own soul's separate
   sense
With infinite and invasive influence
That made strength sweet in him and sweet-
   ness strong,
Being now no more a singer, but a song.

   Till one clear day when brighter sea-wind
   blew   475
And louder sea-shine lightened, for the waves
Were full of godhead and the light that saves,
His father's, and their spirit had pierced him
   through,
He felt strange breath and light all round
   him shed
That bowed him down with rapture; and he
   knew   480
His father's hand, hallowing his humbled
   head,
And the old great voice of the old good time,
   that said:

   "Child of my sunlight and the sea, from
   birth
A fosterling and fugitive on earth;
Sleepless of soul as wind or wave or fire,   485
A manchild with an ungrown god's desire;
Because thou hast loved naught mortal more
   than me,
Thy father, and thy mother-hearted sea;
Because thou hast set thine heart to sing, and
   sold
Life and life's love for song, God's living
   gold;   490
Because thou hast given thy flower and fire of
   youth
To feed men's hearts with visions, truer than
   truth;

455-460. **wild mares in Thessaly,** etc. Boreas, god of the
wind, becoming enamored of some beautiful mares on the
plain of Thessaly, took on the form of an azure-maned steed
and became the sire of twelve female foals. The incident is
related in the *Iliad*, 20, 223 ff., in Virgil's *Georgics*, 3, 275 ff.

459. **levin's,** flash's. 472. **invasive,** penetrating. 478.
father's, Apollo's. Apollo was god of the sun, of music,
and of poetry. Swinburne represents himself as born of
Apollo and the sea nymph Cymothoë. See lines 16-36.
483ff. **Child of my sunlight,** etc. The concluding lines of
the poem are spoken by Apollo.

Because thou hast kept in those world-
    wandering eyes
The light that makes me music of the skies;
Because thou hast heard with world-un-
    wearied ears   495
The music that puts light into the spheres;
Have therefore in thine heart and in thy
    mouth
The sound of song that mingles north and
    south,
The song of all the winds that sing of me,
And in thy soul the sense of all the sea." 500
                         (1880)

From BY THE NORTH SEA

I

'A land that is lonelier than ruin;
    A sea that is stranger than death;
Far fields that a rose never blew in,
    Wan waste where the winds lack breath;
Waste endless and boundless, and flowerless
    But of marsh-blossoms fruitless as free; 6
Where earth lies exhausted, as powerless
    To strive with the sea.

Far flickers the flight of the swallows,
    Far flutters the weft of the grass   10
Spun dense over desolate hollows,
    More pale than the clouds as they pass;
Thick woven as the weft of a witch is
    Round the heart of a thrall that hath sinned,
Whose youth and the wrecks of its riches 15
    Are waifs on the wind.

The pastures are herdless and sheepless,
    No pasture or shelter for herds.
The wind is relentless and sleepless,
    And restless and songless the birds; 20
Their cries from afar fall breathless,
    Their wings are as lightnings that flee;
For the land has two lords that are deathless—
    Death's self, and the sea.

These twain, as a king with his fellow, 25
    Hold converse of desolate speech;
And her waters are haggard and yellow
    And crass with the scurf of the beach;
And his garments are gray as the hoary
    Wan sky where the day lies dim; 30
And his power is to her, and his glory,
    As hers unto him.

In the pride of his power she rejoices,
    In her glory he glows and is glad;

In her darkness the sound of his voice is, 35
    With his breath she dilates and is mad.
"If thou slay me, O death, and outlive me,
    Yet thy love hath fulfilled me of thee."
"Shall I give thee not back if thou give me,
    O sister, O sea?" 40

And year upon year dawns living,
    And age upon age drops dead;
And his hand is not weary of giving,
    And the thirst of her heart is not fed;
And the hunger that moans in her passion, 45
    And the rage in her hunger that roars,
As a wolf's that the winter lays lash on,
    Still calls and implores.

Her walls have no granite for girder,
    No fortalice fronting her stands; 50
But reefs the bloodguiltiest of murder
    Are less than the banks of her sands.
These number their slain by the thousand;
    For the ship hath no surety to be,
When the bank is abreast of her bows and 55
    Aflush with the sea.

No surety to stand, and no shelter
    To dawn out of darkness but one,
Out of waters that hurtle and welter
    No succor to dawn with the sun, 60
But a rest from the wind as it passes,
    Where, hardly redeemed from the waves,
Lie thick as the blades of the grasses
    The dead in their graves.

A multitude noteless of numbers, 65
    As wild weeds cast on an heap;
And sounder than sleep are their slumbers,
    And softer than song is their sleep;
And sweeter than all things and stranger
    The sense, if perchance it may be, 70
That the wind is divested of danger
    And scatheless the sea;

That the roar of the banks they breasted
    Is hurtless as bellowing of herds,
And the strength of his wings that invested
    The wind, as the strength of a bird's; 76
As the sea-mew's might or the swallow's
    That cry to him back if he cries,
As over the graves and their hollows
    Days darken and rise. 80

As the souls of the dead men disburdened
    And clean of the sins that they sinned,
With a lovelier than man's life guerdoned
    And delight as a wave's in the wind,
And delight as the wind's in the billow, 85

---

496. **music ... spheres.** The ancients believed that the
stars made music as they revolved in their spheres.
By the North Sea. See Critical Notes.
10. **weft of the grass,** grass; or the grass itself as a
carpet.

50. **fortalice,** a small fort. 62. **hardly,** with difficulty.
83. **guerdoned,** rewarded.

Birds pass, and deride with their glee
The flesh that has dust for its pillow
   As wrecks have the sea.

When the ways of the sun wax dimmer,
  Wings flash through the dusk like beams;
As the clouds in the lit sky glimmer,   91
  The bird in the graveyard gleams;
As the cloud at its wing's edge whitens
When the clarions of sunrise are heard,
The graves that the bird's note brightens 95
  Grow bright for the bird.

As the waves of the numberless waters
  That the wind cannot number who guides
Are the sons of the shore and the daughters
  Here lulled by the chime of the tides; 100
And here in the press of them standing,
  We know not if these or if we
Live truliest, or anchored to landing
  Or drifted to sea.

In the valley he named of decision,   105
  No denser were multitudes met
When the soul of the seer in her vision
  Saw nations for doom of them set;
Saw darkness in dawn, and the splendor
  Of judgment, the sword and the rod; 110
But the doom here of death is more tender
  And gentler the god.

And gentler the wind from the dreary
  Sea-banks by the waves overlapped,
Being weary, speaks peace to the weary, 115
  From slopes that the tide-stream hath
      sapped;
And sweeter than all that we call so
  The seal of their slumber shall be
Till the graves that embosom them also
  Be sapped of the sea.   120
         (1880)

7

But afar on the headland exalted,
  But beyond in the curl of the bay,
From the depth of his dome deep-vaulted,
  Our father is lord of the day —
Our father and lord that we follow,   5
  For deathless and ageless is he;
And his robe is the whole sky's hollow,
  His sandal the sea.

Where the horn of the headland is sharper,
  And her green floor glitters with fire, 10
The sea has the sun for a harper,

The sun has the sea for a lyre.
The waves are a pavement of amber,
  By the feet of the sea-winds trod
To receive in a god's presence-chamber 15
  Our father, the god.

Time, haggard and changeful and hoary,
  Is master and god of the land;
But the air is fulfilled of the glory
  That is shed from our lord's right hand. 20
O father of all of us ever,
  All glory be only to thee
From heaven, that is void of thee never,
  And earth, and the sea.

O Sun, whereof all is beholden,   25
  Behold now the shadow of this death,
This place of the sepulchers, olden
  And emptied and vain as a breath.
The bloom of the bountiful heather
  Laughs broadly beyond in thy light 30
As dawn, with her glories to gather,
  At darkness and night.

Though the gods of the night lie rotten,
  And their honor be taken away,
And the noise of their names forgotten, 35
  Thou, Lord, art god of the day.
Thou art father and savior and spirit,
  O Sun, of the soul that is free,
And hath grace of thy grace to inherit
  Thine earth and thy sea.   40

The hills and the sands and the beaches,
  The waters adrift and afar,
The banks and the creeks and the reaches
  How glad of thee all these are!
The flowers, overflowing, overcrowded, 45
  Are drunk with the mad wind's mirth;
The delight of thy coming unclouded
  Makes music of earth.

I, last least voice of her voices,
  Give thanks that were mute in me long 50
To the soul in my soul that rejoices
  For the song that is over my song.
Time gives what he gains for the giving
  Or takes for his tribute of me;
My dreams to the wind everliving, 55
  My song to the sea.   (1880)

THE HIGHER PANTHEISM IN A NUT-SHELL

One, who is not, we see; but one, whom we
  see not, is.
Surely this is not that; but that is assuredly
  this.

---

105. **valley . . . decision,** a reference to the prophecy
of Joel regarding the judgment of God upon the enemies of
his people: "Multitudes, multitudes in the valley of decision;
for the day of the Lord is near in the valley of decision" (*Joel*,
3:14).
  4. **Our father,** Phœbus Apollo, god of the sun.

The Higher Pantheism in a Nutshell. This is a parody of
Tennyson's *The Higher Pantheism,* p. 122.

What, and wherefore, and whence? for under
    is over and under;
If thunder could be without lightning, light-
    ning could be without thunder.

Doubt is faith, in the main; but faith, on the
    whole, is doubt.   5
We cannot believe by proof; but could we
    believe without?

Why, and whither, and how? for barley and
    rye are not clover;
Neither are straight lines curves — yet over
    is under and over.

Two and two may be four, but four and four
    are not eight;
Fate and God may be twain, but God is the
    same thing as fate.   10

Ask a man what he thinks, and get from a
    man what he feels;
God, once caught in the fact, shows you a
    fair pair of heels.

Body and spirit are twins; God only knows
    which is which —
The soul squats down in the flesh, like a
    tinker drunk in a ditch.

More is the whole than a part, but half is
    more than the whole;   15
Clearly, the soul is the body — but is not the
    body the soul?

One and two are not one, but one and nothing
    is two;
Truth can hardly be false, if falsehood cannot
    be true.

Once the mastodon was; pterodactyls were
    common as cocks.
Then the mammoth was God; now is He a
    prize ox.   20

Parallels all things are — yet many of these
    are askew;
You are certainly I, but certainly I am not
    you.

Springs the rock from the plain, shoots the
    stream from the rock;
Cocks exist for the hen, but hens exist for
    the cock.

God, whom we see not, is; and God, who is
    not, we see.   25
Fiddle, we know, is diddle; and diddle, we
    take it, is dee.   (1880)

12. **fact,** deed, act.

NEPHELIDIA

From the depth of the dreamy decline of the
    dawn through a notable nimbus of
    nebulous noonshine,
  Pallid and pink as the palm of the flag-
    flower that flickers with fear of the
    flies as they float,
Are the looks of our lovers that lustrously
    lean from a marvel of mystic, mirac-
    ulous moonshine,
  These that we feel in the blood of our
    blushes that thicken and threaten with
    throbs through the throat?
Thicken and thrill as a theater thronged at
    appeal of an actor's appalled agitation,
  Fainter with fear of the fires of the future
    than pale with the promise of pride in
    the past;   6
Flushed with the famishing fullness of fever
    that reddens with radiance of rathe
    recreation,
  Gaunt as the ghastliest of glimpses that
    gleam through the gloom of the gloam-
    ing when ghosts go aghast?
Nay, for the nick of the tick of the time is a
    tremulous touch on the temples of
    terror,
  Strained as the sinews yet strenuous with
    strife of the dead who is dumb as the
    dust-heaps of death;   10
Surely no soul is it, sweet as the spasm of
    erotic emotional exquisite error,
  Bathed in the balms of beatified bliss,
    beatific itself by beatitudes' breath.
Surely no spirit or sense of a soul that was soft
    to the spirit and soul of our senses
  Sweetens the stress of suspiring suspicion
    that sobs in the semblance and sound
    of a sigh;
Only this oracle opens Olympian, in mystical
    moods and triangular tenses —   15
  "Life is the lust of a lamp for the light that
    is dark till the dawn of the day when
    we die."
Mild is the mirk and monotonous music of
    memory, melodiously mute as it may
    be,
  While the hope in the heart of a hero is
    bruised by the breach of men's rapiers,
    resigned to the rod;
Made meek as a mother whose bosom-beats
    bound with the bliss-bringing bulk of
    a balm-breathing baby,
  As they grope through the graveyard of
    creeds, under skies growing green at a
    groan for the grimness of God.   20

Nephelidia. The title means *Cloudlets.* Swinburne here
parodies his own mannerisms of diction and rhythm.
7. **rathe,** quick, fast. 14. **suspiring,** sighing, desiring.
15. **Olympian,** godlike, after the manner of the gods of
Mt. Olympus, in ancient Greece.

Blank is the book of his bounty beholden of
    old, and its binding is blacker than
    bluer;
    Out of blue into black is the scheme of the
      skies, and their dews are the wine of
      the bloodshed of things;
Till the darkling desire of delight shall be free
    as a fawn that is freed from the fangs
    that pursue her,
    Till the heart-beats of hell shall be hushed
      by a hymn from the hunt that has
      harried the kennel of kings.   (1880)

HOPE AND FEAR

Beneath the shadow of dawn's aërial cope,
With eyes enkindled as the sun's own sphere,
Hope from the front of youth in godlike cheer
Looks Godward, past the shades where blind
    men grope
Round the dark door that prayers nor dreams
    can ope,   5
And makes for joy the very darkness dear
That gives her wide wings play; nor dreams
    that fear
At noon may rise and pierce the heart of
    hope.
Then, when the soul leaves off to dream and
    yearn,
May truth first purge her eyesight to discern
What, once being known, leaves time no
    power to appall;   11
Till youth at last, ere yet youth be not, learn
The kind wise word that falls from years that
    fall —
"Hope thou not much, and fear thou not at
    all."   (1882)

ON THE
DEATHS OF THOMAS CARLYLE
AND GEORGE ELIOT

Two souls diverse out of our human sight
Pass, followed one with love and each with
    wonder:
The stormy sophist with his mouth of thunder,
Clothed with loud words and mantled in the
    might
Of darkness and magnificence of night;   5
And one whose eye could smite the night in
    sunder,
Searching if light or no light were thereunder,
And found in love of loving-kindness light.
Duty divine and Thought with eyes of fire,
Still following Righteousness with deep desire,
Shone sole and stern before her and above —

On the Deaths of Thomas Carlyle and George Eliot. Carlyle,
the "stormy sophist," died in 1881; Eliot in 1880.

Sure stars and sole to steer by; but more
    sweet   12
Shone lower the loveliest lamp for earthly
    feet —
The light of little children, and their love.
    (1882)

DICKENS

Chief in thy generation born of men,
    Whom English praise acclaimed as English-
    born,
    With eyes that matched the worldwide eyes
      of morn
For gleam of tears or laughter, tenderest then
When thoughts of children warmed their
    light, or when   5
    Reverence of age with love and labor worn,
    Or godlike pity fired with godlike scorn,
Shot through them flame that winged thy
    swift live pen:
Where stars and suns that we behold not
    burn,
    Higher even than here, though highest was
      here thy place,   10
    Love sees thy spirit laugh and speak and
    shine
With Shakespeare and the soft bright soul of
    Sterne
    And Fielding's kindliest might and Gold-
    smith's grace;
    Scarce one more loved or worthier love
      than thine.   (1882)

ADIEUX À MARIE STUART

I

Queen, for whose house my fathers fought,
    With hopes that rose and fell,
Red star of boyhood's fiery thought,
    Farewell.

They gave their lives, and I, my queen,   5
    Have given you of my life,
Seeing your brave star burn high between
    Men's strife.

The strife that lightened round their spears
    Long since fell still; so long   10
Hardly may hope to last in years
    My song.

Dickens. Swinburne came under the spell of Dickens at
Eton and admired him most of the English novelists.
12. Sterne. Laurence Sterne (1713-68), Henry Fielding
(1707-54), and Oliver Goldsmith (1728-74) were among the
earliest English novelists.
    Adieux à Marie Stuart. The title means Farewells to Mary
Stuart. See Critical Notes.
    1. my . . . fought. Swinburne was proud of the fact that
his ancestors had fought and died in Mary's support. 6.
given . . . life. Swinburne wrote a trilogy of tragedies dealing with Mary Queen of Scots—Chastelard (1865), Bothwell
(1874), and Mary Stuart (1881).

But still through strife of time and thought
    Your light on me too fell;
Queen, in whose name we sang or fought,   15
    Farewell.

2

There beats no heart on either border
    Wherethrough the north blasts blow
But keeps your memory as a warder
    His beacon-fire aglow.   20

Long since, it fired with love and wonder
    Mine, for whose April age
Blithe midsummer made banquet under
    The shade of Hermitage.

Soft sang the burn's blithe notes, that gather
    Strength to ring true;   26
And air and trees and sun and heather
    Remembered you.

Old border ghosts of fight or fairy
    Or love or teen,   30
These they forgot, remembering Mary
    The Queen.

3

Queen once of Scots and ever of ours
    Whose sires brought forth for you
Their lives to strew your way like flowers,   35
    Adieu.

Dead is full many a dead man's name
    Who died for you this long
Time past; shall this too fare the same,
    My song?   40

But surely, though it die or live,
    Your face was worth
All that a man may think to give
    On earth.

No darkness cast of years between   45
    Can darken you;
Man's love will never bid my queen
    Adieu.

4

Love hangs like light about your name
    As music round the shell;   50
No heart can take of you a tame
    Farewell.

Yet, when your very face was seen,
    Ill gifts were yours for giving;

Love gat strange guerdons of my queen   55
    When living.

O diamond heart, unflawed and clear,
    The whole world's crowning jewel!
Was ever heart so deadly dear
    So cruel?   60

Yet none for you of all that bled
    Grudged once one drop that fell;
Not one to life reluctant said
    Farewell.

5

Strange love they have given you, love dis-
    loyal,   65
    Who mock with praise your name,
To leave a head so rare and royal
    Too low for praise or blame.

You could not love nor hate, they tell us,
    You had nor sense nor sting;   70
In God's name, then, what plague befell us
    To fight for such a thing?

"Some faults the gods will give," to fetter
    Man's highest intent;
But surely you were something better   75
    Than innocent!

No maid that strays with steps unwary
    Through snares unseen,
But one to live and die for; Mary,
    The Queen.   80

6

Forgive them all their praise, who blot
    Your fame with praise of you;
Then love may say, and falter not,
    Adieu.

Yet some you hardly would forgive   85
    Who did you much less wrong
Once; but resentment should not live
    Too long.

They never saw your lip's bright bow,
    Your swordbright eyes,   90
The bluest of heavenly things below
    The skies.

Clear eyes that love's self finds most like
    A swordblade's blue,
A swordblade's ever keen to strike,   95
    Adieu.

---

24. Hermitage, a castle on the Hermitage River, a small stream in Roxborough, Scotland. Swinburne spent a day in the vicinity of the castle some years before this poem was written, and his imagination was stirred by the sight of the fortification, the scene of Mary's visit to the wounded Bothwell. **25. burn's,** brook's. **30. teen,** sorrow, grief.

55. guerdons, rewards. **73-76. Some faults ... innocent.** Swinburne believed that a person was the better if he had in him a touch of earth. See Critical Note on title; also *Maud,* I, 80-83, p. 98, and *Lancelot and Elaine,* 132-133, p. 125. **85-86. some ... wrong.** She should be much more ready to forgive those who, like John Knox, were her out-and-out enemies, than those, like the Earl of Murray, who pretended to be her friends.

7

Though all things breathe or sound of fight
  That yet make up your spell,
To bid you were to bid the light
  Farewell.   100

Farewell the song says only, being
  A star whose race is run;
Farewell the soul says never, seeing
  The sun.

Yet, wellnigh as with flash of tears,   105
  The song must say but so
That took your praise up twenty years
  Ago.

More bright than stars or moons that vary,
  Sun kindling heaven and hell,   110
Here, after all these years, Queen Mary,
  Farewell.   (1882)

THE SALT OF THE EARTH

If childhood were not in the world,
  But only men and women grown;
No baby-locks in tendrils curled,
  No baby-blossoms blown;

Though men were stronger, women fairer, 5
  And nearer all delights in reach,
And verse and music uttered rarer
  Tones of more godlike speech;

Though the utmost life of life's best hours
  Found, as it cannot now find, words;   10
Though desert sands were sweet as flowers
  And flowers could sing like birds,

But children never heard them, never
  They felt a child's foot leap and run —
This were a drearier star than ever   15
  Yet looked upon the sun.   (1882)

A CHILD'S LAUGHTER

All the bells of heaven may ring,
All the birds of heaven may sing,
All the wells on earth may spring,
All the winds on earth may bring
  All sweet sounds together;   5
Sweeter far than all things heard,
Hand of harper, tone of bird,
Sound of woods at sundawn stirred,
Welling water's winsome word,
  Wind in warm wan weather,   10

One thing yet there is, that none
Hearing ere its chime be done
Knows not well the sweetest one
Heard of man beneath the sun,
  Hoped in heaven hereafter;   15
Soft and strong and loud and light,
Very sound of very light
Heard from morning's rosiest height,
When the soul of all delight
  Fills a child's clear laughter.   20

Golden bells of welcome rolled
Never forth such notes, nor told
Hours so blithe in tones so bold,
As the radiant mouth of gold
  Here that rings forth heaven.   25
If the golden-crested wren
Were a nightingale — why, then,
Something seen and heard of men
Might be half as sweet as when
  Laughs a child of seven.   (1882)

From SONNETS OF ENGLISH DRA-MATIC POETS (1590-1650)

1. CHRISTOPHER MARLOWE

Crowned, girdled, garbed and shod with light
  and fire,
  Son first-born of the morning, sovereign
    star!
Soul nearest ours of all, that wert most far,
Most far off in the abysm of time, thy lyre
Hung highest above the dawn-enkindled quire
  Where all ye sang together, all that are, 6
  And all the starry songs behind thy car
Rang sequence, all our souls acclaim thee sire.
"If all the pens that ever poets held
  Had fed the feeling of their masters'
    thoughts,"   10
And as with rush of hurtling chariots
The flight of all their spirits were impelled
  Toward one great end, thy glory — nay,
    not then,
  Not yet might'st thou be praised enough
    of men.   (1882)

2. WILLIAM SHAKESPEARE

Not if men's tongues and angels' all in one
  Spake, might the word be said that might
    speak thee.
  Streams, winds, woods, flowers, fields,
    mountains, yea, the sea,

107-108. **twenty years Ago.** See note on line 6.
The Salt of the Earth. Christ calls his disciples "the salt of the earth" in *Matthew,* 5:13.

Sonnets of English Dramatic Poets (1590-1650). The series contains twenty-one sonnets.
Christopher Marlowe. Marlowe (1564-93), the most brilliant of the pre-Shakespearean playwrights, was the morning star that heralded the Elizabethan day. Swinburne found him the most congenial of the Elizabethans.

What power is in them all to praise the sun?
His praise is this — he can be praised of none.
　Man, woman, child, praise God for him;
　　but he　　　　　　　　　　　　　　6
　Exults not to be worshiped, but to be.
He is; and, being, beholds his work well done.
All joy, all glory, all sorrow, all strength, all
　　mirth,　　　　　　　　　　　　　　9
Are his; without him, day were night on earth.
　Time knows not his from time's own period.
All lutes, all harps, all viols, all flutes, all lyres,
Fall dumb before him ere one string suspires.
　All stars are angels; but the sun is God.
　　　　　　　　　　　　　　　　(1882)

3. BEN JONSON

Broad-based, broad-fronted, bounteous, mul-
　　tiform,
　With many a valley impleached with ivy
　　and vine,
　Wherein the springs of all the streams run
　　wine,
And many a crag full-faced against the storm,
The mountain where thy Muse's feet made
　　warm　　　　　　　　　　　　　　5
　Those lawns that reveled with her dance
　　divine
Shines yet with fire as it was wont to shine
From tossing torches round the dance aswarm.

Nor less, high-stationed on the gray grave
　　heights,
High-thoughted seers with heaven's heart-
　　kindling lights　　　　　　　　　　10
　Hold converse; and the herd of meaner
　　things
Knows or by fiery scourge or fiery shaft
When wrath on thy broad brows has risen,
　　and laughed,
　Darkening thy soul with shadow of thun-
　　derous wings.　　　　　　　　　　(1882)

4. BEAUMONT AND FLETCHER

An hour ere sudden sunset fired the west,
　Arose two stars upon the pale deep east.
　The hall of heaven was clear for night's
　　high feast,
Yet was not yet day's fiery heart at rest.
Love leapt up from his mother's burning
　　breast　　　　　　　　　　　　　5

To see those warm twin lights, as day
　　decreased,
Wax wider, till when all the sun had ceased,
As suns they shone from evening's kindled
　　crest.
Across them and between, a quickening fire,
Flamed Venus, laughing with appeased desire.
　Their dawn, scarce lovelier for the gleam
　　of tears,　　　　　　　　　　　　11
Filled half the hollow shell 'twixt heaven and
　　earth
With sound like moonlight, mingling moan
　　and mirth,
Which rings and glitters down the darkling
　　years.　　　　　　　　　　　　(1882)

19. THE MANY

Greene, garlanded with February's few flowers
　Ere March came in with Marlowe's raptur-
　　ous rage;
　Peele, from whose hand the sweet white
　　locks of age
Took the mild chaplet woven of honored
　　hours;
Nash, laughing hard; Lodge, flushed from
　　lyric bowers;　　　　　　　　　　5
　And Lilly, a goldfinch in a twisted cage
　Fed by some gay great lady's pettish page
Till short sweet songs gush clear like short
　　spring showers;
Kid, whose grim sport still gamboled over
　　graves;
　And Chettle, in whose fresh funereal verse
　Weeps Marian yet on Robin's wildwood
　　hearse;　　　　　　　　　　　　11
Cooke, whose light boat of song one soft
　　breath saves,
　Sighed from a maiden's amorous mouth
　　averse;
Live likewise ye — Time takes not you for
　　slaves.　　　　　　　　　　　　(1882)

CHILDREN

Of such is the kingdom of heaven.
　No glory that ever was shed
From the crowning star of the seven
　That crown the north world's head,

Ben Jonson. Jonson (1573?-1637) is praised for the many aspects of his genius. He could carouse with his friends and write delicate lyrics, thunderous blank verse, rollicking comedy, and stately masques (line 8). He was familiar with classic writers (line 10), and his broad experiences in actual life made him a capital satirist (line 13).
Beaumont and Fletcher. Francis Beaumont (1584-1616) and John Fletcher (1579-1625) were joint authors of a number of plays including romantic tragi-comedies. Lines 1-4 suggest that Elizabethan drama had about reached its end when these two came.

The Many. Swinburne indicates the general spirit of each of the men mentioned in this sonnet—Robert Greene (1560-92), Christopher Marlowe (1564-93), George Peele (1558-98), Thomas Nash (1567-1601), Thomas Lodge (1558?-1625), John Lyly (1553?-1606), Thomas Kyd (1558?-94), Henry Chettle (*d.* 1607?), and Joshua Cooke (*fl.* 1614).
　11. **Marian,** Maid Marian, a female character in the old May games, who became attached to the Robin Hood ballads and plays as the outlaw's sweetheart.
　Children. 1. **Of such . . . heaven.** From *Matthew,* 19:14.—"Jesus said, 'Suffer little children, and forbid them not, to come unto me; for of such is the kingdom of heaven.'" Cf. *Matthew,* 18:1-6. 3-4. **crowning star . . . head,** the North Star, the brightest of the seven stars composing the constellation of *Ursa Minor.*

No word that ever was spoken　　　5
  Of human or godlike tongue,
Gave ever such godlike token
  Since human harps were strung.

No sign that ever was given
  To faithful or faithless eyes　　　10
Showed ever beyond clouds riven
  So clear a Paradise.

Earth's creeds may be seventy times seven
  And blood have defiled each creed;
If of such be the kingdom of heaven,　　　15
  It must be heaven indeed.　　　(1882)

CHILD AND POET

You send me your love in a letter,
  I send you my love in a song;
Ah, child, your gift is the better,
  Mine does you but wrong.

No fame, were the best less brittle,　　　5
  No praise, were it wide as earth,
Is worth so much as a little
  Child's love may be worth.

We see the children above us
  As they might angels above;　　　10
Come back to us, child, if you love us,
  And bring us your love.　　　(1882)

ÉTUDE RÉALISTE

1

A baby's feet, like sea-shells pink,
  Might tempt, should heaven see meet,
An angel's lips to kiss, we think,
  A baby's feet.

Like rose-hued sea-flowers toward the heat　5
  They stretch and spread and wink
Their ten soft buds that part and meet.

No flower-bells that expand and shrink
  Gleam half so heavenly sweet
As shine on life's untrodden brink　　　10
  A baby's feet.

2

A baby's hands, like rosebuds furled
  Whence yet no leaf expands,
Ope if you touch, though close upcurled,
  A baby's hands.　　　15

Then, fast as warriors grip their brands
  When battle's bolt is hurled,
They close, clenched hard like tightening
  bands.

Étude Réaliste. The title means *A Realistic Study.*

No rosebuds yet by dawn impearled
  Match, even in loveliest lands,　　　20
The sweetest flowers in all the world —
  A baby's hands.

3

A baby's eyes, ere speech begin,
  Ere lips learn words or sighs,
Bless all things bright enough to win　　　25
  A baby's eyes.

Love, while the sweet thing laughs and lies,
  And sleep flows out and in,
Sees perfect in them Paradise.

Their glance might cast out pain and sin,　　　30
  Their speech make dumb the wise,
By mute glad godhead felt within
  A baby's eyes.

    (1883)

THE ROUNDEL

A roundel is wrought as a ring or a starbright
  sphere,
With craft of delight and with cunning of
  sound unsought,
That the heart of the hearer may smile if to
  pleasure his ear
    A roundel is wrought.

Its jewel of music is carven of all or of
  aught —
Love, laughter, or mourning — remembrance
  of rapture or fear —　　　6
That fancy may fashion to hang in the ear of
  thought.

As a bird's quick song runs round, and the
  hearts in us hear
Pause answer to pause, and again the same
  strain caught,
So moves the device whence, round as a pearl
  or tear,　　　10
    A roundel is wrought.

    (1883)

IN GUERNSEY
(TO THEODORE WATTS)

1

The heavenly bay, ringed round with cliffs
  and moors,
Storm-stained ravines, and crags that lawns
  inlay,

The Roundel. See note on *Rondel,* p. 691.
In Guernsey. Guernsey is one of the largest of the Channel
Islands south of England. Theodore Watts-Dunton (1832-
1914) was an English critic, novelist, and poet. Swinburne
lived in his home after 1879.
2. **lawns,** open spaces.

Soothes as with love the rocks whose guard
    secures
  The heavenly bay.

O friend, shall time take even this away,   5
This blessing given of beauty that en-
    dures,
This glory shown us, not to pass but stay?

Though sight be changed for memory, love
    insures
What memory, changed by love to sight,
    would say —
The word that seals forever mine and yours,
  The heavenly bay.   11

2

My mother sea, my fostress, what new strand,
What new delight of waters, may this be,
The fairest found since time's first breezes
    fanned
  My mother sea?   15

Once more I give me, body and soul, to
    thee,
Who hast my soul forever; cliff and sand
Recede, and heart to heart once more are
    we.

My heart springs first and plunges, ere my
    hand
Strike out from shore; more close it brings
    to me,   20
More near and dear than seems my father-
    land,
  My mother sea.

3

Across and along, as the bay's breadth opens,
    and o'er us
Wild autumn exults in the wind, swift rapture
    and strong
Impels us, and broader the wide waves
    brighten before us   25
  Across and along.

The whole world's heart is uplifted, and
    knows not wrong;
The whole world's life is a chant to the sea-
    tide's chorus;
Are we not as waves of the water, as notes
    of the song?

Like children unworn of the passions and
    toils that wore us,   30
We breast for a season the breath of the seas
    that throng,
Rejoicing as they, to be borne as of old they
    bore us
  Across and along.
                    (1883)

From A MIDSUMMER HOLIDAY

ON A COUNTRY ROAD

Along these low pleached lanes, on such a day,
So soft a day as this, through shade and sun,
With glad grave eyes that scanned the glad
    wild way,
And heart still hovering o'er a song begun,
And smile that warmed the world with
    benison,   5
Our father, lord long since of lordly rime,
Long since hath haply ridden, when the lime
Bloomed broad above him, flowering where
    he came.
Because thy passage once made warm this
    clime,
Our father Chaucer, here we praise thy name.

Each year that England clothes herself with
    May,   11
She takes thy likeness on her. Time hath
    spun
Fresh raiment all in vain and strange array
For earth and man's new spirit, fain to shun
Things past for dreams of better to be won, 15
Through many a century since thy funeral
    chime
Rang, and men deemed it death's most direful
    crime
To have spared not thee for very love or
    shame;
And yet, while mists round last year's mem-
    ories climb,
Our father Chaucer, here we praise thy name.

Each turn of the old wild road whereon we
    stray,   21
Meseems, might bring us face to face with one
Whom, seeing, we could not but give thanks,
    and pray
For England's love our father and her son
To speak with us as once in days long done 25
With all men, sage and churl and monk and
    mime,
Who knew not as we know the soul sublime
That sang for song's love more than lust of
    fame.
Yet, though this be not, yet, in happy time,
Our father Chaucer, here we praise thy name.

Friend, even as bees about the flowering
    thyme,   31
Years crowd on years, till hoar decay begrime
Names once beloved; but, seeing the sun the
    same,

A Midsummer Holiday. The three poems under this title
are in the form of *ballades* (see note on *A Ballad of Dreamland*,
p. 723).
  1. **pleached lanes,** lanes shaded by interwoven boughs.
11. Each year . . . May. Swinburne had great love for
spring. See *A Vision of Spring in Winter*, p. 721.

As birds of autumn fain to praise the prime, 34
Our father Chaucer, here we praise thy name.
                                        (1884)

IN THE WATER

The sea is awake, and the sound of the song
  of the joy of her waking is rolled
From afar to the star that recedes, from anear
  to the wastes of the wild wide shore.
Her call is a trumpet compelling us homeward; if dawn in her east be acold,
From the sea shall we crave not her grace to
  rekindle the life that it kindled before,
Her breath to requicken, her bosom to rock
  us, her kisses to bless as of yore?   5
For the wind, with his wings half open, at
  pause in the sky, neither fettered nor free,
Leans waveward and flutters the ripple to
  laughter; and fain would the twain of
  us be
Where lightly the wave yearns forward from
  under the curve of the deep dawn's dome,
And, full of the morning and fired with the
  pride of the glory thereof and the glee,
Strike out from the shore as the heart in us
  bids and beseeches, athirst for the foam.

Life holds not an hour that is better to live
  in; the past is a tale that is told,   11
The future a sun-flecked shadow, alive and
  asleep, with a blessing in store.
As we give us again to the waters, the rapture
  of limbs that the waters enfold
Is less than the rapture of spirit whereby,
  though the burden it quits were sore,
Our souls and the bodies they wield at their
  will are absorbed in the life they adore —
In the life that endures no burden, and bows
  not the forehead, and bends not the
  knee —   16
In the life everlasting of earth and of heaven,
  in the laws that atone and agree,
In the measureless music of things, in the
  fervor of forces that rest or that roam,
That cross and return and reissue, as I after
  you and as you after me —
Strike out from the shore as the heart in us
  bids and beseeches, athirst for the foam.

For, albeit he were less than the least of
  them, haply the heart of a man may be
  bold   21
To rejoice in the word of the sea, as a mother's
  that saith to the son she bore,
"Child, was not the life in thee mine, and
  my spirit the breath in thy lips from of
  old?
Have I let not thy weakness exult in my
  strength, and thy foolishness learn of
  my lore?

Have I helped not or healed not thine anguish, or made not the might of thy
  gladness more?"   25
And surely his heart should answer, "The
  light of the love of my life is in thee."
She is fairer than earth, and the sun is not
  fairer, the wind is not blither than she.
From my youth hath she shown me the joy
  of her bays that I crossed, of her cliffs
  that I clomb,
Till now that the twain of us here, in desire
  of the dawn and in trust of the sea,
Strike out from the shore as the heart in us
  bids and beseeches, athirst for the foam.

Friend, earth is a harbor of refuge for winter,
  a covert whereunder to flee   31
When day is the vassal of night, and the
  strength of the hosts of her mightier
  than he;
But here is the presence adored of me, here
  my desire is at rest and at home.
There are cliffs to be climbed upon land, there
  are ways to be trodden and ridden; but
  we   34
Strike out from the shore as the heart in us
  bids and beseeches, athirst for the foam.
                                        (1884)

ON THE VERGE

Here begins the sea that ends not till the
  world's end. Where we stand,
Could we know the next high sea-mark set
  beyond these waves that gleam,
We should know what never man hath known,
  nor eye of man hath scanned.
Naught beyond these coiling clouds, that melt
  like fume of shrines that steam,
Breaks or stays the strength of waters till
  they pass our bounds of dream.   5
Where the waste Land's End leans westward,
  all the seas it watches roll
Find their border fixed beyond them, and a
  worldwide shore's control;
These whereby we stand no shore beyond us
  limits — these are free.
Gazing hence, we see the water that grows
  iron round the Pole,
From the shore that hath no shore beyond it
  set in all the sea.   10

Sail on sail along the sea-line fades and
  flashes; here on land
Flash and fade the wheeling wings on wings
  of mews that plunge and scream.
Hour on hour along the line of life and time's
  evasive strand

<hr>

On the Verge. 1. **the sea that ends not,** the North
Sea. 6. **Land's End,** the southwestern extremity of
England.

Shines and darkens, wanes and waxes, slays
    and dies; and scarce they seem
More than motes that thronged and trembled
    in the brief noon's breath and beam.
Some with crying and wailing, some with
    notes like sound of bells that toll,   16
Some with sighing and laughing, some with
    words that blessed and made us whole,
Passed, and left us, and we know not what
    they were, nor what were we.
Would we know, being mortal? Never breath
    of answering whisper stole
From the shore that hath no shore beyond
    it set in all the sea.   20

Shadows, would we question darkness? Ere
    our eyes and brows be fanned
Round with airs of twilight, washed with dews
    from sleep's eternal stream,
Would we know sleep's guarded secret? Ere
    the fire consume the brand,
Would it know if yet its ashes may requicken?
    Yet we deem
Surely man may know, or ever night unyoke
    her starry team,   25
What the dawn shall be, or if the dawn shall
    be not; yea, the scroll
Would we read of sleep's dark scripture,
    pledge of peace or doom of dole.
Ah, but here man's heart leaps, yearning
    toward the gloom with venturous glee,
Though his pilot eye behold nor bay nor
    harbor, rock nor shoal,
From the shore that hath no shore beyond it
    set in all the sea.   30

Friend, who knows if death indeed have life
    or life have death for goal?
Day nor night can tell us, nor may seas
    declare nor skies unroll
What has been from everlasting, or if aught
    shall alway be.
Silence, answering, only strikes response rever-
    berate on the soul
From the shore that hath no shore beyond it
    set in all the sea.   35
               (1884)

NEAP-TIDE

Far off is the sea, and the land is afar.
    The low banks reach at the sky,
    Seen hence, and are heavenward high;
Though light for the leap of a boy they are,
    And the far sea late was nigh.   5

The fair wild fields and the circling downs,
    The bright sweet marshes and meads,
    All glorious with flowerlike weeds,

Neap-Tide. Neap tides are the lowest tides during the
month.

The great gray churches, the sea-washed
    towns,
    Recede as a dream recedes.   10

The world draws back and the world's light
    wanes,
    As a dream dies down and is dead;
    And the clouds and the gleams overhead
Change, and change; and the sea remains,
    A shadow of dreamlike dread.   15

Wild, and woeful, and pale, and gray,
    A shadow of sleepless fear,
    A corpse with the night for bier,
The fairest thing that beholds the day
    Lies haggard and hopeless here.   20

And the wind's wings, broken and spent,
    subside;
    And the dumb waste world is hoar
    And strange as the sea the shore;
And shadows of shapeless dreams abide
    Where life may abide no more.   25

A sail to seaward, a sound from shoreward,
    And the spell were broken that seems
    To reign in a world of dreams
Where vainly the dreamer's feet make for-
    ward
    And vainly the low sky gleams.   30

The sea-forsaken, forlorn, deep-wrinkled,
    Salt, slanting stretches of sand
    That slope to the seaward hand —
Were they fain of the ripples that flashed and
    twinkled
    And laughed as they struck the strand?

As bells on the reins of the fairies ring   36
    The ripples that kissed them rang,
    The light from the sundawn sprang,
And the sweetest of songs that the world may
    sing
    Was theirs when the full sea sang.   40

Now no light is in heaven, and now
    Not a note of the sea-wind's tune
    Rings hither; the bleak sky's boon
Grants hardly sight of a gray sun's brow —
    A sun more sad than the moon.   45

More sad than a moon that clouds beleaguer
    And storm is a scourge to smite,
    The sick sun's shadowlike light
Grows faint as the clouds and the waves wax
    eager,
    And withers away from sight.   50

The day's heart cowers, and the night's heart
    quickens;
    Full fain would the day be dead,

And the stark night reign in his stead;
The sea falls dumb as the sea-fog thickens,
    And the sunset dies for dread.   55

Outside of the range of time, whose breath
    Is keen as the manslayer's knife
And his peace but a truce for strife,
Who knows if haply the shadow of death
    May be not the light of life?   60

For the storm and the rain and the darkness
    borrow
    But an hour from the suns to be,
    But a strange swift passage, that we
May rejoice, who have mourned not today,
    tomorrow,
    In the sun and the wind and the sea. 65
                                    (1889)

ON THE
DEATH OF ROBERT BROWNING

He held no dream worth waking; so he said,
He who stands now on death's triumphal
    steep,
Awakened out of life wherein we sleep
And dream of what he knows and sees, being
    dead.
But never death for him was dark or dread;
"Look forth," he bade the soul, and fear not.
    Weep,   6
All ye that trust not in his truth, and keep
Vain memory's vision of a vanished head
As all that lives of all that once was he
Save that which lightens from his word; but
    we,   10
Who, seeing the sunset-colored waters roll,
Yet know the sun subdued not of the sea,
Nor weep nor doubt that still the spirit is
    whole,
And life and death but shadows of the soul.
                                (1889; 1890)

THE LAKE OF GAUBE

The sun is lord and god, sublime, serene,
    And sovereign on the mountains; earth and
    air
Lie prone in passion, blind with bliss unseen
By force of sight and might of rapture, fair
    As dreams that die and know not what they
    were.   5

The lawns, the gorges, and the peaks, are one
Glad glory, thrilled with sense of unison
In strong compulsive silence of the sun.

Flowers dense and keen as midnight stars
    aflame
    And living things of light like flames in
    flower   10
That glance and flash as though no hand
    might tame
        Lightnings whose life outshone their
        stormlit hour
        And played and laughed on earth, with
        all their power
Gone, and with all their joy of life made long
And harmless as the lightning life of song, 15
Shine sweet like stars when darkness feels
    them strong.

The deep mild purple flaked with moonbright
    gold
    That makes the scales seem flowers of
    hardened light,
The flamelike tongue, the feet that noon
    leaves cold,
    The kindly trust in man, whence once the
    sight   20
    Grew less than strange, and faith bade fear
    take flight,
Outlive the little harmless life that shone
And gladdened eyes that loved it, and was
    gone
Ere love might fear that fear had looked
    thereon.

Fear held the bright thing hateful, even as
    fear,   25
    Whose name is one with hate and horror,
    saith
That heaven, the dark deep heaven of water
    near,
    Is deadly deep as hell and dark as death.
    The rapturous plunge that quickens blood
    and breath
With pause more sweet than passion, ere they
    strive   30
To raise again the limbs that yet would dive
Deeper, should there have slain the soul alive.

As the bright salamander in fire of the noon-
    shine exults and is glad of his day,
The spirit that quickens my body rejoices to
    pass from the sunlight away,
To pass from the glow of the mountain flower-
    age, the high multitudinous bloom,   35

On the Death of Robert Browning. Browning died in Venice
on December 12, 1889. This is the seventh in a series of
sonnets on Browning's death.
    6. **"Look forth."** These words are a translation of
Prospice, the title of one of Browning's poems, p. 317.
    The Lake of Gaube. Swinburne visited the Lake of Gaube,
in the heart of the Pyrenees Mountains, between France and
Spain, in the spring of 1862. See Critical Notes.

6. **lawns**, levels, open spaces. 10. **living . . . light**, salamanders, which were supposed to be able to live unharmed in
fire. See Critical Note on title. 27-28. **That heaven . . .
death**, a reference to the local superstition that death awaited
anyone who dared to bathe in the lake.

Far down through the fathomless night of the
  water, the gladness of silence and
  gloom.
Death-dark and delicious as death in the
  dream of a lover and dreamer may
  be,
It clasps and encompasses body and soul with
  delight to be living and free —
Free utterly now, though the freedom endure
  but the space of a perilous breath,
And living, though girdled about with the
  darkness and coldness and strangeness
  of death —   40
Each limb and each pulse of the body rejoic-
  ing, each nerve of the spirit at rest,
All sense of the soul's life rapture, a passionate
  peace in its blindness blest.
So plunges the downward swimmer, embraced
  of the water unfathomed of man,
The darkness unplummeted, icier than seas
  in midwinter, for blessing or ban;
And swiftly and sweetly, when strength and
  breath fall short, and the dive is done,
Shoots up as a shaft from the dark depth shot,
  sped straight into sight of the sun;   46
And sheer through the snow-soft water, more
  dark than the roof of the pines above,
Strikes forth, and is glad as a bird whose
  flight is impelled and sustained of love.
As a sea-mew's love of the sea-wind breasted
  and ridden for rapture's sake
Is the love of his body and soul for the darkling delight of the soundless lake;   50
As the silent speed of a dream too living to
  live for a thought's space more
Is the flight of his limbs through the still
  strong chill of the darkness from shore
  to shore.
Might life be as this is and death be as life
  that casts off time as a robe,
The likeness of infinite heaven were a symbol
  revealed of the lake of Gaube.

Whose thought has fashioned and measured
  The darkness of life and of death,   56
The secret within them treasured,
  The spirit that is not breath?
Whose vision has yet beholden
  The splendor of death and of life?   60
Though sunset as dawn be golden,
  Is the word of them peace, not strife?
Deep silence answers; the glory
  We dream of may be but a dream,
And the sun of the soul wax hoary   65
  As ashes that show not a gleam.
But well shall it be with us ever
  Who drive through the darkness here,
If the soul that we live by never,
  For aught that a lie saith, fear.   70
  (1899)

EDWARD LEAR (1812-1888)

THE JUMBLIES

They went to sea in a sieve, they did;
  In a sieve they went to sea;
In spite of all their friends could say,
On a winter's morn, on a stormy day,
  In a sieve they went to sea.   5
And when the sieve turned round and round,
And everyone cried, "You'll all be drowned!"
They called aloud, "Our sieve ain't big,
But we don't care a button; we don't care a
  fig—
  In a sieve we'll go to sea!"   10
    Far and few, far and few,
      Are the lands where the Jumblies live.
      Their heads are green, and their hands
        are blue;
      And they went to sea in a sieve.

They sailed away in a sieve, they did,   15
  In a sieve they sailed so fast,
With only a beautiful pea-green veil
Tied with a ribbon, by way of a sail,
  To a small tobacco-pipe mast.
And everyone said who saw them go,   20
"Oh! won't they be soon upset, you know,
For the sky is dark, and the voyage is long;
And, happen what may, it's extremely wrong
  In a sieve to sail so fast."

The water it soon came in, it did;   25
  The water it soon came in.
So, to keep them dry, they wrapped their feet
In a pinky paper all folded neat;
  And they fastened it down with a pin.
And they passed the night in a crockery-jar;
And each of them said, "How wise we are! 31
Though the sky be dark, and the voyage be
  long,
Yet we never can think we were rash or
  wrong,
  While round in our sieve we spin."

And all night long they sailed away;   35
  And, when the sun went down,
They whistled and warbled a moony song
To the echoing sound of a coppery gong,
  In the shade of the mountains brown,
"O Timballoo! how happy we are   40
When we live in a sieve and a crockery-jar!
And all night long, in the moonlight pale,
We sail away with a pea-green sail
  In the shade of the mountains brown."

They sailed to the Western Sea, they did —
  To a land all covered with trees;   46
And they bought an owl, and a useful cart,
And a pound of rice, and a cranberry-tart,

And a hive of silvery bees;
And they bought a pig, and some green jack-
    daws,   50
And a lovely monkey with lollipop paws,
And forty bottles of ring-bo-ree,
    And no end of Stilton cheese.

And in twenty years they all came back—
    In twenty years or more;   55
And everyone said, "How tall they've grown!
For they've been to the Lakes, and the Tor-
    rible Zone,
And the hills of the Chankly Bore."
And they drank their health, and gave them
    a feast
Of dumplings made of beautiful yeast;   60
And everyone said, "If we only live,
We, too, will go to sea in a sieve,
    To the hills of the Chankly Bore."
      Far and few, far and few,
      Are the lands where the Jumblies live.
      Their heads are green, and their hands
      are blue;   66
      And they went to sea in a sieve.
                       (1871)

THE OWL AND THE PUSSY-CAT

The Owl and the Pussy-Cat went to sea
    In a beautiful pea-green boat;
They took some honey, and plenty of money
    Wrapped up in a five-pound note.
The Owl looked up to the stars above,   5
    And sang to a small guitar,
"O lovely Pussy, O Pussy, my love,
    What a beautiful Pussy you are,
        You are,
        You are!   10
    What a beautiful Pussy you are!"

Pussy said to the Owl, "You elegant fowl,
    How charmingly sweet you sing!
Oh! let us be married; too long we have
    tarried;
    But what shall we do for a ring?"   15
They sailed away, for a year and a day,
    To the land where the bong-tree grows;
And there in a wood a Piggy-wig stood,
    With a ring at the end of his nose,
        His nose,   20
        His nose,
    With a ring at the end of his nose.

"Dear Pig, are you willing to sell for one
    shilling
    Your ring?" Said the Piggy, "I will."
So they took it away, and were married next
    day   25
    By the Turkey who lives on the hill.

53. **Stilton cheese**, a popular brand of English cheese, originally sold at Stilton, a parish in Huntingdonshire.

They dined on mince and slices of quince,
    Which they ate with a runcible spoon;
And hand in hand, on the edge of the sand,
    They danced by the light of the moon,
        The moon,   31
        The moon,
    They danced by the light of the moon.
                       (1871)

LIMERICKS

There was an Old Man with a beard,
Who said, "It is just as I feared!—
Two Owls and a Hen, four Larks and a Wren,
Have all built their nests in my beard!"

———

There was an Old Man in a tree,
Who was horribly bored by a Bee;
When they said, "Does it buzz?" he replied,
    "Yes, it does!
It's a regular brute of a Bee!"

———

There was an Old Man of the Coast,
Who placidly sat on a post;
But when it was cold, he relinquished his hold,
And called for some hot buttered toast.

———

There was an Old Man of Berlin,
Whose form was uncommonly thin;
Till he once, by mistake, was mixed up in a
    cake,
So they baked that Old Man of Berlin.

———

There was an old man in a barge,
Whose nose was exceedingly large;
But in fishing by night, it supported a light,
Which helped that old man in a barge.

———

There was an old man on the Border,
Who lived in the utmost disorder;
He danced with the cat, and made tea in his
    hat,
Which vexed all the folks on the Border.
                       (1871)

CHARLES STUART CALVERLEY
(1831-1884)

COMPANIONS

A TALE OF A GRANDFATHER

I know not of what we pondered
    Or made pretty pretense to talk,
As, her hand within mine, we wandered

Toward the pool by the lime-tree walk,
    While the dew fell in showers from the passion
        flowers 5
    And the blush-rose bent on her stalk.

I cannot recall her figure:
    Was it regal as Juno's own?
Or only a trifle bigger
    Than the elves who surround the throne 10
Of the Faëry Queen, and are seen, I ween,
    By mortals in dreams alone?

What her eyes were like I know not:
    Perhaps they were blurred with tears;
And perhaps in yon skies there glow not 15
    (On the contrary) clearer spheres.
No! as to her eyes I am just as wise
    As you or the cat, my dears.

Her teeth, I presume, were "pearly":
    But which was she, brunette or blonde? 20
Her hair, was it quaintly curly;
    Or as straight as a beadle's wand?
That I failed to remark; it was rather dark
    And shadowy round the pond.

Then the hand that reposed so snugly 25
    In mine — was it plump or spare?
Was the countenance fair or ugly?
    Nay, children, you have me there!
My eyes were p'haps blurred; and besides I'd
        heard
    That it's horribly rude to stare. 30

And I — was I brusque and surly?
    Or oppressively bland and fond?
Was I partial to rising early?
    Or why did we twain abscond,
When nobody knew, from the public view 35
    To prowl by a misty pond?

What passed, what was felt or spoken —
    Whether anything passed at all —
And whether the heart was broken
    That beat under that shelt'ring shawl — 40
(If shawl she had on, which I doubt) — has
        gone,
    Yes, gone from me past recall.

Was I haply the lady's suitor?
    Or her uncle? I can't make out;
Ask your governess, dears, or tutor. 45
    For myself, I'm in hopeless doubt
As to why we were there, who on earth we
        were,
    And what this is all about.

(1872)

8. **Juno**, queen of the gods. 11. **ween**, think. 22. **bea-
dle's wand**. court-summoner's staff.

BALLAD

PART 1

The auld wife sat at her ivied door,
    (*Butter and eggs and a pound of cheese*)
A thing she had frequently done before;
    And her spectacles lay on her aproned
        knees.

The piper he piped on the hilltop high, 5
    (*Butter and eggs and a pound of cheese*)
Till the cow said, "I die," and the goose
        asked "Why?"
    And the dog said nothing, but searched for
        fleas.

The farmer he strode through the square
        farmyard;
    (*Butter and eggs and a pound of cheese*) 10
His last brew of ale was a trifle hard,
    The connection of which with the plot one
        sees.

The farmer's daughter hath frank blue eyes;
    (*Butter and eggs and a pound of cheese*)
She hears the rooks caw in the windy skies,
    As she sits at her lattice and shells her
        peas. 16

The farmer's daughter hath ripe red lips;
    (*Butter and eggs and a pound of cheese*)
If you try to approach her away she skips
    Over tables and chairs with apparent ease.

The farmer's daughter hath soft brown hair;
    (*Butter and eggs and a pound of cheese*) 22
And I met with a ballad, I can't say where,
    Which wholly consisted of lines like these.

PART 2

She sat with her hands 'neath her dimpled
        cheeks, 25
    (*Butter and eggs and a pound of cheese*)
And spake not a word. While a lady speaks
    There is hope, but she didn't even sneeze.

She sat with her hands 'neath her crimson
        cheeks;
    (*Butter and eggs and a pound of cheese*) 30
She gave up mending her father's breeks,
    And let the cat roll in her best chemise.

She sat with her hands 'neath her burning
        cheeks,
    (*Butter and eggs and a pound of cheese*)
And gazed at the piper for thirteen weeks; 35
    Then she followed him out o'er the misty
        leas.

31. **breeks**, breeches.

Her sheep followed her, as their tails did them,
  (*Butter and eggs and a pound of cheese*)
And this song is considered a perfect gem;
    And as to the meaning, it's what you
      please.   (1872)

CHARLES LUTWIDGE DODGSON
("Lewis Carroll") (1832-1898)

From *ALICE'S ADVENTURES IN WONDERLAND*

FATHER WILLIAM

"You are old, Father William," the young
  man said,
"And your hair has become very white,
And yet you incessantly stand on your head—
  Do you think, at your age, it is right?"

"In my youth," Father William replied to his
  son,   5
"I feared it might injure the brain;
But now that I'm perfectly sure I have none,
  Why, I do it again and again."

"You are old," said the youth, "as I men-
  tioned before,
  And have grown most uncommonly fat; 10
Yet you turned a back-somersault in at the
  door—
  Pray, what is the reason of that?"

"In my youth," said the sage, as he shook his
  gray locks,
  "I kept all my limbs very supple
By the use of this ointment—one shilling
  the box—   15
  Allow me to sell you a couple."

"You are old," said the youth, "and your
  jaws are too weak
  For anything tougher than suet;
Yet you finished the goose, with the bones
  and the beak;
  Pray, how did you manage to do it?"   20

"In my youth," said his father, "I took to
  the law,
  And argued each case with my wife;
And the muscular strength which it gave to
  my jaw
  Has lasted the rest of my life."

"You are old," said the youth, "one would
  hardly suppose   25
  That your eye was as steady as ever;

Father William. This is a parody on Southey's *The Old Man's Comforts*. See Critical Notes.

Yet you balanced an eel on the end of your
  nose—
  What made you so awfully clever?"

"I have answered three questions, and that
  is enough,"
  Said his father; "don't give yourself airs! 30
Do you think I can listen all day to such
  stuff?
  Be off, or I'll kick you downstairs!" (1865)

THE MOCK TURTLE'S SONG

"Will you walk a little faster?" said a whiting
  to a snail,
"There's a porpoise close behind us, and he's
  treading on my tail.
See how eagerly the lobsters and the turtles
  all advance!
They are waiting on the shingle—will you
  come and join the dance?
  Will you, won't you, will you, won't you,
    will you join the dance?   5
  Will you, won't you, will you, won't you,
    won't you join the dance?

"You can really have no notion how delight-
  ful it will be
When they take us up and throw us, with
  the lobsters, out to sea!"
But the snail replied, "Too far, too far!" and
  gave a look askance—
Said he thanked the whiting kindly, but he
  would not join the dance.   10
  Would not, could not, would not, could
    not, would not join the dance.
  Would not, could not, would not, could
    not, could not join the dance.

"What matters it how far we go?" his scaly
  friend replied,
"There is another shore, you know, upon the
  other side.
The further off from England the nearer is
  to France;   15
Then turn not pale, beloved snail, but come
  and join the dance.
  Will you, won't you, will you, won't you,
    will you join the dance?
  Will you, won't you, will you, won't you,
    won't you join the dance?"   (1865)

From *THROUGH THE LOOKING-GLASS*
JABBERWOCKY

'Twas brillig, and the slithy toves
  Did gyre and gimble in the wabe;
All mimsy were the borogoves,
  And the mome raths outgrabe.

"Beware the Jabberwock, my son!   5
  The jaws that bite, the claws that catch!
Beware the Jubjub bird, and shun
  The frumious Bandersnatch!"

He took his vorpal sword in hand;
  Long time the manxome foe he sought —
So rested he by the Tumtum tree,   11
  And stood awhile in thought.

And, as in uffish thought he stood,
  The Jabberwock, with eyes of flame,
Came whiffling through the tulgey wood,   15
  And burbled as it came!

One, two! One, two! And through and through
  The vorpal blade went snicker-snack!
He left it dead, and with its head
  He went galumphing back.   20

"And hast thou slain the Jabberwock?
  Come to my arms, my beamish boy!
O frabjous day! Callooh! Callay!"
  He chortled in his joy.

'Twas brillig, and the slithy toves   25
  Did gyre and gimble in the wabe;
All mimsy were the borogoves,
  And the mome raths outgrabe.   (1872)

THE WALRUS AND THE CARPENTER

The sun was shining on the sea,
  Shining with all his might;
He did his very best to make
  The billows smooth and bright —
And this was odd, because it was   5
  The middle of the night.

The moon was shining sulkily,
  Because she thought the sun
Had got no business to be there
  After the day was done —   10
"It's very rude of him," she said,
  "To come and spoil the fun!"

The sea was wet as wet could be,
  The sands were dry as dry.
You could not see a cloud, because   15
  No cloud was in the sky;
No birds were flying overhead —
  There were no birds to fly.

The Walrus and the Carpenter
  Were walking close at hand;   20
They wept like anything to see
  Such quantities of sand.
"If this were only cleared away,"
  They said, "it *would* be grand!"

"If seven maids with seven mops   25
  Swept it for half a year,
Do you suppose," the Walrus said,
  "That they could get it clear?"
"I doubt it," said the Carpenter,
  And shed a bitter tear.   30

"O Oysters, come and walk with us!"
  The Walrus did beseech.
"A pleasant walk, a pleasant talk,
  Along the briny beach;
We cannot do with more than four,   35
  To give a hand to each."

The eldest Oyster looked at him,
  But never a word he said;
The eldest Oyster winked his eye,
  And shook his heavy head —   40
Meaning to say he did not choose
  To leave the oyster-bed.

But four young Oysters hurried up,
  All eager for the treat;
Their coats were brushed, their faces washed,
  Their shoes were clean and neat —   46
And this was odd, because, you know,
  They hadn't any feet.

Four other Oysters followed them,
  And yet another four;   50
And thick and fast they came at last,
  And more, and more, and more —
All hopping through the frothy waves,
  And scrambling to the shore.

The Walrus and the Carpenter   55
  Walked on a mile or so,
And then they rested on a rock
  Conveniently low;
And all the little Oysters stood
  And waited in a row.   60

"The time has come," the Walrus said,
  "To talk of many things:
Of shoes — and ships — and sealing-wax —
  Of cabbages — and kings —
And why the sea is boiling hot —   65
  And whether pigs have wings."

"But wait a bit," the Oysters cried,
  "Before we have our chat;
For some of us are out of breath,
  And all of us are fat!"   70
"No hurry!" said the Carpenter.
  They thanked him much for that.

"A loaf of bread," the Walrus said,
  "Is what we chiefly need;
Pepper and vinegar besides   75
  Are very good indeed —

Now, if you're ready, Oysters dear,
  We can begin to feed."

"But not on us!" the Oysters cried,
  Turning a little blue.   80
"After such kindness, that would be
  A dismal thing to do!"
"The night is fine," the Walrus said,
  "Do you admire the view?

"It was so kind of you to come!   85
  And you are very nice!"
The Carpenter said nothing but
  "Cut us another slice.
I wish you were not quite so deaf —
  I've had to ask you twice!"   90

"It seems a shame," the Walrus said,
  "To play them such a trick,
After we've brought them out so far,
  And made them trot so quick!"
The Carpenter said nothing but   95
  "The butter's spread too thick!"

"I weep for you," the Walrus said;
  "I deeply sympathize."
With sobs and tears he sorted out
  Those of the largest size,   100
Holding his pocket-handkerchief
  Before his streaming eyes.

"O Oysters," said the Carpenter,
  "You've had a pleasant run!
Shall we be trotting home again?"   105
  But answer came there none —
And this was scarcely odd, because
  They'd eaten every one.

                      (1872)

From THE HUNTING OF THE SNARK
THE BAKER'S TALE

They roused him with muffins — they roused
  him with ice —
  They roused him with mustard and cress —
They roused him with jam and judicious
  advice —
  They set him conundrums to guess.

When at length he sat up and was able to
  speak,   5
  His sad story he offered to tell;
And the Bellman cried, "Silence! Not even
  a shriek!"
  And excitedly tingled his bell.

    The Baker's Tale. **1. him,** the Baker, who had fainted
when the Bellman, after mentioning the "unmistakable
marks" of snarks, had said, "Some are Boojums."

There was silence supreme! Not a shriek,
  not a scream,
  Scarcely even a howl or a groan,   10
As the man they called "Ho!" told his story
  of woe
In an antediluvian tone.

"My father and mother were honest though
  poor —"
  "Skip all that!" cried the Bellman in haste.
"If it once becomes dark, there's no chance
  of a Snark —   15
We have hardly a minute to waste!"

"I skip forty years," said the Baker, in tears,
  "And proceed without further remark
To the day when you took me aboard of your
  ship
  To help you in hunting the Snark.   20

"A dear uncle of mine (after whom I was
  named)
  Remarked, when I bade him farewell —"
"Oh, skip your dear uncle!" the Bellman
  exclaimed,
  As he angrily tingled his bell.

"He remarked to me then," said that mildest
  of men,   25
  " 'If your Snark be a Snark, that is right;
Fetch it home by all means — you may serve
  it with greens,
  And it's handy for striking a light.

" 'You may seek it with thimbles — and seek
  it with care;
  You may hunt it with forks and hope; 30
You may threaten its life with a railway-
  share;
  You may charm it with smiles and soap—' "

("That's exactly the method," the Bellman
  bold
  In a hasty parenthesis cried,
"That's exactly the way I have always been
  told   35
  That the **capture** of Snarks should be
  tried!")

" 'But oh, beamish nephew, beware of the
  day,
  If your Snark be a Boojum! For then
You will softly and suddenly vanish away,
  And never be met with again!'   40

"It is this, it is this that oppresses my soul,
  When I think of my uncle's last words;
And my heart is like nothing so much as a
  bowl
  Brimming over with quivering curds!

"It is this, it is this — " "We have had that
   before!" 45
The Bellman indignantly said.
And the Baker replied, "Let me say it once
   more.
It is this, it is this that I dread!

"I engage with the Snark — every night after
   dark —
In a dreamy, delirious fight; 50
I serve it with greens in those shadowy scenes,
And I use it for striking a light;

"But if ever I meet with a Boojum, that day,
   In a moment (of this I am sure),
I shall softly and suddenly vanish away — 55
And the notion I cannot endure!" (1876)

WILLIAM SCHWENCK GILBERT
(1836-1911)

THE YARN OF THE *NANCY BELL* —

'Twas on the shores that round our coast
   From Deal to Ramsgate span,
That I found alone on a piece of stone
   An elderly naval man.

His hair was weedy, his beard was long, 5
   And weedy and long was he,
And I heard this wight on the shore recite
   In a singular minor key:

"Oh, I am a cook and a captain bold,
   And the mate of the *Nancy* brig, 10
And a bo'sun tight, and a midshipmite,
   And the crew of the captain's gig."

And he shook his fists and he tore his hair,
   Till I really felt afraid,
For I couldn't help thinking the man had
   been drinking, 15
   And so I simply said:

"Oh, elderly man, it's little I know
   Of the duties of men of the sea,
And I'll eat my hand if I understand
   However you can be 20

"At once a cook, and a captain bold,
   And the mate of the *Nancy* brig,
And a bo'sun tight, and a midshipmite,
   And the crew of the captain's gig."

The *Yarn of the Nancy Bell*. This poem was first offered
to *Punch* but was declined by the editor on the ground that
it was too cannibalistic for his readers' tastes.
   2. Deal, Ramsgate. These are famous watering-places
about ten miles apart on the coast of Kent.

Then he gave a hitch to his trousers, which
   Is a trick all seamen larn, 26
And having got rid of a thumping quid,
   He spun this painful yarn:

" 'Twas in the good ship *Nancy Bell*
   That we sailed to the Indian Sea, 30
And there on a reef we come to grief,
   Which has often occurred to me.

"And pretty nigh all the crew was drowned
   (There was seventy-seven o' soul),
And only ten of the *Nancy's* men 35
   Said 'Here!' to the muster-roll.

"There was me and the cook and the captain
   bold,
And the mate of the *Nancy* brig,
And the bo'sun tight, and a midshipmite,
   And the crew of the captain's gig. 40

"For a month we'd neither wittles nor drink,
   Till a-hungry we did feel,
So we drawed a lot, and, accordin' shot
   The captain for our meal.

"The next lot fell to the *Nancy's* mate, 45
   And a delicate dish he made;
Then our appetite with the midshipmite
   We seven survivors stayed.

"And then we murdered the bo'sun tight,
   And he much resembled pig; 50
Then we wittled free, did the cook and me,
   On the crew of the captain's gig.

"Then only the cook and me was left,
   And the delicate question, 'Which
Of us two goes to the kettle?' arose, 55
   And we argued it out as sich.

"For I loved that cook as a brother, I did,
   And the cook he worshiped me;
But we'd both be blowed if we'd either be
   stowed
In the other chap's hold, you see. 60

" 'I'll be eat if you dines off me,' says Tom;
   'Yes, that,' says I, 'you'll be —'
'I'm boiled if I die, my friend,' quoth I;
   And 'Exactly so,' quoth he.

"Says he, 'Dear James, to murder me 65
   Were a foolish thing to do,
For don't you see that you can't cook *me*,
   While I can — and will — cook *you!*'

"So he boils the water, and takes the salt
   And the pepper in portions true 70

(Which he never forgot) and some chopped
    shalot,
And some sage and parsley too.

" 'Come here,' says he, with a proper pride
    Which his smiling features tell,
' 'Twill soothing be if I let you see   75
    How extremely nice you'll smell.'

"And he stirred it round and round and
    round,
And he sniffed at the foaming froth;
When I ups with his heels, and smothers his
    squeals
    In the scum of the boiling broth.   80

"And I eat that cook in a week or less,
    And — as I eating be
The last of his chops, why, I almost drops,
    For a wessel in sight I see!

.   .   .   .   .

"And I never larf, and I never smile,   85
    And I never lark nor play,
But sit and croak, and a single joke
    I have — which is to say:

" 'Oh, I am a cook and a captain bold,
    And the mate of the *Nancy* brig,   90
And a bo'sun tight, and a midshipmite,
    And the crew of the captain's gig!' " (1866)

THE BISHOP OF RUM-TI-FOO

From east and south the holy clan
Of bishops gathered, to a man;
To Synod, called Pan-Anglican;
    In flocking crowds they came.
Among them was a Bishop, who   5
Had lately been appointed to
The balmy isle of Rum-ti-Foo,
    And Peter was his name.

His people — twenty-three in sum —
They played the eloquent tum-tum   10
And lived on scalps served up in rum —
    The only sauce they knew.
When first good BISHOP PETER came
(For PETER was that Bishop's name),
To humor them, he did the same   15
    As they of Rum-ti-Foo.

His flock, I've often heard him tell
(His name was PETER), loved him well,
And summoned by the sound of bell,
    In crowds together came.   20
"Oh, Massa, why you go away?
Oh, MASSA PETER, please to stay."
(They called him PETER, people say,
    Because it was his name.)

He told them all good boys to be,   25
And sailed away across the sea,
At London Bridge that Bishop he
    Arrived one Tuesday night —
And as that night he homeward strode
To his Pan-Anglican abode   30
He passed along the Borough Road
    And saw a gruesome sight.

He saw a crowd assembled round
A person dancing on the ground,
Who straight began to leap and bound   35
    With all his might and main.
To see that dancing man he stopped,
Who twirled and wriggled, skipped and
    hopped,
Then down incontinently dropped,
    And then sprang up again.   40

The Bishop chuckled at the sight,
"This style of dancing would delight
A simple Rum-ti-Foozle-ite.
    I'll learn it, if I can,
To please the tribe when I get back."   45
He begged the man to teach his knack.
"Right Reverend Sir, in half a crack,"
    Replied that dancing man.

The dancing man he worked away
And taught the Bishop every day —   50
The dancer skipped like any fay —
    Good PETER did the same.
The Bishop buckled to his task
With *battements*, cuts, and *pas de basque*
(I'll tell you, if you care to ask,   55
    That PETER was his name).

"Come, walk like this," the dancer said,
"Stick out your toes — stick in your head,
Stalk on with quick, galvanic tread —
    Your fingers thus extend;   60
The attitude's considered quaint."
The weary Bishop, feeling faint,
Replied, "I do not say it ain't,
    But 'Time!' my Christian friend!"

---

71. **shalot**, a kind of onion.
The Bishop of Rum-Ti-Foo. The imaginary bishopric of Rum-Ti-Foo may be placed in England's island possessions in the South Seas.
3. **Synod . . . Pan-Anglican.** The first General Council of the Pan-Anglican Churches, to which bishops of the Church of England came from all parts of the Empire, met in London, September 25, 1867. Gilbert's poem was published in *Fun* on November 16 of that year.

31. **Borough Road**, a street on the south bank of the Thames, between London Bridge and Lambeth Palace, where the meetings of the Synod were held. 54. **battements . . . basque**, agile dance movements, involving striking the feet together, crossing over, and quick turning.

"We now proceed to something new— 65
Dance as the PAYNES and LAURIS do,
Like this—one, two—one, two—one, two."
    The Bishop, never proud,
But in an overwhelming heat
(His name was PETER, I repeat) 70
Performed the PAYNE and LAURI feat,
    And puffed his thanks aloud.

Another game the dancer planned—
"Just take your ankle in your hand,
And try, my lord, if you can stand— 75
    Your body stiff and stark.
If when revisiting your see,
You learnt to hop on shore—like me—
The novelty must striking be,
    And must excite remark." 80

"No," said the worthy Bishop, "No;
That is a length to which, I trow,
Colonial Bishops cannot go.
    You may express surprise
At finding Bishops deal in pride— 85
But, if that trick I ever tried,
I should appear undignified
    In Rum-ti-Foozle's eyes.

"The islanders of Rum-ti-Foo
Are well-conducted persons, who 90
Approve a joke as much as you,
    And laugh at it as such;
But if they saw their Bishop land,
His leg supported in his hand,
The joke they wouldn't understand— 95
    'Twould pain them very much!"
                                    (1867)

From *TRIAL BY JURY*

THE JUDGE'S SONG

When I, good friends, was called to the Bar,
    I'd an appetite fresh and hearty,
But I was, as many young barristers are,
    An impecunious party.
I'd a swallow-tail coat of a beautiful blue—
    A brief which was brought by a booby— 6

A couple of shirts and a collar or two,
    And a ring that looked like a ruby!

In Westminster Hall I danced a dance,
    Like a semi-despondent fury; 10
For I thought I should never hit on a chance
    Of addressing a British jury—
But I soon got tired of third-class journeys,
    And dinners of bread and water;
So I fell in love with a rich attorney's 15
    Elderly, ugly daughter.

The rich attorney, he wiped his eyes,
    And replied to my fond professions:
"You shall reap the reward of your enterprise,
    At the Bailey and Middlesex Sessions. 20
You'll soon get used to her looks," said he,
    "And a very nice girl you'll find her—
She may very well pass for forty-three
    In the dusk, with a light behind her!"

The rich attorney was as good as his word; 25
    The briefs came trooping gayly,
And every day my voice was heard
    At the Sessions or Ancient Bailey.
All thieves who could my fees afford
    Relied on my orations, 30
And many a burglar I've restored
    To his friends and his relations.

At length I became as rich as the GURNEYS—
    An incubus then I thought her,
So I threw over that rich attorney's 35
    Elderly, ugly daughter.
The rich attorney my character high
    Tried vainly to disparage—
And now, if you please, I'm ready to try
    This Breach of Promise of Marriage! 40
                                    (1875)

From *THE PIRATES OF PENZANCE*

THE POLICEMAN'S LOT

When a felon's not engaged in his employment,
    Or maturing his felonious little plans,
His capacity for innocent enjoyment
    Is just as great as any honest man's.
Our feelings we with difficulty smother 5
    When constabulary duty's to be done.
Ah, take one consideration with another,
    A policeman's lot is not a happy one!

---

66. **Paynes and Lauris**, two families of actors, pantomimists, and dancers. The Paynes, a father and four children, acted in legitimate drama and performed in ballet and harlequinade before distinguished audiences; the Lauris, a brother and two sisters were cheap music-hall entertainers.
The Judge's Song. The remaining poems of Gilbert are taken from his comic operas. The Judge sings this song just after he takes his position on the bench before beginning the trial of a breach-of-promise suit.
6. **brief,** in English law, a condensed statement of the facts of a litigated case drawn up by an attorney for the use of a barrister in conducting proceedings in a court of justice. Only barristers are admitted to plead at the bar; attorneys, or solicitors, institute actions in behalf of their clients and furnish counsel (barristers) with necessary materials, facts, etc.

9. **Westminster Hall,** until 1882 the seat of England's chief law courts. 20. **Bailey,** "Old Bailey," central criminal court of London. **Middlesex,** a criminal court in Westminster. 33. **Gurneys,** a family of wealthy philanthropists.
The Policeman's Lot. The Sergeant, leader of sentimental police, laments that he must apprehend a band of ruthless but magnanimous pirates infesting the shores of Cornwall.

When the enterprising burglar's not a-bur-
       gling,
When the **cut-throat isn't** occupied in
       crime,   10
He loves to hear the little brook a-gurgling,
And listen to the merry village chime.
When the coster's finished jumping on his
       mother,
He loves to lie a-basking in the sun.
Ah, take one consideration with another,   15
The policeman's lot is not a happy one!
                                   (1879)

From *PATIENCE*

"OH, HOLLOW! HOLLOW! HOLLOW!"

What time the poet hath hymned
The writhing maid, lithe-limbed,
   Quivering on amaranthine asphodel,
How can he paint her woes,
Knowing, as well he knows,   5
   That all can be set right with calomel?

When from the poet's plinth
The amorous colocynth
   Yearns for the aloe, faint with rapturous
       thrills,
How can he hymn their throes   10
Knowing, as well he knows,
   That they are only uncompounded pills?

Is it, and can it be,
Nature hath this decree,
   Nothing poetic in the world shall dwell? 15
Or that in all her works
Something poetic lurks,
   Even in colocynth and calomel?
                       I cannot tell.
                                   (1881)

SONG: COLONEL

Colonel

When I first put this uniform on,
   I said, as I looked in the glass,

"It's one to a million
   That any civilian
My figure and form will surpass.   5
   Gold lace has a charm for the fair,
And I've plenty of that, and to spare,
   While a lover's professions,
   When uttered in Hessians,
Are eloquent everywhere!"   10
   A fact that I counted upon,
   When I first put this uniform on!

Chorus of Dragoons

By a simple coincidence, few
   Could ever have reckoned upon,
The same thing occurred to me, too,   15
   When I first put this uniform on!

Colonel

I said, when I first put it on,
   "It is plain to the veriest dunce
   That every beauty
   Will feel it her duty   20
To yield to its glamour at once.
   They will see that I'm freely gold-laced
   In a uniform handsome and chaste"—
   But the peripatetics
   Of long-haired aesthetics   25
Are very much more to their taste—
   Which I never counted upon,
   When I first put this uniform on!

Chorus

By a simple coincidence, few
   Could ever have counted upon,   30
I never thought that would come true,
   When I first put this uniform on!
                                   (1881)

RECITATIVE AND SONG: BUNTHORNE

Am I alone,
   And unobserved?   I am!
Then let me own
   I'm an aesthetic sham!
This air severe   5
   Is but a mere
       Veneer!

---

13. **coster,** a peddler of fruit, vegetables, and fish.
"Oh, Hollow! Hollow! Hollow!" Bunthorne tells the dairy-
maid Patience that this poem, which he has just composed,
"is a wild, weird, fleshly thing; yet very tender, very yearning, very precious. . . . It is the wail of the poet's heart on discovering that everything is commonplace. To understand
it," he concludes, "cling passionately to one another and
think of faint lilies."
   3. **amaranthine asphodel,** purplish lily. 6. **calomel,** a
purgative drug. 7. **plinth,** the block on which a statue or
other architectural unit rests. 8. **colocynth,** a plant of the
gourd family, the fruit of which yields a strong purgative.
9. **aloe,** a plant of the lily family.
Song: Colonel. Young women have spoken disparagingly of
the uniform of a British officer. In this song the Colonel and
the Dragoons defend it.

9. **Hessians,** high military boots, reaching nearly to the
knee. 25. **aesthetics,** aesthetes or persons who aspire
to a cultivated taste for the beautiful in nature or in art.
The Aesthetic Movement, self-consciously dedicated to the
principle of art for art's sake, had sufficiently organized its
forces by the early 1880's to attract much public attention
and ridicule; it was already influencing new fashions in dress
and deportment and at the same time inspiring such satires
as Gilbert's *Patience* and George du Maurier's drawings in
Punch.
   Recitative and Song: Bunthorne. As the Colonel and the
Dragoons depart, Bunthorne enters to deliver this confessional soliloquy in a singsong stage whisper.

This cynic smile
  Is but a wile
    Of guile!   10
This costume chaste
  Is but good taste
    Misplaced!
      Let me confess!
A languid love for lilies does *not* blight me! 15
Lank limbs and haggard cheeks do *not* delight
  me!
  I do *not* care for dirty greens
    By any means.
  I do *not* long for all one sees
    That's Japanese.   20
  I am *not* fond of uttering platitudes
    In stained-glass attitudes.
In short, my mediaevalism's affectation,
Born of a morbid love of admiration!
                                           (1881)

SONG: BUNTHORNE

If you're anxious for to shine in the high
  aesthetic line as a man of culture rare,
You must get up all the germs of the transcendental terms, and plant them everywhere.
You must lie upon the daisies, and discourse
  in novel phrases of your complicated
  state of mind,
The meaning doesn't matter if it's only idle
  chatter of a transcendental kind.
      And everyone will say,   5
        As you walk your mystic way,
"If this young man expresses himself in terms
  too deep for *me*,
Why, what a very singularly deep young man
  this deep young man must be!"

Be eloquent in praise of the very dull old days
  which have long since passed away,
And convince 'em, if you can, that the reign
  of good Queen Anne was Culture's
  palmiest day.   10
Of course you will pooh-pooh whatever's
  fresh and new, and declare it's crude and
  mean,
For Art stopped short in the cultivated court
  of the Empress Josephine.
      And everyone will say,
        As you walk your mystic way,

"If that's not good enough for him which is
  good enough for *me*,   15
Why, what a very cultivated kind of youth
  this kind of youth must be!"

Then a sentimental passion of a vegetable
  fashion must excite your languid spleen,
An attachment *à la* Plato for a bashful young
  potato, or a not-too-French French bean!
Though the Philistines may jostle, you will
  rank as an apostle in the high aesthetic
  band,
If you walk down Piccadilly with a poppy or
  a lily in your mediaeval hand.   20
      And everyone will say,
        As you walk your flowery way,
"If he's content with a vegetable love, which
  would certainly not suit *me*,
Why, what a most particularly pure young
  man this pure young man must be!"
                                           (1881)

From *IOLANTHE*

THE SUSCEPTIBLE CHANCELLOR

The law is the true embodiment
Of everything that's excellent.
It has no kind of fault or flaw,
And I, my lords, embody the law.
The constitutional guardian I   5
Of pretty young wards in Chancery.
All are agreeable girls, and none
Are over the age of twenty-one.
    A pleasant occupation for
    A rather susceptible Chancellor!   10

But though the compliment implied
Inflates me with legitimate pride,
It nevertheless can't be denied
That it has its inconvenient side.
For I'm not so old and not so plain,   15
And I'm quite prepared to marry again;
But there'd be the deuce to pay in the Lords
If I fell in love with one of my wards;
    Which rather tries my temper, for
    I'm *such* a susceptible Chancellor!   20

And everyone who'd marry a ward
Must come to me for my accord;

Song: Bunthorne. Bunthorne was dressed to resemble Oscar
Wilde, the most conspicuous figure among the young aesthetes; in this song he reviews—and caricatures—many of
Wilde's cultivated gestures and enthusiasms. See Biographical
Sketch of Wilde.
10. **reign . . . day.** The reign of Queen Anne (1702-14)
was an important period in the neoclassical movement in
English literature; Gilbert finds its emphasis on form rather
tedious. 12. **Empress Josephine**, first wife of Napoleon I
and empress of the French from 1804 to 1809.

17. **vegetable fashion.** Wilde was a vegetarian. 18.
attachment à la Plato, a Platonic love, which involved
a purely spiritual comradeship. 19. **Philistines**, persons
lacking liberal culture and refinement.
The Susceptible Chancellor. Phyllis, beloved by the half-
fairy Strephon and by the entire House of Lords, is a Ward
of Chancery, and so can marry only with the consent of the
Lord Chancellor, who in this song describes his dilemma.
6. **Chancery**, a branch of the High Court of Justice. The
wardship of infants and minors left without other guardian
comes under its jurisdiction. 17. **Lords**, the House of Lords,
of which the Lord Chancellor is the presiding officer.

So in my court I sit all day,
Giving agreeable girls away —
With one for him, and one for he,   25
And one for you, and one for ye,
And one for thou, and one for thee;
But never, oh, never, a one for me!
    Which is exasperating for   29
    A highly susceptible Chancellor!
                                    (1882)

SAID I TO MYSELF, SAID I

When I went to the Bar as a very young man
    (Said I to myself, said I),
I'll work on a new and original plan
    (Said I to myself, said I).
I'll never assume that a rogue or a thief   5
Is a gentleman worthy implicit belief
Because his attorney has sent me a brief
    (Said I to myself, said I).

I'll never throw dust in a juryman's eyes
    (Said I to myself, said I),   10
Or hoodwink a judge who is not over-wise
    (Said I to myself, said I).
Or assume that the witnesses summoned in
    force
In Exchequer, Queen's Bench, Common Pleas,
    or Divorce
Have perjured themselves as a matter of
    course   15
    (Said I to myself, said I).

Ere I go into court I will read my brief
    through
    (Said I to myself, said I),
And I'll never take work I'm unable to do
    (Said I to myself, said I).   20
My learned profession I'll never disgrace
By taking a fee with a grin on my face
When I haven't been there to attend to the
    case
    (Said I to myself, said I).

In other professions in which men engage   25
    (Said I to myself, said I),
The Army, the Navy, the Church, and the
    Stage
    (Said I to myself, said I),
Professional license, if carried too far,
Your chance of promotion will certainly
    mar;   30
And I fancy the rule might apply to the Bar
    (Said I to myself, said I).   (1882)

THE CONTEMPLATIVE SENTRY

When all night long a chap remains
    On sentry-go, to chase monotony
He exercises of his brains —
    That is, assuming that he's got any.
Though never nurtured in the lap   5
    Of luxury, yet I admonish you,
I am an intellectual chap,
    And think of things that would astonish
    you.
I often think it's comical
    How Nature always does contrive   10
That every boy and every gal,
    That's born into the world alive,
Is either a little Liberal,
    Or else a little Conservative.
        Fal, lal, la!   15

When in that house M.P.'s divide,
    If they've a brain and cerebellum too,
They've got to leave that brain outside
    And vote just as their leaders tell 'em
    to.
But then the prospect of a lot   20
    Of statesmen, all in close proximity,
A-thinking for themselves, is what
    No man can face with equanimity.
Then let's rejoice with loud fal, lal,
    That Nature wisely does contrive   25
That every boy and every gal
    That's born into the world alive
Is either a little Liberal,
    Or else a little Conservative.   29
        Fal, lal, la!
                                    (1882)

From *PRINCESS IDA*

THE DISAGREEABLE MAN

If you give me your attention, I will tell you
    what I am:
I'm a genuine philanthropist — all other
    kinds are sham.
Each little fault of temper and each social
    defect
In my erring fellow-creatures, I endeavor to
    correct.
To all their little weaknesses I open peoples'
    eyes,   5
And little plans to snub the self-sufficient I
    devise;
I love my fellow-creatures — I do all the
    good I can —

Said I to Myself, Said I. The Chancellor refuses to admit
that Strephon may love Phyllis without the Court's permission, even though the "case bubbles over with poetic emotion."
He says, "I have always kept my duty strictly before my eyes,
and it is to this fact that I owe my advancement to my
present distinguished position." He then sings this song.
    7. **attorney . . . brief.** See note on *The Judge's Song*,
line 6, p. 753.   14. **Exchequer . . . Divorce,** branches of the
High Court of Justice.

The Contemplative Sentry. On guard outside the Houses of
Parliament, Private Willis amuses himself with political
speculations.
The Disagreeable Man. The misshapen and adder-tongued
King Gama, who here describes himself, is a professional
cynic; he is later subjected to the ingenious torture of having
all his wants satisfied and hence being left with "nothing to
grumble at."

Yet everybody says I'm such a disagreeable
man!
    And I can't think why!

To compliments inflated I've a withering
reply,   10
And vanity I always do my best to morti-
fy;
A charitable action I can skillfully dissect;
And interested motives I'm delighted to
detect.
I know everybody's income and what everybody earns,
And I carefully compare it with the income-
tax returns;   15
But to benefit humanity, however much I
plan,
Yet everybody says I'm such a disagreeable
man!
    And I can't think why!

I'm sure I'm no ascetic; I'm as pleasant as
can be;
You'll always find me ready with a crushing
repartee;   20
I've an irritating chuckle, I've a celebrated
sneer,
I've an entertaining snigger, I've a fascinating
leer;
To everybody's prejudice I know a thing or
two;
I can tell a woman's age in half a minute —
and I do —
But although I try to make myself as pleasant
as I can,   25
Yet everybody says I'm such a disagreeable
man!
    And I can't think why!   (1884)

From THE MIKADO

THEY'LL NONE OF 'EM BE MISSED

As some day it may happen that a victim must
be found,
    I've got a little list — I've got a little list
Of social offenders who might well be underground,
    And who never would be missed — who
never would be missed!
There's the pestilential nuisances who write
for autographs —   5
All people who have flabby hands and irritating laughs —
All children who are up in dates, and floor
you with 'em flat —
All persons who in shaking hands, shake
hands with you like *that* —

They'll None of 'Em Be Missed. This song is sung by
Ko-Ko, the Lord High Executioner.

And all third persons who on spoiling *tête-à-
têtes* insist —
    They'd none of 'em be missed — they'd
none of 'em be missed!   10

Chorus

He's got 'em on the list — he's got 'em on
the list;
    And they'll none of 'em be missed — they'll
none of 'em be missed!

There's a nigger serenader, and the others of
his race,
    And the piano-organist — I've got him on
the list!
And the people who eat peppermint and puff
it in your face,   15
    They never would be missed — they never
would be missed!
Then the idiot who praises, with enthusiastic
tone,
All centuries but this, and every country
but his own;
And the lady from the provinces who dresses
like a guy,
And "who doesn't think she waltzes, but
would rather like to try"!   20
And that singular anomaly, the lady novelist —
    I don't think she'd be missed — I'm *sure*
she'd not be missed!

Chorus

He's got her on the list — he's got her on
the list;
    And I don't think she'll be missed—I'm
sure she'll not be missed!

And that *Nisi Prius* nuisance, who just now
is rather rife,   25
    The Judicial humorist — I've got *him* on
the list!
All funny fellows, comic men, and clowns of
private life —
    They'd none of 'em be missed — they'd
none of 'em be missed!
And apologetic statesmen of a compromising
kind,
Such as — What d'ye call him — Thing'em
bob, and likewise Never Mind,   30
And 'St — 'st — 'st — and What's-his-name,
and also You-know-who —
    The task of filling up the blanks I'd rather
leave to *you*.

25. **Nisi Prius**, literally, *unless before;* a law term used of
any cause involving issues of fact and appointed to be tried
in the courts of Westminster unless before the day set the
judges tried the cause in the county in which it arose.

But it really doesn't matter whom you put
   upon the list,
  For they'd none of 'em be missed —
    they'd none of 'em be missed!

Chorus

You may put 'em on the list — you may put
   'em on the list;   35
And they'll none of 'em be missed — they'll
   none of 'em be missed!   (1885)

THREE LITTLE MAIDS FROM SCHOOL

Three little maids from school are we,
Pert as a school girl well can be,
Filled to the brim with girlish glee,
    Three little maids from school!

Everything is a source of fun.   5
Nobody's safe, for we care for none!
Life is a joke that's just begun!
    Three little maids from school!

Three little maids who, all unwary,
Come from a ladies' seminary,   10
Freed from its genius tutelary —
    Three little maids from school!

One little maid is a bride, Yum-Yum —
Two little maids in attendance come —
Three little maids is the total sum,   15
    Three little maids from school!

From three little maids take one away —
Two little maids remain, and they —
Won't have to wait very long, they say —
    Three little maids from school!   20

Three little maids who, all unwary,
Come from a ladies' seminary,
Freed from its genius tutelary —
    Three little maids from school!   (1885)

LET THE PUNISHMENT
FIT THE CRIME

A more humane Mikado never
   Did in Japan exist,
    To nobody second,
    I'm certainly reckoned
  A true philanthropist.   5
It is my very humane endeavor
   To make, to some extent,
    Each evil liver
    A running river
Of harmless merriment.   10

My object all sublime
  I shall achieve in time —
To let the punishment fit the crime —
   The punishment fit the crime;
And make each prisoner pent   15
  Unwillingly represent
A source of innocent merriment,
  Of innocent merriment!

All prosy dull society sinners,
  Who chatter and bleat and bore,   20
   Are sent to hear sermons
   From mystical Germans
Who preach from ten to four.
The amateur tenor, whose vocal villainies
  All desire to shirk,   25
   Shall, during off-hours,
   Exhibit his powers
To Madame Tussaud's waxwork.

The lady who dyes a chemical yellow,
  Or stains her gray hair puce,   30
   Or pinches her figger,
   Is blacked like a nigger
With permanent walnut juice.
The idiot who, in railway carriages,
  Scribbles on window panes,   35
   We only suffer
   To ride on a buffer
In Parliamentary trains.

    My object all sublime, etc.

The advertising quack who wearies   40
  With tales of countless cures,
   His teeth, I've enacted,
   Shall all be extracted
By terrified amateurs.
The music hall singer attends a series   45
  Of masses and fugues and "ops"
   By Bach, interwoven
   With Spohr and Beethoven,
  At classical Monday Pops.

The billiard sharp whom any one catches,   50
  His doom's extremely hard —
   He's made to dwell
   In a dungeon cell
On a spot that's always barred.

Three Little Maids from School. This song is sung by Yum-Yum, Peep-Bo, and Pitti-Sing after they have been heralded by a Chorus of Yum-Yum's schoolfellows.
   Let the Punishment Fit the Crime. This song is sung by the Mikado after he has been heralded by a procession and a Chorus.

28. **Madame Tussaud's waxwork,** an exhibition of wax-portrait models of ancient and modern personages and historical tableaux, founded by Marie Tussaud (1760-1850) and located in Marylebone Road, London. 30. **puce,** dark brown. 38. **Parliamentary trains,** trains that each railway company was required to run daily each way over its system for the convenience of third-class passengers at a rate not over one penny a mile. 46. **masses . . . "ops."** A mass is the musical setting of certain portions of the Mass; a fugue is a musical composition developed from one or more given themes according to strict rules; ops are works. 47-48. **Bach . . . Beethoven,** Johann Sebastian Bach (1685-1750), famous German composer and musician; Ludwig Spohr (1784-1859), German composer; and Ludwig van Beethoven (1770-1827), noted Dutch composer, born in Germany. 49. **Monday Pops,** popular concerts of popular music given on Monday. A singer of cheap music is punished by being made to listen to serious music.

And there he plays extravagant matches   55
  In fitless finger-stalls,
    On a cloth untrue
    With a twisted cue,
And elliptical billiard balls!

  My object all sublime, etc.   (1885)

WILLOW, TITWILLOW

On a tree by a river a little tom-tit
  Sang "Willow, titwillow, titwillow!"
And I said to him, "Dicky-bird, why do you
  sit
Singing, 'Willow, titwillow, titwillow'?
Is it weakness of intellect, birdie?" I cried,   5
"Or a rather tough worm in your little inside?"
With shake of his poor little head he replied,
  "Oh, willow, titwillow, titwillow!"

He slapped at his chest, as he sat on that
  bough,
  Singing, "Willow, titwillow, titwillow!"   10
And a cold perspiration bespangled his brow,
  Oh, willow, titwillow, titwillow!
He sobbed and he sighed, and a gurgle he gave,
Then he threw himself into the billowy wave,
And an echo arose from the suicide's grave —
  "Oh, willow, titwillow, titwillow!"   16

Now I feel just as sure as I'm sure that my
  name
  Isn't Willow, titwillow, titwillow,
That 'twas blighted affection that made him
  exclaim,
  "Oh, willow, titwillow, titwillow!"   20
And if you remain callous and obdurate, I
Shall perish as he did, and you will know why,
Though I probably shall not exclaim as I die,
  "Oh, willow, titwillow, titwillow!"   (1885)

ARTHUR WILLIAM EDGAR O'SHAUGHNESSY (1844-1881)

THE FOUNTAIN OF TEARS

If you go over desert and mountain,
  Far into the country of sorrow,
  Today and tonight and tomorrow,
And maybe for months and for years,
  You shall come, with a heart that is bursting
  For trouble and toiling and thirsting,   6
You shall certainly come to the fountain
At length — to the Fountain of Tears.

Very peaceful the place is, and solely
  For piteous lamenting and sighing,   10
  And those who come living or dying
Alike from their hopes and their fears;
  Full of cypress-like shadows the place is,
  And statues that cover their faces;
But out of the gloom springs the holy   15
And beautiful Fountain of Tears.

And it flows and it flows with a motion
  So gentle and lovely and listless,
  And murmurs a tune so resistless
To him who hath suffered and hears —   20
  You shall surely — without a word spoken,
  Kneel down there and know your heart
    broken,
And yield to the long curbed emotion
That day by the Fountain of Tears.

For it grows and it grows, as though leap-
  ing
  Up higher the more one is thinking;   26
  And ever its tunes go on sinking
More poignantly into the ears;
  Yea, so blessèd and good seems that foun-
    tain,
  Reached after dry desert and mountain, 30
You shall fall down at length in your weeping
And bathe your sad face in the tears.

Then, alas! while you lie there a season,
  And sob between living and dying,
  And give up the land you were trying   35
To find 'mid your hopes and your fears;
  — O the world shall come up and pass o'er
    you;
  Strong men shall not stay to care for you,
Nor wonder indeed for what reason
Your way should seem harder than theirs.   40

But perhaps, while you lie, never lifting
  Your cheek from the wet leaves it presses,
  Nor caring to raise your wet tresses
And look how the cold world appears —
  O perhaps the mere silences round you —
  All things in that place grief hath found
    you,   46
Yea, e'en to the clouds o'er you drifting,
May soothe you somewhat through your tears.

You may feel, when a falling leaf brushes
  Your face, as though someone had kissed
    you,   50
  Or think at least someone who missed you
Hath sent you a thought — if that cheers;
  Or a bird's little song, faint and broken,
  May pass for a tender word spoken;
— Enough, while around you there rushes   55
That life-drowning torrent of tears.

---

56. **fitless finger-stalls,** ill-fitting coverings for the fingers.
  Willow, Titwillow. This song is sung by Ko-Ko, the Lord High Executioner of the Town of Titipu, as he tries to convince the elderly lady Katisha that he will "perish on the spot" if she does not accept his love. She had protested that no one had ever died of a broken heart.

13. **cypress-like,** dark and full of the associations of death.

And the tears shall flow faster and faster,
  Brim over, and baffle resistance,
    And roll down bleared roads to each dis-
      tance
Of past desolation and years;   60
  Till they cover the place of each sorrow,
  And leave you no Past and no morrow;
For what man is able to master
And stem the great Fountain of Tears?

But the floods and the tears meet and gather;
  The sound of them all grows like thunder.
   — O into what bosom, I wonder,
Is poured the whole sorrow of years?
  For Eternity only seems keeping
  Account of the great human weeping;   70
May God, then, the Maker and Father —
May He find a place for the tears!   (1870)

From CHAITIVEL

Hath any loved you well, down there,
  Summer or winter through?
Down there, have you found any fair
  Laid in the grave with you?
Is death's long kiss a richer kiss   5
  Than mine was wont to be —
Or have you gone to some far bliss
  And quite forgotten me?

What soft enamoring of sleep
  Hath you in some soft way?   10
What charmed death holdeth you with deep
  Strange lure by night and day?
  — A little space below the grass,
   Out of the sun and shade;
But worlds away from me, alas,   15
  Down there where you are laid?

My bright hair's waved and wasted gold,
  What is it now to thee —
Whether the rose-red life I hold
  Or white death holdeth me?   20
Down there you love the grave's own green,
  And evermore you rave
Of some sweet seraph you have seen
  Or dreamt of in the grave.

There you shall lie as you have lain,   25
  Though in the world above,
Another live your life again,
  Loving again your love.
Is it not sweet beneath the palm?

Is not the warm day rife   30
With some long mystic golden calm
  Better than love and life?

The broad quaint odorous leaves like hands
  Weaving the fair day through,
Weave sleep no burnished bird withstands, 35
  While death weaves sleep for you;
And many a strange rich breathing sound
  Ravishes morn and noon;
And in that place you must have found
  Death a delicious swoon.   40

Hold me no longer for a word
  I used to say or sing;
Ah, long ago you must have heard
  So many a sweeter thing.
For rich earth must have reached your heart
  And turned the faith to flowers;   46
And warm wind stolen, part by part,
  Your soul through faithless hours.

And many a soft seed must have won
  Soil of some yielding thought,   50
To bring a bloom up to the sun
  That else had ne'er been brought;
And, doubtless, many a passionate hue
  Hath made that place more fair,
Making some passionate part of you   55
  Faithless to me down there.   (1872)

ODE

We are the music makers,
  And we are the dreamers of dreams,
Wandering by lone sea-breakers,
  And sitting by desolate streams —
World-losers and world-forsakers,   5
  On whom the pale moon gleams —
Yet we are the movers and shakers
  Of the world forever, it seems.

With wonderful deathless ditties
We build up the world's great cities,   10
  And out of a fabulous story
  We fashion an empire's glory:
One man with a dream, at pleasure,
  Shall go forth and conquer a crown;
And three with a new song's measure   15
  Can trample a kingdom down.

We, in the ages lying
In the buried past of the earth,
Built Nineveh with our sighing,
  And Babel itself in our mirth;   20

Chaitivel. This poem is based freely upon a *lai* of Marie de France, 12th century poet and fabulist. Sarrazine has loved Pharamond and has given him a tress of her golden hair as a token; but he has died in warfare against the Paynims and has been buried with the tress of hair wrapped around him. Thereafter Sarrazine takes a new lover, Chaitivel. One day, in a mood of pity and half-revived love, she sings this song to Pharamond; he listens from his grave.
  23. seraph, angel.

Ode. Cf. Tennyson's *The Poet,* page 16.
  19-20. Built Nineveh, etc. Nineveh, the magnificent capital of the ancient Assyrian Empire, traditionally the greatest city, and Babel, the highest tower in the world, are taken as types of superb projects conceived by dreamers. See *Genesis,* 11:1-9.

And o'erthrew them with prophesying
　To the old of the new world's worth;
For each age is a dream that is dying,
　Or one that is coming to birth.

A breath of our inspiration　　　　　　25
Is the life of each generation;
　A wondrous thing of our dreaming
　Unearthly, impossible seeming —
The soldier, the king, and the peasant
　Are working together in one,　　　　　30
Till our dream shall become their present,
　And their work in the world be done.

They had no vision amazing
Of the goodly house they are raising;
　They had no divine foreshowing　　　　35
　Of the land to which they are going.
But on one man's soul it hath broken,
　A light that doth not depart;
And his look, or a word he hath spoken,
　Wrought flame in another man's heart.　40

And therefore today is thrilling
With a past day's late fulfilling;
　And the multitudes are enlisted
　In the faith that their fathers resisted,
And, scorning the dream of tomorrow,　　45
　And bringing to pass, as they may,
In the world, for its joy or its sorrow,
　The dream that was scorned yesterday.

But we, with our dreaming and singing,
　Ceaseless and sorrowless we!　　　　　50
The glory about us clinging
　Of the glorious futures we see,
Our souls with high music ringing.
　O men! it must ever be
That we dwell, in our dreaming and singing,
　A little apart from ye.　　　　　　　56

For we are afar with the dawning
　And the suns that are not yet high,
And out of the infinite morning
　Intrepid you hear us cry —　　　　　60
How, spite of your human scorning,
　Once more God's future draws nigh,
And already goes forth the warning
　That ye of the past must die.

Great hail! we cry to the comers　　　　65
　From the dazzling unknown shore;
Bring us hither your sun and your summers,
　And renew our world as of yore;
You shall teach us your song's new numbers,
　And things that we dreamed not before —
Yea, in spite of a dreamer who slumbers,　71
　And a singer who sings no more.　(1874)

21. o'erthrew . . . prophesying. O'Shaughnessy calls
the prophets of Israel poets. The destruction of Nineveh
was prophesied by Nahum (2-3), Jonah (1-4), and Zephaniah
(2:13-15); of Babylon by Isaiah (13, 14, 21, 47, etc.) and
Jeremiah (50-51).

SONG

I made another garden, yea,
　For my new love;
I left the dead rose where it lay,
　And set the new above.
Why did the summer not begin?　　　　5
Why did my heart not haste?
My old love came and walked therein,
　And laid the garden waste.

She entered with her weary smile,
　Just as of old;　　　　　　　　　10
She looked around a little while
　And shivered with the cold.
Her passing touch was death to all,
　Her passing look a blight;
She made the white rose-petals fall,　　15
　And turned the red rose white.

Her pale robe clinging to the grass
　Seemed like a snake
That bit the grass and ground, alas!
　And a sad trail did make.　　　　　20
She went up slowly to the gate;
　And there, just as of yore,
She turned back at the last to wait,
　And say farewell once more.　(1874)

ZULEIKA

Zuleika is fled away,
　Though your bolts and your bars were
　　strong;
A minstrel came to the gate today
　And stole her away with a song.
His song was subtle and sweet,　　　　5
It made her young heart beat,
　It gave a thrill to her faint heart's will,
And wings to her weary feet.

Zuleika was not for ye,
　Though your laws and your threats were
　　hard;　　　　　　　　　　10
The minstrel came from beyond the sea,
　And took her in spite of your guard.
His ladder of song was slight,
But it reached to her window height;
　Each verse so frail was the silken rail　15
From which her soul took flight.

The minstrel was fair and young;
　His heart was of love and fire;
His song was such as you ne'er have sung,
　And only love could inspire.　　　　20
He sang of the singing trees,
And the passionate sighing seas,
　And the lovely land of his minstrel band;
And with many a song like these

He drew her forth to the distant wood,   25
  Where bird and flower were gay,
And in silent joy each green tree stood;
  And with singing along the way,
He drew her to where each bird
Repeated his magic word,   30
  And there seemed a spell she could not tell
In every sound she heard.

And singing and singing still,
  He lured her away so far,
Past so many a wood and valley and hill,   35
  That now, would you know where they
    are?
In a bark on a silver stream,
As fair as you see in a dream;
  Lo! the bark glides along to the minstrel's
    song,
While the smooth waves ripple and gleam.   40

And soon they will reach the shore
  Of that land whereof he sings,
And love and song will be evermore
  The precious, the only things;
They will live and have long delight,   45
They two in each other's sight,
  In the violet vale of the nightingale,
And the flower that blooms by night.   (1874)

SONG

When the Rose came I loved the Rose,
  And thought of none beside,
Forgetting all the other flowers,
  And all the others died;
And morn and noon, and sun and showers,   5
And all things loved the Rose,
  Who only half returned my love,
Blooming alike for those.

I was the rival of a score
  Of loves on gaudy wing,   10
The nightingale I would implore
  For pity not to sing;
Each called her his; still I was glad
  To wait or take my part;
I loved the Rose — who might have had   15
  The fairest lily's heart.   (1881)

WILFRID SCAWEN BLUNT
(1840-1922)

From THE LOVE SONNETS OF PROTEUS

From PART I — To MANON

2. COMPARING HER TO A FALCON

Brave as a falcon and as merciless,
With bright eyes watching still the world, thy
  prey,

I saw thee pass in thy lone majesty,
Untamed, unmated, high above the press.
The dull crowd gazed at thee. It could not
  guess   5
The secret of thy proud aërial way,
Or read in thy mute face the soul which lay
A prisoner there in chains of tenderness.
— Lo, thou art captured. In my hand today
I hold thee, and awhile thou deignest to be 10
Pleased with my jesses. I would fain beguile
My foolish heart to think thou lovest me.
  See,
I dare not love thee quite. A little while
And thou shalt sail back heavenwards. Woe
  is me!

3. ON HIS FORTUNE IN LOVING HER

I did not choose thee, dearest. It was Love
That made the choice, not I. Mine eyes
  were blind
As a rude shepherd's who to some lone grove
His offering brings, and cares not at what
  shrine
He bends his knee. The gifts alone were
  mine,   5
The rest was Love's. He took me by the
  hand,
And fired the sacrifice, and poured the wine,
And spoke the words I might not understand.
I was unwise in all but the dear chance
Which was my fortune, and the blind desire 10
Which led my foolish steps to Love's abode,
And youth's sublime unreasoned prescience
Which raised an altar and inscribed in fire
Its dedication: "To the unknown god."

5. ON THE POWER OF HER BEAUTY

I am light-hearted now. An hour ago

The Love Sonnets of Proteus. "The author of these sonnets, styling himself Proteus, acknowledges thereby a natural
mood of change. He here lays bare what was once his heart,
to the public, but what for good or evil is his heart no longer,
thus closing forever his account with youth. He stands
upon the threshold of middle life, and already his dreams are
changed" (from the Preface to the first edition).
  Proteus, in Greek myth, was a sea-god who had the power
of changing his shape with great rapidity. The four parts
of the sonnet-cycle deal frankly with successive love experiences, real or imagined; the first two perhaps relate
to episodes during Blunt's service with the English embassy
at Paris, 1864-68; the last two lead up to his marriage with
the Lady Arabella Noel, granddaughter of Lord Byron, in
1870.
  Blunt uses the word *sonnet* in a rather loose sense.
  Part I. To Manon. Blunt's state of mind, in this section,
recalls that of the Chevalier de Grieux, who, in the Abbé
Prevost's novel (1733), loved the fascinating, selfish Manon
Lescaut not wisely but too well.
  On His Fortune in Loving Her. 14. **To . . . god.** In
addressing the Athenians, Paul said: "As I passed by and
beheld your devotions, I found an altar with this inscription,
TO THE UNKNOWN GOD. Whom therefore ye ignorantly wor-
ship, him declare I unto you" (*Acts*, 17:23).

There was a tempest in my heaven, a flame
Of sullen lightning under a bent brow
And a dull muttering which breathed no
name.
Now all is changed. The very winds are
tame, 5
And the birds sing aloud from every bough.
And my heart leaps. What empire dost thou
claim,
Child, o'er this earth, that nature serves
thee so?
Sublime magician! Well may earth and
heaven
Change at thy bidding, and the hearts of
men. 10
Didst thou but know the power that beauty
hath,
The sea should leave his bed, the rocks be
riven,
And wise men, deeming chaos come again,
Should kneel before thee and conjure thy
wrath.

21. HIS BONDAGE TO MANON IS BROKEN

From this day forth I lead another life,
Another life! A life without a tear!
Today has ended the unequal strife;
My service and my sorrow finish here.
See, my soul cuts her cable of belief 5
And sails toward the ocean. She shall steer
Sublime henceforth o'er accidents of grief.
Her storm has rolled to a new hemisphere.
I have loved too much, too loyally, too long.
Today I am a pirate of the sea. 10
Let others suffer. I have suffered wrong.
Let others love, and love as tenderly.
Oh, Manon, there are women yet unborn
Shall rue thy frailty, else am I forsworn.

From PART II — JULIET

33. REMINDING HER OF A PROMISE

Oh, Juliet, we have quarreled with our fate,
And fate has struck us. Wherefore do we cry?
We prayed for liberty, and now too late
Find liberty is this, to say "good-by."
The winter, which we loved not, has gone by
And spring is come. The gardens, which were
bare 6
When we first wandered through them, you
and I,
The prisoners of our vain wishes, are
Now full of golden flowers. The very lane
Down to the sea is green. The cactus hedge
We saw cut down has sprouted new again, 11

Part II. Juliet. This section concerns a "woman with a
past" and suggests the "young waverer" Romeo, to whom
Friar Laurence said, "These violent delights have violent
ends" (*Romeo and Juliet*, II, 6, 9).

And swallows have their nests on the cliff's
edge
Where we so often sat and dared complain
Because our joy was new, and called it pain.

34. THE SAME CONTINUED

Yes, spring is come, but joy, alas, is gone —
Gone ere we knew it, while our foolish eyes,
Which should have watched its motions every
one
Were looking elsewhere, at the hills, the skies,
Chasing vain thoughts, as children butter-
flies, 5
Until the hour struck and the day was done,
And we looked up in passionate surprise
To find that clouds had blotted out our sun.
Our joys are gone. And what is left to us,
Who loved not even love when it was here?
What but a voice which sobs monotonous 11
As these sad waves upon the rocks, the dear
Fond voice which once made music with our
own,
And which our hearts now ache to think
upon.

39. FAREWELL TO JULIET

Juliet, farewell. I would not be forgiven
Even if I forgave. These words must be
The last between us two in earth or heaven,
The last and bitterest. You are henceforth
free
Forever from my bitter words and me. 5
You shall not at my hand be further vexed
With either love, reproach, or jealousy
(So help me Heaven), in this world or the
next.
Our souls are single for all time to come
And for eternity, and this farewell 10
Is as the trumpet note, the crack of doom,
Which heralds an eternal silence. Hell
Has no more fixed and absolute decree.
And heaven and hell may meet — yet never
we.

53. THE SAME CONTINUED

Farewell, then. It is finished. I forgo
With this all right in you, even that of tears.
If I have spoken hardly, it will show
How much I loved you. With you disappears
A glory, a romance of many years. 5
What you may be henceforth I will not know.
The phantom of your presence on my fears
Is impotent at length for weal or woe.
Your past, your present, all alike must fade
In a new land of dreams where love is not. 10
Then kiss me and farewell. The choice is
made

And we shall live to see the past forgot,
If not forgiven. See, I came to curse,
Yet stay to bless. I know not which is worse.

From PART III — GODS AND FALSE GODS

55. ST. VALENTINE'S DAY

Today, all day, I rode upon the Down,
With hounds and horsemen, a brave com-
    pany.
On this side in its glory lay the sea,
On that the Sussex Weald, a sea of brown.
The wind was light, and brightly the sun
    shone,   5
And still we galloped on from gorse to gorse.
And once, when checked, a thrush sang, and
    my horse
Pricked his quick ears as to a sound unknown.
I knew the spring was come. I knew it even
Better than all by this, that through my
    chase   10
In bush and stone and hill and sea and heaven
I seemed to see and follow still your face.
Your face my quarry was. For it I rode,
My horse a thing of wings, myself a god.

56. TO ONE WHOM HE DARED NOT LOVE

As one who, in a desert wandering
Alone and faint beneath a pitiless sky,
And doubting in his heart if he shall bring
His bones back to his kindred or there die,
Finds at his feet a treasure suddenly   5
Such as would make him for all time a king,
And so forgets his fears and with keen eye
Falls to a-counting each new precious thing —
So was I when you told me yesterday
The tale of your dear love. Awhile I stood   10
Astonished and enraptured, and my heart
Began to count its treasures. Now dismay
Steals back my joy, and terror chills my blood,
And I remember only "We must part."

61. TO ONE EXCUSING HIS POVERTY

Ah! love, impute it not to me a sin
That my poor soul thus beggared comes to
    thee.
My soul a pilgrim was, in search of thine,
And met these accidents by land and sea.
The world was hard, and took its usury,   5
Its toll for each new night in each new inn;

And every road had robber bands to fee;
And all, even kindness, must be paid in coin.
Behold my scrip is empty, my heart bare.
I give thee nothing who my all would give.
My pilgrimage is finished, and I fare   11
Bare to my death, unless with thee I live.
Ah! give, love, and forgive that I am poor.
Ah! take me to thy arms and ask no more.

69. SIBYLLINE BOOKS

When first, a boy, at your fair knees I kneeled,
'Twas with a worthy offering. In my hand
My young life's book I held, a volume sealed,
Which none but you, I deemed, might under-
    stand.
And you I did entreat to loose the band   5
And read therein your own soul's destiny.
But, Tarquin-like, you turned from my
    demand,
Too proudly fair to find your fate in me.
When now I come, alas, what hands have
    turned
Those virgin pages! Some are torn away,   10
And some defaced, and some with passion
    burned,
And some besmeared with life's least holy
    clay.
Say, shall I offer you these pages wet

With blood and tears? And will your sorrow
    read
What your joy heeded not? — Unopened yet
One page remains. It still may hold a fate, 16
A counsel for the day of utter need.
Nay, speak, sad heart, speak quick. The
    hour is late.
Age threatens us. The Gaul is at the gate.

71. THE TWO HIGHWAYMEN

I long have had a quarrel set with Time,
Because he robbed me. Every day of life
Was wrested from me after bitter strife;
I never yet could see the sun go down
But I was angry in my heart, nor hear   5
The leaves fall in the wind without a tear
Over the dying summer. I have known
No truce with Time nor Time's accomplice,
    Death.
The fair world is the witness of a crime
Repeated every hour. For life and breath   10

Part III. Gods and False Gods. Compare Emerson's Give
All to Love.—"When half-gods go, The gods arrive."
St. Valentine's Day. 1. Down, a tract of open upland.
4. Sussex Weald, an extensive oak forest in Sussex and
Kent, counties on the southern coast of England. 6. gorse,
a spiny shrub with yellow flowers. 12. your face, that of
the lady to whom Part III is addressed. (See note on title,
p. 754.)
To One Excusing His Poverty. 9. scrip, wallet or small bag.

Sibylline Books. According to legend, the Cumaean Sibyl
offered to sell nine books of Grecian oracles to Tarquinius
Superbus, traditional seventh king of Rome, for 300 pieces
of gold. On his refusal she burned three books and offered
the remaining six at the same price. Again Tarquin refused.
She destroyed three more and offered the remaining three at
the original price. This time Tarquin accepted.
19. Gaul . . . gate, the cry uttered in Rome when Brennus,
the leader of the Gauls, was discovered at the gates of the city
in 390 B.C. His presence was revealed by the cackling of the
sacred geese in the temple.

Are sweet to all who live; and bitterly
The voices of these robbers of the heath
Sound in each ear and chill the passer-by.
—What have we done to thee, thou mon-
    strous Time?
What have we done to Death that we must
    die?   15

From Part IV — VITA NOVA

91. LAUGHTER AND DEATH

There is no laughter in the natural world
Of beast or fish or bird, though no sad doubt
Of their futurity to them unfurled
Has dared to check the mirth-compelling
    shout.
The lion roars his solemn thunder out   5
To the sleeping woods. The eagle screams
    her cry.
Even the lark must strain a serious throat
To hurl his blest defiance at the sky.
Fear, anger, jealousy have found a voice.
Love's pain or rapture the brute bosoms
    swell.   10
Nature has symbols for her nobler joys,
Her nobler sorrows. Who had dared foretell
That only man, by some sad mockery,
Should learn to laugh who learns that he
    must die?

95. HE IS NOT A POET

I would not, if I could, be called a poet.
I have no natural love of the "chaste muse."
If aught be worth the doing I would do it;
And others, if they will, may tell the news.
I care not for their laurels, but would choose
On the world's field to fight or fall or run. 6
My soul's ambition will not take excuse
To play the dial rather than the sun.
The faith I held I hold, as when a boy
I left my books for cricket-bat and gun.   10
The tales of poets are but scholars' themes,
In my hot youth I held it that a man
With heart to dare and stomach to enjoy
Had better work to his hand in any plan
Of any folly, so the thing were done,   15
Than in the noblest dreaming of mere dreams.

97. CHANCLEBURY RING

Say what you will, there is not in the world
A nobler sight than from this upper Down.

No rugged landscape here, no beauty hurled
From its Creator's hand as with a frown,
But a green plain on which green hills look
    down   5
Trim as a garden plot. No other hue
Can hence be seen, save here and there the
    brown
Of a square fallow, and the horizon's blue.
Dear checker-work of woods, the Sussex
    Weald!
If a name thrills me yet of things of earth, 10
That name is thine. How often have I fled
To thy deep hedgerows and embraced each
    field,
Each lag, each pasture — fields which gave
    me birth
And saw my youth, and which must hold me
    dead.

112. GIBRALTAR

Seven weeks of sea, and twice seven days of
    storm
Upon the huge Atlantic, and once more
We ride into still water and the calm
Of a sweet evening screened by either shore
Of Spain and Barbary. Our toils are o'er,   5
Our exile is accomplished. Once again
We look on Europe, mistress as of yore
Of the fair earth and of the hearts of men.
Aye, this is the famed rock, which Hercules
And Goth and Moor bequeathed us. At this
    door   10
England stands sentry. God! to hear the
    shrill
Sweet treble of her fifes upon the breeze,
And at the summons of the rock gun's roar
To see her red coats marching form the hill.
                                             (1875)

From THE LOVE LYRICS OF PROTEUS

SONG — LOVE ME A LITTLE

Love me a little, love me as thou wilt,
    Whether a draft it be of passionate wine
    Poured with both hands divine,
Or just a cup of water spilt

9. **Sussex Weald.** See note on *St. Valentine's Day*, line 4, p. 756. 13. **lag**, a marshy meadow (Sussex dialect).
112. Gibraltar. Gibraltar is a rocky promontory at the southern extremity of Spain, separated by the Straits of Gibraltar from Morocco, one of the Barbary States of North Africa. According to myth, Hercules placed it in its present position, as one of the pillars of Hercules, in the course of his tenth labor for King Eurystheus. It was conquered in the 5th century by the Visigoths, in the 8th century by the Moors; it is now a British possession.
The Love Lyrics of Proteus. Under this title, in 1892 Blunt grouped a number of lyrics that had been published previously. On the title see note on *The Love Sonnets of Proteus*, p. 754.

Part IV. Vita Nova. The title means *New Life;* compare *Vita Nuova* (c. 1307), in which Dante recorded the varying moods of his love for Beatrice.
97. *Chanclebury Ring*, Chanctonbury Ring, a hill rising 800 feet above the Sussex plain near Steyning. There is an ancient camp on the summit.
2. **Down**, a tract of open upland.

On dying lips and mine.   5
Give me the love thou wilt,
The purity, the guilt,
  So it be thine.

Love me a little. Let it be thy cheek
  With its red signals. That were dear to
      kiss.   10
  Or, if thou mayest not this,
A finger-tip my own to seek
  At nightfall when none guess.
Eyes have the wit to speak,
And sighs send messages;   15
  Even give less.

Love me a little. Let it be in words
Of happy omen heralding thy choice,
  Or in a veiled sad voice
Of warning, like a frightened bird's. 20
  How should I not rejoice,
Though swords be crossed with swords
And discord mar love's chords
  And tears thy voice?

Love me a little. All my world thou art.   25
  Thy much were Heaven; thy little, Earth
      shall be.
  If not Eternity,
Then Time be mine, the human part,
  A single hour with thee.
Love as thou wilt and art,   30
With all or half a heart,
  So thou love me.   (1875)

THE STRICKEN HART

The stricken hart had fled the brake,
His courage spent for life's dear sake.
He came to die beside the lake.

The golden trout leaped up to view,
The moorfowl clapped his wings and flew,   5
The swallow brushed him as she flew.

He looked upon the glorious sun,
His blood dropped slowly on the stone,
He loved the life so nearly won,

And then he died. The ravens found   10
A carcass couched upon the ground,
They said their god had dealt the wound.

The Eternal Father calmly shook
One page untitled from life's book.
Few words. None ever cared to look.   15

Yet woe for life thus idly riven.
He blindly loved what God had given,
And love, some say, has conquered Heaven.
                                    (1875)

The Stricken Hart. 1. **brake**, thicket.

SONG — LILAC AND GOLD AND GREEN

Lilac and gold and green!
  Those are the colors I love the best,
Spring's own raiment untouched and clean,
  When the world is awake and yet hardly
      dressed,
And the stranger sun, her bridegroom shy,   5
Looks at her bosom and wonders why
  She is so beautiful, he so blest.

Lilac and green and gold!
  Those were the colors you wore today;
Robed you were in them fold on fold,   10
  Clothed in the light of your love's de-
      lay.
And I held you thus in my arms, once only,
And wondered still, as you left me lonely,
  How the world's beauty was changed to
      gray.

Lilac and gold and green!   15
  I would die for the truth of those colors
      true!
Lilac for loyalty, gold for my queen,
  And green the faith of my love for you.
Here is a posy of all the three.
My heart is with it. So think of me,   20
  And our weeping skies shall once more be
      blue.   (1875)

THE BROKEN PITCHER

Accursed be the hour of that sad day
  The careless potter put his hand to thee,
And dared to fashion out of common clay
  So pure a shape as thou didst seem to
      me.
An idle boy, when vintage was begun,   5
  I passed and saw thy beauty for my sin,
And poured unheedingly till it was done
  The red wine of my love's first gathering
      in.

And thou, ah! thou didst look at me and
      smile
  To see me give with such ungrudging hand,
As taking all to thy dear heart, the while 11
  It only fell upon the thirsty sand.

Sad pitcher, thou wast broken at the well,
  Ere yet the shepherd's lip had tasted thine.
A god had lost in thee his hydromel,   15
  As I have wasted my poor wealth of wine.

Yet, wherefore wast thou made so fair a
      thing?
  Or why of clay, whose fabric rightly were

The Broken Pitcher. 15. **hydromel**, a drink compounded
of honey and water.

Of finest gold, new-fashioned for a king,
  And framed by some divine artificer?   20

I will not curse thee, thou poor shape of clay,
  That thou art other than thou seemed to be,
Yet I will break thee, that no passer may
  Unthinking break another heart on thee.
                                    (1875)

SONG — YOU HAVE LET THE BEAUTY OF THE DAY GO OVER

You have let the beauty of the day go over,
  You have let the glory of the noon go by.
Clouds from the west have gathered close and
    cover
  All but a remnant now of our proud sky.

Dumbly the rain beats on our darkened faces.
  Hushed are the woods. Alas, for us no bird 6
Shall sing today of pleasure in green places,
  No touch shall thrill, no soul of leaves be
    stirred.

Why did we wait? What faith was ours in
    fortune?
  What was our pride that fate should kneel
    to us?   10
Oh, we were fools. Love loves not to im-
    portune,
  And he is silent here in this sad house.

Alas, dear love, the day for us is ended,
  The pleasure of green fields, of streams, of
    skies.
One hour remains, one only of joy blended   15
  With coming night. Ah, seize it ere it flies.

Draw fast the curtains. Close the door on
    sorrow.
  Shut out the dusk. It only makes us grieve.
Here we may live a life — and then, to-
    morrow,
  If fate still wills it, we may take our
    leave.   (1875)

SONG — COME WITH THE SUMMER LEAVES

Come with the summer leaves, love, to my
    grave,
  And, if you doubt among the quiet dead,
Choose out that mound where greenest grasses
    wave
  And where the flowers grow thickest and
    most red.

Come in the morning while the dews of night,
  Which are fair Nature's tears in darkness
    shed,   6
Rim the sad petals nor are garnered quite,
  Like my last hopes untimely harvested.

Come to my grave — ah, gather, love, those
    flowers!
  Out of my heart they grow for your dear
    head.   10
These are its songs unwritten and all yours,
  The love I loved you with and left unsaid.
                                    (1875)

THE DESOLATE CITY

Dark to me is the earth. Dark to me are the
    heavens.
  Where is she that I loved, the woman with
    eyes like stars?
Desolate are the streets. Desolate is the city,
  A city taken by storm, where none are left
    but the slain!

Sadly I rose at dawn, undid the latch of my
    shutters,   5
  Thinking to let in light, but I only let in
    love.
Birds in the boughs were awake; I listened to
    their chaunting;
  Each one sang to his love; only I was alone.

This, I said in my heart, is the hour of life
    and of pleasure.
  Now each creature on earth has his joy,
    and lives in the sun,   10
Each in another's eyes finds light, the light
    of compassion,
  This is the moment of pity, this is the
    moment of love.

Speak, O desolate city! Speak, O silence in
    sadness!
  Where is she that I loved in my strength,
    that spoke to my soul?
Where are those passionate eyes that ap-
    pealed to my eyes in passion?   15
  Where is the mouth that kissed me, the
    breast I laid to my own?

Speak, thou soul of my soul, for rage in my
    heart is kindled.
  Tell me, where didst thou flee on the day
    of destruction and fear?
See, my arms still enfold thee, enfolding thus
    all heaven,
  See, my desire is fulfilled in thee, for it fills
    the earth.   20

Thus in my grief I lamented. Then turned I
    from the window,
  Turned to the stair, and the open door, and
    the empty street,
Crying aloud in my grief, for there was none
    to chide me,
  None to mock my weakness, none to behold
    my tears.

Groping I went, as blind. I sought her house,
    my belovéd's.   25
  There I stopped at the silent door, and
    listened and tried the latch.
Love, I cried, dost thou slumber? This is no
    hour for slumber,
  This is the hour of love, and love I bring
    in my hand.

I knew the house, with its windows barred,
    and its leafless fig-tree,
  Climbing round by the doorstep, the only
    one in the street;   30
I knew where my hope had climbed to its
    goal and there encircled
  All that those desolate walls once held, my
    belovéd's heart.

There in my grief she consoled me. She loved
    me when I loved not.
  She put her hand in my hand, and set her
    lips to my lips.
She told me all her pain and showed me all
    her trouble.   35
  I, like a fool, scarce heard, hardly returned
    her kiss.

Love, thy eyes were like torches. They
    changed as I beheld them.
  Love, thy lips were like gems, the seal thou
    settest on my life.
Love, if I loved not then, behold this hour
    thy vengeance;
  This is the fruit of thy love and thee, the
    unwise grown wise.   40

Weeping strangled my voice. I called out,
    but none answered;
  Blindly the windows gazed back at me,
    dumbly the door;
She whom I love, who loved me, looked not
    on my yearning,
  Gave me no more hands to kiss, showed
    me no more her soul.

Therefore the earth is dark to me, the sun-
    light blackness,   45
  Therefore I go in tears and alone, by night
    and day;
Therefore I find no love in heaven, no light,
    no beauty,
  A heaven taken by storm, where none are
    left but the slain!   (1889)

THE OLD SQUIRE

I like the hunting of the hare
  Better than that of the fox;

I like the joyous morning air,
  And the crowing of the cocks.

I like the calm of the early fields,   5
  The ducks asleep by the lake,
The quiet hour which nature yields
  Before mankind is awake.

I like the pheasants and feeding things
  Of the unsuspicious morn;   10
I like the flap of the wood-pigeon's wings
  As she rises from the corn.

I like the blackbird's shriek, and his rush
  From the turnips as I pass by,
And the partridge hiding her head in a bush,
  For her young ones cannot fly.   16

I like these things, and I like to ride,
  When all the world is in bed,
To the top of the hill where the sky grows
    wide,
  And where the sun grows red.   20

The beagles at my horse heels trot
  In silence after me;
There's Ruby, Roger, Diamond, Dot,
  Old Slut and Margery —

A score of names well used, and dear,   25
  The names my childhood knew;
The horn, with which I rouse their cheer,
  Is the horn my father blew.

I like the hunting of the hare
  Better than that of the fox;   30
The new world still is all less fair
  Than the old world it mocks.

I covet not a wider range
  Than these dear manors give;
I take my pleasures without change,   35
  And as I lived I live.

I leave my neighbors to their thought;
  My choice it is, and pride,
On my own lands to find my sport,
  In my own fields to ride.   40

The hare herself no better loves
  The field where she was bred,
Than I the habit of these groves,
  My own inherited.

I know my quarries every one,   45
  The meuse where she sits low;

The Old Squire. 12. **corn**, wheat or other grain.
  46. **meuse**, a path made in the grass by rabbits, or a hole
in the hedge (Sussex dialect).

The road she chose today was run
A hundred years ago.

The lags, the gills, the forest ways,
The hedgerows one and all, 50
These are the kingdoms of my chase,
And bounded by my wall;

Nor has the world a better thing,
Though one should search it round,
Than thus to live one's own sole king, 55
Upon one's own sole ground.

I like the hunting of the hare;
It brings me, day by day,
The memory of old days as fair,
With dead men passed away. 60

To these, as homeward still I ply
And pass the churchyard gate,
Where all are laid as I must lie,
I stop and raise my hat.

I like the hunting of the hare; 65
New sports I hold in scorn.
I like to be as my fathers were,
In the days ere I was born. (1889)

HENRY AUSTIN DOBSON
(1840-1921)

INCOGNITA

Just for a space that I met her —
Just for a day in the train!
It began when she feared it would wet her,
That tiniest spurtle of rain;
So we tucked a great rug in the sashes, 5
And carefully padded the pane;
And I sorrow in sackcloth and ashes,
Longing to do it again!

Then it grew when she begged me to reach her
A dressing-case under the seat; 10
She was "really so tiny a creature
That she needed a stool for her feet!"
Which was promptly arranged to her order
With a care that was even minute,
And a glimpse — of an open-work border, 15
And a glance — of the fairyest boot.

Then it drooped, and revived at some hovels —
"Were they houses for men or for pigs?"
Then it shifted to muscular novels,

With a little digression on prigs: 20
She thought *Wives and Daughters* "so jolly";
"Had I read it?" She knew when I had,
Like the rest, I should dote upon "Molly,"
And "poor Mrs. Gaskell — how sad!"

"Like Browning?" "But so-so." His proof lay
Too deep for her frivolous mood, 26
That preferred your mere metrical *soufflé*
To the stronger poetical food;
Yet at times he was good — "as a tonic."
Was Tennyson writing just now? 30
And was this new poet Byronic
And clever, and naughty, or how?

Then we trifled with concerts and croquet,
Then she daintily dusted her face;
Then she sprinkled herself with "Ess Bou-
quet," 35
Fished out from the foregoing case;
And we chattered of Gassier and Grisi,
And voted Aunt Sally a bore;
Discussed if the tight rope were easy,
Or Chopin much harder than Spohr. 40

And oh! the odd things that she quoted,
With the prettiest possible look,
And the price of two buns that she noted
In the prettiest possible book;
While her talk like a musical rillet 45
Flashed on with the hours that flew;
And the carriage, her smile seemed to fill it
With just enough summer — for Two.

Till at last in her corner, peeping
From a nest of rugs and of furs, 50
With the white shut eyelids sleeping
On those dangerous looks of hers,
She seemed like a snow-drop breaking,
Not wholly alive nor dead,
But with one blind impulse making 55
To the sounds of the spring overhead;

And I watched in the lamplight's swerving
The shade of the down-dropped lid,
And the lip-line's delicate curving,

---

49. **lags,** marshy meadows (Sussex dialect). **gills,** rocky
valleys.
Incognita. The title means *An Unknown Woman.*

21. **Wives and Daughters,** an unfinished novel by Mrs.
Gaskell that appeared serially in *The Cornhill Magazine* from
August, 1864, to January, 1866. 23. **"Molly,"** the heroine
of *Wives and Daughters.* 24. **"poor . . . sad."** Elizabeth
Cleghorn Gaskell (1810-1865), English novelist, had recently died. 35. **"Ess Bouquet,"** Essence Bouquet, a
heavy perfume blending the fragrance of several flowers,
particularly of bergamot. 37. **Gassier,** Edouard Gassier
(1822-1871), French baritone who appeared frequently in
London opera. **Grisi,** Giulia Grisi (1811-1869), an Italian
prima-donna who sang much in London opera. 38. **Aunt
Sally,** a game, popular at English summer resorts, in which
balls are thrown at puppets. 40. **Chopin,** Frédéric F.
Chopin (1809-1849), Polish composer for the piano. **Spohr,**
Ludwig Spohr (1784-1859), German violinist and composer.

Where a slumbering smile lay hid,   60
Till I longed that, rather than sever,
   The train should shriek into space,
And carry us onward — forever —
   Me and that beautiful face.

But she suddenly woke in a fidget,   65
   With fears she was "nearly at home,"
And talk of a certain Aunt Bridget,
   Whom I mentally wished — well, at Rome;
Got out at the very next station,
   Looking back with a merry *Bon Soir;*   70
Adding, too, to my utter vexation,
   A surplus, unkind *Au Revoir.*

So left me to muse on her graces,
   To doze and to muse, till I dreamed
That we sailed through the sunniest places 75
   In a glorified galley, it seemed;
But the cabin was made of a carriage,
   And the ocean was Eau-de-Cologne,
And we split on a rock labeled MARRIAGE,
   And I woke — as cold as a stone.   80

And that's how I lost her — a jewel,
   Incognita — one in a crowd,
Not prudent enough to be cruel,
   Not worldly enough to be proud.
It was just a shut lid and its lashes,   85
   Just a few hours in a train,
And I sorrow in sackcloth and ashes,
   Longing to see her again.   *(1866; 1866)*

A DEAD LETTER

"À cœur blessé — l'ombre et le silence."
           — H. DE BALZAC

I

I drew it from its china tomb —
   It came out feebly scented
With some thin ghost of past perfume
   That time and years had lent it.

An old, old letter — folded still!   5
   To read with due composure
I sought the sun-lit window-sill
   Above the gray enclosure,

That, glimmering in the sultry haze,
   Faint-flowered, dimly shaded,   10
Slumbered, like Goldsmith's Madam Blaize,
   Bedizened and brocaded.

A queer old place! You'd surely say
   Some tea-board garden-maker
Had planned it in Dutch William's day   15
   To please some florist Quaker,

So trim it was. The yew-trees still,
   With pious care perverted,
Grew in the same grim shapes; and still
   The lipless dolphin spurted;   20

Still in his wonted state abode
   The broken-nosed Apollo;
And still the cypress-arbor showed
   The same umbrageous hollow.

Only — as fresh young Beauty gleams   25
   From coffee-colored laces —
So peeped from its old-fashioned dreams
   The fresher modern traces;

For idle mallet, hoop, and ball
   Upon the lawn were lying,   30
A magazine, a tumbled shawl,
   Round which the swifts were flying;

And, tossed beside the Guelder rose,
   A heap of rainbow knitting,
Where, blinking in her pleased repose,   35
   A Persian cat was sitting.

"A place to love in — live — for aye,
   If we too, like Tithonus,
Could find some god to stretch the gray
   Scant life the Fates have thrown us;   40

"But now by steam we run our race
   With buttoned heart and pocket;
Our Love's a gilded, surplus grace —
   Just like an empty locket.

" 'The time is out of joint.' Who will,   45
   May strive to make it better;
For me, this warm old window-sill,
   And this old dusty letter."

2

"Dear *John* (the letter ran), it can't, can't be,
   For Father's gone to *Chorley Fair* with
       Sam,   50
And Mother's storing Apples — *Prue* and Me
   Up to our Elbows making Damson Jam;
But we shall meet before a Week is gone —
   ' 'Tis a long Lane that has no Turning,' *John!*

A Dead Letter. "À cœur . . . silence," darkness and
silence for the wounded heart.
   11. **Madam Blaize.** See Oliver Goldsmith's *An Elegy
on That Glory of Her Sex, Mrs. Mary Blaize,* 1759:
     "At church, in silks and satins new,
       With hoop of monstrous size,
     She never slumbered in her pew—
       But when she shut her eyes."

15. **Dutch William,** William of Orange, king of England
(1688-1702); he was of Dutch descent. 22. **Apollo,** a statue
of Apollo, Greek god of music and beauty. 33. **Guelder
rose,** a flowering shrub, sometimes called a "Snowball tree."
38-40. **Tithonus . . . us.** Tithonus, brother of Priam, king
of Troy, was granted immortality by Eos, goddess of the
dawn. See Tennyson's *Tithonus,* page 44. 45. 'The time
. . . joint.' From *Hamlet,* I, 5, 188. 50. **Chorley Fair,**
a weekly market held in Chorley, in North Lancashire.

"Only till Sunday next, and then you'll wait
  Behind the White-Thorn, by the broken
    Stile —   56
We can go round and catch them at the Gate,
All to ourselves, for nearly one long Mile;
Dear *Prue* won't look, and Father he'll go on,
And *Sam's* two Eyes are all for *Cissy, John!*

"*John*, she's so smart — with every Ribbon
  new,   61
Flame-colored Sack, and Crimson Padesoy;
As proud as proud, and has the Vapors too,
Just like My Lady; — calls poor *Sam* a
  Boy,
And vows no Sweetheart's worth the Think-
  ing-on   65
Till he's past Thirty . . . I know better, *John!*

"My Dear, I don't think that I thought of
  much
Before we knew each other, I and you;
And now, why, *John*, your least, least Finger-
  touch
Gives me enough to think a Summer
  through.   70
See, for I send you Something! There, 'tis
  gone!
Look in this corner — mind you find it,
  John!"

3

This was the matter of the note —
  A long-forgot deposit,
Dropped in an Indian dragon's throat,   75
  Deep in a fragrant closet,

Piled with a dapper Dresden world —
  Beaux, beauties, prayers, and poses —
Bonzes with squat legs undercurled,
  And great jars filled with roses.   80

Ah, heart that wrote! Ah, lips that kissed!
  You had no thought or presage
Into what keeping you dismissed
  Your simple old-world message!

A reverent one. Though we today   85
  Distrust beliefs and powers,
The artless, ageless things you say
  Are fresh as May's own flowers,

Starring some pure primeval spring,
  Ere Gold had grown despotic —   90
Ere Life was yet a selfish thing,
  Or Love a mere exotic!

I need not search too much to find
  Whose lot it was to send it,
That feel upon me yet the kind   95
  Soft hand of her who penned it;

And see, through two score years of smoke,
  In by-gone, quaint apparel,
Shine from yon time-black Norway oak
  The face of Patience Caryl —   100

The pale, smooth forehead, silver-tressed;
  The gray gown, primly flowered;
The spotless, stately coif whose crest
  Like Hector's horse-plume towered;

And still the sweet half-solemn look   105
  Where some past thought was clinging,
As when one shuts a serious book
  To hear the thrushes singing.

I kneel to you! Of those you were,
  Whose kind old hearts grow mellow —   110
Whose fair old faces grow more fair
  As Point and Flanders yellow;

Whom some old store of garnered grief,
  Their placid temples shading,
Crowns like a wreath of autumn leaf   115
  With tender tints of fading.

Peace to your soul! You died unwed —
  Despite this loving letter.
And what of John? The less that's said
  Of John, I think, the better.   (1868)

TO "LYDIA LANGUISH"

"Il me faut des émotions."
    — BLANCHE AMORY

You ask me, Lydia, "whether I,
If you refuse my suit, shall die."
  (Now pray don't let this hurt you!)
Although the time be out of joint,
I should not think a bodkin's point   5
  The sole resource of virtue;
Nor shall I, though your mood endure,
Attempt a final Water-cure

---

103. **coif,** a linen cap. 104. **Hector's horse-plume,** described by Homer (the *Iliad*, Book 6, lines 494-5), in connection with Hector's parting from his wife. 112. **Point and
Flanders,** varieties of fine lace.
  To "Lydia Languish." Lydia Languish is the sentimental
lady in R. B. Sheridan's *The Rivals*, 1775.
  "Il . . . émotions," "I must have my thrills," a phrase
which Thackeray gave to Blanche Amory, a character in
The History of Pendennis, Volume 2, Chapter 35.
  4. **time . . . joint.** From *Hamlet*, I, 5, 188. 5. **bodkin's
point.** See *Hamlet*, III, 1, 70-76.—
  "For who would bear the whips and scorn of time, . . .
    When he himself might his quietus make
      With a bare bodkin?"
8. **Water-cure.** The final water-cure is drowning; the
usual water-cure involved bathing in such medicinal springs
as those at Bath and Tunbridge Wells.

---

62. **Padesoy,** a gown made of corded silk. 63. **Vapors,**
melancholy moods, especially fashionable among ladies of
the 18th century. 77. **Dresden world,** a world inhabited by
the daintily sophisticated shepherds and shepherdesses of
Dresden china. 79. **Bonzes,** statuettes of Buddhist monks.

Except against my wishes;
For I respectfully decline   10
To dignify the Serpentine,
And make *hors-d'œuvres* for fishes;
But if you ask me whether I
    Composedly can go,
Without a look, without a sigh,   15
    Why, then I answer — No.

"You are assured," you sadly say
(If in this most considerate way
    To treat my suit your will is),
That I shall "quickly find as fair   20
Some new Neæra's tangled hair —
    Some easier Amaryllis."
I cannot promise to be cold
If smiles are kind as yours of old
    On lips of later beauties;   25
Nor can I, if I would, forget
The homage that is Nature's debt,
    While man has social duties;
But if you ask shall I prefer
    To you I honor so,   30
A somewhat visionary Her,
    I answer truly — No.

You fear, you frankly add, "to find
In me too late the altered mind
    That altering Time estranges."   35
To this I make response that we
(As physiologists agree)
    Must have septennial changes;
This is a thing beyond control,
And it were best upon the whole   40
    To try and find out whether
We could not, by some means, arrange
This not-to-be-avoided change
    So as to change together;
But, had you asked me to allow   45
    That you could ever grow
Less amiable than you are now —
    Emphatically — No.

But — to be serious — if you care
To know how I shall really bear   50
    This much discussed rejection,
I answer you: As feeling men
Behave, in best romances, when
    You outrage their affection; —
With that gesticulatory woe,   55
By which, as melodramas show,
    Despair is indicated;
Enforced by all the liquid grief
Which hugest pocket-handkerchief

11. **the Serpentine**, a body of water in Hyde Park,
London. 21-22. **Neæra . . . Amaryllis**, shepherdesses in
classical Latin pastoral poetry. Cf. Milton's *Lycidas*, 64-69.—
 "Alas what boots it with uncessant care
 To tend the homely, slighted shepherd's trade,
 And strictly meditate the thankless Muse?
 Were it not better done as others use,
 To sport with Amaryllis in the shade,
 Or with the tangles of Neæra's hair?"

Has ever simulated;   60
And when, arrived so far, you say
    In tragic accents, "Go,"
Then, Lydia, then . . . I still shall stay,
    And firmly answer — No.

(*1872; 1872*)

ROSE-LEAVES

"Sans peser. — Sans rester."

A KISS

Rose kissed me today.
    Will she kiss me tomorrow?
Let it be as it may,
Rose kissed me today.
But the pleasure gives way   5
    To a savor of sorrow; —
Rose kissed me today —
    Will she kiss me tomorrow?

CIRCE

In the School of Coquettes
    Madam Rose is a scholar —
Oh, they fish with all nets
In the School of Coquettes!
When her brooch she forgets   5
    'Tis to show her new collar;
In the School of Coquettes
    Madam Rose is a scholar!

A TEAR

There's a tear in her eye —
    Such a clear little jewel!
What *can* make her cry?
There's a tear in her eye.
"Puck has killed a big fly —   5
    And it's *horribly* cruel";
There's a tear in her eye —
    Such a clear little jewel!

A GREEK GIFT

Here's a present for Rose,
    How pleased she is looking!
Is it verse? — is it prose?
Here's a present for Rose!
"*Plats*," "*Entrées*," and "*Rôts*" —   5
    Why, it's "Gouffé on Cooking";

Rose-Leaves. "**Sans . . . rester**," "without pondering,
without waiting." These lyrics are in the medieval French
form known as the triolet, characterized by its lightness and
the set repetition of its lines.
 Circe. Circe was the epic coquette who held the men of
Ulysses in her power; see Homer's *Odyssey*, Book 5.
 A Tear. 5. **Puck**, probably a cat, named from Shakespeare's goblin in *A Midsummer Night's Dream*.
 A Greek Gift. A Greek gift is one that brings profit to the
giver—said of the Trojan Horse.
 5. "**Plats . . . Rôts**," chapter headings on "main dishes,"
"subordinate dishes," and "roasts" in a cook-book. 6.
"**Gouffé on Cooking**," a glorified cook-book, written in
French by Jules Gouffé, chef at the Paris Jockey Club, and
translated by Alphonse Gouffé, head pastry-cook to her
Majesty the Queen, London, 1868.

Here's a present for Rose,
How *pleased* she is looking!

"URCEUS EXIT"

I intended an Ode,
And it turned to a Sonnet.
It began *à la mode*,
I intended an Ode;
But Rose crossed the road   5
In her latest new bonnet;
I intended an Ode,
And it turned to a Sonnet.   (1874)

ARS VICTRIX

(IMITATED FROM THÉOPHILE GAUTIER)

Yes; when the ways oppose —
When the hard means rebel,
Fairer the work outgrows —
More potent far the spell.

O Poet, then, forbear   5
The loosely-sandaled verse,
Choose rather thou to wear
The buskin — straight and terse;

Leave to the tiro's hand
The limp and shapeless style;   10
See that thy form demand
The labor of the file.

Sculptor, do thou discard
The yielding clay — consign
To Paros marble hard   15
The beauty of thy line —

Model thy Satyr's face
In bronze of Syracuse;
In the veined agate trace
The profile of thy Muse.   20

Painter, that still must mix
But transient tints anew,
Thou in the furnace fix
The firm enamel's hue;

Let the smooth tile receive   25
Thy dove-drawn Erycine;

Thy Sirens blue at eve
Coiled in a wash of wine.

All passes. ART alone
Enduring stays to us;   30
The Bust outlasts the throne —
The Coin, Tiberius;

Even the gods must go;
Only the lofty Rime
Not countless years o'erthrow —   35
Not long array of time.

Paint, chisel, then, or write;
But, that the work surpass,
With the hard fashion fight —
With the resisting mass.   40
(1876)

"GOOD-NIGHT, BABETTE!"

"Si vieillesse pouvait! — "

SCENE — *A small neat room. In a high
Voltaire chair sits a white-haired
old gentleman.*

MONSIEUR VIEUXBOIS.   BABETTE.

M. Vieuxbois (turning querulously)

Day of my life! Where *can* she get?
Babette! I say! Babette! — Babette!
Babette (entering hurriedly)
Coming, M'sieu'! If M'sieu' speaks
So loud, he won't be well for weeks!

M. Vieuxbois

Where have you been?

Babette

                      Why, M'sieu' knows —   5
April! . . . Ville d'Avray! . . . Ma'am'-selle
Rose!

M. Vieuxbois

Ah! I am old — and I forget.
Was the place growing green, Babette?

Babette

But of the greenness! — yes, M'sieu'!
And then the sky so blue! — so blue!   10

"*Urceus Exit.*" From Horace's *Art of Poetry*, lines 21-22:
"Amphora coepit institui: currente rota cur urceus exit?"—
"That was a wine-jar when the molding began; why, as the
wheel runs round, does it turn out a pitcher?" (Fairclough's
translation.) Horace is speaking of poems that begin grandly
and end trivially.
Ars Victrix. The title means *Art the Victor.* Gautier
(1811-72) was a noted French poet, novelist, and critic.
9. tiro, novice, beginner. 15. Paros, a Greek island in
the Ægean Sea; famous for its white marble quarries. 17.
Satyr, a sylvan deity represented as part man and part
horse or goat, given to riotous merriment. 18. Syracuse,
the chief Greek city of ancient Sicily, noted for fine work in
bronze. 26. dove-drawn Erycine, Venus, goddess of love,
whose chariot was often represented as drawn by doves.
She was called Erycine from the city of Ceryx, Sicily, one of
her centers of worship.

27. Sirens, sea nymphs said to frequent an island near
the coast of Italy, and by their singing to lure mariners to
destruction. 32. Coin, Tiberius, the coin outlasts the
monarch whose face it bears. Tiberius was emperor of
Rome (14-37 A.D.).
"*Good-Night, Babette!*" "Si . . . pouvait!" From an old
French proverb, adapted by H. Estienne, *Les Premices*, Epigram 191: "Si jeunesse savait! si vieillesse pouvait!"—"If
youth only knew! if age only could!" Voltaire chair, a
deep, low easy-chair with an adjustable back.
6. Ville d'Avray, a quiet suburb down the Seine from
Paris; evidently Rose was buried there.

And when I dropped my *immortelle*,
How the birds sang!
   (*Lifting her apron to her eyes*)
                This poor Ma'am'selle!

M. Vieuxbois

You're a good girl, Babette, but she —
She was an angel, verily.
Sometimes I think I see her yet   15
Stand smiling by the cabinet;
And once, I know, she peeped and laughed
Betwixt the curtains . . .
              Where's the draft?
   (*She gives him a cup*)
Now I shall sleep, I think, Babette —
Sing me your Norman *chansonnette*.   20

Babette (sings)

"*Once at the Angelus*
  (*Ere I was dead*),
Angels all glorious
  Came to my bed;
Angels in blue and white   25
  Crowned on the head."

M. Vieuxbois (drowsily)

"She was an angel" . .   "Once she
  laughed" . . .
What, was I dreaming?
            Where's the draft?

Babette (showing the empty cup)

The draft, M'sieu'?

M. Vieuxbois

             How I forget!
I am so old! But sing, Babette!   30

Babette (sings)

"*One was the friend I left*
  Stark in the snow;
One was the wife that died
  Long — long ago;
One was the love I lost . . .   35
  How could she know?"

M. Vieuxbois (murmuring)

Ah, Paul! . . . old Paul! . . . Eulalie too!
And Rose . . . And O! "the sky so blue!"

Babette (sings)

"*One had my mother's eyes,*
  Wistful and mild;   40
One had my father's face;

---

11. **immortelle**, a daisy-like flower, the everlasting, often used for decorating graves. 20. **chansonnette**, a folk-song. 21. **Angelus**, the bell rung at morning, noon, or evening to summon worshipers to recite the Angelus, a prayer commemorating the Annunciation.

  One was a child:
    All of them bent to me —
  Bent down and smiled!"
(*He is asleep!*)

M. Vieuxbois (almost inaudibly)

          "How I forget!"   45
"I am so old!" . . . "Good night, Babette!"
           (*1876;* 1876)

"YOU BID ME TRY"

You bid me try, BLUE-EYES, to write
A Rondeau. What! — forthwith? — tonight?
  Reflect. Some skill I have, 'tis true;
  But thirteen lines! — and rimed on two!
"Refrain," as well. Ah, hapless plight!   5

Still, there are five lines — ranged aright.
These Gallic bonds, I feared, would fright
  My easy Muse. They did, till you —
    You bid me try!

That makes them eight. The port's in
  sight —   10
'Tis all because your eyes are bright!
  Now just a pair to end in "oo" —
  When maids command, what can't we do?
Behold! — the RONDEAU, tasteful, light,
    You bid me try!   15
              (1876)

THE CURÉ'S PROGRESS

Monsieur the Curé down the street
  Comes with his kind old face —
With his coat worn bare, and his straggling
    hair,
  And his green umbrella-case.

You may see him pass by the little "*Grande*
    Place,"   5
  And the tiny "*Hôtel-de-Ville*";
He smiles as he goes to the *fleuriste* Rose,
  And the *pompier* Théophile.

He turns, as a rule, through the "*Marché*"
    cool,
  Where the noisy fish-wives call;   10
And his compliment pays to the "*belle*
    Thérèse,"
  As she knits in her dusky stall.

"*You Bid Me Try.*" This poem, adapted from the original of the French poet Vincent Voiture (1598-1648), exemplifies its own form—a rondeau, which consists of thirteen lines running on two rimes, and an unrimed refrain taken from the beginning of the first line. The form is of French origin.
7. **Gallic bonds**, the restrictions imposed by the French (Gallic) form.
The Curé's Progress. The title means *The Parish Priest on a Stroll.*
5. "**Grande Place**," the public square. 6. "**Hôtel-de-Ville**," the town hall. 7. **fleuriste**, florist. 8. **pompier**, fireman. 9. "**Marché**," public market. 11. "**belle Thérèse**," beautiful Theresa.

There's a letter to drop at the locksmith's
  shop,
  And Toto, the locksmith's niece,
Has jubilant hopes, for the Curé gropes   15
  In his tails for a *pain d'épice*.

There's a little dispute with a merchant of
  fruit,
  Who is said to be heterodox,
That will ended be with a *"Ma foi, oui!"*
  And a pinch from the Curé's box.   20

There is also a word that no one heard
  To the furrier's daughter Lou;
And a pale cheek fed with a flickering red,
  And a *"Bon Dieu garde M'sieu'!"*

But a grander way for the *Sous-Préfet*,   25
  And a bow for Ma'am'selle Anne;
And a mock "off-hat" to the Notary's cat,
  And a nod to the Sacristan —

For ever through life the Curé goes
  With a smile on his kind old face —   30
With his coat worn bare, and his straggling
  hair,
  And his green umbrella-case.
               (*1878; 1878*)

ON A FAN THAT BELONGED TO THE MARQUISE DE POMPADOUR

Chicken-skin, delicate, white,
  Painted by Carlo Vanloo,
Loves in a riot of light,
  Roses and vaporous blue;
Hark to the dainty *frou-frou!*   5
Picture above, if you can,
  Eyes that could melt as the dew —
This was the Pompadour's fan!

See how they rise at the sight,
  Thronging the *Œil de Bœuf* through   10
Courtiers as butterflies bright,
  Beauties that Fragonard drew,
Talon-rouge, falbala, queue,

Cardinal, Duke — to a man,
  Eager to sigh or to sue —   15
This was the Pompadour's fan!

Ah, but things more than polite
  Hung on this toy, *voyez-vous!*
Matters of state and of might,
  Things that great ministers do;   20
Things that, maybe, overthrew
Those in whose brains they began;
  Here was the sign and the cue —
This was the Pompadour's fan!

Envoy

Where are the secrets it knew?   25
  Weavings of plot and of plan?
— But where is the Pompadour, too?
This was the Pompadour's *fan!*
              (*1878; 1878*)

ON THE HURRY OF THIS TIME

With slower pen men used to write,
Of old, when "letters" were "polite";
  In Anna's, or in George's days,
  They could afford to turn a phrase,
Or trim a straggling theme aright.   5

They knew not steam; electric light
Not yet had dazed their calmer sight; —
  They meted out both blame and praise
    With slower pen.

Too swiftly now the hours take flight!   10
What's read at morn is dead at night;
  Scant space have we for Art's delays,
  Whose breathless thought so briefly stays,
We may not work — ah! would we might! —
    With slower pen.   15
              (*1882; 1882*)

[handwritten margin notes: "art needs time to develope" / "time is being lost"]

THE LADIES OF ST. JAMES'S

A PROPER NEW BALLAD OF THE COUNTRY AND
THE TOWN

The ladies of St. James's
  Go swinging to the play;
Their footmen run before them,
  With a "Stand by! Clear the way!"
But Phyllida, my Phyllida!   5

---

16. **pain d'épice,** piece of gingerbread. 19. "**Ma foi, oui!**" "You're certainly right." 20. **pinch . . . box,** a pinch of snuff. 24. "**Bon . . . M'sieu'!**" "God protect you, sir." 25. **Sous-Préfet,** the highest state official in the arrondissement, or county, to which the town belongs. 28. **Sacristan,** the church functionary who has charge of the sacred vessels and vestments.
On a Fan That Belonged to the Marquise de Pompadour. This is a *ballade* in honor of Jeanne Antoinette Poisson le Normant d'Étioles (1721-1764), mistress of Louis XV of France, and a lady of great political astuteness and power. (For an explanation of the *ballade* form, see note on Swinburne's *A Ballad of Dreamland*, page 713.)
2. **Carlo Vanloo,** a painter (1705-1765), high in the favor of Louis XV and the court. 5. **frou-frou,** the rustling of skirts. 10. **Œil de Bœuf,** a waiting-room in the royal palace at Versailles. 12. **Fragonard,** Jean Honoré Fragonard (1732-1806), fashionable painter of amorous and gay ladies at the French court. 13. **Talon . . . queue,** characteristic details in the aristocratic dress of the period— red heels, plaited flounces, and pigtails.

18. **voyez-vous!** don't you see?
On the Hurry of This Time. This is a rondeau (see note on "*You Bid Me Try*," p. 774).
3. **Anna's . . . George's days,** the Neo-Classic age of English literature, comprising the reigns of Anne (1702-14) and George I (1714-27).
The Ladies of St. James's. St. James is a fashionable district in London with Pall Mall as its principal thoroughfare.
Subtitle. **country . . . town.** London is the "town"; the rest of the British Isles is the "country."

She takes her buckled shoon,
When we go out a-courting
Beneath the harvest moon.

The ladies of St. James's
Wear satin on their backs;   10
They sit all night at *Ombre*,
With candles all of wax.
But Phyllida, my Phyllida!
She dons her russet gown,
And runs to gather May dew   15
Before the world is down.

The ladies of St. James's!
They are so fine and fair,
You'd think a box of essences
Was broken in the air;   20
But Phyllida, my Phyllida!
The breath of heath and furze,
When breezes blow at morning,
Is not so fresh as hers.

The ladies of St. James's!   25
They're painted to the eyes;
Their white it stays forever,
Their red it never dies.
But Phyllida, my Phyllida!
Her color comes and goes;   30
It trembles to a lily —
It wavers to a rose.

The ladies of St. James's!
You scarce can understand
The half of all their speeches,   35
Their phrases are so grand;
But Phyllida, my Phyllida!
Her shy and simple words
Are clear as after rain-drops
The music of the birds.   40

The ladies of St. James's!
They have their fits and freaks;
They smile on you — for seconds,
They frown on you — for weeks.
But Phyllida, my Phyllida!   45
Come either storm or shine,
From Shrove-tide unto Shrove-tide,
Is always true — and mine.

My Phyllida! my Phyllida!
I care not though they heap   50
The hearts of all St. James's,
And give me all to keep;

I care not whose the beauties
Of all the world may be,
For Phyllida — for Phyllida   55
Is all the world to me!   (*1883; 1883*)

ON A NANKIN PLATE

"Ah me, but it might have been!
Was there ever so dismal a fate?" —
Quoth the little blue mandarin.

"Such a maid as was never seen!
She passed, though I cried to her 'Wait' — 5
Ah me, but it might have been!

"I cried, O my Flower, my Queen,
Be mine!' 'Twas precipitate" —
Quoth the little blue mandarin —

"But then . . . she was just sixteen,   10
Long-eyed — as a lily straight —
Ah me, but it might have been!

"As it was, from her palankeen,
She laughed — 'You're a week too late!' "
(Quoth the little blue mandarin.)   15

"That is why, in a mist of spleen,
I mourn on this Nankin Plate.
Ah me, but it might have been!" —
Quoth the little blue mandarin.   (*1883; 1883*)

"IN AFTER DAYS"

In after days when grasses high
O'er-top the stone where I shall lie,
    Though ill or well the world adjust
    My slender claim to honored dust,
I shall not question nor reply.   5

I shall not see the morning sky;
I shall not hear the night-wind sigh;
    I shall be mute, as all men must
        In after days!

6. **shoon**, shoes. 11. **Ombre**, the 18th century equivalent of bridge; for a graphic description of the game, see Pope's *Rape of the Lock*, Canto 3. 14. **russet**, rustic, homespun; made of coarse brown cloth. 47. **Shrove-tide**, the three days just before Lent.

On a Nankin Plate. The Nankin blue-and-white china porcelain, made at the Imperial works at King-te-chin and exported from Nankin, was much in vogue in England at the time; compare Lang's *Ballade of Blue China*, p. 806. Dobson's poem is a villanelle, an old French form of lyric.
3. **mandarin**, a Chinese official of army or state. 13. **palankeen**, an enclosed chair borne on the shoulders of porters.
"In After Days." This is a rondeau (see note on *"You Bid Me Try,"* p. 774. "The old French forms which M. Theodore de Banville has turned to such good use in his *Odes Funambulesques* and *Occidentales* are rather better known at this moment [1877] than when, in the course of 1876, most of these attempts were published. The rondeau (not the first in English by a century or so) is here written upon the model of Voiture; the rondel upon that of Charles of Orleans, but with a (symmetric) deviation in the arrangement of the lines . . ." (Dobson's note).

But yet, now living, fain were I   10
That someone then should testify,
  Saying — "He held his pen in trust
  To Art, not serving shame or lust."
Will none? — Then let my memory die
    In after days!   15
           (*1884;* 1884)

"WHEN BURBADGE PLAYED"

When Burbadge played, the stage was bare
Of fount and temple, tower and stair;
  Two backswords eked a battle out;
  Two supers made a rabble rout;
The throne of Denmark was a chair!   5

And yet, no less, the audience there
Thrilled through all changes of Despair,
  Hope, Anger, Fear, Delight, and Doubt
    When Burbadge played!

This is the Actor's gift: to share   10
All moods, all passions, nor to care
  One whit for scene, so he without
  Can lead men's minds the roundabout
Stirred as of old those hearers were
    When Burbadge played!   15
           (*1885;* 1885)

A DIALOGUE

TO THE MEMORY OF MR. ALEXANDER POPE

"Non injussa cano." — VIRGIL

Poet.   I sing of Pope —
Friend.   What, Pope, the Twitnam Bard,
Whom Dennis, Cibber, Tibbald pushed so
  hard!
Pope of the *Dunciad!* Pope who dared to
  woo,
And then to libel, Wortley-Montagu!   5
Pope of the *Ham-walks* story —
Poet.   Scandals all!
Scandals that now I care not to recall.
Surely a little, in two hundred Years,
One may neglect Contemporary Sneers —
Surely allowance for the Man may make   10
That had all Grub Street yelping in his Wake!
And who (I ask you) has been never Mean,
When urged by Envy, Anger, or the Spleen?

"*When Burbadge Played.*" This is another rondeau (see
note on "*You Bid Me Try,*" p. 774, and on "*In After Days,*"
p. 776. Richard Burbadge (c. 1567-1619) was a business
associate of Shakespeare and the most popular actor of his
time.

A Dialogue to the Memory of Mr. Alexander Pope. "**Non
. . . cano,**" "Not unbidden do I sing"; from Virgil's sixth
Eclogue, line 9.

For a discussion of the literary background of the poem
see Critical Notes.

No; I prefer to look on Pope as one
Not rightly happy till his Life was done;   15
Whose whole Career, romance it as you please,
Was (what he called it) but a "long Disease."
Think of his Lot — his Pilgrimage of Pain,
His "crazy Carcass," and his restless Brain;
Think of his Night-Hours with their Feet of
  Lead,   20
His dreary Vigil and his aching Head;
Think of all this, and marvel then to find
The "crooked Body with a crooked Mind!"
Nay rather, marvel that, in Fate's Despite,
You find so much to solace and delight —   25
So much of Courage, and of Purpose high
In that unequal Struggle *not* to die.
I grant you freely that Pope played his Part
Sometimes ignobly — but he loved his Art;
I grant you freely that he sought his Ends,   30
Not always wisely — but he loved his Friends;
And who for Friends a nobler Roll could
  show —
Swift, St. John, Bathurst, Marchmont, Peter-
  b'ro',
Arbuthnot—
  Friend.   ATTICUS?
  Poet.   Well (*entre nous*),
Most that he said of Addison was *true.*   35
Plain Truth you know —
  Friend.   Is often not polite
(So *Hamlet* thought) —
  Poet.   And Hamlet (*Sir*) was right.
But leave Pope's Life. Today, methinks, we
  touch
The Work too little and the Man too much.
Take up the *Lock,* the *Satires, Eloise* —   40
What Art supreme, what Elegance, what
  Ease!
How keen the Irony, the Wit how bright,
The Style how rapid, and the Verse how
  light!
Then read once more, and you shall wonder
  yet
At Skill, at Turn, at Point, at Epithet.   45
"True Wit is Nature to Advantage dressed"—
Was ever Thought so pithily expressed?
"And ten low Words oft creep in one dull
  Line" —
Ah, what a Homily on Yours . . . and
  Mine!
Or take — to choose at Random — take but
  This —   50
"Ten censure wrong for one that writes
  amiss."
  Friend.   Packed and precise, no Doubt.
  Yet surely those
Are but the Qualities we ask of Prose.
Was he a Poet?
  Poet.   Yes; if that be what
Byron was certainly and Bowles was not;   55

Or say you grant him, to come nearer Date,
What Dryden had, that was denied to Tate —
  Friend. Which means, you claim for him
      the Spark divine,
Yet scarce would place him on the highest
      Line —
  Poet. True, there are classes. Pope was
      most of all   60
Akin to Horace, Persius, Juvenal;
Pope was, like them, the Censor of his Age,
An Age more suited to Repose than Rage;
When Riming turned from Freedom to the
      Schools,
And shocked with License, shuddered into
      Rules;   65
When Phœbus touched the Poet's trembling
      Ear
With one supreme Commandment, *Be thou
      Clear;*
When Thought meant less to reason than
      compile,
And the Muse labored . . . chiefly with the
      File.
Beneath full Wigs no Lyric drew its Breath
As in the Days of great Elizabeth;   71
And to the Bards of Anna was denied
The Note that Wordsworth heard on Duddon-
      side.
But Pope took up his Parable, and knit
The Woof of Wisdom with the Warp of Wit;
He trimmed the Measure on its equal Feet,   76
And Smoothed and fitted till the Line was
      neat;
He taught the Pause with due Effect to fall;
He taught the Epigram to come at Call;
He wrote —
  Friend.   His *Iliad!*
  Poet.   Well, suppose you own   80
You like your *Iliad* in the Prose of Bohn —
Though if you'd learn in Prose how *Homer*
      sang,
'Twere best to learn of Butcher and of Lang —
Suppose you say your Worst of Pope, de-
      clare
His Jewels Paste, his Nature a Parterre,   85
His art but Artifice — I ask once more
Where have you seen such Artifice before?
Where have you seen a Parterre better graced,
Or Gems that glitter like his Gems of Paste?
Where can you show, among your Names of
      Note,
So much to copy and so much to quote?
And where, in Fine, in all our English Verse,

A Style more trenchant and a Sense more
      terse?
So I, that love the old Augustan Days
Or formal Courtesies and formal Phrase,   95
That like along the finished Line to feel
The Ruffle's Flutter and the Flash of Steel;
That like my Couplet as compact as clear;
That like my Satire sparkling though severe,
Unmixed with Bathos and unmarred by
      Trope,   100
I fling my Cap for Polish — and for Pope!
                                    (*1888;* 1888)

ON THE FUTURE OF POETRY

Bards of the Future! you that come
With striding march, and roll of drum,
What will your newest challenge be
To our prose-bound community?

What magic will you find to stir   5
The limp and languid listener?
Will it be daring and dramatic?
Will it be frankly democratic?

Will Pegasus return again
In guise of modern aeroplane,   10
Descending from a cloudless blue
To drop on us a bomb or two?

I know not. Far be it from me
To darken dark futurity;
Still less to render more perplexed   15
The last vagary, or the next.

Leave Pindus Hill to those who list,
Iconoclast or anarchist —
So be it. "They that break shall pay."
I stand upon the ancient way.   20

I hold it for a certain thing,
That, blank or riming, song must sing;
And more, that what is good for verse,
Need not, by dint of rime, grow worse.

I hold that they who deal in rime   25
Must take the standpoint of the time —

---

66. **Phœbus**, Apollo, as adapted by the Romans from the Greeks, god of healing and prophecy and patron of poetry and music. 72. **Bards of Anna**, poets of Queen Anne's reign, 1702-14. 73. **Note . . . Duddon-side**, lyric inspiration from nature; see Wordsworth's *A Series of Sonnets on the River Duddon*, 1820. 85. **Parterre**, a garden with flower beds formally arranged in geometric symmetry.

On the Future of Poetry. "These lines were suggested by a lecture on 'The Future of English Poetry,' delivered by Edmund Gosse, in June, 1913" (Alban Dobson's note). 9. **Pegasus**, the winged horse of Greek mythology, symbolic of poetic inspiration. 17. **Pindus Hill**, a mountain between Thessaly and Epirus in Greece, sacred, like Helicon and Parnassus, to Apollo and the Muses; see Ovid's *Metamorphoses*, 1, 5, 570; Virgil's tenth *Eclogue*; etc.

But not to catch the public ear,
As mountebank or pulpiteer;

That the old notes are still the new,
If the musician's touch be true—   30
Nor can the hand that knows its trade
Achieve the trite and ready-made;

That your first theme is Human Life,
Its hopes and fears, its love and strife—
A theme no custom can efface,   35
Common, but never commonplace;

For this, beyond all doubt is plain:
The Truth that pleased will please again,
And move men as in bygone years   39
When Hector's wife smiled through her tears.
                    (*1913; *1914)

GERARD MANLEY HOPKINS
(1844-1889)

HEAVEN—HAVEN

(A NUN TAKES THE VEIL)

I have desired to go
    Where springs not fail,
To fields where flies no sharp and sided hail
    And a few lilies blow.

And I have asked to be   5
    Where no storms come,
Where the green swell is in the havens dumb,
    And out of the swing of the sea.
                    (*c. 1866; *1918)

THE HABIT OF PERFECTION

Elected Silence, sing to me
And beat upon my whorlèd ear,
Pipe me to pastures still and be
The music that I care to hear.

Shape nothing, lips; be lovely-dumb: 5
It is the shut, the curfew sent
From there where all surrenders come
Which only makes you eloquent.

Be shellèd, eyes, with double dark

And find the uncreated light: 10
This ruck and reel which you remark
Coils, keeps, and teases simple sight.

Palate, the hutch of tasty lust,
Desire not to be rinsed with wine;
The can must be so sweet, the crust   15
So fresh that come in fasts divine!

Nostrils, your careless breath that spend
Upon the stir and keep of pride,
What relish shall the censers send
Along the sanctuary side!   20

O feel-of-primrose hands, O feet
That want the yield of plushy sward,
But you shall walk the golden street
And you unhouse and house the Lord.

And, Poverty, be thou the bride   25
And now the marriage feast begun,
And lily-colored clothes provide
Your spouse not labored-at nor spun.
                    (*1866; *1918)

THE WRECK OF THE DEUTSCHLAND

*To the happy memory of five
Franciscan Nuns exiles by the Falk Laws
drowned between midnight
and morning of Dec. 7th, 1875*

PART THE FIRST

1

Thou mastering me
    God! giver of breath and bread;
    World's strand, sway of the sea;
        Lord of living and dead;
Thou hast bound bones and veins in me,
        fastened me flesh,   5
And after it almost unmade, what with
        dread,
    Thy doing: and dost thou touch me a-
        fresh?
Over again I feel thy finger and find thee.

---

11. **ruck and reel**, crowding and confusion. 27-28. **lily-colored . . . spun.** Cf. *Matthew*, 6:28-29.—". . . Consider the lilies of the field, how they grow; they toil not, neither do they spin: And yet I say unto you, That even Solomon in all his glory was not arrayed like one of these."

The Wreck of the Deutschland. The ship *Deutschland*, which sailed from Bremen, Germany, was wrecked in the mouth of the Thames River.

The Falk Laws, under the direction of Herr Falk, Minister of Worship, closed all monasteries in Prussia in May 1875 and expelled all members of religious orders except those who cared for the sick. For a full account of the bitter struggle between the Roman Catholic Church and the German government, see the entry "Kulturkampf" in *The Catholic Encyclopedia*.

---

40. **Hector's wife . . . tears**, a reference to the scene of tender parting between Hector and Andromache (*Iliad*, Book 6, lines 390-502); her tears were at the thought of losing Hector, her smiles from a sense of their happy love.

Heaven—Haven. This simple lyric, restrained and delicate in tone, conventional in form, affords a sharp contrast to the later work of Hopkins which, seeking to forge a new poetic idiom, breaks with standard metrical practice. See Critical Notes on Hopkins.

The Habit of Perfection. 2. **whorlèd**, having whorls.

2

I did say yes
O at lightning and lashed rod;   10
Thou heardst me truer than tongue con-
     fess
Thy terror, O Christ, O God;
Thou knowest the walls, altar and hour
     and night:
The swoon of a heart that the sweep and
     the hurl of thee trod
Hard down with a horror of height: 15
And the midriff astrain with leaning of, laced
     with fire of stress.

3

The frown of his face
Before me, the hurtle of hell
Behind, where, where was a, where was
     a place?
I whirled out wings that spell   20
And fled with a fling of the heart to the heart
     of the Host.
My heart, but you were dovewinged, I can
     tell,
Carrier-witted, I am bold to boast,
To flash from the flame to the flame then,
     tower from the grace to the grace.

4

I am soft sift   25
In an hourglass—at the wall
Fast, but mined with a motion, a drift,
     And it crowds and it combs to the
     fall;
I steady as a water in a well, to a poise, to
     a pane,
But roped with, always, all the way down
     from the tall   30
Fells or flanks of the voel, a vein
Of the gospel proffer, a pressure, a principle,
     Christ's gift.

5

I kiss my hand
To the stars, lovely-asunder
Starlight, wafting him out of it; and   35
Glow, glory in thunder;
Kiss my hand to the dappled-with-damson
     west:
Since, tho' he is under the world's splendour
     and wonder,

His mystery must be instressed, stressed;
For I greet him the days I meet him, and bless
     when I understand.   40

6

Not out of his bliss
Springs the stress felt
Nor first from heaven (and few know
     this)
Swings the stroke dealt—
Stroke and a stress that stars and storms
     deliver,   45
That guilt is hushed by, hearts are flushed
     by and melt—
But it rides time like riding a river
(And here the faithful waver, the faithless
     fable and miss).

7

It dates from day
Of his going in Galilee;   50
Warm-laid grave of a womb-life grey;
     Manger, maiden's knee;
The dense and the driven Passion, and
     frightful sweat;
Thence the discharge of it, there its swell-
     ing to be,
Though felt before, though in high flood
     yet—   55
What none would have known of it, only the
     heart, being hard at bay,

8

Is out with it! Oh,
We lash with the best or worst
Word last! How a lush-kept plush-capped
     sloe
Will, mouthed to flesh-burst,   60
Gush!—flush the man, the being with it,
     sour or sweet,
Brim, in a flash, full!—Hither then, last or
     first,
To hero of Calvary, Christ's feet—
Never ask if meaning it, wanting it, warned
     of it—men go.

9

Be adored among men,   65
God, three-numberèd form;
Wring thy rebel, dogged in den,
     Man's malice, with wrecking and storm.
Beyond saying sweet, past telling of tongue,
Thou art lightning and love, I found it, a
     winter and warm;   70
Father and fondler of heart thou hast
     wrung:

20. **that spell**, in that brief bout. (This and other readings
draw in part upon the notes of W. H. Gardner to the Oxford
edition of Hopkins's poems.) 31. **voel**, a mountain in North
Wales, where the poem was written. The word *roped* in
line 30 suggests trickles of water running down the sides of
the mountain.

Hast thy dark descending and most art merciful then.

10

With an anvil-ding
 And with fire in him forge thy will 74
Or rather, rather then, stealing as Spring
 Through him, melt him but master
  him still:
Whether at once, as once at a crash Paul,
Or as Austin, a lingering-out swéet skíll,
 Make mercy in all of us, out of us all 79
Mastery, but be adored, but be adored King.

PART THE SECOND

11

'Some find me a sword; some
 The flange and the rail; flame,
Fang, or flood' goes Death on drum,
 And storms bugle his fame.
But wé dream we are rooted in earth—
 Dust! 85
Flesh falls within sight of us, we, though
 our flower the same,
Wave with the meadow, forget that there
 must
The sour scythe cringe, and the blear share
 come.

12

On Saturday sailed from Bremen,
 American-outward-bound, 90
Take settler and seamen, tell men with
 women,
 Two hundred souls in the round—
O Father, not under thy feathers nor ever
 as guessing
The goal was a shoal, of a fourth the doom
 to be drowned;
 Yet did the dark side of the bay of thy
  blessing 95
Not vault them, the millions of rounds of thy
 mercy not reeve even them in?

13

Into the snows she sweeps,
 Hurling the haven behind,

The Deutschland, on Sunday; and so the
 sky keeps,
 For the infinite air is unkind, 100
And the sea flint-flake, black-backed in the
 regular blow,
Sitting Eastnortheast, in cursed quarter,
 the wind;
 Wiry and white-fiery and whirlwind-
  swivellèd snow
Spins to the widow-making unchilding unfa-
 thering deeps.

14

She drove in the dark to leeward, 105
 She struck—not a reef or a rock
But the combs of a smother of sand: night
 drew her
 Dead to the Kentish Knock;
And she beat the bank down with her bows
 and the ride of her keel:
The breakers rolled on her beam with ru-
 inous shock; 110
 And canvas and compass, the whorl and
  the wheel
Idle for ever to waft her or wind her with, these
 she endured.

15

Hope had grown grey hairs,
 Hope had mourning on, 114
Trenched with tears, carved with cares,
 Hope was twelve hours gone;
And frightful a nightfall folded rueful a day
Nor rescue, only rocket and lightship,
 shone,
 And lives at last were washing away:
To the shrouds they took,—they shook in the
 hurling and horrible airs. 120

16

One stirred from the rigging to save
 The wild woman-kind below,
With a rope's end round the man, handy
 and brave—
 He was pitched to his death at a blow,
For all his dreadnought breast and braids of
 thew: 125
They could tell him for hours, dandled the
 to and fro
 Through the cobbled foam-fleece, what
  could he do
With the burl of the fountains of air, buck and
 the flood of the wave?

---

77. **at a crash Paul.** St. Paul, as Saul of Tarsus, was
converted to Christianity suddenly by a vision while he was
on the road to Damascus. For the account see *Acts*, 9:1-9.
78. **Austin**, St. Augustine (354-430), one of the great Fathers
of the Church. The process of his conversion was rational
and leisurely. 88. **share**, the part of a plow which cuts the
ground at the bottom of the furrow. 95. **bay**, used in an
architectural sense. 96. **reeve**, gather.

107. **combs**, ridges. 108. **Kentish Knock**, a sandbank
near the mouth of the Thames River. 111. **whorl**, screw-
propeller. 128. **burl**, fullness. **buck**, sudden plunging and
sudden stopping.

17

They fought with God's cold—
And they could not and fell to the
    deck   130
(Crushed them) or water (and drowned
    them) or rolled
With the sea-romp over the wreck.
Night roared, with the heart-break hearing
    a heart-broke rabble,
The woman's wailing, the crying of child
    without check—
Till a lioness arose breasting the babble,
A prophetess towered in the tumult, a virginal
    tongue told.   136

18

Ah, touched in your bower of bone
Are you! turned for an exquisite smart,
Have you! make words break from me
    here all alone,
Do you!—mother of being in me,
    heart.   140
O unteachably after evil, but uttering truth,
Why, tears! is it? tears; such a melting, a
    madrigal start!
Never-eldering revel and river of youth,
What can it be, this glee? the good you have
    there of your own?

19

Sister, a sister calling   145
A master, her master and mine!—
And the inboard seas run swirling and
    hawling;
The rash smart sloggering brine
Blinds her; but she that weather sees one
    thing, one;
Has one fetch in her: she rears herself to
    divine   150
Ears, and the call of the tall nun
To the men in the tops and the tackle rode
    over the storm's brawling.

20

She was first of a five and came
Of a coifèd sisterhood.
(O Deutschland, double a desperate
    name!   155
O world wide of its good!
But Gertrude, lily, and Luther, are two of a
    town,

Christ's lily and beast of the waste wood:
From life's dawn it is drawn down,
Abel is Cain's brother and breasts they have
    sucked the same.)   160

21

Loathed for a love men knew in them,
Banned by the land of their birth,
Rhine refused them.   Thames would ruin
    them;
Surf, snow, river, and earth
Gnashed: but thou art above, thou Orion of
    light;   165
Thy unchancelling poising palms were
    weighing the worth,
Thou martyr-master: in thy sight
Storm flakes were scroll-leaved flowers, lily
    showers—sweet heaven was astrew
    in them.

22

Five! the finding and sake
And cipher of suffering Christ.   170
Mark, the mark is of man's make
And the word of it Sacrificed.
But he scores it in scarlet himself on his own
    bespoken,
Before-time-taken, dearest prizèd and
    priced—
Stigma, signal, cinquefoil token   175
For lettering of the lamb's fleece, ruddying
    of the rose-flake.

23

Joy fall to thee, father Francis,
Drawn to the Life that died;
With the gnarls of the nails in thee, niche
    of the lance, his
Lovescape crucified   180
And seal of his seraph-arrival! and these
    thy daughters
And five-livèd and leavèd favour and pride,
Are sisterly sealed in wild waters,
To bathe in his fall-gold mercies, to breathe
    in his all-fire glances.

160. **Abel, Cain.** Cain was the eldest son of Adam and
Eve, and the murderer of his brother Abel. For this crime
Cain was condemned to be a fugitive. See *Genesis,* 4:1-12.
163. **them,** the Franciscan nuns. 165. **Orion,** a famous
hunter of giant stature; after his death he became a constellation. God was considered the hunter who drove these Franciscan nuns from their place of shelter in Germany so that
their faith and courage might be tested. 169. **finding,** mark
or device. The number of nuns corresponds with the number
of wounds on the crucified body of Christ. 175. **cinquefoil,**
a decorative design having five points. 177. **Francis,** St.
Francis of Assisi (1181?-1226), founder of the Franciscan
order, to which the nuns belonged. He was one of the most
devout and best loved of all the saints. 180. **Lovescape,** the
pattern of the five wounds of Christ; the stigmata received
by St. Francis.

141. **after,** make after. 150. **fetch,** strategem. 157. **Gertrude,** the German saint and mystic (1256?-1302) who lived
in a convent near Eisleben, the birthplace of Martin Luther
(1483-1546). Luther was excommunicated in 1520 because
he denied the supremacy of the Pope; a year later he was
placed under the ban of the empire.

24

Away in the loveable west,   185
On a pastoral forehead of Wales,
I was under a roof here, I was at rest,
And they the prey of the gales;
She to the black-about air, to the breaker, the thickly
Falling flakes, to the throng that catches and quails   190
Was calling 'O Christ, Christ, come quickly':
The cross to her she calls Christ to her, christens her wild-worst Best.

25

The majesty! what did she mean?
Breathe, arch and original Breath.
Is it love in her of the being as her lover had been?   195
Breathe, body of lovely Death.
They were else-minded then, altogether, the men
Woke thee with a *we are perishing* in the weather of Gennesareth.
Or is it that she cried for the crown then,
The keener to come at the comfort for feeling the combating keen?   200

26

For how to the heart's cheering
The down-dugged ground-hugged grey
Hovers off, the jay-blue heavens appearing
Of pied and peeled May!
Blue-beating and hoary-glow height; or night, still higher,   205
With belled fire and the moth-soft Milky Way,
What by your measure is the heaven of desire,
The treasure never eyesight got, nor was ever guessed what for the hearing?

27

No, but it was not these.
The jading and jar of the cart,   210
Time's tasking, it is fathers that asking for ease

Of the sodden-with-its-sorrowing heart,
Not danger, electrical horror; then further it finds
The appealing of the Passion is tenderer in prayer apart:
Other, I gather, in measure her mind's
Burden, in wind's burly and beat of endragonèd seas.   216

28

But how shall I . . . make me room there:
Reach me a . . . Fancy, come faster—
Strike you the sight of it? look at it loom there,
Thing that she . . . there then! the Master,   220
Ipse, the only one, Christ, King, Head:
He was to cure the extremity where he had cast her;
Do, deal, lord it with living and dead;
Let him ride, her pride, in his triumph, despatch and have done with his doom there.

29

Ah! there was a heart right   225
There was single eye!
Read the unshapeable shock night
And knew the who and the why;
Wording it how but by him that present and past,
Heaven and earth are word of, worded by?—   230
The Simon Peter of a soul! to the blast
Tarpeian-fast, but a blown beacon of light.

30

Jesu, heart's light,
Jesu, maid's son,
What was the feast followed the night
Thou hadst glory of this nun?—   236
Feast of the one woman without stain.
For so conceivèd, so to conceive thee is done;

216. **burly**, bluster. 221. **Ipse**, Himself. 226. **single eye.** Cf. *Matthew*, 6:22—"The light of the body is the eye: if therefore thine eye be single, thy whole body shall be full of light." 231-232. These lines express personal qualities of the nun—steadfast devotion, fear, and supreme example. *Peter*, one of Christ's twelve apostles, was first called Simon, but Jesus changed his name as He said, ". . . That thou art Peter, and upon this rock I will build my church; . . ."—*Matthew*, 16:18. **Tarpeia**, an ancient rock or peak of the Capitoline Hill, Rome. It was named after Tarpeia, a vestal virgin, whose dead body was hurled from it because she was a traitor. 237. **Feast . . . stain,** the Feast of the Immaculate Conception of the Blessed Virgin Mary, December 8, an important holy day in the Roman Catholic Church. 238. **so . . . thee.** The nun also was a virgin.

186. **pastoral forehead,** St. Beuno's College, which stands on a hill in the Vale of Clwyd, in North Wales. 192. **The cross to her.** She identifies her own suffering with that of Christ. 198. **weather of Gennesareth.** See *Matthew*, 14:22-34. When the disciples in a ship on the Lake of Gennesareth (Sea of Galilee) were frightened by the heavy storm, Jesus astonished them by calming the waves and the winds. 208. **treasure . . . hearing.** See *I Corinthians*, 2:9—". . . Eye hath not seen, nor ear heard, neither have entered into the heart of man, the things which God hath prepared for them that love him."

But here was heart-throe, birth of a
    brain,
Word, that heard and kept thee and uttered
    thee outright.   240

31

Well, she has thee for the pain, for the
    Patience; but pity of the rest of them!
Heart, go and bleed at a bitterer vein
    for the
Comfortless unconfessed of them—
No not uncomforted: lovely-felicitous Prov-
    idence   245
Finger of a tender of, O of a feathery deli-
    cacy, the breast of the
Maiden could obey so, be a bell to, ring
    of it, and
Startle the poor sheep back! is the shipwrack
    then a harvest, does tempest carry
    the grain for thee?

32

I admire thee, master of the tides,
    Of the Yore-flood, of the year's fall; 250
The recurb and the recovery of the gulf's
    sides,
    The girth of it and the wharf of it and
    the wall;
Stanching, quenching ocean of a motionable
    mind;
Ground of being, and granite of it: past all
    Grasp God, throned behind   255
Death with a sovereignty that heeds but hides,
    bodes but abides;

33

With a mercy that outrides
    The all of water, an ark
For the listener; for the lingerer with a
    love glides
Lower than death and the dark;   260
A vein for the visiting of the past-prayer,
    pent in prison,
The-last-breath penitent spirits—the utter-
    most mark
Our passion-plungèd giant risen,
The Christ of the Father compassionate,
    fetched in the storm of his strides.

34

Now burn, new born to the world, 265

Double-naturèd name,
    The heaven-flung, heart-fleshed, maiden-
    furled
    Miracle-in-Mary-of-flame,
Mid-numbered He in three of the thunder-
    throne!
Not a dooms-day dazzle in his coming nor
    dark as he came;   270
    Kind, but royally reclaiming his own;
A released shower, let flash to the shire, not a
    lightning of fire hard-hurled.

35

Dame, at our door
    Drowned, and among our shoals,
Remember us in the roads, the heaven-
    haven of the Reward: 275
    Our King back, oh, upon English souls!
Let him easter in us, be a dayspring to the
    dimness of us, be a crimson-cresseted
    east,
More brightening her, rare-dear Britain, as
    his reign rolls,   279
    Pride, rose, prince, hero of us, high-priest,
Our   hearts'   charity's   hearth's   fire,   our
    thoughts' chivalry's throng's Lord.
                            (1876–1889; 1918)

• GOD'S GRANDEUR

The world is charged with the grandeur of
    God.
    It will flame out, like shining from shook
    foil;
    It gathers to a greatness, like the ooze of oil
Crushed.   Why do men then now not reck his
    rod?
Generations have trod, have trod, have trod; 5
    And all is seared with trade; bleared,
    smeared with toil,
    And wears man's smudge and shares man's
    smell—the soil
Is bare now, nor can foot feel, being shod.

And for all this, nature is never spent;
    There lives the dearest freshness deep down
    things;   10
And though the last lights off the black West
    went
    Oh, morning, at the brown brink eastward,
    springs—
Because the Holy Ghost over the bent
    World broods with warm breast and with
    ah! bright wings.
                            (1877; 1918)

250. **Yore-flood.** See *Genesis*, 6-8. 251. **recurb . . . sides,**
the stemming and restemming of wave and tide. Cf. *Job*,
38:8-11. 254. **granite.** The restless mind of man finds peace
only in God. 256. **Death.** See lines 81-84. **bodes,** portends.
264. **fetched.** Its subject is *giant*, line 263.

God's Grandeur. 3-4. **ooze of oil Crushed,** oil from crushed
olives.

THE STARLIGHT NIGHT

Look at the stars! look, look up at the skies!
  O look at all the fire-folk sitting in the air!
  The bright boroughs, the circle-citadels
      there!
Down in dim woods the diamond delves! the
      elves'-eyes!
The grey lawns cold where gold, where quick-
      gold lies!   5
  Wind-beat whitebeam! airy abeles set on a
      flare!
  Flake-doves sent floating forth at a farm-
      yard scare!—
Ah well! it is all a purchase, all is a prize.

Buy then! bid then!—What?—Prayer, pa-
      tience, alms, vows.
Look, look: a May-mess, like on orchard
      boughs!   10
  Look! March-bloom, like on mealed-with-
      yellow sallows!
These are indeed the barn; withindoors house
The shocks. This piece-bright paling shuts
      the spouse
  Christ home, Christ and his mother and all
      his hallows.   (*1877; 1918*)

THE SEA AND THE SKYLARK

On ear and ear two noises too old to end
  Trench—right, the tide that ramps against
      the shore;
  With a flood or a fall, low lull-off or all roar,
Frequenting there while moon shall wear and
      wend.

Left hand, off land, I hear the lark ascend,   5
  His rash-fresh re-winded new-skeinèd score
  In crisps of curl off wild winch whirl, and
      pour
And pelt music, till none 's to spill nor spend.

How these two shame this shallow and frail
      town!
  How ring right out our sordid turbid time,
Being pure! We, life's pride and cared-for
      crown,   11

  Have lost that cheer and charm of earth's
      past prime:
Our make and making break, are breaking,
      down
  To man's last dust, drain fast towards man's
      first slime.   (*1877; 1918*)

The Starlight Night. 6. **whitebeam**, a tree with leaves
white on the underside. **abeles**, white poplars. 10. **May-
mess**, medley, like blossoms in May. 11. **mealed ... sallows**,
willows stained with yellow pollen. 14. **hallows**, saints.

THE WINDHOVER

(TO CHRIST OUR LORD)

I caught this morning morning's minion, king-
  dom of daylight's dauphin, dapple-dawn-
      drawn Falcon, in his riding
Of the rolling level underneath him steady
      air, and striding
High there, how he rung upon the rein of a
      wimpling wing
In his ecstasy! then off, off forth on swing,   5
  As a skate's heel sweeps smooth on a bow-
      bend; the hurl and gliding
Rebuffed the big wind. My heart in hiding
Stirred for a bird—the achieve of, the
      mastery of the thing!

Brute beauty and valor and act, oh, air, pride,
      plume, here
Buckle! AND the fire that breaks from thee
      then, a billion   10
Times told lovelier, more dangerous, O my
      chevalier!

No wonder of it; sheer plod makes plow
      down sillion
Shine, and blue-bleak embers, ah, my dear,
  Fall, gall themselves, and gash gold-ver-
      million,   (*1877; 1918*)

PIED BEAUTY

Glory be to God for dappled things—
  For skies of couple-color as a brinded cow;
  For rose-moles all in stipple upon trout
      that swim;
Fresh-firecoal chestnut-falls; finches' wings;
  Landscape plotted and pieced—fold, fal-
      low, and plow;   5
      And all trades, their gear and tackle
      and trim.

All things counter, original, spare, strange;
  Whatever is fickle, freckled (who knows
      how?)
  With swift, slow; sweet, sour; adazzle,
      dim;
He fathers-forth whose beauty is past
      change—   10
      Praise him.   (*1877; 1918*)

The Windhover. The windhover is a kestrel, or sparrow-
hawk. Hopkins regarded this as his best poem and inscribed
it accordingly as his offering to Christ.
4. **wimpling**, rippling. 12. **sillion**, the ridge between two
furrows of plowed land.
  Pied Beauty. 3. **stipple**, a method in painting of applying colors in dots. 4. **chestnut-falls**, chestnuts newly
stripped of their husks. 5. **plotted and pieced**, divided
into fields. 6. **trim**, equipment. 7. **counter**, contrary to
what is expected. **spare**, rare. 10. **whose ... change**. Cf.
James, 1:17.

HURRAHING IN HARVEST

Summer ends now; now, barbarous in beauty,
    the stooks arise
    Around; up above, what wind-walks! what
      lovely behaviour
    Of silk-sack clouds! has wilder, wilful-wavier
Meal-drift moulded ever and melted across
    skies?

I walk, I lift up, I lift up heart, eyes,   5
    Down all that glory in the heavens to glean
      our Saviour;
    And, éyes, heárt, what looks, what lips yet
      gave you a
Rapturous love's greeting of realer, of rounder
    replies?

And the azurous hung hills are his world-
    wielding shoulder
    Majestic — as a stallion stalwart, very-
      violet-sweet! —   10
These things, these things were here and but
    the beholder
    Wanting; which two when they once meet,
The heart rears wings bold and bolder
    And hurls for him, O half hurls earth for
      him off under his feet.
                        (1877; 1918)

FELIX RANDAL

Felix Randal the farrier, O he is dead then?
    my duty all ended,
Who have watched his mould of man, big-
    boned and hardy-handsome
Pining, pining, till time when reason rambled
    in it and some
Fatal four disorders, fleshed there, all con-
    tended?

Sickness broke him. Impatient he cursed at
    first, but mended   5
Being anointed and all; though a heavenlier
    heart began some
Months earlier, since I had our sweet reprieve
    and ransom
Tendered to him. Ah well, God rest him all
    road ever he offended!

This seeing the sick endears them to us, us too
    it endears.
My tongue had taught thee comfort, touch
    had quenched thy tears,   10
Thy tears that touched my heart, child, Felix,
    poor Felix Randal;

Felix Randal. 1. **farrier**, horseshoer. 8. **all road ever**,
in whatever way.

How far from then forethought of, all thy more
    boisterous years,
When thou at the random grim forge, powerful
    amidst peers,
Didst fettle for the great grey drayhorse his
    bright and battering sandal!
                        (1880; 1918)

SPRING AND FALL

TO A YOUNG CHILD

Márgarét, are you gríeving
Over Goldengrove unleaving?
Leáves, líke the things of man, you
With your fresh thoughts care for, can you?
Áh! ás the heart grows older   5
It wíll come to such sights colder
By and by, nor spare a sigh
Though worlds of wanwood leafmeal lie;
And yet you wíll weep and know why.
Now no matter, child, the name: 10
Sórrow's spríngs áre the same.
Nor mouth had, no nor mind, expressed
What heart heard of, ghost guessed:
It ís the blight man was born for,
It is Margaret you mourn for.   15
                        (1880; 1918)

INVERSNAID

This darksome burn, horseback brown,
His rollback highroad roaring down,
In coop and in comb the fleece of his foam
Flutes and low to the lake falls home.

A windpuff-bonnet of fawn-froth   5
Turns and twindles over the broth
Of a pool so pitchblack, fell-frowning,
It rounds and rounds Despair to drowning.

Degged with dew, dappled with dew
Are the groins of the braes that the brook
    treads through,   10
Wiry heathpacks, flitches of fern,
And the beadbonny ash that sits over the
    burn.

13. **random**, built with stones of irregular shapes and
sizes. 14. **fettle**, make ready.
    Spring and Fall. 8. **wanwood**, decaying woods (suggest-
ing in sound, wormwood). **leafmeal**, leaf by leaf (cf. piecemeal), suggesting also the mealiness of dead leaves. 13.
ghost guessed, i.e., the child has already intuited the meaning of the **blight**, the fall of man, the death in man's world.
    Inversnaid. Inversnaid is a hamlet on one of the finest
points of the eastern shore of Loch Lomond, Scotland.
    1. **burn**, brook. 3. **coop**, hollow place between waves.
comb, crest of wave. 4. **Flutes**, forms streaks or channels.
6. **twindles**, twists, winds. 9. **Degged**, sprinkled. 10. **braes**,
hillsides. · 11. **heathpacks**, clumps of heather. **flitches**,
clumps.

What would the world be, once bereft
Of wet and of wildness? Let them be left,
Oh, let them be left, wildness and wet;   15
Long live the weeds and the wilderness yet.

(*1881*; 1918)

THE LEADEN ECHO AND THE GOLDEN ECHO

(*Maiden's song from St. Winefred's Well*)

THE LEADEN ECHO

How to kéep — is there ány any, is there none
        such, nowhere known some, bow or
        brooch or braid or brace, láce, latch
        or catch or key to keep
Back beauty, keep it, beauty, beauty, beauty,
        . . . from vanishing away?
Ó is there no frowning of these wrinkles,
        rankèd wrinkles deep,
Dówn? no waving off of these most mournful
        messengers, still messengers, sad and
        stealing messengers of grey?
No there's none, there's none, O no there's
        none,   5
Nor can you long be, what you now are,
        called fair,
Do what you may do, what, do what you may,
And wisdom is early to despair:
Be beginning; since, no, nothing can be done
To keep at bay   10
Age and age's evils, hoar hair,
Ruck and wrinkle, drooping, dying, death's
        worst, winding sheets, tombs and
        worms and tumbling to decay;
So be beginning, be beginning to despair.
O there's none; no no no there's none:
Be beginning to despair, to despair,   15
Despair, despair, despair, despair.

THE GOLDEN ECHO

        Spare!
There ís one, yes I have one (Hush there!);
Only not within seeing of the sun,
Not within the singeing of the strong sun,   20
Tall sun's tingeing, or treacherous the tainting
        of the earth's air,
Somewhere elsewhere there is ah well where!
        one,
Óne. Yes I cán tell such a key, I dó know
        such a place,
Where whatever's prized and passes of us,
        everything that's fresh and fast flying
        of us, seems to us sweet of us and
        swiftly away with, done away with,
        undone,

Undone, done with, soon done with, and yet
        dearly and dangerously sweet   25
Of us, wimpled-water-dimpled, not-by-morn-
        ing-matchèd face,
The flower of beauty, fleece of beauty, too
        too apt to, ah! to fleet,
Never fleets móre, fastened with the tenderest
        truth
To its own best being and its loveliness of
        youth: it is an everlastingness of, O
        it is an all youth!
Come then, your ways and airs and looks,
        locks, maiden gear, gallantry and
        gaiety and grace,   30
Winning ways, airs innocent, maiden manners,
        sweet looks, loose locks, long locks,
        lovelocks, gaygear, going gallant, girl-
        grace —
Resign them, sign them, seal them, send them,
        motion them with breath,
And with sighs soaring, soaring síghs deliver
Them; beauty-in-the-ghost, deliver it, early
        now, long before death
Give beauty back, beauty, beauty, beauty,
        back to God, beauty's self and beauty's
        giver.   35
See; not a hair is, not an eyelash, not the
        least lash lost; every hair
Is, hair of the head, numbered.
Nay, what we had lighthanded left in surly
        the mere mould
Will have waked and have waxed and have
        walked with the wind what while we
        slept,
This side, that side hurling a heavyheaded
        hundredfold   40
What while we, while we slumbered.
O then, weary then whý should we tread? O
        why are we so haggard at the heart, so
        care-coiled, care-killed, so fagged, so
        fashed, so cogged, so cumbered,
When the thing we freely fórfeit is kept with
        fonder a care,
Fonder a care kept than we could have kept
        it, kept
Far with fonder a care (and we, we should
        have lost it) finer, fonder   45
A care kept. — Where kept? Do but tell us
        where kept, where. —
Yonder. — What high as that! We follow,
        now we follow. — Yonder, yes yonder,
        yonder,
Yonder.   (*1882;* 1918)

The Leaden Echo and the Golden Echo was written for Hopkins' uncompleted drama *St. Winefred's Well.*
4. **Dówn** goes with "frowning" (line 3). 12. **ruck,** pucker. 17. **Spare,** i.e., cease lamenting.

26. **wimpled,** rippled. 27. **fleece of beauty,** meant (said Hopkins) to suggest "the velvetiness of roseleaves, flesh, and other things." 28. **own best being,** i.e., the resurrected body will take the loveliest form it assumed in life. 38-39. Hopkins glossed these lines: "Nay more: the seed that we so carelessly flung into the dull furrow, and then forgot it, will have come to ear meantime." 42. **fashed,** vexed; **cogged,** deceived or cheated.

CARRION COMFORT

Not, I'll not, carrion comfort, Despair, not
feast on thee;
Not untwist — slack they may be — these
last strands of man
In me ór, most weary, cry *I can no more.* I
can;
Can something, hope, wish day come, not
choose not to be.
But ah, but O thou terrible, why wouldst
thou rude on me 5
Thy wring-world right foot rock? lay a lion-
limb against me? scan
With darksome devouring eyes my bruisèd
bones? and fan,
O in turns of tempest, me heaped there; me
frantic to avoid thee and flee?

Why? That my chaff might fly; my grain
lie, sheer and clear.
Nay in all that toil, that coil, since (seems) I
kissed the rod, 10
Hand rather, my heart lo! lapped strength,
stole joy, would laugh, chéer.
Cheer whom though? the hero whose heaven-
handling flung me, fóot tród
Me? or me that fought him? O which one? is
it each one? That night, that year
Of now done darkness I wretch lay wrestling
with (my God!) my God.
(*1885;* 1918)

NO WORST, THERE IS NONE

No worst, there is none. Pitched past pitch
of grief,
More pangs will, schooled at forepangs, wilder
wring.
Comforter, where, where is your comforting?
Mary, mother of us, where is your relief?

My cries heave, herds-long; huddle in a main,
a chief 5
Woe, world-sorrow; on an age-old anvil wince
and sing —
Then lull, then leave off. Fury had shrieked
'No ling-
ering! Let me be fell: force
I must be brief'.

O the mind, mind has mountains; cliffs of
fall
Frightful, sheer, no-man-fathomed. Hold
them cheap 10
May who ne'er hung there. Nor does long
our small
Durance deal with that steep or deep. Here!
creep,
Wretch, under a comfort serves in a whirlwind: all
Life death does end and each day dies with
sleep. (*1885;* 1918)

I WAKE
AND FEEL THE FELL OF DARK

I wake and feel the fell of dark, not day.
What hours, O what black hoùrs we have
spent
This night! what sights you, heart, saw; ways
you went!
And more must, in yet longer light's delay.
With witness I speak this. But where I
say 5
Hours I mean years, mean life. And my la-
ment
Is cries countless, cries like dead letters sent
To dearest him that lives alas! away.

I am gall, I am heartburn. God's most
deep decree
Bitter would have me taste: my taste was
me; 10
Bones built in me, flesh filled, blood brimmed
the curse.
Selfyeast of spirit a dull dough sours. I see
The lost are like this, and their scourge to be
As I am mine, their sweating selves; but worse.
(*c.* 1885; 1918)

MY OWN HEART
LET ME MORE HAVE PITY ON

My own heart let me more have pity on; let
Me live to my sad self hereafter kind,
Charitable; not live this tormented mind
With this tormented mind tormenting yet.

I cast for comfort I can no more get 5
By groping round my comfortless, than blind

No Worst, There Is None. This sonnet describes the
"dark night of the soul," the despair that comes of the sense
of being deserted by God.
2. **schooled at forepangs,** taught by past experience of
pain. 5. **herds-long,** as numerous and as prolonged as
cries from a whole bleating herd of sheep. 8. **fell,** fierce,
cruel, deadly. **force,** perforce, of necessity.

10-11. **Hold . . . there,** he who never hung on the face of
the mountains may underestimate the terror of the heights.
13. **comfort,** the "carrion comfort" of despair that looks to
death as an end of life's miseries.
I Wake and Feel the Fell of Dark. 14. **but worse,** the
damned are in a worse plight.
My Own Heart Let Me More Have Pity On. 5-7. Robert
Bridges glossed these lines: "I cast for comfort, (which) I
can no more find in my comfortless (world) than a blind man
in his dark world" can find day.

Eyes in their dark can day or thirst can find
Thirst's all-in-all in all a world of wet.

Soul, self; come, poor Jackself, I do advise
You, jaded, let be; call off thoughts awhile 10
Elsewhere; leave comfort root-room; let joy
　　size
At God knows when to God knows what;
　　whose smile
's not wrung, see you; unforeseen times
　　rather — as skies
Betweenpie mountains — lights a lovely mile.
　　　　　　　　　　　　　　(c. 1885; 1918)

THAT NATURE IS A HERACLITEAN FIRE AND OF THE COMFORT OF THE RESURRECTION

Cloud-puffball, torn tufts, tossed pillows |
　　flaunt forth, then chevy on an air-
built thoroughfare: heaven-roysterers, in gay-
　　gangs | they throng; they glitter in
　　marches.
Down roughcast, down dazzling whitewash, |
　　wherever an elm arches,
Shivelights and shadowtackle in long | lashes
　　lace, lance, and pair.
Delightfully the bright wind boisterous |
　　ropes, wrestles, beats earth bare 5
Of yestertempest's creases; | in pool and rut
　　peel parches
Squandering ooze to squeezed | dough, crust,
　　dust; stanches, starches
Squadroned masks and manmarks | treadmire
　　toil there
Footfretted in it. Million-fuelèd, | nature's
　　bonfire burns on.
But quench her bonniest, dearest | to her,
　　her clearest-selvèd spark 10
Man, how fast his firedint, | his mark on mind,
　　is gone!
Both are in an unfathomable, all is in an
　　enormous dark
Drowned. O pity and indignation! Man-
　　shape, that shone
Sheer off, disseveral, a star, | death blots
　　black out; nor mark
　　　　Is any of him at all so stark

But vastness blurs and time | beats level.
　　Enough! the Resurrection, 15
A heart's-clarion! Away grief's gasping, |
　　joyless days, dejection.
　　　　　　Across my foundering deck shone
A beacon, an eternal beam. | Flesh fade, and
　　mortal trash
Fall to the residuary worm; | world's wildfire,
　　leave but ash:
　　　　In a flash, at a trumpet crash,
I am all at once what Christ is, | since he was
　　what I am, and 21
This Jack, joke, poor potsherd, | patch,
　　matchwood, immortal diamond,
　　　　Is immortal diamond.
　　　　　　　　　　　　　　(1888; 1918)

TO R. B.

The fine delight that fathers thought; the
　　strong
Spur, live and lancing like the blowpipe flame,
Breathes once and, quenchèd faster than it
　　came,
Leaves yet the mind a mother of immortal
　　song.
Nine months she then, nay years, nine years
　　she long 5
Within her wears, bears, cares and combs the
　　same:
The widow of an insight lost she lives, with aim
Now known and hand at work now never
　　wrong.
　　Sweet fire the sire of muse, my soul needs
　　　　this;
I want the one rapture of an inspiration. 10
O then if in my lagging lines you miss
The roll, the rise, the carol, the creation,
My winter world, that scarcely breathes that
　　bliss
Now, yields you, with some sighs, our expla-
　　nation.　　　　　　　(1889; 1918)

RICHARD WATSON DIXON
(1833-1900)

ST. MARY MAGDALENE

Kneeling before the altar step,
　　Her white face stretched above her hands;

---

9. **Jackself,** the ordinary helpless self.　11. **size,** adjust.
The passage means: let joy adapt itself to whatever God wills,
whenever God wills it, for joy cannot be forced; "unforeseen," it comes at times to light our way.　14. **Betweenpie,**
mottle, mark out with light and shade (cf. "pied" in *Pied
Beauty,* p. 777).
　That Nature Is a Heraclitean Fire. This poem measures
the changefulness and transience of the world against the
concept of the Resurrection and the immortality of the unchanging Christ. Heraclitus (c. 535-c. 475) taught that all
things were in a state of constant change and flux as mani-
festations of the basic element fire.
　1. **chevy,** race or scamper.　4. **Shivelights,** arrows of
light. **shadowtackle,** trees etched against the sky like the
outlines of a ship's tackle.　5-9. The wind dries out and
turns to dust the ruts and footprints shaped in doughy mud.
14. **disseveral,** distinct and various.

20. **residuary worm,** the worm that inherits all that is left.
23. **Jack,** an ordinary commonplace man. **potsherd,** fragment of a broken pot. **patch,** fool in motley. **diamond,** a
hard and perdurable substance produced by heat and change.
　To R. B. This poem is a tribute to Robert Bridges, Hopkins' closest friend and ultimately his editor.
　St. Mary Magdalene. All four Gospels tell of Mary Magdalene, who, cured of "seven devils" (see *Luke,* 8:2), became
the devoted follower of Jesus, witnessed the crucifixion,
discovered the empty tomb, and was the first to meet the
risen Christ. In Christian tradition she has frequently been
represented as a fallen woman restored to grace by humility
and faith.

In one great line her body thin
Rose robed right upwards to her chin;
Her hair rebelled in golden bands,   5
   And filled her hands;

Which likewise held a casket rare
   Of alabaster at that tide;
Simeon was there and looked at her,
Trancedly kneeling, sick and fair;   10
Three parts the light her features tried,
   She rest implied.

Strong singing reached her from within,
   Discordant but with weighty rhymes;
Her swaying body kept the stave;   15
Then all the woods about her wave,
She heard, and saw, in mystic mimes,
   Herself three times.

Once, in the doorway of a house,
   With yellow lintels painted fair,   20
Very far off, where no men pass,
Green and red banners hung in mass
Above scorched woodwork wormed and bare,
   And spider's snare.

She, scarlet in her form and gold,   25
   Fallen down upon her hands and knees,
Her arms and bosom bare and white,
Her long hair streaming wild with light,
Felt all the waving of the trees,
   And hum of bees.   30

A rout of mirth within the house,
   Upon the ear of madness fell,
Stunned with its dread, yet made intense;
A moment, and might issue thence
Upon the prey they quested well,   35
   Seven fiends of hell.

She grovelled on her hands and knees,
   She bit her breath against that rout;
Seven devils inhabited within,
Each acting upon each his sin,   40
Limb locked in limb, snout turning snout,
   And these would out.

Twice, and the woods lay far behind,
   Gold corn spread broad from slope to slope;
The copses rounded in faint light,   45
Far from her pathway gleaming white,
Which gleamed and wound in narrow scope,
   Her narrow hope.

She on the valley stood and hung,
   Then downward swept with steady haste; 50
The steady wind behind her sent
Her robe before her as she went;

Descending on the wind, she chased
   The form she traced.

She, with her blue eyes blind with flight,   55
   Rising and falling in their cells,
Hands held as though she played a harp,
Teeth glistening as in laughter sharp,
Flew ghostly on, a strength like hell's,
   When it rebels,   60

Behind her, flaming on and on,
   Rushing and streaming as she flew;
Moved over hill as if through vale,
Through vale as if o'er hill, no fail;
Her bosom trembled as she drew   65
   Her long breath through.

Thrice, with an archway overhead,
   Beneath, what might have seemed a tomb;
White garments fallen fold on fold,
As if limbs yet were in their hold,   70
Drew the light further in the gloom,
   Of the dark room.

She, fallen without thought or care,
   Heard, as it were, a ceaseless flow
Of converse muttered in her ear,   75
Like waters sobbing wide and near,
About things happened long ago
   Of utter woe.   (1861)

DREAM

I

With camel's hair I clothed my skin,
   I fed my mouth with honey wild;
And set me scarlet wool to spin,
   And all my breast with hyssop filled;
Upon my brow and cheeks and chin   5
   A bird's blood spilled.

I took a broken reed to hold,
   I took a sponge of gall to press;
I took weak water-weeds to fold
   About my sacrificial dress.   10

I took the grasses of the field,
   The flax was bolled upon my crine;
And ivy thorn and wild grapes healed
   To make good wine.

I took my scrip of manna sweet,   15
   My cruse of water did I bless;
I took the white dove by the feet,
   And flew into the wilderness.

7-9. See *Mark*, 14:3; Dixon apparently identifies Mary
Magdalene with the woman who anointed the head of
Jesus "in the house of Simon the leper."

Dream. 1-2. The dreamer sees himself in the guise of
John the Baptist. Cf. *Mark*, 1:6.—"And John was clothed
with camel's hair, and with a girdle of skin about his loins:
and he did eat locusts and wild honey." 12. **crine**, hair.

II

The tiger came and played;
Uprose the lion in his mane;   20
The jackal's tawny nose
And sanguine dripping tongue
Out of the desert rose
And plunged its sands among;
The bear came striding o'er the desert plain. 25

Uprose the horn and eyes
And quivering flank of the great unicorn,
And galloped round and round;
Uprose the gleaming claw
Of the leviathan, and wound   30
In steadfast march did draw
Its course away beyond the desert's bourn.

I stood within a maze
Woven round about me by a magic art,
And ordered circle-wise: 35
The bear more near did tread,
And with two fiery eyes,
And with a wolfish head,
Did close the circle round in every part.

III

With scarlet corded horn,   40
With frail wrecked knees and stumbling pace,
The scapegoat came:
His eyes took flesh and spirit dread in flame
At once, and he died looking towards my face.
                                      (1861)

DAWNING

Over the hill I have watched the dawning,
I have watched the dawn of morning light,
Because I cannot well sleep by night,
Every day I have watched the dawning.
And today very early my window shook   5
With the cold wind fresh from the ghastly
    brook,
And I left my bed to watch the dawning.
Very cold was the light, very pale, very still,
And the wind blew great clouds over the hill
Towards the wet place of the dying dawn-
    ing;   10
It blew them over towards the east
In heavier charge as the light increased,
From the very death of the dying dawning.
Whence did the clouds come over the hill?
I cannot tell, for no clouds did fill   15
The clear space opposite the dawning

---

30. **leviathan,** a Biblical sea monster. 42. **scapegoat,** in
ancient Jewish practice, the goat allowed to escape into the
wilderness when the high priest had placed the sins of the
people upon its head. See *Leviticus,* 16:5-10.

Right over the hill, long, low, and pearl-grey,
Set in the wind to live as it may;
And as the light increased from the dawning,
The cold, cold brook unto my seeming   20
Did intermit its ghastly gleaming
And ran forth brighter in the dawning.
The wall-fruit stretched along the wall,
The pear-tree waved its banners tall;
Then close beside me in the dawning,   25
I saw thy face so stonily grey,
And the close lips no word did say,
The eyes confessed not in the dawning.
I saw a man ride through the light
Upon the hill-top, out of sight   30
Of me and thee and all the dawning.   (1861)

SONG

The feathers of the willow
Are half of them grown yellow
    Above the swelling stream;
And ragged are the bushes,
And rusty now the rushes,   5
    And wild the clouded gleam.

The thistle now is older,
His stalk begins to moulder,
    His head is white as snow;
The branches all are barer,   10
The linnet's song is rarer,
    The robin pipeth now.   (1864)

WILLIAM ERNEST HENLEY
(1849-1903)

TO MY MOTHER

Chiming a dream by the way
    With ocean's rapture and roar,
I met a maiden today
    Walking alone on the shore;
Walking in maiden wise,   5
    Modest and kind and fair,
The freshness of spring in her eyes
    And the fullness of spring in her hair.

Cloud-shadow and scudding sun-burst
    Were swift on the floor of the sea,   10
And a mad wind was romping its worst,
    But what was their magic to me?
Or the charm of the midsummer skies?
    I only saw she was there,
A dream of the sea in her eyes   15
    And the kiss of the sea in her hair.

I watched her vanish in space;
    She came where I walked no more;
But something had passed of her grace

To the spell of the wave and the shore;   20
And now, as the glad stars rise,
  She comes to me, rosy and rare,
The delight of the wind in her eyes
  And the hand of the wind in her hair.
                                    (*1872;* 1888)

From *IN HOSPITAL*

I. ENTER PATIENT

The morning mists still haunt the stony street;
The northern summer air is shrill and cold;
And, lo, the hospital, gray, quiet, old,
Where Life and Death like friendly chafferers
    meet.
Through the loud spaciousness and drafty
    gloom   5
A small, strange child — so agéd yet so
    young! —
Her little arm besplinted and beslung,
Precedes me gravely to the waiting-room.
I limp behind, my confidence all gone.
The gray-haired soldier-porter waves me on,
And on I crawl, and still my spirits fail;   11
A tragic meanness seems so to environ
These corridors and stairs of stone and iron,
Cold, naked, clean — half-workhouse and
    half-jail.

2. WAITING

A square, squat room (a cellar on promotion),
Drab to the soul, drab to the very daylight;
Plasters astray in unnatural-looking tinware;
Scissors and lint and apothecary's jars.

Here, on a bench a skeleton would writhe
    from   5
Angry and sore, I wait to be admitted;
Wait till my heart is lead upon my stomach,
While at their ease two dressers do their
    chores.

One has a probe — it feels to me a crowbar.
A small boy sniffs and shudders after blue-
    stone.   10
A poor old tramp explains his poor old ulcers.
Life is (I think) a blunder and a shame.

4. BEFORE

Behold me waiting — waiting for the knife.
A little while, and at a leap I storm

The thick, sweet mystery of chloroform,
The drunken dark, the little death-in-life.
The gods are good to me — I have no wife,   5
No innocent child, to think of as I near
The fateful minute; nothing all-too dear
Unmans me for my bout of passive strife.
Yet I am tremulous and a trifle sick,
And, face to face with chance, I shrink a
    little;   10
My hopes are strong, my will is something
    weak.
Here comes the basket? Thank you. I am
    ready.
But, gentlemen my porters, life is brittle;
You carry Cæsar and his fortunes — steady!

5. OPERATION

You are carried in a basket,
Like a carcass from the shambles,
To the theater, a cockpit
Where they stretch you on a table.

Then they bid you close your eyelids,   5
And they mask you with a napkin,
And the anæsthetic reaches
Hot and subtle through your being.

And you gasp and reel and shudder
In a rushing, swaying rapture,   10
While the voices at your elbow
Fade — receding — fainter — farther.

Lights about you shower and tumble,
And your blood seems crystallizing —
Edged and vibrant, yet within you   15
Racked and hurried back and forward.

Then the lights grow fast and furious,
And you hear a noise of waters,
And you wrestle, blind and dizzy,
In an agony of effort,   20

Till a sudden lull accepts you,
And you sound an utter darkness . . .
And awaken . . . with a struggle . . .
On a hushed, attentive audience.

8. STAFF-NURSE: OLD STYLE

The great masters of the commonplace,
REMBRANDT and good SIR WALTER — only
    these
Could paint her all to you: experienced ease

In Hospital. This is a series of poems based upon impressions of the Old Infirmary, Edinburgh, where Henley was
a patient for twenty months, suffering from a tubercular
disease. One foot had been amputated in his youth, and it
was feared that he would lose the other, but it was saved
by the skill of Dr. Joseph Lister (1827-1912), originator of
antiseptic surgery.
  2. Waiting. 10. **bluestone,** cupric sulphate, or blue
vitriol, used as an emetic.

4. Before. 14. **You . . . fortunes,** Julius Caesar's words,
quoted by Plutarch in his *Life of Cæsar.* They were addressed,
during the war with Pompey, to a boatman who had Cæsar
as his passenger.
  5. Operation. 15. **Edged,** sharp.
  8. Staff-Nurse: Old Style. 2. **Rembrandt,** Dutch realistic painter (1606-1669). **Sir Walter,** Sir Walter Scott (1771-
1832), whose graphic word-paintings of Edinburgh characters,
as in *The Heart of Midlothian,* were doubtless in Henley's mind.

And antique liveliness and ponderous grace;
The sweet old roses of her sunken face;   5
The depth and malice of her sly, gray eyes;
The broad Scots tongue that flatters, scolds,
      defies,
The thick Scots wit that fells you like a mace.
These thirty years has she been nursing here,
Some of them under SYME, her hero still.   10
Much is she worth, and even more is made
      of her.
Patients and students hold her very dear.
The doctors love her, tease her, use her skill.
They say "The Chief" himself is half-afraid
      of her.

10. STAFF-NURSE: NEW STYLE

Blue-eyed and bright of face but waning fast
Into the sear of virginal decay,
I view her as she enters, day by day,
As a sweet sunset almost overpast.
Kindly and calm, patrician to the last,   5
Superbly falls her gown of sober gray,
And on her chignon's elegant array
The plainest cap is somehow touched with
      caste.
She talks BEETHOVEN; frowns disapprobation
At BALZAC's name, sighs it at "poor GEORGE
      SAND's";   10
Knows that she has exceeding pretty hands;
Speaks Latin with a right accentuation;
And gives at need (as one who understands)
Draft, counsel, diagnosis, exhortation.

13. CASUALTY

As with varnish red and glistening
Dripped his hair; his feet looked rigid;
Raised, he settled stiffly sideways.
You could see his hurts were spinal.

He had fallen from an engine,   5
And been dragged along the metals.
It was hopeless, and they knew it;
So they covered him, and left him.

As he lay, by fits half sentient,
Inarticulately moaning,   10
With his stockinged soles protruded
Stark and awkward from the blankets,

To his bed there came a woman,
Stood and looked and sighed a little,

And departed without speaking,   15
As himself a few hours after.

I was told it was his sweetheart.
They were on the eve of marriage.
She was quiet as a statue,
But her lip was gray and writhen.   20

14. AVE, CAESAR!

From the winter's gray despair,
From the summer's golden languor,
Death, the lover of Life,
Frees us for ever.

Inevitable, silent, unseen,   5
Everywhere always,
Shadow by night and as light in the day,
Signs she at last to her chosen;
And, as she waves them forth,
Sorrow and Joy   10
Lay by their looks and their voices,
Set down their hopes, and are made
One in the dim Forever.

Into the winter's gray delight,   15
Into the summer's golden dream,
Holy and high and impartial,
Death, the mother of Life,
Mingles all men for ever.

16. HOUSE-SURGEON

Exceeding tall, but built so well his height
Half-disappears in flow of chest and limb;
Moustache and whisker trooper-like in trim;
Frank-faced, frank-eyed, frank-hearted; al-
      ways bright
And always punctual — morning, noon, and
      night;   5
Bland as a Jesuit, sober as a hymn;
Humorous, and yet without a touch of whim;
Gentle and amiable, yet full of fight.
His piety, though fresh and true in strain,
Has not yet whitewashed up his common
      mood   10
To the dead blank of his particular Schism.
Sweet, unaggressive, tolerant, most humane,
Wild artists like his kindly elderhood,
And cultivate his mild Philistinism.

19. SCRUBBER

She's tall and gaunt, and in her hard, sad face
With flashes of the old fun's animation
There lowers the fixed and peevish resignation
Bred of a past where troubles came apace.
She tells me that her husband, ere he died,   5

---

10. **Syme,** James Syme (1799-1870), recognized as the greatest living surgeon in his day. 14. **"The Chief,"** Dr. Lister, successor to Syme as chief surgeon at the Edinburgh Infirmary.
16. *Staff-Nurse: New Style.* 9. **Beethoven,** Ludwig van Beethoven (1770-1827), German musical composer; he was well established in 1872 as an old master. 10. **Balzac,** Honoré de Balzac (1799-1850), French naturalistic writer. Conservative Englishwomen found his stories too frank. **George Sand,** pseudonym of Mme. Aurore Dudevant (1804-1876), French novelist, celebrated also for her romantic love affairs with the poet Musset, the composer Chopin, and others.

16. *House-Surgeon.* 11. **Schism,** sectarian creed. 14. **Philistinism,** middle-class materialism and conventionality, a term made famous by Matthew Arnold in his essay on *Culture and Anarchy,* 1869, but used previously by Carlyle, who adapted it from German university usage.

Saw seven of their children pass away,
And never knew the little lass at play
Out on the green, in whom he's deified.
Her kin dispersed, her friends forgot and gone,
All simple faith her honest Irish mind,
Scolding her spoiled young saint, she labors
    on —
Telling her dreams, taking her patients' part,
Trailing her coat sometimes; and you shall
    find
No rougher, quainter speech, nor kinder heart.

25. APPARITION

Thin-legged, thin-chested, slight unspeakably,
Neat-footed and weak-fingered; in his face —
Lean, large-boned, curved of beak, and
    touched with race,
Bold-lipped, rich-tinted, mutable as the sea,
The brown eyes radiant with vivacity —   5
There shines a brilliant and romantic grace,
A spirit intense and rare, with trace on trace
Of passion and impudence and energy.
Valiant in velvet, light in ragged luck,
Most vain, most generous, sternly critical,   10
Buffoon and poet, lover and sensualist;
A deal of Ariel, just a streak of Puck,
Much Antony, of Hamlet most of all,
And something of the Shorter-Catechist.

27. NOCTURNE

At the barren heart of midnight,
When the shadow shuts and opens
As the loud flames pulse and flutter,
I can hear a cistern leaking.

Dripping, dropping, in a rhythm,   5
Rough, unequal, half-melodious,
Like the measures aped from nature
In the infancy of music;

Like the buzzing of an insect,
Still, irrational, persistent . . .   10
I must listen, listen, listen
In a passion of attention;

Till it taps upon my heartstrings,
And my very life goes dripping,
Dropping, dripping, drip-drip-dropping,   15
In the drip-drop of the cistern.

28. DISCHARGED

Carry me out
Into the wind and the sunshine,
Into the beautiful world.
O the wonder, the spell of the streets!
The stature and strength of the horses,   5
The rustle and echo of footfalls,
The flat roar and rattle of wheels!
A swift tram floats huge on us . . .
It's a dream?
The smell of the mud in my nostrils   10
Blows brave — like a breath of the sea!

As of old,
Ambulant, undulant drapery,
Vaguely and strangely provocative,
Flutters and beckons. O yonder —   15
Is it? — the gleam of a stocking!
Sudden, a spire
Wedged in the mist! O the houses,
The long lines of lofty, gray houses,
Cross-hatched with shadow and light!
These are the streets . . .   20
Each is an avenue leading
Whither I will!

Free . . . !
Dizzy, hysterical, faint,
I sit, and the carriage rolls on with me   25
Into the wonderful world.   (*1872-1875;* 1888)

INVICTUS

Out of the night that covers me,
    Black as the Pit from pole to pole,
I thank whatever gods may be
    For my unconquerable soul.

In the fell clutch of circumstance   5
    I have not winced nor cried aloud.
Under the bludgeonings of chance
    My head is bloody, but unbowed.

Beyond this place of wrath and tears
    Looms but the Horror of the shade,   10
And yet the menace of the years
    Finds, and shall find, me unafraid.

It matters not how strait the gate,
    How charged with punishments the scroll,
I am the master of my fate;   15
I am the captain of my soul.   (*1875;* 1888)

O, GATHER ME THE ROSE

O, gather me the rose, the rose,
    While yet in flower we find it,

25. *Apparition.* This is an accurate sketch of Robert Louis Stevenson, who visited Henley in the hospital, 1875, and became his close friend. Stevenson dedicated his *Virginibus Puerisque* to Henley (1881).
    12. **Ariel,** the airy spirit that executes Prospero's bidding in Shakespeare's *Tempest.* **Puck,** the mischievous spirit of English folklore and of Shakespeare's *Midsummer Night's Dream.* 13. **Antony,** Marcus Antonius (83-30 B.C.), fiery orator in Shakespeare's *Julius Cæsar,* sensualist and lover in *Antony and Cleopatra.* 14. **Shorter-Catechist,** an adherent to strict Calvinistic religious and ethical principles as embodied in the Shorter Catechism, compiled by the Westminster Assembly in 1646-47.

Invictus. The title means *Unconquered.* Cf. Swinburne's *The Garden of Proserpine,* lines 83-84, p. 697.

For summer smiles, but summer goes,
   And winter waits behind it!   4

For with the dream foregone, foregone,
   The deed foreborne for ever,
The worm, regret, will canker on,
   And Time will turn him never.

So well it were to love, my love,
   And cheat of any laughter   10
The fate beneath us and above,
   The dark before and after.

The myrtle and the rose, the rose,
   The sunshine and the swallow,   14
The dream that comes, the wish that goes,
   The memories that follow!   (*1874; 1888*)

I AM THE REAPER

I am the Reaper.
All things with heedful hook
Silent I gather.
Pale roses touched with the spring,
Tall corn in summer,
Fruits rich with autumn, and frail winter
   blossoms —
Reaping, still reaping —
All things with heedful hook
Timely I gather.

I am the Sower.   10
All the unbodied life
Runs through my seed-sheet.
Atom with atom wed,
Each quickening the other,
Fall though my hands, ever changing, still
   changeless.   15
Ceaselessly sowing,
Life, incorruptible life,
Flows from my seed-sheet.

Maker and breaker,
I am the ebb and the flood,   20
Here and Hereafter.
Sped through the tangle and coil
Of infinite nature,
Viewless and soundless I fashion all being.
Taker and giver,
I am the womb and the grave,
The Now and the Ever.   (*1875; 1888*)

THE SANDS ARE ALIVE WITH SUNSHINE

The sands are alive with sunshine,
   The bathers lounge and throng,
And out in the bay a bugle
   Is lilting a gallant song.

The clouds go racing eastward,   5
   The blithe wind cannot rest,
And a shard on the shingle flashes
   Like the shining soul of a jest;

While children romp in the surges,
   And sweethearts wander free,   10
And the Firth as with laughter dimples . . .
   I would it were deep over me! (*1875; 1888*)

TO A. D.

The nightingale has a lyre of gold,
   The lark's is a clarion call;
And the blackbird plays but a boxwood flute,
   But I love him best of all.

For his song is all of the joy of life,   5
   And we in the mad, spring weather,
We two have listened till he sang
   Our hearts and lips together. (*1876; 1888*)

TO K. DE M.

Love blows as the wind blows,
Love blows into the heart.
      — NILE BOAT SONG.

Life in her creaking shoes
Goes, and more formal grows,
A round of calls and cues;
Love blows as the wind blows.
Blows! . . . in the quiet close   5
As in the roaring mart,
By ways no mortal knows
Love blows into the heart.

The stars some cadence use,
Forthright the river flows,   10
In order fall the dews,
Love blows as the wind blows;
Blows! . . . and what reckoning shows
The courses of his chart?
A spirit that comes and goes,   15
Love blows into the heart.   (*1878; 1888*)

I. M.
MARGARITÆ SORORI

A late lark twitters from the quiet skies;
And from the west,
Where the sun, his day's work ended,

7. **shard . . . shingle,** a fragment of pottery or glass on the beach. 11. **Firth,** a narrow arm of the sea.
To A. D. The poem was dedicated to Henry Austin Dobson (1840-1921), poet and essayist, who had expressed great admiration for it. See Alban Dobson, *Some Notes on Austin Dobson*, 1928, p. 157.
To K. de M. This poem was dedicated to Henley's friend and literary protégé, Mrs. Katherine de Mattos, cousin of Robert Louis Stevenson. In some of Henley's poems, as in this one and in *To W. A.*, p. 796, there is no relation between the content and the person to whom it is dedicated.
I. M. Margaritae Sorori. Henley wrote this poem in memory of his wife's sister Margaret.

Lingers as in content,
There falls on the old, gray city   5
An influence luminous and serene,
A shining peace.

The smoke ascends
In a rosy-and-golden haze. The spires
Shine, and are changed. In the valley   10
Shadows rise. The lark sings on. The sun,
Closing his benediction,
Sinks, and the darkening air
Thrills with a sense of the triumphing night —
Night with her train of stars   15
And her great gift of sleep.

So be my passing!
My task accomplished and the long day done,
My wages taken, and in my heart
Some late lark singing,   20
Let me be gathered to the quiet west,
The sundown splendid and serene,
Death.

                      (*1886;* 1888)

TO W. A.

Or ever the knightly years were gone
  With the old world to the grave,
I was a King in Babylon
  And you were a Christian Slave.

I saw, I took, I cast you by,   5
  I bent and broke your pride.
You loved me well, or I heard them lie,
  But your longing was denied.
Surely I knew that by and by
  You cursed your gods and died.   10

And a myriad suns have set and shone
  Since then upon the grave
Decreed by the King of Babylon
  To her that had been his Slave.

The pride I trampled is now my scathe,   15
  For it tramples me again.
The old resentment lasts like death,
  For you love, yet you refrain.
I break my heart on your hard unfaith,
  And I break my heart in vain.   20

Yet not for an hour do I wish undone
  The deed beyond the grave,
When I was a King in Babylon
  And you were a Virgin Slave.

                      (1884)

ON THE WAY TO KEW

On the way to Kew,
By the river old and gray,
Where in the Long Ago
We laughed and loitered so,
I met a ghost today,   5
A ghost that told of you —
A ghost of low replies
And sweet inscrutable eyes,
  Coming up from Richmond
As you used to do.   10

By the river old and gray,
The enchanted Long Ago
Murmured and smiled anew.
On the way to Kew,
March had the laugh of May,   15
The bare boughs looked aglow,
And old immortal words
Sang in my breast like birds,
  Coming up from Richmond
As I used with you.   20

With the life of Long Ago
Lived my thought of you.
By the river old and gray,
Flowing his appointed way,
As I watched I knew   25
What is so good to know —
Not in vain, not in vain,
Shall I look for you again,
  Coming up from Richmond
On the way to Kew.   (1888)

BALLADE
OF A TOYOKUNI COLOR-PRINT

Was I a Samurai renowned,
Two-sworded, fierce, immense of bow?
A histrion angular and profound?
A priest? a porter? — Child, although
I have forgotten clean, I know   5
That in the shade of Fujisan,
What time the cherry-orchards blow,
I loved you once in old Japan.

As here you loiter, flowing-gowned
And hugely sashed, with pins a-row   10
Your quaint head as with flamelets crowned,
Demure, inviting — even so,

To W. A. This poem was probably dedicated to William
Archer (1856-1924), playwright and critic, a member of the
younger literary group in which Henley and Stevenson were
interested. See note on *To K. de M.,* p. 795. The time
indicated in line 1 is a conscious anachronism. Babylon was
in ruins before the 5th century B.C.

On the Way to Kew. Kew, with its famous gardens, and
Richmond are in the environs of London, a short distance up
the Thames.
    Ballade of a Toyokuni Color-Print. Utagawa Toyokuni
(1769-1825) was a popular Japanese painter of women and
actors. On the form of the poem see note on Swinburne's
A Ballad of Dreamland, p. 723.
    1. **Samurai,** a member of the ancient Japanese military
aristocracy. 3. **histrion,** actor. 6. **Fujisan,** Mount Fuji,
which forms a characteristic background for many Japanese
prints. 7. **blow,** bloom. The flowering cherry is a tree common in Japan.

When merry maids in Miyako
To feel the sweet o' the year began,
And green gardens to overflow,   15
I loved you once in old Japan.

Clear shine the hills; the rice-fields round
Two cranes are circling; sleepy and slow,
A blue canal the lake's blue bound
Breaks at the bamboo bridge; and lo!   20
Touched with the sundown's spirit and glow,
I see you turn, with flirted fan,
Against the plum-tree's bloomy snow. . .
I loved you once in old Japan!

ENVOY

Dear, 'twas a dozen lives ago;   25
But that I was a lucky man
The Toyokuni here will show:
I loved you — once — in old Japan.   (1888)

BALLADE OF YOUTH AND AGE

Spring at her height on a morn at prime,
Sails that laugh from a flying squall,
Pomp of harmony, rapture of rime —
Youth is the sign of them, one and all.
Winter sunsets and leaves that fall,   5
An empty flagon, a folded page,
A tumble-down wheel, a tattered ball —
These are a type of the world of Age.

Bells that clash in a gaudy chime,
Swords that clatter in onsets tall,   10
The words that ring and the fames that
    climb —
Youth is the sign of them, one and all.
Hymnals old in a dusty stall,
A bald, blind bird in a crazy cage,
The scene of a faded festival —   15
These are a type of the world of Age.

Hours that strut as the heirs of time,
Deeds whose rumor's a clarion-call,
Songs where the singers their souls sublime —
Youth is the sign of them, one and all.   20
A staff that rests in a nook of wall,
A reeling battle, a rusted gage,
The chant of a nearing funeral —
These are a type of the world of Age.

ENVOY

Struggle and turmoil, revel and brawl —   25
Youth is the sign of them, one and all.
A smoldering hearth and a silent stage —
These are a type of the world of Age.
    (1888)

13. **Miyako**, a Japanese village in the northeastern part of the island of Hondo.
Ballade of Youth and Age. 1. **prime**, nine o'clock. 13. **stall**, bookshop.

BALLADE OF DEAD ACTORS

Where are the passions they essayed,
And where are the tears they made to flow?
Where the wild humors they portrayed
For laughing worlds to see and know?
Othello's wrath and Juliet's woe?   5
Sir Peter's whims and Timon's gall?
And Millamant and Romeo?
Into the night go one and all.

Where are the braveries, fresh or frayed?
The plumes, the armors — friend and foe?   10
The cloth of gold, the rare brocade,
The mantles glittering to and fro?
The pomp, the pride, the royal show?
The cries of war and festival?
The youth, the grace, the charm, the glow?   15
Into the night go one and all.

The curtain falls, the play is played:
The Beggar packs beside the Beau;
The Monarch troops, and troops the Maid;
The Thunder huddles with the Snow.   20
Where are the revelers high and low?
The clashing swords?　The lover's call?
The dancers gleaming row on row?
Into the night go one and all.

ENVOY

Prince, in one common overthrow   25
The Hero tumbles with the Thrall;
As dust that drives, as straws that blow,
Into the night go one and all.   (1888)

DOUBLE BALLADE OF LIFE AND FATE

Fools may pine, and sots may swill,
Cynics gibe and prophets rail,
Moralists may scourge and drill,
Preachers prose, and fainthearts quail.
Let them whine, or threat, or wail!   5
Till the touch of Circumstance
Down to darkness sink the scale,
Fate's a fiddler, Life's a dance.

What if skies be wan and chill?
What if winds be harsh and stale?   10
Presently the east will thrill,
And the sad and shrunken sail,
Bellying with a kindly gale,

Ballade of Dead Actors. 3. **humors**, character peculiarities or obsessions. 6. **Sir Peter (Teazle)**, in Richard Brinsley Sheridan's *School for Scandal*, 1777. **Timon**, the cynic in Shakespeare's *Timon of Athens*. 7. **Millamant**, the heroine of Congreve's *The Way of the World*, 1700. 9. **braveries**, splendid ornaments and attire. 18. **packs**, goes out.
Double Ballade of Life and Fate. A double ballade consists of six stanzas instead of the three of the regular ballade. 4. **prose**, declaim monotonously.

Bear you sunwards, while your chance
Sends you back the hopeful hail! —   15
"Fate's a fiddler, Life's a dance."

Idle shot or coming bill,
Hapless love or broken bail,
Gulp it (never chew your pill!),
And, if Burgundy should fail,   20
Try the humbler pot of ale!
Over all is heaven's expanse.
Gold's to find among the shale.
Fate's a fiddler, Life's a dance.

Dull Sir Joskin sleeps his fill,   25
Good Sir Galahad seeks the Grail,
Proud Sir Pertinax flaunts his frill,
Hard Sir Aeger dints his mail;
And the while by hill and dale
Tristram's braveries gleam and glance,   30
And his blithe horn tells its tale —
"Fate's a fiddler, Life's a dance."

Araminta's grand and shrill,
Delia's passionate and frail,
Doris drives an earnest quill,   35
Athanasia takes the veil;
Wiser Phyllis o'er her pail,
At the heart of all romance
Reading, sings to Strephon's flail —
"Fate's a fiddler, Life's a dance."   40

Every Jack must have his Jill
(Even Johnson had his Thrale!);
Forward, couples — with a will!
This, the world, is not a jail.
Hear the music, sprat and whale!   45
Hands across, retire, advance!
Though the doomsman's on your trail,
Fate's a fiddler, Life's a dance.

ENVOY

Boys and girls, at slug and snail
And their kindred look askance.   50
Pay your footing on the nail;
Fate's a fiddler, Life's a dance.   (1888)

20. **Burgundy**, an expensive wine, from the province of Burgundy, France. 25-36. **Joskin . . . Athanasia.** While many of these names should be associated with varying human types rather than with actual characters, some are capable of identification. Galahad is the central figure of the Grail quest in Arthurian romance; Sir Pertinax is a strutting patriot in Macklin's comedy, *The Man of the World*, 1764; Tristram is famous in Arthurian romance as a knight and the lover of Isolde; Araminta is an extravagant and snobbish woman in Vanbrugh's comedy, *The Confederacy*, 1695; Delia is the fickle and alluring lady to whom the Roman poet Tibullus addressed his poems; Sir Æger may be a character in the 15th century romance, *Sir Eger, Sir Grame, and Sir Graysteel*; Athanasia is possibly St. Anastasia, a Roman girl who entered a nunnery in the 4th century. 37-39. **Phyllis . . . Strephon**, traditional names for a pastoral shepherdess and shepherd; see Virgil's *Eclogues*, Sidney's *Arcadia*, and W. S. Gilbert's *Iolanthe*. 42. **Johnson . . . Thrale.** Mrs. Thrale, later Mrs. Piozzi, was a friend and patron of Dr. Samuel Johnson, the literary dictator of the later 18th century.

WHEN YOU ARE OLD

When you are old, and I am passed away —
Passed, and your face, your golden face, is
                gray —
I think whate'er the end, this dream of mine,
Comforting you, a friendly star will shine
Down the dim slope where still you stumble
                and stray.   5
So may it be: that so dead Yesterday,
No sad-eyed ghost but generous and gay,
May serve you memories like almighty wine,
                When you are old!

Dear Heart, it shall be so. Under the sway 10
Of death the past's enormous disarray
Lies hushed and dark. Yet though there
                come no sign,
Live on well pleased; immortal and divine
Love shall still tend you, as God's angels may,
                When you are old.   15
                                           (1888)

WHAT IS TO COME

What is to come we know not. But we know
That what has been was good — was good to
                show,
Better to hide, and best of all to bear.
We are the masters of the days that were;
We have lived, we have loved, we have suf-
                fered . . . even so.   5

Shall we not take the ebb who had the flow?
Life was our friend. Now, if it be our foe —
Dear, though it spoil and break us! — need
                we care
                What is to come?

Let the great winds their worst and wildest
                blow,   10
Or the gold weather round us mellow slow;
We have fulfilled ourselves, and we can dare
And we can conquer, though we may not share
In the rich quiet of the afterglow
                What is to come.   15
                                           (1888)

LONDON VOLUNTARIES

1. *Grave*

St. Margaret's bells,
Quiring their innocent, old-world canticles,
Sing in the storied air,

When You Are Old. This and the following poem are rondeaus (see note on Dobson's "*You Bid Me Try*," p. 774).
London Voluntaries. 1. *Grave.* A voluntary is an organ solo; *grave* is a slow, solemn movement in music.
1. **St. Margaret's**, the parish church of Westminster, close beside Westminister Abbey. 2. **canticles**, hymns, chants.

All rosy-and-golden, as with memories
Of woods at evensong, and sands and seas 5
Disconsolate for that the night is nigh.
O the low, lingering lights! The large last
  gleam
(Hark! how those brazen choristers cry and
  call!)
Touching these solemn ancientries, and there,
The silent River ranging tide-mark high 10
And the callow, gray-faced Hospital,
With the strange glimmer and glamour of a
  dream!
The Sabbath peace is in the slumbrous trees,
And from the wistful, the fast-widowing sky
(Hark! how those plangent comforters call
  and cry!) 15
Falls as in August plots late roseleaves fall.
The sober Sabbath stir —
Leisurely voices, desultory feet! —
Comes from the dry, dust-colored street,
Where in their summer frocks the girls go
  by, 20
And sweethearts lean and loiter and confer,
Just as they did an hundred years ago,
Just as an hundred years to come they will —
When you and I, dear love, lie lost and low,
And sweet-throats none our welkin shall
  fulfill, 25
Nor any sunset face serene and slow;
But, being dead, we shall not grieve to die.

2. *Andante con moto*

Forth from the dust and din,
The crush, the heat, the many-spotted glare,
The odor and sense of life and lust aflare,
The wrangle and jangle of unrests,
Let us take horse, dear heart, take horse and
  win —
As from swart August to the green lap of
  May —
To quietness and the fresh and fragrant
  breasts
Of the still, delicious night, not yet aware
In any of her innumerable nests
Of that first sudden plash of dawn, 10
Clear, sapphirine, luminous, large,
Which tells that soon the flowing springs of
  day
In deep and ever deeper eddies drawn
Forward and up, in wider and wider way,
Shall float the sands, and brim the shores, 15
On this our lith of the world, as round it
  roars

And spins into the outlook of the sun
(The Lord's first gift, the Lord's especial
  charge),
With light, with living light, from marge to
  marge
Until the course He set and staked be run. 20

Through street and square, through square
  and street,
Each with his home-grown quality of dark
And violated silence, loud and fleet,
Waylaid by a merry ghost at every lamp,
The hansom wheels and plunges. Hark, O
  hark, 25
Sweet, how the old mare's bit and chain
Ring back a rough refrain
Upon the marked and cheerful tramp
Of her four shoes! Here is the Park,
And, oh, the languid midsummer wafts adust,
The tired midsummer blooms! 30
O the mysterious distances, the glooms
Romantic, the august
And solemn shapes! At night this City of
  Trees
Turns to a tryst of vague and strange 35
And monstrous Majesties,
Let loose from some dim underworld to range
These terrene vistas till their twilight sets;
When, dispossessed of wonderfulness, they
  stand
Beggared and common, plain to all the land 40
For stooks of leaves! And lo! the Wizard
  Hour,
His silent, shining sorcery winged with power!
Still, still the streets, between their carcanets
Of linking gold, are avenues of sleep.
But see how gable ends and parapets 45
In gradual beauty and significance
Emerge! And did you hear
That little twitter-and-cheep,
Breaking inordinately loud and clear
On this still, spectral, exquisite atmosphere?
'Tis a first nest at matins! And behold 51
A rakehell cat — how furtive and acold!
A spent witch homing from some infamous
  dance —
Obscene, quick-trotting, see her tip and fade
Through shadowy railings into a pit of shade!
And now! a little wind and shy, 56
The smell of ships (that earnest of romance),
A sense of space and water, and thereby
A lamplit bridge touching the troubled sky,
And look, O look! a tangle of silver gleams 60
And dusky lights, our River and all his
  dreams,
His dreams that never save in our deaths can
  die.

10. **River,** the Thames. 11. **Hospital,** Chelsea Hospital, a short distance up the Thames from St. Margaret's. 15. **plangent,** resounding. **comforters,** the bells of St. Margaret's.
2. *Andante con moto,* with energy or emotion, a musical movement not so slow as *andante* but less rapid than *allegretto.*
16. **lith,** limb, section.

38. **terrene,** earthly. 41. **stooks,** bundles. 43. **carcanets,** golden collars set with jewels—referring to the rows of street-lamps. 51. **matins,** morning songs.

What miracle is happening in the air,
Charging the very texture of the gray
With something luminous and rare?   65
The night goes out like an ill-parceled fire,
And, as one lights a candle, it is day.
The extinguisher, that perks it like a spire
On the little formal church, is not yet green
Across the water; but the housetops nigher,   70
The corner-lines, the chimneys — look how
         clean,
How new, how naked!   See the batch of
         boats,
Here at the stairs, washed in the freshsprung
         beam!
And those are barges that were goblin floats,
Black, hag-steered, fraught with devilry and
         dream!   75
And in the piles the water frolics clear,
The ripples into loose rings wander and flee,
And we — we can behold that could but hear
The ancient River singing as he goes,   79
New-mailed in morning, to the ancient
         Sea.
The gas burns lank and jaded in its glass;
The old Ruffian soon shall yawn himself
         awake,
And light his pipe, and shoulder his tools, and
         take
His hobnailed way to work!

                          Let us too pass —
Pass ere the sun leaps and your shadow
         shows —   85
Through these long, blindfold rows
Of casements staring blind to right and left,
Each with his gaze turned inward on some
         piece
Of life in death's own likeness — Life bereft
Of living looks as by the Great Release —   90
Pass to an exquisite night's more exquisite
         close!

Reach upon reach of burial — so they feel,
These colonies of dreams!   And as we steal
Homeward together, but for the buxom
         breeze,
Fitfully frolicking to heel   95
With news of dawn-drenched woods and
         tumbling seas,
We might — thus awed, thus lonely that we
         are —
Be wandering some dispeopled star,
Some world of memories and unbroken
         graves,
So broods the abounding Silence near and
         far —   100
Till even your footfall craves
Forgiveness of the majesty it braves.

66. ill-parceled, poorly divided or built.

3. Scherzando

Down through the ancient Strand
The spirit of October, mild and boon
And sauntering, takes his way
This golden end of afternoon,
As though the corn stood yellow in all the land,
And the ripe apples dropped to the harvest-
         moon.   6

Lo! the round sun, half-down the western
         slope —
Seen as along an unglazed telescope —
Lingers and lolls, loath to be done with day:
Gifting the long, lean, lanky street   10
And its abounding confluences of being
With aspects generous and bland;
Making a thousand harnesses to shine
As with new ore from some enchanted mine,
And every horse's coat so full of sheen   15
He looks new-tailored, and every 'bus feels
         clean,
And never a hansom but is worth the feeing;
And every jeweler within the pale
Offers a real Arabian Night for sale;
And even the roar   20
Of the strong streams of toil, that pause and
         pour
Eastward and westward, sounds suffused —
Seems as it were bemused
And blurred, and like the speech
Of lazy seas on a lotus-haunted beach —   25
With this enchanted lustrousness,
This mellow magic, that (as a man's caress
Brings back to some faded face, beloved
         before,
A heavenly shadow of the grace it wore
Ere the poor eyes were minded to beseech)   30
Old things transfigures, and you hail and bless
Their looks of long-lapsed loveliness once
         more;
Till Clement's, angular and cold and staid,
Gleams forth in glamour's very stuffs arrayed;
And Bride's, her aëry, unsubstantial charm 35
Through flight on flight of springing, soaring
         stone
Grown flushed and warm,
Laughs into life full-mooded and fresh-blown;
And the high majesty of Paul's

3. Scherzando, a musical movement, light and happy.
1. Strand.   The direct way from St. Paul's Cathedral to
Charing Cross and Trafalgar Square comprises Ludgate Hill,
Fleet Street, and the Strand, each a continuation of the
other.   The Strand was anciently a country road linking
London with the village of Westminster.   2. boon, good;
cf. French bon.   8. unglazed telescope, a tube without
lenses.   23. bemused, in a trance.   24. lotus-haunted,
covered with lotus trees, the fruit of which causes dreaminess
and forgetfulness.   (See Tennyson's The Lotos-Eaters, page
28.)   33. Clement's, St. Clement Danes, a church midway
of the Strand; it was built in 1681 by Sir Christopher Wren.
35. Bride's, a Wren church, just off Fleet Street, with a
tall spire (226 feet).   39. Paul's, St. Paul's Cathedral, at
the head of Ludgate Hill, built (1675-1710) in the Renaissance
style by Wren.

Uplifts a voice of living light, and calls — 40
Calls to his millions to behold and see
How goodly this his London Town can be!

For earth and sky and air
Are golden everywhere,
And golden with a gold so suave and fine 45
The looking on it lifts the heart like wine.
Trafalgar Square
(The fountains volleying golden glaze)
Shines like an angel-market. High aloft
Over his couchant Lions, in a haze 50
Shimmering and bland and soft,
A dust of chrysoprase,
Our Sailor takes the golden gaze
Of the saluting sun, and flames superb,
As once he flamed it on his ocean round. 55
The dingy dreariness of the picture-place,
Turned very nearly bright,
Takes on a luminous transiency of grace,
And shows no more a scandal to the ground.
The very blind man pottering on the curb 60
Among the posies and the ostrich feathers
And the rude voices touched with all the
      weathers
Of the long, varying year,
Shares in the universal alms of light.
The windows, with their fleeting, flickering
      fires, 65
The height and spread of frontage shining
      sheer,
The quiring signs, the rejoicing roofs and
      spires —
'Tis El Dorado — El Dorado plain,
The Golden City! And when a girl goes by,
Look! as she turns her glancing head, 70
A call of gold is floated from her ear!
Golden, all golden! In a golden glory,
Long-lapsing down a golden coasted sky,
The day not dies, but seems
Dispersed in wafts and drifts of gold, and shed
Upon a past of golden song and story 76
And memories of gold and golden dreams.

4. *Largo e mesto*

Out of the poisonous East,
Over a continent of blight,
Like a maleficent Influence released
From the most squalid cellarage of hell,
The Wind-Fiend, the abominable — 5
The Hangman Wind that tortures temper and
      light —

Comes slouching, sullen and obscene,
Hard on the skirts of the embittered night;
And in a cloud unclean
Of excremental humors, roused to strife 10
By the operation of some ruinous change,
Wherever his evil mandate run and range,
Into a dire intensity of life,
A craftsman at his bench, he settles down
To the grim job of throttling London Town. 15

So, by a jealous lightlessness beset
That might have oppressed the dragons of old
      time
Crunching and groping in the abysmal slime,
A cave of cutthroat thoughts and villainous
      dreams,
Hag-rid and crying with cold and dirt and
      wet, 20
The afflicted City, prone from mark to mark
In shameful occultation, seems
A nightmare labyrinthine, dim and drifting,
With wavering gulfs and antic heights, and
      shifting,
Rent in the stuff of a material dark, 25
Wherein the lamplight, scattered and sick and
      pale,
Shows like the leper's living blotch of bale —
Uncoiling monstrous into street on street
Paven with perils, teeming with mischance,
Where man and beast go blindfold and in
      dread, 30
Working with oaths and threats and faltering
      feet
Somewhither in the hideousness ahead;
Working through wicked airs and deadly dews
That make the laden robber grin askance
At the good places in his black romance, 35
And the poor, loitering harlot rather choose
Go pinched and pined to bed
Than lurk and shiver and curse her wretched
      way
From arch to arch, scouting some three-
      penny prey.

Forgot his dawns and far-flushed afterglows,
His green garlands and windy eyots forgot, 41
The old Father-River flows,
His watchfires cores of menace in the gloom,
As he came oozing from the Pit, and bore,
Sunk in his filthily transfigured sides, 45
Shoals of dishonored dead to tumble and rot
In the squalor of the universal shore —
His voices sounding through the gruesome air
As from the Ferry where the Boat of Doom
With her blaspheming cargo reels and rides, 50
The while his children, the brave ships,

---

47. **Trafalgar Square**, an open square, just north of
Charing Cross, containing fountains fed by artesian wells
and a column surmounted by a statue of Lord Nelson, famous
British admiral (1778-1805), and guarded by four bronze
lions, the work of Sir Edwin Landseer. 52. **dust of chrysoprase**, a greenish haze as if composed of particles of green
limestone. 67. **quiring signs**, signs that unite in proclaiming wares. 68. **El Dorado**, the legendary golden city
sought by the Spanish conquerors of America.
4. *Largo e mesto*, slowly and sadly.

22. **occultation**, concealment. 27. **bale**, sorrow, death.
41. **eyots**, small islands. 42. **Father-River**, the Thames.
49. **Ferry . . . Doom**, the boat in which Charon, the ferryman
of Hades, conveys the dead across the river Styx.

No more adventurous and fair,
Nor tripping it light of heel as homebound
    brides,
But infamously enchanted,
Huddle together in the foul eclipse,   55
Or feel their course by inches desperately,
As through a tangle of alleys murder-haunted,
From sinister reach to reach out—out—to sea.

And Death the while—
Death with his well-worn, lean, professional
    smile,   60
Death in his threadbare working trim—
Comes to your bedside, unannounced and
    bland,
And with expert, inevitable hand
Feels at your windpipe, fingers you in the lung,
Or flicks the clot well into the laboring heart,
Thus signifying unto old and young,   66
However hard of mouth or wild of whim,
'Tis time—'tis time by his ancient watch—
    to part
From books and women and talk and drink
    and art.
And you go humbly after him   70
To a mean suburban lodging—on the way
To what or where
Not Death, who is old and very wise, can say;
And you—how should you care
So long as, unreclaimed of hell,   75
The Wind-Fiend, the insufferable,
Thus vicious and thus patient, sits him down
To the black job of burking London Town?

5. *Allegro mæstoso*

Spring winds that blow
As over leagues of myrtle-blooms and may;
Bevies of spring clouds trooping slow,
Like matrons heavy bosomed and aglow
With the mild and placid price of increase!
    Nay,   5
What makes this insolent and comely stream
Of appetence, this freshet of desire
(Milk from the wild breasts of the willful Day!),
Down Piccadilly dance and murmur and
    gleam
In genial wave on wave and gyre on gyre?   10
Why does that nymph unparalleled splash
    and churn
The wealth of her enchanted urn
Till, over-billowing all between
Her cheerful margents, gray and living green,
It floats and wanders, glittering and fleeing, 15

An estuary of the joy of being?
Why should the lovely leafage of the Park
Touch to an ecstasy the act of seeing?
—Sure, sure my paramour, my Bride of
    Brides,
Lingering and flushed, mysteriously abides 20
In some dim, eye-proof angle of odorous dark,
Some smiling nook of green-and-golden shade,
In the divine conviction robed and crowned
The globe fulfills his immemorial round
But as the marrying-place of all things made!

There is no man, this deifying day,   26
But feels the primal blessing in his blood.
There is no woman but disdains—
The sacred impulse of the May
Brightening like sex made sunshine through
    her veins—   30
To vail the ensigns of her womanhood.
None but, rejoicing, flaunts them as she goes,
Bounteous in looks of her delicious best,
On her inviolable quest;
These with their hopes, with their sweet
    secrets those,   35
But all desirable and frankly fair,
As each were keeping some most prosperous
    tryst,
And in the knowledge went imparadised!
For look! a magical influence everywhere,
Look how the liberal and transfiguring air 40
Washes this inn of memorable meetings,
This center of ravishments and gracious
    greetings,
Till, through its jocund loveliness of length
A tidal-race of lust from shore to shore,
A brimming reach of beauty met with
    strength,   45
It shines and sounds like some miraculous
    dream,
Some vision multitudinous and agleam,
Of happiness as it shall be evermore!

Praise God for giving
Through this His messenger among the days 50
His word the life He gave is thrice-worth
    living!
For Pan, the bountiful, imperious Pan—
Not dead, not dead, as impotent dreamers
    feigned,
But the gay genius of a million Mays
Renewing his beneficent endeavor!—   55
Still reigns and triumphs, as he hath tri-
    umphed and reigned
Since in the dim blue dawn of time
The universal ebb-and-flow began,
To sound his ancient music, and prevails,
By the persuasion of his mighty rime,   60

58. reach, the distance sailed on a single tack. **78. burking,** murdering. The word is derived from William Burke, of Edinburgh, who was executed for smothering persons in order to sell their bodies for dissection.

5. *Allegro mæstoso,* quick—but with dignity.

2. may, hawthorn. **7. appetence,** longing. **9. Piccadilly,** a street in the fashionable district of London, lined with hotels, shops, and clubs. **10. gyre,** whirl. **11. nymph,** a statue of a nymph spouting water.

17. Park, Hyde Park, at the end of Piccadilly. **31. vail,** lower. **41-42. inn . . . greetings,** Piccadilly. **45. reach,** extent. **52-53. Pan . . . dead.** See Mrs. Browning's *The Dead Pan,* p. 384.

Here in this radiant and immortal street
Lavishly and omnipotently as ever
In the open hills, the undissembling dales,
The laughing-places of the juvenile earth.
For lo! the wills of man and woman meet, 65
Meet and are moved, each unto each endeared,
As once in Eden's prodigal bowers befell,
To share his shameless, elemental mirth
In one great act of faith; while deep and
strong,
Incomparably nerved and cheered, 70
The enormous heart of London joys to beat
To the measures of his rough, majestic song;
The lewd, perennial, overmastering spell
That keeps the rolling universe ensphered,
And life, and all for which life lives to long, 75
Wanton and wondrous and forever well.

(*1890-1892; 1892*)

PROLOGUE TO *RHYMES AND RHYTHMS*

Something is dead . . .
The grace of sunset solitudes, the march
Of the solitary moon, the pomp and power
Of round on round of shining soldier-stars
Patrolling space, the bounties of the sun — 5
Sovran, tremendous, unimaginable —
The multitudinous friendliness of the sea,
Possess no more — no more.

Something is dead . . .
The autumn rain-rot deeper and wider soaks
And spreads, the burden of winter heavier
weighs, 11
His melancholy close and closer yet
Cleaves, and those incantations of the spring
That made the heart a center of miracles
Grow formal, and the wonder-working hours
Arise no more — no more. 16

Something is dead . . .
'Tis time to creep in close about the fire
And tell gray tales of what we were, and dream
Old dreams and faded, and as we may rejoice
In the young life that round us leaps and
laughs, 21
A fountain in the sunshine, in the pride
Of God's best gift that to us twain returns,
Dear heart, no more — no more. (*1892*)

WHERE FORLORN SUNSETS FLARE AND FADE

Where forlorn sunsets flare and fade
On desolate sea and lonely sand,
Out of the silence and the shade

What is the voice of strange command
Calling you still, as friend calls friend 5
With love that cannot brook delay,
To rise and follow the ways that wend
Over the hills and far away?

Hark to the city, street on street
A roaring reach of death and life, 10
Of vortices that clash and fleet
And ruin in appointed strife,
Hark to it calling, calling clear,
Calling until you cannot stay
From dearer things than your own most dear
Over the hills and far away. 16

Out of the sound of the ebb-and-flow,
Out of the sight of lamp and star,
It calls you where the good winds blow,
And the unchanging meadows are — 20
From faded hopes and hopes agleam,
It calls you, calls you night and day
Beyond the dark into the dream
Over the hills and far away. (*1892*)

MIDSUMMER MIDNIGHT SKIES

Midsummer midnight skies,
Midsummer midnight influences and airs,
The shining, sensitive silver of the sea
Touched with the strange-hued blazonings
of dawn;
And all so solemnly still I seem to hear 5
The breathing of Life and Death,
The secular Accomplices,
Renewing the visible miracle of the world.

The wistful stars
Shine like good memories. The young
morning wind 10
Blows full of unforgotten hours
As over a region of roses. Life and Death
Sound on — sound on . . . And the night
magical,
Troubled yet comforting, thrills
As if the Enchanted Castle at the heart 15
Of the wood's dark wonderment
Swung wide his valves, and filled the dim
sea-banks
With exquisite visitants:
Words fiery-hearted yet, dreams and desires
With living looks intolerable, regrets 20
Whose voice comes as the voice of an only
child
Heard from the grave: shapes of a Might-
Have-Been —
Beautiful, miserable, distraught —
The Law no man may baffle denied and slew.

Rhymes and Rhythms. This is a collection of lyrics published in 1892.

8. **Over . . . away.** See Stevenson's *A Song of the Road*,
4, p. 814. 11. **fleet**, rush.

The spell-bound ships stand as at gaze   25
To let the marvel by. The gray road
   glooms . . .
Glimmers . . . goes out . . . and there, O
   there where it fades,
What grace, what glamour, what wild will,
Transfigure the shadows? Whose,
Heart of my heart, Soul of my soul, but
   yours?   30

Ghosts — ghosts — the sapphirine air
Teems with them even to the gleaming
   ends
Of the wild day-spring! Ghosts,
Everywhere — everywhere — till I and you
At last — dear love, at last! —   35
Are in the dreaming, even as Life and Death
Twin-ministers of the unoriginal Will.

                      (1892)

TO JAMES McNEILL WHISTLER

Under a stagnant sky,
Gloom out of gloom uncoiling into gloom,
The River, jaded and forlorn,
Welters and wanders wearily — wretchedly —
   on;
Yet in and out among the ribs   5
Of the old skeleton bridge, as in the piles
Of some dead lake-built city, full of skulls,
Worm-worn, rat-riddled, moldy with mem-
   ories,
Lingers to babble to a broken tune
(Once, O the unvoiced music of my heart!)   10
So melancholy a soliloquy
It sounds as it might tell
The secret of the unending grief-in-grain,
The terror of Time and Change and Death,
That wastes this floating, transitory world. 15

What of the incantation
That forced the huddled shapes on yonder
   shore
To take and wear the night
Like a material majesty?
That touched the shafts of wavering fire   20
About this miserable welter and wash
(River, O River of Journeys, River of
   Dreams!)
Into long, shining signals from the panes
Of an enchanted pleasure-house,
Where life and life might live life lost in life
For ever and evermore?   26

O Death! O Change! O Time!
Without you, oh, the insufferable eyes
Of these poor Might-Have-Beens,
These fatuous, ineffectual Yesterdays!   30
                      (1892)

FRESH FROM HIS FASTNESSES

Fresh from his fastnesses
Wholesome and spacious,
The North Wind, the mad huntsman,
Halloas on his white hounds
Over the gray, roaring   5
Reaches and ridges,
The forest of ocean,
The chace of the world.
Hark to the peal
Of the pack in full cry,   10
As he thongs them before him,
Swarming voluminous,
Weltering, wide-wallowing,
Till in a ruining
Chaos of energy,   15
Hurled on their quarry,
They crash into foam!

Old Indefatigable,
Time's right-hand man, the sea
Laughs as in joy   20
From his millions of wrinkles;
Laughs that his destiny,
Great with the greatness
Of triumphing order,
Shows as a dwarf   25
By the strength of his heart
And the might of his hands.

Master of masters,
O maker of heroes,
Thunder the brave,   30
Irresistible message:
"Life is worth Living
Through every grain of it,
From the foundations
To the last edge   35
Of the cornerstone, death."   (1892)

SPACE AND DREAD AND THE DARK

Space and dread and the dark —
Over a livid stretch of sky
Cloud-monsters crawling, like a funeral train
Of huge, primeval presences
Stooping beneath the weight   5
Of some enormous, rudimentary grief;
While in the haunting loneliness
The far sea waits and wanders with a sound

To James McNeill Whistler. Whistler was a noted painter and etcher (1834-1903). He was born in America, but lived most of his life in Chelsea, a district of London on the bank of the Thames; there he made a series of paintings and etchings of the river, done at twilight or at night, that show it at its loveliest.

7. **dead . . . city,** a reference to the prehistoric lake-cities built on piles to protect the inhabitants from their enemies. 13. **grief-in-grain,** unfading grief. Grain is a cochineal dye; cloth dyed in grain is unfading.

Fresh from His Fastnesses. 8. **chace,** hunting ground (obsolete form of *chase*).

As of the trailing skirts of Destiny,
Passing unseen   10
To some immitigable end
With her gray henchman, Death.

What larve, what specter is this
Thrilling the wilderness to life
As with the bodily shape of Fear?   15
What but a desperate sense,
A strong foreboding of those dim
Interminable continents, forlorn
And many-silenced, in a dusk
Inviolable utterly, and dead   20
As the poor dead it huddles and swarms and
        styes
In hugger-mugger through eternity?

Life — life — let there be life!
Better a thousand times the roaring hours
When wave and wind,   25
Like the Arch-Murderer in flight
From the Avenger at his heel,
Storm through the desolate fastnesses
And wild waste places of the world!

Life — give me life until the end,   30
That at the very top of being,
The battle-spirit shouting in my blood,
Out of the reddest hell of the fight
I may be snatched and flung
Into the everlasting lull,   35
The immortal, incommunicable dream. (1892)

ENGLAND, MY ENGLAND

What have I done for you,
    England, my England?
What is there I would not do,
    England, my own?
With your glorious eyes austere,   5
As the Lord were walking near,
Whispering terrible things and dear
    As the Song on your bugles blown,
    England —
Round the world on your bugles blown!

Where shall the watchful Sun,   10
    England, my England,
Match the master-work you've done,
    England, my own?
When shall he rejoice again
Such a breed of mighty men   15
As come forward, one to ten,
    To the Song on your bugles blown,
    England —
Down the years on your bugles blown?

Ever the faith endures,
    England, my England —   20

Space and Dread and the Dark. 13. larve, ghost.

"Take and break us; we are yours,
    England, my own!
Life is good, and joy runs high
Between English earth and sky;
Death is death; but we shall die   25
    To the Song on your bugles blown,
    England —
To the stars on your bugles blown!"

They call you proud and hard,
    England, my England;
You with worlds to watch and ward,   30
    England, my own!
You whose mailed hand keeps the keys
Of such teeming destinies
You could know nor dread nor ease
    Were the Song on your bugles blown,
    England —   35
Round the Pit on your bugles blown!

Mother of Ships whose might,
    England, my England,
Is the fierce old Sea's delight,
    England, my own,   40
Chosen daughter of the Lord,
Spouse-in-Chief of the ancient Sword,
There's the menace of the Word
    In the Song on your bugles blown,
    England —
Out of heaven on your bugles blown!   45
                                          (1892)

ANDREW LANG (1844-1912)

TWILIGHT ON TWEED

Three crests against the saffron sky,
    Beyond the purple plain,
The kind remembered melody
    Of Tweed once more again.

Wan water from the border hills,   5
    Dear voice from the old years,
Thy distant music lulls and stills,
    And moves to quiet tears.

Like a loved ghost thy fabled flood
    Fleets through the dusky land;   10
Where Scott, come home to die, has stood,
    My feet returning stand.

A mist of memory broods and floats,
    The border waters flow;

Twilight on Tweed. The Tweed River flows through the
border country of Scotland and England, and hence is
associated with many stirring folk-ballads. Abbotsford, the
home of Sir Walter Scott, was on the bank of the Tweed. In
1831 Scott was induced to cruise in the Mediterranean in
order to regain his health, but when he felt himself dying, he
insisted upon being taken home to Abbotsford.
   1. **Three crests,** three peaks near Abbotsford; the highest of these is Eildon Hill (line 21).

The air is full of ballad notes, 15
  Borne out of long ago.

Old songs that sung themselves to me,
  Sweet through a boy's day-dream,
While trout below the blossomed tree
  Plashed in the golden stream. 20

   .   .   .   .   .

Twilight, and Tweed, and Eildon Hill,
  Fair and too fair you be;
You tell me that the voice is still
  That should have welcomed me. (1872)

BALLADE OF BLUE CHINA

There's a joy without canker or cark,
There's a pleasure eternally new,
'Tis to gloat on the glaze and the mark
Of china that's ancient and blue;
Unchipped, all the centuries through 5
It has passed, since the chime of it rang,
And they fashioned it, figure and hue,
In the reign of the Emperor Hwang.

These dragons (their tails, you remark,
Into bunches of gillyflowers grew) — 10
When Noah came out of the ark,
Did these lie in wait for his crew?
They snorted, they snapped, and they slew,
They were mighty of fin and of fang,
And their portraits Celestials drew 15
In the reign of the Emperor Hwang.

Here's a pot with a cot in a park,
In a park where the peach-blossoms blew;
Where the lovers eloped in the dark,
Lived, died, and were changed into two 20
Bright birds that eternally flew
Through the boughs of the may, as they sang;
'Tis a tale was undoubtedly true
In the reign of the Emperor Hwang.

ENVOY

Come, snarl at my ecstasies, do! 25
Kind critic, your "tongue has a tang";

But — a sage never heeded a shrew
In the reign of the Emperor Hwang.
                        (1883)

BALLADE OF HIS CHOICE OF A SEPULCHER

Here I'd come when weariest!
    Here the breast
Of the Windberg's tufted over
Deep with bracken; here his crest
    Takes the west, 5
Where the wide-winged hawk doth hover.

Silent here are lark and plover;
    In the cover
Deep below, the cushat best
Loves his mate, and croons above her 10
    O'er their nest,
Where the wide-winged hawk doth hover.

Bring me here, life's tired-out guest,
    To the blest
Bed that waits the weary rover — 15
Here should failure be confessed;
    Ends my quest,
Where the wide-winged hawk doth hover!

ENVOY

Friend, or stranger kind, or lover,
Ah, fulfill a last behest, 20
    Let me rest
Where the wide-winged hawk doth hover!
                      (1883)

THE ODYSSEY

As one that for a weary space has lain
Lulled by the song of Circe and her wine
In gardens near the pale of Proserpine,
Where that Ææan isle forgets the main,
And only the low lutes of love complain, 5
And only shadows of wan lovers pine;
As such an one were glad to know the brine
Salt on his lips, and the large air again —
So gladly, from the songs of modern speech
Men turn, and see the stars, and feel the
    free 10
Shrill wind beyond the close of heavy flowers;
And, through the music of the languid hours,

Ballade of Blue China. For a definition of *ballade* see note on Swinburne's *A Ballad of Dreamland,* p. 723. Cf. also Dobson's *On a Nankin Plate,* p. 776.
  1. **cark,** anxiety. 8. **Emperor Hwang,** a mythical emperor, c. 2700 B.C., during whose reign the art of pottery-making is fabled to have been established in China.
  19-20. **lovers . . . flew.** According to the story told to explain the picture common on blue-ware of the willow pattern, Li-chi, the daughter of a mandarin, eloped with Chang, her father's secretary; the two lovers were pursued, beaten, but saved from death by the gods, who changed them into turtle-doves. Neither the willow pattern nor the story is especially oriental. 22. **may.** The Chinese plum, pictured frequently in blue-ware, was taken by Europeans to be hawthorn, or may. 26. **"tongue . . . tang."** From Shakespeare's *The Tempest,* II, 2, 52.—
    "But none of us cared for Kate;
    For she had a tongue with a tang."

Ballade of His Choice of a Sepulcher. 3. **Windberg,** a mountain in the border district of Scotland, fifteen miles south of Selkirk, Lang's birthplace. 4. **bracken,** fern. 9. **cushat,** ring-dove.
  The Odyssey. Lang was greatly interested in Homer. He translated the *Odyssey* and wrote several books on Homeric themes.
  2. **Circe,** a sorceress, living in the isle of Æea who with an enchanted wine changed men into hogs (*Odyssey,* Book 10). 3. **pale of Proserpine.** See Swinburne's *The Garden of Proserpine* and note, p. 697. 11. **close,** enclosed garden.

They hear like ocean on a western beach
The surge and thunder of the Odyssey.

(1883)

SCYTHE SONG

Mowers, weary and brown, and blithe,
  What is the word methinks ye know ·
Endless over-word that the scythe
  Sings to the blades of the grass below?
Scythes that swing in the grass and clover, 5
  Something, still, they say as they pass;
What is the word that, over and over,
  Sings the scythe to the flowers and grass?

Hush, ah hush, the scythes are saying,
  Hush, and heed not, and fall asleep; 10
Hush, they say to the grasses swaying;
  Hush, they sing to the clover deep!
Hush — 'tis the lullaby Time is singing —
  Hush, and heed not, for all things pass;
Hush, ah hush! and the scythes are swinging 15
  Over the clover, over the grass! (1888)

HERODOTUS IN EGYPT

He left the land of youth, he left the young,
The smiling gods of Greece; he passed the isle
Where Jason loitered, and where Sappho
  sung;
He sought the secret-founted wave of Nile,
And of their old world, dead a weary while, 5
Heard the priests murmur in their mystic
  tongue,
And through the fanes went voyaging, among
Dark tribes that worshiped Cat and Croc-
  odile.
He learned the tales of death Divine and
  birth,
Strange loves of Hawk and Serpent, Sky and
  Earth, 10
The marriage, and the slaying of the Sun.

Herodotus in Egypt. Herodotus, Greek traveler and historian, visited Egypt approximately from 460 to 454 B.C., and in Book 2 of his *History* recorded his impressions of Egyptian customs and religion.
2-3. **isle . . . sung.** Jason spent a considerable time on the island of Lemnos, in the Ægean sea, before proceeding on his quest of the Golden Fleece; Sappho (6th century B.C.), Greek lyric poet, lived on the island of Lesbos. 4. **secret-founted . . . Nile.** The source of the Nile was unknown to the ancients, who imagined it to proceed from mysterious underground channels; see Herodotus, Book 2, Section 28. 8. **Cat and Crocodile.** The cat, identified with the goddess Pasht, and the crocodile, identified with the water-god Sobk, were worshiped in Egyptian temples as sacred animals. See Herodotus, Book 2, Sections 67, 69. 9-11. **tales . . . Sun,** references to Egyptian myths. The death of the god Osiris from being locked in a chest and thrown into the sea, and the birth of the god Horus, are celebrated myths. Osiris, identified with the hawk, was the husband of Isis, identified with the serpent. From the marriage of Seb, the earth, and Nut, the sky, was born the race of Egyptian gods. According to one Egyptian legend, Osiris, the primal god of the sun, married Isis, goddess of the moon; he was later slain by his enemy, Set, but restored to life by Isis.

The shrines of gods and beasts he wandered
  through,
And mocked not at their godhead, for he knew
Behind all creeds the Spirit that is One.

(1888)

ON CALAIS SANDS

On Calais Sands the gray began,
  Then rosy red above the gray;
The morn with many a scarlet van
  Leaped, and the world was glad with May!
The little waves along the bay 5
  Broke white upon the shelving strands;
The sea-mews flitted white as they
    On Calais Sands!

On Calais Sands must man with man
  Wash honor clean in blood today; 10
On spaces wet from waters wan
  How white the flashing rapiers play —
Parry, riposte! and lunge! The fray
  Shifts for a while, then mournful stands
The victor; life ebbs fast away 15
    On Calais Sands!

On Calais Sands a little space
  Of silence; then the splash and spray,
The sound of eager waves that ran
  To kiss the perfumed locks astray, 20
To touch these lips that ne'er said "Nay,"
  To dally with the helpless hands,
Till the deep sea in silence lay
    On Calais Sands!

Between the lilac and the may 25
  She waits her love from alien lands;
Her love is colder than the clay
    On Calais Sands!

(1894)

THREE PORTRAITS OF PRINCE CHARLES

1731

Beautiful face of a child,
  Lighted with laughter and glee,

On Calais Sands. Calais, a French seaport across the English Channel from Dover, was a frequent dueling spot for Englishmen. Cf. Arnold's *Dover Beach*, p. 499.
3. **van,** vanguard. 13. **riposte,** a return thrust; like parry and lunge, a term in fencing. 25. **may,** hawthorn.
Three Portraits of Prince Charles. Charles Edward Stuart (1720-88), called the Young Pretender and Bonnie Prince Charlie, grandson of James II of England, made an attempt (1745-46) to gain the British throne with the help of devoted Scottish Highlanders; defeated at Culloden, he solaced himself by notorious debaucheries, spent the last days of his life in Rome, and was buried in St. Peter's. Lang describes actual portraits of the Prince. See Lang's *Prince Charles Edward Stuart, the Young Chevalier*, 1903.

Mirthful and tender and wild,
  My heart is heavy for thee!

1744

Beautiful face of a youth,   5
  As an eagle poised to fly forth
To the old land loyal of truth,
  To the hills and the sounds of the North:
Fair·face, daring and proud,
  Lo! the shadow of doom, even now,   10
The fate of thy line, like a cloud,
  Rests on the grace of thy brow!

1773

Cruel and angry face!
  Hateful and heavy with wine,
Where are the gladness, the grace,   15
  The beauty, the mirth that were thine?

Ah, my Prince, it were well —
  Hadst thou to the gods been dear —
To have fallen where Keppoch fell,
  With the war-pipe loud in thine ear!   20
To have died with never a stain
  On the fair White Rose of renown,
To have fallen, fighting in vain,
  For thy father, thy faith, and thy crown!
More than thy marble pile,   25
  With its women weeping for thee,
Were to dream in thine ancient isle,
  To the endless dirge of the sea!
But the fates deemed otherwise;
  Far thou sleepest from home,   30
From the tears of the northern skies,
  In the secular dust of Rome.

A city of death and the dead,
  But thither a pilgrim came,
Wearing on weary head   35
  The crowns of years and fame:
Little the Lucrine lake
  Or Tivoli said to him,
Scarce did the memories wake
  Of the far-off years and dim,   40
For he stood by Avernus' shore.
  But he dreamed of a northern glen,
And he murmured, over and o'er,
  "For Charlie and his men":
And his feet, to death that went,   45

4. **My . . . thee.** "Charles is loved for his forlorn hope: for his desperate resolve; for his reckless daring, the winning charm that once were his; for bright hair, and brown eyes; above all, as the center and inspirer of old chivalrous loyalty, as one who would have brought back a lost age, an impossible realm of dreams" (Lang's *Prince Charles*, page 4). 18. **gods . . . dear.** An allusion to the Greek proverb "Whom the Gods love die young." 19. **Keppoch**, a Highland chief, leader of the Macdonald clan, killed at Culloden Field. 22. **White Rose**, emblem of the Stuarts. 34. **a pilgrim,** Sir Walter Scott, who used the theme of the "forlorn hope" of Charles Stuart in *Waverley* and *Redgauntlet*. Scott visited Rome in 1831, shortly before his death. 37. **Lucrine lake,** the site of an ancient lake near Rome. 38. **Tivoli,** a town near Rome. 41. **Avernus,** a lake near Rome, regarded by the ancients as the entrance to the lower world.

Crept forth to St. Peter's shrine,
And the latest minstrel bent
  O'er the last of the Stuart line.   (1894)

ALICE CHRISTIANA MEYNELL
(1847-1922)

SONG OF THE NIGHT AT DAYBREAK

All my stars forsake me,
And the dawn-winds shake me;
Where shall I betake me?

Whither shall I run
Till the set of the sun,   5
Till the day be done?

To the mountain-mine,
To the boughs o' the pine,
To the blind man's eyne,

To a brow that is   10
Bowed upon the knees,
Sick with memories.   (1875)

A SONG OF DERIVATIONS

I come from nothing; but from where
Come the undying thoughts I bear?
  Down, through long links of death and birth,
  From the past poets of the earth,
My immortality is there.   5

I am like the blossom of an hour.
But long, long vanished sun and shower
  Awoke my breath i' the young world's air;
  I track the past back everywhere
Through seed and flower and seed and flower.

Or I am like a stream that flows   11
Full of the cold springs that arose
  In morning lands, in distant hills;
  And down the plain my channel fills
With melting of forgotten snows.   15

Voices I have not heard possessed
My own fresh songs; my thoughts are blessed
  With relics of the far unknown;
  And mixed with memories not my own
The sweet streams throng into my breast.   20

Before this life began to be,
The happy songs that wake in me

46. **St. Peter's shrine.** The tomb of the Stuarts is in St. Peter's Cathedral at Rome. 47. **latest minstrel,** Scott, author of *The Lay of the Last Minstrel.*

Woke long ago, and far apart.
Heavily on this little heart
Presses this immortality.   25
                                            (1875)

AFTER A PARTING

Farewell has long been said; I have foregone
    thee;
  I never name thee even.
But how shall I learn virtues and yet shun
    thee?
  For thou art so near heaven
That heavenward meditations pause upon
    thee.   5

Thou dost beset the path to every shrine;
  My trembling thoughts discern
Thy goodness in the good for which I pine;
  And, if I turn from but one sin, I turn
Unto a smile of thine.   10

How shall I thrust thee apart
  Since all my growth tends to thee night
    and day —
To thee faith, hope, and art?   13
  Swift are the currents setting all one
    way;
They draw my life, my life, out of my heart.
                                         (1877; 1890)

RENOUNCEMENT

I must not think of thee; and, tired yet
    strong,
I shun the thought that lurks in all delight —
The thought of thee — and in the blue
    heaven's height,
And in the sweetest passage of a song.
Oh, just beyond the fairest thoughts that
    throng   5
This breast, the thought of thee waits, hid-
    den yet bright;
But it must never, never come in sight;
I must stop short of thee the whole day
    long.
But when sleep comes to close each difficult
    day,
When night gives pause to t e long watch I
    keep,   10
And all my bonds I needs must loose apart,
Must doff my will as raiment laid away —
With the first dream that comes with the
    first sleep
I run, I run, I am gathered to thy heart.
                                         (1877; 1893)

After a Parting. This lyric, like *Renouncement*, was written to the young Catholic priest who had first encouraged her
writing and who had received her into the Catholic Church.

THE SHEPHERDESS

She walks — the lady of my delight —
  A shepherdess of sheep.
Her flocks are thoughts. She keeps them
    white;
  She guards them from the steep;
She feeds them on the fragrant height,   5
  And folds them in for sleep.

She roams maternal hills and bright,
  Dark valleys safe and deep.
Into that tender breast at night
  The chastest stars may peep.   10
She walks — the lady of my delight —
  A shepherdess of sheep.

She holds her little thoughts in sight,
  Though gay they run and leap.
She is so circumspect and right;   15
  She has her soul to keep.
She walks — the lady of my delight —
  A shepherdess of sheep.   (1894)

THE LADY POVERTY

The Lady Poverty was fair;
But she has lost her looks of late,
With change of times and change of air.
Ah, slattern! she neglects her hair,
Her gown, her shoes; she keeps no state   5
As once when her pure feet were bare.

Or — almost worse, if worse can be —
She scolds in parlors, dusts and trims,
Watches and counts. Oh, is this she
Whom Francis met, whose step was free,   10
Who with obedience caroled hymns,
In Umbria walked with Chastity?

Where is her ladyhood? Not here,
Not among modern kinds of men;
But in the stony fields, where clear   15
Through the thin trees, the skies appear,
In delicate spare soil and fen,
And slender landscape and austere.   (1894)

"I AM THE WAY"

Thou art the Way.
Hadst Thou been nothing but the goal,
    I cannot say
If Thou hadst ever met my soul.

The Lady Poverty. 9-12. **Oh . . . Chastity.** St. Francis
(1182-1226), identified with the town of Assisi, in Umbria,
Italy, vowed himself to chastity, obedience, and poverty, and
founded the great Franciscan order of friars.
"I Am the Way." The title is quoted from *John,* 14:6.—
"Jesus saith unto him, I am the way, the truth, and the life:
no man cometh unto the Father, but by me."

I cannot see —   5
I, child of process — if there lies
    An end for me,
Full of repose, full of replies.

I'll not reproach
The road that winds, my feet that err.   10
    Access, Approach
Art Thou, Time, Way, and Wayfarer. (1896)

ROBERT LOUIS STEVENSON
(1850-1894)

TO ALISON CUNNINGHAM

FROM HER BOY

For the long nights you lay awake
And watched for my unworthy sake;
For your most comfortable hand
That led me through the uneven land;
For all the story-books you read;   5
For all the pains you comforted;
For all you pitied, all you bore,
In sad and happy days of yore;
My second Mother, my first Wife,
The angel of my infant life —   10
From the sick child, now well and old,
Take, nurse, the little book you hold!

And grant it, Heaven, that all who read
May find as dear a nurse at need,
And every child who lists my rime,   15
In the bright, fireside, nursery clime,
May hear it in as kind a voice
As made my childish days rejoice!   (1885)

BED IN SUMMER

In winter I get up at night
And dress by yellow candle-light.
In summer, quite the other way,
I have to go to bed by day.

I have to go to bed and see   5
The birds still hopping on the tree,
Or hear the grown-up people's feet
Still going past me in the street.

And does it not seem hard to you,
When all the sky is clear and blue,   10
And I should like so much to play,
To have to go to bed by day?   (1885)

WHOLE DUTY OF CHILDREN

A child should always say what's true
And speak when he is spoken to,
And behave mannerly at table —
At least as far as he is able.   (1885)

PIRATE STORY

Three of us afloat in the meadow by the
    swing,
    Three of us aboard in the basket on the lea.
Winds are in the air, they are blowing in the
    spring,
    And waves are on the meadow like the
      waves that are at sea.

Where shall we adventure, today that we're
    afloat,   5
    Wary of the weather and steering by a
      star?
Shall it be to Africa, a-steering of the boat,
    To Providence, or Babylon, or off to
      Malabar?

Hi! but here's a squadron a-rowing on the
    sea —
    Cattle on the meadow a-charging with a
      roar!   10
Quick, and we'll escape them, they're as mad
    as they can be,
    The wicket is the harbor, and the garden
      is the shore.   (1885)

FOREIGN LANDS

Up into the cherry tree
Who should climb but little me?
I held the trunk with both my hands
And looked abroad on foreign lands.

I saw the next door garden lie,   5
Adorned with flowers, before my eye,
And many pleasant places more
That I had never seen before.

I saw the dimpling river pass
And be the sky's blue looking-glass;   10
The dusty roads go up and down
With people tramping into town.

If I could find a higher tree
Farther and farther I should see,
To where the grown-up river slips   15
Into the sea among the ships,

To where the roads on either hand
Lead onward into fairyland,

---

6. **Of process**, in the meshes of life—queer, changing,
ordered, yet apparently meaningless.
   To Alison Cunningham. This is the dedicatory poem to
A Child's Garden of Verses, from which the following lyrics
through *The Little Land,* p. 813, are taken; Alison Cunningham, or "Cummy," had been Stevenson's nurse during his
sickly childhood.

Pirate Story. **8. Providence,** an island in the Bahamas,
West Indies. **Babylon,** the ancient capital of Assyria.
Malabar, a district in West Madras, India.

Where all the children dine at five,
And all the playthings come alive.   20
                                                      (1885)

TRAVEL

I should like to rise and go
Where the golden apples grow; —
Where below another sky
Parrot islands anchored lie,
And, watched by cockatoos and goats,   5
Lonely Crusoes building boats; —
Where in sunshine reaching out
Eastern cities, miles about,
Are with mosque and minaret
Among sandy gardens set,   10
And the rich goods from near and far
Hang for sale in the bazaar; —
Where the Great Wall round China goes,
And on one side the desert blows,
And with bell and voice and drum,   15
Cities on the other hum; —
Where are forests, hot as fire,
Wide as England, tall as a spire,
Full of apes and cocoanuts
And the negro hunters' huts; —   20
Where the knotty crocodile
Lies and blinks in the Nile,
And the red flamingo flies
Hunting fish before his eyes; —
Where in jungles, near and far,   25
Man-devouring tigers are,
Lying close and giving ear,
Lest the hunt be drawing near,
Or a comer-by be seen
Swinging in a palanquin; —   30
Where among the desert sands
Some deserted city stands,
All its children, sweep and prince,
Grown to manhood ages since,
Not a foot in street or house,   35
Not a stir of child or mouse,
And when kindly falls the night,
In all the town no spark of light.
There I'll come when I'm a man
With a camel caravan;   40
Light a fire in the gloom
Of some dusty dining-room;
See the pictures on the walls,
Heroes, fights and festivals;
And in a corner find the toys   45
Of the old Egyptian boys.   (1885)

Travel. **2. Where . . . grow**, in the fabulous garden of the
Hesperides. **13. Great Wall**, built in the years following
214 B.C., by the emperor Che Hwang-te, to protect the
northern frontier of China from the invasions of the Tartars.
30. palanquin, an enclosed chair borne on the shoulders of
porters. **33. sweep**, chimney-sweep. Cf. Shakespeare's
Cymbeline, IV, 2, 262-63.—
   "Golden lads and girls all must,
   As chimney-sweepers, come to dust."

LOOKING FORWARD

When I am grown to man's estate
I shall be very proud and great,
And tell the other girls and boys
Not to meddle with my toys.   (1885)

AUNTIE'S SKIRTS

Whenever Auntie moves around,
Her dresses make a curious sound;
They trail behind her up the floor,
And trundle after through the door.   (1885)

THE LAND OF COUNTERPANE

When I was sick and lay a-bed,
I had two pillows at my head,
And all my toys beside me lay
To keep me happy all the day.

And sometimes for an hour or so   5
I watched my leaden soldiers go,
With different uniforms and drills,
Among the bedclothes, through the hills;

And sometimes sent my ships in fleets
All up and down among the sheets;   10
Or brought my trees and houses out,
And planted cities all about.

I was the giant great and still
That sits upon the pillow-hill,
And sees before him, dale and plain,   15
The pleasant Land of Counterpane.   (1885)

THE LAND OF NOD

From breakfast on through all the day
At home among my friends I stay,
But every night I go abroad
Afar into the Land of Nod.

All by myself I have to go,   5
With none to tell me what to do —
All alone beside the streams
And up the mountain-sides of dreams.

The strangest things are there for me,
Both things to eat and things to see,   10
And many frightening sights abroad
Till morning in the Land of Nod.

Try as I like to find the way,
I never can get back by day,
Nor can remember plain and clear   15
The curious music that I hear.   (1885)

MY SHADOW

I have a little shadow that goes in and out
with me,
And what can be the use of him is more than
I can see.
He is very, very like me from the heels up to
the head;
And I see him jump before me, when I jump
into my bed.

The funniest thing about him is the way he
likes to grow —   5
Not at all like proper children, which is
always very slow;
For he sometimes shoots up taller like an
india-rubber ball,
And he sometimes gets so little that there's
none of him at all.

He hasn't got a notion of how children ought
to play,
And can only make a fool of me in every sort
of way.   10
He stands so close beside me, he's a coward
you can see;
I'd think shame to stick to nursie as that
shadow sticks to me!

One morning, very early, before the sun was
up,
I rose and found the shining dew on every
buttercup;
But my lazy little shadow, like an arrant
sleepy-head,   15
Had stayed at home behind me and was fast
asleep in bed.
                                              (1885)

SYSTEM

Every night my prayers I say,
And get my dinner every day;
And every day that I've been good,
I get an orange after food.

The child that is not plain and neat,   5
With lots of toys and things to eat,
He is a naughty child, I'm sure —
Or else his dear papa is poor.
                                              (1885)

ESCAPE AT BEDTIME

The lights from the parlor and kitchen shone
out
Through the blinds and the windows and
bars;
And high overhead and all moving about,
There were thousands of millions of stars.
There ne'er were such thousands of leaves on
a tree,   5
Nor of people in church or the Park,

As the crowds of the stars that looked down
upon me,
And that glittered and winked in the dark.

The Dog, and the Plow, and the Hunter, and
all,
And the star of the sailor, and Mars,   10
These shone in the sky, and the pail by the
wall
Would be half full of water and stars.
They saw me at last, and they chased me
with cries,
And they soon had me packed into bed;
But the glory kept shining and bright in my
eyes,   15
And the stars going round in my head.
                                              (1885)

THE COW

The friendly cow all red and white,
I love with all my heart —
She gives me cream with all her might,
To eat with apple-tart.

She wanders lowing here and there,   5
And yet she cannot stray,
All in the pleasant open air,
The pleasant light of day;

And blown by all the winds that pass
And wet with all the showers,   10
She walks among the meadow grass
And eats the meadow flowers.   (1885)

HAPPY THOUGHT

The world is so full of a number of things,
I'm sure we should all be as happy as kings.
                                              (1885)

THE WIND

I saw you toss the kites on high
And blow the birds about the sky;
And all around I heard you pass,
Like ladies' skirts across the grass —
    O wind, a-blowing all day long,   5
    O wind, that sings so loud a song!

I saw the different things you did,
But always you yourself you hid.
I felt you push, I heard you call,
I could not see yourself at all —   10
    O wind, a-blowing all day long,
    O wind, that sings so loud a song!

O you that are so strong and cold,
O blower, are you young or old?

9. **Dog, Plow, Hunter,** names of familiar constellations.
10. **star of the sailor,** the North Star.

Are you a beast of field and tree,   15
Or just a stronger child than me?
　　O wind, a-blowing all day long,
　　O wind, that sings so loud a song! (1885)

GOOD AND BAD CHILDREN

Children, you are very little,
And your bones are very brittle;
If you would grow great and stately,
You must try to walk sedately.

You must still be bright and quiet,   5
And content with simple diet;
And remain, through all bewild'ring,
Innocent and honest children.

Happy hearts and happy faces,
Happy play in grassy places —   10
That was how, in ancient ages,
Children grew to kings and sages.

But the unkind and the unruly,
And the sort who eat unduly,
They must never hope for glory —   15
Theirs is quite a different story!

Cruel children, crying babies,
All grow up as geese and gabies,
Hated, as their age increases,
By their nephews and their nieces.   (1885)

THE LAMPLIGHTER

My tea is nearly ready, and the sun has left
　　the sky;
It's time to take the window to see Leerie
　　going by;
For every night at teatime and before you
　　take your seat,
With lantern and with ladder he comes post-
　　ing up the street.

Now Tom would be a driver and Maria go
　　to sea,   5
And my papa's a banker and as rich as he
　　can be;
But I, when I am stronger and can choose
　　what I'm to do,
O Leerie, I'll go round at night and light the
　　lamps with you!

For we are very lucky, with a lamp before
　　the door,
And Leerie stops to light it as he lights so
　　many more;   10
And O! before you hurry by with ladder and
　　with light,
O Leerie, see a little child and nod to him
　　tonight!   (1885)

Good and Bad Children. 18. **gabies,** dunces.

A birdie with a yellow bill
　　Hopped upon the window-sill,
Cocked his shining eye and said:
　　"Ain't you 'shamed, you sleepy-head!"
　　　　　　　　　　　　　　　　(1885)

THE LAND OF STORY-BOOKS

At evening when the lamp is lit,
Around the fire my parents sit;
They sit at home and talk and sing,
And do not play at anything.

Now, with my little gun, I crawl   5
All in the dark along the wall,
And follow round the forest track
Away behind the sofa back.

There, in the night, where none can spy,
All in my hunter's camp I lie,   10
And play at books that I have read
Till it is time to go to bed.

These are the hills, these are the woods,
These are my starry solitudes;
And there the river by whose brink   15
The roaring lions come to drink.

I see the others far away
As if in firelit camp they lay,
And I, like to an Indian scout,
Around their party prowled about.   20

So, when my nurse comes in for me,
Home I return across the sea,
And go to bed with backward looks
At my dear Land of Story-books.   (1885)

THE LITTLE LAND

When at home alone I sit
And am very tired of it,
I have just to shut my eyes
To go sailing through the skies —
To go sailing far away   5
To the pleasant Land of Play;
To the fairy land afar
Where the Little People are;
Where the clover-tops are trees,
And the rain-pools are the seas,   10
And the leaves like little ships
Sail about on tiny trips;
And above the daisy tree
　　Through the grasses,
High o'erhead the Bumble Bee   15
　　Hums and passes.

In that forest to and fro
I can wander, I can go;
See the spider and the fly,

And the ants go marching by   20
Carrying parcels with their feet
Down the green and grassy street.
I can in the sorrel sit
Where the ladybird alit.
I can climb the jointed grass;   25
    And on high
See the greater swallows pass
    In the sky,
And the round sun rolling by
Heeding no such things as I.   30

Through the forest I can pass
Till, as in a looking-glass,
Humming fly and daisy tree
And my tiny self I see,
Painted very clear and neat   35
On the rain-pool at my feet.
Should a leaflet come to land
Drifting near to where I stand,
Straight I'll board that tiny boat
Round the rain-pool sea to float.   40

Little thoughtful creatures sit
On the grassy coasts of it;
Little things with lovely eyes
See me sailing with surprise.
Some are clad in armor green   45
(These have sure to battle been!);
Some are pied with ev'ry hue,
Black and crimson, gold and blue;
Some have wings and swift are gone; —
But they all look kindly on.   50
When my eyes I once again
Open, and see all things plain:
High bare walls, great bare floor;
Great big knobs on drawer and door;
Great big people perched on chairs,   55
Stitching tucks and mending tears,
Each a hill that I could climb,
And talking nonsense all the time —
    O dear me,
    That I could be   60
A sailor on the rain-pool sea,
A climber in the clover tree,
And just come back, a sleepy-head,
Late at night to go to bed.   (1885)

A SONG OF THE ROAD

The gauger walked with willing foot,
And aye the gauger played the flute;
And what would Master Gauger play
But *Over the hills and far away?*

Whene'er I buckle on my pack   5
And foot it gayly in the track,

O pleasant gauger, long since dead,
I hear you fluting on ahead.

You go with me the selfsame way —
The selfsame air for me you play;   10
For I do think and so do you
It is the tune to travel to.

For who would gravely set his face
To go to this or t'other place?
There's nothing under heav'n so blue 15
That's fairly worth the traveling to.

On every hand the roads begin,
And people walk with zeal therein;
But wheresoe'er the highways tend,
Be sure there's nothing at the end.   20

Then follow you wherever hie
The traveling mountains of the sky,
Or let the streams of civil mode
Direct your choice upon the road;

For one and all, or high or low,   25
Will lead you where you wish to go;
And one and all go night and day
Over the hills and far away!   (1887)

THE HOUSE BEAUTIFUL

A naked house, a naked moor,
A shivering pool before the door,
A garden bare of flowers and fruit
And poplars at the garden foot;
Such is the place that I live in,   5
Bleak without and bare within.

Yet shall your ragged moor receive
The incomparable pomp of eve,
And the cold glories of the dawn
Behind your shivering trees be drawn; 10
And when the wind from place to place
Doth the unmoored cloud-galleons chase,
Your garden gloom and gleam again,
With leaping sun, with glancing rain.
Here shall the wizard moon ascend   15
The heavens, in the crimson end
Of day's declining splendor; here
The army of the stars appear.
The neighbor hollows dry or wet,
Spring shall with tender flowers beset; 20
And oft the morning muser see
Larks rising from the broomy lea,
And every fairy wheel and thread
Of cobweb dew-bediamonded.
When daisies go, shall winter time   25
Silver the simple grass with rime;

A Song of the Road. 1. **gauger,** a revenue officer who measures the contents of casks. 4. **Over . . . away,** the refrain of a popular 17th century song. It is found in Farquhar's *The Recruiting Officer,* in Gay's *The Beggars' Opera,* and elsewhere. Cf. Henley's *Where Forlorn Sunsets,* p. 803.

The House Beautiful. The title was suggested by the wayside palace in Bunyan's *Pilgrim's Progress.*
22. **broomy lea,** a field covered with broom, a shrub with stiff green branches.

Autumnal frosts enchant the pool
And make the cart-ruts beautiful;
And when snow-bright the moor expands,
How shall your children clap their hands!   30
To make this earth our hermitage,
A cheerful and a changeful page,
God's bright and intricate device
Of days and seasons doth suffice.   (1887)

TO ANDREW LANG

Dear Andrew, with the brindled hair,
Who glory to have thrown in air,
High over arm, the trembling reed,
By Ale and Kail, by Till and Tweed —
An equal craft of hand you show   5
The pen to guide, the fly to throw.
I count you happy-starred; for God,
When He with inkpot and with rod
Endowed you, bade your fortune lead
Forever by the crooks of Tweed,   10
Forever by the woods of song
And lands that to the Muse belong;
Or if in peopled streets, or in
The abhorred pedantic sanhedrin,
It should be yours to wander, still   15
Airs of the morn, airs of the hill,
The plovery forest and the seas
That break about the Hebrides,
Should follow over field and plain
And find you at the window-pane;   20
And you again see hill and peel,
And the bright springs gush at your heel.
So went the fiat forth, and so
Garrulous like a brook you go,
With sound of happy mirth and sheen   25
Of daylight — whether by the green
You fare that moment, or the gray;
Whether you dwell in March or May;
Or whether treat of reels and rods
Or of the old unhappy gods —   30
Still like a brook your page has shone,
And your ink sings of Helicon.   (1887)

REQUIEM

Under the wide and starry sky,
Dig the grave and let me lie.
Glad did I live and gladly die,
And I laid me down with a will.

This be the verse you grave for me: 5
Here he lies where he longed to be;
Home is the sailor, home from sea,
And the hunter home from the hill.   (1887)

THE CELESTIAL SURGEON

If I have faltered more or less
In my great task of happiness;
If I have moved among my race
And shown no glorious morning face;
If beams from happy human eyes   5
Have moved me not; if morning skies,
Books, and my food, and summer rain
Knocked on my sullen heart in vain —
Lord, thy most pointed pleasure take
And stab my spirit broad awake;   10
Or, Lord, if too obdurate I,
Choose thou, before that spirit die,
A piercing pain, a killing sin,
And to my dead heart run them in!   (1887)

IN THE STATES

With half a heart I wander here
    As from an age gone by,
A brother — yet though young in years,
    An elder brother, I.

You speak another tongue than mine,   5
    Though both were English born.
I toward the night of time decline;
    You mount into the morn.

Youth shall grow great and strong and free,
    But age must still decay;   10
Tomorrow for the States — for me,
    England and Yesterday.   (1887)

THE SPAEWIFE

Oh, I wad like to ken — to the beggar-wife
        says I —
Why chops are guid to brander and nane sae
        guid to fry,
An' siller, that's sae braw to keep, is brawer
        still to gi'e.
It's gey an' easy spierin', says the beggar-wife
        to me.

Oh, I wad like to ken — to the beggar-wife
        says I —   5
Hoo a' things come to be whaur we find them
        when we try,

To Andrew Lang. See Lang's poem, pp. 796 ff. 2-3. **thrown . . . reed**, cast with a fly-rod; Lang's poems include a section *On Fishing*. 4. **Ale . . . Tweed**, rivers in the border country, northern England and southern Scotland, where Lang was born and bred; see Lang's *Twilight on Tweed*, p. 805. 14. **sanhedrin.** Originally signifying the supreme council of the Jews, the term is here applied to the faculty of the University of St. Andrews, of which Lang was long a member. 18. **Hebrides,** islands on the west coast of Scotland. 21. **peel**, the tower or keep of an ancient border castle. 30. **old unhappy gods.** See Lang's studies in comparative mythology: *Custom and Myth* (1884), *Myth, Ritual, and Religion* (1887); *The Making of Religion* (1898). 32. **your ink . . . Helicon,** your writing is genuinely inspired. Helicon was a Greek mountain sacred to the Muses.
Requiem. The title means *Rest.* It is the first word of a Mass for the dead, "Give eternal rest to them, O Lord."

In the States. Stevenson's first visit to America was from August 1870 to August 1880; most of his time was spent in Monterey and San Francisco. He was in America again from August 1887 to June 1888, largely at Saranac Lake, New York.
The Spaewife. A spaewife is a fortune-teller.
2. **brander**, broil on a gridiron. 3. **siller**, money. **braw**, fine. 4. **It's . . . spierin'**, it's easy enough to ask.

The lasses in their claes an' the fishes in the
　　sea.
It's gey an' easy spierin', says the beggar-wife
　　to me.

Oh, I wad like to ken — to the beggar-wife
　　says I —
Why lads are a' to sell an' lasses a' to buy;　10
An' naebody for dacency but barely twa or
　　three.
It's gey an' easy spierin', says the beggar-wife
　　to me.

Oh, I wad like to ken — to the beggar-wife
　　says I —
Gin death's as shüre to men as killin' is to
　　kye,
Why God has filled the yearth sae fu' o' tasty
　　things to pree.　　　　　　　　　　15
It's gey an' easy spierin', says the beggar-wife
　　to me.

Oh, I wad like to ken — to the beggar-wife
　　says I —
The reason o' the cause an' the wherefore o'
　　the why,
Wi' mony anither riddle brings the tear into
　　my e'e.
It's gey an' easy spierin', says the beggar-wife
　　to me.　　　　　　　　　　　　20
　　　　　　　　　　　　　　(1887)

CHRISTMAS AT SEA

The sheets were frozen hard, and they cut
　　the naked hand;
The decks were like a slide, where a seaman
　　scarce could stand;
The wind was a nor'-wester, blowing squally
　　off the sea;
And cliffs and spouting breakers were the only
　　things a-lee.

They heard the surf a-roaring before the break
　　of day;　　　　　　　　　　　　5
But 'twas only with the peep of light we saw
　　how ill we lay.
We tumbled every hand on deck instanter,
　　with a shout,
And we gave her the maintops'l, and stood by
　　to go about.

All day we tacked and tacked between the
　　South Head and the North;
All day we hauled the frozen sheets, and got
　　no further forth;　　　　　　　　10

7. **claes**, clothes. 14. **Gin**, if. **kye**, cows. 15. **pree**,
taste.
Christmas at Sea. This poem is not autobiographical, although it is connected with many lighthouse-inspection
trips which Stevenson made with his father.

All day as cold as charity, in bitter pain and
　　dread,
For very life and nature we tacked from head
　　to head.

We gave the South a wider berth, for there
　　the tide-race roared;
But every tack we made we brought the
　　North Head close aboard.
So's we saw the cliff and houses and the
　　breakers running high,　　　　　15
And the coastguard in his garden, with his
　　glass against his eye.

The frost was on the village roofs as white as
　　ocean foam;
The good red fires were burning bright in
　　every longshore home;
The windows sparkled clear, and the chim-
　　neys volleyed out;
And I vow we sniffed the victuals as the vessel
　　went about.　　　　　　　　　20

The bells upon the church were rung with a
　　mighty jovial cheer;
For it's just that I should tell you how (of all
　　days in the year)
This day of our adversity was blesséd Christ-
　　mas morn,
And the house above the coastguard's was the
　　house where I was born.

O well I saw the pleasant room, the pleasant
　　faces there,　　　　　　　　　25
My mother's silver spectacles, my father's
　　silver hair;
And well I saw the firelight, like a flight of
　　homely elves,
Go dancing round the china plates that stand
　　upon the shelves.

And well I knew the talk they had, the talk
　　that was of me,
Of the shadow on the household and the son
　　that went to sea;　　　　　　　30
And O the wicked fool I seemed, in every
　　kind of way,
To be here and hauling frozen ropes on blesséd
　　Christmas Day.

They lit the high sea-light, and the dark
　　began to fall.
"All hands to loose topgallant sails," I heard
　　the captain call.
"By the Lord, she'll never stand it," our first
　　mate, Jackson, cried.　　　　　35
. . . "It's the one way or the other, Mr.
　　Jackson," he replied.

She staggered to her bearings, but the sails
　　were new and good,

And the ship smelt up to windward just as
    though she understood;
As the winter's day was ending, in the entry
    of the night,
We cleared the weary headland, and passed
    below the light.   40

And they heaved a mighty breath, every soul
    on board but me,
As they saw her nose again pointing handsome
    out to sea;
But all that I could think of, in the darkness
    and the cold,
Was just that I was leaving home and my
    folks were growing old.   (1888)

I WILL MAKE YOU BROOCHES

I will make you brooches and toys for your
    delight
Of bird-song at morning and star-shine at
    night.
I will make a palace fit for you and me
Of green days in forests and blue days at sea.

I will make my kitchen, and you shall keep
    your room,   5
Where white flows the river and bright blows
    the broom,
And you shall wash your linen and keep your
    body white
In rainfall at morning and dewfall at night.

And this shall be for music when no one else
    is near,
The fine song for singing, the rare song to
    hear!   10
That only I remember, that only you admire,
Of the broad road that stretches and the
    roadside fire.   (1895)

BRIGHT IS THE RING OF WORDS

Bright is the ring of words
    When the right man rings them,
Fair the fall of songs
    When the singer sings them.
Still they are caroled and said —   5
    On wings they are carried —
After the singer is dead
    And the maker buried.

Low as the singer lies
    In the field of heather,   10
Songs of his fashion bring
    The swains together.
And when the west is red

With the sunset embers,
The lover lingers and sings,
    And the maid remembers.   (1895)

SING ME A SONG

Sing me a song of a lad that is gone,
    Say, could that lad be I?
Merry of soul he sailed on a day
    Over the sea to Skye.

Mull was astern, Rum on the port,   5
    Egg on the starboard bow;
Glory of youth glowed in his soul —
    Where is that glory now?

Sing me a song of a lad that is gone,
    Say, could that lad be I?   10
Merry of soul he sailed on a day
    Over the sea to Skye.

Give me again all that was there,
    Give me the sun that shone!
Give me the eyes, give me the soul,   15
    Give me the lad that's gone!

Sing me a song of a lad that is gone,
    Say, could that lad be I?
Merry of soul he sailed on a day
    Over the sea to Skye.   20

Billow and breeze, islands and seas,
    Mountains of rain and sun,
All that was good, all that was fair,
    All that was me is gone.   (1895)

EVENSONG

The embers of the day are red
Beyond the murky hill.
The kitchen smokes; the bed
In the darkling house is spread.
The great sky darkens overhead,   5
And the great woods are shrill.
So far have I been led,
Lord, by thy will;
So far I have followed, Lord, and wondered
    still.
The breeze from the embalmèd land   10
Blows sudden toward the shore,
And claps my cottage door.
I hear the signal, Lord — I understand.
The night at thy command
Comes. I will eat and sleep and will not
    question more.   (1895)

---

38. **smelt**, eased gradually.
I Will Make You Brooches. 6. **broom**, a shrub with stiff,
green branches.

Sing Me a Song. 4-6. **Skye . . . Egg**, islands on the
western coast of Scotland. The route from Mull to Skye is
due north and passes, at the half way point, between Rum
on the left and Egg (or Eigg) on the right; the distance is
about forty miles. Stevenson made this trip in 1874 on
board the schooner *Heron.*

OSCAR WILDE (1854-1900)

IMPRESSION DU MATIN

The Thames nocturne of blue and gold
   Changed to a harmony in gray;
   A barge with ocher-colored hay
Dropt from the wharf: and chill and cold

The yellow fog came creeping down   5
   The bridges, till the houses' walls
   Seemed changed to shadows, and St. Paul's
Loomed like a bubble o'er the town.

Then suddenly arose the clang
   Of waking life; the streets were stirred   10
   With country wagons; and a bird
Flew to the glistening roofs and sang.

But one pale woman all alone,
   The daylight kissing her wan hair,
   Loitered beneath the gas lamps' flare,   15
With lips of flame and heart of stone.
              (1877; 1881)

IMPRESSIONS

1. LES SILHOUETTES

The sea is flecked with bars of gray,
The dull dead wind is out of tune,
And like a withered leaf the moon
Is blown across the stormy bay.

Etched clear upon the pallid sand   5
Lies the black boat; a sailor boy
Clambers aboard in careless joy
With laughing face and gleaming hand.

And overhead the curlews cry,
Where through the dusky upland grass   10
The young brown-throated reapers pass,
Like silhouettes against the sky.   (1877)

2. LA FUITE DE LA LUNE

To outer senses there is peace,
A dreamy peace on either hand,
Deep silence in the shadowy land,
Deep silence where the shadows cease—

Save for a cry that echoes shrill   5
From some lone bird disconsolate;

A corncrake calling to its mate;
The answer from the misty hill.

And suddenly the moon withdraws
Her sickle from the lightening skies,   10
And to her somber cavern flies,
Wrapped in a veil of yellow gauze.   (1877)

THE GRAVE OF KEATS

Rid of the world's injustice, and his pain,
He rests at last beneath God's veil of blue;
Taken from life when life and love were new
The youngest of the martyrs here is lain,
Fair as Sebastian, and as early slain.   5
No cypress shades his grave, no funeral yew,
But gentle violets weeping with the dew
Weave on his bones an ever-blossoming chain.
O proudest heart that broke for misery!
O sweetest lips since those of Mitylene!   10
O poet-painter of our English Land!
Thy name was writ in water—it shall stand;
And tears like mine will keep thy memory
    green,
As Isabella did her Basil-tree.   (1877)

HÉLAS!

To drift with every passion till my soul
Is a stringed lute on which all winds can play,
Is it for this that I have given away
Mine ancient wisdom, and austere control?
Methinks my life is a twice-written scroll   5
Scrawled over on some boyish holiday
With idle songs for pipe and virelay
Which do but mar the secret of the whole.
Surely there was a time I might have trod
The sunlit heights, and from life's disso-
    nance
Struck one clear chord to reach the ears of
    God;   11
Is that time dead? lo! with a little rod
I did but touch the honey of romance—
And must I lose a soul's inheritance? (1881)

The Grave of Keats. Keats, like Shelley, is buried in the lovely English Cemetery at Rome.
5. **Sebastian,** a Christian martyr shot with arrows and beaten to death by order of the emperor Diocletian (288); he is represented in art as a beautiful young man. 6. **cypress** ... **yew,** symbols of mourning. 10. **Mitylene,** a city on the island of Lesbos (in the Ægean Sea) where Sappho, the Greek poetess (6th century B.C.), lived and sang. 12. **name** ... **water,** the epitaph on the tombstone of Keats; it was composed by himself. See Rossetti's sonnet *John Keats,* page 543. 14. **Isabella . . . Basil-tree.** See Keats's *Isabella, or the Pot of Basil,* 1818; the story, retold from Boccaccio's *Decameron,* is of a lady who buried her murdered lover's head in a pot, and planted there a basil-tree which she watered with her tears.
Hélas! The title means *Alas!*
7. **virelay,** an old French lyric form, using only two rimes and composed in short lines with a refrain. 12-13. **a little rod,** etc., a reference to Jonathan's tasting forbidden honey with the end of a rod; see *I Samuel,* 14:27-43.

Impression du Matin. This "impression of the morning" attempts to imitate the paintings of the French Impressionists, who sought, above all, to record the radiance of light.
1-2. **nocturne,** night-piece, and **harmony,** musical terms adopted by Whistler to describe his "aesthetic" canvases. Wilde here sees a "harmony" in yellow and gray.
Impressions. Les Silhouettes means *The Silhouettes. La Fuite de la Lune* means *The Flight of the Moon.*

REQUIESCAT

Tread lightly, she is near
  Under the snow,
Speak gently, she can hear
  The daisies grow.

All her bright golden hair   5
  Tarnished with rust,
She that was young and fair
  Fallen to dust.

Lily-like, white as snow,
  She hardly knew   10
She was a woman, so
  Sweetly she grew.

Coffin-board, heavy stone,
  Lie on her breast,
I vex my heart alone   15
  She is at rest.

Peace, peace, she cannot hear
  Lyre or sonnet,
All my life's buried here,
  Heap earth upon it.   (1881)

IMPRESSION: LE REVEILLON

The sky is laced with fitful red;
The circling mists and shadows flee:
The dawn is rising from the sea,
Like a white lady from her bed.

And jagged brazen arrows fall   5
Athwart the feathers of the night,
And a long wave of yellow light
Breaks silently on tower and hall,

And spreading wide across the wold
Wakes into flight some fluttering bird,   10
And all the chestnut tops are stirred,
And all the branches streaked with gold.
     (1881)

APOLOGIA

Is it thy will that I should wax and wane,
  Barter my cloth of gold for hodden gray,
And at thy pleasure weave the web of pain
  Whose brightest threads are each a wasted
    day?

Is it thy will—Love that I love so well—   5
That my Soul's House should be a tortured
    spot
Wherein, like evil paramours, must dwell
  The quenchless flame, the worm that dieth
    not?

Nay, if it be thy will, I shall endure,
  And sell ambition at the common mart,   10
And let dull failure be my vestiture,
  And sorrow dig its grave within my heart.

Perchance it may be better so—at least
  I have not made my heart a heart of stone,
Nor starved my boyhood of its goodly feast,
  Nor walked where Beauty is a thing un-
    known.   16

Many a man hath done so; sought to fence
  In straitened bonds the soul that should be
    free,
Trodden the dusty road of common sense,
  While all the forest sang of liberty,   20

Not marking how the spotted hawk in flight
  Passed on wide pinion through the lofty air,
To where some steep untrodden mountain
    height
  Caught the last tresses of the Sun God's
    hair;

Or how the little flower he trod upon,   25
  The daisy, that white-feathered shield of
    gold,
Followed with wistful eyes the wandering sun,
  Content if once its leaves were aureoled.

But surely it is something to have been
  The best belovéd for a little while,   30
To have walked hand in hand with Love,
    and seen
  His purple wings flit once across thy smile.

Aye! though the gorgéd asp of passion feed
  On my boy's heart, yet have I burst the
    bars,   34
Stood face to face with Beauty, known indeed
  The Love which moves the Sun and all
    the stars!   (1881)

THE HARLOT'S HOUSE

We caught the tread of dancing feet,
  We loitered down the moonlit street,
And stopped beneath the Harlot's House.

Requiescat. The title means *Let Her Rest.*
Impression: Le Réveillon. Le Réveillon is a term used in painting to designate a strong light-effect against a somber background.
Apologia. The title means *Apology*—a self-justification, as in Newman's *Apologia pro Vita Sua;* Wilde's most complete *apologia* is his *De Profundis.*

24. **Sun God,** Apollo, to whom the daisy (day's eye) was sacred. 25-28. **little flower . . . aureoled.** Cf. Browning's *Rudel to the Lady of Tripoli,* 6-18, p. 201. 36. **Love . . . stars.** Cf. the last line of Dante's *Divine Comedy:* "Love, which moves the sun and the other stars."

Inside, above the din and fray,
We heard the loud musicians play   5
The "Treues Liebes Herz" of Strauss.

Like strange mechanical grotesques,
Making fantastic arabesques,
The shadows raced across the blind.
We watched the ghostly dancers spin,   10
To sound of horn and violin,
Like black leaves wheeling in the wind.

Like wire-pulled Automatons,
Slim silhouetted skeletons
Went sidling through the slow quadrille,   15
Then took each other by the hand,
And danced a stately saraband;
Their laughter echoed thin and shrill.

Sometimes a clock-work puppet pressed
A phantom lover to her breast,   20
Sometimes they seemed to try and sing.
Sometimes a horrible Marionette
Came out and smoked its cigarette
Upon the steps like a live thing.

Then turning to my love I said,   25
"The dead are dancing with the dead,
The dust is whirling with the dust."
But she, she heard the violin,
And left my side and entered in:
Love passed into the House of Lust.   30

Then suddenly the tune went false,
The dancers wearied of the waltz,
The shadows ceased to wheel and whirl,
And down the long and silent street,
The dawn with silver-sandaled feet,   35
Crept like a frightened girl.

                    (*1883;* 1885)

THE SPHINX

TO MARCEL SCHWOB
IN FRIENDSHIP AND ADMIRATION

In a dim corner of my room for longer than my
    fancy thinks
A beautiful and silent Sphinx has watched me
    through the shifting gloom.

Inviolate and immobile she does not rise, she
    does not stir,
For silver moons are naught to her and naught
    to her the suns that reel.

Red follows gray across the air, the waves of
    moonlight ebb and flow,   5
But with the dawn she does not go and in the
    night-time she is there.

Dawn follows Dawn and Nights grow old, and
    all the while this curious cat
Lies couching on the Chinese mat with eyes of
    satin rimmed with gold.

Upon the mat she lies and leers and on the
    tawny throat of her
Flutters the soft and silky fur or ripples to her
    pointed ears.   10

Come forth, my lovely seneschal! so somno-
    lent, so statuesque!
Come forth you exquisite grotesque! half
    woman and half animal!

Come forth my lovely languorous Sphinx! and
    put your head upon my knee!
And let me stroke your throat and see your
    body spotted like the Lynx!

And let me touch those curving claws of yellow
    ivory and grasp   15
The tail that like a monstrous Asp coils round
    your heavy velvet paws!

———

A thousand weary centuries are thine while I
    have hardly seen
Some twenty summers cast their green for
    Autumn's gaudy liveries.

But you can read the Hieroglyphs on the great
    sandstone obelisks,
And you have talked with Basilisks, and you
    have looked on Hippogriffs.   20

O tell me, were you standing by when Isis to
    Osiris knelt?
And did you watch the Egyptian melt her
    union for Antony,

The Harlot's House. **6. Treues Liebes Herz,** "The Heart
of True Love." **Strauss,** Johann Strauss (1825-99), famous
Austrian composer, known as "the Waltz King." **8. arabesques,** intricate designs or postures. **17. saraband,** slow,
stately Spanish dance. **22. Marionette,** a small figure in
human form moved by strings or hand, as in a puppet show.
The Sphinx. In Greek legend the Sphinx was a monster
with the head and breasts of a woman, the body and paws of a
lion, the wings of a bird, the tail of a serpent, and a human
voice. She sat on a high rock by the roadside in Thebes,
Boeotia, and destroyed all passers-by who could not guess her
riddle. The most famous figure of the Sphinx, 172 feet long
and 66 feet high, is near the Great Pyramid, in Egypt.

11. seneschal, a managing official in the castle of a noble
in the Middle Ages. **20. Basilisks,** fearful creatures of ancient
legend, like serpents or dragons. **Hippogriffs,** mythical creatures having the body of a horse, the wings and head of an
eagle, and the forelegs of a lion. **21. Isis,** the chief female
divinity in Egyptian mythology, the sister and wife of Osiris,
the chief god of the underworld. She represented the female
productive force of nature. **22. the Egyptian,** Cleopatra,
queen of Egypt (69-30 B.C.). She was beloved by Mark
Antony (83-30 B.C.), a Roman general. See Shakespeare's
Antony and Cleopatra. **union,** a large pearl of fine quality
and rare beauty.

And drink the jewel-drunken wine, and bend
    her head in mimic awe
To see the huge proconsul draw the salted
    tunny from the brine?

And did you mark the Cyprian kiss white A-
    don on his catafalque?   25
And did you follow Amenalk, the God of He-
    liopolis?

And did you talk with Thoth, and did you hear
    the moon-horned Io weep?
And know the painted kings who sleep be-
    neath the wedge-shaped Pyramid?

Lift up your large black satin eyes which are
    like cushions where one sinks!
Fawn at my feet, fantastic Sphinx! and sing
    me all your memories!   30

Sing to me of the Jewish maid who wandered
    with the Holy Child,
And how you led them through the wild, and
    how they slept beneath your shade.

Sing to me of that odorous green eve when
    crouching by the marge
You heard from Adrian's gilded barge the
    laughter of Antinöus,

And lapped the stream and fed your drouth
    and watched with hot and hungry
    stare   35
The ivory body of that rare young slave with
    his pomegranate mouth!

Sing to me of the Labyrinth in which the two-
    formed bull was stalled!
Sing to me of the night you crawled across the
    temple's granite plinth,

When through the purple corridors the scream-
    ing scarlet Ibis flew
In terror, and a horrid dew dripped from the
    moaning Mandragores,   40

And the great torpid crocodile within the tank
    shed slimy tears,
And tare the jewels from his ears and stag-
    gered back into the Nile,

And the priests cursed you with shrill psalms
    as in your claws you seized the snake,
And crept away with it to slake your passion
    by the shuddering palms.

Who were your lovers? who were they who
    wrestled for you in the dust?   45
Which was the vessel of your Lust? What
    Leman had you, every day?

Did giant Lizards come and crouch before you
    on the reedy banks?
Did Gryphons with great metal flanks leap on
    you in your trampled couch?

Did monstrous hippopotami come sidling to-
    ward you in the mist?
Did gilt-scaled dragons writhe and twist with
    passion as you passed them by?   50

And from the brick-built Lycian tomb what
    horrible Chimera came
With fearful heads and fearful flame to breed
    new wonders from your womb?

Or had you shameful secret quests and did you
    harry to your home
Some Nereid coiled in amber foam with cu-
    rious rock-crystal breasts?

Or did you treading through the froth call to
    the brown Sidonian   55
For tidings of Leviathan, Leviathan or Be-
    hemoth?

---

24. **tunny,** a large marine fish of the mackerel family.
25. **Cyprian,** Venus, goddess of love; she had a temple in
Cyprus. **Adon,** Adonis, a beautiful youth beloved by Venus.
He was killed by a wild boar while hunting. On the very spot
where his blood had been shed, Venus made the anemone grow.
catafalque, a structure supporting the coffin of an eminent
person during a funeral. 26. **Heliopolis,** a famous city of
ancient Egypt, not far from modern Cairo. It was a city of
learning noted for its oracles and temples. 27. **Thoth,** a god
of Egyptian mythology identified by the Greeks with Hermes,
the messenger of the gods. **Io,** in classical myth the beautiful
maiden loved by Jupiter, who changed her into a heifer to
conceal her from his wife, Juno. But Juno knew, and she
sent a gadfly to chase the heifer all over the world. 31. **Jewish
maid,** the Virgin Mary. Warned in a dream, Joseph took
Mary and the young child by night and fled into Egypt,
where they remained until the death of Herod the king—
Matthew, 2. 34. **Adrian,** Hadrian, Roman emperor (117-138),
who invaded Britain in 120. **Antinöus,** a model of manly
beauty, a favorite of Hadrian and his companion in all his
journeys. Antinöus drowned himself in the Nile in 130 A.D.
37. **Labyrinth,** in Greek mythology the bewildering structure built in Crete as a prison for the Minotaur, a monster
with a bull's head and a human body. 38. **plinth,** the
square slab which forms part of the base of certain classical
columns.

39. **Ibis,** a sacred bird of the ancient Egyptians. In the
guise of an ibis, the god Thoth escaped the pursuit of Typhon,
a hundred-headed, fiery-eyed monster who, by some, was
considered the father of the Sphinx. 40. **Mandragores,**
narcotic plants of the nightshade family. 41. **crocodile,** a
symbol of deity among the Egyptians. 46. **Leman,** lover.
48. **Gryphons,** mythical monsters, with the body of a lion
and the head and wings of an eagle. According to Herodotus,
the Greek historian, they guarded the gold in Scythia.
51. **Chimera,** a fabulous monster of Greek mythology, with
a goat's body, a lion's head, and a serpent's tail. It was
born in Lycia, in Asia Minor. 54. **Nereid,** one of the fifty
beautiful and dainty sea nymphs, daughters of the kind sea
god, Nereus, of Greek mythology. 55. **Sidonian,** a native of
Sidon, an ancient seaport of Phoenicia. 56. **Leviathan,** the
name given in the Bible to a mythical sea serpent. See *Job,*
41. **Behemoth,** a large animal described in *Job,* 40:15-24,
probably a hippopotamus.

Or did you when the sun was set climb up the
    cactus-covered slope
To meet your swarthy Ethiop whose body was
    of polished jet?

Or did you while the earthen skiffs dropped
    down the gray Nilotic flats
At twilight, and the flickering bats flew round
    the temple's triple glyphs,   60

Steal to the border of the bar and swim across
    the silent lake
And slink into the vault and make the Pyr-
    amid your lúpanar,

Till from each black sarcophagus rose up the
    painted swathèd dead?
Or did you lure unto your bed the ivory-
    horned Tragelaphos?

Or did you love the god of flies who plagued
    the Hebrew and was splashed   65
With wine unto the waist? or Pasht, who had
    green beryls for her eyes?

Or that young god, the Tyrian, who was more
    amorous than the dove
Of Ashtaroth? or did you love the god of the
    Assyrian,

Whose wings, like strange transparent talc,
    rose high above his hawk-faced head,
Painted with silver and with red and ribbed
    with rods of Oreichalch?   70

Or did huge Apis from his car leap down and
    lay before your feet
Big blossoms of the honey-sweet and honey-
    colored nenuphar?

How subtle-secret is your smile! Did you love
    none then? Nay, I know
Great Ammon was your bedfellow! He lay
    with you beside the Nile!

The river-horses in the slime trumpeted when
    they saw him come   75
Odorous with Syrian galbanum and smeared
    with spikenard and with thyme.

He came along the river bank like some tall
    galley argent-sailed,
He strode across the waters, mailed in beauty,
    and the waters sank.

He strode across the desert sand: he reached
    the valley where you lay:
He waited till the dawn of day: then touched
    your black breasts with his hand.   80

You kissed his mouth with mouth of flame:
    you made the hornèd god your own:
You stood behind him on his throne: you
    called him by his secret name.

You whispered monstrous oracles into the cav-
    erns of his ears:
With blood of goats and blood of steers you
    taught him monstrous miracles.

White Ammon was your bedfellow! Your
    chamber was the steaming Nile!   85
And with your curved archaic smile you
    watched his passion come and go.

With Syrian oils his brows were bright: and
    wide-spread as a tent at noon
His marble limbs made pale the moon and lent
    the day a larger light.

His long hair was nine cubits' span and colored
    like that yellow gem
Which hidden in their garments' hem the
    merchants bring from Kurdistan.   90

His face was as the must that lies upon a vat of
    new-made wine:
The seas could not insapphirine the perfect
    azure of his eyes.

His thick soft throat was white as milk and
    threaded with thin veins of blue:
And curious pearls like frozen dew were
    broidered on his flowing silk.

On pearl and porphyry pedestaled he was too
    bright to look upon: 95
For on his ivory breast there shone the won-
    drous ocean-emerald,

---

60. **glyphs,** vertical grooves in pillars. 62. **lúpanar,** brothel. 64. **Tragelaphos,** a fabulous animal, part stag and part goat. 65. **god of flies,** Beelzebub, whose name is translated most often as *Lord of flies.* 66. **Pasht,** Bast, in Egyptian mythology a lion or cat-headed goddess. 67. **the Tyrian,** Alexander the Great (356-323 B.C.), who became King of Macedon when only twenty years of age. He was known for his amorousness. After a six months' siege he destroyed Tyre, one of the most important cities of Phoenicia, noted at one time for its magnificence and luxury. 68. **Ashtaroth,** Astarte, the Phoenician goddess of sexual love, identified with Venus (Aphrodite), goddess of love and beauty, to whom doves and sparrows were sacred. **god of the Assyrian,** cf. the winged god of Rossetti's *The Burden of Nineveh,* page 502. 70. **Oreichalch,** a gilded copper or brass alloy. 71. **Apis,** a sacred bull of the Egyptians. 72. **nenuphar,** European water lily. 74. **Ammon,** one of the chief deities in Egyptian mythology; as god of life he was represented as having the head of a ram. He had a famous oracle in the Libyan desert, which Alexander the Great visited.

89. **nine cubits' span.** A cubit is a unit of linear measure, 18 inches. 90. **Kurdistan,** a region in West Asia, mostly in Turkey and partly in Iran. 91. **must,** mold. 92. **insapphirine,** dye or make a deeper blue.

That mystic moonlit jewel which some diver of
   the Colchian caves
Had found beneath the blackening waves and
   carried to the Colchian witch.

Before his gilded galiot ran naked vine-
   wreathed corybants,
And lines of swaying elephants knelt down to
   draw his chariot,   100

And lines of swarthy Nubians bare up his litter
   as he rode
Down the great granite-paven road between
   the nodding peacock fans.

The merchants brought him steatite from Sidon in their painted ships:
The meanest cup that touched his lips was
   fashioned from a chrysolite.

The merchants brought him cedar chests of
   rich apparel bound with cords: 105
His train was borne by Memphian lords: young
   kings were glad to be his guests.

Ten hundred shaven priests did bow to Ammon's altar day and night,
Ten hundred lamps did wave their light
   through Ammon's carven house—
   and now

Foul snake and speckled adder with their
   young ones crawl from stone to stone
For ruined is the house and prone the great
   rose-marble monolith!   110

Wild ass or trotting jackal comes and couches
   in the moldering gates:
Wild satyrs call unto their mates across the
   fallen fluted drums.

And on the summit of the pile the blue-faced
   ape of Horus sits
And gibbers while the fig-tree splits the pillars
   of the peristyle.

The god is scattered here and there: deep hidden in the windy sand   115
I saw his giant granite hand still clenched in
   impotent despair.

And many a wandering caravan of stately Ne-
   groes silken-shawled,
Crossing the desert halts appalled before the
   neck that none can span.

And many a bearded Bedouin draws back his
   yellow-striped burnous
To gaze upon the Titan thews of him who was
   thy paladin.   120

Go, seek his fragments on the moor and wash
   them in the evening dew,
And from their pieces make anew thy muti-
   lated paramour!

Go, seek them where they lie alone and from
   their broken pieces make
Thy bruiséd bedfellow! And wake mad passion in the senseless stone!

Charm his dull ear with Syrian hymns! he
   loved your body! oh, be kind, 125
Pour spikenard on his hair, and wind soft rolls
   of linen round his limbs.

Wind round his head the figured coins! stain
   with red fruits those pallid lips!
Weave purple for his shrunken hips! and purple for his barren loins!

Away to Egypt! Have no fear. Only one
   God has ever died.
Only one God has let His side be wounded by
   a soldier's spear.   130

But these, thy lovers, are not dead. Still by
   the hundred-cubit gate
Dog-faced Anubis sits in state with lotus-lilies
   for thy head.

Still from his chair of porphyry gaunt Memnon
   strains his lidless eyes
Across the empty land, and cries each yellow
   morning unto thee.

And Nilus with his broken horn lies in his
   black and oozy bed,   135

98. **Colchian witch,** Medea, a famous enchantress, the
daughter of the king of Colchis, an ancient region on the
coast of the Black Sea. She aided her lover, Jason, in his
quest for the Golden Fleece. 99. **corybants,** mythical attendants of Cybele, goddess of nature, whom they accompanied with wild dances and music. 101. **Nubians,** natives of
Nubia, in northeastern Africa. 104. **chrysolite,** an olive
green mineral, used for gems. 106. **Memphian,** from Mem-
phis, an ancient city in Egypt. 110. **monolith,** a large stone
shaped into a pillar, or statue. 113. **ape of Horus,** in Egyptian mythology the hawk-headed god of day, the rising sun.

119. **Bedouin,** a nomadic Arab of the deserts. **burnous,**
a cloaklike garment and hood woven in one piece. 120. **Titan,**
gigantic. The Titans were fabled giants who fought against
the Olympian gods only to be overthrown. **paladin,** distinguished champion. 130. **one . . . spear,** Christ, who was
crucified. See *John,* 19:34. 132. **Anubis,** in Egyptian mythology a god with the head of a dog or a jackal, who guarded
the tombs and conducted the spirits of the dead to their final
abode. 133. **Memnon,** a prince of the Ethiopians, who was
slain by Achilles in the Trojan War. According to tradition a
colossal statue near ancient Thebes, now Karnak, Upper
Egypt, was supposed to represent Memnon. When struck by
the rays of the rising sun it gave forth a musical note, a
harplike sound. 135. **Nilus,** the river Nile.

And till thy coming will not spread his waters
    on the withering corn.

Your lovers are not dead, I know. They will
    rise up and hear your voice
And clash their cymbals and rejoice and run to
    kiss your mouth! And so,

Set wings upon your argosies! Set horses to
    your ebon car!
Back to your Nile! Or if you are grown sick
    of dead divinities   140

Follow some roving lion's spoor across the
    copper-colored plain,
Reach out and hale him by the mane and bid
    him be your paramour!

Couch by his side upon the grass and set your
    white teeth in his throat
And when you hear his dying note lash your
    long flanks of polished brass,

And take a tiger for your mate, whose amber
    sides are flecked with black,   145
And ride upon his gilded back in triumph
    through the Theban gate,

And toy with him in amorous jests, and when
    he turns, and snarls, and gnaws,
O smite him with your jasper claws! and bruise
    him with your agate breasts!

———

Why are you tarrying? Get hence! I weary
    of your sullen ways,
I weary of your steadfast gaze, your somnolent
    magnificence.   150

Your horrible and heavy breath makes the
    light flicker in the lamp,
And on my brow I feel the damp and dreadful
    dews of night and death.

Your eyes are like fantastic moons that shiver
    in some stagnant lake,
Your tongue is like a scarlet snake that dances
    to fantastic tunes,

Your pulse makes poisonous melodies, and
    your black throat is like the hole 155
Left by some torch or burning coal on Sara-
    cenic tapestries.

Away! The sulphur-colored stars are hur-
    rying through the Western gate!
Away! Or it may be too late to climb their
    silent silver cars!

156. **Saracenic**, made by the Saracens or early Arabs.

See, the dawn shivers round the gray gilt-
    dialed towers, and the rain
Streams down each diamonded pane and blurs
    with tears the wannish day.   160

What snake-tressed fury fresh from Hell, with
    uncouth gestures and unclean,
Stole from the poppy-drowsy queen and led
    you to a student's cell?

———

What songless tongueless ghost of sin crept
    through the curtains of the night,
And saw my taper burning bright, and
    knocked, and bade you enter in?

Are there not others more accursed, whiter
    with leprosies than I?   165
Are Abana and Pharphar dry that you come
    here to slake your thirst?

Get hence, you loathsome mystery! Hideous
    animal, get hence!
You wake in me each bestial sense, you make
    me what I would not be.

You make my creed a barren sham, you wake
    foul dreams of sensual life,
And Atys with his blood-stained knife were
    better than the thing I am.   170

False Sphinx! False Sphinx! By reedy Styx
    old Charon, leaning on his oar,
Waits for my coin. Go thou before, and leave
    me with my crucifix,

Whose pallid burden, sick with pain, watches
    the world with wearied eyes,
And weeps for every soul that dies, and weeps
    for every soul in vain.   (1894)

THE BALLAD OF READING GAOL

I

He did not wear his scarlet coat,
    For blood and wine are red,
And blood and wine were on his hands

161. **snake-tressed fury**, an avenging spirit of classical
mythology. The Furies were attendants of Proserpine, queen
of Hades; their heads were wreathed with serpents.   166.
Abana and Pharphar, rivers of Damascus (2 *Kings*, 5:12).
170. **Atys**, Phrygian god of vegetation. According to one
story he died from self-inflicted wounds. 171. **Styx**, the chief
river of the lower world which had to be crossed by souls
passing to the regions of the dead. It was Charon's duty to
ferry the dead across, and for doing so from the mouth of each
passenger he collected a coin.
    The Ballad of Reading Gaol. The background of the ballad
is the jail at Reading, Berkshire, where Wilde was imprisoned,
1895-97; the central event is the execution, for murder, of a
trooper in the Royal Horse Guards, July 7, 1896. The ballad
was written at Berneval, France, after Wilde's release.

When they found him with the dead,
The poor dead woman whom he loved,   5
  And murdered in her bed.

He walked amongst the Trial Men
  In a suit of shabby gray;
A cricket cap was on his head,
  And his step seemed light and gay;   10
But I never saw a man who looked
  So wistfully at the day.

I never saw a man who looked
  With such a wistful eye
Upon that little tent of blue   15
  Which prisoners call the sky,
And at every drifting cloud that went
  With sails of silver by.

I walked, with other souls in pain,
  Within another ring,   20
And was wondering if the man had done
  A great or little thing,
When a voice behind me whispered low,
  "That fellow's got to swing."

Dear Christ! the very prison walls   25
  Suddenly seemed to reel,
And the sky above my head became
  Like a casque of scorching steel;
And, though I was a soul in pain,
  My pain I could not feel.   30

I only knew what hunted thought
  Quickened his step, and why
He looked upon the garish day
  With such a wistful eye;
The man had killed the thing he loved,   35
  And so he had to die.

Yet each man kills the thing he loves,
  By each let this be heard,
Some do it with a bitter look,
  Some with a flattering word,   40
The coward does it with a kiss,
  The brave man with a sword!

Some kill their love when they are young,
  And some when they are old;
Some strangle with the hands of Lust,   45
  Some with the hands of Gold.
The kindest use a knife, because
  The dead so soon grow cold.

Some love too little, some too long,
  Some sell, and others buy;   50
Some do the deed with many tears,
  And some without a sigh;
For each man kills the thing he loves,
  Yet each man does not die.

7. **Trial Men,** men sentenced by a preliminary court the verdict of which might be appealed.

He does not die a death of shame   55
  On a day of dark disgrace,
Nor have a noose about his neck,
  Nor a cloth upon his face,
Nor drop feet foremost through the floor
  Into an empty space.   60

He does not sit with silent men
  Who watch him night and day;
Who watch him when he tries to weep,
  And when he tries to pray;
Who watch him lest himself should rob   65
  The prison of its prey.

He does not wake at dawn to see
  Dread figures throng his room —
The shivering chaplain robed in white,
  The sheriff stern with gloom,   70
And the governor all in shiny black,
  With the yellow face of Doom.

He does not rise in piteous haste
  To put on convict-clothes,
While some coarse-mouthed doctor gloats,
  and notes   75
  Each new and nerve-twitched pose,
Fingering a watch whose little ticks
  Are like horrible hammer-blows.

He does not know that sickening thirst
  That sands one's throat before   80
The hangman with his gardener's gloves
  Slips through the padded door,
And binds one with three leathern thongs,
  That the throat may thirst no more.

He does not bend his head to hear   85
  The burial office read,
Nor, while the terror of his soul
  Tells him he is not dead,
Cross his own coffin, as he moves
  Into the hideous shed.   90

He does not stare upon the air
  Through a little roof of glass;
He does not pray with lips of clay
  For his agony to pass;
Nor feel upon his shuddering cheek   95
  The kiss of Caiaphas.

2

Six weeks our guardsman walked the yard,
  In the suit of shabby gray.
His cricket cap was on his head,
  And his step seemed light and gay,   100
But I never saw a man who looked
  So wistfully at the day.

96. **kiss of Caiaphas,** the kiss of Judas bought with the money received from Caiaphas, the high priest, for the betrayal of Christ. See *Matthew,* 26.

I never saw a man who looked
  With such a wistful eye
Upon that little tent of blue   105
  Which prisoners call the sky,
And at every wandering cloud that trailed
  Its raveled fleeces by.

He did not wring his hands, as do
  Those witless men who dare   110
To try to rear the changeling Hope
  In the cave of black Despair;
He only looked upon the sun,
  And drank the morning air.

He did not wring his hands nor weep,   115
  Nor did he peek or pine,
But he drank the air as though it held
  Some healthful anodyne;
With open mouth he drank the sun
  As though it had been wine!   120

And I and all the souls in pain,
  Who tramped the other ring,
Forgot if we ourselves had done
  A great or little thing,
And watched with gaze of dull amaze   125
  The man who had to swing.

And strange it was to see him pass
  With a step so light and gay,
And strange it was to see him look
  So wistfully at the day,   130
And strange it was to think that he
  Had such a debt to pay.

For oak and elm have pleasant leaves
  That in the springtime shoot;
But grim to see is the gallows-tree,   135
  With its adder-bitten root,
And, green or dry, a man must die
  Before it bears its fruit!

The loftiest place is that seat of grace
  For which all worldlings try;   140
But who would stand in hempen band
  Upon a scaffold high,
And through a murderer's collar take
  His last look at the sky?

It is sweet to dance to violins   145
  When love and life are fair;
To dance to flutes, to dance to lutes
  Is delicate and rare;
But it is not sweet with nimble feet
  To dance upon the air!   150

So with curious eyes and sick surmise
  We watched him day by day,

118. **anodyne,** a drug that kills pain.

And wondered if each one of us
  Would end the self-same way,
For none can tell to what red hell   155
  His sightless soul may stray.

At last the dead man walked no more
  Amongst the Trial Men,
And I knew that he was standing up
  In the black dock's dreadful pen,   160
And that never would I see his face
  In God's sweet world again.

Like two doomed ships that pass in storm
  We had crossed each other's way;
But we made no sign, we said no word — 165
  We had no word to say —
For we did not meet in the holy night,
  But in the shameful day.

A prison wall was round us both,
  Two outcast men we were.   170
The world had thrust us from its heart,
  And God from out His care;
And the iron gin that waits for Sin
  Had caught us in its snare.

3

In Debtors' Yard the stones are hard,   175
  And the dripping wall is high,
So it was there he took the air
  Beneath the leaden sky,
And by each side a warder walked,
  For fear the man might die.   180

Or else he sat with those who watched
  His anguish night and day;
Who watched him when he rose to weep,
  And when he crouched to pray;
Who watched him lest himself should rob 185
  Their scaffold of its prey.

The governor was strong upon
  The Regulations Act;
The doctor said that death was but
  A scientific fact;   190
And twice a day the chaplain called,
  And left a little tract.

And twice a day he smoked his pipe,
  And drank his quart of beer;
His soul was resolute, and held   195
  No hiding-place for fear;
He often said that he was glad
  The hangman's hands were near.

173. **gin,** trap. 175. **Debtors' Yard,** a division of the exercise ground in Reading Gaol, formerly set apart for debtors. 188. **Regulations Act,** a law placing all prisons under governmental supervision and prescribing humane treatment for prisoners.

But why he said so strange a thing
  No warder dared to ask; 200
For he to whom a watcher's doom
  Is given as his task,
Must set a lock upon his lips,
  And make his face a mask.

Or else he might be moved, and try 205
  To comfort or console —
And what should human Pity do
  Pent up in Murderers' Hole?
What word of grace in such a place
  Could help a brother's soul? 210

With slouch and swing around the ring
  We trod the Fools' Parade!
We did not care — we knew we were
  The Devil's Own Brigade;
And shaven head and feet of lead 215
  Make a merry masquerade.

We tore the tarry rope to shreds
  With blunt and bleeding nails;
We rubbed the doors, and scrubbed the floors,
  And cleaned the shining rails; 220
And, rank by rank, we soaped the plank,
  And clattered with the pails.

We sewed the sacks, we broke the stones,
  We turned the dusty drill;
We banged the tins, and bawled the hymns,
  And sweated on the mill; 226
But in the heart of every man
  Terror was lying still.

So still it lay that every day
  Crawled like a weed-clogged wave; 230
And we forgot the bitter lot
  That waits for fool and knave,
Till once, as we tramped in from work,
  We passed an open grave.

With yawning mouth the yellow hole 235
  Gaped for a living thing;
The very mud cried out for blood
  To the thirsty asphalt ring.
And we knew that ere one dawn grew fair
  Some prisoner had to swing. 240

Right in we went, with soul intent
  On Death and Dread and Doom.
The hangman, with his little bag,
  Went shuffling through the gloom;
And each man trembled as he crept 245
  Into his numbered tomb.

That night the empty corridors
  Were full of forms of Fear,

And up and down the iron town
  Stole feet we could not hear, 250
And through the bars that hide the stars
  White faces seemed to peer.

He lay as one who lies and dreams
  In a pleasant meadow-land,
The watchers watched him as he slept, 255
  And could not understand
How one could sleep so sweet a sleep
  With a hangman close at hand.

But there is no sleep when men must weep
  Who never yet have wept; 260
So we — the fool, the fraud, the knave —
  That endless vigil kept,
And through each brain on hands of pain
  Another's terror crept.

Alas! it is a fearful thing 265
  To feel another's guilt!
For, right within, the sword of Sin
  Pierced to its poisoned hilt,
And as molten lead were the tears we shed
  For the blood we had not spilt. 270

The warders with their shoes of felt
  Crept by each padlocked door,
And peeped and saw, with eyes of awe,
  Gray figures on the floor,
And wondered why men knelt to pray 275
  Who never prayed before.

All through the night we knelt and prayed,
  Mad mourners of a corse!
The troubled plumes of midnight were
  The plumes upon a hearse; 280
And bitter wine upon a sponge
  Was the savor of Remorse.

The gray cock crew, the red cock crew,
  But never came the day;
And crooked shapes of Terror crouched, 285
  In the corners where we lay;
And each evil sprite that walks by night
  Before us seemed to play.

They glided past, they glided fast,
  Like travelers through a mist; 290
They mocked the moon in a rigadoon
  Of delicate turn and twist,
And with formal pace and loathsome grace
  The phantoms kept their tryst.

With mop and mow, we saw them go, 295
  Slim shadows hand and hand;
About, about, in ghostly rout
  They trod a saraband;

217. **We ... shreds.** Prisoners sentenced to hard labor, as Wilde was, were forced to tear ropes to shreds to make oakum for calking vessels.

291. **rigadoon,** a gay, lively dance. 298. **saraband,** a stately Spanish dance.

And the damned grotesques made arabesques,
  Like the wind upon the sand!   300

With the pirouettes of marionettes,
  They tripped on pointed tread;
But with flutes of Fear they filled the ear,
  As their grisly masque they led,
And loud they sang, and long they sang,   305
  For they sang to wake the dead.

"Oho!" they cried, "the world is wide,
  But fettered limbs go lame!
And once, or twice, to throw the dice
  Is a gentlemanly game,   310
But he does not win who plays with Sin
  In the secret House of Shame."

No things of air these antics were,
  That frolicked with such glee;
To men whose lives were held in gyves,   315
  And whose feet might not go free,
Ah! wounds of Christ! they were living things,
  Most terrible to see.

Around, around, they waltzed and wound;
  Some wheeled in smirking pairs;   320
With the mincing step of a demirep
  Some sidled up the stairs;
And with subtle sneer, and fawning leer,
  Each helped us at our prayers.

The morning wind began to moan,   325
  But still the night went on;
Through its giant loom the web of gloom
  Crept till each thread was spun;
And, as we prayed, we grew afraid
  Of the Justice of the Sun.   330

The moaning wind went wandering round
  The weeping prison-wall;
Till like a wheel of turning steel
  We felt the minutes crawl.
O moaning wind! what had we done   335
  To have such a seneschal?

At last I saw the shadowed bars,
  Like a lattice wrought in lead,
Move right across the whitewashed wall
  That faced my three-plank bed,   340
And I knew that somewhere in the world
  God's dreadful dawn was red.

At six o'clock we cleaned our cells,
  At seven all was still,
But the sough and swing of a mighty wing 345
  The prison seemed to fill,
For the Lord of Death with icy breath,
  Had entered in to kill.

He did not pass in purple pomp,
  Nor ride a moon-white steed.   350
Three yards of cord and a sliding board
  Are all the gallows' need;
So with rope of shame the Herald came
  To do the secret deed.

We were as men who through a fen   355
  Of filthy darkness grope —
We did not dare to breathe a prayer,
  Or to give our anguish scope;
Something was dead in each of us,
  And what was dead was Hope.   360

For man's grim Justice goes its way,
  And will not swerve aside:
It slays the weak, it slays the strong,
  It has a deadly stride;
With iron heel it slays the strong,   365
  The monstrous parricide!

We waited for the stroke of eight;
  Each tongue was thick with thirst.
For the stroke of eight is the stroke of Fate
  That makes a man accursed,   370
And Fate will use a running noose
  For the best man and the worst.

We had no other thing to do,
  Save to wait for the sign to come;
So, like things of stone in a valley lone, 375
  Quiet we sat and dumb;
But each man's heart beat thick and quick,
  Like a madman on a drum!

With sudden shock the prison-clock
  Smote on the shivering air,   380
And from all the gaol rose up a wail
  Of impotent despair,
Like the sound that frightened marshes hear
  From some leper in his lair.

And as one sees most fearful things   385
  In the crystal of a dream,
We saw the greasy hempen rope
  Hooked to the blackened beam,
And heard the prayer the hangman's snare
  Strangled into a scream.   390

And all the woe that moved him so
  That he gave that bitter cry,
And the wild regrets, and the bloody sweats,
  None knew so well as I;
For he who lives more lives than one   395
  More deaths than one must die.

4

There is no chapel on the day
  On which they hang a man;

299. **arabesques,** interlaced lines and curves. 301.
pirouettes of marionettes, whirling on their toes, like
dancing puppets. Cf. *The Harlot's House*, p. 819.

386. **crystal . . . dream,** in a dream where, as in the ball
of the crystal-gazer, move uncanny shapes.

The chaplain's heart is far too sick,
  Or his face is far too wan,   400
Or there is that written in his eyes
  Which none should look upon.

So they kept us close till nigh on noon,
  And then they rang the bell,
And the warders with their jingling keys   405
  Opened each listening cell,
And down the iron stair we tramped,
  Each from his separate hell.

Out into God's sweet air we went,
  But not in wonted way,   410
For this man's face was white with fear,
  And that man's face was gray,
And I never saw sad men who looked
  So wistfully at the day.

I never saw sad men who looked   415
  With such a wistful eye
Upon that little tent of blue
  We prisoners called the sky,
And at every careless cloud that passed
  In happy freedom by.   420

But there were those amongst us all
  Who walked with downcast head,
And knew that, had each got his due,
  They should have died instead;
He had but killed a thing that lived,   425
  Whilst they had killed the dead.

For he who sins a second time
  Wakes a dead soul to pain,
And draws it from its spotted shroud,
  And makes it bleed again,   430
And makes it bleed great gouts of blood,
  And makes it bleed in vain!

Like ape or clown, in monstrous garb
  With crooked arrows starred,
Silently we went round and round   435
  The slippery asphalt yard;
Silently we went round and round,
  And no man spoke a word.

Silently we went round and round,
  And through each hollow mind   440
The Memory of dreadful things
  Rushed like a dreadful wind,
And Horror stalked before each man,
  And Terror crept behind.

The warders strutted up and down,   445
  And kept their herd of brutes;
Their uniforms were spick and span,
  And they wore their Sunday suits,

434. **arrows.** The garb of English convicts was marked
with arrows.

But we knew the work they had been at,
  By the quicklime on their boots.   450

For where a grave had opened wide,
  There was no grave at all —
Only a stretch of mud and sand
  By the hideous prison-wall,
And a little heap of burning lime,   455
  That the man should have his pall.

For he has a pall, this wretched man,
  Such as few men can claim;
Deep down below a prison-yard,
  Naked for greater shame,   460
He lies, with fetters on each foot,
  Wrapt in a sheet of flame!

And all the while the burning lime
  Eats flesh and bone away —
It eats the brittle bone by night,   465
  And the soft flesh by day;
It eats the flesh and bone by turns,
  But it eats the heart alway.

For three long years they will not sow
  Or root or seedling there;   470
For three long years the unblessed spot
  Will sterile be and bare,
And look upon the wondering sky
  With unreproachful stare.

They think a murderer's heart would taint
  Each simple seed they sow.   476
It is not true! God's kindly earth
  Is kindlier than men know,
And the red rose would but blow more red,
  The white rose whiter blow.   480

Out of his mouth a red, red rose!
  Out of his heart a white!
For who can say by what strange way,
  Christ brings His will to light,
Since the barren staff the pilgrim bore   485
  Bloomed in the great Pope's sight?

But neither milk-white rose nor red
  May bloom in prison air —
The shard, the pebble, and the flint,
  Are what they give us there;   490
For flowers have been known to heal
  A common man's despair.

So never will wine-red rose or white,
  Petal by petal, fall

456. **pall,** the cloth thrown over a coffin. 485-86. **barren
. . . sight,** a reference to the old German legend of Tannhäuser, which Wagner made the basis for an opera. Tannhäuser, guilty of heinous sin, besought Pope Urban IV (1261-
64) for forgiveness; the pope declared that pardon was as
impossible as for roses to bloom on the pilgrim's staff; after
Tannhäuser left, the staff burst into bloom. Compare Swinburne's *Laus Veneris*, p. 674, and *Ave Atque Vale*, line 157
and note, p. 702, and line 166 and note, p. 702.

On that stretch of mud and sand that lies 495
   By the hideous prison-wall,
To tell the men who tramp the yard
   That God's Son died for all.

Yet though the hideous prison-wall
   Still hems him round and round,   500
And a spirit may not walk by night
   That is with fetters bound,
And a spirit may but weep that lies
   In such unholy ground,

He is at peace — this wretched man —   505
   At peace, or will be soon;
There is no thing to make him mad,
   Nor does Terror walk at noon,
For the lampless Earth in which he lies
   Has neither Sun nor Moon.   510

They hanged him as a beast is hanged;
   They did not even toll
A requiem that might have brought
   Rest to his startled soul,
But hurriedly they took him out,   515
   And hid him in a hole.

They stripped him of his canvas clothes,
   And gave him to the flies;
They mocked the swollen purple throat,
   And the stark and staring eyes;   520
And with laughter loud they heaped the
     shroud
   In which their convict lies.

The chaplain would not kneel to pray
   By his dishonored grave,
Nor mark it with that blessed Cross   525
   That Christ for sinners gave,
Because the man was one of those
   Whom Christ came down to save.

Yet all is well; he has but passed
   To Life's appointed bourne;   530
And alien tears will fill for him
   Pity's long-broken urn,
For his mourners will be outcast men,
   And outcasts always mourn.

5

I know not whether laws be right,   535
   Or whether laws be wrong;
All that we know who lie in jail
   Is that the wall is strong;
And that each day is like a year,
   A year whose days are long.   540

But this I know, that every law
   That men have made for man,
Since first man took his brother's life,
   And the sad world began,

But straws the wheat and saves the chaff 545
   With a most evil fan.

This too I know — and wise it were
   If each could know the same —
That every prison that men build
   Is built with bricks of shame,   550
And bound with bars lest Christ should see
   How men their brothers maim.

With bars they blur the gracious moon,
   And blind the goodly sun;
And they do well to hide their hell,   555
   For in it things are done
That Son of God nor son of Man
   Ever should look upon!

The vilest deeds like poison weeds
   Bloom well in prison-air;   560
It is only what is good in man
   That wastes and withers there.
Pale Anguish keeps the heavy gate,
   And the warder is Despair.

For they starve the little frightened child 565
   Till it weeps both night and day;
And they scourge the weak, and flog the fool,
   And gibe the old and gray,
And some grow mad, and all grow bad,
   And none a word may say.   570

Each narrow cell in which we dwell
   Is a foul and dark latrine,
And the fetid breath of living Death
   Chokes up each grated screen,
And all, but Lust, is turned to dust   575
   In Humanity's machine.

The brackish water that we drink
   Creeps with a loathsome slime,
And the bitter bread they weigh in scales
   Is full of chalk and lime,   580
And Sleep will not lie down, but walks
   Wild-eyed, and cries to Time.

But though lean Hunger and green Thirst
   Like asp and adder fight,
We have little care of prison fare,   585
   For what chills and kills outright
Is that every stone one lifts by day
   Becomes one's heart at night.

With midnight always in one's heart,
   And twilight in one's cell,   590
We turn the crank, or tear the rope,
   Each in his separate hell,
And the silence is more awful far
   Than the sound of a brazen bell.

545. **straws**, throws away.

And never a human voice comes near 595
  To speak a gentle word;
And the eye that watches through the door
  Is pitiless and hard;
And by all forgot, we rot and rot,
  With soul and body marred. 600

And thus we rust Life's iron chain,
  Degraded and alone;
And some men curse, and some men weep,
  And some men make no moan;
But God's eternal laws are kind 605
  And break the heart of stone.

And every human heart that breaks,
  In prison-cell or yard,
Is as that broken box that gave
  Its treasure to the Lord, 610
And filled the unclean leper's house
  With the scent of costliest nard.

Ah! happy they whose hearts can break
  And peace of pardon win!
How else may man make straight his plan 615
  And cleanse his soul from sin?
How else but through a broken heart
  May Lord Christ enter in?

And he of the swollen purple throat,
  And the stark and staring eyes, 620
Waits for the holy hands that took
  The Thief to Paradise;
And a broken and a contrite heart
  The Lord will not despise.

The man in red who reads the law 625
  Gave him three weeks of life,
Three little weeks in which to heal
  His soul of his soul's strife,
And cleanse from every blot of blood
  The hand that held the knife. 630

And with tears of blood he cleansed the hand,
  The hand that held the steel—
For only blood can wipe out blood,
  And only tears can heal—
And the crimson stain that was of Cain 635
  Became Christ's snow-white seal.

6

In Reading gaol by Reading town
  There is a pit of shame,
And in it lies a wretched man
  Eaten by teeth of flame, 640
In a burning winding-sheet he lies,
  And his grave has got no name.

And there, till Christ call forth the dead,
  In silence let him lie.
No need to waste the foolish tear, 645
  Or heave a windy sigh;
The man had killed the thing he loved,
  And so he had to die.

And all men kill the thing they love,
  By all let this be heard, 650
Some do it with a bitter look,
  Some with a flattering word,
The coward does it with a kiss,
  The brave man with a sword!

(1896; 1898)

WILLIAM SHARP ("Fiona Macleod")*
(1855-1905)

THE LAST ABORIGINAL

I see him sit, wild-eyed, alone,
  Amidst gaunt, spectral, moonlit gums;
He waits for death: not once a moan
  From out his rigid fixed lips comes;
His lank hair falls adown a face 5
  Haggard as any wave-worn stone,
And in his eyes I dimly trace
  The memory of a vanished race.

The lofty ancient gum-trees stand,
  Each gray and ghostly in the moon, 10
The giants of an old strange land
  That was exultant in its noon
When all our Europe was o'erturned
  With deluge and with shifting sand,
With earthquakes that the hills inurned 15
And central fires that fused and burned.

The moon moves slowly through the vast
  And solemn skies; the night is still,

609-12. **box . . . nard.** See *Mark,* 14:3-9. While Christ was dining with Simon the leper, a woman came with an alabaster box, broke it open, and poured the contents—the precious ointment, nard—over Christ's head. 621-22. **holy . . . Paradise.** See *Luke,* 23:39-43. Christ said to the repentant thief on the cross: "Today shalt thou be with me in Paradise." 623-24. **broken . . . despise.** From *Psalms,* 51:17.—"A broken and a contrite heart, O God, thou wilt not despise." 625. **man in red,** the judge who passed sentence of death upon the prisoner. Cf. Carlyle's *Sartor Resartus,* I, 9—"Has not your Red hanging-individual a horsehair wig, squirrel skins, and a plush gown; whereby all mortals know that he is a JUDGE?" 635-36. **stain . . . seal.** See *Isaiah,* 1:18. —"Come now, and let us reason together, saith the Lord; though your sins be as scarlet, they shall be as white as snow; though they be red like crimson, they shall be as wool."

*"Fiona Macleod" is the pseudonym which Sharp adopted after 1894 to distinguish his more romantic poetry from that written under his own name, which had preceded. The name is feminine; *Fiona* is the diminutive of *Fionnaghal,* meaning *a fair maid,* and had been borne by the daughter of a Highland clergyman whom Sharp knew.
The Last Aboriginal. This poem is connected with Sharp's voyage to Australia in 1876. This and the following three poems were signed "William Sharp."
11-16. **The giants . . . burned.** Geologists regard Australia as the earliest formed of the continents and the least affected by pre-historic disturbances.

Save when a warrigal springs past
   With dismal howl, or when the shrill   20
Scream of a parrot rings which feels
   A twining serpent's fangs fixed fast,
Or when a gray opossum squeals—
   Or long iguana, as it steals

From bole to bole, disturbs the leaves.   25
   But hushed and still he sits—who knows
That all is o'er for him who weaves
   With inner speech, malign, morose,
A curse upon the whites who came
   And gathered up his race like sheaves   30
Of thin wheat, fit but for the flame—
Who shot or spurned them without shame.

He knows he shall not see again
   The creeks whereby the lyre-birds sing;
He shall no more upon the plain,   35
   Sun-scorched, and void of water-spring,
Watch the dark cassowaries sweep
   In startled flight, or, with spear lain
In ready poise, glide, twist, and creep
Where the brown kangaroo doth leap.   40

No more in silent dawns he'll wait
   By still lagoons, and mark the flight
Of black swans near; no more elate
   Whirl high the boomerang aright
Upon some foe. He knows that now   45
   He too must share his race's night—
He scarce can know the white man's plow
Will one day pass above his brow.

Last remnant of the Austral race,
   He sits and stares, with failing breath;   50
The shadow deepens on his face,
   For 'midst the spectral gums waits death:
A dingo's sudden howl swells near—
   He stares once with a startled gaze,
As half in wonder, half in fear,   55
Then sinks back on his unknown bier.
                              (1884)

HIGH NOON AT MIDSUMMER ON THE CAMPAGNA

High noon,
And from the purple-veiléd hills
To where Rome lies in azure mist,
Scarce any breath of wind
Upon this vast and solitary waste,   5

These leagues of sunscorched grass
Where i' the dawn the scrambling goats main-
   tain
A hardy feast,
And where, when the warm yellow moonlight
   floods the flats,
Gaunt laggard sheep browse spectrally for
   hours   10
While not less gaunt and spectral shepherds
   stand
Brooding, or with hollow vacant eyes
Stare down the long perspectives of the dusk.
Now not a breath:
No sound;   15
No living thing,
Save where the beetle jars his crackling shards,
Or where the hoarse cicala fills
The heavy heated hour with palpitant whirr.
Yet hark!   20
Comes not a low deep whisper from the
   ground,
A sigh as though the immemorial past
Breathed here a long, slow, breath?
Hushed nations sleep below; lost empires here
Are dust; and deeper still,   25
Dim shadowy peoples are the mold that
   warms
The roots of every flower that blooms and
   blows:
Even as we, too, bloom and fade,
Who are so fain
To be as the Night that dies not, but forever
Weaves her immortal web of starry fires;   31
To be as Time itself,
Time, whose vast holocausts
Lie here, deep buried from the ken of men,
Here, where no breath of wind   35
Ruffles the brooding heat,
The breathless blazing heat
Of Noon.   (1891)

THE WHITE PEACOCK

Here where the sunlight
Floodeth the garden,
Where the pomegranate
Reareth its glory
Of gorgeous blossom;   5
Where the oleanders
Dream through the noontides;
And, like surf o' the sea
Round cliffs of basalt,
The thick magnolias   10
In billowy masses
Front the somber green of the ilexes;
Here where the heat lies
Pale blue in the hollows,

---

19. **warrigal**, the Australian wild dog.   24. **iguana**, a
large lizard.   25. **bole**, tree-trunk.   49 **Austral race**, Australian aborigines, steadily diminishing in number.   53.
dingo, the Australian wild dog.
   High Noon at Midsummer on the Campagna. The Campagna is the plain surrounding Rome; see Browning's *Two
in the Campagna,* p. 241.

The White Peacock. 12. **ilexes**, holly-trees.

Where blue are the shadows 15
On the fronds of the cactus,
Where pale blue the gleaming
Of fir and cypress,
With the cones upon them
Amber or glowing 20
With virgin gold;
Here where the honey-flower
Makes the heat fragrant,
As though from the gardens
Of Gulistan, 25
Where the bulbul singeth
Through a mist of roses
A breath were borne;
Here where the dream-flowers
The cream-white poppies 30
Silently waver,
And where the Sirocco,
Faint in the hollows,
Foldeth his soft white wings in the sunlight,
And lieth sleeping 35
Deep in the heart of
A sea of white violets —
Here, as the breath, as the soul of this beauty
Moveth in silence, and dreamlike, and slowly,
White as a snow-drift in mountain valleys 40
When softly upon it the gold light lingers,
White as the foam o' the sea that is driven
O'er billows of azure agleam with sun-yellow,
Cream-white and soft as the breasts of a girl,
Moves the White Peacock, as though through
　　the noontide 45
A dream of the moonlight were real for a
　　moment.
Dim on the beautiful fan that he spreadeth,
Foldeth and spreadeth abroad in the sunlight,
Dim on the cream-white are blue adumbra-
　　tions,
Shadows so pale in their delicate blueness 50
That visions they seem as of vanishing violets,
The fragrant white violets veined with azure,
Pale, pale as the breath of blue smoke in far
　　woodlands.
Here, as the breath, as the soul of this beauty,
White as a cloud through the heats of the
　　noontide, 55
Moves the White Peacock. (1891)

ON A NIGHTINGALE IN APRIL

The yellow moon is a dancing phantom
　　Down secret ways of the flowing shade;
And the waveless stream has a murmuring
　　whisper
　　　Where the alders wave.

Not a breath, not a sigh, save the slow
　　stream's whisper; 5
　　Only the moon is a dancing blade
That leads a host of the Crescent warriors
　　　To a phantom raid.

Out of the lands of Faerie a summons,
　　A long strange cry that thrills through the
　　　glade — 10
The gray-green glooms of the elm are stirring,
　　　Newly afraid.

Last heard, white music, under the olives
　　Where once Theocritus sang and played —
Thy Thracian song is the old new wonder —
　　　O moon-white maid! 16

THE WHITE PEACE

It lies not on the sunlit hill
　　Nor on the sunlit plain;
Nor ever on any running stream
　　Nor on the unclouded main —

But sometimes, through the Soul of Man, 5
　　Slow moving o'er his pain,
The moonlight of a perfect peace
　　Floods heart and brain. (1894)

SHULE, SHULE, SHULE, AGRAH!

His face was glad as dawn to me,
His breath was sweet as dusk to me,
His eyes were burning flames to me,
　　Shule, shule, shule, agrah!

The broad noon-day was night to me, 5
The full-moon night was dark to me,
The stars whirled and the poles span
The hour that God took him far from me.

Perhaps he dreams in heaven now,
Perhaps he doth in worship bow, 10
A white flame round his foam-white brow,
　　Shule, shule, shule, agrah!

I laugh to think of him like this,
Who once found all his joy and bliss
Against my heart, against my kiss, 15
　　Shule, shule, shule, agrah!

Star of my joy, art still the same
Now thou hast gotten a new name?

24-25. gardens Of Gulistan. Gulistan is a town in British Afghanistan; but Sharp associated the term with the
Gulistan, or *Rose-Garden*, a collection of tales and aphorisms
made by the Persian poet Sadi in 1258. **26. bulbul**, the
Persian nightingale. **32. Sirocco**, a hot, dry wind from the
desert.

7. Crescent warriors, Turks. **14. Theocritus**, the third-
century pastoral poet of Sicily. **15. Thracian song.** According to Greek myth, the nightingale is the metamorphosed
form of Philomela, whose sad ravishing occurred in Thrace.
See Arnold's *Philomela*, p. 486, and Swinburne's *Itylus*, p. 685.
The White Peace. This and following poems of Sharp were
signed "Fiona Macleod."
Shule, Shule, Shule, Agrah! The title means *Move, Move,
Move to Me, My Heart* (Sharp's translation of the Gælic).

Pulse of my heart, my Blood, my Flame,
   Shule, shule, shule, agrah!   20
                (1896)

THE ROSE OF FLAME

Oh, fair immaculate rose of the world, rose of
   my dream, my Rose!
Beyond the ultimate gates of dream I have
   heard thy mystical call:
It is where the rainbow of hope suspends and
   the river of rapture flows —
And the cool sweet dews from the wells of
   peace forever fall.

And all my heart is aflame because of the
   rapture and peace,   5
And I dream, in my waking dreams and deep
   in the dreams of sleep,
Till the high sweet wonderful call that shall
   be the call of release
Shall ring in my ears as I sink from gulf to
   gulf and from deep to deep —

Sink deep, sink deep beyond the ultimate
   dreams of all desire —
Beyond the uttermost limit of all that the
   craving spirit knows;   10
Then, then, oh, then I shall be as the inner
   flame of thy fire,
O fair immaculate rose of the world, rose of
   my dream, my Rose!   (1896)

THE WASHER OF THE FORD

There is a lonely stream in a lone dim land;
It hath white dust for shore it has, white
   bones bestrew the strand:
The only thing that liveth there is a naked
   leaping sword;
But I, who a seer am, have seen the whirling
   hand
     Of the Washer of the Ford.   5

A shadowy shape of cloud and mist, of gloom
   and dusk, she stands,
     The Washer of the Ford.
She laughs, at times, and strews the dust
   through the hollow of her hands.
She counts the sins of all men there, and slays
   the red-stained horde —
The ghosts of all the sins of men must know
   the whirling sword   10
     Of the Washer of the Ford.

She stoops and laughs when in the dust she
   sees a writhing limb:

The Rose of Flame. Cf. Yeats' *The Rose of the World*, p. 871.

"Go back into the ford," she says, "and
   hither and thither swim;
Then I shall wash you white as snow, and
   shall take you by the hand,
And slay you there in silence with this my
   whirling brand,   15
And trample you into the dust of this white,
   windless sand" —
     This is the laughing word
     Of the Washer of the Ford
     Along that silent strand.   (1896)

THE VALLEY OF WHITE POPPIES

Between the gray pastures and the dark
   wood
A valley of white poppies is lit by the low
   moon;
   It is the grave of dreams, a holy rood.

It is quiet there; no wind doth ever fall.
Long, long ago a wind sang once a heart-
   sweet rune.   5
Now the white poppies grow, silent and tall.

A white bird floats there like a drifting leaf;
It feeds upon faint sweet hopes and perishing
   dreams
And the still breath of unremembering grief.

And as a silent leaf the white bird passes, 10
Winnowing the dusk by dim forgetful streams.
I am alone now among the silent grasses.
              (1901)

THE VALLEY OF PALE BLUE FLOWERS

In a hidden valley a pale blue flower grows.
It is so pale that in the moonshine it is dimmer than dim gold,
   And in the starshine paler than the palest
   rose.

It is the flower of dream. Who holds it is
   never old.
It is the flower of forgetfulness — and oblivion
   is youth;   5
   Breathing it, flame is not empty air, dust
   is not cold.

Lift it, and there is no memory of sorrow
   or any ruth;
The gray monotone of the low sky is filled
   with light;
   The dim, terrible, impalpable lie wears the
   raiment of truth.

The Valley of White Poppies. The poppy is the flower of oblivion.
   5. **rune,** a song of magic—from association of the primitive Teutonic runic characters with magic spells and incantations.

I lift it, now, for somewhat in the heart of
    the night   10
Fills me with dread. It may be that, as a
    tiger in his lair,
Memory, crouching, waits to spring into
    the light.

No, I will clasp it close to my heart, over-
    droop with my hair;
I will breathe thy frail faint breath, O pale
    blue flower,
And then . . . and then . . . nothing shall
    take me unaware!   15

Nothing: no thought; no fear; only the
    invisible power
Of the vast deeps of night, wherein down a
    shadowy stair
My soul slowly, slowly, slowly, will sink to
    its ultimate hour.   (1901)

THE VALLEY OF SILENCE

In the secret Valley of Silence
    No breath doth fall;
No wind stirs in the branches;
    No bird doth call.
As on a white wall   5
    A breathless lizard is still,
So silence lies in the valley
    Breathlessly still.

In the dusk-grown heart of the valley
    An altar rises white.   10
No rapt priest bends in awe
    Before its silent light;
But sometimes a flight
    Of breathless words of prayer
White-winged enclose the altar,   15
    Eddies of prayer.   (1901)

DIM FACE OF BEAUTY

Dim face of Beauty haunting all the world,
Fair face of Beauty all too fair to see,
Where the lost stars adown the heavens are
    hurled,
    There, there alone for thee
    May white peace be.   5

For here where all the dreams of men are
    whirled
Like sear torn leaves of autumn to and fro,
There is no place for thee in all the world,
    Who driftest as a star,
    Beyond, afar.   10

Beauty, sad face of Beauty, Mystery, Wonder,
What are these dreams to foolish babbling
    men? —

Who cry with little noises 'neath the thunder
    Of ages ground to sand,
    To a little sand.   15
               (1907)

VALE, AMOR!

We do not know this thing
    By the spoken word;
It is as though in a dim wood
    One heard a bird
    Suddenly sing —   5
Then in the twinkling of an eye
A shadow glooms the earth and sky,
And we stand silent, startled, in a changed
    mood.

It is but a little thing
    The leaping sword,   10
When in the startled silence of changed mood
    It comes as when a bird
    Doth suddenly sing.
But thrust of sword or agony of soul
Are alike swift and terrible and strong,   15
And no foot stirs the dead leaves of that
    silent wood.
               (1907)

THE WEAVER OF SNOW

In Polar noons when the moonshine glimmers,
    And the frost-fans whirl,
And whiter than moonlight the ice-flowers
    grow,
And the lunar rainbow quivers and shimmers,
And the Silent Laughers dance to and fro,   5
    A stooping girl
    As pale as pearl
Gathers the frost-flowers where they blow:
And the fleet-foot fairies smile, for they know
    The Weaver of Snow.   10

And she climbs at last to a berg set free,
    That drifteth slow;
And she sails to the edge of the world we
    see,
And waits till the wings of the north wind
    lean
Like an eagle's wings o'er a lochan of green,
    And the pale stars glow   16
    On berg and floe . . .
Then down on our world with a wild laugh
    of glee
She empties her lamp full of shimmer and
    sheen.
And that is the way in a dream I have seen   20
The Weaver of Snow.
               (1907)

Vale, Amor! The title means *Farewell, Love.*
The Weaver of Snow. 15. **lochan**, pond.

DREAMS WITHIN DREAMS

I have gone out and seen the lands of Faery
  And have found sorrow and peace and
    beauty there,
And have not known one from the other, but
    found each
  Lovely and gracious alike, delicate and fair.

"They are children of one mother, she that is
    called Longing,   5
  Desire, Love," one told me; and another,
    "Her secret name
Is Wisdom"; and another, "They are not
    three but one";
  And another, "Touch them not, seek them
    not; they are wind and flame."

I have come back from the hidden, silent
    lands of Faery
  And have forgotten the music of its ancient
    streams;   10
And now flame and wind and the long, gray,
    wandering wave
  And beauty and peace and sorrow are
    dreams within dreams.   (1907)

LIONEL JOHNSON (1867-1902)

BY THE STATUE OF KING CHARLES
AT CHARING CROSS

  Somber and rich, the skies;
  Great glooms, and starry plains.
  Gently the night wind sighs;
  Else a vast silence reigns.

  The splendid silence clings   5
  Around me; and around
  The saddest of all kings
  Crowned, and again discrowned.

  Comely and calm, he rides
  Hard by his own Whitehall.   10
  Only the night wind glides;
  No crowds, nor rebels, brawl.

  Gone too, his Court; and yet,
  The stars his courtiers are —
  Stars in their stations set,   15
  And every wandering star.

  Alone he rides, alone,
  The fair and fatal king;

Dark night is all his own,
That strange and solemn thing.   20

Which are more full of fate —
The stars, or those sad eyes?
Which are more still and great —
Those brows, or the skies?

Although his whole heart yearn   25
In passionate tragedy,
Never was face so stern
With sweet austerity.

Vanquished in life, his death
By beauty made amends;   30
The passing of his breath
Won his defeated ends.

Brief life, and hapless? Nay;
Through death, life grew sublime.
Speak after sentence? Yea —   35
And to the end of time.

Armored he rides, his head
Bare to the stars of doom;
He triumphs now, the dead,
Beholding London's gloom.   40

Our wearier spirit faints,
Vexed in the world's employ;
His soul was of the saints,
And art to him was joy.

King, tried in fires of woe!   45
Men hunger for thy grace;
And through the night I go,
Loving thy mournful face.

Yet, when the city sleeps,
When all the cries are still,   50
The stars and heavenly deeps
Work out a perfect will.

THE LAST MUSIC

Calmly, breathe calmly all your music, maids!
Breathe a calm music over my dead queen.
All your lives long, you have nor heard, nor
    seen,
Fairer than she, whose hair in somber braids
  With beauty overshades   5
Her brow, broad and serene.

By the Statue of King Charles at Charing Cross. At Charing Cross, close to Trafalgar Square in London, stands an equestrian statue of King Charles I, who was beheaded by the Parliamentary party at the close of the Civil War, 1649.
  10. Whitehall, the royal palace near Charing Cross; now only the banquet-hall is left standing.

31-32. passing . . . ends. Popular feeling was so stirred by the dignity and patience with which Charles met his end that the power of Parliament was shaken and the restoration of the monarchy was soon assured. **35. Speak after sentence.** After Charles had been sentenced to death, he asked permission to speak; but John Bradshaw, the president of the court, refused the request because Charles had not recognized the right of the court to try him. **44. art . . . joy.** In his palaces at Richmond and Whitehall, Charles made one of the finest collections of paintings in Europe.

Surely she hath lain so an hundred years;
Peace is upon her, old as the world's heart.
Breathe gently, music! Music done, depart,
And leave me in her presence to my tears, 10
　　With music in mine ears;
　　For sorrow hath its art.

Music, more music, sad and slow! she lies
Dead — and more beautiful than early morn.
Discrowned am I, and of her looks forlorn; 15
Alone, vain memories immortalize
　　The way of her soft eyes,
　　Her musical voice low-borne.

The balm of gracious death now laps her
　　round,　　　　　　　　　　　　　　19
As once life gave her grace beyond her peers.
Strange! that I loved this lady of the spheres,
To sleep by her at last in common ground,
　　When kindly sleep hath bound
　　Mine eyes, and sealed mine ears.

Maidens! make a low music; merely make 25
Silence a melody, no more. This day,
She travels down a pale and lonely way;
Now, for a gentle comfort, let her take
　　Such music, for her sake,
　　As mourning love can play.　　　　　30

Holy my queen lies in the arms of death;
Music moves over her still face, and I
Lean breathing love over her. She will lie
In earth thus calmly, under the wind's
　　breath —
　　The twilight wind, that saith:　　　35
　　Rest! worthy found, to die.　　(1889)

THE CHURCH OF A DREAM

Sadly the dead leaves rustle in the whistling
　　wind,
Around the weather-worn, gray church, low
　　down the vale;
The Saints in golden vesture shake before the
　　gale;
The glorious windows shake, where still they
　　dwell enshrined;
Old Saints by long dead, shriveled hands, long
　　since designed:　　　　　　　　　　5
There still, although the world autumnal be,
　　and pale,
Still in their golden vesture the old saints
　　prevail;
Alone with Christ, desolate else, left by man-
　　kind.
Only one ancient Priest offers the Sacrifice,
Murmuring holy Latin immemorial:　　　10

The Last Music. 15. **forlorn**, robbed.

Swaying with tremulous hands the old censer
　　full of spice,
In gray, sweet incense clouds; blue, sweet
　　clouds mystical:
To him, in place of men, for he is old, suffice
Melancholy remembrances and vesperal.

　　　　　　　　　　　　　　　(1890)

TO MORFYDD

A voice on the winds,
A voice by the waters,
　　Wanders and cries:
Oh! what are the winds?
And what are the waters?　　　　　5
Mine are your eyes!

Western the winds are,
And western the waters,
　　Where the light lies:
Oh! what are the winds?　　　　　10
And what are the waters?
Mine are your eyes!

Cold, cold, grow the winds,
And wild grow the waters,
　　Where the sun dies:　　　　　　15
Oh! what are the winds?
And what are the waters?
Mine are your eyes!

And down the night winds,
And down the night waters,　　　　20
　　The music flies:
Oh! what are the winds?
And what are the waters?
Cold be the winds,
And wild be the waters,　　　　　25
　　So mine be your eyes!

　　　　　　　　　　　　　　　(1891)

LONDON TOWN

Let others chaunt a country praise,
Fair river walks and meadow ways;
Dearer to me my sounding days
　　In *London Town;*
To me the tumult of the street　　　5
Is no less music than the sweet
Surge of the wind among the wheat,
　　By dale or down.

Three names mine heart with rapture hails,
With homage: *Ireland, Cornwall, Wales —* 10

The Church of a Dream. 14. **vesperal**, pertaining to the
evening.
To Morfydd. Morfydd was an Irish girl to whom a number
of Johnson's lyrics are addressed.
London Town. 10. **Ireland . . . Wales.** Johnson made
vacation tours in all of these regions; to their influence he
attributed a Celtic strain in his poetry.

Lands of lone moor, and mountain gales,
   And stormy coast;
Yet *London's* voice upon the air
Pleads at mine heart, and enters there;
Sometimes I well-nigh love and care   15
   For *London* most.

Listen upon the ancient hills —
All silence! save the lark, who trills
Through sunlight, save the rippling rills;
   There peace may be.   20
But listen to great *London!* loud,
As thunder from the purple cloud,
Comes the deep thunder of the crowd,
   And heartens me.

O gray, O gloomy skies! What then?   25
Here is a marvelous world of men;
More wonderful than *Rome* was, when
   The world was *Rome!*
See the great stream of life flow by!
Here thronging myriads laugh and sigh,   30
Here rise and fall, here live and die —
   In this vast home.

In long array they march toward death,
Armies, with proud or piteous breath;
Forward! the spirit in them saith,   35
   Spirit of life.
Here the triumphant trumpets blow;
Here mourning music sorrows low;
Victors and vanquished, still they go
   Forward in strife.   40

Who will not heed so great a sight?
Greater than marshaled stars of night,
That move to music and with light —
   For these are men!
These move to music of the soul,   45
Passions, that madden or control;
These hunger for a distant goal,
   Seen now and then.

Is mine too tragical a strain,
Chaunting a burden full of pain,   50
And labor, that seems all in vain?
   I sing but truth.
Still, many a merry pleasure yet,
To many a merry measure set,
Is ours, who need not to forget   55
   Summer and youth.

Do *London* birds forget to sing?
Do *London* trees refuse the spring?
Is *London* May no pleasant thing?
   Let country fields,   60
To milking maid and shepherd boy,
Give flowers, and song, and bright employ;

42-43. **stars . . . music.** The ancients believed that the
stars made music as they revolved in their spheres.

Her children also can enjoy,
   What *London* yields.

Gleaming with sunlight, each soft lawn   65
Lies fragrant beneath dew of dawn;
The spires and towers rise, far withdrawn,
   Through golden mist.
At sunset, linger beside *Thames;*
See now, what radiant lights and flames!   70
That ruby burns, that purple shames
   The amethyst.

Winter was long and dark and cold;
Chill rains! grim fogs, black fold on fold,
Rough street, and square, and river rolled!   75
   Ah, let it be;
Winter is gone! Soon comes July,
With wafts from hayfields by-and-by,
While in the dingiest courts you spy
   Flowers fair to see.   80

Take heart of grace, and let each hour
Break gently into bloom and flower;
Winter and sorrow have no power
   To blight all bloom.
One day, perchance, the sun will see   85
London's entire felicity,
And all her loyal children be
   Clear of all gloom.

A dream? Dreams often dreamed come true;
Our world would seem a world made new   90
To those, beneath the churchyard yew
   Laid long ago!
When we beneath like shadows bide,
Fair *London,* throned upon *Thames'* side,
May be our children's children's pride;   95
   And we shall know.

                       (1891)

CADGWITH

I

Man is a shadow's dream!
Opulent Pindar saith;
Yet man may win a gleam
Of glory, before death.

Saith golden Shakespeare: *Man*   5
Is a dream's shadow! Yet,
Though death do all death can,
His soul toward life is set.

91. **yew,** a tree, symbolic of sorrow, often planted in
graveyards.
  Cadgwith. Cadgwith is a fishing village in Cornwall. The
poem is dedicated to Lawrence Binyon, a contemporary
British poet.
  1-2. **Man . . . saith.** From Pindar's eighth Pythian Ode,
lines 95-96: "Man is but a dream of a shadow." Pindar
(522-443 B.C.) was a Greek writer of choral odes famous for
their elaborate harmonies. 5-6. **Man . . . shadow.** From
Hamlet, II, 2, 265.—"A dream itself is but a shadow."

I, living with delight
This rich autumnal day, 10
Mark the gulls' curving flight
Across the black-girt bay.

And the sea's working men,
The fisher-folk, I mark
Haul down their boats, and then 15
Launch for the deep sea dark.

Far out the strange ships go,
Their broad sails flashing red
As flame, or white as snow:
The ships, as David said. 20

Winds rush and waters roll;
Their strength, their beauty, brings
Into mine heart the whole
Magnificence of things:

That men are counted worth 25
A part upon this sea,
A part upon this earth,
Exalts and heartens me.

Ah, Glaucus, soul of man!
Encrusted by each tide, 30
That, since the seas began,
Hath surged against thy side:

Encumbering thee with weed,
And tangle of the wave!
Yet canst thou rise at need, 35
And thy strong beauty save!

Tides of the world in vain
Desire to vanquish thee;
Prostrate, thou canst again
Rise, lord of earth and sea! 40

Rise, lord of sea and earth,
And winds, and starry night.
Thine is the greater birth
And origin of light.

2

My windows open to the autumn night,
In vain I watched for sleep to visit me;
How should sleep dull mine ears, and dim my
sight,
Who saw the stars, and listened to the sea?

Ah, how the City of our God is fair! 5
If, without sea, and starless though it be,
For joy of the majestic beauty there,
Men shall not miss the stars nor mourn the
sea.

3

Mary Star of the sea!
Look on this little place;
Bless the kind fisher race,
Mary Star of the sea!

Send harvest from the deep, 5
Mary Star of the Sea!
Mary Star of the Sea!
Let not these women weep.

Mary Star of the Sea!
Give wife and mother joy 10
In husband and in boy,
Mary Star of the Sea!

With intercession save,
Mary Star of the Sea!
Mary Star of the Sea! 15
These children of the wave.

Mary Star of the Sea!
Pour peace upon the wild
Waves, make their murmurs mild,
Mary Star of the Sea! 20

Now in thy mercy pray,
Mary Star of the Sea!
Mary Star of the Sea!
For sailors far away.

Mary Star of the Sea! 25
Now be thy great prayers said
For all poor seamen dead,
Mary Star of the Sea! (1892)

THE PRECEPT OF SILENCE

I know you: solitary griefs,
Desolate passions, aching hours!
I know you: tremulous beliefs,
Agonized hopes, and ashen flowers!

The winds are sometimes sad to me, 5
The starry spaces, full of fear;
Mine is the sorrow on the sea,
And mine the sigh of places drear.

Some players upon plaintive strings
Publish their wistfulness abroad; 10
I have not spoken of these things,
Save to one man, and unto God.

(1893)

20. **David said.** See *Psalms*, 104: 24-26.—"O Lord, how
manifold are thy works! in wisdom hast thou made them all:
the earth is full of thy riches. So is this great and wide sea,
wherein are things creeping innumerable, both small and
great beasts. There go the ships: there is that leviathan,
whom thou hast made to play therein." Cf. *Psalms*, 107:
23-30. 29. **Glaucus**, in Greek mythology a fisherman and
diver who leaped into the sea and rose from it changed into
a sea-god; see Ovid, *Metamorphoses*, 13:906.
Section 2. See *Revelation*, 21: 23—"And the city had no
need of the sun, neither of the moon, to shine in it; for the
glory of God did lighten it, and the Lamb is the light thereof."

THE DARK ANGEL

Dark Angel, with thine aching lust
To rid the world of penitence;
Malicious Angel, who still dost
My soul such subtile violence!

Because of thee, no thought, no thing,   5
Abides for me undesecrate:
Dark Angel, ever on the wing,
Who never reachest me too late!

When music sounds, then changest thou
Its silvery to a sultry fire;   10
Nor will thine envious heart allow
Delight untortured by desire.

Through thee, the gracious Muses turn
To Furies, O mine Enemy!
And all the things of beauty burn   15
With flames of evil ecstasy.

Because of thee, the land of dreams
Becomes a gathering place of fears,
Until tormented slumber seems
One vehemence of useless tears.   20

When sunlight glows upon the flowers,
Or ripples down the dancing sea,
Thou, with thy troop of passionate powers,
Beleaguerest, bewilderest, me.

Within the breath of autumn woods,   25
Within the wintry silences,
Thy venomous spirit stirs and broods,
O Master of impieties!

The ardor of red flame is thine,
And thine the steely soul of ice;   30
Thou poisonest the fair design
Of nature, with unfair device.

Apples of ashes, golden bright;
Waters of bitterness, how sweet!
O banquet of a foul delight,   35
Prepared by thee, dark Paraclete!

Thou art the whisper in the gloom,
The hinting tone, the haunting laugh;
Thou art the adorner of my tomb,
The minstrel of mine epitaph.   40

I fight thee, in the Holy Name!
Yet, what thou dost, is what God saith;

Tempter! should I escape thy flame,
Thou wilt have helped my soul from Death —

The second Death, that never dies,   45
That cannot die, when time is dead;
Live Death, wherein the lost soul cries,
Eternally uncomforted.

Dark Angel, with thine aching lust!
Of two defeats, of two despairs: 50
Less dread, a change to drifting dust,
Than thine eternity of cares.

Do what thou wilt, thou shalt not so,
Dark Angel! triumph over me:
Lonely, unto the Lone I go;   55
Divine, to the Divinity.   (1893)

THE RED WIND

Red Wind from out the East,
Red Wind of blight and blood!
Ah, when wilt thou have ceased
Thy bitter, stormy flood?

Red Wind from over sea,   5
Scourging our lonely land!
What Angel loosened thee
Out of his iron hand?

Red Wind! whose word of might
Winged thee with wings of flame?   10
O fire of mournful night,
What is thy master's name?

Red Wind! who bade thee burn,
Branding our hearts? Who bade
Thee on and never turn,   15
Till waste our souls were laid?

Red Wind! from out the West
Pour winds of Paradise,
Winds of eternal rest,
That weary souls entice.   20

Wind of the East! Red Wind!
Thou witherest the soft breath
Of Paradise the kind,
Red Wind of burning death!

O Red Wind! hear God's voice;   25
Hear thou, and fall, and cease.
Let Inisfail rejoice
In her Hesperian peace.   (1894)

The Dark Angel. 4. **subtile,** insidious. 13. **Furies,** three avenging deities, attendants of Proserpina, queen of Hades. 36. **Paraclete,** advocate—a term applied by St. John to the Holy Spirit as man's guardian angel, but by Johnson to his dark angel.

The Red Wind. 27. **Inisfail,** Ireland. 28. **Hesperian peace,** that of the Hesperian gardens, situated either beyond the setting sun or beyond the north wind, in perpetual sunshine and happiness. Cf. Tennyson's *Hesperides,* p. 19.

ERNEST DOWSON
(1867-1900)

NUNS OF THE PERPETUAL ADORATION

Calm, sad, secure; behind high convent walls,
　These watch the sacred lamp, these watch
　　and pray
And it is one with them when evening falls,
　And one with them the cold return of
　　day.

These heed not time; their nights and days
　they make　　　　　　　　　　　　5
Into a long, returning rosary,
Whereon their lives are threaded for Christ's
　sake;
　Meekness and vigilance and chastity.

A vowed patrol, in silent companies,
　Life-long they keep before the living
　　Christ.　　　　　　　　　　　　10
In the dim church, their prayers and pen-
　ances
　Are fragrant incense to the Sacrificed.

Outside, the world is wild and passionate;
　Man's weary laughter and his sick de-
　　spair
Entreat at their impenetrable gate;　　15
　They heed no voices in their dream of
　　prayer.

They saw the glory of the world displayed;
　They saw the bitter of it, and the sweet;
They knew the roses of the world should
　fade,
　And be trod under by the hurrying feet.　20

Therefore they rather put away desire,
　And crossed their hands and came to
　　sanctuary
And veiled their heads and put on coarse
　attire:
　Because their comeliness was vanity.

And there they rest; they have serene in-
　sight
　Of the illuminating dawn to be;　　26
Mary's sweet Star dispels for them the night,
　The proper darkness of humanity.

Calm, sad secure; with faces worn and
　mild:
　Surely their choice of vigil is the best?　30
Yea! for our roses fade, the world is wild;
　But there, beside the altar, there, is rest.
　　　　　　　　　　　　　(1891)

VITÆ SUMMA BREVIS SPEM NOS VETAT INCOHARE LONGAM

They are not long, the weeping and the
　laughter,
　Love and desire and hate;
I think they have no portion in us after
　We pass the gate.

They are not long, the days of wine and
　roses;　　　　　　　　　　　　5
　Out of a misty dream
Our path emerges for a while, then closes
　Within a dream.

　　　　　　　　　　　　　(1896)

NON SUM QUALIS ERAM BONÆ SUB REGNO CYNARÆ

Last night, ah, yesternight, betwixt her lips
　and mine
There fell thy shadow, Cynara! thy breath
　was shed
Upon my soul between the kisses and the
　wine;
And I was desolate and sick of an old passion,
　Yea, I was desolated and bowed my
　　head —　　　　　　　　　　　5
I have been faithful to thee, Cynara! in my
　fashion.

All night upon mine heart I felt her warm
　heart beat,
Night-long within mine arms in love and
　sleep she lay;
Surely the kisses of her bought red mouth
　were sweet;
But I was desolate and sick of an old passion,
　When I awoke and found the dawn was
　　gray —　　　　　　　　　　　11
I have been faithful to thee, Cynara! in
　my fashion.

I have forgot much, Cynara! gone with the
　wind,
Flung roses, roses riotously with the throng,
Dancing, to put thy pale, lost lilies out of
　mind;　　　　　　　　　　　　15
But I was desolate and sick of an old passion,
　Yea, all the time, because the dance was
　　long —
I have been faithful to thee, Cynara! in my
　fashion.

Vitæ Summa Brevis Spem Nos Vetat Incohare Longam.
The title means *The Short Span of Life Forbids Us to Encour-
age Prolonged Hope* (Horace, *Odes*, Book 1, Ode 4, line 15).
　Non Sum Qualis Eram Bonæ Sub Regno Cynaræ. The
title means *I Am Not What Once I Was in Kind Cynara's Day*
(Horace, *Odes*, Book 4, Ode 1, lines 3-4). Dowson takes the
name of the lady from Horace, but develops a wholly different
idea.

I cried for madder music and for stronger
   wine,
But when the feast is finished and the lamps
   expire,   20
Then falls thy shadow, Cynara! the night
   is thine;
And I am desolate and sick of an old passion
   Yea, hungry for the lips of my desire —
I have been faithful to thee, Cynara! in my
   fashion.   (1896)

AMOR PROFANUS

Beyond the pale of memory,
In some mysterious dusky grove,
A place of shadows utterly,
Where never coos the turtle-dove,
A world forgotten of the sun,   5
I dreamed we met when day was done,
And marveled at our ancient love.

Met there by chance, long kept apart,
We wandered through the darkling glades;
And that old language of the heart   10
We sought to speak — alas! poor shades!
Over our pallid lips had run
The waters of oblivion,
Which crown all loves of men or maids.

In vain we stammered; from afar   15
Our old desire shone cold and dead.
That time was distant as a star,
When eyes were bright and lips were red.
And still we went with downcast eye
And no delight in being nigh,   20
Poor shadows most uncomforted.

Ah, Lalage! while life is ours,
Hoard not thy beauty rose and white,
But pluck the pretty, fleeting flowers
That deck our little path of light;   25
For all too soon we twain shall tread
The bitter pastures of the dead —
Estranged, sad specters of the night.
        (1896)

YVONNE OF BRITTANY

In your mother's apple orchard,
   Just a year ago, last spring —
Do you remember, Yvonne!

The dear trees lavishing
Rain of their starry blossoms   5
   To make you a coronet?
Do you remember, Yvonne?
   As I remember yet.

In your mother's apple orchard,
   When the world was left behind;   10
You were shy, so shy, Yvonne!
   But your eyes were calm and kind.
We spoke of the apple harvest,
   When the cider press is set,
And such-like trifles, Yvonne!   15
   That doubtless you forget.

In the still, soft Breton twilight,
   We were silent; words were few,
Till your mother came out chiding,
   For the grass was bright with dew.   20
But I know your heart was beating,
   Like a fluttered, frightened dove.
Do you ever remember, Yvonne?
   That first faint flush of love?

In the fullness of midsummer,   25
   When the apple-bloom was shed,
Oh, brave was your surrender,
   Though shy the words you said.
I was so glad, so glad, Yvonne!
   To have led you home at last;   30
Do you ever remember, Yvonne!
   How swiftly the days passed?

In your mother's apple orchard
   It is grown too dark to stray,
There is none to chide you, Yvonne!   35
   You are over-far away.
There is dew on your grave grass, Yvonne!
   But your feet it shall not wet —
No, you never remember, Yvonne!
   And I shall soon forget.   40
        (1896)

YOU WOULD HAVE UNDERSTOOD ME

     Ah, dans ces mornes séjours
     Les jamais sont les toujours
        — Paul Verlaine.

You would have understood me, had you
   waited;
   I could have loved you, dear! as well as
     he —
Had we not been impatient, dear! and fated
   Always to disagree.

Amor Profanus. The title means *Profane Love.* The distinction between sacred and profane love—the spiritual and the physical—is one made by Plato and Spenser. It is the theme of one of Titian's famous paintings.
   22. **Lalage,** a lady who is the subject of Horace's fifth Ode, Book 2. **23-24. Hoard . . . flowers.** Cf. Herrick's *Gather Ye Rosebuds While Ye May* and the *Carpe Diem* of Horace, *Odes,* Book 1, Ode 11.
   Yvonne of Brittany. Brittany is a province in the northwestern part of France, originally a Celtic kingdom.

17. **Breton,** of Brittany.
   You Would Have Understood Me. **Ah . . . toujours,** "In these dreary regions, never is forever." Paul Verlaine was a French lyric poet (1844-96) much admired by Dowson; the quotation is from *Reversibilités.*

What is the use of speech? Silence were fitter, 5
  Lest we should still be wishing things
    unsaid.
Though all the words we ever spake were
  bitter,
    Shall I reproach you dead?

Nay, let this earth, your portion, likewise
  cover
  All the old anger, setting us apart.   10
Always, in all, in truth was I your lover;
    Always, I held your heart.

I have met other women who were tender,
  As you were cold, dear! with a grace as rare.
Think you I turned to them, or made sur-
  render,   15
    I who had found you fair?

Had we been patient, dear! ah, had you
  waited,
  I had fought death for you, better than
    he;
But from the very first, dear! we were fated
    Always to disagree.   20

Late, late, I come to you, now death dis-
  closes
  Love that in life was not to be our part;
On your low lying mound between the roses,
    Sadly I cast my heart.

I would not waken you — nay! this is fitter; 25
  Death and the darkness give you unto me;
Here we who loved so, were so cold and
  bitter,
    Hardly can disagree.   (1896)

BEATA SOLITUDO

What land of Silence
  Where pale stars shine
On apple-blossom
  And dew-drenched vine,
    Is yours and mine?   5

The silent valley
  That we will find,
Where all the voices
  Of humankind
    Are left behind.   10

There all forgetting,
  Forgotten quite,
We will repose us,
  With our delight
    Hid out of sight.   15

Beata Solitudo. The title means *Blessed Solitude.*

The world forsaken,
  And out of mind
Honor and labor,
  We shall not find
    The stars unkind.   20

And men shall travail,
  And laugh and weep;
But we have vistas
  Of gods asleep,
    With dreams as deep.   25

A land of Silence,
  Where pale stars shine
On apple-blossoms
  And dew-drenched vine,
    Be yours and mine!   (1896)   30

GRAY NIGHTS

A while we wandered (thus it is I dream!)
Through a long, sandy track of No Man's
  Land,
Where only poppies grew among the sand,
The which we, plucking, cast with scant
  esteem,
And ever sadlier, into the sad stream,   5
Which followed us, as we went, hand in hand,
Under the estrangéd stars, a road unplanned,
Seeing all things in the shadow of a dream.
And ever sadlier, as the stars expired,
We found the poppies rarer, till thine eyes   10
Grown all my light, to light me were too
  tired,
And at their darkening, that no surmise
Might haunt me of the lost days we desired,
After them all I flung those memories!   (1896)

CHANSON SANS PAROLES

In the deep violet air,
  Not a leaf is stirred;
  There is no sound heard,
But afar, the rare
  Trilled voice of a bird.   5

Is the wood's dim heart,
  And the fragrant pine,
  Incense, and a shrine
Of her coming? Apart,
  I wait for a sign.   10

What the sudden hush said,
  She will hear, and forsake,

Gray Nights. **3. poppies.** The poppy is the flower of
oblivion.
Chanson sans Paroles. The title means *A Song without
Words.* It was frequently given by Mendelssohn (1809-47)
to his compositions.

Swift, for my sake,
Her green, grassy bed —
She will hear and awake!   15

She will hearken and glide,
From her place of deep rest,
Dove-eyed, with the breast
Of a dove, to my side;
The pines bow their crest.   20

I wait for a sign:
The leaves to be waved,
The tall tree-tops laved
In a flood of sunshine,
This world to be saved!   25

In the deep violet air,
Not a leaf is stirred;
There is no sound heard,
But afar, the rare
Trilled voice of a bird.   (1896)

CARTHUSIANS

Through what long heaviness, assayed in
what strange fire,
Have these white monks been brought
into the way of peace,
Despising the world's wisdom and the world's
desire,
Which from the body of this death bring
no release?

Within their austere walls no voices penetrate;   5
A sacred silence only, as of death, obtains;
Nothing finds entry here of loud or passionate;
This quiet is the exceeding profit of their
pains.

From many lands they came, in divers fiery
ways;
Each knew at last the vanity of earthly
joys;   10
And one was crowned with thorns, and one
was crowned with bays,
And each was tired at last of the world's
foolish noise.

It was not theirs with Dominic to preach
God's holy wrath,

They were too stern to bear sweet Francis'
gentle sway;
Theirs was a higher calling and a steeper
path,   15
To dwell alone with Christ, to meditate
and pray.

A cloistered company, they are companionless,
None knoweth here the secret of his
brother's heart:
They are but come together for more loneliness,
Whose bond is solitude and silence all
their part.   20

O beatific life! Who is there shall gainsay,
Your great refusal's victory, your little
loss,
Deserting vanity for the more perfect way,
The sweeter service of the most dolorous
Cross.

Ye shall prevail at last! Surely ye shall
prevail!   25
Your silence and austerity shall win at
last;
Desire and mirth, the world's ephemeral
lights shall fail,
The sweet star of your queen is never
overcast.

We fling up flowers and laugh, we laugh
across the wine;
With wine we dull our souls and careful
strains of art;   30
Our cups are polished skulls round which
the roses twine:
None dares to look at Death who leers
and lurks apart.

Move on, white company, whom that has
not sufficed!
Our viols cease, our wine is death, our
roses fail:
Pray for our heedlessness, O dwellers with
the Christ!   35
Though the world fall apart, surely ye
shall prevail.   (1899)

VILLANELLE OF THE POET'S ROAD

Wine and woman and song,
Three things garnish our way;
Yet is day over long.

Carthusians. The Carthusians are an order of monks
founded by St. Bruno in 1084; they wear white robes, observe
strict discipline, and live as hermits in separate dwellings
within common walls. Cf. Arnold's *Stanzas*, p. 491.
11. **bays,** laurel wreaths emblematic of fame won in the
world before entrance into the monastery. 13. **Dominic,**
founder (1216) of the Dominican order of Black Friars, distinguished for their ability as preachers and theologians.

14. **Francis,** St. Francis of Assisi, founder (1210) of the
Franciscan order of Grey Friars, who vow themselves to the
imitation of Christ in gentleness and poverty.
Villanelle of the Poet's Road. A villanelle is an old French
lyric form characterized by the set repetition of lines; compare
Dobson's *On a Nankin Plate*, p. 776.

Lest we do our youth wrong,
  Gather them while we may: 5
Wine and woman and song.

Three things render us strong,
  Vine leaves, kisses, and bay;
Yet is day over long.

Unto us they belong,   10
  Us the bitter and gay,
Wine and woman and song.

We, as we pass along,
  Are sad that they will not stay;
Yet is day over long.   15

Fruits and flowers among,
  What is better than they:
Wine and woman and song?
  Yet is day over long.   (1899)

TO ONE IN BEDLAM

With delicate, mad hands, behind his sordid
    bars,
Surely he hath his posies, which they tear
    and twine;
Those scentless wisps of straw, that miserably
    line
His strait, caged universe, whereat the dull
    world stares,
Pedant and pitiful. Oh, how his rapt gaze wars
With their stupidity! Know they what
    dreams divine   6
Lift his long, laughing reveries like enchanted
    wine,
And make his melancholy germane to the
    stars?
O lamentable brother! if those pity thee,
Am I not fain of all thy lone eyes promise
    me;   10
Half a fool's kingdom, far from men who
    sow and reap,
All their days, vanity? Better than mortal
    flowers,
Thy moon-kissed roses seem: better than
    love or sleep,
The star-crowned solitude of thine oblivious
    hours!   (1899)

A LAST WORD

Let us go hence — the night is now at hand;
  The day is overworn, the birds all flown;
  And we have reaped the crops the gods
    have sown,
Despair and death; deep darkness o'er the
    land,   4

Broods like an owl; we cannot understand
  Laughter or tears, for we have only known
  Surpassing vanity: vain things alone
Have driven our perverse and aimless band.

Let us go hence, somewhither strange and
    cold,
  To Hollow Lands where just men and
    unjust   10
Find end of labor, where's rest for the old,
Freedom to all from love and fear and lust.
Twine our torn hands! O pray the earth
    enfold
Our life-sick hearts and turn them into
    dust.   (1899)

JOHN DAVIDSON (1857-1909)

TO THE NEW WOMEN

Free to look at fact,
Free to come and go,
Free to think and act,
Now you surely know
The wrongs of womanhead   5
At last are fairly dead.

Abler than man to vex,
Less able to be good,
Fiercer in your sex,
Wilder in your mood,   10
Seeking — who knows what?
About the world you grope;
Some of you have thought
Man may be your hope.

Soon again you'll see,   15
Love and love alone,
As simple as can be,
Can make this life atone.

Be bold and yet be bold,
But be not overbold,   20
Although the knell is tolled
Of the tyranny of old.

And meet your splendid doom,
On heaven-scaling wings,
Women, from whose bright womb   25
The radiant future springs!   (1894)

TO THE NEW MEN

Heat the furnace hot;
Smelt the things of thought
Into dross and dew;
Mold the world anew.

---

8. **bay**, the laurel wreath won for excellence in song.
A Last Word. 1. **Let . . . hence.** Cf. Swinburne's *A
Leave-Taking*, line 1 (p. 685).

To the New Women. 19-20. **Be bold . . . overbold.** "Be
bold, be bold, but not too bold" is the inscription over the
door of the robber's castle in the old English folk-tale
Mr. Fox. See also Spenser's *Faerie Queene*, III, xi, 50, 54.

More than earth and sea   5
Is a heart and eye;
Gird yourselves, and try
All the powers that be.

Wicked, cease at once
Troubling; wearied eyes,   10
Rest you now, while suns
Dawn and moons arise.

'Stablish heaven today;
Cleanse the beast-marked brow;
Wipe all tears away.   15
Do it — do it now!

Love, and hope, and know;
Man — you must adore him.
Let the whole past go;
Think God's thought before Him.   20

Knowledge is power? Above
All else, knowledge is love.

Heat the furnace hot;
Smelt the world-old thought
Into dross and dew;   25
Mold the earth anew.   (1894)

A BALLAD OF HEAVEN

He wrought at one great work for years;
    The world passed by with lofty look.
Sometimes his eyes were dashed with tears;
    Sometimes his lips with laughter shook.

His wife and child went clothed in rags,   5
    And in a windy garret starved;
He trod his measures on the flags,
    And high in heaven his music carved.

Wistful he grew, but never feared;
    For always on the midnight skies   10
His rich orchestral score appeared
    In stars and zones and galaxies.

He thought to copy down his score;
    The moonlight was his lamp; he said,
"Listen, my love"; but on the floor   15
    His wife and child were lying dead.

Her hollow eyes were open wide;
    He deemed she heard with special zest:
Her death's-head infant coldly eyed
    The desert of her shrunken breast.   20

"Listen, my love: my work is done;
    I tremble as I touch the page
To sign the sentence of the sun
    And crown the great eternal age.

"The slow *adagio* begins;   25
    The winding-sheets are raveled out
That swathe the minds of men, the sins
    That wrap their rotting souls about.

"The dead are heralded along
    With silver trumps and golden drums,   30
And flutes and oboes, keen and strong,
    My brave *andante* singing comes.

"Then like a python's sumptuous dress
    The frame of things is cast away,
And out of Time's obscure distress,   35
    The thundering *scherzo* crashes Day.

"For three great orchestras I hope
    My mighty music shall be scored;
On three high hills they shall have scope
    With heaven's vault for a sounding-board.

"Sleep well, love; let your eyelids fall;   41
    Cover the child; good-night, and if . . .
What? Speak . . . the traitorous end of all!
    Both . . . cold and hungry . . . cold and stiff!

"But no, God means us well, I trust.   45
    Dear ones, be happy, hope is nigh;
We are too young to fall to dust,
    And too unsatisfied to die."

He lifted up against his breast
    The woman's body, stark and wan;   50
And to her withered bosom pressed
    The little skin-clad skeleton.

"You see you are alive," he cried.
    He rocked them gently to and fro.
"No, no, my love, you have not died;   55
    Nor you, my little fellow; no."

Long in his arms he strained his dead
    And crooned an antique lullaby;
Then laid them on the lowly bed,
    And broke down with a doleful cry.   60

"The love, the hope, the blood, the brain,
    Of her and me, the budding life,
And my great music — all in vain!
    My unscored work, my child, my wife!

"We drop into oblivion,   65
    And nourish some suburban sod;

---

14. **beast-marked**, marked by Antichrist. See *Revelation*, 19:20.—"And the beast was taken, and with him the false prophet that wrought miracles before him, with which he deceived them that had received the mark of the beast, and them that worshiped his image."
A Ballad of Heaven. 7. **flags**, paving stones. 12. **zones**, divisions of the heavens by astronomical parallels. **galaxies**, such swarms of stars as the Milky Way.

25, 32, 36. **adagio, andante, scherzo**, movements in a symphony: slow, moderately rapid, and quick; cf. Henley's *London Voluntaries*, p. 798. 64. **unscored work**, unwritten music.

My work, this woman, this my son,
  Are now no more: there is no God.

"The world's a dustbin; we are due,
  And death's cart waits: be life accurst!" 70
He stumbled down beside the two,
  And clasping them, his great heart burst.

Straightway he stood at heaven's gate,
  Abashed and trembling for his sin;
I trow he had not long to wait, 75
  For God came out and let him in.

And then there ran a radiant pair,
  Ruddy with haste and eager-eyed,
To meet him first upon the stair —
  His wife and child beatified. 80

They clad him in a robe of light,
  And gave him heavenly food to eat;
Great seraphs praised him to the height,
  Archangels sat about his feet.

God, smiling, took him by the hand, 85
  And led him to the brink of heaven;
He saw where systems whirling stand,
  Where galaxies like snow are driven.

Dead silence reigned; a shudder ran
  Through space; Time furled his wearied
      wings; 90
A slow *adagio* then began,
  Sweetly resolving troubled things.

The dead were heralded along;
  As if with drums and trumps of flame,
And flutes and oboes keen and strong, 95
  A brave *andante* singing came.

Then like a python's sumptuous dress,
  The frame of things was cast away,
And out of Time's obscure distress
  The conquering *scherzo* thundered Day. 100

He doubted; but God said, "Even so;
  Nothing is lost that's wrought with tears.
The music that you made below
  Is now the music of the spheres."
                    (1894)

A BALLAD OF HELL

"A letter from my love today!
  Oh, unexpected, dear appeal!"
She struck a happy tear away,
  And broke the crimson seal.

"My love, there is no help on earth, 5
  No help in heaven; the dead-man's bell
Must toll our wedding; our first hearth
  Must be the well-paved floor of hell."

The color died from out her face,
  Her eyes like ghostly candles shone; 10
She cast dread looks about the place,
  Then clenched her teeth and read right on.

"I may not pass the prison door;
  Here must I rot from day to day,
Unless I wed whom I abhor, 15
  My cousin, Blanche of Valencay.

"At midnight with my dagger keen,
  I'll take my life; it must be so.
Meet me in hell tonight, my queen,
  For weal and woe." 20

She laughed although her face was wan;
  She girded on her golden belt;
She took her jeweled ivory fan,
  And at her glowing missal knelt.

Then rose, "And am I mad?" she said. 25
  She broke her fan, her belt untied;
With leather girt herself instead,
  And stuck a dagger at her side.

She waited, shuddering in her room,
  Till sleep had fallen on all the house. 30
She never flinched; she faced her doom:
  The two must sin to keep their vows.

Then out into the night she went,
  And stooping crept by hedge and tree;
Her rose-bush flung a snare of scent, 35
  And caught a happy memory.

She fell, and lay a minute's space;
  She tore the sward in her distress;
The dewy grass refreshed her face;
  She rose and ran with lifted dress. 40

She started like a morn-caught ghost
  Once when the moon came out and stood
To watch; the naked road she crossed,
  And dived into the murmuring wood.

The branches snatched her streaming cloak;
  A live thing shrieked; she made no stay! 46
She hurried to the trysting-oak —
  Right well she knew the way.

Without a pause she bared her breast,
  And drove her dagger home and fell, 50

83. **seraphs**, angels of a superior order. 104. **music . . spheres.** The ancients believed that the stars made music as their spheres revolved.

24. **missal**, a book of the Mass. 41. **morn-caught ghost.** According to folk-belief, spirits may wander abroad in the hours of darkness, but must return to their graves before dawn on penalty of infinite torture. See the folk-ballad *The Wife of Usher's Well*.

And lay like one that takes her rest,
And died and wakened up in hell.

She bathed her spirit in the flame,
And near the center took her post;
From all sides to her ears there came,　55
The dreary anguish of the lost.

The devil started at her side,
Comely, and tall, and black as jet.
"I am young Malespina's bride;
Has he come hither yet?"　60

"My poppet, welcome to your bed."
"Is Malespina here?"
"Not he! Tomorrow he must wed
His cousin Blanche, my dear!"

"You lie, he died with me tonight."　65
"Not he! it was a plot." "You lie."
"My dear, I never lie outright."
"We died at midnight, he and I."

The devil went. Without a groan
She, gathered up in one fierce prayer,　70
Took root in hell's midst all alone,
And waited for him there.

She dared to make herself at home
Amidst the wail, the uneasy stir.
The blood-stained flame that filled the dome,
Scentless and silent, shrouded her.　76

How long she stayed I cannot tell;
But when she felt his perfidy,
She marched across the floor of hell;
And all the damned stood up to see.　80

The devil stopped her at the brink.
She shook him off; she cried, "Away!"
"My dear, you have gone mad, I think."
"I was betrayed; — I will not stay."

Across the weltering deep she ran;　85
A stranger thing was never seen:
The damned stood silent to a man;
They saw the great gulf set between.

To her it seemed a meadow fair;
And flowers sprang up about her feet;　90
She entered heaven; she climbed the stair;
And knelt down at the mercy-seat.

Seraphs and saints with one great voice
Welcomed that soul that knew not fear;
Amazed to find it could rejoice,　95
Hell raised a hoarse half-human cheer.
(1894)

61. **poppet**, darling. 93. **seraphs**, angels of a superior order.

THIRTY BOB A WEEK

I couldn't touch a stop and turn a screw,
And set the blooming world a-work for me,
Like such as cut their teeth — I hope, like
you —
On the handle of a skeleton gold key;
I cut mine on a leek, which I eat it every
week;　5
I'm a clerk at thirty bob, as you can see.

But I don't allow it's luck and all a toss;
There's no such thing as being starred and
crossed;
It's just the power of some to be a boss,
And the bally power of others to be bossed.
I face the music, sir; you bet I ain't a cur; 11
Strike me lucky if I don't believe I'm lost!

For like a mole I journey in the dark,
A-traveling along the underground
From my Pillared Halls and broad Suburban
Park,　15
To come the daily dull official round;
And home again at night with my pipe all
alight,
A-scheming how to count ten bob a pound.

And it's often very cold and wet,
And my missis stitches towels for a hunks;
And the Pillared Halls is half of it to let— 21
Three rooms about the size of traveling
trunks.
And we cough, my wife and I, to dislocate a
sigh,
When the noisy little kids are in their bunks.

But you never hear her do a growl or whine,
For she's made of flint and roses, very odd;
And I've got to cut my meaning rather fine,
Or I'd blubber, for I'm made of greens and
sod.
So p'r'aps we are in Hell for all that I can tell,
And lost and damned and served up hot to
God.　30

I ain't blaspheming, Mr. Silver-tongue;
I'm saying things a bit beyond your art.
Of all the rummy starts you ever sprung,
Thirty bob a week's the rummiest start!
With your science and your books and your
the'ries about spooks,　35
Did you ever hear of looking in your heart?

I didn't mean your pocket, Mr., no —
I mean that having children and a wife,

Thirty Bob a Week. A bob is a shilling—now worth about fourteen cents.
10. **bally**, an intensifying adjective without definite meaning. 18. **count . . . pound**, make ten shillings go as far as a pound (twenty shillings). 20. **hunks**, stingy old man.

With thirty bob on which to come and go,
　　Isn't dancing to the tabor and the fife;　40
When it doesn't make you drink, by Heaven!
　　it makes you think,
　　And notice curious items about life.

I step into my heart and there I meet
　　A god-almighty devil singing small,
Who would like to shout and whistle in the
　　street,　45
And squelch the passers flat against the
　　wall;
If the whole world was a cake he had the
　　power to take,
　　He would take it, ask for more, and eat
　　it all.

And I meet a sort of simpleton beside,
　　The kind that life is always giving beans;
With thirty bob a week to keep a bride　51
　　He fell in love and married in his teens.
At thirty bob he stuck; but he knows it isn't
　　luck;
　　He knows the seas are deeper than tureens.

And the god-almighty devil and the fool　55
　　That meet me in the High Street on the
　　strike,
When I walk about my heart a-gathering
　　wool,
　　Are my good and evil angels if you like.
And both of them together in every kind of
　　weather
　　Ride me like a double-seated bike.　60

That's rough a bit and needs its meaning
　　curled.
　　But I have a high old hot un in my mind —
A most engrugious notion of the world,
　　That leaves your lightning 'rithmetic be-
　　hind:
I give it at a glance when I say "There ain't
　　no chance,　65
　　Nor nothing of the lucky-lottery kind."

And it's this way that I make it out to be:
　　No fathers, mothers, countries, climates —
　　none;
Not Adam was responsible for me,
　　Nor society, nor systems, nary one;　70
A little sleeping seed, I woke — I did, in-
　　deed —
　　A million years before the blooming sun.

I woke because I thought the time had come;
　　Beyond my will there was no other cause;
And everywhere I found myself at home,　75
　　Because I chose to be the thing I was;

And in whatever shape of mollusc or of ape
　　I always went according to the laws.

I was the love that chose my mother out;　79
　　I joined two lives and from the union burst;
My weakness and my strength without a
　　doubt
　　Are mine alone forever from the first;
It's just the very same with a difference in the
　　name
　　As "Thy will be done." You say it if you
　　durst!

They say it daily up and down the land　85
　　As easy as you take a drink, it's true;
But the difficultest go to understand,
　　And the difficultest job a man can do,
Is to come it brave and meek with thirty bob
　　a week,
　　And feel that that's the proper thing for
　　you.　90

It's a naked child against a hungry wolf;
　　It's playing bowls upon a splitting wreck;
It's walking on a string across a gulf
　　With millstones fore-and-aft about your
　　neck;
But the thing is daily done by many and
　　many a one;　95
　　And we fall, face forward, fighting, on
　　the deck.

　　　　　　　　　　　　　　　　(1894)

A BALLAD OF A NUN

From Eastertide to Eastertide
　　For ten long years her patient knees
Engraved the stones—the fittest bride
　　Of Christ in all the diocese.

She conquered every earthly lust;　5
　　The abbess loved her more and more;
And, as a mark of perfect trust,
　　Made her the keeper of the door.

High on a hill the convent hung,
　　Across a duchy looking down,　10
Where everlasting mountains flung
　　Their shadows over tower and town.

The jewels of their lofty snows
　　In constellations flashed at night;
Above their crests the moon arose;　15
　　The deep earth shuddered with delight.

Long ere she left her cloudy bed,
　　Still dreaming in the orient land,

---

63. **engrugious**, egregious, extraordinary.

A Ballad of a Nun. 10. **duchy**, the estate of a duke.

On many a mountain's happy head
  Dawn lightly laid her rosy hand.   20

The adventurous sun took Heaven by storm;
  Clouds scattered largesses of rain;
The sounding cities, rich and warm,
  Smouldered and glittered in the plain.

Sometimes it was a wandering wind,   25
  Sometimes the fragrance of the pine,
Sometimes the thought how others sinned,
  That turned her sweet blood into wine.

Sometimes she heard a serenade
  Complaining sweetly far away: 30
She said, "A young man woos a maid";
  And dreamt of love till break of day.

Then would she ply her knotted scourge
  Until she swooned; but evermore
She had the same red sin to purge,   35
  Poor, passionate keeper of the door!

For still night's starry scroll unfurled,
  And still the day came like a flood:
It was the greatness of the world
  That made her long to use her blood.   40

In winter-time when Lent drew nigh,
  And hill and plain were wrapped in snow,
She watched beneath the frosty sky
  The nearest city nightly glow.

Like peals of airy bells outworn   45
  Faint laughter died above her head
In gusts of broken music borne:
  "They keep the Carnival," she said.

Her hungry heart devoured the town:
  "Heaven save me by a miracle!   50
Unless God sends an angel down,
  Thither I go though it were Hell."

She dug her nails deep in her breast,
  Sobbed, shrieked, and straight withdrew the
      bar;
A fledgling flying from the nest,   55
  A pale moth rushing to a star.

Fillet and veil in strips she tore;
  Her golden tresses floated wide;
The ring and bracelet that she wore
  As Christ's betrothed, she cast aside.   60

"Life's dearest meaning I shall probe;
  Lo! I shall taste of love at last!
Away!" She doffed her outer robe,
  And sent it sailing down the blast.

Her body seemed to warm the wind;   65
  With bleeding feet o'er ice she ran:
"I leave the righteous God behind;
  I go to worship sinful man."

She reached the sounding city's gate;
  No question did the warder ask: 70
He passed her in: "Welcome, wild mate!"
  He thought her some fantastic mask.

Half-naked through the town she went;
  Each footstep left a bloody mark;
Crowds followed her with looks intent;   75
  Her bright eyes made the torches dark.

Alone and watching in the street
  There stood a grave youth nobly dressed;
To him she knelt and kissed his feet;
  Her face her great desire confessed.   80

Straight to his house the nun he led:
  "Strange lady, what would you with me?"
"Your love, your love, sweet lord," she said;
  "I bring you my virginity."

He healed her bosom with a kiss;   85
  She gave him all her passion's hoard;
And sobbed and murmured ever, "This
  Is life's great meaning, dear, my lord.

"I care not for my broken vow;
  Though God should come in thunder soon,
I am sister to the mountains now,   91
  And sister to the sun and moon."

Through all the towns of Belmarie
  She made a progress like a queen.
"She is," they said, "whate'er she be,   95
  The strangest woman ever seen.

"From fairyland she must have come,
  Or else she is a mermaiden."
Some said she was a ghoul, and some
  A heathen goddess born again.   100

But soon her fire to ashes burned;
  Her beauty changed to haggardness;
Her golden hair to silver turned;
  The hour came of her last caress.

At midnight from her lonely bed   105
  She rose, and said, "I have had my will."
The old ragged robe she donned, and fled
  Back to the convent on the hill.

Half-naked as she went before,
  She hurried to the city wall,   110

---

57. **Fillet,** a small band intended to encircle the hair.

85. **healed.** See line 53. 93. **Belmarie,** a name chosen probably because of its pleasant sound.

Unnoticed in the rush and roar
And splendor of the carnival.

No question did the warder ask:
Her ragged robe, her shrunken limb,
Her dreadful eyes! "It is no mask;   115
It is a she-wolf, gaunt and grim!"

She ran across the icy plain;
Her worn blood curdled in the blast;
Each footstep left a crimson stain;
The white-faced moon looked on aghast. 120

She said between her chattering jaws,
"Deep peace is mine, I cease to strive;
Oh, comfortable convent laws,
That bury foolish nuns alive!

"A trowel for my passing-bell,   125
A little bed within the wall,
A coverlet of stones; how well
I there shall keep the Carnival!"

Like tired bells chiming in their sleep,
The wind faint peals of laughter bore;   130
She stopped her ears and climbed the steep,
And thundered at the convent door.

It opened straight: she entered in,
And at the wardress' feet fell prone:
"I come to purge away my sin;   135
Bury me, close me up in stone."

The wardress raised her tenderly;
She touched her wet and fast-shut eyes:
"Look, sister; sister, look at me;
Look; can you see through my disguise?"

She looked and saw her own sad face,   141
And trembled, wondering, "Who art thou?"
"God sent me down to fill your place:
I am the Virgin Mary now."

And with the word, God's mother shone: 145
The wanderer whispered, "Mary, hail!"
The vision helped her to put on
Bracelet and fillet, ring and veil.

"You are sister to the mountains now,
And sister to the day and night;   150
Sister to God."   And on the brow
She kissed her thrice, and left her sight.

While dreaming in her cloudy bed,
Far in the crimson orient land,
On many a mountain's happy head   155
Dawn lightly laid her rosy hand.   (1895)

ECLOGUE: THE MERCHANTMAN

The Markethaunters

Now, while our money is piping hot
From the mint of our toil that coins the
    sheaves,
Merchantman, merchantman, what have you
    got
In your tabernacle hung with leaves?
    What have you got?   5
    The sun rides high;
    Our money is hot;
    We must buy, buy, buy!

The Merchantman

I come from the elfin king's demesne
With chrysolite, hyacinth, tourmaline;   10
I have emeralds here of living green;
    I have rubies, each like a cup of wine;
And diamonds, diamonds that never have
    been
Outshone by eyes the most divine!

The Markethaunters

Jewelry?—Baubles; bad for the soul;   15
Desire of the heart and lust of the eye!
Diamonds, indeed! We wanted coal.
    What else do you sell? Come, sound your
    cry!
    Our money is hot;
    The night draws nigh;   20
    What have you got
    That we want to buy?

The Merchantman

I have here enshrined the soul of the rose
Exhaled in the land of the daystar's birth;
I have casks whose golden staves enclose 25
    Eternal youth, eternal mirth;
And cordials that bring repose,
    And the tranquil night, and the end of the
    earth.

The Markethaunters

Rapture of wine? But it never pays;
We must keep our common-sense alert. 30
Raisins are healthier, medicine says—
    Raisins and almonds for dessert.
    But we want to buy;
    For our money is hot,
    And age draws nigh.   35
    What else have you got?

The Merchantman

I have lamps that gild the luster of noon;
Shadowy arrows that pierce the brain;

---

125. trowel . . . passing-bell, an indication that her long-ing for "life" had ended.

Eclogue: The Merchantman.   10. chrysolite . . . tourma-line, semi-precious stones: olive-green, bluish violet, and vari-colored.

Dulcimers strung with beams of the moon;
　Psalteries fashioned of pleasure and pain; 40
A song and a sword and a haunting tune
　That may never be offered the world again.

The Markethaunters

Dulcimers! psalteries! Whom do you mock?
　Arrows and songs? We have axes to grind!
Shut up your booth and your moldering stock,
　For we never shall deal. — Come away; let
　　us find　　　　　　　　　　　　　46
　　　What the others have got!
　　　We must buy, buy, buy;
　　For our money is hot,
　　　And death draws nigh.　　　50
　　　　　　　　　　　　　(1899)

A RUNNABLE STAG

When the pods went pop on the broom, green
　　broom,
　And apples began to be golden-skinned,
We harbored a stag in the Priory coomb,
　And we feathered his trail up-wind, up-
　　wind,
　We feathered his trail up-wind —　　5
　　A stag of warrant, a stag, a stag,
　　A runnable stag, a kingly crop,
　　Brow, bay and tray and three on top,
　　A stag, a runnable stag.

Then the huntsman's horn rang yap, yap,
　　yap,　　　　　　　　　　　　　10
　And "Forwards" we heard the harborer
　　shout;
But 'twas only a brocket that broke a gap
　In the beechen underwood, driven out,
　From the underwood antlered out.
　　By warrant and might of the stag, the
　　　stag,　　　　　　　　　　　15
　　The runnable stag, whose lordly mind
　　Was bent on sleep, though beamed and
　　　tined
　　He stood, a runnable stag.

So we tufted the covert till afternoon
　With Tinkerman's Pup and Bell-of-the-
　　North;　　　　　　　　　　　20

And hunters were sulky and hounds out of
　tune
Before we tufted the right stag forth,
Before we tufted him forth,
　The stag of warrant, the wily stag,
　The runnable stag with his kingly crop,
　Brow, bay and tray and three on top, 26
　The royal and runnable stag.

It was Bell-of-the-North and Tinkerman's
　Pup
That stuck to the scent till the copse was
　drawn.　　　　　　　　　　　29
"Tally ho! tally ho!" and the hunt was up,
　The tufters whipped and the pack laid on,
　The resolute pack laid on,
　　And the stag of warrant away at last,
　　The runnable stag, the same, the same,
　　His hoofs on fire, his horns like flame, 35
　　A stag, a runnable stag.

"Let your gelding be — if you check or chide
　He stumbles at once and you're out of the
　　hunt;
For three hundred gentlemen, able to ride,
　On hunters accustomed to bear the brunt,
　Accustomed to bear the brunt,　　41
　　Are after the runnable stag, the stag,
　　The runnable stag with his kingly crop,
　　Brow, bay and tray and three on top,
　　The right, the runnable stag."　　45

By perilous paths in coomb and dell,
　The heather, the rocks, and the river-bed,
The pace grew hot, for the scent lay well,
　And a runnable stag goes right ahead.
　The quarry went right ahead —　　50
　　Ahead, ahead, and fast and far;
　　His antlered crest, his cloven hoof,
　　Brow, bay and tray and three aloof,
　　The stag, the runnable stag.

For a matter of twenty miles and more, 55
　By the densest hedge and the highest wall,
Through herds of bullocks he baffled the lore
　Of harborer, huntsman, hounds and all,
　Of harborer, hounds and all —
　　The stag of warrant, the wily stag, 60
　　For twenty miles, and five and five,
　　He ran, and he never was caught alive,
　　This stag, this runnable stag.

When he turned at bay in the leafy gloom,
　In the emerald gloom where the brook ran
　　deep　　　　　　　　　　　65
He heard in the distance the rollers boom,
　And he saw in a vision of peaceful sleep
　In a wonderful vision of sleep,

A stag of warrant, a stag, a stag,
  A runnable stag in a jeweled bed,   70
Under the sheltering ocean dead,
A stag, a runnable stag.

So a fateful hope lit up his eye,
  And he opened his nostrils wide again,
And he tossed his branching antlers high   75
  As he headed the hunt down the Charlock
    glen,
As he raced down the echoing glen —
  For five miles more, the stag, the stag,
  For twenty miles, and five and five,
Not to be caught now, dead or alive,   80
The stag, the runnable stag.

Three hundred gentlemen, able to ride,
  Three hundred horses as gallant and free,
Beheld him escape on the evening tide,
  Far out till he sank in the Severn Sea,   85
Till he sank in the depths of the sea —
  The stag, the buoyant stag, the stag
  That slept at last in a jeweled bed
Under the sheltering ocean spread,
The stag, the runnable stag.   90
               (1906)

SONG

Closes and courts and lanes,
  Devious, clustered thick,
The thoroughfare, mains and drains,
  People and mortar and brick,
Wood, metal, machinery, brains,   5
  Pen and composing stick:
    Fleet Street, but exquisite flame
      In the nebula once ere day and night
    Began their travail, or earth became,
    And all was passionate light.   10

Networks of wire overland,
  Conduits under the sea,
Aerial message from strand to strand
  By lightning that travels free,
Hither in haste to hand   15
  Tidings of destiny
    These tingling nerves of the world's
      affairs
    Deliver remorseless, rendering still
    The fall of empires, the price of shares,
    The record of good and ill.   20

Tidal the traffic goes
  Citywards out of the town;
Townwards the evening ebb o'erflows
  This highway of old renown,

When the fog-woven curtains close,   25
  And the urban night comes down,
    Where souls are spilt and intellects spent
    O'er news vociferant near and far,
    From Hesperus hard to the Orient,
    From dawn to the evening star.   30

This is the royal refrain
  That burdens the boom and the thud
Of omnibus, mobus, wain,
  And the hoofs on the beaten mud,
From the Griffin at Chancery Lane   35
  To the portal of old King Lud —
    Fleet Street, diligent night and day,
    Of news the mart and the burnished
      hearth,
    Seven hundred paces of narrow way,
    A notable bit of the earth.   (1909)

FRANCIS THOMPSON (1859-1907)

THE POPPY

TO MONICA

Summer set lip to earth's bosom bare,
And left the flushed print in a poppy there;
Like a yawn of fire from the grass it came,
And the fanning wind puffed it to flapping
  flame.

With burnt mouth, red like a lion's, it drank 5
The blood of the sun as he slaughtered sank,
And dipped its cup in the purpurate shine
When the eastern conduits ran with wine;

Till it grew lethargied with fierce bliss,
And hot as a swinkéd gypsy is,   10
And drowsed in sleepy savageries,
With mouth wide a-pout for a sultry kiss.

A child and man paced side by side,
Treading the skirts of eventide;
But between the clasp of his hand and hers
Lay, felt not, twenty withered years.   16

She turned, with the rout of her dusk South
  hair,
And saw the sleeping gypsy there;
And snatched and snapped it in swift child's
  whim,
With — "Keep it, long as you live!" — to
  him.   20

---

85. **Severn Sea**, the Bristol Channel, at the mouth of the
Severn River.
Song. 1. **Closes**, enclosed plots of ground. 7. **Fleet
Street**, a short but very busy street in the heart of London.

29. **Hesperus . . . Orient**, far west to far east. 33.
mobus, motorbus. **wain**, wagon. 35. **Griffin . . . Lane**,
an old tavern at the point where Fleet Street, intersected by
Chancery Lane, becomes the Strand. 36. **portal . . . Lud**,
Ludgate, at the eastern extremity of Fleet Street. King
Lud was a mythical king of Britain, the traditional founder
of London.
The Poppy. Monica is the daughter of Wilfrid and Alice
Meynell, Thompson's benefactors.
7. **purpurate**, purple. 10. **swinkéd**, wearied with toil.

And his smile, as nymphs from their laving
    meres,
Trembled up from a bath of tears;
And joy, like a mew sea-rocked apart,
Tossed on the wave of his troubled heart.

For *he* saw what she did not see,   25
That — as kindled by its own fervency —
The verge shriveled inward smolderingly;

And suddenly 'twixt his hand and hers
He knew the twenty withered years —
No flower, but twenty shriveled years.   30

"Was never such thing until this hour,"
Low to his heart he said; "the flower
Of sleep brings wakening to me,
And of oblivion, memory.

"Was never this thing to me," he said,   35
"Though with bruiséd poppies my feet are
    red!"
And again to his own heart very low:
"O child! I love, for I love and know;

"But you, who love nor know at all
The diverse chambers in Love's guest-hall, 40
Where some rise early, few sit long:
In how differing accents hear the throng
His great Pentecostal tongue;

"Who know not love from amity,
Nor my reported self from me;   45
A fair fit gift is this, meseems,
You give — this withering flower of dreams.

"O frankly fickle, and fickly true,
Do you know what the days will do to you?
To your Love and you what the days will do,
O frankly fickle, and fickly true?   51

"You have loved me, Fair, three lives — or
    days;
'Twill pass with the passing of my face.
But where *I* go, your face goes too,
To watch lest I play false to you.   55

"I am but, my sweet, your foster-lover,
Knowing well when certain years are over
You vanish from me to another;
Yet I know, and love, like the foster-mother.

"So, frankly fickle, and fickly true!   60
For my brief life-while I take from you
This token, fair and fit, meseems,
For me — this withering flower of dreams."

---

43. Pentecostal, referring to the gift of speaking in many languages bestowed upon the apostles as they were celebrating the Jewish feast of the Pentecost, (*Acts*, 2:5).

The sleep-flower sways in the wheat its
    head,
Heavy with dreams, as that with bread; 65
The goodly grain and the sun-flushed sleeper
The reaper reaps, and Time the reaper.

I hang 'mid men my needless head,
And my fruit is dreams, as theirs is bread.
The goodly men and the sun-hazed sleeper 70
Time shall reap; but after the reaper
The world shall glean of me, me the sleeper!

Love, love! your flower of withered dream
In leavéd rime lies safe, I deem,
Sheltered and shut in a nook of rime, 75
From the reaper man, and his reaper Time.

Love! I fall into the claws of Time;
But lasts within a leavéd rime
All that the world of me esteems —
My withered dreams, my withered dreams.
                      (1893)

THE MAKING OF VIOLA

1

The Father of Heaven

Spin, daughter Mary, spin,
Twirl your wheel with silver din;
Spin, daughter Mary, spin,
    Spin a tress for Viola.

Angels

Spin, Queen Mary, a   5
Brown tress for Viola!

2

The Father of Heaven

Weave, hands angelical,
Weave a woof of flesh to pall —
Weave, hands angelical —
    Flesh to pall our Viola.   10

Angels

Weave, singing brothers, a
Velvet flesh for Viola!

3

The Father of Heaven

Scoop, young Jesus, for her eyes,
Wood-browned pools of Paradise —
Young Jesus, for the eyes,   15
    For the eyes of Viola.

Angels

Tint, Prince Jesus, a
Duskéd eye for Viola!

The Making of Viola. **8. pall,** cover.

4

The Father of Heaven

Cast a star therein to drown,
Like a torch in cavern brown,   20
Sink a burning star to drown
Whelmed in eyes of Viola.

Angels

Lave, Prince Jesus, a
Star in eyes of Viola!

5

The Father of Heaven

Breathe, Lord Paraclete,   25
To a bubbled crystal meet —
Breathe, Lord Paraclete —
Crystal soul for Viola.

Angels

Breathe, Regal Spirit, a
Flashing soul for Viola!   30

6

The Father of Heaven

Child-angels, from your wings
Fall the roseal hoverings,
Child-angels, from your wings
On the cheeks of Viola.

Angels

Linger, rosy reflex, a   35
Quenchless stain, on Viola!

7

*All things being accomplished, saith the Father
of Heaven:*

Bear her down, and bearing, sing,
Bear her down on spyless wing,
Bear her down, and bearing, sing,
With a sound of Viola.   40

Angels

Music as her name is, a
Sweet sound of Viola!

8

Wheeling angels, past espial,
Danced her down with sound of viol;
Wheeling angels, past espial,   45
Descanting on "Viola."

Angels

Sing, in our footing, a
Lovely lilt of "Viola!"

9

Baby smiled, mother wailed,
Earthward while the sweetling sailed; 50
Mother smiled, baby wailed,
When to earth came Viola.

And her elders shall say:

So soon have we taught you a
Way to weep, poor Viola!

10

Smile, sweet baby, smile,   55
For you will have weeping-while;
Native in your heaven is smile —
But your weeping, Viola?

Whence your smiles, we know, but ah!
Whence your weeping, Viola? —   60
Our first gift to you is a
Gift of tears, my Viola!   (1893)

LITTLE JESUS

*Ex ore infantium Deus et lactentium
perfecisti laudem.*

Little Jesus, wast Thou shy
Once, and just so small as I?
And what did it feel like to be
Out of heaven, and just like me?
Didst Thou sometimes think of *there*,   5
And ask where all the angels were?

I should think that I would cry
For my house all made of sky;
I would look about the air,
And wonder where my angels were;   10
And at waking 'twould distress me —
Not an angel there to dress me!

Hadst Thou ever any toys,
Like us little girls and boys?
And didst Thou play in heaven with all   15
The angels, that were not too tall,
With stars for marbles?   Did the things
Play *Can you see me?* through their wings?

Didst Thou kneel at night to pray,
And didst Thou join Thy hands, this way? 20
And did they tire sometimes, being young,
And make the prayer seem very long?
And dost Thou like it best, that we
Should join our hands to pray to Thee?
I used to think, before I knew,   25
The prayer not said unless we do.
And did Thy Mother at the night

---

25. **Paraclete.** Christ; see note on Johnson's *The Dark Angel*, 36, p. 840. 35. **reflex,** reflection—from the glorious wings of the angels. 46. **Descanting,** singing.

Little Jesus. **Ex . . . laudem,** the Vulgate version of *Psalms,* 8:2; the Authorized Version has: "Out of the mouths of babes and sucklings hast thou ordained strength."

Kiss Thee, and fold the clothes in right?
And didst Thou feel quite good in bed,
Kissed, and sweet, and Thy prayers said?　30

Thou canst not have forgotten all
That it feels like to be small;
And Thou know'st I cannot pray
To thee in my father's way —
When Thou wast so little, say,　35
Couldst Thou talk Thy Father's way?

So, a little Child, come down
And hear a child's tongue like Thy own;
Take me by the hand and walk,
And listen to my baby-talk.　40
To Thy Father show my prayer
(He will look, Thou art so fair),
And say: "O Father, I, Thy Son,
Bring the prayer of a little one."

And He will smile, that children's tongue　45
Has not changed since Thou wast young!
(1893)

THE HOUND OF HEAVEN

I fled Him, down the nights and down the
days;
I fled Him, down the arches of the years;
I fled Him, down the labyrinthine ways
Of my own mind; and in the mist of tears
I hid from Him, and under running laughter.
Up vistaed hopes I sped;　6
And shot, precipitated,
Adown Titanic glooms of chasméd fears,
From those strong Feet that followed, fol-
lowed after.
But with unhurrying chase,　10
And unperturbéd pace,
Deliberate speed, majestic instancy,
They beat — and a Voice beat
More instant than the Feet —
"All things betray thee, who betrayest
Me."　15

I pleaded, outlaw-wise,
By many a hearted casement, curtained red,
Trellised with intertwining charities
(For, though I knew His love Who followéd,
Yet was I sore adread　20
Lest, having Him, I must have naught be-
side);
But, if one little casement parted wide,
The gust of His approach would clash it to.
Fear wist not to evade, as Love wist to pur-
sue.

Across the margent of the world I fled,　25
And troubled the gold gateways of the
stars,
Smiting for shelter on their clangéd bars;
Fretted to dulcet jars
And silvern chatter the pale ports o' the moon.
I said to dawn, Be sudden; to eve, Be soon;　30
With thy young skyey blossoms heap me
over
From this tremendous Lover!
Float thy vague veil about me, lest He see!
I tempted all His servitors, but to find
My own betrayal in their constancy,　35
In faith to Him their fickleness to me,
Their traitorous trueness, and their loyal
deceit.
To all swift things for swiftness did I sue;
Clung to the whistling mane of every wind.
But whether they swept, smoothly
fleet,　40
The long savannahs of the blue;
Or whether, Thunder-driven,
They clanged his chariot 'thwart a
heaven
Plashy with flying lightnings round the spurn
o' their feet —
Fear wist not to evade as Love wist to
pursue.　45
Still with unhurrying chase,
And unperturbéd pace,
Deliberate speed, majestic instancy,
Came on the following Feet,
And a Voice above their beat —　50
"Naught shelters thee, who wilt not
shelter Me."

I sought no more that after which I strayed
In face of man or maid;
But still within the little children's eyes
Seems something, something that replies;
They at least are for me, surely for me!　56
I turned me to them very wistfully;
But, just as their young eyes grew sudden
fair
With dawning answers there,
Their angel plucked them from me by the
hair.　60
"Come then, ye other children, Nature's —
share
With me" (said I) "your delicate fellowship;
Let me greet you lip to lip,
Let me twine with you caresses,
Wantoning　65
With our Lady-Mother's vagrant tresses,
Banqueting
With her in her wind-walled palace,
Underneath her azured daïs,

The Hound of Heaven. "As the hound follows the hare,
never ceasing in its running, ever drawing nearer in the chase
... so does God follow the fleeing soul by his Divine grace"
(O'Conor, *A Study of Francis Thompson's "Hound of Heaven,"*
1912, page 7).
24. wist, knew.

25. margent, edge, boundary. **28-29. Fretted . . .
moon,** troubled the doors of the moon until they vibrated
with sweet sounds. **41. savannahs,** open, level regions.

Quaffing, as your taintless way is,   70
    From a chalice
Lucent-weeping out of the dayspring."
So it was done;
I in their delicate fellowship was one —
Drew the bolt of Nature's secrecies.   75
I knew all the swift importings
    On the willful face of skies;
I knew how the clouds arise
Spuméd of the wild sea-snortings;
    All that's born or dies   80
    Rose and drooped with — made them
        shapers
Of mine own moods, or wailful or divine —
    With them joyed and was bereaven.
I was heavy with the even,
    When she lit her glimmering tapers   85
    Round the day's dead sanctities.
I laughed in the morning's eyes.
I triumphed and I saddened with all weather,
    Heaven and I wept together,
And its sweet tears were salt with mortal
        mine;   90
Against the red throb of its sunset-heart
    I laid my own to beat,
    And share commingling heat;
But not by that, by that, was eased my
        human smart.
In vain my tears were wet on Heaven's gray
        cheek.   95
For ah! we know not what each other says,
    These things and I; in sound I speak —
Their sound is but their stir, they speak by
        silences.
Nature, poor stepdame, cannot slake my
        drouth;
    Let her, if she would owe me,   100
Drop yon blue bosom-veil of sky, and show
        me
    The breasts o' her tenderness;
Never did any milk of hers once bless
    My thirsting mouth.
    Nigh and nigh draws the chase,   105
    With unperturbéd pace,
    Deliberate speed, majestic instancy;
    And past those noiséd Feet
    A voice comes yet more fleet —
"Lo! naught contents thee, who content'st
    not Me."   110

Naked I wait Thy love's uplifted stroke!
My harness piece by piece Thou hast hewn
        from me,
    And smitten me to my knee;
    I am defenseless utterly.
    I slept, me thinks, and woke,   115
And, slowly gazing, find me stripped in
        sleep.
In the rash lustihead of my young powers,

72. Lucent-weeping, dripping with luminous drops.

    I shook the pillaring hours
And pulled my life upon me; grimed with
        smears,
I stand amid the dust o' the mounded years —
My mangled youth lies dead beneath the
        heap.   121
My days have crackled and gone up in smoke,
Have puffed and burst as sun-starts on a
        stream.
    Yea, faileth now even dream
The dreamer, and the lute the lutanist;   125
Even the linked fantasies, in whose blossomy
        twist
I swung the earth a trinket at my wrist,
Are yielding; cords of all too weak account
For earth with heavy griefs so overplussed.
    Ah! is Thy love indeed   130
A weed, albeit an amaranthine weed,
Suffering no flowers except its own to mount?
    Ah! must —
    Designer infinite! —
Ah! must Thou char the wood ere Thou canst
        limn with it?   135
My freshness spent its wavering shower i' the
        dust;
And now my heart is as a broken fount,
Wherein tear-drippings stagnate, spilt down
        ever
    From the dank thoughts that shiver
Upon the sighful branches of my mind.   140
    Such is; what is to be?
The pulp so bitter, how shall taste the rind?
I dimly guess what Time in mists confounds;
Yet ever and anon a trumpet sounds
From the hid battlements of Eternity;   145
Those shaken mists a space unsettle, then
Round the half-glimpséd turrets slowly wash
        again.
    But not ere him who summoneth
    I first have seen, enwound
With glooming robes purpureal, cypress-
        crowned;   150
His name I know, and what his trumpet saith.
Whether man's heart or life it be which yields
    Thee harvest, must Thy harvest fields
    Be dunged with rotten death?

    Now of that long pursuit   155
    Comes on at hand the bruit;
That Voice is round me like a bursting
        sea:
    "And is thy earth so marred,
    Shattered in shard on shard?
Lo, all things fly thee, for thou fliest Me!

118-119. shook . . . me, as Samson shook the pillars of the temple at Gaza and pulled down the roof on his head; see Judges, 16:29-30. 131. amaranthine, immortal, like the amaranth, which grows in the fields of Heaven. 135. limn, draw—as with charcoal. 150. purpureal, purple, as of royalty. cypress-crowned, as a symbol of sorrow and death. 156. bruit, noise, clamor. 159. shard, fragment.

Strange, piteous, futile thing,   161
Wherefore should any set thee love apart?
Seeing none but I makes much of naught"
          (He said),
"And human love needs human meriting,
    How hast thou merited —   165
Of all man's clotted clay the dingiest clot?
    Alack, thou knowest not
How little worthy of any love thou art!
Whom wilt thou find to love ignoble thee
    Save Me, save only Me?   170
All which I took from thee I did but take,
    Not for thy harms,
But just that thou might'st seek it in My
    arms.
    All which thy child's mistake
Fancies as lost, I have stored for thee at
    home;   175
    Rise, clasp My hand, and come!"

    Halts by me that footfall;
    Is my gloom, after all,
Shade of His hand, outstretched caress-
    ingly?
    "Ah, fondest, blindest, weakest,   180
    I am He Whom thou seekest!
Thou dravest love from thee, who dravest
    Me."   (*1891; 1893*)

TO THE DEAD CARDINAL OF
        WESTMINSTER

I will not perturbate
Thy Paradisal state
        With praise
    Of thy dead days;

To the new-heavened say,   5
"Spirit, thou wert fine clay" —
        This do,
    Thy praise who knew.

Therefore my spirit clings
Heaven's porter by the wings,   10
        And holds
    Its gated golds

Apart, with thee to press
A private business —
        Whence,   15
    Deign me audience.

Anchorite, who didst dwell
With all the world for cell,
        My soul
    Round me doth roll   20

A sequestration bare.
Too far alike we were,
        Too far
    Dissimilar.

For its burning fruitage I   25
Do climb the tree o' the sky;
        Do prize
    Some human eyes.

You smelt the heaven-blossoms,
And all the sweet embosoms   30
        The dear
    Uranian year.

Those Eyes my weak gaze shuns,
Which to the suns are Suns,
        Did   35
    Not affray your lid.

The carpet was let down
(With golden moltings strown)
        For you
    Of the angels' blue.   40

But I, ex-Paradised,
The shoulder of your Christ
        Find high
    To lean thereby.

So flaps my helpless sail,   45
Bellying with neither gale,
        Of Heaven
    Nor Orcus even.

Life is coquetry
Of Death, which wearies me,   50
        Too sure
    Of the amour;

A tiring-room where I
Death's divers garments try,
        Till fit   55
    Some fashion sit.

It seemeth me too much
I do rehearse for such
        A mean
    And single scene.   60

The sandy glass hence bear —
Antique remembrancer;
        My veins
    Do spare its pains.

With secret sympathy   65
My thoughts repeat in me

To the Dead Cardinal of Westminster. The Cardinal was
Henry Edward Manning (1808-92), a great preacher and
social reformer.
    17. **Anchorite,** hermit.

21. **sequestration,** medium of separation—i.e., it separated me from the world.   32. **Uranian year,** a year in heaven
(from Urania, the muse of astronomy), equal to 365,000
earthly years (*2 Peter,* 3:8).   48. **Orcus,** the underworld.

Infirm
The turn o' the worm

Beneath my appointed sod;
The grave is in my blood;   70
    I shake
To winds that take

Its grasses by the top;
The rains thereon that drop
    Perturb   75
With drip acerb

My subtly answering soul;
The feet across its knoll
    Do jar
Me from afar.   80

As sap foretastes the spring;
As Earth ere blossoming
    Thrills
With far daffodils,

And feels her breast turn sweet   85
With the unconceivéd wheat;
    So doth
My flesh foreloathe

The abhorréd spring of Dis,
With seething presciences   90
    Affirm
The preparate worm.

I have no thought that I,
When at the last I die,
    Shall reach   95
To gain your speech.

But you, should that be so,
May very well, I know,
    May well
To me in hell   100

With recognizing eyes
Look from your Paradise —
    "God bless
Thy hopelessness!"

Call, holy soul, O call   105
The hosts angelical,
    And say —
"See, far away

"Lies one I saw on earth;
One stricken from his birth   110
    With curse
Of destinate verse.

"What place doth He ye serve
For such sad spirit reserve —
    Given,   115
In dark lieu of Heaven,

"The impitiable Dæmon,
Beauty, to adore and dream on,
    To be
Perpetually   120

"Hers, but she never his?
He reapeth miseries;
    Foreknows
His wages woes;

"He lives detachéd days;   125
He serveth not for praise;
    For gold
He is not sold;

"Deaf is he to world's tongue;
He scorneth for his song   130
    The loud
Shouts of the crowd;

"He asketh not world's eyes;
Not to world's ears he cries;
    Saith — 'These   135
Shut, if you please';

"He measureth world's pleasure,
World's ease, as Saints might measure;
    For hire
Just love entire   140

"He asks, not grudging pain;
And knows his asking vain,
    And cries —
'Love! Love!' and dies,

"In guerdon of long duty,   145
Unowned by Love or Beauty;
    And goes —
Tell, tell, who knows!

"Aliens from Heaven's worth,
Fine beasts who nose i' the earth,   150
    Do there
Reward prepare.

"But are *his* great desires
Food but for nether fires?
    Ah me,   155
A mystery!

"Can it be his alone,
To find, when all is known,
    That what
He solely sought   160

76. acerb, harsh, bitter. 89. spring of Dis, the river
Styx, in the realm of Dis, or Pluto (god of the lower world),
over which the dead must pass. 92. preparate, ready—to
devour the body. 111-12. curse . . . verse, predestined to
sorrow, as was Œdipus when, before his birth, an oracle
foretold in mystic verses his sorrowful end.

117. impitiable Dæmon, pitiless spirit.

"Is lost, and thereto lost
All that its seeking cost?
     That he
     Must finally,

"Through sacrificial tears   165
And anchoretic years,
     Tryst
     With the sensualist?"

So ask; and if they tell
The secret terrible,   170
     Good friend,
     I pray thee send

Some high gold embassage
To teach my unripe age.
     Tell!   175
     Lest my feet walk hell.   (1893)

FIELD-FLOWER

A PHANTASY

God took a fit of Paradise-wind,
    A slip of cœrule weather,
A thought as simple as Himself,
    And raveled them together.
Unto His eyes He held it there,   5
To teach it gazing debonair
    With memory of what, perdie,
A God's young innocences were.
His fingers pushed it through the sod —
It came up redolent of God,   10
Garrulous of the eyes of God
    To all the breezes near it;
Musical of the mouth of God
    To all had ears to hear it;
Mystical with the mirth of God,   15
    That glow-like did ensphere it.
    And — "Babble! babble! babble!" said;
    "I'll tell the whole world one day!"
    There was no blossom half so glad,
    Since sun of Christ's first Sunday.   20

A poet took a flaw of pain,
    A hap of skyey pleasure,
A thought had in his cradle lain,
    And mingled them in measure.
That chrism he laid upon his eyes,   25
And lips, and heart, for euphrasies,
    That he might see, feel, sing, perdie,
The simple things that are the wise.
Beside the flower he held his ways,

And leaned him to it gaze for gaze —   30
He took its meaning, gaze for gaze,
    As baby looks on baby;
Its meaning passed into his gaze,
    Native as meaning may be;
He rose with all his shining gaze   35
    As children's eyes at play be.
    And — "Babble! babble! babble!" said;
    "I'll tell the whole world one day!"
    There was no poet half so glad,
    Since man grew God that Sunday.   40
                      (1897)

ENVOY

Go, songs, for ended is our brief, sweet play;
    Go, children of swift joy and tardy sorrow;
And some are sung, and that was yesterday,
    And some unsung, and that may be to-
        morrow.

Go forth; and if it be o'er stony way,   5
    Old joy can lend what newer grief must
        borrow;
And it was sweet, and that was yesterday,
    And sweet is sweet, though purchaséd with
        sorrow.

Go, songs, and come not back from your far
        way;
    And if men ask you why ye smile and
        sorrow,   10
Tell them ye grieve, for your hearts know
        Today,
    Tell them ye smile, for your eyes know
        Tomorrow.   (1897)

THE KINGDOM OF GOD

"IN NO STRANGE LAND"

O world invisible, we view thee,
O world intangible, we touch thee,
O world unknowable, we know thee,
Inapprehensible, we clutch thee!

Does the fish soar to find the ocean,   5
The eagle plunge to find the air —
That we ask of the stars in motion
If they have rumor of thee there?

Not where the wheeling systems darken,
And our benumbed conceiving soars! —   10

Field-Flower. 1. **fit**, strain, as of music. 2. **cœrule**, heavenly (deep-blue). 7. **perdie**, indeed (originally an Old French oath, *par Dieu*, by God). 22. **hap**, a chance bit. 25. **chrism**, sacred oil, used in the administration of Roman Catholic sacraments. 26. **euphrasies**, magic restoratives, as of the herb euphrasy (eye-bright), fabled to make old eyes young.

Envoy. This poem was printed at the end of a volume of poems entitled *New Poems* (1897).
1. **Go, songs**, a common literary convention, used by Chaucer, Spenser, Southey, and others.
The Kingdom of God. This poem was found among Thompson's papers at his death. **"In . . . land."** See *Exodus*, 2:22.—Zipporah bore Moses a son, "and he called his name Gershom; for he said, 'I have been a stranger in a strange land.'"

The drift of pinions, would we hearken,
Beats at our own clay-shuttered doors.

The angels keep their ancient places —
Turn but a stone and start a wing!
'Tis ye, 'tis your estrangéd faces,   15
That miss the many-splendored thing.

But (when so sad thou canst not sadder)
Cry — and upon thy so sore loss
Shall shine the traffic of Jacob's ladder
Pitched betwixt Heaven and Charing Cross.

Yea, in the night, my Soul, my daughter,   21
Cry — clinging Heaven by the hems;
And lo, Christ walking on the water,
Not of Gennesareth, but Thames!   (1913)

ROBERT SEYMOUR BRIDGES*
(1844-1930)

ELEGY

The wood is bare: a river-mist is steeping
    The trees that winter's chill of life bereaves;
Only their stiffened boughs break silence,
        weeping
        Over their fallen leaves;

That lie upon the dank earth brown and
        rotten,   5
    Miry and matted in the soaking wet —
Forgotten with the spring, that is forgotten
        By them that can forget.

Yet it was here we walked when ferns were
        springing,
    And through the mossy bank shot bud
        and blade —   10
Here found in summer, when the birds were
        singing,
        A green and pleasant shade.

'Twas here we loved in sunnier days and
        greener;
    And now, in this disconsolate decay,
I come to see her where I most have seen
        her,   15
        And touch the happier day.

For on this path, at every turn and corner,
    The fancy of her figure on me falls;
Yet walks she with the slow step of a mourner,
        Nor hears my voice that calls.   20

So through my heart there winds a track of
        feeling,
    A path of memory, that is all her own,
Whereto her phantom beauty ever stealing
        Haunts the sad spot alone.

About her steps the trunks are bare; the
        branches   25
    Drip heavy tears upon her downcast head,
And bleed from unseen wounds that no sun
        staunches,
        For the year's sun is dead.

And dead leaves wrap the fruits that summer
        planted;
    And birds that love the South have taken
        wing.   30
The wanderer, loitering o'er the scene
        enchanted,
        Weeps, and despairs of spring. (1873)

I WILL NOT LET THEE GO

I will not let thee go.
Ends all our month-long love in this?
    Can it be summed up so,
    Quit in a single kiss?
I will not let thee go.   5

I will not let thee go.
If thy words' breath could scare thy deeds,
    As the soft south can blow
    And toss the feathered seeds,
    Then might I let thee go.   10

I will not let thee go.
Had not the great sun seen, I might;
    Or were he reckoned slow
    To bring the false to light,
    Then might I let thee go.   15

I will not let thee go.
The stars that crowd the summer skies
    Have watched us so below
    With all their million eyes,
    I dare not let thee go.   20

I will not let thee go.
Have we not chid the changeful moon,
    Now rising late, and now
    Because she set too soon,
    And shall I let thee go?   25

I will not let thee go.
Have not the young flowers been content,
    Plucked ere their buds could blow,
    To seal our sacrament?
    I cannot let thee go.   30

19. **Jacob's ladder**, that on which Jacob saw angels
going up and down between heaven and earth (*Genesis*, 28:12).
20. **Charing Cross**, a locality near Trafalgar Square, in the
heart of London. 24. **Gennesareth**, the Sea of Galilee;
the incident of Christ's walking on the sea is recorded in
Matthew, 14:25-33.
*Only the early work of Bridges is here represented.

I Will Not Let Thee Go. 28. **blow**, bloom.

I will not let thee go.
I hold thee by too many bands;
  Thou sayest farewell, and lo!
I have thee by the hands,
And will not let thee go.   35
              (1873)

A POPPY GROWS UPON THE SHORE

A poppy grows upon the shore,
  Bursts her twin cup in summer late;
Her leaves are glaucous-green and hoar,
  Her petals yellow, delicate.

Oft to her cousins turns her thought,   5
  In wonder if they care that she
Is fed with spray for dew, and caught
  By every gale that sweeps the sea.

She has no lovers like the red,
  That dances with the noble corn;   10
Her blossoms on the waves are shed,
  Where she stands shivering and forlorn.
              (1873)

TRIOLET

When first we met we did not guess
That Love would prove so hard a master;
Of more than common friendliness
When first we met we did not guess.
Who could foretell this sore distress   5
This irretrievable disaster
When first we met? — We did not guess
That Love would prove so hard a master.
              (1873)

TRIOLET

All women born are so perverse
No man need boast their love possessing.
If naught seem better, nothing's worse;
All women born are so perverse.
From Adam's wife, that proved a curse   5
Though God had made her for a blessing,
All women born are so perverse
No man need boast their love possessing.
              (1873)

From THE GROWTH OF LOVE

4

The very names of things beloved are dear,
And sounds will gather beauty from their
    sense,
As many a face through love's long residence

A *Poppy Grows upon the Shore.* 3. **glaucous-green,**
bluish green.   10. **corn,** wheat.
  Triolet. See note on *Rose-Leaves,* p. 772.
  The Growth of Love. This is a series of sixty-nine sonnets.

Groweth to fair instead of plain and sear;
But when I say thy name it hath no peer,   5
And I suppose fortune determined thence
Her dower, that such beauty's excellence
Should have a perfect title for the ear.
Thus may I think the adopting Muses chose
Their sons by name, knowing none would be
    heard   10
Or writ so oft in all the world as those —
Dan Chaucer, mighty Shakespeare, then for
    third
The classic Milton, and to us arose
Shelley with liquid music in the word.
              (1876)

8

For beauty being the best of all we know
Sums up the unsearchable and secret aims
Of nature, and on joys whose earthly names
Were never told can form and sense bestow;
And man has sped his instinct to outgo   5
The step of science; and against her shames
Imagination stakes out heavenly claims,
Building a tower above the head of woe.
Nor is there fairer work for beauty found
Than that she win in nature her release   10
From all the woes that in the world abound;
Nay with his sorrow may his love increase,
If from man's greater need beauty redound,
And claim his tears for homage of his peace.
              (1876)

16

This world is unto God a work of art,
Of which the unaccomplished heavenly plan
Is hid in life within the creature's heart,
And for perfection looketh unto man.
Ah me! those thousand ages: with what
    slow   5
Pains and persistence were his idols made,
Destroyed and made, ere ever he could know
The mighty mother must be so obeyed.
For lack of knowledge and through little
    skill
His childish mimicry outwent his aim;   10
His effort shaped the genius of his will;
Till through distinction and revolt he came,
True to his simple terms of good and ill,
Seeking the face of Beauty without blame.
              (1876)

20

The world still goeth about to show and hide,
Befooled of all opinion, fond of fame;
But he that can do well taketh no pride,
And see'th his error, undisturbed by shame:
So poor's the best that longest life can do,   5
The most so little, diligently done;
So mighty is the beauty that doth woo,
So vast the joy that love from love hath
    won.

God's love to win is easy, for He loveth
Desire's fair attitude, nor strictly weighs   10
The broken thing, but all alike approveth
Which love hath aim'd at Him — that is
    heaven's praise;
And if we look for any praise on earth,
'Tis in man's love — all else is nothing worth.
                                              (1876)

23

O weary pilgrims, chanting of your woe,
That turn your eyes to all the peaks that
    shine,
Hailing in each the citadel divine
The which ye thought to have entered long
    ago;
Until at length your feeble steps and slow   5
Falter upon the threshold of the shrine,
And your hearts overburdened doubt in fine
Whether it be Jerusalem or no:
Disheartened pilgrims, I am one of you;
For, having worshiped many a barren face   10
I scarce now greet the goal I journeyed to;
I stand a pagan in the holy place;
Beneath the lamp of truth I am found untrue,
And question with the God that I embrace.
                                              (1876)

35

All earthly beauty hath one cause and proof,
To lead the pilgrim soul to beauty above;
Yet lieth the greater bliss so far aloof,
That few there be are weaned from earthly
    love.
Joy's ladder it is, reaching from home to
    home,   5
The best of all the work that all was good;
Whereof 'twas writ the angels aye upclomb,
Down sped, and at the top the Lord God
    stood.
But I my time abuse, my eyes by day
Centered on thee, by night my heart on
    fire —   10
Letting my numbered moments run away —
Nor e'en 'twixt night and day to heaven
    aspire —
So true it is that what the eye seeth not
But slow is loved, and loved is soon forgot.
                                              (1889)

62

I will be what God made me, nor protest
Against the bent of genius in my time,
That science of my friends robs all the best,
While I love beauty, and was born to rime.

Sonnet 35. 7-8. **angels . . . stood,** a reference to Jacob's
ladder, *Genesis,* 28:12-13.—"And he dreamed, and behold a
ladder set up on the earth, and the top of it reached to
heaven; and behold the angels of God ascending and descending on it. And, behold, the Lord stood above it."
    "The argument is partly from Michael Angelo's *Madrigals,*
19" (Bridges's note).

Be they our mighty men, and let me dwell   5
In shadow among the mighty shades of old,
With love's forsaken palace for my cell;
Whence I look forth and all the world be-
    hold,
And say, These better days, in best things
    worse,
This bastardy of time's magnificence,   10
Will mend in fashion and throw off the curse,
To crown new love with higher excellence.
Cursed though I be to live my life alone,
My toil is for man's joy, his joy my own.
                                              (1889)

A PASSER-BY

Whither, O splendid ship, thy white sails
    crowding,
    Leaning across the bosom of the urgent
        West,
That fearest nor sea rising, nor sky clouding,
    Whither away, fair rover, and what thy
        quest?
    Ah! soon, when Winter has all our vales
        opprest,   5
When skies are cold and misty, and hail is
    hurling,
    Wilt thou glide on the blue Pacific, or rest
In a summer haven asleep, thy white sails
    furling.

I there before thee, in the country that well
    thou knowest,
    Already arrived am inhaling the odorous
        air.   10
I watch thee enter unerringly where thou
    goest,
    And anchor queen of the strange shipping
        there,
    Thy sails for awnings spread, thy masts
        bare;
Nor is aught from the foaming reef to the
    snow-capped, grandest
    Peak, that is over the feathery palms
        more fair   15
Than thou, so upright, so stately, and still
    thou standest.

And yet, O splendid ship, unhailed and
    nameless,
    I know not if, aiming a fancy, I rightly
        divine
That thou hast a purpose joyful, a courage
    blameless,
    Thy port assured in a happier land than
        mine.   20
    But for all I have given thee, beauty
        enough is thine,
As thou, aslant with trim tackle and shroud-
    ing,

From the proud nostril curve of a prow's
       line
In the offing scatterest foam, thy white sails
       crowding.

                                    (1879)

I HAVE LOVED FLOWERS THAT FADE

I have loved flowers that fade,
Within those magic tents
Rich hues have marriage made
With sweet unmemoried scents:
A honeymoon delight —   5
A joy of love at sight,
That ages in an hour —
My song be like a flower!

I have loved airs, that die
Before their charm is writ   10
Along a liquid sky
Trembling to welcome it.
Notes, that with pulse of fire
Proclaim the spirit's desire,
Then die, and are nowhere —   15
My song be like an air!

Die, song, die like a breath,
And wither as a bloom;
Fear not a flowery death,
Dread not an airy tomb!   20
Fly with delight, fly hence!
'Twas thine love's tender sense
To feast; now on thy bier
Beauty shall shed a tear.

                                    (1879)

THERE IS A HILL BESIDE THE SILVER THAMES

There is a hill beside the silver Thames,
Shady with birch and beech and odorous pine;
And brilliant underfoot with thousand gems
Steeply the thickets to his floods decline.
       Straight trees in every place   5
       Their thick tops interlace,
And pendant branches trail their foliage fine
       Upon his watery face.

Swift from the sweltering pasturage he flows;
His stream, alert to seek the pleasant shade, 10
Pictures his gentle purpose, as he goes
Straight to the caverned pool his toil has
       made.
       His winter floods lay bare
       The stout roots in the air;
His summer streams are cool, when they
       have played   15
       Among their fibrous hair.

A rushy island guards the sacred bower,
And hides it from the meadow, where in peace
The lazy cows wrench many a scented flower,
Robbing the golden market of the bees;   20
       And laden barges float
       By banks of myosote,
And scented flag and golden flower-de-lys
       Delay the loitering boat.

And on this side the island, where the pool   25
Eddies away, are tangled mass on mass
The water-weeds, that net the fishes cool,
And scarce allow a narrow stream to pass;
       Where spreading crowfoot mars
       The drowning nenuphars,   30
Waving the tassels of her silken grass
       Below her silver stars.

But in the purple pool there nothing grows,
Not the white water-lily spoked with gold;
Though best she loves the hollows, and well
       knows   35
On quiet streams her broad shields to un-
       fold —
       Yet should her roots but try
       Within these deeps to lie,
Not her long reaching stalk could ever hold
       Her waxen head so high.   40

Sometimes an angler comes, and drops his
       hook
Within its hidden depths, and 'gainst a tree
Leaning his rod, reads in some pleasant book,
Forgetting soon his pride of fishery;
       And dreams, or falls asleep,   45
       While curious fishes peep
About his nibbled bait, or scornfully
       Dart off and rise and leap.

And sometimes a slow figure 'neath the trees,
In ancient-fashioned smock, with tottering
       care   50
Upon a staff propping his weary knees,
May by the pathway of the forest fare:
       As from a buried day
       Across the mind will stray
Some perishing mute shadow — and un-
       aware   55
       He passeth on his way.

Else, he that wishes solitude is safe,
Whether he bathe at morning in the stream;
Or lead his love there when the hot hours
       chafe
The meadows, busy with a blurring steam;   60
       Or watch, as fades the light,
       The gibbous moon grow bright,

22. myosote, a plant of the forget-me-not family. 30.
nenuphars, water-lilies. 62. gibbous, convex, as the
moon is when three-fourths full.

Until her magic rays dance in a dream,
   And glorify the night.

Where is this bower beside the silver Thames?
O pool and flowery thickets, hear my vow! 66
O trees of freshest foliage and straight stems,
No sharer of my secret I allow —
   Lest ere I come the while
   Strange feet your shades defile;   70
Or lest the burly oarsman turn his prow
   Within your guardian isle.   (1879)

LONDON SNOW

When men were all asleep the snow came
   flying,
In large white flakes falling on the city brown,
Stealthily and · perpetually settling and
   loosely lying,
   Hushing the latest traffic of the drowsy
   town;
Deadening, muffling, stifling its murmurs
   failing;   5
Lazily and incessantly floating down and
   -down;
   Silently sifting and veiling road, roof, and
   railing;
Hiding difference, making unevenness even,
Into angles and· crevices softly drifting and
   sailing.
   All night it fell, and when full inches
   seven   10
It lay in the depth of its uncompacted
   lightness,
The clouds blew off from a high and frosty
   heaven;
And all woke earlier for the unaccustomed
   brightness
Of the winter dawning, the strange un-
   heavenly glare.
The eye marveled — marveled at the daz-
   zling whiteness;   15
   The ear harkened to the stillness of the
   solemn air;
No sound of wheel rumbling nor of foot
   falling,
And the busy morning cries came thin and
   spare.
   Then boys I heard, as they went to school,
   calling;
They gathered up the crystal manna to
   freeze   20
Their tongues with tasting, their hands with
   snowballing;
   Or rioted in a drift, plunging up to the
   knees;
Or peering up from under the white-mossed
   wonder,
"O look at the trees!" they cried, "O look
   at the trees!"

With lessened load a few carts creak and
   blunder,   25
Following along the white deserted way,
A country company long dispersed asunder;
   When now already the sun, in pale dis-
   play
Standing by Paul's high dome, spread forth
   below
His sparkling beams, and awoke the stir of
   the day.   30
   For now doors open, and war is waged
   with the snow;
And trains of somber men, past tále of
   number,
Tread along brown paths, as toward their
   toil they go;
   But even for them awhile no cares en-
   cumber
Their minds diverted; the daily word is
   unspoken,   35
The daily thoughts of labor and sorrow
   slumber
At the sight of the beauty that greets them,
   for the charm they have broken.

                      (1880)

THE VOICE OF NATURE

I stand on the cliff and watch the veiled sun
   paling
A silver field afar in the mournful sea,
The scourge of the surf, and plaintive gulls
   sailing
   At ease on the gale that smites the shudder-
   ing lea:
   Whose smile severe and chaste   5
June never hath stirred to vanity, nor age
   defaced.
In lofty thought strive, O spirit, forever;
In courage and strength pursue thine own
   endeavor.

Ah! if it were only for thee, thou restless
   ocean
   Of waves that follow and roar, the sweep
   of the tides;   10
Wer't only for thee, impetuous wind, whose
   motion
   Precipitate all o'errides, and turns, nor
   abides;
   For you, sad birds and fair,
Or only for thee, bleak cliff, erect in the
   air —
Then well could I read wisdom in every
   feature,   15
O well should I understand the voice of
   Nature.

29. **Paul's high dome,** the dome of St. Paul's Cathedral,
London. 32. **tale,** count.

But far away, I think, in the Thames valley,
  The silent river glides by flowery banks;
And birds sing sweetly in branches that arch
    an alley
  Of cloistered trees, moss-grown in their
    ancient ranks: 20
    Where if a light air stray,
  'Tis laden with hum of bees and scent of
    may.
Love and peace be thine, O spirit, forever;
Serve thy sweet desire; despise endeavor.

And if it were only for thee, entrancéd river, 25
  That scarce dost rock the lily on her airy
    stem,
Or stir a wave to murmur, or a rush to quiver;
  Wer't but for the woods, and summer asleep
    in them:
    For you my bowers green,
  My hedges of rose and woodbine, with
    walks between,   30
Then well could I read wisdom in every
    feature,
O well should I understand the voice of
    Nature.   (1880)

THE CLOUDS HAVE LEFT THE SKY

The clouds have left the sky,
  The wind hath left the sea,
The half-moon up on high
  Shrinketh her face of dree.

She lightens on the comb   5
  Of leaden waves, that roar
And thrust their hurried foam
  Up on the dusky shore.

Behind the western bars
  The shrouded day retreats,   10
And unperceived the stars
  Steal to their sovran seats.

And whiter grows the foam,
  The small moon lightens more;
And as I turn me home,   15
  My shadow walks before.   (1890)

THE SNOW LIES SPRINKLED ON THE BEACH

The snow lies sprinkled on the beach,
And whitens all the marshy lea;
The sad gulls wail adown the gale;
The day is dark and black the sea.
  Shorn of their crests the blighted waves 5
With driven foam the offing fleck;

22. **may**, hawthorn.
The Clouds Have Left the Sky. 4. **dree**, sorrow, grief.

The ebb is low and barely laves
The red rust of the giant wreck.

On such a stony, breaking beach
My childhood chanced and chose to be; 10
'Twas here I played, and musing made
My friend the melancholy sea.
  He from his dim enchanted caves
With shuddering roar and onrush wild
Fell down in sacrificial waves   15
At feet of his exulting child.

Unto a spirit too light for fear
His wrath was mirth, his wail was glee —
My heart is now too fixed to bow
Though all his tempests howl at me; 20
  For to the gain life's summer saves,
My solemn joy's increasing store,
The tossing of his mournful waves
Makes sweetest music evermore.
          (1890)

I LOVE ALL BEAUTEOUS THINGS

I love all beauteous things,
  I seek and adore them;
God hath no better praise,
  And man in his hasty days
  Is honored for them.   5

I too will something make
  And joy in the making,
Although tomorrow it seem
Like the empty words of a dream
  Remembered on waking.   (1890)

NIGHTINGALES

Beautiful must be the mountains whence ye
    come,
And bright in the fruitful valleys the streams,
    wherefrom
        Ye learn your song.
Where are those starry woods? Oh, might I
    wander there,
Among the flowers, which in that heavenly
    air   5
        Bloom the year long!

Nay, barren are those mountains and spent
    the streams;
Our song is the voice of desire, that haunts our
    dreams,
        A throe of the heart,
Whose pining visions dim, forbidden hopes
    profound,   10
No dying cadence nor long sigh can sound,
        For all our art.

Alone, aloud in the raptured ear of men
We pour our dark nocturnal secret; and then,

As night is withdrawn 15
From these sweet-springing meads and burst-
ing boughs of May,
Dream, while the innumerable choir of day
     Welcome the dawn. (1893)

SO SWEET LOVE SEEMED

So sweet love seemed that April morn,
When first we kissed beside the thorn,
So strangely sweet, it was not strange
We thought that love could never change.

But I can tell — let truth be told — 5
That love will change in growing old;
Though day by day is naught to see,
So delicate his motions be.

And in the end 'twill come to pass
Quite to forget what once he was, 10
Nor even in fancy to recall
The pleasure that was all in all.

His little spring, that sweet we found,
So deep in summer floods is drowned,
I wonder, bathed in joy complete, 15
How love so young could be so sweet.
               (1893)

WINTER NIGHTFALL

The day begins to droop —
  Its course is done;
But nothing tells the place
  Of the setting sun.

The hazy darkness deepens, 5
  And up the lane
You may hear, but cannot see,
  The homing wain.

An engine pants and hums
  In the farm hard by; 10
Its lowering smoke is lost
  In the lowering sky.

The soaking branches drip,
  And all night through
The dropping will not cease 15
  In the avenue.

A tall man there in the house
  Must keep his chair;
He knows he will never again
  Breathe the spring air. 20

His heart is worn with work;
  He is giddy and sick
If he rise to go as far
  As the nearest rick.

Winter Nightfall. 8. **wain**, wagon. 24. **rick**, stack of hay.

He thinks of his morn of life, 25
  His hale, strong years;
And braves as he may the night
  Of darkness and tears.
               (1899)

MY DELIGHT AND THY DELIGHT

My delight and thy delight
Walking, like two angels white,
In the gardens of the night;

My desire and thy desire
Twining to a tongue of fire, 5
Leaping live, and laughing higher;
Through the everlasting strife
In the mystery of life.

Love, from whom the world begun,
Hath the secret of the sun.

Love can tell, and love alone,
Whence the million stars were strewn,
Why each atom knows its own,
How, in spite of woe and death,
Gay is life, and sweet is breath; 15

This he taught us, this we knew,
Happy in his science true,
Hand in hand as we stood
'Neath the shadows of the wood,
Heart to heart as we lay 20
In the dawning of the day.
               (1899)

PATER FILIO

Sense with keenest edge unuséd,
  Yet unsteeled by scathing fire;
Lovely feet as yet unbruiséd
  On the ways of dark desire;
Sweetest hope that lookest smiling 5
  O'er the wilderness defiling!

Why such beauty, to be blighted
  By the swarm of foul destruction?
Why such innocence delighted,
  When sin stalks to thy seduction? 10
All the litanies e'er chaunted
Shall not keep thy faith undaunted.

I have prayed the sainted Morning
  To unclasp her hands to hold thee;
From resignful Eve's adorning 15
  Stol'n a robe of peace to enfold thee;
With all charms of man's contriving
Armed thee for thy lonely striving.

Pater Filio. The title means *Father to Son.*

Me too once unthinking Nature
— Whence Love's timeless mockery took
   me —
Fashioned so divine a creature,
  Yea, and like a beast forsook me.
I forgave, but tell the measure
Of her crime in thee, my treasure.

                  (1899)

MARY ELIZABETH COLERIDGE
(1861-1907)

A MOMENT

The clouds had made a crimson crown
  About the mountains high.
The stormy sun was going down
  In a stormy sky.

Why did you let your eyes so rest on me,   5
  And hold your breath between?
In all the ages this can never be
  As if it had not been.

                  (1896)

"HE KNOWETH NOT THAT THE DEAD ARE THINE"

The weapon that you fought with was a word,
And with that word you stabbed me to the
    heart.
Not once but twice you did it, for the sword
  Made no blood start.

They have not tried you for your life. You go
Strong in such innocence as men will boast. 6
They have not buried me. They do not know
  Life from its ghost.   (1896)

GIFTS

I tossed my friend a wreath of roses, wet
  With early dew, the garland of the morn.
He lifted it — and on his brow he set
  A crackling crown of thorn.

Against my foe I hurled a murderous dart. 5
  He caught it in his hand — I heard him
    laugh —
I saw the thing that should have pierced his
    heart
  Turn to a golden staff.

                  (1896)

"*He Knoweth Not That the Dead Are Thine.*" See *Proverbs,*
9:18. Of the simple-minded man who listens to the call of
a foolish woman, the writer says: "He knoweth not that the
dead are there; and that her guests are in the depths of hell."

THE WITCH

I have walked a great while over the snow,
  And I am not tall nor strong.
My clothes are wet, and my teeth are set,
  And the way was hard and long.
I have wandered over the fruitful earth,   5
  But I never came here before.
Oh, lift me over the threshold, and let me in
    at the door!

The cutting wind is a cruel foe;
  I dare not stand in the blast.
My hands are stone, and my voice a groan,
  And the worst of death is past.   11
I am but a little maiden still;
  My little white feet are sore.
Oh, lift me over the threshold, and let me in
    at the door!

Her voice was the voice that women have, 15
  Who plead for their heart's desire.
She came — she came — and the quivering
    flame
  Sank and died in the fire.
It never was lit again on my hearth
  Since I hurried across the floor,   20
To lift her over the threshold, and let her in
    at the door!   (1896)

A HUGUENOT

Oh, a gallant set were they,
As they charged on us that day,
A thousand riding like one!
  Their trumpets crying,
  And their white plumes flying,   5
And their sabers flashing in the sun.

Oh, a sorry lot were we,
As we stood beside the sea,
Each man for himself as he stood!
  We were scattered and lonely —   10
  A little force only
Of the good men fighting for the good.

But I never loved more
On sea or on shore
The ringing of my own true blade.   15
  Like lightning it quivered,
  And the hard helms shivered,
As I sang, "None maketh me afraid!" (1896)

The Witch. Cf. *The Land of Heart's Desire,* p. 873.
  7. **lift...threshold.** According to a folk belief, no evil
spirit is able to cross the threshold of a house unless lifted over
by an inmate. See S. T. Coleridge's *Christabel,* lines 129 ff.
17-18. **quivering...fire.** The presence of an evil spirit is
betrayed by the action of fire, according to folk-belief. Cf.
Christabel, lines 156 ff.
  A Huguenot. The French Protestants, or Huguenots, were
severely persecuted from the revocation of the Edict of Nantes
in 1685 to the restitution of their civil rights in 1787. This
poem concerns an episode in their heroic resistance to French
dragoons, bent on their annihilation.

L'OISEAU BLEU

The lake lay blue below the hill.
  O'er it, as I looked, there flew
Across the waters, cold and still,
  A bird whose wings were palest blue.

The sky above was blue at last,   5
  The sky beneath me blue in blue.
A moment, ere the bird had passed
  It caught his image as he flew.   (1897)

JEALOUSY

"The myrtle bush grew shady
  Down by the ford." —
"Is it even so?" said my lady.
  "Even so!" said my lord.
"The leaves are set too thick together   5
  For the point of a sword."

"The arras in your room hangs close,
  No light between!
You wedded one of those
  That see unseen." —   10
"Is it even so?" said the King's Majesty.
  "Even so!" said the Queen.   (1897)

SHADOW

Child of my love! though thou be bright as
  day,
  Though all the sons of joy laugh and adore
    thee,
Thou canst not throw thy shadow self away.
  Where thou dost come, the earth is darker
  for thee.

When thou dost pass, a flower that saw the
  sun   5
  Sees him no longer.
The hosts of darkness are, thou radiant one,
  Through thee made stronger.   (1897)

UNWELCOME

We were young, we were merry, we were very
  very wise,
  And the door stood open at our feast,
When there passed us a woman with the
  West in her eyes,
  And a man with his back to the East.

Oh, still grew the hearts that were beating so
  fast,   5
  The loudest voice was still.

L'Oiseau Bleu. The title means *The Blue-Bird.*

The jest died away on our lips as they passed,
  And the rays of July struck chill.

The cups of red wine turned pale on the
  board,
  The white bread black as soot.   10
The hound forgot the hand of her lord,
  She fell down at his foot.

Low let me lie, where the dead dog lies,
  Ere I sit me down again at a feast,
When there passes a woman with the West
  in her eyes,   15
  And a man with his back to the East. (1898)

IN A VOLUME OF AUSTIN DOBSON

The faded perfume of forgotten years,
  The scent of withered rose-leaves sweetly
    faint,
  Old-world imaginations, fancies quaint,
And fun just dancing on the edge of tears;

A boy's delight, a little maiden's fears,   5
  A heroine of the days of patch and paint,
  The gentle visions of an old French saint,
The treachery that repels not but endears.
        (1907)

LORD ALFRED DOUGLAS
(1870-1945)

IMPRESSION DE NUIT: LONDON

See what a mass of gems the city wears
Upon her broad live bosom! row on row
Rubies and emeralds and amethysts glow.
See! that huge circle, like a necklace, stares
With thousands of bold eyes to heaven, and
  dares   5
The golden stars to dim the lamps below,
And in the mirror of the mire I know
The moon has left her image unawares.
That's the great town at night: I see her
  breasts;
Pricked out with lamps they stand like huge
  black towers,   10
I think they move! I hear her panting breath.
And that's her head where the tiara rests.
And in her brain, through lanes as dark as
  death,
Men creep like thoughts . . . The lamps are
  like pale flowers.   (*1894;* 1894)

In a Volume of Austin Dobson. See Dobson's poems, pages
769 ff.
Impression de Nuit: London. The title means *Impression
of a London Night.* The poem was written on the top floor
of a building near Hyde Park.
12. tiara, a coronet—here, a circle of lights.

A SONG

Steal from the meadows, rob the tall green
hills,
  Ravish my orchard's blossoms, let me bind
A crown of orchard flowers and daffodils,
  Because my love is fair and white and kind.

Today the thrush has trilled her daintiest
phrases,   5
  Flowers with their incense have made drunk
the air,
God has bent down to gild the hearts of
daisies,
  Because my love is kind and white and fair.

Today the sun has kissed the rose-tree's
daughter,
  And sad Narcissus, Spring's pale acolyte, 10
Hangs down his head and smiles into the
water,
  Because my love is kind and fair and white.
                  (*1894*)

PLAINTE ETERNELLE

The sun sinks down, the tremulous daylight
dies.
  (Down their long shafts the weary sunbeams glide.)
  The white-winged ships drift with the falling tide;
Come back, my love, with pity in your eyes!

The tall white ships drift with the falling tide.
  (Far, far away I hear the seamews' cries.) 6
Come back, my love, with pity in your eyes!
There is no room now in my heart for pride.

Come back, come back! with pity in your eyes,
  (The night is dark, the sea is fierce and
wide.)   10
  There is no room now in my heart for pride,
Though I become the scorn of all the wise.

I have no place now in my heart for pride.
  (The moon and stars have fallen from the
skies.)
  Though I become the scorn of all the wise,
Thrust, if you will, sharp arrows in my side. 16

Let me become the scorn of all the wise.
  (Out of the East I see the morning ride.)
  Thrust, if you will, sharp arrows in my side,
Play with my tears and feed upon my sighs. 20

Wound me with swords, put arrows in my
side.
  (On the white sea the haze of noon-day
lies.)
  Play with my tears and feed upon my sighs,
But come, my love, before my heart has died.

Drink my salt tears and feed upon my sighs.
  (Westward the evening goes with one red
stride.)   26
Come back, my love, before my heart has
died,
Down sinks the sun, the tremulous daylight
dies.

Come back! my love, before my heart has
died.
  (Out of the South I see the pale moon rise.)
  Down sinks the sun, the tremulous daylight
dies,   31
The white-winged ships drift with the falling
tide.   (c. 1896)

THE DEAD POET

I dreamed of him last night, I saw his face
All radiant and unshadowed of distress,
And as of old, in music measureless,
I heard his golden voice and marked him trace
Under the common thing the hidden grace 5
And conjure wonder out of emptiness,
Till mean things put on beauty like a dress
And all the world was an enchanted place.
And then methought outside a fast locked
gate
I mourned the loss of unrecorded words,   10
Forgotten tales and mysteries half said,
Wonders that might have been articulate,
And voiceless thoughts like murdered singing
birds.
And so I woke and knew that he was dead.
                  (*1901*)

THE GREEN RIVER

I know a green grass path that leaves the field,
And like a running river, winds along
Into a leafy wood where is no throng
Of birds at noon-day, and no soft throats
yield
Their music to the moon. The place is sealed,
An unclaimed sovereignty of voiceless song, 6
And all the unravished silences belong
To some sweet singer lost or unrevealed.
So is my soul become a silent place.
Oh, may I wake from this uneasy night   10

A Song. 10. **Narcissus,** a beautiful youth who fell in love
with his own reflection seen in the water and who pined
away in desire for it; he was changed into the flower that
bears his name. **acolyte,** one who carries the wine, the
water, and the lights at the Mass.
Plainte Eternelle. The title means *Everlasting Lament.*

The Dead Poet. This poem was written about Oscar Wilde
a year after his death. Cf. Keats's sonnet *When I Have
Fears That I May Cease to Be.*

To find a voice of music manifold.
Let it be shape of sorrow with wan face,
Or Love that swoons on sleep, or else delight
That is as wide-eyed as a marigold. (c. 1907)

WILLIAM BUTLER YEATS*
(1865-1939)

THE STOLEN CHILD

Where dips the rocky highland
Of Sleuth Wood in the lake,
There lies a leafy island
Where flapping herons wake
The drowsy water rats;   5
There we've hid our faery vats,
Full of berries,
And of reddest stolen cherries.
Come away, O human child!
To the waters and the wild   10
With a faery, hand in hand,
For the world's more full of weeping than
    you can understand.

Where the wave of moonlight glosses
The dim gray sands with light,
Far off by furthest Rosses   15
We foot it all the night,
Weaving olden dances,
Mingling hands and mingling glances
Till the moon has taken flight;
To and fro we leap   20
And chase the frothy bubbles,
While the world is full of troubles
And is anxious in its sleep.
Come away, O human child!
To the waters and the wild   25
With a faery, hand in hand,
For the world's more full of weeping than
    you can understand.

Where the wandering water gushes
From the hills above Glen-Car,
In pools among the rushes   30
That scarce could bathe a star,
We seek for slumbering trout
And whispering in their ears
Give them unquiet dreams;
Leaning softly out   35
From ferns that drop their tears
Over the young streams.

Come away, O human child!
To the waters and the wild
With a faery, hand in hand,   40
For the world's more full of weeping than
    you can understand.

Away with us he's going,
The solemn-eyed;
He'll hear no more the lowing
Of the calves on the warm hillside   45
Or the kettle on the hob
Sing peace into his breast,
Or see the brown mice bob
Round and round the oatmeal-chest.
For he comes, the human child,   50
To the waters and the wild
With a faery, hand in hand,
From a world more full of weeping than he
    can understand.

(1889)

THE ROSE OF THE WORLD

Who dreamed that beauty passes like a
    dream?
For these red lips, with all their mournful
    pride,
Mournful that no new wonder may betide,
Troy passed away in one high funeral gleam,
And Usna's children died.   5

We and the laboring world are passing by;
Amid men's souls, that waver and give place,
Like the pale waters in their wintry race,
Under the passing stars, foam of the sky,
Lives on this lonely face.   10

Bow down, archangels, in your dim abode.
Before you were, or any hearts to beat,
Weary and kind, one lingered by His seat;
He made the world to be a grassy road
Before her wandering feet.   15

(1893)

THE LAKE ISLE OF INNISFREE

I will arise and go now, and go to Innisfree,
    And a small cabin build there, of clay and
        wattles made,

---

*The first nine poems of William Butler Yeats are reprinted from his *Early Poems and Stories* and *Later Poems* by permission of The Macmillan Company, publishers.
2. **Sleuth . . . lake.** The lake of Glen-Car, surrounded by wooded hills, is in the county of Sligo, province of Connaught, northwestern Ireland. 15. **Rosses**, granite headlands on the Sligo coast; Yeats says in a note that the locality is thought to be a favorite haunt of fairies.

The Rose of the World. Before Yeats, the rose had been used as a symbol of love, as in the medieval *Romance of the Rose*; of the Virgin Mary, called "the mystic rose"; and also of Ireland, as in J. Mangan's *Dark Rosaleen*. Yeats feels that the beauty of a woman suggests all other beautiful things and concepts in the world, and is hence infinitely important.
4. **Troy . . . gleam.** Helen's beauty brought about the Trojan War and the burning of Troy; cf. Symons' *Modern Beauty*, line 8, p. 886. 5. **Usna's children.** The three sons of Usna died for the love of Deirdre, as related in the old Irish epic tales of Cuchulain.
The Lake Isle of Innisfree. Innisfree is an island in Lough Gill, a lake in the county of Sligo, Ireland.
2. **wattles**, interwoven rods and twigs.

Nine bean rows will I have there, a hive for
   the honey bee,
And live alone in the bee-loud glade.

And I shall have some peace there, for peace
   comes dropping slow,   5
   Dropping from the veils of the morning to
   where the cricket sings;
There midnight's all a glimmer, and noon a
   purple glow,
And evening full of the linnet's wings.

I will arise and go now, for always night and
   day
   I hear lake water lapping with low sounds
   by the shore;   10
While I stand on the roadway, or on the
   pavements gray,
I hear it in the deep heart's core.   (1893)

WHEN YOU ARE OLD

When you are old and gray and full of sleep,
And nodding by the fire, take down this book,
And slowly read, and dream of the soft look
Your eyes had once, and of their shadows
   deep;

How many loved your moments of glad
   grace,   5
And loved your beauty with love false or true;
But one man loved the pilgrim soul in you,
And loved the sorrows of your changing face.

And bending down beside the glowing bars
Murmur, a little sadly, how love fled   10
And paced upon the mountains overhead
And hid his face amid a crowd of stars.
     (1893)

CUCHULAIN'S FIGHT WITH THE SEA

A man came slowly from the setting sun,
To Emer, raddling raiment in her dun,
And said, "I am that swineherd whom you bid
Go dwell upon the cliffs and watch the tide;
But now I have no need to watch it more."   5

Then Emer cast the web upon the floor,
And raising arms all raddled with the dye,
Parted her lips with a loud sudden cry.

That swineherd stared upon her face and said,
"Not any god alive, nor mortal dead,   10
Has slain so mighty armies, so great kings,
Nor won the gold that now Cuchulain brings."

"Why do you tremble thus from feet to
   crown?"

He caught his breath and cast him weeping
   down
Upon the web-heaped floor, and thus his
   word: 15
"With him is one sweet-throated like a bird."

"You dare me to my face," and thereupon
She smote with raddled fist, and where her son
Herded the cattle came with stumbling feet,
And cried with angry voice, "It is not meet   20
To idle life away with flocks and herds."

"I have long waited, mother, for those words;
But wherefore now?"

               "There is a man to die;
You have the heaviest arm under the sky."

"No, somewhere under daylight or the stars   25
My father stands amid his battle cars."

"But you have grown to be the taller man."

"Yet somewhere under starlight or the sun
My father stands amid his battle cars."

"But he is old and sad with many wars."   30

"I only ask what way my journey lies.
For He who made you bitter, made you wise."

"The Red Branch gather a great company
Between the game and the horses of the sea.
Go there, and camp upon the forest's rim;   35
But tell your name and lineage to him
Whose blade compels, and bid them send
   you one
Who has a like vow from their triple dun."

Among those feasting kings Cuchulain dwelt,
And his young dear one close beside him knelt;
Stared like the spring upon the ancient
   skies,   41
Upon the mournful wonder of his eyes,

Cuchulain's Fight with the Sea. Cuchulain is the chief hero
of the Ulster or Red Branch cycle of Irish epic lays, dating
from the beginning of the Christian era and preserved in
manuscripts of a much later date or in folk tradition. The
poem relates one of the later incidents of the hero's career:
Emer, who long before the opening of the poem had borne a
son to Cuchulain, is made angry by the news that Cuchulain
has deserted her for a princess, to whom Yeats gives no name;
she sends her son, now grown to manhood, to avenge her
wrong; she instructs him to seek a battle with Cuchulain but
to keep his identity a secret. As a result, the son is slain
by the father. Cf. Arnold's *Sohrab and Rustum,* p. 475.
   In the older versions of the story, such as those in Curtin's
Myths and Folk-Lore of Ireland (which Yeats called his
source) and Lady Gregory's *Cuchulain of Muirthemne,* Emer
is not the name of the jealous queen whom Cuchulain has
deserted, but that of his faithful wife.
   2. **raddling,** coloring with red dye. **dun,** a hill fort.

33. Red Branch, the men of Ulster. **34. Between . . .
sea,** between the forest and the ocean. **38. like vow,** a vow
not to disclose his name until compelled by force of arms.
triple dun, group of three forts.

And pondered on the glory of his days;
And all around the harp-string told his
    praise,
And Concobar, the Red Branch king of kings,
With his own fingers touched the brazen
    strings.   46

At last Cuchulain spake, "Some man has made
His evening fire amid the leafy shade.
I have often heard him singing to and fro,
I have often heard the sweet sound of his
    bow;   50
Seek out what man he is."

                        One went and came.
"He bade me let all know he gives his name
At the sword point, and bade me bring him
    one
Who had a like vow from our triple dun."

"I only of the Red Branch hosted now,"   55
Cuchulain cried, "have made and keep that
    vow."

After short fighting in the leafy shade,
He spake to the young man, "Is there no maid
Who loves you, no white arms to wrap you
    round,
Or do you long for the dim sleepy ground, 60
That you have come and dared me to my
    face?"

"The dooms of men are in God's hidden
    place."

"Your head a while seemed like a woman's
    head
That I loved once."

                        Again the fighting sped,
But now the war rage in Cuchulain woke,   65
And through that new blade's guard the old
    blade broke,
And pierced him.
            "Speak before your breath is done."
"Cuchulain I, mighty Cuchulain's son."

"I put you from your pain. I can no more."

While day its burden on to evening bore,   70
With head bowed on his knees Cuchulain
    stayed,
Then Concobar sent that sweet-throated
    maid,
And she, to win him, his gray hair caressed;
In vain her arms, in vain her soft white breast.
Then Concobar, the subtlest of all men,   75

45. Concobar, king of Ulster. 55. hosted, present in
the army. 62. dooms, fates.

Ranking his Druids round him ten by ten,
Spake thus, "Cuchulain will dwell there and
    brood,
For three days more in dreadful quietude,
And then arise, and raving slay us all.
Chaunt in his ear delusions magical,   80
That he may fight the horses of the sea."
The Druids took them to their mystery,
And chanted for three days.

                        Cuchulain stirred,
Stared on the horses of the sea, and heard
The cars of battle and his own name cried; 85
And fought with the invulnerable tide. (1893)

THE LAND OF HEART'S DESIRE

O Rose, thou art sick.
            — *William Blake.*

PERSONS OF THE PLAY

MAUREEN BRUIN   MARY BRUIN
BRIDGET BRUIN   FATHER HART
SHAWN BRUIN   A FAERY CHILD

*The Scene is laid in the Barony of Kilma-
cowen, in the County of Sligo, and at a remote
time.*

SCENE.—*A room with a hearth on the floor in
the middle of a deep alcove to the Right.
There are benches in the alcove and a table;
and a crucifix on the wall. The alcove is
full of a glow of light from the fire. There
is an open door facing the audience to the
Left, and to the left of this a bench. Through
the door one can see the forest. It is night,
but the moon or a late sunset glimmers
through the trees and carries the eye far off
into a vague, mysterious world. MAUREEN
BRUIN, SHAWN BRUIN, and BRIDGET
BRUIN sit in the alcove at the table or about
the fire. They are dressed in the costume of
some remote time, and near them sits an old
priest, FATHER HART. He may be dressed*

76. **Druids,** priests of the ancient Celts. 86. **fought . . .
tide.** Other versions relate that Cuchulain fought in frenzy
with the waves for three days and nights until he fell from
hunger and exhaustion.
    The Land of Heart's Desire. "The Land of Heart's De-
sire" is the Celtic Otherworld, sometimes called the Isle of
Avalon or the Blessed Isles; it is a land of perpetual youth
and happiness. Irish legends tell of men who have seen it
on the horizon or who have dwelt there; Welsh legends relate
that Arthur is waiting there his time for returning.
    O . . . sick, from William Blake's *The Sick Rose* (*Songs of
Experience,* 1794):
            "O Rose, thou art sick!
                The invisible worm,
            That flies in the night,
                In the howling storm,

            Has found out thy bed
                Of crimson joy,
            And his dark secret love
                Does thy life destroy."

as a friar. There is food and drink upon the table. MARY BRUIN *stands by the door reading a book. If she looks up she can see through the door into the wood.*

BRIDGET.   Because I bid her clean the
  pots for supper
She took that old book down out of the
  thatch;
She has been doubled over it ever since.
We should be deafened by her groans and
  moans
Had she to work as some do, Father Hart;   5
Get up at dawn like me and mend and scour
Or ride abroad in the boisterous night like you,
The pyx and blessed bread under your arm.
SHAWN.   Mother, you are too cross.
BRIDGET.   You've married her,
And fear to vex her and so take her part.   10
MAURTEEN [*to* FATHER HART].   It is but
  right that youth should side with youth;
She quarrels with my wife a bit at times,
And is too deep just now in the old book!
But do not blame her greatly: she will grow
As quiet as a puff-ball in a tree   15
When but the moons of marriage dawn and
  die
For half a score of times.
FATHER HART.   Their hearts are wild,
As be the hearts of birds, till children come.
BRIDGET.   She would not mind the kettle,
  milk the cow,
Or even lay the knives and spread the cloth.   20
SHAWN.   Mother, if only —
MAURTEEN.   Shawn, this is half empty;
Go, bring up the best bottle that we have.
FATHER HART.   I *never* saw her read a
  book before;
What can it be?
MAURTEEN [*to* SHAWN].   What are you
  waiting for?
You must not shake it when you draw the
  cork;   25
It's precious wine, so take your time about it.
[*To Priest*]   [SHAWN *goes.*]
There was a Spaniard wrecked at Ocris Head,
When I was young, and I have still some
  bottles.
He cannot bear to hear her blamed; the book
Has lain up in the thatch these fifty years;   30
My father told me my grandfather wrote it,
And killed a heifer for the binding of it —
But supper's spread, and we can talk and eat.
It was little good he got out of the book,
Because it filled his house with rambling
  fiddlers,   35

And rambling ballad-makers and the like.
The griddle-bread is there in front of you.
Colleen, what is the wonder in that book,
That you must leave the bread to cool?
  Had I
Or had my father read or written books   40
There were no stocking stuffed with yellow
  guineas
To come when I am dead to Shawn and you.
FATHER HART.   You should not fill your
  head with foolish dreams.
What are you reading?
MARY.   How a Princess Edane,
A daughter of a King of Ireland, heard   45
A voice singing on a May Eve like this,
And followed half awake and half asleep,
Until she came into the Land of Faery,
Where nobody gets old and godly and grave,
Where nobody gets old and crafty and wise,   50
Where nobody gets old and bitter of tongue.
And she is still there, busied with a dance
Deep in the dewy shadow of a wood,
Or where stars walk upon a mountain-top.
MAURTEEN.   Persuade the colleen to put
  down the book;   55
My grandfather would mutter just such
  things,
And he was no judge of a dog or a horse,
And any idle boy could blarney him;
Just speak your mind.
FATHER HART.   Put it away, my colleen;
God spreads the heavens above us like great
  wings   60
And gives a little round of deeds and days,
And then come the wrecked angels and set
  snares,
And bait them with light hopes and heavy
  dreams,
Until the heart is puffed with pride and goes
Half shuddering and half joyous from God's
  peace;   65
For it was some wrecked angel, blind with
  tears,
Who flattered Edane's heart with merry
  words.
My colleen, I have seen some other girls
Restless and ill at ease, but years went by
And they grew like their neighbors and
  were glad   70
In minding children, working at the churn,
And gossiping of weddings and of wakes;
For life moves out of a red flare of dreams
Into a common light of common hours,
Until old age bring the red flare again.   75

---

8. **pyx**, the vessel which contains the consecrated bread used in the Roman Catholic Mass. 27. **Spaniard**, Spanish ship. **Ocris Head**, a promontory that separates Sligo Bay from the ocean.

38. **Colleen**, girl. 44. **Princess Edane.** The story is found in Lady Wilde's *Ancient Legends of Ireland* (1886-88). Edain is the King of Munster's daughter; she is lured to the Land of Heart's Desire by Midar, king of the fairies. 46. **May Eve.** According to Irish folk-lore, the fairies are especially powerful on May Eve and frequently steal away newly married mortal women to be their own brides. 72. **wakes**, feasts which precede Irish funerals.

MAURTEEN. That's true — but she's too
young to know it's true.
BRIDGET. She's old enough to know that
it is wrong
To mope and idle.
MAURTEEN. I've little blame for her;
She's dull when my big son is in the fields,
And that and maybe this good woman's
tongue   80
Have driven her to hide among her dreams
Like children from the dark under the bed-
clothes.
BRIDGET. She'd never do a turn if I were
silent.
MAURTEEN. And maybe it is natural upon
May Eve
To dream of the good people. But tell me,
girl,   85
If you've the branch of blessed quicken wood
That women hang upon the post of the door
That they may send good luck into the
house?
Remember they may steal new-married brides
After the fall of twilight on May Eve,   90
Or what old women mutter at the fire
Is but a pack of lies.
FATHER HART. It may be truth.
We do not know the limit of those powers
God has permitted to the evil spirits
For some mysterious end. You have done
right [to MARY];   96
It's well to keep old innocent customs up.

[MARY BRUIN *has taken a bough of quicken
wood from a seat and hung it on a nail in
the door-post. A girl child strangely
dressed, perhaps in faery green, comes out
of the wood and takes it away.*

MARY. I had no sooner hung it on the nail
Before a child ran up out of the wind;
She has caught it in her hand and fondled it;
Her face is pale as water before dawn.   100
FATHER HART. Whose child can this be?
MAURTEEN. No one's child at all.
She often dreams that some one has gone by,
When there was nothing but a puff of wind.
MARY. They have taken away the blessed
quicken wood,
They will not bring good luck into the
house;   105
Yet I am glad that I was courteous to them,
For are not they, likewise, children of God?
FATHER HART. Colleen, they are the
children of the fiend,
And they have power until the end of Time,

When God shall fight with them a great
pitched battle   110
And hack them into pieces.
MARY.   He will smile,
Father, perhaps, and open His great door.
FATHER HART. Did but the lawless angels
see that door
They would fall, slain by everlasting peace;
And when such angels knock upon our
doors,   115
Who goes with them must drive through the
same storm.

[*An arm comes around the door-post and
knocks and beckons. It is clearly seen in
the silvery light.* MARY BRUIN *goes to
door and stands in it for a moment.*
MAURTEEN BRUIN *is busy filling* FATHER
HART'S *plate.* BRIDGET BRUIN *stirs the
fire.*

MARY [*coming to table*]. There's somebody
out there that beckoned me
And raised her hand as though it held a cup,
And she was drinking from it, so it may be
That she is thirsty.

[*She takes milk from the table and carries it
to the door.*

FATHER HART. That will be the child   120
That you would have it was no child at all.
BRIDGET. And maybe, Father, what he
said was true;
For there is not another night in the year
So wicked as tonight.
MAURTEEN. Nothing can harm us   124
While the good Father's underneath our roof.
MARY. A little queer old woman dressed
in green.
BRIDGET. The good people beg for milk
and fire
Upon May Eve — woe to the house that gives,
For they have power upon it for a year.
MAURTEEN. Hush, woman, hush!
BRIDGET.   She's given milk away. 130
I knew she would bring evil on the house.
MAURTEEN. Who was it?
MARY. Both the tongue and face were
strange.
MAURTEEN. Some strangers came last
week to Clover Hill;
She must be one of them.
BRIDGET.   I am afraid.
FATHER HART. The Cross will keep all
evil from the house   135
While it hangs there.

85. **good people,** fairies—so called lest they take offense
and do mortals injury. 86. **blessed . . . wood,** mountain
ash, hung on the door-post to protect the household from
the power of the fairies.

128. **woe . . . gives.** It was formerly said that Irish
peasants never give away fire, water, milk, or salt on May
Eve for fear of falling under a fairy spell.

MAURTEEN. Come, sit beside me, colleen,
And put away your dreams of discontent,
For I would have you light up my last days,
Like the good glow of the turf; and when I die
You'll be the wealthiest hereabout, for,
    colleen,   140
I have a stocking full of yellow guineas
Hidden away where nobody can find it.
    BRIDGET. You are the fool of every
        pretty face,
And I must spare and pinch that my son's
    wife
May have all kinds of ribbons for her head.
    MAURTEEN. Do not be cross; she is a
        right good girl!
The butter is by your elbow, Father Hart.
My colleen, have not Fate and Time and
    Change
Done well for me and for old Bridget there?
We have a hundred acres of good land,   150
And sit beside each other at the fire.
I have this reverend Father for my friend;
I look upon your face and my son's face —
We've put his plate by yours — and here he
    comes,
And brings with him the only thing we have
    lacked,   155
Abundance of good wine.. [SHAWN comes in.]
    Stir up the fire,
And put new turf upon it till it blaze;
To watch the turf-smoke coiling from the fire,
And feel content and wisdom in your heart,
This is the best of life; when we are young   160
We long to tread a way none trod before,
But find the excellent old way through love,
And through the care of children, to the hour
For bidding Fate and Time and Change
    good-by.

[MARY stands for a moment in the door, and
    then takes a sod of turf from the fire and
    goes out through the door. SHAWN follows
    her and meets her coming in.

    SHAWN. What is it draws you to the chill
        o' the wood?   165
There is a light among the stems of the trees
That makes one shiver.
    MARY.   A little queer old man
Made me a sign to show he wanted fire
To light his pipe.
    BRIDGET. You've given milk and fire
Upon the unluckiest night of the year and
    brought,   170
For all you know, evil upon the house.
Before you married you were idle and fine
And went about with ribbons on your head;
And now — no, Father, I will speak my
    mind —
She is not a fitting wife for any man —   175

    SHAWN. Be quiet, mother!
    MAURTEEN. You are much too cross.
    MARY. What do I care if I have given
        this house,
Where I must hear all day a bitter tongue,
Into the power of faeries!
    BRIDGET.   You know well
How calling the good people by that name,   180
Or talking of them over much at all,
May bring all kinds of evil on the house.
    MARY. Come, faeries, take me out of
        this dull house!
Let me have all the freedom I have lost;
Work when I will and idle when I will!   185
Faeries, come take me out of this dull world,
For I would ride with you upon the wind,
Run on the top of the dishevelled tide,
And dance upon the mountains like a flame.
    FATHER HART. You cannot know the
        meaning of your words.   190
    MARY. Father, I am right weary of four
        tongues:
A tongue that is too crafty and too wise,
A tongue that is too godly and too grave,
A tongue that is more bitter than the tide,
And a kind tongue too full of drowsy love, 195
Of drowsy love and my captivity.

[SHAWN BRUIN leads her to a seat at the left
    of the door.

    SHAWN. Do not blame me; I often lie
        awake
Thinking that all things trouble your bright
    head.
How beautiful it is — your broad pale
    forehead   199
Under a cloudy blossoming of hair!
Sit down beside me here — these are too old,
And have forgotten they were ever young.
    MARY. Oh, you are the great door-post
        of this house,
And I the branch of blessed quicken wood,
And if I could I'd hang upon the post,   205
Till I had brought good luck into the house.

[She would put her arms about him, but
    looks shyly at the priest and lets her arms
    fall.

    FATHER HART. My daughter, take his
        hand — by love alone
God binds us to Himself and to the hearth,
That shuts us from the waste beyond His
    peace,
From maddening freedom and bewildering
    light.   210
    SHAWN. Would that the world were mine
        to give it you,
And not its quiet hearths alone, but even

All that bewilderment of light and freedom,
If you would have it.
MARY.   I would take the world
And break it into pieces in my hands   215
To see you smile watching it crumble away.
SHAWN.   Then I would mould a world of
    fire and dew,
With no one bitter, grave or over-wise,
And nothing marred or old to do you wrong,
And crowd the enraptured quiet of the sky 220
With candles burning to your lonely face.
MARY.   Your looks are all the candles
    that I need.
SHAWN.   Once a fly dancing in a beam of
    the sun,
Or the light wind blowing out of the dawn,
Could fill your heart with dreams none other
    knew,   225
But now the indissoluble sacrament
Has mixed your heart that was most proud
    and cold
With my warm heart forever; the sun and moon
Must fade and heaven be rolled up like a
    scroll;   229
But your white spirit still walks by my spirit.
    [A Voice singing in the wood.
MAURTEEN.   There's some one singing.
                    Why, it's but a child.
It sang, "The lonely of heart is withered away."
A strange song for a child, but she sings
    sweetly.
Listen, listen!   [Goes to door.
MARY.   Oh, cling close to me,
Because I have said wicked things tonight. 235
THE VOICE.   The wind blows out of the
    gates of the day,
The wind blows over the lonely of heart,
And the lonely of heart is withered away.
While the faeries dance in a place apart,
Shaking their milk-white feet in a ring,   240
Tossing their milk-white arms in the air;
For they hear the wind laugh and murmur
    and sing
Of a land where even the old are fair,
And even the wise are merry of tongue;
But I heard a reed of Coolaney say,   245
"When the wind has laughed and murmured
    and sung
The lonely of heart is withered away!"
MAURTEEN.   Being happy, I would have
    all others happy,
So I will bring her in out of the cold.
    [He brings in the faery child.

226. indissoluble sacrament, marriage. 228-29. sun
. . . scroll. From the description of the last judgment in
Revelation (5:12, 14)—"the sun became black . . . and the
moon became as blood . . . And the heaven departed as a
scroll when it is rolled together." 245. Coolaney, a lake
some six miles southwest of Kilmacowen. 249. He . . . child.
According to folk-lore, evil spirits were not able to cross a
mortal threshold without being helped. See S. T. Coleridge's
Christabel; also Mary Coleridge's The Witch, p. 868.

THE CHILD.   I tire of winds and waters
    and pale lights.   250
MAURTEEN.   And that's no wonder, for
    when night has fallen
The wood's a cold and a bewildering place,
But you are welcome here.
THE CHILD.   I am welcome here.
For when I tire of this warm little house,
But there is one here that must away, away. 255
MAURTEEN.   O, listen to her dreamy and
    strange talk.
Are you not cold?
THE CHILD.   I will crouch down beside
    you,
For I have run a long, long way this night.
BRIDGET.   You have a comely shape.
MAURTEEN.   Your hair is wet.
BRIDGET.   I'll warm your chilly feet.
MAURTEEN.   You have come indeed   260
A long, long way—for I have never seen
Your pretty face—and must be tired and
    hungry;
Here is some bread and wine.
THE CHILD.   The wine is bitter.
Old mother, have you no sweet food for me?
BRIDGET.   I have some honey.
                    [She goes into the next room.
MAURTEEN.   You have coaxing ways, 265
The mother was quite cross before you came.

    [BRIDGET returns with the honey and fills
    a porringer with milk.

BRIDGET.   She is the child of gentle people;
    look
At her white hands and at her pretty dress.
I've brought you some new milk, but wait a
    while
And I will put it to the fire to warm,   270
For things well fitted for poor folk like us
Would never please a high-born child like you.
THE CHILD.   From dawn, when you must
    blow the fire ablaze,
You work your fingers to the bone, old
    mother.
The young may lie in bed and dream and
    hope,   275
But you must work your fingers to the bone
Because your heart is old.
BRIDGET.   The young are idle.
THE CHILD.   Your memories have made
    you wise, old father;
The young must sigh through many a dream
    and hope,
But you are wise because your heart is old. 280

    [BRIDGET gives her more bread and honey.

MAURTEEN.   Oh, who would think to find
    so young a girl
Loving old age and wisdom?

THE CHILD.   No more, mother.
MAURTEEN. What a small bite! The
  milk is ready now. [*Hands it to her.*]
  What a small sip!
THE CHILD. Put on my shoes, old mother.
For I would like to dance now I have eaten, 285
The reeds are dancing by Coolaney lake,
And I would like to dance until the reeds
And the white waves have danced them-
  selves asleep.

[BRIDGET *puts on the shoes, and the* CHILD
  *is about to dance, but suddenly sees the
  crucifix and shrieks and covers her eyes.*

What is the ugly thing on the black cross?
FATHER HART. You cannot know how
  naughty your words are!
That is our Blessed Lord.
THE CHILD.   Hide it away! 291
BRIDGET. I have begun to be afraid again.
THE CHILD. Hide it away!
MAURTEEN. That would be wickedness!
BRIDGET. That would be sacrilege!
THE CHILD. The tortured thing! Hide it
  away!
MAURTEEN. Her parents are to blame. 295
FATHER HART. That is the image of the
  Son of God.
THE CHILD [*caressing him*]. Hide it away,
  hide it away!
MAURTEEN.   No, no.
FATHER HART. Because you are so young
  and like a bird,
That must take fright at every stir of the
  leaves,
I will go take it down.
THE CHILD.   Hide it away! 300
And cover it out of sight and out of mind!

[FATHER HART *takes crucifix from wall and
  carries it towards inner room.*

FATHER HART. Since you have come into
  this barony,
I will instruct you in our blessed faith;
And being so keen-witted you'll soon learn.
                    [*To the others.*
We must be tender to all budding things, 305
Our Maker let no thought of Calvary
Trouble the morning stars in their first song.
              [*Puts crucifix in inner room.*
THE CHILD. Here is level ground for
  dancing; I will dance.   [*Sings.*]
The wind blows out of the gates of the day,
The wind blows over the lonely of heart, 310
And the lonely of heart is withered away.
                        [*She dances.*

307. morning stars . . . song. From *Job*, 38:7.—"When
the morning stars sang together, and all the sons of God
shouted for joy"; the creation of the world is described.

MARY [*to* SHAWN]. Just now when she
  came near I thought I heard
Other small steps beating upon the floor,
And a faint music blowing in the wind,
Invisible pipes giving her feet the tune.   315
SHAWN. I heard no steps but hers.
MARY.   I hear them now,
The unholy powers are dancing in the house.
MAURTEEN. Come over here, and if you
  promise me
Not to talk wickedly of holy things
I will give you something.   320
THE CHILD. Bring it me, old father.
MAURTEEN. Here are some ribbons that
  I bought in the town
For my son's wife — but she will let me give
  them
To tie up that wild hair the winds have
  tumbled.
THE CHILD. Come, tell me, do you love
  me?   325
MAURTEEN.   Yes, I love you.
THE CHILD. Ah, but you love this fireside.
  Do you love me?
FATHER HART. When the Almighty puts
  so great a share
Of His own ageless youth into a creature,
To look is but to love.
THE CHILD.   But you love Him?
BRIDGET. She is blaspheming.
THE CHILD. And do you love me too? 330
MARY. I do not know.
THE CHILD. You love that young man
  there,
Yet I could make you ride upon the winds,
Run on the top of the dishevelled tide,
And dance upon the mountains like a flame.
MARY. Queen of Angels and kind saints,
  defend us!   335
Some dreadful thing will happen. A while
  ago
She took away the blessed quicken wood.
FATHER HART. You fear because of her
  unmeasured prattle;
She knows no better. Child, how old are
  you?
THE CHILD. When winter sleep is abroad
  my hair grows thin,   340
My feet unsteady. When the leaves awaken
My mother carries me in her golden arms;
I'll soon put on my womanhood and marry
The spirits of wood and water, but who can
  tell
When I was born for the first time? I think
I am much older than the eagle cock   346
That blinks and blinks on Ballygawley Hill,
And he is the oldest thing under the moon.
FATHER HART. Oh, she is of the faery people.
THE CHILD.   One called,

347. Ballygawley Hill, a mountain in Tyrone, Ulster.

I sent my messengers for milk and fire, 350
She called again and after that I came.

[All except SHAWN and MARY BRUIN gather
behind the priest for protection.

SHAWN [rising]. Though you have made
all these obedient,
You have not charmed my sight and won
from me
A wish or gift to make you powerful:
I'll turn you from the house. 355
FATHER HART. No, I will face her.
THE CHILD. Because you took away the
crucifix
I am so mighty that there's none can pass,
Unless I will it, where my feet have danced
Or where I've whirled my finger-tops.

[SHAWN tries to approach her and cannot.

MAURTEEN. Look, look! 360
There something stops him—look how he
moves his hands
As though he rubbed them on a wall of glass!
FATHER HART. I will confront this mighty
spirit alone;
Be not afraid, the Father is with us,
The Holy Martyrs and the Innocents, 365
The adoring Magi in their coats of mail,
And He who died and rose on the third day,
And all the nine angelic hierarchies.

[THE CHILD kneels upon the settle beside
MARY and puts her arm about her.

Cry, daughter, to the Angels and the Saints.
THE CHILD. You shall go with me, newly-
married bride,
And gaze upon a merrier multitude. 370
White-armed Nuala, Aengus of the Birds,
Feacra of the hurtling foam, and him
Who is the ruler of the Western Host,
Finvarra, and their Land of Heart's Desire, 375
Where beauty has no ebb, decay no flood,
But joy is wisdom, Time an endless song.
I kiss you and the world begins to fade.
SHAWN. Awake out of that trance—and
cover up
Your eyes and ears.
FATHER HART. She must both look and
listen, 380
For only the soul's choice can save her now.

Come over to me, daughter; stand beside
me;
Think of this house and of your duties in it.
THE CHILD. Stay and come with me,
newly-married bride,
For if you hear him you grow like the rest; 385
Bear children, cook, and bend above the
churn,
And wrangle over butter, fowl, and eggs,
Until at last, grown old and bitter of tongue,
You're crouching there and shivering at the
grave.
FATHER HART. Daughter, I point you
out the way to Heaven. 390
THE CHILD. But I can lead you, newly-
married bride,
Where nobody gets old and crafty and wise,
Where nobody gets old and godly and grave,
Where nobody gets old and bitter of tongue,
And where kind tongues bring no captivity;
For we are but obedient to the thoughts 396
That drift into the mind at a wink of the eye.
FATHER HART. By the dear Name of the
One crucified,
I bid you, Mary Bruin, come to me.
THE CHILD. I keep you in the name of
your own heart. 400
FATHER HART. It is because I put away
the crucifix
That I am nothing, and my power is nothing.
I'll bring it here again.
MAURTEEN [clinging to him]. No.
BRIDGET. Do not leave us.
FATHER HART. Oh, let me go before it is
too late;
It is my sin alone that brought it all. 405
[Singing outside.
THE CHILD. I hear them sing, "Come,
newly-married bride,
Come to the woods and waters and pale
lights."
MARY. I will go with you.
FATHER HART. She is lost, alas!
THE CHILD [standing by the door]. But
clinging mortal hope must fall from you,
For we who ride the winds, run on the
waves, 410
And dance upon the mountains are more
light
Than dewdrops on the banner of the dawn.
MARY. Oh, take me with you.
SHAWN. Beloved, I will keep you.
I've more than words, I have these arms to
hold you,
Nor all the faery host, do what they please, 415
Shall ever make me loosen you from these
arms.
MARY. Dear face! Dear voice!
THE CHILD. Come, newly-married bride.
MARY. I always loved her world—and
yet—and yet——

357. took . . . crucifix. Fairies partake of the nature of
demons in that their great power fails in the presence of
Christian symbols. 365. Innocents, the young children put
to death by Herod (Matthew, 2:16). 368. nine . . . hierarchies. Heavenly beings are traditionally divided into
nine groups, arranged in order of importance: Seraphim,
Cherubim, Thrones, Dominations, Virtues, Powers, Prin-
cipalities, Archangels, Angels. 372. Nuala, queen of the
Connaught fairies. Aengus, the Celtic god of love; his
kisses changed to birds and flew always about his head.
373. Feacra, "an ancient hero, now . . . a sea-fairy" (Yeats's
note). 375. Finvarra, king of the Connaught fairies.

THE CHILD. White bird, white bird, come with me, little bird.   420
MARY.   She calls me!
THE CHILD.   Come with me, little bird.

[*Distant dancing figures appear in the wood.*

MARY.   I can hear songs and dancing.
SHAWN.   Stay with me.
MARY.   I think that I would stay — and yet — and yet——
THE CHILD.   Come, little bird with crest of gold.
MARY [*very softly*].   And yet——
THE CHILD.   Come, little bird with silver feet!
[MARY BRUIN *dies, and the* CHILD *goes*.
SHAWN.   She is dead!
BRIDGET.   Come from that image; body and soul are gone.   425
You have thrown your arms about a drift of leaves,
Or bole of an ash-tree changed into her image.
FATHER HART.   Thus do the spirits of evil snatch their prey,
Almost out of the very hand of God;
And day by day their power is more and more,   430
And men and women leave old paths, for pride
Comes knocking with thin knuckles on the heart.

[*Outside there are dancing figures and, it may be a white bird, and many voices singing:*

The wind blows out of the gates of the day,
The wind blows over the lonely of heart,
And the lonely of heart is withered away;   435
While the faeries dance in a place apart,
Shaking their milk-white feet in a ring,
Tossing their milk-white arms in the air;
For they hear the wind laugh and murmur and sing
Of a land where even the old are fair,   440
And even the wise are merry of tongue;
But I heard a reed of Coolaney say —
"When the wind has laughed and murmured and sung,
The lonely of heart is withered away." (1894)

INTO THE TWILIGHT

Out-worn heart, in a time out-worn,
Come clear of the nets of wrong and right;
Laugh heart again in the gray twilight,
Sigh, heart, again in the dew of the morn.

420. **White bird,** the symbol of the soul.

Your mother Eire is always young,   5
Dew ever shining and twilight gray;
Though hopes fall from you and love decay,
Burning in fires of a slanderous tongue.

Come, heart, where hill is heaped upon hill;
For there the mystical brotherhood   10
Of sun and moon and hollow and wood
And river and stream work out their will;

And God stands winding His lonely horn,
And time and the world are ever in flight;
And love is less kind than the gray twilight,   15
·And hope is less dear than the dew of the morn.

(1899)

THE HOST OF THE AIR

O'Driscoll drove with a song
The wild duck and the drake
From the tall and the tufted reeds
Of the drear Hart Lake.

And he saw how the reeds grew dark   5
At the coming of night tide,
And dreamed of the long dim hair
Of Bridget his bride.

He heard while he sang and dreamed
A piper piping away,   10
And never was piping so sad,
And never was piping so gay.

And he saw young men and young girls
Who danced on a level place
And Bridget his bride among them,   15
With a sad and a gay face.

The dancers crowded about him,
And many a sweet thing said,
And a young man brought him red wine
And a young girl white bread.   20

But Bridget drew him by the sleeve,
Away from the merry bands,
To old men playing at cards
With a twinkling of ancient hands.

The bread and the wine had a doom,   25
For these were the host of the air;
He sat and played in a dream
Of her long dim hair.

5. **Eire,** Ireland.
The Host of the Air. "This poem is founded on an old Gaelic ballad that was sung and translated for me by a woman at Ballisodare in County Sligo" (Yeats's note).
  The "Host of the Air" is an especially malignant branch of the fairy race.
4. **Hart Lake,** "a gloomy and tree-bordered pond" five miles south of Sligo.

He played with the merry old men
And thought not of evil chance,   30
Until one bore Bridget his bride
Away from the merry dance.

He bore her away in his arms,
The handsomest young man there,
And his neck and his breast and his arms   35
Were drowned in her long dim hair.

O'Driscoll scattered the cards
And out of his dream awoke:
Old men and young men and young girls
Were gone like a drifting smoke;   40

But he heard high up in the air
A piper piping away,
And never was piping so sad,
And never was piping so gay.   (1899)

HE REMEMBERS FORGOTTEN BEAUTY

When my arms wrap you round I press
My heart upon the loveliness
That has long faded from the world;
The jeweled crowns that kings have hurled
In shadowy pools, when armies fled;   5
The love-tales wrought with silken thread
By dreaming ladies upon cloth
That has made fat the murderous moth;
The roses that of old time were
Woven by ladies in their hair;   10
The dew-cold lilies ladies bore
Through many a sacred corridor
Where such gray clouds of incense rose
That only the gods' eyes did not close:
For that pale breast and lingering hand   15
Come from a more dream-heavy land,
A more dream-heavy hour than this;
And when you sigh from kiss to kiss
I hear white Beauty sighing, too,
For hours when all must fade like dew;   20
But flame on flame, deep under deep,
Throne over throne, where in half sleep
Their swords upon their iron knees
Brood her high lonely mysteries.   (1899)

THE WILD SWANS AT COOLE

The trees are in their autumn beauty,
The woodland paths are dry,
Under the October twilight the water
Mirrors a still sky;
Upon the brimming water among the stones   5
Are nine-and-fifty swans.

The nineteenth autumn has come upon me

The Wild Swans at Coole. Reprinted from Yeats's *Collected Poems* by permission of The Macmillan Company, publishers.

Since I first made my count;
I saw, before I had well finished,
All suddenly mount   10
And scatter wheeling in great broken rings
Upon their clamorous wings.

I have looked upon those brilliant creatures,
And now my heart is sore.
All's changed since I, hearing at twilight,   15
The first time on this shore,
The bell-beat of their wings above my head,
Trod with a lighter tread.

Unwearied still, lover by lover,
They paddle in the cold   20
Companionable streams or climb the air;
Their hearts have not grown old;
Passion or conquest, wander where they will,
Attend upon them still.

But now they drift on the still water   25
Mysterious, beautiful;
Among what rushes will they build,
By what lake's edge or pool   28
Delight men's eyes when I awake some day
To find they have flown away?   (1919)

SAILING TO BYZANTIUM

I

That is no country for old men.   The young
In one another's arms, birds in the trees
—Those dying generations—at their song,
The salmon-falls, the mackerel-crowded seas,
Fish, flesh, or fowl, commend all summer long
Whatever is begotten, born, and dies.   6
Caught in that sensual music, all neglect
Monuments of unaging intellect.

2

An aged man is but a paltry thing,
A tattered coat upon a stick, unless   10
Soul clap its hands and sing, and louder sing
For every tatter in its mortal dress,
Nor is there singing school but studying
Monuments of its own magnificence;
And therefore I have sailed the seas and come
To the holy city of Byzantium.   16

3

O sages, standing in God's holy fire
As in the gold mosaic of a wall,

Sailing to Byzantium. Reprinted from Yeats's *Collected Poems* by permission of The Macmillan Company, publishers.
   Byzantium symbolizes the ideal journey's end for old people, since in it were properly combined the forces of body, mind, and spirit; all is at rest in the stillness of eternity, represented by the pure design of Byzantine art.
   4. salmon-falls . . . seas.   During the spawning period, salmon leap up waterfalls and mackerel crowd up streams.

Come from the holy fire, perne in a gyre,
And be the singing-masters of my soul.   20
Consume my heart away; sick with desire
And fastened to a dying animal
It knows not what it is; and gather me
Into the artifice of eternity.

4

Once out of nature I shall never take   25
My bodily form from any natural thing,
But such a form as Grecian goldsmiths make
Of hammered gold and gold enamelling
To keep a drowsy emperor awake;
Or set upon a golden bough to sing   30
To lords and ladies of Byzantium
Of what is past, or passing, or to come.

(1927)

AMONG SCHOOL CHILDREN

1

I walk through the long schoolroom question-
        ing;
A kind old nun in a white hood replies;
The children learn to cipher and to sing,
To study reading-books and history,
To cut and sew, be neat in everything   5
In the best modern way—the children's eyes
In momentary wonder stare upon
A sixty-year-old smiling public man.

2

I dream of a Ledaean body, bent
Above a sinking fire, a tale that she   10
Told of a harsh reproof, or trivial event
That changed some childish day to tragedy—
Told, and it seemed that our two natures blent
Into a sphere from youthful sympathy,
Or else, to alter Plato's parable,   15
Into the yolk and white of the one shell.

3

And thinking of that fit of grief or rage
I look upon one child or t'other there
And wonder if she stood so at that age—
For even daughters of the swan can share   20
Something of every paddler's heritage—

And had that colour upon cheek or hair,
And thereupon my heart is driven wild:
She stands before me as a living child.

4

Her present image floats into the mind—   25
Did Quattrocento finger fashion it
Hollow of cheek as though it drank the wind
And took a mess of shadows for its meat?
And I though never of Ledaean kind
Had pretty plumage once—enough of that,   30
Better to smile on all that smile, and show
There is a comfortable kind of old scarecrow.

5

What youthful mother, a shape upon her lap
Honey of generation had betrayed,
And that must sleep, shriek, struggle to escape
As recollection or the drug decide,   36
Would think her son, did she but see that shape
With sixty or more winters on its head,
A compensation for the pang of his birth,
Or the uncertainty of his setting forth?   40

6

Plato thought nature but a spume that plays
Upon a ghostly paradigm of things;
Solider Aristotle played the taws
Upon the bottom of a king of kings;
World-famous golden-thighed Pythagoras   45
Fingered upon a fiddle-stick or strings
What a star sang and careless Muses heard:
Old clothes upon old sticks to scare a bird.

7

Both nuns and mothers worship images,
But those the candles light are not as those   50
That animate a mother's reveries,
But keep a marble or a bronze repose.
And yet they too break hearts—O Presences
That passion, piety or affection knows,
And that all heavenly glory symbolise—   55
O self-born mockers of man's enterprise;

8

Labour is blossoming or dancing where
The body is not bruised to pleasure soul,

19. perne in a gyre, spool in a circular or a spiral motion.
30. golden bough. "I have read somewhere that in the
Emperor's palace at Byzantium was a tree made of gold and
silver, and artificial birds that sang."—Yeats.
  Among School Children. Reprinted from Yeats's Collected
Poems by permission of The Macmillan Company, publishers.
  9. Ledaean, like Leda, whose arched figure was a frequent
subject of medieval art. Yeats is thinking of his mother.
15. Plato's parable. Plato's Symposium contains a discussion of the nature of man, made up of three sexes: male, female, and a union of the two in spherical form. Because this
creature attacked the gods, it was cut in two. Plato symbolizes the union of mutually sympathetic natures in "the yolk
and white of the one shell."

42. ghostly paradigm, spiritual pattern.   43. Aristotle,
most celebrated of the Greek philosophers (384-322 B.C.).
He was more immediately "realistic" than Plato. played the
taws, used the whip. As a teacher of Alexander the Great
(the "king of kings," 336-323 B.C.), Aristotle once gave the
young prince a whipping.   45. Pythagoras, famous Greek
philosopher of the 6th century B.C., said to have had a golden
thigh. He is credited with the invention of the lyre and with
the creation of the theory of the music of the spheres.   48.
Old . . . bird. All these philosophies—of Plato, of Aristotle,
and of Pythagoras—are in direct contrast to the reality of
birth and death. Cf. Sailing to Byzantium, 9-10, p. 881.
57. Labour, childbirth.

Nor beauty born out of its own despair,
Nor blear-eyed wisdom out of midnight oil. 60
O chestnut-tree, great-rooted blossomer,
Are you the leaf, the blossom or the bole?
O body swayed to music, O brightening glance,
How can we know the dancer from the dance?
(1928)

ARTHUR SYMONS (1865-1945)

JAVANESE DANCERS

Twitched strings, the clang of metal, beaten
    drums,
Dull, shrill, continuous, disquieting;
And now the stealthy dancer comes
Undulantly with cat-like steps that cling;

Smiling between her painted lids a smile, 5
Motionless, unintelligible, she twines
Her fingers into mazy lines;
The scarves across her fingers twine the while.

One, two, three, four glide forth, and, to
    and fro,
Delicately and imperceptibly, 10
Now swaying gently in a row,
Now interthreading slow and rhythmically,

Still, with fixed eyes, monotonously still,
Mysteriously, with smiles inanimate,
With lingering feet that undulate, 15
With sinuous fingers, spectral hands that
    thrill

In measure while the gnats of music whirr,
The little amber-colored dancers move,
Like painted idols seen to stir
By the idolators in a magic grove. 20
(1889; 1892)

ON THE BEACH

Night, a gray sky, a ghostly sea,
The soft beginning of the rain;
Black on the horizon, sails that wane
Into the distance mistily.

The tide is rising, I can hear 5
The soft roar broadening far along;
It cries and murmurs in my ear
A sleepy old forgotten song.

Softly the stealthy night descends,
The black sails fade into the sky. 10
Is not this, where the sea-line ends,
The shore-line of infinity?

I cannot think or dream; the gray
Unending waste of sea and night,

Dull, impotently infinite, 15
Blots out the very hope of day.
(1890; 1892)

BEFORE THE SQUALL

The wind is rising on the sea,
The windy white foam-dancers leap;
And the sea moans uneasily,
And turns to sleep and cannot sleep.

Ridge after rocky ridge uplifts 5
Wild hands, and hammers at the land,
Scatters in liquid dust, and drifts
To death among the dusty sand.

On the horizon's nearing line,
Where the sky rests, a visible wall, 10
Gray in the offing, I divine
The sails that fly before the squall.
(1890; 1892)

EMMY

Emmy's exquisite youth and her virginal air,
Eyes and teeth in the flash of a musical smile,
Come to me out of the past, and I see her
    there
As I saw her once for a while.

Emmy's laughter rings in my ears, as bright,
Fresh, and sweet as the voice of a mountain
    brook, 6
And still I hear her telling us tales that night,
Out of Boccaccio's book.

There, in the midst of the villainous dancing-
    hall,
Leaning across the table, over the beer, 10
While the music maddened the whirling skirts
    of the ball,
As the midnight hour drew near,

There with the women, haggard, painted, and
    old,
One fresh bud in a garland withered and stale,
She, with her innocent voice and her clear
    eyes, told 15
Tale after shameless tale.

And ever the witching smile, to her face be-
    guiled,
Paused and broadened, and broke in a ripple
    of fun,
And the soul of a child looked out of the eyes
    of a child,
Or ever the tale was done. 20

Emmy. 8. **Boccaccio's book,** the *Decameron* (1353), a
collection of a hundred tales, some of them "shameless."

O my child, who wronged you first, and began
First the dance of death that you dance so
    well?
Soul for soul: and I think the soul of a man
Shall answer for yours in hell.   (*1891; 1892*)

AT CARBIS BAY

Out of the night of the sea,
Out of the turbulent night,
A sharp and hurrying wind
Scourges the waters white:
The terror by night.   5

Out of the doubtful dark,
Out of the night of the land,
What is it breathes and broods,
Hoveringly at hand?
The menace of land.   10

Out of the night of heaven,
Out of the delicate sky,
Pale and serene the stars
In their silence reply:
The peace of the sky.   (*1893; 1895*)

EPILOGUE: CREDO

Each, in himself, his hour to be and cease
Endures alone, yet few there be who dare,
Sole with themselves, their single burden bear,
All the long day until the night's release.

Yet, ere the night fall, and the shadows close,
This labor of himself is each man's lot;   6
All a man hath, yet living, is forgot,
Himself he leaves behind him when he goes.

If he have any valiancy within,
If he have made his life his very own,   10
If he have loved or labored, and have known
A strenuous virtue, or a strenuous sin,

Then, being dead, his life was not all vain,
For he has saved what most desire to lose, 14
And he has chosen what the few must choose,
Since life, once lived, returns no more again.

For of our time we lose so large a part
In serious trifles, and so oft let slip
The wine of every moment, at the lip
Its moment, and the moment of the heart. 20

We are awake so little on the earth,
And we shall sleep so long, and rise so late,

If there is any knocking at that gate
Which is the gate of death, the gate of birth.
             (*1894; 1895*)

THE WANDERERS

Wandering, ever wandering,
Their eyelids freshened with the wind of the
    sea
Blown up the cliffs at sunset, their cheeks
    cooled
With meditative shadows of hushed leaves
That have been drowsing in the woods all day
And certain fires of sunrise in their eyes.   6

They wander, and the white roads under them
Crumble into fine dust behind their feet,
For they return not; life, a long white road,
Winds ever from the dark into the dark,   10
And they, as days, return not; they go on
Forever, with the traveling stars; the night
Curtains them, being wearied, and the dawn
Awakens them unwearied; they go on.
They know the winds of all the earth, they
    know   15
The dust of many highways, and the stones
Of cities set for landmarks on the road.
Theirs is the world, and all the glory of it,
Theirs, because they forego it, passing on
Into the freedom of the elements;   20
Wandering, ever wandering,
Because life holds not anything so good
As to be free of yesterday, and bound
Toward a newborn tomorrow; and they go
Into a world of unknown faces, where   25
It may be there are faces waiting them,
Faces of friendly strangers, not the long
Intolerable monotony of friends.

The joy of earth is yours, O wanderers,
The only joy of the old earth, to wake,   30
As each new dawn is patiently renewed,
With foreheads fresh against a fresh young
    sky,
To be a little further on the road,
A little nearer somewhere, some few steps
Advanced into the future, and removed   35
By some few counted milestones from the
    past;
God gives you this good gift, the only gift
That God, being repentant, has to give.

Wanderers, you have the sunrise and the stars;
And we, beneath our comfortable roofs,   40
Lamplight, and daily fire upon the hearth,
And four walls of a prison, and sure food,
But God has given you freedom, wanderers!
             (*1895; 1897*)

At Carbis Bay. Carbis is a bay in Cornwall, southwestern
England, near St. Ives.
  Epilogue: Credo. Cf. Browning's *Two in the Campagna*,
p. 241; Henley's *Invictus*, p. 794; and Kipling's *Tomlinson*,
p. 896.

The Wanderers. Cf. Kipling's *The Explorer.*

ARQUES — AFTERNOON

Gently a little breeze begins to creep
Into the valley, and the sleeping trees
Are stirred, and breathe a little in their sleep,
And nod, half-wakened, to the breeze.

Cool little quiet shadows wander out   5
Across the fields, and dapple with dark trails
The snake-gray road coiled stealthily about
The green hill climbing from the vales.

And faintlier, in this cooler peace of things,
My brooding thoughts, a scattered flock
   grown few,   10
Withdrawn upon their melancholy wings,
Float farther off against the blue.
            (1896; 1897)

OPALS

My soul is like this cloudy, flaming opal ring.
The fields of earth are in it, green and glim-
   mering,
The waves of the blue sky, night's purple
   flower of noon,
The vanishing cold scintillations of the moon,
And the red heart that is a flame within a
   flame.   5
And as the opal dies, and is reborn the same,
And all the fire that is its life-blood seems to
   dart
Through the veined variable intricacies of its
   heart,
And ever wandering ever wanders back again,
So must my swift soul constant to itself
   remain.   10
Opal, have I not been as variable as you?
But, cloudy opal flaming green and red and
   blue,
Are you not ever constant in your varying,
Even as my soul, O captive opal of my ring?
            (1896; 1899)

THE OLD WOMEN

They pass upon their old, tremulous feet,
Creeping with little satchels down the street,
And they remember, many years ago,
Passing that way in silks. They wander, slow
And solitary, through the city ways,   5
And they alone remember those old days
Men have forgotten. In their shaking heads
A dancer of old carnivals yet treads
The measure of past waltzes, and they see
The candles lit again, the patchouli   10
Sweeten the air, and the warm cloud of musk

Enchant the passing of the passionate dusk.
Then you will see a light begin to creep
Under the earthen eyelids, dimmed with sleep,
And a new tremor, happy and uncouth,   15
Jerking about the corners of the mouth.
Then the old head drops down again, and
   shakes,
Muttering.
Sometimes, when the swift gaslight wakes
The dreams and fever of the sleepless town,
A shaking huddled thing in a black gown   21
Will steal at midnight, carrying with her
Violet little bags of lavender,
Into the tap-room full of noisy light;
Or, at the crowded earlier hour of night,   25
Sidle, with matches, up to some who stand
About a stage-door, and, with furtive hand,
Appealing: "I too was a dancer, when
Your fathers would have been young gentle-
   men!"
And sometimes, out of some lean ancient
   throat,   30
A broken voice, with here and there a note
Of unspoilt crystal, suddenly will arise
Into the night, while a cracked fiddle cries
Pantingly after; and you know she sings
The passing of light, famous, passing things,
And sometimes, in the hours past midnight,
   reels   36
Out of an alley upon staggering heels,
Or into the dark keeping of the stones
About a doorway, a vague thing of bones
And draggled hair.   40

And all these have been loved.
And not one ruinous body has not moved
The heart of man's desire, nor has not seemed
Immortal in the eyes of one who dreamed
The dream that men call love. This is the
   end   45
Of much fair flesh; it is for this you tend
Your delicate bodies many careful years,
To be this thing of laughter and of tears,
To be this living judgment of the dead,
An old gray woman with a shaking head.   50
            (1900)

THE UNLOVED

These are the women whom no man has
   loved.
Year after year, day after day has moved
These hearts with many longings, and with
   tears,
And with content; they have received the
   years
With empty hands, expecting no good thing; 5
Life has passed by their doors, not entering.
In solitude, and without vain desire,
They have warmed themselves beside a lonely
   fire;
And, without scorn, beheld as in a glass

The blown and painted leaves of Beauty pass.
Their souls have been made fragrant with the
    spice   11
Of costly virtues lit for sacrifice;
They have accepted Life, the unpaid debt,
And looked for no vain day of reckoning.

Yet   15
They too in certain windless summer hours
Have felt the stir of dreams, and dreamed the
    powers
And the exemptions and the miracles
And the cruelty of Beauty. Citadels
Of many-walled and deeply-moated hearts 20
Have suddenly surrendered to the arts
Of so compelling magic; entering,
They have esteemed it but a little thing
To have won so great a conquest; and with
    haste
They have cast down, and utterly laid waste,
Tower upon tower, and sapped their roots
    with flame;   26
And passed on that eternity of shame
Which is the way of Beauty on the earth.
And they have shaken laughter from its mirth,
To be a sound of trumpets and of horns   30
Crying the battle-cry of those red morns
Against a sky of triumph.

On some nights
Of delicate Springtide, when the hesitant
    lights   34
Begin to fade, and glimmer, and grow warm,
And all the softening air is quick with storm,
And the ardors of the young year, entering in,
Flush the gray earth with buds; when the trees
    begin
To feel a trouble mounting from their roots,
And all their green life blossoming into shoots,
They too, in some obscure, unblossoming
    strife,   41
Have felt the stirring of the sap of life.
And they have wept, with bowed head; in the
    street
They hear the twittering of little feet,
The rocking of the cradles in their hearts.   45

This is a mood, and, as a mood, departs
With the dried tears; and they resume the
    tale
Of the dropt stitches; these must never fail
For a dream's sake; nor, for a memory,
The telling of a patient rosary.   50
                   (*1896; 1900*)

IN THE BAY

The seagulls whiten and dip,
Crying their lonely cry,
At noon in the blue of the bay;
And I hear the slow oars drip,

As the fisherman's boat drifts by,   5
And the cuckoo calls from the hillside far
    away.

The white birds cry for the foam,
O white birds crying to me
The cry of my heart evermore,
By perilous seas to roam   10
To a shore far over the sea,
And I would that my ship went down within
    sight of the shore!   (*1896*)

IN THE WOOD OF FINVARRA

I have grown tired of sorrow and human tears;
Life is a dream in the night, a fear among
    fears,
A naked runner lost in a storm of spears.

I have grown tired of rapture and love's
    desire;
Love is a flaming heart, and its flames aspire
Till they cloud the soul in the smoke of a
    windy fire.   6

I would wash the dust of the world in a soft
    green flood;
Here, between sea and sea, in the fairy wood,
I have found a delicate, wave-green solitude.

Here, in a fairy wood, between sea and sea, 10
I have heard the song of a fairy bird in a tree,
And the peace that is not in the world has
    flown to me.   (*1896; 1900*)

MODERN BEAUTY

I am the torch, she saith, and what to me
If the moth die of me? I am the flame
Of Beauty, and I burn that all may see
Beauty, and I have neither joy nor shame,
But live with that clear life of perfect fire 5
Which is to men the death of their desire.

I am Yseult and Helen, I have seen
Troy burn, and the most loving knight lie
    dead.

In the Wood of Finvarra. This is the last of a group of five
poems under the general title *In Ireland.* The scene of the
poem is a forest on a point of land, near the village of Finvarra,
extending into the Bay of Galway on the western coast of
Ireland. Symons visited the spot in August, 1896. Finvarra
is the name of the king of the Connaught fairies; cf. Yeats's
The Land of Heart's Desire, 375, p. 879.
    Modern Beauty. 7. **Yseult . . . Helen.** The beauty of
Yseult, wife of King Mark of Cornwall, made Sir Tristram
her devoted lover for his lifetime; that of Helen induced
Paris to steal her from her husband and caused the Trojan
War. See Arnold's *Tristram and Iseult,* p. 458; Swinburne's
Tristram of Lyonesse, p. 717; and note on Browning's *Development,* 3, p. 377. 8. **Troy burn.** The burning of Troy by
the victorious Greeks is described in Virgil's *Æneid,* Book 2.
8. **most . . . dead.** When Tristram lay mortally wounded
in Brittany, Yseult sailed from Cornwall to help him; on
her arrival she found him dead.

The world has been my mirror, time has been
My breath upon the glass; and men have said,
Age after age, in rapture and despair,   11
Love's poor few words, before mine image
      there.

I live, and am immortal; in mine eyes
The sorrow of the world, and on my lips
The joy of life, mingle to make me wise;   15
Yet now the day is darkened with eclipse:
Who is there lives for beauty? Still am I
The torch, but where's the moth that still
      dares die?   (*1899;* 1900)

THE LOOM OF DREAMS

I broider the world upon a loom,
I broider with dreams my tapestry;
Here in a little lonely room
I am master of earth and sea,
And the planets come to me.   5

I broider my life into the frame,
I broider my love, thread upon thread;
The world goes by with its glory and shame,
Crowns are bartered and blood is shed;
I sit and broider my dreams instead.   10

And the only world is the world of my dreams,
And my weaving the only happiness;
For what is the world but what it seems?
And who knows but that God, beyond our
      guess,
Sits weaving worlds out of loneliness?   15
                            (*1900;* 1901)

LOVE SONG

O woman of my love, I am walking with you
      on the sand,
And the moon's white on the sand and the
      foam's white in the sea;
And I am thinking my own thoughts, and your
      hand is on my hand,
And your heart thinks by my side, and it's
      not thinking of me.

O woman of my love, the world is narrow and
      wide,   5
And I wonder which is the lonelier of us two:
You are thinking of one who is near to your
      heart, and far from your side;
I am thinking my own thoughts, and they are
      all thoughts of you.   (*1903;* 1906)

TO A SEA-GULL

Bird of the fierce delight,
Brother of foam as white
And winged as foam is,

Wheeling again from flight
To some unfooted height   5
Where your blithe home is;

Bird of the wind and spray,
Crying by night and day
Sorrowful laughter,
How shall man's thought survey   10
Your will or your wings' way,
Or follow after?

What pride is man's, and why,
Angel of air, should I
Joy to be human?   15
You walk and swim and fly,
Laugh like a man and cry
Like any woman.

I would your spirit were mine
When your wings dip and shine   20
Smoothly advancing;
I drink a breathless wine
Of speed in your divine
Aerial dancing.
                            (*1904;* 1906)

NIGHT

The night's held breath,
And the stars' steady eyes:
Is it sleep, is it death,
In the earth, in the skies?

In my heart of hope,   5
In my restless will,
There is that should not stop
Though the earth stood still,

Though the heavens shook aghast,
As the frost shakes a tree,   10
And a strong wind cast
The stars in the sea.
                            (*1905;* 1906)

AMENDS TO NATURE

I have loved colors, and not flowers;
Their motion, not the swallow's wings;
And wasted more than half my hours
Without the comradeship of things.

How is it, now, that I can see,   5
With love and wonder and delight,
The children of the hedge and tree,
The little lords of day and night?

How is it that I see the roads,
No longer with usurping eyes,   10
A twilight meeting-place for toads,
A midday mart for butterflies?

I feel, in every midge that hums,
Life, fugitive and infinite,
And suddenly the world becomes   15
A part of me and I of it.

(1906)

RUDYARD KIPLING (1865-1936)

THE BALLAD OF EAST AND WEST

*Oh, East is East, and West is West, and never
the twain shall meet,*
*Till Earth and Sky stand presently at God's
great Judgment Seat;*
*But there is neither East nor West, Border,
nor Breed, nor Birth,*
*When two strong men stand face to face, though
they come from the ends of the earth!*

Kamal is out with twenty men to raise the
Border side,   5
And he has lifted the Colonel's mare that is
the Colonel's pride.
He has lifted her out of the stable-door
between the dawn and the day,
And turned the calkins upon her feet, and
ridden her far away.
Then up and spoke the Colonel's son that led
a troop of the Guides:
"Is there never a man of all my men can say
where Kamal hides?"   10
Then up and spoke Mohammed Khan, the
son of the Ressaldar:
"If ye know the track of the morning-mist,
ye know where his pickets are.
"At dusk he harries the Abazai — at dawn he
is into Bonair,
"But he must go by Fort Bukloh to his own
place to fare,
"So if ye gallop to Fort Bukloh as fast as a
bird can fly,   15
"By the favour of God ye may cut him off
ere he win to the Tongue of Jagai.
"But if he be past the Tongue of Jagai,
right swiftly turn ye then,
"For the length and the breadth of that
grisly plain is sown with Kamal's men.

"There is rock to the left, and rock to the
right, and low lean thorn between,
"And ye may hear a breech-bolt snick where
never a man is seen."   20
The Colonel's son has taken a horse, and a
raw rough dun was he,
With the mouth of a bell and the heart of
Hell, and the head of the gallows-tree.
The Colonel's son to the Fort has won, they
bid him stay to eat —
Who rides at the tail of a Border thief, he sits
not long at his meat.
He's up and away from Fort Bukloh as fast
as he can fly,   25
Till he was aware of his father's mare in the
gut of the Tongue of Jagai,
Till he was aware of his father's mare with
Kamal upon her back,
And when he could spy the white of her eye,
he made the pistol crack.
He has fired once, he has fired twice, but the
whistling ball went wide.
"Ye shoot like a soldier," Kamal said. "Show
now if ye can ride!"   30
It's up and over the Tongue of Jagai, as
blown dust-devils go,
The dun he fled like a stag of ten, but the
mare like a barren doe.
The dun he leaned against the bit and slugged
his head above,
But the red mare played with the snaffle-
bars, as a maiden plays with a glove.
There was rock to the left and rock to the
right, and low lean thorn between,   35
And thrice he heard a breech-bolt snick tho'
never a man was seen.
They have ridden the low moon out of the
sky, their hoofs drum up the dawn,
The dun he went like a wounded bull, but
the mare like a new-roused fawn.
The dun he fell at a water-course — in a
woeful heap fell he,
And Kamal has turned the red mare back,
and pulled the rider free.   40
He has knocked the pistol out of his hand —
small room was there to strive,
" 'Twas only by favour of mine," quoth he,
"ye rode so long alive:
"There was not a rock for twenty mile, there
was not a clump of tree,
"But covered a man of my own men with his
rifle cocked on his knee.
"If I had raised my bridle-hand, as I have
held it low,   45
"The little jackals that flee so fast were
feasting all in a row.

The Ballad of East and West. From *Departmental Ditties,*
copyright 1892, 1893, and 1899 by Rudyard Kipling.
   The scene of the ballad is the border between Afghanistan
and the Northwest Frontier Province of India; it concerns a
raid made by the Afghans into British territory and a pursuit
into the hostile Afghan wilderness. It is modeled, to a certain extent, on the old ballads of the Scottish border, such as
Kinmont Willie; see Sir Walter Scott's *Minstrelsy of the
Scottish Border.*
   5. Kamal, chief of an Afghan tribe. **6. lifted,** stolen.
8. calkins, shoes. **9. Guides,** the Queen's Own Corps of
Guides, a corps of 1400 men recruited from many different
races, stationed at Mardan, on the border between India
and Afghanistan. **11. Ressaldar,** native captain in an
East-Indian troop. **13. Abazai . . . Bonair,** villages on the
Indian frontier, about forty miles apart. **14. Fort Bukloh,**
a British fort on the border. **16. Tongue of Jagai,** a
mountain ridge in Eastern Afghanistan; see Kipling's *The
Drums of the Fore and Aft.*

20. hear a breech-bolt snick, hear a breech-bolt click as
it is pulled back ready for firing. **32. stag of ten,** a stag
with ten branches on his horns. **34. snaffle-bars,** the two
sections of a jointed bit. **42. 'Twas . . . alive.** Compare
the similar situation in Scott's *The Lady of the Lake,* Canto V,
Sections 8-12 (lines 170-318).

"If I had bowed my head on my breast, as I
    have held it high,
"The kite that whistles above us now were
    gorged till she could not fly."
Lightly answered the Colonel's son: "Do
    good to bird and beast,
"But count who come for the broken meats
    before thou makest a feast.   50
"If there should follow a thousand swords
    to carry my bones away,
"Belike the price of a jackal's meal were
    more than a thief could pay.
"They will feed their horse on the standing
    crop, their men on the garnered grain,
"The thatch of the byres will serve their
    fires when all the cattle are slain.
"But if thou thinkest the price be fair, — thy
    brethren wait to sup,   55
"The hound is kin to the jackal-spawn, —
    howl, dog, and call them up!
"And if thou thinkest the price be high, in
    steer and gear and stack,
"Give me my father's mare again, and I'll
    fight my own way back!"
Kamal has gripped him by the hand and set
    him upon his feet.
"No talk shall be of dogs," said he, "when
    wolf and grey wolf meet.   60
"May I eat dirt if thou hast hurt of me in
    deed or breath;
"What dam of lances brought thee forth to
    jest at the dawn with Death?"
Lightly answered the Colonel's son: "I hold
    by the blood of my clan:
"Take up the mare for my father's gift — by
    God, she has carried a man!"
The red mare ran to the Colonel's son, and
    nuzzled against his breast;   65
"We be two strong men," said Kamal then,
    "but she loveth the younger best.
"So she shall go with a lifter's dower, my
    turquoise-studded rein,
"My 'broidered saddle and saddle-cloth, and
    silver stirrups twain."
The Colonel's son a pistol drew, and held it
    muzzle-end,
"Ye have taken the one from a foe," said he;
    "Will ye take the mate from a friend?"   70
"A gift for a gift," said Kamal straight; "a
    limb for the risk of a limb.
"Thy father has sent his son to me, I'll send
    my son to him!"
With that he whistled his only son, that
    dropped from a mountain-crest —
He trod the ling like a buck in spring, and
    he looked like a lance in rest.
"Now here is thy master," Kamal said, "who
    leads a troop of the Guides,   75

"And thou must ride at his left side as shield
    on shoulder rides.
"Till Death or I cut loose the tie, at camp
    and board and bed,
"Thy life is his — thy fate it is to guard him
    with thy head.
"So, thou must eat the White Queen's meat,
    and all her foes are thine,
"And thou must harry thy father's hold for
    the peace of the Border-line.   80
"And thou must make a trooper tough and
    hack thy way to power —
"Belike they will raise thee to Ressaldar when
    I am hanged in Peshawur."

They have looked each other between the
    eyes, and there they found no fault,
They have taken the Oath of the Brother-in-
    Blood on leavened bread and salt:
They have taken the Oath of the Brother-in-
    Blood on fire and fresh-cut sod,   85
On the hilt and the haft of the Khyber knife,
    and the Wondrous Names of God.
The Colonel's son he rides the mare and
    Kamal's boy the dun,
And two have come back to Fort Bukloh
    where there went forth but one.
And when they drew to the Quarter-Guard,
    full twenty swords flew clear —
There was not a man but carried his feud
    with the blood of the mountaineer.   90
"Ha' done! ha' done!" said the Colonel's son.
    "Put up the steel at your sides!
"Last night ye had struck at a Border thief —
    to-night 'tis a man of the Guides!"

*Oh, East is East, and West is West, and never
    the twain shall meet,
Till Earth and Sky stand presently at God's
    great Judgment Seat;
But there is neither East nor West, Border, nor
    Breed, nor Birth,   95
When two strong men stand face to face,
    though they come from the ends of the earth.*
                  (1889)

DANNY DEEVER

"What are the bugles blowin' for?" said Files-
    on-Parade.
"To turn you out, to turn you out," the
    Colour-Sergeant said.
"What makes you look so white, so white?"
    said Files-on-Parade.

---

54. **byres**, cow-stables. 57. **gear**, equipment. 67. **lifter's**,
horse-thief's. 74. **ling**, heather.
    79. **White Queen's meat**, the rations of Queen Victoria's
soldiers. 82. **Peshawur**, now a city of West Pakistan,
formerly a military center on the northwest frontier of India
near the Khyber Pass. 86. **Khyber knife**, an Afghan
weapon with a three-foot triangular blade.
    Danny Deever. From *The Barrack-Room Ballads*, copyright
1892 and 1899 by Rudyard Kipling.
    1. **Files-on-Parade**, private soldier.

"I'm dreadin' what I've got to watch," the
   Colour-Sergeant said.
For they're hangin' Danny Deever, you
   can hear the Dead March play,   5
The regiment's in 'ollow square — they're
   hangin' him to-day;
They've taken of his buttons off an' cut
   his stripes away,
An' they're hangin' Danny Deever in the
   mornin'.

"What makes the rear-rank breathe so 'ard?"
   said Files-on-Parade.
"It's bitter cold, it's bitter cold," the Colour-
   Sergeant said.   10
"What makes that front-rank man fall
   down?" said Files-on-Parade.
"A touch o' sun, a touch o' sun," the Colour-
   Sergeant said.
They are hangin' Danny Deever, they are
   marchin' of 'im round,
They 'ave 'alted Danny Deever by 'is
   coffin on the ground;
An' 'e'll swing in 'arf a minute for a sneak-
   in' shootin' hound —   15
O they're hangin' Danny Deever in the
   mornin'!

"'Is cot was right-'and cot to mine," said
   Files-on-Parade.
"'E's sleepin' out an' far to-night," the
   Colour-Sergeant said.
"I've drunk 'is beer a score o' times," said
   Files-on-Parade.
"'E's drinkin' bitter beer alone," the Colour-
   Sergeant said.   20
They are hangin' Danny Deever, you
   must mark 'im to 'is place,
For 'e shot a comrade sleepin' — you must
   look 'im in the face;
Nine 'undred of 'is county an' the Reg-
   iment's disgrace,
While they're hangin' Danny Deever in
   the mornin'.

"What's that so black agin the sun?" said
   Files-on-Parade.   25
"It's Danny fightin' 'ard for life," the Colour-
   Sergeant said.
"What's that that whimpers over'ead?"
   said Files-on-Parade.
"It's Danny's soul that's passin' now," the
   Colour-Sergeant said.
For they're done with Danny Deever, you
   can 'ear the quickstep play,
The regiment's in column, an' they're
   marchin' us away;   30
Ho! the young recruits are shakin', an'
   they'll want their beer to-day,
After hangin' Danny Deever in the mornin'.
                              (1890)

TOMMY

I went into a public-'ouse to get a pint o'
   beer,
The publican 'e up an' sez, "We serve no
   red-coats here."
The girls be'ind the bar they laughed an'
   giggled fit to die,
I outs into the street again an' to myself sez
   I:
   O it's Tommy this, an' Tommy that, an'
      "Tommy, go away";   5
   But it's "Thank you, Mister Atkins," when
      the band begins to play,
   The band begins to play, my boys, the
      band begins to play —
   O it's "Thank you, Mister Atkins," when
      the band begins to play.

I went into a theatre as sober as could be,
They gave a drunk civilian room, but 'adn't
   none for me;   10
They sent me to the gallery or round the
   music-'alls,
But when it comes to fightin', Lord! they'll
   shove me in the stalls!
   For it's Tommy this, an' Tommy that,
      an' "Tommy, wait outside";
   But it's "Special train for Atkins" when the
      trooper's on the tide —
   The troopship's on the tide, my boys, the
      troopship's on the tide,   15
   O it's "Special train for Atkins" when the
      trooper's on the tide.

Yes, makin' mock o' uniforms that guard you
   while you sleep
Is cheaper than them uniforms, an' they're
   starvation cheap;
An' hustlin' drunken soldiers when they're
   goin' large a bit
Is five times better business than paradin' in
   full kit.   20
   Then it's Tommy this, an' Tommy that,
      an' "Tommy, 'ow's yer soul?"
   But it's "Thin red line of 'eroes" when the
      drums begin to roll —
   The drums begin to roll, my boys, the drums
      begin to roll,
   O it's "Thin red line of 'eroes" when the
      drums begin to roll.

Tommy. From *The Barrack-Room Ballads*, copyright 1892
and 1899 by Rudyard Kipling.
   2. **publican**, proprietor of a public-house, or "saloon."
6. **Mister Atkins.** Thomas Atkins, originally the hypo-
thetical name used in instructing soldiers how to fill out
account blanks, etc., has become the nickname for a private
in the British army. Cf. Meredith's *"Atkins."* 12. **stalls**,
orchestra seats. 22. **"Thin ... 'eroes."** A war correspondent, W. H. Russell, used this phrase in describing the
93d Highlanders in action at the Battle of Balaklava, Crimean
War. Cf. Tennyson's *The Charge of the Light Brigade*, p. 95.

We aren't no thin red 'eroes, nor we aren't
  no blackguards too,   25
But single men in barricks, most remarkable
  like you;
An' if sometimes our conduck isn't all your
  fancy paints,
Why, single men in barricks don't grow into
  plaster saints;
    While it's Tommy this, an' Tommy that,
      an' "Tommy, fall be'ind,"
    But it's "Please to walk in front, sir," when
      there's trouble in the wind —   30
    There's trouble in the wind, my boys,
      there's trouble in the wind,
    O it's "Please to walk in front, sir," when
      there's trouble in the wind.

You talk o' better food for us, an' schools, an'
  fires, an' all:
We'll wait for extry rations if you treat us
  rational.
Don't mess about the cook-room slops, but
  prove it to our face   35
The Widow's Uniform is not the soldier-man's
  disgrace.
    For it's Tommy this, an' Tommy that, an'
      "Chuck him out, the brute!"
    But it's "Saviour of 'is country" when the
      guns begin to shoot;
    An' it's Tommy this, an' Tommy that, an'
      anything you please;
    An' Tommy ain't a bloomin' fool — you
      bet that Tommy sees!   (1890)

"FUZZY-WUZZY"

(SOUDAN EXPEDITIONARY FORCE)

We've fought with many men acrost the seas,
  An' some of 'em was brave an' some was
    not:
The Paythan an' the Zulu an' Burmese;
  But the Fuzzy was the finest o' the lot.
We never got a ha'porth's change of 'im: 5

'E squatted in the scrub an' 'ocked our
  'orses,
'E cut our sentries up at Sua*kim*,
  An' 'e played the cat an' banjo with our
    forces.
    So 'ere's *to* you, Fuzzy-Wuzzy, at your
      'ome in the Soudan;
    You're a pore benighted 'eathen but a
      first-class fightin' man;   10
    We gives you your certificate, an' if you
      want it signed
    We'll come an' 'ave a romp with you
      whenever you're inclined.

We took our chanst among the Kyber 'ills,
  The Boers knocked us silly at a mile,
The Burman give us Irriwaddy chills,   15
  An' a Zulu *impi* dished us up in style:
But all we ever got from such as they
  Was pop to what the Fuzzy made us swaller;
We 'eld our bloomin' own, the papers say,
  But man for man the Fuzzy knocked us
    'oller.   20
    Then 'ere's *to* you, Fuzzy-Wuzzy, an'
      the missis and the kid;
    Our orders was to break you, an' of
      course we went an' did.
    We sloshed you with Martinis, an' it
      wasn't 'ardly fair;
    But for all the odds agin' you, Fuzzy-
      Wuz, you broke the square.

'E 'asn't got no papers of 'is own,   25
  'E 'asn't got no medals nor rewards,
So *we* must certify the skill 'e's shown
  In usin' of 'is long two-'anded swords:
When 'e 's 'oppin' in an' out among the bush
  With 'is coffin-'eaded shield an' shovel-
    spear,   30
An' 'appy day with Fuzzy on the rush
  Will last an 'ealthy Tommy for a year.
    So 'ere's *to* you, Fuzzy-Wuzzy, an' your
      friends which are no more,
    If we 'adn't lost some messmates we
      would 'elp you to deplore.
    But give an' take's the gospel, an' we'll
      call the bargain fair,   35
    For if you 'ave lost more than us, you
      crumpled up the square!

---

36. **Widow,** an affectionate nickname applied to Queen Victoria by her soldiers.
    "Fuzzy-Wuzzy." From *Departmental Ditties,* copyright 1892, 1893, and 1899 by Rudyard Kipling.
    In 1881 the tribesmen of the Soudan, a territory along the southern border of the Sahara Desert and the upper waters of the Nile, rebelled against English and Egyptian rule. Under the leadership of a prophet called the Mahdi, they defeated an army under General Hicks in 1883, besieged and massacred General Gordon at Khartum in 1885, and remained unconquered until 1898. Because of their long, curly hair, they were called "Fuzzy-Wuzzies" by the British troops.
    Soudan . . . Force, an army, under the leadership of General Graham, sent in 1884 to relieve General Gordon, who was besieged by the Soudanese at Khartum.
    3. **Paythan,** Moslem group in Afghanistan and Pakistan. **Zulu,** natives of southeast Africa, against whom the British conducted a campaign in 1879. **Burmese.** Because of outrages against British subjects in Burma, England conquered and annexed Burma after a brief campaign in 1885; see note on *Mandalay,* p. 893. 5. **ha'porth's change.** A half-penny's worth of change would be reckoned in fractions of a cent.

7. **Suakim,** a seaport on the Red Sea, the headquarters of the British and Egyptian army operating against the Sudanese. 13. **Kyber 'ills,** the mountains on the Afghanistan border; see *The Ballad of East and West,* p. 888. 14. **Boers,** the Dutch settlers in South Africa with whom the British engaged in various minor conflicts before the Boer War of 1899-1902; they were celebrated for their deadliness with the rifle at long range. 15. **Irriwaddy,** the chief river in Burma. 16. **Zulu impi.** The Zulu army, organized into regiments, or *impis,* overwhelmed a British force of 4000 men during the early part of the 1879 campaign in southeast Africa. 23. **Martinis,** British rifles, named after the Swiss inventor. 24. **broke the square,** pierced the hollow square, the favorite British formation in open warfare; the Sudanese accomplished this feat in a battle at Tamai, 1884.

'E rushes at the smoke when we let drive,
  An', before we know, 'e 's 'ackin' at our 'ead;
'E's all 'ot sand an' ginger when alive,
  An' 'e 's generally shammin' when 'e 's
    dead.   40
'E 's a daisy, 'e 's a ducky, 'e 's a lamb!
'E 's a injia-rubber idiot on the spree,
'E 's the on'y thing that doesn't give a damn
  For a Regiment o' British Infantree!
    So 'ere's *to* you, Fuzzy-Wuzzy, at your
      'ome in the Soudan;   45
    You're a pore benighted 'eathen but a
      first-class fightin' man;
    An' 'ere's *to* you, Fuzzy-Wuzzy, with
      your 'ayrick 'ead of 'air —
    You big black boundin' beggar — for
      you broke a British square!
                                      (1890)

GUNGA DIN

You may talk o' gin and beer
When you're quartered safe out 'ere,
An' you're sent to penny-fights an' Aldershot
  it;
But when it comes to slaughter
You will do your work on water,   5
An' you'll lick the bloomin' boots of 'im
  that's got it.
Now in Injia's sunny clime,
Where I used to spend my time
A-servin' of 'Er Majesty the Queen,
Of all them black-faced crew   10
The finest man I knew
Was our regimental bhisti, Gunga Din.
    He was "Din! Din! Din!
  "You limpin' lump o' brick-dust, Gunga Din!
    "Hi! *Slippy hitherao!*   15
  "Water, get it! *Panee lao!*
  "You squidgy-nosed old idol, Gunga Din!"

The uniform 'e wore
Was nothin' much before,
An' rather less than 'arf o' that be'ind,   20
For a piece o' twisty rag
An' a goatskin water-bag
Was all the field-equipment 'e could find.
When the sweatin' troop-train lay
In a sidin' through the day,   25
Where the 'eat would make your bloomin'
  eyebrows crawl,
We shouted "Harry By!"
Till our throats were bricky-dry,
Then we wopped 'im 'cause 'e couldn't serve
  us all.

It was "Din! Din! Din!   30
"You 'eathen, where the mischief 'ave you
  been?
"You put some *juldee* in it
"Or I'll *marrow* you this minute
"If you don't fill up my helmet, Gunga
  Din!"

'E would dot an' carry one   35
Till the longest day was done;
An' 'e didn't seem to know the use o' fear.
If we charged or broke or cut,
You could bet your bloomin' nut,
'E'd be waitin' fifty paces right flank rear. 40
With 'is mussick on 'is back,
'E would skip with our attack,
An' watch us till the bugles made "Retire,"
An' for all 'is dirty 'ide
'E was white, clear white, inside   45
When 'e went to tend the wounded under
  fire!
    It was "Din! Din! Din!"
  With the bullets kickin' dust-spots on the
    green.
    When the cartridges ran out,
    You could 'ear the front-ranks shout,   50
  "Hi! ammunition-mules an' Gunga Din!"

I sha'n't forgit the night
When I dropped be'ind the fight
With a bullet where my belt-plate should 'a'
  been.
I was chokin' mad with thirst,   55
An' the man that spied me first
Was our good old grinnin', gruntin' Gunga
  Din.
'E lifted up my 'ead,
An' 'e plugged me where I bled,
An' 'e guv me 'arf-a-pint o' water green.   60
It was crawlin' and it stunk,
But of all the drinks I've drunk,
I'm gratefullest to one from Gunga Din.
    It was "Din! Din! Din!
  "'Ere's a beggar with a bullet through 'is
    spleen;   65
    "'E's chawin' up the ground,
    "An' 'e's kickin' all around:
  "For Gawd's sake, git the water, Gunga
    Din!"

'E carried me away
To where a dooli lay,   70
An' a bullet come an' drilled the beggar clean.
'E put me safe inside,
An' just before 'e died,
"I 'ope you liked your drink," sez Gunga Din.
So I'll meet 'im later on   75
In the place where 'e is gone —

Gunga Din. From *Departmental Ditties*, copyright 1892, 1893, and 1899 by Rudyard Kipling.
3. **Aldershot it**, live comfortably in Aldershot, a military camp in northeast Hampshire. 12. **bhisti**, a Mohammedan regimental water-carrier; the word means *heavenly one.* 15. **hitherao**, come here. 16. **Panee lao**, bring water quickly. 27. **Harry By**, Oh, brother! 29. **wopped**, hit.

32. **juldee**, speed. 33. **marrow**, hit. 41. **mussick**, water-skin. 70. **dooli**, stretcher for conveying the wounded.

Where it's always double drill and no can-
teen.
'E'll be squattin' on the coals
Givin' drink to poor damned souls,
An' I'll get a swig in hell from Gunga Din! 80
Yes, Din! Din! Din!
You Lazarushian-leather Gunga Din!
Though I've belted you an' flayed you,
By the livin' Gawd that made you,
You're a better man than I am, Gunga
Din!

(1890)

MANDALAY

By the old Moulmein Pagoda, lookin' eastward to the sea,
There's a Burma girl a-settin', and I know
she thinks o' me;
For the wind is in the palm-trees, and the
temple-bells they say:
"Come you back, you British soldier; come
you back to Mandalay!"

Come you back to Mandalay,   5
Where the old Flotilla lay:
Can't you 'ear their paddles chunkin'
from Rangoon to Mandalay?
On the road to Mandalay,
Where the flyin'-fishes play,
An' the dawn comes up like thunder
outer China 'crost the Bay!   10

'Er petticoat was yaller an' 'er little cap was
green,
An' 'er name was Supi-yaw-lat — jes' the
same as Theebaw's Queen,
An' I seed her first a-smokin' of a whackin'
white cheroot,
An' a-wastin' Christian kisses on an 'eathen
idol's foot:

Bloomin' idol made o' mud —   15
Wot they called the Great Gawd Budd —
Plucky lot she cared for idols when I
kissed 'er where she stud!
On the road to Mandalay . . .

When the mist was on the rice-fields an' the
sun was droppin' slow,
She'd git 'er little banjo an' she'd sing
"Kulla-lo-lo!"   20
With 'er arm upon my shoulder an' 'er cheek
agin my cheek
We useter watch the steamers an' the hathis
pilin' teak.

Elephints a-pilin' teak
In the sludgy, squdgy creek,
Where the silence 'ung that 'eavy you
was 'arf afraid to speak!   25
On the road to Mandalay . . .

But that's all shove be'ind me — long ago
an' fur away,
An' there ain't no 'busses runnin' from the
Bank to Mandalay;
An' I'm learnin' 'ere in London what the
ten-year soldier tells:
"If you've 'eard the East a-callin', you won't
never 'eed naught else."   30

No! you won't 'eed nothin' else
But them spicy garlic smells,
An' the sunshine an' the palm-trees an'
the tinkly temple-bells;
On the road to Mandalay . . .

I am sick o' wastin' leather on these gritty
pavin'-stones,   35
An' the blasted Henglish drizzle wakes the
fever in my bones;
Tho' I walks with fifty 'ousemaids outer
Chelsea on the Strand,
An' they talks a lot o' lovin', but wot do
they understand?

Beefy face an' grubby 'and —
Law! wot do they understand?   40
I've a neater, sweeter maiden in a
cleaner, greener land!
On the road to Mandalay . . .

Ship me somewheres east of Suez, where the
best is like the worst,
Where there aren't no Ten Commandments
an' a man can raise a thirst;
For the temple-bells are callin', an' it's there
that I would be —   45
By the old Moulmein Pagoda, looking lazy
at the sea;

On the road to Mandalay,
Where the old Flotilla lay,
With our sick beneath the awnings when
we went to Mandalay!

82. **Lazarushian-leather**, an example of army slang;
Din's skin suggested Russian leather.
Mandalay. From *The Barrack-Room Ballads*, copyright
1892 and 1899 by Rudyard Kipling.
England conquered and annexed Burma in 1885-86, after
which a British force of occupation was stationed there.
The two chief cities are Rangoon, near the mouth of the
Irrawaddy River, and Mandalay, on the river about 375
miles north of Rangoon.
1. **Moulmein Pagoda**, a Buddhist temple in Moulmein
(Maulmain), across the Gulf of Martaban from Rangoon.
6. **old Flotilla**, the boats of the Irrawaddy Flotilla Company, plying from Rangoon to Mandalay. 12. **Theebaw's
Queen.** Thebaw, king of Burma from 1876 to 1885, was
deposed by the English; his wife, Supaiyah Lat, was notorious
for her cruelty. 16. **Budd**, Buddha, worshiped by most
Burmese.

22. **hathis**, elephants, trained to stack logs of teak, a
hard wood used in ship construction, in lumber-yards.
37. **Chelsea**, a district on the Thames above Westminster in
London. **Strand**, a thoroughfare connecting Westminster
with Fleet Street.

On the road to Mandalay!   50
Where the flyin'-fishes play,
An' the dawn comes up like thunder
    outer China 'crost the Bay!   (1890)

THE CONUNDRUM OF THE WORKSHOPS

When the flush of a new-born sun fell first on
    Eden's green and gold,
Our father Adam sat under the Tree and
    scratched with a stick in the mould;
And the first rude sketch that the world had
    seen was joy to his mighty heart,
Till the Devil whispered behind the leaves,
    "It's pretty, but is it Art?"

Wherefore he called to his wife, and fled to
    fashion his work anew —   5
The first of his race who cared a fig for the
    first, most dread review;
And he left his lore to the use of his sons —
    and that was a glorious gain
When the Devil chuckled "Is it Art?" in the
    ear of the branded Cain.

They builded a tower to shiver the sky and
    wrench the stars apart,
Till the Devil grunted behind the bricks:
    "It's striking, but is it Art?"   10
The stone was dropped at the quarry-side
    and the idle derrick swung,
While each man talked of the aims of Art,
    and each in an alien tongue.

They fought and they talked in the North
    and the South; they talked and they
    fought in the West,
Till the waters rose on the pitiful land, and
    the poor Red Clay had rest —
Had rest till the dank blank-canvas dawn
    when the dove was preened to start,   15
And the Devil bubbled below the keel: "It's
    human, but is it Art?"

The tale is as old as the Eden Tree — and
    new as the new-cut tooth —
For each man knows ere his lip-thatch grows
    he is master of Art and Truth;
And each man hears as the twilight nears, to
    the beat of his dying heart,
The Devil drum on the darkened pane: "You
    did it, but was it Art?"   20

We have learned to whittle the Eden Tree to
    the shape of a surplice-peg,
We have learned to bottle our parents twain
    in the yelk of an addled egg,
We know that the tail must wag the dog, for
    the horse is drawn by the cart;
But the Devil whoops, as he whooped of old:
    "It's clever, but is it Art?"

When the flicker of London sun falls faint on
    the Club-room's green and gold,   25
The sons of Adam sit them down and scratch
    with their pens in the mould —
They scratch with their pens in the mould of
    their graves, and the ink and the anguish
    start,
For the Devil mutters behind the leaves:
    "It's pretty, but is it Art?"

Now, if we could win to the Eden Tree where
    the Four Great Rivers flow,
And the Wreath of Eve is red on the turf as
    she left it long ago,   30
And if we could come when the sentry slept
    and softly scurry through,
By the favour of God we might know as much
    —as our father Adam knew!   (1890)

ENVOY

There's a whisper down the field where the
    year has shot her yield,
And the ricks stand grey to the sun,
Singing: "Over then, come over, for the
    bee has quit the clover,
"And your English summer's done."

        You have heard the beat of the off-shore
            wind,   5
        And the thresh of the deep-sea rain;
        You have heard the song — how long?
            how long?
        Pull out on the trail again!
Ha' done with the Tents of Shem, dear lass,
We've seen the seasons through,   10
And it's time to turn on the old trail, our
    own trail, the out trail,
Pull out, pull out, on the Long Trail — the
    trail that is always new!

21. **surplice-peg,** a peg in the sacristy of a church on
which surplices, worn by the clergy and choir, are hung.
29. **Four . . . Rivers,** the rivers that flowed out from the
Garden of Eden (*Genesis*, 2:10-14).
    Envoy. From *Departmental Ditties,* copyright 1892, 1893,
and 1899 by Rudyard Kipling.
    This poem is sometimes published under the title *The
Long Trail.*
    1. **shot her yield,** harvested her crop of grain. 9. **Tents
of Shem,** houses with servants; *Genesis,* 9:27.—"God shall
enlarge Japheth, and he shall dwell in the tents of Shem; and
Canaan shall be his servant."

    The Conundrum of the Workshops. From *Departmental
Ditties,* copyright 1892, 1893, and 1899 by Rudyard Kipling.
    9. **tower,** the tower of Babel, the builders of which were
punished by being forced to talk in different languages; see
Genesis, 11:4-9. 14. **waters rose,** the Flood; see *Genesis,*
7:10-12. 15. **dove,** the one sent out by Noah to discover dry
land (*Genesis,* 8:8-12).

It's North you may run to the rime-ringed
    sun,
  Or South to the blind Horn's hate;
Or East all the way into Mississippi Bay, 15
  Or West to the Golden Gate —
Where the blindest bluffs hold good, dear lass,
  And the wildest tales are true,
And the men bulk big on the old trail, our
    own trail, the out trail,
And life runs large on the Long Trail — the
    trail that is always new.   20

The days are sick and cold, and the skies are
    grey and old,
  And the twice-breathed airs blow damp;
And I'd sell my tired soul for the bucking
    beam-sea roll
  Of a black Bilbao tramp,
With her load-line over her hatch, dear lass,
  And a drunken Dago crew,   26
And her nose held down on the old trail, our
    own trail, the out trail,
From Cadiz south on the Long Trail — the
    trail that is always new.

There be triple ways to take, of the eagle or
    the snake,
  Or the way of a man with a maid;   30
But the sweetest way to me is a ship's upon
    the sea
  In the heel of the North-East Trade.
Can you hear the crash on her bows, dear lass,
  And the drum of the racing screw,
As she ships it green on the old trail, our own
    trail, the out trail,   35
As she lifts and 'scends on the Long Trail —
    the trail that is always new?

See the shaking funnels roar, with the Peter
    at the fore,
  And the fenders grind and heave,
And the derricks clack and grate, as the tackle
    hooks the crate,

And the fall-rope whines through the
    sheave;   40
It's "Gang-plank up and in," dear lass,
  It's "Hawsers warp her through!"
And it's "All clear aft" on the old trail, our
    own trail, the out trail,
We're backing down on the Long Trail — the
    trail that is always new.

O the mutter overside, when the port-fog
    holds us tied,   45
  And the sirens hoot their dread!
When foot by foot we creep o'er the hueless
    viewless deep
  To the sob of the questing lead!
It's down by the Lower Hope, dear lass,
  With the Gunfleet Sands in view,   50
Till the Mouse swings green on the old trail,
    our own trail, the out trail,
And the Gull Light lifts on the Long Trail
    — the trail that is always new.

O the blazing tropic night, when the wake's
    a welt of light
  That holds the hot sky tame,
And the steady fore-foot snores through the
    planet-powdered floors   55
  Where the scared whale flukes in flame!
Her plates are scarred by the sun, dear lass,
  And her ropes are taut with the dew,
For we're booming down on the old trail, our
    own trail, the out trail,
We're sagging south on the Long Trail — the
    trail that is always new.   60

Then home, get her home, where the drunken
    rollers comb,
  And the shouting seas drive by,
And the engines stamp and ring, and the wet
    bows reel and swing,
  And the Southern Cross rides high!
Yes, the old lost stars wheel back, dear lass,
  That blaze in the velvet blue.   66
They're all old friends on the old trail, our
    own trail, the out trail,
They're God's own guides on the Long Trail
    — the trail that is always new.

Fly forward, O my heart, from the Foreland
    to the Start —
  We're steaming all too slow,   70

14. blind Horn, Cape Horn, at the extremity of South
America, dangerous for mariners because of storms. 23.
beam-sea, waves coming at right angles to the ship's course.
24. Bilbao tramp, a slow freight vessel hailing from Bilbao,
a port on the northern coast of Spain. A tramp picks up
cargo wherever it can be found. 25. load-line . . . hatch.
The load-line is a line on the side of the ship to mark the
depth to which the cargo causes her to sink. The hatch, or
opening to the hold, is above the level of the deck. The
load-line is normally at or just above the water-line; hence
a roll bringing the load-line above the hatch would happen
only in a very rough sea. 26. Dago, a term applied by the
British sailor to Latin peoples—French, Spanish, Italian, etc.
28. Cadiz, a peninsula which forms the harbor of Cadiz in
Spain. 29. triple ways. See *Proverbs*, 30:18-19.—"There
be three things which are too wonderful for me, yea, four
which I know not: the way of an eagle in the air; the way of
a serpent upon a rock; the way of a ship in the midst of the
sea; and the way of a man with a maid." 32. North-East
Trade, the regular wind which, in the northern hemisphere,
blows toward the equator. 37. the Peter at the fore, the
Blue Peter, a blue flag with a white square in the center,
hoisted on the foremast head to indicate that the ship is about
to sail.

40. fall-rope . . . sheave. The fall-rope passes from
the hoisting winch through a pulley, or sheave, at the head of
the derrick employed in loading cargo. 49-52. Lower Hope
. . . Gull Light, points on the route from the London docks,
down the Thames River, into the English Channel; the
Mouse is a lightship marking the course. 56. whale . . .
flame. When in tropic seas a whale beats its tail (flukes)
on the water as it dives, the spray thrown up shines in a
brilliant phosphorescent glow. 61. comb, break. 64.
Southern Cross, a constellation visible only in the southern
hemisphere. 69. Foreland . . . Start, capes at the northern
and southern extremities of the Devon coast on the English
Channel.

And it's twenty thousand mile to our little
   lazy isle
Where the trumpet-orchids blow!
You have heard the call of the off-shore wind
And the voice of the deep-sea rain;
You have heard the song. How long? how
   long?   75
   Pull out on the trail again!

The Lord knows what we may find, dear lass,
And The Deuce knows what we may do —
But we're back once more on the old trail,
   our own trail, the out trail,
We're down, hull-down, on the Long Trail—
   the trail that is always new.   80
                    (1892)

TOMLINSON

Now Tomlinson gave up the ghost in his
   house in Berkeley Square,
And a Spirit came to his bedside and gripped
   him by the hair —
A Spirit gripped him by the hair and carried
   him far away,
Till he heard as the roar of a rain-fed ford
   the roar of the Milky Way:
Till he heard the roar of the Milky Way die
   down and drone and cease,   5
And they came to the Gate within the Wall
   where Peter holds the keys.
"Stand up, stand up now, Tomlinson, and
   answer loud and high
"The good that ye did for the sake of men or
   ever ye came to die —
"The good that ye did for the sake of men in
   little earth so lone!"
And the naked soul of Tomlinson grew white
   as a rain-washed bone.   10

"Oh I have a friend on earth," he said, "that
   was my priest and guide,
"And well would he answer all for me if he
   were by my side."
— "For that ye strove in neighbour-love it
   shall be written fair,
"But now ye wait at Heaven's Gate and not
   in Berkeley Square:
"Though we called your friend from his bed
   this night, he could not speak for you,15
"For the race is run by one and one and never
   by two and two."
Then Tomlinson looked up and down, and
   little gain was there,
For the naked stars grinned overhead, and
   he saw that his soul was bare.

The Wind that blows between the Worlds, it
   cut him like a knife,
And Tomlinson took up the tale and spoke
   of his good in life.   20
"O this I have read in a book," he said,
   "and that was told to me,
"And this I have thought that another man
   thought of a Prince in Muscovy."
The good souls flocked like homing doves and
   bade him clear his path,
And Peter twirled the jangling keys in weariness and wrath.
"Ye have read, ye have heard, ye have
   thought," he said, "and the tale is yet
   to run: 25
"By the worth of the body that once ye had,
   give answer — what ha' ye done?"
Then Tomlinson looked back and forth, and
   little good it bore,
For the Darkness stayed at his shoulder-blade
   and Heaven's Gate before: —
"O this I have felt, and this I have guessed,
   and this I have heard men say,
"And this they wrote that another man wrote
   of a carl in Norroway."   30
"Ye have read, ye have felt, ye have guessed,
   good lack! Ye have hampered Heaven's
   Gate;
"There's little room between the stars in idleness to prate!
"O none may reach by hired speech of neighbour, priest, and kin
"Through borrowed deed to God's good meed
   that lies so fair within;
"Get hence, get hence to the Lord of Wrong,
   for the doom has yet to run,   35
"And . . . the faith that ye share with Berkeley Square uphold you, Tomlinson!"

    .   .   .   .   .

The Spirit gripped him by the hair, and sun
   by sun they fell
Till they came to the belt of Naughty Stars
   that rim the mouth of Hell.
The first are red with pride and wrath, the
   next are white with pain,
But the third are black with clinkered sin
   that cannot burn again: 40
They may hold their path, they may leave
   their path, and never a soul to mark,
They may burn or freeze, but they must not
   cease in the Scorn of the Outer Dark.
The Wind that blows between the Worlds, it
   nipped him to the bone,

Tomlinson. From *Departmental Ditties,* copyright 1892,
1893, and 1899 by Rudyard Kipling.
  1. **Berkeley Square,** a residential section in London, distinguished by its eminent respectability.

22. **Muscovy,** Russia. The Prince is sometimes identified with Count Leo Tolstoy (1828-1910), noted for his mildly
radical social doctrines. 30. **carl in Norroway.** This has
been taken to refer to Henrik Ibsen (1828-1906), whose
plays, dealing frankly with social problems, were much discussed in Tomlinson's England. A carl in early times was a
man of the peasantry, or common people. 35. **doom,**
judgment.

And he yearned to the flare of Hell-gate there
    as the light of his own hearth-stone.
The Devil he sat behind the bars, where the
    desperate legions drew,   45
But he caught the hasting Tomlinson and
    would not let him through.
"Wot ye the price of good pit-coal that I
    must pay?" said he,
"That ye rank yoursel' so fit for Hell and ask
    no leave of me?
"I am all o'er-sib to Adam's breed that ye
    should give me scorn,
"For I strove with God for your First Father
    the day that he was born.   50
"Sit down, sit down upon the slag, and answer
    loud and high
"The harm that ye did to the Sons of Men or
    ever you came to die."
And Tomlinson looked up and up, and saw
    against the night
The belly of a tortured star blood-red in
    Hell-Mouth light;
And Tomlinson looked down and down, and
    saw beneath his feet   55
The frontlet of a tortured star milk-white in
    Hell-Mouth heat.
"O I had a love on earth," said he, "that
    kissed me to my fall;
"And if ye would call my love to me I know
    she would answer all."
— "All that ye did in love forbid it shall be
    written fair,
"But now ye wait at Hell-Mouth Gate and not
    in Berkeley Square: 60
"Though we whistled your love from her bed
    to-night, I trow she would not run,
"For the sin ye do by two and two ye must
    pay for one by one!"
The Wind that blows between the Worlds,
    it cut him like a knife,
And Tomlinson took up the tale and spoke
    of his sin in life: —
"Once I ha' laughed at the power of Love
    and twice at the grip of the Grave,   65
"And thrice I ha' patted my God on the head
    that men might call me brave."
The Devil he blew on a brandered soul and
    set it aside to cool: —
"Do ye think I would waste my good pit-
    coal on the hide of a brain-sick fool?
"I see no worth in the hobnailed mirth or the
    jolthead jest ye did
"That I should waken my gentlemen that are
    sleeping three on a grid."   70
Then Tomlinson looked back and forth, and
    there was little grace.
For Hell-Gate filled the houseless soul with
    the Fear of Naked Space.

"Nay, this I ha' heard," quo' Tomlinson,
    "and this was noised abroad;
"And this I ha' got from a Belgian book on
    the word of a dead French lord."
— "Ye ha' heard, ye ha' read, ye ha' got,
    good lack! and the tale begins afresh —
"Have ye sinned one sin for the pride o' the
    eye or the sinful lust of the flesh?"   76
Then Tomlinson he gripped the bars and
    yammered, "Let me in —
"For I mind that I borrowed my neighbour's
    wife to sin the deadly sin."
The Devil he grinned behind the bars, and
    banked the fires high:
"Did ye read of that sin in a book?" said he;
    and Tomlinson said "Ay!"   80
The Devil he blew upon his nails, and the
    little devils ran,
And he said, "Go husk this whimpering thief
    that comes in the guise of a man:
"Winnow him out 'twixt star and star, and
    sieve his proper worth:
"There's sore decline in Adam's line if this be
    spawn of earth."
Empusa's crew, so naked-new they may not
    face the fire,   85
But weep that they bin too small to sin to
    the height of their desire,
Over the coal they chased the Soul, and
    racked it all abroad,
As children rifle a caddis-case or the raven's
    foolish hoard.
And back they came with the tattered Thing,
    as children after play,
And they said: "The soul that he got from
    God he has bartered clean away.   90
"We have threshed a stook of print and book,
    and winnowed a chattering wind
"And many a soul wherefrom he stole, but his
    we cannot find.
"We have handled him, we have dandled him,
    we have seared him to the bone,
"And Sire, if tooth and nail show truth he has
    no soul of his own."
The Devil he bowed his head on his breast
    and rumbled deep and low: —   95
"I'm all o'er-sib to Adam's breed that I
    should bid him go.
"Yet close we lie, and deep we lie, and if I
    gave him place,
"My gentlemen that are so proud would flout
    me to my face;
"They'd call my house a common stews and
    me a careless host,
"And — I would not anger my gentlemen for
    the sake of a shiftless ghost."   100

47. **Wot**, know. 49. **o'er sib**, too closely related. 67. **brandered**, broiled. 70. **grid**, a gridiron used for broiling.

85. **Empusa**, a monster, with one foot of brass and another of an ass, that tormented souls in the Greek underworld. 88. **caddis-case**, a covering made of sticks or stones by the larva of the caddis-fly. 91. **stook**, stack, pile.

The Devil he looked at the mangled Soul that
   prayed to feel the flame,
And he thought of Holy Charity, but he
   thought of his own good name: —
"Now ye could haste my coal to waste, and
   sit ye down to fry.
"Did ye think of that theft for yourself?" said
   he; and Tomlinson said "Ay!"
The Devil he blew an outward breath, for his
   heart was free from care: —   105
"Ye have scarce the soul of a louse," he said,
   "but the roots of sin are there.
"And for that sin should ye come in were I the
   lord alone.
"But sinful pride has rule inside — ay,
   mightier than my own.
"Honour and Wit, fore-damned they sit, to
   each his Priest and Whore;
"Nay, scarce I dare myself go there, and you
   they'd torture sore.   110
"Ye are neither spirit nor spirk," he said; "ye
   are neither book nor brute —
"Go, get ye back to the flesh again for the
   sake of Man's repute.
"I'm all o'er-sib to Adam's breed that I should
   mock your pain,
"But look that ye win to worthier sin ere ye
   come back again.
"Get hence, the hearse is at your door — the
   grim black stallions wait —   115
"They bear your clay to place to-day. Speed,
   lest ye come too late!
"Go back to Earth with a lip unsealed — go
   back with an open eye,
"And carry my word to the Sons of Men or
   ever ye come to die:
"That the sin they do by two and two they
   must pay for one by one,   119
"And . . . the God that you took from a
   printed book be with you, Tomlinson!"
                   (1892)

ENVOY

When Earth's last picture is painted and the
   tubes are twisted and dried,
When the oldest colours have faded, and the
   youngest critic has died,
We shall rest, and, faith, we shall need it —
   lie down for an æon or two,
Till the Master of All Good Workmen shall
   put us to work anew.

And those that were good shall be happy:
   they shall sit in a golden chair;   5
They shall splash at a ten-league canvas with
   brushes of comets' hair.

They shall find real saints to draw from —
   Magdalene, Peter, and Paul;
They shall work for an age at a sitting and
   never be tired at all!

And only the Master shall praise us, and only
   the Master shall blame;
And no one shall work for money, and no one
   shall work for fame,   10
But each for the joy of the working, and
   each, in his separate star,
Shall draw the Thing as he sees It for the
   God of Things as They are!
                   (1892)

THE LAST CHANTEY

"And there was no more sea."

Thus said the Lord in the Vault above the
   Cherubim,
   Calling to the Angels and the Souls in their
      degree:
     "Lo! Earth has passed away
     On the smoke of Judgment Day.
That Our word may be established shall We
   gather up the sea?"   5

Loud sang the souls of the jolly, jolly mar-
   iners:
   "Plague upon the hurricane that made us
     furl and flee!
     But the war is done between us,
     In the deep the Lord hath seen us —
Our bones we'll leave the barracout', and
   God may sink the sea!"   10

Then said the soul of Judas that betrayéd
   Him:
   "Lord, hast Thou forgotten Thy covenant
     with me?
     How once a year I go
     To cool me on the floe?
And Ye take my day of mercy if Ye take
   away the sea."   15

Then said the soul of the Angel of the Off-
   shore Wind:
   (He that bits the thunder when the bull-
     mouthed breakers flee):
     "I have watch and ward to keep

---

111. **spirk**, vegetable.
Envoy. Copyright 1892 by Rudyard Kipling.

The Last Chantey. Copyright 1893 by Rudyard Kipling.
A chantey (pronounced "shanty") is a sailor's ballad to the rhythm of which the anchor is raised and the sails reefed or set.
And . . . sea, from the description in *Revelation* (21:1) of the end of the world. 1. **Cherubim,** a high order of angels. 10. **barracout',** the barracuda, a carnivorous fish of the Pacific and West Indian waters. 13-14. **once . . . floe.** According to legend Judas was released from infernal torment once a year and allowed to spend each Christmas Day on an iceberg. Cf. Arnold's *Saint Brandan,* p. 497. 17. **bits,** checks.

O'er Thy wonders on the deep,
And Ye take mine honour from me if Ye
  take away the sea!"   20

Loud sang the souls of the jolly, jolly mar-
  iners:
  "Nay, but we were angry, and a hasty folk
    are we.
  If we worked the ship together
  Till she foundered in foul weather,
Are we babes that we should clamour for a
  vengeance on the sea?"   25

Then said the souls of the slaves that men
  threw overboard:
  "Kennelled in the picaroon a weary band
    were we;
  But Thy arm was strong to save,
  And it touched us on the wave,
And we drowsed the long tides idle till Thy
  Trumpets tore the sea."   30

Then cried the soul of the stout Apostle Paul
  to God:
  "Once we frapped a ship, and she laboured
    woundily.
  There were fourteen score of these,
  And they blessed Thee on their knees,
When they learned Thy Grace and Glory
  under Malta by the sea!"   35

Loud sang the souls of the jolly, jolly mar-
  iners,
  Plucking at their harps, and they plucked
    unhandily:
  "Our thumbs are rough and tarred,
  And the tune is something hard —
May we lift a Deepsea Chantey such as sea-
  men use at sea?"   40

Then said the souls of the gentlemen-adven-
  turers —
  Fettered wrist to bar all for red iniquity:
  "Ho, we revel in our chains
  O'er the sorrow that was Spain's;
Heave or sink it, leave or drink it, we were
  masters of the sea!"   45

Up spake the soul of a grey Gothavn 'speckshioner —

(He that led the flenching in the fleets of
  fair Dundee):
  "Oh, the ice-blink white and near,
  And the bowhead breaching clear!
Will Ye whelm them all for wantonness that
  wallow in the sea?"   50

Loud sang the souls of the jolly, jolly mariners,
  Crying: "Under Heaven, here is neither
    lead nor lee!
  Must we sing for evermore
  On the windless, glassy floor?
Take back your golden fiddles and we'll beat
  to open sea!"   55

Then stooped the Lord, and He called the
  good sea up to Him,
  And 'stablished His borders unto all eter-
    nity,
  That such as have no pleasure
  For to praise the Lord by measure,
They may enter into galleons and serve Him
  on the sea.   60

*Sun, Wind, and Cloud shall fail not from the
  face of it,*
  *Stinging, ringing spindrift, nor the fulmar
    flying free;*
  And the ships shall go abroad
  To the Glory of the Lord
*Who heard the silly sailor-folk and gave them
  back their sea!*   (1892)

THE KING

"Farewell, Romance!" the Cave-men said;
  "With bone well carved he went away,
"Flint arms the ignoble arrowhead,
  "And jasper tips the spear to-day.
"Changed are the Gods of Hunt and Dance, 5
"And he with these.   Farewell, Romance!"

"Farewell, Romance!" the Lake-folk sighed;
  "We lift the weight of flatling years;
"The caverns of the mountain-side
  "Hold Him who scorns our hutted piers. 10
"Lost hills whereby we dare not dwell,
"Guard ye his rest.   Romance, Farewell!"

27. **picaroon,** a pirate-ship. 32. **frapped a ship.** *Acts* 27 describes how the ship on which St. Paul was a passenger was wrapped about the hull with cable (frapped) to keep it from breaking apart in a storm. **woundily,** excessively. 35. **Malta,** the island in the Mediterranean where Paul's ship was wrecked. 41. **gentlemen-adventurers,** members of the great 16th century trading companies that came often into conflict with Spanish interests in the New World. 44. **sorrow . . . Spain's,** the defeat of the Spanish Armada by the English fleet, 1588. 46. **Gothavn 'speckshioner.** Gothavn is a port in northern Greenland; a specksioneer is the chief harpooner on a whaling vessel who directs the operation of flenching the whale—i.e., cutting the blubber from the bones.

47. **Dundee,** the Scottish whaling port. 49. **bowhead,** the Greenland whale. **breaching,** breaking the water, as by leaping out. 52. **lead nor lee,** a good place neither to go nor to stay. A lead (pronounced "leed") is an open channel ahead of a ship; a lee is a sheltered anchorage. 54. **glassy floor.** See *Revelation,* 4:6.—"And before the throne there was a sea of glass like unto crystal." 62. **spindrift,** spray blown from the crests of waves. **fulmar,** an ocean bird akin to the petrel.
The King. Copyright 1899 by Rudyard Kipling.
5. **Gods . . . Dance.** It is assumed that the gods of prehistoric man were hunting gods and that they were propitiated by ceremonial dances. 7. **Lake-folk.** Many traces remain of prehistoric inhabitants of Switzerland who lived in villages built on piles, or piers (line 10), near the shores of the lakes.

"Farewell, Romance!" the Soldier spoke;
  "By sleight of sword we may not win,
"But scuffle 'mid uncleanly smoke   15
  "Of arquebus and culverin.
"Honour is lost, and none may tell
"Who paid good blows. Romance, farewell!"

"Farewell, Romance!" the Traders cried;
  "Our keels have lain with every sea;   20
"The dull-returning wind and tide
  "Heave up the wharf where we would be;
"The known and noted breezes swell
  "Our trudging sail. Romance, farewell!"

"Good-bye, Romance!" the Skipper said;   25
  "He vanished with the coal we burn.
"Our dial marks full-steam ahead,
  "Our speed is timed to half a turn.
"Sure as the ferried barge we ply   29
"'Twixt port and port. Romance, good-bye!"

"Romance!" the season-tickets mourn,
  "*He* never ran to catch his train,
"But passed with coach and guard and horn—
  "And left the local—late again!"
Confound Romance! . . . And all unseen   35
Romance brought up the nine-fifteen.

His hand was on the lever laid,
  His oil-can soothed the worrying cranks,
His whistle waked the snowbound grade,
  His fog-horn cut the reeking Banks;   40
By dock and deep and mine and mill
The Boy-god reckless laboured still!

Robed, crowned and throned, He wove his
    spell,
  Where heart-blood beat or hearth-smoke
    curled,
With unconsidered miracle,   45
  Hedged in a backward-gazing world:
Then taught his chosen bard to say:
"Our King was with us—yesterday!" (1894)

THE SONG OF THE BANJO

You couldn't pack a Broadwood half a mile—
  You mustn't leave a fiddle in the damp—
You couldn't raft an organ up the Nile,
  And play it in an Equatorial swamp.
I travel with the cooking-pots and pails—5
I'm sandwiched 'tween the coffee and the
    pork—

And when the dusty column checks and tails,
  You should hear me spur the rearguard
    to a walk!

With my "*Pilly-willy-winky-winky popp!*"
  [Oh, it's any tune that comes into my
    head!]   10
So I keep 'em moving forward till they
    drop;
  So I play 'em up to water and to bed.

In the silence of the camp before the fight,
  When it's good to make your will and
    say your prayer,
You can hear my *strumpty-tumpty* over-
    night,   15
  Explaining ten to one was always fair.
I'm the Prophet of the Utterly Absurd,
  Of the Patently Impossible and Vain—
And when the Thing that Couldn't has oc-
    curred,
  Give me time to change my leg and go
    again.   20

With my "*Tumpa - tumpa - tumpa - tumpa-
    tump!*"
  In the desert where the dung-fed camp-
    smoke curled.
There was never voice before us till I led
    our lonely chorus,
  I—the war-drum of the White Man round
    the world!

By the bitter road the Younger Son must
    tread,   25
  Ere he win to hearth and saddle of his
    own,—
'Mid the riot of the shearers at the shed,
  In the silence of the herder's hut alone—
In the twilight, on a bucket upside down,
  Hear me babble what the weakest won't
    confess—   30
I am Memory and Torment—I am Town!
  I am all that ever went with evening dress!

With my "*Tunka-tunka-tunka-tunka-tunk!*"
  [So the lights—the London Lights—grow
    near and plain!]
So I rowel 'em afresh towards the Devil and
    the Flesh,   35
  Till I bring my broken rankers home again.

In desire of many marvels over sea,
  Where the new-raised tropic city sweats
    and roars,
I have sailed with Young Ulysses from the
    quay

16. **arquebus and culverin,** early kinds of firearms.
23. **known . . . breezes.** Scientific charting of the prevailing winds of the world was begun in Germany early in
the 19th century. 40. **reeking Banks,** the foggy Grand Banks
of Newfoundland, setting of Kipling's *Captains Courageous.*
The Song of the Banjo. From *The Seven Seas,* copyright
1896 and 1905 by Rudyard Kipling.
1. **Broadwood,** an English piano.

7. **tails,** straggles. 12. **to water,** to water the horses, one
of the last duties of the day. 35. **rowel 'em,** spur them.
36. **rankers,** soldiers in the ranks. 39. **Young Ulysses.**
See Tennyson's *Ulysses,* page 43.

Till the anchor rumbled down on stranger
  shores. 40
He is blooded to the open and the sky,
  He is taken in a snare that shall not fail,
He shall hear me singing strongly, till he die,
  Like the shouting of a backstay in a gale.

With my *"Hya! Heeya! Heeya! Hullah!*
  Haul!" 45
[Oh the green that thunders aft along the
  deck!]
Are you sick o' towns and men? You must
  sign and sail again,
  For it's "Johnny Bowlegs, pack your kit
  and trek!"

Through the gorge that gives the stars at
  noon-day clear —
  Up the pass that packs the scud beneath
  our wheel — 50
Round the bluff that sinks her thousand
  fathom sheer —
Down the valley with our guttering brakes
  asqueal:
Where the trestle groans and quivers in the
  snow,
  Where the many-shedded levels loop and
  twine,
Hear me lead my reckless children from
  below 55
  Till we sing the Song of Roland to the
  pine!

With my *"Tinka-tinka-tinka-linka-tink!"*
  [Oh the axe has cleared the mountain,
  croup and crest!]
And we ride the iron stallions down to drink,
  Through the cañons to the waters of the
  West! 60

And the tunes that mean so much to you
  alone —
  Common tunes that make you choke and
  blow your nose,
Vulgar tunes that bring the laugh that brings
  the groan —
  I can rip your very heartstrings out with
  those;
With the feasting, and the folly, and the
  fun — 65
  And the lying, and the lusting, and the
  drink,

And the merry play that drops you, when
  you're done,
  To the thoughts that burn like irons if
  you think.

With my *"Plunka-lunka-lunka-lunka-lunk!"*
  Here's a trifle on account of pleasure past, 70
Ere the wit that made you win gives you
  eyes to see your sin
  And — the heavier repentance at the last!

Let the organ moan her sorrow to the roof —
  I have told the naked stars the Grief of
  Man.
Let the trumpet snare the foeman to the
  proof — 75
  I have known Defeat, and mocked it as
  we ran!
My bray ye may not alter nor mistake
  When I stand to jeer the fatted Soul of
  Things,
But the Song of Lost Endeavour that I
  make,
  Is it hidden in the twanging of the strings?

With my *"Ta-ra-rara-rara-ra-ra-rrrp!"* 81
  [Is it naught to you that hear and pass
  me by?]
But the word — the word is mine, when the
  order moves the line
  And the lean, locked ranks go roaring
  down to die!

The grandam of my grandam was the
  Lyre — 85
  [O the blue below the little fisher-huts!]
That the Stealer stooping beachward filled
  with fire,
  Till she bore my iron head and ringing
  guts!
By the wisdom of the centuries I speak — 89
  To the tune of yestermorn I set the truth —
I, the joy of life unquestioned — I, the Greek —
  I, the everlasting Wonder-song of Youth!

With my *"Tinka-tinka-tinka-tinka-tink!"*
  [What d' ye lack, my noble masters? What
  d' ye lack?]
So I draw the world together link by link: 95
  Yea, from Delos up to Limerick and back!
                       (1895)

41. **blooded**, initiated. 44. **backstay**, a wire rope that holds the mast of a ship in place; in a high wind, its vibrations make a clear sound. 45. **Hya!** etc., cries used by sailors when hauling to insure that all will pull in unison. 48. **Johnny . . . trek**, a reference to the Cape-Dutch song, "Pack your kit and trek, Johnny with the limping leg." 50. **scud**, low, thin clouds flying before the wind. 54. **many-shedded levels**, levels covered with sheds to protect railways from snowdrifts and avalanches. 56. **Song of Roland**, the great French epic of the Middle Ages.

87. **the Stealer**, Hermes, the god of theft and protector of thieves; he invented the lyre, which he made out of a sea-shell. 94. **What d'ye lack**, formerly the traditional appeal of London peddlers and shopkeepers to passers-by. 96. **Delos up to Limerick**. Delos, an island off the coast of Greece, was the birthplace of Apollo, god of music. Limerick is a town in the province of Munster, Ireland, that gave its name to a nonsense poem of five lines. Kipling's phrase covers all times and every class of song from the divine music of Apollo to the modern limerick.

THE LAW OF THE JUNGLE

*Now this is the Law of the Jungle — as old and
as true as the sky;
And the Wolf that shall keep it may prosper,
but the Wolf that shall break it must die.*

*As the creeper that girdles the tree-trunk the
Law runneth forward and back —
For the strength of the Pack is the Wolf, and
the strength of the Wolf is the Pack.*

Wash daily from nose-tip to tail-tip; drink
deeply, but never too deep; 5
And remember the night is for hunting, and
forget not the day is for sleep.

The Jackal may follow the Tiger, but, Cub,
when thy whiskers are grown,
Remember the Wolf is a hunter — go forth
and get food of thine own.

Keep peace with the Lords of the Jungle —
the Tiger, the Panther, the Bear;
And trouble not Hathi the Silent, and mock
not the Boar in the lair. 10

When Pack meets with Pack in the Jungle,
and neither will go from the trail,
Lie down till the leaders have spoken — it
may be fair words shall prevail.

When ye fight with a Wolf of the Pack, ye
must fight him alone and afar,
Lest others take part in the quarrel, and the
Pack be diminished by war.

The Lair of the Wolf is his refuge, and where
he has made him his home, 15
Not even the Head Wolf may enter, not even
the Council may come.

The Lair of the Wolf is his refuge, but where
he has digged it too plain,
The Council shall send him a message, and
so he shall change it again.

If ye kill before midnight, be silent, and
wake not the woods with your bay,
Lest ye frighten the deer from the crops, and
the brothers go empty away. 20

Ye may kill for yourselves, and your mates,
and your cubs as they need, and ye can;
But kill not for pleasure of killing, and *seven
times never kill Man!*

If ye plunder his Kill from a weaker, devour
not all in thy pride;
Pack-Right is the right of the meanest; so
leave him the head and the hide.

The Kill of the Pack is the meat of the Pack.
Ye must eat where it lies; 25
And no one may carry away of that meat to
his lair, or he dies.

The Kill of the Wolf is the meat of the Wolf.
He may do what he will,
But, till he has given permission, the Pack
may not eat of that Kill.

Cub-Right is the right of the Yearling. From
all of his Pack he may claim
Full-gorge when the killer has eaten; and
none may refuse him the same. 30

Lair-Right is the right of the Mother. From
all of her year she may claim
One haunch of each kill for her litter; and
none may deny her the same.

Cave-Right is the right of the Father — to
hunt by himself for his own:
He is freed of all calls to the Pack; he is judged
by the Council alone.

Because of his age and his cunning, because
of his gripe and his paw, 35
In all that the Law leaveth open, the word of
the Head Wolf is Law.

*Now these are the Laws of the Jungle, and
many and mighty are they;
But the head and the hoof of the Law and the
haunch and the hump is — Obey!*

(1895)

SESTINA OF THE TRAMP-ROYAL

Speakin' in general, I 've tried 'em all —
The 'appy roads that take you o'er the
world.
Speakin' in general, I 've found them good
For such as cannot use one bed too long,
But must get 'ence, the same as I 've done, 5
An' go observin' matters till they die.

What do it matter where or 'ow we die,
So long as we've our 'ealth to watch it all —

The Law of the Jungle. From *The Second Jungle Book,*
copyright 1895 by Rudyard Kipling.
10. Hathi the Silent, the elephant.

Sestina of the Tramp-Royal. From *The Seven Seas,* copyright 1896 and 1905 by Rudyard Kipling.
A sestina is a poem of six stanzas of six lines each with a
closing envoy. The line-endings of the first stanza recur in
the other stanzas but in different order. The form was first
used by the troubadours, a class of lyric poets who flourished
in southeastern France from the 11th to the 13th centuries.

The different ways that different things are
  done,
An' men an' women lovin' in this world;   10
Takin' our chances as they come along,
An' when they ain't, pretendin' they are
  good?

In cash or credit — no, it aren't no good;
You 'ave to 'ave the 'abit or you'd die,
Unless you lived your life but one day long, 15
Nor didn't prophesy nor fret at all,
But drew your tucker some'ow from the
  world,
An' never bothered what you might ha' done.

But, Gawd, what things are they I 'aven't
  done!
I've turned my 'and to most, an' turned
  it good,   20
In various situations round the world —
For 'im that doth not work must surely die;
But that's no reason man should labour all
'Is life on one same shift — life's none so long.

Therefore, from job to job I've moved along. 25
Pay couldn't 'old me when my time was
  done,
For something in my 'ead upset it all,
Till I 'ad dropped whatever 't was for good,
An', out at sea, be'eld the dock-lights die,
An' met my mate — the wind that tramps the
  world!   30

It's like a book, I think, this bloomin' world,
Which you can read and care for just so long,
But presently you feel that you will die
Unless you get the page you're readin' done,
An' turn another — likely not so good;   35
But what you're after is to turn 'em all.

Gawd bless this world! Whatever she 'ath
  done —
Excep' when awful long — I've found it good.
So write, before I die, " 'E liked it all!"
                   (1896)

RECESSIONAL

God of our fathers, known of old,
  Lord of our far-flung battle-line,
Beneath whose awful Hand we hold

Dominion over palm and pine —
Lord God of Hosts, be with us yet,
Lest we forget — lest we forget!

The tumult and the shouting dies;
  The Captains and the Kings depart:
Still stands Thine ancient sacrifice,
  An humble and a contrite heart.   10
Lord God of Hosts, be with us yet,
Lest we forget — lest we forget!

Far-called, our navies melt away;
  On dune and headland sinks the fire:
Lo, all our pomp of yesterday   15
  Is one with Nineveh and Tyre!
Judge of the Nations, spare us yet,
Lest we forget — lest we forget!

If, drunk with sight of power, we loose
  Wild tongues that have not Thee in awe, 20
Such boastings as the Gentiles use,
  Or lesser breeds without the Law —
Lord God of Hosts, be with us yet,
Lest we forget — lest we forget!

For heathen heart that puts her trust   25
  In reeking tube and iron shard,
All valiant dust that builds on dust,
  And guarding, calls not Thee to guard,
For frantic boast and foolish word —
Thy Mercy on Thy People, Lord!
                   (1897)

THE WHITE MAN'S BURDEN

Take up the White Man's burden —
  Send forth the best ye breed —
Go bind your sons to exile
  To serve your captives' need;
To wait in heavy harness,   5
  On fluttered folk and wild —
Your new-caught, sullen peoples,
  Half-devil and half-child.

22. **work . . . die.** See *2 Thessalonians*, 3:10.—"If any would not work, neither should he eat."
Recessional. From *The Five Nations*, copyright 1903 by Rudyard Kipling.
A recessional is a hymn sung while the clergy and the choir leave the church in procession at the close of a service. Kipling's poem was written as the celebration of Queen Victoria's Diamond Jubilee (the end of her sixtieth year as queen) was drawing to a close. The poem served as an appropriate warning at a time when the British people were dazzled by the pomp and power of empire. Cf. the first lyric of Housman's *A Shropshire Lad*, p. 909, with its reference to the Golden Jubilee (1887).
4. **palm and pine,** a reference to the wide extent of the Empire. 6. **Lest we forget.** See *Deuteronomy*, 6:12.—"Then beware lest thou forget the Lord, which brought thee forth out of the land of Egypt, from the house of bondage." 9-10. **sacrifice . . . heart.** See *Psalms*, 51:17.—"The sacrifices of God are a broken spirit; a broken and a contrite heart, O God, thou wilt not despise." 16. **Nineveh and Tyre.** Nineveh was the famous capital of ancient Assyria; it is now buried under sand. Tyre, in Phoenicia, once a great maritime city, is now an unimportant cotton-shipping port. 21-22. **Gentiles . . . Law.** See *Romans*, 2:14.—"For when the Gentiles, which have not the law, do by nature the things contained in the law, these, having not the law, are a law unto themselves." For Kipling, a Gentile may be anyone not English. 26. **shard,** shell-fragment.
The White Man's Burden. Copyright 1899 by Rudyard Kipling.
This phrase was used at the close of the Spanish-American War, 1898, to describe the responsibility of the United States in caring for Cuba and the Philippines; it thus became the watchword of imperialism.

Take up the White Man's burden —
  In patience to abide,   10
To veil the threat of terror
  And check the show of pride;
By open speech and simple,
  An hundred times made plain,
To seek another's profit,   15
  And work another's gain.

Take up the White Man's burden —
  The savage wars of peace —
Fill full the mouth of Famine
  And bid the sickness cease;   20
And when your goal is nearest
  The end for others sought,
Watch Sloth and heathen Folly
  Bring all your hope to nought.

Take up the White Man's burden —   25
  No tawdry rule of kings,
But toil of serf and sweeper —
  The tale of common things.
The ports ye shall not enter,
  The roads ye shall not tread,   30
Go make them with your living,
  And mark them with your dead.

Take up the White Man's burden —
  And reap his old reward:
The blame of those ye better,   35
  The hate of those ye guard —
The cry of hosts ye humour
  (Ah, slowly!) toward the light: —
"Why brought ye us from bondage,
  "Our loved Egyptian night?"   40

Take up the White Man's burden —
  Ye dare not stoop to less —
Nor call too loud on Freedom
  To cloak your weariness;
By all ye cry or whisper,   45
  By all ye leave or do,
The silent, sullen peoples
  Shall weigh your Gods and you.

Take up the White Man's burden —
  Have done with childish days —   50
The lightly proffered laurel,
  The easy, ungrudged praise.
Comes now, to search your manhood
  Through all the thankless years,
Cold, edged with dear-bought wisdom, 55
  The judgment of your peers!

                  (1899)

BOOTS

(Infantry Columns)

We're foot — slog — slog — slog — sloggin'
  over Africa!
Foot — foot — foot — foot — sloggin' over
  Africa —
(Boots — boots — boots — boots — movin'
  up and down again!)
    There's no discharge in the war!

Seven — six — eleven — five — nine-an'-
  twenty mile to-day —   5
Four — eleven — seventeen — thirty-two
  the day before —
(Boots — boots — boots — boots — movin'
  up and down again!)
    There's no discharge in the war!

Don't — don't — don't — don't — look at
  what's in front of you.
(Boots — boots — boots — boots — movin'
  up an' down again);   10
Men — men — men — men — men go mad
  with watchin' 'em,
    An' there's no discharge in the war!

Try — try — try — try — to think o' something different —
Oh — my — God — keep — me from goin'
  lunatic!
(Boots — boots — boots — boots — movin'
  up an' down again!)   15
    There's no discharge in the war!

Count — count — count — count — the
  bullets in the bandoliers.
If — your — eyes — drop — they will get
  atop o' you!
(Boots — boots — boots — boots — movin'
  up an' down again) —
    There's no discharge in the war!   20

We — can — stick — out — 'unger, thirst,
  an' weariness,
But — not — not — not — not the chronic
  sight of 'em —
Boots — boots — boots — boots — movin'
  up an' down again,
  An' there's no discharge in the war!

'Tain't — so — bad — by — **day because o'**
  company,   25

39-40. **Why . . . night.** When the Israelites were hungry in the wilderness, on their journey from Egypt, they murmured against Moses and Aaron, saying: "Would to God we had died by the hand of the Lord in the land of Egypt, where we sat by the flesh pots, and when we did eat bread to the full" (*Exodus,* 16:2-3).

Boots. From *The Five Nations,* copyright 1903 by Rudyard Kipling.
  The rhythm is that of marching troops. The poem refers particularly to the Boer War, 1899-1902.
4. **There's . . . war.** See *Ecclesiastes,* 8:8.—"There is no man that hath power over the spirit to retain the spirit; neither hath he power in the day of death: and there is no discharge in that war." 17. **bandoliers,** cartridge-belts worn over the shoulder.

But night — brings — long — strings — o'
   forty thousand million
Boots — boots — boots — boots — movin'
   up an' down again.
     There's no discharge in the war!

I — 'ave — marched — six — weeks in 'Ell
   an' certify
It — is — not — fire — devils, dark or anything,   30
But boots — boots — boots — boots — movin' up an' down again,
   An' there's no discharge in the war! (1903)

"CITIES AND THRONES AND POWERS"

"A CENTURION OF THE THIRTIETH"—
PUCK OF POOK'S HILL

Cities and Thrones and Powers
   Stand in Time's eye,
Almost as long as flowers,
   Which daily die:
But, as new buds put forth   5
   To glad new men,
Out of the spent and unconsidered Earth
   The Cities rise again.

This season's Daffodil,
   She never hears   10
What change, what chance, what chill,
   Cut down last year's;
But with bold countenance,
   And knowledge small,
Esteems her seven days' continuance   15
   To be perpetual.

So Time that is o'er-kind,
   To all that be,
Ordains us e'en as blind,
   As bold as she: 20
That in our very death,
   And burial sure,
Shadow to shadow, well persuaded, saith,
   "See how our works endure!"   (1905)

THE CHILDREN'S SONG

PUCK OF POOK'S HILL

Land of our Birth, we pledge to thee
Our love and toil in the years to be;
When we are grown and take our place
As men and women with our race.

Father in Heaven who lovest all,
Oh, help Thy children when they call;
That they may build from age to age
An undefiled heritage.

Teach us to bear the yoke in youth,
With steadfastness and careful truth;   10
That, in our time, Thy Grace may give
The Truth whereby the Nations live.

Teach us to rule ourselves alway,
Controlled and cleanly night and day;
That we may bring, if need arise,   15
No maimed or worthless sacrifice.

Teach us to look in all our ends
On Thee for judge, and not our friends;
That we, with Thee, may walk uncowed
By fear or favour of the crowd.   20

Teach us the Strength that cannot seek,
By deed or thought, to hurt the weak;
That, under Thee, we may possess
Man's strength to comfort man's distress.

Teach us Delight in simple things,   25
And Mirth that has no bitter springs;
Forgiveness free of evil done,
And Love to all men 'neath the sun!

Land of our Birth, our faith, our pride,
For whose dear sake our fathers died;   30
Oh, Motherland, we pledge to thee
Head, heart, and hand through the years to be!
                        (1906)

THE RECALL

"AN HABITATION ENFORCED"—
ACTIONS AND REACTIONS

I am the land of their fathers.
In me the virtue stays.
I will bring back my children,
After certain days.

Under their feet in the grasses   5
My clinging magic runs.
They shall return as strangers.
They shall remain as sons.

Over their heads in the branches
Of their new-bought, ancient trees,   10
I weave an incantation
And draw them to my knees.

Scent of smoke in the evening,
Smell of rain in the night—

The hours, the days and the seasons,   15
Order their souls aright,

Till I make plain the meaning
Of all my thousand years—
Till I fill their hearts with knowledge,   19
While I fill their eyes with tears.   (1909)

From EPITAPHS OF THE WAR

A SERVANT

We were together since the War began.
He was my servant—and the better man.

A SON

My son was killed while laughing at some jest.
        I would I knew
What it was, and it might serve me in a time
        when jests are few.

EX-CLERK

Pity not! The Army gave
Freedom to a timid slave:
In which Freedom did he find
Strength of body, will, and mind:
By which strength he came to prove   5
Mirth, Companionship, and Love:
For which Love to Death he went:
In which Death he lies content.

THE WONDER

Body and Spirit I surrendered whole
To harsh Instructors—and received a soul . . .
If mortal man could change me through and
        through
From all I was—what may The God not do?

THE COWARD

I could not look on Death, which being known,
Men led me to him, blindfold and alone.

A GRAVE NEAR CAIRO

Gods of the Nile, should this stout fellow here
Get out—get out! He knows not shame nor
        fear.

BOMBED IN LONDON

On land and sea I strove with anxious care
To escape conscription. It was in the air!

BATTERIES OUT OF AMMUNITION

If any mourn us in the workshop, say
We died because the shift kept holiday.

COMMON FORM

If any question why we died,
Tell them, because our fathers lied.

A DEAD STATESMAN

I could not dig: I dared not rob:
Therefore I lied to please the mob.
Now all my lies are proved untrue
And I must face the men I slew.
What tale shall save me here among   5
Mine angry and defrauded young?

DESTROYERS IN COLLISION

For Fog and Fate no charm is found
        To lighten or amend.
I, hurrying to my bride, was drowned—
        Cut down by my best friend.
                                (1914–1918)

THE STORM CONE

This is the midnight—let no star
Delude us—dawn is very far.
This is the tempest long foretold—
Slow to make head but sure to hold.

Stand by! The lull 'twixt blast and blast   5
Signals the storm is near, not past;
And worse than present jeopardy
May our forlorn to-morrow be.

If we have cleared the expectant reef,
Let no man look for his relief.   10
Only the darkness hides the shape
Of further peril to escape.

It is decreed that we abide
The weight of gale against the tide
And those huge waves the outer main   15
Sends in to set us back again.

They fall and whelm.   We strain to hear
The pulses of her labouring gear,
Till the deep throb beneath us proves,
After each shudder and check, she moves!   20

She moves, with all save purpose lost,
To make her offing from the coast;
But, till she fetches open sea,
Let no man deem that he is free!   (1932)

Epitaphs of the War. From *The Years Between,* by Rudyard Kipling. Copyright 1919 by Rudyard Kipling, reprinted by permission of Mrs. George Bambridge and Doubleday & Company, Inc.

The Storm Cone. From *Rudyard Kipling's Verse,* by Rudyard Kipling. Copyright 1932 by Rudyard Kipling, reprinted by permission of Mrs. George Bambridge and Doubleday & Company, Inc.

GEORGE WILLIAM RUSSELL*
("A. E.") (1867-1935)

BY THE MARGIN OF THE GREAT DEEP

When the breath of twilight blows to flame
    the misty skies,
All its vaporous sapphire, violet glow and
    silver gleam
With their magic flood me through the
    gateway of the eyes;
    I am one with the twilight's dream.

When the trees and skies and fields are one in
    dusky mood,   5
Every heart of man is rapt within the mother's
    breast;
Full of peace and sleep and dreams in the
    vasty quietude,
    I am one with their hearts at rest.

From our immemorial joys of hearth and home
    and love
Strayed away along the margin of the un-
    known tide,   10
All its reach of soundless calm can thrill me
    far above
    Word or touch from the lips beside.

Aye, and deep and deep and deeper let me
    drink and draw
From the olden fountain more than light or
    peace or dream,
Such primeval being as o'erfills the heart
    with awe,   15
    Growing one with its silent stream.
                   (1894)

THE HERMIT

Now the quietude of earth
Nestles deep my heart within;
Friendships new and strange have birth
Since I left the city's din.

Here the tempest stays its guile,   5
Like a big kind brother plays,
Romps and pauses here awhile
From its immemorial ways.

Now the silver light of dawn
Slipping through the leaves that fleck   10
My one window, hurries on,
Throws its arms around my neck.

*The poems of George William Russell are reprinted from his *Collected Poems* by permission of The Macmillan Company, publishers.
"A. E.," Russell's pen-name, an abbreviation of Æon (age, eternity), the name which Russell used in signing early work.

Darkness to my doorway hies,
Lays her chin upon the roof,
And her burning seraph eyes   15
Now no longer keep aloof.

And the ancient mystery
Holds its hands out day by day,
Takes a chair and croons with me
By my cabin built of clay.   20

When the dusky shadow flits,
By the chimney nook I see
Where the old enchanter sits,
Smiles and waves and beckons me. (1894)

OVERSOUL

I am Beauty itself among beautiful things.
         — *Bhagavad-Gita.*

The East was crowned with snow-cold bloom
And hung with veils of pearly fleece;
They died away into the gloom,
Vistas of peace — and deeper peace.

And earth and air and wave and fire   5
In awe and breathless silence stood;
For One who passed into their choir
Linked them in mystic brotherhood.

Twilight of amethyst, amid
Thy few strange stars that lit the heights,   10
Where was the secret spirit hid?
Where was Thy place, O Light of Lights?

The flame of Beauty far in space —
Where rose the fire: in Thee? in Me?
Which bowed the elemental race   15
To adoration silently?   (1894)

INHERITANCE

As flow the rivers to the sea
Adown from rocky hill or plain,
A thousand ages toiled for thee

15. **seraph.** A seraph is one of an order of heavenly beings regarded as fiery and purifying ministers of Jehovah.
Oversoul. The oversoul is the divine personality, perfect Goodness, Truth, and Beauty. According to the pantheistic or transcendental philosophy, the oversoul is the whole of which individual souls are parts; hence all created things partake of the divine nature. A man may therefore come to understand from observation of his own mind and of external nature something of what constitutes perfect Beauty and perfect Truth, since God is in the dawn and twilight as well as in the mind of man. This conception is to be found in Platonic and in Oriental philosophy, as well as in the poetry of Wordsworth, Shelley, and Emerson. Cf. *Unity* and *Reconciliation,* pp. 908 and 909, and Browning's *"Transcendentalism,"* p. 265. See also Emerson's essay entitled *The Oversoul.*
Bhagavad-Gita, "the song of the holy one": a philosophic episode, expounding Brahmanic philosophy, in the *Mahabharata,* a Hindu epic. The deity Krishna is the speaker.
5. **earth . . . fire,** the four elements of which the universe is composed. 7. **One,** the divine spirit which makes harmony out of naturally discordant elements.

And gave thee harvest of their gain;
And weary myriads of yore   5
Dug out for thee earth's buried ore.

The shadowy toilers for thee fought
In chaos of primeval day
Blind battles with they knew not what;
And each before he passed away   10
Gave clear articulate cries of woe —
Your pain is theirs of long ago.

And all the old heart sweetness sung,
The joyous life of man and maid
In forests when the earth was young,   15
In rumors round your childhood strayed,
The careless sweetness of your mind
Comes from the buried years behind.

And not alone unto your birth
Their gifts the weeping ages bore,   20
The old descents of God on earth
Have dowered thee with celestial lore;
So, wise, and filled with sad and gay
You pass into the further day.

                     (1894)

UNITY

One thing in all things have I seen;
One thought has haunted earth and air;
Clangor and silence both have been
Its palace chambers.   Everywhere

I saw the mystic vision flow   5
And live in men and woods and streams,
Until I could no longer know
The dream of life from my own dreams.

Sometimes it rose like fire in me
Within the depths of my own mind,   10
And spreading to infinity,
It took the voices of the wind;

It scrawled the human mystery —
Dim heraldry — on light and air;
Wavering along the starry sea   15
I saw the flying vision there.

Each fire that in God's temple lit
Burns fierce before the inner shrine,
Dimmed as my fire grew near to it
And darkened at the light of mine.   20

At last, at last, the meaning caught —
The Spirit wears its diadem;
It shakes its wondrous plumes of thought
And trails the stars along with them.

                     (1894)

THE MEMORY OF EARTH

In the wet dusk silver-sweet, ·
Down the violet-scented ways,
As I moved with quiet feet
I was met by mighty days.

On the hedge the hanging dew   5
Glassed the eve and stars and skies;
While I gazed a madness grew
Into thundered battle cries.

Where the hawthorn glimmered white,
Flashed the spear and fell the stroke —   10
Ah, what faces pale and bright
Where the dazzling battle broke!

There a hero-hearted queen
With young beauty lit the van;
Gone! the darkness flowed between   15
All the ancient wars of man.

While I paced the valley's gloom
Where the rabbits pattered near,
Shone a temple and a tomb
With a legend carven clear: 20

"Time put by a myriad fates
That her day might dawn in glory;
Death made wide a million gates
So to close her tragic story."   (1897)

PARTING

As from our dream we died away
Far off I felt the outer things;
Your wind-blown tresses round me play,
Your bosom's gentle murmurings.

And far away our faces met   5
As on the verge of the vast spheres;
And in the night our cheeks were wet,
I could not say with dew or tears.

O gate by which I entered in!
O face and hair! O lips and eyes!   10
Through you again the world I win,
How far away from Paradise!   (1897)

CONTINUITY

No sign is made while empires pass.
The flowers and stars are still His care,
The constellations hid in grass,
The golden miracles in air.

Life in an instant will be rent   5
Where death is glittering blind and wild —
The Heavenly Brooding is intent
To that last instant on Its child.

It breathes the glow in brain and heart,
Life is made magical. Until 10
Body and spirit are apart
The Everlasting works Its will.

In that wild orchid that your feet
In their next falling shall destroy,
Minute and passionate and sweet 15
The Mighty Master holds His joy.

Though the crushed jewels droop and fade
The Artist's labors will not cease,
And of the ruins shall be made
Some yet more lovely masterpiece.   (1897)

A NEW THEME

I fain would leave the tender songs
    I sang to you of old,
Thinking the oft-sung beauty wrongs
    The magic never told;

And touch no more the thoughts, the moods,
    That win the easy praise; 6
But venture in the untrodden woods
    To carve the future ways.

Though far or strange or cold appear
    The shadowy things I tell, 10
Within the heart the hidden seer
    Knows and remembers well.

I think that in the coming time
    The hearts and hopes of men
The mountain tops of life shall climb, 15
    The gods return again.

I strive to blow the magic horn;
    It feebly murmureth;
Arise on some enchanted morn,
    Poet, with God's own breath! 20

And sound the horn I cannot blow,
    And by the secret name
Each exile of the heart will know
    Kindle the magic flame.   (1897)

ALFRED EDWARD HOUSMAN
(1859-1936)

From A SHROPSHIRE LAD

I. 1887

From Clee to heaven the beacon burns,
    The shires have seen it plain;
From north and south the sign returns
    And beacons burn again.

Look left, look right, the hills are bright, 5
    The dales are light between,
Because 'tis fifty years tonight
    That God has saved the Queen.

Now, when the flame they watch not towers
    About the soil they trod, 10
Lads, we'll remember friends of ours
    Who shared the work with God.

To skies that knit their heartstrings right,
    To fields that bred them brave,
The saviors come not home tonight: 15
    Themselves they could not save.

It dawns in Asia, tombstones show
    And Shropshire names are read;
And the Nile spills his overflow
    Beside the Severn's dead. 20

We pledge in peace by farm and town
    The Queen they served in war,
And fire the beacons up and down
    The land they perished for.

'God save the Queen' we living sing, 25
    From height to height 'tis heard;
And with the rest your voices ring,
    Lads of the Fifty-third.

Oh, God will save her, fear you not:
    Be you the men you've been, 30
Get you the sons your fathers got,
    And God will save the Queen.

2

Loveliest of trees, the cherry now
Is hung with bloom along the bough,
And stands about the woodland ride
Wearing white for Eastertide.

Now, of my threescore years and ten, 5
Twenty will not come again,
And take from seventy springs a score,
It only leaves me fifty more.

A Shropshire Lad. Shropshire is a quiet, old-fashioned county of central England, on the border of Wales, with Shrewsbury as its chief city.
Lyric 1. 1887. The year 1887, which marked the completion of Victoria's fiftieth year as queen of England, was celebrated as the Golden Jubilee; compare Kipling's *Recessional,* p. 894.
1. **Clee,** a town in the southern part of Shropshire. 17. **Asia.** From 1878 to 1886 the English fought wars in Afghanistan and Burma; compare the wars of empire referred to in Kipling's "*Fuzzy-Wuzzy,*" page 882. 19. **Nile.** In 1882 the English put down a native revolt in Egypt; in 1881-1898 they fought in the Soudan. 20. **Severn,** a large river flowing through Shropshire. 28. **Fifty-third,** the Shropshire Regiment of Foot, with a history that includes service in the American Revolution and in campaigns in India and in Egypt.

And since to look at things in bloom
Fifty springs are little room, 10
About the woodlands I will go
To see the cherry hung with snow.

4. REVEILLE

Wake: the silver dusk returning
Up the beach of darkness brims,
And the ship of sunrise burning
Strands upon the eastern rims.

Wake: the vaulted shadow shatters, 5
Trampled to the floor it spanned,
And the tent of night in tatters
Straws the sky-pavilioned land.

Up, lad, up, 'tis late for lying:
Hear the drums of morning play; 10
Hark, the empty highways crying
'Who'll beyond the hills away?'

Towns and countries woo together,
Forelands beacon, belfries call;
Never lad that trod on leather 15
Lived to feast his heart with all.

Up, lad: thews that lie and cumber
Sunlit pallets never thrive;
Morns abed and daylight slumber
Were not meant for man alive. 20

Clay lies still, but blood's a rover;
Breath's a ware that will not keep.
Up, lad: when the journey's over
There'll be time enough to sleep.

7

When smoke stood up from Ludlow,
And mist blew off from Teme,
And blithe afield to plowing
Against the morning beam
I strode beside my team, 5

The blackbird in the coppice
Looked out to see me stride,
And hearkened as I whistled
The trampling team beside,
And fluted and replied: 10

'Lie down, lie down, young yeoman;
What use to rise and rise?
Rise man a thousand mornings
Yet down at last he lies,
And then the man is wise.' 15

I heard the tune he sang me,
And spied his yellow bill;

Lyric 7. 2. **Teme,** a river which flows by Ludlow.
11. **yeoman,** a land-owning farmer.

I picked a stone and aimed it
And threw it with a will:
Then the bird was still. 20

Then my soul within me
Took up the blackbird's strain,
And still beside the horses
Along the dewy lane
It sang the song again: 25

'Lie down, lie down, young yeoman;
The sun moves always west;
The road one treads to labor
Will lead one home to rest,
And that will be the best.' 30

10. MARCH

The sun at noon to higher air,
Unharnessing the silver Pair
That late before his chariot swam,
Rides on the gold wool of the Ram.

So braver notes the storm-cock sings 5
To start the rusted wheel of things,
And brutes in field and brutes in pen
Leap that the world goes round again.

The boys are up the woods with day
To fetch the daffodils away, 10
And home at noonday from the hills
They bring no dearth of daffodils.

Afield for palms the girls repair,
And sure enough the palms are there,
And each will find by hedge or pond 15
Her waving silver-tufted wand.

In farm and field through all the shire
The eye beholds the heart's desire;
Ah, let not only mine be vain,
For lovers should be loved again. 20

12

When I watch the living meet,
And the moving pageant file
Warm and breathing through the street
Where I lodge a little while,

If the heats of hate and lust 5
In the house of flesh are strong,
Let me mind the house of dust
Where my sojourn shall be long.

Lyric 10. March. Compare the opening of Chaucer's
Canterbury Tales.
2. **silver Pair,** the Pisces, or Fishes, the sign of the zodiac
through which the sun passes during the month prior to
March 21. 4. **Ram,** Aries, the sign of the zodiac into which
the sun passes on March 21. 5. **storm-cock,** the missel
thrush, called the storm-cock because it sings early in the
spring and is said to presage stormy weather.

In the nation that is not
  Nothing stands that stood before;   10
There revenges are forgot,
  And the hater hates no more;

Lovers lying two and two
  Ask not whom they sleep beside,
And the bridegroom all night through   15
  Never turns him to the bride.

13

When I was one-and-twenty,
  I heard a wise man say,
'Give crowns and pounds and guineas
  But not your heart away;
Give pearls away and rubies   5
  But keep your fancy free.'
But I was one-and-twenty,
  No use to talk to me.

When I was one-and-twenty,
  I heard him say again,   10
'The heart out of the bosom
  Was never given in vain;
'Tis paid with sighs a plenty
  And sold for endless rue.'
And I am two-and-twenty,   15
  And oh, 'tis true, 'tis true.

15

Look not in my eyes, for fear
  They mirror true the sight I see,
And there you find your face too clear
  And love it and be lost like me.
One the long nights through must lie   5
  Spent in star-defeated sighs,
But why should you as well as I
  Perish? gaze not in my eyes.

A Grecian lad, as I hear tell,
  One that many loved in vain,   10
Looked into a forest well
  And never looked away again.
There, when the turf in springtime flowers,
  With downward eye and gazes sad,
Stands amid the glancing showers   15
  A jonquil, not a Grecian lad.

18

Oh, when I was in love with you,
  Then I was clean and brave,
And miles around the wonder grew
  How well did I behave.

And now the fancy passes by,   5
  And nothing will remain,
And miles around they'll say that I
  Am quite myself again.

19. TO AN ATHLETE DYING YOUNG

The time you won your town the race
We chaired you through the market-place;
Man and boy stood cheering by,
And home we brought you shoulder-high.

Today, the road all runners come,   5
Shoulder-high we bring you home,
And set you at your threshold down,
Townsman of a stiller town.

Smart lad, to slip betimes away
From fields where glory does not stay   10
And early though the laurel grows
It withers quicker than the rose.

Eyes the shady night has shut
Cannot see the record cut,
And silence sounds no worse than cheers   15
After earth has stopped the ears:

Now you will not swell the rout
Of lads that wore their honours out,
Runners whom renown outran
And the name died before the man.   20

So set, before its echoes fade,
The fleet foot on the sill of shade,
And hold to the low lintel up
The still-defended challenge-cup.

And round that early-laureled head   25
Will flock to gaze the strengthless dead,
And find unwithered on its curls
The garland briefer than a girl's.

21. BREDON HILL

In summertime on Bredon
  The bells they sound so clear;
Round both the shires they ring them
  In steeples far and near,
  A happy noise to hear.   5

Here of a Sunday morning
  My love and I would lie,
And see the coloured counties,
  And hear the larks so high
  About us in the sky.   10

Lyric 19. To an Athlete Dying Young. 11. **laurel,** used as a symbol of triumph.
Lyric 21. Bredon Hill. Bredon Hill is a rounded hill (961 ft. high), commanding an extensive view, in southern Worcestershire, northeast of Tewkesbury.
8. **counties.** The counties of Worcestershire, Gloucestershire, Herefordshire, Warwickshire, and Oxfordshire may be seen from Bredon Hill.

Lyric 15. 9. **Grecian lad,** Narcissus, who repulsed all who sought his love and was, in retribution, fated to fall in love with his own image in a spring; in hopeless longing he pined away, and was changed into the flower that bears his name.

The bells would ring to call her
  In valleys miles away:
'Come all to church, good people;
  Good people, come and pray.'
But here my love would stay.   15

And I would turn and answer
  Among the springing thyme,
'Oh, peal upon our wedding,
  And we will hear the chime,
And come to church in time.'   20

But when the snows at Christmas
  On Bredon top were strown,
My love rose up so early
  And stole out unbeknown
And went to church alone.   25

They tolled the one bell only,
  Groom there was none to see,
The mourners followed after,
  And so to church went she,
And would not wait for me.   30

The bells they sound on Bredon,
  And still the steeples hum,
'Come all to church, good people,' —
  Oh, noisy bells, be dumb;
I hear you, I will come.   35

25

This time of year a twelvemonth past,
  When Fred and I would meet,
We needs must jangle, till at last
  We fought and I was beat.

So then the summer fields about,   5
  Till rainy days began,
Rose Harland on her Sundays out
  Walked with the better man.

The better man she walks with still,
  Though now 'tis not with Fred: 10
A lad that lives and has his will
  Is worth a dozen dead.

Fred keeps the house all kinds of weather,
  And clay's the house he keeps;
When Rose and I walk out together   15
  Stock-still lies Fred and sleeps.

27

'Is my team ploughing,
  That I was used to drive
And hear the harness jingle
  When I was man alive?'

Ay, the horses trample,   5
  The harness jingles now;

No change though you lie under
  The land you used to plough.

'Is football playing
  Along the river shore,   10
With lads to chase the leather,
  Now I stand up no more?'

Ay, the ball is flying,
  The lads play heart and soul;
The goal stands up, the keeper   15
  Stands up to keep the goal.

'Is my girl happy,
  That I thought hard to leave,
And has she tired of weeping
  As she lies down at eve?'   20

Ay, she lies down lightly,
  She lies not down to weep:
Your girl is well contented.
  Be still, my lad, and sleep.

'Is my friend hearty,   25
  Now I am thin and pine,
And has he found to sleep in
  A better bed than mine?'

Yes, lad, I lie easy,
  I lie as lads would choose;   30
I cheer a dead man's sweetheart,
  Never ask me whose.

28. THE WELSH MARCHES

High the vanes of Shrewsbury gleam
Islanded in Severn stream;
The bridges from the steepled crest
Cross the water east and west.

The flag of morn in conqueror's state   5
Enters at the English gate;
The vanquished eve, as night prevails,
Bleeds upon the road to Wales.

Ages since the vanquished bled
Round my mother's marriage-bed;   10
There the ravens feasted far
About the open house of war:

When Severn down to Buildwas ran,
Coloured with the death of man,
Couched upon her brother's grave   15
The Saxon got me on the slave.

Lyric 28. The Welsh Marches. The border land, or Marches,
between Wales and England was from the 5th to the 13th
century, the scene of bloody conflict between the native
Celts and the Saxon and Norman invaders.
  1. **Shrewsbury**, the county town of Shropshire, located
on the Severn River. 13. **Buildwas**, a town on the Severn,
twelve miles below Shrewsbury.

The sound of fight is silent long
That began the ancient wrong;
Long the voice of tears is still
That wept of old the endless ill. 20

In my heart it has not died,
The war that sleeps on Severn side;
They cease not fighting, east and west,
On the marches of my breast.

Here the truceless armies yet 25
Trample, rolled in blood and sweat;
They kill and kill and never die;
And I think that each is I.

None will part us, none undo
The knot that makes one flesh of two, 30
Sick with hatred, sick with pain,
Strangling — When shall we be slain?

When shall I be dead and rid
Of the wrong my father did?
How long, how long, till spade and hearse 35
Put to sleep my mother's curse?

29. THE LENT LILY

'Tis spring; come out to ramble
The hilly brakes around,
For under thorn and bramble
About the hollow ground
The primroses are found. 5

And there's the windflower chilly
With all the winds at play,
And there's the Lenten lily
That has not long to stay
And dies on Easter day. 10

And since till girls go maying
You will find the primrose still,
And find the windflower playing
With every wind at will,
But not the daffodil, 15

Bring baskets now, and sally
Upon the spring's array,
And bear from hill and valley
The daffodil away
That dies on Easter day. 20

30

Others, I am not the first,
Have willed more mischief than they durst:
If in the breathless night I too
Shiver now, 'tis nothing new.

More than I, if truth were told, 5
Have stood and sweated hot and cold,
And through their reins in ice and fire
Fear contended with desire.

Agued once like me were they,
But I like them shall win my way 10
Lastly to the bed of mould
Where there's neither heat nor cold.

But from my grave across my brow
Plays no wind of healing now,
And fire and ice within me fight 15
Beneath the suffocating night.

31

On Wenlock Edge the wood's in trouble;
His forest fleece the Wrekin heaves;
The gale, it plies the saplings double,
And thick on Severn snow the leaves.

'Twould blow like this through holt and
hanger 5
When Uricon the city stood;
'Tis the old wind in the old anger,
But then it threshed another wood.

Then, 'twas before my time, the Roman
At yonder heaving hill would stare: 10
The blood that warms an English yeoman,
The thoughts that hurt him, they were there.

There, like the wind through woods in riot,
Through him the gale of life blew high;
The tree of man was never quiet: 15
Then 'twas the Roman, now 'tis I.

The gale, it plies the saplings double,
It blows so hard, 'twill soon be gone:
To-day the Roman and his trouble
Are ashes under Uricon. 20

32

From far, from eve and morning
And yon twelve-winded sky,
The stuff of life to knit me
Blew hither: here am I.

Now — for a breath I tarry 5
Nor yet disperse apart —
Take my hand quick and tell me,
What have you in your heart.

Lyric 31. 1. **Wenlock Edge**, a range of hills in southern Shropshire, southeast of Shrewsbury. 2. **the Wrekin**, an isolated extinct volcano southeast of Shrewsbury. 5. **holt**, wood. **hanger**, a thicket on a steep hillside. 6. **Uricon**, Uriconium, an ancient Roman city near the modern Wroxeter, southeast of Shrewsbury; during the Roman occupation (1st to 5th centuries A.D.) it was the capital of Britannia Secunda, one of the four provinces of Britain; it was burned by the Saxons in 584 and is now in ruins.
Lyric 32. 2. **twelve-winded**, having all the winds of heaven.

Lyric 29. 6. **windflower**, the anemone.

Speak now, and I will answer;
  How shall I help you, say;   10
Ere to the wind's twelve quarters
  I take my endless way.

39

'Tis time, I think, by Wenlock town
  The golden broom should blow;
The hawthorn sprinkled up and down
  Should charge the land with snow.

Spring will not wait the loiterer's time   5
  Who keeps so long away,
So others wear the broom and climb
  The hedgerows heaped with may.

Oh tarnish late on Wenlock Edge,
  Gold that I never see;   10
Lie long, high snowdrifts in the hedge
  That will not shower on me.

40

Into my heart an air that kills
  From yon far country blows:
What are those blue remembered hills,
  What spires, what farms are those?

That is the land of lost content,   5
  I see it shining plain,
The happy highways where I went
  And cannot come again.

42. THE MERRY GUIDE

Once in the wind of morning
  I ranged the thymy wold;
The world-wide air was azure
  And all the brooks ran gold.

There through the dews beside me   5
  Behold a youth that trod,
With feathered cap on forehead,
  And poised a golden rod.

With mien to match the morning
  And gay delightful guise   10
And friendly brows and laughter
  He looked me in the eyes.

Oh whence, I asked, and whither?
  He smiled and would not say,

And looked at me and beckoned   15
  And laughed and led the way.

And with kind looks and laughter
  And naught to say beside
We two went on together,
  I and my happy guide.   20

Across the glittering pastures
  And empty upland still
And solitude of shepherds
  High in the folded hill,

By hanging woods and hamlets   25
  That gaze through orchards down
On many a windmill turning
  And far-discovered town,

With gay regards of promise
  And sure unslackened stride   30
And smiles and nothing spoken,
  Led on my merry guide.

By blowing realms of woodland
  With sunstruck vanes afield
And cloud-led shadows sailing   35
  About the windy weald,

By valley-guarded granges
  And silver waters wide,
Content at heart I followed
  With my delightful guide.   40

And like the cloudy shadows
  Across the country blown,
We·two fare on forever,
  But not we two alone.

With the great gale we journey   45
  That breathes from gardens thinned,
Borne in the drift of blossoms
  Whose petals throng the wind;

Buoyed on the heaven-heard whisper
  Of dancing leaflets whirled   50
From all the woods that autumn
  Bereaves in all the world.

And midst the fluttering legion
  Of all that ever died
I follow, and before us   55
  Goes the delightful guide,

With lips that brim with laughter
  But never once respond,
And feet that fly on feathers,
  And serpent-circled wand.   60

Lyric 39. 1. **Wenlock town.** Wenlock is a small town southeast of Shrewsbury. 2. **broom,** a stiff shrub with yellow blossoms. **blow,** bloom. 8. **may,** hawthorn.
Lyric 42. The Merry Guide. 2. **wold,** a low hill. 6. **youth,** Mercury, the messenger of the gods, who guided the souls of the dead to Hades. He carried the caduceus, a staff twined with serpents (line 60), as the symbol of his office.

24. **folded hill,** a hill pastured with sheep. 36. **weald,** open country. 37. **granges,** country houses with surrounding farm lands.

43. THE IMMORTAL PART

When I meet the morning beam,
Or lay me down at night to dream,
I hear my bones within me say,
'Another night, another day.

'When shall this slough of sense be cast,   5
This dust of thoughts be laid at last,
The man of flesh and soul be slain
And the man of bone remain?

'This tongue that talks, these lungs that
   shout,
These thews that hustle us about,   10
This brain that fills the skull with schemes,
And its humming hive of dreams, —

'These to-day are proud in power
And lord it in their little hour:
The immortal bones obey control   15
Of dying flesh and dying soul.

' 'Tis long till eve and morn are gone:
Slow the endless night comes on,
And late to fulness grows the birth
That shall last as long as earth.   20

'Wanderers eastward, wanderers west,
Know you why you cannot rest?
'Tis that every mother's son
Travails with a skeleton.

'Lie down in the bed of dust;   25
Bear the fruit that bear you must;
Bring the eternal seed to light,
And morn is all the same as night.

'Rest you so from trouble sore,
Fear the heat o' the sun no more,   30
Nor the snowing winter wild,
Now you labour not with child.

'Empty vessel, garment cast,
We that wore you long shall last.
— Another night, another day.'   35
So my bones within me say.

Therefore they shall do my will
To-day while I am master still,
And flesh and soul, now both are strong,
Shall hale the sullen slaves along,   40

Before this fire of sense decay,
This smoke of thought blow clean away,
And leave with ancient night alone
The stedfast and enduring bone.

45

If it chance your eye offend you,
   Pluck it out, lad, and be sound:
'Twill hurt, but here are salves to friend you,
   And many a balsam grows on ground.

And if your hand or foot offend you,   5
   Cut it off, lad, and be whole;
But play the man, stand up and end you,
   When your sickness is your soul.

48

Be still, my soul, be still; the arms you bear
   are brittle
Earth and high heaven are fixt of old and
   founded strong.
Think rather, — call to thought, if now you
   grieve a little,
The days when we had rest, O soul, for
   they were long.

Men loved unkindness then, but lightless in
   the quarry   5
   I slept and saw not; tears fell down, I did
   not mourn;
Sweat ran and blood sprang out and I was
   never sorry:
   Then it was well with me, in days ere I
   was born.

Now, and I muse for why and never find the
   reason,
   I pace the earth, and drink the air, and feel
   the sun.   10
Be still, be still, my soul; it is but for a
   season:
   Let us endure an hour and see injustice
   done.

Aye, look: high heaven and earth ail from
   the prime foundation;
   All thoughts to rive the heart are here, and
   all are vain:
Horror and scorn and hate and fear and
   indignation —   15
   Oh, why did I awake? when shall I sleep
   again?

49

Think no more, lad; laugh, be jolly:
   Why should men make haste to die?
Empty heads and tongues a-talking
Make the rough road easy walking,
And the feather pate of folly   5
   Bears the falling sky.

Lyric 45. **1-2. eye . . . sound.** From *Mark,* 9:47.—"If
thine eye offend thee, pluck it out; it is better for thee to
enter into the kingdom of God with one eye, than having
two eyes to be cast into hell fire."
5-6. hand . . . off. From *Mark,* 9:43-45.—"If thy hand
offend thee, cut it off . . . And if thy foot offend thee cut it
off . . ."

Oh, 'tis jesting, dancing, drinking
  Spins the heavy world around.
If young hearts were not so clever,
Oh, they would be young forever.   10
Think no more; 'tis only thinking
  Lays lads underground.

51

Loitering with a vacant eye
Along the Grecian gallery,
And brooding on my heavy ill,
I met a statue standing still.
Still in marble stone stood he,   5
And stedfastly he looked at me.
'Well met,' I thought the look would say,
'We both were fashioned far away;
We neither knew, when we were young,
These Londoners we live among.'   10

Still he stood and eyed me hard,
An earnest and a grave regard:
'What, lad, drooping with your lot?
I too would be where I am not.
I too survey that endless line   15
Of men whose thoughts are not as mine.
Years, ere you stood up from rest,
On my neck the collar prest;
Years, when you lay down your ill,
I shall stand and bear it still.   20
Courage, lad, 'tis not for long:
Stand, quit you like stone, be strong.'
So I thought his look would say;
And light on me my trouble lay,
And I stept out in flesh and bone   25
Manful like the man of stone.

52

Far in a western brookland
  That bred me long ago
The poplars stand and tremble
  By pools I used to know.

There, in the windless night-time,   5
  The wanderer, marvelling why,
Halts on the bridge to hearken
  How soft the poplars sigh.

He hears: no more remembered
  In fields where I was known,   10
Here I lie down in London
  And turn to rest alone.

There, by the starlit fences,
  The wanderer halts and hears
My soul that lingers sighing   15
  About the glimmering weirs.

Lyric 51. 2. **Grecian gallery,** in the British Museum, London. 22. **Stand . . . strong.** Cf. *I Corinthians,* 16:13. *Lyric 52.* 16. **weirs,** pools of water above a dam.

53. THE TRUE LOVER

The lad came to the door at night,
  When lovers crown their vows,
And whistled soft and out of sight
  In shadow of the boughs.

'I shall not vex you with my face   5
  Henceforth, my love, for aye;
So take me in your arms a space
  Before the east is gray.

'When I from hence away am past
  I shall not find a bride,   10
And you shall be the first and last
  I ever lay beside.'

She heard and went and knew not why;
  Her heart to his she laid;
Light was the air beneath the sky   15
  But dark under the shade.

'Oh do you breathe, lad, that your breast
  Seems not to rise and fall,
And here upon my bosom prest
  There beats no heart at all?'   20

'Oh, loud, my girl, it once would knock,
  You should have felt it then;
But since for you I stopped the clock
  It never goes again.'

'Oh, lad, what is it, lad, that drips   25
  Wet from your neck on mine?
What is it falling on my lips,
  My lad, that tastes of brine?'

'Oh like enough 'tis blood, my dear,
  For when the knife has slit   30
The throat across from ear to ear
  'Twill bleed because of it.'

Under the stars the air was light
  But dark below the boughs,
The still air of the speechless night,   35
  When lovers crown their vows.

54

With rue my heart is laden
  For golden friends I had,
For many a rose-lipt maiden
  And many a lightfoot lad.

By brooks too broad for leaping   5
  The lightfoot boys are laid;
The rose-lipt girls are sleeping
  In fields where roses fade.

57

You smile upon your friend to-day,
    To-day his ills are over;
You hearken to the lover's say,
    And happy is the lover.

'Tis late to hearken, late to smile,   5
    But better late than never:
I shall have lived a little while
    Before I die forever.

62

'Terence, this is stupid stuff:
You eat your victuals fast enough;
There can't be much amiss, 'tis clear,
To see the rate you drink your beer.
But oh, good Lord, the verse you make,   5
It gives a chap the belly-ache.
The cow, the old cow, she is dead;
It sleeps well, the horned head:
We poor lads, 'tis our turn now
To hear such tunes as killed the cow.   10
Pretty friendship 'tis to rhyme
Your friends to death before their time
Moping melancholy mad:
Come, pipe a tune to dance to, lad.'

Why, if 'tis dancing you would be,   15
There's brisker pipes than poetry.
Say, for what were hop-yards meant,
Or why was Burton built on Trent?
Oh many a peer of England brews
Livelier liquor than the Muse,   20
And malt does more than Milton can
To justify God's ways to man.
Ale, man, ale's the stuff to drink
For fellows whom it hurts to think:
Look into the pewter pot   25
To see the world as the world's not.
And faith, 'tis pleasant till 'tis past:
The mischief is that 'twill not last.
Oh, I have been to Ludlow fair
And left my necktie God knows where,   30
And carried half-way home, or near,
Pints and quarts of Ludlow beer:
Then the world seemed none so bad,
And I myself a sterling lad;
And down in lovely muck I've lain,   35
Happy till I woke again.
Then I saw the morning sky:
Heigho, the tale was all a lie;
The world, it was the old world yet,
I was I, my things were wet,   40

And nothing now remained to do
But begin the game anew.

Therefore, since the world has still
Much good, but much less good than ill,
And while the sun and moon endure   45
Luck's a chance, but trouble's sure,
I'd face it as a wise man would,
And train for ill and not for good.
'Tis true, the stuff I bring for sale
Is not so brisk a brew as ale: 50
Out of a stem that scored the hand
I wrung it in a weary land.
But take it: if the smack is sour,
The better for the embittered hour;
It should do good to heart and head   55
When your soul is in my soul's stead;
And I will friend you, if I may,
In the dark and cloudy day.

There was a king reigned in the East;
There, when kings will sit to feast,   60
They get their fill before they think
With poisoned meat and poisoned drink.
He gathered all that springs to birth
From the many-venomed earth;
First a little, thence to more,   65
He sampled all her killing store;
And easy, smiling, seasoned sound,
Sate the king when healths went round.
They put arsenic in his meat
And stared aghast to watch him eat;   70
They poured strychnine in his cup
And shook to see him drink it up:
They shook, they stared as white's their shirt:
Them it was their poison hurt.
— I tell the tale that I heard told.   75
Mithridates, he died old.

63

I hoed and trenched and weeded,
    And took the flowers to fair:
I brought them home unheeded;
    The hue was not the wear.

So up and down I sow them   5
    For lads like me to find,
When I shall lie below them,
    A dead man out of mind.

Some seed the birds devour,
    And some the season mars,   10
But here and there will flower
    The solitary stars,

Lyric 62. **18. Burton ... Trent.** In the sixteen breweries of Burton-upon-Trent, a city in Derbyshire, three million barrels of beer are annually produced. More than one peer of England owes his nobility to a fortune made in brewing. **22. justify ... man,** given by Milton as his purpose in writing *Paradise Lost* (Book I, line 26).

51. stem ... hand. Experience is a raw material more painful to handle than the grain from which ale is brewed. **59. a king,** etc. Realizing that his enemies were conspiring to poison him, Mithridates VI, king of Pontus (120-63 B.C.), inured himself to poison by taking it in gradually increased doses until it no longer had any effect upon him; so, at least, Pliny affirms in his *Natural History,* 25:2.

And fields will yearly bear them
  As light-leaved spring comes on,
And luckless lads will wear them   15
  When I am dead and gone.   (1896)

THOMAS HARDY
(1840-1928)

POSTPONEMENT

Snow-bound in woodland, a mournful word,
Dropt now and then from the bill of a bird,
Reached me on wind-wafts; and thus I heard,
  Wearily waiting: —

"I planned her a nest in a leafless tree,   5
But the passers eyed and twitted me,
And said: 'How reckless a bird is he,
  Cheerily mating!'

"Fear-filled, I stayed me till summer-tide,
In lewth of leaves to throne her bride;   10
But alas! her love for me waned and died,
  Wearily waiting.

"Ah, had I been like some I see,
Born to an evergreen nesting-tree,
None had eyed and twitted me,   15
  Cheerily mating!"
           (1866; 1898)

HAP

If but some vengeful god would call to me
From up the sky, and laugh: "Thou suffering
    thing,
Know that thy sorrow is my ecstasy,
That thy love's loss is my hate's profiting!"
Then would I bear it, clench myself, and die, 5
Steeled by the sense of ire unmerited;
Half-eased in that a Powerfuller than I
Had willed and meted me the tears I shed.

But not so. How arrives it joy lies slain,
And why unblooms the best hope ever
    sown?   10
— Crass Casualty obstructs the sun and rain,
And dicing Time for gladness casts a moan . . .
These purblind Doomsters had as readily
    strown
Blisses about my pilgrimage as pain.
           (1866; 1898)

NEUTRAL TONES

We stood by a pond that winter day,
And the sun was white, as though chidden of
    God,

And a few leaves lay on the starving sod;
  — They had fallen from an ash, and were
    gray.
Your eyes on me were as eyes that rove   5
Over tedious riddles of years ago;
And some words played between us to and fro
  On which lost the more by our love.

The smile on your mouth was the deadest
    thing
Alive enough to have strength to die;   10
And a grin of bitterness swept thereby
  Like an ominous bird a-wing. . . .

Since then, keen lessons that love deceives,
And wrings with wrong, have shaped to me
Your face, and the God-curst sun, and a tree,
  And a pond edged with grayish leaves.
           (1867; 1898)

HERESS AND ARCHITECT

FOR A. W. BLOMFIELD

She sought the Studios, beckoning to her side
An arch-designer, for she planned to build.
He was of wise contrivance, deeply skilled
In every intervolve of high and wide —
  Well fit to be her guide.   5

    "Whatever it be,"
    Responded he,
With cold, clear voice, and cold, clear view,
"In true accord with prudent fashionings
For such vicissitudes as living brings,   10
And thwarting not the law of stable things,
  That will I do."

"Shape me," she said, "high halls with tracery
And open ogive-work, that scent and hue
Of buds, and traveling bees, may come in
    through,   15
The note of birds, and singing of the sea,
  For these are much to me."

    "An idle whim!"
    Broke forth from him
Whom naught could warm to gallantries; 20
"Cede all these buds and birds, the zephyr's
    call,

Neutral Tones. Reprinted from Hardy's *Collected Poems*
by permission of The Macmillan Company, publishers.
   Heiress and Architect. Reprinted from Hardy's *Wessex
Poems and Other Verses* by permission of Mrs. Thomas Hardy.
   A. W. Blomfield (1829-1899), an architect, Hardy's first
employer and lifelong friend.
   4. intervolve . . . wide, the interaction of height and
width in the construction of buildings. **14. ogive-work,**
archways. **21. Cede,** abandon the thought of.

Postponement. Reprinted from Hardy's *Collected Poems* by
permission of The Macmillan Company, publishers.

And scents, and hues, and things that falter
all,
And choose as best the close and surly wall,
 For winters freeze."

"Then frame," she cried, "wide fronts of
 crystal glass,   25
That I may show my laughter and my light —
Light like the sun's by day, the stars' by
 night —
Till rival heart-queens, envying, wail, 'Alas,
 Her glory!' as they pass."

  "O maid misled!"   30
   He sternly said
Whose facile foresight pierced her dire;
"Where shall abide the soul when, sick of glee,
It shrinks, and hides, and prays no eye may
 see?
Those house them best who house for secrecy,
 For you will tire."   36

"A little chamber, then, with swan and dove
Ranged thickly, and engrailed with rare
 device
Of reds and purples, for a Paradise
Wherein my Love may greet me, I my Love, 40
 When he shall know thereof?"

  "This, too, is ill,"
   He answered still,
The man who swayed her like a shade.
"An hour will come when sight of such sweet
 nook   45
Would bring a bitterness too sharp to brook,
When brighter eyes have won away his look,
 For you will fade."

Then said she faintly: "Oh, contrive some
 way —
Some narrow winding turret, quite mine
 own,   50
To reach a loft where I may grieve alone!
It is a slight thing; hence do not, I pray,
 This last dear fancy slay!"

  "Such winding ways
   Fit not your days," 55
Said he, the man of measuring eye;
"I must even fashion as the rule declares,
To wit: Give space (since life ends unawares)
To hale a coffined corpse adown the stairs;
 For you will die."   60
    (*1867; 1898*)

HER INITIALS

Upon a poet's page I wrote
Of old two letters of her name;

22. **falter,** prove transitory. 38. **engrailed,** furnished
with a border-design of notched or wavy lines.

Part seemed she of the effulgent thought
Whence that high singer's rapture came.
— When now I turn the leaf the same 5
Immortal light illumes the lay,
But from the letters of her name
The radiance has waned away! (*1869; 1898*)

"WHEN I SET OUT FOR LYONNESSE"

When I set out for Lyonnesse,
 A hundred miles away,
  The rime was on the spray,
And starlight lit my lonesomeness
When I set out for Lyonnesse   5
 A hundred miles away.

What would bechance at Lyonnesse
 While I should sojourn there
  No prophet durst declare,
Nor did the wisest wizard guess   10
What would bechance at Lyonnesse
 While I should sojourn there.

When I came back from Lyonnesse
 With magic in my eyes,
  All marked with mute surmise 15
My radiance rare and fathomless,
When I came back from Lyonnesse
 With magic in my eyes!
      (*1870; 1914*)

SHELLEY'S SKYLARK

(*The neighbourhood of Leghorn: March, 1887*)

Somewhere afield here something lies
In Earth's oblivious eyeless trust
That moved a poet to prophecies —
A pinch of unseen, unguarded dust;

The dust of the lark that Shelley heard, 5
And made immortal through times to be —
Though it only lived like another bird,
And knew not its immortality;

Lived its meek life; then, one day, fell —
A little ball of feather and bone; 10

"*When I Set Out for Lyonnesse.*" Reprinted from Hardy's
Collected Poems by permission of The Macmillan Company,
publishers.
 The poem records a visit made to St. Juliot Rectory in
Cornwall, March, 1870, when Hardy first met Emma Gifford,
who became the first Mrs. Hardy. Lyonesse, in the Arthurian
romances, is an indefinite region in Cornwall. See note on
Tennyson's *Morte d'Arthur*, 4, page 39.
 Shelley's Skylark. Reprinted from Hardy's *Poems of the
Past and the Present* by permission of Mrs. Thomas Hardy.
 Shelley's ode *To a Skylark* was written in Leghorn, on the
northwest coast of Italy, in 1820.
 3. **prophecies.** The last stanza of *To a Skylark* is:
   "Teach me half the gladness
    That thy brain must know,
   Such harmonious madness
    From my lips would flow
  The world should listen then—as I am listening now."

And how it perished, when piped farewell,
And where it wastes, are alike unknown.

Maybe it rests in the loam I view,
Maybe it throbs in a myrtle's green,
Maybe it sleeps in the coming hue   15
Of a grape on the slopes of yon inland scene.

Go find it, faeries, go and find
That tiny pinch of priceless dust,
And bring a casket silver-lined,
And framed of gold that gems encrust;   20

And we will lay it safe therein,
And consecrate it to endless time;
For it inspired a bard to win
Ecstatic heights in thought and rime.
                                   (*1887: 1902*)

A BEAUTY'S SOLILOQUY
DURING HER HONEYMOON

Too late, too late! I did not know my fairness
    Would catch the world's keen eyes so!
How the men look at me! My radiant
        rareness
    I deemed not they would prize so!

That I was a peach for any man's possession 5
    Why did not some one say
Before I leased myself in an hour's obsession
    To this dull mate for aye!

His days are mine. I am one who cannot
        steal her
    Ahead of his plodding pace —   10
As he is, so am I. One doomed to feel her
    A wasted form and face!

I was so blind! It did sometimes just strike
        me
    All girls were not as I,
But, dwelling much alone, how few were like
        me   15
    I could not well descry;

Till, at this Grand Hotel, all looks bend on me
    In homage as I pass
To take my seat at breakfast, dinner — con
        me
    As poorly spoused, alas!   20

I was too young. I dwelt too much on duty;
    If I had guessed my powers
Where might have sailed this cargo of choice
        beauty
    In its unanchored hours!

Well, husband, poor plain man; I've lost
        life's battle! —   25
Come — let them look at me.
O damn, don't show in your looks that I'm
        your chattel
Quite so emphatically!

                                   (*1892; 1922*)

HER DEATH AND AFTER

The summons was urgent; and forth I went —
By the way of the Western Wall, so drear
On that winter night, and sought a gate,
        Where one, by Fate,
        Lay dying that I held dear.   5

And there, as I paused by her tenement,
And the trees shed on me their rime and hoar,
I thought of the man who had left her lone —
        Him who made her his own
        When I loved her, long before.   10

The rooms within had the piteous shine
That home-things wear when there's aught
        amiss;
From the stairway floated the rise and fall
        Of an infant's call,
        Whose birth had brought her to this.   15

Her life was the price she would pay for that
        whine —
For a child by the man she did not love.
"But let that rest forever," I said,
        And bent my tread
        To the bedchamber above.   20

She took my hand in her thin white own,
And smiled her thanks — though nigh too
        weak —
And made them a sign to leave us there,
        Then faltered, ere
        She could bring herself to speak.   25

"Just to see you — before I go — he'll
        condone
Such a natural thing now my time's not
        much —
When Death is so near it hustles hence
        All passioned sense
        Between woman and man as such!   30

"My husband is absent. As heretofore
The City detains him. But, in truth,
He has not been kind. . . . . I will speak no
        blame,

A Beauty's Soliloquy during Her Honeymoon. Reprinted
from Hardy's *Collected Poems* by permission of The Macmillan Company, publishers.

Her Death and After. Reprinted from Hardy's *Wessex
Poems and Other Verses* by permission of Mrs. Thomas Hardy.
    2. **Western Wall**, a street on the outskirts of Dorchester,
southern England, on the site of a Roman wall. 32. **City**,
the financial district of London.

But — the child is lame;
Oh, I pray she may reach his ruth!   35

"Forgive past days — I can say no more —
Maybe had we wed you would. now
  repine! . . .
But I treated you ill. I was punished.
  Farewell!
          — Truth shall I tell?
Would the child were yours and mine!40

"As a wife I was true. But, such my un-
  ease
That, could I insert a deed back in Time,
I'd make her yours, to secure your care;
          And the scandal bear,
          And the penalty for the crime!"   45

— When I had left, and the swinging trees
Rang above me, as lauding her candid say,
Another was I. Her words were enough—
          Came smooth, came rough,
          I felt I could live my day.   50

Next night she died; and her obsequies
In the Field of Tombs where the earthworks
  frowned
Had her husband's heed. His tendance
  spent,
          I often went
          And pondered by her mound.   55

All that year and the next year whiled,
And I still went thitherward in the gloam;
But the Town forgot her and her nook,
          And her husband took
          Another Love to his home.   60

And the rumor flew that the lame lone child
Whom she wished for its safety child of mine,
Was treated ill when offspring came
          Of the new-made dame,
          And marked a more vigorous line.   65

A smarter grief within me wrought
Than even at loss of her so dear
That the being whose soul my soul suffused
          Had a child ill-used,
          While I dared not interfere!   70

One eve as I stood at my spot of thought
In the white-stoned Garth, brooding thus her
  wrong,
Her husband neared; and to shun his nod
          By her hallowed sod
          I went from the tombs among   75

To the Cirque of the Gladiators which
  · faced —
That haggard mark of Imperial Rome,
Whose Pagan echoes mock the chime
          Of our Christian time
          From its hollows of chalk and loam.   80

The sun's gold touch was scarce displaced
From the vast Arena where men once bled,
When her husband followed; bowed, half-
  passed
          With lip upcast;
          Then halting sullenly said: 85

"It is noised that you visit my first wife's
  tomb.
Now, I gave her an honored name to bear
While living, when dead. So I've claim to
  ask
          By what right you task
          My patience by vigiling there?   90

"There's decency even in death, I assume;
Preserve it, sir, and keep away;
For the mother of my first-born you
          Show mind undue!
          — Sir, I've nothing more to say."   95

A desperate stroke discerned I then —
God pardon — or pardon not — the lie;
She had sighed that she wished (lest the child
  should pine
          Of slights) 'twere mine,
          So I said: "But the father I.   100

"That you thought it yours is the way of men;
But I won her troth long ere your day.
You learned how, in dying, she summoned
  me?
          'Twas in fealty.
          — Sir, I've nothing more to say,   105

"Save that, if you'll hand me my little maid,
I'll take her, and rear her, and spare you toil.
Think it more than a friendly act none can;
          I'm a lonely man,
          While you've a large pot to boil.   110

"If not, and you'll put it to ball or blade —
Tonight, tomorrow night, anywhen —
I'll meet you here . . . . But think of it,
          And in season fit
          Let me hear from you again."   115

— Well, I went away, hoping; but naught I
  heard

52. **Field of Tombs**, a cemetery on the southern outskirts
of Dorchester. 72. **Garth**, a piece of enclosed ground;
here, the cemetery.

76. **Cirque ... Gladiators**, Maumbury Ring, the remains
of an ancient Roman amphitheater, near the cemetery in
Dorchester. 111. **put ... blade**, fight a duel with pistol or
sword.

Of my stroke for the child, till there greeted
   me
A little voice that one day came
      To my window-frame
     And babbled innocently: 120

"My father who's not my own, sends word
I'm to stay here, sir, where I belong!"
Next a writing came: "Since the child was
   the fruit
      Of your lawless suit,
     Pray take her, to right a wrong."   125

And I did. And I gave the child my love,
And the child loved me, and estranged us
   none.
But compunctions loomed; for I'd harmed
   the dead
      By what I said
     For the good of the living one.   130

— Yet though, God wot, I am sinner enough,
And unworthy the woman who drew me so,
Perhaps this wrong for her darling's good
      She forgives, or would,
     If only she could know!   135
             (1898)

FRIENDS BEYOND

William Dewy, Tranter Reuben, Farmer
   Ledlow late at plow,
   Robert's kin, and John's, and Ned's,
And the Squire, and Lady Susan, lie in Mell-
   stock churchyard now!

"Gone," I call them, gone for good, that
   group of local hearts and heads;
   Yet at mothy curfew-tide,   5
And at midnight when the noon-heat breathes
   it back from walls and leads,

They've a way of whispering to me — fellow-
   wight who yet abide —
   In the muted, measured note
Of a ripple under archways, or a lone cave's
   stillicide:

"We have triumphed; this achievement turns
   the bane to antidote,   10
   Unsuccesses to success,
Many thought-worn eves and morrows to a
   morrow free of thought.

"No more need we corn and clothing, feel
   of old terrestrial stress;
   Chill detraction stirs no sigh;
Fear of death has even bygone us — death
   gave all that we possess."   15

W. D. — "Ye mid burn the old bass-viol that
   I set such value by."
   Squire. — "You may hold the manse in fee,
You may wed my spouse, may let my
   children's memory of me die."

Lady S. — "You may have my rich brocades,
   my laces; take each household key;
   Ransack coffer, desk, bureau;   20
Quiz the few poor treasures hid there, con
   the letters kept by me."

Far. — "Ye mid zell my favorite heifer, ye
   mid let the charlock grow,
   Foul the grinterns, give up thrift."
Far. Wife. — "If ye break my best blue
   china, children, I shan't care or ho."

All. — "We've no wish to hear the tidings,
   how the people's fortunes shift;   25
   What your daily doings are;
Who are wedded, born, divided; if your
   lives beat slow or swift.

"Curious not the least are we if our intents
   you make or mar,
   If you quire to our old tune,
If the City stage still passes, if the weirs still
   roar afar."   30

— Thus, with very gods' composure, freed
   those crosses late and soon
   Which in life, the Trine allow
(Why, none witteth), and ignoring all that
   haps beneath the moon,

William Dewy, Tranter Reuben, Farmer
   Ledlow late at plow,
   Robert's kin, and John's, and Ned's,   35
And the Squire, and Lady Susan, murmur
   mildly to me now.   (1898)

DRUMMER HODGE

They throw in Drummer Hodge, to rest
   Uncoffined — just as found:
His landmark is a kopje-crest

---

131. **wot,** knows.
Friends Beyond. Reprinted from Hardy's *Wessex Poems and Other Verses* by permission of Mrs. Thomas Hardy.
1. **Tranter.** A tranter is a carrier. 3. **Mellstock,** Hardy's name for Stinsford, a village northeast of Dorchester, Dorsetshire, England. 6. **leads,** the lead covering of roofs. 9. **stillicide,** continual dropping of water.

16. **mid,** may. 17. **hold . . . fee,** buy my house. 22. **charlock,** wild mustard. 23. **grinterns,** compartments in a granary. 24. **ho,** fuss (Dorset dialect). 30. **weirs,** dams. 32. **Trine,** the Trinity: Father, Son, and Holy Spirit.
Drummer Hodge. Reprinted from Hardy's *Poems of the Past and the Present* by permission of Mrs. Thomas Hardy.
   The background of the poem is the Boer War, fought in South Africa, 1899-1902, between the English and the Dutch settlers.
3. **kopje-crest,** the top of a hillock.

That breaks the veldt around;
  And foreign constellations west   5
    Each night above his mound.

Young Hodge the Drummer never knew —
  Fresh from his Wessex home —
The meaning of the broad Karoo,
  The Bush, the dusty loam,   10
And why uprose to nightly view
  Strange stars amid the gloam.

Yet portion of that unknown plain
  Will Hodge forever be;
His homely Northern breast and brain   15
  Grow to some Southern tree,
And strange-eyed constellations reign
  His stars eternally.   (1899)

THE SOULS OF THE SLAIN

The thick lids of Night closed upon me
    Alone at the Bill
    Of the Isle by the Race —
Many-caverned, bald, wrinkled of face
And with darkness and silence the spirit
    was on me   5
    To brood and be still.

No wind fanned the flats of the ocean,
    Or promontory sides,
    Or the ooze by the strand,
Or the bent-bearded slope of the land,   10
Whose base took its rest mid everlong
    motion
    Of criss-crossing tides.

Soon from out of the southward seemed
    nearing
    A whirr, as of wings
    Waved by mighty-vanned flies,   15
Or by night-moths of measureless size,
And in softness and smoothness wellnigh
    beyond hearing
    Of corporal things.

And they bore to the bluff, and alighted —
    A dim-discerned train   20
    Of sprites without mold,
Frameless souls none might touch or might
    hold —

On the ledge by the turreted lantern, far-
    sighted
    By men of the main.

And I heard them say "Home!" and I
    knew them   25
    For souls of the felled
    On the earth's nether bord
Under Capricorn, whither they'd warred,
And I neared in my awe, and gave heed-
    fulness to them
    With breathings inheld.   30

Then, it seemed, there approached from
    the northward
    A senior soul-flame
    Of the like filmy hue;
And he met them and spake: "Is it you,
O my men?" Said they, "Aye! We bear
    homeward and hearthward   35
    To feast on our fame!"

"I've flown there before you," he said then.
    "Your households are well;
    But — your kin linger less
On your glory and war-mightiness   40
Than on dearer things." — "Dearer?" cried
    these from the dead then,
    "Of what do they tell?"

"Some mothers muse sadly, and murmur
    Your doings as boys —
    Recall the quaint ways   45
Of your babyhood's innocent days.
Some pray that, ere dying, your faith had
    grown firmer,
    And higher your joys.

"A father broods: 'Would I had set him
    To some humble trade,   50
    And so slacked his high fire,
And his passionate martial desire;
Had told him no stories to woo him and
    whet him
    To this dire crusade!' "

"And, General, how hold out our sweet-
    hearts,   55
    Sworn loyal as doves?"
    — "Many mourn; many think
It is not unattractive to prink
Them in sables for heroes. Some fickle and
    fleet hearts
    Have found them new loves."   60

"And our wives?" quoth another resignedly,
    "Dwell they on our deeds?"

4. **veldt**, the South-African prairie. 5. **west**, set in the west. 8. **Wessex**. Originally a Saxon kingdom comprising the part of England south of the Thames, Wessex, as Hardy uses the term, corresponds to the county of Dorset. 9. **Karoo**, a desert plateau in South Africa. 10. **Bush**, areas covered with scrubby growth.
The Souls of the Slain. Reprinted from Hardy's *Poems of the Past and the Present* by permission of Mrs. Thomas Hardy. 1. **lids . . . Night.** Cf. *Before Waterloo*, 1, p. 928. 2-3. **Bill . . . Race.** The Isle of Portland extends into the English Channel near Weymouth on the Dorset coast; at its southern extremity are Portland Bill, a rocky promontory, and Portland Race, a dangerous channel with swift tides. 10. **bent-bearded**, covered with bent, a stiff grass. 15. **vanned**, winged.

23. **lantern**, lighthouse. 27. **earth's nether bord**, the other side of the earth. 28. **Under Capricorn**, south of the Tropic of Capricorn—that is, in South Africa, where the Boer War was fought, 1899-1902.

— "Deeds of home; that live yet
Fresh as new — deeds of fondness or fret;
Ancient words that were kindly expressed or
  unkindly, 65
These, these have their heeds."

— "Alas! then it seems that our glory
Weighs less in their thought
Than our old homely acts,
And the long-ago commonplace facts 70
Of our lives — held by us as scarce part of
  our story,
And rated as naught!"

Then bitterly some: "Was it wise now
To raise the tomb-door
For such knowledge? Away!" 75
But the rest: "Fame we prized till today;
Yet that hearts keep us green for old kindness
  we prize now
A thousand times more!"

Thus speaking, the trooped apparitions
Began to disband 80
And resolve them in two:
Those whose record was lovely and true
Bore to northward for home; those of bitter
  traditions
Again left the land,

And, towering to seaward in legions, 85
They paused at a spot
Overbending the Race —
That engulfing, ghast, sinister place —
Whither headlong they plunged, to the
  fathomless regions
Of myriads forgot. 90

And the spirits of those who were homing
Passed on, rushingly,
Like the Pentecost Wind;
And the whirr of their wayfaring thinned
And surceased on the sky, and but left in the
  gloaming 95
Sea-mutterings and me.   (*1899;* 1900)

THE DARKLING THRUSH

I leant upon a coppice gate
  When Frost was specter-gray,
And Winter's dregs made desolate
  The weakening eye of day.
The tangled bine-stems scored the sky 5
  Like strings of broken lyres,
And all mankind that haunted nigh
  Had sought their household fires.

The land's sharp features seemed to be
  The Century's corpse outleant, 10
His crypt the cloudy canopy,
  The wind his death-lament.
The ancient pulse of germ and birth
  Was shrunken hard and dry,
And every spirit upon earth 15
  Seemed fervorless as I.

At once a voice arose among
  The bleak twigs overhead
In a full-hearted evensong
  Of joy illimited; 20
An aged thrush, frail, gaunt, and small,
  In blast-beruffled plume,
Had chosen thus to fling his soul
  Upon the growing gloom.

So little cause for carolings 25
  Of such ecstatic sound
Was written on terrestrial things
  Afar or nigh around,
That I could think there trembled through
  His happy good-night air 30
Some blessed Hope, whereof he knew
  And I was unaware.   (*1900;* 1900)

AUTUMN IN KING'S HINTOCK PARK

Here by the baring bough
  Raking up leaves,
Often I ponder how
  Springtime deceives —
I, an old woman now, 5
  Raking up leaves.

Here in the avenue
  Raking up leaves,
Lords' ladies pass in view,
  Until one heaves 10
Sighs at life's russet hue,
  Raking up leaves!

Just as my shape you see
  Raking up leaves,
I saw, when fresh and free, 15
  Those memory weaves
Into gray ghosts by me,
  Raking up leaves.

Yet, Dear, though one may sigh,
  Raking up leaves, 20
New leaves will dance on high —
  Earth never grieves! —
Will not, when missed am I
  Raking up leaves.   (*1901;* 1909)

93. Pentecost Wind. From *Acts,* 2:2.—"And suddenly
there came a sound from heaven as of a rushing mighty wind."
The Darkling Thrush. Reprinted from Hardy's *Poems of
the Past and the Present* by permission of Mrs. Thomas Hardy.
1. coppice, thicket. 5. bine, a climbing plant.

10. Century's corpse, the recently ended 19th century.
Autumn in King's Hintock Park. Reprinted from Hardy's
Collected Poems by permission of The Macmillan Company,
publishers.
King's Hintock is Hardy's name for Melbury Sampford,
north of Dorchester in Dorsetshire.

GOD-FORGOTTEN

I towered far, and lo! I stood within
The presence of the Lord Most High,
Sent thither by the sons of earth, to win
    Some answer to their cry.

— "The Earth, sayest thou? The Human
    race?   5
By Me created? Sad its lot?
Nay; I have no remembrance of such place—
    Such world I fashioned not." —

— "O Lord, forgive me when I say
Thou spakest the word that made it all." —
"The Earth of men — let me bethink me.....
    Yea!   11
      I dimly do recall

"Some tiny sphere I built long back
(Mid millions of such shapes of mine)
So named . . . It perished, surely — not a
    wrack   15
      Remaining, or a sign?

"It lost my interest from the first,
My aims therefor succeeding ill;
Haply it dies of doing as it durst?" —
    "Lord, it existeth still." —   20

"Dark, then, its life! For not a cry
Of aught it bears do I now hear;
Of its own act the threads were snapt
    whereby
      Its plaints had reached mine ear.

"It used to ask for gifts of good,   25
Till came its severance, self-entailed,
When sudden silence on that side ensued,
    And has till now prevailed.

"All other orbs have kept in touch;
Their voicings reach me speedily.   30
Thy people took upon them overmuch
    In sundering them from me!

"And it is strange — though sad enough —
Earth's race should think that one whose
    call
Frames, daily, shining spheres of flawless
    stuff   35
      Must heed their tainted ball! . . .

"But sayest it is by pangs distraught,
    And strife, and silent suffering? —
Sore grieved am I that injury should be
    wrought
      Even on so poor a thing!   40

God-Forgotten. Reprinted from Hardy's *Poems of the Past and the Present* by permission of Mrs. Thomas Hardy.

"Thou should'st have learnt that *Not to
    Mend*
For Me could mean but *Not to Know*.
Hence, Messengers! and straightway put an
    end
      To what men undergo." . . .

Homing at dawn, I thought to see   45
One of the Messengers standing by.
— Oh, childish thought! . . . Yet often it
    comes to me
      When trouble hovers nigh.

               (1902)

THE LAST CHRYSANTHEMUM

Why should this flower delay so long
    To show its tremulous plumes?
Now is the time of plaintive robin-song,
    When flowers are in their tombs.

Through the slow summer, when the sun 5
    Called to each frond and whorl
That all he could for flowers was being done,
    Why did it not uncurl?

It must have felt that fervid call
    Although it took no heed,   10
Waking but now, when leaves like corpses
    fall,
    And saps all retrocede.

Too late its beauty, lonely thing,
    The season's shine is spent,
Nothing remains for it but shivering   15
    In tempests turbulent.

Had it a reason for delay,
    Dreaming in witlessness
That for a bloom so delicately gay
    Winter would stay its stress?   20

— I talk as if the thing were born
    With sense to work its mind;
Yet it is but one mask of many worn
    By the Great Face behind.

               (1902)

THE TO-BE-FORGOTTEN

I heard a small sad sound,
And stood awhile among the tombs around.
"Wherefore, old friends," said I, "are you
    distrest,
    Now, screened from life's unrest?"

The Last Chrysanthemum. Reprinted from Hardy's *Poems of the Past and the Present* by permission of Mrs. Thomas Hardy.
12. **retrocede**, go down the stalk.
The To-Be-Forgotten. Reprinted from Hardy's *Poems of the Past and the Present* by permission of Mrs. Thomas Hardy.

— "Oh, not at being here;   5
But that our future second death is near;
When, with the living, memory of us numbs,
   And blank oblivion comes!

"These, our sped ancestry,
Lie here embraced by deeper death than we; 10
Nor shape nor thought of theirs can you descry
   With keenest backward eye.

"They count as quite forgot;
They are as men who have existed not;
Theirs is a loss past loss of fitful breath;   15
   It is the second death.

"We here, as yet, each day
Are blest with dear recall; as yet, can say
We hold in some soul loved continuance
   Of shape and voice and glance.   20

"But what has been will be —
First memory, then oblivion's swallowing sea;
Like men foregone, shall we merge into those
   Whose story no one knows.

"For which of us could hope   25
To show in life that world-awakening scope
Granted the few whose memory none lets die,
   But all men magnify?

"We were but Fortune's sport;
Things true, things lovely, things of good
   report   30
We neither shunned nor sought . . . We see
   our bourne,
   And seeing it we mourn."

                (1902)

AT CASTERBRIDGE FAIR

1. The Ballad-Singer

Sing, Ballad-singer, raise a hearty tune;
Make me forget that there was ever a one
I walked with in the meek light of the moon
   When the day's work was done.

Rime, Ballad-rimer, start a country song;   5
Make me forget that she whom I loved well

Swore she would love me dearly, love me
   long,
   Then — what I cannot tell!

Sing, Ballad-singer, from your little book;
Make me forget those heart-breaks, achings,
   fears;   10
Make me forget her name, her sweet sweet
   look —
   Make me forget her tears.

2. Former Beauties

These market-dames, mid-aged, with lips
   thin-drawn,
   And tissues sere,
Are they the ones we loved in years agone,
   And courted here?

Are these the muslined pink young things to
   whom   5
   We vowed and swore
In nooks on summer Sundays by the Froom,
   Or Budmouth shore?

Do they remember those gay tunes we trod
   Clasped on the green;   10
Aye; trod till moonlight set on the beaten sod
   A satin sheen?

They must forget, forget! They cannot
   know
   What once they were,
Or memory would transfigure them, and
   show   15
   Them always fair.

3. After the Club-Dance

Black'on frowns east on Maidon,
   And westward to the sea,
But on neither is his frown laden
   With scorn, as his frown on me!

At dawn my heart grew heavy,   5
   I could not sip the wine,
I left the jocund bevy
   And that young man o' mine.

The roadside elms pass by me —
   Why do I sink with shame   10

30-31. **Things . . . sought.** From *Philippians*, 4:8.—
"Finally, brethren, whatsoever things are true, whatsoever
things are honest, whatsoever things are just, whatsoever
things are pure, whatsoever things are lovely, whatsoever
things are of good report; if there be any virtue, if there be
any praise, think on these things."
   At Casterbridge Fair. Reprinted from Hardy's *Collected
Poems* by permission of The Macmillan Company, publishers.
   Casterbridge is Hardy's name for Dorchester, the county
seat of Dorsetshire, in southern England. To its weekly fair,
or market, came the country people to sell their produce, and
ballad-singers to furnish entertainment.

2. *Former Beauties.* **7. Froom,** the river Frome, which
flows through Dorchester. **8. Budmouth,** Weymouth, a
seaport and summer resort on the Dorset coast.
   3. *After the Club-Dance.* A dance is given by the Dorset
Farmers' Club on the evenings of market-days.
   1. Black'on, Blackdown Hill, an elevation southwest of
Dorchester, on which now stands a monument to Hardy.
Maidon, Maiden Castle, an ancient Celtic fort on a hill
south of Dorchester.

When the birds a-perch there eye me?
They, too, have done the same!

4. THE MARKET-GIRL

Nobody took any notice of her as she stood
    on the causey curb,
All eager to sell her honey and apples and
    bunches of garden herb;
And if she had offered to give her wares and
    herself with them too that day,
I doubt if a soul would have cared to take a
    bargain so choice away.
But chancing to trace her sunburnt grace
    that morning as I passed nigh,   5
I went and I said, "Poor maidy dear! —
    and will none of the people buy?"
And so it began; and soon we knew what the
    end of it all must be,
And I found that though no others had bid,
    a prize had been won by me.

5. THE INQUIRY

And are ye one of Hermitage —
Of Hermitage, by Ivel Road,
And do ye know, in Hermitage
A thatch-roofed house where sengreens grow?
And does John Waywood live there still —   5
He of the name that there abode
When father hurdled on the hill
    Some fifteen years ago?

Does he now speak o' Patty Beech,
The Patty Beech he used to — see,   10
Or ask at all if Patty Beech
Is known or heard of out this way?
— Ask if ever she's living yet,
And where her present home may be,
And how she bears life's fag and fret   15
    After so long a day?

In years agone at Hermitage
This faded face was counted fair,
None fairer; and at Hermitage
We swore to wed when he should thrive.   20
But never a chance had he or I,
And waiting made his wish outwear,
And Time, that dooms man's love to die,
    Preserves a maid's alive.

6. A WIFE WAITS

Will's at the dance in the Club-room below,
    Where the tall liquor-cups foam;

I on the pavement up here by the Bow,
    Wait, wait, to steady him home.

Will and his partner are treading a tune,   5
    Loving companions they be;
Willy, before we were married in June,
    Said he loved no one but me;

Said he would let his old pleasures all go
    Ever to live with his Dear.   10
Will's at the dance in the Club-room below;
    Shivering I wait for him here.

7. AFTER THE FAIR

The singers are gone from the Cornmarket-
    place
    With their broadsheets of rimes,
The street rings no longer in treble and bass
    With their skits on the times,
And the Cross, lately thronged, is a dim
    naked space   5
    That but echoes the stammering chimes.

From Clock-corner steps, as each quarter
    ding-dongs,
    Away the folk roam
By the "Hart" and Grey's Bridge into byways
    and "drongs,"
    Or across the ridged loam;   10
The younger ones shrilling the lately heard
    songs,
    The old saying, "Would we were home."

The shy-seeming maiden so mute in the fair
    Now rattles and talks,
And that one who looked the most swaggering
    there   15
    Grows sad as she walks,
And she who seemed eaten by cankering care
    In statuesque sturdiness stalks.

And midnight clears High Street of all but the
    ghosts
    Of its buried burghees,   20
From the latest far back to those old Roman
    hosts

---

4. *The Market-Girl.* 1. **causey,** the bridge across the Frome River at the east end of Dorchester.
5. *The Inquiry.* 1. **Hermitage,** a village northwest of Dorchester on the road to Yeovil (Ivel). 4. **sengreens,** plants growing on the walls of houses. 7. **hurdled,** made hurdles, movable frames for folding sheep, enclosing land, etc.
6. *A Wife Waits.* 1. **Club-room,** the quarters of the Dorchester Farmers' Club.
3. **Bow,** a curved corner where the main streets of Dorchester cross.
7. *After the Fair.* 1. **Cornmarket-place,** the central market-place in Dorchester. 2. **broadsheets,** ballads, frequently dealing with current events, printed on one side of a large sheet of paper. 5. **Cross,** the intersection of the two main streets at the central market-place. 7. **Clock-corner,** the corner of the market-place next to St. Peter's Church. 9. **"Hart,"** the White Hart, the last inn on the London road out of Dorchester. **Grey's Bridge,** a stone bridge across a branch of the Frome River, near Dorchester on the London road. **"drongs,"** narrow lanes between walls (Dorset dialect). 19. **High Street,** the main east-and-west street of Dorchester. 20. **burghees,** citizens. 21. **Roman hosts.** Dorchester was, during the Roman occupation of Britain, the walled town of Durnovaria; relics of Roman times are preserved in the Dorset County Museum in Dorchester.

Whose remains one yet sees,
Who loved, laughed, and fought, hailed their
　friends, drank their toasts
At their meeting-times here, just as these!
　　　　　　　　　　　　(*1902;* 1909)

SONGS from *THE DYNASTS*

THE NIGHT OF TRAFALGÁR

In the wild October night-time, when the
　wind raved round the land,
And the Back-sea met the Front-sea, and our
　doors were blocked with sand,
And we heard the drub of Dead-man's Bay,
　where bones of thousands are,
We knew not what the day had done for us
　at Trafalgár.
　　　　(*All*) Had done, 　　　　　　·5
　　　　　Had done,
　　　　For us at Trafalgár!

"Pull hard, and make the Nothe, or down we
　go!" one says, says he.
We pulled; and bedtime brought the storm;
　but snug at home slept we.
Yet all the while our gallants after fighting
　through the day, 　　　　　　　　10
Were beating up and down the dark, sou'-
　west of Cadiz Bay.
　　　　　The dark,
　　　　　The dark,
　　　　Sou'-west of Cadiz Bay!

The victors and the vanquished then the
　storm it tossed and tore, 　　　　　15
As hard they strove, those worn-out men,
　upon that surly shore;
Dead Nelson and his half-dead crew, his foes
　from near and far,
Were rolled together on the deep that night
　at Trafalgár!
　　　　　The deep,
　　　　　The deep, 　　　　　　　　20
　　　　That night at Trafalgár! 　(1903)

BUDMOUTH DEARS

When we lay where Budmouth Beach is,
Oh, the girls were fresh as peaches,
With their tall and tossing figures and their
　eyes of blue and brown!
And our hearts would ache with longing
As we paced from our sing-songing, 　　5
With a smart *Clink! Clink!* up the Espla-
　nade and down.

They distracted and delayed us
By the pleasant pranks they played us,
And what marvel, then, if troopers, even of
　regiments of renown,
On whom flashed those eyes divine, O, 　10
Should forget the countersign, O,
As we tore *Clink! Clink!* back to camp above
　the town.

Do they miss us much, I wonder,
Now that war has swept us sunder,
And we roam from where the faces smile to
　where the faces frown? 　　　　　15
And no more behold the features
Of the fair fantastic creatures,
And no more *Clink! Clink!* past the parlors
　of the town?

Shall we once again there meet them?
Falter fond attempts to greet them? 　　20
Will the gay sling-jacket glow again beside
　the muslin gown? —
Will they archly quiz and con us
With a sideway glance upon us,
While our spurs *Clink! Clink!* up the Es-
　planade and down?
　　　　　　　　　　　　　　(1908)

BEFORE WATERLOO

Chorus of the Years (aerial music)

The eyelids of eve fall together at last,
And the forms so foreign to field and tree
Lie down as though native, and slumber fast!

Songs from The Dynasts. Reprinted from Hardy's *The Dynasts* by permission of The Macmillan Company, publishers.
The Dynasts is a long epic-drama, "intended simply for
mental performance, and not for the stage," dealing with the
wars with Napoleon, 1796-1815.
The Night of Trafalgár. The speakers in the poem are
Weymouth boatmen who are awaiting news of the naval battle
of Trafalgar, October 21, 1805. Lord Nelson, who was killed
in the battle, led the English ships victoriously against the
combined French and Spanish fleets in the waters between the
harbor of Cadiz and Cape Trafalgar, northwest of Gibraltar
on the Spanish coast. The men sing a "new ballet that they've
lately had prented here, and were hawking about town last
market-day."
2. **Back-sea . . . Front-sea.** With a storm at high-tide,
the waves from the English Channel (Front-sea) swept over
the barriers and into the harbor of Weymouth (Back-sea). 3.
Dead-man's Bay, West Bay, dangerous because of its rocks
and currents, west of Weymouth on the Dorset coast. 8.
Nothe, a promontory which forms, on one side, the harbor of
Weymouth.

Budmouth Dears. Budmouth is Weymouth, a town on the
Dorset coast, frequented by soldiers and sailors from the
neighboring Portland Roads, a naval anchorage. The song is
sung on the eve of the Battle of Vitoria. The English Army
in the Peninsula and the Spanish and Portuguese allies are
bivouacking on the western side of the plain, about six miles
from town. The Hussar, who sings the song, recalls a previous
visit to Budmouth-Regis.
6. **Esplanade**, a terraced walk following the course of
Weymouth Bay. 21. **sling-jacket**, a jacket worn by
Hussars; it hung loosely over the shoulder and made a
picturesque effect.
Before Waterloo. The English and their allies defeated
Napoleon and the French in the Battle of Waterloo, fought,
June 18, 1815, on a plain south of Brussels in Belgium.
Chorus of the Years. The Years and the Pities (p. 929)
are impersonated abstractions among the characters of the
drama. Hardy explains that the Years stand for "the passion-
less Insight of the Ages," and the Pities for "the Universal
Sympathy of human nature—the spectator idealized."

Chorus of the Pities

Sore are the thrills of misgiving we see
In the artless champaign at this harlequinade,
Distracting a vigil where calm should be!   6

The green seems oppressed, and the Plain
    afraid
Of a Something to come, whereof these are
    the proofs —
Neither earthquake, nor storm, nor eclipse's
    shade!

Chorus of the Years

Yea, the coneys are scared by the thud of
    hoofs,   10
And their white scuts flash at their vanishing
    heels,
And swallows abandon the hamlet-roofs.

The mole's tunneled chambers are crushed
    by wheels,
The larks' eggs scattered, their owners fled;
And the hedgehog's household the sapper
    unseals.   15

The snail draws in at the terrible tread,
But in vain; he is crushed by the felloe-rim;
The worm asks what can be overhead,

And wriggles deep from a scene so grim,
And guesses him safe; for he does not know   20
What a foul red flood will be soaking him!

Beaten about by the heel and toe
Are butterflies, sick of the day's long rheum,
To die of a worse than the weather-foe.

Trodden and bruised to a miry tomb   25
Are ears that have greened but will never be
    gold,
And flowers in the bud that will never bloom.

Chorus of the Pities

So the season's intent, ere its fruit unfold,
Is frustrate, and mangled, and made succumb,
Like a youth of promise struck stark and
    cold! . . .   30

And what of these who tonight have come?

Chorus of the Years

The young sleep sound; but the weather
    awakes

In the veterans, pains from the past that
    numb;

Old stabs of Ind, old Peninsular aches,
Old Friedland chills, haunt their moist mud
    bed,   35
Cramps from Austerlitz; till their slumber
    breaks.

Chorus of Sinister Spirits

And each soul shivers as sinks his head
On the loam he's to lease with the other dead
From tomorrow's mist-fall till Time be sped!
                                      (1908)

THE CURATE'S KINDNESS

A WORKHOUSE IRONY

I thought they'd be strangers aroun' me,
    But she's to be there!
Let me jump out o' wagon and go back and
    drown me
    At Pummery or Ten-Hatches Weir.

I thought: "Well, I've come to the Union — 5
    The workhouse at last —
After honest hard work all the week, and
    Communion
    O' Zundays, these fifty years past.

" 'Tis hard; but," I thought, "never mind
    it —
    There's gain in the end;   10
And when I get used to the place I shall find it
    A home, and may find there a friend.

"Life there will be better than t'other,
    For peace is assured.
The men in one wing and their wives in an-
    other
    Is strictly the rule of the Board."   15

Just then one young Pa'son arriving
    Steps up out of breath
To the side o' the wagon wherein we were
    driving
    To Union; and calls out and saith: 20

34-36. **Ind . . . Austerlitz,** earlier battles and campaigns
in which the armies had engaged. The Indian campaign,
1798-99, included battles in Egypt and Asia Minor; the
Peninsular campaign took place in Portugal and Spain from
1804 to 1814; at Friedland, in East Prussia, Napoleon defeated the Russians and Prussians in 1807; at Austerlitz, in
Austria, he defeated an army of Russians and Austrians in
1805.
The Curate's Kindness. Reprinted from Hardy's *Collected
Poems* by permission of The Macmillan Company, publishers.
4. **Pummery,** Poundbury, an ancient Celtic or Roman
earthwork on an elevation near Dorchester; it contains a
pond. **Ten-Hatches Weir,** a pond held back by a dam in a
meadow near Dorchester. 5. **Union,** a home for the poor,
supported by a union of several neighboring parishes, and
administered by a board of governors.

5. **champaign,** open plain. **harlequinade,** fantastic
show—referring to the coming battle. 10. **coneys,** rabbits.
11. **scuts,** tails. 15. **sapper,** a soldier employed in digging
trenches. 17. **felloe-rim,** the rim of a wheel on a gun-mount
or supply-wagon. 23. **rheum,** sorrow; poetic for tears.

"Old folks, that harsh order is altered,
  Be not sick of heart!
The Guardians they poohed and they pished
  and they paltered
  When urged not to keep you apart.

" 'It is wrong,' I maintained, 'to divide them,
  Near forty years wed.'   25
'Very well, sir.   We promise, then, they shall
  abide them
  In one wing together,' they said."

Then I sank — knew 'twas quite a foredone
  thing
  That misery should be   30
To the end! . . . To get freed of her there was
  the one thing
  Had made the change welcome to me.

To go there was ending but badly;
  'Twas shame and 'twas pain;
"But anyhow," thought I, "thereby I shall
  gladly   35
  Get free of this forty years' chain."

I thought they'd be strangers aroun' me,
  But she's to be there!
Let me jump out o' wagon and go back and
  drown me
  At Pummery or Ten-Hatches Weir.   40
                                        (1909)

LET ME ENJOY

(MINOR KEY)

Let me enjoy the earth no less
Because the all-enacting Might
That fashioned forth its loveliness
Had other aims than my delight.

About my path there flits a Fair,   5
Who throws me not a word or sign;
I'll charm me with her ignoring air,
And laud the lips not meant for mine.

From manuscripts of moving song
Inspired by scenes and dreams unknown,   10
I'll pour out raptures that belong
To others, as they were my own.

And some day hence, towards Paradise
And all its blest — if such should be —
I will lift glad, afar-off eyes,   15
Though it contain no place for me.
                                        (1909)

  Let Me Enjoy. Reprinted from Hardy's *Collected Poems* by
permission of The Macmillan Company, publishers.
  Satires of Circumstance. Reprinted from Hardy's *Collected
Poems* by permission of The Macmillan Company, publishers.

From SATIRES OF CIRCUMSTANCE

1. AT TEA

The kettle descants in a cozy drone,
And the young wife looks in her husband's
  face,
And then at her guest's, and shows in her own
Her sense that she fills an envied place;
And the visiting lady is all abloom,   5
And says there was never so sweet a room.

And the happy young housewife does not
  know
That the woman beside her was first his
  choice,
Till the fates ordained it could not be so . . .
Betraying nothing in look or voice   10
The guest sits smiling and sips her tea,
And he throws her a stray glance yearningly.

3. BY HER AUNT'S GRAVE

"Sixpence a week," says the girl to her lover,
"Aunt used to bring me, for she could confide
In me alone, she vowed.   'Twas to cover
The cost of her headstone when she died.
And that was a year ago last June;   5
I've not yet fixed it.   But I must soon."

"And where is the money now, my dear?"
"Oh, snug in my purse . . . Aunt was so slow
In saving it — eighty weeks, or near." . . .
"Let's spend it," he hints.   "For she won't
  know.   10
There's a dance tonight at the Load of Hay."
She passively nods.   And they go that way.

9. AT THE ALTAR-RAIL

"My bride is not coming, alas!" says the
  groom,
And the telegram shakes in his hand.   "I own
It was hurried!   We met at a dancing-room
When I went to the Cattle-Show alone,
And then, next night, where the Fountain
  leaps,   5
And the Street of the Quarter-Circle sweeps.

"Aye, she won me to ask her to be my wife —
'Twas foolish perhaps! — to forsake the ways
Of the flaring town for a farmer's life.
She agreed.   And we fixed it.   Now she says:

  1. At Tea. 1. **descants**, sings.
  3. By Her Aunt's Grave. 11. **Load of Hay**, a famous inn
on Hampstead Road, London, described by Washington
Irving in his *Tales of a Traveler.*
  9. At the Altar-Rail. 4. **Cattle-Show**, an annual show
held at the Agricultural Hall in Islington, London.   5-6.
Fountain . . . Quarter-Circle, the Fountain of Trafalgar
Square and the Quadrant, a curved portion of Regent Street,
London.

'It's sweet of you, dear, to prepare me a nest, 11
But a swift, short, gay life suits me best.
What I really am you have never gleaned;
I had eaten the apple ere you were weaned.' "

(1911)

BEENY CLIFF

Oh, the opal and the sapphire of that wander-
    ing western sea,
And the woman riding high above with bright
    hair flapping free —
The woman whom I loved so, and who loyally
    loved me.

The pale mews plained below us, and the
    waves seemed far away
In a nether sky, engrossed in saying their
    ceaseless babbling say,   5
As we laughed light-heartedly aloft on that
    clear-sunned March day.

A little cloud then cloaked us, and there flew
    an irised rain,
And the Atlantic dyed its levels with a dull
    misfeatured stain,
And then the sun burst out again, and
    purples prinked the main.

— Still in all its chasmal beauty bulks old
    Beeny to the sky,   10
And shall she and I not go there once again
    now March is nigh,
And the sweet things said in that March say
    anew there by and by?

What if still in chasmal beauty looms that
    wild weird western shore,
The woman now is — elsewhere — whom the
    ambling pony bore,
And nor knows nor cares for Beeny, and will
    laugh there nevermore.   15

(1913; 1914)

BEYOND THE LAST LAMP

(*Near Tooting Common*)

While rain, with eve in partnership,
Descended darkly, drip, drip, drip,
Beyond the last lone lamp I passed

Walking slowly, whispering sadly,
    Two linked loiterers, wan, downcast: 5
Some heavy thought constrained each face,
And blinded them to time and place.

The pair seemed lovers, yet absorbed
In mental scenes no longer orbed
By love's young rays. Each countenance   10
    As it slowly, as it sadly
    Caught the lamplight's yellow glance,
Held in suspense a misery
At things which had been or might be.

When I retrod that watery way   15
Some hours beyond the droop of day,
Still I found pacing there the twain
    Just as slowly, just as sadly,
    Heedless of the night and rain.
One could but wonder who they were,   20
And what wild woe detained them there.

Though thirty years of blur and blot
Have slid since I beheld that spot,
And saw in curious converse there
    Moving slowly, moving sadly   25
    That mysterious tragic pair,
Its olden look may linger on —
All but the couple; they have gone.

Whither? Who knows, indeed . . . And yet
To me, when nights are weird and wet,   30
Without those comrades there at tryst
    Creeping slowly, creeping sadly,
    That lone lane does not exist.
There they seem brooding on their pain,
And will, while such a lane remain.   35

(1914)

"AH, ARE YOU DIGGING ON MY GRAVE?"

"Ah, are you digging on my grave
    My loved one? — planting rue?"
— "No; yesterday he went to wed
One of the brightest wealth has bred.
'It cannot hurt her now,' he said,   5
    'That I should not be true.' "

"Then who is digging on my grave?
    My nearest dearest kin?"
— "Ah, no; they sit and think, 'What use!
What good will planting flowers produce?   10
No tendance of her mound can loose
    Her spirit from Death's gin.' "

Beeny Cliff. Reprinted from Hardy's *Collected Poems* by
permission of The Macmillan Company, publishers.
  Beeny Cliff is a headland on the western Cornish coast, a
little over a mile from St. Juliot, the home, before marriage,
of the first Mrs. Hardy.
  4. mews plained, sea-gulls cried. **12. that March**, in
1870, when Hardy first met Miss Gifford, who became the
first Mrs. Hardy; cf. *"When I Set Out for Lyonnesse,"* page 925.
  Beyond the Last Lamp. Reprinted from Hardy's *Collected
Poems* by permission of The Macmillan Company, publishers.
  Tooting Common, a park on the southern outskirts of
London. Hardy lived near, in Upper Tooting, 1878-80.

"Ah, Are You Digging on My Grave?" Reprinted from
Hardy's *Collected Poems* by permission of The Macmillan
Company, publishers.
  2. rue, an herb with bitter leaves, symbolic of sorrow. **12.
gin,** trap.

"But some one digs upon my grave?
  My enemy? — prodding sly?"
— "Nay; when she heard you had passed the
    Gate   15
That shuts on all flesh soon or late,
She thought you no more worth her hate,
  And cares not where you lie."

"Then, who is digging on my grave?
  Say — since I have not guessed!"   20
— "O it is I, my mistress dear,
Your little dog, who still lives near,
And much I hope my movements here
  Have not disturbed your rest?"

"Ah, yes! *You* dig upon my grave . . .   25
  Why flashed it not on me
That one true heart was left behind!
What feeling do we ever find
To equal among human kind
  A dog's fidelity!"   30

"Mistress, I dug upon your grave
  To bury a bone, in case
I should be hungry near this spot
When passing on my daily trot.
I am sorry, but I quite forgot   35
  It was your resting-place."   (1914)

UNDER THE WATERFALL

"Whenever I plunge my arm, like this,
In a basin of water, I never miss
The sweet sharp sense of a fugitive day
Fetched back from its thickening shroud of
    gray.
        Hence the only prime   5
        And real love-rime
        That I know by heart,
        And that leaves no smart,
Is the purl of a little valley fall
About three spans wide and two spans tall 10
Over a table of solid rock,
And into a scoop of the self-same block;
The purl of a runlet that never ceases
In stir of kingdoms, in wars, in peaces;
With a hollow boiling voice it speaks   15
And has spoken since hills were turfless
    peaks."

"And why gives this the only prime
Idea to you of a real love-rime?
And why does plunging your arm in a bowl
Full of spring water, bring throbs to your
    soul?"   20

"Well, under the fall, in a crease of the stone,
Though where precisely none ever has known,

Jammed darkly, nothing to show how prized,
And by now with its smoothness opalized,
    Is a drinking-glass;   25
    For, down that pass
    My lover and I
    Walked under a sky
Of blue with a leaf-wove awning of green,
In the burn of August, to paint the scene, 30
And we placed our basket of fruit and
    wine
By the runlet's rim, where we sat to dine;
And when we had drunk from the glass
    together,
Arched by the oak-copse from the weather,
I held the vessel to rinse in the fall,   35
Where it slipped, and sank, and was past
    recall,
Though we stooped and plumbed the little
    abyss
With long bared arms.   There the glass still
    is.
And, as said, if I thrust my arm below
Cold water in basin or bowl, a throe   40
From the past awakens a sense of that time,
And the glass we used, and the cascade's
    rime.
The basin seems the pool, and its edge
The hard smooth face of the brook-side ledge,
And the leafy pattern of china-ware   45
The hanging plants that were bathing there.

"By night, by day, when it shines or lours
There lies intact that chalice of ours,
And its presence adds to the rime of love
Persistently sung by the fall above.   50
No lip has touched it since his and mine
In turns therefrom sipped lovers' wine."
                                        (1914)

THE OXEN

Christmas Eve, and twelve of the clock.
  "Now they are all on their knees,"
An elder said as we sat in a flock
  By the embers in hearthside ease.

We pictured the meek mild creatures where 5
  They dwelt in their strawy pen,
Nor did it occur to one of us there
  To doubt they were kneeling then.

So fair a fancy few would weave
  In these years!   Yet, I feel,   10
If someone said on Christmas Eve,
  "Come; see the oxen kneel,

Under the Waterfall. Reprinted from Hardy's *Collected Poems* by permission of The Macmillan Company, publishers.

The Oxen. Reprinted from Hardy's *Collected Poems* by permission of The Macmillan Company, publishers.
A widespread folk-belief is that cattle fall on their knees at midnight of Christmas Eve, as did the ox in the stable at Bethlehem when Christ was born.

"In the lonely barton by yonder coomb
Our childhood used to know,"
I should go with him in the gloom,   15
Hoping it might be so.

(1915; 1917)

IN TIME OF "THE BREAKING OF NATIONS"

(JEREMIAH, 51:20)

Only a man harrowing clods
In a slow silent walk
With an old horse that stumbles and nods
Half asleep as they stalk.

Only thin smoke without flame   5
From the heaps of couch-grass;
Yet this will go onward the same
Though Dynasties pass.

Yonder a maid and her wight
Come whispering by: 10
War's annals will fade into night
Ere their story die.

(1915; 1917)

THE CLOCK-WINDER

It is dark as a cave,
Or a vault in the nave
When the iron door
Is closed, and the floor
Of the church relaid   5
With trowel and spade.

But the parish-clerk
Cares not for the dark
As he winds in the tower
At a regular hour   10
The rheumatic clock
Whose dilatory knock
You can hear when praying
At the day's decaying,
Or at any lone while   15
From a pew in the aisle.

Up, up from the ground,
Around and around
In the turret stair

He clambers, to where   20
The wheelwork is,
With its tick, click, whizz,
Reposefully measuring
Each day to its end
That mortal men spend   25
In sorrowing and pleasuring.
Nightly thus does he climb
To the trackway of Time.

Him I followed one night
To this place without light,   30
And, ere I spoke, heard
Him say, word by word,
At the end of his winding,
The darkness unminding:

"So I wipe out one more,   35
My Dear, of the sore
Sad days that still be,
Like a drying Dead Sea,
Between you and me!"

Who she was no man knew: 40
He had long borne him blind
To all womankind;
And was ever one who
Kept his past out of view.

(1917)

"FOR LIFE I HAD NEVER CARED GREATLY"

For life I had never cared greatly,
As worth a man's while;
Peradventures unsought,
Peradventures that finished in naught,
Had kept me from youth and through man-
hood till lately   5
Unwon by its style.

In earliest years—why I know not—
I viewed it askance;
Conditions of doubt,
Conditions that leaked slowly out,   10
May haply have bent me to stand and to
show not
Much zest for its dance.

With symphonies soft and sweet color
It courted me then,
Till evasions seemed wrong,   15
Till evasions gave in to its song,
And I warmed, until living aloofly loomed
duller
Than life among men.

13. **barton,** farmyard. **coomb,** a valley between steep hills.
In Time of "The Breaking of Nations." Reprinted from Hardy's *Collected Poems* by permission of The Macmillan Company, publishers.
Compare this poem with *Jeremiah,* 51:20—"Thou art my battle axe and weapons of war; for with thee I break in pieces the nations, and with thee will I destroy kingdoms."
The Clock-Winder. Reprinted from Hardy's *Collected Poems* by permission of The Macmillan Company, publishers.

"For Life I Had Never Cared Greatly." Reprinted from Hardy's *Collected Poems* by permission of The Macmillan Company, publishers.

Anew I found naught to set eyes on,
When, lifting its hand,   20
It uncloaked a star,
Uncloaked it from fog-damps afar,
And showed its beams burning from pole to
       horizon
              As bright as a brand.

And so, the rough highway forgetting,   25
I pace hill and dale
Regarding the sky,
Regarding the vision on high,
And thus re-illumed have no humor for letting
       My pilgrimage fail.   (1917)

SNOW IN THE SUBURBS

Every branch big with it,
Bent every twig with it;
Every fork like a white web-foot;
Every street and pavement mute:
Some flakes have lost their way, and grope
       back upward, when   5
Meeting those meandering down they turn
       and descend again.
The palings are glued together like a wall,
And there is no waft of wind with the fleecy
       fall.

A sparrow enters the tree,
Whereon immediately   10
A snow-lump thrice his own slight size
Descends on him and showers his head and
       eyes,
And overturns him,
And near inurns him,
And lights on a nether twig, when its brush
Starts off a volley of other lodging lumps with
       a rush.   16

The steps are a blanched slope,
Up which, with feeble hope,
A black cat comes, wide-eyed and thin;   19
And we take him in.   (1925)

AN ANCIENT TO ANCIENTS

Where once we danced, where once we sang,
       Gentlemen,
The floors are sunken, cobwebs hang,
And cracks creep; worms have fed upon
The doors. Yea, sprightlier times were then 5
Than now, with harps and tabrets gone,
       Gentlemen!

Where once we rowed, where once we sailed,
       Gentlemen,
And damsels took the tiller, veiled   10
Against too strong a stare (God wot
Their fancy, then or anywhen!)
Upon that shore we are clean forgot,
       Gentlemen!

We have lost somewhat, afar and near,   15
       Gentlemen,
The thinning of our ranks each year
Affords a hint we are nigh undone,
That we shall not be ever again
The marked of many, loved of one,   20
       Gentlemen.

In dance the polka hit our wish,
       Gentlemen,
The paced quadrille, the spry schottische,
"Sir Roger."—And in opera spheres   25
The "Girl" (the famed "Bohemian"),
And "Trovatore," held the ears,
       Gentlemen.

This season's paintings do not please,
       Gentlemen,   30
Like Etty, Mulready, Maclise;
Throbbing romance has waned and wanned;
No wizard yields the witching pen
Of Bulwer, Scott, Dumas, and Sand,
       Gentlemen.   35

The bower we shrined to Tennyson,
       Gentlemen,
Is roof-wrecked; damps there drip upon
Sagged seats, the creeper-nails are rust,
The spider is sole denizen;   40
Even she who voiced those rhymes is dust,
       Gentlemen!

We who met sunrise sanguine-souled,
       Gentlemen,
Are wearing weary. We are old;   45
These younger press; we feel our rout
Is imminent to Aïdes' den—
That evening shades are stretching out,
       Gentlemen!

Snow in the Suburbs. Reprinted from Hardy's *Collected Poems* by permission of The Macmillan Company, publishers.
An Ancient to Ancients. Reprinted from Hardy's *Collected Poems* by permission of The Macmillan Company, publishers.

11. **wot,** knows. 25. **"Sir Roger,"** Sir Roger de Coverley, an old-fashioned country dance, beloved by the English people. 26. **The "Girl"...."Bohemian,"** *The Bohemian Girl,* an opera by Balfe, produced in London in 1843. 27. **"Trovatore,"** *Il Trovatore,* an opera by Verdi, 1853. 31. **Etty ... Maclise,** English and Irish painters of the earlier nineteenth century: William Etty (1787-1849), William Mulready (1786-1863), Daniel Maclise (1806-1870). 34. **Bulwer ... Sand,** nineteenth-century English and French novelists: Edward Bulwer-Lytton, 1803-1873; Sir Walter Scott, 1771-1832; Alexander Dumas, 1802-1870; George Sand (Baroness Dudevant), 1804-1876. 36-38. **bower ... wrecked,** a reference to the decline in favor, in certain critical circles, of the poetry of Tennyson after his death. 39. **creeper-nails,** the nails which fasten the vine to the wall. 47. **Aïdes,** Hades, god of the Greek underworld.

And yet, though ours be failing frames,   50
    Gentlemen,
So were some others' history names,
Who trode their track light-limbed and fast
As these youth, and not alien
From enterprise, to their long last,   55
    Gentlemen.

Sophocles, Plato, Socrates,
    Gentlemen,

57-61. **Sophocles . . . Origen.** Greek authors and philosophers and Christian fathers of the church who had in common a profitable old age.

Pythagoras, Thucydides,
Herodotus, and Homer—yea,   60
Clement, Augustin, Origen,
Burnt brightlier toward their setting-day,
    Gentlemen.

And ye, red-lipped and smooth-browed; list,
    Gentlemen;   65
Much is there waits you we have missed;
Much lore we leave you worth the knowing,
Much, much has lain outside our ken:
Nay, rush not: time serves: we are going,   69
    Gentlemen.   (1922)

A LITERARY CHRONOLOGY
1830-1901

ENGLAND	EUROPE	THE UNITED STATES

WILLIAM IV (1830-1837)

	ENGLAND	EUROPE	THE UNITED STATES

1830	Lyell, *Geology*
	Milman, *History of the Jews*
	Tennyson, *Poems, Chiefly*
	   Lyrical
		Hugo, *Hernani*
		Comte, *The Positive*
		   Philosophy	

1831		Stendhal, *The Red and the* *Black* Sand, *Indiana*	
1832	(First Reform Bill) Tennyson, *Poems* (Deaths of Scott and Bentham)	(Death of Goethe) Goethe, *Faust II*	Irving, *Alhambra*
1833	(Oxford Movement begins) Browning, *Pauline*	Balzac, *Eugénie Grandet*	
1834	Carlyle, *Sartor Resartus* Bulwer-Lytton, *Last Days of* *Pompeii* (Death of Coleridge)	Balzac, *Père Goriot*	
1835	Browning, *Paracelsus*	Vigny, *Chatterton*	
1836	Dickens, *Pickwick Papers*	Musset, *Confessions of a Child* *of the Century*	Emerson, *Nature*

VICTORIA (1837-1901)

	ENGLAND	EUROPE	THE UNITED STATES
1837	Carlyle, *French Revolution*	Hugo, poems Gogol, *Dead Souls*	
1838	(Chartist Movement begins) Dickens, *Oliver Twist*	Lamartine, *Fall of an Angel*	
1839	Darwin, *Voyage of the Beagle* Bailey, *Festus*	Stendhal, *Charterhouse of* *Parma*	
1840	Bulwer-Lytton, *Money*		Poe, *Tales of the Grotesque*
1841	Carlyle, *Heroes* Browning, *Pippa Passes* (*Punch* founded)		Emerson, *Essays* Cooper, *The Deerslayer*
1842	Tennyson, *Poems*		Longfellow, *Ballads and Other* *Poems*
1843	Ruskin, *Modern Painters, I* Carlyle, *Past and Present* Mill, *Logic* (Wordsworth becomes poet laureate)		Prescott, *Conquest of Mexico* Whittier, *Lays of My Home*
1844	(Children's Factory Act)	Hebbel, *Maria Magdalena* Verdi, *Ernani* Heine, *New Poems*	

1845	Disraeli, *Sybil*
	Browning, *Dramatic Romances*
	   and Lyrics
		Mérimée, *Carmen*
		Wagner, *Tannhäuser*
			Poe, *The Raven and Other*
			   Poems

1846	(Repeal of Corn Laws) Lear, *Book of Nonsense*		Melville, *Typee*
1847	Tennyson, *The Princess* C. Brontë, *Jane Eyre* E. Brontë, *Wuthering Heights*		Emerson, *Poems* Longfellow, *Evangeline*

1848	(Chartism collapses)
	Thackeray, *Vanity Fair*
	Gaskell, *Mary Barton*
	Macaulay, *History of England*
	Mill, *Principles of Political*
	   Economy
	(Pre-Raphaelites organize)
		(Revolutions in France,
		   Germany, Austria)
			Lowell, *Vision of Sir Launfal*

ENGLAND	EUROPE	THE UNITED STATES
1849 Arnold, *Strayed Reveller* Layard, *Nineveh*		
1850 Pre-Raphaelite *Germ* Tennyson, *In Memoriam* Kingsley, *Alton Locke* Dickens, *David Copperfield* (Wordsworth dies; Tennyson becomes poet laureate)	(Death of Balzac)	Hawthorne, *The Scarlet Letter*

1851 Ruskin, *Stones of Venice, I*
Borrow, *Lavengro*
E. B. Browning, *Casa Guidi
  Windows*
(Great Exhibition)
	Heine, *Romanzero*	Melville, *Moby Dick*
		Parkman, *Conspiracy of
		  Pontiac*

1852 Arnold, *Empedocles* Thackeray, *Henry Esmond* Newman, *Idea of a University*	Gautier, poems (Louis Napoleon becomes emperor of the French)	Stowe, *Uncle Tom's Cabin*
1853 Arnold, *Poems* Dickens, *Bleak House* Gaskell, *Cranford*		
1854 (Crimean War, till 1856) Dickens, *Hard Times*		Thoreau, *Walden*
1855 Tennyson, *Maud* Browning, *Men and Women*		Whitman, *Leaves of Grass*
1856 E. B. Browning, *Aurora Leigh*		
1857 Trollope, *Barchester Towers* (Indian Mutiny)	Baudelaire, *Flowers of Evil* Flaubert, *Madame Bovary*	
1858 Morris, *Defence of Guenevere*		Holmes, *Autocrat of the Breakfast Table*
1859 Tennyson, *Idylls of the King* Eliot, *Adam Bede* Mill, *On Liberty* FitzGerald, *Rubáiyát* Meredith, *Ordeal of Richard Feverel* Darwin, *Origin of Species*		
1860 *Essays and Reviews* Ruskin, *Unto This Last* Eliot, *Mill on the Floss*		Hawthorne, *Marble Faun*
1861 Rossetti, *Early Italian Poets* Reade, *Cloister and the Hearth* (Death of Prince Consort)		(Civil War, 1861-1865)
1862 C. Rossetti, *Goblin Market* Meredith, *Modern Love*	Hugo, *Les Misérables* Flaubert, *Salammbô* Turgenev, *Fathers and Sons*	

1863 Eliot, *Romola*
Kingsley, *Water-Babies*
(Death of Thackeray)
	Renan, *Life of Jesus*
	(Salon des refusés—French
	  impressionism)
		Longfellow, *Tales of a
		  Wayside Inn*

1864 Browning, *Dramatis Personæ* Tennyson, *Enoch Arden* Newman, *Apologia pro Vita Sua*		

1865 Dickens, *Our Mutual Friend*
Arnold, *Essays in Criticism*
Swinburne, *Atalanta in
  Calydon*
Carroll, *Alice's Adventures in
  Wonderland*
	Goncourt, *Germinie Lacerteux*
	Wagner, *Tristan and Isolde*	

1866 Swinburne, *Poems and Ballads* Ruskin, *Crown of Wild Olive* Newman, *Dream of Gerontius*	Dostoevsky, *Crime and Punishment* Tolstoi, *War and Peace*	
1867 (Second Reform Bill) Carlyle, *Shooting Niagara* Robertson, *Caste* Morris, *Life and Death of Jason*	Ibsen, *Peer Gynt* Marx, *Das Kapital I* Turgenev, *Smoke*	

	ENGLAND	EUROPE	THE UNITED STATES
1868	Browning, *The Ring and the Book* Collins, *Moonstone*		Alcott, *Little Women*
1869	Arnold, *Culture and Anarchy* Blackmore, *Lorna Doone*	Verlaine, poems Flaubert, *Sentimental Education*	Twain, *Innocents Abroad*
1870	Rossetti, *Poems, House of Life* Morris, *Earthly Paradise* O'Shaughnessy, *An Epic of Women* (Death of Dickens)	(Franco-Prussian War begins) (Italian unity completed)	Harte, *Luck of Roaring Camp*
1871	Swinburne, *Songs before Sunrise* Darwin, *Descent of Man*	(German empire established) Rimbaud, *Bateau ivre*	Whitman, *Democratic Vistas* Lowell, *My Study Windows*
1872	Eliot, *Middlemarch* Butler, *Erewhon*	Nietzsche, *Birth of Tragedy*	
1873	Pater, *Renaissance* Trollope, *Eustace Diamonds* Mill, *Autobiography*	Rimbaud, *Season in Hell*	
1874	Thomson, *City of Dreadful Night* Morley, *On Compromise*	Hugo, *Ninety-three*	
1875	Hopkins, *Wreck of the Deutschland* (pub. 1918)	Tolstoi, *Anna Karenina*	Stedman, *Victorian Poets*
1876	Bradley, *Ethical Studies*	Mallarmé, *Afternoon of a Faun*	Twain, *Tom Sawyer* Bancroft, *History of the United States*
1877	Mallock, *New Republic* Patmore, *Unknown Eros* (Victoria becomes empress of India)	Zola, *L'Assommoir* (Russo-Turkish War, 1877-1878)	Lanier, *Poems*
1878	Hardy, *Return of the Native*	(Congress of Berlin)	
1879	Meredith, *The Egoist*	Ibsen, *A Doll's House*	James, *Daisy Miller* George, *Progress and Poverty*
1880	Gissing, *Workers in the Dawn* Tennyson, *Ballads and Other Poems*	Maupassant, *Tales* Dostoevsky, *Brothers Karamazov*	
1881	Rossetti, *Ballads and Sonnets* Blunt, *Love Sonnets of Proteus* Wilde, *Poems* Gilbert and Sullivan, *Patience* (Death of Carlyle)	Ibsen, *Ghosts*	James, *Portrait of a Lady*
1882	Swinburne, *Tristram of Lyonesse* (Deaths of Darwin and Rossetti)	C. F. Meyer, *Poems* Wagner, *Parsifal*	Howells, *A Modern Instance*
1883	Trollope, *Autobiography* Stevenson, *Treasure Island*	Nietzsche, *Thus Spake Zarathustra*	
1884	Tennyson, *Becket* (Third Reform Bill)	Huysmans, *Against the Grain*	Twain, *Huckleberry Finn*
1885	Gilbert and Sullivan, *The Mikado* Pater, *Marius, the Epicurean* Stevenson, *Child's Garden of Verses*		Howells, *Rise of Silas Lapham*
1886	Kipling, *Departmental Ditties* Froude, *Oceana*		James, *Bostonians*
1887	Stevenson, *Underwoods* Pater, *Imaginary Portraits* (Golden Jubilee)		Dewey, *Psychology*
1888	Doughty, *Arabia Deserta* Henley, *Book of Verses* Moore, *Confessions of a Young Man*		Bellamy, *Looking Backward*

ENGLAND	EUROPE	THE UNITED STATES
1888 Ward (Mrs.), *Robert Elsmere* (Death of Arnold)		
1889 Pater, *Appreciations* Tennyson, *Demeter* (Death of Browning) Browning, *Asolando* Yeats, *Wanderings of Oisin*		
1890 Morris, *News from Nowhere* Wilde, *Dorian Gray* Frazer, *Golden Bough I*	George, *Hymns* France, *Thaïs*	Dickinson, *Poems* James, *Principles of* *Psychology*

1891 Hardy, *Tess of the*
  D'Urbervilles
Gissing, *New Grub Street*
		Garland, *Main-Travelled*
		  Roads

1892 Kipling, *Barrack-Room* *Ballads* Shaw, *Widowers' Houses* Tennyson, *Death of Œnone* (Death of Tennyson)		Crane, *Maggie*

1893 Yeats, *Celtic Twilight*
Meynell, *Poems*
Gissing, *The Odd Women*
Bradley, *Appearance and*
  Reality
Pinero, *Second Mrs.*
  Tanqueray		

1894 Davidson, *Ballads and Songs* Moore, *Esther Waters*	France, *Red Lily* D'Annunzio, *Triumph of* *Death*	
1895 Wilde, *Importance of Being* *Earnest* Hardy, *Jude the Obscure* Conrad, *Almayer's Folly*		Crane, *Red Badge of Courage*
1896 Housman, *A Shropshire Lad* Dowson, *Verses*	Hauptmann, *The Sunken Bell*	Santayana, *The Sense of* *Beauty*
1897 (Diamond Jubilee)	Rostand, *Cyrano de Bergerac*	Robinson, *Children of Night*
1898 Hardy, *Wessex Poems*		
1899 (Boer War, 1899-1902)	Chekhov, *Uncle Vanya*	Norris, *McTeague*
1900 Yeats, *The Shadowy Waters* Conrad, *Lord Jim*	Tolstoi, *Resurrection*	Dreiser, *Sister Carrie*
1901 Kipling, *Kim* (Death of Victoria; accession of Edward VII)	Mann, *Buddenbrooks*	Moody, *Poems* James, *The Sacred Fount*

BIBLIOGRAPHIES, BRIEF BIOGRAPHIES, LISTS OF WORKS, CRITICISMS, AND CRITICAL NOTES

The following bibliographies are meant to serve as convenient, though by no means exhaustive, reference lists for a study of Victorian poetry. They should be supplemented by the current "Victorian Bibliography," which appears each year in the June issue of *Victorian Studies*, and by *Bibliographies of Studies in Victorian Literature*, collected in 1945 by W. D. Templeman and in 1956 by Austin Wright. The student will also find a useful guide to research on all the major poets of this text, and many of the minor ones, in *The Victorian Poets*, edited by Frederic E. Faverty.

The General Bibliography below lists background books and discussions of literary movements in the Victorian period. It is followed by bibliographical material and biographical sketches of the poets in the order in which they appear in the text. The biographical sketches supply only the essential facts of the lives of the poets, with emphasis on their writings; each concludes with a list of principal publications and the dates of first appearance. The introductory criticisms are presented as suggestive, rather than necessarily definitive, estimates; many reflect late-Victorian or early twentieth-century opinion, which the present-day reader, with a longer and possibly clearer perspective, may wish to question or qualify.

GENERAL BIBLIOGRAPHY

SOCIAL AND POLITICAL HISTORY

Asquith, H.H., *Some Aspects of the Victorian Age*, London, Oxford Univ. Press, 1918

Boon, John, *Victorians, Edwardians, and Georgians*, London, Hutchinson, 1928

Brinton, C., *English Political Thought in the Nineteenth Century*, 2d ed., Cambridge, Harvard Univ. Press, 1949

Bryant, A., *The Pageant of England, 1840-1940*, New York, Harper, 1941

Cambridge Modern History, The, 14 vols., ed. by A.W. Ward, G.W. Prothero, and S. Leathes, Vols. 11 and 12, New York, Macmillan, 1909-1910

Clark, G.K., *The Making of Victorian England*, Cambridge, Harvard Univ. Press, 1962

Gladstone, W.E., *Gleanings of Past Years, 1843-1878*, 7 vols., New York, Scribner, 1879

Gretton, R.H., *A Modern History of the English People: 1880-1922*, New York, Dial Press, 1930

Halévy, E., *Victorian Years, 1841-1895*, Vol. 4, *History of the English People in the Nineteenth Century*, tr. from the French by E.I. Watkin, London, Benn, 1951

Hayward, A.L., *The Days of Dickens; a Glance at Some Aspects of Early Victorian Life in London*, New York, Dutton, 1926

Heaton, H., *Economic History of Europe*, New York, Harper, 1948

Inge, W.R., *The Victorian Age*, London, Cambridge Univ. Press, 1922

Low, S. and L.C. Sanders, *The Political History of England, 1837-1901*, London, Longmans, 1907

McCarthy, J., *A History of Our Own Times*, 5 vols., New York, Harper, 1905

Metz, R., *A Hundred Years of British Philosophy*, tr. by J.W. Harvey, T.E. Jessop, and Henry Sturt, ed. by J.H. Muirhead, New York, Macmillan, 1938

Petrie, Sir Charles, *The Victorians*, London, Eyre and Spotiswood, 1960

Social England, 6 vols., ed. by H.D. Traill and J.S. Mann, Vol. 6, New York, Putnam, 1899

Strachey, G. Lytton, *Eminent Victorians*, London, Chatto, 1918

Strachey, G. Lytton, *Queen Victoria*, New York, Harcourt, 1921

Temperley, H.W.V., *The Victorian Age in Politics, War, and Diplomacy*, London, Cambridge Univ. Press, 1928

Trevelyan, G.M., *British History in the Nineteenth Century, 1782-1901*, London, Longmans, 1922

Victorian England, 2d ed., ed. by G.M. Young, New York, Oxford Univ. Press, 1953

Wingfield-Stratford, E., *The Victorian Cycle*, 3 studies, New York, Morrow, 1935

Woodward, E.L., *The Age of Reform, 1815-1870*, Oxford, Clarendon Press, new ed., 1962

HISTORY OF LITERATURE AND IDEAS

Altick, R.D., *The English Common Reader: A Social History of the Mass Reading Public, 1800-1900*, Chicago, Univ. of Chicago Press, 1957

Andrews, C.E. and M.O. Percival, eds., *Poetry of the Nineties*, New York, Harcourt, 1926

Appleman, Philip, et al., eds., *1859: Entering an Age of Crisis*, Bloomington, Indiana Univ. Press, 1959

Archer, William, *Poets of the Younger Generation*, London, Lane, 1902

Batho, E.C. and B. Dobrée, *The Victorians and After, 1830-1914*, New York, Dover, 1952

Baumann, A.A., *The Last Victorians*, Philadelphia, Lippincott, 1927

Boyd, E.A., *Ireland's Literary Renaissance*, New York, Knopf, 1922

Brandes, G., *Main Currents in Nineteenth Century Literature*, 6 vols., New York, Boni & Liveright, 1923

Brooke, S.A., *Four Victorian Poets*, New York, Putnam, 1908

Buckley, J.H., *The Victorian Temper: a Study in Literary Culture*, Cambridge, Mass., Harvard Univ. Press, 1951

Burdett, O., *The Beardsley Period*, London, Lane, 1925

Bush, D., *Mythology and the Romantic Tradition in English Poetry*, Cambridge, Mass., Harvard Univ. Press, 1937

Cambridge History of English Literature, The, 14 vols., ed. by A.W. Ward and A.R. Waller, Vols. 12-14, New York, Putnam, 1908

Chesterton, G.K., *The Victorian Age in Literature*, New York, Holt, 1913

Church, R.W., *The Oxford Movement*, London, Macmillan, 1894

Croce, B., *European Literature in the Nineteenth Century*, tr. by D. Ainslie, London, Chapman, 1924

Cunliffe, J.W., *English Literature during the Last Half-Century*, New York, Macmillan, 1923

Cunliffe, J.W., *Leaders of the Victorian Revolution*, New York, Appleton, 1934

Daiches, D., *Poetry and the Modern World: a Study of Poetry in England between 1900 and 1939*, Chicago, Univ. of Chicago Press, 1940

Dowden, E., *New Studies in Literature*, London, Paul, 1895

Dowden, E., *Studies in Literature, 1789-1877*, London, Paul, 1922

Drinkwater, J., *Victorian Poetry*, New York, Doran, 1924

Ehrsam, T.G., R.H. Deily, and R.M. Smith, comps., *Bibliographies of Twelve Victorian Authors*, New York, Wilson, H.W., 1936

Ellis, S.M., *Mainly Victorian*, London, Hutchinson, 1925

Elton, O., *Modern Studies*, London, Arnold, 1907

Elton, O., *A Survey of English Literature, 1780-1880*, 4 vols., New York, Macmillan, 1920

Evans, B.I., *English Poetry in the Later Nineteenth Century*, London, Methuen, 1933

Fairchild, Hoxie, N., *Religious Trends in English Poetry*, vol. 4, 1830-1880, and vol. 5, 1880-1920, New York, Columbia Univ. Press, 1957, 1962

Faverty, Frederic E., ed., *The Victorian Poets: A Guide to Research*, Cambridge, Mass., Harvard Univ. Press, 1956

Foakes, R.A., *The Romantic Assertion: A Study of the Language of Nineteenth Century Poetry*, New Haven, Yale Univ. Press, 1958

Ford, George H., *Keats and the Victorians*, New Haven, Yale Univ. Press, 1944

Granville-Barker, H., ed., *The Eighteen-Seventies*, essays by Fellows of the Royal Society of Literature, New York, Macmillan, 1929

Grierson, H.J.C., *Lyrical Poetry from Blake to Hardy*, New York, Harcourt, 1929

Harrison, F., *Studies in Early Victorian Literature*, London, Arnold, 1895

Hearn, L., *Pre-Raphaelite and Other Poets*, New York, Dodd, 1922

Hicks, G., *Figures of Transition: a Study of British Literature at the End of the Nineteenth Century*, New York, Macmillan, 1939

Hough, G., *The Last Romantics*, London, Duckworth, 1949

Houghton, W.E., *The Victorian Frame of Mind, 1830-1870*, New Haven, Yale Univ. Press, 1957

Hudson, W.H., *A Short History of English Literature in the Nineteenth Century*, London, Bell, 1918

Hunt, W.H., *Pre-Raphaelitism and the Pre-Raphaelite Brotherhood*, New York, Macmillan, 1905-1906

Hutton, R.H., *Brief Literary Criticisms*, London, Macmillan, 1906

Irvine, William, *Apes, Angels and Victorians*, New York, McGraw Hill, 1955

Jackson, H., *The Eighteen Nineties*, New York, Kennerley, 1914

Johnson, E.D.H., *The Alien Vision of Victorian Poetry*, Princeton, Princeton Univ. Press, 1952

Knickerbocker, W.S., *Creative Oxford: Its Influence in Victorian Literature*, Syracuse, N.Y., Syracuse Univ. Press, 1925

Langbaum, Robert, *The Poetry of Experience: The Dramatic Monologue in Modern Literary Tradition*, New York, Random House, 1957

Leavis, F.R., *New Bearings in English Poetry; a Study of the Contemporary Situation*, New York, Stewart, 1950

Le Gallienne, R., *The Romantic '90's*, New York, Doubleday, 1925

Lucas, F.L., *Ten Victorian Poets*, 3d ed., New York, Macmillan, 1948

Madeleva, Sister Mary, "The Religious

Poetry of the Nineteenth Century," *Chaucer's Nuns and Other Essays*, New York, Appleton, 1925

Manly, J.M., and Edith Rickert, *Contemporary British Literature*, New York, Harcourt, 1928

Mégroz, R.L., *Modern English Poetry, 1882-1932*, London, Nicholson, 1933

Muddiman, B., *The Men of the Nineties*, London, Danielson, 1920

Neff, E.E., *A Revolution in European Poetry, 1660-1900*, New York, Columbia Univ. Press, 1940

Oliphant, Mrs. M., *The Victorian Age of English Literature*, 2 vols., New York, Tait, 1892

Peckham, Morse, *Beyond the Tragic Vision: The Quest for Identity in the Nineteenth Century*, New York, Braziller, 1962

Peters, R.L., "Whistler and the English Poets of the 1890's," *Modern Language Quarterly*, 1957, 18:251-261

Phelps, W.L. *The Advance of English Poetry in the Twentieth Century*, New York, Dodd, 1918

Pinto, V. de S., *Crisis in English Poetry, 1880-1940*, New York, Longmans, 1951

Roppen, Georg, *Evolution and Poetic Belief*, Oxford, Blackwell, 1956

Routh, H.V., *Towards the Twentieth Century*, New York, Macmillan, 1937

Saintsbury, G., *A History of Nineteenth Century Literature*, London, Macmillan, 1896

Saintsbury, G., *The Later Nineteenth Century*, Edinburgh, Blackwood, 1907

Shorter, C.K., *Victorian Literature*, New York, Dodd, 1897

Somervell, D.C., *English Thought in the Nineteenth Century*, London, Longmans, Green, 1929

Stedman, E.C., *Victorian Poets*, Boston, Houghton, 1903

Symons, A., "The Decadent Movement in Literature," *London Quarterly Review*, 1918, 129:89-103

Templeman, W.D., ed., *Bibliographies of Studies in Victorian Literature . . . 1932-1944*, Urbana, Univ. of Ill. Press, 1945

Tindall, W.Y., *Forces in Modern British Literature, 1885-1946*, New York, Knopf, 1947

Walker, H., *The Greater Victorian Poets*, New York, Macmillan, 1895

Walker, H., *The Literature of the Victorian Era*, London, Cambridge Univ. Press, 1910

Warren, A.H., Jr., *English Poetic Theory, 1825-1865*, Princeton, N.J., Princeton Univ. Press, 1950

Waugh, A., "Some Movements in Victorian Poetry," *Reticence in Literature*, London, Wilson, 1915

Welby, T.E., *The Victorian Romantics*, London, Howe, 1929

Willey, Basil, *More Nineteenth Century Studies*, New York, Columbia Univ. Press, 1955

Willey, Basil, *Nineteenth Century Studies*, New York, Columbia Univ. Press, 1950

Williams, C., *Poetry at Present*, studies of Hardy, Bridges, Housman, Kipling, Yeats, New York, Oxford Univ. Press, 1930

Williams, Raymond, *Culture and Society, 1780-1950*, New York, Columbia Univ. Press, 1958

Williams, S.T., *Studies in Victorian Literature*, New York, Dutton, 1923

Woodberry, G.E., *Literary Memoirs of the Nineteenth Century*, New York, Harcourt, 1921

Wright, Austin, ed., *Victorian Literature: Modern Essays in Criticism*, New York, Oxford Univ. Press, 1961

Yeats, William Butler, *Autobiography*, New York, Macmillan, 1953

Young, G.M., *Victorian England: Portrait of an Age*, London, Oxford Univ. Press, 1936

JOHN HENRY NEWMAN, p. 1

STANDARD EDITIONS

Verses on Various Occasions, London, Burns, 1880

The Dream of Gerontius and Other Poems, London, Oxford Univ. Press, 1914

The Dream of Gerontius, ed. w. an intro. by W.P. Stockley, London, Crandon, 1923

Essays and Sketches, 3 vols., ed. w. a pref. and an intro. by C.F. Harrold, New York, Longmans, 1948

Essays, Critical and Historical, 2 vols., London, Pickering, 1871

Apologia pro Vita Sua, ed. by C.F. Harrold, New York, Longmans, 1947

The Idea of a University, Defined and Illustrated, ed. w. a pref. and an intro, by C.F. Harrold, New York, Longmans, 1947

Selections from the Prose Writings, ed. w. an intro. by L.E. Gates, New York, Holt, 1895

Letters and Correspondence, 2 vols., London, Longmans, 1892

Letters and Diaries, about 30 vols., ed. by C.S. Dessain, London, Nelson, 1961- (in process)

The Essential Newman, ed. by V.F. Blehl, New York, New American Library, 1963

BIOGRAPHY

Abbott, E.A., *The Anglican Career of Cardinal Newman*, 2 vols., London, Macmillan, 1902

Atkins, G.G., *Life of Cardinal Newman*, New York, Harper, 1931

Barry, William, *Newman*, Literary Lives, New York, Scribner, 1904

De Vere, A., "Some Recollections of Cardinal Newman," *Nineteenth Century*, 1896, 40: 395-411

George, R.E.G. (Robert Sencourt, pseud.), *Life of Newman*, London, Dacre Press, 1948

Goyau, Mme. Lucie F.F., *Newman; Sa Vie et Ses Oeuvres*, Paris, Perrin, 1901

Harrold, C.F., *John Henry Newman*, New York, Longmans, 1945

Hutton, R.H., *Cardinal Newman*, Boston, Houghton, 1891

May, J.L., *Cardinal Newman*, New York, Dial Press, 1930

Moody, J., *John Henry Newman*, New York, Sheed, 1945

Newman, B., *Cardinal Newman; a Biographical and Literary Study*, New York, Century, 1925

Ross, J.E., *John Henry Newman: Anglican Minister, Catholic Priest, Roman Cardinal*, New York, Norton, 1933

Trevor, Meriol, *Newman: Light in Winter*, New York, Doubleday, 1962

Trevor, Meriol, *Newman: The Pillar of the Cloud*, New York, Doubleday, 1962

Ward, M., *Young Mr. Newman*, New York, Sheed, 1948

Ward, W.P., *The Life of John Henry, Cardinal Newman; Based on His Private Journals and Correspondence*, London, Longmans, 1937

CRITICISM

Barstow, H.H., "Lead, Kindly Light," *Homiletic Review*, 1923, 86:152-157

Birrell, A., "Cardinal Newman," *More Obiter Dicta*, London, Heinemann, 1924

Brickel, A.G., "Cardinal Newman and Gilbert K. Chesterton," *Catholic World*, 1919, 109:744-752

Brilioth, Y.T., *The Anglican Revival*, London, Longmans, 1925

Cadman, S.P., *The Three Religious Leaders of Oxford and Their Movements*, New York, Macmillan, 1916

Castle, W.R., Jr., "Newman and Coleridge," *Sewanee Review*, 1909, 17:139-152

Church, R.W., *The Oxford Movement*, London, Macmillan, 1894

Cronin, J.F., *Cardinal Newman: His Theory of Knowledge*, Washington, D.C., Catholic Univ. of America Press, 1935

Doyle, Sir F.H.C., "Dr. Newman's *The Dream of Gerontius*," *Lectures*, London, Macmillan, 1869

Fletcher, J.B., "Newman and Carlyle," *Atlantic Monthly*, 1905, 95:669-679

Flood, J.M., *Cardinal Newman and Oxford*, London, Nicholson, 1933

Froude, J.A., "The Revival of Romanism," *Short Studies*, 3d s., New York, Scribner, 1892

Fuller, E., "Arnold, Newman, and Rossetti," *Critic*, 1904, 45:273-276

Genung, J.F., "John Henry Newman as a Writer," *New England Magazine*, 1890, n.s., 3:199-205

Hall, S., *A Short History of the Oxford Movement*, New York, Longmans, 1906

Harrold, C.F., *John Henry Newman*, New York, Longmans, 1945

Houghton, W.E., *The Art of Newman's Apologia*, New Haven, Conn., Yale Univ. Press, 1945

Hutton, R.H., "Newman and Tennyson," *Brief Literary Criticisms*, London, Macmillan, 1906

Hutton, R.H., "The Two Great Oxford Thinkers, Cardinal Newman and Matthew Arnold," *Essays on Some of the Modern Guides of English Thought in Matters of Faith*, London, Macmillan, 1887

Inge, W.R., "Cardinal Newman," *Outspoken Essays*, London, Longmans, 1921

Johnson, L., "Cardinal Newman," *Post Liminium*, London, Mathews, 1911

Lovett, R.M., "Cardinal Newman's Poetry," *Harvard Monthly*, 1891, 11:191-200

Mearns, J., "*Lead, Kindly Light*: Its Sources and Its Meanings," *Catholic World*, 1913, 96:500-523

Meynell, W., "Cardinal Newman and His Contemporaries," *Contemporary Review*, 1890, 59:313-332

Middleton, R.D., *Newman at Oxford: His Religious Development*, New York, Oxford Univ. Press, 1950

More, P.E., "Cardinal Newman," *The Drift of Romanticism*, 8th s., Shelburne Essays, Boston, Houghton, 1913

Pick, John, "Newman the Poet," *Renascence*, 1956, 8:127-135

Reilly, J.J., *Newman as a Man of Letters*, New York, Macmillan, 1925

Ruggles, E., *Journey into Faith*, New York, Norton, 1944

Ryan, J.K., and E.D. Benard, eds., *American Essays for the Newman Centennial*, Washington, D.C., Catholic Univ. of America Press, 1947

Shafer, R., *Christianity and Naturalism*, New Haven, Conn., Yale Univ. Press, 1926

Stephen, L., "Newman's Theory of Belief," *An Agnostic's Apology*, London, Smith, 1893

Stockley, W.F.P., " 'At the Hour of Our Death': Notes by a Reader of *The Dream of Gerontius*," *Dublin Review*, 1918, 162: 87-111

Tymms, T.V., "Lead, Kindly Light," *Good Words*, 1893, 34:665-669

Webb, C.C.J., *Religious Thought in the Oxford Movement*, New York, Macmillan, 1928

BIOGRAPHICAL SKETCH

The verse of John Henry, Cardinal Newman (1801-1890), was the by-product of a life intensely devoted to a quest for a satisfactory personal religion and to a warfare against what he deemed irreligious tendencies in society. From early childhood his mind was set on the unseen. Through Scott's novels he lived imaginatively in the Middle Ages; from the Bible he peopled his world with angels; and he felt with great vividness the presence of God. In 1816 came the mystic experience which he described in his *Apologia* as an "inward conversion," a dedication to a religious purpose from which he never deviated. After taking his degree at Oxford, he was ordained a clergyman in the Church of England; and in 1828 he was made vicar of the Church of St. Mary's at Oxford, where his sermons were to be of much influence in coming years. With a group of Oxford friends, including Hurrell Froude, John Keble, and Edward Pusey, he began to feel intense dissatisfaction with the emotional coldness and the dependence on rationalism of the English Church, and sought to make it more spiritual and at the same time more socially powerful. Before any public movement was launched, however, Newman's health failed, and he was persuaded in the winter of 1832 to make a tour of southern Europe.

In Rome he began, in what has been called "a lyrical interlude between the prose chapters of a working life," his *Lyra Apostolica*, in which he voiced his religious turmoil and his hatred of English Liberalism. He hurried home to take up the battle in behalf of a conservative sacramental form of piety and theology. A great movement in the Church of England, known as the Oxford Movement, was the result. The Movement was launched by a sermon of Keble's in 1833, by a series of ninety *Tracts for the Times* (published at Oxford) of which Newman wrote twenty-nine, and by Newman's sermons at St. Mary's. These sermons, which Matthew Arnold called "religious music," together with Newman's clear and compelling style in his *Tracts* and the magic force of his personality, won sympathy for the cause and deeply affected religious and social ideas in England. Newman came more and more to feel that his ideal in religion, with its emphasis on tradition and on an imagination that transcends reason, could never be satisfied in the English Church. He retired, therefore, from St. Mary's in 1843, and in 1845 he became a Roman Catholic. The last half of Newman's life was less public than the first. He continued to write: from lectures delivered at the short-lived Catholic University of Dublin came, in 1852, his humanistic *Idea of a University;* in answer to an attack made by Charles Kingsley on Catholic ethics came, in 1864, his autobiographic *Apologia pro Vita Sua*. He was made a cardinal in 1879. He lived for the most part in somewhat lonely retirement at his oratory in Edgbaston where he died in 1890.

Newman's principal writings were: *The Arians of the Fourth Century*, 1833; *Lyra Apostolica*, 1834; *Tracts for the Times* (contributions), 1834-1841; *Lectures on the Prophetical Office of the Church*, 1837; *Parochial Sermons*, 1837-1842; *Sermons Bearing on Subjects of the Day*, 1843; *The Idea of a University*, 1852; *Verses on Religious Subjects*, 1853; *Callista*, 1856; *Apologia pro Vita Sua*, 1864; *The Dream of Gerontius*, 1865; *Verses on Various Occasions*, 1868; *Grammar of Assent*, 1870.

INTRODUCTORY CRITICISMS

"Newman was a writer almost by accident. He was essentially a leader of men, an ecclesiastical prince, who used literature as an instrument of his rule. But he was also a mystic and a poet, gifted with literary power of the most winning and magnetic kind. His influence upon pure literature has therefore been great. His medieval cast of mind, his passionate perception of the beauty of the symbolism embodied in the medieval church, united with Ruskin's devotion to medieval art to influence a remarkable group of young painters and poets known as the 'Pre-Raphaelites.' " —Moody and Lovett, *A History of English Literature*, p. 342.

"Both by his moralistic minimizing of himself as a poet, and by his deprecatory view of his own poetry, he [Newman]—some will say unnecessarily—condemned himself to an inferior rank among English poets. . . . A 'tragic chorus' entitled 'The Elements,' . . . bears comparison with one of the great choruses in the *Antigone:* . . . 'The Dream of Gerontius' has a simple, sometimes a severe, beauty which is easily lost on the 'common reader.' To recognize the artistry of the poem one must examine its stanzaic variety, the occasional, almost Miltonic, grandeur of its blank verse, its skillfully managed contrasts, its boldness of imagination. . . . Although the sacrifice of visual effect leads to a loss of interest and tension in the central part of the poem, this loss is retrieved at the end where Newman's own *feeling* creates some of the most moving lyrics in the whole work. Newman realized to what extent he had depended on hearing, and thus proposed that 'Gerontius' might be set to music; those who have heard Sir Edward Elgar's oratorio will know the justness of Newman's suggestion."—Charles Frederick Harrold, *John Henry Newman*, pp. 271-283.

ALFRED, LORD TENNYSON, p. 13

STANDARD EDITIONS

Works, 6 vols., annot. by Alfred, Lord Tennyson, ed. by Hallam, Lord Tennyson, New York, Macmillan, 1908
Poetic and Dramatic Works, 7 vols., Boston, Houghton, 1929
Complete Poetical Works, Cambridge ed., Boston, Houghton, 1947
Poetical Works, Including the Plays, enl. ed., Oxford Standard Authors, London, Oxford Univ. Press, 1954
Works, w. notes by the author, ed. w. a mem. by Hallam, Lord Tennyson, London, Macmillan, 1913
The Poems and the Plays, New York, Modern Lib., 1938
Representative Poems, sel. and ed. by S.C. Chew, New York, Odyssey, 1941
Selected Poems, ed. by Marjorie H. Nicolson, Boston, Houghton, 1924
Selected Poetry, ed. w. an intro. by D. Bush, New York, Modern Lib., 1951
Selections from [His] Poems, sel. and w. an intro. by W.A. Auden, New York, Doubleday, 1944
Poems of Tennyson, ed. by J.H. Buckley, Boston, Houghton Mifflin, 1958
Unpublished Early Poems, ed. by Sir Charles Tennyson, London, Macmillan, 1931
Idylls of the King, ed. w. notes and an intro. by W.H. Wilcox, Philadelphia, Lippincott, 1920
Idylls of the King, ed. w. an intro. by Elizabeth Nitchie, New York, Macmillan, 1928
In Memoriam, The Princess, and Maud, ed. w. intro., coms., and notes, by J.C. Collins, London, Methuen, 1902
The Devil and the Lady, ed. by Sir Charles Tennyson, London, Macmillan, 1930

BIOGRAPHY

Benson, A.C., *Alfred Tennyson*, London, Methuen, 1904
Brookfield, F.A., "Alfred Tennyson," *The Cambridge Apostles*, New York, Scribner, 1906

Faussett, H.I'A., *Tennyson, a Modern Portrait*, London, Selwyn, 1923
Knowles, J., "A Personal Reminiscence of Tennyson," *Nineteenth Century*, 1893, 33: 164-188
Lounsbury, T.R., *The Life and Times of Tennyson*, New Haven, Yale Univ. Press, 1915
Lyall, Sir A.C., *Tennyson*, English Men of Letters Series, New York, Macmillan, 1902
Nicolson, Sir Harold, *Tennyson; Aspects of His Life, Character, and Poetry*, new ed., London, Constable, 1949
Rader, R.W., "Tennyson and Rosa Baring," *Victorian Studies*, 1962, 5:224-260
Rader, R.W., *Tennyson's "Maud": The Biographical Genesis*, Berkeley, Univ. of California Press, 1963
Rawnsley, H.D., *Memories of the Tennysons*, Glasgow, Mac Lehose, 1900
Rawnsley, H.D., "Personal Recollections of Tennyson," *Nineteenth Century*, 1925, 97: 109, 190-196
Richardson, Joanna, *The Pre-Eminent Victorian: A Study of Tennyson*, London, Cape, 1962
Ritchie, Anne T., *Records of Tennyson, Ruskin, and the Brownings*, New York, Harper, 1892
Symonds, J.A., "Recollections of Tennyson," *Century Magazine*, 1893, 46:32-37
Tennyson, Sir Charles, *Alfred Tennyson*, New York, Macmillan, 1949
Tennyson, Sir Charles, "The Somersby Tennysons," *Victorian Studies*, Christmas Supplement, 1963
Tennyson, Hallam, *Alfred, Lord Tennyson; a Memoir by His Son*, 2 vols., New York, Macmillan, 1897
Tennyson, Hallam, *Tennyson and His Friends*, London, Macmillan, 1911
Weld, Agnes G., *Glimpses of Tennyson and of Some of His Relations and Friends*, London, Williams, 1902

CRITICISM

Alford, Henry, "The Idylls of the King," *Contemporary Review*, 1870, 13:104-125
Atkins, G.G., "The Entangled Soul—*Idylls of the King*," "Faith and Doubt—*In Memoriam*," *Reinspecting Victorian Religion*, New York, Macmillan, 1928
Bagehot, W., "Wordsworth, Tennyson, and Browning," *Literary Studies*, 3 vols., London, Longmans, 1895
Baker, A.E., *A Concordance to the Poetical and Dramatic Works of Alfred, Lord Tennyson*, New York, Macmillan, 1914
Baker, A.E., *A Tennyson Dictionary*, New York, Dutton, 1916

Ball, Patricia M., "Tennyson and the Romantics," *Victorian Poetry*, 1963, 1:7-16

Baum, P.F., *Tennyson Sixty Years After*, Chapel Hill, Univ. of N.C. Press, 1948

Benton, R.P., "Tennyson and Lao Tzu," *Philosophy East and West*, 1962, 12:233-240

Bishop, Jonathan, "The Unity of *In Memoriam*," *Victorian Newsletter*, 1962, 21:9-14

Boas, F.S., "*The Idylls of the King* in 1921," *Nineteenth Century*, 1921, 90:819-830

Bowden, Marjorie, *Tennyson in France*, Manchester, Eng., Manchester Univ. Press, 1930

Bradley, A.C., *A Commentary on Tennyson's "In Memoriam,"* London, Macmillan, 1901

Bradley, A.C., *The Reaction Against Tennyson*, English Association Pamphlet No. 39, London, Oxford Univ. Press, 1917

Brooke, S.A., *Tennyson, His Art and Relation to Modern Life*, London, Isbister, 1900

Buckley, Jerome H., *Tennyson: The Growth of a Poet*, Cambridge, Mass., Harvard Univ. Press, 1960

Carr, A.J., "Tennyson as a Modern Poet," *University of Toronto Quarterly*, 1950, 19: 361-382

Chapman, Elizabeth R., *A Companion to "In Memoriam,"* New York, Macmillan, 1888

Chesterton, G.K., "Tennyson," *The Uses of Diversity*, London, Methuen, 1920

Collins, J.C., *Illustrations of Tennyson*, London, Chatto, 1891

Crawford, A.W., "Tennyson's *Maud*," *Canadian Magazine*, 1914, 43:29-36

Cressman, E.D., "Classical Poems of Tennyson," *Classical Journal*, 1928, 24:98-111

Cross, T.P., "Alfred Tennyson as a Celticist," *Modern Philology*, 1921, 18:485-492

DeMott, Benjamin, "The General, the Poet, and the Inquisition," *Kenyon Review*, 1962, 24:442-456

Dixon, J.M., *The Spiritual Meaning of "In Memoriam,"* New York, Abingdon Press, 1920

Dowden, E., "Mr. Tennyson and Mr. Browning," *Studies in Literature*, London, Paul, 1882

Drinkwater, John, "Tennyson's Diction," "Tennyson's Influence," *"The Idylls of the King,"* *Victorian Poetry*, London, Hodder, 1923

Eidson, J.O., *Tennyson in America*, Athens, Univ. of Ga. Press, 1943

Eliot, T.S., "In Memoriam," *Essays, Ancient and Modern*, New York, Harcourt, 1936

Elsdale, H., *Studies on Tennyson's "Idylls of the King,"* London, Paul, 1877

Elton, O., "Tennyson; an Inaugural Lecture," *Modern Studies*, London, Arnold, 1907

Faguet, E., "Centenary of Tennyson," *Quarterly Review*, 1909, 210:305-328

Franklin, H.C.T., "Tennyson as a Sea-Poet," *Temple Bar*, 1902, 125:185-191

Gatty, A., *A Key to Tennyson's "In Memoriam,"* London, Bell, 1905

Genung, J.F., *Tennyson's "In Memoriam"; Its Purpose and Its Structure*, Boston, Houghton, 1884

Gibson, Walker, "Behind the Veil: A Distinction between Poetic and Scientific Language in Tennyson, Lyell, and Darwin," *Victorian Studies*, 1958, 2:60-68

Gladstone, W.E., "Tennyson," *Gleanings of Past Years, 1843-1878*, 7 vols., New York, Scribner, 1879

Gordon, W.C., *The Social Ideals of Alfred Tennyson as Related to His Time*, Chicago, Univ. of Chicago Press, 1906

Gosse, E., "Tennyson—and After," *Questions at Issue*, London, Heinemann, 1893

Granville-Barker, H., "Some Victorians Afield: the Poet as Dramatist," *Fortnightly Review*, 1929, 131:655-672

Grendon, F., "Influence of Keats upon the Early Poems of Tennyson," *Sewanee Review*, 1907, 15:285-296

Grierson, H.J., "The Tennysons," *Cambridge History of English Literature*, Vol. 13, Ch. 2, New York, Putnam, 1908

Groom, B., *On the Diction of Tennyson, Browning and Arnold*, New York, Oxford Univ. Press, 1939

Gwynn, S.L., *Tennyson; a Critical Study*, London, Blackie, 1899

Hallam, A.H., "On Some Characteristics of Modern Poetry and on the Lyrical Poems of Alfred Tennyson," *Literary Remains*, Boston, Ticknor, 1863

Harrison, F., "Tennyson," *Tennyson, Ruskin, Mill, and Other Literary Estimates*, New York, Macmillan, 1900

Henley, W.E., "Tennyson," *Views and Reviews*, London, Macmillan, 1921

Hutton, R.H., "Newman and Tennyson," "Browning and Tennyson," *Brief Literary Criticisms*, London, Macmillan, 1906

Hutton, R.H., "Tennyson," *Literary Essays*, London, Macmillan, 1892

James, H., "Tennyson's Drama," *Views and Reviews*, Boston, Ball, 1908

Japikse, Cornelia G., *The Dramas of Alfred, Lord Tennyson*, London, Macmillan, 1926

Johnson, E.D.H., *Alien Vision of Victorian Poetry*, Princeton, N.J., Princeton Univ. Press, 1952

Johnson, E.D.H., "*In Memoriam:* The Way of the Poet," *Victorian Studies*, 1958, 2:139-148

Johnson, E.D.H., "The Lily and the Rose: Symbolic Meaning in Tennyson's *Maud*," *PMLA*, 1949, 64:1222-1227

Jones, H., *The Immortality of the Soul in the Poems of Tennyson and Browning*, Boston, Am. Unitar., 1907

Jones, R., *The Growth of "The Idylls of the King,"* Philadelphia, Lippincott, 1895

Killham, John, ed., *Critical Essays on the Poetry of Tennyson*, London, Routledge & Kegan Paul, 1960

Killham, John, *Tennyson and "The Princess": Reflections of an Age*, London, Athlone Press, 1958

Layard, G.S., *Tennyson and His Pre-Raphaelite Illustrators*, London, Stock, 1894

Littledale, H., Essays on Lord Tennyson's *"Idylls of the King,"* London, Macmillan, 1907

Lockhart, J.G., "Tennyson's Poems," *Quarterly Review*, 1833, 49:81-96. Adverse criticism of the 1832 volume

Lockyer, N., and W.L., *Tennyson as a Student and Poet of Nature*, London, Macmillan, 1910

Luce, M., *A Handbook to the Works of Alfred, Lord Tennyson*, London, Bell, 1908

MacCallum, M.W., *Tennyson's "Idylls of the King" and Arthurian Story from the Sixteenth Century*, Glasgow, Mac Lehose, 1894

Mackail, J.W., "Theocritus and Tennyson," *Lectures on Greek Poetry*, London, Longmans, 1910

Mackie, A., "Tennyson as Botanist, Entomologist, Ornithologist, Geologist," *Nature Knowledge in Modern Poets*, London, Longmans, 1906

Marshall, George O., *A Tennyson Handbook*, New York, Twayne, 1964

Masterman, C.F.G., *Tennyson as a Religious Teacher*, London, Methuen, 1900

Mattes, E.B., *In Memoriam: the Way of a Soul*, New York, Exposition Press, 1951

Maynadier, G.H., *The Author of the English Poets*, Boston, Houghton, 1907

Metzger, Lore, "The Eternal Process: Parallels between Goethe's *Faust* and *In Memoriam*," *Victorian Poetry*, 1963, 1-189-196

Meynell, Alice C., "Some Thoughts of a Reader of Tennyson," *Hearts of Controversy*, London, Burns, 1918

Mill, J.S., "Tennyson's Poems," *Early Essays*, London, Bell, 1897

Miller, Betty, "Tennyson and the Sinful Queen," *Twentieth Century*, 1955, 158:355-363

Moore, Carlisle, "Faith, Doubt, and Mystical Experience in *In Memoriam*," *Victorian Studies*, 1963 7:155-169

More, P.E., "Tennyson, Poet of National Life," *Shelburne Essays*, 7th s., New York, Putnam, 1910

Mustard, W.P., *Classical Echoes in Tennyson*, New York, Macmillan, 1904

Myers, F.W.H., "Tennyson as a Prophet," *Science and a Future Life*, London, Macmillan, 1893

Nicoll, W.R. and T.J. Wise, "The Building of the *Idylls*," *Literary Anecdotes of the Nineteenth Century*, New York, Dodd, 1895-1896

Nitchie, E., "Tennyson and the Victorians," *Vergil and the English Poets*, New York, Columbia Univ. Press, 1919

Noyes, A., "Tennyson and Some Recent Critics," *Some Aspects of Modern Poetry*, London, Hodder, 1924

Paden, W.D., *Tennyson in Egypt*, Lawrence, Univ. of Kan., 1942

Palgrave, F.T., "The Landscape of Alfred, Lord Tennyson," *Landscape in Poetry*, London, Macmillan, 1897

Pettigrew, John, "Tennyson's 'Ulysses': A Reconciliation of Opposites," *Victorian Poetry*, 1963, 1:27-45

Pitt, Valerie, *Tennyson Laureate*, London, Barrie & Rockliff, 1962

Priestley, F.E.L., "Tennyson's Idylls," *Univ. of Toronto Quarterly*, 1949, 19:35-49

Pyre, J.F.A., *The Formation of Tennyson's Style*, Madison, Univ. of Wisconsin Studies, No. 12, 1921

Rader, W., *The Elegy of Faith; a Study of Alfred Tennyson's "In Memoriam,"* New York, Crowell, 1902

Rhys, John, *Studies in the Arthurian Legend*, London, Oxford Univ. Press, 1891

Robinson, Edna M., *Tennyson's Use of the Bible*, Baltimore, Furst, 1917

Roppen, Georg, " 'Ulysses' and Tennyson's Sea-Quest," *English Studies*, 1959, 40:77-90

Rosenberg, John D., "The Two Kingdoms of *In Memoriam*," *Journal of English and Germanic Philology*, 1959, 8:228-240

Royce, J., "Tennyson and Pessimism," *Studies of Good and Evil*, New York, Appleton, 1898

Ryals, Clyde de L., *Theme and Symbol in Tennyson's Poems to 1850*, Philadelphia, University of Pennsylvania Press, 1964

Saintsbury, G., "Tennyson," *Corrected Impressions*, New York, Dodd, 1895. In *Collected Essays and Papers*, 4 vols., New York, Dutton, 1923–1924

Salt, H.S., *Tennyson as a Thinker*, London, Fifield, 1909

Sanders, Charles R., "Carlyle and Tennyson," *PMLA*, 1961, 76:82-97

Scaife, C.H.O., *The Poetry of Alfred Tennyson*, London, Cobden-Sanderson, 1930

Shanks, E., "The Return of Tennyson," *Second Essays in Literature*, London, Collins, 1927

Shannon, E.F., *Tennyson and the Reviewers*, Cambridge, Mass., Harvard Univ. Press, 1952

Shepherd, H.E., *A Commentary upon Tennyson's "In Memoriam,"* New York, Neale, 1908

Sneath, E.H., *The Mind of Tennyson*, New York, Scribner, 1900

Spedding, J., "Tennyson's Poems," *Reviews and Discussions*, London, Paul, 1879

Stange, G.R., "Tennyson's Garden of Art: a Study of 'The Hesperides,' " *PMLA*, 1952, 67:732-743

Stange, G.R., "Tennyson's Mythology: a Study of 'Demeter and Persephone,' " *ELH*, 1954, 21:67-80

Starnes, D.W.T., "The Influence of Carlyle upon Tennyson," *Texas Review*, 1921, 6: 316-336

Stedman, E.C., "Alfred Tennyson," "Tennyson and Theocritus," *Victorian Poets*, Boston, Houghton, 1887

Steffen, P., *Die Alliteration bei Tennyson*, Kiel, Fiencke, 1905

Sterling, J., "Tennyson's Poems," *Essays and Tales*, 2 vols., London, Parker, 1848

Svaglic, Martin J., "A Framework for Tennyson's *In Memoriam*," *Journal of English and Germanic Philology*, 1962, 61:810-825

Swinburne, A.C., "Tennyson and Musset," *Miscellanies*, London, Chatto, 1886

Swinburne, A.C., *Under the Microscope*, in *Complete Works*, 20 vols., London, Heinemann, 1925-1927

Tennyson, Sir Charles, *Six Tennyson Essays*, London, Cassell, 1954

Thomas, G., "Tennyson and the Georgians," *London Quarterly Review*, 1923, 140: 45-55

Thomson, J.C., "Suppressed Poems of Tennyson," *Harper's Magazine*, 1903, 108: 70-74

Traill, D.H., "Aspects of Tennyson," *Nineteenth Century*, 1892, 32:952-966

Turner, Paul, "Some Ancient Light on Tennyson's *Oenone*," *Journal of English and Germanic Philology*, 1962, 61:52-72

Van Dyke, H., *Studies in Tennyson*, New York, Scribner, 1921

Ward, W., "Tennyson's Religious Poetry," *Dublin Review*, 1909, 145:306-322

Watkins, W., *The Birds of Tennyson*, London, Porter, 1903

Watson, A., *Tennyson*, London, Jack, 1913

Watts-Dunton, T., "Tennyson as a Nature Poet," *Nineteenth Century*, 1893, 33:836-856

Weatherhead, L.D., "Tennyson's After-world," *London Quarterly Review*, 1925, 144:157-174

Whitman, W., "A Word about Tennyson," *Rivulets of Prose*, New York, Greenberg Publishers, 1928

Wilmot, Mabel E., *Idylls of the King*, New York, Globe Bk., 1921

Wilson, John (Christopher North, pseud.), "Tennyson's Poems," *Essays, Critical and Imaginative*, 4 vols., Edinburgh, Blackwood, 1856-1857

Wise, T.J., *A Bibliography of the Writings of Alfred, Lord Tennyson*, 2 vols., London, Clay, 1908

BIOGRAPHICAL SKETCH

The first period of Alfred Tennyson's life (1809-1892), from his birth in 1809 in the quiet rectory of Somersby, in Lincolnshire, to the death of his father in 1831, was sheltered from the storms of the outside world, yet troubled by the tensions of a close and passionate family. His natural taste for poetry developed early in the cultured environment of his home. He wrote lyrics at five, and at eight, blank verse in the manner of Thomson's *Seasons;* he imitated Scott and Moore, and at the death of Byron in 1824 he "thought everything was over and finished for everyone—that nothing else mattered." With his brother Charles he published a volume entitled *Poems by Two Brothers* in 1827 that clearly shows the influence of his first poetic masters. After entering Trinity College, Cambridge, in 1828, he shifted his allegiance to Wordsworth, Coleridge, Shelley, and Keats, and wrote poems that were extravagantly admired by his circle of college friends. Most of these friends, including Arthur Henry Hallam, belonged to a club called "The Apostles," which met periodically to discuss the problems of religion, ethics, and science that were then beginning to trouble society. The members of the club looked up to the handsome and romantic Tennyson as their poet-prophet.

He was hence somewhat spoiled by praise when, after 1831, his life became less easy. His father's death brought new responsibilities. The public reception of *Poems, Chiefly Lyrical* (1830) and of the 1832 volume of *Poems*, despite the inclusion of *The Palace of Art*, *The Lotos-Eaters*, and *The Lady of Shalott*, was cool; and Tennyson, always unusually sensitive to adverse criticism, was hurt by vitriolic reviews that appeared in *Blackwood's Magazine* and the *Quarterly Review*. Another blow came in 1833 with the death of Hallam in Vienna, a sudden end to an unusually intimate friendship. Tennyson suffered also from the want of money and was forced to postpone indefinitely his marriage with Emily Sellwood, to whom he became engaged in 1836.

In meeting these reverses Tennyson showed what Carlyle later called "a right valiant, true-fighting, victorious heart; strong as a lion's, yet gentle, loving, and full of music." He consoled himself for Hallam's death by beginning the long series of elegies that were brought together in 1850 as *In Memoriam A. H. H.* He resolutely set about perfecting himself in the art of poetry; for ten years he wrote almost continuously, revising again and again both his new work and that which had already been published, until he made himself an expert craftsman in verse. Finally, in 1842, he published his popular *Poems* and at once had his reward; the volume was well received by the general public. Eased of his financial burden in 1845 by a government pension of £200 a year and heartened by the great success of *In Memoriam*, in 1850 he married Emily Sellwood. In the same year he was appointed to succeed Wordsworth as poet laureate, and from that date until his death he remained the official poetic voice of Victorian England.

In order to indulge his love for retirement, for being alone with his moods, he purchased in 1853 the estate of Farringford on the Isle of Wight; there he lived quietly, working in his garden, tramping across the moors, writing poetry, or talking with a few intimates amid clouds of tobacco smoke in a tiny room at the top of the house. He also kept up his Latin and Greek and his early habit of reading by which he continued to inform himself of new discoveries in the physical sciences; his wide reading during his life included not only English poetry but French, German, and Italian poetry as well. Meanwhile he had written the *Ode on the Death of the Duke of Wellington* (1852), the popular *The Charge of the Light Brigade* (1854), and a series of dramatic monologues and lyrics entitled *Maud* (1855). A journey to Wales, where he visited the spots associated with the Arthurian legends, reawakened his interest in the theme that had fascinated him from boyhood and which had furnished material for *The Lady of Shalott* (1832), *Morte d'Arthur* (1842), and other early poems. This enthusiasm resulted in 1859 in the publication of the first group of *The Idylls of the King*, to be followed by others in 1869 and 1872, with the entire group rearranged and published as a complete series in 1888. In 1864 appeared the *Enoch Arden* volume containing the *Northern Farmer*, the first of his humorous pieces in dialect. In 1868 Tennyson built Aldworth, a Gothic structure in Surrey,

near the Sussex border, which thereafter served as an alternate home with Farringford. In 1875 he began a series of poetic dramas, the most important of which were *Queen Mary* (1875), *Harold* (1876), and *Becket* (1884), constituting a "trilogy of English history."

More honors, which did little to disturb the essential simplicity of his character, came with advancing years. His elevation to the peerage, which he was prevailed upon to accept in 1884, only "for the sake of literature," was a tribute not only from the queen but also from all English-speaking peoples to a poet whom they regarded also as a prophet, a great ethical teacher. His writing continued, almost undiminished in excellence. After *Tiresias and Other Poems* (1885) came the vigorous *Locksley Hall Sixty Years After* (1886), his literary autobiography, *Merlin and the Gleam* (1889), and *Crossing the Bar* (1889), which by his wish stands last in all editions of his collected works. In 1892 he died peacefully at Aldworth and was buried in Westminster Abbey beside Robert Browning.

Tennyson's principal publications were: *Poems by Two Brothers*, 1827; *Poems, Chiefly Lyrical*, 1830; *Poems*, 1832; *Poems*, 1842; *The Princess*, 1847; *In Memoriam*, 1850; *Ode on the Death of the Duke of Wellington*, 1852; *Maud, and Other Poems*, 1855; *Idylls of the King* (*Enid, Vivien, Elaine, Guinevere*), 1859; *Enoch Arden and Other Poems*, 1864; *The Holy Grail, and Other Poems* (*The Coming of Arthur, The Holy Grail, Pelleas and Ettarre, The Passing of Arthur*), 1869; *Gareth and Lynette*, etc., 1872; *Queen Mary*, 1875; *Harold*, 1876; *Ballads, and Other Poems*, 1880; *Becket*, 1884; *Tiresias, and Other Poems*, 1885; *Locksley Hall Sixty Years After*, 1886; *Demeter, and Other Poems*, 1889; *The Death of Œnone, Akbar's Dream, and Other Poems*, 1892.

INTRODUCTORY CRITICISMS

"Tennyson more than any other writer of his day interpreted the Victorian Age to itself. It was an age of rapid change and palpable transition. Political revolutions, social upheavals, moral rebellions, intellectual insurrections, religious revolts, were transforming the old and stable world into a chaos whence a new order could not, by many anxious watchers, be seen to emerge. Tennyson was keenly sensitive to the movements of the time. He took an absorbed interest in current politics; he sympathized with social reform; he kept in close touch with the new science; and, in particular, seized with quick comprehension and eager welcome the novel and (at first appearance) disquieting doctrine of evolution; he was profoundly religious, and he recognized the necessity, both for himself and for his generation, of reconciling if possible the new knowledge with the old faith. He first convinced himself and then he showed his fellows—in poems such as *In Memoriam, The Ancient Sage, Silent Voices,* and *Crossing the Bar*—how the perplexities of the moment could be resolved, and how the essentials of the ancient creeds could be restated in terms of the most modern science. He made it clear to many doubtful and troubled minds that, in spite of the triumphs of naturalism, it was still possible, and indeed necessary, to hold fast to faith in human freedom, in Divine immanence, and in personal immortality. He based his convictions ... not on external evidences which criticism can question or skepticism assail, but on intuitions and revelations peculiar to the patient and expectant soul ... It was because he *felt* so accurately the perplexities of the age, and because he wrestled with them faithfully and resolved them hopefully, that he made so strong an appeal to the conservative culture of his generation."—F. J. C. Hearnshaw, *Spectator,* Oct. 6, 1917, p. 352.

"It is the perfection of his artistry which is, for our age even more than for his own, the enduring grandeur of Tennyson. No modern poet has labored more truly on his work or believed more sincerely in the greatness of his art or has striven more nobly for perfection than did Tennyson. The writing of poetry was to him not a mere exercise, nor, on the other hand, the result of fine fervor; it was a vocation in which he toiled as laboriously as any worker in metals or precious gems. The whirligig of time has brought in its revenges so far as his position as the voice of the English people is concerned; but if we have lost the old worship of the prophet, we have gained a new understanding and admiration of the artist. 'The labor of the file' was Tennyson's labor. At his worst, we can bring no charge against him more serious than sentimentality, a comfortable conservatism, a too-easy faith; at his best he is one of the greatest glories of the English tongue."—Marjorie H. Nicolson, Introduction to *Selected Poems,* pp. 20-21.

"Whatever he sets out to do, he succeeds in doing, ... He had the finest ear of any English poet since Milton.... *Maud* and *In Memoriam* are each a series of poems, given form by the greatest lyrical resourcefulness that a poet has ever shown.... Tennyson is the great master of metric as well as of melancholia; ... the saddest of all English poets, among the Great in Limbo, the most

instinctive rebel against the society in which he was the most perfect conformist."—T. S. Eliot, *Essays Ancient and Modern,* pp. 175-189.

CRITICAL NOTES

THE POET, p. 16

This poem expresses Tennyson's early ideas concerning his life mission. Later he would not have desired rites and forms to melt "before his eyes," because he came to regard them as necessary and felt that they should be modified or superseded very slowly. Cf. *You Ask Me, Why,* p. 37; *Of Old Sat Freedom,* p. 37; *Love Thou Thy Land,* p. 38; *In Memoriam,* 33, p. 57; and *Freedom,* p. 166.

THE LADY OF SHALOTT, p. 17

This is Tennyson's first published poem on an Arthurian subject. The source of the poem is an Italian romance, *Donna di Scalotta* (Lady of Scalott). Tennyson says that he substituted *Shalott* for *Scalott* because of the softer sound. The word is the same as *Astolat,* the name of the heroine's home in Malory's version of the story in *Morte Darthur,* which was Tennyson's source for the idyll *Lancelot and Elaine* (p. 123). Tennyson stated that the key to the symbolical meaning of *The Lady of Shalott* is found in the closing lines of Part 2: "The new-born love for something, for someone in the wide world from which she has been so long excluded, takes her out of the region of shadows into that of realities." The poem was first published in 1832; it was virtually rewritten in 1842 with many modifications and improvements and with great gain in poetic dignity. The wealth of sensuous beauty in the poem suggests Keats.

ŒNONE, p. 20

The story of Œnone is found in Ovid, Euripides, and other classical writers. But though the poem is classical in theme and outline, it is modern in sentiment; the speech of Pallas (ll. 142 ff.) expresses Tennyson's own philosophy of life. The descriptions of scenery in the poem belong to the Pyrenees Mountains, visited by Tennyson in 1830, rather than to Mt. Ida. Part of *Œnone* was written in the valley of Cauteretz, in the Pyrenees.

THE PALACE OF ART, p. 24

This poem is an allegory embodying the poet's belief that "the Godlike life is with man and for man." Though it was written under the influence of the Cambridge Apostles, Tennyson from the beginning had high ethical impulses and was always concerned with questions involving the conduct of life. Like Wordsworth he wished "to be regarded as a teacher or as nothing." The poem teaches that qualities of mind and heart, noble in themselves, become ignoble unless they are shared with others.

The poem contains a series of notable descriptions, each one conceived as a finished picture—clear and distinct, and yet rich and suggestive.

LADY CLARA VERE DE VERE, p. 27

This poem illustrates a curious obsession of Tennyson—a sentimental interest in a poor youth who loves above his station and fortune. The expression of current democratic sympathies won instant popularity for the piece, although in politics Tennyson was a conservative in the tradition of Edmund Burke and Coleridge. Cf. *You Ask Me, Why*, p. 37.

THE LOTOS-EATERS, p. 28

The lotos-eaters were a people who lived on the flowery fruit of the lotos tree, which produced forgetfulness of home. The poem is based upon a brief passage in Book 9 of Homer's *Odyssey*, which tells how Ulysses and his mariners came to the land of the lotos-eaters and how Ulysses escaped by binding his men to the boats. The underlying theme of the poem is similar to that of *The Palace of Art*, p. 24.

YOU ASK ME, WHY, THOUGH ILL AT EASE, p. 37

This poem and the two following poems show Tennyson's interest in contemporary political and social questions. Being conservative, the poet had little sympathy with radical reforms, at home or abroad, especially those which were promoted by overzealous factions and seemed to threaten the nice balance of constitutional government.

Aubrey de Vere states that the first two poems were probably suggested by some popular demonstration connected with the rejection of the Reform Bill of 1832 by the House of Lords. (See *Memoir*, I, 506.)

MORTE D'ARTHUR, p. 39

This poem was written and published before Tennyson had conceived the plan for *The Idylls of the King*. It is pure narrative, without allegorical intent. It was later incorporated, with additions, in *The Passing of Arthur*, the last of *The Idylls*. The source of the poem is Sir Thomas Malory's *Morte Darthur*, Book 21.

W. S. Landor, who saw the poem in 1837, said, "It is more Homeric than any poem of our time, and rivals some of the noblest parts of the Odyssea."

For a full statement regarding *The Idylls of the King*, see pp. 955–958.

ULYSSES, p. 43

Ulysses is the hero of Homer's *Odyssey*, but Tennyson's poem is based upon a passage in Canto 26 of Dante's *Inferno*, in which Ulysses tells Dante and Virgil how he had set out from Circe's island, driven by an ardor to gain experience of the world, with one vessel only and a small group of loyal companions. They were old and slow when they came to the Straits of Gibraltar, in ancient imaginings the strait that marked the limit of the world, beyond which none might go. "O brothers," said Ulysses to his mariners, "who through a thousand perils have reached the West, to this so little vigil of your senses that remains be ye unwilling to deny the experience, following the sun, of the world that hath no people. Consider ye your origin; ye were not made to live as brutes, but for pursuit of virtue and knowledge." Unlike Dante, however, Tennyson has Ulysses start from his home in Ithaca.

Tennyson said that the poem was written soon after the death of his friend Arthur Hallam and gave expression to the poet's need of "going forward and braving the struggle of life perhaps more simply than anything in *In Memoriam*" (*Memoir*, I, 196).

Critics have been generous in their praise of this poem, emphasis being placed especially upon its dignity and nobility of conception, its beauty and power of expression, and its imaginative fervor. The reading of this poem and of *Locksley Hall* is said to have led Sir Robert Peel to give Tennyson a pension in 1845.

Compare Hotspur's four famous lines in Shakespeare's *Henry IV*, Part One, V, 2, 82 ff.—

O gentlemen, the time of life is short!
To spend that shortness basely were too long,
If life did ride upon a dial's point,
Still ending at the arrival of an hour.

LOCKSLEY HALL, p. 45

The speaker in this poem is a young man whose love has been denied by a woman of superior fortune. Despite his spleen and bombast, he makes knowing allusions to recent discoveries in astronomy and electricity and to current social problems. In the sequel, *Locksley Hall Sixty Years After*, the same character appears as an old man whose experience has mellowed his outlook upon life and at the same time has given him a disillusioned view of the present to supplant his vague dreams of future progress.

SIR GALAHAD, p. 50

Galahad, the son of Lancelot and Elaine (the daughter of King Pelleas, not the maid of Astolat), takes the place of Percivale in the later legends of the quest for the Holy Grail. The Grail, originally a magic vessel of Celtic mythology, became, under the influence of the church, the cup from which Christ drank at the Last Supper, and in which Christ's blood was caught by Joseph of Arimathea at the Crucifixion. The cup was supposed to have been brought to Glastonbury, England, by Joseph. It was visible only to the pure in heart and vanished when approached by any other. In medieval romances the finding of the Grail was the great aim of many knights, but Sir Galahad was the only one who achieved the quest. For various accounts of the quest, see Tennyson's *The Holy Grail*, p. 140. Sir Galahad is here portrayed as a mystic, the counterpart of the nun in *Saint Agnes' Eve*, p. 37.

Page 51, lines 69-72. This passage describes an experience familiar to Tennyson himself, one which he calls "a kind of waking trance, I have frequently had, quite up from boyhood, when I have been all alone" (*Memoir*, I, 320). In *The Holy Grail*, 907-915 (p. 150), the experience is transferred to King Arthur. Cf. *In Memoriam*, 95, p. 80.

THE VISION OF SIN, p. 51

This poem presents two contrasted revels: the first, a drunken orgy in a palace; the second, a senile debauch in a ruined inn. Since the youth is riding a winged horse (Pegasus), he seems to represent the typical poet. The poem accordingly is related in theme to *The Palace of Art*.

THE PRINCESS, p. 54

The Princess, first published in 1847, is a half-serious, half-burlesque narrative poem. It tells the story of a princess who founded a college for the purpose of emancipating woman by educating her in complete isolation from man. The prince and two of his companions disguise themselves as girls and gain admission to the college, but they are finally discovered and ejected. The father of the prince prepares to attack the college with an army, and warriors rush to the defense of the princess and her maidens. A combat is arranged between fifty followers of each side, and the prince is defeated. Finally the princess is overcome with sympathy for the wounded prince and gives up her purpose, and marries him.

The poem asserts the supremacy of normal human affections over any arbitrary or mechanical scheme to suppress them. By implication, Princess Ida stands for the art-for-art's-sake artist in retreat from life, like the Soul in *The Palace of Art*. Ida's thwarted sympathies, however, are awakened by a child whom she holds in her arms during the tournament and who links her with true womanhood. It was to bring the child still more into prominence that additional songs were inserted between the parts of the poem in the edition of 1850. Of this latter group Tennyson wrote to S. E. Dawson in 1882: "I may tell you that the songs were not an afterthought. Before the first edition came out, I deliberated with myself whether I should put songs in between the separate divisions of the poem; again I thought the poem will explain itself; but the public did not see that the child, as you say, was the heroine of the piece, and at last I conquered my laziness and inserted them." In the poem the songs appear without titles.

The following songs appeared in the original edition: *Tears, Idle Tears; O Swallow, Swallow; Now Sleeps the Crimson Petal;* and *Come Down, O Maid.*

TEARS, IDLE TEARS, p. 55

Tennyson told James Knowles that this song was written at Tintern Abbey "when the woods were all yellowing with autumn seen through the ruined windows. It is what I have always felt even from a boy, and what as a boy I called the 'passion of the past.' And so it is always with me now; it is the distance that charms me in the landscape, the picture and the past, and not the immediate today in which I move."—*Nineteenth Century*, January 1893.

IN MEMORIAM, p. 57

This poem was written in memory of Tennyson's dearest friend, Arthur Henry Hallam, the gifted son of the famous historian Henry Hallam. Arthur Hallam was born in London, February 1, 1811. He became acquainted with Tennyson at Trinity College,

Cambridge, in 1828, where they belonged to the same club—The Apostles—and the two promising youths soon became devoted friends. They made summer trips together— to the Pyrenees in 1830 and down the Rhine in 1832. The intimacy increased when Hallam became engaged to Tennyson's sister Emily. After graduation Hallam began the study of law with his father in London. He visited the Continent in August 1833 and died suddenly in Vienna on September 15. His body was taken to England and was buried on January 3, 1834 in the chancel of Clevedon Church in Somersetshire.

The main action of the poem covers less than five years, beginning with the death of Hallam in the fall of 1833 and extending into the spring of 1838, but the "Epilogue" concerns the wedding of Tennyson's sister Cecilia in 1842. The lyrics, written without any view of being woven into a whole, were composed over a period of seventeen years and reveal various degrees of sorrow and various attitudes toward life, death, and immortality. The opening section, which stresses Tennyson's final conviction that faith alone can uncover the eternal purpose of God and solve the problem of immortality, was written last.

Tennyson said of the poem: "It must be remembered that this is a poem, *not* an actual biography . . . It was meant to be a kind of *Divina Commedia*, ending with happiness . . . The different moods of sorrow as in a drama are dramatically given, and my conviction that fear, doubts, and suffering will find answer and relief only through Faith in a God of Love. *I* is not always the author speaking of himself, but the voice of the human race speaking through him" (*Memoir*, I, 304-305).

The stanza form, which Tennyson at first believed was his own invention, was used in the Elizabethan period by Sidney, Jonson, and others, and by a number of later poets. Tennyson had used it before in *Love Thou Thy Land*, p. 38, and in other poems.

The main divisions of the poem are marked by the three Christmas sections—28, 78, and 104. Tennyson suggested nine groups of the sections as follows: 1-8, 9-20; 21-27; 28-49; 50-58; 59-71; 72-98; 99-103; 104-131. The turning point in the poem, where sorrow gives way to acceptance, may be placed at section 85.

In Memoriam should be compared with Milton's *Lycidas*, Shelley's *Adonais*, and Arnold's *Thyrsis*, p. 493.

"*In Memoriam* is the whole poem. It is unique: it is a long poem made by putting together lyrics, which have only the unity and continuity of a diary, the concentrated diary of a man confessing himself. It is a diary of which we have to read every word." —T. S. Eliot, *Essays Ancient and Modern*, p. 183.

MAUD, p. 96

Maud was Tennyson's favorite poem for reading aloud. He said of it: "This poem is a little *Hamlet*, the history of a morbid poetic soul, under the blighting influence of a recklessly speculative age. He is the heir of madness, an egotist with the makings of a cynic, raised to sanity by a pure and holy love which elevates his whole nature, passing from the height of triumph to the lowest depth of misery, driven into madness by the loss of her whom he has loved, and, when he has at length passed through the fiery furnace, and has recovered his reason, giving himself up to work for the good of mankind through the unselfishness born of his great passion . . . The peculiarity of this poem is that different phases of passion in one person take the place of different characters" (*Memoir*, I, 396).

"As a masterpiece of rhythm," writes J. C. Collins, the poem "must rank among the wonders of art"; but it was greeted with hostile criticism by many of Tennyson's contemporaries, and some later critics have regarded it as a "splendid failure."

Page 110, Part Two, Section IV. Tennyson regarded this lyric as "the most touching of his works," and Swinburne called it "the poem of deepest charm and fullest delight of pathos and melody ever written by Mr. Tennyson." A version of this section first appeared as "Stanzas" in a volume entitled *The Tribute,* published in 1837. It has been stated that *Maud* grew out of a suggestion of Sir John Simeon regarding this early poem— that to make it fully intelligible a preceding poem was necessary (*Memoir*, I, 379). See note on *In the Garden at Swainston*, p. 123.

MILTON, p. 114

Tennyson considered Milton superior to Virgil as a stylist and said that there was nothing in English to equal the splendor of his finest passages. This poem is one of a group which Tennyson called "experiments in quantity." It imitates, as far as can be done in English, a classical form of prosody invented by Alcaeus, a Greek lyric poet of 600 B.C., and used by Horace and other ancient poets. In English prosody, a four-line strophe of one form of Alcaics may be scanned thus—

```
∪ — ∪ — ⌣ ‖ — ∪∪ —∪∪
∪ — ∪ — ⌣ ‖ —∪∪ —∪∪
∪ — ∪ — ‖ ∪ — —∪ — ∪
—∪∪ —∪∪‖ — ∪ — ∪
```

THE HIGHER PANTHEISM, p. 122

Pantheism identifies the universe, taken as a whole, with God; it asserts that the combined forces and laws manifested in the universe are God. The poem expresses what Tennyson regards as a higher truth than this doctrine; it declares that God lives in the world but transcends it; that men have their being in him but that the human spirit is consciously distinct from the Divine Spirit.

Hallam Tennyson writes of his father: "He said again to us with deep feeling in January 1869: 'Yes, it is true that there are moments when the flesh is nothing to me, when I feel and know the flesh to be the vision, God and the Spiritual the only real and true. Depend upon it, the Spiritual *is* the real; it belongs to one more than the hand and the foot. You may tell me that my hand and my foot are only imaginary symbols of my existence, I could believe you; but you never, never can convince me that the *I* is not an eternal Reality, and that the Spiritual is not the true and real part of me'" (*Memoir*, II, 90).

THE IDYLLS OF THE KING, p. 123

The Idylls of the King consists of twelve narratives that deal with the history of King Arthur and the Knights of the Round Table.

The first important treatment of Arthur appears in Geoffrey of Monmouth's *Historia Regum Britanniæ* (1147), which purports to tell the story of the British kings from the founding of Britain to the year 689. Arthur there appears as the great chieftain who defended his country against the invading Saxons. Geoffrey's work became a storehouse for other writers, who made the material widely known. Of the medieval poets who treated the Arthur story, Layamon (*c.* 1200) was the first to make Arthur the hero of the English, as distinct from the Welsh, people; he also gave for the first time a full account of the founding of the Round Table and of the death of Arthur. In the fifteenth century Sir Thomas Malory selected material from various earlier sources and produced a complete history of the Knights of the Round Table from the birth of Arthur to his last great battle and death. He made Arthur the great central figure of a unified narrative, and his *Morte Darthur* became at once the great treasury of Arthurian romance.

When he was a mere boy, Tennyson happened upon Malory's book, and he at once became interested in the Arthurian legend. In 1832 he published *The Lady of Shalott* (p. 17), his first Arthurian poem. Other early poems dealing with the material were *Morte d'Arthur* (p. 39), *Sir Lancelot and Queen Guinevere*, and *Sir Galahad* (p. 50).

The material for all but two of the idylls was gained from Malory's *Morte Darthur*, published in 1485. For *The Marriage of Geraint* and *Geraint and Enid* Tennyson used *The Mabinogion*, a collection of old Welsh tales translated by Lady Charlotte Guest and published in 1838-1849. Tennyson made many changes in his material to suit his allegorical or symbolic intent and unified it around the rise and fall of the Round Table. He deliberately "moralized" his materials so that his work as a whole became a study in social ethics, the record of a culture which is ultimately betrayed by what is false within.

Although the writing of *The Idylls* was not completed until 1885, as early as 1835 Tennyson projected a possible allegorical scheme for the story of Arthur. In the final section, *To the Queen* (p. 160), he states that the poems constitute an

> . . . old imperfect tale,
> New-old, and shadowing Sense at war with Soul.

The progress of the twelve idylls (as arranged in their final order in 1888) corresponds to the course of the months and seasons of the year, from the coming of Guinevere in the spring, through the knightly successes of summer, to the last tournament in autumn, and to Arthur's last battle in December.

Following is a list of the poems in their final order, and the dates of their original publication:

SUMMARY OF THE IDYLLS OF THE KING

The Coming of Arthur

The Coming of Arthur relates how Arthur, son of Uther, legendary king of the Britons, wooed the princess Guinevere (daughter of Leodogran, king of Cameliard) and won her as his wife. Indirectly we are also told how Arthur was secretly reared by the wizard Merlin, how at a strategic moment Merlin set him on Uther's throne and proclaimed him king, and how Arthur had dedicated himself to the high purpose of making chaotic Britain a coherent and law-abiding nation. For this end he had gathered about him his Round Table, a body of knights exemplifying the finest qualities of chivalry. Chief among them was the great Lancelot, Arthur's friend; it was he whom Arthur sent to escort Guinevere from her home in Cameliard to Camelot for the marriage. At the close of the idyll, the reign of law in Britain has well begun; yet in the background lurks the figure of Modred, Arthur's traitorous nephew, from the beginning intent on working harm.

In the four subsequent tales, the Round Table is at the peak of its achievement.

Gareth and Lynette

Gareth and Lynette tells how young Gareth, nephew of King Arthur, longed to leave his home and prove himself at Arthur's Court. His mother, loving and fearful, strove to keep him with her; yet his persistence persuaded her at last to let him go, on condition that he, disguised, serve a year in Arthur's kitchen before asking for knighthood. With his identity at Camelot concealed from all but Arthur, Gareth endured his position and by his industry and cheerfulness won the respect of Arthur, who promised him an early opportunity to show his true worth. That opportunity came with the arrival of the fair but sharp-tongued Lynette, with the request that Arthur send a knight to liberate her sister from captivity. When Gareth, still in his kitchen clothes, was given the quest, she was indignant; and her indignation continued for many a long mile on the journey to her sister's castle. Finally, however, Gareth's good-natured humility under her scornful sarcasm and his prowess in overcoming successive foes, symbolizing the terrors of life and death, won her gradual admiration and at length her love.

The Marriage of Geraint

The Marriage of Geraint describes another sort of courtship—how the polished and handsome Geraint met and loved humble Enid. Riding on a quest to chastise a discourteous knight, Geraint asked lodging for the night at a ruined castle. Signs of poverty were everywhere, but what little the inmates of the castle had they offered to Geraint with a cheeriness and graciousness that won his heart. Especially was he pleased with Enid, the daughter of his host. Her faded gown and the menial tasks that she performed could not obscure her charm. In the course of an evening during which Geraint followed Enid everywhere with his eyes, he learned that the discourteous knight whom he had come to chastise was the one who had reduced his host to his present poverty, that a tournament was to be held the next day in which he would have an opportunity to meet his foe, but that he must be accompanied by a lady in order to enter the tournament. Impulsively Geraint proposed that he satisfy this requirement by taking Enid with him as his destined bride. The parents were overjoyed at so high an alliance for Enid; she, shrinking at first from the suddenness of the proposal, saw it also as an honor and obeyed. In the tournament Geraint was victor; the title and lands of Enid's father were restored; and Enid prepared for the journey to Camelot and her marriage by exchanging her old garments for more new and splendid ones. But Geraint insisted that she ride with him in her ancient gown, and she, obedient, complied.

Geraint and Enid

Geraint and Enid portrays Enid as the ideal wife and Geraint as a very human husband. Alarmed by the influence which the growing intimacy between Lancelot and Guinevere might have on Enid's mind, Geraint took Enid from the Court to his own country. There he lost himself in the pleasures of marriage; giving up his mighty exercises, he lived only for Enid. Far from being joyful at Geraint's exclusive devotion, Enid became increasingly distressed and felt herself the cause of his inaction. Her distress was at last apparent to Geraint; misinterpreting it as a sign that she loved him no longer, he angrily donned his armor and left the castle, ordering Enid to ride before him and not to speak to him whatever might betide. Enid obeyed, except when Geraint's safety was concerned; twice, much to his ostensible anger, she spoke to warn him against foes in the path. As they rode on, Geraint's impulsive anger began to ebb in spite of his efforts to preserve it, until he almost forgot to berate Enid when she disobeyed his command once more to warn him of a plot against his life. In the next encounter Geraint was seriously wounded; when he woke from his swoon to find Enid weeping over him, he found his anger wholly gone. The tale ends with Enid mounted behind Geraint on his great charger, complete confidence established between them as a result of their adventures together, and Geraint's life again made purposeful. They lived on together, in their own land, united in a resolve to cooperate with Arthur in making England a peaceful and compact society.

Balin and Balan

In *Balin and Balan* the interest of the story centers in Balin, surnamed "the Savage," who came to Camelot, in the company of his older and more developed brother Balan, to acquire courtesy as a cure for the violent moods that often assailed him. For a time the influence of Lancelot and Guinevere, whom he worshiped as examples of the perfect courtesy that he lacked, succeeded in holding his roughness in check; but when his brother, going on a quest to rid a forest of a demon that haunted it, left him alone, he came to despair of attaining an ideal too high above him. He credited, too, scandalous stories about the relationship of Lancelot and Guinevere which Vivien, the "wily wanton" of the Court and Merlin's mistress, came to Camelot to spread. Discouraged and disillusioned, he rode impetuously out from Camelot and met, as the first victim of his rage, his own brother, who took him for the demon he had gone out to subdue. Without recognizing each other, they fought and died tragically at each other's hands.

Merlin and Vivien

The snake in the paradise of Camelot, the enchantress Vivien, found another victim in the crafty Merlin, the magician and the prophet of the Court, as the tale of *Merlin and Vivien* relates. During his long life Merlin had attained fame and had become invaluable to the state through his supernatural wisdom and foresight. Yet the evil charm of Vivien was more than his wisdom could conquer. Even though he saw through her wiles and understood the consequences of yielding to her desires, his emotions overbore his reason. Thus beguiled, he revealed to Vivien the charm that was the secret of his power, and she immediately used it upon him.

> And in the hollow oak he lay as dead,
> And lost to life and use and name and fame.

Lancelot and Elaine

Two tragedies are related in the idyll of *Lancelot and Elaine*. In the one, the lovable Elaine, who had been brought up in seclusion, saw the great Lancelot, adored him, guarded his shield as he rode away to fight in disguise at Camelot, nursed him after he had been wounded, offered her love to him, found her love hopeless, and died like a wilting flower. The other tragedy is that of Lancelot, whom, had it not been for his unfortunate vows exchanged with Guinevere, Elaine could have made happy.

The Holy Grail

The disintegration of the Table Round, foreshadowed in previous tales, proceeds in *The Holy Grail*. Here the force that undermines the stability of the society which Arthur has established is a falsely conceived religious fervor which leads to an evasion of social duty. Carried away by their desire for an unearthly holiness that only a few unusual men could attain, the knights of Arthur let the kingdom shift for itself while they rode away to seek the Grail. Galahad, the pure, sought and attained. Percival and Bors caught glimpses of the splendor. Lancelot was kept by his sinful love of Guinevere from realizing a holiness that, in his great sincerity of heart, he much desired. Gawain and the other knights merely wasted their efforts in a quest beyond their scope; meanwhile Camelot crumbled into ruins, and the kingdom of God on earth suffered from the absence of those who should have maintained it.

Pelleas and Ettarre

The story of *Pelleas and Ettarre* gives further indication that the ideals of faithfulness and purity on which the stability of the Table Round depended were losing their strength. The young Pelleas, inexperienced and idealistic, believed that all men, like Lancelot, were loyal and that all women, like Guinevere, were pure. His first disillusionment came from loving the self-centered Ettarre, who accepted his devotion only until he had won for her in a tournament the title of "Queen of Beauty," and then scorned him utterly. Trusting Gawain to plead his cause before Ettarre, Pelleas suffered another disillusionment in discovering that Gawain used the mission only as a pretext for winning the love of Ettarre for himself; and the later discovery that Lancelot and Guinevere were also guilty effectually destroyed his faith in humanity. Maddened, he rushed to Camelot, fought with Lancelot, and though defeated made the lovers feel his scorn. "And each foresaw the dolorous day to be."

The Last Tournament

The love of Lancelot for Guinevere is ironically paralleled in *The Last Tournament* by the love of Tristram for Isolt, wife of King Mark of Cornwall. Lancelot and Guinevere, however guilty, were still noble; Tristram loved Isolt, abandoned her to marry in Brittany, and then returned, lured by the memory of her black eyes. On the way he stopped at Camelot, where he found Arthur's court changed from its ancient purity into a place of lightness and revelry, observed the unhappiness of Lancelot and Guinevere in having, by their unwitting example, led the world astray, saw Arthur baffled by the failure of his ideals, and won, in a last tournament, a string of rubies for his love. Riding on, he came to Tintagel and Isolt. She reproached him for his treason, hated and yet loved him; he placed the rubies around her neck and sang her a last song before the sword of King Mark struck him down from behind.

Guinevere

In *Guinevere* the end of the Table Round has come. Before the opening of the tale Modred had forced upon Arthur the knowledge of Lancelot's love for Guinevere, Lancelot had fled to France, Arthur had pursued him, and Modred had seized the kingdom in Arthur's absence. To escape Modred, Guinevere took refuge in a house of nuns at Almesbury, sorrowing for her part in the disruption of the kingdom, goaded to despair by the innocent prattling of a novice with her tales of the wicked queen. There Arthur came to take a last farewell before his battle with the traitors. As, noble in his sorrow, Arthur stood before her, reproachful but forgiving, Guinevere for the first time realized that she loved him with a higher love than ever she had loved Lancelot. But the discovery came too late.

The Passing of Arthur

The Passing of Arthur records the last great battle between the remnant of the Round Table and the rebels under Modred, the destruction of both armies, the death of Modred at Arthur's hand, the fatal wounding of Arthur, and the last scene of his life when only Bedivere is left with him. Wishing to restore his mystic sword Excalibur to the Lady of the Lake, from whom it had come, Arthur commanded Bedivere to throw it into the waters; twice the beauty of the sword caused Bedivere to disobey; the third time he flung it, and a white arm came out of the water to seize it. Remorseful for his delay, he then carried Arthur to the edge of the sea. There came a barge, and in the barge three queens who received the king and bore him out of Bedivere's sight to Avalon, the happy island of the blessed. As he went, Arthur gave as a last word the hope that the order of the future might accomplish what the old order had nobly attempted—to subdue the bestial element in man and to make society coherent and high-minded.

LANCELOT AND ELAINE, p. 123

Lancelot, the son of King Ban of Brittany, was stolen in infancy by Vivien, the Lady of the Lake, who threw him into the water; hence he was called "Lancelot of the Lake." His guilty love for Guinevere, wife of King Arthur, was the initial cause of the disruption of the Court. Astolat, the home of Elaine, according to Malory was Guildford, in Surrey. The poem is based upon Malory's *Morte d'Arthur*, Book 18, Chs. 8-20.

This poem should be compared with *The Lady of Shalott*, p. 17.

Page 139, lines 1417-1418. Malory relates that when Lancelot heard of the last great battle in which Arthur was wounded, he set out to seek forgiveness for the wrong done his king. But he was too late; Arthur was dead. After uttering a devout prayer for Arthur's soul, Lancelot sought Guinevere. He found her in a nunnery at Almesbury, and after taking a last farewell of her he expressed repentance in a lonely chapel and thereafter led a life of prayer and fasting. When Guinevere died, Lancelot buried her by the side of King Arthur in Glastonbury Abbey. Thereafter he refused food and drink, and within a few weeks he died.

THE HOLY GRAIL, p. 140

For a statement regarding the origin and the significance of the Grail, see Critical Note on *Sir Galahad*, p. 952.

Tennyson represents the quest for the Holy Grail by the multitude as mistaken zeal. The quest is properly reserved for a select few. The source of the poem is Malory's *Morte D'Arthur*, Books 11-17.

Pages 145-146, lines 489-539. Tennyson regarded this passage and lines 763-849 as among the best blank verse he ever wrote.

THE LAST TOURNAMENT

Tennyson's bitter *Idyll* stands in sharp contrast to more romantic celebrations of the love of Tristram and Iseult, especially Wagner's passionate opera and Swinburne's ecstatic *Tristram of Lyonesse* (the Prelude of which will be found on page 717). It may be compared with Arnold's *Tristram and Iseult*, though the poems differ markedly in intention. *The Last Tournament* as the tenth of the twelve *Idylls* depicts with great intensity and skill the decadence of the Arthurian world; the King must fight the brutal Red Knight and see his own men resort to uncontrolled violence. Tristram, who has come too late to Camelot to take its idealism seriously, is a mere opportunist, intent only on the satisfaction of selfish desire. By the end of the poem the autumn gloom pervades the whole kingdom, Guinevere has fled, and Dagonet the fool can see no cause for any future smile.

THE REVENGE, p. 162

The main source of this poem was a report of the famous battle written in 1591 by Sir Walter Raleigh, a cousin of Grenville, the hero of the incident. Stevenson calls the poem "one of the noblest ballads in the English language." Cf. Browning's *Hervé Riel*, p. 365.

Sir Richard Grenville was a British naval hero of the sixteenth century. In 1585 he had charge of a fleet that set out to colonize Virginia. In 1591 he was put in command of the *Revenge*, one of the best ships in the small fleet under Lord Thomas Howard sent to the Azores, islands west of Portugal, to intercept the Spanish treasure ships returning from the West Indies. The king of Spain sent a powerful fleet of fifty-three warships against the English. The Earl of Cumberland, coasting along Portugal, sent a warning to Howard as he lay at anchor off Flores, the most westerly island of the Azores. Howard escaped with five of the six ships, but Grenville delayed to take his sick men aboard. He then tried to pass through the entire Spanish fleet, and the fight occurred. It lasted fifteen hours, and Grenville surrendered only after all but twenty of his men were killed. He was mortally wounded in the fight and died a few days later.

RIZPAH, p. 164

This poem was suggested by a story, found in a current magazine, of a young man who had been hanged in chains in the eighteenth century for robbing the mail (*Memoir*, II, 250). The date 17—, prefixed to the poem, places the poem as of the eighteenth century, when it was the custom for bodies of criminals to be left hanging until they became skeletons.

The title of the poem is Biblical, being taken from 2 *Samuel*, 21:8-10.—"But the king took the two sons of Rizpah . . . And he delivered them into the hands of the Gibeon-ites, and they hanged them in the hill before the Lord: . . . And Rizpah the daughter of Aiah took sackcloth, and spread it for her upon the rock, from the beginning of harvest until water dropped upon them out of heaven, and suffered neither the birds of the air to rest on them by day, nor the beasts of the field by night."

The poem is a dramatic monologue spoken by a mad mother, on her deathbed in the hospital, to a visiting lady, clearly a sort of evangelical missionary.

VASTNESS, p. 167

No conviction was so constantly forced upon Tennyson as that expressed in the theme of this poem. He said: "What matters anything in this world without full faith in the Immortality of the Soul and of Love?" —*Memoir*, II, 343. Cf. *In Memoriam*, Section 34, p. 65, and *Locksley Hall Sixty Years After*, ll. 60-72.

The style of this poem and of *To Virgil* (p. 166) resembles that of Whitman.

AKBAR'S DREAM, p. 176

Akbar was the great Mogul ruler of India from 1556 to 1605. He invented a religion that aimed to incorporate the best of all beliefs. In the poem he relates a dream about building a temple where all people of all creeds might worship and in which might dwell "Truth, and Peace, and Love, and Justice." He saw himself killed and the temple destroyed; he saw also some people come from the West who restored toleration and abolished objectionable practices. The "Hymn," addressed to the sun, stands at the end of the poem.

ROBERT BROWNING, p. 176

STANDARD EDITIONS

Complete Works, 12 vols., ed. w. intros. and notes by Charlotte Porter and Helen A. Clarke, New York, Crowell, 1898

Works, 9 vols., w. intros. by F.G. Kenyon, Centenary ed., London, Smith

Complete Poetic and Dramatic Works, Cambridge ed., Boston, Houghton, 1895

Complete Poetical Works, New York, Macmillan, 1915

The Poetical Works; Complete from 1833 to 1868 and the Shorter Poems Thereafter, Oxford Standard Authors, New York, Oxford Univ. Press, 1941

New Poems of Robert Browning and Elizabeth Barrett Browning, ed. by F.G. Kenyon, New York, Macmillan, 1915

A Blot in the 'Scutcheon and Other Dramas, ed. by Arlo Bates, Boston, Heath, 1904

The Ring and the Book, w. an intro. by M.J. Moses, and crit. notes by Helen A. Clarke, New York, Crowell, 1927

The Ring and the Book, w. an intro. by E. Dowden and notes by A.K. Cook, Oxford Standard Authors, New York, Oxford Univ. Press, 1940

Letters, collected by Thomas J. Wise, ed. by T.L. Hood, New Haven, Conn., Yale Univ. Press, 1933

The Letters of Robert Browning and Elizabeth Barrett Browning, 1845-1846, 2 vols., New York, Harper, 1899

Letters of Robert Browning to Miss Isa Blagden, Waco, Texas, Baylor Univ. Press, 1923

New Letters, ed. w. an intro. and notes by W.C. DeVane and K.L. Knickerbocker, New Haven, Conn., Yale Univ. Press, 1950

Letters of the Brownings to George Barrett, ed. by P.N. Landis and R.E. Freeman, Urbana, Univ. of Illinois Press, 1958

The Best of Browning, ed. w. notes by W.H. Rogers, New York, Ronald Press, 1942

Poems, ed. w. notes by Donald Smalley, Boston, Houghton Mifflin, 1956

BIOGRAPHY

Browning, Fannie Barrett, *Some Memories of Robert Browning*, Boston, Jones, 1928

Burdett, O., *The Brownings*, Boston, Houghton, 1929

Chesterton, G.K., *Robert Browning*, English Men of Letters Series, New York, Macmillan, 1925

Clarke, Helen A., *Browning and His Century*, New York, Doubleday, 1912

Dowden, E., *The Life of Robert Browning*, New York, Dutton, 1917

Griffin, W.H., *The Life of Robert Browning*, 3d ed., rev. and enl., London, Methuen, 1938

Herford, C.H., *Robert Browning*, New York, Dodd, 1905

James, H., ed., *W.W. Story and His Friends*, Boston, Houghton, 1903

Kenyon, F.G., ed., *Robert Browning and Alfred Domett*, London, Smith, 1906

Loth, D.G., *The Brownings; a Victorian Idyll*, New York, Brentano's, 1929

Lounsbury, T.R., *The Early Literary Career of Robert Browning*, New York, Scribner, 1911

Marzials, F.T., *Browning*, London, Bell, 1905

Miller, Betty B.S., *Robert Browning; a Portrait*, New York, Scribner, 1953

Orr, Mrs. A., *Life and Letters of Robert Browning*, Boston, Houghton, 1908

Ritchie, Anne T., *Records of Tennyson, Ruskin, and the Brownings*, New York, Harper, 1892

Waugh, A., *Robert Browning*, Boston, Small, 1900

Whiting, Lilian, *The Brownings; Their Life and Art*, Boston, Little, 1917

Winwar, F., *The Immortal Lovers: Elizabeth Barrett and Robert Browning*, New York, Harper, 1950

CRITICISM

Altick, Richard D., "'A Grammarian's Funeral': Browning's Praise of Folly," *Studies in English Literature*, 1963, 3:449-460

Assad, Thomas J., "Browning's 'My Last Duchess,'" *Tulane Studies in English*, 1961, 10:117-128

Atkins, G.G., "*Cleon*," "*Abt Vogler*, and *Saul*," "*The Ring and the Book*," *Reinspecting Victorian Religion*, New York, Macmillan, 1928

Bagehot, W., "Wordsworth, Tennyson, and Browning," *Literary Studies*, 3 vols., ed. by R.H. Hutton, London, Longmans, 1895

Barrett, Elizabeth, "Miss Elizabeth Barrett's Criticism of Her Future Husband's Poems," *New Poems of Robert Browning and Elizabeth Barrett Browning*, ed. by F.G. Kenyon, New York, Macmillan, 1915

Berdoe, E., *The Browning Cyclopædia*, 2d ed., New York, Macmillan, 1950

Berdoe, E., *A Primer of Browning*, New York, Dutton, 1904

Birrell, A., "On the Alleged Obscurity of Mr. Browning's Poetry," "Robert Browning," *Collected Essays and Addresses*, 3 vols., London, Dent, 1922

Boas, G., *Tennyson and Browning*, New York, Nelson, 1925

Bonnell, J.K., "Touch Images in the Poetry of Robert Browning," *PMLA*, 1922, 37:574-598

Brockington, A.A., *Browning and the Twentieth Century*, New York, Oxford Univ. Press, 1932

Brooke, S.A., *The Poetry of Robert Browning*, New York, Crowell, 1902

Broughton, L.N. and B.F. Stelter, *A Concordance to the Poems of Robert Browning*, New York, Stechert, 1924

Burton, R., "Renaissance Pictures in Browning's Poetry," *Literary Likings*, Boston, Copeland, 1898

Campbell, Lily B., *The Grotesque in the Poetry of Robert Browning*, thesis, Austin, Univ. of Tex., 1907

Cassidy, J., *A Study of Browning's "The Ring and the Book,"* Boston, Houghton, 1924

Charlton, H.B., *Browning as Dramatist*, Manchester, Eng., John Rylands, 1939

Charlton, H.B., *Browning as Poet of Religion*, Manchester, Eng., Manchester Univ. Press, 1943

Charlton, H.B., *Browning's Ethical Poetry*, Manchester, Eng., Manchester Univ. Press, 1943

Clarke, G.H., "*The Ring and the Book;* an Appreciation," *Canadian Magazine*, 1911, 36:325-335, 444-455

Clarke, Helen A., *Browning's England; a Study of English Influences in Browning*, New York, Baker, 1908

Clarke, Helen A., *Browning's Italy*, New York, Baker, 1907

Collins, J.C., "Browning and Butler," "Browning and Montaigne," "Browning and Lessing," *Posthumous Essays*, ed. by L.C. Collins, London, Dent, 1912

Compton-Rickett, A., *Robert Browning: Humanist*, London, Jenkins, 1924

Cook, A.K., *A Commentary upon Browning's "The Ring and the Book,"* London, Oxford Univ. Press, 1920

Corrigan, Beatrice, *Curious Annals: New Documents Relating to Browning's Roman Murder Story*, Toronto, Univ. of Toronto Press, 1956

Crawford, A.W., "Browning's *Cleon*," *Journal of English and Germanic Philology*, 1927, 26:485-490

Crawford, A.W., "Browning's *Saul*," *Queen's Quarterly*, 1927, 34:448-454

Cressman, E.D., "Classical Poems of Robert Browning," *Classical Journal*, 1927, 23:198-207

Cunliffe, J.W., "Elizabeth Barrett's Influence on Browning's Poetry," *PMLA*, 1908, 23:169-183

Curry, S.S., *Browning and the Dramatic Monologue*, Boston, Expression Co., 1908

De Reul, P., "Art and Thought of Robert Browning," *Rice Institute Pamphlets*, 1926, 13:227-304

DeVane, W.C., *A Browning Handbook*, New York, Crofts, 1955

DeVane, W.C., *Browning's "Parleyings,"* New Haven, Conn., Yale Univ. Press, 1927

DeVane, W.C., "The Landscape of Browning's *Childe Roland*," *PMLA*, 1925, 40:426-432

DeVane, W.C., "*Sordello's* Story Retold," *Studies in Philology*, 1930, 27:1-24

Dickson, A., "Browning's Source for *The Pied Piper of Hamelin*," *Studies in Philology*, 1926, 23:327-336

Drachmann, A.G., "Alloy and Gold," *Studies in Philology*, 1925, 22:418-424

Drinkwater, J., "Browning's Diction," *Victorian Poetry*, New York, Doran, 1924

Duffin, H.C., *Amphibian: A Reconsideration of Browning*, Cambridge, Eng., Bowes and Bowes, 1956

Elliott, G.R., "The Whitmanism of Browning," *The Cycle of Modern Poetry*, Princeton, N.J., Princeton Univ. Press, 1929

Firkins, O.W., "Paradoxical Ethics of Browning," *Poet Lore*, 1912, 23:348-359

Fleisher, David, "'Rabbi Ben Ezra,' 49-72," *Victorian Poetry*, 1963, 1:46-52

Flower, B.O., "Browning's *Rabbi Ben Ezra*," *Arena*, 1908, 40:334-341

Fonblanque, E. de, "Influence of Italy on the Poetry of the Brownings," *Fortnightly Review*, 1909, 92:327-344

Fuson, B.W., *Browning and His English Predecessors in the Dramatic Monolog*, Iowa City, Univ. of Iowa Press, 1948

Gleason, Katherine F., *The Dramatic Art of Robert Browning*, Boston, Badger, 1927

Glicksman, H., "The Legal Aspects of Browning's *The Ring and the Book*," *Modern Language Notes*, 1920, 35:473-479

Golder, H., "Browning's *Childe Roland*," *PMLA*, 1924, 39:963-978

Goodwin, F.D., "*The Ring and the Book*," *Poet Lore*, 1925, 36:577-582

Grant, P.S., "Browning's Art in Monologue," *Essays*, New York, Harper, 1922

Greer, L., *Browning and America*, Chapel Hill, Univ. of N.C. Press, 1952

Groom, B., *On the Diction of Tennyson, Browning and Arnold*, New York, Oxford Univ. Press, 1939

Hardy, I., "Browning's *Childe Roland*," *Poet Lore*, 1913, 24:53-58

Hatcher, H.H., *The Versification of Robert Browning*, Columbus, Ohio State Univ. Press, 1928

Havens, R.D., "Blake and Browning," *Modern Language Notes*, 1926, 41:464-466

Hermann, E.A., *The Faith of Robert Browning*, Boston, Sherman, 1916

Hickey, E., "Study of Browning's *Saul*," *Catholic World*, 1911, 94:320-336

Hogrefe, Pearl, *Browning and Italian Art and Artists*, Lawrence, Univ. of Kan. Bulletin, 1914

Honan, Park, *Browning's Characters: A Study in Technique*, New Haven, Conn., Yale Univ. Press, 1961

Hood, T.L., "Browning's Ancient Classical Sources," *Harvard Studies in Classical Philology*, 1922, 33:79-188

Horne, R.H., "Robert Browning," *A New Spirit of the Age, 1844*, ed. by W. Jerrold, London, Oxford Univ. Press, 1907

Hutton, R.H., "Mr. Browning," *Literary Essays*, London, Macmillan, 1892

Hutton, R.H., "Robert Browning," "Browning and Tennyson," *Brief Literary Criticisms*, London, Macmillan, 1906

Inge, W.R., "The Mysticism of Robert Browning," *Studies of English Mystics*, London, Murray, 1906

James, H., "Browning in Westminster Abbey," *Essays in London and Elsewhere*, New York, Harper, 1903

James, H., "The Novel in *The Ring and the Book*," *Notes on Novelists*, New York, Scribner, 1914

James, H., "On a Drama of Browning," *Views and Reviews*, Boston, Ball, 1908

Jerman, B.R., "Browning's Witless Duke," *PMLA*, 1957, 72:488-493

Johnson, E.D.H., *Alien Vision of Victorian Poetry*, Princeton, N.J., Princeton Univ. Press, 1952

Jones, H., *Browning as a Philosophical and Religious Teacher*, Glasgow, Mac Lehose, 1899

Jones, H., *The Immortality of the Soul in the Poems of Tennyson and Browning*, Boston, Am. Unitar. Assoc., 1907

Jones, H., "Robert Browning and Elizabeth Barrett Browning," *Essays on Literature*, London, Hodder, 1924. Same article in *Cambridge History of English Literature*, Vol. 13, Ch. 3

Jones, R.M., *Mysticism in Robert Browning*, New York, Macmillan, 1924

Kelman, John, "Robert Browning, the Hebrew," "Robert Browning, the Greek," *Prophets of Yesterday and Their Message for Today*, Cambridge, Mass., Harvard Univ. Press, 1924

Kenmare, D. (pseud.), *Ever a Fighter: a Modern Approach to the Works of Robert Browning*, London, Barrie, J., 1952

Ker, W.P., "Browning," *Collected Essays*, 2 vols., London, Macmillan, 1925

Kernahan, C., "One Aspect of Browning," *Wise Men and a Fool*, London, Ward, 1901

King, Roma A., Jr., *The Bow and the Lyre: The Art of Robert Browning*, Ann Arbor, Univ. of Michigan Press, 1957

Kingsland, W.G., *Robert Browning, Chief Poet of the Age*, London, Jarvis, 1887

Kirkconnell, W., "The *Epilogue* to *Dramatis Personæ*," *Modern Language Notes*, 1926, 41:213-219

Knickerbocker, Kenneth L., "A Tentative Apology for Browning," *University of Tennessee Studies in the Humanities*, 1956, I, 75-82

Langbaum, Robert, *The Poetry of Experience: The Dramatic Monologue in Modern Literary Tradition*, New York, Random House, 1957

Lomax, J.A., "*Karshish* and *Cleon*," *Sewanee Review*, 1911, 19:441-449

Loudon, K.M., *Browning's "Sordello"; a Commentary*, New York, Macmillan, 1906

Lounsbury, T.R., "A Philistine View" (on *A Blot in the 'Scutcheon*), *Atlantic Monthly*, 1899, 84:764-773

Lubbock, P., "Browning's Work," *Quarterly Review*, 1912, 217:437-457

Lynd, R., "Browning: the Poet of Love," *Old and New Masters*, London, Unwin, 1919

Lyttleton, A.T., "Browning," *Modern Poets of Faith, Doubt, and Paganism*, London, Murray, 1904

McAleer, E.C., "Browning's 'Cleon' and Auguste Comte," *Comparative Literature*, 1956, 8:142-145

Machen, Mrs. Minnie, *The Bible in Browning*, New York, Macmillan, 1903

Massey, B.W.A., "Browning's Vocabulary," *Notes and Queries*, 1925, 149:96-99, 114-116, 186-190, 256-259

Mayne, E.C., *Browning's Heroines*, London, Chatto, 1913

Molineux, Marie A., *A Phrase Book from the Poetic and Dramatic Works of Robert Browning*, Boston, Houghton, 1896

More, P.E., "Why Is Browning Popular?" *Shelburne Essays*, 3d s., New York, Putnam, 1905

Nettleship, J.T., *Robert Browning; Essays and Thoughts*, London, Mathews, 1890

Nicoll, W.R., and T.J. Wise, "Materials for a Bibliography of the Writings of Robert Browning," *Literary Anecdotes of the Nineteenth Century*, 2 vols., London, Hodder, 1895

Noel, R., "Robert Browning," *Essays on Poetry and Poets*, London, Paul, 1886

Old Yellow Book, The, in photoreproduction, w. trans., essay, and notes by C.W. Hodell, Washington, Carnegie Institution of Washington, 1916

Old Yellow Book, The, a new trans. w. notes and crit. chap. by J.M. Gest, Boston, Chipman Law Pub., 1925

Orr, Mrs. A., *A Handbook to the Works of Robert Browning*, London, Bell, 1902

Palmer, G.H., "The Monologue of Browning," *Harvard Theological Review*, 1918, 11:121-144

Pater, W., "Robert Browning," *Essays from "The Guardian*," London, Macmillan, 1901

Phelps, W.L., *Robert Browning, How to Know Him*, Indianapolis, Bobbs, 1915

Priestley, F.E.L., "Blougram's Apologetics," *University of Toronto Quarterly*, 1946, 15:139-147

Raymond, W.O., "Browning and Higher
Criticism," *PMLA*, 1929, 44:590-621

Raymond, W.O., *Infinite Moment, and Other
Studies in Robert Browning*, Toronto, Univ.
of Toronto Press, 1950

Rhys, E., *Browning and His Poetry*, London,
Harrap, 1918

Russell, Frances T., *One Word More on
Browning*, Stanford, Calif., Stanford Univ.
Press, 1927

Saintsbury, G., "Browning," *Corrected Impressions*, 1895; in *The Collected Essays
and Papers*, 4 vols., New York, Dutton,
1923-1924

Sanders, Charles R., "Carlyle, Browning, and
the Nature of a Poet," *Emory University
Quarterly*, 1960, 16:197-209

Santayana, G., "The Poetry of Barbarism,"
Interpretations of Poetry and Religion,
New York, Scribner, 1900

Scudder, Vida D., "Browning as a Humorist,"
*The Life of the Spirit in the Modern Eng-
lish Poets*, Boston, Houghton, 1901

Sessions, Ina Beth, "The Dramatic Monologue," *PMLA*, 1947, 42:503-516

Shanks, E., "Robert Browning," *Second
Essays on Literature*, London, Collins,
1927

Sim, Mrs. Frances M., *Robert Browning, the
Poet and the Man, 1833-1846*, New York,
Appleton, 1923

Sim, Mrs. Frances M., *Robert Browning: Poet
and Philosopher, 1850-1889*, London, Unwin, 1923

Smith, Charles W., *Browning's Star-Imagery*,
Princeton, N.J., Princeton Univ. Press,
1941

Somervell, D.C., "The Reputation of Robert
Browning," *Essays and Studies*, Vol. 15:
122-138, London, Oxford Univ. Press,
1929

Starkman, Miriam, "The Manichee in the
Cloister: A Reading of Browning's 'Solil-
oquy of the Spanish Cloister,' " *Modern
Language Notes*, 1960, 75:399-405

Stephen, L., "Browning's Casuistry," *Living
Age*, 1903, 236:257-271

Stockley, W.F.P., "Faith and Morals in
Robert Browning," *Thought*, Dec. 1926

Stowell, R.S., *The Significance of "The Ring
and the Book,"* Boston, Poet Lore, 1903

Symons, A., *An Introduction to the Study of
Browning*, London, Dent, 1906

Van Dyke, H., "The Glory of the Imperfect,"
Companionable Books, New York, Scribner, 1922

Walker, H., "Browning," "Tennyson and
Browning," *The Greater Victorian Poets*,
New York, Macmillan, 1895

Weatherhead, W.D., "Browning and Man's

Final Destiny," *London Quarterly Review*,
1929, 151:72-87

Whitla, William, *The Central Truth: The
Incarnation in Browning's Poetry*, Toronto, Univ. of Toronto Press, 1964

Wise, T.J., *A Complete Bibliography of the
Writings in Prose and Verse of Robert
Browning*, London, privately printed, 1897

BIOGRAPHICAL SKETCH

Robert Browning (1812-1889) was de-
scended on his father's side from English-
Creole stock, his grandfather having married
Margaret Tittle, a Creole from the West
Indies. His mother was the daughter of a
Hamburg German who married a Scottish
woman and settled in Dundee, Scotland.
Until the age of twenty-one Browning lived
in Camberwell, on the outskirts of London.
Except for two unimportant years in the
University of London, his principal education
came from private tutors and from his father,
a well-to-do official of the Bank of England,
who dabbled pleasantly in arts and letters,
and who had gathered about him a library of
six thousand volumes, most of which Browning soon mastered. His taste for painting
and music, as well as for poetry and the
theater, was developed in early years; then,
as always, he lived vigorously. Byron was
the first model for Browning's attempts at
verse; when he was fourteen, he discovered
Shelley's *Queen Mab* in a bookshop; with his
mother's help he acquired Shelley's complete
works, and under this influence wrote his
Pauline (1833). While on a visit to St. Peters-
burg, Russia, in the winter of 1833, he wrote
Porphyria's Lover and *Johannes Agricola*,
the earliest of his dramatic lyrics.

During the next two years Browning's
thought and art underwent a considerable
change. He was too independent and
original of mind to be imitative long. His
next poem, *Paracelsus* (1835), was abstruse in
theme and manner, dramatic rather than
lyric in its method, a psychological study and
a defense of an ethical principle; it marked,
therefore, the direction that his later poetry
was to take. At the suggestion of the actor
Macready, Browning now tried his hand
at drama and wrote *Strafford* (1837), a
tragedy that proved poorly adapted to the
stage. He then spent two years in Italy,
where he acquired local color and background
for his long poem *Sordello* (1840) and became
enamored of the country and interested in
her struggle for liberty from Austria. *Sordello*,
the most difficult of Browning's poems to
read because of its intricacies of style and
phrasing, gave the author an unfortunate

reputation for obscurity and for nearly twenty years lost him the sympathy of English readers. During the next six years Browning published a series entitled *Bells and Pomegranates* (1841-1846), in which in drama, lyric, and romance he struck the note that was to dominate the rest of his poetry. The dramas in the series, including *Pippa Passes* (1841), *A Blot in the 'Scutcheon* (1843), *Colombe's Birthday* (1844), and *A Soul's Tragedy* (1846), were hardly more successful as plays than *Strafford;* but in the short dramatic monologues, including such poems as *In a Gondola, Pictor Ignotus, The Bishop Orders His Tomb at St. Praxed's Church,* and the first part of *Saul* (which combined the psychological acuteness of *Sordello* with the objective directness of his plays), Browning had at last found his proper field.

Browning was not yet a popular poet when he was prompted, by reading a volume of poems published in 1844, to write its author, Miss Elizabeth Barrett, a letter of praise. She replied; other letters, a meeting, and an engagement followed. In spite of the obstacles due to her physical weakness and the opposition of her father, they were married in 1846 and went to Italy. The experience returned Mrs. Browning to at least partial health; a son was born, and she lived for fifteen years to give Browning happiness and encouragement. Their home, with the exception of visits in England and France, was the villa of Casa Guidi in Florence. Concern for his wife's health, the entertainment of interesting visitors from England and America, excursions into art and music kept Browning from writing extended poems; but the series of shorter dramatic monologues published as *Men and Women* in 1855 marked in many ways the summit of his achievement.

The death of Mrs. Browning in 1861 changed the pattern of Browning's life. With great difficulty he overcame an impulse to live in unproductive solitude. He returned to England, assumed the responsibility of educating his son, and by degrees began to find pleasure in his friendships, especially those with women. *The Ring and the Book,* which had been conceived before Mrs. Browning's death as the result of finding the record of a seventeenth-century murder trial for sale in the Florentine market place, occupied his time for some years and was at last published in 1868 and 1869. The interest in Greek literature which had been encouraged by Mrs. Browning's devotion to Euripides resulted in a series of poems on classical subjects from 1871 to 1877. In the last years of his life, his long-deferred popularity enlarged his contacts with the social and artistic life of his time. He regarded with somewhat amused tolerance the formation of Browning Clubs in England and America dedicated to his adulation. His later poetry consisted of realistic dramas in verse, such as *Red Cotton Night-Cap Country* (1873) and *The Inn Album* (1875), or poems in which his political and ethical opinions were conveyed with great indirectness and subtlety through the self-confession of a protagonist, as in *Prince Hohenstiel-Schwangau* (1871) and *Fifine at the Fair* (1872). The difficulty of these poems staggered his admirers but could not wholly discourage them. His last two years he spent at Asolo, where he had written *Pippa Passes* during his first visit to Italy, and at Venice, where his son, now married, had a villa and studio. There he died in 1889. His last poems, collected under the title of *Asolando* (1889), showed that his vigor of mind and his buoyancy were unabated to the end.

Browning's principal publications were: *Pauline,* 1833; *Paracelsus,* 1836; *Strafford,* 1837; *Sordello,* 1840; *Bells and Pomegranates,* 1841-1846; *Christmas-Eve and Easter-Day,* 1850; *In a Balcony,* 1855; *Men and Women,* 1855; *Dramatis Personæ,* 1864; *The Ring and the Book,* 1868-1869; *Balaustion's Adventure,* 1871; *Prince Hohenstiel-Schwangau,* 1871; *Fifine at the Fair,* 1872; *Red Cotton Night-Cap Country,* 1873; *Aristophanes' Apology,* 1875; *The Inn Album,* 1875; *Pacchiarotto and How He Worked in Distemper, with Other Poems,* 1876; *La Saisiaz,* 1878; *Dramatic Idyls,* 1879-1880; *Jocoseria,* 1883; *Ferishtah's Fancies,* 1884; *Parleyings with Certain People of Importance,* 1887; *Asolando,* 1890.

INTRODUCTORY CRITICISMS

"The first and perhaps the final impression we receive from the work of Robert Browning is that of a great nature, an immense personality. The poet in him is made up of many men. He is dramatist, humorist, lyrist, painter, musician, philosopher, and scholar, each in full measure, and he includes and dominates them all. In richness of nature, in scope and penetration of mind and vision, in energy of passion and emotion, he is probably second among English poets to Shakespeare alone. In art, in the power or the patience of working his native ore, he is surpassed by many; but few have ever held so rich a mine in fee. So large, indeed, appear to be his natural endowments, that we cannot feel as if the whole vast extent of his work has come near to exhausting them."—Arthur Symons, *An Introduction to the Study of Browning,* p. 1.

The characters in Browning's dramas "are impervious to outward influence, except in so far as it serves to discharge what is already within. Within the inner realm of passions, emotions, volitions, ambitions, and the world which these catch up in their career, there is no lack of movement. A plenitude of powers, all active, are revealed by him: they cooperate, sever, mingle, collide, combine, and are all astrain—but they are all psychical. Browning places us in the parliament of the mind. It is the powers of the mind to which we listen in high debate. . . . The tendency towards dwelling upon ideal issues rather than upon outer deeds, on the significance of facts for souls, and the insignificance of all things save in the soul's context, was always present in Browning; so, also, was the tendency towards monologue, with its deliberate, ordered persistency. And both of these tendencies grew. External circumstance became, more and more, the mere garb of the inner mood; deeds, more and more, the creatures of thoughts; and all real values were, more and more, undisguisedly ideal ministrants to man's need of beauty, or goodness, or love and happiness."—Henry Jones, *Cambridge History of English Literature*, Vol. 13, pp. 67-68.

"Browning's chief influence, other than what is purely artistic, upon a reader is towards establishing a connection between the known order of things in which we live and move and that larger order of which it is a part. He plays upon the will, summoning it from lethargy to activity. He spiritualizes the passions by showing that they tend through what is human towards what is divine. He assigns to the intellect a sufficient field for exercise, but attaches more value to its efforts than its attainments. His faith in an unseen order of things creates a hope which persists through the apparent failures of earth. In a true sense he may be named the successor of Wordsworth, not indeed as an artist but as a teacher."—Edward Dowden, *The Life of Robert Browning*, p. 396.

"In the course of his long career as a poet he [Browning] had suffered more than most poets from the excesses of both contumely and laudation. He triumphed over both at last, but not before the laudation had done damage to the quality of his poetic achievement. To his later contemporaries his poetry and his presence had become the very symbols of heartiness, courage, and faith. Some of his spirit has lingered to us who live in a disenchanted world. Yet the critics of our own day are inclined to disregard what Browning says, and to fasten intently upon how he says it. He is now seen to have been a pioneer and a revolutionist in the art of the new psychological poetry, a century before his time; and this aspect, at least, of his present fame would have delighted Robert Browning."—William Clyde DeVane, *A Browning Handbook*, p. 36.

CRITICAL NOTES

PARACELSUS, p. 176

Paracelsus, named after the hero, is a poem of five scenes, each representing a critical moment in the life of a famous Swiss physician (1493-1541) who, in spite of his charlatanism, has been termed "the father of modern chemistry." In the poem, Paracelsus, at twenty, aspires to attain knowledge, which he regards as the highest good, and contrary to the advice of two friends—Festus and his wife Michal—he decides to gain his end through untried methods and in unfamiliar places; he will give up love and pleasures of life in order to succeed. After nine years of study Paracelsus admits defeat, and as he reflects upon his sad condition, he hears the poet Aprile reveal his passion for love and beauty and the life of art. But Aprile admits failure in life because he has not knowledge; Paracelsus realizes that his plans could not succeed because he lacked the quality of love. Five years later, outwardly successful as a teacher and a physician, Paracelsus confides to Festus that his life is a failure because he has contented himself with low aims; he has lost the human qualities of love, hope, fear, and faith. His students desert him, and he is denounced as a quack; but he still aspires—he will combine pleasure with knowledge; he will try all experiences of life, no matter how evil. Festus warns him in vain against this course of action; in the last scene Paracelsus lies dying in a hospital, conscious of all his mistakes, but he expresses his confidence in these words:

> "If I stoop
> Into a dark tremendous sea of cloud,
> It is but for a time; I press God's lamp
> Close to my breast; its splendor, soon or late,
> Will pierce the gloom: I shall emerge one day.
> You understand me? I have said enough!"

In spite of its abstruseness of subject and manner, this poem is interesting and valuable in that it foreshadows much of Browning—his thought, his style, his high moral purpose, his lyrical power, and his ability to present critical moments of life poignantly in a form that anticipated his distinctive dramatic monologue.

HEAP CASSIA, SANDAL-BUDS, AND STRIPES, p. 176

This song is sung by Paracelsus to his friend Festus in Scene 4. Deserted and despised, Paracelsus sets out again in quest of knowledge, with all the enthusiasm of his youth—with the old aims, but not the same means. He speaks of the beauty of these aims; he calls them dreams and has them pass in song.

OVER THE SEA OUR GALLEYS WENT, p. 176

This song, a parable of "the men who proudly clung to their first fault, and withered in their pride," also is sung by Paracelsus in Scene 4. It explains his attitude toward "airy projects" that urged him to give over his wild courses of pleasure and hold to a "noble purpose."

THUS THE MAYNE GLIDETH, p. 177

This song, in Scene 5, is sung by Festus as he tries to comfort the dying and half-delirious Paracelsus. The song of the river they both knew so well restored the heart and mind of the listener as David's music restored the mind of Saul. (See *Saul*, p. 223.)

PIPPA PASSES, p. 179

Mrs. Orr reports (*A Handbook to the Works of Robert Browning*, p. 55) that "Mr. Browning was walking alone, in a wood near Dulwich, when the image flashed upon him of someone walking thus alone through life; one apparently too obscure to leave a trace of his or her passage, yet exercising a lasting though unconscious influence at every step of it; and the image shaped itself into the little silk-winder of Asolo, Felippa, or Pippa."

"The dramas of Browning," says Arlo Bates, "are inward. His temperament led him to select as the *motiv* of a play a theme so spiritual that its completeness could not be visible even to those of fairly acute perception in that swift first view which is all the stage allows. When he had worked out this theme, moreover, he took no trouble to complete the outward story. The result in representation was sure to be disconcerting and episodical. Striking examples of this are *Pippa Passes* and *In a Balcony*, where as far as outward events are concerned nothing is finished, and an audience must inevitably feel that it has seen only part of the play. Yet each is complete in the spiritually dramatic sense. The theme of the first, for instance, is the influence of Pippa upon other lives, unseen and unseeing; and this is fully shown. What happens as a consequence of the influence is not part of the spiritual theme. The drama, however, demands the completeness of the visible, whereas Browning was content with the working out of the spiritual."—*A Blot in the 'Scutcheon and Other Dramas*, Introduction, p. xvi.

RUDEL TO THE LADY OF TRIPOLI, p. 201

Geoffrey de Rudel was a Provençal troubadour of the twelfth century. Although he had never seen the Countess of Tripoli, he had heard of her great beauty, and in the true spirit of chivalric love of the Middle Ages he set out to visit her in her home in northern Africa. When he arrived at Tripoli, he was deathly sick, and when the Countess went on board the ship to see him, he died in her arms. In the poem the *Mount* is the Lady, the *Sun* is Love, and the *Flower* is Rudel.

IN A GONDOLA, p. 204

When Browning heard of a picture by Daniel Maclise (1806-1870) entitled *The Serenade*, he wrote the first stanza of this poem to stand as the description of the picture in an art catalog. Later, when he saw the picture, he thought it merited better treatment and wrote the rest of the poem.

THE LABORATORY, p. 211

The first water-color painting of Dante Gabriel Rossetti was an illustration of this poem and had as its title line 4—"Which is the poison to poison her, prithee?" Arthur Symons refers to the poem as "one of the very finest examples of Browning's unique power of compressing and concentrating intense emotion into a few pregnant words, each of which has its own visible gesture and audible intonation."—*An Introduction to the Study of Browning*, p. 86.

"HOW THEY BROUGHT THE GOOD NEWS FROM GHENT TO AIX," p. 213

Browning said that there was no historical foundation for this poem. "I wrote it," he states, "under the bulwark of a vessel, off the African coast, after I had been at sea long enough to appreciate even the fancy of a gallop on the back of a certain good horse 'York,' then in my stable at home."

THE LOST LEADER, p. 214

The following letter was written by Browning in reply to a question whether this poem refers to Wordsworth after he abandoned the liberal views of his youth:

19 Warwick-Crescent, W., Feb. 24, '75
DEAR MR. GROSART: I have been asked the question you now address me with, and as duly answered it, I can't remember how many times; there is no sort of objection to one more assurance or rather confession, on my part, that I *did* in my hasty youth presume to use the great and venerated personality of Wordsworth as a sort of painter's model; one from which this or the other particular feature may be selected and turned to account; had I intended more, above all, such a boldness as portraying the entire man, I should not have talked about "handfuls of silver and bits of ribbon." These never influenced the change of politics in the great

poet, whose defection, nevertheless, accompanied as it was by a regular face-about of his special party, was to my juvenile apprehension, and even mature consideration, an event to deplore. But just as in the tapestry on my wall I can recognize figures which have *struck out* a fancy, on occasion, that though truly enough thus derived, yet would be preposterous as a copy, so, though I dare not deny the original of my little poem, I altogether refuse to have it considered as the "very effigies" of such a moral and intellectual superiority.

Faithfully yours,
ROBERT BROWNING.

THE BISHOP ORDERS HIS TOMB AT SAINT PRAXED'S CHURCH, p. 222

This poem has won high praise for the way in which it re-creates the temper of the Renaissance period. Ruskin says of the poem: "Robert Browning is unerring in every sentence he writes of the Middle Ages; always vital, right, and profound; so that in the matter of art, with which we have been specially concerned, there is hardly a principle connected with the medieval temper that he has not struck upon in those seemingly careless and too rugged rhymes of his. . . . I know no other piece of modern English prose or poetry in which there is so much told, as in these lines, of the Renaissance spirit—its worldliness, inconsistency, pride, hypocrisy, ignorance of itself, love of art, of luxury, and of good Latin. It is nearly all that I said of the central Renaissance in thirty pages of the *Stones of Venice*, put into as many lines, Browning's being also the antecedent work. The worst of it is that this kind of concentrated writing needs so much *solution* before the reader can fairly get the good of it, that people's patience fails them, and they give the thing up as insoluble; though, truly, it ought to be to the current of common thought like Saladin's talisman, dipped in clear water, not soluble altogether, but making the element medicinal."—*Modern Painters*, Vol. IV, ch. 20, sec. 32, 34.

SAUL, p. 223

The first nine stanzas of this poem were published in 1845; the rest were written in Rome in 1853-1854, after his marriage. The advance in religious fervor noticeable in the second part has been said to be due to the influence of Mrs. Browning.

A GRAMMARIAN'S FUNERAL, p. 247

Compare these comments on *A Grammarian's Funeral*:

Stopford Brooke says: "This is the artist at work, and I doubt whether all the laborious prose written, in history and criticism, on the revival of learning, will ever express better than this short poem the inexhaustible thirst of the Renaissance in its pursuit of knowledge, or the enthusiasm of the pupils of a New Scholar for his desperate strife to know in a short life the very center of the universe."—*The Poetry of Robert Browning*, p. 155.

Richard D. Altick writes: "The grammarian's biography, as revealed by the students, is one of progressive detachment from life and increasing neglect of his duty to society at large: a course of which Browning, and not alone the youthful Browning of *Paracelsus*, could hardly have approved. . . . To have wasted God-given physical attributes, to have scorned the rich potentialities of youth and talent and preferred instead the dusty existence of a hermitic philosopher may be admirable in the eyes of the students, but not, one would suppose, in those of the poet who wrote 'Fra Lippo Lippi.' . . . The students praise their master's heroic passion for learning, but to Browning it is a misdirected passion insofar as it contravenes God's intention that life be used for living. The grammarian put the cart before the horse; while acknowledging the desirability of living, he pedantically chose to read about it first. . . . The grammarian's choice was, in effect, a denial of the very premise and spirit of Renaissance humanism, which Browning so much admired: the harmonious blending of living and learning, the study of the classics not as an end in itself but as a guide to a richer life."— " 'A Grammarian's Funeral': Browning's Praise of Folly?" in *Studies in English Literature*, III (1963), 449-460.

THE STATUE AND THE BUST, p. 249

The characters and the places mentioned in this poem are historical. The statue is that of Ferdinand I (1549-1609), Grand Duke of Florence. It stands in the Piazza della Santa Annunziata, a famous square in Florence named after the church on one side of it. The statue looks toward the palace once owned by a noble family named Riccardi and now called the Palazzo Antinori. The bust, which existed only in fancy, was that of the wife of the head of the Riccardi family; it is represented as having been placed beneath the window of the palace which the statue faces.

The Duke's palace, situated in the Via Larga (line 34), was built by Cosimo de' Medici in 1430. In 1659 it was sold by the Medici family to Marchese Riccardi and has since been known as the Palazzo Riccardi. It should not be confused with the original Riccardi palace, in which the lady was kept prisoner.

A correspondent of an American paper once asked the following questions regarding this poem:

1. When, how, and where did it happen? Browning's divine vagueness lets one gather only that the lady's husband was a Riccardi. 2. Who was the lady? who the duke? 3. The magnificent house wherein Florence lodges her préfet is known to all Florentine ball-goers as the Palazzo Riccardi. It was bought by the Riccardi from the Medici in 1659. From none of its windows did the lady gaze at her more than royal lover. From what window, then, if from any? Are the statue and the bust still in their original positions?

The letter fell into the hands of Thomas J. Wise; he sent it to Browning, and received the following answer:

Jan. 8, 1887.

DEAR MR. WISE: I have seldom met with such a strange inability to understand what seems the plainest matter possible: "ball-goers" are probably not history-readers, but any guide-book would confirm what is sufficiently stated in the poem. I will append a note or two, however. 1. "This story the townsmen tell"; "when, how, and where," constitutes the subject of the poem. 2. The lady was the wife of Riccardi; and the duke, Ferdinand, just as the poem says. 3. As it was built by, and inhabited by, the Medici till sold, long after, to the Riccardi, it was not from the duke's palace, but a window in that of the Riccardi, that the lady gazed at her lover riding by. The statue is still in its place, looking at the window under which "now is the empty shrine." Can anything be clearer? My "vagueness" leaves what to be "gathered" when all these things are put down in black and white? Oh, "ball-goers"!

Page 252, lines 214–250. "Mr. Santayana in his most interesting book *Interpretations of Poetry and Religion* . . . describes the poetry of Browning most truly as the poetry of barbarism, by which he means the poetry which utters the primeval and indivisible emotions. 'For the barbarian is the man who regards his passions as their own excuse for being, who does not domesticate them either by understanding their cause, or by conceiving their ideal goal.' Whether this be or be not a good definition of the barbarian, it is an excellent and perfect definition of the poet. It might, perhaps, be suggested that barbarians, as a matter of fact, are generally highly traditional and respectable persons who would not put a feather wrong in their head-gear, and who generally have very few feelings and think very little about those they have. It is when we have grown to a greater and more civilized stature that we begin to realize and put to ourselves intellectually the great feelings that sleep in the depths of us. Thus it is that the literature of our day has steadily advanced toward a passionate simplicity, and we become more primeval as the world grows older until Whitman writes huge and chaotic psalms to express the sensations of a schoolboy out fishing, and Maeterlinck embodies in symbolic dramas the feelings of a child in the dark."—G. K. Chesterton, *Robert Browning*, pp. 183-184.

"CHILDE ROLAND TO THE DARK TOWER CAME," p. 252

This poem is based upon Edgar's mad song in *King Lear*, III, 4, 187-189.—

"Child Rowland to the dark tower came,
His word was still—Fie, foh, and fum,
I smell the blood of a British man."

Mrs. Orr (*A Handbook to the Works of Robert Browning*, p. 274, note) ventures to state that the picturesque materials in the poem "included a tower which Mr. Browning once saw in the Carrara Mountains, a painting which caught his eye years later in Paris, and the figure of a horse in the tapestry in his own drawing room—welded together in the remembrance of the line from *King Lear*."

In an article describing a visit to Browning, J. W. Chadwick speaks of the tapestry and writes as follows:

"Upon the lengthwise wall of the room, above the Italian furniture, somber and richly carved, there was a long, wide band of tapestry, on which I thought I recognized the miserable horse of Childe Roland's pilgrimage:—

'One stiff blind horse, his every bone a-stare,
Stood stupefied, however he came there:
Thrust out past service from the devil's stud!'

I asked Mr. Browning if the beast of the tapestry was the beast of the poem; and he said yes, and descanted somewhat on his lean monstrosity. But only a Browning could have evolved the stanzas of the poem from the woven image. I further asked him if he had ever said that he only wrote *Childe Roland* for its realistic imagery, without any moral purpose—a notion to which Mrs. Sutherland Orr has given currency; and he protested that he never had. When I asked him if constancy to an ideal—'He that endureth to the end shall be saved'—was not a sufficient understanding of the central purpose of the poem, he said, 'Yes, just about that.' "—"An Eagle-Feather," *The Christian Register*, Jan. 19, 1888, 67:37.

G. K. Chesterton writes of the poem: "It is the hint of an entirely new and curious type of poetry, the poetry of the shabby and hungry aspect of the earth itself. Daring poets who wished to escape from conventional gardens and orchards had long been in the habit of celebrating the poetry of rugged and gloomy landscapes, but Browning is not content with this. He insists upon celebrating the poetry of mean landscapes. That sense of scrubbiness in nature, as of a man unshaved, had never been conveyed with this enthusiasm and primeval gusto before:

'If there pushed any ragged thistle-stalk
Above its mates, the head was chopped; the bents
Were jealous else. What made those holes and rents
In the dock's harsh swarth leaves, bruised as to balk
All hope of greenness? 'tis a brute must walk
Pashing their life out, with a brute's intents.'

"This is a perfect realization of that eerie sentiment which comes upon us, not so often among mountains and waterfalls, as it does on some half-starved common at twilight, or in walking down some gray mean street. It is the song of the beauty of refuse; and Browning was the first to sing it. Oddly enough it has been one of the poems about which most of those pedantic and trivial questions have been asked, which are asked by those who treat Browning as a science instead of a poet. 'What does the poem of *Childe Roland* mean?' The only genuine answer to this is 'What does anything mean?' Does the earth mean nothing? Do gray skies and wastes covered with thistles mean nothing? Does an old horse turned out to graze mean nothing? If it does, there is but one further truth to be added—that everything means nothing."—*Robert Browning*, p. 159.

IN A BALCONY, p. 255

"The real core of the play is this development of the love of Constance. She allows herself to be loved; she delights in the pretty play of intrigue; she is proud of the devotion of this man who is shaping the destinies of the kingdom; she is even great enough to be ready to make to the Queen the highest sacrifice of which her nature as it then is can be capable: but she is not touched by the flame of that passion which makes the very soul of Norbert incandescent. The great *motiv* of *In a Balcony* is the awakening of the inmost consciousness of Constance to the greatness of the love of Norbert and her quick response to that call which this perception makes to her highest and most feminine nature. . . . To call the drama incomplete—'equivalent to the third or fourth act of what might prove a tragedy or a drama,' is Mrs. Sutherland Orr's way of putting it—or to consider of importance what comes after the closing words of Constance, is to ignore the fact that the aim is to picture the regeneration of the soul of Constance from intellectual love to supreme passion, her rise from intellectual self-sacrifice to that complete self-surrender which is the highest phase of human love; and to fail to consider how this aim is completely accomplished before the curtain falls."—Arlo Bates, *A Blot in the 'Scutcheon and Other Dramas*, Introduction, pp. xxix, xxxi.

A contrasting view of this drama is given in the following quotation from Stopford Brooke:

"I do not believe that Browning meant to make self-sacrifice the root of Constance's doings. If he did he has made a terrible mess

of the whole thing. He was much too clear-headed a moralist to link self-sacrifice to systematic lying. Self-sacrifice is not self-sacrifice at all when it sacrifices truth. It may wear the clothes of Love, but, in injuring righteousness, it injures the essence of love. It has a surface beauty, for it imitates love, but if mankind is allured by this beauty, mankind is injured. It is the false Florimel of self-sacrifice. Browning, who had studied self-sacrifice, did not exhibit it in Constance. There is something else at the root of her actions, and I believe it to be jealousy. The very first lie she urges her lover to tell (that is, to let the Queen imagine he loves her) is just the thing a jealous woman would invent to try her lover and the Queen, if she suspected the Queen of loving him, and him of being seduced from her by the worldly advantage of marrying the Queen."—*The Poetry of Robert Browning*, pp. 341-342.

BISHOP BLOUGRAM'S APOLOGY, p. 268

Bishop Blougram speaks his "apology"—his defense of his faith and his way of life—to Gigadibs, a vulgar journalist who has maligned him and now seeks sensational new material for a magazine article. The subtle bishop, a superb logician, thoroughly exposes the superficiality of the skeptic by making ironic concessions to the rationalistic point of view; yet at the same time he manages to suggest the profound psychological basis of his own belief. The irony of course plays over the character of Bishop Blougram, too; and though we are expected to reject the naïveté of Gigadibs, we must be cautious in assuming that Browning wholly endorses Blougram's arguments. Some of the latter, however, are much closer in form and tone to Browning's own brand of liberal Protestantism than to orthodox Roman Catholicism. Thus, though Browning admitted that Cardinal Wiseman, leader of the Roman Catholic Church in England, was the original of his Blougram, it is not surprising that Wiseman, reviewing the poem, failed to recognize the portrait.

FRA LIPPO LIPPI, p. 283

"This picture of the harum-scarum monk painter of the fifteenth century, historical in its framework but with Browning's usual freedom of psychologic interpretation, is instinct with the pagan joy of life which is in dramatic contrast with the conventual medieval conception. Aside from its pictorial and human values—and these suffice to place it high among the monologues—it has much interest as an expression of the so-called realistic philosophy of art, put into the mouth of Lippo, one of the strongest of arguments for those who find the reproduction of God's world in art an all-sufficient object."—Richard Burton, *Select Poems of Robert Browning*, p. 319. The poem is probably Browning's defense of his own poetic "realism."

ANDREA DEL SARTO, p. 288

This poem was written as an interpretation of a picture by Andrea del Sarto representing the painter and his wife in the Pitti Palace, Florence. John Kenyon, a cousin of Mrs. Browning, had asked Browning to secure for him a copy of the picture; being unable to find a satisfactory copy, Browning sent him the poem instead.

The early paintings of Andrea del Sarto are regarded as his best work. A. C. Swinburne says of them: "These are the first fruits of his flowering manhood, when the bright and buoyant genius in him had free play and large delight in its handiwork; when the fresh interest of invention was still his, and the dramatic sense, the pleasure in the play of life, the power of motion and variety; before the old strength of sight and of flight had passed from weary wing and clouding eye, the old pride and energy of enjoyment had gone out of hand and heart.

"How the change fell upon him, and how it wrought, anyone may see who compares his later with his earlier work. . . . The time came when another than Salome [referring to Andrea del Sarto's picture of Salome dancing before Herod] was to dance before the eyes of the painter; and she required of him the head of no man, but his own soul; and he paid the forfeit into her hands. . . . In Mr. Browning's noblest poem—his noblest, it seems to me—the whole tragedy is distilled into the right words, the whole man raised up and reclothed with flesh. One point only is but lightly touched upon—missed it could not be by an eye so sharp and skillful—the effect upon his art of the poisonous solvent of love. How his life was corroded by it, and his soul burnt into dead ashes we are shown in full; but we are not shown in full what as a painter he was before, what as a painter he might have been without it."—"Notes on Designs of the Old Masters at Florence," *Complete Works*, Vol. 15, pp. 190-193.

PROSPICE, p. 317

This poem is a defiant statement of Browning's faith in personal immortality. In 1876 he said in a letter to a friend: "Dante wrote what I will transcribe from my wife's Testament wherein I recorded it fourteen years ago, 'Thus I believe, thus I affirm, thus I am certain it is, that from this life I shall pass to another, there where that lady lives of whom my soul was enamored.' "—W. H. Griffin, *The Life of Robert Browning*, p. 297. To another correspondent he wrote: "Why, *amico mio*, you know as well as I that death is life, just as our daily, our momentarily, dying body is none the less alive and ever recruiting new forces of existence. Without death, which is our crape-like churchyardy word for change, for growth, there could be no prolongation of that which we call life. . . . Never say of me that I am dead."

THE RING AND THE BOOK, p. 320

This is Browning's longest if not his greatest work, the triumph of the dramatic monologue. It consists of twelve books totaling over twenty thousand lines, which present from different points of view the story of a famous murder that occurred in Italy in 1698.

As recorded in *The Old Yellow Book*, the source of Browning's poem, the story is as follows: Guido Franceschini (born 1658), a Florentine nobleman of depleted fortune, was married at Rome in 1693 to Pompilia (born July 17, 1680), brought up as the daughter and heir of Pietro and Violante Comparini, who were thought to possess considerable property. All three went to live with Guido in his home at Arezzo. Unable to endure the bitter feeling shortly aroused, the Comparini returned to Rome (March-April 1694) and gave out the report that Pompilia was not their child, Violante having purchased her as a baby from a disreputable mother. On this ground Pietro brought suit against Guido to recover the marriage dowry. The case, first decided in favor of Guido, was appealed and never settled, much to Guido's mortification.

Because of domestic unhappiness, partly due to Guido's jealousy aroused by the friendship between Pompilia and Giuseppe Caponsacchi (born 1673), a young Canon in the church, Pompilia fled with the Canon for Rome—on April 29, 1697. They arrived on the following evening at Castelnuovo, a hamlet about fifteen miles from Rome, and stayed all night at the inn, where they were overtaken by Guido next morning. On his complaint they were arrested and taken to prison. They were tried before the Tribunal of the Governor, and in September a decision was announced. Pompilia was sent to a convent, and Caponsacchi was suspended for three years and banished to Civita Vecchia, a seaport near Rome. Expecting the birth of a child, Pompilia was allowed to go to the house of the Comparini in Rome. Both Guido and Pompilia had entered suit for divorce, but before either case could be considered, Pompilia gave birth to a son, on December 18, 1697. On the night of January 2, 1698, Guido and four of his confederates gained entrance to the house, murdered the aged Comparini, and left Pompilia for dead; she lived four days. The murderers were caught, tried before the Court, and sentenced to be executed. Guido's appeal to the Pope for clemency was denied, and the execution took place on February 22, 1698.

Browning became interested in the story in 1860, when by chance he came upon a parchment-bound book in Florence containing a collection of documents—some printed and some written—bearing upon the case; he bought the volume for eightpence. This collection is now known as *The Old Yellow Book;* it was Browning's chief source of material, and furnished the "Book" part of the title of his poem. The other part of the title was derived from a ring worn by Mrs. Browning, and after her death by Browning himself on his watch chain.

Book I, called *The Ring and the Book*, explains the title of the poem by pointing out the analogy between the process of manufacturing a ring and the process of transforming the collection of crude facts into a finished poem. As the jeweler adds an alloy to permit the desired workmanship on the ring, so Browning mixes his poetic fancy with the simple legal evidence contained in the *Yellow Book* to make possible an artistic whole. A summary of the story is given as Browning imagines it after his fancy has vitalized the characters into living personalities. In the end, however, as with the ring, the alloy must be removed, leaving only the refashioned product. To accomplish this result, the characters will appear in the poem and tell their own stories.

Book II, *Half Rome*, presents the view of persons who take Guido's side—that of a husband deceived and imposed upon from the beginning. The scene is in the church where the dead bodies of the Comparini lie exposed to the view of the curious multitude. The story, up to the point of the murder, is told by a partisan who suggests that as Violante had deceived her husband regarding the child, it was natural for her to deceive Guido since she desired a noble husband for the girl. After the foster parents left Guido's home and announced that Pompilia was not their child, Guido took the view that all this was done to defraud him. Naturally he was resentful, especially when the Court gave such slight

punishment to Pompilia and the priest. What Guido did, therefore, he did in defense of his honor.

Book III, *The Other Half Rome*, presents the view of the other half of the public, in favor of Pompilia, dying in the hospital from her wounds. The action of the Comparini is excused, and it is Guido who is charged with treachery and deceit and cruelty. It is pointed out that guilty persons would not flee, much less stop before they reached their destination. This half of the public denies the husband the right to act as judge and executioner of his own case.

Book IV, *Tertium Quid*, presents the opinion of a disinterested critic, the spokesman of the superior class, who cleverly tries to avoid offending the prejudices of his distinguished listeners. Both parties in the action are blamed, both excused. Which sinned more was hard to tell.

Book V, *Count Guido Franceschini*, gives Guido's defense. Tortured into confessing the murder, Guido seeks to justify his whole course of action. He tells the Court of his ancient and honored family, of its service to the state and to the church. In seeking a wife with a dowry he followed a laudable course, advised by loyal friends. He had dealt fairly, but had been cheated. Besides, Pompilia and her foster parents had maligned his character and had made him the laughingstock of the town. His resentment was natural when his wife was referred to as the bastard of a nameless strumpet and when he found Caponsacchi loitering about her windows. Then one morning he found the servants drugged, his money stolen, and his wife gone with the priest. When he overtook the fugitives, he did not, as was his right, exact immediate vengeance by killing them, but called upon the law for help; and all he got was mild punishment for the offenders. When he heard of the release of Pompilia, of the birth of her son, and of the theft of the child he had longed for, he could not endure the shame longer. With four loyal servants he went to Rome. They arrived on Christmas Eve, and for nine days he prayed against temptation to avenge the wrongs. He confessed the murder, but after it was committed he slept soundly; he had done God's bidding—what the Court should have done before—and as the law's defender he demands thanks and his freedom.

Book VI, *Giuseppe Caponsacchi*, gives the story of the priest, the facts that he had related at his own trial six months before. Then the Court laughed at him; now it listens soberly. He stresses the sanctity of his priestly vows and tells how he first saw Pompilia, the "sad, strange lady," at the theater; how letters were brought to him, purported to have been written by her, imploring sympathy and aid. Though conscious of the trick being played by Guido, the priest talked with Pompilia and learned that the letters were forgeries since she could neither read nor write; and together they planned the escape and rode continuously until they reached Castelnuovo, near Rome. All night he kept guard over Pompilia, but early in the morning they were overtaken by Guido and his band, and later tried and punished. He reminds the Court of the forged letters and points out that if he and Pompilia were guilty they would not have taken flight as they did. He reasserts his innocence, and with all the sincerity and pathos of his nature begs the Court to be just.

Book VII, *Pompilia*, gives the life story of Pompilia as she told it on her deathbed in the presence of the nuns and of her confessor. Conscious of her impending death from Guido's twenty-two dagger wounds, she rejoices that she has been a mother if only for two weeks. She tells of her happy child life with the Comparini, of the mysteriousness of her marriage with Guido, of the unfortunate deceit practiced upon him by Violante, and of his cruel treatment and false charges. When she was told that the priest had written her letters, she begged that he be entreated to write no more. Unable to endure the torture in Guido's home, she had appealed first to the Archbishop, then to the Governor of the city, and when aid was denied, she asked Caponsacchi to take her to her foster parents at Rome. She tells of the flight, of being overtaken by Guido, and of the horrors of the fatal night of the murder. Though she could not love her husband, she forgives him. At the last she blesses Caponsacchi and commits her soul to God.

Book VIII, *Dominus Hyacinthus de Archangelis*, gives the plans of Guido's lawyer, who sees in the case a great opportunity for self-exploitation. He is in his study preparing for the defense. He plans to astonish the Pope with his eloquence, and to ridicule the Latin of his opponent, whose argument he endeavors to anticipate. He will object to the method used to force a confession from Guido on the ground that a nobleman is exempt from torture. If Guido had not confessed, it would have been easy to charge the murder to Caponsacchi. In his speech to the Court he plans to quote authorities who say that a man's honor is inviolable, and he will insist that Guido acted within his rights. He also plans to speak for the four accomplices. His account is interspersed with remarks regarding family matters, especially his liking for rich foods.

Book IX, *Juris Doctor Johannes-Baptista Bottinius*, introduces Pompilia's lawyer as he prepares the case of the state against Guido and his confederates. He plans to make light of the charges against Pompilia and Caponsacchi and to admit the possibility of many of them being true. He will praise the priest for defending Pompilia after the Archbishop and the Governor had refused to aid her. He will adorn his speech with learned literary allusions and will take pains to criticize his opponent's method of living.

Book X, *The Pope*, presents the final judgment, made by the Pope, to whom the decision of the Court had been appealed. After a detailed study of the evidence in the case the Pope finds nothing good in Guido, and denounces him for his dastardly acts, especially since he had had every opportunity for right living and had not shown any signs of repentance for what he had done. Pompilia and Caponsacchi, both champions of truth, are found worthy of praise. In full consciousness of performing his duty to God he signs the order for the execution of Guido and his accomplices.

The Pope calls Pompilia "perfect in whiteness . . . my flower, my rose, I gather for the breast of God." Of Caponsacchi he says—

> "And surely not so very much apart,
> Need I place thee, my warrior priest."

Book XI, *Guido*, presents the final plea by the condemned man in his prison cell awaiting execution. He protests his innocence and implores the aid of the Cardinal and the Abate who have come to be with him to the end. He denounces the Pope for his lack of mercy and refuses to repent. He seeks to justify all his acts and regrets that Pompilia lived long enough to tell her story; otherwise he would have been free. He makes a final frantic appeal for his life as he hears approaching the Brothers of Mercy, who have come to chant the Office of the Dying at his cell door and to attend his death on the scaffold.

Book XII, *The Book and the Ring*, gives the report of the execution and comments of persons regarding it. The first is contained in a letter from a Venetian who had visited Rome and witnessed the public execution; he describes the events of the day and states that before his death Guido asked forgiveness of God. One letter is from Guido's lawyer to friends of the Court telling them of the fine quality of his client and stating that he does not care how soon the old Pope dies. The third letter is from Pompilia's lawyer who regrets that he had not been on the other side, since the case was so easy that he had had no opportunity to show his skill. He objects to public statements made by Pompilia's confessor and vows to even things up when he defends the nuns in their suit for Pompilia's property. A decision of the Pope, however, restores the character of Pompilia and dismisses the suit of the nuns. No record was found of Pompilia's son.

MUCKLE-MOUTH MEG, p. 377

This poem is related to the folklore theme of the "loathly lady" who is frequently a bespelled mortal waiting for some courageous hero to kiss her and break the charm that keeps her ugly. See Morris's *The Lady of the Land*, p. 643. It was once the practice in England to allow criminals their freedom if they would marry disreputable women. See Feste's statement in *Twelfth Night*, I, 5, 20: "Many a good hanging prevents a bad marriage." The story told in this poem is to be found in Sir Thomas Dick Lauder's *Scottish Rivers*. It is based upon a feud that had existed for a long time between the Murrays and the Scotts. William Scott, son of the head of the family of Harden, was caught, with his followers, stealing cattle from Sir Gideon Murray and was given the choice, as stated in the poem, of either marrying Sir Gideon's daughter, muckle-mouthed Meg, or hanging. He chose the daughter. Sir Walter Scott, who was always proud of his Border ancestry, was descended from this marriage.

ELIZABETH BARRETT BROWNING
p. 379

STANDARD EDITIONS

Complete Works, 6 vols., ed. w. an intro. and notes by Charlotte Porter and Helen A. Clarke, New York, Crowell, 1900

Poetical Works, ed. by Sir F.G. Kenyon, Globe ed., New York, Macmillan, 1897

Complete Poetical Works, ed. by Harriet Waters Preston, Cambridge ed., Boston, Houghton, 1900

New Poems by Robert Browning and Elizabeth Barrett Browning, ed. by Sir F.G. Kenyon, New York, Macmillan, 1915

Poetical Works; with Two Prose Essays, New York, Oxford Univ. Press, 1951

The Letters of Elizabeth Barrett Browning, 2 vols. in 1, ed. w. biog. additions by Sir F.G. Kenyon, New York, Macmillan, 1899

The Letters of Robert Browning and Elizabeth Barrett Browning, 1845-1846, 2 vols., New York, Harper, 1899

Elizabeth Barrett Browning: Letters to Her Sister, ed. by L. Huxley, London, Murray, 1929

Elizabeth Barrett to Mr. Boyd, letters, ed. by Barbara McCarthy, New Haven, Conn., Yale Univ. Press, 1955

BIOGRAPHY

Burdett, O., *The Brownings*, Boston, Houghton, 1929

Clarke, Isabel C., *Elizabeth Barrett Browning*, London, Hutchinson, 1929

Creston, Dormer (Dorothy J. Baynes, pseud.), *Andromeda in Wimpole Street; the Romance of Elizabeth Barrett Browning*, London, Butterworth, T., 1929

Hewlett, D., *Elizabeth Barrett Browning, a Life*, New York, Knopf, 1952

Loth, D.G., *The Brownings; a Victorian Idyll*, New York, Brentano's, 1929

Lubbock, P., *Elizabeth Barrett Browning in Her Letters*, London, Smith, 1906

Marks, Jeanette, *The Family of the Barrett*, New York, Macmillan, 1938

Merlette, Germaine Marie, *Etude sur la Vie et les Oeuvres d'Elizabeth Barrett Browning*, Paris, Colin, 1904

Miller, Betty B.S., *Robert Browning; a Portrait*, New York, Scribner, 1953

Taplin, Gardner B., *The Life of Elizabeth Barrett Browning*, New Haven, Conn., Yale Univ. Press, 1957

Willis, Irene Cooper, *Elizabeth Barrett Browning*, London, Howe, 1928

Winwar, F., *The Immortal Lovers: Elizabeth Barrett and Robert Browning*, New York, Harper, 1950

CRITICISM

Bald, M.A., "Mrs. Browning," *Women Writers of the Nineteenth Century*, London, Cambridge Univ. Press, 1923

Benson, A.C., "Elizabeth Barrett Browning," *Essays*, New York, Macmillan, 1896

Blackwood's Magazine, "Mrs. Barrett Browning—Aurora Leigh," 1857, 81:23-41

Chesterton, G.K., "Elizabeth Barrett Browning," *Varied Types*, New York, Dodd, 1903

Conway, E., "Elizabeth Barrett Browning," *Anthony Munday and Other Essays*, New York, privately printed, 1927

Dawson, W.J., "The Humanitarian Movement in Poetry—Thomas Hood and Mrs. Browning," *Makers of Poetry*, New York, Revell, 1906

Fonblanque, E. de, "The Influence of Italy on the Poetry of the Brownings," *Fortnightly Review*, 1909, 92:327-344

Gould, Elizabeth P., *The Brownings and America*, Boston, Poet Lore, 1904

Hayter, Alethea, *Mrs. Browning*, London, Faber, 1963

Royds, Kathleen E., *Elizabeth Barrett Browning and Her Poetry*, London, Harrap, 1918

Tidderman, L.E., "Elizabeth Barrett Browning; the Woman and Her Work" *Westminster Review*, 1907, 167:82-92

Wedmore, F., "The Brownings," *Certain Comments*, London, Selwyn, 1925

Whiting, Lilian, *A Study of Elizabeth Barrett Browning*, Boston, Little, 1899

Woolf, Virginia, "Aurora Leigh," *The Second Common Reader*, New York, Harcourt, 1932

BIOGRAPHICAL SKETCH

Elizabeth Barrett Browning (1806-1861) was from her girlhood devoted to literature. Without any regular education, she yet contrived to pick up from her brother's tutor a knowledge of Greek, Latin, and the modern languages; Homer and Pope were her earliest passions. Her father, who combined a despotic desire to rule unconditionally in his family with a pride in the achievements of his children, had Elizabeth's premature epic on the Battle of Marathon privately printed in 1819. Her exercises in verse became her chief amusement when, in 1821, she fell while she was saddling her pony and suffered an injury to her spine; this injury and the later shock of her brother's death by drowning confined her for many years to a darkened room. From her invalid's room she wrote many letters and a good deal of verse. In 1844 she published a volume which not only established her poetic reputation but also moved Robert Browning, then rising to fame, to write her a letter of praise. A correspondence followed and a meeting in 1845. Under the stimulus of Browning's companionship, Miss Barrett found new life. The record of the experience is in her *Sonnets from the Portuguese* (1850). Her health so improved that marriage seemed possible; however, there was one obstacle, the fanatical opposition of her father. But she showed a strength of purpose as great as his, married Browning secretly, and soon after left with him for France and Italy. During the next fifteen years, Mrs. Browning's home, except for occasional visits to France and England, was the villa of Casa Guidi at Florence, where her son was born in 1849, her books written, and artists and writers from England and America hospitably entertained. Among these guests was Hawthorne, who has left a description of Mrs. Browning's delicacy, her slender hands, black ringlets, and pale, eager face. Her impulsive sympathy made her an ardent champion of the Italian struggle for independence from Austria; a strain of mysticism in her nature made her a convert to spiritualism. Yet her life was largely centered in a passionate love for her home, her husband, and her boy. Her health, always precarious, at length failed in 1861.

Mrs. Browning's principal works were: *An Essay on Mind, with Other Poems*, 1826; *Prometheus Bound, and Miscellaneous Poems*, 1833; *The Seraphim, and Other Poems*, 1838; *Poems*, 1844; *Sonnets from the Portuguese*, 1850; *Casa Guidi Windows*, 1851; *Aurora Leigh*, 1857; *Poems before Congress*, 1860; *Last Poems*, 1862.

INTRODUCTORY CRITICISM

"Elizabeth Barrett had a strength really rare among women poets—the strength of phrase. She excelled in her sex, in epigram, almost as much as Voltaire in his. Pointed phrases like: 'Martyrs by the pang without the palm'—or 'Incense to sweeten a crime and myrrh to embitter a curse,' these expressions, which are witty after the old fashion of the conceit, came quite freshly and spontaneously to her quite modern mind. But the first fact is this, that these epigrams of hers were never so true as when they turned on one of the two or three pivots on which contemporary Europe was really turning. She is by far the most European of all the English poets of that age; all of them, even her own much greater husband, look local beside her. Tennyson and the rest are nowhere."—Gilbert Chesterton, *The Victorian Age in Literature*, pp. 177-178.

CRITICAL NOTES

SONNETS FROM THE PORTUGUESE, p. 387

This is a sonnet sequence (not a translation as the name implies) celebrating the love and courtship of Robert Browning and Elizabeth Barrett.

The sonnets were meant to be private, but were published at the urgent suggestion of Browning, who once said, "I dared not reserve to myself the finest sonnets written in any language since Shakespeare." For some unexplained reason Mrs. Browning selected the title *Sonnets Translated from the Bosnian*, but Browning suggested *Sonnets from the Portuguese* because of his admiration of her earlier love poem *Catarina to Camoëns*. Camoëns (1524-1580) was a famous Portuguese poet.

CASA GUIDI WINDOWS, p. 395

The home of the Brownings overlooked a portion of the city of Florence that was the scene of many stirring events associated with the cause of Italian freedom, with which Mrs. Browning was in profound sympathy. She wrote the first part of *Casa Guidi Windows* during the heroic year of 1848, which marked a popular but vain uprising against Austria; the second part was completed in 1851. The poem deals especially with the earlier phases of the movement.

EMILY BRONTË, p. 399

STANDARD EDITIONS

Complete Works of Emily Brontë, London, Hodder, 1910-1911

Emily Brontë; Poems, London, Selwyn, 1923

Complete Poems, ed. by C. Shorter, w. bibliog. and notes by C.W. Hatfield, New York, Doran, 1924

The Complete Poems, ed. by C.W. Hatfield, New York, Columbia Univ. Press, 1941

Brontë Poems; Selection from the Poetry of Charlotte, Emily, Anne, and Branwell Brontë, ed. w. an intro. by A.C. Benson, New York, Putnam, 1915

Emily Brontë, Augustan Books of Modern Poetry, London, Benn, 1926

BIOGRAPHY

Clarke, Isabel, *Haworth Parsonage; a Picture of the Brontë Family,* London, Hutchinson, 1927

Crandall, Norma, *Emily Brontë: A Psychological Portrait,* Rindge, N.H., Smith, 1957

Hanson, L. and E., *The Four Brontës,* New York, Oxford Univ. Press, 1949

Hinkley, L.L., *The Brontës: Charlotte and Emily,* New York, Hastings House, 1945

Moore, V., *The Life and Eager Death of Emily Brontë,* London, Rich, 1936

Ratchford, F.E., *The Brontës' Web of Childhood,* New York, Columbia Univ. Press, 1941

Shorter, C., *The Brontës and Their Circle,* New York, Dutton, 1914

Shorter, C., *The Brontës; Life and Letters,* New York, Scribner, 1908

Simpson, C., *Emily Brontë,* New York, Scribner, 1930

Sinclair, May, *The Three Brontës,* Boston, Houghton, 1914

Sugden, K.A.R., *A Short History of the Brontës,* London, Oxford Univ. Press, 1929

White, W.B., *The Miracle of Haworth,* New York, Dutton, 1939

Wright, J.C., *The Story of the Brontës,* London, Parsons, 1925

CRITICISM

Bald, M.A., "The Brontës," *Woman Writers of the Nineteenth Century,* London, Cambridge Univ. Press, 1923

Clutton-Brock, A., "The Brontës," *Essays on Books,* London, Metheun, 1920

Cooke, D., "Emily Brontë's Poems," *Nineteenth Century,* 1926, 100:248-262

Dimnet, E., *The Brontë Sisters,* tr. from the French by Louise M. Sill, New York, Harcourt, 1928

Dodds, M.H., "Gondaliand," *Modern Language Review,* 1923, 18:9-21, and 1926, 21:373-379

Drinkwater, J., "The Brontës as Poets," *Prose Papers,* London, Mathews, 1917

Haldane, R.B., "Emily Brontë's Place in Literature," *Brontë Society Publications,* Vol. 2, Part 12

Harrison, G.E.S., *The Clue to the Brontës,* London, Methuen, 1948

Kaulman, R., *Natur-Paganismus in der Weltanschauung von Emily Brontë,* Bonn dissertation, 1926

Masson, J., "The Brontës as Seen through French Eyes," *London Quarterly,* 1919, 131:62-72

Meynell, Alice, "Charlotte and Emily Brontë," *Hearts of Controversy,* London, Burns, 1918

Powys, J.C., "Emily Brontë," *Suspended Judgments,* New York, Shaw, A.W., 1916

Ralli, A., "Emily Brontë; the Problem of Personality," *Critiques,* London, Longmans, 1927

Read, H., "Charlotte and Emily Brontë," *Reason and Romanticism,* London, Faber, 1926

Smith, J.C., "Emily Brontë," *Essays and Studies,* Vol. 5, London, Oxford Univ. Press, 1914

Swinburne, A.C., "Emily Brontë," *Miscellanies,* London, Chatto, 1886

Symons, A., "Emily Brontë," *Dramatis Personæ,* Indianapolis, Bobbs, 1923

Wise, T.J., *A Bibliography of the Writings in Prose and Verse of the Members of the Brontë Family,* London, Clay, 1917

Wood, B., "A Bibliography of the Works of the Brontë Family," *Brontë Society Publications,* Vol. 1, Parts 1 and 6

BIOGRAPHICAL SKETCH

Emily Brontë (1818-1848) was born and brought up in a church parsonage at Haworth, among the bleak Yorkshire moors, which she loved with fervent and almost hysterical passion. She attended school for short unhappy intervals, first at Cowan's Bridge, depicted as Lowood School by her sister Charlotte in *Jane Eyre;* later at Roe Head, where Charlotte also studied. In 1842 Emily went with Charlotte to Brussels to study but returned before the end of the year. She had brief and bitter experiences as a governess before finally relapsing definitely into secluded home life at Haworth. She died in 1848 of the family scourge, tuberculosis.

Emily Brontë wrote under a pseudonym—Ellis Bell. Her poems were first published in 1846 with those of her sisters, who also used pseudonyms, in *Poems by Currer, Ellis, and Acton Bell;* her only other book was *Wuthering Heights,* a novel, published in 1847.

INTRODUCTORY CRITICISMS

"When we turn to Emily's poetry, the genius of it becomes instantly apparent. She was speaking her own natural language. Her verse is often obscured by its plainness and directness, its apparent indifference to all artistic charm. It is full of weak and conventional rhymes, careless assonances, vague and broken rhythms. Very few of her poems are accurately constructed. But there is an immense feeling of reality and observation. The power of the Brontës lay in their capacity for multiplying the significance of what would seem the small and trivial incidents and emotions; and Emily seems to have turned upon nature and life an unflinching vision, and to have really seen for herself the things which familiarity is apt to blur."—A. C. Benson, Introduction to *Brontë Poems,* pp. xi-xii.

Matthew Arnold, in *Haworth Churchyard,* speaks thus of Emily Brontë and her last poem, *No Coward Soul Is Mine* (p. 400):

(How shall I sing her?) whose soul
Knew no fellow for might,
Passion, vehemence, grief,
Daring, since Byron died,
That world-famed son of fire—she, who sank
Baffled, unknown, self-consumed;
Whose too bold dying song
Stirred, like a clarion-blast, my soul.

AUBREY THOMAS DE VERE, p. 401

STANDARD EDITIONS

Poetical Works, London, Paul, 1884-1889
Poetical Works, 7 vols., London, Macmillan, 1898
Selections from the Poems, ed. w. a pref. by G.E. Woodberry, New York, Macmillan, 1894
May Carols and Other Poems, London, Macmillan, 1897
Essays, Chiefly on Poetry, 2 vols., London, Macmillan, 1887
Essays Chiefly Literary and Ethical, London, Macmillan, 1889
Recollections, New York, Arnold, 1897

BIOGRAPHY AND CRITICISM

Brégy, Katherine, "The Poetry of De Vere," *Catholic World,* 1907, 84:788-801
Dublin Review, "De Vere's *Poems,*" 1855, 38:300-321
Gunning, J.P., *Aubrey de Vere; a Memoir,* Limerick, Ireland, Guy, 1902
Pijpers, Th. A., *Aubrey de Vere as a Man of Letters,* Nijmegen, Netherlands, Dekker and Vande Vegt, 1941
Quarterly Review, "The Poetry of the De Veres," 1896, 183:310-338
Reilly, Sister Mary Paraclita, *Aubrey de Vere: Victorian Observer,* Lincoln, Univ. of Neb. Press, 1953
Thompson, F., "Aubrey de Vere," *A Renegade Poet, and Other Essays,* Boston, Ball, 1910
Towle, E.A., "*Recollections* of Aubrey de Vere," *Sewanee Review,* 1899, 7:271-286
Ward, W.P., *Aubrey de Vere; a Memoir,* London, Macmillan, 1904
Woodberry, G.E., "Aubrey de Vere, Poet and Critic," *Studies of a Littérateur,* New York, Harcourt, 1921

BIOGRAPHICAL SKETCH

Aubrey Thomas de Vere (1814-1902), the son of an Irish baronet and poet of the same name, was born at Curragh Chase in County Limerick, Ireland, and educated at Trinity College, Dublin. Upon visits in England, he became the fast friend of Tennyson, Henry Taylor, and other English men of letters. His early interest in poetry was dominated first by Byron, then by Wordsworth; but *The Search after Proserpine,* published in 1843, shows influence of Shelley and the Greeks. De Vere was interested in Irish political and economic problems of his time, and after witnessing the horrors of the Irish famine of 1846, inclined toward Catholicism; he was finally received into the Catholic Church in 1851. From that time on, as he tells us, his poems were almost exclusively "intended to illustrate religious philosophy or early Irish history." For a few years he taught under Father Newman in the new Catholic University at Dublin but resigned in 1858 for permanent retirement at Curragh Chase.

The principal publications of De Vere were: *The Waldenses,* 1842; *The Search after Proserpine,* 1843; *May Carols,* 1857; *The Sisters, Inisfail, and Other Poems,* 1861; *The Legends of St. Patrick,* 1872; *Poetical Works,* 1884; *Critical Essays,* 3 vols., 1887-1889.

INTRODUCTORY CRITICISM

"The qualities of Aubrey de Vere's poetry are not far to seek. Lyrical in verse, strong in style, mainly historical in theme, heroic or spiritual in substance, above all placid, it stirs and tranquillizes the soul in the presence of lovely scenes, high actions, and those 'great ideas that man was born to learn'; and its outlook is upon the field of the soul regenerate, where suffering is remembered only through its purification, blessed in issues of sweetness, dignity, and peace. It takes wide range, but is predominantly either Bardic or Christian. The sympathy of the poet with the ancient Irish spirit must have been fed with patriotic fervor, akin to renewed inspiration, to permit him to render the old lays of his country with such fidelity to their native genius."—G. E. Woodberry, *Studies of a Littérateur*, p. 159.

WILLIAM BARNES, p. 402

STANDARD EDITIONS

The Poems of William Barnes, ed. by Bernard Jones, 2 vols., Carbondale, Southern Illinois Univ. Press, 1962

Selected Poems, chosen and ed. w. a pref. by T. Hardy, London, Oxford Univ. Press, 1908

Selected Poems, ed. by G. Grigson, Cambridge, Mass., Harvard Univ. Press, 1950

Poems of Rural Life in the Dorset Dialect; a Selection, London, Paul, 1909

Twenty Poems in Common English, ed. w. an intro. by John Drinkwater, New York, Duffield, 1925

Poems of Rural Life in Common English, Boston, Roberts, 1869

Poems of Rural Life in the Dorset Dialect, London, Macmillan, 1887

BIOGRAPHY AND CRITICISM

Baxter, Lucy E., *The Life of William Barnes, Poet and Philologist*, London, Macmillan, 1887

Drinkwater, J., "William Barnes," *A Book for Bookmen*, London, Dulau, 1926

Dugdale, G., *William Barnes of Dorset*, London, Cassell, 1953

Edinburgh Review, "The Life and Poems of William Barnes," 1888, 168:119-138

Hardy, T., "The Rev. William Barnes, B. D.," *Athenaeum*, Oct. 16, 1886, pp. 501-502. Reprinted in Johnson's *The Art of Thomas Hardy*, Dodd, 1923

Jacobs, W.D., *William Barnes, Linguist*, Albuquerque, Univ. of N. Mex. Press, 1952

Levy, William T., *William Barnes: The Man and the Poems*, Dorchester, Eng., Longmans, 1960

Patmore, C., "An English Classic, William Barnes," *Fortnightly Review*, 1886, 46: 659-670

Powys, L., "William Barnes, the Dorset Poet," *The Freeman*, 1922, 5:415-416

Woodberry, G.E., "William Barnes, the Dorsetshire Poet," *Literary Memoirs of the Nineteenth Century*, New York, Harcourt, 1921

BIOGRAPHICAL SKETCH

William Barnes (1801-1886) was born and lived practically the whole of his life in Dorsetshire, the southern county of England in which his ancestors had for centuries been farmers. Far from seeking to free himself from his local environment, he cultivated it and interpreted it to the world. In spite of poverty, he made the most of Dorsetshire schools and of opportunities for self-education, gained after ten years of work *in absentia* a degree from Cambridge, and became a scholar with a wide reputation especially in mathematics, archaeology, and philology. In the intervals of his employment as teacher and country parson, he wrote verse, pried into the Celtic and Roman ruins about Dorchester, and wrote on the Dorset dialect and on the relations between English and other Teutonic tongues; his most remarkable crotchet was his defense of "purity" in English against the use of Latin derivatives and his employment of such terms as "wheelsaddle" and "sunprint" in place of "bicycle" and "photograph." Well-read in many literatures, admiring Petrarch and the Persian poet Saadi above all other writers, he yet confined the materials of his poetry to the limits of Dorchester. His first descriptions of his neighbors appeared in 1833, in local newspapers; his *Poems of Rural Life in the Dorset Dialect*, published in 1844, was followed by three other groups of "hand-writs," the last "in common English." The praise of Patmore, Tennyson, and Allingham did nothing to alter his essential homeliness and serenity; as much a part of the Dorset countryside as the thatched houses, he worked vigorously in school and parish and study until well over eighty. Hardy, his successor as the laureate poet of Dorsetshire, has described him as an old man, plodding into Dorchester on a market day "attired in a caped cloak, knee-breeches, and buckled shoes, with a leather satchel slung over his shoulders, and a stout staff in his hand," keeping the middle of the road, and pausing before the town clock to set his ancient watch to London time.

Barnes's principal publications were: *Poems of Rural Life in the Dorset Dialect*, 1844; *A Philological Grammar*, 1854; *Hwomely Rhymes*,

1858; *Notes on Ancient Britain and the Britons*, 1858; *Tiw: a View of the Roots and Stems of the English as a Teutonic Tongue*, 1862; *A Grammar and Glossary of the Dorset Dialect*, 1863; *Poems of Rural Life in the Dorset Dialect: Third Collection*, 1863; *Poems of Rural Life in Common English*, 1868; *An Outline of English Speechcraft*, 1878; *An Outline of Redecraft or Logic*, 1878.

INTRODUCTORY CRITICISM

"Readers will observe that Barnes is no untutored minstrel, that he is, indeed, a highly skilled technician, weaving all sorts of structural fancies into his verse ... Barnes had a lyric heart, but he was a grave gentleman, a scholar, and in the most agreeable sense a precisian, and he delighted to exercise his singing gift in the terms of a very agile and conscious art. It will be noted, too, that this poet, who as a parish priest had more than an amateur knowledge of the seamy side of life, chose to be unashamedly on the side of the angels in his poetry."—John Drinkwater, Introduction to Barnes's *Twenty Poems in Common English*, p. 9.

CHARLES KINGSLEY, p. 405

STANDARD EDITIONS

Life and Works, 19 vols., London, Macmillan, 1901-1903
Poems, London, Macmillan, 1902
Charles Kingsley: His Letters and Memories of His Life, ed. by his wife, 2 vols., London, Macmillan, 1901

BIOGRAPHY

Brown, W.H., *Charles Kingsley: the Work and Influence of Parson Lot*, London, Unwin, 1924
Martin, Robert B., *The Dust of Combat: A Life of Charles Kingsley*, London, Faber, 1960
Pope-Hennessy, Dame Una B., *Canon Charles Kingsley*, New York, Macmillan, 1949
Stubbs, C.W., *Charles Kingsley and the Christian Social Movement*, London, Blackie, 1899

CRITICISM

Baldwin, S.E., *Charles Kingsley*, Ithaca, N.Y., Cornell Univ. Press, 1934
Harrison, F., "Charles Kingsley," *Studies in Early Victorian Literature*, London, Arnold, 1895
Hearn, L., "Charles Kingsley as a Poet," *Appreciations of Poetry*, London, Dodd, 1916
Kendall, G., *Charles Kingsley and His Ideas*, London, Hutchinson, 1947

Lang, A., "Charles Kingsley," *Essays in Little*, London, Henry, 1891
Living Age, "Charles Kingsley as a Lyric Poet," 1855, 46:315-316
Russell, G.W.E., "Charles Kingsley," *Selected Essays on Literary Subjects*, London, Dent, 1914
Thorp, M.F., *Charles Kingsley, 1819-1875*, Princeton, N.J., Princeton Univ. Press, 1937
Waugh, A., "Charles Kingsley," *Reticence in Literature*, London, Wilson, 1915

BIOGRAPHICAL SKETCH

Charles Kingsley (1819-1875), known as the proponent of "muscular Christianity," was the son of a clergyman but was himself at first attracted more by physical sports than by the church. At Clovelly, on the western coast of Devon, he learned to swim and row, and acquired an almost scientific knowledge of coastal plants and rocks; at the University of Cambridge, which he entered in 1838, he boxed, rowed on his college crew, and tramped on long geological and botanical excursions. His generous if somewhat excitable sympathies becoming concerned with the hardships of the poor, he was prompted, after his graduation, to enter the church as a means to alleviating social distress; he took parishes where there was the most work to do in the least congenial surroundings. With the same end, he espoused the cause of "Christian Socialism," which aimed to combine the teachings of Christ with the teachings of socialism in their application to life; he delivered lectures and wrote pamphlets designed to promote a better understanding between landlords and tenants, employers and laborers; and in 1848-1851 published his novels *Alton Locke* and *Yeast*, which further promulgated his views. Another novel, *Hypatia*, in 1853, reflected his interest not only in the intellectual crises of his time but also in historical studies; his *Westward Ho!*, written in 1855 during a vacation near his boyhood home in Clovelly, combined a romantic love of the past with a delight in vigorous adventure. The life of animals and plants about the seashore gave him his material for *Glaucus* in 1855 and *The Water-Babies* in 1863. His poems, which he began writing early in his boyhood and published in 1858-1875, embodied all his varied and energetic interests. Advancing years brought no abatement in his zest for living, even though ill health and a constitutional restlessness kept him from working long in any one direction. From 1860 to 1863 he delivered lectures on history at Cambridge, more remarkable for their interest than their accuracy. In later life he held important positions in the church. He became involved in 1864 in an unfortunate religious controversy with Cardinal Newman and was signally defeated. For the sake of his health, he traveled in 1874 through the western states of America; returning to England, he sank rapidly and died in 1875 at the country parish of which he had long been rector. Villagers and local huntsmen mingled with great soldiers and statesmen at his funeral.

Kingsley's principal publications were: *Alton Locke*, 1850; *Yeast*, 1851; *Hypatia*, 1853; *Alexandria and Her Schools*, 1854; *Sermons for the Times*, 1855; *Westward Ho!*, 1855; *Glaucus, or the Wonders of the Shore*, 1855; *The Heroes, or Greek Fairy Tales*, 1856; *Two Years Ago*, 1857; *Andromeda, and Other Poems*, 1858; *The Water-Babies*, 1863; *Hereward the Wake*, 1866; *Madam How and Lady Why*, 1869; *At Last*, 1871; *Prose Idylls*, 1873; *Plays and Puritans*, 1873; *Health and Education*, 1874; *Lectures Delivered in America*, 1875.

INTRODUCTORY CRITICISM

"Emotional, intuitive, spontaneous, 'temperamental,' he [Kingsley] diagnosed himself, according to nineteenth century psychology, as a poet and the conviction was strengthened by his knack of versifying. His too fluent utterance needed external restraint; he thought most effectively, therefore, within the imposed barriers of verse. . . . He worked best within a set simple form. A melody heard or imagined would set his invention going and his invention was always fertile in the production of tales, pathetic, exciting or lurid. As a poet he succeeds best with the ballad . . ."—Margaret Farrand Thorp, *Charles Kingsley, 1819-1875*, p. 137.

CRITICAL NOTES

THE SANDS OF DEE, p. 406

Page 406, lines 20-21. In discussing the pathetic fallacy, Ruskin cites lines 20 and 21 of this poem as an example of "fallacy caused by an excited state of the feelings, making us, for the time, more or less irrational." He says: "The foam is not cruel, neither does it crawl. The state of mind which attributes to it these characters of a living creature is one in which the reason is unhinged by grief. All violent feelings have the same effect. They produce in us a falseness in all our impressions of external things, which I would generally characterize as 'the pathetic fallacy.'" —*Modern Painters*, Vol. 3, pt. 4, ch. 12, sec. 5.

ARTHUR HUGH CLOUGH, p. 409

STANDARD EDITIONS

Poems and Prose Remains, w. a sel. fr. his letters and a mem., ed. by his wife, 2 vols., London, Macmillan, 1869

Poems, ed. by H.F. Lowry and others, New York, Oxford Univ. Press, 1952

Poems, w. an intro. by Charles Whibley, New York, Macmillan, 1913

The Bothie and Other Poems, ed. by E. Rhys, London, Scott, 1896

Prose Remains, w. letters and a mem., London, Macmillan, 1888

Correspondence, ed. by F.L. Mulhauser, 2 vols., New York, Oxford Univ. Press, 1957

BIOGRAPHY

Chorley, Lady Katharine, *Arthur Hugh Clough: The Uncommitted Mind*, Oxford, Clarendon Press, 1962

Levy, G., *Arthur Hugh Clough*, London, Sidgwick, 1938

Osborne, James I., *Arthur Hugh Clough*, London, Constable, 1920

Woodward, Frances J., *The Doctor's Disciples: A Study of Four Pupils of Thomas Arnold of Rugby*, London, Oxford Univ. Press, 1954

CRITICISM

Bagehot, W., "Mr. Clough's Poems," *Literary Studies*, 3 vols., ed. by R.H. Hutton, London, Longmans, 1895

Brooke, S.A., "Arthur Hugh Clough," *Four Victorian Poets*, New York, Putnam, 1908

Chapman, E.M., "The Doubters and the Mystics," *English Literature in Account with Religion*, Boston, Houghton, 1910

Emerson, R.W., "Arthur Hugh Clough," *Uncollected Writings*, New York, Lamb, 1912

Garrod, H.W., "Clough," *Poetry and the Criticism of Life*, Cambridge, Mass., Harvard Univ. Press, 1931

Hewlett, M., "Teufelsdröckh in Hexameters," *Nineteenth Century*, 1922, 91:68-75

Houghton, Walter E., *The Poetry of Clough*, New Haven, Conn., Yale Univ. Press, 1963

Hudson, W.H., "Clough," *Studies in Interpretation*, New York, Putnam, 1896

Hutton, R.H., "Amiel and Clough," "The Unpopularity of Clough," *Brief Literary Criticisms*, London, Macmillan, 1906

Hutton, R.H., "Arthur Hugh Clough," *Literary Essays*, London, Macmillan, 1892

Lucas, F.L., *Eight Victorian Poets*, London, Cambridge Univ. Press, 1930

Lyttleton, A.T., "The Poetry of Doubt (Arnold and Clough)," *Modern Poets of Faith, Doubt, and Paganism, and Other Essays*, London, Murray, 1904

Palmer, F.W., *The Relation of Arthur Hugh Clough to the Intellectual Movements of His Time*, parts of Univ. of Iowa thesis, 1939 [n. p., 1944]

Patmore, C., "Arthur Hugh Clough," *Principle in Art*, London, Bell, 1889

Robertson, J.M., "Clough," *New Essays Towards a Critical Method*, London, Lane, 1897

Ryals, Clyde de L., "An Interpretation of Clough's *Dipsychus*," *Victorian Poetry*, 1963, 1:182-188

Shackford, Martha H., "The Clough Centenary: his *Dipsychus*," *Sewanee Review*, 1919, 27:401-410

Sidgwick, H., "The Poems and Prose Remains of Arthur Hugh Clough," *Miscellaneous Essays and Addresses*, London, Macmillan, 1904

Symonds, John A., "Arthur Hugh Clough," *Last and First*, New York, Brown, 1919

Timko, Michael, "The Satiric Poetry of Arthur Hugh Clough," *Victorian Poetry*, 1963, 1:104-114

Timko, Michael, "The 'True Creed' of Arthur Hugh Clough," *Modern Language Quarterly*, 1960, 21:208-222

Turner, A.M., "A Study of Clough's *Mari Magno*," *PMLA*, 1929, 44:569-589

Waddington, Samuel, *Arthur Hugh Clough*, London, Bell, 1883

Welby, T.E., "Clough," *Back Numbers*, London, Constable, 1929

Wolfe, H., "Arthur Hugh Clough," in *The Eighteen-Sixties*, ed. by John Drinkwater, New York, Macmillan, 1932

BIOGRAPHICAL SKETCH

Arthur Hugh Clough (1819-1861), born in Liverpool of Welsh and Yorkshire stock, was a natural student from childhood, the early days of which he spent in Charleston, South Carolina, where he read Pope's *Homer* and many of Scott's novels; at the age of seven he is said to have mastered the lives of Columbus and Cortez. Returned to England he attended Rugby (1829-1837) where he became the "ideal pupil" of Dr. Thomas Arnold. He entered Oxford during the stormy days of the Oxford Movement and soon came under the influence of Newman. A fellowship in Oriel College, accepted after his graduation, was resigned in 1848 because of his inability to subscribe any longer to the tenets of the Church of England, and, as his friend Matthew Arnold wrote, "Thyrsis of his own will went away." Brief travels in France and Italy brought no respite to his troubled spirit. Meantime he had been appointed Head of University Hall, London; had pub-lished *The Bothie of Tober-na-Vuolich* (1848), a "long-vacation pastoral," written like his *Amours de Voyage* (1849 f.) in English hexameters; and had collaborated with his friend Thomas Burbidge on a small volume of verse entitled *Ambarvalia* (1849). Wearying of the restriction of thought imposed by his new position in London, Clough in 1852 accepted a proposal of Emerson to visit America and crossed the Atlantic with Lowell and Thackeray as traveling companions. Despite the welcome accorded him in Boston and Cambridge, where he won the friendship of Emerson, Lowell, Charles Eliot Norton, and Longfellow, his efforts to support himself at tutoring and writing proved a failure, and he returned a year later to become an examiner in the Education Office, London. Married in 1854 to a cousin of Florence Nightingale, he thereafter took a lively interest in Miss Nightingale's work during and after the Crimean War. His health, not for some years very strong, took him to Florence, Italy, where he died in 1861. Clough is immortalized in Arnold's *The Scholar-Gypsy* (p. 487) and *Thyrsis* (p. 493), based upon a friendship formed at Rugby and Oxford.

The principal publications of Clough were: *The Bothie of Tober-na-Vuolich*, 1848; *Ambarvalia* (with T. Burbidge), 1849; *Poems*, 1862; *Poems and Prose Remains*, in 2 vols., ed. by Mrs. Clough, 1869.

INTRODUCTORY CRITICISMS

"He [Clough] was not a great poet, because uppermost in him was the spirit of criticism. He suppressed his evident talent of observation that he might discuss in meter the vexed questions of the moment. And though he was ever intent to criticize life, he was no stern critic of his own poetry. Even though he kept some of his own poems long enough to satisfy Horace, he spared the use of the file.... The need of expression was too active in him. His thoughts clamored so loudly for utterance that he could not control them, and instead of a great poet, he became, so to say, the mouthpiece of his own doubting age. In other words, he was so faithful to the 'movements' of his time that he appears already somewhat antiquated and out of fashion. But if his shorter poems are not written with the exact care which art demands, they set forth with a loyal accuracy the experiences of his mind and soul.... Clough was in trouble always concerning his waning faith.... He hankered after the solution of the problems of life, and was driven back upon doubt. It was this frame of mind, which many have borne with equanimity, that Clough attempted to express in verse. 'Eat, drink, and die,' he wrote in his *Easter Day*, which most clearly reflects the sad candor of his skepticism. And even though, when he wrote these lines, in 1849, he had exchanged the human atmosphere of Oxford for the dismal solitude of University Hall, he could still take comfort in the security of Truth. So he turned back, with a kind of comfort, to a poetic exposition of his skepticism."—C. Whibley, Introduction to *Poems of Arthur Hugh Clough*, pp. xxii-xxiii.

"But my own belief is that the struggle, which was absorbing and was finally to destroy Clough's originality, was a much more personal one. It was in my view the agony of the innate satirical genius of Clough seeking in vain to rid itself of the swaddling-clothes of Arnoldism, and of all the honourable and clogging pieties of the period."—Humbert Wolfe, "Arthur Hugh Clough," in *The Eighteen-Sixties*, ed. by John Drinkwater, p. 29.

"But if we consider *The Bothie, Amours de Voyage* and *Dipsychus* dispassionately it seems to me that we have overwhelming proof that in Clough a great natural satirist and storyteller was smothered not by his own doubts but by the doubts thrust upon him by his friends. Born in a happier time, a less superficially introspective time, he would, I believe, have found a place beside Dryden and Byron as one of the greatest of the English in the satiric mode." Humbert Wolfe, "Arthur Hugh Clough," in *The Eighteen-Sixties*, ed. by J. Drinkwater, p. 50.

See Arnold's *The Scholar-Gypsy* (p. 487) and *Thyrsis* (p. 493).

The present text of the poems follows early published editions, which often supplied titles not found in Clough's manuscripts. The dating, however, owes much to the Oxford edition of 1952, prepared by H. F. Lowry, A. L. P. Norrington, and F. L. Mulhauser, the actual text of which frequently returns to manuscript readings.

CRITICAL NOTES

DIPSYCHUS, p. 415

This poem is generally ranked as Clough's most ambitious work. Miss Shackford says of it: "Dipsychus . . . is the most satiric of all of Clough's poems. It is the reverse side of his own life, the negative aspect of his positive action. It presents in loosely dramatic scenes the spiritual irresolution of the typical young Oxford man who, visiting Venice and delighting in all the shimmering beauty of the city, fascinated by the gay life,

is, however, continually debating whether the appeal of the easy and conventional is the appeal of materialism or of good, honest common sense. The higher and the lower natures are in constant interplay, the remonstrant voice of the aspiring, mystical mood of Dipsychus is answered by the satiric spirit of conformity, the spirit of *laissez-faire* in the world of moral duty, until Dipsychus gives himself over to the care of the Mephisto within himself."—*Sewanee Review*, Oct. 1919, pp. 405-406.

The scene of Part I is Venice, that of Part II, London. The poem, left unfinished, was not published during Clough's lifetime.

The selections on pp. 415-419 of this text are in the same order as they were in the first edition (1865). The 1952 edition rearranges the text.

EDWARD FITZGERALD, p. 425

STANDARD EDITIONS

Variorum and Definitive Edition, Poetical and Prose Writings, 7 vols., incl. a complete bibliog., w. an intro. by Edmund Gosse, New York, Doubleday, 1902-1903

Rubáiyát of Omar Khayyám, showing variants in the 5 orig. printings, New York, Crowell, 1921

FitzGerald's Rubáiyát, Centennial Edition, ed. by Carl J. Weber, w. intro., Waterville, Me., Colby College Press, 1959

Rubáiyát of Omar Khayyám, intro. by Jerome H. Buckley, New York, Collier Books, 1962

Letters and Literary Remains, ed. by W.A. Wright, 3 vols., London, Macmillan, 1889

Letters of Edward FitzGerald to Fanny Kemble, 1871-1883, ed. by W.A. Wright, New York, Macmillan, 1895

More Letters, London, Macmillan, 1901

Some New Letters, ed. by F.R. Barton, London, Williams, 1923

Edward FitzGerald and Bernard Barton; Letters Written by FitzGerald, 1839-1856, ed. by F.R. Barton, New York, Putnam, 1924

Letters from Edward FitzGerald to Bernard Quaritch, 1853 to 1883, ed. by C.Q. Wrentmore, London, Quaritch, 1926

FitzGerald: Selected Works, ed. by Joanna Richardson, London, Hart-Davis, 1962

BIOGRAPHY

Benson, A.C., *Edward FitzGerald*, English Men of Letters Series, New York, Macmillan, 1925

Terhune, A.M., *The Life of Edward FitzGerald*, New Haven, Conn., Yale Univ. Press, 1947

Wright, T., *The Life of Edward FitzGerald*, 2 vols., New York, Scribner, 1904

CRITICISM

Arberry, Arthur J., *Omar Khayyám*, New Haven, Conn. Yale Univ. Press, 1952

Arberry, Arthur J., *The Romance of the Rubáiyát*, New York, Macmillan, 1959

Bradford, G., "Edward FitzGerald," *Bare Souls*, New York, Harper, 1924

Groome, F.H., *Edward FitzGerald: an Aftermath*, Portland, Me., Mosher, 1902

Harris, May, "A Victorian Pagan," *Sewanee Review*, 1926, 34:309-317

Hearn, L., "Edward FitzGerald and the Rubáiyát," *Interpretations of Literature*, 2 vols., New York, Dodd, 1915

Heron-Allen, Edward, *Edward FitzGerald's Rubáiyát of Omar Khayyám and their Original Persian Sources*, London, Quaritch, 1899

Hutton, R.H., "A Great Poet of Denial and Revolt," *Brief Literary Criticisms*, London, Macmillan, 1906

Johnson, L.P., "Lucretius and Omar," *Post Liminium*, London, Mathews, 1911

More, P.E., "Kipling and FitzGerald," *Shelburne Essays*, 2d s., New York, Putnam, 1905

Phelps, W.L., "Schopenhauer and Omar," *Essays on Books*, New York, Macmillan, 1914

Platt, A., "Edward FitzGerald," *Nine Essays*, London, Cambridge Univ. Press, 1928

Ralli, A., "Edward FitzGerald and His Times," *Critiques*, London, Longmans, 1927

Tutin, J.R., *A Concordance to FitzGerald's Translation of the Rubáiyát of Omar Khayyám*, London, Macmillan, 1900

Weir, T.H., "Omar Khayyám," *Quarterly Review*, 1925, 245:63-81

Welby, T.E., "FitzGerald," *Back Numbers*, London, Constable, 1929

Wheeler, C.V.C,. *A Bibliography of Edward FitzGerald*, 3 vols., Washington, 1919

Wolff, Michael, "The *Rubáiyát*'s Neglected Reviewer: A Centennial Recovery," *Victorian Newsletter*, 1960, 17:4-6

BIOGRAPHICAL SKETCH

Edward FitzGerald (1809-1883), born Edward Purcell, came into the name by which he is known when upon the death of his maternal grandfather in 1818 the family assumed the name FitzGerald. After graduation from Trinity College, Cambridge, where he became intimate with Thackeray, and a brief visit to Paris, where he had lived a short time as a boy, FitzGerald settled down to the easy pleasant life of a country gentleman and something of a recluse, devoted to flowers, the ocean, literature, and the friendship of men like Carlyle and Tennyson. His placid seclusion was diversified only by various changes of residence and a very brief, unsatisfactory marriage. Many free adaptations from the Persian, Spanish, and Greek are the record of FitzGerald's more than dilettante fondness for exotic literature, and his delicacy in re-dressing it for English readers. Most of his work appeared anonymously.

FitzGerald's principal publications were: *Euphranor*, 1851; *Polonius*, 1852; *Six Dramas of Calderon* (freely translated), 1853; *Salaman and Absal*, 1856; *The Rubáiyát of Omar Khayyám*, 1859; *The Mighty Magician* and *Such Stuff as Dreams Are Made of* (freely translated from the Spanish), 1865; *The Downfall and Death of King Œdipus*, 1880.

INTRODUCTORY CRITICISM

"Whether his version of the *Rubáiyát*, with its sensuous fatalism, its ridicule of asceticism and renunciation, and its bewildering kaleidoscope of mysticism that becomes materialist, and materialism that becomes mystical, has not indirectly had influences, practical and literary, the results of which would have been more abhorrent to FitzGerald than to almost anyone else, may be suggested. But the beauty of the poem as a poem is unmistakable and altogether astounding. The melancholy richness of the rolling quatrain with its unicorn rhymes, the quaint mixture of farce and solemnity, passion and playfulness, the abundance of the imagery, the power of the thought, the seduction of the rhetoric, make the poem actually, though not original or English, one of the greatest of English poems."—G. Saintsbury, *A History of Nineteenth Century Literature*, p. 209.

CRITICAL NOTES

THE RUBAIYAT OF OMAR KHAYYAM, p. 425

FitzGerald became interested in Persian poetry as early as 1854; he read Omar in 1857 and was at once fascinated by the form and thought of his verse. The result was an English poem of 75 quatrains founded upon Omar and arranged to produce a continuous train of thought. Published in 1859, the poem was ignored until two years later when a remaindered copy was called to the attention of Dante Gabriel Rossetti. Upon his suggestion FitzGerald in 1868 published a completely revised edition, which consisted of 110 stanzas; later editions of 1872 and 1879 rearranged the stanzas and reduced the number to 101.

Some of the changes made in the second and third editions of the poem were improvements, but it is generally thought that the first stanza was best in its original form:

Awake! for Morning in the Bowl of Night
Has flung the Stone that puts the Stars to Flight;
And Lo! the Hunter of the East has caught
The Sultán's Turret in a Noose of Light.

FitzGerald thus describes Omar's verses and his own: "The original Rubáiyát are independent Stanzas, consisting each of four Lines of equal, though varied, Prosody; sometimes all rhyming, but oftener (as here imitated) the third line a blank, sometimes as in the Greek Alcaic, where the penultimate line seems to lift and suspend the Wave that falls over in the last. As usual with such kind of Oriental Verse, the Rubáiyát follow one another according to Alphabetic Rhyme—a strange succession of Grave and Gay. Those here selected are strung into something of an Eclogue, with perhaps a less than equal proportion of the 'Drink and make-merry,' which (genuine or not) occurs over frequently in the Original. Either way, the Result is sad enough: saddest perhaps when most ostentatiously merry: more apt to move Sorrow than Anger toward the old Tent-maker, who, after vainly endeavoring to unshackle his Steps from Destiny, and to catch some authentic Glimpse of *Tomorrow*, fell back upon *Today* (which has outlasted so many Tomorrows!) as the only Ground he's got to stand upon, however momentarily slipping from under his Feet."

In the text, FitzGerald's capital letters have been preserved.

MATTHEW ARNOLD, p. 431

STANDARD EDITIONS

Works, 15 vols., London, Macmillan, 1903-1904, bibliog., Vol. 15, pp. 341-388

Poetical Works, London, Macmillan, 1929

Poetical Works, new ed., ed. by C.B. Tinker and H.F. Lowry, New York, Oxford Univ. Press, 1950

Prose and Poetry, ed. by A.L. Bouton, New York, Scribner, 1927

Essays and Poems, w. an intro. by F.W. Roe, New York, Harcourt, 1928

Complete Prose Works, ed. by R.H. Super, Ar Arbor, Univ. of Michigan Press, 1960 (in process)

Selected Essays, ed. w. intro. and crit. annot.

by H.G. Rawlinson, London, Macmillan, 1924

Culture and Anarchy, ed. by W.S. Knickerbocker, New York, Macmillan, 1925

Discourses in America, New York, Macmillan, 1902

Essays in Criticism, 2 vols., London, Macmillan, 1925

Essays in Criticism, 3d s., w. an intro. by E.J. O'Brien, Boston, Ball, 1910

Literature and Dogma, New York, Macmillan, 1902

Letters of Matthew Arnold, 1848-1888, 2 vols., col. and arr. by G.W.E. Russell, New York, Macmillan, 1895

Unpublished Letters, ed. by A. Whitridge, New Haven, Conn., Yale Univ. Press, 1923

Note-books, ed. by H.F. Lowry and others, New York, Oxford Univ. Press, 1952

Poetry and Criticism, ed. by A. Dwight Culler, Boston, Houghton Mifflin, 1961

BIOGRAPHY

Bonnerot, Louis, *Matthew Arnold, Poète; Essai de Biographie Psychologique*, Paris, Didier, 1947

Chambers, E.K., *Matthew Arnold*, London, Oxford Univ. Press, 1947

Fitch, J., *Thomas and Matthew Arnold and Their Influence on English Education*, New York, Scribner, 1897

Jump, J.D., *Matthew Arnold*, London, Longmans, Green, 1955

Kingsmill, H., *Matthew Arnold*, New York, Dial Press, 1928

Knickerbocker, W.S., "Matthew Arnold at Oxford," *Sewanee Review*, 1927, 35:399-418

Paul, H.W., *Matthew Arnold*, English Men of Letters Series, London, Macmillan, 1925

Russell, G.W.E., *Matthew Arnold*, New York, Scribner, 1904

Saintsbury, G., *Matthew Arnold*, New York, Dodd, 1899

Ward, M.A., "The Family of Fox How," *A Writer's Recollections*, New York, Harper, 1918

CRITICISM

Baum, Paull F., *Ten Studies in the Poetry of Matthew Arnold*, Durham, N.C., Duke Univ. Press, 1958

Bickley, Francis L., *Matthew Arnold and His Poetry*, New York, Dodge, 1911

Birrell, A., "Matthew Arnold," *Collected Essays and Addresses*, 3 vols., London, Dent, 1922

Boyer, C.V., "A Study of Matthew Arnold's

Idea of Perfection," *International Journal of Ethics*, 1923, 33:263-290

Brick, Allan, "Equilibrium in the Poetry of Matthew Arnold," *University of Toronto Quarterly*, 1960, 30:45-56

Brooke, S.A., "Matthew Arnold," *Four Victorian Poets*, New York, Putnam, 1908

Brown, E.K., *Matthew Arnold; a Study in Conflict*, Chicago, Univ. of Chicago Press, 1948

Buckley, Vincent, *Poetry and Morality*, London, Chatto and Windus, 1959

Collins, J.C., "Matthew Arnold," *Posthumous Essays*, ed. by L.C. Collins, London, Dent, 1912

Connell, W.F., *The Educational Thought and Influence of Matthew Arnold*, London, Routledge, 1950

Courtney, Mrs. Janet E., "Matthew Arnold," *Freethinkers of the Nineteenth Century*, London, Chapman, 1920

Dawson, W.H., *Matthew Arnold and His Relation to the Thought of Our Time*, New York, Putnam, 1904

Dixon, J.M., *Matthew Arnold*, New York, Eaton, 1906

Drinkwater, J., "Arnold's Diction," *Victorian Poetry*, London, Hodder, 1923

Dudley, F.A., "Matthew Arnold and Science," *PMLA*, 1942, 57:275-294

Duffin, Henry C., *Arnold the Poet*, London, Bowes and Bowes, 1962

Eells, J.S., *The Touchstones of Matthew Arnold*, New York, Bookman Associates, 1955

Elliott, G.R., "The Arnoldian Lyric Melancholy," *The Cycle of Modern Poetry*, Princeton, N.J., Princeton Univ. Press, 1929

Fairclough, G.T., "*A Fugitive and Gracious Light*": The Relation of Joseph Joubert to Matthew Arnold's Thought, Lincoln, Univ. of Nebraska Press, 1961

Faverty, F.E., *Matthew Arnold, the Ethnologist*, Evanston, Ill., Northwestern Univ. Press, 1951

Foerster, N., "Matthew Arnold and American Letters Today," *Sewanee Review*, 1922, 30:298-306

Garrod, H.W., *Poetry and the Criticism of Life*, Cambridge, Mass., Harvard Univ. Press, 1931

Goldmark, Ruth, "The Hellenism of Matthew Arnold," *Studies in the Influence of the Classics on English Literature*, New York, Columbia Univ. Press, 1918

Gottfried, Leon, *Matthew Arnold and the Romantics*, London, Routledge & Kegan Paul, 1963

Grierson, H.J.C., "Lord Byron, Arnold and Swinburne," *The Background of English Literature*, London, Chatto, 1925

Groom, B., *On the Diction of Tennyson, Browning, and Arnold*, New York, Oxford Univ. Press, 1939

Hanley, E.A., *Stoicism in Major English Poets of the Nineteenth Century*, abridgement of thesis, New York, New York Univ., 1948

Harrison, F., "Matthew Arnold," *Tennyson, Ruskin, Mill, and Other Literary Estimates*, New York, Macmillan, 1900

Henley, W.E., "Arnold," *Views and Reviews*, London, Macmillan, 1921

Houghton, R.E.C., *The Influence of the Classics on the Poetry of Matthew Arnold*, Oxford, Eng., Blackwell, 1923

Houghton, Walter E., "Arnold's 'Empedocles on Etna,'" *Victorian Studies*, 1958, 1:311-336

Houston, P.H., "The Modernism of Arnold," *Sewanee Review*, 1927, 35:187-197

Hutton, R.H., "Matthew Arnold," *Essays in Literary Criticism*, Philadelphia, Coates, 1876

Hutton, R.H., "The Poetic Place of Matthew Arnold," "Matthew Arnold's Popularity," "Our Great Elegiac Poet," *Brief Literary Criticisms*, London, Macmillan, 1906

Hutton, R.H., "The Poetry of Matthew Arnold," *Literary Essays*, London, Macmillan, 1892

Hutton, R.H., "The Two Great Oxford Thinkers, Cardinal Newman and Matthew Arnold," *Essays on Some of the Modern Guides of English Thought in Matters of Faith*, London, Macmillan, 1887

James, D.G., *Matthew Arnold and the Decline of English Romanticism*, London, Oxford Univ. Press, 1961

Johnson, E.D.H., *Alien Vision of Victorian Poetry*, Princeton, N.J., Princeton Univ. Press, 1952

Johnson, L.P., "Matthew Arnold," *Post Liminium*, London, Mathews, 1911

Johnson, W. Stacy, *The Voices of Matthew Arnold*, New Haven, Conn., Yale Univ. Press, 1961

Kelso, A.P., *Matthew Arnold on Continental Life and Literature*, Oxford, Blackwell, 1914

Ker, W.P., "Matthew Arnold," *The Art of Poetry*, London, Oxford Univ. Press, 1923

Knickerbocker, W.S., "Matthew Arnold's Theory of Poetry," *Sewanee Review*, 1925, 33:440-450

Knight, G. Wilson, "*The Scholar-Gypsy*: An Interpretation," *Review of English Studies*, 1955, 6:53-62

Krieger, Murray, " 'Dover Beach' and the Tragic Sense of Eternal Recurrence," *University of Kansas City Review*, 1956, 23:73-79

Leach, H.G., *"The Forsaken Merman," Essays in Memory of Barrett Wendell*, Cambridge, Mass., Harvard Univ. Press, 1926

Lovett, R.M., "Matthew Arnold Today," *Forum*, 1924, 71:666-669

Lyttleton, A.T., "The Poetry of Doubt (Arnold and Clough)," *Modern Poets of Faith, Doubt, and Paganism, and Other Essays*, London, Murray, 1904

Macdonald, I., *The Buried Self; a Background to the Poems of Matthew Arnold*, London, Davies, 1949

Monroe, H., "Matthew Arnold's Centenary," *Poetry*, 1923, 21:206-210

Montague, C.E., "Matthew Arnold," *London Mercury*, 1929, 19:278-284

Omond, T.S., "Arnold and Homer," *English Association Essays and Studies*, Vol. 3, London, Oxford Univ. Press, 1912

Parrish, Stephen M., *A Concordance to the Poems of Matthew Arnold*, Ithaca, Cornell Univ. Press, 1959

Quiller-Couch, A., "Matthew Arnold," *Studies in Literature*, 3 vols., New York, Putnam, 1918

Raleigh, John H., *Matthew Arnold and American Culture*, Berkeley, Univ. of California Press, 1957

Renwanz, J., *Matthew Arnold und Deutschland*, Griefswald, Abel, 1927

Robbins, William, *The Ethical Idealism of Matthew Arnold*, Toronto, Univ. of Toronto Press, 1959

Robertson, J.M., "Matthew Arnold," *Modern Humanists Reconsidered*, London, Watts, 1927

Romer, V.L., "Matthew Arnold and Some French Poets," *Nineteenth Century and After*, 1926, 99:869-890

Roper, A.H., "The Moral Landscape of Arnold's Poetry," *PMLA*, 1962, 77:289-296

Saintsbury, G., "Matthew Arnold," *Corrected Impressions (1895)*, in *Collected Essays and Papers*, 4 vols., New York, Dutton, 1923-1924

Sells, I.E., *Matthew Arnold and France: the Poet*, New York, Macmillan, 1935

Shafer, Robert, "Matthew Arnold," *Christianity and Naturalism*, New Haven, Conn., Yale Univ. Press, 1926

Sherman, S.P., *Matthew Arnold, How to Know Him*, Indianapolis, Bobbs, 1917

Stanley, C.W., *Matthew Arnold*, Toronto, Univ. of Toronto Press, 1938

Stevenson, Lionel, "Matthew Arnold's Poetry: A Modern Appraisal," *Tennessee Studies in Literature*, 1959, 4:31-41

Swinburne, A.C., "Matthew Arnold's New Poems," *Essays and Studies*, London, Chatto, 1875; from *Fortnightly Review*, 1867, 8:414-445

Tillotson, G., *Criticism and the Nineteenth Century*, New York, Barnes & Noble, 1952

Tinker, C.B., and H.F. Lowry, *The Poetry of Matthew Arnold*, New York, Oxford Univ. Press, 1940

Trawick, Buckner, "The Sea of Faith and the Battle by Night in 'Dover Beach,'" *PMLA*, 1950, 65:1282-1284

Trilling, L., *Matthew Arnold*, 2d ed., New York, Columbia Univ. Press, 1949

Tristram, H., "Newman and Matthew Arnold," *Cornhill Magazine*, 1926, 60:309-319

Walbrook, H.M., "The Marguerite Poems," *London Mercury*, 1922, 5:414-415

Warren, T.H., "Matthew Arnold," *Essays of Poets and Poetry, Ancient and Modern*, London, Murray, 1909

White, H.C., "Matthew Arnold and Goethe," *PMLA*, 1921, 36:436-453

Wilkinson, W.C., "Matthew Arnold as Critic," "Matthew Arnold as Poet," *Some New Literary Valuations*, New York, Funk, 1909

Williams, S.T., "The Poetical Reputation of Matthew Arnold," "Matthew Arnold and His Contemporaries," "Three Aspects of Matthew Arnold's Poetry," "Theory and Practice in the Poetry of Matthew Arnold," *Studies in Victorian Literature*, New York, Dutton, 1923

Woods, Margaret, "Matthew Arnold," *Essays and Studies by Members of the English Association*, Vol. 15, London, Oxford Univ. Press, 1929

BIOGRAPHICAL SKETCH

Matthew Arnold (1822-1888), austere poet and brilliant essayist and critic, was the eldest son of Dr. Thomas Arnold, famous headmaster of Rugby, from whom he inherited his high sense of duty and rigid intellectual honesty. Arnold continued the family tradition by attending Rugby and Oxford and then being elected Fellow of Oriel College. At Oxford he formed a friendship with Arthur Hugh Clough and came under the spell of the personal charm of Newman, though not of his intellectual and spiritual influence. Arnold soon abandoned his fellowship and from 1847 to 1851 was secretary to Lord Lansdowne, who then appointed him to an inspectorship of schools, a position Arnold retained until within two years of his death.

Always fond of children and genuinely interested in the welfare of teachers, Arnold made a rich contribution to England through his arduous labors in the field of education, particularly by his reports and studies on foreign school systems, which he investigated, as foreign assistant commissioner on education, in France, Holland, Belgium, Switzerland, and Piedmont.

Arnold had already published two volumes of poetry—*The Strayed Reveller, and Other Poems* (1849) and *Empedocles on Etna, and Other Poems* (1852)—the fruits of Greek inspiration both in matter and in style. Two other volumes of verse (1853, 1855) were followed in 1858 by Arnold's appointment as professor of poetry at Oxford. Save for the volume of *New Poems*, which appeared in 1867, the rest of Arnold's published work consisted of prose essays, some delivered as lectures at Oxford, on literature, criticism, education, religion, etc. His important editorial work included *Six Chief Lives* from Johnson's *Lives of the Poets* in 1878; *Poems of Wordsworth* in 1879, and *Poetry of Byron* in 1881. A lecturing tour in America in 1883 yielded *Discourses in America*, the book of all his writings, Arnold told a friend, by which he "most desired to be remembered." He died suddenly in Liverpool in 1888.

In his lectures and prose writings Arnold, like Carlyle and Ruskin, was an apostle of the higher life. Permeated with classical culture, he sought to impress upon his generation ideals which should save society from "Philistinism," defined as narrow-mindedness, self-complacency, and vulgarity. His creed called for a vigorous "pursuit of our total perfection by means of getting to know ... the best that has been thought and said in the world." He found the most stimulation among the Greeks, and he possessed the rare ability of assimilating the Greek spirit—its simplicity, its lucidity, its chasteness. He was deeply influenced by the Bible, by St. Augustine, by Shakespeare and Wordsworth and Byron, but more significantly by Goethe, whom he read and absorbed as he did the Greek classics in his youth. Sweeping aside the old personal school of literary criticism, Arnold announced "disinterestedness" as the first requisite of a critic and set up "high seriousness" as a touchstone of great literature. With this ethical rather than aesthetic standard of judgment, he looked upon poetry as "a criticism of life" and regarded himself as an exponent of the classical temper in poetry as opposed to the excesses of romanticism, which then seemed to him to be dominant in England.

Arnold's principal publications were: *The Strayed Reveller, and Other Poems*, 1849; *Empedocles on Etna, and Other Poems*, 1852; *Poems*, 1853; *Poems, Second Series*, 1855; *Merope*, a tragedy, 1858; *On Translating Homer*, 1861; *Essays in Criticism*, 1865-1881; *On the Study of Celtic Literature*, 1867; *New Poems*, 1867; *Schools and Universities on the Continent*, 1868; *Culture and Anarchy*, 1869; *St. Paul and Protestantism*, 1870; *Literature and Dogma*, 1873 ff.; *Mixed Essays*, 1879; *Irish Essays and Others*, 1882; *Discourses in America*, 1885.

INTRODUCTORY CRITICISMS

"There is no Victorian poet, perhaps there is no Victorian thinker, more significant in position than Matthew Arnold. Agnosticism of thought and feeling, with all its vagueness, finds in him an exquisitely accurate exponent. No other poet has been so clear in his understanding of confusion, so positive in an unstable equilibrium. In the union of definiteness of technique with vagueness of theme the charm of his work resides. Unsatisfied desire, evasive regret, indecision, doubt, all that has not yet translated itself from the dim twilight of the feeling to the daylight world of the deed—this Arnold gives us with delicate precision of touch. His poems are like gray shadows cast along some temple-floor, shadowy alike in clean purity of outline, and in dim uncertainty of content."—Vida D. Scudder, *The Life of the Spirit in the Modern English Poets*, p. 247.

"No poet in the roll of our literature, unless it be Milton, has been so essentially saturated to the very bone with the classical genius [as has Arnold]. His poetry, however, is 'classical' only in a general sense, not that all of it is imitative of ancient models, or has any affectation of archaism. It is essentially modern in thought, and has all that fetishistic worship of natural objects which is the true note of our Wordsworthian school. But Arnold is 'classical' in the serene self-command, the harmony of tone, the measured fitness, the sweet reasonableness of his verse. This balance, this lucidity, this Virgilian dignity and grace, may be said to be unfailing. Whatever be its shortcomings and its limitations, Arnold's poetry maintains this unerring urbanity of form. There is no thunder, no rant, no discord, no honey, no intoxication of mysticism or crash of battle in him. Our poet's eye doth glance from heaven to earth, from earth to heaven; but it is never caught 'in a fine frenzy rolling.' It is in this sense that Arnold is classical, that he has, and has uniformly and by instinct, some touch of that 'liquid clearness of an Ionian sky' which he felt in Homer. Not but what he is, in thought and by suggestion, one of the most truly modern, the most frankly contemporary, of all our poets."—F. Harrison, *Tennyson, Ruskin, Mill, and Other Literary Estimates*, p. 106.

"Arnold is . . . in a certain sense a unique poet—in the sense that many of his poems succeed with us out of all proportion to their specifically poetic success. For with him we do more than tolerate the dryness of tone into which he occasionally falls, or his reliance upon statement rather than upon the translation of emotion or idea into music and image: we come to have an affection for what are usually accounted faults, to think of them as being the marks of the directness of Arnold's communication with us."—Lionel Trilling, *The Portable Matthew Arnold*, p. 40.

CRITICAL NOTES

SOHRAB AND RUSTUM, p. 475

Arnold quotes in a note the following story of Sohrab and Rustum as told in Sir John Malcolm's *History of Persia*, 2 vols., London, Murray, 1815:

"The young Sohrab was the fruit of one of Rustum's early amours. He had left his mother, and sought fame under the banners of Afrasiab, whose armies he commanded, and soon obtained a renown beyond that of all contemporary heroes but his father. He had carried death and dismay into the ranks of the Persians, and had terrified the boldest warriors of that country, before Rustum encountered him, which at last that hero resolved to do, under a feigned name. They met three times. The first time they parted by mutual consent, though Sohrab had the advantage; the second, the youth obtained a victory, but granted life to his unknown father; the third was fatal to Sohrab, who, when writhing in the pangs of death, warned his conqueror to shun the vengeance that is inspired by parental woes, and bade him dread the rage of the mighty Rustum, who must soon learn that he had slain his son Sohrab. These words, we are told, were as death to the aged hero; and when he recovered from a trance, he called in despair for proofs of what Sohrab had said. The afflicted and dying youth tore open his mail, and showed his father a seal which his mother had placed on his arm when she discovered to him the secret of his birth, and bade him seek his father. The sight of his own signet rendered Rustum quite frantic; he cursed himself, attempting to put an end to his existence, and

was only prevented by the efforts of his expiring son. After Sohrab's death, he burnt his tents and all his goods, and carried the corpse to Seistan, where it was interred; the army of Turan was, agreeably to the last request of Sohrab, permitted to cross the Oxus unmolested. To reconcile us to the improbability of this tale, we are informed that Rustum could have no idea his son was in existence. The mother of Sohrab had written to him her child was a daughter, fearing to lose her darling infant if she revealed the truth; and Rustum, as before stated, fought under a feigned name, an usage not uncommon in the chivalrous combats of those days." Malcolm summarizes the story (Vol. 1, p. 37, note) as told by Firdausi.

THE SCHOLAR-GYPSY, p. 487

Arnold quotes in a note the following account from Joseph Glanvil's *Vanity of Dogmatizing*, 1661, ch. 20:

"There was very lately a lad in the University of Oxford, who was by his poverty forced to leave his studies there; and at last to join himself to a company of vagabond gypsies. Among these extravagant people, by the insinuating subtility of his carriage, he quickly got so much of their love and esteem as that they discovered to him their mystery. After he had been a pretty while exercised in the trade, there chanced to ride by a couple of scholars, who had formerly been of his acquaintance. They quickly spied out their old friend among the gypsies; and he gave them an account of the necessity which drove him to that kind of life, and told them that the people he went with were not such impostors as they were taken for, but that they had a traditional kind of learning among them, and could do wonders by the power of imagination, their fancy binding that of others: that himself had learned much of their art, and when he had compassed the whole secret, he intended, he said, to leave their company, and give the world an account of what he had learned." The quotation omits some phrases and sentences.

THYRSIS, p. 493

Arnold was devoted to Oxford and its environs, where his enduring friendship for Clough was formed. In 1885 he said in a letter to his daughter: "I think Oxford is still, on the whole, the place in the world to which I am most attached." In a letter to his sister, Oct. 18, 1885, he said: "On Friday I got out to Hinksey and up the hill to within sight of the Cumner firs. I cannot describe the effect which this landscape always has on me—the hillside with its valleys, and Oxford in the great Thames valley below."

In a letter to his mother, April 7, 1866, he states that the diction of the poem was modeled on that of Theocritus, whom he had much read during the two years in which the poem was forming itself. He says: "The images are all from actual observation.... The cuckoo on the wet June morning I heard in the garden at Woodford, and all those three stanzas you like are reminiscences of Woodford. Edward [his brother] has, I think, fixed on the two stanzas I like best myself in 'O easy access' and 'And long the way appears.' I also like 'Where is the girl?' and the stanza before it, but it is because they bring certain places and moments before me.... It is probably too *quiet* a poem for the general taste, but I think it will stand wear."

Swinburne says of this poem: "The *Thyrsis* of Mr. Arnold makes a third with *Lycidas* and *Adonais*. It is not so easy as those may think who think by rote and praise by prescription to strike the balance between them. The first, however, remains first, and must remain; its five opening lines are to me the most musical in all known realms of verse; there is nothing like them; and it is more various, more simple, more large and sublime than the others ... The least pathetic of the three is *Adonais*, which indeed is hardly pathetic at all; it is passionate, subtle, splendid; but *Thyrsis*, like *Lycidas*, has a quiet and tender undertone which gives it something of sacred. Shelley brings fire from heaven, but these bring also 'the meed of some melodious tear.' There is a grace ineffable, a sweet sound and sweet savor of things past, in the old beautiful use of the language of shepherds, of flocks and pipes: the spirit is none the less sad and sincere because the body of the poem has put on this dear familiar raiment of romance; because the crude and naked sorrow is veiled and chastened with soft shadows and sounds of a 'land that is very far off'; because the verse remembers and retains a perfume and an echo of Grecian flutes and flowers."
—*Essays and Studies* (*Complete Works*), Vol. 15, p. 92.

CHARLES TENNYSON TURNER, p. 505

STANDARD EDITIONS

A Hundred Sonnets, ed. by John Betjeman and Sir Charles Tennyson, London, Hart-Davis, 1960

Charles Tennyson-Turner (Augustan Books of Poetry), London, Benn, 1931

Collected Sonnets, Old and New, ed. by Hallam,

Lord Tennyson, w. an essay by James Spedding, New York, Macmillan, 1898

Poems by Two Brothers, New York, Macmillan, 1893

BIOGRAPHY AND CRITICISM

Bayne, T., "Charles Tennyson Turner," *Fraser's Magazine*, 1881, 104:790-799

Grosart, A.B., "The Rev. Charles (Tennyson) Turner," *Leisure Hour*, 1875, 24:711-716

Hewlett, H.G., "English Sonneteers: Mr. Charles Turner," *Contemporary Review*, 1873, 22:633-642

Nicolson, H.G., *Tennyson's Two Brothers*, New York, Macmillan, 1947

Palgrave, F.T., "The Landscape of Browning, Arnold, Barnes, and Charles Tennyson," *Landscape in Poetry*, London, Macmillan, 1897

BIOGRAPHICAL SKETCH

Charles Tennyson Turner (1808-1879), the elder brother of Alfred, Lord Tennyson, changed his name to Turner in memory of a great-uncle from whom he inherited property. He shared his brother Alfred's tastes in literature and collaborated with him in the production of an early volume of verse, *Poems by Two Brothers*, in 1827. In 1836 he married the sister of Emily Sellwood, who became Alfred Tennyson's wife, and lived quietly as a clergyman in country parishes until ill health forced his retirement from professional work. Country life, flowers, horses, and dogs appealed greatly to his gentle nature; his life was happy and serene. Poetry was his principal avocation. A collection of sonnets in 1830 was praised by Coleridge; other collections in 1864, 1868, 1873, and 1880 gave him a contemporary reputation as a writer of sonnets almost equal to Wordsworth's. With the sonnets in these various collections were included a few short lyrics in other forms.

INTRODUCTORY CRITICISM

"His [Turner's] verse is saturated with the sense of his duties and his position as a parish priest ... In reading the sonnets we can see him moving about in his parish, succoring the poor, consoling the sick, cheering the aged folk, and speaking kindly to the children; thinking, as he goes, of the news that had that day reached him from the great world, and with an eye ever open to new beauties and new phases of nature.... The slightest incident, the most ordinary event of his daily life, is enough to stir his retiring muse; the first budding green of the spring, the later yellowing leaves of autumn still clinging to the trees, the harvest-field, the first note of cuckoo or nightingale, the coming of the swallows, the first ice in winter, the beautiful play of light through the lattice, the setting free of a prisoned bird, the impression made on his children by some new book—these are his themes; and he treats them with simplicity, grace, and occasional sustained beauty of phrase."—A. H. Japp, in *The Poets and the Poetry of the Century*, ed. by A. H. Miles, Vol. 4, pp. 47-48.

DANTE GABRIEL ROSSETTI, p. 505

STANDARD EDITIONS

Collected Works, 2 vols., ed. w. pref. and notes by W.M. Rossetti, London, Ellis, 1890

Works, 7 vols., London, Ellis, 1900-1901

Complete Poetical Works, ed. w. pref. and notes by W.M. Rossetti, Boston, Little, 1903

Poems, Ballads and Sonnets, ed. by P.F. Baum, New York, Doubleday, 1937

Poems, ed. by Oswald Doughty, London, Dent, 1957

The House of Life, w. an intro. and notes by P.F. Baum, Cambridge, Mass., Harvard Univ. Press, 1928

Family Letters, 2 vols., w. a mem. by W.M. Rossetti, London, Ellis, 1895

Letters to William Allingham, 1854-1870, ed. by G.B. Hill, New York, Stokes, 1898

Letters to Fanny Cornforth, ed. by P.F. Baum, Homewood, Baltimore, Johns Hopkins Press, 1940

Letters of Dante Gabriel Rossetti to His Publisher, ed. w. an intro. and notes by O. Doughty, London, Scholartis, 1928

The Rossetti-Macmillan Letters, ed. by Lona M. Packer, Berkeley, Univ. of California Press, 1963

Rossetti Papers, 1862 to 1870, a compil. by W.M. Rossetti, London, Sands, 1902

The Germ, 5 parts, w. an intro. by W.M. Rossetti, London, Stock, 1901

BIOGRAPHY

Angeli, H.R., *Dante Gabriel Rossetti, His Friends and Enemies*, London, Hamilton, 1949

Beerbohm, Max, *Rossetti and His Circle*, caricatures, London, Heinemann, 1922

Benson, A.C., *Rossetti*, English Men of Letters Series, London, Macmillan, 1904

Burne-Jones, Georgiana, *Memorials of Edward Burne-Jones*, 2 vols., New York, Macmillan, 1904

Caine, H., *Recollections of Rossetti*, London, Cassell, 1928

Cary, Elisabeth L., *The Rossettis*, New York, Putnam, 1907

Doughty, O., *Dante Gabriel Rossetti, a Victorian Romantic*, New Haven, Conn., Yale Univ. Press, rev. ed., 1960

Dunn, H.T., *Recollections of Dante Gabriel Rossetti and His Circle*, ed. by Gale Pedrick, London, Mathews, 1904

Gilchrist, H.H., "Recollections of Rossetti," *Lippincott's Magazine*, 1901, 68:571-576

Hunt, W.H., *Pre-Raphaelitism and the Pre-Raphaelite Brotherhood*, 2 vols., New York, Dutton, 1914

Knight, J., *Life of Dante Gabriel Rossetti*, w. bibliog., London, Scott, 1887

Marillier, H.C., *Dante Gabriel Rossetti: an Illustrated Memorial of His Art and Life*, London, Bell, 1890

Rossetti, Helen M.M., *The Life and Work of Dante Gabriel Rossetti*, London, Virtue, 1902

Rossetti, W.M., *Dante Gabriel Rossetti as Designer and Writer*, London, Cassell, 1889

Rossetti, W.M., ed., *Pre-Raphaelite Diaries and Letters*, London, Hurst, 1900

Rossetti, W.M., ed., *Ruskin: Rossetti: Pre-Raphaelitism; Papers, 1854 to 1862*, London, Allen, G., 1899

Sharp, W., *Dante Gabriel Rossetti; a Record and a Study*, London, Macmillan, 1882

Waugh, Evelyn, *Rossetti, His Life and Works*, London, Duckworth, 1928

Winwar, Frances, *Poor Splendid Wings: the Rossettis and Their Circle*, Boston, Little, 1933

Wood, Esther, *Dante Rossetti and the Pre-Raphaelite Movement*, London, Low, 1894

CRITICISM

Bateman, A.B., "Rossetti, the Pre-Raphaelites, and a Moral," *London Quarterly*, 1928, 149:223-233

Bowra, C.M., "The House of Life," *The Romantic Imagination*, Cambridge, Mass., Harvard Univ. Press, 1947

Buchanan, R.W., *The Fleshly School of Poetry and Other Phenomena of the Day*, London, Strahan, 1872. An article by Buchanan in *Contemporary Review*, 1871, 18:334-350, was answered by Rossetti in "The Stealthy School of Criticism," *Athenæum*, Dec. 16, 1871, pp. 792-794; Buchanan replied in *Athenæum*, Dec. 30, 1871, p. 887. Buchanan's pamphlet was reviewed in *Athenæum*, May 25, 1872, pp. 650-651

Buchanan, R.W., "A Note on Dante Rossetti," *A Look Round Literature*, London, Ward, 1887

Burgum, E.B., "Rossetti and the Ivory Tower," *Sewanee Review*, 1929, 37:431-446

Cassidy, J.A., "Robert Buchanan and the Fleshy Controversy," *PMLA*, 1952, 67: 65-93

Dowden, E., "The Collected Works of Dante Gabriel Rossetti," *Academy*, 1887, 31: 85-86

Forman, H.B., "Dante Gabriel Rossetti," *Our Living Poets*, London, Tinsley, 1871

Fredeman, William E., *Pre-Raphaelitism: A Bibliocritical Study*, Cambridge, Mass., Harvard Univ. Press, 1964

Gray, N.M.B., *Rossetti, Dante, and Ourselves*, London, Faber, 1947

Hamilton, G.R., "Dante Gabriel Rossetti; a Review of His Poetry," *Criterion*, 1928, 7:91-103

Hamilton, Walter, "The Pre-Raphaelites," "The Germ," "Dante Gabriel Rossetti," "Buchanan's Attack on Rossetti," *The Aesthetic Movement in England*, London, Reeves, 1882

Hearn, L., "Studies in Rossetti," *Pre-Raphaelite and Other Poets*, New York, Dodd, 1922

Hodgson, F., "Dante Gabriel Rossetti," *Church Quarterly Review*, 1928, 106:353-362

Hueffer, Ford Madox, *Rossetti; a Critical Essay on His Art*, London, Duckworth, 1902

Lauter, Paul, "The Narrator of 'The Blessed Damozel,'" *Modern Language Notes*, 1958, 73:344-348

Lynd, R., "Rossetti and Ritual," *Old and New Masters*, London, Unwin, 1919

Mégroz, R.L., *Dante Gabriel Rossetti, Painter Poet of Heaven in Earth*, London, Faber, 1928

Monroe, H., "Rossetti," *Poetry*, 1928, 32: 270-277

Mourey, Gabriel, *D. G. Rossetti et les Pré-raphaélites anglais*, Paris, Laurens, 1909

Myers, F.W.H., "Rossetti and the Religion of Beauty," *Essays: Modern*, London, Macmillan, 1908

Pater, W., "Dante Gabriel Rossetti," *Appreciations*, London, Macmillan, 1889

Patmore, C., "Rossetti as a Poet," *Principle in Art*, London, Bell, 1889

Preston, K., *Blake and Rossetti*, London, Moring, 1944

Robillard, Douglas J., "Rossetti's 'Willowwood Sonnets' and the Structure of *The House of Life*," *Victorian Newsletter*, 1962, 22:5-9

Rossetti, W.M., *Bibliography of the Works of Dante Gabriel Rossetti*, London, Ellis, 1905

Rossetti, W.M., "Dante Gabriel Rossetti as Translator," *Sewanee Review*, 1909, 17: 405-408

Shanks, E., "Dante Gabriel Rossetti," *London Mercury*, 1928, 18:67-78

Shine, H., "The Influence of Keats upon Rossetti," *Englische Studien*, 1927, 61: 183-210

Stephens, F.G., *Dante Gabriel Rossetti*, London, Seeley, 1894

Swinburne, A.C., "The Poems of Dante Gabriel Rossetti," *Essays and Studies*, London, Chatto, 1875, and *Fortnightly Review*, 1870, 13:551-579

Symons, A., "Dante Gabriel Rossetti," *Figures of Several Centuries*, London, Constable, 1916

Symons, A., "Rossetti," *Studies in Strange Souls*, London, Sawyer, 1929

Tisdel, F.M., "Rossetti's *House of Life*," *Modern Philology*, 1917, 15:257-276

Trombly, A.E., *Rossetti the Poet*, Austin, Univ. of Texas Bulletin, No. 2060, 1920

Turner, A.M., "Rossetti's Reading and His Critical Opinions," *PMLA*, 1927, 42:465-491

Vaughan, C.W., *Bibliographies of Swinburne, Morris and Rossetti*, English Association Pamphlet, No. 29, London, Oxford Univ. Press, 1914

Wallerstein, R.C., "Personal Experience in Rossetti's *House of Life*," *PMLA*, 1927, 42:492-504

Watts-Dunton, T., "The Truth about Rossetti," *Nineteenth Century*, 1883, 13:404-423

Waugh, E., "D.G. Rossetti: a Centenary Criticism," *Fortnightly Review*, 1928, 129: 595-604

Westminster Review, "The Poetical Writings of Mr. Dante Gabriel Rossetti," 1871, 95:55-92

Willoughby, L.A., *Dante Gabriel Rossetti and German Literature*, London, Oxford Univ. Press, 1912

BIOGRAPHICAL SKETCH

Dante Gabriel Rossetti (1828-1882) was both a poet and a painter, and expressed his romantic and emotional nature similarly in the two arts. His background was Italian; for his father, poet and student of Dante, and an exile from Italy because of his antagonism to Austrian rule, made his London home a gathering place for Italian artists and musicians. Rossetti's boyhood was rich in cultural associations, but largely undisciplined. "As soon as a thing is imposed on me as an obligation," he later said, "my aptitude for doing it is gone." Becoming an art student at the Royal Academy in 1846, he found the training onerous and reacted violently against classical principles in contemporary painting, which he found conventional and uninspired. Taking as his master the radical painter, Ford Madox Brown, and associating himself with Holman Hunt and John Everett Millais, kindred spirits at the art school, he studied medieval painting and organized in 1848 the Pre-Raphaelite Brotherhood, which sought to combine a realistic fidelity in detail with a romantic mysticism in the general effect of their paintings. With his flowing brown hair and dark eyes, an almost ascetic devotion to his work, and magnetic personal charm, Rossetti easily dominated the group. Its first paintings were labeled by the critics as "mere eccentricity"; but when John Ruskin, then a leader of public taste, defended them in two letters to *The Times*, 1850, they became generally admired. In 1856 three young Oxford men, Burne-Jones, Swinburne, and William Morris, were drawn into the Brotherhood. Essentially antagonistic to Rossetti in character, Morris. yet found Rossetti's personality for a time irresistible; the two read the *Morte d'Arthur* together and talked in Rossetti's studio, littered with designs and manuscripts, until three o'clock of many mornings.

Meanwhile Rossetti had periodically abandoned painting for poetry, had written at fever heat such poems as *The Blessed Damozel*, and had returned with equal vigor to his other art. Much of his early poetry, including *The Blessed Damozel* and *My Sister's Sleep*, was printed in *The Germ*, a periodical founded by the Brotherhood in 1850 as an outlet for their writing and art. Rossetti's stimulus at this time came from the writings of Browning and Edgar Allan Poe, from the English folk ballads, and from the medieval poets of Italy; he published in 1861 a collection of translations from the *Early Italian Poets*, later called *Dante and His Circle*. In many ways the decade from 1850 to 1860 was Rossetti's greatest period in both his arts.

In 1850 he became passionately attached to Elizabeth Siddal, a milliner's assistant with abilities in poetry and water-color painting, and a bemused, otherworldly beauty that was an embodiment of the Pre-Raphaelite ideal. She served Rossetti as the model for many of his greatest paintings, inspired many of the sonnets in *The House of Life*, and became his wife in 1860, although she was already doomed by tuberculosis. Rossetti's impatience and the irregularities of his life made his marriage hardly a placid one; yet, at his wife's death in 1862, he was so profoundly afflicted that he enclosed with her body in the coffin his most valuable possession, a bundle of manuscript poems that existed in no other form. He consented, however, to their disinternment in 1869; they formed the basis of his published collection of poems in 1870 and established his poetic reputation.

As his reputation grew, his income increased, and he was able to indulge his fondness for luxury without counting the notes that slipped through his fingers; yet his only relaxation from work was occasional dissipation. The result was insomnia; and, unable to bear the consequent lowering of his efficiency, he began to take chloral in gradually increasing doses. The drug brought on physical deterioration and distressing hallucinations. He came to feel the spirit of his dead wife near him in the form of birds; he was tormented by persecutory illusions, which were encouraged by a bitter attack on his morality in Buchanan's *Fleshly School of Poetry*, so that he felt himself insulted by passing strangers and broke with Browning, who had cast oblique aspersion upon his work in *Fifine at the Fair*. With William Morris at Kelmscott and in the society of the friends which his charm still assured him, he found passing happiness; his genius still continued active and could inspire, even in his last tragic years, such poems as *The White Ship* and *The King's Tragedy*, published in 1881 as *Ballads and Sonnets*. But his great physical strength wore away until his death came finally as a relief in 1882.

INTRODUCTORY CRITICISMS

"Consecrated, from his Italian parentage, to learning, art, and song—reared in a household over which the mediæval spirit has brooded—he [Rossetti] is thoroughly at home among romantic themes and processes, while a feeling like that of Dante exalts the maturer portion of his emblematic verse. . . . Throughout his poetry we discern a finesse, a regard for detail, and a knowledge of color and sound, that distinguish this master of the Neo-Romantic school. His end is gained by simplicity and sure precision of touch. He knows exactly what effect he desires, and produces it by a firm stroke of color, a beam of light, a single musical tone. . . . His lyrical faculty is exquisite; not often swift, but chaste, and purely English. . . . His verse is compact of tenderness, emotional ecstasy, and poetic fire. The spirit of the master whose name he bears clothes him as with a white garment. And we should expect his associates to be humble lovers of the beautiful, first of all, and through its ministry to rise to the lustrous upper heaven of spiritual art."—E. C. Stedman, *Victorian Poets*, pp. 360-366.

"His [Rossetti's] method of writing is as conscious as his choice of theme. He deliberately chooses different manners for different subjects; his narrative poetry is in the simple, coloured concrete, angular style of the Pre-Raphaelites; his sonnets in a majestic, poly-syllabic, abstract, Latinized diction, which rather recalls Milton. But both styles are conscious styles, . . . we are never uncon-scious of the artist vigilantly at work."—Lord David Cecil, "Gabriel Charles Dante Ros-setti," in *The Great Victorians*, ed. by H. J. Massingham and Hugh Massingham, p. 431.

CRITICAL NOTES

The Pre-Raphaelites

The term Pre-Raphaelites was first applied to a group of young German artists who early in the nineteenth century formed a brother-hood in Rome for the purpose of restoring Christian art to the medieval purity of the masters in the age preceding the great Italian painter Raphael (1483-1520). The organization was short-lived, however, and the term was later used to designate the school in England originated by the following seven young men: Dante Gabriel Rossetti and his brother William Michael Rossetti, John Everett Millais, William Holman Hunt, Frederick George Stephens, James Collinson, and Thomas Woolner. They formed the Pre-Raphaelite Brotherhood in 1848, and in 1850 published four issues of *The Germ*, a magazine in which they announced their principles and displayed some of their poetical work.

The group reacted against the neoclassic imitative tendencies of much of the art of their own day and sought to attain the directness, the simplicity, the serious intention of Italian art before Raphael. Both their paintings and their writings were characterized by a self-conscious simplicity of style, love of sensuous beauty, minuteness of detail, and vaguely in definite symbolism. These characteristics find their fullest expression in the highly colored, mystical, imaginative early poems of Rossetti, in much of the work of William Morris, and in some of Swinburne's.

THE BLESSED DAMOZEL, p. 505

There are three versions of this poem, which was written in 1847, when Rossetti was eighteen years of age: one published in *The Germ* in 1850; one in *The Oxford and Cambridge Magazine*, 1856; and one in the *Poems* of 1870. Changes appearing in the second and third versions are regarded as distinct improvements; but Swinburne states that the original readings were often so good that no-body without Rossetti's "insatiable passion

for the best" would have been dissatisfied with them.

"Though at first sight," says A. C. Benson, "the delicate archaic handling of language is a great attraction, yet it is the combination of vastness and nearness in the poem which lends it an incomparable charm."—*Rossetti*, p. 114.

MARY MAGDALENE, p. 524

Rossetti gives the following description of the oil painting of 1865, the theme of which was the basis of this sonnet:

"The scene represents two houses opposite each other, one of which is that of Simon the Pharisee, where Christ and Simon, with other guests, are seated at table. In the opposite house a great banquet is held, and feasters are trooping to it dressed in cloth of gold and crowned with flowers. The musicians play at the door, and each couple kiss as they enter. Mary Magdalene has been in this procession, but has suddenly turned aside at the sight of Christ, and is pressing forward up the steps of Simon's house, and casting the roses from her hair. Her lover and a woman have followed her out of the procession and are laughingly trying to turn her back. The woman bars the door with her arm. Those nearest the Mag-dalene in the group of feasters have stopped short in wonder and are looking after her, while a beggar girl offers them flowers from her basket. A girl near the front of the pro-cession has caught sight of Mary and waves her garland to turn her back. Beyond this, the narrow street abuts on the highroad and river. The young girl seated on the steps is a little beggar who has had food given her from within the house, and is wondering to see Mary go in there, knowing her as a famous woman in the city. Simon looks disdainfully at her, and the servant who is setting a dish on the table smiles, knowing her too. Christ looks toward her from within, waiting till she shall reach him."

THE SONNET, p. 526

In 1880, Rossetti presented his mother on her birthday with a volume of English sonnets in which he had drawn a design illustrating his *Sonnet on the Sonnet*. He thus explained its symbolism in an accompanying letter:

"I have no doubt that your discerning eyes plucked out the heart of the mystery in the little design. In it the Soul is instituting the 'memorial to one dead deathless hour,' a ceremony easily effected by placing a winged hour-glass in a rosebush, at the same time that she touches the fourteen-stringed harp of the Sonnet, hanging round her neck. On the rose-branches trailing over in the opposite corner is seen hanging the Coin, which is the second symbol used for the Sonnet. Its 'face' bears the Soul, expressed in the butterfly; its 'converse,' the Serpent of Eternity enclosing the Alpha and Omega."

THE KING'S TRAGEDY, p. 553

Lines 316-322 of the poem are adapted from Stanza 34 of *The King's Quair* (The King's Book), as follows:

Worschippeth, 3e that loueris bene, this May,
    For of your blisse the kalendis are begonne,
And sing with vs, away, Winter, away!
    Cum, Somer, cum, the suete sesoun and sonne!
    Awake for schame! that haue 3oure hevynnis wonne,
And amorously lift vp 3our hedis all,
Thank Lufe that list 3ou to his merci call.

Lines 327-330 are from Stanza 40.
Lines 331-332 are from Stanza 42.
Lines 339-345 are from Stanza 193.
Lines 346-352 are from Stanza 187.
Lines 370-376 are from Stanza 162.
Lines 379-380 are from Stanza 14.

CHRISTINA ROSSETTI, p. 562

STANDARD EDITIONS

Poetical Works, ed., w. a mem. and notes by W.M. Rossetti, London, Macmillan, 1924
Poems, w. an intro. by Alice Meynell, London, Blackie, 1923
Sing Song, a Nursery Rhyme Book, and Other Poems for Children, New York, Macmillan, 1924
Christina Rossetti, London, Benn, 1926
Commonplace and Other Short Stories, London, Ellis, 1870
Family Letters of Christina Georgina Rossetti, ed. by W.M. Rossetti, New York, Scribner, 1908
Three Rossettis; Unpublished Letters to and from Dante Gabriel, Christina, William, ed. by J.C. Troxell, Cambridge, Mass., Harvard Univ. Press, 1937

BIOGRAPHY

Bell, H.T.M., *Christina Rossetti, a Biographical and Critical Study*, w. a bibliog. by J.P. Anderson, pp. 377-390, Boston, Roberts, 1898
Cary, Elisabeth L., *The Rossettis: Dante Gabriel and Christina*, New York, Putnam, 1900
Hueffer, F.M., "Christina Rossetti and Pre-Raphaelite Love," *Memories and Impressions*, New York, Harper, 1911
Packer, Lona, M., *Christina Rossetti*, Berkeley, Univ. of California Press, 1963

Rossetti Papers, 1862 to 1870, comp. by W.M. Rossetti, London, Sands, 1903
Sandars, M.F., *The Life of Christina Rossetti*, London, Hutchinson, 1930
Sawtell, Margaret, *Christina Rossetti: Her Life and Religion*, London, Mowbray, 1955
Stuart, D.M., *Christina Rossetti*, English Men of Letters, n. s., New York, Macmillan, 1930
Watts-Dunton, T., "Reminiscences of Christina Rossetti," *Nineteenth Century*, 1895, 37:355-366
Zaturenska, M.A., *Christina Rossetti; a Portrait with Background*, New York, Macmillan, 1949

CRITICISM

Bald, M.A., "Christina Rossetti," *Women Writers of the Nineteenth Century*, London, Cambridge Univ. Press, 1923
Benson, A.C., "Christina Rossetti," *Essays*, New York, Macmillan, 1896
Birkhead, E., *Christina Rossetti and Her Poetry*, London, Harrap, 1930
Catholic World, "Christina Rossetti's *Poems*," 1876, 24:122-129
Chambers, E.K., "Christina Rossetti's Verses," *Academy*, 1894, 45:162-164
De la Mare, W., "Christina Rossetti," *The Royal Society of Literature; Essays by Divers Hands*, n. s., Vol. 6, New York, Oxford Univ. Press, 1926
Johnson, L., "Miss Rossetti's *New Poems*," *Academy*, 1896, 50:59-60
Lowther, G., "Christina Rossetti," *Contemporary Review*, 1913, 104:681-689
Meynell, A., "Christina Rossetti," *New Review*, 1895, 12:201-206
More, P.E., "Christina Rossetti," *Shelburne Essays*, 3d s., New York, Putnam, 1905
Noble, J.A., "The Burden of Christina Rossetti," *Impressions and Memories*, London, Dent, 1895
Packer, Lona M., "Symbol and Reality in Christina Rossetti's 'Goblin Market,'" *PMLA*, 1958, 73:375-385
Robb, N.A., *Four in Exile*, London, Hutchinson, 1948
Shove, F., *Christina Rossetti*, New York, Macmillan, 1931
Swann, Thomas B., *Wonder and Whimsy: The Fantastic World of Christina Rossetti*, London, Marshall Jones, 1960
Thomas, E.W., *Christina Georgiana Rossetti*, New York, Columbia Univ. Press, 1931
Waugh, A., "Christina Rossetti," *Reticence in Literature*, London, Wilson, J.G., 1915

BIOGRAPHICAL SKETCH

Christina Georgina Rossetti (1830-1894)

was the younger sister of Dante Gabriel Rossetti, and the earlier period of her life was closely intertwined with his. Reared in the same cultured environment as he and influenced by his artistic principles, she contributed verses to the Pre-Raphaelite organ, *The Germ*, and published in 1862 her romantic *Goblin Market and Other Poems*. Her pale, serious beauty made her a favorite model for her brother in his paintings of the Virgin. Excursions into the country gave her an intimate acquaintance with scenes within a fifty-mile radius of London; she made friends with all animals, even snakes and toads; she symbolized every object that she encountered, and found ethical principles embodied in bits of glass and fragments of stone. After she visited the Continent in 1861 and 1866, her life grew restricted; she cared for her father and mother in prolonged illnesses, and thereafter found other invalid relatives to claim her care. Devout from childhood, she became increasingly preoccupied with religious thoughts. In 1866 she refused a suitor whom she loved, because he was "either not a Christian at all, or else he was a Christian of undefined or heterodox views." Her later poetry was designed almost wholly for religious instruction. Her health was precarious, and in 1871 she acquired a disease that gave her portliness and confined her to her house in Bloomsbury, London. In a small upper back bedroom she did her writing, closing her eyes to evoke mental pictures; she conducted regular household devotions and prayed half an hour each night before retiring. Blessed with a quaint humor and great moral courage, she never alluded in conversation to her illness. At length, a cancer sapped her strength and ended her life.

Christina Rossetti's principal publications were: *Goblin Market and Other Poems*, 1862; *The Prince's Progress*, 1866; *Commonplace*, 1870; *Sing-Song*, 1872; *Seek and Find*, 1879; *A Pageant*, 1881; *Called to Be Saints*, 1881; *Letter and Spirit*, 1882; *Time Flies*, 1885; *The Face of the Deep*, 1892; *Verses*, 1893; *New Poems*, ed. by W. M. Rossetti, 1896.

INTRODUCTORY CRITICISMS

"A power of seeing finely beyond the scope of ordinary vision; that, in a few words, is the note of Miss Rossetti's genius, and it brings with it a subtle . . . power of expressing subtle . . . conceptions; always clearly, always simply, with a singular and often startling homeliness, which is the sincerity of a style that seems to be innocently unaware of its own beauty. This power is shown in every division of her poetry; in the peculiar witchery of the poems

dealing with the supernatural, in the exaltation of the poems of devotion, in the lyrical quality of the songs of children, birds, and corn, in the special variety and the special excellence of the poems of passion and meditation. The union of homely yet always select literalness of treatment with mystical visionariness, or visionariness which is sometimes mystical, constitutes the peculiar quality of her poetry."—A. Symons, *Studies in Two Literatures*, p. 139.

"Miss Rossetti, in her sacred poems, brings together all the elements of art's excellence and of a Christian faith. Their chief note, their unique interest and delight, is a tenderness in them, a tremulous and wistful beauty of adoration, rising and passing, at times, into something like a very joyous adoration of friend by friend. . . . And with this sense of attaining and perceptive faith comes a further sense, of absolute reality. . . . The Paradisal imageries, crowns, palms, flames, all the 'furniture of heaven,' becomes to us in her poetry as real, visible, tangible as altars upon earth; the golden trumpets and harps, the multitudinous music of the Saints and Angels, ring through the triumphing chaunts of her later verse."—Lionel Johnson, *Academy*, July 25, 1896, 50:59.

CRITICAL NOTES

GOBLIN MARKET, p. 568

This poem, says J. A. Noble, "may be read and enjoyed merely as a charming fairy-fantasy, and as such it is delightful and satisfying; but behind the simple story of the two children and the goblin fruit-sellers is a little spiritual drama of love's vicarious redemption, in which the child redeemer goes into the wilderness to be tempted of the devil, that by her painful conquest she may succor and save the sister who has been vanquished and all but slain."—*Impressions and Memories*, p. 59.

COVENTRY PATMORE, p. 576

STANDARD EDITIONS

Works, 5 vols., London, Bell, 1907
Poems, w. an intro. by B. Champneys, London, Bell, 1906
The Poems, ed. w. an intro. by F. Page, New York, Oxford Univ. Press, 1949
Mystical Poems of Nuptial Love, Boston, Humphries, 1938
Selected Poems, ed. w. an intro. by Derek Patmore, London, Chatto, 1931

The Angel in the House, London, Cassell, 1898
The Angel in the House; the Victories of Love, w. an intro. by Alice Meynell, London, Routledge, 1905
Principle in Art, Religio Poetæ and Other Essays, London, Duckworth, 1913
Principle in Art, London, Bell, 1898
Religio Poetæ, Etc., London, Bell, 1907

BIOGRAPHY

Champneys, B., *Memoirs and Correspondence of Coventry Patmore,* 2 vols., London, Bell, 1900
Gosse, E., *Coventry Patmore,* New York, Scribner, 1905
Patmore, D., *The Life and Times of Coventry Patmore,* New York, Oxford Univ. Press, 1950

CRITICISM

Brégy, K., "Coventry Patmore," *Catholic World,* 1910, 90:796-806; 91:14-27
Burdett, O., "Coventry Patmore," *Mercury,* 1923, 8:279-291
Burdett, O., *The Idea of Coventry Patmore,* London, Oxford Univ. Press, 1921
Church, R., "The Devout Amorist," *Spectator,* 1928, 141:237-238
De Vere, A., "Coventry Patmore's Poetry," *Essays Chiefly Literary and Ethical,* London, Macmillan, 1889
Egan, M.F., "The Ode Structure of Coventry Patmore," *Studies in Literature,* St. Louis, Herder, 1899
Gardner, W.H., "The Status of Coventry Patmore," *Month,* 1958, 20:205-219
Garvin, L., "Coventry Patmore: the Praise of the Odes," *Fortnightly Review,* 1897, 67:207-217
Haddow, G.C., "A Neglected Poet," *Queen's Quarterly,* 1924, 31:289-297
Johnson, L., "Coventry Patmore's Genius," *Post Liminium,* London, Mathews, 1911
Lubbock, P., "The Poetry of Patmore," *Quarterly Review,* 1908, 208:356-376
Page, F., "The Centenary of Coventry Patmore," *Dublin Review,* 1923, 173:24-37
Page, F., "Coventry Patmore's *Unknown Eros,*" *Catholic World,* 1917, 105:775-785
Page, F., *Patmore: a Study in Poetry,* New York, Oxford Univ. Press, 1933
Quiller-Couch, A., "Coventry Patmore," *Studies in Literature,* 3 vols., New York, Putnam, 1918
Read, H., "Coventry Patmore," *Collected Essays in Literary Criticism,* 2d ed., London, Faber, 1951
Shuster, G.N., "Poetry and Three Poets," *The Catholic Spirit in Modern English Literature,* New York, Macmillan, 1922

Symons, A., "Coventry Patmore," *Figures of Several Centuries,* London, Constable, 1916
Wedmore, F., "Coleridge and Patmore," *Certain Comments,* London, Selwyn, 1925
Wheaton, L., "Emily Honoria Patmore and Coventry Patmore's Poetry," *Dublin Review,* 1918, 163:207-233

BIOGRAPHICAL SKETCH

Coventry Patmore (1823-1896) had a somewhat unfortunate youth which tended to develop in him self-centered eccentricities. By a father who followed literature as a profession but was regarded socially as a cad, and by doting relatives, he was fatuously praised; he early learned to repeat the familiar words: "Coventry is a clever fellow." Beneath his display of arrogance, however, lay a tenderness that was quick to love and to receive love; and beneath his intellectual self-sufficiency was a mysticism that inclined him, as he grew older, toward transcendental philosophy and fervent religious experience. Tall, angular, and shy, he unveiled his attractive soul only to his friends, to the women whom he loved, and to the readers of his poetry. Among his friends, Tennyson was of the most influence; to him was due the gradual improvement of Patmore's technique in verse; the Pre-Raphaelites accepted him as champion and adviser. Among the women whom he idealized, the most important was Emily Andrews, exquisite in person and sympathetic in mind, whom he married in 1847. Their relationship was the embodiment of an almost religious conception of wedded love which became the theme of *The Angel in the House.* The last part of this poem, *The Victories of Love,* reflects Mrs. Patmore's lingering illness and his anticipations of her early death. *The Angel in the House,* printed in parts from 1854 to 1862, won Patmore a gradually increasing popularity with the reading public until it became a conspicuous best seller. His wife's death in 1862 turned Patmore's thoughts toward religion even more strongly than before, until, under the influence of a Miss Byles whom he married in 1864, he became a Roman Catholic. His second wife brought him wealth, with which he retired to an estate in Sussex; there, no longer dependent on his public, he began a vast and mysterious poem, of a more mystical and transcendental order than his previous writings; of this work nine odes printed in 1868 are the fragments. At Hastings, where he removed in 1875, he carried the work still farther and wrote, under the stimulus of what he called "a flash of spiritual health" and an exaltation of imaginative fervor, the odes, which were published as *The Unknown Eros* in 1877. Edmund Gosse has described him walking by the sea, a gale blowing back his coat from his erect, thin figure, while he meditated on the great mysteries of spiritual love. Somewhat isolated in his last years by the receding of fame, but mellowed by congenial friendships, he lived on with unimpaired mind until 1896.

Patmore's principal publications were: *Poems*, 1844; *Tamerton Church Tower*, 1853; *The Angel in the House*, 1854-1862; *Odes*, 1868; *Collected Works*, including *The Unknown Eros and Other Odes*, 1877; *Amelia*, 1878; *Principle in Art*, 1889; *Religio Poetæ*, 1893; *Rod, Root and Flower*, 1895.

INTRODUCTORY CRITICISMS

"The trivial realism of the narrative in *The Angel in the House* attracted a multitude of readers and at the same time obscured the splendor of the essential part of the poem, so that the very popularity of Patmore's great undertaking delayed and falsified his ultimate success. That success consisted, not in the mild adventures of Honoria and her spouse, but in the magnificence of the philosophical episodes, in which the psychology of love is illustrated in language of great originality and with turns of the most felicitous fancy. . . . More charming are the odes devoted to sentiments of remorse, of recollection, or of poignant *desiderium*, the hopeless longing for a vanished face. . . . But some parts of *The Unknown Eros* . . . are more abstruse. In the sacramental odes Patmore is often metaphysical and sometimes dark with excess of ingenuity. His mystical Catholic poetry is inspired by a study of St. Thomas Aquinas among the ancients and of St. John of the Cross among the moderns. As he pursued his lonely meditations, his odes became more and more exclusively occupied with the religious symbolism of sex. . . . Perhaps in the latest of all his poems . . . written in 1880, Patmore carries his mystical ecstasy to its most transcendental height, where few can follow him." —Edmund Gosse, *The English Poets*, ed. by T. H. Ward, Vol. 5, pp. 231-234.

"*The Angel in the House* first appeared in 1854 and may be said to be . . . a kind of half-conscious, half-unconscious revolt against both Tennyson and Browning, but especially against the former. Revolt, indeed, may seem too fierce a word for the mild domesticities of Patmore's poem. . . . The poem contained, even at the first, much pretty verse; as it went on, it was to contain not a little that is positively beautiful. But its ambling versification—somniferous to some of those whom it did not merely please, and positively irritating to others—the deliberate banality of the subject; and the equally deliberate adoption of language outgoing even Wordsworth, even Crabbe, in its avoidance of poetic diction, though they conciliated a large part of contemporary taste, produced a by no means conciliatory effect upon another part which, in the long run, has prevailed. When a man writes

Our witnesses the cook and groom,
We signed the lease for seven years more,

it is not unreasonable to think that Apollo, if he thought it worth his while, must have twitched the poet's ear rather sharply and that attention should have been paid to the twitch. The scornful allusion 'idylls of the dining-room and the deanery,' though its author, Swinburne, was courteous enough not to name the idyllist, expressed a good deal of the younger and youngest opinion of the time."—G. Saintsbury, *Cambridge History of English Literature*, Vol. 13, pp. 190-191.

"It will be seen that the Patmorean ode is, in short, an iambic measure (like that of *The Angel in the House*), which, however, breaks away from the regularity of the octosyllabic couplet or quatrain to indulge in what Patmore himself called 'the fine irregular rock of the free tetrameter.' The verse in these Odes moves 'in long undulating strains' which are modulated by pauses and irregularly occurring rhymes, the rhymed words determining the length of the lines which vary arbitrarily from two to ten or even twelve syllables. It is therefore a metre of extraordinary freedom and impetuous force—which only needed the internal freedom introduced by Patmore's friend Hopkins to give us all the constituents of modern free verse."—Herbert Read, "Coventry Patmore," in *Collected Essays in Literary Criticism*, pp. 322-323.

CRITICAL NOTES

THE TOYS, p. 580

Mrs. Patmore died in 1862, and after that date the five children of the family formed Patmore's "principal solicitude." Edmund Gosse says: "He loved them and they seem to have been both intelligent and well-behaved. But he suffered cruelly from the utterly impossible standard of conduct which he placed before them. . . .

"The constant strain of responsibility for these young motherless creatures was very trying to his nerves. He gave the subject a consideration too constant, and he lost, in his lonely excitement, a sense of proportion. All the little wayward errors which a mother deals with so patiently, corrects so gently and says nothing about, took monstrous proportions to this austere idealist, with his impossible expectations. He was driven to an exaggeration which must make us smile. He wrote: 'I have indeed very little respect for children. Their so-called innocence is want of practice rather than inclination, and all bad passions seem to me to be more violent in children than in men and women, and more wicked because in more immediate conjunction with the divine vision.' . . .

"It was at this time, and after one of these painful moods, that he wrote the ode called *The Toys*, which illustrates, with more delicacy and truth of analysis than any biographer can hope to seize, the ceaseless oscillation of his spirit between severity and tenderness. It is a 'document' of the highest possible value to us in forming a just notion of the temperament of Patmore."—*Coventry Patmore*, pp. 99-100.

JAMES THOMSON, p. 5m2

STANDARD EDITIONS

Poetical Works, 2 vols., ed. by B. Dobell, w. a mem. of the author, London, Reeves, 1895
Poems, sel. and ed. by G.H. Gerould, New York, Holt, 1927
The City of Dreadful Night, and Other Poems, London, Dobell, 1910
Poems, Essays, and Fragments, ed. by J.M. Robertson, London, Fifield, 1905
Poems and Some Letters, ed. by Anne Ridler, London, Centaur Press, 1963
Essays and Phantasies, London, Reeves, 1881
Biographical and Critical Studies, London, Reeves, 1896

BIOGRAPHY

Dobell, B., *The Laureate of Pessimism*, London, Dobell, 1910
Meeker, J.E., *The Life and Poetry of James Thomson*, New Haven, Conn., Yale Univ. Press, 1917
Salt, H.S., *The Life of James Thomson*, London, Watts, 1914

CRITICISM

Forsyth, R.A., "Evolutionism and the Pessimism of James Thomson (B.V.)," *Essays in Criticism*, 1962, 12:148-166
Hearn, L., "Pessimists and Their Kindred," *Interpretations of Literature*, 2 vols., New York, Dodd, 1915
Hoffman, H., "An Angel in the City of Dreadful Night," *Sewanee Review*, 1924, 32:317-335

Le Roy, G.C., "James Thomson," *Perplexed Prophets*, Philadelphia, Univ. of Pa. Press, 1953
Marks, J., "Disaster and Poetry; a Study of James Thomson," *North American Review*, 1920, 212:93-109
Peyre, R., "Les Sources du Pessimisme de Thomson," *Revue Anglo-Américaine*, 1924, pp. 152-156; 1925, pp. 217-231
Schaefer, W.D., "The Two Cities of Dreadful Night," *PMLA*, 1962, 77:609-615
Symons, A., "James Thomson," *Studies in Two Literatures*, London, Secker, Martin, 1924
Walker, I.B., *James Thomson (B.V.), a Critical Study*, Ithaca, N.Y., Cornell Univ. Press, 1950
Welby, T.E., "James Thomson," *Back Numbers*, London, Constable, 1929

BIOGRAPHICAL SKETCH

James Thomson (1834-1882) symbolized the romantic quality of his genius by signing his poems "Bysshe Vanolis" or "B.V.," in honor of Shelley and of Novalis, the pen name of Friedrich Leopold von Hardenberg (1772-1801), German romantic poet and novelist. Thomson's personality was tragically complex. He was at times one of the most attractive of men—friendly, gay-hearted, alert, sensitive; at other times he was mastered by a melancholy that drove him to dissipation and despair. Perhaps an inheritance from his father, this morbidity was encouraged by certain events of his life. He was left an orphan at the age of eight, and he suffered a real measure of poverty throughout most of his youth. Yet he showed a quick mind, and his guardians had him trained as an army schoolmaster. During his army service in Ireland he fell tragically in love with a young girl named Matilda Weller, whose early death shadowed his whole philosophy. Moreover, having lost the religious faith of his childhood, he could find only a dreary atheism to replace it. Nevertheless his early poems, written for liberal journals, often show the gaiety and the courage that won him a wide circle of devoted friends. Early in the seventies he spent some months with a mining company in Colorado and a short time in Spain as correspondent for a New York newspaper. But he was more and more the victim of a deep melancholia, tormented by insomnia. And at the lowest ebb of spirits, in 1874, he wrote his masterpiece, *The City of Dreadful Night*. For the next seven years he composed practically nothing. In 1880, the first publication of his poems as a volume and the cordial praise that Meredith and others gave him restored his hope. He began in the next year once more to write poetry in his gayest vein. A visit with friends in Leicestershire, during the winter of 1881-1882, was one of the happiest episodes of his life. Yet his melancholy returned; he drank himself into madness, wandered homelessly in London alleys, and died from exhaustion in 1882.

Thomson's principal publications were: *The City of Dreadful Night, and Other Poems*, 1880; *Vane's Story, Weddah and Om-el-Bonain, and Other Poems*, 1881; *Essays and Phantasies*, 1881; *A Voice from the Nile, and Other Poems*, 1884; *Satires and Profanities*, 1884; *Poems, Essays, and Fragments*, 1892.

INTRODUCTORY CRITICISMS

"There is no need at this time of day to argue for or against the philosophy of life in which James Thomson took refuge. His despair was inevitable in a man of his temperament, born and circumstanced as he was. ...*The City of Dreadful Night* is not a comfortable poem, nor is it addressed to 'the hopeful young,' or those to whom 'the shows of life' suffice, or those who find comfort in a heaven above or a heaven on earth. Such persons are expressly warned off by the poet himself. It is, however, the most faithful and magnificent expression of the spirit of despair in all modern poetry; it is brave, and it is supremely honest. It should be read as *Ecclesiastes* or Æschylus should be read, not for the sustenance of faith and hope, but for purification through pity and fear."—G. H. Gerould, Introduction to *Poems of James Thomson*, pp. xvii ff.

"Of lighter strain, written when the poet could still be happy, are *Sunday at Hampstead* and *Sunday up the River*, ... and one or two others ... such as *The Fire That Filled My Heart of Old*. ... Even against these the charge of a monotonous, narrow, and irrational misery has been brought. But what saves Thomson is the perfection with which he expresses the negative and hopeless side of the sense of mystery, of the Unseen; just as Miss Rossetti expresses the positive and hopeful one. No two contemporary poets perhaps ever completed each other in a more curious way than this Bohemian atheist and this devout lady."—G. Saintsbury, *A History of Nineteenth Century Literature*, p. 298.

GEORGE MEREDITH, p. 599

STANDARD EDITIONS

Works, 36 vols., London, Constable, 1914

Poetical Works, w. notes by G.M. Trevelyan, New York, Scribner, 1928
Last Poems, New York, Scribner, 1909
Essay on Comedy, ed. w. an intro. and notes by Lane Cooper, New York, Scribner, 1918
Modern Love, w. an intro. by C. Day Lewis, London, Hart-Davis, 1948
Letters, 2 vols., col. and ed. by his son, New York, Scribner, 1912
Letters to E. Clodd and C.K. Shorter, London, privately printed, 1913
Letters to Alice Meynell, London, Nonesuch Press, 1923

BIOGRAPHY

Butcher, Lady, *Memories of George Meredith*, London, Constable, 1919
Clodd, E., "Meredith: Some Recollections," *Fortnightly Review*, 1909, 92:19-31
Ellis, S.M., "George Meredith: His Association with the Pre-Raphaelites," *London Bookman*, 1928, 73:253-257
Ellis, S.M., *George Meredith; His Life and Friends in Relation to His Work*, London, Richards, Ltd., 1920
Gretton, Mary (Sturge), *The Writings and Life of George Meredith*, London, Oxford Univ. Press, 1926
Hardy, T., "George Meredith: a Reminiscence," *Nineteenth Century*, 1928, 103: 145-148
Lindsay, Jack, *George Meredith: His Life and Work*, London, Bodley Head, 1956
Nicoll, W.R., "Memories of Meredith," *A Bookman's Letters*, London, Hodder, 1913
Priestley, J.B., *George Meredith*, English Men of Letters Series, New York, Macmillan, 1926
Sassoon, S.L., *Meredith*, New York, Viking, 1948
Sencourt, R.E., *The Life of George Meredith*, New York, Scribner, 1929
Stevenson, L., *The Ordeal of George Meredith*, New York, Scribner, 1953

CRITICISM

Armstrong, M., "The Poetry of George Meredith," *North American Review*, 1921, 213: 354-361
Austin, Deborah, "Meredith on the Nature of Metaphor," *University of Toronto Quarterly*, 1957, 27:96-102
Bailey, E.J., "Meredith's *Modern Love*," *Forum*, 1908, 40:245-254
Bailey, John, "Poetry of Meredith," *Fortnightly Review*, 1909, 92:32-46
Barrie, J.M., *George Meredith, a Tribute*, London, Constable, 1922
Bartlett, Phyllis, "George Meredith: Early Manuscript Poems in the Berg Collection,"

Bulletin of the New York Public Library, 1957, 61:396-415

Beach, J.W., *The Comic Spirit in George Meredith*, New York, Longmans, 1911

Bennett, A., "Meredith," *Books and Persons*, London, Chatto, 1917

Brocklehurst, J.H., "George Meredith—an Appreciation," *Manchester Quarterly*, 1928, 187:167-180

Chesterton, G.K., "George Meredith," *The Uses of Diversity*, New York, Dodd, 1921

Clutton-Brock, A., "George Meredith," *More Essays on Books*, New York, Dutton, 1921

Cress, J.H.E., *Meredith Revisited, and Other Essays*, London, Cobden-Sanderson, 1921

Curle, R.H.P., *Aspects of George Meredith*, London, Routledge, 1908

Davidson, J., "George Meredith's Odes," *The Man Forbid, and Other Essays*, Boston, Ball Publishing Co., 1910

Dowden, E., "Mr. Meredith in His Poems," *New Studies in Literature*, London, Paul, 1895

Edgar, P., "Poetry of George Meredith," *Living Age*, 1907, 255:744-751

Esdaile, A.J.K., *A Chronological List of George Meredith's Publications*, London, Constable, 1914

Foote, G.W., "George Meredith: Free Thinker," *English Review*, 1913, 13:602-616

Forman, M.B., *A Bibliography of the Writings in Prose and Verse of George Meredith*, Edinburgh, Dunedin Press, 1922

Granville-Barker, H., "Some Victorians Afield," *Theatre Arts Monthly*, 1929, 13:256-264

Hammerton, J.A., *George Meredith, His Life and Art in Anecdote and Criticism*, Edinburgh, Grant, J., 1911

Hearn, L., "The Poetry of George Meredith," *Pre-Raphaelite and Other Poets*, New York, Dodd, 1922

Henley, W. E., "Meredith," *Views and Reviews*, London, Macmillan, 1921

Jackson, H., "The Ideas of George Meredith," *All Manner of Folk*, London, Richards, Ltd., 1912

Jerrold, W.C., *George Meredith; an Essay towards Appreciation*, London, Greening, 1902

Kelvin, Norman, *A Troubled Eden: Nature and Society in the Works of George Meredith*, Stanford, Calif., Stanford Univ. Press, 1961

Le Gallienne, R., "George Meredith's Poetry," *Forum*, 1910, 43:441-447

Lowes, J.L., "An Unacknowledged Imagist," *Nation*, 1916, 102:217-219

Mayer, F.P., "George Meredith: an Obscure Comedian," *Virginia Quarterly Review*, 1925, 1:409-422

Monkhouse, A., "Mr. Meredith's Poems," *Books and Plays*, London, Lane, 1896

Monroe, H., "Meredith as a Poet," *Poetry*, 1928, 32:210-216

Noyes, A., "George Meredith," *The Opalescent Parrot*, London, Sheed, 1929

Peel, R., *The Creed of a Victorian Pagan*, Cambridge, Mass., Harvard Univ. Press, 1931

Petter, G.B., *George Meredith and His German Critics*, London, Witherby, 1939

Pigou, A.C., "Optimism of Browning and Meredith," *Living Age*, 1905, 246:415-422

Quiller-Couch, A., "The Poetry of George Meredith," *Studies in Literature*, 3 vols., New York, Putnam, 1918

Revell, W.F., "George Meredith's Nature Poetry," *Westminster Review*, 1894, 142:506-523

Reynolds, G.F., "Two Notes on the Poetry of George Meredith," *University of Colorado Studies*, 1925, 15:1-12

Robertson, L.C., "Meredith the Poet," *English Review*, 1927, 44:463-471

Sawin, H.L., "George Meredith: A Bibliography of Meredithiana, 1920-1953," *Bulletin of Bibliography*, 1955, 21:186-191, 215-216

Sherman, S.P., "The Humanism of George Meredith," *On Contemporary Literature*, New York, Holt, 1917

Sinclair, M., "George Meredith," *Outlook*, 1909, 92:413-418

Stratton, C., "On Rereading Meredith," *Sewanee Review*, 1918, 26:153-167

Strong, A.T., *Three Studies in Shelley and an Essay on Nature in Wordsworth and Meredith*, London, Oxford Univ. Press, 1921

Symons, A., "George Meredith as a Poet," *Figures of Several Centuries*, London, Constable, 1916

Trevelyan, G.M., *The Poetry and Philosophy of George Meredith*, London, Constable, 1912

Welby, T.E., "George Meredith," *Back Numbers*, London, Constable, 1929

Westminster Review, "Swinburne and Meredith," 1909, 172:29-35

Woods, Alice, *George Meredith as Champion of Women and of Progressive Education*, Oxford, England, Blackwell, 1937

Wright, W.F., *Art and Substance in George Meredith*, Lincoln, Univ. of Neb. Press, 1953

BIOGRAPHICAL SKETCH

George Meredith (1828-1909) was early in his youth made self-dependent by the extravagance of his father, a rakish tailor of Portsmouth. His formal education was cut short after a year in 1843-1844 at a German school; during an apprenticeship with a London lawyer, he lived precariously on a bowl of porridge a day and continued his education by his own efforts. In 1848 he turned to journalism and began to contribute poetry to periodicals. Handsome, with an athletic build and chestnut-red hair, and gifted with extraordinary brilliance in conversation, he was welcomed in London bohemian circles. In 1849 he made an unfortunate match with the beautiful but flighty daughter of Thomas Love Peacock, from whom he separated in 1858. Their gradual estrangement is studied in Meredith's poem *Modern Love*, which he published with other verse in 1862. Meanwhile he had published in 1859 *The Ordeal of Richard Feverel*, the first of his novels.

His more serious work not proving profitable, Meredith continued to support himself by what he called "the Egyptian bondage" of journalism and reading for publishers. After a journey in the Alps and an unsuccessful attempt to share a London house with Swinburne and Rossetti, he married in 1864 the charming Marie Vulliamy and established a permanent home at Flint Cottage, near Box Hill in Surrey, where the scenery had a romantic quality rare in England. In the hills behind his house he put up a Norwegian chalet, slung a hammock from the beams, and lived there while he wrote novels and his *Poems and Lyrics of the Joy of Earth*, published in 1883. Fastidious, an excellent judge of wine and cigars, he combined social graces with a passion for the out-of-doors and made long tramps over the hills to keep fresh his contact with the primal earth, which he loved as the stern but wholesome mother of mankind.

With the publication of *The Egoist* in 1879 and *Diana of the Crossways* in 1885, Meredith was surprised to find himself at last famous and Box Hill invaded by curious visitors. Whatever joy he might have taken in this long-deferred fame was destroyed by his own ill health and the mortal illness of his wife; he was forced to give up walking; and, as he said: "When I ceased to walk briskly, part of my life was ended." Under these somber circumstances he published his *Poems of Tragic Life* in 1887 and *A Reading of Earth* in 1888. In 1894 he closed his work as a novelist with *The Amazing Marriage* but continued to write and publish volumes of verse. He served in his last years as literary arbiter to the world; his critical opinions were widely quoted and much respected. Crippled, he yet insisted on being wheeled out-of-doors in his chair, in sunshine or rain. When he died, he was buried in the quiet cemetery at Dorking instead of at Westminster Abbey; for, as he said, "better the green grass turf than Abbey pavements."

Meredith's principal publications were: *Poems*, 1851; *The Shaving of Shagpat*, 1856; *The Ordeal of Richard Feverel*, 1859; *Evan Harrington*, 1861; *Modern Love and Poems of the English Roadside*, 1862; *Rhoda Fleming*, 1865; *Vittoria*, 1867; *Beauchamp's Career*, 1876; *On the Idea of Comedy, and of the Uses of the Comic Spirit*, 1877; *The Egoist*, 1879; *Poems and Lyrics of the Joy of Earth*, 1883; *Diana of the Crossways*, 1885; *Ballads and Poems of Tragic Life*, 1887; *A Reading of Earth*, 1888; *One of Our Conquerors*, 1891; *Poems*, 1892; *Lord Ormont and His Aminta*, 1894; *The Amazing Marriage*, 1895; *Odes in Contribution to the Song of French History*, 1898; *A Reading of Life*, 1901; *Last Poems*, 1909; *Celt and Saxon*, 1910; *Up to Midnight*, 1913.

INTRODUCTORY CRITICISMS

"To Meredith poetry has come to be a kind of imaginative logic, and almost the whole of his later work is a reasoning in verse. He reasons, not always clearly to the eye, and never satisfyingly to the ear, but with a fiery intelligence which has more passion than most poets put into frankly emotional verse. He reasons in pictures, every line having its imagery, and he uses pictorial words to express abstract ideas. Disdaining the common subjects of poetry, as he disdains common rhythms, common rhymes, and common language, he does much by his enormous vitality to give human warmth to arguments concerning humanity. He does much, though he attempts the impossible."—A. Symons, *Figures of Several Centuries*, p. 151.

"Though no one speaks less from a chair or pulpit, Mr. Meredith stands to be judged as a teacher and prophet. He is not content to be an observer. . . . Mr. Meredith's ethic is best applied in his prose and best expounded in his verse, though his verse comes, far less often than his prose, to rightness of form. He has his own divinity, pagan by name. Where other writers appeal to God or to Humanity, he speaks, somewhat insistently, of the Earth; and the Earth is not the malign step-mother of pessimistic theory, but a stern genial mother, if at times something of a governess. . . . Earth lends us our bodies, our fund of power, and our capital of instinct, which may be turned to uses fruitful or sterile. Our life is the adjustment and realization of the forces that Earth has given us. It is love, rightly understood, that tasks and rewards our power of directing those forces. Such love helps us, in its better forms, to the vision of 'nobler races.' . . . The creed is not unlike Carlyle's in its courage, but it is more possible, less savage, and less solitary."—Oliver Elton, *Modern Studies*, p. 241.

WILLIAM MORRIS, p. 619

STANDARD EDITIONS

Collected Works, 24 vols., w. intros. by May Morris, London, Longmans, 1910-1915
Poetical Works, 11 vols., London, Longmans, 1896-1898
The Defence of Guenevere and Other Poems, London, Longmans, 1903
The Earthly Paradise, London, Longmans, 1896
The Life and Death of Jason, ed. w. intro. and notes by E. Maxwell, London, Milford, 1914
The Story of Sigurd the Volsung, New York, Longmans, 1904
Prose and Poetry, 1856-1870, London, Oxford Univ. Press, 1913
Letters to His Family and Friends, ed. w. an intro. and notes by P. Henderson, New York, Longmans, 1950
William Morris, Artist, Writer, Socialist; Unpublished and Hitherto Inaccessible Writings, 2 vols., ed. by May Morris, Oxford, England, Blackwell, 1936

BIOGRAPHY

Bloomfield, P., *Life and Work of William Morris*, London, Royal Soc. of Arts, 1934
Clutton-Brock, A., *William Morris, His Work and Influence*, New York, Holt, 1914
Compton-Rickett, A., *William Morris, a Study in Personality*, London, Jenkins, 1913
Eshleman, L.W. (Lloyd E. Grey, pseud.), *William Morris, Prophet of England's New Order*, London, Cassell, 1949
Glasier, J.B., *William Morris and the Early Days of the Socialist Movement*, New York, Longmans, 1921
Godwin, E.F., and S.A. Godwin, *Warrior Bard, the Life of William Morris*, London, Harrap, 1948
Mackail, J.W., *The Life of William Morris*, London, Longmans, 1922
Mackail, J.W., *William Morris and His Circle*, London, Oxford Univ. Press, 1907
Meynell, Esther, *Portrait of William Morris*, London, Chapman, 1947
Noyes, A., *William Morris*, English Men of Letters Series, London, Macmillan, 1908
Shaw, G.B., *William Morris as I Knew Him*, New York, Dodd, 1936

Sparling, H.H., *The Kelmscott Press and William Morris, Master-Craftsman*, London, Macmillan, 1924
Thompson, Edward P., *William Morris, Romantic to Revolutionary*, New York, Monthly Review Press, 1962
Weekley, M., *William Morris*, London, Duckworth, 1934
See also books on Pre-Raphaelitism listed under Dante Gabriel Rossetti.

CRITICISM

Apgar, G., "Morris's *The Lady of the Land*," *Poet Lore*, 1922, 33:274-285
Bartels, H., *William Morris, The Story of Sigurd the Volsung and the Fall of the Niblungs; eine Studie über das Verhältnis des Epos zu den Quellen*, Münster, Westfalen, Schöningh, 1906
Chesterton, G.K., "William Morris and His School," *Varied Types*, New York, Dodd, 1903
Clutton-Brock, A., "The Later Poems of William Morris," *Living Age*, 1906, 251: 241-245
Crane, W., *William Morris to Whistler*, London, Bell, 1911
Drinkwater, John, *William Morris, a Critical Study*, London, Secker, Martin, 1912
Evans, B.I., *William Morris and His Poetry*, London, Harrap, 1925
Forman, H.B., *The Books of William Morris Described*, London, Hollings, Frank, 1897
Grennan, M.R., *William Morris, Medievalist and Revolutionary*, New York, King's Crown Press, 1945
Hamilton, Walter, "William Morris," *The Æsthetic Movement in England*, London, Reeves, 1882
Hearn, L., "William Morris," *Pre-Raphaelite and Other Poets*, New York, Dodd, 1922
Herford, C.H., *Norse Myth in English Poetry*, London, Longmans, 1919
Hoare, D.M., *The Works of Morris and Yeats in Relation to Early Saga Literature*, New York, Macmillan, 1937
Hough, G., *The Last Romantics*, New York, Macmillan, 1950
Jackson, H., *William Morris, Craftsman-Socialist*, London, Cape, 1926
James, H., "The Poetry of William Morris," *Views and Reviews*, Boston, Ball Publishing Co., 1908
Knickerbocker, W.S., "Afterglow," *Creative Oxford, Its Influence in Victorian Literature*, Syracuse, N.Y., Syracuse Univ. Press, 1925
Lang, A., "Mr. Morris's Poems," *Adventures among Books*, London, Longmans, 1905

Lubbock, P., "The Poetry of William Morris," *Quarterly Review*, 1911, 215:482-504

McDowell, G.T., "The Treatment of the Volsungasaga by William Morris," *Scandinavian Studies and Notes*, 1923, 7:151-168

Mackail, J.W., "William Morris," *Studies of English Poets*, London, Longmans, 1926

March-Phillips, L., "Pre-Raphaelitism and the Present," *Contemporary Review*, 1906, 89:709-713

Maurer, O., "Morris's Treatment of Greek Legend in *The Earthly Paradise*," *University of Texas, Studies in English*, 1954, 33: 103-118

Maynadier, G.H., *The Arthur of the English Poets*, Boston, Houghton, 1907

Myers, F.W.H., "Modern Poets and the Meaning of Life," *Nineteenth Century*, 1893, 33:93-111

Ormerod, J., *The Poetry of William Morris*, Derby, England, Public Libraries, 1938

Parry, J.J., "Note on the Prosody of William Morris," *Modern Language Notes*, 1929, 44:306-309

Pater, W., "Æsthetic Poetry," *Appreciations*, London, Macmillan, 1889

Perrine, Laurence, "Morris's Guenevere: An Interpretation," *Philological Quarterly*, 1960, 39:234-241

Phelan, Mrs. Anna A. (Von Helmholtz), *The Social Philosophy of William Morris*, Durham, N.C., Duke Univ. Press, 1927

Pundt, H., *Dante Gabriel Rossetti's Einfluss auf die Gedichte des jungen William Morris*, Breslau, 1920

Ralli, A., "*The Earthly Paradise*," *Critiques*, London, Longmans, 1927

Scott, T., *A Bibliography of the Works of William Morris*, London, Bell, 1897

Shaw, G.B., "William Morris as a Socialist," *London Daily Chronicle*, Oct. 6, 1896

Swinburne, A.C., "Morris's *Life and Death of Jason*," *Essays and Studies*, London, Chatto, 1875

Symons, A., "William Morris," *Studies in Two Literatures*, London, Secker, 1924

Vaughan, C.E., *Bibliographies of Swinburne, Morris, and Rossetti*, English Association Pamphlet No. 29, London, Oxford Univ. Press, 1914

Westminster Review, "Poems by William Morris," 1868, 90:300-312

Wilson, S.P., "William Morris and France," *South Atlantic Quarterly*, 1924, 23:242-255

Yeats, W.B., "The Happiest of the Poets," *Ideas of Good and Evil*, London, Bullen, 1903

BIOGRAPHICAL SKETCH

For William Morris (1834-1896) poetry was the relaxation of a life seriously devoted to great aims in painting, architecture, craftsmanship, and the improvement of human society. He was born in London, the son of a well-to-do broker. As a child he became familiar with the Waverley novels, and by the time he was fourteen he had developed a taste for architecture and a love for the medieval. He learned as a schoolboy, he said, "most of what was to be known about English Gothic." Influenced by the Oxford Movement,[1] he entered Exeter College, Oxford, in 1853 with the intention of taking holy orders; for a time he thought of founding a monastery where he could devote himself to the production of religious art. His Oxford career brought him into intimate contact with Burne-Jones, Rossetti, and other Pre-Raphaelites and greatly enlarged his interests; he learned to appreciate Chaucer and Malory and made his first acquaintance with northern mythology and epic. In 1855, while on a tour in northern France with Burne-Jones, he became so impressed with the glories of the French cathedrals that he abandoned his plan to enter the church and decided to devote himself to art; he gave himself first to architecture, then to painting. It was while he was employed with Rossetti and Burne-Jones in frescoing the walls of the Oxford Union that he met Jane Burden, whom he married in 1859.

Morris had already attracted attention as a poet. Early in his career at Oxford he had written verse of great originality and had published some of his poems, with several remarkable prose tales, in *The Oxford and Cambridge Magazine* (1856), an undergraduate publication which he had founded and supported. Then at London, under the stimulation of Rossetti, he published in 1858 *The Defence of Guenevere, and Other Poems*, a volume that clearly showed Pre-Raphaelite influences. He gave up poetry, however, for the following seven years to plunge into a new project designed to elevate the artistic standards of articles manufactured for use in common life. In company with the Pre-Raphaelites and other friends, he built workshops for the production of many articles, from furniture and glassware to cotton goods and wallpaper, marked by a new beauty of color and design.

In 1866, when this business was operating smoothly, Morris again began to write poetry, this time in a manner more simple, more Chaucerian, than his earlier "Pre-Raphaelite" style. During four years he produced the successive parts of *The Earthly Paradise* (1868-1870), writing with fluency and pleasure;

[1]See the Biographical Sketch of Cardinal Newman, p. 944.

one portion, growing too large for inclusion with the others, he published separately in 1867 as *The Life and Death of Jason*, which proved him a master of romantic narrative. When these Greek and Norse legends had been retold, Morris became fascinated with the Icelandic sagas, studied the language under a tutor, published his translation of the *Volsunga Saga* in 1870, made a journey to Iceland in the following year, and returned so much in the mood of the old skalds that he made other translations in 1874 and published his *Story of Sigurd the Volsung and the Fall of the Niblungs* in 1876.

Morris's literary activities were again interrupted by the pressure of other interests. At his home at Kelmscott Manor House near London, he set up a press dedicated to artistic printing, the crowning achievement of which was the Kelmscott edition of Chaucer, issued in 1896. During the eighties his chief concern, however, was with industrial organization, which was of such a sort, he felt, that true craftsmanship was impossible. He therefore came to advocate state socialism as a corrective for the dehumanization of industry, worked as an ardent leader in radical workingmen's societies, and delivered addresses in halls and in the streets in an effort to make his views prevail. The finest expression of his attitude is his *Dream of John Ball*, published in 1888. By 1890 Morris had come to believe that the victories of socialism were remote, but he did not cease to expound the theory, so clearly involved with his standards of art, until his death.

After 1889 Morris found leisure to withdraw from strenuous actuality for an occasional excursion into prose romance. His *News from Nowhere* (1890) is a socialistic romance of the future; his series of prose tales, interspersed with lyrics, began with *A Tale of the House of the Wolfings* in 1889 and included *The Well at the World's End* in 1896. In 1895 his health declined under the pressure of his work; and his strenuous, high-minded, and singularly devoted life ended in the following year.

Morris's principal publications were: *The Defence of Guenevere, and Other Poems*, 1858; *The Life and Death of Jason*, 1867; *The Earthly Paradise*, 1868-1870; *Love Is Enough*, 1872; *Three Northern Love Songs* (with E. Magnusson), 1875; *The Æneids of Virgil*, 1875; *The Story of Sigurd the Volsung and the Fall of the Niblungs*, 1876; *Hopes and Fears for Art*, 1882; *The Odyssey of Homer*, 1887; *A Dream of John Ball*, 1888; *Signs of Change*, 1888; *A Tale of the House of the Wolfings*, 1889; *News from Nowhere*, 1890; *Poems by the Way*, 1891; *Gothic*

Architecture, 1893; *The Tale of a Beowulf* (with A. J. Wyatt), 1895; *The Well at the World's End*, 1896; *Old French Romances*, 1896; *The Sundering Flood*, 1897; *Architecture, Industry and Wealth*, collected papers, 1902.

INTRODUCTORY CRITICISMS

"One thinks of Morris as a man who wished to make the world as beautiful as an illuminated manuscript. He loved the bright colors, the gold, the little strange insets of landscape, the exquisite craftsmanship of decoration, in which the genius of the medieval illuminators expressed itself. His Utopia meant the restoration, not so much of the soul of man, as of the selected delights of the arts and crafts of the Middle Ages."—R. Lynd, *The Art of Letters*, p. 150.

"There are two important characteristics that individualize Morris's poetic work, and differentiate it from that of his contemporaries. The most obvious thing about his work as an artist, whether the work be a wall-paper or an epic, is . . . spaciousness of design. Large effects, ample spaces of beauty, diffusion rather than concentration, were what he aimed at. . . . It is this quality of workmanship that makes quotation from Morris unsatisfactory. . . . The second characteristic is directness of method. . . . Without it his spaciousness of design might have spelt mere prolixity and incoherence; . . . it gives lucidity . . . to his work. . . . It is a part of the old-world atmosphere he brought into modern literature, and shows how fully he had incorporated into blood and marrow the old legends and sagas."—A. Compton-Rickett, *William Morris*, pp. 114-119.

"Thus for Morris to collect the old stories, to accept them as they come, and to tell them again in a style that removes them as far as possible from the troubled actuality of life, is to perform the proper function of the poet. It is a curiously incomplete aesthetic. It would exclude tragedy and emotional realism. It explains some of Morris's odd but persistent views about poetry—that anybody who is any good ought to be able to compose it while weaving a tapestry at the same time, that the writing of poetry is a relaxation from the arduous practical business of life."—Graham Hough, *The Last Romantics*, pp. 125-126.

CRITICAL NOTES

Some of the poems in Morris's first volume of verse—*The Defence of Guenevere, and Other Poems*—show influences of Pre-Raphaelitism. (See note on the Pre-Raphaelites, p. 991.) Morris early became associated with Rossetti and Burne-Jones and shared with them an enthusiasm for attempting to identify art with life. Fascinated as he was by medieval life, its illuminated manuscripts, its beauty of architectural design, it was but natural that his early poetry especially should bear the inevitable Pre-Raphaelite characteristics of richness of decorative color and psychic bewilderment. Poems on pp. 619-640, inclusive, of this book appeared in Morris's first volume.

THE DEFENCE OF GUENEVERE, p. 619

Guenevere, the wife of King Arthur, being charged with adultery and twice under sentence of death by fire, speaks in this poem in her own defense. Two important incidents, as related by Malory in *Morte d'Arthur*, 19-20, lie back of the poem—(1) While Guenevere was enjoying a holiday with her unarmed knights, she was carried off by Sir Meliagrance and his band (ll. 168 ff.) to Meliagrance's castle, *la Fausse Garde*, and held prisoner until she was rescued by Lancelot. In gaining entrance to Guenevere's chamber one night, Lancelot cut his arm on the bars of the window; the blood that Meliagrance discovered the next morning on the bed came from Lancelot's wound, although Meliagrance charged the Queen with having received one of her wounded knights who had been close by in the castle. Lancelot agreed to prove the Queen's innocence later in a combat with Meliagrance. While Lancelot was being shown about the castle, he stepped upon a trap (l. 190) and fell into a cave full of straw. He managed to escape in time to keep his appointment at the combat, in which he killed Meliagrance and saved Guenevere from the fire. (2) At a later time, Lancelot was found in Guenevere's chamber by fourteen knights who had previously laid a trap to catch the lovers. Lancelot killed thirteen of the knights, including Gawaine's two sons and brother Agravaine; Modred, a half brother of Gawaine, escaped. After this episode, Guenevere was again condemned to be burned. It is at this second trial that she speaks in this poem.

Morris follows Malory's account rather closely except in two details—Gawaine was not present at the fight in the Queen's chamber, and he was not an accuser of the Queen; on the contrary, he spoke most vigorously in her defense. For some unexplained reason Morris presents Gawaine as an accuser. (See G. H. Maynadier's *The Arthur of the English Poets*, pp. 357-360.)

Page 622, line 242. The story of the fight in Guenevere's chamber is thus related by Malory, Book 20, Chapter 4:

And therewith Sir Launcelot wrapped his mantle about his arm well and surely; and by then they had gotten a great form out of the hall, and therewithal they rashed at the door. Fair lords, said Sir Launcelot, leave your noise and your rashing, and I shall set open this door, and then may ye do with me what it liketh you. Come off then, said they all, and do it, for it availeth thee not to strive against us all; and therefore let us into this chamber, and we shall save thy life until thou come to King Arthur. Then Launcelot unbarred the door, and with his left hand he held it open a little, so that but one man might come in at once; and so there came striding a good knight, a much man and large, and his name was Colgrevance of Gore, and he with a sword struck at Sir Launcelot mightily; and he put aside the stroke and gave him such a buffet upon the helmet, that he fell grovelling dead within the chamber door. And then Sir Launcelot with great might drew that dead knight within the chamber door; and Sir Launcelot with help of the queen and her ladies was lightly armed in Sir Colgrevance's armour. And ever stood Sir Agravaine and Sir Modred crying: Traitor knight, come out of the queen's chamber. Leave your noise, said Sir Launcelot unto Sir Agravaine, for wit you well, Sir Agravaine, ye shall not prison me this night; and therefore an ye do by my counsel, go ye all from this chamber door, and make not such crying and such manner of slander as ye do; for I promise you by my knighthood, an ye will depart and make no more noise, I shall as to-morn appear afore you all before the king, and then let it be seen which of you all, outher else ye all, that will accuse me of treason; and there I shall answer you as a knight should, that hither I came to the queen for no manner of mal engine, and that will I prove and make it good upon you with my hands. Fie on thee, traitor, said Sir Agravaine and Sir Modred, we will have thee maugre thy head, and slay thee if we list; for we let thee wit we have the choice of King Arthur to save thee or to slay thee. Ah sirs, said Sir Launcelot, is there none other grace with you? then keep yourself. So then Sir Launcelot set all open the chamber door, and mightily and knightly he strode in amongst them; and anon at the first buffet he slew Sir Agravaine. And twelve of his fellows after, within a little while after, he laid them cold to the earth, for there was none of the twelve that might stand Sir Launcelot one buffet. Also Sir Launcelot wounded Sir Modred, and he fled with all his might. And then Sir Launcelot returned again unto the queen, and said: Madam, now wit you well all our true love is brought to an end, for now will King Arthur ever be my foe; and therefore, madam, an it like you that I may have you with me, I shall save you from all manner adventures dangerous. That is not best, said the queen; meseemeth now ye have done so much harm, it will be best ye hold you still with this. And if ye see that as to-morn they will put me unto death, then may ye rescue me as ye think best. I will well, said Sir Launcelot, for have ye no doubt, while I am living I shall rescue you. And then he kissed her, and either gave other a ring; and so there he left the queen, and went until his lodging.

RAPUNZEL, p. 623

Rapunzel was included in Morris's first volume of poetry—*The Defence of Guenevere, and Other Poems* (1858). Alfred Noyes calls it "the most bewitching of all the poems in this book. Its elaborate metrical scheme is in itself a complete refutation of what has been said about Morris's lack of technique; and it is a most brilliantly successful voyage across the perilous sea that washes fairylands forlorn, full of delicate beauty, and deliciously mediæval."—*William Morris*, by Alfred Noyes, p. 29.

The story of Rapunzel belongs to folklore. It is told as follows in the Grimm brothers' collection of fairy tales: A man and his wife, eagerly looking forward to the birth of their long-desired child, lived near the house and garden of a witch. To satisfy his wife's craving the man stole some vegetables from the garden but was caught by the witch who demanded the unborn child as payment for the theft. The man agreed, and the new-born girl was delivered to the witch, who named her Rapunzel, and at the end of twelve years confined her in a lonely tower with no opening except a small window at the top. Through this, at the command of the witch, Rapunzel daily let down her long golden hair for the witch to use in climbing to the window.

It happened that a prince, passing through the forest surrounding the tower, saw the beautiful girl and loved her. Observing the method used by the witch to gain entrance to the tower, he used it also, and thereafter paid nightly visits to Rapunzel. The witch soon discovered their secret, cut off the golden hair of Rapunzel, and carried her away to the desert. She awaited in the tower a visit from the prince, who was ignorant of what had happened, and so frightened him that he fell from the window into a thorn bush and was blinded. After wandering about for a time, he finally came to Rapunzel, whose tears of joy fell upon his eyes and restored their sight. They then set out for the prince's dominion, where they lived happily ever after.

THE BLUE CLOSET, p. 635

John Drinkwater characterizes this poem with *The Tune of Seven Towers* (p. 636) and *Two Red Roses Across the Moon* (p. 638) as "essays in color without any attempt at concrete significance." "It is wrong," he adds, "to say that these poems have no meaning. They mean exactly the colors that they themselves create. It would be as wise to say that a sunset or a blue distance of mountains is meaningless."—*William Morris*, by John Drinkwater, pp. 65-66.

Noyes describes these poems as "vague and somewhat chaotic mediæval scraps of windmusic."—*William Morris*, by Alfred Noyes, p. 21.

THE LIFE AND DEATH OF JASON, p. 640

Because of its romantic nature, the old Greek legend of the quest of the Golden Fleece was especially interesting to Morris. He originally planned to use it as a theme of one of the narrative poems of *The Earthly Paradise* (p. 642), but his enthusiasm soon outran his first design, and the poem was published separately in 1867 as *The Life and Death of Jason*. It won instant popularity. Following is a brief summary of the story:

Jason was the son of Aeson and nephew of Pelias, King of Iolcos, in Thessaly. To keep Jason from his rightful throne, Pelias sent him in quest of the Golden Fleece, which had been taken from the ram that bore Phrixus, about to be sacrificed to Zeus, through the air to Colchis in Asia. Aeetis, King of Colchis, had

placed the Fleece in a grove where it was guarded by a sleepless dragon. With the aid of the gods, Jason built an enchanted ship, the *Argo*, and accompanied by fifty of the noblest heroes of Greece—including Castor and Pollux, Orpheus, Hercules, Theseus, and Nestor—set out on the perilous undertaking and finally arrived at Colchis. The King promised Jason the Fleece if he would harness two fire-breathing, brazen-hoofed bulls to a plow; plow a field sacred to Mars, sow it with dragons' teeth, and kill the crop of armed men that would spring up; and slay the dragon guarding the Fleece. Jason performed all these tasks with the aid of the King's daughter Medea, a powerful sorceress who had fallen in love with him; after the Fleece was secured he fled with Medea to the ship and sailed back to Iolcos. With the aid of Medea's wiles, Pelias was slain, and Jason and Medea lived happily in Corinth until Jason fell in love with Glauce, the daughter of Creon, King of Corinth. Medea destroyed her rival with a magic robe of death and fled to Athens. Not long after, Jason fell asleep on the seashore and next morning was found dead.

THE EARTHLY PARADISE, p. 642

The Earthly Paradise is a cycle of twenty-four tales told in verse and bound together, after the manner of Chaucer, by a connecting link that forms the subject of the *Prologue*. In the *Prologue*, Morris tells how certain gentlemen and wanderers, driven from their homes in Norway by the great pestilence that spread over Europe in the middle of the fourteenth century, set out to find the fabled Earthly Paradise. After many years they reach a "Western land" inhabited by descendants of the ancient Greeks, who entertain them with semimonthly feasts for a year. At each feast a tale is told, alternately by one of the inhabitants and by one of the visitors. The inhabitants tell stories of Greek mythology; the visitors, stories of Norse or Romance origin. The prologue, the narrative links connecting the tales, and eight of the tales themselves are written in ten-syllabled couplets; seven tales are in eight-syllabled couplets; the rest, together with the lyrics for the various months, are written in seven-lined stanzas. Following is the Table of Contents of the cycle:

THE LADY OF THE LAND, p. 643

The following account of *The Lady of the Land* appears in Cap. IV of *The Voiage and Travaile of Sir John Maundeville*:

Some Men seyn, that in the Ile of Lango[1] is zit the Doughtre of Ypocras, in forme and lykeness of a gret Dragoun, that is a hundred Fadme of lengthe, as Men seyn: For I have not seen hire. And thei of the Isles callen hire, Lady of the Lond. And sche lyethe in an olde castelle, in a Cave, and schewethe twyes of thryes in the Zeer. And sche dothe none harm to no Man, but zif Men don hire harm. And sche was thus chaunged and transformed, from a fair Damysele, in to lykenesse of a Dragoun, be a Goddesse, that was clept Deane.[2] And Men seyn, that sche schalle so endure in that forme of a Dragoun, unto the tyme that a Knyghte come, that is so hardy, that dar come to hire and kiss hire on the Mouthe: And then schalle sche turne azen to hire owne Kynde, and ben a Woman azen: But aftre that sche schalle not liven longe. And it is not long siththen, that a Knyghte of the Rodes, that was hardy and doughty in Armes, seyde that he wolde kyssen hire. And whan he was upon his Coursere, and wente to the Castelle, and entred into the Cave, the Dragoun lifte up hire Hed azenst him. And whan the Knyghte saw hire in that Forme so hidous and so horrible he fleyghe awey. And the Dragoun bare the Knyghte upon a Roche, mawgre his Hede; and from that Roche, sche caste him in to the See: and so was lost bothe Hors and Man. And also a zonge Man, that wiste not of the Dragoun, wente out of a Schipp, and wente thorghe the Ile, til that he come to the Castelle, and cam in to the Cave: and wente so longe, til that he fond a Chambre, and there he saughe a Damysele, that kembed hire Hede, and lokede in a Myrour; and sche hadde meche Tresoure abouten hire: and he trowed, that sche hadde ben a comoun Woman, that dwelled there to resceyve Men to Folye. And he abode, tille the Damysele saughe the Schadewe of him in the Myrour. And sche turned hire toward him, and asked hym, what he wolde. And he seyde, he wolde ben hire Lemman or Paramour. And sche asked him, zif that he were a Knyghte. And he seyde, nay. And than sche seyde, that he myghte not ben hire Lemman: But sche bad him gon azen unto his Felowes, and make him Knyghte, and come azen upon the Morwe, and sche scholde come out of the Cave before him; and thanne come an kysse hire on the mowthe, and have no Drede; for I schalle do the no maner harm, alle be it that thou see me in Lykenesse of a Dragoun. For thoughe thou see me hidouse and horrible to loken onne, I

do the to wytene,[3] that it is made be Enchauntement. For withouten doute, I am non other than thou seest now, a Woman; and therfore drede the noughte. And zif thou kysse me, thou schalt have all this Tresoure, and be my Lord, and Lord also of all that Ile. And he departed fro hire and wente to his Felowes to Shippe, and leet make him Knyghte, and cam azen upon the Morwe, for to kysse this Damysele. And when he saughe hire comen out of the Cave, in forme of a Dragoun, so hidouse and so horrible, he hadde so grete drede, that he fleyghe azen to the Schippe; and sche folewed him. And when sche saughe, that he turned not azen, she began to crye, as a thing that hadde meche Sorwe: and thanne sche turned azen, in to hire Cave; and anon the Knyghte dyede. And siththen hidrewards, myghte no Knyghte se hire, but that he dyede anon. But when a Knyghte comethe, that is so hardy to kisse hire, he schalle not dye; but he schall turne the Damysele in to hire righte Forme and kyndely Schapp, and he schal be Lord of alle the Contreyes and Iles aboveseyd.

THE STORY OF SIGURD THE VOLSUNG, p. 651

Sigurd the Volsung is a verse rendering of the prose *Volsunga Saga*, written in Iceland during the twelfth century. Morris had previously translated it in prose. This saga is the oldest form of the Teutonic epic, the story of Siegfried (or Sigurd) and the Niblungs, best known through the *Nibelungenlied* and Wagner's opera cycle, *Der Ring des Nibelungen*.

The general outlines of the Scandinavian and the German forms of the story are the same, but names and details vary. The hero of the Scandinavian version is Sigurd, the son of Sigmund and the grandson of Volsung, a king of the Huns. Sigmund was slain in battle before the birth of Sigurd, who subsequently became king of the Volsungs. He was reared and trained by Regin, a blacksmith, who incited him to slay the dragon Fafnir and gain possession of his hoard of gold. After plighting troth to Brynhild, one of the Valkyrie, Sigurd visited the court of the Burgundians, called the Niblungs, and under the spell of a love potion married Gudrun, daughter of the Niblung king. Then by a stratagem he aided Gudrun's brother Gunnar to secure Brynhild as his wife. In a jealous rage Brynhild persuaded Gudrun's brother Guttorm to kill Sigurd, and then she took her own life. Gudrun later married Atli (Attila), king of the Huns, who slew her brothers when they visited him. She soon avenged their death by setting fire to the hall and killing Atli and his children.

Morris tells the story in four books, entitled *Sigmund, Regin, Brynhild,* and *Gudrun.*

Book I—Sigmund

Sigmund tells of the early days of the Volsungs before the birth of Sigurd, the last of the race. Volsung, king of the Huns, gave his daughter Signy in marriage to Siggeir, king of the Goths. Jealous of the Volsungs Sig-

---

[1] The Isle of Cos, where Hippocrates (400 B.C.), the famous Greek physician, was born.
[2] Diana, goddess of the moon.

[3] I take thee to witness.

geir invited them to his court, and his band slew all of the visitors except Volsung's son Sigmund, who soon planned vengeance. Assuming the form of another woman Signy went to Sigmund and became the mother of his son Sinfiotli, who later was poisoned by Borghild, Sigmund's first wife. For this deed Borghild was driven from home, and Sigmund then married Hiordis; later he was killed in a battle with the chieftain Lyngi, who also had loved Hiordis. Sigurd was born after the death of Sigmund.

Book II—Regin

Sigurd was reared and trained by Regin, the blacksmith, who told him a story of ancient wrongs and incited him to kill Fafnir the dragon in order to secure a great treasure. Regin stated that upon the death of his brother Otter at the hands of Loki (the Norse god of destruction), Regin's father (Reidmar) demanded as recompense the traditional hoard of gold in the possession of the dwarf Andvari, who lived in the sea in the form of a pike. Loki got the treasure, including a magic ring that had the power to produce gold, but Andvari put a curse upon the ring and the treasure and upon anybody who should possess either. In a quarrel between Regin and his brother Fafnir for possession of the gold, Fafnir got it by killing his father. After inducing Sigurd to slay Fafnir, Regin forged for the exploit a magic sword named the Wrath of Sigurd. Armed with this weapon, Sigurd slew both Fafnir and Regin, seized the golden treasure, and rode away on his horse Greyfell. After a time he came to the Hill of Hindfell, where he found Brynhild the Valkyrie in a trance, placed there by Odin for disobedience and destined to fall in love with a mortal. Sigurd and Brynhild plighted their troth, and Sigurd gave her the fated ring of Andvari.

Book III—Brynhild

Brynhild tells of the deeds of Sigurd, of his sojourn with the Niblungs, or Burgundians, and of his death. After visiting Brynhild in her palace in the Land of Lymdale, Sigurd came to the Land of the Niblungs and made an alliance with King Giuki; through a magic potion given him by Grimhild, the King's wife, Sigurd forgot Brynhild and wedded Gudrun, the daughter of Giuki and Grimhild. Gunnar, who succeeded his father Giuki as king of the Niblungs, loved Brynhild but could not pass the flames that surrounded her magic house in Lymdale. Thereupon Sigurd took the form of Gunnar and rode on Greyfell through the flames. He plighted troth with Brynhild, but during the night he "laid 'twixt him and the body of Brynhild his bright blue battle-blade." As Sigurd departed the next morning Brynhild placed upon his finger the fated ring of the treasure. Shortly after the marriage of Gunnar and Brynhild, Gudrun and Brynhild engaged in a quarrel, and Gudrun tauntingly revealed the truth of Gunnar's wooing. Overcome with grief and rage, Brynhild listened to the declarations of love by Sigurd, then awakened from the effect of Grimhild's potion, and replied, "I will not wed thee, Sigurd, nor any man alive." At the suggestion of Brynhild, the Niblungs accomplished the death of Sigurd through Guttorm, Gunnar's brother, who had not sworn peace with Sigurd at the time of his arrival. Brynhild took her own life after a last request that she be burned on the funeral pyre of Sigurd. With the death of Sigurd the fated treasure of gold passed into the hands of the Niblungs.

Book IV—Gudrun

Gudrun tells of the fateful days of the Niblungs after they slew Sigurd and of their destruction by King Atli and his followers. After the death of Sigurd, Gudrun married King Atli from beyond the sea and incited him to gain the ancient treasure as a means of avenging Sigurd. Atli invited the Niblungs to visit him and after they arrived he captured Gunnar and his brother Hogni and killed all their followers. He then killed Hogni and placed Gunnar in a pit with serpents. For a short time Gunnar charmed them with his playing and singing, but finally one of them stung him to death. To avenge her brothers, Gudrun killed Atli and burned the hall; then she leaped into the sea.

A DREAM OF JOHN BALL, p. 660

A Dream of John Ball is a prose socialistic romance that contrasts English society when the feudal system was breaking up with that of Morris's own day and faintly suggests what the future may present. The author dreams that he is in the county of Kent, where he meets a group of ardent reformers including John Ball, the "mad priest," who was a leader in the Peasants' Revolt of 1381. Former experiences are lived through again, and in discussing "the struggle against tyranny for the freedom of life," the two enthusiasts find much in common. The poem in the text was sung early in the story by a young man of the company as a kind of signal for John Ball to appear.

ALGERNON CHARLES SWINBURNE, p. 664

STANDARD EDITIONS

Complete Works, 20 vols., ed. by E.W. Gosse and T.J. Wise, London, Heinemann, 1925-1927

The Best of Swinburne, ed. by C.K. Hyder and L. Chase, New York, Nelson, 1937

Collected Poetical Works, 2 vols., London, Heinemann, 1924

Works, 2 vols., Philadelphia, McKay, 1910

Atalanta in Calydon, and Erechtheus, w. notes by Marion C. Wier, Ann Arbor, Mich., Wahr, 1922

Lesbia Brandon, ed. by R. Hughes, New York, British Bk. Centre, 1952

Selected Poems, w. an intro. by H. Hare, London, Heinemann, 1950

Swinburne: A Selection, ed. by Dame Edith Sitwell, London, Weidenfeld and Nicolson, 1960

Letters, w. some pers. recol. by T. Hake and A. Compton-Rickett, London, Murray, 1918

The Swinburne Letters, ed. by Cecil Lang, 6 vols., New Haven, Conn., Yale Univ. Press, 1959-1962

Essays and Studies, London, Chatto, 1875

Miscellanies, London, Chatto, 1886

Studies in Prose and Poetry, London, Chatto, 1907

The Age of Shakespeare, New York, Harper, 1908

A Study of Shakespeare, London, Chatto, 1909

BIOGRAPHY

Beerbohm, M., "No. 2, The Pines, Reminiscences of Swinburne," *And Even Now*, New York, Dutton, 1921

Gosse, E.W., *The Life of Algernon Charles Swinburne*, New York, Macmillan, 1917

Hare, H., *Swinburne*, London, Witherby, 1949

Kernahan, C., *In Good Company; Some Personal Recollections*, London, Lane, 1917

Kernahan, C., *Swinburne as I Knew Him*, London, Lane, 1919

Lafourcade, G., *La Jeunesse de Swinburne, 1837-67*, 2 vols., London, Oxford Univ. Press, 1928

Lafourcade, G., *Swinburne; a Literary Biography*, London, Bell, G., 1932

Lang, Cecil, "Swinburne's Lost Love," *PMLA*, 1959, 74:123-130

Nicolson, H.G., *Swinburne*, English Men of Letters Series, London, Macmillan, 1926

Pound, E., "Swinburne versus Biographers," *Poetry*, 1918, 11:322-329

Watts-Dunton, Clara J., *The Home Life of Swinburne*, London, Philpot, 1922

Watts-Dunton, T., "My Recollections of Swinburne," *Nineteenth Century*, 1921, 90: 219-229, 438-447

CRITICISM

Arvin, N., "Swinburne as a Critic," *Sewanee Review*, 1924, 32:405-412

Bennett, A., "Swinburne," *Books and Persons*, London, Chatto, 1917

Buchanan, R.W., *The Fleshly School of Poetry and Other Phenomena of the Day*, London, Strahan, 1872

Chew, S.C., *Swinburne*, Boston, Little, 1929

Connolly, T.E., "Swinburne on 'The Music of Poetry,' " *PMLA*, 1957, 72:680-688

Davison, W.T., "Poetic Agnosticism: Meredith and Swinburne," *London Quarterly*, 1909, 112:127-130

Drinkwater, J., *Swinburne, an Estimate*, London, Dent, 1924

Eliot, T.S., "Swinburne as Poet," *The Sacred Wood*, London, Methuen, 1920

Freeman, A.E., "The Psychological Basis of Swinburne's Convictions," *Poet Lore*, Winter 1928, 38:579-589

Granville-Barker, H., "Some Victorians Afield: the Poet as Dramatist," *Theatre Arts Monthly*, 1929, 13:361-372

Grierson, H.J.C., "Lord Byron, Arnold, and Swinburne," *The Background of English Literature*, London, Chatto, 1925

Harding, A.T., "Shelley's *Adonais* and Swinburne's *Ave Atque Vale*," *Sewanee Review*, 1919, 27:32-42

Hearn, L., "Studies in Swinburne," *Pre-Raphaelite and Other Poets*, New York, Dodd, 1922

Hearn, L., "Swinburne's *Hertha*," *Interpretations of Literature*, 2 vols., New York, Dodd, 1915

Hyder, C.K., *Swinburne's Literary Career and Fame*, Durham, N.C., Duke Univ. Press, 1933

Kellett, E.E., "Swinburne," *Reconsiderations*, London, Cambridge Univ. Press, 1928

Keys, F.V., "Elizabethans and Swinburne," *North American Review*, 1909, 189:53-60

Lafourcade, G., "Swinburne and Baudelaire," *Revue Anglo-Américaine*, 1924, 2:183-196

Lafourcade, G., "Swinburne and Walt Whitman," *Modern Language Review*, 1927, 22: 84-86

Lafourcade, G., *Swinburne's Hyperion and Other Poems; with an Essay on Swinburne and Keats*, London, Faber, 1927

Lyall, A.C., "Characteristics of Mr. Swinburne's Poetry," *Studies in Literature and History*, London, Murray, J., 1915

Mackail, J.W., "Swinburne," *Studies of English Poets*, London, Longmans, 1926

Marks, Jeanette, "Stigmata," *Genius and Disaster*, New York, Adelphi Press, 1925

Meynell, Alice, "Swinburne's Lyrical Poetry," *Hearts of Controversy*, London, Burns, 1918

Michaelides, C.C., "Mr. Swinburne and the Sea," *Independent Review*, 1906, 8:69-80

More, P.E., "Swinburne," *Shelburne Essays*, 3d s., New York, Putnam, 1905

Nash, J.V., "The Religion of Swinburne," *Open Court*, 1923, 37:65-77

Nicolson, H.G., "Swinburne and Baudelaire," *Transactions of the Royal Society of Literature*, n. s., Vol. 6, London, Milford, Humphrey, 1926

Patmore, C., "Mr. Swinburne's Selections," *Principle in Art*, London, Bell, 1889

Peters, Robert L., "Swinburne and the Use of Integral Detail," *Victorian Studies*, 1962, 5:289-302

Pound, Olivia, *On the Application of the Principles of Greek Lyric Tragedy in the Classical Dramas of Swinburne*, University of Nebraska Studies, Vol. 13, No. 4, Lincoln, 1913

Ratchford, F.E., "The First Draft of Swinburne's *Hertha*," *Modern Language Notes*, 1924, 39:22-26

Ratchford, F.E., "Swinburne at Work," *Sewanee Review*, 1923, 31:353-362

Rossetti, W.M., *Swinburne's Poems and Ballads, a Criticism*, London, Hotten, 1866

Rummons, C., "The Ballad Imitations of Swinburne," *Poet Lore*, 1922, 33:58-84

Russell, C.E., "Swinburne and Music," *North American Review*, 1907, 186:427-441

Saintsbury, G., "Mr. Swinburne," *Corrected Impressions*, in *Collected Essays and Papers*, 4 vols., London, Dent, 1923

Serner, Gunnar, *On the Language of Swinburne's Lyrics and Epics*, Lund, Sweden, Berlingska, 1910

Shepherd, R.H., *The Bibliography of Swinburne (1857-1887)*, London, Redway, 1889

Squire, J.C., "Swinburne's Defects," *Books in General*, 3d s., London, Hodder, 1921

Symons, A., "Swinburne," *Studies in Strange Souls*, London, Sawyer, 1929

Thomas, E., *Algernon Charles Swinburne, a Critical Study*, New York, Kennerley, 1912

Thomson, J.C., *Bibliographical List of the Writings of Algernon Charles Swinburne*, Wimbledon, Thomson, 1905

Van Doorn, W., "An Enquiry into the Causes of Swinburne's Failure as a Narrative Poet," *Neophilologus*, 1924, 1925, 10:36-42, 120-125, 199-213, 273-286

Welby, T.E., *A Study of Swinburne*, New York, Doran, 1926

Westminster Review, "Swinburne and Meredith," 1909, 172:29-35

Wier, Marion C., *The Influence of Æschylus and Euripides on the Structure and Content of Swinburne's "Atalanta in Calydon" and "Erechtheus,"* Ann Arbor, Mich., Wahr, 1920

Wise, T.J., *A Bibliography of the Writings in Prose and Verse of Algernon Charles Swinburne*, London, Clay, 1919-1920

Woodberry, G.E., *Swinburne*, New York, McClure, 1905

BIOGRAPHICAL SKETCH

Algernon Charles Swinburne (1837-1909) acquired before his majority practically all the knowledge, abilities, ideas, and tendencies which he utilized during the remainder of his life. By his mother, Lady Jane, and his grandfather, Sir John, he was early introduced to the literatures of France and Italy; at Eton he read everything, especially Elizabethan plays, and, in his impetuous way, adored Landor, Shelley, and Corneille, but loathed Euripides and Racine; at Oxford he became a freethinker in religion, an ardent supporter of Italian and French struggles for political liberty, and a source of anxiety to Benjamin Jowett, the benevolent and learned head of his college, because of the irregularities of his life. With his large head and slender, nervous body, he was no less extraordinary in his physical appearance than in the breadth and vigor of his conversation; consequently, when he came to London after leaving Oxford without a degree in 1861, he attracted a circle of friends, including Dante Gabriel Rossetti and the other Pre-Raphaelites. Under Rossetti's wise guidance his lyrical powers greatly expanded; the influence of FitzGerald's *Rubáiyát* and of the French poets Hugo and Baudelaire was also important in the development of his poetry. A few of his characteristic lyrics—*Faustine* (1862), *The Triumph of Time* (1866), *Laus Veneris* (1866), *Itylus* (1866)—some in the Pre-Raphaelite manner, were written in 1862-1863; and *Atalanta in Calydon* (1865), hailed by Ruskin as "the grandest thing ever done by a youth—though he is a demoniac youth," made him famous.

This fame was soon changed to notoriety. His dissipations became elaborated in popular rumor; and his *Poems and Ballads*, published in 1866, was denounced by the critics and avidly bought by the public. His picture was displayed in shopwindows, and gossip played havoc with his name. For a time Swinburne appeared eager to live up to his reputation, but the strain on his nervous although wiry constitution brought illness, epileptic attacks, and necessitated long periods of recuperation. His thoughts, too, were directed into new channels by the influence of Màzzini, the Italian liberator, for whom in 1868 Swinburne wrote the *Hymn of Man* and devoted three years to *Songs before Sunrise* (1871). Under the care of such friends as Rossetti, Meredith, and Jowett, his health was sufficient to allow him to engage in spirited controversies with political and literary enemies, to make a series of enthusiastic studies in Elizabethan drama, and to write the lyrics which were issued in 1878 as a second series of *Poems and Ballads*. He was near death in the following year, yet was restored to health and given thirty years more of productivity by the almost paternal care of his friend Theodore Watts-Dunton. To the turmoil of Swinburne's preceding life succeeded a great calm. He lived in ordered routine at Watts-Dunton's suburban home; he walked daily over the same path, pausing to talk with children or to admire babies; because of increasing deafness, he seldom visited the larger world. In spite of the inhibiting influence of Watts-Dunton, Swinburne continued to produce some good work and showed his creative vigor and his marvelous lyrical sense through a long list of publications; of this period Tennyson said: "Swinburne is a reed through which all things blow into music." His literary likings he expressed in many appreciative essays. He died of pneumonia in his seventy-third year.

Swinburne's principal publications were: *The Queen Mother and Rosamund*, 1860; *Atalanta in Calydon*, 1865; *Chastelard*, 1865; *Poems and Ballads*, 1866; *Notes on Poems and Reviews*, 1866; *A Song of Italy*, 1867; *William Blake*, 1867; *Songs before Sunrise*, 1871; *Under the Microscope*, 1872; *Bothwell*, 1874; *Essays and Studies*, 1875; *George Chapman*, 1875; *Erechtheus*, 1876; *Poems and Ballads: Second Series*, 1878; *A Study of Shakespeare*, 1880; *Songs of the Springtides*, 1880; *Studies in Song*, 1880; *Mary Stuart*, 1881; *Tristram of Lyonesse, and Other Poems*, 1882; *A Century of Roundels*, 1883; *A Midsummer Holiday, and Other Poems*, 1884; *Marino Faliero*, 1885; *A Study of Victor Hugo*, 1886; *Miscellanies*, 1886; *Locrine*, 1887; *Poems and Ballads: Third Series*, 1889; *A Study of Ben Jonson*, 1889; *The Sisters*, 1892; *Astrophel, and Other Poems*, 1894; *Studies in Prose and Poetry*, 1894; *The Tale of Balen*, 1896; *Rosamund, Queen of the Lombards*, 1890; *A Channel Passage, and Other Poems*, 1904; *The Duke of Gandia*, 1908; *The Age of Shakespeare*, 1908; *Lesbia Brandon*, 1952.

INTRODUCTORY CRITICISMS

"He [Swinburne] broke in on that rather agreeably tedious Victorian tea-party with the effect of some pagan creature, at once impish and divine, leaping on to the sleek lawn, to stamp its goat-feet in challenge, to deride with its screech of laughter the admirable decorum of the conversation. The disorder that followed remains indescribable; and, knowing what we do of the real character of many of the startled company, it is not now quite easy to understand. Few of them were really so tame as they seemed, in that August of 1866, when the summer was so suddenly smitten with strange air, and keen, wild scents and hot, artificial odors of the alcove overwhelmed the temperate perfumes of the insular garden. Even their typical poet, Tennyson, if you considered him closely, when he was off duty, had in him, at any rate as a man, something farouche and acrid, a reminder that, if he now wrote *Enoch Arden*, and the like, he had been, not so long ago, in his lucky, unguarded hour, the author of *Maud*. But, for the time being, he was complacent, and rather somnolent, and a trifle official. There was rather too much suavity in the setting he and they had contrived for themselves, too even a gloss on that cultured society. It had genius and talent in abundance, and was concerned with many matters, of which, however, it now spoke with the emphasis of habit rather than of constantly renewed conviction; but it had become inhospitable to new ideas, suspicious of all instincts which did not bring with them a certificate from some reputable authority. Admirably, it had decided, with the Laureate, to let the ape and tiger die, at any rate as subjects of discussion, but it had fallen into a certain zoölogical confusion, whereby many permanent, if you like deplorable, human characteristics have been assumed to be simian or feline, and it was sure they could be eradicated by a conspiracy of silence."—T. E. Welby, *A Study of Swinburne*, pp. 30-31.

"Swinburne . . . represented, in its most flamboyant shape, revolt against the concessions and the hypocrisies of the Mid-Victorian era. . . . An extraordinary exhilaration accompanied his presence, something uplifted, extravagant, and yet unselfish. No one has ever lived who loved poetry more passionately, found in it more inexhaustible sources of pleasure, cultivated it more thoroughly for itself, more sincerely for nothing which it might be persuaded to offer as a side issue. Half Swinburne's literary influence depended upon little, unregarded matters, such as his unflinching attitude of worship towards the great masters, his devotion to unpopular causes, his uncompromising arrogance in the face of conventionality. It is becoming difficult to recapture even the thrill he caused by his magic use of 'unpoetic' monosyllables, such as 'bleat,' 'pinch,' 'rind,' 'fang,' 'wince,' embedded in the very heart of his ornate melody. But his meteoric flight across the literary heavens, followed by the slow and dignified descent of the glimmering shower of sparks, will long excite curiosity, even when the sensation it caused has ceased to be quite intelligible."—E. W. Gosse, *Portraits and Sketches*, pp. 57-58.

"Reading ... Swinburne on a high rock around which the sea is washing, one is struck by the way in which these cadences, in their unending, ever-varying flow, seem to harmonize with the rhythm of the sea.... The whole essence of Swinburne seems to be made by the rush and soft flowing impetus of the sea. The sea has passed into his blood like a passion, and into his verse like a transfiguring element. It is actually the last word of many of his poems, and it is the first and last word of his poetry."—A. Symons, *Figures of Several Centuries*, p. 161.

"... the words which we use to state our grounds of dislike or indifference cannot be applied to Swinburne as they can to bad poetry. The words of condemnation are words which express his qualities. You may say 'diffuse.' But the diffuseness is essential; had Swinburne practised greater concentration his verse would be, not better in the same kind, but a different thing. His diffuseness is one of his glories. That so little material as appears to be employed in *The Triumph of Time* should release such an amazing number of words, requires what there is no reason to call anything but genius. You could not condense *The Triumph of Time*. You could only leave out."—T. S. Eliot, "Swinburne as Poet," in *Selected Essays, 1917-1932*, p. 282.

CRITICAL NOTES

A SONG IN TIME OF ORDER, p. 664

The date of 1852, accompanying the title of this poem, marked the period of domination of tyrannical forces in Europe. It is against such power that the three republicans of the poem are revolting.

The contagion of the French Revolution of February 1848, which established the Second French Republic, spread throughout the continent of Europe and greatly heartened organized enemies of monarchy and repression. In Germany the forces of democracy clamored for political independence; in Italy and Hungary sporadic uprisings endeavored to throw off the despotic yoke of Austria. A new republic was proclaimed in Florence in February 1849, and on the same day a popular assembly at Rome deposed the Pope from temporal power and proclaimed the Republic of Rome. By his public condemnation of the war for Italian freedom and by his refusal to sanction certain liberal acts of legislation, Pope Pius IX had earlier lost favor with the people and had fled to the Neapolitan fortress at Gaeta. France, however, had already begun proceedings which resulted in the reinstatement of the Pope on July 14, 1849, and his return to Rome in 1850.

The so-called "Papal Aggression" stirred England in 1850, when the Pope issued a bull setting up a hierarchy of bishops for England with titles to be derived from English sees created by the bull rather than as formerly from extinct dioceses in Asia Minor. A statement by Cardinal Wiseman that "Catholic England had been restored to its orbit in the ecclesiastical firmament from which its light had been long vanished" added fuel to the excitement, which eventuated in the burning of effigies and the passing of the Ecclesiastical Titles Bill in 1851, which aimed directly at the provisions of the papal bull.

In December 1851, Lord Palmerston, foreign secretary in England, outraged public opinion by unofficially approving the notorious coup d'état by which Louis Napoleon, who had been elected president of the French Republic, overthrew the government and a year later proclaimed himself Emperor of the French.

FAUSTINE, p. 665

Swinburne gives the following explanation of the origin and the meaning of this poem:

"*Faustine* is the reverie of a man gazing on the bitter and vicious loveliness of a face as common and as cheap as the morality of reviewers, and dreaming of past lives in which this fair face may have held a nobler or fitter station; the imperial profile may have been Faustina's, the thirsty lips a Mænad's, when first she learnt to drink blood or wine, to waste the loves and ruin the lives of men; through Greece and again through Rome she may have passed with the same face which now comes before us dishonored and discrowned. Whatever of merit or demerit there may be in the verses, the idea that gives them such life as they have is simple enough; the transmigration of a single soul, doomed as though by accident from the first to all evil and no good, through many ages and forms, but clad always in the same type of fleshly beauty. The chance which suggested to me this poem was one which may happen any day to any man—the sudden sight of a living face which recalled the well-known likeness of another dead for centuries: in this instance, the noble and faultless type of the elder Faustina, as seen in coin and bust. Out of that casual glimpse and sudden recollection these verses sprang and grew."—*Notes on Poems and Reviews*, in Vol. 16 of the *Complete Works*, pp. 364-365.

ATALANTA IN CALYDON, p. 667

Atalanta in Calydon is a drama in which Swinburne attempted, as he said, "to do something original in English which might in some degree reproduce for English readers the likeness of a Greek tragedy with something of its true poetic life and charm." Although the play diverges from the exact formulas of a Greek drama, it nevertheless accomplishes what the author intended.

The theme concerns the story of the famous hunt for the wild boar that in ancient legend devastated the country in Calydon, a province in northwestern Greece. The story is as follows: Œneus, king of Calydon, had offended Artemis, goddess of the moon, by neglecting her in his rituals, and she sought vengeance by inciting war against him and by sending a wild boar that laid waste the country of his people. In the expedition organized to slay the boar was Atalanta, the beautiful Arcadian huntress, daughter of Zeus and beloved of Artemis. Meleager, a young hero who had taken part in the quest for the Golden Fleece, the son of Œneus and Althaea, fell in love with Atalanta and when the boar was killed presented her with the spoils of victory. Toxeus and Plexippus, brothers of Queen Althaea, resented this action and in attempting to deprive Atalanta of her prize were both killed by Meleager. At the time of the birth of Meleager, Althaea had been warned by the Fates that he would live only so long as the brand in the fire before her remained unconsumed; in order to protect his life she snatched the brand from the flames and carefully preserved it. When she heard of the tragic death of her brothers, she became angry at her son and plunged the brand into the fire; as it was consumed the life of Meleager wasted away.

The Invocation, calling upon Artemis and Apollo to aid the enterprise of the hunt, is the opening section of the drama.

LAUS VENERIS, p. 674

Laus Veneris is a rehandling, or rather an extension, of the Tannhäuser legend. In the medieval story, the knight, who had been enamored of Venus, went to Rome to secure pardon for his sinful love from Pope Urban; denied his request, he returned to Venus. Swinburne thus explains his purpose:

"Of the poem in which I have attempted once more to embody the legend of Venus and her knight, I need say only that my first aim was to rehandle the old story in a new fashion. To me it seemed that the tragedy began with the knight's return to Venus—began at the point where hitherto it had seemed to leave off. The immortal agony of a man lost after all repentance—cast down from fearful hope into fearless despair—believing in Christ and bound to Venus—desirous of penitential pain, and damned to joyless pleasure—this, in my eyes, was the kernel and nucleus of a myth comparable only to that of the foolish virgins and bearing the same burden. The tragic touch of the story is this: that the knight who has renounced Christ believes in him; the lover who has embraced Venus disbelieves in her. Vainly and in despair would he make the best of that which is the worst—vainly remonstrate with God, and argue on the side he would fain desert. Once accept or admit the least admixture of pagan worship, or of modern thought, and the whole story collapses into froth and smoke."—*Notes on Poems and Reviews*, in Vol. 16 of the *Complete Works*, p. 365.

Page 677, lines 181ff. With these lines compare the following passage from the famous Old French love story of Aucassin and Nicolette. The opposition of the father of Aucassin to his love for the beautiful Saracen captive Nicolette led to her being confined in a high chamber in the castle of the Viscount, her godfather. When told that marriage with Nicolette would lose him Paradise, Aucassin replied: "What have I to do in Paradise? I seek not to enter there; but let me have Nicolette, my most sweet friend whom I love so much. Into Paradise none go except the sort of people I will tell you of. There go those old priests and those lame and crippled ones who all day and all night grovel before altars and in old crypts; and those clothed in old, worn cloaks and in old rags; those who are naked and barefoot and full of sores; those who die of hunger and of thirst and of cold, and of miseries. These go to Paradise; with them have I nothing to do; but into hell I wish to go. For into hell go the goodly clerks and the goodly knights, who have died in the tourneys and in the great wars; and the good soldier and the true man. With these do I wish to go. And there go also the fair, courteous ladies who have two loves or three besides their lords.

And there go also the gold and the silver and the rich furs; and there go also the harper and minstrel and the Kings of the world. With these I wish to go, only let me have Nicolette, my most sweet friend, with me."

IN MEMORY OF WALTER SAVAGE LANDOR, p. 691

Swinburne had the faculty of being both a hard hater and a violent lover, which often led him to express extravagant blame or praise with equal facility. Antagonism engendered by the intensity of his attacks and controversies was paralleled by ridicule when he engaged in what he called "the noble pleasure of praising." Hero worship became with him, as Nicolson says (*Swinburne*, p. 69), "a deep and persistent religion, and the most potent of his incantations was ever 'Let us now praise famous men.'" The exaggerations of his critical utterances correlate with such incidents as his kneeling before the aged Landor when they first met in Italy in 1864 or his carrying a footstool to a dinner given in honor of Browning so that he might sit at Browning's feet.

DOLORES, p. 692

Swinburne says of this poem:

"I have striven here to express that transient state of spirit through which a man may be supposed to pass, foiled in love and weary of loving, but not yet in sight of rest; seeking refuge in those 'violent delights' which 'have violent ends,' in fierce and frank sensualities which at least profess to be no more than they are. This poem, like *Faustine*, is so distinctly symbolic and fanciful that it cannot justly be amenable to judgment as a study in the school of realism. The spirit, bowed and discolored by suffering and by passion (which are indeed the same thing and the same word), plays for awhile with its pleasures and its pains, mixes and distorts them with a sense half-humorous and half-mournful, exults in bitter and doubtful emotions:

> Moods of fantastic sadness, nothing worth.

It sports with sorrow, and jests against itself; cries out for freedom and confesses the chain; decorates anew with the name of goddess, crowns anew as the mystical Cotytto, some woman, real or ideal, in whom the pride of life with its companion lusts is incarnate. In her lover's half-shut eyes, her fierce unchaste beauty is transfigured, her cruel sensual eyes have a meaning and a message; there are memories and secrets in the kisses of her lips. She is the darker Venus, fed with burnt-offering and blood-sacrifice; the veiled image of that pleasure which men impelled by satiety and perverted by power have sought through ways as strange as Nero's before and since his time; the daughter of lust and death, and holding of both her parents; Our Lady of Pain, antagonist alike of trivial sins and virtues: no Virgin, and unblessed of men; no mother of the Gods or God; no Cybele, served by sexless priests or monks, adored of Origen or Atys; no likeness of her in Dindymus or Loreto." —*Notes on Poems and Reviews*, in Vol. 16 of the *Complete Works*, pp. 360-361.

Swinburne's poetry lent itself easily to parody, as he himself demonstrated in his own *Nephelidia* (p. 735). One of the most famous parodies is the following poem by Arthur Clement Hilton (1851-1877):

Octopus

BY ALGERNON CHARLES SIN-BURN

Strange beauty, eight-limbed and eight-handed,
　Whence camest to dazzle our eyes?
With thy bosom bespangled and banded
　With the hues of the seas and the skies;
Is thy home European or Asian,
　O mystical monster marine?
Part molluscous and partly crustacean,
　Betwixt and between.

Wast thou born to the sound of sea trumpets,
　Hast thou eaten and drunk to excess　　　　10
Of the sponges—thy muffins and crumpets,
　Of the seaweed—thy mustard and cress?
Wast thou nurtured in caverns of coral,
　Remote from reproof or restraint?
Art thou innocent, art thou immoral,　　　　15
　Sinburnian or Saint?

Lithe limbs, curling free, as a creeper
　That creeps in a desolate place,
To enroll and envelop the sleeper
　In a silent and stealthy embrace,　　　　20
Cruel beak craning forward to bite us,
　Our juices to drain and to drink,
Or to whelm us in waves of Cocytus,
　Indelible ink!

O breast, that 'twere rapture to writhe on!　25
　O arms 'twere delicious to feel
Clinging close with the crush of the Python,
　When she maketh her murderous meal!
In thy eight-fold embraces enfolden,
　Let our empty existence escape;　　　　30
Give us death that is glorious and golden,
　Crushed all out of shape!

Ah! thy red lips, lascivious and luscious,
　With death in their amorous kiss,
Cling round us, and clasp us, and crush us,　35
　With bitings of agonized bliss;
We are sick with the poison of pleasure,
　Dispense us the potion of pain;
Ope thy mouth to its uttermost measure
　And bite us again!　　　　(1872)

Page 692, lines 49-52. These four lines are quoted by Muller, the Forest Officer, in Kipling's story "In the Rukh," first printed in *Many Inventions* (1893) and later included in *The Jungle Book*. To Muller, the *rukh*, or jungle, was older than the gods, and he spent many a long evening smoking and staring into the darkness as he meditated upon his paganism and repeated his favorite quotations. One quiet midnight he was heard to address these words to the *rukh*, delivered with deep feeling:

"Dough we shivt und bedeck und bedrape us,
　Dou art noble und nude und andeek;
Libidina dy moder, Briapus
　Dy fader, a god und a Greek.

Now I know dot Bagan *or* Christian, I shall nefer know der inwardness of der *rukh*."

Page 693, lines 67-68. Of these lines G. K. Chesterton says:

"Swinburne, ... when he wrote the couplet—

'From the lilies and languors of virtue
To the raptures and roses of vice,'

wrote what is nothing but a bad imitation of himself, an imitation that seems indeed to have the wholly unjust and uncritical object of proving that the Swinburnian melody is a mechanical scheme of initial letters."—*Robert Browning*, p. 142.

AVE ATQUE VALE, p. 700

The imagery of *Ave Atque Vale* is largely and fittingly drawn from Baudelaire's *Les Fleurs du Mal* (*The Flowers of Evil*), the following lines of which Swinburne quoted as a kind of motto for his poem:

Nous devrions pourtant lui porter quelques fleurs;
Les morts, les pauvres morts, ont de grandes douleurs,
Et quand Octobre souffle, émondeur des vieux arbres,
Son vent mélancolique á l'entour de leurs marbres,
Certes, ils doivent trouver les vivants bien ingrats.

The lines may be translated as follows: "Yet we should bear him some flowers; the dead, the unhappy dead, have great sorrows, and when October, pruner of ancient trees, blows its melancholy wind about their tombs, surely they must deem the living very ingrates."

Swinburne was early attracted to the great French poet and critic and once spoke of him as "one of the most exquisite, most delicate, and most perfect poets of the century—perfect in sound, in color, in taste of meter, and in tone of emotion." A laudatory review of *Les Fleurs du Mal*, published by Swinburne in 1862, was later retracted as overpraise of Baudelaire's poem.

Ave Atque Vale is generally regarded as Swinburne's highest achievement in elegy and as one of his noblest poems. Nicolson says of it:

"Swinburne pictures himself as standing under 'the veiled porches of the Muse funereal,' actually beside the bier of the dead poet. This almost physical contact throws over the lines a bitter breath of the macabre, gives to them the chilling throb of awe. For this is no Christian ritual which he is celebrating, but rather some despairing Pagan libation, and the salt courageous savor of Roman pessimism gives to the lines that astringent quality which is the secret of their appropriateness and of their strength."—*Swinburne*, p. 159.

HYMN OF MAN, p. 709

Lines 21 ff. With these lines compare the following passage from *The Birds* of Aristophanes:

"Upon the infinite bosom of Erebus an egg filled with gas was deposited to begin with by black-winged Night. From this in the hour ordained was Love, the longed-for, brought forth. His back was aflash with two wings all golden, that whirled like the breezes. He with winged Chaos mated by night in wide Tartarus and begot our breed and first led them into the light of day. At first there was no race of men until Love mixed all things together."

The same idea is found also in Plato's *Symposium* and in Spenser's *Hymn to Heavenly Love*.

TO WALT WHITMAN IN AMERICA, p. 714

When this poem was written, Swinburne regarded Whitman as the inspired poet and prophet of democracy in the New World. A year later he praised Whitman highly in *Under the Microscope* and elsewhere referred to his *O Captain, My Captain* as "the most sonorous anthem ever chanted in the church of the world." Under the chilling influence of Theodore Watts-Dunton, however, Swinburne later swung to the opposite extreme, and in *Whitmania* (1887), in discussing Whitman's display of physical emotion in poetry, says: "Mr. Whitman's Eve is a drunken applewoman, indecently sprawling in the slush and garbage of the gutter amid the rotten refuse of her overturned fruit-stall; but Mr. Whitman's Venus is a Hottentot wench under the influence of cantharides and adulterated rum. Cotytto herself would repudiate the ministration of such priestesses as these."—*Complete Works*, Vol. 15, p. 316.

TRISTRAM OF LYONESSE, p. 717

The story of Tristram and Iseult had intrigued Swinburne when he was at Eton (1849-1853); and during his Oxford period (1856-1860) he began a romance, *Queen Yseult*, which was intended to consist of ten cantos, only six of which were written. One canto was published in 1858; the others not until 1918. About 1860 he wrote "Joyeuse Garde," included in *A Lay of Lilies and Other Poems*, printed by T. J. Wise in 1918. After the publication of Tennyson's *Holy Grail* in 1869, Swinburne gave serious attention to the subject and wrote the Prelude to *Tristram of Lyonesse;* this Prelude was published in 1871 with a Dedicatory Epistle in which he said:

"My aim was simply to present that story, not diluted and debased as it had been in our own time by other hands, but undefaced by improvement and undeformed by transformation, as it was known to the age of Dante wherever the chronicles of romance found hearing from Ercildoune[1] to Florence; and not in the epic or romantic form of sustained or continuous narrative, but mainly through a succession of dramatic scenes or pictures with descriptive settings or backgrounds."

Using as his chief source the Middle English version of *Sir Tristram,* Swinburne worked at his poem intermittently until it was finally completed and published in 1882. "In contrast to the ingenuous encyclopedic manner of the medieval story-tellers," says Chew, "he presents a series of salient episodes, the significant moments in the love story, connected by narrative passages. The fundamental purpose is to sustain the theme of the 'Prelude,' which is Love: in the first canto, the dawn of passion; in the second, the fulfillment of love-longing; in the third, the yearning of Iseult for her absent lover; in the fourth, reunion; in the fifth [the marvelous 'Iseult at Tintagel,' which is the climax of the poem], the renewed yearning of Iseult to the choral accompaniment of wind and sea. The sixth canto, like much of the third, is pitched in a lower key. In the seventh a new *motif*—Fate—is introduced, but here also the theme of Love continues, this time the love of Iseult of the Fair Hands, love changed to jealousy and hate. The eighth canto is devoted to the life of Tristram in absence from Iseult of Ireland; and the last of Love-in-Death. Throughout, the interest is thus centered upon the love theme with a directness and exclusiveness equaled only by Wagner."—*Swinburne,* pp. 170-171.

With Swinburne's poem compare Tennyson's *Last Tournament,* p. 150, and Arnold's *Tristram and Iseult,* p. 458.

THALASSIUS, p. 726

Thalassius is one of many poems by Swinburne that reveal his deep affection for the sea, which he constantly regarded as the symbol of liberty. Swinburne's father was an admiral in the British navy, and from him the poet inherited his love of the sea which was expressed so poignantly as to win for him the title of "laureate of the sea." In a letter writ-

[1]Modern Earlston, Berwickshire, Scotland, traditionally the residence of Thoṁas the Rhymer, legendary Scottish bard and prophet.

ten to E. C. Stedman on February 20, 1875, Swinburne says:

"As for the sea, its salt *must* have been in my blood before I was born. I can remember no earlier enjoyment than being held up naked in my father's arms and brandished between his hands, then shot like a stone from a sling through the air, shouting and laughing with delight, head foremost into the coming wave—which could only have been the pleasure of a very little fellow. I remember being afraid of other things, but never of the sea. But this is enough of infancy; only it shows the *truth* of my endless passionate returns to the sea in all my verse."

BY THE NORTH SEA, p. 733

The locality described in *By the North Sea* is Dunwich on the coast of Suffolk. Once a strong, rich Saxon seaport, it was gradually engulfed by the sea. The last important ruin, a church tower, collapsed about 1916. In the Dedicatory Epistle, prefixed to his collected poems, Swinburne writes of "the dreary beauty, inhuman if not unearthly in its desolation, of the innumerable creeks and inlets, lined and paven with seaflowers, which make of the salt marshes a fit and funereal setting, a fatal and appropriate foreground, for the supreme desolation of the relics of Dunwich; the beautiful and awful solitude of a wilderness on which the sea has forbidden man to build or live, overtopped and bounded by the tragic and ghastly solitude of a headland on which the sea has forbidden the works of human charity and piety to survive."

ADIEUX À MARIE STUART, p. 736

Mary Queen of Scots captured the boyish imagination of Swinburne, and in spite of the liberal and democratic principles of his mature years, he did not modify his early loyalty to the House of Stuart.

This ill-fated queen has been a favorite theme of novelists and poets—Scott, Schiller, Drinkwater, Bjornson, and others—but none has presented her with the completeness, the historical accuracy, the subtlety, and the mastery that mark Swinburne's famous trilogy —*Chastelard* (1865), *Bothwell* (1874), and *Mary Stuart* (1881).

Mary Stuart became queen of Scotland upon the death of her father, James V, in 1542, when she was one week old. At the age of fifteen she was married to the dauphin of France, and she became queen of that country when he ascended to the throne as Francis II in 1559. Left a widow in 1561 she returned to Scotland and in 1565 married James Stuart, Lord Darnley. During her absence in France, the Protestant Reformation, for which John Knox and others had long labored, had become established in Scotland, and being a staunch Roman Catholic she found herself at odds with her Protestant subjects. Angered by her favoritism toward her lowborn Italian secretary, David Rizzio, the Scotch lords and her husband conspired in the murder of Rizzio. After the birth of Mary's son, who became James I, of England, Darnley was murdered, and Mary was charged with the deed. Three months later she married the Earl of Bothwell, who had been exposed as one of Darnley's assassins. Forced to abdicate in 1568 in favor of her son, she sought protection of her cousin, Queen Elizabeth, who promptly made her a prisoner. For the next nineteen years Mary's name was involved in plots for escape and for the overthrow of Elizabeth. She was finally tried, convicted, and executed in 1587.

Swinburne had only scorn for those persons who saw no wrong in Mary and who defended her "at the expense of her intelligence and her courage." He believed that her crimes were great, and his purpose in writing his plays, he says, was "to vindicate her from the imputation of her vindicators." For a complete statement regarding his attitude, see his *Note on the Character of Mary Queen of Scots*, printed in his volume of prose *Miscellanies*, published in 1886.

THE LAKE OF GAUBE, p. 744

The following passage from Swinburne's *Notes of Travel—Alps and Pyrenees* (1894) is quoted as a parallel account of the poet's recollections of Lake Gaube:

"Of all great poets that ever lived, with the one possible and doubtful exception of Dante, Victor Hugo is the one who would have seemed most fit to describe and most capable of describing the lake of Gaube; . . . The fiery exuberance of flowers among which the salamanders glide like creeping flames, radiant and vivid, up to the very skirt of the tragic little pine wood at whose heart the fathomless little lake lies silent, with a dark dull gleam on it as if of half-tarnished steel; the deliciously keen and exquisite shock of a first plunge under its tempting and threatening surface, more icy cold in spring than the sea in winter; the ineffable and breathless purity of the clasping water in which it seems to savor of intrusive and profane daring that a swimmer should take his pleasure till warned back by fear of cramp when but half way across the length of it, and doubtful whether his stock of warmth would hold out for a return from the far edge opposite, to which no favoring magic

can be expected to transport the clothes left behind him on the bank off which he dived; the sport of catching and taming a salamander till it became the pleasantest as well as the quaintest of dumb four-footed friends; the beauty of its purple-black coat of scaled armor inlaid with patches of dead-leaf gold, its shining eyes and its flashing tongue—these things, of which a humbler hand could write at greater length than this, would require such a hand as Hugo's to do them any sort of justice."—*Complete Works*, Vol. 13, pp. 320-321.

EDWARD LEAR, p. 745

STANDARD EDITIONS

Complete Nonsense, ed. and w. an intro. by H. Jackson, New York, Dover, 1951

Nonsense Omnibus, w. an intro. by Sir. E. Strachey, New York, Warne, 1943

Queery Leary Nonsense, ed. by Lady Strachey, intro. by the Earl of Cromer, London, Mills, 1911

The Nonsense A B C, New York, Macmillan, 1928

A Book of Nonsense, col. by E. Rhys, New York, Dutton, 1928. Contains verses by Carroll and others

Letters, ed. by Lady Strachey, w. an intro. by H. Strachey, London, Unwin, 1907

Later Letters, ed. by Lady Strachey, New York, Duffield, 1911

BIOGRAPHY AND CRITICISM

Cammaerts, E., *The Poetry of Nonsense*, London, Routledge, 1925

Davidson, A., *Edward Lear; Landscape Painter and Nonsense Poet*, New York, Dutton, 1939

Lear, Edward, "A Leaf from the Journals of a Landscape Painter," w. biog. intro. by F. L., *Macmillan's Magazine*, 1897, 75: 410-430

Lushington, F., "Memoir of Edward Lear," in Lear's *Illustrations to Tennyson, Nonsense Songs and Stories*, London, Warne, 1888

Malcolm, I., "The Literary Work of Edward Lear," *Cornhill Magazine*, 1908, 97:25-36

Quarterly Review, "Nonsense as a Fine Art," 1888, 167:335-365

Selwyn, E.C., "Later Letters of Edward Lear," *Cornhill Magazine*, 1910, 101: 389-398

Sewell, E., *Field of Nonsense*, London, Chatto, 1952

BIOGRAPHICAL SKETCH

Edward Lear (1812-1888), traveler, painter, and friend of Tennyson, was gifted with a boisterous sense of humor which overflowed during his rare idle moments into his nonsense rhymes. Early in his career, a set of his bird paintings caught the fancy of the Earl of Derby and led to an invitation to paint the birds and animals on the Earl's estate. While there, Lear amused everyone with his impromptu limericks, especially Edward Stanley, the Earl's grandson for whom Lear wrote his first *Book of Nonsense* (1846). Taking up landscape painting, Lear traveled in remote regions—Albania, the desert of Sinai, the Nile Valley—in search of subjects, embodying his experiences in his *Illustrated Journal of a Landscape Painter* (1869) and making light of his hardships. He retired at length to a villa at San Remo in Italy, and there occupied himself with a set of two hundred drawings to illustrate the poetry of Tennyson, but this project was never completed.

Lear's principal publications were: *A Book of Nonsense*, 1846; *The Illustrated Journal of a Landscape Painter*, 1869; *Nonsense Drolleries*, 1889; *The Jumblies and Other Nonsense Verses*, 1900.

INTRODUCTORY CRITICISM

"The parent of modern nonsense-writers he [Lear] is distinguished from all his followers and imitators by the superior consistency with which he has adhered to his aim—that of amusing his readers by fantastic absurdities, as void of vulgarity or cynicism as they are incapable of being made to harbor any symbolical meaning. . . . He has a genius for coining absurd names and words, which, even when they are suggested by the exigencies of his meter, have a ludicrous appropriateness to the matter in hand. His verse is, with the exception of a certain number of cockney rimes, wonderfully flowing and even melodious—or, as he would say, *meloobious*—while to all these qualifications for his task must finally be added the happy gift of pictorial expression, enabling him to double, nay often to quadruple, the laughable effect of his text by an inexhaustible profusion of the quaintest designs."—*Spectator*, September 17, 1887, p. 1251.

CHARLES STUART CALVERLEY, p. 746

STANDARD EDITIONS

Complete Works, w. a biog. notice by Sir W.J. Sendall, London, Bell, 1910
Works, 4 vols., London, Bell, 1896-1898
Verses, Translations, and Fly Leaves, London, Bell, 1904

Literary Remains, w. a mem. by Sir W.J. Sendall, London, Bell, 1886

BIOGRAPHY AND CRITICISM

Babington, P.L., *Browning and Calverley; or Poem and Parody, an Elucidation*, London, Castle, 1925
Ince, R.B., *Calverley and Some Cambridge Wits of the Nineteenth Century*, London, Cayme Press, 1929

BIOGRAPHICAL SKETCH

Charles Stuart Calverley (1831-1884), the son of a Worcestershire clergyman, was celebrated during his undergraduate days at Cambridge for his cleverness, his laziness, and his charm. That he succeeded at Cambridge was due to the efforts of his loyal friends, who dragged him from his bed before the morning was over and locked him in his room with his books. But once aroused, Calverley's mind worked with great brilliance; he won many prizes and medals for his facility in the classics, and great social popularity with the grace of his conversation and the aptness of his impromptu parodies and rhymes. On leaving college, he began the practice of law on the Northern Circuit. The success of his professional career, in which his social talents well supplemented his imperfect knowledge of the law, was cut short by an unfortunate accident: he fell on his head while skating in the winter of 1866-1867 and was never afterwards able to work or read, although he could still compose an occasional set of verses. He lingered on, suffering from pain and depression, until February 17, 1884, when he died in London.

Calverley's publications were: *Verses and Translations*, 1862; *Translations into English and Latin*, 1866; *Theocritus Translated into English Verse*, 1869; *Fly Leaves*, 1872.

INTRODUCTORY CRITICISM

"Calverley had . . . the trained sense of form and finish; the dexterity which flings the verse into just the right form for suggesting and aiding the airy effect of the humor, which fledges and tips the line to carry the point of wit like an arrowshaft; the felicitous turn which brings diction and meter pat on the quick of the jest, and tickles you into instant laughter. Of these qualities all feel the effect, but only a student of technique will realize the cunning art of them. . . . Mastery—mastery of form and technique—is the thing which obviously differentiates him from most before him and many after him. . . . Calverley is surely the first of parodists. He may almost be called the founder of a new dynasty in parody. To an extent not previously approached, his parodies are likewise criticisms, and very keen criticisms, of a poet's weaker side. One grudges to call them parodies, so close and refined is the imitation, so inclusively does he catch and reflect all the elements of a writer's style."—*Spectator*, July 13, 1901, pp. 28-29.

CHARLES LUTWIDGE DODGSON ("Lewis Carroll"), p. 748

STANDARD EDITIONS

Complete Works, w. John Tenniel's illus. and an intro. by A. Woollcott, New York, Random House, 1937

Logical Nonsense; Complete Works, ed. by P.C. Blackburn and L. White, w. an intro., biog., notes, and bibliog., Garden City, N.Y., Garden City Pub. Co., 1942

Collected Verse, w. an intro. by J.F. McDermott, and a bibliog., New York, Dutton, 1929

Songs from Alice in Wonderland, and Through the Looking Glass, music by Lucy E. Broadwood, London, Black, 1921

Further Nonsense Verse and Prose, New York, Appleton, 1926

Alice's Adventures in Wonderland; Through the Looking Glass; and The Hunting of the Snark, w. illus. by John Tenniel, New York, Boni & Liveright, 1925

Alice's Adventures in Wonderland, illus. by Arthur Rackham, w. a poem by Austin Dobson, New York, Doubleday, 1907

The Hunting of the Snark, New York, Macmillan, 1929

Through the Looking Glass, illus. by Gertrude A. Kay, and w. the 50 orig. draw. by John Tenniel, Philadelphia, Lippincott, 1929

The Diaries, ed. by R.L. Green, New York, Oxford Univ. Press, 1954

BIOGRAPHY

Bowman, Isa, *The Story of Lewis Carroll*, London, Dent, 1899

Collingwood, S.D., *The Life and Letters of Lewis Carroll*, w. a bibliog., London, Nelson, 1912

De La Mare, W.J., *Lewis Carroll*, London, Faber, 1932

Green, R.L., *The Story of Lewis Carroll*, New York, Schuman, 1950

Hudson, D., *Lewis Carroll*, New York, Macmillan, 1954

Kelley, W.V., *With the Children in Lewis Carroll's Company*, New York, Abingdon Press, 1917

Lennon, F.B., *Victoria through the Looking Glass; the Life of Lewis Carroll*, New York, Simon & Schuster, 1945

Moses, Belle, *Lewis Carroll in Wonderland and at Home*, New York, Appleton, 1910

Reed, L., *The Life of Lewis Carroll*, London, Foyle, 1932

Tollemache, L.A., "Reminiscences of Lewis Carroll," *Among My Books*, ed. by H.D. Traill, New York, Longmans, 1898

CRITICISM

Ayres, H.M., *Carroll's Alice*, New York, Columbia Univ. Press, 1936

Cammaerts, E., *The Poetry of Nonsense*, London, Routledge, 1925

Gardner, Martin, *The Annotated Alice*, New York, Potter, 1960

Gardner, Martin, *The Annotated Snark*, New York, Simon & Schuster, 1962

Hubbell, G.S., "The Sanity of Wonderland," *Sewanee Review*, 1927, 35:387-398

Hudson, Derek, *Lewis Carroll*, London, Longmans, 1958

Milner, F., "The Poems in *Alice in Wonderland*," *Bookman*, 1903, 18:13-16

Parry, Judge, "The Early Writings of Lewis Carroll," *Cornhill Magazine*, 1924, 56:455-468

Sewell, E., *Field of Nonsense*, London, Chatto, 1952

Taylor, A.L., *White Knight, a Study of C.L. Dodgson (Lewis Carroll)*, Edinburgh, Oliver, 1952

Vail, R.W.G., "*Alice in Wonderland*: the Manuscript and Its Story," *Bulletin of the New York Public Library*, 1928, 32:783-785

Welby, T.E., "Lewis Carroll," *Back Numbers*, London, Constable, 1929

Williams, S.H., *A Bibliography of the Writings of Lewis Carroll*, New York, Bowker, 1924

Williams, S.H., *Some Rare Carrolliana*, privately printed, 1925

Williams, S.H., and F. Madan, *The Lewis Carroll Handbook*, New York, Oxford Univ. Press, 1962

BIOGRAPHICAL SKETCH

Charles Lutwidge Dodgson (1832-1898) to a certain extent lived a dual life; he was known under his own name as a suggestive if somewhat unreliable writer on mathematical problems and under the name of Lewis Carroll as the author of whimsical nonsense stories and rhymes. Shy, stammering, fastidious, eccentric, he lived a solitary life at Oxford, where he held a post as mathematical lecturer and made few friends among his colleagues. Among children, however, he was thoroughly at home. By means of proper introductions to the parents, it was his habit to seek the acquaintance of every attractive child whom he met; and after separation, to keep up the friendship with his charming letters. One such little friend, the dainty Alice Liddell, was his favorite; he took her one day for a boat ride on the river Isis near Oxford and told for her entertainment an imaginative story of her own adventures in a marvelous subterranean world—the story that he expanded into *Alice in Wonderland* (1865). *Alice* made Lewis Carroll famous; Dodgson, who dreaded fame, spent the rest of his life in keeping his identity a doubtful secret, writing in addition to a sequel to *Alice* other contributions to nursery literature, his letters to his vicarious children, and mathematical works that scholars could not be persuaded to read as seriously as they deserved.

Dodgson's principal publications were: *Syllabus of Plane Algebraical Geometry*, 1860; *Alice's Adventures in Wonderland*, 1865; *An Elementary Treatise on Determinants*, 1867; *Through the Looking-Glass*, 1871; *Phantasmagoria and Other Poems*, 1876; *The Hunting of the Snark*, 1876; *Euclid and His Modern Rivals*, 1879; *The Principles of Parliamentary Representation*, 1884; *A Tangled Tale*, 1885; *Silvie and Bruno*, 1889-1893; *Curiosa Mathematica*, 1888-1893; *Symbolic Logic*, 1896.

INTRODUCTORY CRITICISM

"In the kingdom of inspired nonsense there is none greater than Lewis Carroll. His nonsense is like no other man's. It is not ironic and cynical and elaborated like Mr. Gilbert's, nor is it of grotesque, madcap drollery all compact like Edward Lear's. The strange humor never runs riot. It startles and bewilders and delights; it has a flavor to be tasted nowhere else, and that never grows insipid on the palate; yet it is hardly the humor that bubbles and sparkles and evokes irresistible laughter. Lewis Carroll has not Lear's high spirits. Amid his wildest whimsicalities, his most preposterous inversions of fact and reason, he preserves a singular restraint in his manner. He exhibits a sedateness in absurdity, a precision in inconsequence, which give an exquisite incongruity, a delightful piquancy to the writing.... The writer's style is worthy of his humor. Never has nonsense been more neatly turned in prose or rime, more indelibly sealed with the seal of literature."—W. Whyte, *The Poets and the Poetry of the Century*, ed. A. H. Miles, Vol. 9, pp. 443-444.

CRITICAL NOTES

FATHER WILLIAM, p. 748

Father William is a parody on the following poem by Robert Southey:

The Old Man's Comforts

And How He Gained Them

"You are old, Father William," the young man cried,
  "The few locks which are left you are gray;
You are hale, Father William, a hearty old man,
  Now tell me the reason, I pray."

"In the days of my youth," Father William replied,
  "I remembered that youth would fly fast,
And abused not my health, and my vigor at first,
  That I never might need them at last."

"You are old, Father William," the young man cried,
  "And pleasures with youth pass away;
And yet you lament not the days that are gone,
  Now tell me the reason, I pray."

"In the days of my youth," Father William replied,
  "I remembered that youth could not last;
I thought of the future, whatever I did,
  That I never might grieve for the past."

"You are old, Father William," the young man cried,
  "And life must be hastening away;
You are cheerful, and love to converse upon death,
  Now tell me the reason, I pray."

"I am cheerful, young man," Father William replied,
  "Let the cause be thy attention engage;
In the days of my youth I remembered my God!
  And He hath not forgotten my age."   *(1799; 1799)*

JABBERWOCKY, p. 748

These definitions are given by Humpty Dumpty in *Through the Looking-Glass;* the last one is found in the Preface to *The Hunting of the Snark.*

Brillig. Four o'clock in the afternoon—the time when you begin broiling things for dinner.
Slithy. "Lithe and slimy." "Lithe" is the same as "active." ... it's like a portmanteau—there are two meanings packed up into one word.
Toves. Something like badgers—they're something like lizards—and they're something like corkscrews.... they make their nests under sun-dials—also they live on cheese.
Gyre. To go round and round like a gyroscope.
Gimble. To make holes like a gimblet.
Wabe. The grass-plot round a sun-dial, ... called ... because it goes a long way before it, and a long way behind it—And a long way beyond it on each side.
Mimsy. "Flimsy and miserable" ... another portmanteau ...
Borogove. A thin, shabby-looking bird with its feathers sticking out all round—something like a live mop.
Mome. Humpty says, "'mome' I'm not certain about. I think it's short for 'from home'—meaning that they'd lost their way ..."
Rath. A sort of green pig.
Outgrabe. (Past tense of *outgribe.*) "Outgribing" is something between bellowing and whistling, with a kind of sneeze in the middle.
Frumious. Another portmanteau word combining *fuming* and *furious.*

SIR WILLIAM SCHWENCK GILBERT, p. 751

STANDARD EDITIONS

Bab Ballads and Songs of a Savoyard, London, Macmillan, 1924

More "Bab" Ballads, London, Macmillan, 1925

The Savoy Operas; Being Complete Text of the Gilbert and Sullivan Operas as Originally Produced in the Years 1875-1896, London, Macmillan, 1926

Authentic Libretti of the Gilbert and Sullivan Operas, New York, Crown, 1939

The Complete Plays of Gilbert and Sullivan, ed. by B.A. Cerf and D.S. Klopfer, New York, Modern Lib., 1936

The Complete Plays of Gilbert and Sullivan, Garden City, N.Y., Garden City Pub. Co., 1938

Original Plays, London, Chatto, 1902-1911, 1st s., 1902; 2d s., 1903, 1920; 3d s., 1903; 4th s., 1911

Selected Operas, 2 vols., London, Macmillan, 1928

The Pinafore Picture Book, New York, Macmillan, 1908

The Mikado and Other Operas, w. an intro. by W.P. Eaton, New York, Macmillan, 1929

BIOGRAPHY

Browne, Edith A., *W. S. Gilbert*, London, Lane, 1907

Cellier, F.A., and C. Bridgeman, *Gilbert, Sullivan, and D'Oyly Carte; Reminiscences of the Savoy and the Savoyards*, London, Pitman, 1927

Dark, S., and R. Grey, *W. S. Gilbert, His Life and Letters*, w. a bibliog., London, Methuen, 1924

Gilbert, W.S., "An Autobiography," *The Theatre*, London, 1883, 13:217-224

Gilbert, W.S., "My Maiden Brief," *Cornhill Magazine*, 1863, 8:725-732

Pearson, H., *Gilbert and Sullivan*, New York, Harper, 1935

Pearson, H., *Gilbert: His Life and Strife*, London, Methuen, 1957

CRITICISM

Bailey, L., *The Gilbert and Sullivan Book*, New York, British Bk. Centre, 1952

Chesterton, G.K., "Gilbert and Sullivan," *G. K. C. as M. C.*, ed. by J.P. de Fonseka, London, Methuen, 1929

Darlington, W.A., *The World of Gilbert and Sullivan*, New York,, Crowell, 1950

Dunhill, T.F., *Sullivan's Comic Operas*, London, Arnold, 1928

Dunn, G.E., *Gilbert and Sullivan Dictionary*, New York, Oxford Univ. Press, 1936

FitzGerald, S.J.A., *The Story of the Savoy Opera in Gilbert and Sullivan Days*, w. an intro. by T.P. O'Connor, New York, Appleton, 1925

Godwin, A.H., *Gilbert and Sullivan; a Critical Appreciation of the Savoy Operas*. w. an intro. by G.K. Chesterton, London, Dent, 1926

Goldberg, I., *The Story of Gilbert and Sullivan*, w. an annot. list of bks. upon Gilbert and Sullivan, New York, Simon, 1928

Jacobs, A., *Gilbert and Sullivan*, London, Parrish, 1952

Mander, Raymond, and Joe Mitchenson, *A Picture History of Gilbert and Sullivan*, London, Vista, 1962

Moore, Frank L., ed., *The Handbook of Gilbert and Sullivan*, New York, Crowell, 1962

Purdy, C.L.S., *Gilbert and Sullivan*, New York, Messner, 1947

Quiller-Couch, A., "W.S. Gilbert," *Studies in Literature*, 3 vols., New York, Putnam, 1918

Rowland-Brown, H., "The Gilbertian Idea," *Cornhill Magazine*, 1922, 125:503-512

Walbrook, H.M., *Gilbert and Sullivan Opera, a History and a Comment*, London, White, 1922

Williamson, A., *Gilbert and Sullivan Opera: a New Assessment*, New York, Macmillan, 1953

BIOGRAPHICAL SKETCH

William Schwenck Gilbert (1836-1911) was born in London and was educated at London University. As an officer in the Gordon Highlanders, a clerk in a government office, and a practicing barrister in London, he found material for later satires on the army, the civil service, and the law; he also prepared for life-work by contributing verses to his college magazine and by training himself in the art of drawing. In 1861 he began writing for the humorous journal *Fun*, to which in 1867 he contributed his first illustrated ballad, "General John"; his verse and drawing became a weekly feature and bore out his theory that "all humor is based upon a grave and quasi-respectful treatment of the ludicrous." These *Bab Ballads*, so called from Gilbert's childhood nickname, were issued as volumes in 1869 and 1873. Connected from 1863 with the stage as dramatic critic and friend of actors, Gilbert in 1866 wrote his first play, a Christmas piece called *Dulcamara, or the Little Duck and the Great Quack*. Other travesty successes followed with equally fascinating subtitles; among them was *The Princess* (1870), a parody of Tennyson's poem, which he later expanded into his opera *Princess Ida* (1884). In 1870 he began more serious comedies and dramas, the mingled humor and sentiment of which caught the public taste. His most conspicuous successes, however, came with the light operas written for the music provided by Sir Arthur Sullivan, already a noted composer when Gilbert met him in 1871. The first of the series, *Trial by Jury*, expanded from a "Bab Ballad" which had appeared much earlier in *Fun*, was produced in 1875. *The Sorcerer* (1877), *H. M. S. Pinafore* (1878), and *The Pirates of Penzance* (1879) quickly followed; English and American audiences went wild with enthusiasm; the Savoy Opera House was built in London expressly for Gilbert and Sullivan productions. *The Mikado*, produced in 1885, ran two years in London and brought Gilbert thirty thousand pounds. The partnership with Sullivan continued until 1896. In his later years Gilbert lived as a genial country gentleman, kept bees, raised vegetables, and served as justice of the peace. He was knighted in 1907.

Gilbert's principal publications and stage productions were: *Bab Ballads*, 1869; *The Princess*, 1870; *Pygmalion and Galatea*, 1871; *More Bab Ballads*, 1873; *Charity*, c. 1874; *Trial by Jury*, 1875; *The Sorcerer*, 1877; *H. M. S. Pinafore*, 1878; *The Pirates of Penzance*, 1879; *Patience*, 1881; *Iolanthe*, 1882; *Princess Ida*, 1884; *The Mikado*, 1885; *Ruddigore*, 1887; *The Yeomen of the Guard*, 1888; *The Gondoliers*, 1889; *Songs of a Savoyard* (lyrics from the operas), 1890; *Foggerty's Fairy and Other Tales*, 1890; *Utopia Limited*, 1893; *The Grand Duke*, 1896; *The Hooligan*, 1911.

INTRODUCTORY CRITICISM

"Gilbert . . . was a born ironist. From beginning to end *The Bab Ballads* are irony set to a popular tune. Few Englishmen have sustained this dangerous method of satire on a higher level and with fewer lapses into serious instruction. . . . In the operas, Gilbert invented a world of his own, a world of satire and paradox, in which the ordinary standards of morals and experience are reversed. Thus he laughed at all the pompous institutions of the country. . . . In one quality Gilbert differed profoundly from all his rivals: he was a poet. . . . For variety of effect and courage in metrical experiment he is undefeated in his own craft of opera. The lyrics . . . have the true singing quality. Though they may be read with pleasure, yet they are meant to be sung, and Gilbert, juggler with words as he was, has made them fit for musical expression. . . . He was more genuinely inspired with the comic spirit than anyone else of his time, and in the years to come his comedies and operas will interpret the Victorian Age to grave historians."
—*Blackwood's Magazine*, July 1911, pp. 121 ff.

ARTHUR WILLIAM EDGAR O'SHAUGHNESSY, p. 759

STANDARD EDITIONS

Poems, sel. and ed. by W.A. Percy, New Haven, Yale Univ. Press, 1923
Lays of France, London, Ellis, 1872
Music and Moonlight, London, Chatto, 1874

BIOGRAPHY AND CRITICISM

Clarke, G.H., "Arthur O'Shaughnessy's Poetry," *Sewanee Review*, 1923, 31:486-489
Contemporary Review, "Arthur O'Shaughnessy's Poems," 1924, 126:125-128
Gosse, E., "Arthur O'Shaughnessy," *Silhouettes*, London, Heinemann, 1925
Hamilton, Walter, "Arthur W. E. O'Shaughnessy," *The Aesthetic Movement in England*, London, Reeves, 1882
Lucas, F.L., "Arthur O'Shaughnessy's Poetry," *New Statesman*, 1923, 21:596-598
Moulton, Louise C., *Arthur O'Shaughnessy, His Life and His Work, with Selections from His Poems*, Chicago, Stone, 1894

BIOGRAPHICAL SKETCH

Arthur William Edgar O'Shaughnessy (1844-1881), whose dreamy temperament made romantic poetry his natural expression, was from 1861 until his premature death an assistant, like Gosse and Patmore, in the British Museum and was forced to study means of preserving fishes rather than the old French literature that he loved. Unsuspected by his associates, to whom he was an aloof figure with bushy whiskers and a frock coat, he practiced his poetic art and surprised them in 1870 with his limpid *Epic of Women and Other Poems* which won him Swinburne's praise and Rossetti's friendship. Not unlike Rossetti in his tastes, in 1873 he married a lady whose beauty had the Pre-Raphaelite quality. As he found more leisure, established closer contacts with the literary circles of France and England, and published subsequent volumes of verse, his life seemed to promise much; but the death of his wife in 1879 was a great blow, and two years later a chill caught in leaving a theater caused his death.

O'Shaughnessy's principal publications were: *Epic of Women and Other Poems*, 1870; *Lays of France*, 1872; *Music and Moonlight*, 1874; *Toyland* (with Mrs. O'Shaughnessy), 1875; *Songs of a Worker*, 1881.

INTRODUCTORY CRITICISM

"If we take his [O'Shaughnessy's] poetry at its best and analyze what distinguishes it from the work of other poets, we are struck by its lyrical art—soft, tremulous, and rich; this poet has the voice of the blackbird, not that of the nightingale or the lark. It is a flute-music, not strong in quality, nor wide in range, but of a piercing tenderness. There is never any searching after strange epithets or violent phrases, but the stream of melody flows on without effort and without interruption to its appointed close."—E. Gosse, *Silhouettes*, p. 178.

WILFRID SCAWEN BLUNT, p. 762

STANDARD EDITIONS

Poetical Works, 2 vols., London, Macmillan, 1928

Poems, London, Macmillan, 1923

Poetry, sel. and arr. by W.E. Henley and G. Wyndham, London, Heinemann, 1898

Poems, sel. by Floyd Dell, New York, Knopf, 1923

My Diaries, New York, Knopf, 1921

BIOGRAPHY AND CRITICISM

Adams, W.S., *Edwardian Portraits*, London, Secker and Warburg, 1957

Assad, Thomas J., Three Victorian Travellers (Blunt, Doughty, Burton), London, Routledge and Kegan Paul, 1964

Chew, S.C., "Wilfrid Scawen Blunt: An Intimate View," *North American Review*, 1923, 217:664-675

Chew, S.C., "Wilfrid Blunt: Self-Determinist," *New Republic*, 1920, 23:240-250

Fenlon, J.F., "Wilfrid Scawen Blunt," *Catholic World*, 1922, 116:357-369

Finch, Edith, *Wilfrid Scawen Blunt*, London, Cape, 1938

Going, William T., "Oscar Wilde and Wilfrid Blunt," *Victorian Newsletter*, Spring, 1958, pp. 27-28

Graham, R.B.C., "Wilfrid Scawen Blunt," *English Review*, 1922, 35:486-492

Gregory, Lady I.A., "Notes on Wilfrid Scawen Blunt," *Nation*, 1921, 113:660-661

Harris, F., "Wilfrid Scawen Blunt," *Contemporary Portraits*, Fourth Series, New York, Brentano, 1923

O'Connor, T.P., "Wilfrid Scawen Blunt," *Living Age*, 1922, 315:157-163

Poetry Review, "The Poetry of Wilfrid Scawen Blunt," 1921, 12:193-204

Reinehr, Sister Mary Joan, *Wilfrid Scawen Blunt, an Introduction and Study*, Milwaukee, Marquette Univ. Press, 1941

Rogers, C., "The Uncrowned King of Sussex," *Saturday Review of Literature*, 1925, 2:133-134

Shuster, G.N., "Inheritors," *The Catholic*

Spirit in Modern English Literature, New York, Macmillan, 1922

Spectator, "Proteus Unbound," 1889, 63:758-760

Symons, A., "Wilfrid Scawen Blunt," *The Double Dealer*, 1922, 3:37-41

Tynan, Katherine, "Wilfrid Scawen Blunt," *Catholic World*, 1888, 47:370-378

Watson, W., "Poetry by Men of the World," *National Review*, 1889, 14:520-529; same article in *Living Age*, 1890, 184:85-90

White, N.I., "Wilfrid Blunt's Diaries," *South Atlantic Quarterly*, 1922, 21:360-364

BIOGRAPHICAL SKETCH

Wilfrid Scawen Blunt (1840-1922), an impulsive and generous advocate of unpopular causes, was the son of an officer who had distinguished himself in the Napoleonic Wars. Educated in the best Roman Catholic schools, he entered the diplomatic service in 1858 and served at Athens, Madrid, Paris, Lisbon, and in South America; because of his handsome presence and romantic bearing, his career was socially brilliant but not wholly satisfactory to his more sedate superiors. He married in 1869 the beautiful granddaughter of Lord Byron, the Lady Anne Noel, left the diplomatic service, and in 1872 succeeded to the family estate of Crabbet Park in Sussex. There he bred and rode Arab horses and wrote his half-dramatic, half-personal *Love Sonnets of Proteus* (1880) with their frank allusions to his escapades before marriage. Tired of country diversions, he embarked with Lady Anne upon a long series of travels and adventures in Africa, India, and the Near East; became an ardent sympathizer with native viewpoints and an opponent of the British imperialistic policy in India, Egypt, and the Sudan; and wrote, in his *Future of Islam* (1882), *The Wind and the Whirlwind* (1883), and *Ideas about India* (1885), dire predictions, since partly realized, of native revolts. Returning home for a period in 1885-1887, he espoused, with his customary fervor, the nationalist cause in Ireland, ran unsuccessfully for Parliament as an advocate of Home Rule, and, for fiery speeches, was arrested and imprisoned two months in Irish jails. Shortly before his death, he published his *Diaries* (1920), in which he repeated his aversion to the colonial policies that Kipling and Henley had upheld.

Blunt's principal publications were: *Love Sonnets of Proteus*, 1881; *The Future of Islam*, 1882; *The Wind and the Whirlwind*, 1883; *Ideas about India*, 1885; *In Vinculis*, 1889; *A New Pilgrimage*, 1889; *Esther*, 1892; *The Stealing of the Mare*, 1892; *Griselda*, 1893;

Satan Absolved, 1899; *Seven Golden Odes of Pagan Arabia*, 1903; *The Secret History of the British Occupation of Egypt*, 1907; *India under Ripon*, 1909; *Gordon at Khartoum*, 1911; *The Land War in Ireland*, 1912; *Poetical Works*, 1914; *My Diaries*, 1919-1920.

INTRODUCTORY CRITICISM

"[Mr. Blunt] has put more of himself and his sole experience into his verse than any writer of his time.... He comes, in fact, ... straight from the Byron of 'Don Juan'.... In truth, Mr. Blunt, for all his gift, is not a poet in the sense that Shakespeare and Herrick, that Milton and Keats are poets. There are dissonances in his music—little faults of time and tune: as a cheap rhyme, a strained construction, a piece of dubious syntax. But, when all's said, his verse moves with a sort of natural elegance—a careless, high-bred swing; and there is ever a personal and easy touch of distinction in his style."— W.E. Henley, "Prefatory," *The Poetry of Wilfrid Blunt*, pp. v-vi.

HENRY AUSTIN DOBSON, p. 769

STANDARD EDITIONS

Complete Poetical Works, ed. by Alban Dobson, w. a bibliog. index, London, Milford, 1924
Selected Poems, The World's Classics, London, Milford, 1925
Austin Dobson, poems, London, Benn, 1926

BIOGRAPHY AND CRITICISM

Dobson, Alban, *A Bibliography of the First Editions of Published and Privately Printed Books and Pamphlets of Austin Dobson*, London, First Edition Club, 1925
Dobson, Alban, *Austin Dobson: Some Notes*, w. chaps. by Sir Edmund Gosse and George Saintsbury, London, Oxford Univ. Press, 1928
Ellis, S.M., "Austin Dobson," *Mainly Victorian*, London, Hutchinson, 1925
Gosse, E., "Austin Dobson," *Silhouettes*, London, Heinemann, 1925
Henley, W.E., "Dobson," *Views and Reviews*, London, Macmillan, 1921
Johnson, L., "Austin Dobson," *Reviews and Critical Papers*, London, Mathews, 1921
Kernahan, C., "Austin Dobson," *Celebrities*, London, Hutchinson, 1923
Lipscombe, H.C., "Horace and the Poetry of Austin Dobson," *American Journal of Philology*, 1929, 50:1-20
Monroe, H., "From Queen Anne to George the Fifth," *Poetry*, 1921, 19:90-94

Noyes, A., "The Poems of Austin Dobson," *Some Aspects of Modern Poetry*, London, Hodder, 1924
Robinson, J.K., "A Neglected Phase of the Aesthetic Movement: English Parnassianism," *PMLA*, 1953, 68:733-754
Robinson, J.K., "Austin Dobson and the Rondeliers," *Modern Language Quarterly*, 1953, 14:31-42
Symons, A., "Austin Dobson," *Studies in Prose and Verse*, London, Dent, 1904
Welby, T.E., "Austin Dobson," *Back Numbers*, London, Constable, 1929
Weygandt, C., "Austin Dobson, Augustan," *Tuesdays at Ten*, Philadelphia, Univ. of Pa. Press, 1928
Woodberry, G.E., "Austin Dobson," *Studies of a Littérateur*, New York, Harcourt, 1921

BIOGRAPHICAL SKETCH

Henry Austin Dobson (1840-1921) had the latter part of his elementary education in Strasbourg, then a French city, and was thus brought into direct contact with the literature that he always so much esteemed. Returning to England at the age of sixteen, he began work as a clerk in the Board of Trade, where Edmund Gosse also was employed; this post he held for almost fifty years but always regarded it as a necessary means to a livelihood rather than his true profession. This profession was increasingly that of a man of letters. As a scholar, he was interested primarily in the eighteenth century, wrote biographies of its principal figures, edited some fifty of its masterpieces, and composed a series of charming studies of its manners and literature. As a poet, he was impressed originally by the style of the Pre-Raphaelites; but under the influence of Théodore de Banville, whose "Little Treatise" on the older French lyrics attracted his attention in 1874, and of Tennyson, who in 1877 recommended the study of Horace's *Odes*, he developed a style as polished and graceful as the minuets of the century that he most admired. He said that "Pope taught him rhythm, Prior ease, Praed buoyancy and banter." Until 1884 his work was largely in verse, thereafter in prose. A shy, nervous man, fastidious and even prudish in his tastes, continually concerned lest his devotion to literature should offend his business superiors, he welcomed his retirement in 1901 as a relief from drudgery, lived aloof from the turmoil of London in a congenial, scholarly world, loved old books, old friends, old wine.

Dobson's principal publications were: *Vignettes in Rhyme*, 1873; *The Civil Service Handbook of English Literature*, 1874; *Proverbs in Porcelain*, 1877; *William Hogarth*, 1879; *Field-*

ing, 1883; *Old World Idylls*, 1883; *At the Sign of the Lyre*, 1885; *Richard Steele*, 1886; *Oliver Goldsmith*, 1888; *Four Frenchwomen*, 1890; *Horace Walpole*, 1890; *Eighteenth Century Vignettes*, 1892, 1894, 1896; *The Ballad of Beau Brocade*, 1892; *The Story of Rosina*, 1895; *Poems on Several Occasions*, 1895; *Miscellanies*, 1898, 1901; *A Paladin of Philanthropy*, 1899; *Carmina Votiva*, 1901; *Side-Walk Studies*, 1902; *Samuel Richardson*, 1902; *Fanny Burney*, 1903; *De Libris*, 1908; *Old Kensington Palace*, 1910; *At Prior Park*, 1912; *Poems on the War*, 1915; *Rosalba's Journal*, 1915; *A Bookman's Budget*, 1917; *Later Essays*, 1921.

INTRODUCTORY CRITICISM

"Austin Dobson's style both in prose and verse was ever beautifully clear, urbane, and prudent. . . . He was an excellent craftsman and contriver. His verses are often as bright, smooth, and caressable as precious snuff-boxes, and like them they sometimes contain a little pungent dust which can bring water to the eyes. . . . In knowledge of the social and literary life of the eighteenth century he was without a rival, unless that rival might be Dr. Birkbeck Hill; and he knew that saner society and the famous characters who composed it as if he had been, not our, but their contemporary. . . . His standards of good sense and good taste were those of his favorite period, tempered by an exceptional kindliness, and every book he published was a fastidious model of light learning. He never wooed the Muse of introspection or her of the woeful countenance. His own was a Dresden shepherdess, yet in one respect she was not of the eighteenth century; for there was no malice or license in her. She was demure and she wore, I think, a little flowered bonnet."—J. C. Squire, *New Statesman*, Sept. 10, 1921, p. 623.

See Henley's *To A. D.*, p. 795; also Mary Elizabeth Coleridge's *In a Volume of Austin Dobson*, p. 869.

CRITICAL NOTES

A DIALOGUE, p. 777

This poem is full of allusions to the life and writings of Pope and to his contemporaries. The *Friend* of line 2, eager to exhibit the darker side of Pope, who was called "the Twitnam Bard" because of his retirement after 1719 to his villa at Twickenham up the Thames from London, reviews the acrimony with which Pope attacked his contemporaries, such as the critic John Dennis, the playwright and actor Colley Cibber, and the Shakespearian editor Lewis Theobald, in the *Dunciad* (1728-1743) and other personal satires; the

fickleness that led him to profess an exalted friendship for the brilliant Lady Mary Wortley Montagu from 1717 to 1723 and then to attack her bitterly for the rest of his life; and the sorry figure which he cut in a scandalous pamphlet, *A Pop upon Pope*, 1728, that recounted how he was soundly whipped by his victims as he strolled in Ham Walks near Twickenham. The Poet defends Pope.

The explanations necessary for the understanding of this poem and *A Postscript to "Retaliation"* are so numerous that they could not easily be included in the footnotes and are grouped here instead.

Page 777. 11. *Grub Street*, the hack writers who inhabited garrets in Grub Street, now Milton Street, in London.

17. *"long Disease."* See Pope's *Epistle to Dr. Arbuthnot*, ll. 131-132:

"The Muse but served to ease some friend, not wife,
To help me through this long disease, my life."

An illness in childhood left Pope deformed, seldom without pain, for the rest of his life.

23. *"crooked . . . Mind!"* "Mens curva in corpore curvo." Said of Pope by Lord Orrery (Dobson's note).

33-34. *Swift . . . Arbuthnot*, authors and noblemen of the Tory party, with whom Pope was closely associated. Jonathan Swift and Dr. John Arbuthnot joined with Pope in the Scriblerus Club to ridicule false tastes in learning. Henry St. John (pronounced Sinjun), Viscount Bolingbroke, was until 1714 a leader of the Tory party and thereafter a writer on history and politics. Allen, Earl of Bathurst; Patrick Hume, Earl of Marchmont; and Charles Mordaunt, Earl of Peterborough, were other literary noblemen who were frequent visitors at Twickenham.

34. *Atticus*, Joseph Addison (1672-1719), famous essayist, whom Pope attacked in the *Epistle to Dr. Arbuthnot*, ll. 193-214, under the name of Atticus.

37. *So . . . thought.* Many of Hamlet's speeches are veiled or equivocal. Cf. the one to Guildenstern.—"I am but mad north-north-west: when the wind is southerly I know a hawk from a handsaw" (II, 2, 396-398).

40. *Lock . . . Eloise*, works of Pope: *The Rape of the Lock*, 1712-1714, a mock-epic social satire; *Satires*, 1733-1738, including *Epistle to Dr. Arbuthnot*, Pope's masterpiece in personal invective; *Eloïsa to Abelard*, c. 1717, a neo-classic version of the romantic passion between the nun Héloïse and the philosopher Abelard in the twelfth century.

46. *"True . . . dressed."* From Pope's *Essay on Criticism*, l. 297.

48. *"And . . . Line."* From *Essay on Criti-*

cism, l. 347. The sound of Pope's line is here, as he said, "an echo to the sense."

51. *"Ten . . . amiss."* From *Essay on Criticism*, l. 6.

55. *Byron . . . Bowles.* William Lisle Bowles, who wrote sonnets (1789) admired by Wordsworth and Coleridge, later engaged in a controversy with Lord Byron in which Bowles questioned the poetic merits of Pope and defined poetry in accordance with the new romantic principles.

⟋ **Page 777.** 57. *Tate*, Nahum Tate, a mediocre poet (1652-1715), who collaborated with Dryden in the second part of *Absalom and Achitophel* and who succeeded him, after an interval, as poet laureate.

61. *Horace . . . Juvenal*, the three principal satirists in Roman literature. Horace's satire on Augustan Rome is urbane; the satires of Persius and Juvenal on the Rome of Nero and of Domitian are violent.

64-69. *When . . . File*, an accurate characterization of the prevailing mood and spirit of the writing of Pope's day.

80. *Iliad*, Pope's translation (1715-1720) of Homer's epic, not close to the letter or spirit of the original, but superbly adapted to the taste of the eighteenth century.

81. *Bohn*, the publisher of *Bohn's Classical Library* in which a literal prose translation of Homer by T. A. Buckley was included.

83. *Butcher . . . Lang, The Odyssey of Homer Done into English Prose* by S. H. Butcher and Andrew Lang, 1879.

100. *Bathos*, a descent from the sublime to the ridiculous. See *On Bathos: or, Of the Art of Sinking in Poetry*, in the *Works of Alexander Pope*, 1751, Vol. 6, pp. 195 ff. *Trope*, a word used figuratively rather than precisely. Chapter 10 of *On Bathos* concerns *Tropes and Figures*.

GERARD MANLEY HOPKINS, p. 779

STANDARD EDITIONS

Poems, 3d ed., w. notes and biog. intro. by W.H. Gardner, w. pref. by R. Bridges, New York, Oxford Univ. Press, 1948

Poems, ed. w. notes by R. Bridges, London, Oxford Univ. Press, 1918

A Hopkins Reader, sel. and w. an intro. by John Pick, New York, Oxford Univ. Press, 1953

A Vision of the Mermaids, London, Oxford Univ. Press, 1929

The Letters of Gerard Manley Hopkins to Robert Bridges; the Correspondence of Gerard Manley Hopkins and Richard Watson Dixon, 2 vols., ed. by C.C. Abbott, New York, Oxford Univ. Press, 1935

Journals and Papers, ed. by H. House and G. Storey, London, Oxford Univ. Press, 1959

BIOGRAPHY

Brégy, K., "Gerard Hopkins: an Epitaph and an Appreciation," *Catholic World*, 1909, 88:433-447

Gardner, W.H., *Gerard Manley Hopkins*, *(1844-1889)*, 2 vols., New Haven, Conn., Yale Univ. Press, 1948-1949

Lahey, G.F., *Gerard Manley Hopkins*, New York, Oxford Univ. Press, 1938

Pick, J., *Gerard Manley Hopkins, Priest and Poet*, New York, Oxford Univ. Press, 1942

Richards, I.A., "Gerard Hopkins," *Dial*, 1926, 81:195-203

Ritz, Jean-Georges, *Robert Bridges and Gerard Hopkins, 1863-1889: A Literary Friendship*, London, Oxford Univ. Press, 1960

Robinson, H.M., "Gerard Manley Hopkins: a Preface," *Commonweal*, 1927, 7:869-872

Ruggles, E., *Gerard Manley Hopkins*, New York, Norton, 1944

CRITICISM

Baum, Paull F., "Sprung Rhythm," *PMLA*, 1959, 74:418-425

Boyd, Robert, *Metaphor in Hopkins*, Chapel Hill, Univ. of North Carolina Press, 1961

Charney, M., "A Bibliographical Study of Hopkins Criticism, 1918-1940," *Thought*, 1950, v. 14, 97:297-326

Cohen, S.J., "The Poetic Theory of Gerard Manley Hopkins," *Philological Quarterly*, 1947, 26:1-20

Downes, David A., *Gerard Manley Hopkins: A Study of his Ignatian Spirit*, New York, Bookman Associates, 1959

Drew, E.A., *Discovering Poetry*, New York, Norton, 1933

Empson, W., *Seven Types of Ambiguity*, New York, Harcourt, 1931

Gardner, W.H., "The Wreck of the *Deutschland*," *Essays and Studies*, (English Association, London), Vol. 21, New York, Oxford Univ. Press, 1936, pp. 124-152

Harrison, T.P., "The Birds of Gerard Manley Hopkins," *Studies in Philology*, 1957, 54:968-978

Heuser, Alan, *The Shaping Vision of Gerard Manley Hopkins*, New York, Oxford Univ. Press, 1958

Holloway, Sister M.M., *Prosodic Theory of Gerard Manley Hopkins*, Washington, D.C., Catholic Univ. of America, 1947

Kelly, B., *The Mind and Poetry of Gerard Manley Hopkins*, Boston, Humphries, 1935

Kenyon Review (periodical), *Gerard Manley Hopkins*, Norfolk, Conn., New Directions, 1946

Lappin, H.A., "Gerard Hopkins and His Poetry," *Catholic World*, 1919, 109:501-512

McNamee, M.B., "Mastery and Mercy in *The Wreck of the Deutschland*," *College English*, 1962, 23:267-276

Murry, J.M., "Gerard Manley Hopkins," *Aspects of Literature*, London, Collins, 1920

Myers, John A., Jr., "Intimations of Mortality: An Analysis of Hopkins's 'Spring and Fall,'" *English Journal*, 1962, 51:585-587

Peters, W.A., *Gerard Manley Hopkins*, New York, Oxford Univ. Press, 1948

Phare, E.E., *The Poetry of Gerard Manley Hopkins*, New York, Macmillan, 1933

Scrinivasa Iyengar, K.R., *Gerard Manley Hopkins, the Man and the Poet*, New York, Oxford Univ. Press, 1949

Shuster, G.N., "Poetry and Three Poets," *The Catholic Spirit in Modern English Literature*, New York, Macmillan, 1922

Stempel, Daniel, "A Reading of 'The Windhover,'" *College English*, 1962, 23:305-307

Weyand, N.T., and R.V. Schoder, eds., *Immortal Diamond: Studies in Gerard Manley Hopkins*, London, Sheed, 1949

Zabel, M.D., "Gerard Manley Hopkins; Poetry as Experiment and Unity," *Poetry*, 1930, 37:152-161

Zabel, M.D., "Hopkins in His Letters," *Poetry*, 1935, 46, 4:210-219

BIOGRAPHICAL SKETCH

Gerard Manley Hopkins (1844-1889), orthodox in religion, radical in his artistic principles, wrote tense and fervent poems as a child and received an early education intended to prepare him for the English Church. However, in 1866 he came under the magnetic influence of Father Newman and was filled with a religious enthusiasm that resulted in his becoming a Roman Catholic. For a time he studied at Oxford with Walter Pater as his tutor; but in 1868 he entered the Jesuit order as a novice, burned his early poetry, went to live for several months with Newman in Birmingham, saw much of Coventry Patmore, and then went to serve as a missionary in the slums of Liverpool. By nature extremely sensitive and by training fastidious, he was violently shocked by the vice and dirt of Liverpool; he fled shortly to London, received a church in Oxford, and was later appointed to the staff of the University of Dublin. His poetical work, interrupted for seven years by his religious preoccupation, was his chief pleasure in Ireland, where he was little at home and felt by his associates to be a rather unaccountable fellow; his poetic style, already highly individual, became increasingly unorthodox, in diction and form. After five years in Dublin, he died suddenly from a contagious fever. He had published nothing; his manuscript poems passed into the keeping of Robert Bridges, who edited them for the press in 1918. His influence since that time has been enormous. Hopkins has been properly recognized as one of the greatest poets of the nineteenth century and one of the most intense religious lyrists in the language.

INTRODUCTORY CRITICISMS

"Some of his [Hopkins's] meters are woven with such tortuous subtlety, with such tremulous ingenuity, that the endurance of most readers will faint and fail before the task of penetrating through them to what lies beyond; one must tear oneself through thorns and briars, as it were, and not many suffer willingly so stern a trial of onset. Sometimes so opulently obscure is his imagery that only the most painstaking lovers of poetry can hope to win their difficult way to his thought. . . . Yet from the pen of this poet there also came poems and lyrics as crystal-clear as the globèd dew, as musical and unlabored as the song of a thrush among the leaves."—H. A. Lappin, *Catholic World*, July 1919, pp. 511-512.

"Prizing singularity and encouraged by Duns Scotus, its philosopher, Hopkins called the essence and the underlying design of a thing its 'inscape.' His endeavor to be true to his inscape and his themes, making him singular and, he feared, repulsive at first reading, demanded those distortions of syntax, the ellipses, the grammatical improvisations, that make his poetry difficult. In this interest and for intensity he condensed as he distorted. So made and charged with the profound experiences of his faith, his poems seem not recollections in tranquillity but experience in progress. Songs of becoming, not of being, they are opposite in kind to the perfections of Yeats."—William York Tindall, *Forces in Modern British Literature, 1885-1946*, p. 215.

CRITICAL NOTES

The poems of Hopkins become less difficult to read when we understand something of his principle of metrics. Some of his poems are written in what he calls "Sprung Rhythm," which is measured by feet of one to four syllables, with the stress always on the first syllable of the foot. He says, too, that this rhythm provides greater flexibility in the verse by allowing any one kind of foot to follow any other kind. "It is natural in Sprung Rhythm," he adds, "for the lines to be *rove over*, that is, for the scanning of each line immediately to take up that of the one before, so that if the first has one or more syllables at its end the other must have so many the less at its beginning; and in fact the scanning runs on without break from the beginning, say, of a stanza to the end and all the stanza is one long strain, though written in lines asunder."—Quoted by R. Bridges in his edition of Hopkins's *Poems*, Preface, p. 4.

RICHARD WATSON DIXON, p. 789

STANDARD EDITIONS

Christ's Company and Other Poems, London, Smith Elder, 1861
Historical Odes and Other Poems, London, Smith Elder, 1864
Mano, a Poetical History, London, Routledge, 1883
Last Poems, ed. by Robert Bridges, London, Henry Frowde, 1905
The Correspondence of Gerard Manley Hopkins and Richard Watson Dixon, ed. by C.C. Abbott, New York, Oxford Univ. Press, rev. ed., 1955

BIOGRAPHY AND CRITICISM

Beeching, H.C., "R.W. Dixon," *Supplement to Dictionary of National Biography*, 1901
Mackail, J.W., *The Life of William Morris*, London, Longmans, 1922
Mackail, J.W., *William Morris and His Circle*, London, Oxford Univ. Press, 1907
Sambrook, James, *A Poet Hidden: The Life of Richard Watson Dixon*, London, Athlone Press, 1962
Welby, T. Earle, *The Victorian Romantics, 1850-70*, London, Howe, 1929

BIOGRAPHICAL SKETCH

Largely neglected in his own lifetime, Richard Watson Dixon (1833-1900) is now remembered, if at all, primarily as the steadfast friend and sympathetic correspondent of Gerard Manley Hopkins. His work, however, as both poet and historian has its intrinsic merits, and his associations with the Pre-Raphaelites as well as with Hopkins should not be forgotten. Born at Islington, he met the future painter Edward Burne-Jones at school in Birmingham. Later at Oxford with William Morris he projected the *Oxford and Cambridge Magazine*, and he joined Morris and Burne-Jones in helping Rossetti paint frescoes in the Oxford Union.

Ordained in 1858 to a curacy in Lambeth, he officiated at the wedding of Morris and Jane Burden. Not surprisingly, his early work in poetry everywhere bore traces of Pre-Raphaelite influence. Before long he was lost to the Rossetti circle, however, for in 1862 he accepted a post as schoolmaster in remote Carlisle, where six years later he became a minor canon of the cathedral. He then devoted himself to scholarly studies in the growth of the Church of England which ultimately produced a monumental six-volume history. Isolated and lonely, he found new stimulus in his correspondence with Hopkins, who, having been his pupil in London long before, wrote in 1878 to praise several of Dixon's poems. Through Hopkins, Dixon soon came to know Robert Bridges, and the three poets, each seeking an audience in the other two and all finding much needed encouragement, exchanged many spirited letters. Deeply saddened by the death of Hopkins in 1889 and in poor health, he gave more of his energies to his prose work. Belatedly—in fact, only a month before his death—Oxford conferred upon him an honorary degree in recognition of his scholarship. Nine years later, hoping to fix Dixon's reputation as a poet, Bridges edited a careful selection of his verse.

Dixon's principal publications were: *Christ's Company and Other Poems*, 1861; *Historical Odes and Other Poems*, 1864; *The Life of James Dixon*, 1874; *History of the Church of England from the Abolition of the Roman Jurisdiction*, 1878-1902; *Mano, a Poetical History*, 1883; *Odes and Eclogues*, 1884; *Lyrical Poems*, 1887; *Songs and Odes*, 1896; *Last Poems*, 1905.

WILLIAM ERNEST HENLEY, p. 791

STANDARD EDITIONS

Works, 7 vols., London, Nutt, 1908
Works, 5 vols., London, Macmillan, 1921
Poems, New York, Scribner, 1928
Plays, written in col. w. Robert Louis Stevenson, London, Macmillan, 1921

BIOGRAPHY

Cornford, L.C., *William Ernest Henley*, London, Constable, 1913
Low, S., "Memories and Impressions of Henley," *Living Age*, 1903, 239:150-158
Robertson, J.H. (J. Connell, pseud.), *W. E. Henley*, New York, Macmillan, 1949
Stephen, H., "William Ernest Henley as a Contemporary and an Editor," *Mercury*, 1926, 13:387-400

Williamson, K., *W. E. Henley, a Memoir*, London, Shaylor, 1930

CRITICISM

Buckley, J.H., *William Ernest Henley; a Study in the Counter-decadence of the 'Nineties*, Princeton, N.J., Princeton Univ. Press, 1945

Drinkwater, J., "William Ernest Henley," *The Muse in Council*, Boston, Houghton, 1925

Hind, C.L., "W. E. Henley," *Authors and I*, New York, Lane, 1921

Neff, M., "The Place of Henley," *North American Review*, 1920, 211:555-563

Nichols, W.B., "The Influence of Henley," *Living Age*, 1921, 310:88-92

Noyes, A., "The Poetry of W. E. Henley," *Some Aspects of Modern Poetry*, London, Hodder, 1924

Parker, Gilbert, " 'The New Poetry' and Mr. W. E. Henley," *Lippincott's Magazine*, 1893, 52:109-116

Shanks, E., "W. E. Henley," *First Essays on Literature*, London, Collins, 1923

Squire, J.C., "Henley," *Books Reviewed*, New York, Doran, 1922

Symons, A., "Modernity in Verse," *Studies in Two Literatures*, London, Secker, Martin, 1924

Symons, A., "Some Makers of Modern Verse," *Forum*, 1921, 66:476-488

Thompson, F., "William Ernest Henley," *A Renegade Poet, and Other Essays*, Boston, Ball, 1910

Watson, H.B.M., "Living Critics: W. E. Henley," *Bookman*, 1895, 2:186-188

Yeats, W.B., *Autobiography*, New York, Macmillan, 1938

BIOGRAPHICAL SKETCH

William Ernest Henley (1849-1903), whose admiration for heroism is one of the dominant motives of his thought and poetry, was himself the hero of a lifelong contest against physical handicaps. After an elementary education at the Crypt Grammar School at Gloucester, where the Manx poet T. E. Brown gave his literary ambitions a great impetus, he contracted a tubercular disease which necessitated the amputation of a foot. When his doctors later advised the amputation of the other foot, he journeyed in 1873 to Edinburgh, placed himself under the care of Dr. Joseph Lister, the discoverer of antiseptic surgery, and was restored to at least partial health. During his twenty-month confinement in the Edinburgh Infirmary, he recorded his impressions in his *In Hospital*, reflected his defiantly courageous mood in his *Invictus*, and began a long friendship with Robert Louis Stevenson, who came on several occasions to talk at his bedside. Discharged from the hospital, Henley, after a term of hack writing in Edinburgh, in 1877 settled in London, writing essays and reviews for periodicals and collaborating with Stevenson on a series of plays. He worked his way up to the editorship, successively, of three important journals. As editor he was on terms of hearty friendship with his contributors, among whom were Kipling, Brown, Lang, Yeats, and, until an unfortunate disagreement, Stevenson; he championed new movements in literature and art, the painting of Whistler, the sculpture of Rodin, and the poetry of Blunt and Hardy; he joined with Kipling in advocating English imperialism in opposition to the pacific policies of Gladstone and in vehemently supporting the Boer War. In his poetry, composed in the intervals of his editorial work, he departed from traditional principles and wrote independently with a joyous acceptance of life as it is. Powerful in frame, crippled but indomitable, with his leonine head and keen blue eyes, he was not unlike Stevenson's portraits of him as John Silver in *Treasure Island* and Burly in *Talk and Talkers;* with his forceful conversation and trenchant criticism, he dominated his group in London and exerted a wide influence on the new literature of "romantic realism."

Henley's principal publications were: *Deacon Brodie* (with R. L. Stevenson), 1880; *Beau Austin, Admiral Guinea* (with R. L. Stevenson), 1884; *Macaire* (with R. L. Stevenson), 1885; *A Book of Verses*, 1888; *Views and Reviews*, 1890; *The Song of the Sword and Other Verses*, 1892; *For England's Sake*, 1900; *Hawthorne and Lavender*, 1901; *A Song of Speed*, 1903.

INTRODUCTORY CRITICISM

"Mr. Henley, of all the poets of the day, is the most strenuously certain that life is worth living, the most eagerly defiant of fate, the most heroically content with death. There is, indeed, something of the spirit of Walt Whitman in his passion for living. . . . His special 'note,' in the earlier work particularly, is a manly Bohemianism, a refreshingly reckless joy in the happy accidents of existence. . . . His outlook on life is joyous, in spite of misfortune; his outlook on destiny and death is grave, collected, welcoming. . . . Revolutionary always, Mr. Henley has had a wholesome but perilous discontent with the conventions of language and of verse. . . . What Mr. Henley has brought into the language of poetry is a certain freshness, a daring straightforwardness and pungency of epithet, very refreshing in contrast with the traditional limpidness and timidity of the respectable verse of the day. One feels at times that the touch is a little rough, the voice a trifle loud, the new word just a little unnecessary. But with these unaccustomed words and tones Mr. Henley does certainly succeed in flashing the picture, the impression upon us, in realizing the intangible, in saying new things in a new and fascinating manner."—Arthur Symons, *Fortnightly Review*, August 1892, pp. 183 ff.

ANDREW LANG, p. 805

STANDARD EDITIONS

Poetical Works, 4 vols., ed. by Mrs. Lang, London, Longmans, 1923
Andrew Lang, poems, London, Benn, 1926

BIOGRAPHY AND CRITICISM

Beerbohm, M., "Two Glimpses of Andrew Lang," *Life and Letters*, 1928, 1:1-11
Chislett, W., Jr., "Andrew Lang, Scholar-Critic," *Moderns and Near Moderns*, New York, Grafton, 1928
Gordon, G.S., *Andrew Lang*, a lecture, Dec. 1, 1927, London, Oxford Univ. Press, 1928
Gosse, E., "Andrew Lang," *Silhouettes*, London, Heinemann, 1925
Green, R.L., *Andrew Lang; a Critical Biography*, Toronto, Nelson, 1946
Hutchinson, H.G., "Andrew Lang's Poetry," *Edinburgh Review*, 1923, 238:270-286
Jacobs, J., "Andrew Lang as Man of Letters and Folk-Lorist," *Journal of American Folk-Lore*, 1913, 26:367-372
Murray, G., *Andrew Lang the Poet*, London, Oxford Univ. Press, 1948
Ormerod, J., *The Poetry of Andrew Lang*, Derby, England, Derby Corp., 1943
Quarterly Review, "Andrew Lang; a Symposium," 1913, 218:299-329
Repplier, Agnes, "Andrew Lang," *Catholic World*, 1912, 96:289-297
Saintsbury, G., "Andrew Lang in the Seventies—and After," *The Eighteen-Seventies*, ed. by H. Granville-Barker, London, Cambridge Univ. Press, 1929
Saintsbury, G., "Poems of Andrew Lang," *Quarterly Review*, 1923, 240:262-275
Webster, A.B., *Andrew Lang's Poetry*, New York, Oxford Univ. Press, 1937

BIOGRAPHICAL SKETCH

Andrew Lang (1844-1912), like Robert Louis Stevenson, whom he much resembled in physical appearance, grew up in the Border country of Scotland. Many of the themes of his prose and verse have their origin in his boyhood interests—in fishing along the Teviot and the Tweed, in the Border ballads and folk legends, in the lost cause of the Stuarts, in Sir Walter Scott, who had been his father's friend. From the Edinburgh Academy, where he was converted by Homer to a liking for Greek, he went to Oxford, where he was much influenced by Matthew Arnold, then a lecturer on poetry, as well as by the Pre-Raphaelites. Morris's example guided his reading into early French literature; he published in 1872 his first poetry, *Ballads and Lyrics of Old France*. His *Ballades in Blue China*, eight years later, was a further fruit of such studies and much encouraged the revival, inaugurated by Swinburne and Banville, of the old French lyric forms. Meanwhile, too restless for the academic life, he had traveled abroad, married, and begun in London and Scotland a vigorous literary career. He turned his mind and pen in an astonishing variety of directions. After writing for the *Encyclopædia Britannica* articles which ranged from "Crystal-gazing" to "Prometheus," he began with his *Custom and Myth* in 1884 a series of studies in folklore; with his translations of Homer and his *Homer and the Epic* in 1893, his researches in Greek literature; with his *Prince Edward Stuart* in 1900, his books on Scottish history; he wrote also abundant biographies and criticisms, lectured on history at St. Andrews, collected fairy tales for children in "Books, Yellow, Red, and Green, and Blue," expressed himself on all subjects except personal religion and party politics, and yet found time for cricket and fishing. His verse, much of which was written during the intervals of cricket matches, concerns his favorite places and heroes, Scottish and Greek, and has the broad background natural to a man who has been called "the greatest bookman of his age."

Lang's principal publications were: *Ballads and Lyrics of Old France*, 1872; *Odyssey* (trans., with S. H. Butcher), 1879; *Ballades in Blue China*, 1880-1881; *Helen of Troy*, 1882; *Iliad* (trans., with W. Leaf and E. Myers), 1883; *Rhymes à la Mode*, 1884; *Custom and Myth*, 1884; *The Mark of Cain*, 1886; *Letters to Dead Authors*, 1886; *Books and Bookmen*, 1886; *Myth, Ritual, and Religion*, 1887; *Grass of Parnassus*, 1888; *Angling Sketches*, 1891; *Essays in Little*, 1891; *Letters on Literature*, 1893; *Homer and the Epic*, 1893; *Ban and Arrière Ban*, 1894; *Life of Lockhart*, 1896; *Modern Mythology*, 1897; *The Making of Religion*, 1898; *Prince Charles Edward*, 1900; *History of Scotland*, 1900-1907; *The Mystery of Mary Stuart*, 1901; *John Knox and the Reformation*, 1905; *Adventures among Books*, 1905; *Homer and His Age,* 1906; *The Maid of France,* 1908; *The World of Homer,* 1910; *Shakespeare, Bacon, and the Great Unknown,* 1912; *History of English Literature,* 1912.

INTRODUCTORY CRITICISM

"Mr. Lang's is not the sentiment that may be bawled from the roof-tops: it is the sentiment of old romance, of dim memories, all the more beautiful for their vagueness (as the reflection is often more beautiful than the mirrored object), the sentiment of wet spring woods and birds singing in the early dawn. . . . Somewhat in the vein of Thackeray are his lighter pieces: there is much the same spirit of half-humorous, half-sad, but wholly manly, acceptance of the losses and regrets that must inevitably be the shadow cast by life, much the same tenderness toward youth and laughter."—G. R. Tomson, *Academy,* June 2, 1894, p. 451.

See Stevenson's *To Andrew Lang,* p. 815.

ALICE CHRISTIANA MEYNELL, p. 808

STANDARD EDITIONS

Prose and Poetry, centenary vol., ed. by F. Page and others, w. a biog. and crit. intro. by V. Sackville-West, London, Cape, 1947
The Poems, ed. by Frederick Page, Oxford Standard Authors, New York, Oxford Univ. Press, 1940
Poems, ed. by Sir Francis Meynell, London, Hollis & Carter, 1948
Last Poems, London, Burns, 1923
Alice Meynell, poems, London, Benn, 1926
Essays, New York, Scribner, 1914; London, Harrap, 1923
Hearts of Controversy, London, Burns, 1918

BIOGRAPHY AND CRITICISM

Archer, W., "Mrs. Meynell," *Poets of the Younger Generation,* London, Lane, 1902
Brégy, K., "Mrs. Meynell: an Appreciation," *Catholic World,* 1911, 92:494-504
Burdett, O., "The Poems of Alice Meynell," *Critical Essays,* London, Faber, 1925
Chesterton, G.K., "Alice Meynell," *Dublin Review,* 1923, 172:1-12
Connolly, T.L., ed., *Alice Meynell Centenary Tribute, 1847-1947,* Boston, Humphries, 1948
Drinkwater, J., "Alice Meynell," *The Muse in Council,* Boston, Houghton, 1925
Eldridge, R., "The Poetry of Alice Meynell," *Catholic World,* 1922, 116:150-160
Hind, C.L., "Alice Meynell," *Authors and I,* New York, Lane, 1921

Letters of George Meredith to Alice Meynell, London, Nonesuch Press, 1923
Marks, J., "The Multitude: an Appreciation of Alice Meynell," *North American Review,* 1923, 217:365-373
Maynard, T., "Alice Meynell," *Our Best Poets,* New York, Brentano's, 1924
Meynell, Viola, *Alice Meynell; a Memoir,* reissue, London, Cape, 1947
Monroe, H., "Of Two Poets," *Poetry,* 1923, 21:262-267
Noyes, A., "Alice Meynell," *Some Aspects of Modern Poetry,* London, Hodder, 1924
Patmore, C., "Mrs. Meynell, Poet and Essayist," *Fortnightly Review,* 1892, 58:761-776
Repplier, Agnes, "Alice Meynell," *Catholic World,* 1923, 116:721-730
Scott, D., "The Art of Mrs. Meynell," *Men of Letters,* London, Hodder, 1923
Shuster, G.N., "Inheritors," *The Catholic Spirit in Modern English Literature,* New York, Macmillan, 1922
Squire, J.C., "Alice Meynell," *London Mercury,* 1923, 7:285-295
Tuell, Anne K., *Mrs. Meynell and Her Literary Generation,* New York, Dutton, 1925
Tynan, Katharine, "Mrs. Meynell and Her Poetry," *Catholic World,* 1913, 97:668-678

BIOGRAPHICAL SKETCH

Alice Christiana Thompson (1847-1922) grew up in a delightfully artistic and untidy household in Italy, where her mother painted sunsets and her father, a dilettante in many fields, devoted himself to his children's education. While still young, she became a Roman Catholic, and other members of the family followed her. The example of Christina Rossetti and Mrs. Browning set her to writing poetry in her early girlhood; her *Preludes,* published in 1875, won the praise of the greatest literary figures of the time: Rossetti, George Eliot, Ruskin, and Browning. Like Elizabeth Barrett, she attracted her future husband first of all by her poems; Wilfrid Meynell, then a promising young writer of reviews in London, read her sonnets and sought an introduction; after a short engagement, they were married in 1877. For many years Mrs. Meynell wrote little poetry. In the intervals of bearing eight children, she attached herself passionately to humanitarian causes: the prevention of cruelty to animals, the amelioration of conditions in London slums, the extension of political suffrage and industrial rights to women. One of her many acts of kindness for which the world loved her was her rescue of Francis Thompson from poverty and the opium habit and her wise care of him in later years. Encouraged by the hearty interest of W. E. Henley, she began writing reviews and essays in prose; she contributed a weekly column to the *Pall Mall Gazette* and published in magazines her sensitive essays, the earliest of which she collected and published under the titles of *The Rhythm of Life* (1893), *The Color of Life* (1896), and *The Spirit of Place* (1899). Her life was rounded out by a final poetic period, beginning with the World War and ending with her *Last Poems* in 1923. Mrs. Meynell's life was enriched with many interesting friendships; Patmore and Meredith both owed much to her helpful spirit.

Mrs. Meynell's principal publications were: *Preludes*, 1875; *Poems*, a reprint, with additions, of *Preludes*, 1893; *The Rhythm of Life*, 1893; *The Color of Life*, 1896; *London Impressions*, 1898; *The Spirit of Place*, 1899; *John Ruskin*, 1900; *Ceres' Runaway*, 1909; *A Father of Women*, 1917; *Hearts of Controversy*, 1917; *The Second Person Singular, and Other Essays*, 1921; *Last Poems*, 1923.

INTRODUCTORY CRITICISM

"The motives of her [Mrs. Meynell's] poems are neither obvious nor far-fetched; they never quite lack the charm of things familiar, and yet they always possess the charm of things that are new, not with the novelty of inherent strangeness, but with the finer, rarer novelty of strongly individualized apprehension and presentation. In her landscape the poet sees what we ourselves have seen, but sees it with a difference that at once recalls and supplements our own remembrance; in her moods of emotion or reflection she feels and thinks as we may have thought or felt, and yet by the imaginative individuality of the thinking or feeling gives to the utterance of it a certain uniqueness which touches us to delightful surprise."—J. A. Noble, *The Poets and the Poetry of the Century*, ed. by A. H. Miles, Vol. 8, p. 422.

ROBERT LOUIS STEVENSON, p. 810

STANDARD EDITIONS

Works, 35 vols., London, Heinemann, 1924
Works, 32 vols., New York, Scribner, 1925
Complete Poems, New York, Scribner, 1923
Collected Poems, ed. w. an intro. and notes by J.A. Smith, London, Hart-Davis, 1948
R. L. S., an Omnibus, sel. and ed. by G.B. Stern, London, Cassell, 1950
Selected Writings, ed. by S. Commins, New York, Modern Lib., 1950
Letters, 5 vols., ed. by S. Colvin, London, Heinemann, 1924

BIOGRAPHY

Aldington, Richard, *Portrait of a Rebel: The Life and Work of Robert Louis Stevenson*, London, Evans, 1957

Balfour, G., *The Life of Robert Louis Stevenson*, New York, Scribner, 1915

Bermann, R.A., *Home from the Sea*, Indianapolis, Bobbs, 1939

Carré, Jean Marie, *La Vie de Robert Louis Stevenson*, Paris, Gallimard, 1929

Colvin, S., "Robert Louis Stevenson," *Memories and Notes of Persons and Places* New York, Scribner, 1921

Cornford, L.C., *Robert Louis Stevenson*, New York, Dodd, 1900

Cunningham, Alison, *Cummy's Diary*, London, Chatto, 1926

Dalglish, D.N., *Presbyterian Pirate; a Portrait of Stevenson*, New York, Oxford Univ. Press, 1937

Dark, S., *Robert Louis Stevenson*, London, Hodder, 1931

Elwin, M., *The Strange Case of Robert Louis Stevenson*, London, Macdonald & Co., 1950

Fisher, A.B., *No More a Stranger*, Stanford, Calif., Stanford Univ. Press, 1946

Furnas, J.C., *Voyage to Windward; the Life of Robert Louis Stevenson*, New York, Sloane, 1951

Hellman, G.S., *The True Stevenson*, Boston, Little, 1925

Hinkley, L.L., *The Stevensons: Louis and Fanny*, New York, Hastings House, 1950

Issler, A.R., *Our Mountain Hermitage; Silverado and Robert Louis Stevenson*, Stanford, Calif., Stanford Univ. Press, 1950

McGaw, Sister, *Stevenson in Hawaii*, Honolulu, Univ. of Hawaii Press, 1950

McLaren, M.D.S., *Stevenson and Edinburgh*, London, Chapman, 1950

Masson, Rosaline O., *The Life of Robert Louis Stevenson*, Edinburgh, Chambers, 1924

Moors, H.J., *With Stevenson in Samoa*, Boston, Small, 1910

Morris, D.B., *Robert Louis Stevenson and the Scottish Highlanders*, Stirling, Scotland, Mackay, 1929

Osbourne, K.D., *Robert Louis Stevenson in California*, Chicago, McClurg, 1911

Osbourne, L., *An Intimate Portrait of R. L. S.*, New York, Scribner, 1924

Simpson, Evelyn B., *Robert Louis Stevenson's Edinburgh Days*, London, Hodder, 1898

Smith, Janet A., ed., *Henry James and Robert Louis Stevenson*, New York, Macmillan, 1949

Smith, Janet A., *R. L. Stevenson*, London, Duckworth, 1937

Steuart, J.A., *Robert Louis Stevenson; a Critical Biography*, 2 vols., London, Low, 1926

Stevenson, Mrs. Fanny, *The Cruise of the "Janet Nicol" among the South Sea Islands; a Diary*, New York, Scribner, 1914

CRITICISM

Beinecke, E.J., *Stevenson Library*, 3 vols., New Haven, Conn., Yale Univ. Lib., 1951

Chesterton, G.K., *Robert Louis Stevenson*, New York, Dodd, 1928

Colvin, S., E. Gosse, Neil Munro, and others, *Robert Louis Stevenson*, London, Hodder, 1924

Cooper, L.U., *Robert Louis Stevenson*, Denver, Swallow, 1948

Cowell, H.J., *Robert Louis Stevenson*, London, Epworth, 1945

Daiches, D., *Robert Louis Stevenson*, Norfolk, Conn., New Directions, 1947

Dawson, W.J., "The Religion of Robert Louis Stevenson," *Bookman*, 1910, 32:89-93

Fergusson, A.S., "Stevenson the Dreamer," *Queen's Quarterly*, 1922, 30:26-36

Garrod, H.W., "The Poetry of R. L. Stevenson," *The Profession of Poetry, and Other Lectures*, Oxford, Clarendon Press, 1929

Gwynn, S., "Mr. Robert Louis Stevenson: a Critical Study," *Fortnightly Review*, 1894, 62:776-792

Hammerton, J.A., ed., *Stevensoniana*, London, Richards, 1903

Henley, W.E., "R. L. S.," *Pall Mall Magazine*, 1901, 25:505-514

James, H., "Robert Louis Stevenson," *Partial Portraits*, London, Macmillan, 1888

Jessop, A., "The Poetry of Stevenson," *Poet Lore*, 1907, 18:396-401

Kiely, Robert, *Robert Louis Stevenson and the Fiction of Adventure*, Cambridge, Harvard Univ. Press, 1964

Nicoll, W.R., and G.K. Chesterton, *Robert Louis Stevenson*, London, Hodder, 1906

Noyes, A., "Stevenson," *Some Aspects of Modern Poetry*, London, Hodder, 1924

Pinero, A.W., *Robert Louis Stevenson as a Dramatist*, w. an intro. by C. Hamilton, New York, Dramatic Museum of Columbia Univ., 1914

Prideaux, W.F., *A Bibliography of the Works of Robert Louis Stevenson*, London, Hollings, 1917

Rice, R.A., *Robert Louis Stevenson; How to Know Him*, Indianapolis, Bobbs, 1916

Saintsbury, G., "Stevenson and the Problem of Style," *Times Literary Supplement*, Jan. 20, 1921

Slater, J.H., *Robert Louis Stevenson; a Bibliography of His Complete Works*, London, Bell, 1914

Starrett, V., ed., *In Praise of Stevenson; an Anthology*, Chicago, Bookfellows, 1919

Stephen, L., "The Style and Genius of Stevenson," *Studies of a Biographer*, 4 vols., New York, Putnam, 1907

Swinnerton, Frank, *R. L. Stevenson; a Critical Study*, New York, Doran, 1923

Symons, A., "Robert Louis Stevenson," *Studies in Prose and Verse*, London, Dent, 1904

Woolf, L., "The Fall of Stevenson," *London Nation and Athenaeum*, 1924, 34:517; 35:86

BIOGRAPHICAL SKETCH

Robert Louis Stevenson (1850-1894), born in Edinburgh, was an invalid from his earliest youth to the end of life and yet contrived to live abundantly. He was kept alive in his boyhood chiefly through the diligence of his nurse, Alison Cunningham, whom he called "Cummy." He could attend school only for short periods and yet absorbed from various sources a wide knowledge of men and books. From his father and grandfather, both engineers and builders of lighthouses along the rugged Scottish coast, Stevenson learned to love the sea air and the vigorous hardships of an out-of-door life. He at first intended to adopt the family profession, made inspection trips with his father to lighthouses, and studied engineering at the University of Edinburgh; but his interests became gradually centered in literature. He posed as an idler, took pleasure in the Bohemian society of Edinburgh, and acted the gay vagabond; yet he was in reality, in the intervals of illness, continually practicing the art of writing and making himself the master of a highly individual prose style. He contributed to journals, in the years following 1876, a series of essays later collected as *Virginibus Puerisque* (1881) and *Familiar Studies of Men and Books* (1882), and such stories as *A Lodging for the Night* and *The Sire de Malétroit's Door*. For health and adventure he went alone or with friends on many gypsy wanderings: in a sailboat through the Western Islands, in a canoe along the rivers of Belgium and France, and with a donkey in the mountains of southern France. Returning, he wrote *An Inland Voyage* (1878), *Travels with a Donkey* (1879), and other travel sketches. In France he met Mrs. Fanny Osbourne, fell in love with her, and in 1879 followed her to California, where a dangerous lung attack would have ended his life had it not been for her careful nursing. In 1880 they were married, but tuberculosis had taken so strong a hold on him that he could only defer the end by will power and by a restless search for a healthful climate. For a time he lived near John Addington

Symonds at Davos in the Swiss Alps and there spun out of an imagination that had always a sympathy with the child mind the tale that brought him fame, *Treasure Island* (1882). In southern France, at Bournemouth on the English coast, in the Adirondacks of New York, Stevenson successively sought health and continued his writing. At his house of Skerryvore at Westbourne he wrote *A Child's Garden of Verses* (1885), another volume of poetry, *Underwoods* (1887), and collaborated with W. E. Henley in the writing of four plays. From California in 1888 he departed on his last quest for health, a leisurely voyage in the schooner *Casco* among the islands of the Pacific, writing his novels, his tales, and his *Ballads* (1890) under a tropic sun. At length, delighted by the scenery and the primitive native life, he settled in Samoa on his mountainside plantation of Vailima; there he enjoyed a temporary return of health, ruled his natives like a beneficent feudal lord, and wrote with an energy born of a realization that the end must soon come. It came in 1894, sudden and painless. By his wish, he was buried on a mountain peak overlooking the sea.

One of the most conspicuous qualities of Stevenson was his versatility. He was the foremost essayist since Lamb, a master of fiction in two fields (romance and the short story), a dramatist, and a poet. He was animated by a genuine enthusiasm for literature as a fine art. A great ethical purpose underlay most of his work. Regarding romance as a necessary element in life, he revived the romantic novel, in which he exalted fine conduct based upon a thoughtful sense of duty. His was a gospel of the joy of life, and his heroic acceptance of the wholesomeness of human effort without any idea of gain permeated his thought and action.

Stevenson's principal publications were: *An Inland Voyage*, 1878; *Travels with a Donkey*, 1879; *Virginibus Puerisque*, 1881; *Familiar Studies of Men and Books*, 1882; *New Arabian Nights*, 1882; *Treasure Island*, 1882; *Silverado Squatters*, 1883; *Prince Otto*, 1885; *A Child's Garden of Verses*, 1885; *More New Arabian Nights, The Dynamiter*, 1885; *The Strange Case of Dr. Jekyll and Mr. Hyde*, 1886; *Kidnapped*, 1886; *The Merry Men*, 1886; *Underwoods*, 1887; *Memories and Portraits*, 1887; *The Black Arrow*, 1888; *The Wrong Box* (with L. Osbourne), 1889; *The Master of Ballantrae*, 1889; *Father Damien*, 1890; *Ballads*, 1890; *Across the Plains*, 1892; *The Wrecker* (with L. Osbourne), 1892; *Island Nights' Entertainments*, 1893; *Catriona* (David Balfour), 1893; *The Ebb Tide* (with L. Osbourne), 1894; *Vailima Letters*, 1895; *Weir of Hermiston*, 1896; *Songs of Travel*, 1896; *St. Ives* (completed by A. T. Quiller-Couch), 1897.

INTRODUCTORY CRITICISM

"The first thing which struck the reader of *A Child's Garden* was the extraordinary clearness and precision with which the immature fancies of eager childhood were reproduced in it.... It gives us a unique thing, a transcript of that child-mind which we have all possessed and enjoyed, but of which no one, except Mr. Stevenson, seems to have carried away a photograph.... Many authors have achieved brilliant success in describing children, in verbally caressing them, in amusing, in instructing them; but only two, Mrs. Ewing in prose, and Mr. Stevenson in verse, have sat down with them without disturbing their fancies, and have looked into the world of 'make-believe' with the children's own eyes.

"In ... a second volume, this time of grown-up verses, Mr. Stevenson has ventured on a bolder experiment. His *Underwoods*, with its title openly borrowed from Ben Jonson, ... is plainly the work of the same fancy that described the Country of Counterpane and the Land of Storybooks, but it has grown a little sadder and a great deal older. There is the same delicate sincerity, the same candor and simplicity, the same artless dependence on the good faith of the public.... The book is occupied with friendship, with nature, with the honorable instincts of man's moral machinery. Above all, it enters with great minuteness, and in a very confidential spirit, into the theories and moods of the writer himself. It will be to many readers a revelation of the everyday life of an author whose impersonal writings have given them so much and so varied pleasure. ... The same characteristics are displayed in the poems, the same suspicion of 'the abhorred pedantic sanhedrin,' the same fulness of life, the same bright felicity of epithet as in the essays and romances."—E. Gosse, *Questions at Issue*, pp. 241 ff.

OSCAR WILDE, p. 818

STANDARD EDITIONS

Writings, 15 vols., London, Keller, 1907
Works of Oscar Wilde, New York, Dutton, 1954
Complete Works, 10 vols., ed. by R. Ross, New York, Bigelow, 1921
Complete Works, 12 vols., w. an intro. by R. Le Gallienne, New York, Wise, 1927
The Portable Oscar Wilde, sel. and ed. by R. Aldington, New York, Viking, 1946
Poetical Works, w. a biog. intro. by N.H. Dole, New York, Crowell, 1913
De Profundis, ed. by V. Holland, New York, Philosophical Lib., 1950

The Letters of Oscar Wilde, ed. by R. Hart-Davis, London, Hart-Davis, 1962

BIOGRAPHY

Brasol, B.L., *Oscar Wilde, the Man, the Artist, the Martyr*, New York, Scribner, 1938

Bremont, Countess Anna, de, *Oscar Wilde and His Mother*, London, Everett, 1914

Broad, C.L., *The Friendship and Follies of Oscar Wilde*, New York, Crowell, 1955

Davray, H.D., "Oscar Wilde et la Vie de Prison en Angleterre," *Mercure de France*, 1926, 191:313-335

Douglas, Lord A.B., *Oscar Wilde, a Summing Up*, 2d ed., London, Richards Press, 1950

Douglas, Lord A.B., *Oscar Wilde and Myself*, New York, Duffield, 1914

Douglas, Lord A.B., *Without Apology*, London, Secker, Martin, 1938

Gide, A., *Oscar Wilde*, tr. from the French by B. Freditman, London, Kimber, 1951

Harris, Frank, *Oscar Wilde; His Life and Confessions*, 2 vols., London, Pearson, 1920

Holland, Vyvyan, *Oscar Wilde, a Pictorial Biography*, London, Thames and Hudson, 1960

Holland, Vyvyan, *Son of Oscar Wilde*, New York, Dutton, 1954

Hyde, H. Montgomery, *Oscar Wilde: The Aftermath*, London, Methuen, 1963

Kernahan, C., *In Good Company*, London, Lane, 1917

O'Sullivan, V., *Aspects of Wilde*, New York, Holt, 1936

Pearson, H., *The Life of Oscar Wilde*, 5th ed., London, Methuen, 1951

Renier, G.J., *Oscar Wilde*, New York, Appleton, 1933

Sherard, R.H., *The Life of Oscar Wilde*, w. a bibliog., New York, Dodd, 1928

Wilson, T.G., *Victorian Doctor; Being the Life of Sir William Wilde*, New York, Fischer, 1946

Winwar, F., *Oscar Wilde and the Yellow 'Nineties*, New York, Harper, 1940

Wyndham, H., *Speranza: a Biography of Lady Wilde*, New York, Philosophical Lib., 1952

CRITICISM

Agate, J.E., *Oscar Wilde and the Theatre*, London, Curtain Press, 1947

Davray, H.D., "L'Histoire de la Ballade de la Geôle de Reading," *Mercure de France*, 1927, 195:68-101

Dial, "The Poetry of an Aesthete," 1881, 2:82-85

Ervine, St. John G., *Oscar Wilde*, London, Allen, G., 1951

Fehr, B., *Studien zu Oscar Wildes Gedichten*, Berlin, Mayer, 1922

Glaenzer, R.B., "The Story of the *Ballad of Reading Gaol*," *Bookman*, 1911, 33:376-381

Hughes, M.Y. "The Immortal Wilde," *University of California Chronicle*, 1928, 30:305-324

Hutchinson, H.G., "The 'Aesthetes,' and Oscar Wilde," *Portraits of the Eighties*, London, Unwin, 1920

Jackson, H., "Oscar Wilde: the Last Phase," *The Eighteen Nineties*, New York, Knopf, 1922

Le Gallienne, R., "Oscar Wilde," *Touchstone*, 1918, 4:212-221

Le Roy, G.C., "Oscar Wilde," *Perplexed Prophets*, Philadelphia, Univ. of Pa. Press, 1953

Lynd, R., "Oscar Wilde," *The Art of Letters*, London, Unwin, 1920

Mainsard, J., "L'Esthétisme de Walter Pater et d'Oscar Wilde," *Études*, 1928, 525-552

Mason, S., *Bibliography of Oscar Wilde*, London, Laurie, 1914

Maurois, A., *Études Anglaises—Dickens, Walpole, Ruskin, et Wilde*, Grasset, Paris, 1927

Millard, C.S., *Bibliography of Oscar Wilde*, London, Richards, 1907

More, P.E., "Decadent Wit," *With the Wits*, Boston, Houghton, 1919

Powys, J.C., "Oscar Wilde," *Suspended Judgments*, New York, Shaw, 1916

Ransome, A., *Oscar Wilde, a Critical Study*, London, Secker, Martin, 1912

Richter, Helene, "Oscar Wilde's Persönlichkeit in Seinen Gedichten," *Englische Studien*, 1920, 54:201-276

Roditi, E., *Oscar Wilde*, Norfolk, Conn., New Directions, 1947

Rudwin, M., "Oscar Wilde et Barbey d'Aurévilly," *Revue Anglo-Américaine*, 1927, p. 340

Scott-James, R.A., "The Decadents," *Modernism and Romance*, London, Lane, 1908

Shanks, E., "Oscar Wilde," *Second Essays on Literature*, London, Collins, 1927

Symons, A., "An Artist in Attitudes: Oscar Wilde," *Studies in Prose and Verse*, London, Dent, 1904

Woodbridge, H.E., "Oscar Wilde as a Poet," *Poet Lore*, Winter 1908, 19:439-457

Woodcock, G., *The Paradox of Oscar Wilde*, New York, Macmillan, 1950

Yeats, W.B., *Autobiography*, New York, Macmillan, 1938

BIOGRAPHICAL SKETCH

Oscar Fingall O'Flahertie Wills Wilde (1854-1900), wit and aesthete, was born in Dublin of a father who loved many women and a mother who loved clever talk. Precocious and brilliant, he won a gold medal at Dublin for an essay on the Greek comic poets; before he left Oxford in 1878, his wit, his aestheticism, his eccentricities were already widely known. Preaching loudly the doctrine of "art for art's sake," averring that "all good art is useless," affecting long hair, a velvet coat, a sunflower, and an air of elegant indolence, filling his rooms with peacock plumes and blue china, he exaggerated the tendencies that the Pre-Raphaelites had set going, and drew after him a host of young admirers. After leaving Oxford, still bent on astounding the middle classes, he curled his hair in imitation of the emperor Nero and indulged his passion for effete beauty by wearing delicately tinted gloves and a green carnation. His poetry, of which he published a volume in 1881, he threw off with careless grace. "I have given my genius to my life," he said; "to my work only my talent." His notoriety was now enhanced by Gilbert's caricature in *Patience*. After a lecture tour in America, during which he sought to convert his audiences from their vulgar taste for ornamented stoves and scrollwork, he wrote a series of sophisticated tales ostensibly for children, and his *Picture of Dorian Gray* (1891), which with its subtle undercurrent of suggestion has been called "the only French novel written in England." Affirming that "industry is the root of all ugliness," Wilde nevertheless worked harder than he cared to admit from 1892 to 1895, producing a series of "trivial comedies for serious people" with plots then thought shocking and dialogue almost unparalleled for cleverness. Wilde was at the height of his vogue, lionized for his wit by dowagers at teas and idolized by the younger Bohemian set not only for his brilliance but also for an essential kindliness that underlay his posing, when his glory suddenly departed. Enraged by aspersions on his character, he sued the Marquis of Queensberry for libel; the suit failed; countercharges were made, and in 1895 Wilde was found guilty of homosexual conduct and sentenced to two years of hard labor. At the jail in Reading he meditated suicide and composed his confessions in a document of forty-five thousand words, the pathetic *De Profundis*, published in part in 1905 and in full forty-five years later. He found few friends left him when he was liberated. Although he wrote in 1898, while recuperating at Berneval in France, his most effective poem, *The Ballad of Reading Gaol*, his degeneration was rapid. No longer the elegant dandy of his happier days, he slouched about Paris with frayed cuffs and soiled collar, drinking himself into sodden insensibility, sitting at his table all night in futile efforts to compose. A short illness ended his life in 1900.

Wilde's principal publications were: *Poems*, 1881; *The Happy Prince and Other Tales*, 1888; *The Picture of Dorian Gray*, 1891; *Intentions*, 1891; *A House of Pomegranates*, 1892; *Lady Windermere's Fan*, 1892; *A Woman of No Importance*, 1893; *Salome* (in French), 1893; *The Sphinx*, 1894; *The Ideal Husband*, 1895; *The Importance of Being Earnest*, 1895; *The Ballad of Reading Gaol*, 1898; *De Profundis*, 1905, 1950.

INTRODUCTORY CRITICISMS

"... *The Ballad of Reading Gaol* ... must be pronounced his best poem. ... It contains few or no rhetorical flourishes; its diction is simple and poignant; ... it is passionately sincere. In reading most of Wilde's poems we cannot rid ourselves of the impression that the poet has a very delicious sense of his own cleverness and his own imaginative wealth, and that he is thinking about these things quite as much as about the subject he happens to be treating. In *The Ballad of Reading Gaol* he is desperately in earnest: the bitterness of his own prison experience is still in his mouth, and his pity for the condemned man is passionately genuine."—H. E. Woodbridge, *Poet Lore*, Winter 1908, pp. 440-453.

"While still an undergraduate at Oxford in the late seventies, he [Wilde] incurred the loathing of honest men by talking of Baudelaire and the beauty of evil. *Poems* (1881), though generally in the English romantic tradition, shows some traces of Baudelaire, especially *Impression du Matin*, one of the few successful poems in the volume. ... 'The Harlot's House,' written during the eighties, combines the macabre, the urban, and the grotesque with a sudden, disconcerting prettiness, more horrible than what preceded it. From this discord comes surprise and with it poetry. Even the bizarre rhymes, which in Wilde commonly occur for their own sake, conspire toward the intended effect. He had captured the externals of Baudelaire, and he was no less successful in 'The Sphinx' (1894)." —William York Tindall, *Forces in Modern British Literature, 1885-1946*, p. 239.

See Douglas's *The Dead Poet*, p. 860.

WILLIAM SHARP ("Fiona Macleod"), p. 831

STANDARD EDITIONS

Writings of "Fiona Macleod," 7 vols., ar. by Mrs. Sharp, New York, Duffield, 1909-1910

Selected Writings, 4 vols., ar. by Mrs. Sharp, New York, Duffield, 1912
Flower o' the Vine, w. an intro. by Mrs. T.A. Janvier, New York, Webster, 1892
Songs and Poems, London, Stock, 1909
Deirdre and the Sons of Usna, Portland, Maine, Mosher, 1903

BIOGRAPHY AND CRITICISM

Balfour, C., "Fiona Macleod and Celtic Legends," *Dublin Review*, 1911, 149:329-340

Chislett, W., Jr., "William Sharp on the Celtic Revival," *Moderns and Near Moderns*, New York, Grafton, 1928

Goddard, E., "The Winged Destiny and Fiona Macleod," *Fortnightly Review*, 1904, 82: 1037-1044

Janvier, C.A., "Fiona Macleod and Her Creator, William Sharp," *North American Review*, 1907, 184:718-732

Kelman, J., "Celtic Revivals of Paganism," *Among Famous Books*, London, Hodder, 1912

King, G.G., "Fiona Macleod," *Modern Language Notes*, 1918, 33:352-356

Le Gallienne, R., "The Mystery of Fiona Macleod," *Forum*, 1911, 45:170-179

More, P.E., "Fiona Macleod," *The Drift of Romanticism*, Boston, Houghton, 1913

Rhys, E., "The New Mysticism," *Fortnightly Review*, 1900, 73:1045-1056

Rhys, E., "William Sharp and Fiona Macleod," *Century Magazine*, 1907, 74:111-117

Rolt-Wheeler, Ethel, "Fiona Macleod, the Woman," *Fortnightly Review*, 1919, 112: 780-790

Sharp, Elizabeth A., *William Sharp (Fiona Macleod)*, 2 vols., w. a bibliog., New York, Duffield, 1912

Yeats, W.B., "The Later Work of Fiona Macleod," *North American Review*, 1902, 175: 473-485

BIOGRAPHICAL SKETCH

William Sharp (1855-1905), who expressed the more mystic side of his personality under the pseudonym of Fiona Macleod, was born in Paisley at the foot of the Scottish Highlands. Even as William Sharp, before the invention of the extraordinary Fiona, there was little that was commonplace about his career. Restless under discipline, he ran away three times from school, attempted to stow away on an ocean vessel, browsed in the library of the University of Glasgow in preference to attending classes, and after his graduation, spent two months with a band of gypsies. Still vagrant, he used a threatened attack of consumption as the excuse for a voyage to Australia; on his return, he lost several positions in London, fell in with Rossetti and his circle, studied art in Rome, made journeys to America, Germany, and North Africa, married his cousin, and learned to earn a livelihood by his pen. His earliest poems, including *Earth's Voices* (1884), *Romantic Ballads* (1888), and *Sospiri di Roma* (1891), dealt with "Mother Nature and her inner mysteries" and earned him a considerable reputation as a poet of the Swinburne school. In 1890, however, he developed a new sort of romanticism. The Celtic ballads and legends which he had learned from his Highland nurse in boyhood and from other Highlanders in later visits began to haunt his mind until he became at times a seer who saw in trances and in fervent inner vision another world of transcendent beauty. Encouraged by an Italian lady who sympathized with these strange moods and put him "in touch with ancestral memories," he began to describe his visions in prose and verse, and signed these new writings with the name of a Highland girl he once had known, Fiona Macleod. *Pharais, a Romance of the Isles*, in 1894, was the first volume so produced and was succeeded by a series that created for the mythical Fiona a reputation quite independent of that which William Sharp had previously gained. At the same time he wrote other volumes of verse, fiction, and essays in his old manner over his true name. This amazing duality Sharp continued for the rest of his life; his connection with the "Fiona" literature was unsuspected; indeed the volume of *Who's Who* for 1906, the last one that contained Sharp's biography, had also an account of Fiona Macleod's career, in which her diversions were described as "sailing, hillwalks, and listening." In his more ordinary life, at his editorial desk or in his study, he was William Sharp; in the hills with the sweep of the wind fresh against his face and in his dreams and trances, he was Fiona. This "continued play of two faces" in his personality, added to the strain of upholding two separate literary reputations, broke down his health; after some years of restless wandering, he died in Italy. He left a letter in which his connection with Fiona Macleod and the adoption of her name were explained.

William Sharp's principal publications were: *Life of Rossetti*, 1882; *The Human Inheritance*, 1882; *Earth's Voices*, 1884; *Romantic Ballads and Poems of Phantasy*, 1888; *Sospiri di Roma*, 1891; *Vistas*, 1894; *The Gypsy Christ*, 1895; *Ecce Puella*, 1896; *Wives in Exile*, 1896; *Silence Farm*, 1899; *The Progress of Art in the Century*, 1902; *Literary Geography*, 1904; *Essays*, two vols., 1912.

Fiona Macleod's principal publications were: *Pharais*, 1894; *The Mountain Lovers*, 1895; *The Washer of the Ford*, 1896; *Green Fire*, 1896; *From the Hills of Dream*, 1896; *The Laughter of Peterkin*, 1897; *The Divine Adventure, and Other Essays*, 1900; *The House of Usna*, 1900; *The Immortal Hour*, 1900; *The Winged Destiny*, 1904; *Where the Forest Murmurs*, 1906.

INTRODUCTORY CRITICISM

"The 'Fiona' literature . . . ranges through the domain of pure fantasy, of fable and allegory, of speculation, of aesthetic discussion, of symbolized fiction, and of verse. The voice has spoken many tongues, but always the accent of the mystic has persisted, has persisted and increased in poignancy and aloofness; so that in her later work it is frankly, and without the palliation of pictorial or symbolical setting, the speech and vision of the dreaming mind that is offered us. One will miss the essential note of this writing if one fails to see in it, as its prime possession, the confession and aspirations of a spirit swayed, beyond any other impulse, by a passionate consciousness and a special revelation of all beauty. . . . The sense of it is, for her, a perpetual touchstone for the apperception of . . . that miraculous and supersensuous world in which the spirit of the mystic has its intensest life. . . . One must not neglect to note the authentic presence of Celtic 'magic'; . . . it is movingly and persistently present in the writing of Fiona Macleod, where it is touched with the profound and poignant nostalgia, the wistful ecstasy of the 'Eternal Dreamer.' As she herself has said, through each poem 'goes the wind of the Gaelic spirit, which everywhere desires infinitude; but, in the penury of things as they are, turns to the dim enchantment of dreams.'"—L. Gilman, *North American Review*, October 1906, pp. 674-676.

LIONEL JOHNSON, p. 836

STANDARD EDITIONS

Poetical Works, w. pref. by Ezra Pound, London, Mathews, 1915
Complete Poems, ed. by Iain Fletcher, London, Unicorn Press, 1953
Poems, selections, London, Mathews, 1927
Twenty-One Poems, sel. by W.B. Yeats, Portland, Maine, Mosher, 1908
Ireland, with Other Poems, London, Mathews, 1897
Post Liminium, Essays and Critical Papers, London, Mathews, 1911

BIOGRAPHY AND CRITICISM

Boyd, E.A., "Lionel Johnson," *Ireland's Literary Renaissance*, New York, Knopf, 1922
Bronner, M., "The Art of Lionel Johnson," *Bookman*, 1912, 36:183-185
Chislett, W., Jr., "Lionel Johnson: the Classicist as Celt," "A Note on Lionel Johnson," *Moderns and Near Moderns*, New York, Grafton, 1928
Colby, E., "The Poetry and Prose of Lionel Johnson," *Catholic World*, 1913, 96:721-732; 97:52-63
Fletcher, Iain, "Lionel Johnson: 'The Dark Angel,'" in *Interpretations*, ed. by John Wain, London, Routledge, 1955
Harris, F., "Lionel Johnson," *Contemporary Portraits*, 2d s., New York, Harris, 1919
Hind, C.L., "Lionel Johnson," *More Authors and I*, New York, Lane, 1922
More, P.E., "Two Poets of the Irish Movement," *Shelburne Essays*, 1st s., New York, Putnam, 1904
Patrick, A.W., *Lionel Johnson (1867-1902), Poète et Critique*, Paris, Rodstein, 1939
Pick, John, "Divergent Disciples of Walter Pater," *Thought*, 1948, 23:114-128
Scott, D., "Lionel Johnson's Prose," *Men of Letters*, London, Hodder, 1923
Shorter, C.K., *Lionel Johnson*, Vigo Cabinet Series, No. 34, London, Mathews, 1908
Tynan, K., "A Catholic Poet," *Dublin Review*, 1907, 141:327-344
Tynan, K., "Lionel Johnson, Wykehamist," *Catholic World*, 1921, 113:507-513
Waugh, A., "Lionel Johnson," *Tradition and Change*, London, Chapman, 1919
Weygandt, C., "Lionel Johnson, English Irishman," *Tuesdays at Ten*, Philadelphia, Univ. of Pa. Press, 1928

BIOGRAPHICAL SKETCH

Lionel Pigot Johnson (1867-1902) had the distinction of being the only important figure in the Irish literary revival who was not an Irishman. Descended from a distinguished family of soldiers and educated at Winchester and Oxford, he came first in contact with Celtic life through vacation jaunts in Wales and Cornwall. Although his principal literary interest was in poetry, he was forced through the pressure of debts contracted by his expensive tastes in books and prints to write reviews for journals; and the habit once formed, he continued as a facile and intelligent reviewer for the rest of his career. By 1892, however, he found leisure for poetry. His themes were related to the two dominant interests of his life, Roman Catholicism and Ireland. Swayed by the beauty of the Roman

Catholic tradition and ritual, in 1891 he became a Roman Catholic. Already susceptible to Celtic influences through contacts with Wales, he became in consequence of a visit to Ireland in 1893 an ardent champion of Irish nationalism and a contributor to the revival of Irish literature. After 1900 his health failed from intemperance and a too sedulous devotion to writing; he died in 1902.

Johnson's principal publications were: *The Art of Thomas Hardy*, 1894; *Poems*, 1895; *Ireland, with other Poems*, 1897; *Post Liminium; Essays and Critical Papers*, 1911.

INTRODUCTORY CRITICISMS

"What differentiates Johnson's verses from those of his Irish contemporaries is a certain classic hardness of outline, and a restraint not usually found in the loose reveries and wistful outpourings of the Irish muse. Johnson's Greek and Latin studies, his admiration for Pater, who was his tutor, could not but influence his own writing. Whether the theme be English or Celtic, there is always an aloofness in the passion of the poet; he does not abandon himself utterly to his mood. It was easier for Johnson to be reserved than it was for most of the Irish poets. Classical education, for instance, has rarely been their lot."— Ernest Boyd, *Ireland's Literary Renaissance*, pp. 190-193.

"The fundamental conflict in his [Johnson's] verse is between a classical and a Christian ideal of human perfection. . . . It is the same dichotomy that runs through Hopkins's poetry: but the mere mention of Hopkins shows us where Johnson fails. The contrast may be ultimately in strength of nature: with more of Hopkins's terrifying iron control Johnson might have had a similar career to his: but for literature the point lies in Johnson's failure in expression, the inability to find language to match the intensity of his experience."—Graham Hough, *The Last Romantics*, pp. 213-214.

ERNEST DOWSON, p. 841

STANDARD EDITIONS

Complete Poems, New York, The Medusa Head, 1928

Poems, w. a mem. by A. Symons, London, Lane, 1915

The Poems of Ernest Dowson, London, Unicorn Press, 1946

The Poetical Works, ed. w. an intro. by D. Flower, London, Cassell, 1950

Cynara [His] Complete Lyrics, Mt. Vernon, N.Y., Peter Pauper, 1938

The Stories of Ernest Dowson, ed. by M. Longaker, Philadelphia, Univ. of Pa. Press, 1947

BIOGRAPHY AND CRITICISM

Brégy, Katherine, "Ernest Dowson, an Interpretation," *Catholic World*, 1914, 100:193-205

Fletcher, Iain, "Some Unpublished Letters of Ernest Dowson to Herbert Horne," *Notes and Queries*, 1962, 9:100-105

Harris, F., "Ernest Dowson," *Contemporary Portraits*, 2d s., New York, Harris, 1919

Longaker, M., *Ernest Dowson*, Philadelphia, Univ. of Pa. Press, 1944, 1945

Netzer, A.M., "The Poetry of Ernest Dowson," *Texas Review*, 1920, 5:204-208

Osage, A.R., "Ernest Dowson," *Readers and Writers*, London, Allen, 1922

Plarr, V.G., *Ernest Dowson, 1888-1897*, reminiscences, unpub. letters, and marginalia, w. a bibliog. by H.G. Harrison, New York, Gomme, 1914

Symons, A., "Ernest Dowson," *Studies in Prose and Verse*, London, Dent, 1904. Same article in *Fortnightly Review*, 1900, 73:947-957

Thomas, W.R., "Ernest Dowson at Oxford," *Nineteenth Century*, 1928, 103:560-566

BIOGRAPHICAL SKETCH

Ernest Christopher Dowson (1867-1900), the profligate author of delicately lovely lyrics, was the son of a dilettante poet whose precarious health compelled him to reside abroad, in Paris and on the Riviera; Dowson's education was therefore Continental and much interrupted until he came to Oxford. There he read the Latin erotic poets and took hashish for the sake of the vivid dreams that it induced. Leaving Oxford in 1887 without a degree, he went to London, associated with Symons, Yeats, and Lionel Johnson in meetings of the Rhymers' Club at the Cheshire Cheese, made arrangements with a publisher for translations from Baudelaire, Verlaine, and other French poets at a definite weekly stipend, and spent most of his money in stimulants that gave him transient poetic inspiration. Pathetically hungry for love and beauty, he adored from afar the daughter of a French restaurant keeper in London, followed her with his eyes as he sat at his table until the restaurant closed for the night, and then went home to drink and write lyrics in which she was the central figure. As his resources and health ebbed away, he lurked in dismal quarters about the London docks or the Paris markets, shunning his friends and writing his poems in low taverns on the backs of smudgy envelopes; yet, in all his dissipation, he retained a certain dilapidated refinement, and his face still had a delicacy like that of Keats. In 1900 he went home from Paris to die. A friend, finding him unconscious, took him to his house; on his last night Dowson read Dickens and talked until five in the morning about the poems which he was still to write.

Dowson's principal publications were: *A Comedy of Masks* (with Arthur Moore), 1893; *Dilemmas*, 1895; *Verses*, 1896; *The Pierrot of the Minute*, 1897; *Adrian Rome* (with Arthur Moore), 1899; *Decorations*, 1900.

INTRODUCTORY CRITICISM

"Dowson . . . was quite Latin in his feeling for youth, and death, and 'the old age of roses,' and the pathos of our little hour in which to live and love; Latin in his elegance, reticence, and simple grace in the treatment of these motives; Latin, finally, in his sense of their sufficiency for the whole of one's mental attitude. He used the commonplaces of poetry frankly, making them his own by his belief in them: the Horatian Cynara or Neobule[1] was still the natural symbol for him when he wished to be most personal. I remember his saying to me that his ideal of a line of verse was the line of Poe: 'The viol, the violet, and the vine'; and the gracious, not remote or unreal beauty, which clings about such words and such images as these, was always to him the true poetical beauty. There never was a poet to whom verse came more naturally, for the song's sake; his theories were all æsthetic, almost technical ones, such as a theory, indicated by his preference for the line of Poe, that the letter 'v' was the most beautiful of the letters, and could never be brought into verse too often. For more abstract theories he had neither tolerance nor need. Poetry as a philosophy did not exist for him; it existed solely as the loveliest of the arts. He loved the elegance of Horace, all that was most complex in the simplicity of Poe, most bird-like in the human melodies of Verlaine. He had the pure lyric gift, unweighted or unballasted by any other quality of mind or emotion; and a song, for him, was music first, and then whatever you please afterwards, so long as it suggested, never told, some delicate sentiment, a sigh or caress."— Arthur Symons, *Studies in Prose and Verse*, pp. 274-275.

[1] A devotee of Venus and the subject of Horace's twelfth *Ode* in Book 3.

JOHN DAVIDSON, p. 845

STANDARD EDITIONS

Selected Poems, London, Lane, 1905
Poems, w. an intro. by R.M. Wenley, New York, Boni & Liveright, 1924
John Davidson: A Selection of his Poems, ed. by Maurice Lindsay, w. pref. by T.S. Eliot and essay by Hugh McDiarmid, London, Hutchinson, 1961
The Man Forbid and Other Essays, Boston, Ball, 1910
Plays, London, Mathews, 1894

BIOGRAPHY AND CRITICISM

Archer, W., "John Davidson," *Poets of the Younger Generation*, London, Lane, 1902
Bronner, M., "John Davidson, Poet of Anarchy," *Forum*, 1910, 44:305-320
Colum, P. "The Poet of Armageddon: John Davidson," *New Republic*, 1915, 13:310-312
Fineman, H., *John Davidson; a Study of the Relation of His Ideas to His Poetry*, w. a bibliog., Philadelphia, Univ. of Pa. thesis, 1916
Harris, F., "John Davidson," *Contemporary Portraits*, 1st s., New York, Kennerley, 1915
Hind, C.L., "John Davidson," *More Authors and I*, New York, Lane, 1922
Jackson, H., "John Davidson," *The Eighteen Nineties*, New York, Knopf, 1922
Jones, H.M., "A Minor Prometheus," *The Freeman*, 1922, 6:153-155
Lester, John A., Jr., "Prose-Poetry Transmutation in the Poetry of John Davidson," *Modern Philology*, 1958, 56:38-54
Macleod, Robert D., *John Davidson: A Study in Personality*, London, Holmes, 1957
Mories, A.S., "The Religious Significance of John Davidson," *Westminster Review*, 1913, 180:75-85
Petzold, Gertrud von, *John Davidson und sein geistiges Werden unter dem Einfluss Nietzsches*, Leipzig, Tauchnitz, 1928
Scott-James, R.A., "The Self-Conscious Poet," *Modernism and Romance*, London, Lane, 1908
Townsend, J. Benjamin, *John Davidson, Poet of Armageddon*, New Haven, Conn., Yale Univ. Press, 1961
Traill, H.D., "Two Modern Poets," *Fortnightly Review*, 1895, 63:393-407

BIOGRAPHICAL SKETCH

John Davidson (1857-1909), the son of a Scotch evangelical minister, early developed an interest in science through his employment as chemical analyst in a sugar house. Later he became interested in philosophy, during his career as teacher in several Scotch public and private schools. After writing five plays, he went in 1889 to London with the intention of making his fortune by writing; he made a meager living by journalism and fiction, but gave his talents their freest expression in poetry. His two collections of *Fleet Street Eclogues* and three series of ballads, published from 1891 to 1899, were the amusements of a man who otherwise had few pastimes and little relief from struggles against poverty. With the turn of the century, Davidson abandoned poetry to preach, in a series of "Testaments," a philosophic gospel not unlike that of Nietzsche, applying the doctrine of evolution to society and defending imperialism and self-aggrandizement as the means to human progress. Before he could complete a series of plays to be called *God and Mammon*, in which his doctrine was the central theme, he was driven by poverty and ill health into a fit of depression and was prompted, while living at Penzance, to drown himself in Mount's Bay.

Davidson's principal publications were: *Bruce*, 1886; *Scaramouch in Naxos*, 1889; *Perfervid*, 1890; *In a Music Hall and Other Poems*, 1891; *Fleet Street Eclogues*, 1893; *Sentences and Paragraphs*, 1893; *Ballads and Songs*, 1894; *Fleet Street Eclogues: Second Series*, 1896; *New Ballads*, 1897; *The Last Ballad*, 1899; *The Testament of a Vivisector*, 1901; *The Testament of a Man Forbid*, 1901; *The Testament of an Empire Builder*, 1902; *Holiday and Other Poems*, 1906; *The Triumph of Mammon*, 1907; *Mammon and His Message*, 1908; *The Testament of John Davidson*, 1908; *Fleet Street and Other Poems*, 1909.

INTRODUCTORY CRITICISM

"The most immediately felt charm of Mr. Davidson's verse is its goodly energy and force, its excellent vitality: there is life-blood in the strong and vehement lines. He has not a trace of waterish sentiment and prettiness. . . . Each poem has lived in the poet's life, and issues from a living fire of passion, imagination, thought. . . . And the defects of its qualities are not lacking: a certain feverishness at times, an unpruned wealth of words, a rapidity which makes the verse pant for want of breath. . . . In each poem a situation, an emotion, has been faced and wrestled with and mastered: the solutions are triumphant and satisfying. Where Browning would have written psychological studies, with parry and fence, cut and thrust, of encountering emotions, Mr. Davidson chooses rather to throw his problem into a romantic ballad; applying, to subtile and spiritual themes, the direct

narrative vigor and pictorial charm of the ancient ballad story."—Lionel Johnson, *Academy*, Jan. 5, 1895, pp. 6, 7.

FRANCIS THOMPSON, p. 853

STANDARD EDITIONS

Works, 3 vols., ed. by W. Meynell, London, Burns, 1913
Complete Poetical Works, New York, Modern Lib., 1919
Selected Poems, w. a biog. note by W. Meynell, New York, Scribner, 1930
Poems, Oxford Press Series, New York, Oxford Univ. Press, 1937
The Poems, London, Hollis & Carter, 1946
Francis Thompson, collected works, ed. by W. Meynell, Westminster, Md., Newman Bkshop., 1947
Francis Thompson, poems, London, Benn, 1927
A Renegade Poet and Other Essays, w. an intro. by E.J. O'Brien, Boston, Ball Pub. Co., 1910
Literary Criticism, ed. by T.L. Connolly, New York, Dutton, 1948

BIOGRAPHY

Blunt, W.S., "How Wilfrid Meynell Discovered Francis Thompson," *Catholic World*, 1926, 122:678-680
Connolly, T.L., *Francis Thompson: in His Paths*, Milwaukee, Bruce Pub. Co., 1944
Danchin, Pierre, *Francis Thompson: la vie et l'oeuvre*, Paris, Nizet, 1959
Meynell, E., *The Life of Francis Thompson*, New York, Scribner, 1926
Meynell, V., *Francis Thompson and Wilfrid Meynell*, New York, Dutton, 1952
Peterson, E.L., "Francis Thompson: a Picture Biography," *Virginia Quarterly Review*, 1928, 4:244-252
Reid, John C., *Francis Thompson: Man and Poet*, London, Routledge, 1959

CRITICISM

Allen, H.A., "The Poet of the Return to God," *Catholic World*, 1918, 107:289-304
Archer, W., "Francis Thompson," *Poets of the Younger Generation*, London, Lane, 1902
Barnes, G.W., "Francis Thompson," *Poet Lore*, 1915, 26:229-257
Brégy, Katherine, "The Poetry of Francis Thompson," *Catholic World*, 1905, 81:605-614
Chapman, J.A., "Shelley and Francis Thompson," *Papers on Shelley, Wordsworth, and Others*, London, Oxford Univ. Press, 1929
Cock, A.A., "The Poetry of Francis Thompson," *Dublin Review*, 1911, 149:247-277

Contemporary Review, "William Barnes and Francis Thompson," 1909, 95: sup. 19-21

Craig, J., "Francis Thompson and His Poetry," *Catholic World*, 1922, 115:655-667

Finberg, H.P.R., "Francis Thompson," *English Review*, 1925, 41:822-831

Freeman, J., "Coventry Patmore and Francis Thompson," *Moderns*, New York, Crowell, 1917

Gerrard, T.J., "Francis Thompson, Poet," *Catholic World*, 1908, 86:613-628

Hind, C.L., "Francis Thompson," *Authors and I*, New York, Lane, 1921

Jackson, H., "Francis Thompson," *The Eighteen Nineties*, New York, Knopf, 1922

Johnson, L., "Modern Mysticism," *Quarterly Review*, 1914, 220:220-246

Kelman, J., "The Hound of Heaven," *Among Famous Books*, London, Hodder, 1912

La Gorce, A., *Francis Thompson*, tr. by H.F. Kynaston-Snell, London, Burns, 1933

Le Buffe, F.P., *"The Hound of Heaven," an Interpretation*, New York, Macmillan, 1921

Lewis, C.M., "The Poetry of Thompson," *Yale Review*, 1914, n. s., 4:99-114

McNabb, V.J., *Francis Thompson, and Other Essays*, Boston, Humphries, 1936

Madeleva, Sister Mary, "The Prose of Francis Thompson," *Chaucer's Nuns, and Other Essays*, New York, Appleton, 1925

Mégroz, R.L., *Francis Thompson: the Poet of Earth in Heaven*, London, Faber, 1927

More, P.E., "Francis Thompson," *Shelburne Essays*, 7th s., New York, Putnam, 1910

O'Donnell, C.L., *Francis Thompson*, Notre Dame, Ind., Notre Dame Univ. Press, 1906

Patmore, C., "Mr. F. Thompson, a New Poet," *Fortnightly Review*, 1894, 61:19-24

Pope, Myrtle P., "A Critical Bibliography of Works by and about Francis Thompson," *Bulletin of the New York Public Library*, 1958, 62:571-576; 1959, 63:40-49, 155-161, 195-204

Shuster, G.N., "Francis Thompson the Master," *The Catholic Spirit in Modern English Literature*, New York, Macmillan, 1922

Symons, A., "Francis Thompson," *Dramatis Personæ*, Indianapolis, Bobbs, 1923

Thompson, J., *Francis Thompson, Poet and Mystic*, London, Simpkin, 1923

Tynan, K., "Thompson's Place in Poetry," *Fortnightly Review*, 1910, 93:349-360

Wright, T.H., *"The Hound of Heaven," Biblical Poetry*, London, Harrap, 1927

BIOGRAPHICAL SKETCH

Francis Thompson (1859-1907), one of the most innocent and childlike of men, with a child's gaiety and sensitiveness to religious and social impressions, was the son of a provincial doctor, a Catholic, and was designed to follow in his father's profession. He was, however, by temperament and early inclination, a poet. Sent to the best Catholic colleges, he read poetry instead of science; given money to begin his professional work in London, he "idled" in libraries until his father, uncomprehending and exasperated, cut off his allowance. With no notions of how to earn a living, discharged for unpunctuality by a shoemaker with whom he found chance employment, he barely kept alive; the few pennies he earned by selling matches and calling cabs at theater doors, he spent for laudanum to deaden his misery. In the midst of this wretched life, untouched by anything approaching moral degradation, he thought in terms of poetry; on an impulse one day he scribbled verses and an essay on *Paganism New and Old* on dirty scraps of paper, slipped them through the mail slot of the *Merry England* office, and returned to the streets. The editor of *Merry England*, Wilfrid Meynell, left the verses long untouched; when at length he read them, he was astonished. He began a search for the author, found him after great difficulty, and invited him to his home. Thompson's first meeting with Alice Meynell and her two charming children was the turning point of his life. The Meynells reclaimed him from the opium habit and established him in London lodgings. Under their wise care his natural good spirits and the poetic impulse returned, *Poems* (1893) being the first fruit of his new life. For the Meynell daughters, who laughed at his quaint ways and adored him, he wrote his *Sister Songs* in 1895; and in 1897 he published a volume entitled *New Poems*, influenced by close association with Coventry Patmore. This volume closed his brief poetic career. Asked why he wrote no more verse, he replied that he had said all that he had to say. For the rest of his life he lived cheerfully and devoutly, filled a hundred notebooks with merry observations on life, contributed essays on literature to the journals, saw much of the Meynells and of Wilfrid Scawen Blunt, played cricket, until at length his frail body gave way under an attack of consumption.

Thompson's principal publications were: *Poems*, 1893; *Sister Songs*, 1895; *New Poems*, 1897; *Health and Holiness*, 1905.

INTRODUCTORY CRITICISM

"Francis Thompson was one of the few poets now or lately living in whom there was some trace of that divine essence which we best symbolize by fire. Emptiness he had and extravagances, but he was a poet, and he had made of many influences a new beauty. . . .

When he chanted in his chapel of dreams, the airs were often airs which he had learned from Crashaw and Patmore. They came to life again when he used them, and he made for himself a music which was part strangely familiar and part of his own.... When he put these dreams and this music into verse, with a craft which he had perfected for his own use, the poetry was for the most part a splendid rhetoric, imaginative and passionless, as if the moods went by, wrapped in purple, in a great procession.... The genius of Francis Thompson was Oriental, exuberant in color woven into elaborate patterns, and went draped in old silken robes that had survived many dynasties. The spectacle of him was an enchantment; he passed like a wild vagabond of the mind, dazzling our sight. He had no message, but he dropped sentences by the way, cries of joy or pity, love of children, worship of the Virgin and saints and of those who were patron saints to him on earth; his voice was heard like a wandering music, which no one heeded for what it said, but which came troublingly into the mind, bringing it the solace of its old recaptured melodies. Other poets of his time have had deeper things to say, and a more flawless beauty; others have put more of their hearts into their song; but no one has been a torch waved with so fitful a splendor over the gulfs of our darkness."—Arthur Symons, *Dramatis Personæ*, pp. 180-184.

ROBERT SEYMOUR BRIDGES, p. 861

STANDARD EDITIONS

Poetical Works, 6 vols., London, Oxford Univ. Press, 1920
Poetical Works, London, Milford, Humphrey, 1913
Robert Bridges, poems, London, Benn, 1925
The Testament of Beauty, London, Clarendon Press, 1929
Collected Essays and Papers, 4 vols., London, Oxford Univ. Press, 1927-1929

BIOGRAPHY AND CRITICISM

Bailey, John, "The Poetry of Robert Bridges," *Quarterly Review*, 1913, 219:231-255
Braithwaite, W.S., "The Lyrical Poetry of the New Laureate," *Forum*, 1913, 50:877-890
Bronner, M., "Robert Bridges as Lyrist," *Bookman*, 1913, 38:42-45
Davison, E., *Some Modern Poets*, New York, Harper, 1928, pp. 79-111
De Sélincourt, E., *Oxford Lectures on Poetry*, New York, Oxford Univ. Press, 1934, pp. 207-256

De Sélincourt, E., "The Testament of Beauty," *Hibbert Journal*, 1930, 28:416-435
Dowden, E., "The Poetry of Robert Bridges," *New Studies in Literature*, London, Paul, K., 1895
Elton, O., *Robert Bridges and The Testament of Beauty*, New York, Oxford Univ. Press, 1932, 15 pp.
Fox, A.W., "Robert Bridges: Poet Laureate," *Manchester Quarterly*, 1923, 167:135-155
Garrod, H.W., *Poetry and the Criticism of Life*, Cambridge, Mass., Harvard Univ. Press, 1931
Guerard, A.J., *Robert Bridges; a Study of Traditionalism in Poetry*, Cambridge, Mass., Harvard Univ. Press, 1942
Hind, C.L., "Robert Bridges," *More Authors and I*, New York, Lane, 1922
Kellett, E.E., "Poems of Robert Bridges," *London Quarterly Review*, 1915, 124:232-248
Kelshall, T., *Robert Bridges*, London, Scott, 1924
McKay, G.L., *A Bibliography of Robert Bridges*, New York, Columbia Univ. Press, 1933
Miles, L.W., "The Poetry of Robert Bridges," *Sewanee Review*, 1915, 23:129-139
Ritz, Jean-Georges, *Robert Bridges and Gerard Hopkins, 1863-1889: A Literary Friendship*, London, Oxford Univ. Press, 1960
Symons, A., "Robert Bridges," *Studies in Prose and Verse*, London, Dent, 1904
Thompson, E.J., *Robert Bridges, 1844-1930*, London, Oxford Univ. Press, 1944
Trevelyan, R.C., "Prosody and the Poet Laureate," *New Statesman*, 1924, 24:296-298
Twitchett, E., "The Poetry of Robert Bridges," *London Mercury*, 1929, 21:136-145
Warren, T.H., *Robert Bridges*, lecture, Nov. 8, 1913, Oxford, Clarendon Press, 1913
Wright, E.C., *Metaphor, Sound and Meaning in Bridges' The Testament of Beauty*, Philadelphia, Univ. of Pa. Press, 1951
Young, F.E.B., *Robert Bridges; a Critical Study*, London, Secker, Martin, 1914

BIOGRAPHICAL SKETCH

Robert Seymour Bridges (1844-1930), classical scholar, conscious craftsman in verse, and poet laureate of England, was born on the coast of Kent and as his favorite childhood diversion enjoyed lying on the cliffs, with his daydreams as his comrades, and watching the restless sea below. Shelley and Keats were his first examples in poetry. After Eton he proceeded to Oxford, where his strength and skill as an oarsman won him the position of stroke on his victorious college crew. At Oxford he formed a close friendship with Gerard Manley Hopkins, whose poetry he was to give to the world more than fifty years later. He educated himself in medicine and after a prolonged tour on the Continent and in the East settled in London as a physician and practiced there for fifteen years. Restive in the hurry and noise of the city and longing for quiet country life, he retired in 1882 to a suburban residence. After his marriage in 1884, he moved to a Berkshire manor house with a lovely garden and natural surroundings that provided a setting for many of his poems. As early as 1873 he had begun publishing the shorter lyrics with an Elizabethan flavor for which he is chiefly known, and he continued to write them, in the intervals of his larger labors, for the rest of his life. He was, however, chiefly concerned with a series of Greek and Shakespearean masks and plays which he issued from 1883 to 1905 and with experiments in the classic meters. Appointed laureate to succeed Alfred Austin in 1913, he wrote odes of courage during the war and a song of victory at its close, and exerted his influence in favor of phonetic spelling and the purification of English diction and pronunciation. His last utterance in verse was *The Testament of Beauty* in 1929.

Bridges's principal publications were: *Poems*, 1873; *Sonnets*, 1876; *Poems*, 1879; *Poems*, 1880; *Prometheus the Firegiver*, 1883; *Poems*, 1884; *Eros and Psyche*, 1885; *Nero*, 1885; *Sonnets (The Growth of Love)*, 1889; *The Feast of Bacchus*, 1889; *Achilles in Scyros*, *Palicio, The Return of Ulysses, The Christian Captives*, 1890; *Shorter Poems*, collected from earlier publications, with additions, 1890-1899; *Humors of the Court, and Other Poems*, 1893; *Nero, Part II*, 1894; *New Poems*, 1899; *Milton's Prosody*, 1901; *Peace*, 1903; *Now in Wintry Delights*, 1903; *Demeter*, 1905; *The Present State of English Pronunciation*, 1913; *Ibant Obscuri, an Experiment on the Classical Hexameter*, 1916; *The Spirit of Man*, an anthology, 1916; *The Necessity of Poetry*, 1918; *Britannia Victrix*, 1918; *October and Other Poems*, 1920; *New Verse*, 1925; *The Influence of the Audience on Shakespeare's Drama*, 1927; *Collected Essays*, 1928; *The Testament of Beauty*, 1929.

INTRODUCTORY CRITICISM

"Mr. Bridges's poems are seldom outcries of passion; they do not often explore the heights and depths of thought; they are in general of faultless evolution, but their design is rarely . . . complex and of large dimensions. Elements of many and various kinds enter into his . . . poems—delicate observation, delight in external nature, delight in art, delight in love, gladness and grief, ethical seri-

ousness, pensive meditation, graceful play of fancy. But all are subdued to balance, measure, harmony; and sometimes our infirmity craves for some dominant note, some fine extravagance, even some splendid sins. Mr. Bridges's audacities are to be found in occasional phrases—often felicitous and of true descriptive or interpretative power, sometimes not felicitous—and in his metrical experiments. But in his metrical experiments there is nothing revolutionary; they are extensions of a true tradition in English verse; they amount to little more than nicely calculated variations of stress. No writer of verse understands his business better than Mr. Bridges; and if finer and subtler harmonies are attained unconsciously or half-unconsciously by greater poets, our ear soon adapts itself to the delicate surprises and delicate satisfactions which he has thought out and felt as a skilled craftsman." —E. Dowden, *Fortnightly Review*, July 1, 1894, pp. 45-46.

MARY ELIZABETH COLERIDGE, p. 868

STANDARD EDITIONS

Poems, w. a pref. by H. Newbolt, London, Mathews, 1918
Gathered Leaves, w. a mem. by Edith Sichel, London, Constable, 1910

BIOGRAPHY AND CRITICISM

Bridges, R., "The Poems of Mary Coleridge," *Cornhill Magazine*, 1907, 96:594-605
Holland, R.H., "The Poems of Mary Elizabeth Coleridge," *Living Age*, 1908, 257: 348-352
Welby, T.E., "Mary Coleridge," *Back Numbers*, London, Constable, 1929

BIOGRAPHICAL SKETCH

Mary Elizabeth Coleridge (1861-1907) followed her great-granduncle, Samuel Taylor Coleridge, in cultivating a taste for the romantic and the supernatural. Educated at her London home partly under the care of William Johnson Cory, she read and wrote mystically romantic poetry and tales; in 1881 she had her first essays published in periodicals, and in 1893 she issued her first novel, *The Seven Sleepers of Ephesus*, which Stevenson highly praised. Her verse, some of it dating from childhood, remained hidden in manuscript until the future laureate, Robert Bridges, became interested in it and persuaded her to publish a volume, *Fancy's Following*, in 1896; the volume was privately printed in a limited edition and made her poetic talents known only to the appreciative few to whom she sent copies. In the following year a novel, *The*

King with Two Faces, made her famous among a wider public. She continued to write essays and novels for the rest of her life. She did not write much but unselfishly devoted most of her time to the working women of London; she gave lectures on literature in the Working-Women's College and taught the women in their homes. After her sudden death in 1907, Henry Newbolt published her poems; in 1910 extracts from her interesting letters and diaries were issued under the title of *Gathered Leaves*.

Miss Coleridge's principal publications were: *The Seven Sleepers of Ephesus*, 1893; *Fancy's Following*, 1896; *The King with Two Faces*, 1897; *Non Sequitur*, 1900; *The Fiery Dawn*, 1901; *The Shadow on the Wall*, 1904; *The Lady on the Drawing-room Floor*, 1906; *Life of Holman Hunt*, 1907; *Poems*, 1907; *Gathered Leaves*, 1910.

INTRODUCTORY CRITICISM

"Besides her bold and somewhat capricious imagination, with its natural and simple expression, the qualities which Mary Coleridge brought to her poetry . . . were a great literary appetite, knowledge, and memory—a wide sympathy, tenderness of feeling, and profound spirituality—and a humor without which such seriousness and devotion of life as were hers can hardly be made palpable in literature. . . . She did not write poems because she had learned the grammar of verse, nor because she thought she had valuable moral lessons for well-intentioned people. Her poetry is the irrepressible song of a fancy whose vagaries she would have thought it impertinent to analyze. . . ."—Robert Bridges, *Cornhill Magazine*, November 1907, p. 595.

LORD ALFRED DOUGLAS, p. 869

STANDARD EDITIONS

Complete Poems, London, Secker, Martin, 1928
Lord Alfred Douglas, poems, London, Benn, 1926
Lyric, London, Rich, 1935
Sonnets, London, Richards Press, 1943

BIOGRAPHY AND CRITICISM

Bends, E., "Lord Alfred Douglas's *Apologia*," *Englische Studien*, 1916, 49:377-402
Croft-Cooke, Rupert, *Bosie: The Story of Lord Alfred Douglas, his Friends and Enemies*, London, Allen, 1963
Ellis, S.M., "An Authentic Poet: Lord Alfred Douglas," *Mainly Victorian*, London, Hutchinson, 1925
Freeman, W., *Life of Lord Alfred Douglas*, London, Joseph, 1948

Stopes, M.C.C., *Lord Alfred Douglas*, London, Richards Press, 1949

BIOGRAPHICAL SKETCH

Lord Alfred Douglas (1870-1945), the second son of the eighth Marquis of Queensberry, was one of the young Oxford men who attended in the rôle of admirers and imitators the meteoric career of Oscar Wilde. Under Wilde's influence, Lord Alfred early experimented in verse of the aesthetic stamp, particularly in the sonnet form, and acquired considerable technical skill. When Oscar Wilde was brought to trial at the instigation of the Marquis of Queensberry and was sentenced to hard labor at Reading Gaol, Lord Alfred was implicated in the scandal stirred up by the trial and for the rest of his life largely occupied in bringing libel suits against his detractors, attacking them in satiric verse, and defending himself in autobiographical writings remarkable for their lack of reticence. He was founder and editor of two magazines, *Plain Speech* and *Plain English*, dedicated to attacks on public men and the refutation of attacks on himself. Besides the sonnets on which his literary fame largely depends and his satiric pieces, he wrote nonsense poetry, unusual in its polish and sophistication.

Douglas's principal publications were: *Tails with a Twist*, 1893; *The City of the Soul*, 1899; *The Pongo Papers*, 1907; *Sonnets*, 1909; *Oscar Wilde and Myself*, 1914; *The Rhyme of F Double E*, 1914; *The Rossiad*, 1916; *Eve and the Serpent*, 1917; *The Devil's Carnival*, 1922; *In Excelsis*, 1924; *The Duke of Berwick, and Other Rhymes*, 1925; *Autobiography*, 1929; *Oscar Wilde—a Summing Up*, 1940.

INTRODUCTORY CRITICISM

"His [Douglas's] output is small, but his wares are never shoddy. . . . His language is at times archaic, but is never forced. He owes much to the old English ballad-writers. He is indebted in a great measure, without being their bondsman, to such poets as Baudelaire. . . . Whatever may be his personal eccentricities, he sublimates them in art. In spite of private quarrels and public scandals, in spite of political feuds and literary vendettas, malice cannot gainsay the vigor of his diction and the loftiness of his lyric vision."—G. S. Viereck, Introduction to Douglas's *Perkin Warbeck, and Other Poems*, pp. 5-14.

WILLIAM BUTLER YEATS, p. 871

STANDARD EDITIONS

Collected Works, 8 vols., w. a bibliog. by A. Wade, London, Chapman, 1908

Collected Poems, reissue, 2d ed., New York, Macmillan, 1952

Variorum Edition of the Poems, ed. by Peter Allt and R.K. Alspach, New York, Macmillan, 1957

Selected Poems, Lyrical and Narrative, London, Macmillan, 1930

Collected Plays, new ed. w. 5 additional plays, New York, Macmillan, 1953

Autobiographies, New York, Macmillan, 1927

The Autobiography, reissue, 3 vols. in 1, New York, Macmillan, 1953

Letters on Poetry to Dorothy Wellesley, New York, Oxford Univ. Press, 1940

BIOGRAPHY

Ellmann, R., Yeats: the Man and the Masks, New York, Macmillan, 1948

Ervine, St. J.G., "W. B. Yeats," Some Impressions of My Elders, New York, Macmillan, 1922

Hone, J.M., W. B. Yeats, 1865-1939, New York, Macmillan, 1943

McGrath, J., "Yeats and Ireland," Westminster Review, 1911, 176:1-11

Masefield, J., Some Memories of W. B. Yeats, New York, Macmillan, 1940

Moore, George, Hail and Farewell, 3 vols., New York, Appleton, 1911-1914

Pollock, J.H., William Butler Yeats, London, Duckworth, 1935

Ussher, A., Three Great Irishmen: Shaw, Yeats, Joyce, New York, Devin-Adair, 1953

Yeats, J.B., Early Memories, Churchtown, Dundrum, Cuala Press, 1923

CRITICISM

Adams, Hazard, Blake and Yeats: The Contrary Vision, Ithaca, Cornell Univ. Press, 1955

Archer, W., "William Butler Yeats," Poets of the Younger Generation, London, Lane, 1902

Bjersby, B., The Interpretation of the Cuchulain Legend in the Works of W. B. Yeats, Cambridge, Mass., Harvard Univ. Press, 1951

Boyd, E.A., "William Butler Yeats: the Poems; the Plays; the Prose Writings," Ireland's Literary Renaissance, New York, Knopf, 1922

Brooks, C., Modern Poetry and the Tradition, Chapel Hill, Univ. of N.C. Press, 1939

Brown, F.G., "Mr. Yeats and the Supernatural," Sewanee Review, 1925, 33:323-330

Chislett, W., Jr., "The Influence of Lady Gregory on William Butler Yeats," Moderns and Near Moderns, New York, Grafton, 1928

Colum, P., "Mr. Yeats' Plays and Later Poems," Yale Review, 1925, n. s., 14:381-385

Daly, J.J., "The Paganism of Mr. Yeats," Catholic World, 1922, 113:595-605

Ellis-Fermor, U.M., The Irish Dramatic Movement, London, Methuen, 1939

Ellmann, R., The Identity of Yeats, New York, Oxford Univ. Press, 1954

Engelberg, Edward, The Vast Design: Patterns in W. B. Yeats's Aesthetic, Toronto, Univ. of Toronto Press, 1964

Gurd, Patty, The Early Poetry of William Butler Yeats, Lancaster, Pa., New Era, 1916

Gwynn, S.L., ed., Scattering Branches; Tributes to the Memory of W. B. Yeats, New York, Macmillan, 1941

Hall, J., and M. Steinmann, eds., The Permanence of Yeats, New York, Macmillan, 1950

Henn, T.R., The Lonely Tower, Studies in the Poetry of W. B. Yeats, New York, Pellegrini & Cudahy, 1952

Hoare, D.M., The Works of Morris and of Yeats in Relation to Early Saga Literature, New York, Macmillan, 1937

Hough, G., The Last Romantics, New York, Macmillan, 1950

Huneker, J., "A Poet of Visions," The Pathos of Distance, New York, Scribner, 1913

Jeffares, A.N., W. B. Yeats, Man and Poet, New Haven, Conn., Yale Univ. Press, 1949

Kavanagh, P., Story of the Abbey Theatre, New York, Devin-Adair, 1950

Koch, V., W. B. Yeats: the Tragic Phase, Baltimore, Johns Hopkins Press, 1952

MacNeice, L., The Poetry of W. B. Yeats, New York, Oxford Univ. Press, 1941

Menon, V.K.N., The Development of William Butler Yeats, Edinburgh, Oliver, 1942

Monroe, H., "Mr. Yeats and the Poetic Drama," Poetry, 1920, 16:32-38

Moore, Virginia, The Unicorn: William Butler Yeats's Search for Reality, New York, Macmillan, 1954

More, P.E., "Two Poets of the Irish Movement," Shelburne Essays, 1st s., New York, Putnam, 1904

Morris, L.R., The Celtic Dawn, New York, Macmillan, 1917

Morton, D., The Renaissance of Irish Poetry, New York, Washburne, 1929

Murry, J.M., "Mr. Yeats' Swan Song," Aspects of Literature, London, Collins, 1920

O'Donnell, J.P., Sailing to Byzantium; a Study in the Development of the Later Style and Symbolisms in the Poetry of William Butler Yeats, Cambridge, Mass., Harvard Univ. Press, 1939

Parkinson, T.F., W. B. Yeats, Self-Critic; a

Study of His Early Verse, Berkeley, Univ. of Calif. Press, 1951

Parkinson, T.F., *W. B. Yeats: The Later Poetry*, Berkeley, Univ. of California Press, 1964

Parrish, Stephen M., ed., *A Concordance to the Poems of William Butler Yeats*, Ithaca, Cornell Univ. Press, 1963

Paul-Dubois, L., "M. Yeats et le Mouvement poétique en Irlande," *Revue des Deux Mondes*, 1929, 53:558-583

Reid, Benjamin L., *William Butler Yeats: The Lyric of Tragedy*, Norman, Univ. of Oklahoma Press, 1961

Russell, G.W., "Yeats's Early Poems," *Living Age*, 1925, 327:464-466

Shanks, E., "The Later Poetry of Mr. W. B. Yeats," *First Essays on Literature*, London, Collins, 1923

Southern Review, The, Memorial Number, Winter 1942, Vol. 7, No. 3

Starkie, W., "William Butler Yeats," *Nuova Antologia*, 1924, 234:238-245

Stauffer, D.A., *The Golden Nightingale; Essays on Some Principles of Poetry in the Lyrics of William Butler Yeats*, New York, Macmillan, 1949

Stock, Amy G., *W. B. Yeats: His Poetry and Thought*, Cambridge, England, Cambridge Univ. Press, 1961

Sturgeon, M.C., "W. B. Yeats," *Studies of Contemporary Poets*, London, Harrap, 1920

Symons, A., "Mr. W. B. Yeats," *Studies in Prose and Verse*, London, Dent, 1904

Symons, A.J.A., *A Bibliography of the First Editions of Books by William Butler Yeats*, London, First Edition Club, 1924

Tennyson, C., "Irish Plays and Playwrights," *Quarterly Review*, 1911, 215:223-227

Townshend, G., "Yeats' Dramatic Poems," *Drama*, 1912, 5:192-208

Unterecker, John, *A Reader's Guide to William Butler Yeats*, New York, Noonday Press, 1959

Ure, Peter, *Towards a Mythology; Studies in the Poetry of W. B. Yeats*, Liverpool, Univ. Press of Liverpool, 1946

Wade, A., *Bibliography of the Writings of W. B. Yeats*, New York, British Bk. Centre, 1952

Weygandt, C., "Mr. William Butler Yeats," *Irish Plays and Playwrights*, Boston, Houghton, 1913

Weygandt, C., "With Yeats in the Woods of Coole," *Tuesdays at Ten*, Philadelphia, Univ. of Pa. Press, 1928

Wilson, Edmund, *Axel's Castle*, New York, Scribner, 1931

Wilson, F.A.C., *W. B. Yeats and Tradition*, New York, Macmillan, 1958

Winters, Ivor, "The Poetry of W. B. Yeats," *Twentieth Century Literature*, 1960, 6:3-24

BIOGRAPHICAL SKETCH

William Butler Yeats (1865-1939), the principal leader of the Irish Literary Revival, was born near Dublin of Anglo-Irish stock; his father was a portrait painter with Pre-Raphaelite leanings and a fervent interest in the Irish Nationalist cause. A mystic from childhood, Yeats absorbed from the Sligo countryside, where he spent holidays with his grandparents, the fairy lore of Ireland and in his school days gleaned from Sinnett's *Esoteric Buddhism* and other works of transcendental philosophy a sense of the divine mystery in all material things. In these theosophical studies, he was joined by G. W. Russell, whom he met at the Dublin Art School, and by other young men who formed the core of the literary movement, which was both patriotic and mystical. His first poems had to do with "Arcadia and the India of Romance," but a study of Sir Samuel Ferguson's poetry prompted him to write in 1889 *The Wanderings of Oisin*, an epic retelling of Celtic hero tales which his reading in the collections of Irish folklorists had made familiar. Meanwhile Yeats in 1887 had begun a residence in London and had become intimate with Lionel Johnson and Arthur Symons in meetings of the Rhymers' Club and learned from them to appreciate the symbolic poetry of William Blake and of the French symbolists such as Paul Verlaine; this new symbolism, added to that which Yeats had already evolved from his study of Irish legends, burdened his next poetry with a mystical significance that made it highly esoteric. "The old tales" he said, "were still alive for me, indeed, but with a new, strange, half-unreal life, as if in a wizard glass." This preoccupation with symbolism and the "Secret Rose" did not prevent Yeats, who was always practical even when most romantic, from encouraging the growth of the Irish Revival; he helped to organize simultaneously in 1892 the Irish Literary Society in London and the Irish National Literary Society in Dublin and worked hard to guide the new literature away from merely Nationalist propaganda to a purer art, continuing the tradition established by William Allingham and Sir Samuel Ferguson. "An Irish romantic movement," he said, "should make Ireland, as Ireland and all other lands were in ancient times, a holy land to its own people." This purpose, added to the sane influence of Lady Gregory, gradually brought him out of his elaborately symbolic period into one which was no less romantic but more perspicuous.

In 1899 he turned, among other interests, to drama and established with George Moore and other associates the Irish Literary Theatre, which became the Abbey Theatre in 1904; his plays, however, stood somewhat apart from the main current of the Irish drama, which was realistic rather than romantic and legendary as were his *The Land of Heart's Desire* (1894) and *The Shadowy Waters* (1900). As a practical leader he guided many later developments in Irish literature and politics with great energy. He became a senator of the Irish Free State in 1922 and in the following year was awarded the Nobel prize for literature. On the occasion of his seventieth birthday he was hailed by his countrymen as the greatest living Irishman, and by this time he was generally regarded as the major English-speaking poet of the twentieth century.

Yeats's principal publications were: *Mosada*, 1886; *The Wanderings of Oisin*, 1889; *John Sherman*, 1891; *The Countess Kathleen*, 1892; *The Celtic Twilight*, 1893; *The Poems of William Blake* (ed.), 1893; *The Land of Heart's Desire*, 1894; *Poems*, 1895; *The Secret Rose*, 1897; *The Wind among the Reeds*, 1899; *The Shadowy Waters*, 1900; *Cathleen ni Houlihan*, 1902; *Ideas of Good and Evil*, 1903; *In the Seven Woods*, 1903; *Hour Glass and Other Plays*, 1904; *The King's Threshold*, 1904; *Deirdre*, 1907; *The Green Helmet and Other Poems*, 1910; *J. M. Synge and the Ireland of His Time*, 1911; *Plays for an Irish Theatre*, 1912; *Responsibilities*, 1914; *Reveries over Childhood and Youth*, 1915; *Per Amica Silentia Lunae*, 1918; *The Cutting of an Agate*, 1919; *The Wild Swans at Coole*, 1919; *Michael Robartes and the Dancer*, 1921; *Seven Poems and a Fragment*, 1922; *The Trembling of the Veil*, 1922; *Later Poems*, 1922; *A Vision*, 1925; *The Tower*, 1928; *Three Things*, 1929; *The Winding Stair and Other Poems*, 1929; *The King of the Great Clock Tower*, 1934; *New Poems*, 1938.

INTRODUCTORY CRITICISMS

"The distinction of Mr. Yeats, as an Irish poet, is his ability to write Celtic poetry, with all the Celtic notes of style and imagination, in a classical manner. . . . When he takes a Celtic theme, some vast and epic legend, or some sad and lyrical fancy, he does not reflect the mere confused vastness of the one, the mere flying vagueness of the other; his art is full of reason. . . . It is not the subjects alone, nor the musical skill alone, nor the dominant mood alone, but all these together that make these poems so satisfying and so haunting. They have that natural felicity which belongs to beautiful things in nature, but a felicity under the control of art."—Lionel Johnson, *Academy*, Oct. 1, 1892, p. 278.

"It is by means of dramatic symbols . . . that Mr. Yeats weaves about the simplicity of moods that elaborate web of atmosphere in which the illusion of love, and the cruelty of pain, and the gross ecstasy of hope, became changed into beauty. . . . To a poet who is also a mystic there is a great simplicity in things, beauty being really one of the foundations of the world, woman a symbol of beauty, and the visible moment, in which to love or to write love songs is an identical act, really as long or as short as eternity. Never, in these love songs, concrete as they become through the precision of their imagery, does an earthly circumstance divorce ecstasy from the impersonality of vision. This poet cannot see love except as the absolute beauty, cannot distinguish between the mortal person and the eternal idea. Every rapture hurries him beyond the edge of the world and beyond the end of time. The conception of lyric poetry which Mr. Yeats has perfected . . . may be clearly defined. . . . A lyric is an embodied ecstasy, and an ecstasy so profoundly personal that it loses the accidental qualities of personality, and becomes a part of the universal consciousness. Itself, in its first, merely personal stage, a symbol, it can be expressed only by symbol; and Mr. Yeats has chosen his symbolism out of Irish mythology, which gives him the advantage of an elaborate poetic background, new to modern poetry."—Arthur Symons, *Studies in Prose and Verse*, pp. 232-234.

"His [Yeats's] collected poems are so rounded and ardent and brimming that in spite of the seeming smallness of the lyric form, they seek their parallels in the Medici chapel or the Beethoven quartettes more readily than in, say, the jewelled and metal art of Cellini. What qualities led to such accomplishment? Passionate thought, consistent technique, controlled concentration, deliberate delight in the exercise of art. . . . Governing them all is a fifth trait—the lyrical bent—which Yeats did not so much cultivate as inherit. In the cradle, Apollo touched his mouth with honey. . . . Yeats trained his extensive natural gifts with a cool and continued ferociousness."—Donald A. Stauffer, *The Golden Nightingale*, p. 123.

"There are some poets whose poetry can be considered more or less in isolation, for experience and delight. There are others whose poetry, though giving equally experience and delight, has a larger historical importance. Yeats was one of the latter: he was one of those few whose history is the history of their own time, who are a part of the consciousness of an age which cannot be understood without them."—T. S. Eliot, in *The Permanence of Yeats*, ed. by James Hall and Martin Steinmann, p. 343.

ARTHUR SYMONS, p. 883

STANDARD EDITIONS

Collected Works, 16 vols., London, Secker, Martin, 1925
Figures of Several Centuries, London, Constable, 1916
The Romantic Movement in English Poetry, New York, Dutton, 1909
Studies in Prose and Verse, London, Dent, 1904
Studies in Seven Arts, New York, Dutton, 1925
Studies in Strange Souls, London, Sawyer, 1929
The Symbolist Movement in Literature, London, Constable, 1908

BIOGRAPHY AND CRITICISM

Archer, W., "Arthur Symons," *Poets of the Younger Generation*, London, Lane, 1902
Harris, F., "Arthur Symons," *Contemporary Portraits*, 3d s., New York, Harris, 1920
Lewisohn, L., "The Poetic Work of Symons," *Bookman*, 1919, 48:555-556
Llombreaud, Roger, *Arthur Symons: His Life and Letters*, London, Unicorn Press, 1962
More, P.E., "Arthur Symons: the Two Illusions," *Shelburne Essays*, 1st s., New York, Putnam, 1904
Murdock, W.G., *The Work of Arthur Symons: an Appreciation*, Edinburgh, Gray, 1907
Orange, A.R., "Beardsley and Arthur Symons," *Readers and Writers*, London, Allen, 1922
Symons, A., "Notes on Some of My Wanderings," *English Review*, 1914, 18: 404-414
Urban, W.M., "Arthur Symons and Impressionism," *Atlantic Monthly*, 1914, 114:384-393
Wedmore, F., "With Arthur Symons," *Certain Comments*, London, Selwyn, 1925
Welby, T.E., *Arthur Symons, a Critical Study*, London, Philpot, 1925

BIOGRAPHICAL SKETCH

Arthur Symons (1865-1945), poet, critic, and devotee of the arts, was born in Wales of Cornish parents whose conservative ethical and religious principles did not prevent their allowing him liberty to do as he liked. "I wanted to want to be good," he later confessed; "but all I really wanted was to be clever." His first verses were religious, but at the age of thirteen he was writing metrical tales in imitation of Byron's *Don Juan*, which had first attracted him because of its local reputation for appalling wickedness. Hating his middle class environment and shrinking from adopting any profession that would offend his acutely developed sensibilities, he began going up to London for prolonged visits, fell in with such congenial spirits as Wilde and Dowson, attended meetings of the Rhymers' Club, contributed to *The Yellow Book*, the organ of the decadents, edited its brilliant successor, *The Savoy*, haunted the theaters and concert halls, and was intoxicated with the thronging impressions of city life. His greatest joy, he said, was being alone in the midst of a crowd. An eager student of all that interested him, he acquired a knowledge of Elizabethan drama that qualified him in his early twenties to edit Shakespeare and other dramatists, and an acquaintance with the arts that enabled him to earn his livelihood by critical writing. He was one of the first Englishmen to appreciate the French poets Baudelaire and Verlaine and to introduce them to English readers; their example, along with the precepts of Walter Pater, was paramount in developing his own poetic style. To enlarge his experience with life and his store of colorful impressions, he lived in Paris, Rome, Venice, and Seville as he had lived in London, studying the people and the arts. In 1901 he married a lady who, like himself, "possessed some hardly conscious instinct which turns towards beauty unerringly," and in 1905 he rather surprisingly established a permanent home in the quiet environment of Wittersham, where he continued for many years to write and rewrite his "aesthetic" essays and his memories of the colorful nineties.

Symons's principal publications were: *An Introduction to the Study of Browning*, 1886; *Days and Nights*, 1889; *Silhouettes*, 1892; *London Nights*, 1895; *Amoris Victima*, 1897; *Studies in Two Literatures*, 1897; *The Symbolist Movement in Literature*, 1899; *Images of Good and Evil*, 1900; *Plays, Acting, and Music*, 1903; *Cities*, 1903; *Studies in Prose and Verse*, 1904; *Spiritual Adventures*, 1905; *A Book of Twenty Songs*, 1905; *The Fool of the World, and Other Poems*, 1906; *Studies in Seven Arts*, 1906; *William Blake*, 1907; *Cities of Italy*, 1907; *The Romantic Movement in English Poetry*, 1909; *Knave of Hearts*, 1913; *Figures of Several Centuries*, 1916; *Tragedies*, 1916; *Tristan and Iseult*, 1917; *Cities and Sea Coasts and Islands*, 1918; *Color Studies in Paris*, 1918; *The Toy Cart*, 1919; *Studies in Elizabethan Drama*, 1920; *Charles Baudelaire*, 1921; *Dramatis Personæ*, 1923; *Translations from Bau-*

delaire, 1925; *Studies in Strange Souls*, 1929; *Confessions*, 1930; *Wanderings*, 1931.

INTRODUCTORY CRITICISMS

"If there ever was a religion of the eyes, I have devoutly practised that religion. I noted every face that passed me on the pavement; I looked into the omnibuses, the cabs, always with the same eager hope of seeing some beautiful or interesting person, some gracious movement, a delicate expression, which would be gone if I did not catch it as it went. This search without an aim grew to be almost a torture to me; my eyes ached with the effort, but I could not control them. At every moment, I knew, some spectacle awaited them; I grasped at all these sights as a dog that I once saw standing in an Irish stream and snapping at the bubbles that ran continually past him on the water. Life ran past me continually, and I tried to make all its bubbles my own."—A. Symons, "A Prelude to Life," in *Spiritual Adventures*, p. 32.

"His [Symons's] . . . poems deal very often with works of art, and with the highly artificial . . . beauty of the modern urban landscape. . . . He is very largely a poet of the artificial. . . . It is not that he objects to nature. He could from the very first appreciate certain aspects of her, and he came in time to have a very individual feeling for her. But nature, in his early poems, stirs him only where it is an intruder among artificial things. . . . His is the attitude, it has been often enough said, of a decadent poet. . . . His aim was, with the utmost economy, to suggest momentary impressions, transient moods; the impressions to be, of preference, those of one gazing at things themselves artificial or seen under an artificial light, the moods to be not only fleeting but frivolous or perverse. . . . Certain effects of color, which might have been brushed off a moth's wings and which the first breath will scatter; certain movements, of a dancer seen perhaps from the wings; certain notes of a just audible music; certain moods which flutter through the mind and are gone, have been seized delicately, firmly, and perpetuated without any of that incongruous mason's art which too often mars the propriety of 'a moment's monument.' "—T. E. Welby, *Arthur Symons, a Critical Study*, pp. 5-6, 21-22.

RUDYARD KIPLING, p. 888

STANDARD EDITIONS

The Collected Works, 28 vols., Burwash ed., New York, Doubleday, 1941

Complete Works, 35 vols., Sussex ed., London, Macmillan, 1937

Writings in Prose and Verse, 30 vols., New York, Scribner, 1897-1923

A Choice of Kipling's Verse, made by T.S. Eliot, w. an essay on Rudyard Kipling, New York, Scribner, 1943

Collected Verse, New York, Doubleday, 1946

Something of Myself; for My Friends Known and Unknown, New York, Doubleday, 1937

Letters of Travel, 1892-1913, New York, Doubleday, 1920

BIOGRAPHY

Beresford, G.C., *Schooldays with Kipling*, New York, Putnam, 1936

Brown, Hilton, *Rudyard Kipling*, w. a foreword by F. Swinnerton, New York, Harper, 1945

Carpenter, L.R., *Rudyard Kipling, a Friendly Profile*, Chicago, Argus, 1942

Carrington, C.E., *Rudyard Kipling*, New York, Doubleday, 1955

Ferguson, J.D., "The Education of Rudyard Kipling," *Education*, 1924, 45:171-183

Hopkins, R.T., *The Kipling Country*, London, Palmer, 1924

Mansfield, M.F., *A Kipling Notebook*, New York, Mansfield, 1899-1900. Issued also under the title of *Kiplingiana*

Munson, Arley, *Kipling's India*, New York, Doubleday, 1915

Rice, H.C., *Rudyard Kipling in New England*, rev. ed., Brattleboro, Vt., Bk. Cellar, 1951

Worster, W., *Merlin's Isle; a Study of Rudyard Kipling's England*, London, Gyldendal, 1920

CRITICISM

Archer, W., "Rudyard Kipling," *Poets of the Younger Generation*, London, Lane, 1902

Braddy, N., *Rudyard Kipling, Son of Empire*, New York, Messner, 1941

Braybrooke, P., *Kipling and His Soldiers*, Lippincott, Philadelphia, 1926

Bridges, R., "Kipling," *Outlook*, 1899, 61:281-284, 490-491

Chesterton, G.K., "On Mr. Rudyard Kipling and Making the World Small," *Heretics*, New York, Lane, 1905

Chevrillon, A., "Rudyard Kipling's Poetry," *Three Studies in English Literature*, tr. from the French by F. Simmonds, New York, Doubleday, 1923

Croft-Cooke, R., *Rudyard Kipling*, London, Home & Van Thal, 1948

Danchin, F.C., "Songs of the Sea," *Les Langues Modernes*, 1928, pp. 314-324

Davray, H.D., "Rudyard Kipling et Son

Temps," *Mercure de France*, 1929, 215: 257-293

Dowden, E., "The Poetry of Kipling," *The Critic*, 1901, 38:219-224

Durand, R.A., *A Handbook to the Poetry of Rudyard Kipling*, London, Hodder, 1917

Gilmer, H.W., "The Classical Element in the Poems of Rudyard Kipling," *Classical Weekly*, 1921, 14:178-181

Hopkins, R.T., *Rudyard Kipling's World*, London, Holden, 1925

Jackson, H., "Rudyard Kipling," *The Eighteen Nineties*, New York, Knopf, 1922

James, H., *Views and Reviews*, Boston, Ball, 1908

Johnson, L., "Rudyard Kipling: *Barrack-Room Ballads*," *Reviews and Critical Papers*, London, Mathews, 1921

Kernahan, C., "Rudyard Kipling," *Six Famous Living Poets*, London, Butterworth, 1922

Knowles, F.L., *A Kipling Primer*, Boston, Brown, 1899

Lee, V., "Kipling's Handling of Words," *English Review*, 1910, 5:599-607

Livingston, Flora V., *Bibliography of the Works of Rudyard Kipling*, New York, Wells, 1927

MacMunn, G.F., *Rudyard Kipling: Craftsman*, new rev. ed., Toronto, Ryerson Press, 1938

Martindell, E.W., *A Bibliography of the Works of Rudyard Kipling, (1881-1923)*, London, Lane, 1923

Maurice, A.B., "Rudyard Kipling's United States," *Bookman*, 1913, 38:156-163

Millard, B., "Why Women Dislike Kipling," *Bookman*, 1914, 40:328-333

Moore, G., "The Literary Style of Kipling," *Lippincott's Magazine*, 1904, 73:99-103

More, P.E., "Kipling and FitzGerald," *Shelburne Essays*, 2d s., New York, Putnam, 1905

Rutherford, Andrew, ed., *Kipling's Mind and Art*, Stanford, Stanford Univ. Press, 1964

Saxton, E.F., *The Kipling Index*, New York, Doubleday, 1911

Schuyler, M., "Rudyard Kipling as a Poet," *Forum*, 1896, 22:406-413

Shanks, E.B., *Rudyard Kipling; a Study in Literature and Political Ideas*, New York, Doubleday, 1940

Squire, J.C., "Mr. Kipling's Later Verse," *Books in General*, 3d s., London, Hodder, 1921

Stedman, E.C., "Kipling's Ballads of *The Seven Seas*," *Genius and Other Essays*, New York, Moffat, 1911

Stewart, James, *Rudyard Kipling: A Bibliographical Catalogue*, Toronto, Univ. of Toronto Press, 1959

Tompkins, J.M.S., *The Art of Rudyard Kipling*, London, Methuen, 1960

Waterhouse, F.A , "The Literary Fortunes of Kipling," *Yale Review*, 1921, n. s., 10: 817-831

Welby, T.E., "Mr. Kipling," *Back Numbers*, London, Constable, 1929

Weygandt, A.M., *Kipling's Reading and Its Influence on His Poetry*, Philadelphia, Univ. of Pa. Press, 1939

Wilson, E., *The Wound and the Bow*, Boston, Houghton, 1941

Young, W.A., *A Dictionary of the Characters and Scenes in the Stories and Poems of Rudyard Kipling*, London, Routledge, 1921

BIOGRAPHICAL SKETCH

Rudyard Kipling (1865-1936) was born in Bombay, where his father, a writer of verse as well as an artist, was professor of architectural sculpture in the British School of Art. From his native nurse Kipling learned to speak Hindustani as soon as English; until he was six India was practically the only world that he knew. In 1871, however, his parents took him to England and left him with friends to be educated, while they returned to India. In the course of time, he entered the United Services College at Bideford to be fitted for a governmental position in India; his poor eyesight disqualifying him for such a position and his tastes turning toward reading and writing, his friends were easily reconciled to his becoming an author. In this ambition he was encouraged by the praise he received for early poems published in London journals and privately printed by his father in Bombay, and also by the interest of his uncle, Sir Edward Burne-Jones, who as a member of the Pre-Raphaelite Brotherhood introduced him to William Morris and other writers. In 1882 he sailed for India and became subeditor of the *Civil and Military Gazette* at Lahore, where his family was then living; the gruff editor-in-chief, while exacting hard day labor, called him a "clever pup" and allowed him rather a free hand in his contributions; accordingly he submitted poems and stories, later collected as *Departmental Ditties* (1886) and *Plain Tales from the Hills* (1887), along with his regular assignments. This discipline in journalism and this early practice in turning his shrewd observations of English and native life in India into prose and verse "that should take with the English public" were of the highest importance in determining the bent of his literary career. In 1887 he graduated to the editorial staff of a larger paper, the *Pioneer* at Allahabad, and as traveling correspondent began a series of journeys to all parts of India; he saw the fighting on the Afghanistan border and in 1889 embarked on a trip around the world, described in *From Sea to Sea* (1899). Arriving, by way of America, in London, he was somewhat surprised to find himself unknown. A reissue, from English presses, of his works published in India gratified him by its immense success; the English public, it seemed, was hungry for just the graphic impressions of Indian life which he had to offer. A short pause, and he was off once more: to South Africa, where he enlarged his acquaintance with the far-flung empire and cultivated the friendship of Cecil Rhodes; to Australia, Ceylon, and back to India, where he wrote his *Barrack-Room Ballads* (1892). Marrying an American girl in 1892, he embarked with her on new wanderings which led them, by way of Japan, to Brattleboro, Vermont; there Kipling made his first prolonged residence in many years, wrote the *Jungle Books* (1894-1895) and *Just So Stories* (1902) for his two children, and added a not wholly sympathetic acquaintance with American life to his enormous fund of literary material. After returning to England in 1896, Kipling made one more journey to South Africa and another to America; he then settled down to a comparatively uneventful life in the manor house of Bateman's Burwash in Sussex, keeping bees and prize cattle, fishing and tramping over the downs, and drawing from his store of memories the material for his poetry and fiction, the expression of his robust philosophy. The smooth current of his life was broken by the World War, in which he lost his only son; his work took on a new bitterness born of a painful awareness of the tragedy of mechanized warfare. He was often mentioned in connection with the laureateship but never appointed; his highest reward for his work was the Nobel prize for literature in 1907. His later work, though received with less enthusiasm than his early volumes, was no less marked by vigor of content and energy of style.

Kipling's principal publications were: *Departmental Ditties*, 1886; *Plain Tales from the Hills*, 1887; *Soldiers Three, In Black and White, The Story of the Gadsbys, Under the Deodars, The Phantom 'Rickshaw, Wee Willie Winkie*, 1888-1889; *Life's Handicap*, 1890; *The Light That Failed*, 1891; *Barrack-Room Ballads*, 1892; *Many Inventions*, 1893; *The Jungle Book*, 1894; *Second Jungle Book*, 1895; *The Seven Seas*, 1896; *Captains Courageous*, 1897; *The Day's Work*, 1898; *Stalky & Co.*, 1899; *From Sea to Sea*, 1899; *Kim*, 1901; *Just So Stories*, 1902; *The Five Nations*, 1903;

Traffics and Discoveries, 1904; *Puck of Pook's Hill*, 1906; *Actions and Reactions*, 1909; *Rewards and Fairies*, 1910; *Songs from Books*, 1912; *The New Army in Training*, 1914; *France at War*, 1915; *Fringes of the Fleet*, 1915; *Sea Warfare*, 1916; *A Diversity of Creatures*, 1917; *The Years Between*, 1919; *Inclusive Verse*, 1919; *Letters of Travel*, 1920; *Debits and Credits*, 1926; *A Book of Words*, 1928; *Something of Myself*, 1937.

INTRODUCTORY CRITICISMS

"The greatest thing in the world for Kipling is Power at work—whether it is exhibited by a humble man, a huge engine, or an empire. That is why he has made such a strong impression upon strong men everywhere. The age is one of great schemes, industrial, commercial, and political; the achievements of science are marvelous—and yet until Kipling came the people who write were saying that it was an unromantic age; that poetry had been killed the world over by steam, and that romance was dead because republicanism had leveled all men to a common pattern. Kipling had the advantage of living in his impressionable youth where the new civilization was imposing itself upon one that was old and worn out. He saw part of the empire in making. He was looking at the raw edges of the work, and he grasped the full meaning of the new forces behind it. Never has the executive power of man so revealed itself as in the nineteenth century. Instead of looking upon it as prosaic, and turning back to other times and countries for a field of romance, Kipling saw that he and we are truly living in an age of romance. He set to work to reveal the age to itself."—Robert Bridges, *Outlook*, Feb. 4, 1899, pp. 281-282.

"In some of his finest pieces Mr. Kipling is a prey to the grandiose aspect of things. . . . We know that England is great, that Englishmen have done great things, that the fame of her glory has filled the corners of the earth; but we have no occasion to shriek about it, to wax hysterically wroth with those who deny it. Shakespere's great burst of loyal pride, Milton's solemn utterance, Wordsworth's noble verses, Browning's *Home Thoughts from Abroad*, Tennyson's stately lyrics, do not brag and bluster and protest. . . . The occasion on which the verses were written may justify some of this agitated declamation; but the tone is habitual with Mr. Kipling."—Lionel Johnson, *Academy*, May 28, 1892, p. 510.

"What is unusual about Kipling's ballads is his singleness of intention in attempting to convey no more to the simple minded than can be taken in on one reading or hearing. They are best when read aloud, and the ear requires no training to follow them easily. With this simplicity of purpose goes a consummate gift of word, phrase, and rhythm. There is no poet who is less open to the charge of repeating himself. . . . The variety of form ·which Kipling manages to devise for his ballads is remarkable: each is distinct, and perfectly fitted to the content and the mood which the poem has to convey. Nor is the versification too regular: there is the monotonous beat only when the monotonous is what is required; and the irregularities of scansion have a wide scope."—T. S. Eliot, "Rudyard Kipling," in *A Choice of Kipling's Verse*, pp. 10-11.

GEORGE WILLIAM RUSSELL ("A. E."), p. 908

STANDARD EDITIONS

Collected Poems, London, Macmillan, 1926
The House of the Titans, and Other Poems, New York, Macmillan, 1934
Selected Poems, New York, Macmillan, 1935
Some Irish Essays, Dublin, Maunsel, 1906

BIOGRAPHY AND CRITICISM

Bose, A.C., *Three Mystic Poets*, Bombay, School & College Bookstall, 1945
Boyd, E.A., "George W. Russell," *Ireland's Literary Renaissance*, New York, Knopf, 1922
Chislett, W., Jr., "Ideas of Good and Evil in the Poetry of A. E., " *Moderns and Near Moderns*, New York, Grafton, 1928
Colum, P., "A. E., Poet, Painter, and Economist," *New Republic*, 1918, 15:172-174
Current Opinion, "The Spiritual Leader of New Ireland," 1922, 72:74-77
Eglinton, J., "A. E. and His Story," *Dial*, 1927, 82:271-281
Elton, O., "Living Irish Literature," *Modern Studies*, London, Arnold, 1907
Ervine, St. J.G., "A. E.," *Some Impressions of My Elders*, New York, Macmillan, 1922
Feld, R.C., "The Opinions of A. E." *Century Magazine*, 1921, 103:2-9
Ferrar, W.J., "Some Aspects of A.E.," *London Quarterly Review*, 1928, 1950:232-240
Figgis, D., *A. E. (George W. Russell)*, Dublin, Maunsel, 1918
Gibbon, Monk, "A. E.: The Years of Mystery, 1884-1890," *Dublin Magazine*, 1956, 31:8-21
Hind, C.L., "G. W. Russell," *More Authors and I*, New York, Lane, 1922

Living Torch, A. E., The, ed. by M. Gibbon w. an intro. essay, New York, Macmillan, 1938
Magee, W.K., *A Memoir of A. E., George William Russell*, New York, Macmillan, 1937
Morris, L.R., "Four Irish Poets," *Columbia University Quarterly*, 1916, 18:332-344
Nevinson, H.L., "A. E." *Books and Personalities*, London, Lane, 1905
Téry, S., "A. E.," *L'Île des Bards*, Paris, Flammarion, 1925
Welby, T.E., "Æ," *Back Numbers*, London, Constable, 1929
Weygandt, C., "Mr. George W. Russell," *Irish Plays and Playwrights*, Boston, Houghton, 1913

BIOGRAPHICAL SKETCH

George William Russell (1867-1935), whose original theosophist pen name of "Æon" was abbreviated by a hasty printer into "A. E.," the name by which as poet and visionary he was thereafter best known, was born of peasant stock at Lurgan, county Armagh, in Ulster. After acquiring experience with the recalcitrant Irish soil that was of use to him in his later career, and after a brief education in local schools, he journeyed to Dublin with the intention of becoming an artist and thus giving substance to his vivid imaginative life, nursed on Celtic legends. At the art school he met W. B. Yeats and through him was introduced to the group of ardent young Irishmen who were dreaming of a national literature separate from that of England. This group formed a club, later called the Hermetic Society, for the reading of Oriental and transcendental philosophy and theosophist literature, the mysticism of which, joined with the otherworldly quality of the native Celtic tradition, had much to do with the nature of the Irish Literary Revival. To the theosophist journals edited by the group Russell contributed his first poems, collected in 1894 under the title *Homeward: Songs by the Way*. Meanwhile he developed a style in painting as mystical as that of his poems. His belief in the divinity of man resulted in a passion for democracy and social uplift; his love of the old Celtic legends, with their reflection of an heroic age, led him to conceive that the salvation of Ireland lay in a return, with scientific modifications, to the social conditions of the older time. These beliefs he preached to crowds on the hillsides above Dublin, towering before his audience, with his wild hair and giant frame, like a demigod returned from the Celtic past. His essays, his poems, his paintings in divers ways all tended to the same purpose; visionary to a remarkable degree, he yet was able to lead his dreams into constructive channels; from expeditions into the country to see fairies, he returned to lecture on coöperation before agricultural societies. As editor of the *Irish Homestead* he wielded a great influence on Irish economic reform; and as a political leader he had an important part in the movement which resulted in the formation of the Irish Free State. Refusing office under the new government, he preferred to wield his influence upon Irish life through the editorial pages of *The Irish Statesman* and through his personal contacts. To the Sunday evening gatherings at his home, dominated by his towering figure and personality, came the social and literary masters of Ireland. He wrote social and economic works, and for recreation painted his mystic pictures in the wild mountains of Donegal. In his last years his impatience with the politicians of the new Ireland drove him to a self-imposed exile in England, where he died in 1935.

Russell's principal publications were: *Homeward: Songs by the Way*, 1894; *The Earth Breath*, 1897; *Literary Ideals in Ireland* (with others), 1899; *Ideals in Ireland* (with others), 1901; *The Nuts of Knowledge*, 1903; *The Divine Vision*, 1904; *The Mark of Apollo*, 1904; *New Poems*, 1904; *By Still Waters*, 1906; *Irish Essays*, 1906; *Deirdre*, 1907; *The Hero in Man*, 1909; *The Renewal of Youth*, 1911; *Co-operation and Nationality*, 1912; *Gods of War*, 1915; *Imaginations and Reveries*, 1915; *The National Being, Thoughts on an Irish Polity*, 1916; *The Candle of Vision*, 1918; *The Interpreters*, 1922; *Voice of the Stones*, 1925; *The Dark Weeping*, 1929; *Enchantment and Other Poems*, 1930; *Vale and Other Poems*, 1931; *Song and Its Fountains*, 1932; *The House of Titans and Other Poems*, 1934.

INTRODUCTORY CRITICISM

" 'I know I am a spirit, and that I went forth in old time from the Self-ancestral to labors yet unaccomplished; but, filled ever and again with homesickness, I made these homeward songs by the way.' These words, with which A. E. introduced his first book of verse, should serve as a superscription to the *Collected Poems*, so completely do they summarize the whole message and tendency of his poetry. All his life he has sung of this conviction of man's identity with the Divine Power, the Ancestral Self of Eastern philosophy, from whom we are but temporarily divided. The occasion of his poems are those moments of rapture when the seer glimpses some vision reminding him of his immortal destiny, his ˷rption into Universal Being. The hours ⸝ilight and dawn are those which most find the poet rapt in 'divine vision,'

and to this circumstance must be attributed numerous landscapes whose beauty is undiminished by their being so frequently seen in the same light. . . . A. E.'s verse is not so much the utterance of a poet as the song of a prophet, and its importance is to be measured in other than purely literary terms. He often falls below the standard of technical perfection which was set by Yeats, and is the latter's most valuable gift to Irish poetry. But depth and sincerity, coupled with a general high level of workmanship, enable A. E. to take his place in the first rank. . . . We know that he has aspired to give us a revelation of Divine Beauty, and we are grateful that this should be his unique preoccupation."—Ernest Boyd, *Ireland's Literary Renaissance*, pp. 223-231.

ALFRED EDWARD HOUSMAN, p. 909

STANDARD EDITIONS

The Collected Poems, New York, Holt, 1940
More Poems, New York, Knopf, 1936
The Name and Nature of Poetry, New York, Macmillan, 1933
A Shropshire Lad; Last Poems, London, Richards Press, 1929
A Shropshire Lad, w. an apprec. of biog. material gath. by C.J. Weber, New York, Heritage, 1951
Complete Poems, ed. by T.B. Haber, New York, Holt, Rinehart & Winston, 1959

BIOGRAPHY AND CRITICISM

Archer, W., "A. E. Housman," *Poets of the Younger Generation*, London, Lane, 1902
Brenner, R., "Alfred Edward Housman," *Ten Modern Poets*, New York, Harcourt, 1930
Bronowski, J., *The Poet's Defence*, New York, Macmillan, 1939
Drinkwater, J., "A. E. Housman's *Last Poems*," *The Muse in Council*, Boston, Houghton, 1925
Ehrsam, T.G., *A Bibliography of Alfred Edward Housman*, Boston, Faxon, 1941
Ellis, S.M., "A. E. Housman," *Mainly Victorian*, London, Hutchinson, 1925
Garrod, H.W., "Mr. A. E. Housman," *The Profession of Poetry*, London, Oxford Univ. Press, 1929
Gorman, H.S., "Hardy and Housman," *The Procession of Masks*, Boston, Brummer, 1923
Gow, S.F., *A. E. Housman, a Sketch*, New York, Macmillan, 1936
Haber, T.B., "Housman's Poetic Method: His Lectures and His Notebooks," *PMLA*, 1954, 69:1000-1016

Hamilton, Robert, *Housman the Poet*, London, Lee, 1953

Harper, G.M., "Housman," *The Spirit of Delight*, New York, Holt, 1928

Housman, Laurence, *My Brother, A. E. Housman: Personal Recollections Together with Thirty Hitherto Unpublished Poems*, New York, Scribner, 1938

Jones, H.M., "A. E. Housman, Last of the Romans," *Double Dealer*, 1922, 3:136-141

Hyder, C.K., ed., *A Concordance to the Poems of A. E. Housman*, Lawrence, Univ. of Kan. Press, 1940

Jarrell, R., "Texts from Housman," *The Kenyon Review*, Summer 1939, 1,3:260-271

MacDonald, J.F., "The Poetry of A. E. Housman," *Queen's Quarterly*, 1923, 31:114-137

Marlow, Norman, *A. E. Housman: Scholar and Poet*, Minneapolis, Univ. of Minn. Press, 1958

Priestley, J.B., "Mr. A. E. Housman," *Figures in Modern Literature*, New York, Dodd, 1924

Richards, G., *Housman, 1897-1936*, New York, Oxford Univ. Press, 1942

Robinson, O., *Angry Dust: the Poetry of A. E. Housman*, Boston, Humphries, 1950

Stallman, R. W., comp., "Annotated Bibliography of A. E. Housman," *PMLA*, 1945, 60:463-502

Watson, G.L., *A. E. Housman: A Divided Life*, Boston, Beacon Press, 1958

Wilson, E., *The Triple Thinkers*, New York, Harcourt, 1938

Withers, P., *A Buried Life; Personal Recollections of A. E. Housman*, London, Cape, 1940

BIOGRAPHICAL SKETCH

Alfred Edward Housman (1859-1936) was born in Worcestershire, although nearby Shropshire is the principal setting for his poems. He was the eldest of seven children, three of whom adopted literary or artistic careers. Educated at a private school in Worcestershire and at Oxford, he excelled in classical studies, yet he failed to graduate with distinction from the University, and at the age of twenty-two, with some disappointment, he went to London as a clerk in the Patent Office and there submitted to a monotonous routine for ten years. During that period he spent many long evenings reading Latin and Greek in the British Museum and preparing studies in the minor Latin poets, which were later published. As a result of this work he was appointed in 1892 to a professorship in Latin in University College, London, and in 1911 to the Chair of Latin at the University of Cambridge. Between 1886 and 1905 Housman

lived in Highgate, London, and there wrote *A Shropshire Lad*. Most of the poems were composed in 1895, during a great burst of creative activity. The publisher who had accepted the manuscript with some reluctance soon had reason to consider the book a success and asked when a second volume could be expected. Twenty-eight years later Housman completed the second volume—a volume he called, with characteristic finality, *Last Poems*. This was published in 1922. "It is not likely," he said in his foreword, "that I shall ever be impelled to write much more." In the autumn of 1936, the year of his death, his final work, *More Poems*, was issued by his brother Laurence. Apparently little interested in the popularity and influence of his volumes, Housman lived for the most part in seclusion and was singularly averse to talking about himself or his poetry. But despite the meagerness of his output, he attained in his own lifetime a place of distinction among English poets.

Housman's principal publications were: *A Shropshire Lad*, 1896; *Manilius, Book I*, 1903; *Juvenal*, 1905; *Manilius, Book II*, 1912; *Book III*, 1916; *Book IV*, 1920; *Last Poems*, 1922; *Lucan*, 1926; *The Name and Nature of Poetry*, 1933; *More Poems*, 1936.

INTRODUCTORY CRITICISMS

"Mr. Housman has three main topics: a stoical pessimism; a dogged rather than an exultant patriotism; and what I may call a wistful cynicism.... Mr. Housman's melancholy is inveterate and not to be shaken off, but there is nothing whining about it; rather, it is bracing, invigorating.... His patriotism is local rather than national or imperial.... He dwells, not harshly but with compassion, upon the mutability of human feeling, the ease with which the dead are forgot, the anguish of love unrequited, and the danger that long life may mean slow degradation.... One of Mr. Housman's strongest and rarest qualities is his unerring dramatic instinct.... It is long since we have caught just this note in English verse—the note of intense feeling uttering itself in language of unadorned precision, uncontorted truth.... He eschews extrinsic and factitious ornament because he knows how to attain beauty without it. It is good to mirror a thing in figures, but it is at least as good to express the thing itself in its essence.... Mr. Housman has this talent in a very high degree; and cognate and complementary to it is his remarkable gift of reticence.... He will often say more by a cunning silence than many another poet by pages of speech. That is how he has contrived to get into this tiny volume so much of the very essence and savor of life."—William Archer, *Fortnightly Review*, August 1898, pp. 265-271.

"Housman's Shropshire, like Hardy's Wessex, is a part of England full of historic memories and still comparatively free from the taint of industrialism, but, unlike Hardy, Housman has no real contact with a traditional popular culture. He himself admitted that he 'never spent much time there,' but he made some exquisite poetry out of his appreciation of its landscape and used about twenty of its place names very effectively. Out of his memories of the West Country, he constructed a curious dreamworld . . . in which Shropshire Lads drink beer, play football, commit murders, enlist. . . . This pseudo-pastoral fantasy seems partly to conceal and partly to symbolize a profound emotional disturbance in the poet's life of which nothing is known."— Vivian de Sola Pinto, *Crisis in English Poetry, 1880-1940*, pp. 55-56.

THOMAS HARDY, p. 918

STANDARD EDITIONS

Works, 37 vols., London, Macmillan, 1919-1920
Poetical Works, 2 vols., London, Macmillan, 1920-1924
Collected Poems, New York, Macmillan, 1953
Selected Poems, ed. w. an intro. by G.M. Young, New York, Macmillan, 1940
The Dynasts, London, Macmillan, 1927
Winter Words in Various Moods and Metres, New York, Macmillan, 1928
The Short Stories, London, Macmillan, 1928

BIOGRAPHY

Blunden, E.C., *Thomas Hardy*, New York, Macmillan, 1952
Brennecke, E., *The Life of Thomas Hardy*, New York, Greenberg Publishers, 1925
Hardy, E., *Thomas Hardy*, New York, St. Martins, 1954
Hardy, Florence E., *The Early Life of Thomas Hardy, 1840-1891*, London, Macmillan, 1928
Hardy, Florence E., *The Later Years of Thomas Hardy, 1892-1928*, New York, Macmillan, 1930
Harper, C.G., *The Hardy Country*, London, Black, 1925
Hopkins, R.T., *Thomas Hardy's Dorset*, London, Palmer, 1922
Lea, H., *Thomas Hardy's Wessex*, London, Macmillan, 1926
Weber, C.J., *Hardy of Wessex; His Life and Literary Career*, New York, Columbia Univ. Press, 1940

Windle, B.C.A., *The Wessex of Thomas Hardy*, London, Lane, 1926

CRITICISM

Abercrombie, L., *Thomas Hardy, a Critical Study*, New York, Viking, 1927
Bailey, J.O., *Thomas Hardy and the Cosmic Mind: A New Reading of The Dynasts*, Chapel Hill, N.C., Univ. of North Carolina Press, 1956
Beach, J.W., *The Technique of Thomas Hardy*, Chicago, Univ. of Chicago Press, 1922
Beerbohm, M., "Thomas Hardy as a Panoramatist," *Living Age*, 1904, 240:507-510
Bensusan, S.L., "Thomas Hardy," *Quarterly Review*, 1929, 253:313-329
Brash, W.B., "Thomas Hardy," *London Quarterly Review*, 1928, 149:145-157
Braybrooke, P., *Thomas Hardy and His Philosophy*, London, Daniel, 1928
Brennecke, E., *Thomas Hardy's Universe*, New York, Columbia Univ. Press, 1926
Cassidy, J.A., "The Original Source of Hardy's *Dynasts*," *PMLA*, 1954, 69:1085-1100
Cecil, Lord D., *Hardy, the Novelist*, Indianapolis, Bobbs, 1946
Chang Hsin-hai, "A Chinese Estimate of Hardy's Poetry," *Hibbert Journal*, 1928, 27:78-92
Chase, Mary Ellen, *Thomas Hardy from Serial to Novel*, Minneapolis, Univ. of Minn. Press, 1927
Chesterton, G.K., "On Thomas Hardy," *Generally Speaking*, New York, Dodd, 1929
Chew, S.C., *Thomas Hardy, Poet and Novelist*, New York, Knopf, 1928, bibliog. pp. 185-196
Child, H.H., *Thomas Hardy*, London, Nisbet, 1925
Collins, Vere H., *Talks with Thomas Hardy at Max Gate, 1920-22*, London, Duckworth, 1928
Columbine, W.B., "The Poems of Thomas Hardy," *Westminster Review*, 1899, 152:180-184
Dickinson, T.H., "Thomas Hardy's *The Dynasts*," *North American Review*, 1912, 195:526-542
Duffin, H.C., *Thomas Hardy, a Study of the Wessex Novels, the Poems, and the Dynasts*, 3d ed., rev. and enl., New York, Longmans, 1937
Elliott, A.P., *Fatalism in the Works of Thomas Hardy*, Philadelphia, Univ. of Pa. Press, 1935
Elliott, G.R., "Spectral Etching by Thomas Hardy," *The Cycle of Modern Poetry*, Princeton, N.J., Princeton Univ. Press, 1929

Ellis, S.M., "Thomas Hardy, His Lyrics," *Mainly Victorian*, London, Hutchinson, 1925

Fairley, B., "Notes on the Form of *The Dynasts*," *PMLA*, 1919, 34:401-415

Fletcher, J.G., "The Spirit of Thomas Hardy," *Yale Review*, 1924, n. s., 13:322-333

Fletcher, J.G., "Thomas Hardy's Poetry: an American View," *Poetry*, 1920, 16:43-49

Forsyth, P.T., "The Pessimism of Thomas Hardy," *Living Age*, 1912, 275:458-473

Garwood, H., *Thomas Hardy, an Illustration of the Philosophy of Schopenhauer*, Philadelphia, Winston, 1911

Guerard, A.J., *Thomas Hardy: the Novels and Stories*, Cambridge, Mass., Harvard Univ. Press, 1949

Harper, G.M., "Hardy, Hudson, Housman," *The Spirit of Delight*, New York, Holt, 1928

Hawkins, D., *Thomas Hardy*, London, Barker, 1951

Hickson, C., *The Versification of Thomas Hardy*, Philadelphia, Univ. of Pa. Press, 1931

Holland, C., *Thomas Hardy's Wessex Scene*, Dorchester, Longmans, Ltd., 1948

Hone, J.M., "The Poetry of Mr. Hardy," *London Mercury*, 1922, 5:396-405

Hynes, Samuel L., *The Pattern of Hardy's Poetry*, Chapel Hill, Univ. of North Carolina Press, 1961

Johnson, L.P., *The Art of Thomas Hardy*, w. a chap. on his poetry by J.E. Barton and a bibliog. by John Lane, New York, Dodd, 1923

King, R.W., "The Lyrical Poems of Thomas Hardy," *London Mercury*, 1926, 15:157-170

King, R.W., "Verse and Prose Parallels in the Work of Thomas Hardy," *Review of English Studies*, 1962, 13:52-61

Knickerbocker, F.W., "The Victorianness of Thomas Hardy," *Sewanee Review*, 1928, 36:310-325

Knowles, D., "The Thought and Art of Thomas Hardy," *Dublin Review*, 1928, 183:208-218

Lee, V., "Hardy's Handling of Words," *English Review*, 1911, 9:231-241

Lowes, J.L., "Two Readings of Earth," *Yale Review*, 1926, n. s., 15:515-539

MacDowall, A.S., *Thomas Hardy, a Critical Study*, London, Faber, 1931

Martin, G.C., "Thomas Hardy and the English Bible," *London Bookman*, 1928, 74:24-26

Maxwell, D., *The Landscape of Thomas Hardy*, London, Cassell, 1928

Maynard, T., "The Poetry of Thomas Hardy," *Catholic World*, 1926, 123:46-54

Monroe, H., "Thomas Hardy," *Poetry*, 1928, 31:326-332

Murry, J.M., "The Poetry of Mr. Hardy," *Aspects of Literature*, New York, Knopf, 1921

Murry, J.M., "The Supremacy of Thomas Hardy," *New Adelphi*, 1928, 1:219-224

Nevinson, H.W., *Thomas Hardy*, London, Allen, G., 1941

Newton, A.E., *Thomas Hardy, Novelist or Poet?* Philadelphia, privately printed, 1929

Noyes, A., "The Poetry of Hardy," *North American Review*, 1911, 194:96-105

Perkins, David, "Hardy and the Poetry of Isolation," *English Literary History*, 1959, 26:253-270

Purdy, R.L., *Thomas Hardy: a Bibliographical Study*, New York, Oxford University Press, 1954

Quiller-Couch, A., "The Poetry of Thomas Hardy," *Studies in Literature*, 3 vols., New York, Putnam, 1918

Ransom, John Crowe, "Thomas Hardy's Poems and the Religious Difficulties of a Naturalist," *Kenyon Review*, 1960, 22:169-193

Rutland, W.R., *Thomas Hardy; a Study of His Writings and Their Background*, Oxford, England, Blackwell, 1938

Saxelby, F.O., *A Thomas Hardy Dictionary*, London, Routledge, 1911

Shafer, Robert, "Thomas Hardy," *Christianity and Naturalism*, New Haven, Conn., Yale Univ. Press, 1926

Sime, Jessie G., *Thomas Hardy of the Wessex Novels*, Montreal, Carrier, 1928

Smith, R.M., "Philosophy in Thomas Hardy's Poetry," *North American Review*, 1924, 220:330-340

Southern Review, The, "Thomas Hardy Centennial Issue," essays by distinguished modern critics, Summer 1940, Vol. 6, No. 1:1-224

Southworth, J.G., *The Poetry of Thomas Hardy*, New York, Columbia Univ. Press, 1947

Symons, A., *A Study of Thomas Hardy*, London, Sawyer, 1927

Tomlinson, H.M., *Thomas Hardy*, New York, Random House, 1929

Van Doren, Mark, "The Poems of Thomas Hardy" in *Four Poets on Poetry*, ed. by D.C. Allen, Baltimore, Johns Hopkins Press, 1959

Weber, C.J., *Hardy in America*, Waterville, Me., Colby College Press, 1946

Weber, C.J., bibliog. comp., *The First Hundred Years, Thomas Hardy, 1840-1940*, Waterville, Me., Colby College Library, 1942

Webster, H.C., *On a Darkling Plain; the Art and Thought of Thomas Hardy*, Chicago, Univ. of Chicago Press, 1947

Wedmore, F., "Thomas Hardy's Poems," *Certain Comments*, London, Selwyn, 1925

Whibley, C., "The Work of Hardy," *Blackwood's Magazine*, 1913, 193:823-831

Whitmore, C.E., "Mr. Hardy's *Dynasts* as Tragic Drama," *Modern Language Notes*, 1924, 39:455-460

Woolf, V., "Half of Thomas Hardy," *New Republic*, 1928, 57:70-72

BIOGRAPHICAL SKETCH

Thomas Hardy (1840-1928) was born in Dorsetshire, a southern county of England that became the principal background of his fiction and poetry. His father was a building constructor; his mother was intellectually ambitious and so developed his mind that he became even in childhood an analytical although sympathetic observer of life around him. From Dorchester schools he learned little, but when in 1856 he was apprenticed to John Hicks, a local architect, he began the study of Latin and Greek with a fellow apprentice and wrote poems, later destroyed, under the influence of William Barnes, the bard of Dorsetshire, his friend and adviser. His architectural training under Hicks he supplemented in 1862 by study and work in London under Sir Arthur Blomfield; although he perfected himself in architecture to a degree that won him a prize offered by the Royal Institute in 1863 and that gave him a feeling for structure which strongly influenced his literary craftsmanship, he was more interested in the evening classes that he attended at the University of London, in music, plays, and painting, in theological and philosophic discussions with his few friends, and in his poetry. Poetry he wrote in abundance, and all of it, including much that he published in 1898 under the title of *Wessex Poems*, came promptly back from the publishers to whom he submitted it. In 1870, as a consequence of his engagement to Emma Gifford, whom he had met while repairing a church in Cornwall, he felt the need of money and, despairing of selling his poems, began the composition of novels. Working under the helpful advice of George Meredith, he wrote *Desperate Remedies* (1871), *Under the Greenwood Tree* (1872), and *Far from the Madding Crowd* (1874), each novel the work of a year and each showing a rapid advance in technique. By one of life's ironies, it was through these novels, in which he had an interest slight in comparison with his devotion to his poetry, that he achieved fame. For almost thirty years he wrote his verse in private, and for the public he wrote a long series of novels which reached a climax of favor with the publication of *Tess of the D'Urbervilles* in 1891. During this time his philosophic conception of chance as a malignant force ruling the universe, already developed in 1865 when he wrote the first of his *Wessex Poems*, had deepened under the influence of Schopenhauer and other German thinkers; his last novel, *Jude the Obscure* (1895), estranged the general public by its insistent embodiment of this theme. In 1898, settled for some time in a house of his own designing near Dorchester, and financially independent, Hardy was at last enabled to give over his writing of novels and to devote himself to his favorite means of literary expression. In that year he published *Wessex Poems, and Other Verses;* in 1902, *Poems of the Past and the Present;* and other collections followed. The work which he regarded as his masterpiece, the culmination to which all his work and thought had been leading, was his vast Napoleonic epic drama, *The Dynasts,* published in three parts from 1903 to 1908. The remainder of Hardy's life was not anticlimactic. In his later poems and also in the quiet influence that radiated from his Dorset homestead, he continued to impress his personality upon the art and life of the modern world.

Hardy's principal publications were: *Desperate Remedies,* 1871; *Under the Greenwood Tree,* 1872; *A Pair of Blue Eyes,* 1872-1873; *Far from the Madding Crowd,* 1874; *The Hand of Ethelberta,* 1876; *The Return of the Native,* 1878; *The Trumpet-Major,* 1880; *A Laodicean,* 1880-1881; *Two on a Tower,* 1882; *The Mayor of Casterbridge,* 1885-1886; *The Woodlanders,* 1886-1887; *Wessex Tales,* 1888; *A Group of Noble Dames,* 1891; *Tess of the D'Urbervilles,* 1891; *Life's Little Ironies,* 1894; *Jude the Obscure,* 1895; *The Well-Beloved,* 1897; *Wessex Poems, and Other Verses,* 1898; *Poems of the Past and the Present,* 1902; *The Dynasts,* 1903-1908; *Poems of William Barnes* (ed.), 1908; *Time's Laughingstocks and Other Verses,* 1909; *Satires of Circumstance,* 1911-1914; *A Changed Man and Other Stories,* 1913; *Moments of Vision,* 1917; *Late Lyrics,* 1922; *The Queen of Cornwall,* 1923; *Human Shows,* 1925; *Yuletide in a Younger World,* 1927; *Winter Words,* 1928.

INTRODUCTORY CRITICISM

"People call me a pessimist; and if it is pessimism to think, with Sophocles, that 'not to have been born is best,' then I do not reject the designation. I never could understand why the word 'pessimism' should be such a red rag to many worthy people; and I believe, indeed, that a good deal of the robustious, swaggering optimism of recent literature is at bottom cowardly and insincere. I do not see that we are likely to improve the world by asseverating, however loudly, that black is white. . . . But my pessimism, if pessimism it be, does not involve the assumption that the world is going to the dogs. . . . On the contrary, my practical philosophy is distinctly meliorist. What are my books but one plea against 'man's inhumanity to man'—to woman—and to the lower animals? . . . Whatever may be the inherent good or evil of life, it is certain that men make it much worse than it need be. When we have got rid of a thousand remediable ills, it will be time enough to determine whether the ill that is irremediable outweighs the good."—Hardy's answer to his critics, recorded by William Archer, *Pall Mall Magazine*, April 1901, p. 533.

"Earth is to Hardy a haunted spot. . . . I know no poetry so pervaded as his with a sense of the continued presence of the dead, nor is there another body of verse in the world, I think, in which that sense is conveyed to us with such intolerable poignancy and beauty. It is a strange paradox. No living poet is, in his sharp breach with tradition, so intensely of his time as Thomas Hardy; and no poet writing today would have been so utterly at home on earth a thousand years ago."—John Livingston Lowes, *Yale Review*, April 1926, p. 522.

"The reader will look in vain in these poems for the rich, sensuous music of the great Victorian poets, who were always trying to follow Keats's advice to 'load every rift with ore' and to surprise with 'a fine excess' of visual beauty and melody. Hardy's aim was quite different; like Browning, the only Victorian poet by whom he was strongly influenced, and Donne, whose work he greatly admired, he was trying to produce a dramatic rather than a pictorial or musical effect. He differed from Browning, however, in avoiding the romantic and the picturesque, and in his deliberate use of commonplace and contemporary subject matter."—Vivian de Sola Pinto, *Crisis in English Poetry, 1880-1940*, p. 40.

ACKNOWLEDGMENTS

The poems of Robert Bridges are reprinted from his *Poetical Works* (1912) by permission of Oxford University Press, New York.

The poems of Thomas Edward Brown are reprinted from his *Collected Poems* (1900) by permission of The Macmillan Company, New York, publishers.

The poems of John Davidson are reprinted by permission of Dodd, Mead and Company, New York, American publishers.

The poems of Henry Austin Dobson are reprinted from his *Complete Poetical Works* (1923) by permission of his son, Mr. A. T. A. Dobson, and of Humphrey Milford, Oxford University Press, London, publishers.

The poems of Lord Alfred Douglas are reprinted from his *Complete Poems* (1928) by permission of Martin Secker, London.

The poems of Ernest Dowson are reprinted from his *Complete Poems* (1928) by permission of Dodd, Mead and Company, New York, American publishers.

The poems of W. S. Gilbert from his *Patience* (1909) are reprinted by permission of Macmillan & Co. Ltd., London, and of Messrs. Horne & Birkett, London.

The poems of William Ernest Henley are reprinted from his *Poems* (1919) by permission of Charles Scribner's Sons, New York.

The poems of Gerard Manley Hopkins are reprinted from his *Poems* (1918) and *Collected Poems of Gerard Manley Hopkins* (1948) by permission of his heirs and of Humphrey Milford, Oxford University Press, London, publishers.

The poems of A. E. Housman are reprinted from the Centennial Edition of his *Complete Poems* (1959) by permission of Holt, Rinehart and Winston, Inc., New York.

The poems of Rudyard Kipling are reprinted from *Rudyard Kipling's Verse, Inclusive Edition* (1927) by permission of the author; of A. P. Watt and Son, London, Agents; and of Doubleday, Doran and Company, Inc., Garden City, publishers.

The poems of George Meredith are reprinted from his *Poetical Works* (1928) by permission of Charles Scribner's Sons, New York.

The poems of Alice Meynell are reprinted from her *Poems* (1923) by permission of Charles Scribner's Sons, New York.

The poems of George William Russell ("A. E.") are reprinted from his *Collected Poems* (1927) by permission of the author and of The Macmillan Company, New York, publishers.

The poems of William Sharp are reprinted from his *Poems* (1912) and his *Fiona Macleod's Poems* (1910) by permission of Duffield and Company, New York.

The poems of Robert Louis Stevenson are reprinted from his *Complete Poems* (1923) by permission of Charles Scribner's Sons, New York.

The poems of Algernon Charles Swinburne are reprinted from his *Complete Works* (1925) by permission of William Heinemann, Ltd., London.

The poems of Arthur Symons are reprinted from his *Collected Works* (1924) by permission of the author.

The poems of Alfred, Lord Tennyson selected from *Unpublished Early Poems* (1931) are reprinted by permission of Sir Charles Tennyson.

The poems of Francis Thompson are reprinted from his *Complete Poetical Works* (1919) by permission of The Modern Library, Inc., New York.

INDEX OF AUTHORS

INDEX OF TITLES

1064

1068

INDEX OF FIRST LINES

1076